Electrical Machinery

Theory, Performance and Applications

Electrical Machinery

Theory, Performance and Applications

Dr. P. S. Bimbhra
Ph.D., M.E. (Hons.), F.I.E. (India), M.I.S.T.E.
Ex-Dean, Ex. Prof. and Head of Electrical and Electronics Engg. Dept.
Thapar Institute of Engineering and Technology
PATIALA - 147004

KHANNA BOOK PUBLISHING CO. (P) LTD.
Publisher of Engineering and Computer Books
4C/4344, Ansari Road, Darya Ganj, New Delhi-110002
Phone : 011-23244447-48 **Mobile:** +91-9910909320
E-mail : contact@khannabooks.com
Website : www.khannabooks.com

Dear Readers,

To prevent the piracy, this book is secured with HIGH SECURITY HOLOGRAM on the front title cover. In case you don't find the hologram on the front cover title, please write us to at contact@khannabooks.com or whatsapp us at +91-99109 09320 and avail special gift voucher for yourself.

Specimen of Hologram on front Cover title:

Moreover, there is a SPECIAL DISCOUNT COUPON for you with EVERY HOLOGRAM.

How to avail this SPECIAL DISCOUNT:

Step 1: Scratch the hologram
Step 2: Under the scratch area, your "coupon code" is available
Step 3: Logon to www.khannabooks.com
Step 4: Use your "coupon code" in the shopping cart and get your copy at a special discount
Step 5: Enjoy your reading!

Thanks,
Khanna Publishing House

Price: ₹785.00

ISBN: 978-93-89139-10-5

ELECTRICAL MACHINERY
by **P. S. Bimbhra**

First Edition: 2021
Reprint: 2024

To view complete list of books, please scan the QR Code:

Published by:
Khanna Book Publishing Co. (P) Ltd.
CIN: U22110DL1998PTC095547

Visit us at: www.khannabooks.com
Write us at: contact@khannabooks.com

Printed in Bharat,

To my wife

Surinder

and sons

Amitpal and *Panchampal*

Preface

The objective of writing this book continues to be to provide the reader with a text that presents a lucid and comprehensive treatment of transformers and more common types of rotating electrical machines. The philosophy of the book is to emphasize the physical understanding of the basic principles underlying the operation of electrical machines. In order to achieve this goal, the theory is developed from elementary ideas in such a style that their physical concepts are highlighted. The magnetic flux view point has been employed throughout this book, as this approach is easily understood and appreciated by the students. In addition, this approach provides a deep insight into the internal behaviour of electrical machines, so important that these concepts only show the way to creative engineering and become the most valuable asset of student's education. Each chapter takes off from the first fundamentals and is so developed progressively that an average student can grasp it easily. Clarity of presentation is further augmented by an appropriate use of illustrative figures and a wide variety of worked examples. Each chapter concludes with numerous unsolved problems with answer, conceptual questions and hints to the relatively difficult ones.

This volume is designed as a text for degree students on one hand and as a tool for self-study for practicing engineers on the other.

The book begins with basic principles of electrical machines where applications of Faraday and Ampere laws to electromagnetic devices are illustrated. Chapter 1 deals with the treatment of transformers, for an understanding of transformer behaviour is essential to the study of electromechanical - energy conversion process in machines in general, and the circuit model and phasor diagram of a polyphase induction motor in particular. A brief introduction to three-phase transformers is also included in chapter 1. Chapter 2 is concerned with the basic principles of electromechanical - energy conversion. It is emphasized in this chapter that the reaction of the coupling field is essential for the interconversion of energy from one to another form. This chapter shows how the energy stored in the coupling magnetic field can be expressed in terms of circuit parameters L, M or both; this forms the basis of generalized theory of electrical machines. The material covered in this chapter is so presented that level of mathematics required is not too sophisticated. In chapter 3, basic principles of voltage generation and torque production are developed which are applicable to both A.C. and D.C. machines. The applicability of general-voltage and torque expressions to both A.C. and D.C. machines leads to their unified treatment and shows that electrical machines operate on the same basic principles. Chapter 3 also includes practical issues common to all electrical machines types; such as losses, efficiency, cooling and rating. Engineering considerations underlying machine applications, in general, are also discussed in this chapter. Chapters 4 to 6 pertain to the in-depth treatment of three basic types: the D.C. machines, synchronous machines and induction machines. The steady-state model of each machine is developed with due stress on the underlying assumptions. After this, the power flow and operating characteristics of each machine are described at the end of these chapters. Three-phase induction generator is included in chapter 6 as the use of this generator for harnessing wind energy is on the rise. Heart of all rotating electrical machinery is the armature winding. If the heart fails, rotating electrical machinery comes to a grinding halt. The last chapter is thus devoted to these windings where a reasonably detailed account of both D.C. and A.C. machine windings is given. A meaningful knowledge of these windings appears to be indispensable for the Electrical Engineers.

During the last about two to three decades, many new subjects like control systems, power electronics, microprocessors etc. have appeared in the electrical engineering curriculum. These all subjects are, however, peripheral to electrical engineering. It is because an electrical engineer primarily, must be well- conversant with the technology and engineering aspects pertaining to generation, transmission, distribution and utilization of electrical energy. For acquiring skills and sufficient knowledge in these areas, the author feels that at least three courses on electrical machines and three courses on power systems must be taught to the students pursuing degree in electrical engineering.

Some alterations have been made in appendix A, whereas appendices B and D are there as in the previous edition. Appendix C on multiple choice questions has been thoroughly revised, enlarged and updated. Some topics have been re-worded and re-written for making the presentation more lucid and comprehensive. In addition, many more illustrative examples mainly from I.A.S., I.E.S. and GATE have been included. The problem material at the end of each chapter had also been considerably enlarged.

Suggestions made by several colleagues and readers of this book have been included in the present edition. The author would continue to welcome the advice and suggestion for improving the text as well as its usefulness to the readers of the book.

Dr. P. S. Bimbhra

Contents

Basic Principles of Electrical Machines

All rotating electrical machines are electromechanical energy conversion devices. A machine that converts mechanical energy into electrical energy is called a **generator**. The machine that converts electrical energy into mechanical energy is known as a **motor**. In rotating machines, the coupling between electrical and mechanical systems is through the magnetic field. In a transformer also, the primary and secondary windings are coupled through magnetic field. Transformers and all rotating electrical machines are electromagnetic devices. The principles applicable to these electromagnetic devices are primarily related to Faraday and Ampere.

0.1. FARADAY'S LAW

Faraday's law of electromagnetic induction states that an emf is induced in a coil when the magnetic flux linking this coil changes with time. It is expressed as

$$e = \frac{d\Psi}{dt} = N\frac{d\phi}{dt} \qquad \text{...(0.1)}$$

where e = emf induced, volts;

N = number of turns in the coil,

$\psi = N\phi$ = flux linkages with coil, Wb-turns

ϕ = magnetic flux, Wb

t = time, seconds.

Lenz's law. As stated above, changing magnetic flux linking a coil induces an emf in the coil. When the coil circuit is closed, a current begins to flow in the coil. The direction of this induced emf, or induced current is governed by Lenz's law. According to this law, the direction of induced emf and therefore induced current is in such a direction that the induced current develops a flux which always opposes the change in flux responsible for inducing this emf or current.

In order to take into consideration the fact that the induced emf or induced current opposes the change in flux, a negative sign is added to Eq. (0.1).

$$\therefore \qquad e = -\frac{d\psi}{dt} = -N\frac{d\phi}{dt} \qquad \text{...(0.2)}$$

Lenz's law is the outcome of natural law ; for every action, there is an equal and opposite reaction. Lenz's law in short is, **effect opposes the cause.**

Change in flux linkages. Eq. (0.1) shows that induced emf in a coil requires changes in flux, or flux linkages, with respect to time. This change in the flux linking a coil can be obtained by any of the four methods outlined below:

(i) Magnetic flux is constant and stationary, but coil rotates (or conductor moves). Flux-cutting action occurs and emf so induced is known as **speed emf, motional emf, rotational emf or dynamically induced emf.** This principle is used in all dc machines and in synchronous machines with field winding on the stator.

(ii) Coil is stationary, but dc electromagnet (or permanent magnet) is rotated. Here also flux-cutting action generates speed emf. This principle is used in large-sized synchronous generators.

(iii) Coil is stationary, but the flux passing through the coil changes with time. This induced emf is called **transformer emf or statically induced emf**.

(iv) Reluctance of the magnetic circuit varies with rotor rotation. As a consequence, flux variation occurs and emf is generated. This principle is used in inductor alternators.

Faraday's law is associated with two different processes for developing emfs; these are termed *(i)* speed, motional, rotational or dynamically induced emf and *(ii)* statically induced emf or transformer emf. These are now discussed further.

0.1.1. Speed emf or motional emf

Consider a single conductor of length l meter moving at right angle to uniform magnetic field between N and S poles shown in Fig. 0.1. The magnetic field has uniform flux density B tesla. Conductor velocity v m/s is perpendicular to its length and flux density B. Let the conductor travel a small distance dx in a time dt, from position 1 to position 2, Fig. 0.1*(a)*.

Therefore , area swept by the conductor in time $dt = l.dx$ m^2

Flux cut by conductor in time dt

= [Uniform flux density] × [Area swept by conductor normal to field in time dt]

= $[B] . [l.dx] = B\, l\, dx = d\,\phi$ Wb

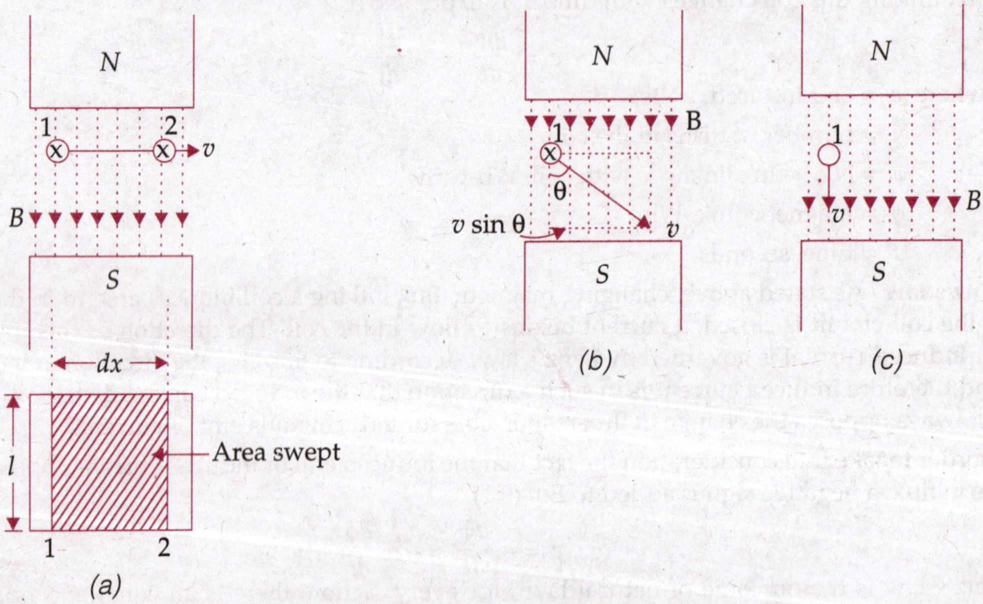

Fig 0.1: Pertaining to the generation of speed emf in a conductor.

As per Faraday's law, magnitude of induced emf e, from Eq. (0.1), is

$$e = \frac{d\phi}{dt} = \frac{Bl.dx}{dt} = Bl.\frac{dx}{dt}$$

Since $\frac{dx}{dt}$ = velocity of conductor v in m/s, the emf induced in one conductor is given by

$$e = Blv \qquad ...(0.3)$$

Now let the conductor move at an angle θ to the direction of magnetic field as shown in Fig. 0.1*(b)*. Now component of velocity perpendicular to magnetic field is $v \sin\theta$.

$$\therefore \qquad e = Blv \sin\theta \qquad ...(0.4)$$

In Fig. 0.1(*c*), conductor moves parallel to the flux lines, no flux is cut and therefore induced emf is zero. In case $\theta = 0$ in Fig. 0.1(*b*), $e = 0$, the case is the same as in Fig. 0.1(*c*).

Eq. (0.4) can also be expressed as

$$\frac{e}{l} = B\, v \sin\theta$$

or

$$\overline{E} = \overline{v} \times \overline{B} \text{ v/m} \quad \text{...(0.5)}$$

where $\overline{E}$ = electric field intensity in volts per meter. Here $\overline{E}$ is in a direction normal to the plane containing $\overline{v}$ and $\overline{B}$. Cross product of $\overline{v}$ and $\overline{B}$ indicates the direction of $\overline{E}$. For this purpose, stretch four fingers of right hand along $\overline{v}$, now move these fingers from $\overline{v}$ towards $\overline{B}$, then outstretched thumb gives the direction of $\overline{E}$. In Fig. 0.2(*a*), $\overline{v}$ and $\overline{B}$ are in *x*-*y* plane and $\overline{E}$ is along *z*-axis, normal to the plane containing $\overline{v}$ and $\overline{B}$. If this rule is applied to Fig. 0.1(*a*), direction of generated emf would be into the paper which can be denoted by cross. Same is true for Fig. 0.1(*b*).

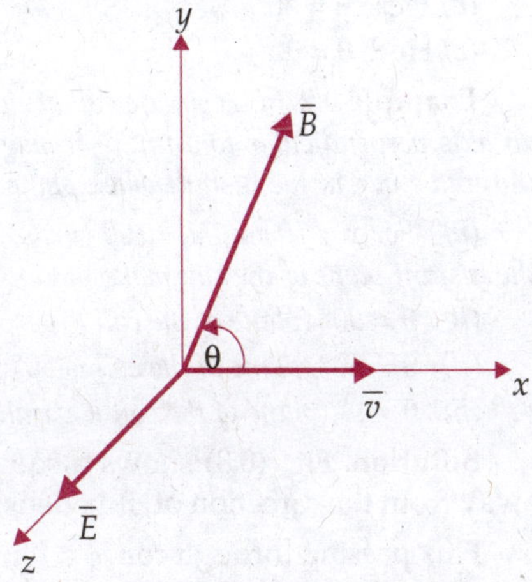

Fig 0.2: (*a*) Pertaining to the direction of electric field intensity $\overline{E}$.

The direction (polarity) of motional, or speed, emf can also be determined by using Fleming's right-hand rule (FRHR). This rule states as under :

Hold the thumb, the first (or forefinger) and the second (or middle) finger of the right-hand at right angles to each other. If First finger points in the direction of Field and the thuMb in the direction of Motion, then the sEcond (or middle) finger, held at right angles to both the thumb and first finger, points in the direction of induced Emf. Fig. 0.2(*b*) is helpful in the application of FRHR.

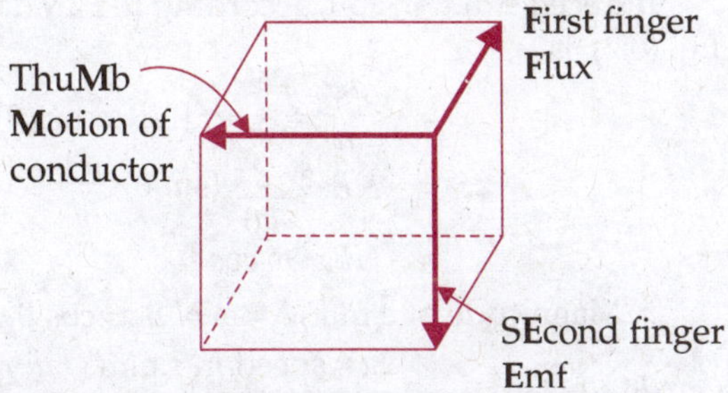

Fig 0.2: (*b*) Fleming's right-hand rule (FRHR), direction of speed emf.

0.1.2. Transformer E.m.f.

The magnitude of transformer e.m.f. is given by Eq. (0.1), or in general, by Eq. (0.2). The coil is stationary (or fixed), but flux is time-varying in nature.

Note that in motional or speed e.m.f., motion or rotation is involved. Therefore, speed e.m.f. is associated with *energy conversion* from electrical to mechanical or mechanical to electrical. The transformer e.m.f. does not involve any motion of the coil. Therefore, transformer e.m.f. is not associated with energy conversion; it is, however, associated with *energy transfer* only.

0.1.3. General case of Induced E.m.f.

Suppose there is a relative movement between coil and the magnetic flux and at the same time, flux is changing with time. Under these conditions, both speed and transformer e.m.fs. would be induced in the coil. Thus, total e.m.f. *e* in the coil would now be given by

$$e = \text{speed or rotational e.m.f., } e_r + \text{transformer e.m.f., } e_t$$

Example 0.1. *A conductor 80 cm long moves at right angle to its length at a constant speed of 30 m/s in a uniform magnetic field of flux density 1.2 T. Find the e.m.f. induced in case the conductor motion is (a) normal to the field flux (b) at an angle of 30° from the direction of field and (c) parallel to the field flux.*

Solution. The e.m.f. induced in conductor, in general, is given by Eq. (0.4), *i.e.*, $e = Blv \sin \theta$, where θ = angle between the direction of motion and field flux

(*a*) Here $\theta = 90°$, $e = Blv \sin 90° = 1.2 \times 0.8 \times 30 \times 1 = 28.8$ V

(*b*) Here $\theta = 30°$, $e = 1.2 \times 0.8 \times 30 \times \sin 30° = 14.4$ V

(*c*) Here $\theta = 90°$, $e = 1.2 \times 0.8 \times 30 \times \sin 0° = 0$

Example 0.2. *(a) A square coil of side x meters and with N turns rotates at a speed of ω rad/sec, around an axis perpendicular to a uniform magnetic field of the flux density B tesla. Derive an expression for the induced e.m.f. at the instant when plane of the coil is at θ radians to the magnetic field.*

(b) For x = 10 cm, N = 100 turns, speed = 1000 r.p.m., B = 1.0 Wb/m², calculate the induced e.m.f. at the instant plane of the coil makes an angle

(i) θ = 90° (plane of the coil is perpendicular to field)

(ii) θ = 30° (plane of the coil is 30° to the field)

(iii) θ = 0° (plane of the coil is parallel to the field)

Solution. Fig. (0.3) shows a square coil with its plane θ° away from the direction of flux density *B*. Area of coil = x^2 m²

Flux passing through coil, ϕ = Flux density B × Area of coil perpendicular to B

$$\phi = (B) \times (x^2 \sin \theta) = Bx^2 \sin \theta \text{ Wb}$$

∴ Flux linkages with coil, $\psi = N\phi = NB\,x^2 \sin \theta$ Wb turns.

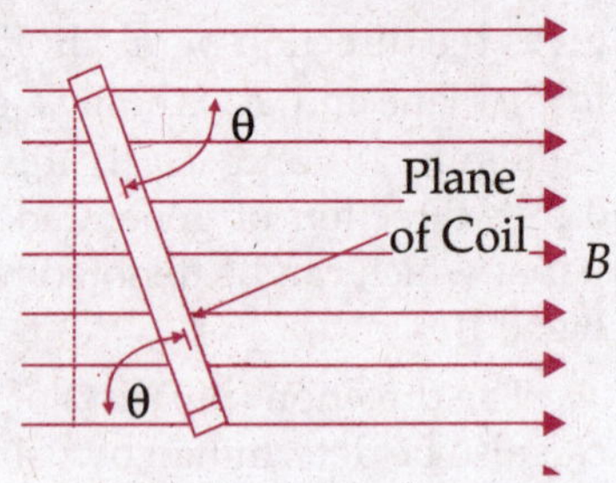

Fig 0.3: Pertaining to Example 0.2

Induced e.m.f. in coil, according to Faraday's law given by Eq. (0.2), is

$$e = -\frac{d\psi}{dt} = -\frac{d}{dt}[NB\,x^2 \sin \theta]$$

$$= -NBx^2 \frac{d}{d\theta}(\sin \theta)\frac{d\theta}{dt} = -NBx^2 \cos \theta \frac{d\theta}{dt}$$

$$= -NBx^2\,\omega \cos \theta \qquad \left[\because \frac{d\theta}{dt} = \text{speed in rad/sec}\right]$$

∴ Magnitude of e.m.f., $e = \omega\,N\,B\,x^2 \cos \theta$

(*b*) (*i*) Here $\omega = \dfrac{2\pi \times \text{speed in r.p.m.}}{60} = \dfrac{2\pi \times 1000}{60} = \dfrac{100\pi}{3}$ rad/s

$N = 100$, $x = 0.1$ m, $\theta = 90°$

∴ $e = \omega\,NB\,x^2 \cos \theta = \dfrac{100\pi}{3} \times 100 \times 1 \times (0.1)^2 \cos 90° = 0$

(*ii*) $\theta = 30°$, $e = \dfrac{100\pi}{3} \times 100 \times 1 \times (0.1)^2 \times \cos 30° = 90.687$ V

(*iii*) $\theta = 0°$, $e = \dfrac{100\pi}{3} \times 100 \times 1 \times (0.1)^2 \times \cos 0° = 104.72$ V

Example 0.3. *A conductor 50 cm long is along y-axis and flux density of 1.2 T along the x-axis. In which direction the conductor should be moved so that maximum e.m.f. is induced in the conductor? If this velocity is 2 m/s, find the value of e.m.f. in the conductor.*

Solution. In the expression, $e = Blv$, the three terms should be perpendicular to each other for maximum induced e.m.f. in the conductor. So the motion of conductor should be along the *z*-axis as $\overline{B}$ and *l* are in the *x*-*y* plane, Fig. 0.4. Magnitude of e.m.f. in conductor,

$$e = Blv = 1.2 \times 0.5 \times 2 = 1.2 \text{ V}$$

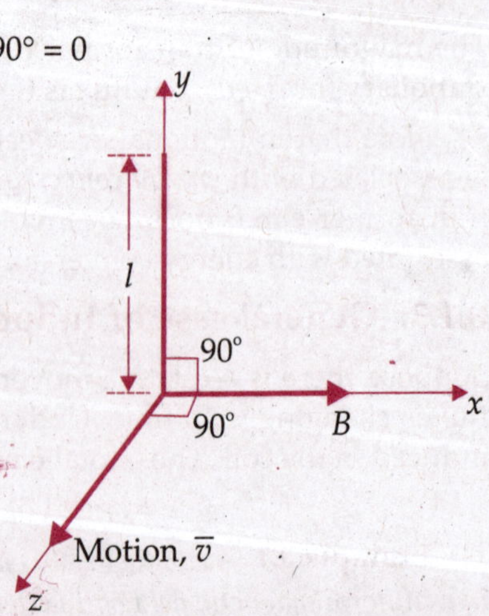

Fig 0.4: Pertaining to Example 0.3

Example 0.4. *A horizontal disc of radius r, pivoted on a vertical spindle, rotates at speed ω rad/sec in a vertically directed magnetic flux density B as shown in Fig. 0.5. Derive an expression for the e.m.f. available across two brushes, one on the spindle at a and the other at b.*

Solution. Area of spindle $= \pi r^2 \text{ m}^2$

Flux passing through the circular spindle, $\phi = \pi r^2 . B$ Wb

The e.m.f. picked up by the two brushes at a and b is actually the e.m.f. induced in one conductor obtained by joining a to b.

For a speed of ω rad/sec, ω radians take 1 second. In other words, ω radians require a time = 1 second

1 radian would require a time $= \frac{1}{\omega}$ s

∴ One revolution or 2π radians would need a time, $t = \frac{2\pi}{\omega}$ s

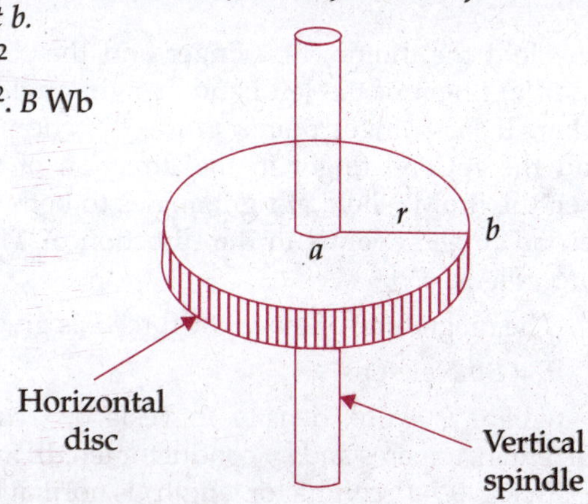

Fig 0.5: Pertaining to Example 0.4

In one revolution, however, flux cut by one conductor, $\phi = \pi r^2 B$ Wb

∴ E.m.f. picked up by brushes = rate of flux cutting by one conductor ab

$$e = \frac{\text{flux cut in one revolution}}{\text{time of one revolution}} = \frac{\phi}{t} = \frac{\pi r^2 B}{2\pi/\omega} \text{ volts}$$

$$\therefore \quad e = \frac{r^2 B\omega}{2} \text{ volts}$$

0.2. FORCE ON CURRENT CARRYING CONDUCTOR

Consider a conductor of length l (perpendicular to paper) carrying a current I into the page, Fig. 0.6*(a)*. This current sets up magnetic flux around the conductor in clockwise direction*. In Fig. 0.6*(b)*, field flux lines between two poles *N*, *S* are shown. If conductor of Fig. 0.6*(a)* is placed in between two poles, then the conductor flux assists the pole flux above the conductor but opposes it below the conductor, Fig. 0.6 *(c)*. As a result, the number of flux lines above the conductor is more than the number below. The resultant flux has the shape as shown in Fig. 0.6*(c)*.

It is known that magnetic flux lines behave like stretched rubber bands, the conductor in Fig. 0.6*(c)*, therefore, experiences a downward force.

If direction of current in conduction is reversed, then the resultant flux distribution is as shown in Fig. 0.6*(d)*. The conductor now experiences an upward force, Fig. 0.6*(d)*. In both Figs. 0.6*(c)* and *(d)*, the magnetic force *F* is in a direction **normal to both conductor and field.**

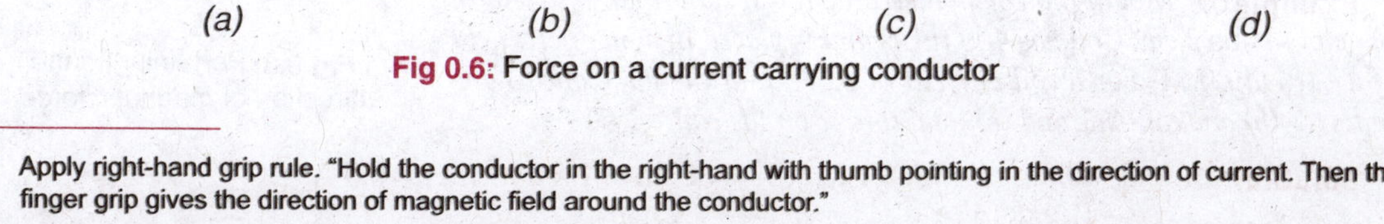

Fig 0.6: Force on a current carrying conductor

* Apply right-hand grip rule. "Hold the conductor in the right-hand with thumb pointing in the direction of current. Then the finger grip gives the direction of magnetic field around the conductor."

The direction of magnetic force can be determined by Fleming's left-hand rule (FLHR) which is stated below.

Hold the thumb, first finger and the second (or middle) finger of the left hand at right angle to each other. If First finger points in the direction of Field and the seCond finger in the direction of Current, then the thuMb, held at right angles to both first and second fingers, points in the direction of Motion or force, Fig. 0.6(*e*).

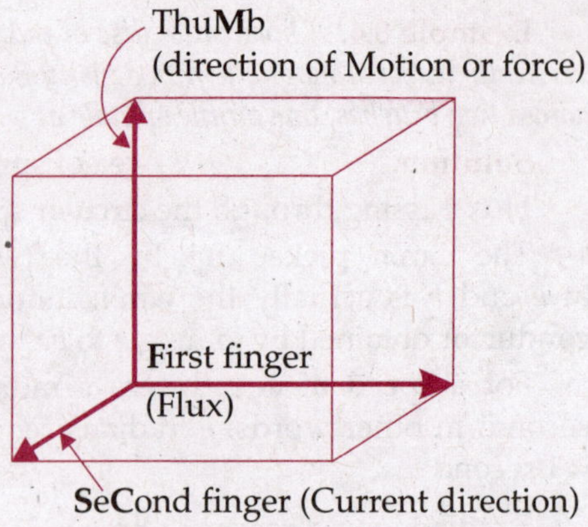

Fig 0.6: (*e*) Fleming's left-hand rule (FLHR)

The magnitude of magnetic force F is given by

$F = BIl$ Newtons ...(0.6)

where B = flux density in Tesla, I = conductor current in amperes and l = conductor length in metres.

In Fig. 0.7(*a*), conductor length l is normal to field flux lines and the force = BIl. In case conductor is displaced by an angle θ from flux lines, then effective conductor length is $l \sin \theta$. Therefore, now the magnitude of magnetic force is $F = BIl \sin \theta$ ...(0.7)

Eq. (0.7) can also be expressed as $\overline{F} = l\,[\overline{I} \times \overline{B}]$ ...(0.8)

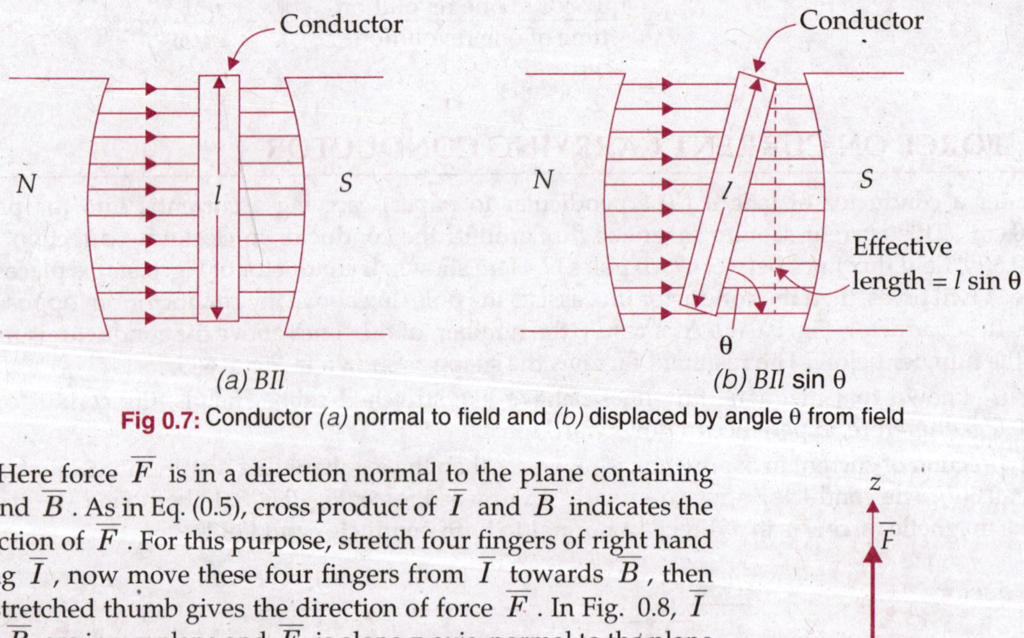

Fig 0.7: Conductor (*a*) normal to field and (*b*) displaced by angle θ from field

Here force $\overline{F}$ is in a direction normal to the plane containing $\overline{I}$ and $\overline{B}$. As in Eq. (0.5), cross product of $\overline{I}$ and $\overline{B}$ indicates the direction of $\overline{F}$. For this purpose, stretch four fingers of right hand along $\overline{I}$, now move these four fingers from $\overline{I}$ towards $\overline{B}$, then outstretched thumb gives the direction of force $\overline{F}$. In Fig. 0.8, $\overline{I}$ and $\overline{B}$ are in x-y plane and $\overline{F}$ is along z-axis, normal to the plane containing $\overline{I}$ and $\overline{B}$.

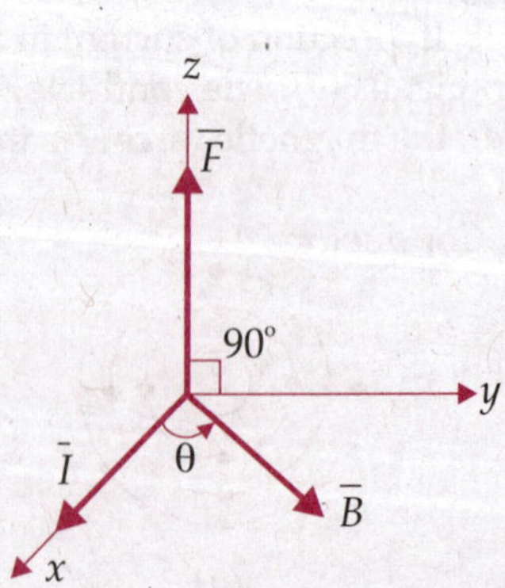

Fig 0.8: Pertaining to the direction of magnetic force

If this rule is applied to Figs. 0.6(*c*) and (*d*), the direction of force is downward in Fig. 0.6(*c*) and upward in Fig. 0.6(*d*).

Example 0.5. *Moving coil of an instrument is rectangular with length 4 cm and radius 2 cm. Coil has 400 turns and is placed in a magnetic field of flux density 0.8T. For a coil current of 0.5A, find the force on (a) one conductor (b) one coil-side and (c) total torque on the coil.*

Solution. Here B = 0.8T, conductor length l = 4 cm = 4×10^{-2} m, I = 0.5 A (*a*) Force on one conductor $F = BIl = 0.8 \times 0.5 \times 4 \times 10^{-2} = 0.016$ N

(*b*) Number of turns = 400. One coil has two coil-sides. Therefore, number of conductors in each coil side = 400

∴ Force on one coil-side = force on one conductor × number of conductors in one coil-side

$$= 0.016 \times 400 = 6.4 \text{ N}$$

(*c*) Here $r = 2 \text{ cm} = 2 \times 10^{-2} \text{ m},$

∴ Total torque on the coil = (force on each coil-side) × 2 coil sides × radius

$$= 6.4 \times 2 \times (2 \times 10^{-2}) = 0.256 \text{ Nm.}$$

0.3. OVERVIEW OF ELECTRICAL MACHINES

The world abounds in umpteen forms of energies. From time immemorial, human-beings have been striving hard in harnessing these energies for improving their living standards. Energy thus serves as the life-blood for the perpetual growth and progress of human civilization. In the energy hierarchy, electrical energy holds the top rank. It is because electrical energy is easily adaptable for all human needs and interests, in an economic and efficient manner. At the same time, electrical energy can be easily controlled and is pollution free at the consumer premises. It is truly said that per-capita energy consumption in any country is an index of the living standard of the people in that country.

At present, environment pollution problems are on the rise. In order to minimize the effects of pollution, the government now compels the users of non-electrical energy to switch over to the use of electrical energy in future. The increasing use of electrical energy in different fields of daily life has been primarily due to the availability of a vast variety of electrical machinery for the purpose of generation, transmission, distribution and utilization.

Electrical energy is generated in thermal, hydroelectric and nuclear power stations. These stations consist primarily of turbines mechanically coupled with large synchronous generators. In addition, generating stations have auxiliary equipment for efficient generation and control of electrical energy. Now-a-days, much attention is given to the generation of electrical energy from natural sources like solar and wind. The energy obtained from solar and wind sources does supplement the energy generated by coal, hydro and nuclear power stations.

The output voltage from synchronous generators is 26 kV in India. In developed countries, it may be 33 kV or even more. This generated voltage is stepped up to 220 kV, 400 kV, 765 V or 865 kV by large size step-up three-phase transformers. Power transmission at high voltage reduces the transmission losses and makes the energy system more efficient.

When power is required at the load end, high voltage is stepped-down by large size step-down three-phase transformers to a voltage level suitable for consumers.

For industrial use, the most widely used motor is three-phase induction motor. Synchronous motors and dc motors are also used for special purposes. For agriculture sector, again three-phase induction motor is the main choice. For domestic and commercial use, single-phase induction and commutator motors are quite common. From above, it may be stated that electrical machines like alternators, transformers and motors form an integral part of any energy system.

0.4. CLASSIFICATION OF ELECTRICAL MACHINES

Electrical machinery can be mainly classified as dc machines and ac machines. D.C. machines can operate as generators and motors, same is true for ac machines.

0.4.1. D.C Machines

In D.C. machines, the field poles are on the stator called yoke. Armature winding and commutator are on the rotor. Fig. 0.9 gives cross-sectional view of a 2-pole D.C. machine. Brushes press on to the commutator surface for collecting the power from a D.C. generator or for feeding D.C. power to the armature of a D.C. motor. D.C. machines are of three types; series, shunt and compound. D.C. series machine has field winding in series with armature circuit, D.C. shunt machine has field winding across the armature circuit whereas a D.C. compound machine has two field windings, one field winding across the armature and second field winding in series with armature.

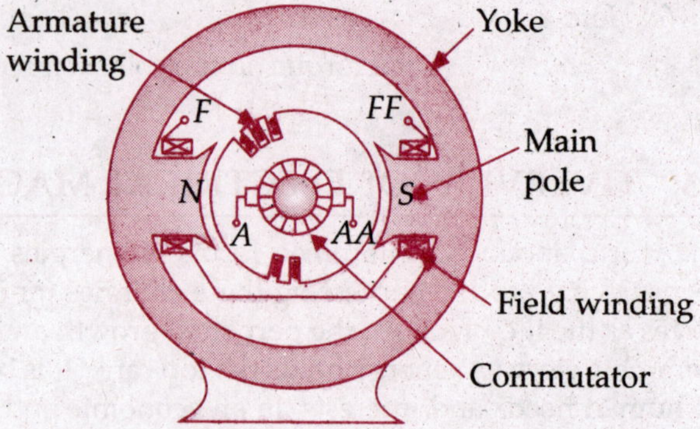

Fig 0.9: Cross-sectional view of a two-pole D.C. machine

D.C. machines are also fitted with interpoles. Large D.C. machines have also compensating windings embedded in the pole faces of main poles.

D.C. machines possess versatile operating characteristics. D.C. motor is easily adaptable for speed control and electric braking.

0.4.2. A.C. Machines

These are further classified as transformers, synchronous machines, induction machines and A.C. commutator machines.

(a) **Transformers.** A transformer is not an electromechanical converter. It is used in almost all the devices energized from A.C. source. It usually steps up or step down electrical energy from one voltage level to another voltage level. However, it is also employed with unity turns ratio for isolation purposes.

In small sizes, single-phase transformers are used. For large ratings, 3-phase transformers are more common.

(b) **Synchronous machines.** In these machines, the field poles may be on stator or rotor. In bigger sizes, field poles are always on the rotor. Fig.0.10 shows cross-sectional view of a two-pole synchronous machine. Field winding on rotor is excited with D.C. whereas stator winding handles three-phase A.C. power. Rotor runs at synchronous speed N_S. Frequency f of the e.m.f generated in armature is given by

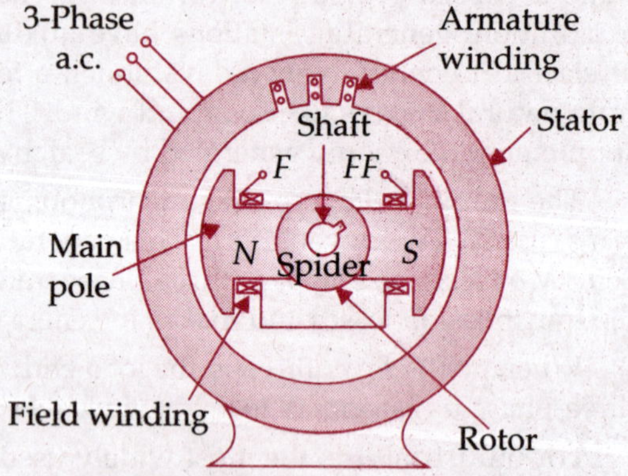

Fig 0.10: Cross-sectional view of a two-pole synchronous machine.

$$f = \frac{PN_s}{120} \text{ Hz}$$

where P = number of field poles

A synchronous machine is a doubly-excited machine. It is employed as an alternator for the generation of three-phase power at all the generating stations. It is also used as a synchronous motor for special applications.

(c) **Induction machines.** These are of two types, three-phase induction machines and single-phase induction machines. Both types are singly-excited in the sense that stator of 3-phase induction motor is fed from three-phase A.C. source whereas stator of single-phase induction motor is energized from 1-phase A.C. source.

Three-phase induction machines. The stator winding of a three-phase induction motor, connected to 3-phase mains, carries both load current and field-producing exciting current. The field produced rotates at synchronous speed in the air gap but rotor speed is always less than synchronous speed. Two types of 3-phase induction motors are as under :

(i) **SCIM.** Rotor carries copper, or aluminum, bars embedded in rotor slots. These bars are short-circuited by two end rings, one at each end. SCIM has the most rugged construction and is used where control of starting torque or speed is not needed.

(ii) **SRIM.** Its stator is similar to the stator of SCIM, but rotor carries 3-phase winding with three leads connected to three slip rings mounted on the shaft. Brushes pressing on the slip rings allow the insertion of external resistances in the rotor circuit. SRIMs are used where speed, or torque, control is required.

A 3-phase induction motor, connected to 3-phase source, can operate as a 3-phase induction generator when driven above synchronous speed. This, however, has not become commercially popular due to certain limitations.

Single-phase induction machines. In addition to 3-phase induction machines discussed above, single-phase induction motors are used where single-phase low voltage (230 V, 50 Hz) is available, as in homes, offices, class rooms, shops etc.

(d) **A.C. Commutator machines.** As the name suggests, these machines are fed from A.C. source and are fitted with commutators. A large variety of A.C. commutator machines are reported in the literature. Only three-phase Schrage motors and single-phase series motors have withstood the onslaught of time. For wide speed control, 3-phase Schrage motor is reliable and introduces no harmonics into the supply system as are produced by inverter-fed three-phase induction motors.

Single-phase series motors are indispensable where high starting torque and light weight is desirable as in sewing machines, food processors, vacuum cleaners and small hand tools. In small sizes, this motor gives the highest power output per rupee cost, though it makes more noise. In addition, this motor is easily adaptable to speed or torque control through the use of power-electronics based 1-phase voltage controllers.

0.5. SPECIAL MACHINES

Many electrical machines having novel constructional features have been developed for special applications. Inductor alternators generate high-frequency voltages and are in use for eddy-current heating. Power selsyns and pilot selyns are used in process industries like paper, steel, textile etc. A.C. machines for speed and position control include synchros, 2-phase control motors and tachometers. Linear motors find use in railway traction, restricted linear motion devices etc. Magnetically levitated machines are also under development for high-speed railway traction. Dynamometers for speed and torque measurement of motors, engines etc., reluctance motors for positioning systems in nuclear reactors and hysteresis motors for driving low-power drives like gyros are also in use.

A large variety of motors have recently appeared in the market. These are stepping motors, brushless D.C. motors (also called PM A.C. motors), variable-reluctance motors, permanent magnet D.C. motors etc. These motors have special applications in computer peripherals, numerically controlled machines, line printers, paper-feed motors in typewriters and printers, VCRs, video cameras, CD players, MP3 systems, precision position control required in robotics etc. PM BLDC motors are already being used in ac inverters. Application of PM BLDMs are also being explored for their use in traction, automobiles and robotics.

0.6. ENERGY EFFICIENCY OF ELECTRICAL MACHINERY

With dwindling sources of fossil fuels (coal, oil and natural gas), cost of energy is going up with the passage of time. Availability of cheap energy promotes its wastage. In order that electrical energy is used prudently, increasing tariffs are being implemented the world over. Under such circumstances, it becomes imperative that electrical energy is utilized judiciously.

In the generation of electric power; electrical machinery, converting mechanical energy into electrical energy, is found to be quite efficient. Therefore, for overall improved efficiency of the energy system, electrical energy conversion to other useful forms (mechanical, thermal etc.) must be carried out as efficiently as possible. Since major portion of the generated power is consumed in electric drives, emphasis must be laid on the efficient use of these drives. High efficiency electric drives can be achieved by

(a) judicious design of electrical machinery and

(b) proper matching of motor-load combination.

I. Judicious design

For an electrical device,

$$\text{power efficiency} = \frac{\text{power output}}{\text{power output} + \text{losses}}$$

$$\text{and energy efficiency} = \frac{(\text{power output}) \times H\,[\text{number of hours or days in service}]}{(\text{power output} + \text{losses}) \times H}$$

It is seen from above that for obtaining an optimum energy efficiency of an electrical machine, its losses (I^2R loss + core loss + friction and windage loss) must be minimized.

I^2R losses can be minimised as under :

(i) Use reduced current density in conductors. This will require more conductor area and therefore reduced winding resistance. Reduced current density would, however, increase the volume and therefore weight of conductor required.

Core loss can be minimized as under :

(i) Use lower value of average flux density in the air gap. This would result in increased volume and weight of stator and rotor iron. Core loss in watts/kg would be less; iron weight would, however, go up. In view of this, the machine design must be so realized that there is an overall reduction in total core loss.

(ii) Use high resistivity steel and thinner iron laminations to reduce the eddy-current loss.

(iii) Use high grade electrical steel to reduce hysteresis loss.

The friction and windage (*F* and *W*) loss can be reduced as under :

(i) Design the rotor fans with improved aerodynamics to minimize the windage loss.

(ii) Use good-quality bearings to reduce the friction loss.

It is observed from above that electrical machinery with improved efficiency requires more iron and conductor materials. High energy-efficient machines are, therefore, more expensive. Users normally go for an electrical machine that has the lowest cost. However, users can be persuaded to purchase only high energy-efficient machines if it is proved to them that (increased capital cost + interest on this capital) would be more than compensated by the energy savings made over the expected long life-span of energy-efficient machines.

In addition, energy-efficient machines would

(i) entail much lower maintenance charges and

(ii) suffer less outages thus increasing the industrial output and less loss of labour hours.

II. Proper matching

Several factors must be taken into consideration for the choice of an energy-efficient electric drive. The most important of these factors is the proper matching of load with the motor so far as their performance requirements are concerned. For example, an efficient 20 kW, 3-phase induction motor, if selected for driving a 10 kW load, would be operating with a lower efficiency, indicating a mismatch of motor with the load. During the selection of motors, usually an over-rated motor is chosen by the application engineer just to cover up any design or manufacturing unforeseen lapses. Therefore, careful attention on the choice of energy-efficient electric drives is justifiable.

0.7. HISTORICAL

Brief historical facts of electrical machines are presented below.

(i) **Transformers.** In 1831, Michael Faraday discovered the most important fact that changing flux can induce an emf in a coil. This law, now known as Faraday's law of electromagnetic induction, forms the basis of operation of transformers. So, it can be stated that transformer was invented by M. Faraday in 1831.

(ii) **D.C. Machines.** D.C. machines were the first rotating electrical machines invented. An elementary dc motor was developed in 1839*. It took another forty years to build a commercially viable dc motor.

(iii) **Three-phase Induction Machines.** Nikola Tesla patented two-phase and three-phase induction motors in 1888. At Frankfurt (Germany) exhibition, N. Tesla exhibited a crude type of polyphase induction motor in 1891. Two years later, in 1893, Dobrowolsky presented a three-phase induction motor with cage rotor and distributed stator winding**.

(iv) **Synchronous Machines.** Nikola Tesla patented two-phase and three-phase synchronous generators and motors in 1888*.

(v) **Single-phase A.C. Commutator Motors.** Galileo Ferraris invented single-phase ac commutator induction motor***.

PROBLEMS

0.1. (a) State Faraday's law of electromagnetic induction. Write an emf expression based on this law and state the symbols used. Why is negative sign used in the emf expression?

(b) Explain the four methods used for changing the flux linking a coil. State also the practical application made from each of these methods.

0.2. (a) Derive an expression for dynamically induced emf. What are the factors on which this emf depends? Express this expression as $\overline{E} = \overline{v} \times \overline{B}$ and explain how this expression is used in determining the direction of induced emf.

(b) Explain Fleming's right-hand rule.

---

* "Electrical Technology" by Edward Hughes.

** "Alternating Current Machines" by M.G. Say.

*** "Google."

0.3. On the periphery of a 60 cm diameter rotor, there is a conductor of length 50 cm. The rotor rotates at 1200 rpm. The flux density under the poles is 0.8 T. Find the emf induced in one conductor. **[Ans.** 15.08 V]

0.4. A conductor 60 cm long moves at right angle to its length at a constant speed of 40 m/sec in a uniform field of density 0.8T. Find the emf induced in case conductor motion is *(a)* perpendicular to field *(b)* at an angle of 30° to the direction of field and *(c)* parallel to field flux. **[Ans.** *(a)* 19.2 V *(b)* 9.6 V *(c)* zero V]

0.5. *(a)* A current carrying conductor is placed in a magnetic field produced by two poles. How will you find the direction of magnetic force acting on the conductor from a consideration of magnetic flux lines.

(b) Write an expression for the force acting on a current-carrying conductor in a magnetic field. State the symbols used and their units.

(c) Explain Fleming's left-hand rule (FLHR).

0.6. *(a)* Derive an expression for the force acting on a current-carrying conductor displaced at an angle θ from the magnetic field. Express this expression as $\overline{F} = l\,[\overline{I} \times \overline{B}]$ and explain how this expression can be used in determining the direction of force.

(b) What is right-hand grip rule? Describe its use.

0.7. A coil with 200 turns has axial length 20 cm and diameter 16 cm. This coil is placed in a uniform radial field of flux density 0.02 T.

(a) Find the emf induced in the coil if it rotates at 30 rps.

(b) Find the force on each conductor, each coil-side and torque acting on the coil, if coil current is 5 A. **[Ans.** *(a)* 24.128V *(b)* 0.02N, 4N, 0.64 Nm]

0.8. A conductor 50 cm long carries a current of 10 A. The conductor is perpendicular to magnetic field of flux density 1 Wb/m^2. *(a)* Find force on one conductor and *(b)* find the mechanical work required to move the conductor at a speed of 10 m/sec.

[Ans. *(a)* 5N *(b)* 50W]

0.9. A copper disc of diameter 300 mm rotates at 600 rpm about a vertical axis through its centre. Plane of copper disc is horizontal. If vertical component of earth's magnetic field is 20 μT, calculate the emf between the circumference of the disc and its vertical axis.

[Hint: $e = \frac{r^2 B\omega}{2}$ from Example 0.4]. **[Ans.** 14.137μV]

0.10. *(a)* Repeat part *(a)* of Example 0.2 in case the coil is circular with radius a metre.

(b) Repeat part *(b)* of Example 0.2 if radius a = 10 cm.

[Ans. *(a)* $\omega NB.\ \pi a^2.\ \cos\theta$ *(b)* 0V, 284.90V, 328.987V]

0.11. An aircraft, with a total wing span of 40 m, is flying horizontally at 900 kmph. Vertical component of earth's magnetic field is 4×10^{-5} T. Calculate the emf generated between the two wing tips of the aircraft. **[Ans.** 0.4V]

1 Chapter

Transformers

A transformer is a static electric device. Basically, a transformer consists of two or more electric circuits, insulated from each other, but coupled by mutual magnetic flux. Electrical energy from one electric circuit is transferred to another electrical circuit (or circuits), through the medium of magnetic field and without a change in the frequency. The electric circuit connected to an alternating voltage source is called **primary winding** and the other circuit which delivers electrical energy to the load is called the **secondary winding**.

1.1. PRINCIPLE OF TRANSFORMER OPERATION

A transformer works on the principle of **electromagnetic induction** (or **mutual induction**) between two (or more) coils. According to this principle, an emf is induced in a coil if it links time-varying* magnetic flux.

Fig.1.1*(a)* shows schematic diagram of a two-winding transformer. Primary winding has N_1 turns and secondary winding has N_2 turns. When primary is connected to an alternating voltage source V_1, an alternating current I_m begins to flow through N_1 turns. This alternating current establishes alternating flux ϕ in the magnetic circuit. The mean path of this flux ϕ is shown by the dotted line in Fig.1.1*(a)*. This alternating magnetic flux ϕ links both primary and secondary windings. As a result, this time-varying flux induces emf E_1 in the primary P across terminals 1 and 2, and emf E_2 in the secondary S across terminals 3 and 4. In Fig.1.1*(a)*, if switch SW is closed, load gets connected to secondary winding. Now secondary delivers power to load. This shows that electrical energy can be transferred from the alternating-voltage source to the load through the medium of coupling magnetic field. Alternatively, it can be said that the electrical energy received by primary is transferred by **transformer action** to the secondary winding and to the load.

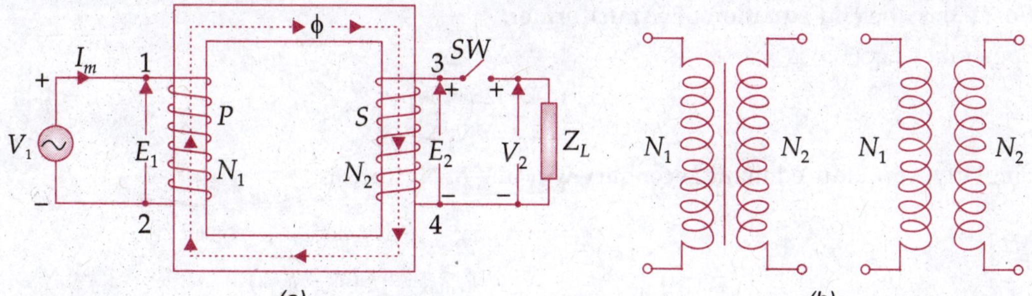

Fig 1.1: Single-phase two-winding transformer *(a)* schematic diagram and *(b)* circuit symbol.

* Changing with time

It is seen from above that transformer is an electromagnetic energy conversion device. It is because the energy received by the primary is first converted to magnetic-field energy; it is then reconverted back to useful electrical energy in the secondary winding.

If a voltmeter is connected across primary terminal 1 and secondary terminal 3, the voltmeter would read zero. This shows that secondary winding is electrically isolated from the primary winding but magnetically coupled through the medium of common magnetic field.

Circuit symbol for single-phase transformer is either of the two circuits shown in Fig. 1.1*(b)*.

1.2. EMF EQUATION OF A TRANSFORMER

Let the voltage applied to primary winding in Fig. 1.1*(a)* be sinusoidal. As a result; current I_m, called **magnetizing current,** would also be sinusoidal. Mmf $N_1 . I_m$ and therefore magnetic flux ϕ would also vary sinusoidally with time as shown in Fig.1.2*(b)*.

Let this flux in the magnetic core of transformer of Fig.1.1*(a)*, at any instant be given by

$$\phi = \phi_{max} \sin \omega t \qquad \text{...(1.1)}$$

where ϕ = instantaneous value of flux, Wb

ϕ_{max} = maximum value of flux, Wb

$\omega = 2\pi f$ = supply frequency in rad/sec

f = supply frequency in Hz.

The emf e_1 induced in the primary winding of N_1 turns by the alternating flux ϕ is given by

$$e_1 = -N_1 \frac{d\phi}{dt} = -N_1 \frac{d}{dt}(\phi_{max} \sin \omega t)$$

$$= -N_1 \omega \phi_{max} \cos \omega t$$

or $$e_1 = N_1 \omega \phi_{max} \sin (\omega t - \pi/2)$$

Its maximum value $E_{1.max}$ occurs when $\sin(\omega t - \pi/2) = 1$

$\therefore$ $$E_{1max} = N_1 \omega \phi_{max} = 2\pi f . N_1 \phi_{max}$$

and $$e_1 = E_{1.max} \sin (\omega t - \pi/2) \qquad \text{...(1.2)}$$

$\therefore$ Rms value of emf E_1 induced in primary winding is given by

$$E_1 = \frac{E_{1.max}}{\sqrt{2}} = \frac{2\pi}{\sqrt{2}} f N_1 . \phi_{max}$$

or $$E_1 = \sqrt{2}\, \pi f N_1 . \phi_{max} \qquad \text{...(1.3)}$$

Eq. (1.3) is the **emf equation of a transformer**.

Sometimes Eq. (1.3) is written as

$$E_1 = 4.44283 f N_1 \phi_{max} \qquad \text{... } (\because \sqrt{2}\,\pi = 4.44283)$$

or $$E_1 = 4.44 f N_1 \phi_{max} \qquad \text{...(1.3)}$$

Similarly, emf induced in the secondary winding of N_2 turns is

$$e_2 = -N_2 \frac{d\phi}{dt} = -N_2\, \omega . \phi_{max} . \cos \omega t$$

$$= N_2\, \omega . \phi_{max} . \sin (\omega t - \pi/2)$$

or $$e_2 = E_{2max} . \sin (\omega t - \pi/2) \qquad \text{...(1.4)}$$

Rms value of E_2 induced in the secondary winding is given by

$$E_2 = \frac{E_{2.max}}{\sqrt{2}} = \sqrt{2}\, \pi f N_2 \phi_{max} \qquad \text{...(1.5)}$$

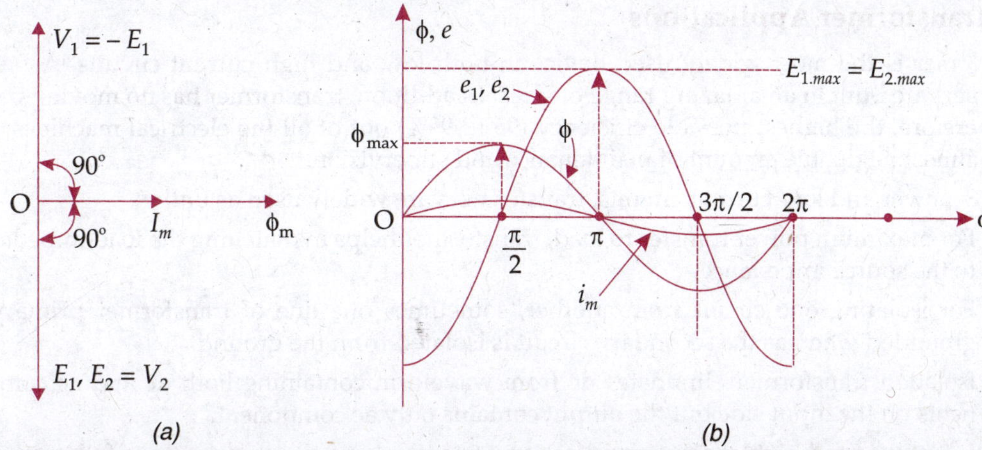

Fig 1.2: *(a)* Phasor diagram showing ϕ_m, I_m, E_1, E_2 and *(b)* time variations of ϕ, e_1, e_2 and I_m.

Variation of flux ϕ from Eq. (1.1), emf e_1 from Eq. (1.2) and emf e_2 from Eq. (1.4) are shown in Fig. 1.2*(b)*. Its phasor diagram is drawn in Fig.1.2*(a)*.

From Eqs. (1.3) and (1.5), we get

$$\frac{E_1}{E_2} = \frac{N_1}{N_2} \qquad ...(1.6)$$

or

$$\frac{E_1}{N_1} = \frac{E_2}{N_2} = \sqrt{2}\,\pi f \phi_{max} \qquad ...(1.7)$$

or emf per turn in primary $\left(\frac{E_1}{N_1}\right)$ = emf per turn in secondary $\left(\frac{E_2}{N_2}\right)$.

Relation expressed by Eq. (1.7) is very significant and must always be remembered.

1.3. TRANSFORMER FEATURES

Here some engineering aspects of transformers are presented.

1.3.1. Step-up/ Step-down Transformers

A transformer with secondary output voltage more than the input voltage is called **a step-up transformer**.

A transformer with secondary output voltage less than the input voltage is called **step-down transformer**.

In step-up transformers, primary is low-voltage (*l.v.*) winding but secondary is high-voltage (*h.v.*) winding. As per Eq. (1.7), emf per turn in both windings is equal, therefore, in step-up transformers, primary turns N_1 are less than the secondary N_2 turns, i.e. $N_1 < N_2$.

In step-down transformers, primary is *h.v.* winding whereas secondary is *l.v.* winding. In other words, in step-down transformers, primary N_1 turns are more than the secondary N_2 turns, i.e., $N_1 > N_2$.

The same transformer can be used as a step-down or step-up transformer depending upon its use in the circuit. For example, consider a single-phase 2200 V / 230 V transformer. If *l.v.* winding of 230 V is connected to ac voltage source, this transformer becomes a step-up transformer. In case *h.v.* 2200 V winding is connected to ac voltage source, this transformer becomes a step-down transformer.

In some transformers, primary turns N_1 = secondary turns N_2; in other words, in this transformer, output voltage = input or source voltage. Such transformers are called **isolating transformers**. These are used for isolating two electric circuits and their use in power systems is very rare.

1.3.2. Transformer Applications

A transformer is the most widely used device in both low and high current circuits. As such, transformers are built in an amazing range of sizes. In addition, transformer has no moving parts, it has, therefore, the highest possible efficiency (95 to 99%) out of all the electrical machines and requires almost negligible amount of maintenance and supervision.

In low-power and low-current circuits, transformers are widely used as under:

1. For maximum power transfer to load, transformer helps in matching the load impedance to the source impedance.
2. For isolating one circuit from another, sometimes one line of transformer primary is grounded whereas the secondary circuit is isolated from the ground.
3. Isolation transformer eliminates dc from waveform containing both dc and ac components on the input side but the output contains only ac component.

For high-power and high-current circuits, transformers play a significant role as follows:

1. It permits the electric generator to generate at the most economical voltage, at about 22 kV or so.
2. Transformers are used to transfer this energy at the most economical transmission voltages, 400 kV or 750 kV. This results in reduction of the transmission losses and increases the power transfer capacity of the transmission lines.
3. Transformers are used to step down the high transmission voltage in many stages to safe values of 400/230 V for use in domestic, commercial and industrial applications.

1.3.3. Energy Conversion

An electromechanical energy conversion device is one which converts energy from electrical to mechanical or from mechanical to electrical. The coupling between the electrical and mechanical systems is through the magnetic field. In a transformer also, the coupling between the primary and secondary windings is by means of the coupling magnetic field. In both electromechanical energy conversion devices and transformers, the coupling magnetic field behaves in a similar manner. Thus, the fundamental principles involved in the analysis of a transformer are much more common in the analysis of electromechanical energy conversion devices.

The transformer is a static piece of electrical machinery and concepts about its behaviour can be understood in a comparatively simpler manner. In view of the above, the analysis of transformer must serve as a prelude to the study of electromechanical energy conversion devices. At the same time, a transformer is one of the most important and useful energy conversion device ever invented and, therefore, a detailed study of its behaviour is justified.

1.4. TYPES AND CONSTRUCTION OF SINGLE-PHASE TRANSFORMERS

There are two general types of transformers, the core-type and shell-type. These two types differ from each other by the manner in which the windings are wound around their magnetic core.

The magnetic core is a stack of thin silicon-steel laminations about 0.35 mm thick for 50 Hz (or 60 Hz) transformers. In order to reduce the eddy-current losses, these laminations are insulated from one another by thin layers of varnish. For reducing the core losses, nearly all transformers have their magnetic core made from cold-rolled-grain-oriented (C.R.G.O.) sheet steel. This material, when magnetized in the rolling direction, has low core-loss and high permeability.

Construction of the two types of single-phase transformers is now described.

1.4.1. Core-type Transformers

Fig.1.3*(a)* shows the constructional details of a single-phase core-type transformer. It consists of two vertical **limbs** or **legs** and two horizontal sections, called **yokes**. Both low voltage and high voltage windings are divided into two equal halves. Half of the low voltage (*l.v.*) winding is placed over one leg and its other half over the second leg. For the high voltage (*h.v.*) winding also, half of the winding is put on one leg and its other half over the second leg as shown in Fig.1.3*(a)*. Placing of half of each winding over each leg ensures better magnetic coupling between primary and secondary windings; this further leads to low leakage flux. L.V. winding is placed adjacent to the steel core and *h.v.* winding outside, in order to minimize the amount of insulation required.

Both *l.v.* and *h.v.* windings have the same centre. These windings are, therefore, called **concentric** or **cylindrical windings**. In core-type transformers, the magnetic flux ϕ has single path around the legs and yokes as shown by dotted line in Fig.1.3*(a)*. In this type, the windings surround a considerable part of steel core as depicted in Fig.1.3*(a)*.

1.4.2. Shell-type Transformers

Fig.1.3*(b)* shows the constructional details of a single-phase shell-type transformer. It consists of one central limb and two outer limbs. Both low-voltage and high-voltage windings are wound on the central limb. Also, both *l.v.* and *h.v.* windings are subdivided into sections. The *l.v.* and *h.v.* subsections or coils are put on the central limb alternately to form sandwich winding. Note that bottom and top *l.v.* coils are of half the size of other *l.v.* coils. Winding on the central limb is called **sandwiched** or **interleaved winding**.

In shell-type transformer, flux ϕ in the central limb divides equally and returns through the outer two legs as shows in Fig.1.3*(b)*. In this type, core surrounds the windings whereas in core-type, windings surround the core.

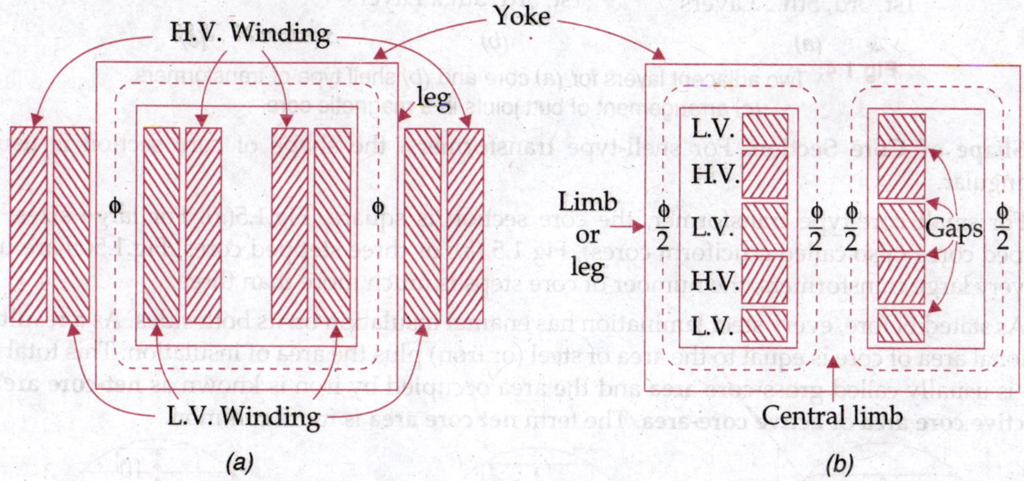

Fig 1.3: Constructional details of single-phase *(a)* core-type transformer and *(b)* shell-type transformer

Shape of Laminations. In single-phase core-type transformer, the shape of laminations may be *L*-type or *U* and *I* type. In Fig.1.4*(a)*, only *L*-type laminations in first, third, ... and second, fourth, ... layers are shown.

For single-phase shell type transformer, the shape of laminations may be of *E* and *I* shape or *U* and *T* shape. In Fig.1.4*(b)*, only *E* and *I* type laminations in first, third, ... and second, fourth, ... layers are shown.

The steel core is assembled in such a manner that the butt joints in adjacent layers are staggered as illustrated in Fig.1.4*(c)*. The staggering of the butt joints avoids continuous air gap and, therefore, the reluctance of the magnetic circuit is not increased. At the same time continuous air gap would reduce the mechanical strength of the core and, therefore, the staggering of butt joints is essential.

During the transformer construction, first the primary and secondary windings are wound. Then the laminations are pushed through the coil openings, layer by layer and the steel core is prepared. The laminations are then tightened by means of clamps and bolts.

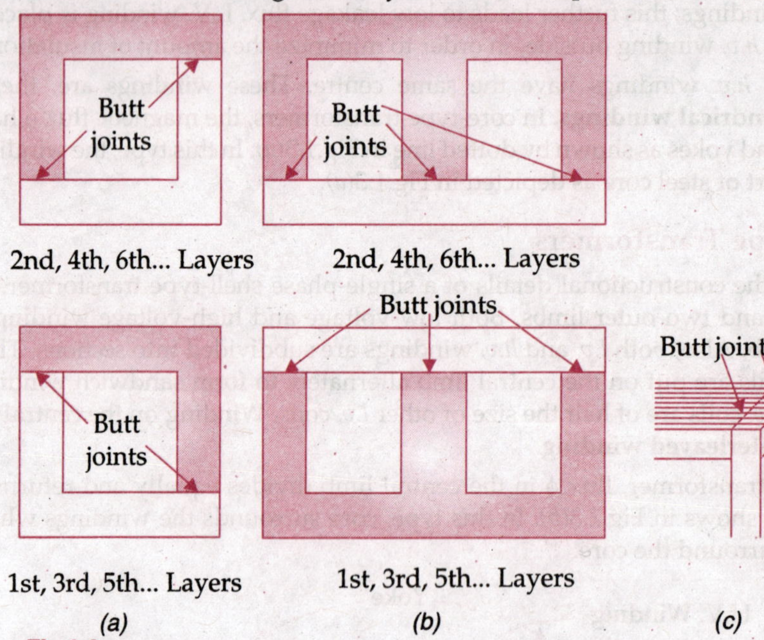

Fig 1.4: Two adjacent layers for *(a)* core and *(b)* shell type of transformers *(c)* arrangement of butt joints in a magnetic core

Shape of Core Section. For shell-type transformers, the shape of core section is usually rectangular.

For small core-type transformer, the core section is square, Fig.1.5*(a)*. For large sizes, two stepped cores (also called cruciform cores), Fig 1.5 *(b)*; or three stepped cores, Fig.1.5*(c)* are used. For very large transformers, the number of core steps is much more than three.

As stated before, every steel lamination has enamel insulation on its both sides. As a result, the sectional area of core is equal to the area of steel (or iron) plus the area of insulation. This total core area is usually called **gross-core area** and the area occupied by iron is known as **net-core area** A_i, **effective core area** or **active core-area**. The term **net core area** is more common.

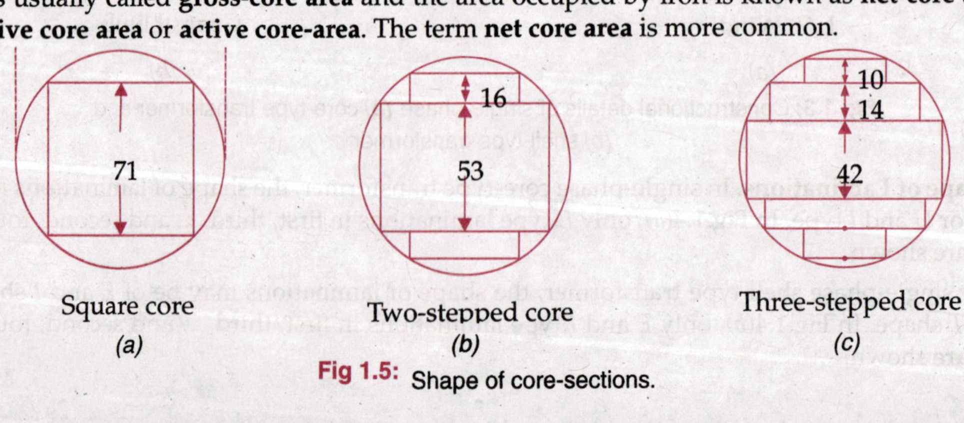

Fig 1.5: Shape of core-sections.

The ratio $\frac{\text{net core area}}{\text{gross core area}}$ is called **iron-factor** or **stacking factor**.

Its value is usually taken equal to 0.9.

Low-power transformers are air-cooled whereas large power transformers are immersed in oil for better cooling. In oil-cooled transformers, the oil serves *(i)* as a coolant and also *(ii)* as an insulating medium.

For power frequency range of 25 to 400 Hz, transformers are constructed with 0.35 mm thick silicon-steel laminations. For audio-frequency range of 20 to 20,000 Hz, iron core with suitable refinements is used. For high frequencies employed in communication circuits, core is made up of powdered ferromagnetic alloys, called ferrites. In special cases, the magnetic circuit of a transformer may be made of non-magnetic material and in such a case, the transformer is referred as an air-core transformer. The air-core transformer is primarily used in radio devices and in certain types of measuring and testing instruments.

1.4.3. Comparison between Core and Shell type Transformers.

1. In core type, the windings are wound around two legs of the magnetic core. In shell type, the windings are wound around central limb of a three-legged magnetic core.
2. For given rating, core-type transformer requires less iron but more conductor material as compared to shell-type transformer.
3. Core-type transformer has two-legged core whereas shell-type has three-legged core.
4. Core-type construction is used for high-voltage, high-current power transformers whereas shell-type transformers are preferred for low-voltage, low-power level transformers.
5. Core-type transformer uses concentric coils whereas shell-type transformer uses sandwiched coils.

1.5. IDEAL TWO-WINDING TRANSFORMER

In the beginning, a transformer is assumed to be an ideal one, merely for obtaining an easier explanation of what happens in a transformer. For a transformer to be an ideal one, the following assumptions are made:

1. Winding resistances are negligible.
2. All the flux set up by the primary winding links the secondary winding, *i.e.*, all the flux is confined to the magnetic core.
3. The core losses (hysteresis and eddy-current losses) are negligible.
4. The core has very high permeability so that a negligible mmf is required to establish the core flux.

At a later stage, the effect of these assumptions will be taken up one by one.

It has been stated before that the words 'primary' and ' secondary' should not be associated with the two windings of a transformer. It is because a transformer has one *l.v.* winding and the other *h.v.* winding. However, it has been found convenient to use these terms during the transformer analysis. But it should be kept in mind that these are arbitrary terms as explained before. Henceforth, subscripts 1 and 2 would be associated respectively with the primary and secondary windings of a transformer.

1.5.1. Ideal Transformer on No Load

Transformer at no load means load, or secondary current I_2, is zero.

When alternating voltage V_1 is applied to primary of a transformer, a magnetizing current I_m begins to flow in the primary winding, Fig 1.1 *(a)*. As per assumption (4), the magnitude of I_m is vanishingly small because negligible mmf is to be established. The function of current I_m is to set up magnetic flux ϕ linking both the windings, *i.e.*, its function is to magnetize the magnetic core, that is why it is called **magnetizing current**. Current I_m lags V_1 by 90°. Flux ϕ induces emfs E_1 and E_2 in the primary and secondary windings respectively.

As per Eqs. (1.1), (1.2) and (1.4), both emfs e_1 and e_2 lag flux by 90°, Fig.1.2*(b)*.

Induced emf E_1 and applied voltage V_1 are equal and opposite, *i.e.*, $V_1 = -E_1$.

Flux ϕ, I_m, E_1, V_1 and E_2 are shown in the phasor diagram of Fig.1.2*(a)*.

Here it is assumed that $N_1 = N_2$ and therefore $E_1 = E_2$.

For an ideal transformer, $E_2 = V_2$. Fig.1.2*(a)* shows phasor diagram of an ideal transformer at no load with phasor I_m infinitesimally small.

1.5.2. Ideal Transformer on Load

In Fig.1.6*(a)*, if the switch SW is closed, load impedance Z_L gets connected across the secondary terminals *m*, *n*. Since the secondary winding resistance is zero, $V_2 = E_2$. According to Lenz's law, the direction of secondary winding current I_2 should be such that the secondary mmf F_2 $(= I_2 N_2)$ is opposite to mutual flux in the core. For F_2 to be directed against ϕ, the current I_2 must leave the terminal *n*, pass through the load and enter the terminal *m*, Fig.1.6*(a)*. The secondary winding behaves like a voltage source, therefore, terminal *n* must be treated as positive and terminal *m* as negative. This means that when terminal b is positive with respect to terminal c in Fig.1.6*(a)*, terminal *n* is positive with respect to m at the same time. This forms the basis for polarity markings in transformers, Art 1.14. If secondary winding is wound in a manner opposite to that shown in Fig.1.6*(a)*, then terminal *m* would be positive with respect to terminal *n*. This implies that polarity markings of the windings in transformers depend upon the manner in which the windings are wound around the legs with respect to each other.

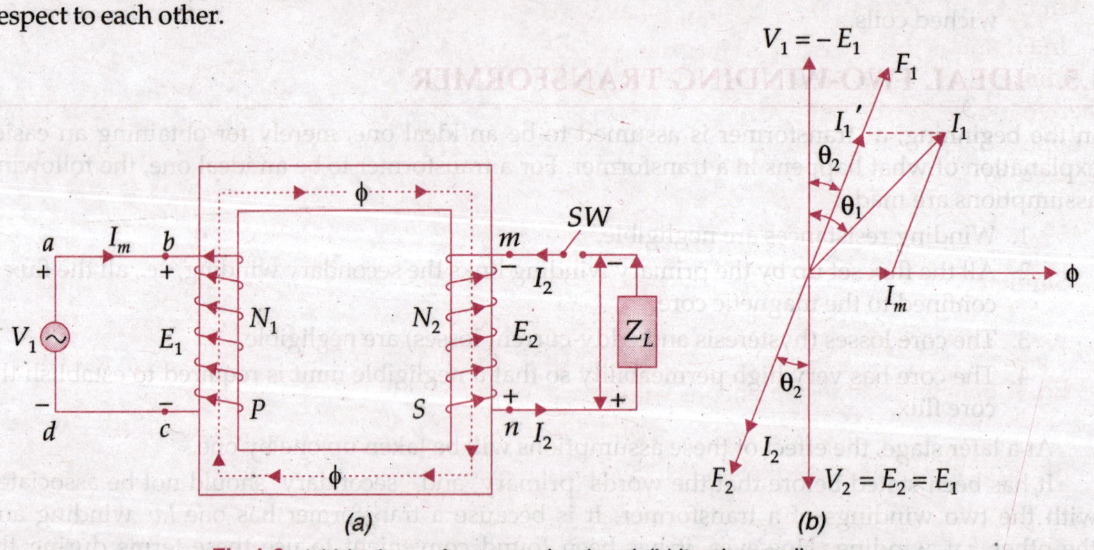

Fig 1.6: *(a)* Ideal transformer on load and *(b)* its phasor diagram.

In Fig.1.6*(a)*, the secondary mmf F_2, being opposite to ϕ, tends to reduce the alternating mutual flux ϕ. Any reduction in ϕ would reduce E_1. For an ideal transformer, $V_1 = -E_1$. If the applied voltage V_1 is constant, E_1 and therefore, mutual flux ϕ in the core must remain constant, as per Eq. (1.3). This can happen only if the primary draws more current I_1' from the source, in order to neutralize the demagnetizing effect of F_2. In this manner, I_2 causes the primary to take more current I_1' from source, in addition to negligible I_m such that

$$I_1' N_1 = I_2 N_2 \qquad \text{...(1.8)}$$

or compensating primary mmf, F_1 = secondary mmf, F_2

Any change in the secondary current is at once reflected by a corresponding change in the primary current so that core flux remains unaltered.

In the above expression, I_1' is called the **load component** of primary current I_1. It is thus seen that core flux in an ideal transformer remains constant and is independent of the load current.

Assuming current I_2 to lag behind V_2 by an angle θ_2, the phasor diagram under load for an ideal transformer can be drawn as shown in Fig.1.6(*b*). Since mmf F_1 and F_2 tend to magnetize the core in opposite directions, these are shown in phase opposition in Fig.1.6(*b*).

The total primary current I_1 is the phasor sum of I_1' and I_m, *i.e.*,

$$I_1 = I_1' + I_m$$

The power factor on the primary side of the ideal transformer is $\cos\theta_1$.

As the magnetizing current I_m is negligibly small, we can put $I_m = 0$ in Eq.(1.8). As a result, we get

$$I_1 N_1 = I_2 N_2 \qquad \text{...(1.9)}$$

i.e., Primary ampere turns = Secondary ampere turns

Thus, for an ideal transformer, with $I_m = 0$, we have

$$\frac{V_1}{V_2} = \frac{E_1}{E_2} = \frac{N_1}{N_2} = \frac{I_2}{I_1} \qquad \text{...(1.10)}$$

and $$E_1 I_1 = E_2 I_2$$

or $$V_1 I_1 = V_2 I_2 \qquad \text{...(1.11)}$$

i.e., Primary voltamperes = Secondary voltamperes

In Eqs. (1.10) and (1.11); V_1, V_2, I_1, I_2 have rms values.

In Fig.1.6(*a*), the current I_m in the primary is assumed to flow along the path *a b c d a*. The emf e_1 induced in N_1 turns must be in such a direction as to oppose the cause *i.e.* I_m as per Lenz's law. Therefore, the direction of emf e_1 is as shown by the arrows in the primary N_1 turns and it is seen to oppose v_1. Since the primary winding resistance is zero, e_1 at every instant, must be equal and opposite to v_1,

i.e., $$v_1 = -e_1 = N_1 \frac{d\phi}{dt} \qquad \text{...(1.12)}$$

Similarly $$v_2 = N_2 \frac{d\phi}{dt}$$

$\therefore$ $$\frac{v_1}{N_1} = \frac{v_2}{N_2} = \frac{d\phi}{dt} \qquad \text{...(1.13a)}$$

Eq. (1.9) in terms of instantaneous values is

$$i_1 N_1 = i_2 N_2 \qquad \text{...(1.13b)}$$

Multiplication of Eqs. (1.13*a*) and (1.13*b*) gives

$$v_1 i_1 = v_2 i_2 \qquad \text{...(1.14)}$$

This means that instantaneous power input into primary equals the instantaneous power output from the secondary. This relation is a consequence of the assumptions (1)–(3) made for an ideal transformer.

Distinction between $v_1 = -e_1$ and $v_1 = e_1$. If Kirchhoff's voltage law is applied to the primary winding circuit *a b c d a* of Fig.1.6(*a*), then terminal *b* must be positive with respect to terminal *c*. It is because current I_m can flow from a higher potential to a lower potential only.

$\therefore$ For the circuit *a b c d a*, the K.V.L. gives

$$v_1 - e_1 = 0 \text{ or } v_1 = e_1$$

From Eq. (1.12), $$v_1 = N_1 \frac{d\phi}{dt}, \quad \therefore e_1 = N_1 \frac{d\phi}{dt} \qquad ...(1.15)$$

Here the emf e_1 is treated as a **voltage drop** in the direction of current I_m and its instantaneous value is given by Eq. (1.15).

In Fig.1.6*(a)*, current I_m flows from *b* to *c*, through the primary winding. If I_m and therefore, flux ϕ is increasing, then e.m.f. e_1 induced in the primary should be in such a direction that if e_1 acted alone, it would establish a current opposite to I_m as per Lenz's law. Accordingly, the direction of e_1 is indicated by arrows in the primary winding, terminal *b* is again positive with respect to terminal *c* and e_1 is seen to be acting opposite to v_1. This physical fact, e_1 opposing v_1, is written in mathematical form as

$$v_1 = -e_1 = N_1 \frac{d\phi}{dt}$$

where e_1 is treated as a reaction e.m.f., counter e.m.f. or generated e.m.f.

The approach which led to the relation $e_1 = N_1 \frac{d\phi}{dt}$ is usually referred to as the circuit view point. The second approach which gave the relation $e_1 = -N_1 \frac{d\phi}{dt}$ is referred to as the field or flux view-point. Any of the two view-points may be followed. Since the field view-point gives better physical concepts of the internal behaviour of a transformer, it is adopted in this book.

Example 1.1. *The emf per turn for a single-phase, 2310/220 N, 50 Hz transformer is approximately 13 volts. Calculate (a) the number of primary and secondary turns and (b) the net cross-sectional area of the core, for a maximum flux density of 1.4T.*

Solution. Emf per turn, $E_t = 13$ volts

(a) Number of secondary turns, $N_2 = \dfrac{\text{Secondary voltage, } V_2}{E_t} = \dfrac{220}{13} = 16.92$

Now the number of turns cannot be a fraction, therefore, $N_2 = 17$ (nearest whole number).

For $N_2 = 17$, number of primary turns, $N_1 = N_2 \left(\dfrac{V_1}{V_2}\right) = 17\left[\dfrac{2310}{220}\right] = 178.5$

This shows that N_2 cannot be equal to 17 turns. The other nearest integers are 16 or 18. It is preferable to take $N_2 = 18$.

$$\therefore \qquad N_1 = 18\left[\frac{2310}{220}\right] = 18 \times 10.5 = 189 \text{ turns.}$$

Thus the required values of N_1 and N_2 are 189 and 18 turns respectively.

(b) New value of emf per turn, $E_t = \dfrac{220}{18}$ volts

The net core area can be obtained from the relation

$$\sqrt{2}\pi f \phi_{max} = E_t$$

$$\sqrt{2}\pi f B_m A_i = E_t = \frac{220}{18}$$

Here $\underline{B_m}$ = maximum value of core flux density in Wb/m² or Teslas and A_i = net core area.

$$\therefore \qquad \sqrt{2}\pi (50)(1.4 A_i) = \frac{220}{18} \qquad \therefore A_i = 393 \text{ cm}^2$$

It may be seen that if N_2 is taken equal to 16, the emf per turn increases and net core area is more. As a consequence, more iron for core and more conductor material are required; this all is not desirable.

Example 1.2. *A single-phase 50 Hz transformer has three windings : a 220-V primary, a 600-V secondary and a centre-tapped 11-0-11 V tertiary. For a net core area of 75 cm², calculate the number of turns in the three windings. The maximum value of flux density is 1.2T.*

Solution. Emf per turn = $\sqrt{2}\pi f.B_m.A_i = \sqrt{2}\pi(50)(1.2)(75)\times 10^{-4} = 2.00$ volts.

$\therefore$ Number of turns in each half of the tertiary winding, $N_3 = \frac{11}{2} = 5.5$ turns.

So take $N_3 = 6$ turns. New value of emf per turn = $\frac{11}{6}$ V = E_t

Total number of turns in tertiary = 2 × 6 = 12.

Turns in the 600 V secondary winding, $N_2 = \frac{V_2}{E_t} = 600 \times \frac{6}{11} = 327$

and turns in the 220 V primary winding, $N_1 = \frac{V_1}{E_1} = \frac{220 \times 6}{11} = 120.$

Example 1.3. *A transformer is designed to have hot-rolled steel laminations, with a flux density of 1.2T and the weight of core and conductor is found to be 100 kg and 80 kg respectively. If the transformer is redesigned with cold-rolled grain oriented (CRGO) steel laminations, which permit a higher flux density of 1.6T; find the saving in core and conductor materials. The two types of core materials have the same densities and the total flux remains the same. Make suitable assumptions wherever required.*

Solution. **With hot-rolled steel lamination :**

$$\text{Total flux, } \phi_{max} = \text{Flux density } B_{m1} \times \text{Area } A_1$$

or
$$\phi_{max} = 1.2\,A_1,\ \text{or } A_1 = \frac{\phi_{max}}{1.2} m^2$$

The diameter of the circle around the core is given by (assuming circular core),

$$\frac{\pi}{4}d_1^2 = A_1 = \frac{\phi_{max}}{1.2} \quad \text{or } d_1 = \sqrt{\frac{4}{\pi}\cdot\frac{\phi_{max}}{1.2}}$$

Length of one turn around the core is

$$L_1 = \pi\, d_1 = \pi\,.\sqrt{\frac{4}{\pi}\cdot\frac{\phi_{max}}{1.2}}$$

With CRGO laminations : $\phi_{max} = 1.6\,A_2$ or $A_2 = \frac{\phi_{max}}{1.6} m^2$

Diameter of the circle around the core is

$$d_2 = \sqrt{\frac{4}{\pi}\cdot\frac{\phi_{max}}{1.6}}$$

Length of one turn around the core is

$$L_2 = \pi\, d_2 = \pi\,.\sqrt{\frac{4}{\pi}\cdot\frac{\phi_{max}}{1.6}}$$

Now for laminations,

$$\frac{\text{Weight of CRGO laminations } (W_2)}{\text{Weight of h.r. laminations } (W_1)} = \frac{(\text{Core volume})_2\,(\text{Density})}{(\text{Core volume})_1\,(\text{Density})}$$

or
$$\frac{W_2}{W_1} = \frac{(A_2)\,(\text{Height of the limb})}{(A_1)\,(\text{Height of the limb})} = \frac{\phi_{max}/1.6}{\phi_{max}/1.2} = \frac{1.2}{1.6} = \frac{3}{4}$$

Assuming same height of the limbs in both types,

$$W_2 = \frac{3}{4}(W_1) = \frac{3}{4}(100) = 75 \text{ kg}$$

$$\therefore \quad \text{Percentage saving in core material} = \frac{100-75}{100} \times 100 = 25\%$$

Now for conductor material,

$$\frac{\text{Weight of conductor when using CRGO laminations } (w_2)}{\text{Weight of conductor when using h.r. laminations } (w_1)} = \frac{(L_2)\text{ (Conductor cross-section) (Turns)}}{(L_1)\text{ (Conductor cross-section) (Turns)}}$$

$$= \frac{\pi.\sqrt{\frac{4}{\pi}.\phi_{max}/1.6}}{\pi.\sqrt{\frac{4}{\pi}.\phi_{max}/1.2}} = \frac{\sqrt{3}}{2} = 0.866$$

$\therefore \qquad w_2 = 80 \times 0.866 = 69.28$ kg.

Percentage saving in conductor material $= \frac{80 - 69.28}{80} \times 100 = 13.4\%$

Conductor cross-section and the number of turns are assumed equal in both the cases.

Example 1.4. *A single phase transformer is designed to operate at 240/120 V, 50 Hz. Calculate the secondary no load voltage and its frequency if the h.v. side of the transformer is connected to :*

(a) 240 V, 40 Hz; (b) 120 V, 25 Hz; (c) 120 V, 50 Hz; (d) 480 V, 50 Hz; (e) 240 V, dc.

Solution. Primary voltage V_1 at frequency f_1 is $V_1 = \sqrt{2}\,\pi f_1 \phi_{max1} N_1$.

Let the primary voltage at frequency f_2 be V_{11} so that $V_{11} = \sqrt{2}\,\pi f_2 \phi_{max2} N_1$.

$$\therefore \qquad \frac{V_{11}}{V_1} = \frac{f_2 \phi_{max2}}{f_1 \phi_{max1}} \qquad ...(i)$$

(a) From Eq. (i), $\qquad \frac{240}{240} = \frac{(40)(\phi_{max2})}{(50)(\phi_{max1})}$

or $\qquad \phi_{max2} = 1.25\phi_{max1}$.

Secondary no load voltage at frequency f_1 is

$$E_2 = \sqrt{2}\,\pi f_1 \phi_{max1} N_2$$

and at frequency f_2 is $E_{22} = \sqrt{2}\,\pi f_2 \phi_{max2} N_2$

$$\therefore \qquad \frac{E_{22}}{E_2} = \frac{f_2 \phi_{max2}}{f_1 \phi_{max1}} \qquad ...(ii)$$

$$E_{22} = 120 \left(\frac{40 \times 1.25\phi_{max1}}{50 \times \phi_{max1}}\right) = 120 \text{ volts at 40 Hz.}$$

This shows that the magnitude of the secondary voltage remains unaffected, in case only the supply frequency changes.

(b) From Eq. (i), $\qquad \frac{120}{240} = \frac{(25)(\phi_{max2})}{(50)(\phi_{max1})}$ or $\phi_{max2} = \phi_{max1}$

From Eq. (ii), $\qquad E_{22} = 120 \times \frac{(25)(\phi_{max1})}{(50)(\phi_{max1})} = 60$ volts at 25 Hz.

(c) From Eq. (i), $\qquad \frac{120}{240} = \frac{(50)(\phi_{max2})}{(50)(\phi_{max1})}$ or $\phi_{max2} = 0.5\,\phi_{max1}$

From Eq. (ii), $\qquad E_{22} = 120 \times \frac{50 \times 0.5\,\phi_{max1}}{(50) \times (\phi_{max1})} = 60$ V at 50 Hz

(d) From Eq. (i), $\qquad \frac{480}{240} = \frac{50 \times (\phi_{max2})}{50 \times (\phi_{max1})}$ or $\phi_{max2} = 2\,\phi_{max1}$

For the same core area, the flux density is doubled, the magnetizing current becomes quite large (refer to B-H curve) and the transformer may get damaged.

(e) The direct current is alternating current at zero frequency. In other words, there is no change of flux with time. As a result, secondary induced emf, $E_{22} = 0$. Further the counter emf E_1, which opposes the applied voltage V_1 is also zero. Therefore, the primary no load current is limited only by the primary winding resistance r_1. Since r_1 is quite small, the current $240/r_1$ will be tremendously high and transformer will definitely get burnt.

1.6. REAL TRANSFORMER

The purpose of first considering an ideal transformer *i.e.* a transformer with no core losses, no winding resistances, no magnetic leakage flux and very high permeability, is merely to highlight the most important aspects of transformer action.

Magnetization curve of a real transformer is non-linear and its effect is to introduce higher-order harmonics in the magnetizing current. Since all the quantities in a phasor diagram must be of the same frequency, these higher-order harmonics (whose frequencies are odd multiples of fundamental frequency) cannot be represented in the phasor diagram. So a linear magnetization curve for the transformer core will be assumed.

A real transformer (also called **practical or actual** transformer) differs from an ideal transformer. A real transformer has winding resistances, it has iron loss in the magnetic core. There is also magnetic leakage flux in an actual transformer. For the study of a real transformer, all these imperfections must be taken into consideration. This is done in what follows.

1.6.1. Effect of core loss

The magnetic core of a transformer goes through cyclic magnetizaton. The term cyclic magnetization means that the magnetic flux in the core is in clockwise direction during positive half cycle of I_m and in anticlockwise direction during negative half cycle of I_m. This cyclic magnetization causes the appearance of hysteresis and eddy-current loss in the transformer core. Sum of hysteresis and eddy-current loss is called **iron loss** or **core loss**. The effect of core loss can be taken into consideration by core-loss current I_c in the primary winding. But magnetizing current I_m is already flowing in the primary winding. There sum, i.e. $\bar{I}_c + \bar{I}_m$ is called the **no-load current**, or **exciting current**, I_o of a transformer, *i.e.* $\bar{I}_o = \bar{I}_c + \bar{I}_m$. It can be stated from above that function of exciting or no-load current is two fold; current I_c provides core loss in the magnetic circuit and the current I_m produces the required core flux.

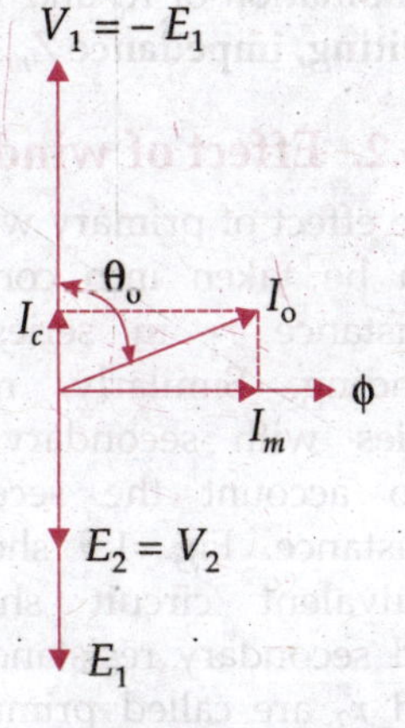

Fig 1.7: Phasor diagram of a single-phase transformer at no load

The current I_c is in phase with V_1 so that $V_1 I_c$= core loss P_c. Current I_m lags V_1 by 90°. In almost all transformers, magnitude of I_c is quite small as compared to I_m. As a result, no-load power factor angle θ_o is around 70° to 80°.

Currents I_c and I_m are shown in the phasor diagram of Fig. 1.7 of a transformer at no load. It is seen from the phasor diagram that

$$I_c = I_o \cos \theta_o$$

$$I_m = I_o \sin \theta_o$$

$$I_o = \sqrt{I_c^2 + I_m^2} \quad \text{...(1.15)}$$

No-load power factor,

$$\cos \theta_o = \frac{I_c}{I_o}$$

Core loss, $P_c = V_1 I_o \cos\theta_o = V_1 I_c$

Reactive power, $V_1 I_o \sin\theta_o = V_1 I_m$ ...(1.16)

Sometimes I_c is called active component or power-component of no-load current. Also, I_m is called reactive component or wattless component of I_o. But the terms core-loss current for I_c and magnetizing current for I_m are more common.

No-load equivalent circuit. The current I_c is in phase with V_1 in Fig. 1.7 and the product $V_1 I_c$ gives core loss. Since I_c is in phase with V_1, core loss can be taken care of by resistance R_c such that

core loss, $$P_c = I_c^2 R_c = \frac{V_1^2}{R_c} \quad ...(1.17)$$

and $$R_c = \frac{V_1}{I_c} \quad ...(1.18)$$

Since magnetizing current I_m logs V_1 by 90°, this can be represented by a reactance X_m such that

$$X_m = \frac{V_1}{I_m} \quad ...(1.19)$$

R_c and X_m are shown in Fig.1.8, in which the effect of core loss and magnetizing current are only shown. Here R_c and X_m are called **core-loss** resistance and magnetizing reactance respectively. Parallel combination of R_c and X_m is called **shunt branch**, or **exciting, impedance** Z_m.

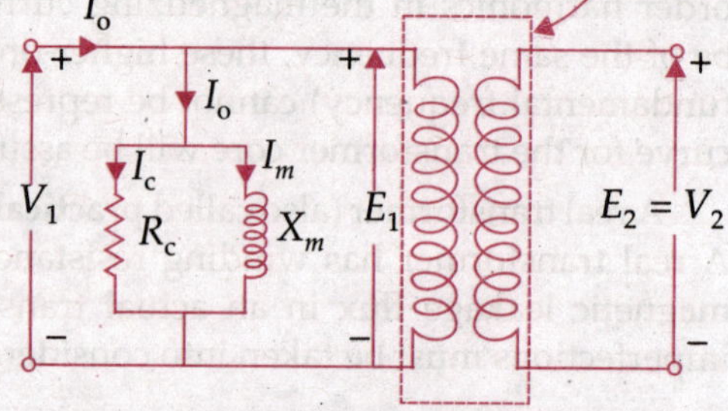

Fig 1.8: No-load equivalent circuit of a transformer showing only R_c and X_m

1.6.2. Effect of winding resistance

The effect of primary winding resistance can be taken into consideration by a resistance r_1 in series with primary winding. Similarly, resistance r_2 in series with secondary winding takes into account the secondary winding resistance. Fig. 1.9 shows transformer equivalent circuit showing primary and secondary resistances only. Here r_1 and r_2 are called primary-winding and secondary resistances respectively.

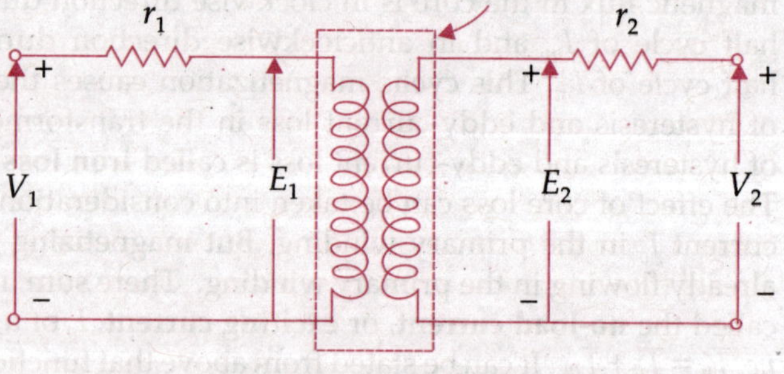

Fig 1.9: Transformer resistances shown.

1.6.3. Effect of leakage flux

The flux paths in a transformer are shown in Fig.1.10*(a)*. The mutual flux ϕ links both primary and secondary windings. There is, however, a small amount of flux that links only one winding, this is called **leakage flux**. Primary leakage flux ϕ_{l1} links only primary winding. Similarly, secondary leakage flux ϕ_{l2} links secondary winding only. These leakage fluxes are shown in Fig. 1.10*(a)*. The path of leakage flux is mainly in air (and oil). Since the reluctance offered by air is constant, the primary leakage flux (mmf/reluctance) varies linearly with primary current. Similarly, the secondary leakage flux varies linearly with secondary current.

It is seen from Fig.1.10*(a)* that there are three fluxes in an actual transformer. These are mutual flux ϕ linking both primary and secondary windings; primary leakage flux ϕ_{l1} linking only primary winding and secondary leakage flux ϕ_{l2} linking only the secondary winding. Mutual flux is created by the joint action of primary and secondary mmfs.

In Fig.1.10.*(b)*, primary winding turns N_1 and secondary winding turns N_2 are shown twice just for analysis purposes only. Turns N_1 are linked by mutual flux ϕ. Also, primary leakage flux ϕ_{l1} linking N_1 turns is depicted separately merely for convenience.

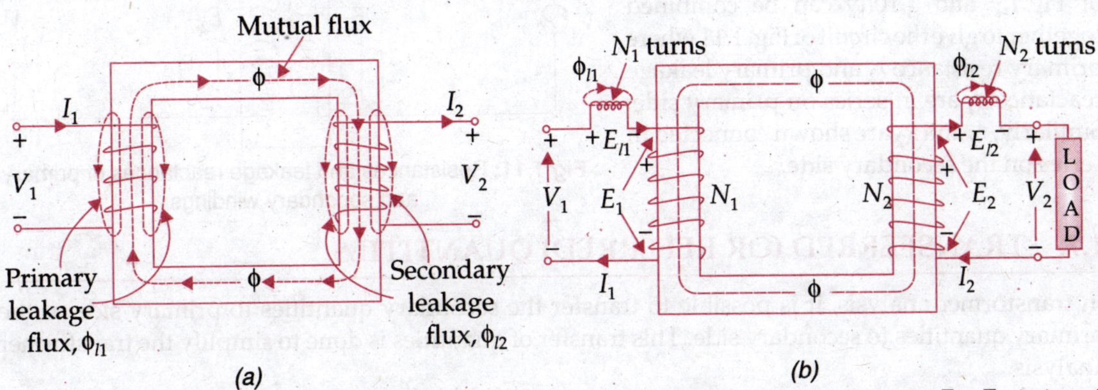

Fig 1.10: *(a)* Mutual flux and two leakage fluxes *(b)* Emfs E_1, E_2 induced by mutual flux and E_{l1}, E_{l2} induced by primary and secondary leakage fluxes

Mutual flux induces emf E_1 in primary winding and it is given by

$$E_1 = \sqrt{2}\,.\pi.\,f\,.\,N_1.\,\phi_{max} \qquad ...(1.3)$$

Similarly, primary leakage flux ϕ_{l1} linking N_1 turns must also induce an emf E_{l1} in the primary winding, just like E_1 is induced by mutual flux ϕ_{max} in N_1 turns. The voltage induced by ϕ_{l1}, Fig.1.10*(b)*, in primary N_1 turns is given by

$$E_{l1} = \sqrt{2}\,\pi f\, N_1(\sqrt{2}\,.\,\phi_{l1}) \qquad ...(1.20)$$

Here $\sqrt{2}\,\phi_{l1}$ is the maximum value of primary leakage just as ϕ_{max} appears in emf expressions E_1 and E_2. Primary leakage inductance l_1 is defined as

$$l_1 = \frac{\text{leakage flux linkages with primary winding}}{\text{primary winding current}}$$

$$\therefore \qquad l_1 = \frac{N_1.\phi_{l1}}{I_1} \quad \text{or} \quad \phi_{l1} = \frac{I_1 l_1}{N_1}$$

Substituting this value of ϕ_{l1} in Eq. (1.20), we get

$$E_{l1} = \sqrt{2}\,\pi f\, N_1\left[\frac{\sqrt{2} I_1 l_1}{N_1}\right]$$

$$= [2\pi f\, l_1]\, I_1 = x_1 I_1 \qquad ...(1.21)$$

where $x_1 = \omega.l_1$ is called **primary leakage reactance**. It is seen from above that E_{l1} is actually a voltage drop across x_1. This shows that primary leakage flux ϕ_{l1} is taken care of by primary leakage reactance x_1 in series with primary winding, Fig.1.10*(c)*.

Similarly, the effect of secondary leakage flux ϕ_{l2} can be taken into account by secondary leakage reactance x_2 connected in series with secondary winding, as shown in Fig.1.10*(c)*.

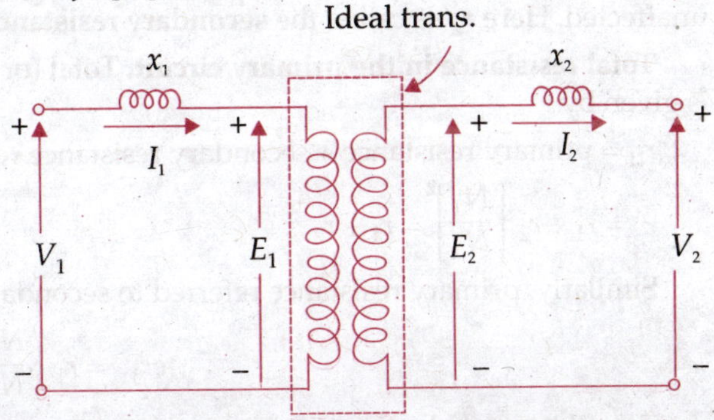

Fig 1.10: *(c)* Primary leakage repentance x_1 and secondary leakage reactance x_2.

Note that x_1 and x_2 are fictitious quantities merely introduced to represent the effect of primary and secondary leakage fluxes respectively. Electrical circuits of Fig.1.9 and 1.10*(c)* can be combined together to give the circuit of Fig. 1.11 where primary resistance r_1 and primary leakage reactance x_1 are in series on primary side. Similarly, r_2 and x_2 are shown connected in series on the secondary side.

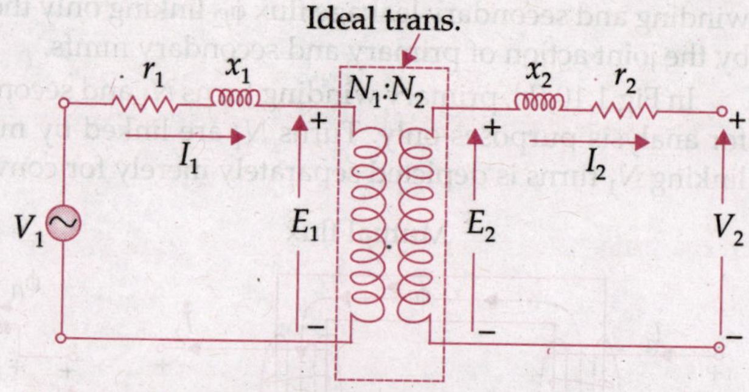

Fig 1.11: Resistances and leakage reactances of primary and secondary windings

1.7. TRANSFERRED (OR REFERRED) QUANTITIES

In transformer analysis, it is possible to transfer the secondary quantities to primary side or the primary quantities to secondary side. This transfer of quantities is done to simplify the transformer analysis.

1.7.1. Transferring Resistance

Suppose the secondary winding resistance r_2 is to be referred (or transferred) to primary side. Let r_2' be the resistance of secondary winding referred to primary winding. This referred resistance r_2' on primary side should produce the same effect as r_2 produces in the secondary circuit. Comparing the power consumed by r_2' when carrying primary current I_1' with the power consumed by r_2 when carrying secondary current I_2, we get

$$(I_1')^2\, r_2' = I_2^2 \cdot r_2$$

or

$$r_2' = \left[\frac{I_2}{I_1'}\right]^2 r_2$$

Secondary current I_2 gets reflected as I_1' in primary such that $I_1'\, N_1 = I_2\, N_2$.

$$\therefore \qquad \left[\frac{I_2}{I_1'}\right] = \frac{N_1}{N_2}$$

$$\therefore \qquad r_2' = \left[\frac{N_1}{N_2}\right]^2 . r_2 \qquad ...(1.22)$$

Note from Eq. (1.22) that when referred to **primary**, primary turns N_1 appear in the **numerator.** If resistance r_2' is placed in the primary circuit, the relation between V_1 and V_2, Fig.1.9, remains unaffected. Here r_2' is called the **secondary resistance referred to primary side.**

Total resistance in the primary circuit. Total (or equivalent) resistance on the primary side r_{l1} is given by

r_{l1} = primary resistance + secondary resistance referred to primary side

$$= r_1 + r_2 \left[\frac{N_1}{N_2}\right]^2 = r_1 + r_2' \qquad ...(1.23)$$

Similarly, primary resistance referred to secondary side is

$$r_1' = r_1 \left(\frac{N_2}{N_1}\right)^2$$

Total (or equivalent) resistance r_{l2} referred to secondary side is r_{l2} = secondary resistance + primary resistance referred to secondary side

$$\therefore \qquad r_{l2} = r_2 + r_1\left(\frac{N_2}{N_1}\right)^2 = r_2 + r_1' \qquad ...(1.24)$$

Eq. (1.24) shows that when referred to **secondary side,** secondary turns appear in the numerator.

1.7.2. Transferring Leakage Reactance

In reactance, reactive power, in general, is given by

$$Q = V\,I\sin\theta = (IZ).\,I\sin\theta = (IZ)\,(I)\left[\frac{X}{Z}\right] = I^2 X \text{ var}$$

Let x_2' be the leakage reactance of secondary winding referred to primary side. This referred leakage reactance x_2' on the primary side must produce the same effect as produced by x_2 on the secondary side. Thus, comparing the reactive volt-amperes on both sides, we get

var on primary side = var on secondary side

$$[I_1']^2 .\, x_2' = I_2^2 .\, x_2$$

$$\therefore \qquad x_2' = \left[\frac{I_2}{I_1'}\right]^2 = \left[\frac{N_1}{N_2}\right]^2 .\, x_2 \qquad ...(1.25)$$

Here x_2' is called **Secondary leakage reactance referred to primary.** Total leakage reactance on the primary side is

x_{e1} = (primary leakage reactance) + (secondary leakage reactance referred to primary)

$$= x_1 + x_2\left(\frac{N_1}{N_2}\right)^2 = x_1 + x_2' \qquad ...(1.26)$$

Similarly, primary leakage reactance referred to secondary side is

$$x_1' = x_1\left(\frac{N_2}{N_1}\right)^2$$

Total leakage reactance on the secondary side is

x_{e2} = (secondary leakage reactance) + (primary leakage reactance referred to secondary)

$$= x_2 + x_1\left(\frac{N_2}{N_1}\right)^2 = x_2 + x_1' \qquad ...(1.27)$$

From above, it can be concluded that total leakage impedance referred to primary is

$$z_{e1} = r_{e1} + j\,x_{e1}$$

Similarly, total leakage impedance referred to secondary is

$$z_{e2} = r_{e2} + j\,x_{e2}$$

Also, total leakage impedance on primary side is

$$z_{e1} = r_{e1} + j\,x_{e1} = \sqrt{r_{e1}^2 + x_{e1}^2} = z_{e2}\left(\frac{N_1}{N_2}\right)^2$$

Similarly, total leakage impedance on seconday side is

$$z_{e2} = r_{e2} + j\,x_{e2} = \sqrt{r_{e2}^2 + x_{e2}^2} = z_{e1}\left(\frac{N_2}{N_1}\right)^2$$

Example 1.5. *(a) A 2200/220 V, 50 Hz, single-phase transformer has exciting current of 0.6 A and a core loss of 361 watts, when its h.v. side is energised at rated voltage. Calculate the two components of the exciting current.*

(b) If the transformer of part (a), supplies a load current of 60 A at 0.8.p.f. lag on its l.v. side, then calculate the primary current and its power factor. Ignore leakage impedance drops.

Solution. *(a)* Exciting current $I_o = 0.6$ A

Supply voltage $V_1' = 2200$ V;

Core loss $P_c = 361$ watts.

$\therefore$ Core loss component $I_c = \dfrac{P_c}{V_1'}$

$$= \frac{361}{2200} = 0.164 \text{ A.}$$

From Eq. (1.15),

Magnetising component

$I_m = \sqrt{I_o^2 - I_c^2} = \sqrt{(0.60)^2 - (0.164)^2} = 0.577$ A.

(b) The primary current component I_1', required to neutralise the effect of secondary current $I_2 = 60$ A, is given by

$$I_1' N_1 = I_2 N_2$$

$$I_1' = \frac{220}{2200}(60) = 6 \text{ A.}$$

Note that $\dfrac{V_2}{V_1} = \dfrac{N_2}{N_1}$

The currents I_0, I_2, I_1' and I_1 are indicated in the phasor diagram of Fig.1.12.

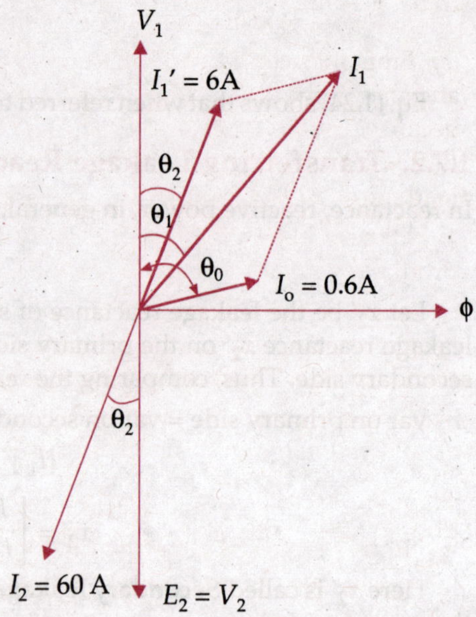

Fig 1.12: Phasor diagram for Example 1.5

The vertical component of $I_0 = I_c = 0.164$ A

The horizontal component of $I_0 = I_m = 0.577$ A.

$\therefore$ Vertical component of $I_1 = I_1 \cos\theta_1 = I_1' \cos\theta_2 + I_c$

$$= 6 \times 0.8 + 0.164 = 4.964 \text{ A.}$$

Horizontal component of $I_1 = I_1 \sin\theta_1 = I_1' \sin\theta_2 + I_m = 6 \times 0.6 + 0.577 = 4.177$ A

$\therefore$ Primary current $I_1 = \sqrt{(I_1\cos\theta_1)^2 + (I_1\sin\theta_1)^2} = \sqrt{(4.964)^2 + (4.177)^2} = 6.488$

Primary power factor $= \cos\theta_1 = \dfrac{I_1\cos\theta_1}{I_1} = \dfrac{4.964}{6.488} = 0.7651$ lagging.

Example 1.6. *An ideal transformer has three windings : 100 turns on primary winding P, 160 turns on secondary winding S and 60 turns on tertiary winding T, Fig.1.13 (a). Winding S feeds 10 A to a resistive load whereas a pure-capacitance load across winding T takes 20 A.*

(a) Calculate the current in the primary winding and its pf in case transformer magnetizing current is neglected.

(b) With the polarity markings on P as shown, mark the polarities on windings S and T also.

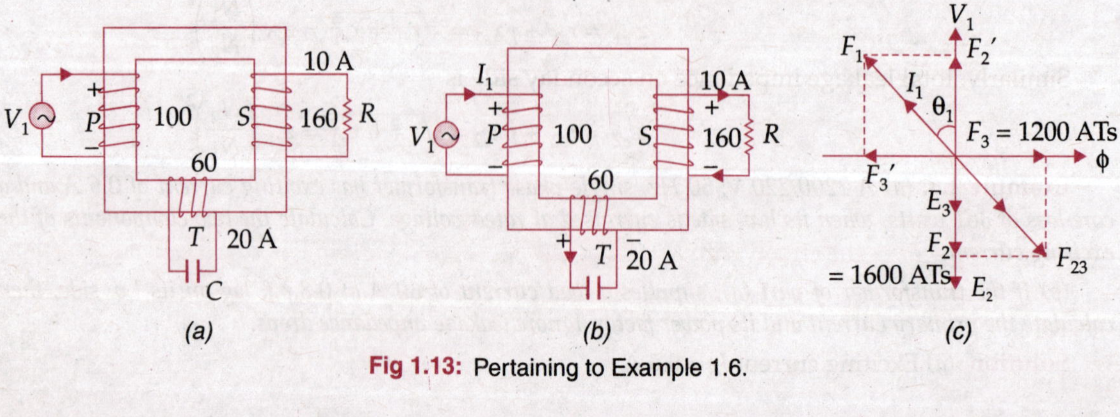

Fig 1.13: Pertaining to Example 1.6.

Solution. Applied voltage V_1 and mutual flux ϕ are shown in the phasor diagram of Fig.1.13 *(c)*. Emfs induced in windings S and T are indicated as E_2 and E_3 respectively. Current $I_2 = 10$ A and therefore secondary winding mmf $F_2 = I_2 N_2 = 10 \times 160 = 1600$ ATs is shown in phase with E_2 because load is resistive in nature. Likewise, current $I_3 = 20$ A and therefore tertiary winding mmf $F_3 = I_3 N_3 = 20 \times 60 = 1200$ ATs must lead E_3 by 90° as the load is a pure capacitance. Resultant of load mmfs F_2 and F_3 gives $F_{23} = \sqrt{1200^2 + 1600^2} = 1 = 2000$ ATs.

Principle of transformer action requires that primary winding must balance the load mmf F_{23} produced by the combined action of currents in two windings S and T.

$\therefore$ Primary winding mmf, $F_1 = F_{23} = 2000$ ATs

Current in primary winding, $I_1 = \dfrac{F_1}{N_1} = \dfrac{2000}{100} = 20$ A

Power factor on the primary side = $\cos\theta_1 = \dfrac{F_2'}{F_1} = \dfrac{1600}{2000} = 0.8$ leading.

Power factor can also be calculated as under :

Power input to primary = power delivered to load.

$V_1 . I_1 \cos\theta_1$ = power delivered to R is $\left[\dfrac{V_1}{N_1} \times N_2\right] \times 10$ + power delivered to C.

$V_1 . I_1 \cos\theta_1 = \dfrac{V_1}{100} \times 160 \times 10$ + power delivered to C is zero.

$\cos\theta_1 = \dfrac{160 \times 10}{100 \times 20} = 0.8$ leading

(b) Polarity markings and direction of currents are indicated on the secondary and tertiary windings in Fig. 1.13*(b)*.

Example 1.7. *A single-phase source, equivalent to 16 V with internal resistance of 2 k Ω, feeds a resistive load of 80 Ω through an ideal transformer. Calculate the turns ratio of the transformer so that maximum power is transferred to load.*

Under the conditions of maximum power transfer, calculate (a) load voltage across 80 Ω (b) load current on the secondary side (c) power delivered to load (d) power delivered by source and the efficiency.

Solution. Fig.1.14*(a)* shows 16 V source connection to load of 80 Ω through an ideal transformer. For transfer of maximum power to load; the load resistance, when transferred to primary side, must be equal to internal resistance of source. Therefore, for maximum power transfer,

$$\text{internal source resistance} = \left(\frac{N_1}{N_2}\right)^2 \times \text{load resistance}$$

or

$$2000 = \left(\frac{N_1}{N_2}\right)^2 \times 80$$

$$\therefore \quad \frac{N_1}{N_2} = \sqrt{\frac{2000}{80}} = 5$$

$\therefore$ The transformer turns ratio is $\dfrac{N_1}{N_2} = 5$.

Fig.1.14*(b)* gives the circuit with $R_L \left[= 80 \times \left(\dfrac{5}{1}\right)^2\right]$ referred to primary side. Here the current I_1 is

$$I_1 = \frac{16}{2000 + 2000} = \frac{16}{4000} \text{ A}$$

(a) In Fig.1.14 (b), $I_1.R = \frac{16}{4000} \times 2000 = 8$ V = load voltage on primary side. This voltage when referred to secondary side is given by

$$\frac{8V}{N_1} = \frac{V_2}{N_2} \text{ or } V_2 = 8 \times \frac{N_2}{N_1} = \frac{8}{5} = 1.6 \text{ V = load voltage across } R_L$$

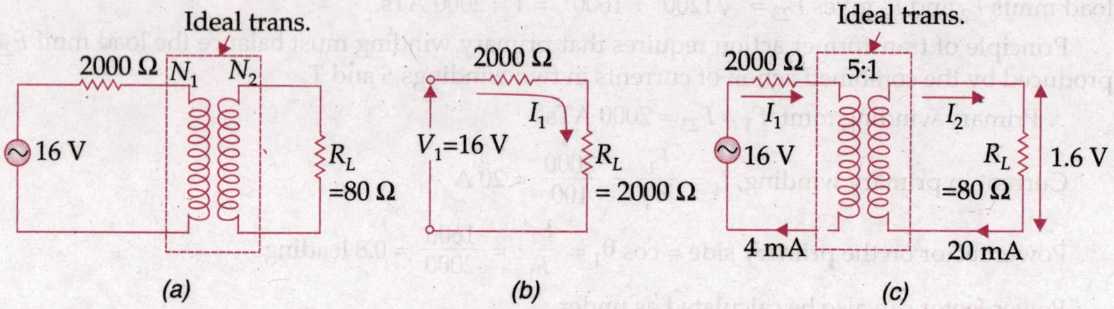

Fig 1.14: Pertaining to Example 1.7.

(b) Load current on secondary side, $I_2 = \frac{V_2}{R_L} = \frac{1.6}{80} = 0.02$ A = 20 mA.

Also, $I_1 N_1 = I_2 N_2 \therefore I_2 = I_1 \times \frac{N_1}{N_2} = \frac{16}{4000} \times 5 = 20$ mA

(c) Power delivered to load = $I_2^2 . R_L = (20 \times 10^{-3})^2 \times 80 = 32$ mW

Also, power delivered to load = $\frac{V_2^2}{R_L} = \frac{(1.6)^2}{80} = 32$ mW

(d) Power delivered by source, from Fig.1.14(b), is

$$I_1^2 [\text{source resistance} + R_L] = \left[\frac{16}{4000}\right]^2 (2000 + 2000) = 64 \text{ mW}$$

$$\therefore \text{ Efficiency} = \frac{\text{Power delivered to load}}{\text{Power delivered by source}} = \frac{32}{64} \times 100 = 50\%$$

Example 1.8. *A 2200/400 V, single-phase transformer has the following resistances and leakage reactances :*

$r_1 = 1.2\ \Omega$, $r_2 = 0.3\ \Omega$, $x_1 = 4.00\ \Omega$, $x_2 = 1.00\ \Omega$

A load of resistance 4 Ω and inductive reactance 3 Ω is connected across the secondary terminals. Calculate the load voltage, load power factor and power consumed by the load.

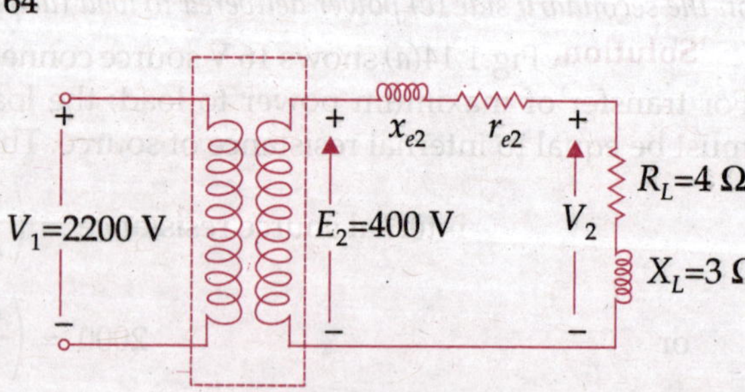

Fig 1.15: Equivalent circuit referred to secondary side, Example 1.8.

Solution. If would be better to do the calculations by referring all the parameters to secondary side. The equivalent circuit so obtained is shown in Fig.1.15, where

$$r_{e2} = r_2 + r_1 = \left(\frac{N_2}{N_1}\right)^2$$

Here $$\frac{N_1}{N_2} = \frac{E_1}{E_2} = \frac{2200}{400}$$

$$\therefore \quad r_{e2} = 0.3 + 1.2 \left[\frac{400}{2200}\right]^2$$

$$= 0.33967 \simeq 0.34\ \Omega$$

$$x_{e2} = x_2 + x_1 \left[\frac{N_2}{N_1}\right]^2$$

$$= 1.0 + 4 \left[\frac{400}{2200}\right]^2 = 1.132\ \Omega$$

$$\therefore \quad z_{e2} = r_{e2} + j\,x_{e2} = 0.34 + j\,1.132\ \Omega$$

$$Z_L = 4 + j\,3\ \Omega$$

Total impedance is secondary circuit, $Z = z_{e2} + Z_L = 4.34 + j\,4.132\ \Omega = \sqrt{4.34^2 + 4.132^2} = 5.9924\ \Omega$

$\therefore$ Load current, $I_2 = \dfrac{E_2}{Z} = \dfrac{400}{5.9924} = 66.75$ A

Load voltage, $V_2 = I_2 . Z_2 = 66.75 \times \sqrt{4^2 + 3^2} = 333.75$ V

Load power factor, $\cos\theta_2 = \dfrac{R}{Z_L} = \dfrac{4}{5} = 0.8$ lagging

Load power $= V_2 I_2 \cos\theta_2 = 333.75 \times 66.75 \times 0.8 = 17822.25$ W

Also, load power $= I_2^2 R_L = (66.75)^2 \times 4 = 17822.25$ W

1.8. RATING OF TRANSFORMERS

The manufacturer of transformers fixes a name plate on the transformer, on which are recorded the rated output, the rated voltages, the rated frequency etc. of a particular transformer. A typical name plate rating of a single phase transformer is as follows : 20 kVA, 3300/220 V, 50 Hz. Here 20 kVA is the rated output at the secondary terminals.* Note that the rated output is expressed in kilo-volt-amperes (kVAs) rather than in kilowatts (kWs). This is due to the fact that rated transformer output is limited by heating and hence by the losses in the transformer. The two types of losses in a transformer are core loss and ohmic ($I^2 r$) loss. The core loss depends on transformer voltage and ohmic loss on the transformer current. As these losses depend on transformer voltage (V) and current (I) and are almost unaffected by the load pf, the transformer rated output is expressed in VA ($V \times I$) or in kVA and not in kW. For example, a transformer working on rated voltage and rated current with load pf equal to zero has rated losses and rated kVA output but delivers zero power to load. This shows that transformer rating must be expressed in kVA.

For any transformer :

$$\left\{\begin{array}{l}\text{Rated input in kVA at}\\ \text{the primary terminals}\\ (\cos\theta_1)\end{array}\right\} = \left\{\begin{array}{l}\text{Rated output in kVA}\\ \text{at the secondary}\\ \text{terminals } (\cos\theta_2)\end{array}\right\} + \text{Losses}$$

Since the transformer operates at a very high efficiency, losses may be ignored. Further, the primary p.f. $\cos\theta_1$ and the secondary p.f. $\cos\theta_2$ are nearly equal. Therefore, the rated kVA marked on the nameplate of a transformer, refers to both the windings, *i.e.*, the rated kVA of the primary winding and the secondary winding are equal.

The voltage 3300/220 V refers to the design voltages of the two windings. Either of the two may serve as primary or secondary. If it is a step down transformer, then 3300 V is the rated primary voltage and refers to the voltage applied to the primary winding. The voltage of 220 V is the rated secondary voltage and refers to the voltage developed between output terminals at no load, with rated voltage applied to the primary terminals.

* A terminal is that part of an electrical engineering device, which is intended to receive the external connections

Rated primary and secondary currents are calculated from the rated kVA and the corresponding rated voltages. For example, for 3300/220 V, 20 kVA, single-phase transformer, we have rated (or full-load) primary current = $\frac{20,000}{3300}$ = 6.06 A and rated (or full-load) secondary current = $\frac{20,000}{220}$ = 90.91 A.

Note that the rated primary and secondary currents refer to the currents for which the windings are designed.

Rated frequency refers to the frequency for which the transformer is designed to operate.

The ratios $\frac{E_1}{E_2}$ and $\frac{N_1}{N_2}$ are called the voltage ratio and turns ratio respectively. These two ratios are equal as seen from Eq.1.6. At no load, V_1 and E_1 are nearly equal in magnitude for large transformers, therefore, their no-load voltage ratio is

$$\frac{V_1}{E_2} = \frac{N_1}{N_2}, \quad i.e., \quad \frac{\text{Rated primary voltage}}{\text{Rated secondary voltage}} = \frac{N_1}{N_2}.$$

1.9. EQUIVALENT CIRCUIT OF A TRANSFORMER

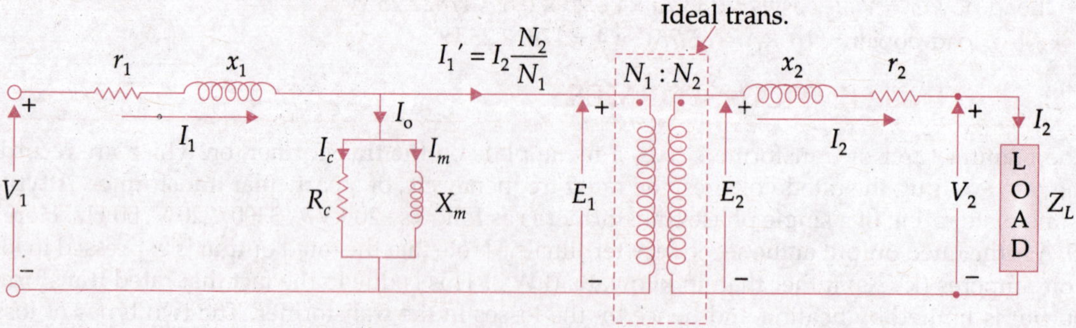

Fig 1.16: Exact equivalent circuit of a single-phase transformer

The equivalent circuit for any electrical engineering device may consist of a combination of resistances, inductances, capacitances, voltages etc. Such an equivalent circuit, or circuit model, can be analyzed by direct application of electric circuit theory. The circuit model can also be investigated further for any modifications required in the transformer.

For developing the transformer equivalent circuit, we consider first the primary winding, then the magnetic core and finally the Fig. 1.16 secondary winding.

The exact, or complete, equivalent circuit of a single-phase transformer is shown in Fig.1.16. In this circuit, the primary winding has r_1 = primary winding resistance and x_1 = primary leakage reactance. Here x_1 takes into account the primary leakage flux as explained before. Further, V_1, I_1 are applied voltage and current respectively. The primary current I_1 consists of two components, one component I_1' counteracts the secondary mmf $I_2 N_2$ such that $I_1' N_1 = I_2 N_2$ or $I_1' = I_2 \frac{N_2}{N_1}$. The other components of I_1 is no-load current I_0. The exciting current I_0 is further composed of two components, I_c and I_m *i.e.*, $\bar{I}_0 = \bar{I}_c + \bar{I}_m$. Current I_c is in phase with E_1 and E_1. I_c = core loss. Core loss P_c can be represented by resistance R_c in parallel with E_1 so that

$$\left.\begin{aligned} P_c &= I_c^2\, R_c = E_1 . I_c = \frac{E_1^2}{R_c} \\ \text{and} \quad R_c &= \frac{E_1}{I_c} \end{aligned}\right\} \quad \text{...(1.28)}$$

Here I_c is called core-loss current

Magnetizing current I_m lags E_1 by 90°, Fig.1.7. This can be represented in the equivalent circuit by an inductive reactance X_m, such that

$$X_m = \frac{E_1}{I_m} \quad ...(1.29)$$

R_c and X_m are shown in parallel in Fig.1.16. Here R_c is called magnetizing resistance or core-loss resistance and X_m the magnetizing reactance. Parallel combination of R_c and X_m is called exciting impedance Z_m. Emfs E_1 and E_2 pertain to ideal transformer. Primary applied voltage and current are V_1 and I_1 respectively and $\overline{I}_1 = \overline{I}_1' + \overline{I}_o = I_2 \frac{N_2}{N_1} + \overline{I}_o$. For primary circuit consisting of E_1, V_1, r_1 etc., KVL gives $V_1 - I_1 (r_1 + j x_1) - E_1 = 0$ or $V_1 = E_1 + I_1 (r_1 + j x_1)$.

To the equivalent circuit so developed, we now add the representation of the secondary winding. Emf E_2 is induced in N_2 turns of the ideal transformer. Just like primary leakage impedance, secondary winding leakage impedance consists of x_2 and r_2 in series as shown in Fig.1.16. Here x_2 takes into account the secondary leakage flux and r_2 is the resistance of secondary winding. Also; V_2, I_2 are the load voltage and current respectively. Z_L is the load impedance. KVL for the secondary circuit gives $E_2 = V_2 + I_2 (r_2 + j x_2)$.

1.9.1. Equivalent Circuit Referred to Primary

If the secondary quantities are transferred to primary side, an exact equivalent circuit referred to primary is obtained. Secondary parameters r_2, x_2, Z_L are $r_2 \left(\frac{N_1}{N_2}\right)^2$, $X_2 \left(\frac{N_1}{N_2}\right)^2$, $Z_L \left(\frac{N_1}{N_2}\right)^2$ on the primary side. Emf E_2 becomes $E_2 \frac{N_1}{N_2}$ and I_2 is reflected on the primary side as $I_1' = I_2 \frac{N_2}{N_1}$. Fig.1.17 shows an exact equivalent circuit with all secondary parameters referred to primary. This circuit is called **exact equivalent circuit of a transformer referred to primary**. Also $\overline{I}_1 = \overline{I}_1' + \overline{I}_0$. The exact equivalent circuit of Fig.1.17 is also known as *T*-circuit of a transformer. Similarly, *T*-circuit of transformer referred to secondary can be obtained.

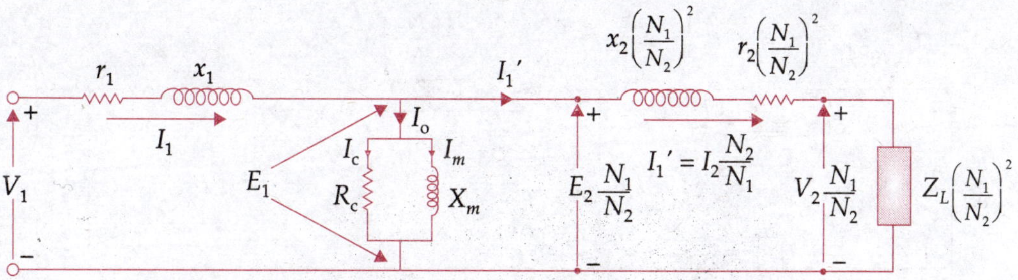

Fig 1.17: Exact equivalent circuit of a transformer referred to primary.

1.9.2. Approximate Equivalent Circuit Referred to Primary

The no-load current I_o of a transformer is about 2 to 6% of a full-load primary current. For practical purposes, the voltage drop $I_o (r_1 + j x_1)$ is quite small and can, therefore, be neglected. Thus, it does not make any material difference whether the exciting impedance $R_c \,||\, X_m$ is connected before the primary leakage impedance $(r_1 + j x_1)$ or after it. With this change, currents I_c and I_m are not greatly affected. Thus, an approximate equivalent circuit referred to primary is obtained from Fig.1.17 by shifting the shunt branch $R_c \,||\, X_m$ to the primary input terminals as shown in Fig.1.18. From this circuit of Fig.1.18; r_{e1}, x_{e1}, z_{e1} are as follows :

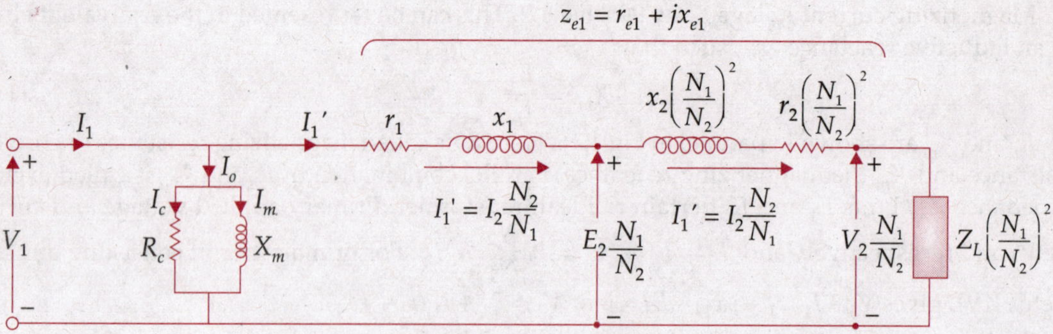

Fig 1.18: Approximate equivalent circuit of a transformer referred to primary.

$$r_{e1} = r_1 + r_2\left(\frac{N_1}{N_2}\right)^2, \; x_{e1} = x_1 + x_2\left(\frac{N_1}{N_2}\right)^2$$

Total leakage impedance on primary side, $z_{e1} = r_{e1} + jx_{e1}$

Current I_1' is given by

$$I_1' = \frac{V_1}{z_{e1} + Z_L\left(\frac{N_1}{N_2}\right)^2} \quad ...(1.30)$$

and primary current

$$\bar{I}_1 = \bar{I}_1' + \bar{I}_o. \quad ...(1.31)$$

1.9.3. Approximate Equivalent Circuit Referred to Secondary

If all the primary quantities from Fig. 1.16 are transferred to secondary side, an approximate equivalent circuit referred to secondary is obtained; this is shown in Fig.1.19.

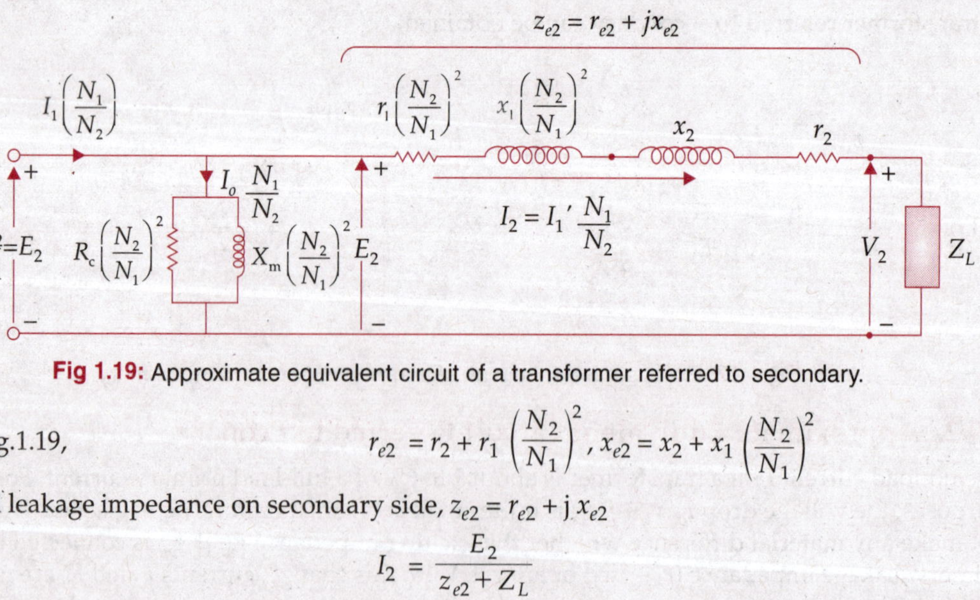

Fig 1.19: Approximate equivalent circuit of a transformer referred to secondary.

In Fig.1.19, $r_{e2} = r_2 + r_1\left(\frac{N_2}{N_1}\right)^2, \; x_{e2} = x_2 + x_1\left(\frac{N_2}{N_1}\right)^2$

Total leakage impedance on secondary side, $z_{e2} = r_{e2} + j\,x_{e2}$

$$\therefore \quad I_2 = \frac{E_2}{z_{e2} + Z_L}$$

$$V_1\frac{N_2}{N_1} = E_2 = V_2 + I_2 . z_{e2} \quad ...(1.32)$$

and

$$I_1\frac{N_1}{N_2} = I_2 + I_0\frac{N_1}{N_2} \quad ...(1.33)$$

1.9.4. Further Simplification of Approximate Equivalent Circuit

The no-load current of a transformer is about 2 to 6% of full-load current. As such, effect of no-load current on transformer operation can be neglected without causing any appreciable error. Therefore, for all practical purposes, the exciting branch $R_c \parallel X_m$ can be omitted from Fig.1.19 and this leads to simplified equivalent circuit referred to secondary side as shown in Fig.1.20*(a)*. This simplification is justifiable in large transformers, say over 100 kVA or so. For transformers having ratings near 500 kVA or more, the equivalent resistance r_{e2} is quite small as compared with equivalent leakage reactance x_{e2}. Consequently, r_{e2} may be omitted from Fig.1.20*(a)* leading to the equivalent circuit of Fig.1.20*(b)*. Thus, when a large power system is studied, a transformer is usually replaced by its equivalent circuit of the form shown in Fig.1.20*(b)*.

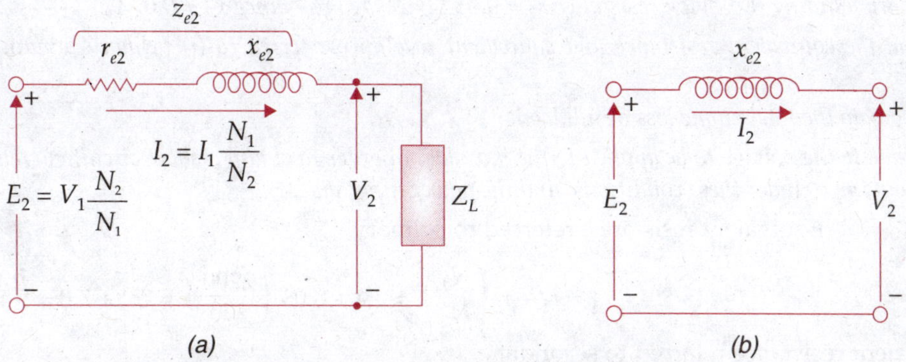

Fig 1.20: *(a)* Simplified equivalent circuit of a transformer referred to secondary *(b)* Equivalent circuit used in high kVA rated transformers.

It may be interesting at this stage to draw the phasor diagram for the equivalent circuit of Fig.1.16 from a knowledge of electric circuit theory. Assume that the secondary load voltage V_2, load current I_2 and angle θ_2 by which I_2 lags V_2, are known. First of all, draw I_2 lagging V_2 by load power-factor angle θ_2. Add $\overline{I}_2 (r_2 + j\,x_2)$ to V_2 to obtain E_2.

Now assume $N_1 = N_2$, then $E_1 = E_2$ and $I_1' = I_2$. The magnetizing current I_m must lag E_1 by 90°. Further, core-loss current I_c must be in phase with E_1. The phasor sum of I_c and I_m gives no load current I_o. Phasor sum of I_1' or I_2 and I_o gives primary current $\overline{I}_1$, as shown in Fig.1.21. The voltage drop $\overline{I}_1(r_1 + j\,x_1)$ is now added to E_1 to obtain V_1; this is shown in Fig.1.21. The secondary power factor is cos θ_2 lagging and primary power factor is cos θ_1 lagging.

The voltage drops $I_1\,(r_1 + jx_1)$ and $I_2\,(r_2 + jx_2)$ have been drawn to a much larger scale in comparison with V_1 or V_2, just for the sake of clarity.

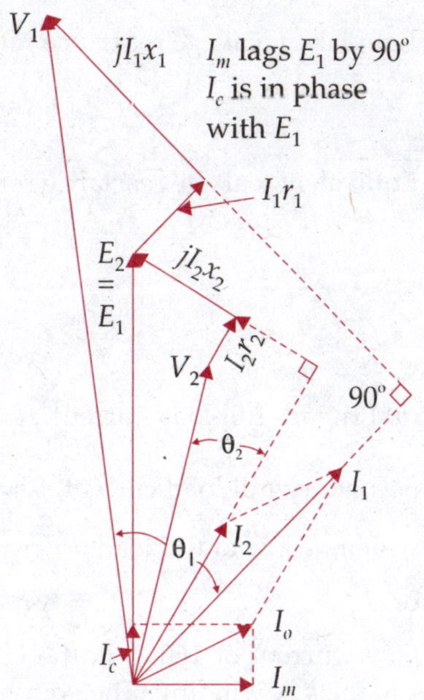

Fig 1.21: Phasor diagram for exact equivalent circuit of Fig. 1.16

Example 1.9. *For a two winding transformer, derive an expression for the total ohmic loss, in terms of the equivalent resistance, referred to either side.*

Solution. Total ohmic loss in a transformer

$$P_{oh} = (I_1^2 r_1 + I_2^2 r_2) \text{ watts}$$

Expressing I_2 in terms of I_1 gives

$$P_{oh} = I_1^2 r_1 + \left[I_1\left(\frac{N_1}{N_2}\right)\right]^2 r_2 = I_1^2\left[r_1 + r_2\left(\frac{N_1}{N_2}\right)^2\right] = I_1^2 r_{e1}$$

If P_{oh} is expressed in terms of I_2, then

$$P_{oh} = \left[I_2\left(\frac{N_2}{N_1}\right)\right]^2 r_1 + I_2^2 r_2 = I_2^2\left[\left(\frac{N_2}{N_1}\right)^2 r_1 + r_2\right] = I_2^2 r_{e2}$$

Thus the total ohmic loss in a transformer = (Equivalent resistance referred to either side) (Square of the current on that side).

Example 1.10. *A 33 kVA, 2200/220 V, 50 Hz single-phase transformer has the following parameters:*

Primary winding (h.v. side): resistance $r_1 = 2.4\ \Omega$; leakage reactance $x_1 = 6.00\ \Omega$.

Secondary winding (l.v. side): resistance $r_2 = 0.03\ \Omega$; leakage reactance $x_2 = 0.07\ \Omega$.

(a) Find the equivalent resistance and equivalent reactance referred to (i) primary winding and (ii) secondary.

(b) Calculate the total ohmic loss at full load.

(c) Calculate the voltage to be applied to the h.v. side, in order to obtain a short circuit current of 160A in the l.v. winding. Under these conditions, find the power input also.

Solution. *(a)* Equivalent resistance referred to primary,

$$r_{e1} = r_1 + r_2\left(\frac{N_1}{N_2}\right)^2 = 2.4 + 0.03\left(\frac{2200}{220}\right)^2 = 2.4 + 3.0 = 5.4\ \Omega$$

Equivalent resistance referred to secondary,

$$r_{e2} = r_2 + r_1\left(\frac{N_2}{N_1}\right)^2 = 0.03 + 2.4\left(\frac{220}{2200}\right)^2 = 0.03 + 0.024 = 0.054\ \Omega$$

Equivalent leakage reactance referred to primary,

$$x_{e1} = x_1 + x_2\left(\frac{N_1}{N_2}\right)^2 = 6 + 0.07\left(\frac{2200}{220}\right)^2 = 6 + 7 = 13\ \Omega$$

Equivalent leakage reactance referred to secondary,

$$x_{e2} = x_2 + x_1\left(\frac{N_2}{N_1}\right)^2$$

$$= 0.07 + 6\left(\frac{220}{2200}\right)^2 = 0.07 + 0.06 = 0.13\Omega$$

(b) Primary full-load current, $I_1 = \dfrac{33000}{2200} = 15$ A

Secondary full-load current, $I_2 = \dfrac{33000}{220} = 150$ A

$\therefore$ Ohmic loss at full load $= I_1^2 r_{e1} = (15)^2 \times 5.4 = 1215$ W

or $= I_2^2 r_{e2} = (150)^2 \times 0.054 = 1215$ W

(c) A current of 160 A in the *l.v.* winding is equivalent to 16 A in the *h.v.* winding. The equivalent circuit of transformer during short circuit with parameters referred to *h.v.* side is illustrated in Fig. 1.22. From this figure, equivalent leakage impedance referred to *h.v.* side is

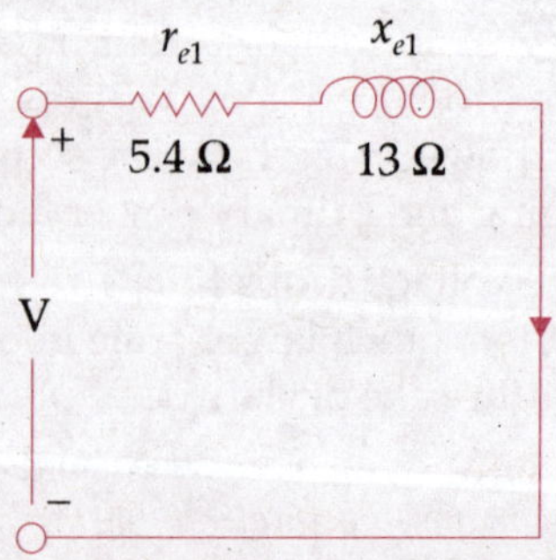

Fig 1.22: Equivalent circuit referred to h.v. side, Ex. 1.9

$$z_{e1} = 5.4 + j\,13 = \sqrt{(5.4)^2 + (13)^2} = 14.08\ \Omega$$

∴ The voltage to be applied to the *h.v.* side,

$$V = 16\, z_{e1} = 16 \times 14.08 = 225.28 \text{ volts.}$$

$$\text{Power input } = I_1^2\, r_{e1} = 16^2 \times 5.4 = 1382.4 \text{ W}$$

or

$$\text{Power input } = VI \cos\theta = (225.28)(16) \times \frac{5.4}{14.08} = 1382.4 \text{ W}$$

Example 1.11. *A 10 kVA, 2500/250 V, single phase transformer has resistances and leakage reactances as follows :*

$$r_1 = 4.8\ \Omega \qquad r_2 = 0.048\ \Omega$$

$$x_1 = 11.2\ \Omega \qquad x_2 = 0.112\ \Omega$$

Subscripts 1 and 2 denote high voltage and low voltage windings respectively.

With primary supply voltage held constant at 2500 V, calculate the secondary terminal voltage, when

(a) the l.v. winding is connected to a load impedance of $5 + j\,3.5\ \Omega$.

(b) the transformer delivers its rated current at 0.8 p.f. lagging on the l.v. side.

Solution. *(a)* All the quantities may be referred to either the *h.v.* side or the *l.v.* side. In this example, *l.v.* winding is the secondary winding since load is connected across it. With all the quantities referred to the *l.v.* side, the equivalent circuit of Fig.1.23 *(a)* is obtained, where

$$r_{e2} = r_2 + r_1 \left(\frac{N_2}{N_1}\right)^2 = 0.048 + 4.8 \left(\frac{1}{10}\right)^2 = 0.096\ \Omega.$$

and

$$x_{e2} = x_2 + x_1 \left(\frac{N_2}{N_1}\right)^2 = 0.112 + 11.2 \left(\frac{1}{10}\right)^2 = 0.224\ \Omega.$$

The transformer leakage impedance $r_{e2} + jx_{e2}$ and the load impedance are in series. Therefore, the total impedance in the secondary winding circuit is,

$$z = 5.096 + j\,3.724 = 6.31 \angle\ 36.2°.$$

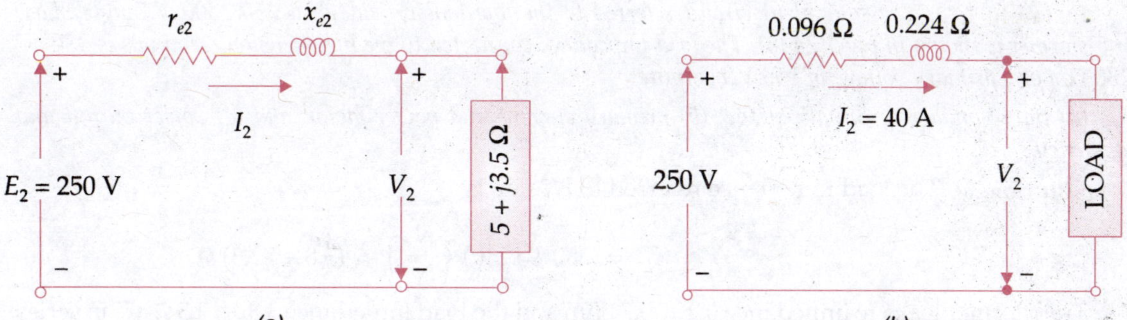

Fig 1.23: Equivalent circuit for Example 1.11.

Hence the load current,

$$I_2 = \frac{250}{6.31} = 39.65 \text{ A.}$$

The secondary terminal voltage E_2 is $V_2 = I_2 Z_L$

$$= (39.65)\left[\sqrt{(5)^2 + (3.5)^2}\right] = (39.65)\,(6.1) = 242 \text{ V.}$$

(b) The equivalent circuit with all the quantities referred to *l.v.* side is given in Fig.1.23 *(b)*. The rated current on the *l.v.* side is

$$I_2 = \frac{10{,}000}{250} = 40 \text{ A.}$$

The phasor diagram for Fig.1.23 *(b)* is illustrated in Fig. 1.23 *(c)*.

From the geometry of this diagram,

$$OB^2 = OA^2 + AB^2$$

or $$(250) = \sqrt{(V_2 \cos\theta_2 + I_2 r_{e2})^2 + (V_2 \sin\theta_2 + I_2 x_{e2})^2}$$

or $$(250) = \sqrt{(0.8V_2 + 3.84)^2 + (0.6V_2 + 8.96)^2}$$

or $$(250)^2 = V_2^2 + 16.90V_2 + 95.55$$

or $$V_2^2 + 16.90V_2 - 62{,}404 = 0$$

$$\therefore V_2 = \frac{-16.90 + \sqrt{286 + 249{,}616}}{2} = 241.55 \text{ V.}$$

Alternatively, the secondary terminal voltage V_2 can be obtained as follows :

From the phasor diagram, it may be seen that OD is approximately equal to OB = 250 volts.

$$\therefore \quad V_2 = OD - CD = 250 - CD.$$

Now $$CD = CE + ED$$

$$= I_2 r_{e2} \cos\theta_2 + I_2 x_{e2} \sin\theta_2$$

$$= (3.84)(0.8) + (8.96)(0.6)$$

$$= 8.448 \cong 8.45 \text{ volts.}$$

$\therefore$ Secondary terminal voltage,

$$V_2 = 250 - 8.45 = 241.55 \text{ V.}$$

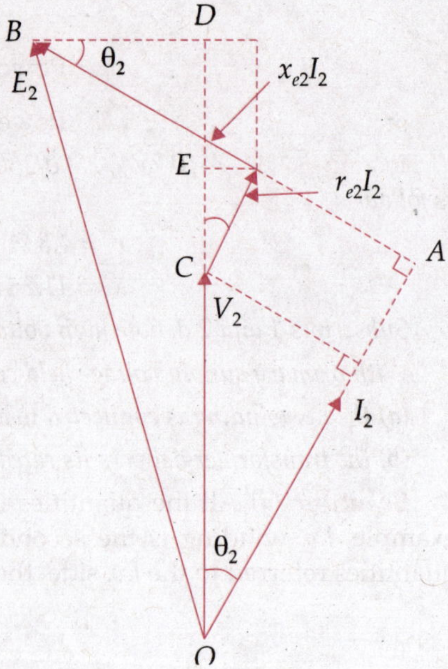

Fig 1.23: *(c)* Phasor diagram for circuit of Fig. 1.23*(b)*

The magnitude of the secondary voltage V_2 turns out to be same in both the methods. However, the computational labour in the second method is less than in the first method, therefore, the second method should be preferred.

Example 1.12. *The equivalent circuit referred to the low-tension side of a 250/2500 V single phase transformer is shown in Fig.1.24 (a). The load impedance connected to the high-tension terminals is 380 + j 230 Ω. For a primary voltage of 250 V, compute*

(a) the secondary terminal voltage, (b) primary current and power factor, and (c) power output and efficiency.

Solution. *(a)* The load impedance referred to *l.t.* side is

$$Z_L' = (380 + j\,230)\left(\frac{N_1}{N_2}\right)^2 = (3.8 + j\,2.3)\ \Omega.$$

Transformer leakage impedance 0.2 + *j*0.7 ohm and the load impedance 3.8 + *j* 2.3 Ω are in series as shown in Fig. 1.24 *(b)*. Therefore, total series impedance is $4 + j\,3 = 5\angle 36.9°$.

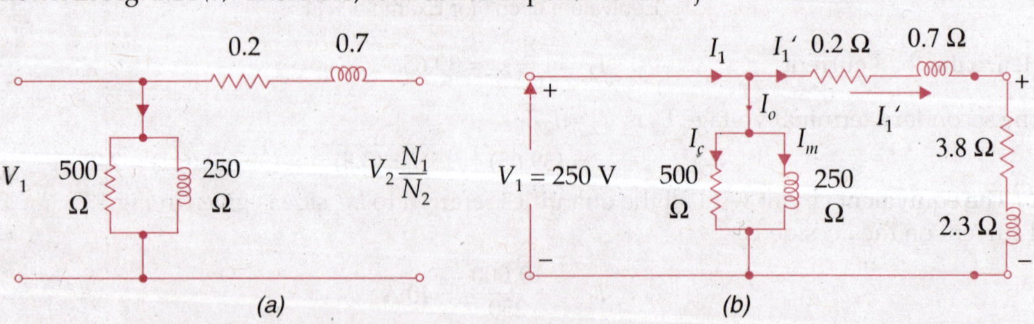

Fig 1.24: *(a)* Transformer equivalent circuit for Example 1.12. *(b)* Pertaining to Example 1.12.

Taking V_1 as the reference phasor $\overline{V}_1 = 250 \angle 0°$.

$$\because \quad \overline{I}_1' = \frac{250\angle 0°}{5\angle 3.69°} = 50 \angle -36.9°$$

$$= 50 (\cos 36.9° - j \sin 36.9°) = (40 - j\,30) \text{ A.}$$

or $\quad I_1' = 50 \text{ A and } I_2 = I_1' \frac{N_1}{N_2} = 50 \times \frac{1}{10} = 5 \text{ A}$

$\therefore \quad$ Secondary terminal voltage $= I_2 Z_L$

$$= 5\,[380^2 + 230^2]^{½} = 5 \times 444 = 2220 \text{ V}$$

(b) The core loss current $\overline{I}_c = \dfrac{\overline{V}_1}{R_c} = \dfrac{250\angle 0°}{500\angle 0°} = 0.5 \angle 0° = 0.5 + j\,0$

The magnetizing current $\overline{I}_m = \dfrac{\overline{V}_1}{jX_m} = \dfrac{250\angle 0°}{250\angle 90°} = 1\angle -90° = 0 - j\,1$

$\therefore$ Exciting current $\overline{I}_o = \overline{I}_c + \overline{I}_m = (0.5 - j1)$ A.

Hence total primary current $\overline{I}_1 = \overline{I}_1' + \overline{I}_o = (40 - j30) + (0.5 - j1) = 40.5 - j\,31 = 51 \angle -37.4°$

$\therefore$ Primary current $I_1 = 51$ A and primary p.f. $= \cos \theta_1 = \cos 37.4° = 0.794$ lagging.

(c) Load p.f. $= \cos \theta_2 = \dfrac{380}{[380^2 + 230^2]^{½}} = 0.855$ lagging.

Power output $= V_2 I_2 \cos \theta_2 = 2220 \times 5 \times 0.855 = 9500$ watts.

Also power output $= (I_1')^2 R_L = (50)^2 (3.8) = 9500$ watts.

Core loss $P_c = \dfrac{V_1^2}{R_c} = \dfrac{(250)^2}{500} = 125$ watts.

or $P_c = I_c^2 R_c = (0.5)^2 (500) = 125$ watts.

Ohmic loss $P_{oh} = (I_1')^2 r_{e1} = (50)^2 (0.2) = 500$ watts.

Power input $= V_1 I_1 \cos \theta_1 = (250)(51)(0.794) = 10{,}125$ watts.

Also power input = Power output + Losses = 9500 + 125 + 500 = 10,125 watts.

$$\therefore \text{Efficiency} = \frac{\text{Output}}{\text{Input}} = \frac{\text{Input} - \text{Losses}}{\text{Input}} = 1 - \frac{\text{Losses}}{\text{Input}} = 1 - \frac{500 + 125}{10{,}125} = 0.9383 \text{ p.u. or } 93.83\%.$$

1.10. OPEN-CIRCUIT AND SHORT-CIRCUIT TESTS

These two tests on a transformer, help to determine *(i)* the parameters of the equivalent circuit of Fig. 1.18 or 1.19, *(ii)* the voltage regulation and *(iii)* efficiency. Complete analysis of the transformer can be carried out, once its equivalent circuit parameters are known.

The power required during these two tests is equal to the appropriate power loss occurring in the transformer.

Open circuit (or No-load) test. The circuit diagram for performing open circuit test on a single phase transformer is given in Fig. 1.25 *(a)*. In this diagram, a voltmeter, wattmeter and an ammeter are shown connected on the low voltage side of the transformer. The high voltage side, is left open circuited. The rated frequency voltage applied to the primary, *i.e.*, low voltage side, is varied with the help of a variable ratio auto-transformer. When the voltmeter reading is equal to the rated voltage of the *l.v.* winding, all the three instrument readings are recorded.

The ammeter records the no-load current or exciting current I_0. Since I_0 is quite small (2 to 6% of rated current), the primary leakage impedance drop is almost negligible, and for all practical purposes, the applied voltage V_1 is equal to the induced emf E_1. Consequently, the equivalent circuit of Fig.1.17 gets modified to that shown in Fig.1.25 *(b)*.

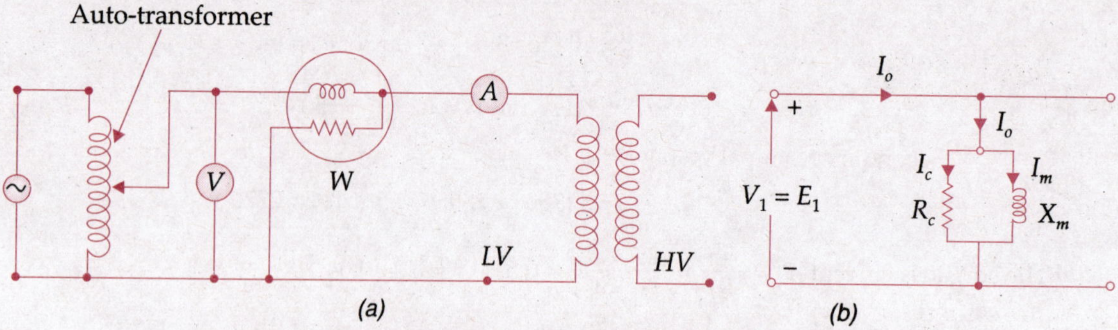

Fig 1.25: *(a)* Circuit diagram for open-circuit test on a transformer and *(b)* approximate equivalent circuit at no load.

The input power given by the wattmeter reading consists of core loss and ohmic loss. The exciting current being about 2 to 6 per cent of the full load current, the ohmic loss in the primary $(= I_0^2 r_1)$ varies from 0.04 per cent $\left(\frac{2}{100} \times \frac{2}{100} \times 100\right)$ to 0.36 per cent of the full-load primary ohmic loss. In view of this fact, the ohmic loss during open circuit test is negligible in comparison with the normal core loss (approximately proportional to the square of the applied voltage). Hence the wattmeter reading can be taken as equal to transformer core loss. A negligible amount of dielectric loss may also exist. Error in the instrument readings may be eliminated if required. Let

V_1 = applied rated voltage on *l.t.* side,

I_0 = exciting current (or no-load current),

and P_c = core loss. ...(1.34)

Then $P_c = V_1 I_0 \cos \theta_0$

$$\therefore \quad \text{No load p.f.} = \cos \theta_0 = \frac{P_c}{V_1 I_0}$$

From the phasor diagram of Fig. 1.7 *(c)*, it follows that

$$I_c = I_0 \cos \theta_0 \text{ and } I_m = I_0 \sin \theta_0$$

From Fig.1.25. *(b)*, $I_c = \frac{P_c}{V_1}$

$$\therefore \quad \text{Core loss resistance } R_{CL} = \frac{V_1}{I_c} = \frac{V_1}{I_0 \cos \theta_0}$$

$$= \frac{V_1^2}{V_1 I_0 \cos \theta_0} = \frac{V_1^2}{P_c} \qquad \text{...(1.35 a)}$$

Also $I_c^2 R_{CL} = P_C$

$$\therefore \quad R_{CL} = \frac{P_c}{I_c^2} = \frac{P_c}{(I_0 \cos \theta_0)^2} \qquad \text{...(1.35 b)}$$

Magnetizing reactance,

$$X_{mL} = \frac{V_1}{I_m} = \frac{V_1}{I_0 \sin \theta_0} \qquad \text{...(1.36)}$$

The subscript L with R_c and X_m is used merely to emphasize that these values are for the l.t. side.

This must be kept in mind that the values of R_c and X_m, in general, refer to the side, in which the instruments are placed (the *l.t.* side in the present case). A voltmeter is sometimes used at the open-circuited secondary terminals, in order to determine the turns ratio.

Thus the open-circuit test gives the following information : *(i)* core loss at rated voltage and frequency, *(ii)* core-loss current and magnetizing current, *(iii)* the shunt branch parameters of the equivalent circuit, *i.e.* R_C and X_m and *(iv)* turns ratio of the transformer.

Short-circuit test. The low voltage side of the transformer is short-circuited and the instruments are placed on the high voltage side, as illustrated in Fig.1.26 *(a)*. The applied voltage is adjusted by auto-transformer, to circulate rated current in the high voltage side. In a transformer, the primary mmf is almost equal to the secondary mmf, therefore, a rated current in the *h.v.* winding causes rated current to flow in the *l.v.* winding.

A primary voltage of 2 to 12% of its rated value is sufficient to circulate rated currents in both primary and secondary windings. From Fig. 1.26 *(b)*, it is clear that the secondary leakage impedance drop appears across the exciting branch (R_c and X_m in parallel). About half (1 to 6%) of the applied voltage appears across the secondary leakage impedance and, therefore, across the exciting branch. The core flux induces the voltage across the exciting branch and since the latter is 1 to 6% of rated voltage, the core flux is also 1 to 6% of its rated value. Hence the core loss, being approximately proportional to the square of the core flux, is 0.01 per cent $\left(= \frac{1}{100} \times \frac{1}{100} \times 100\right)$ to 0.36 per cent $\left(= \frac{6}{100} \times \frac{6}{100} \times 100\right)$ of its value at rated voltage. The wattmeter, in short circuit test, records the core loss and the ohmic loss in both the windings. Since the core loss has been proved to be almost negligible in comparison with the rated-voltage core loss, the wattmeter can be taken to register only the ohmic losses in both the windings.

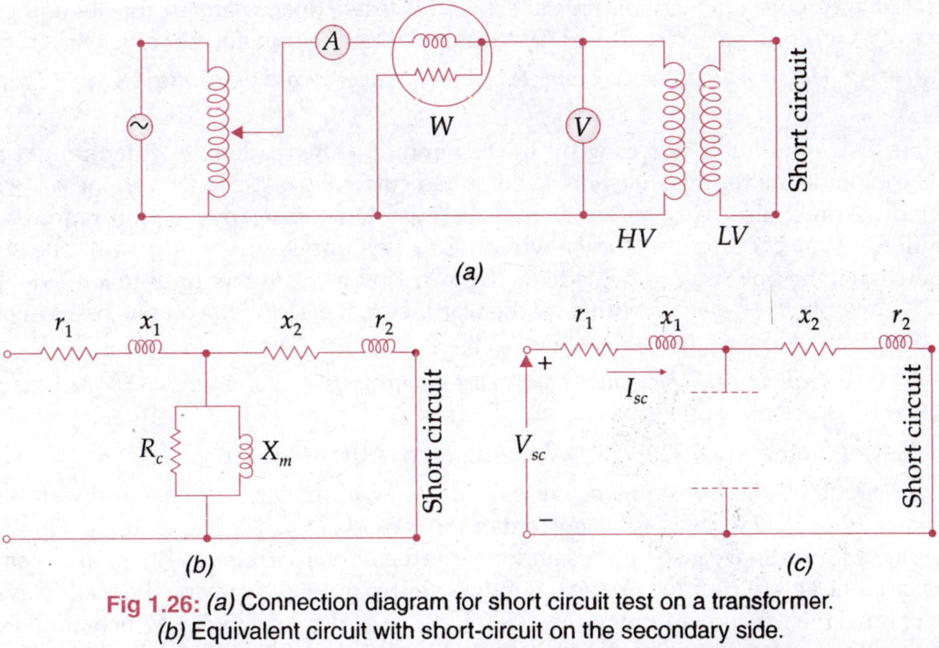

Fig 1.26: *(a)* Connection diagram for short circuit test on a transformer.
(b) Equivalent circuit with short-circuit on the secondary side.
(c) Transformer equivalent circuit with secondary short-circuited.

At rated voltage, the exciting current is 2 to 6% of full load current. When the voltage across the exciting branch is 1 to 6% of rated voltage, the exciting current may be 0.02 per cent $\left(= \frac{2}{100} \times \frac{1}{100} \times 100\right)$ to 0.36% per cent $\left(= \frac{6}{100} \times \frac{6}{100} \times 100\right)$ of its full-load current and can, therefore, be safely ignored. As a result of this, the equivalent circuit of Fig. 1.17, with the secondary short-circuited, gets modified to that shown in Fig.1.26 *(c)*. The instrument readings may be corrected, if required. Let V_{sc}, I_{sc}* and P_{sc} be the voltmeter, ammeter and wattmeter readings; then from Fig. 1.26 *(c)*, equivalent leakage impedance referred to h.v. side,

$$z_{eH} = \frac{V_{SC}}{I_{SC}} \qquad \text{...(1.37 (a))}$$

equivalent resistance referred to *h.v.* side, $r_{eH} = \frac{P_{SC}}{I_{SC}^2}$ ...(1.37 *(b)*)

and equivalent leakage reactance referred to *h.v.* side,

$$x_{eH} = \sqrt{z_{eH}^2 - r_{eH}^2} \qquad \text{...(1.38)}$$

In r_{eH}, x_{eH} and z_{eH}, the subscript *H* is used to indicate that these quantities are referred to *h.v.* side. These parameters can, however, be referred to the *l.v.* side, if required.

In the analysis of transformer equivalent circuit, the values of equivalent resistance and equivalent leakage reactance referred to either side, are used. However, if the leakage impedance parameters for both primary and secondary are required separately, then it is usual to take $r_1 = r_2 = \frac{1}{2} r_e$ and $x_1 = x_2 = \frac{1}{2} x_e$, referred to the same side.

Thus, the short-circuit test gives the following information : *(i)* ohmic loss at rated current and frequency and *(ii)* the equivalent resistance and equivalent leakage reactance.

Voltage regulation of a transformer can be determined from the data obtained from short-circuit test. Data of both open-circuit and short-circuit tests is necessary *(i)* for obtaining all the parameters of exact equivalent circuit and *(ii)* for calculating the transformer efficiency.

Example 1.13. *How can a wattmeter, connected on the h.v. side, record the ohmic loss in the l.v. winding also?*

Solution. This question may spring up in the mind of some readers. A little thought process provides the explanation for this question. When rated current is made to flow in the *h.v.* winding, the *l.v.* winding must also carry rated current, because the transformer action requires $I_1N_1 = I_2N_2$. The flow of rated current in the *l.v.* winding causes ohmic loss, which must be supplied from somewhere. The only way to provide *l.v.* winding loss is from the input to *h.v.* side. But the entire input power to *h.v.* side is recorded by the wattmeter, therefore, the ohmic losses in both the windings are given by the wattmeter reading.

Example 1.14. *Explain why open-circuit and short-circuit tests are performed on the l.v. side and h.v. side respectively.*

Solution. Consider a 3300/220 V, 33 kVA, single-phase transformer.

For open-circuit test on low voltage side, the ranges of voltmeter, ammeter and wattmeter are 220 V (rated value), 6 A (2 to 6% of rated current of 150 A) and 6 A, 220 V respectively. These are the standard ranges for ordinary instruments and, therefore, more accurate readings can be obtained. If the open circuit test is performed on the h.v. side, a source of 3300 V may not be readily available. At the same time, the instrument ranges are 3300 V, 0.4 A and 0.4 A, 3300 V which are not within the range of ordinary instruments and the results obtained may not be so accurate. Also it may not be safe to work on the high voltage side.

* The short-circuit current I_{sc} should be, either equal to or near to the rated current.

For a short-circuit test on the h.v. side, the instrument ranges are 165 V (2 to 12% of rated voltage of 3300 V), 10 A (rated current) and 10 A, 165 V which are well within the range of the ordinary instruments. On the other hand, instrument ranges, for a short-circuit test on l.v. side are 11 V, 150 A, and 150 A, 11 V. Instruments of such ranges and auto-transformer capable of handling 150 A, may not be readily available and at the same time, the results may not be so accurate. It is for these reasons that the open-circuit and short-circuit tests are conducted on l.v. and h.v. sides respectively.

Example 1.15. *A 20 kVA, 2500/250 V, 50 Hz, single-phase transformer gave the following test results :*

Open-circuit test (on l.v. side) : 250 V, 1.4 A, 105 watts.

Short-circuit test (on h.v. side) : 104 V, 8 A, 320 watts.

Compute the parameters of the approximate equivalent circuit referred to high-voltage and low-voltage sides. Also draw the exact equivalent circuit referred to the low-voltage side.

Solution. From open-circuit test : No-load power factor $= \cos\theta_0 = \dfrac{105}{250 \times 1.4} = 0.3$

$\therefore \quad \theta_0 = 75.55°$ and $\sin\theta_0 = 0.954$.

$$\therefore \quad I_c = I_0 \cos\theta_0 = 1.4 \times 0.3 = 0.42 \text{ A}$$

and $$I_m = I_0 \sin\theta_0 = 1.4 \times 0.954 = 1.336 \text{ A}.$$

Hence $R_{cL} = \dfrac{V_1}{I_c} = \dfrac{250}{0.42} = 595\ \Omega$ and $X_{mL} = \dfrac{V_1}{I_m} = \dfrac{250}{1.336} = 187\ \Omega$.

Alternatively, the value of R_{cL} and X_{mL} can be determined as follows :

$$R_{cL} = \frac{V_1^2}{P_c} = \frac{(250)^2}{105} = 595\ \Omega$$

Now $I_c = \dfrac{V_1}{R_{cL}} = \dfrac{250}{595} = 0.42$ A and $I_m = \sqrt{I_0^2 - I_c^2} = \sqrt{(1.4)^2 - (0.42)^2} = 1.336$ A

$$\therefore \quad X_{mL} = \frac{V_1}{I_m} = \frac{250}{1.336} = 187\ \Omega.$$

From short-circuit test : $z_{eH} = \dfrac{V_{sc}}{I_{sc}} = \dfrac{104}{8} = 13\ \Omega$

$$r_{eH} = \frac{P_{sc}}{I_{sc}^2} = \frac{320}{(8)^2} = 5\ \Omega$$

$$\therefore \quad x_{eH} = \sqrt{z_{eH}^2 - r_{eH}^2} = \sqrt{(13)^2 - (5)^2} = 12\ \Omega$$

Equivalent circuit parameters referred to l.v. side are

$R_{cL} = 595\ \Omega$, $X_{mL} = 187\ \Omega$; $r_{eL} = 5\left(\dfrac{1}{10}\right)^2 = 0.05\ \Omega$; $x_{eL} = 12\left(\dfrac{1}{10}\right)^2 = 0.12\ \Omega$.

This equivalent circuit is shown in Fig.1.27 *(a)*.

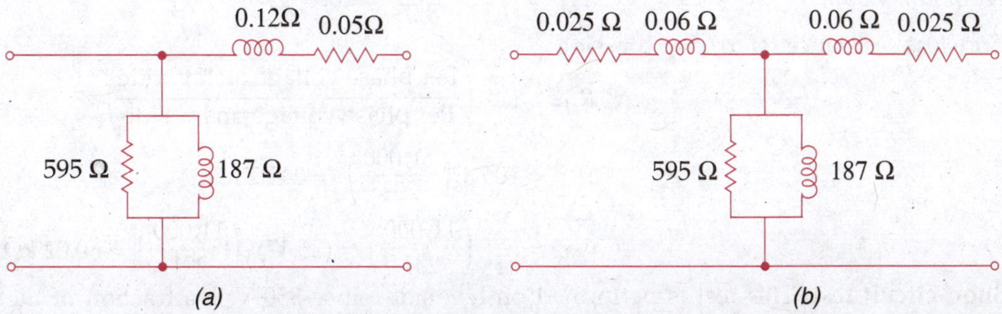

Fig 1.27: *(a)* Approximate equivalent circuit referred to l.v. side and *(b)* exact equivalent circuit referred to l.v. side.

Equivalent circuit parameters referred to h.v. side are

$$R_{cH} = 595\,(10)^2 = 59{,}500\ \Omega$$
$$X_{mH} = 187\,(10)^2 = 18{,}700\ \Omega$$
$$r_{eH} = 5\ \Omega\ ;\ x_{eH} = 12\ \Omega.$$

An equivalent circuit showing these parameters can easily be drawn.

Exact equivalent circuit parameters referred to l.v. side are

$$r_{1L} = r_{1H}' = \frac{1}{2}\,r_{eL} = \frac{1}{2}\,(0.05) = 0.025\ \Omega$$
$$x_{1L} = x_{1H}' = \frac{1}{2}\,x_{eL} = \frac{1}{2}\,(0.12) = 0.06\ \Omega$$
$$R_{cL} = 595\ \Omega \text{ and } X_{mL} = 187\ \Omega.$$

The exact equivalent circuit is shown in Fig. 1.27 *(b)*.

Example 1.16. *A 200 kVA, 11000/400 V, delta-star distribution transformer gave the following test results :*

Open circuit test : 400 V, 9 A, 1.50 kW.

Short circuit test : 350 V, rated current, 2.1 kW.

Calculate the equivalent circuit parameters referred to the h.v. side and its efficiency at half full load of unity power factor.

Solution. Problems relating to 3-phase balanced system are solved by reducing all the quantities to per phase values and so is done here.

Open-circuit test. This circuit is performed on the l.v. side, since the applied voltage for this test is equal to the rated voltage on the l.v. side, which is star connected.

$\therefore$ Per phase applied voltage $\quad V_1 = \dfrac{400}{\sqrt{3}} = 231$ V.

Per phase exciting current $\quad I_o = 9$ A.

Per phase core loss $\quad P_c = \dfrac{1500}{3} = 500$ W.

Now $\quad V_1 I_o \cos\theta_0 = P_c$

$\therefore$ Core loss current $\quad = I_o \cos\theta_0 = I_c = \dfrac{P_c}{V_1} = \dfrac{500}{231} = 2.165$ A.

Magnetizing current $\quad I_m = \sqrt{I_o^2 - I_c^2} = \sqrt{9^2 - (2.165)^2} = 8.73$ A.

From Eq. (1.35), $\quad R_{cL} = \dfrac{V_1}{I_c} = \dfrac{231}{2.165} = 106.8\ \Omega$

From Eq. (1.36), $\quad X_{mL} = \dfrac{V_1}{I_m} = \dfrac{231}{8.73} = 26.47\ \Omega$

Core loss resistance referred to h.v. side

$$R_{cH} = R_{cL}\left(\frac{\text{Per phase voltage on h.v. side}}{\text{Per phase voltage on l.v. side}}\right)^2$$
$$= 106.8\left(\frac{11{,}000}{231}\right)^2 = 242.2\ \text{k}\Omega.$$
$$X_{mH} = X_{cL}\left(\frac{11{,}000}{231}\right)^2 = (26.47)\left(\frac{11{,}000}{231}\right)^2 = 60.02\ \text{k}\Omega.$$

Short-circuit test. This test is performed on h.v. side, since 350 V is a fraction of the rated voltage on h.v. side, which is in delta.

$\therefore$ Applied voltage/phase $\quad V_{sc} = 350$ V

Current/phase $\quad I_{sc} = \text{Rated current} = \dfrac{200{,}000}{3 \times 11{,}000} = 6.06 \text{ A}.$

Ohmic loss per phase $\quad P_{sc} = \dfrac{2100}{3} = 700 \text{ W}$

$$\therefore \quad z_{eH} = \frac{V_{sc}}{I_{sc}} = \frac{350}{6.06} = 57.8\ \Omega$$

$$r_{eH} = \frac{P_{sc}}{I_{sc}^2} = \frac{700}{(6.06)^2} = 19.06\ \Omega$$

$$x_{eH} = \sqrt{(57.8)^2 - (19.06)^2} = 54.6\ \Omega$$

Efficiency at half full load,

$$\eta = 1 - \frac{\text{Per phase losses}}{\text{Per phase output + Per phase losses}}$$

$$= 1 - \frac{500 + \left(\frac{1}{2}\right)^2 700}{\frac{1}{2}\left(\frac{200}{3} \times 1000 \times 1\right) + 500 + \left(\frac{1}{2}\right)^2 (700)}$$

$$= 1 - \frac{675}{34{,}008} = 0.9802 \text{ p.u. or } 98.02\%.$$

1.11. THE PER UNIT SYSTEM

For electrical machines or electrical machine systems, the various calculations are commonly done by using the per unit quantities. In this article, the method of expressing volts, amperes, ohms etc. in per unit quantities, is explained.

For any system, the per unit values are obtained by choosing a set of certain base values, which can be chosen arbitrarily. However, it is common and preferable to choose the rated quantities of the device as its base values.

For any system or device, the per unit quantity is related to the base quantity by the following relation :

$$\text{Per unit quantity} = \frac{\text{Actual value of the quantity in any unit}}{\text{Base value of that quantity in the same unit}}$$

In this article, attention is directed to single phase 2-winding transformer, for which the base quantities are selected as follows. The subscripts B, L and H denote base, l.v. side and h.v. side respectively.

For high voltage side :

Base voltage $\quad V_{BH} = \text{Rated voltage on h.v. side}$

Base current $\quad I_{BH} = \text{Rated current on h.v. side}$

$$= \frac{\text{Transformer rated VA}}{\text{Rated voltage on h.v. side}}$$

Base impedance $\quad Z_{BH} = \dfrac{V_{BH}}{I_{BH}}\ \Omega = \dfrac{V_{BH} \times V_{BH}}{I_{BH} \times V_{BH}} = \dfrac{(\text{rated voltage on } HV \text{ side})^2}{\text{rated VA}}$

Dividing the numerator and denominator by $(1000)^2$, we get

$$Z_{BH} = \frac{\left(\dfrac{V_{BH}}{1000}\right)^2}{\dfrac{\text{rated VA}}{(1000)^2}} = \frac{(kV)^2_{BH}}{(MVA)_{BH}} \qquad \text{...(1.39 } a)$$

$$\therefore \quad (r_{eH}, x_{eH}, z_{eH})_{p.u.} = \frac{\text{Actual value of } r_{eH}, x_{eH} \text{ and } z_{eH} \text{ in ohms}}{Z_{BH} \text{ in ohms}} \quad ...(1.39\ b)$$

For low-voltage side :

Base voltage $\quad V_{BL}$ = rated voltage on low voltage side.

$$\text{Base current} \quad I_{BL} = \text{rated current on l.v. side} = \frac{\text{Rated } VA \text{ of transformer}}{\text{Rated voltage on l.v. side}}$$

$$\text{Base impedance} \quad Z_{BL} = \frac{V_{BL}}{I_{BL}}\ \Omega = \frac{(\text{rated voltage on } LV \text{ side})^2}{\text{rated VA}}$$

Z_{BH}, as per Eq. (1.39a), can also be expressed as

$$Z_{BL} = \frac{(kV)^2_{BL}}{(MVA)^2_{BL}} \quad ...(1.40\ a)$$

$$\therefore \quad (r_{eL}, x_{eL}, z_{eL})_{p.u.} = \frac{\text{Actual value of } r_{eL}, x_{eL} \text{ and } z_{eL} \text{ in ohms}}{Z_{BL} \text{ in ohms}} \quad ...(1.40\ b)$$

$$\text{Per unit rated voltage on } h.v. \text{ side} = \frac{\text{Rated voltage on } h.v. \text{ side}}{V_{BH}} = 1.$$

$$\text{Per unit rated current on } h.v. \text{ side} = \frac{\text{Rated current on } h.v. \text{ side}}{I_{BH}} = 1.$$

Thus the per unit values of the rated quantities of a device are equal to unity. Note also that the per unit quantities are dimensionless whereas the base quantities have a dimension.

$$\text{Now} \quad (z_{eL})_{p.u.} = \frac{z_{eL} \text{ in ohms}}{Z_{BL} \text{ in ohms}} = \frac{z_{eL}\, I_{BL}}{Z_{BL}\, I_{BL}}$$

$$= \frac{\text{Voltage drop across } z_{eL} \text{ at rated current}}{V_{BL}} \quad ...(1.41)$$

Eq. (1.41) shows that the p.u. value of z_{eL}(or z_{eH}) gives information about the leakage impedance drop on the l.v. (or h.v.) side. For example, in a single-phase transformer of 2300/230 V having z_{eH} = 0.03 p.u., the voltage drop across the h.v. leakage impedance will be 3% of 2300, *i.e.*, (0.03) (2300) = 69 volts.

$$\text{Also} \quad (r_{eL})_{p.u.} = \frac{r_{eL} \text{ in ohms}}{Z_{BL} \text{ in ohms}}$$

$$\text{or} \quad \frac{r_{eL}\, I_{BL}}{Z_{BL}\, I_{BL}} = \frac{r_{eL}\, I_{BL}}{V_{BL}} = \frac{I^2_{BL}\, r_{eL}}{V_{BL}\, I_{BL}}$$

$$\therefore \quad (r_{eL})_{p.u.} = \frac{\text{Ohmic loss at rated current}}{\text{Rated VA}} \quad ...(1.42)$$

Thus the p.u. value of r_{eL} or r_{eH} also furnishes the information about the ohmic or resistance loss at rated current occurring in the transformer. For example, in a single-phase transformer of 10 kVA, 2300/230 V having r_{eH} = 0.018 p.u., the ohmic loss at rated current is 1.8% of 10 kVA or.(0.018) (10,000) = 180 watts.

From Eqns. (1.39) and (1.40), it can be written that

$$Z\ (pu) = \frac{Z(\Omega)\,(MVA)_B}{(kV)^2_B}$$

In case base values $(kV)_B$ and $(MVA)_B$ are modified, then we get

$$Z(pu)_{old} = \frac{Z(\Omega)\,(MVA)_{B.old}}{(kV)^2_{B.old}}$$

$$Z(pu)_{new} = \frac{Z(\Omega)\,(MVA)_{B.new}}{(kV)^2_{B.new}}$$

Taking their ratios, $$\frac{Z(pu)_{new}}{Z(pu)_{old}} = \frac{(MVA)_{B.new}}{(MVA)_{B.old}} \cdot \frac{(kV)^2_{B.old}}{(kV)^2_{B.new}}$$

$$\therefore \quad Z(pu)_{new} = Z(pu)_{old} \cdot \frac{(MVA)_{B.new}}{(MVA)_{B.old}} \cdot \frac{(kV)^2_{B.old}}{(kV)^2_{B.new}} \quad ...(1.43)$$

Example 1.17. *Show that the per-unit values of r_{eL}, x_{eL} and z_{eL} are equal to the per-unit values of r_{eH}, x_{eH} and z_{eH}. Subscripts L and H denote l.v. and h.v. windings respectively.*

Solution. $$(r_{eL})_{p.u} = \frac{r_{eL} \text{ in ohms}}{Z_{BL} \text{ in ohms}} \quad ...(i)$$

But $$r_{eL} = r_{eH}\left(\frac{N_L}{N_H}\right)^2 \Omega$$

where N_L and N_H are the number of turns in the l.v. and h.v. windings respectively. Substitution of the value of r_{eL} in Eq. *(i)* gives :

$$(r_{eL})_{p.u.} = \frac{r_{eH}}{Z_{BL}}\left(\frac{N_L}{N_H}\right)^2 = \frac{r_{eH}}{Z_{BL}\left(\frac{N_H}{N_L}\right)^2} = \frac{r_{eH}}{Z_{BH}}$$

$$\left[\because Z_{BH} = Z_{BL}\left(\frac{N_H}{N_L}\right)^2\right]$$

$$= (r_{eH})_{p.u.}$$

Similarly $(x_{eL})_{p.u.} = (x_{eH})_{p.u.}$ and $(z_{eL})_{p.u.} = (z_{eH})_{p.u.}$

Hence the required result has been proved.

Example 1.18. *(a) A 20 kVA, 2500/250 V, single phase transformer has equivalent leakage impedance of $z_{eH} = 2.6 + j\,4.3\ \Omega$ when referred to h.v. side. Find the p.u. value of z_{eH} referred to (i) h.v. side and (ii) l.v. side. Find also the total leakage impedance drop referred to each side.*

(b) If the transformer of part (a) has an exciting current of 4.8 A on the h.v. side, find its p.u. value on the (i) h.v. side and (ii) l.v. side.

Solution. *(a) (i) H.V. side :*

Base voltage $$V_{BH} = 2500 \text{ V}$$

Base current $$I_{BH} = \frac{20{,}000}{2500} = 8 \text{ A.}$$

$\therefore$ Base impedance $$Z_{BH} = \frac{V_{BH}}{I_{BH}} = \frac{2500}{8} = 312.5\ \Omega$$

Per unit value of equivalent leakage impedance referred to h.v. side,

$$(z_{eH})_{p.u.} = \frac{z_{eH} \text{ in ohm}}{Z_{BH} \text{ in ohm}} = \frac{2.6 + j\,4.3}{312.5} = 0.00832 + j\,0.01376.$$

(ii) L.V. side : Equivalent leakage impedance referred to l.v. side

$$z_{eL} = z_{eH}\left(\frac{N_L}{N_H}\right)^2 = z_{eH}\left(\frac{V_L}{V_H}\right)^2 = (2.6 + j\,4.3)\left(\frac{250}{2500}\right)$$

$$= 0.026 + j\,0.043\ \Omega$$

Now $$V_{BL} = 250 \text{ V}, I_{BL} = \frac{20{,}000}{250} = 80 \text{ A.}$$

$$\therefore \quad \text{Base impedance } Z_{BL} = \frac{V_{BL}}{I_{BL}} = \frac{250}{80} = 3.125\ \Omega$$

$$\because \quad (z_{eL})_{p.u.} = \frac{z_{eL} \text{ in ohm}}{Z_{BL} \text{ in ohm}} = \frac{0.026 + j\,0.043}{3.125} = 0.00832 + j\,0.01376.$$

The magnitude of $(z_{eL})_{p.u.}$ or $(z_{eH})_{p.u.} = \sqrt{(0.00832)^2 + (0.01376)^2} = 0.01607$

Total leakage impedance drop on h.v. side = (0.01607) (2500) = 40.175 V

and total leakage impedance drop on l.v. side = (0.01607) (250) = 4.0175 V.

(b) (i) P.u. value of exciting current referred to h.v. side

$$= \frac{I_{eH}}{I_{BH}} = \frac{4.8}{8} = 0.6 \text{ p.u.}$$

(ii) Exciting current when referred to l.v. winding

$$I_{eL} = (4.8)\left(\frac{2500}{250}\right) = 48 \text{ A.}$$

$$(I_{eL})_{p.u.} = \frac{I_{eL} \text{ in Amp.}}{I_{BL} \text{ in Amp.}} = \frac{48}{80} = 0.6$$

The p.u. value of exciting current is seen to be same on both the sides.

Example 1.19. *A 10 kVA, 2000/200 V, single-phase transformer has following parameters :*

$$r_1 = 3.6\ \Omega \qquad x_1 = 5.2\ \Omega$$

$$r_2 = 0.04\ \Omega \qquad x_2 = 0.056\ \Omega$$

Subscripts 1 and 2 denote high voltage and low voltage windings respectively.

Find the p.u. values of r_{e1}, r_{e2}, x_{e1} and x_{e2}.

Solution. *H.V. side.*

Base Voltage $V_{BH} = 2000$ V

Base current $I_{BH} = \dfrac{10{,}000}{2000} = 5$ A

∴ Base impedance $Z_{BH} = \dfrac{2000}{5} = 400\ \Omega$

$$r_{1p.u} = \frac{3.6}{400} = 0.009$$

$$x_{1p.u} = \frac{5.2}{400} = 0.013$$

$$r_{e1} \text{ in ohms} = r_1 + r_2\left(\frac{N_1}{N_2}\right)^2 = (3.6) + 0.04\,(10)^2 = 7.6\ \ \Omega$$

$$r_{e1\,p.u.} = \frac{7.6}{400} = 0.019$$

$$x_{e1p.u.} = \frac{1}{Z_{BH}}\left[x_1 + x_2\left(\frac{N_1}{N_2}\right)^2\right] = \frac{1}{400}\,[5.2 + 0.056\,(10)^2] = 0.027.$$

L.V. side. Base voltage $V_{BL} = 200$ V

Base current $I_{BL} = \dfrac{10{,}000}{200} = 50$ A

∴ Base impedance $Z_{BL} = \dfrac{200}{50} = 4\ \Omega$

$$r_{2\,p.u.} = \frac{0.04}{4} = 0.01$$

$$x_{2\,p.u.} = \frac{0.056}{4} = 0.014.$$

$$r_{e2\,p.u.} = \frac{1}{Z_{BL}}\left[r_2 + r_1\left(\frac{N_2}{N_1}\right)^2\right] = \frac{1}{4}\left[0.04 + 3.6\left(\frac{1}{10}\right)^2\right] = 0.019$$

Similarly, $x_{e2p.u.,} = 0.027.$

Note that in p.u. system $r_{e1\,p.u.} = r_{e2\,p.u.} = r_{1\,p.u.} + r_{2\,p.u.}.$

and $x_{e1\,p.u.} = x_{e2\,p.u.} = x_{1\,p.u.} + x_{2\,p.u.}.$

This example shows that the transformer equivalent parameters in p.u. system are equal on both sides.

The foregoing examples illustrate the advantages of p.u. system and these are now summarised below :

(i) The calculations in per unit quantities are easy, since during the transformer analysis, one need not bother whether the parameters are referred to h.v. or l.v. side. This advantage is more significant when a circuit consists of many transformers of different turn ratios.

(ii) The p.u. parameters of different sizes of transformers (and other types of electrical machines) lie within a narrow range. For example, the magnetizing current of transformers normally lies between 0.02 and 0.05 p.u., the equivalent resistance between 0.005 p.u. (large transformers) and 0.02 p.u. (small transformers) and the equivalent reactance usually varies from 0.05 (large transformers) to 0.1 (small transformers). Thus from a knowledge of the p.u. parameters of a transformer (or any other electrical machine), one can know about its design and performance characteristics. This information further facilitates in the comparison of units of a given size made by the various manufacturers.

Example 1.20. *For a 200 kVA, 4000/1000 V, single-phase transformer, draw the equivalent circuit referred to l.v. side and insert all the values. It is given that the transformer efficiency at unity power factor is 97% both at full load and at 60% of full load. The no-load pf is 0.25 and the full-load regulation at a lagging pf of 0.8 is 5%.*

Solution. Total losses in a transformer $= \left(\frac{1}{0.97} - 1\right)(200{,}000) = 6185.5$ W

At full load, $P_c + P_{oh} = 6185.5$ W ... *(i)*

At 60% of full load, $P_c + (0.6)^2 . P_{oh} = 6185.5 \times 0.6$ W

or $P_c + 0.36\,P_{oh} = 3711.3$ W ...*(ii)*

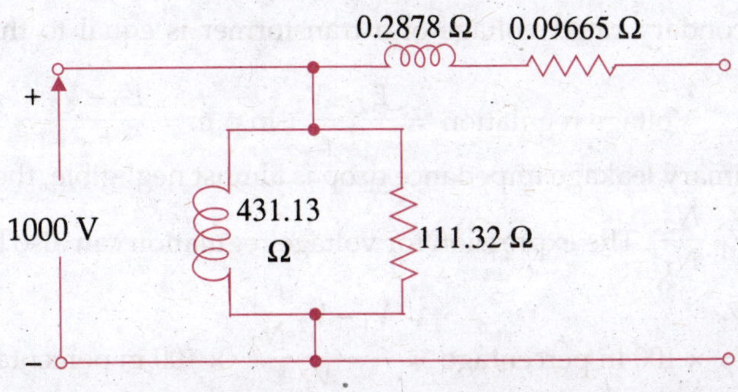

Fig 1.28: Pertaining to Example 1.20

From Eqns. *(i)* and *(ii)*, ohmic losses,

$$P_{oh} = \frac{6185.5 - 3711.3}{(1 - 0.36)} = 3866 \text{ W}$$

and core loss, $P_c = 6185.5 - 3866 = 2319.5$ W

Parameters are required on the low-voltage side. From Eqn. (1.42)

$$(r_{e2})_{p.u.} = \frac{3866}{200{,}000} = 0.01933 \text{ or } 1.933\%$$

But per unit voltage regulation from Eq. (1.46 *a*) is

$$0.05 = (r_{e2})_{p.u.} \cos\theta_2 + (x_{e2})_{p.u.} \sin\theta_2$$
$$= (0.01933 \times 0.8 + (x_{e2})_{p.u.} \times 0.6)$$

or $(x_{e2})_{p.u.} = 0.05756$

$$r_{e2} \text{ in ohms} = (r_{e2})_{p.u.} \times Z_{BL} = 0.01933 \times \frac{(1000)^2}{200{,}000} = 0.09665\ \Omega$$

and similarly x_{e2} in ohms = 0.2878 Ω

Core-loss resistance, $R_c = \frac{(1000)^2}{2319.5} = 431.13\ \Omega$

Exciting current, $I_o = \frac{P_c}{V_2 \cos\theta_0} = \frac{2319.5}{1000 \times 0.25} = 9.278$ A

and core-loss current, $I_c = \frac{2319.5}{1000} = 2.3195$ A

Magnetizing current, $I_m = \sqrt{9.278^2 - 2.3195^2} = 8.9834$ A

∴ Magnetizing reactance, $X_m = \frac{1000}{8.9834} = 111.32\ \Omega$

The approximate equivalent circuit referred to l.v. side is shown in Fig. 1.28.

1.12. VOLTAGE REGULATION OF A TRANSFORMER

It is defined as the change in magnitude of the secondary terminal voltage, expressed as a percentage (or per unit) of the secondary rated voltage, when load at a given power factor is reduced to zero, with primary applied voltage held constant.

If V_2 = secondary terminal voltage at any load,

and E_2 = secondary terminal voltage at no load,

then at a given power factor and specified load, the voltage regulation is given by

$$\text{Voltage regulation} = \frac{E_2 - V_2}{\text{Secondary rated voltage}} \text{ in p.u.}$$

As per IS, the secondary rated voltage of a transformer is equal to the secondary terminal voltage at no load, *i.e.* E_2.

$$\therefore \quad \text{Voltage regulation} = \frac{E_2 - V_2}{E_2} \text{ in p.u.} = \frac{E_2 - V_2}{E_2} \times 100 \text{ in percentage.}$$

At no load, the primary leakage impedance drop is almost negligible, therefore, the secondary no load voltage $E_2 = V_1 \frac{N_2}{N_1}$. The expression for voltage regulation can also be written as

$$\frac{V_1 \frac{N_2}{N_1} - V_2}{V_1 \frac{N_2}{N_1}} \times 100 \text{ in percentage} = \frac{V_1 - V_2 \frac{N_1}{N_2}}{V_1} \times 100 \text{ in percentage.}$$

Here V_1 is the primary applied voltage.

The change in secondary terminal voltage with load current is due to the primary and secondary leakage impedances of the transformer. The magnitude of this change depends on the load pf, load current, total resistance and total leakage reactance of the transformer.

A distribution transformer should have a small value of voltage regulation (*i.e.* good voltage regulation), so that the terminal voltage at the consumers' premises does not vary widely as the load changes. For a transformer of large voltage regulation (*i.e.* poor voltage regulation), the voltage at the consumers' terminals will fall appreciably with the increase in load—this has a detrimental effect on the operation of the fluorescent tubes, T.V. sets, refigerator motors etc. since these are designed to operate satisfactorily at a constant voltage. Thus the distribution transformers should be designed to have a low value of leakage impedance.

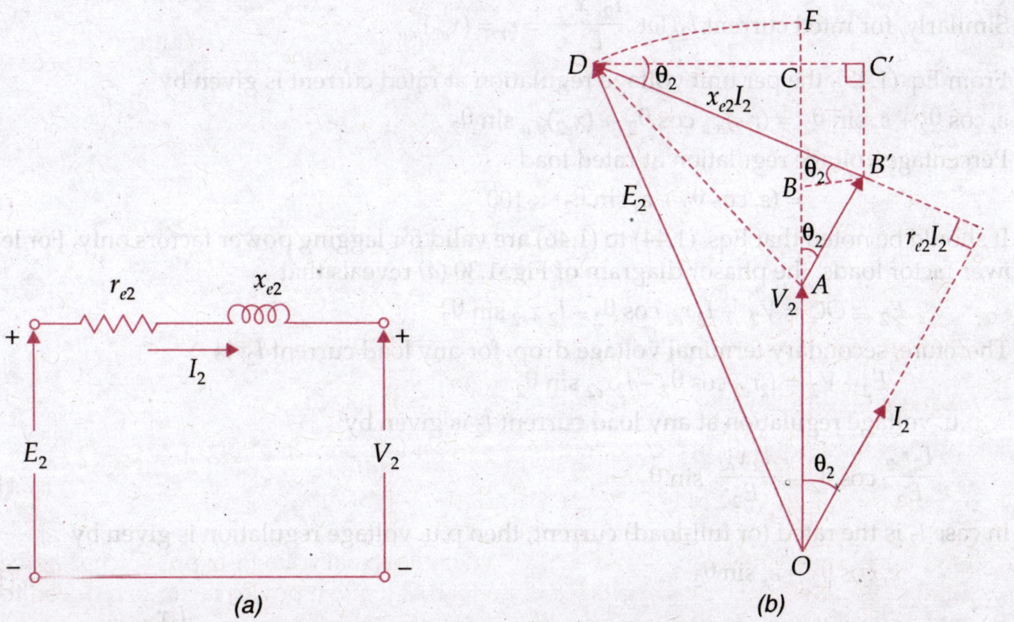

Fig 1.29: *(a)* Approximate equivalent circuit of a 2-winding transformer, referred to secondary *(b)* the phasor diagram of the circuit of Fig. 1.29 *(a)* for a lagging power factor load.

The voltage regulation of a transformer can be obtained from its approximate equivalent circuit referred to primary or secondary. Fig. 1.29 *(a)* illustrates the approximate equivalent circuit of a transformer referred to the secondary side and the phasor diagram for this circuit is drawn in Fig. 1.29 *(b)* for a lagging power factor load. For the calculation of voltage regulation, draw an arc of radius *OD* meeting the extension of line *OA* in *F*. It may be seen from Fig. 1.29 *(b)* that $OF\ (= E_2)$ is approximately equal to *OC*.

$$\therefore \quad E_2 \cong OC = OA + AB + BC \text{ (or } B'C') = OA + AB' \cos\theta_2 + DB' \sin\theta_2$$
$$= V_2 + I_2 r_{e2} \cos\theta_2 + I_2\, x_{e2} \sin\theta_2.$$

Thus the voltage drop in the secondary terminal voltage

$$= E_2 - V_2 = I_2\, r_{e2} \cos\theta_2 + I_2\, x_{e2} \sin\theta_2 \qquad \text{...(1.44)}$$

Note carefully that $E_2 - V_2$ is not equal to AD, i.e., $I_2\, z_{e2}$. The change in secondary terminal voltage is equal to the magnitude of E_2 minus the magnitude of V_2.

In Eq. (1.44), per unit voltage regulation for any load current I_2 is

$$\frac{E_2 - V_2}{E_2} = \frac{I_2 r_{e2}}{E_2} \cos\theta_2 + \frac{I_2 x_{e2}}{E_2} \sin\theta_2 \qquad \text{...(1.45)}$$

In case I_{2r} is the rated current, then from Eq. (1.41),

$$(r_{e2})_{p.u.} = \frac{I_{2r}\, r_{e2}}{E_2} = \frac{\text{Voltage drop across } r_{e2} \text{ at rated current}}{\text{Rated (=base) voltage } E_2}$$

$$= \text{p.u. equivalent resistance or p.u. resistance drop}$$

$$= \varepsilon_r \text{ (say)}$$

Also $\varepsilon_r = \dfrac{I_{2r}\, r_{e2}}{E_2} = \dfrac{I_{2r}^2\, r_{e2}}{E_2 I_{2r}} = \dfrac{\text{Ohmic loss at rated current}}{\text{Rated } VA}$

Note that ε_r here and $(r_{eL})_{p.u.}$ in Eq. (1.42) are identical.

Similarly, for rated current I_2, let $\dfrac{I_{2r}\, x_{e2}}{E_2} = \varepsilon_r = (x_{e2})_{p.u.}$

From Eq. (1.45), the per unit voltage regulation at rated current is given by

$$\varepsilon_r \cos\theta_2 + \varepsilon_x \sin\theta_2 = (r_{e2})_{p.u} \cos\theta_2 + (x_{e2})_{p.u} \sin\theta_2 \quad \text{...(1.46 a)}$$

Percentage voltage regulation at rated load

$$= (\varepsilon_r \cos\theta_2 + \varepsilon_x \sin\theta_2) \times 100 \quad \text{...(1.46 b)}$$

It should be noted that Eqs. (1.44) to (1.46) are valid for lagging power factors only. For leading a power factor loads, the phasor diagram of Fig. 1.30 *(a)* reveals that

$$E_2 \cong OC = V_2 + I_2 r_{e2} \cos\theta_2 - I_2 x_{e2} \sin\theta_2$$

Therefore, secondary terminal voltage drop, for any load current I_2, is

$$E_2 - V_2 = I_2 r_{e2} \cos\theta_2 - I_2 x_{e2} \sin\theta_2 \quad \text{...(1.47)}$$

$\therefore$ p.u. voltage regulation at any load current I_2 is given by

$$\frac{I_2 r_{e2}}{E_2} \cos\theta_2 - \frac{I_2 x_{e2}}{E_2} \sin\theta_2 \quad \text{...(1.48 a)}$$

In case I_2 is the rated (or full-load) current, then p.u. voltage regulation is given by

$$\varepsilon_r \cos\theta_2 - \varepsilon_x \sin\theta_2 \quad \text{...(1.48 b)}$$

1.12.1. Voltage regulation at unity power factor load.

Transformer phasor diagram at unity power factor load is shown in Fig.1.29 *(c)*. From this phasor diagram,

$$E_2 = \sqrt{(V_2 + I_2 r_{e2})^2 + (I_2 x_{e2})^2}$$

Exact voltage regulation $= \dfrac{E_2 - V_2}{E_2}$

At unity pf load, $\cos\theta_2 = 1$ and $\sin\theta_2 = 0$

Therefore, voltage regulation for unity power-factor load, from Eq. 1.46 *(b)* is

$$\text{V.R.} = \varepsilon_r \times 1 + \varepsilon_x (0) = \varepsilon_r = r_{e2pu} = \frac{I_2 r_{e2}}{E_2} \quad \text{...(1.49)}$$

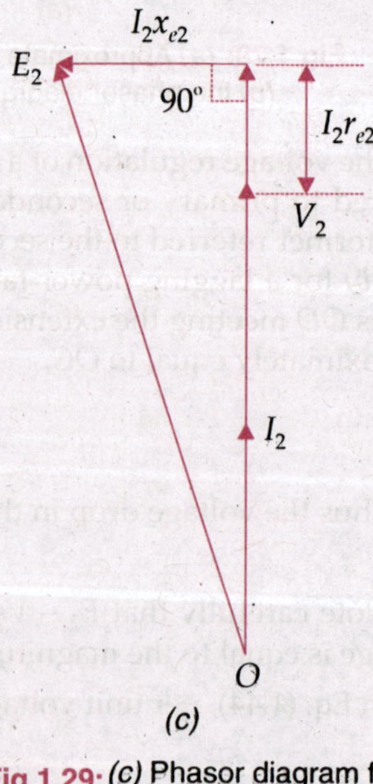

(c)

Fig 1.29: *(c)* Phasor diagram for 1-phase transformer at unity pf load

1.12.2. Condition for Zero Voltage Regulation

It is seen from Eq. (1.46) that voltage regulation varies with load power factor. If load power factor is varied with constant values of load current and secondary e.m.f., then zero voltage regulation will occur when

$$\varepsilon_r \cos\theta_2 + \varepsilon_x \sin\theta_2 = 0$$

or

$$\tan\theta_2 = -\frac{\varepsilon_r}{\varepsilon_x} = -\frac{\dfrac{I_2 r_{e2}}{E_2}}{\dfrac{I_2 x_{e2}}{E_2}} = -\frac{r_{e2}}{x_{e2}}$$

$\therefore$ Magnitude of load p.f., $\cos\theta_2 = \dfrac{x_{e2}}{z_{e2}}$.

The negative value of $\tan\theta_2$ indicates a leading power factor. Therefore, zero voltage regulation occurs when load p.f. is $\dfrac{x_{e2}}{z_{e2}}$ leading. For leading p.f.s. greater than $\dfrac{x_{e2}}{z_{e2}}$, voltage regulation will be negative, *i.e.* the voltage will rise from its no load value, as the transformer load is increased.

1.12.3. Condition for Maximum Voltage Regulation

$$\text{P.u. voltage regulation} = \varepsilon_r \cos\theta_2 + \varepsilon_x \sin\theta_2.$$

The condition for maximum voltage regulation is obtained by differentiating the above expression with respect to θ_2 and equating the results to zero. Here again the load current and secondary e.m.f. are assumed to remain constant.

$$\therefore \qquad \frac{d}{d\theta_2}(\text{p.u. regulation}) = -\varepsilon_r \sin\theta_2 + \varepsilon_x \cos\theta_2 = 0$$

or

$$\tan\theta_2 = \frac{\varepsilon_x}{\varepsilon_r} = \frac{x_{e2}}{r_{e2}}$$

any

$$\cos\theta_2 = \frac{r_{e2}}{z_{e2}}.$$

Here $\tan\theta_2$ is positive, therefore, maximum voltage regulation occurs at a lagging load p.f. equal to $\dfrac{r_{e2}}{z_{e2}}$. In other words, maximum voltage regulation occurs when load power-factor angle θ_2 is equal to the leakage impedance angle ϕ of the transformer.

$\therefore$ The magnitude of maximum voltage regulation

$$= \varepsilon_r \cdot \frac{r_{e2}}{z_{e2}} + \varepsilon_x \cdot \frac{x_{e2}}{z_{e2}}$$

$$= \frac{I_2 \cdot r_{e2}}{E_2} \cdot \frac{r_{e2}}{z_{e2}} + \frac{I_2 x_{e2}}{E_2} \cdot \frac{x_{e2}}{z_{e2}}$$

$$= \frac{I_2}{E_2 z_{e2}}(r_{e2}^2 + x_{e2}^2) = \frac{I_2 \cdot z_{e2}}{E_2} = z_{e2} \text{ p.u.}$$

Thus the magnitude of maximum voltage regulation is equal to the p.u. value of equivalent leakage impedance of the transformer. For example, if a transformer has $z_{e2} = 0.054$, then magnitude of maximum possible voltage regulation is 5.4%.

Phasor diagrams for a single-phase transformer for different operating power factors are illustrated in Fig. 1.30. In Fig. 1.30 *(a)*, $E_2 < V_2$, voltage regulation (V.R.) is therefore negative. In Fig. 1.30 *(b)*, $E_2 = V_2$, V.R. is zero. Fig. 1.30 *(c)* is drawn under the condition of maximum V.R., because here load power-factor angle θ_2 = leakage-impedance angle ϕ of the transformer where $\phi = \tan^{-1}(x_{e2}/r_{e2}) = \cos^{-1}(r_{e2}/z_{e2})$. It is seen from Fig. 1.30 *(c)* that for greatest or maximum voltage regulation, V_2 is in phase with E_2, therefore, $E_2 - V_2 = I_2 \cdot z_{e2}$.

$\therefore$ Magnitude of maximum voltage regulation $= \dfrac{I_2 \cdot z_{e2}}{E_2}$.

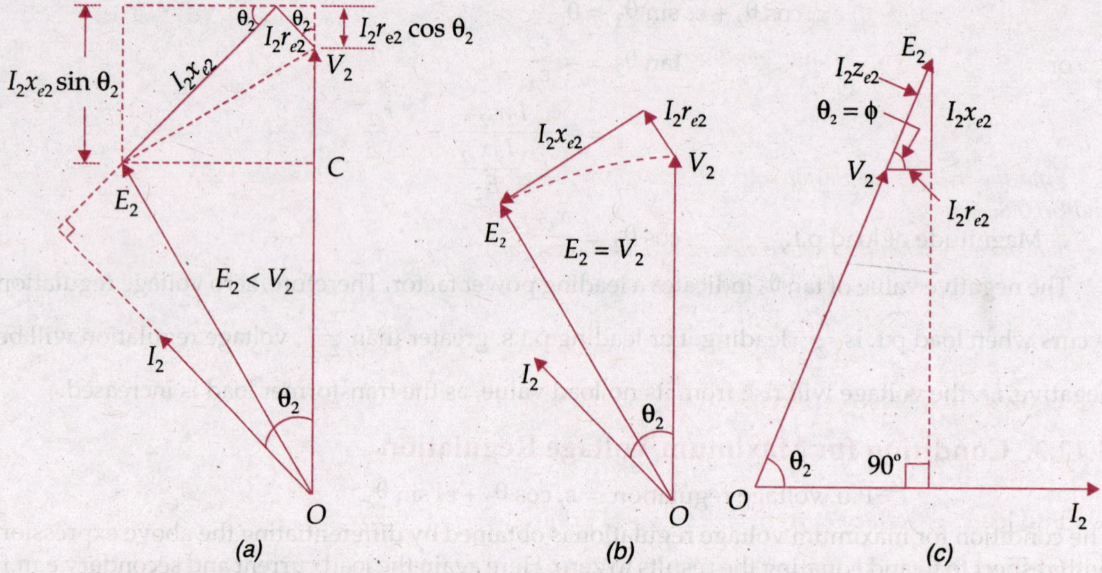

Fig 1.30: Phasor diagrams for 1-phase transformer for *(a)* negative voltage regulation (V.R.) *(b)* zero V.R. and *(c)* maximum V.R.

Example 1.21. *Show that the per unit voltage regulation of a transformer is given by* $\frac{V_{sc}}{E_2}\cos(\theta_{sc}-\theta_2)$ *where* V_{sc} *is the voltage required to circulate rated current on short-circuit,* θ_{sc} *is the p.f. angle on short-circuit and* θ_2 *is the load power factor angle.*

Solution. The transformer equivalent circuit under short-circuit is illustrated in Fig. 1.26 *(c)* and by referring to it, the phasor diagram of Fig. 1.31 is drawn. From these figures, it is seen that

$$V_{sc} = I_{rated}\, z_{e2} = I_{sc}\, z_{e2}$$

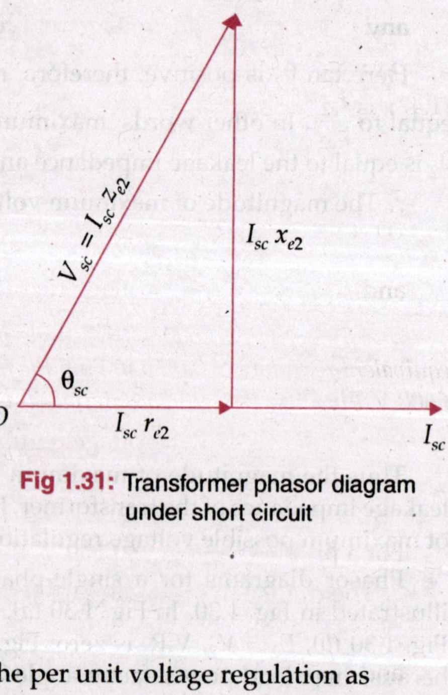

Fig 1.31: Transformer phasor diagram under short circuit

Fig. 1.31 also reveals that

$$I_{sc}\, r_{e2} = I_{sc}\, z_{e2}\cos\theta_{sc}$$

and $$I_{sc}\, x_{e2} = I_{sc}\, z_{e2}\sin\theta_{sc}$$

Division of these two relations by E_2 gives

$$\frac{I_{sc}\, r_{e2}}{E_2} = \varepsilon_r = \frac{I_{sc}}{E_2}\cdot\frac{r_{e2}}{z_{e2}} z_{e2}$$

$$= \frac{I_{sc} z_{e2}}{E_2}\cos\theta_{sc}$$

and $$\frac{I_{sc}\, x_{e2}}{E_2} = \varepsilon_x = \frac{I_{sc}\, z_{e2}}{E_2}\sin\theta_{sc}$$

P.u. voltage regulation = $\varepsilon_r\cos\theta_2 + \varepsilon_x\sin\theta_2$.

Substitution of the values ε_r and ε_x, from above, gives the per unit voltage regulation as

$$\frac{I_{sc}\, z_{e2}}{E_2}\cdot[\cos\theta_{sc}\cos\theta_2 + \sin\theta_{sc}\sin\theta_2] = \frac{V_{sc}}{E_2}\cos(\theta_{sc}-\theta_2) \quad ...(1.50)$$

Hence the required result has been proved.

Example 1.22. *A 20 kVA, 2500/500 V, single-phase transformer has the following parameters :*

h.v. winding	*l.v. winding*
$r_1 = 8\ \Omega$	$r_2 = 0.3\ \Omega$
$x_1 = 17\ \Omega$	$x_2 = 0.7\ \Omega$

Find the voltage regulation and the secondary terminal voltage at full load for a p.f. of (a) 0.8 lagging and (b) 0.8 leading.

The primary voltage is held constant at 2500 V.

Solution. Equivalent resistance referred to l.v. or secondary winding.

$$r_{e2} = 0.3 + 8\left(\frac{500}{2500}\right)^2 = 0.62\ \Omega$$

Equivalent reactance referred to secondary winding,

$$x_{e2} = 0.7 + 17\left(\frac{1}{25}\right) = 1.38\ \Omega$$

Full load secondary current = $\dfrac{20{,}000}{500}$ = 40 A.

(a) From Eq. (1.44), the full-load voltage drop in the secondary terminal voltage, for a lagging p.f., is

$$E_2 - V_2 = I_2\, r_{e2} \cos\theta_2 + I_2\, x_{e2} \sin\theta_2$$

$$= 40\ (0.62)\ (0.8) + 40\ (1.38)\ (0.6) = 52.96\ \text{V}.$$

$\therefore$ Secondary terminal voltage $V_2 = 500 - 52.96 = 447.04$ V

and voltage regulation $= \dfrac{E_2 - V_2}{E_2} = \dfrac{52.96}{500} = 0.1059$ or 10.59%.

(b) For a leading p.f., the full-load voltage drop in the secondary terminal voltage, from Eq. (1.47), is

$$E_2 - V_2 = I_2\, r_{e2} \cos\theta_2 - I_2\, x_{e2} \sin\theta_2$$

$$= 19.84 - 33.12 = -13.28\ \text{V}$$

$\therefore$ $V_2 = 500 + 13.28 = 513.28$ V

and voltage regulation $= \dfrac{E_2 - V_2}{E_2} = -\dfrac{13.28}{500} = -0.02656$ or -2.656%.

Example 1.23. *A 6600/440 V, single-phase transformer has an equivalent resistance of 0.02 p.u. and an equivalent reactance of 0.05 p.u. Find the full-load voltage regulation at 0.8 p.f. lag, if the primary voltage is 6600 V. Find also the secondary terminal voltage at full load.*

Solution. P.u. voltage regulation $= \varepsilon_r \cos\theta_2 + \varepsilon_x \sin\theta_2 = (0.02)\ (0.8) + (0.05)\ (0.6) = 0.046$

$$\therefore \quad \frac{E_2 - V_2}{E_2} = 0.046$$

For a primary voltage of 6600 V, the secondary no load voltage E_2 is 440 V.

$\therefore$ The change in the secondary terminal voltage

$$E_2 - V_2 = 440\ (0.046) = 20.25\ \text{V}$$

and secondary terminal voltage $V_2 = 440 - 20.25 = 419.75$ V.

Example 1.24. *A short-circuit test, when performed on the h.v. side of a 10 kVA, 2000/400 V, single-phase transformer gave the following data :*

60 V, 4 A, 100 watts.

If the l.v. side is delivering full load (or rated) current at 0.8 p.f. lag and at 400 V, find the voltage applied to h.v. side.

Solution. From short circuit data $r_{eH} = \dfrac{P_{sc}}{I_{sc}^2} = \dfrac{100}{(4)^2} = 6.25\ \Omega$

$$z_{eH} = \frac{V_{sc}}{I_{sc}} = \frac{60}{4} = 15\ \Omega$$

$$\therefore \quad x_{eH} = \sqrt{z_{eH}^2 - r_{eH}^2} = \sqrt{(15)^2 - (6.25)^2} = 13.61\ \Omega$$

For the l.v. side, the parameters are $r_{eL} = 6.25\left(\dfrac{1}{5}\right)^2 = 0.25\ \Omega$

$$x_{eL} = 13.61\left(\frac{1}{5}\right)^2 = 0.544\ \Omega$$

Full load secondary current $I_{2L} = \dfrac{10{,}000}{400} = 25$ A.

Now $E_2 - V_2 = I_{2L}\, r_{eL} \cos\theta_2 + I_{2L}\, x_{eL} \sin\theta_2$

$$= (25)(0.25)(0.8) + 25(0.544)(0.6) = 13.16 \text{ V.}$$

For $V_2 = 400$ V, $E_2 = 400 + 13.16 = 413.16$ V.

$\therefore$ The voltage applied to the primary is $= 413.16 \times \dfrac{2000}{400} = 2065.8$ V.

Example 1.25. *A single-phase load is fed through a 33-kV feeder whose impedance is 30 + j 120 Ω and a 33/3.3 kV transformer of equivalent leakage impedance 0.3 + j 1.4 Ω referred to l.v. side. For a load of 100 kW at pf 0.8 leading at 3.3 kV terminals, compute*

(a) voltage at the sending end of the feeder,

(b) voltage at the primary terminals of the transformer,

(c) active and reactive powers and also the power factor at the sending end of the feeder.

Solution. *(a)* For the transformer and feeder, equivalent circuit referred to l.v. side is shown in Fig. 1.32. In this figure, feeder impedance referred to l.v. side is given by

$$(30 + j\,120) \times \left(\frac{3.3}{33}\right)^2 = 0.30 + j\,1.2\ \Omega$$

Load current, $I_2 = \dfrac{100{,}000}{3300 \times 0.8} = 37.88$ A

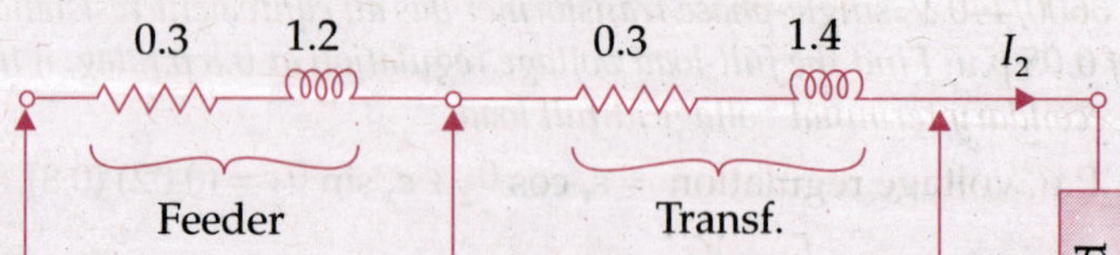

Fig 1.32: Equivalent circuit referred to l.v. side, Example 1.25

It is seen from Fig. 1.32. that for a leading pf load, voltage V_s at the sending end of the feeder and referred to *l.v.* side as per Eq. (1.47) is given by

$$V_s = V_2 + I_2 (R \cos\theta_2 - X \sin\theta_2)$$

where $R = 0.3 + 0.3 = 0.6\ \Omega$ and $X = 1.2 + 1.4 = 2.6\ \Omega$

$\therefore$ $V_s = 3300 + 37.88\ (0.6 \times 0.8 - 2.6 \times 0.6)$

$= 3259.09$ V on the l.v. side.

Voltage at the sending end of the feeder = 3259.09 × 10 = 32590.9 V

(b) From Fig. 1.32, $V_1 = [3300 + 37.88\ (0.3 \times 0.8 - 1.4 \times 0.6)] = 3277.3$ V

$\therefore$ Voltage at the primary terminals of transformer

$$V_1 = 3277.3 \times 10 = 32773 \text{ V}$$

(c) Active power loss = $(37.88)^2 \times 0.6 = 860.94$ W

Reactive power loss = $(37.88)^2 \times 2.6 = 3730.73$ var

Complex power at load end = $100 - j\,100 \tan(\cos^{-1} 0.8)$

$= (100 - j\,75)$ kVA

Complex power at the sending end

$= (100 - j\,75) + (0.86 + j\,3.730) = (100.86 - j\,71.27)$ kVA

Therefore, active and reactive powers at the sending end of the feeder are 100.86 kW and 71.27 kvar respectively.

Power factor at the sending end = $\cos \tan^{-1} \dfrac{71.27}{100.86} = 0.8167$ leading.

Example 1.26. *A 10 kVA, 2000/200 V, 50 Hz, 1-phase transformer, when working on rated voltage at no load, takes an input of 125 W at 0.15 pf. Its per cent leakage impedance, based on its own kVA rating, is (0.5 + j 1). If the transformer delivers 10 kW at 200 V at pf 0.8 lagging on its l.v. side, determine the input power and power factor.*

Solution. Base impedance on H.V. side $Z_{BH} = \dfrac{(kV)_B^2}{(MVA)_B} = \dfrac{2^2}{10 \times 10^{-3}} = 400\ \Omega$

Leakage impedance on h.v. side, $Z_{e1} = (0.5 + j\,1)\dfrac{400}{100} = 2 + j\,4\ \Omega$

Shunt branch parameters on the h.v. side are calculated as under :

Core-loss resistance, $R_c = \dfrac{V_1^2}{P_c} = \dfrac{2000^2}{125} = 32000\ \Omega$

No-load current, $I_o = \dfrac{125}{2000 \times 0.15} = 0.4167$ A

$\cos\theta_0 = 0.15$ and $\sin\theta_0 = 0.98869$

$\therefore$ Magnetizing reactance, $X_m = \dfrac{V_1}{I_o \sin\theta_0} = \dfrac{2000}{0.4167 \times 0.98869} = 4854.4\ \Omega$

The transformer equivalent circuit referred to h.v. side is shown in Fig. 1.33.

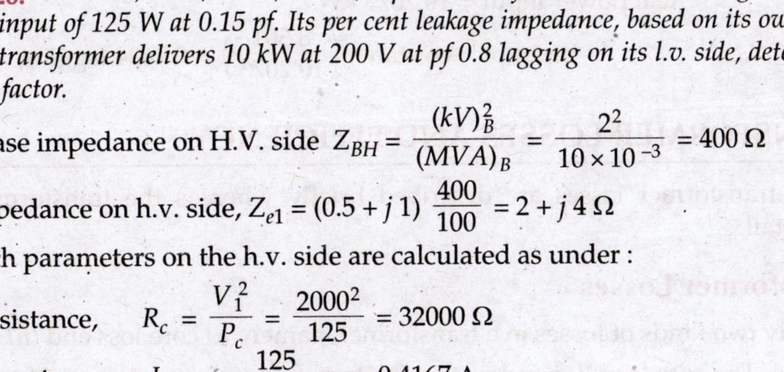

Fig 1.33: Pertaining to Example 1.26

Secondary load current, $I_2 = \dfrac{10,000}{0.8 \times 2000} = 62.5$ A

Primary load currrent, $I_1 = \dfrac{62.5}{10} = 6.25$ A

Load $pf = \cos \theta_2 = 0.8 = \cos \theta_1$

Primary input voltage, $V_1 = V_1' + I_1 (r_{e1} \cos \theta_1 + x_{e1} \sin \theta_1)$

$= 2000 + 6.25 (2 \times 0.8 + 4 \times 0.6) = 2025$ V

Active power loss in series resistance = $(6.25)^2 \times 2 = 78.125$ W

Reactive power loss in series reactance = $(6.25)^2 \times 4 = 156.25$ var

Active power loss in core-loss resistance = $\dfrac{(2025)^2}{32000} = 128.145$ W

Reactive power loss in magnetizing reactance = $\dfrac{(2025)^2}{4854.4} = 844.72$ var

Complex power at load end = $10 [1 + j \tan (\cos^{-1} 0.8)] = (10 + j\, 7.5)$ kVA

Complex power input to transformer = $(10 + 0.07813 + 0.12815) + j\, (7.5 + 0.15625 + 0.8447)$

$= (10.2073) + j\, (8.501)$ kVA

$\therefore$ Real power input = 10.2073 kW

Input pf = $\cos \tan^{-1} \left(\dfrac{8.501}{10.2073}\right) = 0.7684$ lagging

1.13. TRANSFORMER LOSSES AND EFFICIENCY

In this article, transformer losses are described briefly whereas the transformer efficiency is discussed in detail.

1.13.1. Transformer Losses

There are mainly two kinds of losses in a transformer, namely *(i)* core loss and *(ii)* ohmic loss.

(i) **Core loss.** The core loss P_c occurring in the transformer iron, consists of two components, hysteresis loss P_h and eddy current loss P_e, *i.e.*

$$P_c = P_h + P_e$$

The hysteresis and eddy current losses in the core have been found to be given by the expressions

$$P_h = K_h f B_m^{\,x}$$

and

$$P_e = K_e f^2 B_m^{\,2} \qquad \text{...(1.51)}$$

where K_h = proportionality constant which depends upon the volume and quality of the core material and the units used.

K_e = proportionality constant whose value depends on the volume and resistivity of the core material, thickness of laminations and the units employed.

B_m = maximum flux density in the core.

and f = frequency of the alternating flux.

The value of the exponent x (called Steinmetz's constant) varies from 1.5 to 2.5, depending upon the magnetic properties of the core material. Therefore, the total core loss is

$$P_c = K_h f B_m^{\,x} + K_e f^2 B_m^{\,2} \qquad \text{...(1.52)}$$

If it is required to express the core loss in terms of voltage, frequency etc., the procedure is given below.

The applied voltage V is almost equal to the induced e.m.f. given by the Eq. (1.3), *i.e.*

$$V = \sqrt{2}\,\pi f N \phi_{max} = \sqrt{2}\,\pi f N B_m A_i$$

where A_i is the net core area and N is the number of turns. Substitution of the value of B_m gives hysteresis loss as

$$P_h = K_h f \left(\frac{1}{\sqrt{2}\pi N A_i}\right)^x \left(\frac{V}{f}\right)^x$$

For a transformer N and A_i are constant

$$\therefore \qquad P_h = k_h V^x f^{1-x} \qquad ...(1.53)$$

Thus the hysteresis loss depends on both the applied voltage and its frequency.

The eddy current loss P_e is given by $P_e = K_e f^2 \left(\frac{1}{\sqrt{2}\pi N A_i}\right)^2 \left(\frac{V}{f}\right)^2 = k_e V^2$ ...(1.54)

The eddy current loss is, therefore, proportional to the square of the applied voltage and is independent of frequency f. According to Eq. (1.3); for any given voltage ($\propto B_m f$), if f decreases B_m increases correspondingly and if f increases B_m decreases correspondingly.

Hence the eddy current loss P_e, *at any given voltage*, is independent of frequency f.

The total core loss P_c, in terms of voltage and frequency is

$$P_c = k_h V^x f^{1-x} + k_e V^2 \qquad ...(1.55)$$

(ii) **Ohmic loss.** When a transformer is loaded, ohmic loss (I^2R) occurs in both the primary and secondary winding resistances. Since the standard operating temperature of electrical machines is 75°C, the ohmic loss should be calculated at 75°C.

In addition to the core and ohmic losses, the following two losses are also present in a transformer :

Stray load loss. Leakage fields present in a transformer induce eddy currents in conductors, tanks, channels, bolts etc. and these eddy currents give rise to stray load loss.

Dielectric loss. This loss occurs in the insulating materials, *i.e.*, in the transformer oil and the solid insulation of *h.v.* transformers.

The stray load loss and dielectric loss are small and are, therefore, neglected.

1.13.2. Transformer Efficiency

The efficiency of a transformer (or any other device) is defined as the ratio of output power to input power.

Thus

$$\text{Efficiency } \eta = \frac{\text{Output power}}{\text{Input power}} = \frac{V_2 I_2 \cos\theta_2}{V_2 I_2 \cos\theta_2 + P_c + I_2^2 r_{e2}} \qquad ...(1.56)$$

where P_c = total core loss,

$I_2^2 r_{e2}$ = total ohmic losses,

$V_2 I_2$ = output VA,

and $\cos\theta_2$ = load p.f.

As described before, stray load losses and dielectric losses are small and have been ignored. The efficiency can also be expressed as

$$\eta = \frac{\text{Output power}}{\text{Input power}} = \frac{\text{Input power} - \text{Losses}}{\text{Input power}} = 1 - \frac{\text{Losses}}{\text{Input power}} \qquad ...(1.57)$$

The efficiencies of power and distribuiton transformers are usually very high (95 to 99%). It is, therefore, more accurate to determine the efficiency from the measurement of losses from Eq. (1.57) than from the measurement of output from Eq. (1.56). Reference to Art. 3.9 is also helpful.

Due to primary leakage impedance drop, the emf E_1 (or E_2) and therefore, the mutual flux ϕ decreases for lagging power factor loads and may increase for leading power factor loads. Under normal operating conditions, the variation in the mutual flux ϕ is not more than 2 or 3%. Consequently the core losses can be assumed constant at all loads. In other words, it can be stated that transformer core loss is almost independent of load current. The ohmic losses depend on the load current. For example, if $I^2 r_e$ is the ohmic loss at full load, then at half full load, the ohmic loss will be $\frac{1}{4} I^2 r_e$.

Efficiency of a transformer can also be expressed in per unit parameters. In Eqn. (1.56), dividing both numerator and denominator by $V_2 I_2$, we get

$$\eta = \frac{\cos\theta_2}{\cos\theta_2 + \frac{P_c}{V_2 I_2} + \frac{I_2^2 r_{e2}}{V_2 I_2}}$$

$$= \frac{\text{load } pf}{\text{load } pf + p.u. \text{ core loss} + p.u. \text{ equivalent resistance}} \quad \text{...(1.57 a)}$$

It can also be shown that

$$\eta = 1 - \frac{p.u.P_c + p.u.r_e}{\text{load } pf + p.u.P_c + p.u.r_e} \quad \text{...(1.57 b)}$$

Efficiency given by Eqns. (1.57 *a*) and (1.57 *b*) is at rated current only. Efficiency at load current I_2', different from rated load current I_2, is given by

$$\eta = 1 - \frac{p.u.P_c + \left(\frac{I_2'}{I_2}\right)^2 (p.u.r_e)}{\left(\frac{I_2'}{I_2}\right)^2 .\text{load } pf + p.u.P_c + \left(\frac{I_2'}{I_2}\right)^2 p.u.r_e} \quad \text{...(1.57 c)}$$

Condition for maximum efficiency. In Eq. (1.56), P_c is constant and the load voltage V_2 remains practically constant. At a specified value of load p.f. $\cos\theta_2$, the efficiency will be maximum when $\frac{d\eta}{dI_2} = 0$. Therefore, $\frac{d\eta}{dI_2}$ for Eq. (1.56) is

$$\frac{d\eta}{dI_2} = \frac{\left[\begin{array}{c}(V_2 I_2 \cos\theta_2 + P_c + I_2^2 r_{e2})(V_2\cos\theta_2) \\ - V_2 I_2 \cos\theta_2 (V_2 \cos\theta_2 + 2 I_2 r_{e2})\end{array}\right]}{[V_2 I_2 \cos\theta_2 + P_c + I_2^2 r_{e2}]^2} = 0$$

or $\quad [V_2 I_2 \cos\theta_2 + P_c + I_2^2 r_{e2}]\, V_2 \cos\theta_2 = V_2 I_2 \cos\theta_2 (V_2 \cos\theta_2 + 2 I_2 r_{e2})$

$$I_2^2 r_{e2} = P_c \quad \text{...(1.58)}$$

or $\quad$ Variable ohmic loss, $I_2^2 r_{e2}$ = Constant core loss, P_c

Hence the maximum efficiency occurs when the variable ohmic loss $I_2^2 r_{e2}$ is equal to the fixed core loss P_c. From Eq. (1.58) the load current I_{2m} at which maximum efficiency occurs is given by

$$I_{2m} = \sqrt{\frac{P_c}{r_{e2}}} = I_{fl}\sqrt{\frac{P_c}{I_{fl}^2 r_{e2}}} \quad \text{...(1.58 a)}$$

If both sides of above equation are multiplied by $E_2/1000$, we get

$$\frac{E_2 I_{2m}}{1000} = \frac{E_2 I_{fl}}{1000}\sqrt{\frac{P_c}{\text{Full load ohmic losses}}}$$

$\therefore$ kVA load for maximum η

$$= (\text{rated transformer kVA}) \times \sqrt{\frac{\text{Core loss}}{\text{Ohmic losses at rated current}}}$$

or $$(\text{kVA})_{\max \cdot \eta} = (\text{kVA}) \sqrt{\frac{P_c}{I_{fl}^2 r_{e2}}} \quad ...(1.59)$$

Determination of the transformer efficiency without loading it. The transformer efficiency can be calculated if the total losses in the transformer are known. It has already been pointed out that the wattmeter reading in the open circuit test records the core loss P_c, and during the short circuit test at rated current, it registers the full load ohmic loss P_{sc}. Thus the total losses $(P_c + P_{sc})$ at full load are known from these two tests without loading the transformer and the efficiency can be calculated as follows :

From Eq. (1.57), $$\eta \text{ at full load } = 1 - \frac{P_c + P_{sc}}{(\text{Rated VA}) \cos \theta_2 + P_c + P_{sc}}$$

At any other load current, say nI_{fl}, the efficiency is given by

$$\eta = 1 - \frac{P_c + n^2 P_{sc}}{n(\text{Rated VA}) \cos \theta_2 + P_c + n^2 P_{sc}} \quad ...(1.60)$$

As before, maximum efficiency occurs when variable ohmic loss = Constant core loss, *i.e.*

$$n^2 P_{sc} = P_c$$

or $$n = \sqrt{\frac{P_c}{P_{sc}}} \quad ...(1.61)$$

Eq. (1.59) can now be re-written as

$$(\text{kVA})_{\max \cdot \eta} = (n)\,(\text{kVA})_{\text{rated}} \quad ...(1.59)$$

Example 1.27. *In a transformer if the load current is kept constant, find the power factor at which the maximum efficiency occurs.*

Solution. For a constant load current, the ohmic losses P_{sc} are constant. Core loss P_c is already a fixed quantity. Therefore, total transformer losses are constant for a constant load current. Now the efficiency is

$$\eta = \frac{V_2 I_2 \cos \theta_2}{V_2 I_2 \cos \theta_2 + \text{constant losses (C)}}$$

The power factor at which maximum efficiency occurs can be obtained by equating $\frac{d\eta}{d\theta_2} = 0$. From the above expression for efficiency, we get

$$\frac{d\eta}{d\theta_2} = \frac{[V_2 I_2 \cos \theta_2 + C] V_2 I_2 (-\sin \theta_2) - (V_2 I_2 \cos \theta_2) V_2 I_2 (-\sin \theta_2)}{[V_2 I_2 \cos \theta_2 + C]^2} = 0$$

or $$(V_2 I_2)^2 \sin \theta_2 \cos \theta_2 + C.V_2 I_2 \sin \theta_2 = (V_2 I_2)^2 \sin \theta_2 \cos \theta_2$$

or $$\sin \theta_2 = 0$$

$\therefore$ Power factor $$\cos \theta_2 = 1.$$

Thus the maximum efficiency, for a constant load current, occurs at unity power factor.

It is seen from Eqn. (1.58 (*a*)) that the load current at which maximum efficiency occurs does not depend upon the load power factor because P_c and r_{e2} are almost unaffected by a variation in the load power factor.

A reduction in the load power factor reduces the transformer output and therefore the transformer efficiency is also reduced accordingly. Fig. 1.34 illustrates the effect of p.f. on efficiency.

Note that transformer efficiency is maximum at the same load current regardless of variation in the load power factor.

Energy Efficiency. Power transformers are used at the sending and receiving ends of a long, high-voltage power transmission line for stepping up or stepping down the voltage. These transformers are manipulated to operate almost always at or near their rated capacity (kVA rating). Therefore, power transformers are disconnected during light load periods. In view of this, a power transformer is designed to have maximum efficiency at or near its full load (rated) kVA. Hence the choice of a power transformer, out of a large numbers of competing transformers, should be based on full load efficiency.

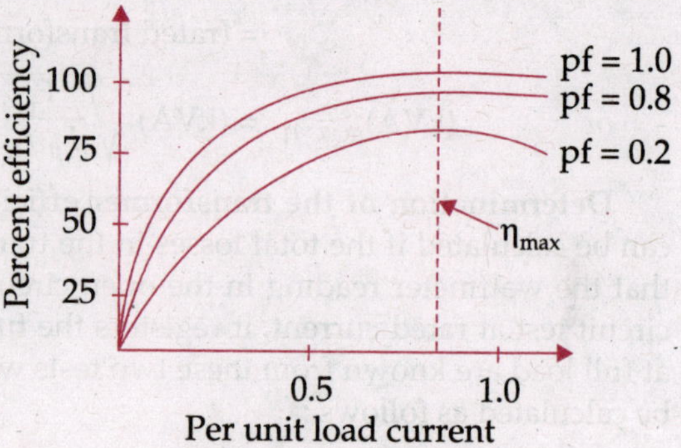

Fig 1.34: Effect of load p.f. on transformer efficiency curves

Distribution transformers are those which change the voltage to a level suitable for utilisation purposes at the consumer's premises. A power transformer does not come in direct contact with the consumer's terminals, whereas a distribution transformer must have its secondary directly connected with the consumer's terminals. The load on a distribution transformer varies over a wide range during a 24 hour day. For example, a distribution transformer in a residential colony may have practically little or no load during a considerable portion of the day time, but in the evenings, the load (illumination load etc.) may be near its rated capacity. Note that the primary of distribution transformers are always energized and, therefore, the core loss takes place continuously. In view of this, the distribution transformers are designed to have very low value of core loss. But for reduced core loss P_c, the maximum efficiency may occur at about one-half of its rated kVA, as per Eqs. (1.61) and (1.59). Thus a distribution transformer should not be judged by its full load efficiency, which is usually much less than its maximum efficiency. However, the choice of a distribution transformer, out of a large number of competing transformers, can be based on energy efficiency, defined as follows :

Energy efficiency of a transformer is defined as the ratio of total energy output for a certain period to the total energy input for the same period.

The energy efficiency can be computed for any length of load cycle, provided its load variations are known. When energy efficiency is computed for a day of 24 hours, it is called *all day efficiency.*

$$\therefore \quad \text{All day } \eta = 1 - \frac{\text{Daily losses in kWh}}{\text{Daily input in kWh}} \qquad \text{...(1.62)}$$

Example 1.28. *In a transformer, the core loss is found to be 52 watts at 40 Hz and 90 watts at 60 Hz ; both losses being measured at the same peak flux density. Compute the hysteresis and eddy current losses at 50 Hz.*

Solution. From Eq. (1.52), the total core loss is $P_c = K_h f B_m^{\,x} + K_e f^2 B_m^{\,2}$

For constant flux density $\quad P_c = K_h f + k_e f^2$

where constant $\quad k_h = K_h B_m^{\,x}$ and constant $k_e = K_e B_m^{\,2}$

$\therefore$ At 40 Hz, $\quad 52 = k_h (40) + k_e (40)^2$

and at 60 Hz, $\quad 90 = k_h (60) + k_e (60)^2$

or $\quad 52 = 40 k_h + 1600 k_e$

and $\quad 90 = 60 k_h + 3600 k_e$.

From the above two equations, k_h and k_e are found to be

$$k_h = \frac{9}{10} \text{ and } k_e = \frac{1}{100}.$$

Thus at 50 Hz, the hysteresis loss $P_h = k_h f = \frac{9}{10}(50) = 45$ watts.

and eddy current loss $P_e = k_e f^2 = \frac{1}{100}(50)^2 = 50$ watts.

Example 1.29. *A 220 V, 60 Hz, single-phase transformer has hysteresis loss of 340 watts and eddy current loss of 120 watts. If the transformer is operated from 230 V, 50 Hz supply mains, then compute its total core loss. Assume Steinmetz's constant equal to 1.6.*

Solution. The operating voltage $V_1 = \sqrt{2}\pi f_1 B_{m1} A_i N$ and $V_{11} = \sqrt{2}\pi f_2 B_{m2} A_i N$

$$\therefore \quad \frac{V_1}{V_{11}} = \frac{f_1 B_{m1}}{f_2 B_{m2}} \quad \text{or} \quad \frac{220}{230} = \left(\frac{60}{50}\right)\left(\frac{B_{m1}}{B_{m2}}\right)$$

$$\therefore \quad B_{m2} = \left(\frac{60}{50}\right)\left(\frac{230}{220}\right) B_{m1} = 1.255\, B_{m1}.$$

From Eq. (1.51), hysteresis loss $P_h = K_h f B_m{}^x$

$$\therefore \quad \frac{P_{h2}}{P_{h1}} = \frac{f_2 B_{m2}{}^x}{f_2 B_{m1}{}^x} = \frac{50}{60}(1.255)^{1.6}$$

or $$P_{h2} = (340)\left(\frac{5}{6}\right)(1.255)^{1.6} = (340)\left(\frac{5}{6}\right)(1.438) = 408 \text{ W}.$$

From Eq. (1.51), eddy current loss $P_e = K_e f^2 B_m{}^2$

$$\therefore \quad \frac{P_{e2}}{P_{e1}} = \left(\frac{f_2}{f_1}\right)^2 \left(\frac{B_{m2}}{B_{m1}}\right)^2 = \left(\frac{50}{60}\right)^2 (1.255)^2$$

or $$P_{e2} = (120)\left(\frac{5}{6}\right)^2 (1.255)^2 = 131.3 \text{ W}$$

$\therefore$ Total core loss $P_{c2} = P_{h2} + P_{e2} = 408 + 131.3 = 539.3$ W.

Example 1.30. *The ohmic, hysteresis and eddy current losses in a transformer at 50 Hz are 1.6%, 0.9% and 0.6% respectively. For a Steinmetz's coefficient of 1.6 find*

(a) these losses at 60 Hz, for the same system voltage and current and

(b) the output at 60 Hz, for the total losses to remain the same as on 50 Hz.

Solution. *(a)* Subscripts 1 and 2 will be used to refer to 50 and 60 Hz quantities respectively.

Since the voltage and current at both the frequencies of 50 Hz and 60 Hz are the same, the output also remains the same.

The ohmic loss depends on the current and here it is given that the current at both the frequencies are equal. Therefore, ohmic losses in watts remain unchanged and for the same output, the percentage ohmic losses are again 1.6%. Thus

Ohmic loss at 50 Hz P_{oh1} = Ohmic loss at 60 Hz, $P_{oh2} = 1.6\%$.

As before $$\frac{V_1}{V_2} = \frac{f_1 B_{m1}}{f_2 B_{m2}} \text{ or } 1 = \frac{50\, B_{m1}}{60\, B_{m2}} \text{ or } B_{m2} = \frac{5}{6} B_{m1}$$

From Eq. (1.51), hysteresis loss, $P_h = K_h f B_m{}^x$

$$\therefore \quad \frac{P_{h2}}{P_{h1}} = \frac{f_2}{f_1}\left(\frac{B_{m2}}{B_{m1}}\right)^x$$

or $$P_{h2} = P_{h1}\left(\frac{60}{50}\right)\left(\frac{5}{6}\right)^{1.6} = P_{h1}(0.833)^{0.6} = 0.896\, P_{h1}.$$

or $$\frac{P_{h2}}{\text{Output}} = 0.896 \frac{P_{h1}}{\text{Output}} = 0.896\ (0.9) = 0.806\%$$

From Eq. (1.51), eddy current loss, $P_e = K_e f^2 B_m^2$

$$\therefore \qquad \frac{P_{e2}}{P_{e1}} = \left(\frac{f_2}{f_1}\right)^2 \left(\frac{B_{m2}}{B_{m1}}\right)^2$$

or $$P_{e2} = P_{e1}\left(\frac{60}{50}\right)^2\left(\frac{5}{6}\right)^2 = P_{e1}$$

For the same output, percentage P_{e1} = percentage P_{e2} = 0.6%.

Thus the ohmic, hysteresis and eddy current losses at 60 Hz are 1.6%, 0.806% and 0.6% respectively.

(b) The core loss depends on voltage and frequency only. Therefore, P_{c1} = 1.5% (= 0.9 + 0.6) and P_{c2} = 1.406% = (0.806 + 0.6) can't be changed for given values of voltage and frequency. For the total losses to remain the same, the ohmic loss alone can be varied.

$$\therefore \qquad \text{Total losses at 50 Hz} = \text{Total losses at 60 Hz}$$

or $$3.1\ (= 1.6 + 0.9 + 0.6) = 1.406 + \text{New ohmic losses.}$$

∴ Permissible value of ohmic losses at 60 Hz = 3.1 – 1.406 = 1.694%

Since the ohmic losses are proportional to the square of the current, we have

$$\left(\frac{\text{New permissible current}}{\text{Original current}}\right)^2 = \frac{\text{New ohmic losses}}{\text{Original ohmic losses}} = \frac{1.694}{1.60}$$

$$\therefore \qquad \text{New permissible current} = \sqrt{\frac{1.694}{1.60}}\ \text{(original current)}$$

$$= (1.028)\ \text{(original current)}$$

For the same voltage, output at 60 Hz = (1.028) (output at 50 Hz)

It is, therefore, seen that output at a higher-frequency operation is increased for the same total loss.

Example 1.31. *A 11/0.4 kV, 25 Hz, single-phase transformer has ohmic, hysteresis and eddy current losses of 1.8, 0.8 and 0.3% respectively. What do these losses become if the transformer is operated from 22 kV, 50 Hz supply system. The current is assumed to remain the same in both the cases.*

Also calculate the efficiency in each case.

Solution. Subscripts 1 and 2 are used to denote 11 kV, 25 Hz and 22 kV, 50 Hz systems respectively.

At 50 Hz, the voltage is doubled $\left(= \frac{22}{11}\right)$. For the same current, therefore, the output P_2 at 50 Hz is double the output P_1 at 25 Hz, *i.e.* $P_2 = 2P_1$. It is given that

$$\frac{P_{oh1}}{P_1} = 1.8\%; \quad \frac{P_{h1}}{P_1} = 0.8\%; \quad \frac{P_{e1}}{P_1} = 0.3\%$$

Ohmic loss. Since the current is same at both the frequencies and voltages, the ohmic losses in watts remain unaltered, *i.e.* $P_{oh2} = P_{oh1}$.

Percentage ohmic loss at higher frequency $= \frac{P_{oh2}}{P_2} = \frac{P_{oh1}}{2P_1} = \frac{1}{2}(1.8) = 0.9\%$

Core loss. The voltage is related to f, B_m etc. by the expression

$$V = \sqrt{2}\,\pi f B_m A_i N$$

$$\therefore \quad \frac{V_1}{V_2} = \left(\frac{f_1}{f_2}\right)\left(\frac{B_{m1}}{B_{m2}}\right) \quad \text{or} \quad \frac{11{,}000}{22{,}000} = \left(\frac{25}{50}\right)\frac{B_{m1}}{B_{m2}}$$

$$\text{or} \quad \frac{1}{2} = \frac{1}{2}\left(\frac{B_{m1}}{B_{m2}}\right)$$

$$\therefore \quad B_{m2} = B_{m1}$$

The hysteresis loss $P_h = K_h f B_m^{\,x}$ watts

$$\therefore \quad \frac{P_{h2}}{P_{h1}} = \left(\frac{f_2}{f_1}\right)\left(\frac{B_{m2}}{B_{m1}}\right)^x$$

$$\text{or} \quad P_{h2} = P_{h1}\left(\frac{50}{25}\right)(1)^x = 2(1)^x P_{h1} = 2P_{h1}.$$

Percentage hysteresis loss at f_2, V_2 is $= \dfrac{P_{h2}}{P_2} = \dfrac{2P_{h1}}{2P_1} = 0.8\%.$

The eddy current loss $P_e = K_e f^2 B_m^{\,2}$ watts

$$\therefore \quad \frac{P_{e2}}{P_{e1}} = \left(\frac{f_2}{f_1}\right)^2\left(\frac{B_{m2}}{B_{m1}}\right)^2$$

$$\text{or} \quad P_{e2} = P_{e1}\left(\frac{50}{25}\right)^2 (1)^2 = 4\,P_{e1}$$

Percentage eddy current loss at f_2, V_2 is $\dfrac{P_{e2}}{P_2} = \dfrac{4P_{e1}}{2P_1} = 2\left(\dfrac{P_{e1}}{P_1}\right) = 2\,(0.3) = 0.6\%$

Efficiency at f_1, V_1

$$\eta = 1 - \frac{\text{Losses}}{\text{Output} + \text{Losses}} = 1 - \frac{\text{Losses/Output}}{1 + \text{Losses/Output}}$$

$$= 1 - \frac{\text{P.u. losses}}{1 + \text{P.u. losses}} = 1 - \frac{0.018 + 0.008 + 0.003}{1 + 0.018 + 0.008 + 0.003}$$

$$= 1 - \frac{0.029}{1.029} = 0.97182 \text{ or } 97.182\%$$

Efficiency at f_2, V_2

$$\eta = 1 - \frac{0.009 + 0.008 + 0.006}{1 + 0.009 + 0.008 + 0.006}$$

$$= 1 - \frac{0.023}{1.023} = 0.97755\% \text{ or } 97.755\%$$

Example 1.32. *A 10 kVA, 2500/250 V, single-phase transformer gave the following test results :*

Open-circuit test	*250 V*	*0.8 A*	*50 W*
Short-circuit test	*60 V*	*3 A*	*45 W*

(a) Calculate the efficiency at $\frac{1}{4}, \frac{1}{2}, 1$ *and* $1\frac{1}{4}$ *of full load at 0.8 p.f.*

(b) Calculate the load (kVA output) at which maximum efficiency occurs and also the value of maximum efficiency at 0.8 p.f.

(c) Compute the voltage regulation and the secondary terminal voltage under rated load at power factors of (i) 0.8 lagging and (ii) 0.8 leading.

Solution. It may be noted that

(i) Open-circuit test has been conducted on l.v. side, because 250 V during this test is equal to the rated voltage on l.v. side.

(ii) Short-circuit test has been performed on h.v. side, since 60 V is a fraction (2 to 12%) of the rated voltage on h.v. side.

(a) Full load (or rated) current on h.v. side = $\dfrac{10,000}{2500} = 4$ A

Ohmic loss of 45 watts is due to a short-circuit current of 3 A.

∴ Ohmic loss at full load current of 4 A

$$P_{sc} = 45\left(\frac{4}{3}\right)^2 = 80 \text{ Watts}$$

Fixed core loss $\qquad P_c = 50$ watts.

At 0.8 p.f. and at $\frac{1}{4}$ full load, the core loss $P_c = 50$ W, ohmic loss = $\left(\frac{1}{4}\right)^2 P_{sc} = \left(\frac{1}{4}\right)^2 (80) = 5$ W

and output = $\frac{1}{4}$ (10,000) (0.8) = 2000 W.

$$\therefore \qquad \eta \text{ at } \frac{1}{4} \text{ full load } = 1 - \frac{50+5}{2000+50+5} = 0.9732 \text{ or } 97.32\%.$$

$$\text{Similarly } \eta \text{ at } \frac{1}{2} \text{ full load } = 1 - \frac{50 + \left(\frac{1}{2}\right)^2 80}{\frac{1}{2}(10,000)(0.8) + 50 + \frac{80}{4}} = 0.9828 \text{ or } 98.28\%$$

At full load
$$\eta = 1 - \frac{80+50}{8000+50+80} = 0.984 \text{ or } 98.4\%$$

At $1\frac{1}{4}$ full load,
$$\eta = 1 - \frac{50 + \left(\frac{5}{4}\right)^2 80}{\frac{5}{4}(10,000)(0.8) + 50 \left(\frac{5}{4}\right)^2 80} = 0.9828 \text{ or } 98.28\%.$$

The efficiencies calculated above are the same whether the load p.f. is 0.8 lagging or 0.8 leading.

(b) Let the maximum efficiency occur at n times the rated kVA.

∴ Ohmic loss at maximum $\eta = n^2$ (80) watts.

But maximum η occurs when ohmic loss = core loss

i.e. $\qquad n^2 (80) = 50$ or $n = \sqrt{\dfrac{50}{80}} = 0.79$

∴ kVA output at maximum $\qquad \eta = n\,(10) = (0.79)\,(10) = 7.9$ kVA.

Note that the kVA output at maximum efficiency does not depend on the load p.f.

For maximum efficiency, ohmic loss = core loss = 50 watts.

∴ Total losses at maximum η = 50 + 50 = 100 W.

$$\text{The magnitude of maximum efficiency } = 1 - \frac{100}{(7900)(0.8) + 100} = 0.98443 \text{ or } 98.443\%.$$

(c) From short-circuit test,

$$r_{eH} = \frac{45}{9} = 5\ \Omega$$

$$z_{eH} = \frac{60}{3} = 20\ \Omega$$

$$\therefore \qquad x_{eH} = \sqrt{(20)^2 - (5)^2} = 19.35\ \Omega$$

$$\therefore \qquad \varepsilon_r = \frac{I_H \cdot r_{eH}}{V_H} = \frac{4 \times 5}{2500} = 0.008 \text{ p.u.}$$

$$\varepsilon_x = \frac{I_H \cdot x_{eH}}{V_H} = \frac{4 \times 19.35}{2500} = 0.031.$$

$\therefore$ Voltage regulation at 0.8 p.f. lagging $= \varepsilon_r \cos\theta_2 + \varepsilon_x \sin\theta_2$

$= 0.008\,(0.8) + 0.031\,(0.6) = 0.0250$ p.u. or 2.5%

[**Check.** From Eq. (1.50), voltage regulation for a lagging p.f. is $\frac{V_{sc}}{E_2}\cos(\theta_{sc} - \theta_2)$ p.u.

$$\text{Now } V_{sc} \text{ for full load current} = 60 \times \frac{\text{Full load current}}{\text{Current during } sc \text{ test}}$$

$$= 60 \times \frac{4}{3} = 80 \text{ V on } h.v. \text{ side} = 8 \text{ V on } l.v. \text{ side}$$

$$V_{sc} I_{sc} \cos\theta_{sc} = P_{sc} = 80 \text{ W}$$

$$\therefore \quad \cos\theta_{sc} = \frac{80}{80 \times 4} = 0.25$$

or $\theta_{sc} = 75.5°$ and $\theta_2 = \cos^{-1}(0.8) = 36.9°$

$$\therefore \quad \text{Voltage regulation at 0.8 p.f. lag} = \frac{8}{250}\cos(75.5° - 36.9°)$$

$$= \frac{8}{250}\cos 38.6 = 0.025 \text{ p.u.]}$$

$$\text{Now} \quad \frac{E_2 - V_2}{E_2} = 0.025 \text{ or } V_2 = 0.975\,E_2.$$

$\therefore$ Secondary terminal voltage at full load $= 0.975\,E_2$

or $V_2 = (0.975)\,(250) = 243.75$ V.

Voltage regulation at 0.8 p.f. leading $= \varepsilon_r \cos\theta_2 - \varepsilon_x \sin\theta_2$

$= (0.008)\,(0.8) - (0.031)\,(0.6) = -0.0122$ or -1.22%.

[**Check.** Per unit voltage regulation at leading p.f.

$$= \frac{V_{sc}}{E_2}\cos(\theta_{sc} + \theta_2) = \frac{8}{250}\cos(75.5° + 36.9°)$$

$$= -\frac{8}{250}\sin 22.4° = -0.0122 \text{ p.u.]}$$

$$\text{Now} \quad \frac{E_2 - V_2}{E_2} = -0.0122 \text{ or } V_2 = 1.0122\,E_2.$$

$\therefore$ Secondary terminal voltage at full load 0.8 p.f. lead,

$$V_2 = 1.0122\,E_2 = 1.0122\,(250) = 253.05 \text{ V}.$$

Example 1.33. *The efficiency of a 20 kVA, 2500/250 V, single-phase transformer at unity p.f. is 98% at rated load and also at half rated load. Determine*

(a) the transformer core loss and ohmic losses; and

(b) the p.u. value of the equivalent resistance of the transformer.

Solution. *(a)*

$$\eta = 1 - \frac{\text{Losses}}{\text{Output + Losses}}$$

At full load,

$$0.98 = 1 - \frac{P_c + P_{sc}}{(20{,}000)(1) + P_c + P_{sc}}$$

or

$$\frac{P_c + P_{sc}}{(20{,}000) + P_c + P_{sc}} = 0.02$$

or

$$(P_c + P_{sc}) = \frac{400}{0.98} = 408 \text{ W}$$

At $\frac{1}{2}$ full load,
$$0.98 = 1 - \frac{P_c + \left(\frac{1}{2}\right)^2 P_{sc}}{\frac{1}{2}(20{,}000)(1) + P_c + \left(\frac{1}{2}\right)^2 P_{sc}}$$

or
$$\frac{P_c + \frac{1}{4}P_{sc}}{10{,}000 + P_c + \frac{1}{4}P_{sc}} = 0.02$$

or
$$\left(P_c + \frac{1}{4}P_{sc}\right) = \frac{200}{0.98} = 204 \text{ W.}$$

But
$$P_c + P_{sc} = 408 \text{ W}$$

∴
$$\frac{3}{4} P_{sc} = 204 \text{ W}$$

or
$$P_{sc} = (204)\left(\frac{4}{3}\right) = 272 \text{ W.}$$

and
$$P_c = 204 - \frac{272}{4} = 136 \text{ W.}$$

(*b*) From Eq. (1.42) p.u. value of $r_e = \frac{\text{Ohmic losses}}{\text{Rated VA}} = \frac{272}{20{,}000} = \mathbf{0.0136.}$

Example 1.34. *The maximum efficiency of a 100 kVA, single phase transformer is 98% and occurs at 80% of full load at 0.8 p.f. If the leakage impedance of the transformer is 5%, find the voltage regulation at rated load of 0.8 p.f. lagging.*

Solution. Efficiency
$$\eta = \frac{\text{Output}}{\text{Output + Losses}}$$

or
$$\frac{\text{Output + Losses}}{\text{Output}} = \frac{1}{\eta} = 1 + \frac{\text{Losses}}{\text{Output}}$$

∴
$$\text{Losses} = \left(\frac{1}{\eta} - 1\right) \text{Output}$$

Output at maximum $\eta = (100{,}000)\ (0.8)\ (0.8) = 64{,}000$ W.

$$\text{Total transformer losses} = \left(\frac{1}{0.98} - 1\right)(64{,}000) = 1308 \text{ watts.}$$

At maximum η, ohmic losses = core loss $P_c = \frac{1308}{2} = 654$ W

These ohmic losses of 654 W occur at 80% of full load current.

∴
$$\text{Ohmic losses at full load} = 654\left(\frac{100}{80}\right)^2 = 1022 \text{ W.}$$

From Eq. (1.42),
$$r_{e.p.u.} = \frac{1022}{100{,}000} = 0.01022 = \varepsilon_r$$

It is given that
$$z_{e.p.u.} = 0.05$$

$$x_{e.p.u.} = \sqrt{(0.05)^2 - (0.01022)^2} = 0.0489 = \varepsilon_x$$

$$\text{Voltage regulation} = \varepsilon_r \cos\theta_2 + \varepsilon_x \sin\theta_2$$
$$= (0.01022)\ (0.8) + (0.0489)\ (0.6) = \mathbf{(0.0375)} \text{ or } \mathbf{3.75\%}.$$

Example 1.35. *The full-load voltage drops in a single-phase transformer are 2% and 4% due respectively to resistance and leakage reactance. The full-load ohmic loss is equal to the iron loss. Calculate*

(a) the efficiency on full load at unity p.f.

(b) the full-load p.f. at which voltage drop is maximum and

(c) the load p.f. at which voltage drop is zero.

Solution. Percentage full-load voltage drop in resistance $= \dfrac{I_2 r_{e2}}{E_2} \times 100 = 2$

Percentage full-load voltage drop in leakage reactance $= \dfrac{I_2 x_{e2}}{E_2} \times 100 = 4$

(a) From above, $\dfrac{I_2^2 r_{e2}}{I_2 E_2} = 0.02$

$\therefore$ Full-load ohmic loss = 0.02 × Rated VA = Iron loss (given)

Full-load
$$\eta = \frac{\text{Rated VA} \times 1}{\text{Rated VA} \times 1 + I_2^2 r_{e2} + \text{Iron loss}} \times 100$$
$$= \frac{\text{Rated VA} \times 100}{\text{Rated VA} + 0.02 \times \text{Rated VA} + 0.02 \times \text{Rated VA}}$$
$$= \frac{100}{1.04} = 96.154\%$$

(b) Maximum voltage drop means maximum voltage regulation. Therefore, full-load p.f. at which voltage drop is maximum

$$= \frac{r_{e2}}{z_{e2}} = \frac{\text{percentage } r_{e2}}{\text{percentage } z_{e2}} = \frac{2}{\sqrt{2^2+4^2}} = 0.4472 \text{ lagging.}$$

(c) Load p.f. at which voltage drop is zero

$$= \frac{x_{e2}}{z_{e2}} = \frac{\text{percentage } x_{e2}}{\text{percentage } z_{e2}} = \frac{4}{\sqrt{2^2+4^2}} = 0.8944 \text{ leading.}$$

Example 1.36. *When a 20 kVA, 3300/220 V, 50 Hz transformer is operated on rated voltage at no load, its power input is 160 watts at a p.f. of 0.15. Under rated load conditions, the voltage drops in the total resistance and total leakage reactance are, respectively, 1 and 3 per cent of rated voltage. Determine input power and p.f. when the transformer delivers 14.96 kW at 220 V at 0.8 p.f. lagging to a load on the LV side.*

Solution. Load current, $I_2 = \dfrac{14{,}960}{220 \times 0.8} = 85$ A

Rated current on *LV* side $= \dfrac{20{,}000}{220}$ A

It is given that $\dfrac{\text{Rated current} \times r_{e2}}{E_2} = 0.01$

$\therefore$ $r_{e2} = \dfrac{0.01 \times 220 \times 220}{20{,}000} = 0.0242\ \Omega$

and $x_{e2} = \dfrac{0.03 \times 220 \times 220}{20{,}000} = 0.0726\ \Omega$

Ohmic loss = (load current)$^2 \times r_{e2} = (85)^2 \times 0.0242 = 174.85$ W

$\therefore$ Input power = 14960 + 174.85 + 160 = 15294.85 W

With load current I_2 as reference phasor, Fig. 1.29 *(b)*,

$$\overline{I}_2 = 85 + j\,0$$

and $\overline{V}_2 = 220\,(0.8 + j\,0.6) = 176 + j\,132$

$\therefore$ $\overline{E}_2 = \overline{V}_2 + \overline{I}_2 \overline{z}_{e2} = 176 + j\,132 + 85\,(0.0242 + j\,0.0726)$

$= 178.057 + j\,138.171 = 225.38\ \angle 37.81°$ V

If E_2 is taken as reference for convenience, then I_2 can be written as

$$\bar{I}_2 = 85\angle{-37.81} = 67.155 - j\,52.11 \text{ A and } \bar{E}_2 = 225.38\angle 0°$$

From no-load values,

$$I_0 = \frac{160}{0.15 \times 220} = 4.848 \text{ A}$$

$$I_c = I_0 \cos\theta_0 = \frac{160}{220} = 0.727 \text{ A}$$

$$I_m = \sqrt{(4.848)^2 - (0.727)^2} = 4.793 \text{ A}$$

Note that voltage E_2 appears across R_c and X_m in parallel. As a result, I_c is in plase with E_2 and I_m lags E_2 by 90°. Therefore, no-load current with E_2 as reference, can be written as

$$\bar{I}_0 = 0.727 - j\,4.793$$

$$\therefore \quad \text{Input current} = \bar{I}_2 + \bar{I}_0 = 67.155 - j\,52.11 + 0.727 - j\,4.793$$

$$= 67.882 - j\,56.903 = 88.577\angle{-39.972°}$$

$$\therefore \quad \text{Input p.f.} = \cos(39.972°) = 0.7663 \text{ lag}$$

Strictly speaking,

$$I_c = 0.727 \times \frac{225.38}{220} = 0.745 \text{ A}$$

and

$$I_m = 4.793 \times \frac{225.38}{220} = 4.910 \text{ A}$$

as E_2 appears across R_c, X_m. The results are modified as under :

$$\text{Input current} = 67.155 - j52.11 + 0.745 - j\,4.910$$

$$= 67.9 - j57.02 = 88.666\angle{-40.022°}$$

$$\text{Input p.f.} = \cos(40.022°) = 0.7658 \text{ lag}$$

$$\text{Input power} = 14960 + 174.85 + 160 \times \frac{225.38}{220} = 15302.77 \text{ W.}$$

Example 1.37. *The maximum efficiency of a 1-phase, 11000/400 V, 500 kVA transformer is 98% and occurs at 80% full load, unity power factor. The percentage impedance is 4.5%. Load power factor is now varied while load current and the supply voltage are held constant at their rated values. Determine the load power factor at which the secondary terminal voltage is minimum and find the value of the later.*

Solution. Total losses in transformer $= \left(\frac{1}{0.988} - 1\right) \times 500{,}000 \times 0.8 = 4858.3$ W

These losses are under the condition of maximum efficiency. Therefore, core losses = ohmic losses at 80% full load $= \frac{1}{2} \times 4858.3 = 2429.15$ W

$$\text{Full-load ohmic losses} = 2429.15\left(\frac{100}{80}\right)^2 = 3795.55 \text{ W}$$

From Eq. (1.42),

$$r_{e2} = \frac{3795.55}{500{,}000} \times 100 = 0.759\%$$

$$x_{e2} = \sqrt{z_{e2}^2 - r_{e2}^2} = [4.5^2 - 0.759^2]^{1/2} = 4.4355\%$$

It is already proved that load p.f. at which voltage regulation is maximum, or the load p.f. at which secondary terminal voltage is minimum, is given by

$$\cos\theta_2 = \frac{r_{e2}}{z_{e2}} = \frac{0.759}{4.5} = 0.1687 \text{ lag}$$

Now

$$\frac{E_2 - V_2}{E_2} = (r_{e2}\cos\theta_2 + x_{e2}\sin\theta_2) \text{ in per unit}$$

$$\therefore \quad \frac{E_2 - V_2}{E_2} \times 100 = (0.759 \times 0.1687 + 4.4355 \times 0.98567) = 4.5$$

or

$$V_2 = E_2(1 - 0.045) = 400 \times 0.955 = 382 \text{ V}$$

$\therefore$ Secondary terminal voltage = 382 V

Example 1.38. *A 5 kVA, single-phase transformer has a core loss of 40 watts and full load ohmic loss of 100 watts. The daily variation of load on the transformer is as follows :*

7 A.M. to 1 P.M.: *3 kW at p.f. 0.6*

1 P.M. to 6 P.M.: *2 kW at p.f. 0.8*

6 P.M. to 1 A.M.: *6 kW at p.f. 0.9*

1 A.M. to 7 A.M.: *No load.*

Determine the all day efficiency of the transformer.

Solution. Note that core loss remains fixed at 40 W, whereas ohmic losses vary as the square of the kVA load.

7 A.M. to 1 P.M., $\quad \text{kVA load} = \dfrac{3}{0.6} = 5 \text{ kVA}$

$\therefore \quad \text{Ohmic losses for 6 hours} = (100)\left(\dfrac{5}{5}\right)^2 = 100 \text{ W}$

1 P.M. to 6 P.M. ; $\quad \text{kVA load} = \dfrac{2}{0.8} = 2.5 \text{ kVA}$

$\therefore \quad \text{Ohmic losses for 5 hours} = (100)\left(\dfrac{2.5}{5.0}\right)^2 = 25 \text{ W}$

6 P.M. to 1 A.M. ; $\quad \text{kVA load} = \dfrac{6}{0.9} = \dfrac{20}{3} \text{ kVA}$

$\therefore \quad \text{Ohmic losses for 7 hours} = (100)\left(\dfrac{20}{3 \times 5}\right)^2 = 177.8 \text{ W.}$

1 A.M. to 7 A.M. ; $\quad \text{Ohmic losses} = 0$

$$\therefore \quad \text{Daily energy lost as ohmic losses} = \frac{1}{1000}[(100)(6) + (25)(5) + (177.8)(7)]$$

$$= \frac{1969.6}{1000} = 1.97 \text{ kWh}$$

$$\text{Daily energy lost as core loss} = \frac{40 \times 24}{1000} = 0.960 \text{ kWh.}$$

$$\therefore \quad \text{Total kWh lost} = 1.970 + 0.960 = 2.93 \text{ kWh.}$$

$$\text{Daily kWh output} = [3 \times 6 + 2 \times 5 + 6 \times 7 + 0] = 70 \text{ kWh.}$$

$$\therefore \text{All day} \quad \eta = 1 - \frac{\text{Daily losses in kWh}}{(\text{Daily output + Daily losses}) \text{ in kWh}}$$

$$= 1 - \frac{2.93}{72.93} = 0.9598 \text{ or } 95.98\%.$$

1.13.3. Separation of Hysteresis and Eddy Current Losses

In this article is given a method for separating the transformer core loss into its two components of hysteresis and eddy-current losses.

For a sine flux wave, the transformer core loss, from Eq. (1.52) is

$$P_c = K_h f B_m^x + K_e f^2 B_m^2 \qquad \text{...(1.52)}$$

It may be seen from this equation that hysteresis loss varies linearly with frequency whereas the eddy current loss varies as the square of the frequency.

Division of both sides of Eq. (1.52) by f, gives,

$$\text{Core loss per cycle} = \frac{P_c}{f} = K_h B_m^x + K_e f B_m^2 \qquad \text{...(1.63)}$$

Eq. (1.63) shows that hysteresis loss per cycle is independent of frequency whereas eddy current loss per cycle is proportional to frequency.

Now $$V \cong E = \sqrt{2}\,\pi f N \phi_{max}$$

or $$\frac{V}{f} = \sqrt{2}\,\pi N \times \phi_{max} = \sqrt{2}\,\pi N B_m A_i$$

For any transformer N and A_i are constant, therefore, $B_m \propto \frac{V}{f}$. For a particular value of $\frac{V}{f}$ or of maximum flux density B_m, Eq. (1.63) can be written as

$$\frac{P_c}{f} = K_1 + K_2 f \qquad ...(1.64)$$

where constant $K_1 = K_h B_m^x$ and constant $K_2 = K_e B_m^2$.

Equation (1.64) is the equation of a straight line. Consequently, the plot of P_c/f against frequency f, results in a straight line, as shown in Fig. 1.35

The values of K_1 and K_2 in Eq. (1.64) can be determined by performing open circuit test on the transformer. During this test, the applied voltage V and frequency f are varied together so as to keep V/f (and therefore B_m) almost constant. In the laboratory, the ratio V/f can be maintained constant by a d.c. motor-driven alternator feeding the transformer on open circuit. An adjustment of the speed of the alternator and its excitation help in keeping ratio V/f constant. A wattmeter during the open circuit test registers the core loss. After P_c, V and f are recorded, the core loss per cycle is plotted against frequency f. The intercept of the straight line on the vertical axis, gives the value of constant K_1 and the slope of the line AB gives constant K_2. Once K_1 and K_2 are known, the hysteresis and eddy current losses can be determined separately.

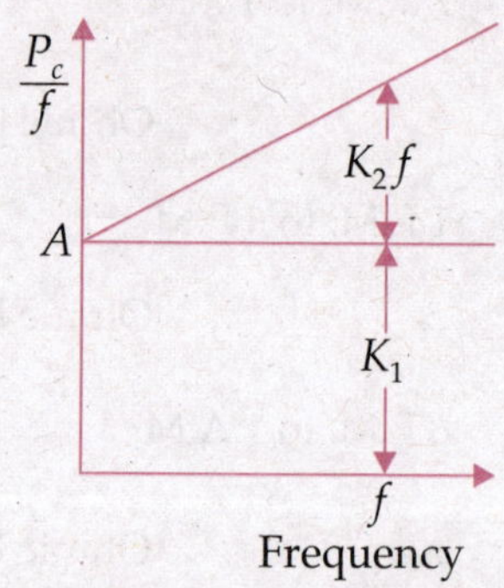

Fig 1.35: Plot of core losses per cycle against frequency

From Eq. (1.64), $$P_c = K_1 f + K_2 f^2 = P_h + P_e$$

$\therefore$ $$P_h = K_1 f$$

and $$P_e = K_2 f^2 \qquad ...(1.65)$$

For the separation of core loss of a three-phase transformer, the readings should be changed to per phase values, before plotting $\frac{P_c}{f}$ against f.

Example 1.39. *An open circuit test when performed on the delta side of a bank of three-phase transformer gave the following data :*

Terminal voltage in V	214	171.00	128.4	85.6
Frequency in Hz	50	40	30	20
Power input in W	100	72.5	50	30

Determine the hysteresis and eddy current losses at :

(a) 60 Hz and (b) 40 Hz

Solution. First of all the readings are changed to per phase values, as given below :

Per phase voltage in V	214	171.00	128.40	85.6
Per phase power in W, i,e. P_c	33.3	24.2	16.67	10

It may be seen that the ratio $\frac{V}{f}$ has a constant value of 4.28. Therefore, Eq. (1.64) can be used for separating the hysteresis and eddy current losses.

The core loss per cycle, *i.e.* $\frac{P_c}{f}$ is calculated in a tabular form as follows :

$\frac{P_c}{f}$	0.667	0.605	0.556	0.50
f	50	40	30	20

In Fig. 1.36, $\frac{P_c}{f}$ is plotted against f. The straight line so obtained intersects the vertical axis at the point A. The intercept OA gives the value of K_1 equal to 0.39. The slope of the line AB can be obtained at any frequency, say 50 Hz.

$$\therefore \qquad K_2\,(50) = 0.667 - 0.39 = 0.277$$

$$\text{or} \qquad K_2 = \frac{0.277}{50} = 0.00554.$$

From Eq. (1.64),

(*a*) P_h per phase = (0.39) (60) = 23.4 W

P_e per phase = (0.00554) $(60)^2$ = 19.95 W

∴ Total hysteresis and eddy-current losses at 60 Hz are 23.4 × 3 = 70.2 W and 59.85 W respectively.

(*b*) P_h per phase = (0.39) (40) = 15.6 W

P_e per phase = (0.00554) $(40)^2$ = 8.86 W.

Total hysteresis and eddy-current losses at 40 Hz are 46.8 W and 26.58 W respectively.

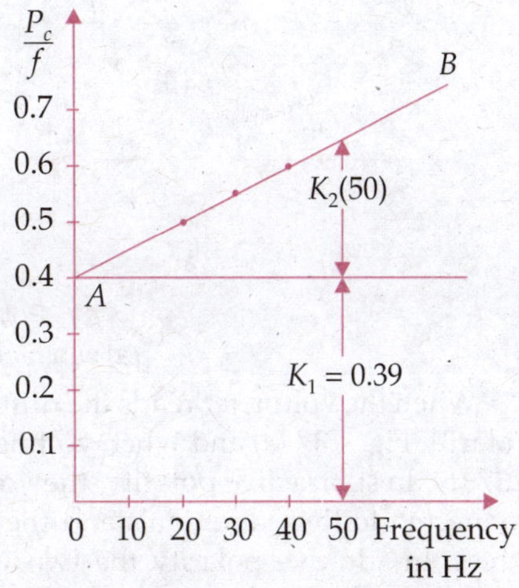

Fig 1.36: Pertaining to Example 1.39

1.14. TESTING OF TRANSFORMERS

A wide variety of tests can be performed on a transformer and in this article, only a few of them are dealt with. The tests to be described here, are simple, can be performed easily in the laboratory and are helpful in gaining a better physical insight into the transformer behaviour.

(*a*) **Polarity test.** On the primary side of a two-winding transformer, one terminal is positive with respect to the other terminal at any one instant. At the same instant, one terminal of the secondary winding is positive with respect to the other terminal. These relative polarities of the primary and secondary terminals at any instant must be known if the transformers are to be operated in parallel or are to be used in a polyphase circuit.

When viewed from the h.v. side, the terminals are marked A_1 and A_2, the former, *i.e.* A_1 being on the extreme right, as per IS–2026. Terminals A_1 and A_2 are marked plus and minus arbitrarily in Fig. 1.37. Now terminal A_1 is connected to one end of the secondary winding and a voltmeter is connected between A_2 and other end of the secondary winding. A voltage of suitable value is now applied to the h.v. winding. Let E_1 and E_2 be the emfs induced on h.v. and l.v. sides respectively. If the voltmeter reading is equal to $E_1 - E_2$, then secondary terminal connected to A_1 is positive and is marked a_1, the l.v. terminal connected to A_2 through the voltmeter is negative and is marked a_2 as shown in Fig. 1.37 (*a*). If voltmeter reading is equal to $E_1 + E_2$, then the terminals connected to A_1 and A_2 are negative and positive and are marked a_2 and a_1 respectively as shown in Fig. 1.37 (*b*). The subscript numbers 1, 2 on the h.v. and l.v. windings are so arranged that when A_2 is negative with respect to A_1, a_2 is also negative with respect to a_1 at the same instant. In other words, if the instantaneous emf is directed from A_2 to A_1 in h.v. winding, it is at the same time directed from a_2 to a_1 in the l.v. winding.

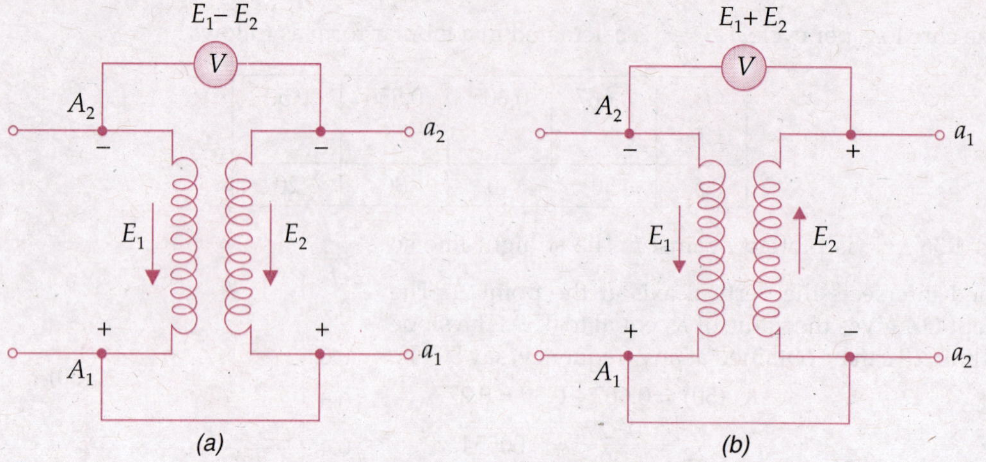

Fig 1.37: Polarity test on a two winding transformer *(a)* subtractive polarity and *(b)* additive polarity.

When the voltmeter reads the difference $E_1 - E_2$, the transformer is said to possess a subtractive polarity Fig. 1.37 (*a*) and when voltmeter reads $E_1 + E_2$, the transformer has additive polarity Fig. 1.37 *(b)*. In subtractive polarity, the voltage between A_2 and a_2 (or A_1 and a_1) is reduced. The leads connected to these terminals and the two windings are, therefore, not subjected to high voltage stress. In additive polarity the two windings and the leads connected to A_1, A_2, a_1 and a_2 are subjected to high voltage stresses. On account of these reasons, subtractive polarity is preferable to additive polarity.

(b) **Open circuit and** *(c)* **Short circuit tests.** These two tests have already been described in detail in Art. 1.10.

(d) **Load test (Back to back or Sumpner's test).** A load test on a transformer is necessary if its maximum temperatures rise is to be determined. A small transformer can be put on full load by means of a suitable load impedance. But for large transformers, full load test is difficult, since it involves considerable waste of energy and a suitable load, capable of absorbing full load power, is not easily available. However, large transformers can be put on full load by means of Sumpner's or back to back test. The Sumpner's test can also be used for calculating the efficiency of a transformer, though the latter can be determined accurately from open-circuit and short-circuit tests.

The back to back test on single-phase transformers requires two identical units. Fig. 1.38 illustrates the circuit for two single-phase transformers, where two primaries connected in parallel, are energised at rated voltage and rated frequency. With secondaries open, the wattmeter W_1 records the core losses of both the transformers. The two secondaries are connected in series with their polarities in phase opposition, which can be checked by means of a voltmeter. The range of this voltmeter connected across terminals *ab*, Fig. 1.38, should be double the rated voltage of either transformer secondary. Zero voltmeter reading ($V_{ab} = 0$) indicates the secondaries are connected in opposition. Now, if the terminals *ab* are short-circuited, the current in the secondary would be zero because $V_{ab} = 0$ and the wattmeter reading W_1 remains unaltered. In case the voltmeter reads the sum of the two secondary voltages, the secondaries are in the same phase. In order to bring them in phase opposition, terminals *ad* should be joined together to result in zero voltage across terminals *bc*.

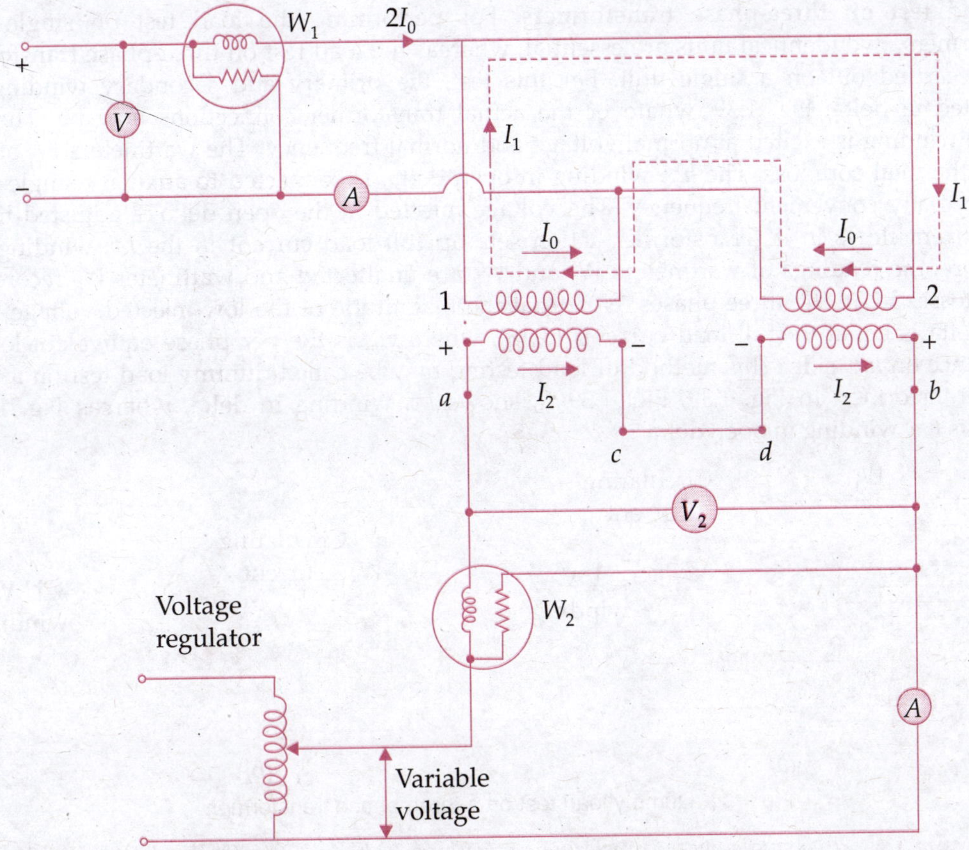

Fig 1.38: Sumpner's (or back to back) test on two identical single-phase transformers.

In Fig. 1.38, it is assumed that voltage across *ab* is zero and the two secondaries are in phase opposition. Now a voltage is injected in the secondary circuit by means of a voltage regulator, fed from the source connected to the primaries or from a separate source. The injected voltage is adjusted till rated current flows in the two series-connected secondaries. By transformer action, primary windings also carry rated current. Note that the full load current in the primaries, completes its path through the main bus bars (shown dotted) and, therefore, the reading of wattmeter W_1 remains unaffected. It may be seen that the reading of voltmeter V_2 is equal to the sum of leakage impedance drops in both the transformers. The low-injected voltage has given rise to full load currents in primary and secondary windings, therefore, the full load ohmic losses of both the transformers are measured by the wattmeter W_2 (Fig. 1.38). If P_c and P_{sc} are the core and ohmic losses in each transformer, then the reading of wattmeter $W_1 = 2P_c$ and that of wattmeter $W_2 = 2P_{sc}$. The efficiency can now be determined by using Eq. (1.57) or Eq. (1.60).

It is seen from above that in Sumpner's test, even though the transformers are not supplying any load current, yet full iron-loss occurs in their cores and full-load ohmic-loss occurs in their windings. Net power input to the two transformers is $(2P_c + 2P_{sc})$. If temperature rise of the two transformers is to be measured, then the two transformers are kept under rated loss conditions for several hours till maximum stable temperature is reached.

If $2I_0$ is the no load current, then for the assumed directions of I_0 and I_2, the primary current of transformer 1 is less (difference of $\overline{I}_1$ and $\overline{I}_0$) than the primary current of transformer 2 (sum of $\overline{I}_1$ and $\overline{I}_0$). Therefore, the two transformers do not operate under identical conditions–one may have slightly less temperature than the other.

Load test on three-phase transformers. For performing the load test on single-phase transformers, two identical units are essential, whereas the load test on three-phase transformers can be carried out on a single unit. For this test, the primary and secondary windings are connected in delta, Fig. 1.39, whatever the actual transformer connections may be. The low-voltage winding is excited at normal voltage and normal frequency. The wattmeters W_1 and W_2 record the total core loss. The *h.v.* winding in open delta, is connected to auxiliary single-phase supply of any convenient frequency. The voltage injected in the open delta is adjusted till full load current flows in it. Transformer action sets up full load current in the *l.v.* winding also. As before, the readings of wattmeters W_1 and W_2 are unaffected and wattmeter W_3 records the ohmic losses in all the three phases. Note that the magnitude of the low-injected voltage in the open delta is equal to (full load current) ($3z_{eH}$), where z_{eH} is the per phase equivalent leakage impedance on *h.v.* side. This method of load testing may be called dummy load test on a three-phase transformer. In Fig. 1.39, Fig. 1.39*(a)*, shows *l.v.* winding in delta, whereas Fig. 1.39*(b)* shows its *h.v.* winding in open delta.

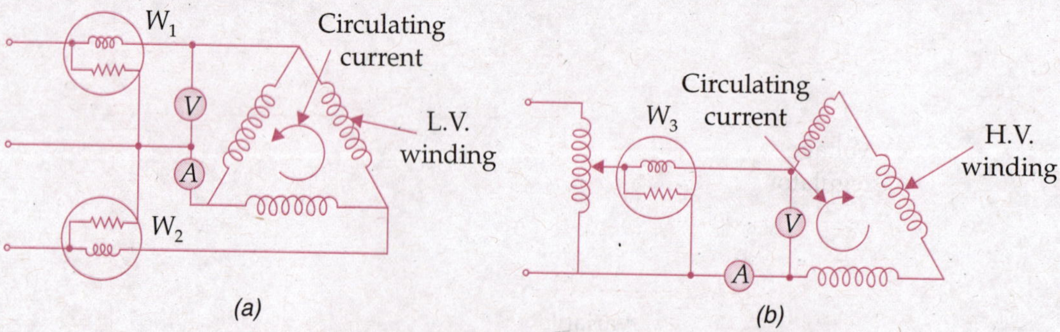

Fig 1.39: Dummy load test on a three-phase transformer.

Example 1.40. *Two single-phase transformers of ratings 10 kVA, 230/400 V and 10 kVA, 230/410 V are employed for back to back test. The l.v. side is fed from 230 V supply mains whereas a voltage regulator connected to the same 230 V mains feeds 25 A in the series connected h.v. windings. For a core loss of 200 W in each transformer, calculate the reading of the wattmeter connected on the l.v. side. Each transformer has its reluctance equal to three times its resistance.*

Solution. Had the voltage ratios of the two transformers been equal, the wattmeter on the *l.v.* side would read 400 W. But this is not the case in the present example.

A current of 25 A induces the following currents in the primaries of Fig. 1.40 :

$$\text{Primary current of transformer 1} = \frac{25 \times 400}{230} = \frac{1000}{23} \text{ A}$$

$$\text{and primary current of transformer 2} = \frac{25 \times 410}{230} = \frac{1025}{23} \text{ A}$$

These two primary currents, caused by 25 A in the secondary winding, are shown in Fig. 1.40. Kirchoff's current law at the junction *K* of this figure shows that $\frac{1025}{23} - \frac{1000}{23} = \frac{25}{23}$ A must flow through ammeter A_1 and the current coil of wattmeter W_1. Thus the reading of wattmeter W_1 is affected by an amount equal to $230 \times \frac{25}{23} \times \cos\theta_{sc}$.

Now

$$\cos\theta_{sc} = \text{p.f. during transformer short-circuit}$$

$$= \frac{r_e}{Z_e} = \frac{r_e}{\sqrt{r_e^2 + x_e^2}} = \frac{r_e}{\sqrt{r_e^2 + (3r_e)^2}} = \frac{1}{\sqrt{10}}$$

$\therefore$ The amount by which reading of wattmeter W_1 is affected

$$= 230 \times \frac{25}{23} \times \frac{1}{\sqrt{10}} = 79.1 \text{ watts.}$$

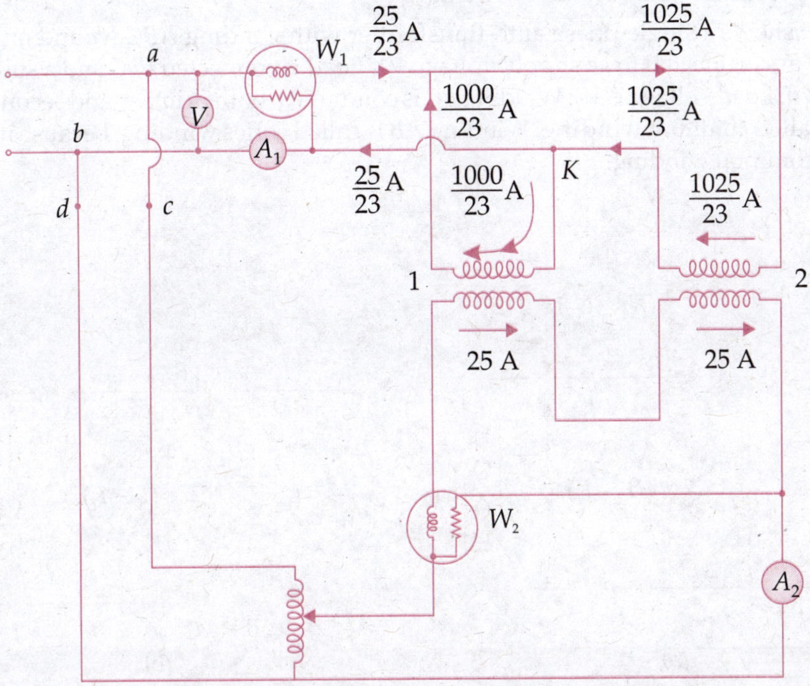

Fig 1.40: Pertaining to Example 1.40

With terminal *a* connected to *c* and terminal *b* to *d*, the currents 25/23 A and I_0 flow in the same direction in the current coil of wattmeter W_1. Therefore, the wattmeter reading is increased to (400 + 79.1) = 479.1 watts.

If *c* is connected to *b* and *d* to *a*, it will be seen that 25/23 A and I_0 flow opposite to each other and consequently the reading of wattmeter W_1 is reduced to (400 – 79.1) = 320.9 watts.

Hence the reading of wattmeter W_1 may be 479.1 watts or 320.9 watts, depending on the arrangement of connections.

Example 1.41. *A 300 kVA, 3300/400 V, three-phase transformer has its primary and secondary windings connected in delta for a dummy load test. For circulating full load current, the magnitude of the voltage injected in the open delta of h.v. windings, is 360 V. Calculate the leakage impedance per phase in ohms and in per unit system.*

Solution. The voltage across each phase of the *h.v.* winding $= \frac{360}{3} = 120\ V = V_{sc}$

On the *h.v.* side, $\quad V_{ph} = 3300$ V

and $$I_{ph} = \frac{300 \times 10^2}{3 \times 3300} = \frac{100}{3.3} \text{ A} = I_{sc}$$

$$\therefore \quad z_{eH} \text{ in ohms} = \frac{V_{sc}}{I_{sc}} = \frac{120}{100/3.3} = 3.96\ \Omega.$$

$$Z_{base} = \frac{V_{base}}{I_{base}} = \frac{\text{rate } V_{ph}}{\text{rated } I_{ph}} = \frac{3300}{100/3.3} = 108.9\ \Omega$$

$$\therefore \quad z_{eH} \text{ in p.u.} = \frac{z_{eH} \text{ in } \Omega}{Z_{base}} = \frac{3.96}{108.9} = 0.0364 \text{ p.u.}$$

1.15. SINGLE-PHASE AUTO TRANSFORMERS

A single-phase auto-transformer is **one winding transformer** in which a part of the winding is common to both primary and secondary circuits.

Fig. 1.41 *(a)* shows a single-phase auto-transformer with winding *ABC* wound on an iron core. Terminals *A*, *C* are connected to ac supply voltage V_1. Load is connected to *C* and a suitable tapping point *B* as shown. Load voltage is V_2. Winding *BC* is common to both primary and secondary circuits; it is therefore called **common winding**. Winding *AB* is called series winding, because it is connected in series with common winding.

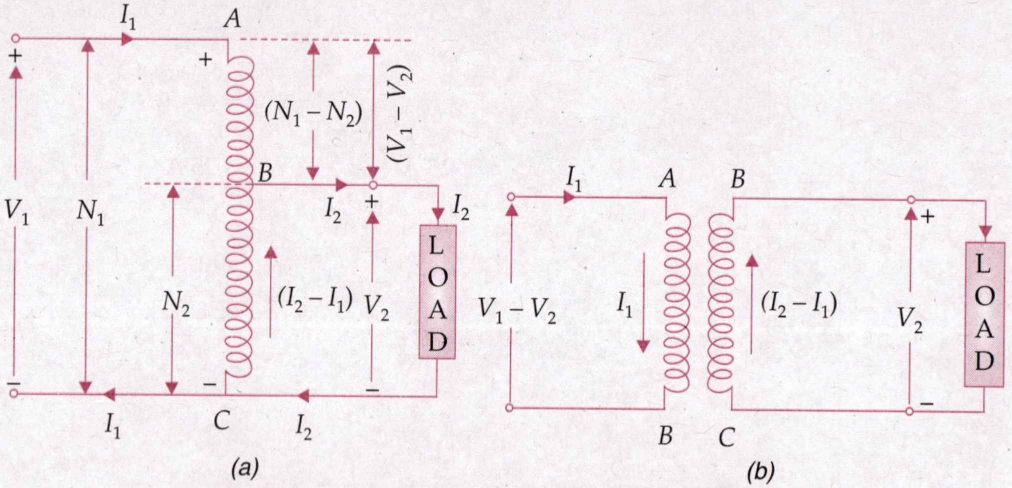

Fig 1.41: *(a)* Single-phase step-down auto-transformer
(b) auto-transformer of Fig. 1.41*(a)* connected as a two-winding transformer.

When winding *ABC* is energized from source V_1, working flux induces emf E_1 in winding *ABC*. At the same time, an emf E_2 is induced in between terminals *B* and *C*. Therefore, $(E_1/N_1) = (E_2/N_2)$. If terminal *B* can be moved up or down, *i.e.* if terminal *B* is a sliding contact, the output voltage V_2 can be varied. Voltage across terminals *A* and *B* is $(V_1 - V_2)$.

1.15.1. Step-down Autotransformer.

A step-down auto-transformer is one in which secondary voltage is less than the primary input voltage. A simple arrangement of a step-down auto-transformer is shown in Fig. 1.41*(a)* because here $V_2 < V_1$. Neglecting losses, input power, $V_1 I_1 \cos\theta_1$ = output power, $V_2 I_2 \cos\theta_2$. For an ideal auto-transformer (losses and voltage drops neglected), $\cos\theta_1 = \cos\theta_2$; therefore $V_1 I_1 = V_2 I_2$ and $I_1 N_1 = I_2 N_2$.

$$\therefore \quad \frac{V_2}{V_1} = \frac{I_1}{I_2} = \frac{N_2}{N_1} = k \qquad \text{...(1.66)}$$

Here *k* is less than unity. The relations expressed by Eq. (1.66) are identical with a two-winding transformer, see Eq. (1.10).

Let the terminal *A* in Fig. 1.41*(a)* be positive with respect to terminal *C*, at the instant shown. Then, at no load, the exciting current flows from *A* to *C*. As a result, winding *ABC* creates a working flux vertically downward in the core. When winding *BC* is connected to load, current must flow from *C* to *B* in order to oppose the working flux as per Lenz's law. But working flux in a transformer remains almost constant at its no-load value. Therefore, primary must draw an additional current I_1 from source in order to neutralise the effect of current I_{CB}. Thus, current in winding *ABC* is I_1

from A to B and B to C and current I_2 from C to B. Here $I_2 > I_1$, because $V_2 > V_1$. KCL at node B gives $I_{CB} + I_1 - I_2 = 0$ or $I_{CB} = I_2 - I_1$.

Mmf of winding $AB = I_1 (N_1 - N_2)$

$$= (I_2 - I_1) N_2 \qquad ...[\because I_1 N_1 = I_2 N_2]$$

$$= I_{CB} \cdot N_2 = \text{mmf of winding } CB$$

This shows that transformer action takes place between winding AB and winding BC. In other words, voltamperes across winding AB are transferred by transformer action to the load connected across winding BC.

$$\therefore \quad \text{Transformed } VA = V_{AB} I_{AB} = (V_1 - V_2) I_1$$

$$\text{Also transformed } VA = V_{CB} I_{CB} = V_2 (I_2 - I_1)$$

Total input VA to auto-transformer = $V_1 I_1$= output $VA = V_2 I_2$

$$\therefore \quad \frac{\text{Transformed VA}}{\text{Input VA to auto-transformer}} = \frac{(V_1 - V_2) I_1}{V_1 I_1} = 1 - \frac{V_2}{V_1} = (1 - k) \qquad ...(1.67)$$

Out of the total input volt-amperes $V_1 I_1$ to auto-transformer, only $V_{AB} I_{AB} = (V_1 - V_2) I_1$ are delivered to the output by transformer action. The rest of the voltamperes required for the output are **conducted** directly from the input.

$$\therefore \quad \text{Conducted VA} = \text{Total input VA} - \text{transformed VA}$$

$$= V_1 I_1 - (V_1 - V_2) I_1 = V_2 I_1$$

$$\therefore \quad \frac{\text{Conducted VA}}{\text{Input VA to auto-transformer}} = \frac{V_2 I_1}{V_1 I_1} = k \qquad ...(1.68\ a)$$

Neglecting internal impedance drops and losses, Eqs. (1.67) and (1.68) become,

$$\frac{\text{Transformed power}}{\text{Input power to auto-transformer}} = 1 - k \qquad ...(1.69)$$

$$\text{and} \quad \frac{\text{Conducted power}}{\text{Input power to auto-transformer}} = k \qquad ...(1.68\ b)$$

Eq. (1.69) may be written as

$$\frac{\text{Inductively transformed power}}{\text{Total input power to auto-transformer}} = (1 - k) = \frac{V_1 - V_2}{V_1} = \frac{\text{High voltage} - \text{Low voltage}}{\text{High voltage}}$$

It is seen from above that auto-transformer of Fig. 1.41*(a)* is equivalent to two-winding transformer, with winding AB acting as primary and winding BC as the secondary, see Fig. 1.41*(b)*. Output of this equivalent two-winding transformer = rating of $AB = (V_1 - V_2) I_1$ = rating of $BC = (I_2 - I_1) V_2$.

For auto-transformer of Fig. 1.41*(a)*, output VA = $V_2 I_2$

$$\left.\begin{aligned} \therefore \quad \frac{\text{Output VA of auto-transformer}}{\text{Output VA of equivalent two-winding transformer}} &= \frac{V_2 I_2}{(V_1 - V_2) I_1} = \frac{1}{1-k} \\ \text{or} \quad \frac{V_2 I_2}{(I_2 - I_1) V_2} &= \frac{1}{1-k} \end{aligned}\right\} \qquad ...(1.70)$$

Since k is less than one, $\left(\frac{1}{1-k}\right)$ is more than unity. Eq. (1.70) shows that a two-winding transformer connected as a step-down auto-transformer would have its VA rating $\left[\frac{1}{1-k}\right]$ times the rating of two-winding transformer. This increment in rating becomes more pronounced as k approaches unity. Ideally, if $k = 1$, then Eq. (1.68 *b*) shows that conducted power is equal to the entire input power and Eq. (1.69) shows that transformed power is zero. This shows that there is no need of an auto-transformer if $k = 1$.

If $k = 0.8$, Eq. (1.70) gives VA rating of auto-transformer $= \dfrac{1}{1-0.8} = 5 \times$ VA rating of 2-winding transformer. This implies that a two-winding 1000 VA transformer with $k = 0.8$ would give an output of 5000 VA when connected as an auto-transformer.

1.15.2. Step-up Auto-transformer

Fig. 1.42 shows a single-phase step-up auto-transformer. The number of turns in winding ABC is N_2 and in winding BC, it is N_1. Therefore, winding AB has $(N_2 - N_1)$ turns.

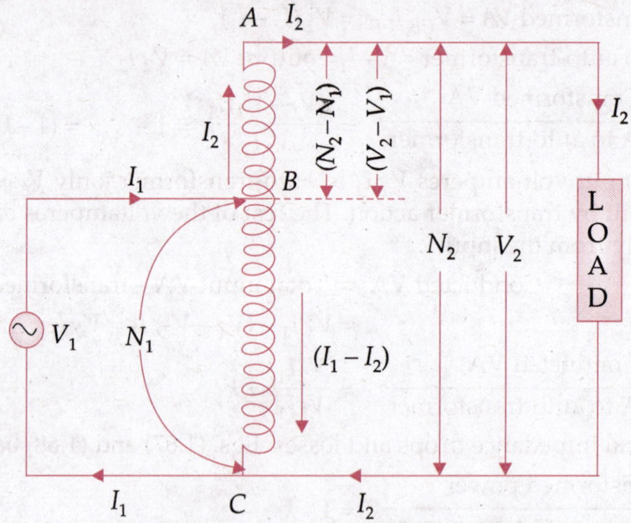

Fig 1.42: Single-phase step-up auto-transformer

Here $V_2 > V_1$ and $I_2 < I_1$. Current I_2 is the load current. Current in winding BC is $(I_1 - I_2)$ downward. Assuming ideal conditions,

$$\frac{V_1}{V_2} = \frac{I_2}{I_1} = \frac{N_1}{N_2} = \text{k (less than one)}$$

Mmf of winding $AB = I_2 (N_2 - N_1) = I_1 N_1 - I_2 - N_1$

$= (I_1 - I_2)N_1 = I_{BC}. N_1$

$=$ mmf of winding BC.

This shows that transformer action occurs between windings BC and AB as in a step-down auto-transformer. As before, voltamperes across BC are transferred by transformer action as voltamperes to winding AB.

If the windings BC and AB are used as primary and secondary windings of an equivalent two-winding transformer, then output VA of equivalent two-winding transformer = VA across AB = $(V_2 - V_1) I_2$. Also output VA of step-up auto-transformer of Fig. 1.42 is $V_2 I_2$.

$$\therefore \frac{\text{Output VA of step-up auto-transformer}}{\text{Output VA of equivalent two-winding transformer}} = \frac{V_2 I_2}{(V_2 - V_1) I_2} = \frac{1}{1-k} \quad \text{...(1.71)}$$

Eq. (1.71) shows that enhanced power rating of step-up auto-transformer is also of the same order as in a step-down auto-transformer. Further analysis of step-up auto-transformer can be carried out as done in a step-down auto-transformer.

1.15.3. Saving of Conductor Material in Auto-transformer

The cross-section of a conductor is proportional to the current carried by it. Length of conductor in a winding is proportional to the number of turns in the winding. Thus, the weight of conductor in a winding is proportional to the product of current and number of turns in the winding.

For an auto-transformer of Fig. 1.41*(a)*, winding *AB* carries a current I_1 and has $(N_1 - N_2)$ turns.

$\therefore$ Weight of conductor for winding $AB \propto (N_1 - N_2)\, I_1$

Winding *BC* carries a current $(I_2 - I_1)$ and has N_2 turns

$\therefore$ Weight of conductor for winding $BC \propto (I_2 - I_1)\, N_2$

Hence, total weight of conductor in an auto-transformer is

$$\propto I_1(N_1 - N_2) + (I_2 - I_1)\, N_2$$
$$\propto 2\,(I_1 N_1 - I_1 N_2)$$
$$\propto 2\,(N_1 - N_2)\, I_1$$

If the weight of conductor in an auto-transformer and ordinary two-winding transformer is to be compared, the two types must have the same input $(V_1 I_1)$, same output $(V_2 I_2)$ and same voltage ratio V_1/V_2. Therefore, an ordinary transformers must have voltages V_1, V_2 and currents I_1, I_2 for its primary and secondary windings respectively. If peak flux density and core area are assumed equal, then emf per turn E_t (= $\sqrt{2}\,\pi f B_m A_i$) in the two types of transformers, is the same. Thus a two-winding transformer must have $N_1 \left(= \dfrac{V_1}{E_t}\right)$ and $N_2 \left(= \dfrac{V_2}{E_t}\right)$ turns in its primary and secondary windings respectively.

$\therefore$ Total weight of conductor in a two-winding transformer

$$\propto I_1 N_1 + I_2 N_2$$
$$\propto 2\, I_1 N_1 \text{ or } (2\, I_2 N_2)$$

$$\therefore \frac{\text{Weight of conductor in auto-transformer}}{\text{Weight of conductor in two-winding transformer}} = \frac{2(N_1 - N_2) I_1}{2\, N_1 I_1} = \left(1 - \frac{N_2}{N_1}\right) = 1 - k$$

$\therefore$ [Conductor weight in auto-transformer]

= $(1 - k)$ [Conductor weight in two-winding transformer]

or [Conductor weight in two-winding transformer] – [Conductor weight in auto-transformer]

= k [Conductor weight in two-winding transformer]

$\therefore$ [Saving in conductor material if auto-transformer is used]

= k [Conductor material in a two winding transformer] ...(1.72)

Eq. (1.72) shows that use of an auto-transformer in place of two-winding transformer results in conductor (copper or aluminium), saving to the extent of k times the weight of conductor in a two-winding transformer.

If $k = 0.1$, saving of conductor material is only 10% and for $k = 0.9$, saving of conductor material is 90%. Hence the use of auto-transformer is more economical only when the voltage ratio k is more nearer to unity. In practice, the auto-transformers are used only when k is more than 1/3.

1.15.4. Connecting Two-winding Transformer as an Auto-transformer

A two-winding transformer can be connected as an auto-transformer. For this purpose, consider a conventional 3000/600 V two-winding transformer to be connected as an auto-transformer. This two winding transformer is shown in Fig. 1.43*(a)*. Its *h.v.* terminals are marked *A*, *B* and *l.v.* terminals *C*, *D*. Dots shown in Fig.1.43 *(a)* indicate that when *A* is positive with respect to *B*, *C* is also positive with respect to D at the same instant. Plus and minus polarities are also marked in Fig. 1.43 *(a)* for convenience.

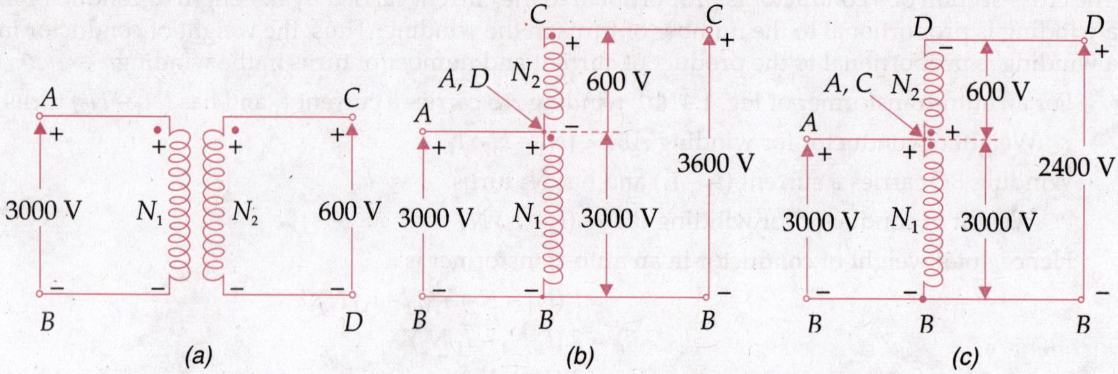

Fig 1.43: *(a)* Single-phase two-winding transformer *(b)* 1-phase step-up auto-transformer with additive polarity and *(c)* 1-phase step-down auto-transformer with subtractive polarity.

Additive polarity. Additive polarity means that the two windings of transformer are so connected to form an auto-transformer that output voltages get **added up**. Therefore, output voltage is more than input voltage for additive polarity and thus, a step-up auto-transformer is obtained. In Fig. 1.43 *(b)*, if terminals A and D are connected together, then input terminals are A, B and output terminals are BC. If we trace the path from B to D and then from D to C, the output voltage across BC is found to be the sum of 3000 V and 600 V *i.e.* 3600 V. Thus, Fig. 1.43 *(b)* gives a step-up auto-transformer.

Subtractive polarity. A subtractive polarity means that the output voltages get subtracted. This scheme, therefore, gives step-down auto-transformer. In Fig. 1.43 *(c)*; A, C are connected together so that input terminals are A, B and output terminals are B, D. As before, travel from B to C and then from C to D. This gives an output voltage equal to the difference of two voltages, *i.e.* 3000 – 600 = 2400 V. Thus, Fig. 1.43 *(c)* gives a step-down auto-transformer.

1.15.5. Advantages, Disadvantages and Applications of Auto-transformers

An auto-transformer uses less conductor material and reduced core material as compared to a two-winding transformer. It has, therefore, the following advantages over a two-winding transformer.

1. Auto-transformer uses less material for its construction, it has, therefore, smaller size as compared to a two-winding transformer.
2. Since auto-transformer uses less conductor and core material, it has lower cost.
3. A reduction in conductor and core material leads to lower ohmic and core losses. Auto-transformer is, therefore, more efficient.
4. Since auto-transformer uses one winding, it has reduced winding resistance and leakage reactance. As a result, auto-transformer has superior voltage regulation than a two-winding transformer of the same output.

Disadvantages

(i) If the ratio of transformation k differs far from unity, the economic advantages of auto-transformer over two-winding transformer decrease.

(ii) The main disadvantage of an auto-transformer is due to the direct electrical connection between the low-voltage and high voltage sides. If primary is supplied at high voltage, then an open circuit in the common winding BC would result in the appearance of dangerously high voltage on the *l.v.* side. This high voltage may be detrimental to the load and the persons working there. Thus, a suitable protection must be provided against such an occurrence.

(iii) Auto-transformer has lower leakage impedance. Therefore, short-circuit current in an auto-transformer is higher than that in a corresponding two-winding transformer.

Applications

1. These are used for obtaining continuously variable ac voltage at the output terminals.
2. These are used for interconnecting power systems having voltage ratios, not differing far from unity; e.g., 132 kV and 220 kV.
3. Auto-transformers are used for the starting of induction motors and synchronous motors.
4. Auto-transformers are also used for the boosting or bucking of supply voltage by a small amount.

1.15.6. Variable Ratio Auto-transformers

For obtaining variable output voltages, variable ratio auto-transformers are used. Variable ratio auto-transformers are known by their trade names, such as variac, dimmerstat, autostat etc.

A variable ratio transformer (or variac) has toroidal core and toroidal winding. A sliding contact with the winding is made by carbon brush, see Fig.1.44. The position of the sliding contact can be varied by handwheel and with this, the output voltage gets changed. A variac used for starting induction motors and synchronous motors is commonly called an auto-transformer starter or a starting compensator.

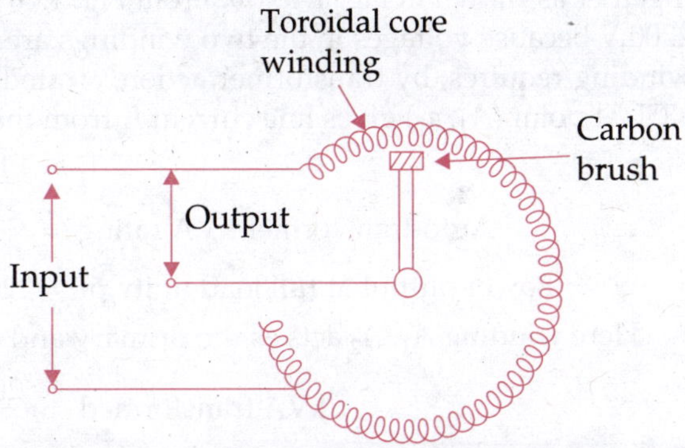

Fig 1.44: Single-phase variable ratio auto-transformer

Schematic diagrams for single-phase and three-phase variable ratio auto-transformers are illustrated in Fig. 1.45.

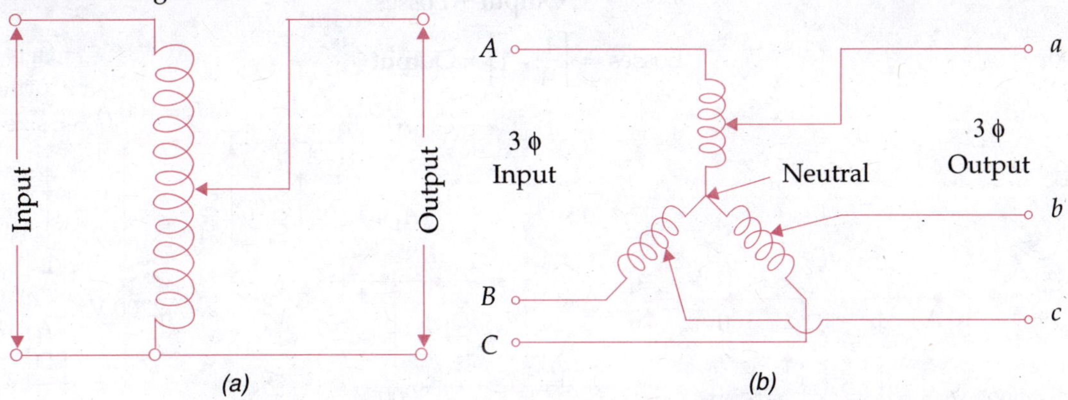

Fig 1.45: Schematic diagram for (a) single-phase variac and (b) three-phase variac.

When auto-transformer is used for supplying *l.v.* system, then its common point, such ac C in Fig. 1.42 in case of single-phase system or the neutral in case of 3-phase system, must be earthed otherwise there is a risk of serious shock.

Example 1.42. *A 20 kVA, 2000/200 V, two-winding transformer is to be used as an auto-transformer to obtain the following voltages:*

(a) 2000 V on primary and 2200 V on secondary,

(b) 2000 V on primary and 1800 V on secondary and

(c) 200 V on primary and 1800 V on secondary.

At full-load unity power factor, calculate the power output, power transformed and power conducted. If the efficiency of two-winding transformer at 0.6 pf is 96%, find the auto-transformer efficiency at the same power factor.

Solution. A two-winding 2000/200 V transformer is shown in Fig. 1.46 *(a)*, where *h.v.* terminals are marked A_1, A_2 and *l.v.* terminals a_1, a_2. Rated currents of *h.v.* and *l.v.* windings of this transformer are respectively,

$$I_1 = \frac{20{,}000}{2000} = 10 \text{ A and } I_2 = \frac{20{,}000}{200} = 100 \text{ A}$$

(a) For obtaining output voltage of 2200 V, terminal A_1 (positive) and a_2 (negative) are connected together as shown in Fig. 1.46 *(b)*. From Fig. 1.46 *(b)*, output voltage (from A_2 to a_1) is 2000 + 200 = 2200 V because voltages in the two windings are in series aiding. Rated current of 100 A in the *l.v.* winding requires, by transformer action, a rated current of 10 A in the 2000 V primary winding. KCL at point (A_1, a_2) gives line current I_1 from the source to be equal to

$$I_1 = 100 + 10 = 110 \text{ A}$$

$$\therefore \quad \text{Auto-transformer kVA rating} = \frac{2200 \times 100}{1000} = \frac{2000 \times 110}{1000} = 220 \text{ kVA}$$

$$\therefore \quad \text{Power output at full load unity pf} = 220 \text{ kW.}$$

Here winding A_1, A_2 acts as the primary and a_1, a_2 as the secondary.

$$\therefore \quad \text{kVA transformed} = \frac{200 \times 100}{1000} = \frac{2000 \times 10}{1000} = 20 \text{ kVA}$$

and $\quad$ power transformed = 20 kW

kVA conducted = 220 − 20 = 200 kVA

and $\quad$ power conducted = 200 kW

Now efficiency
$$\eta = \frac{\text{Output}}{\text{Output} + \text{Losses}}$$

or
$$\text{Losses} = \left[\frac{1}{\eta} - 1\right] \times \text{Output}$$

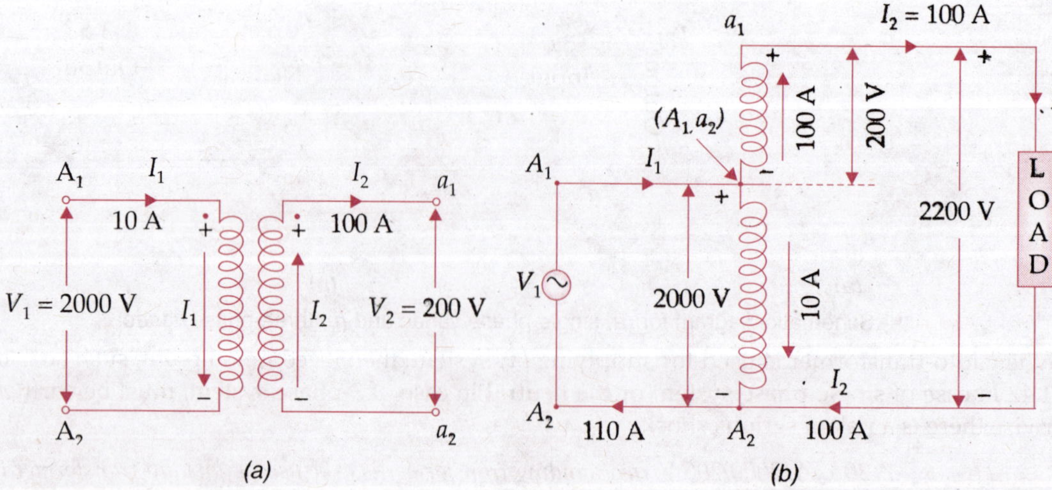

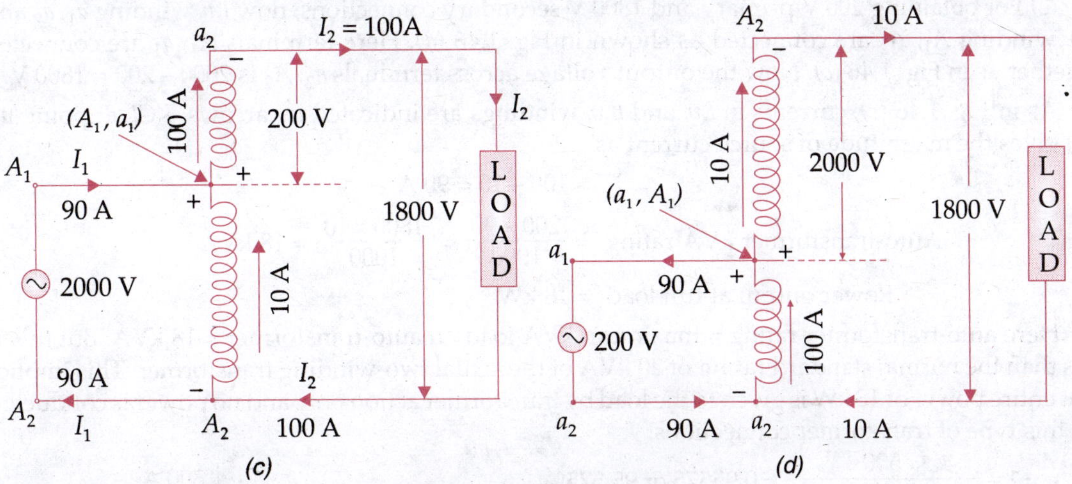

Fig 1.46: Pertaining to Example 1.42

$$\therefore \quad \text{Losses in two-winding transformer} = \left[\frac{1}{0.96} - 1\right] \times 20{,}000 \times 0.6 = 500 \text{ W}.$$

Since auto-transformer operates at rated voltage and rated current, total losses in auto-transformer operation also remain constant at 500 W.

∴ Efficiency of auto-transformer for an output of 220 kVA is

$$\eta = 1 - \frac{\text{losses}}{\text{input}} = 1 - \frac{500}{220{,}000 \times 0.6 + 500}$$

$$= 0.99623 \text{ or } 99.623\%$$

(b) For obtaining an output voltage of 1800 V, *l.v.* polarities a_1, a_2 are reversed from those given in Fig. 1.46 *(b)*. This is shown in Fig. 1.46 *(c)*. Physically, the two connection diagrams look identical, but the reversal of l.v. polarities makes a marked difference in the auto-transformer output. In Fig. 1.46 *(c)*, terminals A_1, a_1 are connected together. Now the output voltage (from A_2 to a_2) is 2000 – 200 = 1800 V, because the two emfs in the two windings are opposing each other. As before, the current in the *h.v.* and *l.v.* windings are equal to their rated values 10 A and 100 A respectively.

Since the secondary or *l.v.* winding a_1, a_2 in Fig. 1.46 *(c)* is reversed, its mmf also gets reversed. As load current I_2 = 100 A cannot reverse, it is the current of 10 A in the primary or *h.v.* winding A_1, A_2 that gets reversed as shown in Fig. 1.46 *(c)*. Now *KCL* at point (A_1, a_1) gives line current I_1 as

$$I_1 = 100 - 10 = 90 \text{ A}$$

$$\therefore \quad \text{Auto-transformer kVA rating} = \frac{2000 \times 90}{1000} = \frac{1800 \times 100}{1000} = 180 \text{ kVA}$$

$$\text{Power output at full load} = 180 \text{ kW}$$

Here, again winding A_1, A_2 acts as the primary and winding a_1, a_2 as the secondary.

$$\therefore \quad \text{Transformed kVA} = 200 \times 100 = 2000 \times 10 = 20{,}000 \text{ VA} = 20 \text{ kVA}$$

and $\quad$ power transformed = 20 kW

$$\text{kVA conducted} = 180 - 20 = 160 \text{ kVA}$$

and $\quad$ power conducted = 160 kW

$$\eta = 1 - \frac{500}{180{,}000 \times 0.6 + 500} = 0.99539 \text{ or } 99.54\%$$

(c) For obtaining 200 V primary and 1800 V secondary connections, now *l.v.* winding a_1, a_2 and *h.v.* winding A_1, A_2 are connected as shown in Fig. 1.46 *(d)*. Here terminals A_1, a_1 are connected together as in Fig. 1.46 *(c)*. Now the output voltage across terminals a_2, A_2 is 2000 – 200 = 1800 V.

As in Fig. 1.46 *(c)*, currents in *l.v.* and *h.v.* windings are indicated by arrows. *KCL* at point (a_1, A_1) gives the magnitude of source current as

$$I_1 = 100 - 10 = 90 \text{ A}$$

$$\therefore \quad \text{Auto-transformer kVA rating} = \frac{200 \times 90}{1000} = \frac{1800 \times 10}{1000} = 18 \text{ kVA}$$

$$\text{Power output at full load} = 18 \text{ kW}$$

Here auto-transformer rating = maximum kVA load on auto-transformer = 18 kVA. But this is less than the normal standard rating of 20 kVA of the actual two-winding transformer. This implies that entire power of 18 kW is given to the load by transformer action only and no power is conducted for this type of transformer connections.

$$\eta = 1 - \frac{500}{18{,}000 \times 0.6 + 500} = 0.95575 \text{ or } 95.575\%.$$

Example 1.43. *A 2000/1000/500 V, single-phase, three-winding transformer is to be used as an auto-transformer, with supply voltage of 3000 V. Two loads, one of 1050 kVA at 3500 V and the other of 180 kVA at 1000 V, are to be energised from this auto-transformer output. Draw a suitable diagram of connections and find the currents in various parts of the circuit. Assume the loads to have the same power factor.*

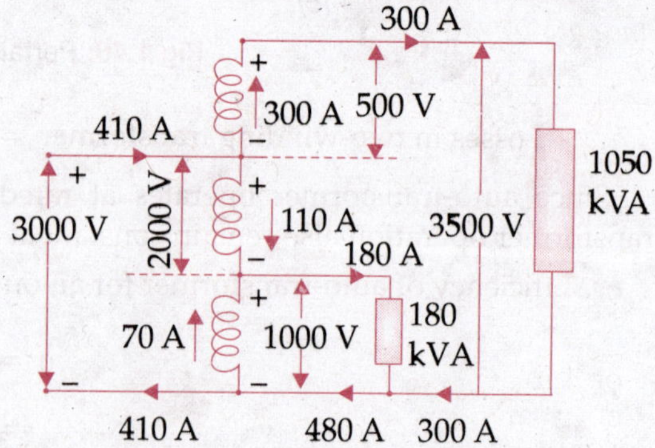

Fig 1.47: Pertaining to Example 1.43

Solution. The arrangement of the three-windings, to suit the voltages of 3000 V, 3500 V and 1000 V, is shown in Fig. 1.47.

The current through the load of 1050 kVA at 3500 V is $= \dfrac{1{,}050{,}000}{3500} = 300$ A.

The current through the load of 180 kVA at 1000 V is $= \dfrac{180{,}000}{1000} = 180$ A

The total kVA supplied = 1050 + 180 = 1230 kVA.

$\therefore$ The total current taken from the supply mains is $= \dfrac{1{,}230{,}000}{3000} = 410$ A.

The application of Kirchoff's current law at the appropriate points gives the distribution of currents in all parts of the circuit as shown in Fig. 1.47.

Example 1.44. *A 10 kVA, 2500/250 V, single-phase, two-winding transformer is used as an auto-transformer to raise the supply voltage of 2500 V to an output voltage of 2625 V. The l.v. winding of the two-winding transformer consists of two equal parts of 125 V each. If both parts of the low voltage winding are used, determine*

(a) auto-transformer kVA output and (b) kVA transformed and conducted.

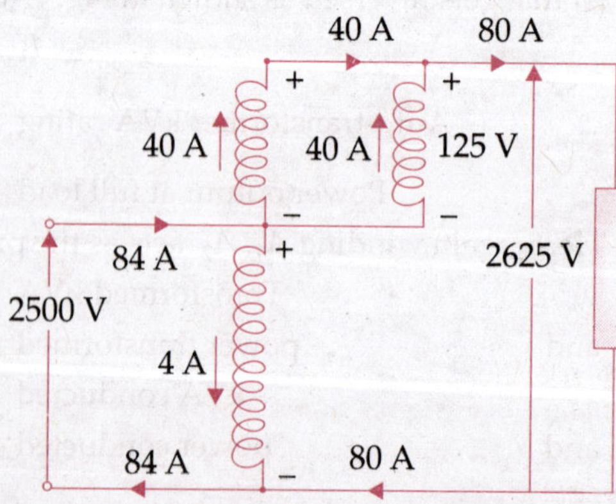

Fig 1.48: Pertaining to Example 1.44

Solution. The two parts of the *l.v.* winding are first connected in parallel and then in series with the *h.v.* winding, so that the output voltage is 2500 + 125 = 2625 V. The scheme of connections, with proper polarity markings, is illustrated in Fig. 1.48.

The rated current of *l.v.* winding is 40 A $\left(= \frac{10,000}{250}\right)$

$\therefore$ Total output current is 40 + 40 = 80 A.

$$\therefore \quad \text{Auto-transformer kVA rating} = \frac{80 \times 2625}{1000} = 210 \text{ kVA}$$

The rated current of h.v. winding is 4 A. Therefore, the current drawn from the supply is 84 A.

$$(b) \qquad \text{kVA transformed} = \frac{80 \times 125}{1000} = 10 \text{ kVA}$$

and kVA conducted = 210 – 10 = 200 kVA.

Example 1.45. *A 3-Phase star-connected auto-transformer, supplies a balanced 3-phase load of 40 kW at 380 V and at 0.8 p.f. lagging. If the supply voltage is 440 V, determine the currents in the various branches of the auto-transformer. Exciting current and internal voltage drops are neglected.*

Solution. The load current $I_2 = \frac{40,000}{(\sqrt{3})(380)(0.8)} = 75.9$ A.

For a balanced 3-phase load, the problem can be solved on per phase basis. Since exciting current and internal voltage drops ae neglected, per phase kVA input = per phase kVA output

$$\text{or} \qquad \frac{440}{\sqrt{3}} I_1 = \frac{380}{\sqrt{3}} I_2$$

$$\text{or} \qquad I_1 = \frac{380}{440} \times 75.9 = 65.6 \text{ A}.$$

$\therefore$ The current flowing from neutral *N* to the tapping points *a*, *b*, *c* is (75.9 – 65.6) = 10.3 A.

The magnitude and direction of the currents in the various branches of the 3-phase auto-transformer is shown in Fig. 1.49.

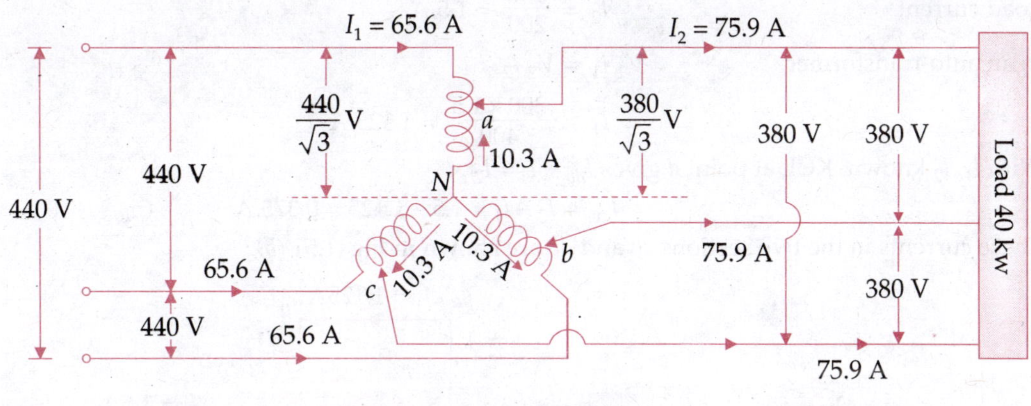

Fig 1.49: Pertaining to Example 1.45.

Example 1.46. *A single-phase ideal transformer has 1000 turns and 400 turns for its primary and secondary windings respectively. The secondary winding delivers a resistive load of 600 kW between terminals A and C and a load of 60 + j 60 Ω between terminals A and B. Between A and B, there are 300 turns and between B and C, there are 100 turns so that between A and C, there are total 400 secondary turns. For a primary voltage of 30 kV, find the primary current and primary input.*

Solution. The arrangement of primary and secondary windings and the loads is as shown in

Fig. 1.50. Voltage between terminals A and C is $V_{ac} = \frac{30{,}000}{1000} \times 400 = 12{,}000$ V and load current

$I_2 = \frac{600{,}000}{12{,}000} = 50$ A

Similarly, $V_{ab} = 30 \times 300 = 9000$ V

Load current $I_2' = \frac{9{,}000}{60 + j60} = \frac{150}{\sqrt{2}} \angle -45°$

$\therefore \overline{I}_{BA} = \overline{I}_2 + \overline{I}_2'$

$= 50 + j\,0 + \frac{150}{\sqrt{2}}(\cos 45° - j \sin 45°)$

$= (125 - j\,75)$ A

Secondary m.m.f. $= I_{BA} \times 300 + I_{CB} \times 100$

$= (125 - j\,75) \times 300 + 50 \times 100$

$= 42500 - j\,22500$

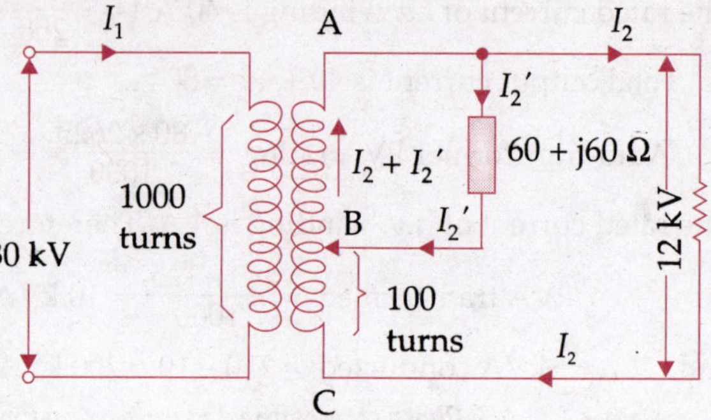

Fig 1.50: Pertaining to Example 1.46

$\therefore$ Primary current $I_1 = \frac{42500 - j\,22500}{1000} = (42.5 - j\,22.5)$ A $= 48.088 \angle -27.897°$

Primary input $= 30 \times 48.088 \times \cos 27.897° = 1274.991$ kW

Power factor at primary terminals $= \cos 27.897° = 0.8838$ lagging.

Example 1.47. *A 1-phase auto-transformer with taps at 0%, 25%, 75% and 100% positions is connected to 400 V primary supply and feeds two secondary load resistors connected as shown in Fig. 1.51 (a). Find the currents in the three sections of the winding, assuming an ideal core.* [I.A.S., 1989]

Solution. This example can be solved easily by considering one load at a time and then superimposing the two results.

In Fig. 1.51 *(b)*, load of resistance 200 Ω is shown connected across terminals *bd*. In this figure, secondary voltage, $V_2 = 0.75 \times 400 = 300$ V.

Load current $\qquad I_2 = \frac{300}{200} = 1.5$ A

In an auto-transformer, $\qquad V_1 I_1 = V_2 I_2$

$\therefore \qquad I_1 = \frac{300 \times 1.5}{400} = 1.125$ A

With I_1, I_2 known, KCL at point d gives $I_{db} + I_1 = I_2$

or $\qquad I_{db} = I_2 - I_1 = 1.5 - 1.125 = 0.375$ A

These currents in the two sections *ab* and *db* are shown in Fig. 1.51 *(b)*.

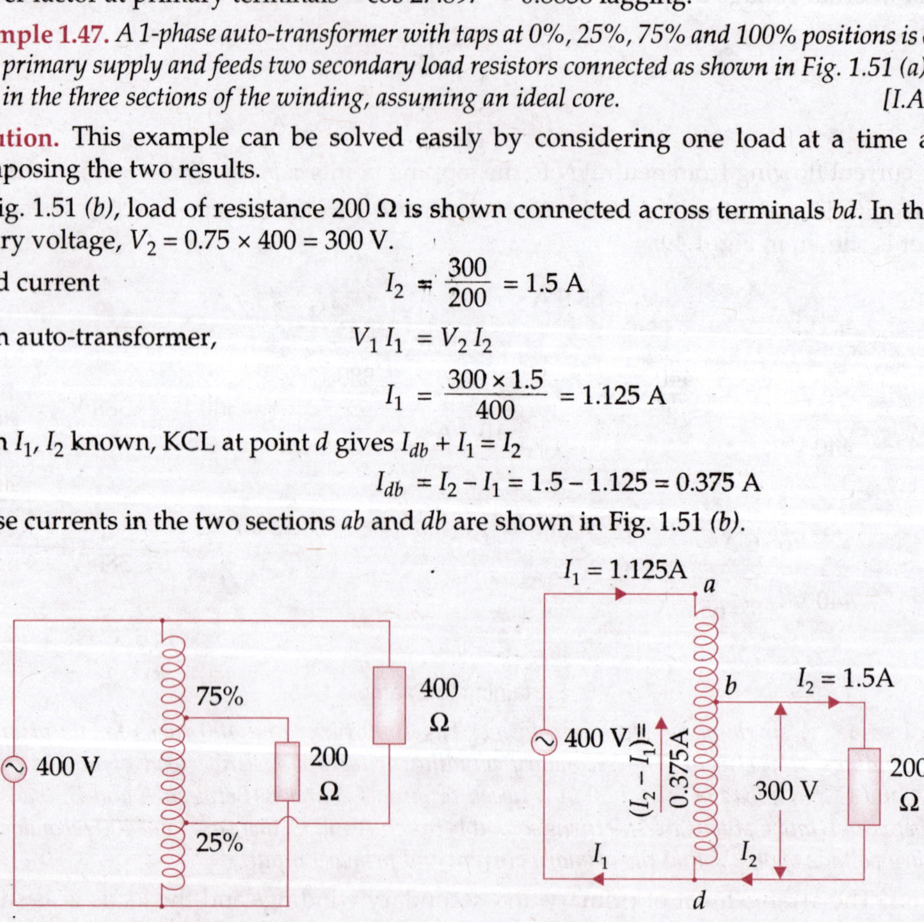

(a) *(b)*

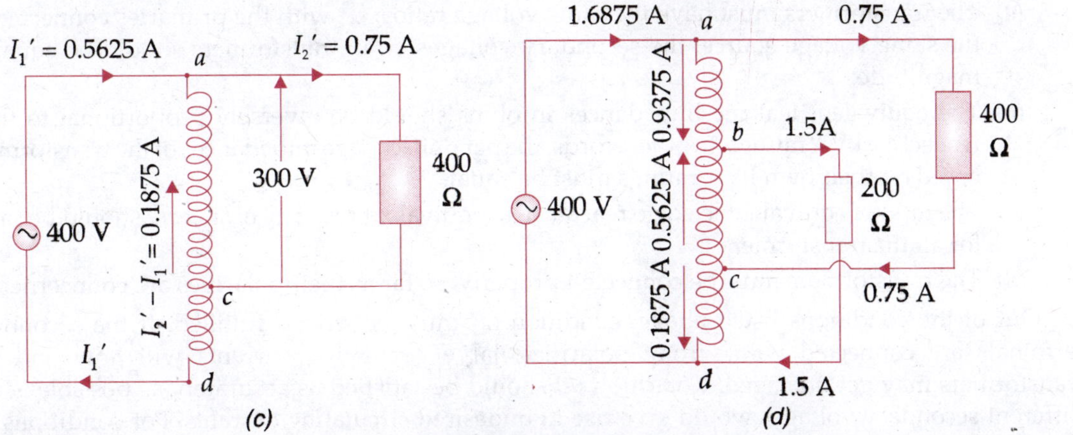

Fig 1.51: Pertaining to Example 1.47

In Fig. 1.51 *(c)*, load of resistance 400 Ω is shown connected across terminals *ac*. In this figure, secondary voltage = 300 V and the secondary current $I_2' = 300/400 = 0.75$ A.

Now $$V_1 I_1' = V_2 I_2'$$

or $$I_1' = \frac{300 \times 0.75}{400} = 0.5625 \text{ A}$$

KCL at *a* gives $$I_{ca} = I_2' - I_1' = 0.75 - 0.5625 = 0.1875 \text{ A}$$

Currents in the sections *ac* and *cd* are shown in Fig. 1.51 *(c)*. Superimposing the results of Figs. 1.51 *(b)* and *(c)*, currents in the three sections of the windings are shown in Fig. 1.51 *(d)*.

1.16. PARALLEL OPERATION OF SINGLE-PHASE TRANSFORMERS

When electric power is supplied to a locality, city or an area, a single transformer, capable of handling the required power demand, is installed. In some cases, it may be preferable to install two or more transformers in parallel, instead of one large unit. Though two or more transformers may be expensive than one large unit, yet this scheme possesses certain advantages described below:

(i) With two or more transformers, the power system becomes more reliable. For instance if one transformer develops fault, it can be removed and the other transformers can maintain the flow of power, though at a reduced level.

(ii) Transformers can be switched off or on, depending upon the power demand. In this manner, the transformer losses decrease and the system becomes more economical and efficient in operation.

(iii) The cost of a standby (or spare) unit is much less when two or more transformers are installed.

In any case, with the passage of time, electric power demand may become more than the rated kVA capacity of the already existing transformer or transformers. Under such circumstances, the need for extra transformer arises. Since the supply voltage has to remain constant, the extra unit must be connected in parallel.

Note that the parallel operation of transformers requires that their primary windings, as well as their secondary windings, are connected in parallel. In this article, only the parallel operation of single-phase transformers is considered.

The various conditions which must be fulfilled for the satisfactory parallel operation of two or more single-phase transformers, are as follows:

(a) The transformers must have the same voltage ratios, *i.e.* with the primaries connected to the same voltage source, the secondary voltages of all transformers should be equal in magnitude.

(b) The equivalent leakage impedances in ohms should be inversely proportional to their respective kVA ratings. In other words, the per unit leakage impedances of the transformers based on their own kVA ratings must be equal.

(c) The ratio of equivalent leakage reactance to equivalent resistance, *i.e.* x_e/r_e should be same for all the transformers.

(d) The transformers must be connected properly, so far as their polarities are conncerned.

Out of the conditions listed above, condition *(d)* must be strictly fulfilled. If the secondary terminals are connected with wrong polarities, large circulating currents will flow and the transformers may get damaged. Condition *(a)* should be satisfied as accurately as possible; since different secondary voltages would give rise to undesired circulating currents. For conditions *(b)* and *(c)*, some deviation is permissible. Thus the fulfilment of condition *(d)* is essential, whereas the fulfilment of other conditions is desirable.

Fig. 1.52 shows two single-phase transformers in parallel, connected to the same voltage source on the primary side. Terminals with proper polarity markings have been connected both on the h.v. and l.v. sides. A further check on the polarities can be applied by connecting a voltmeter V in series with the two secondaries. If voltmeter reads the sum of the two secondary voltages, the polarities are improper and can be corrected by reversing the secondary terminals of any one transformer. In case voltmeter reading is zero, the two transformers have proper polarities. Now the voltmeter V is removed and load can be put on two transformers in parallel.

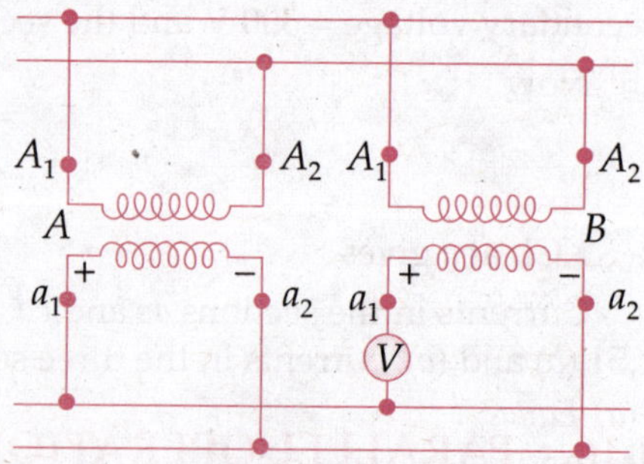

Fig 1.52: Two single-phase transformers in parallel

1.16.1. No-load operation

If the no-load secondary voltages E_a and E_b for transformers A and B, are equal in magnitude and are in time phase, then $\overline{E}_a - \overline{E}_b = 0$ and no current can circulate in the transformer windings. If E_a and E_b are unequal or are out of phase, then the resultant voltage $\overline{E}_a - \overline{E}_b$ will circulate a current I_c given by the expression,

$$\overline{I}_c = \frac{\overline{E}_a - \overline{E}_b}{\overline{z}_{ea} + \overline{z}_{eb}} \quad ...(1.73)$$

In Eq. (1.73), z_{ea} and z_{eb} are the equivalent leakage impedances in ohms, referred to the secondaries of transformers A and B respectively.

Since z_{ea} and z_{eb} are usually small, even a low value of $\overline{E}_a - \overline{E}_b$ may produce a rather large circulating current. Note that due to transformer action, the circulating current will flow both in the primaries and secondaries–this being indicated by dotted lines in Fig. 1.53 *(a)*, where E_a is assumed in phase with and greater than E_b. The circulating current gives rise to additional ohmic losses in the transformers and, therefore, reduces the efficiency of the parallel-connected transformers. It is usual in practice to keep the circulating current less than 10% of the rated current, consequently the transformer turns ratios must be as nearly equal as is possible.

The terminal voltage V on the secondary side of both the transformers, must be same. It is seen from Fig. 1.53 *(a)* that I_c and E_a are in the same direction, whereas I_c and E_b are in opposite directions. Therefore, if the secondary circuits of transformer A and B are traversed, then

$$\overline{E}_a - \overline{I}_c\overline{z}_{ea} = \overline{E}_b + \overline{I}_c\overline{z}_{eb} = \overline{V} \quad ...(1.74)$$

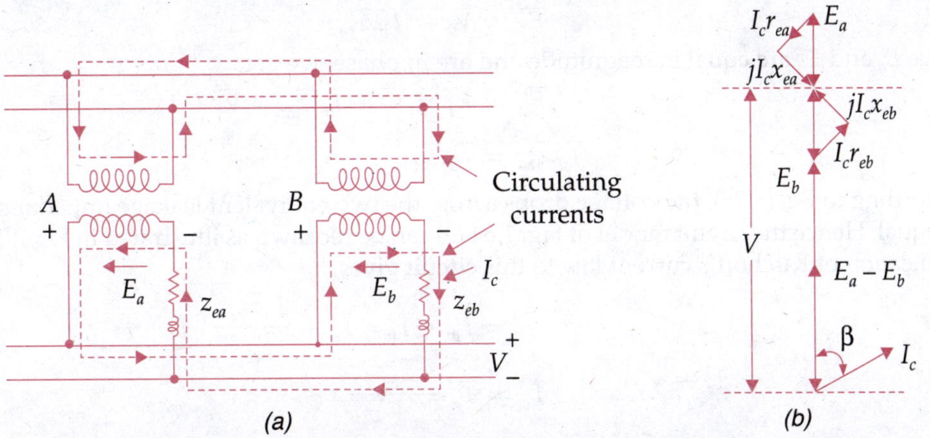

Fig 1.53: Two transformers in parallel *(a)* Path of circulating currents at no load *(b)* Phasor diagram illustrating the effect of I_c at no load.

Eq. (1.74) is depicted in phasor diagram of Fig. 1.53 *(b)*. The angle β by which I_c lags $(E_a - E_b)$ is given by

$$\beta = \tan^{-1} \frac{x_{ea} + x_{eb}}{r_{ea} + r_{eb}}$$

Fig. 1.53 *(b)* illustrates that at no load, the effect of circulating current I_c is to boost the lower voltage E_b to V and to reduce the higher voltage E_a to V.

1.16.2. On-load operation

(a) Equal voltage ratios. When the transformers have equal voltage ratios, the magnitudes of the secondary no-load voltages are equal. Further if the primary leakage impedance drops due to exciting currents are also equal, then $\overline{E}_a = \overline{E}_b$ and the circulating current at no load is zero.

The equivalent circuit of a single-phase transformer of Fig. 1.20 *(a)*, helps in representing two transformers in parallel by the equivalent circuit of Fig. 1.54 *(a)*. In this figure, transformer A is represented by its no-load secondary voltage E_a in series with its leakage impedance z_{ea}. Transformer B is also represented in a similar manner. The common secondary load voltage is V and load current I is shared as I_a and I_b by the transformers A and B respectively. The load impedance is Z ohms.

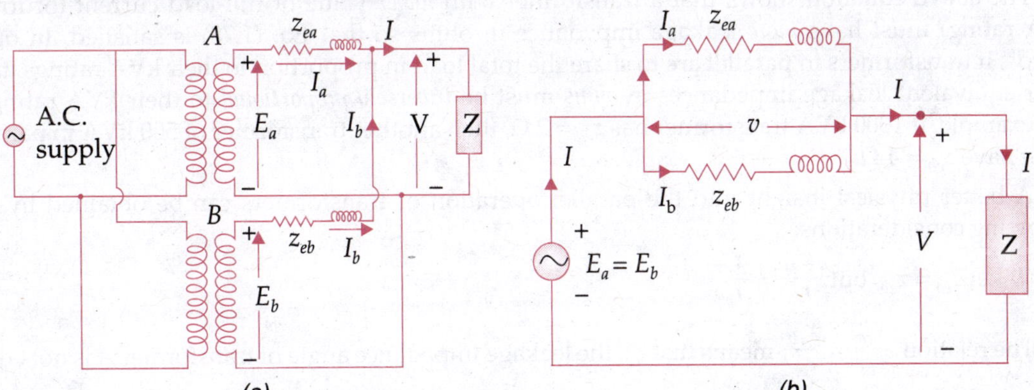

Fig 1.54: *(a)* and *(b)* Circuit modelling of two 1-phase transformers in parallel.

From Fig. 1.54 *(a)*, the voltage equations for transformers A and B are

$$\overline{E}_a = \overline{V} + \overline{I}_a . \overline{z}_{ea}$$

and $$\overline{E}_b = \overline{V} + \overline{I}_b.\overline{z}_{eb}$$

Since E_a and E_b are equal in magnitude and are in phase, we get

$$\overline{E}_a = \overline{E}_b = \overline{V} + \overline{I}_a.\overline{z}_{ea} = \overline{V} + \overline{I}_b.\overline{z}_{eb}$$

or $$\overline{I}_a.\overline{z}_{ea} = \overline{I}_b.\overline{z}_{eb} \quad ...(1.75)$$

According to Eq. (1.75), the voltage drops across the two equivalent leakage impedances z_{ea} and z_{eb} are equal. Hence the circuit model of Fig. 1.54 *(a)* can be redrawn as illustrated in Fig. 1.54 *(b)* and the application of Kirchoff's current law to this circuit gives,

$$\overline{I} = \overline{I}_a + \overline{I}_b = \overline{I}_a + \frac{\overline{I}_a\overline{z}_{ea}}{\overline{z}_{eb}}$$

$\therefore$ $$\overline{I}_a = \overline{I}\,\frac{\overline{z}_{eb}}{\overline{z}_{ea} + \overline{z}_{eb}} \quad ...(1.76\ a)$$

Similarly, $$\overline{I}_b = \overline{I}\,\frac{\overline{z}_{ea}}{\overline{z}_{ea} + \overline{z}_{eb}} \quad ...(1.76\ b)$$

Multiplying both sides of Eqs. (1.76 *a*) and (1.76 *b*) by the terminal voltage V, we get

$$\overline{S}_a = \overline{S}\,\frac{\overline{z}_{eb}}{\overline{z}_{ea} + \overline{z}_{eb}} \quad ...(1.77\ a)$$

and $$\overline{S}_b = \overline{S}\,\frac{\overline{z}_{ea}}{\overline{z}_{ea} + \overline{z}_{eb}} \quad ...(1.77\ b)$$

Here $$\overline{S}_a = \overline{V}\,\overline{I}_a,\ \overline{S}_b = \overline{V}\,\overline{I}_b \text{ and } \overline{S}_a = \overline{V}\,\overline{I}$$

Note that $\overline{V}, \overline{I}, \overline{S}$ etc. are phasor quantities.

When more than two transformers are operated in parallel, then voltage equation for these transformers, say *A, B, C, D*..., can be written by referring to Fig. 1.54 *(a)* as under:

$$E_a - I_a\,z_{ea} = E_b - I_b \cdot z_{eb} = E_c - I_c\,z_{ec} = E_d - I_d \cdot z_{ed} = ... = V = IZ$$

If no-load emfs of these transformers are equal, *i.e.*, $E_a = E_b = E_c = E_d = ... = E_2$ (no-load secondary voltage), then from above,

$$E_2 - V = I_a\,z_{ea} = I_b\,z_{eb} = I_c\,z_{ec} = I_d \cdot z_{ed} = ... = v \quad ...(1.78)$$

The above equation shows that a transformer with *lower* value of full-load current (or lower kVA rating) must have *more* leakage impedance in ohms so that Eq. (1.78) is satisfied. In other words, if transformers in parallel are to share the total load in proportion to their kVA ratings, then their equivalent leakage impedances in *ohms* must be *inversely proportional* to their kVA ratings.* For example, if 1000 kVA transformer has $z_{ea} = 2\ \Omega$, then another transformer of 500 kVA in parallel must have $z_{eb} = 4\ \Omega$.

A better physical insight into the parallel operation of transformers can be obtained by the following considerations:

(i) Let $z_{ea} = z_{eb}$, but $\dfrac{x_{ea}}{r_{ea}} \neq \dfrac{x_{eb}}{r_{eb}}$

The relation $\dfrac{x_{ea}}{r_{ea}} \neq \dfrac{x_{eb}}{r_{eb}}$ means that ϕ_a, the leakage impedance angle of transformer *A* is not equal to ϕ_b, the leakage impedance angle of transformer *B*. Here $\phi_a = \tan^{-1}\dfrac{x_{ea}}{r_{ea}}$ and $\phi_b = \tan^{-1}\dfrac{x_{eb}}{x_{eb}}$.

* This statement is already made as (b) where four conditions for the parallel operation of two or more 1-phase transformers are reported.

For equal voltage ratios under consideration, $\overline{E}_a = \overline{E}_b$ and as per Fig. 1.54 *(b)*, the leakage impedance drops are equal, *i.e.* $I_a\, z_{ea} = I_b\, z_{eb} = v$. Since z_{ea} is taken equal to z_{eb}, $I_a = I_b$. The current I_a lags v by an angle ϕ_a and I_b lags v by angle ϕ_b, see Fig. 1.55 *(a)*, where it is assumed that $\phi_b > \phi_a$.

The secondary terminal quantities V, I and power factor $\cos\theta_2$ are taken to be known. In order to determine I_a and I_b, draw $I_a = I_b$ with an angle $\phi_b - \phi_a$ between them, Fig. 1.55 *(b)*. The phasor sum of I_a and I_b gives I which is a known quantity–therefore, I_a and I_b can be computed. Phasor sum of $V, I_a\, z_{ea}$ and $V, I_b\, z_{eb}$ gives $E_a = E_b$. Fig. 1.55 *(b)* reveals that transformer A operates at a better *p.f.* (cosine of angle between E_a and I_a) and transformer B at a poor *p.f.* (cosine of angle between E_b and I_b) as compared to the load *p.f.*

Here $z_{ea} = z_{eb}$ and $I_a = I_b$; therefore, as per Eq. (1.77), the kVA shared by transformers A and B are equal. The total output kVA, proportional to I, is reduced; because I is the phasor sum, and not the arithmetic sum of I_a and I_b. In other words, $I_a < \frac{I}{2}$ and $I_b < \frac{I}{2}$ and the total kVA output is less than the sum of kVA ratings of the individual transformers. In general when reactance to resistance ratios are not equal, their full load kVA output is less than the sum of their individual transformer kVA ratings. It is also concluded that a transformer with greater leakage impedance angle operates at a poor *p.f.* as compared to the other with a lower leakage impedance angle.

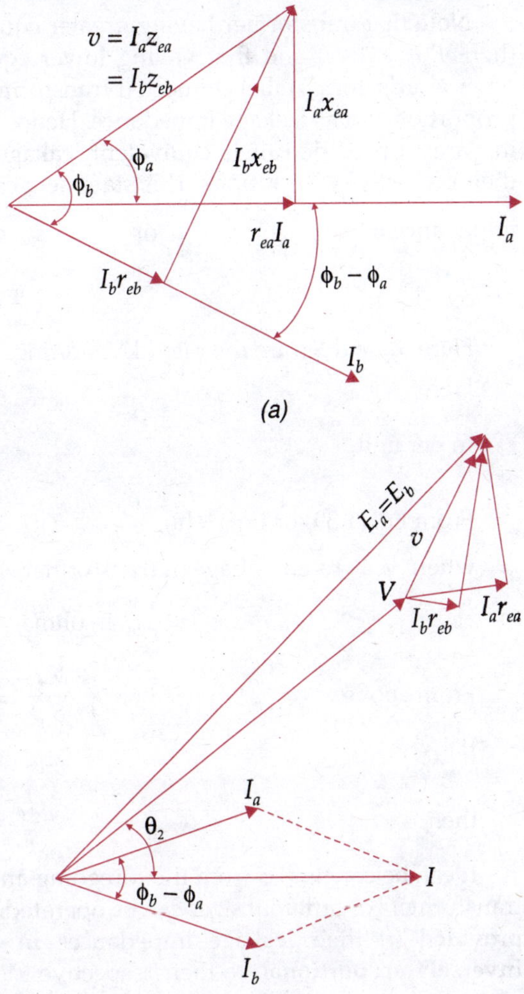

Fig 1.55: *(a) and (b)* Parallel operation with $z_{ea} = z_{eb}$ but $\frac{x_{ea}}{r_{ea}} \neq \frac{x_{eb}}{r_{eb}}$

(ii) Let $z_{ea} > z_{eb}$, but $\frac{x_{ea}}{r_{ea}} = \frac{x_{eb}}{r_{eb}}$.

When $\overline{E}_a = \overline{E}_b$, $I_a\, z_{ea} = I_b z_{eb}$ and since $z_{ea} > z_{eb}$, $I_a < I_b$. The relation $\frac{x_{ea}}{r_{ea}} = \frac{x_{eb}}{r_{eb}}$ means that $\phi_a = \phi_b$. The phasor diagram of Fig. 1.55 *(b)* gets modified to that shown in Fig. 1.56, where I_a and I_b have been drawn proportional to the reciprocal of z_{ea} and z_{eb} respectively. Both the transformers are seen to operate at the same power factor and the total output kVA is increased. Since I is the arithmetic sum of I_a and I_b for $\phi_a = \phi_b$, the total output kVA is equal to the sum of kVA ratings of the individual transformers.

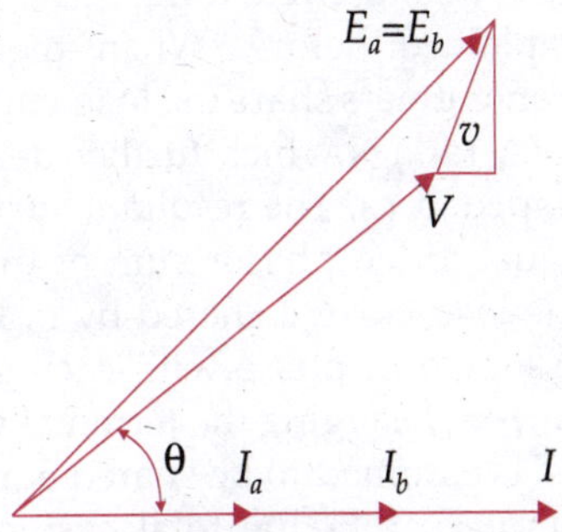

Fig 1.56: Parallel operation of transformers with $z_{ea} > z_{eb}$ but $\frac{x_{ea}}{r_{ea}} = \frac{x_{eb}}{r_{eb}}$.

The kVA supplied by transformers A and B are $E_a I_a \times 10^{-3}$ and $E_b I_b \times 10^{-3}$ respectively. Here $z_{ea} > z_{eb}$, $I_a < I_b$, therefore, $E_a I_a < E_b I_b$; it means that kVA shared by transformer A is less than that shared by transformer B.

Note that transformer having greater equivalent leakage impedance (here z_{ea}) shares less kVA (here $E_a I_a \times 10^{-3}$) and that having lower equivalent leakage impedance shares greater kVA. In other words, for parallel connected transformers, the kVA shared by each transformer is inversely proportional to its leakage impedance. Hence transformers of different kVA ratings can be operated in parallel provided their equivalent leakage impedances *in ohms* are inversely proportional to their respective kVA ratings. This statement can be expressed mathematically as equivalent leakage

impedance $\propto \dfrac{1}{\text{kVA rating}}$ or $z_{ea} \propto \dfrac{1}{S_{ar}}$ and $z_{eb} \propto \dfrac{1}{S_{br}}$

$$\therefore \quad \frac{z_{ea}}{z_{eb}} = \frac{S_{br}}{S_{ar}}$$

Here S_{ar} and S_{br} are the rated kVA ratings of transformers A and B respectively.

Here $$I_a . z_{ea} = I_b . z_{eb}$$

In per unit, $$z_{ea.pu} = \frac{z_{ea} \text{ in ohms}}{\text{base impedance } Z_{BA}}$$

From Eq. (1.39) or Eq. (1.40), $$Z_{BA} = \frac{V_r^2}{S_{ar}}$$

where V_r = rated voltage of transformer A

$$\therefore \quad z_{ea} \text{ in ohms} = z_{ea.pu} \frac{V_r^2}{S_{ar}}$$

From above, $$I_a . z_{ea.pu} \frac{V_r^2}{S_{ar}} = I_b\, z_{eb.pu} \frac{V_r^2}{S_{br}}$$

If $$z_{ea.pu} = z_{eb.pu} \text{ and } \phi_a = \phi_b$$

then, $$\frac{I_a}{I_b} = \frac{S_{ar}}{S_{br}} \qquad \text{...(1.79)}$$

It can be concluded from the foregoing analysis that transformers of different sizes can be operated in parallel provided *(i)* their leakage impedances **in ohms** are **inversely proportional** to their respective kVA ratings, or *(ii)* their **per unit** leakage impedances based on their own kVA rating are equal in magnitude and quality (*i.e.* the impedance angle ϕ).

(b) Unequal voltage ratios. Unequal secondary e.m.f.s give rise to circulating current on no load as has been explained before. When the load is connected, the transformers share the load current in proportion to their kVA ratings which further depends upon their leakage impedances. The resultant current in any transformer is equal to the phasor sum of the circulating current and the load current shared by it. In Fig. 1.57, E_a and E_b are assumed in phase with each other, with $E_a > E_b$. Load current I, lagging the terminal voltage V by load *pf* angle θ_2, is assumed to be shared equally by the transformers. Since $E_a > E_b$ the total current shared by transformer A is the phasor sum of $I/2$ and I_c and that shared by transformer B is the phasor difference of $I/2$ and I_c, *i.e.*

$$\bar{I}_a = \frac{\bar{I}}{2} + \bar{I}_c \text{ and } \bar{I}_b = \frac{\bar{I}}{2} - \bar{I}_c .$$

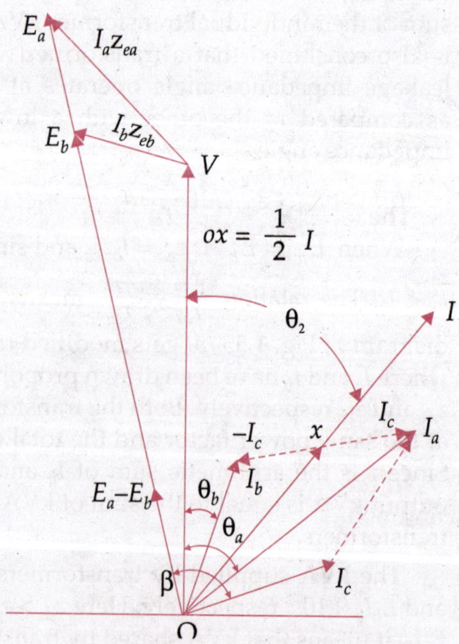

Fig 1.57: On-load parallel operation of two transformers with $E_a > E_b$.

It is seen from the phasor diagram of Fig. 1.57 that the effect of circulating current is to reduce the power factor and increase the current shared by the transformer having greater no-load induced e.m.f. At the same time, the power factor of the secondary transformer with smaller no-load induced e.m.f. is increased and the current shared by it is decreased.

An analytrical solution for the currents I_a and I_b can be obtained by writing down the Kirchoff's voltage equations for Fig. 1.54 *(a)*.

$$\therefore \quad \bar{E}_a - \bar{I}_a \bar{z}_{ea} = (\bar{I}_a + \bar{I}_b)\,\bar{Z} = \bar{V} \quad \text{...(1.80 a)}$$

and

$$\bar{E}_b - \bar{I}_b \bar{z}_{eb} = (\bar{I}_a + \bar{I}_b)\,\bar{Z} = \bar{V} \quad \text{...(1.80 b)}$$

From these equations, I_a and I_b are to be obtained. Assume $E_a > E_b$ as before.

Subtraction of Eq. (1.80 *b*) from Eq. (1.80 *a*) gives

$$\bar{E}_a - \bar{E}_b = \bar{I}_a \bar{z}_{ea} - \bar{I}_b \bar{z}_{eb}$$

$$\therefore \quad \bar{I}_b = \frac{\bar{I}_a \bar{z}_{ea} - (\bar{E}_a - \bar{E}_b)}{\bar{z}_{eb}}$$

Substitution of I_b in Eq. (1.80 *a*) gives

$$\bar{E}_a - \bar{I}_a \bar{z}_{ea} = \bar{I}_a \bar{Z} + \frac{\bar{I}_a \bar{z}_{ea} \bar{Z}}{\bar{z}_{eb}} - \frac{(\bar{E}_a - \bar{E}_b)\bar{Z}}{\bar{z}_{eb}}$$

or

$$\bar{I}_a = \frac{\bar{E}_a}{\bar{z}_{ea} + \bar{Z} + \dfrac{\bar{Z}\bar{z}_{ea}}{\bar{z}_{eb}}} + \frac{\bar{E}_a - \bar{E}_b}{\bar{z}_{ea} + \bar{z}_{eb} + \dfrac{\bar{z}_{ea}\bar{z}_{eb}}{\bar{Z}}} \quad \text{...(1.81 a)}$$

Also,

$$I_a = \frac{E_a \cdot z_{eb} - (\bar{E}_a - \bar{E}_b)Z}{z_{ea}\, z_{eb} + Z(z_{ea} + z_{eb})} \quad \text{...(1.81 b)}$$

Similarly,

$$\bar{I}_b = \frac{\bar{E}_b}{\bar{z}_{eb} + \bar{Z} + \dfrac{\bar{Z}\bar{z}_{eb}}{\bar{z}_{ea}}} - \frac{\bar{E}_a - \bar{E}_b}{\bar{z}_{ea} + \bar{z}_{eb} + \dfrac{\bar{z}_{ea}\bar{z}_{eb}}{\bar{Z}}} \quad \text{...(1.81 c)}$$

Also,

$$I_b = \frac{E_b \cdot z_{ea} - (\bar{E}_a - \bar{E}_b)Z}{z_{ea}\, z_{eb} + Z(z_{ea} + z_{eb})} \quad \text{...(1.81 d)}$$

The load current I is given by $\quad I = I_a + I_b =$ Eqn. (1.74 *b*) + Eqn. (1.81 *d*)

$$\therefore \quad I = \frac{E_a \cdot z_{eb} + E_b \cdot z_{ea}}{z_{ea} \cdot z_{eb} + Z(z_{ea} + z_{eb})} \quad \text{...(1.82)}$$

Terminal voltage, $\quad V = IZ$

$$= \frac{E_a \cdot z_{eb} + E_b \cdot z_{ea}}{\dfrac{z_{ea} \cdot z_{eb}}{Z} + (z_{ea} + z_{eb})} \quad \text{...(1.83)}$$

In the expressions for I_a and I_b, the second term represents the circulating current under load conditions in case E_a and E_b are not equal. This circulating current I_c, from Eqn. (1.81 *a*), is given by

$$I_c = \frac{E_a - E_b}{z_{ea} + z_{eb} + \dfrac{z_{ea} z_{eb}}{Z}} \quad \text{...(1.84)}$$

Terminal voltage V can also be obtained as follows:

$$\bar{V} = \bar{I}\,\bar{Z} = (\bar{I}_a + \bar{I}_b)\bar{Z} = \left(\frac{\bar{E}_a - \bar{V}}{\bar{z}_{ea}} + \frac{\bar{E}_b - \bar{V}}{\bar{z}_{eb}}\right)\bar{Z}$$

On simplification this gives,

$$\overline{V}\left(\frac{1}{\bar{z}_{ea}}+\frac{I}{\bar{z}_{eb}}+\frac{I}{\overline{Z}}\right)=\frac{\overline{E}a}{\bar{z}_{ea}}+\frac{\overline{E}b}{\bar{z}_{eb}}$$

For more than two transformers in parallel,

$$\overline{V}\left(\frac{1}{\bar{z}_{ea}}+\frac{I}{\bar{z}_{eb}}+\frac{I}{\bar{z}_{ec}}+\ldots+\frac{I}{\overline{Z}}\right)=\frac{\overline{E}a}{\bar{z}_{ea}}+\frac{\overline{E}b}{\bar{z}_{eb}}+\frac{\overline{E}c}{\bar{z}_{ec}}+\ldots \qquad \ldots(1.85)$$

Eqn. (1.85) is applicable to any number of transformers (or generators) in parallel and is usually called *parallel-generator theorem.*

If it is required to express I_a and I_b in terms of the load current I, then Eqs. (1.80 *a*) and (1.80 *b*) can be handled as follows:

$$\overline{E}_a-\overline{I}_a\bar{z}_{ea}=\overline{E}_b-\overline{I}_b\bar{z}_{eb}$$

$$\overline{I}_a\bar{z}_{ea}=\overline{E}_a-\overline{E}_b+\overline{I}_b\bar{z}_{eb}$$

Addition of $\overline{I}_a\bar{z}_{eb}$ to both sides, gives

$$\overline{I}_a(\bar{z}_{ea}+\bar{z}_{eb})=(\overline{I}_a+\overline{I}_b)\bar{z}_{eb}+\overline{E}_a-\overline{E}_b$$

But $\overline{I}_a+\overline{I}_b=\overline{I}$

$$\therefore \quad \overline{I}_a=\overline{I}\,\frac{\bar{z}_{eb}}{\bar{z}_{ea}+\bar{z}_{eb}}+\frac{\overline{E}_a-\overline{E}_b}{\bar{z}_{ea}+\bar{z}_{eb}} \qquad \ldots(1.86\ a)$$

Similarly,

$$\overline{I}_b=\overline{I}\,\frac{\bar{z}_{ea}}{\bar{z}_{ea}+\bar{z}_{eb}}+\frac{\overline{E}_a-\overline{E}_b}{\bar{z}_{ea}+\bar{z}_{eb}} \qquad \ldots(1.86\ b)$$

In case $E_a = E_b$, Eq. (1.86) reduces to Eq. (1.76) from which load current I as shared by transformers A and B can be computed. When $E_a > E_b$, then the currents shared by transformers A and B are given by Eq. (1.86). Since $E_a > E_b$, I_a is more than I_b as is evident from Eq. (1.86). The circulating current is equal to the difference of e.m.fs. divided by the local circuit impedance.

Example 1.48. *Two transformers have equal voltage ratios. The magnitude of their equivalent leakage impedances are equal but their reactance to resistance ratios are 9 and 3. Find the ratio of full load kVA delivered, to the sum of their individual kVA ratings.*

Solution. For this example, refer to Fig. 1.55. The difference between the angles of the transformer equivalent leakage impedance is

$$\phi_b-\phi_a=\tan^{-1}\frac{x_{eb}}{r_{eb}}-\tan^{-1}\frac{x_{ea}}{r_{ea}}=\tan^{-1}9-\tan^{-1}3=12.14°$$

Here $z_{ea} = z_{eb}$, $\therefore I_a = I_b$

The load current I, from Fig. 1.55, is given by

$$I=2I_a\cos\frac{\phi_b-\phi_a}{2}=2I_a\cos(6.07)=2I_a(0.994)$$

$$\therefore \quad \frac{\text{Numerical sum, }2I_a}{\text{Phasor sum, }I}=\frac{1}{\cos 6.07}=\frac{1}{0.994}=1.007.$$

It is thus seen that the numerical sum of I_a and I_b, *i.e.* $2I_b$ or $2I_a$ is nearly equal to their phasor sum I. This shows that for parallel connected transfomers, the requirement of keeping reactance to resistance ratios equal is not of much importance.

$$\therefore \quad \frac{\text{Full-load kVA delivered}}{\text{Sum of their kVA ratings}}=\frac{VI\times10^{-3}}{(VI_a+VI_b)10^{-3}}$$

$$=\frac{2I_a\cos(6.07°)}{2I_a}=\cos 6.07°=0.994.$$

Example 1.49. *A number of transformers with equal voltage ratios are operating in parallel. The magnitude of their leakage impedance voltage drops at rated currents are not equal. What will be the total kVA output of these transformers, without any one of them being overloaded?*

Solution. Let $(Iz_e)_{fl1}$, $(Iz_e)_{fl2}$, $(Iz_e)_{fl3}$ .... be the magnitude of equivalent impedance voltage drops at rated currents for transformers 1, 2, 3, ... Further let the kVA ratings of the transformers 1, 2, 3, ... be $(\text{kVA})_1$, $(\text{kVA})_2$, $(\text{kVA})_3$, ... respectively. Assume that the transformer 1 has the lowest magnitude of the equivalent impedance voltage drop.

Since the transformers have equal voltage ratios, their equivalent impedances are connected in parallel as in Fig. 1.54 *(b)* and the voltage drop across z_{e1}, z_{e2}, z_{e3} ... must be the same. As the load on the parallel-connected transformers is increased, the current shared by each transformer also increases. When the voltage drop across equivalent leakage impedances becomes equal to $(Iz_e)_{fl1}$, then transformer 1 is fully loaded and is carrying the rated current. But the other transformers are not loaded to their full-load capacity, because $(Iz_e)_{fl1}$ is of the lowest magnitude.

When transformer 1 is fully loaded, the voltage drop across other leakage impedances is also $(Iz_e)_{fl1}$. For transformer 2, full load voltage drop $(Iz_e)_{fl2}$ would cause it to deliver its rated $(\text{kVA})_2$. For voltage drop $(Iz_e)_{fl1}$ across transformer 2, the load shared by it is given by $\dfrac{(Iz_e)_{fl1}}{(Iz_e)_{fl2}} \times (\text{kVA})_2$.

Similarly load shared by transformer 3 = $\dfrac{(Iz_e)_{fl1}}{(Iz_e)_{fl3}} \times (\text{kVA})_3$

The total kVA output from the parallel-connected transformers is almost equal to the numerical sum of their individual output, as is shown in Ex. 1.48.

$$\therefore \quad (\text{kVA})_T = (\text{kVA})_1 + \frac{(Iz_e)_{fl1}}{(Iz_e)_{fl2}} (\text{kVA})_2 + \frac{(Iz_e)_{fl1}}{(Iz_e)_{fl3}} (\text{kVA})_3 \quad ...(1.87)$$

In Eq. (1.87), $(\text{kVA})_T$ is the total kVA output that can be delivered to the load without overloading transformer 1, which has been assumed to have minimum full-load impedance voltage drop.

The leakage impedance voltage drops may be expressed in volts, in per cent or in per unit.

Example 1.50. *Three 400 kVA, 11,000/6600 V, 50 Hz single-phase transformers gave the following data, when operated at rated current with their l.v. windings short circuited.*

Transformer 1	:	*360 V, 3025 watts*
Transformer 2	:	*400 V, 3200 watts*
Transformer 3	:	*480 V, 3250 watts*

These three transformers are operating in parallel with their primary voltage held constant at 11 kV.

(a) What is the greatest load at unity p.f. that can be put on these three transformers in parallel without overloading any of them?

(b) What is the secondary terminal voltage under the condition of part (a).

Solution. *(a)* Here $(Iz_e)_{fl1} = 360$ V, $(Iz_e)_{fl2} = 400$ V

and $(Iz_e)_{fl3} = 480$ V.

Transformer 1 is loaded first to its rated capacity, because $(Iz_e)_{fl1}$ has lowest magnitude. Thus the greatest load that can be put on these transformers without overloading any one of them is,

$$(\text{kVA})_T = (\text{kVA})_1 + \frac{(Iz_e)_{fl1}}{(Iz_e)_{fl2}} (\text{kVA})_2 + \frac{(Iz_e)_{fl1}}{(Iz_e)_{fl3}} (\text{kVA})_3 + ...$$

$$= 400 + \frac{360}{400} \times 400 + \frac{360}{480} \times 400 = 1060 \text{ kVA}.$$

The total load operates at unity p.f. and it is nearly true to say that transformer 1 is also operating at unity p.f.

(b) Secondary rated current $= \frac{400}{6.6} = 60.6$ Amp

Since transformer 1 is fully loaded, its secondary carries the rated current of 60.6 A.

For transformer 1, $r_{e2} = \frac{3025}{(60.6)^2} = 0.825\ \Omega$

Full-load voltage drop for transformer 1,

$$E_2 - V_2 = I_2 r_{e2} \cos\theta_2 + I_2 x_{e2} \sin\theta_2$$
$$= (60.6)(0.825)(1) + 0 = 50 \text{ V}$$

$\therefore$ Secondary terminal voltage $V_2 = 6600 - 50 = 6550$ V.

Example 1.51. *The short-circuit tests on two single phase transformers gave the following results:*

200 kVA : 3% rated voltage ; rated current at 0.25 p.f. lag.

500 kVA : 4% rated voltage ; rated current at 0.3 p.f. lag.

(a) These two transformers are connected in parallel. How do they share a load of 560 kW at 0.8 p.f. lag?

(b) If their voltage ratings are 11,000/400 V, calculate the secondary terminal voltage at the load given in part (a).

Solution. $I_{rated} = I_{base} = 1.00$

$$V_{rated} = V_{base} = 1.00$$

Under short circuit, $I_{sc}\, z_{e1} = V_{sc}$

Since $I_{sc} = I_{rated}$; $1\, z_{e1} = (0.03)(1)$

or $z_{e1} = 0.03$

Short-circuit p.f., $\cos\theta_{sc} = 0.25,$

$\therefore$ $\sin\theta_{sc} = 0.968.$

In complex notation, $\bar{z}_{e1} = 0.03\,(0.25 + j\,0.968) = (0.0075 + j\,0.029)$ p.u.

Similarly $\bar{z}_{e2} = 0.04\,(0.3 + j\,0.953) = 0.012 + j\,0.0381$ p.u.

(a) When using p.u. system, the values of z_{e1} and z_{e2} should be referred to the common base kVA. Here the common base kVA may be 200 kVA, 500 kVA or any other suitable base kVA. Choosing 500 kVA base arbitrarily, we get

$$\bar{z}_{e1} = \frac{500}{200}(0.0075 + j\,0.029)$$
$$= 0.01875 + j\,0.0725 = 0.075\angle 75.52^\circ$$
$$\bar{z}_{e2} = \frac{500}{500}(0.012 + j\,0.0381) = 0.04\angle 72.54^\circ$$
$$\bar{z}_{e1} + \bar{z}_{e2} = 0.03 + j\,0.11 = 0.114\angle 74.74^\circ.$$

Total kVA, $S = \frac{560}{0.8} = 700$ kVA

$\therefore$ $\bar{S} = 700\ \angle -\cos^{-1} 0.8 = 700\ \angle -36.9^\circ$

From Eq. (1.77), $\bar{S}_1 = \bar{S}\,\frac{\bar{z}_{e2}}{\bar{z}_{e1} + \bar{z}_{e2}}$

$$= (700\ \angle -36.9)\,\frac{0.04\angle 72.54^\circ}{0.114\angle 74.74^\circ} = 245.0\angle -39.1^\circ \text{kVA}$$

$\therefore$ $S_1 = (245)(\cos 39.1^\circ)$ at p.f. of $\cos 39.1^\circ$ lag

$$= 190 \text{ kW at } 0.776 \text{ p.f. lag}$$

$$\bar{S}_2 = (700\angle -36.90)\ \frac{0.075\angle 75.52°}{0.114\angle 74.74°} = 460\angle -36.1°\ \text{kVA}$$

$$\therefore \quad S_2 = (460)\ (\cos 36.1°) \text{ at p.f. of } \cos 36.1 \text{ lag}$$

$$= 372 \text{ kW at p.f. of } 0.808 \text{ lag.}$$

[**Check.** Total power = 190 + 372 = 562 kW, almost equal to 560 kW]

(b) Current shared by transformer 1 $= \dfrac{245}{200} = 1.225$ p.u.

Transformer 1 is, therefore, overloaded by 22.5%, *i.e.* 45 kVA

Current shared by transformer 2 $= \dfrac{460}{500} = 0.92$ p.u.

transformer 2 is, therefore, under loaded by 8%, *i.e.* 40 kVA.

Voltage regulation, from Eq. (1.46), is given by $\varepsilon_r \cos\theta_2 + \varepsilon_x \sin\theta_2$.

For transformer 1, the voltage regulation at 1.225 p.u. current is

$$= 1.225\ (\varepsilon_r \cos\theta_2 + \varepsilon_x \sin\theta_2)$$

$$= 1.225\ (0.0075 \times 0.776 + 0.0290 \times 0.631)$$

$$= 1.225\ (0.024119) = 0.029546$$

or
$$\frac{E_2 - V_2}{E_2} = 0.029546$$

or
$$V_2 = (0.970454)\ (400) = 388.182 \text{ volts.}$$

From part *(a)* of this example, two points may be observed. Firstly, the sum of kVA shared by each transformer (245 + 460 = 705 kVA) is slightly greater than the load kVA (= 700 kVA). Secondly, the two transformers operate at different power factors ; one at a p.f. greater and the other at a p.f. lower than the load p.f. These two points have already been discussed in Fig. 1.55.

Example 1.52. *Two single-phase transformers rated 1000 kVA and 500 kVA have per unit leakage impedance of (0.02 + j 0.06) and (0.025 + j 0.08) respectively. What is the largest kVA load that can be delivered by the parallel combination of these two transformers without overloading any one?*

Solution. For transformer 1 of 1000 kVA,

$$\bar{z}_{e1} = (0.02 + j\,0.06) \text{ p.u.}$$

For transformer 2 of 500 kVA, $\quad \bar{z}_{e2} = (0.025 + j\,0.08)$ p.u.

Choose a base of 1000 kVA.

$$\bar{z}_{e1} = 0.02 + j\,0.06 = 0.06325\ \angle 71.565°$$

$$\bar{z}_{e2} = \frac{1000}{500}\ (0.025 + j\,0.08) = 0.16763\ \angle 72.646°$$

$$\bar{z}_{e1} + \bar{z}_{e2} = 0.07 + j\,0.22 = 0.2309\ \angle 72.35°$$

Now
$$S_1 = \frac{z_{e2}}{z_{e1} + z_{e2}} \cdot S$$

$\therefore$ Total kVA load,
$$S = 1000 \times \frac{0.2309}{0.16763} = 1377.44 \text{ kVA}$$

Similarly,
$$S = 500 \times \frac{0.2309}{0.06325} = 1825.3 \text{ kVA}$$

On per unit basis, z_{e1} (= 0.06325) based on its own kVA rating is less than z_{e2} (= 0.0838) based on its own kVA rating. Therefore, as the load on the parallel combination is increased, transformer 1 reaches its load of 1000 kVA first. So transformer 2 shares a load of 1377.44 – 1000 = 377.44 kVA.

$\therefore$ Largest possible load on two transformers is 1377.44 kVA.

This example can also be solved by using Eq. (1.87). For this, z_{e1} and z_{e2} should not be referred to a common base kVA. As $z_{e1} < z_{e2}$, transformer 1 reaches its rated kVA first.

Largest kVA load on both the transformers, from Eq. (1.87), is

$$(\text{kVA})_T = 1000 + \frac{0.06325}{0.0838} \times 500 = 1377.34 \text{ kVA}.$$

Example 1.53. *Two 1-phase transformers have the following data :*

A : 100 kVA, 6600/230 V, $z_{ea} = 1.5 + j\,4\%$

B : 200 kVA, 6600/220 V, $z_{eb} = 1 + j\,5\%$

These two transformers are connected in parallel and 6600 V is applied to h.v. bus bars. Calculate

(a) no-load circulating current and the ohmic loss caused by it and

(b) no-load terminal voltage.

Solution. *(a)* Leakage impedance should be expressed in ohms on the secondary side.

Full-load secondary current of transformer $A = \dfrac{100{,}000}{230}$ A

$$\therefore \quad z_{ea} \text{ in ohms} = (0.015 + j\,0.04)\frac{(230)^2}{100{,}000} = 0.00794 + j\,0.0212\ \Omega$$

Full-load secondary current of transformer $B = \dfrac{200{,}000}{220}$ A

$$\therefore \quad z_{eb} \text{ in ohms} = (0.01 + j\,0.05)\frac{(220)^2}{200{,}000} = 0.00242 + j\,0.0121\ \Omega$$

$$z_{ea} + z_{eb} = (0.00794 + j\,0.0212) + (0.00242 + j\,0.0121)$$

$$= 0.01036 + j\,0.0333 = 0.03487\ \angle 72.72°\ \Omega$$

From Eqn. (1.73), circulating current at no-load is given by

$$I_c = \frac{E_a - E_b}{z_{ea} + z_{eb}} = \frac{230 - 220}{0.03487\angle 72.72°} = 286.78\ \angle -72.72° \text{A}$$

$\therefore$ Circulating current, $I_a = 286.78$ A and $I_b = -286.78$ A

Ohmic loss due to circulating current $= I_c^2\,(r_{ea} + r_{eb}) = (286.78)^2 \times 0.01036 = 852.04$ W

No-load secondary terminal voltage, $V = E_a - I_a\,z_{ea}$

or $V = 230 - (286.78\ \angle -72.72°)(0.00794 + j\,0.0212)$

$= 230 - (286.78\ \angle -72.72°)(0.02264\ \angle 69.45°)$

$= 230 - 6.482 + j\,0.370 = 223.518 + j\,0.370 = 223.5183$ V.

Example 1.54. *A 500 kVA, 1-phase transformer A having 0.015 pu resistance, 0.05 p.u. leakage reactance is to share a load of 750 kVA at 400 V and at 0.8 p.f. lagging with another 250 kVA, 1-phase transformer having 0.01 p.u. resistance and 0.05 p.u. leakage reactance. Their secondary no-load e.m.f.s are 405 V and 415 V respectively. Find*

(a) circulating current at no load

(b) current supplied by each transformer and

(c) kVA, kW and p.f. of each transformer.

Solution. For such numerical problems, it is more convenient to work in ohmic values.

$$z_{ea} \text{ in ohms} = (0.015 + j\,0.05) \times \frac{400^2}{500{,}000}$$

$$= 0.0048 + j\,0.016\ \Omega = 0.167\ \angle 73.3°\ \Omega$$

$$z_{eb} \text{ in ohms} = (0.01 + j\,0.05) \times \frac{400^2}{250,000}$$
$$= 0.0064 + j\,0.032\ \Omega = 0.0326\ \angle 78.69°\ \Omega$$

Load current, $I = \dfrac{750,000}{400} = 1875$ A

Load impedance, $Z = \dfrac{V}{I} = \dfrac{400}{1875} = 0.2133\ \Omega$ at p.f. 0.8 lag

$$\bar{Z} = 0.2133\ \angle 36.87°\ \Omega$$
$$z_{ea} + z_{eb} = 0.0112 + j\,0.048 = 0.0493\ \angle 76.87°\ \Omega$$

(a) Circulating current at no-load

$$I_b = -I_a = \frac{E_b - E_a}{z_{ea} + z_{eb}} = \frac{415 - 405}{0.0493\angle 76.87°}$$
$$= 202.84\ \angle -76.87°\ \text{A}$$

∴ Circulating current at no load is 202.84 A at a p.f. of cos 76.87° = 0.227 lag.

(b)
$$z_{ea} \cdot z_{eb} = 0.0167\ \angle 73.3° \times 0.036\ \angle 78.69°$$
$$= 0.000544\ \angle 151.99° = -0.00048 + j\,0.0002555\ \Omega$$
$$Z(z_{ea} + z_{eb}) = (0.2133\ \angle 36.87°)(0.0493\ \angle 76.87°)$$
$$= 0.01052\ \angle 113.74° = -0.004235 + j\,0.00963\ \Omega$$
$$E_a \cdot z_{eb} = 405 \times 0.0326\ \angle 78.69°$$
$$= 13.203\ \angle 78.69° = 2.589 + j\,12.947$$
$$E_b \cdot z_{ea} = 415 \times 0.0167\ \angle 73.3° = 6.93\ \angle 73.3° = 1.99 + j\,6.637$$

Current shared by transformer *A*, from Eqn. (1.81 (*b*)), is

$$I_a = \frac{E_a \cdot z_{eb} + (E_a - E_b)Z}{z_{ea} \cdot z_{eb} + Z(z_{ea} + z_{eb})}$$
$$= \frac{2.589 + j\,12.947 + (405 - 415)(0.2133\angle 36.87°)}{-0.00048 + j\,0.0002555 - 0.004235 + j\,0.00963}$$
$$= \frac{0.8826 + j\,11.667}{-0.004715 + j\,0.009866} = \frac{11.7\angle 85.67°}{0.010953\angle 115.5°}$$
$$= 1068.2\ \angle -29.83°\ \text{A}$$

From Eqn. (1.81 (*d*)),
$$I_b = \frac{1.99 + 6.637 + 1.7064 + j\,1.28}{0.010953\angle 115.5°} = \frac{3.6964 + j\,7.917}{0.010953\angle 115.5°}$$
$$= \frac{8.7374\angle 64.97°}{0.010953\ \angle 115.5°} = 797.72\ \angle -50.53°$$

∴ Currents supplied by transformer *A* and *B* are respectively 1068.2 A and 797.72 A.

(c) kVA shared by transformer $A = \dfrac{1068.2 \times 400}{1000} = 427.28$ kVA

kVA shared by transformer $B = \dfrac{797.72 \times 400}{1000} = 319.1$ kVA

kW shared by transformer *A* = 427.28 × cos 29.83°

= 370.67 kW at p.f. = 0.8675 lagging

kW shared by transformer *B* = 319.1 × cos 50.53

= 202.85 kW at p.f. = 0.6357 lagging

A slight difference in the no-load e.m.f.s and per unit leakage impedances have resulted in unequal load sharing and different operating p.f.s. Transformer *A* is underloaded by (500 – 427.28) = 72.72 kVA whereas transformer *B* is overloaded by (319.1 – 250) = 69.1 kVA and their operating p.f.s are 0.8675 lagging and 0.6357 lagging respectively.

Example 1.55. *Two 1-phase transformers A and B have the following data:*

Transformer A : leakage impedance referred to sec, $z_{ea} = 0.4 + j\,2.2\ \Omega$*, no- load secondary e.m.f.,* $E_a = 510V$

Transformer B : leakage impedance referred to sec, $z_{eb} = 0.6 + j\,1.7\ \Omega$*, no-load secondary e.m.f.,* $E_b = 500V$

These two transformers, operated in parallel, are connected to a load of impedance $(5 + j\,3)\ \Omega$*. Calculate the reactance to be connected in series with transformer B so that load current is shared equally between the two.*

Solution. Here $z_{ea} = 0.4 + j\,2.2\ \Omega$

Let the total reactance of transformer *B* be $x\ \Omega$. This gives

$$z_{eb} = 0.6 + jx\ \Omega$$

From Eqns. (1.81 (*b*)) and (1.81 (*d*)), we get

$$\frac{I_a}{I_b} = \frac{E_a \cdot z_{eb} + (E_a - E_b)Z}{E_b \cdot z_{ea} - (E_a - E_b)Z}$$

$$1 = \frac{510(0.6 + j\,x) + (510 - 500)(5 + j3)}{500(0.4 + j\,2.2) - (510 - 500)(5 + j3)}$$

Dividing the numerator and denominator by 500, we get

$$1 = \frac{1.02(0.6 + j\,x) + 0.02(5 + j3)}{(0.4 + j\,2.2) - 0.02(5 + j3)}$$

or $$1 = \frac{0.712 + j\,(1.02x + 0.06)}{0.3 + j2.14}$$

or $$0.712 + j\,(1.02x + 0.06) = 0.3 + j\,2.14$$

$$0.712^2 + (1.02x + 0.06)^2 = 0.3^2 + (2.14)^2$$

$$1.02x + 0.06 = \sqrt{4.163} = 2.0403$$

or $$x = 1.9415\ \Omega$$

∴ External reactance to be connected in series with the transformer

$$B = x - 1.7 = 1.9415 - 1.7 = 0.2415\ \Omega.$$

1.17. TAP-CHANGERS ON TRANSFORMERS

The modern equipment, utilising electrical energy, are designed to operate satisfactorily at one voltage level. It is, therefore, of paramount importance to keep the consumers' terminal voltage within the prescribed limits. The transformer output voltage and hence the consumers' terminal voltage can be controlled by providing taps either on the primary or on the secondary.

The principle of regulating the secondary output voltage is based on changing the number of turns in the primary or secondary. Let V_1, N_1 and V_2, N_2 be the primary and secondary quantities. If N_1 is decreased, e.m.f. per turn on primary (= V_1/N_1) increases, therefore, secondary output voltage $(V_1/N_1)\,N_2$ also increases. On the other hands, if N_2 is increased keeping N_1 constant, the secondary output voltage $(V_1/N_1)\,N_2$ also increases. In other words, decreasing primary turns N_1 has the same effect as that of increasing the secondary turns N_2.

The taps which help in altering the turns ratio, may be placed on the primary or secondary side. The choice between the two sides should be based on maintaining the voltage per turn constant, as far as possible. If primary voltage per turn decreases, the core flux decreases and this results in poor utilisation of the core, though core losses are reduced. On the other hand, if primary voltage per turn increases, the core flux increases and this results in magnetic saturation of the core, more core losses, increased magnetizing current and pronounced third harmonic. In transformers at the generating stations, the primary voltage can be kept almost constant, consequently the taps should be provided on the secondary side. If transformer is energised from a variable voltage source, as at the receiving end of a transmission line, the taps should be provided on the primary side.

Other factors, described below, may also be taken into consideration, while deciding upon the side to be provided with taps.

(i) Transformer with large turns ratio, are tapped on the h.v. side, since this enables a smoother control of the output voltage. On the other hand, taps on the l.v. winding, vary output voltage in large steps, which is usually undesirable.

(ii) Tap-changing gear on the h.v. side will have to handle low currents, though more insulation will have to be provided.

(iii) It is difficult to tap the l.v. winding, since it is placed next to the core due to insulation considerations. The h.v. winding, placed outside the l.v. winding, is easily accessible and can, therefore, be tapped without any difficulty.

A consideration of the foregoing points can help in deciding upon the side of the transformer to be tapped.

A further question arises about whether the transformer winding should be tapped at the end or in the middle. In order to investigate this, refer to Fig. 1.58 *(a)*, where the currents in the primary and secondary coils must flow in opposite directions. These currents interact with leakage flux in between the two coils and produce a radial force, repelling each other.

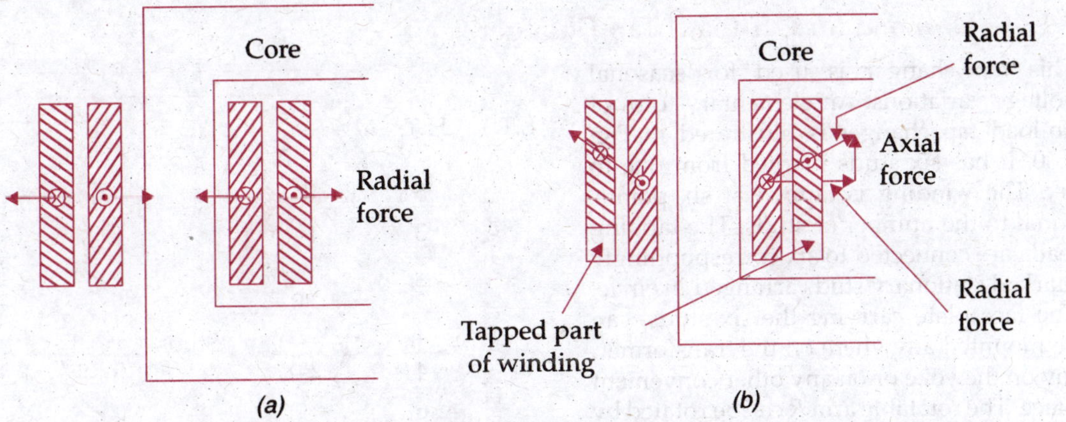

Fig 1.58: *(a)* Radial force, *(b)* Effect of providing tapped coils at the end of a winding.

This radial force tends to compress the inner coil on to the core and burst the outer coil away from the core. The repelling force may be regarded as acting along the line joining the centres of gravity of the primary and secondary coils.

Suppose the winding is tapped at one end. When some of the turns are cut out by tap changer as shown in Fig. 1.58 *(b)*; axial forces, in addition to radial forces, are also developed. Under short circuit conditions, the axial forces tending to compress the coils axially, are very large. In order to obviate this, physical position of the tapped coils should be in the middle of winding, so that no axial forces arise after some turns are cut out. Electrically the tapchanger is connected where the voltage to neutral is minimum. For example, in a star-connected transformer, the tapped end of the windings are connected to form the star point, though physically the tapped coils are placed in the middle of the winding, see Fig. 1.59. This however is not possible in case of delta-connected transformers, where it is electrically essential to provide the tapped coils, in the middle so that the tap-changing gear is far removed from the line and lightning surges.

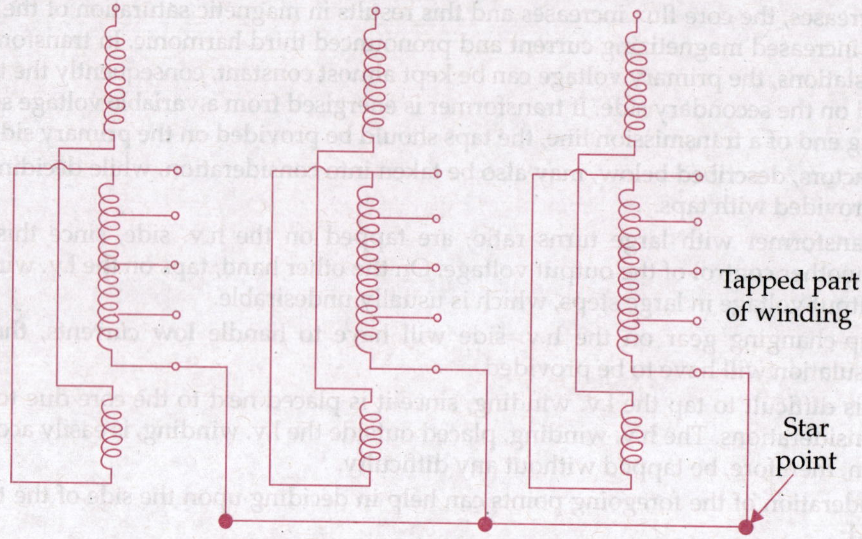

Fig 1.59: Star connection of the tapped coils.

If the tap-changer is designed to operate with the transformer out of circuit, it is then called *off load* (or no-load) *tap-changer.* A tap-changer designed to operate with the transformer in circuit, is called *on-load tap-changer*.

1.17.1. No-Load (or Off-load) Tap Changer

This tap changer is used for seasonal voltage variations. An elementary form of no-load tap changer is illustrated in Fig. 1.60. It has six studs marked from one to six. The winding is tapped at six points, equal to the number of studs. The tapping leads are connected to six correspondingly marked stationary studs arranged in circle. The face plate carrying the six studs, can be mounted anywhere on the transformer, say on the yoke or on any other convenient place. The rotatable arm R can be rotated by means of handwheel, from outside the tank.

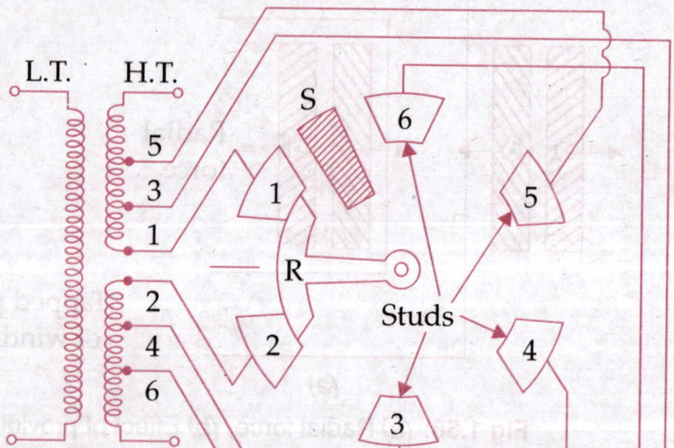

Fig 1.60: No-load tap changer.

If the winding is tapped at 2.5% intervals, then with the rotatable arm R;

(*i*) at studs 1, 2; full winding is in circuit;

(*ii*) at studs 2, 3 ; 97.5% of the winding is in circuit ;

(*iii*) at studs 3, 4 ; 95% of the winding is in circuit ;

(*iv*) at studs 4, 5 ; 92.5% of the winding is in circuit ; and

(*v*) at studs 5, 6 ; 90% of the winding is in circuit.

Stop S fixes the final position and prevents the arm R from being rotated clockwise. In the absence of stop S, the arm R may come in contact with studs 1 and 6. In such a case, only the lower part of the winding is cut out of circuit and this is undesirable from mechanical stress considerations.

The tap-changing must be carried out only after the transformer is disconnected from the supply. Suppose arm *R* is at studs 1 and 2. For bringing arm R at studs 2 and 3, the transformer is first de-energised and then the arm R is rotated to bridge studs 2 and 3. After this, transformer is switched on to the supply and now 97.5% of the winding remains in circuit.

1.17.2. On-load Tap-changer

This tap-changer is used for daily or short period voltage alterations. The output voltage can be regulated with the changer, without any supply interruptions. During the operation of an on-load tap changer ;

(i) the main circuit should not be opened otherwise dangerous sparking will occur and

(ii) no part of the tapped winding should get short-circuited.

One form of elementary on load tap-changer is illustrated in Fig. 1.61 *(a)*. The centre tapped reactor C prevents the tapped winding from getting short-circuited. The transformer tappings are connected to the correspondingly marked segments 1 to 5. Two movable fingers *A* and *B*, connected to centre-tapped reactor *via* switches *x* and *y*, make contact with any one of the segments under normal operation.

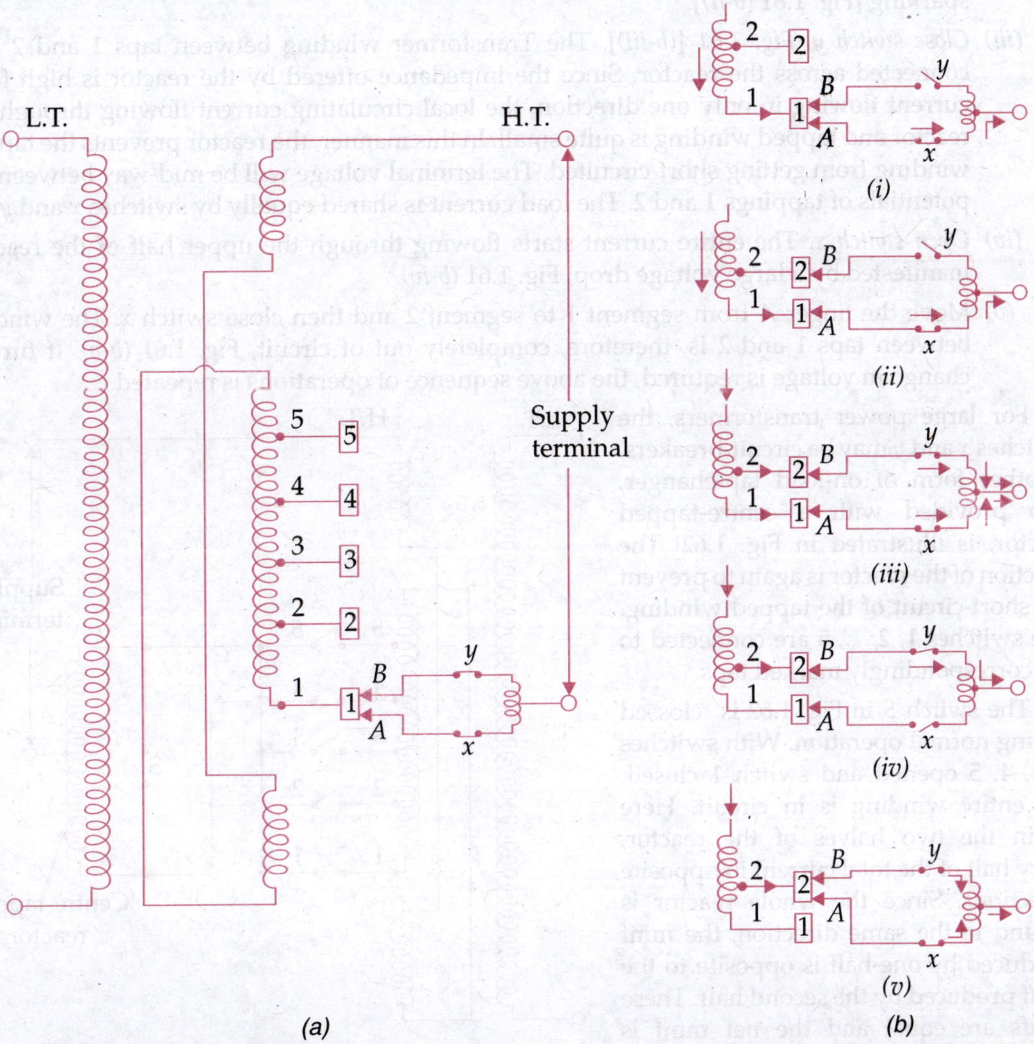

Fig 1.61: *(a)* On-load tap-changer *(b)* Sequence of operations from tapping 1 to tapping 2.

In Fig. 1.61 *(a)*, both the fingers are in contact with segment 1 and full winding is in circuit. Switches *x, y* are closed. One half of the total current flows through *x*, lower half of the reactor and then to the external circuit. The other half of the total current flows through *y*, upper half of the reactor and then to the external circuit. It is seen that currents in the upper and lower halves of the reactor flow in opposite directions. Since the whole reactor is wound in the same direction, the m.m.f. produced by one-half is opposite to the m.m.f. produced by the second half. These m.m.fs. are equal and the net m.m.f. is practically zero ; therefore, the reactor is almost non-inductive and the impedance offered by it is very small. Consequently the voltage drop in the centre-tapped reactor is negligible.

When a change in voltage is required, the fingers *A* and *B* can be brought to segment 2, by adopting the following sequence of operations :

(i) *Open switch y, Fig. 1.61 (b-i).* The entire current must now flow through the lower half of the reactor. It, therefore, becomes highly inductive and there is a large voltage drop. It should be noted that the reactor must be designed to handle full load current, momentarily.

(ii) The finger *B* carries no current and can, therefore, be moved to segment 2, without any sparking [Fig. 1.61 *(b-ii)*].

(iii) *Close switch y, Fig. 1.61* [*(b-iii)*]. The Transformer winding between taps 1 and 2 gets connected across the reactor. Since the impedance offered by the reactor is high for a current flowing in only one direction, the local circulating current flowing through the reactor and tapped winding is quite small. In this manner, the reactor prevents the tapped winding from getting short-circuited. The terminal voltage will be mid-way between the potentials of tappings 1 and 2. The load current is shared equally by switches *x* and *y*.

(iv) *Open switch x.* The entire current starts flowing through the upper half of the reactor, manifested by a large voltage drop, Fig. 1.61 *(b-iv)*.

(v) Move the finger *A* from segment 1 to segment 2 and then close switch *x*. The winding between taps 1 and 2 is, therefore, completely out of circuit, Fig. 1.61 *(b-v)*. If further change in voltage is required, the above sequence of operations is repeated.

For large power transformers, the switches *x* and *y* may be circuit-breakers. Another form of on-load tap-changer, also provided with a centre-tapped reactor, is illustrated in Fig. 1.62. The function of the reactor is again to prevent the short-circuit of the tapped winding. The switches 1, 2, ..., 5 are connected to the correspondingly marked taps.

The switch *S* in Fig. 1.62 is clossed during normal operation. With switches 2, 3, 4, 5 opened and switch 1 closed, the entire winding is in circuit. Here again the two halves of the reactor, carry half of the total current in opposite directions. Since the whole reactor is wound in the same direction, the mmf produced by one-half is opposite to the mmf produced by the second half. These mmfs are equal and the net mmf is practically zero; therefore, the reactor is

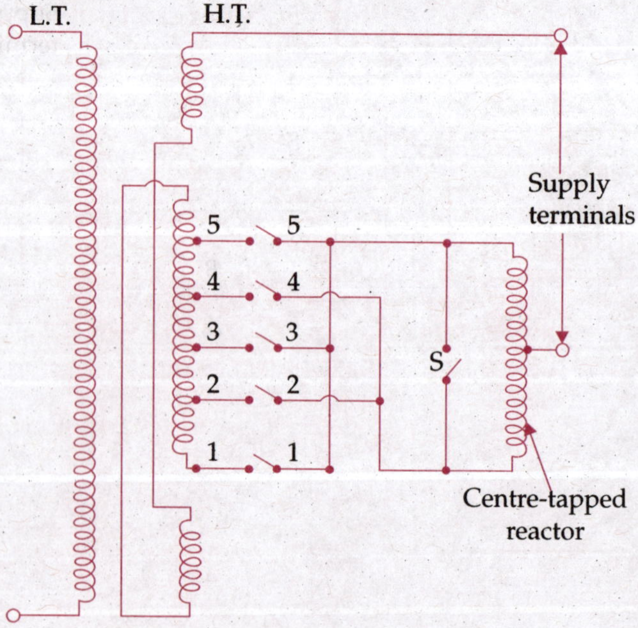

Fig 1.62: On-load tap-changer.

almost non-inductive and the impedance offered by it is very small. Consequently, the voltage drop in the center-tapped reactor is negligible. In changing from tap 1 to tap 2, the following sequence of operations is carried out :

(i) *Open switch S.* Now total current flows through the upper half of the reactor and there is more voltage drop.

(ii) *Close switch 2.* Winding between taps 1 and 2 is connected across the reactor.

(iii) *Open switch 1.* The entire current now flows through the lower half of the reactor and there is more voltage drop.

(iv) *Close switch S.* The total current now flows equally between the upper and lower halves of the reactor and now voltage drop in reactor is negligible as explained before.

For further change in voltage; the sequence, as explained above must be followed for every change in tap position. At present, tap changing is done automatically in large power transformers so as to maintain almost constant secondary output voltage.

For distribution transformers, tap changing is carried out manually.

Example 1.56. *A 100 kVA transformer is provided with tap-changer on the primary side. Find out the tap-setting for maintaining rated voltage on the secondary side for loads of (a) 90 kVA at 0.8 p.f. lag and (b) 100 kW at 0.8 p.f. lag.*

The per unit leakage impedance of the transformer is 0.0075 + j 0.09.

Solution. *(a)* Taking rated kVA of the transformer as the base kVA, a load of 90 kVA is equivalent to a load of 90/100 = 0.9 p.u. Therefore, the voltage drop at 90 kVA will be 0.9 times the voltage drop at 100 kVA for the same load p.f.

$$\therefore \text{P.u. voltage drop or p.u. voltage regulation} = 0.9\,[r_{p.u.} \cos\theta_2 + x_{p.u.} \sin\theta_2]$$
$$= 0.9\,[0.0075 \times 0.8 + 0.09 \times 0.6]$$
$$= 0.9\,[0.06] = 0.054 \text{ p.u. or } 5.4\%.$$

Thus the number of turns in the primary winding should be tapped down by 5.4%.

(b) A load of 100 kW or 100/0.8 = 125 kVA is equivalent to a load of 1.25 p.u.

$$\therefore \text{P.u. voltage drop or p.u. voltage regulation} = 1.25\,[0.0075 \times 0.8 + 0.09 \times 0.6] = 0.075 \text{ or } 7.5\%.$$

Thus the number of turns in the primary winding should be tapped down by 7.5%.

Example 1.57. *A delta-star 11/0.433 kV transformer is provided with a tap changer. A three-phase star-connected load of 10 kVA at 400 V and at 0.8 p.f. lagging, is supplied by the transformer through leads of impedance 0.5 + j 1 Ω per lead. The leakage impedance of l.v. winding is 0.2 + j 1 Ω per phase and that of h.v. winding is 300 + j 1500 Ω per phase. In order to maintain a voltage of 400 V at the load terminals, find the tap setting.*

Solution.
$$\frac{\text{Per phase h.v.}}{\text{Per phase l.v.}} = \frac{11{,}000}{433/\sqrt{3}} = \frac{11{,}000}{250} = 44.$$

$$\therefore \text{H.V. leakage impedance referred to l.v. side} = (300 + j\,1500)\left(\frac{1}{44}\right)^2 = (0.155 + j\,0.775)\,\Omega \text{ per phase.}$$

Total per phase impedance between the transformer secondary and the load

$$= (0.155 + j\,0.775) + (0.2 + j\,1) + (0.5 + j\,1) = 0.855 + j\,2.775\,\Omega = R + jX.$$

$$\text{Per phase load current} \qquad I_L = \frac{10{,}000}{\sqrt{3}(400)} = 14.43 \text{ A.}$$

$$\text{Total impedance drop per phase} = I_L\,[R \cos\theta_2 + X \sin\theta_2]$$
$$= 14.43\,[0.855 \times 0.8 + 2.775 \times 0.6]$$
$$= 14.43\,(2.359) = 34.05 \text{ V.}$$

Per phase voltage to be maintained at the load terminals = $\dfrac{400}{\sqrt{3}}$ = 231 V.

Per phase voltage that must be maintained at transformer l.v. terminals = 231 + 34.05 = 265.05 V

At no load, the transformer l.v. terminal voltage = $\dfrac{433}{\sqrt{3}}$ = 250 V.

∴ The voltage boost that the tap-changer must provide = 265.05 – 250 = 15.05 V.

$$\therefore \quad \text{Tap setting} = \frac{15.05}{250} \times 100 = 6.02\%$$

Tap down if the tapped coils are on the h.v. side or tap up if the tapped coils are on the l.v. side.

1.18. TRANSFORMER AS A MAGNETICALLY COUPLED CIRCUIT

The transformer is a device with magnetic coupling between primary and secondary windings. Here the equivalent circuit of a transformer is derived by treating it as a mutually coupled circuit. The present treatment of transformer gives a better physical significance of the equivalent circuit parameters in terms of transformer magnetic fields. This article supplements the presentation of Art. 1.9 and perhaps leads to a better appreciation of the parameters involved in the transformer equivalent circuit.

In Fig. 1.63, a two-winding transformer is shown, where r_1 and r_2 are resistances of primary and secondary winding respectively. The applied voltage v_1 establishes current i_1 in the primary winding. With current i_1 acting alone, total flux ϕ_1 is produced. This flux ϕ_1 links all the primary turns and is made up of two component fluxes ϕ_{m1} and ϕ_{l1}, i.e., $\phi_1 = \phi_{m1} + \phi_{l1}$, see Fig. 1.63. Flux ϕ_1 produced by i_1 alone is called the **mutual flux** since it links both primary and secondary windings. Flux ϕ_{l1} links only the primary winding and is therefore called **primary leakage flux.**

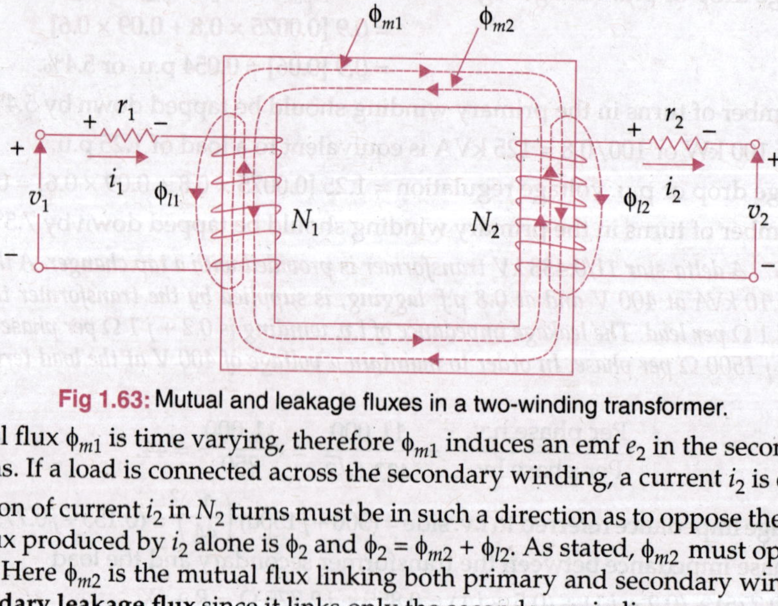

Fig 1.63: Mutual and leakage fluxes in a two-winding transformer.

The mutual flux ϕ_{m1} is time varying, therefore ϕ_{m1} induces an emf e_2 in the secondary winding, having N_2 turns. If a load is connected across the secondary winding, a current i_2 is established.

The direction of current i_2 in N_2 turns must be in such a direction as to oppose the flux ϕ_{m1} as per Lenz's law. Flux produced by i_2 alone is ϕ_2 and $\phi_2 = \phi_{m2} + \phi_{l2}$. As stated, ϕ_{m2} must oppose ϕ_{m1} in the core, Fig. 1.63. Here ϕ_{m2} is the mutual flux linking both primary and secondary windings whereas ϕ_{l2} is the **secondary leakage flux** since it links only the secondary winding.

When primary current i_1 and secondary current i_2 are flowing together, both ϕ_{m1} and ϕ_{m2} are produced in the magnetic core. As ϕ_{m2} opposes ϕ_{m1}, Fig. 1.63, the **resultant mutual flux** ϕ linking both primary and secondary windings is $\phi = \phi_{m1} - \phi_{m2}$.

Total flux linkage with primary winding ψ_1 is given by ψ_1 = [Resultant mutual flux linkages with primary] + [Leakage flux linkages with primary]

$$= N_1 \phi + N_1 \phi_{l1} = N_1 (\phi_{m1} - \phi_{m2}) + N_1 \phi_{l1}.$$
$$= N_1 (\phi_{m1} + \phi_{l1}) - N_1 \phi_{m2} = N_1 \phi_1 - N_1 \phi_{m2}$$

Now KVL gives the voltage equation for the primary winding circuit in Fig. 1.63 as

$$v_1 = r_1 i_1 + \frac{d\Psi_1}{dt} \qquad ...(1.88)$$

Substitution of ψ_1 in Eq. (1.88) gives $v_1 = r_1 i_1 + \frac{d}{dt} [N_1 \phi_1 - N_1 \phi_{m2}]$ ...(1.89)

The **self-inductance** of a winding is defined as the total flux linkage with a winding per ampere in the same winding. Therefore, the self-inductance L_1 of primary winding is

$$L_1 = \frac{N_1 \phi_1}{i_1} \quad \text{or} \quad N_1 \phi_1 = L_1 . i_1$$

The **mutual inductance** is defined as the flux linkage with a winding per ampere in another mutually coupled winding. Thus, the mutual inductance of primary winding is

$$M_{12} = \frac{N_1 \phi_{m2}}{i_2}$$

Current i_2 produces mutual flux ϕ_{m2} in secondary winding and it links primary winding having N_1 turns. So here $N_1 \phi_{m2}$ is the flux linkage with primary winding due to current i_2 in the secondary winding.

Similarly $$M_{21} = \frac{N_2 \phi_{m1}}{i_1}$$

For mutually-coupled circuits with common iron core,

$$M_{12} = M_{21} = M.$$

$$\therefore \quad N_1 \phi_{m2} = M . i_2 \text{ and } N_2 \phi_{m1} = M . i_1 \qquad ...(1.90)$$

Substitution of the values of $N_1 \phi_1$ and $N_1 \phi_{m2}$ in Eq. (1.89) gives

$$v_1 = r_1 i_1 + \frac{d}{dt} [L_1 i_1 - M i_2]$$

or $$v_1 = r_1 i_1 + L_1 . \frac{di_1}{dt} - M \frac{di_2}{dt} \qquad ...(1.91)$$

The flux linkages with the secondary winding ψ_2 is given by

ψ_2 = [Resultant mutual flux linkages with secondary] + [Leakage flux linkages with secondary]

$$= N_2 \phi + N_2 (-\phi_{l2}) = N_2 (\phi_{m1} - \phi_{m2}) - N_2 \phi_{l2}$$
$$= N_2 \phi_{m1} - N_2 (\phi_{m2} + \phi_{l2}) = N_2 \phi_{m1} - N_2 \phi_2$$

The minus sign before ϕ_{l2} is due to the fact that ϕ_{l2} is opposing the resultant mutual flux ϕ. Voltage equation for the secondary circuit, from Fig. 1.63, is

$$\frac{d\Psi_2}{dt} = r_2 i_2 + v_2$$

or $$\frac{d}{dt} [N_2 \phi_{m1} - N_2 \phi_2] = r_2 i_2 + v_2$$

Similar to L_1, self-inductance L_2 of secondary winding is

$$L_2 = \frac{N_2 \phi_2}{i_2}. \text{ Also } M = \frac{N_2 \phi_{m1}}{i_1}$$

or $$N_2 \phi_2 = L_2 i_2 \quad \text{and} \quad N_2 \phi_{m1} = M . i_1$$

Substitution of the values of $N_2 \phi_2$ and $N_2 \phi_{m1}$ in the above equation gives

$$\frac{d}{dt} (M i_1 - L_2 i_2) = r_2 i_2 + v_2$$

or $$M \frac{di_1}{dt} = L_2 . \frac{di_2}{dt} + r_2 i_2 + v_2 \qquad ...(1.92)$$

A magnetically coupled circuit satisfying Eqn. (1.91) and (1.92) is illustrated in Fig. 1.64 *(a)*.

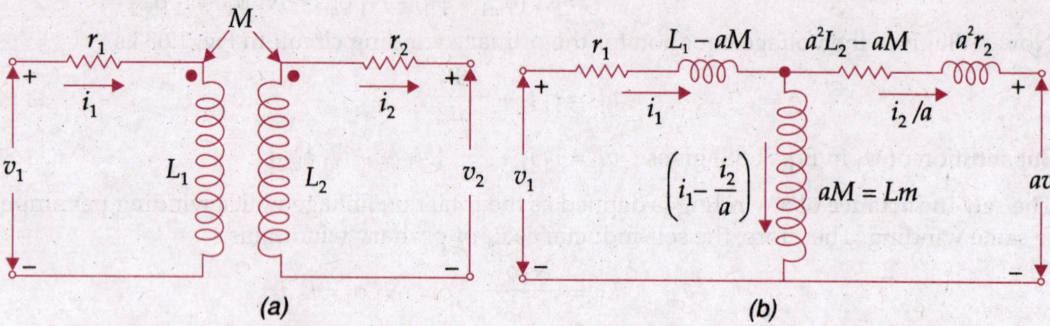

Fig 1.64: *(a)* Magnetically-coupled circuit and *(b)* Conductively coupled circuit of a transformer.

Voltage Eq. (1.92) is for the secondary side of transformer. This can be referred to primary by multiplying it with the turns ratio $\frac{N_1}{N_2} = a$. Therefore, Eq. (1.92), when referred to primary side is

$$a\,M.\frac{di_1}{dt} = a^2.L_2.\frac{d}{dt}\left(\frac{i_2}{a}\right) + a^2\,r_2\left(\frac{i_2}{a}\right) + a\,v_2 \quad \text{...(1.93)}$$

Here $\frac{i_2}{a} = \frac{i_2.N_2}{N_1}$ is the secondary current referred to primary side and is the same as I_1' in Fig. 1.6 *(b)* or Fig. 1.17.

Subtracting $a\,M.\frac{d}{dt}\left(\frac{i_2}{a}\right)$ from left hand term and from the first term on the right side of Eq. (1.93), we get

$$a\,M.\frac{d}{dt}\left[i_1 - \frac{i_2}{a}\right] = [a^2\,L_2 - a\,M]\,\frac{d}{dt}\left(\frac{i_2}{a}\right) + a^2\,r_2\left(\frac{i_2}{a}\right) + a\,v_2 \quad \text{...(1.94)}$$

Now voltage Eq. (1.91) can be written as $v_1 = r_1\,i_1 + L_1.\frac{di_1}{dt} - a\,M.\frac{d}{dt}\left(\frac{i_2}{a}\right)$

To the right hand side of above equation, subtract $a\,M\frac{di_1}{dt}$ from second term and add it to the third term.

$$\therefore \quad v_1 = r_1\,i_1 + (L_1 - a\,M)\,\frac{di_1}{dt} + a\,M.\frac{d}{dt}\left[i_1 - \frac{i_2}{a}\right] \quad \text{...(1.95)}$$

A conductively coupled circuit for a two-winding transformer, satisfying Eqs. (1.94) and (1.95) is illustrated in Fig. 1.64 *(b)*.

The term $a\,M$ in Eqs. (1.94) and (1.95), or Fig. 1.64 *(b)*, must be examined further.

$$\therefore \quad a\,M = \frac{N_1}{N_2}.\frac{N_2\phi_{m1}}{i_1} = \frac{N_1\phi_{m1}}{i_1} \quad \text{...(1.96 a)}$$

The mutual flux linkages (here $N_1\,\phi_{m1}$) with a winding per ampere in the same winding is called **magnetizing inductance**, symbol L_m.

$$\therefore \quad a\,M = \frac{N_1\phi_{m1}}{i_1} = L_m \quad \text{...(1.96 b)}$$

Also $$L_1 - a\,M = L_1 - L_m = \frac{N_1\phi_1}{i_1} - \frac{N_1\phi_{m1}}{i_1} = \frac{N_1}{i_1}\,[\phi_1 - \phi_m] = \frac{N_1\phi_{l1}}{i_1}$$

The **leakage inductance** is defined as the leakage flux linkages (here $N_1\,\phi_{l1}$) with a winding per ampere in the same winding.

$$\therefore \quad L_1 - a\,M = L_1 - L_m = \frac{N_1\phi_{l1}}{i_1} = l_1 = \text{primary leakage inductance} \quad \text{...(1.97 a)}$$

Similarly, $$(a^2\,L_2 - a\,M) = a^2\left[L_2 - \frac{M}{a}\right]$$

$$= a^2 \left[L_2 - \frac{N_2}{N_1} \cdot \frac{N_1 \phi_{m2}}{i_2}\right] = a^2 \left[L_2 - \frac{N_2 \phi_{m2}}{i_2}\right]$$

$$= a^2 [L_2 - L_m]$$

$$= a^2 \text{ (Secondary leakage inductance)} = a^2 .l_2 \quad ...(1.97\ b)$$

The current flowing through magnetizing inductance $a\ M$ or L_m of Fig. 1.64 *(b)* is equal to (primary current i_1 – secondary current referred to primary, *i.e.*, $i_2 \dfrac{N_2}{N_1}$ or $\dfrac{i_2}{a}$). Since core loss is neglected, $\left(i_1 - \dfrac{i_2}{a}\right)$ must be equal to the transformer magnetizing current i_m, *i.e.*, $\left(i_1 - \dfrac{i_2}{a}\right) = i_m$.

In view of the foregoing discussion, Eqs. (1.94) and (1.95) can be written as follows:

From Eq. (1.94),

$$L_m \cdot \frac{di_m}{dt} = a^2 l_2 \cdot \frac{d}{dt}\left(\frac{i_2}{a}\right) + a^2 r_2 \left(\frac{i_2}{a}\right) + a\, v_2 \quad ...(1.98)$$

and from Eq. (1.95),

$$v_1 = r_1 i_1 + l_1 \cdot \frac{di_1}{dt} + L_m \cdot \frac{di_m}{dt} \quad ...(1.99)$$

From Eqs. (1.98) and (1.99), equivalent circuit of Fig. 1.65 *(a)* is obtained. For sinusoidal applied voltage V_1, Eq. (1.99) may be expressed in terms of rms values as

$$\overline{V}_1 = r_1 \overline{I}_1 + j\,\omega l_1 I_, + j\,\omega\, L_m I_m$$

or

$$\overline{V}_1 = r_1 \overline{I}_1 + j\,x_1 \overline{I}_1 + j\,X_m \overline{I}_m \quad ...(1.100)$$

Similarly, Eq. (1.98) can be written as

$$j\,\omega\, L_m I_m = a.\, j\,\omega\, l_2 . \overline{I}2 + a\, r_2 \overline{I}2 + a\, \overline{V}2$$

or

$$j\,X_m I_m = j\,x_2 I_2 .\, a + a r_2 I_2 + a\, \overline{V}2$$

But

$$a = \frac{N_1}{N_2} \quad \text{and} \quad \frac{N_2}{N_1} \cdot \frac{N_1}{N_2} = 1$$

$$\therefore j\,X_m \overline{I}_m = j\,x_2 . \overline{I}_2 \left(\frac{N_2}{N_1} \cdot \frac{N_1}{N_2}\right) \cdot \frac{N_1}{N_2} + r_2 \overline{I}_2 \left(\frac{N_2}{N_1} \cdot \frac{N_1}{N_2}\right) \cdot \frac{N_1}{N_2} + \frac{N_1}{N_2} \cdot \overline{V}_2$$

$$= j\left[x_2 \left(\frac{N_1}{N_2}\right)^2\right] \cdot \overline{I}_2 \cdot \frac{N_2}{N_1} + r_2 \left(\frac{N_1}{N_2}\right)^2 \cdot \overline{I}_2 \cdot \frac{N_2}{N_1} + \frac{N_1}{N_2} V_2$$

But $I_2 = I_1' \dfrac{N_1}{N_2}$ or $I_2 \dfrac{N_2}{N_1} = I_1'$ (See Example 1.5 *(b)*)

$$\therefore \quad j\,X_m \overline{I}_m = j\,x_2 \left(\frac{N_1}{N_2}\right)^2 . I_1' + r_2 \left(\frac{N_1}{N_2}\right)^2 . I_1' + \frac{N_1}{N_2} . \text{V}_2 \quad ...(1.101)$$

From Eqs. (1.100) and (1.101), equivalent circuit of Fig. 1.65 *(b)* can be drawn.

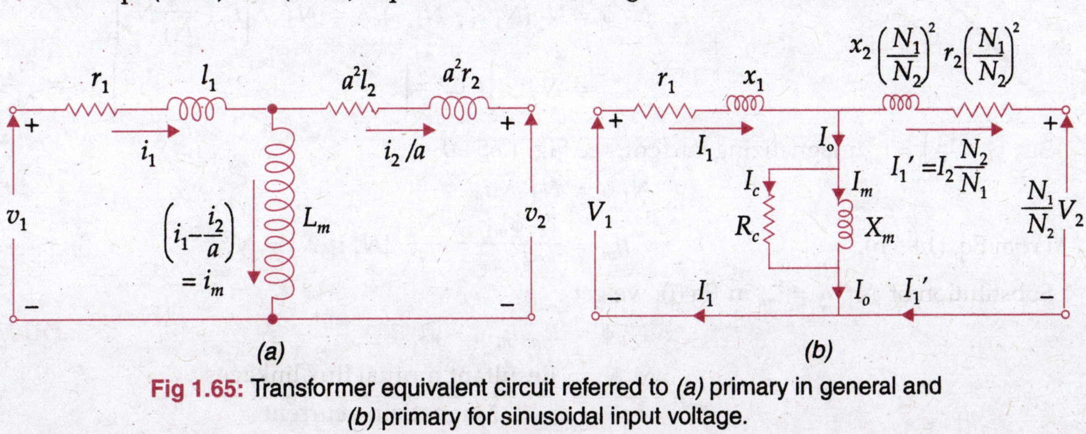

Fig 1.65: Transformer equivalent circuit referred to *(a)* primary in general and *(b)* primary for sinusoidal input voltage.

The effect of core loss P_c can be shown in Fig. 1.65 *(b)* by a resistance $R_c \left(=\frac{P_c}{I_c^2}\right)$ in parallel with X_m. Here I_c is the core-loss component of no-load current I_0. It is thus seen that equivalent circuit of a transformer, Fig. 1.65 *(b)*, derived by treating it as a mutually coupled circuit is identical with that already obtained in Fig. 1.17.

The present treatment, however, gives a clear physical significance of the elements of equivalent circuit of Fig. 1.65 as under:

(i) Effect of magnetic leakage fluxes ϕ_{l1} and ϕ_{l2} is shown by leakage inductances l_1 and l_2 respectively.

(ii) Resultant core flux ϕ magnetizes the iron core. Its effect is taken care of by magnetizing inductance L_m.

Note : In Fig. 1.63, if voltage v_2 is applied to the winding having N_2 turns, then current i_2 is set up. If the current establishes mutual flux ϕ_{m2} in the direction of ϕ_{m1}, then the resultant mutual flux ϕ linking both the primary and secondary windings is $\phi = \phi_{m1} + \phi_{m2}$ and Eqs. (1.91) and (1.92) become

$$v_1 = r_1 i_1 + L_1 \frac{di_1}{dt} + M\frac{di_2}{dt} \qquad \text{...(1.102 a)}$$

and

$$v_2 = r_2 i_2 + L_2 \frac{di_2}{dt} + M\frac{di_1}{dt} \qquad \text{...(1.102 b)}$$

It may be recalled that Eqs. (1.102 *a*) and (1.102 *b*) are true only when the magnetic saturation is neglected. Similar equations are used quite frequently in generalized theory of electrical machines and in Chapter 2 on electro-mechanical energy conversion principles.

Example 1.58. *Prove that magnetizing inductance L_m in the transformer equivalent circuit takes care of the resultant flux in the magnetic core.*

Solution. The mutual flux ϕ_{m1} produced by current i_1 acting alone is given by ϕ_{m1} = (mmf due to i_1) (core permeance $\wedge$, offered to the mutual flux).

$$\therefore \qquad \phi_{m1} = \frac{N_1 i_1}{\text{core reluctance}} = N_1\, i_1 . \wedge$$

Similarly the mutual flux ϕ_{m2} with i_2 acting alone is

$$\phi_{m2} = \frac{N_2 i_2}{\text{core reluctance}} = N_2 .\, i_2 . \wedge$$

$\therefore$ Resultant core flux, $\qquad \phi = \phi_{m1} - \phi_{m2} = (N_1\, i_1 - N_2\, i_2). \wedge$

Resultant mutual flux linkages with primary winding is

$$N_1\, \phi = N_1\, (N_1\, i_1 - N_2\, i_2). \wedge = N_1^2 . \wedge \left[i_1 - \frac{i_2}{N_1} N_2\right]$$

$$= N_1^2 . \wedge \left[i_1 - \frac{i_2}{a}\right] \qquad \text{...} \left[\because a = \frac{N_1}{N_2}\right]$$

But $\left(i_1 - \frac{i_2}{a}\right) = i_m$, magnetizing current, see Fig. 1.65 *(a)*

$$\therefore \qquad N_1\, \phi = N_1^2 \wedge i_m \qquad \text{...(i)}$$

From Eq. (1.96 b), $\qquad L_m = \frac{N_1 \phi_{m1}}{i_1} = \frac{N_1}{i}\, [N_1\, i_1 \wedge] = N_1^2 . \wedge$

Substitution of $N_1^2 \wedge = L_m$ in Eq (i), we get

$$N_1\, \phi = L_m .\, i_m \qquad \text{...(1.103)}$$

$$\therefore \qquad L_m = \frac{N_1 \phi}{i_m} = \frac{\text{Resultant mutual flux linkages}}{\text{Magnetizing current}}$$

Hence, the magnetizing inductance L_m takes care of resultant mutual flux in the magnetic core of a transformer.

Example 1.59. *Voltage equation for the primary winding of a single-phase transformer is given by*

$$v_1 = r_1 i_1 + l_1 \cdot \frac{di_1}{dt} + L_m \cdot \frac{di_m}{dt}$$

Write this equation for sinusoidal applied voltage and hence show that its third term is equal to emf E_1 induced in the transformer primary.

Solution. For sinusoidal applied voltage V_1, primary voltage equation can be expressed in terms of rms values as

$$\overline{V}_1 = r_1 \overline{I}_1 + j\omega l_1 . \overline{I}_1 + j\omega . L_m . \overline{I}_m$$

$$= \overline{I}_1 (r_1 + j x_1) + j \overline{I}_m X_m$$

From Eq. (1.103), $L_m = \dfrac{N_1 \phi}{I_m}$. Here I_m = r.m.s value of magnetizing current and therefore ϕ is also rms value of core flux.

∴ Rms value of mutual flux linkages is

$$N_1 \phi = L_m I_m$$

In the term $N_1 \phi$, ϕ is the rms value of flux. If ϕ_{max} is the maximum value of core flux, then $\phi = \dfrac{\phi_{max}}{\sqrt{2}}$ and the term $\omega L_m I_m = \omega N_1 \phi$ can be written as

$$X_m I_m = \omega N_1 \phi = 2\pi f N_1 . \frac{\phi_{max}}{\sqrt{2}} = \sqrt{2}\, \pi f N_1 . \phi_{max}$$

This is the same expression as in Eq. (1.3).

∴ $\omega L_m I_m = X_m I_m = \omega N_1 \phi = \sqrt{2}\, \pi f N_1 \phi_{max} = E_1$, emf induced in the primary winding. This indicates that emf E_1 can be shown across X_m in 1.65 *(b)* as it is indicated in Fig. 1.17.

1.18.1. Co-efficient of Coupling

Current i_1 in primary winding produces a total flux $\phi_1 = \phi_{m1} + \phi_{l1}$. Here ϕ_{m1} links both primary and secondary windings, it is, therefore, called mutual flux produced by current i_1 alone. The coupling factor k_1 for primary winding is defined as

$$k_1 = \frac{\text{Mutual flux produced by } i_1 \text{ alone, } \phi_{m1}}{\text{Total flux produced by } i_1 \text{ alone, } \phi_1}$$

$$= \frac{\phi_{m1}}{\phi_1} = \frac{\phi_1 - \phi_{l1}}{\phi_1} \quad ...(1.104)$$

Here k_1 indicates the degree of coupling between two windings.

Similarly, coupling factor k_2 for secondary winding is defined as

$$k_2 = \frac{\text{Mutual flux produced by } i_2 \text{ alone, } \phi_{m2}}{\text{Total flux produced by } i_2 \text{ alone, } \phi_2}$$

$$= \frac{\phi_{m2}}{\phi_2} = \frac{\phi_2 - \phi_{l2}}{\phi_2} \quad ...(1.105)$$

The coefficient of coupling k between two coupled coils is defined as the geometric mean of the coupling factors k_1 and k_2.

$$\therefore \quad k = \sqrt{k_1 . k_2} = \left[\left(\frac{\phi_{m1}}{\phi_1} \right) \cdot \left(\frac{\phi_{m2}}{\phi_2} \right) \right]^{1/2}$$

From Eq. (1.90), $\phi_{m1} = \dfrac{M.i_1}{N_2}$ and $\phi_{m2} = \dfrac{Mi_2}{N_1}$

$$\therefore \qquad k = \left[\left(\frac{Mi_1}{\phi_1.N_2}\right)\cdot\left(\frac{M.i_2}{\phi_2.N_1}\right)\right]^{1/2}$$

$$= \left[\left(\frac{Mi_1}{\phi_1.N_1}\right)\cdot\left(\frac{M.i_2}{\phi_2.N_2}\right)\right]^{1/2}$$

But self inductance $L_1 = \dfrac{N_1\phi_1}{i_1}$ and $L_2 = \dfrac{N_2\phi_2}{i_2}$

$$\therefore \qquad k = \left[\left(\frac{M}{L_1}\right)\cdot\left(\frac{M}{L_2}\right)\right]^{1/2} = \frac{M}{\sqrt{L_1L_2}}$$

or
$$M = k\sqrt{L_1.L_2} \qquad ...(1.106)$$

The coefficient of coupling may vary from 0.01 (for radio coils) to 0.98 (for iron-cored transformers).

The coefficient of coupling measures how closely the magnetic fields of two windings are interlinked or coupled.

For zero leakage flux, from Eqs. (1.104) and (1.105), $k_1 = 1.0$, $k_2 = 1.0$ and $k = 1$. Circuits with low value of leakage flux are called closely-coupled circuits.

For closely coupled circuits, the following relations may be written.

For $k_1 \cong 1$,
$$k_1 = \frac{\phi_{m1}}{\phi_1} = \frac{N_1\dfrac{\phi_{m1}}{i_1}}{N_1\dfrac{\phi_1}{i_1}} = \frac{L_m}{L_1}$$

But, $L_m = a\,M$,
$$\therefore \quad k_1 = \frac{a\,M}{L_1} = \frac{N_1}{N_2}\cdot\frac{M}{L_1}$$

For $k_1 \cong 1$, $\dfrac{N_1}{N_2}\cdot\dfrac{M}{L_1} = 1$
$$\therefore \quad \frac{N_1}{N_2} = \frac{L_1}{M} \qquad ...(1.107)$$

For $k_2 \cong 1$,
$$k_2 = \frac{\phi_{m2}}{\phi_2} = \frac{(N_1\phi_{m2})/i_2}{(N_1\phi_2)/i_2}$$

From Eq. (1.90),
$$M = \frac{N_1\phi_{m2}}{i_2}$$

$$\therefore \quad k_2 = \frac{M}{(N_2\,\phi_2/i_2).\dfrac{N_1}{N_2}} = \frac{N_2}{N_1}\cdot\frac{M}{L_2} \qquad \left[\because L_2 = \frac{N_2\phi_2}{i_2}\right]$$

For $k_2 \cong 1$,
$$\frac{N_1}{N_2} = \frac{M}{L_2} \qquad ...(1.108)$$

From Eqs. (1.107) and (1.108),
$$\left(\frac{N_1}{N_2}\right)^2 = \frac{L_1}{M}\cdot\frac{M}{L_2}, \quad \therefore \quad \frac{N_1}{N_2} = \sqrt{\frac{L_1}{L_2}}$$

Hence, for closely coupled circuits,
$$\frac{N_1}{N_2} \cong \frac{L_1}{M} \cong \frac{M}{L_2} \cong \sqrt{\frac{L_1}{L_2}} \qquad ...(1.109)$$

1.18.2. Methods of Increasing the Coefficient of Coupling

This may also be called as the "methods of reducing the leakage flux."

Eqs. (1.104) and (1.105) reveal that the coupling factors and the coefficient of coupling can be increased by reducing the leakage fluxes pertaining to the two circuits. In two-winding transformers, coefficient of coupling can be increased or the leakage flux reduced by the following methods :

(a) *By increasing the window height.* In a transformer the window area $H \times W$ is governed by the conductor cross-sectional area of primary and secondary windings and the insulation. For a given area if window height H is increased, the length of leakage flux path becomes more. This has the effect of increasing the reluctance offered to the leakage flux paths and for a given m.m.f., the leakage flux is reduced. Usually the ratio H/W does not exceed 4.

(b) *By arranging the primary and secondary windings concentrically.* Fig. 1.66 *(a)* shows primary winding on one limb and secondary winding on the other limb or leg. In Fig. 1.66 *(b)*, half of the primary and secondary windings are on one leg and their other halves are on the second leg. Since the primary and secondary windings in Fig. 1.66 *(b)* are more close to each other, leakage flux is reduced and the coefficient of coupling increased. Reduction of leakage flux in Fig. 1.66 *(b)* may also be explained as follows :

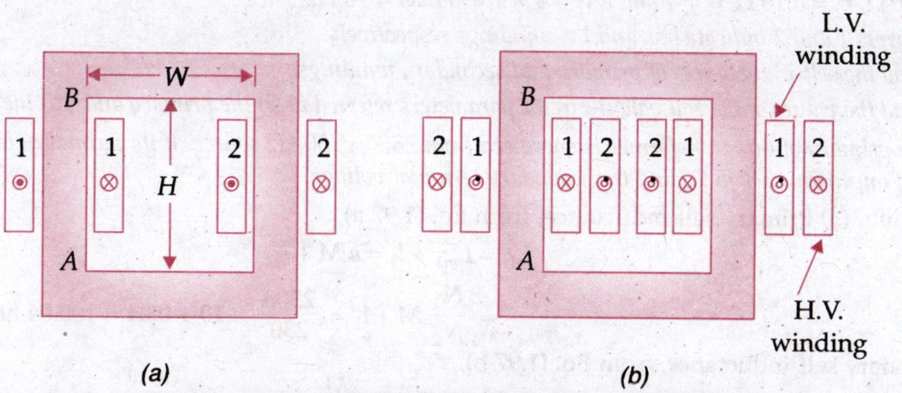

Fig 1.66: *(a)* Primary and secondary winding on each limb or leg
(b) Concentric primary and secondary windings.

In Fig. 166 *(a)*, the magnetic potential difference between points A, B is $I_1 N_1$, whereas in Fig. 1.66 *(b)* its value is $\frac{I_1 N_1}{2}$. Since the leakage flux depends upon the magneic potential difference between points A, B its value in Fig. 1.66 *(b)* is about half of that in Fig. 1.66 *(a)*.

(c) *By sandwiching the primary and secondary windings.* Fig. 1.67 shows the winding 2 in two sections and winding 1 in four sections. On each leg, winding 2 is sandwiched by two sections of winding 1. The aim of sandwiching is again to arrange the primary and secondary windings as close to each other as is possible, so that the leakage flux is reduced.

The leakage flux can be reduced further by using more sandwiched sections for both primary and secondary windings.

Fig 1.67: Winding 2 is sandwiched between sections of winding 1.

(d) *By using shell-type construction*. In shell-type transformers the l.v. and h.v. windings are sandwiched as shown in Fig. 1.3 *(b)*. This arrangement of using sandwiched coils causes more closeness of the primary and secondary windings and the leakage flux is, therefore, considerably reduced.

In addition to the reduction in leakage flux by sandwiching in shell-type construction, iron surrounds both the windings. In view of this, the fluxes produced by primary and secondary windings tend to follow the least-reluctance iron path around them, rather than the high-reluctance air path. In this manner the leakage flux is further reduced and the coefficient of coupling is increased.

Example 1.60. *A 10 kVA, 2300/230 V, single-phase transformer has the following parameters :*

$r_1 = 10\,\Omega$, $r_2 = 0.10\,\Omega$, $l_1 = 40$ mH, $l_2 = 4 \times 10^{-4}$ H, $M = 10$ H.

Subscripts 1 and 2 indicate h.v. and l.v. windings respectively.

(a) Find the self-inductances of primary and secondary windings.

(b) Find the values of the equivalent-circuit parameters referred to (i) the primary and (ii) the secondary.

(c)The primary of this transformer is energised from 2300 V, 50 Hz source. If its secondary is connected to a load of impedance $5 + j5\,\Omega$, find the secondary terminal voltage.

Solution. *(a)* Primary self-inductance, from Eq. (1.97 a),

$$L_1 = L_{m1} + l_1 = a\,M + l_1$$

$$= \frac{N_1}{N_2} M + l_1 = \frac{2300}{230} \times 10 + 0.04 = 100.04 \text{ henrys.}$$

Secondary self-inductance, from Eq. (1.97 b),

$$L_2 = L_{m2} + l_2 = \frac{M}{a} + l_2$$

$$= M\frac{N_2}{N_1} + l_2 = 10 \times \frac{1}{10} + 4 \times 10^{-4} = 1.0004 \text{ H}$$

(b) Parameters referred to primary winding are :

$$r_1 = 10\ \Omega\,;\ r_2 = 0.1 \times \left(\frac{N_1}{N_2}\right)^2 = 0.1 \times (10)^2 = 10\,\Omega$$

$$l_1 = 40 \text{ mH}\,;\ l_2 = 4 \times 10^{-4}\left(\frac{N_1}{N_2}\right)^2 = 4 \times 10^{-4}\,(10)^2 = 40 \text{ mH.}$$

$$L_{m1} = M\frac{N_1}{N_2} = 10 \times 10 = 100 \text{ H.}$$

Parameters referred to secondary winding are :

$$r_1 = 10 \times \left(\frac{1}{10}\right)^2 = 0.10\,\Omega\,;\ r_2 = 0.1\,\Omega$$

$$l_1 = 40 \times 10^{-3}\left(\frac{1}{10}\right)^2 = 4 \times 10^{-4} \text{ H}\,;\ l_2 = 4 \times 10^{-4} \text{ H.}$$

$$L_{m2} = M\frac{N_2}{N_1} = 10 \times \frac{1}{10} = 1.00 \text{ H.}$$

(c) The equivalent circuit referred to secondary is as shown in Fig. 1.68 *(a)*.

For 50 Hz supply, the equivalent circuit of Fig. 1.68 *(a)* gets modified to that shown in Fig. 1.68 *(b)*, where

$$x_1 = 2\pi f\,l_1 = 2\pi(50)\,(4 \times 10^{-4}) = 0.1256\,\Omega$$

$$x_2 = 0.1256\,\Omega.$$

and

$$X_{m2} = 2\pi f\,L_{m2} = 2\pi(50)\,(1.00) = 314\,\Omega.$$

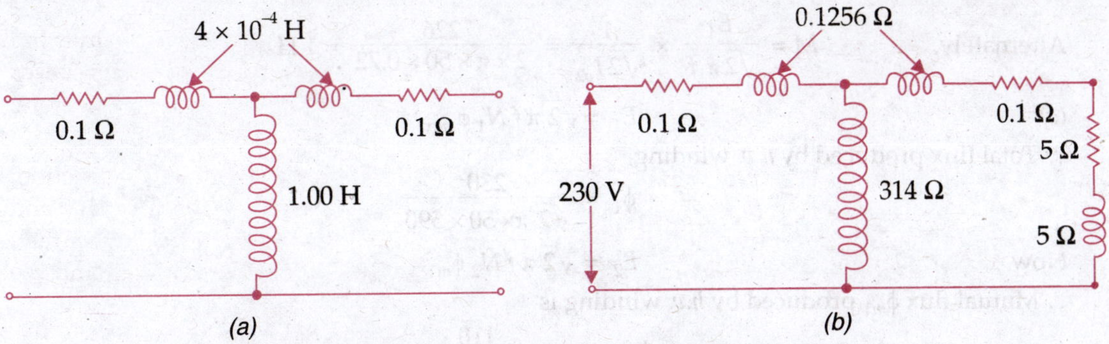

Fig 1.68: Equivalent circuit referred to secondary, Example 1.60.

The current flowing through X_{m2} is much smaller as compared to that in 5.1 + j 5.1256 Ω connected in parallel with it.

$$\therefore \quad \text{Secondary terminal voltage} = \frac{230}{5.2 + j\,5.2512} \times (5 + j5)$$

$$= \frac{230}{\sqrt{(5.2)^2 + (5.2512)^2}} \times \sqrt{(5)^2 \times (5)^2} = 220.7 \text{ V}$$

Example 1.61. *A single-phase two winding transformer gave the following test results :*

(i) H.V. winding (590) turns when energised from 230 V, 50 Hz supply, takes a no-load current of 0.35 A and induced e.m.f. across open circuited l.v. winding is 110 V.

(ii) L.V. winding (295 turns) when energised from 115 V, 50 Hz supply takes a no-load current of 0.72 A and induced e.m.f. across open circuited h.v. winding is 226 V.

Calculate (a) self-inductances of h.v. and l.v. windings (b) the mutual inductance between h.v. and l.v. windings (c) coupling factors k_1 and k_2 for h.v. and l.v. winidings respectively and the coefficient of coupling k. Neglect core loss and winding resistances.

Solution.

$$E = \sqrt{2}\,\pi f N \phi_{max} = \sqrt{2}\,\pi f \psi_{max}$$

where ψ_{max} = maximum flux linkages

(a) For *h.v.* winding,

$$E_1 = \sqrt{2}\,\pi f N_1 \phi_{max} = \sqrt{2}\,\pi f \psi_{max1}$$

$$230 = \sqrt{2}\,\pi \times 50 \times \psi_{m1}$$

$$\therefore \text{ Maximum flux linkages with } h.v. \text{ winding, } \psi_{m1} = \frac{230}{\sqrt{2}\pi \times 50}$$

$$\therefore \text{ Self-inductance of } h.v. \text{ winding, } L_1 = \frac{\Psi_{m1}}{\sqrt{2}I} = \frac{230}{\sqrt{2} \times \pi \times 50} \times \frac{1}{\sqrt{2} \times 0.35} = 2.0918 \text{ H}$$

For *l.v.* winding,

$$E_2 = \sqrt{2}\,\pi f \psi_{m2}$$

$$\therefore \text{ Maximum flux linkages with } l.v. \text{ winding, } \psi_{m2} = \frac{115}{\sqrt{2}\pi \times 50}$$

$$\therefore \text{ Self-inductance of } l.v. \text{ winding, } L_2 = \frac{\Psi_{m2}}{\sqrt{2}I} = \frac{115}{\sqrt{2}\pi \times 50} \times \frac{1}{\sqrt{2} \times 0.72} = 0.5084 \text{ H}$$

(b) Here $\sqrt{2}\,\pi f$ × maximum value of mutual flux linkages = secondary induced emf, E_2

$$\therefore \text{ Maximum value of mutual flux linkages} = \frac{E_2}{\sqrt{2} \times \pi \times f} = \frac{110}{\sqrt{2}\pi \times 50}$$

$$\therefore \text{ Mutual inductance } M = \frac{\text{Maximum value of mutual flux linkages}}{\sqrt{2} \times I_{o1}} = \frac{110}{\sqrt{2}\pi \times 50} \cdot \frac{1}{\sqrt{2} \times 0.32} = 1 \text{ H}$$

Alternately, $$M = \frac{E_1}{\sqrt{2}\pi f} \times \frac{1}{\sqrt{2} I_{o2}} = \frac{226}{2 \times \pi \times 50 \times 0.72} = 1 \text{ H}$$

(c) $$E_1 = \sqrt{2}\, \pi f N_1 \phi_{max}$$

∴ Total flux produced by *h.v.* winding,

$$\phi_1 = \frac{230}{\sqrt{2}\, \pi \times 50 \times 590}$$

Now $$E_2 = \sqrt{2}\, \pi f N_2 \phi_{m1}$$

∴ Mutual flux ϕ_{m1} produced by *h.v.* winding is

$$\phi_{m1} = \frac{110}{\sqrt{2} \times \pi \times 50 \times 295}$$

∴ $$k_1 = \frac{\phi_{m1}}{\phi_1} = \frac{110}{\sqrt{2} \times \pi \times 50 \times 295} \times \frac{\sqrt{2}\, \pi \times 50 \times 590}{230} = 0.95652$$

Total flux produced by *l.v.* winding, $$\phi_2 = \frac{115}{\sqrt{2}\, \pi \times 50 \times 295}$$

Mutual flux ϕ_{m2} produced by *l.v.* winding = $\dfrac{E_1}{\sqrt{2}\pi f N_1}$

∴ $$\phi_{m2} = \frac{226}{\sqrt{2}\, \pi \times 50 \times 590}$$

∴ $$k_2 = \frac{\phi_{m2}}{\phi_2} = \frac{226}{\sqrt{2}\, \pi \times 50 \times 590} \times \frac{\sqrt{2}\, \pi \times 50 \times 295}{115} = 0.9826$$

Coefficient of coupling, $$k = \sqrt{k_1 \times k_2} = \sqrt{0.95652 \times 0.9826} = 0.9695$$

Check. $M = k\sqrt{L_1 L_2} = 0.9695\sqrt{(2.0918)(0.5084)} = 1.00 \text{ H}$

Alternately, part (c) can be calculated as under.

$$k_1 = \frac{N_1}{N_2} \cdot \frac{M}{L_1} = \frac{590}{295} \times \frac{1}{2.0918} = 0.95611$$

$$k_2 = \frac{N_2}{N_1} \cdot \frac{M}{L_2} = \frac{295}{590} \times \frac{1}{0.5084} = 0.98348$$

∴ $$k = \sqrt{k_1 \times k_2} = \sqrt{0.95611 \times 0.98348} = 0.9696$$

Example 1.62. *The self and mutual inductances of a two-winding transformer are*

$$L_1 = 4 \text{ mH}, L_2 = 6 \text{ mH}, M_{12} = M_{21} = 1.8 \text{ mH}.$$

Calculate the current which would flow in the winding 1 when this winding is connected to a 130-volt, (500/π) Hz supply and the load of 0.2 mH inductance is connected across the winding 2. Assume power losses in the windings and the magnetic circuit to be negligible. *(I.E.S., 1982)*

Solution. Here $L_1 = 4$ mH, $L_2 = 6$ mH, $M_{12} = M_{21} = 1.8$ mH, $r_1 = r_2 = 0$

For the parameters given, equivalent circuit of Fig. 1.64 (*b*) should be used.

Take here $a = \dfrac{N_1}{N_2} = 1$ for convenience.

∴ $$L_1 - aM = 4 - 1.8 = 2.2 \text{ mH}, aM = 1.8 \text{ mH}$$

$$a^2 L_2 - aM = 6 - 1.8 = 4.2 \text{ mH}$$

Load inductance referred to primary = $a^2 L_2 = 0.2$ mH

Observation of Fig. 1.64 (*b*) shows that $(a^2 L_2 - aM + a^2 L)$ is in parallel with $L_m = aM$.

∴ Total inductance seen by the primary applied voltage

$$= (L_1 - a\,M) + \frac{(a\,M)[a^2 L_2 - a\,M + a^2 L]}{a\,M + a^2 L_2 - a\,M + a^2 L}$$

$$= 2.2 \times 10^{-3} + \frac{(1.8 \times 10^{-3})(4.2 + 0.2) \times 10^{-3}}{(1.8 + 4.2 + 0.2) \times 10^{-3}}$$

$$= 3.4774 \times 10^{-3}\text{ H}$$

Total reactance at the primary terminals $= 2\pi \times \frac{500}{\pi} \times 3.4774 \times 10^{-3} = 3.4774\ \Omega$

∴ Current in the primary winding 1 $= \frac{130}{3.4774} = 37.384$ A

1.19. PULSE TRANSFORMERS

The transformers which handle voltages and currents in the form of pulses are called pulse transformers. The use of such transformers is quite common in radar, television, digital computer and thyristor systems. The functions of pulse transformers are :

(i) for changing the amplitude of a voltage pulse,

(ii) for inverting the polarity of a pulse,

(iii) for affecting dc isolation between source and load,

(iv) for coupling different stages of pulse amplifiers.

The input voltage to pulse transformers is of discontinuous nature as shown in Fig. 1.69 *(a)*. The most important requirement of these transformers is that input pulse at the primary should be reproduced as accurately as possible at its secondary terminals. Fig. 1.69 *(b)* shows a square wave pulse at the input terminals. The pulse width varies from a fraction of a microsecond to about 25 microseconds. Usually, a sufficient time elapses before the next pulse appears. The waveform of the output voltage at the secondary terminals can be determined through the use of equivalent circuit of the pulse transformer.

A typical output voltage pulse is shown in Fig. 1.70, where pulse transformer parameters are also defined. The rise time is the time interval required for the output to rise from 0.1 to 0.9 of its final value. The distortions present in the output pulse can be determined through the transient analysis of its equivalent circuit.

The transformer analysis is usually carried out by dividing its solution into three parts. The first part gives the response near the front edge of the pulse, the second part gives, the response during the flat-top and the third part gives the response after the termination of the pulse.

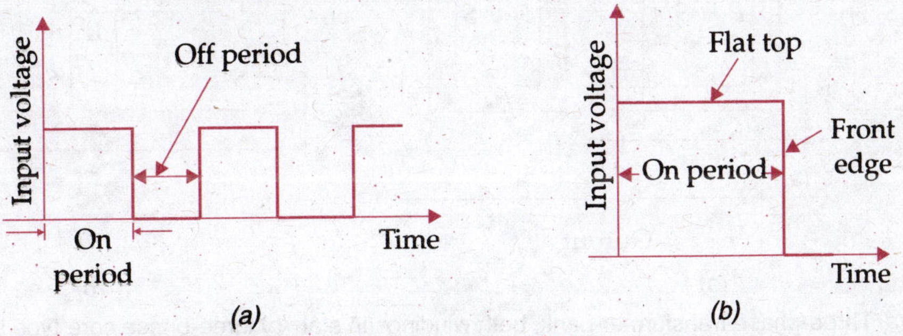

Fig 1.69: *(a)* Train of input-voltage pulses and *(b)* Square-wave input voltage pulse

For leading edge of the input pulse analysis, stray capacitance is included in the equivalent circuit. In order to keep the rise time within limits, the leakage inductance of the transformer should be kept to a minimum.

The transformer response to the flat-top portion of the input pulse is carried out by using the low-frequency equivalent circuit. The output voltage is seen to have downward tilt, or drop-off, during its pulse duration time. The output voltage cannot remain flat as this would mean D.C. passing through a transformer which is not possible. The droop-off of the pulse can be kept as small as possible by having high magnetizing inductance for the transformer.

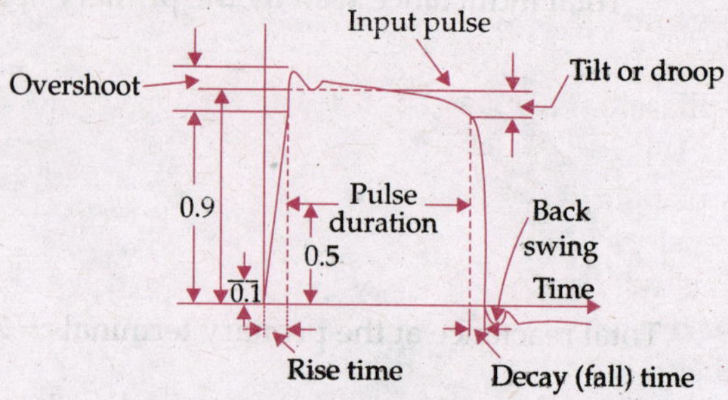

Fig 1.70: Waveform of output voltage pulses for a pulse transformer.

When the input pulse is zero, the output pulse does not reduce to zero instantaneously because of the magnetic energy stored in the transformer inductance. The fall, or decay, time for the output pulse is shown in Fig. 1.70. There is a backswing of the output voltage and because of transformer inductance and stray capacitance, damped oscillations and a long-duration negative overshoot are observed after the decay time of the pulse.

It is seen from Figs. 1.69 *(a)* and 1.70 that differences between input voltage pulse and output voltage are caused by *(i)* a finite rise time, *(ii)* tilt, *(iii)* a finite decay or fall time and *(iv)* a backswing.

Pulse transformers are quite small in size. Both primary and secondary windings have comparatively few turns so that leakage inductance is minimum. In order that transformer has maximum magnetizing inductance, its core is made of ferrites or from high permeability alloys such as permalloy. As the off-period (time interval between successive pulses) is usually quite large as compared with on-period, the transformer can handle high pulse-power levels.

1.20. THREE-PHASE TRANSFORMERS

Generation, transmission and distribution of electric energy is invariably done through the use of three-phase* systems because of its several advantages over single-phase systems. As such, a

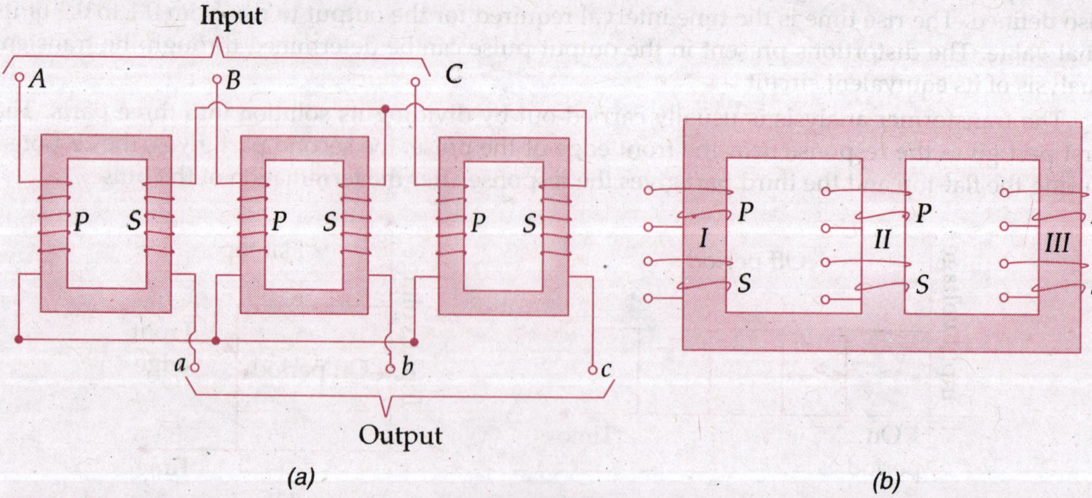

Fig 1.71: *(a)* Three-phase transformer bank, both windings in star *(b)* three-phase core-type transformer.

* For relationship between line and phase quantities in delta and star connected systems, the reader may refer to Appendix-B.

large number of three-phase transformers are inducted in a 3-phase energy system for stepping-up or stepping-down the voltage as required. For 3-phase up or down transformation, three units of 1-phase transformers or one unit of 3-phase transformer may be used.

When three identical units of 1-phase transformers are used, Fig. 1.71 *(a)*, the arrangement is usually called a bank of three transformers or a 3-phase transformer bank. A single 3-phase transformer unit may employ 3-phase core-type construction, Fig. 1.71 *(b)* or 3-phase shell-type construction (not shown). A single-unit 3-phase core-type transformer uses a three-limbed core, one limb for each phase winding as shown in Fig. 1.71 *(b)*. Actually, each limb has the l.v. winding placed adjacent to the laminated steel core and then h.v. winding is placed over the l.v. winding. Appropriate insulation is placed in between the core and l.v. winding and also in between the two windings.

A 3-phase core-type transformer costs about 15% less than a bank of three 1-phase transformers. Also, a single unit occupies less space than a bank.*

1.20.1. Three-phase Transformer Connections

Three-phase transformers may have the following four standard connections :

(a) star-delta (Y – Δ) *(b)* delta-star (Δ – Y)

(c) delta-delta (Δ – Δ) *(d)* star-star (Y – Y)

These connections are shown in Figs. 1.72 and 1.73, where V and I are taken as input line voltage and line current respectively. Primary and secondary windings of one phase are drawn parallel to each other. With phase turns ratio from primary to secondary as $N_1/N_2 = a$, the voltages and currents in the windings and lines are shown in Figs. 1.72 and 1.73. The various connections are now described briefly.

***(a)* Star-delta (*Yd*) connection** : This connection is commonly used for stepping down the voltage from a high level to a medium or low level. The insulation on the h.v. side of the transformer is stressed only to 57.74% $\left(= \frac{1}{\sqrt{3}} \times 100\right)$ of line to line voltage.

For per-phase m.m.f. balance, $I_2 N_2 = I_1 N_1$

Here primary phase current, I_1 = primary line current I

∴ Secondary phase current, $I_2 = \frac{N_1}{N_2} \cdot I_1 = aI$

Secondary line current $= \sqrt{3} I_2 = \sqrt{3} \cdot aI$

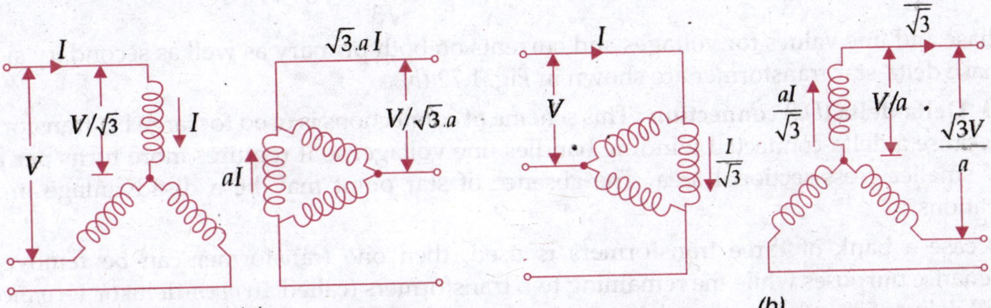

Fig 1.72: *(a)* Star-delta connection and *(b)* delta-star connection of 3-phase transformers.

* For more details of 3-phase transformers, see Chapter 8 of the book, "Generalized Theory of Electrical Machines" by the same author.

Also, voltage per turn on primary = voltage per turn on secondary

$$\frac{V}{\sqrt{3}}\cdot\frac{1}{N_1} = \frac{V_2}{N_2}$$

$\therefore$ Secondary phase voltage, $V_2 = \dfrac{N_2}{N_1}\cdot\dfrac{V}{\sqrt{3}} = \dfrac{V}{a.\sqrt{3}}$

Secondary line voltage = Secondary phase voltage = $\dfrac{V}{a\sqrt{3}}$

$$\text{Input VA} = 3\frac{V}{\sqrt{3}}I = \sqrt{3}\,VI = \text{output VA} = 3\cdot\frac{V}{a\sqrt{3}}\cdot\sqrt{3}\,aI = \sqrt{3}\,VI$$

Phase and line values for voltages and currents on both primary and secondary sides of star-delta transformer are shown in Fig. 1.72 *(a)*.

(b) Delta-Star (*Dy*) connection : This type of connection is used for stepping up the voltage to a high level. For example, these are used in the beginning of h.v. transmission lines so that insulation is stressed to about 57.74% of line voltage.

Delta-star transformers are also generally used as distribution transformers for providing mixed line to line voltage to high-power equipment and line to neutral voltage to 1-phase low-power equipment. For example, 11 kV/400 V, delta-star distribution transformer is used to distribute power to consumers by 3-phase four-wire system. Three-phase high-power equipment is connected to 400 V, three line wires, whereas 1-phase low-power equipment is energised from 231 V line to neutral circuits.

For per-phase m.m.f. balance, $I_2N_2 = I_1N_1$

Here primary phase current, $I_1 = \dfrac{1}{\sqrt{3}}$ (primary line current I)

Secondary phase current, $I_2 = \dfrac{N_1}{N_2}\cdot I_1 = a\dfrac{I}{\sqrt{3}}$ = Secondary line current

Also, $\dfrac{V_2}{N_2} = \dfrac{V_1}{N_1}$

Secondary phase voltage, $V_2 = \dfrac{N_2}{N_1}\cdot V_1 = \dfrac{V}{a}$

Secondary line voltage $= \sqrt{3}\cdot\dfrac{V}{a}$

$$\text{Input } VA = 3\cdot V\cdot\frac{I}{\sqrt{3}} = \sqrt{3}\,\text{VI} = \text{output VA} = 3\cdot\frac{\text{V}}{\text{a}}\cdot\text{a}\frac{\text{I}}{\sqrt{3}} = \sqrt{3}\cdot\text{VI}$$

Phase and line values for voltages and currents on both primary as well as secondary sides of a 3-phase delta-star transformer are shown in Fig. 1.72 *(b)*.

(c) Delta-delta (*Dd*) connection : This scheme of connections is used for large l.v. transformers. It is because a delta-connected winding handles line voltage, so it requires more turns per phase but of smaller cross-sectional area. The absence of star point may be a disadvantage in some applications.

In case a bank of three transformers is used, then one transformer can be removed for maintenance purposes while the remaining two transformers (called an *open*-delta or *V-connection*) can still deliver 58% of the power delivered by the original 3-phase transformer bank.

For per-phase m.m.f. balance, $I_2N_2 = I_1N_1$

Primary phase current, $I_1 = \dfrac{1}{\sqrt{3}}$ (primary line current I)

Secondary phase current, $$I_2 = \frac{N_1}{N_2} \cdot I_1 = \frac{aI}{\sqrt{3}}$$

Secondary line current $$= \sqrt{3} \cdot \left(\frac{aI}{\sqrt{3}}\right) = aI$$

Also, $$\frac{V_2}{N_2} = \frac{V_1}{N_1}$$

Secondary phase voltage, $$V_2 = \frac{N_2}{N_1} \cdot V_1 = \frac{V}{a} \quad \text{(Here, } V_1 = V\text{)}$$

Secondary line voltage $$= V_2 = \frac{V}{a}$$

$$\text{Input } VA = 3 \cdot V \cdot \frac{I}{\sqrt{3}}$$

$$= \sqrt{3}\, VI = \text{output } VA = 3 \cdot \frac{V}{a} \cdot \frac{aI}{\sqrt{3}} = \sqrt{3} \cdot VI$$

Phase and line values for voltages and currents on both primary and secondary sides of a 3-phase delta-star transformer are shown in Fig. 1.73 *(a)*.

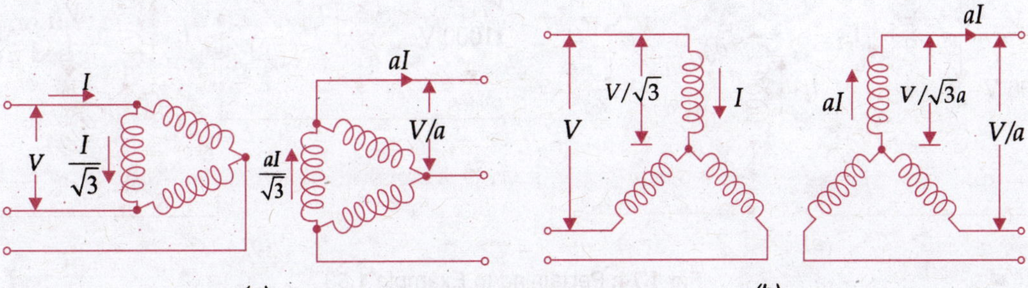

Fig 1.73: *(a)* Delta-delta connection and *(b)* Star-star connection of three-phase transformers.

***(d)* Star-star (*Yy*) connection :** This connection is used for small h.v. transformers. As stated before, with star connection, turns per phase are minimum and the winding insulation is stressed to 57.74% of line voltage. Star-star connection is rarely used in practice because of oscillatory neutral problems.*

For per-phase m.m.f. balance, $$I_2N_2 = I_1N_1$$

Primary phase current, $$I_1 = \text{primary line current, } I$$

Secondary phase current, $$I_2 = \frac{N_1}{N_2} \cdot I_1 = aI = \text{secondary line current}$$

Secondary phase voltage, $$V_2 = \frac{N_2}{N_1} \cdot V_1 = \frac{V}{\sqrt{3}a} \quad \ldots\left(\text{Here, } V_1 = \frac{V}{\sqrt{3}}\right)$$

Secondary line voltage $$= \sqrt{3}\, V_2 = \sqrt{3} \cdot \frac{V}{\sqrt{3}a} = \frac{V}{a}$$

$$\text{Input VA} = 3 \cdot \frac{V}{\sqrt{3}} \cdot I = \sqrt{3}\, VI = \text{output VA} = 3 \cdot \frac{V}{\sqrt{3}a} \cdot aI = \sqrt{3} \cdot VI$$

As before, phase and line values of voltages and currents on both the sides of a star-star transformer are shown in Fig. 1.73 *(b)*.

* For more details, see Chapter 8 of the book, "Generalized Theory of Electrical Machines" by the same author.

Example 1.63. *A 3-phase transformer is used to step-down the voltage of a 3-phase, 11 kV feeder line. Per-phase turns ratio is 12. For a primary line current of 20 A, calculate the secondary line voltage, line current and output kVA for the following connections :*

(a) star-delta (b) delta-star (c) delta-delta (d) star-star. Neglect losses.

Solution. *(a)* Three-phase transformer with star-delta connection is shown in Fig. 1.74 *(a)*

Phase voltage on primary, $V_{p1} = \frac{V_{L1}}{\sqrt{3}} = \frac{11000}{\sqrt{3}}\text{ V}$

Phase current on primary, $I_{p1} = I_{L1} = 20\text{ A}$

Here, $\frac{V_{p1}}{12} = \frac{V_{p2}}{1}$ and $I_{p1} \times 12 = I_{p2} \times 1$

$\therefore$ Phase voltage on secondary, $V_{p2} = \frac{11000}{\sqrt{3}\times 12} = 529.25\text{ V}$

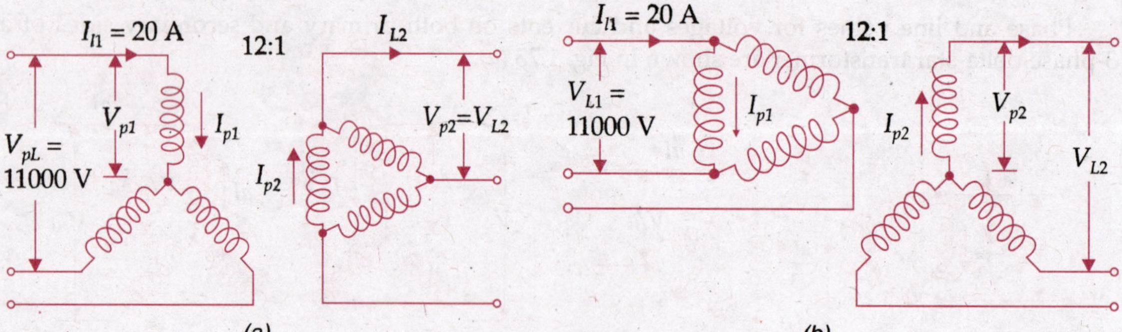

Fig 1.74: Pertaining to Example 1.63

Line voltage on secondary, $V_{L2} = V_{p2} = 529.25\text{ V}$

Phase current on secondary, $I_{p2} = 12 I_{p1} = 12 \times 20 = 240\text{ A}$

Line current on secondary, $I_{L2} = \sqrt{3}\ I_{p2} = \sqrt{3}\ \times 240 = 415.68\text{ A}$

Output $\text{kVA} = \frac{3V_{p2}.I_{p2}}{1000} = 3\cdot\frac{11000}{\sqrt{3}\times 12}\times 240\times\frac{1}{1000} = 381.04\text{ kVA}.$

(b) Delta-star connection of 3-phase transformer is shown in Fig. 1.74 *(b)*.

Phase voltage on secondary, $V_{p2} = \frac{V_{p1}}{12} = \frac{V_{L1}}{12} = \frac{11000}{12}\text{ V} = 916.67\text{ V}$

Line voltage on secondary, $V_{L2} = \sqrt{3}\ V_{p2} = \sqrt{3}\times\frac{11000}{12} = 1587.67\text{ V}$

Phase current on primary, $I_{p1} = I_{L1} / \sqrt{3} = \frac{20}{\sqrt{3}}\text{ A}$

Phase current on secondary, $I_{p2} = 12\ I_{p1} = 12 \times \frac{20}{\sqrt{3}} = 138.568\text{ A}$

Line current on secondary, $I_{L2} = I_{p2} = 138.568\text{ A}$

Output $\text{kVA} = 3 \times \frac{11000}{12}\times\frac{12\times 20}{1000\times\sqrt{3}} = 381.04\text{ kVA}$

(*c*) Delta-delta connection of 3-phase transformer is shown in Fig. 1.75 (*c*).

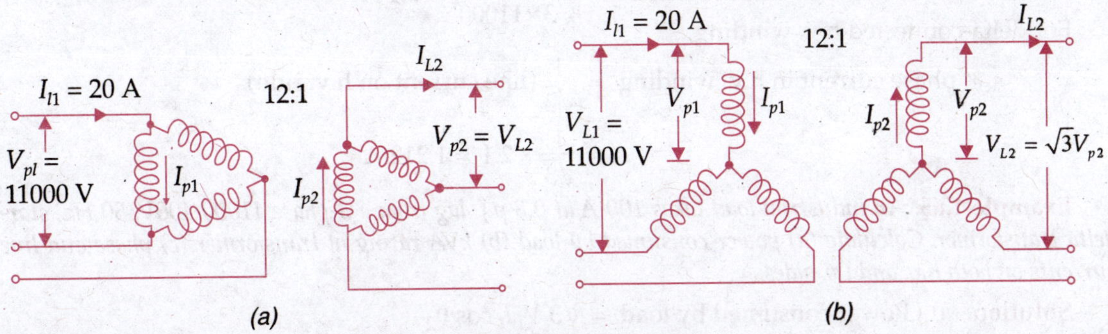

Fig 1.75: Pertaining to Example 1.63.

Phase voltage on secondary, $V_{p2} = \dfrac{V_{p1}}{12} = \dfrac{V_{L1}}{12} = \dfrac{11000}{12}\text{ V} = 6351\text{ V}$

Line voltage on secondary, $V_{L2} = V_{p2} = 6351\text{ V}$

Phase current on primary, $I_{p1} = \dfrac{20}{\sqrt{3}}\text{ A}$

Phase current on secondary, $I_{p2} = 12\,I_{p1} = 12 \times \dfrac{20}{\sqrt{3}}\text{ A}$

Line current on secondary, $I_{L2} = \sqrt{3}\,I_{p2} = \sqrt{3}\cdot\dfrac{12\times 20}{\sqrt{3}} = 240\text{ A}$

Output $\text{kVA} = \dfrac{3V_{p2}I_{p2}}{1000} = 3\times\dfrac{11000}{12}\times\dfrac{240}{\sqrt{3}} = 381.04\text{ kVA}$

(*d*) 3-phase transformer with star-star connection is shown in Fig. 1.75 (*d*).

Phase voltage on secondary, $V_{p2} = \dfrac{V_{p1}}{12} = \dfrac{11000}{\sqrt{3}\times 12}\text{ V}$

Line voltage on secondary, $V_{L2} = \sqrt{3}\,V_{p2} = \sqrt{3}\cdot\dfrac{11000}{\sqrt{3}\times 12} = \dfrac{11000}{12}\text{ V}$

Phase current on primary, $I_{p1} = I_{L1} = 20\text{ A}$

Phase current on secondary, $I_{p2} = 12\,I_{p1} = 12\times 20 = 240\text{ A}$

Line current on secondary, $I_{L2} = I_{p2} = 240\text{ A}$

Output $\text{kVA} = \dfrac{3\times 11000}{\sqrt{3}\times 12}\times\dfrac{240}{1000} = 381.04\text{ kVA}$

Example 1.64. *A 11000/415 V, delta-star transformer feeds power to a 30 kW, 415 V, 3-phase induction motor having an efficiency of 90% and full-load p.f. 0.833. Calculate the transformer rating and phase and line currents on both high and low voltage sides.*

Solution. Transformer kVA rating $= \dfrac{30}{0.9\times 0.833} = 40\text{ kVA}$

Line current on l.v. side of transformer $= \dfrac{\text{Total load in VA}}{\sqrt{3}\times\text{line voltage}} = \dfrac{40{,}000}{\sqrt{3}\times 415} = 55.65\text{ A}$

For star-connected l.v. winding, phase current in l.v. winding

= line current on l.v. side = 55.65 A

$$\text{Line current on h.v. side of transformer} = \frac{40,000}{\sqrt{3}\times 11000} = 2.1 \text{ A}$$

For delta-connected h.v. winding,

$$\text{phase current in h.v. winding} = \frac{1}{\sqrt{3}}(\text{line current on h.v. side})$$

$$= \frac{1}{\sqrt{3}} \times 2.1 = 1.212 \text{ A}$$

Example 1.65. *An industrial load takes 100 A at 0.8 p.f. lag from a 3-phase 11000/400V, 50 Hz, star-delta transformer. Calculate (a) power consumed by load (b) kVA rating of transformer (c) phase and line currents on both h.v. and l.v. sides.*

Solution. *(a)* Power consumed by load $= \sqrt{3}\, V_l I_l \cos\theta_2$

$$= \sqrt{3} \times 400 \times 100 \times 0.8 \times \frac{1}{1000} = 55.424 \text{ kW}$$

(b) kVA rating of transformer $= \sqrt{3} \times 400 \times 100 \times \frac{1}{1000} = 69.28 \text{ kVA}$

(c) Phase current or line current on star-connected h.v. side $= \frac{69.28}{\sqrt{3}\times 11} = 3.636 \text{ A}$

Line current on l.v. secondary side $I_l = 100 \text{ A}$

Phase current on delta-connected secondary side $= \frac{I_l}{\sqrt{3}} = \frac{100}{\sqrt{3}} = 57.73 \text{ A}$

1.21. INSTRUMENT TRANSFORMERS

Voltages upto about 765 kV and currents in the range of thousands of amperes exist in 50 Hz (or 60 Hz) power systems. It is usually necessary to measure these high values of voltages and currents with the help of standard low-range instruments; 0-110 V for voltmeters and 0-1 A or 0-5 A for ammeters. For this purpose, specialized accurate ratio transformers have been developed. These special transformers are known as instrument transformers or instrumentation transformers.

In general, function of instrument transformers is to reduce high values of voltages and currents to lower safe values to be used in ac power circuits to supply instruments, protective relays or control circuits. Accuracy of measurement is more important in instrument transformers.

Instrument transformers are of two types: *(i)* current transformers and *(ii)* potential transformers.

Advantages of Instrument Transformers :

(1) Ammeters and voltmeters used with instrument transformers are usually standardized. Its value is 1 A or 5 A for ammeters and 110 V for voltmeters.

(2) The measuring instruments, placed far away from h.v. circuits, offer safety to the operator.

(3) The wires connecting instrument transformers to ammeters or voltmeters may be of smaller cross-section.

(4) High current flowing in a conductor can be measured by clip-on type current transformer without breaking the circuit.

Both types of instrument transformers are precisely built so that these behave like ideal transformers. These are, therefore, designed to operate at low flux densities so that their magnetizing current is small.

1.21.1. Current Transformers

A current transformer has primary and secondary winding as in an ordinary transformer. The primary of current transformer (CT) consists of a few turn of thick wire connected in series with high-current load, Fig. 1.76 *(a)*. Sometimes the primary is just one bar or conductor passing through the core as shown in Fig. 1.76 *(b)*.

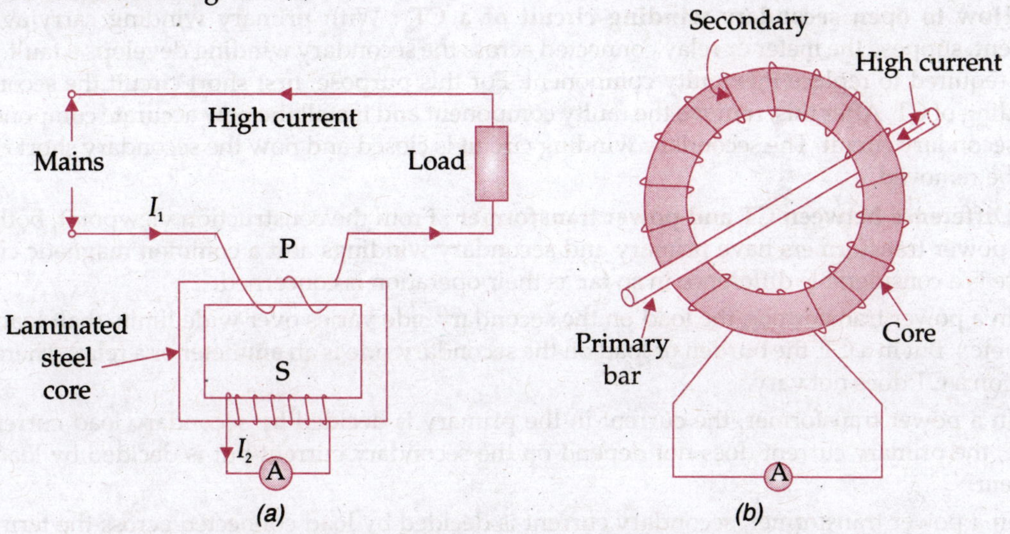

Fig 1.76: Current transformer *(a)* with wound primary and *(b)* with bar primary.

The secondary winding has large number of turns, Fig. 1.76 *(a)*. The secondary may be uniformly wound around core with large number of turns of thin wire, Fig. 1.76 *(b)*. The secondary winding is designed to handle usually 5 A (or 1A). Insulation between primary and secondary windings should be sufficient to withstand high line to neutral voltage.

Cores of CTs are made up of silicon steel laminations. For obtaining high degree of accuracy in the measurements, core may be made by using mumetal or permalloy.

The function of a CT is to step-down higher value of current to a lower value which can be easily measured by a low-range ammeter, 0-1 A or 0-5 A. Another function of CT is to supply a small current to the operating coil of a relay for the protection of transmission lines or equipment.

Burden of a CT : The load connected across the secondary terminals of a CT is called its burden. Its units are in volt-amperes (VA).

Effect of opening secondary winding of a CT : In a CT, the secondary mmf opposes the primary mmf as in other types of transformers. In practice, the secondary mmf is a little less than the primary mmf. This difference is due to some mmf required for magnetizing the core of CT. For an accurate CT, this difference in mmfs should be as small as possible. This is achieved by designing CT with large magnetizing impedance.

In case secondary of a CT gets open circuited during its operation, there would be no secondary mmf. Now, the large current in primary, equal to load current, would act as the magnetizing current since secondary current $I_2 = 0$. This large magnetizing current produces large core flux. This flux in the magnetic core is many times more than for which the core is designed. As a consequence, large core flux in the magnetic circuit of CT would result in the following :

(a) It would cause the production of large core losses resulting in heating of the core and insulation leading to its damage.

(b) It would induce a high voltage across open-circuited secondary terminals. This high voltage may be dangerous to life and equipment and may even cause break-down of insulation.

(c) It would cause the presence of residual flux in the core leading to inaccurate future readings.

This shows that secondary circuit of a CT should never be left open-circuited when the primary circuit is carrying the load current.

How to open secondary winding circuit of a CT : With primary winding carrying load current, suppose the meter or relay connected across the secondary winding develops a fault. Now it is required to replace this faulty component. For this purpose, first short circuit the secondary winding of CT. After this, remove the faulty component and install the new accurate component in the secondary circuit. The secondary winding circuit is closed and now the secondary short circuit can be removed.

Difference between CT and power transformer : From the construction viewpoint, both CTs and power transformers have primary and secondary windings and a common magnetic circuit. There is a considerable difference in so far as their operation is concerned.

In a power transformer, the load on the secondary side varies over wide limits (half load, full load etc.). But in a CT, the burden or load on the secondary side is an ammeter or a relay. Therefore, load on a CT does not vary.

In a power transformer, the current in the primary is decided by secondary load current. In a CT, the primary current does not depend on the secondary current but is decided by load line current.

In a power transformer, secondary current is decided by load connected across the terminals of secondary winding. In a CT, secondary current depends upon the primary line current and the turns ratio.

In a power transformer, the maximum flux density used may be as high as 1.6 T. But in a CT, the flux density used is quite small so as to lower its magnetizing current.

A power transformer handles large amounts of power. A CT handles only a small amount of power because their only loads are simple ammeters, relays etc.

1.21.2. Potential Transformers

A potential transformer is a **step-down** transformer with large number of primary turns as compared to secondary turns. The primary winding of PT is connected across the high voltage to be measured. Its secondary winding is connected to a voltmeter or the potential coil of a wattmeter or energy meter. Thus, load on the secondary circuit of PT is only the impedance of the instrument pressure coil. These are, therefore, designed for very small current carrying capacities. The secondary winding of a PT is usually designed for 110 V.

Potential transformers are made from high quality magnetic core. These are designed at very low flux densities so that their magnetizing current is quite small. It is required in PT that *(i)* variation of voltage ratio with load is minimum and *(ii)* phase shift between input and output voltages is also minimum. In addition, insulation between primary and secondary windings must be large enough to withstand high line voltage.

The connections of a potential transformer for measuring high voltage are shown in Fig. 1.77. It is usual practice to ground the secondary of PT. This is done to protect the operator from high voltage risks in case of insulation breakdown.

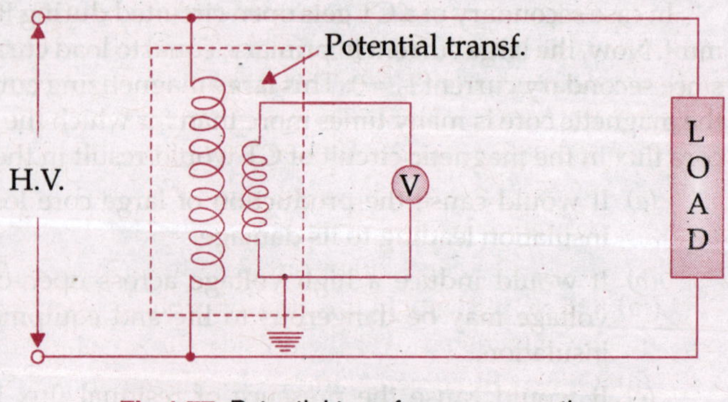

Fig 1.77: Potential transformer connections

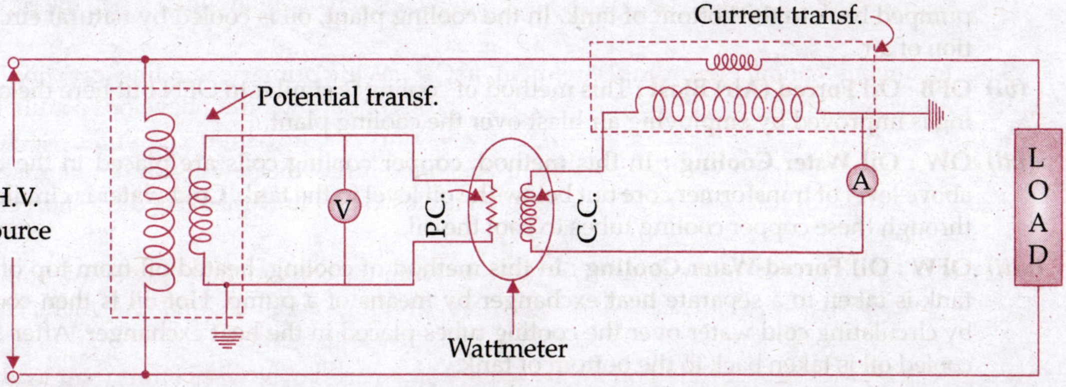

Fig 1.78: Use of PT and CT for the measurement of voltage, current and power in a 1-phase ac circuit.

Use of PT and CT for the measurement of voltage, current and power in a single-phase h.v. ac circuit is shown in Fig. 1.78. Note that one terminal of PT and one terminal of CT are grounded for the sake of safety to the operator.

1.22. TRANSFORMER COOLING

When transformer is in operation, core losses and $I^2 R$ losses occur in the core and windings respectively. These losses cause heating and therefore temperature rise of the transformer. Thus, a transformer must be cooled so that temperature rise of the core and windings remain within their specified limits.

The various methods of cooling of transformers are classified below in standard code language.

(i) **AN : Air Natural :** In this type of cooling, transformer core and windings are open to air surrounding the transformer. Air cools the core and coils by natural circulation without any external device. Sometimes, a sheet metal enclosure is provided to protect the windings from any mechanical damage. This method is suitable for low-voltage transformers up to about 25 kVA.

(ii) **AB : Air Blast :** In this method, cooling is improved by a continuous blast of cool air instead of natural circulation. The blast is produced by a fan. The air must be filtered before passing it through the windings.

(iii) **ON : Oil Natural :** These days, most of the transformers have their windings and core immersed in oil. The oil acts as a cooling medium and also as an insulating medium. A steel tank is used to contain oil and the transformer.

The mineral oil takes away the heat generated in the core and windings. Heated oil then rises and its place is taken by cool oil from the bottom of tank. Heated oil transfers its heat to the tank walls by natural circulation. Heat from the tank walls gets transferred to the surrounding air by means of radiation and convection. The oil becomes cooler and falls to the bottom of tank. Thus, a continuous natural circulation of oil is set up in the tank which takes away heat from heated parts and transfers it to the surrounding air.

Plain tank surface provides good dissipation of heat. For large size transformers, cooling surface area of tank must be increased. This is achieved by providing corrugations, fins, tubes (see Fig. 1.79) or radiators to the tank.

(iv) **OB : Oil Blast :** In this type of cooling, better cooling of ON type transformer is achieved by blasting air over the outside surface of the tank containing oil.

(v) **OFN : Oil Forced Natural :** In this method of cooling, a motor driven pump draws hot oil from top of the tank and forces the oil to a separate cooling plant. The cooled oil is then

pumped back to the bottom of tank. In the cooling plant, oil is cooled by natural circulation of air.

(vi) **OFB : Oil Forced (Air) Blast :** This method of cooling is similar to OFN but here the cooling is improved by employing air blast over the cooling plant.

(vii) **OW : Oil Water Cooling :** In this method, copper cooling coils are placed in the tank above level of transformer core but below the oil level in the tank. Cold water is circulated through these copper cooling tubes to cool the oil.

(viii) **OFW : Oil Forced Water Cooling :** In this method of cooling, heated oil from top of the tank is taken to a separate heat exchanger by means of a pump. Hot oil is then cooled by circulating cold water over the cooling tubes placed in the heat exchanger. After this, cooled oil is taken back to the bottom of tank.

Eight simple cooling methods are listed above. In addition, there are several mixed cooling methods like ON/OB, ON/OFN, ON/OFB, ON/OB/OFB etc. When transformers employ more than one method of cooling, then the transformer has two or three MVA ratings depending upon the cooling methods employed.

1.23. CONSERVATOR, BREATHER AND BUCHHOLZ RELAY

Transformer oil should not be allowed to come in contact with atmospheric air which may contain moisture. When air full of moisture comes in contact with oil, the insulating properties of oil get spoiled. In addition, air may lead to the formation of acidity and sludging of oil. The acidity and sludging deteriorates the cooling process of windings and tank. In order that oil does not lose its properties, a conservator is used. Function of conservator is to take care of expansion or contraction of oil in the transformer tank during its operation.

A conservator is an air-tight cylindrical metal drum connected near the top of tank by means of a pipe. The level of conservator is above the level of tank top as shown in Fig. 1.79. The main tank is filled with oil in such a manner that conservator is partially filled, Fig. 1.79. The conservator does not allow the atmospheric air from coming in contact with the oil.

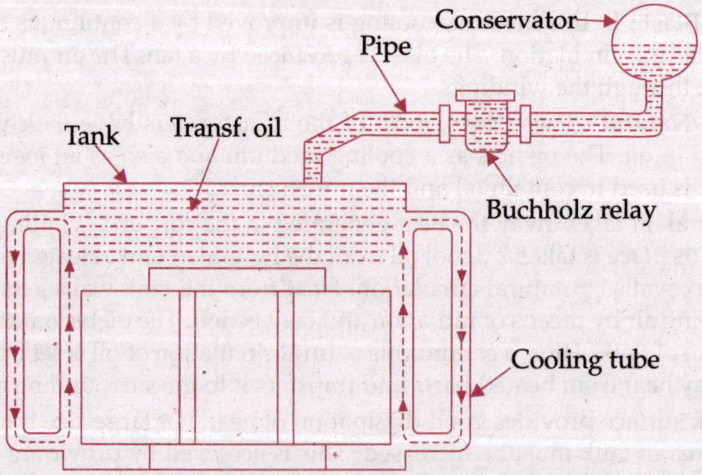

Fig 1.79: Conservator and Buchholz relay fitted to transformer tank.

When the oil expands due to heat, some oil comes into conservator from tank. Now oil level in conservator rises and some air from conservator is pushed out. When the transformer cools, some oil flows back to the tank from conservator. As a result, oil level in conservator falls and some air is drawn in from the atmosphere. This is called **breathing** . The air, coming in, is passed through an apparatus, called **breather**. The function of breather is to extract moisture from the air going into the conservator. The breather is small container filled with silica gel which extracts the moisture from atmospheric air. Silica gel should be checked regularly, dried and replaced when the need arises.

Note that the breather has to handle both the incoming air from atmosphere and the outgoing air to the atmosphere.

Buchholz Relay : Buchholz Relay (BR) is used for the protection of oil-filled transformers from incipient (beginning to happen) faults.

B.R. consists of a vessel or container, normally full of oil. This chamber contains two floats A and B which are hinged and can move up or down depending on the oil pressure Fig. 1.80 *(a)*. Activation of this relay is dependent on the generation of gas in the transformer tank.

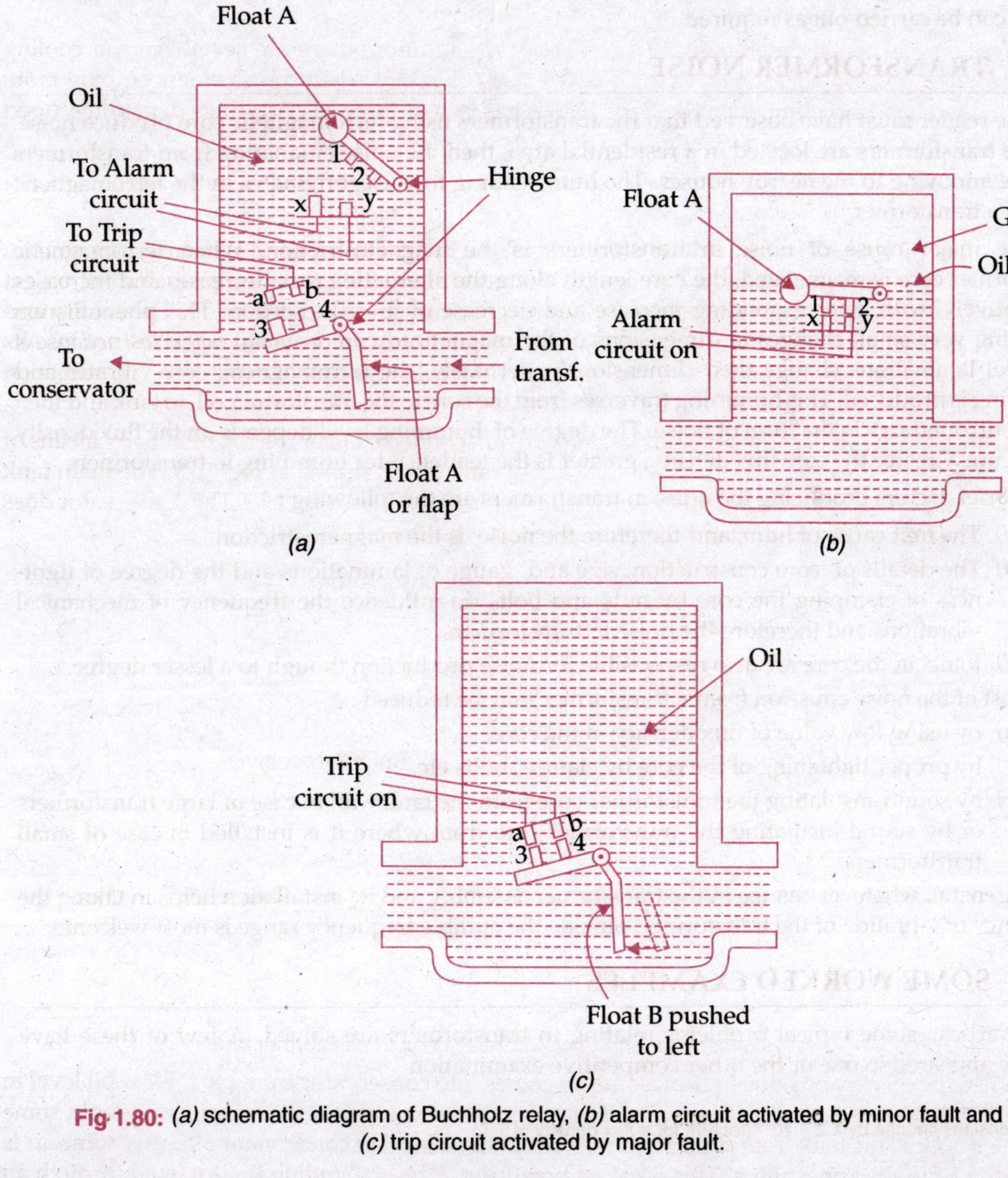

Fig 1.80: *(a)* schematic diagram of Buchholz relay, *(b)* alarm circuit activated by minor fault and *(c)* trip circuit activated by major fault.

When a fault occurs, gas bubbles are generated in the transformer tank. These bubbles rise in the tank, travel the pipe line towards the conservator. These bubbles, or gas, get trapped in the upper part of the B.R. vessel. As a result, oil level falls, float A also sinks and eventually float contracts 1, 2 get connected with stationary contacts x, y, Fig. 1.80 *(b)*. As soon as 1, 2 come in contact with x, y, a switch closes the alarm circuit. This alarm activation indicates some fault in the transformer. The transformer is now disconnected and repaired accordingly.

If the rate of gas generation is small, lower float B is not affected. In case of major fault within the transformer, gas production is violent. As a result, oil displacement by violet gas is so strong that it causes abnormal flow of oil along the pipe line tilting the float B to left, Fig. 1.80 *(c)*. This tilt causes contacts 3, 4 to come in touch with stationary a, b contacts. This completes the circuit of trip coil of circuit breaker and eventually transformer is disconnected on both h.v. and l.v. sides. Now repair can be carried out as required.

1.24. TRANSFORMER NOISE

The reader must have observed that the transformers using ferromagnetic core produce noise. In case transformers are located in a residential area, then the noise emanating from transformers may be annoying to the nearby houses. The hum, leading to noise, originates in the ferromagnetic core of a transformer.

The major cause of noise in transformers is the magnetostriction. When ferromagnetic transformer core is magnetized, the core length along the alternating flux decreases and increases alternatively, with a corresponding increase and decrease of its cross-section. This phenomenon involving very small changes in dimensions of the magnetized core is called *magnetostriction*. As the steel laminations change their dimensions* alternately, the ferromagnetic core vibrates and humming is produced. This humming traverses from the core to the transformer oil, to tank and then to the surroundings in the form of noise. The degree of humming level depends on the flux density in the core. Greater the core flux density, greater is the tendency for humming in transformers.

In brief, factors producing the noise in transformers are the following :

(i) The first cause of hum, and therefore the noise, is the magnetostriction.

(ii) The details of core construction, size and gauge of laminations and the degree of tightness of clamping the core by nuts and bolts do influence the frequency of mechanical vibrations and therefore the noise in transformers.

(iii) Joints in the core are also responsible for noise production though to a lesser degree.

Most of the noise emission from a transformer may be reduced :

(a) by using low value of flux density in the core,

(b) by proper tightening of the core by clamps, bolts etc.

(c) by sound-insulating the transformer core from the tank wall in case of large transformers or by sound-insulating the transformer core from where it is installed in case of small transformers.

In general, whatever change in the transformer assembly and its installation helps in taking the frequency of vibration of the transformer, outside the audible frequency range is most welcome.

1.25. SOME WORKED EXAMPLES

In this article, some typical problems relating to transformers are solved. A few of these have already appeared in one or the other competitive examination.

* Dimensions change by 1.2×10^{-4} percent for a flux density of 1 T.

Example 1.66. *A single-phase transformer has its core dimensions in centimeters as shown in Fig. 1.81. The core is square in cross-section. For a maximum flux density of 1.2 T in the core, the magnetic-field internsity is 600 A/m and the core loss is 2 W/kg at 50 Hz. Core density is 7.8 g/cm³.*

For an applied voltage of 1200 V, 50 Hz at primary terminals, calculate

(a) the number of primary turns

(b) current, p.f. and power on the primary side under no-load conditions.

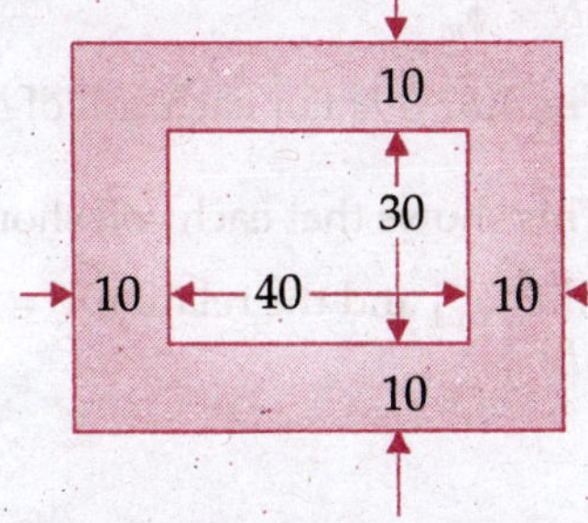

Fig 1.81: Pertaining to Example 1.66

Solution. *(a)* Gross core area = $10 \times 10 \times 10^{-4} = 0.01$ m²

Net core area = gross core area × stacking (or iron) factor

$$A_i = 0.01 \times 0.9 = 0.009 \text{ m}^2$$

Maximum value of core flux, $\phi_{max} = A_i \times B_m = 0.009 \times 1.2 = 0.0108$ Wb

From Eqn. (1.3), $E_1 = \sqrt{2}\, \pi f N_1 \phi_{max}$

∴ Number of turns in primary, $N_1 = \dfrac{1200}{\sqrt{2}\,\pi \times 50 \times 0.0108} = 500.25 \cong 500$ turns.

(b) Mean length of flux path, $L = [(40 + 10) + (30 + 10)] \times 2 = 180$ cm.

m.m.f. for the core = $H.L = 600 \times 1.80 = 1080$ ATs.

Maximum value of magnetizing current $= \dfrac{\text{core m.m.f.}}{N_1} = \dfrac{1080}{500} = 2.16$ A

R.m.s. value of magnetizing current, $I_m = \dfrac{2.16}{\sqrt{2}} = 1.528$ A

Core volume $= L \times A_i = 1.80 \times 0.009 = 0.0162$ m³

Weight of core = $0.0162 \times 7.8 \times 10^6 \times 10^{-3} = 126.36$ kg

Total core (or iron) loss, $P_c = 126.36 \times 2 = 252.72$ W

Core loss component of primary current.

$$I_c = \frac{P_c}{V_1} = \frac{252.72}{1200} = 0.2106 \text{ A}$$

∴ No load current, $I_0 = \sqrt{I_c^2 + I_m^2} = \sqrt{0.2106^2 + 1.528^2} = 1.542$ A

No-load p.f., $\cos\theta^\circ = \dfrac{I_m}{I_0} = \dfrac{0.2106}{1.542} = 0.1366$

Power at no-load = core loss = 252.72 W

Also, power input at no load = $V_1 I_0 \cos\theta^\circ = 1200 \times 1.542 \times 0.1366 = 252.76$ W.

Example 1.67. *The magnetic circuit of a 1-phase core-type transformer is energised in three different configurations shown in Fig. 1.80, but from the same voltage V and frequency f. In Fig. 1.80 (a), the magnetizing current is 4 A, maximum flux density in core is 1 T and e.m.f. induced in secondary winding is 100 V.*

Find these values for Figs. 1.80 (b) and (c). Magnetic saturation and core loss may be neglected.

Solution. Fig. 1.82 *(a)* $V = \sqrt{2}\,\pi f N \phi_{m1}$ or $\phi_{m1} = \dfrac{V}{\sqrt{2}\,\pi f N}$

For flux ϕ_{m1} in the core, maximum core flux density is $B_{m1} = \dfrac{\phi_{m1}}{A_i} = 1$ T (given), where A_i = net core area.

Flux ϕ_{m1} is produced by primary m.m.f. $I_{m1} \cdot N_1$, where magnetizing current $I_{m1} = 4$ A (given), *i.e.*, $4N \propto \phi_m$

Fig. 1.82 *(b)* : For each coil of *N* turns, $V = \sqrt{2}\,\pi f N \phi_{m2}$ or $\phi_{m2} = \dfrac{V}{\sqrt{2}\,\pi f N} = \phi_{m1}$

This shows that each coil should produce a flux $\dfrac{\phi_{m1}}{2}$ so that both the coils produce a combined core flux ϕ_{m1} and the relation $V = \sqrt{2}\,\pi f N\phi_{m1}$ is satisfied for each coil. For flux ϕ_{m1} in the core in Fig. 1.82 *(b)*

$$B_{m2} = \frac{\phi_{m2}}{A_i} = \frac{\phi_{m1}}{A_i} = 1\text{ T}$$

The two coils are identical, therefore each coil has the same magnetizing current, *i.e.*, $I_{m2}' = I_{m2}''$.

For upper coil, $I_{m2}' N \propto \dfrac{\phi_{m1}}{2}$

and for lower coil, $I_{m2}'' N \propto \dfrac{\phi_{m1}}{2}$

Adding, we get $(I_{m2}' + I_{m2}'')N \propto \phi_{m1}$

But $4N \propto \phi_{m1}$

$\therefore$ $(I_{m2}' + I_{m2}'') = 4$ A

Magnetizing current of each coil, $I_{m2}' = I_{m2}'' = 2$ A.

Total magnetizing current $I_{m2} = I_{m2}' + I_{m2}'' = 4$ A

For core flux ϕ_{m1}, e.m.f. induced in secondary winding is 100 V as in Fig. 1.82 *(a)*.

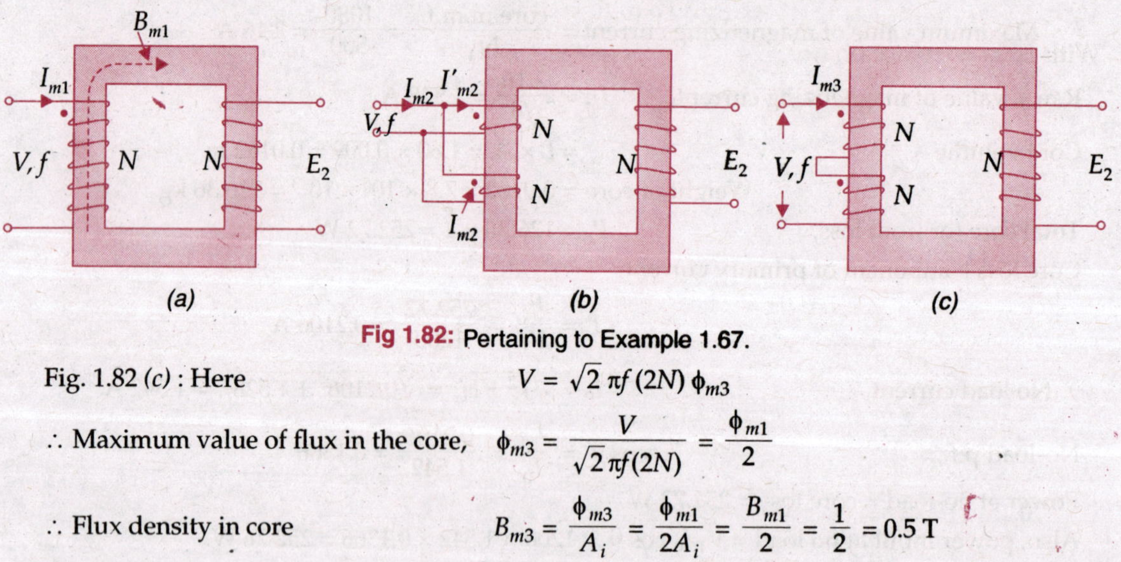

Fig 1.82: Pertaining to Example 1.67.

Fig. 1.82 *(c)* : Here $V = \sqrt{2}\,\pi f\,(2N)\,\phi_{m3}$

$\therefore$ Maximum value of flux in the core, $\phi_{m3} = \dfrac{V}{\sqrt{2}\,\pi f(2N)} = \dfrac{\phi_{m1}}{2}$

$\therefore$ Flux density in core $B_{m3} = \dfrac{\phi_{m3}}{A_i} = \dfrac{\phi_{m1}}{2A_i} = \dfrac{B_{m1}}{2} = \dfrac{1}{2} = 0.5$ T

Also, $I_{m3}\,(2N) \propto \phi_{m3}$ or $I_{m3}\,(2N) \propto \dfrac{\phi_{m1}}{2}$

From Fig. 1.82 *(a)*, $4N \propto \phi_{m1}$.

$$\therefore \quad \frac{I_{m3}(2N)}{4N} = \frac{\phi_{m1}}{2} \times \frac{1}{\phi_{m1}} = \frac{1}{2} \text{ or } I_{m3} = \frac{4}{2} \times \frac{1}{2} = 1\text{ A}$$

$\therefore$ Magnetizing current for both series connected coils = 1 A. For a core flux of $\dfrac{\phi_{m1}}{2}$, e.m.f. induced in secondary = $\dfrac{100}{2} = 50$ V.

Example 1.68. *A 20 kVA, 250/125 V, 1-phase transformer has the following data :*

$$r_1 = 0.15\ \Omega,\ x_1 = 0.25\ \Omega,\ r_2 = 0.03\ \Omega,\ x_2 = 0.4\ \Omega$$

Subscripts 1 and 2 denote h.v. and l.v. windings respectively.

When this transformer is fully loaded, the magnitude of e.m.f. induced in primary at full load is found to be equal to the primary terminal voltage. Calculate the load voltage, load p.f. and load power. Neglect the magnetizing current.

Solution. With secondary parameters referred to primary, the equivalent circuit is as shown in Fig. 1.83 *(a)*.

Primary full load current $\quad I_1 = \dfrac{20,000}{250} = 80\text{ A}$

Voltage drop between primary terminal voltage V_1 and primary induced e.m.f. E_1 can be written by referring to Eq. (1.44) as under :

$$V_1 - E_1 = I_1 (r_1 \cos \theta_1 + x_1 \sin \theta_1)$$

In the above equation, E_1 is taken as reference and θ_1 is the phase angle between E_1 and I_1, see Fig. 1.29.

But $\quad V_1 = E_1$ (given), $\quad \therefore\ 0 = r_1 \cos \theta_1 + x_1 \sin \theta_1$

$$\theta_1 = -\tan^{-1} \frac{r_1}{x_1} = -\tan^{-1} \frac{0.15}{0.25} = -30.96°$$

Negative sign for θ_1 indicates that I_1 leads E_1 [similar to I_2 leading V_2 in Fig. 1.30 *(a)*] by 30.96° as shown in Fig. 1.83 *(b)*. This figure shows that

$V_2' - \overline{E}_1 - \overline{I}_1 (r_2' + j x_2'),\ \overline{V}_2' = \overline{E}_1 - \overline{I}_1 (0.12 + j\,0.16)$

With E_1 as reference phasor,

$$\overline{I}_1 = 80 \angle 30.96°$$

$$V_2' = 250 \angle 0° - 80 \angle 30.96\ (0.12 + j0.16)$$

$$= 250 - 80 \angle 30.96 \times 0.2 \angle 53.13°$$

$$= 250 - 16 \angle 84.09° = 248.35 - j15.915$$

$$\therefore \quad \overline{V}_2' = 248.86 \angle -3.67°$$

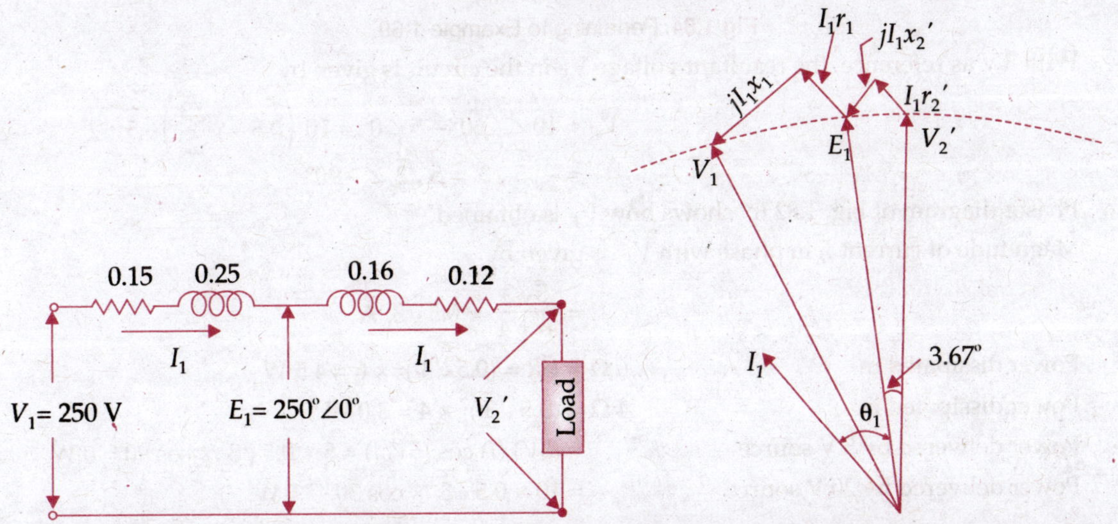

Fig 1.83: *(a)* Equivalent circuit and corresponding phasor diagram for example 1.68.

$\overline{V}_2'$ lags E_1 by 3.67° as shown in Fig. 1.83 *(b)*. This figure also reveals that I_1 leads load voltage V_2' by $\theta_1 + 3.67° = 30.96° + 3.67° = 34.63°$.

$\therefore$ Load p.f. $= \cos(\theta_1 + 3.67)$

$= \cos 34.63° = 0.8228$ leading $= \cos\theta_2$

Load voltage $V_2 = \dfrac{248.86}{2} = 124.43$ V

Secondary full load current, $I_2 = \dfrac{20{,}000}{125} = 160$ A

Load power $V_2 I_2 \cos\theta_2 = 124.43 \times 160 \times 0.8228 = 16380.961$ W.

Example 1.69. *In Fig. 1.84 (a), calculate*

(a) the power delivered by each source,

(b) the power dissipated in each resistor *[GATE, 1991]*

Solution. Secondary parameters 16 Ω and $20\angle -60°$ when transferred to primary side become $16 \times \frac{1}{4} = 4\ \Omega$ and $20\angle -60° \times \frac{1}{2} = 10\angle -60°$ V respectively. The circuit of Fig. 1.82 *(b)* becomes the equivalent circuit of Fig. 1.82 *(a)*.

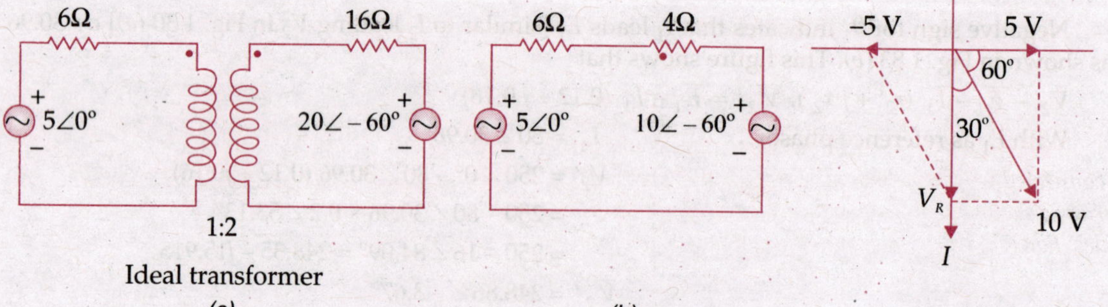

Fig 1.84: Pertaining to Example 1.69.

With 5 V as reference, the resultant voltage V_R in the circuit is given by

$$V_R = 10\angle -60° - 5\angle 0° = 10\left(0.5 - j\frac{\sqrt{3}}{2}\right) - 5$$

$$= -j5\sqrt{3} = 5\sqrt{3}\angle -90°$$

Phasor diagram of Fig. 1.82 *(c)* shows how V_R is obtained.

Magnitude of current I, in phase with V_R, is given by

$$I = \frac{5\sqrt{3}}{6+4} = 0.5\sqrt{3}\ \text{A}$$

Power dissipated in $6\ \Omega = I^2R = (0.5\sqrt{3})^2 \times 6 = 4.5$ W

Power dissipated in $4\ \Omega = (0.5\sqrt{3})^2 \times 4 = 3.0$ W

Power delivered by 5 V source $= (5V)(I)\cos(5V, I) = 5 \times 0.5\sqrt{3} \times \cos 90 = 0$ W

Power delivered by 20 V source $= 10 \times 0.5\sqrt{3} \times \cos 30°$ 7.5 W.

Example 1.70. *Fig. 1.85 (a) shows the approximate equivalent circuit of a 1.2 kVA, 240/110 V single-phase transformer referred to the primary. Evaluate its efficiency and regulation when it delivers full load at rated voltage and unity power factor.* (GATE, 1992)

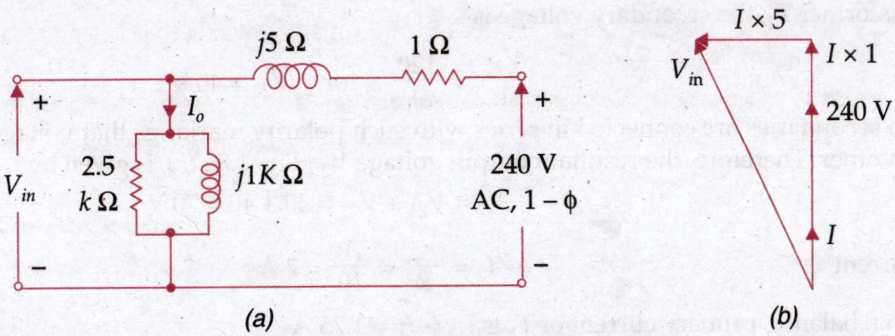

Fig 1.85: Pertaining to Example 1.70

Solution. Primary full-load current, $I_1 = \frac{1200}{240} = 5$ A

With 240 V as the reference, phasor diagram to obtain V_{in} is shown in Fig. 1.85 *(b)*.

$$\therefore \qquad V_{in} = \sqrt{(240 + 5 \times 1)^2 + (5 \times 5)^2} = 246.27 \text{ V}$$

$$I^2R \text{ loss} = 5^2 \times 1 = 25 \text{ W}$$

$$\text{Core loss} = \frac{V_{in}^2}{R_c} = \frac{(246.27)^2}{2500} = 24.26 \text{ W}$$

$$\text{Efficiency at full load} = \frac{1200 \times 1 \times 100}{1200 \times 1 + 25 + 24.26} = 96.057\%$$

$$\text{Voltage regulation} = \frac{V_{in} - V_1}{V_{in}} = \frac{246.27 - 240}{246.27} \times 100 = 2.546\%.$$

Example 1.71. *Fig. 1.86 (a) shows two 1-phase ideal transformers T_1 and T_2 of turns ratio 4 : 1 and 3 : 1 connected with their primaries in parallel across a 120 V, 50 Hz source. Their secondaries are connected in series as shown. The dot-points indicate terminals of the corresponding polarity on the primary and secondary sides. For R = 10 Ω, determine the current taken from the source, primary input impedance and power input.*

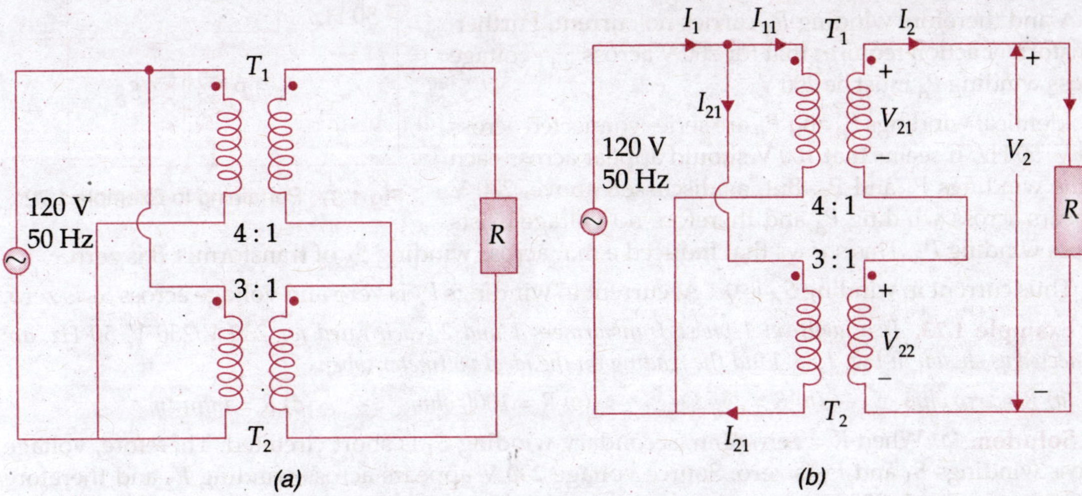

Fig 1.86: Pertaining to Example 1.71.

Solution. For transformer T_1, the secondary voltage is

$$\frac{V_{21}}{1} = \frac{120}{4} \quad \text{or} \quad V_{21} = 30 \text{ V}$$

For transformer T_2, the secondary voltage is

$$\frac{V_{22}}{1} = \frac{120}{4} \quad \text{or} \quad V_{22} = 40 \text{ V}$$

The two secondaries are connected in series with such polarity markings that voltages V_{21} and V_{22} aid each other. Therefore, the resultant output voltage V_2, Fig. 1.86 *(b)*, is given by

$$V_2 = V_{21} + V_{22} = 30 + 40 = 70 \text{ V}$$

Load current $$I_2 = \frac{V_2}{R} = \frac{70}{10} = 7 \text{ A}$$

For m.m.f. balance, primary current of T_1 is $I_{11} = \frac{7}{4} = 1.75$ A

and primary current of T_2 is $I_{21} = \frac{7}{3} = 2.333$ A

∴ Source current $$I_1 = I_{11} + I_{21} = 1.75 + 2.333 = 4.083 \text{ A}$$

Primary input impedance $$= \frac{120}{4.083} = 29.3902 \text{ A}$$

Power input to primary $$= 120 \times 4.083 \cong 70 \times 7 = 490 \text{ Watts.}$$

Example 1.72. *Two identical 200 V/200 V, 50 Hz single-phase transformers A and B have negligible power losses and negligible leakage fluxes. The magnetizing current taken by either transformer when fed from rated voltage is 0.1 A. If the windings of A and B are connected as shown in Fig. 1.87, estimate the currents drawn by P_A and S_A and the open circuit voltage across S_B. P_A and S_A are the two windings of transformer A, while P_B and S_B are the two windings of transformer B.* *[I.A.S., 1991]*

Solution. A careful examination of Fig. 1.87 reveals that winding S_A is directly connected across 200 V, 50 Hz supply. For 200 V across S_A, the magnetizing current needed to establish the required flux (and therefore the rated voltage 200 V) must flow through the winding S_A. This means that winding S_A carries the magnetizing current of 0.1 A and therefore winding P_A carries no current. Further, transformer action requires that for 200 V across S_A, voltage across winding P_A must be 200 V.

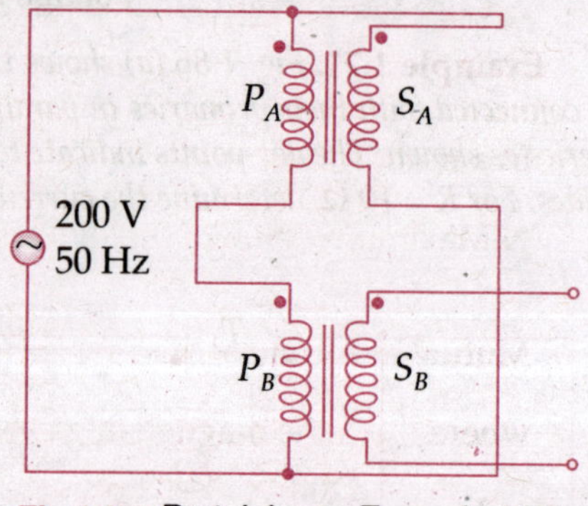

Fig 1.87: Pertaining to Example 1.72.

Identical windings P_A and P_B are series connected across 200 V, 50 Hz. It seems that 100 V should appear across each of the windings P_A and P_B. But, as discussed above, 200 V appears across winding P_A and therefore no voltage exists across winding P_B. This shows that induced e.m.f. across winding S_B of transformer B is zero.

Thus current in winding S_A is 0.1 A, current in windings P_A is zero and voltage across S_B is zero.

Example 1.73. *Two identical 1-phase transformers 1 and 2, each rated for 230 V/230 V, 50 Hz, are connected as shown in Fig. 1.88. Find the reading on the ideal voltmeter when*

(a) R = zero ohm *(b) R = 115 Ω* *(c) R = 1000 ohm* *(d) R = infinity.*

Solution. *(a)* When R = zero ohm, secondary winding S_1 is short circuited. Therefore, voltage across windings S_1 and P_1 is zero. Source voltage 230 V appears across winding P_2 and therefore voltmeter reading is 230 V.

(b) For R = 115 Ω, current through R should be 115/115 = 1 A. This current causes windings P_1 and P_2 to carry 1 A. Thus voltage across winding P_2 = magnetizing impedance of transformer 2 × 1 A acting as its magnetizing current because winding S_2 carries no current. As magnetizing impedance is large, the voltage across P_2 rises much above 115 V and that across P_1 collapses. It

shows that voltage across S_1 is much less than 115 V and likewise current through R is less than 1 A. However, the voltmeter reading is much more than 115 V but less than 230 V. Let this voltmeter reading be denoted by V_b.

(c) For R = 1000 Ω, current is reduced in both S_1 and P_1. Likewise, current in winding P_2 is also reduced. Therefore, voltage across winding P_2 is now less than its value in part (b). Even then, the voltmeter reading is more than 115 V say V_c but V_c is less than V_b obtained in part (b).

(d) For R equal to infinity, winding S_1 behaves as open-circuited winding. As expected, voltmeter reading is now 115 V.

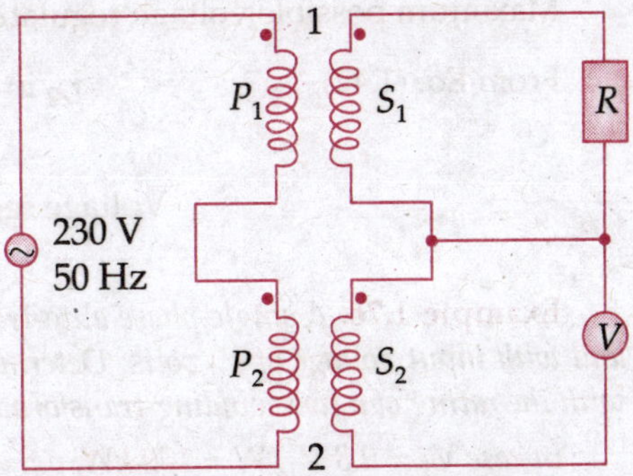

Fig 1.88: Pertaining to Example 1.73.

Example 1.74. *A 4 kVA, 50 Hz, single-phase transformer has a ratio 200/400 V. The data taken on the l.v. side at the rated voltage show that the open circuit input wattage is 80 W. The mutual inductance between the primary and secondary windings is 1.91 H. What value will be the current taken by the transformer, if the no-load test is conducted on the h.v. side at rated voltage? Neglect the effect of winding resistances and leakage reactances.* (GATE, 1995)

Solution. Open-circuit input wattage = core loss in transformer = 80 W

But core loss $I_{c1} V = 80$ W

Core loss in a transformer remains unaltered whether it is energized from l.v. side or h.v. side.

∴ Core-loss current when energized from h.v. side,

$$I_{c2} = \frac{80}{400} = 0.2 \text{ A}$$

In a transformer,

$$E = \sqrt{2}\,\pi f N \phi_{max} = \sqrt{2}\,\pi f \psi_{max}$$

∴ Maximum value of flux linkages ψ_{max} with l.v. winding $= \dfrac{V_1}{\sqrt{2}\pi f}$

$$\text{Mutual inductance, } M = \frac{\text{Flux linkages with l.v. winding}}{\text{Current in h.v. winding}} = \frac{V_1}{\sqrt{2}\,\pi f}\cdot\frac{1}{\sqrt{2}\,I_{m2}} = 1.91 \text{ H (given)}$$

where I_{m2} is the magnetizing current in h.v. winding.

$$\therefore I_{m2} = \frac{200}{\sqrt{2}\pi \times 50}\cdot\frac{1}{\sqrt{2}\times 1.91} = 0.3333 \text{ A}$$

The current taken by transformer when energized on h.v. side, as per Eq. (1.15), is

$$I_o = \sqrt{I_{c2}^2 + I_{m2}^2} = [0.2^2 + 0.3333^2]^{1/2} = \mathbf{0.3887\ A.}$$

Example 1.75. *A 100 kVA, 11 kV/400 V, 3-phase transformer has its maximum possible efficiency of 98%, when it delivers 80 kVA at unity p.f. and rated voltage. The maximum possible voltage regulation of the transformer is 4%. Find the efficiency and voltage regulation of the transformer for rated kVA output at 0.8 p.f. lagging.* (I.A.S., 1994)

Solution. Total losses in transformer $= \left(\frac{1}{\eta} - 1\right)$ output $= \left(\frac{1}{0.98} - 1\right) \times 80{,}000 = 1632.65$ W

∴ Core losses = ohmic losses = 1632.65/2 = 816.325 W

$$\text{Rated-load ohmic losses} = \left(\frac{1}{0.8}\right)^2 \times 816.325 = 1275.51 \text{ W}$$

$$\text{Transformer efficiency} = \frac{100{,}000 \times 0.8}{80{,}000 + 816.325 + 1275.51} \times 100 = 97.452\%$$

Maximum possible voltage regulation of a transformer is equal to z_{e2} in p.u. = 0.04 p.u.

From Eq. (1.42), r_{e2} in per unit $= \dfrac{1275.51}{100,000} = 0.01278$

$\therefore$ $x_{e2} = [0.04^2 - 0.1278^2]^{½} = 0.0379$ p.u.

$$\text{Voltage regulation} = [r_{e2} \cos \theta_2 + x_{e2} \sin \theta_2]$$
$$= [0.0128 \times 0.8 + 0.0397 \times 0.6] \times 100 = 3.298\%.$$

Example 1.76. *A single-phase auto-transformer is to deliver a power of W kW at unity p.f. at V_2 volts and with input voltage of V_1 volts. Determine the kVA rating of each section of the winding and compare it with the rating of a two-winding transformer assuming an efficiency of η in both cases.*

In case $V_2 = 0.8\ V_1$, W = 100 kW, p.f. = 1.00, η = 0.96, determine their ratings.

Solution. *Two-winding transformer:*

$$\text{Secondary winding rating} = \frac{W \text{ in kW}}{\text{p.f.}} = W \text{ kVA}$$

$$\text{Primary winding rating} = \frac{W}{\eta} \times \frac{1}{p.f.} = \frac{W}{\eta} \text{ kVA}$$

Here *p.f.* on primary side is assumed the same as on the secondary side.

Auto-transformer. Assuming it a step-down transformer, as in Fig. 1.41, the voltage rating of section $AB = V_1 - V_2$ and its current rating is $I_1 = \dfrac{W}{\eta} \cdot \dfrac{1}{V_1}$.

$$\therefore \quad \text{kVA rating of section } AB = I_1(V_1 - V_2) = \frac{W}{\eta} \cdot \frac{1}{V_1}(V_1 - V_2) = \frac{W}{\eta}(1 - \text{k})$$

where k = ratio of transformation $= \dfrac{V_2}{V_1}$

The voltage across section $BC = V_2$ and its current rating is $(I_2 - I_1) = \dfrac{W}{V_2} - \dfrac{W}{\eta V_1}$

$$\therefore \text{ kVA rating of section } BC = V_2 (I_2 - I_1) = V_2 \left[\frac{1}{V_2} - \frac{1}{\eta V_1}\right] W = W \left[1 - \frac{k}{\eta}\right]$$

For two-winding transformer, secondary rating = 100 kVA and primary rating

$$= \frac{100}{0.96} = 104.167 \text{ kVA.}$$

For auto-transformer, rating of section

$$AB = \frac{100}{0.96} [1 - 0.8] = 20.833 \text{ kVA}$$

and rating of section $BC = 100 \left[1 - \dfrac{0.8}{0.96}\right] = 16.667$ kVA

1.26. SUMMARY

Transformer is a static device and no electromechanical energy conversion is involved in it. However, it is preferable to study the transformer first and then the rotating electrical machines, since electrical behaviour of transformers and rotating machines is similar in many respects. The coupling between the primary and secondary windings of a transformer is through the magnetic field. Similarly, in rotating electrical machines, the coupling between electrical and mechanical systems (or stator and rotor windings) is through the magnetic field. In view of this, many of the relevant equations and the conclusions drawn in the transformer theory, are applicable to the analysis of A.C. machines and to some extent to D.C. machines also. These points of similarity are discussed below :

(*i*) In transformers, the resultant mutual flux is confined to the core, it therefore links both the primary and secondary windings. Similarly, in rotating machines, the resultant mutual flux crosses the air-gap and links both the stator and rotor windings.

The resultant mutual flux in transformer is produced by the combined action of primary and secondary currents. Similarly the resultant mutual air-gap flux in rotating machine is produced by the combined action of stator and rotor currents.

(ii) In transformers, the supply voltage is alternating, therefore the resultant mutual flux linkages are changing with time and e.m.f.s are induced in stationary primary and secondary windings. In rotating machines, the resultant air-gap flux linkages are made to change with time by rotor rotation and then speed e.m.f.s are induced in the armature windings. The existence of speed e.m.f.s due to mechanical motion is essential for electromechanical energy conversion.

(iii) The resultant mutual flux in both transformers and rotating machines, is the useful flux, since it takes part in the energy-conversion process. In addition to this useful flux, leakage fluxes linking one winding and not the other, are also present in both. In both, transformer and rotating machines, the leakage fluxes are accounted for by leakage reactances. In both, the leakage fluxes are largely in air, consequently the leakage reactances are unaffected by the magnetic saturation and are assumed constant.

(iv) In transformers, the applied voltage has to overcome the primary leakage impedance drop and the counter e.m.f. induced in the primary by the resultant core flux. Similarly in A.C. windings of motors, the applied voltage has to overcome the leakage impedance drop and the counter e.m.f. generated by the resultant mutual air-gap flux.

The leakage impedance drops are usually small, therefore in both transformers and rotating machines, the applied voltage is approximately equal to the counter e.m.f. Consequently constant applied voltage and frequency requires constant counter e.m.f. and therefore a constant value of resultant mutual flux. Hence in A.C. electromagnetic devices having small leakage impedance drops, the resultant mutual flux is determined by the applied voltage and frequency. Since, for constant applied voltage and frequency the resultant mutual flux is constant, the currents in all the windings must adjust themselves so as to create this constant flux.

It may be concluded from the above discussion that the transformers, induction motors, synchronous motors and the alternators connected to infinite bus-bars, may be regarded as constant-flux machines.

(v) Losses in rotating machines are the same as in transformers, except for the friction and windage losses.

(vi) An open-circuit, or no-load, test helps in knowing the excitation requirements and core loss (and friction and windage loss in rotating machines). Short-circuit test helps in determining the ohmic loss and the leakage impedances of the windings. In rotating electrical machines, however, D.C. resistance measurement is needed. Both open-circuit and short-circuit tests help in the calculation of efficiency of both transformers and rotating electrical machines.

PROBLEMS

1.1. *(a)* Define a transformer. How is the energy transferred from one circuit to another? Distinguish between primary and secondary windings.

(b) Transformer is the main reason for the wide-spread popularity of A.C. systems over D.C. systems. Explain.

(c) Give some transformer applications in electronic and control circuits.

(d) Describe the two general types of transformers. Why is the low-voltage winding placed near the core? Why are the butt joints in the adjacent layers staggered?

1.2. (a) Why is iron used for the construction of transformer-core?

(b) Why is the transformer core laminated?

(c) Is it possible to use any winding of the transformer as its primary? Explain.

(d) Distinguish between step-up and step-down transformers. State clearly the quantities which remain unaltered or get stepped-up or stepped-down.

1.3. (a) Explain the principle of transformer action.

(b) Derive an expression for the e.m.f. induced in a transformer winding. Show that e.m.f. per turn in priamry is equal to e.m.f. per turn in the secondary.

(c) A 6300/210 V, 50 Hz, single-phase transformer has per turn e.m.f. of about 9 volts and maximum flux density of 1.2 T. Find the number of high-voltage and low-voltage turns and the net cross-sectional area of the core. **[Ans.** 720 turns, 24 turns, 328.3 cm^2]

1.4. (a) Draw and explain the no-load phasor diagram of a 1-phase transformer. Discuss how primary leakage flux is accounted for in the phasor diagram.

(b) Expain how the primary current increases as the current on the secondary side of the transformer is increased.

(c) A single-phase 50 Hz transformer has four windings : a 230 V primary, a 900 V winding with a centre tapping, a 6 V winding with a centre tapping and an 8 V winding. For a net core area of 20 cm^2, find the number of turns on each winding. The maximum value of flux density is not to exceed 1.2 T.

[**Hint.** A centre-tapped winding must have even number of turns. First calculate the number of turns in the lowest-voltage winding, here 6 V winding.]

[Ans. 12, 16, 1800, 460 (primary)]

1.5. Give the concept of single-phase ideal transformer. Describe its performance with the help of e.m.f. equations, its phasor diagrams at no load and on load.

Discuss how core flux in an ideal transformer is independent of load current.

1.6. (a) In an ideal transformer, discuss how impedance is transferred from secondary to primary or vice-versa.

(b) Ideal transformers A and B are designed to work at 50 Hz and 10 kHz respectively. For the same e.m.f. per turn and for the same core flux densities, compare their core areas.

[Ans. (b) $A : B = 200 : 1$]

1.7. (a) The primary winding of a single-phase transformer is energized from fixed sinusoidal voltage with secondary open-circuited. If the shaded portion of the iron core is removed, Fig. 1.89, discuss what would happen to the magnitudes of its exciting current, core flux and the no-load power factor.

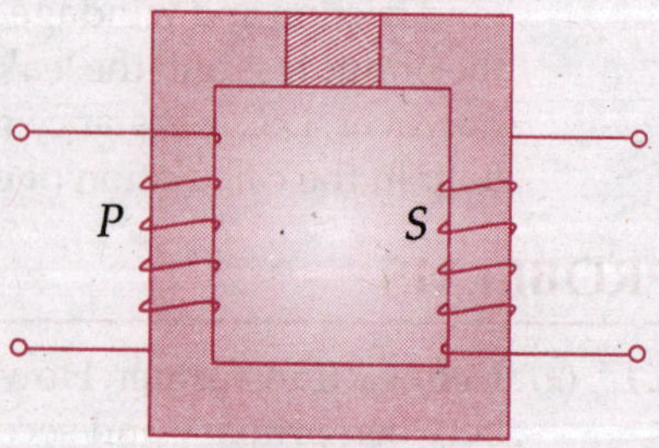

Fig 1.89: Pertaining to Problem 1.7 (a)

(b) A single-phase, 50 Hz transformer has voltage rating of 11000/400 V based on its winding turns ratio. Its leakage and magnetizing inductances, during tests, are found to be 0.2 H and 80 H respectively on its primary (h.v.) side. For primary applied voltage of 11000 V at 50 Hz, calculate the open-circuit secondary voltage.

[Ans. (a) Exciting current increases, core flux remains constant and no-load power factor is worsened. (b) 399 V]

1.8. *(a)* A single-phase transformer is designed to operate at rated primary voltage 230 V and at rated frequency 50 Hz. If its primary voltage is increased by 10% on no load, discuss what would happen to the transformer operation?

(b) Discuss the advantages of using CRGO laminations in transformers.

(c) A 10 kVA, 440/220 V, 400 Hz transformer is desired to be used at frequency of 60 Hz. Find the voltage as well as the kVA rating of the transformer at this reduced frequency.

[**Ans.** *(a)* Magnetizing current, core loss and exciting current increase, third harmonics in exciting current is more pronounced. *(c)* 66/33 V, 1.5 kVA]

1.9. *(a)* Explain why transformer rating is expressed in kVA or VA. Describe the significance of all the items mentioned on the name-plate of a single-phase transformer.

(b) A 1-phase transformer has the following data :

Peak flux density in core = 1.40 T ; Net core area = 0.012 m^2

Current density in conductors = 2.5 MA/m^2 ;

Conductor dia. = 2.0 mm; Primary voltage = 230 V, 50 Hz.

Calculate the kVA rating of the transformer and the number of turns on the primary winding. [**Ans.** *(b)* 1.80642 kVA, 62 turns]

1.10. A 100 kVA, 2400/240 V, 50 Hz single phase transformer has an exciting current of 0.64 A and a core loss of 700 watts, when its high-voltage side is energised at rated voltage and frequency. Calculate the two components of the exciting current.

If the above transformer supplies a load current of 40 amperes at 0.8 power factor lag on its *l.v.* side, then calculate the primary current and its power factor. Ignore leakage impedance drops. [**Ans.** 0.292 A; 0.569 A; 4.584 A, p.f. = 0.762 lagging]

1.11. *(a)* What current flows in the transformer primary when its secondary is open? What is its function? Give its order of magnitude.

(b) In a transformer, core flux depends on voltage, whereas the leakage fluxes depend on the currents. Explain.

(c) Three cores made up of iron, aluminium and wood have the same dimensions and are wound with the same number of turns. If these cores are fed from the same voltage at a fixed frequency, then write the names of the materials in an order relating to the magnitudes of *(i)* magnetizing current, *(ii)* hysteresis loss and *(iii)* eddy-current loss. Give a brief description for each answer.

[**Hint.** Iron is ferro-magnetic material, aluminium is paramagnetic material ($\mu_r = 1.002$) and wood is non-magnetic material with $\mu_r = 1.00$. Flux produced is same in all the three cores.]

Ans. *(c)* *(i)* Wood, aluminium and iron
(ii) Iron, aluminium and wood
(iii) Aluminium, iron and wood
} in decreasing order

1.12. When the primary of a transformer is energised at rated voltage of 11,000 V and at rated frequency of 50 Hz, it takes 3.2 A and 2400 watts at no-load. Another transformer has all its core dimensions $\sqrt{2}$ times the corresponding core dimensions of the first transformer. Number of primary turns, type of core material and lamination thickness are the same in both the transformers. If the primary of the second transformer is energised from 22,000 V, 50 Hz supply, calculate the no-load current and power drawn by it.

[**Hint:** Core loss ∝ Core volume

$$\therefore \quad P_{c2} = (\sqrt{2})^3 (P_{c1}) = (\sqrt{2})^3 (2400) = 6780 \text{ watts.}$$

Core loss component $I_{c2} = (\sqrt{2})^3\ I_{c1}$

$$I_{c2} = 2\sqrt{2}\left(\frac{2400}{11,000}\right) = 2\sqrt{2}\ (0.2182) = 0.617 \text{ A}$$

Magnetizing component, $I_{m1} = \sqrt{I_{01}^2 - I_{c1}^2} = \sqrt{(3.2)^2 - (0.2182)^2} = 3.193$ A

Now reluctance $R_{l2} = \dfrac{Rl_1}{\sqrt{2}},\ \phi_{m1} = \dfrac{11,000}{\sqrt{2}\pi f N_1}$

and $\phi_{m2} = \dfrac{22,000}{\sqrt{2}\pi f N_1} = 2\phi_{m1}$

But $\phi_{m1} = \dfrac{\text{m.m.f.}}{\text{Reluctance}} = \dfrac{I_{m1}N_1}{Rl_1}$

Also $\dfrac{I_{m2}N_1}{Rl_2} = \phi_{m2} = 2\phi_{m1} = \dfrac{2I_{m1}N_1}{Rl_1}$

$\therefore$ $I_{m2} = \dfrac{Rl_2}{Rl_1}(2I_{m1}) = \sqrt{2}\,I_{m1} = \sqrt{2}\ (3.193) = 4.515$ A etc.]

[Ans. 4.557 A, 6780 watts.]

1.13. *(a)* Draw the exact equivalent circuit of a transformer and describe briefly the various parameters involved in it.

(b) A 50 Hz, 3-phase core-type star-delta transformer has a line voltage ratio of 11,000/440 volts. The cross-section of the core is square with a circumscribing circle of 0.4 m diameter. Determine the number of turns per phase on high-voltage and low-voltage windings for a maximum flux density of 1.25 T. Assume that the insulation occupies 10% of the total core area.

[Hint. Net core area $A_i = (0.4 \cos 45°)^2\ (0.9)$

Low-voltage per phase turns = $\dfrac{440}{\text{e.m.f. per turn}}$ etc.] **[Ans.** 318, 22]

1.14. A single-phase transformer has 1000 primary turns and 80 secondary turns wound around a core of net cross-sectional area 40 cm^2. The r.m.s. value of flux density in the core is limited to 1.4 T. Calculate the maximum 50 Hz r.m.s. primary voltage that can be applied on the primary side without reaching saturation.

The core has a mean length of 160 cm and its relative permeability is 6000. Find the value of exciting current if the transformer primary is energised from the voltage calculated above. Calculate, also the magnetizing reactance as seen from primary and secondary sides.

[Hint. $\phi_{max} = \dfrac{(\sqrt{2}I_m N_1)\mu_0 \cdot \mu_r \cdot A_i}{L}$] **[Ans.** 1758.76 V, 0.2971 A, 5919.76 Ω, 37.886 Ω]

1.15. *(a)* How the no-load current of a single-phase transformer is taken care of in the equivalent circuit of a transformer.

(b) A 400/100 V, ideal 1-phase transformer is connected to a load of 8 + *j* 6 Ω and its primary is fed from 400 V, 50 Hz source. Calculate the current, power factor and power on both primary and secondary sides. Neglect magnetizing current.

[Ans. *(a)* By $R_c \parallel X_m$ *(b)* 10 A, 0.8 lag, 800 W ; 2.5 A, 0.8 lag, 800 W]

1.16. *(a)* How many fluxes are there in an actual 1-phase transformer? How is their effect shown in the equivalent circuit of a transformer?

(b) A 50 kVA, 6600/230 V, single-phase transformer has h.v. and l.v. winding resistances of 7 Ω and 0.008 Ω respectively. With l.v. winding open, a current of 0.3 A at a p.f. of 0.3 (lagging) is recorded on h.v. side with the application of full rated voltage. Calculate efficiency at full load and 0.8 p.f. lagging. Determine also the load current at which maximum efficiency occurs. **[Ans.** *(a)* Three fluxes *(b)* 96.68%, 189.74 A]

1.17. *(a)* What is the basis for transferring resistances and leakage reactances, from primary to secondary or from secondary to primary, in a transformer. Hence derive expressions for

(i) total resistance on primary side and also on secondary side,

(ii) total leakage reactance on primary side and also on secondary side.

(b) the constants of a single phase 50 Hz, 2200/220 V transformer are as follows :

h.v. side : $r_1 = 0.21\ \Omega$, $x_1 = 3.84\ \Omega$, $R_{c1} = 4800\ \Omega$, $X_{m1} = 3500\ \Omega$

h.v. side : $r_2 = 0.006\ \Omega$, $x_2 = 0.022\ \Omega$.

Find the equivalent circuit parameters referred to *(i)* h.v. side and *(ii)* l.v. side.

[Ans. *(a)* Referred quantities to one side should produce the same effect as on the previous side

(b) (i) $r_{e1} = 0.81\ \Omega$, $x_{e1} = 6.04\ \Omega$, $R_{c1} = 4800\ \Omega$, $X_{m1} = 3500\ \Omega$

(ii) $r_{e2} = 0.0081\ \Omega$, $x_{e2} = 0.0604\ \Omega$, $R_{c2} = 48\ \Omega$, $X_{m2} = 35\ \Omega$]

1.18. Draw the exact equivalent circuit of a 1-phase transformer. From this, derive the approximate and simplified equivalent circuits of the transformer. State the various assumptions made.

Also draw the phasor diagram from the exact equivalent circuit of a transformer, assuming primary turns = secondary turns.

1.19. *(a)* Give the equivalent circuit of a transformer and define its various parameters. Clearly state the assumptions involved in the applicability of this equivalent circuit.

(b) How will the equivalent circuit be modified if the transformer is an air-cored transformer?

(c) A 100 kVA, 1000/400 volts, single-phase transformer, when excited at rated voltage on h.v. side, draws a no-load current of 3.0 A at 0.5 lagging power factor. If it is excited from the l.v. side at rated voltage, determine the no-load current, power factor and power input.

[Hint. *(a)* Assumptions : *(i)* No saturation, *(ii)* Equivalent circuit parameters remain constant for minor changes in supply voltage and frequency.]

[Ans. *(b)* Omit R_c from Fig. 1.16 *(c)* 7.5 A, 0.5 lag, 1500 W]

1.20. *(a)* In open-circuit test, the ohmic losses are negligible in comparison with normal core loss. Explain.

(b) In short-circuit test, the core loss is negligible in comparison with full-load ohmic losses. Explain.

(c) A 5 kVA, 1000/200 V, 50 Hz single-phase transformer gave the following test results :

Open-circuit test (l.v. side) : 200 V, 1.2 A, 90 W

Short-circuit test (h.v. side) : 50 V, 5 A, 110 W.

Compute the parameters of the approximate equivalent circuit referred to l.v. side. Also draw the exact equivalent circuit referred to l.v. side.

[Ans. Approx. equivalent circuit : $R_{c2} = 444.44\ \Omega$, $X_{m2} = 179.86\ \Omega$, $r_{e2} = 0.176\ \Omega$, $x_{e2} = 0.3592\ \Omega$ Exact equivalent circuit : $R_{c2} = 444.44\ \Omega$, $X_{m2} = 179.86\ \Omega$, $r_2 = r_1' = 0.088\ \Omega$, $x_2 = x_1' = 0.1796\ \Omega$]

1.21. *(a)* Show that leakage fluxes in a transformer are dependent upon the currents in the windings.

(b) A 10 kVA, 500/250 V, single-phase transformer gave the following test results :

S.C. test (h.v. side) : 60 V, 20 A, 150 W.

The maximum efficiency occurs at unity p.f. and at 1.2 full-load current. Determine full load efficiency at 0.8 p.f. Also calculate the maximum efficiency. [**Ans.** 95.625%, 96.525%]

1.22. (a) What parameters of the equivalent circuit of a transformer can be determined from open-circuit and short-circuit tests? Explain.

(b) Explain why open-circuit and short-circuit tests should be performed on l.v. and h.v. sides respectively.

(c) Show that per unit value of equivalent resistance r_{eL} or r_{eH}, can be obtained from the following relation :

$$r_{eL} \text{ or } r_{eH} = \frac{\text{Ohmic losses at rated current}}{\text{Rated VA}}$$

Subscripts *L* and *H* denote l.v. and h.v. sides respectively.

1.23. A 5 kVA, 2200/220 V, single-phase transformer has the following parameters :

h.v. side : $r_1 = 3.4\ \Omega$, $x_1 = 7.2\ \Omega$

l.v. side : $r_2 = 0.028\ \Omega$, $x_2 = 0.060\ \Omega$

(a) The transformer is made to deliver rated current at 0.8 lagging power factor, to a load connected on the l.v. side. If the load voltage is 220 V, calculate the terminal voltage on the h.v. side.

(b) Repeat part *(a)* for a load p.f. of 0.8 leading.

(c) For a core loss of 30 watts at rated voltage and frequency, find the efficiency under the conditions of part *(a)* and *(b)*.

(d) The transformer exciting current is 3% of full-load current. Calculate voltmeter, ammeter and wattmeter readings for open-circuit test at rated voltage and short-circuit test at rated current. The instruments are connected on l.v. side for open-circuit test and on h.v. side for short circuit test. [**Ans.** *(a)* 2229.27 *(b)* 2193.27 V *(c)* 98.47%

(d) O.C. test : 220 V, 0.682 A, 30 W; S.C. test : 33.14 V, 2.273 A, 32.10 W]

1.24. (a) Define voltage regulation of a transformer.

(b) What causes ∝ change in secondary terminal voltage of a transformer, as it is loaded? Enumerate the factors which influence the magnitude of this change.

(c) A 50 Hz, single-phase transformer draws a short-circuit current of 30 A at 0.2 p.f. lag when connected to 16 V, 50 Hz source. What will be the short-circuit current, and its p.f., when the same transformer is energised from 16 V, 25 Hz source?

Hint. (c) $\dfrac{r_e}{z_e} = \dfrac{r_e}{\sqrt{r_e^2 + x_e^2}} = 0.2$ or $24r_e^2 = x_e^2$

$$30 = \frac{16}{\sqrt{r_e^2 + x_e^2}} = \frac{16}{5r_e}$$

∴ $r_e = 0.1067\ \Omega$ and $x_e = 0.523\ \Omega$

At 25 Hz, $x_e = 0.2615\ \Omega$ and $r_e = 0.1067\ \Omega$ etc.] [**Ans.** 56.65 A, 0.3778 lag]

1.25. (a) For a lagging p.f. load, show that per unit voltage regulation of a transformer can be obtained from the expression

$$z_{e2pu} \cdot \cos(\phi - \theta_2)$$

where ϕ = leakage impedance angle and θ_2 = load power-factor angle.

(*b*) Find also the condition under which maximum voltage regulation occurs.

(*c*) A 10 kVA, 2500/250 V, single-phase transformer has full load ohmic loss of 300 W. The maximum possible voltage drop in the transformer-secondary voltage is 20 V. Find voltage regulation of this transformer for rated kVA output at 0.8 p.f. lagging. **[Ans.** (*c*) 6.852%]

1.26. (*a*) Voltage regulation of a transformer varies with power factor. Validate this statement through suitable derivations. At what power factor will the regulation be (*i*) maximum and (*ii*) zero.

Does the maximum efficiency of a transformer also depend on power factor? Discuss.

(*b*) A 25 kVA, 2000/200 V, 50 Hz transformer has maximum efficiency at 80% of full load. Its per unit resistance and impedance are 0.012 and 0.05 respectively. Determine its efficiency and voltage regulation at half of the full load and at 0.8 p.f. lagging.

[Ans. (*b*) 97.4%, 1.9362%]

1.27. (*a*) The full-load voltage drops in a transformer are 2% and 4% due respectively to resistance and leakage reactance. The full-load ohmic loss is equal to iron loss. Calculate

(*i*) the efficiency on half load at unity p.f.

(*ii*) the lagging p.f. on full-load ouput at which the voltage drop is a maximum and

(*iii*) the maximum percentage voltage drop.

(*b*) A single-phase transformer has percentage regulation of 4 and 4.4 for lagging power factor of 0.8 and 0.6 respectively. The full-load ohmic loss is equal to iron loss. Calculate

(*i*) the lagging p.f. at which full-load regulation is maximum,

(*ii*) the full-load efficiency at unity p.f.

[Ans. (*a*) 95.24%, 0.4472 lag, 4.472% (*b*) 0.4472 lag, 96.154%]

1.28. (*a*) Is the voltage regulation at power factor 0.8 lagging better or worse than its value at power factor 0.6 lagging for the same kVA output? Give appropriate reasons.

(*b*) A 3300/1100 V, single-phase transformer has leakage impedance of $4 + j\,40\ \Omega$ referred to its h.v. side. When unity power factor load of 20 kW is connected on the l.v. side, the secondary terminal voltage measured is 1050 V. Calculate the voltage and power factor as measured on its h.v. terminals. **[Ans.** (*b*) 3185.5 V, 0.9968 lag]

1.29. (*a*) Derive an expression for computing the per unit voltage regulation of a transformer both for lagging and leading power factors.

(*b*) A 3300/230 V, single phase transformer has an equivalent resistance of 0.015 p.u. and an equivalent leakage reactance of 0.04 p.u. Find the secondary terminal voltage at full load and 0.8 p.f. lag, for a primary voltage of 3300 V. **[Ans.** 221.72 V]

1.30. (*a*) Describe a test on a 1-phase transformer that gives its ohmic losses. Discuss the determination of the equivalent circuit parameters which can be obtained from this test.

(*b*) A single-phase transformer has a regulation of 10% when delivering full load at unity p.f. and 15% when delivering the same load at 0.8 p.f. lagging. What would be the regulation if the transformer is delivering half-load at 0.8 p.f. leading? **[Ans.** 0.5%] (*I.E.S., 1981*)

1.31. (*a*) Describe a test on a 1-phase transformer that gives its core losses. Discuss the determination of the equivalent circuit parameters which can be obtained from this test.

(*b*) The maximum efficiency of a 500 kVA, 3300/500 V, 50 Hz single-phase transformer is 97% and occurs at 3/4 full load, unity power factor. If the impedance is 10%, calculate the regulation at full load, power factor 0.8 lagging. **[Ans.** 7.5206%] (*I.A.S., 1986*)

1.32. *(a)* In a 1-phase transformer, the core flux remains substantially constant and is independent of the load current. Explain.

(b) In a transformer, find the load current at which maximum efficiency occurs. State the assumptions made.

(c) When a transformer with data given in Prob. 1.23 is loaded, it is found that secondary voltage at no load and full load remains unchanged. Determine the transformer loading under rated current conditions. Neglect the magnetizing current.

[**Ans.** p.f. = 0.905 leading, 4.525 kVA]

1.33. *(a)* For constant values of load voltage and load p.f., obtain the condition for maximum efficiency in a 1-phase transformer. Hence, derive therefrom the relation

$$(\text{kVA})_{\text{max. }\eta} = (\text{kVA})_{\text{rated}} \cdot \sqrt{\frac{\text{core losses}}{\text{rated ohmic losses}}}$$

(b) The leakage impedance of a 10 kVA, 3300/220 V transformer as given on its name phate is 10%. Determine *(i)* the voltage that must be applied on HV side to circulate rated current with LV side shorted and *(ii)* the maximum possible voltage regulation.

[**Ans.** *(i)* 330 V; *(ii)* 10%]

1.34. *(a)* A non-sinusoidal voltage $v = 150 \sin 314t - 75 \sin 1570t$ is applied to the 250 turns winding of a transformer. Find the core flux as a function of time.

(b) A voltage $v = 200 \sin 314t$ is applied to the transformer winding in a no-load test. The resulting current is found to be $i = 3 \sin (314t - 60°)$. Determine the core loss and r.m.s. value of the exciting current.

(c) A transformer has the following test data :

Test No. 1 : 100% voltage, 6% current, p.f. = 0.2

Test No. 2 : 8% voltage, 100% current, p.f. = 0.3

Identify the tests. Calculate efficiency and percentage regulation at full load unity p.f. and at 0.8 p.f. lagging.

[**Hint.** *(c)* core loss = 0.012, full-load ohmic loss = 0.024, z = 0.08 etc.]

[**Ans.** *(a)* $(-1.911 \cos 314\, t + 0.1911 \cos 1570t)$ mWb.
(b) 150 watts, 2.122 A *(c)* 96.525%, 95.694%; 2.4%, 6.498%]

1.35. *(a)* Describe briefly the various losses in a transformer and explain how each loss varies with the load current.

(b) Express the total core loss in terms of voltage and frequency.

1.36. *(a)* A transformer is operated at rated frequency but at a voltage higher than its rated value. Explain how the following quantities would change :

(i) No-load current. *(ii)* Hysteresis loss and *(iii)* Eddy current loss.

(b) A 200 V, 60 Hz single-phase transformer has hysteresis and eddy current losses of 250 watts and 90 watts respectively. If the transformer is now energised from 230 V, 50 Hz supply, calculate its core losses. Assume Steinmetz's constant equal to 1.6.

[**Ans.** *(a) (i)* Increases *(ii)* Increases, $P_h \propto (V)^x$ *(iii)* Increases, $P_e \propto (V)^2$. *(b)* 467.83 watts.]

1.37. A 1-phase, 11/66 kV, 50 MVA transformer has primary and secondary leakage impedances of $0.01 + j0.06$ per unit each. The shunt branch impedance in p.u. is $80 + j\,0$ in parallel with $0 + j90$. All quantities are in per unit on the transformer base. Calculate, in ohms, the parameters of primary and secondary windings and the shunt branch referred to low-voltage side.

[**Ans.** $r_1 = r_2' = 0.0242\ \Omega$; $x_1 = x_2' = 0.1452\ \Omega$; $R_c = 193.6\ \Omega$, $X_m = 217.8\ \Omega$]

1.38. Fig 1.90 illustrates the equivalent circuit referred to the l.v. side of a 400/3200 V, 1-phase, 50 Hz, 16 kVA transformer. With primary voltage held fixed at 400 V, the h.v. is loaded to its rated current at p.f. 0.8 lag at its terminals. Compute

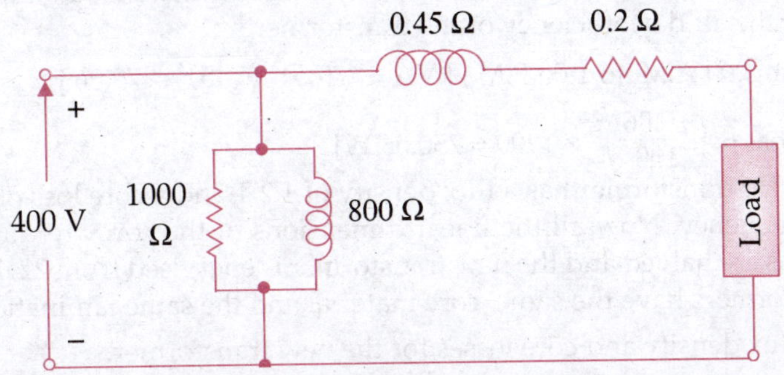

Fig 1.90: Pertaining to Problem 1.38.

(*a*) the terminal voltage at the h.v. terminals

(*b*) the l.v. input current and its p.f. and

(*c*) the efficiency.

[Ans. (*a*) 3062.4 V (*b*) 40.635 A, 0.78316 lag (*c*) 96.229%]

1.39. (*a*) Suggest a suitable test to predetermine the regulation of a transformer and explain it.

(*b*) A 200 kVA, 1-phase, 50Hz, 2300/230 V transformer has a core loss of 300 W. At full load, I^2R loss is 800 W and the leakage reactance is 0.032 p.u. Calculate the total loss and the voltage regulation for (*a*) 1.2 p.u. load at p.f. 0.8 lagging and (*b*) 0.70 p.u. load at p.f. 0.6 leading.

[Ans. (*a*) 1452 W, 0.02688 p.u. (*b*) 692 W, – 0.01624 p.u.]

1.40. A single-phase load is fed through a 66 kV feeder of impedance 100 + *j* 320 ohms and a 66/6.6 kV transformer of equivalent leakage impedance 0.3 + *j* 1.2 ohms referred to l.v. side. For a load of 200 kW at p.f. 0.8 leading at 6.6 kV, calculate

(*a*) voltage at the sending end of the feeder,

(*b*) voltage at the primary terminals of the transformer and

(*c*) active and reactive powers and p.f. at the sending end of the feeder.

[Ans. (*a*) 65394 V (*b*) 65818 V (*c*) 201.8654 kW, 143.6865 kVAr, 0.8147 leading.]

1.41. A 100kVA, 50 Hz, 440/11000 V, 1-phase transformer has an efficiency of 98.5% when supplying full-load current at 0.8 p.f. and an efficiency of 99% when supplying half-full load current at unity p.f. Find the iron losses and ohmic losses corresponding to full load current. At what value of load current will the maximum efficiency be attained?

[Ans. 267.37 W, 950.93 W, 120.523 A] [*I.A.S., 1987*]

1.42. (*a*) What are the approximations involved in obtaining the equivalent circuit parameters from open-circuit and short-circuit tests? Discuss the validity of these tests.

(*b*) Discuss the effect of frequency and voltage on the equivalent circuit parameters of a transformer.

1.43. (*a*) Distinguish between distribution and power transformers.

(*b*) Define energy efficiency and all day efficiency.

(*c*) The daily variation of load on a 100 kVA transformer is as follows:

8.00 A.M. to 1.00 P.M. : 65 kW, 45 kVAr

1.00 P.M. to 6.00 P.M. : 80 kW, 50 kVAr

6.00 P.M. to 1.00 A.M. : 30kW, 30 kVAr

1.00 A.M. to 8.00 A.M. : No load

This transformer has no-load core loss of 370 watts and a full load ohmic loss of 1200 watts. Determine the all-day efficiency of the transformer.

[**Hint.** From 8.00 A.M. to 1.00 P.M., kVA = $\sqrt{(65)^2 + (45)^2} = 79.06$]

$\therefore$ Ohmic loss = $\left(\frac{79.06}{100}\right)^2 \times 1200 = 750.06$ W] **[Ans.** 97.959%]

1.44. A 11,000 V, 50 Hz transformer has a flux density of 1.2 T and a core loss of 3000 watts at rated voltage and frequency. Now all the linear dimensions of the core are doubled; primary and secondary turns are halved and the new transformer is energised from 22,000 V, 50 Hz supply. Both the transformers have the same core material and the same lamination thickness.

Calculate the flux density and core losses for the new transformer.

[**Hint.** $V_1 = \sqrt{2}\,\pi f_1 B_{m1} A_1 N_1$ and $V_2 = \sqrt{2}\,\pi f_1 B_{m2}\,.4A_1 . \frac{N_1}{2}$. $\therefore \frac{V_1}{V_2} = \frac{11,000}{22,020} = \frac{B_{m1}}{2B_{m2}}$ etc.]

[Ans. 1.2 T, 24,000 watts]

1.45. *(a)* Describe the method by which the separation of the core losses of a transformer is achieved.

(b) In a test for the determination of losses of a 440 V, 50 Hz transformer, the total iron losses were found to be 2500 watts at normal voltage and frequency. When the applied voltage and frequency were 220 V and 25 Hz, the iron losses were found to be 850 watts. Calculate the eddy current and hysteresis losses at normal voltage and frequency.

[Ans. 1600 watts, 900 watts]

1.46. *(a)* How can the polarity test be performed on a single-phase two-winding transformer? Explain how the subtractive polarity is preferable to additive polarity in transformers.

(b) Fig. 1.91 illustrates four terminals *AB* and *CD* of a two-winding transformer. When a voltage of 100 V is applied across *AB* with *BD* short circuited, voltage across terminals *AC* is found to be 100 V. Find the polarity and turns ratio of the transformer.

[Ans. *A* and *C* (or *B* and *D*) have same polarity.

Turns ratio from *AB* to *CD* is 1 : 2.]

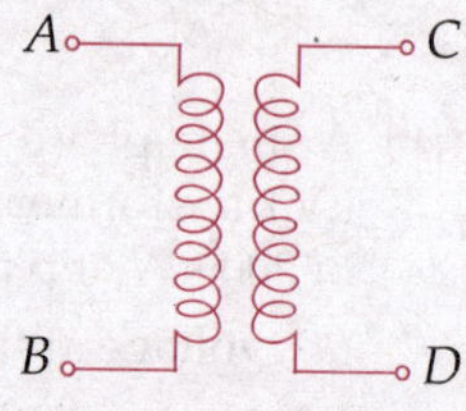

Fig 1.91: Pertaining to Problem 1.46*(b)*.

1.47. *(a)* In each of the diagrams of Fig. 1.92 , the instantaneous polarity of the primary winding of an ideal transformer is as shown. Indicate:

(i) the direction of flux in the core.

(ii) the polarity of the instantaneous voltage induced in the secondary.

(iii) the directions of the instantaneous currents existing in the primary and secondary windings when each secondary is connected to a resistive load.

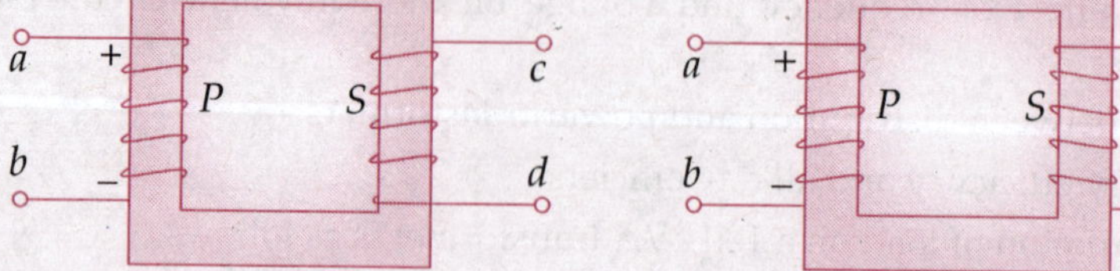

(a) *(b)*

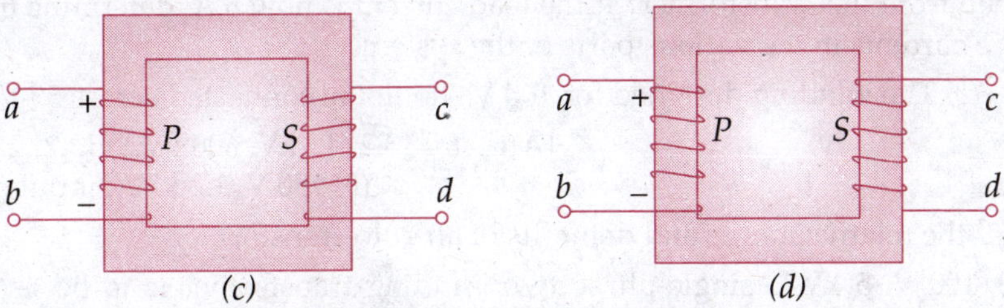

Fig 1.92: Pertaining to Problem 1.47*(a)*.

(b) *A*, *B* and *C* are the three windings of a transformer having 200, 100 and 60 turns respectively. When a voltage of 100 V is applied across *A*, find the voltage that develops across *x y*, as shown in Fig 1.93.

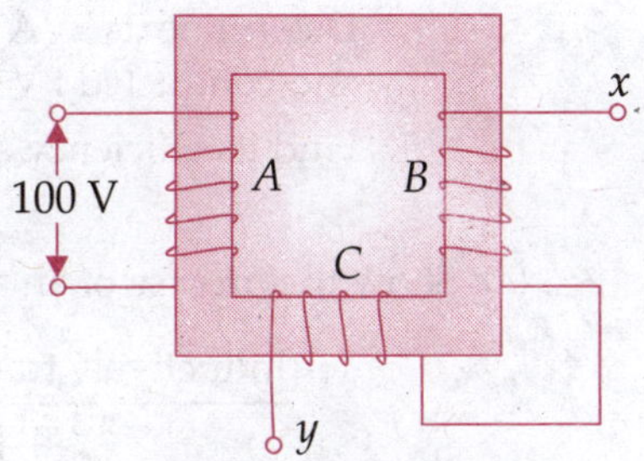

Fig 1.93: Pertaining to Problem 1.47*(b)*

[**Ans.** *(a)* *A (i)* Clockwise *(ii)* d positive and c negative *(iii)* From a to b and from c to d.
B (i) Clockwise *(ii)* c positive and d negative *(iii)* From a to b and from d to c.
C (i) Anti-clockwise *(ii)* c positive and d negative *(iii)* From a to b and from d to c.
D (i) Anti-clockwise *(ii)* d positive and c negative *(iii)* From a to b and from c to d. *(b)* 20 volts.]

1.48. *(a)* In back to back test, show that one transformer may have slightly less temperature rise than the other.

(b) In Sumpner's test, the reading of the wattmeter recording the core losses, remains unaffected when low-voltage is injected in the secondary series circuit. Explain.

(c) In Sumpner's test, the frequency of the voltage injected in the secondary circuit, may not be equal to the rated frequency. Explain.

[*(c)* **Hint.** Secondary short-circuit current $I_{sc} = \dfrac{V}{Z_{sc}}$. Here I_{sc} is made equal to the rated current for any value of frequency merely by adjusting V. Since the ohmic losses are equal to $(I_{sc})^2 \times$ (Resistance), some variation of frequency from rated value, will not vary the winding resistance and, therefore, the ohmic losses.]

1.49. *(a)* The temperature of a transformer determined under either no-load condition or short-circuit condition, does not give true temperature rise experienced in practice. Discuss this and explain a suitable method of determining the temperature rise of a transformer.

(b) Two similar 40 kVA, single-phase transformers gave the following results when tested by the back to back method:

W_1 in the supply line: 800 watts.

W_2 in the secondaries series circuit at rated current: 1000 watts.

Calculate the efficiency of each transformer at unity p.f. [**Ans.** *(b)* 97.8%]

1.50. *(a)* Define an auto-transformer. A single-phase two winding transformer is rated 11000/2200 V, 100 kVA. If the two windings are connected in series to form an auto-transformer, find its voltage and current ratings.

(b) A 200/100 V, single-phase transformer is rated 10 kVA. If this transformer is connected as an auto-transformer across a 50-V supply, what is the maximum output voltage that can be

obtained from this transformer? If the load current is now 8 A, determine the kVA output and the currents in the various parts of the system.

[**Hint.** *(b)* The winding designed for 100 V should be connected across 50 V supply.]

[**Ans.** *(a)* 13.2/11 kV, 600 kVA; 13.2/2.2 kV, 120 kVA
(b) 150 V, 1.2 kVA, input current = 24 A]

1.51. *(a)* Discuss the relative merits and demerits of an auto-transformer.

(b) A 400/100 V, 5 kVA, single-phase two winding transformer is to be used as an auto-transformer to supply 400 volts from a 500 V voltage source. When tested as a two-winding transformer at rated load and 0.8 p.f. lagging, its efficiency was found to be 0.95.

(i) Determine its kVA rating as an auto-transformer. Also calculate the transformed kVA and conducted kVA.

(ii) Find its efficiency as an auto-transformer at rated load and at 0.8 p.f. lagging.

[**Ans.** *(b) (i)* 25 kVA, 5 kVA and 20 kVA. *(iii)* 98.958%)

1.52. *(a)* Show that in case of an auto-transformer,

$$\frac{\text{Inductively transferred power}}{\text{Total power}} = \frac{\text{High voltage} - \text{Low voltage}}{\text{High voltage}}$$

(b) A 10,000/5,000 V single-phase transformer is rated at 100 kVA as a two-winding transformer. It is desired to connect the two windings of the transformer in series across 15,000 volts supply and operate it as an auto-transformer. Explain the connections for achieving the same. What are the possible voltage ratios and the corresponding maximum outputs? [**Ans.** *(b) (i)* Voltage ratio : 1/3, 150 kVA output.

(ii) Voltage ratio : 2/3, 300 kVA output.]

1.53. *(a)* In an auto-transformer, the power transfer from primary circuit to the secondary circuit is partly by transformer action and partly by direct conduction. Justify this statement.

(b) A 11000/2200 V, 100 kVA, single-phase two-winding transformer is to be used as an auto-transformer by connecting the two windings in series. Give the possible values of voltage ratios and kVA outputs.

[**Ans.** *(b) (i)* 13200/2200 V or 2200/13200 V; kVA = 120
13200/11000 V or 11000/13200 V; kVA = 600]

1.54. An ideal transformer has its secondary winding labelled as *a, b, c*. The primary has 100 turns. The number of turns on the secondary side are 400 between *a, b* and 200 between *b, c* so that total turns between *a, c* are 600. The transformer supplies a resistive load of 6 kW between a and c. In addition, a load of impedance $1000\angle 45^\circ\ \Omega$ is connected between *a* and *b*. For a primary voltage of 1000 V, compute the primary current and the primary input.

[**Ans.** 20.691 A, 17.32 kW]

1.55. A single-phase ideal transformer has 400 primary turns and 600 secondary turns. The primary is connected to 800 V source. The full secondary has a resistive load of 24 kW. The secondary is tapped at 500 turns across which there is a pure inductive load of 20 kVA. Find the primary current, its power factor and the power input to primary.

[**Ans.** 39.051 A, 0.7682 lagging, 23.999 kW]

1.56. *(a)* Two resistive loads R_1 and R_2 each of 200 Ω are to be supplied with voltages of 100 V and 300 V respectively, from the available 400 V supply. To this end, one auto-transformer connected as shown in Fig. 1.94 is designed.

Assuming the auto-transformer to be ideal, calculate the currents in its windings. What is the VA rating of a two winding transformer which would have approximately the same size as the auto-transformer?

(b) It is proposed to connect R_1 between terminals *d* and *a* suitable tap *c* on the winding, instead of across *a* and *b*, could it lead to a more economical design of the auto-transformer? Explain.
(I.E.S., 1979)

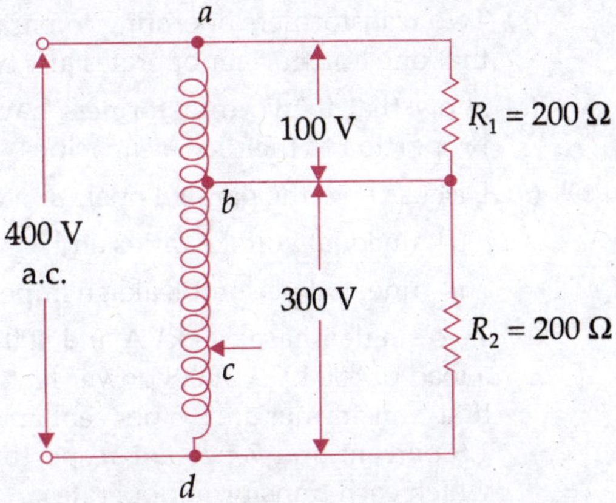

Fig 1.94: Pertaining to Problem 1.56.

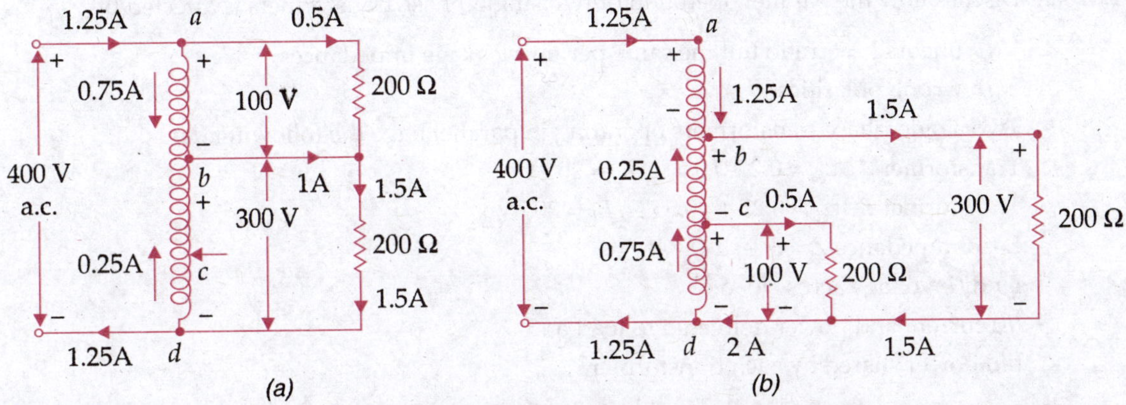

Fig 1.95: Pertaining to the solution of Problem 1.56.

[Ans. *(a)* Currents in the windings are as shown in Fig. 1.95 *(a)* 0.75 VA]
(b) With the proposed connections, the currents in the windings are as shown in Fig. 1.95 *(b)*. The scheme of Fig. 1.95 *(b)* would not be economical, because the windings have to handle more currents and would, therefore, be thicker in cross-section and more conductor material would be required.]

1.57. A single-phase transformer has three windings and each winding is designed for 300 V, 50 Hz. If supply voltage available is 300 V, 50 Hz, then determine the possible output voltages below and above 300 V, 50 Hz. **[Ans.** 100 V, 150 V, 200 V, and 450 V, 600 V, 900 V]

1.58. *(a)* Why is it preferable to install two or more transformers in parallel than one large unit?

(b) Explain why parallel operation of transformers is necessary.

(c) State the essential and desirable conditions which should be satisfied before two single phase transformers may be operated in parallel.

(d) Under what conditions, the no-load circulating current is zero in two single-phase transformers operating in parallel?

1.59. *(a)* Discuss the effect of circulating current at no-load, in two single phase transformers operating in parallel.

(b) Two transformers operating in parallel have different reactance to resistance ratios. Show that one transformer operates at a better p.f. than the other.

(c) Show that if two transformers have same p.u. impedances, they will share the load in proportion to their kVA capacities.

1.60. (a) Discuss how the parallel operation of two single-phase transformers is affected by

(i) unequal voltage ratios and

(ii) unequal per unit leakage impedances but same x_e/r_e ratio.

(b) Two single-phase 500 kVA and 400 kVA transformers are connected in parallel to supply a load of 800 kVA at 0.8 power factor lagging. The resistance and leakage reactance of the first transformer are 2.5 per cent and 6 percent respectively and of the second transformer 1.6 percent and 7 percent respectively. Calculate the kVA loading and power factor at which each transformer operates.

[**Ans.** (b) 465.6 kVA at p.f. = 0.84 lag and 337.2 kVA at p.f. = 0.737 lag]

1.61. (a) Discuss how the parallel operation of two single-phase transformers is affected by

(i) unequal $\frac{x_e}{r_e}$ ratio but the same per unit leakage impedances,

(ii) wrong polarities.

(b) Two single-phase transformers operating in parallel have the following data :

Transformer $A : z_{ea} = 0.2 + j\,0.6\ \Omega$, $E_a = 208$ V

Transformer $B : z_{eb} = 0.25 + j\,0.55\ \Omega$, $E_b = 205$ V

Load impedance $Z = 3 + j\,2\ \Omega$.

Find (i) voltage across load

(ii) current and power delivered to load and

(iii) power shared by each transformer.

[**Hint.** (b) Calculate $\frac{1}{z_{ea}} + \frac{1}{z_{eb}} + \frac{1}{Z} = 3.464 \angle -65.87°$; $\frac{E_a}{z_{ea}} + \frac{E_b}{z_{eb}} = 667.08 \angle -68.51°$ and use Eq. (1.85) for load voltage V. Further, use Eq. (1.80 (a)) for $I_a = \frac{E_a - V}{z_{ea}}$ and I_b. Load current $\bar{I} = \bar{I}_a + \bar{I}_b$ etc.]

[**Ans.** (b) (i) 192.725 V (ii) 53.31 A, 8554.6 W (iii) 4221.58 W, 4332.78 W]

1.62. (a) 'Two transformers to be operated in parallel should have the same capacity.' Justify whether this statement is correct or not.

(b) Following is the data for short-circuit tests on four 2000/200 V single-phase transformers :

Transformer	*Rating*	*Short-circuit data*		
		V_{sc}	I_{sc}	P_{sc}
A	100 kVA	125 V	48 A	1100 W
B	200 kVA	117 V	90 A	2050 W
C	300 kVA	147 V	140 A	3800 W
D	400 kVA	156 V	190 A	5000 W

Out of these, which two transformers would operate most successfully in parallel?

[**Ans.** Transformers A and B]

1.63. (a) Two single-phase transformers with unequal voltage ratios are operating in parallel.

Discuss, with the help of phasor diagrams, the load current shared by each and their operating power factors. State the assumptions made.

(*b*) Two 1-phase, 6600/2200 V transformers have the following short-circuit data :

Transformer A (200 kVA) : 62 V, 30.3 A, 370 W

Transformer B (400 kVA) : 66 V, 60.6 A, 650 W

These transformers are put in parallel and connected to a load of 0.8 p.f. lag with primary voltage held fixed at 6600 V.

(*i*) Calculate the maximum kW load that can be supplied by these transformers without causing the load voltage to fall below 2150 V.

(*ii*) For the condition of part (*i*), find kVA shared by each transformer.

[**[Hint.** (*b*) (*i*) Current shared by transformer A = 32.765 A

$$\text{Maximum kW load} = \frac{32.765}{30.3}\left(200 + \frac{62}{66} \times 400\right) \times 0.8 \Bigg]$$

[**Ans.** (*b*) (*i*) 498.08 kW (*ii*) 216.27 kVA, 406.33 kVA]

1.64. (*a*) Explain why in testing large transformers the open-circuit test is carried out with the high-voltage winding open and the short-circuit test with the low-voltage winding shorted.

(*b*) A 100 kVA transformer having 1% resistance and 4% leakage reactance is operated in parallel with a 200 kVA transformer having 1% resistance and 6% leakage reactance. If the total load delivered is 300 kVA at unity p.f., calculate the kVA load on each transformer as well as the operating p.f. of each transformer. (*I.E.S., 1975*)

[**Ans.** (*b*) 127.445 kVA at p.f. 0.9989 leading. 172.776 kVA at p.f. 0.9994 lagging]

1.65. (*a*) Discuss the conditions necessary for the successful parallel operation of single-phase transformers. How can you check these conditions?

(*b*) Two single-phase transformers in parallel supply a load of 500 amperes at 0.8 p.f. lagging and at 400 volts. Their equivalent impedances referred to secondary windings are $(2 + j\,3)$ ohms and $(2.5 + j\,5)$ ohms. Compute the current and kVA supplied by each transformer and the corresponding power factors.

[**Ans.** (*b*) 304.51 A, 121.804 kVA and p.f. 0.8282 lagging;
196.431 A, 78.572 kVA and p.f. 0.7524 lagging]

1.66. Determine the largest value of load that can be delivered by the parallel combination of two transformers described in Problem 1.64 (*b*) without overloading any of them.

[**Ans.** 235.56 kVA]

1.67. (*a*) Two single-phase transformers having identical voltage ratings but unequal kVA ratings are to be opereated in parallel. Under what conditions can the two transformers supply a total kVA equal to the sum of their individual kVA ratings without any transformer getting overloaded? Derive the conditions mentioned.

(*b*) Two single-phase, 11000-440 V transformers have kVA ratings of 200 kVA and 100 kVA respectively. The equivalent resistance and reactance of the 200 kVA transformer are respectively 1.0 and 5.0 ohms, when referred to the 11,000 V side. The equivalent reactance of 100 kVA transformer referred to the 11,000 V side is 9.0 ohms.

(*i*) What should be the equivalent resistance of 100 kVA transformer if each transformer is to supply load in proportion to its kVA rating when operated in parallel?

(*ii*) What is the maximum combined kVA that can be supplied by the transformers in parallel without overloading any one transformer? (*I.E.S., 1978*)

[**Hint.** *(b) (i)* $\frac{z_{ea}}{z_{eb}} = \frac{S_{br}}{S_{ar}}$ or $\sqrt{\frac{1+5^2}{r_{eb}^2+9^2}} = \frac{100}{200}$ etc.]

(iii) Since $z_{eb} = 2z_{ea}$, each transformer shares load equal to its kVA rating and because $\frac{x_{ea}}{r_{ea}} \neq \frac{x_{eb}}{r_{eb}}$, the angle between I_a and I_b [Fig. 1.55 *(b)*], or between 100 kVA and 200 kVA is $(\phi_a - \phi_b)$. Thus the maximum combined kVA is given by

$$\sqrt{[200 + 100\cos(\phi_a - \phi_b)]^2 + [100\sin(\phi_a - \phi_b)]^2}$$

$$= \sqrt{[200 + 100\cos 16.74]^2 + [100\sin 16.74]^2} = 297.16 \text{ kVA}]$$

[**Ans.** *(a) (i)* $\frac{z_{ea}}{z_{eb}} = \frac{S_{br}}{S_{ar}}$ and *(ii)* $\frac{x_{ea}}{r_{ea}} = \frac{x_{eb}}{r_{eb}}$ *(b) (i)* 4.796 ohms *(ii)* 297.16 kVA]

1.68. *(a)* Describe the principle of regulating the voltage with the help of tap-changers.

(b) Discuss whether the winding should be tapped on h.v. side or on l.v. side.

(c) Explain why the transformer winding should be tapped in the middle.

1.69. *(a)* Why should the tap-changer be connected near the neutral? What about delta-connected transformers?

(b) What is the difference between no-load and on-load tap-changers?

(c) Describe no-load tap-changer with a suitable diagram.

1.70. *(a)* What precautions should be observed during the operation of on-load tap-changers?

(b) Explain the function of centre-tapped reactor in on-load tap changer.

(c) Describe one type of on-load tap-changer, with proper sequence of operation for changing the voltage.

1.71. *(a)* A 11/33 kV, delta/star tap-changer transformer supplies a star-connected load of 1200 kW at 0.8 p.f. lag. Per-phase leakage impedances for l.v. winding and h.v. windings are respectively $0.5 + j5\ \Omega$ and $2.0 + j\ 15\ \Omega$. Each line conductor has impedance of $2 + j\ 5\ \Omega$. If l.v. winding is energised at 11 kV, find the tap-changer setting to give load terminal voltage of 33 kV. [**Ans.** Tap up by 3.5%]

1.72. Derive the transformer equivalent circuit, treating it as a magnetically coupled circuit.

1.73. *(a)* A single-phase transformer, with its secondary winding open, is energised from 220 V DC. It is assumed that exciting current in primary winding is less than its rated current.

If a small portion of the iron core is removed by making appropriate cuts in the iron core, discuss what would happen to *(i)* exciting current in the primary winding and *(ii)* the magnitude of core flux.

(b) A two-winding 2000/200 V transformer has the following parameters : $L_1 = 15$ H, $l_1 = 0.5$ H, $l_2 = 0.01$ H

(i) Calculate the mutual inductance of the transformer.

(ii) Find the self-inductance of the secondary winding.

[**Ans.** *(a)* Exciting current remains constant but core flux is reduced.

(b) (i) $M = 1.45$ H *(ii)* $L_2 = 0.155$ H]

1.74. *(a)* Define mutual inductance and discuss the methods of increasing it between two circuits.

(b) Show that if two circuits are linked with the same magnetic circuit, the mutual inductance is $M = k\sqrt{L_1 L_2}$, where k is the coefficient of coupling and L_1, L_2 are the self-inductances of the two circuits.

1.75. (a) Define self-inductance, magnetizing inductance and leakage inductance. Express self-inductance in terms of the other two.

(b) Define co-efficient of coupling. How can it be increased in two magnetically coupled coils?

1.76. An air-core transformer gave the following data for two tests conducted on it :

Test 1. When 20 volts at 400 Hz is applied to winding 1 with winding 2 open-circuited, the current and power in winding 1 are 2 A and 20 watts and voltage across winding 2 is 15 V.

Test 2. When 24 V at 400 Hz is applied to winding 2 with winding 1 open-circuited, the current and power in winding 2 are 1.5 A and 18 watts.

(a) Find the values of r_1, r_2, L_1, L_2 and M.

(b) Winding 1 is energised from a 30 V, 400 Hz source and winding 2 is connected to a load of 20 Ω resistance. Find the current in winding 1.

[**Ans.** (a) 5 Ω, 8 Ω, 1.99 mH, 3.183 mH, 2.984 mH (b) 3.664 A]

1.77. A 100/400 V, 2 kVA single-phase transformer has 5% impedance. If it is connected as a 500/400 V auto-transformer, deduce from fundamentals its kVA rating and percentage impedance as an auto-transformer. *[I.A.S., 1994]* [**Ans.** 10 kVA 1%]

1.78. An ideal transformer feeds a load of 100 Ω from a voltage source which can be represented by an internal e.m.f. of 10 V with an internal resistance of 2000 Ω.

(a) Find the turns ratio so that maximum power is transferred to load.

(b) Under the condition of part (a), find the current, voltage and power in the load.

[**Ans.** (a) 4.472 (b) 11.18 mA, 1.118 V, 12.5 mW]

1.79. (a) For a single-phase auto-transformer, derive, from ab-initio, the relation between input power, conducted power and transformed power in terms of high and low voltages.

(b) Discuss the advantages and disadvantages of an auto-transformer as compared to a two-winding transformer.

1.80. A 2400/240 V, 200 kVA, 1-phase transformer has a core loss of 1.8 kW at rated voltage. Its equivalent resistance is 1.1 percent. Find the transformer efficiency at p.f. of 0.9 at full load. Find also the kVA load at which maximum efficiency occurs. Calculate, also, the maximum efficiency at p.fs. of 0.8, 0.9 and unity. [**Ans.** 97.826%, 181 kVA, 97.574%, 97.838%, 98.05%]

1.81. In a 1-phase transformer, zero-voltage regulation occurs at p.f. of 0.94 leading, whereas its maximum possible voltage regulation is 4%. Find its voltage regulation at p.f. 0.8 lagging.

If its ohmic losses are 136.5 W, find kVA of the transformer. [**Ans.** 3.348%, 10 kVA]

1.82. For a 2000/200 V, 20 kVA single-phase transformer, the load current at which maximum efficiency occurs is 90 A. Its equivalent resistance is 0.015 p.u. Find its half-rate load efficiency at p.f. 0.8.

Also, calculate its voltage regulation at full load unity p.f. [**Ans.** 96.177%, 1.5%]

1.83. For a 2300/230 V, 1-plase transformer, maximum possible voltage regulation is 5% and occurs at a p.f. of 0.25. Find its load voltage at full-load power factors of 0.8 lead and 0.8 lag.

[**Ans.** 234.38 V, 220.98 V]

1.84. A single-phase transformer has eddy current loss of 100 W and hysteresis loss of 120 W. For the same supply voltage, if both lamination thickness and operating frequency are reduced by 10%, find the new value of core losses. Take Steinmetz's constant = 2. [**Ans.** 214.33 W]

1.85. (a) For a 1-phase transformer, equivalent resistance is 1.5%. Its per unit core loss is 0.01. Find efficiency of this transformer at p.f. 0.8.

(b) A 1-phase transformer has the ratio $\frac{x_{e2}}{r_{e2}} = 3$ and equivalent resistance is 1.5%. Find the full-load p.f. at which voltage regulation is 4%. Find the maximum full-load efficiency of this transformer at the p.f. calculated above.

[Ans. *(a)* 96.97% *(b)* 0.7764 lag, 96.28%]

1.86. *(a)* Describe four possible ways of connections of 3-phase transformers with relevant relations amongst voltages and currents on both h.v. and l.v. sides.

(b) A bank of three single-phase transformers has its h.v. terminals connected to 3-wire, 3-phase, 11 kV system. Its l.v. terminals are connected to a 3-wire, 3-phase load rated at 1500 kVA, 2200 V. Specify the voltage, current and kVA ratings of each transformer for both h.v. and l.v. windings for the following connections :

(i) $Y - \Delta$ *(ii)* $\Delta - Y$ *(iii)* $\Delta - \Delta$ *(iv)* $Y - Y$.

The first symbol indicates h.v. winding and the second symbol l.v. winding.

[Ans. Each transformer rating = 500 kVA *(i)* 6351/2200 V, 78.37/227.27 A *(ii)* 11000/1270.2 V, 45.45/393.64 A *(iii)* 11000/2200 V, 45.45/227.27 A *(iv)* 6351/1270.2 V, 78.37/393.64 A]

1.87. *(a)* Explain the reasons why distribution transformers are designed for minimum core loss rather than ohmic loss.

(b) For the circuit shown in Fig. 1.96, find

(i) the turns ratio from primary to secondary for maximum power transformer *(mpt)* to load,

(ii) the value of X_c in Ω for *mpt*,

(iii) load voltage under *mpt*,

(iv) maximum power delivered to load.

[Hint. *(b) (i)* $10 = \left(\frac{N_1}{N_2}\right)^2 \times 1.6$ etc.]

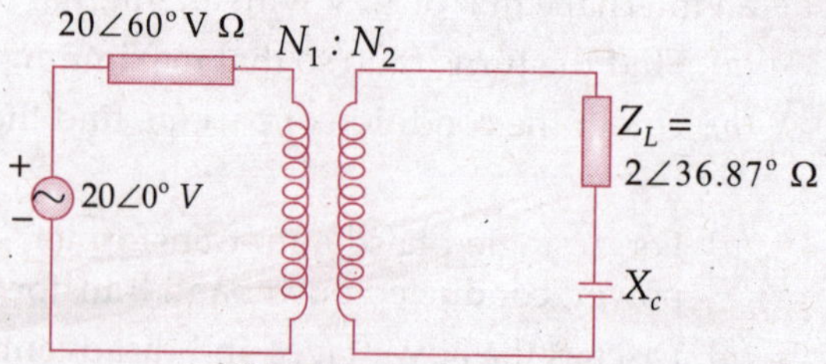

Fig 1.96: Pertaining to Problem 1.87*(b)*

[Ans. *(b) (i)* 2.5 *(ii)* 3.9712 Ω *(iii)* $5\angle 36.87°$ V *(iv)* 10 W]

1.88. The efficiency at unity p.f., of a 6600/384 V, 200 kVA single-phase transformer is 98%, both at full-load and at half full-load. The power factor at no-load is 0.2 lagging and the full-load regulation at a lagging p.f. of 0.8 is 4%. Draw the equivalent circuit referred to LV side and insert all values. *[I.E.S., 2002]*

[Ans. $R_C = 108.381\ \Omega$, $X_m = 22.124\ \Omega$, $r_{e2} = 0.01\ \Omega$, $x_{e2} = 0.03578\ \Omega$]

1.89. *(a)* Flux in the core of a transformer is 0.003 sin 314 *t* Wb. If this transformer has 100 primary turns, determine the voltage induced in the primary as a function of time.

(b) A voltage $v = 200 \sin 314t + 20 \sin 942t$ is applied to the primary winding of a transformer having 100 turns. Determine the instantaneous and rms values of core flux. Neglect leakage flux.

[Hint. *(b)* Use $v = N\frac{d\phi}{dt}$]

[Ans. *(a)* 94.2 cos 314 *t* volts *(b)* (– 6.3694 cos 314 *t* – 0.2123 cos 942 *t*) mWb ; 4.5063 mWb]

1.90. *(a)* Discuss the points of similarity in transformers and rotating electrical machines.

(b) What is the major cause of noise in transformers? Discuss the steps which may help in reducing it.

2

Chapter Electromechanical Energy Conversion Principles

Conversion of other forms of energies into electrical energy is a common practice. The main advantage of this conversion is that energy in electrical form can be transmitted, utilized and controlled more easily, reliably and efficiently. Energy conversion devices are required first for converting other forms of energies into electrical energy and then for converting electrical energy into the required useful forms, such as sound, light, heat or mechanical energy. In other words, energy conversion devices are required at both ends of an electrical system, since energy is neither available and nor required in electrical form. One typical example illustrating the processing of energy is a hydroelectric plant where energy is converted to electrical form. It is then transmitted and distributed over lines and finally converted to mechanical energy in an electric motor for final use. Another example is the conversion of sound energy into electrical energy at the talker's end, its transmission over lines in electrical form and its final conversion to sound waves at the listener's end.

An electro-mechanical energy conversion device is one which converts electrical energy into mechanical energy or mechanical energy into electrical energy. Operating principles of energy conversion devices are similar, but their structural details differ depending upon their function. Various electromechanical energy conversion devices may be categorised as under :

(i) The first category of devices, involving small motion, processes only low-energy signals from electrical to mechanical or vice versa. These include telephone receivers, loud-speakers, microphone, pickups, and sensors. These devices, working under linear input-output conditions and involving small motions, require low-signals and are usually called **transducers.**

(ii) The second category consists of **force-, or, torque-producing devices** with limited mechanical motion. Examples of such devices are electromagnets, relays, moving-iron instruments, moving-coil instruments, solenoids etc.

(iii) The third category includes **continuous energy conversion devices** such as motors and generators; these are used primarily for bulk energy conversion and utilization. In a machine acting as a **motor**, energy is converted from electrical to mechanical; whereas in a **generator**, energy is converted from mechanical to electrical.

Energy conversion process is basically a reversible process. However, in practice, devices may be designed and constructed to suit one particular mode of conversion or the other.

All these energy conversion devices operate on similar physical principles, but their constructional details differ. The coupling between the electrical and mechanical systems of these devices is through the magnetic or electric field. The object of this chapter is to develop the electromechanical-energy conversion principles with field energy as the basis. The analysis of energy conversion devices by field-energy concept is more general and broad-based, since it is applicable to all devices possessing rotational, linear or vibratory motions. Other advantages of this approach are as follows :

(i) It can deal with both steady state and transient analysis of all electromechanical energy converters.

(ii) It gives more physical insight into the operation of all these devices, which is indispensable.

(iii) This approach leads physically to the generalized theory of electrical machines.

(iv) The conventional approach can be introduced at any stage, to study the effect of saturation, commutation etc.

Electromechanical energy conversion devices pertaining to transducers and force, or, torque producing devices are discussed in this chapter. Continuous energy conversion devices are treated in other chapters of this book.

The present chapter begins with the principle of conservation of energy and then expressions for forces and torques are developed in terms of field variables. The essential conditions for the energy conversion from electrical to mechanical form or *vice versa*, are clearly brought out in this chapter.

The energy storing capacity of the magnetic field is much greater (about 25,000 times) than that of the electric field. In view of this fact, electromechanical energy conversion devices with magnetic field as the coupling medium between electrical and mechanical systems are more common in commercial applications. As such more emphasis is given to these devices. However, devices using electric field as the coupling medium are also discussed in this chapter.

2.1. PRINCIPLE OF ENERGY CONVERSION

When energy is converted from one form into another, the *principle of conservation of energy* can be invoked. According to this principle, energy can neither be created nor destroyed, it can merely be converted from one form into another.

In an energy conversion device, out of the total input energy, some energy is converted into the required form, some energy is stored and the rest is dissipated. In view of this, the energy balance equation must include these four energy terms and for a motor, it can be written as

(Total electrical energy input)

= (Mechanical energy output) + (Total energy stored) + (Total energy dissipated) ...(2.1)

The principle of energy conversion is based on energy balance Eq. (2.1). It should be noted that Eq. (2.1) is written for motor action where electrical energy input and mechanical energy output are treated as positive terms. For generator action,

(Total mechanical energy input)

= (Electrical energy output) + (Total energy stored) + (Total energy dissipated)

The various forms of energies involved in Eq. (2.1) for an electromechanical energy conversion device, are now described below :

(i) Total electrical energy input from the supply mains is W_{ei}.

(ii) The mechanical energy output is W_{mo}.

(iii) Total energy stored in any device = Energy stored in magnetic field, W_{es} + Energy stored in mechanical system, W_{ms}.

(iv) Total energy dissipated = Energy dissipated in electric circuit as ohmic losses + Energy dissipated as magnetic core loss (hysteresis and eddy-current losses) + Energy dissipated in mechanical system (friction and windage losses etc.).

Thus the energy balance Eq. (2.1) can be written in more specific terms as

$W_{ei} = W_{mo} + (W_{es} + W_{ms})$ + (Ohmic energy losses + Coupling field energy losses) + (Energy losses in mechanical system).

The subscripts *e*, *m*, *i*, *s* and *o* stand for electrical, mechanical, input, stored and output respectively. For example, subscript *ei* denotes electrical input (energy), subscript *ms* denotes mechanical stored (energy).

If the appropriate terms are grouped together, then the energy balance equation becomes,

$(W_{ei}$ – Ohmic energy losses)

$$= (W_{mo} + W_{ms} + \text{Mechanical energy losses}) + (W_{es} + \text{Coupling field energy losses}) \quad ...(2.2a)$$

or

$$W_{elec} = W_{mech} + W_{fld} \quad ...(2.2b)$$

Eq. (2.2) leads to the electromechanical energy conversion model of Fig. 2.1. The various losses, *i.e.* I^2R losses, coupling field losses and the friction and windage losses are irreversible, and these are therefore dissipated as heat. Energy stored in the coupling field W_{es}, is dealt with later in Art. 2.2(*b*). The energy stored in the mechanical system W_{ms}, is the kinetic energy $\frac{1}{2}$ (mass) u^2 for a linear-motion system or $\frac{1}{2}J\omega_r^2$ for a rotary-motion system. Here *u* is the linear velocity in m/sec and ω_r is the angular velocity in radians per second. Note that the coupling field is associated with e.m.f. *e* and current *i* on the electrical side and torque *T* (or force *F*) and speed ω_r (or *u*) on the mechanical side.

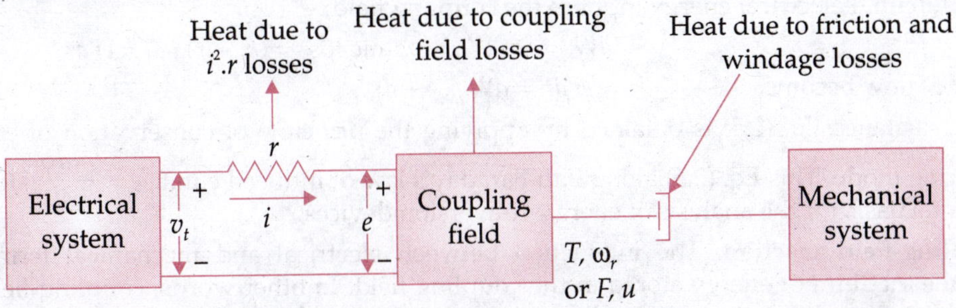

Fig 2.1: General representation of electromechanical energy conversion device.

In Eq. (2.2*b*), W_{elec} is the net electrical energy input to the coupling field. W_{mech} is the total energy converted to mechanical form and it is equal to the sum of useful mechanical energy W_{mo}, mechanical energy stored W_{ms} and mechanical energy losses. W_{fld} is the total energy absorbed by the coupling field and it is equal to the sum of both the stored field energy W_{es} and the coupling field energy losses.

It is evident from above that electrical losses (ohmic and coupling-field losses) as well as mechanical losses (friction and windage losses), though always present, play no basic role in the energy conversion process. Neglect of these losses in the representation of Fig. 2.1 leads to Fig. 2.2(*a*) for motoring-mode and Fig. 2.2(*b*) for generating mode. In Fig. 2.2, lossless energy-conversion region is associated with electrical quantities *e* and *i* at electrical terminals and mechanical quantities *T* and ω_r (or *F* and *u*) at mechanical terminal. The advantage of this model is that direct attention can be focused on the process of energy conversion, so important in understanding the action and reaction of coupling field on electrical and mechanical terminals. It must, however, be kept in mind that electrical and mechanical losses are an integral part of electromechanical energy conversion device and must, therefore, be considered in determining the input or output of an energy-conversion system.

For the lossless conversion system of Fig. 2.2(*a*), Eq. (2.2) can be written in differential form as

$$dW_{elec} = dW_{mech} + dW_{fld} \quad ...(2.3)$$

where dW_{elec} = differential electrical energy input to couping field

dW_{mech} = differential mechanical energy output

dW_{fld} = differential change in energy stored in the coupling field.

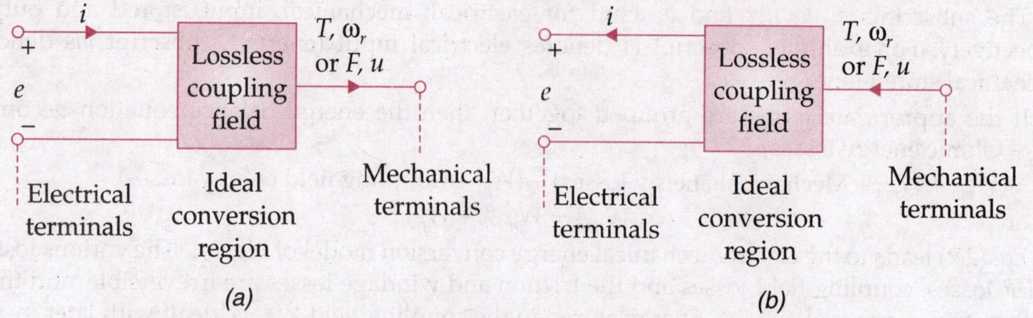

Fig 2.2: Representation of lossless electromechanical energy conversion device *(a)* motoring mode and *(b)* generating mode.

From Fig. 2.1, the differential electrical energy input in time dt is

$$dW_{ei} = v_t\, i\, dt$$

Ohmic loss in resistance r in time dt is $i^2r\, dt$.

∴ Differential electrical energy input to the coupling field,

$$dW_{elec} = dW_{ei} - \text{ohmic loss} = (v_t - ir)\, i\, dt = ei\, dt \qquad \text{...(2.4)}$$

Eq. (2.3) now becomes

$$ei\, dt = dW_{mech} + dW_{fld} \qquad \text{...(2.5)}$$

Energy balance Eq. (2.5) is obtained by applying the principle of conservation of energy to the motoring mode. This Eq. (2.5) alongwith Faraday's law of induced e.m.f., $e = -\frac{d\psi}{dt}$, forms the fundamental basis for the analysis of energy-conversion devices.

Coupling-field reaction. The interaction between electrical and mechanical terminals is through the medium of energy stored in the coupling field. In other words, coupling field is the link between electrical and mechanical systems. In order that a moving member can rotate, or move, with respect to stationary member, an air gap must exist in between the stator and rotor. This energy stored in the coupling field must produce action and reaction on the electrical and mechanical systems for the conversion of energy from electrical to mechanical (motoring mode) or from mechanical to electrical (generating mode).

If the output is mechanical, as in a motor, the coupling field must react with the electrical systems in order to absorb electrical energy from it. In a motor, this reaction is the counter e.m.f. e, Fig. 2.2 (a), similar to the e.m.f. induced in the primary winding of a transformer. The coupling field extracts energy proportional to $e \cdot i$ from the electrical system, converts and delivers energy proportional to $T \cdot \omega_r$ (or $F \cdot u$) to the mechanical system.

If the output is electrical, as in a generator, the coupling field must react with the mechanical system so as to absorb mechanical energy from it. In a generator, this reaction is the counter-torque T, opposite to the applied mechanical torque of the prime-mover. This counter-torque is produced through the interaction of conductor current i and the coupling field. In this manner, the coupling field extracts mechanical energy proportional to [(reaction torque) × (speed)] from the mechanical system, converts and delivers it as electrical energy proportional to $e \cdot i$ to the electrical system. It may be seen from above that coupling field serves as the energy conversion region.

Thus, the reaction of the coupling field on the electrical or mechanical system is essential for electromechanical energy conversion process. Since induced e.m.f. e and torque T are associated with the coupling field, these are usually called electromechanical coupling terms.

Electromechanical energy conversion devices are slow-moving devices because of the inertia associated with mechanical components. Therefore, the coupling field necessary for the energy conversion must be slowly varying and as such the nature of this field is *quasi-static*. Electromagnetic radiation from the coupling field is almost negligible.

2.2. SINGLY EXCITED MAGNETIC SYSTEMS

In this article, the expressions for electric energy input, magnetic field energy stored, mechanical work done and the mechanical force are developed for singly excited magnetic systems.

(a) Electric energy input. Consider a simple magnetic* system of a toroid, excited by a single coil as shown in Fig. 2.3. The instantaneous voltage equation for the electric circuit is written by applying Kirchhoff's voltage law.

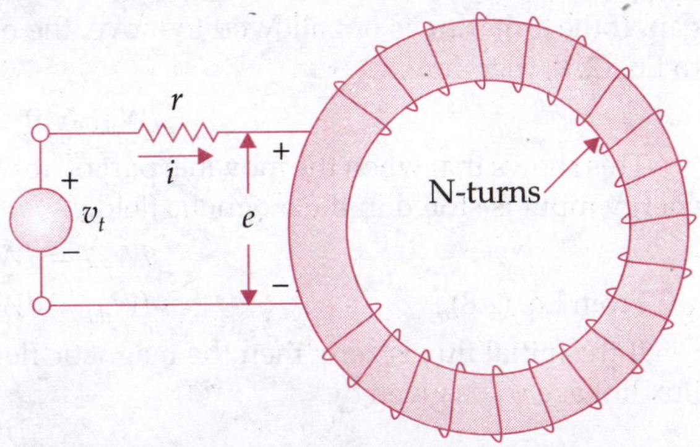

Fig 2.3: Toroidal core excited from single source.

$\therefore \quad v_t = ir + e$

where e is the reaction e.m.f. taken as a voltage drop in the direction of current i, refer to Art. 1.3.

$$\therefore \qquad e = \frac{d\psi}{dt}$$

and
$$v_t = ir + \frac{d\psi}{dt} \qquad ...(2.6)$$

Here ψ is the instantaneous flux linkages with the circuit. Multiplying both sides of Eq. (2.6) by idt, we get

$$v_t\, idt = ri^2\, dt + i\, d\psi$$

or
$$(v_t - ir)\, idt = i\, d\psi$$

or
$$e\, idt = i\, d\psi$$

In view of Eq. (2.4),
$$dW_{elec} = e\, idt = i \cdot d\psi \qquad ...(2.7)$$

If the toroidal core is made of ferromagnetic material, then most of the flux would be confined to the core. Assuming that flux ϕ links all the N turns of the coil in Fig. 2.3, the flux linkages ψ are equal to $N\phi$ Wb-turns. Therefore, from Eq. (2.7),

$$dW_{elec} = i \cdot d\psi = iN\, d\phi = F\, d\phi \qquad ...(2.8)$$

In Eq. (2.8), ϕ is the instantaneous value of the coil flux and $F = iN$ is the instantaneous coil m.m.f.

Eq. (2.7) or (2.8) shows that for the toroid to extract energy from the supply system, the flux linkages of the magnetic field must change. These changing flux linkages cause the generation of reaction e.m.f. e. As stated before, the flow of charges or current against the reaction e.m.f. e causes the extraction of energy from the electrical system.

(b) Magnetic field energy stored. Consider a simple electromagnetic relay of Fig. 2.4 *(a)*. Initially the armature is in the open position. When switch S is closed, current i is established in the N-turn coil. The flux set up depends on m.m.f. Ni and the reluctance

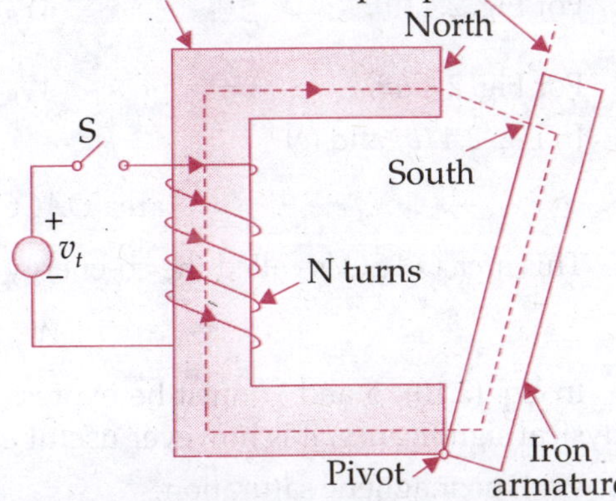

Fig 2.4: *(a)* Simple electromagnetic relay

* The reader is advised to go through Appendix A to know more about magnetic circuits..

of the magnetic path. The magnetic field thus produced, creates north and south poles as shown in Fig. 2.4. *(a)*, and as a result of it, there is established a magnetic force tending to shorten the air-gap. If the armature is not allowed to move, the mechanical work done, dW_{mech} is zero. According to Eq. (2.3), therefore,

$$dW_{elec} = 0 + dW_{fld}$$

This shows that when the movable part of any physical system is kept fixed, the entire electrical energy input is stored in the magnetic field.

$$\therefore \qquad dW_{fld} = dW_{elec}$$

From Eq. (2.8),

$$dW_{fld} = dW_{elec} = i \cdot d\psi = F \cdot d\phi \qquad \text{...(2.9a)}$$

If the initial flux is zero, then the magnetic field energy stored W_{fld}, in establishing a flux ϕ_1 or flux linkage ψ_1, is given by

$$W_{fld} = \int_0^{\psi_1} i \cdot d\psi = \int_0^{\phi_1} F \cdot d\phi \qquad \text{...(2.9b)}$$

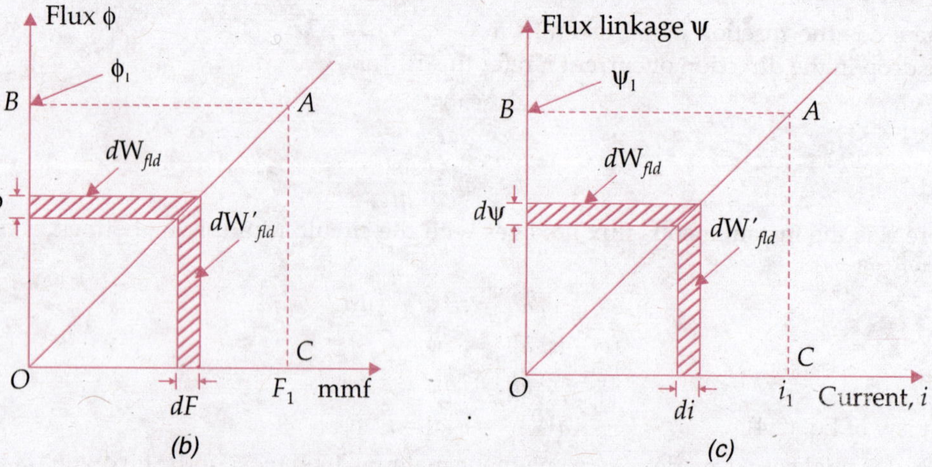

Fig 2.4: Pertaining to field energy and co-energy for a linear magnetic circuit.

In Eq. (2.9 *b*), i and F must be expressed in terms of ψ and ϕ respectively.

When the armature is held in open position in Fig. 2.4 *(a)*, then most of the m.m.f. is consumed in the air gap and it is likely that magnetic saturation may not occur as shown in Fig. 2.4 *(b)* and *(c)*.

For Fig. 2.4 *(b)*,

$$W_{fld} = \int_0^{\phi_1} dW_{fld} = \int_0^{\phi_1} F \,.\, d\phi = \text{area } OABO.$$

For Fig. 2.4 *(c)*,

$$W_{fld} = \int_0^{\psi_1} dW_{fld} = \int_0^{\psi_1} i\, d\psi = \text{area } OABO.$$

In Fig. 2.4 *(b)* and *(c)*

$$\text{area } OACO = \int d\,W'_{fld} = \int_0^{F_1} \phi\, dF = \int_0^{i_1} \psi\, di$$

This area *OACO* is called the co-energy W'_{fld}.

$$\therefore \qquad W'_{fld} = \int_0^{F_1} \phi\, dF = \int_0^{i_1} \psi\, di \qquad \text{...(2.10)}$$

In Eq. (2.10), ϕ and ψ must be expressed in terms of F and i respectively. Co-energy has no physical significance, it is however useful in calculating the magnetic forces.

With no magnetic saturation,

$$\text{Area } OABO = \text{area } OACO$$

or

$$W_{fld} = W'_{fld}$$

and $$W_{fld} + W'_{fld} = \text{area } OCABO = \phi_1 F_1 = \psi_1 i_1$$

In general, for a linear magnetic circuit,

$$W_{fld} = W'_{fld} = \frac{1}{2}\psi i = \frac{1}{2}F\phi \quad \text{...(2.11)}$$

The magnetic stored energy and co-energy can also be expressed in terms of reluctance and permeance of the magnetic path.

Now m.m.f. = (flux) (reluctance)

or $$F = (\phi)\, Rl = \frac{\Phi}{\text{Permeance}, \Delta}$$

$$\therefore \quad W_{fld} = W'_{fld} = \frac{1}{2}\phi^2 Rl = \frac{1}{2}\frac{\phi^2}{\Delta}$$

Also $$W_{fld} = W'_{fld} = \frac{1}{2}F^2\Delta = \frac{1}{2}\frac{F^2}{Rl}.$$

The self-inductance L is defined as the magnetic flux-linkages per ampere, *i.e.*,

$$L = \frac{\psi}{i}$$

$\therefore$ From Eq. (2.11), $$W_{fld} = W'_{fld} = \frac{1}{2}Li^2 = \frac{1}{2}\frac{\psi^2}{L}$$

Summarising the results obtained for a linear magnetic circuit, the stored magnetic energy W_{fld} and co-energy W'_{fld} can be written as follows :

$$W_{fld} = W'_{fld} = \frac{1}{2}F\phi = \frac{1}{2}\psi i = \frac{1}{2}\phi^2 Rl = \frac{1}{2}\frac{\phi^2}{\Delta}$$

$$= \frac{1}{2}\frac{F^2}{Rl} = \frac{1}{2}F^2\Delta = \frac{1}{2}Li^2 = \frac{1}{2}\frac{\psi^2}{L} \text{ joules} \quad \text{...(2.12)}$$

In the simple magnetic relay of Fig. 2.4 *(a)*, path of the magnetic flux is through the yoke, armature and air-gap. Since the reluctance offered by the air-gap is much larger than that of the iron, a major part of the m.m.f. Ni is required to overcome the air gap reluctance. Accordingly, most of the magnetic energy W_{fld} is stored in the air gap.

If W_{fld1} and W_{fld2} are respectively the magnetic energies stored in iron and air gap of Fig. 2.4 *(a)*, then total energy stored $W_{fld} = W_{fld1} + W_{fld2}$. The magnetic stored-energy density w_{fld1} for the iron is given by

$$w_{fld1} = \frac{W_{fld1}}{\text{(Length of the magnetic path through iron)}\ \text{(Iron area normal to the magnetic flux)}}$$

$$= \frac{W_{fld1}}{\text{(Length)(Area)}} = \frac{1}{2}\frac{F_1\phi}{\text{(Length)(Area)}}$$

$$= \frac{1}{2}\left(\frac{F_1}{\text{Length}}\right)\left(\frac{\phi}{\text{Area}}\right) = \frac{1}{2}H_1 B \text{ joules/m}^3.$$

Here F_1 is the m.m.f. required to overcome the iron reluctance and H_1 is the magnetic-field intensity in ampere-turns per metre length of the iron path. B is the flux density in Wb/m² or tesla.

But $$B = \mu_1 H_1$$

$$\therefore \quad w_{fld1} = \frac{1}{2}\mu_1 H_1^2 = \frac{1}{2}\frac{B^2}{\mu_1} \text{ joules/m}^3.$$

Similarly for the air-gap, the magnetic stored energy density w_{fld2} is

$$w_{fld2} = \frac{1}{2} H_2 B = \frac{1}{2} \mu_0 H_2^2 = \frac{1}{2} \frac{B^2}{\mu_0} \text{ joules/m}^3.$$

Here μ_1 and μ_0 are the permeabilities of iron and air gap respectively.

In general, the magnetic stored energy density w_{fld} is given by

$$w_{fld} = \frac{1}{2} HB = \frac{1}{2} \mu H^2 = \frac{1}{2} \frac{B^2}{\mu_0} \text{ joules/m}^3.$$

where H is the magnetic-field intensity in ampere-turns per metre at point where the permeability is μ.

For a linear magnetic circuit,

$$w_{fld}' = w_{fld} = \frac{1}{2} \mu H^2 = \frac{1}{2} \frac{B^2}{\mu} = \frac{1}{2} HB \text{ joules/m}^3 \quad ...(2.13)$$

Here w_{fld}' is the co-energy density.

An examination of Eq. (2.12) reveals that the magnetic field energy can be expressed in terms of field variables F, ϕ, ψ and parameters Rl, Δ or in terms of inductance parameter L and current variable i. This fact that field energy can be expressed in terms of circuit parmeter L, clears the way for electric circuit approach to the analysis of electrical machines, *i.e.* the generalized theory of electrical machines. Thus the field-energy approach serves as the physical basis for the generalized theory of electrical machines.

(c) Mechanical work done. Consider the simple magnetic relay of Fig. 2.4 *(a)* again. In Fig. 2.5 *(a)*, the movable end of the armature is assumed to be held in open position. When the switch S is closed, the exciting current increases from zero to $i_1 = V_t/r$ and the flux linkages increases from zero to ψ. Here r is the coil resistance. As explained before, the magnetic energy stored W_{fld} in the field is given by the cross-hatched area $OABO$. Area OAi_1O is equal to co-energy W'_{fld}.

In Fig. 2.5 *(b)*, the movable end of the armature is assumed in the closed position, so that the air-gap is zero. When the switch S is closed, the exciting current again rises from zero to $i_1 = V_t/r$ whereas the flux linkages increase from zero to ψ_2. Here the flux linkages ψ_2 must be greater than ψ_1, since the reluctance of the magnetic path is considerably reduced for the same m.m.f. The energy W_{fld} stored in the magnetic field is now given by the cross-hatched area $OCDO$. As before, area OCi_1O is equal to co-energy W'_{fld}.

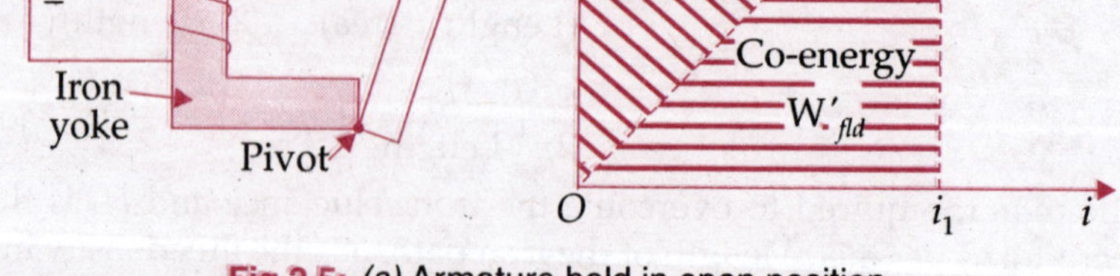

Fig 2.5: *(a)* Armature held in open position.

With the armature in the open position, the exciting current i_1 sets up field in the magnetic circuit. This field creates magnetic force, due to which the free end of the armature moves to the closed position. During the armature movement, from its open position, the reluctance of the magnetic path decreases, thereby increasing the flux linkages from its initial value of ψ_1. These increments in flux linkages induce a counter e.m.f. in the coil, which opposes the flow of exciting current i, *i.e.*

$$i = \frac{V_t - \text{counter e.m.f. induced in the coil during armature movement}}{\text{Coil impedance}}$$

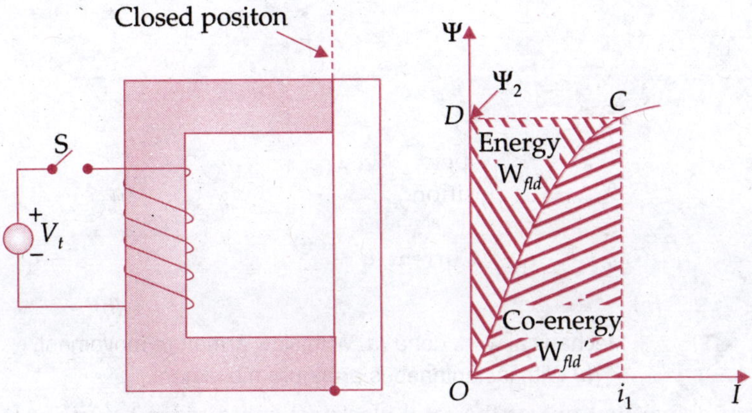

Fig 2.5: *(b)* Armature held in closed position.

The magnitude of counter e.m.f. induced in the exciting coil depends on how fast the armature moves. The two extreme cases of armature motion are considered further:

I. Slow movement. With the armature in the open position, the exciting current is i_1 the flux linkage are ψ_1 and the operating point is A, [Fig. 2.6 *(a)*]. In the closed armature position, the flux linkages are ψ_2, current is i_1 and the operating point is C. The slow movement of the armature from open position causes almost a negligible amount of counter e.m.f. $\left(= \dfrac{\psi_2 - \psi_1}{\text{Time}}\right)$ in the coil. As a result of it, the exciting current i_1 remains substantially constant during the armature movement from open to closed position and accordingly the operating point A reaches the new operating point C along the vertical line AC as shown in Fig. 2.6 *(a)*.

Now change in the stored energy of magnetic field W_{fld}, during the time armature moves from open (point A) to the closed position (point C) is given by,

$$W_{fld} = \text{(Magnetic energy stored in the closed position)} - \text{(Magnetic energy stored in open position)}$$

or $$W_{fld} = \text{area } OA'CDFO - \text{area } OAA'FO.$$

Electric energy input during this change is

$$W_{elec} = \int_{\psi_1}^{\psi_2} i_1\, d\psi = i_1\,(\psi_2 - \psi_1) = \text{area } ACDFA'A$$

But $$W_{elec} = W_{fld} + W_{mech}$$

$\therefore$ $$\text{area } ACDFA'A = \text{area } OA'CDFO - \text{area } OAA'FO + W_{mech}$$

or $$W_{mech} = \text{area } OACDFO - \text{area } OA'CDFO$$

$$= \text{area } OACA'O \quad ...(2.14)$$

Eq. (2.14) shows that the mechanical work done is equal to the area enclosed between the two magnetization curves at open and closed positions and the vertical ψ–i locus during the slow armature movement. This is shown by cross-hatched area in Fig. 2.6 *(a)*.

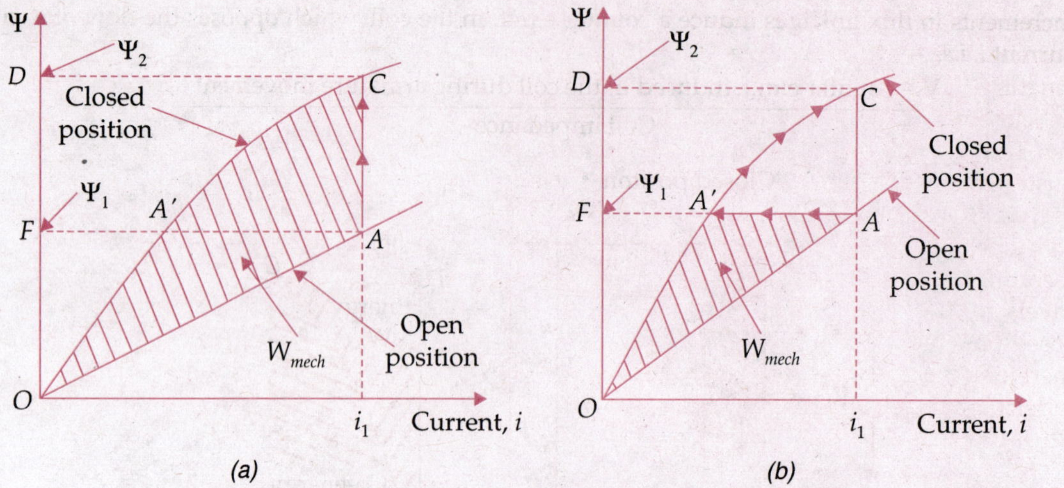

Fig 2.6: Mechanical work done *(a)* With slow armature movement. *(b)* With instantaneous armature movement.

It is seen from above that out of the total electrical energy input during slow movement of the armature, some energy gets stored in the magnetic field and the remaining is outputted as mechanical energy. It is shown in Example 2.1 that with saturation ignored, half of the electrical energy input gets stored in the magnetic field and the other half appears as mechanical energy output during slow armature movement.

II. Instantaneous movement. Here the armature is assumed to move from the open to closed position instantaneously. According to the *constant flux linkage theorem*, the flux linkages with an inductive circuit can't change suddenly. So here also, during the fast movement of the armature, the flux linkages don't change and remain constant at ψ_1. The operating point, therefore, travels horizontally from A to A'. After the armature has closed, the operating point travels from A' to C along the closed-position magnetization curve [Fig. 2.6 *(b)*], since the final operating point has to be C.

During the time instantaneous movement of the armature occurs from open (point A) to closed position (point A'), we have

(i) Change in the magnetic stored energy,

$$W_{fld} = \text{area } OA'FO - \text{area } OAA'FO$$

and *(ii)*

$$W_{elec} = \int_{\psi_1}^{\psi_1} i d\psi = 0$$

But

$$W_{elec} = W_{fld} + W_{mech}$$

$\therefore$

$$O = \text{area } OA'FO - \text{area } OAA'FO + W_{mech}$$

or

$$W_{mech} = \text{area } OAA'O \quad ...(2.15)$$

Eq. (2.15) shows that the mechanical work done is equal to the area enclosed between the two magnetization curves at open and closed positions and the horizontal ψ–i locus during the instantaneous movement of armature. This is indicated by cross-hatched area in Fig. 2.6 *(b)*.

During fast armature movement, it is seen from above that *(i)* there is no electrical energy input *(ii)* mechanical energy output is at the expense of field energy stored, *i.e.*, mechanical energy output = reduction in the magnetic stored energy.

III. Transient movement. The armature movement will neither be too slow nor too fast, but will lie somewhere in between the two extreme limits discussed above. The flux linkage-current locus will accordingly be in between the two locii shown in Fig. 2.6 *(a)* and *(b)*. Initially the armature movement is slow and as it is nearing the closed position, its movement becomes fast. The ψ–i locus will, therefore, be $AC'C$ as illustrated in Fig. 2.7. The operating point A reaches C' during the time armature moves from open to closed position. Since the final operating point has to be C, the operating point travels further from point C' to C along the closed-position magnetization curve $OA'C'C$. Therefore, the armature when allowed to move under the influence of magnetic force, has ψ–i locus $AC'C$ as shown in Fig. 2.7.

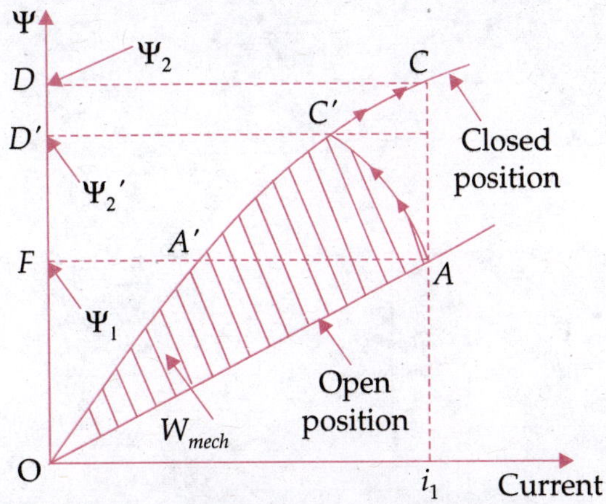

Fig 2.7: Flux linkage-current locus during transient movement of armature.

During the time armature moves from open (point A) to closed position (point C'), we have

(i) Change in the magnetic stored energy,

W_{fld} = Energy stored in the closed position – Energy stored in the open position

= area $OA'C'D'FO$ – area $OAA'FO$

(ii) $$W_{elec} = \int_{\psi_1}^{\psi_2'} i d\psi = \text{area } AC'D'FA'A.$$

But $$W_{elec} = W_{fld} + W_{mech}.$$

$\therefore$ $$\text{Area } AC'D'FA'A = \text{area } OA'C'D'FO - \text{area } OAA'FO + W_{mech}$$

or $$W_{mech} = (\text{area } OAA'FO + \text{area } AC'D'FA'A) - \text{area } OA'C'D'FO$$

$$= \text{area } OAC'A'O \qquad ...(2.16)$$

Eq. (2.16) again shows that the energy converted to mechanical (or mechanical work done) is equal to the area enclosed between the two magnetization curves at open and closed positions and the ψ–i locus during the transient movement of armature.

(d) Determination of magnetic force. In Fig. 2.5 *(a)*, the magnetic force tending to shorten the air gap increases as the gap length decreases. In view of this, the magnitude of average magnetic force $f_{e(av)}$ can be obtained from the relation,

$$f_{e(av)} = \frac{\text{Mechanical work done during armature movement}}{\text{Distance travelled during armature movement}} \qquad ...(2.17)$$

From Figs. 2.5 *(a)* and (2.7), $$f_{e(av)} = \frac{\text{Area } OAC'A'O}{\text{Gap length, } g}$$

In order to obtain a suitable expression for the magnetic force developed, a differential armature movement of magnitude dx must be imagined in the direction of the magnetic force f_e. This movement or displacement dx need not be a real one. For this reason, the displacement dx is referred to as the virtual displacement and the expression $f_e\,dx$ as the virtual work. This method of determining the magnetic force is called the *principle of virtual work*. According to this principle, the movable (or rotatable) part is allowed a virtual displacement dx (or $d\theta$) in the direction of magnetic force f_e (or torque T_e). Then its effect on the energy balance Eq. (2.3) is investigated in order to obtain the magnitude and direction of magnetic force f_e or magnetic torque T_e.

In Fig. 2.8 *(a)*, assume the armature to be at a distance g_1 from the open position. Then a virtual displacement dx in the direction of magnetic force f_e is considered. The two magnetization curves for the armature positions g_1 and $(g_1 + dx)$ have been shown in Fig. 2.8 *(b)*.

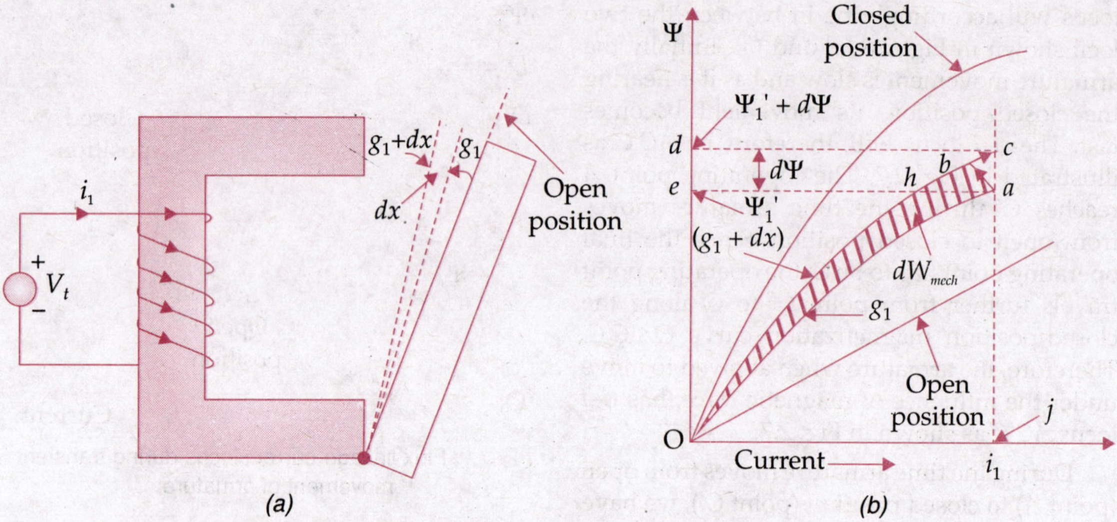

Fig 2.8: Mechanical work done for differential movement of armature.

The flux linkage-current locus during the differential displacement dx is abc. Here a is the operating point at position g_1, and ψ_1' and i_1 are corresponding values. The operating point at (g_1 + dx) is c and the corresponding values are $\psi_1' + d\psi$ and i_1.

As explained before, the mechanical work done in the virtual displacement dx is

$$\text{area } oabho = f_e\, dx \qquad \text{...(2.18)}$$

The area $oabho$ differs from the area $oaho$ by the triangular area abh. Since the displacement dx is infinitesimally small, the triangular area abh may be ignored as dx approaches zero. Alternatively, the armature movement over the virtual displacement dx may be taken as instantaneous. Note that the final operating point at ($g_1 + dx$) must be c, as explained in Art. 2.2 (c).

Now $$dW_{elec} = \int_{\psi_1'}^{\psi_1'} i\, d\psi = 0\,;\; dW_{mech} = f_e\, dx.$$

Substitution of the values in Eq. (2.3) gives

$$0 = f_e\, dx + dW_{fld} \text{ at constant } \psi$$

or $$f_e\, dx = -\, dW_{fld} \text{ at constant } \psi \qquad \text{...(2.19)}$$

The electrical energy flow during the virtual displacement dx is zero for constant ψ, as shown above. Thus the mechanical work $f_e\, dx$ is done at the expense of the field energy stored and this is indicated by a negative sign before dW_{fld} in Eq. (2.19).

∴ From Eq. (2.19), $$f_e = -\left(\frac{d\,W_{fld}}{dx}\right) \text{ at constant } \psi$$

or $$f_e = -\left(\frac{dW_{fld}}{dx}\right)_{\psi = \text{constant}} \qquad \text{...(2.20)}$$

Also $$f_e = -\left(\frac{dW_{fld}}{dx}\right)_{\phi = \text{constant}}$$

Note that W_{fld} must be expressed in terms of ψ and x or ϕ and x. Here ψ and x are referred to as **state variables**. It is because their values decide the state function W_{fld}. In view of this, Eq. (2.20) leads to the parametric equations for magnetic force as,

$$f_e = -\frac{\partial\, W_{fld}(\psi, x)}{\partial x} = -\frac{\partial\, W_{fld}(\phi, x)}{\partial x} \qquad \text{...(2.21)}$$

In the above expression for magnetic force, ψ or ϕ are independent variables. As voltage is equal to the derivative of ψ, this expression gives f_e for a *voltage-controlled system*. In Eq. (2.21), partial derivative is taken while keeping flux linkages ψ, or flux ϕ, constant.

Similarly, the area *oabho* differs from the area *oacbho* by the triangular area *abc*. Here again area *oabho* may be taken equal to the area *oacbho* as dx approaches zero. Alternatively, slow movement of the armature may be assumed over the virtual displacement dx, so that the operating point moves vertically from *a* to *c*.

Here $$dW_{elec} = \int_{\psi_1'}^{\psi_1' + d\psi} i_1 d\psi = i_1 d\psi = \text{area } acdea.$$

For obtaining dW_{fld}, Fig. 2.8 *(b)* reveals that

area *acdea* = area *ojcdo* – area *ojaeo*.

= [(Magnetic stored energy + Co-energy) at position $(g_1 + dx)$]

– [(Magnetic stored energy + Co-energy) at position g_1]

In other words, area *acdea* represents the differential increase in field energy dW_{fld} and co-energy dW_{fld}', from rectangular area *ojaeo* to rectangular area *ojcdo*, during the virtual displacement dx. In view of this,

$$\text{area } acdea = dW_{fld} + dW_{fld}'$$

But it is already seen that area *acdea* = $dW_{elec} = i_1 d\psi$.

$$\therefore \quad dW_{fld} + dW_{fld}' = i_1 d\psi = \text{area } acdea$$

Thus the differential change in field energy dW_{fld} is given by

$$dW_{fld} = i_1 d\psi - dW_{fld}'.$$

Also $$dW_{mech} = f_e dx$$

Substitution of the values of $dW_{elec} = i_1 d\psi$, $dW_{fld} = i_1 d\psi - dW_{fld}'$ and $dW_{mech} = f_e dx$ in Eq. (2.3) gives,

$$i_1\, d\psi = f_e dx + i_1 d\psi - dW_{fld}'$$

or $$f_e\, dx = + dW_{fld}' \text{ at constant } i \qquad ...(2.22)$$

The positive sign before dW_{fld}' indicates that during the virtual displacement dx, the mechanical work $f_e\, dx$ is equal to the increase in co-energy at constant current.

$$\therefore \quad f_e = + \frac{dW_{fld}'}{dx} \text{ at constant } i.$$

Since W_{fld}' must be expressed in terms of (i, x) or (F, x) ; the parametric equations for the magnetic force are

$$f_e = \frac{\partial W_{fld}'}{\partial x}(i, x) = \frac{\partial W_{fld}'}{\partial x}(F, x) \qquad ...(2.23)$$

In Eq. (2.23), partial derivative is taken while holding i, or F, constant. As before, here i and x (or F and x) are referred to as state variables.

Eqs. (2.21) and (2.23) give the magnitude of electro-magnetic force f_e because the armature movement is linear. For angular movements of armature, the electromagnetic torque T_e can be obtanied from parametric Eq. (2.21) as

$$T_e = -\frac{\partial W_{fld}(\psi, \theta)}{\partial \theta} = -\frac{\partial W_{fld}(\phi, \theta)}{\partial \theta} \qquad ...(2.24)$$

and from parametric Eq. (2.23) as

$$T_e = \frac{\partial W_{fld}'}{\partial \theta}(i, \theta) = \frac{\partial W_{fld}'}{\partial \theta}(F, \theta) \qquad ...(2.25)$$

Eq. (2.23) for magnetic force and Eq. (2.25) for magnetic torque are applicable to systems in which current is an independent variable. In other words, these two force and torque expressions are applicable to *current-controlled systems*.

It can be stated that any physical device will develop electromagnetic force or torque, if its magnetization curve is affected by a differential displacement of its movable (or rotatable) part, the other part remaining fixed.

It must be borne in mind that Eqs. (2.21) to (2.25) hold good even when the magnetic path is saturated. In case the magnetic saturation is neglected, *i.e.* the graph between ψ and i or ϕ and F is considered linear, then

$$W_{fld} = W_{fld}'.$$

Invoking the relations of Eq. (2.23), we get

$$\left.\begin{aligned} f_e &= \frac{\partial W_{fld}'}{\partial x}(i, x) = \frac{\partial W_{fld}}{\partial x}(i, x) \\ \text{and} \quad f_e &= \frac{\partial W_{fld}'}{\partial x}(F, x) = \frac{\partial W_{fld}}{\partial x}(F, x) \end{aligned}\right\} \quad \text{...(2.26)}$$

Now $W_{fld} = \frac{1}{2}\phi^2 Rl$. Therefore, from Eq. (2.21),

$$f_e = -\frac{1}{2}\phi^2 \frac{dRl}{dx} \quad \text{...(2.27)}$$

Also $W_{fld} = \frac{1}{2}F^2 \Delta = \frac{1}{2} i^2 L = \frac{1}{2}\frac{\psi^2}{L}$ and from Eq. (2.26),

$$f_e = \frac{1}{2}F^2 \frac{d\Delta}{dx} = \frac{1}{2} i^2 \frac{dL}{dx} = \frac{1}{2}\psi^2 \cdot \frac{d}{dx}\left[\frac{1}{L}\right] \quad \text{...(2.28)}$$

The magnetic stored energy is also expressed as $W_{fld} = \frac{1}{2} i\psi$. If current i is expressed in terms of ψ and x, then from Eq. (2.21),

$$f_e = -\frac{1}{2}\psi \frac{\partial i}{\partial x}(\psi, x) \quad \text{...(2.29)}$$

In case ψ is expressed in terms of i and x, then from Eq. (2.26),

$$f_e = \frac{1}{2} i \frac{\partial \psi}{\partial x}(i, x) \quad \text{...(2.30)}$$

Similarly for electromagnetic torque T_e, we have

$$\begin{aligned} T_e &= \frac{1}{2}\phi^2 \frac{dRl}{d\theta} = \frac{1}{2}F^2 \frac{d\Delta}{d\theta} = \frac{1}{2} i^2 \frac{dL}{d\theta} \\ &= -\frac{1}{2}\psi \frac{\partial i}{\partial \theta}(\psi, \theta) = \frac{1}{2} i \frac{\partial \psi}{\partial \theta}(i, \theta) \end{aligned} \quad \text{...(2.31)}$$

From an examination of Eqs. (2.21) to (2.31), it can be stated that electromagnetic force or torque developed in any physical system, acts in such a direction as to tend to

(i) decrease the magnetic stored energy at constant ψ or ϕ, see Eqs. (2.21) and (2.24) ;

(ii) increase both field energy stored and co-energy at constant current or m.m.f. Eq. (2.26);

(iii) decrease the reluctance, [Eqs. (2.27) and (2.31)] ;

(iv) increase the permeance and inductance, Eqs. (2.28) and (2.31) ;

(v) decrease current i at constant flux linkages ψ, Eq. (2.29) or increase ψ at constant i, Eq. (2.30).

The foregoing expressions obtained for f_e and T_e are equally applicable to magnetic fields produced by permanent magnets ; because f_e and T_e do not depend upon the source of the field.

Alternative method : Alternatively, the results obtained in Eqs. (2.19) and (2.22) can be arrived at as under :

In Fig. 2.8 (a), assume the relay to be at position g_1 so that the relay operating point is a in Fig. 2.9. Magnetization curves for positions g_1 and $(g_1 + dx)$ are shown in Fig. 2.9.

Assume virtual displacement dx from position g_1 to position $(g_1 + dx)$ in the direction of force f_e at constant flux linkages $\psi = oe$ in Fig. 2.9 *(a)*. In other words, movement from g_1 to $(g_1 + dx)$ is assumed fast. Observation of Fig. 2.9*(a)* shows that field energy stored **decreases** from area *oaheo* to area *oheo*. Now area $oaho = f_e.dx$.

$\therefore$ $f_e\,dx$ = area *oaho*

= **decrease** in field energy stored after virtual displacement dx in the direction of f_e, at constant ψ.

or $$f_e\,dx = -\,dW_{fld} \text{ with } \psi \text{ constant} \qquad ...(2.19)$$

The negative sign before dW_{fld} indicates *reduction* in the field energy stored at constant flux linkages.

For obtaining Eq. (2.22), assume virtual displacement dx from position g_1 to position $(g_1 + dx)$ in the direction of f_e and at constant current $i_1 = oj$ in Fig. 2.9 *(b)*. In other words, the movement from g_1 to $(g_1 + dx)$ is assumed slow. Observation of Fig. 2.9 *(b)* reveals that co-energy **increases** from area *ojao* to area *ojcho*.

$\therefore$ $f_e\,dx$ = area *oacho*

= **increase** in co-energy after virtual displacement dx in the direction of f_e, at constant current

or $$f_e\,dx = +\,dW_{fld}' \text{ at constant current} \qquad ...(2.22)$$

The positive sign before dW_{fld}' indicates an increase in the co-energy at constant current.

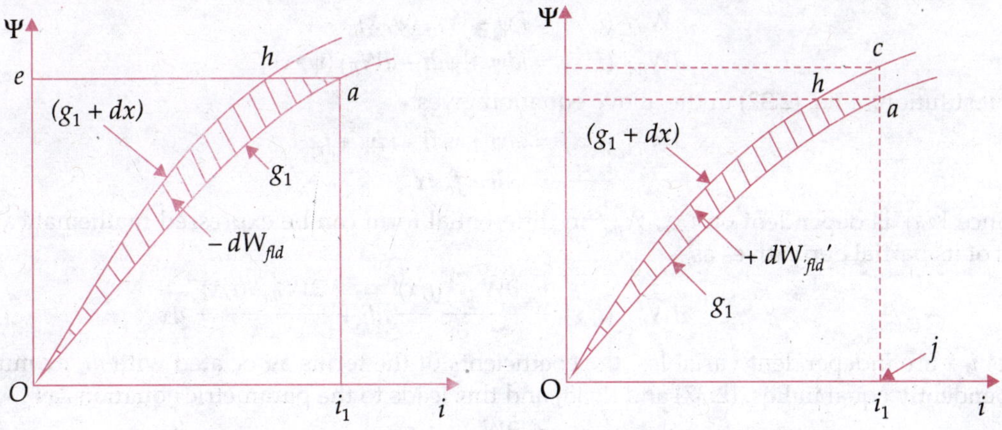

Fig 2.9: *(a)* Decrease of energy with displacement *dx*, at constant flux-linkages.
(b) Increase of co-energy with displacement *dx*, at constant current.

Second alternative method : Another method for obtaining the expressions (2.19) and (2.22) for the magnetic force f_e in terms of field energy and co-energy is as under :

Consider magnetic relay of Fig. 2.4 *(a)*, where the magentic field energy is primarily stored in air gap. If air gap varies, then x measured from the open position also varies and as a consequence, field energy stored changes. From this, it can be stated that W_{fld} is a function of two independent variables ψ and x (or ϕ and x).

Mechanical work done in differential movement dx in the direction of magnetic force f_e is

$$dW_{mech} = f_e\, dx$$

From Eq. (2.7), $$dW_{elec} = i\, d\psi$$

Substituting these values in Eq. (2.3) gives

$$i d\psi = f_e\, dx + dW_{fld}(\psi, x)$$

or $$dW_{fld}(\psi, x) = i\, d\psi - f_e\, dx \quad ...(2.32)$$

This equation is more general than Eq. (2.9). For example, if armature is assumed stationary, $dx = 0$ and therefore

$$dW_{fld} = i\, d\psi$$

This is the same as Eq. (2.9).

Since W_{fld} is dependent on ψ, x ; W_{fld} in differential form can be expressed mathematically in terms of its two partial derivatives as

$$dW_{fld}(\psi, x) = \frac{\partial W_{fld}(\psi, x)}{\partial \psi}\, d\psi + \frac{\partial W_{fld}(\psi, x)}{\partial x}\, dx \quad ...(2.33)$$

Since ψ, x are independent variables, the coefficients of the terms associated with $d\psi$ and dx in Eqs. (2.32) and (2.33) must be equal.

$$\therefore \quad i = \frac{\partial W_{fld}(\psi, x)}{\partial \psi} \quad ...(2.34)$$

and $$f_e = -\frac{\partial W_{fld}(\psi, x)}{\partial x} \quad ...(2.35)$$

Eq. (2.35) is the same as Eq. (2.21).

It is clear from Fig. 2.4 *(c)* that co-energy W_{fld}' depends on i and x, and is given by

$$W_{fld}'(i, x) = i\,\psi - W_{fld}(\psi, x) \quad ...(2.36)$$

or $$dW_{fld}'(i, x) = i d\psi + \psi di - dW_{fld}(\psi, x)$$

Substitution of Eq. (2.32) in the above equation gives

$$dW_{fld}'(i, x) = i d\psi + \psi di - i d\psi + f_e dx$$

$$= \psi di + f_e\, dx \quad ...(2.37)$$

Since W_{fld}' is dependent on i, x; W_{fld}' in differential form can be expressed mathematically in terms of its partial derivatives as

$$dW_{fld}'(i, x) = \frac{\partial W_{fld}'(i,x)}{\partial i}\, di + \frac{\partial W_{fld}'(i,x)}{\partial x}\, dx \quad ...(2.38)$$

As i, x are independent variables, the coefficients of the terms associated with di, dx must be independently equal in Eqs. (2.37) and (2.38) and this leads to the parametric equations as

$$\psi = \frac{\partial W_{fld}'(i,x)}{\partial i} \quad ...(2.39)$$

and $$f_e = \frac{\partial W_{fld}'(i,x)}{\partial x} \quad ...(2.40)$$

Eq. (2.40) is the same as Eq. (2.23).

We have derived the expressions for mechanical work done, the magnetic force f_e etc ; by taking an elementary example of a simple magnetic relay merely for convenience. The reader should not come to the conclusion that all these expressions are applicable only to the simple magnetic relay alone. Actually the various expressions obtained so far, have broad significance and apply equally well to all physical systems having coupling magnetic field as the link between stationary and moving parts. If it is required to calculate f_e or T_e for any physical system, then its movable part is imagined to be given a virtual displacement dx or $d\theta$ in the direction of f_e or T_e – use of Eqs. (2.21), (2.23) or (2.31) then gives the required results.

When Eqs. (2.21), (2.23), (2.24) and (2.25) are used, one should keep in mind firstly the algebraic sign and secondly the variables in which energy and co-energy functions W_{fld} and W_{fld}' are expressed. The choice between W_{fld} and W_{fld}' depends upon the initial description of the physical magnetic system under consideration.

Example 2.1. *For a certain relay, the magnetization curves for open and closed positions of the armature are linear. If the armature of the relay moves from open to closed position at constant current (i.e. very slowly), show that the electrical energy input is shared equally between field energy stored and the mechanical work done.*

Solution. With the relay in the open position, assume the operating point to be A, so that the current and flux linkage are i_1 and ψ_1 respectively, Fig. 2.10.

In the closed position, the operating point is B, so that the current is i_1 and the flux linkage is ψ_2.

The armature movement from open to closed position is at constant current, therefore, the ψ-i locus is along the vertical line AB.

During the movement from open to closed position, the electrical energy input is

$$W_{elec} = \int_{\psi_1}^{\psi_2} i_1 d\psi = i_1 (\psi_2 - \psi_1)$$

The mechanical work done W_{mech} is given by the cross-hatched area $OABCO$.

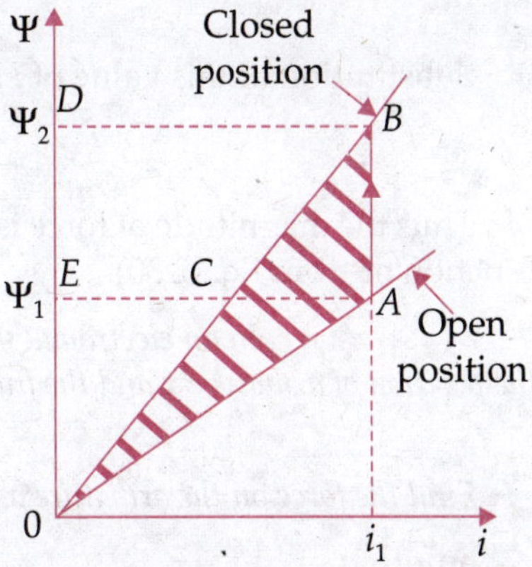

Fig 2.10: Pertaining to Example 2.1.

$\therefore$ $$W_{mech} = \text{triangular area } OABCO = \frac{1}{2}(\psi_2 - \psi_1)i_1$$

Magnetic stored energy $$W_{fld} = \text{triangular area } OCBDEO - \text{triangular area } OACEO$$

$$= \frac{1}{2}\psi_2 i_1 - \frac{1}{2}\psi_1 i_1 = \frac{1}{2}(\psi_2 - \psi_1)\, i_1$$

It is seen from above that $$W_{fld} = W_{mech} = \frac{1}{2} W_{elec}$$

This proves the required result.

Example 2.2. *For the simple magnetic relay of Fig. 2.4 (a), the variation of flux linkage ψ in terms of current i and displacement x from the open position is given by the relation $\psi = ix^{1/2}$. Obtain an expression for the magnetic force.*

Solution. The electromagnetic force f_e can be obtained by taking the partial derivative of either the field energy function W_{fld} or co-energy function W_{fld}'.

From magnetic stored energy considerations, the magnetic force is

$$f_e = -\frac{\partial W_{fld}(\psi, x)}{\partial x} \quad ...(2.21)$$

From Eq. (2.9), $$W_{fld}(\psi, x) = \int_0^{\psi} i d\psi = \int_0^{\psi} \frac{\psi}{x^{1/2}} d\psi = \frac{1}{x^{1/2}} \cdot \frac{\psi^2}{2}$$

$\therefore$ $$f_e = -\frac{\partial}{\partial x}\left[\frac{1}{x^{1/2}} \cdot \frac{\psi^2}{2}\right] = -\frac{\psi^2}{2}\left(-\frac{1}{2}\right)x^{-3/2} = \frac{\psi^2}{4} \cdot \frac{1}{x^{3/2}} \quad ...(2.41)$$

From the co-energy considerations

$$f_e = \frac{\partial W_{fld}'}{\partial x}(i, x) \quad ...(2.23)$$

But from Eq. (2.10), $\quad W_{fld}'(i, x) = \int_0^i \psi di = \int_0^i ix^{1/2} di = x^{1/2} \cdot \frac{i^2}{2}$

$$\therefore \quad f_e = \frac{\partial}{\partial x}\left[x^{1/2} \cdot \frac{i^2}{2}\right] = \frac{i^2}{2} \cdot \frac{1}{2} \cdot x^{-1/2} = \frac{i^2}{4} \cdot \frac{1}{x^{1/2}} \quad ...(2.41\ a)$$

Also, from Eq. (2.30), $\quad f_e = \frac{1}{2} i \frac{\partial \psi}{\partial x}(i, x)$

$$= \frac{1}{2} i \frac{\partial}{\partial x}(ix^{1/2}) = \frac{i^2}{4} \cdot \frac{1}{x^{1/2}} \quad ...(2.41\ b)$$

But $\quad \psi = ix^{1/2} \quad$ or $\quad i = \frac{\psi}{x^{1/2}}$

Substitution of this value of i in Eq. 2.41 *(a)* gives,

$$f_e = \frac{\psi^2}{x} \cdot \frac{1}{4} \cdot \frac{1}{x^{1/2}} = \frac{\psi^2}{x} \cdot \frac{1}{x^{3/2}} \quad ...(2.41\ c)$$

Thus the magnitude of force is the same, whether it is calculated from field-energy or co-energy function or from Eq. (2.30).

Example 2.3. *In an electromagnetic relay, functional relation between the current i in the exciting coil, the position of armature x and the flux linkages ψ is given by*

$$i = 2\psi^3 + 3\psi(1 - x + x^2),\ x > 0.5$$

Find the force on the armature as a function of ψ.

Solution. $\quad i = 2\psi^3 + 3\psi(1 - x + x^2)$

Field energy stored, $\quad W_{fld}(\psi, x) = \int_0^\psi i d\psi = \int_0^\psi [2\psi^3 + 3\psi(1 - x + x^2)] d\psi$

$$= \frac{2\psi^4}{4} + 3\frac{\psi^2}{4}(1 - x + x^2)$$

Magnetic force is given by Eq. (2.21).

$$\therefore \quad f_e = -\frac{\partial W_{fld}(\psi, x)}{\partial x} = -\frac{\partial}{\partial x}\left[\frac{\psi^4}{2} + \frac{3\psi^2}{2}(1 - x + x^2)\right]$$

$$= -\left[0 + \frac{3\psi^2}{2}(0 - 1 + 2x)\right] = \frac{3\psi^2}{2}(1 - 2x).$$

For $x > 0.5$, f_e is negative, therefore f_e acts to decrease the field energy stored at constant flux linkage.

Example 2.4. *The simple magnetic relay of Fig. 2.4 (a) gave the following ψ-i characteristics:*

(i) Open position, $\psi = 0.04\ i$ Wb-turn for all values of current i,

(ii) Closed position, $\psi = 0.06i \quad 0 \le i \le 20;\ \psi = 1.2 + 0.03(i - 20)\ i > 20$.

For an armature movement from open to closed position, find the magnitude of average magnetic force. The air-gap length is 2 cm and the current during armature movement is assumed to remain constant at 40A.

Solution. The variations of flux linkage with current are sketched in Fig. 2.11, both for open and closed positions of the armature. *B* is the operating point for open position and C is the operating point for the closed position. The ψ-*i* locus during the armature movement is along the vertical line *BC*, since current remains constant at 40 A.

The mechanical work done during the armature movement

= area $OABCDO$ = area $ODCFEO$ – area $OABFEO$

$= \left[\frac{1}{2}(20)(1.2)+\frac{1}{2}(1.2+1.8)(20)\right]-\left[\frac{1}{2}(40)(1.6)\right]$

= 42 – 32 = 10 joules.

Average electromagnetic force,

$$f_{e\,(av)} = \frac{10}{2\times10^{-2}} = 500 \text{ newtons.}$$

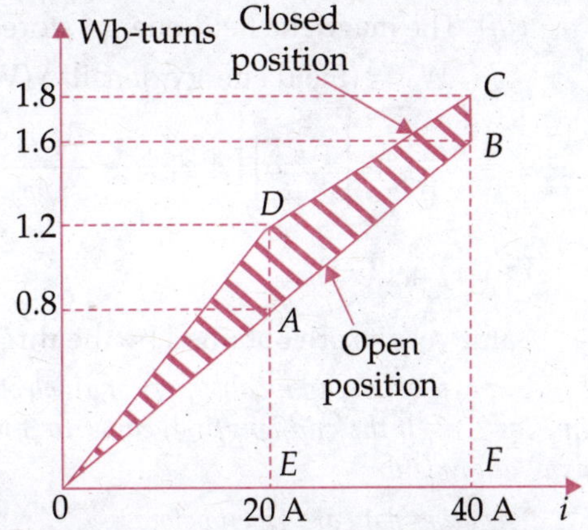

Fig 2.11: ψ-*i* characteristics, Example 2.4.

Example 2.5. *For the electromagnet shown in Fig. 2.12 (a), obtain an expression for the magnetic force f_e. The reluctance is assumed to be offered by the air gap alone. Magnetic leakage and fringing is neglected.*

Solution. The solution of this example will be illustrated by three alternative methods.

(i) For a gap length g, reluctance is given by

$$Rl_g = \frac{g}{\mu_0 A}$$

From Eq. (2.27),

$$f_e = -\frac{1}{2}\cdot\phi_g^2\frac{dRl_g}{dg}$$

∴

$$f_e = -\frac{1}{2}\phi_g^2\frac{d}{dg}\left[\frac{g}{\mu_0 A}\right] = -\frac{1}{2}\phi_g^2\frac{1}{\mu_0 A} \quad ...(i)$$

Air-gap flux density,

$$B_g = \frac{\text{Air-gap flux, } \phi_g}{\text{Area, } A} \quad \text{or} \quad \phi_g = B_g.A$$

Substituting the value of ϕ_g in Eq. (i), we get

$$f_e = -\frac{1}{2}\cdot B_g^2.A^2\frac{1}{\mu_0 A} = -\frac{1}{2}\cdot\frac{B_g^2.A}{\mu_0}\text{ N}$$

(ii) Air-gap permeance,

$$\Lambda_g = \frac{1}{Rl_g} = \frac{\mu_0 A}{g}$$

From Eq. (2.28),

$$f_e = \frac{1}{2}F^2\frac{d\Lambda_g}{dg} = \frac{1}{2}F^2\frac{d}{dg}\left[\frac{\mu_0 A}{g}\right] = -\frac{1}{2}F^2\frac{\mu_0 A}{g^2}$$

or

$$f_e = -\frac{1}{2}(iN)^2.\frac{\mu_0 A}{g^2} \quad ...(ii)$$

Now, air-gap mmf, $iN = H_g \times g = \frac{B_g}{\mu_0}\times g$

Substituting the value of iN in Eq. (ii), we get

$$f_e = -\frac{1}{2}\left[\frac{B_g^2.g^2}{\mu_0^2}\right]\times\frac{\mu_0 A}{g^2} = -\frac{1}{2}\frac{B_g^2.A}{\mu_0}$$

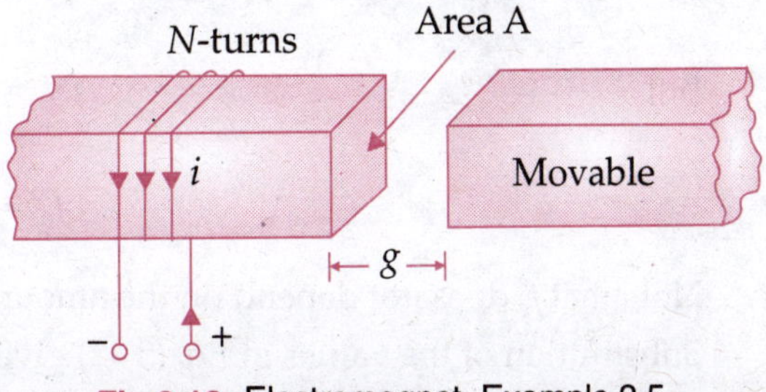

Fig 2.12: Electromagnet, Example 2.5.

(iii) The magnetic field-energy stored in air-gap of length g is given by

$$W_{fld} = \text{(Field energy density) (Volume of the magnetic field in the air-gap)}$$

$$= \left[\frac{1}{2}\frac{B_g^2}{\mu_0}\right][A.g] = \frac{1}{2}\frac{B_g^2.A.g}{\mu_0}$$

From Eq. (2.21), $$f_e = -\frac{\partial W_{fld}(\phi, g)}{\partial g} = -\frac{\partial}{\partial g}\left[\frac{1}{2}\cdot\frac{B_g^2.A}{\mu_0}\times g\right] = -\frac{1}{2}\frac{B_g^2.A}{\mu_0}$$

Same results are obtained by the three methods illustrated above.

Example 2.6. *A movable part of an electromagnet is displaced axially by an amount of 1 mm as shown in Fig. 2.13. If the gap-length g, equal to 3 mm, is held constant, find the force tending to bring them into axial alignment.*

The other data are given below :

Pole width, w_p = 6 mm

Flux density in the air-gap = 0.8 Wb/m^2 or tesla.

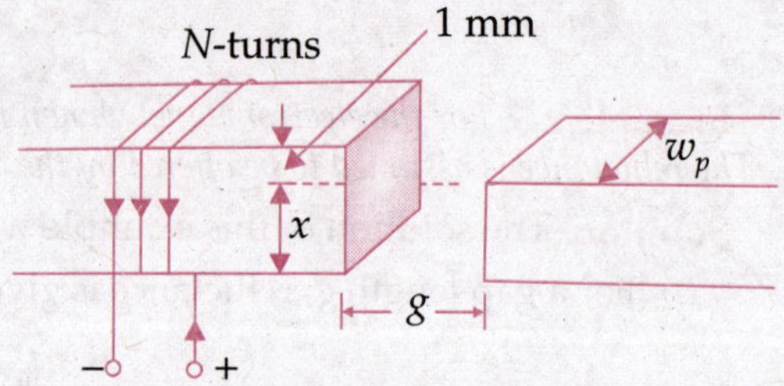

Fig 2.13: Electromagnet, Example 2.6.

Solution. Assume that all the field energy is contained in overlapping surfaces of the pole faces. Let the overlapping height be x as shown in Fig. 2.13. Then reluctance of the overlapping region is

$$Rl_g = \frac{g}{\mu_0 x w_p}$$

Here xw_p = area of the overlapping surface.

and $$W_{fld} = \frac{1}{2}\phi_g^2 Rl_g$$

$$= \frac{1}{2}\phi_g^2 \frac{g}{\mu_0 x w_p}$$

$\therefore$ $$f_e = -\frac{\partial W_{fld}}{\partial x}(\phi, x) = \frac{1}{2}\phi_g^2 \frac{g}{\mu_0 w_p x^2}$$

Now $$\phi_g = B_g w_p x$$

$\therefore$ $$f_e = \frac{1}{2}\frac{B_g^2 w_p^2 x^2 g}{\mu_0 w_p x^2} = \frac{1}{2}\frac{B_g^2 w_p g}{\mu_0} \quad \text{...(2.42)}$$

Alternatively, $$W_{fld} = \frac{1}{2}F^2 \Delta_g = \frac{1}{2}(iN)^2 \frac{\mu_0 w_p x}{g}$$

$\therefore$ $$f_e = \frac{\partial W_{fld}}{\partial x}(i, x) = \frac{1}{2}(iN)^2 \cdot \frac{\mu_0 w_p}{g}$$

But $$iN = \frac{B_g}{\mu_0}g$$

$\therefore$ $$f_e = \frac{1}{2}\left(\frac{B_g}{\mu_0}g\right)^2 \frac{\mu_0 w_p}{g} = \frac{1}{2}\frac{B_g^2 w_p g}{\mu_0} \quad \text{...(2.42 a)}$$

Note that f_e does not depend on the amount of axial displacement.

Substitution of the values in Eq. (2.42) gives

$$f_e = \frac{1}{2}\frac{(0.8)^2(6\times10^{-3})(3\times10^{-3})}{4\pi\times10^{-7}} = 4.584 \text{ newtons.}$$

Example 2.7. *A coil and plunger magnet is shown in Fig. 2.14. The coil has 1500 turns and carries a constant current of 3 amperes. All the reluctance is assumed to be offered by the air-gap g. Magnetic leakage and fringing is neglected.*

(a) For gap lengths of 2.0, 1.50, 1.00 and 0.5 cm, find air-gap flux densities and coil inductances.

(b) Find the energy stored in the magnetic field for different gap-lengths given in part (a).

(c) Compute the electromagnetic forces for the corresponding gap lengths.

(d) Find the mechanical work done, if the plunger is allowed to move slowly from g = 2.0 cm to g = 0.5 cm.

(e) If the coil resistance is neglected, find the electrical energy supplied by the source for the conditions of part (d).

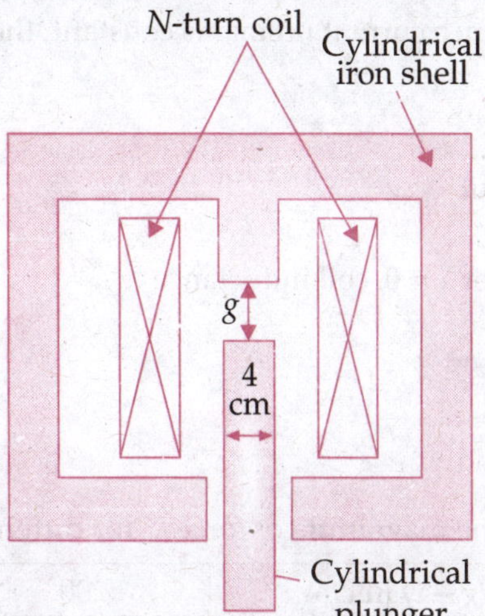

Fig 2.14: Coil and plunger magnet, Example 2.7.

Solution. *(a)* Consider the plunger to move by a small displacement x in the direction of magnetic force, so that the new air-gap length becomes $(g - x)$. Then m.m.f. per unit air-gap length is

$$H_g = \frac{iN}{g-x}$$

∴ Air-gap flux density for any gap length is

$$B_g = \mu_0 H_g = \frac{\mu_0 iN}{(g-x)} \text{ Wb/m}^2$$

Now inductance
$$L = \frac{\text{Flux linkages}}{\text{Current}} = \frac{N}{i}(\phi) = \frac{N}{i}\left(\frac{\text{m.m.f.}}{\text{Reluctance}}\right)$$

$$= \frac{N}{i}\left(\frac{Ni}{\text{Reluctance}}\right) = N^2 \,.\, \text{Permeance}$$

For gap length $(g - x)$, the coil inductance L_x is given by

$$L_x = N^2 \frac{\mu_0 A}{(g-x)}$$

The values of B_g and L_x are given below in tabular form for different gap lengths.

x in cm	0	0.5	1.0	1.50
(g – x) in cm (gap length)	2.00	1.50	1.00	0.50
B_g in Wb/m²	0.2827	0.377	0.565	1.131
L in henries	0.178	0.237	0.3553	0.7106

(b) Energy stored in the magnetic field,

$$W_{fld} = \frac{1}{2} i^2 L$$

Since current remains constant at 3 A, W_{fld} for different gap lengths is

W_{fld} : 0.8, 1.067, 1.60, 3.2 watt-sec.

(c) Magnetic force
$$f_e = \frac{\partial W_{fld}}{\partial x}(\phi, x) = \frac{\partial W_{fld}}{\partial x}(i, x)$$

Since current i remains constant, the second relation must be used.

$$\therefore \qquad f_e = \frac{\partial W_{fld}}{\partial x}(i, x) = \frac{1}{2} i^2 \frac{dL_x}{dx}$$

But $$L_x = \frac{N^2}{\text{Reluctance}} = N^2 \frac{\mu_0 A}{(g-x)}$$

For $x = 0$, coil inductance $$L = N^2 \frac{\mu_0 A}{g} = 0.178 \text{ H.}$$

$$\therefore \qquad L_x = \frac{gL}{(g-x)}$$

and $$f_e = \frac{1}{2} i^2 \frac{d}{dx}\left(\frac{gL}{g-x}\right) = \frac{1}{2} i^2 \frac{gL}{(g-x)^2}$$

The magnitude of force f_e, for different gap lengths, is given below in tabular form.

$(g - x)$ in cm	2.00	1.50	1.00	0.50
f_e in Newtons	40	71.2	160	640

(d) For a virtual displacement dx in the direction of the electromagnetic force f_e, the mechanical work done is

$$f_e\, dx = \frac{1}{2} i^2 \frac{gL}{(g-x)^2} \times dx$$

$\therefore$ Total mechanical work done W_{mech}, as the plunger is allowed to move from $g = 2.0$ cm to $g = 0.5$ cm, is given by

$$W_{mech} = \frac{1}{2} i^2 gL \int_0^{1.5} \frac{1}{(g-x)^2} \cdot dx = \frac{1}{2} i^2 gL \left[\frac{1}{(g-x)}\right]_0^{1.5}$$

$$= \frac{1}{2} (3)^2 (2) (0.178) \left[\frac{1}{0.5} - \frac{1}{2}\right] = 2.4 \text{ watt-sec}$$

(e) $$dW_{elec} = eidt = id\,\psi_x$$

Now flux linkages $$\psi_x = i\,L_x = \frac{gL}{(g-x)}\, i$$

$$\therefore \qquad \frac{d\psi_x}{dx} = \frac{gL}{(g-x)^2} \cdot i$$

Thus $$dW_{elec} = i \cdot \frac{d\psi_x}{dx}\, dx = i^2 \frac{gL}{(g-x)^2}\, dx$$

and $$W_{elec} = i^2 gL \int_0^{1.5} \frac{dx}{(g-x)^2}$$

$$= (3)^2 (2) (0.178) \left[\frac{1}{(g-x)}\right]_0^{1.5} = 4.8 \text{ watt sec.}$$

Now the total energy supplied by source is 4.8 watt-sec and mechanical work done is 2.4 watt-sec. The rest of the energy, according to Eq. (2.3), is stored in the magnetic field. That is half of the electric energy supplied is converted to mechanical energy and the remaining half is stored in the magnetic field. In other words, the mechanical work done is equal to the energy stored in the magnetic field at constant current (here it is 3 A).

From part *(b)*, it is seen that the field energy stored at gap length 2.00 cm is 0.8 watt-sec and at gap length 0.5 cm, its value is 3.2 watt-sec. Therefore, increase in magnetic energy stored as gap length changes from 2.00 to 0.5 cm, is equal to (3.2 – 0.8) = 2.4 watt-sec.

This verifies the above statement.

Example 2.8. *For the mechanical configuration shown in Fig. 2.15, assume that all the field energy is present in the overlaping regions. The radius r is much greater than air-gap length g. Calculate the magnitude of torque, when the maximum flux density in the air-gap is limited to 2.2 T. The other data are as follows :*

Radius, $r = 50$ *mm ;*

Gap length, $g = 2$ *mm ;*

Length normal to radius r is $l = 10$ *mm.*

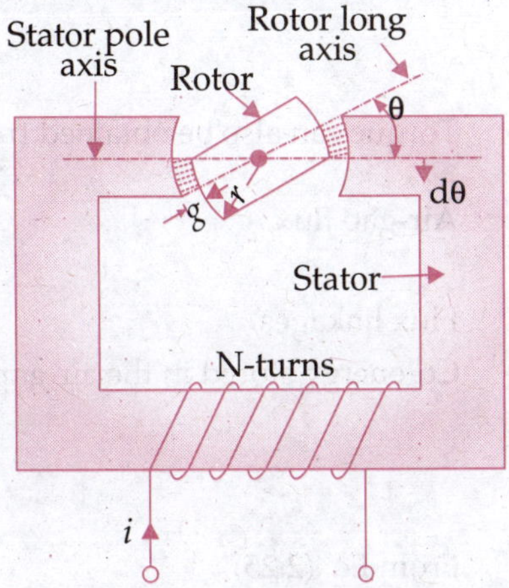

Fig 2.15: Pertaining to Example 2.8.

Solution. Let the angle of overlap be θ radians.

The reluctance of two air-gaps in series is

$$Rl_g = \frac{2g}{\mu_0 (r\theta) l}$$

$$\therefore \quad T_e = -\frac{1}{2}\phi_g^2 \frac{d}{d\theta}(Rl_g)$$

$$= -\frac{1}{2}\phi_g^2 \frac{d}{d\theta}\left[\frac{2g}{\mu_0 (r\theta) l}\right]$$

$$= \phi_g^2 \frac{g}{\mu_0 r l \theta^2}$$

But air-gap flux, $\phi_g = B_g A = B_g (r\theta l)$

$$\therefore \quad T_e = B_g^2 (r\theta l)^2 \frac{g}{\mu_0 r l \theta^2} = \left(\frac{B_g^2 g\, rl}{\mu_0}\right)$$

Alternatively, $T_e = \frac{1}{2}F^2 \frac{d\Lambda_g}{d\theta} = \frac{1}{2}(iN)^2 \frac{d}{d\theta}\left(\frac{\mu_0 r\theta l}{2g}\right) = (iN)^2\left(\frac{\mu_0 rl}{4g}\right)$

But m.m.f., $iN = \frac{2B_g g}{\mu_0}$

$$\therefore \quad T_e = \left(\frac{2B_g g}{\mu_0}\right)^2 \cdot \frac{\mu_0 rl}{4g} = \left(\frac{B_g^2\, grl}{\mu_0}\right)$$

The torque T_e acts in such a direction as to reduce the air-gap reluctance, *i.e.* rotor long axis tends to align itself with the stator-pole axis.

Substitution of the numerical values in the torque expression derived above, gives

$$T_e = \frac{(2.2)^2 (2\times 10^{-3})(50\times 10^{-3})(10\times 10^{-3})}{4\pi\times 10^{-7}} = 3.8515 \text{ N-m.}$$

Example 2.9. *Repeat Example 2.8 in case air-gap length is not negligible as compared to rotor radius.*

Solution. Average gap radius $= \left(r + \frac{1}{2}g\right)$

Area normal to flux path, $A_g = \left[\left(r + \frac{1}{2}g\right)\theta\right] \cdot l.$

Reluctance offered by two air gaps,

$$Rl_g = \frac{2g}{\mu_0 A_g} = \frac{2g}{\mu_0\left(r + \frac{1}{2}g\right)\theta l}$$

$$T_e = -\frac{1}{2}\phi_g^2 \frac{d}{d\theta}[Rl_g] = -\frac{1}{2}\phi_g^2 \frac{d}{d\theta}\left[\frac{2g}{\mu_0\left(r+\frac{1}{2}g\right)\theta\cdot l}\right] = \phi_g^2 \frac{g}{\mu_0\left(r+\frac{1}{2}g\right)l\cdot\theta^2}$$

But air-gap flux,
$$\phi_g = B_g \cdot A_g = B_g \cdot \left(r + \frac{1}{2}g\right)\theta \cdot l$$

$$\therefore \quad T_e = \left[B_g \cdot \left(r+\frac{1}{2}g\right)\theta l\right]^2 \frac{g}{\mu_0\left(r+\frac{1}{2}g\right)l \cdot \theta^2} = B_g^2 \frac{gl\left(r+\frac{1}{2}g\right)}{\mu_0}$$

Torque can also be obtained from the derivative of co-energy $W_{fld}' = \frac{1}{2}\psi i$ from Eq. (2.10).

Air-gap flux,
$$\phi_g = \frac{\text{m.m.f.}}{Rl_g} = \frac{i \cdot N}{2g} \cdot \mu_0 \left(r+\frac{1}{2}g\right)\theta \cdot l$$

Flux linkages,
$$\psi_g = N\phi_g = \frac{iN^2}{2g} \cdot \mu_0\left(r+\frac{1}{2}g\right)\theta \cdot l$$

Co-energy stored in the air-gap field,
$$W_{fld}' = \frac{1}{2}\psi_g i = \frac{1}{2} \cdot \frac{i^2N^2}{2g} \mu_0 \left(r+\frac{1}{2}g\right)\theta l$$

From Eq. (2.25),
$$T_e = \frac{\partial W_{fld}'(i \cdot \theta)}{\partial \theta} = \frac{1}{4}\frac{i^2N^2}{g}\mu_0\left(r+\frac{1}{2}g\right)l \quad ...(i)$$

But
$$B_g = \frac{\phi_g}{A_g} = \left[\frac{Ni}{2g} \cdot \mu_0\left(r+\frac{1}{2}g\right)\theta \cdot l\right] \times \frac{1}{\left(r+\frac{1}{2}g\right) \cdot \theta l} \quad ...(ii)$$

$$B_g = \frac{\mu_0 \cdot iN}{2g}$$

Substituting the value of $iN = \frac{2g \cdot B_g}{\mu_0}$ in Eq. *(i)* gives

$$T_e = \frac{1}{4}\left[\frac{B_g \cdot 2g}{\mu_0}\right]^2 \frac{1}{g} \cdot \mu_0 \left(r+\frac{1}{2}g\right)l = B_g^2 \frac{gl\left(r+\frac{1}{2}g\right)}{\mu_0}$$

Substitution of the numerical values in the torque expression derived above gives

$$T_e = (2.2)^2 \frac{(2\times10^{-3})(10\times10^{-3})(50+1) \cdot 10^{-3}}{4\pi\times10^{-7}} = 3.929 \text{ Nm}$$

2.3. RELUCTANCE MOTOR

An elementary form of a single-phase reluctance motor is illustrated in Fig. 2.16. It has saliency (salient poles) both on the stator and rotor. The reluctance or permeance of the magnetic circuit depends on the relative angular position of the rotor and stator. Single-phase voltage applied to *N*-turn coil establishes stator pulsating flux, which crosses the air-gap along the stator pole axis. In Fig. 2.16, the axis of the stator flux is indicated by a horizontal dotted line–this axis of the stator poles is called stator direct axis (or *d*-axis). An axis 90° away from the *d*-axis is called quadrature axis. Angle θ_r in Fig. 2.16 *(b)*, is the space angle between stator *d*-axis and the long rotor-axis. When space angle $\theta_r = 0$, *i.e.* when long rotor-axis is coincident with stator *d*-axis, the reluctance offered to the stator flux, by two small air gaps in series with high permeability iron, is minimum. Let this minimum reluctance be designated by Rl_d. When the rotor long-axis is along the *q*-axis, *i.e.* when the space angle $\theta_r = 90°$, the reluctance offered to the stator flux, by two very large air gaps in series with high-permeability iron, is maximum–let it be designated by Rl_q. It may be seen from Fig. 2.16 that when $\theta_r = 0, \pi, 2\pi$, etc, the reluctance offered to the stator flux is Rl_d and when

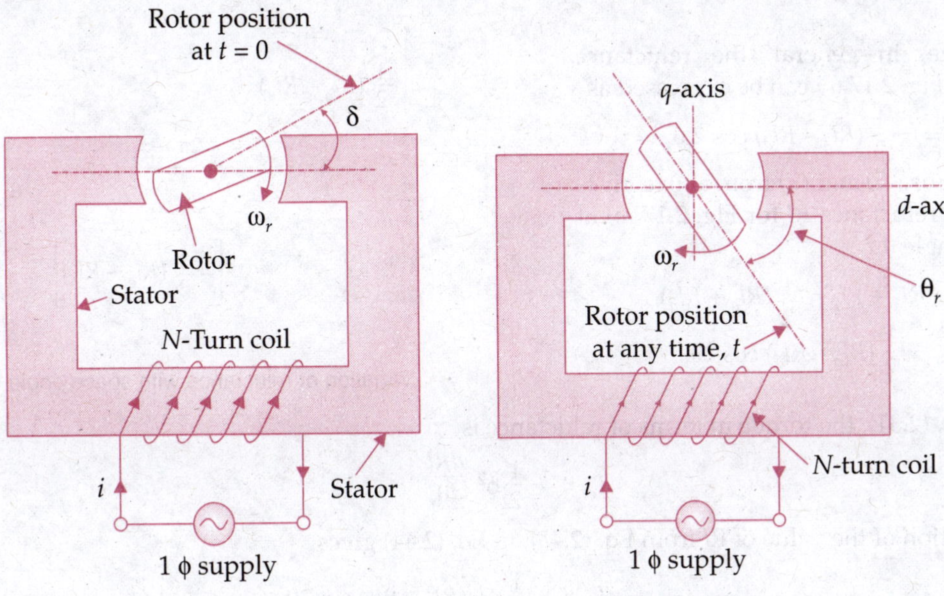

Fig 2.16: Single-phase reluctance motor.

$\theta_r = \frac{\pi}{2}, \frac{3\pi}{2}$ etc., the reluctance offered is Rl_q. The parameters Rl_d and Rl_q are called direct-axis and quadrature-axis reluctances respectively. The variation of reluctance Rl with θ_r depends on the shape of the stator and rotor poles and here this variation is assumed to be a sine function of space angle θ_r as shown in Fig. 2.17 *(a)*.

An examination of Fig. 2.17 *(a)* reveals that the reluctance variation Rl with space angle θ_r can be thought of as composed of Figs. 2.17 *(b)* and 2.17 *(c)*. In Fig. 2.17 *(b)*, reluctance is constant, therefore Rl_1 can be expressed as

$$Rl_1 = \frac{1}{2}(Rl_q + Rl_d) \quad \text{...(i)}$$

In Fig. 2.17 *(c)*, reluctance Rl_2 varies sinusoidally. It can be expressed as under :

At $\theta_r = 0$, $\quad Rl_2 = -\frac{1}{2}(Rl_q - Rl_d)$

or $\quad Rl_2 = -\frac{1}{2}(Rl_q - Rl_d)\cos 0°$

At $\theta_r = 45°, Rl_2 = 0$

or $\quad Rl_2 = -\frac{1}{2}(Rl_q - Rl_d)\cos 2(\pi/4)$

At $\theta_r = 90° = \pi/2$, $\quad Rl_2 = \frac{1}{2}(Rl_q - Rl_d) = -\frac{1}{2}(Rl_q - Rl_d)\cos 2(\pi/2)$

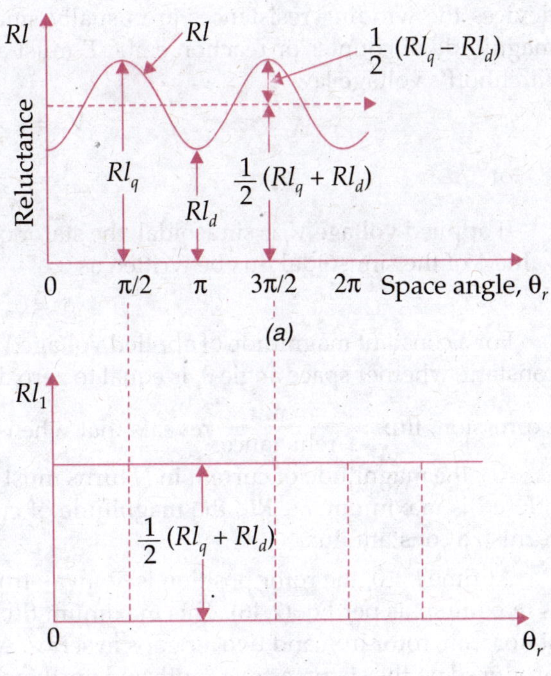

Fig 2.17: *(a)* to *(b)* Variation of reluctance with space angle θ_r.

Therefore, in general, the reluctance variation in Fig. 2.17 *(c)* can be expressed as

$$Rl_2 = -\frac{1}{2}(Rl_q - Rl_d)\cos 2\theta_r \quad \text{...(ii)}$$

Sum of Eqs., *(i)* and *(ii)* from above gives the value of reluctance Rl for Fig. 2.17 *(a)* at any space angle θ_r.

$$\therefore \quad Rl = Rl_1 + Rl_2 = \frac{1}{2}(Rl_q + Rl_d) - \frac{1}{2}(Rl_q - Rl_d)\cos 2\theta_r \quad \text{...(2.43)}$$

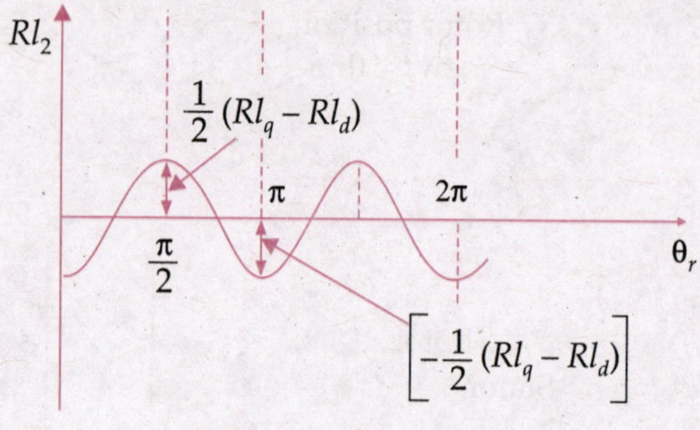

(c)

Fig 2.17: *(c)* Variation of reluctance with space angle θ_r.

From Eq. (2.31), the torque in terms of reluctance is

$$T_e = -\frac{1}{2}\phi^2 \frac{dRl}{d\theta_r} \quad \text{...(2.44)}$$

Substitution of the value of Rl from Eq. (2.43), in Eq. (2.44) gives

$$T_e = -\frac{1}{2}\phi^2 (Rl_q - Rl_d)\sin 2\theta_r \quad \text{...(2.45)}$$

Assume that the flux produced by coil m.m.f. iN is confined to the stator core. The stator winding resistance in Fig. 2.16 may be neglected, because in well-designed energy-conversion devices the winding resistances are usually small. As a consequence of these assumptions, the magnitude of counter or reaction e.m.f. E must always be equal to the applied voltage V_t, as per Kirchhoff's voltage law.

$$\therefore \quad V_t = E = \sqrt{2}\pi f N \phi_{max}$$

or

$$\phi_{max} = \frac{V_t}{\sqrt{2}\pi f N}.$$

If applied voltage V_t is sinusoidal, the stator core flux is also a sine wave. Let the instantaneous value ϕ of the sinusoidal flux be written as

$$\phi = \phi_{max}\cos \omega t \quad \text{...(2.46)}$$

For a constant magnitude of applied voltage V_t, the magnitude of stator flux ϕ must also remain constant, whether space angle θ_r is equal to zero degree, 90° or has any other value in Fig. 2.16. The expression, flux $= \dfrac{\text{m.m.f.}}{\text{reluctance}}$ reveals that when reluctance offered to constant flux is minimum, *i.e.*, Rl_d, the magnitude of current in N turns must also be minimum. Similarly when the reluctance offered is maximum, *i.e.* Rl_q, the magnitude of current in N turns must be maximum, in order to furnish a constant flux.

At time $t = 0$, the rotor position is $\delta°$ away from stator d-axis as shown in Fig. 2.16 *(a)* and flux is maximum as per Eq. (2.46). This maximum flux produced by stator, completes its path through stator iron, rotor iron and two air gaps in series. As a result of this flux path, north and south poles produced on the stator, attract south and north poles induced on the rotor–the torque so developed turns the rotor in the assumed direction of rotation *i.e.* clockwise. An alternative way of describing the above happenings is that the stator flux has a tendency to follow a minimum reluctance path (or has a tendency to shorten its magnetic path). The minimum reluctance position can be attained only if the rotor turns clockwise. If δ is taken on the other side of stator d-axis, *i.e.* opposite to that shown in Fig. 2.16 *(a)*, the rotor would rotate in an anti-clockwise direction.

For the instantaneous position of the rotor at any time t as shown in Fig. 2.16 *(b)*, the space angle θ_r can be expressed as

$$\theta_r = (\omega_r t - \delta) \quad ...(2.47)$$

where ω_r is the shaft angular velocity in rad/sec. Actually the torque developed by a singly excited reluctance motor fluctuates considerably and, therefore, the instantaneous speed is not constant. Here the torque expression is derived by assuming the rotor to be running at a constant angular velocity of ω_r rad/sec.

The difference between the time angular velocity ω (supply frequency in rad/sec. *i.e.* $\omega = 2\pi f$) and the shaft angular velocity ω_r $(= 2\pi n)$ must be kept in mind. Here n is the shaft speed in r.p.s.

Substitution of the values of ϕ and θ_r from Eqs. (2.46) and (2.47) respectively; in Eq. (2.45), gives instantaneous value of torque as

$$T_e = \frac{1}{2}\phi_{max}^2 \cos^2 \omega t\,(Rl_q - Rl_d) \sin(2\omega_r t - 2\delta)$$

Now $\cos^2 \omega t = \frac{1}{2}(1 + \cos 2\omega t)$

$$\therefore \quad T_e = -\frac{1}{4}\phi_{max}{}^2 (Rl_q - Rl_d)\,[\sin(2\omega_r t - 2\delta) + \cos 2\omega t \sin(2\omega_r \cdot t - 2\delta)] \quad ...(2.48)$$

But $\sin A \cos B = \frac{1}{2}[\sin(A + B) + \sin(A - B)]$

Therefore Eq. (2.48) can be written as

$$T_e = -\frac{1}{4}\phi_{max}{}^2 (Rl_q - Rl_d)\,[\sin(2\omega_r t - 2\delta) + \frac{1}{2}\sin(2\omega_r t + 2\omega t - 2\delta) + \frac{1}{2}\sin(2\omega_r \cdot t - 2\omega t - 2\delta)] \quad ...(2.49)$$

Eq. (2.49) gives the instantaneous value of the torque. The average value of the torque can be obtained by finding the average value of Eq. (2.49) over a complete cycle. When the shaft angular velocity ω_r is not equal to the time angular velocity ω, then average torque over the complete cycle is zero, since all the three sine terms within the bracket are varying with time.

$$\therefore \quad T_{e\,(av)} = 0 \text{ when } \omega_r \neq \omega.$$

However, if the rotor speed is such that $\omega_r = \omega$, then instantaneous torque is

$$T_e = -\frac{1}{4}\phi_{max}{}^2 (Rl_q - Rl_d)\,[\sin(2\omega t - 2\delta) + \frac{1}{2}\sin(4\omega t - 2\delta) + \frac{1}{2}\sin(-2\delta)] \quad ...(2.50)$$

In Eq. (2.50), the first two terms within the brackets are seen to vary at twice and four times the line frequency respectively. Therefore, their average value over a complete cycle is zero. However, the last term within the bracket, *i.e.*, $\frac{1}{2}\sin(-2\delta)$ does not vary with time.

$$\therefore \quad T_{e\,(av)} = -\frac{1}{4}\phi_{max}{}^2 (Rl_q - Rl_d)\left[\frac{1}{2}\sin(-2\delta)\right]$$

$$= +\frac{1}{8}\phi_{max}{}^2 (Rl_q - Rl_d) \sin 2\delta \quad ...(2.51)$$

This shows that reluctance motor can develop torque only at one speed, *i.e.* the synchronous speed. Reluctance motor, as usual, is therefore not a self-starting motor. A winding put in the rotor pole-faces, serves to produce induction motor torque during starting and as the shaft speed approaches synchronous speed, rotor pulls into step and continues running at synchronous speed.

Maximum average torque is

$$T_{e\,(av)} = \frac{1}{8}\phi_{max}{}^2 (Rl_q - Rl_d) \text{ and occurs when } \delta = 45°$$

The average torque given by Eq. (2.51) can alternatively be expressed as follows :

Direct-axis inductance, $$L_d = \frac{N^2}{Rl_d}$$

and quadrature axis inductance, $$L_q = \frac{N^2}{Rl_q}$$

$$\therefore \quad T_{e\,(av)} = \frac{\phi_{max}^{\;2}}{8}\left(\frac{N^2}{L_q} - \frac{N^2}{L_d}\right)\sin 2\delta$$

$$= \frac{1}{8}\,\omega\,\phi_{max}^{\;2}\,N^2\left(\frac{1}{\omega L_q} - \frac{1}{\omega L_d}\right)\sin 2\delta.$$

Now $\omega L_d = X_d$ is called the direct-axis reactance

and $\omega L_q = X_q$, the q-axis reactance.

Further $V_t = \sqrt{2}\,\pi f N\,\phi_{max}$

or $$N\,\phi_{max} = \frac{V_t}{\sqrt{2}\,\pi f} = \frac{\sqrt{2}V_t}{\omega}$$

$$\therefore \quad T_{e\,(av)} = \frac{V_t^2}{4\omega}\left(\frac{1}{X_q} - \frac{1}{X_d}\right)\sin 2\delta \qquad ...(2.52)$$

Also $$T_{e\,(av)} = \frac{V_t}{4\omega}\left(\frac{V_t}{X_q} - \frac{V_t}{X_d}\right)\sin 2\delta$$

or $$T_{e\,(av)} = \frac{V_t}{4\omega}(I_q - I_d)\sin 2\delta \qquad ...(2.53)$$

Here I_q, I_d are the currents taken from the supply when the rotor is held in minimum and maximum reluctance positions respectively.

Reluctances Rl_d and Rl_q depend on the geometry of the magnetic circuit and are, therefore, constant for a given motor. If the magnitude of supply voltage is constant, flux ϕ_{max} is constant, therefore, the only variable in Eq. (2.51) is the angle δ. A plot giving the variation of torque $T_{e\,(av)}$ with δ is depicted in Fig. 2.18. If load torque on the motor changes, then the angle δ adjusts itself till reluctance torque becomes equal to the load torque–in view of this, angle δ is usually called the load-angle. With the increase of load on the motor, load angle δ increases till it reaches its maximum value of 45°. Any further increase in load on the motor, would cause it to stall (fall out of step or loose synchronism).

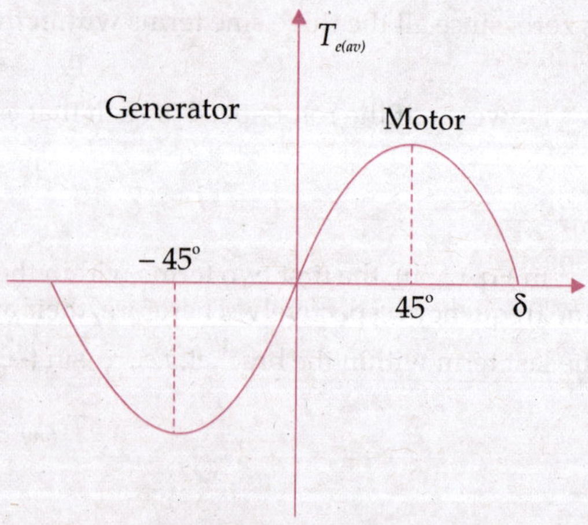

Fig 2.18: Torque-load angle characteristics of reluctance motor.

The single-phase reluctance machine can be made to work as a generator also. For this purpose, the machine must be driven first as a reluctance motor and then mechanical power is supplied to the shaft from the prime-mover. As the mechanical power input to the shaft is increased, the space position of the rotor advances so that angle δ first decreases and then becomes negative. As soon as δ becomes negative, the machine starts working as a generator converting the mechanical power input to electrical power output, (Fig. 2.18).

Single-phase reluctance motors are used extensively in driving electric clocks and other timing devices, because they operate at constant synchronous speed in case the supply frequency remains constant.

In the singly-excited motor, illustrated in Fig. 2.16, the reluctance torque is developed because the reluctance seen by the stator flux varies with rotor movement. If the salient pole rotor of Fig. 2.16 is replaced by a cylindrical rotor as shown in Fig. 2.19 *(a)* the reluctance offered to the stator flux remains constant for all rotor positions–consequently no reluctance torque is developed. It may thus be concluded that the reluctance torque is present only in those electrical machines in which the reluctance seen by the working flux varies with rotor movement. For example, in Fig. 2.19 *(b)* (a synchronous machine), the reluctance torque is present, because the reluctance offered to the stator-produced working flux is a function of space angle θ_r. In Fig. 2.19 *(c)*, the reluctance seen by the rotor-produced working flux is invariant or constant, therefore, no reluctance torque is developed.

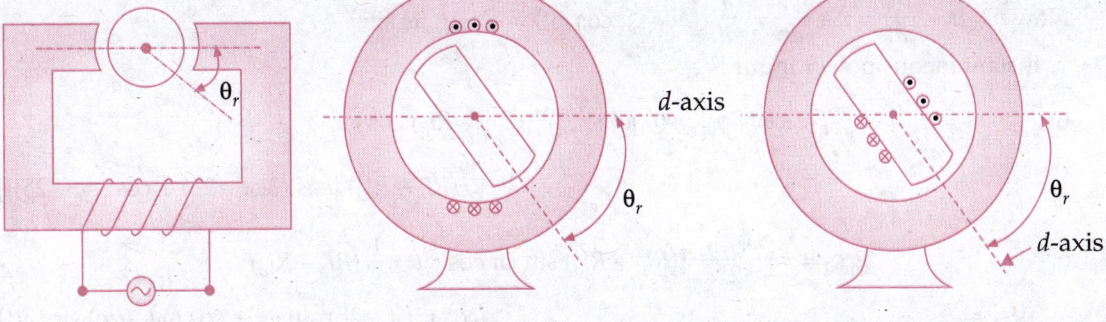

Fig 2.19: *(a)* Salient pole rotor of Fig. 2.16 is replaced by cylindrical rotor *(b)* Reluctance torque is present *(c)* Reluctance torque is absent.

Example 2.10. *For the single-phase reluctance motor illustrated in Fig. 2.16, find an expression for the intantaneous current i in terms of reluctance, maximum flux ϕ_{max}, ω, t and δ.*

If the winding resistance is neglected, develop an expression for the average electromagnetic torque in terms of reluctance and maximum flux.

Solution. The variation of reluctance with rotor angular position θ_r is illustrated in Fig. 2.17. An expression giving the value of reluctance for any space angle θ_r is given by Eq. (2.43) and it is repeated here for convenience.

$$Rl = \frac{1}{2}(Rl_q + Rl_d) - \frac{1}{2}(Rl_q - Rl_d)\cos 2\theta_r \quad ...(2.43)$$

As before, let the instantaneous value of flux be given by

$$\phi = \phi_{max} \cos \omega t \quad ...(2.46)$$

Neglecting the m.m.f. required for the iron path, the total m.m.f. around the closed magnetic path of Fig. 2.16 is given by

Total m.m.f. = coil m.m.f., $iN = \phi Rl$

or
$$i = \frac{\phi \cdot Rl}{N} \quad ...(2.54)$$

Substitution of the values of ϕ and Rl in Eq. (2.54) gives

$$i = \frac{\phi_{max}\cos \omega t}{N}\left[\frac{1}{2}(Rl_q + Rl_d) - \frac{1}{2}(Rl_q - Rl_d)\cos 2\theta_r\right]$$

As before, let $\theta_r = \omega_r t - \delta$.

$$\therefore \qquad i = \frac{\phi_{max} \cos \omega t}{2N} [(Rl_q + Rl_d) - (Rl_q - Rl_d) \cos (2\omega_r t - 2\delta)]$$

With rotor angular velocity ω_r equal to the time angular velocity ω, the expression for the instantaneous current i becomes

$$i = \frac{\phi_{max}}{2N} [(Rl_q + Rl_d) \cos \omega t - (Rl_q - Rl_d) \cos (2\omega t - 2\delta) \cos \omega t]$$

Now $\quad \cos A \cos B = \frac{1}{2} [\cos (A + B) + \cos (A - B)]$

$$\therefore \qquad i = \frac{\phi_{max}}{2N} \cdot \left[(Rl_q + Rl_d) \cos \omega t - \frac{1}{2}(Rl_q - Rl_d) \{\cos(3\omega t - 2\delta) + \cos(\omega t - 2\delta)\}\right]$$

This is the required expression for the instantaneous current i.

It is seen from current i expresion that stator coil current contains a third harmonic component.

Now $v = ir + \frac{d\psi}{dt} = 0 + \frac{d\psi}{dt} = \frac{d}{dt} (N \phi_{max} \cos \omega t) = -N\phi_{max} \omega \sin \omega t.$

$\therefore$ Instantaneous power input $P_{\text{inst}} = vi$

or
$$P_{\text{inst}} = -\omega N \phi_{max} \sin \omega t \cdot \frac{\phi_{max}}{2N} [(Rl_q + Rl_d) \cos \omega t - \frac{1}{2} (Rl_q - Rl_d) \{\cos (3\omega t - 2\delta) + \cos (\omega t - 2\delta)\}]$$

or
$$P_{\text{inst}} = -\frac{\omega \phi_{max}^2}{2} [(Rl_q + Rl_d) \sin \omega t \cos \omega t - \frac{1}{2} (Rl_q - Rl_d) \{\cos (3\omega t - 2\delta) \sin \omega t + \cos (\omega t - 2\delta) \sin \omega t\}]$$

But $\sin A \cos B = \frac{1}{2} [\sin (A + B) + \sin (A - B)]$

$$\therefore \qquad P_{\text{inst}} = -\frac{\omega \phi_{max}^2}{2} \left[\frac{Rl_q + Rl_d}{2} \sin 2\omega t - \frac{1}{4} (Rl_q - Rl_d) \{\sin (4\omega t - 2\delta) + \sin (-2\omega t + 2\delta) + \sin (2\omega t - 2\delta) + \sin 2\delta\}\right]$$

Since $\sin (-2\omega t + 2\delta) + \sin (2\omega t - 2\delta) = 0$, we get

$$P_{\text{inst}} = -\frac{\omega \phi_{max}^2}{2} \left[\frac{Rl_q + Rl_d}{2} \sin 2\omega t - \frac{1}{4} (Rl_q - Rl_d) \{\sin (4\omega t - 2\delta) + \sin 2\delta\}\right]$$

The first two sine terms within the bracket vary at twice and four times the line frequency respectively–their average value is, therefore, zero. The third sine term does not vary with time. Therefore, average value of the above equation is

$$P_{\text{inst}} = -\frac{\omega \phi_{max}^2}{2} \left[-\frac{1}{4}(Rl_q - Rl_d) \sin 2\delta\right] = \frac{\omega \phi_{max}^2}{8} (Rl_q - Rl_d) \sin 2\delta$$

$$\therefore \qquad T_{e\,(av)} = \frac{P}{\omega} = \frac{\phi_{max}^2}{8} (Rl_q - Rl_d) \sin 2\delta$$

This torque expression agrees with that already obtained in Eq. (2.51).

Example 2.11. *For the electromagnetic device shown in Fig. 2.20, the cross-sectional area normal to the flux is A and the reluctance is offered by air gap alone. Compute the average force on the movable member in terms of N, x, A etc. when*

(a) $i = I_m \cos \omega t$ *(b)* $v = V_m \cos \omega t$

Solution. *(a)* Reluctance offered by air gap $= \frac{x}{\mu_0 A}$.

$$\therefore \qquad L_x = \frac{N^2 \mu_0 A}{x}$$

$$W_{fld}'(i, x) = \frac{1}{2} i^2 L_x = \frac{1}{2} i^2 \frac{N^2 \mu_0 A}{x}$$

From Eq. (2.26),

$$f_e = \frac{\partial W_{fld}'(i,x)}{\partial x} = -\frac{1}{2} i^2 \frac{N^2 \mu_0 A}{x^2}$$

$$= -\frac{1}{2} \frac{N^2 \mu_0 A}{x^2} I_m^2 \cos^2 \omega t$$

$$= -\frac{1}{2} \frac{N^2 \mu_0 A}{x^2} I_m^2 \left[\frac{1+\cos 2\omega t}{2}\right]$$

$$\therefore \qquad f_{e\,(av)} = -\frac{1}{4} \frac{N^2 \mu_0 A}{x^2} I_m^2$$

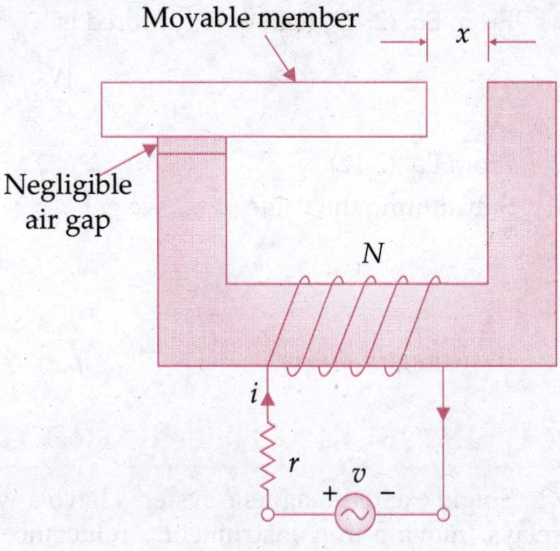

Fig 2.20: Pertaining to Example 2.11.

(b) From Eq. (2.31),

$$f_e = -\frac{1}{2} \phi^2 \frac{dRl}{dx} = -\frac{1}{2} \phi^2 \frac{1}{\mu_0 A} \qquad \ldots(i)$$

For the electric circuit, $\qquad v = ir + L_x \dfrac{di}{dt}$

For $v = V_m \cos \omega t$, its steady state solution is

$$\bar{I} = \frac{V_m}{\sqrt{r^2 + \omega^2 L_x^2}} \angle -\tan^{-1} \frac{\omega L_x}{r}$$

$$\therefore \qquad i = \frac{V_m}{\sqrt{r^2 + \omega^2 L_x^2}} \cos\left(\omega t - \tan^{-1} \frac{\omega L_x}{r}\right)$$

Now

$$\phi = \frac{Ni}{Rl} = \frac{N V_m \mu_0 A}{x\sqrt{r^2 + \omega^2 L_x^2}} \cos\left(\omega t - \tan^{-1} \frac{\omega L_x}{r}\right)$$

Substituting this value of ϕ in force expression *(i)*,

$$f_e = -\frac{1}{2} \frac{N^2 V_m^2 \mu_0^2 A^2 \cos^2\left(\omega t - \tan^{-1} \frac{\omega L_x}{r}\right)}{\mu_0 A\left[x^2 (r^2 + \omega^2 L_x^2)\right]}$$

Substitution of $L_x = \dfrac{N^2 \mu_0 A}{x}$ gives

$$f_e = -\frac{1}{2} \frac{N^2 V_m^2 \mu_0 A}{\left[r^2 x^2 + (\omega N^2 \mu_0 A)^2\right]} \cos^2\left(\omega t - \tan^{-1} \frac{\omega L_x}{r}\right)$$

$$\therefore \qquad f_{e\,(av)} = -\frac{1}{4} \frac{V_m^2 N^2 \mu_0 A}{\left[(rx)^2 + (\omega N^2 \mu_0 A)^2\right]}$$

Part *(b)* of this example can also be solved as under :

$$L_x = \frac{N^2 \cdot \mu_0 A}{x}$$

$$\psi_x = N\phi = \frac{N^2 V_m \mu_0 A}{x\sqrt{r^2 + \omega^2 L_x^2}} \cos\left(\omega t - \tan^{-1} \frac{\omega t}{r}\right)$$

From Eq. (2.12), field energy stored is

$$W_{fld} = \frac{1}{2}\frac{\Psi_x^2}{L_x} = \frac{1}{2}\frac{\Psi_x^2 \cdot x}{N^2\mu_0 A}$$

From Eq. (2.12),

$$f_e = -\frac{\partial W_{fld}(\Psi, x)}{\partial x} = -\frac{1}{2}\frac{\Psi_x{}^2}{N^2\mu_0 A}$$

Substituting the value of ψ_x, we get

$$f_e = -\frac{1}{2}\frac{N^2 V_m^2 \mu_0 A}{r^2x^2 + (\omega N^2\mu_0 A)^2}\cos^2\left(\omega t - \tan^{-1}\frac{\omega L}{r}\right)$$

Its average value is

$$f_{e\text{-}(av)} = -\frac{1}{4}\frac{N^2 V_m^2 \mu_0 A}{(rx)^2 + (\omega N^2\mu_0 A)^2}$$

2.4. DOUBLY-EXCITED MAGNETIC SYSTEMS

Singly excited magnetic systems have a wide variety of applications, such as electromagnets, relays, moving-iron instruments, reluctance motors etc. Most of the electromagnetic energy conversion devices belong to doubly-excited or multiply-excited magnetic systems. A doubly-excited magnetic system is one which has two independent sources of excitations, examples are synchronous machines, loudspeakers, tachometers, d.c. shunt machines etc.

Fig. 2.21 illustrates a simple model of a doubly-excited magnetic system. This model consists of stator iron, rotor iron and both are of the salient pole type. The stator with N_s turns is energised from source 1 and the rotor with N_r turns is excited from source 2. The m.m.fs. produced by both the stator and rotor windings are in the same direction and magnetic torque T_e is in the anticlockwise direction as shown in Fig. 2.21. For convenience, magnetic saturation and hysteresis are neglected.

The differential electrical energy input to a single-excited magnetic system, from Eq. (2.7), is given by

$$dW_{elec} = i d\psi$$

Therefore, the differential electrical energy input dW_{elec} from two energy sources 1 and 2, in Fig. 2.21, is

$$dW_{elec} = i_s d\psi_s + i_r d\psi_r \qquad ...(2.55)$$

Here ψ_s and ψ_r are the instantaneous total flux linkages of stator and rotor windings respectively. Since the magnetic saturation is neglected, ψ_s and ψ_r can be expressed in terms of self and mutual inductances.

$$\therefore \quad \left.\begin{aligned} \psi_s &= L_s i_s + M_{sr}\, i_r \\ \text{and} \quad \psi_r &= L_r i_r + M_{rs}\, i_s \end{aligned}\right\} \qquad ...(2.56)$$

where L_s = self-inductance of stator winding

L_r = self-inductance of rotor winding

and $M_{sr} = M_{rs}$ = mutual inductance between stator and rotor windings.

In Fig. 2.21, initially the space angle between rotor and stator axes is θ_r and both the currents i_s and i_r are assumed zeros. Now the stator and rotor coils are switched on to their respective energy sources, so that the currents rise from zero to i_s and i_r respectively. If the rotor is not allowed to move, then dW_{mech} is zero and Eq. (2.3) becomes

$$dW_{elec} = 0 + dW_{fld}$$

Thus, with the rotor held fixed, all the electric energy supplied by the two supply sources, is stored in the magnetic field.

From Eq. (2.55),

$$\begin{aligned} dW_{fld} &= dW_{elec} = i_s d\psi_s + i_r d\psi_r \\ &= i_s d(L_s i_s + M_{sr} i_r) + i_r d(L_r i_r + M_{rs} i_s) \end{aligned} \qquad ...(2.57)$$

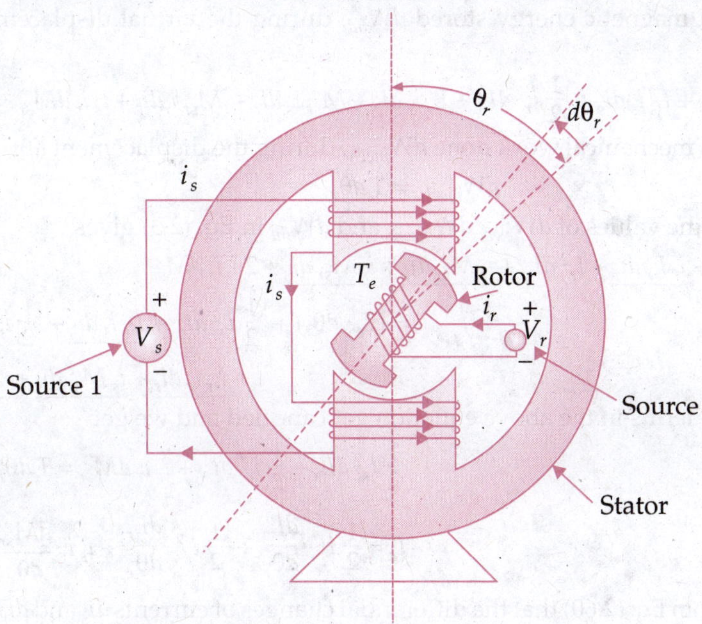

Fig 2.21: Doubly-excited magnetic system.

From Example (2.7), $$L_s = \frac{N_s^2}{Rl_s}, L_r = \frac{N_r^2}{Rl_r}$$

From Eq. (1.90), $$M = \frac{N_1\Phi_2}{i_2} = \frac{N_1}{i_2}\cdot\frac{N_2 i_2}{Rl} = \frac{N_1 N_2}{Rl}$$

Similarly, $$M_{sr} = M_{rs} = \frac{N_s N_r}{Rl_{sr}}$$

where Rl_s = reluctance seen by the stator flux

Rl_r = reluctance seen by the rotor flux

and Rl_{sr} = reluctance seen by the resultant of stator and rotor fluxes.

Since the rotor is not allowed to move, the reluctances and therefore the inductances are constant. In view of this, the differential changes in inductances, *i.e.* dL_s, dL_r and dM_{sr} in Eq. (2.57) are all zeros.

Therefore, from Eq. (2.57), $$dW_{fld} = i_s L_s di_s + i_s M_{sr} di_r + i_r L_r di_r + i_r M_{sr} di_s$$
$$= i_s L_s di_s + i_r L_r di_r + M_{sr} d\,(i_s i_r)$$

The magnetic field energy stored in establishing the currents from zero to i_s and i_r is given by

$$W_{fld} = L_s \int_0^{i_s} i_s\, di_s + L_r \int_0^{i_r} i_r\, di_r + M_{sr} \int_0^{i_s i_r} d(i_s i_r).$$

$$= \frac{1}{2} i_s^2 L_s + \frac{1}{2} i_r^2 L_r + M_{rs}\, i_s\, i_r \quad ...(2.58)$$

For obtaining the magnetic torque T_e, assume the rotor to move through a virtual displacement $d\theta_r$ in the direction of T_e as shown in Fig. 2.21. With rotor movement, reluctances Rl_s, Rl_r, Rl_{sr}, and therefore inductances L_s, L_r, M_{sr} must vary. Therefore, the differential electrical energy input $dW_{elec.}$ during virtual displacement $d\theta_r$, from Eq. (2.57) is,

$$dW_{elec} = i_s\, d\,[L_s\, i_s + M_{sr}\, i_r] + i_r\, d\,[L_r\, i_r + M_{sr}\, i_s]$$
$$= i_s\, L_s\, di_s + i_s^2\, dL_s + i_s\, M_{sr}\, di_r + i_s\, i_r\, dM_{sr} + i_r\, L_r\, di_r + i_r^2\, dL_r + i_r\, M_{sr}\, di_s + i_r i_s\, dM_{sr}$$

The differential magnetic energy stored dW_{fld}, during the virtual displacement $d\theta_r$, from Eq. (2.58), is

$$dW_{fld} = \frac{1}{2} i_s^2\, dL_s + L_s\, i_s\, di_s + \frac{1}{2} i_r^2\, dL_r + L_r\, i_r\, di_r + M_{sr}\, i_s\, di_r + M_{sr}\, i_r di_s + i_s\, i_r\, dM_{sr}$$

The differential mechanical work done dW_{mech}, during the displacement $d\theta_r$, is

$$dW_{mech} = T_e d\theta_r$$

Substitution of the values of dW_{elec}, dW_{mech} and dW_{fld} in Eq. (2.3) gives

$$\underline{i_s L_s di_s} + i_s^2\, dL_s + \underline{i_r L_r di_r} + i_r^2\, dL_r + \underline{i_s M_{sr} di_r} + \underline{i_r M_{sr} di_s} + 2\, i_s i_r\, dM_{sr}$$
$$= (T_e \cdot d\theta_r) + \frac{1}{2} i_s^2\, dL_s + \underline{L_s\, i_s\, di_s} + \frac{1}{2} i_r^2\, dL_r$$
$$+ \underline{L_r\, i_r\, di_r} + \underline{i_s\, M_{sr}\, di_r} + \underline{i_r\, M_{sr} di_s} + i_s\, i_r\, dM_{sr}$$

The underlined terms in the above equation get canceled and we get

$$\frac{1}{2} i_s^2\, dL_s + \frac{1}{2} i_r^2\, dL_r + i_s\, i_r\, dM_{sr} = T_e d\theta_r \qquad ...(2.59)$$

or

$$T_e = \frac{1}{2} i_s^2 \frac{dL_s}{d\theta_r} + \frac{1}{2} i_r^2 \frac{dL_r}{d\theta_r} + i_s\, i_r \frac{dM_{sr}}{d\theta_r} \qquad ...(2.60)$$

It can be seen from Eq. (2.60) that the differential changes of currents di_s and di_r do not contribute to the production of magnetic torque T_e. It may therefore be stated that torque T_e depends on *(i)* the instantaneous values of currents i_s and i_r and *(ii)* the angular rate of change of inductances.

If Eq. (2.58) for W_{fld} is differentiated with respect to the space angle θ_r, but with constant currents, the right hand side of Eq. (2.60) is obtained. Therefore, magnetic torque T_e can also be obtained from the space derivative of field energy expression, *i.e.*

$$T_e = \frac{\partial W_{fld}'}{\partial \theta_r} (i_s, i_r, \theta_r) \qquad ...(2.61)$$

Here W_{fld} must be expressed in terms of i_s, i_r and θ_r and when partial derivative is taken, currents are kept constant.

Integration of Eq. (2.57) for W_{elec}, with constant currents, gives

$$W_{elec} = i_s^2\, L_s + i_r^2\, L_r + 2 i_s\, i_r\, dM_{sr} \qquad ...(2.62)$$

For a linear magnetic circuit, $W_{fld} = W_{fld}'$, therefore Eq. (2.61) can be written as

$$T_e = \frac{\partial W_{fld}'}{\partial \theta_r} (i_s, i_r, \theta_r) \qquad ...(2.62a)$$

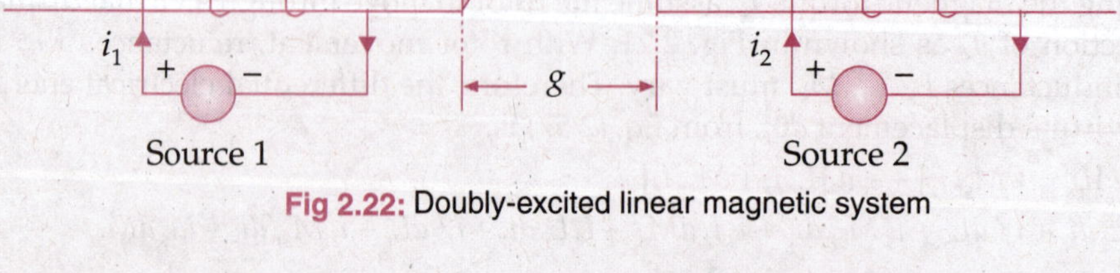

Fig 2.22: Doubly-excited linear magnetic system

Comparison of Eqs. (2.58), (2.59) and (2.62) reveals that if the electrical energy input takes place at constant currents as given by Eq. (2.62), then half of it is converted to mechanical energy, Eq. (2.59) and the remaining half is stored in the magnetic field at constant currents, Eq. (2.58). In other words, the magnetic energy stored at constant currents is equal to the mechanical work done.

The linear magnetic force f_e, for a doubly-excited magnetic system can be obtained by referring to Fig. 2.22.

The differential electrical energy input dW_{elec}, from two energy sources is

$$dW_{elec} = i_1\, d\psi_1 + i_2\, d\psi_2$$

Here $\psi_1 = L_1 i_1 + M_{12} i_2$

and $\psi_2 = L_1 i_2 + M_{21} i_1$

also $M_{12} = M_{21}$

The magnitude of magnetic force f_e can be obtained by adopting the procedure as followed for magnetic torque T_e. It will be found to have the expression

$$f_e = \frac{1}{2} i_1^2 \frac{dL_1}{dx} + \frac{1}{2} i_2^2 \frac{dL_2}{dx} + i_1 i_2 \frac{dM_{12}}{dx} \qquad \text{...(2.63a)}$$

or

$$f_e = \frac{\partial W_{fld}}{\partial x}(i_1, i_2, x) \qquad \text{...(2.63b)}$$

$$= \frac{\partial W_{fld}'}{\partial x}(i_1, i_2, x) \qquad \text{...(2.63c)}$$

An examination of Eqs. (2.61) and (2.63) reveals that the magnetic torques and forces act in such a direction as to tend to increase the field energy at constant currents.

2.4.1. Electromagnetic and Reluctance Torques

The total torque developed by the doubly-excited magnetic system is given by Eq. (2.60). This torque expression will now be examined in detail and some interesting conclusions will be obtained.

In Fig. 2.21, if $i_r = 0$, then from Eq. (2.60),

$$T_e = \frac{1}{2} i_s^2 \frac{dL_s}{d\theta_r} \qquad \text{...(2.64a)}$$

and if

$$i_s = 0,\ T_e = \frac{1}{2} i_r^2 \frac{dL_r}{d\theta_r} \qquad \text{...(2.64b)}$$

Eq. (2.64*a*) shows that even with $i_r = 0$, the torque can be developed, because the reluctance Rl_s seen by the stator-produced flux changes with rotor position. A change of Rl_s varies the stator self-inductance L_s with θ_r. Similarly, Eq. (2.64*b*) shows that with $i_s = 0$, the torque can be developed, because L_r is a function of rotor position. In view of this, the torque expressions given by Eq. (2.64) are called reluctance torques. Therefore, in Fig. (2.21), the reluctance torque is present with any one of the currents acting alone. The physical concepts about the development of reluctance torques in Fig. (2.21) is also important. If only the stator is excited, then the stator flux would have a tendency to follow a minimum reluctance path and for doing this, the rotor turns anticlockwise. Now if only the rotor is excited, the rotor flux would have a tendency to follow a minimum reluctance path and for achieving this, the rotor again turns anticlockwise.

In Fig. 2.21, suppose the salient pole rotor is replaced by cylindrical rotor and is excited as before, by current i_r. Then torque expression from Eq. (2.60) becomes

$$T_e = \frac{1}{2} i_r^2 \frac{dL_r}{d\theta_r} + i_s i_r \cdot \frac{dM_{sr}}{d\theta_r} \qquad \text{...(2.65)}$$

The reluctance torques term $\frac{1}{2} i_s^2 \frac{dL_s}{d\theta_r}$ disappears, because now the reluctance Rl_s seen by the stator flux does not vary with rotor movement. Consequently L_s is constant and $\frac{dL_s}{d\theta_r}$ is zero.

Thus the first two terms in Eq. (2.60), involving the angular rate of change of self-inductances L_s and L_r, represent reluctance torques for the mechanical structure of Fig. 2.21.

The last term $i_s i_r \frac{dM_{sr}}{d\theta_r}$ represents that component of total torque, which depends on the currents in both the stator and rotor windings and also on the angular rate of change of mutual inductance M_{sr}. This component of torque is commonly called the *electromagnetic torque* of electromagnetic-energy conversion devices. An examination of $i_s i_r \frac{dM_{sr}}{d\theta_r}$ reveals that the electromagnetic torque can exist only if *(i)* the two windings, one on stator and the other on the rotor, are mutually coupled and *(ii)* both the windings carry currents.

The physical concept about the development of electromagnetic torque in Fig. 2.21 is as follows. The north, south poles produced on stator by i_s and south, north poles produced on rotor by i_r, attract each other tending to align their fields. The torque so developed by the interaction of stator and rotor magnetic fields is the electromagnetic or interaction torque.

It should be noted that the reluctance torque $\left(\frac{1}{2} i_s^2 \frac{dL_s}{d\theta_r} \text{ or } \frac{1}{2} i_r^2 \frac{dL_r}{d\theta_r}\right)$ does not depend on the direction of currents in stator or rotor windings. But the interaction torque $[i_s i_r \frac{dM_{sr}}{d\theta_r}]$ does depend on the direction of currents i_s and i_r. In Fig. 2.21, with the given direction of currents i_s and i_r, the electromagnetic, or interaction, torque is anticlockwise as shown. If direction of current, say i_r, is reversed in Fig. 2.21, the interaction torque would be opposite to that shown in Fig. 2.21, *i.e.* in the clockwise direction; but the direction of reluctance torque would still be in the same direction as before *i.e.* anticlockwise.

2.5. ELEMENTARY SYNCHRONOUS MACHINES

In this article torque expressions, in case of elementary synchronous machines, are derived from a consideration of the magnetic field energy stored.

(a) **Single-phase cylindrical rotor machine.** The basic form of an elementary single-phase synchronous machine of cylindrical rotor type is shown in Fig. 2.23 *(a)*. The variation of stator to rotor mutual inductance M_{sr} can be determined by connecting a single-phase supply to stator winding and a voltmeter across rotor winding. When $\theta_r = 0$, the flux linkages with the rotor are maximum and this is indicated by a maximum voltmeter reading, therefore, mutual inductance between stator and rotor is maximum, *i.e.*, $M_{sr} = M_{max}$ for $\theta_r = 0$. When $\theta_r = \frac{\pi}{2}$, the voltmeter reading is zero, because the stator winding axis is perpendicular to the rotor winding axis–therefore the mutual inductance M_{sr} is zero for $\theta_r = \pi/2$. When $\theta_r = \pi$, the rotor flux linkages are again maximum but in the reversed direction. Consequently the polarity of the rotor induced e.m.f. is also reversed and therefore the mutual inductance is maximum but negative, *i.e.*, $M_{sr} = -M_{max}$ for $\theta_r = \pi$. The variation of M_{sr} from $\theta_r = 0$ to $\theta_r = \pi$ is assumed to be a cosine function of θ_r and this is shown in Fig. 2.23 *(b)*.

The reluctance seen by the stator flux does not depend on the rotor movement, therefore L_s is constant. Similarly L_r is also constant, Fig. 2.23 (*b*). It is seen from Fig. 2.23 (*b*) that the mutual inductance M_{sr} at any angle θ_r can be expressed as

$$M_{sr} = M_{max} \cos \theta_r.$$

Here θ_r is the space angle between stator and rotor field axes.

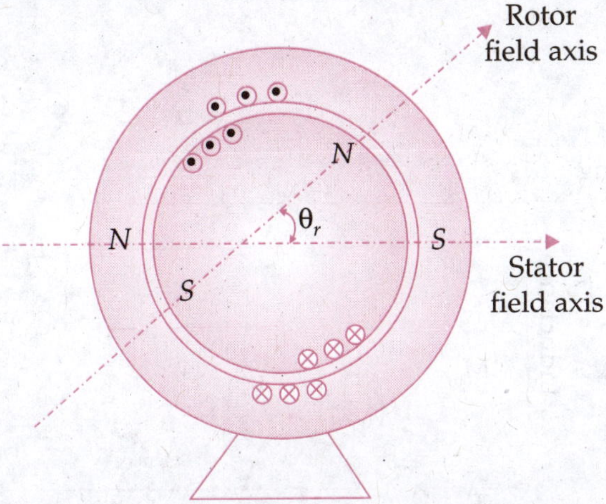

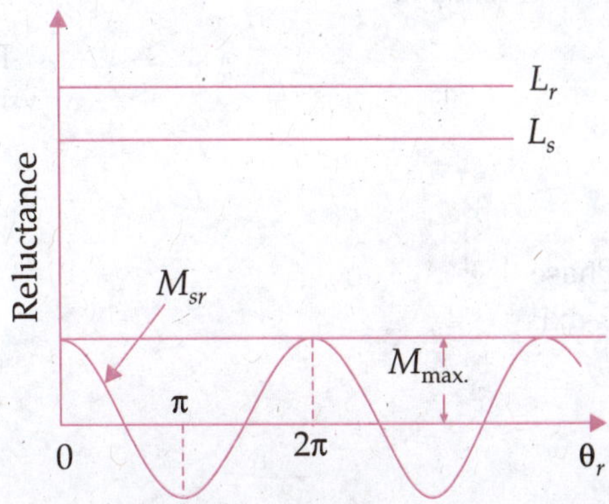

Fig 2.23: *(a)* Single-phase cylindrical rotor synchronous machine. *(b)* Inductance variations with space angle θ_r.

Let the stator and rotor instantaneous currents be i_s and i_r respectively, then

$$W_{fld}(i_s, i_r, \theta_r) = \frac{1}{2} i_s^2 L_s + \frac{1}{2} i_r^2 L_r + i_s i_r M_{sr}$$

$$= \frac{1}{2} i_s^2 L_s + \frac{1}{2} i_r^2 L_r + i_s i_r M_{max} \cos\theta_r$$

$$\therefore \quad \text{Torque, } T_e = \frac{\partial W_{fld}}{\partial \theta_r}(i_s, i_r, \theta_r)$$

$$= 0 + 0 - i_s i_r M_{max} \sin\theta_r = - i_s i_r M_{max} \sin\theta_r.$$

Negative sign indicates that the torque T_e tends to reduce the angle θ_r. This torque expression is applicable whether the rotor is revolving or stationary. In a synchronous machine, D.C. excitation is applied either to stator winding or to the rotor winding.

Let $\quad i_r = I_{dc}, \quad i_s = I_m \cos\omega t$

and $\quad \theta_r = \omega_r t - \delta.$

Here $\quad \omega_r$ = rotor angular velocity in rad/sec.

δ = rotor angular position at time $t = 0$

and $\quad I_m = \sqrt{2} I$, is the maximum value of stator current

$$\therefore \quad T_e = - I_{dc} I_m M_{max} \cos\omega t \sin(\omega_r t - \delta)$$

$$= - I_{dc} I_m M_{max} \frac{1}{2} [\sin(\omega_r t + \omega t - \delta) + \sin(\omega_r t - \delta - \omega t)]$$

If $\omega_r \neq \omega$, then $T_{e(av)} = 0$. If rotor runs at synchronous speed, *i.e.*, $\omega_r = \omega$ then

$$T_e = -\frac{I_{dc} I_m M_{max}}{2} [\sin(2\omega t - \delta) + \sin(-\delta)]$$

$$\therefore \quad T_{e\,(av)} = \frac{I_{dc} I_m M_{max}}{2} \sin\delta \qquad \text{...(2.66)}$$

(*b*) **Two-phase cylindrical rotor synchronous machine.** Fig. 2.24 (*a*) illustrates an elementary two-phase cylindrical rotor synchronous machine where two phase armature windings are designated by α, β. The space angle θ_r is the angle between field winding axis and phase α-axis.

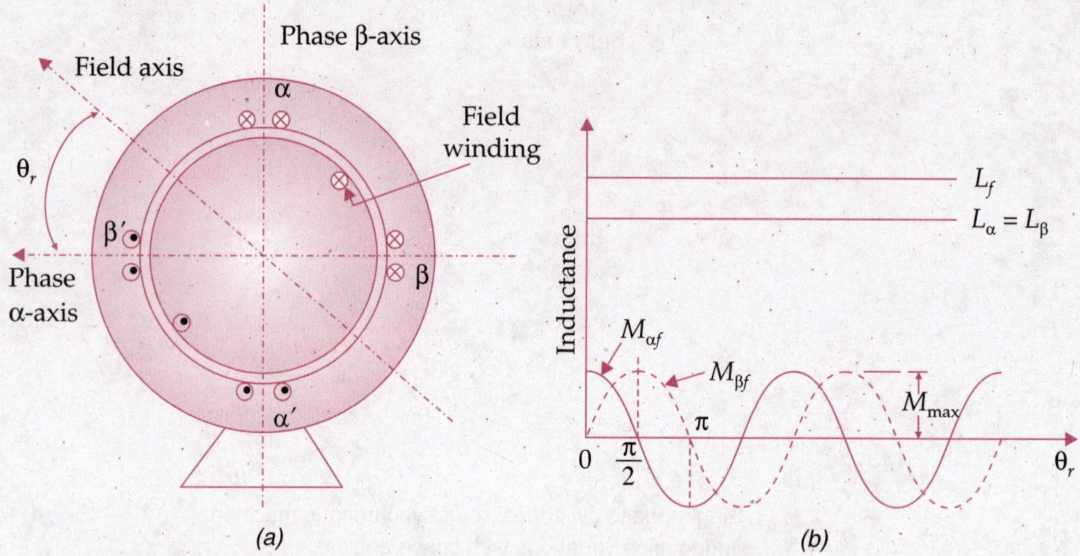

Fig 2.24: *(a)* Two-phase cylindrical rotor synchronous machine.
(b) Its inductance variations with space angle θ_r.

The variation of mutual inductance $M_{\alpha f}$ between phase α and field winding *f* and $M_{\beta f}$ between phase β and field winding *f*, can be determined by connecting a single-phase supply to rotor winding and two voltmeters, one across each phase winding of the stator. When $\theta_r = 0$, mutual flux linkages with phase α are maximum, but with phase β the flux linkages are zero. This is indicated by maximum voltmeter reading across phase α and zero voltmeter reading across phase β. Hence $M_{\alpha f} = M_{max}$ and $M_{\beta f} = 0$ for $\theta_r = 0$. When $\theta_r = \pi/2$, it can be shown that $M_{\alpha f} = 0$ and $M_{\beta f} = M_{max}$. For $\theta_r = \pi$, it can also be shown that $M_{\alpha f} = -M_{max}$ and $M_{\beta f} = 0$, [Fig. 2.24 (*b*)].

The reluctance offered to the fluxes produced by phase α and β windings does not vary with rotor movement. Therefore, self-inductance L_α, L_β for phases α, β respectively are constant and are equal to each other. Similarly, self-inductance L_f of the field winding is constant. Since the axes of phase α and phase β windings are normal to each other and air-gap is uniform, the mutual inductance $M_{\alpha\beta}$ between α, β windings is zero.

From Fig. 2.24 (*b*), $\quad M_{\alpha f} = M_{max} \cos\theta_r$

and $\quad M_{\beta f} = M_{max} \sin\theta_r$.

Let i_α, i_β be the phase currents and i_f the field current. The magnetic field energy stored is

$$W_{fld}(i_\alpha, i_\beta, i_f, \theta_r) = \frac{1}{2} i_\alpha^2 L_\alpha + \frac{1}{2} i_\beta^2 L_\beta + \frac{1}{2} i_f^2 L_f + i_\alpha i_\beta M_{\alpha\beta} + i_\alpha i_f M_{\alpha f} + i_\beta i_f M_{\beta f}$$

$$= \frac{1}{2} i_\alpha^2 L_\alpha + \frac{1}{2} i_\beta^2 L_\beta + \frac{1}{2} i_f^2 L_f + i_\alpha i_\beta M_{\alpha\beta} + i_\alpha i_f M_{max}\cos\theta_r + i_\beta i_f M_{max}\sin\theta_r$$

∴ The electromagnetic torque T_e is

$$T_e = \frac{\partial W_{fld}}{\partial \theta_r}(i_\alpha, i_\beta, i_f, \theta_r)$$

$$= -i_\alpha i_f M_{max}\sin\theta_r + i_\beta i_f M_{max}\cos\theta_r.$$

Let $\quad i_f = I_f$ (direct current in field winding)

$$i_\alpha = I_m \cos\omega t,\ i_\beta = I_m \sin\omega t$$

and $\quad \theta_r = \omega_r t - \delta$.

$$\therefore \quad T_e = -I_f I_m M_{max} \sin(\omega_r t - \delta)\cos\omega t + I_f \cdot I_m M_{max}\cos(\omega_r t - \delta)\sin\omega t$$

$$= I_f I_m M_{max}[\sin\omega t\cos(\omega_r t - \delta) - \sin(\omega_r t - \delta)\cos\omega t]$$

$$= I_f I_m M_{max}[\sin(\omega t - \omega_r t + \delta)] \quad \text{...(2.67)}$$

When $\omega_r \neq \omega$, $T_{e\,(av)} = 0$.

If the rotor is runnning at synchronous speed, then $\omega_r = \omega$.

$$\therefore \quad T_e = I_f I_m M_{max}[\sin(\omega t - \omega t + \delta)]$$

$$= I_f I_m M_{max}\sin\delta. \quad \text{...(2.68)}$$

This shows that torque T_e in a 2-phase synchronous machine is constant at all instants of time.

The voltage equation for phase α can be written as

$$v_\alpha = r_\alpha i_\alpha + p\psi_\alpha$$

But $\psi_\alpha = L_\alpha i_\alpha + M_{\alpha f} I_f = L_\alpha I_m \cos\omega t + M_{max} I_f \cos(\omega t - \delta)$

$$\therefore \quad v_\alpha = r_\alpha \cdot \sqrt{2}\, I\cos\omega t - \omega L_\alpha I_m \sin\omega t - \omega M_{max} I_f \sin(\omega t - \delta)$$

For phase β, $v_\beta = r_\beta i_\beta + p\psi_\beta$

But $\psi_\beta = L_\beta i_\beta + M_{\beta f} I_f = L_\beta \cdot I_m \sin\omega t + M_{max} I_f \sin(\omega t - \delta)$

$$\therefore \quad v_\beta = r_\beta \cdot \sqrt{2}\, I\sin\omega t + \omega L_\beta I_m \cos\omega t + \omega M_{max} I_f \cos(\omega t - \delta)$$

(c) **Two-phase salient-pole synchronous machine.** An elementary form of two-phase salient-pole synchronous machine is illustrated in Fig. 2.25. Its two-phase armature windings are designated by α, β. The space angle θ_r is the angle between field-winding axis (or rotor axis) and phase α-axis.

The variation of self-inductances L_α, L_β and mutual inductances $M_{\alpha f}$, $M_{\beta f}$ can be determined as outlined in the previous articles *(a)* and *(b)*. These inductance variations with respect to space angle θ_r are depicted in Fig. 2.26.

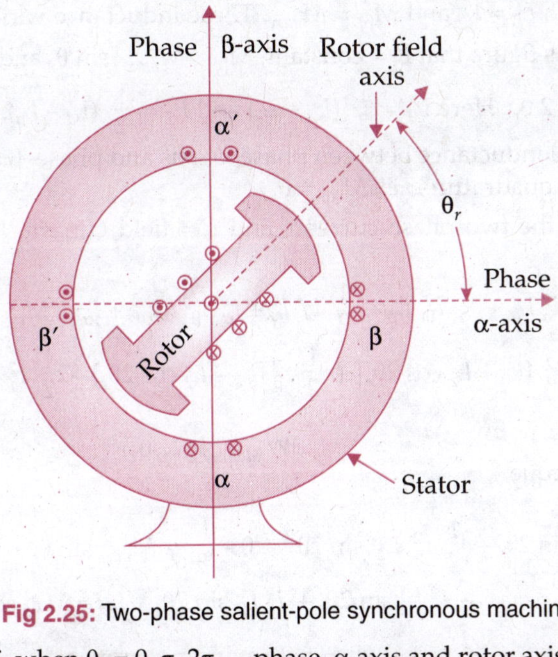

Fig 2.25: Two-phase salient-pole synchronous machine.

Phase α. In Fig. 2.25, when $\theta_r = 0, \pi, 2\pi, \ldots$, phase–α axis and rotor axis coincide, self inductance $L_\alpha = L_d$. Mutual inductance between phase–α and field winding is $M_{\alpha f} = M_{max}$ at $\theta_r = 0$, $M_{\alpha f} = 0$ at $\theta_r = \frac{\pi}{2}$, $M_{\alpha f} = -M_{max}$ at $\theta_r = \pi$ and so on. Field self-inductance L_f = constant.

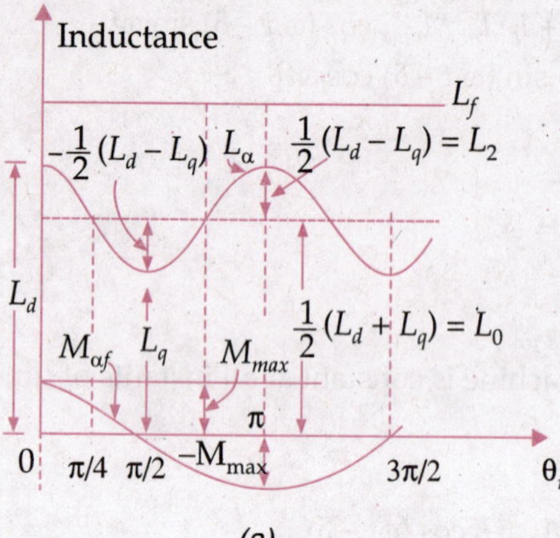

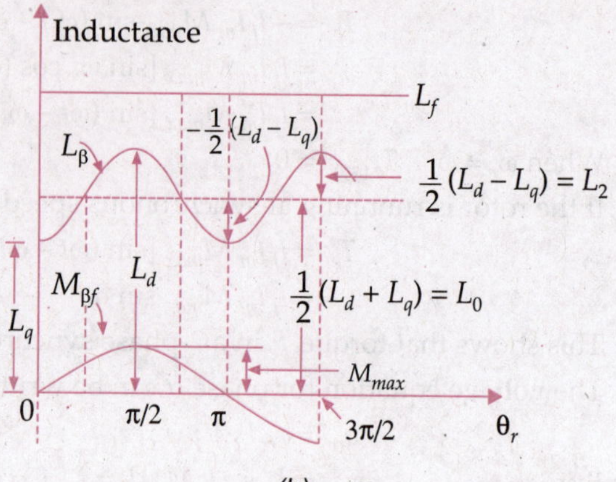

Fig 2.26: Inductance variations with space angle θ_r for Fig. 2.25.

When $\theta_r = \frac{\pi}{2}, \frac{3\pi}{2}, \frac{5\pi}{2}, ...,$ phase α axis is 90° away from rotor axis, therefore self-inductance is minimum, *i.e.* $L_\alpha = L_q$. As before, $M_{\alpha f} = 0$ at $\theta_r = \frac{\pi}{2}$. These inductance variations are shown in Fig. 2.26(*a*). It is seen from this figure that field self-inductance L_f = constant ; mutual inductance $M_{\alpha f} = M_{max} \cos \theta_r$ and phase–α self-inductance $L_\alpha = \frac{1}{2}(L_d + L_q) + \frac{1}{2}(L_d - L_q) \cos 2\theta_r = L_0 + L_2 \cos 2\theta_r$.

Phase β. In Fig. 2.25, when $\theta_r = 0, \pi, 2\pi, ...,$ plase–β axis is 90° away from rotor field axis, ∴ $L_\beta = L_q$, L_f = constant and mutual inductance $M_{\beta f} = 0$ at $\theta_r = 0°$, $M_{\beta f} = M_{max}$ at $\theta_r = \frac{\pi}{2}$, $M_{\beta f} = 0$ at $\theta_r = \pi$ and so on.

When $\theta_r = \frac{\pi}{2}, \frac{3\pi}{2}, ...,$ $L_\beta = L_d$ and $M_{\beta f} = M_{max}$. These inductance variations are shown in Fig. 2.26 *(b)*. It is seen from this figure that L_f = constant, $M_{\beta f} = M_{max} \cdot \sin \theta_r$ and $L_\beta = \frac{1}{2}(L_d + L_q) - \frac{1}{2}(L_d - L_q) \cos 2\theta_r = L_0 - L_2 \cos 2\theta_r$. Here $L_0 = \frac{1}{2}(L_d + L_q)$ and $L_2 = \frac{1}{2}(L_d - L_q)$.

Note here that mutual inductance between phase–α axis and phase–β axis is zero. It is because their magnetic axis are in quadrature, *i.e.*, $M_{\alpha\beta} = 0$.

Torque. Let i_α, i_β be the two-phase currents and i_f = field current. Now the magnetic field energy stored is

$$W_{fld}(i_\alpha, i_\beta, i_f, \theta_r) = \frac{1}{2} i_\alpha^2 L_\alpha + \frac{1}{2} i_\beta^2 L_\beta + \frac{1}{2} i_f^2 L_f + i_\alpha \cdot i_\beta \cdot M_{\alpha\beta} + i_\alpha \cdot i_f M_{\alpha f} + i_\beta i_f M_{\alpha f}.$$

$$= \frac{1}{2} i_\alpha^2 [L_0 + L_2 \cos 2\theta_r] + \frac{1}{2} i_\beta^2 [L_0 - L_2 \cos 2\theta_r] + \frac{1}{2} i_f^2 \cdot L_f + 0 + i_\alpha i_f M_{max} \cos \theta_r + i_\beta i_f M_{max} \sin \theta_r$$

∴ Electromagnetic torque, $$T_e = \frac{\partial W_{fld}(i_\alpha, i_\beta, i_f, \theta_r)}{\partial \theta_r}$$

$$\therefore T_e = -\frac{1}{2} i_\alpha^2 \cdot L_2 \cdot 2 \sin 2\theta_r + \frac{1}{2} i_\beta^2 L_2 \cdot \sin 2\theta_r + 0 - i_\alpha \cdot i_f \cdot M_{max} \sin \theta_r + i_\beta \cdot i_f M_{max} \cos \theta_r$$

$$- i_\alpha^2 L_2 \sin 2\theta_r + i_\beta^2 L_2 \sin 2\theta_r + i_\beta i_f \cdot M_{max} \cos \theta_r - i_\alpha i_f \cdot M_{max} \sin \theta_r$$

Let
I_f = field-winding current,
$i_\alpha = I_m \cos \omega t,$
$i_\beta = I_m \sin \omega t$ and $\theta_r = \omega_r t - \delta.$

$$\therefore T_e = -I_m^2 L_2 \cos^2 \omega t \cdot \sin 2\theta_r + I_m^2 L_2 \cdot \sin^2 \omega t \cdot \sin 2\theta_r + M_{max} I_f I_m \sin \omega t \cos \theta_r - M_{max} I_f I_m \cos \omega t \sin \theta_r.$$

$$= -I_m^2 L_2 \left[\frac{1+\cos 2\omega t}{2}\right] \sin (2\omega_r t - 2\delta) + I_m^2 L_2 \left[\frac{1-\cos 2\omega t}{2}\right] \sin (2\omega_r t - 2\delta) + M_{max} \cdot I_f I_m [\sin \omega t \cdot \cos (\omega_r t - \delta) - \cos \omega t \cdot \sin (\omega_r t - \delta)]$$

$$= -\frac{I_m^2 \cdot L_2}{2} \sin (2\omega_r t - 2\delta) - \frac{I_m^2 \cdot L_2}{2} \cos 2\omega t \cdot \sin (2\omega_r t - 2\delta) + \frac{I_m^2 L_2}{2} \sin (2\omega_r t - 2\delta) - \frac{I_m^2 \cdot L_2}{2} \cos 2\omega t \cdot \sin (2\omega_r t - 2\delta) + M_{max} \cdot I_f I_m [\sin (\omega t - \omega_r t + \delta)].$$

Here $\sin (A - B) = \sin A \cos B - \cos A \sin B$ is used.

Also $$\sin A \cos B = \frac{1}{2} [\sin (A - B) + \sin (A + B)]$$

$$\therefore \quad T_e = -\frac{I_m^2 L_2}{2} [\sin (2\omega_r t - 2\omega t - 2\delta) + \sin (2\omega_r t + 2\omega t - 2\delta)] + M_{max} \cdot I_f I_m \sin (\omega t - \omega_r t + \delta)$$

When $\omega_r \neq \omega$, $\quad T_{e\,(av)} = 0$

If rotor is running at synchronous speed, then $\omega_r = \omega$

$$\therefore \quad T_e = -\frac{I_m^2 L_2}{2} [\sin (-2\delta) + \sin (4\omega t - 2\delta)] + I_f I_m M_{max} \sin \delta$$

$$\therefore \quad T_{e\,(av)} = \frac{I_m^2 L_2}{2} \sin 2\delta + I_f \cdot I_m M_{max} \cdot \sin \delta$$

Substituting the value of $L_2 = \frac{1}{2} (L_d + L_q)$, we get

$$T_{e\,(av)} = \frac{1}{4} I_m^2 (L_d - L_q) \sin 2\delta + M_{max} I_f \cdot I_m \sin \delta \qquad ...(2.69)$$

If field current is reduced to zero, then

$$T_{e\,(av)} = \frac{1}{4} I_m^2 (L_d - L_q) \sin 2\delta \qquad ...(2.70)$$

Eq. (2.70) gives the reluctance torque of a salient-pole synchronous machine. The other component of torque, *i.e.* $M_{max} I_f \cdot I_m \sin \delta$ is the electromagnetic or interaction torque of the salient-pole machine.

Example 2.12. *For the doubly excited magnetic system shown in Fig. 2.21, plot the nature of the inductance variations with different rotor angular positions.*

Solution. The variation of mutual inductance M_{sr} with different rotor angular positions, can be investigated by adopting the procedure outlined in Art. 2.5 *(a)*. The inductance variations with space angle θ_r are assumed to be sinusoidal.

(i) When $\theta_r = 0$, air-gap length and therefore reluctance is minimum. Consequently the stator self-inductance $L_s \left(= \frac{N_s^2}{Rl}\right)$ and rotor self-inductance $L_r \left(= \frac{N_r^2}{Rl}\right)$ are maximum. Since the magnetic axis of both the stator and rotor coils coincide for $\theta_r = 0$, the mutual inductance is also maximum and let it be positive so that $M_{sr} = + M_{max}$.

(ii) When $\theta_r = \frac{\pi}{2}$, the air-gap length and therefore the reluctance is maximum. Therefore L_s and L_r are minimum (but not negative). The mutual inductance M_{sr} is zero, because the stator and rotor axes are normal to each other.

(iii) When $\theta_r = \pi$, air-gap length is again minimum and therefore L_s and L_r are maximum. The mutual inductance is again maximum but negative, *i.e.* $M_{sr} = -M_{max}$, as explained in Art. 2.5 *(a)*.

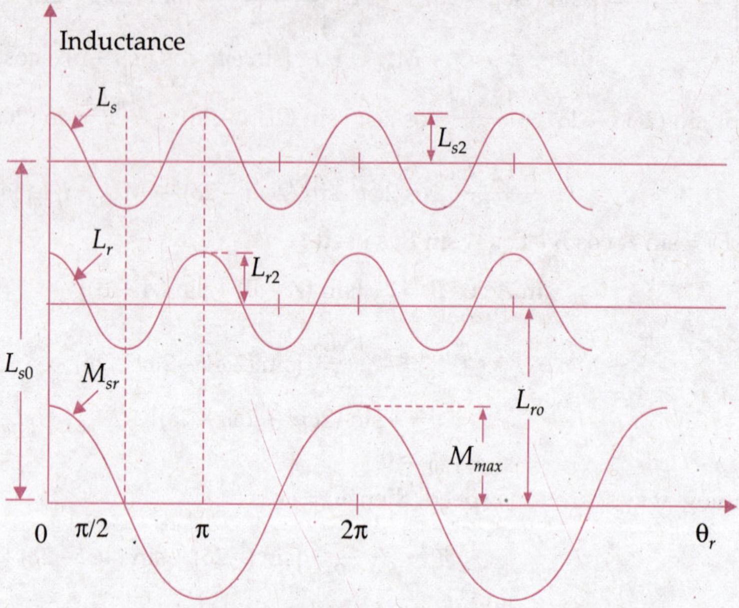

Fig 2.27: Inductance variations of Fig. 2.21, Example 2.12.

The variations of L_s, L_r and M_{sr} with different rotor angular positions θ_r, are illustrated in Fig. 2.27. The expressions for L_s, L_r and M_{sr} are

$$L_s = L_{s0} + L_{s2} \cos 2\theta_r$$

$$L_r = L_{r0} + L_{r2} \cos 2\theta_r$$

and

$$M_{sr} = M_{max} \cos \theta_r.$$

Here L_{s0}, L_{s2}, L_{r0} and L_{r2} are indicated in Fig. 2.27.

Example 2.13. *The self and mutual inductances of a doubly excited magnetic system of Fig. 2.21, are as follows.*

$$L_s = 0.6 + 0.20 \cos 2\theta_r \cdot H.$$

$$L_r = 0.75 + 0.30 \cos 2\theta_r \cdot H.$$

and

$$M_{sr} = 0.8 \cos \theta_r\, H.$$

The winding resistances are negligible.

(a) For stationary rotor at an angular position of $\theta_r = 60°$, find the magnitude and direction of torque when the currents in the arrow directions of Fig. 2.21 are :

(i) $i_s = 20$ *A d.c. and* $i_r = 10$ *A d.c.*

(ii) $i_s = 20$ *A d.c. and* $i_r = -10$ *A d.c.*

(iii) $i_s = 20$ *A d.c. and* $i_r = 0$ *A.*

(b) The rotor winding is now short-circuited and a sinusoidal current of 20 A r.m.s. flows in stator winding. Find again the magnitude and direction of torque for stationary rotor at $\theta_r = 60°$.

(c) Repeat part (b), if the voltage applied to stator winding is sinusoidal and is of the magnitude of 314 V r.m.s. at 50 Hz.

(d) For the values of currents given in part (a i), write the stator and rotor voltage equations. Assume a rotor speed of 20 rad/sec for this part only.

Solution. For $\theta_r = 60°$; L_s, L_r, M_{sr} and their derivatives with respect to θ_r have the following values:

$$L_s = 0.6 + 0.2 \cos 120° = 0.50 \text{ H}$$

$$L_r = 0.75 + 0.3 \cos 120° = 0.60 \text{ H}$$

$$M_{sr} = 0.8 \cos 60° = 0.40 \text{ H}$$

$$\frac{dL_s}{d\theta_r} = -2 \times 0.2 \sin 2 \times 60° = -0.3464$$

$$\frac{dL_r}{d\theta_r} = -(0.3)(2) \sin 120° = -0.52$$

and
$$\frac{dM_{sr}}{d\theta_r} = -0.8 \sin 60° = -0.693$$

(a) (i) From Eq. (2.60)

$$T_e = \frac{1}{2} i_s^2 \frac{dL_s}{d\theta_r} + \frac{1}{2} i_r^2 \frac{dL_s}{d\theta_r} + i_s i_r \frac{dM_{sr}}{d\theta_r}$$

Substitution of the numerical values gives

$$T_e = \frac{1}{2}(20)^2(-0.3464) + \frac{1}{2}(10)^2(-0.52) + (20)(-10)(-0.693)$$
$$= -233.88 \text{ N-m.}$$

Since torque is negative, it acts in such a direction as to decrease θ_r, *i.e.* in counter-clockwise direction of Fig. 2.21.

(ii)
$$T_e = \frac{1}{2}(20)^2(-0.3464) + \frac{1}{2}(-10)^2(-0.52) + (20)(-10)(-0.693)$$
$$= -69.28 - 26 + 138.6 = 43:32 \text{ N-m.}$$

Since torque is positive, it acts in clockwise direction.

(iii)
$$T_e = \frac{1}{2}(20)^2(-0.3464)$$
$$= -69.28 \text{ N-m. (counter-clockwise)}$$

(b) For rotor circuit,
$$v_r = r_r i_r + \frac{d\psi_r}{dt}$$

Since rotor winding is short-circuited, $v_r = 0$

$$\therefore \quad 0 = 0 + \frac{d\psi_r}{dt}$$

But
$$\psi_r = L_r i_r + M_{sr} i_s$$

$$\therefore \quad \frac{d}{dt}(\psi_r) = \frac{d}{dt}(L_r i_r + M_{sr} i_s) = 0$$

or
$$\frac{d}{dt}(L_r i_r) = -\frac{d}{dt}(M_{sr} i_s)$$

or
$$L_r i_r = -M_{sr} i_s$$

i.e.
$$i_r = -\frac{M_{sr}}{L_r} i_s \qquad \text{...(2.71)}$$

It is given that $i_s = \sqrt{2}\,(20) \sin \omega t$. Therefore, from Eq. (2.71),

$$i_r = -\frac{M_{sr}}{L_r}\sqrt{2}\,(20)\sin\omega t = -\frac{0.40}{0.60}\sqrt{2}\,(20)\sin\omega t$$

$$= -\frac{40}{3}\sqrt{2}\sin\omega t$$

Substitution of the values in Eq. (2.60) gives

$$T_e = \frac{1}{2}(20\sqrt{2}\sin\omega t)^2(-0.3464) + \frac{1}{2}\left(\frac{40\sqrt{2}}{3}\sin\omega t\right)^2(-0.52)$$

$$+ (20\sqrt{2})\left(\frac{-40\sqrt{2}}{3}\right)(-0.693)\sin^2\omega t$$

$$= [-138.56 - 92.45 + 369.60]\sin^2\omega t = 138.59\left(\frac{1-\cos 2\omega t}{2}\right)$$

$$\therefore \quad T_{e\,(av)} = 69.295 \text{ N-m (clockwise)}$$

(c) Now the voltage impressed on the stator winding is

$$v_s = (\sqrt{2})\,314\sin\omega t$$

But
$$v_s = r_s i_s + \frac{d\psi_s}{dt} = \frac{d\psi_s}{dt}$$

Also
$$\psi_s = L_s i_s + M_{sr} i_r$$

Substitution of i_r from Eq. (2.71), gives

$$\psi_s = L_s i_s - \frac{M_{sr}^2}{L_r} i_s = \left(L_s - \frac{M_{sr}^2}{L_r}\right) i_s = L_s' i_s$$

where L_s' is called the short-circuit inductance of stator winding.

$$\therefore \quad L_s' = \left(L_s - \frac{M_{sr}^2}{L_r}\right) = \left[0.5 - \frac{(0.4)^2}{0.6}\right] = 0.23 \text{ H.}$$

$$\therefore \quad v_s = \frac{d\psi_s}{dt} = \frac{d}{dt}(i_s L_s') = 314\sqrt{2}\sin\omega t$$

or
$$i_s L_s' = \int 314.\sqrt{2}\sin\omega t \cdot dt = -\frac{314\sqrt{2}}{\omega}\cos\omega t$$

$$= -\frac{314\sqrt{2}}{314}\cos 314\,t = -\sqrt{2}\cos 314\,t.$$

$$\therefore \quad i_s = -\frac{1.414}{0.23}\cos 314\,t = -6.15\cos 314\,t$$

From Eq. (2.71)
$$i_r = -\frac{M_{sr}}{L_r} i_s = +\frac{0.4}{0.6}(6.15)\cos 314\,t = 4.1\cos 314\,t$$

For $\theta_r = 60°$,
$$T_e = \frac{1}{2}(-6.15\cos 314\,t)^2(-0.3464) + \frac{1}{2}(4.1\cos 314\,t)^2(-0.52)$$

$$+ (-6.15\cos 314\,t)(4.1\cos 314\,t)(-0.693)$$

$$= -6.55\cos^2 314\,t - 4.37\cos^2 314\,t + 17.48\cos^2 314\,t$$

$$= 6.56\cos^2 314\,t = 6.56\left(\frac{1+\cos 628\,t}{2}\right)$$

$$\therefore \quad T_{e\,(av)} = \frac{6.56}{2} = 3.28 \text{ N-m (clockwise)}$$

(d) Stator and rotor voltage equations are $v_s = r_s i_s + \dfrac{d\psi_s}{dt}$

and
$$v_r = r_r i_r + \frac{d\psi_r}{dt}$$

Now $\psi_s = L_s i_s + M_{sr} i_r$

$$= (0.6 + 0.20 \cos 2\theta_r)(20) + (0.8 \cos \theta_r)10$$
$$= 12 + 4 \cos 2\theta_r + 8 \cos \theta_r$$

and $\psi_r = L_r i_r + M_{sr} i_r$

$$= (0.75 + 0.30 \cos 2\theta_r)10 + (0.8 \cos \theta_r)20$$

∴ Stator voltage equation is $v_s = 0 + \frac{d}{dt}(12 + 4 \cos 2\theta_r + 8 \cos \theta_r)$

$$= -(4 \sin 2\theta_r)\, 2\frac{d\theta_r}{dt} - 8 \sin \theta_r \frac{d\theta_r}{dt}.$$

But $\frac{d\theta_r}{dt} = \omega_r = 20 \text{ rad/sec.}$

∴ $v_s = -160 \sin 2\theta_r - 160 \sin \theta_r = -160(\sin \theta_r + \sin 2\theta_r)$

Rotor voltage equation is $v_r = 0 + \frac{d}{dt}(7.5 + 3 \cos 2\theta_r + 16 \cos \theta_r)$

$$= -(3 \sin 2\theta_r)\, 2 \times 20 - (16 \sin \theta_r)\, 20$$
$$= -120 \sin 2\theta_r - 320 \sin \theta_r = -40(8 \sin \theta_r + 3 \sin 2\theta_r).$$

Example 2.14. *A dynamometer type moving coil instrument can be represented by two coils as shown in Fig. 2.28 (a). The self and mutual inductances of the two coils are:*

$L_1 = 0.20$ *mH,* $L_2 = 0.15$ *mH and* $M_{12} = 0.08 \sin \theta$ *mH.*

The fixed and moving coils are conneted in series and the current flowing through them is $I_m \sin \omega t$. *The controlling torque produced by the helical restraining spring varies in direct proportion to the deflection angle θ and its value is 0.0144 N-m at θ = 90°.*

(a) Find an expression for torque in terms of the angular position θ.

(b) Find the time average torque in terms of θ.

(c) For I = 5, 10 and 15 amperes, sketch the variation of average torque with angle θ.

(d) Sketch also a curve showing the variation of current with θ.

(e) If the instrument is designed to read a maximum of 15 Amps, give the range of pointer deflection.

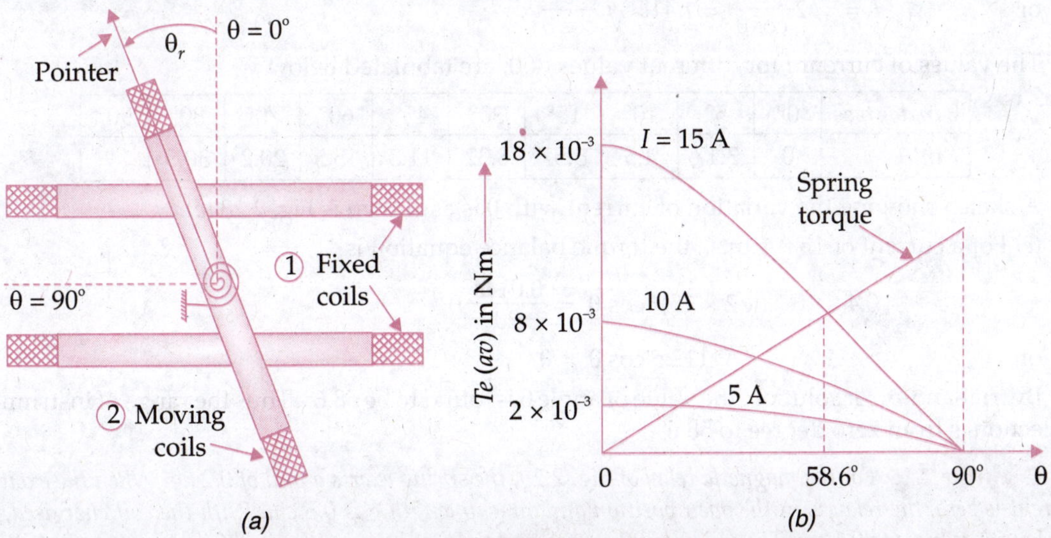

Fig 2.28: *(a)* Dynamometer type moving coil instrument.
(b) Variation of torque $T_{e(av)}$ with θ.

Solution. *(a)* The magnetic torque is given by

$$T_e = \frac{1}{2}i_1^2\frac{dL_1}{d\theta} + \frac{1}{2}i_2^2\frac{dL_2}{d\theta} + i_1 i_2\frac{dM_{12}}{d\theta}$$

Here $i_1 = i_2 = I_m \sin \omega t$, because the two coils are connected in series.

$$\therefore \quad T_e = 0 + 0 + (I_m \sin \omega t)^2 \frac{d}{d\theta}(0.08 \sin \theta)\, 10^{-3}$$

$$= 0.8 \times 10^{-4} I_m^2 \sin^2 \omega t \cos \theta \text{ N-m.}$$

(b)
$$T_e = 0.8 \times 10^{-4} I_m^2 \left(\frac{1-\cos 2\omega t}{2}\right) \cos \theta$$

$$\therefore \quad T_{e\,(av)} = 0.4 \times 10^{-4} I_m^2 \cos \theta \text{ N-m.}$$

(c) For $I = 5$ A r.m.s., $T_{e\,(av)} = (0.4 \times 10^{-4})\,(\sqrt{2} \times 5)^2 \cos \theta = 2 \times 10^{-3} \cos \theta$ N-m.

For $I = 10$ A r.m.s., $T_{e\,(av)} = 8 \times 10^{-3} \cos \theta$ N-m.

For $I = 15$ A r.m.s., $T_{e\,(av)} = 18 \times 10^{-3} \cos \theta$ N-m.

The variation of $T_{e\,(av)}$ with different values of θ is shown in Fig. 2.28 *(b)*.

(d) Let k_s be the spring constant. Then for a deflection of 90°,

$$k_s\,(90°) = 0.0144 \text{ N-m}$$

$$\therefore \quad k_s = \frac{0.0144}{90} \text{ N-m/degree.}$$

For any current I and deflection θ, the torque balance equation is given by

Spring restraining torque = deflecting torque

$$\frac{0.0144}{90}(\theta) = 0.4 \times 10^{-4}\, I_m^2 \cos \theta$$

or
$$I^2 = \frac{0.0144 \times 10^4}{90 \times 0.4 \times 2} \cdot \frac{\theta}{\cos \theta}$$

or
$$I = \sqrt{2\frac{\theta}{\cos \theta}} = 1.414\sqrt{\frac{\theta}{\cos \theta}}$$

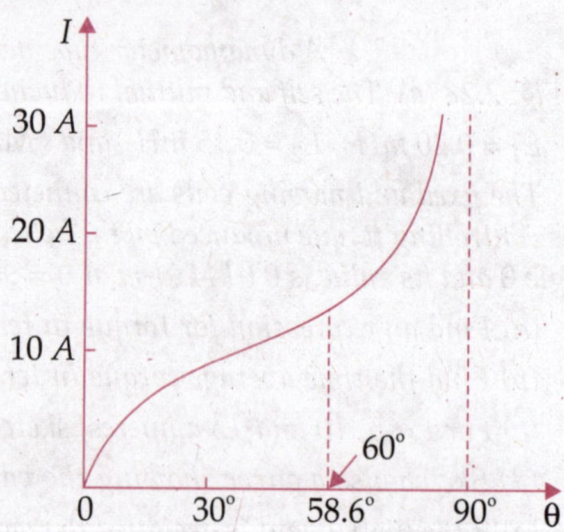

Fig 2.28: *(c)* Variation for current with angle θ.

The values of current I for different values of θ, are tabulated below :

θ in degrees	0°	5°	10°	15°	30°	45°	60°	70°	80°	90°
I in A	0	3.17	4.5	5.57	8.32	11.3	15.5	20.2	30.5	∝

A sketch showing the variation of current with θ is as shown is Fig. 2.28 *(c)*.

(e) For a current of 15 A r.m.s., the torque balance equation is

$$0.4 \times 10^{-4}\,(\sqrt{2} \times 15)^2 \cos \theta = \frac{0.0144}{90}\theta$$

or
$$112.5 \cos \theta = \theta$$

By trial-and-error solution, the value of angle θ is found to be 58.6°. Thus the range of instrument deflection is from zero degree to 58.6°.

Example 2.15. *For the magnetic relay of Fig. 2.29, the spring exerts a pull of 0.2 kg. When the exciting current is zero, the relay is in the open position and air-gap length g is 0.5 cm. With the coil energised, the gap length reduces to 0.1 cm. The coil has 2000 turns and the magnetic leakage and fringing is neglected. The magnetization curve for the relay core material is given further.*

B in T	0.20	0.40	0.60	0.80	1.00	1.20
H in ATs/m	50	100	160	225	300	400

The mean length of magnetic iron path is 20 cm and its area of cross-section throughout is 0.2 cm^2.

(a) When the relay is in open position, calculate the magnitude of the exciting current required to close it.

(b) What should be the magnitude of exciting current to keep it in the closed position?

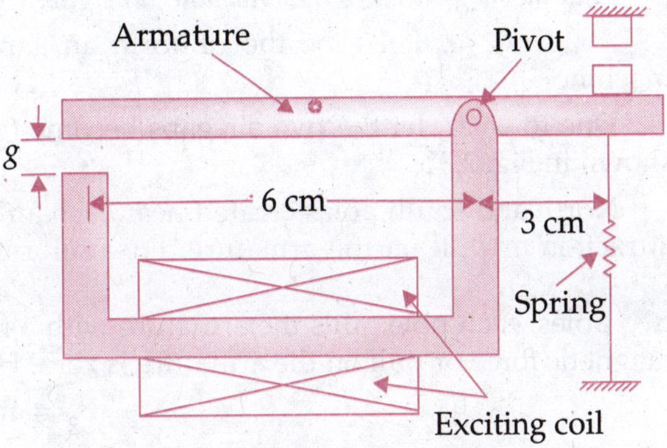

Fig 2.29: Magnetic Relay, Example 2.15.

Solution. *(a)* The electromagnetic force f_e across the gap length can be obtained from the force-balance equation, *i.e.*

$$f_e \times 6 = (0.2 \times 9.81) \times 3$$

$$\text{or} \quad f_e = \frac{(0.2 \times 9.81) \times 3}{6} = 0.981 \text{ newtons.}$$

If B_g is the air-gap flux density, then

$$f_e = \frac{1}{2}\frac{B_g^2 A}{\mu_0} = 0.981$$

$$\therefore \quad B_g^{\,2} = \frac{2 \times 0.981 \times 4\pi \times 10^{-7}}{0.2 \times 10^{-4}} = 0.1233$$

$$\text{or} \quad B_g = \sqrt{0.1233} = 0.351 \text{ T}$$

From B-H curve of Fig. 2.30, AT/m. for a flux density of 0.351 T are 87.7. Therefore total ampere-turns for iron length

$$= 0.20 \times 87.7 = 17.54$$

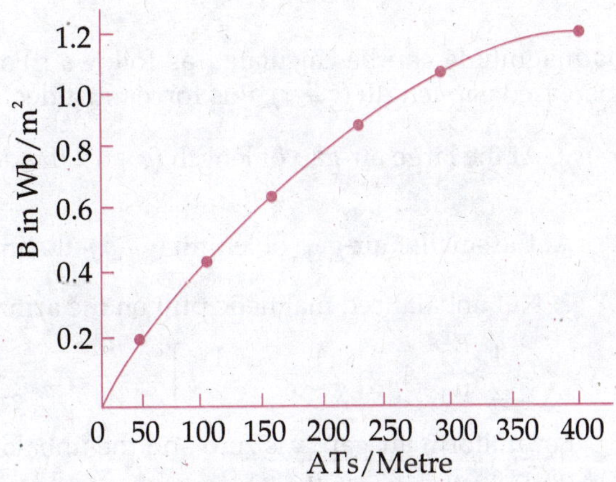

Fig 2.30: B-H curve, Example 2.15.

$$\text{Ampere-turns for air-gap} = \frac{B_g}{\mu_0} \cdot g$$

$$= \frac{(0.351)(0.5 \times 10^{-2})}{4\pi \times 10^{-7}} = 1396.58$$

$\therefore$ Total ATs for the magnetic path for an air-gap length of 0.5 cm = 1396.58 + 17.54 = 1414.12

$\therefore$ Exciting current required to close the armature relay is

$$= \frac{1414.2}{2000} = 0.7071 \text{ A.}$$

(b) Air-gap ampere-turns, for g = 0.1 cm, are

$$= \frac{(0.351)(0.1 \times 10^{-2})}{4\pi \times 10^{-7}} = 279.32$$

Total ATs for the magnetic path, for g = 0.1 cm, are

$$= 279.32 + 17.54 = 296.86.$$

$$\therefore \text{ Exciting current required to keep the armature closed} = \frac{296.86}{2000} = 0.1484 \text{ A}$$

Example 2.16. *(a) The air-gap under the poles of a D.C. machine is not uniform, due to wear of the bearings. Find an expression for the unbalanced magnetic pull on the armature. For this example, an elementary two-pole D.C. machine of Fig. 2.31 may be considered.*

(b) A 2-pole D.C. machine has its armature displaced by an amount of 0.1 mm. Other data are as follows.

Air-gap flux density : 0.8 T

Area under each pole : 200 cm²

Uniform air-gap length : 0.6 cm.

Find the magnitude of the unbalanced magnetic pull on the armature.

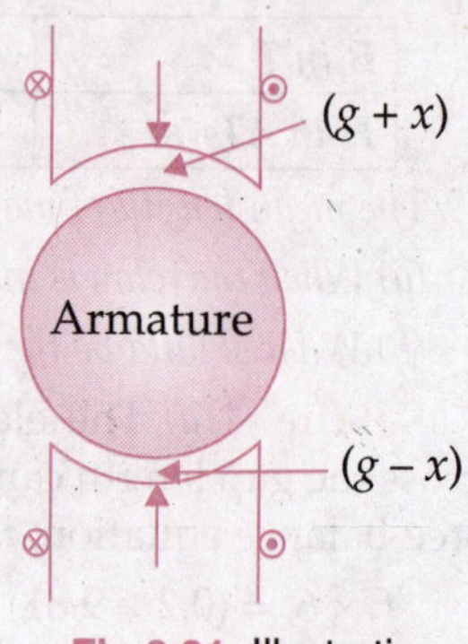

Fig 2.31: Illustrating unbalanced magnetic pull, Example 2.16.

Solution. *(a)* Let g be the uniform air-gap length of the D.C. machine.

Due to wear, let the two air-gaps become $(g + x)$ and $(g - x)$, as shown in Fig. 2.31.

North and south poles created near each air-gap, exert a force of attraction or pull on the armature. For uniform air-gaps under the two poles, each pole pulls the armature with a force of $\frac{1}{2}\frac{B_g^2}{\mu_0}A_p$ newtons, therefore the balanced magnetic force or pull on the armature is zero. Here

B_g = air-gap flux density under each pole

and A_p = area under each pole.

When the two air-gaps become unequal, the unbalanced magnetic pull comes into play and its magnitude can be calculated as follows : For air-gap length g, force of pull = $\frac{1}{2}\frac{B_g^2}{\mu_0}A_p$. For increased gap length $(g + x)$, this force must decrease.

$\therefore$ At the large air-gap of length $(g + x)$, the decreased force of pull = $\frac{1}{2}\frac{B_g^2}{\mu_0}A_p\frac{g}{g+x}$

At the smaller air-gap of length $(g - x)$, the increased force of pull = $\frac{1}{2}\frac{B_g^2}{\mu_0}A_p\frac{g}{g-x}$

$\therefore$ Net unbalanced magnetic pull on the armature of a 2-pole D.C. machine is

$$= \frac{1}{2}\frac{B_g^2}{\mu_0}A_p g\left[\frac{1}{g-x}-\frac{1}{g+x}\right] = \frac{B_g^2}{\mu_0}A_p\frac{gx}{g^2-x^2} \text{ newtons} \quad ...(2.72)$$

For uniform air-gap, x is zero and the unbalanced magnetic pull is also zero.

(b) Substitution of the numerical values in Eq. (2.72), gives the magnitude of unbalanced magnetic pull as

$$= \frac{(0.8)^2}{4\pi\times10^{-7}}(200\times10^{-4})\frac{6\times0.1}{36-0.01} = 169.76 \text{ N}$$

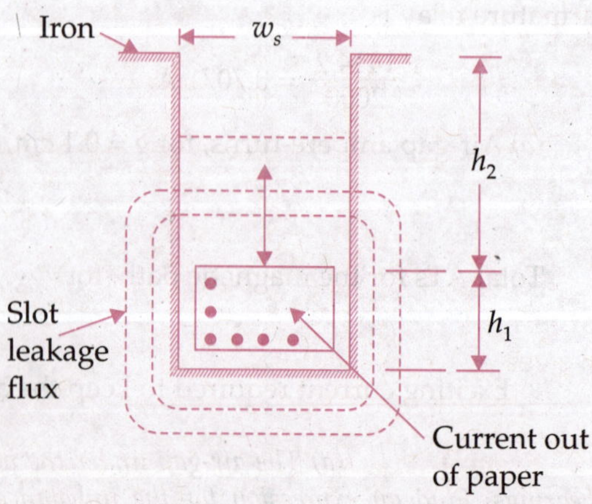

Fig 2.32: Slot leakage flux, Example 2.17

Example 2.17. *Fig. 2.32 shows a slot containing z_s conductors and each conductor carries a current of i amperes. The iron part of the magnetic circuit is assumed to have infinite permeability.*

(a) Find the variation of the flux density in the part of the slot (i) above the conductor portion and (ii) occupied by the conductor.

(b) Find an expression for the leakage flux above the conductor portion.

(c) Find the electromagnetic force F_e, created by the slot leakage flux present above the conductor portion.

(d) For $i = \sqrt{2}\,(1000) \sin 314t$, find the direction and magnitude of magnetic force found in part (c). There are two conductors in the slot, embedded length is 1 metre and slot width is 5 cm.

Solution. *(a)* Since reluctance of the iron path is assumed to be negligible, all the m.m.f. is expended in the slot width w_s only.

(i) If H_s is the magnetic field intensity above conductor portion in ATs per unit length, then

$$H_s w_s = i z_s$$

or $$H_s = \frac{i z_s}{w_s}$$

$\therefore$ Flux density $$B_s = \mu_0 H_s = \frac{\mu_0 i z_s}{w_s}$$

Since the current enclosed is constant, the flux density B_s over the conductor portion is also constant as shown in Fig. 2.33.

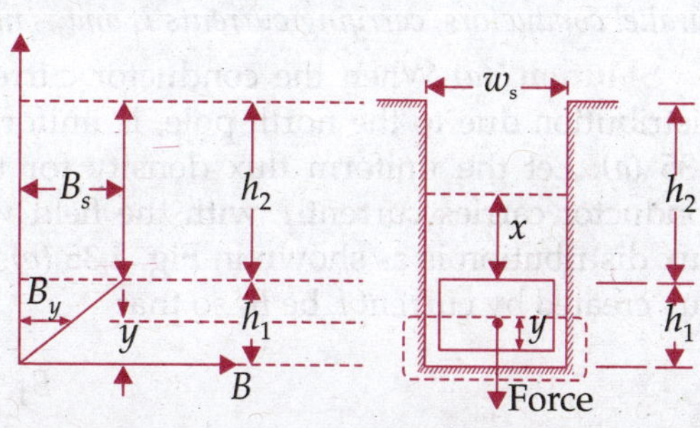

Fig 2.33: Flux density variation over the slot depth.

(ii) For the conductor, let H_y be the magnetic field intensity at a height y from the bottom of the conductor, then

$$H_y w_s = i z_s \frac{y}{h_1} \quad \text{or} \quad H_y = \frac{i z_s}{w_s} \cdot \frac{y}{h_1}$$

Flux density $$B_y = \mu_0 H_y = \frac{\mu_0 i z_s}{w_s} \cdot \frac{y}{h_1}$$

The nature of the flux density variation over the slot depth $(h_1 + h_2)$ is illustrated in Fig. 2.33.

(b) Slot leakage flux ϕ_s above the conductor region is

$$\phi_s = B_s (h_2 l) = \frac{\mu_0 i z_s}{w_s} h_2 l \text{ Wb.}$$

Here l is the embedded length of conductor normal to the plain of paper. Expression for ϕ_s reveals that the slot leakage flux is directly proportional to the slot depth, slot length and inversely proportional to slot width.

(c) Consider a slot depth of height x, just above h_1 as shown in Fig. 2.33. Then the magnetic field energy stored by the slot leakage flux ϕ_s for the slot depth of height x is given by

$$W_{fld} = \frac{1}{2} \frac{B_s^2}{\mu_0} x l w_s$$

Substitution of the value of B_s gives

$$W_{fld}(i, x) = \frac{1}{2} \frac{\mu_0 i^2 z_s^2}{w_s} \cdot xl$$

$\therefore$ Electromagnetic force $$f_e = \frac{\partial W_{fld}}{\partial x}(i, x) = \frac{1}{2} \frac{\mu_0 i^2 z_s^2}{w_s} l$$

= force created by slot leakage flux present above the conductor portion.

(d) The direction of the force f_e is towards the bottom of the slot, irrespective of the direction of current (use Fleming's left hand rule). Substituting the numerical values in the expression for f_e, we get

$$f_e = \frac{1}{2} \frac{4\pi \times 10^{-7} (2)^2 \times 1}{5 \times 10^{-2}} (\sqrt{2} \times 1000)^2 \sin^2 \omega t = 32\pi \left(\frac{1 - \cos 2\omega t}{2}\right)$$

$$f_{e\,(av)} = \frac{32\pi}{2} = 50.265 \text{ newtons.}$$

Example 2.18. *(a) For a two-pole D.C. machine, a conductor on the armature carries a current of i amperes, as shown in Fig. 2.34. Derive an expression for the electromagnetic force f_e on the conductor.*

(b) Use the result obtained in part (a), to determine the force between two parallel conductors, carrying currents i_1 and i_2 in the same direction.

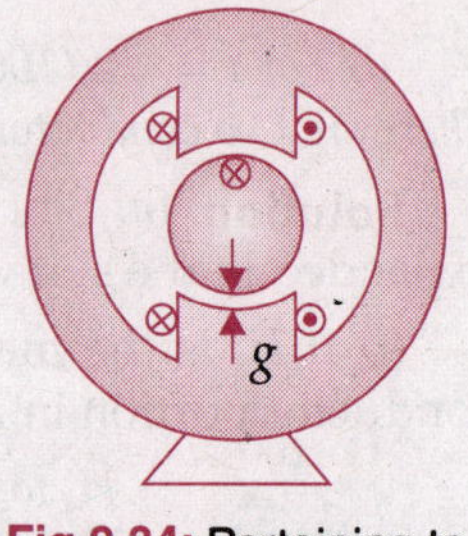

Fig 2.34: Pertaining to Example 2.18.

Solution. *(a)* When the conductor current is zero, the air-gap flux distribution due to the north pole, is uniform over the pole width, Fig. 2.35 *(a)*. Let the uniform flux density for this stator flux be B. If the conductor carries current i, with the field winding unexcited, then the flux distribution is as shown in Fig. 2.35 *(b)*. Let the flux density, due to flux created by current i, be B_1 so that

$$B_1 = \frac{\mu_0 i}{2g}$$

Here the reluctance is assumed to be offered by the air-gap alone. Note that the conductor flux has to traverse the air-gap twice as shown.

When both the field winding and conductor carry current, then the resultant flux distribution is obtained by superimposing the flux distribution of Figs. 2.35 *(a)* and *(b)*. The flux density to the right of conductor is seen to be $B + B_1$ and to the left of it, $B - B_1$. If the conductor moves a small displacement x to the right, then the change in magnetic stored energy in the air-gap is given by

$$W_{fld} = \left[\frac{1}{2}\frac{(B+B_1)^2}{\propto_0} - \frac{1}{2}\frac{(B-B_1)^2}{\propto_0}\right] glx$$

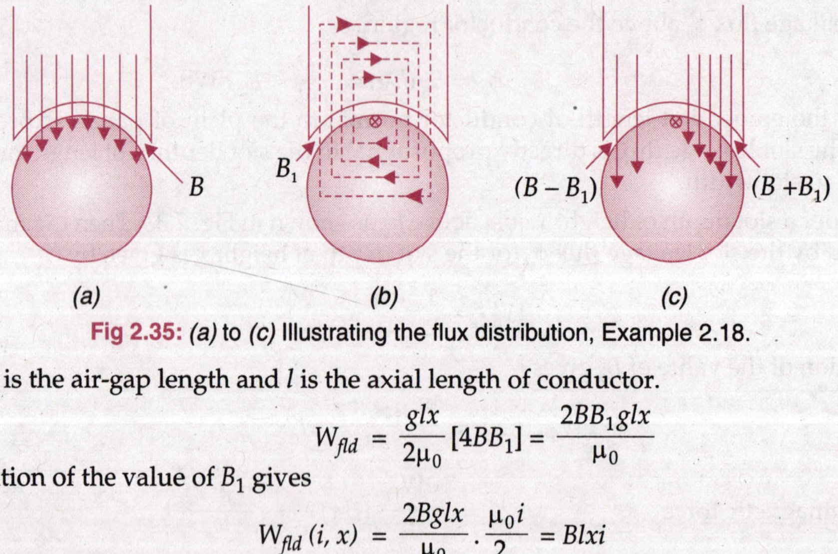

Fig 2.35: *(a)* to *(c)* Illustrating the flux distribution, Example 2.18.

where g is the air-gap length and l is the axial length of conductor.

$$W_{fld} = \frac{glx}{2\mu_0}[4BB_1] = \frac{2BB_1 glx}{\mu_0}$$

Substitution of the value of B_1 gives

$$W_{fld}(i, x) = \frac{2Bglx}{\mu_0} \cdot \frac{\mu_0 i}{2_g} = Blxi$$

$\therefore$ Force on the current carrying conductor is

$$f_e = \frac{\partial W_{fld}}{\partial x}(i, x) = Bli \qquad ...(2.73)$$

(b) Let d be the distance between the two conductors carrying current i_1 and i_2 in the same direction, as shown in Fig. 2.36.

The magnetic field intensity H_1 at the conductor 2, created by current i_1, is

$$H_1 \cdot 2\pi d = \text{total current enclosed} = i_1$$

$\therefore \qquad H_1 = \dfrac{i_1}{2\pi d}$

$\therefore$ Flux density B_1 at the conductor 2 is

$$B_1 = \mu_0 H_1 = \frac{\mu_0 i_1}{2\pi d} T$$

$\therefore$ Force of attraction between the two conductors

$$= B_1 l\, i_2 = \frac{\mu_0 i_1 i_2 l}{2\pi d} \text{ newtons.}$$

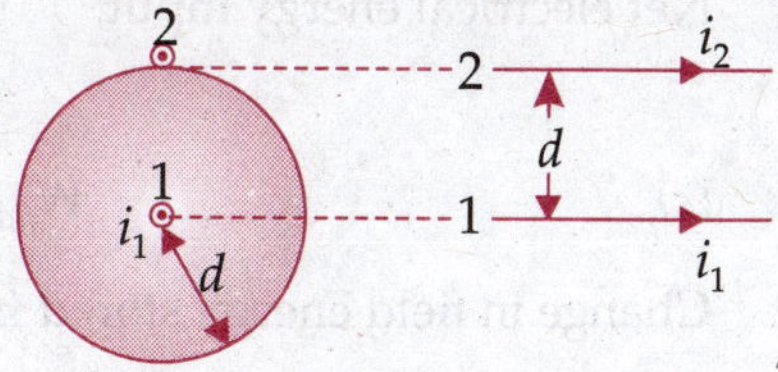

Fig 2.36: Illustrating force between two current carrying conductors.

Example 2.19. *Self- and mutual-inductances in henrys of two coupled coils are*

$$L_1 = 3 + \frac{1}{2x}, L_2 = 2 + \frac{1}{2x}, M_{12} = M_{21} = \frac{1}{2x}$$

over a certain displacement x in metres. The coil resistances are the negligible.

For constant currents of $I_1 = 10$ A and $I_2 = -5$ A, compute

(a) the mechanical work done in decreasing x from 1 m to 0.5 m,

(b) the energy supplied by each electrical source in part (a),

(c) change in field energy in part (a).

Hence verify that sum of the energies associated with mechanical work done and field energy is equal to the energy supplied by both sources during the motion from x = 0.5 to x = 1 m.

Solution. For a linear case,

$$W_{fld}(i_1, i_2, x) = \frac{1}{2} L_1 i_1^2 + \frac{1}{2} L_2 i_2^2 + i_1 i_2 M$$

$$= \frac{1}{2}\left(3+\frac{1}{2x}\right)100 + \frac{1}{2}\left(2+\frac{1}{2x}\right)25 + (-50)\left(\frac{1}{2x}\right) = 175 + \frac{25}{4x}$$

(a) From Eq. (2.26), $\qquad f_e = \dfrac{\partial W_{fld}(i_1, i_2, x)}{\partial x} = -\dfrac{25}{4x^2}$

$$\therefore \qquad W_{mech} = \int_{0.5}^{1.0} f_e\, dx = \int_{1.0}^{0.5} -\frac{25}{4x^2}\, dx = \frac{25}{4}\left|\frac{1}{x}\right|_1^{0.5} = +\frac{25}{4} \text{ watt-sec}$$

(b) $\qquad dW_{elec} = i_1\, d\psi_1 + i_2\, d\psi_2$

Here $\qquad \psi_1 = L_1 i_1 + M i_2 = \left(3+\dfrac{1}{2x}\right)10 + (-5)\left(\dfrac{1}{2x}\right) = 30 + \dfrac{5}{2x}$

$$\psi_2 = L_2 i_2 + M i_1 = \left(2+\frac{1}{2x}\right)(-5) + \frac{1}{2x}(10) = -10 + \frac{5}{2x}$$

Energy supplied by source 1, $\qquad W_{elec1} = \displaystyle\int_{\psi_1(x=1.0)}^{\psi_2(x=0.5)} i_1\, d\psi_1$

$$= 10\left[\left(30+\frac{5}{2x}\right)\Bigg|_{x=0.5} - \left(30+\frac{5}{2x}\right)\Bigg|_{x=1.0}\right] = 25 \text{ watt-sec}$$

Similarly, energy supplied by source 2 is

$$W_{elec2} = \int_{\psi_1(x=1.0)}^{\psi_2(x=0.5)} i_2\, d\psi_2$$

$$= (-5)\left[\left(-10+\frac{5}{2x}\right)\Bigg|_{x=0.5} - \left(-10+\frac{5}{2x}\right)\Bigg|_{x=1.0}\right]$$

$$= -12.5 \text{ watt-sec}$$

Net electrical energy input,

$$W_{elec} = W_{elec1} + W_{elec2} = 25 - 12.5 \text{ watt-sec} = 12.5 \text{ watt-sec}$$

(c) $$W_{fld}(i_1, i_2, x) = 175 + \frac{25}{4x}$$

Change in field energy stored from $x = 1.0$ to $x = 0.5$ m

$$W_{fld} = (W_{fld} \text{ at } x = 0.5) - (W_{fld} \text{ at } x = 1.0)$$

$$= \left(175 + \frac{25}{2}\right) - \left(175 + \frac{25}{4}\right) = + \frac{25}{4} \text{ watt-sec}$$

Here $$W_{fld} + W_{mech} = \frac{25}{4} + \frac{25}{4} = 12.5 = W_{elec}$$

This verifies the required result.

Example 2.20. *For the two coils of Example 2.19, compute the value of average magnetic force at $x = 0.5$ m if*

(a) both coils are connected in parallel across a voltage of 220 cos 314 t volts,

(b) both coils are connected in series across a voltage of 220 cos 314 t volts,

(c) coil 2 is shorted and coil 1 is connected to the same voltage as in part (a).

(d) both coils in series carry a current of 0.5 cos 314 t A.

Solution. For a linear case,

$$W_{fld}(i_1, i_2, x) = \frac{1}{2} L_1 i_1^2 + \frac{1}{2} L_2 i_2^2 + i_1 i_2 M$$

$$= \frac{1}{2}\left(3 + \frac{1}{2x}\right) i_1^2 + \frac{1}{2}\left(2 + \frac{1}{2x}\right) i_2^2 + i_1 i_2 \left(\frac{1}{2x}\right)$$

$$f_e = \frac{\partial W_{fld}(i_1, i_2, x)}{\partial x} = -\frac{1}{4x^2} i_1^2 - \frac{1}{4x^2} i_2^2 - i_1 i_2 \frac{1}{2x^2}$$

For $x = 0.5$ m, $$f_e = -i_1^2 - i_2^2 - 2i_1 i_2$$

(a) $$\psi_1 = L_1 i_1 + M i_2 = \left(3 + \frac{1}{2x}\right) i_1 + \frac{1}{2x} i_2$$

$$\psi_2 = M i_1 + L_2 i_2 = \frac{1}{2x} i_1 + \left(2 + \frac{1}{2x}\right) i_2$$

At $x = 0.5$ m, $$\psi_1 = 4i_1 + i_2 \quad \text{and} \quad \psi_2 = i_1 + 3i_2$$

As the coils are in parallel, $$v = \frac{d\psi_1}{dt} = \frac{d\psi_2}{dt}$$

or $$4\frac{di_1}{dt} + \frac{di_2}{dt} = \frac{di_1}{dt} + 3\frac{di_2}{dt}$$

or $$\frac{di_2}{dt} = \frac{3}{2}\frac{di_1}{dt} \quad \text{or} \quad i_2 = \frac{3}{2} i_1$$

∴ $$220 \cos 314t = 4\frac{di_1}{dt} + \frac{di_2}{dt} = \frac{11}{2} \cdot \frac{di_1}{dt}$$

or $$\frac{di_1}{dt} = 40 \cos 314t \quad \text{or} \quad i_1 = \frac{40}{314} \sin 314t$$

∴ $$i_2 = \frac{60}{314} \sin 314t$$

Substituting the value of i_1, i_2 in the expression for f_e gives

$$f_e = \frac{-1}{(314)^2}\,[(40)^2 + (60)^2 + 2(60)(40)]\sin^2 314t$$

$$= -\,0.101424 \sin^2 314t$$

$$\therefore \qquad f_{e\,(av)} = -\,0.050712 \text{ N}$$

(b)
$$v = \frac{d\psi_1}{dt} + \frac{d\psi_2}{dt} = \left(4\frac{di_1}{dt} + \frac{di_2}{dt}\right) + \left(\frac{di_1}{dt} + 3\frac{di_2}{dt}\right)$$

For series connected coils, $i_1 = i_2 = i$

$$\therefore \qquad 220 \cos 314\,t = 9\frac{di}{dt} \quad \text{or} \quad i = \frac{220}{9 \times 314}\sin 314t$$

$$\therefore \qquad f_e = -4\left(\frac{220}{9 \times 314}\right)^2 \sin^2 314t$$

or
$$f_{e\,(av)} = -\,0.01212 \text{ N}$$

(c) With coil 2 shorted and coil 1 connected to voltage source,

$$v = 4\frac{di_1}{dt} + \frac{di_2}{dt}$$

$$0 = \frac{di_1}{dt} + 3\frac{di_2}{dt} \quad \text{or} \quad \frac{di_1}{dt} = -3\frac{di_2}{dt}$$

$$\therefore \qquad 220 \cos 314t = v = -\frac{12di_2}{dt} + \frac{di_2}{dt} = -\frac{11di_2}{dt}$$

or
$$i_2 = -\frac{20}{314}\sin 314t \quad \text{and} \quad i_1 = \frac{60}{314}\sin 314t$$

$$\therefore \qquad f_e = \frac{-1}{(314)^2}\,[(60)^2 + (20)^2 - 2(20)(60)]\sin^2 314t$$

$$= -\left(\frac{40}{314}\right)^2 \sin^2 314t$$

or
$$f_{e\,(av)} = -\,0.00811 \text{ N.}$$

Example 2.21. *Two magnetic surfaces separated by distance g have a flux density of 1.6 T in between them. This value is usually the saturation level for ferromagnetic materials. Find the force between these two surfaces for area A = 1 m².*

Solution. Let A be the area of the magnetic surfaces which are separated by a distance g. The field energy stored is given by

$$W_{fld}(B, g) = \frac{1}{2}\frac{B^2}{\mu_0}(A.\,g)$$

From Eq. (2.21)
$$f_e = -\frac{\partial W_{fld}(B,g)}{\partial g} = -\frac{1}{2}\frac{B^2 A}{\mu_0}$$

$$= -\frac{1}{2}\frac{(1.6)^2 \times 1}{4\pi \times 10^{-7}} = -\frac{0.32}{\pi} \times 10^7 \text{ N}$$

Negative sign indicates that force tends to reduce the gap length.

2.6. SINGLY-EXCITED ELECTRIC FIELD SYSTEMS

The electric field as a coupling medium between electrical and mechanical systems can be treated in a manner similar to magnetic field discussed earlier. Here also the terms energy and co-energy will be introduced to obtain the expressions for force or torque. Charge and voltage associated with electric field are analogous, respectively, to flux linkages and current in a magnetic field.

(a) **Electric field energy stored.** A singly-excited energy conversion device using electric field as the coupling medium is represented in Fig. 2.37 by a parallel plate condenser with fixed and movable plates. A current source feeds the condenser. Leakage current of the condenser is represented by conductance *G*. This means that electric field between the two plates is conservative, *i.e.* all energy supplied is recoverable from the device. The energy flow in an electric field system is also governed by Eq. (2.3) as in a magnetic field system.

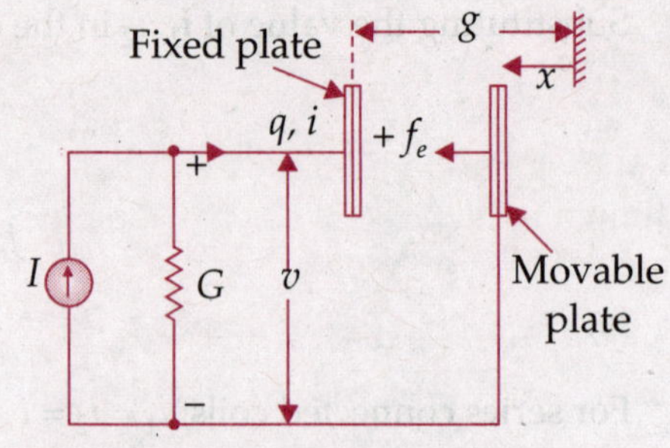

Fig 2.37: Singly-excited electric-field energy conversion device.

When current source is connected, current and charge flow into the device of Fig. 2.37 and the differential electrical energy input to the condenser in time *dt* is

$$dW_{elec} = vidt = vdq \qquad \text{...(2.74)}$$

The mechanical work done in time *dt* by the force f_e is

$$dW_{mech} = f_e\, dx \qquad \text{...(2.75)}$$

where *dx* is the displacement of movable plate in the direction of f_e during time *dt*.

Eq. (2.3) in terms of Eqs. (2.74) and (2.75) is

$$vdq = dW_{fld} + f_e\, dx \qquad \text{...(2.76)}$$

If the movable plate is not allowed to move, then $f_e\, dx = 0$ and Eq. (2.76) becomes

$$dW_{elec} = dW_{fld} = vdq \qquad \text{...(2.77)}$$

Note that in Eq. (2.77), *v* is constant and charge builds up from zero to *q*.

$$\therefore \qquad W_{fld} = \int_0^q vdq$$

For a linear electric field, $C = \dfrac{q}{v}$ = capacitance of the device.

$$\therefore \qquad W_{fld} = \frac{1}{C}\int_0^q qdq = \frac{1}{2}\frac{q^2}{C} \qquad \text{...(2.78 a)}$$

Also $\qquad W_{fld} = \dfrac{1}{2}\dfrac{q^2}{C} = \dfrac{1}{2}vq \qquad \text{...(2.78 b)}$

Capacitance *C* depends on the distance between the two plates and can be written as

$$C = \frac{\varepsilon_0 A}{(g - x)}$$

where *A* = plate area and ε_0 = permittivity of free space.

Thus, the field energy W_{fld} is a function of two independent variables *q* and *x*, *i.e.*

$$W_{fld}(q, x) = \frac{1}{2}\frac{q^2}{C(x)} = \frac{(g - x).q^2}{2\,\varepsilon_0 A} \qquad \text{...(2.79)}$$

Eq. (2.79) reveals that electric field energy can be changed electrically by changing *q* or mechanically by changing *x* (i.e. by drift of the movable plate).

The energy density in electric field is given by

$$W_{fld} = \int_0^D E \cdot dD = \int_0^D \frac{D}{\varepsilon_0}\cdot dD$$

$$= \frac{1}{\varepsilon_0}\int_0^D D.dD = \frac{1}{2}\cdot\frac{D^2}{\varepsilon_0} \qquad \text{...(2.80)}$$

where D = electric field flux density, Coulombs/m^2

E = electric field intensity or potential gradient, volts/m = $\frac{D}{\varepsilon_0}$

(b) **Coenergy.** For a linear case, the variation of q with v is as shown in Fig. 2.38. As in a magnetic system, coenergy W_{fld}' is the area $OACO$. Compare this figure with Fig. 2.4 (c).

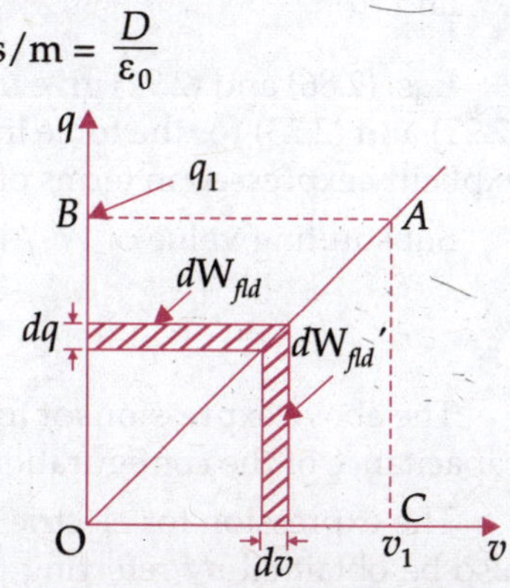

Fig 2.38: Electric field energy and coenergy in a linear circuit

$$\therefore \quad \text{Area } OACO = \int_0^{v_1} q \cdot dv = C\int_0^{v_1} v\, dv$$

$$W_{fld}' = \frac{1}{2}Cv_1^2$$

In general,
$$W_{fld}'(v, x) = \frac{1}{2}C(x)\, v^2 \qquad ...(2.81)$$

Coenergy density,
$$w_{fld}' = \int_0^E D.dE = \int_0^E \varepsilon_0 \cdot E.dE$$
$$= \varepsilon_0 \int_0^E E \cdot dE = \frac{1}{2}\varepsilon_0 E^2 \qquad ...(2.82)$$

(c) **Calculation of force.** The force produced by electric field can be obtained by the use of field energy or coenergy functions as in the case of magnetic systems. The field energy stored is dependent on q, x and as such, Eq. (2.76) can be expressed as

$$dW_{fld}(q, x) = vdq - f_e\, dx \qquad ...(2.83)$$

The field enegy $W_{fld}(q, x)$ can also be expressed mathematically in terms of its two partial derivatives as

$$dW_{fld}(q, x) = \frac{\partial W_{fld}}{\partial q} dq + \frac{\partial W_{fld}}{\partial x} \cdot dx \qquad ...(2.84)$$

The field energy in Eq. (2.83) and (2.84) is same, therefore the coefficients associated with dq and dx must be equal in both these equations.

$$\therefore \quad v = \frac{\partial W_{fld}(q,x)}{\partial q} \qquad ...(2.85)$$

and
$$f_e = -\frac{\partial W_{fld}(q,x)}{\partial x} \qquad ...(2.86)$$

It is seen from Fig. 2.38 that coenergy is given by

$$W_{fld}' = q_1 v_1 - W_{fld}.$$

In general,
$$W_{fld}'(v, x) = qv - W_{fld}(q, x)$$

In differential form,
$$dW_{fld}'(v, x) = d(qv) - dW_{fld}(q, x) \qquad ...(2.87)$$

Substitution of Eq. (2.83) in Eq. (2.87) gives

$$dW_{fld}'(v, x) = qdv + vdq - vdq + f_e\, dx$$
$$= qdv + f_e\, dx \qquad ...(2.88)$$

As W_{fld}' is dependent on v, x ; it can be expressed mathematically in terms of its partial derivatives as

$$dW_{fld}'(v, x) = \frac{\partial W_{fld}'(v,x)}{\partial v} dv + \frac{\partial W_{fld}'(v,x)}{\partial x} dx \qquad ...(2.89)$$

The coefficients of dv, dx on the right hand side of Eqs. (2.88) and (2.89) must be equal and this yields the charge and force expressions as

$$q = \frac{\partial W_{fld}'(v,x)}{\partial v} \qquad ...(2.90)$$

and $$f_e = \frac{\partial W_{fld}'(v,x)}{\partial x} \quad ...(2.91)$$

Eqs. (2.86) and (2.91) give the force expressions for electric field system ; corresponding, to Eqs. (2.21) and (2.23) for the force in magnetic field system. Note that field energy in Eq. (2.86) must be explicitly expressed in terms of q and x and co-energy in Eq. (2.91) in terms of v and x.

Substituting value of $W_{fld}'(v, x)$ from Eq. (2.81) in Eq. (2.91), we get

$$f_e = \frac{1}{2} v^2 \frac{dC(x)}{dx} \quad ...(2.92)$$

The above expression for force states that electric force acts in such a direction as to increase the capacitance of the configuration.

The expression for electric force, as given by Eq. (2.86), can also be obtained by referring to Fig. 2.39. In this figure, when switch is closed, capacitor gets charged to source voltage V_s. Switch S is then opened. Now the upper plate is given a virtual displacement dx in the direction of electric force. During this displacement, charge on capacitor, $q = CV_s$ remains constant. As the switch S is open, during virtual displacement electrical energy input, $dW_{elec} = 0$ and the mechanical work done, $dW_{mech} = f_e \cdot dx$.

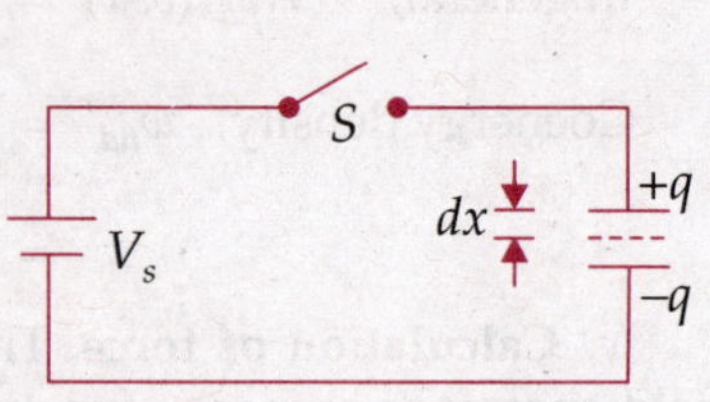

Fig 2.39: Capacitor charged with constant q.

From Eq. (2.3), $0 = f_e \cdot dx + dW_{fld}$ at constant q.

$$\therefore \quad f_e = -\frac{\partial W_{fld}(q,x)}{\partial x} \quad ...(2.86)$$

In Eq. (2.86), field energy stored in the electric field must be explicitly expressed in terms of q and x.

Example 2.22. *Two parallel plates, each of area $A = 1\ m^2$, are separated by a distance g. The electric field intensity between the plates is $3 \times 10^6 V/m$, a value equal to the breakdown strength of air. Find force between the two plates. Use both energy and co-energy methods.*

Solution. For a distance g between the two plates, a plate movement x in the direction of force, reduces the plate distance to $(g - x)$. For this space, electric field energy stored is

$$W_{fld}(q, x) = \frac{1}{2}\frac{q^2}{C} = \frac{1}{2}\frac{q^2(g-x)}{A\varepsilon_0}$$

From Eq. (2.86), $$f_e = -\frac{\partial W_{fld}(q,x)}{\partial x} = \frac{1}{2}\frac{g^2}{A\varepsilon_0}$$

For $$q = DA = \varepsilon_0 EA,$$
$$f_e = E^2 \varepsilon_0 A$$

The coenergy is given by $$W_{fld}'(v, x) = \frac{1}{2}Cv^2 = \frac{1}{2}v^2 \frac{A\varepsilon_0}{g-x}$$

From Eq. (2.91) $$f_e = -\frac{\partial W_{fld}'(v,x)}{\partial x} = \frac{1}{2}v^2 \frac{A\varepsilon_0}{(g-x)^2}$$

For $$v = E(g-x), f_e = \frac{1}{2}[E(g-x)]^2 \frac{A\varepsilon_0}{(g-x)^2} = \frac{1}{2}E^2 \varepsilon_0 A$$

$$\therefore \quad f_e = \frac{1}{2}(3 \times 10^6)^2 \left(\frac{10^{-9}}{36\,\pi}\right) \times 1 = \frac{1}{8\pi} \times 10^3 \text{ N.}$$

Both the methods give the same force. It is as expected. It may be interesting at this stage to compare the force produced by magnetic field when B is near the saturation level with the force produced by electric field when E is equal to its breakdown value.

$$\therefore \quad \frac{f_e \text{ per unit area in magnetic field (Example 2.21)}}{f_e \text{ per unit area in electric field (Example 2.22)}} = \frac{0.32 \times 10^7 \times 8\neq}{\neq \times 10^3} = 25600.$$

This shows that force density in the magnetic field is 25,600 times its value in the electric field at the maximum possible field strengths assumed.

This in fact is the reason why all practical energy conversion devices make use of the magnetic field rather than the electric field as the coupling medium. Electric field devices operating at very low-power levels are sometimes used for relatively high frequency applications.

Example 2.23. *In Fig. 2.40, certain voltage is applied between a fixed plate and a movable plate. A counter weight of 5 gms. in the balance keeps the bar horizontal. Calculate the magnitude of voltage applied between the two plates having cross-sectional area of 30 cm². Distance between the two plates is 1 cm.*

Solution. Co-energy stored between the two plates, $W_{fld}' = \frac{1}{2}CV^2$. Here $C = \frac{\varepsilon_0 A}{x}$ where x = distance between the two plates.

$$\therefore \quad W_{fld}'(V, x) = \frac{1}{2}V^2 \frac{\varepsilon_0 A}{x}$$

Force between the two plates, $$f_e = \frac{\partial W_{fld}'(V,x)}{\partial x} = -\frac{1}{2}V^2 \frac{\varepsilon_0 A}{x^2} \text{ N}$$

Negative sign indicates that electric force f_e acts in such a direction as to reduce the distance between the two plates. For the bar to remain horizontal in Fig. 2.40, electrostatic force

$$f_e \times 8 = 5 \times 10$$

or $$f_e = \frac{50}{8} = \frac{25}{4} \text{ gms.} = \frac{25}{4} \times \frac{1}{1000} \times 9.81 \text{ N}$$

But the magnitude of force between the two plates is

$$f_e = \frac{1}{2}V^2 \frac{\varepsilon_0 A}{x^2} \text{ N}$$

$$\therefore \quad \frac{25}{4} \times \frac{9.81}{1000} = \frac{1}{2}V^2 \left(\frac{10^{-9}}{36\,\pi}\right) \frac{30 \times 10^{-4}}{(1 \times 10^{-2})^2}$$

or $$V = \left[\frac{25 \times 2 \times 36\,\pi \times 10^4 \times 9.81}{4000 \times 10^{-9} \times 30 \times 10^{-4}}\right]^{1/2}$$

$$= 21500.822 \text{ V} \simeq 21.50 \text{ kV}$$

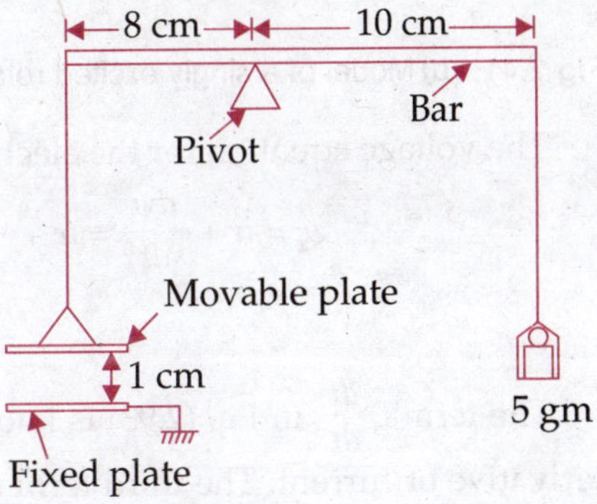

Fig 2.40: Pertaining to Example 2.23.

Thus the voltage applied between the two plates is 21.50 kV.

The basic principle demonstrated in this example may be used for the measurement of high voltages quite accurately.

2.7. DYNAMIC EQUATIONS

The electromechanical-energy-conversion devices operate with electrical system on one side and mechanical system on the other side. It is the behaviour of the entire electromechanical system that is important, because a particular system may operate satisfactorily under steady state conditions but may fail miserably under the electromechanical transients. In view of this, the operation of the entire system, comprising of electrical system, conversion device and mechanical system, should be investigated in detail during the electromechanical system planning. Thus the complete analysis of a physical system involves electric circuit equations, energy conversion relations and equations of motions.

Simple models of singly excited electro-mechanical systems are illustrated in Figs. 2.41 *(a)* and *(b)*. Model of Fig. 2.41 *(a)* is applicable only to restricted linear movements, because of the presence of a spring. Similarly the model illustrated in Fig. 2.41 *(b)* is for the restricted rotary motions only. If spring K is replaced by a mechanical load torque in Fig. 2.41 *(b)*, it becomes the model of a rotating electrical mechine with energy conversion from electrical to mechanical.

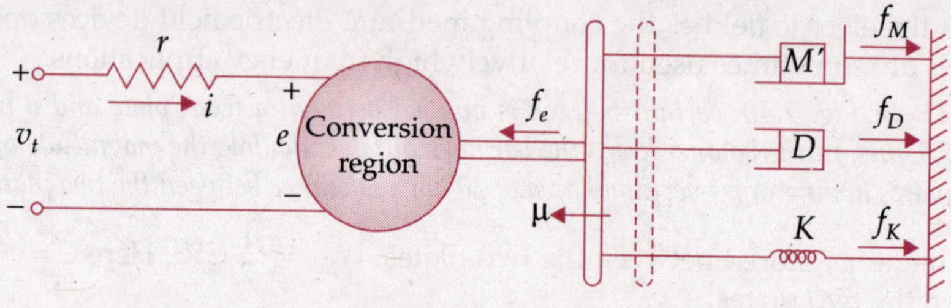

Fig 2.41: *(a)* Model of a singly excited translational electromechanical system, involving restricted linear movement.

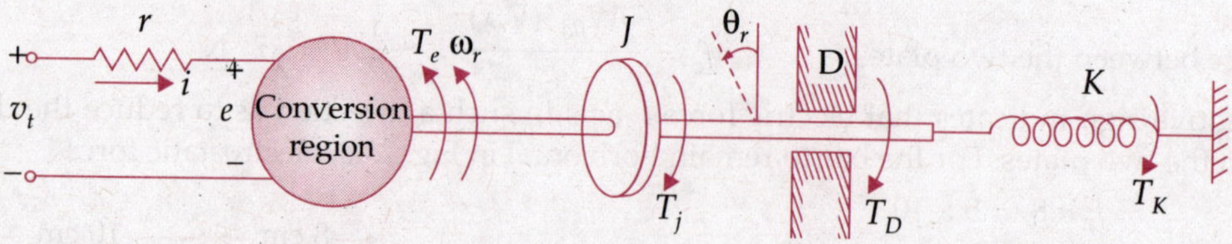

Fig 2.41: *(b)* Model of a singly excited rotational electromechanical system, involving restricted rotary motion.

The voltage equation for the electrical system of both Figs. 2.41 *(a)* and *(b)* is,

$$v_t = ir + \frac{d\psi}{dt} = ir + \frac{d}{dt}(Li) = ir + L\frac{di}{dt} + i\left(\frac{dL}{d\theta_r}\right)\frac{d\theta_r}{dt}$$

$$= ir + L\frac{di}{dt} + i\left(\frac{dL}{d\theta_r}\right)\omega_r \quad ...(2.93)$$

The term $L\frac{di}{dt}$ in Eq. (2.93) is known as the transformer voltage, because it involves the time derivative of current. The third term of Eq. (2.93) is the speed or rotational voltage term, because of the presence of speed ω_r in it. Note that it is the speed voltage term that determines the flow of energy between electrical and mechanical systems.

In Fig. 2.41 *(a)*, the magnetic force f_e is opposed by inertia force f_M, damping force f_D and restraining spring force f_K. Therefore the force balance equation is

$$f_e = f_M + f_D + f_K = M\frac{du}{dt} + Du + K\int u\,dt$$

or

$$f_e = M\frac{d^2x}{dt^2} + D\frac{dx}{dt} + Kx \quad ...(2.94)$$

where M = mass in kgs,

D = coefficient of friction or damping constant in newtons per metre per sec.,

K = linear spring constant in newtons per metre displacement,

and $u = \frac{dx}{dt}$, linear velocity in metres/sec.

In Fig. 2.41 *(b)*, the magnetic torque T_e is opposed by inertia torque T_j, damping torque T_D and restraining spring torque T_K. Therefore the torque-balance equation is

$$T_e = T_j + T_D + T_K = J\frac{d\omega_r}{dt} + D\omega_r + K\int \omega_r\, dt$$

or

$$T_e = J\frac{d^2\theta_r}{dt^2} + D\frac{d\theta_r}{dt} + K\theta_r \qquad ...(2.95)$$

where J = moment of inertia in kg m^2

D = damping constant in N-m per rad/sec.

K = rotary spring constant in N-m per radian

and $\omega_r = \frac{d\theta_r}{dt}$, angular velocity in rad/sec.

The dynamic equation for a rotating electric motor, from Eq. (2.95), is

$$T_e = J\frac{d^2\theta_r}{dt^2} + D\frac{d\theta_r}{dt} + T_L \qquad ...(2.96)$$

where T_L is the load torque opposing the magnetic torque T_e.

The magnetic force f_e or torque T_e can be calculated from the partial derivative of W_{fld} as explained before.

Thus both the Eqs. (2.93) and (2.94) describe the total behaviour of a linear electromechanical system and both the Eqs. (2.93) and (2.95) that of a rotary electromechanical system.

For illustrating the formulation of dynamic equations for a system, consider the configuration shown in Fig. 2.42. Reluctance of the two air gaps in series is

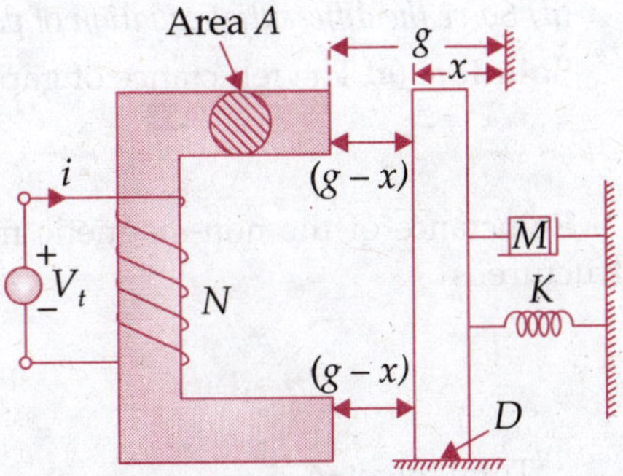

Fig 2.42: Typical electromechanical system.

$$Rl = \frac{2(g-x)}{\mu_0 A}$$

Assuming the iron to have infinite permeability, self-inductance of the configuration is

$$L(x) = \frac{N^2}{Rl} = \frac{N^2\cdot\mu_0 A}{2(g-x)}$$

From Eq. (2.28),

$$f_e = \frac{1}{2}i^2\frac{dL(x)}{dx} = \frac{1}{2}i^2\frac{N^2\cdot\mu_0 A}{2(g-x)^2} = i^2\frac{N^2\cdot\mu_0 A}{4(g-x)^2}$$

Therefore, the two differential equations governing the system dynamic performance are as under :

From Eq. (2.93),

$$v_t = ir + \frac{N^2\cdot\mu_0 A}{2(g-x)}\times\frac{di}{dt} + i\frac{N^2\cdot\mu_0 A}{2(g-x)^2}\times\frac{dx}{dt} \qquad ...(2.97)$$

From Eq. (2.94),

$$f_e = i^2\frac{N^2\cdot\mu_0 A}{4(g-x)^2} = M\frac{d^2x}{dt^2} + D\cdot\frac{dx}{dt} + K\cdot x \qquad ...(2.98)$$

Eqs. (2.97) and (2.98) are non-linear differential equations which can be solved numerically on a digital computer. These equations can, however, be linearised for small movements about the equilibrium, or operating, point and then can be solved for dynamic or steady-state conditions as desired.

Example 2.24. *For the plunger magnet shown in Fig. 2.43, the reluctance of the iron portion is neglected. The coil has N turns. The spring constant is K newtons per unit displacement. Neglect the coil-resistance, magnetic leakage and fringing. Movement of the iron plunger is assumed frictionless. The coil is excited from sinusoidal voltage so that the air-gap flux at any time t is given by*

$$\phi = \phi_{max} \cos \omega t$$

The plunger is executing a simple harmonic motion.

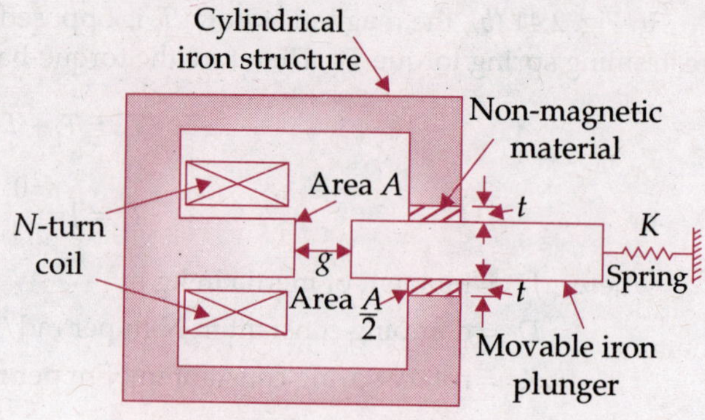

Fig 2.43: Plunger magnet, Example 2.24.

(a) Derive an expression for the magnetic force f_e acting on the movable iron plunger, in terms of ϕ_{max}, ω and t.

(b) Find an expression for the coil voltage as a function of ϕ_{max}, N, ω and t.

(c) Write the differential equation of the iron plunger movement in terms of ϕ_{max}, ω and t.

(d) Solve the differential equation of part (c) for the sinusoidal steady-state operation.

Solution. *(a)* The reluctance of gap length *g* is given by

$$Rl_1 = \frac{g}{\mu_0 A}$$

Reluctance of the non-magnetic material between the iron plunger and the cylindrical iron structure is

$$Rl_2 = \frac{t}{\mu_0 . A/2} = \frac{2t}{\mu_0 A}$$

∴ Total reluctance

$$Rl = \left(\frac{g}{\infty_0 A} + \frac{2t}{\infty_0 A} \right) = \frac{g+2t}{\mu_0 A}$$

∴ Magnetic force,

$$f_e = -\frac{1}{2}\phi^2 \frac{dRl}{dg} = -\frac{1}{2}\phi^2 \frac{d}{dg}\left(\frac{g+2t}{\mu_0 A}\right) = -\frac{1}{2}\phi^2 \frac{1}{\mu_0 A}$$

Here negative sign indicates force tends to reduce gap length.

For $\phi = \phi_{max} \cos \omega t$,

$$f_e = \frac{1}{2}\phi^2_{max} \frac{1}{\mu_0 A} \cos^2 \omega t = \frac{1}{4}\frac{\phi^2_{max}}{\mu_0 A}(1 + \cos 2\omega t)$$

(b)

$$e = -\frac{d\psi}{dt} = -\frac{d}{dt}(N \phi_{max} \cos \omega t)$$

∴

$$e = \omega N \phi_{max} \sin \omega t.$$

(c) The magnetic force f_e has to overcome the forces due to

(i) spring *(ii)* friction and *(iii)* mass *M*.

Now *K* is the spring constant in newtons per unit displacement. For any displacement *x*,

$$f_K = Kx \text{ newtons}$$

and

$$f_D = D\frac{dx}{dt} \text{ newtons}$$

where *D* is the coefficient of friction of the movable part in newtons per metre per sec. and $\frac{dx}{dt}$ is the velocity in m/sec.

$$f_M = M\frac{d^2x}{dt^2} \text{ newtons}$$

and here M is the mass of the movable iron plunger in kg and $\frac{d^2x}{dt^2}$ is the acceleration in metres per sec^2.

Therefore, the force-balance equation is $f_e = f_M + f_D + f_K$

or $$\frac{1}{4}\frac{\phi^2{}_m}{\mu_0 A}(1+\cos 2\omega t) = M\frac{d^2x}{dt^2} + 0 + Kx$$

(d) Normally the solution of such an equation shall consist of a complementary function and particular integral. A C.F. gives the transient part of the solution and P.I. gives the steady-state solution of the equation. Since here only steady-state solution is required, the C.F. will not be obtained. Therefore,

$$M\frac{d^2x}{dt^2} + Kx = \frac{\phi_m^2}{4\mu_0 A}(1+\cos 2\omega t) \qquad ...(2.99)$$

The right hand side of Eq. (2.99) is the forcing function and it is seen to consist of constant and double frequency components. Therefore, the steady-state solution of this equation must contain similar components. In view of this, let the steady-state solution of Eq. (2.99) be given by

$$x = P + Q\cos 2\omega t \qquad ...(2.100)$$

then $$\frac{dx}{dt} = -2\omega Q \sin 2\omega t \text{ and } \frac{d^2x}{dt^2} = -4\,\omega^2 Q\cos 2\omega t.$$

The values of P and Q are obtained by substituting the values of x and $\frac{d^2x}{dt^2}$ in Eq. (2.99). Therefore,

$$-4\,\omega^2 QM\cos 2\omega t + KP + KQ\cos 2\omega t = \text{C}\,(1+\cos 2\omega t) \qquad ...(2.101)$$

where $$\text{C} = \frac{\phi_m^2}{4\mu_0 A}$$

Comparison of the terms on right and left hand sides of Eq. (2.101), gives

$$KP = \text{C}, \quad \therefore\ P = \frac{\text{C}}{K}$$

and $$KQ - 4\omega^2 QM = \text{C}, \quad \therefore\ \text{Q} = \frac{\text{C}}{K - 4\omega^2 M}$$

Substitution of the values of P and Q in Eq. (2.100) gives the steady-state solution as

$$x = \frac{\text{C}}{K} + \frac{\text{C}\cos 2\omega t}{K - 4\omega^2 M} = \frac{\phi_m^2}{4\mu_0 AK}\left[1 + \frac{K\cos 2\omega t}{K - 4\omega^2 M}\right]$$

If the transient part of the solution is required, then additional terms like $A_1 e^{-t/T_1}$ and $A_2\, e^{-t/T_2}$ shall be added to the steady-state solution obtained above.

2.8. SOME WORKED EXAMPLES

The object of this article is to solve some typical problems pertaining to the principles of electromechanical energy conversion.

Example 2.25. *An inductor is made from magnetic core with two air-gaps of equal length g, as shown in Fig. 2.44. The exciting coil has 1000 turns, A = 5 cm × 5 cm and g = 1 cm. Core is assumed to have infinite permeability and fringing is neglected.*

(a) Find the coil inductance.

In case coil current is 5 A, find the magnetic energy stored in the inductor. Find also the force on the armature.

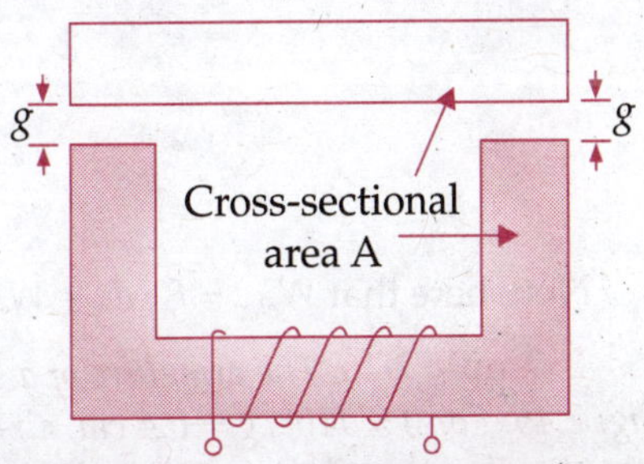

Fig 2.44: Pertaining to Example 2.25.

(b) With coil current held fixed at 5 A, find the electrical energy supplied by source if the gap length decreases from 1 cm to 0.5 cm.

(c) For part (b), find the mechanical work done.

Solution. *(a)* For two air-gaps in series, reluctance

$$Rl = \frac{2g}{\mu_0 A}$$

Coil inductance,
$$L = \frac{N^2}{Rl} = \frac{N^2 \mu_0 A}{2g} = \frac{a}{2g}$$
$$= \frac{(1000)^2 (4\pi \times 10^{-7})(0.05)^2}{2 \times 0.01} = 0.15708 \text{ H}$$

where
$$a = N^2 \mu_0 A = (1000)^2 (4\pi \times 10^{-7})(0.05)^2 = \pi \times 10^{-3}$$

Field energy stored in inductor
$$= \frac{1}{2} LI^2 = \frac{1}{2} \times 0.15708 (5)^2 = 1.9635 \text{ watt-sec}$$

Field energy stored,
$$W_{fld} = \frac{1}{2} i^2 \cdot L = \frac{1}{2} \cdot i^2 \cdot \frac{a}{2g} = \frac{1}{4} i^2 \frac{a}{g}$$

Force on the armature,
$$f_e = \frac{\partial W_{fld}(i, g)}{\partial g}$$

or
$$f_e = \frac{1}{4} i^2 a \cdot \frac{\partial}{\partial g}\left[\frac{1}{g}\right] = -\frac{1}{4} \cdot \frac{i^2 a}{g^2}$$

Negative sign indicates that force tends to reduce the gap length g.

Magnitude of force on the armature,
$$f_e = \frac{1}{4} (5)^2 \times \frac{\pi \times 10^{-3}}{(0.01)^2} = 196.35 \text{ N}$$

(b) Electrical energy input at constant-current movement

$$W_{elec} = (\psi_2 - \psi_1) I. \text{ But } L = \frac{\psi}{I} \text{ or } \psi = LI$$

$\therefore W_{elec} = [L_2 - L_1] I^2 = [L_2$ when gap has reduced to 0.5 cm $- L_1$ when gap length = 1 cm$] I^2$

$$= \left[\frac{a}{2g} (= L) \text{ when } g = 0.5 \text{ cm} - \frac{a}{2g} \text{ when } g = 1 \text{ cm}\right] I^2$$

$$= \frac{a}{2}\left[\frac{1}{0.005} - \frac{1}{0.01}\right] I^2 = \frac{\pi \times 10^{-3}}{2}\left[\frac{1}{0.005} - \frac{1}{0.01}\right] \times 5^2 = 3.927 \text{ watt-sec.}$$

(c) Mechanical work done
$$= \int_{1.0}^{0.5} f_e . dg = \int_{1.0}^{0.5} -\frac{1}{4} i^2 a . \frac{1}{g^2} \cdot dg$$

$$= -\frac{1}{4} i^2 a \left| -\frac{1}{g} \right|_{1}^{0.5} = \frac{i^2 a}{4} \left| \frac{1}{g} \right|_{1.0}^{0.5}$$

$$= \frac{1}{4} \times 5^2 \times (\pi \times 10^{-3}) \left[\frac{1}{0.005} - \frac{1}{0.01}\right]$$

$$= 1.9635 \text{ watt-sec.}$$

Note here that $W_{elec} = f_e \cdot dx + W_{fld}$

Example 2.26. *The armature of a 2-pole D.C. machine is inadvertently displaced axially as shown in Fig. 2.45. For $\theta = 110°$, $g = 0.4$ cm, air-gap flux density = 0.5 T, armature diameter = 30 cm, find the axial force tending to pull the armature into alignment with the field structure.*

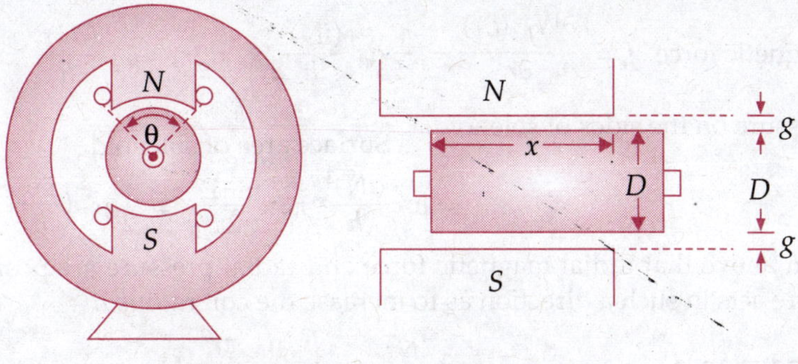

Fig 2.45: Pertaining to Example 2.26.

Solution. The magnetic stored energy per unit volume = $\frac{1}{2}\frac{B^2}{\mu_0}$. The magnetic energy stored in the two air-gaps,

$$W_{fld} = \text{[Energy density] [Volume of two air-gaps]}$$

$$= \frac{1}{2}\frac{B^2}{\mu_0}\left[\frac{D}{2}\cdot\theta\cdot x\cdot g\cdot 2\right]$$

∴ Force that tends to pull the armature into alignment,

$$f_e = \frac{\partial W_{fld}}{\partial x} = \frac{1}{2}\frac{B^2}{\mu_0} D\cdot\theta\cdot g$$

$$\therefore \qquad f_e = \frac{1}{2}\frac{(0.5)^2\times 0.3\times 110\times \neq \times 0.4\times 10^{-2}}{4\neq\times 10^{-7}\times 180} = 229.17 \text{ N.}$$

Example 2.27. *A solenoid of height h and radius r has N turns. For a solenoid current i, calculate*

(a) the energy stored inside the solenoid

(b) the radial magnetic force tending to burst out the solenoid

(c) the radial pressure on the sides of solenoid

(d) the solenoid inductance.

Assume no flux outside the solenoid.

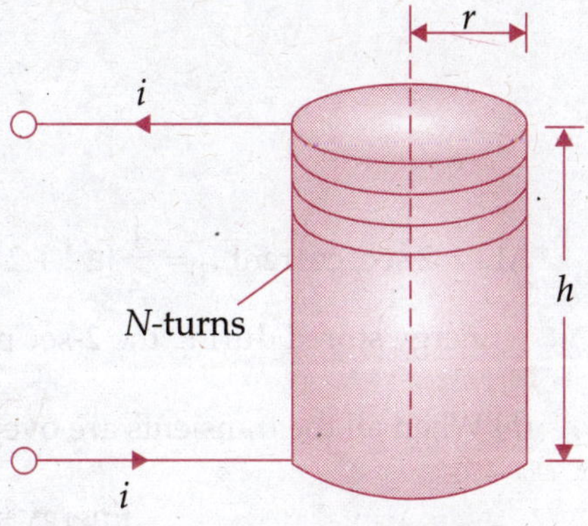

Fig 2.46: Pertaining to Example 2.27.

Solution. *(a)* For the direction of current i shown in Fig. 2.46, the magnetic field inside the solenoid is directed axially upward.

∴ Magnetic field intensity inside the solenoid,

$$H = \frac{i\cdot N}{h} \text{ AT/m}$$

Flux density $B = \mu_0 H = \mu_0 \frac{iN}{h}$ Wb/m^2

Field energy density inside the solenoid

$$w_{fld} = \frac{1}{2}\frac{B^2}{\mu_0} = \frac{1}{2}\mu_0\left(\frac{iN}{h}\right)^2 \text{ J/m}^3$$

Field energy stored inside the solenoid,

$$W_{fld} = w_{fld}\times \text{volume of solenoid}$$

$$= \frac{1}{2}\mu_0\left(\frac{iN}{h}\right)^2\times\pi r^2 h = \frac{1}{2}\mu_0\frac{(iN)^2}{h}\times\pi r^2$$

(b) Radial magnetic force, $f_e = \dfrac{\partial W_{fld}(i,r)}{\partial r} = \dfrac{1}{2}\mu_0 \dfrac{(iN)^2}{h} \times \pi(2r) = \mu_0 \dfrac{(iN)^2}{h} \pi r$ N

(c) Radial pressure on the sides of solenoid $= \dfrac{f_e}{\text{Surface area of solenoid}}$

$$= \mu_0 \frac{(iN)^2}{h} \pi r \times \frac{1}{2\pi rh} = \frac{1}{2}\mu_0 \left(\frac{iN}{h}\right)^2 \text{ N/m}^2$$

It is seen from above that radial magnetic force and radial pressure are positive. This means that radial pressure acts in such a direction as to increase the coil radius *r*.

(d) Solenoid inductance $L = \dfrac{N^2}{Rl} = \dfrac{N^2 \cdot \mu_0 \cdot \pi r^2}{h}$ H

Example 2.28. *An inductor of resistance 4 Ω and inductance 2 H is switched on to a voltage source which varies linearly from zero to 8 V in 2 sec and then stays constant. Find the energy stored in inductor (a) during the 2-sec period (b) after all the transients are over.*

Solution. (a) Applied voltage at any time $= \dfrac{8}{2}t = 4t$

$$\therefore \quad 4t = Ri + L\frac{di}{dt} = 4i + 2\frac{di}{dt}$$

Its Laplace transform gives, $\dfrac{4}{s^2} = I(s)\,[4 + 2s]$ or $I(s) = \dfrac{4}{s^2(2s+4)} = \dfrac{2}{s^2(s+2)}$

Let $$\frac{2}{s^2(s+2)} = \frac{K_{o1}}{s^2} + \frac{K_{o2}}{s} + \frac{K_1}{s+2}$$

Constants K_{o1}, K_{o2} and K_1 can be determined in the usual method.

$$\therefore \quad K_{o1} = 1,\ K_{o2} = -\frac{1}{2} \text{ and } K_1 = \frac{1}{2}$$

$$\therefore \quad I(s) = \left[\frac{1}{s^2} - \frac{1}{2s} + \frac{1}{2}\cdot\frac{1}{s+2}\right]$$

$$\therefore \quad i(t) = \left[t - \frac{1}{2} + \frac{1}{2}e^{-2t}\right] = \frac{1}{2}[e^{-2t} + 2t - 1]$$

At $t = 2$ sec, current $I_1 = \dfrac{1}{2}[e^{-4} + 2 \times 2 - 1] = 1.51$ A

Energy stored during the 2-sec period $= \dfrac{1}{2}LI_1^2 = \dfrac{1}{2} \times 2 \times 1.51^2 = 2.2801$ J

(b) When all the transients are over, $I = \dfrac{V}{R} = \dfrac{8}{4} = 2$ A

$$\text{Energy stored} = \frac{1}{2} \times 2 \times 2^2 = 4 \text{ J.}$$

Example 2.29. *For the magnetic circuit of Fig. 2.47, length of iron path = 120 cms., g = 0.5 cm, area of cross-section of iron = 5 × 5 cm², μ_r = 1500, I = 2 A, N = 1000 turns.*

Calculate and compare the field-energy stored and field-energy density in iron as well as in air-gap. Neglect fringing and leakage flux.

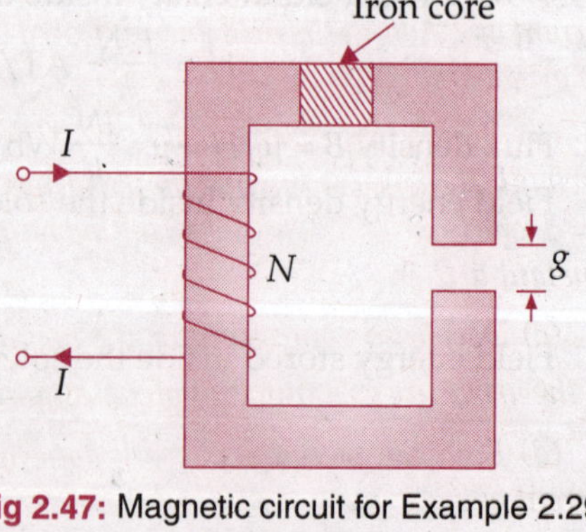

Fig 2.47: Magnetic circuit for Example 2.29.

Solution. Total reluctance $= \dfrac{\text{Length of iron path}}{\propto_0 \propto_r \times \text{Area}} + \dfrac{\text{Gap length}}{\mu_0 \times \text{Area}}$

$$= \frac{120 \times 10^{-2}}{4\pi \times 10^{-7} \times 1500 \times 25 \times 10^{-4}} + \frac{0.5 \times 10^{-2}}{4\pi \times 10^{-7} \times 25 \times 10^{-4}}$$

$$= \frac{10^9}{4\pi \times 25}\left[\frac{120}{1500} + \frac{0.5}{1}\right] = 1.8462 \times 10^6 \text{ A/Wb}$$

Flux, $\phi = \frac{NI}{Rl} = \frac{1000 \times 2}{1.8462 \times 10^6} \times 10^3 = 1.0833 \text{ mWb}$

Field energy stored in iron $= \frac{1}{2}\phi^2 \times$ reluctance offered by iron path

$$= \frac{1}{2}[1.0833 \times 10^{-3}]^2 \times \frac{120 \times 10^{-2}}{4\pi \times 10^{-7} \times 1500 \times 25 \times 10^{-4}}$$

$$= 0.14942 \text{ J}$$

Field energy stored in air-gap $= \frac{1}{2}\phi^2 \times$ reluctance of air-gap

$$= \frac{1}{2}[1.0833 \times 10^{-3}]^2 \times \frac{0.5 \times 10^{-2}}{4\pi \times 10^{-7} \times 25 \times 10^{-4}} = 0.93387 \text{ J}$$

Energy density in iron $= \frac{\text{Energy stored in iron}}{\text{Volume of iron}}$

$$= \frac{0.14942}{120 \times 10^{-2} \times 25 \times 10^{-4}} = 49.807 \text{ J/m}^3$$

Energy density in air-gap $= \frac{0.93387}{0.5 \times 10^{-2} \times 25 \times 10^{-4}} = 74709.6 \text{ J/m}^3$

$$\frac{\text{Energy stored in air gap}}{\text{Energy stored in iron}} = \frac{0.93387}{0.14942} = 6.25$$

$$\frac{\text{Energy density in air gap}}{\text{Energy density in iron}} = \frac{74709.6}{49.807} = 1499.98 \simeq 1500$$

This example demonstrates that most of the field energy is stored in the air-gap.

Example 2.30. *For the electromagnetic relay of Fig. 2.48, the exciting coil has N = 1200 turns and core area A = 6 cm × 5 cm. The relay is made from infinitely permeable magnetic material. Neglect fringing effects.*

(a) Find the coil inductance for x = 1 cm. For a coil current of 2 A, find the field energy stored and force on the armature.

(b) Find the mechanical work done (or the mechanical energy output) as the armature moves from x = 1 cm to x = 0.5 cm with coil current remaining constant at 2 A.

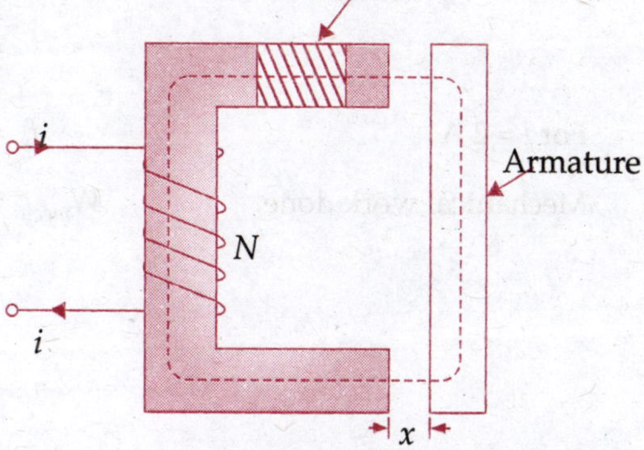

Fig 2.48: Pertaining to Example 2.30.

(c) Derive an expression for the magnetic force f_e on the armature as a function of x assuming constant coil current of 2 A. Hence find $\int_1^{0.5} fe \cdot dx$.

(d) Find the mechanical work done in part (b) if the flux linkages are maintained constant at a coil current of 2 A.

(e) Repeat part (d) using the expression $\int\left[-\frac{\partial W_{fld}(\psi, x)}{\partial x}\right]dx$.

Solution. *(a)* Reluctance of two air-gaps, $Rl = \dfrac{2x}{\mu_0 A}$

Coil inductance, $L(x) = \dfrac{N^2}{Rl} = \dfrac{N^2 \mu_0 A}{2x}$

For $x = 1$ cm, $L_1 = \dfrac{(1200)^2 \times 4\pi \times 10^{-7} \times 30 \times 10^{-4}}{2 \times 1 \times 10^{-2}} = 0.2714$ H

Field energy stored, $W_{fld} = \dfrac{1}{2} i_1^2 L_1 = \dfrac{1}{2} \times 2^2 \times 0.2714 = 0.5428$ J

Force on armature,
$$f_e = +\frac{\partial W_{fld}(i,x)}{\partial x} = \frac{1}{2} i^2 \frac{dL(x)}{dx}$$
$$= \frac{1}{2} i^2 \frac{d}{dx}\left[\frac{N^2 \mu_0 A}{2x}\right] = -\frac{1}{2} i^2 \frac{N^2 \mu_0 A}{2x^2}$$

For $x = 1$ cm,
$$f_e = -\frac{1}{2} \times 2^2 \times \frac{(1200)^2 \times 4\pi \times 10^{-7} \times 30 \times 10^{-4}}{2 \times 1 \times 10^{-4}}$$
$$= -54.287 \text{ N.}$$

(b) When $x = 1$ cm, flux linkages,
$$\psi_1 = i_1 L_1 = 2 \times 0.2714 = 0.5428 \text{ Wbt}$$

When $x = 0.5$ cm, coil inductance
$$L_2 = 2L_1 = 2 \times 0.2714 = 0.5428 \text{ H}$$
$$\therefore \quad \psi_2 = i_1 L_2 = 2 \times 0.5428 = 1.0856 \text{ Wbt.}$$

∴ Mechanical energy output or mechanical work done
$$= \frac{1}{2}(\psi_2 - \psi_1) i_1 = \frac{1}{2}(1.0856 - 0.5428) \times 2 = 0.5428 \text{ J.}$$

(c)
$$f_e = \frac{\partial W_{fld}(i,x)}{\partial x} = \frac{1}{2} i^2 \frac{dL(x)}{dx} = \frac{1}{2} i^2 \frac{N^2 \mu_0 A}{2x^2}$$
$$= -\frac{1}{4} i^2 \frac{N^2 \mu_0 A}{2x^2}$$

For $i = 2$ A,
$$f_e = -\frac{1}{4} \times 2^2 \times \frac{N^2 \mu_0 A}{2x^2} = -\frac{N^2 \mu_0 A}{x^2}$$

Mechanical work done,
$$W_{mech} = \int_1^{0.5} f_e \cdot dx$$
$$= -\frac{N^2 \mu_0 A}{1} \int_{0.01}^{0.005} \frac{1}{x^2} dx = \frac{N^2 \mu_0 A}{1} \left| \frac{1}{x} \right|_{0.01}^{0.005}$$
$$= (1200)^2 \times 4\pi \times 10^{-7} \times 30 \times 10^{-4} \left[\frac{1}{0.005} - \frac{1}{0.01}\right]$$
$$= 0.5248 \text{ J.}$$

(d) Flux linkages for $x = 1$ cm and $i_1 = 2$ *A*, $\psi_1 = 0.5428$ (as in part *(b)*)

When x reduces to 0.5, the flux linkages are again 0.5428 Wbt (given).

∴ Current that can produce 0.5428 Wbt, when $x = 0.5$ cm is given by
$$i_2 L_2 = 0.5428$$

or
$$i_2 = \frac{0.5428}{0.5428} = 1 \text{ A}$$

∴ Mechanical work done if the flux linkages are maintained constant

$$= \frac{1}{2}\psi_1(i_1 - i_2) = \frac{1}{2} \times 0.5428\,(2-1) = 0.2714 \text{ J.}$$

(e) Electromagnetic force, $f_e = -\dfrac{\partial W_{fld}(\psi, x)}{\partial x}$

But $W_{fld} = \dfrac{1}{2}L(x)\cdot i^2$ and $\psi = L(x)\cdot i$ or $i = \dfrac{\psi}{L(x)}$

∴ $$W_{fld} = \frac{1}{2}L(x)\cdot\left[\frac{\psi}{L(x)}\right]^2 = \frac{1}{2}\frac{\psi^2}{L(x)}$$

Here $$L(x) = \frac{N^2}{Rl} = \frac{N^2.\mu_0 A}{2x}$$

∴ $$W_{fld} = \frac{1}{2}\frac{\psi^2.2x}{N^2\mu_0 A} = \frac{x\cdot\psi^2}{N^2\mu_0 A}$$

$$f_e = -\frac{\partial W_{fld}(\psi,x)}{\partial x} = -\frac{\partial}{\partial x}\left[\frac{x\cdot\psi^2}{N^2\mu_0 A}\right] = -\frac{\psi^2}{N^2\mu_0 A}$$

For $x = 1$ cm, $$\psi = L(x)\cdot i = \frac{N^2\mu_0 A}{2x}\cdot i$$

$$= \frac{(1200)^2 \times 4\pi\times10^{-7}\times 30\times10^{-4}}{2\times1\times10^{-2}} = 0.5428 \text{ Wbt}$$

Mechanical energy output, $$W_{mech} = \int_1^{0.5} f_e\cdot dx$$

$$= -\int_1^{0.5}\frac{\psi^2}{N^2\mu_0 A}dx = -\frac{\psi^2}{N^2\mu_0 A}[0.005 - 0.01] = \frac{0.005\,\psi^2}{N^2\mu_0 A}$$

Substituting the values, we get $$W_{mech} = \frac{0.005\times(0.5428)^2}{(1200)^2\times 4\pi\times10^{-7}\times 30\times10^{-4}} = 0.2714 \text{ J.}$$

Example 2.31. *For the cylindrical solenoid magnet shown in Fig. 2.49, the iron has infinite permeability. Neglect coil resistance, magnetic leakage and fringing.*

(a) If N-turn coil carries dc steady current I, derive an expression for the magnetic force on the movable iron plunger.

(b) In case I = 5 A, N = 500 turns, g = 6 mm, b = 21 mm, a = 2 mm and l = 40 mm, calculate the magnitude of force acting on the plunger.

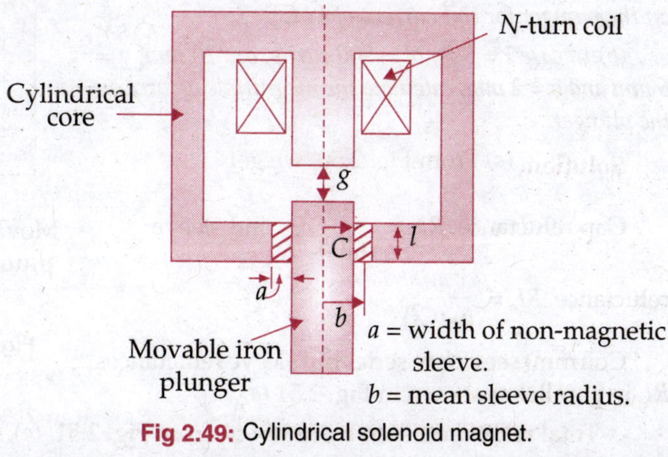

Fig 2.49: Cylindrical solenoid magnet.

Solution. (a) Reluctance of gap of length g, $Rl_g = \dfrac{g}{\mu_0(\pi C^2)}$

Reluctance of non-magnetic sleeve, $Rl_s = \dfrac{a}{\mu_0(2\pi\, bl)}$

Total reluctance $$Rl = Rl_g + Rl_s = \frac{g}{\mu_0(\pi C^2)} + \frac{a}{\mu_0(2\pi\, bl)}$$

$$= \frac{1}{\pi\mu_0}\left[\frac{g}{C^2} + \frac{a}{2\,bl}\right] = \frac{1}{\mu_0\pi}[k_1 \cdot g + k_2]$$

where $$k_1 = \frac{1}{C^2} \text{ and } k_2 = \frac{a}{2\,bl}$$

Coil inductance, $$L = \frac{N^2}{Rl} = \frac{N^2 \cdot \mu_0 \cdot \pi}{[k_1\, g + k_2]}$$

∴ Magnetic force, $$f_e = \frac{1}{2}i^2\frac{dL}{dg} = \frac{1}{2}i^2\frac{d}{dg}\left[\frac{\mu_0\pi N^2}{k_1 g + k_2}\right] = -\frac{1}{2}\frac{i^2 N^2\,\pi\,\mu_0 k_1}{[k_1 g + k_2]^2}$$

For steady current I, $$f_e = -\frac{1}{2}I^2\frac{N^2\mu_0\pi\, k_1}{[k_1 g + k_2]^2}\ \text{N}$$

(b) Here $I = 5$ A, $N = 500$, $g = 6$ mm, $k_1 = \frac{1}{C^2}$. Fig. 2.49 reveals that plunger radius $C = b - \frac{a}{2}$ $= 21 - \frac{2}{2} = 20$ mm, $a = 2$ mm, $l = 40$ mm, $b = 21$ mm

∴ $$k_1 = \frac{1}{C^2} = \frac{1}{[20\times 10^{-3}]^2} = 2500$$

and $$k_2 = \frac{a}{2\,bl} = \frac{2}{2\times 21\times 40\times 10^{-3}} = 1.19$$

∴ Magnitude of force acting on the plunger is

$$f_e = \frac{1}{2}(5)^2 \times \frac{(500)^2\times 4\neq \times 10^{-7}\times \neq \times 2500}{[2500\times 6\times 10^{-3} + 1.19]^2} = 117.667\ \text{N}$$

Example 2.32. *A solenoid with a core of square cross-section is shown in Fig. 2.50. Magnetic leakage, fringing and iron-portion reluctance are neglected.*

(a) Derive expressions for coil inductance and force on the plunger for coil current of I (dc).

(b) In case I = 5 A, N = 500 turns, c = 20 mm, g = 6 mm and b = 2 mm, calculate the magnitude of force on the plunger.

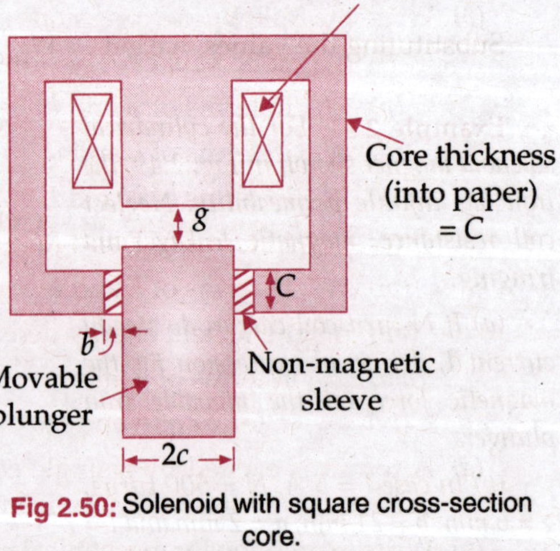

Fig 2.50: Solenoid with square cross-section core.

Solution. *(a)* From Fig. 2.50, we get

Gap reluctance, $Rl_g = \frac{g}{\mu_0(2C^2)}$ and sleeve reluctance, $Rl_s = \frac{b}{\mu_0(C^2)}$.

Coil mmf sees Rl_g in series but sleeve reluctances Rl_s in parallel as shown in Fig. 2.51 *(a)*.

∴ Total reluctance seen by mmf *i.N*, from Fig. 2.51. *(a)*, is

$$Rl = Rl_g + \frac{Rl_s}{2} = \frac{g}{\mu_0.2\,C^2} + \frac{b}{\mu_0.2\,C^2} = \frac{1}{\mu_0.2\,C^2}[g+b]$$

$\therefore$ Inductance $\quad L = \dfrac{N^2}{Rl} = \dfrac{2N^2\mu_0.C^2}{(g+b)}$.

$\therefore$ Force $f_e = \dfrac{1}{2}i^2\dfrac{dL}{dg} = -\dfrac{1}{2}i^2\dfrac{2N^2\mu_0.C^2}{(g+b)^2}$

$$= -\frac{\mu_0 N^2 i^2 C^2}{(g+b)^2}$$

For d.c. current I, $\quad f_e = -\dfrac{\mu_0 N^2 I^2 C^2}{(g+b)^2}$

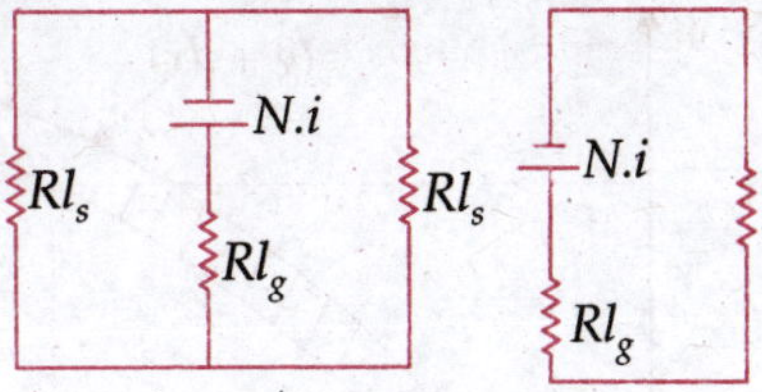

Fig 2.51: Electrical equivalent of the magnetic circuit of Fig. 2.50

(*b*) Substituting the values, the magnitude of force is

$$f_e = \frac{4\pi\times10^{-7}\times500^2\times5^2\times[20\times10^{-3}]^2}{[(6+2)\times10^{-3}]^2} = 49.088 \text{ N}$$

PROBLEMS

2.1. (*a*) State the advantages of analysing energy-conversion devices by field-energy concept.

(*b*) Describe the principle of energy-conversion. From a consideration of the various energies involved, develop the model of an electromechanical energy-conversion device.

(*c*) Show that the reaction of coupling magnetic field on the electrical or mechanical system is essential for the electromechanical-energy-conversion process.

2.2. (*a*) Draw and explain fully the general block-diagram representation of an electromechanical energy-conversion device.

(*b*) For a singly excited magnetic system, derive the relation for the magnetic stored energy in terms of reluctance.

2.3. (*a*) Based on the principle of conservation of energy, write an energy balance equation for a motor. Discuss briefly about the four energy terms involved.

(*b*) Write the following expressions :

(*i*) magnetic field energy stored W_{fld} in terms of ϕ and Rl

(*ii*) W_{fld} in terms of ψ and i

(*iii*) W_{fld} in terms of L and i

(*iv*) W_{fld} in terms of ψ and L

(*v*) W_{fld} in terms of F and Rl

(*vi*) W_{fld} in terms of F and ϕ

(*vii*) magnetic field energy density w_{fld} in terms of B and H

(*viii*) w_{fld} in terms of μ and B

(*ix*) w_{fld} in terms of μ and H. **[Ans.** (*b*) See Art. 2.2**]**

2.4. (*a*) A toroid is excited by a single coil. Discuss the conditions under which this toroid can extract energy from the supply system.

(*b*) Write expression for mechanical work done $f_e \cdot dx$ from a physical consideration of Fig. 2.52 (*a*) and hence find an expression for the magnetic force f_e. (*c*) Repeat part (*b*) for Fig. 2.52 (*b*).

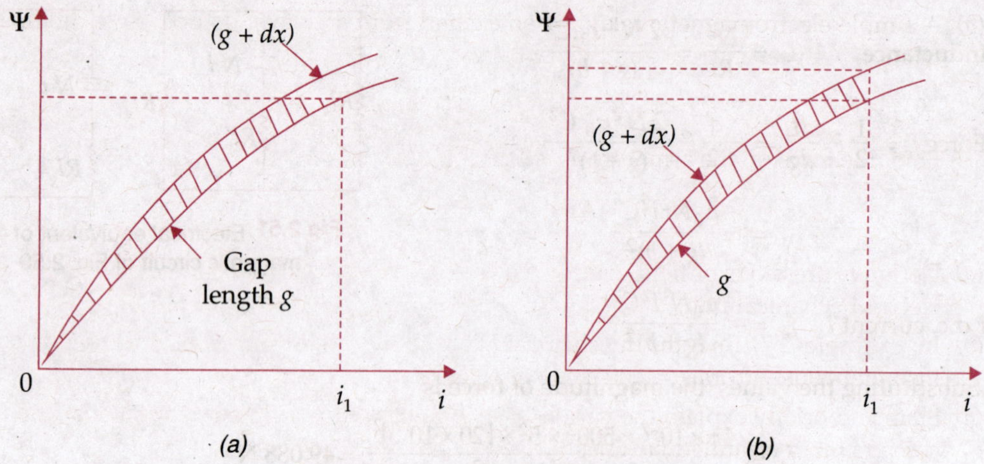

Fig 2.52: Pertaining to Prob. 2.4.

[**Ans.** (b) $f_e \cdot dx = - dW_{fld}$ with constant ψ, $f_e = -\dfrac{\partial W_{fld}}{\partial x}(\psi, x)$; (c) $f_e \cdot dx = + dW_{fld}'$ with constant i, $f_e = +\dfrac{\partial W_{fld}'}{\partial x}(i, x)$]

2.5. (a) For a linear magnetic circuit, derive the following relations for the stored magnetic energy W_{fld} and co-energy W_{fld}'

$$W_{fld} = W_{fld}' = \frac{1}{2}F\phi = \frac{1}{2}\psi i = \frac{1}{2}\phi^2 Rl = \frac{1}{2}\frac{\phi^2}{\Delta} = \frac{1}{2}\cdot\frac{F^2}{Rl} = \frac{1}{2}Li^2 = \frac{1}{2}\frac{\psi^2}{L} \text{ joules.}$$

Hence show that the magnetic stored energy density w_{fld} is given by $\dfrac{1}{2}\dfrac{B^2}{\mu}$ joules/m^3.

(b) A 10 kW, 1440 r.p.m. D.C. shunt generator has a time constant L_f/r_f of 0.2 sec for its field winding. Under normal operating conditions, the $I_f^2\, r_f$ loss in the field winding is 400 watts. Compute the energy stored in the magnetic field produced by the field winding, under normal operating conditions. [**Ans.** 40 watt-sec.] [*I.E.S.*, 1985]

2.6. For an electromagnetic system, show that the mechanical work done is equal to the area enclosed between the two magnetization curves at open and closed positions of the armature and the ψ-i locus during the armature movement.

2.7. (a) Describe the principle of virtual work and hence show that the magnetic force f_e is given by the expression

$$f_e = -\frac{\partial W_{fld}}{\partial x}(\psi, x) = -\frac{\partial W_{fld}}{\partial x}(\phi, x)$$

(b) The functional relationship of m.m.f. F, flux ϕ and the position co-ordinate x of a device is given by $F = \phi^3 x^3$. Compute the stored energy and the magnetic force acting in the x-direction. Does this force tend to increase or decrease x? Verify your result by the use of co-energy function.

[**Ans.** (b) $\dfrac{1}{4}\phi^4 x^3, \left(-\dfrac{3}{4}\phi^4 x^2\right)$, decrease x]

2.8. (a) What is the principle of virtual work? Illustrate its use to show that magnetic force f_e developed in an elementary magnetic relay is given by

$$f_e = \frac{\partial W_{fld}'}{\partial x}(i, x) = \frac{\partial W_{fld}'}{\partial x}(F, x)$$

(*b*) A simple electromagnetic relay, when excited from a voltage source, gave the following relation between current and flux linkages :

$$i = \psi^2 + \psi \left(1 - \frac{x}{2}\right)^2 ; x < 1$$

Find the force on the armature as a function of ψ.

[**Ans.** (*b*) $-\frac{1}{2}\psi^2\left(1-\frac{x}{2}\right)$; force tends to increase x for $x < 1$]

2.9. (*a*) Derive expressions of field energy, co-energy and the magnetic force in a singly-excited electromechanical unit.

(*b*) In Example 2.7, find the mechanical work done, if the plunger is allowed to move instantaneously from $g = 2.00$ cm to $g = 0.5$ cm. [**Ans.** (*b*) 0.60 Joules]

2.10. (*a*) State and briefly explain the various phenomena useful for the electromechanical energy conversion in rotating machines.

(*b*) Derive an expression for reluctance torque in a rotating electrical machine.

[(*a*) **Hint:** (*i*) Current-carrying conductor in a magnetic field experiences a force. Also force exists between current-carrying circuits, because of the interaction of their magnetic fields. (*ii*) A ferromagnetic material when placed in a magnetic field, experiences a force which tends to bring it into the minimum reluctance position.]

2.11. (*a*) Show that the torque developed in a doubly excited magnetic system is equal to the rate of increase of field energy with respect to displacement at constant currents.

Hence or otherwise, derive an expression for the torque developed in a cylindrical rotor machine with one rotor winding excited with D.C. and another winding on the stator connected to an A.C. source. State the assumptions made for obtaining the torque expression.

2.12. (*a*) A simplified reluctance motor is illustrated in Fig. 2.16 (*b*). Assume sinusoidal inductance variation with θ_r and designate,

L_d = maximum inductance when long axis of movable iron slug is in the direct axis, *i.e.* when $\theta_r = 0$ and π

and L_q = minimum inductance when long axis of movable iron slug is in quadrature axis, *i.e.*, when $\theta_r = \frac{\pi}{2}$ and $\frac{3\pi}{2}$.

Note that L_d and L_q must remain positive. (*a*) Write an expression for the variable inductance in terms of L_d, L_q and θ_r.

(*b*) Find an expression for the instantaneous torque on the rotating element. Assume $\theta_r = \omega_{rt} - \delta$ and $i = I_m \cos \omega t$.

(*c*) If the movable iron slug speed ω_r is made equal to the time angular speed ω, is a non-zero time-average torque possible? If yes, find its expression.

[**Hint:** For this problem, refer to Art. 2.5 (*c*)].

[**Ans.** (*a*) $\frac{1}{2}(L_d + L_q) + \frac{1}{2}(L_d - L_q)\cos 2\theta_r$

(*b*) $T_e = -\frac{1}{4} I_m^2 (L_d - L_q)\left[\sin(2\omega_r t - 2\delta) + \frac{1}{2}\sin(2\omega_r t + 2\omega t - 2\delta) + \frac{1}{2}\sin(2\omega_r t - 2\omega t - 2\delta)\right]$

(*c*) $T_{e\,(av)} = \frac{1}{8} I_m^2 (L_d - L_q)\sin 2\delta$]

2.13. (*a*) For the reluctance motor shown in Fig. 2.16 (*b*), derive an expression for the emf induced in stator winding at synchronous speed, if stator current is $i = I_m \sin \omega t$. Neglect stator resistance. Take $\theta_r = \omega_r t - \delta$.

(b) Why does the emf expression obtained in part (a) contain third harmonic emf component?

[**Hint:** (a) $e = \dfrac{d\psi_s}{dt}$, $\psi_s = i\,[L_0 + L_2 \cos 2\,\theta_r]$ etc.]

[**Ans.** (a) $e = \omega\, L_0\, I_m \cos \omega t - \dfrac{1}{2}\, \omega\, L_2\, I_m \cos (\omega t - \delta) + \dfrac{3}{2}\, \omega L_2\, I_m \cos (3\omega t - 2\delta)$
(b) Stator flux contains third harmonic component of flux.]

2.14. Two windings, one on stator and the other on rotor, has the following parameters :

$r_s = 2.5\ \Omega \quad L_s = 0.03\ \text{H} \qquad r_r = 3.00\ \Omega \quad L_r = 0.12\ \text{H} \qquad M_{sr} = 0.06 \cos \theta_r$

where θ_r is the space angle between stator and rotor winding axes.

The two windings are connected in parallel and the rotor is locked at $\theta_r = 90°$. With the currents initially zero, the windings are switched on to a voltage source of 30 volts D.C. at time $t = 0$.

(a) Find i_s, i_r as functions of time.

(b) Find an expression for the magnetic torque T_e as a function of time.

[**Ans.** (a) $i_s = 12(1 - e^{-83.3t})$, $i_r = 10(1 - e^{-25t})$ (b) $T_e = -7.2(1 - e^{-83.3t} - e^{-25t} + e^{-108.3t})$]

2.15. Two sinusoidally distributed current sheets are placed, one on the stator and the other on the rotor of an idealised rotating electrical machine, with smooth air-gap. The parameters of the machine are :

$$L_s = 1.0\ \text{H},\ L_r = 0.3\ \text{H},\ M_{sr} = 0.5 \cos \theta_r$$

where θ_r is the relative angle between the current sheets.

Stator and rotor resistances are considered negligible. The stator is excited by a sinusoidal current $I_m \cos \omega t$, while the rotor is short-circuited.

(a) With the machine at standstill, compute the instantaneous torque developed as a function of θ_r and t.

(b) If the rotor is allowed to rotate, at what angle it will come to rest.

[(b) **Hint:** $T_{e\,(av)} = 0.2083\ I_m^2 \sin 2\theta_r$.

For $\theta_r = 0°$, $T_{e\,(av)} = 0$. For $\theta_r = 1°$, torque is positive, therefore, torque tends to increase θ_r, *i.e.* torque tends to take the rotor away from $\theta_r = 0°$ position. Thus a slight disturbance at $\theta_r = 0°$ position will take the rotor away from this position. In view of this, position of $\theta_r = 0°$ is unstable one.

For $\theta_r = 90°$, $T_{e\,(av)} = 0$. For $\theta_r = 89°$, torque is positive, therefore, torque tends to increase the angle from 89°, *i.e.*, the torque has a tendency to increase the angle from 89° to 90°. For $\theta_r = 91°$, torque is negative, therefore, torque tends to decrease the angle from 91° to 90°. Thus, between $\theta_r = 0°$ and $\theta_r = 180°$, stable rest position is 90°.]

[**Ans.** (a) $0.2083\ I_m^2 \sin 2\theta_r\,(1 + \cos 2\,\omega t)$.
(b) Between $\theta_r = 0°$ and 180°, stable rest position is at 90°.
Between $\theta_r = 180°$ and 360°, the stable rest position is at 270°]

2.16. (a) Find an expression for the magnetic force developed in a doubly excited translational magnetic system.

(b) Two air-cored coils have their magnetic axes coincident. Their parameters are :

$L_1 = 0.4$ H, $L_2 = 0.2$ H

$M_{12} = M_{21} = 0.1\, e^{-4x}$ H

where x is the distance between the two coils.

For steady current of $I_1 = 10$ A and $I_2 = 5$ A, calculate the magnetic force developed. Does this force tend to increase or decrease x? Calculate the magnitude of force for $x = 2.5$ cm.

[**Ans.** $(-20e^{-4x})$ N ; decrease x ; – 18.097 N]

2.17. A doubly excited rotating machine has following self and mutual inductances :

$r_s = 40\ \Omega \quad L_s = 0.16$ H

$r_r = 2\ \Omega \quad L_r = 0.04 + 0.02 \cos 2\theta_r$ H

$M_{sr} = 0.08 \cos \theta_r$

where θ_r is the space angle between coil axes. The rotor is revolving at a speed of 100 rad/sec. For $i_s = 10$ A D.C. and $i_r = 2$ A D.C.

(*a*) derive expressions for the instantaneous voltages applied to the stator and rotor windings.

(*b*) obtain expressions for magnetic torque and the corresponding electrical power.

For both the parts (*a*) and (*b*), find their values for $\theta_r = 90°$.

[**Ans.** (*a*) $400 - 16 \sin \theta_r$; 384 V ; $4 - 8 \sin 2\theta_r - 80 \sin \theta_r$; – 76 V.
(*b*) $-0.08 \sin 2\theta_r - 1.6 \sin \theta_r$; – 1.6 N-m ; $-8 \sin 2\theta_r - 160 \sin \theta_r$; –160 watts.]

2.18. The doubly-excited magnetic system of Fig. 2.21 has the following self and mutual inductances:

$$L_s = L_r = 3 + \cos 2\theta, M = 2 \cos \theta$$

where θ is the angle between the axis of stator and rotor coils. The coils, connected in series, carry a current of $i = \sqrt{2}\, I \cos \omega t$. Determine the time-average torque as a function of angle θ.

[**Ans.** $-2I^2 (\sin 2\theta + \sin \theta)$]

2.19. (*a*) The electromagnetic relay shown in Fig. 2.48 is wound with two coupled coils having the following parameters : $L_1 = \dfrac{2}{x}, L_2 = \dfrac{3}{x}, M = \dfrac{4}{x}$

Obtain an expression for the force on the armature as a function of time if $i_1 = I_{m1} \sin \omega_1 t$ and $i_2 = I_{m2} \sin \omega_2 t$. Find the magnitude of average force in case (*a*) $\omega_1 \neq \omega_2$ and (*b*) $\omega_1 = \omega_2$.

[**Ans.** $-\dfrac{1}{x^2} I_{m1}^2 \sin^2 \omega_1 t - \dfrac{3}{2} \cdot \dfrac{1}{x^2} I_{m2}^2 \sin^2 \omega_2 t - I_{m1} I_{m2} \dfrac{4}{x^2} \sin \omega t_1 \sin \omega t_2$

(*a*) $-\dfrac{1}{2x^2}\left[I_{m1}^2 + \dfrac{3}{2} I_{m2}^2\right]$ (*b*) $-\dfrac{1}{2x^2}\left[I_{m1}^2 + \dfrac{3}{2} I_{m2}^2 + 4\, I_{m1} I_{m2}\right]$

2.20. (*a*) Define field energy and co-energy. Give the significance of co-energy in the derivation of torque or force in an electromechanical energy conversion device.

(*b*) All practical energy conversion devices make use of the magnetic field as a coupling medium rather than an electric field. Discuss.

2.21. (*a*) Prove that energy and co-energy in a linear magnetic system are given by identical expressions.

(*b*) An electric machine has cylindrical stator and salient-pole rotor. Justify the correctness or otherwise of the following statements :

(*i*) Reluctance torque is produced when exciting winding is on rotor.

(*ii*) Reluctance torque is produced when exciting winding is on stator.

(*iii*) When stator and rotor both carry exciting winding, electromagnetic torque is produced.

(*iv*) When stator and rotor both carry exciting windings, electromagnetic as well as reluctance torques are produced.

[**Ans.** (*b*) (*i*) Incorrect (*ii*) Correct (*iii*) Incorrect (*iv*) Correct.]

2.22. Fig. 2.53 shows an electromagnet used to lift an iron piece. If $N = 1000$, $i = 1$ Amp., $x = 0.5$ mm, $A = 1\ \text{cm}^2$, calculate (*a*) coil inductance, (*b*) stored magnetic field energy and (*c*) the force *F* on the iron piece. ($\mu_0 = 4\,\pi \times 10^{-7}$ H/m) [*GATE*, 1988]

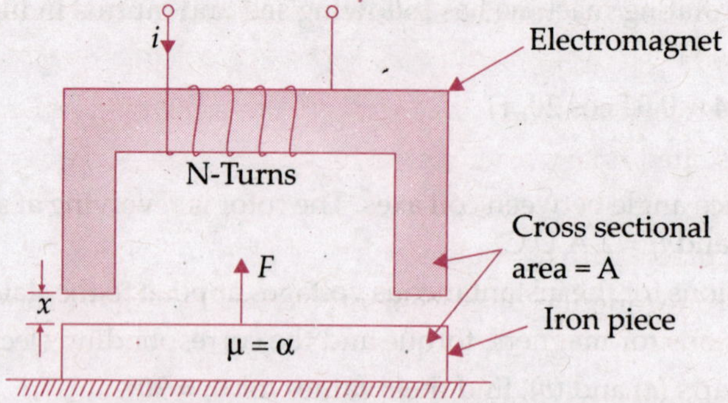

Fig 2.53: Pertaining to Problem 2.22.

[**Ans.** (*a*) 0.125664 H (*b*) 0.062832 W-sec (*c*) 125.664 N]

2.23. For the electromagnet shown in Fig. 2.53, N = 300 turns, coil resistance = 5 Ω and cross-sectional area $A = 20\ \text{cm}^2$.

(*a*) Find the coil voltage required to lift a 120-kg slab of iron from a distance of x = 1 cm.

(*b*) When the iron slab is in contact with electromagnet, there is a minimum air-gap of x = 0.5 mm. Calculate the minimum voltage required to lift this slab.

[**Ans.** (*a*) 228.13 V (*b*) 11.406 V]

2.24. A voltage $V_m \cos \omega t$ is applied to the N-turn coil of the electromagnet shown in Fig. 2.53. Coil resistance is R Ω. For air-gap length x as shown, find

(*a*) the average value of magnetic energy stored in the inductor

(*b*) voltage-source power output as a function of time and its average value.

[**Hint:** Proceed as in Example 2.11] [**Ans.** (*a*) $\frac{1}{2} \frac{V_m^2 N^2 \mu_0 A x}{(2xR)^2 + (\omega N^2 \mu_0 . A)^2}$ J

(*b*) $\frac{V_m^2}{\sqrt{R^2 + (\omega L_x)^2}^2} \left[\cos^2 \omega t \cos \theta + \frac{\sin 2\omega t}{2} \sin \theta\right]$, $\frac{1}{2} \frac{V_m^2}{R^2 + \left(\frac{\omega N^2 \mu_0 A}{2x}\right)} \cos \theta$

where $\theta = \tan^{-1} \frac{\omega N^2 \mu_0 A}{2xR}$]

2.25. Fig. 2.54 shows a singly-excited electromechanical device having a stationary core (stator) carrying N turns and an unwound rotating core (rotor). A voltage $e = 200\sqrt{2}\ \sin (100\ \pi t)\ V$ is applied across the stator winding while the rotor is rotating at 100π rad/s such that its position θ at any instant is given by θ = 100 πt + δ, where δ is the position at t = 0. Rotor surface is shaped such that the air-gap reluctance is of the form

$$\frac{R_q + R_d}{2} - \frac{R_q - R_d}{2} \cos 2\theta$$

(*a*) Write the numerical expression for the core flux ϕ due to the applied voltage (neglect winding resistance, leakage and fringing flux) as a function of time if N = 1000 turns.

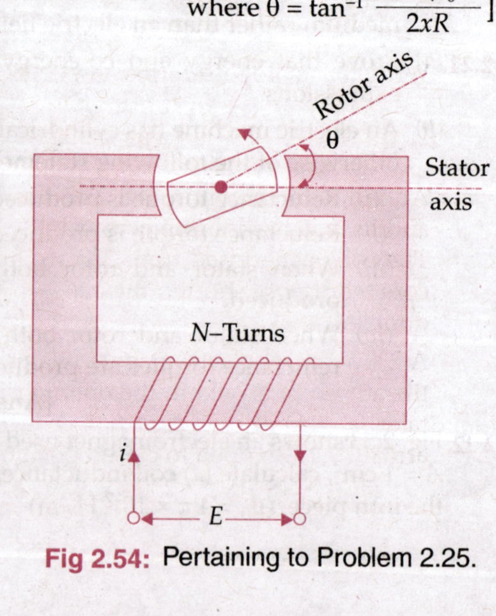

Fig 2.54: Pertaining to Problem 2.25.

(*b*) Calculate the average torque develcped as a function of δ, if $R_d = 10^8/4\pi$ and $R_q = 3R_d$.

[*GATE*, 1988] [**Ans.** (*a*) 0.9002 cos (100 πt) mWb (*b*) 1.61258 sin 2δ Nm]

2.26. (*a*) Distinguish between singly-excited and doubly-excited magnetic systems.

(*b*) In a doubly-excited rotary machine, the inductance co-efficients are

$L_{11} = (1.1 + 0.4 \cos 2\theta)$; $L_{22} = (0.03 + 0.005 \cos 2\theta)$; $L_{12} = 0.2 \cos \theta$.

The exciting currents are $i_1 = 8$ A and $i_2 = 50$ A.

Obtain the torque/angular displacement relation. Derive the expression used, if any.

[*I.A.S.*, 1994] [**Ans.** (*b*) (– 38.1 sin 2θ – 80 sin θ) Nm]

2.27. Derive an expression for the torque in a doubly-excited magnetic system having salient-pole type of stator as well as rotor. Hence show that differential changes of currents do not contribute to the production of magnetic torque.

2.28. For a certain relay, the magnetization curves for open and closed positions of armature are linear as shown in Fig. 2.55. At armature open, air-gap length is 1 cm.

(*a*) For very slow movement of armature, calculate the mechanical work done in moving the armature from open to closed position. Where does this energy come from?

(*b*) Repeat part (*a*) in case the armature moves very fast.

(*c*) Calculate the magnitude of average magnetic force on the armature during (*i*) slow armature movement and (*ii*) fast armature movement.

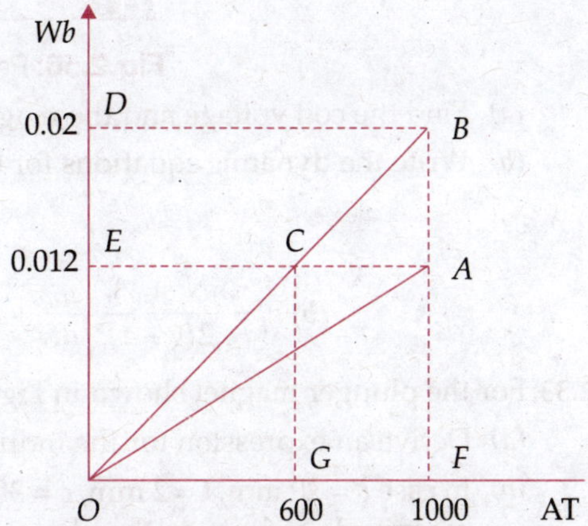

Fig 2.55: Pertaining to Problem 2.28.

[**Ans.** (*a*) 4 W-sec (*b*) 2.4 W-sec (*c*) 400 N, 240 N]

2.29. The following terms and expressions pertain to the magnetic field system. Symbols used have their usual meaning :

$$\psi, i, B, \frac{1}{2}\, i\, \psi, \frac{1}{2}\frac{\psi^2}{L(x)}, \frac{1}{2}\frac{B^2}{\mu_0}, f_e = -\frac{\partial W_{fld}}{\partial x}(\psi, x), f_e = \frac{\partial W_{fld}'(i,x)}{\partial x}$$

Write the analogous terms and expressions for the electric field system.

$$\text{[Ans. } q, v, D, \frac{1}{2}vq, \frac{1}{2}\frac{q^2}{C(x)}, \frac{1}{2}\frac{D^2}{\varepsilon_0}, f_e = -\frac{\partial W_{fld}(q,x)}{\partial x}, f_e = \frac{\partial W_{fld}'(v,x)}{\partial x}\text{]}$$

2.30. An inductor shown in Fig. 2.47 has $N = 1000$ turns , $A = 5$ cm × 5 cm, gap length = 0.5 cm and its iron has infinite permeability. Coil is assumed to have no resistance and leakage flux. The coil is energised from 230 V, 50 Hz. Calculate the time-average force acting on the iron core tending to shorten the air-gap. What would happen to this force if air-gap length were doubled? [**Ans.** – 85.305 N, Magnetic force would remain constant.]

2.31. A 230 V, 50 Hz electromagnet relay takes a current of 3 A at power factor of 0.2 lagging when the armature is held in the open position. When the armature is in closed position, the relay takes a current of 1 A at power factor of 0.08 lagging. Find the work done in moving the armature from open to closed position.

[**Hint:** Find $Z_1 = \frac{230}{3}\ \Omega$, $X_1 = Z_1 \sin\theta_1 = 2\pi \times 50 \times L_1$, energy stored $= \frac{1}{2} L_1 I_1^2$ etc.]

[**Ans.** 0.711 J]

2.32. For the electromechanical system shown in Fig. 2.56, coil resistance is negligible and air-gap flux density under steady operating condition is $B = B_m \sin \omega t$.

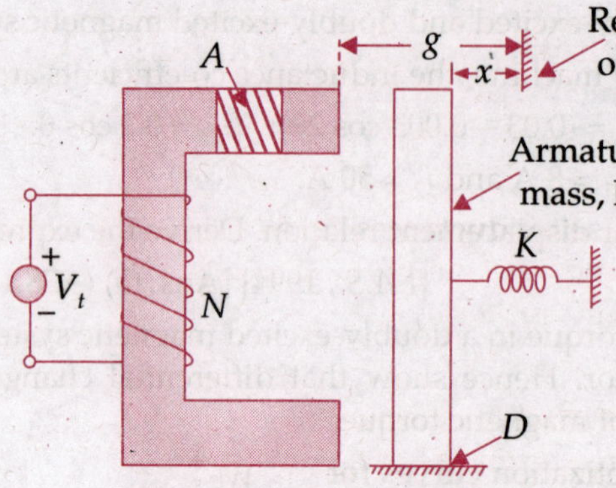

Fig 2.56: Pertaining to Problem 2.32.

(a) Find the coil voltage and the magnetic force as a function of time.

(b) Write the dynamic equations for the system shown.

[**Ans.** *(a)* $-\omega N B_m A \cos \omega t$; $\frac{1}{\mu_0} A B_m^2 \sin^2 \omega t$

(b) $v_t = \frac{N^2 \mu_0 A}{2(g-x)} \cdot \frac{di}{dt} + \frac{N^2 \mu_0 A}{2(g-x)^2} \cdot \frac{dx}{dt}, \frac{1}{2} i^2 \frac{N^2 \cdot \mu_0 A}{2(g-x)^2} = M \frac{d^2 x}{dt^2} + D \frac{dx}{dt} + K \cdot x$]

2.33. For the plunger magnet shown in Fig. 2.57, reluctance of ferromagnetic circuit is neglected.

(a) Derive an expression for the inductance of coil and magnetic force on the plunger.

(b) In case $b = 20$ mm, $t = 2$ mm, $c = 30$ mm, $x = 6$ mm, $N = 500$ turns and $I = 5$ A (d.c.), find the magnitude of force on the plunger.

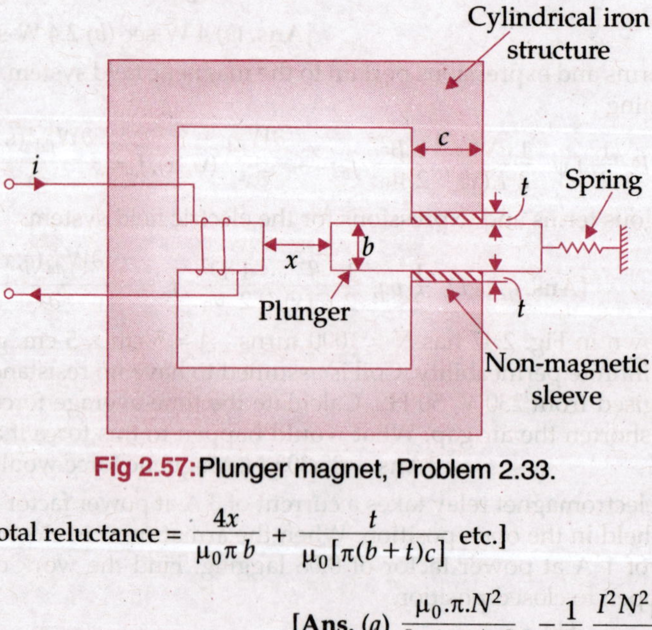

Fig 2.57: Plunger magnet, Problem 2.33.

[**Hint:** *(a)* Total reluctance = $\frac{4x}{\mu_0 \pi b} + \frac{t}{\mu_0 [\pi (b+t) c]}$ etc.]

[**Ans.** *(a)* $\frac{\mu_0 . \pi . N^2}{[x k_1 + k_2]}, -\frac{1}{2} \frac{I^2 N^2 \mu_0 \pi k_1}{(x k_1 + k_2)^2}$ *(b)* 31.054 N]

2.34. Fig. 2.58 shows a two-winding magnetic circuit with one fixed member having N_1 turns and the other movable element having N_2 turns. Both air-gap lengths remain equal as the movable element moves.

(a) Derive expressions for self-inductances of the two windings and the mutual inductance between them in terms of number of turns.

(b) Find expression for $W_{fld}'(i_1, i_2, g)$.

(c) Derive expression for force acting on the movable element in terms of currents.

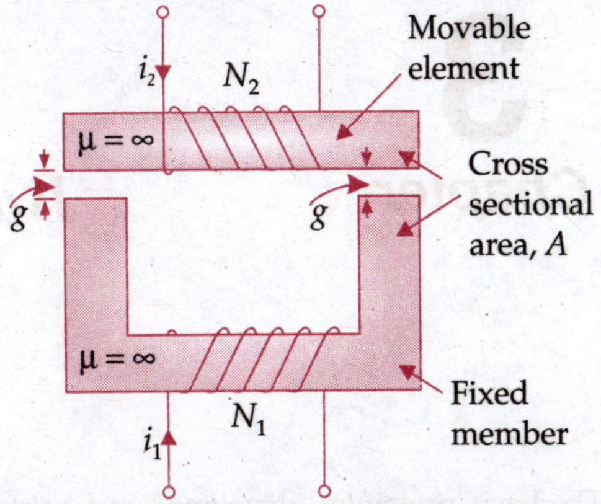

Fig 2.58: Two-winding magnetic circuit, Problem 2.34.

$$\textbf{[Ans.} \ (a)\ L_1 = \frac{\mu_0 . N_1^2 A}{2g},\ L_2 = \frac{\mu_0 . N_2^2 A}{2g},\ M = \frac{\mu_0 . N_1 N_2 A}{2g}$$

$$(b)\ \frac{\mu_0 A}{4g}\ [(N_1 i_1 + N_2 i_2)^2],\ (c)\ -\frac{\mu_0 A}{4g^2}\ [(N_1 i_1 + N_2 i_2)^2]\textbf{]}$$

2.35. (a) A three-phase synchronous machine has two salient poles on the rotor. The rotor pole axis makes an angle θ_r with the axis of phase '*a*' winding. Derive an expression for the self-inductance of phase '*a*' in terms of θ_r.

(b) In case rotor has four salient poles, repeat part (a).

[Hint: (a) Refer to Art. 2.5(c).**]**

$$\textbf{[Ans.}\ (a)\ L_a = L_0 + L_2 \cos 2\theta_r, \text{ where } L_0 = \frac{1}{2}(L_d + L_q) \text{ and } L_2 = \frac{1}{2}(L_d - L_q)$$

$$(b)\ L_a = L_0 + L_2 \cos 4\,\theta_r\textbf{]}$$

3 Chapter

Basic Concepts of Rotating Electrical Machines

The basic principles, developed in Chapter 2 for describing the behaviour of electromechanical energy conversion devices, apply equally well to rotating electrical machines. The purpose of this chapter is to develop general expressions for electromagnetic torque and generated e.m.fs. in rotating machines and to make use of the basic principles of Chapter 2. These basic torque and e.m.f. expressions are applicable to both D.C. and A.C. machines, because the fundamental principles underlying their operation, are the same. The constructional features of the various types of rotating machines are also described, so that the general torque and e.m.f. expressions are modified to suit the particular construction of a machine. It must be emphasized at the outset that both D.C. and A.C. machines work on the same basic principles; they differ only in construction. The final forms of the generated e.m.f. and torgue expressions for the two types (A.C. and D.C.) of electrical machines differ, only because their constructional details are different.

3.1. PHYSICAL CONCEPTS OF TORQUE PRODUCTION

At the beginning of this chapter, a brief resume of the physical concepts of torque production in rotating electrical machines is presented.

3.1.1. Electromagnetic (or Interaction) Torque

Fig. 3.1 *(a)* illustrates a salient-pole stator with 2 poles and a cylindrical rotor with one conductor. When stator coils are energised, stator magnetic flux is set up and its path is as shown in Fig. 3.1 *(a)*, with no current in the rotor conductor. If rotor conductor carries a current indicated by, say dot, then the magnetic flux picture is as depicted in Fig. 3.1 *(b)*, with no current in the stator coil. When stator coils and rotor conductor, both carry currents, then the flux produced by the rotor current interacts with the stator-produced flux, giving the resultant magnetic flux distribution as illustrated in Fig. 3.1 *(c)*. Since the magnetic flux lines behave like stretched rubber bands, the rotor conductor experiences a force in the upward direction. The clockwise torque developed due to the interaction of stator and rotor magnetic fields, is called **interaction** or **electromagnetic torque.**

Consider now one current-carrying coil on the rotor. The direction of current in the coil is indicated by dot under stator-north pole and by cross under stator south pole, [Fig. 3.1 *(d)*]. The rotor current produces rotor flux and this creates two poles on the rotor. The stator *S* pole attracts rotor *N* pole and repels rotor *S* pole, resulting in clockwise torque. Similarly stator *N* pole attracts rotor *S* pole and repels rotor *N* pole, resulting again in clockwise torque. The total torque developed in this manner, Fig. 3.1 *(d)*, is called **interaction** or **electromagnetic torque**. A brief review of Art. 2.4.1 supplements the foregoing presentation.

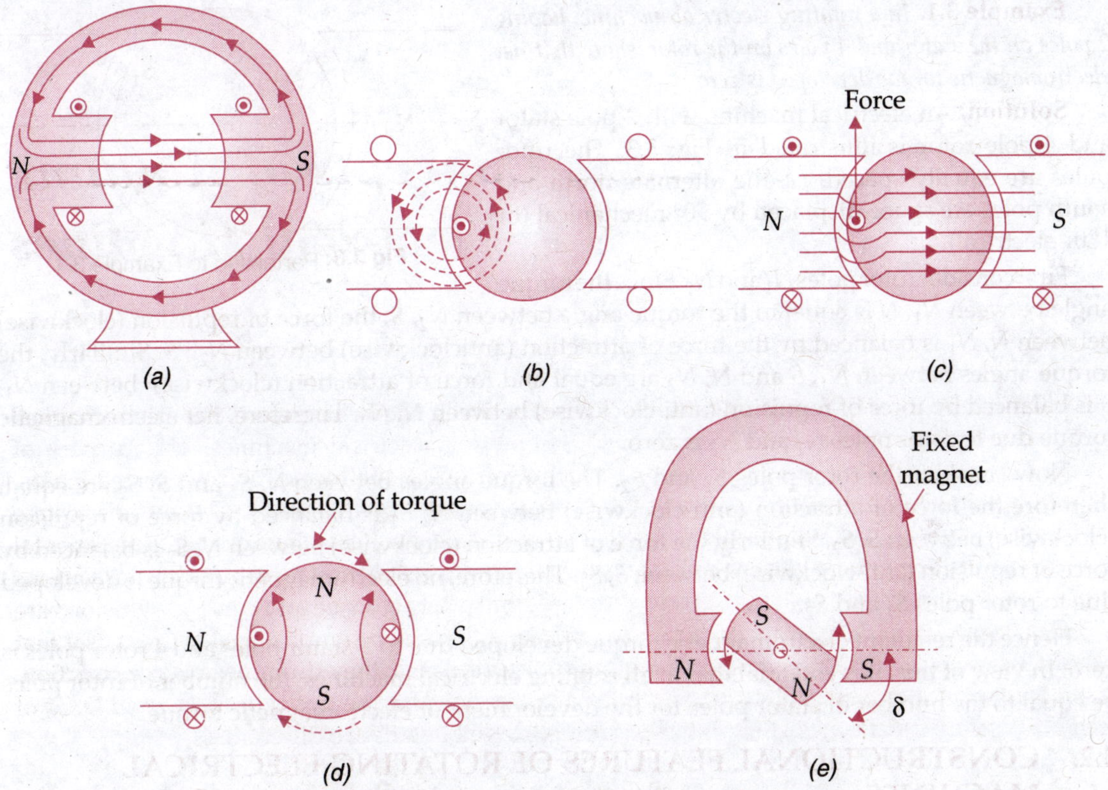

Fig 3.1: Illustrating the production of interaction torque.

The physical understanding of interaction torque can further be highlighted by referring to Fig. 3.1 *(e)*. In this figure, one permanent magnet free to rotate, is placed in the field of a stationary magnet. The tendency of the two fields to align themselves in the same direction is called interaction torque. The angle between stator-field axis and rotor-field axis is called the torque angle δ [Fig. 3.1 *(e)*]. Note that the torque angle δ in Fig. 3.1 *(d)* is 90°. The magnitude of electromagnetic or interaction torque in all rotating machines is given by

$$T_e \propto \text{(Stator field strength) (Rotor field strength)} \sin \delta.$$

3.1.2. Reluctance (or Alignment) Torque

In Fig. 3.1 *(a)*, the path of the magnetic flux is shown when the stator coils carry current. If a ferromagnetic rotor is suitably placed in this magnetic field, the path of stator-produced flux is affected considerably as shown in Fig. 3.2. Since the magnetic flux has a tendency to follow a minimum reluctance path or has a tendency to shorten its flux path, the rotor experiences a counter-clockwise torque, called the **reluctance or alignment torque**. When the long rotor axis coincides with the stator polar axis, the reluctance torque is reduced to zero. Note that the reluctance or alignment torque can be produced only when the reluctance seen by the working flux changes with the rotor movement, see Art. 2.3.

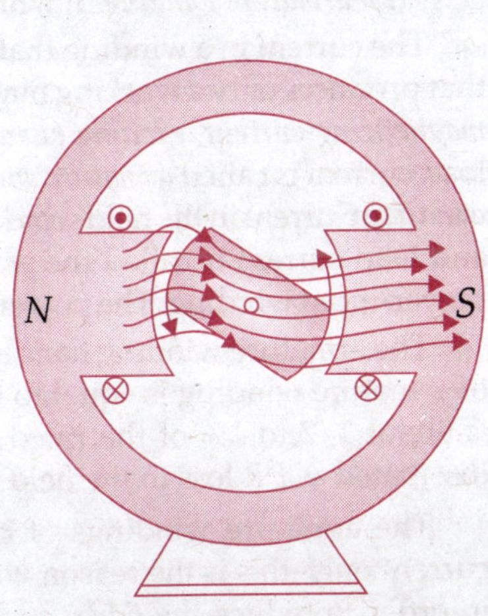

Fig 3.2: Production of reluctance torque.

Example 3.1. *In a rotating electrical machine, having 2 poles on the stator and 4 poles on the rotor, show that net electromagnetic torque developed is zero.*

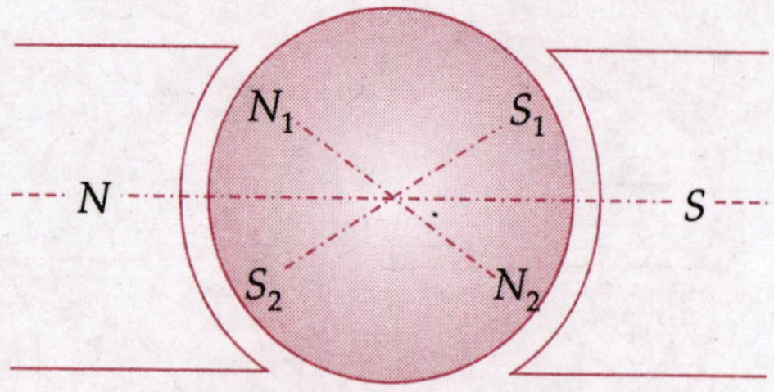

Fig 3.3: Pertaining to Example 3.1.

Solution. An electrical machine with 2-pole stator and 4-pole rotor is illustrated in Fig. 3.3. The rotor poles are equally spaced, *i.e.* the alternate north and south poles are space-displaced by 90° mechanical (or 180° electrical).

First consider rotor poles N_1 and N_2. Since the torque angle between N_1, N is equal to the torque angle between N_2, S; the force of repulsion (clockwise) between N, N_1 is balanced by the force of attraction (anticlockwise) between N_2 , S. Similarly, the torque angles between N_1, S and N, N_2 are equal and force of attraction (clockwise) between N_1, S is balanced by force of repulsion (anti-clockwise) between N, N_2. Therefore, net electromagnetic torque due to rotor poles N_1 and N_2 is zero.

Now consider the rotor poles S_1 and S_2. The torque angles between N, S_1 and S, S_2 are equal, therefore the force of attraction (anti-clockwise) between N, S_1 is balanced by force of repulsion (clockwise) between S, S_2. Similarly the force of attraction (clockwise) between N, S_2 is balanced by force of repulsion (anti-clockwise) between S, S_1. Therefore, no electromagnetic torque is developed due to rotor poles S_1 and S_2.

Hence the resultant electromagnetic torque developed due to 2-stator poles and 4 rotor poles is zero. In view of this, it is essential that in all rotating electrical machines, the number of rotor poles be equal to the number of stator poles for the development of electromagnetic torque.

3.2. CONSTRUCTIONAL FEATURES OF ROTATING ELECTRICAL MACHINES

All the rotating electrical machines, used for generation purposes, electric drives or for control systems, have many common essential features from the construction point of view. For example, every rotating electrical machine must possess *(i)* stator (stationary member) *(ii)* rotor (rotating member) *(iii)* air-gap separating the stator and rotor and *(iv)* shaft, bearing, foundation etc. In addition to it, every electrical machine usually has

(a) *exciting or field winding*, which produces the working flux and

(b) *armature winding* in which the working e.m.f is induced by the working flux.

The current in a winding that varies as the machine is loaded is called **load current**. The current that produces only a working magnetic flux and does not vary with the load on the machine is called *magnetizing current, exciting current* or *field current*. The winding on the machine that carries only load current is called *armature winding*. The winding that handles only exciting current is called *field winding*. Current in the field winding is always dc. A winding which handles both the exciting current and load current is called the *primary winding* of that device. The primary winding is usually the power-input winding. The power-output winding for such machines is called the *secondary winding*.

The armature winding handles all the power that is being converted or transformed. The rating of armature winding is equal to the power rating of the machine. The field winding power rating is about 1/2 to 2% of the rated power of the machine. The power input to dc field winding is dissipated as I^2R loss in the field winding (once the required field current is established.)

The armature windings of both the D.C. and A.C. machines have to deal with alternating current only–this is the reason why the armature structures of all rotating machines are laminated in order to reduce the eddy current losses. Further, almost all the rotating machines have even number of alternate N and S poles (called hetropolar structure). If power is fed to or taken from the rotor, it is obvious that sliding contacts are essential. All types of large rotating machines are provided with radial and axial ventilating ducts for cooling purposes.

In this article, important constructional features of more common types of rotating electrical machines are described.

3.2.1. Polyphase Induction Machines

Polyphase induction machine can work as an induction generator, but for most of the applications, it is used as a motor. In view of this, attention is directed mainly towards polyphase induction motors.

Stator. The stator of an induction motor consists of stator frame, stator core, polyphase (3- or 2-phase) distributed winding, two end-covers, bearings etc. The stator core is a stack of cylindrical steel laminations which are slotted along their inner periphery for housing the 3-phase winding. The stator core fits closely in the cast-iron stator frame. The two end-covers made of cast-iron and the stator frame, provide only mechanical support to the stator core and are not designed to carry the stator flux.

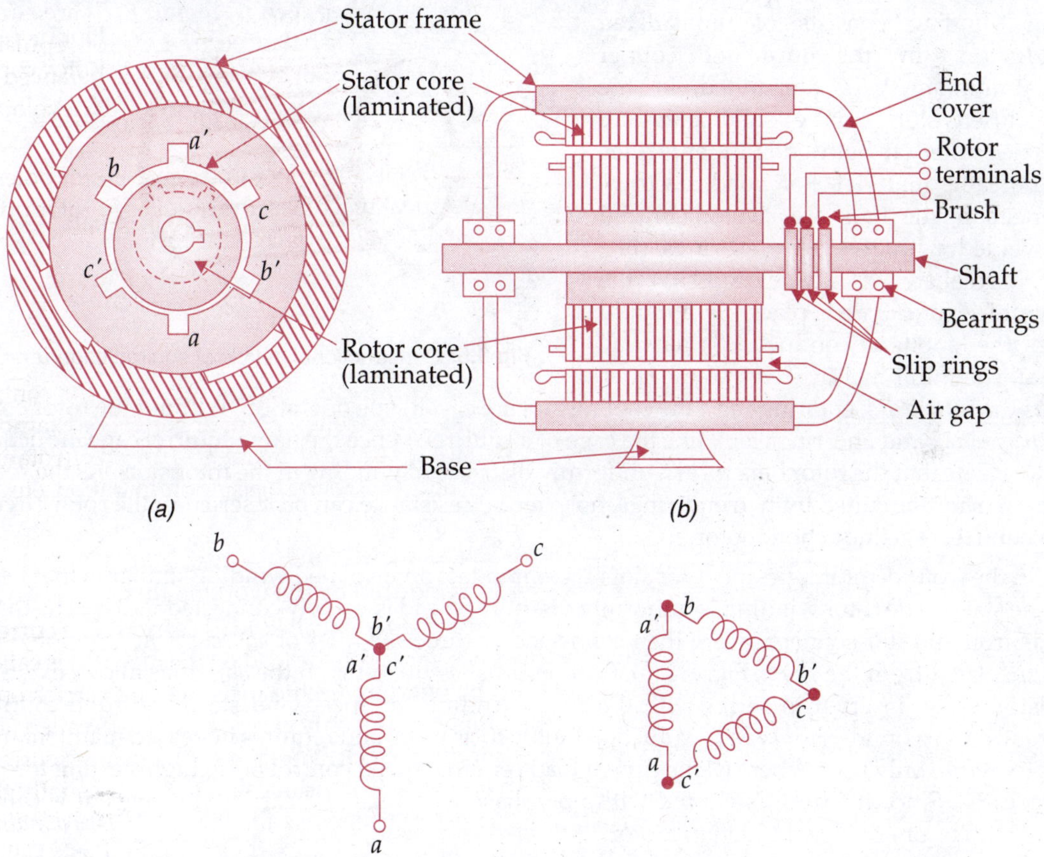

Fig 3.4: Constructional features of polyphase induction motors.

The essential parts of a 3-phase induction motor are illustrated in Fig. 3.4 *(a)* and *(b)*. For simplicity, the stator is shown to have 6 slots, though actually the number of stator slots is far more than six, depending upon the three-phase winding design. Three coils *aa′*, *bb′* and *cc′* represent the windings of the three phases *a*, *b* and *c* respectively. Three windings are space displaced by 120°

electrical and may be connected in star or delta as illustrated in Fig. 3.4 *(c)*. Many a time, the six ends of the three phase windings are brought out to the terminal box on the stator frame. The six ends are suitably marked to indicate the starting and finishing ends of the three-phase windings. Note that three-phase winding in the stator slots is uniformly distributed along the air-gap periphery.

Large size motors use open slots so that already prepared and properly insulated coils can be easily inserted in open slots. Small size induction motors use semiclosed slots so as to reduce the effective gap length between stator and rotor.

The air gap between stator and rotor should be as small as is mechanically possible; this will

(i) reduce the leakage flux between stator and rotor and

(ii) lead to better operating power factor of the induction motor.

Rotor. The induction motor has two types of rotors; the squirrel cage rotor and the wound-rotor. Both types of rotors, make use of circular laminations tightly assembled on the shaft or on the cast-iron spider carried by the shaft.

For the squirrel cage type, the rotor winding consists of uninsulated conductors, in the form of copper or aluminium bars embedded in the semiclosed slots. These solid bars are short-circuited at both ends by end-rings of the same material. For good electrical connection, the bars are riveted, brazed or welded with the two end-rings (Fig. 3.5). In smaller sizes, say below 40 kW, the assembled rotor core is placed in a mould and the molten conducting material, usually aluminium, is forced into the slots. Thus the rotor bars, end rings and the cooling fan, are cast in one operation. Without the rotor core, the rotor bars and end-rings look like the cage of a squirrel, hence the name squirrel cage induction motor. Note that the rotor bars form a uniformly distributed winding in the rotor slots. As the rotor bars are short-circuited by two end-rings, no external resistance can be inserted in the rotor circuit of a squirrel cage induction motor.

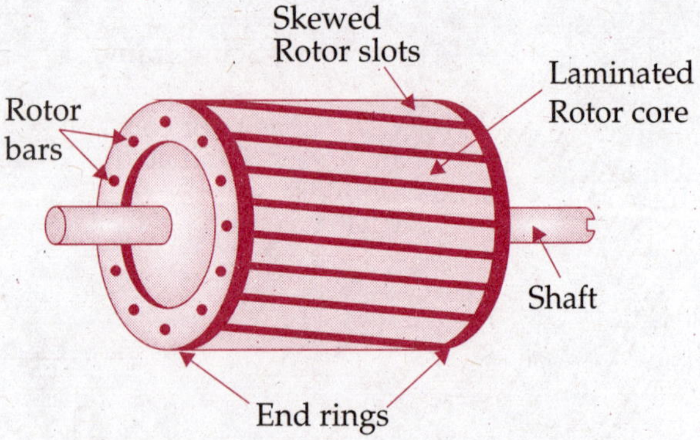

Fig 3.5: Constructional details of squirrel cage rotor.

In the wound-rotor type, the rotor slots accommodate an insulated winding similar to that used on the stator. The rotor winding is uniformly distributed and is usually connected in star. The three leads from the star connection are then connected to three *slip rings* or *collector rings* mounted on but insulated from the shaft, Fig. 3.4 *(b)*. Carbon brushes pressing on the *slip* rings allow, external resistors to be inserted in series with the rotor winding for speed and starting-torque control. Actually, the wound-rotor type of induction motor costs more and requires increased maintenance; it is therefore only used where *(i)* the driven load requires speed control or *(ii)* high starting torque is required. Since the rotor is wound with polyphase windings and carries slip rings, it is called wound-rotor or slip-ring induction motor.

In both the types, the rotor slots are not parallel to the shaft axis, *i.e.*, the rotor slots are skewed for obtaining a quieter and smoother operation of the induction motor.

The squirrel cage type is simpler and more economical in construction than the wound-rotor type. Further the cage type is more rugged and requires less maintenance than the wound-rotor type, since the former does not require slip rings and carbon brushes.

A polyphase induction motor receives electrical energy from one alternating voltage source; it is, therefore called a singly excited machine. The stator carries the field winding, armature winding is on the rotor. The stator winding connected to the supply, is called the primary winding, similar to the transformer primary winding. The rotor winding is called the secondary winding, since it receives energy from the stator by mutual flux, as in the case of a transformer. In other words, an induction motor may be regarded as a generalized transformer with electric power transformation from stator to rotor, along with a change in frequency and a flow of mechanical power, see Art. 6.1.

This motor has come to be called as induction motor, because stator delivers energy to rotor by means of induction (*i.e.* transformer action). The type of the rotor used, decides the name of the particular type of induction motor.

3.2.2. Synchronous Machines

In synchronous machines, the armature winding either exports A.C. power (synchronous generator) or imports A.C. power (synchronous motor), whereas the field winding is alway energised from a D.C. source. In other words, the synchronous machines are doubly excited energy-conversion devices. The generation of e.m.f., in general, depends on the relative motion between field flux and armature winding. In view of this, an A.C. *generator, alternator or synchronous generator* may have either rotating field poles and stationary armature, or rotating armature and stationary field poles. Nevertheless, synchronous machines are invariably constructed with high-power armature winding on the stator and low-power field winding on the rotor; though small synchronous machines with the reverse arrangement may also be built.

The advantages of providing the field winding on rotor and armature winding on the stator are given below:

(*a*) *More Economical*. It is economical to have armature winding on the stator and field winding on the rotor. In order to illustrate this, consider a 3-phase, star-connected, 200 MVA, 11 kV, synchronous machine. Its line current is $\dfrac{200 \times 10^3}{\sqrt{3} \times 11} = 10{,}500$ A. If the armature winding is placed on the rotor, three slip rings, each capable of handling 10,500 A, would be required. Further each slip ring must be properly insulated from the shaft for a voltage of $11/\sqrt{3}$, *i.e.* 6.35 kV. The star-point of the 3 phase winding must also be brought out through fourth slip-ring, in order to connect it to a grounded metal plate through a resistance for the purpose of protection.

Assume now that the low-power required for the field winding is 1 MW at 500 volts. Then the exciting or field current is $\dfrac{1000}{0.5} = 2000$ A. Only two slip rings, each capable of handling 2000 A, are required. Also each slip ring should be insulated from the shaft for a voltage of 500 volts only. This shows that it is cheaper to have field winding on the rotor rather than the armature winding. Thus the construction of synchronous machine with armature winding on the stator and field winding on the rotor is much more economical.

(*b*) *More Efficient*. With armature winding on the stator and field winding on the rotor, only two slip rings are required in a synchronous machine. There are, therefore, reduced slip ring losses and a more efficient synchronous machine.

(*c*) *Better Insulation*. Stationary armature windings can be insulated satisfactorily for higher voltages, allowing the construction of high-voltage, say 33 kV, synchronous machines.

(*d*) *Efficient Cooling*. Stationary armature winding can be cooled more efficiently, thus permitting the construction of large synchronous machines, say 1000 MW or above.

(*e*) *More Output*. Low-power field winding on the rotor gives a lighter rotor and, therefore, low centrifugal forces. In view of this, higher rotor speeds are permissible, thus increasing the synchronous machine output for given dimensions.

(f) *Lesser Rotor Weight and Inertia*. Field winding on the rotor requires less amount of copper and insulation. This reduces overall weight of rotor and its inertia. Reduced rotor weight allows the use of low-priced bearings and also their longer life because of minimal wear and tear.

(g) *Rigid and Convenient Construction*. Three-phase armature winding, capable of handling hight voltage and hight current, can be more easily braced against electromagnetic forces when it is placed in stator slots. In addition, flexible water tube connection for water cooling can be installed more conveniently on stator than on the rotor. This all results in a rigid and convenient construction of a synchronous machine.

(h) *More Armature Tooth Strength*. High-current synchronous machines require more armature copper for each slot. Greater amount of copper can be accommodated by making the slots deeper so that wider and stronger teeth are prepared for the armature. Armature on stator would have wider and stronger teeth whereas the armature on rotor would lead to narrower and weaker teeth. Strong teeth also results in less noise due to vibration and are less likely to be damaged during fabrication and use. Therefore, armature winding must be provided on the stator and field winding on the rotor.

Synchronous machines are of two types depending upon the geometrical structure of the rotor, *viz., (a) salient-pole type* and *(b) cylindrical-rotor, round-rotor* or *non-salient pole type*. Salient means standing out, sticking out or projecting and in Fig. 3.6 *(a)*, four salient poles are shown on the rotor. The field winding on the salient poles is a concentrated winding. In case of cylindrical rotor, the field winding is a distributed winding housed in the rotor slots, Fig. 3.7 *(b)*. A further distinction between the two types is that the salient pole synchronous machines have non-uniform air-gap–under the pole centres it is minimum and in between the poles, the air-gap is maximum, Fig. 3.6 *(a)*. In cylindrical rotor synchronous machine, the air-gap is uniform throughout, neglecting the slot-openings.

The stators of both the types of synchronous machines are similar to the induction motor stator. That is the synchronous-machine stator consists of a cast iron stator frame, a cylindrical laminated and uniformly slotted stator core, a polyphase distributed winding placed in the stator slots, bearings, base etc., Fig 3.6 *(a)*. As in a polyphase induction motor, the stator frame and end-covers serve merely as a mechanical support to the stator core and are not designed to carry the magnetic flux.

Synchronous generators are usually of 3-phase type because of the several advantages associated with 3-phase generation, transmission and high-power utilization. Nevertheless, single-phase alternators are also constructed for specific requirements. For the generation of three-phase voltage, at least three coils (one coil per phase), phase displaced by 120 electrical degrees in space, are required. In the elementary synchronous machine of Fig. 3.6 *(a)*, the armature has a total of 12 slots, *i.e.*, 4 slots per phase; though the stator of an actual machine has much larger number of armature slots; depending on the 3-phase winding design. In Fig. 3.6 *(a)*, each phase is shown to possess two coils. For example, phase *a* coils are designated as a_1, a_1' and a_2, a_2'. The two coils of each phase are connected in series so that their voltages add. Then the 3-phases may be connected in star or delta as shown in Fig. 3.6 *(b)*. In this figure, the three terminals are designated by letters a_1, b_1, c_1. The two coils of phase *a* may be connected in parallel with a_1, a_2 as one terminal and a_1', a_2' as the second terminal. Similarly, the coils of phases *b* and *c* can be connected. The parallel connection of two coils will increase the current per parallel path to double the value. These parallel-connected coils with six terminals may be interconnected in star or delta. Star connection of parallel connected coils is shown in Fig. 3.6 *(c)*.

The frequency of the generated e.m.f., from Eq. (3.5), is

$$f = \frac{PN}{120} \text{ Hz.}$$

In India and many other countries, alternators feeding the power systems, generate a frequency of 50 Hz.

$$\therefore \text{ Number of poles, } \quad P = \frac{6{,}000}{\text{Speed in r.p.m., } N} \quad \text{...(3.1)}$$

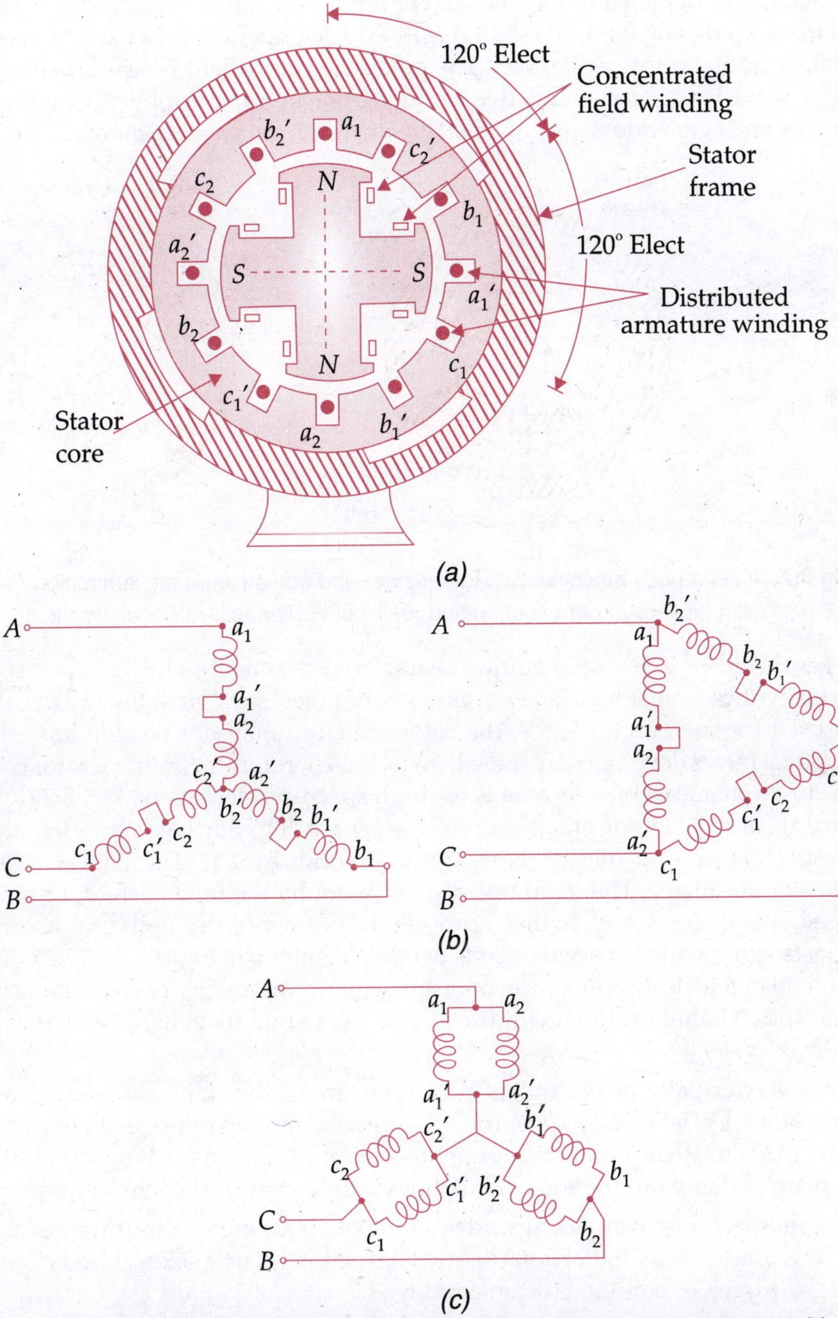

Fig 3.6: *(a)* 4-pole, 3-phase salient pole construction of synchronous machine.
(b) Schematic diagram of star and delta connections with coils in series.
(c) Schematic diagram of star connection with coils in parallel.

Oil engines and hydraulic turbines operate best at relatively low speeds, therefore, the alternators driven by these prime-movers, must have relatively large number of poles, Eq. (3.1). For accommodating large number of poles, the rotor diameter must be comparatively increased and from mechanical considerations, salient pole construction has been found to suit best for low-speed prime-movers. Salient pole rotor structure is also employed for comparatively small synchronous machines as depicted in Fig. 3.6 *(a)*. For larger machines, the laminated salient poles are dove-tailed to the spider keyed to the shaft, Fig. 3.7 *(a)*. Damper bars are usually inserted in the pole shoe, to damp out the rotor oscillations. The pole shoe of a salient pole is suitably shaped so as to obtain a sine wave for the radial flux density along the air-gap periphery. Commercially, the salient pole synchronous generators are called *hydro-alternators* or *hydrogenerators*.

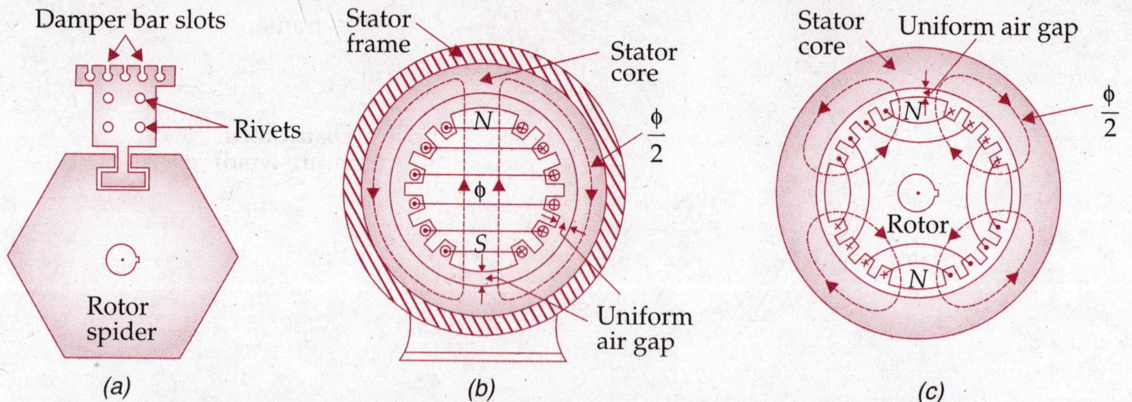

Fig 3.7: Synchronous machine. *(a)* Rotor spider and one salient-pole lamination *(b)* 2-pole cylindrical-rotor construction and *(c)* 4-pole cylindrical-rotor construction.

Steam and gas turbines have best operating characteristics at relatively high speeds, therefore, alternators driven by these, must have a fewer number of poles, say 2 or 4, Eq. (3.1). If salient pole construction is used for such high speeds, the rotor structure may not be able to withstand the enormous centrifugal forces developed by the salient poles. Therefore, cylindrical rotor construction is best suited from mechanical considerations, for high speed primemovers. Fig. 3.7 *(b)* illustrates a 2-pole cylindrical rotor, made of one piece, solid steel forging. For large core lengths, rotor is fabricated from several pieces of solid steel forgings placed side by side. The axial slots are cut only in a part of the rotor periphery. The main poles are created, by the field current, in the unslotted rotor surface, as shown in Fig. 3.7 *(b)*. In this figure, a total of 6 concentric coils are shown. A 4-pole cylindrical-rotor structure with 2 concentric coils per pole is shown in Fig. 3.7 *(c)*. The radial air-gap flux density wave in cylindrical rotor synchronous machine is more nearer to a sine wave than in salient pole machines. Commercially, cylindrical rotor synchronous generators are called *turbo-alternators* or *turbogenerators*.

Synchronous motors, usually of the salient pole type, are of the same general construction as salient pole generators. Under steady state, the synchronous motors operate at constant speed as determined by Eq. (3.5). In salient-pole synchronous motors, the functions of damper bars (embedded in the pole faces) are to damp out the rotor oscillations and to start the synchronous motors.

For synchronous machines of large sizes, adequate cooling arrangements must be incorporated to dissipate the heat produced by the various losses. For relatively large sizes, closed circuit cooling, using air, water, hydrogen or helium, is often employed.

A synchronous machine is usually connected to an energy system, fed by other alternators. In a synchronous generator, the frequency of the generated e.m.f. depends on the rotational speed and poles. Thus a synchronous machine can be connected to an energy system, only when the frequency or rotational speed of the synchronous machine is equal to the frequency of the supply system. In other words, for successful operation, the rotational speed of the synchronous machine must synchronize with the frequency of the energy system and this is the reason for naming it a synchronous machine.

A single synchronous generator may operate at any frequency or speed, since it is not to be synchronized with any energy system. However, a single synchronous motor fed from an energy system must synchronize its rotational speed with the system frequency.

3.2.3. Direct Current Machines

In a D.C. machine, the field winding is on the stator and the armature winding is on the rotor. The constructional features of a typical two-pole D.C. machine are depicted in Fig. 3.8.

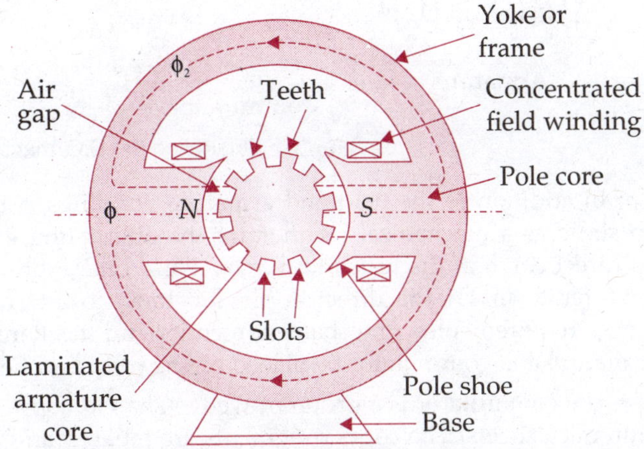

Fig 3.8: Constructional features of a 2-pole D.C. machine.

Stator. The stator consists of *(i)* yoke (or frame) made of unlaminated ferromagnetic material, *(ii)* the salient field poles bolted to the inner periphery of the yoke and *(iii)* bearings, brushrigging carrying brush-holders, end-covers etc. The yoke rests on a supporting base and is made of cast iron for small machines. In larger machines, the yoke is made of fabricated steel which has higher permeability than cast iron. In modern D.C. motors to be driven through power-electronic converters, the yoke is constructed from laminations in order to reduce the eddy-current loss.

The field poles are made of a stack of steel plates (1 to 1.5 mm thick), rivetted together. The pole core, where the exciting or field winding is wound, is usually of smaller cross-section than the pole shoe (or pole face), due to the following reasons :

(a) The reduced cross-section of the pole core requires less copper for the field winding.

(b) The large pole shoe area increases the flux per pole entering the armature, due to the reduction in air-gap reluctance.

(c) Pole shoes provide mechanical strength and support to the field winding.

From economic considerations, the yoke and poles of smaller machines may be made of cast-iron.

The concentrated field winding, when excited with direct current, produces alternate north and south poles, called hetropolar construction. It may be seen from Fig. 3.8 that both the armature core and yoke, carry half of the flux per pole.

The brush rigging *B*, as shown in Fig. 3.9 consists of a group of brush-holders and their attachment to the yoke or end-cover. Stationary carbon brushes are housed in brush holders and are kept pressed on to the commutator surface by means of tension controlled springs. Thus the connection of the armature winding to the external circuit is through the commutator and brushes.

Rotor. The armature core consists of a stack of circular steel laminations about 0.4 to 0.6 mm thick. The periphery of these laminations is slotted to receive the distributed armature winding, Fig. 3.8. These laminations are insulated from one another so as to decrease the eddy-current losses. In case of small machines, the laminations are assembled tightly on the shaft, but on the cast-iron spider in case of large machines.

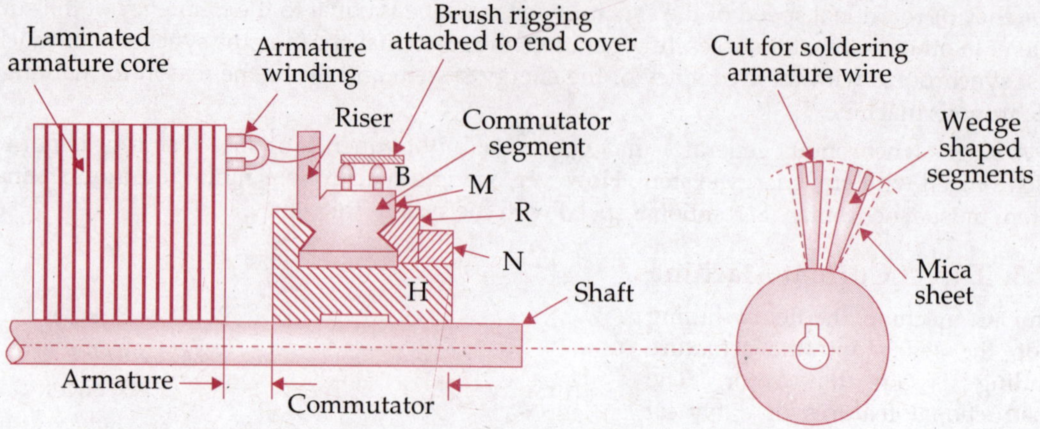

Fig 3.9: Illustrating the D.C. machine construction.

In addition to the field and armature windings, a D.C. generator must have a commutator, to serve as a mechanical rectifier for the alternating e.m.f. generated in the armature winding to direct e.m.f. at the brush terminals. For a D.C. motor, the commutator serves as a mechanical inverter to invert the direct applied voltage to alternating voltage in the armature winding. These requirements of mechanical-rectifier and mechanical-inverter operations demand that the armature and commutator be placed on the rotor and field winding on the stator.

The commutator is a group of wedge-shaped copper segments, insulated from each other by thin mica sheets. The copper segments are tapered and arranged side by side to form a cylinder. Fig. 3.9 illustrates a hard-drawn copper segment, with two *V*-shaped grooves, insulated properly by micanite *M*, from cast-iron sleeve or hub *H* and from ring *R*. The *V*-shaped construction prevents the commutator segments from flying out due to centrifugal force. The threaded ring R tightens the various components together and is kept in position by nut *N*. The hub *H* is keyed to the shaft, taking care that the commutator is kept some distance away (for the armature over-hang), from the armature core. One end of each commutator segment is projected to form a riser. The commutator is so placed that riser is facing the armature core, see Fig. 3.9. Two armature wires are soldered to each riser.

It may be seen that a D.C. machine is equivalent to an A.C. machine plus a mechanical rectifier, *i.e.*, commutator. Since the armature winding is closed on itself, D.C. generator can operate as a delta-connected three-phase alternator, if the armature winding is tapped at intervals of 120 electrical degrees, from the other side of the commutator.

3.3. CONCEPTS OF GENERAL TERMS PERTAINING TO ROTATING MACHINES

Some of the terms, like pole-pitch, electrical and mechanical degrees etc., are used quite frequently in the literature pertaining to rotating electrical machines. The purpose of this article is to make the reader familiar with these terms.

Fig. 3.10 *(a)* shows an elementary two-pole machine, with its 2 field coils excited by direct current. The flux density at the point *a* in between the 2 poles will be zero. Under the centre of the pole indicated by point *b*, the flux density would be maximum say positive; at *c* it is zero and at point *d* it is again maximum but negative. Note that the flux entering the stator or leaving the rotor is considered positive. In other words, south pole on the stator or north pole on the rotor, produces positive flux density. According to this convention. the variation of flux density *B*, along the air-gap periphery is depicted in Fig. 3.10 *(b)*. If this variation of *B*, along the air-gap circumference is assumed sinusoidal as shown in Fig. 3.10 *(b)* ; then it is said that "in the elementary machine of Fig. 3.10 *(a)*, the flux density is sinusoidally distributed in space."

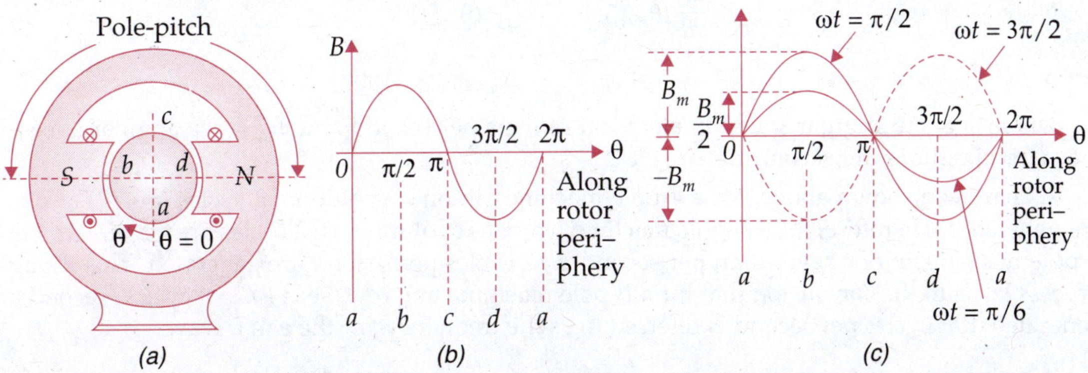

Fig 3.10: *(a)* Elementary two pole machine, *(b)* Flux density variation along air-gap periphery and *(c)* Pulsating flux

Suppose the field coils of Fig. 3.10 *(a)* are excited with alternating current $i = I_m \sin \omega t$. Then, at $\omega t = 0$, current is zero and no field flux is produced. At $\omega t = \pi/6$, $i = I_m/2$ and maximum flux density under the pole is $B_m/2$. At this instant of $\omega t = \pi/6$, the variation of flux density wave along the air-gap periphery is also sine wave as shown in Fig. 3.10 *(c)*. At $\omega t = \pi/2$, the flux density under the poles is B_m. After $\omega t = \pi/2$, the flux density wave starts decreasing. At $\omega t = \pi$, the flux density is again zero. After $\omega t = \pi$ is crossed, the direction of current in the field coils is reversed and consequently field poles of reversed polartiy are created. At $\omega t = 3\pi/2$, the flux density is $-B_m$. Note that the axis of field flux remains along *bd*. Such a flux is called alternating or pulsating-stationary flux.

Note that the pulsating flux at any instant is distributed sinusoidally along the air-gap periphery.

Electrical and mechanical degrees. The e.m.f. induced in a conductor is given by Faraday's law of electro-magnetic induction, which can be expressed in many different forms. In one form, the generated e.m.f. *e* is given by *Blv* volts ; where flux density *B* in *T*, length of the conductor *l* in metres and velocity *v* in m/sec, are orthogonal or normal to each other. If a conductor of constant length *l*, moves with a constant velocity *v*, the e.m.f. *e*, induced in the conductor, has the waveform of flux-density variation. That is, for square flux-density wave, e.m.f. waveform is square ; for rectangular flux-density wave, e.m.f. waveform is rectangular and for sine flux-density wave, e.m.f. waveform is also a sine wave.

In Fig. 3.10 *(a)*, assume that one conductor rotates at uniform angular velocity. When the conductor is at *a*, conductor e.m.f. is zero (because *B* is zero), at *b* the conductor e.m.f. is maximum (because *B* is maximum) and so on. In one revolution, one cycle of conductor e.m.f. is generated, as shown in Fig. 3.11 *(a)*. Assume now the conductor rotating in a 4 pole machine of Fig. 3.11 *(c)*. When the conductor is at *a*, e.m.f. is zero ; at *b*, e.m.f. is maximum ; at *c* e.m.f. is zero and so on. In one complete revolution, two cycles of e.m.f. are generated as shown in Fig. 3.11 *(b)*. Since one cycle of e.m.f. or current is equal to 360° electrical, in one revolution of 360 mechanical degrees, 2 cycles are equivalent to 720° electrical for a 4-pole machine. In other words, 720 electrical degrees in a 4-pole machine can be related to 360 mechanical degrees as follows :

$$720 \text{ electrical degrees} = \frac{4}{2}(360 \text{ mechanical degrees})$$

or

$$\theta_{elect} = \frac{4}{2}\theta_{mech}$$

For a *P*-pole machine, $\frac{P}{2}$ cycles of e.m.f. will be generated in one revolution. Thus for a *P*-pole machine,

$$\theta_{elect} = \frac{P}{2}\theta_{mech} \qquad \text{...(3.2)}$$

Now
$$\frac{d}{dt}(\theta_{elect}) = \frac{P}{2}\cdot\frac{d}{dt}(\theta_{mech})$$

or
$$\omega = \frac{P}{2}\omega_m \qquad \text{...(3.3)}$$

where ω is the angular speed in electrical radians per second and ω_m is the angular speed in mechanical radians per second.

As has been shown above, for a 4-pole machine ; in one revolution, 2 cycles (= 4/2) of e.m.f. are generated. Therefore, for a P-pole machine ; in one revolution, $P/2$ cycles are generated. For a P-pole machine, in one revolution per second, $P/2$ cycles per second are generated. This thought process leads to the conclusion that for a P-pole machine, in n rev./sec., $P/2 \cdot n$ cycles/second are generated. But cycles per second is referred to as the frequency f of the e.m.f. wave.

$\therefore$
$$f = \frac{Pn}{2} \text{ cycles per second or Hertz} \qquad \text{...(3.4)}$$

If the speed N is in r.p.m., then

$$f = \frac{PN}{120} \text{ Hz} \qquad \text{...(3.5)}$$

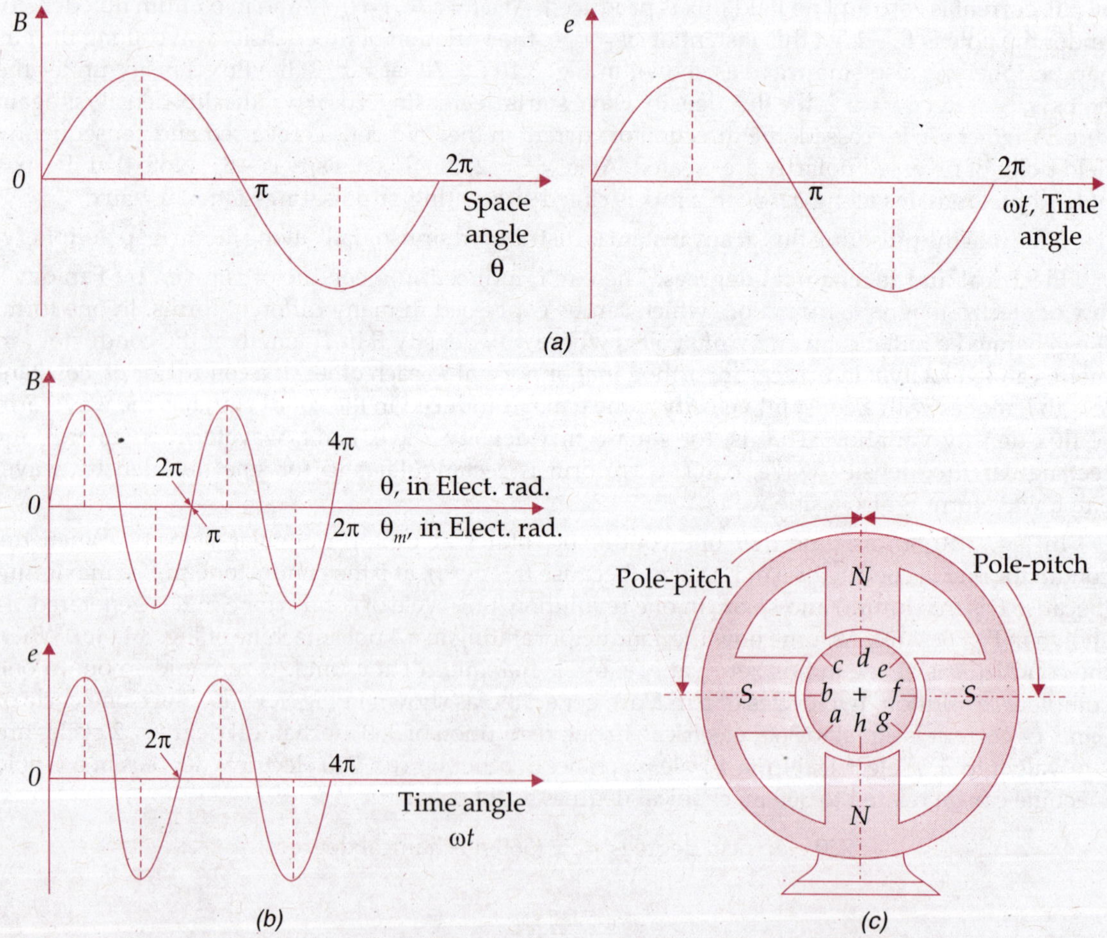

Fig 3.11: Flux-density variation with space angle θ and corresponding e.m.f. variation with time angle ωt *(a)* For two-pole machine and *(b)* For 4-pole machine *(c)* An elementary 4-pole machine.

Note that the left hand diagram of Fig. 3.11 *(a)* and upper diagram of Fig. 3.11 *(b)* give the variation of flux density B as a function of the space angle θ measured along the air-gap periphery. The right hand diagram of Fig. 3.11 *(a)* and lower diagram of Fig. 3.11 *(b)* give the variation of e.m.f. e as a function of time angle ωt. Since rotor rotation involves time, it may be stated that space variable quantity B is transformed to time variable quantity e, on account of rotor rotation.

Pole-pitch. The peripheral distance between two adjacent poles, is called pole-pitch. Pole-pitch is always expressed in electrical degrees, rather than in mechanical degrees. It can, therefore, be inferred that pole pitch is always equal to 180 electrical degrees or π electrical radians. Pole pitches are indicated in Fig. 3.10 *(a)* and Fig. 3.11 *(c)*.

Coil. Fig. 3.12 *(a)* illustrates a 2-pole machine, with one coil a, a' housed in two stator slots. Its developed view, with coil laid out flat is illustrated in Fig. 3.12 *(b)*. Fig. 3.12 *(c)* gives the plan of the coil a, a'. Fig. 3.12 *(c)* reveals that coil a, a' has one turn. The e.m.f. is generated in active lengths AB and CD only. These active lengths are called the two *coil-sides* of a coil. For the coil of Fig. 3.12 *(c)*, each coil-side has one conductor. Thus it is seen that one turn consists of two conductors and one coil is made up of two coil-sides. In Fig. 3.12 *(c)*, the two coil-sides AB and CD are connected in series by end connection so that the e.m.f. at coil terminals 1, 2 is the summation of two coil-side e.m.fs.

If the plan of the coil a, a' is as depicted in Fig. 3.12 *(d)*, then this coil is seen to have 2 turns. It can alternatively be stated that Fig. 3.12 *(d)* represents single two-turn coil. Each coil-side has two conductors and total conductors in the coil are 4, Fig. 3.12 *(d)*. If one coil has N turns, then it is termed as single N-turn coil, with N conductors in each coil side and $2N$ conductors in the coil. Fig. 3.12 *(f)* illustrates one N-turn or multi-turn coil.

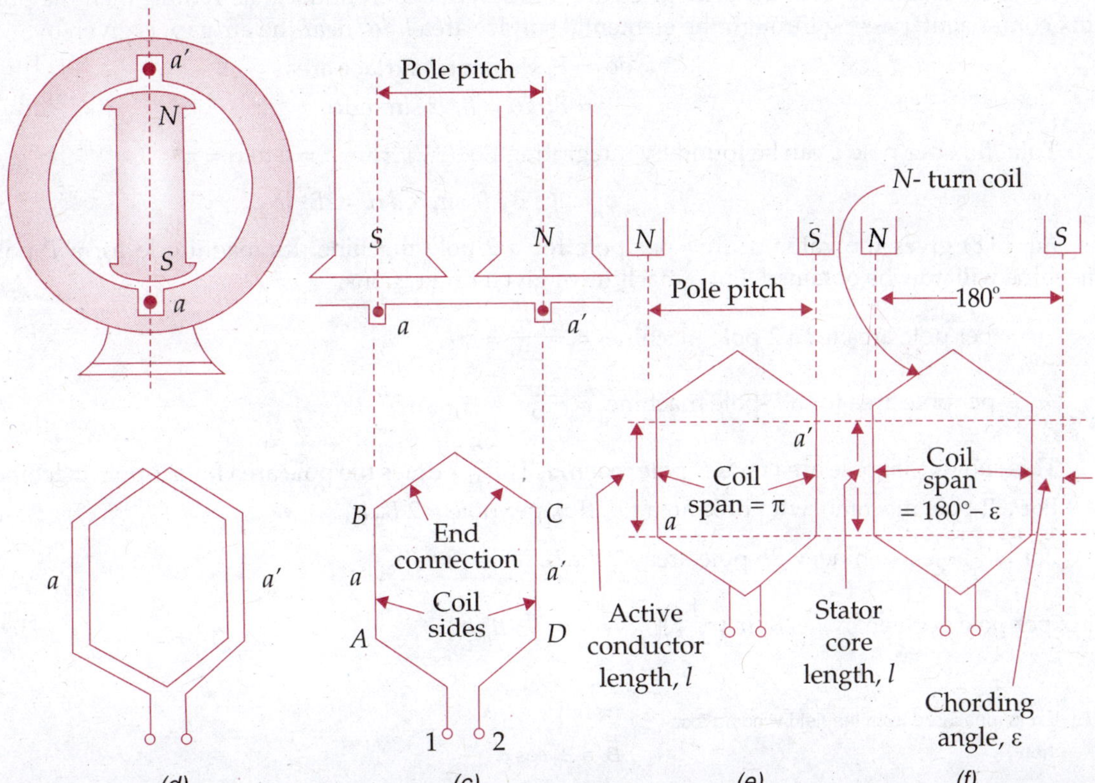

Fig 3.12: *(a)* Elementary 2-pole machine with one coil. *(b)* Its developed view. *(c)* One-turn coil. *(d)* Two-turn coil. *(e)* Full-pitch coil. *(f)* N-turn chorded coil.

A coil, with two coil-sides 180 electrical space degrees apart (or one pole-pitch apart), is called a *full-pitch coil.* A full-pitch coil can alternatively be defined as a coil whose two coil-sides span one pole-pitch. It may be seen from Fig. 3.12 *(a)* that coil *a, a′* is a full-pitch coil, since its two coil-sides are one pole-pitch apart. Thus a full-pitch coil is a coil, with coil-pitch or coil-span equal to 180 electrical space degrees. *Coil-span* (or coil-pitch) is defined as the distance between the two coil-sides of one coil. Coil-span is measured in terms of electrical degrees, coil-sides or slots. In Fig. 3.12 *(e)*, coil span = 180° electrical space degrees, this coil is, therefore, termed a full-pitch coil. In Fig. 3.12 *(f)*, coil span is less than 180° ; this coil is, therefore, called a short-pitch, or chorded coil. A *chording angle* ε is defined as the angle by which coil-span departs from 180° electrical space degrees. In Fig. 3.12 *(f)*, chording angle is ε°, therefore chorded *N*-turn coil of this figure has a coil-span = 180° – ε.

Flux per pole. For calculating the flux per pole, consider Fig. 3.13 *(a)* and *(b)* ; where the field windings are taken on the rotor and stator respectively. Field winding in these figures is depicted on the cylindrical structure and note that it does not make any difference if the field winding were on the salient pole structure. In both the figures, the origin for space angle α, for convenience, is taken 90° away from field winding axis. In view of this, when α = 0°, the flux density *B* is zero, when α = 90°, *B* is maximum say B_p, when α = 180°, *B* is again zero. This variation of flux density with space angle α is illustrated in Fig. 3.13 *(c)* and if this variation is assumed sinusoidal, then the flux density *B* can be expressed as,

$$B = B_p \sin \alpha \qquad \text{...(3.6)}$$

In order to calculate the flux per pole, consider an elemental angle $d\alpha$, α degrees away from zero of the flux density wave, Fig. 3.13.

If *l* is the axial length of the armature core (normal to paper) and *r* is its radius, then the pole flux component passing through the elemental surface area $lrd\alpha$, near the air-gap, is given by

$$d\phi = B.\ \text{elemental surface area}$$

$$= Blrd\alpha = B_p\, lr \sin \alpha\, d\alpha \qquad \text{...(3.7)}$$

Total flux per pole ϕ can be found by integrating Eq. (3.7) from α = 0 to α = π*

$$\therefore \quad \phi = \int_0^{\pi} B_p\, lr \sin \alpha\, d\,\alpha = 2B_p\, lr \qquad \text{...(3.8)}$$

Eq. (3.8) gives the value of flux per pole for a 2-pole machine. Its magnitude for a *P*-pole machine will now be obtained. For a machine of given dimensions,

$$\text{per pole area for a 2-pole machine} = \frac{2\pi rl}{2} = \pi rl$$

$$\text{per pole area for a } P\text{-pole machine} = \frac{2\pi rl}{P} = \frac{2}{P}(\pi rl)$$

This shows that pole area for a *P*-pole machine is $\left(\frac{2}{P}\right)$ times the pole area for a 2-pole machine.

For a 2-pole machine, with pole area πrl, flux per pole = 2 $B_p\, lr$.

For a *P*-pole machine, with pole area $\frac{2}{P}(\pi rl)$,

$$\text{flux per pole is given by,} \quad 2B_p\, lr\left(\frac{1}{\neq rl}\right)\left(\frac{2}{P}\neq rl\right) = \frac{4}{P} B_p\, lr \qquad \text{...(3.9)}$$

---

* If α is measured from the field winding axis

then $B = B_p \cos \alpha$

and $\phi = \int_{-\neq/2}^{\neq/2} B_p\, lr \cos \alpha\, d\alpha = 2B_p\, lr$

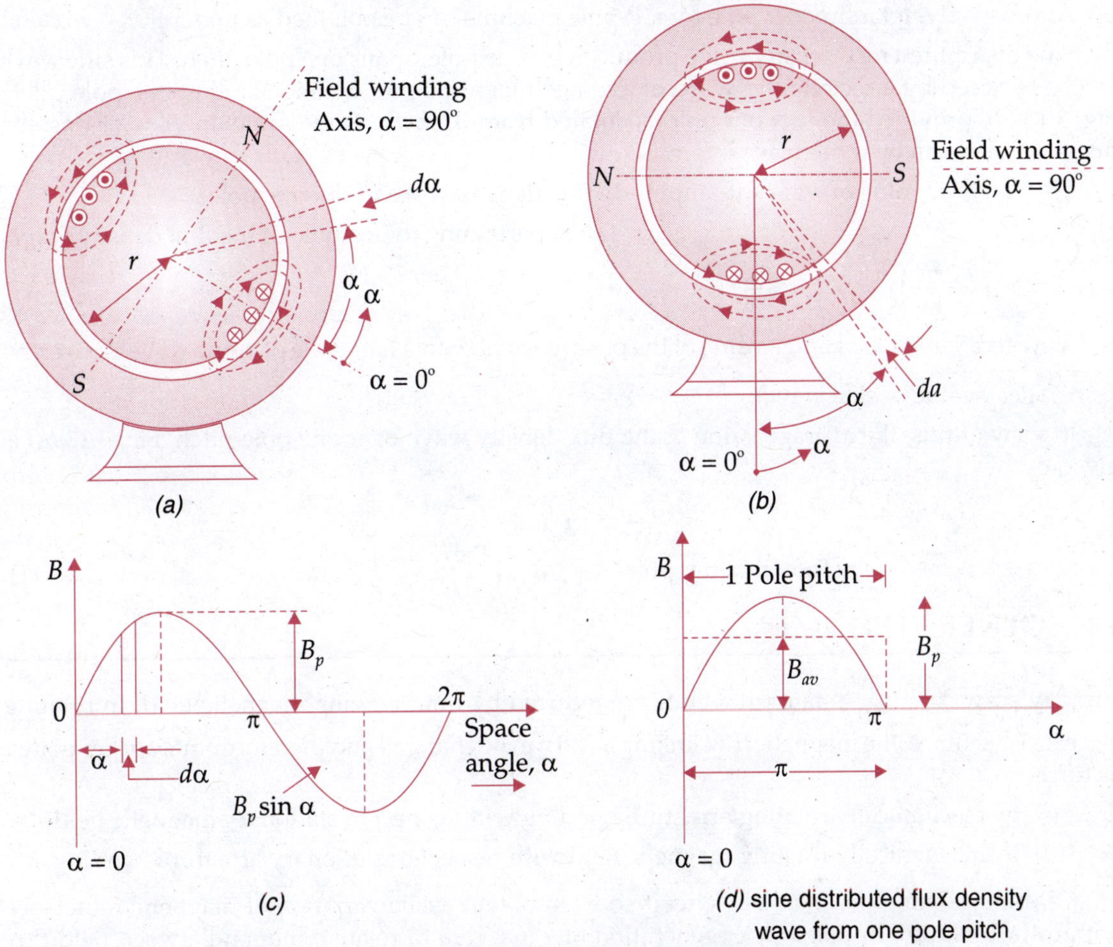

Fig 3.13: Pertaining to flux per pole.

Another method of obtaining Eq. (3.9) is as under :

For a P-pole machine, the variation of flux density B with space angle α will again be similar to that shown in Fig. 3.13 *(c)* and will be given by Eq. (3.6). For obtaining the flux per pole, the elemental angle must be expressed in mechanical degrees. So consider an elemental space angle $d\,\alpha_m$ in mechanical degrees (similar to $d\alpha$ in Fig. 3.13 (*a*)). The flux passing through the elemental mechanical surface area $lrd\alpha_m$ is given by

$$d\phi = Blrd\alpha_m = B_p\, lr \sin\alpha \cdot d\alpha_m \qquad ...(3.10)$$

Here subscript p is used to denote peak value.

From Eq. (3.2), electrical degrees $= \frac{P}{2}$ (mechanical degrees)

$$\alpha = \frac{P}{2}\,\alpha_m \quad \text{or} \quad d\alpha = \frac{P}{2}\,d\alpha_m$$

Substituting the value of $d\alpha_m$ in Eq. (3.10), we get elemental flux $d\phi$ as

$$d\phi = \frac{2}{P} \cdot B_p \cdot lr \sin\alpha \cdot d\alpha$$

Total flux per pole,

$$\phi = \frac{2}{P} \cdot B_p \cdot lr \int_0^{\pi} \sin\alpha\, d\alpha = \frac{4}{P} \cdot B_p\, lr \qquad ...(3.11)$$

Alternatively, total flux per pole for a P-pole machine can be obtained as under :

Sine distributed flux density wave produced by one pole, spans one pole pitch. This sine wave can be replaced by a rectangular wave of average magnitude B_{av} again spanning one pole pitch, Fig. 3.13 *(d)*, provided the flux per pole calculated from B_p or B_{av} is the same. In view of this, the flux per pole ϕ can be written as

ϕ = (Average value of constant-amplitude flux density wave under one pole)

× (Area pertaining to one pole of the flux density wave)

$$= (B_{av})\left(\frac{2\pi rl}{P}\right)$$

Now recall that the average value of the positive or negative half cycle of a sine wave is given by $\frac{2}{\pi}$ (Peak value of sine wave).

In view of this, the average value of the flux density wave over one pole-pitch, Fig. 3.13 *(d)* is given by

$$B_{av} = \frac{2}{\pi}B_p$$

$$\therefore \qquad \text{Total flux per pole} = \left(\frac{2}{\pi}B_p\right)\left(\frac{2\pi rl}{P}\right) = \frac{4}{P}B_p\,rl \qquad ...(3.11)$$

3.4. GENERATED EMFs

Faraday's law $e = -\frac{d\psi}{dt}$ states that emfs are induced by time-varying magnetic field. In rotating electrical machines, the magnetic flux linking a coil can be changed and therefore emfs are generated as further :

(i) by mechanically rotating armature winding with respect to stationary magnetic field,

(ii) by mechanically rotating magnetic field with respect to stationary armature winding,

or *(iii)* by designing the magnetic circuit so as to obtain cyclic variation of magnetic reluctance with rotor rotation*. In this article, generation of e.m.f. due to relative motion between field flux and armature winding is only considered. Elementary forms of rotating machines, depicted in Fig. 3.14, are used in deriving the generated e.m.f. expressions. It does not make any difference whether the field poles are created on the cylindrical rotor of Fig. 3.14 *(a)* or on the salient pole rotor of Fig. 3.14 *(b)*. Similarly the field poles created by the cylindrical stator of Fig. 3.14 *(c)*, may be produced by a salient pole stator of Fig. 3.14 *(d)*. It is the relative motion between field flux and armature winding that matters. The distribution of the flux-density wave in the air-gap is assumed a sine wave.

In Fig. 3.14 *(a)* and *(b)*, stator-coil (or armature coil) axis is stationary while field-winding (or field) axis rotates. In Fig. 3.14 *(c)* and *(d)*, field axis is stationary but armature-coil axis rotates with the rotor.

3.4.1. Generated e.m.f. in a Full-pitched Coil

In Fig. 3.14, the two coil-sides *a, a′* of one coil, are diametrically opposite to each other, *i.e.*, the coil spans 180 electrical space degrees. For simplicity, two-pole machines, with one N-turn full pitched armature coil are considered first in Fig. 3.14. Actually an electrical machine consists of a large number of properly connected armature coils. The resultant armature voltage in any machine is obtained by adding the individual coil e.m.fs. in a manner decided by the armature winding design.

* Inductor alternators work on this principle, see the book, "Generalized Theory of Electrical Machines" by the same author.

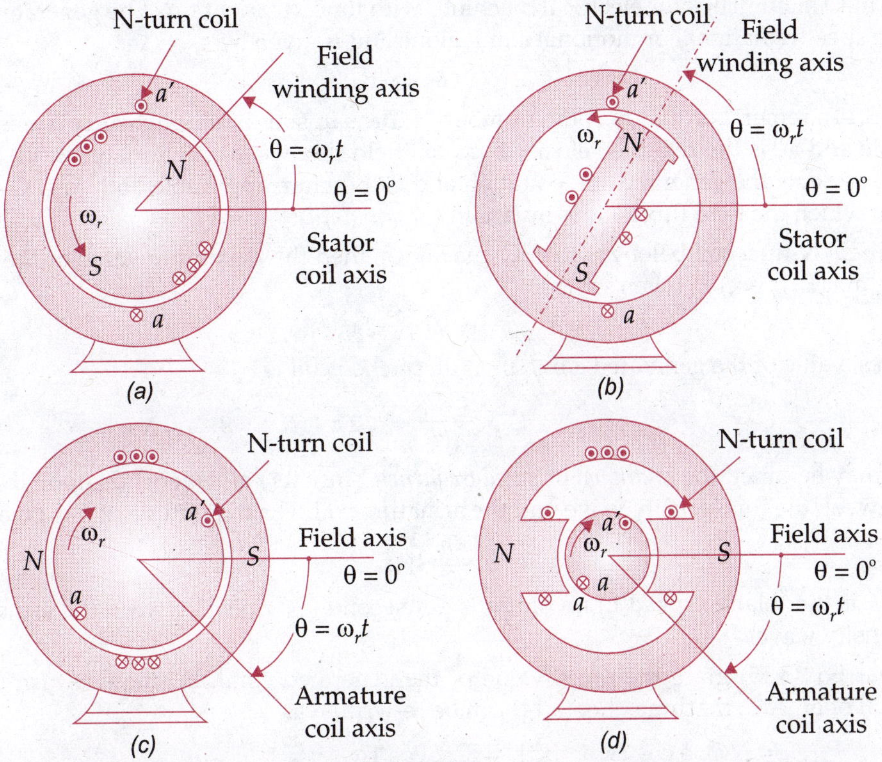

Fig 3.14: Pertaining to the generation of e.m.f. in single N-turn full-pitched coil

In Fig. 3.14, the time origin is chosen arbitrarily, at the instant coil axis coincides with the field winding axis. That is at the time origin $t = 0$, time angle $\theta = \omega_r t = 0$ and the field winding axis and coil axis are coincident. Here ω_r is the angular velocity in radians per second, at which the rotor rotates. An examination of Fig. 3.14 reveals that at the instant $\theta = 0$, the flux passing through (or linking) the coil is maximum ($= \phi \cos 0^\circ$). In other words, at $\theta = 0$, the entire flux ϕ produced by one pole, is passing through the coil. When time angle $\theta = \omega_r t = 90^\circ$, the field winding axis becomes in quadrature with the armature coil axis and, therefore, the flux passing through the coil is zero ($= \phi \cos 90^\circ$). For $\theta = \omega_r t = 180^\circ$, the flux passing through the coil is again maximum ($= \phi \cos 180^\circ$), but reversed in direction. In view of the above thought process, an expression giving the variation of flux passing through the coil can be written as $\phi \cos \theta$ or $\phi \cos \omega_r t$. Therefore, the flux linkages ψ with the full-pitch N-turn armature coil, at any time t, are :

$$\psi = N \text{ (flux passing through the coil at any time } t)$$

$$= N \phi \cos \omega_r t \qquad ...(3.12)$$

By Faraday's law, the e.m.f. induced in N-turn armature coil is given by

$$e = -\frac{d\psi}{dt} = N \phi \omega_r \sin \omega_r t - N \frac{d\phi}{dt} \cos \omega_r t \qquad ...(3.13)$$

In Eq. (3.13), $N \phi \omega_r \sin \omega_r t$ is the **speed-voltage** term, because it contains speed ω_r in it.

The second term $N \dfrac{d\phi}{dt} \cos \omega_r t$ is **transformer-voltage** term, because it involves the time derivative of the flux ϕ. If the field flux ϕ is time-invariant (*i.e.* ϕ not varying with time), the transformer e.m.f. in Eq. (3.13) reduces to zero and the generated e.m.f. is equal to the speed voltage (or speed e.m.f.) alone. Thus for electrical machines with time invariant flux, the generated e.m.f. is equal to the speed, rotational or motional e.m.f. alone and is given by

$$e = N \omega_r \phi \sin \omega_r t \quad ...(3.14)$$

In Eq. (3.14), remember that N is the number of turns in single full pitched coil, ϕ is the total flux per pole and ω_r is the relative velocity between field flux wave and armature coil. Note that Eq. (3.14) represents the general e.m.f. equation and is therefore applicable both to D.C. and A.C. machines in which the field flux is time-invariant (or constant).

If the single N-turn coil belonges to A.C. machines, then the maximum value of the speed or generated e.m.f. E_{max} occurs when $\sin \omega_r t = 1$.

$$\therefore \quad E_{max} = \omega_r N \phi = 2\pi f_r N \phi$$

The r.m.s. value of the generated e.m.f. in a full pitched coil is

$$E = \frac{E_{max}}{\sqrt{2}} = \sqrt{2}\pi f_r N \phi = 4.44 f_r N \phi \quad ...(3.15)$$

Here f_r may be called the *rotational* or *speed frequency*, since its value depends upon the relative velocity between the flux-density wave and the armature coil. The magnitude of f_r is given by

$$f_r = \frac{P n_r}{2} \text{ Hz}$$

where n_r is the relative speed in revolutions per second (*i.e.* r.p.s.) between the armature coil and flux-density wave.

Note that Eq. (3.15) gives the r.m.s. value of the generated e.m.f. in single N-turn full-pitch armature coil of an A.C. machine. Eq. (3.14) can be re-written as

$$e = N \omega_r \phi \cos\left(\omega_r t - \frac{\pi}{2}\right) = E_{max} \cos\left(\omega_r t - \frac{\pi}{2}\right) \quad ...(3.16)$$

An examination of Eqs. (3.12) and (3.16) reveals that the speed or generated e.m.f. lags by 90° the flux that generates it. This statement is true when the flux is time-invariant and is sine distributed in space. Nothing has been said about whether the armature coil moves or the flux-density wave travels. It is the relative velocity between flux-density wave and the coil that matters.

3.4.2. Generated e.m.f. in a Short-pitched Coil

Let the N-turn armature coil be short-pitched by ε electrical space degrees, so that the coil-pitch or coil-spane is $(180 - \varepsilon)$ electrical space degrees. For the short-pitched or chorded coil, Fig. 3.14 *(b)* is redrawn as shown in Fig. 3.15 *(a)*. The chording angle ε is shown as $\varepsilon/2$ at two places, in order that coil axis and field winding axis coincide. A *chording angle*, as already defined, is that angle by which the coil pitch departs from 180° electrical. Chording angle is also sometimes called *short-pitching angle*. It is obvious that the flux passing through the fractional pitch or chorded coil of Fig. 3.15 *(a)* is less than the flux passing through the full-pitched coil of Fig. 3.14 *(b)*.

Note that the total flux per pole is again equal to $2B_p lr$ for a 2-pole machine and $\frac{4}{P} B_p lr$ for a P-pole machine. The origin of space angle α is again taken as 90° away from the field axis. In order to determine the flux passing through or linking the coil, Eq. (3.7) should be integrated from $\alpha = \frac{\varepsilon}{2}$ to $\alpha = \pi - \frac{\varepsilon}{2}$, refer to Figs. 3.15 *(a)* and *(b)*.

$\therefore$ Flux passing through the chorded coil of Fig. 3.15 *(a)*

$$= \int_{\varepsilon/2}^{\pi-\varepsilon/2} B_p lr \sin \alpha \, d\alpha = 2B_p lr \cos \frac{\varepsilon}{2}$$

But $\quad 2B_p lr = \phi$

$\therefore$ Flux passing through the chorded coil $= \phi \cos \frac{\varepsilon}{2}$.

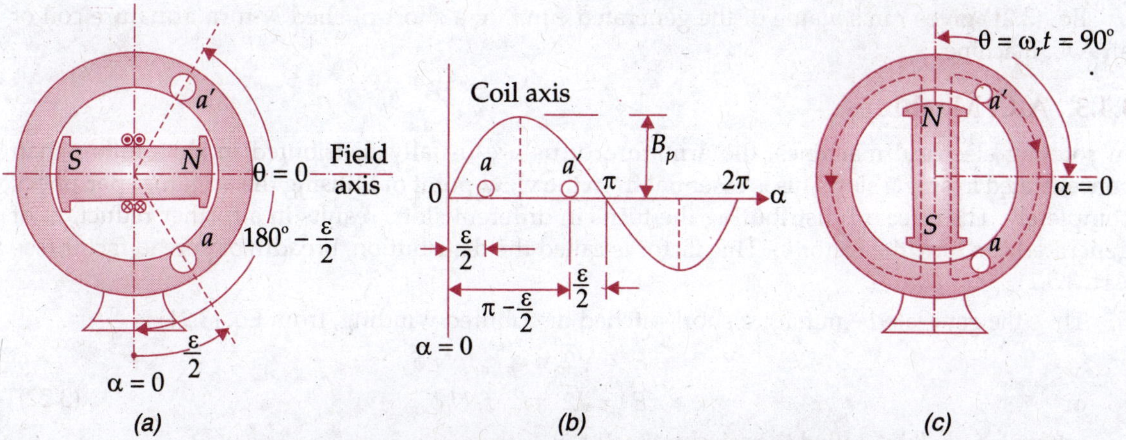

Fig 3.15: Pertaining to the generated e.m.f. in a short-pitched coil.

The time origin, as before, is at the instant field winding axis and armature coil axis coincide. Therefore, when $\theta = \omega_r t = 0$, refer to Fig. 3.15 *(a)*, the flux passing through the coil is maximum and is equal to $\phi \cos \frac{\varepsilon}{2} \left(= \phi \cos \frac{\varepsilon}{2} \cos 0°\right)$. When $\theta = \omega_r t = 90°$, refer to Fig. 3.15 *(c)*, the flux passing through the coil is zero $\left(= \phi \cos \frac{\varepsilon}{2} \cos 90°\right)$.

In Fig. 3.15 *(c)*, though one flux line is shown around coil *aa′*, the flux passing through the coil is zero. This fact may further be ascertained by observing that the coil magnetic axis and the field winding axis are 90° away from each other. For $\theta = \omega_r t = 180°$, the flux linking the coil would again be maximum $\left(= \phi \cos \frac{\varepsilon}{2} \cos 180°\right)$, but in the reversed direction. Therefore, a general expression for the flux passing through the chorded coil is $\phi \cos \frac{\varepsilon}{2} \cos \theta$ or $\phi \cos \frac{\varepsilon}{2} \cos \omega_r t$.

∴ The flux-linkages with short-pitched *N*-turn coil are

$$\psi = N \phi \cos \frac{\varepsilon}{2} \cos \omega_r t \qquad ...(3.17)$$

By Faraday's law, the e.m.f. induced in *N*-turn short-pitched armature coil is given by

$$e = -\frac{d\psi}{dt} = N \phi \, \omega_r \cos \frac{\varepsilon}{2} \sin \omega_r t \qquad ...(3.18)$$

In Eq. (3.18), flux ϕ is considered time-invariant.

The maximum value of the speed voltage E_{max} occurs when $\sin \omega_r t = 1$.

$$\therefore \quad E_{max} = N \phi \, \omega_r \cos \frac{\varepsilon}{2}$$

Its r.m.s value is

$$E = \frac{E_{max}}{\sqrt{2}} = \sqrt{2}\, \pi f_r N \phi \cos \frac{\varepsilon}{2} \qquad ...(3.19)$$

It may be seen from Eqs. (3.15) and (3.19) that the effect of short-pitched coil is to reduce the generated e.m.f. An examination of these equations reveals that this reduction factor is $\cos \frac{\varepsilon}{2}$ and is referred to as *coil pitch factor, coil-span factor* or *pitch factor*, symbol k_p.

∴ Pitch factor,

$$k_p = \cos \frac{\varepsilon}{2} \qquad ...(3.20)$$

Eq. (3.19) can be re-written as

$$E = \sqrt{2}\, \pi k_p f_r N \phi \qquad ...(3.21)$$

Eq. (3.21) gives r.m.s. value of the generated e.m.f. in a short-pitched N-turn armature coil of an A.C. machine.

3.4.3. A.C. Machines

In rotating electrical machines, the armature turns are usually distributed in slots rather than concentrated in single slot. This is essential from the view-point of utilising the armature periphery completely. The effect of distributing the turns in different slots, results in a further reduction of generated e.m.f. by the factor k_d. This factor is called the distribution, breadth or spread factor (see Art. 3.5.1).

Thus the generated e.m.f. for a short-pitched distributed winding, from Eq. (3.21) is

$$E = \sqrt{2}\ \pi\, k_p\, k_d f_r\, N\, \phi$$

or

$$E = \sqrt{2}\ \pi\, k_w\, f_r\, N\, \phi \qquad ...(3.22)$$

where $k_w (= k_p\, k_d)$ is called the winding factor.

In Eq. (3.22), note that N is the number of distributed turns in series.

The basic expression for the generated e.m.f. in A.C. machines is given by Eq. (3.22). This expression is now modified for the more common types of A.C. machines, in which the air-gap flux ϕ is constant in amplitude.

(i) Synchronous machines

(a) Armature winding. Two or three phase (*i.e.* poly-phase) armature winding is distributed in the slots along the armature periphery. The field winding is excited with D.C., therefore, the amplitude of the field flux wave does not vary with time. If N_{ph} is the total number of series turns per phase of the polyphase armature winding, then the e.m.f. generated in any one phase, from Eq. (3.22), is given by

$$E = \sqrt{2}\ \pi\, k_w\, f_r\, N_{ph}\, \phi \qquad ...(3.23)$$

If time origin is taken at the instant when flux linkages with phase a are maximum, then e.m.f. e_a for phase a can be written as

$$e_a = \sqrt{2}\, E \sin \omega t$$

For a phase sequence a, b, c ; voltages for phases b, c can be expressed as

$$e_b = \sqrt{2}\, E \sin (\omega t - 120°)$$

and

$$e_c = \sqrt{2}\, E \sin (\omega t - 240°)$$

These expressions for e_a, e_b, e_c are phase voltages and can be measured between line terminal and neutral for a star-connected alternator. For a delta-connected alternator ; e_a, e_b, e_c represent phase as well as line e.m.fs.

A synchronous machine can run only at synchronous speed. Consequently the relative velocity between the flux-density wave and the armature winding must be synchronous speed. The rotational frequency f_r is equal to $\frac{Pn_r}{2}$. In a synchronous machine, $\frac{P\text{(synchronous speed in r.p.s.)}}{2}$, *i.e.* $\frac{Pn_s}{2}$ is equal to the frequency f in Hz, for which the synchronous machine is designed.

Thus the generated e.m.f. in any one phase of a synchronous machine is given by

$$E_{ph} = \sqrt{2}\ \pi\, f\, k_w\, N_{ph}\, \phi \qquad ...(3.24)$$

Eq. (3.24) for a synchronous machine and Eq. (1.3) for a transformer, are of identical nature. In a transformer, core flux is varying with time and e.m.fs. are induced in the stationary primary and secondary coils. In a rotating machine, the relative motion between armature coil and the flux-density wave, causes flux linking the coil to vary with time and as a result, an e.m.f. is induced in the armature coil. In the transformer e.m.f. expression, the flux ϕ_{max} is the maximum value of the core flux, whereas in a synchronous machine, flux ϕ is the total flux per pole. In a transformer, the windings are concentrated, whereas in a synchronous machine, the armature winding is distributed and the reduction factor k_w must appear in the e.m.f. expression.

***(b)* Field-winding.** The field winding of a synchronous machine is always energised with direct current. Under steady-state conditions, the field or exciting current is given by

$$I_r = \frac{V_f}{r_f} \quad ...(3.25)$$

where V_f = direct voltage applied to the field winding

and r_f = field winding resistance.

***(ii)* Induction Machines**

(a) Stator. The polyphase stator winding of an induction machine is similar to the armature winding of a sychronous machine. When balanced polyphase voltages are applied to the stator winding, a rotating magnetic field of constant amplitude is produced in the air-gap. The speed of this rotating field is referred to as the synchronous speed and is given by Eq. (3.69).

Since there is relative velocity between the constant amplitude rotating field and the stationary stator winding, an e.m.f. is induced in the stator winding. The magnitude of this e.m.f., in any one phase is given by Eq. (3.24), which is repeated here, for convenience as

$$E_s = \sqrt{2}\,\pi\, f k_w N_{phs}\, \phi \quad ...(3.26)$$

For induction motor, f is the frequency of the applied voltages and N_{phs} is the stator series turns per phase. The stator induced e.m.f. E_s differs from the stator applied voltage by an amount equal to the stator leakage impedance drop–this phenomenon being similar to what happens in the primary winding of a transformer. Thus E_s given by Eq. (3.26) represents the counter e.m.f. in the stator winding. Actually the stator winding of a polyphase induction motor may be treated like the primary winding of a transformer.

***(b)* Rotor.** The rotating magnetic field in the air gap of an induction motor, travels at a synchronous speed of $\omega\left(=\frac{4\pi f}{P}\right)$ rad/sec, determined by the supply frequency f of the currents and the number of stator poles P. Assume that the rotor runs at a speed ω_r $(= \pi\, Pn_r)$ less than the rotating field speed ω. If the rotor revolves in the direction of rotating field, then the relative speed between the rotating flux wave and rotor is $(\omega - \omega_r)$ rad/sec. It has been shown before that the relative velocity between the coil and flux-density wave, determines the magnitude of induced e.m.f. in the coil. In view of this, the induced or generated e.m.f. in one rotor coil of N-turns is given by (refer to Eq. 3.14),

$$e = N(\omega - \omega_r)\, \phi \sin (\omega - \omega_r)t \quad ...(3.27)$$

The e.m.f. induced in one phase of the rotor distributed winding is

$$e = N_{phr}(\omega - \omega_r)k_w\, \phi \sin (\omega - \omega_r)t \quad ...(3.28)$$

where N_{phr} is the rotor series turns per phase.

In Eq. (3.28), the relative speed between rotor and rotating flux wave, *i.e.* $(\omega - \omega_r)$, is referred to as the *slip speed* in rad/sec.

$$\therefore \quad \text{Slip speed} = (\omega - \omega_r) \text{ rad/sec}$$

But it is more convenient to work with the ratio $\frac{\omega - \omega_r}{\omega}$, since it is a dimensionless quantity.

$$\therefore \quad \text{Slip } s = \frac{\omega - \omega_r}{\omega} = \frac{\text{Synchronous speed} - \text{Rotor speed}}{\text{Synchronous speed}} \quad ...(3.29a)$$

$$= \frac{n_s - n_r}{n_s} = \frac{N_s - N_r}{N_s} \quad ...(3.29\,b)$$

$$\therefore \quad \omega_r = \omega\,(1 - s)\,;\, n_r = n_s\,(1 - s)$$

$$\text{or} \quad N_r = N_s\,(1 - s) \quad ...(3.30)$$

Here n_s and N_s are the synchronous speeds in r.p.s and r.p.m. respectively. Further n_r and N_r are the rotor speeds in r.p.s and r.p.m. respectively.

Eq. (3.28) can now be re-written as,

$$e = s\omega\, N_{phr}\, k_w\, \phi \sin s\omega t \quad ...(3.31)$$

Its r.m.s. value is

$$E = 1/\sqrt{2}\,[s\,(2\pi f)\, N_{phr}\, k_w\, \phi]$$

$$= \sqrt{2}\,\pi\, s\, f\, k_w\, N_{phr}\, \phi \quad ...(3.32)$$

An examination of Eq. (3.31) reveals that the frequency of the e.m.f. generated in the rotor winding is ωs rad/sec or sf Hz. It is thus seen that the slip s effects both the magnitude and frequency of the rotor e.m.f. The frequency of the rotor e.m.f. sf, is called the *slip frequency* in Hz.

If the rotor is made to revolve in a direction opposite to the rotating flux wave, then the relative velocity between the rotor winding and the rotating flux wave becomes $(\omega + \omega_r)$ and the e.m.f. induced in one phase of the rotor is given by [from Eq. (3.14)].

$$e = (\omega + \omega_r)\, N_{phr}\, k_w\, \phi \sin (\omega + \omega_r)t \quad ...(3.33)$$

Now

$$\omega + \omega_r = \omega + \omega\,(1 - s) = \omega\,(2 - s)$$

∴ Eq. (3.33) becomes

$$e = \omega\,(2 - s)\, N_{phr}\, k_w\, \phi \sin (2 - s)\,\omega t \quad ...(3.34)$$

Its r.m.s. value is

$$E = \sqrt{2}\,\pi\, f\,(2 - s)\, N_{phr}\, k_w\, \phi \quad ...(3.35)$$

Eq. (3.34) indicates that the frequency of the e.m.f. generated in the rotor circuit is $f\,(2 - s)$ Hz. It can thus be concluded that a polyphase induction motor of the slip-ring or wound-rotor type can be used as a *frequency converter* (or changer) for changing the supply frequency f to other frequencies sf or $(2 - s)\,f$ at the slip-ring terminals.

3.4.4. Generated e.m.f. in D.C. Machines

Before deriving the e.m.f. equation for a D.C. machine, it is worthwhile to know the difference in the construction and operation of an A.C. generator and D.C. generator. Elementary forms of an A.C. generator and a D.C. generator are illustrated in Fig. 3.16 *(a)* and *(b)* respectively.

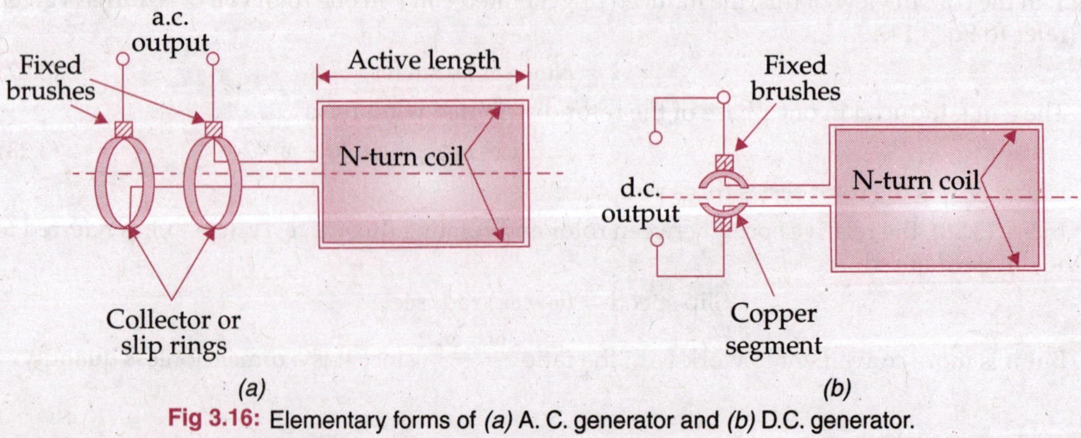

Fig 3.16: Elementary forms of *(a)* A. C. generator and *(b)* D.C. generator.

Fig. 3.16 *(a)* illustrates a two-pole alternator, with single *N*-turn full-pitched coil. The two ends of the *N*-turn coil are connected to two slip rings mounted on, but insulated from the shaft. Two carbon brushes, stationary in space, rub on these rotating *collector rings, or slip rings*, for collecting the alternating e.m.f. directly.

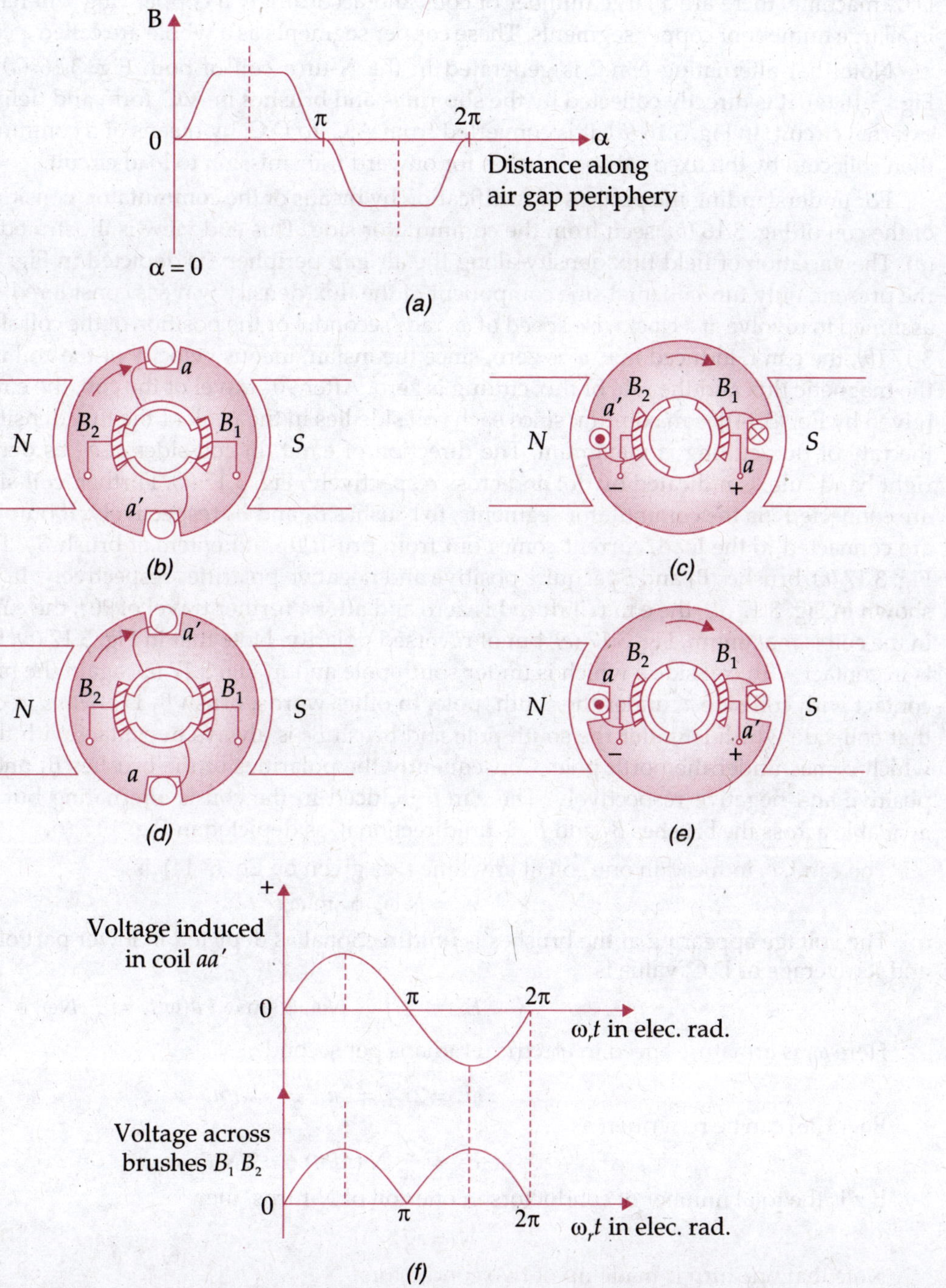

Fig 3.17: Rectification of A.C. to D.C. by means of commutator

For the 2-pole D.C. machine, one full pitched N-turn coil is shown in Fig. 3.16 *(b)*. One copper ring is split into two portions, which are insulated from each other and also from the shaft on which these are mounted. The two ends of the coil are connected to these two copper segments, on which two stationary carbon brushes are resting under suitable spring pressure. For an actual D.C. machine, there are a large number of coils and accordingly a copper ring will have to be cut in a large number of copper segments. These copper segments as a whole are called a commutator.

Note that alternating e.m.f. is generated in the N-turn coil of both Fig. 3.16 *(a)* and *(b)*. In Fig. 3.16 *(a)*, it is directly collected by the slip rings and brushes in A.C. form and delivered to the external circuit. In Fig. 3.16 *(b)*, it is converted from A.C. to D.C. by means of a commutator and is then collected by the fixed carbon brushes for onward transmission to load circuit.

For understanding the process of rectification by means of the commutator, consider end-view of the coil of Fig. 3.16 *(b)*, seen from the commutator side. This end view is illustrated in Fig. 3.17 *(b)*. The variation of field flux density along the air gap periphery is depicted in Fig. 3.17 *(a)*. For the present, only fundamental sine component of the flux-density wave is considered. The rotor is assumed to revolve at a clockwise speed of ω_r rad/second. For the position of the coil shown in Fig. 3.17 *(b)*, the e.m.f. induced in a, a' is zero, since the instantaneous velocity of the coil is parallel to the magnetic flux and the rate of flux cutting is zero. After 90° travel of the coil, the e.m.f. induced [given by Eq. (3.14)] is maximum, since each coil side lies in the peak of the flux density wave and the rate of flux-cutting is maximum. The direction of e.m.f. in coil-sides a, a', as determined by right hand rule, is indicated by dot and cross respectively, Fig. 3.17 *(c)*. Further, coil-sides a and a' are connected via the commutator segments, to brushes B_1 and B_2 respectively. If output terminals are connected to the load, current comes out from brush B_1 and enters at brush B_2. Therefore, in Fig. 3.17 *(c)*, brushes B_1 and B_2 acquire positive and negative polarities respectively. In the position shown in Fig. 3.17 *(d)*, the e.m.f. induced is zero and after a further travel of 90°, the e.m.f. induced in the coil is maximum, Fig. 3.17 *(e)*, but of reversed polarity. Note that in Fig. 3.17 *(c)*, the brush B_1 is in contact with coil side a which is under south pole and in Fig. 3.17 *(e)*, again the brush B_1 is in contact with coil-side a' under the south pole. In other words, brush B_1 is always in contact with that coil-side which is under the south pole and brush B_2 is always in contact with that coil-side which comes under the north pole. Consequently the polarities of the brushes B_1 and B_2 remain positive and negative respectively. The e.m.f. induced in the coil is alternating but the voltage available across the brushes B_1 and B_2 is unidirectional, as depicted in Fig. 3.17 *(f)*.

The e.m.f. e_c induced in one coil at any time t, as given by Eq. (3.14), is

$$e_c = N\,\omega_r\,\phi \sin \omega_r t$$

The voltage appearing at the brushes is unidirectional as depicted in lower part of Fig. 3.17 *(f)* and its average or D.C. value is

$$E_c = \frac{1}{\pi}\int_0^{\pi} N\omega_r\,\phi \sin \omega_r t\, d(\omega_r t) = \frac{2}{\pi} N\omega_r\,\phi \qquad ...(3.36)$$

Here ω_r is armature speed in electrical radians per second.

$$\therefore \qquad \omega_r = 2\pi f_r = 2\pi \frac{Pn}{2} = \pi Pn.$$

Eq. (3.36) can be re-written as

$$E_c = \frac{2}{\pi} N(\pi Pn)\,\phi = 2\,N\,Pn\,\phi \qquad ...(3.37)$$

If z is the total number of conductors in one coil of N-turns, then

$$N = \frac{z}{2}.$$

Note that one turn is made up of two conductors.

Substituting the value of N, Eq. (3.37) becomes

$$E_c = Pn\,\phi\,z \qquad ...(3.38)$$

E.m.f. per turn, from Eq. (3.37) $= \frac{1}{N}(2NPn\,\phi) = 2Pn\,\phi$ ...(3.39)

Average E.m.f. per conductor, from Eq. (3.38) or from Eq. (3.37)

$$E_z = \frac{1}{z}(Pn\phi z) = Pn\phi \qquad ...(3.40)$$

For a single coil of N-turns, or of z conductors, Eq. (3.38) gives the average or D.C. value of the e.m.f. available across the two brushes. Actually the armature winding consists of several coils uniformly distributed at the armature surface–this has the effect of increasing the voltage appearing across the armature terminals and of reducing the ripple in the output voltage. Eq. (3.38) can be used to determine the terminal voltage for a practical D.C. machine, provided z is now replaced by the number of series conductors between the brushes. If Z is the total number of armature conductors arranged in a parallel paths, then series conductors between brushes are $\frac{Z}{a}$. Thus the voltage E_a* appearing between the brushes, from Eq. (3.40), is

E_a = (average e.m.f. per conductor) (number of conductors in each parallel path)

$$E_a = (Pn\phi)\left(\frac{Z}{a}\right) = \frac{\phi ZnP}{a} \qquad ...(3.41)$$

or

$$E_a = K_e\,\phi n \qquad ...(3.42)$$

where constant

$$K_e = \frac{ZP}{a} \qquad ...(3.43)$$

Now speed in mech. rad/sec. $\omega_m = 2\pi n$.

Substitution of the value of n in Eq. (3.41) gives

$$E_a = \frac{\phi ZP}{a}\cdot\frac{\omega_m}{2\pi} = \frac{ZP}{2\pi a}\,\phi\,\omega_m = K_a\,\phi\,\omega_m \qquad ...(3.44)$$

where constant

$$K_a = \frac{ZP}{2\pi a} \qquad ...(3.45)$$

Constants K_e and K_a depend upon the armature winding design.

It should be remembered that for D.C. machines, the armature winding is always a double layer winding and is of two types, namely *lap-connected type* and *wave-connected type.*

In lap winding, the number of parallel paths a is equal to the number of field poles, *i.e.* $a = P$.

In wave winding, the number of parallel paths a is always 2 irrespective of the number of field poles, *i.e.*, $a = 2$ whatever the number of field poles may be. It should be noted that Eq. (3.14) forms the starting point for obtaining the e.m.f. expression for both D.C. and A.C. machines.

The voltage available across the brushes is unidirectional. For the same value of peak flux density B_p, it is easy to see that average value of brush voltage would be more for a flat-topped flux density wave of Fig. 3.17 *(a)* than for a sinusoidal flux density wave of Fig. 3.13 *(c)*. It is because of this reason that dc machines are designed with flat-topped B-wave.

Example 3.2. *A D.C. generator has 24 armature conductors. Average e.m.f. induced in one conductor is 2 V and each conductor is designed to handle a current of 5 A. Calculate the rating of this generator if number of parallel paths in this machine are (a) 2 (b) 4 and (c) 6.*

Solution. The arrangement of 24 conductors for parallel paths 2, 4 and 6 is illustrated in Fig. 3.18 *(a)*, *(b)* and *(c)* respectively. Here each conductor is treated like a 2-V cell with current-carrying capacity of 5 A.

---

* See Example 3.2

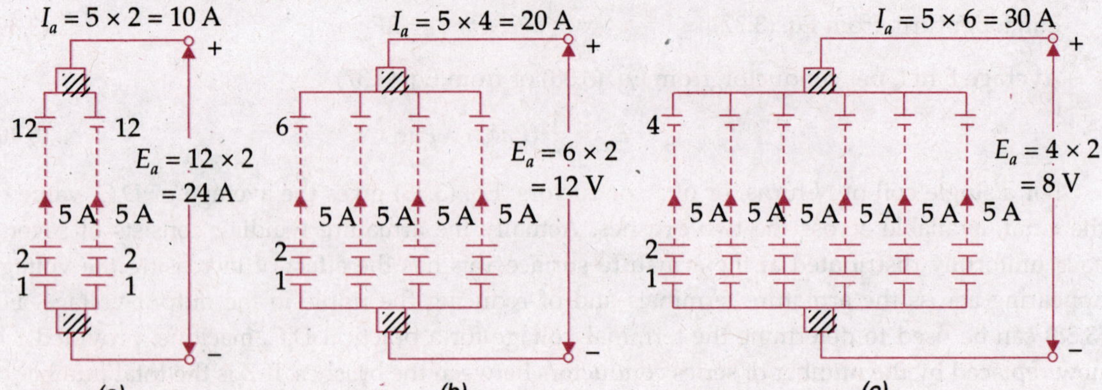

Fig 3.18: Pertaining to Example 3.2 *(a)* Two-parallel paths *(b)* Four-parallel paths *(c)* Six-parallel paths.

(a) For two-parallel paths, there are 12 $\left(=\frac{Z}{a}=\frac{24}{2}\right)$ series-connected conductors in each path. In other words, conductors between the two brushes are 12.

$\therefore$ Output voltage, E_a = (Number of series-connected conductors between two brushes) × (Average e.m.f. per conductor)

$= 12 \times 2 = 24$ V

Output current, I_a = (Current per path) × (Number of parallel paths)

$= 5 \times 2 = 10$ A

$\therefore$ Power rating $= E_a I_a = 24 \times 10 = 240$ W

(b) For four-parallel paths, there are 6 $\left(=\frac{24}{4}\right)$ conductors in each parallel path.

$\therefore$ Output voltage $= 6 \times 2 = 12$ V

Output current $= 5 \times 4 = 20$A

Power rating $= 12 \times 20 = 240$ W

(c) For 6-parallel paths, $E_a = 4 \times 2 = 8$, $I_a = 5 \times 6 = 30$ A,

Power rating $= E_a I_a = 8 \times 30 = 240$ W.

This example demonstrates that *(i)* the power rating of a D.C. machine does not depend on its number of parallel paths and *(ii)* the voltage between output brushes = (average generated e.m.f. per conductor) × (conductors per parallel path).

Example 3.3. *A 4-pole machine has 60 slots and 8 conductors per slot. The total flux per pole is 20 mWb. For a relative speed of 1500 r.p.m. between field flux and armature winding, calculate the generated armature voltage if the machine is*

(a) a D.C. machine with lap-connected winding and

(b) a three-phase star-connected machine with winding factor equal to 0.96. All the turns in each phase are in series.

Solution. *(a)* For lap-connected winding, $a = P = 4$.

Total number of conductors $Z = 60 \times 8 = 480.$

$$\text{Speed in r.p.s.} = \frac{1500}{60} = 25.$$

From Eq. (3.41), the generated e.m.f. $E_a = \dfrac{\phi ZnP}{a} = \dfrac{(20\times10^{-3})(480)(25)(4)}{4} = 240$ volts.

(b) Total number of turns $= \frac{480}{2} = 240.$

Number of series turns per phase, $N_{ph} = \frac{240}{3} = 80.$

Generated e.m.f. frequency, $f = \frac{Pn}{2} = 4 \times \frac{25}{2} = 50$ Hz.

From Eq. (3.24), the generated e.m.f. per phase is

$$E_{ph} = \sqrt{2}\,\pi f N_{ph}\, k_w\, \phi = \sqrt{2}\,\pi(50)(80)(0.96)(20 \times 10^{-3})$$

$$= 341 \text{ volts.}$$

Generated e.m.f. between line terminals $= \sqrt{3}\,E_{ph} = \sqrt{3}\,(341) = 591$ volts.

Example 3.4. *A 4-pole, 3-phase, slip-ring induction motor is coupled mechanically with a 6-pole synchronous motor. The induction motor stator and synchronous motor are energised from the same 50 Hz voltage source.*

(a) What will be the frequency of the e.m.fs. at the rotor slip rings if the synchronous motor is driven (i) in a direction opposite to the rotating field produced by the induction motor stator (ii) in the direction of the induction motor rotating field.

(b) If the frequency of the 3-phase rotor terminal voltage is required to be 150 Hz. calculate the number of poles that the induction motor must have.

(c) If the induction motor is assumed to have 8 poles, calculate the number of synchronous motor poles, for obtaining 3-phase, 150 Hz voltages at the induction motor slip rings.

Solution. *(a)* Synchronous motor runs always at synchronous speed of $\frac{120f}{P}$ r.p.m.

$\therefore$ Synchronous-motor speed $= \frac{(120)(50)}{6} = 1000$ r.p.m.

Speed of the rotating field, produced by induction motor stator

$$= \frac{120f}{P} = \frac{(120)(50)}{6} = 1500 \text{ r.p.m.}$$

(i) When the induction motor rotor is driven in a direction opposite to the rotating field, the relative velocity between induction motor rotor conductors and its rotating field is

$$(1500 + 1000) = 2500 \text{ r.p.m.}$$

$\therefore$ Frequency of the e.m.f. at rotor slip ring terminals

$$= \frac{(\text{Rotor poles})(\text{Relative velocity in r.p.m})}{120}$$

$$= \frac{(4)(2500)}{120} = 83\frac{1}{3} \text{ Hz.}$$

Note that the rotor poles, equal to the stator poles, are 4.

(ii) When the induction motor rotor is driven in the direction of the rotating field, then relative velocity is

$$(1500 - 1000) = 500 \text{ r.p.m.}$$

$\therefore$ Frequency of the e.m.f. at rotor terminals

$$= \frac{4 \times 500}{120} \text{ Hz} = 16\frac{2}{3} \text{ Hz.}$$

(b) For obtaining a frequency of 150 Hz at induction-motor rotor terminals, the rotating field and rotor must run in opposite directions.

$\therefore$ The relative speed between rotor and rotating field = [Rotor speed + Rotating field speed]

$$= \left[1000 + \frac{120 \times 50}{P_{im}}\right]$$

where P_{im} = number of poles on the induction motor.

$\therefore$ Frequency of the e.m.f. at rotor terminals is given by $\dfrac{P_{im}\left[1000 + \dfrac{6000}{P_{im}}\right]}{120} = 150$ or $P_{im} = 12$ poles.

(c) Relative speed between rotor and rotating field must be equal to $\left[\dfrac{(120)(50)}{P_{sm}} + \dfrac{(120)(50)}{8}\right]$

Here P_{sm} is the number of poles on the synchronous motor.

$\therefore$ Frequency of the rotor e.m.f. is $\dfrac{8\left[120 \times \dfrac{50}{P_{sm}} + 750\right]}{120} = 150$ or $P_{sm} = 4$ poles.

Example 3.5. *A 3-phase, 4-pole, 50 Hz slip-ring induction motor has 420 stator turns and 240 rotor turns. The magnitude of the rotating flux per pole is 30 m Wb. The winding factors for both stator and rotor windings are 0.96. Calculate frequency and the magnitude of per phase e.m.fs. in the stator and rotor windings when the rotor is*

(a) stationary

(b) revolving in the direction of rotating flux wave at a speed of 1440 r.p.m. and

(c) revolving opposite to the direction of rotating flux wave at a speed of 1440 r.p.m.

Solution. (a) Per phase e.m.f. induced in the stator winding is given by Eq. (3.26).

$\therefore$ Stator per phase e.m.f.,

$$E_s = \sqrt{2}\,\pi f k_w N_{phs}\phi = \sqrt{2}\,\pi\,(50)\,(0.96)\left(\frac{420}{3}\right)(30 \times 10^{-3})$$

$$= 310 \text{ volts at 50 Hz.}$$

From Eq. (3.32), the rotor per phase e.m.f. is

$$E_r = \sqrt{2}\,\pi s f k_w N_{phr}\,\phi$$

At standstill,

$$\text{slip, } s = \frac{n_s - 0}{n_s} = 1$$

$\therefore$

$$E_r = \sqrt{2}\,\pi\,(50 \times 1)\,(0.96)\left(\frac{240}{3}\right)(30 \times 10^{-3})$$

$$= 310 \times \frac{80}{140} = 177 \text{ volts at } 50\ (= sf) \text{ Hz.}$$

(b) Stator per phase e.m.f. is unaffected with the rotation of the rotor.

$$E_s = 310 \text{ volts at 50 Hz.}$$

The speed at which rotating flux wave travels is given by

$$N_s = \frac{120f}{P} \text{ r.p.m.} = \frac{120 \times 50}{4} = 1500 \text{ r.p.m.}$$

For rotor speed of 1440 r.p.m. in the direction of rotating flux wave,

$$\text{slip, } s = \frac{1500 - 1440}{1500} = 0.04.$$

From Eq. (3.32), the rotor per phase e.m.f. is

$$E_r = \sqrt{2}\,\pi\,(0.04)\,(50)\,(0.96)\,(80)\,(30 \times 10^{-3}) = 0.04 \times 177$$

$$= 7.08 \text{ volts at a frequency of } 0.04 \times 50\ (= sf) \text{ i.e. } 2 \text{ Hz.}$$

(c) When the rotor revolves at 1440 r.p.m. opposite to the direction of rotating flux wave,

$$\text{slip, } s = \frac{1500 + 1440}{1500} = 1.96.$$

From Eq. (3.32),

$$E_r = \sqrt{2}\,\pi s f\, k_w\, N_{phr}\, \phi$$

$$= \sqrt{2}\,\pi\,(1.96)\,(50)\,(0.96)\,(80)\,(30 \times 10^{-3}) = 1.96 \times 177$$

$$= 346.92 \text{ volts at a frequency of } 1.96 \times 50, \textit{ i.e. } 98 \text{ Hz.}$$

3.5. E.M.F. POLYGON

This article develops the physical concepts of e.m.f. polygon and these concepts are then extended to derive the expressions for distribution and pitch factors.

Consider Fig. 3.19 *(a)* in which 8 conductors housed in 8 slots are shown. The field current produces two poles on the rotor and the field flux is assumed to be sine-distributed in space, *i.e.*, along the air-gap periphery. At the instant shown in Fig. 3.19 *(a)*, the conductor is being cut by the maximum flux, say ϕ_m, therefore emf induced in it is also maximum, say E_m. This emf can be represented by a phasor whose projection on the vertical axis must be equal to the rms value of the emf generated in conductor 1. This is shown in Fig. 3.19 *(a)* by a phasor $\overline{E}_1 = E_m/\sqrt{2}$ along the vertical axis.

Conductor 2 is being cut by a flux (= $\phi_m \cos\gamma$) less than ϕ_m, accordingly the magnitude of generated emf is less than E_m. This emf in conductor 2 is indicated by phasor $\overline{E}_2$ (= E_1) whose vertical component $E_2 \cos\gamma$ is equal to the rms generated emf in conductor 2. Note that E_2 is displaced from E_1 by an angle γ, equal to the angle between adjacent slots. This angle γ (gamma) is usually called the **angular slot pitch** and is given by

$$\gamma = \frac{\pi . P}{\text{Total number of slots}} \cdot \text{Elect. radians}$$

$$= \frac{180 . P}{\text{Total number of slots}} \cdot \text{Elect. degree}$$

$$= \frac{180}{\text{Slots per pole}} \cdot \text{Elect. degree}$$

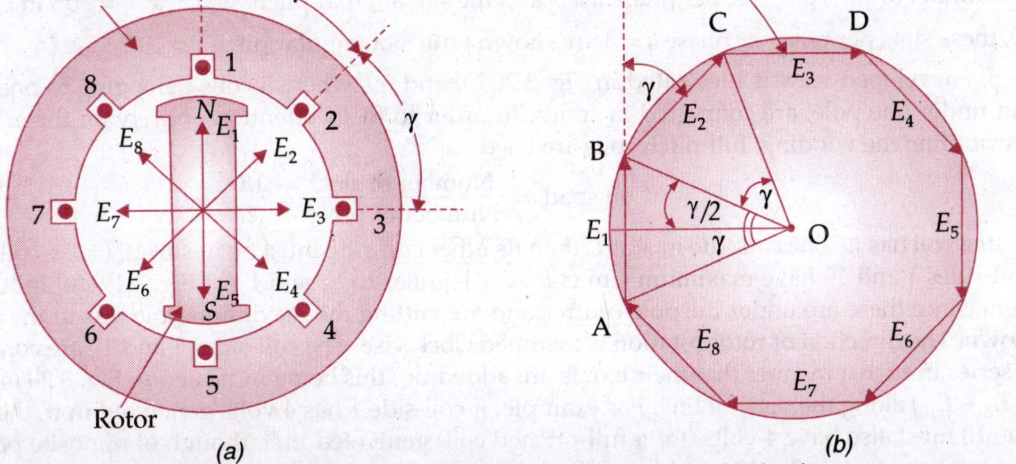

Fig 3.19: *(a)* Emf induced in various conductors and *(b)* e.m.f. polygon. The various phasor e.m.fs E_1, E_2,.... E_8 may be called star of conductor emfs or star of slot emfs.

In Fig. 3.19 *(a)*, γ is equal to 45°. The emf generated in conductor 3 can similarly be represented in Fig. 3.19 *(a)* by phasor $\overline{E}_3$ (= E_1) whose vertical component $E_3 \cos 2\gamma$ is equal to the rms generated emf in conductor 3. Note that E_3 is displaced from E_1 by 2γ and from E_2 by γ.

At the instant shown in Fig. 3.19 *(a)*, it may be seen that conductor 3 is not cutting any magnetic flux and therefore no emf is generated in this conductor, therefore, emf phasor $\overline{E}_3$ (= E_1) must have zero vertical projection (= $E_m \cos 2\gamma = E_m \cos 90°$). The same thought process can further be used for conductor emfs E_4, E_5,...., E_8. Note that all phasors E_1, E_2,...., E_8 are of equal lengths. Their projections on the vertical axis, determine the magnitude of rms generated emfs in the various conductors.

In Fig. 3.19 *(b)*, E_1 (= *AB*) is drawn parallel to $\overline{E}_1$ of Fig. 3.19 *(a)*. At the point *B*, *BC* = E_2 is drawn parallel to $\overline{E}_2$ of Fig. 3.19 *(a)* and so on. It will be found that conductor emfs E_1, E_2,......,E_8 constitute a closed **emf polygon**. The perpendicular bisectors of each of the conductor emfs E_1, E_2,......,E_8 (*i.e. AB, BC, CD* etc.) will pass through a point *O*, indicating that if a circle with *O* as centre and *OA* as radius is drawn, it must pass through the points *A, B, C, D* etc. The angle subtended by each phasor emf at the centre *O* is seen to be equal to the slot angular pitch γ.

Starting from the front end of conductor 1, join the back ends of conductors 1 and 2 in Fig. 3.19 *(a)*. Further, join conductors 2 and 3 by a connection at the front end, 3 and 4 at the back end and so on. The resultant emf appearing between the starting front end of conductor 1 and the finishing end of conductor 8 (*i.e.*, after having gone through all the conductors once), will be found to be zero. This is evident from Fig. 3.19 *(b)* by the phasor addition of emf phasors E_1, E_2,......,E_8.

3.5.1. Distribution, Breadth or Belt Factor

The e.m.f. generated in a full-pitched armature coil of *N*-turns is given by Eq. (3.14). In rotating electrical machines, however, the armature winding is not concentrated in a single slot, but distributed uniformly along the air gap periphery. The advantages of distributing the winding in slots are :

(i) reduction of the harmonics in the generated e.m.f. wave, thus making it approach a sine wave, see Prob. 3.30 *(a)*.

(ii) full utilisation of the armature iron and copper and

(iii) adding rigidity and mechanical strength to the winding.

For obtaining a general expression for the distribution factor, the stator of Fig. 3.19 *(a)* is assumed to have 18 slots. In these slots, a single-layer, 2-pole, 3-phase winding is placed, so that the number of slots per pole per phase *q* is 3 and the slot angular pitch γ is $\frac{2\times180}{18} = 20°$. In Fig. 3.20 *(a)*, these slots per pole per phase $q = 3$ are shown with slot angular pitch $\gamma = 20°$.

Its developed view is illustrated in Fig. 3.20 *(b)* and *(c)*, where 3 coils belonging to one phase and under one pole, are connected in series. In order to focus attention entirely on the effects of distributing the winding, full-pitch coils are used.

$$\therefore \quad \text{Coil span} = \frac{\text{Number of slots}}{\text{Number of poles}} = \frac{18}{2} = 9.$$

If a coil has its one coil side in slot 1, then its other coil-side must be in slot 10 (= 1 + coil span). Coil-sides 1 and 10 have maximum e.m.fs E_1, E_{10} [similar to E_1 and E_5 of Fig. 3.19 *(a)*] induced in them, since these are under the pole centres and are cutting the maximum pole flux at the instant shown. The direction of rotor rotation is assumed clockwise. The coil-sides 1 and 10 are connected in series in such a manner that their e.m.fs are added up; this being indicated in Fig. 3.20 *(d)* by *ab* (= $E_1 + E_{10}$) along the vertical line. For example, if coil-side 1 has 4 volts generated in it, then coil-side 10 must also have 4 volts (for a full-pitched coil) generated in it; though of opposite polarity. The total e.m.f. in coil 1-10 would be 8 (= 4+ 4) volts. The e.m.f. generated in coil-sides 2 and 11 are E_2 and E_{11}, similar to E_2 and E_6 of Fig. 3.19 *(a)*. The total e.m.f. in coil 2-11 is given by the sum of E_2 and E_{11}, this e.m.f. being indicated in Fig. 3.20 *(d)* by *bc*, phase displaced from the maximum e.m.f. position by slot-angular pitch γ. The vertical projection of *bc* gives the rms value of the emf generated in coil 2-11. Similarly, the total emf $(E_3 + E_{12})$ generated in coil 3-12, is indicated in Fig. 3.20 *(d)* by *cd*, phase displaced from the maximum emf position by an angle 2γ.

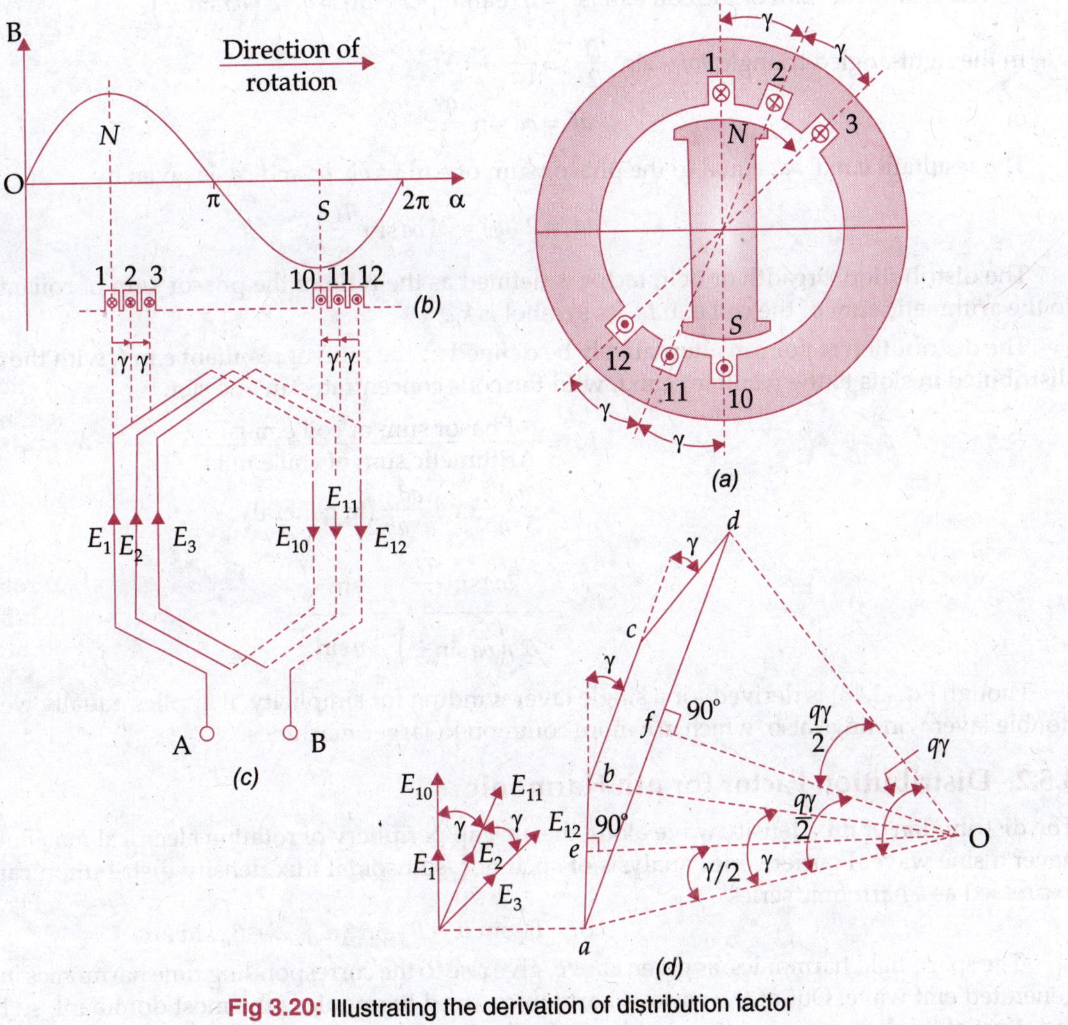

Fig 3.20: Illustrating the derivation of distribution factor

The resultant e.m.f. appearing between the terminals *AB* of the three (or in general *q*) coils 1-10, 2-11 and 3-12 is the phasor sum of the e.m.f. phasors *ab*, *bc* and *cd* and this resultant is seen to be equal to *ad* in the right hand side of Fig. 3.20 *(d)*. Here *q* denotes the slots per pole per phase.

As indicated earlier, the right bisector of phasors *ab*, *bc* and *cd* must meet at a point *o* and the points, *a*, *b*, *c*, *d* would lie on a circle with *oa* as radius. Now draw perpendiculars *oe* and *of* to *ab* and *ad* respectively. From Fig. 3.20 *(d)*, it is seen that, in general, angle *aob* is equal to the slot angular pitch γ, angle $aod = q\gamma$ and angle $aof = \dfrac{q\gamma}{2}$

In the right-angled triangle *aoe*.

$$\sin\frac{\gamma}{2} = \frac{ae}{oa}$$

or $$ae = oa \sin \frac{\gamma}{2}$$

$\therefore$ $$\text{e.m.f. per coil} = ab = bc = cd = 2(ae) = 2\left(oa \sin \frac{\gamma}{2}\right)$$

The arithmetic sum of the coil e.m.fs. $= q$ (e.m.f. per coil) $= q \cdot 2\left(oa \sin \frac{\gamma}{2}\right)$

In the right-angled triangle *aof*, $\sin \frac{q\gamma}{2} = \frac{af}{oa}$

or $$af = oa \sin \frac{q\gamma}{2}$$

The resultant e.m.f. *ad*, equal to the phasor sum of e.m.f.s *ab*, *bc* and *cd*, is given by

$$ad = 2\,(af) = 2\left(oa \sin \frac{q\gamma}{2}\right)$$

The distribution, breadth or belt, factor is defined as the ratio of the phasor sum of coil e.m.fs. to the arithmetic sum of the coil e.m.fs. Its symbol is k_d.

The distribution factor can alternatively be defined as the ratio of resultant e.m.f. with the coils distributed in slots to the resultant e.m.f. with the coils concentrated in one slot.

$\therefore$
$$k_d = \frac{\text{Phasor sum of coil e.m.fs.}}{\text{Arithmetic sum of coil e.m.fs.}}$$

$$= \frac{ad}{3 \cdot ab} \text{ or } \frac{ad}{q \cdot ab} \text{ (in general)}$$

$$= \frac{2oa \sin \frac{q\gamma}{2}}{2q\left(oa \sin \frac{\gamma}{2}\right)} = \frac{\sin \frac{q\gamma}{2}}{q \sin \frac{\gamma}{2}} \quad ...(3.46)$$

Though Eq. (3.46) is derived for a single layer winding for simplicity, it applies equally well to double layer windings also, which are more common in larger machines.

3.5.2. Distribution Factor for nth Harmonic

The distribution of flux density wave along the air-gap periphery of rotating electrical machines is never a sine wave. Fourier series analysis of such non-sinusoidal flux density distribution can be expressed as a harmonic series

$$B = B_1 \sin \alpha + B_3 \sin 3\alpha + ... + B_n \sin n\alpha$$

The space-field harmonics, as given above, give rise to the corresponding time harmonics in the generated emf wave. Out of the various harmonics, third harmonic is the most dominant, so here the effect of this harmonic is only considered. In Fig. 3.21 *(a)*, fundamental and third harmonic flux density waves are shown. It is seen from this figure that third harmonic B-wave makes the resultant flux-density wave a flat-topped B-wave. A third harmonic component of the flux density wave, may be imagined as produced by 3 poles as compared to one pole for the fundamental component, this is illustrated in Fig. 3.21 *(a)*. In view of this, the slot-angular pitch γ on the fundamental scale, would become 3γ for the third harmonic component and hence $n\gamma$ for the nth harmonic component. Thus the distribution factor for the nth harmonic, from Eq. (3.46) is

$$k_{dn} = \frac{\sin \frac{qn\gamma}{2}}{q \sin \frac{n\gamma}{2}} \quad ...(3.47\ a)$$

Examples will show that k_{dn} is less than k_{d1}. This has the effect of reducing the nth harmonic emf in comparison with fundamental emf. This is certainly an advantage of distributing the windings in slots. When the slot angular pitch γ is less than about 15° electrical (or slots per pole per phase tends to be large), the distribution factor approaches,

from Eq. (3.46),
$$k_d = \frac{\sin\frac{q\gamma}{2}}{\frac{q\gamma}{2}} \qquad \text{...(3.47 b)}$$

and from Eq. (3.47 *a*),
$$k_{dn} = \frac{\sin\frac{qn\gamma}{2}}{\frac{qn\gamma}{2}} \qquad \text{...(3.47 c)}$$

In Fig. 3.20 *(b)* or *(c)*, if adjoining coil-sides 1, 2, 3 (or 10, 11, 12) belong to the same phase, then this phase group in adjacent slots is called a **phase belt** or **phase band**. If slots per pole per phase is a whole number, then all the phase belts are alike. The peripheral angular distance of a phase belt is called its **phase spread** σ (= *q*γ) in electrical space degrees. Now Eq. (3.46) can be re-written to include phase spread σ (sigma) as

$$k_d = \frac{\sin\frac{\sigma}{2}}{q\sin\frac{\sigma}{2q}} \qquad \text{...(3.48)}$$

From Eq. (3.47 *a*),
$$k_{dn} = \frac{\sin\frac{n\sigma}{2}}{q\sin\frac{n\sigma}{2q}} \qquad \text{...(3.48 a)}$$

For γ < 15° electrical, from Eq. (3.47 *b*),
$$k_d = \frac{\sin\frac{\sigma}{2}}{\frac{\sigma}{2}} \qquad \text{...(3.48 b)}$$

and from Eq. (3.47 *c*),
$$k_{dn} = \frac{\sin\frac{n\sigma}{2}}{\frac{n\sigma}{2}} \qquad \text{...(3.48 c)}$$

The above expression for distribution factor for fundamental component and for γ < 15° electrical can also be derived by referring to Fig. 3.21 *(b)*. This figure shows that when *q* = slots per pole per phase tends to be large, the slot angular pitch γ tends to be small for a given phase spread σ. The phasor diagram for coil emfs now becomes an arc of a circle whose chord *ab* is the resultant emf as shown in Fig. 3.21 *(b)*. The distribution factor is therefore

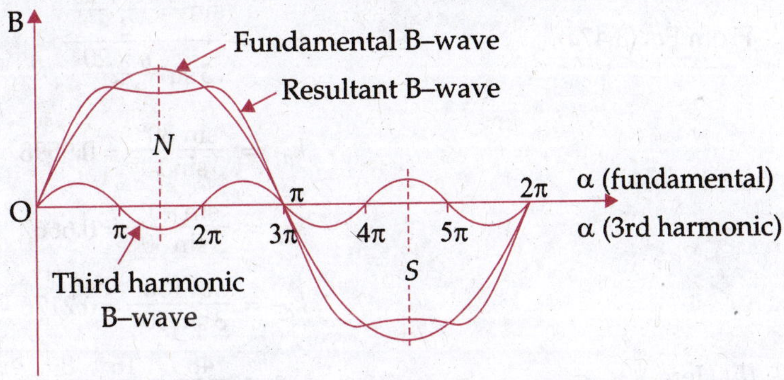

Fig 3.21: *(a)* Fundamental and third harmonic B-waves in an electrical machine.

$$k_d = \frac{\text{Phasor sum of coil e.m.fs}}{\text{Arithmetic sum of coil e.m.fs}} = \frac{\text{chord } abc}{\text{arc } ab}$$

$$= \frac{2.oa\sin\frac{\sigma}{2}}{oa\cdot\sigma} = \frac{\sin\frac{\sigma}{2}}{\frac{\sigma}{2}} \qquad \text{...(3.48 b)}$$

When $q > 5$ or $\gamma < 15°$ electrical, the winding is called **uniformly distributed winding.**

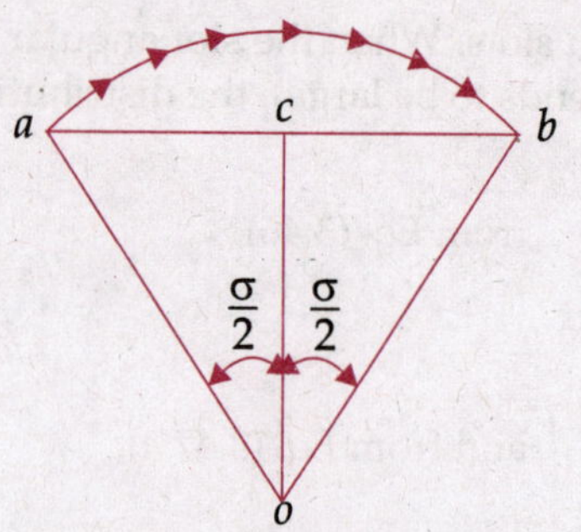

Fig 3.21: *(b)* Coil emf for uniformly distributed winding.

In fractional-slot windings (discussed in chapter 7),

$$q = \frac{S}{mP} = \frac{S/m}{P}$$

is not a whole number. Here S is the number of slots and m, the number of phases. If k is the highest common factor between S/m and P, then q can be written as

$$q = \frac{S/m}{P} = \frac{k \cdot S_k}{k \cdot P_k} = \frac{S_k}{P_k}$$

The distribution factor for fractional-slot windings is obtained by replacing q by S_k in Eq. (3.48 *a*).

$$\therefore \quad k_{dn} = \frac{\sin\frac{n\sigma}{2}}{S_k \sin\frac{n\sigma}{2S_k}} \qquad \text{...(3.48 } d\text{)}$$

One pole pitch is equivalent to 180 electrical space degrees and in a 3-phase machine, the winding is so distributed as to give a phase spread of 60 electrical space degrees. In other words, each phase group or each phase belt occupies 60° (= σ) electrical, under each pole for a 3-phase machine and 90° (= σ) electrical under each pole for a 2-phase machine.

Example 3.6. *Calculate the fundamental, third and fifth harmonic belt factors for a stator having*

(a) 54 slots, 3-phase, 6 poles

(b) 48 slots, 3-phase, 6 poles with narrow spread winding.

Solution. *(a)* Slots per pole per phase, $q = \frac{54}{3 \times 6} = 3$

Slot angular pitch, $\gamma = \frac{P \times 180}{S} = \frac{6 \times 180}{54} = 20°$

From Eq. (3.47*a*), $k_{dn} = \frac{\sin\frac{n \times 3 \times 20}{2}}{3\sin\frac{n \times 20}{2}}$

$$\therefore \quad k_{d1} = \frac{\sin 30°}{3\sin 10°} = 0.9598$$

$$k_{d3} = \frac{\sin 90°}{3\sin 30°} = 0.6667$$

$$k_{d5} = \frac{\sin 150°}{3\sin 50°} = 0.2176$$

(b) Here $q = \frac{48}{3 \times 6} = \frac{16}{6} = \frac{8}{3} = \frac{S_k}{P_k}$

From Eq. (3.48 *c*), $k_{dn} = \frac{\sin\frac{n \times 60}{2}}{8\sin\frac{n \times 60}{2 \times 8}}$

$$\therefore \quad k_{d1} = \frac{\sin 30°}{8\sin 3.75°} = 0.9556$$

$$k_{d3} = \frac{\sin 90°}{8 \sin 11.25°} = 0.6407$$

$$k_{d5} = \frac{\sin 150°}{8 \sin 18.75°} = 0.1944$$

This example demonstrates that $k_{d5} < k_{d3} < k_{d1}$.

3.5.3. Pitch (or Coil-span) Factor

An expression for the pitch factor has already been derived in Eq. (3.20). An alternative way of obtaining Eq. (3.20) is presented here, for it leads to better physical concepts of pitch factor.

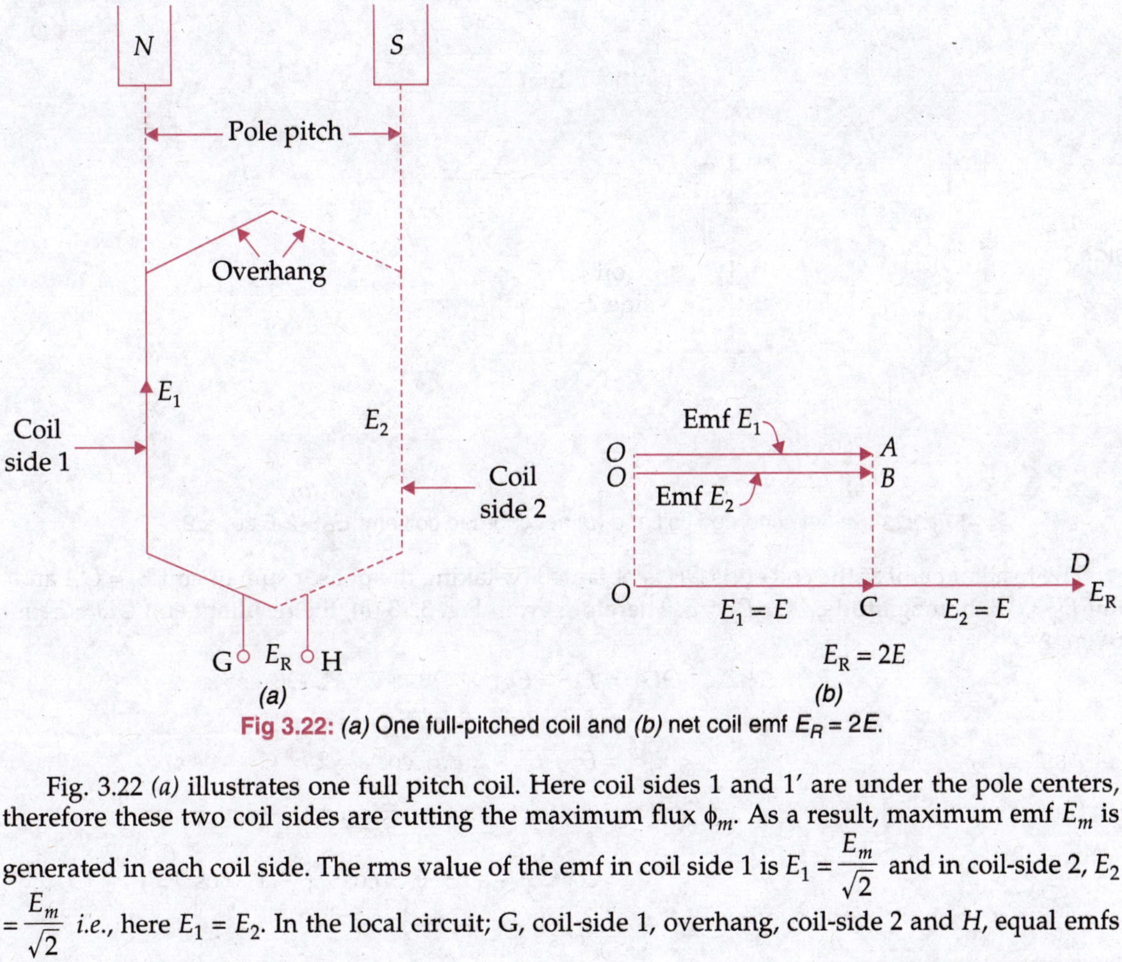

Fig 3.22: *(a)* One full-pitched coil and *(b)* net coil emf $E_R = 2E$.

Fig. 3.22 *(a)* illustrates one full pitch coil. Here coil sides 1 and 1′ are under the pole centers, therefore these two coil sides are cutting the maximum flux ϕ_m. As a result, maximum emf E_m is generated in each coil side. The rms value of the emf in coil side 1 is $E_1 = \frac{E_m}{\sqrt{2}}$ and in coil-side 2, $E_2 = \frac{E_m}{\sqrt{2}}$ *i.e.*, here $E_1 = E_2$. In the local circuit; G, coil-side 1, overhang, coil-side 2 and H, equal emfs $OA = E_1$ and $OB = E_2$, are aiding each other and are in phase as shown in Fig. 3.22 *(b)*. Therefore, the resultant e.m.f. E_R can be obtained by the phasor sum of emfs $OA = E_1$ and $OB = E_2$.

∴ Net emf at the coil ends $GH \doteq E_R = OA + OB = OC + CD = E_1 + E_2$. Since $E_1 = E_2 = E$, $E_R = E + E = 2E$ = arithmetic sum of coil-side emfs of a full-pitched coil.

Fig. 3.23 *(a)* shows a short-pitched or chorded coil with chording angle equal to ε° electrical. Here coil side 1 is cutting the maximum flux ϕ_m, therefore maximum emf E_m is generated in it. Other coil-side 2 is cutting a flux $\phi_m \cos ε°$ (for ε° = 0, flux = ϕ_m), as a result, emf generated in coil-side 2 is $E_m \cos ε°$. Therefore, rms values of emf in coil-side 1 and 2 are $OA = E_1 = \frac{E_m}{\sqrt{2}} = E$ and $OB =$

$E_2 = \frac{E_m}{\sqrt{2}} \cos \varepsilon = E \cos \varepsilon$ respectively. Therefore, these emfs OA in coil side 1 and emf OB in coil side 2 are displaced from each other by chording angle ε as shown in Fig. 3.23 (*b*).

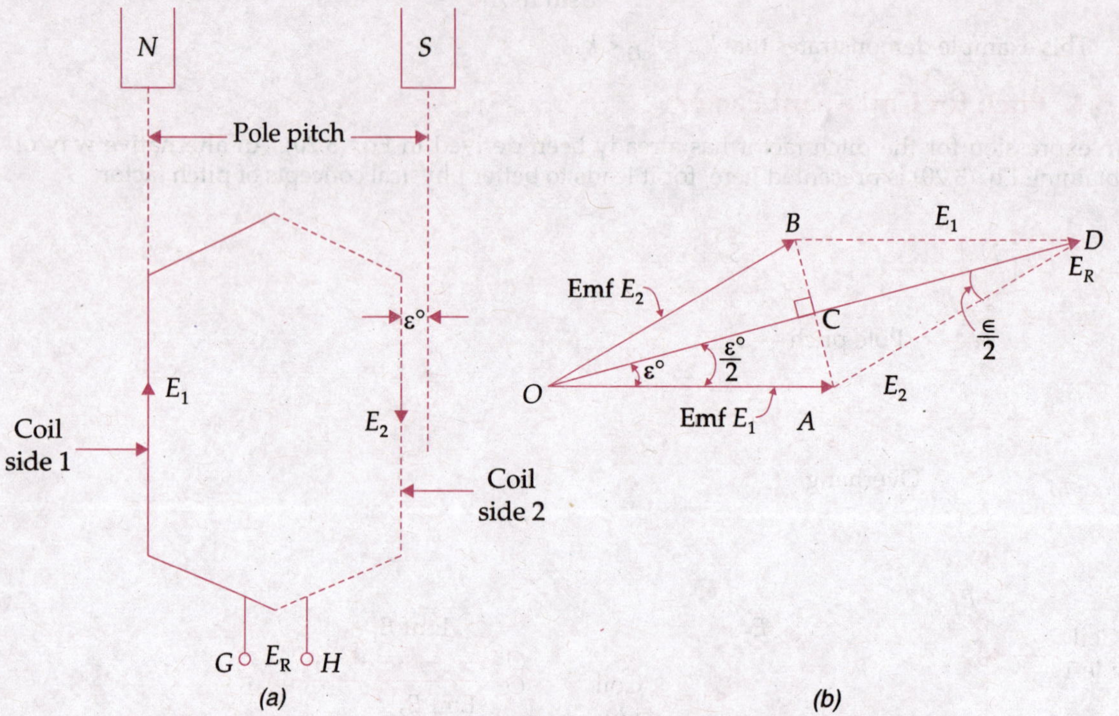

Fig 3.23: (*a*) One chorded coil and (*b*) net chorded coil emf $E_R = 2\,E \cos \varepsilon/2$.

The resultant emf at the coil ends GH is obtained by taking the phasor sum of emf $E_1 = OA$ and emf $E_2 = OB$. In magnitude, $E_1 = E_2 = E$. Therefore, from Fig. 3.23 (*b*), the resultant emf $OD = E_R$ is given by

$$OD^2 = E_R{}^2 = OA^2 + OB^2 + 2\,OA.\,OB.\cos \varepsilon$$

$$= E_1{}^2 + E_2{}^2 + 2\,E_1.\,E_2.\cos \varepsilon$$

As $E_1 = E_2$,
$$E_R{}^2 = E^2 + E^2 + 2.\,E.E.\cos \varepsilon = 2\,E^2\,(1 + \cos \varepsilon)$$

But
$$\cos \varepsilon = \cos\left(\frac{\varepsilon}{2} + \frac{\varepsilon}{2}\right) = \cos \frac{\varepsilon}{2} \cdot \cos \frac{\varepsilon}{2} - \sin \frac{\varepsilon}{2} \cdot \sin \frac{\varepsilon}{2}$$

$$= \cos^2 \frac{\varepsilon}{2} - \sin^2 \frac{\varepsilon}{2} = \cos^2 \frac{\varepsilon}{2} - (1 - \cos^2 \frac{\varepsilon}{2})$$

$$= 2\cos^2 \frac{\varepsilon}{2} - 1.$$

∴
$$E_R{}^2 = 2E^2\,[1 + 2\cos^2 \frac{\varepsilon}{2} - 1] = 4\,E^2 . \cos^2 \frac{\varepsilon}{2}$$

∴
$$E_R = 2\,E \cos \frac{\varepsilon}{2}$$

Also, E_R can be obtained from Fig. 3.23 (*b*) as under :

$$E_R = OD = OC + CD = OA \cos \frac{\varepsilon}{2} + AD \cos \frac{\varepsilon}{2} = E \cos \frac{\varepsilon}{2} + E \cos \frac{\varepsilon}{2} = 2E \cos \frac{\varepsilon}{2}.$$

The *pitch factor* is defined as the ratio of resultant e.m.f. of a chorded coil to the resultant e.m.f. had the same coil been full-pitched, symbol k_p.

Thus $$k_p = \frac{\text{Resultant e.m.f. of a chorded coil}}{\text{Resultant e.m.f. of a full pitched coil}} = \frac{2E\cos\frac{\varepsilon}{2}}{2E} = \cos\frac{\varepsilon}{2} \qquad ...(3.20)$$

The chording angle is ε° for fundamental flux wave and for *nth* space field harmonic, the chording angle becomes $n\varepsilon°$ electrical. Therefore, the pitch factor for *nth* harmonic is

$$k_{pn} = \cos\frac{n\varepsilon}{2} \qquad ...(3.49)$$

The advantages of using fractional-pitch winding are :

(*i*) reduction in the copper for overhang, this results in less cost of the machine.

(*ii*) reduction of harmonics in the generated e.m.f. wave, thereby rendering the output e.m.f. wave almost a sine wave.

It may be seen that the use of short-pitched coils reduces the output voltage by the factor cos ε/2. In order to compensate this reduction in output voltage, more turns and, therefore, more copper is essential. Since the advantage of reducing the higher order harmonics in the e.m.f. wave is much more important than the disadvantage of higher initial cost, the use of chorded coils is justified.

Winding factor. The product of distribution factor k_d and the pitch factor k_p is referred to as the winding factor, symbol k_w.

∴ $$k_w = k_d \times k_p \qquad ...(3.50)$$

In case of three-phase alternators, the third harmonic e.m.f. can be suppressed by star or delta connection, as in the case of 3-phase transformers. Hence at the time of winding design, the attention is mainly directed for the attenuation of 5th and 7th order harmonics, by adopting a suitable chording angle. A chording angle of ε = 30° (coil pitch = 150° electrical) is most useful, since it gives the following pitch factors :

0.966 for fundamental, 0.707 for 3rd harmonic, 0.259 for 5th and 7th harmonics, 0.707 for 9th harmonic.

Three-phase alternators are invariably star-connected to eliminate 3rd and 9th (*i.e.*, multiples of 3, called triplen) harmonics from line e.m.fs. ; though 5th and 7th harmonic e.m.fs. of reduced magnitude are present in the lines.

From Eq. (3.24), the fundamental e.m.f. per phase is

$$E_{ph1} = \sqrt{2}\,\pi f k_{w1} N_{ph} \phi_1$$

For third harmonic, e.m.f. per phase is

$$E_{ph3} = \sqrt{2}\,\pi (3f) k_{w3} N_{ph} \phi_3$$

In general, for *nth* harmonic, e.m.f. per phase is

$$E_{phn} = \sqrt{2}\,\pi nf k_{wn} N_{ph} \phi_n$$

Here subscripts 1, 3 and *n* denote fundamental, third and *nth* harmonics respectively.

From E_{phn} and E_{ph1} expressions, the *nth* harmonic and fundamental r.m.s. phase e.m.fs. are related as

$$\frac{E_{phn}}{E_{ph1}} = \frac{k_{wn}}{k_{w1}} \cdot \frac{n\phi_n}{\phi_1} \qquad ...(3.51\ a)$$

Also, ϕ_1 = Total value of fundamental flux per pole

= (Average flux density) (Area under one pole)

$$= \left(\frac{2}{\pi}B_1\right)\left(\frac{\pi DL}{P}\right) = \frac{2DL}{P}B_1$$

where B_1 = Peak value of fundamental component of flux density wave

D = Air-gap diameter of armature

and L = Core length of armature

Similarly, $$\phi_3 = \frac{2DL}{3P} B_3$$

In general, for *nth* harmonic, $$\phi_n = \frac{2DL}{nP} B_n$$

From above, $$\frac{\phi_n}{\phi_1} = \left[\frac{2DL.B_n}{nP}\right] \times \left[\frac{P}{2DL.B_1}\right] = \frac{1}{n} \cdot \frac{B_n}{B_1}$$

Eq. (3.51 *a*) in terms of B_1, B_n becomes

$$\frac{E_{phn}}{E_{ph1}} = \frac{k_{wn}}{k_{w1}} \cdot \frac{B_n}{B_1} \qquad ...(3.51\ b)$$

The r.m.s. phase e.m.f. is $$E_{ph} = [E^2{}_{ph1} + E^2{}_{ph3} + ... + E^2{}_{phn}]^{1/2}$$

The line e.m.f. in star connection does not include triplen harmonics.

3.5.4. Elimination of Harmonics from Alternator e.m.f. waveforms

In this part of section, the methods of eliminating or suppressing harmonics from the e.m.f. waveform of an alternator are discussed briefly.

In alternators, the primary source, or cause, of harmonics in the e.m.f. waveform is due to the non-sinusoidal field flux waveform. In case the field flux waveform is a sine wave, there would be no harmonics in the alternator generated e.m.f. Thus, first an attempt is made to have almost sinusoidal field flux wave and then the means to reduce the harmonics from the e.m.f. waveform should be adopted.

Field flux waveform can be made as much sinusoidal as possible by the following methods :

(*i*) Small air gap at the pole centre and large air gap towards the pole ends in salient-pole synchronous machines tends to make the field flux sinusoidal.

(*ii*) Skew the pole faces if possible.

(*iii*) In turbo-alternators, the air gap is uniform. So field winding is distributed in the slots in such a manner as to make the field flux waveform almost a sine wave.

In spite of all these attempts, field flux waveform along the air-gap periphery is not sinusoidal. As a result, harmonic e.m.fs. are always generated in an alternator. These can, however, be eliminated or suppressed as follows :

(*iv*) **Distribution:** The distribution of the armature winding along the air-gap periphery tends to make the e.m.f. waveform sinusoidal, see Prob. 3.30.

(*v*) **Chording:** With coil-span less than pole pitch, the harmonics can be eliminated, see Eq. (3.49).

(*vi*) **Skewing:** By skewing the armature slots, only tooth harmonics or slot harmonics can be eliminated, see Example 3.6 in this chapter and Art 5.15.4*.

(*vii*) **Fractional slot winding:** An introduction to fractional-slot windings is given in Art. 7.8 in this book. In fractional-slot windings, the space relation between teeth and slots under a given pole face is not the same as under the next and the succeeding pole faces. It follows that the pulsation of flux and the emf produced in the coils under one of the poles are more or less neutralized by other out of phase pulsations in the remaining coils of the winding.

* 'Generalized Theory of Electrical Machines' by the same Author.

(viii) **Alternator connections:** Star or delta connections of alternators suppress triplen harmonics from appearing across the lines, see Art 8.4.2.*

Example 3.7. *In an alternator, show that the output e.m.f. wave can't contain even harmonics.*

Solution. Fig. 3.24 illustrates one full-pitch coil a, a'. The fundamental component of the field flux wave induces maximum e.m.f. in coil-sides a, a', since these are cutting the maximum flux ϕ_{m1}. If r.m.s. value of the e.m.f. in each coil-side is E_1, then the resultant e.m.f. of the fundamental frequency across the coil ends A, B is $2E_1$, as explained before.

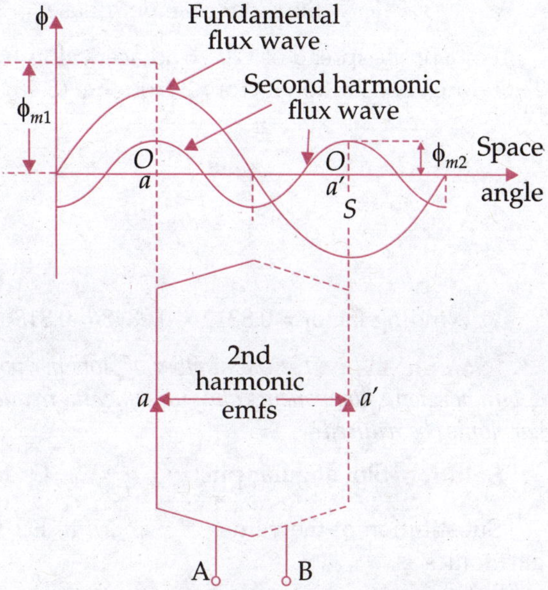

Fig 3.24: Pertaining to Example 3.7.

The second harmonic component of field flux wave also induces maximum e.m.fs. in coil-sides a, a', because these are cutting the maximum flux ϕ_{m2} at the instant shown. The direction of the second harmonic e.m.fs. is indicated by arrows in the lower diagram of Fig. 3.24. The resultant of the second harmonic e.m.f. between coil terminals A, B is seen to be zero, since the two second harmonic e.m.fs. are opposing each other in the coil circuit.

This shows that the second harmonic e.m.fs. or in general, even harmonic e.m.fs., cannot be generated in an alternator. Consequently the output e.m.f. wave is free from even harmonic e.m.fs.

This example demonstrates that even if the field flux wave contains second harmonic component, the output voltage is free from second harmonic e.m.fs. It should however be noted that field flux wave is symmetrical, *i.e.*, field flux wave has equal positive and negative half cycles and as a consequence field flux wave can't contain even field-space harmonics. Thus no even harmonics can be generated–hence the output e.m.f. is free from even harmonics.

In case, even-space-harmonics are present in the field flux wave, the positive and negative half cycles will not be identical, which however is never the case in rotating electrical machines.

Example 3.8. *For a 3-phase winding with coil span of 160°, determine the distribution and winding factors in case the winding has a phase spread of 120°. Take the three-phase winding (a) to be uniformly distributed and (b) to have 9 slots per pole.*

Solution. (*a*) When the winding is uniformly distributed, the distribution factor k_d from Eq. (3.48 *b*) is

$$k_d = \frac{\sin\frac{\sigma}{2}}{\sigma/2} = \frac{\sin\frac{120}{2}}{\frac{120}{2}\times\frac{\pi}{180}} \quad \frac{3\sin 60^\circ}{\pi} = 0.827$$

Chording angle $\quad \varepsilon = 180 - 160^\circ = 20^\circ$

∴ Coil-span factor, $\quad k_p = \cos\frac{\varepsilon}{2} = \cos 10^\circ = 0.9848$

∴ $\quad$ Winding factor $= k_d \cdot k_p = 0.827 \times 0.9848 = 0.8144$

* 'Generalized Theory of Electrical Machines' by the same Author.

(*b*) Slot angular pitch $= \dfrac{180}{9} = 20°$

Slots per pole per phase $= \dfrac{9}{3} = 3$

For a phase spread of 120°, 6 adjacent slots [$6 \times \gamma = 6 \times 20 = 120°$] must belong to the same phase. Therefore, distribution factor k_d, from Eq. (3.48) is

$$k_d = \frac{\sin\dfrac{\sigma}{2}}{q\sin\dfrac{\sigma}{2q}} = \frac{\sin\dfrac{120}{2}}{6\sin\dfrac{120°}{2\times 6}}$$

$$= \frac{\sin 60°}{6\sin 10°} = 0.8312$$

∴ Winding factor = 0.8312 × 0.9848 = 0.8186.

Example 3.9. *If Q is the number of slots per pole, show that the distribution and pitch factors for (2Q ± 1)th harmonic components and fundamental frequency components are equal. How can these higher order harmonics be reduced?*

Solution. Slot angular pitch $\gamma = \dfrac{\pi}{Q}$. Order of harmonics, $n = (2Q \pm 1)$

Substitution of the values of γ and n in Eq. (3.47 *a*) gives the distribution factor for (2*Q* ± 1)th harmonics as

$$k_{d\,(2Q\pm1)} = \frac{\sin\dfrac{q}{2}(2Q\pm1)\dfrac{\neq}{Q}}{q\sin\dfrac{1}{2}(2Q\pm1)\dfrac{\neq}{Q}} = \frac{\sin\left(q\neq \pm \dfrac{q\neq}{2Q}\right)}{q\sin\left(\neq \pm \dfrac{\neq}{2Q}\right)}$$

$$= \frac{\sin q\neq \cos\dfrac{q\neq}{2Q} \pm \cos q\neq \sin\dfrac{q\neq}{2Q}}{q\left[\sin\neq\cos\dfrac{\neq}{2Q} \pm \cos\neq\sin\dfrac{\neq}{2Q}\right]}$$

In the above expression, sin $q\pi$ in the numerator and sin π in denominator, are always zero for any value of q (the number of slots per pole per phase). In view of this, the distribution factor becomes

$$k_{d\,(2Q\pm1)} = \frac{\pm\cos q\neq \sin\dfrac{q\neq}{2Q}}{\pm q\cos\neq\sin\dfrac{\neq}{2Q}}$$

The value of cos π is always equal to (–1) and that of cos $q\pi$ is equal to 1 or –1, depending upon the value of q. Thus the magnitude of the distribution factor for (2*Q* ± 1)th order of harmonic is

$$k_{d\,(2Q\pm1)} = \frac{\sin\dfrac{q\neq}{2Q}}{q\sin\dfrac{\neq}{2Q}}$$

For the fundamental component, the distribution factor, from Eq. (3.47*a*) is

$$k_{d1} = \frac{\sin\dfrac{q\neq}{2Q}}{q\sin\dfrac{\neq}{2Q}} = k_{d\,(2Q\pm1)}$$

The pitch factor for $(2Q \pm 1)$th harmonic, from Eq. (3.49), is

$$k_{p\,(2Q \pm 1)} = \cos \frac{(2Q \pm 1)\varepsilon}{2}$$

Here, Q is the number of slots per pole. As one pole covers an angle of 180° electrical or π electrical radians, the angle covered by Q slots is π radians. In view of this, expression for $k_{p(2Q \pm 1)}$ can be written as

$$k_{p\,(2Q \pm 1)} = \cos \frac{(2\pi \pm 1)\varepsilon}{2} = \cos\left(\pi\varepsilon \pm \frac{\varepsilon}{2}\right)$$

$$= \cos \pi\varepsilon \cos \frac{\varepsilon}{2} \pm \sin \pi\varepsilon \sin \frac{\varepsilon}{2}$$

For any value of chording angle ε in electrical degrees, $\sin \pi\varepsilon = 0$ and $\cos \pi\varepsilon$ is equal to + 1 or –1. Therefore,

$$k_{p\,(2Q \pm 1)} = \cos \frac{\varepsilon}{2} = k_{p1}$$

These higher order harmonics of the order of $(2Q \pm 1)$, are referred to as the slot harmonics, tooth harmonics, slot ripples or tooth ripples. These harmonics are attenuated by skewing the slots.

Example 3.10. *An alternator, with full-pitched uniformly distributed winding, is wound as follows :*

(a) Single phase winding placed in (i) two-thirds of the slots and (ii) all the slots.

(b) All the slots are wound with (i) single phase and (ii) 3-phase windings.

(c) All the slots are wound with (i) two-phase and (ii) 3-phase windings.

For each of the above cases, calculate the ratio of outputs and the amount of copper required.

Solution. (*a*) When two-third of the slots are wound, the phase spread σ, for single phase winding is $\sigma = \frac{2}{3}(180) = 120°$. From Eq. (3.48 *c*), the distribution factor for the fundamental component is

$$k_{d1} = \frac{\sin \frac{120}{2}}{\frac{120}{2} \times \frac{\pi}{180}} = 0.827$$

$\therefore$ Output voltage with two-third of the slots wound is $\propto \left(\frac{2}{3}\right)(0.827)$.

When all the slots are wound, phase spread $\sigma = 180°$ and from Eq. (3.48 *c*),

$$k_{d1} = \frac{\sin \frac{180}{2}}{\frac{180}{2} \times \frac{\pi}{180}} = 0.637$$

$\therefore$ Output voltage with all the slots wound is $\propto$ (1) (0.637).

In all the cases, it is assumed that frequency f, flux per pole ϕ and the conductor cross-section are the same.

$$\therefore \text{ The ratio of outputs} = \frac{[(\text{Current})(\text{Voltage})]\text{with all the slots wound}}{[(\text{Current})(\text{Voltage})]\text{with two-third slots wound}} = \frac{1 \times 0.637}{\frac{2}{3} \times (0.827)} = 1.15.$$

$$\text{Corresponding ratio of copper required} = \frac{1}{2/3} = 1.5.$$

It is thus seen that for 50% increase in copper, the output is increased by 15% only. This is the reason why approximately two-thirds of the slots are wound in case of single-phase induction machines.

(*b*) For a 3-phase winding, the usual phase spread σ is 60° (narrow-spread).

$$\therefore \qquad k_{d1} = \frac{\sin \frac{60}{2}}{\frac{60}{2} \times \frac{\pi}{180}} = 0.955$$

When all the slots are wound with single-phase winding, then $k_{d1} = 0.637$, from part (*a*).

$\therefore$ Ratio of outputs

$$= \frac{[(\text{Current})(\text{Voltage})]\text{for a 3-phase winding with all slots wound}}{[(\text{Current})(\text{Voltage})]\text{for a single phase winding with all slots wound}} = \frac{(1)(0.955)}{(1)(0.637)} = 1.5.$$

$$\text{Ratio of copper required} = \frac{1}{1} = 1.$$

Thus for the same amount of copper, the output for a 3-phase winding is 50% more than for a single-phase winding with all the slots wound.

(*c*) For a two-phase winding, the phase spread σ is 90°.

$$\therefore \quad k_{d1} = \frac{\sin\frac{90}{2}}{\frac{90}{2}\times\frac{\pi}{180}} = 0.90$$

Distribution factor for 3-phase winding, as calculated in part (*b*) is 0.955.

$$\therefore \quad \text{Ratio of output} = \frac{\text{Output for a 3-phase winding}}{\text{Output for a 2-phase winding}} = \frac{(1)(0.955)}{(1)(0.90)} = 1.06.$$

$$\text{Ratio of copper required} = \frac{1}{1} = 1.$$

Example 3.11. *(a) A 3-phase, 6 pole, 1000 r.p.m. alternator has an air-gap diameter of 28 cm and a core length 23 cm. A two-layer narrow-spread (σ = 60°) winding is employed and the winding is accommodated in 4 slots per pole per phase, with 8 conductors per slot. The coils are short-pitched by one slot. When the flux density wave covering two pole pitches, is analysed into space harmonics, the fundamental is found to have an amplitude of 0.87 T and the 3rd and 5th harmonics to have amplitudes of 0.24 and 0.14 T respectively. Estimate the resultant phase and line voltages on no load if the alternator is (i) star-connected and (ii) delta-connected.*

(b) If per phase reactance of the alternator at 50 Hz is 10 Ω, calculate the circulating current when the machine is delta connected. Neglect alternator resistance.

The effect of slot ripples should be ignored.

Solution. $$\text{Pole pitch} = \frac{\pi D}{P} = \frac{\pi(0.28)}{6}\text{ m}$$

In the presentation leading to Eq. (3.51 *b*), it is shown that

$$\phi_1 = \frac{2DL}{P}B_1 = \frac{2\times 0.28\times 0.23}{6}\times 0.87 = 0.0187\text{ Wb}$$

Also, $$\phi_3 = \frac{2DL}{3P}B_3 = \frac{2\times 0.28\times 0.23}{3\times 6}\times 0.24 = 0.00172\text{ Wb}$$

$$\phi_5 = \frac{2DL}{5P}B_5 = \frac{2\times 0.28\times 0.23}{5\times 6}\times 0.14 = 0.0006\text{ Wb.}$$

Slot per pole per phase, $q = 4$.

Slot-angular pitch or slot angle

$$\gamma = \frac{180°}{\text{Slots per pole}} = \frac{180}{4\times 3} = 15°$$

The distribution factors from Eq. (3.47 *a*) are

$$k_{d1} = \frac{\sin\frac{q\gamma}{2}}{q\sin\frac{\gamma}{2}} = \frac{\sin\frac{60}{2}}{4\sin\frac{15}{2}} = 0.9576$$

$$k_{d3} = \frac{\sin\frac{3q\gamma}{2}}{q\sin\frac{3\gamma}{2}} = \frac{\sin\frac{3\times 60}{2}}{4\sin\frac{3\times 15}{2}} = 0.6533$$

$$k_{d5} = \frac{\sin\frac{5q\gamma}{2}}{q\sin\frac{5\gamma}{2}} = \frac{\sin\frac{5\times 60}{2}}{4\sin\frac{5\times 15}{2}} = 0.2053$$

The coil is short-pitched by one slot. This gives a chording angle of

$$\varepsilon = \frac{180}{12} = 15° = \gamma$$

The coil-span factors from Eq. (3.49) are

$$k_{p1} = \cos\frac{\varepsilon}{2} = \cos\frac{15}{2} = 0.991$$

$$k_{p3} = \cos\frac{3\varepsilon}{2} = \cos\frac{45}{2} = 0.9238$$

and

$$k_{p5} = \cos\frac{5\varepsilon}{2} = \cos\frac{75}{2} = 0.793$$

∴ The winding factors are

$$k_{w1} = k_{p1} \times k_{d1} = 0.991 \times 0.9576 = 0.949$$

$$k_{w3} = k_{d3} \times k_{p3} = 0.6533 \times 0.9238 = 0.6035$$

and

$$k_{w5} = k_{d5} \times k_{p5} = 0.2053 \times 0.793 = 0.163.$$

Subscripts 1, 3, 5 are used to denote fundamental, third and fifth harmonics respectively.

$$\text{Total number of slots} = 4 \times 3 \times 6 = 72.$$

$$\text{Total number of turns} = \frac{72 \times 8}{2} = 288.$$

∴ Series turns per phase,

$$N_{ph} = \frac{288}{3} = 96.$$

From Eq. (3.24), the fundamental e.m.f. per phase is

$$E_{ph1} = \sqrt{2}\,\pi f k_{w1} N_{ph} \phi_1$$

$$= \sqrt{2}\,\pi\,(50)\,(0.949)\,(96)\,(0.0187) = 378.4 \text{ volts.}$$

For third harmonic component, Eq. (3.51 *a*) gives

$$E_{ph3} = E_{ph1}\frac{k_{w3}}{k_{w1}}\frac{3\phi_3}{\phi_1}$$

$$= 378.4 \times \frac{0.6035}{0.949} \times \frac{3 \times 0.00172}{0.0187} = 66.40 \text{ volts.}$$

Similarly, $$E_{ph5} = E_{ph1}\frac{k_{w5}}{k_{w1}}\frac{5\phi_5}{\phi_1}$$

$$= 378.4 \times \frac{0.163}{0.949} \times \frac{5 \times 0.0006}{0.0187} = 10.427 \text{ volts.}$$

(*i*) For star-connected alternator, the magnitude of the per phase e.m.f. is

$$E_{ph} = \sqrt{E^2_{ph1} + E^2_{ph3} + E^2_{ph5}}$$

$$= \sqrt{(378.4)^2 + (66.4)^2 + (10.427)^2} = 384.32 \text{ volts.}$$

Recall that for star-connected alternator, the third frequency e.m.fs. don't appear between the lines.

$$\therefore \quad E_{line} = \sqrt{3}\sqrt{E^2_{ph1} + E^2_{ph5}}$$

$$= \sqrt{3}\sqrt{(378.4)^2 + (10.427)^2} \cong \sqrt{3}(378.54) = 655.63 \text{ volts}$$

(*ii*) For delta-connected alternator, the third harmonic e.m.fs. are short-circuited by the closed delta and consequently don't appear in the lines.

$$\therefore \quad E_{ph} = E_{line} = \sqrt{(378.4)^2 + (10.427)^2} \cong 378.54 \text{ volts.}$$

(*b*) When the alternator is delta connected, the resultant of fundamental and 5th harmonic e.m.fs. in the closed delta is zero, but the resultant of 3rd harmonic e.m.fs. is $3E_3$. This e.m.f. $3E_3$ gives rise to a circulating current determined by the total 3rd harmonic reactance of $3 \times (3 \times 10)\ \Omega$ at 150 Hz.

$$\therefore \text{ Third harmonic circulating current} = \frac{3E_3}{3 \times (3 \times 10)} = \frac{3 \times 66.4}{3 \times (3 \times 10)} = 2.213 \text{ A.}$$

Example 3.12. *For a 3-phase winding with 3 slots per pole per phase and coil span of 8 slots, compute the breadth and pitch factors.*

The flux density wave in the air gap of this machine is found to have 20% third harmonic. Calculate percentage increase in per phase r.m.s. e.m.f. due to this harmonic.

Solution. Slot per pole per phase, $q = 3$, Slot per pole $= 3 \times 3 = 9$

Slot angular pitch, $$\gamma = \frac{180}{9} = 20°$$

$$\therefore \quad k_{d1} = \frac{\sin\frac{q\gamma}{2}}{q\sin\frac{\gamma}{2}} = \frac{\sin 30°}{3\sin 10°} = 0.9598$$

For a coil span of 8 slots, the coil is short-pitched by one slot and the chording angle is

$$\varepsilon = \gamma = 20°$$

$$\therefore \quad k_{p1} = \cos\frac{\varepsilon}{2} = \cos 10° = 0.985$$

$$\therefore \quad k_{w1} = 0.9598 \times 0.985 = 0.9454$$

$$k_{d3} = \frac{\sin 90}{3\sin 30} = 0.667$$

$$k_{p3} = \cos 30° = 0.866$$

$$k_{w3} = 0.667 \times 0.866 = 0.5776$$

From Eq. (3.51 *b*), $$E_{ph3} = E_{ph1}\frac{0.5776}{0.9454} \times 0.20 = 0.1222\, E_{ph1}$$

$$\therefore \qquad E_{ph} = \sqrt{E^2_{ph1} + (0.1222E_{ph1})^2} = 1.00744\ E_{ph1}$$

Therefore, percentage increase in generated e.m.f. due to third harmonic flux density component

$$= \frac{1.00744 - 1.0}{1.0} \times 100 = 0.744\%.$$

Example 3.13. *A 6-pole, 50 Hz alternator has 42 slots with two-layer winding. The flux per pole is 0.012 Wb and each full-pitch coil has 8 turns. Determine the phase and line e.m.fs. in case the narrow-spread coils are connected to form (a) 2-phase winding and (b) 3-phase star-connected winding.*

Solution. (*a*) Slots per pole per phase, $q = \frac{S/m}{P} = \frac{42/2}{6} = \frac{3\times 7}{3\times 2} = \frac{7}{2}$

As q is not an integer, the 2-phase winding is a fractional-slot winding with $S_k = 7$. Its distribution factor for the fundamental from Eq. (3.48 *d*), is

$$k_d = \frac{\sin\frac{90}{2}}{7\sin\frac{1}{2}\frac{90}{7}} = 0.9022$$

$$k_w = 0.9022 \text{ as } k_p = 1$$

Per phase series turns, $N_{ph} = \frac{42\times 8}{2} = 168$

$$\therefore \qquad E_{ph} = \sqrt{2}\,\pi f k_w N_{ph}\,\phi$$

$$= \sqrt{2}\,\pi\,(50)\,(0.9022)\,(168)\,(0.012) = 403.98 \text{ V}$$

$$E_l = \sqrt{2} \times E_{ph} = 571.23 \text{ V}$$

(*b*) $q = \frac{42/3}{6} = \frac{2\times 7}{2\times 3} = \frac{7}{3}$

From Eq. (3.48 *d*), $k_d = \frac{\sin\frac{60}{2}}{7\sin\frac{1}{2}\cdot\frac{60}{7}} = 0.9558$

$$N_{ph} = \frac{42\times 8}{3} = 112$$

$$\therefore \qquad E_{ph} = \sqrt{2}\,\pi\,(50)\,(0.9558)\,(112)\,(0.012) = 285.322 \text{ V}$$

$$E_l = \sqrt{3} \times 285.322 = 494.18 \text{ V}.$$

Example 3.14. *A 3-phase star-connected alternator has 81 slots, 6 poles and double-layer narrow-spread winding with coil-span equal to 13 slot pitches. The flux density distribution in the air gap is given by* $B(\theta) = \sin\theta + 0.4\sin 3\theta + 0.25\sin 5\theta$.

Determine the r.m.s. value of third and fifth harmonic phase e.m.fs. in terms of fundamental phase e.m.f. Also, calculate the ratio of resultant line e.m.f. to the resultant phase e.m.f.

Solution. Slots per pole per phase, $q = \frac{81/3}{6} = \frac{3\times 9}{3\times 2} = \frac{9}{2}$

Angular slot pitch, $\gamma = \frac{6\times 180}{81} = \left(\frac{40}{3}\right)^\circ$

Coil span, $13\gamma = \frac{13\times 40}{3} = \left(\frac{520}{3}\right)^\circ$

Chording angle, ε = (one pole pitch) – (coil span) $= 180 - \frac{520}{3} = \left(\frac{20}{3}\right)^\circ$

From Eq. (3.48 *d*),

$$k_{d1} = \frac{\sin\frac{60}{2}}{9\sin\frac{1}{2}\cdot\frac{60}{9}} = 0.9555,$$

$$k_{p1} = \cos\frac{\varepsilon}{2} = \cos\frac{20}{3\times 2} = 0.9988$$

$$k_{d3} = \frac{\sin 90°}{9\sin\frac{60}{6}} = 0.6399,$$

$$k_{p3} = \cos\left(\frac{10}{3}\times 3\right) = 0.9848.$$

$$k_{d5} = \frac{\sin 150}{9\sin\frac{300}{18}} = 0.1937,$$

$$k_{p5} = \cos\left(\frac{10}{3}\times 5\right) = 0.958$$

$\therefore$

$$k_{w1} = 0.9555 \times 0.9983 = 0.9539$$

$$k_{w3} = 0.6399 \times 0.9848 = 0.6302$$

$$k_{w5} = 0.1937 \times 0.958 = 0.1856$$

From Eq. (3.51 *b*),

$$E_{ph3} = E_{ph1}\frac{0.6302}{0.9539} \times 0.4 = 0.2643\ E_{ph1}$$

$$E_{ph5} = E_{ph1}\frac{0.1856}{0.9539} \times 0.25 = 0.0486\ E_{ph1}$$

Resultant phase e.m.f., $E_{ph} = [E^2_{ph1} + E^2_{ph3} + E^2_{ph5}]^{1/2} = 1.0355\ E_{ph1}$

Resultant line e.m.f.,

$$E_l = \sqrt{3}\,[E^2_{ph1} + E^2_{ph5}]^{1/2} = 1.734\ E_{ph1}$$

$$\frac{E_l}{E_{ph}} = \frac{1.734}{1.0355} = 1.675$$

Note that line e.m.f. is not equal to $\sqrt{3}$ times the phase e.m.f. It is because of the presence of third harmonic e.m.f. in the phase voltage.

Example 3.15. *The flux density distribution along the air-gap periphery of a salient-pole machine is rectangular as shown in Fig. 3.25 (a). Draw one complete cycle of the e.m.f. generated in a single-turn coil of coil-span 150° electrical. The coil moves with a velocity of 20 m/sec in a peak flux density of 1 T. The effective length of armature conductor is 0.8 m. Calculate r.m.s. value of the voltage in the single-turn coil.*

Solution. The flux density distribution is shown in Fig. 3.25 (*a*). With coil-span of 180°, the waveform of the e.m.f. generated in a single-turn coil will be similar to *B*-waveform. For coil-span less than 180°, the generated e.m.f. waveform will be different from *B*-waveform. The waveshape of the e.m.f. generated in the coil with coil-span of 150° electrical is sketched in Fig. 3.25 (*b*) as follows :

(*i*) For $0° < \theta < 30°$, instant 1, coil *aa′* is shown moving in zero *B*-wave. Therefore, e.m.f. in the coil for this range is zero as shown.

(*ii*) For $30° < \theta < 60°$, instant 2, coil-side *a* is cutting through $B_p = 1$ T but coil-side *a′* is cutting zero *B*-wave. The resultant e.m.f. across the single-turn coil is

$$e = Blv = 1 \times 0.8 \times 20 = 16 \text{ V}$$

(*iii*) For $60° < \theta < 150°$, instant 3, both coil-sides are cutting through 1 T. Therefore, net e.m.f. generated in conductors of single-turn coil is

$$e = 2Blv = 2 \times 1 \times 0.8 \times 20 = 32 \text{ V}$$

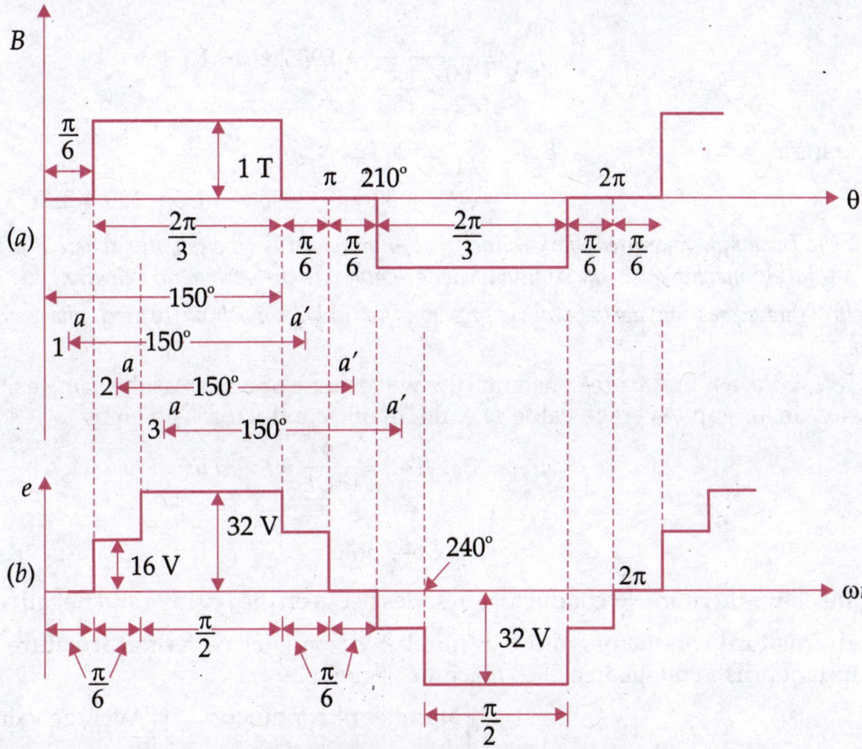

Fig 3.25: Pertaining to Example 3.15.

In this manner, e.m.f. waveform of Fig. 3.25 (*b*) is sketched. RMS value of this generated e.m.f. in one single-turn coil

$$\left[\frac{1}{\neq}\left\{16^2 \times \frac{\neq}{6} \times 2 + 32^2 \times \frac{\neq}{2}\right\}\right]^{1/2} = 24.44 \text{ V}$$

Example 3.16. *A 50 Hz, salient-pole alternator has the field flux-density waveform of Fig. 3.25 (a). This alternator has the following data :*

Total turns = 360, phase spread = 60°, pole-pitch = 0.6 m

Stator length = 0.8 m, coil-span = 150° electrical

Calculate r.m.s. value of the fundamental e.m.f. per phase.

Solution. The fundamental value of peak flux density, by Fourier series analysis, is

$$B_1 = \frac{4}{\pi} B_m \cos \varepsilon = \frac{4}{\pi} \times 1 \times \cos\frac{\pi}{6} = 1.10266 \text{ T}$$

Pole pitch

$$= \frac{\pi D}{P} = \frac{2\pi r}{P} = 0.6 \text{ and } r = \frac{P \times \text{pole pitch}}{2\pi}$$

Fundamental air-gap flux per pole, from Eq. (3.11), is

$$\phi_1 = \frac{4}{P} B_1 l r = \frac{4}{P} B_1 l \frac{P \times \text{pole pitch}}{2\pi} = \frac{2}{\pi} \cdot B_1 l \text{ (pole pitch)}$$

$$= \frac{2}{\pi} \times 1.10266 \times 0.8 \times 0.6 = 0.33695 \text{ Wb}$$

Taking the winding as uniformly distributed,

$$k_{d1} = \frac{\sin\frac{60}{2}}{\frac{60}{2}\times\frac{\pi}{180}} = 0.955,\ k_{p1} = 1$$

Per-phase e.m.f., $E_{ph1} = \sqrt{2}\,\pi f \phi_1 k_{w1} N_{ph}$

$$= \sqrt{2}\,\pi \times 50 \times 0.33695 \times 0.955 \times 120 = 8576.7 \text{ V}.$$

Example 3.17. *The e.m.f. generated in a conductor at any instant is given by Blv, where B is the air-gap flux density in a rotating machine, l is the conductor length and v is the peripheral velocity.*

With the help of this expression, derive e.m.f. expressions for (a) D.C. machine (b) three-phase synchronous machine.

Solution. In $e = Blv$, as l and v are constants, the waveshape of e.m.f. e is the same as that of the flux-density wave in air gap. Average value of e.m.f. in one conductor is given by

$$E_{av} = B_{av}\cdot l \cdot v = \frac{\phi}{\frac{\pi D l}{P}} \times l \times \pi D n = P\phi n$$

where ϕ = flux per pole

For a D.C. machine, there are $\frac{Z}{a}$ conductors in series between the positive and negative brushes. Here Z = total armature conductors and a = number of parallel paths for armature winding. Therefore, output of brush voltage in a D.C. machine is given by

$$E = \begin{bmatrix}\text{Number of conductors}\\ \text{in each parallel path}\\ \text{between the two brushes}\end{bmatrix}\begin{bmatrix}\text{Average value of}\\ \text{e.m.f. generated}\\ \text{in one conductor}\end{bmatrix}$$

$$= \frac{Z}{a}\cdot(P\phi n) = \frac{\phi Z n P}{a}$$

Here n is the armature speed in r.p.s. The above e.m.f. expression is the required expression for a D.C. machine.

(*b*) From above, average e.m.f. generated in one conductor,

$$E_{av} = (P\phi n) = 2f\phi, \text{ where } f = \frac{Pn}{2}$$

Now $\frac{\text{r.m.s. value}}{\text{average value}}$ = form factor

Assuming the waveshape of flux-density wave sinusoidal, its form factor is

$$FF = \frac{\frac{1}{\sqrt{2}}B_m}{\frac{2}{\pi}B_m} = \frac{\pi}{2\sqrt{2}}$$

Also $\frac{\text{r.m.s. value of e.m.f. per conductor}}{\text{average value of e.m.f. per conductor}} = FF$

$\therefore$ R.m.s. value of e.m.f. generated in one conductor.

$$E_{rms} = FF \times E_{av} = \frac{\pi}{2\sqrt{2}} \times 2f\phi = \frac{\pi}{\sqrt{2}} f\phi$$

E.m.f. per turn $= 2\left(\frac{\pi}{\sqrt{2}} f\phi\right) k_p = \sqrt{2}\,\pi f\phi\, k_p$

where k_p is the coil-span factor.

Per-phase generated e.m.f. $= \sqrt{2}\,\pi f\phi N_{ph} k_p k_d = \sqrt{2}\,\pi f\phi N_{ph} k_w$

where N_{ph} = series turns per phase

Another way of obtaining phase-e.m.f. expression is as under :

Maximum e.m.f. per conductor, $E_{max} = B_m lv$

For a sinusoidal flux density wave,

$$E_{max} = \frac{\pi}{2}(B_{av})\, l \cdot v = \frac{\pi}{2}\left(\frac{\pi}{\frac{\pi DL}{P}}\right) l \cdot \pi Dn = \pi\phi f$$

R.m.s. value of e.m.f. generated in one conductor $= \dfrac{E_{max}}{\sqrt{2}} = \dfrac{\pi}{\sqrt{2}}\phi f$

Now proceed as above.

Example 3.18. *A 6-pole alternator, with 54 slots, runs at a speed of 1000 r.p.m. Two 80-turn coils A and B are placed in slots as under :*

Coil A : coil-sides in slots 1 and 11.

Coil B : coil-sides in slots 2 and 10.

Flux per pole is 0.015 Wb. Find the resultant e.m.f. if coils A and B are connected in series (a) aiding (b) opposing.

Solution. Pole pitch $= \dfrac{54}{6} = 9$ slots $= 180°$

Slot-angular pitch, $\gamma = \dfrac{6 \times 180}{54} = 20°$

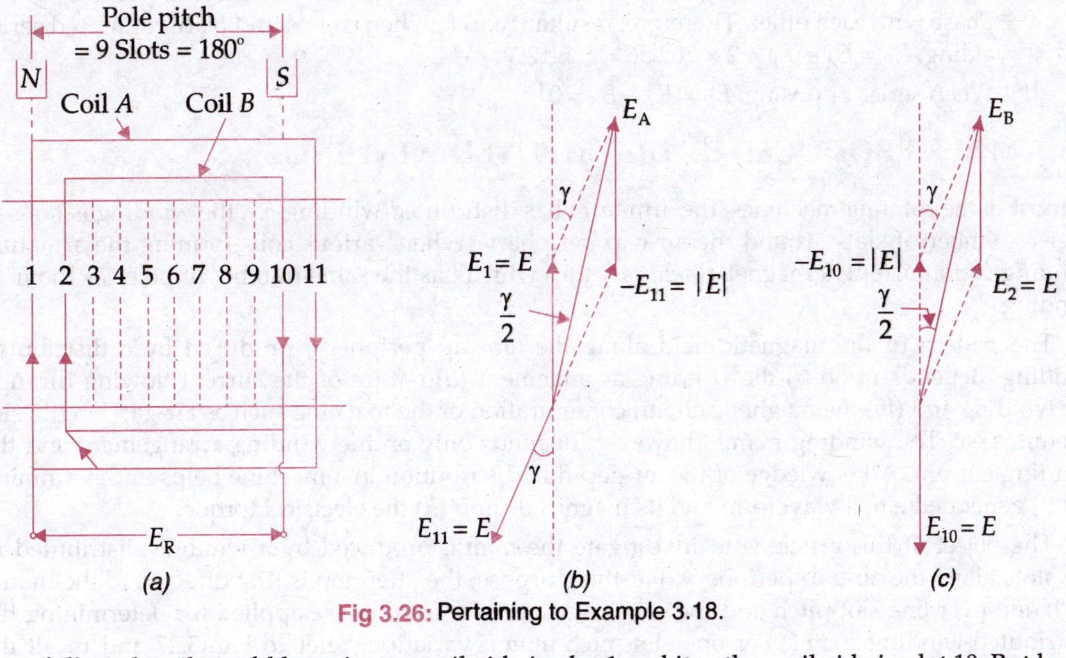

Fig 3.26: Pertaining to Example 3.18.

A full-pitch coil would have its one coil-side in slot 1 and its other coil-side in slot 10. But here coil *A* is overpitched by one slot because this coil has its coil-sides in slot 1 and 11, Fig. 3.26 (*a*). Likewise, coil *B* is short-pitched by one slot (= 20°), because its coil-sides are placed in slots 2 and 10, Fig. 3.26 (*a*).

In Fig. 3.26 (*a*), e.m.fs generated in coil-sides 1 and 10 of a full-pitch coil would be maximum but of opposite sign. Phasor diagram for e.m.fs generated in coil-sides 1 and 11 is shown in Fig. 3.26 (*b*), while that for e.m.fs generated in coil-sides 2 and 10 is shown in Fig. 3.26 (*c*).

One coil-side of 80-turn coil has 80 conductors. R.m.s. value of generated e.m.f. in one conductor, from Example 3.17, is $\frac{\pi}{\sqrt{2}} f\phi$.

∴ E.m.f. generated in one coil-side of coil *A* or coil *B* having 80 conductors is given by

$$\frac{\pi}{2} f\phi \text{ (conductors in one coil-side)}$$

$$E_1 = \frac{\pi}{2} \times 50 \times 0.015 \times 80 = 133.306 \text{ V}$$

This e.m.f. $E_1 = E = 133.306$ V, generated in coil-side 1 of coil *A* is shown by vertical phasor E_1. E.m.f. generated in coil-side 11 of coil *A* is shown as $E_{11} = E = 133.306$ V; $(180 + \gamma)$ degrees away from E_1, because coil-span of this coil is equal to $(180 + \gamma)$ degrees (electrical), see Fig. 3.26 (*b*). Resultant of e.m.f. in coil *A* is obtained by reversing phasor E_{11} and adding to phasor E_1, Fig. 3.26 (*b*), (as done during the derivation of pitch factor).

∴ Resultant e.m.f. generated in coil *A* is

$$E_A = 2\,E \cos\frac{\gamma}{2} = 2 \times 133.306 \times \cos 10° = 262.56 \text{ V}$$

E.m.f. generated in coil-side placed in slot 2 is shown as $E_2 = E$, slot-angular pitch (= 20°) lagging behind E_1. Similarly, e.m.f. E_{10} is shown leading E_{11} by $\gamma = 20°$, because here coil-span of coil *B* is 160°. As in coil *A*, resultant of e.m.f. in coil *B* is

$$E_B = 2\,E \cos\frac{\gamma}{2} = 2 \times 133.306 \times \cos 10° = 262.56 \text{ V}$$

(*a*) An examination of Figs. 3.26 (*b*) and (*c*) reveals that resultant e.m.fs. E_A and E_B are in phase with each other. Therefore, resultant e.m.f., when coils *A* and *B* are connected series aiding, $E_R = E_A + E_B = 2 \times 262.56 = 525.12$ V.

(*b*) When series opposing, $E_R = E_A - E_B = 0$.

3.6. M.M.F. PRODUCED BY DISTRIBUTED WINDINGS

In most of the rotating machines, the armature has distributed winding, *i.e.* the winding is housed over a number of slots around the air-gap periphery. When various coils forming the armature winding carry current, a magnetic field is set up which has the same number of poles as the field winding.

The pattern of the magnetic field along the air gap periphery, produced by a distributed winding, depends upon (*i*) the winding arrangement (*ii*) nature of the current flowing through the winding and (*iii*) the magnetic circuit configuration of the machine such as air-gap length, slot openings etc. The winding m.m.f., however, depends only on the winding arrangement and the winding current. A knowledge of the air-gap flux distribution in a machine helps in determining the (*i*) generated e.m.f. waveform and its magnitude and (*ii*) the electrical torque.

The object of this article is to investigate the m.m.f. produced by a winding distributed in the slots along the air-gap periphery. For this purpose, the attention is first directed to the m.m.f. variation over one slot-pitch and the conclusions drawn from it, are applied for determining the distributed-winding m.m.f. For one slot-pitch-m.m.f. variation, refer to Fig. 3.27 and recall the Ampere's Circuital Law. According to this law, the m.m.f. acting on any closed path is equal to the total current enclosed by that path. In Fig. 3.27 (*a*), each slot is assumed to contain 9 conductors and each conductor carries a current *i*. If path 1 is traversed, the ampere-conductors enclosed are 3*i* and this is therefore the m.m.f. change as shown in Fig. 3.27 (*b*). If path 2 is traversed, the current enclosed is 6*i* and for the path 3, the total current enclosed is 9*i*. This m.m.f. variation is sketched in Fig. 3.27 (*b*) and it is seen that the m.m.f. changes linearly from zero to 9*i* over the slot portion or slot width. If the tooth is traversed, the enclosed current remains 9*i* till one slot-pitch is covered. When the three conductors of the adjoining slot are covered, the enclosed current is again $3i$ as shown in Fig. 3.27 (*b*). It can, therefore, be concluded that the m.m.f. changes linearly over the slot portion and does not change for the tooth portion as shown in Fig. 3.27 (*b*).

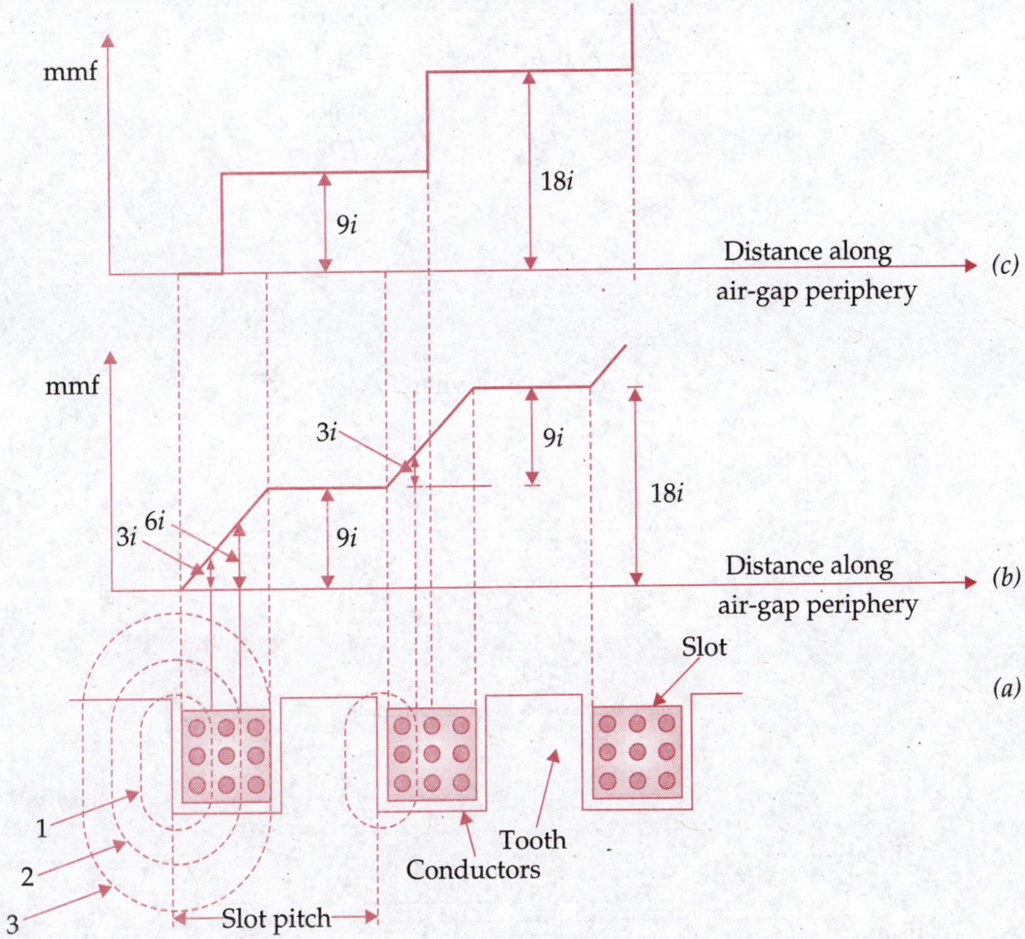

Fig 3.27: Variation of m.m.f. along air-gap periphery.

In order to make the analysis simpler, the change in m.m.f. over the slot portion is taken as stepped at the middle of the slot width. In other words, the total change of m.m.f. [*i.e.*, $9i$ in Fig. 3.27 (*b*)] over the slot portion, is taken to occur at the centre of the slot, as depicted in Fig. 3.27 (*c*).

3.6.1. M.m.f. of a coil

Consider one full-pitched coil on the stator of a 2-pole uniform air-gap machine, Fig. 3.28 (*a*). The coil consists of N turns and each turn carries a current i. The direction of current in the two coil-sides is indicated by a cross and a dot (cross-current away from the reader; dot current towards the reader). The magnetic flux set up by this coil current is shown by the dotted lines in Fig. 3.28 (*a*) and its developed view (stator and rotor peripheries laid out flat) is illustrated in Fig. 3.28 (*b*).

In order to determine the coil m.m.f. the following assumptions are made for simplicity :

(*i*) The permeability of stator and rotor irons is much greater than that of the air. In view of this, it may be assumed here that the stator and rotor cores have infinite permeability. This means that the reluctance to the magnetic flux is offered by the air-gap alone.

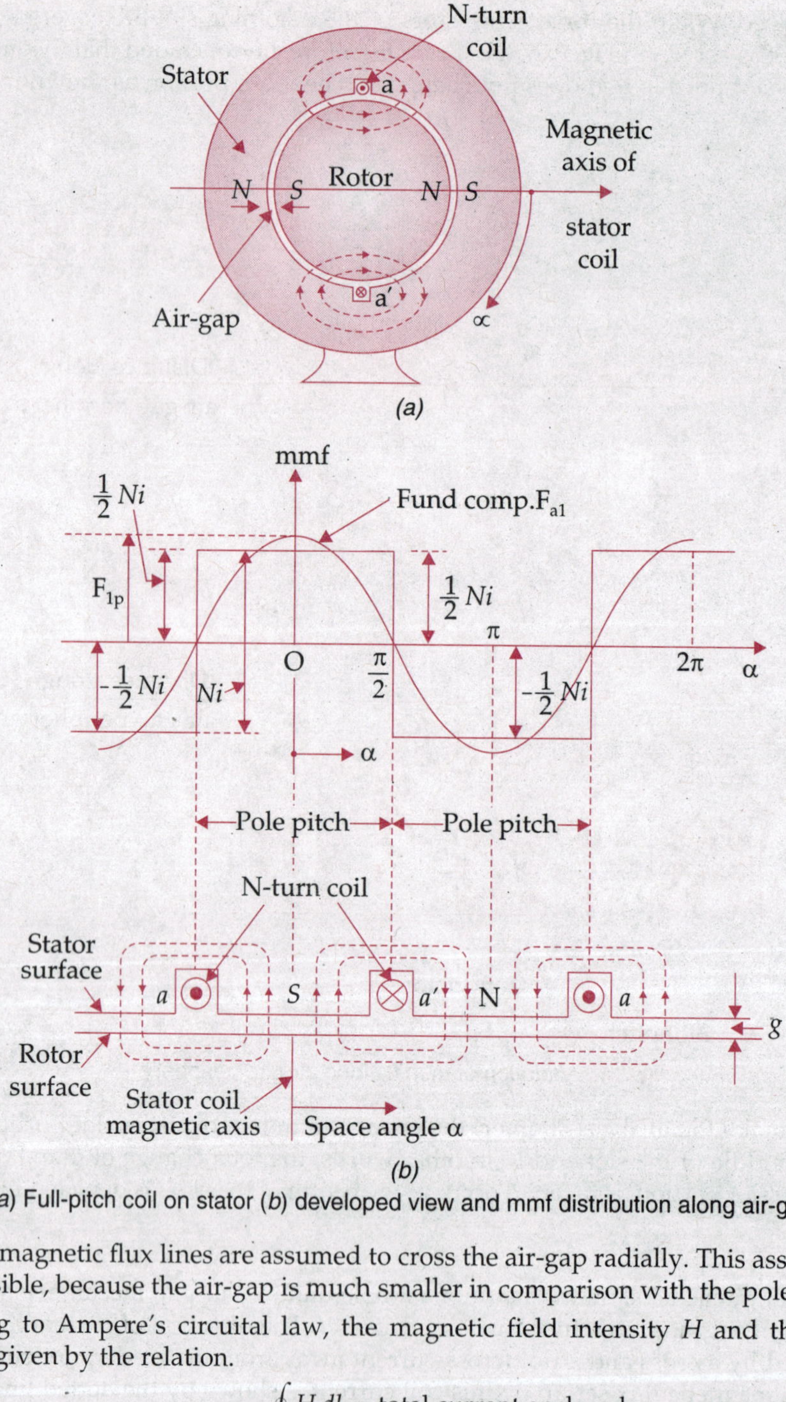

Fig 3.28: (*a*) Full-pitch coil on stator (*b*) developed view and mmf distribution along air-gap periphery.

(*ii*) The magnetic flux lines are assumed to cross the air-gap radially. This assumption is permissible, because the air-gap is much smaller in comparison with the pole pitch.

According to Ampere's circuital law, the magnetic field intensity H and the total current enclosed are given by the relation.

$$\oint H\,dl = \text{total current enclosed.}$$

If any of the dotted closed path in Fig. 3.28 (*a*) or (*b*) is traversed around any one coil-side, then

$$2gH = Ni$$

or

$$gH = \frac{Ni}{2} \qquad \text{...(3.52)}$$

Thus the magnetic potential difference or mmf gH across each gap (there are two air-gaps in series) is $\frac{1}{2}$ Ni. Since any closed path around any coil-side, satisfies Eq. (3.52), the variation of mmf along the air-gap periphery is of rectangular waveform and of magnitude $\frac{1}{2}$ Ni. Mmf or flux leaving the rotor is assumed positive.

Therefore, the variation of mmf along the air-gap periphery is as shown in Fig. 3.28 (*b*). It is seen that the air-gap mmf at any instant is rectangular. If D.C. is applied to the stator coil, mmf or field produced would be constant. The magnitude of this mmf wave does not change with time. Therefore, when D.C. is applied to single N-turn coil,

(*i*) mmf of constant magnitude is produced and

(*ii*) axis of magnetic flux or mmf remains fixed in position along the stator coil axis.

If an alternating current is applied to the stator coil, the magnetic field or mmf would be alternating in nature. But its magnetic axis would always remain along the stator coil axis. This type of field with A.C. in stator coil is called **pulsating magnetic field**.

The rectangular m.m.f. wave of magnitude $\frac{1}{2}$ Ni can be resolved by Fourier series into its fundamental and higher order harmonic components. The fundamental component of rectangular wave is found to be

$$F_{a1} = \frac{4}{\pi} \cdot \frac{Ni}{2} \cos \alpha = F_{1p} \cos \alpha \qquad \text{...(3.53 } a\text{)}$$

where α is electrical space angle measured from the magnetic axis of the stator coil as shown in Fig. 3.28. Here F_{1p}, the peak value of the sine m.m.f. wave for a 2-pole machine is given by

$$F_{1p} = \frac{4}{\pi} \cdot \frac{Ni}{2} \text{ ATs per pole} \qquad \text{...(3.53 } b\text{)}$$

This peak m.m.f., F_{1p} is always aligned along the magnetic axis of the coil.

If i is alternating current, then peak value of the fundamental sine component varies in accordance with i. That is when i is zero, F_{1p} is zero, when i is maximum, F_{1p} is maximum and so on. When $i = I_{max} = \sqrt{2}\, I$, then time maximum of the peak m.m.f. for a 2-pole machine is,

$$F_{1pm} = \frac{4}{\pi} \frac{N\sqrt{2I}}{2} \text{ ATs per pole} \qquad \text{...(3.54)}$$

and for a P-pole machine,

$$F_{1pm} = \frac{4}{\pi} \frac{N\sqrt{2I}}{P} \text{ ATs per pole} \qquad \text{...(3.55)}$$

3.6.2. M.m.f. of Distributed Windings

Fig. 3.29 (*a*) depicts three full-pitched coils of a distributed winding on the stator and Fig. 3.29 (*c*) illustrates the developed view of 3.29 (*a*). Each coil has N_c turns and each turn carries i amperes.

By referring to Fig. 3.28 (*b*), the mmf variation due to coil 1,1′ alone is seen to be a rectangular wave of magnitude $\pm\frac{1}{2}$ $N_c\, i$ as shown in Fig. 3.29 (c-*i*). Similarly, the mmf variations due to coils 2,2′ and 3, 3′ are shown in Fig. 3.29 (c-*ii*) and (c-*iii*) respectively. The combined mmf produced by the three coils can be obtained by summing up the ordinates of the individual coil mmfs. For example, to the left of coil-side 1, the combined mmf is $-\frac{3}{2}N_c i$, between the coil-sides 1 and 2 the combined m.m.f. is $-\frac{1}{2}N_c i$, between the coil-sides 2 and 3 the combined m.m.f. is + $\frac{1}{2}$ $N_c\, i$; between coil-sides 3 and 1′ the combined m.m.f. is $3/2\, N_c\, i$ and so on. This resultant m.m.f variation along the air-gap periphery is depicted in Fig. 3.29 (c-*iv*). It should be noted that the effect of winding distribution has changed the shape of the m.m.f. wave, from rectangular to stepped.

When the machine has more than three slots per pole per phase, as is usually the case, the steps are neglected and m.m.f. variation is taken as smooth over these slots. As a consequence, stepped m.m.f. wave changes to trapezoidal m.m.f. wave as shown in Fig. 3.29 (c-*iv*).

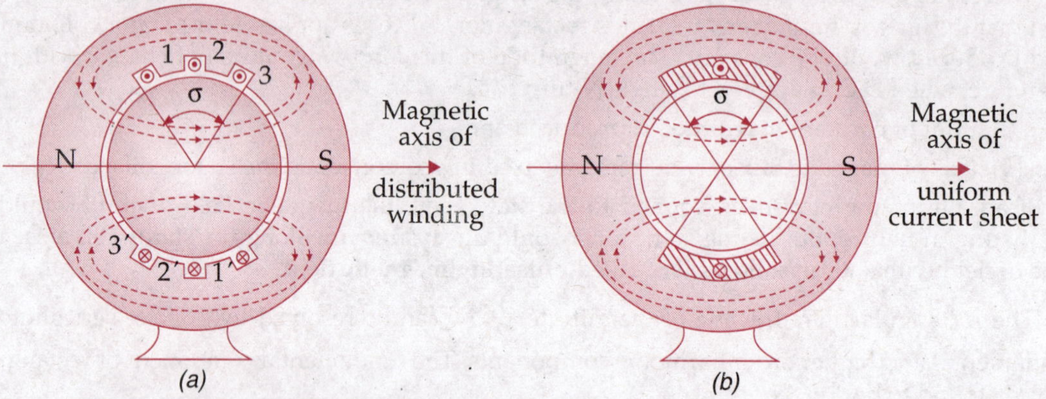

Fig 3.29: Pertaining to the mmf produced by *(a)* a distributed winding and *(b)* an equivalent current sheet.

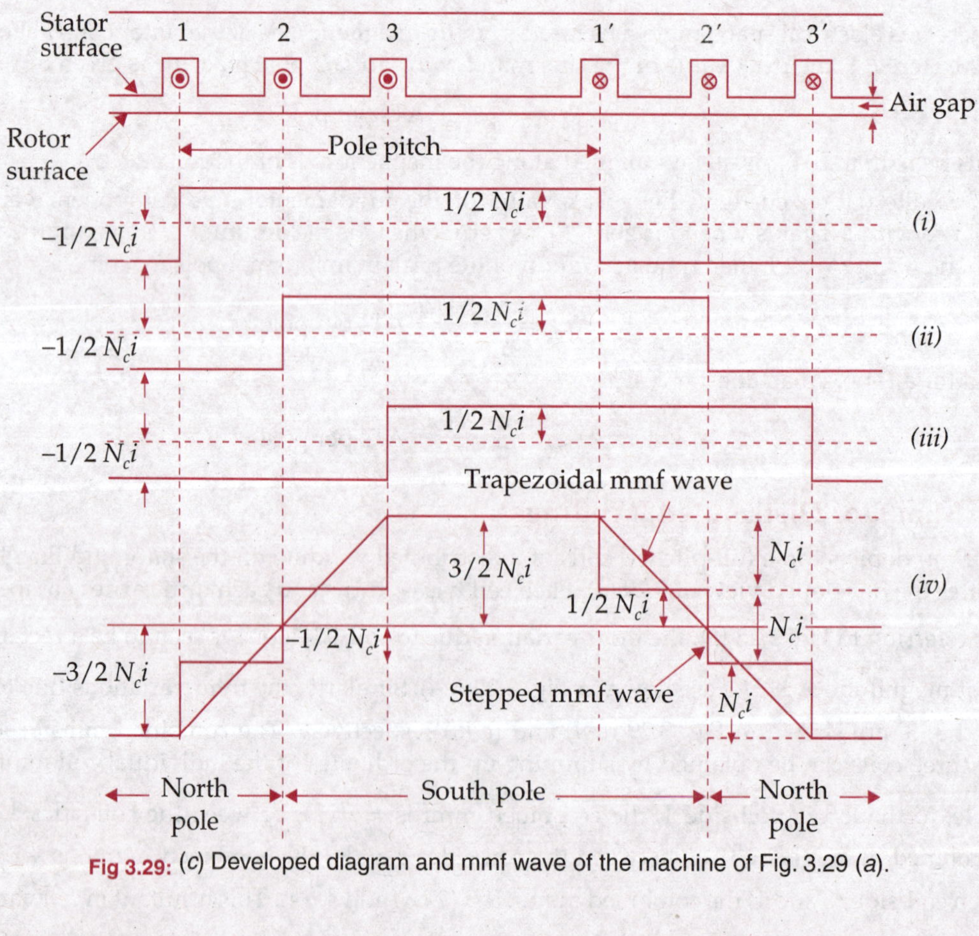

Fig 3.29: *(c)* Developed diagram and mmf wave of the machine of Fig. 3.29 *(a)*.

The smooth variation of m.m.f. over 3 slots per pole per phase in Fig. 3.29 (*c*) may be assumed to be produced by a uniformly distributed current sheet placed on the inner periphery of the stator as shown in Fig. 3.29 (*b*). The current sheet is, therefore, a thin strip of conducting material attached to the stator and is used here to replace the uniformly distributed winding in the slots of Fig. 3.29 (*a*). In other words, the m.m.f. produced by uniformly distributed current sheet of Fig. 3.29 (*b*) is indentical, in all respects, with the m.m.f. produced by uniformly distributed winding of Fig. 3.29 (*a*). If the distributed winding in the slots is on the rotor, then the uniformly distributed current sheet would be wrapped around the rotor accordingly.

Actually, the m.m.f. distribution along the air-gap periphery depends on the nature of slots, winding and the exciting current. In case the m.m.f. produced by uniformly distributed winding is sinusoidally distributed in space, then the equivalent current sheet must also be sinusoidally distributed in space.

In Fig. 3.29 (*a*), the total ampere conductors in the band covering an angle σ are $3N_c i$ and, therefore, the angular current density is $J = \frac{3N_c i}{\sigma}$. The trapezoidal m.m.f. wave of amplitude $\frac{3N_c i}{2}$ $\left(= \frac{1}{2} J\sigma\right)$ of Fig. 3.29 (*c*), can therefore be obtained as illustrated in Fig. 3.30 (*a*) by a uniform current sheet of density $J = \frac{3N_c i}{\sigma}$. Note that the m.m.f. at the middle of uniform current sheet is zero and is maximum $\left(= \frac{1}{2} J\sigma\right)$ at the end of the uniform current sheet. Further note that m.m.f. varies linearly over the angle σ from $-\frac{1}{2} J\sigma$ to $+\frac{1}{2} J\sigma$, because the current sheet is uniformly distributed. In case the current sheet is sinusoidal, then the m.m.f. wave is also sinusoidally distributed in space as shown in Fig. 3.30 (*b*). But note from this figure that sinusoidal m.m.f. wave is displaced by 90° (electrical) from sinusoidal current sheet.

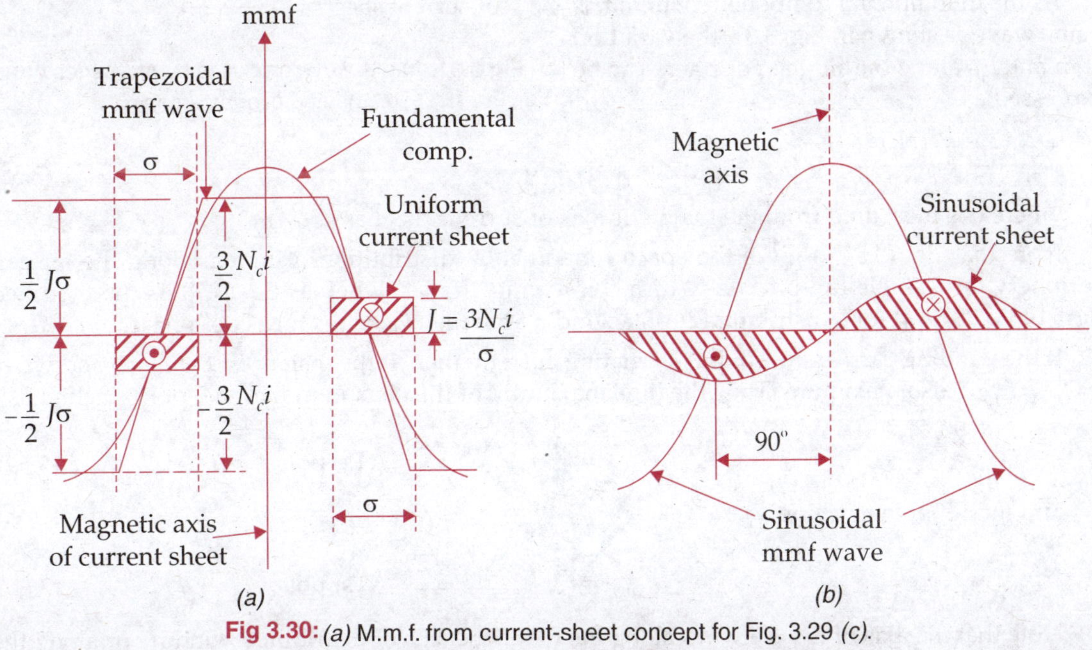

Fig 3.30: *(a)* M.m.f. from current-sheet concept for Fig. 3.29 *(c)*.
(b) M.m.f. wave produced by a sinusoidal current sheet.

In general, for N_{ph} full-pitched series turns per phase, distributed over an angle σ under each pole, the angular current density is $J = \frac{N_{ph}i}{\sigma}$. The amplitude of magnetic potential difference or m.m.f. across each gap is $\frac{1}{2}J\sigma = \frac{1}{2}\frac{N_{ph}i}{\sigma}\sigma = \frac{1}{2}N_{ph}\cdot i$ as shown in Fig. 3.31.

The Fourier-series analysis of trapezoidal m.m.f. wave of Fig. 3.31, gives the peak value of the fundamental sine-component as,

$$F_{1p} = \frac{4}{\pi}\cdot\frac{\sin\sigma/2}{\sigma/2}\left(\frac{1}{2}N_{ph}\cdot i\right)\text{ATs per pole} = \frac{4}{\pi}\cdot k_d\frac{N_{ph}\cdot i}{2}\text{ ATs/pole} \quad ...(3.56)$$

For F_{1p}, the subscripts 1 an p stand for fundamental and peak respectively.

Note that the effect of distributing the turns in the various slots, has resulted in the introduction of breadth factor k_d in Eq. (3.56). If the winding is fractional-pitch winding then the coil-span factor k_p must also be introduced ; modifying the peak value of the m.m.f. given by Eq. (3.56) as,

$$F_{1p} = \frac{4}{\pi}\cdot k_d k_p\frac{N_{ph}\cdot i}{2}\text{ ATs/pole}$$

$$= \frac{4}{\pi}k_w\frac{N_{ph}\cdot i}{2}\text{ ATs/pole.}$$

For P-pole machine,

$$F_{1p} = \frac{4}{\pi}\cdot k_w\frac{N_{ph}\cdot i}{P}\text{ ATs/pole} \quad ...(3.57)$$

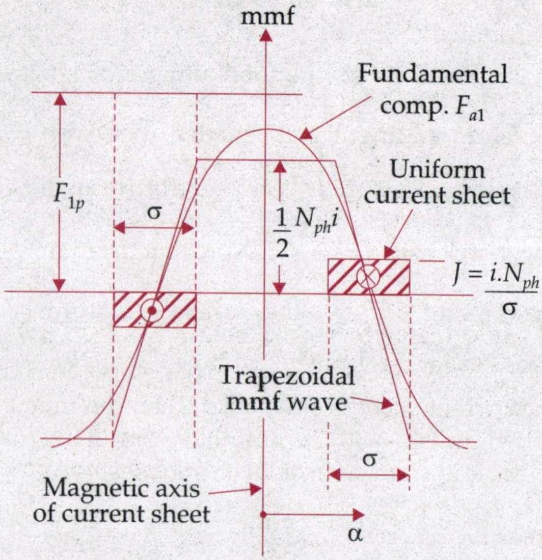

Fig 3.31: M.m.f. wave produced by N_{ph} series turns distributed over an angle σ.

As the fundamental component of m.m.f. is a sine wave as shown in Fig. 3.31, the variation of m.m.f. F_{a1} along the air gap periphery can be expressed as

$$F_{a1} = \frac{4}{\pi}k_w\frac{N_{ph}\cdot i}{P}\cos\alpha = F_{1p}\cos\alpha \quad ...(3.58)$$

where α is measured from the magnetic axis of current sheet as shown.

Note that Eq. (3.53 *a*) gives the space fundamental distribution of m.m.f. along the air-gap periphery for a single full-pitched N-turn coil having 2 poles, whereas Eq. (3.58) is the modified form of Eq. (3.53 *a*) for a distributed P-pole winding having N_{ph} series turns per phase.

If the winding carries sinusoidal alternating current, then at the instant $i = 0$, $F_{1p} = 0$ and when $i = I_{max}$, F_{1p} is also maximum. Thus the time maximum of the peak m.m.f. for a 2-pole machine is

$$F_{1pm} = \frac{4}{\pi}k_w\frac{N_{ph}\cdot\sqrt{2}I}{2}\text{ ATs/pole} \quad ...(3.59)$$

and for a P-pole machine,

$$F_{1pm} = \frac{4}{\pi}k_w\frac{N_{ph}\cdot\sqrt{2}I}{P}\text{ ATs/pole} \quad ...(3.60)$$

Note that the axis of F_{1p} is always along the magnetic axis of distributed winding or along the magnetic axis of the current sheet as shown in Figs. 3.30 and 3.31.

The field winding in a cylindrical-rotor synchronous machine is distributed in rotor slots as shown in Fig. 3.7 (*b*) for a 2-pole machine. The number of turns per slot can be varied in order to minimise the harmonics in the field flux waveform. Like the armature winding m.m.f. given by Eq. (3.60), the peak value of fundamental m.m.f. wave F_{1f} produced by field winding in a P-pole machine can be expressed as

$$F_{1f} = \frac{4}{\pi} k_f \frac{N_f I_f}{P} \text{ ATs/pole} \qquad ...(3.61)$$

where N_f = total number of field turns

I_f = field-winding current

k_f = field-winding factor

Single-phase winding. The m.m.f. produced by single-phase winding on the stator, or rotor, is alternating or pulsating in nature. This can be demonstrated by referring to Fig. 3.32 where

(i) a single-phase winding is represented by a uniform current sheet of spread σ and

(ii) only the fundamental sine component of trapezoidal m.m.f. wave is considered.

The time origin of current in single-phase winding is taken at the instant current is positive and maximum as shown in Fig. 3.32 *(a)*. At $\omega t_1 = 0$, $i_1 = I_{max}$ and the m.m.f waveform along the air-gap periphery is sinusoidal with a peak value of F_{p1} (= F_m) proportional to maximum current I_{max}. At ωt_2, the current in single-phase winding is i_2 and the m.m.f. waveform is again sinusoidal with a peak value F_{p2} proportional to i_2, see Fig. 3.32. Note that the peaks F_{p1}, F_{p2} are always along the axis of single-phase winding. At $\omega t_3 = \frac{\pi}{2}$, $i_3 = 0$ and therefore no m.m.f. is produced. At $\omega t_4 = \pi$, $i_4 = -I_{max}$ and m.m.f. waveform is sinusoidal with peak $-F_{p4}$ as shown. If the space angle α along the air-gap periphery is measured from the axis of single-phase winding as shown, then, at ωt_1, m.m.f. F_1 at any space angle α can be expressed as

$$\left.\begin{aligned} & & F_1 &= F_{p1} \cos \alpha \\ &\text{Similarly at } \omega t_2, & F_2 &= F_{p2} \cos \alpha \\ &\text{At } \omega t_3, & F_3 &= F_{p3} \cos \alpha = 0 \\ &\text{At } \omega t_4, & F_4 &= -F_{p4} \cos \alpha \end{aligned}\right\} \qquad ...(3.62)$$

In Eq. (3.62), subscript p indicates peak value and subscripts 1, 2, 3... denote the instants 1, 2, 3...

Remember that the amplitudes of various m.m.fs F_{p1}, F_{p2}, F_{p3}... vary with time in accordance with current variations i_1, i_2, i_3.... But the currents i_1, i_2, i_3... vary sinusoidally with time, consequently the m.m.fs. F_{p1}, F_{p2}, F_{p3}... must also vary sinusoidally with time.

In Fig. 3.32 *(a)*, the time origin of current i is taken at the instant of its passing through maximum positive value. Therefore, at $\omega t_1 = 0$, $i_1 = I_{max}$.

This gives peak value of m.m.f. at instant ωt_1 as

$$F_{p1} \propto \text{(single-phase winding turns)} (I_{max} \cdot \cos \omega t_1)$$

$$\propto N I_{max} \cdot \cos \omega t_1$$

or $$F_{p1} = F_m \cos \omega t_1 = F_m \cos 0 = F_m$$

where $$F_m \propto N\, I_{max}.$$

At ωt_2, $$i_2 = I_{max} \cos \omega t_2. \text{ This gives}$$

$$F_{p2} = F_m \cos \omega t_2$$

Similarly $$F_{p3} = F_m \cos \omega t_3$$

$$F_{p4} = -F_m \cos \omega t_4$$

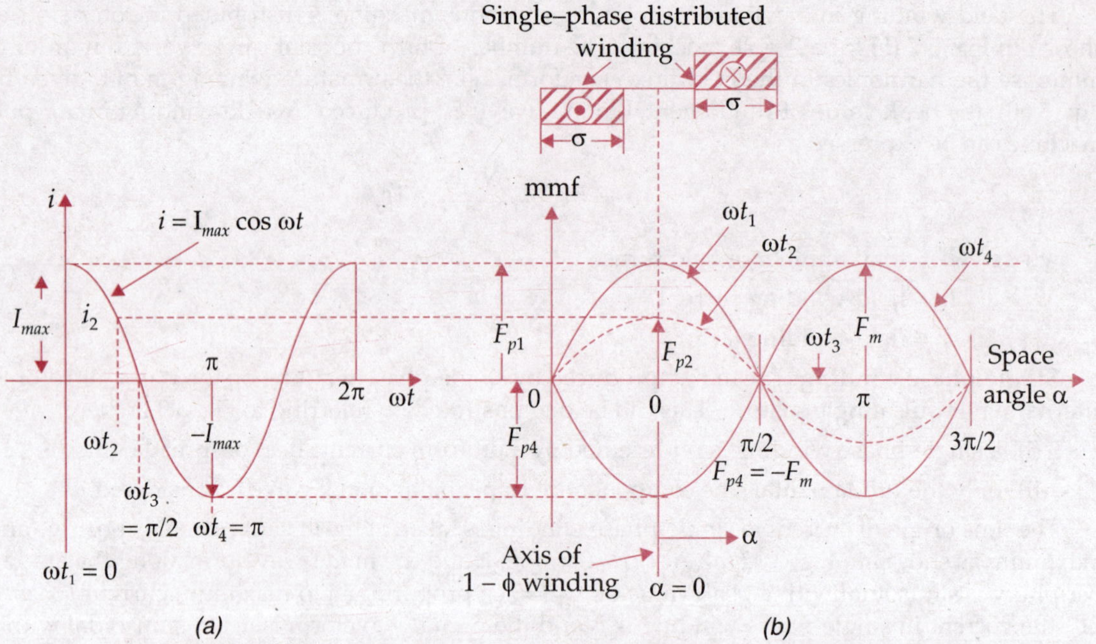

Fig 3.32: Pertaining to pulsating mmf produced by single-phase distributed winding.

Substitution of the values of F_{p1}, F_{p2} ..., as given above, in Eq. (3.62) gives the pulsating m.m.f. wave as

$$\left.\begin{aligned} &\text{at } \omega t_1, && F_1 = F_m \cos \omega t_1 \cos \alpha = F_m \cos 0 \cos \alpha \\ &\text{at } \omega t_2, && F_2 = F_m \cos \omega t_2 \cos \alpha \\ &\text{at } \omega t_3, && F_3 = F_m \cos \omega t_3 \cos \alpha \\ &\text{and at } \omega t_4, && F_4 = F_m \cos \omega t_4 \cos \alpha \end{aligned}\right\} \quad ...(3.63)$$

In Eq. (3.63), F_3 is zero because at $\omega t_3 = \frac{\pi}{2}$, current is zero. An examination of Eq. (3.63) reveals that a general expression for the *stationary (or standing) pulsating m.m.f.* wave, set up by a single-phase distributed winding carrying alternating current, can be expressed in terms of both time angle ωt and space angle α as,

$$F(\alpha, t) = F_m \cos \omega t \cos \alpha \quad ...(3.64)$$

In Eqs. 3.63 and 3.64, F_m is the m.m.f. per pole corresponding to the maximum current I_{max} and is equal to F_{1pm} as given by Eq. (3.59) for a 2-pole machine or by Eq. (3.60) for a *P*-pole machine. In Eq. (3.64), the term cos ω*t* indicates that m.m.f. varies cosinusoidally (or sinusoidally) with time and the term cos α denotes its cosinusoidal, or sinusoidal, distribution in space along the air-gap periphery.

In order to give physical significance to Eq. (3.64), the reader should assume himself/herself seated at α = 0°, *i.e.*, on the axis of the single-phase winding in Fig. 3.32 *(b)*. Now at time $t = 0$, $\omega t = 0$ and the m.m.f. seen by the reader, as per Eq. (3.64) is maximum (cos α = cos 0° = 1). As the time progresses, ω*t* changes and the m.m.f. seen by the reader also changes.

At ω*t* = 60°, the reader sitting at α = 0° sees $\frac{1}{2} F_m$; at ω*t* = 90°, the m.m.f. seen is zero ; at ω*t* = 180°, the m.m.f. seen is $-F_m$ and at ω*t* = 270°, m.m.f. seen is zero. This shows that the reader seated at α = 0° on the axis of single-phase winding, where cos α is always unity, comes across an m.m.f. pulsating between $+F_m$ and $-F_m$. Suppose the reader is sitting at 60° away from the phase axis, *i.e.*, at $\alpha = 60°$, then at $\omega t = 0°$, the m.m.f. seen by the reader is $F_m \cdot \cos 0°. \cos 60° = \frac{1}{2} F_m$ and at $\omega t = 180°$, the m.m.f. seen is $-\frac{1}{2} F_m$. Thus the m.m.f. seen by the reader at $\alpha = 60°$ is again pulsating between $+\frac{1}{2} F_m$ and $-\frac{1}{2} F_m$, but now he/she can never see maximum m.m.f. F_m. If the reader is sitting at $\alpha = 90°$, the m.m.f. seen by the reader is always zero for all times to come, because cos 90° is always zero.

Example 3.19. *A 3-phase, 2-pole stator has double-layer full-pitched winding with 5 slots per pole per phase. If each coil has N_c turns and i is the conductor current, then sketch the m.m.f. waveform produced by phase a alone. For $N_c = 4$ and per-phase current 20 A, determine the maximum, as well as r.m.s., value of the peak of fundamental m.m.f. wave.*

Solution. A 2-pole stator structure with 5 slots per pole per phase is shown in Fig. 3.33 *(a)*. The angle subtended by 5 slots is $\sigma = 5\gamma = 5 \times \frac{180}{15} = 60°$. The slots of phase *a* are numbered 1, 2, ... 5 and 1′, 2′, ... 5′. For double-layer winding, each slot contains 2 coil-sides or $2N_C$ conductors. Slots pertaining to phases *b* and *c* are also shown. Note that sequence of phase belts is *a c′ b a′ c b′* clockwise and each belt has phase spread σ of 60 degrees electrical. Current flow in coil-sides is indicated by dots and crosses.

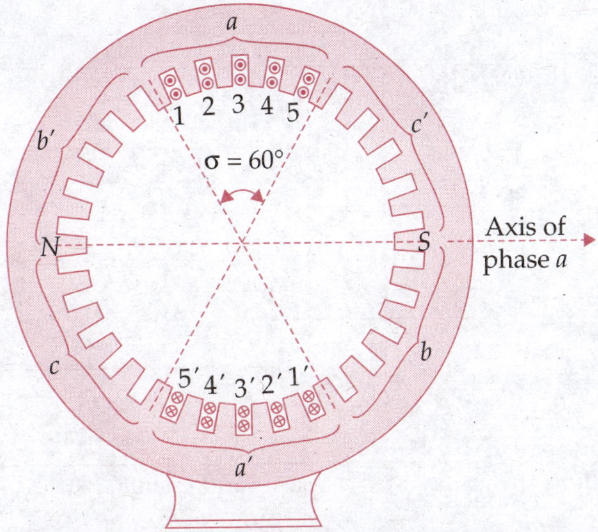

Fig 3.33: *(a)* A 3-phase, 2-pole stator with double layer winding having 5 slots per pole per phase.

Developed view of Fig. 3.33 *(a)* is shown in Fig. 3.33 *(b)*. For any closed path around slot 1, the total current enclosed is $2N_C\, i$ ampere conductors, therefore magnetic potential difference across each gap is $\frac{1}{2}[2N_c\, i] = N_c\, i$. Thus, the m.m.f. variation from $-N_c\, i$ to $+N_c\, i$ shown at the middle of slot 1 in Fig. 3.33 (*c i*). Like slot 1, the m.m.f. variation for slot 1′ is from $+N_c\, i$ to $-N_c\, i$ as shown. Thus, m.m.f. variation for coil 11′ is of rectangular waveform with amplitude $\pm N_c\, i$. Similarly, the rectangular m.m.f. waveforms of amplitude $\pm N_c\, i$ are sketched for the coils 22′, ..., 55′ in Fig. 3.33 (*c ii*) to Fig. 3.33 (*c v*). The combined m.m.f. produced by 5 coils is obtained by adding the ordinates of the individual coil m.m.fs. The resultant m.m.f. waveform shown in Fig. 3.33 (*c vi*) consists of a series of steps each of height $2N_c\, i$ = (conductors per slot) (conductor current). The amplitude of the resultant m.m.f. wave is $5N_c\, i$. This amplitude of m.m.f. can also be obtained as further :

Uniform current density,

$$J = \frac{[\text{Ampere conductors in one slot}][\text{Number of adjacent slots in one phase–belt}]}{\text{Angle covered by adjacent slots (i.e. phase spread)}}$$

$$J = \frac{[2N_c i][5]}{\sigma} = \frac{10N_c i}{\sigma}$$

$$\text{Resultant amplitude of m.m.f.} = \frac{1}{2} J\sigma = \frac{1}{2}\,\frac{10N_C \cdot i}{\sigma} \cdot \sigma = 5N_c\, i \text{ AT/pole}$$

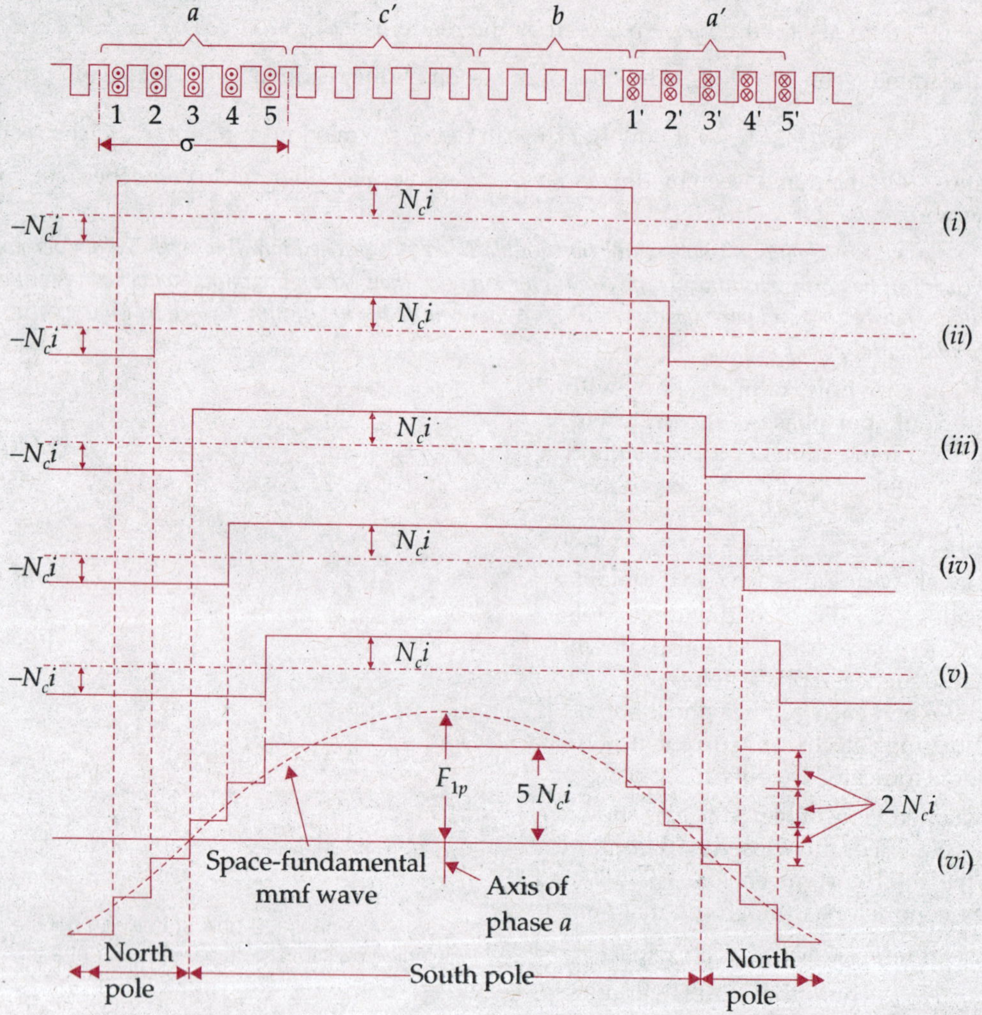

Fig 3.33: Pertaining to Example 3.19 *(b)* developed view of Fig. 3.33 *(a)* and *(c)* m.m.f. waveforms.

As before, the resultant m.m.f waveform of Fig. 3.33 (*c vi*) can be resolved into fundamental and a series of odd harmonics. The peak value of fundamental sine component is

$$F_{1p} = \frac{4}{\pi} \cdot \frac{\sin\frac{\sigma}{2}}{\sigma/2} \, [5N_c \, i] = \frac{4}{\pi} \cdot k_d \, [5N_c \, i] \text{ AT/pole}$$

For $N_c = 4$, $I_{max} = \sqrt{2} \times 20$ A. This gives the maximum value (here I_{max} is used) of the peak of resultant m.m.f. wave as

$$F_{1pm} = \frac{4}{\pi} \cdot \frac{\sin\frac{60}{2}}{30\times\frac{\pi}{180}} \cdot [5 \times 4 \sqrt{2} \times 20] = 687.687 \text{ AT/pole}$$

R.m.s. value of this peak is given by

$$F_{1p} = \frac{4}{\pi} \cdot \frac{3}{\pi} \cdot [5 \times 4 \times 20] = 486.342 \text{ AT/pole.}$$

Example 3.20. *Each belt of a 2-pole, 3-phase balanced winding is considered to consist of current sheet of uniform density. Trace out the m.m.f. variation due to phase-a belt alone.*

In case this machine has 300 full-pitched turns with phase current of 24 A, then calculate

(a) peak amplitude of the m.m.f. wave.

(b) peak as well as r.m.s. value of the fundamental m.m.f. wave.

Solution. The six phase belts of a 2-pole, 3-phase machine are shown as *ac′ b a′ cb′* in Fig. 3.34. The current in the belt *a* is assumed towards the reader and is therefore indicated by dot. Likewise, the current in belt *a′* is shown by cross. The m.m.f. variation due to uniform current sheet in phase-*a* belts is drawn by referring to Fig. 3.30 *(a)*. The m.m.f. is zero at the middle of current sheet and varies uniformly over the spread of phase-belts. In between the phase-belts carrying cross and dot direction of current, the m.m.f. is positive ; this is as expected. The m.m.f. variation thus obtained has trapezoidal waveform as shown in Fig. 3.34.

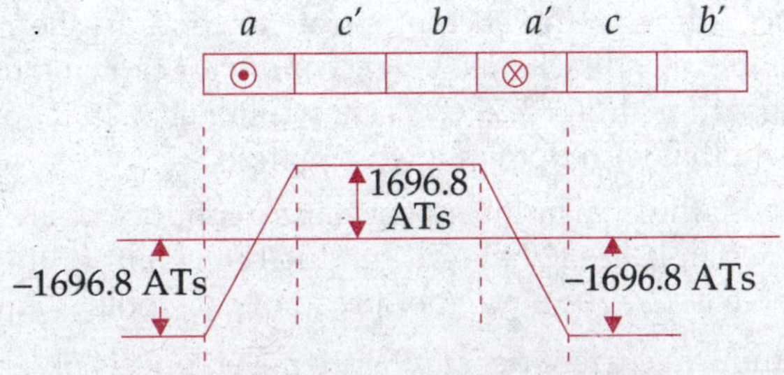

Fig 3.34: Pertaining to Example 3.20.

(*a*) Peak value of uniform current density

$$J = \frac{N_{ph} \cdot \sqrt{2} I}{\text{Phase spread of one belt}}$$

Series turns per phase, $N_{ph} = \dfrac{300}{3} = 100$

Phase spread, $\sigma = 60°.$

$$\therefore \quad J = \frac{100 \times \sqrt{2} \times 24}{60 \times \frac{\pi}{180}} = \frac{2400 \times 3 \times \sqrt{2}}{\pi} \text{ AT/rad}$$

Peak amplitude of trapezoidal m.m.f. wave $= \dfrac{1}{2} J\sigma$

$$= \frac{1}{2} \times \frac{2400 \times 3 \times \sqrt{2}}{\pi} \times \frac{\pi}{3} = 1200 \times \sqrt{2} = 1696.8 \text{ ATs/pole.}$$

(*b*) Peak value of fundamental m.m.f. wave, from Eq. (3.56), is

$$F_{1pm} = \frac{4}{\pi} \cdot \frac{\sin\frac{\sigma}{2}}{\sigma/2} \cdot [\text{Peak value of trapezoidal m.m.f. wave}]$$

$$= \frac{4}{\pi} \cdot \frac{\sin\frac{60}{2}}{30 \times \frac{\pi}{180}} [1200 \times \sqrt{2}\,] = 2063.06 \text{ ATs/pole}$$

R.m.s. value of the fundamental m.m.f. wave $= \dfrac{1}{\sqrt{2}} F_{1pm} = \dfrac{4}{\pi} \times \dfrac{3}{\pi} [1200] = 1459.025$ ATs/pole

3.6.3. M.m.f. Waveform of Commutator Machines

The armature winding of all the commutators machines are on the rotor, because of the necessity of commutator action. Fig. 3.35 (*a*) illustrates the cross-section of a 2-pole commutator machine of both A.C. and D.C. types. In this figure, current directions are shown by crosses and dots. The direction of current in any conductor is in one direction and after it crosses the brush width, the direction of current in it gets reversed, see Art. 4.1. Thus the direction of current as shown under each pole, remains unaltered despite the rotor movement. The m.m.f. established by the armature currents is always perpendicular to the main-field axis as shown. Since the current direction under each pole remains unaltered, the uniformly distributed armature winding of Fig. 3.35. (*a*), may be replaced by a uniformly distributed current sheet wrapped around the rotor as shown in Fig. 3.35 (*b*). Now according to the current sheet concept, all the conductors under each pole are equivalent to a uniformly distributed single conductor carrying the whole current under each pole. The developed diagram of Fig. 3.35 (*b*) is shown in Fig. 3.35 (*c*), where current sheet with cross is shown positive and that with dot is shown negative.

If the total number of armature conductors is Z, then for a P-pole machine, the conductors under each pole are Z/P. For a conductor current i_z, the total current uniformly distributed under each pole is $(Z/P)\, i_z$. Since the spread of each pole is equivalent to π electrical radians, the magnitude of uniform current density J under each pole is given by $J = \frac{1}{\pi}\frac{Z}{P}\, i_z$ Ampere conductors per electrical rad.

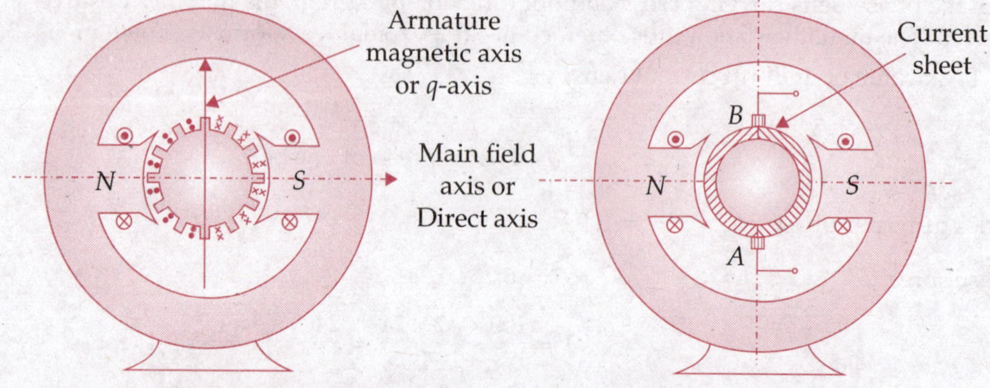

(a) (b)

Fig 3.35: Two-pole commutator machine *(a)* its cross-section and *(b)* current sheet replaces armature winding.

By referring to Fig. 3.30 (*a*), the m.m.f. wave produced by the constant current sheet in Fig. 3.35 (*c*) is seen to be a triangular m.m.f. wave. If i is the total current at the armature terminals, then for a parallel paths, i/a is the current in each conductor. Since the commutator winding has a phase spread of $\sigma = \pi$ radians, the peak of the triangular m.m.f. wave, as per Fig. 3.30 (*c*) and Eq. 3.64, is given by

$$\frac{1}{2} J\sigma = \frac{1}{2}\left(\frac{1}{\pi}\frac{Z}{P}\frac{i}{a}\right)\pi = \frac{1}{2}\frac{Z}{P}\frac{i}{a} \text{ AT/pole} \quad \text{...(3.65)}$$

For a D.C. commutator machine, the peak of the triangular m.m.f. wave becomes $\frac{Z}{2P}\cdot\frac{I_a}{a}$ AT/ per pole, where I_a is the total current at the armature terminals. For a single phase commutator machine, the peak value of the triangular m.m.f. wave becomes $\frac{Z}{2P}\frac{\sqrt{2}I}{a} = \frac{1}{\sqrt{2}}\frac{ZI}{Pa}$ AT per pole, where I is the r.m.s. value of the total armature current.

The fundamental sine component of the triangular m.m.f. wave, obtained by Fourier-series analysis, is found to be equal to $8/\pi^2$ (peak value of the triangular m.m.f. wave). Therefore, the peak value of the fundamental sine component F_a for a D.C. machine [Fig. 3.35 (*d*)],

$$F_a = \frac{8}{\pi^2}\left(\frac{Z}{2P}\cdot\frac{I_a}{a}\right) = \frac{8}{\pi^2}\left(\frac{N}{P}\frac{I_a}{a}\right) \text{ AT/pole} \qquad ...(3.66)$$

Here N is the total number of armature turns.

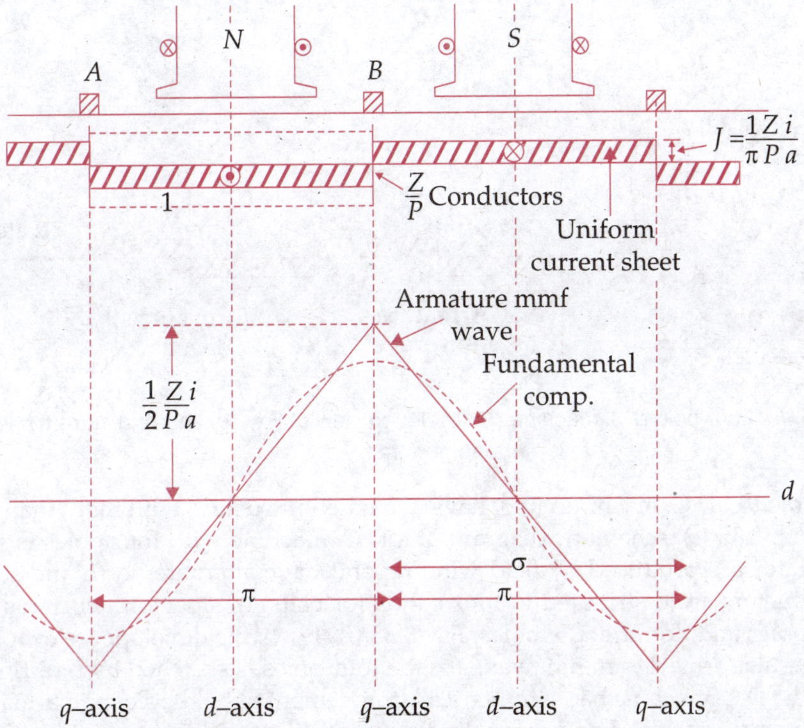

Fig 3.35: *(c)* and *(d)*. Pertaining to the m.m.f. wave produced by the current sheet of a commutator machine.

The peak value of the fundamental sine component for a single-phase commutator machine; [Fig. 3.35 (*d*)] is

$$F_a = \frac{8}{\pi^2}\left(\frac{Z}{2P}\cdot\frac{\sqrt{2}I}{a}\right) = \frac{8\sqrt{2}}{\pi^2}\cdot\frac{N}{P}\cdot\frac{I}{a} \text{ AT/pole} \qquad ...(3.67)$$

Here also N is the total number of armature turns.

Alternatively, Eq. (3.65) can also be obtained as under :

Take the integral around the dotted closed path 1 shown in Fig. 3.35 (*c*). As per Ampere's circuital law,

$$\oint H.dl = \text{[conductors per pole] [current per conductor]} = \left[\frac{Z}{P}\right]\cdot\left[\frac{i}{a}\right]$$

where i = total armature current,

a = number of parallel path in armature winding,

and $\frac{i}{a}$ = current per conductor.

Since the closed dotted path traverses the air gap twice, peak value of triangular armature mmf is

$$\frac{1}{2}\cdot\frac{Z}{P}\cdot\frac{i}{a} \text{ AT/pole} \qquad ...(3.65)$$

In a D.C. machine, armature current does not vary with time. Therefore, the armature m.m.f. wave for a D.C. machine remains constant in amplitude and does not depend on the armature speed. In case of single-phase commutator machine, the armature m.m.f. wave, unaffected by the armature speed, is stationary in space, but pulsates at the supply frequency.

Fig. 3.35 (*d*) reveals that peaks of the triangular m.m.f. wave and its fundamental sine component, coincide with the brush axis or *q*-axis.

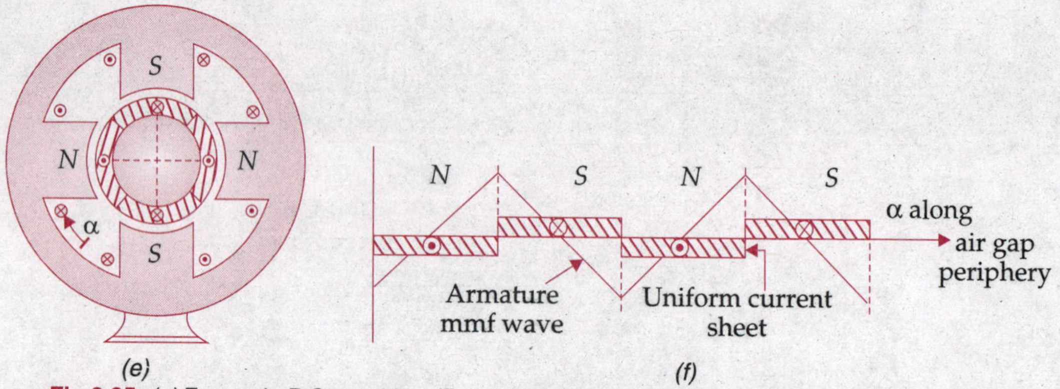

Fig 3.35: *(e)* Four-pole D.C. machine *(f)* developed view of Fig. *(e)* showing current sheet and armature m.m.f. wave.

In actual practice, D.C. machines may have a magnetic structure with more than two poles on the stator. In Fig. 3.35 (*e*), schematic diagram of a D.C. machine with four poles is shown. These poles on the stator are produced by field winding and have alternate north and south polarity. Armature conductors are distributed in four bands (or belts) of slots with currents indicated by cross under *S* poles and dot under *N* poles. Fig. 3.35 (*f*) shows the developed view of Fig. 3.35 (*e*), where the triangular armature m.m.f. wave for the four poles is sketched by referring to Fig. 3.35 (*c*) and (*d*). As the D.C. machine has symmetrical arrangement of field poles and armature winding around its periphery, the m.m.f. and magnetic circuit conditions under one pole-pair repeat under the next pole-pair.

3.7. ROTATING MAGNETIC FIELD

When balanced polyphase currents flow in balanced polyphase windings, a rotating magnetic field is produced. In other words, all polyphase A.C. machines are associated with rotating magnetic fields in their air-gaps. Consequently, a knowledge of the rotating field produced by a polyphase winding is essential for understanding the theory of polyphase A.C. machines such as polyphase synchronous and induction machines. As three-phase machines are more common, attention will primarily be focused on the production of rotating field in these machines.

For a 3-phase machine, the three windings are displaced from each other by 120 electrical space degrees along the air-gap periphery. Fig. 3.36 (*a*) illustrates a 2-pole 3-phase stator winding. Note that each phase is distributed or spread over 60° electrical (called phase-spread σ), under each pole. For convenience, the three-phase winding *a, b, c* is represented by three full pitched coils, *aa′*, *bb′*, *cc′* as illustrated in Fig. 3.36 (*b*). For instance, the concentrated full-pitched coil *aa′* represents phase *a* winding in all respects. A current in phase *a* winding establishes magnetic flux directed along the magnetic axis of coil *aa′*. Positive currents are assumed to be flowing as indicated by crosses in coil-sides *a′*, *b′*, *c′*. It means that when phase *a* alone carries positive current, the flux produced by this phase is directed horizontally from left to right–if phase *a* current is negative, the flux produced is directed horizontally from right to left. The three-phase currents flowing in the three-phase windings, are varying sinusoidally with time as depicted in Fig. 3.36 (*c*). In order to have better physical insight into the production of rotating magnetic field, graphical analysis involving magnetic-flux plot as well as space-phasor representation will be presented here. It should be noted that the resultant flux, in the air gap of a 3-phase machine, is due to the combined action of all the three-winding fluxes.

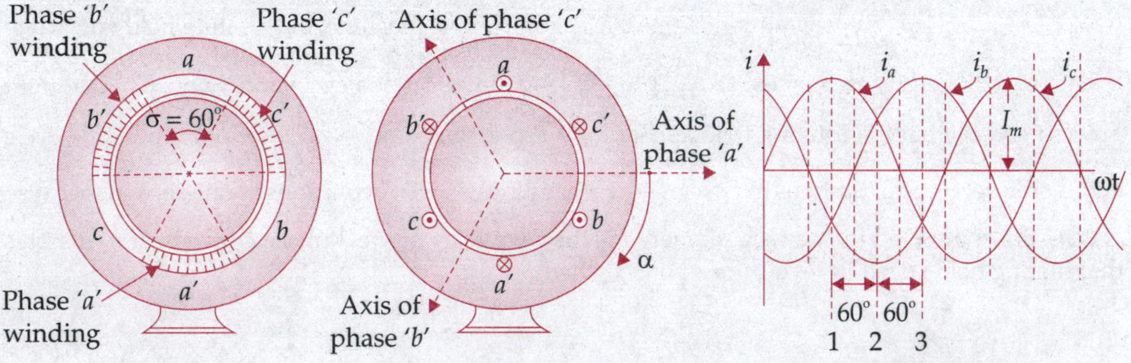

(a) *(b)* *(c)*

Fig 3.36: *(a)* 3-phase winding space displaced by 120 degrees electrical, from each other, *(b)* 3-coils *aa'*, *bb'*, *cc'* represent three-phase winding and *(c)* 3-phase instantaneous currents.

Graphical analysis–magnetic flux plot. At the instant 1, [Fig. 3.36 (*c*)], the current in phase *a* is positive and maximum, say I_m and this current is represented by cross and dot in coil-sides *a'* and *a* respectively in Fig. 3.37 (*a*). Currents i_b and i_c are both negative and equal to $\frac{I_m}{2}$, *i.e.* $i_b = i_c = -\frac{I_m}{2}$. Since i_b and i_c are negative, crosses must be shown in coil-sides *b*, *c* and dots in coil-sides *b'*, *c'*. Right hand grip rule gives the distribution of flux at instant 1, as shown in Fig. 3.37 (*a*). Note that two poles are created on the stator. At instant 2, $i_a = \frac{I_m}{2}$, $i_b = \frac{I_m}{2}$ and $i_c = -I_m$. Therefore, crosses must be shown in coil-sides *a'*, *b'* and *c* [Fig. 3.37 (*b*)] and the resultant flux distribution is found to be as shown in Fig. 3.37 (*b*). Note that two poles are created again, but the axis of the resultant flux has turned clockwise through 60 electrical degrees in space. At instant 3, $i_a = -\frac{I_m}{2}$, $i_b = I_m$ and $i_c = -\frac{I_m}{2}$.

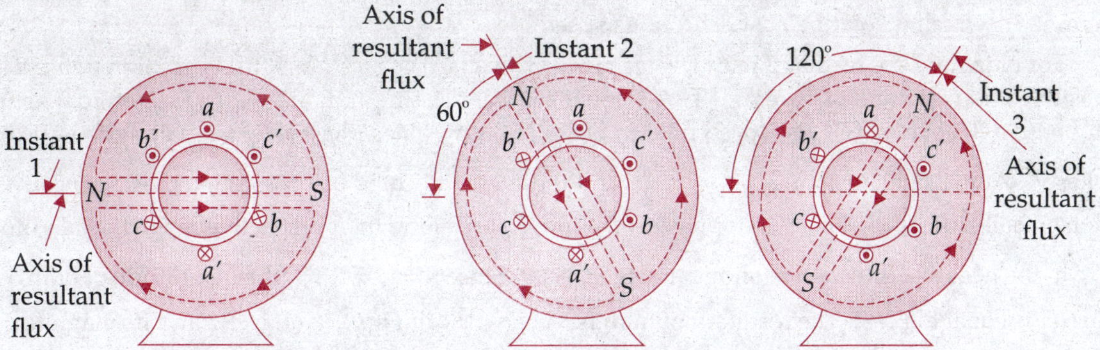

(a) *(b)* *(c)*

Fig 3.37: Production of rotating magnetic field illustrated by magnetic flux plot.

Therefore, the crosses and dots are as shown in Fig. 3.37 (*c*) and the 2 poles produced by the resultant flux are seen to have turned through further 60 electrical space degrees. At other instants of time, *i.e.*, as the time elapses, the two poles rotate further. In this manner, a rotating magnetic field is produced. Note that the space angle traversed by rotating flux is equal to the time angle traversed by currents. In one cycle, the two poles must come to the position indicated in Fig. 3.37 (*a*). Thus in a 2-pole machine, the rotating field travels a distance covered by two poles (*i.e.*, two pole pitches) in one cycle. For a 4-pole machine, the rotating field will travel a distance covered by two poles, *i.e.* $\frac{1}{2}\left(=\frac{1}{4/2}\right)$ revolution in one cycle. For a 6-pole machine, the rotating field will travel a distance covered by two poles, *i.e.*, $\frac{1}{3}\left(=\frac{1}{6/2}\right)$ revolution in one cycle and so on. This thought process reveals that the rotating field speed, for a *P*-pole machine, is $\frac{1}{P/2}$ revolution in one cycle and therefore $\frac{f}{P/2}$ revolutions in *f* cycles—in other words $\frac{f}{P/2}$ revolutions in one second, because *f* cycles are completed in one second. Here *f* is the frequency of the 3 phase currents. If n_s denotes the rotating field speed in revolutions per sec, then

$$n_s = \frac{f}{P/2} = \frac{2f}{P} \quad ...(3.68)$$

or

$$N_s = \frac{120f}{P} \text{ r.p.m.} \quad ...(3.69)$$

The speed at which rotating magnetic field revolves is called the *synchronous speed.*

The graphical analysis presented above brings out clearly the production of rotating magnetic field, but it fails to establish that the magnitude of rotating flux remains constant at all instants of time. The graphical analysis given below, proves this fact.

Graphical analysis–space phasor representation. When phase *a* alone carries current, an m.m.f. is established along its magnetic axis. Neglecting space harmonics, the m.m.f. is sinusoidally distributed along the air-gap periphery. Further, phase *a* m.m.f. wave is stationary but pulsating in nature. For convenience, this sinusoidally distributed m.m.f. is represented by a space phasor $\overline{F}_a$ directed along the axis of phase *a*. Note that the magnitude of $\overline{F}_a$ is proportional to current i_a and is directed from left to right with positive i_a and from right to left with negative i_a (Fig. 3.38). In other words, the space phasor F_a is oscillating along the axis of phase *a*. Same state of affairs exist, when phase *b* alone or phase *c* alone carry currents. When currents i_a, i_b, i_c flow in their respective phase windings, then the three stationary pulsating m.m.fs. $\overline{F}_a$, $\overline{F}_b$, $\overline{F}_c$ combine to give the resultant m.m.f. $\overline{F}_R$ which is rotating at synchronous speed.

For obtaining the resultant m.m.f, refer to Fig. 3.36 (*c*). At the instant 1, the current in phase *a* is positive and maximum, *i.e.*, $i_a = I_m$. This current sets up maximum m.m.f. F_m [= F_{1pm} of Eq. (3.59)] in phase *a*. This m.m..f. F_m is represented in Fig. 3.38 (*a*) by space phasor $\overline{F}_a = F_m$ along the axis of phase *a*. At the same instant, $i_b = i_c = -\frac{I_m}{2}$ and these are indicated by crosses in coil-sides *b*, *c* and dots in coil-sides *b′*, *c′*. The m.m.f. phasors $\overline{F}_b$ and $\overline{F}_c$ are along their respective magnetic axis, but are in the negative direction as shown in Fig. 3.38 (*a*). Since $i_b = i_c = -\frac{I_m}{2}$, the magnitude of both F_b and F_c is equal to $F_m/2$. The resultant of m.m.fs. $\overline{F}_a$, $\overline{F}_b$, $\overline{F}_c$ in Fig. 3.38 (*a*) is $\overline{F}_R$ and its magnitude is given by

$$F_R = F_m + \frac{2F_m}{2} \cos 60° = \frac{3}{2} F_m$$

The vertical component of $\overline{F}_b$ and $\overline{F}_c$ cancel each other.

Note that at instant 1, current in phase *a* is maximum and the resultant m.m.f. $F_R = \frac{3}{2} F_m$, directed along the phase *a* axis, is sinusoidally distributed in space.

At instant 2, Fig. 3.36 (*c*), $i_a = i_b = \frac{I_m}{2}$ and $i_c = -I_m$. The m.m.f. phasors $\overline{F}_a$ and $\overline{F}_b$ both equal to $\frac{F_m}{2}$ in magnitude, are along their respective magnetic axis in the positive direction. The m.m.f. $\overline{F}_c$ $= F_m$, in phase *c*, is indicated in the negative direction, but along the phase *c*-axis. The amplitude of the resultant m.m.f. F_R is again found to be equal to $\frac{3}{2}F_m$ but it is seen to rotate by a space angle of 60° clockwise.

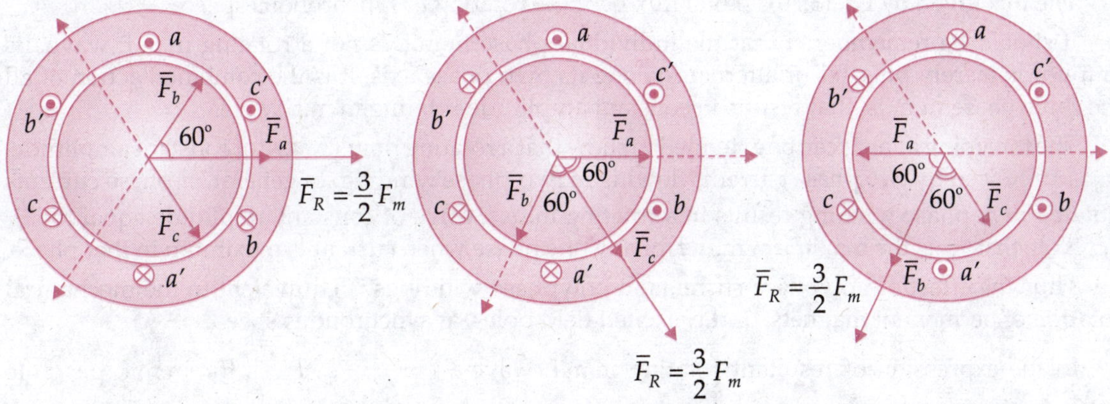

Fig 3.38: Production of rotating magnetic field illustrated by space phasor m.m.fs .

At instant 3, $i_a = i_c = \frac{-I_m}{2}$ and $i_b = I_m$. The m.m.f. phasors $\overline{F}_a$, $\overline{F}_b$, $\overline{F}_c$ are as shown in Fig. 3.38 (*c*) and the amplitude of resultant m.m.f. F_R is again $\frac{3}{2}F_m$ directed along phase *b*-axis. In other words, the resultant m.m.f. has turned through a further space angle of 60° from its position occupied at instant 2. At other instants of time, *i.e.*, as the time passes, the resultant m.m.f. revolves further, but its amplitude remains equal to $\frac{3}{2}F_m$. In this manner a constant-amplitude rotating m.m.f. or rotating field is produced in the air-gap of a three phase machine.

Note that at instant 3, current in phase *b* is maximum and the resultant m.m.f. $F_R = \frac{3}{2}F_m$ is directed along the axis of phase *b*. It may be summarised from above that resultant m.m.f. $F_R = \frac{3}{2}F_m$ *(or peak of rotating m.m.f. wave) is directed along the axis of that phase which carries the maximum current at that instant.* Fig. 3.38 reveals that rotating m.m.f. revolves from phase *a* towards phase *b* and then phase *c* in case the phase sequence of supply currents is *abc*. A reversal of the phase sequence of supply currents will reverse the direction of rotation of the resultant m.m.f. wave.

The speed of this rotating field, as shown above, is given by Eq. (3.68) or Eq. (3.69).

Sinusoidal rotating m.m.f. wave creates in-phase sinusoidal rotating flux-density wave in the air gap. With negligible reluctance of the iron path, the peak value of *B*-wave is given by

$$B_p = \frac{\mu_0 F_R}{g} = \frac{3}{2}\frac{\mu_0 F_m}{g}$$

The resultant m.m.f. F_R crosses one air-gap length *g*. The expression for the flux per pole rotating at synchronous speed, from Eq. (3.11), is given by

$$\phi = \frac{4}{P}\cdot l \cdot r \cdot \frac{3}{2}\frac{\mu_0 F_m}{g} = \frac{6}{P}\frac{\mu_0 rl\, F_m}{g}$$

Substituting the value of F_m from Eq. (3.59), the expression for the fundamental flux per pole is given by

$$\phi = \frac{6}{P}\cdot\frac{\mu_0 rl}{g}\cdot\frac{4}{\pi}\cdot k_w\cdot\frac{N_{ph}\sqrt{2}I}{P}$$

$$= \frac{24\sqrt{2}}{\pi g P^2}\cdot \mu_0\, rl\, k_w\, N_{ph}\, I \qquad \text{...(3.70)}$$

The flux given by Eq. (3.70) is total flux per pole rotating at synchronous speed.

It should be remembered that the individual phase m.m.f. is not a rotating m.m.f. wave, its amplitude merely pulsates or alternates along its own phase axis. It is the combined action of all the three phase m.m.fs. that results in constant amplitude rotating m.m.f. wave.

The foregoing analsis can be extended to show that a rotating m.m.f. wave of constant amplitude. F_m is produced by two phase currents flowing in two-phase winding. In general, m-phase currents flowing in m-phase winding results in a rotating m.m.f. wave of constant amplitude equal to $\frac{m}{2}$ F_m. Note that F_m is the maximum m.m.f. of any one phase when current is maximum in that phase.

Thus the effect of polyphase currents in polyphase windings is equivalent to the mechanical rotation of permanent magnets, or d.c. excited field poles, at synchronous speed.

In the expression of resultant rotating m.m.f. wave $F_R = \frac{3}{2}F_m$, F_m is the m.m.f. per pole corresponding to maximum current I_m and its value is given by Eq. (3.59). If this value of F_m is substituted in $F_R = \frac{3}{2}F_m$, then the amplitude of rotating m.m.f. wave, in terms of series turns per phase N_{ph}, r.m.s. current I etc., is given by

$$F_R = \frac{3}{2}F_m = \frac{3}{2}\frac{4\sqrt{2}}{\pi}k_w\frac{N_{ph}I}{P} \text{ ATs/pole}$$

$$= 3\,\frac{2\sqrt{2}}{\pi}k_w\frac{N_{ph}I}{P} \text{ ATs/pole} \qquad \text{...(3.71 a)}$$

$$= 2.7\,k_w\frac{N_{ph}I}{P} \text{ ATs/pole} \qquad \text{...(3.71 b)}$$

For m-phase machine

$$F_R = m\,\frac{2\sqrt{2}}{\pi}k_w\frac{N_{ph}I}{P} \text{ ATs/pole} \qquad \text{...(3.72 a)}$$

$$= 0.90\,\frac{m\,k_w N_{ph}\,I}{P} \text{ ATs/pole} \qquad \text{...(3.72 b)}$$

In the foregoing analysis, only the fundamental component of the m.m.f. produced by each phase of a 3-phase winding has been considered. If the space harmonics are also taken into account in the single phase m.m.f. waves, then the resultant m.m.f. produced by 3-phase currents flowing in three phase windings, will consist of the following components :

(i) Constant amplitude fundamental m.m.f. wave rotating in the air-gap at synchronous speed.

(ii) Space harmonics of the order of 3, 9, 15 ....., *i.e.* triplen harmonics are absent.

(iii) Fifth harmonic m.m.f. wave–sinusoidally distributed in space with its amplitude constant and equal to one-fifth of that of the fundamental component. Constant amplitude fifth harmonic m.m.f. wave rotates in a direction opposite to that of the fundamental component and at a speed of one-fifth of that of the fundamental synchronous speed.

(iv) Seventh harmonic m.m.f. wave–sinusoidally distributed in space with its amplitude constant and equal to one-seventh of that of the fundamental component. Constant amplitude seventh harmonic m.m.f. wave rotates in the direction of the fundamental component and at a speed equal to one-seventh of that of the fundamental synchronous speed.

In general, it may be stated for *n*th harmonic m.m.f. waves that these are sinusoidally distributed in space with their constant amplitude [refer to Eq. (3.71 *b*)] equal to

$$F_n = \frac{1}{n}\left[2.7\, k_{wn} \frac{N_{ph} I}{P}\right] \text{ ATs/pole}$$

where F_n is the constant amplitude of *n*th harmonic component and k_{wn} is the winding factor for *n*th space harmonic. Note that *n* can be equal to $6k \pm 1$ only, where *k* is an integer 1, 2, 3 .... Space harmonics of the order of $6k + 1$ (7, 13, 19........) have their constant amplitude equal to $\frac{1}{6k+1} F_1$ and rotate in the direction of fundamental component F_1 at a speed of $\frac{1}{6k+1}$ of the fundamental synchronous speed. Space harmonics of the order of $6k - 1$ (5, 11, 17......) have their constant amplitude equal to $\frac{1}{6k-1} F_1$ and rotate in a direction opposite to that of the fundamental m.m.f. wave ; at a speed of $\frac{1}{6k-1}$ of the fundamental synchronous speed.

Example 3.21. *When single-phase winding is excited by an alternating current, a pulsating m.m.f. wave is produced. Show that this stationary m.m.f. wave can be resolved into two constant amplitude travelling m.m.f. waves rotating in opposite directions at synchronous speed.*

Solution. It is seen from Fig. 3.31 that when single-phase winding having N_{ph} turns is excited by current *i*, trapezoidal m.m.f. wave is produced. The fundamental component of this m.m.f. wave is sinusoidally distributed along the air-gap periphery and is given by Eq. (3.58) as

$$F_{a1} = \frac{4}{\pi} k_w \frac{N_{ph}}{P} i \cos \alpha \qquad ...(i)$$

If single-phase winding carries sinusoidally varying current $i = I_{max} \cos \omega t$, then m.m.f. distribution, from Eq. *(i)*, is

$$F_{a1} = \frac{4}{\pi} k_w \cdot \frac{N_{ph}}{P} \cdot I_{max} \cos \omega t \cos \alpha$$

$$= F_m \cos \alpha \cos \omega t \qquad ...(ii)$$

where

$$F_m = \frac{4}{\pi} \cdot k_w \cdot \frac{N_{ph}}{P} \cdot I_{max} \qquad ...(iii)$$

Eq. *(ii)* is the same as Eq. (3.64) and F_m as given by Eq. *(iii)* is equal to F_{1pm} of Eq. (3.59). As stated earlier, F_m is the m.m.f. per pole corresponding to maximum current I_{max}. As exciting current varies, magnitude of F_m also varies accordingly, but its axis remains along the magnetic axis of single-phase winding.

In Eq. *(ii)*, cos α indicates that m.m.f. is sinusoidally distributed in space along the air-gap periphery and cos ω*t* implies that m.m.f. amplitude varies sinusoidally in time at frequency ω as shown in Fig. 3.32 *(b)*.

By using the trigonometric identity, $\cos a \cos b = \frac{1}{2}\cos(a-b) + \frac{1}{2}\cos(a+b)$, Eq. *(ii)* can be re-written in the form Fig. 3.39. Total m.m.f. of single-phase winding resolved into two counter-rotating mmf waves.

$$F_{a1} = \frac{1}{2} F_m \cos(\alpha - \omega t) + \frac{1}{2} F_m \cos(\alpha + \omega t) = F_f + F_b \qquad ...(iv)$$

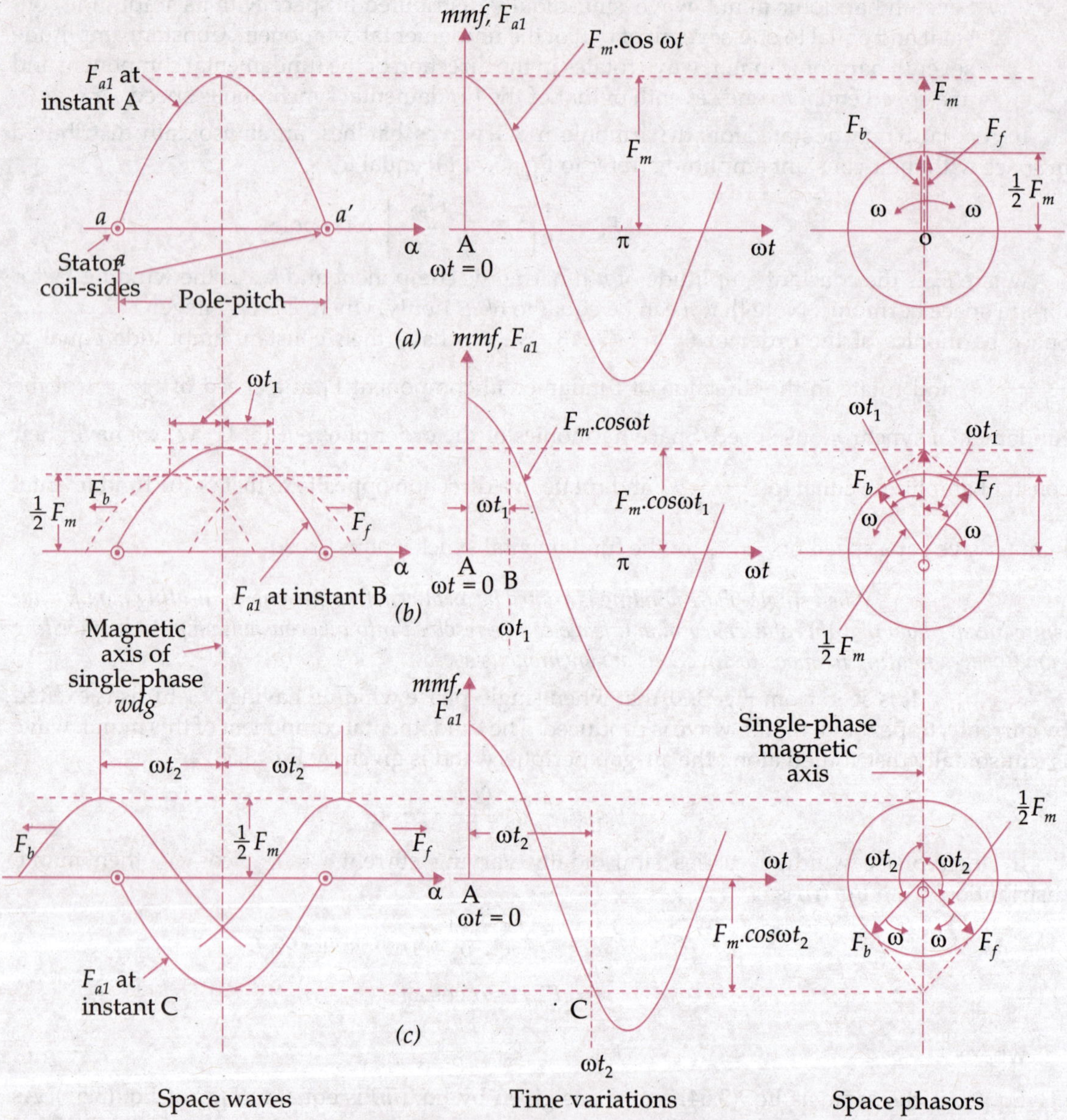

Fig 3.39: Total m.m.f. of single-phase winding resolved into two counter-rotating m.m.f. waves.

Here $F_f = \frac{1}{2} F_m \cos(\alpha - \omega t)$ represents a rotating m.m.f. wave travelling in the forward (positive α) direction at synchronous speed ω. The other component $F_b = \frac{1}{2} F_m \cos(\alpha + \omega t)$ is also a rotating m.m.f. wave but travelling in the backward (negative α) direction at synchronous speed ω. The amplitude of both F_f and F_b is $\frac{1}{2} F_m$ which is half of the amplitude F_m of the pulsating m.m.f. wave.

A physical picture of the two counter-rotating m.m.f. waves can be gained by referring to Fig. 3.39, where single-phase winding is by one full pitch coil *aa′* on stator. When i = maximum current I_{max}, the amplitude of m.m.f. is $F_{a1} = F_m$ as along the axis of single-phase winding at $\omega t = 0$ as shown at instant A in Fig. 3.39 *(a)*. The m.m.f. F_m is resolved into $F_f = F_b = \frac{1}{2} F_m$ as shown. Both forward m.m.f. and backward m.m.f. waves travel at synchronous speed ω in opposite directions, see space-phasor diagram of Fig.3.39(a) on the extreme right.

At instant B, at an angle ωt_1 from $\omega t = 0$, the amplitude of m.m.f. wave is $F_m \cos \omega t_1$ and the two counter-rotating m.m.f. waves of amplitude $\frac{1}{2} F_m$ travel by an angle ωt_1 from the stator winding axis. However, their resultant, equal to $F_m \cos \omega t_1$, is still along the stator winding axis, Fig. 3.39(b). In the m.m.f. space wave shown in Fig. 3.39(b), the m.m.f. Fa_1 at instant B has been resolved into two sinusoidal m.m.f. waves marked F_f and F_b. Both forward and backward m.m.f. waves have travelled through an angle ωt_1, forward F_f wave to the right and backward m.m.f. wave F_b to the left. In the space-phasor diagram of Fig. 3.39(b), F_f has rotated clockwise (forward) by an angle ωt_1 and F_b has rotated anticlockwise (backward) by angle ωt_1.

An instant C, at an angle ωt_2 from instant A ($\omega t = 0$), the two half amplitude components $F_f = F_b = \frac{1}{2} F_m$ would travel or rotate through an angle ωt_2 as shown respectively in space-wave and space-phasor diagrams of Fig. 3.39(c). But their resultant mmf $F_m \cos \omega t_2$ remains along the magnetic axis of the stator winding.

It must be kept in mind that single-phase winding when excited by an alternating current does not produce two counter-rotating m.m.f. waves. It always produces one stationary m.m.f. wave pulsating along its magnetic axis. It is the decomposition of the m.m.f. of a single-phase winding into two counter-rotating m.m.f. waves ; this is a very important concept which helps in the understanding of a.c. electrical machinery to a great extent.

Example 3.22. *A single-phase winding, when excited by an alternating current, produces one pulsating m.m.f. wave which can be decomposed into two counter-rotating m.m.f. waves travelling at synchronous speed. Use this concept to prove that a rotating magnetic field of constant amplitude is produced when 3-phase balanced winding is excited by three phase balanced currents.*

Solution. A three-phase rotating electrical machine is wound with three windings *a, b, c* displaced from each other by a space angle of 120° as shown in Fig. 3.36 *(b)*. Consider that these windings are excited respectively by three-phase balanced currents given by

$$\left.\begin{aligned} i_a &= I_{max} \cos \omega t \\ i_b &= I_{max} \cos (\omega t - 120°) \\ i_c &= I_{max} \cos (\omega t - 240°) \end{aligned}\right\} \quad ...(i)$$

These currents in phase winding *a, b, c* set up three pulsating m.m.f. waves in the air-gap. These m.m.fs are directed along the magnetic axis of phases *a, b, c* as indicated in Fig. 3.36 *(b)*. For the currents given by Eq. *(i)* and with the magnetic axis of 3-phase winding displaced in space by 120°, the three m.m.fs F_a, F_b and F_c can be expressed mathematically as

$$\begin{aligned} F_a &= F_m \cos \alpha \cos \omega t \\ F_b &= F_m \cos (\alpha - 120°) \cos (\omega t - 120°) \\ F_c &= F_m \cos (\alpha - 240°), \cos (\omega t - 240°) \end{aligned}$$

Note that angle α is measured from the axis of phase *a* as shown in Fig. 3.36 *(b)*. As in Example 3.21, the pulsating m.m.f. of phase *a* can be expressed as

$$F_a = \frac{1}{2} F_m \cos (\alpha - \omega t) + \frac{1}{2} F_m \cos (\alpha + \omega t) \quad ...(ii)$$

Similarly, for phases *b* and *c*,

$$F_b = \frac{1}{2} F_m \cos (\alpha - 120° - \omega t + 120°) + \frac{1}{2} F_m \cos (\alpha - 120° + \omega t - 120°)$$

$$F_b = \frac{1}{2} F_m \cos (\alpha - \omega t) + \frac{1}{2} F_m \cos (\alpha + \omega t - 240°) \quad ...(iii)$$

$$F_c = \frac{1}{2} F_m \cos(\alpha - 240° - \omega t + 240°) + \frac{1}{2} F_m \cos(\alpha - 240° + \omega t - 240°)$$

$$= \frac{1}{2} F_m \cos(\alpha - \omega t) + \frac{1}{2} F_m \cos(\alpha + \omega t - 120°) \quad ...(iv)$$

The resultant m.m.f. $F_R(\alpha, t)$ can be obtained by adding the three m.m.f.s given by Eqs. *(ii)*, *(iii)* and *(iv)*.

$$\therefore F_R(\alpha, t) = F_a + F_b + F_c$$

$$= \frac{1}{2} F_m [\cos(\alpha - \omega t) + \cos(\alpha + \omega t) + \cos(\alpha - \omega t) + \cos(\alpha + \omega t - 240°) + \cos(\alpha - \omega t) + \cos(\alpha + \omega t - 120°)]$$

$$= \frac{3}{2} F_m \cos(\alpha - \omega t) + \frac{1}{2} F_m [\cos(\alpha + \omega t) + \cos(\alpha + \omega t - 120°) + \cos(\alpha + \omega t - 240°)] \quad ...(v)$$

But $\frac{1}{2} F_m \cos(\alpha + \omega t)$, $\frac{1}{2} F_m \cos(\alpha + \omega t - 120°)$, $\frac{1}{2} F_m \cos(\alpha + \omega t - 240°)$ represent three m.m.f. sinusoids displaced in phase by 120°. Therefore, their sum must be zero, *i.e.*,

$$\frac{1}{2} F_m [\cos(\alpha + \omega t) + \cos(\alpha + \omega t - 120) + \cos(\alpha + \omega t - 240)] = 0$$

Eq. *(v)*, therefore, reduces to $F_R(\alpha, t) = \frac{3}{2} F_m \cdot \cos(\alpha - \omega t)$ ...*(vi)*

It can be shown that Eq. *(vi)* represents a travelling m.m.f. wave of constant amplitude $\frac{3}{2} F_m$.

At $\omega t = 0°$, $F_R(\alpha, t) = \frac{3}{2} F_m \cos\alpha$

At $\omega t = 45°$, $F_R(\alpha, t) = \frac{3}{2} F_m \cos(\alpha - 45°)$

At $\omega t = 90°$, $F_R(\alpha, t) = \frac{3}{2} F_m \cos(\alpha - 90°) = \frac{3}{2} F_m \sin\alpha$

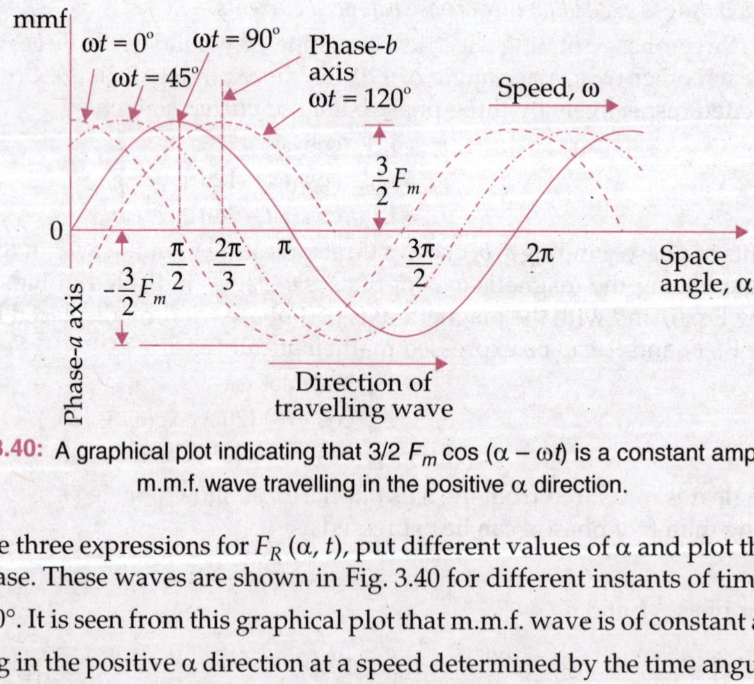

Fig 3.40: A graphical plot indicating that 3/2 $F_m \cos(\alpha - \omega t)$ is a constant amplitude m.m.f. wave travelling in the positive α direction.

In the above three expressions for $F_R(\alpha, t)$, put different values of α and plot these three waves with α as the base. These waves are shown in Fig. 3.40 for different instants of time corresponding to 0°, 45° and 90°. It is seen from this graphical plot that m.m.f. wave is of constant amplitude $\frac{3}{2} F_m$ and is travelling in the positive α direction at a speed determined by the time angular frequency ω.

Thus, the space angle α in Eq. *(vi)* means that the m.m.f. wave at any moment is sinusoidally distributed in space along the air-gap periphery. The time angle ωt in Eq. *(vi)* means that the entire waveform is travelling along the air-gap circumference at a constant angular $\omega = 2\pi f$ electrical radians per second (called synchronous speed). For a *P*-pole machine, the synchronous speed ω_m, from Eq. (3.3), is

$$\omega_m = \frac{2}{P}\,\omega = \frac{4\pi f}{P} \text{ rad/sec}$$

or
$$n_s = \frac{2\pi f}{P} \text{ r.p.s.}$$

or
$$N_s = \frac{120f}{P} \text{ r.p.m.}$$

An examination of Eq. *(vi)* and Fig. 3.40 reveals that

(i) when $\omega t = 0°$ and $\alpha = 0°$, current in phase *a* is maximum [Eq. *(i)*] and peak of travelling m.m.f. wave $\frac{3}{2}F_m$ is along the axis of phase *a*,

(ii) when $\omega t = 120°$ and $\alpha = 120°$, current i_b is maximum and peak of travelling m.m.f. wave is along the axis of phase *b* ; because from Eq. *(vi)*, $F_R = \frac{3}{2}F_m \cos(120° - 120°) = \frac{3}{2}F_m$.

(iii) Similarly, when $\omega t = 240°$ and $\alpha = 240°$, peak of travelling m.m.f. wave is aligned along the axis of phase *c*.

In general, it can be stated that peak of rotating m.m.f. wave travels from phase *a*, to phase *b* and then to phase *c* [*i.e.* clockwise in Fig. 3.36 *(b)*] when phase sequence of three phase supply is *abc*.

Example 3.23. *In a uniform air-gap (non-salient pole) machine, show that the space harmonics present in the rotating m.m.f. wave, generate only fundamental frequency voltages in the stator winding.*

Solution. Flux = m.m.f. × permeance

Neglecting magnetic saturation, the permeance offered to the magnetic flux is constant for a uniform air-gap machine. Thus the flux is proportional to the m.m.f. In view of this, *n*th space harmonic m.m.f. wave will produce *n*th space hamonic flux wave.

Let the speed of the fundamental component of rotating flux wave be N_{s1}. Then speed of the *n*th harmonic flux wave $= \frac{1}{n}N_{s1}$.

Now number of harmonic poles, produced by *n*th harmonic

= *n* (poles *P*, produced by the fundamental flux wave) = *nP*

Frequency of the generated e.m.f. in the stator winding, due to fundamental rotating flux wave having *P* poles is given by

$$f = \frac{(\text{Relative speed})(\text{Poles } P)}{120} = \frac{N_{s1}P}{120}$$

Frequency of the generated e.m.f. in the stator winding, due to *n*th space harmonic rotating m.m.f. wave having *nP* poles is given by

$$\frac{(\text{Relative velocity})(\text{Harmonic poles})}{120} = \frac{\left(\frac{1}{n}N_{s1}\right)(nP)}{120} = \frac{N_{s1}P}{120} = f$$

This proves the required result.

Example 3.24. *Find the amplitude of m.m.f. produced by a squirrel cage winding.*

Solution. A squirrel cage winding, as described before, consists of one bar in each slot and these bars are short-circuited by end rings at both the sides. If rotor has *S* slots, then there are *S* bars or *S* conductors. In effect *S* bars are equivalent to $\frac{S}{2}$ phases, each phase having single full-pitched turn. Since the winding factor of single full-pitched turn is unity, the amplitude of resultant m.m.f. wave, from Eq. (3.72 *b*) is

$$F_R = 0.90\,\frac{S}{2}\,\frac{(1)(1)I}{P}\ \text{ATs/pole} = 0.45\,\frac{SI}{P}\ \text{ATs/pole}$$

Here I is the r.m.s. value of the bar current.

Example 3.25. *Three-phase voltages are applied to the three windings of an electrical machine. If any two supply terminals are interchanged, show that the direction of rotating m.m.f. wave is reversed, though its amplitude remains unaltered.*

Solution. For this example, either graphical or mathematical analysis may be used. For better physical concepts, first mathematical and then graphical analysis are given here.

The m.m.f. for phase a, pulsating with time and stationary in space, can be written by referring to Eq. (3.64) as

$$F_a = F_m \cos \omega t \cos \alpha.$$

Suppose the supply terminals to phases b and c are interchanged, then for phase b, the space angle displacement remains at 120°, but time phase angle must now become 240° instead of 120°. In other words, $\cos\left(\omega t - \frac{2\pi}{3}\right)$ must be replaced by $\cos\left(\omega t - \frac{4\pi}{3}\right)$ for phase b m.m.f., because supply terminals b and c are interchanged. In view of this, phase b m.m.f. F_b should be written as

$$F_b = F_m \cos\left(\omega t - \frac{4\pi}{3}\right) \cos\left(\alpha - \frac{2\pi}{3}\right)$$

Similar reasoning leads to phase c m.m.f. as

$$F_c = F_m \cos\left(\omega t - \frac{2\pi}{3}\right) \cos\left(\alpha - \frac{4\pi}{3}\right)$$

The resultant of three pulsating m.m.f. waves is

$$F_R(\alpha, t) = F_a + F_b + F_c$$

$$= F_m \left[\cos \omega t \cos \alpha + \cos\left(\omega t - \frac{4\pi}{3}\right)\cos\left(\alpha - \frac{2\pi}{3}\right) + \cos\left(\omega t - \frac{2\pi}{3}\right)\cos\left(\alpha - \frac{4\pi}{3}\right)\right]$$

$$= \frac{F_m}{2}\,[\cos(\alpha - \omega t) + \cos(\alpha + \omega t) + \cos(\alpha - \omega t - 120 + 240) + \cos(\alpha + \omega t - 2\pi)$$
$$+ \cos(\alpha - \omega t - 240 + 120) + \cos(\alpha + \omega t - 2\pi)]$$

But $\cos(\alpha + \omega t - 2\pi) = \cos(\alpha + \omega t)$ and $\cos(\alpha - \omega t + 120°) = \cos(\alpha - \omega t - 240°)$

$$\therefore\ F_R(\alpha, t) = \frac{F_m}{2}\,[\cos(\alpha - \omega t) + \cos(\alpha + \omega t) + \cos(\alpha - \omega t - 240°) + \cos(\alpha + \omega t)$$
$$+ \cos(\alpha - \omega t - 120) + \cos(\alpha + \omega t)]$$

Now $\cos(\alpha - \omega t) + \cos(\alpha - \omega t - 120) + \cos(\alpha - \omega t + 240) = 0$

$$\therefore \qquad F_R(\alpha, t) = \frac{3}{2} F_m \cos(\alpha + \omega t) \qquad ...(i)$$

A plot of Eq. *(i)* shows that the resultant m.m.f. is of constant amplitude $\frac{3}{2} F_m$, but it is travelling in the negative α direction, Fig. 3.41 *(a)*. If the phases b and c were not interchanged, then the m.m.f. would travel in the positive α direction as depicted in Fig. 3.40.

This proves that if any two supply terminals are interchanged, the amplitude of rotating field remains unaltered, but its direction of rotation is reversed. This procedure (reversing any two supply lines) is adopted in a 3-phase induction motor if its direction of rotation is to be reversed.

For graphical analysis, refer to Fig. 3.36 *(c)* and Fig. 3.38. At instant 1, $i_a = I_m$, $i_b = i_c = -\frac{I_m}{2}$. Since i_b and i_c are interchanged, $i_b = i_c = -\frac{I_m}{2}$ and the resultant m.m.f. is directed along the phase a axis, as shown in Fig. 3.38 *(a)*. At instant 2, $i_a = \frac{I_m}{2}$, $i_b = \frac{I_m}{2}$ and $I_c = -I_m$. After supply terminals of phases b and c are interchanged, current $\frac{I_m}{2}$ flows in phase winding c (indicated by cross in c' and dot in c) and current $-I_m$ flows in phase winding b (indicated by dot in b' and cross in b), Fig. 3.41 *(b)*. As a result of it, the resultant m.m.f. wave is as shown in Fig. 3.41 *(b)*. Note that the resultant m.m.f. has rotated anti-clockwise through an angle of 60 electrical space degrees. At instant 3, F_R will travel further by an angle of 60 electrical space degrees. This shows that if any two supply terminals to 3-phase winding are interchanged, the direction of rotating m.m.f. wave gets reversed. If supply terminals to phases b and c were not interchanged, then rotating m.m.f. wave would travel in the clockwise direction, as shown in Fig. 3.38. Thus graphical analysis also proves the required result.

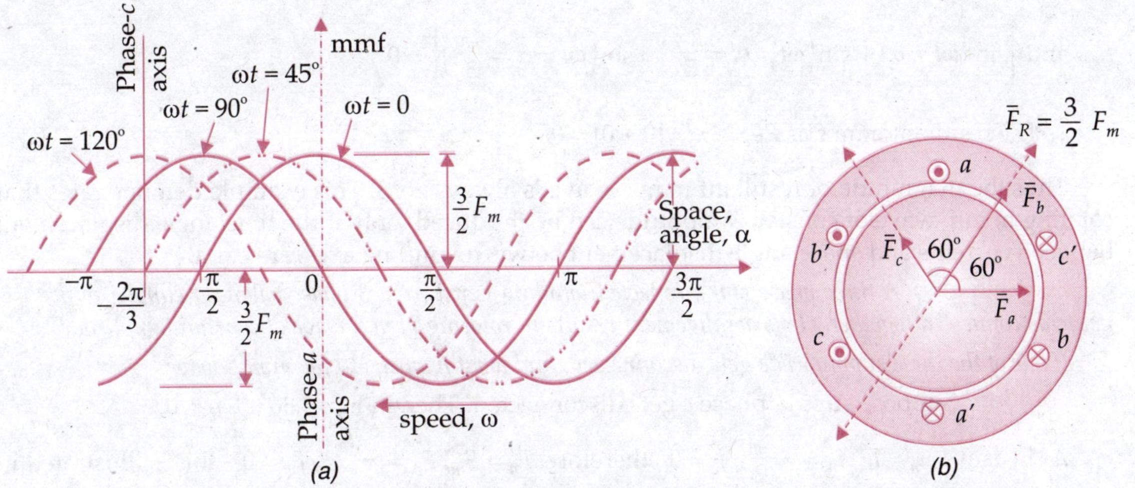

Fig 3.41: Pertaining to Example 3.25.

Example 3.26. *Fig. 3.42 shows three coils a, b, c ; with their magnetic axis coincident. Coils a, b, c are excited by three phase balanced currents*

$$I_m \sin \omega t,\ I_m \sin\left(\omega t - \frac{2\pi}{3}\right) \text{ and } I_m \sin\left(\omega t - \frac{4\pi}{3}\right)$$

respectively. Find the magnitude of resultant m.m.f. wave.

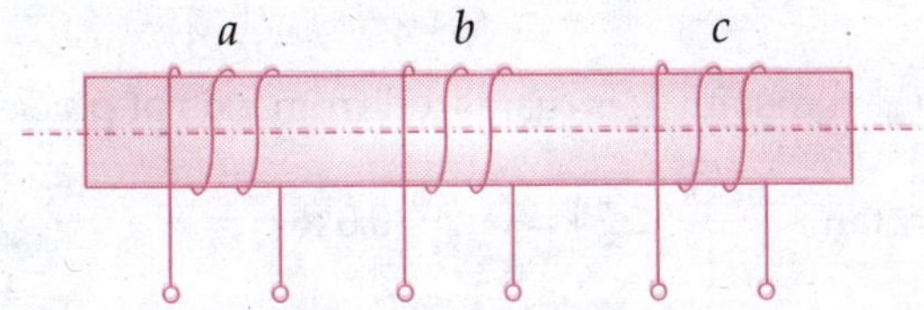

Fig 3.42: Pertainig to Example 3.26.

Solution. The m.m.fs. produced by three coils a, b, c are proportional to their respective currents. These can, therefore, be expressed as

$$F_a = F_m \sin \omega t \cos \alpha,\ F_b = F_m \sin\left(\omega t - \frac{2\pi}{3}\right) \cos \alpha \text{ and } F_c = F_m \sin\left(\omega t - \frac{4\pi}{3}\right) \cos \alpha.$$

The three currents are displaced in time phase by 120° or $2\pi/3$ radians, but the angle of space displacement between the magnetic axes of the three coils is zero as shown in Fig. 3.42. It is due to this reason that cos α appears in all the three m.m.f. expressions given above.

Their resultant m.m.f. is

$$F_R(\alpha, t) = F_a + F_b + F_c$$

$$= F_m \left[\sin \omega t \cos \alpha + \sin\left(\omega t - \frac{2\pi}{3}\right)\cos \alpha + \sin\left(\omega t - \frac{4\pi}{3}\right)\cos \alpha\right]$$

$$= \frac{F_m}{2}\left[\sin(\omega t + \alpha) + \sin(\omega t - \alpha) + \sin\left(\omega t + \alpha - \frac{2\pi}{3}\right) + \sin\left(\omega t - \alpha - \frac{2\pi}{3}\right)\right.$$
$$\left. + \sin\left(\omega t + \alpha - \frac{2\pi}{3}\right) + \sin\left(\omega t - \alpha - \frac{4\pi}{3}\right)\right]$$

But $\left[\sin(\omega t + \alpha) + \sin\left(\omega t + \alpha - \frac{2\pi}{3}\right) + \sin\left(\omega t + \alpha - \frac{4\pi}{3}\right)\right] = 0$

and $\left[\sin(\omega t - \alpha) + \sin\left(\omega t - \alpha - \frac{2\pi}{3}\right) + \sin\left(\omega t - \alpha - \frac{4\pi}{3}\right)\right] = 0$

$\therefore$ The resultant m.m.f. is $F_R = \frac{F_m}{2}[0 + 0] = 0.$

Thus the magnitude of resultant m.m.f. wave is always zero. This example demonstrates that rotating m.m.f. wave of constant amplitude can be produced, only if the time angle displacement between currents and space angle displacement between winding axes, are equal.

Example 3.27. *A three phase star-connected winding is fed from 3-phase balanced supply, with their neutrals connected together. (This arrangement results in rotating m.m.f. wave of constant amplitude).*

If one of the three supply leads gets disconnected, find what happens to the m.m.f. wave.

Solution. Suppose supply phase c gets disconnected. Then in Fig. 3.36 (*c*), $i_c = 0$.

At instant 1, $i_a = I_m$, $i_b = -\frac{I_m}{2}$, $i_c = 0$; therefore, $F_a = F_m$, $F_b = -\frac{F_m}{2}$, $F_c = 0$ – this is illustrated in Fig. 3.43 (*a*). The amplitude of the resultant m.m.f. wave is

$$F_R = \sqrt{(\text{Horizontal comp.})^2 + (\text{Vertical comp.})^2}$$

$$= \sqrt{\left(F_m + \frac{F_m}{2}\cos 60°\right)^2 + \left(\frac{F_m}{2}\sin 60°\right)^2}$$

$$= \sqrt{\left(\frac{5}{4}F_m\right)^2 + \left(\frac{\sqrt{3}}{4}F_m\right)^2} = \frac{\sqrt{7}}{4}F_m = 1.32\, F_m.$$

Resultant m.m.f. 1.32 F_m at instant 1, is displaced from axis of phase a, by an angle given by

$$\tan^{-1}\left(\frac{\text{Vert. comp.}}{\text{Horiz. comp}}\right) = \tan^{-1}\left(\frac{\sqrt{3}}{4} \times \frac{4}{5}\right) = \tan^{-1}(0.3464) = 19.1°$$

At an instant 30° away from instant 1, $i_a = \frac{\sqrt{3}}{2} I_m$, $i_b = 0$, $i_c = 0$, therefore, $F_a = \frac{\sqrt{3}}{2} F_m$, $F_b = F_c = 0$, Fig. 3.43 (*b*). Thus the amplitude of the resultant m.m.f. wave is $\frac{\sqrt{3}}{2} F_m = 0.866\, F_m$ and it is centred along phase a-axis.

From instant 1 to instant 30° away from it, the time-phase angle covered is 30°, whereas the space angle covered is only 19.1°. This means that between these two instants, rotating m.m.f. has changed its amplitude from 1.32F_m to 0.866 F_m and travels at a speed less than the synchronous speed given by Eq. (3.69).

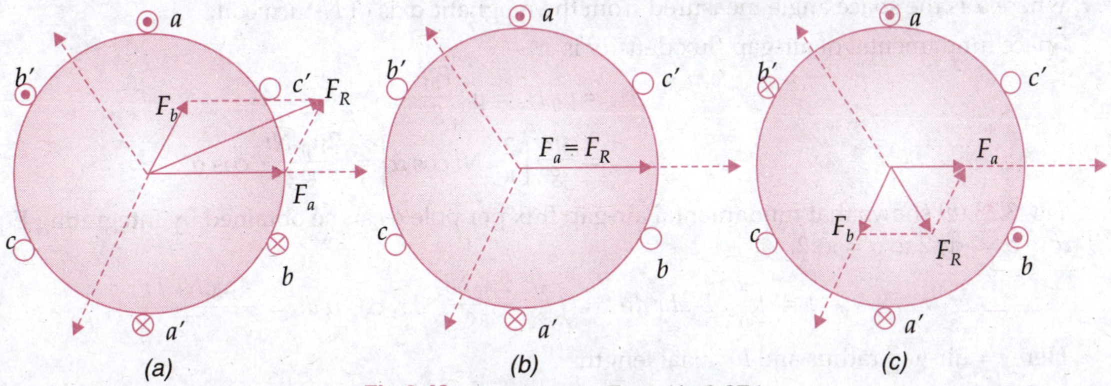

Fig 3.43: Pertaining to Example 3.27.

At instant 2, $$i_a = i_b = \frac{I_m}{2}, i_c = 0$$

and $$F_a = F_b = \frac{F_m}{2}, F_c = 0, \text{Fig. 3.43 } (c).$$

$$\therefore F_R = \sqrt{(\text{Horiz. comp.})^2 + (\text{Vert. comp.})^2} = \sqrt{\left(\frac{F_m}{2} - \frac{F_m}{2}\cos 60°\right)^2 + \left(\frac{F_m}{2}\sin 60°\right)^2}$$

$$= \sqrt{\left(\frac{F_m}{4}\right)^2 + \left(\frac{\sqrt{3}}{4}F_m\right)^2} = \frac{F_m}{2}.$$

The resultant m.m.f. F_R at instant 2 is displaced from phase *a*-axis, by an angle given by

$$\tan^{-1}\left\{\frac{\sqrt{3}}{4} \times \frac{4}{1}\right\} = \tan^{-1}(\sqrt{3}) = 60°$$

From an instant 30° away from instant 1 and upto instant 2, the time-angle covered is 30°, whereas the space angle covered is 60°. This means that between these two instants, the rotating m.m.f. wave has changed its amplitude from $0.866F_m$ to $0.5F_m$ and travels faster than the synchronous speed given by Eq. (3.69).

At instant 3, the resultant m.m.f. wave will be found to be $1.32F_m$ and it will be seen that from instant 2 to instant 3, the time phase angle covered is 60°, whereas the space phase angle travelled is more than 60°.

Thus, with one supply phase disconnected, a rotating m.m.f. wave of varying amplitude is produced. Note that the varying-amplitude-rotating m.m.f. wave does not travel at constant synchronous speed given by Eq. (3.69), but at a speed fluctuating around the synchronous speed.

In case the three-phase winding is delta connected or star-connected without neutral, then disconnection of one of the supply leads, results in single-phase operation of the machine, *i.e.* the m.m.f. becomes stationary and pulsating in nature.

Example 3.28. *Derive an expression for the self-inductance of a single N-turn full-pitched coil belonging to a uniform air-gap machine of gap length g, radius r and core length l. Saturation and leakage flux are neglected.*

Solution. A single *N*-turn full-pitched coil, Fig. 3.28 *(a)*, produces rectangular m.m.f. wave of magnitude $\frac{1}{2}Ni$ as shown in Fig. 3.28 *(b)*.

Its fundamental component is given by Eq. (3. 53 *a*) as

$$F_{a1} = \frac{4}{\pi} \cdot \frac{Ni}{2} \cos\alpha \text{ ATs/pole}$$

where α is the space angle measured from the magnetic axis of N-turn coil.

Space fundamental of air-gap flux density is

$$B_g = \mu_0 H_g = \mu_0 \frac{F_{a1}}{g}$$

$$= \frac{\mu_0}{g}\left[\frac{2}{\pi}\cdot Ni\cos\alpha\right] = \frac{2\mu_0.Ni}{\pi.g}\cos\alpha \quad ...(i)$$

Fig. 3.28 *(b)* shows that fundamental air-gap flux per pole ϕ can be obtained by integrating Eq. *(i)* from $\alpha = -\pi/2$ to $\alpha = \pi/2$.

$$\therefore \quad \phi = \int_{-\pi/2}^{\pi/2} B_g.l.r\, d\alpha = \int_{-\pi/2}^{\pi/2} \frac{2\mu_0 Ni}{\pi g}.l.r.\cos\alpha\, d\alpha = \frac{4\mu_0.Ni.\,l\,r}{\pi g} \quad ...(ii)$$

Here r = air-gap radius and l = axial length

$\therefore$ Self-inductance of N-turn full-pitched coil is

$$L = \frac{\text{flux linkage with this coil}}{\text{current in this coil}} = \frac{N\phi}{i}$$

$$= \frac{N}{i}\left[\frac{4\mu_0.Ni.\,l\,r}{\pi g}\right] = \frac{4\mu_0.N^2.l.r}{\pi g}$$

Example 3.29. *(a) A uniform air-gap machine of gap length g, core length l and radius r, has distributed winding having N_{ph} series turns per phase with winding factor k_w. Show that self-inductance of these series turns is given by*

$$L = \frac{16\mu_0 rl}{\pi g P^2}(k_w N_{ph})^2$$

Saturation and leakage flux are neglected.

Hence show that self-inductance of phase winding, with uniformly distributed full-pitched coils is given by

(i) $L_\alpha = L_\beta = \frac{128\,\mu_0 rl}{\pi^3 g P^2}\cdot N_{ph}^2$ *for a 2-phase machine and*

(ii) $L_a = L_b = L_c = \frac{144\,\mu_0 rl}{\pi^3 g P^2}\cdot N_{ph}^2$ *for a 3-phase machine.*

(b) Show that the mutual inductance between stator phase winding with N_{phs} series per phase and rotor phase winding with N_{phr} series turns per phase is given by

$$M = \frac{16\mu_0 rl}{\pi g P^2}[(k_{ws}\cdot N_{phs})(k_{wr} N_{phr})]$$

Solution. *(a)* For a P-pole machine, the peak value of fundamental sine component of m.m.f. with N_{ph} series turns is given by Eq. (3.57) as

$$F_{1p} = \frac{4}{\pi}k_w\frac{i.N_{ph}}{P}\text{ ATs/pole}$$

$$\therefore \quad B_p = \mu_0\frac{F_{1p}}{g} = \frac{\mu_0}{g}\left[\frac{4}{\pi}k_w.\frac{i.N_{ph}}{P}\right]$$

From Eq. (3.11), the flux per pole is $\phi = \frac{4}{P}rl.B_p = \frac{4}{P}rl\left[\frac{\mu_0}{g}\left(\frac{4}{\pi}\cdot k_w\cdot\frac{i.N_{ph}}{P}\right)\right]$

$$= \frac{16\mu_0 rl}{\pi g P^2}(k_w\cdot i\,N_{ph})$$

∴ Stator self-inductance, $L = \dfrac{(\text{Effective stator turns}).\phi}{i}$

∴ $$L = \left[\frac{k_w.N_{ph}}{i}\right]\left[\frac{16\,\mu_0 rl}{\pi g P^2}\cdot k_w.i.N_{ph}\right]$$

$$= \frac{16\,\mu_0 rl}{\pi g P^2}\,(k_w\,N_{ph})^2$$

(i) For uniformly distributed full-pitched winding, $k_p = 1$. For a two-phase winding, the phase spread σ is 90°

$$k_d = \frac{\sin\frac{\sigma}{2}}{\frac{\sigma}{2}} = \frac{\sin\frac{90}{2}}{\frac{90}{2}\times\frac{\pi}{180}} = \frac{2\sqrt{2}}{\pi}.$$

∴ $$k_w = k_p \times k_d = \frac{2\sqrt{2}}{\pi}.$$

∴ Self-inductance for any one phase of a two-phase machine is

$$L_\alpha = L_\beta = \frac{16\mu_0 rl}{\pi g P^2}\left(\frac{2\sqrt{2}}{\pi}\cdot N_{ph}\right)^2 = \frac{128\mu_0 rl}{\pi^3 g P^2}\cdot N_{ph}^{\,2}$$

(ii) For full-pitched coils, $k_p = 1$. For a three-phase winding, the phase spread σ is usually 60°.

∴ $$k_d = \frac{\sin\frac{60}{2}}{\frac{60}{2}\times\frac{\pi}{180}} = \frac{3}{\pi}.$$

∴ $$k_w = k_p \times k_d = \frac{3}{\pi}$$

∴ Self-inductance for any one phase of a three-phase machine is

$$L_a = L_b = L_c = \frac{16\mu_0 rl}{\pi g P^2}\left[\frac{3}{\pi}\cdot N_{pl}\right]^2 = \frac{144\mu_0 rl}{\pi^3 g P^2}\,N_{ph}^{\,2}.$$

(b) Current i_s in the stator series turns per phase $N_{ph.s}$ produce a fundamental sine flux ϕ_s, [from part *(a)*] is given by

$$\phi_s = \frac{16\mu_0 rl}{\pi g P^2}\,[k_{ws}\,N_{ph.s}]\,i_s$$

Mutual inductance $M = \dfrac{\phi_s\,(\text{effective rotor turns})}{i_s}$

$$= \frac{16\mu_0 rl}{\pi g P^2}\,(k_{ws}\,.\,N_{phs})\,i_s\left[\frac{k_{wr}.N_{phr}}{i_s}\right]$$

$$= \frac{16\mu_0 rl}{\pi g P^2}\,[(k_{ws}.N_{ph.s})(k_{wr}.N_{phr})]$$

Example 3.30. *A 6-pole, 50 Hz, 3-phase induction motor has a stator bore diameter of 1.2 metres. Its stator is cut and laid out flat, so that rotating m.m.f. wave now becomes a travelling m.m.f. wave. Find the linear velocity of the travelling m.m.f. wave in metres per second.*

Solution. Speed of rotating m.m.f. wave $= \dfrac{2f}{P}$ r.p.s.

But in one revolution, a peripheral distance of πD metres is traversed.

$$\therefore \quad \text{Speed of travelling m.m.f. wave} = \frac{2f}{P}(\pi D)\ \text{m/sec} = 2f\left(\frac{\pi D}{P}\right)\ \text{m/sec.}$$

$$= 2f\,(\text{pole-pitch}) = f\,(\lambda)\ \text{m/sec.}$$

Here λ is the wavelength of the travelling m.m.f. wave and is equal to two pole-pitches.

For a diameter $D = 1.2$ m, the speed of travelling m.m.f. wave

$$= 2f\left(\frac{\pi \times 1.2}{6}\right) = 100\left(\frac{\pi \times 1.2}{6}\right) = 62.82\ \text{m/sec.}$$

Example 3.31. *Sketch the resultant m.m.f. wave for a 2-pole, 3-phase balanced winding when phase a carries (i) maximum current I_m (ii) I_m cos 30° and (iii) I_m cos 60°. Consider each belt of the winding as a current sheet of uniform density.*

Solution. The stator shown in Fig. 3.36 *(a)* is cut and laid out flat as shown in Fig. 3.44 *(a)*. Note that the sequence of phase belts is *a, c′, b, a′, c, b′*.

(i) When $i_a = I_m$, $i_b = i_c = -I_m/2$. These currents are indicated in Fig. 3.44 *(a)* by dots and crosses. For convenience, phase belts, *a, c′, b* etc. are shown in the same plane. Note that dots and crosses in Fig. 3.44 *(a)* are identical to that in Fig. 3.38 *(a)*. By referring to Fig. 3.30, m.m.f. for phase *a* is as shown. For I_m, maximum m.m.f. is F_m as given by Eq. (3.59). For phases *b* and *c*, the maximum m.m.f. is $F_m/2$ as $|i_b| = |i_c| = \frac{1}{2} I_m$. Note that for phase belt with dot, the m.m.f. variation has positive slope and for phase belt with cross, the m.m.f. variation has negative slope. Summation of the ordinates in Fig. 3.44 *(b)*, *(c)*, *(d)* gives the resultant m.m.f. variation as shown in Fig. 3.44. *(e)*.

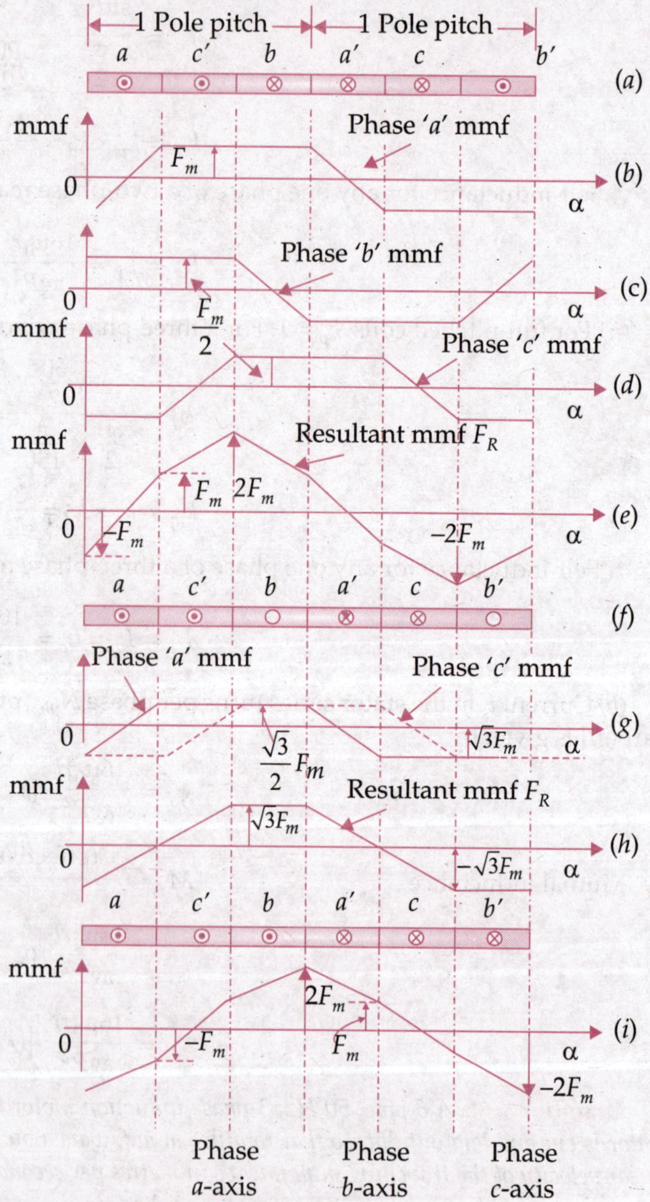

Fig 3.44: Pertaining to Example 3.31.

(*ii*) When $i_a = I_m \cos 30° = \frac{\sqrt{3}}{2} I_m$, $i_b = 0$ and $i_c = -\frac{\sqrt{3}}{2} I_m$. These currents are shown in Fig.3.44 (*f*), m.m.f. variation for phase *a* is shown by solid line and for phase *c* by dotted line in Fig. 3.44 (*g*). Phase *b* produces no m.m.f. as $i_b = 0$. Resultant m.m.f. variation is shown in Fig. (3.44 *h*).

(*iii*) For $i_a = I_m \cos 60° = \frac{1}{2} I_m$, $i_b = \frac{1}{2} I_m$ and $i_c = -I_m$. The m.m.fs. for individual phases *a, b, c* can be drawn accordingly ; this is left as an exercise for the reader. The resultant m.m.f., however, is shown in Fig. 3.44 (*i*).

3.8. PRODUCTION OF TORQUE IN NON-SALIENT POLE MACHINES

The purpose of this article is to derive a general torque expression for rotating electrical machines, in terms of two magnetic fields, one produced by stator currents and the other by rotor currents. In order to obtain this torque expression, an elementary two-pole uniform air-gap (or non-salient pole) machine, shown in Fig. 3.45 (*a*), is considered.

Currents in the stator winding produce stator m.m.f., which is assumed sinusoidally distributed in space, *i.e.*, along the air-gap periphery. The peak value of the stator m.m.f. F_s is directed along stator magnetic axis. In Fig. 3.45 (*a*), the stator magnetic axis is taken to be horizontal, with F_s directed from left to right. Similarly, currents in the rotor winding produce rotor m.m.f. which is also assumed a spatial sine wave. The peak value of rotor m.m.f. F_r is directed along the rotor magnetic axis as shown in Fig. 3.45 (*a*). Note that F_s and F_r are the peak values of the stator and rotor m.m.fs. per pole (or per air-gap crossing) respectively. If stator or rotor has more than one winding then F_s is the resultant stator m.m.f. per pole produced by all stator windings and F_r is the resultant rotor m.m.f. per pole produced by all rotor windings. These two m.m.fs. F_s and F_r, in effect, cause the appearance of stator and rotor poles, along their respective magnetic axis–this is illustrated in Fig. 3.45 (*a*). The stator and rotor poles so produced, have a tendency to align their magnetic axis and in this manner, electromagnetic torque is developed. It is shown in this article that the magnitude of electromagnetic torque is proportional to the product of stator m.m.f., rotor m.m.f., and sine of the angle between their magnetic axis.

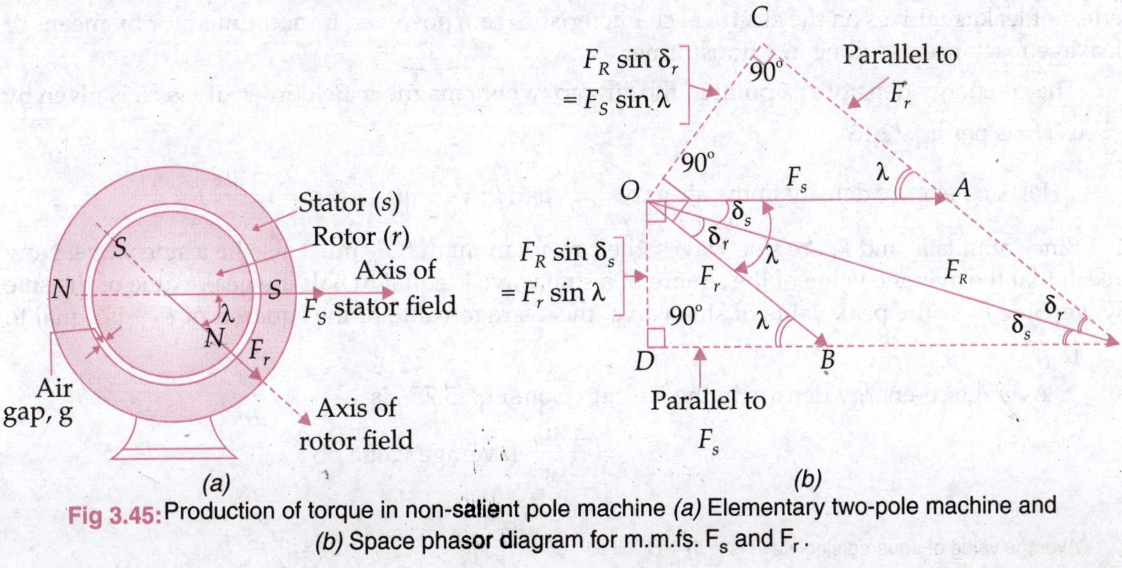

Fig 3.45: Production of torque in non-salient pole machine (*a*) Elementary two-pole machine and (*b*) Space phasor diagram for m.m.fs. F_s and F_r.

In Fig. 3.45. *(a)*, the length of the radial air-gap is g and the average radius (average of stator and rotor radii) is r. The effective axial length is l. For deriving a general torque expression, the following assumptions are made :

(i) The stator and rotor iron is assumed to have infinite permeability. This also means that the saturation and hysteresis are neglected.

(ii) Tangential (along the air-gap periphery) component of the magnetic field is negligible as compared with its radial (along the radius) component. In other words, mutual flux path across the gap length g is radial.

(iii) The length g of the air-gap is assumed much smaller in comparison with average radius r. This effectively means that there is negligible difference between the flux density at the stator surface, at the rotor surface or at any radial distance in the air-gap.

(iv) Only the fundamental sine components of the stator and rotor m.m.f. waves are considered.

Since the m.m.fs. F_s and F_r are spatial sine waves, these can be represented by space phasors $\overline{F}_s$ and $\overline{F}_r$ directed along their respective magnetic axis in Fig. 3.45 *(a)*.

The phasor sum of $\overline{F}_s$ and $\overline{F}_r$ gives the peak value of the resultant m.m.f. wave F_R acting across one air-gap. The magnitude of F_R is given by

$$F_R = \sqrt{F_s^2 + F_r^2 + 2F_s F_r \cos\lambda} \quad \text{...(3.73)}$$

Here λ is the space angle between peak values of stator m.m.f. F_s and rotor m.m.f. F_r.

Resultant field intensity H, produced by m.m.f. wave F_R, is sinusoidal along the air-gap periphery. As stated before, F_R acts across one air-gap, therefore, peak value of magnetic field intensity H_p is given by

$$H_p = \frac{F_R}{g} \quad \text{...(3.74)}$$

Resultant m.m.f. F_R crossing the air gap, gives rise to resultant flux, called *resultant mutual flux* per pole. Some stator flux may not cross the air-gap–this flux linking the stator winding but not the rotor winding, is called the *stator leakage flux*. Similarly, the rotor produced flux, not linking the stator winding, is called the *rotor leakage flux*. Note that leakage fluxes do not take part in the production of torque, it is the resultant mutual flux that produces the electromagnetic torque. The effect of leakage fluxes on the electrical characteristics can, however, be accounted for by means of leakage reactances, as done in a transformer.

The co-energy density at a point in the air gap, where magnetic field intensity is H, is given by $\frac{1}{2}\mu_0 H^2$ as per Eq. (2.13).

$$\therefore \text{ Peak co-energy density in the air-gap} = \frac{1}{2}\mu_0 H_p^2 = \frac{1}{2}\mu_0\left(\frac{F_R}{g}\right)^2 = \frac{1}{2}\frac{\mu_0}{g^2}F_R^2 \quad \text{...(3.75)}$$

Since m.m.fs F_s and F_r are sine waves, their resultant m.m.f. F_R must also be a sine wave. Now recall that the average value of the square of a sine wave is equal to half the peak value of the sine wave. Sine F_R is the peak value of sine wave, the average value of the squared of F_R * is equal to $\frac{1}{2}(F_R)^2$.

$\therefore$ Average co-energy density in the air-gap, from Eq. (3.75), is

$$= \frac{1}{2}\frac{\mu_0}{g^2}\left(\text{average value of } F_R^2\right)$$

* Average value of squared sine wave is $\frac{1}{\pi}\int_0^{\pi}(F\sin\theta)^2\,d\theta = \frac{F^2}{\pi}\int_0^{\pi}\frac{(1-\cos\theta)}{2}\,d\theta = \frac{1}{2}F^2$

$$= \frac{1}{2}\frac{\mu_0}{g^2}\left(\frac{1}{2}F_R^2\right) = \frac{1}{4}\mu_0\left(\frac{F_R}{g}\right)^2 \quad ...(3.76)$$

Total magnetic field co-energy stored in the air gap is

W_{fld}' = (average co-energy density in air-gap) (volume of air gap)

$$= \frac{1}{4}\cdot\mu_0\left(\frac{F_R}{g}\right)^2 (2\pi rlg) = \frac{1}{2}\frac{\mu_0 \pi rl}{g}\cdot F_R^2 \text{ Joules}$$

W_{fld}' in terms of peak values of stator and rotor m.m.f. waves is given as

$$W_{fld}' = \frac{1}{2}\frac{\mu_0 \pi rl}{g}(F_s^2 + F_r^2 + 2F_s F_r \cos\lambda) \quad ...(3.77)$$

For a 2-pole machine, the number of electrical degrees are equal to the number of mechanical degrees. Thus, for a 2-pole machine, the electromagnetic torque, as per Eq. (2.62 (*a*)), can be obtained as

$$T_e = \frac{\partial W_{fld}'}{\partial \lambda}(F_s, F_r, \lambda)$$

In general, for a *P*-pole machine,

$$T_e = \frac{\partial W_{fld}'}{\partial \lambda_m}(F_s, F_r, \lambda_m) = \frac{\partial W_{fld}'}{\partial \lambda}(F_s, F_r, \lambda)\cdot\frac{d\lambda}{d\lambda_m}$$

But, for a *P*-pole machine, electrical angle λ is related to the mechanical angle λ_m by the relation of Eq. (3.2) as

$$\lambda = \frac{P}{2}\lambda_m \text{ or } d\lambda = \frac{P}{2}\, d\lambda_m$$

$$\therefore \quad \frac{d\lambda}{d\lambda_m} = \frac{P}{2}$$

From above, torque is given as

$$T_e = \frac{P}{2}\cdot\frac{\partial W_{fld}'}{\partial \lambda}(F_s, F_r, \lambda)$$

$$= \frac{P}{2}\cdot\frac{\mu_0 \pi rl}{2g}\cdot\frac{\partial}{\partial \lambda}(F_s^2 + F_r^2 + 2F_s\cdot F_r\cdot\cos\lambda)$$

$$= -\frac{P}{2}\cdot\frac{\mu_0 \pi rl}{g}\cdot F_s\cdot F_r\cdot\sin\lambda \text{ Nm} \quad ...(3.78)$$

It is seen from the torque expression Eq. (3.78) that the electromagnetic torque depends upon the number of poles, machine dimensions at the air-gap, peak value of stator and rotor m.m.f.'s and sine of the angle between the axes of the two fields (or m.m.fs). The negative sign in the torque expression (3.78) indicates that the two m.m.fs, one on stator and the other on rotor, tend to reduce the angle λ between them. In other words, the torque acts in such a direction as to align the two m.m.fs F_s and F_r.

Electromagnetic torque given by Eq. (3.78) acts on both stator and rotor in opposite directions. As stator is fixed, it is the rotor that revolves. If it is assumed that rotor is held fixed and stator is free to move, then stator would turn in a direction opposite to that in which rotor had rotated with stator held fixed. In other words, stator and rotor experience equal and opposite torques as given by Eq. (3.78). In practice, electromagnetic torque acting on the stator is transmitted to ground through its foundation and the rotor rotates.

In Fig. 3.45 (*b*), $OA = F_s, OB = F_r$

Now $F_s\cdot\sin\lambda = OC$. But component $F_s \sin\lambda$ (= OC) is normal to F_r. Similarly, component $F_r \sin\lambda$ (= OD) is normal to F_s.

Hence it can be stated from Eq. (3.78) that electromagnetic torque can develop only when one of the two m.m.fs (here F_s or F_r) has a component (here $F_s \sin \lambda$ or $F_r \sin \lambda$) perpendicular to the other m.m.f. or flux.

It is usually more convenient to express Eq. (3.78) in terms of resultant m.m.f. wave F_R. In order to obtain this expression, refer to Fig. 3.45 *(b)* which gives

$$OC = F_s \cdot \sin \lambda = F_R \sin \delta_r$$

and

$$OD = F_r \sin \lambda = F_R \sin \delta_s$$

Substituting these values in Eq. (3.78), we get

$$\left.\begin{aligned} T_e &= -\frac{P}{2} \cdot \frac{\mu_0 \pi r l}{g} \cdot F_s \cdot F_R \cdot \sin \delta_s \\ \text{or} \quad T_e &= -\frac{P}{2} \cdot \frac{\mu_0 \pi r l}{g} \cdot F_r \cdot F_R \cdot \sin \delta_r \end{aligned}\right\} \quad ...(3.79)$$

An examination of Eq. (3.79) reveals that the torque is proportional to the product of one m.m.f. (here F_s or F_r) and a normal component of the resultant m.m.f. F_R.

Note the difference between the torque expressions given by Eqs. (3.78) and (3.79). In Eq. (3.78), torque is proportional to the product of two m.m.fs (or fields) produced by their respective currents and sine of the angle between them. In Eq. (3.79), torque is proportional to the product of resultant m.m.f. (or field), one of the two m.m.fs and sine of the angle between them.

Torque expressions given by Eqs. (3.78) and (3.79) contain fields in terms of their peak m.m.f. waves. When magnetic saturation is neglected, it is permissible to express fields in terms of their peak flux density waves. For this, refer to Eq. (3.74) from which peak value of resultant m.m.f. F_R is

$$F_R = g \cdot H_p = g \frac{B_p}{\mu_0}$$

where B_p = peak value of flux density wave due to peak resultant m.m.f. wave F_R.

Substitution of this value of F_R in Eq. (3.79) gives

$$\left.\begin{aligned} T_e &= -\frac{P}{2} \cdot \pi r l \cdot B_p \cdot F_s \sin \delta_s \\ T_e &= -\frac{P}{2} \cdot \pi r l \cdot B_p \cdot F_r \sin \delta_r \end{aligned}\right\} \quad ...(3.80)$$

During the design of rotating electromagnetic devices, a final check is that flux density in teeth should not exceed 1.8 to 2.2. *T*. This check imposes a limit on the peak value B_p of the resultant flux density wave in Eq. (3.80). The maximum value of m.m.f. in Eq. (3.80) is also limited from a consideration of the temperature rise. Thus, Eq. (3.80) is quite suitable to the designer of electromagnetic devices as it contains important design parameters.

An alternative form of torque expression can be obtained in terms of total flux per pole ϕ. For a *P*-pole machine, total flux per pole, from Eq. (3.11), is

$$\phi = \frac{4}{P} \cdot B_p \cdot l \cdot r$$

or

$$B_p = \frac{P\phi}{4lr} \quad ...(3.81)$$

Substitution of B_p from Eq. (3.81) in Eq. (3.80) gives

$$T_e = -\frac{\pi}{8} P^2 \phi F_s \sin \delta_s \text{ Nm} \quad ...(3.82a)$$

or

$$T_e = -\frac{\pi}{8} P^2 \phi F_r \sin \delta_r \text{ Nm} \quad ...(3.82b)$$

The interpretation of Eqs. (3.82*a*) and (3.82*b*) must be clearly understood. Here P is the number of poles. The total or resultant air-gap flux per pole ϕ, is produced by the combined effect of stator and rotor m.m.fs F_s and F_r. The m.m.f. F_s is resultant of all the stator m.m.fs; similarly F_r is the resultant of all the rotor m.m.fs. For example, in a 3-phase rotating electrical machine, F_s is the resultant stator m.m.f. due to all the three stator m.m.fs. ; F_r is the resultant rotor m.m.f. due to the combined effect of all the three rotor winding m.m.f.'s.

The electrical space angle λ between stator and rotor m.m.fs is called the *torque angle;* whereas the electrical space angle δ_s between F_s and F_R ; and δ_r between F_r and F_R, are called *load angles.* The various torque expressions, derived above, reveal that the electromagnetic torque is proportional to the product of interacting fields and the sine of electrical space angle between their magnetic axis. The negative sign in the torque expressions indicates that electromagnetic torque acts in such a direction as to reduce the space angle between the interacting fields.

If load angle δ_r is time-varying, say $\delta_r = \theta t$ then instantaneous electromagnetic torque from Eq. (3.82 *b*) is,

$$T_{e.inst} = -\frac{\pi}{8}P^2 \phi \, F_r \sin \theta t$$

The average torque over a complete cycle is zero. $\therefore\ T_e = 0.$

This shows that for the development of electromagnetic torque T_e, it is essential that space phase angle δ_r (δ_s or λ) must remain constant with time. If F_r is a travelling m.m.f. wave at some speed, then ϕ must also be a travelling flux wave at the same speed, so that space phase angle δ_r between F_r and ϕ remains unaltered with time. Further, if F_r is a stationary m.m.f. wave, then ϕ must also be a stationary flux wave for δ_r to remain time-invariant.

Torque in Basic Machine Types. The general torque expressions derived above, apply equally well to all types of rotating electrical machines. In order to obtain torque expressions, identical with those already obtained by conventional methods, different pairs of axes are considered for different machines.

D.C. Machines. For D.C. machines, use Eq. (3.78), *i.e.* the magnitude of torque for a D.C. machine is (replacing F_s and F_r by F_f and F_a respectively),

$$T_e = \frac{P}{2} \frac{\mu_0 \pi r l}{g} F_f F_a \sin \lambda_{af} \qquad ...(3.83)$$

Here F_f is the peak value of the field m.m.f. per pole and F_a is the peak value of the armature m.m.f. per pole. Angle λ_{af} is the torque angle between F_f and F_a. The peak value of the flux density B_f under each pole is

$$B_f = \mu_0 H_f = \frac{\mu_0}{g} F_f$$

The total field flux per pole ϕ_f, from Eq. (3.11), is

$$\phi_f = \frac{4}{P} B_p lr = \frac{4}{P} \cdot B_f lr = \frac{4}{P} \frac{\mu_0}{g} F_f lr$$

or

$$F_f = \frac{\phi_f}{4} \frac{P}{\mu_0} \frac{g}{lr} \qquad ...(3.84)$$

Substitution of the value of F_f from Eq. (3.84) in Eq. (3.83) gives

$$\left.\begin{aligned} T_e &= \frac{P}{2} \frac{\mu_0 \pi r l}{g} \frac{\phi_f P g}{4 \mu_0 l r} F_a \sin \lambda_{af} \\ &= \frac{\pi}{8} P^2 \phi_f F_a \sin \lambda_{af} \text{ Nm} \end{aligned}\right\} \qquad ...(3.85)$$

AC machines. For synchronous and induction machines, Eq. (3.82*b*) is preferable. For polyphase A.C. machines, the basic torque expression (3.82*b*) can be expressed in a more useful form, by including the voltage and current in it. This is done as follows :

The rotor m.m.f. F_r, from Eq. (3.72 *a*) is

$$F_r = m\frac{2\sqrt{2}}{\pi}k_w\frac{N_{ph}I}{P}\text{ ATs/pole.}$$

and the resultant air-gap flux per pole, from Eq. (3.24) is

$$\phi = \frac{E_{ph}}{\sqrt{2}\pi f\, N_{ph}k_w}$$

Substitution of the values of F_r and ϕ in Eq. (3.82*b*) gives the magnitude of electromagnetic torque T_e as

$$T_e = \frac{\pi}{8}P^2\left(\frac{E_{ph}}{\sqrt{2}\pi f\, N_{ph}k_w}\right)\left(m\frac{2\sqrt{2}}{\pi}k_w\frac{N_{ph}I}{P}\right)\sin\delta_r$$

$$= \frac{P}{4\pi f}m\,E_{ph}\,I\sin\delta_r$$

For an A.C. machine,

$$\begin{bmatrix}\text{Speed in mechanical}\\ \text{radians per second}\end{bmatrix} = \frac{2}{P}\begin{bmatrix}\text{Speed in electrical}\\ \text{radians per second}\end{bmatrix}$$

i.e. $$\omega_m = \frac{2}{P}\omega = \frac{2}{P}(2\pi f) = \frac{4\pi f}{P} \quad ...(3.86a)$$

$\therefore$ $$T_e = \frac{1}{\omega_m}m\,E_{ph}\,I\sin\delta_r \quad ...(3.86)$$

Note that E_{ph} is the per phase voltage induced in the armature by air-gap flux ϕ and I is the per phase armature current.

Load angle δ_r will be shown to be equal to $(90 + \theta)$ degrees, where θ is the time-phase angle between E_{ph} and I. In view of this, Eq. (3.86) becomes,

$$T_e = \frac{1}{\omega_m}m\,E_{ph}\,I\cos\theta$$

or $$T_e\,\omega_m = m\,E_{ph}\,I\cos\theta.$$

or Mechanical power developed = Electrical power developed.

The power balance in case of D.C. machines is demonstrated in the chapter on D.C. machines.

Example 3.32. *A 2-pole, 50 Hz cylindrical-rotor machine has the following data :*

$D = 1.6$ m, $l = 1.8$ m, $g = 12$ mm

Peak value of sinusoidal rotor and stator m.m.fs. are 4000 AT/pole and 6000 AT/pole respectively. Rotor m.m.f. leads stator m.m.f. by 140° and both run at synchronous speed. Calculate

(a) resultant peak gap m.m.f. *(b) peak gap flux density*

(c) total gap co-energy *(d) electromagnetic torque and* *(e) electromagnetic power*

Solution. (*a*) Resultant peak gap m.m.f F_R, from Eq. (3.73), is given by

$$F_R = [4000^2 + 6000^2 + 2\times 4000\times 6000\times\cos 140°]^{1/2}$$

$$= 3902.55 \text{ ATs/pole.}$$

(*b*) Peak gap flux density,

$$B_p = \mu_0 H_p$$

$$= \mu_0\frac{F_R}{g} = \frac{4\pi\times 10^{-7}\times 3902.55}{12\times 10^{-3}} = 0.4087\ T$$

(*c*) Total gap co-energy $= \frac{1}{2} \frac{\mu_0 \pi r l}{g} F^2{}_R$

$$= \frac{1}{2} \frac{4\pi^2 \times 10^{-7} \times 0.8 \times 1.8}{12 \times 10^{-3}} (3902.55)^2 = 3607.51 \text{ Joules}$$

(*d*) From Eq. (3.78), magnitude of electromagnetic torque,

$$T_e = \frac{P}{2} \cdot \frac{\mu_0 \pi r l}{g} F_s F_r \sin \lambda$$

$$T_e = \frac{2}{2} \cdot \frac{4\neq \times 10^{-7} \times \neq \times 0.8 \times 1.8}{12 \times 10^{-3}} \times 4000 \times 6000 \times \sin 140°$$

$$= 7308.36 \text{ Nm}$$

(*e*) Synchronous speed, $\omega_m = \frac{4\pi f}{P} = \frac{4\pi \times 50}{2} = 100\pi \text{ rad/sec}$

Electromagnetic power, $P = T_e \cdot \omega_m = 7308.36 \times 100\,\pi = 2296.05 \text{ kW}$

Example 3.33. *A uniform air-gap machine has the following dimensions :*

$$D = 0.8 \text{ m}, l = 0.5 \text{ m}, g = 5 \text{ mm}$$

When stator and rotor are energized, the stator and rotor windings produce sinusoidal current sheets of peak density $A_s = 10{,}000$ A/m and $A_r = 6000$ A/m respectively. Magnetic axes of stator and rotor are so displaced as to give a torque angle of 60°. The iron in the machine is assumed to have infinite permeability.

Determine the torque in case the machine windings are designed to produce (a) a 2-pole field and (b) a 6-pole field.

Solution. (*a*) Peak value of stator m.m.f. per pole, from Eq. (3.87 *a*), is

$$F_s = \frac{A_s \cdot D}{P} = \frac{1}{2} \times 10{,}000 \times 0.8 = 4000 \text{ AT}$$

Similarly, $F_r = \frac{A_r \cdot D}{P} = \frac{1}{2} \times 6000 \times 0.8 = 2400 \text{ AT}$

From Eq. (3.78), $T_e = -\frac{P}{2} \frac{\mu_0 \pi r l}{g} F_s \cdot F_r \cdot \sin \lambda$

$$= -\frac{2}{2} \frac{4\neq \times 10^{-7} \times \neq \times 0.4 \times 0.5}{5 \times 10^{-3}} \times 4000 \times 2400 \sin 60°$$

$$= 1312.83 \text{ Nm}$$

(*b*) When $P = 6$, then $F_s = \frac{1}{6} \times 10000 \times 0.8 = \frac{4000}{3} \text{ AT}$

$$F_r = \frac{1}{6} \times 6000 \times 0.8 = 800 \text{ AT}$$

$$\therefore \quad T_e = -\frac{6}{2} \cdot \frac{4\neq \times 10^{-7} \times \neq \times 0.4 \times 0.5}{5 \times 10^{-3}} \times \frac{4000}{3} \times 800 \sin 60°$$

$$= 437.61 \text{ Nm}$$

Example 3.34. *In rotating electrical machines, the component of rotor m.m.f. normal to the stator m.m.f. (or component of stator m.m.f. normal to rotor m.m.f.) gives rise to the production of electromagnetic torque. Explain the function of rotor m.m.f. component in phase with the stator m.m.f. (or stator m.m.f. component in phase with rotor m.m.f.).*

Solution. Refer to Fig. 3.45 (*a*). Stator m.m.f. F_s causes the appearance of *N*, *S* poles on the stator. The rotor m.m.f. component $F_r \cos \lambda$ in phase with F_s, also cause the appearance of *N*, *S* poles on the rotor, as illustrated in Fig. 3.46. Now stator poles produced by F_s attract the rotor poles produced by $F_r \cos \lambda$, thus causing the appearance of radial (*i.e.*, along the radius) forces in opposite directions. If the two air-gaps encountered by m.m.fs. F_s and $F_r \cos \lambda$ are of equal radial lengths, then opposing radial forces are equal. In case the air-gaps are different, the two radial opposing forces are unequal and their difference gives rise to unbalanced magnetic pull, rapid wear of the bearings, noisy performance etc. Poor workmanship or wear of the bearings with the passage of time, may be the causes of different air gaps around the periphery.

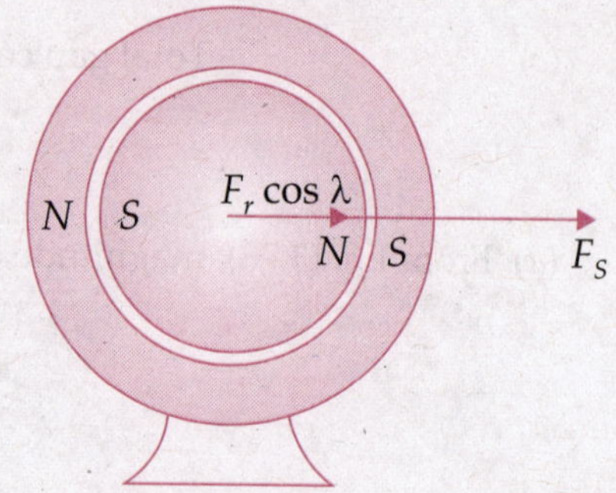

Fig 3.46: Pertaining to Example 3.34.

In view of this, component of rotor m.m.f. in phase with stator m.m.f. (or component of stator m.m.f. in phase with rotor m.m.f.) is detrimental to the operation of rotating electrical machines and should therefore be made as small as possible (and therefore $F_r F_s \sin \lambda$ as large as possible).

When a machine is switched on, a large thud is heard only because of the presence of $F_r F_s \cos \lambda$ in an electrical machine.

Example 3.35. *A 4-pole, 3-phase, star-connected, 50 Hz turbo alternator has the following data :*

Field winding has 12 concentric coils distributed in slots with slot-angular pitch of 8°.

Turns per field coil = 6, Series armature turns per phase = 28

Armature radius = 0.6m, Armature length = 4 m

Gap length = 0.06 m

Winding factor for armature winding = 0.96

Field current = 1000 A.

Calculate :

(a) peak value of fundamental m.m.f. produced by field winding,

(b) peak value of fundamental air-gap flux-density wave,

(c) the fundamental value of air-gap flux per pole and

(d) r.m.s. values of phase and line e.m.fs at no load and at rated speed.

Solution. (*a*) There are 12 concentric coils for 4 poles. This means there are three concentric coils distributed in slots to create one pole. So here $q = 3$ and $r = 8°$ (given). Therefore, distribution factor for field winding from Eq. (3.46) is

$$k_d = \frac{\sin \frac{3 \times 8}{2}}{3 \sin \frac{8}{2}} = 0.9935$$

Coil-span factor, $\quad k_p = 1$

Winding factor for field winding, $\quad k_f = k_d \times k_p = 0.9935$

Number of field turns, $\quad N_f = 6 \times 12 = 72$

From Eq. (3.61), the peak value of fundamental m.m.f. produced by field winding is

$$F_{1f} = \frac{4}{\pi} \times 0.9935 \times \frac{72 \times 1000}{4} = 22769.3 \text{ ATs/pole}$$

(*b*) Peak value of fundamental flux density wave is

$$B_{1p} = \mu_0 H = \frac{\mu_0 F_{1f}}{g} = \frac{4\pi \times 10^{-7} \times 22769.3}{0.06} = 0.4769 \text{ T}$$

(c) From Eq. (3.11), fundamental value of air-gap flux per pole is

$$\phi = \frac{4}{P} B_{1p} \cdot l \cdot r = \frac{4}{4} \times 0.4769 \times 4 \times 0.6 = 1.1446 \text{ Wb}$$

(d) Per phase e.m.f., $E_{ph} = \sqrt{2}\,\pi \times 50 \times 1.1446 \times 28 \times 0.96 = 6833.64$ V

Line e.m.f., $E_1 = \sqrt{3}\, E_{ph} = \sqrt{3} \times 6833.64 = 11835.86$ V.

Example 3.36. *A 3-phase, 6-pole, 50 Hz, star-connected cylindrical-rotor alternator develops an open-circuit e.m.f. of 415 V. The armature has 36 slots with two-layer winding of full-pitched coils with 4 turns each. The alternator has mean air-gap diameter 0.18 m, core length 0.4 m and a gap length 2 mm. The field winding has 42 turns with winding factor of 0.96. Calculate*

(a) the peak value of fundamental flux-density wave in air gap,

(b) the peak value of fundamental m.m.f. wave produced by the field winding and the D.C. field current.

In case this alternator develops a torque of 114 Nm at a torque angle of 146° and at rated voltage, then calculate

(c) peak value of the fundamental armature m.m.f. wave per pole and the resultant m.m.f. wave per pole and

(d) the r.m.s. value of armature current and its power factor.

Solution. (a) Series turns per phase, $N_{ph} = \frac{36 \times 4}{3} = 48$

Slots per pole per phase, $q = \frac{36}{6 \times 3} = 2$

Slot angular pitch, $\gamma = \frac{180}{6} = 30°$

$$k_d = \frac{\sin \frac{60}{2}}{2 \sin \frac{30}{2}} = 0.966, \; k_p = 1$$

Per-phase e.m.f., $E_{ph} = \sqrt{2}\,\pi f N_{ph} \cdot \phi \cdot k_w$

Flux per pole, $\phi = \frac{415}{\sqrt{3} \times \sqrt{2} \times \pi \times 50 \times 48 \times 0.966} = 0.0233$ Wb

But $\phi = \frac{4}{P} \cdot B_{1P} \cdot l \cdot r$

∴ Peak value of fundamental flux-density wave,

$$B_{1P} = \frac{P\phi}{4lr} = \frac{6 \times 0.0233}{4 \times 0.4 \times 0.09} = 0.971 \text{ T}$$

(b) $B_{1P} = \mu_0 H_f = \frac{\mu_0 \cdot F_{1f}}{g}$

∴ Peak value of fundamental field m.m.f. wave,

$$F_{1f} = \frac{g \cdot B_{1p}}{\mu_o} = \frac{2 \times 10^{-3} \times 0.971}{4\pi \times 10^{-7}} = 1545.4 \text{ ATs per pole}$$

From Eq. (3.61), $I_f = \frac{\pi \cdot F_{1f} \cdot P}{4k_f N_f} = \frac{\pi \times 1545.4 \times 6}{4 \times 0.96 \times 42} = 180.62$ A (*c*) From Eq. (3.83), the magnitude of torque is given by

$$T_e = \frac{P}{2} \cdot \frac{\mu_0 \cdot \pi r l}{g} F_{1f} \cdot F_{1a} \cdot \sin \lambda_{af}$$

∴ Peak value of fundamental armature m.m.f. is

$$F_{1a} = \frac{114 \times 2 \times 2 \times 10^{-3}}{6 \times 4\neq \times 10^{-7} \times \neq \times 0.09 \times 0.4 \times 1545.4 \sin 146°}$$

$$= 618.8 \text{ ATs/pole}$$

Resultant value of peak m.m.f. per pole,

$$F_R = [F_{1f}^2 + F_{1a}^2 + 2 F_{1f} \cdot F_{1a} \cdot \cos \lambda_{af}]^{1/2}$$
$$= [1545.4^2 + 618.8^2 + 2 \times 1545.4 \times 618.8 \times \cos 146°]^{1/2}$$
$$= 1088.84 \text{ ATs/pole}$$

(*d*) In a 3-phase synchronous machine, the peak value of rotating m.m.f wave is given by

$$F_{1a} = \frac{3}{2} F_m = \frac{3}{2} \cdot \frac{4}{\pi} \cdot k_w \cdot \frac{N_{ph} \cdot \sqrt{2} I_a}{P} \text{ ATs/ pole}$$

This gives rms value of armature current as $I_a = \dfrac{618.8 \times 2\pi \times 6}{12 \times 0.966 \times 48\sqrt{2}} = 29.65$ A

For power balance, $\sqrt{3} \times 415\, I_a \cos\theta = T_e \cdot \omega_m,$

where $\omega_m = \dfrac{2\pi \times 1000}{60} = \dfrac{100\pi}{3}$ rad/s

∴ Power factor, $\cos\theta = \dfrac{114 \times 100\pi}{3 \times \sqrt{3} \times 415 \times 29.65} = 0.5602$

As $F_R < F_{1f}$ here and F_r (similar to F_R) < F_f (similar to F_{1f}), the p.f. is 0.562 lagging.

3.9. LOSSES AND EFFICIENCY

In electrical machines, the power input (mechanical or electrical) is always more than the power output. The difference between power input and power output, under steady state conditions, is called power loss in watts. Thus, in accordance with the law of conservation of power (or energy),

Power input = power output + power loss

or power loss = power input – power output

Power loss in a machine does not perform any useful work, it leads only to heating of the electrical machine.

A consideration of the power losses in electrical machines is essential for the following three reasons :

(*i*) Losses influence the operating cost of electrical machines. For example, a machine with lower efficiency has more losses and therefore increased operating cost.

(*ii*) Losses cause heating of the machine and therefore its temperature rise. Greater the loss, more is the temperature rise and therefore, faster is the deterioration of the machine insulation. Temperature rise determines the machine rating through its effect on the life of winding insulation. It can, therefore, be stated that temperature rise, and hence the losses determine the rating, or safe power output, of electrical machines.

(*iii*) Voltage drop *IR* is associated with ohmic loss whereas current component, like core-loss current, pertains to the iron loss in electrical machines. Obviously, this suggests that losses associated with voltage drops or current-components must be appropriately taken into account in the equivalent circuit of a machine so that electrical-machine analysis can be carried out as desired.

Machine efficiency is defined as

$$\text{Efficiency } \eta = \frac{\text{Output}}{\text{Input}} \quad \text{...(3.87)}$$

or

$$\eta = \frac{\text{Input} - \text{Output}}{\text{Input}} = 1 - \frac{\text{Losses}}{\text{Input}} \quad \text{...(3.88)}$$

For computing the efficiency, an electrical machine may be subjected to direct load test and its output and input measured simultaneously. Eq. (3.88*a*) then gives the machine efficiency. It is however much difficult to perform the actual load test, because of the cost of providing large inputs and difficulty of dissipating the large outputs. Moreover, a small error in the measurement of either output or input, causes about the same amount of error in the computed efficiency.

Since the losses are a small percentage of output or input, these can be measured more conveniently and economically. Even more important is the fact that a small percentage of error in the measurement of losses, results in a still smaller percentage of error in the computation of efficiency. This is now illustrated with an example. Assume an electrical machine to have an input of 1000 watts and output of 900 watts, so that the total losses are 100 watts and the efficiency is 90%. Suppose there is an error of 10% less, in the measurement of output, then efficiency is given by

$$\frac{810}{1000} \times 100 = 81\%.$$

If there is 10% error (loss) in the measurement of losses, then

$$\eta = \left(1 - \frac{90}{1000}\right) \times 100 = 91\%.$$

Thus a given percentage of error in the measurement of output (here 10%) results in almost the same percentage of error, in the calculation of efficiency. But a given percentage of error in the measurement of losses (here 10%), causes about one tenth (here 1%) of that percentage error, in the computation of efficiency. In view of this, the efficiency is computed by measuring the losses in a given machine.

When a machine is to be selected from a large number of available machines, then their methods of loss measurement should be same. A machine having larger efficiency and , therefore, less energy losses is then selected. But a highly efficient machine is more expensive and, therefore, involves more fixed charges such as interest, taxes and insurance. It should, however, be kept in mind that a more efficient machine is likely to give better performance, with more reliability, less breakdowns, less running charges and minimum maintenance cost, as compared to a less efficient machine.

The various machine losses may be classified as (*a*) electrical losses and (*b*) mechanical losses. These are described below :

(*a*) **Electrical Losses :**

(*i*) **Resistance losses or I^2R losses.** When current flows through various machine winding, I^2R losses occur. The resistance *R*, by convention, is taken as the D.C. resistance of the machine windings at the operating temperature of 75°C. Actually, effective winding resistance R_{eff}, which is more than its D.C. value R_{dc}, should be used in computing the I^2R loss. The effective winding resistance depends on the operating frequency and actual flux conditions existing in the conductor. This increment of loss, equal to ($I^2R_{eff} - I^2R_{dc}$), is usually included in the stray load loss discussed further. In the field circuits of D.C. and synchronous machines, only the resistance loss in the field winding is included for computing their efficiency. The I^2R loss in their field rheostats and other losses in the sources supplying the field winding are, however, included while calculating the system efficiency.

In addition to I^2R loss in the windings, there is brush contact loss at the contacts between the brushes and commutator (D.C. machines) or between the brushes and slip rings (synchronous and induction machines). In D.C. machines, the conduction of current between brushes and commutator is through the short arcs in the tiny air gaps which are inherent in such a contact. As the voltage drop across an arc remains substantially constant, the brush voltage drop in a D.C. machine is taken as constant at 1 to 2 volts total. Thus, the brush contact loss in a D.C. machine is proportional to its armature current. In case of synchronous and induction machines, the brush contact loss is usually neglected for all practical purposes.

(*ii*) **No-load core loss.** This loss, also called open-circuit core loss, consists of hysteresis and eddy-current losses. These losses are present in rotating electrical machines—in case their stator and rotor irons carry an alternating, or time varying, flux under the condition that only the main field (or exciting) winding is energized. In a transformer, therefore core losses are always present. In rotating machines, the hysteresis and eddy current losses can be determined from Eq. (1.46), but here f should be the frequency of the magnetic flux reversals to which a given piece of stator or rotor iron is subjected in one second. Physical understanding of hysteresis and eddy current losses in rotating electrical machines is presented below :

Hysteresis loss. For a 2-pole machine, consider a small iron piece such as AB, subjected to alternating flux as it rotates under N and S poles, Fig. 3.47. When the small iron piece is under N-pole, main pole flux passes through it from A to B, causing the appearance of S-pole at A and N-pole at B. After half a revolution, the iron piece comes under the influence of main S-pole and now main flux passes through it from B to A, causing the appearance of S-pole at B and N-pole at A. Thus in half a revolution, the magnetism of iron piece AB is reversed. When the armature rotates, there are continuous magnetic reversals of such small iron pieces and power required for their reversals is called hysteresis loss. It may be seen that hysteresis loss is directly proportional to the number of magnetic reversal per second or the speed.

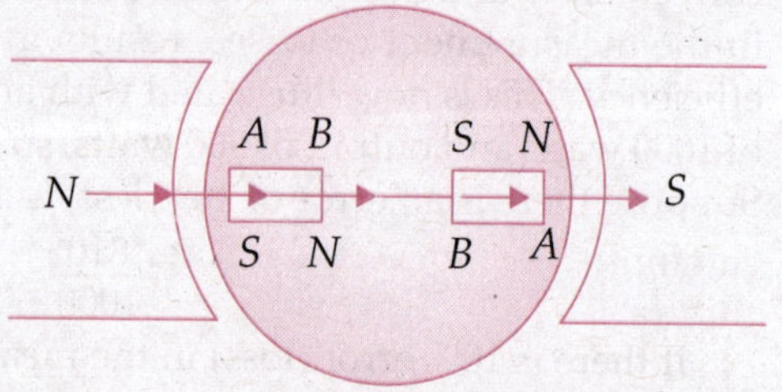

Fig 3.47: Illustrating hysteresis loss.

Eddy current loss. Consider again a 2-pole machine with solid rotor iron. When the rotor rotates, e.m.fs. are generated in the rotor iron in exactly the same way as they are induced in the rotor conductors. In Fig. 3.48 (*a*), these e.m.fs are indicated by dots and crosses. Another view of this figure (plan) is given in Fig. 3.48 (*b*). The e.m.fs generated in the solid iron give rise to circulating currents which are called eddy currents. These eddy currents are of large magnitude, because the resistance offered by the rotor iron is quite small. The power loss equal to (eddy currents)^2 (resistance offered to the flow of eddy currents), is referred to as eddy current loss.

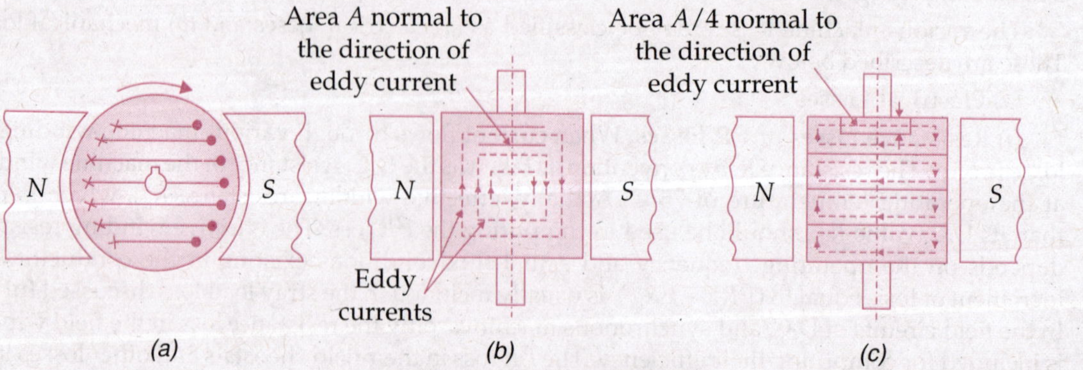

Fig 3.48: Illustrating eddy current loss.

This loss can be minimised by using thin laminations for the rotor structure. This can be illustrated by referring to Fig. 3.49 (c), where only 4 laminations are shown for simplicity. The flux linking each lamination is one-fourth of that linking with solid iron ; therefore, the e.m.f. induced in one lamination is one-fourth of that induced in solid iron. At the same time, the area normal to the direction of eddy currents is reduced to one-fourth of that for solid iron, therefore, resistance R_{lnd} offered to eddy currents in laminated iron is four times the resistance R_{sld} offered in the solid iron, *i.e.*, $R_{lnd} = 4\ R_{sld}$. Here subscripts *lnd* and *sld* stand for laminated and solid respectively. In view of this,

$$\frac{\text{Eddy current loss per lamination}}{\text{Eddy current loss in solid iron}} = \frac{(\text{e.m.f. per lamination})^2 / R_{lnd}}{(\text{e.m.f. in solid core})^2 / R_{sld}}$$

$$= \left(\frac{1}{4}\right)^2 \frac{R_{sld}}{R_{lnd}} = \left(\frac{1}{4}\right)^2 \left(\frac{1}{4}\right) = \frac{1}{64}.$$

$$\therefore \quad \frac{\text{Eddy current loss in laminated rotor}}{\text{Eddy current loss in solid rotor}} = \left(\frac{1}{64}\right)\left(\frac{4}{1}\right) = \left(\frac{1}{4}\right)^2$$

If axial length of the solid rotor core is unity, then the lamination thickness in Fig. 3.48 (*c*) is $\frac{1}{4}$. Thus it can be concluded from above that eddy current loss is proportional to the square of the lamination thickness. If there are more laminations for a given axial length, the lamination thickness decreases and hence eddy current losses are also decreased. Thus the use of thin laminations minimises the eddy current loss. The usual lamination thickness is 0.4 mm to 0.5 mm. If lamination thickness is made less than 0.4 mm, the reduction in eddy current losses is achieved, but at the cost of additional labour charges in assembling the rotor.

The eddy current loss has been found to be given by Eq. (1.46). In case the effect of lamination thickness *t* is to be taken into account, then the eddy current loss P_e can be expressed as

$$P_e = k_e (t \cdot f B_m)^2 \qquad \text{...(3.89)}$$

For both the expressions for P_h and P_e, the frequency *f* and B_m can be replaced respectively by speed and voltage, if required.

In D.C. and synchronous machines, the core loss occurs mainly in the armature iron. It is because the armature in both these machines is subjected to alternating flux as it rotates under the effect of main field poles. With the slotted armature passing across the field poles, the flux density wave pulsates in magnitude as shown in Fig. 3.49 and Fig. 3.50. In Fig. 3.49, slot is under the middle of field pole and the flux density is *AB*. With the relative motion between armature and field poles, tooth may come under the middle of pole as shown in Fig. 3.50. Under this condition, air-gap flux density is *A′B′*. The field m.m.f. is same in both these figures. Here *A′B′* > *AB*, as the air gap length along the middle of pole is less in Fig. 3.50 than in Fig. 3.49. These pulsations in flux density wave arising from slot openings cause losses in the field iron, particularly in the pole faces (or pole shoes). This loss in the pole shoes occurring due to relative motion between field poles and slotted armature is referred to as *pulsation loss*. In order to reduce this loss, pole shoes in D.C. and synchronous machines are laminated. The pulsation loss is composed of hysteresis and eddy current losses in the field-pole shoes. As these losses occur in the pole-faces of field poles, these are also called *pole-face losses*. In induction machines, the stator has core loss, whereas rotor core loss is almost negligible because of reduced frequency of the flux reversals (equal to slip frequency, sf) in the rotor.

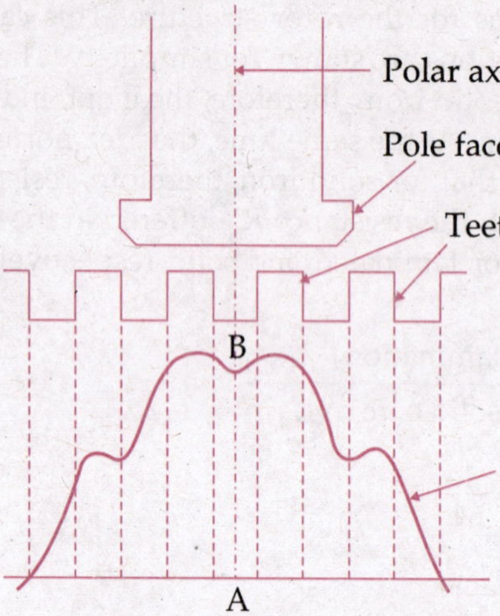

Fig 3.49: Main field-flux distribution, when slot and polar-axis coinside

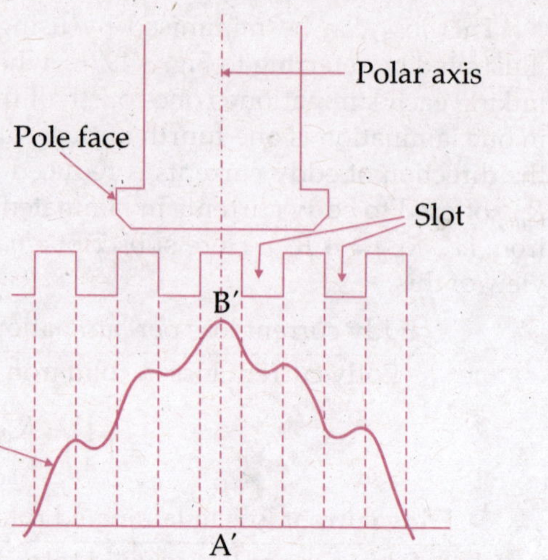

Fig 3.50: Main field-flux distribution, when tooth and polar-axis coinside

(*iii*) **Stray load loss.** When a machine is loaded, the load current establishes an m.m.f. which appreciably changes the space distribution of air-gap flux density wave. This leads to an increase in the core loss from no load to full load. This increment in core loss caused by distortion of the air-gap flux plus the increment in I^2R loss due to non-uniform distribution of conductor current is called stray load loss. In other words, stray load loss consists of two components, one originating in iron parts and the other in the armature conductors. In iron parts, the stray load loss consists of (*a*) the eddy current loss in the stator frame, end covers etc. caused by the armature leakage flux under load and (*b*) the increased teeth loss due to distortion of the flux density wave. In the conductors, the stray load loss is due to the circulating currents set up in the conductors by the alternating leakage flux produced by load current. These circulating, or eddy currents make the conductor current distribution non-uniform and as a result effective resistance of conductor increases. This gives rise to additional conductor loss, called stray load loss. In D.C. machines, stray load loss also occurs in the coils undergoing commutation. This loss is usually taken as proportional to square of the load current. Stray load loss cannot be determined accurately. In D.C. machines, by convention, it is taken as 1% of the rated output for rating above 150 kW. For synchronous and induction machines, it is taken as 0.5% of their rated output.

(*b*) **Mechanical loss.** This loss consists of bearing-friction, brush-friction and windage losses. The windage (wind-friction) loss includes the power required to circulate air through the machine and ventilating ducts and is approximately proportional to square of the speed.

Brush-friction loss occurs in machines fitted with brushes, for example D.C. machines, synchronous machines, wound-rotor induction machines etc. Squirrel-cage induction motors have no brush-friction loss. This loss depends on the brush pressure, coefficient of friction and speed.

Bearing-friction loss is approximately proportional to speed. This loss further depends on the type of bearings, their lubrication etc.

Mechanical loss (sum of friction and windage losses) can be determined by measuring the input to an unexcited and unloaded machine by running it at rated speed. Mechanical loss is primarily frictional in nature.

The mechanical loss and open-circuit core loss combined together are caused by rotor rotation, their sum is therefore referred to as *no-load rotational loss*. This loss can be determined by running the electrical machine as an unloaded motor (the machine may be a generator or a motor) at rated speed or frequency and with armature voltage equal to the normal generated e.m.f. The total power input to the unloaded motor minus a small no-load armature ohmic loss (no load stator ohmic loss in case of induction motor) gives the magnitude of no-load rotational loss. For efficiency computations, the no-load rotational loss need not be split into mechanical and open-circuit core losses.

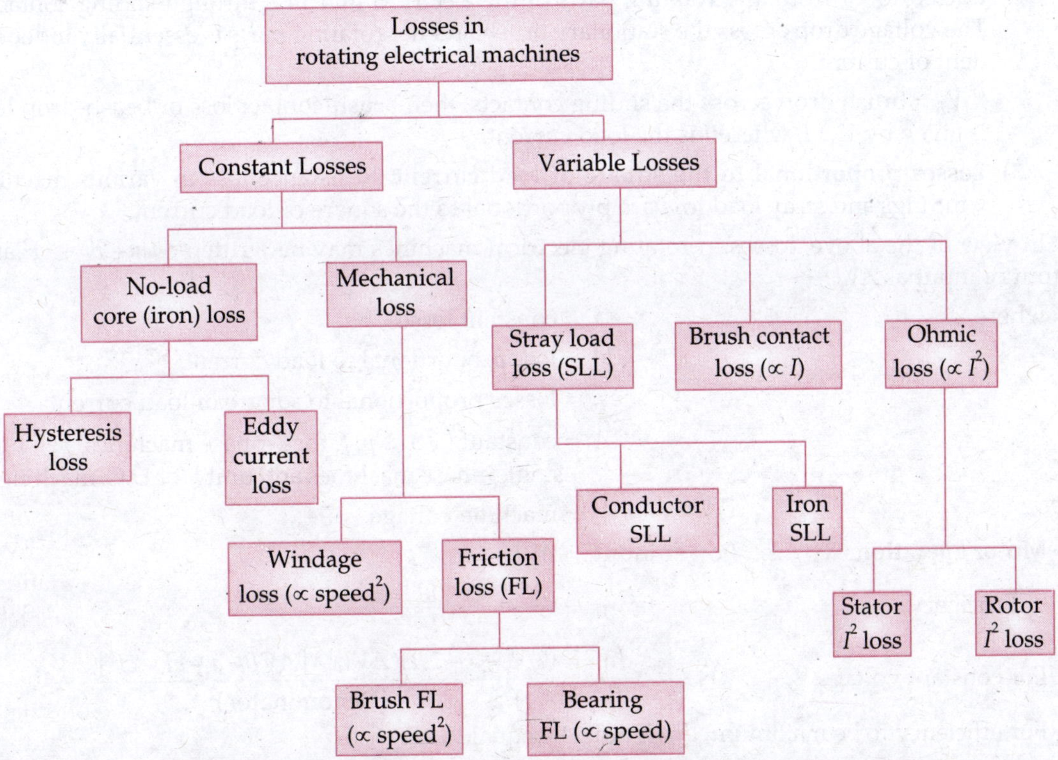

Fig 3.51: Various losses in rotating electrical machines.

For the sake of a quick overview of the various losses occuring in rotating electrical machines, a tree-diagram of Fig. 3.51 is quite helpful. It is seen that various losses are on account of the presence of voltages, currents and rotation of the rotor. This diagram also represents almost all the losses that occur in a transformer in case the losses associated with rotor rotation are neglected.

Maximum efficiency. It is seen from above that rotating electrical machines have constant as well as variable losses. At light loads, output is low, variable loss is low, the efficiency is also low because of the presence of constant losses. The machine efficiency, however, rises progressively with the load. But at a particular load, depending upon the design of the machine, the efficiency is maximum. Beyond this load, efficiency diminishes. Further, efficiency varies with the rating (or size) of the machine; for example, efficiency is nearly 75% for 1-kW machine, 90% for 35 kW, 93% for 350 kW and as high as 97% for 3500 kW machine.

The amount of conductor and iron materials required for a machine of given rating is inversely proportional to its speed. This means that a low-speed machine would require more material whereas a high-speed machine less material for the same rating. More iron and conductor would entail more losses. As a consequence, it can be inferred that for the same rating, efficiency of low-speed machines is lower than that of high-speed machines, the total spread being 3 to 4%.

For qualitative purposes, the various losses in rotating electrical machines, operating at nearly constant voltage and speed, may be grouped into three main losses :

(1) Constant, or fixed, losses. These losses do not depend on the load current. The sum of no-load core loss, friction and windage loss (*i.e.* no-load rotational loss) constitute constant losses unless there is an appreciable variation in speed.

(2) Loss proportional to load current. Brush-contact loss occurs when current is to be conducted to, or from, the rotating parts of the electrical machine through sliding contacts. The voltage drop across the stationary brush and the rotating parts is essentially independent of current.

If V_b = brush drop across the sliding contacts, then brush-contact loss or brush-drop loss is given by $V_b \cdot I$, where I is the load current.

(3) Losses proportional to the square of load current. Resistance loss in various machine windings and stray load loss are proportional to the square of load current.

In view of the above, losses in rotating electrical machines may be written as $a + bI + cI^2$ and output or input as AVI

where a = constant losses,

bI = loss proportional to load current,

cI^2 = losses proportional to square of load current,

A = constant ($\sqrt{3} \times p.f.$ for 3-phase machines, $p.f.$ for single-phase machines and unity for D.C. machines),

V = machine voltage.

Motor operation. Power input $= AVI$

$\therefore$ Efficiency,

$$\eta = \frac{AVI - a - bI - cI^2}{AVI} \qquad ...(3.90)$$

For constant voltage V,

$$\frac{d\eta}{dI} = \frac{(AV - b - 2cI)(AVI) - [AVI - a - bI - cI^2](AV)}{(\text{Denominator})^2}$$

For efficiency to be maximum, $d\eta/dI$ must be equal to zero.

$$\therefore \quad (AV - b - 2cI)\,(AVI) = (AVI - a - bI - CI^2)\,(AV)$$

Its simplification gives,

$$cI^2 = a \qquad ...(3.91)$$

Thus, the motor efficiency is maximum at a load when variable loss cI^2 is equal to constant loss a.

Generator operation. Power output $= AVI$

$\therefore$ Efficiency,

$$\eta = \frac{AVI}{AVI + a + bI + cI^2} \qquad ...(3.92)$$

For constant V,

$$\frac{d\eta}{dI} = \frac{(AV)(AVI + a + bI + cI^2) - (AVI)(AV + b + 2cI)}{(\text{Denominator})^2}$$

For maximum efficiency, $d\eta/dI = 0$ and its simplification gives $cI^2 = a$

i.e. losses proportional to square of current = constant losses

It is seen from above that for both motors and generators, machine efficiency is maximum when variable losses are equal to constant losses.

The variable loss, proportional to square of load current, depends upon the current density, specific resistance and volume of conductor material. Similarly, the constant loss is dependent on flux density, specific density and volume of iron used in a machine. As variable and constant losses must be equal to obtain maximum efficiency, the value of maximum efficiency is governed by the amount of iron and conductor materials used in a machine. It is thus seen that maximum efficiency at a particular load (near the rated load) can be obtained by suitably proportionating the amount and quality of iron and conductor materials used in a machine.

Maximum output. The power output P_0 for a motor can be expressed as

$$P_0 = AVI - a - bI - cI^2$$

The loss proportional to current I (usually brush-contact loss) is quite small, it can therefore be neglected without any appreciable error. In fact, this loss is regarded as zero in industrial A.C. machines. Under these conditions,

$$P_0 = AVI - a - cI^2$$

The motor will have maximum efficiency when

$$\frac{dP_0}{dI} = AV - 2cI = 0 \quad \text{or} \quad I = AV/2c$$

The maximum power output P_{om} is, therefore, given by

$$P_{om} = AV\left(\frac{AV}{2c}\right) - a - c\left(\frac{AV}{2c}\right)^2$$

$$= \frac{(AV)^2}{2c} - a - \frac{(AV)^2}{4c} = \frac{(AV)^2}{4c} - a$$

As the machine power input is $AVI = (AV)^2/2c$, the efficiency under the condition of maximum power output is given by

$$\eta = \left[\frac{\frac{(AV)^2}{4c} - a}{(AV)^2/2c}\right] \times 100 = 50 - \frac{200\text{A.C.}}{(AV)^2}$$

It is thus seen that efficiency at maximum power output is less than 50%. This means that there are more than about 50% losses occuring in the machine. In other words, about half of the power input appears as loss under maximum power output conditions. Such a situation would cause temperature of the power devices to be much more than the specified allowable temperature rise. Hence, it may be inferred from above that electromechanical energy conversion devices used in power systems are never operated to deliver maximum power output. In practice, these are operated at a load, somewhat less than rated load, at which the efficiency is maximum. This, however, is not the situation in electronic equipments which are usually low-power devices. The electronic systems are designed to operate to deliver maximum power output. As the total power handled is very small, efficiency is of little significance in electronic devices.

Example 3.37. *(a) The transformer output in VA is given by*

$$S = K\, B_m\, \delta\, A_i\, A_w$$

where B_m is the core flux density in T, δ is the current density in A/m^2, A_i is the net core area, A_w is the window area and K is a constant.

Compare the ratings and losses of two transformers, the linear dimensions of one being m times those of the other. The flux and current densities are the same.

Hence show that larger the tranformer rating, greater is its efficiency.

(b) Transformer A has a full-load efficiency of 95%. Transformer B has all its linear dimensions 2 times those of the transformer A. Calculate the full-load efficiency of transformer B.

Solution. (*a*) For first transformer, the rating is

$$S_1 = K\, B_m\, \delta\, A_{i1}\, A_{w1}$$

For second transformer, core area $A_{i2} = m^2 A_{i1}$

and window area $A_{w2} = m^2 A_{w1}$.

$\therefore$ The rating of second transformer, $S_2 = K\, B_m\, \delta\, A_{i2}\, A_{w2} = K\, B_m\, \delta\, (m^2 A_{i1})\,(m^2 A_{w1}) = m^4 S_1$.

The core or iron loss $\propto$ volume.

$\therefore$ Second transformer core losses $= m^3$ (core losses in first transformer)

Now $$I^2R = (a\delta)^2 \cdot \frac{\rho L}{a}$$

First transformer $$I^2R \text{ loss} = (a_1\delta)^2 \frac{\rho L_1}{a_1}$$

Second transformer $$I^2R \text{ loss} = (m^2 a_1\delta)^2 \cdot \frac{\rho \cdot mL_1}{m^2 a_1} = m^3 \text{ (First transformer } I^2R \text{ loss)}.$$

$\therefore$ Total losses in second transformer $= m^3$ (Total losses in first transformer).

Now $$\text{efficiency} = \frac{\text{Output}}{\text{Output} + \text{Losses}} = \frac{S_1(p.f.)}{S_1(p.f.) + \text{Losses}W_1}$$

For second transformer, efficiency $$= \frac{m^4[S_1(p.f.)]}{m^4[S_1(p.f.)] + m^3 W_1} = \frac{S_1(p.f.)}{S_1(p.f.) + \dfrac{W_1}{m}} \quad ...(3.93)$$

Eq. (3.93) shows that greater the value of m, greater is the size of transformer and larger is the transformer efficiency, because $\dfrac{W_1}{m}$ gets reduced.

It can be shown for rotating electrical machines also that larger their size, greater is their efficiency.

(*b*) For transformer *A*, efficiency $$\eta_A = \frac{\text{Output}}{\text{Output} + \text{Losses}} = \frac{S_1(p.f.)}{S_1(p.f.) + W_1}$$

$\therefore$ Losses $$W_1 = \left(\frac{1}{\eta_A} - 1\right)[S_1(p.f.)] = \left(\frac{1}{0.95} - 1\right)[S_1(p.f.)] = \frac{0.05}{0.95}[S_1(p.f.)]$$

Efficiency of transformer *B*, from Eq. (3.93) is given by

$$\eta_B = \frac{S_1(p.f.)}{S_1(p.f.) + \dfrac{W_1}{m}} = \frac{S_1(p.f.)}{S_1(p.f.) + \dfrac{1}{2} \times \dfrac{0.05}{0.95}[S_1(p.f.)]}$$

$$= \frac{1}{1 + 0.0263} = 0.9744 \text{ or } 97.44\%.$$

3.10. MACHINE RATINGS

A name-plate fixed to the outside frame of an electrical machine records the data pertaining to its rating. A machine rating specifies the voltage, current, speed, excitation, pf, efficiency, power output etc. under which it can operate satisfactorily. Here satisfactory operation implies that temperature rise of the machine above ambient (or surrounding) temperature does not exceed a specified temperature when machine operates in accordance with the data on the name-plate. For all types of A.C. motors and D.C. machines, output power rating is given in kW (kilowatt). Older practice was to specify the power output of A.C. and D.C. motors in horse-power (1 h.p. = 746 watts). For A.C. generators, rating is in kVA or MVA.

Electrical machines are rated on the basis of their temperature rise resulting from the power losses in iron and conductor. The temperature rise mentioned on the name-plate is the temperature difference between the hottest part of the winding under specified conditions of load, speed, voltage, excitation, cooling and the ambient temperature. For reliable and satisfactory operation of an electrical machine, it should be ensured that its temperature rise remains within specified limits. The temperature rise not only affects the insulation of an electrical machine but also its mechanical parts ; however, the extent of damage is more detrimental to insulating materials than to the mechanical parts.

Deterioration of insulation depends on the temperature as well as the time. It has been found that time to failure for organic insulation is reduced to half for every 8 to 10°C rise in machine temperature.

Insulating materials, more commonly employed in industrial machines, are classified as Class E, Class B, Class F and Class H. Other classes of insulation are not of much commercial interest. These classes of insulation can withstand the following maximum temperatures as per IS.

Insulation class :	E	B	F	H
Maximum temp. °C	120	130	155	180

The figures given above relate to 20-year working life of an electrical machine under average conditions. These classes of insulation consist of the following materials :

Class E : Synthetic-resin enamels, cotton and paper laminates with formaldehyde bonding, etc.

Class B : Mica, glass fibre, asbestos etc. with suitable bonding substances.

Class F : The materials of class *B* with more thermally-resistant bonding materials.

Class H : Silicone elastomet and combinations of mica, glass fibre, asbestos etc. in various forms with silicon resins as bonding substance.

The rating of an electrical machine, from the viewpoint of temperature rise, is governed by the load conditions or load duty cycle. The more common machine ratings are as under.

Continuous rating. It defines the output which a machine can deliver continuously without exceeding a specified temperature rise above the ambient (40°C as per I.S.I.).

Short-time rating. The output which a machine can supply for a specified period (5, 15, 20, 30 or 60 minutes) without exceeding its permissible temperature limit is called short-time rating. The machine is assumed to start from cold.

Intermittent rating. It is the output that a machine can give continuously without exceeding the specified temperature for a train of identical duty cycles consisting of loading and rest periods.

The continuous, short-time as well as intermittent ratings depend upon the cooling and thermal capability of the machine. Out of these, continuous rating is the most common. The loading period for a continuously-rated motor is so large that all parts of the machine attain almost a steady temperature. Continuously-rated motors are used for fans, centrifugal pumps, lathes, conveyors etc. In short-time rated motors, the loading period is so short that machine does not attain steady temperature while the rest period is long enough for the machine to cool to ambient temperature. Short-time rated motors are used for opening and closing weirs, battery-charging unit, sluice gates, lock gates and bridges etc. The machines with intermittent rating are loaded with a train of identical duty cycles so that finally the rise and fall in temperature during each duty cycle are equal. Motors used for hoisting mechanisms, trams, trolley-buses etc. are subjected to intermittent duty.

Short-time rated motors are designed with higher values of flux and current densities in iron and conductor respectively. As a consequence, these motors have better torque producing capability but lower thermal capacity as compared to continuous-rated motors.

A provision is usually made in continuous rated motors that they operate successfully for ± 10% variation in rated voltage and ± 5% variation in rated frequency. The combined variation in rated voltage and frequency should, in no case, exceed ± 10%. Continuous rated motors are expected to have ample safety margin so that these can withstand short-time over-load of 25% at 90% of rated voltage without any damage to the machine.

3.10.1. Choice of Power of Electric Machines

The choice of power rating of a motor for any type of load depends upon the load-time graph. For loads remaining substantially constant with time, the power rating P can be determined from the expression,

$$P = \frac{T\omega_m}{1000\eta} \text{ kW}$$

where T = load torque in Nm ; ω_m = operating speed in rad/sec

and η = product of the efficiencies of transmitting device (gear, belt etc.) and the driven equipment (fan, conveyors etc.).

In many industrial applications, the load requirements vary periodically and over a wide range. For example, during upward journey of a hoist, the motor is fully-loaded but during downward journey, the motor is almost unloaded. The problem is now to choose a continuous-rated (C.R.) motor for such widely varying load cycles of periodic nature. A crude, yet quite often used, method is based on the assumption that losses and therefore heating of the motor is proportional to square of the kW load. This assumption overemphasises the role of I^2R losses as compared to the constant core loss. According to this method, rating of C.R. Motor = average loss, or average heating, of the motor over a periodic duty cycle.

So, for using this method, obtain kW load-time curve. Then rating of C.R. motor = average value of (kW load)^2 – time curve over one periodic load cycle. A little thought process would reveal that rating of C.R. motor = r.m.s. value of kW load – time periodic curve.

As such, this method of estimating the power rating of C.R. motor for periodically varying loads has come to be called *r.m.s. power* method. Thus, according to this method,

$$\text{r.m.s. power } = \text{rating of C.R. motor} = \left[\frac{\sum (kW)^2 \times \text{time}}{\sum \text{time}}\right]^{1/2}$$

Here kW represents the motor-loading profile in a period of duty cycle. Note that this technique is the same as used for obtaining r.m.s. value of periodically varying currents or voltages. If standstill time is also a part of the duty cycle (as in a lift, crane etc.), the above relation is modified as under :

$$\text{r.m.s. power } = \left[\frac{\sum (kW)^2 \times \text{time}}{\text{running time} + (\text{standstill time}/k)}\right]^{1/2} \quad ...(3.94)$$

Here the constant k accounts for the poor ventilation during the standstill time when there is no forced cooling. For open-type motors, $k = 4$ and for closed motors, $k = 1$. It is important to note that r.m.s.-power method can be used only if period of duty cycle is small as compared to the time for the motor to attain a steady temperature.

Though r.m.s.-power method does not give precise results, yet it is used quite often. The error involved in using this method is partially offset by choosing a higher standard rating of the motor. Thus the need for precise computations is avoided with the rounding of calculated r.m.s.-power rating to a higher commercially available motor size. For example, if r.m.s. power method gives motor rating as 46 kW, then a motor with continuous rating of 50 kW should be selected.

For duty cycles with high-torque peaks, a motor selected on the basis of r.m.s.-power method cannot furnish such torques. For these types of duty cycles, short-time rated motors are better suited as they possess better torque producing capabilities.

A continuous-rated motor can deliver higher power output for short-time rating. Let P_r be the power of a continuous-rated motor. Under rated loading P_r, it will be heated up to permissible temperature rise θ_f as shown in Fig. 3.52. The temperature rise at any time t is given by

$$\theta = \theta_f (1 - e^{-t/\tau_h}) \qquad ...(3.95)$$

where τ_h = Heating time constant.

Let the short-time load be P_x and its duration t_x as shown. If continuous-rated motor is run as a short-time rated motor with load P_r for time t_x, it would attain a final temperature rise AB, which is much less than the permissible temperature rise $\theta_f = AC$. After period t_x, short-time rated motor cools down to ambient temperature. During the next short-time loading P_r for duration t_x, the final temperature rise would again be AB. This means that continuous rated motor, when used with load P_r for short-time duration t_x, is underutilized. For full utilization of the motor, the temperature rise during short-time loading should follow the curve $AB'C'$ so that final temperature during t_x is AC. The curve $AB'C'$ can be followed only if load during short-time rating t_x is more than P_r. Let this load be P_x which is more than P_r. In case the period for short-time loading is less than t_x, a load still higher than P_x can be delivered by the motor for the permissible temperature rise AC. It can thus be inferred that as the loading period is reduced, the short-time rating of the continuous-rated motor rises.

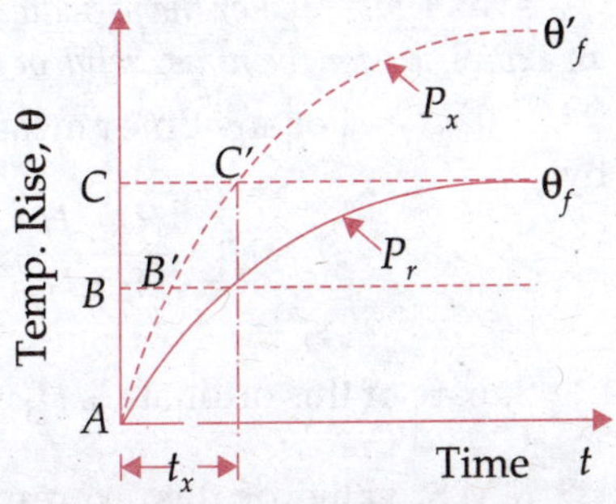

Fig 3.52: Pertaining to continuous and short-time ratings.

If the motor is made to deliver short-time rated load P_x continuously, the final temperature rise would be θ_f' as shown in Fig. 3.52. But temperature rise, in this case, would be $\theta_f = AC$ after time t_x. This can be expressed as

$$\theta_f = \theta_f' (1 - e^{-t_x/\tau_h})$$

or

$$\frac{\theta_f}{\theta_f'} = [1 - \exp(-t_x/\tau_h)] \qquad ...(3.96)$$

Here temperature rise θ_f' is never attained by the motor.

As heating, or temperature rise, of the motor depends on loss, Eq. (3.96) can be written as

$$\frac{\theta_f}{\theta_f'} = \frac{W_r}{W_x} = [1 - \exp(-t_x/\tau_h)] \qquad ...(3.97)$$

where losses W_r and W_x are corresponding to loads P_r and P_x respectively. Loss W_r at rated load P_r is given by

$$W_r = \text{core loss}, W_c + \text{ohmic loss}, W_0$$

Let the ratio (W_c/W_0) be α. Then

$$W_r = \alpha W_0 + W_0 = (1 + \alpha) W_0 \qquad ...(3.98)$$

But ohmic loss is proportional to current squared. As load on motor is proportional to current (except series motor), it follows that ohmic loss is proportional to square of load. As a result,ohmic loss at load P_x can be written as proportional to $(P_x)^2$. Since W_0 is the ohmic loss at rated load P_r, total losses W_x at load P_x can be expressed as

$$W_x = W_c + W_0 (P_x/P_r)^2 = \alpha W_0 + W_0 (P_x/P_r)^2$$
$$= [\alpha + (P_x/P_r)^2] W_0 \qquad ...(3.99)$$

From Eqs. (3.97) to (3.99),

$$\frac{W_x}{W_r} = \frac{\alpha + (P_x/P_r)^2}{1+\alpha} = \frac{1}{1 - \exp(-t_x/\tau_h)} \qquad ...(3.99\ a)$$

or

$$P_x = P_r \left[\frac{1+\alpha}{1 - \exp(-t_x/\tau_h)} - \alpha\right]^{1/2} \qquad ...(3.100)$$

In case core loss W_c is neglected, then $\alpha = 0$ and Eq. (3.100) becomes

$$P_x = P_r \left[\frac{1}{1 - \exp(-t_x/\tau_h)}\right]^{1/2} \qquad ...(3.101)$$

From Eqs. (3.100) and (3.101), short-time rating P_x for duration t_x can be obtained for a motor with continuous rating P_r and heating time constant τ_h.

Example 3.38. *For the periodic load-time plot shown in Fig. 3.53, find an expression for the r.m.s. value over the periodic time T.*

Solution. For any time t measured from t_1, the ordinate is given by

$$H_1 + \frac{H_2 - H_1}{t_2 - t_1} t = H_1 + \frac{H_2 - H_1}{T_1} t.$$

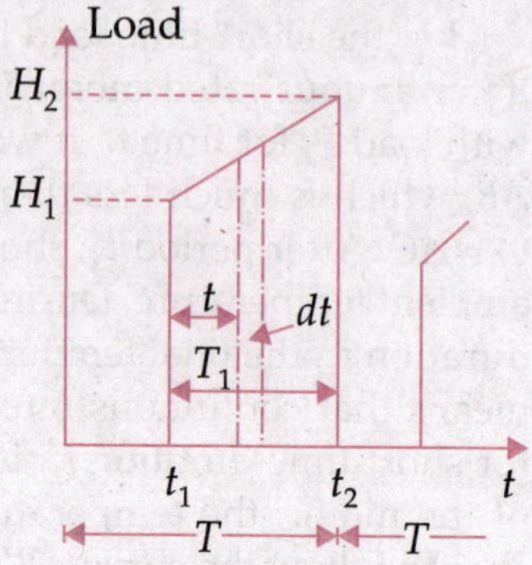

Fig 3.53: Pertaining to Example 3.38.

Square of this ordinate is $H_1^2 + \frac{(H_2 - H_1)^2 t^2}{(T_1^2)} + \frac{2H_1(H_2 - H_1)}{T_1} t$

R.M.S. value of this expression is obtained by integrating it from t_1 to t_2, *i.e.* from 0 to T_1 ; dividing it by periodic time T and then taking its square root.

$$\text{r.m.s. value} = \sqrt{\frac{1}{T}\left[\int_0^{T1} \left\{H_1^2 dt + \frac{(H_2 - H_1)^2 t^2}{T_1^2} dt + \frac{2H_1(H_2 - H_1)t}{T_1} dt\right\}\right]}$$

$$= \left[\frac{1}{T}\left\{H_1^2 T_1 + (H_2^2 + H_1^2 - 2H_1 H_2)\frac{T_1}{3} + (H_1 H_2 - H_1^2)T_1\right\}\right]^{1/2}$$

$$= \left[\frac{1}{T}\{(H_1^2 + H_2^2 + H_1 H_2)T_1/3\}\right]^{1/2}.$$

Example 3.39. *A motor driving a coal-mine equipment has to supply a load rising uniformly from zero to maximum of 2000 kW in 30 seconds during the accelerating period, 1000 kW for 60 seconds during the full load period. During deceleration period of 10 seconds when regenerative braking takes place, the kW returned to the mains falls from an initial value of 600 kW to zero uniformly. The interval for decking before the next load cycle starts is 20 seconds. Estimate a suitable kW rating of the motor based on r.m.s. -power method.*

Solution. The variation of load power over a duty cycle of 120 seconds is illustrated in Fig. 3.54. The r.m.s. value of this cycle gives the kW rating of a continuous-rated motor.

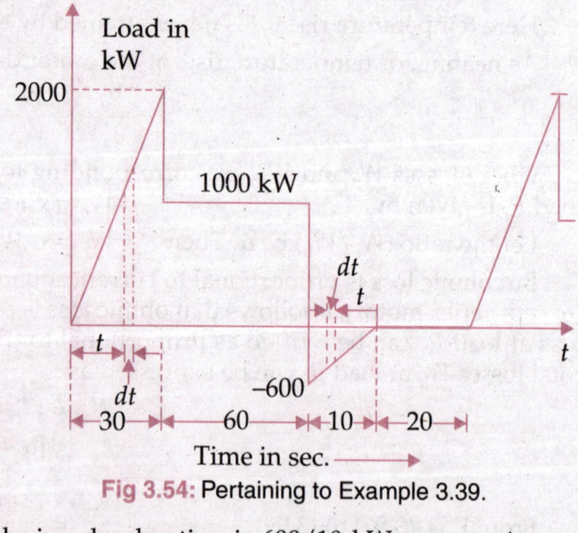

Fig 3.54: Pertaining to Example 3.39.

The slope of the load-time curve during acceleration is 2000/30 kW per sec. and that during deceleration is 600/10 kW per sec. At any time t measured from the zero of the load-time curve, the load kW is $\left(\frac{200}{3}t\right)$ kW and $(60t)$ kW respectively during acceleration and deceleration periods. The r.m.s. value is therefore given by

r.m.s. power

$$= \left[\frac{1}{120}\left\{\int_0^{30} \left(\frac{200}{3}t\right)^2 dt + (1000)^2 \times 60 + \int_0^{10} (60t)^2 \times dt + 0 \times 20\right\}\right]^{1/2}$$

$$= \left[\frac{1}{120}\left\{\left(\frac{200}{3}\right)^2 \times \frac{(30)^3}{3} + 60 \times 10^6 + 1200 \times 10^3\right\}\right]^{1/2} = 918.33 \text{ kW.}$$

So choose a motor of rating above 918.33 kW, say 950 kW.

Example 3.40. *Points on the motor-duty cycle, estimated on the basis of the proposed rolling schedule and previous experience with rolling mills, are given in the following table :*

Time, sec	*0*	*5*	*36*	*39*	*55*	*80*	
Output, kW	*150*	*1000*	*1400*	*300*	*150*	*150*	*Repeat cycle*

The complete curve can be obtained by joining these points with straight lines.

Specify the continuous kW-rating of the motor.

Solution. The load-time curve for one duty cycle is shown in Fig. 3.55 for this example. Continuous kW-rating can be obtained by taking the r.m.s. value of this load-time cycle. From Example 3.38, the r.m.s. power can be obtained as under :

0 – 5 sec ; $H_1 = 150, H_2 = 1000$

5 – 36 sec ; $H_1 = 1000, H_2 = 1400$

and so on.

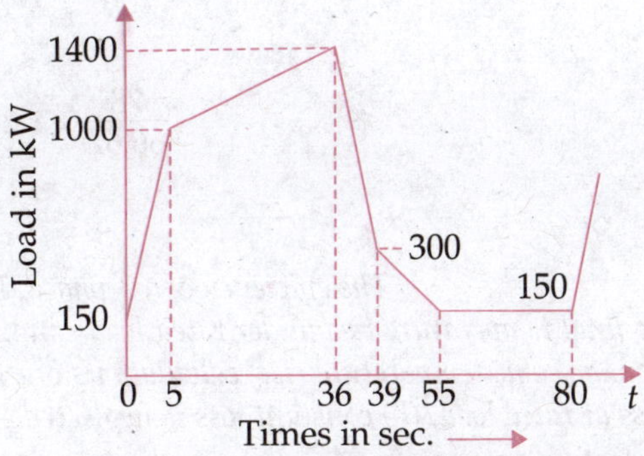

Fig 3.55: Load time graph for Example 3.40.

$$\therefore \text{ r.m.s.-power} = \left[\frac{1}{80}\left\{\frac{5}{3}(150^2 + 1000^2 + 150 \times 1000) + \frac{31}{3}(1000^2 + 1400^2 + 1000 \times 1400) + \frac{3}{3}\right.\right.$$

$$\left.\left.(1400^2 + 300^2 + 1400 \times 300) + \frac{16}{3}(300^2 + 150^2 + 300 \times 150) + 25 \times - 150\right\}\right]^{1/2}$$

$$= \left[\frac{1}{80}\{1954{,}166.6 + 45{,}053{,}333 + 2470{,}000 + 840{,}000 + 3{,}750\}\right]^{1/2}$$

$$= 793.105 \text{ kW}$$

$\therefore$ Choose a motor with continuous rating of 800 kW.

Example 3.41. *(a) Temperature rise of a 200 kVA transformer, having unity pf full-load efficiency of 98%, was found to be 20°C after one hour and 34°C after 2 hours on rated load. The full-load ohmic loss is 3 times the iron loss. What is the final steady temperature rise of the transformer on rated load?*

(b) If the transformer cooling is improved by using a fan so that the effective heat dissipation is increased by 20%, find the new kVA rating (i) for the same final temperature rise as above and (ii) for a temperature rise of 78°C.

Solution. (*a*) From Eq. (3.95), $20 = \theta_f(1 - e^{-1/\tau h})$

and $34 = \theta_f(1 - e^{-2/\tau h})$

$$\therefore \quad \frac{34}{20} = \frac{1 - e^{-2/\tau h}}{1 - e^{-1/\tau h}} = 1 + e^{-1/\tau h}$$

Its simplification gives $\tau_h = 2.804$ hrs.

$$\therefore \quad \theta_f = \frac{20}{1 - \exp(-1/2.804)} = 66.67°\text{C}$$

Here θ_f is final steady temperature rise of the transformer on rated load.

(*b*) (*i*) For the same temperature rise, with increased heat dissipation, new allowable losses W_x are $W_x = 1.2\, W_r$. Here $\alpha = W_c/W_0 = 1/3$

From Eq. (3.99 a), $$\frac{W_x}{W_r} = \frac{\alpha + (P_x/P_r)^2}{1+\alpha}$$

or $$1.2 = \frac{\left(\frac{1}{3}\right) + (P_x/P_r)^2}{1+\frac{1}{3}}$$

$\therefore$ $$P_x = 1.1255 \times 200 = 225.1 \text{ kVA}$$

(*ii*) For allowable temperature rise of 78°C, the new permissible losses are

$$W_x = \frac{78}{66.67} \times 1.2\, W_r \quad \text{As in part } (i),$$

$$\frac{78}{66.67} \times 1.2 = \frac{\frac{1}{3} + (P_x/P_r)^2}{1+\frac{1}{3}}$$

or $$P_x = 1.241 \times 200 = 248.2 \text{ kVA.}$$

Example 3.42. *The efficiency of a 3-phase, 100 kW, 440 V, 50 Hz induction motor is 90% at rated load. Its final temperature rise under rated load conditions is 40°C and its heating time constant is 180 minutes. For the same temperature rise, calculate its one hour rating in case (a) constant loss is equal to the variable loss at rated load, (b) constant loss is neglected.*

Solution. Here $$\tau_h = 3 \text{ hours.}$$

(*a*) $$\alpha = 1$$

From Eq. (3.100), $$P_x = 100\left[\frac{1+1}{1-\exp(-1/3)} - 1\right]^{1/2} = 246 \text{ kW}$$

(*b*) From Eq. (3.101), $$P_x = 100\left[\frac{1}{1-\exp(-1/3)}\right]^{1/2} = 187.8 \text{ kW}$$

This example demonstrates that neglect of core loss gives pessimistic results for the allowable one-hour rating.

Example 3.43. *One hour rating of a machine is twice its continuous rating. Its final steady temperature rise, if operated on one-hour rating, is twice of that under rated load. Find the ratio of core loss to ohmic loss at rated load.*

Solution. From Eqs. (3.97) and (3.99 *a*), we get

$$\frac{\theta_f}{\theta_f'} = \frac{W_r}{W_x} = \frac{1+\alpha}{\alpha + (P_x/P_r)^2} \quad \text{or} \quad \frac{1}{2} = \frac{1+\alpha}{\alpha + (2)^2} \quad \text{or} \quad \alpha = 2.$$

Thus, the ratio of core loss to ohmic loss is 2.

3.11. COOLING (LOSS DISSIPATION)

Cooling of electrical machines is essential for dissipating the heat generated by various losses and thus to prolong the life of insulating materials. In small electrical machines, natural cooling is adequate. In these machines, cooling by natural radiation and convection associated with random air circulation inside the machine body is enough to keep their temperature within limits. However, as the machine size increases, cooling becomes more difficult. The following example illustrates this fact.

Example 3.44. *A rotating electrical machine has its linear dimensions m times the linear dimensions of another machine. Compare their losses and cooling. Both the machines have same flux and current densities.*

Solution. In a rotating electrical machine, core or iron loss depends on the weight of iron used. As the weight = volume of iron × its density, it can be stated that

$$\text{Core loss} \propto \text{Volume}$$

$\therefore$ First machine core loss, $P_{c1} \propto \text{(volume)}$

Second machine core loss, $P_{c2} \propto m^3 \text{(volume)}$

$\therefore$ $P_{c2} = m^3 P_{c1}$

Now $$I^2R \text{ loss} = (a\delta)^2 \frac{\rho L}{a}$$

$$\text{First machine } I^2R \text{ loss} = (a_1\delta)^2 \frac{\rho L_1}{a_1}$$

$$\text{Second machine } I^2R \text{ loss} = (m^2 a_1\delta)^2 \frac{\rho m L_1}{m^2 a_1} = m^3 \text{ (first machine } I^2R \text{ loss)}$$

$\therefore$ Total losses in second machine = m^3 (total losses in first machine)

Cooling surface area of second machine = m^2 (cooling surface area of first machine)

For second rotating electrical machine of bigger size, the losses per unit area

$$= \frac{\text{Losses in second machine}}{\text{Surface area of second machine}}$$

or losses per unit area in second machine $$= \frac{m^3 \text{(losses in first machine)}}{m^2 \text{(cooling area of first machine)}}$$

$$= m \text{ (losses per unit area in first machine)}$$

This shows that for second machine of bigger size ($m > 1$), the loss per unit area is m times that in first machine. In other words, heat to be dissipated per unit area rises as the machine rating, or size, increases. It may therefore be stated that larger machines are difficult to cool than smaller ones and hence require more elaborate cooling arrangements.

Forced air cooling is used for large machines. In this scheme, air is first passed through cleaning filter and then forced into the machine for cooling purposes. A still better method of providing clean cooled air is the *closed-circuit* ventilation system. This is used for small-rating turboalternators. In closed-circuit scheme, hot air from the machine is cooled by means of a water-cooled heat-exchanger and then returned to the machine by a fan. In order that heat arising from the losses is removed more efficiently, cooling ducts are provided in large machines along their core length.

Hydrogen-cooling. Large-rating turbogenerators require compactness from the view-point of economy and transportation. For such generators, closed air-circuit ventilation system is not sufficient to cool the machine effectively. The fan size required to circulate air also increases considerably making the air cooling of large turbogenerators an uneconomical proposition. For such machines, therefore, a better coolant should replace the air. Hydrogen has been found a well-suited cooling medium and is more common in the totally enclosed ventilating system of large turbogenerators. Hydrogen as a coolant has the following advantages over air :

(*i*) **Efficiency and noise.** Hydrogen density is only about 0.07 that of air at the same temperature and pressure. There are, therefore, much less windage and ventilation losses. As a result, machine efficiency is more.

Since the revolving parts rotate in low-density hydrogen, the noise produced is less.

(*ii*) **Cooling.** On an equal-weight basis, specific heat of hydrogen is about 14.5 times that of air. Heat storing capacity is given by

$$\text{mass } (m) \times \text{specific heat } (s) \times \text{temperature rise } (\theta)$$

If heat stored in air is $m\,s\,\theta$, then heat stored in hydrogen is given by

$$(0.07m)\,(14.5s)\,(\theta) = ms\,\theta$$

This shows that for the same temperature and pressure, heat storing capacity per unit volume is same for both hydrogen and air. But heat transfer between hot parts of the machine and the cooling gas is about 1.5 times with hydrogen than with air. This means that cooling with hydrogen is more rapid.

(iii) **Life.** When air is used in high-voltage machines, then during corona discharge the oxygen and nitrogen in air may form ozone, nitric acid and other chemical compounds which may react with organic insulating material. This reaction may harm the insulation, thus reducing the life of insulating material.

When hydrogen is used as a coolant, ozone and other chemical compounds due to corona discharge cannot be formed because of the absence of oxygen. The life of insulation is therefore increased and the maintenance expenses are reduced.

(iv) **Fire Hazard.** Fire hazard inside the machine is minimised because hydrogen-air mixture does not explode so long as the hydrogen content is more than 70%.

(v) **Rating.** Hydrogen pressure inside the machine system is maintained at a pressure above atmospheric. With this, the air cannot leak into hydrogen circuit to form an explosive mixture. However, hydrogen leakage can only be outward. Hydrogen cooling at 1, 2 and 3 times the atmospheric pressure can raise the rating of the machine by 15, 30 and 40% respectively above its air-cooled rating.

The stator of hydrogen cooled machine must be gas tight and explosion proof. For this purpose, oil-filled gas-seals at the rotor shaft ends are necessary.

Direct cooling. It is also referred to as *conductor cooling* or *inner cooling*. The turbogenerator output can be increased by raising the hydrogen pressure inside the machine. But beyond a certain pressure, the increase in output is not economical with the rise in hydrogen pressure. This led to the development of direct cooling of large machines.

With direct cooling of turbogenerators, it is possible almost to double their output with the same physical size. In other words, for the same output, the physical size of the turbogenerator can almost be reduced to half. Here the coolant (liquid or gas) is forced through ducts inside the conductors. Thus the thermal barrier presented by the insulating material is largely overcome and conductor losses are very effectively absorbed by the coolant.

(*a*) **Direct gas cooling.** Large stator cores for turbogenerators are provided with both axial and radial cooling ducts as shown in Fig. 3.56. For rotor of 100 MW or above, the rotor conductor consists of hollow rectangular tubes as shown in Fig. 3.57. The hydrogen gas is admitted to these tubes through insulating flexible connections at the ends.

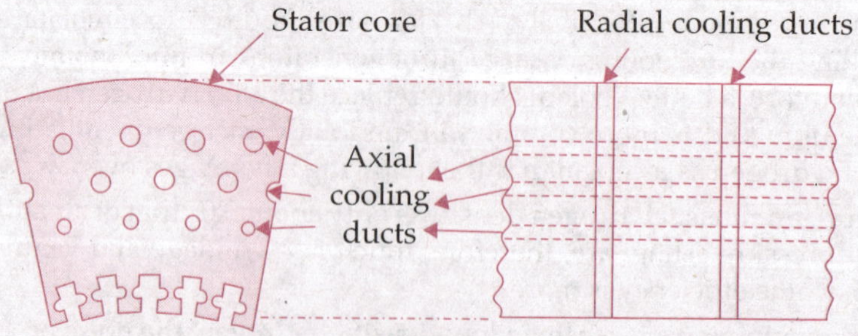

Fig 3.56: Radial and axial cooling ducts in stator cores of large machines.

Direct water cooling. With ratings of 1000 MW or so, hydrogen cooling is not sufficient to cope with the dissipation of large losses. For such ratings, the volume of hydrogen required is so large that its use becomes uneconomical. As the rotor core length increases for large ratings, the middle portion may not be cooled efficiently even with the use of hydrogen. These limitations of hydrogen cooling can be overcome by employing water cooling.

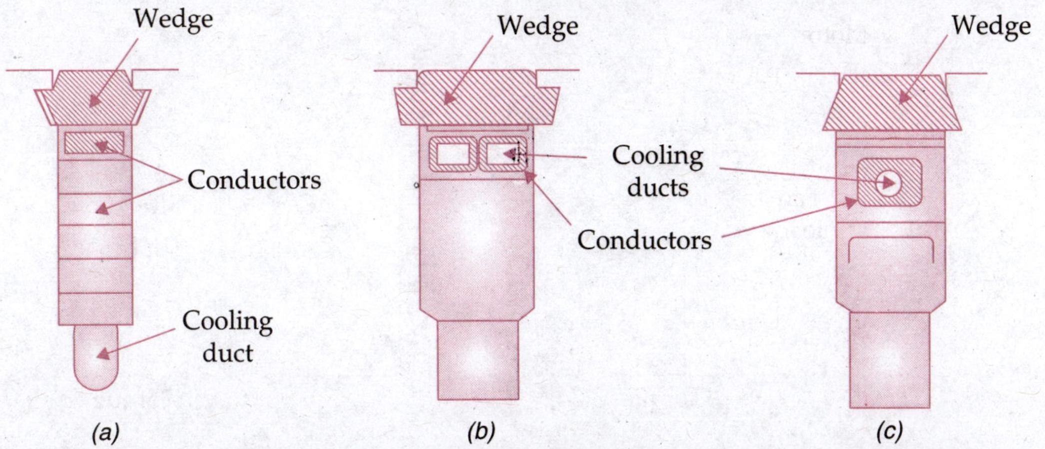

Fig 3.57: Turbo-rotor conductor cooling : (*a*) conventional (*b*) direct gas (*c*) direct water.

Turbogenerators of the highest ratings are likely to have hydrogen-cooled stator cores and direct water cooled stator and rotor windings. The advantages of using water over hydrogen are as under :

(*i*) Thermal capacity of water is several times higher than that of hydrogen ; water can, therefore, carry away more heat.

(*ii*) Though water speed in the cooling ducts is limited to about 2.5 m/sec for avoiding erosion and cavitation, yet water cooling is more efficient than hydrogen.

(*iii*) The duct area for water may be small, this permits more space for copper in the slot.

The disadvantages of direct water cooling are that (*i*) cost of cooling system becomes more and (*ii*) water should be highly purified and distilled.

3.12. MACHINE APPLICATIONS

Machine application means choice of an electrical machine well-suited to meet the demand of a load. A judicious selection of a machine for a given load requires that machine terminal characteristics and load characteristics are known to a fair degree of accuracy. In addition, it is essential that machine and load characteristics are compatible with each other for stable and efficient operation of the machine-load combination.

For many industrial applications, electric motor is usually fed from a constant voltage source. A motor connected to such a source would have one speed-torque curve as shown in Fig. 3.58 (*a*) for a 3-phase induction motor. The load requires torque that may, or may not, vary with speed. In Fig. 3.58 (*a*), the speed-torque curve for a fan type load is shown by a dotted curve. The steady operating point P is obtained where the load characteristic intersects the motor characteristic. At this point P, the torque developed by the motor electromagnetically is equal to the torque absorbed by the load mechanically.

The torque required by a mechanical load, in general, depends upon the type of driven equipment. The speed-torque characteristic of a load represents the change in speed as the load torque is varied. For various driven mechanisms, the speed-torque characteristics may broadly be classified as under :

(*a*) **Speed-torque characteristics independent of speed.** For some driven mechanisms, load torque T_L does not depend upon the operating speed. This is indicated by curve 1 in Fig. 3.58 (*b*). Examples of such loads are cranes during hoisting and loads in which friction is dominant like reciprocating pumps, air compressors etc.

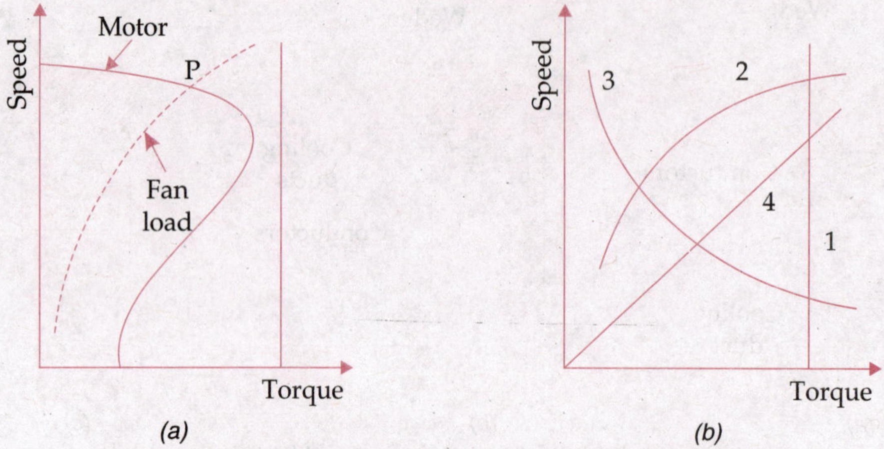

Fig 3.58: (*a*) Speed-torque characteristics of a motor-load system,
(*b*) Speed-torque curves of various types of mechanical loads.

(*b*) **Parabolic speed-torque characteristics.** This is illustrated by curve 2 in Fig. 3.58 (*b*). In such driven equipments, the load torque is proportional to some power of speed. Examples of such loads are fans, centrifugal pumps, propellers in ships etc. In fans, the load torque is almost proportional to square of speed.

(*c*) **Hyperbolic speed-torque characteristics.** These type of characteristics are illustrated by curve 3 in Fig. 3.58 (*b*). For such loads, the driven equipment requires a torque that is inversely proportional to speed. In other words, the load torque required is low at high speeds and high at low speeds. Such type of characteristics are possessed by lathes, milling machines, machine tools, winches etc. Since these loads are associated with high torque at low speeds and low torque at high speeds, the power required to drive such loads remains substantially constant.

(*d*) **Linear speed-torque characteristics.** These type of characteristics are indicated by straight line 4 in Fig. 3.58 (*b*). Such characteristics are possessed by viscous friction and loads in which loading torque is directly proportional to speed. Calendering machines, eddy-current brakes and generators feeding fixed resistors display such type of speed-torque characteristics.

In all types of mechanical loads discussed above, the motor must be able to supply the starting as well as the running torques within specified limits of current and temperature rise.

The electromagnetic torque developed by a motor may remain constant with load or may vary with it. Based on this, the speed-torque characteristics of motors may be classified as under :

(*a*) **Flat-type characteristics.** Some motors develop electro-magnetic torque which does not depend on their operating speed. Such a characteristic is indicated by curve 1 in Fig. 3.59 (*a*). These type of characteristics are possessed by synchronous and hysteresis motors.

(*b*) **Shunt-type characteristics.** In motors possessing shunt type characteristics, the speed drops from no-load to full-load by a few percent as shown by curve 2 in Fig. 3.59 (*a*). Examples of such motors are A.C. induction motors and D.C. shunt motors.

(*c*) **Series-type characteristics.** In some motors, high electromagnetic torque is associated with low speed but low electrical torque with high speed. Such characteristics, indicated by curve 3 in Fig. 3.59 (*a*), are referred to as series-type characteristics. A.C. series (also called universal motors in small sizes) and D.C. series motors possess these types of characteristics.

The speed-torque characteristics shown in Fig. 3.59 (*a*) can be raised or lowered in adjustable-speed drives. D.C. motors are best suited for such speed-controlled drives than A.C. motors.

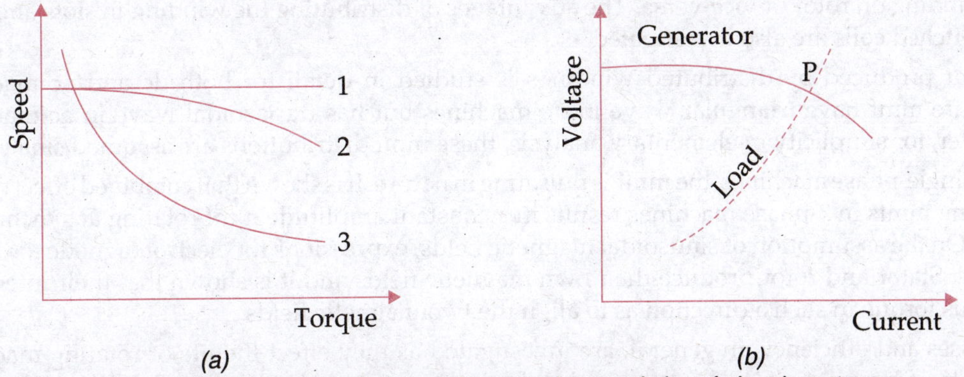

Fig 3.59: *(a)* Various types of speed-torque characteristics of electric motors. *(b)* Volt-ampere characteristics of generator-load combination.

Just as in a motor, the operating point in generator-load combination is obtained where there characteristics intersect each other. In Fig. 3.59 (*b*), solid curve shows variation of output voltage of a generator (D.C. shunt generator or alternator) as its load current is increased. The voltage-current graph for a load is shown in this figure by dotted curve. When this generator feeds power to this load, operating point *P* is obtained by the intersection of their *V-I* characteristics. At point *P*, the power given out by the generator is equal to the power absorbed by the load. When several generators are operated in parallel, as in power generating stations, it is desired that terminal voltage should remain almost constant over a wide variation of load. However, when a motor is fed from a single generator, the output voltage of the generator may be adjusted in a particular fashion so as to obtain a wide speed-control of the motor.

It is seen from above that the most outstanding features of electrical machines are the torque-speed characteristics for a motor and *V-I* characteristics for a generator. Equally important are the limits between which these characteristics can be varied without any damage to the electrical machine. Other relevant economic features are efficiency, p.f., initial cost and effect of losses on operating cost, heating and ratings of electrical machines. Several of these important features are discussed for the common types of electrical machines in the present book.

Steady state performance of electrical machines has been discussed in detail in this book. However, the role played by rotating electrical machines in modern technology has become so wide that an understanding of their transient and dynamic behaviour is of paramount importance. For this purpose, the mechanical features such as shaft elasticity, system moment of inertia and friction must be included in the equations governing the performance of a machine-load system. Such an analysis, being quite complex, is beyond the scope of the present book. This type of analysis is, however, presented in the companion volume "Generalized Theory of Electrical Machines" written by the author of the present book.

3.13. SUMMARY

In this chapter, general expressions for electromagnetic torque and generated emfs are derived. Constructional features of basic types of rotating machines, *i.e.* induction, synchronous and dc machines are presented; this helps in modifying the general torque and emf expressions for a particular machine under consideration. Expressions for generated emf in dc and ac machines are derived from Faraday's law. It is shown that for time-varying magnetic flux, both speed and transformer emfs are generated in armature coils. It is emphasized that it is the relative motion between field flux and armature winding that matters ; the armature winding may be on stator and field winding on rotor or vice-versa. The advantages of distributing the winding in slots and using short-pitched coils are also investigated.

Mmf produced by distributed windings is studied in detail for both dc and ac machines. Armature mmf have triangular wave in dc machines but has trapezoidal wave in ac machines. However, for simplicity in elementary analysis, these mmf distributions are assumed sine waves.

In single-phase machines, the mmf is pulsating in nature. It is shown that combined effect of three pulsating mmfs in 3-phase machines results in a constant amplitude mmf rotating at synchronous speed. On the assumption of sinusoidal magnetic fields, expressions for electromagnetic torque are derived. Stator and rotor produce their own magnetic fields and it is shown that their interaction develops torque in such a direction as to align the two magnetic fields.

Losses and efficiency, in general, are investigated as they effect the life of rotating machines. Concepts of hysteresis, eddy-current and pulsation losses are also presented. Different machine ratings are discussed briefly.

General expressions for electromagnetic torque and generated emfs developed in this chapter are useful for further analysis of the basis rotating machine types in the ensuing chapters.

PROBLEMS

3.1. *(a)* Give the physical concepts about the production of electromagnetic and reluctance torque in rotating electrical machines.

(b) Show that the net electromagnetic torque developed is zero if the rotating electrical machine has different number of poles on its stator and rotor.

3.2. *(a)* Explain the production of torque through the concept of interaction of magnetic fields. Using this concept, show that no electromagnetic torque is produced if (*i*) stator has 4 poles and rotor has 2 poles, (*ii*) stator has 6 poles and rotor has 2 poles.

(b) Explain the concept of alignment torque. Using this concept, discuss the condition under which reluctance torque will be developed in an electrical machine having cylindrical stator and salient-pole rotor. [**Ans.** (*b*) The exciting winding must be on stator]

3.3. *(a)* From the construction point of view, enumerate the common essential features of rotating electrical machines.

(b) Describe the constructional features of both types of polyphase induction motors. Why has induction motor come to be called so?

3.4. *(a)* Describe the advantages of providing field winding on the rotor and armature winding on the stator in case of large synchronous machines.

(b) Give the constructional features of both types of sychronous machines. Why has synchronous machine come to be called so?

3.5. Give the constructional features of D.C. machines. With a suitable diagram, describe the constructional details of a commutator also.

3.6. Explain, with suitable diagrams, the following :

(a) stator of a 3-phase induction machine and the different materials used for its construction,

(b) squirrel-cage rotor of a 3-phase induction motor and the different materials used for its construction,

(c) wound-rotor of a 3-phase induction motor alongwith the various materials used,

(d) 2-pole, 3-phase salient-pole stator of alternator with armature having 6 slots,

(e) 4-pole, 3-phase salient-pole stator of alternator with armature having 12 slots, two parallel paths with windings in star.

(*f*) rotor spider having four salient poles with damper bars, cylindrical rotor having four-pole field winding and the materials used for their construction,

(*g*) different parts of a D.C. machine stator and the materials used for their construction,

(*h*) different parts of a D.C. machine rotor and the materials used for their construction.

3.7. (*a*) In what respect are A.C. and D.C. generators (*i*) similar and (*ii*) different.

(*b*) How can a D.C. generator be converted into a 3-phase delta-connected alternator?

(*c*) What is yoke, pole core, pole-shoe in a D.C. machine? What purpose do they serve?

(*d*) Why is pole-shoe area more than the pole-core area in D.C. machines?

(*e*) What is a commutator? What purpose does it serve in a D.C. generator and motor?

(*f*) Distinguish between armature winding and field winding.

(*g*) Distinguish between load current and exciting current.

3.8. (*a*) Why are some parts of electrical machines laminated?

(*b*) Which parts of the following machines are laminated and which are not? DC machines, 3-phase synchronous machines, 3-phase induction machines.

(*c*) Why is yoke laminated in some DC motors?

(*d*) Which type of rotor of a 3-phase induction motor permits the insertion of external resistance in its circuit?

(*e*) Why are rotor bars skewed in a squirrel-cage rotor?

3.9. (*a*) Give the physical concepts of the following :

(*i*) Flux-density wave is sinusoidally distributed in space.

(*ii*) Pulsating-stationary flux.

(*b*) Distinguish clearly between the electrical and mechanical degrees. Show that

$$\omega = \frac{P}{2}\,\omega_m \text{ and } f = \frac{PN}{120}\text{ Hz.}$$

3.10. (*a*) Explain the following terms with respect to rotating electrical machines :

Pole-pitch, coil, coil-side, full-pitch coil, chorded-coil, chording angle, coil span.

(*b*) Show that for a *P*-pole machine, the total flux per pole is given by

$$\phi = \frac{4}{P}\,B_p \cdot l.r$$

(*c*) Define the terms : conductor, end-connection, turn, two-turn coil.

3.11. (*a*) Derive an expression for the e.m.f. generated in one *N*-turn full-pitch coil because of its relative motion with respect to time-invariant flux ϕ. Hence show that the generated e.m.f. lags by 90° the flux that produces it.

(*b*) Calculate the phase and line voltages of a three-phase star-connected 4-pole small alternator having a total flux per pole 0.30 Wb. Each phase has a concentrated winding of 10 full-pitched turns and the relative velocity between armature winding and field flux is 1500 r.p.m. **[Ans.** 666.33 V, 1154.1 V]

3.12. (*a*) Show that e.m.f. generated in a short-pitched coil is reduced by a factor $\cos\frac{\varepsilon}{2}$ where ε is the chording angle.

(*b*) Using the *Blv* concept, show that average value of e.m.f. generated in one conductor of a rotating machine is $P\,\phi\,n$ where P = number of poles, ϕ = total flux per pole and n = relative speed between flux and conductor. Hence derive an expression for the e.m.f. generated in the armature winding of a synchronous machine.

(*c*) Write a set of voltage equations, as a function of time, for the three phases of synchronous machine with phase order *a*, *b*, *c*. Take time origin at the instant flux linkages with phase *a* are (*i*) zero and (*ii*) maximum.

(*d*) Under the conditions of (*c*), wite a set of voltage equations as a function of time for the line e.m.fs for a star-connected alternator. Show that line voltages are also displaced from each other by a time angle of 120°.

[**Hint:** (*d*) Line voltage $e_{ab} = e_a - e_b$ etc.]

[**Ans.** (*c*) (*i*) $e_a = \sqrt{2}\, E \cos \omega t$, $e_b = \sqrt{2}\, E \cos (\omega t - 120°)$, $e_c = \sqrt{2}\, E \cos (\omega t - 240°)$
(*ii*) $e_a = \sqrt{2}\, E \sin \omega t$, $e_b = \sqrt{2}\, E \sin (\omega t - 120°)$ etc.
(*d*) (*i*) $e_{ab} = \sqrt{3}\, E_m \cos (\omega t + 30°)$, $e_{bc} = \sqrt{3}\, E_m \cos (\omega t - 90°)$,
$e_{ca} = \sqrt{3}\, E_m \cos (\omega t + 150°)$; $E_m = \sqrt{2}\, E$
(*ii*) $e_{ab} = \sqrt{3}\, E_m \sin (\omega t + 30°)$, $e_{bc} = \sqrt{3}\, E_m \sin (\omega t - 90°)$,
$e_{ca} = \sqrt{3}\, E_m \sin (\omega t + 150°)$]

3.13. One *N*-turn coil on cylindrical stator is short-pitched by ε electrical space degrees and salient-pole rotor has 2-pole structure which produces sinusoidal flux along the air-gap periphery. Derive general expression for the flux lingkages with the chorded coil in terms of peak flux density and core dimensions. Find also the ratio of fractional-pitch coil flux linkages to that of the full-pitch coil. [**Ans.** $2\, B_p \cdot l.r. \cos \varepsilon/2, \cos \varepsilon/2$]

3.14. One *N*-turn full-pitched coil rotates with an angular velocity of ω_r rad/sec with respect to field flux.

Give an expression for the flux linkages with the coil as a function of time *t* and hence derive therefrom an expression for the e.m.f. generated in the coil. Discuss nature of the e.m.f. expression so obtained.

3.15. The stator of a 4-pole, 3-phase, 50 Hz induction machine is supplied from 3-phase, 50 Hz supply. The slip rings of the machine are open circuited. It is desired that frequency of the voltage across slip rings is (*a*) 50 Hz (*b*) 75 Hz (*c*) 100 Hz (*d*) 25 Hz. Find the speed of the rotor to obtain these frequencies.

[**Ans.** (*a*) Zero speed, (*b*) 750 r.p.m. against the direction of rotating field,
(*c*) 1500 r.p.m. against the direction of rotating field,
(*d*) 750 r.p.m. in the direction of rotating field.]

3.16. (*a*) Explain how a polyphase induction motor of the slipring type can be used as a frequency changer.

(*b*) The frequency of the e.m.f. in the stator circuit of a 3-phase, 6-pole induction motor is 50 Hz. If rotor circuit e.m.f. has a frequency of 2 Hz, then find :

(*i*) the direction in which the rotor is revolving with respect to the rotating field.

(*ii*) the slip and the rotor speed.

[**Ans.** (*b*) (*i*) in the direction of rotating field, (*ii*) 0.04, 960 r.p.m.]

3.17. (*a*) Explain how A.C. generated in the armature circuit of a D.C. machine, is rectified to D.C. by means of a commutator.

(*b*) Derive an expression for the e.m.f. generated in a D.C. machine.

3.18. (*a*) A 10 kW, 250 V, 8-pole, 600 r.p.m. lap-connected D.C. generator has 400 armature conductors. At rated voltage and current, armature ohmic losses are 150 watts. Compute the useful flux per pole.

(*b*) A 6-pole D.C. generator has a rated speed of 800 r.p.m. Calculate frequency of the e.m.f. (*i*) generated in the armature conductors and (*ii*) at the brushes.

[**Hint:** (*a*) $I_a^2 r_a$ = 150 watts. Calculate E_a from the relation $E_a = V_t + I_a r_a$ and then the flux per pole.] [**Ans.** (*a*) 0.06344 Wb (*b*) 40 Hz ; 0 Hz].

3.19. (*a*) What are the advantages of distributing the windings in slots?

(*b*) Define distribution factor and show that its expression for the fundamental frequency component is given by $\dfrac{\sin q\gamma/2}{q\sin\gamma/2}$.

(*c*) Define the terms phase-band and phase-spread. In 3-phase A.C. machines, explain why a phase-spread of 60° is preferred to a phase spread of 120°.

[**Hint:** (c) For σ = 60°, k_{d1} = 0.955 and for σ = 120°, k_{d1} = 0.827. Thus the phase e.m.f. is reduced and for a given armature current, A.C. machine output is also reduced. For a narrow phase-spread of 60°, the phase e.m.f. and output for a given current are $\dfrac{0.955}{0.827}$ = 1.15 times their corresponding values for the wide phase-spread of 120°. Also for σ = 60, k_{d3} = 0.637 and for σ = 120°, k_{d3} = 0. Though σ = 120° eliminates third harmonics completely from the phase and line e.m.fs., yet 60° phase-spread is almost always employed, because third harmonics can be suppressed from the lines by connecting the phases in star or delta.]

3.20. (*a*) Enumerate the advantages of fractional pitch winding.

(*b*) Define pitch factor and derive an expression for it.

(*c*) What should be the value of chording angle for eliminating (*i*) third harmonics, (*ii*) 5th harmonics and (*iii*) 7th harmonics from the phase e.m.fs.

(*d*) Define winding factor. What is its value for

(*i*) full-pitched distributed winding and

(*ii*) short-pitched concentrated winding? [**Ans.** (*c*) 60°, 36°, 25.71°, (*d*) k_d, k_p]

3.21. (*a*) Discuss the effect of pitch and distribution factors in an alternator.

(*b*) A 3-phase star-connected alternator has a rating of 810 kVA at 2.5 kV and has 12 poles. Rated speed is 500 r.p.m. There are three slots per pole per phase and number of conductors per slot is 5. For a full-pitched winding, compute the flux per pole to give rated terminal voltage at no load. [**Ans.** (*b*) 0.07522 Wb]

3.22. (*a*) For a 3-phase winding having 3-slots per pole per phase, calculate the breadth factor in case phase spread is (*i*) 60° (*ii*) 120°.

(*b*) An alternator has 3 slots per pole per phase. For a coil span of 8 slots, find the winding factor. [**Ans.** (*b*) 0.9598, 0.8312 (*b*) 0.9452]

3.23. (*a*) A full-pitched one-turn coil, the ends of which are connected to slip-rings, is wound on a cylindrical iron core and rotates in a two-pole field, the pole arc being 75% of the pole pitch. Sketch and account for the waveform of the e.m.f. for one revolution of the coil allowing for (*i*) fringing of the flux on the pole tips and (*ii*) no fringing of the flux on the pole tips. [*I.A.S.*, 1980]

(*b*) A 3-phase, 50 Hz, 8-pole, star-connected alternator has 120 stator slots and each slot has 10 conductors. The coil span is 12 slots. If the flux per pole is 0.12 Wb, calculate the induced e.m.f. between lines. Which of the e.m.f. harmonics is eliminated? (*I.A.S.*, 1982)

[**Ans.** (*a*) With no fringing, e.m.f. is zero for first 22.5° and the last 22.5°. For 75% of pole pitch or 135°, the e.m.f. wave is identical with B-wave. (*b*) 8400.3 V, 5th harmonic.]

3.24. A 3-phase, delta-connected, 4-pole, 50 Hz, 415 V induction motor has 36 stator slots and 10-turn coils, each short-pitched by one slot. If stator leakage impedance is neglected, find the flux per pole of the rotating flux-density wave in case the stator of induction motor has *(a)* single-layer winding *(b)* double-layer winding. **[Ans.** *(a)* 0.03295 Wb *(b)* 0.016473 Wb]

3.25. A 4-pole, 50 Hz, delta-connected induction motor is supplied from 415 V, 3-phase source. It has 36 stator slots with double-layer winding and 8-turn coil chorded by one slot. Its stator length is 30 cm, mean air-gap radius 10 cm and air-gap length 1 mm.

(a) For negligible stator impedance, find the flux per pole of the rotating flux density wave.

(b) Find the line current drawn by the motor in case no-load losses are 1400 watts.

[Hint: *(b)* Use Eq. 3.60] **[Ans.** *(a)* 0.0206 Wb *(b)* 15.5672 A]

3.26. A 3-phase, 4-pole, 50 Hz, star-connected turbogenerator has distributed field winding of 140 turns and winding factor is 0.96. Its other data is as under :

Armature series turns per phase = 42

Armature radius = 0.4 m, Armature length = 4m, Gap length = 2 cm.

Winding factor for armature winding = 0.955

For no-load armature e.m.f. of 11 kV, find the value of field current required.

[Ans. 165.74 A]

3.27. A 3-phase, 8-pole, narrow-spread double-layer winding of the armature of an alternator is accommodated in 72 slots with 2 coil-sides per slot. Select a coil span to reduce 5th harmonic e.m.f. as much as possible and calculate the winding factor for fundamental and fifth harmonic e.m.fs.

What slot harmonics do you expect in e.m.f. wave? What would be their winding factor?

[Hint: Order of slot harmonics = $6q \pm 1$ etc.]

[Ans. Coil span = 140° ; k_{w1} = 0.9024, k_{w5} = 0.037786 ; 17 and 19, 0.9024]

3.28. *(a)* How do the winding factors affect the waveform of the output voltage of a synchronous generator?

(b) The line to line voltage of a 3-phase star-connected alternator, having rectangular space distribution of field flux, is observed to have no third or fifth harmonic component.

(i) What are the most likely reasons for the absence of these harmonics? Why?

(ii) By how much could be the fundamental component of voltage be increased by allowing full fifth harmonic in voltage wave?

[Ans. *(b)* *(i)* Star connection eliminates third harmonics ; chording angle of 36° eliminates fifth harmonics. *(ii)* 5.1525%]

3.29. The total flux per pole in the air gap of a 50 Hz A.C. generator is 0.069 Wb. If the flux density distribution is given by $B = B_1 \sin\theta + B_3 \sin 3\theta + B_5 \sin 5\theta$

where $B_3 = \frac{1}{3} B_1$ and $B_5 = \frac{1}{5} B_1$ and θ is the angle measured from interpolar axis, then determine the r.m.s. value of the e.m.f. per turn. The coil span is $\frac{4}{5}$th of a pole pitch.

[Hint: $\varepsilon = \left(1 - \frac{4}{5}\right) 180° = 36°$

$$\therefore \quad k_{p1} = \cos\frac{\varepsilon}{2} = 0.951$$

$$k_{p3} = \cos 3 \times 18 = 0.588, \; k_{p5} = 0$$

From the presentation leading to Eq. (3.51 *b*),

$$\phi_3 = \frac{1}{9}\,\phi_1,\ \phi_5 = \frac{1}{25}\,\phi_1$$

$$\therefore \text{ Total flux per pole } \phi = \phi_1 + \phi_3 + \phi_5 = \phi_1\left(1+\frac{1}{9}+\frac{1}{25}\right) = 1.151\,\phi_1$$

$$\therefore \text{ Fundamental flux per pole} \quad \phi_1 = \frac{0.069}{1.151} = 0.06 \text{ Wb}$$

$$\text{E.m.f. per turn,} \quad E_1 = \sqrt{2}\,\pi f k_{p1}\,\phi_1 = 12.674 \text{ V}$$

$$\text{From Eq. (3.51 } b\text{),} \quad E_3 \text{ per turn } = 12.674 \times \frac{0.588}{0.951} \times \frac{1}{3} = 2.612 \text{ V}$$

$$E_3 = 0$$

$$\text{Total e.m.f. per turn} \quad E = \sqrt{E_1^2 + E_3^2 + E_5^2} = 12.94 \text{ volts]}$$

3.30. (*a*) "Even though the field flux density wave of an alternator is non-sinusoidal, the alternator voltage can be made sinusoidal by dirtributing the armature winding in slots". Illustrate your answer with e.m.f. waveforms.

[**Hint:** (*a*) Non-sinusoidal distribution of field flux-density wave along the air-gap periphery is shown in Fig. 3.60 (*a*). If one full-pitch coil rotates with respect to this flux-density wave, then e.m.f. generated in that coil has the same waveform as that of the inducing flux-density wave–this is illustrated in Fig. 3.60 (*b*).

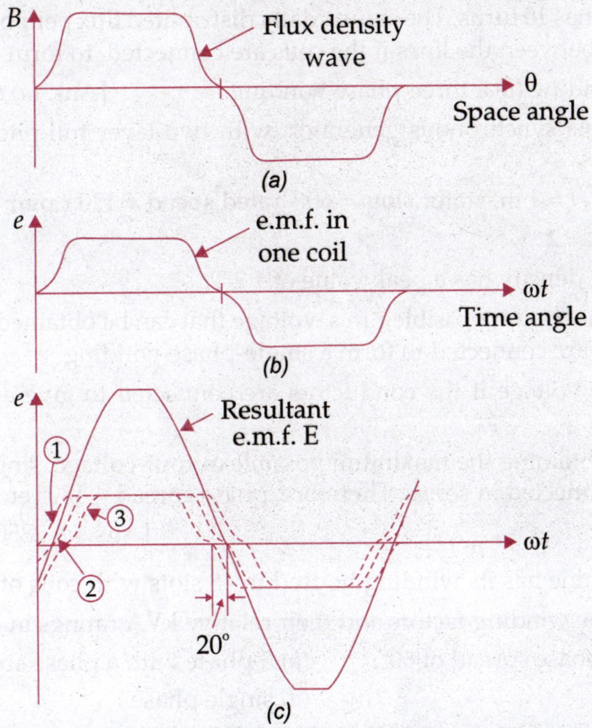

Fig 3.60: Effect of distributing the winding. Problem 3.30.

Suppose there are three slots per pole per phase, *i.e.*, there are 3 coils in the phase-belt or phase-band. Then waveforms of the e.m.f.s. generated in the coils numbered 1, 2 and 3 are as shown in Fig. 3.60 (*c*). Note that the zero-crossing of the e.m.f. waveforms is displaced from each other by a time angle of 20° (= slot angular pitch of 20°).

The e.m.f. waveform for each coil is of the same wave-shape as that of the flux-density wave. Since, in a phase belt, the coils are connected in series, the resultant e.m.f. can be obtained by adding the vertical ordinates of the three waveforms. Fig. 3.60 (*c*) illustrates that the resultant e.m.f. wave E approaches a sine wave. This shows that even though the flux-density wave of an alternator is non-sinusoidal, the alternator voltage can be made sinusoidal by distributing the armature winding in the slots along the air-gap periphery. If the winding consists of fractional-pitch coils, the resultant e.m.f. waveform can be made to approach a better sine wave.]

(*b*) The field-flux distribution of a 3-phase star-connected alternator is given by

$$100 \sin \theta + 30 \sin 3\theta + 20 \sin 5\theta.$$

where θ is the angle measured from the interpolar axis.

The alternator has 9 slots per pole and coil-span is from 1 to 9. If r.m.s. value of the fundamental phase voltage is V_1, then compute :

(*i*) r.m.s. value of the phase voltage and

(*ii*) r.m.s. value of the line voltage.

$\left[\textbf{Hint. } V_3 = V_1 \dfrac{k_{\omega 3}}{k_{\omega_1}} \cdot \dfrac{3\phi_3}{\phi_1} \text{ etc.}\right]$ **[Ans.** (*a*) 1.1507 V_1 (*b*) 1. 751 V_1]

3.31. A 50-Hz, 4-pole synchronous generator with 24 stator slots is wound with two layer winding. Each full-pitch coil has 10 turns. The sinusoidally distributed flux per pole is 0.02 Wb. Calculate the induced e.m.f. between the lines if the coils are connected to form

(*a*) a two-phase winding (*b*) a three-phase winding. [Ans. (*a*) 686.65 V (*b*) 594.693 V]

3.32. A 50-Hz salient-pole synchronous generator, with two-layer full-pitched winding, has the following data :

$$D = 7 \text{ m}, l = 1 \text{ m}, \text{stator slots} = 600, \text{rated speed} = 120 \text{ r.p.m.}$$

conductors per slot = 2.

The sinusoidal flux density has a peak value of 1.2 T.

(*a*) Calculate the maximum possible r.m.s. voltage that can be obtained from this generator if the conductors are connected to form a single-phase winding.

(*b*) Find the phase voltage if the conductors are connected to give a balanced three-phase winding.

[**Hint:** (*a*) For obtaining the maximum possible output voltage, single-phase winding has all the turns connected in series. Therefore, phase spread = 180° etc.]

[**Ans.** (*a*) 28506.24 V (*b*) 14294.47 V]

3.33. A 4-pole A.C. machine has its winding housed in 48 slots with coils of span $\frac{11}{12}$ th of a pole-pitch. Determine the winding factors and their relative kVA ratings in case this winding is

(*a*) 3-phase with a phase spread of 60°, (*b*) 3-phase with a phase spread of 120°,

(*c*) two phase, (*d*) single phase

[**Ans.** Winding factors : (0.9495, 0.8222, 0.895, 0.633), kVA : (100, 86.593, 94.24, 66.27)]

3.34. The flux density distribution for a 50-Hz cylindrical-rotor alternator is

$$B = \sin \theta + 0.3 \sin 3\theta + 0.2 \sin 5\theta + 0.1 \sin 7\theta$$

where θ is measured from neutral axis. Alternator has pole-pitch = 40 cm and core length = 35 cm. Stator coilspan is four-fifth of pole-pitch. Find equation for the e.m.f. generated in one-turn coil and its r.m.s. value.

[**Ans.** $e = 26.61 \sin \theta + 4.935 \sin 3\theta - 1.645 \sin 7\theta$; 19.1762 V]

3.35. An 8-pole alternator with single layer winding and full pitch coils, has 12 slots per pole. Each coil has 30 turns. The flux is sinusoidally distributed in space and its value per pole is 0.03 Wb. The machine is rotated at a speed of 750 r.p.m. The current per conductor is 50 A. For negligible internal voltage drops, find the kVA output available from the stator if the winding is connected as :

(*a*) single phase and (*b*) three phase.

[**Hint:** In single layer winding ,

$$\text{number of coils} = \frac{1}{2}(\text{number of slots}).$$

$$\therefore \quad \text{Total number of turns} = \left(\frac{12 \times 8}{2}\right)(30) = 1440 \text{ turns etc.}]$$

[**Ans.** (*a*) 305.424 kVA (*b*) 9.465 kVA]

3.36. A 3-phase, 50 Hz, 10 pole alternator with 90 slots has star-connected winding to give a generated e.m.f. of 11 kV at no load. The coils are chorded by one slot. If the flux per pole is 0.110 Wb, compute the number of series turns required for each phase of this alternator.

[**Hint:** Conductors per slot must be a whole number.] [**Ans.** 270]

3.37. A 3-phase, 3 kV, 50 Hz, 300 r.p.m. alternator has the following data :

Armature diameter = 1.90 m, core length = 0.39 m

Peak air-gap flux density = 0.95 T

Number of stator slots = 180

Air-gap length = 1 cm

This alternator has single-layer winding and two circuits per phase. Find the total armature turns per phase. Assume sinusoidal flux distribution. The winding is short pitched by one slot. Calculate also the peak value of fundamental field m.m.f.

In case current per conductor is 100 A, estimate kVA rating of the alternator.

[**Ans.** 240, 7559.9 At/pole, 1039.2 kVA]

3.38. The yoke of a 6-pole D.C. machine has its external and internal diameters of 90 and 76 cms respectively and axial length of 30 cms. The armature is wave connected with 72 slots and 6 conductors per slot. The flux density in the yoke is 0.86 T. Calculate the generated e.m.f. at the machine terminals for an armature speed of 900 r.p.m.

[**Hint :** Flux per pole = 2 (yoke flux), see Fig. 3.8] [**Ans.** 702.173 V]

3.39. A 3-phase delta-connected induction motor has 6 poles, 36 slots, 2-layer winding and 12-turn coils short-pitched by one slot. Find the flux per pole of the rotating flux density wave, with stator connected to 400 V, 50 Hz, 3-phase supply. The magnitude of voltage drop in stator leakage impedance is assumed to be 1% of supply voltage. [**Ans.** 0.01327 Wb]

3.40. (*a*) Using *Blv* concept, show that average e.m.f. generated in one conductor is $2 f \phi$. Hence prove that per-phase e.m.f. generated in an alternator is given by $\sqrt{2}\, \pi f \phi\, k_w \cdot N_{ph}$.

(*b*) A 3-phase, 8-pole, 750 r.p.m. star-connected alternator has 144 slots with 6 conductors per slot. Flux per pole is 0.06 Wb and coils are full-pitched. Calculate the phase and line e.m.fs.

What will be the phase and line e.m.fs if the coils are reconnected to form a balanced 2-phase winding? **[Ans.** 1834.8 V, 3177.9 V ; 2595.02 V, 3669.36 V]

3.41. *(a)* Show that the m.m.f. changes linearly over the slot width and remains unaltered over the tooth width.

(b) A uniform air-gap machine consists of one full-pitch coil on the stator. If the coil has N turns, then for a current of i amperes in each turn, show that the m.m.f. along the air-gap periphery is of rectangular waveform with its magnitude equal to $\frac{1}{2}Ni$.

3.42. *(a)* A concentrated winding produces a rectangular m.m.f. waveform. Had this winding been distributed, show that the m.m.f. waveform would change from rectangular to stepped. Hence introduce the concept of current sheet.

A single-phase distributed winding carries alternating current. Show that the time-maximum of the peak m.m.f. for a P-pole machine is given by

$$F_{1pm} = \frac{4}{\pi} k_w \frac{N_{ph}\sqrt{2}I}{P} \text{ ATs per pole.}$$

(b) What would be the magnitude of the fundamental component of m.m.f. produced by the field winding of a uniform air-gap 2-pole machine wound with 16 concentric coils and with a slot angle of 7.5°? Each coil has 13 turns and the conductor current is 200 A.

[Ans. *(b)* 21917.65 ATs/pole]

3.43. In a balanced 3-phase stator winding, each phase belt of phase a has 100 ampere-conductors at the instant of its carrying maximum current. Sketch the m.m.f. wave for this phase in case slots per pole per phase (q) are 1, 2, 3 and 4. Find the amplitude of m.m.f. wave for this phase and comment upon the change in m.m.f. as q is increased.

[Hint : For $q = 1$, m.m.f. amplitude $= \frac{1}{2}(Ni) = 50$ etc.]

[Ans. 50, 100, 150 and 200 m.m.f. wave become more closer to sinusoidal m.m.f. as q is increased].

3.44. A 2-pole, 3-phase A.C. winding has 24 slots. Each slot carries 10 conductors. At the instant phase a carries maximum current of 16 A, do the following :

(a) Sketch m.m.f. wave of phase a only in a developed view of the slots. Comment upon the m.m.f. waveshape and indicate its amplitude in the sketch.

(b) Calculate the amplitude of the fundamental component of the m.m.f. wave.

[Hint: Refer to Fig. 3.29 *(c)*] **[Ans.** *(a)* Stepped m.m.f. wave ; 320 ATs *(b)* 390.2 ATs/pole]

3.45. A 3-phase, 100 kW, 6-pole, 50 Hz, delta-connected induction motor has 20 conductors per slot arranged in 72 slots. For a line current of 76 A, compute the peak value of the fundamental m.m.f. wave of any phase. Also, calculate the peak value of the resultant m.m.f. wave and its speed. The winding is short-pitched by one slot.

[Ans. 3000.8 AT/pole ; 4501.2 AT/pole, 1000 r.p.m.]

3.46. *(a)* Show that the pulsating m.m.f. can be expressed in terms of space angle α and time angle ωt as

$$F(\alpha, t) = F_m \cos \omega t \cos \alpha$$

where F_m is the m.m.f. corresponding to the maximum current I_m.

(b) Show that the m.m.f. produced by the armature winding of a commutator machine is of triangular waveform with its peak value equal to $\frac{1}{2}\frac{Z}{P}\frac{i}{a}$ ATs/ pole.

3.47. Two-phase windings space displaced from each other by 90° electrical, are connected to 2-phase supply. If the currents in the two windings are displaced from each other by a time-phase angle of 90° electrical, prove that a synchronously rotating m.m.f. wave of constant amplitude $I_m N$ is produced. Here N is equal to the series turns per phase.

Hence show that m-phase currents in m-phase windings would produce a synchronously rotating m.m.f. wave of constant amplitude of $\frac{m}{2}$ times the maximum m.m.f. of any one phase.

[**Hint :** Proceed as outlined in Art. 3.7]

3.48. For a non-salient pole machine, derive the general torque expression in terms of the interacting stator and rotor m.m.fs., stating the various assumptions made. Hence show that the electromagnetic torque can exist only when one of the two m.m.fs. has a component normal to the other m.m.f.

3.49. For a non-salient pole machine, derive the general torque expression in terms of total air gap flux per pole ϕ, number of poles P and rotor m.m.f. Hence show that electromagnetic torque can develop only when the load angle or torque angle remains constant with time.

3.50. The armature m.m.f. and field flux density vary sinusoidally with respect to angular position in the air gap of a rotating electrical machine having 4 poles and a rated speed of 960 r.p.m. At rated load conditions, the flux per pole is 20 m Wb, the amplitude of the armature m.m.f. wave is 530 ampere turns and the space displacement between the two waveforms is 36.685°. Estimate the power rating of the machine deriving the necessary relations. [*I.E.S.*, 1979)

[**Ans.** 4kW]

3.51. A 4-pole cylindrical machine has the following data :

Rotor diameter = 0.4 m, l = 1 m, stator bore diameter = 0.41 m

Peak value of sinusoidal gap flux density = 1 T

Calculate the air-gap reluctance, peak air-gap m.m.f., flux per pole and total air-gap energy.

[**Ans.** 12665.15 AT/Wb, 3978.87 ATs, 0.2 Wb, 1250 J]

3.52. A single-phase winding when excited by A.C., produces pulsating-stationary m.m.f. wave which can be decomposed into two constant amplitude counter-rotating m.m.f. waves. Using this concept, prove that when two-phase balanced winding is excited by two-phase balanced currents, a travelling m.m.f. wave of constant amplitude is produced.

3.53. Three coils a, b, c have their magnetic axis coincident. These coils a, b, c are excited by three-phase balanced currents $I_m \cos \omega t$, $I_m \cos (\omega t - 120°)$ and $I_m \cos (\omega t - 240°)$ respectively. Find the magnitude of resultant m.m.f. wave.

3.54. (*a*) Why is it essential to know the power losses in electrical machines? Show that the calculation of efficiency by the measurement of losses is more accurate than by measuring the output.

(*b*) What are no-load rotational losses? How can these be measured?

3.55. (*a*) Enumerate the various power losses in electrical machines. Which of these losses are affected by (*i*) rotor rotation (*ii*) the value of flux (*iii*) the load directly and (*iv*) square of the load.

(*b*) What happens to the power losses in electrical machines? Are these reversible?

(*c*) What is the efficiency of a generator or motor at no load?

[**Ans.** (*a*) (*i*) No-load rotational loss (*ii*) Hysteresis and eddy-current losses (*iii*) Brush contact loss (*iv*) I^2R losses and stray load loss. (*c*) Efficiency is zero.]

3.56. Output of rotating electrical machines is given by

$$S = K D^2 L B_{av} \cdot \overline{ac} \cdot n$$

where D = stator bore diameter, L = core length, n = rotor speed in r.p.s. B_{av} = average flux density in T, $\overline{ac}$ = ampere conductors per unit length of air-gap periphery and K is a constant. Compare the ratings and losses of two rotating electrical machines, the linear dimensions of one being x times those of the other. The flux and current densities in both are the same. Hence show that larger the size of the machine, greater is its efficiency.

[**Hint:** For first machine, $\overline{ac_1} = \dfrac{a\delta \cdot Z}{\pi D}$. Therefore $\overline{ac_2} = x \cdot \overline{ac_1}$ etc.]

[**Ans.** $x^4 S_1$, $x^3 W_1$ where S_1 and W_1 are the rating and losses respectively in the first rotating electrical machine.]

3.57. (*a*) What are the various electrical losses in rotating electrical machines? Give a physical understanding of hysteresis and eddy-current losses and show that the use of thin laminations minimises the eddy-current loss.

(*b*) What loss is designated as stray load loss? How is this caused in electrical machines?

(*c*) Show that maximum efficiency occurs when constant loss is equal to variable loss.

3.58. (*a*) The proposed load schedule for a small rolling mill is as under :

Billet in the rolls, 500 kW for 30 sec.

Billet out of the rolls, 80 kW for 40 sec.

Find a continuous kW rating of the motor.

(*b*) The operating cycle for a lift is as under :

Load going up (1 min) = 60 kW

Loading period at top (2 min) = 10 kW

Load going down (1 min) = – 50 kW (power pumped back to supply)

Loading period at bottom (2 min) = 10 kW

On the basis of heating, select a suitable motor rating out of the following available sizes: 25, 30, 35, 40, 50 and 60 kW. [**Ans.** (*a*) 350 kW (≈ 332.866 kW) (*b*) 35 kW (≈ 32.94 kW)]

3.59. (*a*) What is meant by one-hour rating of an electrical motor? Discuss.

(*b*) A motor driving a colliery winding equipment has the following points on its load duty cycle.

Time, sec	0	20	20	60	60	70	90	Repeat
Output, kW	0	1000	1000 to 500	500	500 to –200	0	0	cycle

The complete load cycle curve can be obtained by joining these points with straight lines. Specify a continuous kW rating of the motor for this load cycle.

[**Ans.** 450 kW (≈ 432.045 kW)]

3.60. (*a*) A continuous-rated motor can deliver higher power outputs for short-time duty. Discuss.

(*b*) A 10 kW, 3-phase induction motor has a heating time constant of 2 hours and attains a final steady temperature rise of 50°C with continuous loading. Find the time for which this motor may be safely loaded at 20 kW. The full-load ohmic loss is twice the core loss and ambient temperature is 30°C. [**Ans.** 0.811 hr]

3.61. (*a*) Explain the significance of machine ratings.

(*b*) Describe more common types of machine ratings based on thermal considerations.

(c) Explain the method of determining the power rating of electric motors for driving the loads requiring almost constant torque.

(d) Describe the method used for the determination of electric-motor rating for a periodically varying load.

3.62. (a) An induction motor has a final steady temperature rise of 40°C when running at its rated output of 20 kW. Determine its half-hour rating for the same temperature rise if the ohmic losses at rated output are 1.25 times its constant losses. The heating time constant is 90 minutes.

(b) For the motor of part (a), the motor cooling is improved by 20% because of its installation in the hills. Find its new continuous power rating (i) for the same temperature rise (ii) for a temperature rise of 50°C. **[Ans.** (a) 47.17 kW (b) 23.324 kW, 27.57 kW]

3.63. (a) What are the more commonly employed classes of insulation in electrical machines? Discuss these with respect to the maximum temperature, materials etc.

(b) An electric motor with continuous rating P_r can deliver much higher output P_x for a short-time duration t_x. Develop a relation that gives the short-time rating P_x in terms of P_r, t_x, heating time constant etc.

3.64. (a) Differentiate between short-time rated and continuous rated motors.

(b) Temperature rise of an electric motor at rated load of 30 kW was found to be 20°C after one-hour run and 50°C after three-hour run. In case its full-load ohmic loss is 1.5 times the constant loss, calculate its one-hour rating without exceeding the specified temperature rise.

(c) In case temperature rise of 10% is allowed for motor in part (b), find its new continuous rating. **[Ans.** (a) 88.74 kW (b) 32.4 kW]

3.65. (a) The temperature rise of an 80 kW motor is 25°C after 0.5 h and 40°C after 1.0 h on full load. The motor I^2R loss on full load is twice the core loss. When this motor is fitted with a fan to improve the cooling, the final full-load temperature is found to be 48°C. Estimate the motor rating for the final temperature rise to be that obtained without fan.

Derive the formula used for obtaining this rating.

(b) For the motor of part (a), determine its one-hour rating (i) without fan and (ii) with fan.

[Ans. (a) 96.44 kW (b) 108.63 kW, 130.95 kW]

3.66. (a) What is pulsation loss? Discuss how this loss is caused in rotating electrical machines.

(b) Describe the advantages of using hydrogen as a coolant in large turbo-generators.

(c) Discuss where direct cooling is preferred over hydrogen cooling.

(d) Describe the various types of speed-torque characteristics as possessed by driven equipments and electric motors.

(e) Answer the following :

(i) Most outstanding feature of a generator and a motor.

(ii) Economic features of rotating electrical machines.

(iii) Factors leading to the progress in electrical machinery.

[Ans. (e) (i) V—I and speed-torque characteristics, (ii) Efficiency, p.f., initial cost etc. (iii) Improvements in the quality and characteristics of steel, conductor and insulating materials and also in the cooling of machines.]

4

Chapter

D.C. Machines

D.C. machine is a highly versatile energy conversion device. It can meet the demand of loads requiring high starting torques, high accelerating and decelerating torques. At the same time, D.C. machine is easily adaptable for drives requiring wide-range speed control and quick reversals. These inherent characteristics can further be modified, if desired, by feedback circuits. In view of these outstanding features, D.C. machine possesses a high degree of flexibility. These are therefore widely used in industry, particularly for tough jobs as are encountered in steel-mill drives—inspite of their higher initial cost.

D.C. machines discussed in this chapter have hetropolar field system (alternate *N* and *S* poles) and armature-commutator system. In normal D.C. machines, stator core is not laminated ; armature core is, however, always laminated to reduce eddy-current losses. Direct-current machines used in control systems have their magnetic circuit completely laminated. This is done to minimise the effect of eddy-current damping on the fast response required in D.C. machines employed in controlled systems.

At present, the annual production of D.C. machines is about 40% of the rupee volume in electrical-machine production and sales. This is on account of the fact that most highway vehicles use batteries for the storage of electric energy. In these vehicles and automobiles, D.C. motors are used as starter motors, windshield-wiper motors, fan motors and for driving other accessories in the vehicles. For these purposes, almost millions of D.C. motors are built each year. In industrial applications requiring accurate control of speed and/or torque, D.C. motor is unrivalled. Therefore, D.C. motors are almost universally employed in steel and aluminium rolling mills, power shovels, electric elevators, railroad locomotives and large earth-moving equipment.

The constructional features of D.C. machines have already been described in Chapter 3. It has been stated there that field winding is a concentrated winding on salient poles bolted to the stator frame and armature winding is a distributed winding housed in the slots around the periphery of the cylindrical rotor. Basis principles underlying the torque production and e.m.f. generation in D.C. machines are also outlined in Chapter 3. The object of this chapter is to present the physical concepts regarding the steady state behaviour of D.C. machines.

Example 4.1. *(a) Sketch a 6-pole D.C. machine. Indicate the flux path for the six poles.*

(b) Draw neat diagram of a D.C. machine. Label all its parts and mention the material used for each part.

Solution. The object of this example is to supplement the constructional details already described in Art 3.2.3. The reader must go through this article before studying the following presentation.

(a) Sketch of a 6-pole D.C. machine is shown in Fig. 4.1. In this figure, iron from the bottom of armature teeth to the shaft diameter is the armature core. The flux paths for the six poles are also shown. It is observed from this figure that

(i) each pole carries a flux ϕ (say),

(ii) yoke handles half of the pole flux *i.e.* $\phi/2$,

(iii) armature core also handles a flux $\phi/2$.

Examination of Fig. 4.1 reveals that main flux ϕ starts from a north pole, crosses the air-gap and then travels down to the armature core. There, it divides into two equal ($\phi/2$) halves, each half enters the nearby south pole, each half then passes through the yoke and reaches the starting point of north pole so as to complete the flux path. Each flux line crosses the air-gap twice. Some flux lines may not enter the armature; this flux, called the leakage flux, is not shown in Fig. 4.1.

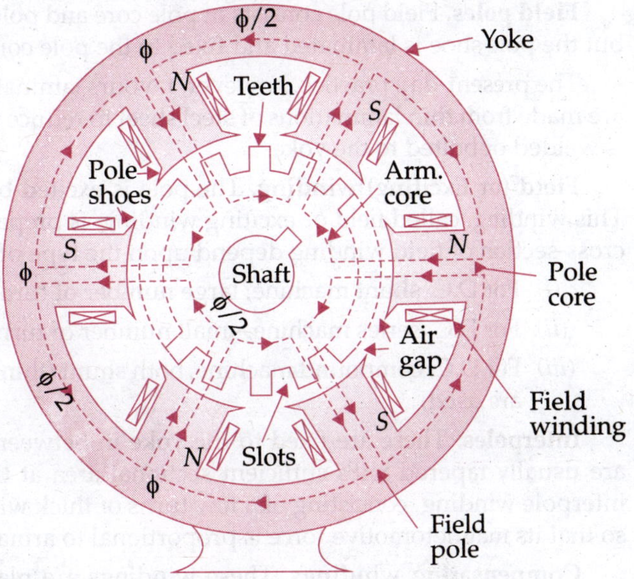

Fig 4.1: Flux paths in a 6-pole D.C. machine.

(b) Various parts of a 6-pole D.C. machine are shown in Fig. 4.1. Commutator forms the most important component of a D.C. machine. In Fig. 4.2 *(a)*, various parts of a 4-pole D.C. machine along with its commutator are labelled.

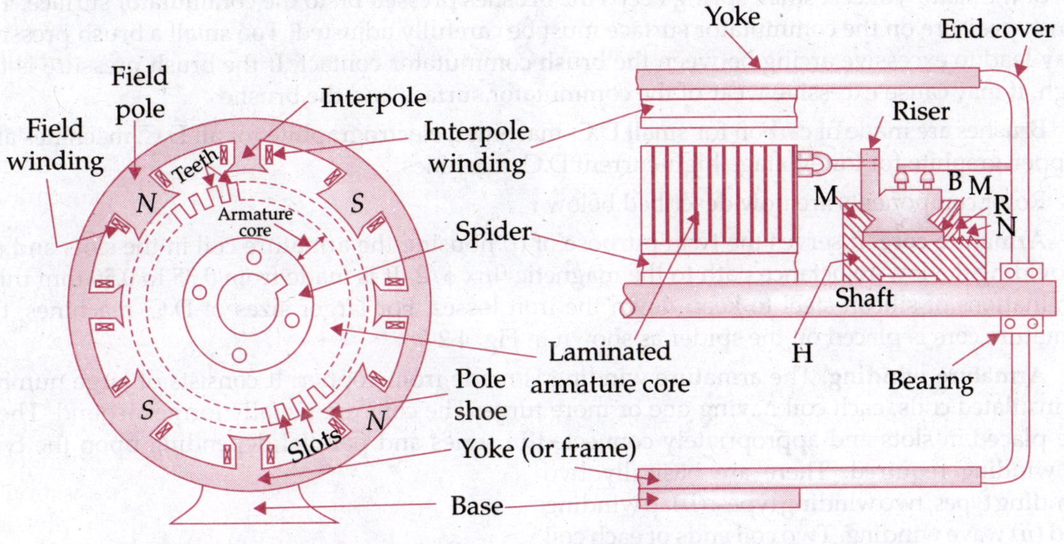

Fig 4.2: *(a)* Constructional features of 4-pole D.C. machine and commutator.

Stator of a D.C. machine consists of yoke (or frame), field windings, interpoles, compensating winding, brushes and end covers. Rotor consists of armature core, armature winding, commutator and shaft. Stator components are described first.

Yoke. It has two functions : *(i)* it provides path for the pole flux ϕ and carries half of it, *i.e.*, $\phi/2$ *(ii)* it provides mechanical support to the whole machine. Since the flux carried by yoke is stationary (*i.e.* constant), it is not laminated. As stated before, cast iron is used for small D.C. machines and fabricated steel for large D.C. machines. In case D.C. motor is to be operated through a power-electronics converter, the yoke is laminated to reduce the eddy-current losses.

Field poles. Field pole consists of pole core and pole shoe. The pole core is made from cast steel but the pole shoe is laminated and fixed to the pole core appropriately.

The present-day practice, however, favours laminated pole. Thus, both pole core and pole shoe are made from thin laminations of steel sheet to reduce the eddy-current losses. The laminated pole is welded or bolted to the yoke.

Field (or Exciting) winding. The pole is excited by a winding wound around the pole core. This winding, called field or exciting winding, is prepared from copper. The number of turns and cross-section of field winding depend upon the type of D.C. machine as under :

(i) For D.C. shunt machine, large number of turns of small cross-section are used.

(ii) For D.C. series machine, small number of turns of large cross-section are used.

(iii) For D.C. compound machine, both shunt (thin wire) and series (thick wire) field windings are used.

Interpoles. These are fixed to the yoke in between the main poles of a D.C. machine. These are usually tapered with sufficient sectional area at the root to avoid magnetic saturation. The interpole winding, consisting of a few turns of thick wire, is connected in series with the armature so that its magnetomotive force is proportional to armature current.

Compensating windings. These windings are placed in the slots cut in the pole faces of a D.C. machine. Compensating winding is also connected in series with the armature circuit. This winding is, however, used in large D.C. machines only.

Brushes. Brushes are housed in box-type brush holders attached to the stator end cover, Fig. 4.2 *(a)*, or the stator yoke. A small spring keeps the brushes pressed on to the commutator surface. The brush pressure on the commutator surface must be carefully adjusted. Too small a brush pressure may lead to excessive arcing between the brush commutator contact. If the brush pressure is too high, it may cause excessive wear of the commutator surface and the brushes.

Brushes are made of carbon for small D.C. machines, electrographite for all D.C. machines and copper-graphite for low-voltage high-current D.C. machines.

Rotor components are now described below :

Armature core. It serves the twin purpose of *(i)* housing the armature coil in the slots and *(ii)* providing the low-reluctance path to the magnetic flux $\phi/2$. It is made from 0.35 to 0.50 mm thick laminations of silicon steel to keep down the iron losses. For larger sizes of D.C. machines, the armature core is placed on the spider as shown in Fig. 4.2 *(a)*.

Armature winding. The armature winding is made from copper. It consists of large number of insulated coils, each coil having one or more turns. The coils are usually former wound. These are placed in slots and appropriately connected in series and parallel depending upon the type of winding required. There are basically two winding types: two winding types: *(i)* lap winding and *(ii)* wave winding. Two coil ends of each coil are then connected to the riser of segments of a commutator, Fig. 4.2 *(a)*.

Commutator. It is of cylindrical structure. It is built up of wedge-shaped segments of high conductivity hard-drawn copper to reduce its wear and tear. Segments are insulated from each other by 0.8 mm thick mica sheets. The segments are tapered as shown in Fig. 4.2 *(b)* so that their assembly results in circular shape. Hub *H* and

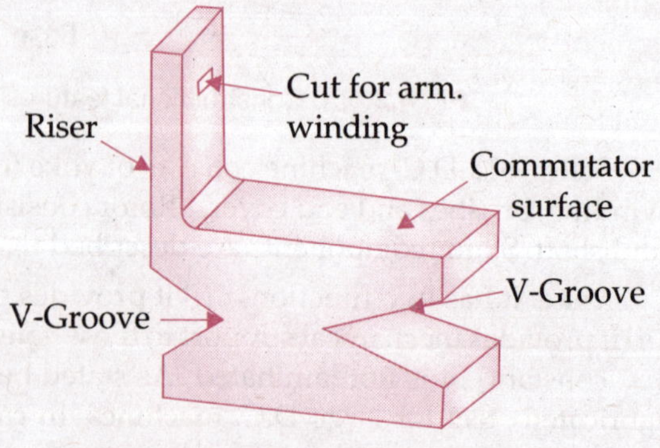

Fig 4.2: *(b)* One commutator segment.

ring R are insulated from commutator segments by mica sheet M and V-shaped so as to prevent the segments from flying out due to centrifugal forces, Fig. 4.2 *(a)*. Each commutator segment, Fig. 4.2 *(b)*, has a riser where conductors from the armature winding are connected.

Shaft. On armature shaft are mounted *(i)* hub H of commutator, *(ii)* spider in big machines or armature core in small machines and *(iii)* bearings. End covers are connected to the yoke on one side and to the bearings and shaft on the other side, Fig. 4.2 *(a)*.

4.1. ACTION OF COMMUTATOR

A commutator performs two important functions in a D.C. machine—the first one is to convert alternating quantities to direct quantities or *vice-versa* and the second function is to keep the rotor or armature m.m.f. stationary in space. The first commutator function of rectifying the alternating quantities in the armature winding to direct quantities at the output brushes of a D.C. generator, has already been explained in Art. 3.4.4. In case of a D.C. motor, the direct quantities at the brushes are converted to alternating quantities (voltage and current) in the armature winding. Thus a commutator can act both as a convertor or rectifier (A.C. to D.C.) and as an inverter (D.C. to A.C.).

The stator of the D.C. machine carries salient poles, which produce stationary air-gap flux. For the development of electromagnetic torque, the armature m.m.f. wave must also be stationary in space. The commutator in a D.C. machine carries out this second important function of rendering the armature m.m.f. wave stationary in space, inspite of the armature rotation. In the present article, this action of the commutator is examined in detail.

Fig. 4.3 shows a 2-pole D.C. machine, with four full-pitched coils housed in 4 slots. The four commutator segments, numbered 1 to 4, are insulated from each other and from the shaft. The centre line of the poles around which the field coil (or coils) is wound, is called the *direct axis* of the machine. The shape of the coil end-connections, makes it necessary to place the two carbon brushes along the direct axis or field axis, as depicted in Fig. 4.3.

In an actual D.C. machine, there are a large number of coils and slots and the number of poles is usually greater than 2, except for small D.C. machines. Therefore the D.C. machine illustrated in Fig. 4.3 differs much from a real machine, but it serves well in explaining the commutator action. It may also be noted that the brushes make contact with the outside periphery of the commutator, though in Fig. 4.3, these are shown inside the commutator segments, for the sake of clarity.

Coil sides in the slots are represented by small circles with crosses and dots in them, indicating currents away and towards the reader, respectively. In Fig. 4.3 *(a)*, there are two parallel paths between the two brushes. One parallel path may be traced as follows–terminal A to right hand carbon brush and commutator segment 1, upper coil-side in slot 1, back end connection 1, lower coil-side in slot 3, commutator segment 2, upper coil-side in slot 2, coil 2, lower coil-side in slot 4, commutator segment 3 and back to the terminal B. The second parallel path is from commutator segment 1, lower coil-side in slot 2, back coil end-connection 4, top coil-side in slot 4, commutator segment 4, lower coil-side of slot 1 and so on till terminal B is reached. The current entering at the right hand carbon brush divides equally between the two parallel paths described above. The effect of current in the armature coils is to set up an armature m.m.f. that is vertically upward along an axis 90° away from *d-axis*. This axis, which is space displaced by an angle of 90° from the *d*-axis, is called the *quadrature axis*. At the rotor surface, armature m.m.f. creates N-pole at the top and S-pole at the bottom of the rotor. The S-pole on the stator, attracts rotor N-pole and repels rotor S-pole. Similarly, N-pole on the stator attracts rotor S-pole and repels rotor N-pole. The torque produced by the interaction of field and armature poles is called *electromagnetic torque*. If this machine is working as a motor, the rotor would rotate in the direction of electromagnetic torque, *i.e.*, in the clockwise direction in Fig. 4.3. In case the machine is working as a generator, then the rotor must be driven by the prime-mover against the direction of electromagnetic torque for proper energy conversion. In Fig. 4.3, this direction of rotation for generator operation must be anticlockwise.

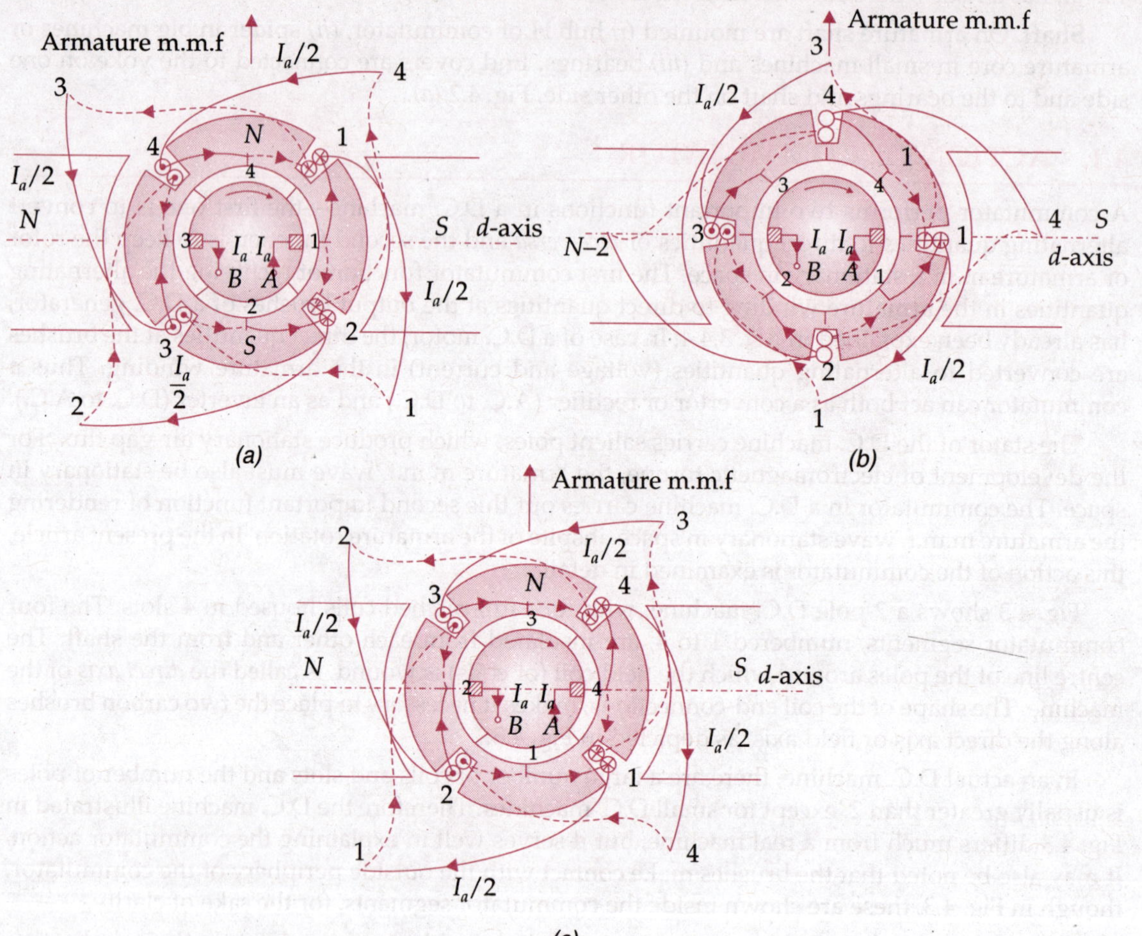

Fig 4.3: Armature m.m.f. is kept stationary in space along interpolar axis by action of the commutator.

Fig. 4.3 *(b)* illustrates the conditions when the rotor has turned through 45° clockwise. There are again two parallel paths, one through coil 1 and the second through coil 3. It may be seen that coils 1, 3 (housed in slots 1, 3) have maximum e.m.fs. generated in them ; because these coils are cutting the maximum flux. Coils 2, 4 are short-circuited by the brushes and carry no currents, because e.m.fs. induced in these coils are zero. Currents in coil-sides pertaining to slots 1, 3 in Fig. 4.3 *(b)*, again establish armature m.m.f. that is directed vertically upward. Note that coil current in each parallel path is again $I_a/2$ as it is in Fig. 4.3 *(a)*.

Fig. 4.3 *(c)* depicts the condition when the rotor has turned through by further 45° from the position of Fig. 4.3 *(b)*. One parallel path is now through coils 4, 1 and the second parallel path is through coils 3, 2. Coils in each parallel path carry again $I_a/2$ as it is in Fig. 4.3 *(a)* and *(b)*. The armature m.m.f. is again directed vertically upward. Hence it can be concluded that **armature m.m.f. is always stationary in space and is directed along the interpolar or quadrature axis,** even though the armature rotates. For a motor, the electromagnetic torque is always acting in the clockwise direction, (Fig. 4.3) and the rotation continues. For a generator, the armature must be driven in anticlockwise direction (Fig. 4.3), for the necessary energy conversion from mechanical to electrical.

An examination of Fig. 4.3 reveals as under :

1. Before 2 and 4 are short circuited by the brushes in Fig. 4.3 *(b)*, current in coil 2 flows as given below, see Fig. 4.3 *(a)*.

   From segment 2 to top coil-side 2, to bottom coil-side 4, and then to segment 3, current in coil 2 is $I_a/2$.

2. After the short circuit of coils 2 and 4 is over, current in coil 2 follows the path as under, see Fig. 4.3 *(c)*.

   From segment 3 to bottom coil-side 4, to top coil-side 2, and then to segment 2, i.e., opposite to the previous current flow. Therefore, current is now $-\frac{I_a}{2}$.

It is seen from above that coil carry current $I_a/2$ (or in general I_a/a) in one direction before these are short circuited. Soon after the short-circuit, these coils carry current $-I_a/2$ (or in general $-I_a/a$) in the reversed direction. Here *a* is the number of parallel paths and in Fig. 4.3, *a* is equal to 2. Thus, during the time of short-circuit, the currents in the short-circuited coils, in general, must be reduced from I_a/a to zero and then built up to $-I_a/a$. This process of current reversal in the coils short-circuited by the brushes is called *commutation* and the time during which it takes place is called *commutation period*. If the current variation with time is uniform from I_a/a to $-I_a/a$ as depicted in Fig. 4.4, a *linear commutation* is obtained.

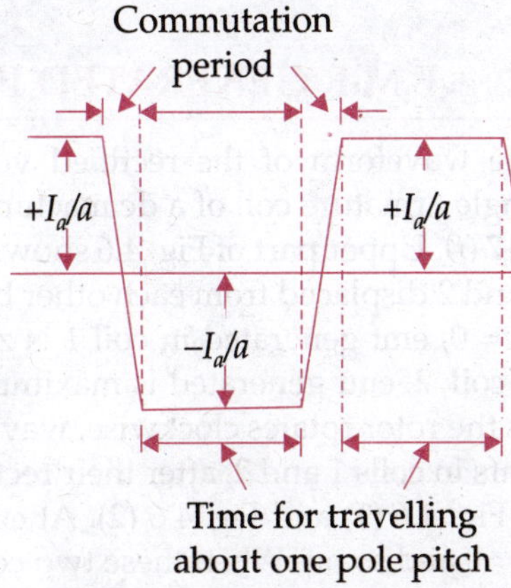

Fig 4.4: Variation of armature-coil current with linear commutation.

Another important conclusion from the foregoing analysis is that the magnitude of current in the coils under each pole, remains constant and equal to I_a/a, (Fig. 4.4). But the magnitude of e.m.fs. induced in the coils under each pole is not constant – coil under the pole centre has maximum e.m.f. induced in it, whereas the other coils have their e.m.f. magnitudes proportional to the flux density wave present there.

The coil short-circuited by the brushes during commutation process must have their coil sides in the zero flux density region so that e.m.f.s. induced in them are zero. In other words, the coils undergoing commutation must have their coil sides in the magnetic neutral axis of the field poles, *i.e.,* in the interpolar or quadrature axis. For example, coils 2 and 4 undergoing commutation in Fig. 4.3 *(b)* have their coil-sides in the magnetic neutral axis or interpolar axis. The shape of the coil end connections is such that the brush-axis is aligned along the field pole or direct axis. For convenience in the schematic diagram of a D.C. machine, the brushes are shown along the quadrature axis, *i.e.,* in the position of the coils which are short-circuited by the brushes and are undergoing commutation—this schematic diagram for a 2-pole D.C. machine is shown in Fig. 4.5 *(a)*. Hence it may be stated that the armature m.m.f. is always directed along the brush axis, which now coincides with the interpolar or quadrature axis of the D.C. machine. The circuit representation, more commonly employed for a D.C. machine with any number of poles is as illustrated in Fig. 4.5 *(b)*. In this figure, circular symbol represents the armature and two small rectangles or squares at the opposite sides of circle represent the two brushes.

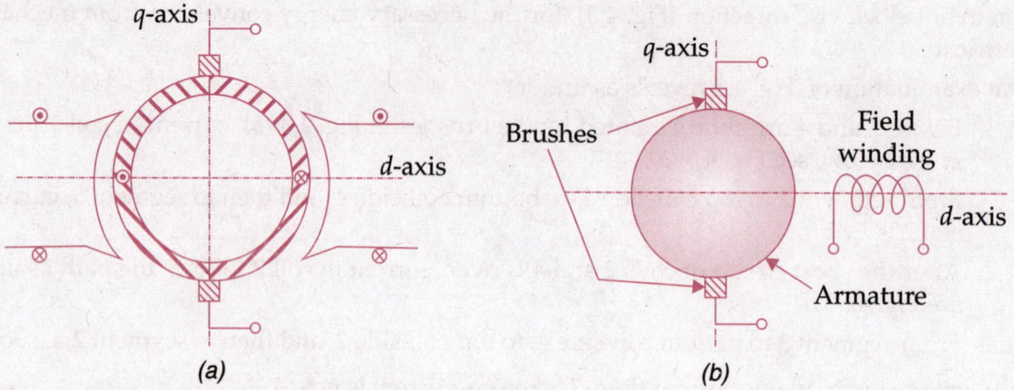

Fig 4.5: Schematic diagram of *(a)* 2-pole D.C. machine and *(b)* D.C. machine with any number of poles.

4.2. E.M.F. GENERATED IN THE ARMATURE

The waveform of the rectified voltage induced in a single armature coil of a dc machine is depicted in Fig. 3.17 *(f)*. Upper part of Fig. 4.6 shows two armature coils 1 and 2 displaced from each other by 90°. At the instant $\omega t = 0$, emf generated in coil 1 is zero, Fig. 4.6 (1) and in coil 2, emf generated is maximum (E_m), Fig. 4.6 (2). As the rotor rotates clockwise, waveforms of generated emfs in coils 1 and 2, after their rectification, are drawn in Fig. 4.6 (1) and Fig. 4.6 (2). At $\omega t = \pi/2$, $e_1 = E_m$ and $e_2 = 0$ and so on. When these two coils are connected in series in between the two brushes as shown in Fig. 4.3, the resultant rectified voltage wave across two brushes is obtained by adding the ordinates of the individual rectified voltage waves e_1 and e_2. This is illustrated in the resultant brush voltage waveform e_R as shown in Fig. 4.6 (3). It is seen from this figure that minimum voltage is E_m and maximum voltage is $\sqrt{2}\ E_m$.

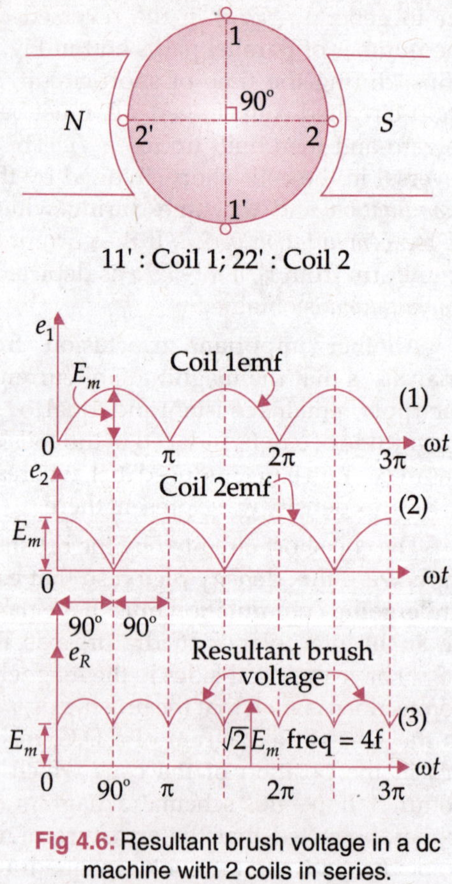

Fig 4.6: Resultant brush voltage in a dc machine with 2 coils in series.

Upper part of Fig. 4.7 shows three coils 1, 2, 3; displaced from each other by 120°. Waveforms of rectified voltage generated in coil 1 is shown as e_1 in Fig. 4.7 (1), in coil 2 is shown as e_2 in Fig. 4.7 (2) and in coil 3 it is shown as e_3 in Fig. 4.7 (3). At $\omega t = 0°$, $e_1 = 0$, $e_2 = E_m \sin 120° = 0.866\ E_m$ and $e_3 = E_m \sin 60° = 0.866\ E_m$. At $\omega t = 30°$, $e_1 = E_m \sin 30° = 0.5\ E_m$, $e_2 = E_m \sin 90° = E_m$ and $e_3 = E_m \sin 30° = 0.5\ E_m$ and so on.

When these three coils are connected in series in between the two brushes, the resultant rectified brush voltage e_R shown in Fig. 4.7 (4) is obtained by adding the ordinates of three rectified voltage waves e_1, e_2 and e_3. It is seen from Fig 4.7 (4) that at $\omega t = 0°$, result and brush voltage e_R is $e_1 + e_2 + e_3 = 0 + 0.866\ E_m + 0.866\ E_m = 1.732\ E_m = \sqrt{3}\ E_m$; at $\omega t = 30°$, $e_R = E_m \sin 30° + E_m \sin 90° + E_m \sin 30° = 2\ E_m$; at $\omega t = 60°$, $e_R = \sqrt{3}\ E_m$ and so on. It is observed from above that with three coils in series *(i)* the resultant brush voltage has increased *(ii)* the frequency of brush voltage has increased and *(iii)* ripple in the rectified voltage has reduced considerably as compared to their corresponding values with two coils in series between the brushes. As the number of series coils between the brushes is increased, *(i)* the magnitude of dc output voltage increases *(ii)* brush frequency becomes quite high so that *(iii)* ripple content in output voltage gets drastically reduced. Actually, there are several coils in series in between the two brushes resulting in an improved waveform for the rectified voltage at the brushes. Strictly speaking, the brush voltage waveform can't reach a pure direct voltage obtainable from a storage battery.

It is seen from Fig. 3.17 *(f)* that ripple voltage with one coil between brushes is $E_m - 0 = E_m$. Ripple voltage with two coils in series, from Fig. 4.6 (3) is $\sqrt{2}\ E_m - E_m = 0.414\ E_m$. With three coils in series, ripple voltage, from Fig. 4.7 (4) is given by $2\ E_m - \sqrt{3}\ E_m = 0.268\ E_m$. This shows that ripple content in output voltage gets reduced as the number of series coils between two brushes is increased.

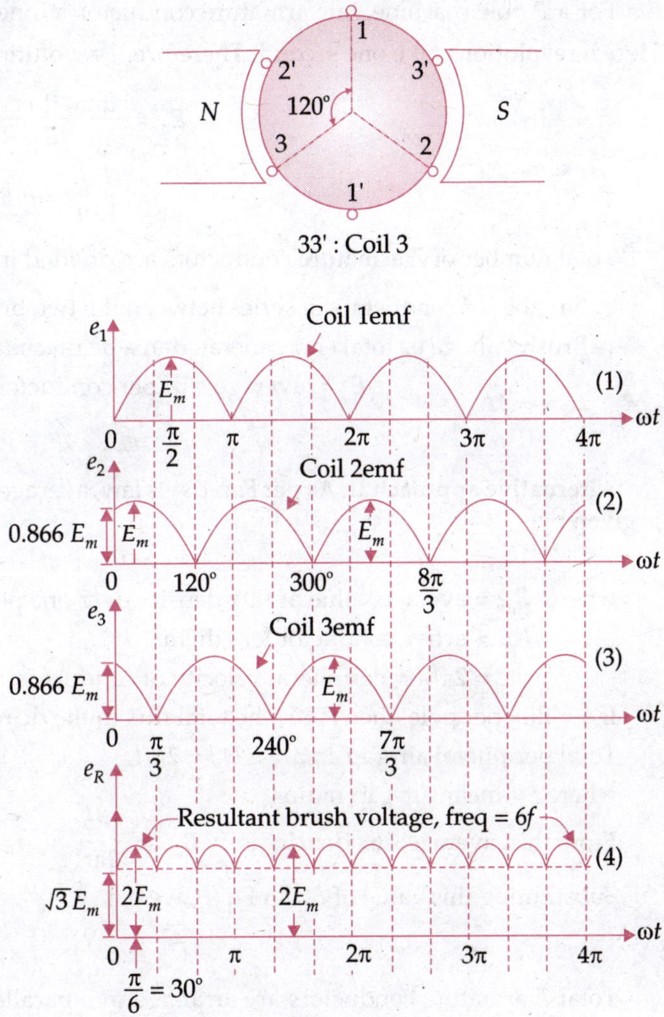

Fig 4.7: Resultant brush voltage in a dc machine with 3 coils in series.

4.2.1. Expression for Generated emf

An expression for the voltage available across the brushes of a dc machine has already been derived in Eq. (3.44). This emf expression, sometimes called **emf equation for a dc machine**, can also be obtained as follows :

Approach I. In a dc machine,

let P = number of poles ;

ϕ = flux per pole, W_b;

n = speed in rps,

a = number of parallel paths in the armature and

Z = total number of armature conductors.

According to Faraday's law,

$$\left.\begin{array}{r}\text{average emf generated}\\ \text{in one conductor, } E_z\end{array}\right| = \frac{\text{total flux cut by the conductor}}{\text{time, in seconds, required to cut that total flux}}$$

For a P pole machine, one armature conductor in one revolution will cut a total flux $P\,\phi$ Wb. Here n revolutions take one second. Therefore, 1 revolution would take $\frac{1}{n}$ sec.

$$\therefore \qquad E_z = \frac{\text{total flux cut in one revolution}}{\text{time for one revolution}}$$

$$= \frac{P\phi}{1/n} = P\,\phi\,n \qquad \text{...(4.1)}$$

Total number of Z armature conductors are divided into a parallel path between two brushes.

$\therefore$ Number of conductors in series between the two brush $= \frac{Z}{a}$

$\therefore$ Brush voltage or total emf generated in a dc machine is

$$E_a = (\text{average emf per conductor}) \times (\text{series conductors between brushes})$$

$$= E_z \times \frac{Z}{a} = P\,\phi\,n \times \frac{Z}{a} = \frac{\phi Znp}{a} \qquad \text{...(4.2)}$$

Alternative approach II. As per Faraday's law, average value of generated emf in one conductor is given by

$$E_z = B_{av}.\, l.\, v^* \qquad \text{...}(i)$$

where B_{av} = average value of flux density over one pole pitch as shown in Fig. 4.8 *(b)*, T

l = active conductor length, m

v = $2\pi rn$ = peripheral velocity of conductor, *m/sec*

If ϕ = flux per pole, then $P\,\phi$ is the total flux in the dc machine.

Total peripheral air-gap area = $\pi\, D.l = 2\pi rl$,

where r = mean air-gap radius.

From this, average flux density is $\quad B_{av} = \frac{P\phi}{2\pi rl}$

Substituting this value of B_{av} in Eq *(i)*, we get

$$E_z = \frac{P\phi}{2\pi rl} \times l \times 2\pi rn = P\,\phi\,n \qquad \text{...(4.1)}$$

Total Z armature conductors are arranged in a parallel paths. Therefore, conductors in series between the two brushes are $\frac{Z}{a}$.

$\therefore$ Voltage generated in the armature of a dc machine is

$$E_a = (\text{average emf per conductor}) \times (\text{series conductors in each parallel path})$$

$$= (P\,\phi\,n)\left(\frac{Z}{a}\right) = \frac{\phi Znp}{a} \qquad \text{...(4.2)}$$

Now, speed in mechanical radians/sec, $\omega_m = 2\pi n$

Substitution of the value of n in Eq. (4.1) gives

$$E_a = \frac{\phi ZP}{a} \times \frac{\omega_m}{2\pi} = \frac{ZP}{2\pi a}\cdot \phi\omega_m = K_a\,\phi\,\omega_m \qquad \text{...(4.3)}$$

where constant $K_a = \frac{ZP}{2\pi a}$ is called **armature constant.**

It should be noted that in D.C. machines, the field flux may not be a spatial-sine wave. In order to get the maximum e.m.f. generated in the armature, the total flux should be as large as possible, though limited by commutation considerations. The aim of obtaining high generated e.m.f., leads to the field from which is usually a flat-topped waveform illustrated in Fig. 3.17 *(a)*.

* Read 0.1.1.

4.3. TORQUE IN D.C. MACHINES

The electromagnetic torque in case of D.C. machines, has been expressed in terms of the interaction of main field flux ϕ_f and armature m.m.f. $\dot{F}_a$ in Eq. (3.85). Since the armature m.m.f. is always directed along the q-axis, the torque angle λ_{af} between the axes of field flux and armature m.m.f. is 90°. Therefore, Eq. (3.85) becomes,

$$T_e = \frac{\pi}{8} P^2 \phi F_a \qquad \text{...(4.4)}$$

Now the peak value of the fundamental sine component F_a for a D.C. machine is given by Eq. (3.66), *i.e.*,

$$F_a = \frac{8}{\pi^2}\left(\frac{Z}{2P} \cdot \frac{I_a}{a}\right) \text{ ATs/pole} \qquad \text{...(4.5)}$$

Substitution of the value of F_a in Eq. 4.4 gives

$$T_e = \frac{\pi}{8} P^2 \phi \frac{8}{\pi^2}\left(\frac{Z}{2P} \cdot \frac{I_a}{a}\right)$$

$$\therefore \quad T_e = \frac{PZ}{2\pi a} \phi I_a = K_a \phi I_a \qquad \text{...(4.6)}$$

where constant $K_a = \frac{ZP}{2\pi a}$, as given by Eq. (3.45), is called the *armature constant*.

Note that in case of generator, the electromagnetic torque T_e opposes the primemover torque and in case of motor, T_e rotates the driven equipment.

From Eq. (4.2), $\phi = \frac{a.E_a}{ZnP}$. Substituting this value ϕ in Eq. (4.6) gives

$$T_e = \frac{PZ}{2\pi a} \times \frac{a.E_a}{ZnP} I_a = \frac{E_a I_a}{2\pi n}$$

But $2\pi n = \omega_m$ rad/sec.

$$\therefore \quad T_e = \frac{E_a I_a}{\omega_m}$$

or

$$T_e.\omega_m = E_a I_a \qquad \text{...(4.7)}$$

Power balance Eq. (4.7) states that mechanical power developed is equal to the electrical power developed.

$$\therefore \text{ Electromagnetic torque} \quad T_e = \frac{1}{\omega_m} E_a I_a \qquad \text{...(4.8)}$$

Torque expression of Eq. (4.6), can alternatively be obtained as follows :

The electromagnetic torque, from Eq. (4.8), is $T_e = \frac{1}{\omega_m} (E_a I_a)$

Substitution of the values of E_a and ω_m gives

$$T_e = \frac{1}{2\pi n}\left(\frac{\phi ZnP}{a} \cdot I_a\right) = \frac{ZP}{2\pi a} \cdot \phi I_a = K_a \phi I_a \qquad \text{...(4.6)}$$

The torque given by Eq. (4.6) is also called the torque developed or total developed torque. Physical interpretation of Eq. (4.6) reveals that for a given D.C. machine, K_a is constant and, therefore, torque T_e is directly proportional to field flux and armature current. The product $E_a I_a$ is called the **electromagnetic power** or internal armature power.

Torque expression for a D.C. machine can also be obtained by referring to Fig. 4.8. In Fig. 4.8 *(a)* is shown a 2-pole D.C. machine and top of Fig. 4.8 *(b)* is its developed view. The current under south pole is indicated by a cross and that under north pole by a dot. It has been shown earlier that direction of conductor current under the poles remains unaltered even though the armature rotates.

This means that force on the conductors under each pole of a D.C. machine remains unidirectional. Force on a conductor is given by *Bll*. It has been brought out in section 4.1 (Fig.

4.4) that magnitude of current in conductors under each pole remains constant ($= \frac{I_a}{a}$). This shows that each armature conductor, as it moves under the influence of pole flux, experiences a force, or torque, whose time variation is a replica of the B-wave. This is shown in Fig. 4.8 *(b)*.

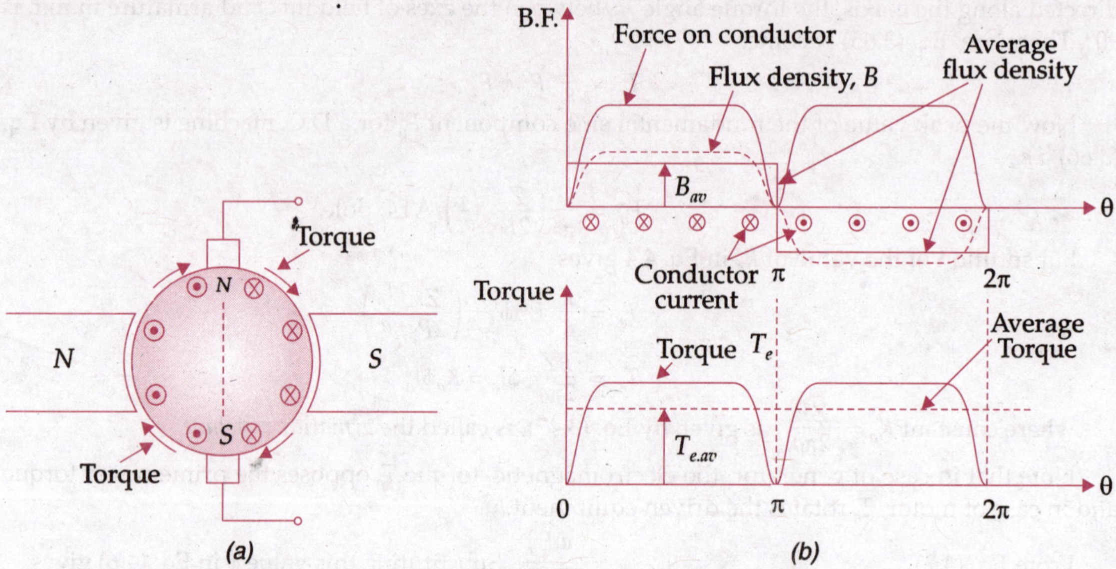

Fig 4.8: Production of torque in a D.C. machine.

Average force on one conductor,

$$f_{av} = B_{av} \cdot I \cdot l$$

As this force is unidirectional, total force acting on Z conductors is

$$F = f_{av} \cdot Z = B_{av} \cdot I \cdot l \cdot Z$$

Since B_{av} over a pole-pitch is constant as shown in Fig. 4.8 *(b)*, and I, l and Z are also constant, electromagnetic force F is also constant. For r = mean air-gap radius, the electromagnetic, or motor, torque is given by

$$T_e = F \cdot r = B_{av} \cdot IlZr$$

But $$B_{av} = \frac{P\phi}{2\pi rl}$$

$\therefore$ $$T_e = \frac{P\phi}{2\pi rl} \cdot Il \cdot Zr = \frac{PZ}{2\pi}\phi I = \frac{P\phi}{2\pi a} \cdot \phi I_a \text{ Nm} \quad \text{...(4.6)}$$

where I = conductor current = current in each parallel path

$$= \frac{I_a}{a} = \frac{\text{Armature current}}{\text{Number of parallel paths}}$$

It is thus seen that average electromagnetic torque for given flux per pole and armature current has uniform profile as shown in Fig. 4.8 *(b)*. Eq. (4.6) also shows that motor torque in a D.C. machine is independent of waveshape of B-curve. Motor torque, however, depends upon the flux per pole for a given armature current.

Torque expression given by Eq. (4.4) emphasizes the interaction of main field flux ϕ with armature m.m.f. F_a for the production of electromagnetic torque. From this, torque expression of Eqn. (4.6) is derived.

Torque expression derived from Fig. 4.8 begins with a force on armature conductor. This is a convenient way of deriving the torque expression, Eq. (4.6). Mechanism of torque production, however, is different in an actual machine where the conductors are placed in the armature slots.

In order to understand the physical process of torque production, refer to Fig. 4.9. In Fig. 4.9 *(a)* is shown the distribution of main field flux in the absence of any armature current in the slots. It is seen from this figure that magnetic flux produced by north pole passes the armature mainly through teeth because slot portion has long air-gap and therefore high reluctance. Fig. 4.9 *(b)* shows the distribution of flux produced by armature current alone. Currents in the conductors are indicated by dots. The armature-produced flux is upwards to the right of slot and downwards to the left of slot.

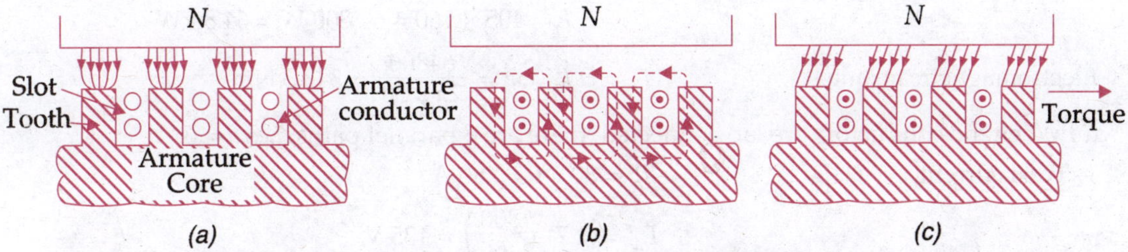

Fig 4.9: Magnetic flux distribution *(a)* due to main pole alone *(b)* due to armature currents alone *(c)* when both main-pole flux and armature flux are present.

When both main-field flux and armature flux are present, main field flux distribution gets distorted as shown in Fig. 4.9 *(c)*. Just above the slot, the armature flux flows from right to left. This distorts the resultant flux distribution from right to left as shown. These tilted lines tend to shorten their path and in doing so, a tangential torque from left to right is produced. It can therefore be stated that the interaction of the main flux with the armature current causes the resultant flux to act on the armature teeth and in doing so, electromagnetic torque is produced in the clockwise direction in Fig. 4.9 *(c)*. It is indeed fortunate that there is very little force on the armature conductors. If all the magnetic force were to act on the conductors, it would harm the insulation between the conductors and slots.

Example 4.2. *The armature of a 4-pole lap-wound D.C. machine has core length = 30 cm, diameter = 40 cm, total conductors = 500, speed = 1200 r.p.m and current = 20 A. For an average flux density of 0.5 T, find the electromagnetic (or gross mechanical) power developed and the internal torque.*

Solution. Here $l = 0.3$ m, $r = 0.20$ m, speed, $n = \frac{1200}{60} = 20$ r.p.s.

It is known that
$$B_{av} = \frac{P\phi}{2\pi rl}$$

$\therefore$ Flux per pole
$$\phi = \frac{0.5 \times 2\pi \times 0.2 \times 0.3}{4} = 0.04712 \text{ Wb}$$

Generated e.m.f.,
$$E_a = \frac{\phi ZnP}{a} = \frac{0.04712 \times 500 \times 20 \times 4}{4} = 471.2 \text{ V}.$$

Gross mechanical power developed, $E_a I_a = 471.2 \times 20 = 9424$ W.

Internal torque,
$$T_e = \frac{E_a I_a}{\omega_m} = \frac{9424}{2\pi \times 20} = 74.994 \text{ Nm} \simeq 75 \text{ Nm}.$$

Example 4.3. *A 6-pole D.C. machine has 300 conductors and each conductor is capable of carring 80 A without excessive temperature rise. The flux per pole is 0.015 Wb and the machine is driven at 1800 rpm. Compute the total current, e.m.f. power developed in the armature and electromagnetic torque, if the armature conductors are : (a) wave connected and (b) lap connected.*

Solution. Here $P = 6, Z = 300, \phi = 0.015$ Wb

Speed, $n = \dfrac{1800}{60} = 30$ r.p.s

The average e.m.f. per conductor $= P\phi n = 6 \times 30 \times 0.015 = 2.7$ V

(a) When the conductors are wave connected, there are only 2 parallel paths, *i.e.*, $a = 2$.

$\therefore$ Total current, I_a = current per conductor $\times a = 80 \times 2 = 160$ A

$$\text{e.m.f. } E_a = (\text{e.m.f. per conductor}) \cdot \frac{Z}{a} = (2.7)\left(\frac{300}{2}\right) = 405 \text{ V}$$

Power developed in the armature or electromagnetic power

$$= E_a I_a = 405 \times 160 = 64{,}800 \text{ W} = 64.8 \text{ kW}$$

Electromagnetic torque, $T_e = E_a I_a / \omega_m = \dfrac{64800}{2\pi \times 30} = 343.5$ Nm

(b) When the conductors are lap connected, there are 6 parallel paths, *i.e.*, $a = 6$.

$\therefore$ Total current, $I_a = 80 \times 6 = 480$ A

$$E_a = (2.7)\left(\frac{300}{6}\right) = 135 \text{ V}$$

Power developed in the armature $= E_a I_a = 135 \times 480 = 64800$ W $= 64.8$ kW

Electromagnetic torque, $T_e = \dfrac{E_a I_a}{\omega_m} = \dfrac{64800}{2\pi \times 30} = 343.5$ Nm

This example demonstrates that D.C. machine rating, in terms of electromagnetic power and internal torque remains unaltered whether the armature winding is lap connected or wave connected.

4.4. CIRCUIT MODEL OF D.C. MACHINES

In D.C. machines, all parallel paths in the armature are symmetrical. Each path has a generated e.m.f. E_a and a resistance r_p as indicated in Fig. 4.10 *(a)* where, for the sake of simplicity, four parallel paths are shown. Viewing from machine terminals (use Thevenin's theorem), the armature circuit of Fig. 4.10 *(a)* can be replaced by circuit model of Fig. 4.10 *(b)* where series resistance $r_a = r_p/a$ and 'a' is the number of parallel paths.

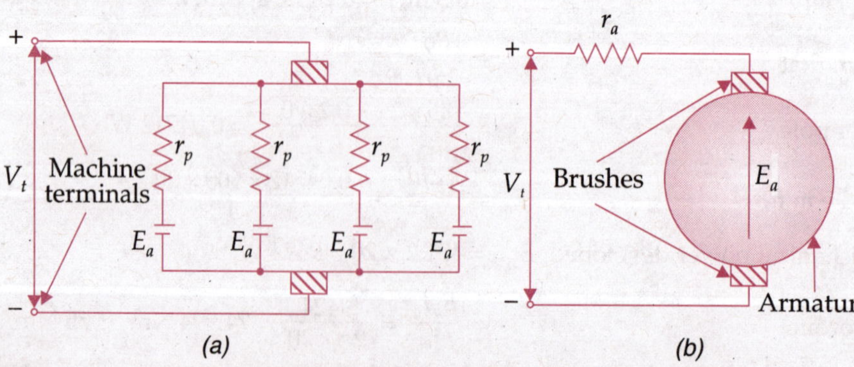

Fig 4.10: Pertaining to the armature circuit of a D.C. machine.

The field winding of a D.C. machine must also be represented in the circuit model. Therefore, the schematic representation, or *circuit model*, of D.C. machines is as shown in Fig. 4.11 *(a)* for a

D.C. generator and in Fig. 4.11 *(b)* for a D.C. motor. It is seen from this figure that for a generator, electromagnetic torque T_e is opposite to the rotor rotation, *i.e.*, T_e opposes the prime-mover torque. This is essential for the conversion of energy from mechanical to electrical. This torque T_e may, therefore, be called counter-torque in a D.C. generator. The magnitude of this counter-torque is given by Eq. (4.6). For motor, the electromagnetic torque T_e is in the direction of rotor rotation.

Generating Mode. When armature current I_a is in the direction of generated e.m.f. E_a, D.C. machine operates in the generating mode. Electromagnetic power is $E_a I_a$ watts and the electrical power output or load power is equal to terminal power $V_t I_a$ watts, Fig. 4.11 *(a)*.

For a D.C. generator, shaft power input $= E_a I_a$ + no-load rotational loss

and $$V_t = E_a - I_a r_a \quad \text{...(4.9)}$$

where V_t = armature terminal voltage, V

I_a = armature current, A

r_a = armature circuit resistance, ohm

Brush contact drop is usually taken as constant at 1 or 2 V. This drop is independent of armature current as the conduction process is primarily through numerous short arcs. Taking this drop as 2V, Eq. (4.9) can be written as

$$V_t = E_a - I_a r_a - 2$$

or $$V_t I_a = E_a I_a - I_a^2 r_a - 2I_a$$

or Electrical power output = Electromagnetic power – Ohmic losses – Brush contact loss ...(4.10)

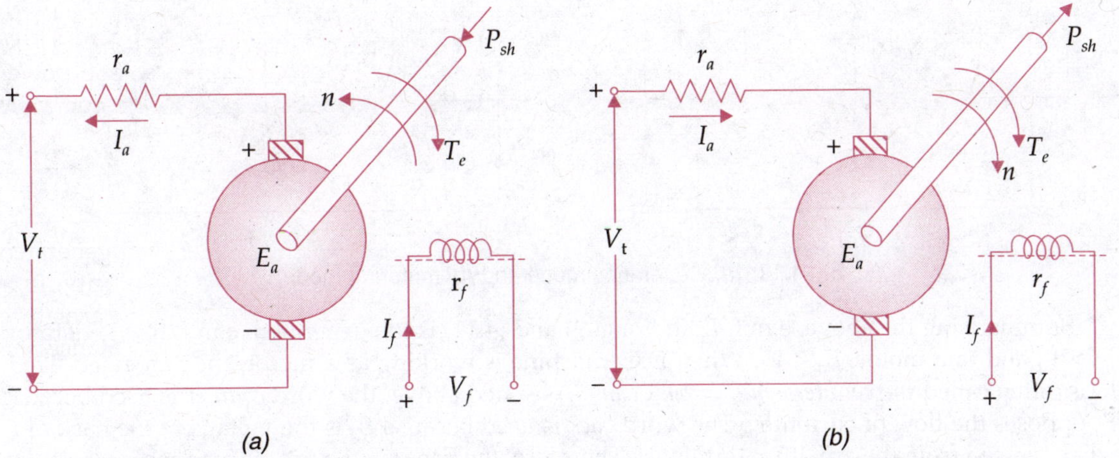

Fig 4.11: Circuit model of a D.C. machine for *(a)* generating mode and *(b)* motoring mode.

Motoring Mode. When armature current I_a flows in opposition to generated e.m.f. E_a as in Fig. 4.11 *(b)*, D.C. machine operates in motoring mode.

For a D.C. motor, shaft power output $= E_a I_a$ – no-load rotational loss

and $$V_t = E_a + I_a r_a + 2 \quad \text{...(4.11)}$$

or $$V_t I_a = E_a I_a + I_a^2 r_a + 2I_a$$

or Electrical power input = Electromagnetic power + Ohmic losses + Brush contact loss ...(4.12)

It is stated above that for generator operation, the e.m.f. and current in a conductor are in the same direction. This is shown in a 2-pole D.C. generator of Fig. 4.12 *(a)*. In this figure, for anti-clockwise rotation of armature, generated e.m.fs. are indicated by crosses and dots below the circles in the slots (use right-hand rule). For assumed anticlockwise rotation, *S* and *N* poles indicated on the rotor in Fig. 4.12 *(a)* must be created by armature currents. This magnetic polarity demands the current directions in the conductors to be indicated by crosses under S pole and by dots under N pole. Current directions in slots are indicated by crosses and dots within the circles in Fig. 4.12 *(a)*. This shows that generated e.m.fs. and currents in a conductor are in the same direction for a D.C. machine working as a generator.

Fig. 4.12 *(b)* shows motoring-mode operation of a D.C. machine. Direction of currents in the armature conductors is indicated by crosses and dots within the circles in the slots. These currents establish N and S poles on the rotor and their interaction with the stator N and S poles results in clockwise rotation of armature. With the armature rotation, the conductors cut the same flux that gives rise to motor torque. This flux cutting action thus causes the generation of e.m.f. in the very same conductors that experience motor action. The generated e.m.fs. in Fig. 4.12 *(b)* are indicated by crosses and dots below the circles in the slots (use right hand rule). It is seen that generated e.m.fs. are in directions opposite to the flow of conductor current. Since this generated e.m.f. opposes the flow of current, it is called counter electromotive force or **counter e.m.f.** Note that counter e.m.f. E_a can never be equal to applied voltage V_t. E.m.f. E_a must always be less than V_t because direction of current, as per Eq. (4.11), first determines the direction of rotation and then the direction of counter e.m.f. The magnitude of counter e.m.f. is governed by Eq. (4.2).

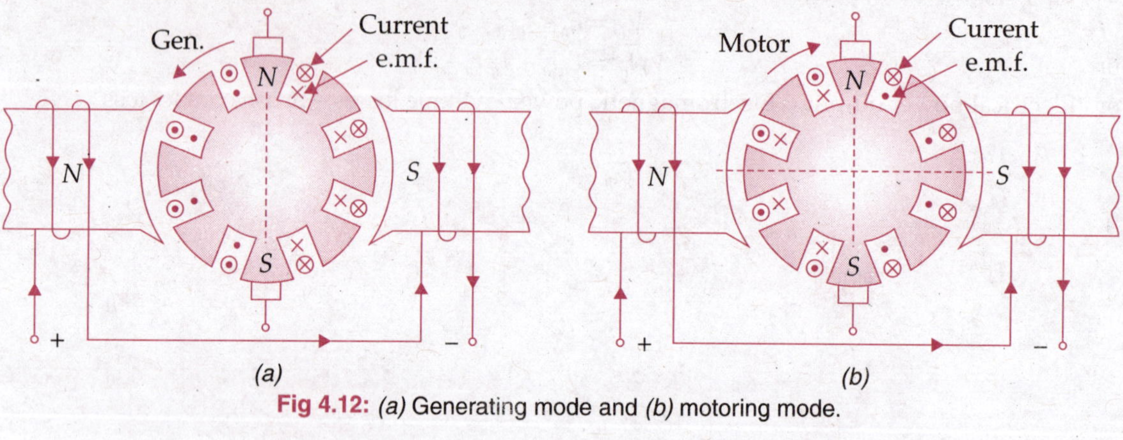

Fig 4.12: *(a)* Generating mode and *(b)* motoring mode.

Summarising the above, e.m.f. E_a in Eq. (4.9) and (4.11) is the generated e.m.f. In a generator, $E_a > V_t$ and in a motor, $E_a < V_t$. When D.C. machine is working as a motor, the generated e.m.f. E_a is often called the *counter e.m.f.* or *back e.m.f.* As stated above, the word *counter* is used because E_a opposes the flow of current I_a. The word *back* is used because E_a is the voltage at the back of r_a when viewed from the armature terminals. Therefore, the generated e.m.f. E_a for a motor may also be called *voltage behind armature circuit resistance.*

Example 4.4. *A 6-pole lap-wound D.C. generator has 240 coils of 2 turns each. Resistance of one turn is 0.03 ohm. The armature is 50 cm long and 40 cm diameter. Air-gap flux density of 0.6 T is uniform over pole shoe. Each pole subtends an angle of 40° mechanical. For armature speed of 1200 rpm, find (a) generated e.m.f. at no-load and (b) the terminal voltage at full load armature current of 40 A.*

Solution. We know that,
$$\theta_{elec} = \frac{P}{2}\,\theta_{mech}$$

Therefore, pole shoe subtends an angle $40 \times \frac{6}{2} = 120°$ electrical.

Flux per pole = (air-gap area under one pole shoe) × (uniform flux density)

$$= \left(\frac{2\pi rl}{P} \times \frac{120}{180}\right) \times 0.6 = \frac{2\pi \times 0.2 \times 0.5}{6} \times \frac{2}{3} \times 0.6 = 0.042 \text{ Wb}$$

Total armature turns =240 × 2 = 480. This gives total armature conductors.

$$Z = 480 \times 2 = 960.$$

Speed, $n = \frac{1200}{60} = 20$ r.p.s, $P = 6, a = 6$

Generated e.m.f. at no-load, $E_a = \frac{\phi ZnP}{a} = \frac{0.042 \times 960 \times 20 \times 6}{6} = 806.4$ V

(b) Number of armature turns per path $= \frac{480}{6} = 80$

Resistance of one path $= 80 \times 0.03 = 2.4\ \Omega$

For 6-pole lap-wound D.C. generator, there are $a = 6$ parallel paths.

$\therefore$ Resistance of armature circuit $= \frac{\text{Resistance of one path}}{\text{Number of parallel paths}} = \frac{2.4}{6} = 0.4\ \Omega$

For D.C. generator, terminal voltage at full load,

$$V_t = E_a - I_a r_a$$

or $$V_t = 806.4 - 40 \times 0.4 = 790.4 \text{ V}$$

4.5. METHODS OF EXCITATION

A D.C. machine can work as an electromechanical energy converter only when its field winding is excited with direct current, except for small D.C. machines employing permanent magnets.

There are, in general, two methods of exciting the field windings of D.C. machines.

(a) Separate excitation and

(b) Self-excitation.

D.C. machines may have one or more field windings and their method of excitation, determines the performance characteristics of the D.C. machines. In Fig. 4.13, the left hand side diagrams give the physical details of the internal connections for a 2-pole machine; whereas the right hand side diagrams give the schematic representation of D.C. machines with the method of excitation specified.

(a) **Separate excitation.** The separately excited field winding consists of several hundred turns of fine wire and is connected to a separate or external D.C. source, Fig. 4.13 *(a)*. The voltage of the external D.C. source has no relation with the armature voltage, *i.e.*, the field winding energised from a separate supply can be designed for any convenient voltage.

(b) **Self-excitation.** When the field winding is excited by its own armature, the machine is said to be a *self-excited* D.C. *machine*. In these machines, the field poles must have a residual magnetism, so that when the armature rotates, a residual voltage appears across the brushes. This residual voltage should establish a current in the field winding so as to reinforce the residual flux.

A self-excited D.C. machine can be sub-divided as follows :

(i) **Series excitation.** The field winding consists of a few turns of thick wire and is connected in series with the armature, Fig. 4.13 *(b)*. In other words, the series field current depends on the armature current and in view of this, a series field may be called a *current-operated field*.

(ii) **Shunt excitation.** The field winding consists of a large number of turns of fine wire and is connected in parallel (or in shunt) with the armature, Fig. 4.13 *(c)*. Therefore, the voltage across the armature terminals and the shunt field is the same and it is for this reason that a shunt field may be called a *voltage-operated field*.

Remember that series and shunt field windings are characterised by low and high resistances respectively.

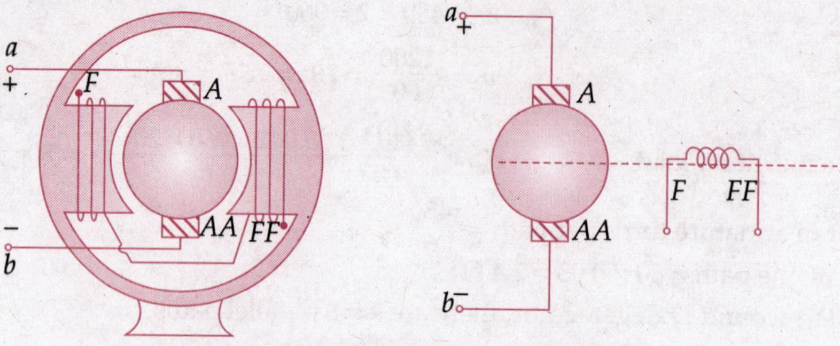

(a) Separately excited D.C. machine

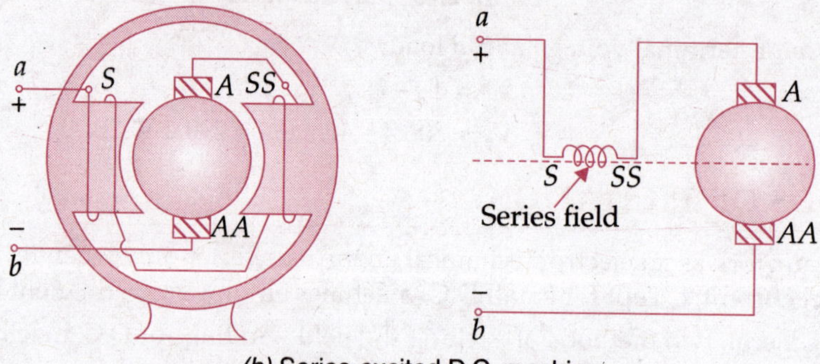

(b) Series-excited D.C. machine

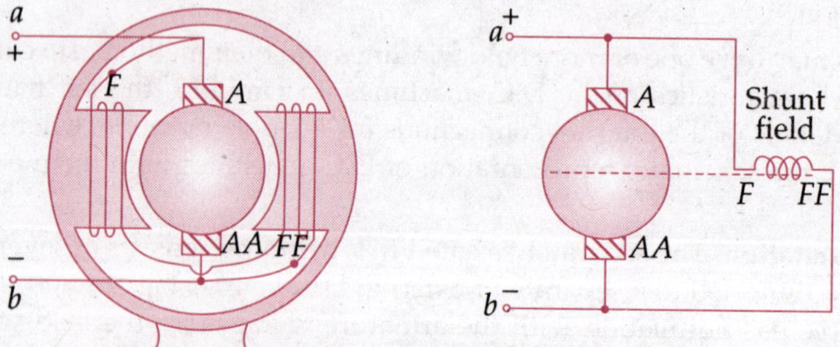

(c) Shunt-excited D.C. machine

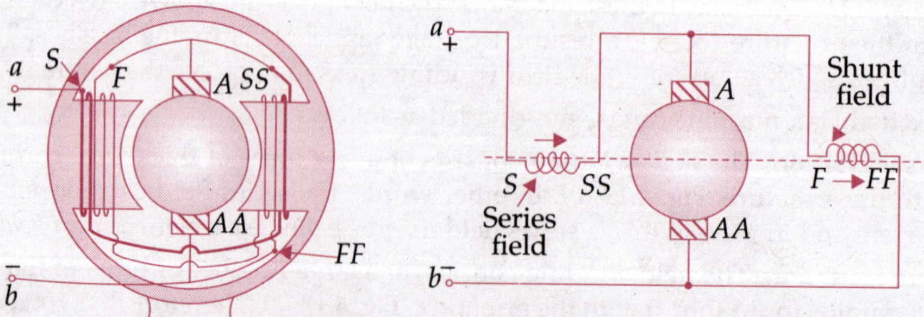

(d) Compound excited D.C. machine

Fig 4.13: Methods of excitation of D.C. machines.

(iii) **Compound excitation.** A compound excitation involves both the series excited winding and the shunt-excitation winding. In some applications, a shunt-excited winding may be replaced by a separately-excited winding. Here a D.C. compound machine, with series and shunt field windings will be discussed.

If the series field flux aids the shunt field flux, so that the resultant air-gap flux per pole is increased, the machine is called a *cumulatively compounded* D.C. machine as shown in Fig. 4.13 *(d)*. In this figure, direction of arrows corresponds to the direction of magnetic flux produced by shunt and series field winding. As the two arrows are in the same direction in Fig. 4.13 *(d)*, this figure is for a cumulatively compounded D.C. machine. In case the series field flux opposes the shunt field flux, so that the resultant air-gap flux per pole is decreased, the machine is called a *differentially compounded* D.C. machine as shown in Fig. 4.14 *(a)*. In this figure, direction of arrows indicate that the two fields are opposing each other.

From the view-point of connections, a D.C. compound machine may have short-shunt connection or a long-shunt connection. In short-shunt connection of Fig. 4.14 *(a)*, the shunt field or voltage-excited winding is connected across the armature terminals. In long-shunt connection, the shunt field winding is connected across the machine or line terminals as shown in Fig. 4.14 *(b)*. In order to remember the difference between short-shunt and long-shunt connections, one may examine Fig. 4.14 a little more carefully. A short-shunt connection requires a wire of short length for connecting *B* to *A*, whereas in long shunt connection, a wire of long length is required for connecting *B* to *A*. However, there is no appreciable difference in the operating characteristics of short-shunt and long-shunt connections. The choice between the two types, depends on mechanical considerations of connections or of reversing switches.

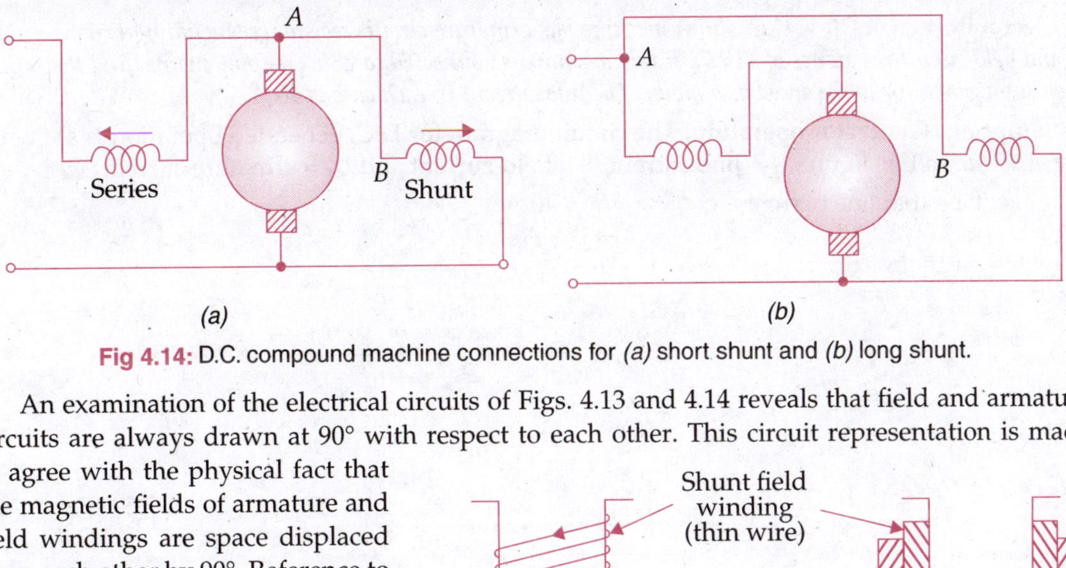

Fig 4.14: D.C. compound machine connections for *(a)* short shunt and *(b)* long shunt.

An examination of the electrical circuits of Figs. 4.13 and 4.14 reveals that field and armature circuits are always drawn at 90° with respect to each other. This circuit representation is made to agree with the physical fact that the magnetic fields of armature and field windings are space displaced from each other by 90°. Reference to Fig. 4.5 *(b)* is also helpful.

In Fig. 4.13 *(d)*, each pole of the compound machine is shown to possess shunt and series field windings. Fig. 4.14 *(c)* illustrates how these windings are arranged

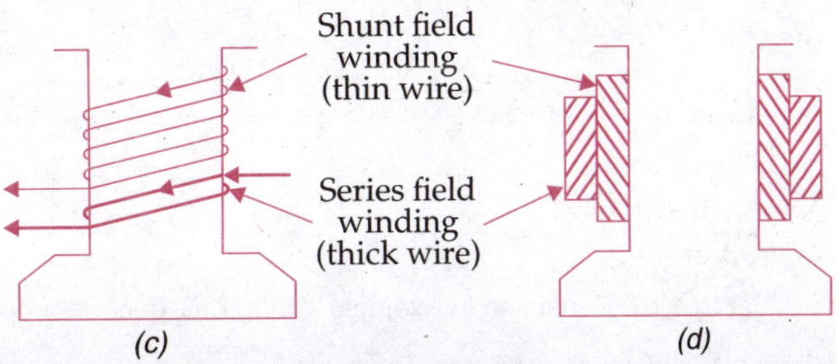

Fig 4.14: Series and shunt field windings on one pole of a D.C. compound machine.

on one pole of a D.C. machine. In this figure, shunt field coil is placed near the yoke and series field coil near the pole shoe just for the sake of clarity. Actual physical arrangement of these coils is as shown in Fig. 4.14 *(d)*. It is seen from this figure that first shunt field coil is wound around the pole body and over it is then wound the series field coil. The reasons for placing the series field coil outside are *(i)* convenience in construction and *(ii)* for its better cooling.

Example 4.5. *A 24 kW, 250 V, 1600 r.p.m. separately-excited D.C. generator has armature circuit resistance of 0.1 Ω. The machine is first run at rated speed and the field current is adjusted to give an open circuit voltage of 260 V. Now, when the generator is loaded to deliver its rated current, the speed of the driving motor is found to be 1500 r.p.m. Compute the terminal voltage of the generator under these conditions. Field flux remains unaltered.*

Solution. It is seen from Eq. (4.2) that generated voltage is $E_a \propto n\phi$

At no-load, $$260 \propto 1600 \times \phi \qquad ...(i)$$

Rated armature current, $$I_a = \frac{24000}{250} = 96 \text{ A}$$

If the generated voltage under rated load is E_{a1}, then

$$E_{a1} \propto 1500 \times \phi \qquad ...(ii)$$

From *(i)* and *(ii)*, $$\frac{E_{a1}}{260} = \frac{1500 \times \phi}{1600 \times \phi}$$

$$E_{a1} = 243.75 \text{ V}$$

From Eq. (4.9), the terminal voltage is

$$V_t = E_{a1} - I_a r_a = 243.75 - 96 \times 0.1 = 234.15 \text{ V.}$$

Example 4.6. *A 230 V D.C. shunt machine has armature circuit resistance (including brushes) of 0.5 Ω and field circuit resistance of 115 Ω. If this machine is connected to 230 V supply mains, find the ratio of speed as a generator to the speed as a motor. The line current in each case is 40 A.*

Solution. Generator operation. The circuit diagram for D.C. generated operation is shown in Fig. 4.15 *(a)*. In this figure, I_L = line current, I_f = field current and I_{a1} = armature current.

It is given that line current, $$I_L = 40 \text{ A}$$

Field current, $$I_f = \frac{230}{115} = 2 \text{ A}$$

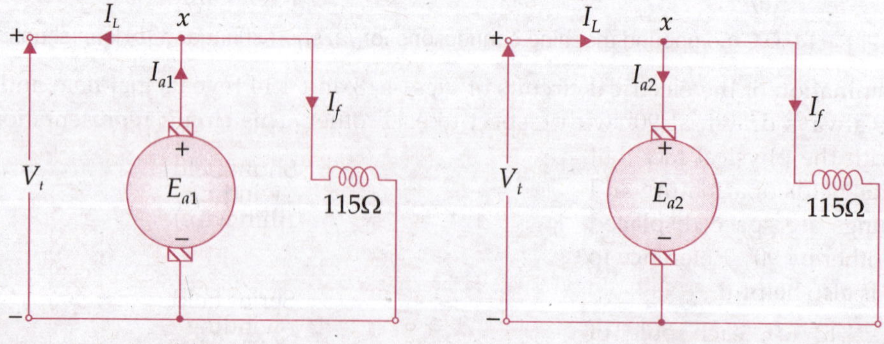

Fig 4.15: Pertaining to Example 4.5 *(a)* D.C. generator operation and *(b)* D.C. motor operation.

KCL at point *x* in Fig. 4.15 *(a)* gives armature current,

$$I_{a1} = I_L + I_f = 40 + 2 = 42 \text{ A.}$$

$\therefore$ Generated e.m.f., $\quad E_{a1} = V_t + I_{a1} r_a = 230 + 42 \times 0.5 = 251$ V

$$\therefore \quad 251 \propto n_g \times \phi \quad ...(i)$$

where n_g is the generator speed and ϕ is the field flux per pole proportional to I_f.

Motor operation. The circuit diagram for D.C. motor operation is given in Fig. 4.15 *(b)*. In this figure, I_{a2} = armature current = 40 A and field current = 2 A as before.

KCL at point x in Fig. 4.15 *(b)* gives D.C. motor armature current

$$I_{a2} = I_L - I_f = 40 - 2 = 38 \text{ A}$$

$\therefore$ Motor counter e.m.f., $E_{a2} = V_t - I_{a2} \cdot r_a = 230 - 38 \times 0.5 = 211$ V

But $$E_{a2} = 211 \propto n_m \times \phi \quad ...(ii)$$

where n_m is the motor speed.

From Eqns. *(i)* and *(ii)*,

$$\frac{E_{a1}}{E_{a2}} = \frac{251}{211} = \frac{n_g \times \phi}{n_m \times \phi}$$

$$= \frac{n_g}{n_m} = 1.1896.$$

Thus the ratio of speed as a generator to the speed as a motor is 1.1896.

4.6. M.M.F. AND FLUX DENSITY WAVEFORMS IN D.C. MACHINES

It has been shown in Art. 4.1 that the current distribution under each pole of a D.C. machine is uniform and is equivalent to a constant current sheet of proper polarity. The space distribution of m.m.f. produced by the armature winding is triangular, with its peak value along the quadrature or brush axis (or 90° away from the main field axis) as shown in Fig. 3.35. The effect of armature m.m.f. on the main-field flux distribution in the air-gap is called *armature reaction*. In this article, armature reaction and its effects are dealt with in detail.

4.6.1. Armature Reaction

The armature m.m.f. produces two undesirable effects on the main field flux and these are :

(i) net reduction in the main field flux per pole and

(ii) distortion of the main field flux wave along the air-gap periphery.

Reduction in the main flux per pole reduces the generated voltage and torque, whereas the distortion of the main-field flux influences the limits of successful commutation in D.C. machines. The purpose of this article is to investigate these effects and to discuss the methods of minimising the problems arising from armature reaction effects.

Fig. 4.16 *(a)* shows the flux path for the main poles of a 2-pole D.C. machine at no-load, *i.e.*, with no armature currents. This main field flux, produced by field m.m.f. $I_f N_f$, is shown by horizontal phasor $OA = \phi_f$ on the right hand side of Fig. 4.16 *(a)*. When the D.C. machine is loaded, currents flow in the armature winding. These currents are shown in Fig. 4.16 *(b)*, by dots under main S pole and by crosses under main N-pole. These armature currents set up armature flux shown by vertical flux lines in Fig. 4.16 *(b)*, with field winding un-excited. In this figure is also shown armature flux ϕ_a by a vertical phasor OB. Flux ϕ_a is produced by armature m.m.f. $I_a N_a$. If the D.C. machine of Fig. 4.16 is working as a motor, then its armature must rotate anti-clockwise, because of the fact that N, S poles of the main field must attract armature produced S, N poles. In case D.C. machine is working as a generator, then its armature must be driven clockwise by the prime-mover.

An examination of Fig. 4.16 *(a)* and *(b)* reveals that the path of armature flux ϕ_a is perpendicular to the main flux path ϕ_f. In other words, the path of the armature flux *crosses* the path of the main-field flux. Thus the effect of armature flux on the main field is entirely *cross-magnetizing* and it is for this reason that the flux created by the armature m.m.f. is called *cross-flux*.

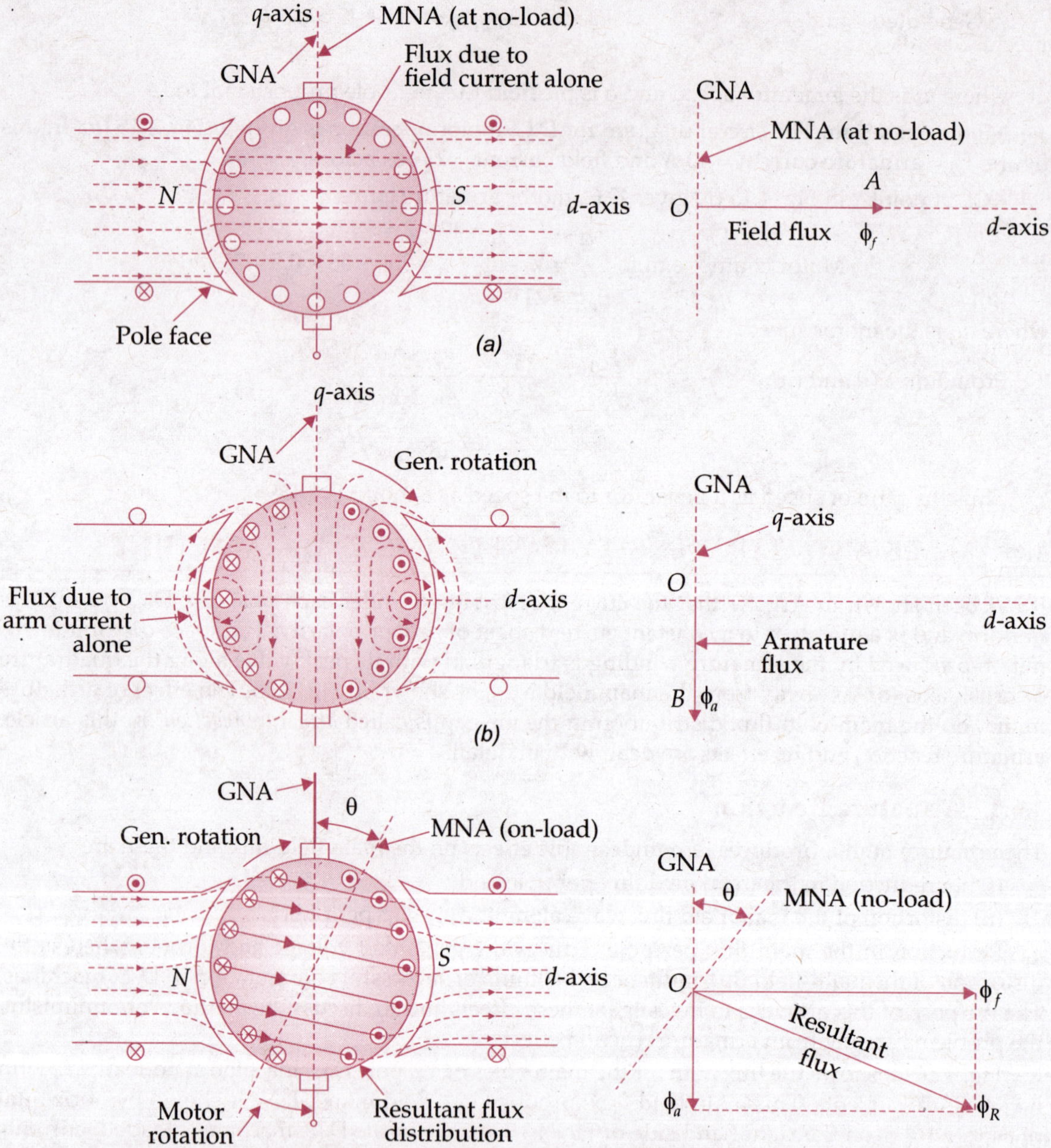

Fig 4.16: Illustrating the space distribution of *(a)* main-pole flux *(b)* armature flux and *(c)* resultant of both main-field and armature fluxes.

When current flows in both the armature and field windings, the resultant flux distribution is obtained by superimposing the two fluxes of Fig. 4.16 *(a)* and *(b)*. This is illustrated on left-hand side of Fig. 4.16 *(c)*. It is seen that armature flux aids the main field flux at upper end of *N*-pole and at the lower end of *S*-pole, therefore, at these two pole ends (or tips), the armature flux strengthens the main field flux. Likewise, the armature flux weakens the main field flux at lower end of *N*-pole and at upper end of *S*-pole. If there is no magnetic saturation, then the amount of strengthening and weakening of the main field flux are equal and the resultant flux per pole remains unaltered from its no-load value. Actually, magnetic saturation does occur and as a consequence, the strengthening effect is less as compared to the weakening effect and the resultant flux is decreased from its no-load value. This is called *demagnetizing effect* of armature flux.

In the phasor diagram of Fig. 4.16 *(c)*, phasor sum of field flux ϕ_f and armature flux ϕ_a gives net flux ϕ_R. This resultant flux ϕ_R is seen to be more than the main-field flux ϕ_f at no-load. This is, however, not true because of magnetic saturation in one of the pole tips of each pole. A geometric neutral axis (GNA) is along the quadrature axis of the D.C. machine. Magnetic neutral axis (MNA) is always perpendicular to the axis of resultant field flux. It is seen from Fig. 4.16 *(a)* that MNA at no-load coincide with the GNA or q-axis. When the D.C. machine is loaded, Fig. 4.16 *(c)* reveals that MNA is shifted from GNA. This shift is dependent upon the magnitude of armature current. Thus, greater the magnitude of armature (or load) current, greater is the shift of MNA from GNA. It may, therefore, be stated from above that net effect of armature flux on the main-field flux is

(i) to distort the main-field flux thereby causing non-uniform distribution of flux under the main poles,

(ii) to shift the MNA *in the direction of rotation for a generator and against the direction of rotation for a motor*, and

(iii) to reduce the main-field flux from its no-load value due to magnetic saturation.

Graphical picture of armature reaction. For better understanding of the interaction between main-field flux and armature flux, it is preferable and convenient to draw the developed diagram of armature conductors and poles. The developed view of Fig. 4.16 *(a)*, with no armature currents under each pole, is shown in Fig. 4.17 *(a)*. The brushes are along the interpolar axes midway between the main-pole axes. Dotted lines in Fig. 4.17 *(a)* show the distribution of main-field flux in the air-gap with no armature currents.

In Fig. 4.17 *(b)*, the variation of main field-flux density along the air-gap periphery is shown by a solid line.

In Fig. 4.17 *(c)*, currents are indicated by dots under S pole and crosses under N pole. These armature currents, with field winding unexcited, produce magnetic flux as shown in Fig. 4.17 *(c)*. As the armature flux produced by armature currents alone is normal to the main-field flux, as before, it is called *cross-flux*. The m.m.f. created by armature currents in a D.C. machine, as per Fig. 3.35 *(d)*, is triangular in nature and is depicted accordingly by a solid line in Fig. 4.17 *(d)*. The air-gap flux due to armature m.m.f. is given by $\dfrac{\text{armature m.m.f.}}{\text{air-gap reluctance}}$. Under the poles, the air-gap is uniform, therefore, the air-gap flux variation under the poles is proportional to armature m.m.f. and is shown in Fig. 4.17 *(d)*. In between the poles, *i.e.*, in the interpolar region, the long air-gap offers large reluctance, consequently the armature flux is much smaller in this region, in spite of a large value of m.m.f. The armature flux density waveform created by armature currents is, therefore, saddle-shaped* as depicted by dotted curve in Fig. 4.17 *(d)*. It is observed from this figure that armature flux-density waveform has *(i)* zero value at the centre of the pole *(ii)* increases from zero to maximum value at the pole tips and then *(iii)* decreases rapidly to a minimum value at the middle of main poles.

When both armature and field windings carry currents, the resultant flux distribution is obtained by superimposing the two fluxes, field flux of Fig. 4.17 *(a)* and armature cross-flux of Fig. 4.17 *(c)*. The resultant flux distribution, so obtained, is shown in Fig. 4.17 *(e)*. This figure reveals the strengthening of the resultant flux at one pole tip and weakening at the other pole tip of each pole. As expected, this agrees with Fig. 4.16 *(c)*.

* Shape of a cycle-saddle.

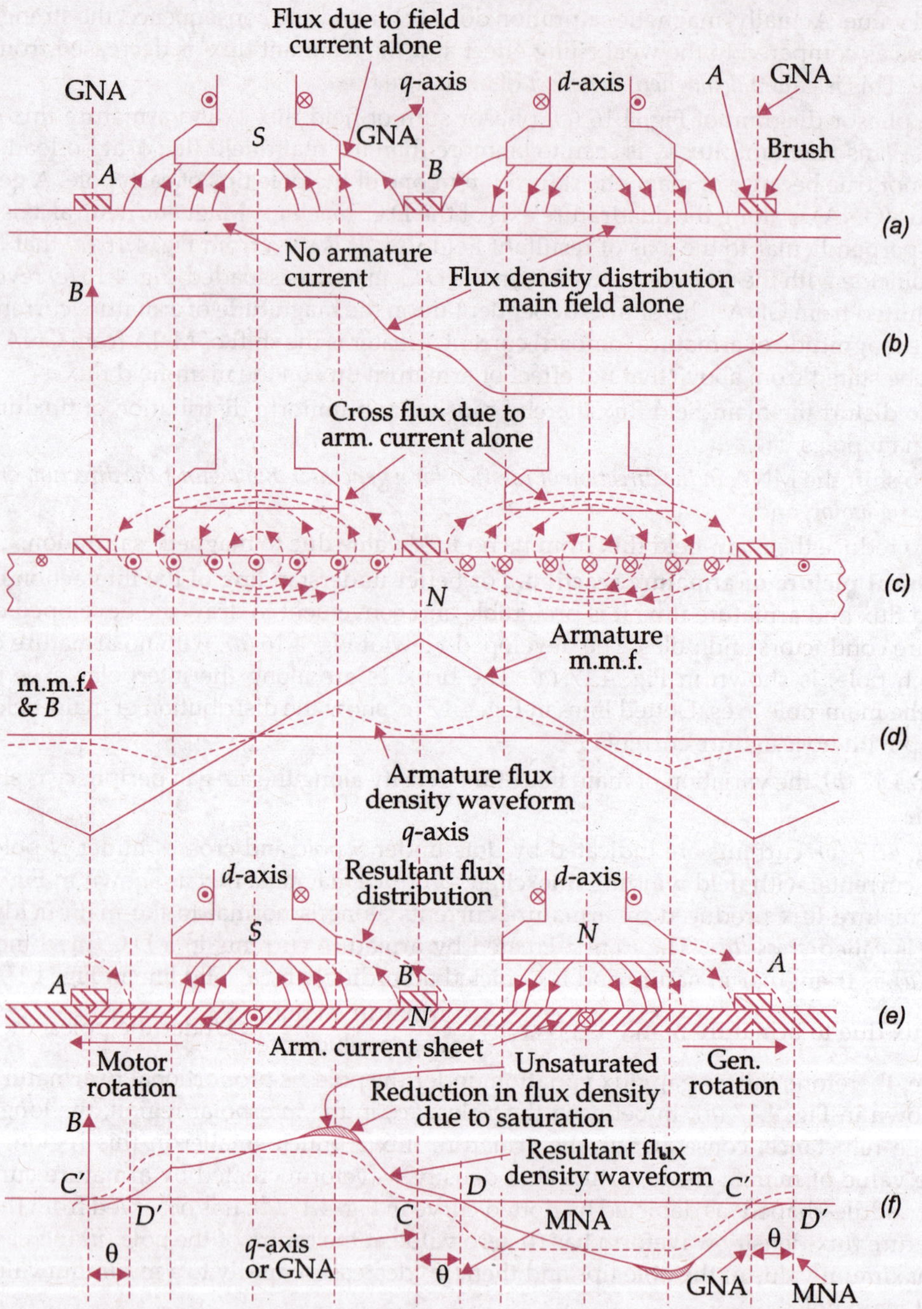

Fig 4.17: Flux distribution and flux-density waveforms respectively due to *(a)*, *(b)* field current alone *(c)*, *(d)* armature current alone and *(e)*, *(f)* both field and armature currents.

For obtaining the resultant air-gap flux density waveform, when both field and armature windings carry currents, add the corresponding flux-density ordinates of Fig. 4.17 *(b)* and 4.17 *(d)* at every point along the air-gap periphery. The resultant flux-density distribution in the air-gaps is shown by the solid curve in Fig. 4.17 *(f)*. It may be seen from the resultant flux-density distribution curve that the effect of cross-magnetizing armature m.m.f. is to decrease the flux density under the leading pole tips* and to increase it under the trailing pole tips for generator operation. Actually, the magnetic saturation in the iron does occur and its effect is to increase the flux density under the trailing pole tips by a smaller amount than the decrease under the leading pole tips. Saturation effect is indicated by cross-hatched areas in Fig. 4.17 *(f)*. Thus, under unsaturated conditions, the amount of flux increase under trailing pole tips is almost equal to the decrease under leading pole tips and the total flux per pole on load remains almost unchanged from its no-load value. Under saturated conditions, the amount of increase in flux is less than the decrease and therefore total flux per pole on load is less than its no-load value. Hence, under saturated conditions, the effect of cross-magnetizing armature m.m.f., *i.e.*, cross-flux, is to demagnetize the main field. But note that the demagnetizing effect of cross-flux is due to saturation only.

Fig. 4.17 *(f)* reveals that point of zero flux density has shifted through an angle θ from *C*, *C′* to *D*, *D′* respectively. In other words, MNA has shifted from GNA by an angle θ.

For a motor, a dot under south pole and a cross under north pole results in an anticlockwise rotation in Fig. 4.16. Therefore, above results are also applicable to D.C. motor. Since the direction of rotation is reversed, the leading pole tips for a motor are the trailing pole tips for a generator. Hence for a motor, the effect of cross-magnetizing armature m.m.f. is to decrease the flux under the trailing pole tips and to increase it under the leading pole tips.

Note from above that for a generator, the effect of armature reaction is to distort the flux and shift the zero crossing of the flux density wave in the direction of rotation. In the case of motor, the distortion of the flux and zero crossing of the flux-density wave is shifted against the distortion of rotation. In constant flux D.C. machines, such as shunt machines, the flux distortion is much more prominent under heavy loads. In series and compound machines, the flux distortion is minimum, because with the increase of armature m.m.f., there is a corresponding increase in the field m.m.f.

The effects of armature m.m.f. described above, may be summarised as follows :

(i) Armature flux path is normal to flux path of main poles. That is why armature flux is called *cross-flux* or *cross-magnetizing flux*.

(ii) The armature reaction distorts the main-field flux distribution along the air-gap periphery. This distortion is in the direction of rotation for a D.C. generator and opposite to the direction of rotation for a D.C. motor. This also means that MNA is shifted in the direction of rotation for a generator and against the direction of rotation for a motor. This shift of MNA from GNA depends upon the magnitude of load (or armature) current.

(iii) The demagnetizing effect of armature m.m.f. reduces the total flux per pole. This reduction has been found to be 1 to 5% from no-load to full-load.

Example 4.7. *Explain how the demagnetizing effect of armature m.m.f. on the main-field flux can be investigated through the use of magnetization curve of a D.C. machine.*

Solution. The effect of magnetic saturation on the reduction of main-field flux caused by armature reaction can be visualized with the help of Fig. 4.18. In this figure, magnetization curve, triangular armature m.m.f. variation and *S* pole of a D.C. machine are shown. The brushes are in the GNA. For field current I_f, the field m.m.f. is AT_f. At no-load, the flux density B_o, under the entire pole shoe is *ab* for a field m.m.f. AT_f. For armature current I_a, armature m.m.f. is $+ AT_a$ under pole tip *Q* and $- AT_a$ under pole tip *P*. The net m.m.f. under pole tip *Q* is $(AT_f + AT_a)$ and that under pole tip *P* is $(AT_f - AT_a)$ as shown. The m.m.f. $(AT_f + AT_a)$ under pole tip *Q* corresponds to a flux density B_1. Under pole tip *P*, net m.m.f. $(AT_f - AT_a)$ corresponds to a flux density B_2. It is observed from Fig.

* If one travels along the assumed direction of rotation (i.e., from left to right for generator operation and from right to left for motor operation), the pole tip that comes first is called the *leading pole tip*. Obviously, the other pole tip is the *trailing pole tip*.

4.18 that increase in Flux at pole tip Q, proportional to $(B_1 - B_0)$ is less than the decrease in flux under pole P, proportional to $(B_0 - B_2)$. This shows that under saturated conditions, the resultant flux per pole is reduced from its no-load value. Therefore, the field excitation has to be increased under loaded conditions if the field flux is to be kept constant at its no-load value.

Note that the flux density at the middle of pole face is not affected by armature m.m.f.

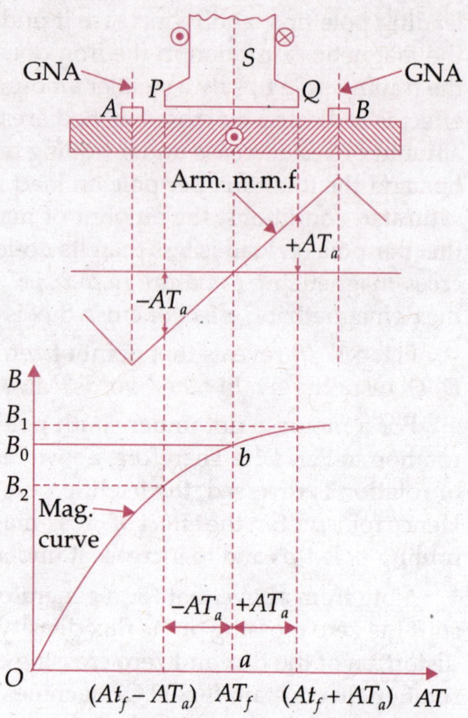

Fig 4.18: Demagnetizing effect of armature m.m.f. on the main-field flux.

Example 4.8. *Discuss the detrimental effects of armature reaction in D.C. machines.*

Solution. It has already been stated that effect of armature m.m.f. on the main field flux is two fold, *(i)* distortion of the main field flux and *(ii)* net reduction of the main field flux.

Distortion of the main field flux gives rise to three detrimental effects and reduction in field flux leads to one bad effect. Rise in iron losses, poor commutation and sparking are caused by distortion of main field flux, whereas the reduction in field flux influences the cost of field winding. These are discussed briefly below.

(i) **Iron losses.** These losses depend on the maximum value of flux density in teeth and in the pole shoes. The armature reaction, by distorting the main field flux waveform, increases the flux density considerably over its corresponding no-load value. As a result ; iron losses, particularly in teeth, are much greater on load than on no-load. In addition, high degree of saturation in teeth forces the flux to stray into the core-end plates, end covers etc. This all leads to more eddy-current and hysteresis losses. Roughly, iron losses at full-load is taken to be 1.5 times its value at no-load.

(ii) **Commutation.** At no-load, zero-crossing of the flux density wave is along the GNA such as point C, C'. Under loaded conditions of the D.C. machine, zero-crossing of the flux density wave is shifted by an angle θ, which depends on the magnitude of armature current.

For good commutation, the coils short-circuited by the brushes should have zero e.m.f. induced in them. The brushes are usually placed along the GNA. Since zero-crossing of the flux density wave is shifted from GNA or q-axis, the coils undergoing commutation do not have zero e.m.f. induced in them. The induced e.m.f. in the commutated coils delays the reversal of armature current in the short-circuited coils ; this may result in detrimental sparking, or poor commutation, at the brushes.

(iii) **Sparking.** Under heavy load, the flux density waveform is distorted considerably. If the two coil-sides of a coil are under the maximum flux density points, a much greater voltage ($\propto Blv$) may be generated in this coil. If this rotational voltage between adjacent commutator segments exceeds 30 or 40 V, a spark may occur between these adjacent segments. Sometimes, this spark may spread around the commutator in the form of a ring fire.

(iv) **Cost of field winding.** Demagnetizing effect of cross-magnetizing armature m.m.f. is to reduce the total flux per pole from its no-load value due to magnetic saturation. In a generator, the magnitude of the e.m.f. generated in the armature decreases with increase in load. In a motor, electromagnetic torque is decreased as the flux per pole is reduced under load. In order to compensate for this reduction in total flux, the field m.m.f. must be augmented. This is possible *(i)*

by increasing the number of turns in the field winding or *(ii)* by using a thick wire for field winding. Either of these schemes entails more copper and, therefore, more cost of the field winding.

4.6.2. Methods of Limiting the Effects of Armature Reaction

The cross-magnetizing effect of armature m.m.f. can be minimised at the design and construction stage of a D.C machine. Various methods of mitigating the effects of armature reaction are discussed below.

(a) **High-reluctance pole tips.** If the reluctance of the pole tips is increased, then the magnitude of armature cross-flux is reduced and the distortion of the resultant flux density wave is minimised. The reluctance of the pole tips can be augmented by using chamfered or eccentric pole shoes. A machine fitted with chamfered or eccentric pole face has short air-gap length at the pole center and longer air-gap lengths under the pole tips, *i.e.* the profile of the pole shoe is not concentric with the armature core as shown in Fig. 4.19 *(a)*.

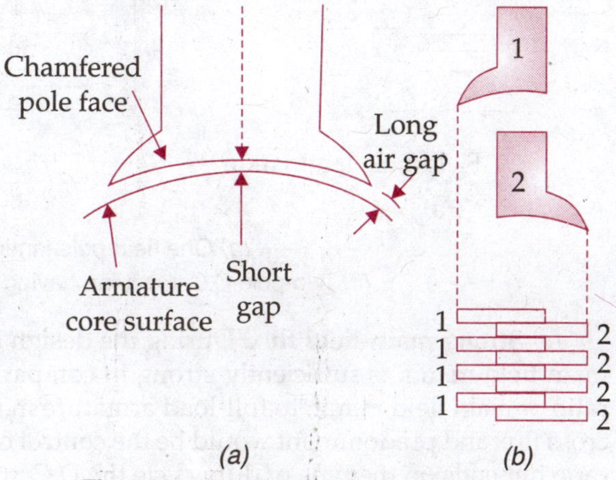

Fig 4.19: *(a)* Chamfered or eccentric pole *(b)* Laminations 1 and 2 are stacked alternatively to give a pole-face view as shown.

Another method of increasing the reluctance to cross-flux is to assemble alternatively the pole laminations depicted in Fig. 4.19 *(b)*. That is, if the first lamination has the pole tip to the left, the second lamination has its pole tip to the right, the third lamination pole tip to the left and so on, until the required pole depth is developed. Since the iron area under the pole tips is almost halved, the reluctance under the pole tips is considerably increased.

The two constructional techniques mentioned above reduce the main field flux to some extent. In order to maintain it constant, the main field m.m.f. must be raised accordingly. But the influence of increased pole-tip reluctance is more pronounced on the cross-flux than on the main-field flux.

In D.C. machines, the short air-gap at the pole centre and longer air-gaps at the pole tips are kept only to limit the effect of cross-magnetizing armature m.m.f. on the main pole flux. The distribution of the flux density wave along the air-gap periphery need not be a sine wave in D.C. machines. But in synchronous machines, the air-gap at the pole centre is short and at the pole tips it is larger from the view point of obtaining sine wave for the flux density wave. In synchronous machines of the salient-pole type, the non-uniform air-gap under the pole faces has nothing to do with the armature reaction.

(b) **Reduction in armature Flux.** Another constructional technique of reducing the armature cross-flux is to create more reluctance in the path of armature flux without reducing the main field flux noticeably. This is achieved by using field-pole laminations having several rectangular holes punched in them. One such lamination having four holes or slots is shown in Fig. 4.20 *(a)*. It is seen from Fig. 4.20 *(b)* that reluctance offered to armature flux is increased due to four air-gap openings introduced in the path of cross-flux. As a result, armature cross-flux is reduced considerably, whereas the main-field flux remains almost unaffected.

Combination of the constructional features described in Fig. 4.19 and 4.20 may be used most effectively in reducing the armature cross flux.

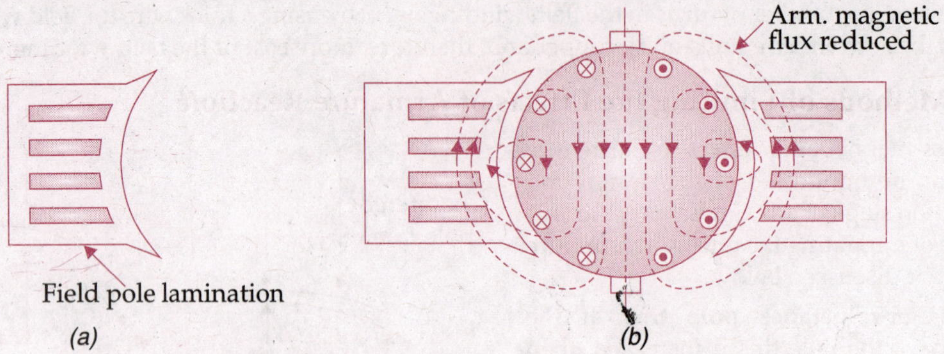

Fig 4.20: *(a)* One field-pole lamination with four punched holes
(b) Two-pole D.C. machine having punched field-pole laminations.

(c) **Strong main-field flux.** During the design of a D.C. machine, it should be ensured that the main field m.m.f. is sufficiently strong in comparison with full-load armature m.m.f. Greater the ratio of main field m.m.f. to full-load armature m.m.f., less is the distortion produced by armature cross flux and predominant would be the control of field m.m.f. over the air-gap flux. Actually, this ratio depends on the type of duty cycle the D.C. machine has to perform.

(d) **Interpoles.** The effect of armature reaction in the **interpolar zone** can be overcome by interpoles, placed in between the main poles. The magnetic axis of interpole winding is in line with the quadrature axis. Interpole winding is connected in series with armature so that interpole m.m.f. is able to neutralize the effect of armature m.m.f. in the interpolar zone at all levels of load current not exceeding the safe limit.

(e) **Compensating winding.** The effect of armature reaction under the **pole shoes** can be limited by using compensating winding. This winding is embedded in slots cut in the pole faces of the D.C. machine. This is the best, but the most expensive method. This is described in detail in Art. 4.9.

4.7. EFFECT OF BRUSH SHIFT

It is seen from Fig. 4.16 or Fig. 4.17 that armature reaction shifts the MNA in the direction of rotation in a generator and against the direction of rotation in a motor. The brushes are along the GNA. The coils undergoing commutation have, therefore, rotational e.m.f. generated in them. As a consequence, sparking and poor commutation occurs. If the brushes are given a shift through an angle θ, no rotational e.m.f. would be generated in the coils undergoing commutation ; this would result in smooth commutation. This shows that for obtaining good commutation, the brushes should be given a forward or backward shift so as to ensure good commutation. In this section, the effect of brush shift in the direction of rotation (called forward shift) or opposite to the direction of rotation (called backward shift) is investigated.

In Fig. 4.16 *(c)*, the brushes are at GNA. Let the brushes be given a forward shift in a generator or backward shift in a motor, so that brush axis is now along the MNA, Fig. 4.21 *(a)*. In other words, the brushes are given a shift through an angle θ and occupy a position *PQ* as shown. The armature flux $\phi_a = OB$ must be along the brush axis as before. Flux ϕ_a can now be decomposed into two components ; *OC* and *OD* as shown in Fig. 4.21 *(b)*. The component $OC = \phi_a \sin\theta$ is opposing the main field flux ϕ_f. Therefore, *OC* has a demagnetizing effect on the main-field flux. The other component *OD*, being perpendicular to the main flux ϕ_f, is the cross-magnetizing armature flux. Note that the resultant flux ϕ_R is obtained from the phasor sum of ϕ_f and ϕ_a, *i.e.*, $\phi_R = \phi_F + \phi_a$. It is observed from Fig. 4.21 (b) that with brush shift, the resultant flux gets reduced from its no-load value even if there is no magnetic saturation.

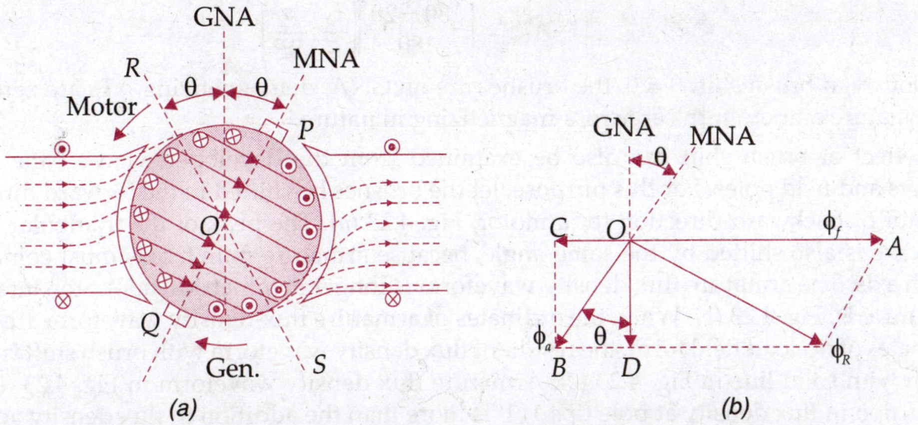

Fig 4.21: Effect of brush shift on the resultant flux in a D.C. machine.

Draw RS making an angle θ with respect to GNA and on the other side of brush shift, Fig. 4.21 *(a)*. The total armature ampere turns can now be divided into two groups as illustrated in Fig. 4.22. The conductors shown in angle *ROP* and *QOS* or the conductors lying in angle 4θ for every 360° electrical (or 2θ for every 180° electrical) are producing a flux opposite to the main field flux. This can be verified by the right-hand grip rule. Hence the ampere turns due to the conductors contained in 4θ degrees for every 360° electrical are demagnetizing in nature.

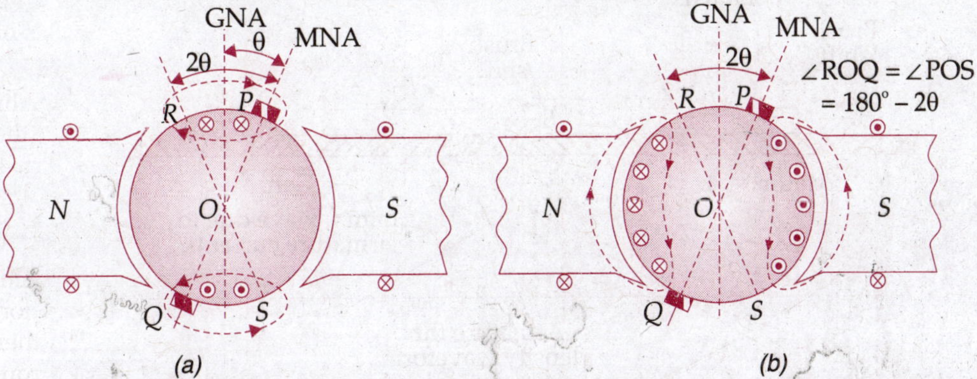

Fig 4.22: Effect of brush shift *(a)* de-magnetizing ampere turns and *(b)* cross-magnetizing ampere turns.

∴ Demagnetizing or back ampere turns/pole AT_d are

$$= \frac{4\theta}{360} \text{ [ATs per pole]}, AT_d = \frac{4\theta}{360}\left[\frac{I_a}{a}\cdot\frac{Z}{2P}\right]$$

or

$$AT_d = \frac{2\theta}{180}\left[\frac{I_a}{a}\cdot\frac{Z}{2P}\right] \quad ...(4.13)$$

In the above expression for AT_d, angle θ is in electrical degrees. In Fig. 4.22 *(b)*, the conductors lying in angle *ROQ* and *POS* produce flux perpendicular to the main-field flux as shown. Therefore, ampere turns produced by the conductors lying within angle (360° – 4θ) for every 360° electrical (or for every pole pair) produce cross-magnetizing ampere turns.

∴ Cross-magnetizing or distorting ampere turns per pole AT_c

$$= \left[\frac{360-4\theta}{360}\right]\left[\frac{I_a}{a}\cdot\frac{Z}{2P}\right]$$

or
$$AT_c = \left[\frac{180 - 2\theta}{180}\right]\left[\frac{I_a}{a} \cdot \frac{Z}{2P}\right] \qquad \text{...(4.14)}$$

Obviously, if brush shift $\theta = 0$, the brushes are on GNA, demagnetizing ATs are zero and the entire armature ampere turns are cross-magnetizing in nature.

The effect of brush shift can also be examined from the developed view of the armature conductors and field poles. For this purpose, let the brushes be shifted in the forward direction for a generator or backward direction for a motor, Fig. 4.23 *(a)*. The peak of the triangular armature m.m.f. wave is also shifted by the same angle, because armature m.m.f. axis must coincide with the brush axis. The armature flux density waveform is longer symmetrical about the interpolar or quadrature axis, Fig. 4.23 *(b)*. When the ordinates of armature flux-density waveform are added to the ordinates of no-load field form, the resultant flux density waveform with brush shift is obtained as shown with solid line in Fig. 4.23 *(c)*. Armature flux density waveform in Fig. 4.23 *(b)* reveals that reduction in flux density at pole tips 1, 1′ is more than the addition in flux density at pole tips 2, 2′. For comparison purposes, the resultant flux density waveform without any brush shift is also drawn with dash-dot line. An examination of Fig. 4.23 *(c)* shows that the ordinates of resultant flux density waveform with brush shift are smaller as compared with the ordinates of resultant flux density waveform with zero brush shift. Consequently, the *flux per pole is reduced if the brushes are given a forward shift in case of a generator or backward shift in case of a motor*. This reduction in flux causes a decrease in the generator terminal voltage or an increase in the motor speed.

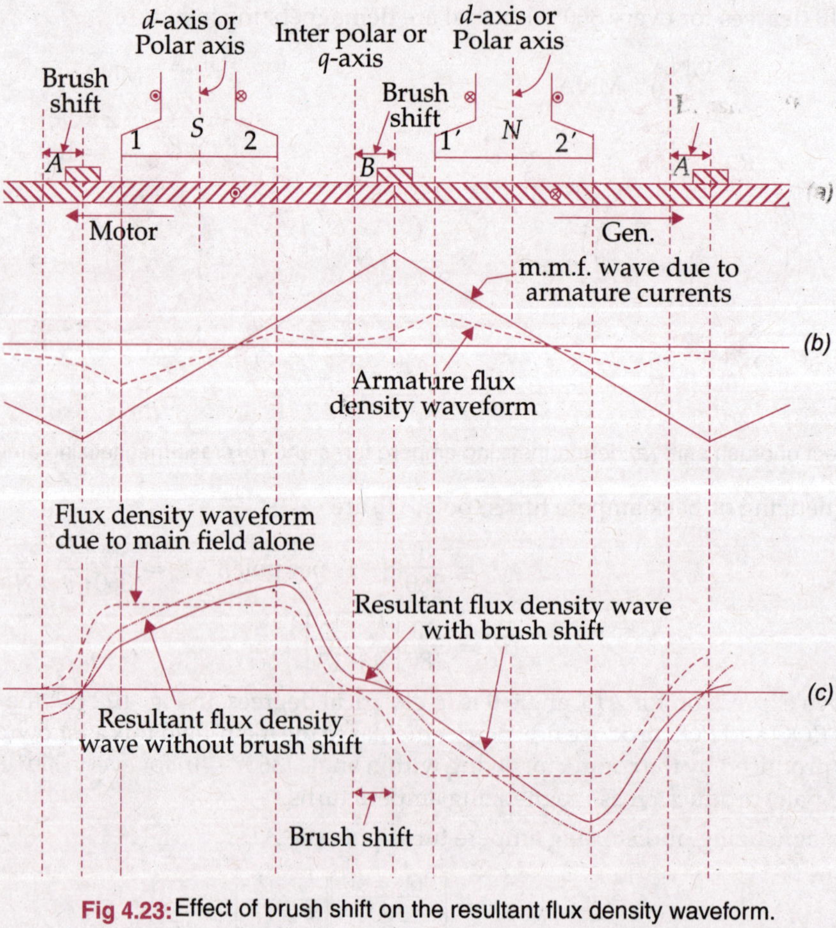

Fig 4.23: Effect of brush shift on the resultant flux density waveform.

If the brushes are given a backward shift in a generator or forward shift in a motor, the flux per pole becomes more and as a result of it, the generator terminal voltage rises and the motor speed falls.

Prior to the invention of interpoles, brush shift was carried out to improve the commutation-forward in a generator and backward in a motor. Now-a-days brush shift is never carried out. However, during the assembly of a D.C. machine, the brushes may be displaced from the quadrature axis unknowingly. Loose brushes in the holders or non-uniform brush pressure may also shift the brush axis from q-axis. Then the question arises as to how to detect whether the brushes are placed correctly along the quadrature axis or not. For this purpose, the following procedure may be adopted.

Run the machine at rated speed as a D.C. generator, first in one direction and then in the opposite direction. For the same field and armature currents, if the terminal voltages for both the directions of rotation are the same, then the brushes are placed correctly along the quadrature axis.

Alternatively, run the machine as a D.C. motor, first in one direction and then in opposite direction. For the same field and armature currents, if the rotor speed turns out to be the same for both directions of rotation, then the brushes are placed correctly along the quadrature axis.

If the brushes get shifted inadvertently from the quadrature axis, then the terminal voltages in case of generator or speeds in case of motor, for both the directions of rotation, would not be equal.

Example 4.9. *A 6-pole, 148 A D.C. shunt generator has 480 conductors and is wave-wound. Its field current is 2 A. Find the demagnetizing and cross-magnetizing ampere turns per pole at full load if*

(a) brushes are on GNA,

(b) brushes are shifted from GNA by 5° electrical,

(c) brushes are shifted from GNA by 5° mechanical.

Solution. Here $a = 2$, $P = 6$, $I_a = I_L + I_f = 148 + 2 = 150$ A, $Z = 480$.

(a) With brushes on GNA, $\theta = 0$, therfore demagnetizing ATs/pole = 0.

The entire armature reaction is cross-magnetizing in nature.

$$\therefore \quad \text{Cross-magnetizing ATs/pole} = \frac{I_a}{a} \cdot \frac{Z}{2P} = \frac{150}{2} \times \frac{480}{2 \times 6} = 3000 \text{ ATs/pole}$$

(b) Here $\theta = 5°$ electrical.

From. Eqn. (4.13),

$$\text{demagnetizing ATs/pole} = \frac{2 \cdot \theta}{180} \cdot \frac{I_a Z}{a \cdot 2P} = \frac{2 \times 5}{180} \times 3000 = 166.67 \text{ ATs/pole}$$

$$\text{Cross-magnetizing ATs/pole} = 3000 - 166.67 = 2833.33 \text{ ATs/pole.}$$

(c) Here $\quad \theta_{elec} = \frac{P}{2} \cdot \theta_{mech}, \therefore \theta = \frac{6}{2} \times 5 = 15°$ electrical

$$\text{Demagnetizing ATs/pole} = \frac{2 \times 15}{180} \times 3000 = 500 \text{ ATs/pole}$$

$$\text{Cross-magnetizing ATs/pole} = 3000 - 500 = 2500 \text{ ATs/pole.}$$

4.8. COMMUTATION

In Fig. 4.24 *(a)*, current in coil C is indicated by cross in coil-side a and dot in coil-side a'. After the coil has traversed the brush width, current in coil C gets reversed ; it is now indicated by dot in coil-side a and cross in coil-side a', Fig. 4.24 *(b)*. In other words, just before the armature coil reaches the brush, it carries current I_a/a

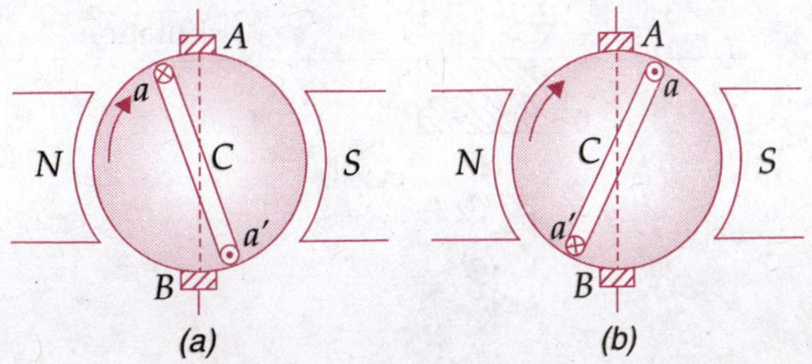

Fig 4.24: Current reversal in coil C.

in one direction. Soon after the armature coil has traversed the brush width, the coil current gets reversed to $-I_a/a$. The reversal of current in the armature coil by means of brush and commutator bars is called **commutation** or **commutation process**. Good commutation means no sparking at the brushes and with commutator surface remaining unaffected during continuous operation of the dc machine. A machine is said to have poor commutation if there is sparking at the brushes and the commutator surface gets damaged during continuous operation of the machine.

The poor commutation may be caused by mechanical or electrical conditions. The mechanical conditions include uneven commutator surface, non-uniform brush pressure, vibration of the brushes in the holders etc. The electrical conditions include an increase in the voltage between commutator segments, an increase in the current density at the trailing edge of the brush etc.

In order to have physical concepts of the commutation process, dc machine coils and commutator bars are represented as shown in Fig. 4.24 *(c)* to Fig. 4.24 *(g)*. In other words, Figs. 4.24 *(c)* to 4.24 *(g)* show the position of coil undergoing commutation at five different instants during the commutation period. Here the two ends of the coil are connected to adjacent bars (lap-connected winding is assumed). Attention will be focused on the reversal of current in coil 1, whose two coil-ends are connected to bars 1 and 2. For simplicity, it is assumed that

(i) the brush width is equal to bars width and

(ii) the mica insulation between the bars (or segments) is of negligible thickness.

In Fig. 4.24 *(c)*, the brush is fully on bar 1. Coil 1 carries current I_c $(= I_a/a)$ from L (left) to R (right). Coil 2 current is I_c from R to L. Therefore, current entering bar 1 is $2\,I_c$ and brush output is also $2\,I_c$. The direction of armature and commutator rotation is taken from L to R.

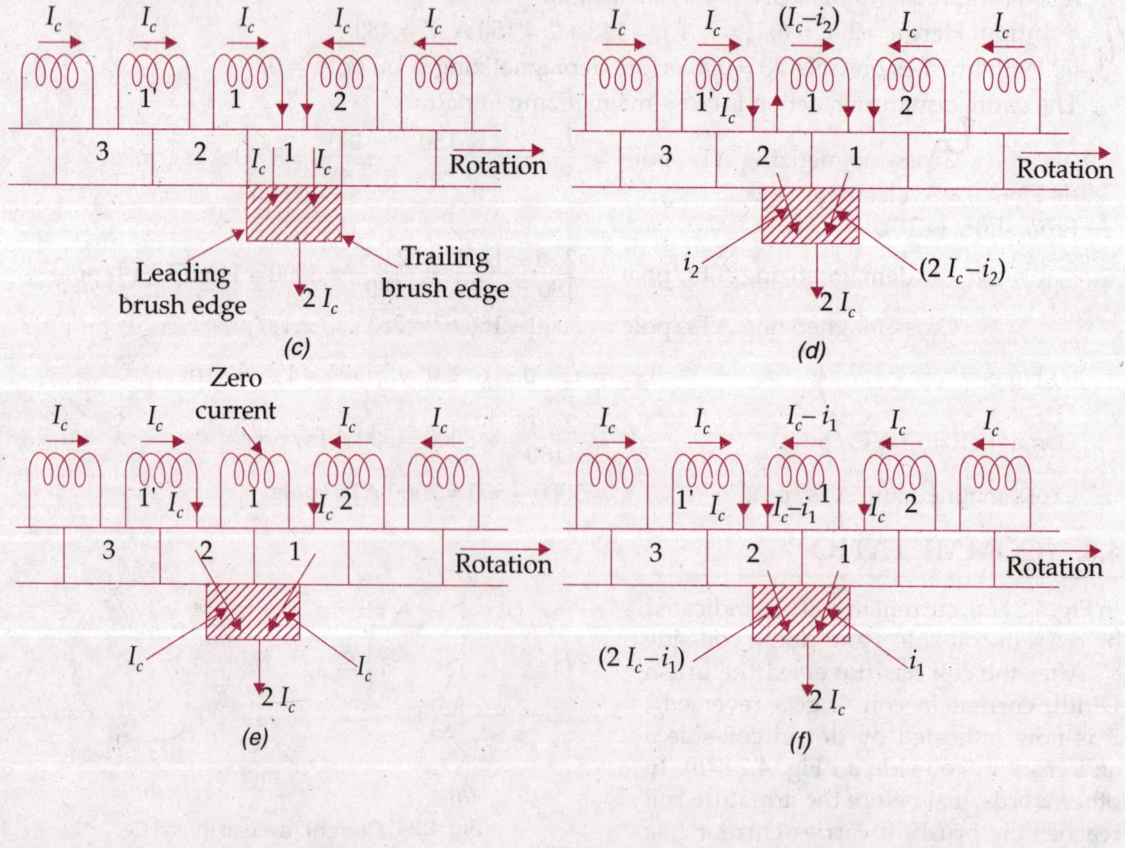

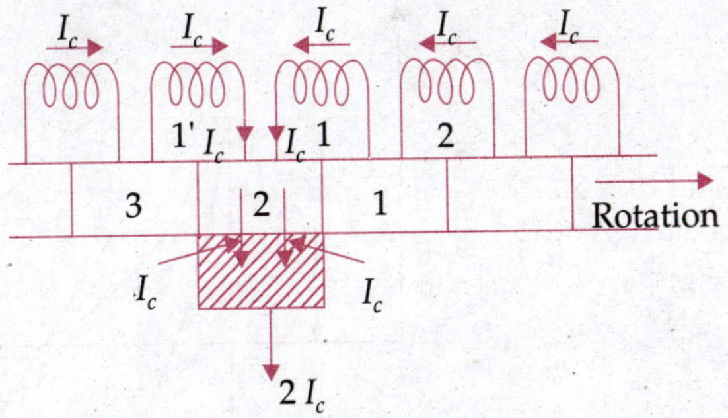

(g)

Fig 4.24: Pertaining to commutation in dc machines.

A little later, as soon as the brush makes contact with bar 2, coil 1 gets short circuited, Fig. 4.24 *(d)*. As a result, current in coil 1 begins to decrease from I_c. At the same time, current from bar 2 to-brush begins to build up from zero, let this current be i_2 (say), Fig. 4.24 *(d)*. Current I_c from coil 1′ enters bar 2, a part i_2 of this current goes to the brush. The remaining current from coil 1′, *i.e.*, $I_c - i_2$ begins to flow in coil 1 from *L* to *R*, Fig. 4.24 *(d)*. Now the current entering bar 1 are $(I_c - i_2)$ from coil 1 and I_c from coil 2. Therefore, bar 1 handles $(2I_c - i_2)$. Currents entering the brush are $(2I_c - i_2)$ from bar 1 and i_2 from bar 2, so that brush current and output current is again equal to $2\,I_c$.

If resistance between brush surface and bars decides the distribution of current, then current i_2 from bar 2 would increase* and current $(2I_c - i_2)$ from bar 1 would decrease linearly with the armature rotation. When brush makes equal area of contacts with bars 1 and 2, then

resistance between bar 1 and brush = resistance between bar 2 and brush

∴ Current from bar 1 to brush = current from bar 2 to brush = I_c

Thus, now each bar delivers I_c to the brush so that the output current is again $2I_c$. Now coil 1 carries no current, Fig. 4.24 *(e)*. Coil 2 current I_c flows to bar 1 and to the brush. Similarly, coil 1′ current I_c flows to bar 2 and then to brush. With further rotation, brush breaks contact with bar 1. Now the brush is fully on bar 2, the short circuit of coil 1 is over and it carries current I_c from *R* to *L* as shown in Fig. 4.24 *(g)*. The time required by the coil current to change from $+I_c$ (from *L* to *R*) to $-I_c$ (from *R* to *L*) is called the **commutation period** T_c. In other words, the commutation period may be defined as the time measured from the instant the brush is fully on bar 1, to the instant the brush is fully on bar 2. It can be computed from the relation

$$T_c = \frac{\text{Brush width}}{\text{Commutator peripheral speed}}$$

Commutation curve is a plot of current in the short-circuited coil undergoing commutation as a function of commutation period. Under the assumption that contact resistance between brush and bar decides the distribution of current, commutation curve is a straight line from $+I_c$ to $-I_c$, as shown in Fig. 4.25 *(a)*. This commutation type is called **straight-line** or **linear commutation**.

Types of commutation. Change of current through a coil undergoing commutation may occur in the manner shown by the curves in Fig. 4.25 *(b)*. These are called commutation curves.

Curve 1. It indicates **linear commutation** or straight-line commutation. This type of commutation requires that coil resistance must be negligible as compared with brush contact resistance.

In other words, brush contact resistance should be the only factor deciding the current flow during commutation. This is explained in Figs. 4.24 *(c)* to *(g)*.

* It is because contact surface area increases with armature rotation, brush contact resistance falls and therefore, more current is shared by bar 2.

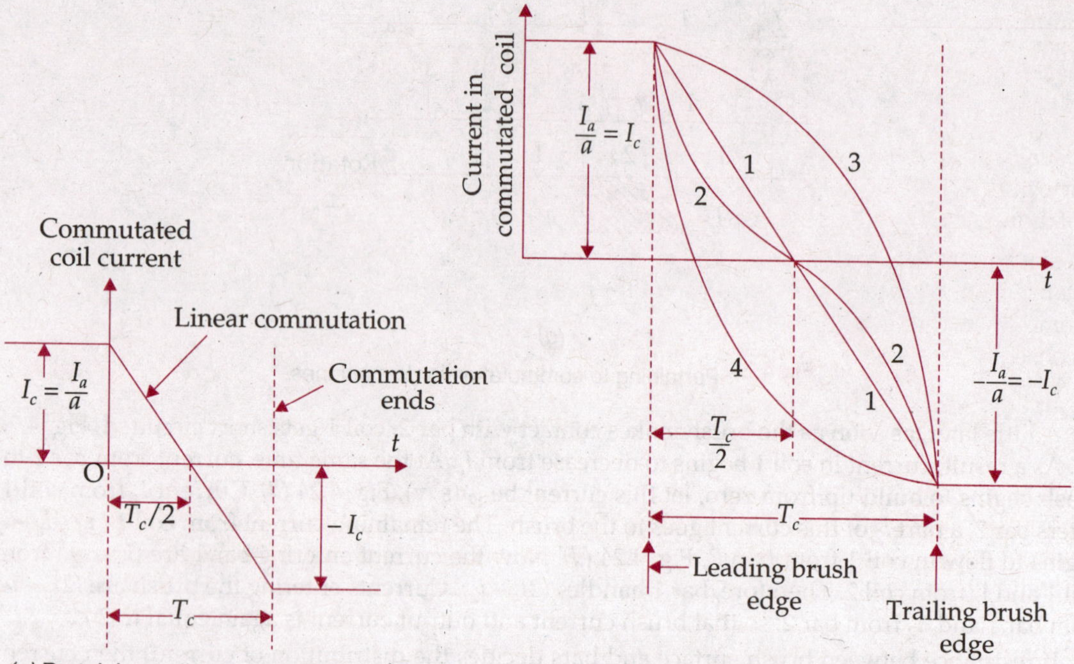

(a) Pertaining to linear commutation. (b) Different types of commutation.

Fig 4.25

Curve 2. If resistance of short-circuited coil is not negligible as compared to brush contact resistance; then curve 2, called **resistance commutation** is achieved. It is seen from this curve that at the leading brush edge or tip, slope of curve 2 is more than that of curve 1. This means that coil resistance enhances the current reversal or helps in the commutation process during the period zero to $T_c/2$. At the trailing brush edge coil resistance retards the current reversal during the period $T_c/2$ to T_c. It is observed from resistance commutation curve 2 that slope of commutation curve, called **current density** is higher at both leading and trailing brush edges.

Curve 3. Commutation curve denoted by 3 is called **under-commutation** or retarded commutation. In the coil undergoing commutation, some voltages (discussed further) are induced which delay the current reversal. The retarded commutation has very high slope of commutation curve near the end of T_c. As a result, it may lead to sparking at the trailing brush edge. This sparking may cause deterioration of brush and bar materials.

Curve 4. This curve denoted as 4 in Fig. 4.25 *(b)* is called **over-commutation**. This type of commutation is achieved by the use of interpoles (discussed further). The curve 4 shows that rate of change of current at the end of commutation period is almost zero. In other words, the current in the coil undergoing commutation has almost reached $-\frac{I_a}{a}$ before the coil leaves the brush. This results in no sparking at the trailing edge of the brush. Therefore, overcommutation gives the most favourable condition for good and satisfactory commutation.

4.8.1. Qualitative Discussion

In the commutated or short-circuited coil undergoing commutation, several emfs are induced. The effect of these emfs on commutation is now examined qualitatively.

(I) **Delayed commutation.** In the commutated coil, the current changes from $+ I_c\left(= \frac{I_a}{a}\right)$ to $- I_c$

in commutation period T_c. During this current change in small interval of time T_c (2 m-sec or less), an e.m.f. e_c is induced in the coil due to its self-inductance L_c and its magnitude is given by

$$e_c = L_c \frac{di_c}{dt}$$

Usually the brush covers more than one bar and the commutated coil may have e.m.f. induced in it due to mutual flux produced by the neighbouring coils. The sum of the two e.m.fs., one due to self-flux of the coil and the other due to the mutual flux of the neighbouring coils, is called *reactance voltage*.

According to Lenz's law, *the effect opposes the cause*. Here the effect is the reactance voltage and cause is the reversal of current. Thus the reactance voltage opposes the reversal of current in the commutated coil. As a result of it, the reversal of current in the short circuited coil is delayed and consequently it lags in time, the values of current it would attain by the linear commutation. For example at $t = \frac{T_c}{2}$, the coil current is zero with linear commutation, but because of reactance voltage, the coil current will be zero after $t > \frac{T_c}{2}$ as shown in Fig. 4.26 (*b*).

This type of commutation is called *under commutation or delayed commutation*. If the current in the short-circuited coil has not reached $-I_c$ by the time brush breaks contact with bar 1, then (*i*) the coil current is $(I_c - i)$ and (*ii*) current *i* from bar 1 to brush is broken which appears in the form of arc at the trailing brush tip as shown in Fig. 4.26 (*a*). As soon as arc is broken, the current through coil 1 rises rapidly from $(I_c - i)$ to I_c as shown in Fig. 4.26 (*b*). Thus, the effect of reactance voltage is to cause sparking, heating of the trailing brush tip and temperature rise of the commutator.

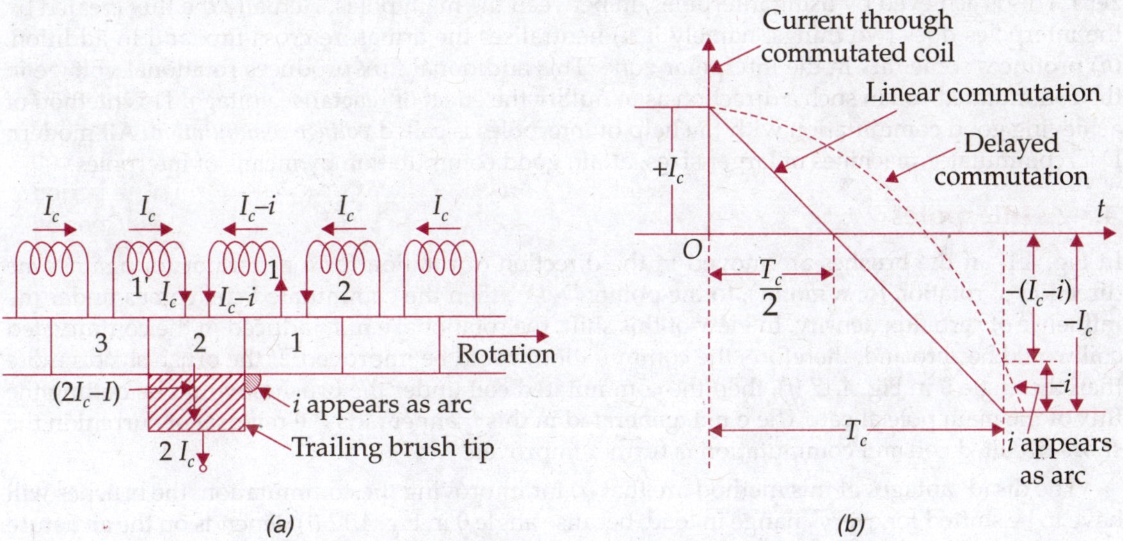

Fig 4.26: Pertaining to delayed commutation.

Good commutation means linear commutation as shown in Figs. 4.25 and 4.26 (*b*). Two ways, tending to promote good commutation are (*i*) resistance commutation and (*ii*) voltage commutation. In fact, resistance commutation always lends a marginal support to voltage commutation so as to secure good commutation. These two methods are now discussed next.

(II) **Resistance Commutation.** It is seen from above that the presence of reactance voltage in the coil undergoing commutation leads to delayed commutation. Therefore, for securing good commutation, reactance voltage must be kept to as low a value as possible. It has been found that the magnitude of reactance voltage is approximately proportional to the armature core length, coil pitch of the winding and square of the number of turns per coil. In view of this, the reactance voltage in the commutated coil can be minimised by using (*i*) small length of armature core by resorting to multipolar design (*ii*) chorded-armature coils and (*iii*) smallest number of armature turns per coil. The effect of reactance voltage in delaying commutation is also minimised if the voltage drop across the brush-contact resistance is sufficiently large as compared with the reactance voltage. The fact that carbon brushes possess significant brush-contact voltage drop, is perhaps one of the main reasons for their use in D.C. machines. This method of achieving good commutation through the use of carbon brushes having significant resistance drops is called *resistance commutation*. In practice, this method of securing good commutation is primarily the domain of fractional-kW commutator machines.

(III) **Voltage commutation.** It will be seen from Fig. 4.17 (*f*), that the armature reaction shifts the zero crossing of the flux density wave from C, C' to D, D'. Thus, as the coil being commutated is under the brushes at C, C' and is cutting the flux whic has the polarity of the main pole S pole at C left behind for a generator. The coil has, therefore, rotational e.m.f. generated in it and must be indicated by dot as per the right-hand rule of e.m.f. generation. This rotational e.m.f. encourages the maintenance of current in the same old direction *i.e* dot and consequently opposes the reversal of current just like the reactance voltage. For a motor the commutated coil is cutting the flux which has the polarity of the main pole S pole at C ahead. According to the right hand rule for e.m.f. generation, the rotational e.m.f. generated in the commutated coil at C, C' is opposite (cross) to what it is (dot) under the main pole ahead. Thus, for both generator and motor, the rotational e.m.f. generated in the commutated coil always opposes reversal of current just like the reactance voltage. In order to cancel the effect of rotational voltage, the flux density in the interpolar zone should be reduced to zero. This is achieved by using interpoles, in between the main poles. Actually the flux created by the interpoles does two things, namely it (*i*) neutralises the armature cross flux and in addition, (*ii*) produces some flux in the interpolar zone. This additional flux produces rotational voltage in the commutated coil in such a direction as to nullify the effect of reactance voltage. This method of achieving good commutation with the help of interpoles is called *voltage commutation*. All modern D.C. commutator machines of larger sizes, attain good commutation by means of interpoles.

4.8.2. Interpoles

In Fig. 4.17, if the brushes are moved in the direction of rotation for a generator (or against the direction of rotation for a motor), to the points D, D' ; then the commutated coil comes under the influence of zero flux density. In view of this shift, the rotational e.m.f. induced in the commutated coil would be zero and, therefore, the commutation would be improved. If the brush shift is more than the angle θ in Fig. 4.17 (*f*), then the commutated coil under the brushes would be cutting the flux of the main pole ahead. The e.m.f. generated in this manner aids the reversal of current in the short-circuited coil and commutation is further improved.

The disadvantages of this method are that (*i*) for improving the commutation, the brushes will have to be shifted for every change in load, because angle θ in Fig. 4.17 (*f*) depends on the armature (or load) current and (*ii*) for larger shift of the brushes in the direction of rotation for a generator and against the direction of rotation for a motor, the demagnetizing ampere-turns increase and the main flux is reduced considerably (see Art. 4.7). This reduced flux may jeopardise the operation of the generator or motor to a noticeable extent. This method of shifting the brushes for improving the commutation was employed before the invention of interpoles.

The interpoles are narrow poles placed exactly midway between the main poles. The interpoles are fitted to the yoke and are also known as *commutation poles or compoles*. In order to make the flux density zero under the brush at C in Fig. 4.17 (*f*), the interpole must have a north polarity. At C', the interpole must have south polarity. From this, it may be concluded that *for a generator, the polarity of the interpole must be the same as that of the main pole ahead of it, in the direction of rotation. For a motor, the polarity of the interpole must be the same as that of the main pole behind it.*

In practice, the interpoles of appropriate polarity are strengthened so that in interpolar zone ; the armature cross flux is neutralized and in addition some flux is produced there. This additional flux in the interpolar zone induces rotational e.m.f. in the commutated coil in such a direction as to oppose the reactance voltage. If this rotational e.m.f. due to the additional interpolar-flux is equal and opposite to the reactance e.m.f., then the resultant e.m.f. in the commutated coil would be zero and therefore zero current in that coil would amount to sparkless commutation. This is the reason why interpoles are designed to provide more m.m.f. than the armature m.m.f. in the commutating zone. In practice, the interpole m.m.f. may be 1.2 to 1.3 times the armature m.m.f. per pole.

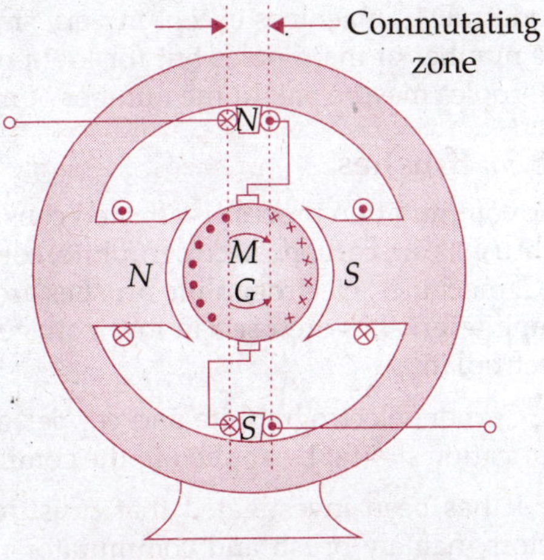

Fig 4.27: Interpoles for D.C. machine.

If the armature current increases, the armature reaction and, therefore, the rotational and reactance e.m.fs. in the commutated coil increase. In order to enable the interopoles to do their duty faithfully with the variation of armature current ; the interpole winding is connected in series with the armature. Fig. 4.27 shows the series connection of armature and compoles. Note from this figure also that the interpole m.m.f. is opposite to the armature m.m.f. in the commutating zone.

Resultant flux density waveform is shown by solid curve in Fig. 4.17 (*f*). When interpoles of proper polarity are fitted to the yoke, the resultant flux density waveform is as illustrated in Fig. 4.28. An examination of this figure reveals that the commutation of the coil now takes place in the field, the polarity of which is the same as that of the main field ahead for a generator. In view of this, the rotational e.m.f. generated and, therefore, the current in the commutated coil is of the same sign (cross) as under the main poles ahead. This helps in the reversal of current in the commutated coil and thus the commutation is improved in a D.C. generator.

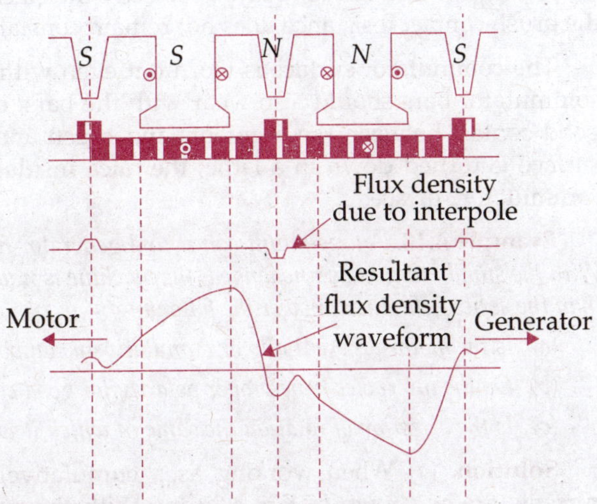

Fig 4.28: Resultant flux density waveform with interpoles of proper polarity for motor mode and generator mode.

In case of D.C. motor, the commutation of the coil takes place in the field, the polarity of which is opposite to the main poles ahead. In view of this, rotational e.m.f. induced in the commutated coil by generator action (apply right hand rule for generator action) is of the same sign (dot) as it would be under the main poles ahead. The current due to this rotational e.m.f. is also of the same sign (dot) as it is under the main poles ahead. This helps in the reversal of the current in the commutated coil and this improves the commutation in a D.C. motor.

In order to avoid saturation in the interpoles, air-gaps under these poles are kept longer than under the main poles. All modern D.C. machines fitted with interpoles, can operate over wide range without sparking. It has, therefore, become a common practice to install the interpoles in modern D.C. machines except in very small D.C. machines. The number of interpoles is equal to the number of main poles but for low-power D.C. machines, say less than 3 or 4 kW, number of interpoles may be half of the number of main poles.

4.8.3. Brushes

The commutation process is affected considerably by the type of brush material. The various types of brushes are carbon, electrographite, copper graphite etc. Carbon brushes are used for very small D.C. machines, electrogaphite brushes are used more frequently in all D.C. machines and copper-graphite brushes are used in low voltage (up to 30 V) heavy current D.C. machines, as used for electroplating.

Carbon, electrographite and copper-graphite brushes are self-lubricating. In view of this, no lubrication should be applied to the commutator surface.

It has been investigated that brush contact resistance is non-linear and depends on many factors, namely brush and commutator materials, current density, brush pressure, commutator speed, current direction, temperature, moisture in the air and atmospheric pressure. In view of this, it is quite difficult to analyse correctly the electrical behaviour of the commutated coil, since the brush contact resistance does not remain constant.

The commutator surface is worn out even with soft material brushes. The mica between the commutator bars should also wear with the bars, otherwise high mica insulation will not allow good contact between the segments and brush and sparking will occur. When the commutator surface is turned down in a lathe, the mica insulation should be undercut to a level below the commutator surface.

Example 4.10. *A long-shunt compound generator fitted with interpoles is cumulatively compounded. With the supply terminals unchanged, the machine is now run as compound motor. If shunt field is stronger than the series field, then answer the following :*

(a) Is the motor differentially or cumulatively compounded?

(b) Do the interpoles have proper polarity for good commutation?

(c) Is the direction of rotation the same in which it was driven as a generator?

Solution. (*a*) When working as a cumulatively compounded generator, the directions of currents are as shown in Fig. 4.29 (*a*). With the supply terminals unchanged, the directions of currents, when running as a motor, are as shown in Fig. 4.29 (*b*). Since the series field opposes the shunt field in Fig. 4.29 (*b*), it becomes a differentially compounded motor.

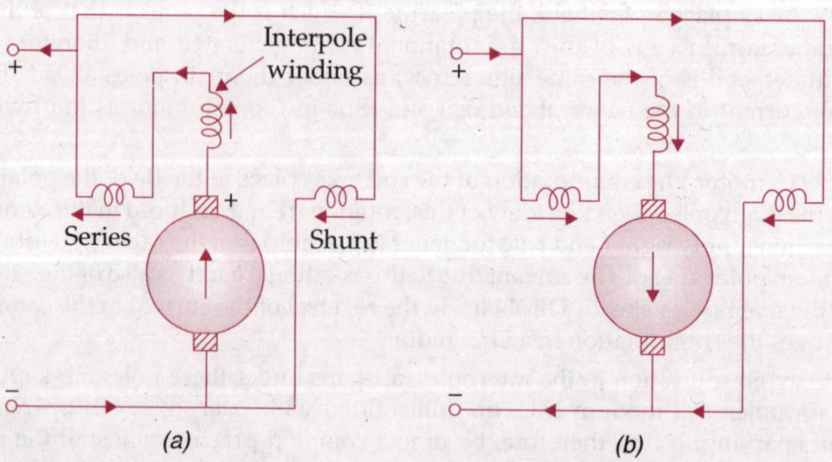

(*a*) (*b*)

(c) (d)

Fig 4.29: Pertaining to Example 4.10.

(*b*) For cumulatively compounded generator, the directions of currents in the armature and interpole windings are as shown in Fig. 4.29 (*a*). When running as a motor, the directions of currents, both in the armature and interpole windings, get reversed. Thus the interpoles have proper polarity for good commutation.

(*c*) For the direction of current in the armature and main *N*, *S* poles as shown in Fig. 4.29 (*c*) for a generator, the armature must be driven in anticlockwise direction. Since the shunt field is stronger than the series field, the main poles polarity remains unchanged for a motor. The direction of armature current, however, gets reversed for a motor as shown in Fig. 4.29 (*d*). Now the main *N*, *S* poles must attract *S*, *N* poles created on the armature. The rotation is thus anticlockwise, the same in which it was driven as a generator.

Example 4.11. *A 4-pole, 100 kW, 200 V lap-connected D.C. machine has 256 conductors. Find the number of turns required on each interpole, if interpolar air-gap is 1 cm and interpolar flux-density is 0.25 T. Neglect the effect of iron parts of the circuit and of the leakage.*

Solution. The interpolar m.m.f. per pole F_{cp} should be equal to the combination of armature m.m.f. per pole F_a and the air-gap m.m.f. In view of this,

$$F_{cp} = F_a + \frac{B_{cp}}{\mu_0} g_{cp}$$

where B_{cp} and g_{cp} are the interpolar flux density and air-gap length respectively.

Full load current $I_a = \frac{100,000}{200} = 500 \text{ A}$

$\therefore$ $F_{cp} = \frac{I_a Z}{2aP} + \frac{B_{cp}}{\mu_0} \cdot g_{cp}$

or $I_a N_{cp} = \frac{500 \times 256}{2(4)(4)} + \frac{0.25}{4\pi \times 10^{-7}} \times 1 \times 10^{-2} = 4000 + 1989 = 5989$

or $N_{cp} = \frac{5989}{500} = 12$ turns per pole.

Thus the turns on each interpole should be equal to 12.

Note. Since the interpoles are designed to provide more m.m.f. than the combination of armature and air-gap m.m.fs., the number of turns on each interpole should be more than 12.

4.9. COMPENSATING WINDINGS

The interpole winding m.m.f. is effective only in the commutating zone. In other words, the armature reaction effects are overcome only under the interpoles and the resultant flux density under the pole faces remains distorted as illustrated in Fig. 4.28.

If a D.C. machine is subjected to heavy overloads or if it operates with a weak main field (as in a motor intended for wide speed control), then the resultant field waveform is extremely distorted, as shwon in Fig. 4.30. Any coil, whose two coil-sides are under the influence of these peak flux densities will have a large rotational e.m.f. induced in it. In Fig. 4.30, at any instant, the coil sides *a* and *a′* are shown under the peak flux densities. If the rotational or speed voltage induced in coil *aa′* exceeds about 30 V (maximum permissible limit is of the order of 30 to 40 V), the air between the adjacent commutator segments to which the coil *aa′* is connected, may breakdown resulting in an arc. Such an arc may then extend to nearby commutator segments and eventually spread rapidly round the entire commutator periphery. This is because the air near the commutator surface is fairly ionised to result in conditions favourable for flashover. Such a flashover is detrimental both to the commutator and the supply line, since the latter is directly short-circuited by the flashover.

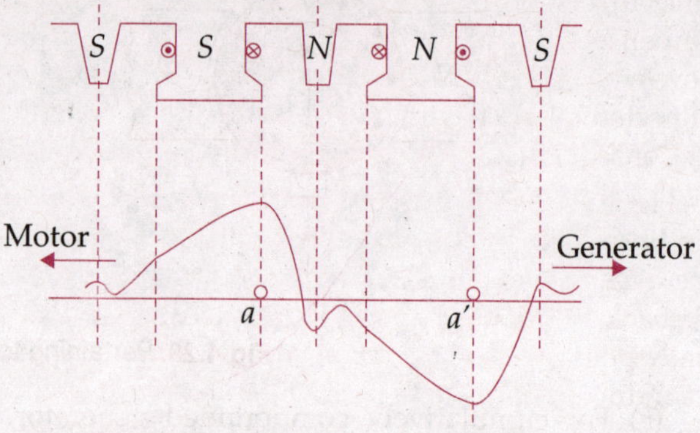

Fig 4.30: Extremely distorted flux density waveform without compensating winding and its effect on coil, *a*, *a′*.

There is another factor which may cause voltage between adjacent segments to exceed 30 V (30 to 40 V). This is associated with the time-variation of armature flux caused by sudden rise or fall of the load current. For understanding this, consider a D.C. machine subjected to rapidly changing loads of wide range. Let us first investigate its operation as a D.C. generator. The distribution of armature reaction flux or cross flux alone, is depicted in Fig. 4.17 (*c*) and also in Fig. 4.17 (*d*). It may be seen that a coil under the pole centres has maximum cross flux around it and consequently has maximum cross flux linkages. Therefore, the effect of rapidly changing flux caused by rapidly changing loads, is more pronounced on the coil under the pole centres and naturally the attention will be focused on this very coil.

When the load on the generator rises suddenly from a low to a high value, the cross flux grows. This growth of cross flux induces an e.m.f.* in the coil in such a direction as to oppose its growth. Thus under *S* pole, this induced e.m.f. must be indicated by a cross *i.e.*, opposite to the rotational e.m.f. already existing in Fig. 4.17 (*c*). Therefore, the resultant e.m.f. in the coil under the pole centres is reduced if the load is suddenly increased on the generator. When the load on the generator falls suddenly from a high to a low value, the armature reaction flux tends to decay. This flux decay is opposed by an e.m.f. induced in this coil. A little consideration will show that this e.m.f. under *S*-pole must be indicated by a dot, *i.e.* it must be shown as aiding the rotational e.m.f. already existing. Therefore, the resultant e.m.f. in coil under the pole centres is increased if the load on the generator is suddenly thrown off. If this combined e.m.f. in the coil exceeds about 30 V, the arc across the air near the mica sheet separating the adjacent commutator bars (to which the coil is connected) may occur, resulting in flashover between positive and negative brushes.

The reader may use the same thought process and come to the conclusion that arcing may occur if the load is suddenly increased from a low to a large value in case of a D.C. motor.

The trouble of flashover which is due to the distortion of flux density wave under the pole shoes or due to the rapidly changing loads, can be effectively overcome by neutralizing or compensating the armature m.m.f. under the pole faces. The best way to achieve this compensation, is by means

* Note that this is transformer e.m.f.

of pole face winding or compensating winding embedded in slots in the pole faces. The armature and compensating windings are connected in series so that their m.m.fs. are proportional to the same current. Further, in order that their m.m.fs. oppose each other, the direction of currents in the compensating winding must be opposite to that in the armature winding just below the pole faces as shown in Fig. 4.31. Half of the compensating winding conductors, say on the right side of a pole are connected in series with half of the conductors on the left hand side of the adjoining pole, Fig. 4.31 (*a*). Consequently the pole-face winding or the compensating winding is a concentric type winding.

Fig. 4.31 (*b*) shows the physical arrangement of connections of armature circuit and compensating winding (CW). In this figure, top brush is connected to back end of the CW conductor 1 in *N*-pole face. The front end of this conductor 1 is connected to front end of CW conductor 1′ in *S*-pole face. The back end of 1′ is connected to back end of 2 in *N*-pole face and so on till back end of conductor 4 in *N*-pole face is reached. Now, front end of conductor 4 in *N*-pole face is connected to front end of conductor 4′ in *S*-pole face. The back end of conductor 4′ is finally brought out and connected to line terminal *B* as shown in Fig. 4.31 (*b*).

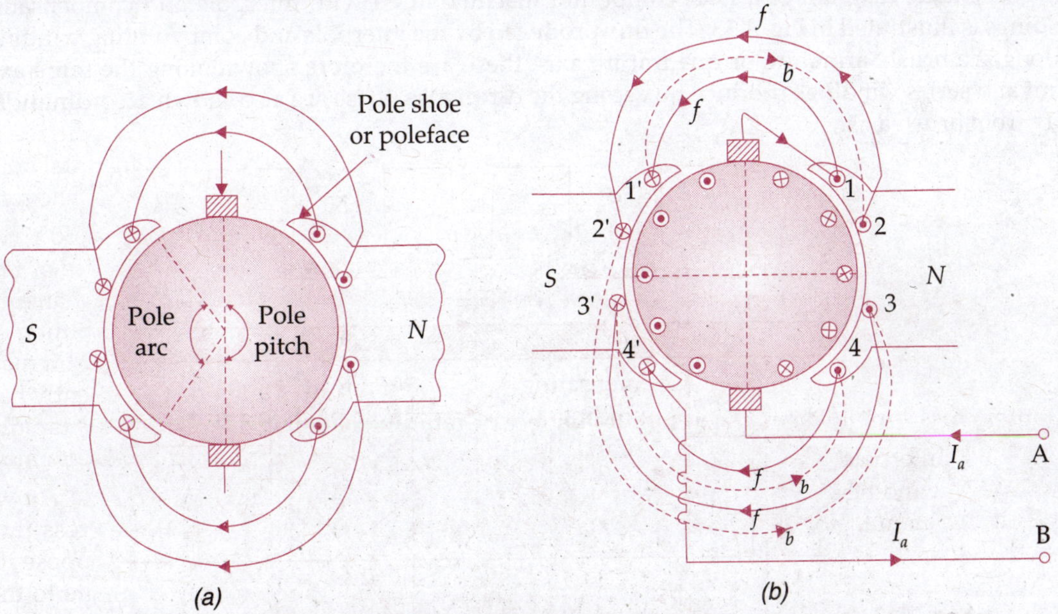

Fig 4.31: Compensating windings embedded in slots in the pole faces.

Fig. 4.32 illustrates how the compensating winding m.m.f. neutralizes the armature m.m.f. under the pole faces. In the interpolar region, the compensating winding m.m.f. and interpole winding m.m.f., both oppose armature m.m.f. The resultant of these three m.m.fs. in the commutating zone should not be zero, from the view point of cancelling the reactance e.m.f. Under the pole faces, compensating winding m.m.f. neutralizes the armature winding m.m.f. Therefore the resultant flux density waveform under the pole faces is seen to be independent of load current and is of the same waveform as produced by the main field alone. This means that the field windings have full control over the air-gap flux. Since the compensating winding

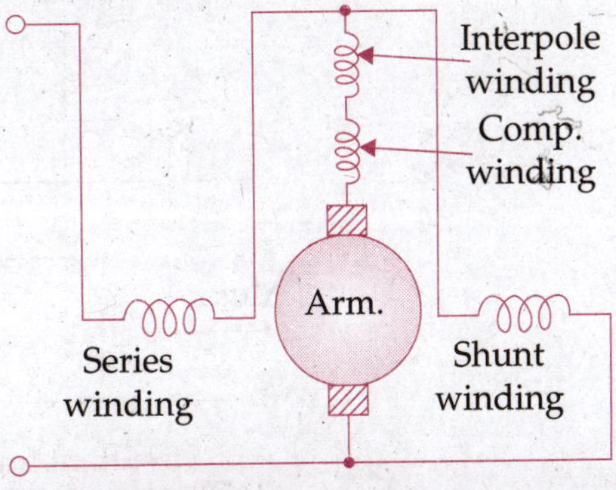

Fig 4.32: Schematic diagram of a D.C. compound machine fitted with interpole and compensating windings

neutralizes the armature m.m.f. under the main poles, the armature flux linkages are reduced. This has the effect of reducing the armature inductance. Thus the armature-circuit time constant is reduced and this results in quicker dynamic response of the D.C. machine.

Since the compensating winding m.m.f. neutralizes the armature m.m.f. only under the main pole-faces, the compensating winding m.m.f. per pole AT_c is given by

$$AT_c = \frac{\text{Pole arc}}{\text{Pole pitch}} \times \text{Armature m.m.f. per pole} = \frac{\text{Pole arc}}{\text{Pole pitch}} \times \frac{I_a Z}{2aP} \quad \text{...(4.17 a)}$$

As compensating winding carries I_a, the compensating winding conductors Z_{cw} can be calculated as under :

$$AT_c = \frac{Z_{cw} \cdot I_a}{2} = \frac{\text{Pole arc}}{\text{Pole pitch}} \times \frac{I_a Z}{2aP}$$

or

$$Z_{cw} = \frac{\text{Pole arc}}{\text{Pole pitch}} \times \frac{Z}{aP} \quad \text{...(4.17 b)}$$

A schematic diagram of a D.C. compound machine fitted with interpole and compensating windings is illustrated in Fig. 4.33. The flux produced by the interpole and compensating windings is along the brush, armature or quadrature axis, these are therefore shown along the same axis. Shunt and series windings produce flux along the direct axis, these are also shown accordingly 90° away from brush axis.

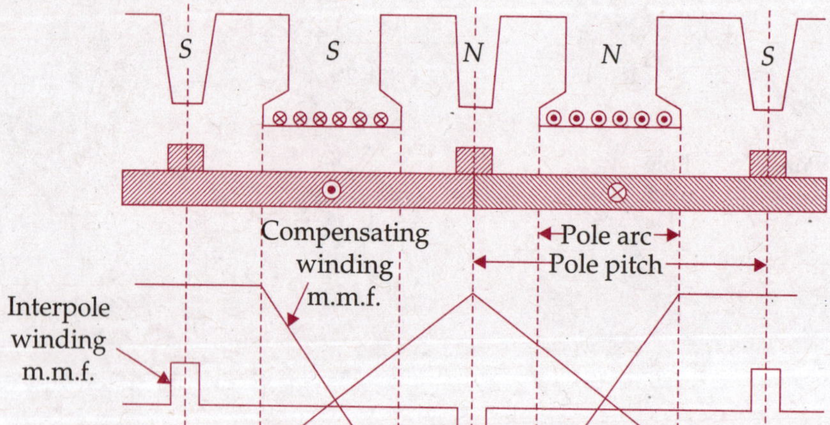

Fig 4.33: Resultant flux density waveform with compensating winding and interpoles.

The compensating winding increases the cost of D.C. machines, these are therefore used in D.C. machines subjected to heavy over-loads or rapidly changing loads (*e.g.* steel mills) or in motors intended for wide speed range by shunt field control.

Summarizing, the methods of improving commutation in D.C. machines are as follows :

(*a*) By increasing the brush contact resistance. This causes more voltage drop at the brush-bar contacts as compared with the reactance voltage and the commutation is improved. This method called resistance commutation is employed in fractional kW DC machines.

(*b*) By shifting the brushes, forward in a generator or backward in a motor. This method was employed for commutation improvement before the invention of interpoles.

(*c*) By providing interpoles. This method is employed in almost all sizes of D.C. machines, except in very small (less than about 0.3 or 0.4 kW) D.C. machines.

(*d*) By providing compensating winding. Since the D.C. machines with compensating winding are more expensive, these are used in those D.C. machines only which have to perform severe duty cycles in industry.

Example 4.12. *A commutator with a diameter of 50 cm rotates at 1000 r.p.m. For a brush width of 1.5 cm, find the time of commutation.*

Solution. Peripheral velocity of commutator,

$$v = \pi DN = \pi \times 50 \times \frac{1000}{60} \text{ cm/s}$$

But $\quad v \times$ time of commutation = brush width

$$\therefore \quad \text{Time of commutation} = \frac{1.5 \times 60}{\pi \times 50 \times 1000} = 0.573 \text{ ms.}$$

Example 4.13. *A single-turn coil has an inductance of 0.02 mH in the commutating zone. Find the value of commutating field required for obtaining straight line commutation for an armature current of 120 A for 4-pole lap-wound dc machine.*

Solution. For straight line or linear commutation, the transformer e.m.f. E_t in the coil undergoing commutation must be neutralized by the speed, or rotational, e.m.f. E_r in the commutating coil.

Transformer e.m.f. in coil, $\quad E_t = L\dfrac{di}{dt}$

Here change of current during commutation $= \dfrac{I_a}{a} \times 2 = \dfrac{120}{4} \times 2 = 60$ A.

Refer to Fig. 4.4. Let dt be denoted by t_c = time of commutation.

$$\therefore \quad E_t = L\frac{di}{dt} = 0.02 \times 10^{-3}\frac{60}{t_c}$$

The speed or rotational e.m.f. in a single-turn coil is given by

$$E_r = 2 \text{ (average emf per conductor)} = 2\,(B_{av} \cdot l \cdot v)$$

If x = brush width, then $\quad v = \dfrac{\text{brush width}}{\text{time of commutation}} = \dfrac{x}{t_c}$

$$\therefore \quad E_r = 2B_{av} \cdot l \cdot \frac{x}{t_c} = 2\frac{\phi_c}{t_c}$$

where ϕ_c = average value of flux in the commutating zone.

For linear commutation, $\quad E_r = E_t$

$$2\frac{\phi_c}{t_c} = 0.02 \times 10^{-3}\frac{60}{t_c} \text{ or } \phi_c = 0.5 \text{ m Wb.}$$

Example 4.14. *A 2000 kW, 400 V, 14-pole D.C. machine has a lap wound armature with 1100 conductors. The pole arc to pole-pitch ratio is 0.7. Compute the number of pole-face conductors of the compensating winding in each pole, so as to obtain uniform air-gap flux density under the pole faces.*

Solution. For a lap-connected armature, $a = P = 14$

Full load armature current $I_a = \frac{2000\times10^3}{400} = 5000$ A

$$\text{Armature ampere conductors per pole} = \frac{I_a Z}{aP} = \frac{5000\times1100}{14\times14}$$

Ampere conductors per pole to be compensated by pole face winding

$$= \frac{\text{Pole arc}}{\text{Pole pitch}} \times \frac{5000\times1100}{14\times14} = 0.7 \times \frac{(5000)(1100)}{14\times14}$$

The compensating winding carries the entire armature current of 5000 A.

$$\therefore \text{ Compensating winding conductors per pole} = \frac{0.7\times1100\times5000}{14\times14\times5000} = 4.$$

Example 4.15. *A compensated D.C. machine has 15,000 armature ampere turns per pole. The ratio of pole arc to pole pitch is 0.68. Interpolar air gap length and flux density are respectively 1 cm and 0.25 teslas. For rated armature current of 850 A, calculate the compensating winding conductors per pole and the number of turns on each interpole.*

Solution. From Eq. (4.17), compensating winding ampere turns per pole are

$$AT_c = 0.68 \times 15000 = 10{,}200 \text{ ATs.}$$

$$\therefore \text{ Compensating winding conductors per pole} = 2 \times \frac{10200}{850} = 24.$$

m.m.f. required for the air gap under the interpole

$$= \frac{B_{cp}}{\mu_0} g_{cp} = \frac{0.25}{4\pi\times10^{-7}} \times 1 \times 10^{-2} = 1989 \text{ ATs.}$$

Without compensating winding, the interpole m.m.f. must be equal to 15,000 + 1989 ATs. But compensating winding has already neutralized 10,200 ATs. In view of this, the ampere turns that must be furnished by each interpole are 15,000 + 1989 – 10,200 = 6790 = 6800 ATs.

$$\therefore \text{ Number of turns on each interpole} = \frac{6800}{850} = 8.$$

4.10. BASIC PERFORMANCE EQUATIONS FOR D.C. MACHINES

For D.C. machines, the expressions for the armature generated e.m.f. E_a and electromagnetic torque T_e, have already been derived in Eqs. (4.3) and (4.6) respectively. These expressions are re-written below, for convenience.

$$E_a = \frac{\phi Z n P}{a} = K_a \phi \omega_m \qquad ...(4.3)$$

and $$T_e = K_a \phi I_a \qquad ...(4.6)$$

where $\omega_m = 2\pi n$ rad/sec.

and $$K_a = \frac{ZP}{2\pi a}$$

In Eqs. (4.3) and (4.6), note that ϕ is the total direct axis flux per pole.

A careful examination of Fig. 4.14 (*a*) leads to the electrical equivalent circuit of D.C. compound machine of Fig. 4.34 (*a*). In this equivalent circuit, armature of the D.C. machine has been replaced by generated e.m.f. E_a and the armature resistance r_a in series with it. Note that the armature resistance r_a = armature winding resistance + compensating winding resistance, if present + interpole winding resistance, if present + brush contact resistance.

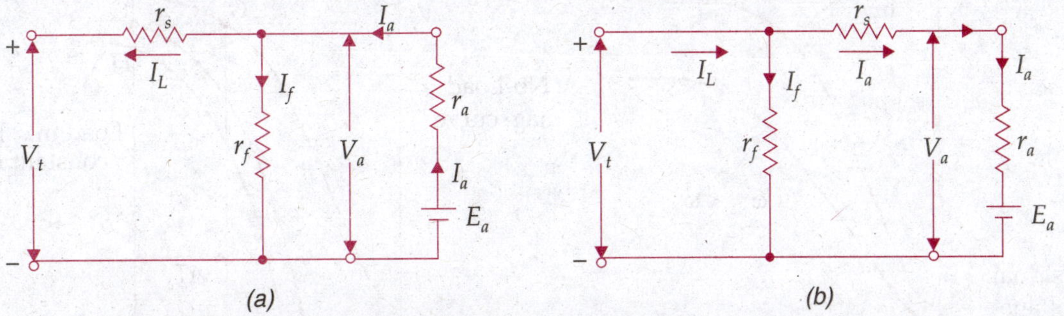

Fig 4.34: Equivalent circuits for (*a*) D.C. compound generator (short-shunt) and (*b*) D.C. compound motor (long-shunt).

In the equivalent circuits, I_a is the armature current, I_f the shunt field current, I_L the line current, V_a the armature terminal voltage, V_t the machine terminal voltage, r_s the series field resistance and r_f the shunt field resistance.

For D.C. compound generator (short-shunt), the voltage and current equations can be written by applying Kirchhoff's voltage and current laws to Fig. 4.34 (*a*). Therefore,

$$V_a = E_a \pm I_a r_a \quad ...(4.18)$$

$$V_t = V_a \pm I_L r_s = E_a \pm I_a r_a \pm I_L r_s \quad ...(4.19)$$

and
$$I_L = I_a \pm I_f \quad ...(4.20)$$

where plus sign is used for a motor and minus sign for a generator.

For the long-shunt compound machine of Fig. 4.34 (*b*).

$$V_a = E_a \pm I_a r_a \quad ...(4.21)$$

$$V_t = V_a \pm I_a r_s = E_a \pm I_a (r_a + r_s) \quad ...(4.22)$$

and
$$I_L = I_a \pm I_f \quad ...(4.23)$$

Here also plus sign is used for a motor, minus sign for a generator. From Eqs. (4.18) to (4.23), neglect those terms which are not required for the specified D.C. machine under consideration. For example, for a D.C. shunt machine, neglect the terms pertaining to series field winding. For a D.C. series machine, neglect those terms which are relevant to shunt field winding.

4.10.1. Magnetisation Curve

In addition to basic performance equations given above, the magnetisation curve is also essential for determining the performance of D.C. machines.

The magnetisation curve is the relationship between air-gap flux ϕ and the field winding m.m.f. or field winding current. From Eq. (4.3), it is seen that for constant speed ω_m, the armature generated e.m.f. E_a at no-load, is proportional to air-gap flux ϕ only. In view of this, a plot between air-gap flux ϕ or $K_a \phi \omega_m$ *i.e.*, E_a and the field winding current or m.m.f., at a given speed, gives the magnetisation curve. This curve is also called *no-load* or *open circuit characteristic*, or *saturation curve*. Fig. 4.35 (*a*) illustrates a typical magnetisation curve at a given speed, with only one field winding excited. The magnetisation curve for any other speed, can be obtained from Eq. (4.3) *i.e.*,

$$\frac{E_a}{\omega_m} = \frac{E_{a1}}{\omega_{m1}} = K_a \phi \quad \text{or} \quad E_{a1} = \frac{E_a}{\omega_m} \cdot \omega_{m1} \quad ...(4.24)$$

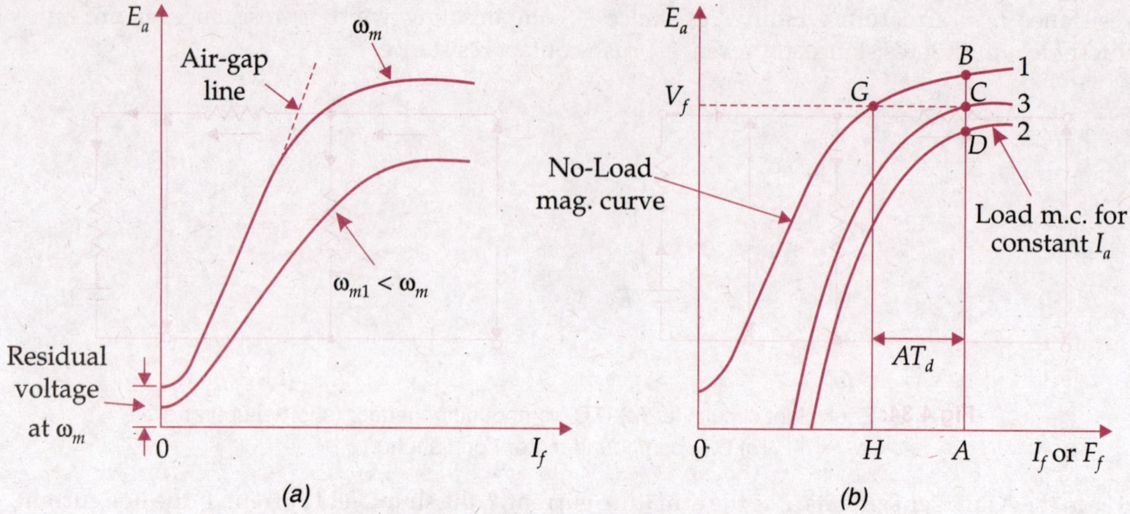

Fig 4.35: (*a*) Typical magnetization curve for a D.C. machine
(*b*) pertaining to the calculation of armature reaction m.m.f. AT_d.

This is illustrated in Fig. 4.35 (*a*) for speed $\omega_{m1} < \omega_m$. For D.C. compound machines, the magnetization curve is obtained with current in the shunt field winding only. During the D.C. compound machine analysis, the series field m.m.f. must also be taken into account as follows :

If N_f are shunt field turns per pole and N_s series-field turns per pole, then

total *d*-axis m.m.f. per pole = $N_f I_f \pm N_s I_s$ ...(4.25)

Plus sign is used for cumulatively compounded machines and minus sign, for differentially compounded machines. Since the magnetization curve is given with current in the shunt field alone, the equivalent shunt field current that would produce the same total m.m.f. given by Eq. (4.25), can be obtained by dividing Eq. (4.25) by N_f.

∴ Equivalent current in the shunt field winding

$$= \frac{N_f I_f \pm N_s I_s}{N_f} = I_f \pm \frac{N_s}{N_f} I_s \quad \text{...(4.26)}$$

The dashed straight line, tangent to the straight line portion of magnetisation curve at speed ω_m, is called **air-gap line** as shown in Fig. 4.35 (*a*).

4.10.2. Effect of Armature m.m.f. on D.C. Machine Calculations

It has been described in Art. 4.6 that the cross-magnetizing effect of armature reaction produces demagnetizing effect on the main pole flux. Since this effect is due to saturation, it can't be included by a simple mathematical expression in the D.C. machine calculations. However, the following method may be used to include the effect of armature m.m.f. on the performance of D.C. machines.

No-load magnetization curve is the graph between armature generated e.m.f. E_a and field current I_f (or field m.m.f. F_f) with constant armature speed ω_m. Load-magnetization curve is the graph between terminal voltage V_t and I_f (or F_f) with constant armature speed ω_m and constant armature current I_a. In Fig. 4.35 (*b*), the no-load and load magnetization curves are sketched in one diagram and are respectively marked 1 and 2. In order to obtain curve 3, add armature resistance drop $I_a r_a$ to each ordinate of curve 2. Here r_a includes the brush contact resistance also. For any field excitation equal to *OA*, *AB* is the armature generated e.m.f. at no-load. For load current I_a, *CD* is the voltage drop equal to $I_a r_a$ as per the construction. Therefore out of the total voltage drop

BD, voltage drop BC is caused by armature reaction. However, no-load e.m.f. $HG = AC$ can be obtained by an excitation equal to $OH = OA - AH$ and in this manner the voltage drop BC due to armature reaction, has been considered in terms of I_f or F_f. In view of this, the armature reaction demagnetizing m.m.f. AT_d is equal to $AH = GC$ and is expressed on the field current or field m.m.f. scale.

The magnitude of demagnetizing m.m.f. AT_d, which accounts for the cross-magnetizing armature reaction, should be calculated at the anticipated terminal voltage, because saturation effects the value of AT_d considerably. However, over the normal operating range of the voltage, the demagnetizing m.m.f. AT_d, accounting for the armature reaction, is taken as proportional to armature current. With this, the net field m.m.f. acting on each pole along the d-axis is given by

$$\text{Net m.m.f.} = N_f I_f \pm N_s I_s - AT_d \quad \text{...(4.27)}$$

The basic equation underlying the analysis of D.C. machines are Eqs. (4.3), (4.6), (4.18) to (4.23), the magnetization curve and power balance Eqs. (4.9) to (4.12). The armature m.m.f. can be accounted for as explained above in Fig. 4.35 (*b*).

Example 4.16. *A 250 V, 10 kW D.C. shunt generator has 1400 turns on each pole. At rated speed, a shunt field current of 2 A produces a no-load voltage of 250 V, but at rated load the same load voltage of 250 V can be produced by a field current of 2.2 amp. It is required, not to change the field current for maintaining load voltage constant, but add a series field winding. Calculate the number of series field turns per pole required for long-shunt connection.*

Solution. Total m.m.f. required at rated load

$$= 2.2 \times 1400 = 3080 \text{ ATs.}$$

The m.m.f. at no-load $= 2 \times 1400 = 2800$ ATs.

∴ The m.m.f. to be supplied by series field winding

$$N_s I_s = 3080 - 2800 = 280 \text{ ATs.}$$

But series field current at full-load

$$I_s = \frac{10{,}000}{250} = 40 \text{ A.}$$

$$\therefore \quad \text{Series field turns} = \frac{280}{40} = 7 \text{ turns.}$$

Example 4.17. *A 230 V, 10 kW D.C. shunt generator gave the following data for the magnetization curve at rated speed of 1500 r.p.m :*

I_f, amp.	0	0.2	0.4	0.6	1.00	1.40	1.80	2.00
E_a, volts	6	40	80	120	194	246	269	274

The resistances of the shunt field and armature circuit (including brushes) are 184 ohms and 0.443 ohms respectively.

At rated load and speed, a field current of 1.7 amp. is required to maintain rated terminal voltage. Find the demagnetizing effect of armature reaction at rated load and speed.

Solution. Full- load current

$$I_L = \frac{10{,}000}{230} = 43.4 \text{ A.}$$

∴ Total armature current at rated load, $I_a = I_L + I_f = 43.4 + 1.7 = 45.1$ A

Total armature resistance drop $= I_a r_a = 45.1 \times 0.443 = 20$ V

For a field current of 1.7 A, point A in Fig. 4.36, represents rated terminal voltage of 230 V. This point A lies on the load magnetization curve, refer to Fig. 4.36. AB is made equal to the total armature resistance drop of 20 V. Through B is drawn a horizontal line meeting the magnetization curve at C. Then BC is the demagnetizing effect of armature reaction in terms of shunt field current.

$\therefore$ Demagnetizing effect due to armature reaction = BC = 0.25 equivalent shunt field current in amperes.

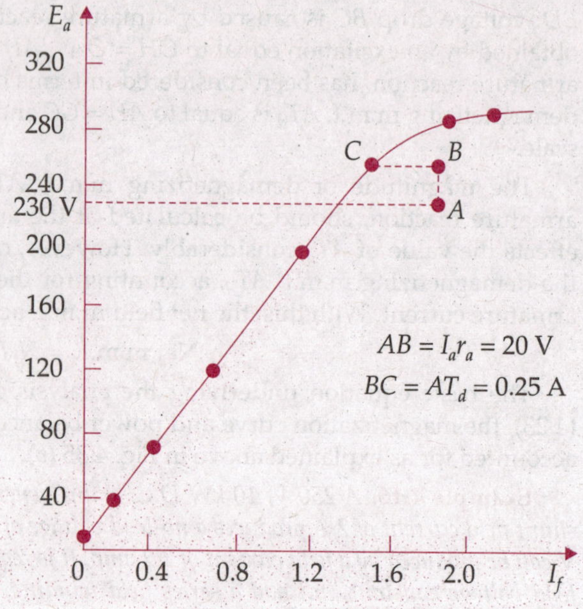

Fig 4.36: Pertaining to Example 4.17.

Example 4.18. *A D.C. shunt generator has a total of 100 Ω in the shunt circuit, including the field winding as well as the regulator. Its terminal voltage is 50 V when the generator is run at 1000 r.p.m., 225 V at 2000 r.p.m. and 405 V at 3000 r.p.m. Draw magnetization curve at 2000 r.p.m. and hence determine the terminal voltage at this speed, if the resistance of the shunt circuit is reduced to (i) 80 Ω and (ii) 70 Ω.*

Solution. For a terminal voltage of 50 V at 1000 r.p.m., the field current is 50/100 = 0.5 A.

At 2000 r.p.m., the terminal voltage is $= 50 \times \dfrac{2000}{1000} = 100$ V at the same field current. Similarly, for a field current of 405/100 = 4.05 A, the terminal voltage of 405 V at 3000 r.p.m. is equivalent to 405 × (2000/3000) = 270 V at 2000 r.p.m. The magnetization curve at 2000 r.p.m. is thus drawn. Resistance lines for 80 Ω and 70 Ω are seen to meet the magnetization curve in Fig. 4.37 at C and P to give the terminal voltages of BC = 253 V and QP = 268 V.

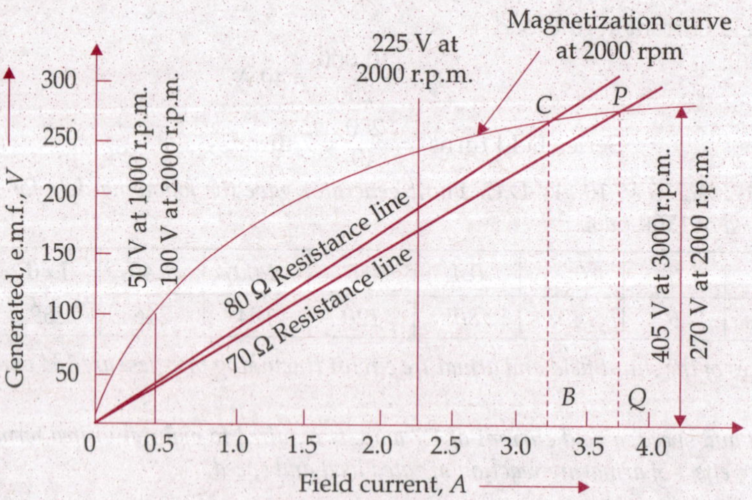

Fig 4.37: Pertaining to Example 4.18.

4.11. OPERATING CHARACTERISTICS OF D.C. GENERATORS

The operating characteristics of D.C. generators present graphically, the relationship between the basic quantities relevant to generator operation. These basic quantities are terminal voltage V_t, armature current I_a, excitation current I_f and speed n. The speed of the generator is constant and is usually fixed by the prime-mover speed.

More important characteristics of D.C. generators are four in number and these are given below:

(i) **No-load characteristic :** The plot of no-load terminal voltage as a function of field current at constant speed is known as no-load characteristic; *i.e.*, $E_a = f(I_f)$ with speed n constant. This characteristic is also called saturation curve, open-circuit characteristic, magnetization curve or no-load magnetization curve.

(ii) **Load characteristic :** It gives the relationship between terminal voltage and field current at constant values of load current and speed; *i.e.*, $V_t = f(I_f)$ with both I_L and n constant. This characteristic is also called load magnetization curve.

(iii) **External characteristic :** The plot of voltage across armature terminals, as a function of load current at constant values of both speed and field current, is called external characteristic; *i.e.* $V_t = f(I_L)$ with both I_f and n constant.

(iv) **Armature characteristic :** A plot showing the variation of field current with load current at constant values of terminal voltage and speed is called armature characteristic; *i.e.*, $I_f = f(I_L)$ with both V_t and n constant. It is also called regulation curve.

The shape of these characteristics depends upon the method of exciting the field windings. Note that in all the D.C. generator characteristics listed above, speed is held constant by the prime-mover. These characteristics are now described in detail for different types of D.C. generators.

4.11.1. Separately-excited generators

These generators are used when a wide range of output voltage is required.

The field winding is now energised and the exciting current I_f is increased in steps—at each step E_a and I_f are recorded. Field current I_f is increased till E_a is about 1.1 to 1.25 times the rated voltage. The graph between E_a and I_f, called no-load characteristic or saturation curve, is shown in Fig. 4.38 *(b)*. If the field current is now decreased from *OB*, E_a versus I_f plot will not follow the original curve *AC*, but will lie above it due to hysteresis.

The magnetization curve for low values of I_f is a straight line, because the entire field m.m.f. is almost spent in forcing the flux through the air gap and the m.m.f. required by the iron is almost negligible. With increased values of I_f and above a certain value of field flux, saturation sets in and m.m.f. required by the iron increases more rapidly than the flux. The knee of the no-load characteristic is at the point *D*, Fig. 4.38 *(b)*.

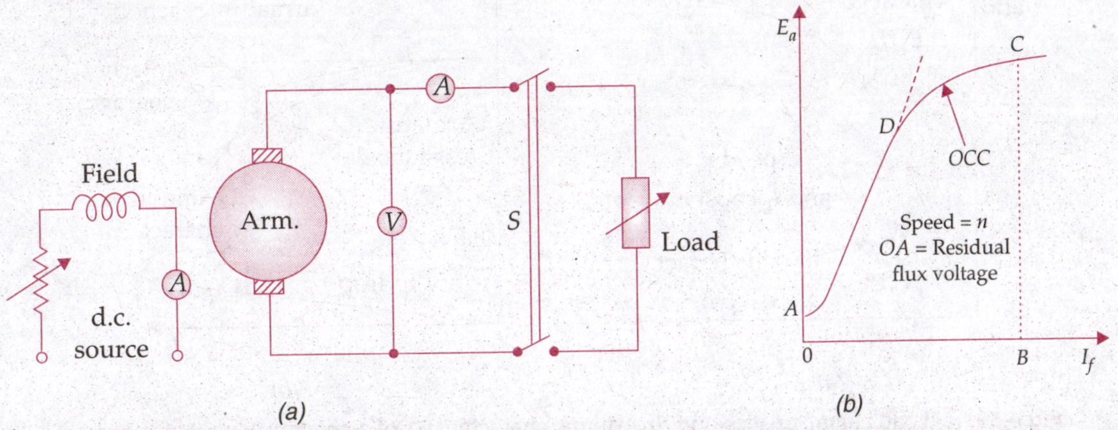

Fig 4.38: Separately excited generator *(a)* connection diagram and *(b)* its no-load characteristic.

(i) **No-load characteristic.** This characteristic gives the variation of armature generated e.m.f. E_a with field current I_f, for zero armature current and constant speed.

The connection diagram for obtaining the no-load characteristic is illustrated in Fig. 4.38 *(a)*. The armature is driven at rated speed by the prime-mover and switch *S* is kept always open. It will be seen that even though the field winding is not energised, the voltmeter indicates a small voltage (2 to 6 volts), due to the presence of residual flux in the main poles. This residual flux voltage is shown by *OA* in Fig. 4.38 *(b)*.

(ii) **Load characteristic.** This characteristic gives the relationship between the terminal voltage V_t and field current I_f for constant I_L and speed. In order to plot it, refer to Fig. 4.38 *(a)*. Run the armature at constant rated speed and close the switch *S*. Adjust the field current till I_L is equal to rated armature current (or any other specified current) and take the instrument readings. In Fig. 4.38 *(a)* load current I_L = armature current I_a. Vary the load and field currents in such a manner that armature current I_a and speed *n* remain constant, but terminal voltage V_t changes. Repeat this process till sufficient number of points for the graph, Fig. 4.39 *(a)*, are obtained. If the load resistance is made zero (*i.e.*, short circuit), then $V_t = 0$ and point *a* on the load characteristic is obtained. With the help of no-load and load magnetization curves, demagnetizing effect of armature reaction can be found out, as explained in Fig. 4.35 *(b)*.

(iii) **External characteristic.** This characteristic gives the variation of armature terminal voltage V_t with load current I_L for constant speed and fixed field current. External or *volt-ampere characteristic* can be obtained experimentally by using the connection diagram of Fig. 4.38 *(a)*. The generator is run at rated speed and its field winding is excited to give rated terminal voltage at no-load. Now close the switch *S*, vary load resistance in steps and for each step, note terminal voltage and load current. A typical external characteristic is shown in Fig. 4.39 *(b)*, by curve 1. The decrease in terminal voltage with increase in load is due to the voltage drops caused by armature reaction and armature circuit resistance. Curve 2 in Fig. 4.39 *(b)*, obtained by adding $I_a r_a$ drop to the ordinates of curve 1, is known as *internal characteristic.* The internal characteristic gives the variation of armature no-load generated e.m.f. E_a minus the voltage drop due to armature reaction, with load current I_L or I_a. In other words, internal characteristic gives the relationship between internally generated e.m.f. and the load current for constant speed and field current. Note that r_a includes the brush contact resistance also and for separately-excited generator $I_a = I_L$. In Fig. 4.39 *(b)*, *OA* is the no-load terminal voltage E_a.

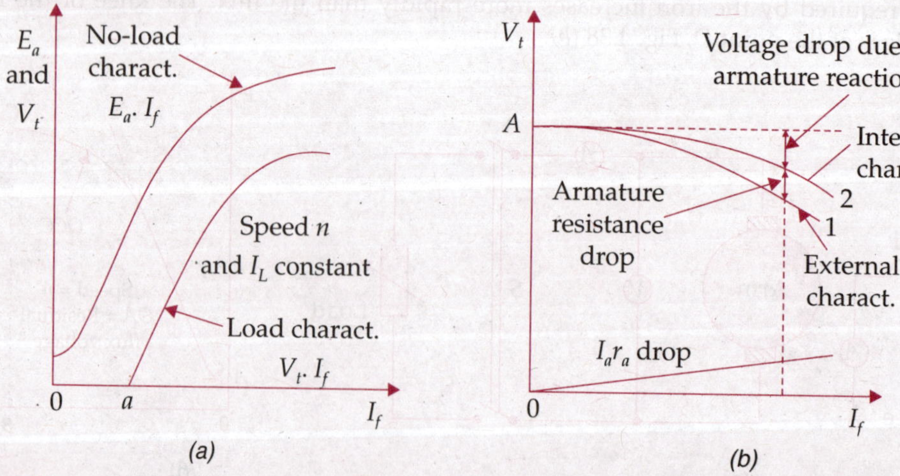

Fig 4.39: *(a)* Load characteristics and *(b)* external characteristic, of a separately excited generator.

The performance of a D.C. generator is gauged by its voltage regulation. It is defined as the change in armature terminal voltage, expressed as a percentage of full-load terminal voltage, when full-load is gradually reduced to zero with speed and field current remaining unchanged.

$$\therefore \text{ Percentage voltage regulation} = \frac{E_a - V_r}{V_r} \times 100$$

where E_a = no-load generated voltage

V_r = rated (or full-load) armature voltage.

(iv) **Armature characteristic or regulation curve.** A plot giving the variation of field current I_f with load current I_L, for constant terminal voltage and speed, is called armature characteristic or regulation curve.

At no-load, the field current is adjusted to give rated terminal voltage of the machine, Fig. 4.38 *(a)*. The load current is now increased in steps and at each step, the field current is adjusted to keep the terminal voltage constant. The regulation curve is then plotted as shown in Fig. 4.40. In the beginning, the curve is almost a straight line and as the saturation sets in, it bends upwards.

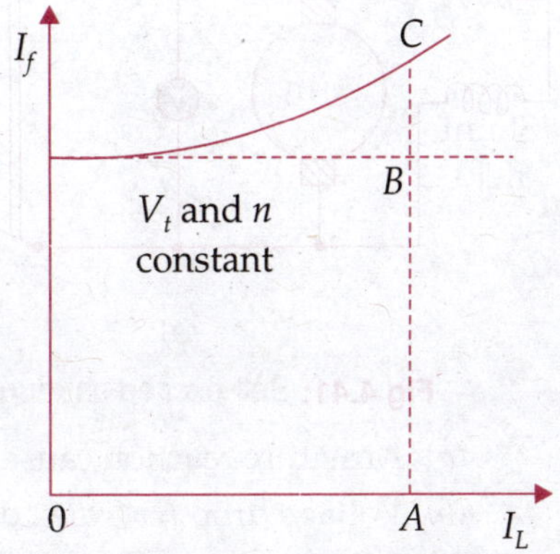

Fig 4.40: Armature characteristic of a separately excited generator.

This characteristic can be employed for calculating the number of series turns for any degree of compounding, in D.C. compound machines. For example, for level compounding, the additional shunt fleld ampere turns *(CB)* × N_f must be furnished by series field armature turns *(OA)* × N_s.

$$\therefore \text{ Series field turns, } \quad N_s = \frac{CB}{OA} \cdot N_f \qquad \text{...(4.28)}$$

4.11.2. Shunt Generators

These generators are most frequently employed, because no separate source for excitation is required. However, the load current must be well below the maximum current for avoiding large dips in the terminal voltage.

(i) **No-load characteristic.** This characteristic for the self-excited shunt generator, can be plotted with the help of connection diagram of Fig. 4.41 *(a)* and by keeping the switch *S* open. If the field winding circuit of the shunt generator is disconnected from the armature circuit and separately excited, then the no-load characteristic with separate excitation will not differ from that obtained with shunt excitation. This is due to the fact that small amount of current (1 to 3% of rated current) flowing in the armature of the shunt generator, has negligible effect on the main flux. It will rather be more convenient to run the shunt generator as a separately-excited generator, as in Fig. 4.38 *(a)*, for obtaining its saturation curve. The saturation or magnetization curve so obtained can be used for shunt generator analysis without any appreciable error.

(ii) **Load characteristic.** The load characteristic can be obtained in the same manner as for the separately-excited generator. Actually the load characteristics obtained both for separate and shunt excitation, are the same. The slight difference is due to the different armature currents, $I_a = I_L + I_f$ for shunt generator and $I_a = I_L$ for separately-excited generator. Different armature currents result in different armature reaction, giving slightly different voltage drops in the two cases.

(iii) **External characteristic.** The shunt generator is connected as shown in Fig. 4.41 *(a)*. The generator is run at rated speed and the field current is adjusted to give rated voltage (or any other suitable voltage) at no-load. Switch *S* is closed, the load is gradually increased in steps and the instrument readings at each step are recorded. A plot of the terminal voltage V_t and load current I_L, with preset value of field current and speed, gives the external characteristic curve 1 in Fig. 4.41 *(b)*. The drop in terminal voltage V_t is due to the following three reasons :

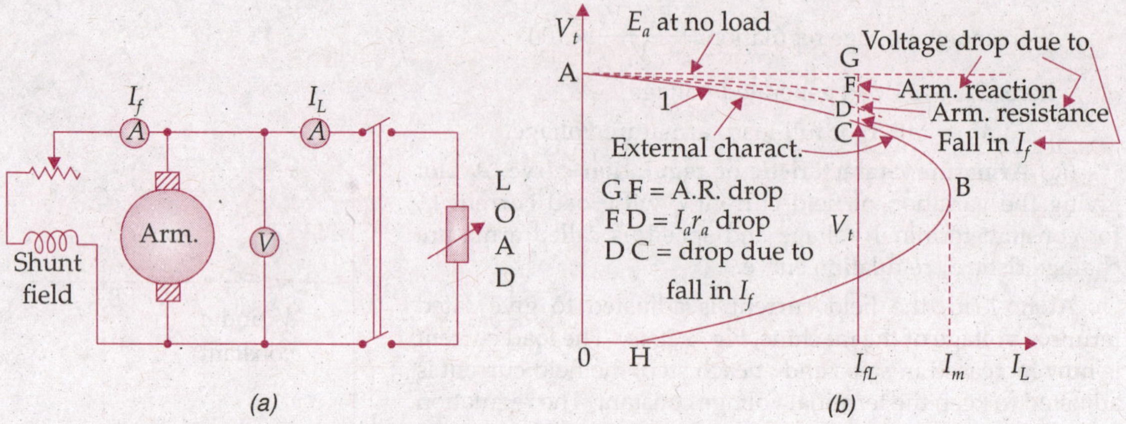

Fig 4.41: Self-excited shunt generator *(a)* connection diagram and *(b)* external characteristic.

(a) Armature reaction causes a reduction in the main flux.

(b) Voltage drop $I_a r_a$ caused by armature resistance.

(c) As the terminal voltage V_t has decreased because of the first two effects listed in parts *(a)* and *(b)*, the field current $\left(=\frac{V_t}{r_f}\right)$ gets reduced.

A reduction in the field current causes the flux and therefore the generated emf to decrease. Thus, the terminal voltage of the generator for a given load current, will be lower when shunt excited than when separately excited, provided no-load voltage is same in both the cases. In Fig. 4.41 *(b)*, *GF* = voltage drop due to armature reaction, $FD = I_a r_a$ = voltage drop due to armature resistance and *DC* = voltage drop due to reduction in the field current. The total voltage drop, from no-load generated voltage *OA*, is given by *GC* ; consequently the terminal voltage at full load is *OA* minus *GC*.

As the load resistance is decreased (load current increased), the terminal voltage drops until point *B* is reached. If load resistance is further decreased, the load current increases momentarily. This momentary increase in load current, produces more armature reaction thus causing a reduction in the terminal voltage and field current. The net reduction in terminal voltage is so large that the load current decreases and the external characteristic turns back. In case the machine is short circuited, the curve terminates at point *H*. Here, *OH* is the load current due to the voltage generated by the residual flux.

Over the normal operating range, the *internal characteristic* (not shown) can be obtained by adding $I_a r_a$ drop to the ordinates of external characteristic, *i.e.*, curve 1.

***(iv)* Armature characteristic.** Shunt generator armature characteristic is obtained by running it as a separately excited generator. The test is carried out as explained before in the case of separately excited generator.

Voltage build up in shunt generators. Consider an unloaded shunt generator as illustrated in Fig. 4.42 *(a)*. In Fig. 4.42 *(b)*, the straight line *Oa* is the graphical plot of Ohm's law for the field circuit. In other words, the slope of the line *Oa*, drawn through origin, represents the field resistance, *i.e.*,

$$\tan \angle aOb = \frac{\text{Voltage } ba}{\text{Current } Ob} = \text{field resistance } r_f \text{ in ohms.}$$

When the armature is driven at a speed for which the magnetisation curve is given, the residual pole flux generates a small voltage *Oc*, with switch *S* open, *i.e.*, with zero field current. When switch *S* is closed, residual flux voltage *Oc* produces a small field current. If the flux produced by this small field current, adds to the residual flux, still larger voltages are generated. In order to understand this, refer to Fig. 4.42 *(b)*, where residual flux voltage *Oc* is shown to produce a small field current equal to *Od*, which in turn raises the generated voltage, to *de*. This voltage *de*, raises the field current to *Of*, which further raises the generated e.m.f. to *fg*, now e.m.f. *fg* raises the field current to *Oh*, which in turn increases the generated e.m.f. to *hj* and so on, till stable point *n* is reached. Note that stable point *n* is determined by the intersection of field resistance line *Oa* and the magnetisation or saturation-curve. Beyond the point *n*, the generated e.m.f. given by the magnetization curve is less than that required to maintain the corresponding field current, therefore, point *n* is the stable point. If the voltage build up from *Oc* to *np* fails, owing to small field current opposing the residual flux, then reverse the shunt field terminals to obtain the voltage build up.

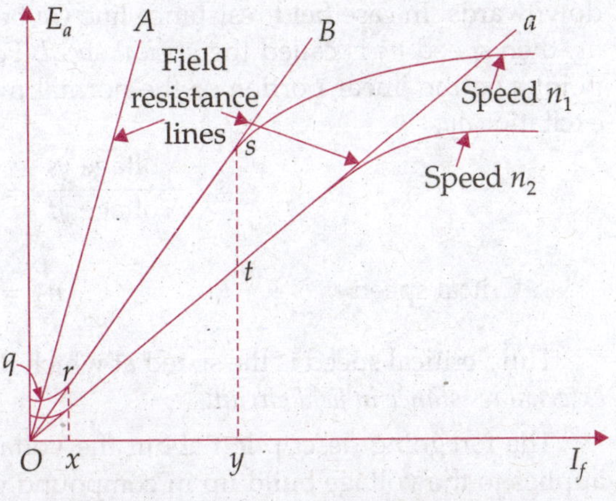

Fig 4.42: Pertaining to critical field resistance and critical speed for a *dc* shunt generator.

If shunt field resistance is increased to *OA* (slope of the field resistance line increased), Fig. 4.43, then the field resistance line and the magnetization curve intersect at point *q*, therefore, the voltage will not build up further than point *q*. If shunt field resistance is such that *OB* represents the field resistance line, then the intersection may be anywhere between points *r* and *s*. The generated voltage in such a case, would vary between the voltage *xr* and *ys*, resulting in unstable conditions. Note that field resistance line *OB* is tangent to the magnetization curve and the field resistance represented by line *OB* is called the *critical field resistance* at given speed n_1. If shunt field resistance is more than the critical field resistance such as given by line *OA*, there will be no voltage build up. In order to calculate the critical field resistance at any speed, a line is drawn through origin *O* and touching the maximum straight line portion of the magnetization curve. The slope of the line is the critical field resistance at a speed for which the magnetization curve has been drawn.

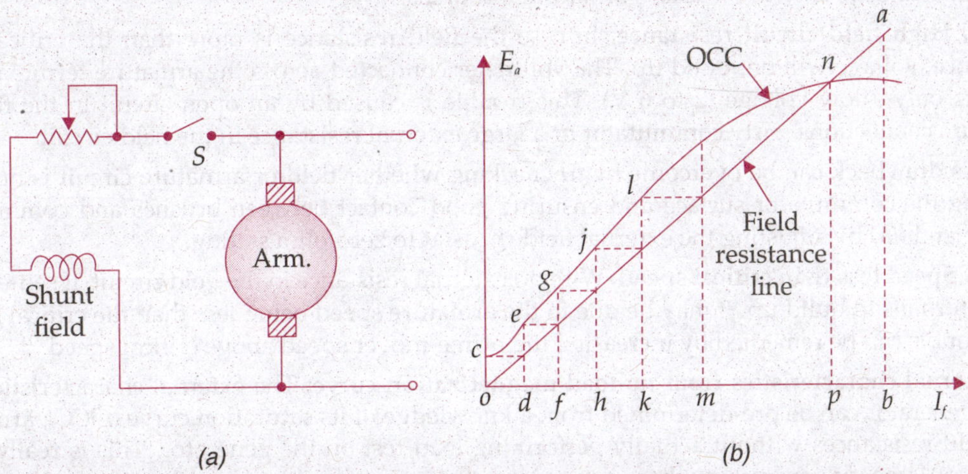

Fig 4.43: Self-excited shunt generator *(a)* connection diagram and *(b)* voltage build-up process.

In Fig. 4.43, suppose the line *Oa* represents the field resistance line with zero external resistance in the field circuit. If speed is reduced from n_1 to n_2, the magnetization curve shifts bodily downwards. In case field resistance line *Oa* becomes tangent to the magnetization curve at speed n_2, then speed n_2 is called the *critical speed*. For calculating critical speed n_2, choose any suitable point *s* on the linear portion of the normal magnetization curve at speed n_1. Then, for the same excitation *oy*,

$$\frac{\text{Voltage } ys}{\text{Voltage } yt} = \frac{\text{Speed } n_1}{\text{Critical speed } n_2}$$

∴ Critcal speed $$n_2 = \frac{\text{Voltage } yt}{\text{Voltage } ys} \times n_1 \qquad \text{...(4.29)}$$

Thus, critical speed is the speed at which the D.C. shunt generator just fails to build up *with no external resistance in field circuit.*

The foregoing description about the voltage build up process for the shunt generators, also applies to the voltage build up in compound generators. In the long-shunt compound generator, the m.m.f. produced by the series field turns is negligibly small.

Failure to build-up. If the self-excited generators fail to built-up the voltage at no-load, it may be due to any one of the following reasons.

(i) **No-residual magnetism.** The voltage build up process can start only if there is residual magnetism in the magnetic circuit of the generator. In case of new machine or the one that has lost its residual magnetism due to aging or jarring in transportation, self-excited generator will fail to build up the voltage. This difficulty can be overcome by exciting the field winding from a separate D.C. source for a few seconds with the armature at rest. After the separate D.C. source is disconnected, the main poles possess residual flux and voltage build up can take place.

The process of connecting the shunt-field winding to a separate D.C. source for creating the necessary residual magnetism in the main poles is called *field flashing*.

(ii) **Field connections reversed.** The small voltage due to residual magnetism, should circulate current in the field coils in such a direction as to produce flux lines aiding the residual flux. If the field connections are incorrect, the flux produced by small field current would oppose the residual flux and the generated voltage would decrease to zero. This trouble can be remedied by reversing the field connections with respect to armature terminals.

(iii) **High field circuit resistance.** In case the field resistance is more than the critical field resistance, voltage will not build up. The voltmeter connected across the armature terminals will indicate only a low voltage (2 to 6 V). This trouble is caused by an open circuit in the field or armature connections, dirty commutator or a large external resistance in the field circuit.

This drawback can be overcome by *(i)* checking whether field or armature circuit is open *(ii)* cleaning the commutator surface and ensuring good contact between brushes and commutator surface and *(iii)* by adjusting the external field rheostat to zero-ohm setting.

(iv) **Speed less than critical speed.** With no external resistance in the field circuit, if self-excited generator fails to build up, it may be due to the armature speed being less than the critical speed. This trouble can be remedied by increasing the prime-mover speed above critical speed.

External characteristics from no-load magnetization curve. The external characteristics of a shunt generator can be pre-determined from a knowledge of its saturation curve *(OCC)*, armature and field resistances without actually performing load test on the generator. This is really done in case of large dc generators where actual load test is not feasible. Here the **effect of armature reaction is neglected**.

In the left of Fig. 4.44, curve 1 is the no-load **magnetization** (E_a versus I_f) and *OA* is the field resistance line (V_t versus I_f). At no-load, *BA* is the armature generated e.m.f. E_a for a field current equal to OB. Under steady state operation and with armature reaction neglected, the vertical distance between the saturation curve 1 and field resistance line OA is equal to armature resistance drop. For example, for field current OC, CD is the armature generated e.m.f. E_a, DD' is the armature resistance drop $I_a r_a$ and CD' is the terminal voltage V_t. That is

$$DD' = CD - CD' \text{ or } I_a r_a = E_a - V_t \quad \text{...(4.30 } a\text{)}$$

or

$$I_a = \frac{E_a - V_t}{r_a} \quad \text{...(4.30 } b\text{)}$$

Eq. (4.30 *a*) reveals that for a known value of I_a, $I_a r_a$ drop and therefore V_t is known.

For plotting the external characteristic, cut OG equal to $I_a r_a$ for any assumed armature current I_a. Draw GH parallel to the field resistance line OA intersecting the magnetization curve at points M and D. From M and D draw vertical lines meeting the field resistance line at M' and D' respectively. In the right hand side of Fig. 4.44, make $O'x$ = load current = assumed armature current $\left(\frac{OG}{r_a}\right)$ minus shunt field current OC. A vertical line at x and horizontal line through points D', M' meet at points d, m. These two points d, m lie on the external characteristic of the shunt generator. Similarly other points on the external characteristic can be plotted. Note that maximum armature current can be found by drawing a line LN, tangent to the magnetization curve and parallel to the field resistance line OA. The magnitude of maximum armature current will be given by $\frac{OL}{r_a}$ and maximum load current is equal to $\frac{OL}{r_a}$ minus OC'. When the terminals are short circuited, $O'K$ is the load current due to the e.m.f. OF generated by the residual flux.

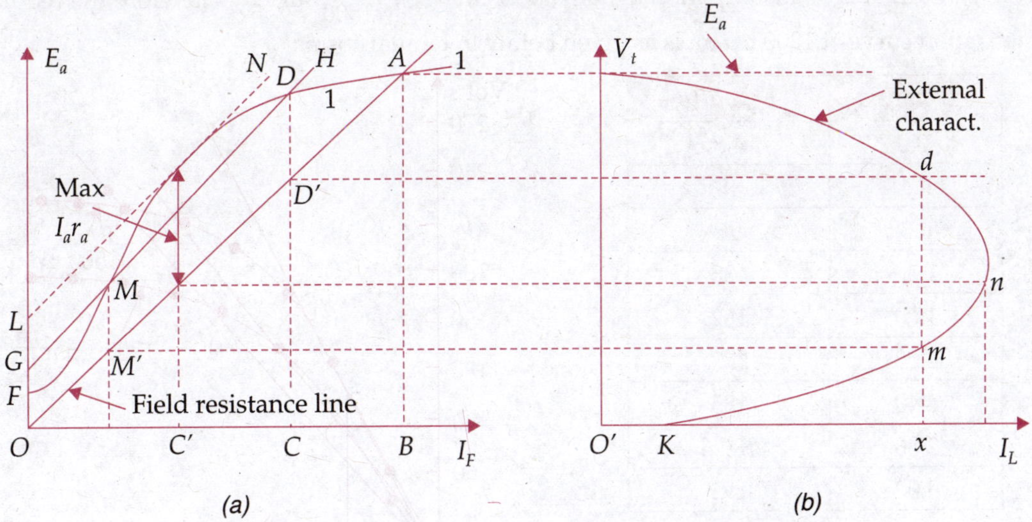

Fig 4.44: Determination of the external characteristic from no-load magnetization curve (armature reaction neglected).

Example 4.19. *The following data pertain to the magnetization curve of a D.C. shunt generator at 1500 r.p.m.*

I_f, amp.	0	0.4	0.8	1.20	1.60	2.00	2.40	2.80	3.00
E_a, volts	6	60	120	172.5	202.5	221	231	237	240

For this generator, obtain

(a) the voltage on open circuit to which the machine will build up (i.e., no-load e.m.f.) for a total shunt field resistance of 100 Ω ;

(b) the critical value of shunt field resistance at 1500 r.p.m. ;

(c) the critical speed for the shunt field resistance of 100 Ω ;

(d) the magnetization curve at 1200 r.p.m. and therefore the open circuit voltage for a field resistance of 100 Ω ;

(e) the terminal voltage of the generator if the total armature resistance is 0.3 Ω, armature current is 50 A and the speed is 1500 r.p.m. Neglect armature reaction.

Solution. *(a)* The magnetisation curve at 1500 r.p.m. is drawn in Fig. 4.45. The field resistance line for 100 Ω is drawn, passing through the origin and say 240 volts, 2.4 amp. point *A*. The field resistance line meets the magnetization curve at the point *B*, giving no-load e.m.f. of 230 volts.

(b) For determining the critical field resistance at 1500 r.p.m., draw a line *OF* passing through origin and the straight line portion of the magnetization curve. The slope of this line is found to be $\frac{180}{1.2} = 150\ \Omega$, which is the critical resistance of the shunt field circuit at 1500 r.p.m.

(c) For determining the critical speed, choose any suitable point *S* on the straight line portion of the magnetization curve. A vertical line from *S*, meets the field resistance line at *t* and the horizontal lien at *y*. From this vertical line and from Eq. (4.29), critical speed

$$n_2 = \frac{60}{90} \times 1500 = 1000 \text{ r.p.m.}$$

(d) The data for the magnetization curve at 1200 r.p.m. can be obtained by multiplying, each of the voltage ordinates of 1500 r.p.m. magnetization curve by $\frac{1200}{1500}$ or $\frac{4}{5}$. Therefore the required magnetization curve at 1200 r.p.m. is as given below in tabular form :

I_f, amp.	E_a, volts
0.0	4.8
0.4	48
0.8	96
1.20	138
1.60	162
2.00	177
2.40	185
2.80	189.6
3.00	192

This magnetization curve is drawn in Fig. 4.45 and is seen to intersect the field resistance line of 100 Ω at the point *C*. This point of intersection gives a no-load generated e.m.f. of 165 volts.

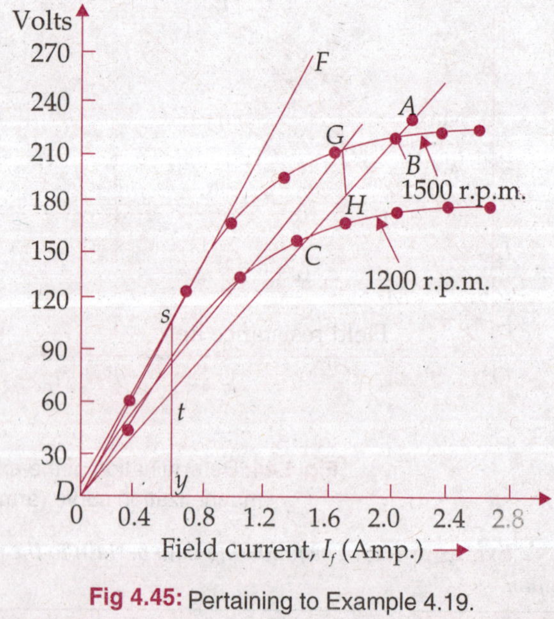

Fig 4.45: Pertaining to Example 4.19.

(e) For an armature resistance drop 50 × 0.3 = 15 volts, cut *OD* equal to $I_a r_a$ drop *i.e.*, 15 volts. Draw *DG* parallel to the field resistance line of 100 Ω *i.e. line OA*. From *G* draw a vertical line meeting the field resistance line at *H*, which gives the terminal voltage equal to 207 volts. Note that *GH* = *OD* = 15 volts and E_a = 207 + 15 = 222 volts.

Example 4.20. *A separately excited generator gave the following data for open circuit characteristic at 1000 r.p.m.*

I_f, amp	0	0.20	0.40	0.60	0.80	1.00	1.20	1.40
E_a, volts	5	50	100	140	170	190	200	205

The armature resistance, including brushes, is 0.5 Ω. If the generator is now shunt connected and is driven at 1100 r.p.m., then, for a total shunt field resistance of 180 Ω, calculate.

(a) no-load e.m.f. ;

(b) the output current and shunt field current for a terminal voltage of 190 V ;

(c) the maximum output current and the corresponding terminal voltage ;

(d) steady state short circuit current.

For the above parts, neglect armature reaction.

(e) In case no-load voltage of 210 V is required, find the additional resistance that must be inserted in the field circuit.

(f) For a shunt field resistance of 150 Ω, the terminal voltage was found to be 180 V at a certain load at 1100 r.p.m. Find the load supplied by the generator and the generated e.m.f. Assume that flux is reduced by 4% due to armature reaction.

Solution. *(a)* The magnetization curve at 1100 r.p.m., from Eq. (4.24) is given by the table below:

I_f, amp.	0	0.2	0.4	0.6	0.80	1.00	1.20	1.40
E_a, volts	5.5	55	110	154	187	209	220	225.5

This curve is plotted in Fig. 4.46. The field resistance line of 180 Ω is drawn as *OA*. It is seen to meet the saturation curve at 221 volts, which is the no-load e.m.f.

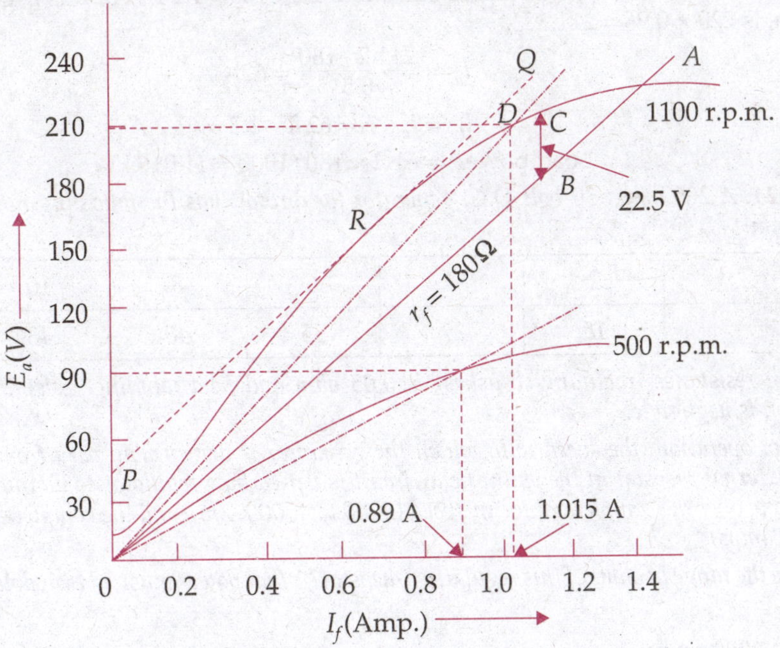

Fig 4.46: Pertaining to Example 4.20.

(b) Terminal voltage of 190 V is indicated by point *B* on the field resistance line. The vertical difference *BC* between the magnetization curve and the field resistance line at the point *B* is 22.5 V, which is equal to the total armature resistance drop $I_a r_a$.

$$\therefore \quad I_a = \frac{22.5}{0.5} = 45 \text{ Amp.}$$

The shunt field current corresponding to the terminal voltage of 190 V is given by

$$I_f = \frac{V_t}{r_f} = \frac{190}{180} = 1.06 \text{ Amp.}$$

$\therefore$ Output current $\quad I_L = I_a - I_f = 45 - 1.06 = 43.94$ Amp.

(c) For maximum output current, draw a line *PQ* tangent to the magnetization curve but parallel to the field resistance line *OA*. The intercept *OP* equal to 46.5 volts represents the entire armature resistance drop.

$$\therefore \quad I_a = \frac{46.5}{0.5} = 93 \text{ Amp.}$$

The tangent point *R* gives a field current of 0.635 amp and the corresponding no-load e.m.f. of 160.5 volts.

$\therefore$ Maximum output current = 93 – 0.635 = 92.365 A

and the corresponding terminal voltage = 160.5 – *OP* = 160.5 – 46.5 = 114 V.

(d) Under steady state short circuit, the terminal voltage is zero and the short circuit current is decided by the residual flux e.m.f. of 5.5 volts and the armature resistance only.

$$\therefore \quad \text{Steady state short cirucit current} = \frac{5.5}{0.5} = 11 \text{ A}$$

(e) The no-load e.m.f. of 210 V meets the saturation curve at *D*. The field current read from the graph is 1.015 A. Thus line *OD* represents a field resistance of $\frac{210}{1.015} = 206.9\ \Omega$. Therefore, additional resistance required in the field circuit = 206.9 – 180 = 26.9 Ω.

(f) Terminal voltage of 180 V gives a field current of 180/150 = 1.2 A. For this I_f, generated e.m.f. E_a at 1100 r.p.m. is 220 × 0.96 = 211.2 V.

$$\therefore \quad I_a = \frac{211.2 - 180}{0.5} = 62.4 \text{ A}$$

$$I_L = I_a - I_f = 62.4 - 1.2 = 61.2 \text{ A}$$

$$\text{Load power} = 61.2 \times 180/1000 = 11.016 \text{ kW.}$$

Example 4.21. *A 200 amp., 30 volt D.C. generator for aircraft has the following no-load saturation curve at 2200 r.p.m.*

I_f, *amp*	2	4	6	8	10	12
E_a, *volts*	15	27	35	40	43	45

The armature resistance (including brushes) is 0.03 ohm and field winding resistance is 2.4 ohms. Armature reaction is negligible.

Under normal operation, the speed with which the generator is driven may vary from 2200 r.p.m. to 4500 r.m.p. An external rheostat in the shunt field circuit is varied by a regulator to maintain the terminal voltage at 28.0 volts over the complete range in speed (2200 to 4500 r.p.m.) and the complete range of output current (0 to 200 amps).

What must be the range in ohms of this regulating rheostat? What power must it be capable of dissipating?

(Ranchi Univ.)

Solution. At 2200 r.p.m.,

A no-load, E_a = 28 + 0 = 28 volts. For this voltage, the field current required, from the magnetization curve of Fig. 4.47 is I_f = 4.23 A.

$\therefore$ Total shunt field resistance

$$= \frac{28}{4.23} = 6.62\ \Omega$$

∴ External resistance

$$R = 6.62 - 2.4 = 4.22\ \Omega$$

At full-load, $E_a = 28 + 200 \times 0.03 = 34.0$ V and the corresponding field current is 5.67 A.

∴ Total field resistance $= \frac{28}{5.67} = 4.94\ \Omega$

and external resistance

$$R = 4.94 - 2.4 = 2.54\ \Omega.$$

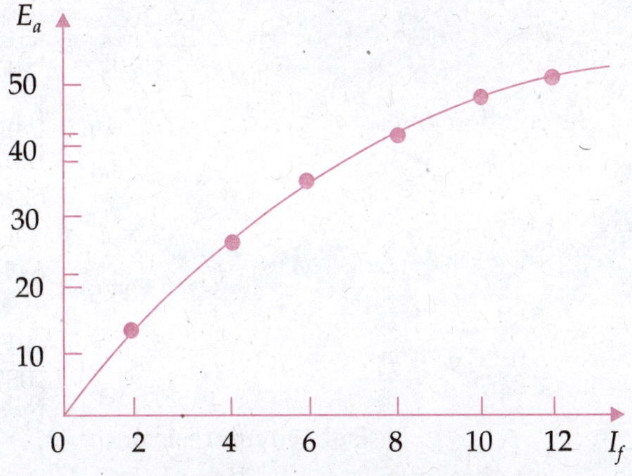

Fig 4.47: Pertaining to Example 4.21.

At 4500 r.p.m.,

At no-load, $E_a = 28$ volts at 4500 r.p.m.

∴ E_a at 2200 r.p.m. $= 28 \times \frac{2200}{4500} = 13.7$ V

From magnetization curve at 2200 r.p.m., 13.7 V corresponds to $I_f = 1.833$ A.

∴ Total field resistance $= \frac{28}{1.833} = 15.27\ \Omega$

and external resistance $= 15.27 - 2.4 = 12.87\ \Omega$.

At full-load $E_a = 28 + 200 \times 0.03 = 34.0$ V at 4500 r.p.m.

∴ E_a at 2200 r.p.m. $= 34 \times \frac{2200}{4500} = 16.62$ V.

From saturation curve at 2200 r.p.m., 16.62 V is produced by a field current of 2.17 A.

∴ External resistance required $= \frac{28}{2.17} - 2.4 = 10.5\ \Omega$.

It is seen from above that the minimum value of external resistance is 2.54 Ω and the maximum value is 12.87 Ω. Thus the range of the regulating resistance is from 2.54 Ω to 12.87 Ω.

Maximum power that must be dissipated by regulating rheostat

$$= (5.67)^2\,(2.54) = 81.66 \text{ watts.}$$

Example 4.22. *A 2-pole D.C. shunt generator charges a 100-V battery of negligible internal resistance. The armature of the machine is made up of 1000 conductors, each of 2 milli-ohm resistance. The charging currents are found to be 10 A and 20 A for generator speeds of 1055 and 1105 rpm respectively. Find the field-circuit resistance and flux per pole of the generator. Neglect armature reaction effects.* (I.E.S., 1979)

Solution. Armature circuit resistance

$$= [\text{conductors per path} \times \text{resistance of each conductor}] \times \frac{1}{\text{number of paths}}$$

$$= 500 \times 2 \times 10^{-3} \times \frac{1}{2} = 0.5\ \Omega$$

Let I_f be the shunt field current.

The generated e.m.f. at 1055 rpm is given by

$$E_{a1} = V_t + (I_L + I_f) \times 0.5 = 100 + (10 + I_f) \times 0.5$$

At 1105 rpm, $E_{a2} = 100 + (20 + I_f) \times 0.5$

But $E_{a1} \propto$ field current × speed $\propto I_f \times 1055$

and $E_{a2} \propto I_f \times 1105$

∴ $I_f \times 1055 \propto 100 + (10 + I_f) \times 0.5$

and $I_f \times 1105 \propto 100 + (20 + I_f) \times 0.5$

$$\therefore \quad \frac{I_f \times 1055}{I_f \times 1105} = \frac{100+(10+I_f)\times 0.5}{100+(20+I_f)\times 0.5}$$

Its solution gives $\qquad I_f = 1$ A

$\therefore \qquad E_{a1} = 100 + (10 + 1) \times 0.5 = 105.5$ volts at 1055 rpm

Now $\qquad E_{a1} = \dfrac{\phi ZnP}{a}$

or $\qquad 105.5 = \dfrac{\phi \times 100 \times 1055 \times 2}{60 \times 2}$

or $\qquad \phi = \dfrac{105.5 \times 60}{1000 \times 1055} = 0.006$ Wb

$\therefore \qquad$ Field circuit resistance $= \dfrac{V_t}{I_f} = \dfrac{100}{1} = 100\ \Omega$

Flux per pole $=$ 6 milliweber.

Example 4.23. *(a) The generator of Example 4.20 is driven at 500 r.p.m. and its field coils are grouped in two parallel circuits. A regulating resistance is included in the field circuit and the machine builds up to a voltage of 90 V. What is the value of the resistance in the regulator?*

(b) A D.C. generator is fitted with the following two field windings :

(i) A separately excited winding of 800 turns per pole and resistance of 160 Ω supplied from a constant voltage source of 220 V.

(ii) A shunt winding of 500 turns per pole and resistance of 200 Ω. The open circuit magnetization at 500 r.p.m. is given by the data as under :

Armature voltage, V	*154*	*302*	*396*	*458*	*505*	*538*
Field ATs per pole	*500*	*1,000*	*1,500*	*2,000*	*2,500*	*3,000*

Determine the no-load terminal voltages at 500 and 600 r.p.m., in case both windings are connected to their respective source at both the speeds and their ATs are in the same direction.

Solution. *(a)* In Fig. 4.46, magnetization curve at 500 r.p.m. is drawn as shown. For a generated e.m.f. of 90 V, the field current is found to be 0.89 A. Thus the total resistance in the field winding is 90/0.89 = 101.12 Ω. When field coils are grouped in two parallel circuits, the shunt-winding resistance reduces from 180 Ω to 45 Ω$\left(= \dfrac{90 \times 90}{90+90}\right)$. For one field coil, field current is I_f. When the field circuit is arranged in parallel paths, the current for each path is I_f and total field current is 2 I_f. Therefore, the value of the resistance R_1 in the regulator is given by $2\,I_f\,(45 + R_1) = 90$

or $\qquad R_1 = \dfrac{90}{2 \times 0.89} - 45 = 5.562\ \Omega.$

(b) ATs of separately-excited winding $= \dfrac{220}{160} \times 800 = 1100$ ATs/pole.

ATs of shunt-field winding for any generated e.m.f. E are given by

$$\frac{E}{200} \times 500 = 2.5E \text{ ATs/pole.}$$

$\therefore$ Total ATs due to both field windings = 1100 + 2.5E ATs/pole.

For 500 r.p.m., the calculations in tabular form are as under :

Generated e.m.f. E, V	*154*	*302*	*396*	*458*	*505*	*538*
(1100 + 2.5E), ATs/pole	*1485*	*1855*	*2090*	*2245*	*2362.5*	*2445*
Field ATs per pole	*500*	*1000*	*1500*	*2000*	*2500*	*3000*

From the above table, a plot between field ATs/pole and E gives the magnetization curve. Plot between (1100 + 2.5E) and E gives the variation of resultant field ATs/pole and generated voltage E. Their intersection at point P, Fig. 4.48, gives the no-load terminal voltage of 490 V at 500 r.p.m.

The computations at 600 r.p.m. are as below :

Emf E,V	*(1100 + 2.5E), ATs/pole*	*Field ATs per pole*
184.8	1562	500
362.4	2006	1000
475.2	2288	1500
549.6	2474	2000
606	2615	2500
645.6	2714	3000

These values are also plotted in Fig. 4.48. The plot between E and (1100 + 2.5E) at 600 r.p.m. is seen to be coincident with that at 500 r.p.m. The point Q gives the no-load voltage as 621 V at 600 r.p.m.

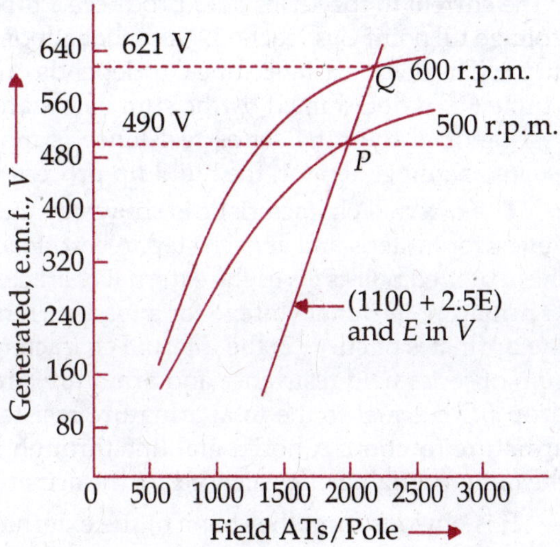

Fig 4.48: Pertaining to Example 4.23 *(b)*.

4.11.3. Series Generators

These generators are used mainly as series boosters connected in the line, to neutralise the effect of line ohmic drop.

(i) **No-load characteristic (no-load magnetization curve).** In a series generator, the armature winding, field winding and load resistance are connected in series, therefore the field current is equal to the armature or load current. In view of this, the no-load magnetization curve can only be obtained by separately exciting its field from a low voltage source as shown in Fig. 4.38 *(a)*, so that armature current is always zero. The magnetization curve at one speed for a series generator is illustrated by curve 1 in Fig. 4.49 *(a)*.

(ii) **Load characteristic (load magnetization curve).** This characteristic also, can only be obtained by separately exciting the series field winding. The shape of this characteristic is identical with that of the separately excited generator.

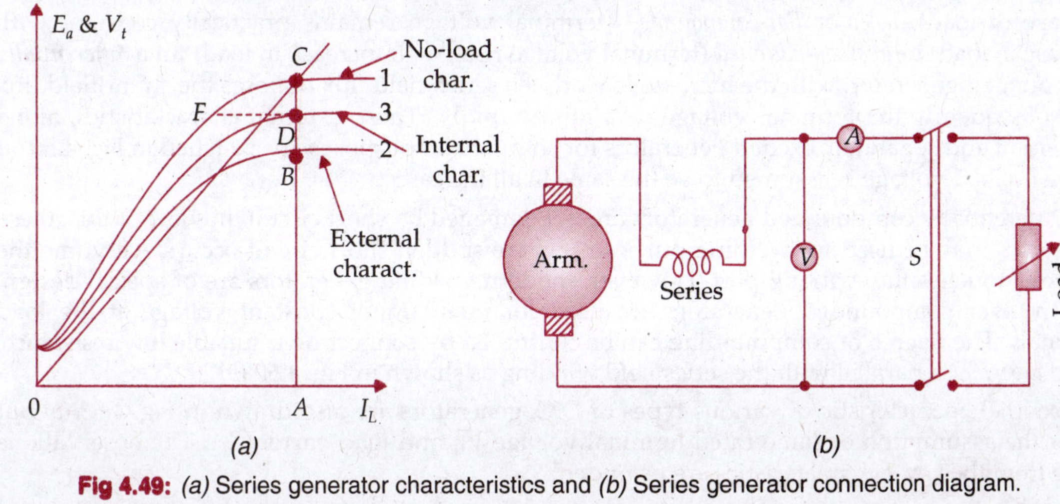

Fig 4.49: *(a)* Series generator characteristics and *(b)* Series generator connection diagram.

(iii) **External characteristic.** For obtaining the external characteristic, connections of Fig. 4.49 *(b)* are used. With the switch *S* open, the small voltage due to residual flux will be indicated by the voltmeter. When the switch *S* is closed, field current equal to the load current, starts flowing. If the current in the series field produces a flux aiding the residual flux, the generator will built up voltage till point *C* is reached. Note that at point *C*, the field resistance line *OC* meets the saturation curve. The field resistance line *OC* depends on the total resistance in the series circuit *i.e.*, the slope of line *OC* is determined by the sum of armature circuit resistance, series field resistance and load resistance. If the total series resistance is more than the critical field resistance, just like a self-excited shunt generator, the build up process will not begin.

The external characteristic is shown by curve 2 in Fig. 4.49 *(a)*. Increase the load on D.C. series generator in steps and at each step, record load voltage and load current. A curve passing through these plotted points gives the external characteristic of curve 2. In this figure, *AB* is the load voltage or armature-terminal voltage for a load current equal to *OA*. If total resistance drop $I_a r$ is added to the ordinates of curve 2, the internal characteristic shown by curve 3 is obtained. Note that *r* is the sum of series field resistance and armature circuit resistance (including brushes). Thus the voltage drop *BD* is equal to the total armature resistance drop $I_a r$ and the voltage drop *CD* is due to the armature reaction. A horizontal line through *D* meets the magnetization curve at *F* and *DF* gives the demagnetizing effect caused by the armature reaction for a load current equal to *OA*.

It is obvious from the shape of the external characteristic that the series generator is a variable voltage generator—it is therefore never used as a voltage source.

4.11.4. Compound Generators

Cumulatively compounded generators are more common because these can furnish almost constant voltage from no-load to full-load.

(i) **No-load characteristic.** For the no-load characteristics, same current flows through the series field and shunt field turns in case of a long-shunt compound generator. Since the number of series field turns is far less than that of the shunt field turns, the effect of series field m.m.f. may be neglected in comparison with the shunt field m.m.f. at no-load. For a short-shunt compound generator, series field carries no current when obtaining its no-load characteristic. Thus the no-load characteristic of a long-shunt or short-shunt compound generator is the same as if it were a shunt generator.

(ii) **External characteristic.** The external characteristics of a compound generator are shown in Fig. 4.50 *(a)*. In a cumulatively compounded generator, with the increase of load current, the series field flux aids the shunt field flux. Depending upon the number of series field turns, the cumulatively compounded generator may be *under-compounded* (terminal voltage falls with increase of load), *level* or *flat-compounded* (terminal voltage remains practically constant with increase in load) or *overcompounded* (terminal voltage rises with increase in load). In a *differentially* compounded generator, with the increase in load, the series-field flux opposes the shunt-field flux and consequently the terminal voltage falls more rapidly. These external characteristics, along with shunt and separately excited generators for comparison purposes are sketched in Fig. 4.50 *(a)* where no-load voltage is assumed to be the same in all the cases.

Differentially compounded generators are not damaged by short circuit. In view of this, these generators may be used for welding purposes, where sudden short circuit occurs everytime the electrode touches the working part. However, modern welding generators are of special design. Slightly over compounded generators are used for maintaining constant voltage at the load terminals. The degree of compounding can be controlled by connecting a suitable low resistance, called *diverter*, in parallel with the series field winding as shown in Fig. 4.50 *(b)*.

External characteristic of various types of D.C. generators are also drawn in Fig. 4.50 *(c)* but under the assumption of same rated terminal voltage V_{tr} and load current I_{Lr}. The observations made from these V-*I* characteristics are us under :

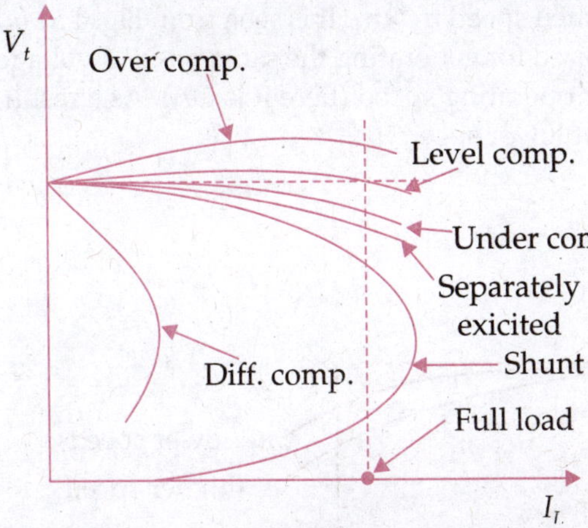

(a)

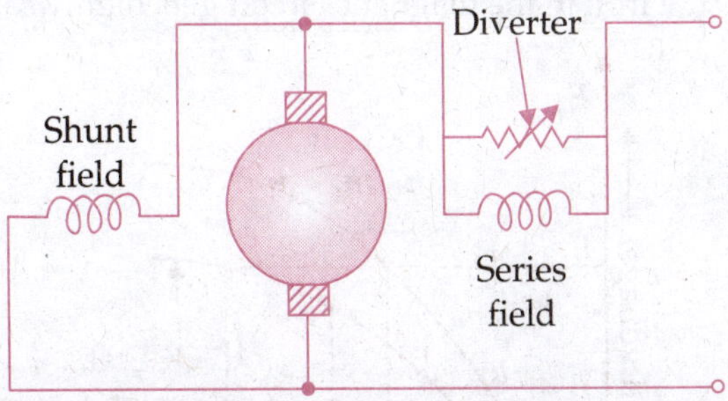

(b)

Fig 4.50: *(a)* External characteristics of various types of D.C. generators and *(b)* circuit diagram of a compound generator with diverter.

(i) For series generator, curve 1, the terminal voltage rises rapidly with load current. At overloads, terminal voltage begins to decrease owing to saturation, armature reaction etc.

(ii) For cumulative overcompounded generator, curve 2, no-load voltage is less than V_{tr}.

(iii) For level, or flat, compounded generator, curve 3, the no-load and full-load voltages are equal. However, terminal voltage at light load is more than V_{tr} but at overloads it falls below V_{tr}.

(iv) For cumulative undercompounded generator, curve 4, no-load voltage is more than V_{tr}.

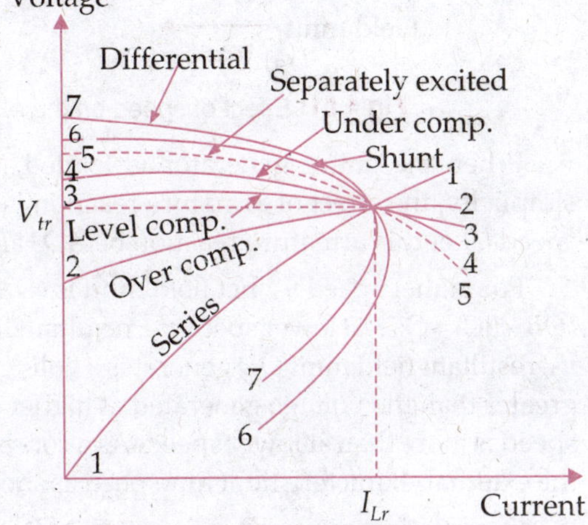

Fig 4.50: *(c)* External characteristics of D.C. generators.

(vi) For both separately-excited (curve 5) and shunt (curve 6) generators, V_{tr} is less than no-load voltage. Voltage variation from no-load to full-load is less in separately-excited generator than in a shunt generator.

(vi) For differential compounded generator, no-load voltage is much higher than V_{tr}.

Fig. 4.50 *(c)* reveals that voltage variation from no-load to full-load is quite high in series and differentially compounded generators.

4.11.5. Effect of Speed on External Characteristics

The external characteristics of shunt and compound generators are affected considerably by the operating speed of the driving motor. In this section, this effect is investigated first for a D.C. shunt generator and then for a cumulative compound generator.

Shunt generators. In Fig. 4.51 *(a)*, magnetisation curves for two different speeds n_1 and n_2 are drawn for a D.C. shunt generator. For the same no-load generated e.m.f. E, shunt-field current or m.m.f. is OB for speed n_1 and OA for speed n_2 where rated speed $n_2 > n_1$. It is seen from Fig. 4.51 *(a)* that at lower operating speed, flux or field m.m.f. required for generating the same no-load voltage is much greater (here OB) than that required at higher operating speed (here it is OA). As a result, the iron in the magnetic circuit gets highly saturated at lower speed n_1.

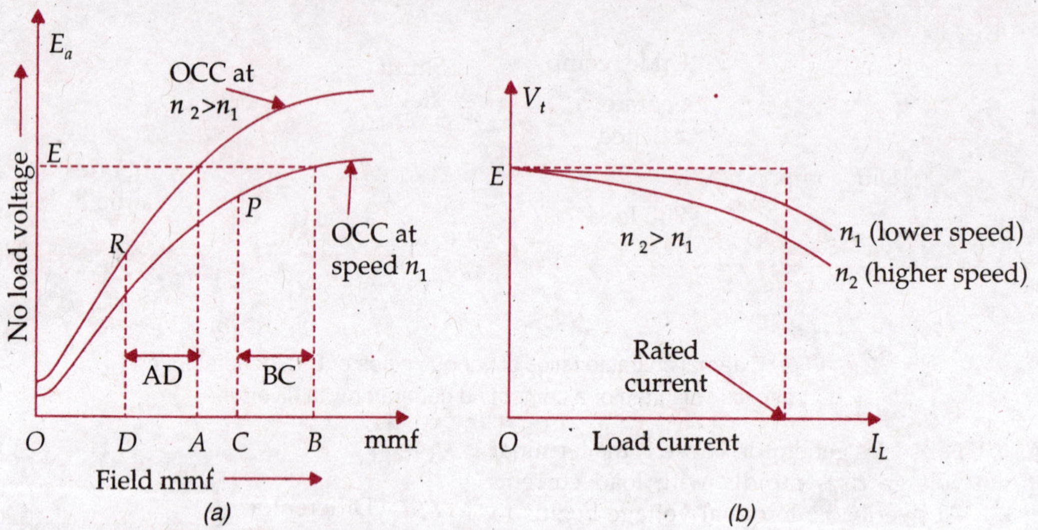

Fig 4.51: Effect of speed on the external characteristics of a dc shunt generator.

When the shunt generator is loaded, armature reaction comes into play. For the sake of simplicity, the effect of armature reaction is taken to be the same for both high and low operating speeds. Let this armature reaction be $AD = BC$ as shown in Fig. 4.51 *(a)*.

For higher speed n_2, net field mmf is $(OA - AD) = OD$ and for lower speed n_1, net field m.m.f. is $(OB - BC) = OC$. At lower speed n_1, resultant field mmf OC generates a voltage CP and at higher speed n_2, resultant field mmf OD generates a voltage DR. Note that voltage at lower speed n_1 has value CP, greater than the voltage generated at higher speed n_2, *i.e.*, DR. This shows that voltage drop at high speed is more than at lower speed. As a consequence, external characteristic at high speed lies below the external characteristic at low speed as shown in Fig. 4.51 *(b)*.

Cumulative compound generators. It is already explained that open-circuit characteristic or magnetization curve for a D.C. compound generator is the same as that obtained for a dc shunt generator. In Fig. 4.52 *(a)* ; two magnetization curves, one at speed n_1 and the other at speed n_2 are drawn. Here rated speed $n_2 > n_1$. As in a D.C. shunt generator, field m.m.f. required at lower speed would be much higher (here OB) for a given generated e.m.f. E than the field m.m.f. required (here OA) at normal speed n_2.

For a particular load current in a dc compound generator, series field mmf (proportional to load current × series field turns) would be the same at both higher and lower operating speeds n_2 and n_1. Here series field at higher speed is AA' and its magnitude is BB' at lower speed. As stated above, mmf AA' = mmf BB'. For a cummulative compound generator, series field mmf must add to shunt field mmf. Therefore, total field mmf at high speed n_2 is $(OA + AA') = OA'$ and at low speed n_1, resultant field mmf is $(OB + BB') = OB'$ as shown in Fig. 4.52 *(a)*. Resultant mmf OA' at rated speed n_2 generates a voltage $A'C$ greater than the voltage $B'D$ generated by total mmf OB' at lower speed n_1. Increased generated voltage $A'C$ further boosts the shunt field current by a greater extent than due to lower voltage $B'D$. This shows that the compounding action is more at higher speed than at lower speed. Thus, external characteristic at higher speed lies above the external characteristic at lower speed as illustrated in Fig. 4.52 *(b)*.

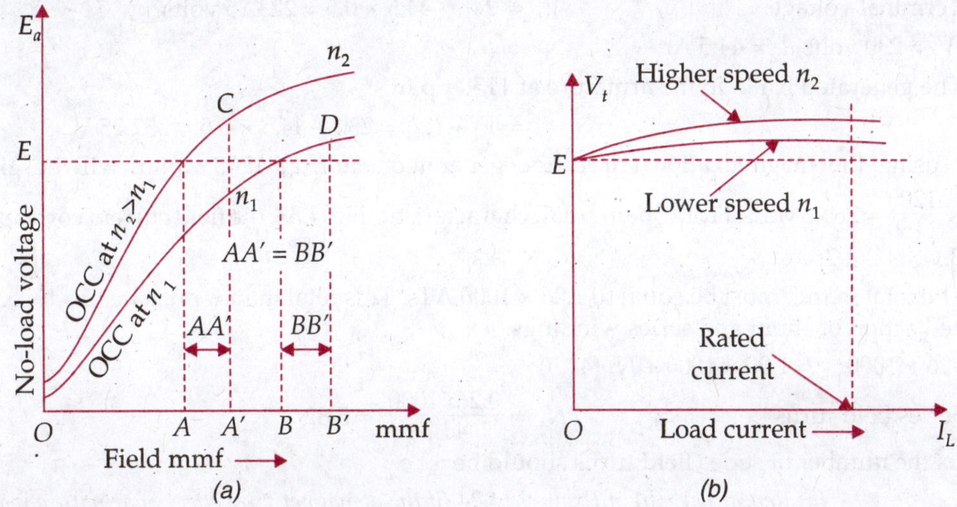

Fig 4.52: *Effect of speed on external characteristics of a dc cumulative compound generator.*

It is seen from Fig. 4.51 and Fig. 4.52 that the effect of speed on external characteristics of a cumulative compound generator is opposite to that in a D.C. shunt generator.

Example 4.24. *A 230 V, 10 kW long-shunt compound generator gave the following data for magnetization curve at 1200 r.p.m.*

I_f, amp.	0.0	0.2	0.4	0.6	0.8	1.0	1.20	1.40	1.60	1.80
E_a, volts	6	53	106	160	209	241	258	272	282	288

The combined resistance of the series winding and armature winding (including brushes) is 0.5 Ω. The shunt winding has 1000 turns. At rated output current, the speed is 1150 r.p.m. and shunt field current is 1.00 A. For negligible armature reaction, calculate

(a) the terminal voltage at rated output current, if the series field has 4 turns and

(b) the number of series field turns per pole for converting it into a flat-compounded generator.

Solution. *(a)* Rated output current $I_L = \frac{10000}{230} = 43.5$ A.

∴ Armature current at rated load $I_a = I_L + I_f = 43.5 + 1.00 = 44.5$ A.

For long shunt compound generator, the series field current I_s = armature current, $I_a = 44.5$ A.

Since the compound generator is cumulatively compounded, the total pole m.m.f. is $N_f I_f + N_s I_s$, *i.e.*, $(1000 \times 1.00 + 4 \times 44.5)$ ampere turns.

∴ The equivalent shunt field current is given by $\frac{1}{N_f}(N_f I_f + N_s I_s)$ or $1.00 + \frac{4 \times 44.5}{1000}$ = 1.18 A. For this field current, the generated e.m.f. from the magnetization curve of Fig. 4.53, is 257 volts. For a speed of 1150 r.p.m. the actual generated e.m.f. E_a is

$$E_a = 257 \times \frac{1150}{1200} = 246 \text{ volts.}$$

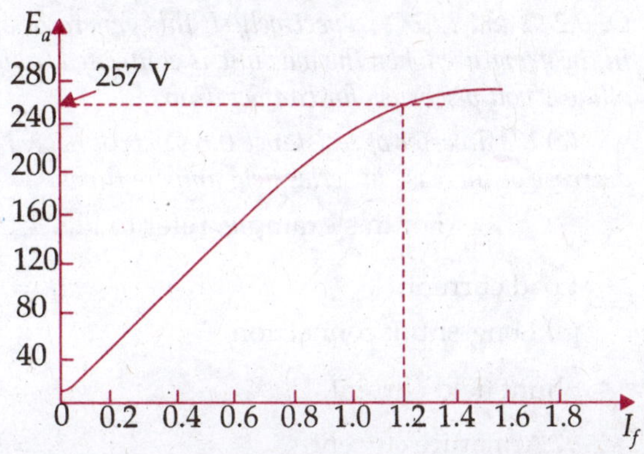

Fig 4.53: Pertaining to Example 4.24

∴ Terminal voltage $V_t = 246 - 44.5 \times 0.5 = 223.75$ volts.

(b) $V_t = 230$ volts, $I_a = 44.5$ A.

∴ The generated e.m.f. in the armature at 1150 r.p.m.

$$= V_t + I_a r_a = 230 + 44.5 \times 0.5 = 252.25 \text{ V}.$$

For using the magnetization curve, the generated e.m.f. at 1200 r.p.m. will be given by $252.25 \times \frac{1200}{1150} = 263.3$ volts. From open circuit characteristic, Fig. 4.53, the field current corresponding to 263.3 volts is 1.26 A.

∴ The total m.m.f. must be equal to 1.26 × 1000 ATs. This total m.m.f. must be produced by the combined action of shunt and series windings.

$$\therefore 1.26 \times 1000 = 1.00 \times 1000 + N_s\,(44.5)$$

∴ Series field turns $N_s = \frac{0.26 \times 1000}{44.5} = 5.82$

Thus the number of series field turns should be 6.

Example 4.25. *(a) Repeat part (b) of Example 4.24, if the demagnetizing effect of armature reaction in terms of equivalent shunt field current is $0.0022 I_a$. Here I_a is the armature current.*

(b) If the series field winding has 10 turns, explain how the desired performance as a flat compounded generator, can be achieved. Assume the series field resistance to be 0.05 Ω.

Solution. *(a)* When the demagnetizing effect is accounted for, then from Eq. (4.27), we get

$$1.26 \times 1000 = 1.0 \times 1000 + N_s \times 44.5 - 0.0022 \times 44.5 \times 1000$$

or $$N_s = \frac{0.3578 \times 1000}{44.5} = 8 \text{ turns}.$$

(b) If there are 10 series field turns, then from Eq. (4.27),

$$1.26 \times 1000 = 1.00 \times 1000 + 10\, I_s - 0.0022\, I_s \times 1000$$

or $$I_s = \frac{0.26}{0.0078} = 33.3 \text{ A}.$$

Out of total armature current of 44.5 A, only 33.3 A should pass through the series field. This can be achieved by putting a resistor, Fig. 4.50 *(b)*, in parallel with the series field winding.

Therefore, $$33.3 = \frac{44.5 \times R_{di}}{0.05 + R_{di}} \quad \text{or} \quad R_{di} = \frac{0.05}{0.3363} = 0.1487\ \Omega.$$

Thus the resistance of the diverter R_{di} should be 0.1487 Ω.

Example 4.26. *A 250 V compound generator has armature, series-field and shunt-field resistances of 0.4 Ω, 0.2 Ω and 125 Ω respectively. If this generator supplies 10 kW at rated voltage, find the e.m.f. generated in the armature when the machine is connected (a) long shunt (b) short shunt. Ignore armature reaction and allow 1 volt per brush for contact drop.*

(c) If a diverter of resistance 0.3 Ω is connected in parallel with series-field winding, find the percentage decrease or increase in series field ampere turns.

Solution. For this example, refer to Fig. 4.14.

Load current, $I_L = \frac{10{,}000}{250} = 40$ A

(a) Long-shunt connection :

Shunt field current, $I_f = \frac{250}{125} = 2$ A

∴ Armature current, $I_a = I_L + I_f = 42$ A

Series-field winding also carries 42 A.

$\therefore$ Generated e.m.f. in armature, $E_a = V_t + I_a(r_s + r_a)$ + total brush contact drop.

The D.C. machine may be lap or wave wound and for any number of poles, total brush contact drop is taken as equal to 2 times the contact drop per brush.

$$\therefore \quad E_a = 250 + 42\,(0.6) + 2 = 277.2 \text{ V}$$

(b) Short-shunt connection :

Voltage across shunt-field and armature terminals = $V_t + I_L \cdot r_s = 250 + 40 \times 0.2 = 258$ V

Shunt field current, $$I_f = \frac{258}{125} = 2.064 \text{ A}$$

$$\therefore \quad I_a = I_L + I_f = 42.064 \text{ A}$$

$$E_a = (V_t + I_L r_s) + I_a r_a + 2 \times \text{contact drop per brush}$$
$$= 258 + 42.064 \times 0.4 + 2 \times 1 = 276.8256 \text{ V.}$$

(c) Series-field ampere-turns are proportional to series-field current *I*.

$$\text{Series-field current with diverter} = \frac{\text{diverter resistance } R_d}{R_d + r_a} \times I = \frac{0.3}{0.5} \times I = 0.6I$$

$\therefore$ Series-field ampere-turns with diverter $\propto 0.6I$

Percentage reduction in series field ampere-turns = $\dfrac{I - 0.6I}{I} \times 100 = 40\%$.

4.12. OPERATING CHARACTERISTICS OF D.C. MOTORS

The basic equations underlying the D.C. motor analysis are, Eqs. (4.3), (4.6), (4.11), (4.18) to (4.23), the no-load magnetization curve and power balance Eq. (4.12). The armature m.m.f. can be taken into account as explained in Fig. 4.35 *(b)*.

In a D.C. motor, e.m.f. E_a generated in the armature is called *back* or *counter e.m.f.* as explained before.

For D.C. motors, the supply voltage is usually constant and the quantities of common interest are speed, torque etc. The following are the three important operating characteristics of D.C. motors:

(i) Speed-armature current characteristic

(ii) Torque-armature current characteristic and

(iii) Speed-torque characteristic.

The object of this article is to describe these operating characteristics for different types of D.C. motors.

4.12.1. D.C. Shunt Motor

For constant supply voltage, the field current is constant. At small values of armature current the demagnetizing effect of armature reaction is almost negligible and therefore the air gap flux is unaffected. For larger values of armature (or load) currents, the demagnetizing effect of armature reaction, decreases the air gap flux slightly.

The speed of a D.C. motor, from Eq. (4.3) is given by

$$\omega_m = \frac{E_a}{K_a \phi} \qquad \text{...(4.33)}$$

But $$E_a = V_t - I_a r_a$$

$$\therefore \quad \omega_m = \frac{V_t - I_a r_a}{K_a \phi} \qquad \text{...(4.34)}$$

(i) **Speed-current characteristic.** For constant supply voltage V_t and constant field current I_f, the motor speed is affected by $I_a r_a$ drop and demagnetizing effect of armature reaction. With

the increase of I_a, the demagnetizing effect of armature reaction increases which reduces the field flux—therefore the motor speed tends to increase. But with the increase of I_a, voltage drop $I_a r_a$ increases and the numerator $(V_t - I_a r_a)$ decreases—therefore the motor speed tends to decrease. With the increase of I_a, the numerator decrement is more than the denominator decrement; in view of this, the speed of D.C. shunt motor with increase of I_a drops only slightly from its no-load speed ω_{mo}. Since I_a at no-load is negligibly small, the shunt motor no-load speed ω_{mo} is given by

$$\omega_{m0} = \frac{V_t}{K_a \phi} \qquad ...(4.35)$$

In case the effect of armature reaction (AR) is neglected, then the denominator of Eq. (4.34) is constant. As a consequence, speed drops faster with I_a. Fig. 4.54 *(a)* illustrates speed-current characteristics of a shunt motor with and without *AR*. The curve marked speed is with *AR* included.

(ii) **Torque-current characteristic.** The expression $T_e = k_a \phi I_a$ reveals that if the flux ϕ is constant as in a shunt motor, the torque would increase linearly with armature current I_a. However, for larger I_a, the net flux decreases due to the demagnetizing effect of armature reaction. In view of this, the torque current characteristic deviates from the straight line, as illustrated in Fig. 4.54 *(a)*. In case the effect of *AR* is neglected, T_e versus I_a characteristic would be a straight line as shown.

(iii) **Speed-torque characteristic.** The speed-torque characteristic is also called the mechanical characteristic and under steady state conditions, it can be obtained as follows :

From Eq. (4.34), $$\omega_m = \frac{V_t - I_a r_a}{K_a \phi}$$

But $$T_e = K_a \phi I_a \quad \text{or} \quad I_a = \frac{T_e}{K_a \phi}$$

Substituting this value of I_a in Eq. (4.34)

$$\omega_m = \frac{1}{K_a \phi}\left[V_t - \frac{T_e r_a}{K_a \phi}\right] = \frac{V_t}{K_a \phi} - r_a \frac{T_e}{K_a^2 \phi^2} = \omega_{mo} - r_a \frac{T_e}{K_a^2 \phi^2} \qquad ...(4.36)$$

It is seen from Eq. (4.36) that with increase of T_e, the speed drops. Note that for larger T_e, larger I_a is required and this has the effect of reducing the air gap flux ϕ, due to saturation and armature reaction. Since with increase of T_e, ϕ is reduced, T_e/ϕ^2 increases at a faster rate and the speed drops more rapidly with the increase of torque in a shunt motor as shown in Fig. 4.54 *(b)*.

If effect of *AR* is neglected, then $(K_a \phi)^2$ in Eq. (4.36) remains constant. As a result, the speed drop with T_e is slow as shown in Fig. (4.54) *(b)*.

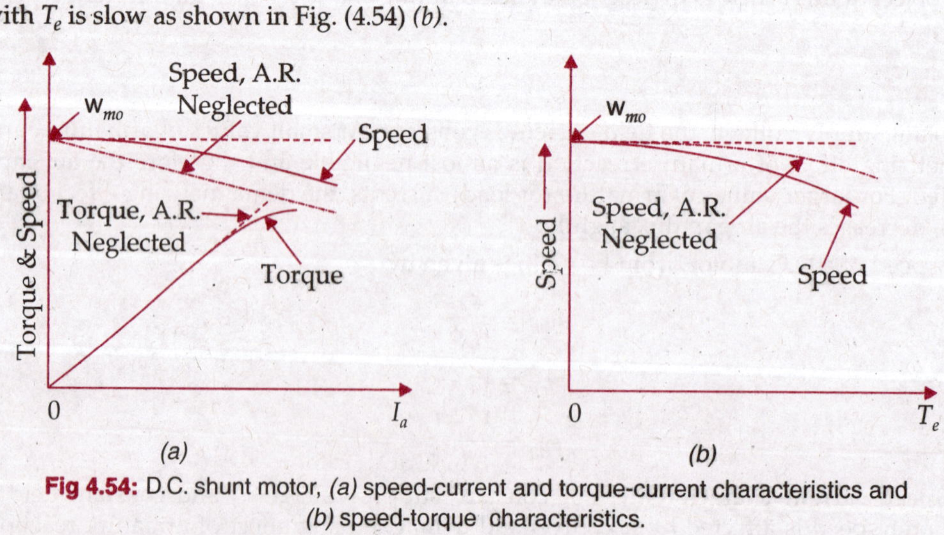

Fig 4.54: D.C. shunt motor, *(a)* speed-current and torque-current characteristics and *(b)* speed-torque characteristics.

4.12.2. D.C. Series Motor

For a series motor, the field current is equal to the armature current.

(i) **Speed-current characteristic.** If saturation and armature reaction are neglected, then main flux ϕ is directly proportional to armature current I_a. Therefore, it may be written that $\phi = CI_a$, where C is any constant.

Now $$E_a = K_a \phi \omega_m = V_t - I_a (r_a + r_s)$$

or $$\omega_m = \frac{V_t}{K_a \phi} - \frac{I_a (r_a + r_s)}{K_a \phi} \quad ...(4.37)$$

or $$\omega_m = \frac{V_t}{K_a C I_a} - \frac{(r_a + r_s)}{K_a C} \quad ...(4.38)$$

It is seen from Eq. (4.38) that with saturation and armature reaction neglected, the speed-current characteristic of a series motor is a hyperbola, as illustrated by solid line in Fig. 4.55 *(a)*.

Let us now investigate the effect of including saturation and armature reaction. At increased values of I_a, the flux ϕ should increase with I_a, but due to the demagnetizing effect of armature reaction and saturation, the air gap flux ϕ tends to remain approximately constant. An examination of Eq. (4.37) reveals that for constant ϕ, the term $\frac{V_t}{K_a \phi}$ is constant and the term $\frac{I_a (r_a + r_s)}{K_a \phi}$ increases linearly with I_a. Thus the speed-current characteristic of a series motor, for larger values of I_a, approaches a straight line, as illustrated by dotted portion of the curve in Fig. 4.55 *(a)*.

At no-load, the armature current is very small, because the power input to motor has to overcome the no-load losses only. Thus the voltage drop $I_a (r_a + r_s)$ at no-load, is almost negligible as compared with V_t and from Eq. (4.37), the no-load speed ω_{mo} is

$$\omega_{mo} = \frac{V_t}{K_a \phi} = \frac{V_t}{K_a C I_a} \quad ...(4.39)$$

Since ω_{mo} is inversely proportional to I_a, the no-load speed of the series motor becomes dangerously high due to small no-load current. In view of this, the series motor must always start and operate under load mechanically coupled with it.

(ii) **Torque-current characteristic.** With saturation and armature reaction neglected,

$$\phi = CI_a$$

$$\therefore \quad T_e = K_a \phi I_a = K_a C I_a^2 = C_1 I_a^2 \quad ...(4.40)$$

Eq. (4.40) shows that the torque is proportional to the square of I_a and, therefore, torque-current characteristic is a parabola. But for larger I_a, the net flux tends to remain approximately constant (as explained in speed-current characteristic). Consequently the torque-current characteristic approaches a straight line for larger values of I_a, Fig. 4.55 *(a)*.

(iii) **Speed-torque characteristic.** If saturation and armature reaction are neglected, then from Eq. (4.40),

$$I_a = \sqrt{\frac{T_e}{K_a C}}$$

Substituting this value of I_a, in Eq. (4.38), $\omega_m = \frac{V_t}{\sqrt{K_a C T_e}} - \frac{r_a + r_s}{K_a C} \quad ...(4.41)$

Thus with negligible saturation and armature reaction, the speed-torque characteristic is a hyperbola, as shown by solid curve in Fig. 4.55 *(b)*.

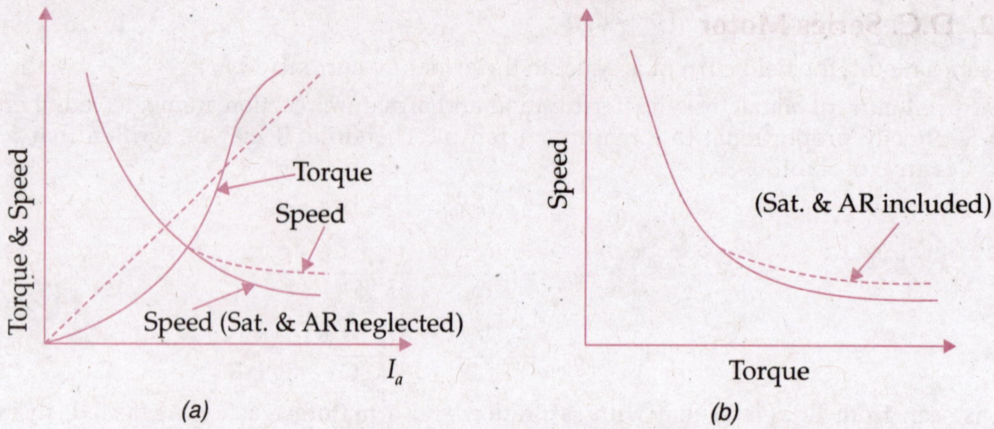

Fig 4.55: D.C. series motor (a) speed-current and torque-current characteristics and (b) speed-torque characteristics.

With saturation and armature reaction included, large torques require large currents and these large currents tend to make air gap flux ϕ constant as explained before. This has the effect of making T_e approximately proportional to I_a (*i.e.*, $T_e = K_a I_a$) and in view of this, Eq. (4.37) becomes,

$$\omega_m = \frac{V_t}{K_a\phi} - \frac{T_e(r_a + r_s)}{K_a^2\phi}$$

Thus, above a certain value of T_e, when air-gap flux ϕ remains approximately constant due to armature reaction and saturation; speed-torque characteristic approaches a straight line as illustrated by dotted curve in Fig. 4.55 *(b)*. It is seen from this figure that for a series motor, the speed drop at increased load torques is almost negligible.

4.12.3. D.C. Compound Motor

A differential compound motor is rarely used in practice. So, the performance characteristics of cumulative compound motor are mainly described in this section.

(i) **Speed-current characteristic.** For a long-shunt compound motor,

$$V_t = E_a + I_a(r_a + r_s)$$

and $\quad E_a = K_a\phi\omega_m = K_a(\phi_{sh} + \phi_{se})\,\omega_m$

where ϕ_{sh} and ϕ_{se} are respectively the fluxes created by shunt and series field windings.

$$\therefore \quad \omega_m = \frac{1}{K_a(\phi_{sh} + \phi_{se})}[V_t - I_a(r_a + r_s)] \qquad ...(4.42)$$

With increase in I_a, ϕ_{se} increases; as a consequence, denominator of Eq. (4.42) increases but its numerator decreases. Thus, with increase in I_a, the speed drops at a faster rate in cumulative compound motor than in a shunt motor. This fact is indicated in Fig. 4.56 where speed-current characteristic of cumulative compound motor is shown below the speed-current characteristic of a D.C. shunt motor. Here no-load speed is assumed to be the same. For comparison purposes, speed-current curve of a D.C. series motor is also sketched in Fig. 4.56.

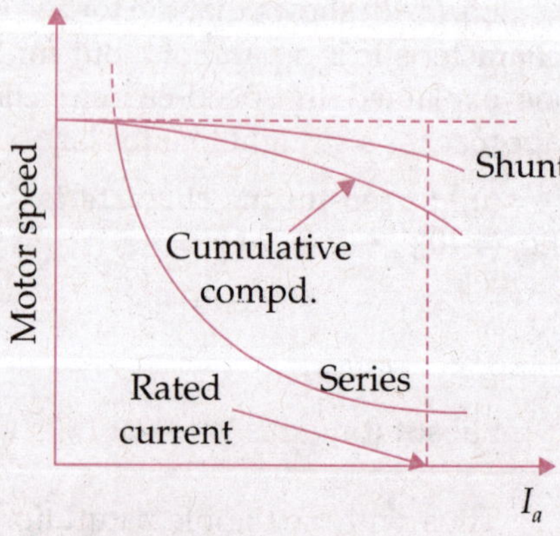

Fig 4.56: Comparison of speed-current characteristics of different dc motors.

(ii) **Torque-current characteristic.** The electromagnetic torque T_e is

$$T_e = K_a \phi I_a = K_a (\phi_{sh} + \phi_{se}) I_a \quad ...(4.43)$$

At no-load, $I_a = 0$, $\phi_{se} = 0$ and therefore $T_e = 0$. As the armature current I_a rises with load, shunt field ϕ_{sh} remains almost constant but series field ϕ_{se} rises. As a result, motor torque T_e also rises as per Eq. (4.43). Shunt motor produces torque = $K_a \phi_{sh} \cdot I_a$; this shows that cumulative compound motor develops a torque (= $K_a (\phi_{sh} + \phi_{se}) I_a$) higher than that developed in a D.C. shunt motor (= $K_a \phi_{sh} \cdot I_a$). This is shown in Fig. 4.57. For comparison purposes, D.C. series motor torque-current characteristic is also sketched in Fig. 4.57.

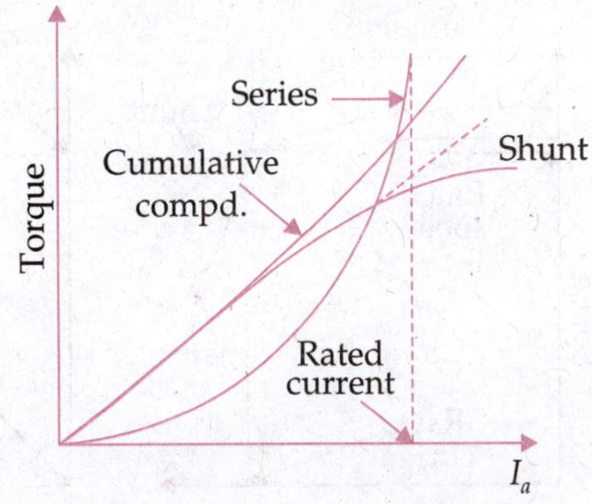

Fig 4.57: Comparison of torque-current characteristics of different dc motors.

(iii) **Speed-torque characteristic.** From Eq. (4.43)

$$I_a = \frac{T_e}{K_a(\phi_{sh} + \phi_{se})}$$

Substitution of this value of I_a in Eq. (4.42) gives

$$\omega_m = \frac{1}{K_a(\phi_{sh} + \phi_{se})}\left[V_t - \frac{T_e(r_a + r_s)}{K_a(\phi_{sh} + \phi_{se})}\right]$$

$$= \frac{V_t}{K_a(\phi_{sh} + \phi_{se})} - (r_a + r_s)\frac{T_e}{K_a^2(\phi_{sh} + \phi_{se})^2} \quad ...(4.44)$$

With increase in motor torque T_e, armature current rises, with this series-field flux ϕ_{se} rises. Eq. (4.44) shows that first term gets reduced and the second term becomes somewhat more (particularly near saturation where $(\phi_{sh} + \phi_{se})$ would tend to remain constant). Consequently, speed drop in a cumulative compound motor is more than it is in a D.C. shunt motor, see Eq. (4.36). Thus, the speed-torque characteristic in a cumulative compound motor is more drooping than in a D.C. shunt motor. Fig. 5.58 shows these characteristics along with D.C. series motor characteristic for the sake of comparison.

The characteristics presented in Figs. 4.56 to 4.58 are sketched on the assumption of same no-load values for torque and speed. Electrical machinery is usually specified in terms of its rated, or full-load, values. In view of this, the curves of Figs. 4.56 to 4.58 are redrawn in Fig. 4.59 with their rated values for speed, torque and current. Characteristics compiled in this figure are suitable in so far as comparison of D.C. motors of the same specification is concerned. Fig. 4.59 *(a)* gives speed-current curves, Fig. 4.59 *(b)* is for torque-current characteristics and Fig. 4.59 *(c)* compares speed-torque characteristics of D.C. series, shunt and cumulative compound motors. For obtaining the curves of Fig. 4.59, push down or push up bodily the various curves of Figs. 4.56 to 4.58.

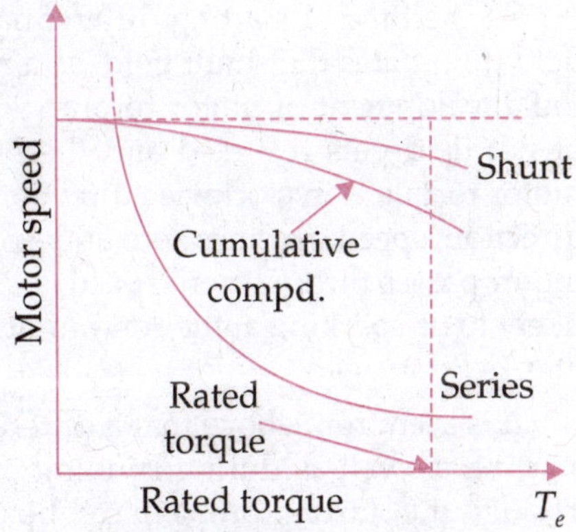

Fig 4.58: Comparison of speed-torque characteristics of D.C. motors.

It is seen from Fig. 4.59 *(b)* that for armature current I_a below rated current, shunt motor develops the largest torque ; but for I_a above the rated current, series motor develops the largest torque. The maximum permissible current at the starting of D.C. motors is limited to about 1.5

times the rated current. Thus, for loads requiring high starting torque such as for hoists, cranes and traction-type loads, series motors are the most suited machines.

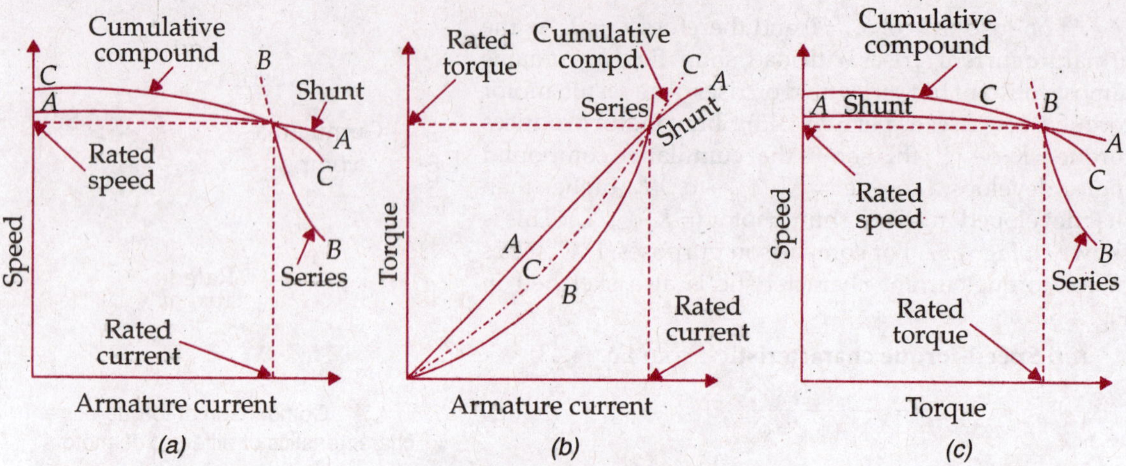

Fig 4.59: *(a)* Speed-current *(b)* torque-current and *(c)* speed-torque characteristics of D.C. motors for comparison at rated load.

In a *differential compound motor*, series-field flux ϕ_{se} opposes the shunt-field flux ϕ_{sh}. Therefore, Eq. (4.42) and (4.43) for this motor become

$$\omega_m = \frac{V_t - I_a(r_a + r_s)}{K_a(\phi_{sh} - \phi_{se})} \quad \text{...(4.45 a)}$$

and

$$T_e = K_a(\phi_{sh} - \phi_{se})\, I_a \quad \text{...(4.45 b)}$$

With increase in load on this motor, I_a rises, ϕ_{se} increases, the numerator decreases but denominator, proportional to $(\phi_{sh} - \phi_{se})$, decreases faster. Therefore, the motor speed rises, Eq. (4.45 *a*). With decrease in $(\phi_{sh} - \phi_{se})$, the motor takes increased I_a as per Eq. (4.45 *b*). Therefore ϕ_{se} rises and speed rises still further putting more load on the motor. This cumulative process makes the motor speed dangerously high.

At the time of starting differential compound motor, more armature current is drawn, series field dominates the shunt field, as a result, motor runs in one direction (say anticlockwise) due to the development of motor torque. Soon after, shunt field dominates series field, so the direction of net field gets reversed and therefore the motor torque is also reversed. Therefore, now the motor torque is in clockwise direction. As a consequence, motor speed falls from its anticlockwise direction, speed becomes zero and eventually motor begins to run in clockwise direction. When the motor passes through zero speed, armature current $I_a = (V_t/r_a)$ becomes dangerously high, there is likely to be sparking at the commutator surface. As a result, the commuator and armature winding may get damaged.

It is seen from above that a differential compound motor possesses inherent instability during starting as well as during running conditions. This motor is, therefore, rarely used in industry. Though the starting problem can be overcome by short-circuiting the series-field winding during starting, yet the instability during running conditions cannot be avoided.

Example 4.27. *A 230-V, D.C. shunt motor, takes an armature current of 3.33 A at rated voltage and at a no-load speed of 1000 r.p.m. The resistances of the armature circuit and field circuit are respectively 0.3 Ω and 160 Ω. The line current at full load and rated voltage is 40 A. Calculate, at full load, the speed and the developed torque in case the armature reaction weakens the no-load flux by 4%.*

Solution. At no-load, the counter e.m.f. is

$$E_{a1} = V_t - I_{a1} r_a = 230 - 3.33 \times 0.3 = 229 \text{ V}.$$

Field current, $$I_f = \frac{230}{160} = 1.44 \text{ A}.$$

At full load, $$I_{a2} = I_L - I_f = 40 - 1.44 = 38.56 \text{ A}.$$

$\therefore$ Counter e.m.f. at full load is $$E_{a2} = 230 - 38.56 \times 0.3 = 218.43 \text{ volts}.$$

At full load, the field flux is $\phi_2 = 0.96\,\phi_1$ (given).

The counter e.m.f. E_a is given by $$E_a = K_a \phi \omega_m$$

$$\therefore \quad \frac{E_{a1}}{E_{a2}} = \frac{K_a \phi_1 \omega_{m1}}{K_a \phi_2 \omega_{m2}} = \frac{\phi_1 n_1}{\phi_2 n_2}$$

or $$\frac{229}{218.43} = \frac{1000 \times \phi_1}{n_2 (0.96 \phi_1)}$$

$\therefore$ Full load speed, $$n_2 = 953.58 \text{ r.p.m.}$$

At full load, $$E_{a2} = K_a \phi_2 \omega_m \text{ or } K_a \phi_2 = \frac{218.43 \times 60}{2\pi \times 953.58}$$

$\therefore$ Electromagnetic, or developed, torque at full load,

$$T_e = K_a \phi_2 I_{a2}$$

$$= \frac{218.43 \times 60}{2\pi \times 953.58} \times 38.56 = 84.346 \text{ Nm}.$$

Example 4.28. *A 220-V D.C. shunt motor has an armature circuit resistance of 0.2 Ω and field resistance of 110 Ω. At no-load the motor takes 5 A and runs at 1500 r.p.m. If the motor draws 52 A at rated voltage and rated load, calculate the motor speed and its rated shaft torque in Nm. The rotational losses at no-load and full-load are the same. Neglect armature reaction.*

Solution. The shunt field current $$I_f = \frac{220}{110} = 2 \text{ A}.$$

At no-load, armature current $$I_{a1} = 5 - 2 = 3 \text{ A}.$$

Counter e.m.f. $$E_{a1} = 220 - 3 \times 0.2 = 219.4 \text{ V}.$$

$\therefore$ Rotational losses $$= E_{a1} I_{a1} = 219.4 \times 3 = 658.2 \text{ watts}.$$

At full load, armature current $$I_{a2} = I_L - I_f = 52 - 2 = 50 \text{A}.$$

$\therefore$ Counter e.m.f. $$E_{a2} = 220 - 50 \times 0.2 = 210 \text{ V}.$$

Here ϕ_1 (no load flux) = ϕ_2 (full load flux), because the field current is constant at 2 A and effect of *AR* is neglected.

$$\therefore \quad \frac{E_{a1}}{E_{a2}} = \frac{n_1 \phi_1}{n_2 \phi_2}$$

or $$n_2 = \frac{n_1 \phi_1}{\phi_1} \times \frac{E_{a2}}{E_{a1}} = \frac{(1500)(210)}{219.4} = 1435 \text{ r.p.m.}$$

Shaft power, $$P_{sh} = \text{Electromagnetic power} - \text{Rotational losses}$$

$$= 210 \times 50 - 658.2 = 9841.8 \text{ watts}.$$

$\therefore$ Shaft torque $$= \frac{P_{sh}}{\omega_m} = \frac{9841.8 \times 60}{2\pi \times 1435} = 65.4 \text{ Nm}.$$

Example 4.29. *A D.C. shunt machine has total armature circuit resistance of 0.4 Ω and field-circuit resistance of 200 Ω. Its open-circuit voltage at 1500 r.p.m. is 230 V for a field current of 1.1 A and 210 V for a field current of 0.9 A.*

If this machine is made to run as a D.C. shunt motor from 230 V supply mains at its full-load armature current of 24 A and at 1500 r.p.m., find the external resistance that must be inserted in the field circuit. Neglect armature reaction.

Solution. For the D.C. shunt motor, the counter or generated e.m.f. E_a at 1500 r.p.m. and at full load is given by

$$E_a = V_t - I_a r_a = 230 - 24 \times 0.4 = 220.4 \text{ V}.$$

For generated e.m.f., E_a = 230 V, the field current I_f is 1.1 A and for E_a = 210 V, I_f = 0.9 A. The change in generated e.m.f. is 20 V for a field current variation of 0.2 A and this change is linear. Therefore, for a generated e.m.f. of 220.4 V at 1500 r.p.m., the field current is given by

$$\left(0.9 \text{ A for } 210 \text{ V} + \frac{0.2}{20} \times 10.4 \text{ for the remaining } 10.4 \text{ V}\right) = 1.004 \text{ A}.$$

For a terminal voltage of 230 V across shunt field winding, a field current of 1.004 A requires a total shunt field resistance of $\frac{230}{1.004} = 229.084\ \Omega$.

∴ External resistance that must be inserted in shunt field circuit

$$= 229.084 - 200 = 29.084\ \Omega.$$

Example 4.30. *A 250-V, 4 pole, shunt motor has two circuit armature winding with 500 conductors. The armature circuit resistance is 0.25 Ω, field resistance is 125 Ω and the flux per pole is 0.02 Wb. Armature reaction is neglected. If the motor draws 14 A from the mains, then compute*

(a) speed and the internal (total or gross) torque developed,

(b) the shaft power, shaft torque and efficiency with rotational losses equal to 300 watts.

Solution.

$$P = 4,\ Z = 500,\ r_a = 0.25\ \Omega,$$

$$r_f = 125\ \Omega,\ \phi = 0.02 \text{ Wb}.$$

Constant shunt field current $= \frac{250}{125} = 2$ A.

(*a*) Armature current $I_a = 14 - 2 = 12$ A.

∴ Counter e.m.f. $E_a = V_t - I_a r_a = 250 - 12 \times 0.25 = 247$ V.

But $E_a = \frac{\phi Z n P}{a}$

or $247 = \frac{0.02 \times 500 \times n \times 4}{2}$

∴ $n = \frac{247.0 \times 2}{10 \times 4} = \frac{247}{20}$ r.p.s. = 741 r.p.m.

Electromagnetic power $P_e = E_a I_a = 247 \times 12 = 2964$ watts.

∴ Internal torque developed $= \frac{P_e}{\omega_m} = \frac{2964 \times 60}{2\pi \times 741} = 38.30$ Nm.

(*b*) Shaft power $P_{sh} = P_e -$ Rotational losses $= 2964 - 300 = 2664$ watts.

Shaft torque $= \frac{P_{sh}}{\omega_m} = \frac{2664 \times 60}{2\pi \times 741} = 34.4$ Nm.

Efficiency $= \frac{\text{Output at the shaft}}{\text{Power input}} = \frac{2664}{250 \times 14} = 0.762 = 76.2\%$.

Example 4.31. *A fan has the following speed-power characteristics :*

Speed, r.p.m.	700	800	900	1000	1100	1200
Input, kW	4.5	8.5	14.00	21.1	30.00	40.75

This fan is driven by a 4-pole, 230 V D.C. shunt motor having an armature winding with two parallel paths and 600 conductors. The flux per pole is 0.01 Wb and the armature circuit resistance is 0.25 Ω. The no load rotational losses are 500 watts. Find the shaft power output, operating speed, armature current and motor efficiency.

Solution. The e.m.f. generated in the armature of D.C. motor is

$$E_a = \frac{\phi ZnP}{60a} \text{ if } n \text{ is in r.p.m.}$$

$$\therefore \quad \text{Counter e.m.f. } E_a = \frac{(0.01)(600)n(4)}{60 \times 2} = 0.2n \text{ volts.}$$

Now

$$V_t = E_a + I_a r_a$$

$$I_a = \frac{V_t - E_a}{r_a} = \frac{230 - 0.2n}{0.25} = (920 - 0.8n) \text{ Amp}$$

$\therefore$ Shaft power output in watts,

$$P_{sh} = E_a I_a - \text{Rotational losses}$$
$$= (0.2n)(920 - 0.8n) - 500$$
$$= 184n - 0.16n^2 - 500$$

or

$$P_{sh} = (0.18n - 1.6 \times 10^{-4} n^2 - 0.5) \text{ kW.}$$

For different speeds, the shaft power output P_{sh} of the motor calculated from the above expression, is given in tabular form as follows :

n, r.p.m.	*700*	*800*	*900*	*1000*	*1100*
P_{sh}, kW	*49.9*	*44.3*	*33.5*	*23.5*	*8.3*

The shaft power output versus speed of the motor are plotted on the graph in Fig. 4.60. On the same graph is plotted the power input versus speed characteristic of the fan. The intersection of these two curves gives the required operating point, from which it is found that the operating speed is 1012 r.p.m. and power output of the motor or power input to the fan is 22 kW.

$\therefore$ Armature current is

$$I_a = (920 - 0.8n)$$
$$= (920 - 0.8 \times 1012) = 110.4 \text{ A.}$$

Armature $I_a^2 r_a$ loss

$$= (110.4)^2 \times 0.25 = 3050 \text{ watts.}$$

$\therefore$ Power input

= Power output loss + Rotational losses $+ I_a^2 r_a$

= 22000 + 500 + 3050 = 25,550 watts.

$$\therefore \text{Motor efficiency} = \frac{22{,}000}{25{,}550} \times 100 = 86.2\%.$$

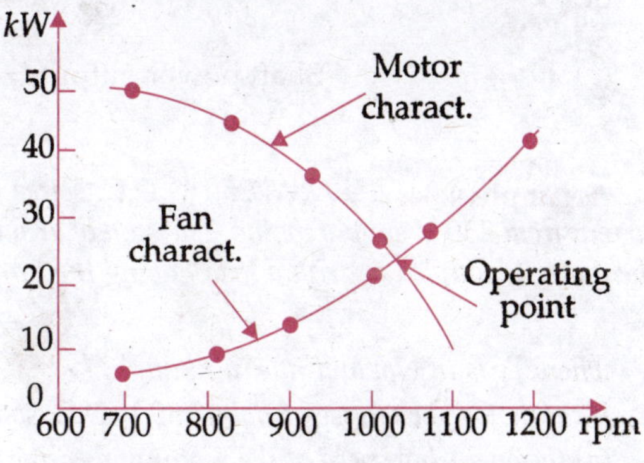

Fig 4.60: Pertaining to Example 4.28.

Example 4.32. *A 230-V D.C. series motor has an armature circuit resistance of 0.2 Ω and field resistance of 0.1 Ω. At rated voltage, the motor draws a line current of 40 amps and runs at a speed of 1000 r.p.m. Find the speed of the motor for a line current of 20 A at 230 V. Assume that the flux at 20 A line current is 60% of the flux at 40 A line current.*

Solution. For 40 A line current, $E_{a1} = V_t - I_a(r_a + r_s) = 230 - 40(0.2 + 0.1) = 218$ V.

For a line current of 20 A, $E_{a2} = 230 - 20(0.3) = 224$ volts.

Now flux at 20 A, *i.e.* $\phi_2 = 0.6$ times the flux at 40 A i.e. $\phi_2 = 0.6\,\phi_1$

$$\therefore \quad \frac{E_{a1}}{E_{a2}} = \frac{n_1\phi_1}{n_2\phi_2}$$

$$\text{or} \quad \frac{218}{224} = \frac{(1000)(\phi_1)}{n_2(0.6\phi_1)} \quad \text{or} \quad n_2 = \frac{1000 \times 224}{218 \times 0.6} = 1713 \text{ r.p.m.}$$

Example 4.33. *A 15 kW, 230 V, 80 A, 1000 r.p.m. D.C. series motor has the following full load losses expressed in percentage of motor input :*

Armature circuit ohmic loss (including brush loss) = 2.8%

Field ohmic loss = 2.6%

Rotational loss = 2.2%

Neglect the armature reaction and magnetic saturation and assume the rotational loss to remain constant. If the motor draws half the rated current at rated voltage, determine

(a) speed in r.p.m. and *(b) shaft power output*

Solution. Full load input = 230 × 80 = 18400 watts.

$$\therefore \quad \text{Total ohmic losses} = I_L^2\,(r_a + r_s) = (18400)\left(\frac{5.4}{100}\right)$$

$$\text{or} \quad (80)^2\,(r_a + r_s) = 994 \quad \text{or} \quad (r_a + r_s) = \frac{994}{6400} = 0.155\ \Omega.$$

(a) $\therefore \quad E_{a1} = 230 - 80 \times 0.155 = 217.6$ volts

and $\quad E_{a2} = 230 - 40 \times 0.155 = 223.8$ V.

Since the magnetic saturation is neglected, $\phi_1 \propto 80$ A and $\phi_2 \propto 40$ A.

$$\therefore \quad \frac{E_{a1}}{E_{a2}} = \frac{n_1\phi_1}{n_2\phi_2}$$

$$\text{or} \quad \frac{217.6}{223.8} = \frac{(1000)(80)}{n_2(40)} \quad \text{or } n_2 = \frac{(1000)(80)(223.8)}{(40)(217.6)} = 2055 \text{ r.p.m.}$$

(b) $\quad$ Shaft power output $= E_{a2} I_{a2}$ – Rotational loss

$$= 223.8 \times 40 - (18400)\left(\frac{2.2}{100}\right) = 8952 - 405 = 8547 \text{ watts.}$$

Example 4.34. ***A 40 kW, 250 V D.C. series motor, runs at a speed of 1500 r.p.m. while taking rated current from 250 V supply mains. The sum of armature circuit resistance and series field resistance is 0.2 Ω. The motor is coupled to drive a load having the torque speed characteristic given by***

$$T_L = 5\sqrt{n}$$

where T_L is in Nm and n is in r.p.m.

If the motor is energised from a 250 V D.C. source, find

(a) the operating speed of the motor and connected load and (b) the current drawn from the source. Neglect magnetic saturation, armature reaction and rotational losses.

Solution. (a) $\quad$ Rated current $= \dfrac{40,000}{250} = 160$ A

At rated load, $\quad E_a = 250 - 160 \times 0.2 = 218$ V.

The rated electromagnetic torque of the motor is

$$T_e = \frac{E_a I_a}{\omega_m} = \frac{(218)(160)}{2\pi \times 1500} \times 60 = 222 \text{ Nm.}$$

Now the relation giving the torque-speed characteristic of the series motor, must be developed.

Since the magnetic saturation is neglected.

$$T_e = K_a \phi I = K_1 I_a^2$$

$$\therefore \quad K_1 = \frac{222}{(160)^2}$$

Also, $$E_a = K_2 \phi n = K_2 I_a n$$

$$\therefore \quad K_2 = \frac{218}{(160)(1500)} = 0.000908.$$

Note that the values of constants K_1 and K_2 are obtained from rated conditions.

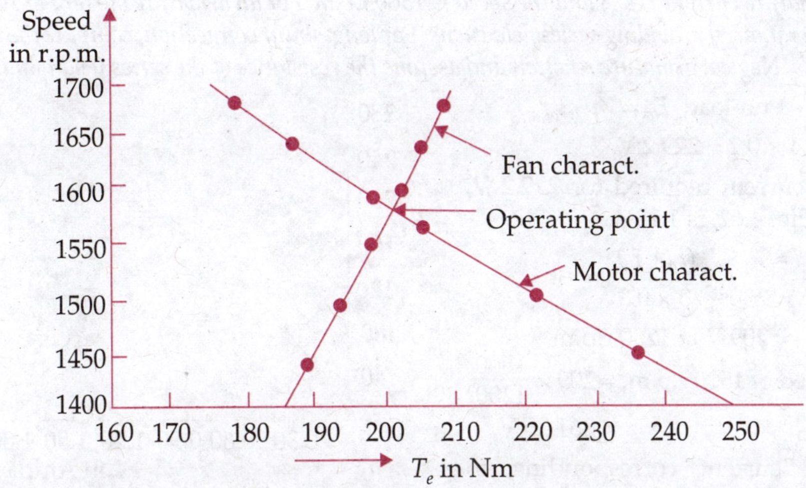

Fig 4.61: Pertaining to Example 4.34.

The armature current at any speed is

$$I_a = \frac{V_t - E_a}{r_a} = \frac{250 - K_2 I_a n}{0.2}$$

$$= 1250 - 5\,(0.000908)\, I_a n = 1250 - 0.00454\, I_a n$$

or $$I_a = \frac{1250}{1 + 0.00454n}$$

$$\therefore \quad T_e = K_1 I_a^2 = \frac{222}{(160)^2} \cdot \frac{(1250)^2}{(1 + 0.00454n)^2} = \frac{13530}{(1 + 0.00454n)^2}$$

The above expression gives the speed-torque characteristic of the series motor.

The various points in the series-motor characteristic are tabulated below and then plotted in Fig. 4.61.

n, r.p.m.	1400	1450	1500	1550	1600	1650	1700
T_e, Nm	250	234	221	209	197.8	186.8	177.8

Speed-torque characteristic of the load, obtained from expression $T_L = 5\sqrt{n}$, is tabulated below and then plotted in Fig. 4.61.

n, r.p.m.	1400	1450	1500	1550	1600	1650	1700
T_L, Nm	186	192	193.5	196.5	200	203	206

The intersection of the series motor and load characteristics, gives the operating point, from which it is seen that the operating speed of the motor and load is 1591 r.p.m. and the torque is 199.5 Nm.

(*b*) Current drawn from the source $I_a = \dfrac{1250}{1 + 0.00454 \times 1591} = 151.8$ A.

Example 4.35. *A 15 kW, 230 V, D.C. shunt motor has the following data for its magnetization curve at 1500 r.p.m.*

I_f, *amp*	0	0.2	0.4	0.6	0.8	1.02	1.15	1.32	1.56	1.92	2.40
E_a, *volt*	6	40	80	120	160	200	220	240	260	280	300

The armature circuit resistance is 0.2 Ω and the shunt field has 1000 turns per pole. At rated voltage and no load, the armature current is 4 A and the speed is 1500 r.p.m. For an armature current of 70 A, the speed is reduced to 1200 r.p.m. by providing series field turns. For long-shunt connection, compute the number of these series field turns. Neglect armature reaction and assume the resistance of the series field winding to be 0.1 Ω.

Solution. At no-load, $E_a = V_t - I_a r_a$

$E_a = 230 - 4 \times 0.2 = 229.2$ V.

The field current required for 229.2 V, from O.C.C., Fig. 4.62, is 1.23 A.

At load, $E_a = V_t - I_a(r_a + r_s)$

$= 230 - 70 \times 0.3$

$= 209$ V at 1200 r.p.m.

E_a at a speed of 1500 r.p.m. $= 209 \times \dfrac{1500}{1200}$

$= 261.25$ V.

The field current corresponding to 261.25 V, from Fig. 4.62, is 1.575 A.

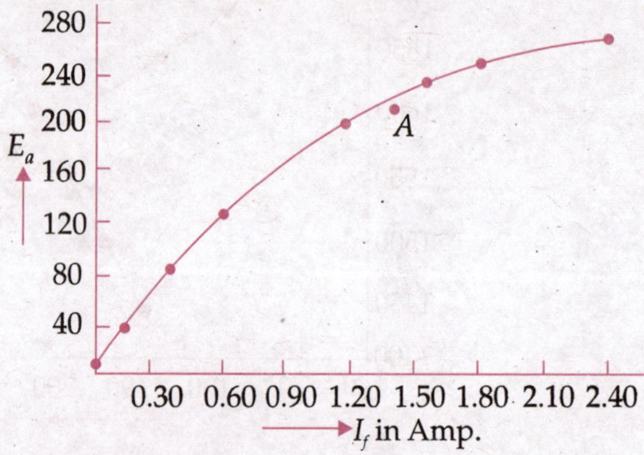

Fig 4.62: Pertaining to Example 4.32 and 4.33.

From Eq. (4.25),

Main field m.m.f., $\quad 1.575 \times 1000 = 1.23 \times 1000 + N_s (70)$

∴ Series field turns, $\quad N_s = \dfrac{0.345 \times 1000}{70} = 5$ turns.

Example 4.36. *D.C. shunt machine of this example, has the same magnetization curve at 1500 r.p.m. as that given in Example 4.35.*

The armature circuit resistance (including brushes) is 0.2 Ω and shunt field has 2000 turns per pole. The shunt motor speed, both at no-load and rated load is 1500 r.p.m. The motor armature current at rated load is 36 A.

(a) For a no-load speed of 1500 r.p.m., determine the shunt field current of the motor when connected to 230 V mains. Neglect armature circuit resistance drop and armature reaction at no-load.

(b) Determine the effective armature reaction at full load in ampere turns per pole.

(c) At rated voltage and at rated armature current of 36 A, the speed is to be reduced to 1350 r.p.m. by providing the shunt motor with series field winding. Calculate the required number of series field turns. Assume the series field resistance to be 0.05 Ω and the motor to be cumulatively compounded.

(d) If the series field winding has 20 turns per pole, determine the speed at rated armature current and at rated voltage of 230 V. Assume series field resistance to be 0.05 Ω.

(e) If series field turns installed are 20, find the internal starting torque in case the starting armature current is limited to 50 A and the shunt field current is 1.23 A. Assume the demagnetizing effect of armature reaction to be 200 ampere turns per pole.

Solution. (*a*) At no-load, $E_a = V_t = 230$ V as it is given that armature circuit resistance drop is neglected.

Therefore, constant shunt field current I_f, from O.C.C. of Fig. 4.62 is 1.23 A corresponding to $E_a = 230$ V.

(*b*) At full load, $I_a = 36$ A. $\therefore E_a = 230 - 36 \times 0.2 = 222.8$ volts

In Fig. 4.62, point A is plotted with $E_a = 222.8$ V and $I_f = 1.23$ amp. The horizontal distance between point A and the magnetization curve, gives the effective armature reaction in terms of shunt field current. Its value is 0.06 A.

$\therefore$ Armature reaction in ampere-turns per pole = 0.06 × 2000 = 120

(*c*) At rated load, with series field winding in circuit,

$$E_a = 230 - 36\,(0.2 + 0.05) = 221 \text{ V at 1350 rpm}$$

$$\therefore \quad E_a \text{ at 1500 r.p.m.} = 221 \times \frac{1500}{1350} = 245.5 \text{ V.}$$

From Fig. 4.62, $E_a = 245.5$ V requires $I_f = 1.365$ A. From Eq. (4.27),

$$1.365 \times 2000 = 1.23 \times 2000 + N_s\,(36) - 120$$

$\therefore$ Series field turns, $N_s = \dfrac{65}{6} \cong 11$ turns per pole.

(*d*) If series field winding has 20 turns, then net field m.m.f. from Eq. (4.27) is

$$(1.23 \times 2000 + 20 \times 36 - 120) \text{ ATs.}$$

$\therefore$ The net field m.m.f. in terms of the equivalent shunt field amperes is

$$I_f = \frac{1.23 \times 2000 + 20 \times 36 - 120}{2000} = 1.23 + 0.36 - 0.06 = 153 \text{ A.}$$

From Fig. 4.62, the value of E_a corresponding to $I_f = 1.53$ A is 258 V at 1500 r.p.m. But counter e.m.f. E_a corresponding to rated voltage and rated current is 230 – 36 (0.2 + 0.05) = 221 volts. Therefore, the motor speed n corresponding to $E_a = 221$ V is

$$\frac{221}{258} = \frac{n}{1500} \quad \text{or} \quad n = \frac{221}{258} \times 1500 = 1285 \text{ r.p.m.}$$

(*e*) The net main field m.m.f. = 1.23 × 2000 + 20 × 50 – 200

$\therefore$ The net field m.m.f. in equivalent shunt field current is

$$I_f = \frac{1.23 \times 2000 + 20 \times 50 - 200}{2000} = 1.63 \text{ A.}$$

From Fig. 4.62, corresponding to 1.63 A field current, E_a at 1500 r.p.m. is 264 volts. But

$$E_a = K_a \phi \omega_m$$

$$\therefore \quad K_a\phi = \frac{264 \times 60}{2\pi \times 1500} = \frac{264}{50\pi}$$

$\therefore$ Starting torque, $T_{est} = K_a \phi I_a = \dfrac{264}{50\pi} \times 50 = 89$ Nm.

Example 4.37. *A 230 V, 250 rpm, 100 A separately-excited D.C. motor has an armature resistance of 0.5 Ω. The motor is connected to 230 V D.C. supply and rated D.C. voltage applied to the field winding. It is driving a load whose torque-speed characteristic is given by $T_L = 500 - 10\omega$, where ω is the rotational speed expressed in rad/sec and T_L is the load torque in Nm. Find the steady state speed at which the motor will drive the load and the armature current drawn by it from the source. Neglect the rotational losses of the machine.*

[GATE, 2002]

Solution. At rated load, motor counter e.m.f., $E_a = V_t - I_a r_a$

or $K_m \cdot \omega_r = 230 - 100 \times 0.5 = 180$ V

where ω_r = rated motor speed in rad/sec

$\therefore$ Motor constant, $K_m = \dfrac{180 \times 60}{2\pi \times 250}$ V-s/rad

Armature current at any speed ω is given by

$$I_a = \frac{V_t - E_a}{r_a} = \frac{230 - K_m \cdot \omega}{0.5} \quad ...(i)$$

$\therefore$ Motor torque, $T_e = K_m I_a = \dfrac{K_m}{0.5}[230 - K_m \cdot \omega]$

Under steady state, motor torque T_e = load torque, T_L

or $$\frac{K_m}{0.5}[230 - K_m \cdot \omega] = 500 - 10\omega$$

or $$\frac{230}{0.5} \times \frac{180 \times 60}{2\pi \times 250} - \frac{1}{0.5}\left(\frac{180 \times 60}{2\pi \times 250}\right)^2 \cdot \omega = 500 - 10\omega$$

or $$3162.73 - 94.545\omega = 500 - 10\omega$$

$$\omega = \frac{3162.73 - 500}{84.545} = 31.495 \text{ rad/sec}$$

$\therefore$ $$\text{Speed} = \frac{31.495 \times 60}{2\pi} = 300.75 \text{ rpm}$$

From Eq. (*i*), armature current is $I_a = \dfrac{1}{0.5}\left[230 - \dfrac{180 \times 60}{2\pi \times 250} \times 31.495\right] = 26.913$ A.

4.13. D.C. MOTOR STARTING

At the time of starting, the motor speed is zero, therefore, counter e.m.f. E_a (= $K_a \phi \omega_m$) is also zero. Consequently, for the armature circuit, the voltage equation is $V_t = 0 + I_a r_a$ for shunt motor and $V_t = 0 + I_a (r_a + r_s)$ for both series and compound motors. With rated applied voltage the starting armature current is, therefore, $\dfrac{V_t}{r_a}$ for shunt motor and $\dfrac{V_t}{r_s + r_a}$ for both series and compound motors. Since the resistance r_a and $(r_a + r_s)$ are much smaller, the motor draws large starting armature current from the supply mains. For example, a 10 kW, 250 V shunt motor may have armature circuit resistance equal to 0.2 Ω. If switched on directly, its starting armature current would be $\dfrac{250}{0.2}$ = 1250 A, whereas the rated armature current is only 40 A. Such heavy inrush of starting current taken by the motor may result in

(*i*) detrimental sparking at the commutator,

(*ii*) damage to the armature winding and deterioration of the insulation due to overheating,

(*iii*) high starting torque and quick acceleration—which may damage the rotating parts of the motor and the load connected to the motor shaft and

(*iv*) large dips in the supply voltage.

In view of this, the armature current must be limited to a value that can be commutated safely, by inserting a suitable external resistance in the armature circuit. As the motor accelerates, counter e.m.f. E_a is generated in the armature and this decreases the armature current to a small value. Thus the external resistance inserted in the armature circuit should be gradually decreased, as the armature accelerates. If this additional resistance inserted is left in the armature circuit, it would result in

(*i*) reduced operating speed of the motor than its normal speed and

(*ii*) additional energy loss and, therefore, reduced efficiency.

A precaution should be observed while starting shunt and compound motors. In these motors, at the time of starting the field excitation should be kept at maximum value, because of the two reasons given below :

(i) A large field current would result in low operating speed. Consequently the time required from standstill to this low speed is less and, therefore, there is less heating of the armature during starting.

(ii) Motor torque required to overcome the friction and load torque is proportional to the product of I_f and I_a. Since I_f is kept at its maximum permissible value, the armature current required during starting would be minimum for a given load torque. This minimum starting current would further result in improved commutation during motor and load acceleration. Thus the rheostat, in series with the shunt field winding, should be at zero resistance position at the time of starting the D.C. shunt and compound motors. In case of small D.C. motors, no starting resistance in the armature circuit may be required.

4.13.1. Shunt and Compound Motor Starters

The primary function of a starter is to *limit the starting current* in the armature circuit during starting and *accelerating time* of the motor. The simplest type of starter consists of a rheostat inserted in series with the armature circuit as shown in Fig. 4.63. The simple starter is however modified to include a few protective devices, such as overcurrent release, no-volt release etc. There are two standard types of starters for shunt and compound motors. These are, three-point starter and four-point starter. The four-point starter is used when wide range of speed by shunt field control is required. When no (or a little) speed control is required, either type of starter may be employed.

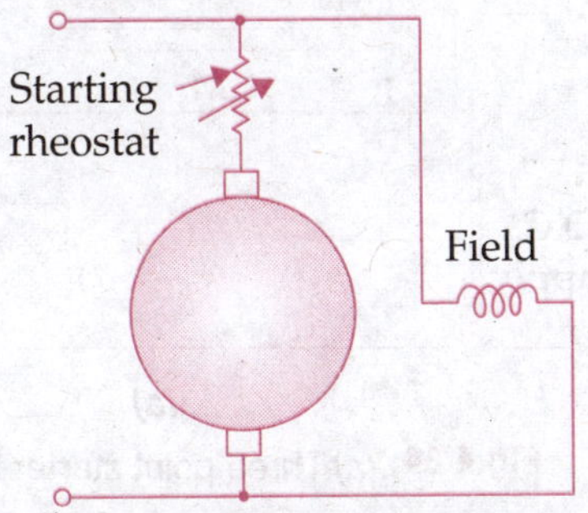

Fig 4.63: Starting rheostat in the armature circuit of a D.C. shunt motor.

Three-point Starter. A three-point starter, with its electrical connections and protective features is illustrated in Fig. 4.64 *(a)*, within the dotted lines. The starter is shown connected with the supply mains and dc shunt motor. Since only three terminals (*L, A, F*) are available from the starter, it is called **three-point starter**. The starter terminals *L* (line), *A* (armature) and *F* (field) must be connected respectively to the supply terminal (positive or negative), motor armature terminal (any of the two armature terminals) and shunt field terminal (any of the two field terminals). The starter handle *H* is fitted with spiral spring and a soft-iron keeper as shown in Fig. 4.64 *(a)*.

When the motor is at rest, starter handle *H* is kept in the off position by a strong spiral spring. One stud marked "OFF" in Fig. 4.64 *(a)* indicates that motor is disconnected from the dc supply. The starting resistance is connected between contact studs 1, 2, 3, 4, ... 6. For starting the motor, the handle is rotated to come in contact with stud 1. As soon as handle *H* touches stud 1, the shunt field and holding coil *HC* get connected in series across the supply, whereas the armature gets connected in series with the entire starting resistance. Since the current begins to flow in both the field and armature windings, the motor begins to rotate. After the armature has picked up sufficient speed, the handle *H* is moved to stud 2, thereby cutting out the resistance between studs 1 and 2. Movement of the handle is continued **slowly** till the soft-iron keeper touches the holding magnet *HC*. With the movement of handle *H*, as the starting resistance is cut out of the armature circuit, it gets inserted in the field winding circuit. In the final position, handle *H* is at stud ON. The entire starting resistance is cut out of the armature circuit but is put in series with field circuit. So now armature is directly connected to dc source. However, field winding, through *HC* and starting resistance gets connected to dc supply as shown in Fig. 4.64 *(a)*. With handle *H* at stud ON, a current flowing through *HC* produces electromagnetic force of attraction greater than the spring pull. As a result, handle *H* is held in ON stud by *HC*.

The holding magnet or holding coil *HC* is also called **no-volt release** or **low-voltage release** and has the following functions:

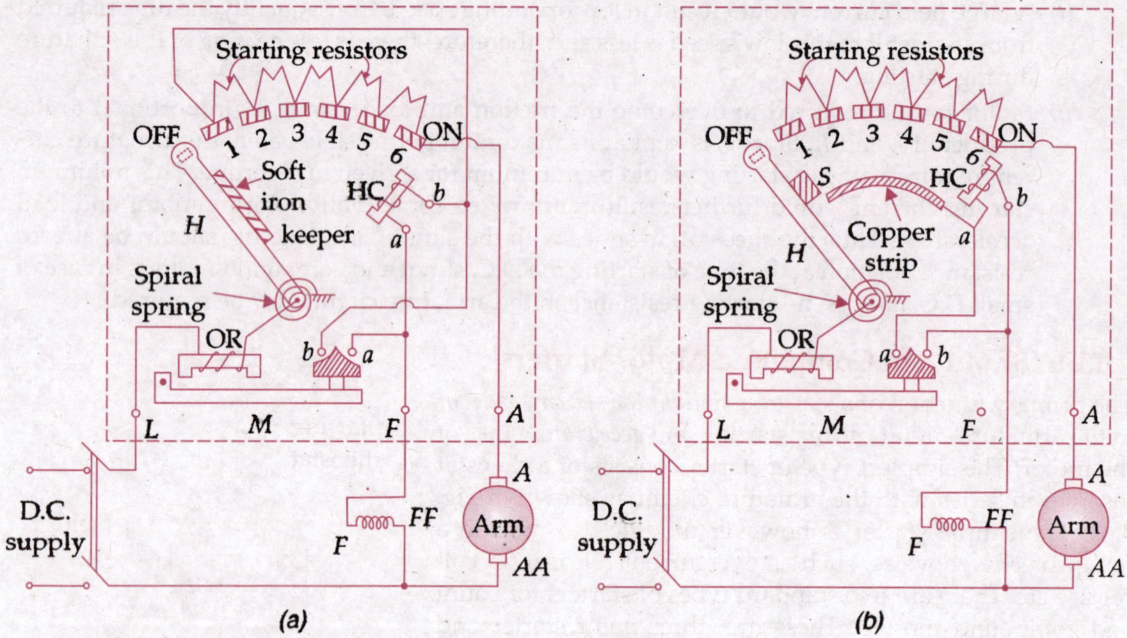

Fig 4.64: *(a)* Three-point starter for a dc shunt motor and *(b)* an alternative scheme of 3-point starter.

(i) In case of power failure, electromagnet *HC* gets demagnetized and the spiral spring brings the handle back to its OFF position. If, during the power failure, the handle fails to return to OFF position, the motor might be damaged in case the power is restored because then there would be no starting resistance in the armature circuit. The holding coil in association with spiral spring takes care of this danger automatically.

(ii) If the shunt field becomes open circuited accidentally, *HC* gets demagnetized and the starter handle is returned by spring pull to the OFF position. In case the stater handle is not released, the speed starts increasing with the decaying of field flux. The small residual flux will result in dangerously high speed. At the same time, for providing a given load torque ; the armature current starts increasing and in case the fuse or circuit breaker does not disconnect the motor from dc supply mains, the armature may get damaged. The holding coil in association with spiral spring takes care of this hazard automatically.

(iii) With this arrangement, the starting resistance in the armature circuit can either be zero or full. The handle cannot be left on any intermediate stud willingly or unwillingly.

An examination of Fig. 4.64 *(a)* reveals that under running conditions, the field winding, holding coil *HC* and the starting resistance are in series. Since the starting resistance is much smaller in comparison with shunt field resistance, its effect on the shunt field current is negligible. But the starting resistance does influence field circuit, at the time of switching off the dc motor. With the method of connection of Fig. 4.64 *(a)*, when the motor is disconnected from dc supply, field winding comes in series with holding coil, starting resistance and armature circuit with handle *H* still at stud ON. For very small time (a few seconds), handle *H* remains at ON stud. During this small time, most of the electromagnetic energy stored in field winding is discharged through this total resistance when magnetic force of holding coil *HC* decays, spring force pulls the handle *H* from ON position. As the handle *H* flies back (negligible time) from ON stud to stud 1, field winding remains closed through *HC* coil, starting resistance and armature circuit. Thus, there is no break in the field current and by the time, handle *H* reaches stud 1, field current decays to nearly zero value. As a result, when starter handle leaves stud 1, there is no danger of high voltage induced in the field winding and of any sparking at stud 1.

Another protective device *OR*, known as the **overload release** is a small magnet. This *OR* carries the total current drawn by motor. In case the load current exceeds a present value due to overload, *OR* becomes more strong magnet and attracts the movable soft iron *M* pivoted at one end. As the soft iron *M* is attracted, two terminals *a, b* of the no-volt release *HC* get short circuited. In this manner, *HC* gets demagnetized and the starter arm *H* is pulled back to OFF position by the spiral spring—the motor is thus automatically disconnected from the mains in case of overload. The motor current, at which the overload release *OR* should operate, can be adjusted merely by varying the distance between the electromagnet and the movable soft iron *M*.

An alternative scheme* of three-point starter is shown in Fig. 4.64 *(b)*. Here starting is carried out as in Fig 4.64 *(a)*. When handle *H* comes in contact with stud 1, field winding gets energized through copper strip and holding coil *HC*, whereas armature circuit is connected to dc supply through starting resistance. In the final position, handle *H* is at stud ON. *HC* produces electromagnetic force greater than the spring pull. As a results, handle *H* is held in ON position by *HC*. Now armature circuit is directly connected to dc supply as in Fig. 4.64 *(a)*. Field winding gets connected to D.C. supply through holding coil *HC*. Under running conditions, starting resistance is not in any of the two circuits.

For stopping the motor, dc supply is switched off. Now the field winding comes in series with *HC* and armature circuit with handle *H* at stud ON. During the very small time handle remains at stud ON *(i)* starting resistance plays no role *(ii)* as the total series resistance is lesser and most of the magnetic field energy stored has to be dissipated, it would take a little longer time as compared to that in the starter of Fig. 4.64 *(a)*.

When handle *H* begins to leave stud ON, starting resistance, step by step, comes in series with field circuit, *HC* coil and armature circuit. Therefore, during the period handle *H* flies back (negligible time), from stud ON to stud 1, field circuit is kept closed. Therefore, when handle *H* leaves stud 1, there is no danger of any hazardous sparking at stud 1.

From above, it may be stated as under.

(i) Both circuit diagrams for three-point starter are correct.

(ii) Fig. 4.64 *(b)* uses copper strip and Fig. 4.64 *(a)* uses a copper wire; therefore three-point starter of Fig. 4.64 *(b)* is relatively expensive.

(iii) In Fig. 4.64 *(a)*, effect of starting resistance is much smaller in comparison with field winding resistance, therefore its effect on shunt field current is insignificant.

(iv) During running conditions, there is [field current]^2 × starting resistance loss in Fig. 4.64*(a)*, but this is negligibly small.

Disadvantages. In case of a three-point starter, the field circuit and the hold coil are in series. If speeds above the normal are to be obtained, the field current must be reduced. At a certain value of reduced field current (therefore, increased motor speed), the electromagnetic pull of the holding coil may become less than the spring force. In such a case, the starter handle returns to the OFF position and the motor stops. Thus a three-point starter can't be used where wide range of speed control, by shunt field control (or field weakening method) is required. This undesirable feature can be overcome in four-point starters.

Four-point starter. As the name suggests, four terminals (*L, L, F, A*) are available from this starter. In Fig. 4.65, a four-point starter is shown connected to D.C. supply mains and a D.C. shunt motor. Under normal running conditions with starter handle in the ON position, the holding coil *HC* is in series with the starting resistance and an additional resistance *R* as shown in Fig. 4.65. The

* Feedback from a reader ; "giving dc supply to field winding through starting resistance, during running conditions, is not correct, Fig. 4.64 *(b)* is the correct figure."

function of resistance R is to prevent short circuit of the supply mains, in case the overload release OR operates. When HC gets short circuited by OR, the current through R is limited by its own resistance and the starting resistance.

The other components of the four-point starter are the same as in a three-point starter. The shunt field winding in series with the starting resistance, now permits wide speed control by field rheostat (not shown) inserted in the field circuit. Note that four-point starter permits the change of field current by field rheostat, without affecting the holding coil current. Therefore, the pull of the holding magnet is unaffected and remains more than the spring pull for any value of speed. In view of this, four-point starters are more popular with speed controlled motors. When little or no speed control is desired, either three- or four-point starter may be used.

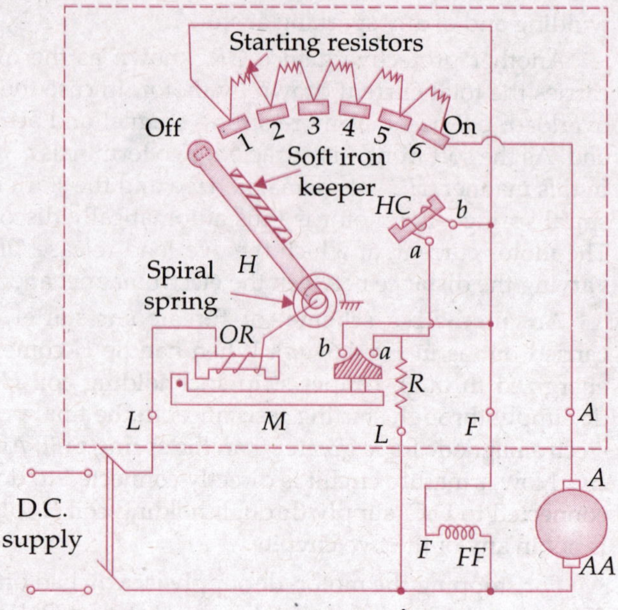

Fig 4.65: Four-point starter connected to a shunt motor.

4.13.2. Series Motor Starters

In series motors also, a starting resistance is inserted in series with the armature, for limiting the starting current to a safe value. As usual, this starting resistance is cut out gradually as the motor accelerates. Fig.4.66 *(a)* illustrates a series motor starter used in applications, where the removal of load is remote. Holding coil in series with protective resistance R, acts as no-volt release, like the no-volt release of three-point or four-point starter. In view of this, starter of Fig. 4.66 *(a)* is referred to as the *no-volt release type of starter*.

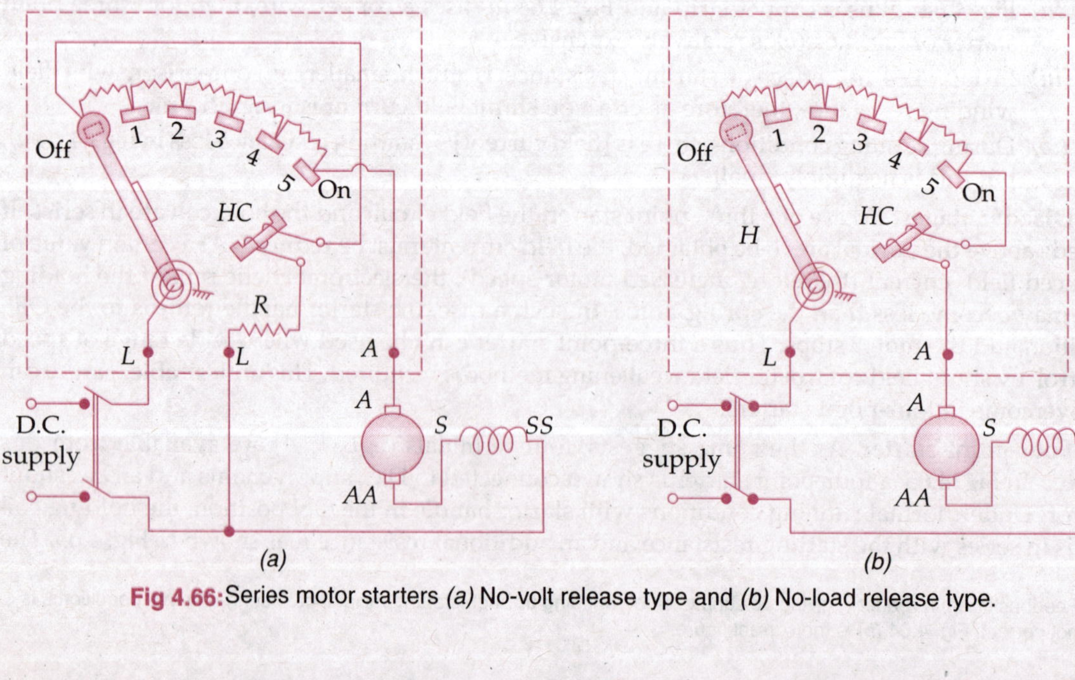

Fig 4.66: Series motor starters *(a)* No-volt release type and *(b)* No-load release type.

In case there is a possibility of removal of or reduction in load, starter illustrated in Fig. 4.66 *(b)* may be used. In this, the load current passes through the series field, armature and holding coil. The holding coil consists of a few turns which are capable of carrying the load current. In case of removal of load or reduction in load below a safe value, the line current flowing through the holding coil is reduced. This reduced value of current decreases the strength of the holding magnet and the spring pull brings the starter handle to off position. This type of starter is, therefore, referred to as the *no-load release type of starter*.

Note. A D.C. motor should not be stopped by forcing the starter handle to the off position. If it is done, then dangerous sparking is caused at stud 1, because here the field circuit is broken and the entire stored magnetic field energy is dissipated in the form of heavy spark.

Automatic Starters. Push-button type of automatic starters are used quite often in industry. Even an inexperienced operator, with the help of auto-starters, can start and stop the motor without any difficulty.

The operation of these automatic starters depends upon, either the time delay or the counter e.m.f. developed across the armature terminals. Here only the basic principles of the counter e.m.f., automatic starter are presented.

Counter e.m.f. starter. When the motor is switched on, the counter e.m.f. developed across the armature terminals is zero. Contractors* 1 *A* and 1 *B* are normally open and, therefore, starting resistances R_1 and R_2 are in series with the armature at the time of starting. As the motor accelerates, the counter e.m.f. increases. When counter e.m.f. becomes equal to the operating voltage of the voltage-sensitive relay *A*, it operates and closes the normally open contact 1 *A*, thus cutting out the starting resistance R_1. With the motor speed still rising, the counter e.m.f. increases till the operating voltage of voltage-sensitive relay *B* is reached. At this instant, relay B operates and it closes the normally open contact 1 *B*. Consequently the starting resistor R_2 is cut out and the armature gets connected directly across the supply mains as shown in Fig. 4.67.

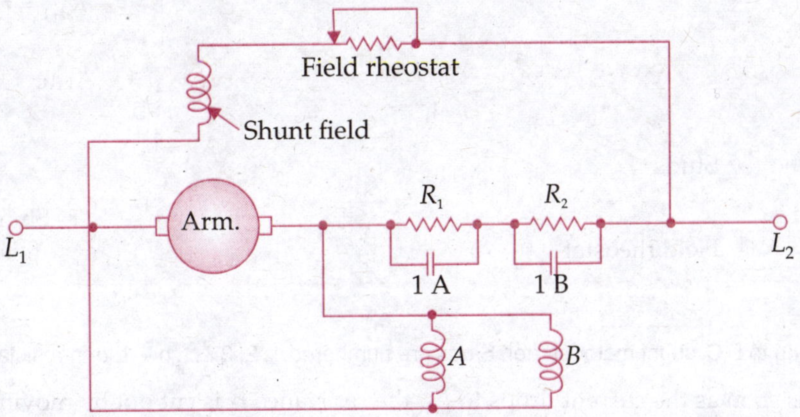

Fig 4.67: Counter e.m.f. automatic starter connected to D.C. shunt motor.

The disadvantage of counter e.m.f. automatic starter is that if the motor fails to start, the counter e.m.f. remains zero, the voltage-sensitive relays can't operate and as a result of it, the starting resistance may burn. Such occurrences can be avoided by employing definite time-limit starters but this will not be described here.

D.C. Shunt motor starter design. Starting resistances between the various studs of a shunt motor starter, should be graded and not made equal. This grading of starting resistances is essential in order to avoid the abnormal rush of armature current on the last few steps, particularly on the last stud.

* A contactor is heavy duty relay designed to open or close an electrical power circuit.

During the starting process, as the starting resistance elements are cut out manually or automatically, the maximum armature current I_{a1} should be such that it can be commutated satisfactorily by the brushes and commutator. At the same time, the minimum armature current I_{a2} should be able to develop electromagnetic torque T_e sufficient to accelerate the load torque T_L. In other words, the armature current during starting process is taken to fluctuate between fixed limits I_{a1} (maximum) and I_{a2} (minimum). The armature reaction and the armature inductance are neglected during the motor starter design.

Fig. 4.68 illustrates a D.C. shunt motor with n resistance elements or $(n + 1)$ studs. Therefore, this starter is called n-section, n-element, n-step or $(n + 1)$ stud starter. The "off" stud has not been included in $n + 1$ studs. Note that resistance $R_1 = r_1 + r_2 + r_3 + ... + r_n + r_a$; $R_2 = r_2 + r_3 + ... + r_n + r_a$ and so on and $R_{n+1} = r_a$, armature circuit resistance (including brushes).

At the instant the motor is switched on, the total armature circuit resistance R_1 should be equal to

$$R_1 = \frac{\text{Terminal voltage}}{\text{Maximum permissible armature current}} = \frac{V_t}{I_{a1}} = r_1 + r_2 + r_3 + ... + r_n + r_a \qquad ...(4.46)$$

With the handle on stud 1, the motor accelerates, counter e.m.f. develops and as a result of it, the armature current starts decreasing from I_{a1}. When the current has dropped to minimum current I_{a2}, then the counter e.m.f., with the handle on stud 1, is given by,

$$E_{a1} = V_t - I_{a2}R_1 \quad \text{or} \quad R_1 = \frac{V_t - E_{a1}}{I_{a2}} \qquad ...(4.47)$$

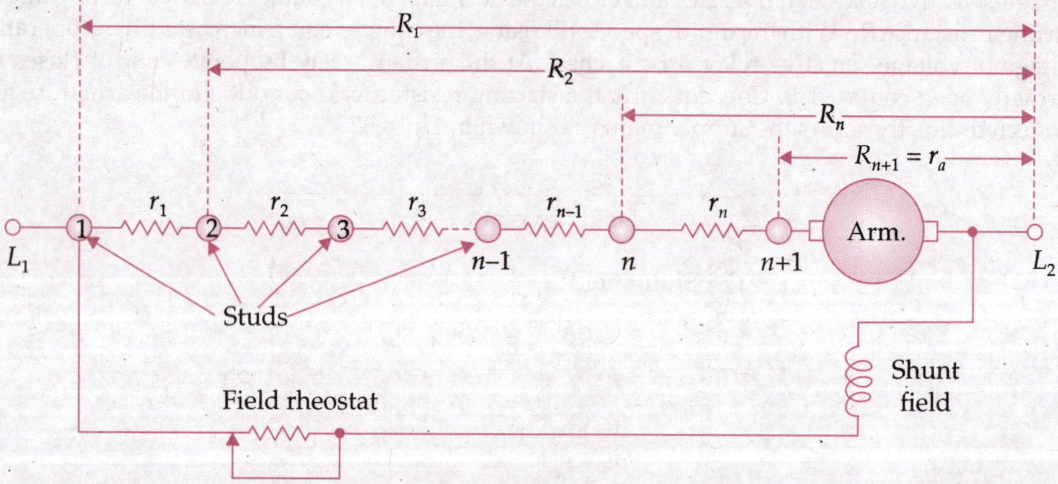

Fig 4.68: Pertaining to D.C. shunt motor starter. Studs are numbered 1, 2, 3 ...... n + 1 for n resistance elements.

At stud 1, as soon as the current drops to I_{a2}, the resistance r_1 is cut out by moving the handle to stud 2. During the *notching-up process* (process of cutting out a resistance) from stud 1 to stud 2, the speed and, therefore E_{a1} ($\propto \omega_m \phi$) do not change. At stud 2, just after r_1 is cut out, the current shoots up again to I_{a1}. Therefore,

$$R_2 = \frac{V_t - E_{a1}}{I_{a1}} = r_2 + r_3 + ... + r_n + r_a \qquad ...(4.48)$$

From Eqs. (4.47) and (4.48),

$$\frac{R_2}{R_1} = \frac{I_{a2}}{I_{a1}} = \frac{\text{Minimum armature current}}{\text{Maximum armature current}}$$

otor starter can be carried out as under :

(*i*) Compute R_1 from Eq. (4.46).

(ii) From Eq. (4.50), compute the number of steps n choosing the nearest whole number.

(iii) Now use Eq. (4.54) for computing the magnitude of various resistance elements r_1, r_2, etc.

The design of D.C. series-motor starter, being somewhat more involved, is not dealt within this book.

Example 4.38. *In a 230 V, 10 kW D.C. shunt motor, it is required that the starting armature current should not exceed twice its rated armature current. During the starting of the motor, the starting resistance is cut out in steps, as soon as the armature current drops to its rated value. The field resistance is 115 Ω and the total armature circuit resistance is 0.348 Ω. Neglect armature inductance.*

(a) Find the external resistance required at the time of starting the motor.

(b) Determine the value of the first resistance element that must be cut out, when the armature current drops to rated value.

(c) Find the external resistance to be cut out in the second step.

(d) Find the total number of steps required and their resistance values.

Solution. Constant shunt field current $= \dfrac{230}{115} = 2$ A.

$$\text{Rated armature current} = \frac{10{,}000}{230} - 2 = 41.4 \text{ A.}$$

(a) External resistance required at the time of starting

$$= r_1 + r_2 + \ldots + r_n = \frac{V_t}{2 \times 41.4} - r_a$$

$$= \frac{230}{2 \times 41.4} - 0.348 = 2.432\ \Omega.$$

(b) When the armature current drops to rated current, at stud 1, then the counter e.m.f. is

$$E_{a1} = V_t - 41.4 \text{ (external resistance at stud 1} + r_a)$$

$$= 230 - 41.4\,(2.432 + 0.348) = 114.9 \text{ V.}$$

At the instant the handle is moved to stud 2, armature current shoots up to 2 (41.4) A, but the counter e.m.f. remains at 114.9 volts.

Therefore, at the second stud, $r_2 + r_3 + \ldots + r_n + r_a = \dfrac{V_t - E_{a1}}{2 \times 41.4} = \dfrac{230 - 114.9}{82.8} = 1.39\ \Omega.$

∴ External resistance $r_2 + r_3 + \ldots + r_n = 1.39 - r_a = 1.042\ \Omega.$

∴ The resistance that must be cut out in first step is $r_1 = 2.432 - 1.042 = 1.39\ \Omega.$

(c) At second stud, when armature current drops to rated current, then counter e.m.f. E_{a2} is

$$E_{a2} = V_t - 41.4\,(r_2 + r_3 + \ldots + r_n + r_a)$$

$$= 230 - 41.4\,(1.39) = 172.4 \text{ V.}$$

When the handle is moved to third stud, E_{a2} remains at 172.4 V, but armature current becomes 82.8 A.

$$\therefore \quad r_3 + \ldots + r_n + r_a = \frac{V_t - E_{a2}}{2 \times 41.4} = \frac{230 - 172.4}{82.8} = 0.695\ \Omega$$

∴ The resistance that must be cut out in second step is

$$r_2 = 1.39 - 0.695 = 0.695\ \Omega$$

(d) At third stud, when armature current falls to 41.4 A, then

$$E_{a3} = V_t - 41.4\,(r_3 + \ldots + r_n + r_a)$$

$$= 230 - 41.4\,(0.695) = 201.15 \text{ V}$$

When the handle is moved to 4th stud, then

$$r_4 + \ldots + r_n + r_a = \frac{V_t - E_{a3}}{2 \times 41.4} = \frac{28.85}{82.8} = 0.348\ \Omega. = r_a$$

Therefore, when the handle is moved to fourth stud, the armature resistance $r_a = 0.348\ \Omega$, is sufficient to limit the current to 82.8 A.

Since there are four studs, three resistance elements are required.

The resistance of the third elements is $= 0.695 - r_a = 0.347\ \Omega$.

Thus the resistance of the three steps or elements r_1, r_2, r_3 are respectively 1.39 Ω, 0.695 Ω, 0.347 Ω.

Example 4.39. *A 240 V, 50 A, 1500 r.p.m. D.C. shunt motor has an armature resistance of 0.2 Ω. For this example, shunt field current is neglected.*

(a) For a four step starter (four resistance elements and five studs), calculate the values of the various steps, with armature current not exceeding 1.40 p.u.

(b) If counter e.m.f. starter is employed, find the voltages at which the contractors should close.

(c) Sketch the approximate variations of armature current and speed, during the accelerating process of the motor.

Solution. Base voltage $V_t = 240 \text{ V} = 1 \text{ p.u}$

Base armature current $I_a = 50 \text{ A} = 1 \text{ p.u}$

Base resistance $R_b = \dfrac{\text{Base voltage}}{\text{Base current}} = \dfrac{240}{50} = 4.80\ \Omega.$

∴ Per unit armature resistance $R_a = \dfrac{0.2}{4.80} = 0.0417.$

(a) At the instant the motor is switched on, the total resistance R_1, in the armature circuit should be given by $R_1 = \dfrac{V_t}{I_{a1}} = \dfrac{1}{1.4} = 0.714$ p.u. or $0.714 \times 4.80 = 3.43\ \Omega$.

From Eq. (4.50) ; $\alpha = \left(\dfrac{r_a}{R_1}\right)^{1/n} = \left(\dfrac{0.0417}{0.714}\right)^{1/4} = 0.492.$

From Eq. (4.51) ; $r_1 = R_1 (1 - \alpha) = 0.714 (0.508) = 0.363$ p.u. or 1.742 Ω.

From Eq. (4.52) ; $r_2 = \alpha\, r_1 = 0.492 (0.363) = 0.1788$ p.u. or 0.858 Ω.

Similarly $r_3 = \alpha\, r_2 = 0.492 (0.1788) = 0.089$ p.u. or 0.427 Ω.

and $r_4 = \alpha\, r_3 = 0.492 (0.089) = 0.0438$ p.u. or 0.210 Ω.

(b) $\alpha = \dfrac{I_{min}}{I_{max}} = \dfrac{I_{a2}}{I_{a1}} = 0.492$

∴ $I_{a2} = 0.492 \times 1.4 = 0.689$ p.u. or $I_{a2} = 34.45$ A.

Let the time be reckoned from the instant the motor is switched on. At stud 1, suppose the armature current drops to $I_{a2} = 0.689$ p.u. after time t_1. Then the counter e.m.f. at t_1 is

$$E_{a1} = V_t - I_{a2} R_1 = 1 - 0.689 \times 0.714 = 0.508 \text{ p.u.}$$

∴ Voltage across the armature terminals at instant t_1 is

$$V_{at1} = E_{a1} + I_{a2}\, r_a = 0.508 + 0.689 \times 0.0417$$
$$= 0.537 \text{ p.u. or } 129.00 \text{ volts.}$$

Therefore, the first contactor should close at 129 volts.

At stud 2, suppose the current falls to I_{a2} after time t_2, then the counter e.m.f. is

$$E_{a2} = V_t - I_{a2} R_2 = V_t - I_{a2} (R_1 - r_1)$$
$$= 1.00 - 0.689 (0.714 - 0.363) = 0.758 \text{ p.u.}$$

∴ $$V_{at2} = E_{a2} + I_{a2}\, r_a = 0.758 + 0.02870$$
$$= 0.787 \text{ p.u. or } 187.2 \text{ volts.}$$

At stud 3, when the current reduces to I_{a2} after time t_3, the counter e.m.f. is

$$E_{a3} = V_t - I_{a2} R_3 = V_t - I_{a2} (R_2 - r_2)$$
$$= 1.00 - 0.689 (0.351 - 0.179) = 0.881$$

$\therefore$ $$V_{at3} = E_{a3} + I_{a2} r_a = 0.881 + 0.02870 = 0.91 \text{ or } 218.5 \text{ volts.}$$

Similarly at stud 4, $$E_{a4} = V_t - I_{a2} R_4 = V_t - I_{a2} (R_3 - r_3)$$
$$= 1.00 - 0.689 (1.172 - 0.089) = 0.9428$$

and $$V_{at4} = E_{a4} + I_{a2} r_a = 0.972 \text{ p.u. or } 233 \text{ volts.}$$

Finally, with the motor running at full load,

$$E_a = V_t - I_a r_a = 1 - 1.0 \times 0.0417 = 0.958 \text{ p.u.}$$

Thus the contactors, say 1*A*, 1*B*, 1*C* and 1*D*, should close at 129, 187.2, 218.5 and 233 volts respectively.

(*c*) At full load, counter e.m.f. $E_a = 0.958$ p.u. corresponds to rated speed of 1500 r.p.m.

Now $$E_a = K_a \phi \omega_m$$

But $$n = 1500 \text{ r.p.m.} = 1 \text{ p.u.}$$

$\therefore$ $$0.958 \propto K_a \phi \cdot 1$$

At time t_1, $$E_{a1} \propto K_a \phi n_1$$

$\therefore$ $$n_1 = \frac{E_{a1}}{E_a} = \frac{0.508}{0.958} = 0.531 \text{ p.u.} = 796 \text{ r.p.m.}$$

Similarly $$n_2 = \frac{0.758}{0.958} = 0.792 \text{ p.u.} = 1189 \text{ r.p.m.}$$

$$n_3 = \frac{0.881}{0.958} = 0.92 \text{ p.u.} = 1380 \text{ r.p.m.}$$

and $$n_4 = \frac{0.9428}{0.958} = 0.984 \text{ p.u.} = 1477 \text{ r.p.m.}$$

Approximate shapes of armature current (and electromagnetic torque also, because $T_e \propto I_a$ for constant flux motor) and speed, with respect to time are shown in Fig. 4.69.

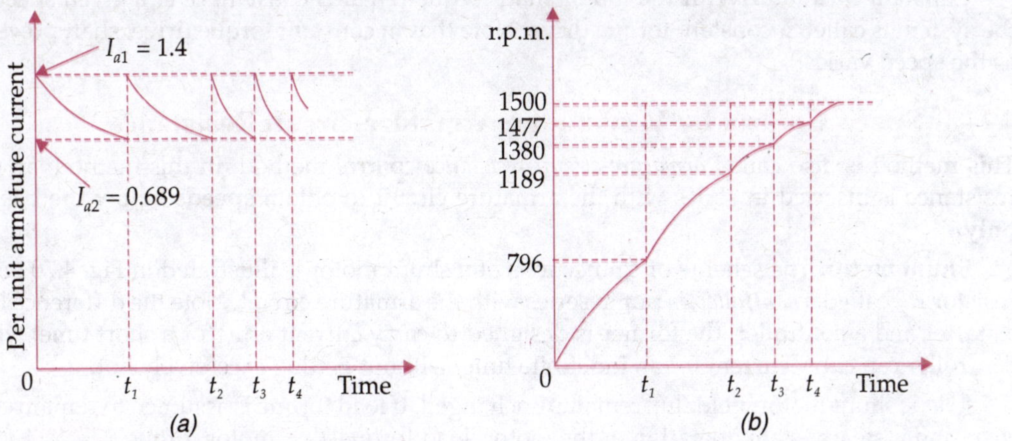

Fig 4.69: Variation of *(a)* armature current and *(b)* speed; with respect to the starting time of a D.C. shunt motor of Example 4.36.

4.14. SPEED CONTROL OF D.C. MOTORS

The term 'speed control' stands for intentional speed variation, carried out manually or automatically. Natural speed change due to load, is not included in the term 'speed control'.

D.C. motors are most suitable for wide range speed control and are, therefore, indispensable for many adjustable speed drives.

The speed of a D.C. motor is given by Eq. (4.34) and it is re-written here for convenience, *i.e.*,

$$\omega_m = \frac{V_t - I_a r_a}{K_a \phi} \qquad ...(4.34)$$

where armature constant $K_a = \frac{PZ}{2\pi a}$ and ϕ is the field flux per pole.

It follows from Eq. (4.34) that for a D.C. motor, there are basically three methods of speed control and these are :

(i) Variation of resistance in the armature circuit,

(ii) Variation of the field flux, and

(iii) Variation of the armature terminal voltage.

Before describing these methods, it is preferable to define the terms base speed, speed regulation, speed range, constant power drive and constant torque drive.

Base speed. It is defined as the speed at which a motor runs at rated armature voltage and rated field current. Base speed is equal to the rated speed or nameplate speed of the motor.

Speed regulation. If the speed-change from full-load to no-load is $\Delta\omega_m$, then speed regulation is defined as the ratio of $\Delta\omega_m$ to rated speed (or base speed) ω_m.

$$\therefore \quad \text{Per cent speed regulation} = \frac{\Delta\omega_m}{\omega_m} \times 100 \qquad ...(4.57)$$

Speed range. It is defined as the ratio of the maximum allowable speed to minimum allowable speed of the motor. When the speed range of a motor is specified, it must be mentioned whether this speed range is at no-load, full load or a fraction of full load.

Constant power drive. If the motor shaft power (shaft torque × speed) remains constant over a given speed range, the system is called a constant power drive. Note that in constant power drive, higher torques are available at lower speeds and lower torques at higher speeds. The motor size is always decided by the highest torque requirement at the lowest speed.

Constant torque drive. If the motor shaft torque remains constant over a given speed range, the system is called a constant torque drive. Note that in constant torque drive, shaft power varies as the speed varies.

4.14.1. Speed Control by Varying the Armature-circuit Resistance

This method is also called *armature-circuit-resistance* control method. In this method, an external resistance is inserted in series with the armature circuit to obtain **speeds below the base speed only**.

Shunt motor. The scheme of connections of a shunt motor is illustrated in Fig. 4.70 *(a)*, where resistor R_g, called a *controller*, is put in series with the armature circuit. Note the difference between a starter and a controller, the former is designed to carry current only for a short time, whereas a controller can carry current for an indefinite time, without getting excessively hot.

In a dc shunt motor, field flux remains unchanged. If load torque is assumed to remain constant, then under steady-state operation of the motor, load torque T_L = motor torque $T_e = K_a \phi I_a$. As the flux in shunt motor is substantially constant, value of armature current I_a = (constant torque)/(K_a × constant flux) would remain constant.

From Eq. (4.34),

$$\omega_{m1} = \frac{V_t - I_a r_a}{K_a \phi} = \frac{E_{a1}}{K_a \phi}$$

When external resistance R_g is inserted in the armature circuit, armature current remains constant and Eq. (4.34) gives new speed ω_{m2} as

$$\omega_{m2} = \frac{V_t - I_a(r_a + R_g)}{K_a\phi} = \frac{E_{a2}}{K_a\phi}$$

From above, we get

$$\frac{\omega_{m2}}{\omega_{m1}} = \frac{n_2}{n_1} = \frac{V_t - I_a(r_a + R_g)}{V_t - I_a r_a} \quad ...(4.58)$$

It is seen from Eq. (4.58) that $n_2 < n_1$.

With the insertion of external resistance R_g in armature circuit, back emf $E_{a2} = [V_t - I_a (r_a + R_g)]$ is reduced. But $E_{a2} = K_a \phi \omega_m$. With constant excitation, reduction in back emf E_{a2} is possible only through reduction in motor speed ω_m. This shows that insertion of external resistance in the armature circuit results in decreased motor speed. Thus, by armature circuit resistance, speed can be controlled below base speed only.

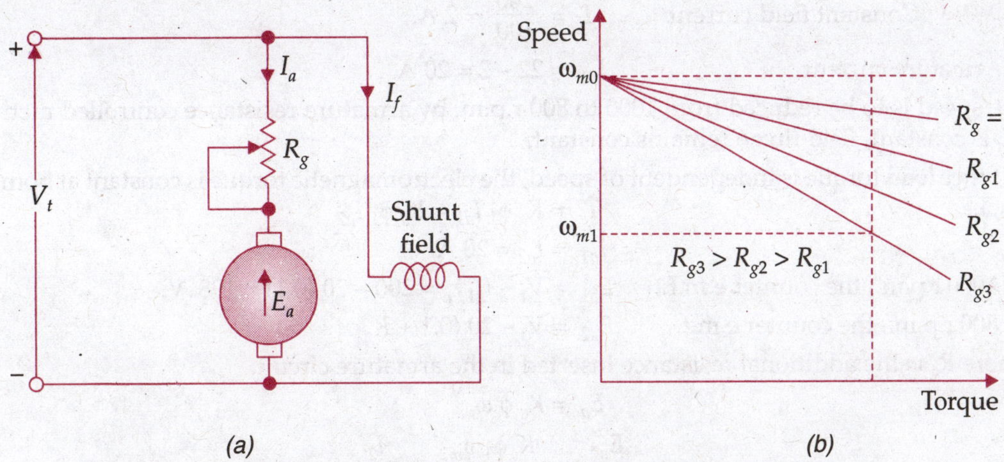

Fig 4.70: Shunt motor speed control by varying the armature circuit resistance *(a)* Schematic circuit diagram and *(b)* speed-torque characteristics.

Thus, for this type of speed control and with a constant load torque, it can be concluded as follows :

(a) The armature current drawn from the supply remains constant. Also the power delivered from the supply mains to the motor does not change and remains constant at $P_1 = V_t I_a$, whether R_g is in the armature circuit or not.

(b) Power delivered to load is $P_2 = E_{a2} I_a = [V_t - I_a (r_a + R_g)] I_a$ or P_2 = (constant load torque) × ω_m. It is thus seen that the power P_2 delivered to load decreases in proportion to the decrease in speed.

The efficiency of this method of speed control is

$$\eta = \frac{P_2}{P_1} = \frac{[V_t - I_a(r_a + R_g)I_a]}{V_t I_a} = \left[1 - \frac{R_a + R_g}{V_t} I_a\right]$$

If R_g is increased to obtain lower operating speeds, the motor efficiency is lowered and this results in higher operational costs.

The disadvantages of this method are : *(i)* lower efficiency and higher operational costs at reduced speeds as proved above and *(ii)* poor speed regulation with fixed controller resistance R_g in the armature circuit. For example, for a controller resistance equal to R_{g3} the speed is ω_{m1} at a certain load torque and for the same R_{g3}, the speed becomes almost ω_{m0} at no load as shown in Fig. 4.70 *(b)*.

The principal advantage of this method is that speeds below base speed down to creeping speeds of only a few r.p.m., are easily obtainable. But, because of considerable waste of energy at reduced speeds ; this method is economically viable where only short time or intermittent slow downs are required.

Example 4.40. *A 200 V D.C. shunt motor takes 22 amperes at rated voltage and runs at 1000 rpm. Its field resistance is 100 Ω and armature circuit resistance (including brushes) is 0.1 Ω. Compute the value of additional resistance required in the armature circuit to reduce the speed to 800 rpm; when*

(a) the load torque is independent of speed (as in a reciprocating pump),

(b) the load torque is proportional to speed,

(c) the load torque varies as the square of the speed (as in a fan-type load),

(d) the load torque increases as the cube of the speed.

Solution. Constant field current $I_f = \dfrac{200}{100} = 2\text{ A}.$

∴ Armature current $I_{a1} = 22 - 2 = 20\text{ A}.$

The speed is to be reduced from 1000 to 800 r.p.m. by armature resistance controlled method. Since I_f is constant, field flux ϕ remains constant.

(a) Since load torque is independent of speed, the electromagnetic torque is constant at both the speeds, *i.e.,* $T_e = K_a \phi_1 I_{a1} = K_a \phi_1 I_{a2}$

or $I_{a1} = I_{a2} = 20\text{ A}.$

At 1000 r.p.m., the counter e.m.f., $E_{a1} = V_t - I_{a1} r_a = 200 - 20\,(0.1) = 198.\text{ V}.$

At 800 r.p.m., the counter e.m.f. $E_{a2} = V_t - 20\,(0.1 + R_g)$

where R_g is the additional resistance inserted in the armature circuit.

Now $E_a = K_a \phi\, \omega_m$

$$\therefore \quad \frac{E_{a2}}{E_{a1}} = \frac{K_a \phi_1 \omega_{m2}}{K_a \phi_1 \omega_{m1}} = \frac{n_2}{n_1}$$

$$\text{or} \quad \frac{200 - 20\,(0.1 + R_g)}{198} = \frac{800}{1000}$$

Its solution gives $R_g = 1.98\ \Omega$

Loss in $R_g = (20)^2\,(1.98) = 792$ watts.

(b) Here load torque $T_L \propto$ speed n.

But electromagnetic torque, $T_e = K_a \phi I_a.$

Under steady state, $T_e = T_L$

i.e. $K_a\phi_1 I_{a1} \propto n_1$ and $K_a\phi_1 I_{a2} \propto n_2$

$$\text{or} \quad \frac{I_{a2}}{I_{a1}} = \frac{n_2}{n_1} \quad \text{or} \quad I_{a2} = 20\left(\frac{800}{1000}\right) = 16\text{ A}.$$

Now $E_{a2} = 200 - 16\,(0.1 + R_g)$ and $E_{a1} = 198$ V.

$$\therefore \quad \frac{E_{a2}}{E_{a1}} = \frac{200 - 16\,(0.1 + R_g)}{198} = \frac{800}{1000}$$

Its solution gives $R_g = 2.5\ \Omega.$

Loss in $R_g = (16)^2 \cdot (2.5) = 640$ watts.

(c) Here load torque $T_L \propto (\text{speed})^2$

Now as in part *(b)*, $K_a\phi_1 I_{a1} \propto n_1^2$

and $$K_a\phi_1 I_{a2} \propto n_2^2 \text{ or } \frac{I_{a2}}{I_{a1}} = \left(\frac{n_2}{n_1}\right)^2$$

∴ $$I_{a2} = (20)\left(\frac{800}{1000}\right)^2 = 12.8 \text{ A.}$$

Now $$E_{a2} = 200 - 12.8\,(0.1 + R_g)$$

Thus $$\frac{E_{a2}}{E_{a1}} = \frac{200 - 12.8\,(0.1 + R_g)}{198} = \frac{800}{1000}$$

Its solution gives $R_g = 3.15\ \Omega$.

Loss in $R_g = (12.8)^2\,(3.15) = 517$ watts.

(*d*) Here load torque ∝ (speed)^3

As in part (*b*) ; $$K_a\phi_1 I_{a1} \propto (n_1)^3$$

and $$K_a\phi_1 I_{a2} \propto (n_2)^3 \quad \text{or} \quad I_{a2} = (20)\left(\frac{800}{1000}\right)^3 = 10.24 \text{ A.}$$

∴ $$\frac{E_{a2}}{E_{a1}} = \frac{200 - 10.24\,(0.1 + R_g)}{198} = \frac{800}{1000}.$$

Its solution gives $R_g = 3.96\ \Omega$.

Loss in $R_g = (10.24)^2\,(3.96) = 415$ watts.

This example illustrates that if the armature resistance control method is employed for loads whose torque requirement varies as the square or cube of the speed, the loss in R_g is reduced considerably, resulting in higher operating efficiency at reduced speeds. Even then it can't be stated whether this method is economical enough for such type of loads, if reduced speeds for longer periods are required.

Example 4.41. *A 240 V, 50 A, 800 rpm D.C. shunt motor has armature circuit resistance of 0.2 Ω. If load torque is reduced to 60% of its full-load value and a resistance of 2 Ω is inserted in series with armature circuit, find the motor speed. Armature reaction weakens the field flux by 4% at full load and by 2% at 60% of full load.*

Solution. At rated load, $$E_{a1} = V_t - I_{a1} r_a = 240 - 50 \times 0.2 = 230 \text{ V}$$

Also $$E_{a1} \propto N_1\,\phi_1$$

Rated torque $$T_{L1} = K_a\,\phi_1\,I_{a1} = K_a\,\phi_1 \times 50$$

New torque $$T_{L2} = 0.6\,T_{L1} = K_a\,\phi_2\,I_{a2}$$

It is given that $\phi_1 = 0.96\phi$ and $\phi_2 = 0.98\,\phi$ where ϕ is the main field flux at no-load.

∴ $$\frac{T_{L1}}{T_{L2}} = \frac{T_{L1}}{0.6\,T_{L1}} = \frac{1}{0.6} = \frac{K_a \times 0.96\phi \times 50}{K_a \times 0.98\phi \times I_{a2}}$$

∴ $$I_{a2} = 50 \times 0.6 \times \frac{0.96}{0.98} = 29.39 \text{ A}$$

New counter e.m.f., $$E_{a2} = 240 - 29.39\,(2 + 0.2) = 175.342 \text{ V}$$

∴ $$\frac{E_{a1}}{E_{a2}} = \frac{N_1\phi_1}{N_2\phi_2} \text{ or } \frac{230}{175.342} = \frac{800 \times 0.96\phi}{N_2 \times 0.98\phi}$$

∴ Motor speed, $$N_2 = \frac{800 \times 175.342 \times 0.96}{230 \times 0.98} = 597.44 \text{ r.p.m.}$$

Series motor. In case of series motor, if wide range of speed control is required, it is usually carried out by this method.

Fig. 4.71 *(a)* illustrates the schematic diagram of a D.C. series motor for its speed control by varying the armature circuit resistance.

Before the introduction of resistor R_g, $V_t = k_a\phi\omega_{m1} + I_{a1}(r_a + r_s)$

If saturation is neglected, then field flux is proportional to the armature current.

Let $\phi = CI_a$ so that $\phi_1 = CI_{a1}$

$$\therefore \quad V_t = [k_a C\omega_{m1} + (r_a + r_s)]\, I_{a1} = [k\omega_{m1} + (r_a + r_s)]I_{a1}$$

where $k = k_a C$

$$\therefore \quad \omega_{m1} = \frac{V_t - I_{a1}(r_a + r_s)}{kI_{a1}} \quad \text{...}(i)$$

After the resistor R_g is inserted in series with the armature circuit as shown in Fig. 4.71 *(a)*,

$$V_t = [k_a C\omega_{m2} + (r_a + r_s + R_g)]I_{a2}$$

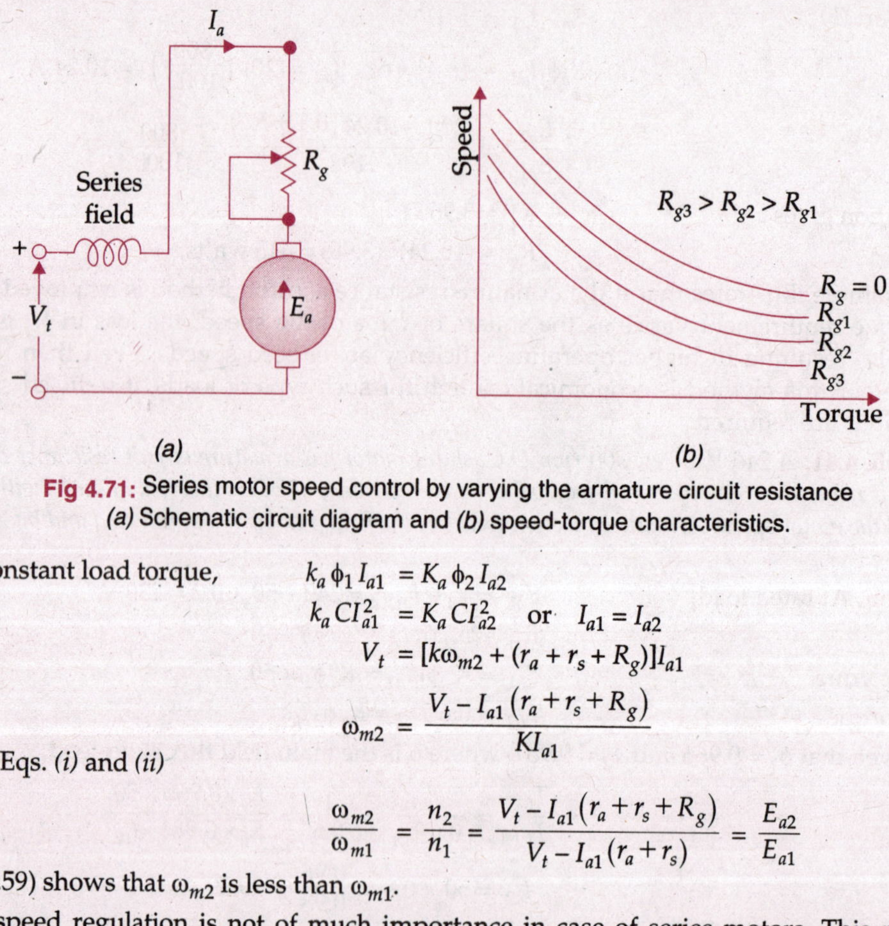

Fig 4.71: Series motor speed control by varying the armature circuit resistance *(a)* Schematic circuit diagram and *(b)* speed-torque characteristics.

For constant load torque, $\quad k_a \phi_1 I_{a1} = K_a \phi_2 I_{a2}$

or $\quad k_a CI_{a1}^2 = K_a CI_{a2}^2 \quad$ or $\quad I_{a1} = I_{a2}$

$$\therefore \quad V_t = [k\omega_{m2} + (r_a + r_s + R_g)]I_{a1}$$

and

$$\omega_{m2} = \frac{V_t - I_{a1}(r_a + r_s + R_g)}{KI_{a1}} \quad \text{...}(ii)$$

From Eqs. *(i)* and *(ii)*

$$\therefore \quad \frac{\omega_{m2}}{\omega_{m1}} = \frac{n_2}{n_1} = \frac{V_t - I_{a1}(r_a + r_s + R_g)}{V_t - I_{a1}(r_a + r_s)} = \frac{E_{a2}}{E_{a1}} \quad \text{...}(4.59)$$

Eq. (4.59) shows that ω_{m2} is less than ω_{m1}.

Poor speed regulation is not of much importance in case of series motors. This method of speed control is employed chiefly for series motors driving cranes, hoists, trains etc. The resistors employed for limiting the armature starting current, may be used for speed control purposes also.

In order to fully utilise the motor capacity at all speeds, the armature current is kept equal to the allowable armature current, *i.e.*, the rated armature current. For shunt motor, the field flux is obviously constant. For series motor, the field flux is also constant, because it is produced by armature current which is maintained equal to its rated value. Since field flux remains constant in both types of motors, armature-current-resistance control method is usually referred to as a *constant torque* [(constant field flux) (rated armature current)] *drive* method.

Example 4.42. *A D.C. series motor, running a fan at 1000 r.p.m., takes 50 A from 250 V mains. The armature plus field resistance is 0.6 Ω. If an additional resistance of 4.4 Ω is inserted in series with the armature circuit, find the motor speed in case the field flux is proportional to the armature current.*

Solution. For a fan, load torque, $T_L \propto n^2$.

Electromagnetic torque, $T_e = K_a \phi I_a$.

Since field flux $\phi \propto I_a, T_e \propto I_a^2$.

Under study state, $T_e = T_L$ or $I_{a1}^2 \propto n_1^2$ and $I_{a2}^2 \propto n_2^2$

$$\therefore \quad I_{a2} = I_{a1}\left(\frac{n_2}{n_1}\right) = 50\,\frac{n_2}{1000} = \frac{n_2}{20} \text{ Amp.}$$

Now counter e.m.f. $E_{a1} = 250 - 50\,(0.6) = 220$ V

and counter e.m.f. $E_{a2} = 250 - \frac{n_2}{20}\,(4.4 + 0.6) = \left(250 - \frac{n_2}{4}\right)$ volts.

Now $$\frac{E_{a2}}{E_{a1}} = \frac{n_2\phi_2}{n_1\phi_1}$$

$$\therefore \quad \frac{250 - \frac{n_2}{4}}{220} = \frac{n_2 \cdot \frac{n_2}{20}}{(1000)(50)} \quad \text{or} \quad n_2^2 + 1137n_2 - 11.37 \times 10^5 = 0$$

Its solution gives $n_2 = 641$ r.p.m.

Shunted-armature method. Speed control by armature-circuit resistance control can be carried out easily, but it suffers from poor speed regulation. This disadvantage can be overcome by shunted-armature method, which is a modification of the armature-circuit resistance control method. In this modified method, external resistances are inserted both in series and in parallel with the armature, as shown in Fig. 4.72 *(a)* for a shunt motor and in Fig. 4.72 *(b)* for a series motor. In effect, combination of R_1 and R_2 acts as a potential divider and the voltage across R_2 is applied to the armature.

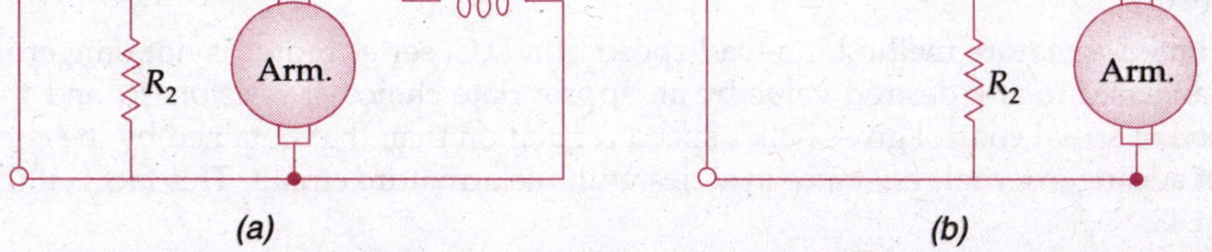

Fig 4.72: Shunted armature method of speed control *(a)* for shunt motor and *(b)* for series motor.

For a D.C. shunt motor, shunt field current is unaffected by R_1 and R_2. Applying Thevenin's theorem at the armature terminals, the Thevenin's equivalent circuit for Fig. 4.72 *(a)* is as illustrated in Fig. 4.73 *(a)*, where the shunt field winding is not shown. From this equivalent circuit,

$$E_a = K_a\phi\,\omega_m = \left[V_t \frac{R_2}{R_1 + R_2} - I_a \cdot \frac{R_1 R_2}{R_1 + R_2} - I_a r_a\right]$$

$$\therefore \qquad \omega_m = \frac{1}{K_a\phi}[AV_t - AR_1I_a - I_ar_a]$$

$$= \frac{1}{K_a\phi}[AV_t - I_a(AR_1 + r_a)] \qquad ...(4.60)$$

where $$A = \frac{R_2}{R_1 + R_2}.$$

Electromagnetic torque $$T_e = K_a\phi I_a$$

$$\therefore \qquad \omega_m = \frac{1}{K_a\phi}\left[AV_t - \frac{T_e(AR_1 + r_a)}{K_a\phi}\right]$$

By varying both R_1 and R_2 and therefore A, speed ω_m can be controlled.

For a series motor, Thevenin's equivalent circuit looking from the armature terminals is as shown in Fig. 4.73 *(b)*. From this equivalent circuit,

$$E_a = K_a\phi\omega_m = V_tB - (r_s + R_1)BI_a - r_aI_a$$

or $$\omega_m = \frac{1}{K_a\phi}[V_tB - (r_s + R_1)BI_a - r_aI_a]$$

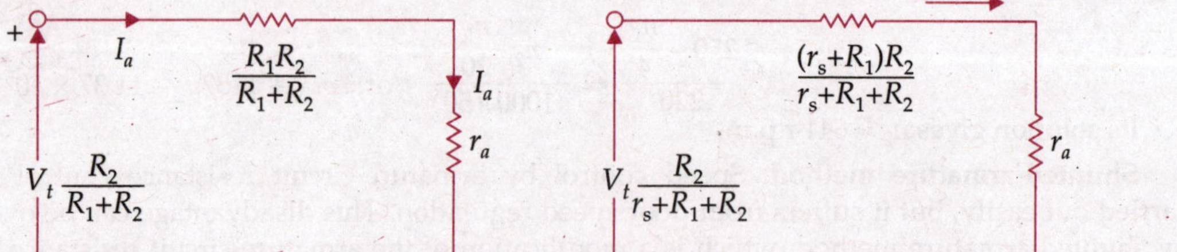

Fig 4.73: Thevenin's equivalent circuits *(a)* for Fig. 4.72 *(a)* and *(b)* for Fig. 4.72 *(b)*.

or $$\omega_m = \frac{1}{K_a\phi}[V_tB - I_a\{(r_s + R_1)B + r_a\}] \qquad ...(4.61)$$

where $$B = \frac{R_2}{r_s + R_1 + R_2}$$

By varying both R_1 and R_2 and therefore B, the speed control can be carried out as is evident from Eq. (4.61).

By shunted-armature method, no-load speed of a D.C. series motor is not dangerously high; it can be adjusted to any desired value by an appropriate choice of resistors R_1 and R_2. Further, this method of speed control gives better speed regulation than that obtained by the conventional method of adding external resistance in series with the armature circuit. This fact is illustrated by Example 4.43.

Example 4.43. *A 230 V D.C. shunt motor runs at 900 r.p.m. at no-load, while taking an armature current of 2 A. The armature resistance including brushes is 0.5 Ω. At rated load and rated voltage, the armature current is 20 A. Find the speed regulation if*

(a) 2 Ω is placed in series with armature and 3 Ω in parallel with it.

(b) only 3 Ω is inserted in series with the armature.

Neglect rotational losses and armature reaction.

Solution. At no load, $E_a = V_t - I_a r_a = 230 - 2 \times 0.5 = 229$ volts.

$\therefore$ $E_a = K_a\phi\, \omega_m = K_a \phi \dfrac{2\pi \times 900}{60} = 229$ V

or $K_a\phi = \dfrac{229}{30\pi} = 2.43$ V-s/rad.

(a) $A = \dfrac{R_2}{R_1 + R_2} = \dfrac{3}{2+3} = 0.6$

$\therefore$ No-load speed from Eq. (4.60) is $\omega_{m0} = \dfrac{1}{K_a\phi}\,[AV_t - I_a(AR_1 + r_a)]$

$$= \frac{1}{2.43}\,[0.6 \times 230 - 2\,(0.6 \times 2 + 0.5)] = 55.4 \text{ rad/sec.}$$

Full load speed, $\omega_m = \dfrac{1}{2.43}\,[138 - 20(1.7)] = 42.80$ rad/sec.

$\therefore$ Per cent speed regulation $= \dfrac{\omega_{m0} - \omega_m}{\omega_m} \times 100 = \dfrac{55.4 - 42.80}{42.80} \times 100 = 29.44\%$

(b) No load speed, $\omega_{m0} = \dfrac{V_t - I_a(r_a + R_1)}{K_a\,\phi} = \dfrac{230 - 2(0.5+3)}{2.43} = 91.77$ rad/sec.

Full load speed, $\omega_m = \dfrac{230 - 20(0.5+3)}{2.43} = 65.84$ rad/sec.

$\therefore$ Per cent speed regulation $= \dfrac{91.77 - 65.84}{65.84} \times 100 = 39.38$

This example illustrates that speed regulation in case of shunted-armature method is better than in the case of armature-circuit-resistance control method.

4.14.2. Speed Control by Varying the Field Flux

This method of speed control, also called *field-weakening method* or field-current control method, gives **speed above the base speed only**.

Shunt motor. The arrangement of connections is shown in Fig. 4.74 *(a)*. The field flux and hence the speed of a shunt motor, can be controlled easily by varying the field regulating resistance. This is one of the simplest and economical methods and is, therefore, used extensively in modern electric drives.

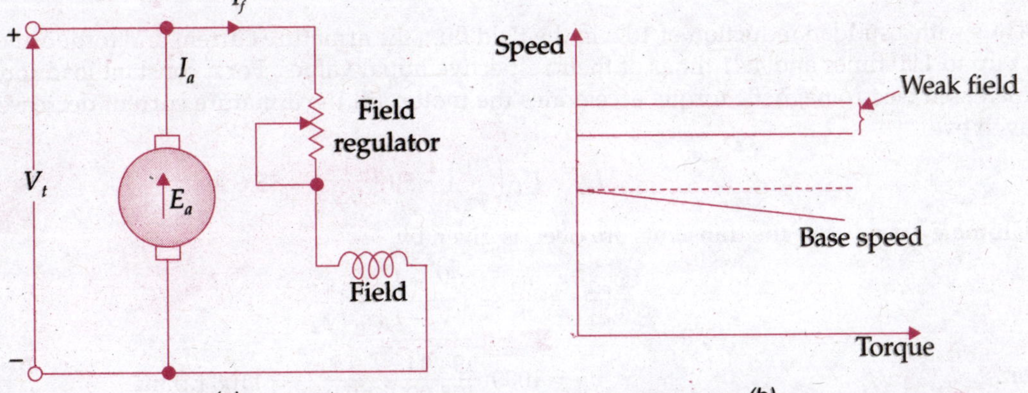

Fig 4.74: Shunt motor speed control by varying field flux. *(a)* Schematic connection diagram and *(b)* Speed-torque characteristics.

Under steady running conditions, if field circuit resistance is increased, the field current I_f and the field flux ϕ are reduced. Since the rotor speed can't change suddenly due to its inertia, a decrease in field flux causes a reduction of counter e.m.f. As a result of it, more current flows through the armature [$I_a = (V_t - \text{counter e.m.f.})/r_a$]. The percentage increase in I_a is much more than the percentage decrease in the field flux. In view of this, the electromagnetic torque is increased and this being more than the load torque, the motor gets accelerated. With this, the counter e.m.f. rises and I_a starts decreasing till electromagnetic torque becomes equal to the constant load torque.

If armature current is I_{a1} for flux ϕ_1, and I_{a2} when the flux is changed to ϕ_2, then for a constant load torque,

$$I_{a1} = \frac{T_e(=T_L)}{K_a\phi_1}, \quad \omega_{m1} = \frac{V_t - I_{a1}r_a}{K_a\phi_1}$$

$$I_{a2} = \frac{T_e(=T_L)}{K_a\phi_2}, \quad \omega_{m2} = \frac{V_t - I_{a2}r_a}{K_a\phi_2}$$

The above phenomenon describing the changes in speed and armature current as the field flux is varied, can be better illustrated with an example.

Example 4.44. *A 200-V D.C. shunt motor, with an armature resistance of 0.1 Ω, is running at 1000 r.p.m. and takes an armature current of 50 A. If the field flux is suddenly reduced by 10%, obtain (a) the maximum value of current at this instant and the corresponding torque and (b) ultimate speed and armature current after the transients are over. Assume constant load torque and negligible armature inductance.*

Solution. *(a)* Initial counter e.m.f., $E_a = V_t - I_a r_a = 200 - 50\,(0.1) = 195$ V.

With a sudden reduction in field flux by 10%, the speed remains at 1000 r.p.m., due to motor inertia, therefore, the new counter e.m.f. becomes 195 × 0.90 = 175.5 V.

∴ The maximum value of armature current

$$= \frac{200-175.5}{0.1} = 245 \text{ A} = \frac{245}{50} \text{ (initial current of 50 A)}$$

$$= 4.9 \text{ (initial current of 50 A)}$$

and the corresponding torque

$$= \left(\frac{\text{Maximum current}}{\text{Initial current}} \times \frac{\text{New flux}}{\text{Initial flux}}\right) \times \text{(Initial torque)}$$

$$= \left(\frac{245}{50}\right)(0.9)\text{ (Initial torque)} = 4.41 \text{ (initial torque)}$$

Thus with a sudden reduction of 10% in the field flux, the armature current and torque at once shoot up to 4.90 times and 4.41 times of their respective initial values. For a constant load torque, the increased electromagnetic torque accelerates the motor, till the armature current decreases to I_{a2} given by

$$I_{a2} = I_{a1}\left(\frac{\phi_1}{\phi_2}\right) = 50\left(\frac{1}{0.9}\right) = 55.6 \text{ A}$$

Ultimate speed after the transients are over, is given by

$$\frac{\omega_{m2}}{\omega_{m1}} = \frac{n_2}{n_1} = \left(\frac{V_t - I_{a2}r_a}{V_t - I_{a1}r_a}\right)\frac{\phi_1}{\phi_2}$$

or

$$n_2 = 1000\,\frac{194.44}{195.00} \times \frac{\phi_1}{0.9\phi_1} = 1108 \text{ r.p.m.}$$

This example shows that in order to avoid objectionable armature current surges, the field resistance should be increased gradually, *i.e.* in small steps.

For a constant load torque, power input to motor $V_t(I_a + I_f)$ [approximately 200 × 50 watts before and 200 × 55.6 watts after the change in field flux] increases almost in proportion to the armature current. The counter e.m.f. (195 V and 194.44 V) remains approximately constant. In view of this, the motor output, *i.e.*, $E_a I_a$ also increases in proportion to the armature current. With simultaneous increase of motor input and motor output, the motor efficiency remains substantially constant. This method is, therefore, the most economical method and at the same time gives smooth speed control. At any particular setting of the field regulator, the speed remains nearly constant between no-load and full load, Fig. 4.74 *(b)*. This method of speed control gives a speed range of 2 : 1 to 4 : 1.

The disadvantages of this method are as follows :

(a) Top speeds are obtained with very weak field. This weak field at top speeds causes the armature current to increase for the development of certain load torque. With increased armature current associated with weak main field, the resultant field waveform is badly distorted as shown in Fig. 4.30. Now consider a coil *aa′* with its coilsides under the peak flux densities as shown. If rotational voltage induced in coil *aa′* exceeds 30 V, the air between the adjacent segments, to which the coil *aa′* is connected, may breakdown resulting in arcing or flashover. Such an arc may extend to nearby commutator segments giving rise to flashover between positive and negative brushes and this leads to direct short circuit on the line. This shows that commutation is very poor when high speeds are obtained with a very weak main field.

(b) The armature may get overheated at high speeds, because the increased armature current results in more ohmic losses whereas cooling by ventilation does not improve proportionally.

(c) If the field flux is weakened considerably, the speed becomes very high and due to these changes, the motor operation may become unstable. For example, when the field flux is weakened heavily, a constant torque load demands an increased armature current. The demagnetizing armature reaction m.m.f. may reduce the already weakened field flux, to such an extent that the electromagnetic torque becomes less than the load torque, inspite of increased I_a–consequently the motor slows down. Constant torque $\left(T_e = \frac{\text{Power}}{\omega_m} = \frac{E_a I_a}{\omega_m}\right)$ requires less I_a at reduced speed, because E_a remains substantially constant. A decrease in I_a and, therefore, a decrease in the demagnetizing armature reaction, causes the field flux to rise from its weakened value. As a result of it, the electromagnetic torque ($\propto \phi\, I_a$) starts growing, even though I_a has become less. If motor torque becomes greater than the load torque, the motor accelerates and its speed may again become very high; due to this, the above happening may re-occur resulting in periodic speed fluctuations, *i.e.* hunting of the motor. A weak series-field winding, (called *stabilizing winding*) assisting the shunt field may avoid this unstable operation at hight speeds. A stabilizing winding allows wider speed range and is added in all the D.C. motors intended for adjustable speed operation. Use of compensating winding further increases this speed range.

Example 4.45. *In Example 4.44, after the transients are over, the reduced field flux is suddenly increased to its value ϕ_1. Calculate the armature current before the speed starts changing.*

Solution. With a sudden increase in field flux from $0.9\phi_1$ to ϕ_1 the counter e.m.f. rises to

$$194.44 \times \frac{\phi_1}{0.9\phi_1} = 216 \text{ V}.$$

The current taken from the supply $= \dfrac{200 - 216}{0.1} = -160$ A.

Since the armature current is now negative, the machine acts momentarily as a generator and feeds the power to the supply, at the expense of its kinetic energy. The speed reduces rapidly till counter e.m.f. becomes less than the supply voltage, so that motor action takes place and torque balance is obtained.

Example 4.44 and 4.45 conclude that the field regulator resistance must be varied in very small steps.

Series motor. The field flux and, therefore, the speed of a series motor can be varied *(a)* by placing a resistor, called a *diverter*, in parallel with the series field winding as shown in Fig. 4.75 *(a)*; *(b)* by tapping the series field winding as shown in Fig. 4.75 *(b)*, and *(c)* by changing the field coil connections from series to parallel, Fig. 4.75 *(c)*.

(a) **Diverter field control.** When the diverter resistance is varied, the current in the series field winding is changed, Fig. 4.75 *(a)* and there is, therefore, a corresponding change in field flux and the speed.

(b) **Tapped-field control.** When the field winding is tapped, Fig. 4.75 *(b)*, the number of series field turns is changed and, therefore, the series field m.m.f. and the speed are changed.

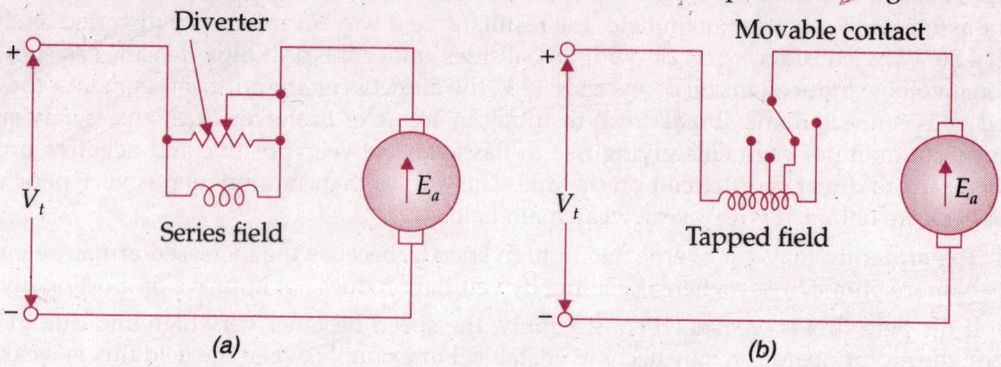

Fig 4.75: Series motor speed control *(a)* by a diverter and *(b)* by tapped field.

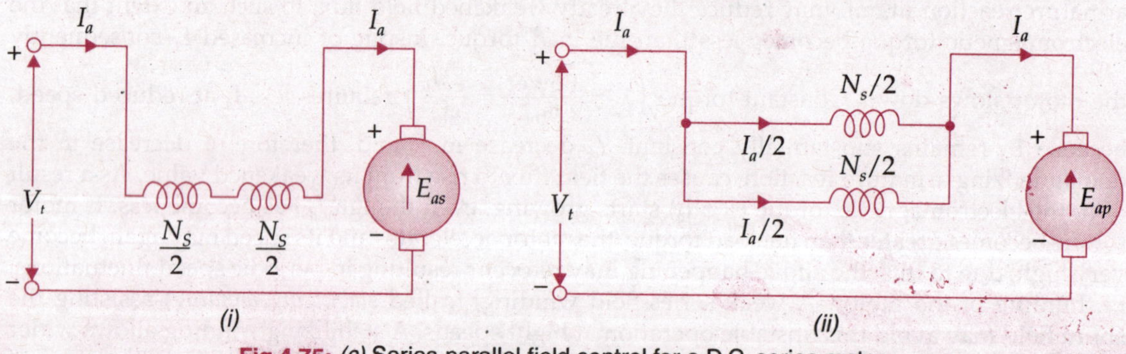

Fig 4.75: *(c)* Series-parallel field control for a D.C. series motor.

If the series motor is to work under violently varying loads, then the diverter resistance should be highly inductive. For example, when the series motor is used for traction purposes, the current collector may lose contact with the overhead wire. After this, the motor continues running due to inertia, but the current and, therefore, the series field flux may collapse. After a short while, when the contact with overhead wire is re-established, the entire current may pass through the resistive diverter due to the large inductance of the series field winding. Since the current in series field is almost zero due to its high inductance, the counter e.m.f. developed by the motor would be zero and this would result in heavy in-rush of armature current when the contact is re-established. In view of this, the diverter resistance should also be highly inductive, as stated before. This difficulty is, however, not present in tapped field control which is, therefore, preferable for series traction motors.

(c) **Series-parallel field control.** In this method, the series field winding is divided into two equal halves. When these two halves are in series, Fig. 4.75 *(c i)*, then for an armature current of I_a, total field m.m.f. F_s is,

$$F_s = I_a\left(\frac{N_s}{2}+\frac{N_s}{2}\right) = I_a N_s$$

Counter e.m.f. $$E_{as} = V_t - I_a(r_s + r_a)$$

When the two halves of field winding are connected in parallel as shown in Fig. 4.75 *(c ii)*, then for the same I_a, each parallel path shares $I_a/2$ and total field m.m.f. F_p is

$$F_p = (I_a/2)\,(N_s/2)\,2 = \frac{I_a N_s}{2}$$

Counter e.m.f. $$E_{ap} = V_t - I_a\left(\frac{r_s}{4}+r_a\right)$$

For no magnetic saturation,

$$\frac{E_{ap}}{E_{as}} = \frac{n_2(I_a N_s/2)}{n_1(I_a N_s)} \quad \text{or} \quad n_2 = 2n_1\frac{E_{ap}}{E_{as}}$$

This shows that parallel connection of field coils results in higher operating speed of the series motor.

For a constant load torque, a decrease in field flux, gives increased I_a and increased speed. Thus power input $V_t I_a$ and power output (= constant load torque × speed) increase and, therefore, efficiency remains almost unchanged.

For both shunt and series motor control, the counter e.m.f. E_a remains substantially constant, because a decrease in field flux is compensated by a corresponding increase in speed. If the armature current I_a is kept equal to the motor rated (or nameplate) current for its full utility, the power output $I_a E_a$ remains approximately constant and for this reason, field-flux speed-control method may be called a *constant power drive* method.

Since $E_a I_a$ remains approximately constant, the maximum torque is obtained when the D.C. motor runs at the lowest speed. In view of this, field-flux control method is suitable to drives requiring large torques at low speeds. In case the field-flux control method is used to drive a load requiring constant torque over the entire speed range, then motor rating and size are decided by the product of constant torque and the highest possible speed, thus motor rating in kW is high. Obviously, such a motor operating at low speed would have low power output (= constant torque × low speed) and would, therefore be underutilized.

Example 4.46. *A 4-pole D.C. series fan motor takes an armature current of 60 amperes, when running steadily at 2000 r.p.m. on a 220 V supply. The four field coils are now connected in two parallel groups of two in series. Assuming that the flux produced is directly proportional to the exciting current and the load torque increases as the square of the speed, find the new speed and the armature current. Neglect losses and assume constant supply voltage.*

Solution. Electromagnetic torque, $T_e \propto \phi I_a$

and load torque, $T_L \propto n^2$ (given)

Under steady state conditions,

$$T_L = T_e \quad \text{or} \quad n^2 \propto \phi I_a$$

If I_{a1} is the armature current with four field coils in series, then

$$n_1^2 \propto \phi_1 I_{a1} \quad \text{or} \quad n_1^2 \propto I_{a1}^2 \text{ as } \phi_1 \propto I_{a1}$$

If I_{a2} is the armature current when four field coils are connected in two parallel groups, then

$$n_2^2 \propto \phi_2 I_{a2} \quad \text{or} \quad n_2^2 \propto \frac{I_{a2}}{2} I_{a2}, \text{ as } \phi_2 \propto \frac{I_{a2}}{2}$$

$$\therefore \quad \left(\frac{n_1}{n_2}\right)^2 = \frac{I_{a1}^2}{I_{a2}^2/2} \quad \text{or} \quad \left(\frac{2000}{n_2}\right)^2 = 2\left(\frac{60}{I_{a2}}\right)^2 \quad \text{or} \quad I_{a2} = \frac{30\sqrt{2}\,n_2}{1000}$$

Counter e.m.f. with all the four coils in series, $E_{as} = V_t - I_{a1}(r_a + r_s) \propto n_1 \phi_1$

and with the four coils in two parallel groups, $E_{ap} = V_t - I_{a2}\left(r_a + \frac{r_s}{4}\right) \propto n_2 \phi_2$

Since r_a and r_s are not given, $$\frac{220}{220} = \frac{n_1 I_{a1}}{n_2 (I_{a2}/2)}$$

or $$n_2 \cdot \frac{30\sqrt{2}\, n_2}{2 \times 1000} = 2000 \times 60 \quad \text{or} \quad n_2 = 2378.4 \text{ r.p.m.}$$

$\therefore$ $$I_{a2} = \frac{30\sqrt{2} \times 2378.4}{1000} = 100.9 \text{ A.}$$

Example 4.47. *A shunt motor connected to a constant D.C. voltage source, drives a load requiring constant electromagnetic torque. Prove that, if counter e.m.f. $E_a > 1/2\, V_t$, the speed decreases with an increase in flux (or vice versa) and if $E_a < 1/2\, V_t$, the speed increases with an increase in flux. Here V_t is the armature terminal voltage.*

Solution. From Eq. (4.34), $$\omega_m = \frac{V_t - I_a r_a}{K_a \phi} \qquad \text{...(4.34)}$$

If an external resistance R_g is inserted in series with armature circuit, Eq. (4.34) becomes

$$\omega_m = \frac{V_t - I_a(r_a + R_g)}{K_a \phi} \qquad \text{...(4.62)}$$

Now electromagnetic torque $T_e = K_a \phi I_a$. Substituting the value of I_a in Eq. (4.62) ;

$$\omega_m = \frac{V_t}{K_a \phi} - \frac{(r_a + R_g) T_e}{K^2 \phi^2} \qquad \text{...(4.63)}$$

For a constant electromagnetic torque T_e,

$$\frac{d\omega_m}{d\phi} = -\frac{V_t}{K_a \phi^2} + 2\frac{(r_a + R_g) T_e}{K_a^2 \phi^3} \qquad \text{...(4.64)}$$

With an increase in flux, if the speed decreases as is usually case, then the term $\frac{d\omega_m}{d\phi}$ must be treated as negative, *i.e.*, $\frac{d\omega_m}{d\phi} < 0$.

Therefore, from Eq. (4.64), $-\frac{V_t}{K_a \phi^2} + 2\frac{(r_a + R_g) T_e}{K_a^2 \phi^3} < 0$

or $$-\frac{V_t}{K_a} + 2\frac{(r_a + R_g)(K_a \phi I_a)}{K_a^2 \phi} < 0 \quad \text{or} \quad V_t - 2(r_a + R_g)\, I_a > 0$$

or $$V_t - I_a(r_a + R_g) > I_a(r_a + R_g)$$

i.e., Counter e.m.f. E_a > (total armature circuit resistance drop)

Also $$E_a + E_a > [I_a(r_a + R_g) + E_a]$$

or $$2E_a > V_t, \text{ because } V_t = [E_a + I_a(r_a + R_g)]$$

or $$E_a > \frac{1}{2} V_t.$$

Thus the speed decreases with an increase in flux (or *vice versa*) for a D.C. shunt motor only if the counter e.m.f. E_a > total armature circuit resistance drop or $E_a > \frac{1}{2} V_t$.

With an increase in flux, if the speed increases then $\frac{d\omega_m}{d\phi}$ must be positive, *i.e.* $\frac{d\omega_m}{d\phi} > 0$.

Therefore, from Eq. (4.64), $-\dfrac{V_t}{K_a\phi^2}+2\dfrac{(r_a+R_g)T_e}{K_a^2\phi^3}>0$

or $\quad -V_t+2\,(r_a+R_g)\,I_a>0$ or $V_t-I_a\,(r_a+R_g)<I_a\,(r_a+R_g)$

or $\quad E_a<I_a\,(r_a+R_g)$ or $2E_a<I_a\,(r_a+R_g)+E_a$

or $\quad 2E_a<V_t$ or $E_a<\dfrac{1}{2}V_t$.

Thus the speed increases with an increase in field flux for a D.C. shunt motor, if the counter e.m.f. E_a < total armature circuit resistance drop or $E_a<\dfrac{1}{2}V_t$.

Example 4.48. *A 230-V D.C. shunt motor has an armature-circuit resistance of 0.4 Ω and field resistance of 115 Ω. This motor drives a constant torque load and takes an armature current of 20 A at 800 r.p.m. If motor speed is to be raised from 800 to 1000 rpm, find the resistance that must be inserted in the shunt-field circuit. Assume magnetization curve to be a straight line.*

Solution. At 800 r.p.m, $\quad T_{e1}\propto\phi_1 I_{a1}$

At 1000 r.p.m, $\quad T_{e2}\propto\phi_2 I_{a2}$

$$\therefore\quad \frac{T_{e1}}{T_{e2}}=1=\frac{\phi_1\times 20}{\phi_2 I_{a2}}$$

$$\therefore\quad I_{a2}=20\,\frac{\phi_1}{\phi_2}=20k$$

where $\quad k=\dfrac{\phi_1}{\phi_2}$

At 800 r.p.m., $\quad E_{a1}=230-20\times 0.4=222$ V.

At 1000 r.p.m., $\quad E_{a2}=230-20k\times 0.4=230-8k$

Now $\quad \dfrac{E_{a1}}{E_{a2}}=\dfrac{N_1\phi_1}{N_2\phi_2}$

$$\therefore\quad \frac{222}{230-8k}=\frac{800\times\phi_1}{1000\times\phi_2}=0.8k$$

or $\quad 222=230\times 0.8k-6.4k^2$ or $k^2-28.75k+34.69=0$

$$\therefore\quad k=\frac{28.75\pm\sqrt{826.5625-138.76}}{2}=27.49\text{ or }1.26$$

Higher value of 27.49 is not feasible.

$$\therefore\quad k=\frac{\phi_1}{\phi_2}=1.26$$

Since magnetization curve is linear, $\dfrac{\phi_1}{\phi_2}=\dfrac{I_{f1}}{I_{f2}}=1.26$

But $\quad I_{f1}=\dfrac{230}{115}=2$ A

$$\therefore\quad I_{f2}=\frac{2}{1.26}=1.587\text{ A}$$

New shunt-field circuit resistance

$$=\frac{V_t}{I_{f2}}=\frac{230}{1.587}=144.93\ \Omega$$

External resistance that must be inserted in shunt-field circuit

$$=144.93-115=29.93\ \Omega.$$

Example 4.49. *A 250 V D.C. shunt motor has an armature resistance of 0.5 Ω and a field resistance of 250 Ω. When driving a constant torque load at 600 rpm, the motor draws 21 A. What will be the new speed of the motor if an additional 250 Ω resistance is inserted in the field circuit.* (GATE, 1988)

Solution. Field current, $I_{f1} = \frac{250}{250} = 1 \text{ A}$

Armature current, $I_{a1} = 21 - 1 = 20 \text{ A}$

Counter e.m.f., $E_{a1} = 250 - 20 \times 0.5 = 240 \text{ V}$

$$I_{f2} = \frac{250}{250+250} = 0.5 \text{ A}$$

Neglecting magnetic saturation, $\phi_1 \propto I_{f1}$ or $\frac{\phi_1}{\phi_2} = \frac{I_{f1}}{I_{f2}} = \frac{1}{0.5}$

For constant load torque, $T_{L1} = T_{L2}$ or $T_{e1} = T_{e2}$ $\quad K_a \phi_1 I_{a1} = K_a \phi_2 I_{a2}$

$$\therefore \quad I_{a2} = I_{a1} \times \frac{\phi_1}{\phi_2} = I_{a1} \times \frac{I_{f1}}{I_{f2}} = 20 \times \frac{1}{0.5} = 40 \text{ A}$$

New counter e.m.f., $E_{a2} = 250 - 40 \times 0.5 = 230 \text{ V}$

Now $$\frac{E_{a1}}{E_{a2}} = \frac{N_1\phi_1}{N_2\phi_2} \text{ or } \frac{240}{230} = \frac{600}{N_2}\cdot\frac{\phi_1}{\phi_2} = \frac{600}{N_2} \times \frac{I_{f1}}{I_{f2}} = \frac{600}{0.5\, N_2}$$

$\therefore$ Motor speed, $N_2 = \frac{600 \times 230}{240 \times 0.5} = 1150 \text{ r.p.m.}$

Example 4.50. *A D.C. shunt motor takes 50 A on full load from 250 V mains. Its speed is to be raised by 40% by weakening of the field flux. If the torque at the increased speed is 20% more than that at the initial speed, find the percentage change in field flux. The armature resistance (including brushes) is 0.5 Ω.*

Solution. Electromagnetic torque at the initial speed is $T_{e1} \propto \phi_1 I_{a1}$ and at the increased speed, $T_{e2} \propto \phi_2 I_{a2}$.

$$\therefore \quad \frac{T_{e1}}{T_{e2}} = \frac{I_{a1}\phi_1}{I_{a2}\phi_2} \text{ or } \frac{1}{1.2} = \frac{50\phi_1}{I_{a2}\phi_2}$$

$$\therefore \quad I_{a2} = (50)\,(1.2)\,\frac{\phi_1}{\phi_2} = 60\,\frac{\phi_1}{\phi_2} = 60a$$

where $a = \frac{\phi_1}{\phi_2}$.

At the initial speed, $E_{a1} = 250 - 50 \times 0.5 = 225$ V and at the increased speed,

$$E_{a2} = 250 - 60a(0.5) = (250 - 30a) \text{ V.}$$

Now $$\frac{E_{a1}}{E_{a2}} = \frac{n_2\phi_2}{n_1\phi_1}$$

$$\therefore \quad \frac{250 - 30a}{225} = \frac{1.4n_1 \cdot \phi_2}{n_1(\phi_2 \cdot a)} = \frac{1.4}{a}.$$

or $$250a - 30a^2 = 315.0 \text{ or } a^2 - 8.33a + 10.5 = 0$$

Its solution gives $a = 1.547 = \frac{\phi_1}{\phi_2}$

$\therefore$ Field flux at the increased speed, $\phi_2 = \frac{\phi_1}{1.547} = 0.647\,\phi_1$.

$\therefore$ Percentage reduction in field flux $= \frac{\phi_1 - 0.647\phi_1}{\phi_1} \times 100 = 35.3\%$.

Example 4.51. *A 250 V D.C. shunt motor has the following magnetization curve at 1200 r.p.m.*

E_a *in V*	125	180	215	250	275	300
I_f *in A*	0.38	0.58	0.80	1.10	1.36	1.76

The shunt field winding has 1000 turns per pole. At no-load, the motor runs at 1200 r.p.m. with negligible armature current. Find the number of series turns per pole required to reduce the speed to 900 r.p.m. when the full load armature current is 100 A. The series field will have a resistance of 0.2 Ω and the armature resistance including brushes is 0.1 Ω. Assume that the armature reaction at full load is equivalent to 4% reduction in main field m.m.f.

Solution. At no-load, the armature resistance drop is zero. Therefore, the counter e.m.f. at no-load speed of 1200 r.p.m. is 250 V, which requires a shunt field current of 1.1 A, Fig. 4.76, or shunt field ATs of 1100.

At full-load, the counter e.m.f.

$$= 250 - 100\,(0.3) = 220 \text{ V}.$$

This counter e.m.f. of 220 V corresponds to a full-load speed of 900 r.p.m. Since, the magnetising curve is given for 1200 r.p.m., the counter e.m.f. of 220 V should be $\frac{220}{900} \times 1200 =$ 293.3 V at 1200 r.p.m.

Now corresponding to this e.m.f. of 293.3 V, the field current from Fig. 4.76 is 1.62 A.

Since the armature reaction at full-load is equivalent to 4% reduction in main field m.m.f., the total field m.m.f. required is $1.62 \times 1000 \times \frac{100}{96} = 1690$ ATs. Shunt field is already furnishing 1100 ATs.

$\therefore$ Series field ATs $= 1690 - 1100 = 590$

$\therefore$ Series field turns $= \frac{590}{100} \cong 6.$

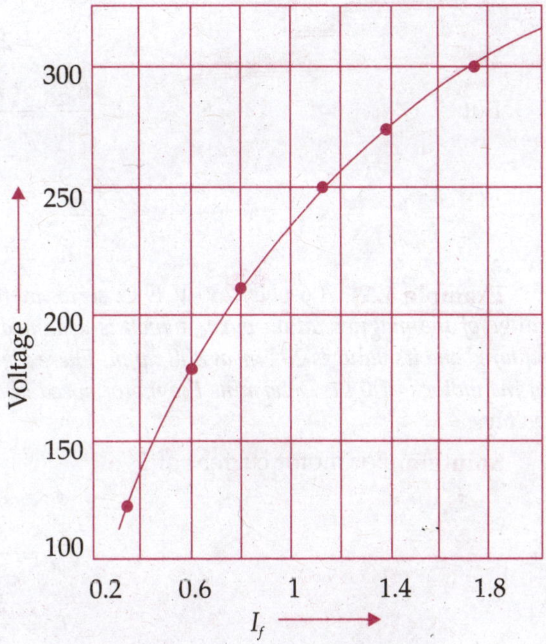

Fig 4.76: Magnetization curve pertaining to Example 4.51.

Example 4.52. *A D.C. series motor, running a friction load at 1000 r.p.m., takes 40 A from 240 V supply mains. Its field resistance is 0.2 Ω and that of the armature is 0.25 Ω. If a diverter of 0.3 Ω resistance, is put in parallel with the series field winding, find the motor speed. Assume the field flux to be proportional to field current.*

Solution. Note that the torque required by a friction load (*e.g.*, a reciprocating pump) at different speeds remains constant. Now electromagnetic torque $T_e \propto \phi I_a$.

Since ϕ has been assumed proportional to I_a, $T_e \propto I_a^2$.

$$\therefore \qquad T_{e1} \propto (40)^2.$$

With a diverter in parallel with the field winding, the field current is reduced. Therefore, if new armature current is I_{a2}, then only a part of it passes through the series field. Thus the new field current is given by

$$I_{a2}\,\frac{R_{div}}{R_{div} + r_s} = I_{a2}\,\frac{0.3}{0.3 + 0.2} = 0.6 I_{a2}.$$

New value of field flux $\phi_2 \propto (0.6 I_{a2})$

Thus $T_{e2} \propto (\phi_2) I_{a2} \propto (0.6 I_{a2}) I_{a2} \propto 0.6 I_{a2}^2$

$\therefore$ $\frac{T_{e2}}{T_{e1}} = 1 = \frac{0.6 I_{a2}^2}{(40)^2}$ or $I_{a2} = \sqrt{\frac{1600}{0.6}} = 51.6$ A.

Now $E_{a1} = V_t - I_{a1}(r_a + r_s) = 240 - 40(0.25 + 0.2) = 222$ V.

When diverter is put in parallel with r_s, then

$$E_{a2} = V_t - I_{a2}\left[r_a + \frac{r_s \cdot R_{div}}{r_s + R_{div}}\right]$$

$$= 240 - 51.6\left[0.25 + \frac{(0.2)(0.3)}{0.5}\right] = 220.9 \text{ V}$$

But $$\frac{E_{a2}}{E_{a1}} = \frac{n_2 \phi_2}{n_1 \phi_1}$$

$\therefore$ $$\frac{220.9}{222} = \frac{n_2(0.6 \times 51.6)}{(1000)(40)}$$

$\therefore$ $$n_2 = 1285 \text{ r.p.m.}$$

Example 4.53. *A 6-pole, 230 V D.C. series motor has a flux per pole of 4 mWb/Amp over the working range of the magnetization curve which is assumed to be linear. The load torque is proportional to speed squared and its value is 20 Nm at 800 r.p.m. There are 432 wave-connected conductors and the total resistance of the motor is 1.0 Ω. Determine the motor speed and current when this motor is connected to rated supply voltage.*

Solution. For motor current of I_a,

$$\phi = 4 \times 10^{-3} I_a \text{ Wb}$$

$\therefore$ $$E_a = \frac{\phi Z n P}{60a} = \frac{4 \times 10^{-3} I_a \times 432 \times n \times 6}{60 \times 2} = 0.0864 n I_a \quad ...(i)$$

$$T_e = \frac{E_a I_a}{\omega_m} = \frac{0.0864\, n I_a \cdot I_a}{2\pi n} \times 60 = 0.825 I_a^2 \quad ...(ii)$$

But $$E_a = V_t - I_a(r_a + r_s) = 230 - I_a \quad ...(iii)$$

From *(i)* and *(iii)*, $$0.0864\, n I_a = 230 - I_a$$

or $$I_a = \frac{230}{1 + 0.0864n} \quad ...(iv)$$

Substituting the values of I_a in *(ii)*, $$T_e = 0.825\left(\frac{230}{1 + 0.864n}\right)^2$$

It is given that $T_L \propto n^2$ or $T_L = Kn^2$ or $20 = K(800)^2$

$\therefore$ $$K = 20/(800)^2 = 3.125 \times 10^{-5} \text{ Nm/r.p.m.}$$

Under steady state conditions, $T_L = T_e$ or $Kn^2 = T_e$

or $$3.125 \times 10^{-5} n^2 = 0.825\left(\frac{230}{1 + 0.864n}\right)^2$$

Its solution gives $$n = 651.888 \cong 652 \text{ r.p.m.}$$

From *(iv)*, $$I_a = \frac{230}{1 + 0.0864 \times 654} = 4.01166 \cong 4.012 \text{ A.}$$

Example 4.54. *A 230 V, 1000 r.p.m. D.C. shunt motor has field resistance of 115 Ω and armature circuit resistance of 0.5 Ω. At no-load, the motor runs at 1000 r.p.m. with armature current of 4 A and with full field flux.*

(a) For a load requiring 80 Nm, compute armature current and speed of the motor.

(b) If it is desired that motor develops 8 kW at 1250 r.p.m., determine the value of external resistance that must be inserted in series with the field winding. Saturation and armature reaction are neglected.

Solution. At no-load, $E_a = 230 - 4 \times 0.5 = K_a\phi\omega_m$

or $K_a\phi = \dfrac{228 \times 60}{2\pi \times 1000} = 2.177 \text{ V-sec/rad}$

(a) Now $T_e = K_a\phi I_a$

$\therefore$ $I_a = \dfrac{80}{2.177} = 36.75 \text{ A}$

For this armature current, $E_a = 230 - 36.75 \times 0.5 = K_a \phi\, \omega_m$

$\therefore$ $\omega_m = \dfrac{211.625}{2.177} = 97.21 \text{ rad/sec} = \dfrac{2\pi n}{60}$

or $n = 928.3$ r.p.m.

(b) Motor developed power $= E_{a1} I_{a1} = 8000$ watts or $(230 - I_{a1} \times 0.5)\, I_{a1} = 8000$

Its solution gives $I_{a1} = 422.1$ A or 37.9 A. The higher value of I_{a1} is redundant, so take $I_{a1} = 37.9$ A.

For a field current of $\dfrac{230}{115} = 2$ A, $K_a\phi = 2.177$ V-s/rad.

$\therefore$ For $I_f = 2$ A, $K_a\phi = 2.177$ V-s/rad

For $I_f = 1$ A, $K_a\phi = \dfrac{2.177}{2}$ V-s/rad

For $I_f = I_{f1}$, $(K_a\phi)_1 = \dfrac{2.177}{2} \cdot I_{f1}$ V-s/rad

Now $E_{a1} = 230 - 37.9 \times 0.5 = (K_a\phi)_1 \cdot \omega_{m1}$

or $211.05 = \dfrac{2.177}{2} I_{f1} \dfrac{2\pi \times 1250}{60}$ or $I_{f1} = 1.481$ A

$\therefore$ $r_{f1} = 230/1.481 = 155.3\ \Omega$.

So, the resistance that must be inserted in series with the field winding

$$= r_{f1} - r_f = 155.3 - 115 = 40.3\ \Omega.$$

Example 4.55. *A 250-V D.C. series motor has armature and series-field resistances of 0.25 Ω and 0.15 Ω respectively.*

(a) Calculate the current for developing a torque of 80 Nm at 1200 r.p.m.

(b) Calculate the percentage reduction in flux when the motor runs at 1800 r.p.m. at half the current obtained in part (a).

Solution. *(a)* For a D.C. motor, developed torque,

$$T_e = \frac{E_a I_a}{\omega} \quad \text{or} \quad T_e \cdot \omega = E_a I_a = [V_t - I_a (r_a + r_s)]\, I_a$$

Substituting the values, we get

$$80 \times \frac{2\pi \times 1200}{60} = [250 - I_a \times 0.4]\, I_a \text{ or } I_a^2 - 625 I_a + 25132.74 = 0$$

Its solution gives $I_a = 43.2$ A

(b) For this part, let 43.2 A be denoted by I_{a1}.

New value of current, $I_{a2} = \dfrac{I_{a1}}{2} = 21.6$ A

Counter e.m.f., $E_{a1} = 250 - 43.2 \times 0.4 = 232.72$ V

Counter e.m.f., $E_{a2} = 250 - 21.6 \times 0.4 = 241.36$ V

Now $\dfrac{E_{a1}}{E_{a2}} = \dfrac{N_1\phi_1}{N_2\phi_2}$ or $\dfrac{\phi_2}{\phi_1} = \dfrac{1200}{1800} \times \dfrac{241.36}{232.76} = 0.6914$

Percentage reduction in flux $= \dfrac{\phi_1 - \phi_2}{\phi_1} \times 100 = (1 - 0.6914) \times 100 = 30.86\%.$

Example 4.56. *A 230-V D.C. series motor develops its rated output at 1500 r.p.m. while taking 20 A. Armature and series field resistances are 0.3 Ω and 0.2 Ω respectively. Neglecting saturation. determine the resistance that must be added to obtain rated torque (a) at starting and (b) at 1000 r.p.m..*

Solution. Motor torque, $T_e = K_a\phi I_a$

As magnetic saturation is neglected, $\phi \propto I_a$ and therefore $T_e = KI_a^2$.

Rated armature current, $I_{a1} = 20$ A

(*a*) At starting, $E_a = 0$ and $V_t = I_{a1}(r_a + r_s + R_{ex1})$

∴ External resistance to be added in the motor armature circuit,

$$R_{ex1} = \frac{230}{20} - (0.5) = 11\ \Omega.$$

(*b*) For developing rated torque at 1000 r.p.m., current remains the same, *i.e.* at 1000 r.p.m., armature current $I_{a2} = I_{a1} = 20$ A.

$$\frac{E_{a2}}{E_{a1}} = \frac{N_2\phi_2}{N_1\phi_1} = \frac{N_2 I_{a2}}{N_1 I_{a1}} = \frac{N_2}{N_1}$$

$$E_{a1} = 230 - 20 \times 0.5 = 220 \text{ V}$$

∴ $\dfrac{E_{a2}}{220} = \dfrac{1000}{1500}$ or $E_{a2} = \dfrac{2}{3} \times 220 = 146.67$ V

Also $E_{a2} = V_t - I_{a2}(r_a + r_s + R_{ex2})$

$146.67 = 230 - 20\,(0.5 + R_{ex2})$ or $R_{ex2} = 4.167 - 0.5 = 3.667\ \Omega.$

Example 4.57. *A D.C. series motor drives a fan at 800 r.p.m. and takes 20 A when fed from rated voltage of 230 V. The motor resistance is 0.4 Ω. The motor speed is to be raised to 1000 r.p.m. by voltage control. Find the voltage and current in case magnetic circuit is (a) saturated and (b) unsaturated.*

Solution. At 800 r.p.m., $E_{a1} = 230 - 20 \times 0.4 = 222$ V

For a fan, $T_L \propto N^2$ or $T_L = K_1 N^2$

For the motor, $T_e = K_a\phi I_a$

(*a*) When magnetic circuit is saturated, ϕ = constant and $T_e = KI_a$. Under steady state,

$$T_e = T_L \text{ or } KI_a = K_1 N^2$$

or $\dfrac{KI_{a2}}{KI_{a1}} = \dfrac{K_1 N_2^2}{K_1 N_1^2}$ or $I_{a1} = 20\left(\dfrac{1000}{800}\right)^2 = 31.25$ A

$$E_{a2} = V_{t2} - 31.25 \times 0.5 \qquad ...(i)$$

Now $\dfrac{E_{a2}}{E_{a1}} = \dfrac{N_2\phi_2}{N_1\phi_1} = \dfrac{N_2}{N_1}$ as ϕ = constantx

∴ $E_{a2} = 222 \times \dfrac{1000}{800} = 277.5$ V

From (*i*), $V_{t2} = 277.5 + 31.25 \times 0.5 = 293.125$ V

(*b*) When magnetic circuit is not saturated,

$$\phi \propto I_a \quad \text{and} \quad T_e = K_2 I_a^2$$

As $T_e = T_L$, $$K_2 I_a^2 = K_1 N^2 \quad \text{or} \quad \left(\frac{I_{a3}}{I_{a1}}\right)^2 = \left(\frac{N_3}{N_1}\right)^2$$

or $$I_{a3} = I_{a1}\frac{N_3}{N_1} = 20 \times \frac{1000}{800} = 25 \text{ A}$$

$$E_{a3} = V_{t3} - 25 \times 0.5 \quad \text{...(ii)}$$

Also $$\frac{E_{a3}}{E_{a1}} = \frac{N_3\phi_3}{N_1\phi_1} = \frac{N_3 I_{a3}}{N_1 I_{a1}}$$

or $$E_{a3} = 222 \times \frac{1000}{800} \times \frac{25}{20} = 346.87 \text{ V}$$

From (*ii*), $$V_{t3} = 346.87 + 25 \times 0.5 = 359.375 \text{ V}.$$

4.14.3. Speed Control by Varying the Armature Terminal Voltage

Reference to Eq. (4.34) shows that if the armature terminal voltage V_t is varied, counter e.m.f. ($V_t - I_a r_a$) changes almost proportionally and for a constant-flux motor (*e.g.*, a.d.c. shunt motor), the speed approximately in the same proportion as V_t. At present, the bulk power is usually available as alternating voltage. So, for driving a D.C. motor, A.C. must be converted to D.C. and then only fed to. D.C. motor armature for its speed control. D.C. motor speed control by varying the armature terminal voltage is obtained by (*a*) Ward-Leonard system (*b*) controlled rectifiers and (c) series-parallel armature control.

An examination of Eq. (4.34) reveals that addition of external resistance in the armature circuit is equivalent to the variation of armature terminal voltage. But the behaviour of motor with added resistance in the armature circuit is quite different from its behaviour with armature terminal voltage control method. Consequently this method of speed control is considered separately.

(*a*) **Ward-Leonard system.** The schematic diagram of this system is illustrated in Fig. 4.77. In this figure, *M* is the separately excited D.C. motor whose speed is to be controlled and *G* is the separately excited generator driven by a three-phase driving motor (usually an induction motor). The combination of A.C. driving motor and the D.C. generator is called motor-generator set and it converts A.C. into .D.C., which is fed to the main motor *M*. If no supply is available, the three phase motor can be replaced by some prime-mover.

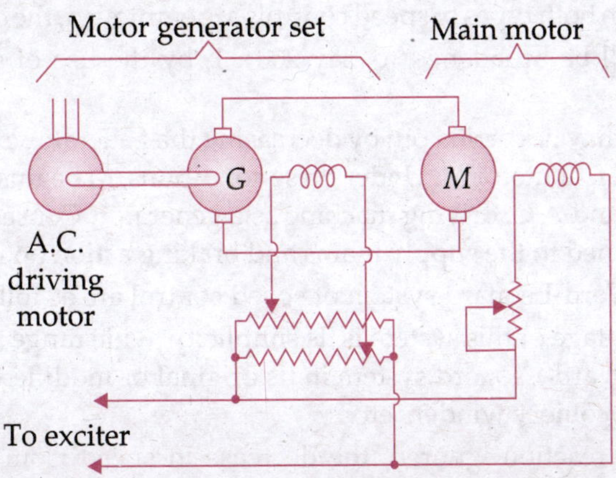

Fig 4.77: Schematic diagram of Ward-Leonard system of speed control.

For starting motor M, its field circuit is first energised and then the generator output voltage is adjusted to a low value by decreasing its field excitation. This is done in order to limit the starting current to a safe value but it should be ensured at the same time that enough starting torque is produced to accelerate the motor and the load. In view of this, no starting rheostats are necessary and, therefore, considerable amount of energy is saved during starting. A change in the generator field current varies the voltage applied to the motor armature and, therefore, the motor speed is changed. Thus the motor speed control is obtained merely by changing the generator field current.

In order to achieve wider speed control range, speeds below base speed are obtained by voltage control and above base speed, by field flux control. For better utility of motor M, its current I_a is maintained equal to its rated current during its speed control.

Speeds, from the lowest possible speed up to base speed, are obtained by increasing the generator output voltage, with constant motor field flux. Since the speed control is carried out with rated current I_a and with constant motor field flux ϕ, a constant torque ($\propto \phi I_a$) up to base speed is obtained. Power (= torque × speed) increases in proportion to speed. Thus *constant torque and variable power drive* is obtained up to base speed, with armature-terminal voltage control method as shown in Fig. 4.78.

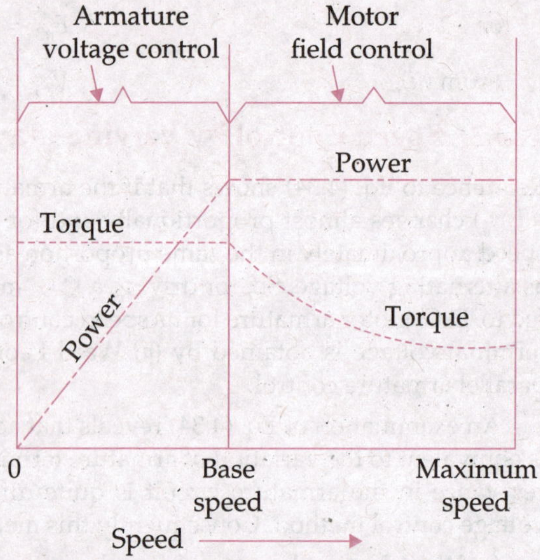

Fig 4.78: Torque-speed and power-speed characteristics for Ward-Leonard system of speed control.

Speeds above base speed are obtained by decreasing the motor field flux with constant generator voltage. As before, the armature current I_a is kept equal to its rated value. Under these conditions, $V_t I_a$ or $E_a I_a$ remains constant and the electromagnetic torque proportional to ϕI_a decreases as the field flux is decreased. Thus, weakening of the motor field flux results in *constant power and variable torque drive* above base speed, Fig. 4.78.

The speed range with armature voltage control exclusively is 10 : 1, the lowest speed being limited mainly by the residual magnetism of the generator. The speed range with motor field control alone, is 3 : 1 to 4 : 1, the highest speed being limited by poor commutation, armature heating and unstable operation. When both types of speed controls are employed, the overall speed range is 40 : 1.

Speed range can still be broadened to, say 200 : 1, by the use of amplidynes incorporating closed-loop system.

Braking of motor M may be carried out by decreasing the generator excitation so that its e.m.f. is less than the counter e.m.f. of motor M. Under these conditions, M begins to work momentarily as a generator, G as a motor and A.C. driving machine as a generator. Consequently the kinetic energy of M and its load is returned to the supply mains and braking action on main motor M takes place.

The advantages of Ward-Leonard system of speed control are as follows :

(i) The main advantage of this system is its simplicity, wide range and smooth speed control. Consequently Ward-Leonard system in its original or modified form, is used extensively in rolling mills, colliery winders etc.

(ii) With armature reaction ignored, the decrease in speed from no-load to rated load, is mainly due to the resistance drops in both the generator armature and motor armature.

The speed regulation is, therefore, quite good.

(iii) The direction of main motor rotation can be changed merely by reversing the generator field current.

(iv) Speed control is carried out through the field circuits of generator and motor. Since these field circuits are low-power circuits, the control apparatus is not costly.

(v) The efficiency at low speeds, is higher than that obtained by other methods of speed control.

The only disadvantage of this method is its higher initial cost, because three machines having rating equal to the full load output, are required.

Example 4.58. *An adjustable speed D.C. shunt motor has speed range 4 : 1. If motor takes an armature current of 60 A at speed n; then calculate the armature current at speed 4n when speed control is obtained by (a) field flux control and (b) armature-voltage control. The motor is driving a load requiring*

(i) constant power and *(ii) constant torque.*

Ignore all losses and armature reaction.

Solution. (a) **Field-flux control.** (i) When load requires constant power, then $E_a I_a$ or torque × speed must remain constant.

At speed n, let the field flux be ϕ, so that $E_a \propto \phi n$.

With field-flux control, the counter e.m.f. E_a remains approximately constant, because a reduction in flux ϕ is compensated by a corresponding increase in speed n. Thus the product $\phi \times n$ remains constant in field-flux control. Therefore, at speed $4n$, field-flux must be $\phi/4$, so that E_a remains unchanged.

∴ For constant power drive ($E_a I_a$ constant) the armature current at $4n$ is equal to $I_a = 60$ A.

(ii) For constant load torque, $T_e \propto \phi\, I_a$ must remain constant and from part (a, i), it is seen that field flux at $4n$ must be $\phi/4$. In view of this, the armature current for constant torque $\left(\phi I_a = \frac{\phi}{4} \times 4I_a\right)$ must be $4I_a = 4 \times 60 = 240$ A.

(b) **Armature-voltage control.** (i) For load requiring constant power, $V_t I_a = E_a I_a$ is constant.

If the armature voltage is V_t at speed n, then at speed $4n$, the armature voltage must be $4V_t$ (field flux is constant), since speed is approximately proportional to V_t, Eq. (4.34).

∴ For constant power drive, the armature current $\left(V_t I_a = 4V_t \times \frac{I_a}{4}\right)$ is $\frac{I_a}{4} = \frac{60}{4} = 15$ A.

(ii) For constant load torque, $T_e \propto \phi I_a$ must remain constant. At speed $4n$, armature voltage is 4 V_t *i.e.*, the counter e.m.f. now becomes $4E_a$. But $4E_a \propto (4n)(\phi)$ *i.e.*, the field flux remains unchanged at both the speeds n and $4n$. Consequently for constant torque, the armature current is 60 A.

Part (b, ii) can alternatively be explained as follow :

For constant torque, ϕI_a is constant. In armature-voltage control method, ϕ is left untouched, *i.e.*, ϕ remains constant. In view of this, I_a must remain constant at 60 A in order to furnish constant torque ($\propto \phi I_a$).

Example 4.59. *For a Ward-Leonard system, two identical 220 V, 15 A D.C. machines are used. Total armature resistance of each machine is 0.4 Ω and the magnetization curve for each machine at 1500 r.p.m. is as given below :*

E_a in V	120	160	197	210	220	228	232	236	243	248
I_f in A	0.3	0.4	0.5	0.6	0.7	0.8	0.9	1.00	1.20	1.45

The generator of the Ward-Leonard system is driven at a constant speed of 1500 r.p.m.

(a) The generator field current is varied from 0.15 A to 1.4 A, while the motor field current is maintained constant at 0.6 A. Find the speed range (i) for full load armature current of 15 A and (ii) for no-load. Assume the armature current to be negligible at no-load.

(b) The maximum speed obtained in part (a) at full load armature current, is to be doubled with the help of field flux control. If the generator field current is not allowed to exceed 1A, find the minimum motor field current required.

Solution. *(a) (i)* For generator, $I_f = 0.15\text{A}$, $E_a = 60$ V from magnetization curve. Full load voltage drop in two armature resistances in series = 15 (0.4 + 0.4) = 12 V.

∴ Actual counter e.m.f. of the motor, when the generator field current is 0.15 A = $E_a - I_a(2r_a) = 60 - 12 = 48$ V.

But the motor counter e.m.f. for a field current of 0.6 A at 1500 r.p.m., from the magnetization curve of Fig. 4.79 is 210 V.

∴ Minimum motor speed

$$= \frac{48}{210} \times 1500 = 343 \text{ r.p.m.} \cong 345 \text{ r.p.m.}$$

For $I_f = 1.4$ A, the generator e.m.f. E_a is 247 V.

∴ Motor counter e.m.f. = 247 – 12 = 235 V.

∴ Maximum motor speed

$$= \frac{235}{210} \times 1500 = 1680 \text{ r.p.m.}$$

Thus the speed range is 1680 : 345 or 4.87 : 1.

(ii) For no-load, armature current $I_a = 0$

∴ Motor counter e.m.f. = generator e.m.f.

When the generator field current is minimum, *i.e.*, 0.15 A, the motor counter e.m.f. E_a is 60 V.

∴ Minimum motor speed at no-load

$$= \frac{60}{210} \times 1500 \cong 430 \text{ r.p.m.}$$

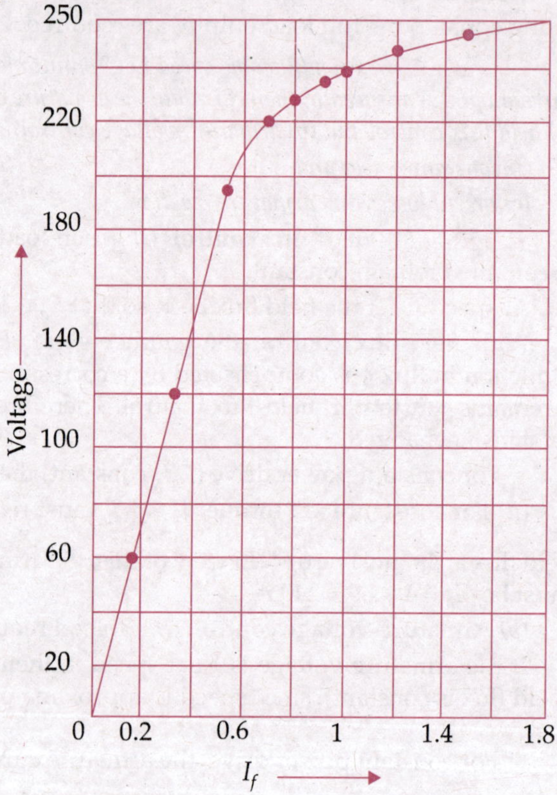

Fig 4.79: Magnetization curve pertaining to Example 4.59.

∴ Per cent speed drop from no-load to full-load = $\dfrac{430 - 345}{430} \times 100 = 19.78\%$

When the generator field current is maximum, *i.e.* 1.4 A, the generator e.m.f. is 247 V. Therefore, the motor counter e.m.f. at no-load is also 247 V.

∴ Maximum motor speed at no-load for the condition of minimum speed

$$= \frac{247}{210} \times 1500 = 1762 \text{ r.p.m.}$$

Thus the speed range at no-load is 1762 : 430 or 4.1 : 1.

Per cent speed drop from no-load to full-load for the condition of maximum speed

$$= \frac{1762 - 1680}{1762} \times 100 = 4.65\%$$

It is seen from above that speed regulation is poor under the condition of minimum speed setting of motor. But under the setting of maximum speed, the speed regulation is better.

(b) For generator field current of 1 A, the e.m.f. generated in the generator armature is E_a = 236 V.

$\therefore$ Motor counter e.m.f. at full load = 236 – 12 = 224 V.

This motor counter e.m.f. of 224 V must correspond to 2 × 1680 = 3360 r.p.m. Therefore, motor counter e.m.f. at 1500 r.p.m. is = $\frac{224}{3360} \times 1500 = 100$ V

From the magnetization curve of Fig. 4.79, the motor field current for E_a = 100 V is 0.25 A. Thus minimum field current required is 0.25 A. Note that the overall speed range with both armature voltage control and field flux control becomes 3360 : 345 or 9.74 : 1.

(b) **Speed control with controlled rectifiers.** Controlled rectifier D.C. supply can be used in place of motor-generator set of the Ward-Leonard system. Now-a-days the silicon controlled rectifiers (or thyristors) have made the SCR–D.C. motor scheme much more economical and its other advantages are less floor space, higher efficiency and quicker control of the output voltage.

Single-phase controlled rectifiers using thyristors are used for the speed control of D.C. motors below base speed. These are suitable up to about 15 kW rating.

For a single-phase full converter, the speed is given by

$$\omega_m = \frac{\frac{2V_m}{\pi}\cos\alpha}{K_a\phi} - \frac{r_a}{(K_a\phi)^2}\cdot T_e \quad ...(4.65)$$

where V_m = maximum value of 1-phase source voltage

and α = firing-angle delay.

There is usually a small voltage drop in conducting thyristors. If this voltage drop is taken as constant and equal to v_r, then Eq. (4.65) becomes,

$$\omega_m = \frac{\frac{2V_m}{\pi}\cos\alpha - v_r}{K_a\cdot\phi} - \frac{r_a}{(K_a\phi)^2}\cdot T_e \quad ...(4.66)$$

For D.C. motor ratings above 15 kW, 3-phase controlled rectifiers using thyristors are used. The speed in case of 3-phase full converter is given by $\omega_m = \frac{\frac{3V_{ml}}{\pi}\cos\alpha - v_r}{K_a\cdot\phi} - \frac{r_a}{(K_a\phi)^2}\cdot T_e$ ...(4.67)

where V_{ml} = maximum value of line voltage.

It is seen from Eqs. (4.65) to (4.67) that by varying the firing angle delay α, the motor speed can be controlled. For detailed analysis of single-phase and 3-phase full converters or other types of controlled converters, the relevant literature may be consulted.

The use of single-phase and three-phase controlled converters has made possible the precise speed control of D.C. motors and has opened up new vistas for their widespread applications in industry.

(c) **Series-parallel armature control.** This method of armature voltage control requires two identical D.C. motors coupled together mechanically to a common load. It is usual to employ this method for D.C. series motors, though it can be used for D.C. shunt and compound motors also.

In Fig. 4.80, the connections for series-parallel control of two identical D.C. motors are shown. When the armatures are in series as in Fig. 4.80 *(a)*, the voltage across each armature is $E_{as} = \frac{V_t}{2}$ and the field flux ϕ is established by current $I_{as} = I_L$. This gives motor counter e.m.f. (= $K_a\,\phi\omega_m$) as

$E_{as} = \frac{V_t}{2} = KI_L\omega_s$, where ω_s is the motor speed when motors are connected in series and flux $\phi \propto I_{as}$ because magnetic saturation is neglected. Subscript s stands for series connection.

When the armatures are in parallel as shown in Fig. 4.80 *(b)*, voltage across each armature is V_t and the field flux is established by current $I_{ap} = \frac{I_L}{2}$. This gives motor counter e.m.f. $E_{ap} = V_t = K\cdot\frac{I_L}{2}\cdot\omega_p$ where ω_p is the motor speed when motors are in parallel. Subscript p stands for parallel.

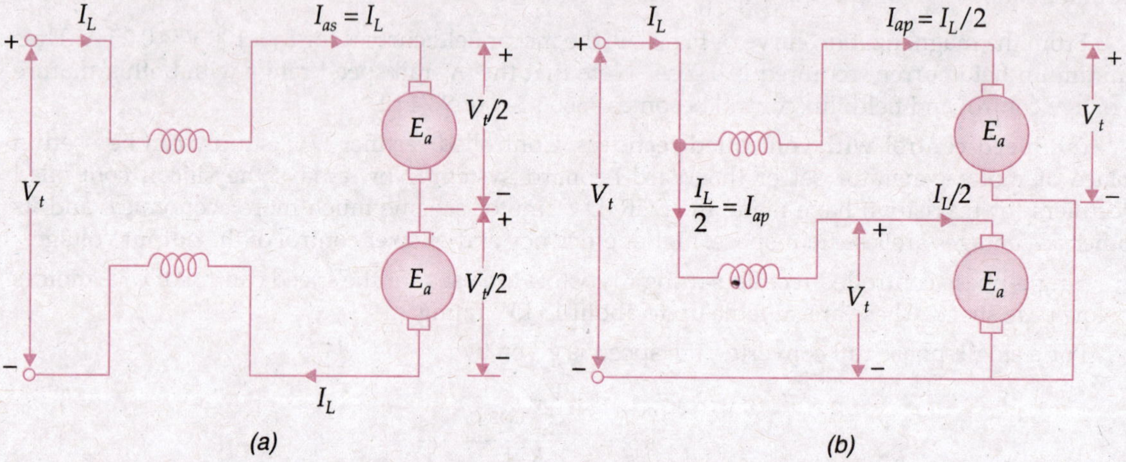

Fig 4.80: Series-parallel speed control of two D.C. series motors *(a)* armatures in series and *(b)* armatures in parallel.

$$\therefore \quad \frac{E_{ap}}{E_{as}} = \frac{V_t}{V_t/2} = \frac{K\cdot\frac{I_L}{2}\cdot\omega_p}{KI_L\cdot\omega_s} = \frac{\omega_p}{2\omega_s} \text{ or } \frac{\omega_p}{\omega_s} = 4.$$

Electromagnetic torque, $T_e = K_a\,\phi\,I_a$ or $T_e = CI_a^2$ $(\because \phi \propto I_a)$

When in series, $T_{es} = KI_L^2$ because $I_{as} = I_L$

When in parallel, $T_{ep} = K\left(\frac{I_L}{2}\right)^2 = K\cdot\frac{I_L^2}{4}$ because $I_{ap} = \frac{I_L}{2}$

$$\therefore \quad \frac{T_{ep}}{T_{es}} = \frac{K\cdot\frac{I_L^2}{4}}{K\,I_L^2} = \frac{1}{4}$$

This shows that for the conditions specified in Fig. 4.80, the ratio of speeds with motors in parallel to that with motor in series is 4, *i.e.*, speed range is 4. The ratio of torques with motors in parallel to that when in series is $\frac{1}{4}$. For constant power input V_tI_L from D.C. source, Fig. 4.80 offers constant power drive.

It is seen from above that series-parallel armature control method offers only two discrete speeds. This method is commonly employed for the speed control of D.C. series traction motors.

Example 4.60. *A 4 kW, 230 V, 1000 r.p.m. separately excited D.C. motor is fed from 260 V A.C. source through a single-phase full converter. At no-load and with zero firing angle delay, the motor draws 2 A and runs at 1100 r.p.m. The armature circuit resistance is 0.5 Ω. Voltage drop in conducting thyristors is 2 V. For a firing angle delay of 30° and rated armature current of 20 A, compute*

(a) the motor torque and *(b) motor speed.*

Solution. With zero firing angle delay, $\alpha = 0°$

$$\therefore \quad \frac{2V_m}{\pi} = E_a + I_a r_a + 2$$

$$\text{or} \quad K_a \phi \omega_m = \frac{2\sqrt{2} \times 260}{\pi} - 2 \times 0.5 - 2 = 231.08$$

$$\therefore \quad K_a \phi = \frac{231.08 \times 60}{2\pi \times 1100} = 2.006 \text{ V-sec/rad}$$

(a) Motor torque,

$$T_e = K_a \phi I_a = 2.006 \times 20 = 40.12 \text{ Nm}$$

(b) From Eq. (4.67),

$$\omega_m = \frac{\dfrac{2\sqrt{2} \times 260 \times \cos 30}{\pi} - 2}{2.006} - \frac{0.5}{(2.006)^2} \times 40.12$$

$$= 95.072 \text{ rad/sec} = \frac{2\pi n}{60}$$

$$\therefore \quad n = 907.87 \text{ r.p.m.} \cong 908 \text{ r.p.m.}$$

Example 4.61. *The magnetization curve of a 4-pole D.C. series motor was obtained by running the machine as a separately excited generator, field and armature currents being adjusted to the same value. The following test data were recorded at a constant speed of 800 r.p.m. :*

Terminal voltage, V	*200*	*375*	*443*	*485*	*510*	*518*
Field current, A	*15*	*30*	*45*	*60*	*75*	*90*

(a) Plot the speed torque and current-torque curves for this series motor when connected to 600 V D.C. source. The resistance of the armature circuit is 0.3 Ω and that of the field winding is 0.25 Ω. Find also the speed and current for a torque of 300 Nm.

(b) In case a diverter of resistance 0.25 Ω is connected across series field winding, calculate the speed and torque for armature currents of 30 and 60 amperes.

(c) With no diverter, if the field winding is tapped at 80% of full series turns, compute the speed and torque for an armature current of 75 A.

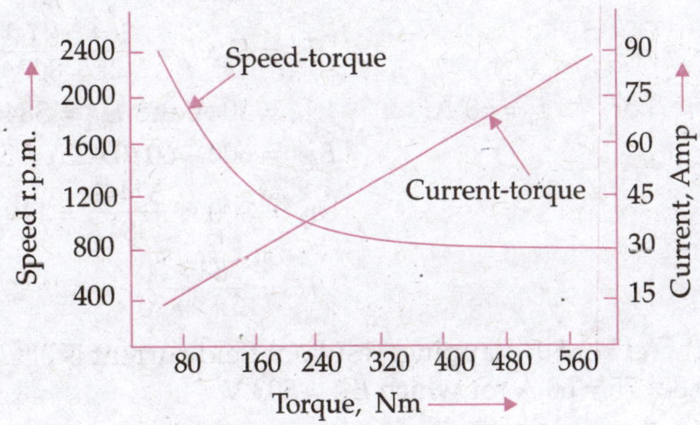

Fig 4.81: Pertaining to Example 4.61.

Solution. (a) The solution of this example is given in tabular form below. The given data is for the terminal voltage V_t and the generated e.m.f. E_{a1}, which would be given by $E_{a1} = V_t + I_a r_a$ as the field and armature currents are equal. With applied voltage as 600 V, $E_{a2} = 600 - I_a (r_a + r_s)$. Now $E_{a1} \propto n_1 \phi_1$ and $E_{a2} \propto n_2 \phi_1$.

$$\therefore \quad \frac{E_{a1}}{E_{a2}} = \frac{800}{n_2} \quad \text{or} \quad n_2 = 800 \frac{E_{a2}}{E_{a1}}$$

$$\text{Also,} \quad T_e = \frac{E_{a2} I_a}{\omega_{m2}} = \frac{E_{a2} I_a}{2\pi n_2} \times 60 = \frac{E_{a2} I_a \times 60}{2\pi} \times \frac{E_{a1}}{800 E_{a2}} = \frac{3}{80\pi} E_{a1} I_a$$

$I_f = I_a$	15	30	45	60	75	90, A
V_t	200	375	443	485	510	518, V

$E_{a1} = V_t + I_a r_a$	204.5	384	456.5	503	532.5	545, V
$E_{a2} = 600 - I_a (r_a + r_s)$	591.75	583.5	575.25	567	558.75	550.5, V
$n_2 = 800 \dfrac{E_{a2}}{E_{a1}}$	2315	1216	1008	902	839	808, r.p.m.
$T_e = \dfrac{3}{80\pi} E_{a1} I_a$	36.62	137.5	245.2	360.2	476.7	585.5, Nm.

The speed-torque and current-torque curves are plotted in Fig. 4.81. For a torque of 300 Nm, the speed and current are found to be 940 r.p.m. and 52.5 A respectively from the graph of Fig. 4.81.

(*b*) For $I_a = 30$ A, $\quad I_f = I_a \left(\dfrac{\text{Diverter resistance, } R_d}{R_d + r_s}\right) = 30 \left(\dfrac{0.25}{0.50}\right) = 15$ A

For $I_f = 15$ A, $\quad E_{a1} = 204.5$ V (given)

Now $\quad E_{a2} = 600 - I_a \left(r_a + \dfrac{R_d r_s}{R_d + r_s}\right) = 600 - 30\,(0.3 + 0.125) = 587.25$ V

$\therefore \quad n_2 = 800 \times \dfrac{E_{a2}}{E_{a1}} = 800 \times \dfrac{587.25}{204.5} = 2297.3$ r.p.m.

For $I_f = 15$ A, $\quad K_a\phi = \dfrac{E_{a1} \times 60}{2\pi \times 800}$

$\therefore \quad T_e = K_a\phi\, I_a = \dfrac{204.5 \times 60}{2\pi \times 800} \times 30 = 73.23$ Nm

For $I_a = 60$ A, $\quad I_f = 30$ A and $E_{a1} = 384$ V

$E_{a2} = 600 - 60\,(0.425) = 574.5$ V

$\therefore \quad n_2 = 800 \times \dfrac{574.5}{384} = 1196.87$ r.p.m.

$T_e = \dfrac{384 \times 60}{2\pi \times 800} \times 60 = 275.02$ Nm.

(*c*) For 80% tapping, resultant field current is 0.8 I_a. For $I_a = 75$ A, the equivalent field current is 0.8 × 75 = 60 A for which $E_{a1} = 503$ V

For $I_a = 75$ A, $\quad E_{a2} = 600 - 75\,(0.3 + 0.8 \times 0.25) = 562.5$ V

$\therefore \quad n_2 = 800 \times \dfrac{562.5}{503} = 894.6$ r.p.m.

$T_e = \dfrac{503 \times 60}{2\pi \times 800} \times 75 = 450.3$ Nm.

Example 4.62. *A D.C. shunt motor, with an armature circuit resistance of 0.3 Ω, operates an hoist whose efficiency is 70%. Calculate size of the D.C. motor for raising a load of 800 kgs at a speed of 3 m/sec.*

In case the supply voltage falls from its initial value of 230 V to 190 V, calculate the hoist speed.

Solution. Here 800 kgs is the weight to be lifted up, therefore, the resisting force due to gravitational pull = 800 × 9.81 = 7848 kgm/sec^2 = 7848 Newtons.

Power required for lifting the load = 7848 × 3 Nm/s or W

$\therefore$ Power rating of D.C. motor = input power to hoist = $\dfrac{7848 \times 3}{\text{hoist efficiency}}$

$$= \frac{7848 \times 3}{0.7} = 33634 \text{ W} = 33.634 \text{ kW}$$

For supply voltage of 230 V, motor counter e.m.f., $E_a = (230 - I_a \times 0.3)$

$\therefore \quad E_a I_a$ = Developed power in D.C. motor = 33634

or $\quad I_a[230 - 0.3 I_a] = 33634 \quad$ or $\quad 0.3 I_a^2 - 230 I_a + 33634 = 0$

Its solution gives, $\quad I_a = 196.70$ A

For supply voltage of 190 V, $\quad E_a = (190 - 196.7 \times 0.3) = 130.99$ V

Assuming the armature current the same as before,

$$E_a I_a = 130.99 \times 196.70 = \frac{800 \times v \times 9.81}{0.7}$$

where v is the new speed of hoist. $\quad v = \dfrac{130.99 \times 196.70 \times 0.7}{800 \times 9.81} = 2.298$ m/s.

Example 4.63. *A D.C. series motor hoists a load at 6 m/sec while taking 60 A at 600 V from D.C. mains. The total resistance of the motor is 0.5 Ω. Calculate the resistance to be added in the motor circuit in order to slow the hoisting speed from 6 m/s to 4 m/s. Assume no magnetic saturation.*

Solution. Motor generated e.m.f., $E_a = (600 - 60 \times 0.5) = 570$ V

Let K be the load in kgs to be lifted up. Under steady state,

motor electromagnetic power = power required for lifting up the load

$$E_a I_a = K \times 9.81 \times 6$$

or $\quad 570 \times 60 = K \times 9.81 \times 6 \qquad ...(i)$

At lower hoisting speed, let R_{ex} be the external resistance be to added in the motor circuit. Then

$$60\,[600 - 60\,(R_{ex} + 0.5)] = K \times 9.81 \times 4 \qquad ...(ii)$$

From *(i)* and *(ii)*, $\quad \dfrac{60[600 - 60(R_{ex} + 0.5)]}{60 \times 570} = \dfrac{K \times 4 \times 9.81}{K \times 6 \times 9.81}$

or $\quad 600 - 60\,(R_{ex} + 0.5) = 380$

or $\quad R_{ex} = 3.167\ \Omega.$

Example 4.64. *A 4-pole D.C. motor runs at 600 r.p.m. on full load and takes 25 A at 450 V. The armature is lap wound with 500 conductors and flux per pole is given by $\phi = (1.7 \times 10^{-2}) \cdot I^{0.5}$ Weber, where I is the motor current. If the supply voltage and torque both are halved, calculate the speed at which the motor will run. Neglect stray losses.* (I.A.S., 1984)

Solution. Here $\quad \phi = 0.017\sqrt{I}$

For $I = 25$ A, $\quad \phi = 0.017\sqrt{25} = 0.085$ Wb

$$E_a = \frac{\phi Z n P}{a} = \frac{0.085 \times 500 \times 600 \times 4}{60 \times 4} = 425 \text{ V}$$

For D.C. motor, $\quad V_t = E_a + I_a r_a$

$$450 = 425 + 25 \times r_a$$

$\therefore$ Armature circuit resistance, $\quad r_a = 1\ \Omega$

Motor torque, $\quad T_e = K_a \phi I_a$

or $\quad T_e = K_a \times 0.017\sqrt{I} \cdot I = K_a \times 0.017\, I^{1.5}$

$$\frac{T_e}{2} = K_a \times 0.017\, I_2^{1.5}$$

$$\therefore \quad \frac{T_e}{T_{e/2}} = \frac{K_a \times 0.017\,(25)^{1.5}}{K_a \times 0.017\,(I_2)^{1.5}} = \left(\frac{25}{I_2}\right)^{1.5} = 2 \text{ or } I_2 = \frac{25}{2^{2/3}} = 15.75 \text{ A}$$

Therefore, new armature current, $I_{a2} = I_2 = 15.75$ A

$$E_{a2} = 225 - 15.75 \times 1 = 209.25 \text{ V}$$

$$E_{a1} = 425 \text{ V}, N_1 = 600 \text{ r.p.m}, \phi_1 = 0.085 \text{ Wb}$$

$$\phi_2 = 0.017\,(15.75)^{1.5} = 0.0675 \text{ Wb} \qquad \frac{E_{a2}}{E_{a1}} = \frac{\phi_1 N_2}{\phi_1 N_1}$$

or
$$\frac{209.25}{425} = \frac{0.0675 \times N_2}{0.085 \times 600}$$

or
$$N_2 = \frac{209.25 \times 0.085}{425 \times 0.0675} \times 600 = 372 \text{ r.p.m.}$$

Example 4.65. *A D.C. shunt motor is required to drive (i) constant power load (ii) constant torque load and (iii) the load whose torque requirement varies with the speed.*

Under rated conditions, the D.C. shunt motor takes rated armature current and runs at rated speed. Find the speed and current, if the following changes are made.

(a) Armature terminal voltage V_t halved, field current I_f unchanged

(b) V_t unchanged, I_f halved and

(c) Both V_t and I_f halved.

Neglect saturation and all the machine losses.

Solution. *(i)* Constant power drive means constant $E_a I_a \cong V_t I_a$.

(a) With V_t halved and I_f unchanged, speed $\left(n \propto \frac{V_t}{I_f}\right)$ is reduced to half, *i.e.*, $n = \frac{1}{2}$ p.u.

Further with V_t halved, E_a is halved and, therefore, for constant power drive, armature current I_a must be doubled, *i.e.*, $I_a = 2$ p.u.

Alternatively,
$$V_{t1} I_{a1} = \frac{V_{t1}}{2} I_{a2}$$

∴
$$I_{a2} = 2I_{a1} = 2 \text{ p.u.}$$

(b) With V_t unchanged and I_f halved, the speed is doubled, *i.e.* $n = 2$ p.u. Further with V_t unchanged, E_a remains constant and, therefore, I_a remains unchanged, *i.e.*, $I_a = 1$ p.u.

(c) With both V_t and I_f halved, speed remains unchanged, *i.e.*, $n = 1$ p.u. Further with both V_t and I_f halved,

$$V_{t1} I_{a1} = \frac{V_{t1}}{2} I_{a2} \quad \therefore I_{a2} = 2I_{a1} = 2 \text{ p.u.}$$

(ii) Constant torque drive means constant $\phi\, I_a$ or constant $I_f I_a$, because saturation is neglected.

As in part *(i)*, the speeds for parts *(a)*, *(b)* and *(c)* are respectively $\frac{1}{2}$ p.u., 2 p.u. and 1 p.u.

(a) With V_t halved and I_f unchanged, current I_a remains unchanged because torque $\propto I_f I_a$ must remain constant.

Therefore,
$$I_a = 1 \text{ p.u.}$$

(b) With V_t unchanged and I_f halved, constant torque drive requires I_a to be doubled, *i.e.*,

$$I_a = 2 \text{ p.u.}$$

(c) With both V_t and I_f halved, constant torque drive requires I_a to be equal to 2 p.u.

(iii) Load torque $T_L \propto n$ and electromagnetic torque $T_e \propto \phi I_a$ or $\propto I_f I_a$. Therefore $I_f I_a \propto n$.

As in part *(i)*, the speeds for parts *(a)*, *(b)* and *(c)* are respectively $\frac{1}{2}$ p.u., 2 p.u. and 1 p.u.

(a) With V_t halved and I_f unchanged, speed is halved.

∴
$$I_{f1} I_{a1} \propto n \text{ and } I_{f1} I_{a2} \propto \frac{n}{2}$$

$$\therefore \quad I_{a2} = \frac{I_{a1}}{2} = \frac{1}{2} \text{ p.u.}$$

(b) With V_t unchanged and I_f halved, speed is doubled.

$$\therefore \quad I_{f1} I_{a1} \propto n \text{ and } \frac{I_{f1}}{2} I_{a2} \propto 2n$$

$$\therefore \quad I_{a2} = 4I_{a1} = 4 \text{ p.u.}$$

(c) With both V_t and I_f halved, speed remains unchanged.

$$\therefore \quad I_{f1} I_a \propto n \text{ and } \frac{I_{f1}}{2} I_{a2} \propto n$$

$$\therefore \quad I_{a2} = 2I_{a1} = 2 \text{ p.u.}$$

Example 4.66. *A 4-pole D.C. series motor has flux per pole $\phi = 4 \times 10^{-3} I_a$ Wb where I_a is the armature current. The motor drives a fan requiring 30 Nm at 1000 r.p.m. The wave-connected armature has 480 conductors and its resistance is 1 Ω.*

Find the motor speed and armature current if it is fed from 230 V D.C. mains.

Solution. For a fan, load torque $\quad T_L \propto N^2$

For a speed of 1000 r.p.m., load torque requires 30 Nm

For a speed of N r.p.m.,

$$\text{load torque required} = 30 \left(\frac{N}{1000}\right)^2 \text{ Nm}$$

Motor torque
$$T_e = \frac{PZ}{2\pi a} \cdot \phi I_a = \frac{4 \times 480}{2\pi \times 2} \times 4 \times 10^{-3} I_a^2$$

Under steady state,
$$T_e = T_L \quad \text{or} \quad \frac{4 \times 480}{2\pi \times 2} \times 4 \times 10^{-3} I_a^2 = 30\left(\frac{N}{1000}\right)^2$$

or
$$I_a = N\left[\frac{30}{1000^2} \times \frac{2\pi \times 2}{4 \times 480 \times 4 \times 10^{-3}}\right]^{1/2} = 0.007 \text{ N} \quad \text{...(i)}$$

Counter e.m.f.,
$$E_a = V_t - I_a r_a = \frac{\phi Z n P}{a}$$

or
$$230 - I_a \times 1 = \frac{4 \times 10^{-3} \times 480 \times N \times 4}{60 \times 2} \quad \text{...(ii)}$$

Substituting the volume of $I_a = 0.007N$ in Eq. *(ii)*, we get

$$230 - 0.007N = \frac{16 \times 480 \times 10^{-3} N}{120} = 0.064N$$

∴ Motor speed,
$$N = \frac{230}{0.071} = 3239.44 \text{ r.p.m.}$$

Motor armature current,
$$I_a = 0.007 \times 3239.44 = 22.676 \text{ A.}$$

4.15. EFFICIENCY AND TESTING OF D.C. MACHINES

It is preferable to refer to Art. 3.9, where losses and efficiency in electrical machines have been described in general. For D.C. machines, the various losses are as follows :

1. No-load Rotational loss. This loss is made up of two losses, namely *(a)* the iron loss at working flux and speed and *(b)* the mechanical loss, *i.e.*, friction and windage losses at the operating speed. Let the no-load rotational loss be represented by W_o.

2. I²R loss. *(a)* Armature circuit loss $I_a^2\ r_a$, where r_a includes the resistances of brush contacts, armature winding, interpole winding and compensating winding, if present.

(b) Field ohmic loss $V_f\ I_f$. Note that this loss includes the field-rheostat loss also. In series machines, field ohmic loss forms a part of the armature circuit loss.

3. Stray load losses. These are produced by *(a)* the distortion of the air-gap flux due to the armature reaction and *(b)* the currents in the commutated coil. It is difficult to measure the stray load losses. In small machines, the losses are neglected, but for machines of about 150 kW or more, they are assumed to be 1% of the rated output.

In Fig. 4.82 *(a)* and *(b)*, power flow diagrams for D.C. compound generator and motor are shown respectively. The symbols used in this figure are the same as used in Fig. 4.34 *(b)*. An examination of Fig. 4.82 shows that these power flow diagrams are for long shunt D.C. compound machines. For short-shunt D.C. compound machines, the entry of series and shunt field losses should be interchanged in Fig. 4.82. In case series or shunt field is absent in a D.C. machine, it is accordingly omitted in Fig. 4.82.

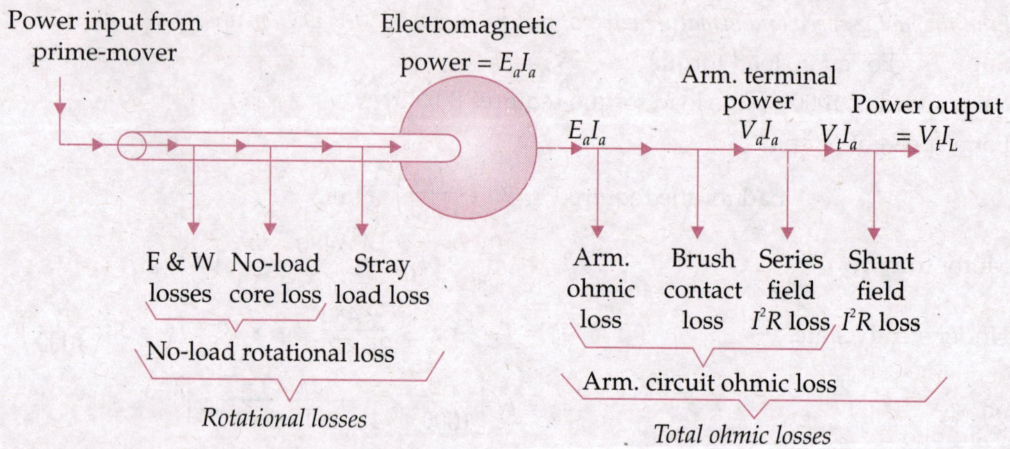

(a)

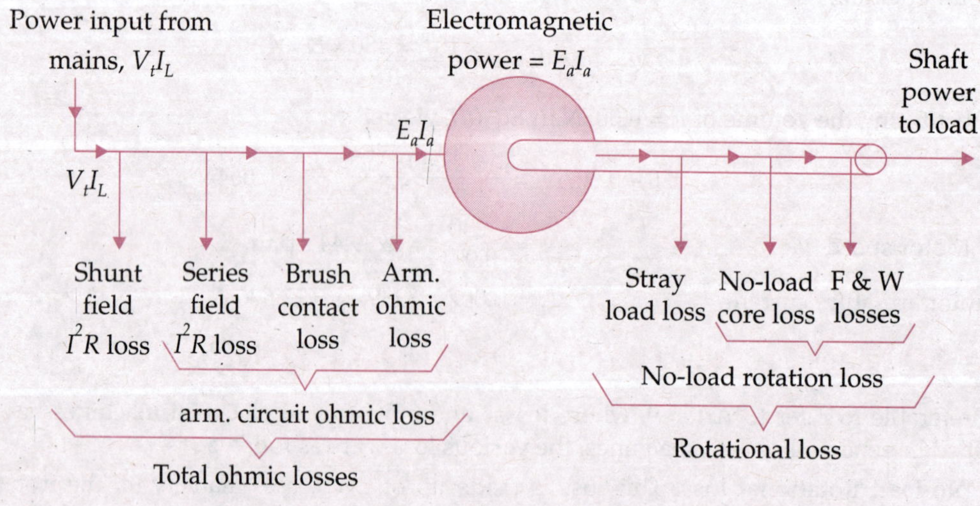

(b)

Fig 4.82: Power flow diagrams for long-shunt *(a)* D.C. compound generator and *(b)* D.C. compound motor.

The electromagnetic power is associated with the generated e.m.f. E_a in the armature of a D.C. machine. The sum of no-load rotational loss and stray-load loss is sometimes called **rotational loss.** The rotational loss when added to, or subtracted from, electromagnetic power gives respectively the shaft-power input to D.C. generators and shaft-power output from D.C. motors. Also, the total ohmic losses when added to, or subtracted from, electromagnetic power give respectively the total electrical power input to D.C. motor or electrical power output from the D.C. generator.

4.15.1. Efficiency of D.C. Machines

In general, the efficiency is given by

$$\eta = 1 - \frac{\text{Losses}}{\text{Input}}$$

For a generator, $$\eta_g = 1 - \frac{\text{Losses}}{V_t I_L + \text{Losses}}$$

or $$\eta_g = 1 - \frac{I_a^2 r_a + V_f I_f + W_o}{V_t I_L + I_a^2 r_a + V_f I_f + W_o} \quad ...(4.68)$$

where V_t and I_L are the output voltage and output current respectively and W_o is the no-load rotational loss.

For a motor, $$\eta_m = 1 - \frac{I_a^2 r_a + V_f I_f + W_o}{V_t I_L} \quad ...(4.69)$$

where V_t and I_L are the input quantities.

Maximum efficiency. The field winding loss $V_f I_f$ and the no-load rotational losses W_o remain approximately constant. The maximum efficiency, as before, occurs when variable losses $I_a^2 r_a$ are equal to the constant losses $V_f I_f + W_o$. This can, however, be proved as follows :

Generator efficiency, $$\eta_g = \frac{V_t I_L}{V_t I_L + I_a^2 r_a + V_f I_f + W_o}$$

In shunt or compound machines, assume that the field current I_f is negligible as compared with the line current I_L. With this assumption, $I_L = I_a$ and generator efficiency becomes

$$\eta_g = \frac{V_t I_L}{V_t I_L + I_L^2 r_a + V_f I_f + W_o}$$

For a given value of V_t, the maximum efficiency occurs, when

$$\frac{d\eta_g}{dI_L} = \frac{[V_t I_L + I_L^2 r_a + V_f I_f + W_o]V_t - V_t I_L [V_t + 2I_L r_a]}{[\text{Denominator}]^2} = 0$$

or $$[V_t I_L + I_L^2 r_a + V_f I_f + W_o]\, V_t = V_t I_L [V_t + 2I_L r_a] \quad \text{or} \quad I_L^2 r_a = V_f I_f + W_o$$

or Variable armature circuit loss = Constant loss.

Same conclusion can be arrived at, from Eq. (4.69) for a D.C. motor.

Example 4.67. *A 10 kW, 250 V D.C. shunt generator has total no-load rotational loss of 400 watts. The armature circuit (including brushes) and shunt field resistances are 0.5 Ω and 250 Ω respectively. Calculate the shaft power input and the efficiency at rated load. Also calculate the maximum efficiency and the corresponding power output.*

Solution. Constant shunt field current $I_f = \frac{250}{250} = 1$ A

∴ Constant losses = Shunt field losses + No-load rotational losses

= 250 × 1 + 400 = 650 watts.

Generator output current at rated output $I_L = \frac{10,000}{250} = 40$ A

$\therefore$ Generator armature current $I_a = I_L + I_f = 40 + 1 = 41$ A.

Armature circuit loss $= I_a^2 r_a = (41)^2 \times 0.5 = 840$ W.

Generator losses $= 650 + 840 = 1490$ W

$\therefore$ Generator shaft power input $= 10,000 + 650 + 840 = 11490$ watts.

$\therefore$ At rated load, $\eta_g = \left(1 - \frac{1490}{11490}\right) \times 100 = 87.02\%$

Maximum efficiency occurs when

Variable losses = Constant losses = 650 W.

$\therefore$ Total losses at maximum efficiency = 650 + 650 = 1300 watts.

But variable losses $= I_a^2 r_a = 650$ W.

$\therefore$ Armature current at maximum efficiency is, $I_a = \sqrt{\frac{650}{0.5}} = 36$ A

Generator output current $= I_a - I_f = 35$ A.

$\therefore$ Generator output power $= 250 \times 35 = 8750$ W

Generator input $= 8750 + 1300 = 10050$ W

$\therefore$ Maximum $\eta = \left(1 - \frac{1300}{10050}\right) \times 100 = 87.07\%$.

Example 4.68. *A 250 V, 15 kW, shunt motor has a maximum efficiency of 88% and a speed of 700 r.p.m, when delivering 80% of its rated output. The resistance of its shunt field is 100 Ω. Determine the efficiency and speed when the motor draws a current of 78 A from the mains.*

Solution. Rated output = 15 kW

$$\text{Efficiency } \eta = \frac{\text{Output}}{\text{Output} + \text{Losses}}$$

or

$$\text{Total losses} = \left(\frac{1}{\eta} - 1\right) \text{Output}$$

$$= \left(\frac{1}{0.88} - 1\right) \times 0.8 \times 15,000 = 1636 \text{ W.}$$

At maximum efficiency, Constant losses

= (No-load rotational losses + Shunt field losses)

= Variable armature circuit losses $I_a^2 r_a$

$$= \frac{1636}{2} = 818 \text{ W.}$$

$\therefore$ Input to motor at maximum efficiency $= 0.8 \times 15000 + 1636 = 13636$ W.

Input line current $I_{L1} = \frac{13,636}{250} = 54.6$ A

$\therefore$ Armature current $I_{a1} = 54.6 - \frac{250}{100} = 52.1$ A

But $I_a^2 r_a = (52.1)^2 \times r_a = 818$ W

$\therefore$ Armature circuit resistance $r_a = \frac{818}{(52.1)^2} = 0.301\ \Omega$

Now motor input current, $I_{L2} = 78$ A

$\therefore$ $I_{a2} = 78 - 2.5 = 75.5$ A.

Now $I_{a2}^2 r_a$ loss $= (75.5)^2 \times 0.301 = 1718$ W

Total power input $= 78 \times 250 = 19{,}500$ W

Total losses $= 1718 + 818 = 2536$ W

$\therefore$ Motor efficiency for a line current of 78 A is

$$= \left(1 - \frac{2536}{19{,}500}\right) \times 100 = 87\%.$$

Now counter e.m.f. $E_{a1} = V_t - I_{a1} r_a = 250 - 52.1 \times 0.301 = 234.32$ V

$$E_{a2} = 250 - 75.5 \times 0.301 = 227.28 \text{ V}$$

But $\dfrac{E_{a1}}{E_{a2}} = \dfrac{234.32}{227.28} = \dfrac{n_1 \phi_1}{n_2 \phi_2} = \dfrac{700 \times \phi_1}{n_2 \times \phi_2}$

For constant field current $\phi_1 = \phi_2$

$\therefore$ $n_2 = \dfrac{700 \times 227.28}{234.32} = 678$ r.p.m.

Example 4.69. *A 10 kW, 900 r.p.m., 400 V D.C. shunt motor has armature circuit resistance (including brushes) of 1 Ω and shunt field resistance of 400 Ω. If efficiency at rated load is 85%, then calculate :*

(a) the no-load armature current,

(b) the speed when the motor draws 20 A from the mains and

(c) the armature current, when the total (or internal) torque developed is 98.5 Nm.

Assume the flux to remain constant.

Solution. Total losses $= \left(\dfrac{1}{\eta} - 1\right) \times$ rated output

$$= \left(\frac{1}{0.85} - 1\right) \times 10{,}000 = 1765 \text{ W}.$$

(a) Total input $= 10{,}000 + 1765 = 11{,}765$ W.

$\therefore$ Line current $I_L = \dfrac{11{,}765}{400} = 29.41$ A.

Armature current at rated load $I_a = 29.41 - \dfrac{400}{400} = 28.41$ A.

Armature circuit loss $= I_a^2 r_a = (28.41)^2 \times 1 = 810$ W.

Shunt field losses $= I_f V_f = 1 \times 400 = 400$ W.

No-load rotational loss $W_o = \text{Total losses} - I_a^2 r_a - I_f V_f$

$$= 1765 - 810 - 400 = 555 \text{ W}.$$

But $W_o = V_t I_{ao} - I_{ao}^2 r_a$ or $555 = 400 I_{ao} - I_{ao}^2 \times 1$

If armature circuit loss at no-load is neglected, the value of no-load armature current will not differ appreciably.

$\therefore$ No-load armature current, $I_{ao} = \dfrac{555}{400} = 1.39$ A

(b) At rated load, $E_{a1} = 400 - 28.41 = 371.59$ V.

For motor line current of 20 A, the armature current is

$$I_a = 20 - I_f = 20 - 1 = 19 \text{ A}.$$

$\therefore$ $E_{a2} = 400 - 19 \times 1 = 381$ V.

The speed at rated load is 900 r.p.m.

$$\therefore \quad \frac{E_{a1}}{E_{a2}} = \frac{371.59}{381} = \frac{n_1\phi_1}{n_2\phi_2} = \frac{900 \times \phi_1}{n_2 \times \phi_1}$$

$$\therefore \quad n_2 = \frac{381}{371.59} \times 900 = 924 \text{ r.p.m.}$$

(c) At rated load,
$$E_{a1} = K_a\phi_1\,\omega_m = 371.59 \text{ V}$$

$$\therefore \quad K_a\phi_1 = \frac{371.59 \times 60}{2\pi \times 900} = 3.94.$$

Now electromagnetic torque
$$T_e = K_a\phi_1 I_a = 98.5 \text{ Nm}$$

∴ Armature current
$$I_a = \frac{98.5}{3.94} = 25 \text{ A.}$$

Example 4.70. *A 10 kW, 240 V D.C. shunt motor draws a line current of 5.2 A while running at no-load speed of 1200 r.p.m. from a 240 V D.C. supply. It has an armature resistance of 0.25 Ω and a field resistance of 160 Ω. Estimate the efficiency of the motor when it delivers rated load.* (GATE, 1993)

Solution. Constant shunt field current $= \frac{240}{160} = 1.5$ A

No-load armature current, $I_{ao} = 5.2 - 1.5 = 3.7$ A

Constant no-load rotational loss,

$$W_o = V_t I_{ao} - I_{ao}^2 r_a = 240 \times 3.7 - (3.7)^2 \times 0.25 = 884.6 \text{ W}$$

$$E_a = V_t - I_a r_a = (240 - 0.25\, I_a)$$

Electromagnetic power $= E_a I_a =$ shaft power + no-load rotational loss

$$(240 - I_a \times 0.25)\, I_a = 10{,}000 + 884.6 \quad \text{or} \quad 0.25\, I_a^2 - 240\, I_a + 10884.6 = 0$$

Its solution gives $I_a = 47.73$ A

Motor input $= E_a I_a$ + full-load $I_a^2 r_a$ loss + shunt field loss

$$= 10884.6 + (47.73)^2 \times 0.25 + 1.5 \times 240 = 11814.14 \text{ W}$$

$$\therefore \quad \text{Motor efficiency} = \frac{10{,}000}{11{,}814.14} \times 100 = 84.64\%.$$

Example 4.71. *A 440 V D.C. shunt motor has a no-load ($I_a = 0$) speed of 2000 r.p.m. It is running at 1000 r.p.m at full load torque, reduced armature voltage and full field. If load torque is reduced to 50% of rated value with armature voltage and field voltage held constant at previous values, the speed increases to 1050 r.p.m. Find the armature voltage drop at full load. Neglect effect of armature reaction.* (GATE, 1994)

Solution. Let I_{a1} be the armature current at full-load torque.

Counter e.m.f. E_{a1} at full-load torque is

$$E_{a1} = (440 - I_{a1}\, r_a) \propto N_1\,\phi_1 \quad ...(i)$$

Motor torque,
$$T_{e1} = K_a\,\phi_1\, I_{a1}$$

Now
$$\frac{T_{e1}}{2} = K_a\,\phi_2\, I_{a2}$$

As the field voltage is held constant, $\phi_2 = \phi_1$

$$\therefore \quad \frac{T_{e1}}{T_{e1}/2} = \frac{K_a\phi_1 I_{a1}}{K_a\phi_1 I_{a2}} = 2$$

$$\therefore \quad I_{a2} = \frac{I_{a1}}{2}$$

Counter e.m.f. E_{a2} at half rated torque is

$$E_{a2} = \left(400 - \frac{1}{2} I_{a1} \cdot r_a\right) \propto N_2 \phi_2 \quad ...(ii)$$

From *(i)* and *(ii)*,

$$\frac{E_{a1}}{E_{a2}} = \frac{N_1 \phi_1}{N_2 \phi_2}$$

$$\frac{440 - I_{a1} r_a}{440 - \frac{1}{2} I_{a1} r_a} = \frac{1000 \times \phi_1}{1050 \times \phi_1} = \frac{20}{21}$$

or $\quad 440 \times 21 - 21\, I_{a1}\, r_a = 440 \times 20 - 10 I_{a1} r_a \quad$ or $\quad I_{a1} r_a = \frac{440}{11} = 40$ V.

$\therefore$ Armature voltage drop at full load $= I_{a1}\, r_a = 40$ V.

Example 4.72. *A D.C. shunt motor, with armature circuit resistance of 0.1 Ω, runs at 1600 r.p.m. while taking an armature current of 100 A from 230 V D.C. source. The friction and windage loss is 300 W, no-load core losses are 1200 W and the total I^2R loss is 2500 W. Stray load loss equals 1.0% of the output.*

Find the shaft torque of the motor and its efficiency.

Solution. Motor counter e.m.f., $E_a = 230 - 100 \times 0.1 = 220$ V

Electromagnetic power $= E_a I_a = 220 \times 100 = 22{,}000$ W

No-load rotational loss $= 300 + 1200 = 1500$ W

Subtracting no-load rotational loss from electromagnetic power, we get

$$22000 - 1500 = 20500 \text{ W.}$$

Let P_{sh} be the shaft power output.

$\therefore$ Stray load loss $= 0.01 P_{sh}$

$\therefore$ $20500 - 0.01\, P_{sh} = P_{sh}$

Shaft power, $\quad P_{sh} = \frac{20500}{1.01} = 20297$ W

Shaft torque, $\quad T_{sh} = \frac{P_{sh}}{\omega_m} = \frac{20297 \times 60}{2\pi \times 1600} = 121.14$ Nm

Power input to motor = electromagnetic power + total I^2R loss

$= 22000 + 2500 = 24500$ W

$\therefore$ Motor efficiency $= \frac{\text{motor shaft power}}{\text{motor input power}} = \frac{20297}{24500} \times 100 = 82.845\%$

4.15.2. Testing of D.C. Machines

D.C. machines can be tested by three different methods—namely, direct method, indirect method and regenerative method. These methods are now described briefly.

Direct Method. This method is suitable only for small D.C. machines. In direct method, the D.C. machine is subjected to rated load and the entire output power is wasted. The ratio of output power to input power gives the efficiency of a D.C. machine. For a D.C. generator, the rated output power is wasted in resistors.

For a D.C. motor, a *brake test* is carried out as illustrated in Fig. 4.83. A belt around the air- or water-cooled pulley has its ends attached to spring balances S_1 and S_2. The belt tightening hand wheels H_1 and H_2, help in adjusting the load

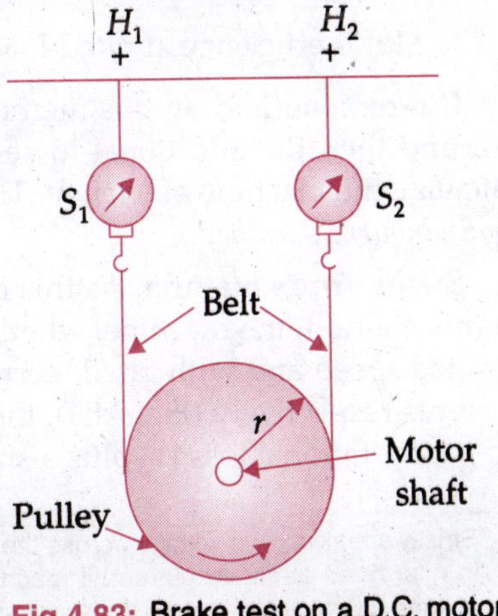

Fig 4.83: Brake test on a D.C. motor.

on the pulley and, therefore, on the motor. If spring balances are calibrated in kilograms, the motor output is given by,

Motor output = $\omega (S_1 - S_2)\, r \times 9.81$ watts.

where S_1 and S_2 are the tensions on the tight and slack sides of the belt, r is the effective radius of the brake-pulley in metres (= $\frac{1}{2}$ outside pulley diameter + $\frac{1}{2}$ belt thickness) and $\omega(= 2\pi n)$ is the motor speed in rad/sec.

If V_t is the motor terminal voltage and I_L is the line current, then power input to motor = $V_t I_L$ watts, and percentage motor efficiency,

$$\eta_m = \frac{\omega(S_1 - S_2) r \times 9.81}{V_t I_L} \times 100 \qquad \text{...(4.70)}$$

For a series motor, the brake should be sufficiently tight before the motor is switched on to the supply.

The size of the motor that can be tested by this method, is limited from the consideration of the heat that can be dissipated at the brake drum or pulley.

The disadvantages of this method are that *(i)* the spring balance readings are not steady and *(ii)* the friction torque, at a particular setting of the handwheels H_1 and H_2, does not remain constant.

Example 4.73. *A full-load brake test on a small D.C. shunt motor, gave the following data :*

Spring balance readings	*25 kg and 9 kg*
Outside pulley diameter	*19.5 cm*
Belt thickness	*0.50 cm*
Motor speed	*1500 r.p.m.*
Applied voltage	*230 V*
Line current	*12.5 A.*

Calculate the shaft torque, shaft power and the motor efficiency at rated load.

Solution. Shaft torque $= (S_1 - S_2) \times$ Effective radius

$$= (25 - 9)\left(\frac{19.5}{2} + \frac{0.5}{2}\right)\frac{1}{100} \text{ kg-m}$$

$$= 16 \times 0.1 \times 9.81 \text{ Nm} = 15.7 \text{ Nm}$$

$$\text{Shaft power} = \omega \times \text{Shaft torque} = \frac{2\pi \times 1500}{60} \times 15.7 = 2470 \text{ W}$$

$$\text{Motor input} = V_t I_L = 230 \times 12.5 = 2875 \text{ W}$$

$\therefore$ Motor efficiency at rated load $\quad \eta_m = \dfrac{2470}{2875} \times 100 = 85.6\%.$

Indirect method. In this method, the no-load machine losses are first measured by a suitable test and then the additional losses on load are determined from the machine data, in order to calculate the machine efficiency. The simplest method of measuring the no-load machine losses is by *Swinburne's method*.

Swinburne's method. As this is a no-load test, it cannot be performed on a D.C. series motor. In this method, the machine, whether it is a motor or a generator, is run as a no-load shunt motor at rated speed and with rated* terminal voltage V_t. If I_{ao} and I_f are the no-load armature and field currents respectively (Fig. 4.84), then the power absorbed by the armature (= $V_t I_{ao}$) is equal to the no-load rotational loss W_o plus a small amount of armature circuit loss $I_{ao}^2 r_a$.

* Strictly speaking, the voltage across the armature terminals should be equal to rated terminal voltage V_t + voltage drop in r_a at rated armature current, if machine under test is a generator. In case the machine under test is a motor, the voltage across the armature terminals should be = V_t – voltage drop in r_a at rated armature current.

$\therefore$ No-load rotational loss $W_o = V_t I_{ao} - I_{ao}^2 r_a$.

Here armature circuit resistance r_a includes the brush contact resistance also.

$$\text{Shunt field loss} = V_t \cdot I_f$$

Let I_L be the load current at which the machine efficiency is required.

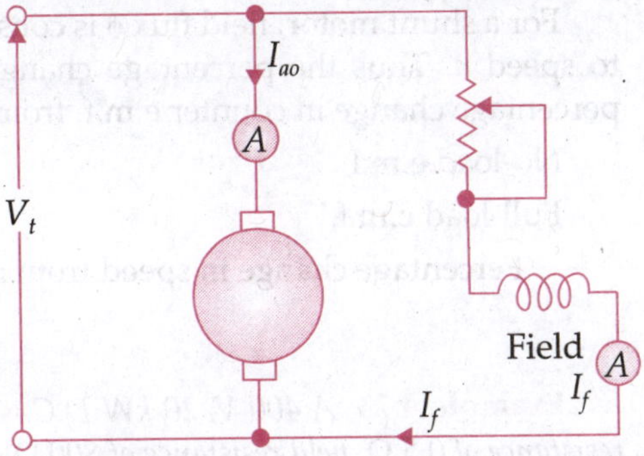

Fig 4.84: Swinburne's method of measuring no-load losses of a dc motor

Generator efficiency. Generator output = $V_t I_L$

Armature current $\quad I_a = I_L + I_f$

$$\text{Armature circuit loss} = I_a^2 r_a$$

Note that here r_a is the armature circuit resistance when hot.

$$\text{Shunt field losses} = I_f V_t$$

$$\text{Total losses} = W_o + I_a^2 r_a + I_f V_t$$

$$\therefore \quad \eta_g = 1 - \frac{W_o + I_a^2 r_a + I_f V_t}{V_t I_L + W_o + I_a^2 r_a + I_f V_t}$$

Motor efficiency. When the machine is working as a motor then $I_a = I_L - I_f$.

$$\text{Motor input} = V_t I_L$$

$$\therefore \quad \eta_m = 1 - \frac{W_o + I_a^2 r_a + I_f V_t}{V_t I_L}$$

The advantages of Swinburne's method are *(a)* low power required for testing even large machines, since only no-load losses are to be supplied from the mains and *(b)* the efficiency of the machine can be calculated at any desired load.

Since the D.C. machine is Swinburne's method is running at no-load, the disadvantages of this method are : *(a)* stray load losses can't be accounted for and *(b)* the actual performance of the machine on rated load can't be checked. For example, Swinburne's test gives no indication about whether the commutation on rated load is satisfactory or whether the temperature rise on rated load is within the specified limits.

Example 4.74. *A 400-V D.C. shunt motor takes 5 A at no-load. Its armature resistance (including brushes) is 0.5 Ω and shunt field resistance is 200 Ω. Estimate the kW output and efficiency when the motor takes 50 A on full load.*

Find also the percentage change in speed from no-load to full-load.

Solution. Constant shunt field current $I_f = \dfrac{400}{200} = 2$ A

$\therefore$ No-load armature current, $\quad I_{ao} = 5 - 2 = 3$ A.

Constant no-load rotational loss, $\quad W_o = V_t I_{ao} - I_{ao}^2 r_a = 400 \times 3 - (3)^2 \times 0.5 = 1194.5$ W

At full load, the armature current $\quad I_a = 50 - I_f = 50 - 2 = 48$ A.

$\therefore$ Full load armature circuit loss $= I_a^2 r_a = (48)^2 (0.5) = 1152$ W

Constant shunt field losses $= V_t I_f = 400 \times 2 = 800$ W

$\therefore$ Total losses at full load $= 1194.5 + 1152 + 800 = 3146.5$ W

Motor input at full load $= 50 \times 400 = 20{,}000$ W.

$\therefore$ Motor efficiency $= \left(1 - \dfrac{3146.5}{20{,}000}\right) \times 100 = 84.27\%$.

For a shunt motor, field flux ϕ is constant, therefore, the motor counter e.m.f. E_a is proportional to speed n. Thus the percentage change in speed from no-load to full-load is the same as the percentage change in counter e.m.f. from no-load to full-load.

No-load e.m.f. $\quad E_{ao} = V_t - I_{ao} r_a = 400 - 3 \times 0.5 = 398.5$ V

Full-load e.m.f. $\quad E_a = 400 - 48 \times 0.5 = 376$ V

$\therefore$ Percentage change in speed from no-load to full-load

$$= \frac{398.5 - 376}{398.5} \times 100 = 5.65\%.$$

Example 4.75. *A 400 V, 20 kW D.C. shunt motor takes 2.5 A when running light. For an armature resistance of 0.5 Ω, field resistance of 800 Ω and brush drop of 2 V, find the full-load efficiency.*

Solution. Field current, $\quad I_f = \frac{400}{800} = 0.5$ A

No-load armature current, $\quad I_{ao} = 2.5 - 0.5 = 2.0$ A

Constant no-load rotational loss, $\quad W_o = V_t I_{ao} - I_{ao}^2 r_a - V_b I_a = 400 \times 2.0 - 2^2 \times 0.5 - 2 \times 2$

or $\quad W_o = 794$ W

$$\text{Total constant losses} = W_o + V_t \cdot I_f = 794 + 400 \times 0.5 = 994 \text{ W}$$

At full load, let $\quad I_L = \text{line current} = I_a + I_f$

$$\text{Power input} = \text{Power output} + \text{total losses}$$

$$V_t \cdot I_L = 20{,}000 + 994 + I_a^2 r_a + V_b I_a$$

$$400\,(I_a + 0.5) = 20{,}000 + 994 + 0.5\,I_a^2 + 2I_a$$

or
$$0.5\,I_a^2 - 398 I_a + 20794 = 0$$

$$I_a = \frac{398 \pm \sqrt{398^2 - 4 \times 0.5 \times 20794}}{1} = 56.22 \text{ A}$$

$$\text{Armature ohmic loss} = 56.22^2 \times 0.5 = 1580.34 \text{ W}$$

$$\text{Brush-drop loss} = 56.22 \times 2 = 112.44 \text{ W}$$

$\therefore$
$$\text{Total losses} = 994 + 1580.34 + 112.44 = 2686.78 \text{ W}$$

$$\text{Power input} = 20{,}000 + 2686.78 = 22686.78 \text{ W}$$

$$\text{Full-load efficiency of shunt motor} = \frac{20000}{22686.78} \times 100 = 88.157\%.$$

Example 4.76. *Find an expression for the maximum steady state power output of a D.C. shunt motor with an armature resistance r_a, if the applied voltage V_t and the shunt-field current I_f are kept constant. Neglect rotational losses and assume that the theoretical maximum power output will not overload the motor.*

Solution. Power output P of a D.C. shunt motor is given by

$$P = \text{Power input} - \text{total losses}$$
$$= V_t I_L - I_a^2 r_a - V_t I_f - V_b I_a - \text{rotational losses}$$

But $I_a = I_L - I_f$ and it is given that rotational losses are neglected.

$\therefore$
$$P = V_t (I_L - I_f) - I_a^2 r_a - V_b I_a = V_t I_a - I_a^2 r_a - V_b I_a \quad \text{...(i)}$$

In the above expression, it is given that applied voltage V_t is constant. The only variable in above expression for power output P is I_a. Therefore, differentiating it with respect to I_a, we get

$$\frac{dP}{dI_a} = V_t - 2I_a r_a - V_b = 0$$

Thus, armature current under the condition of maximum power output is

$$I_{am} = \frac{V_t - V_b}{2r_a}$$

Substituting this value of armature current in *(i)*, we get the maximum output power.

$$\therefore \quad P_{max} = \frac{V_t(V_t - V_b)}{2r_a} - \frac{(V_t - V_b)^2}{4r_a^2} r_a - \frac{V_b(V_t - V_b)}{2r_a}$$

$$= \frac{V_t^2 - V_t V_b - V_t V_b + V_b^2}{2r_a} - \frac{V_t^2 + V_b^2 - 2V_t V_b}{4r_a}$$

$$= \frac{2V_t^2 - 4V_t V_b + 2V_b^2 - V_t^2 - V_b^2 + 2V_t V_b}{4r_a}$$

$$P_{max} = \frac{V_t^2 + V_b^2 - 2V_t V_b}{4r_a} = \frac{(V_t - V_b)^2}{4r_a}$$

In case brush contact loss $V_b I_a$ is neglected, then $P_{max} = \frac{V_t^2}{4r_a}$

Regenerative or Hopkinson's Method. In this method, two identical D.C. machines are coupled, both mechanically and electrically and are tested simultaneously. One of the machines is made to run as a motor and it drives the other machine as a generator. In this section, the regenerative test on two identical D.C. shunt machines is described.

For performing Hopkinson's test, Fig. 4.85, machine I is started as a D.C. shunt motor by a starter (not shown) and brought up to rated speed with switch S open. Both the machines I and II run at the same speed, because these are mechanically coupled. The field current I_{f2} of the second machine is now adjusted and when the voltmeter across switch S reads zero, switch S is closed. The magnitude of the armature currents I_1 and I_2 can be adjusted to any value by varying the field currents I_{f1} and I_{f2}. The machine with a lower value of field current runs as a motor, because its counter e.m.f. would be less than the e.m.f. generated in the armature of the other machine. In Fig. 4.85, I_{f2} is greater than I_{f1}, then machine I acts as a motor and machine II as a generator. Thus machine I running as a motor drives machine II as a generator. Since both the machines are coupled electrically, the power output of generator II is fed to the motor I and it is for this reason that Hopkinson's method is called a *regenerative method*. Consequently the power drawn from the dc supply should only be sufficient to overcome the losses in both the machines. The speed of the set should be equal to the rated speed. If the speed falls, it can be corrected by decreasing motor field current I_{f1} — this has the effect of decreasing E_{a1} and increasing $I_2 = \frac{E_{a2} - E_{a1}}{2r_a}$ and, therefore, $I_1 (= I + I_2)$ also increases. Increase in I_1 more than compensates the decrease in I_{f1}, therefore, motor torque $\propto I_1 I_{f1}$ increases and speed of the set becomes more. If E_{a1} is made greater than E_{a2} by increasing I_{f1} and decreasing I_{f2}, the functions of the two machines can be interchanged, *i.e.* machine I can be made to work as a generator and machine II as a motor.

In Fig. 4.85, I_1 and I_2 are the armature currents of motor and generator respectively and V_t is the terminal voltage of both the machines, *i.e.*, V_t = D.C. supply voltage.

$\therefore$ Input to motor armature $= V_t I_1$

If η_m is the motor efficiency, then the motor output $= \eta_m V_t I_1$

Generator output $= V_t I_2$.

If η_g is the generator efficiency,

Then, the generator input $= \frac{V_t I_2}{\eta_g}$

Since the generator is driven by motor, Fig. 4.85 reveals that motor output,

$$V_t \cdot I_1 \cdot \eta_m = \text{generator input}, \ \frac{V_t I_2}{\eta_g} \quad \text{or} \quad \eta_m \eta_g = \frac{I_2}{I_1}$$

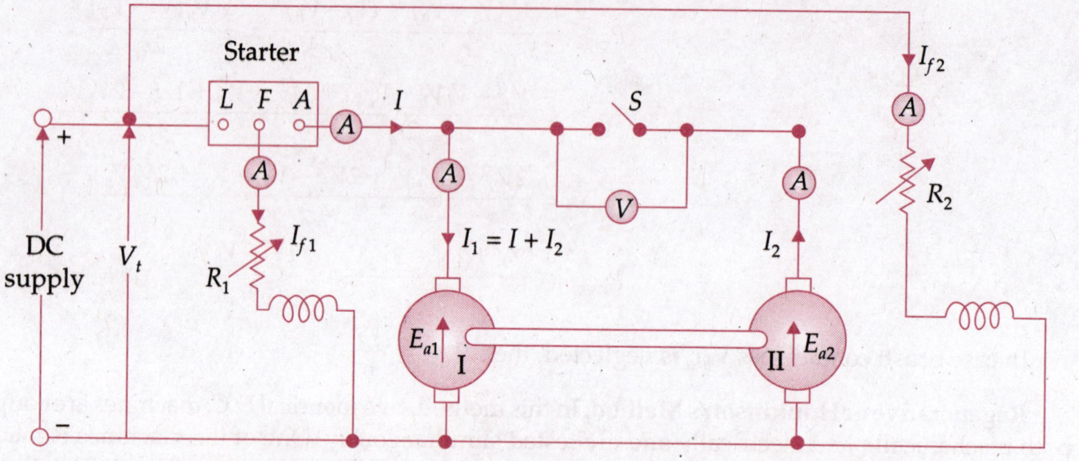

Fig 4.85: Regenerative or Hopkinson's test on two D.C. shunt machines.

If the efficiencies of the two machines are assumed equal, *i.e.*, $\eta_m = \eta_g = \eta$, then

$$\eta = \sqrt{\frac{I_2}{I_1}} = \sqrt{\frac{\text{Generator armature current}}{\text{Motor armature current}}} \quad ...(4.71)$$

Actually the efficiencies of the two machines are not equal, because of the following two reasons :

(*a*) The motor armature current I_1 (= $I + I_2$) is greater than the generator armature current I_2 and thus the armature circuit loss in motor is more than the armature circuit loss in generator.

(*b*) The generator field current is greater than the motor field current. Since both machines are running at the same speed, the generator iron losses (∝ speed and flux) are more than the motor iron losses.

For calculating the efficiencies, the above two reasons can be taken into consideration as follows: If r_a is the hot resistance of each armature circuit, then

armature circuit loss in generator (II) $= I_2^2 r_a$

and armature circuit loss in motor (I) $= I_1^2 r_a$

Power drawn from the supply (excluding the field losses in both the machines) = $V_t I$

∴ No-load rotational loss in two machines,

$$W_o = V_t I - r_a (I_1^2 + I_2^2)$$

In case resistance of generator armature circuit is not equal to the resistance of motor armature circuit, then

$$W_o = V_t I - I_1^2 r_{am} - I_2^2 r_{ag}$$

where r_{am} = resistance of motor armature circuit

and r_{ag} = resistance of generator armature circuit

Assume that the no-load rotational losses for each machine are the same.

∴ No-load rotational loss for each machine = $\dfrac{W_o}{2}$.

$$\text{Generator output} = V_t I_2$$

Generator loss, $$W_g = \frac{W_o}{2} + V_t I_{f2} + I_2^2 r_a$$

$\therefore$ Generator efficiency, $$\eta_g = \left(1 - \frac{W_g}{V_t I_2 + W_g}\right)$$

Motor input $$= V_t (I_1 + I_{f1})$$

Total motor losses, $$W_m = \frac{W_o}{2} + V_t I_{f1} + I_1^2 r_a$$

$\therefore$ Motor efficiency, $$\eta_m = \left[1 - \frac{W_m}{V_t(I_1 + I_{f1})}\right]$$

The iron losses depend on the e.m.f. generated in the armature, therefore iron losses in generator are more than the motor iron losses. The motor with low field current has more armature current, consequently the distortion of the field flux in motor is more than in the generator. In view of this, the stray load losses in motor are more (iron losses are less) than in the generator (more iron losses). Thus the assumption of equal division of rotational losses (including the effect of stray load losses also) is quite valid.

The advantages of this method are : *(a)* the method can be used for large size machines because the power drawn from the D.C. source has to furnish only the losses in the two machines, *(b)* the machines can be tested under rated load conditions and thus the temperature rise and commutation process can be checked and *(c)* the efficiency is being determined under rated load conditions, therefore, the stray load losses are included.

The main disadvantage lies in the requirements of two identical D.C. machines.

Example 4.77. *Two identical D.C. shunt machines when tested by Hopkinson's method, gave the following data :*

Line voltage 230 V ; line current excluding both the field currents 30 A ; motor armature current 230 A, field currents 5 A and 4 A.

If the armature resistance of each machine (including brushes) is 0.025 Ω, calculate efficiency of both the machines.

Solution. For this example, refer to Fig. 4.85.

Since the motor armature current I_1 is 230 A, the generator armature current is

$$I_2 = I_1 - I = 230 - 30 = 200 \text{ A}.$$

$\therefore$ Armature circuit loss in generator $= (200)^2 (0.025) = 1000$ W

Armature circuit loss in motor $= (230)^2 (0.025) = 1322$ W.

Power drawn from the supply (excluding the field loss in two machines)

$$= V_t I = 230 \times 30 = 6900 \text{ W}.$$

$\therefore$ No-load rotational loss in both the machines

$$W_o = V_t I - r_a (I_1^2 + I_2^2) = 6900 - (1322 + 1000) = 4578 \text{ W}$$

$\therefore$ No-load rotational loss for each machine $= \frac{W_o}{2} = 22889$ W

For generator, output $= V_t I_2 = 230 \times 200 = 46{,}000$ W

Total losses, $$W_g = \frac{W_o}{2} + V_t I_{f2} + I_2^2 r_a$$

$$= 2289 + 230 \times 5 + 1000 = 4439 \text{ W}$$

$\therefore$
$$\eta_g = \left(1 - \frac{4439}{46{,}000 + 4439}\right) \times 100 = 91.2\%$$

For motor,
$$\text{input} = V_t (I_1 + I_{f1}) = 230\,(230 + 4) = 53{,}800 \text{ W}$$

Total losses,
$$W_m = \frac{W_o}{2} + I_1^2 r_a + V_t I_{f1}$$
$$= 2289 + 1322 + 230 \times 4 = 4531 \text{ W}$$

$\therefore$
$$\eta_m = \left(1 - \frac{4531}{53{,}800}\right) \times 100 = 91.58\%$$

In case both the machines are assumed to have the same efficiency, then

$$\eta_m = \eta_g = \sqrt{\frac{I_2}{I_1}} = \sqrt{\frac{200}{230}} = 0.93 \text{ or } 93\%.$$

Field's test for series machines. In this method, two identical D.C. series machines are required which are then mechanically and electrically coupled together. This test gives efficiencies of both the machines. The scheme of connections is illustrated in Fig. 4.86. Machine M acting as a motor drives machine G as a generator. The series fields of both M and G are connected in series with the motor armature. In order that the load is not thrown off accidentally, the generator armature is connected to load directly without any switch.

The motor M is started in the usual manner and the generator output is wasted in the variable resistive load. The voltage V_2 across the motor terminals, should be equal to its rated value. Consequently the supply voltage V_t should be equal to V_2 plus voltage drop across the generator field.

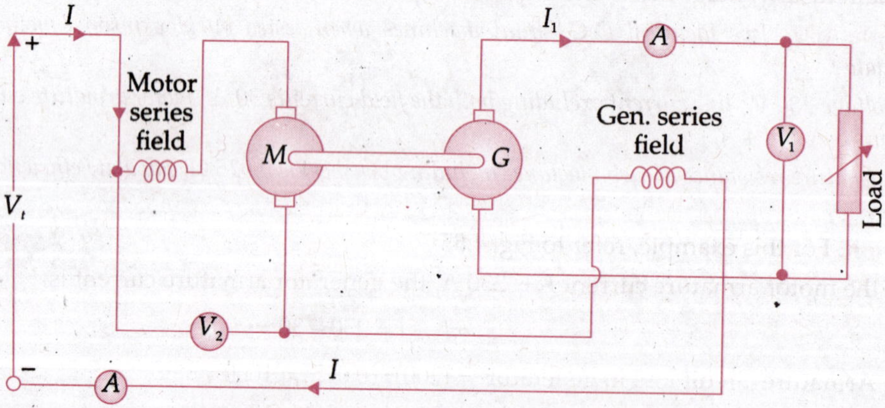

Fig 4.86: Field's test on two D.C. series machines.

Since the motor and generator fields are in series, the iron losses in both machines are the same. The resistance of the various windings can be measured easily.

Let V_t = supply voltage

I = motor input current

V_1 = generator terminal voltage

and I_1 = generator output current.

$\therefore$ Power input to the whole set $= V_t I$

Power output of the generator $= V_1 I_1$

$\therefore$ Total losses in the whole set, $W = V_1 I - V_1 I_1$

Total ohmic losses, $W_c = I^2 (r_{am} + r_{sm} + r_{sg}) + I_1^2 r_{ag}$.

Here the subscripts g and m denote generator and motor respectively. For example, r_{am} is the motor armature circuit resistance, r_{sg} is the generator series field resistance, etc.

No-load rotational loss of both the machines,

$$W_0 = W - W_c$$

$\therefore$ No-load rotational loss of each machine $= \dfrac{W_0}{2}$.

$$\text{Motor power input} = V_2 I.$$

$\therefore$ Motor efficiency,

$$\eta_m = 1 - \frac{\dfrac{W_0}{2} + I^2 (r_{am} + r_{sm})}{V_2 I}$$

Generator input

$$= V_1 I_1 + \frac{W_0}{2} + I^2 r_{sg} + I_1^2 r_{ag}$$

$\therefore$ Generator efficiency,

$$\eta_g = 1 - \frac{\dfrac{W_0}{2} + I^2 r_{sg} + I_1^2 r_{ag}}{V_1 I_1 + \dfrac{W_0}{2} + I^2 r_{sg} + I_1^2 r_{ag}}$$

Note that the Field's test (known after Mr. M.B. Field) is not a regenerative one, because the generator output is wasted in load resistance and not fed to the motor.

The accuracy of this test depends on the accuracy with which the motor input and generator output are measured.

Brake test on series motors is possible in case of small machines. Swinburne's method of testing is not possible, because series motors have the tendency of attaining dangerous speeds at no-load. In view of this, the Field's test is quite suitable for D.C. series machines. At the same time, there is no difficulty in obtaining two similar D.C. series machines, because these motors used for traction purposes, are usually available in pairs.

Example 4.78. *A Field's test on two similar series machines gave the following data :*

Motor :	*armature current*	= 60 A
	voltage across armature	= 500 V
	voltage across field	= 40 V
Generator :	*terminal voltage*	= 450 V
	output current	= 46 A
	voltage across field	= 40 V

Armature resistance (including brushes) of each machine is 0.25 Ω. Calculate efficiency of both the machines.

Solution. Power input to the whole set $= (500 + 40 + 40)\,(60) = 34{,}800$ W

Generator output $= 450 \times 46 = 20{,}700$ W.

$\therefore$ Total losses in the whole set $= 34{,}800 - 20{,}700 = 14{,}100$ W

Total ohmic losses $= (60)^2 \times 0.25 + 60\,(40 + 40) + (46)^2 \times 0.25 = 6230$ W

$\therefore$ No-load rotational loss of each machine

$$= \frac{14{,}100 - 6230}{2} = 3935 \text{ W}$$

Motor power input $= (500 + 40)\,(60) = 32{,}400$ watts.

Total motor losses = Armature circuit loss + Field circuit loss + No-load rotational loss

$$= (60)^2 \times 0.25 + 60 \times 40 + 3935 = 7235 \text{ W}.$$

$\therefore$ Motor efficiency, $\quad \eta_m = \left(1 - \dfrac{7235}{32,400}\right) \times 100 = 77.68\%.$

Total generator losses = Armature circuit loss + Field circuit loss + No-load rotational loss

$$= (46)^2 (0.25) + 60 \times 40 + 3935 = 6865 \text{ watts}.$$

$$\text{Generator input} = 20,700 + 6865 = 27,005 \text{ W}.$$

$\therefore$ Generator efficiency, $\quad \eta_g = \left(1 - \dfrac{6865}{27,005}\right) \times 100 = 74.49\%.$

4.16. ROTATING AMPLIFIERS

Electronic amplifiers can give outputs economically up to a certain power level and for large amplified power outputs, rotating amplifiers are used. These amplifiers are in common use in modern automatic electric drives, because they possess high power gain and can work favourably under transient conditions.

There are three types of rotating amplifiers, namely, *(a)* machines with self-excited tuned fields, *(b)* machines with a highly saturated magnetic circuit and *(c)* cross-field machines. Since the rotating amplifiers of the cross-field type are more common, only these are described in this article.

Ordinarily, a separately excited D.C. generator, driven at constant speed, is a single-stage rotating amplifier, the power gain being $\dfrac{\text{power output}}{\text{field power}}$, but the term rotating amplifier is not applied to it. The power amplification of 20 : 1 to 100 : 1 is obtained in one D.C. generator according to its size. For larger power gain, two cascaded machines as shown in Fig. 4.87 are used, the overall power gain being the product of the power gain of each machine. Only a small power is required by the field of the first generator (called exciter) and the power output of the second generator is sufficiently large to give a high overall power gain. In such a scheme, if ordinary D.C. machines are used as shown in Fig. 4.87, the transient response of the system is very sluggish, because of the large field winding inductances. However, the two stages of amplification, can be combined in one machine as shown in Fig. 4.88 *(a)*, in which one armature winding behaves as two separate armatures superimposed. The time constants of such a machine are considerably less, giving quick response to control. Such two stage generators are called rotating amplifiers and in these the armature reaction m.m.f. of the first stage is made to act as field flux for the second stage. It should be noted that one armature winding can behave as two separate armatures only if there are two fluxes electrically in quadrature and two sets of brushes per pole-pair. The armature reaction m.m.f. is sometimes called the cross-reaction of the armature and it is for this reason that the two-stage generators are also called *cross field machines*.

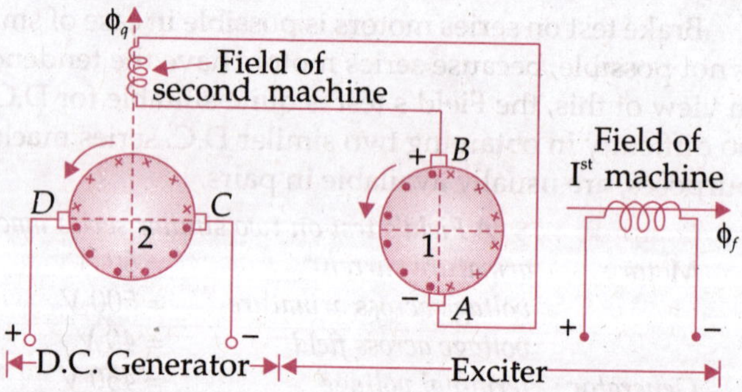

Fig 4.87: Two D.C. generators connected electrically in cascade.

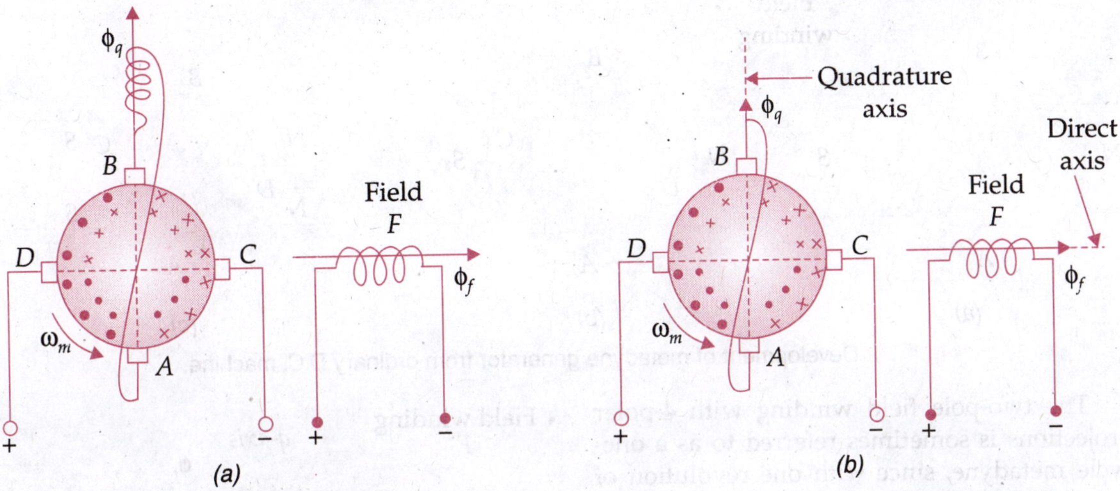

Fig 4.88: Cross-field or metadyne generators *(a)* with ampliator and *(b)* its schematic representation.

4.16.1. Cross-field or Metadyne Generators

The brush axes of the exciter and D.C. generator of Fig. 4.87, are purposely shown in quadrature, so that the superposition of the two armatures results in the cross-field generator or metadyne generator of Fig. 4.88 *(a)*. The field winding *F* produces a flux ϕ_f along the *d*-axis. When the armature rotates in the flux ϕ_f, an e.m.f. appears across brushes *AB* and this e.m.f. circulates current in the *q*-axis field winding, called an *ampliator winding*. The flux ϕ_q set up by the ampliator winding, generates a second e.m.f. across the output brushes C and D which are connected to the load.

Note that the *q*-axis flux ϕ_q is produced due to both the ampliator winding m.m.f. and the armature reaction m.m.f. If the armature m.m.f. alone is sufficient to produce the desired flux ϕ_q, the brushes *A*, *B* may be joined together to give the schematic representation of cross-field generator of Fig. 4.88 *(b)*. In ordinary D.C. generator, the armature reaction is a troublesome feature but in cross-field generator it is put to advantage as the field flux of the second stage. Note also that the generation of e.m.f. across brushes *A*, *B* due to flux ϕ_f, is the first stage of generation and the generation of e.m.f. across brushes *C*, *D* due to the flux ϕ_q, forms the second stage of generation.

Construction. The pole structure of a cross-field generator is different from that of the D.C. machine, the pole configuration for the latter, for a 2-pole machine being shown in Fig. 4.89 *(a)*. If the same pole structure is used for the metadyne, Fig. 4.89 *(b)*, then the coil (undergoing commutation) short-circuited by the output brushes *C*, *D* would be cutting the maximum *d*-axis flux ϕ_f and would have, therefore, maximum rotational e.m.f. generated in it. As a result of it, a large circulating current may flow in this short-circuited coil, giving rise to poor commutation. The flux density at the position of the output brushes *C*, *D* can be reduced (and, therefore, rotational e.m.f. reduced) by making a cut in the middle of the pole face as shown in Fig. 4.89 *(c)*. Interpoles are normally required along the output brushes and even after this cut shown in Fig. 4.89 *(c)*, there is no space to fit the interpoles. Thus, in order to provide space for interpoles, one pole is split into two separate parts, giving the appearance of 4 poles for a two-pole cross-field machine as shown in Fig. 4.89 *(d)*.

For deciding the polarity of interpoles near the brushes C and *D*, attention should be given to *d*-axis m.m.f. produced by armature. The armature currents, indicated by inner crosses and dots on the armature, produce *N* pole near *D* and *S* pole near *C*. In order to make the flux density zero under the brush at *D*, the interpole near brush *D* must have *N* polarity. Similarly, the interpole near brush C must have *S* polarity.

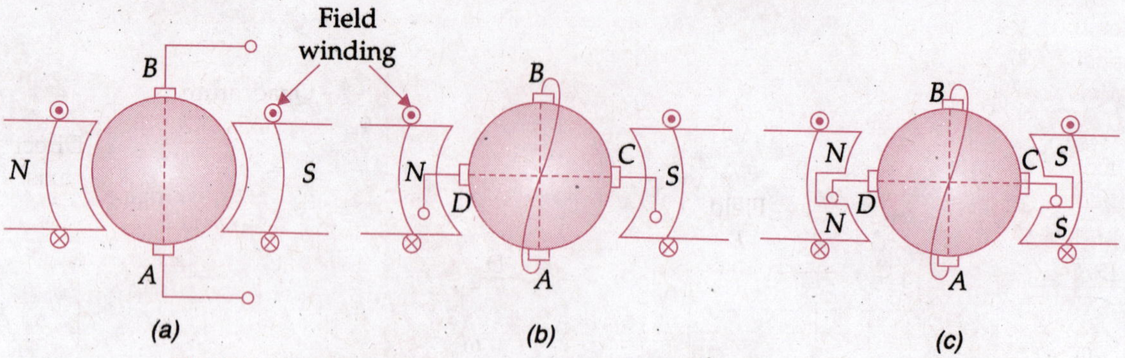

Fig 4.89: Development of metadyne generator from ordinary D.C. machine.

The two-pole field winding with 4-polar projections is sometimes referred to as a one-cycle metadyne, since with one revolution of the armature, one cycle of e.m.f. is generated.

In Fig. 4.89 *(d)*, the rotor has one commutator and one armature winding designed for two poles. The field or control winding F is wound on two-polar projections, belonging to one pole. The main flux ϕ_f, leaves the pole projections 1 and 2 and enters the polar projections 4 and 3.

E.M.F. Equations. The field winding flux ϕ_f is directed along the horizontal axis or direct axis and the lines of force enter the armature radially from pole segments 1 and 2 and leave radially into the pole segments 3 and 4. The rotation of the armature in the main flux ϕ_f generates an e.m.f. E_{q1} between the q-axis brushes AB, and its magnitude is given by

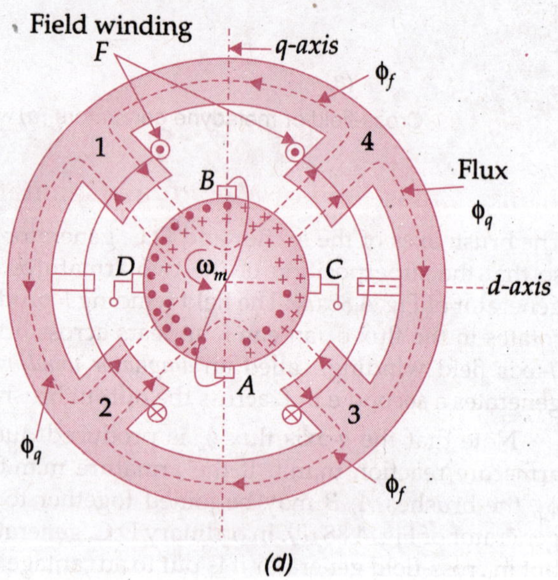

Fig 4.89: Development of 2-pole metadyne generator from ordinary D.C. machine.

$$E_{q1} = \frac{\phi_f Z Pn}{a} = K_a \omega_m \phi_f$$

or $\quad E_{q1} = K_{qf} I_f$, provided saturation is ignored.

Here K_{qf} = voltage generated across q-axis brushes/field ampere at speed ω_m.

ϕ_f = total d-axis field flux per pole, which is proportional to field (or control) current I_f.

Since brushes AB are short-circuited, a large armature current, shown by outer crosses and dots in Fig. 4.89 *(d)*, starts flowing and this establishes a stationary magnetic flux ϕ_q centred along the brushes A, B. This flux ϕ_q is directed upward and it is seen that ϕ_q and ϕ_f are in the same direction in polar projections 2 and 4, and are in the opposite direction in the polar projections 1 and 3. If saturation is ignored, ϕ_f remains unaltered.

Rotation of the armature in ϕ_q generates e.m.f. E_d across brushes C, D and it is given by

$$E_d = \frac{\phi_q ZnP}{a} = K_a \omega_m \phi_q = K_{dq} I_q.$$

Here K_{dq} is the e.m.f. generated across the d-axis brushes/q-axis armature current at speed ω_m. When load is connected across the output brushes C, D, the load current starts flowing in the armature and it is indicated by the inner crosses and dots in Fig. 4.89 *(d)*. It must be clearly understood that e.m.fs. and currents exist simultaneously in the same armature conductors and the position of two pairs of brushes only separate them out. Note that the armature currents are additive between brushes *B*, *C* and *A*, *D* and they are subtractive between brushes *B*, *D* and *A*, *C*.

When the *d*-axis armature current I_d flows, the inner crosses and dots establish a flux ϕ_d due to *d*-axis armature m.m.f., opposite to the *d*-axis field flux ϕ_f. It is due to this reason that metadyne is called a two-stage power amplifier, with *negative current feedback* with respect to the main flux.

With the first stage of generation, *q*-axis armature flux ϕ_q is established 90° away (and in the direction of rotation) from the field flux ϕ_f. Second stage of generation establishes ϕ_d, 90° away (and in the direction of rotation) from ϕ_q, *i.e.*, 180° away, in the direction of rotation from ϕ_f. In other words, the direct axis armature flux ϕ_d opposes the main field flux ϕ_f. If the direction of rotation is reversed, in the first stage ϕ_q is directed downward 90° away from ϕ_f and in the second stage ϕ_d is shifted 90° away from ϕ_q, *i.e.*, 180° away from main field flux ϕ_f. This shows that even with reversed direction of rotation of the armature, the polarity of the output brushes *C*, *D* remains unaltered and this fact is used in a Rosenberg generator for train lighting purposes.

In order to obtain better visualisation of the output voltage across brushes *C*, *D*; the spatial phasor diagram of Fig. 4.90 is of considerable help. In this figure, arrows between $\phi_f, I_q; E_{q1}, \phi_f; I_d, E_d$ etc. indicate the dependence of former on the later. For example ϕ_f depends on I_f, E_{q1} on ϕ_f and so on.

As already explained, the voltage generated across *q*-axis brushes *A*, *B* (in the first stage) is,

$$E_{q1} = K_{af} I_f, \text{ due to } I_f \text{ acting alone.}$$

The *d*-axis armature current I_d establishes *d*-axis armature flux ϕ_d which opposes the control field flux ϕ_f. Rotation of armature in this flux ϕ_d generates an e.m.f. E_{q2} across brushes *A*, *B*. Its magnitude is given by

$$E_{q2} = K_{qd} I_d$$

where K_{qd} is the *q*-axis armature voltage/*d*-axis armature current at speed ω_m.

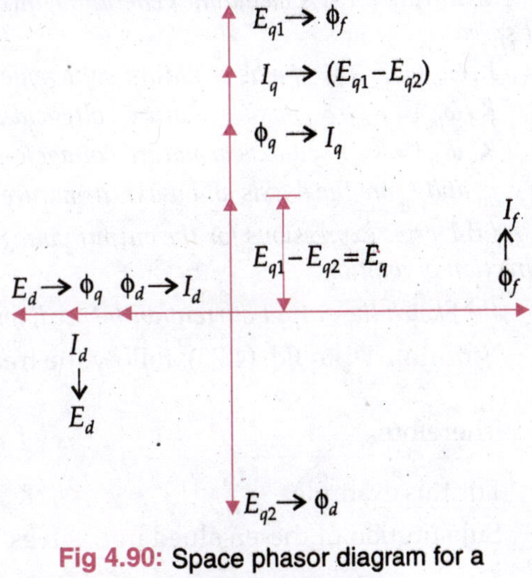

Fig 4.90: Space phasor diagram for a metadyne generator.

Since the two e.m.fs. E_{q1} and E_{q2} across brushes *A*, *B* are in opposite sense as shown in Fig. 4.90, the resultant *q*-axis generated voltage is,

$$E_q = E_{q1} - E_{q2} = (K_{qf} I_f - K_{qd} I_d) \text{ volts.}$$

The *q*-axis armature current is $$I_q = \frac{E_{q1} - E_{q2}}{r_q} = \frac{K_{qf} I_f - K_{qd} I_d}{r_q}$$

where r_q = armature resistance across brushes *A*, *B*.

The voltage equation for the second stage, from the *q*-axis armature circuit to *d*-axis armature circuit is

$$E_d = K_{dq} I_q = \frac{K_{dq} K_{qf} V_f}{r_q r_f} - \frac{K_{dq} K_{qd}}{r_q} I_d.$$

At no-load, $I_d = 0$. Therefore, the output voltage at no-load is

$$E_{d0} = \frac{K_{dq} K_{qf} V_f}{r_q r_f} \qquad \text{...(4.72)}$$

$\therefore$ Voltage amplification, $\dfrac{E_{d0}}{V_f} = \dfrac{K_{dq}K_{qf}}{r_q r_f} = A$

Let $\dfrac{K_{dq}K_{qd}}{r_q}$ be K_1, then $E_d = AV_f - K_1 I_d$. ...(4.73)

In Eq. (4.73), the presence of term $K_1 I_d$ is due to the negative current feedback.

When load is connected, the output voltage is

$$V_d = E_d - I_d r_d = AV_f - I_d(K_1 + r_d) \quad \text{...(4.74)}$$

Here r_d is the d-axis armature resistance.

Also V_d = load voltage = $V_L = I_L R_L$ and $I_d = I_L$.

$$\therefore \quad I_L R_L = AV_f - I_d(K_1 + r_d)$$

or $$I_d = I_L = \frac{AV_f}{r_d + R_L + K_1}.$$

Example 4.79. *A metadyne generator (uncompensated cross-field generator) has the following constants at speed ω_m.*

$K_f\omega_m (= K_{qf})$ = q-axis armature voltage/field amp.

$K_d\,\omega_m (= K_{qd})$ = q-axis armature voltage/d-axis armature current.

$K_q\,\omega_m (= K_{dq})$ = d-axis armature voltage/q-axis armature current.

r_d and r_q are the d-axis and q-axis armature resistances respectively.

(a) Derive expressions for the output voltage and current and show that these are interdependent of the direction of rotation.

(b) Sketch the output current with speed, for a resistive load R_L across the output terminals.

Solution. Upto Eq. (4.73), follow the treatment that has been adopted for its derivation.

Therefore, $$E_d = AV_f - K_1 I_d = \frac{K_{dq}K_{qf}}{r_q r_f}\cdot V_f - \frac{K_{dq}K_{qd}}{r_q} I_d.$$

For this example, $K_{qf} = K_f\omega_m$, $K_{dq} = K_q\omega_m$ and $K_{qd} = K_d\omega_m$.

Substitution of these valued in E_d gives

$$E_d = \frac{K_f K_q \cdot \omega_m^2}{r_q} I_f - \frac{K_d K_q \cdot \omega_m^2}{r_q} I_d \quad \text{...(4.75)}$$

From Eq. (4.75), $$I_d = \frac{K_f}{K_d} I_f - \frac{r_q}{K_d K_q \omega_m^2} E_d \quad \text{...(4.76)}$$

In an ordinary D.C. generator, if the direction of rotation is reversed, the polarity of the output voltage is also reversed, because the speed term ω_m appears only once in its e.m.f. expression. For a metadyne generator, the presence of ω_m^2 in Eq. (4.75) indicates that the polarity of the output voltage remains unaltered with the reversal of direction of rotation. Eq. (4.76) also shows that the direction of output current is unaffected by the speed reversal, because ω_m^2 exists in this expression.

(b) The load voltage $V_d = E_d - I_d r_d = I_d R_L$

$$\therefore \quad I_d(r_d + R_L) = E_d = \frac{K_f K_q \omega_m^2}{r_q} I_f - \frac{K_d K_q \omega_m^2}{r_q} I_d$$

or $$I_d = \frac{K_q K_f I_f}{K_d K_q + \dfrac{r_q(r_d + R_L)}{\omega_m^2}} \quad \text{...(4.77)}$$

At $\omega_m = 0$, the denominator of Eq. (4.77) is equal to infinity and, therefore, I_d is zero. With the increase in ω_m, the term $\dfrac{r_q(r_d + R_L)}{\omega_m^2}$ decreases and, therefore, I_d rises. For relatively larger speeds, the term $\dfrac{r_q(r_d + R_L)}{\omega_m^2}$ would tend to a negligible value, showing thereby that output current I_d is limited to

$$I_d = \frac{K_q K_f}{K_d K_q} I_f = \frac{K_f}{K_d} I_f$$

The sketch showing the variation of I_d with ω_m is given in Fig. 4.91. The cross-field-generator, which possesses these characteristics is the Rosenberg generator and it is employed extensively for lighting trains and other vehicles.

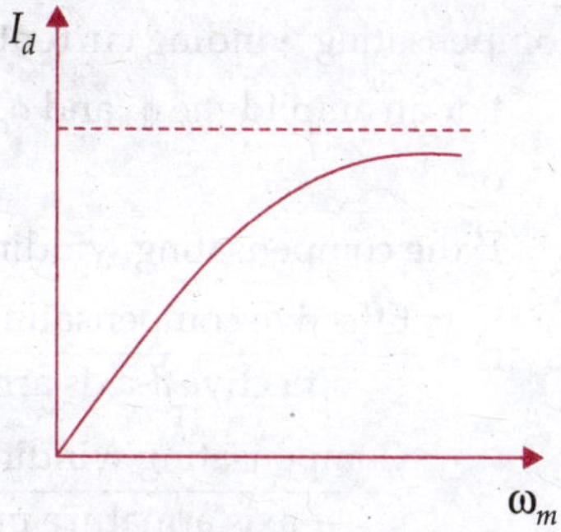

Fig 4.91: Variation of output current I_d with speed ω_m, for a cross-field generator with no compensating winding and supplying a resistive load.

4.16.2. Amplidyne

An amplidyne is a metadyne generator provided with a compensating winding, on the stator d-axis. The compensating winding is connected in series with the d-axis armature circuit. Fig. 4.92 gives the schematic representation of an amplidyne. It is essential in an ampidyne that the compensating winding flux ϕ_c neutralizes the flux ϕ_d produced by the d-axis armature current, at all possible load currents. It may be stated here that amplidyne is one manufacturer's trade name for a fully compensated cross-field generator.

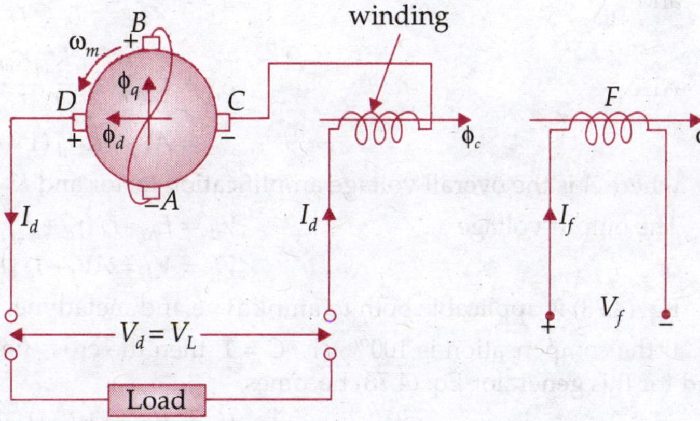

Fig 4.92: Schematic representation of an amplidyne.

Fig. 4.90 is repeated here in Fig. 4.93, but with certain additions.

The flux ϕ_c produced by the compensating winding, opposes the d-axis armature flux ϕ_d and, therefore, assists the field flux ϕ_f as shown in Figs. 4.92 and 4.93. Rotation of the armature in the flux ϕ_c generates an e.m.f. $E_{q3} = K_{qc} I_d$ across the brushes A, B. Thus, the rotational e.m.fs. appearing across brushes A, B are E_{q1} due to ϕ_f, E_{q2} due to ϕ_d and E_{q3} due to ϕ_c, Fig. 4.93. Here K_{qc} is the q-axis armature voltage/

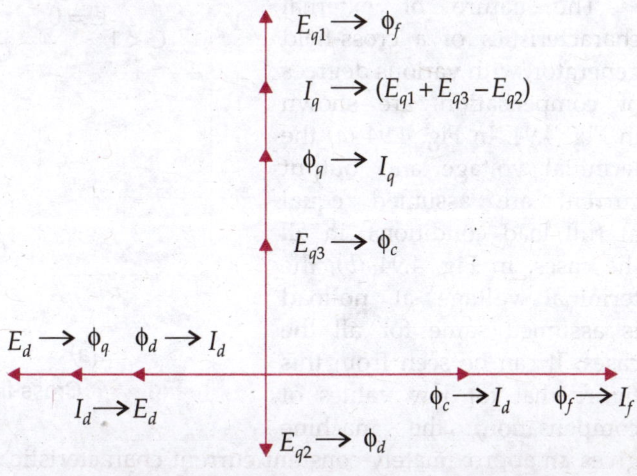

Fig 4.93: Space phasor diagram for an amplidyne.

compensating winding current equal to I_d, at speed ω_m.

For an amplidyne ϕ_d and ϕ_c are equal, *i.e.*, $E_{q2} = E_{q3}$

or $$K_{qd} I_d = K_{qc} I_d \quad \text{or} \quad K_{qd} = K_{qc}$$

If the compensating winding ATs are not equal to *d*-axis armature ATs, then let

$$C = \frac{\text{Effective compensating winding turns, } N_c}{\text{Effective } d\text{-axis armature turns, } N_a} = \frac{N_c \cdot I_d/\text{Rel.}}{N_a I_d/\text{Rel.}}$$

$$= \frac{\text{Compensating winding m.m.f./Rel.}}{d\text{-axis armature m.m.f./Rel.}} = \frac{\phi_c}{\phi_d} = \frac{E_{q3}}{E_{q2}}$$

or $$E_{q3} = CE_{q2}, \text{ i.e., } K_{qc} = CK_{qd}$$

Fig. 4.93 reveals that the sense of e.m.f. E_{q2} is opposite to that of e.m.fs. E_{q1} and E_{q3}. So the resultant *q*-axis generated e.m.f. is

$$E_q = E_{q1} - E_{q2} + E_{q3}$$
$$= K_{qf} I_f - K_{qd} I_d + K_{qc} I_d$$
$$= K_{qf} I_f - K_{qd}(1 - C) I_d$$

and $$I_q = \frac{E_q}{r_q} = \frac{K_{qf}}{r_q} \cdot \frac{V_f}{r_f} - \frac{K_{qd} I_d}{r_q}(1 - C)$$

Also $$E_d = K_{dq} I_q = \frac{K_{dq} K_{qf}}{r_q \cdot r_f} V_f - \frac{K_{dq} K_{qd}}{r_q}(1 - C) I_d$$
$$= AV_f - K_1 I_d (1 - C)$$

where A is the overall voltage amplification factor and K_1 is a constant, as before.

The output voltage $$V_d = E_d - I_d(r_d + r_c) = V_L$$

or $$V_d = V_L = AV_f - I_d[K_1(1 - C) + r_d + r_c] \quad \text{...(4.78)}$$

Eq. (4.78) is applicable both to amplidyne and metadyne.

If the compensation is 100%, *i.e.*, C = 1, then the cross-field generator is known as amplidyne and for this generator Eq. (4.78) becomes,

$$V_d = V_L = AV_f - I_d(r_d + r_c) \quad \text{...(4.79)}$$

If C = 0, less than or greater than one, the cross-field generator is called a metadyne.

The nature of external characteristics of a cross-field generator, with various degrees of compensation, are shown in Fig. 4.94. In Fig. 4.94 *(a)* the terminal voltage and output current are assumed equal at full load conditions, in all the cases. In Fig. 4.94 *(b)*, the terminal voltage at no-load is assumed same for all the cases. It can be seen from this figure that for low values of compensation, the machine gives an approximately constant current characteristic, while for degree of compensation of the order of unity, the machine gives approximately constant voltage characteristics. Therefore,

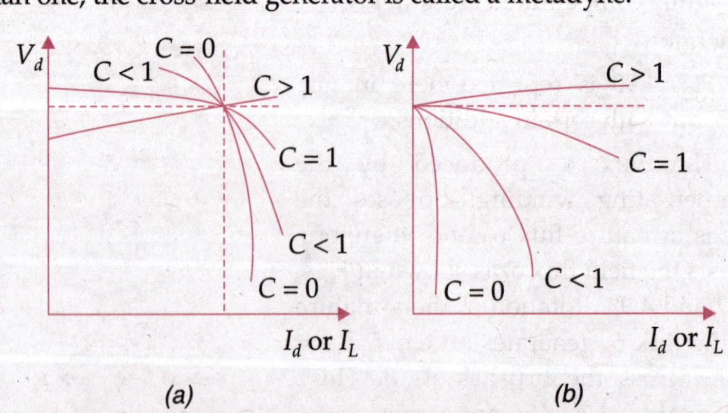

Fig 4.94: Cross-field generator characteristics for different compensations.

un-compensated metadyne is usually called a constant current source and a fully compensated metadyne *i.e.*, an amplidyne, a constant voltage source.

Comparison of voltage Eq. (4.79) for an amplidyne and Eq. (4.74) for a metadyne, shows that the negative feedback effect $K_1 I_d$ of the output current is cancelled in amplidyne and the resultant d-axis flux is equal to the field flux. In other words, the d-axis flux is under complete control of the field winding and is unaffected by the d-axis armature current I_d.

It must be understood that larger power gains are obtained at the expense of the mechanical energy of the prime-mover. Power gains of the order of 20,000 : 1 are possible with amplidyne. Since the power required by the field, or control, winding is very small, amplidyne field winding can be fed directly from an electronic amplifier. If an ampliator winding is provided, then for the given d-axis output voltage ($K_a \omega_m \phi_q$), *i.e.*, for the given q-axis flux ϕ_q, the current I_q is reduced thereby resulting in improved commutation along the q-axis.

At no-load, with constant V_f, the output voltage, from Eq. (4.79), is $E_{d0} = AV_f$, is independent of speed reversal as explained before. Also E_{d0} is proportional to ω_m^2 since both K_{dq} and K_{qf} vary in direct proportion to speed ω_m. It is also seen from E_{d0} expression [Eq. (4.72)] that with the reversal of field current, the polarity of the output voltage gets reversed.

For control applications, a cross-field generator is fitted with more than one field winding.

Armature ohmic loss. For a 2-pole machine, there are two parallel paths. Fig. 4.95 shows the distribution of armature currents I_d and I_q in the armature circuit of a 2-pole cross-field generator. If r_a is the armature resistance, then the resistance of each parallel path will be $2r_a$. If I_a is the effective armature current, then the armature ohmic loss, as seen from Fig. 4.95, is

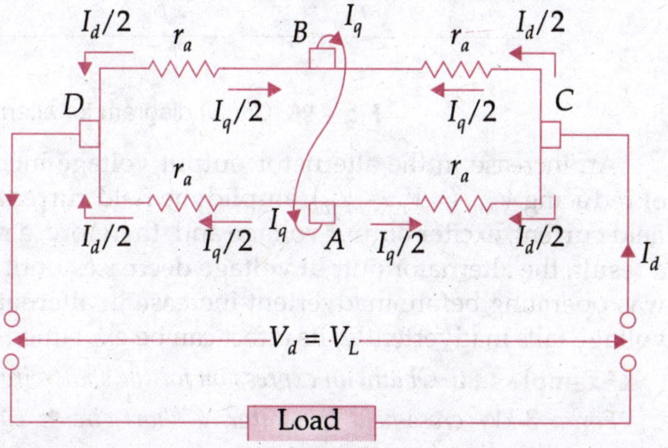

Fig 4.95: Simplified diagram showing the distribution of armature current, in the armature of a 2-pole cross-field generator.

$$I_a^2 r_a = [½ (I_d - I_q)]^2 \times 2r_a + [½(I_d + I_q)]^2 \times 2r_a \quad \text{or} \quad I_a = \sqrt{I_d^2 + I_q^2}$$

$$\therefore \quad \text{Armature ohmic loss} = \left(I_d^2 + I_q^2\right) \times r_a.$$

Applications of the amplidyne. An amplidyne is widely used for various purposes, particularly in feedback control systems where the regulated power requirement is in the range of 1 to 50 kW. It may sometimes be found economical to feed the field winding of an alternator directly from the amplidyne in case excitation requirements are within the range of amplidyne rating. It can also serve as a generator in a Ward-Leonard system of speed control provided the controlled D.C. motor rating is not high. In these feedback systems, the controlled quantity is compared with a fixed quantity and the difference between the two (*i.e.* the error signal) is made to actuate the controlled mechanism in such a manner as to tend to eliminate the error.

Here only an elementary closed loop scheme for regulating the alternator (ac generator) output voltage is described.

Alternator voltage-regulation. When the application of an ampliydne is shown in a circuit configuration, its compensating winding is not shown just for the sake of convenience.

Fig. 4.96 illustrates the use of amplidyne for regulating the output voltage of an alternator. The dc exciter feeds the alternator field whereas its own field current is obtained from the amplidyne output brushes. A linear rectifier converts alternating voltage from three-phase ac generator to dc voltage V_{fb}. This voltage V_{fb} is compared with a fixed reference voltage V_{ref} so that their difference $(V_{ref} - V_{fb}) = V_{amf}$ is applied to the amplidyne field (or control) winding.

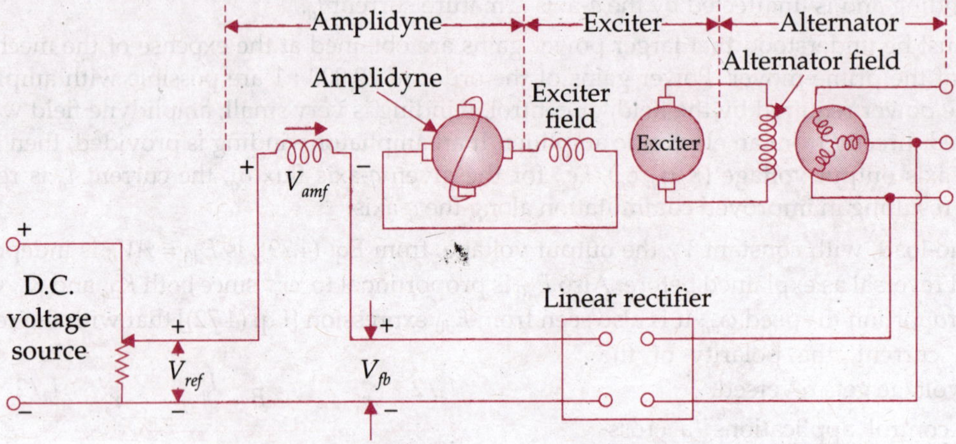

Fig 4.96: Circuit diagram for alternator voltage regulation.

An increase in the alternator output voltage increases V_{fb} proportionally. This has the effect of reducing V_{amf} (= $V_{ref} - V_{fb}$), amplidyne field current and flux, amplidyne output voltage, exciter field current, exciter output voltage and, therefore, a reduction in the field current of alternator. As a result, the alternator output voltage decreases until it comes down to its initial value at which it was operating before inadvertent increase in alternator output voltage. In case alternator output voltage falls inadvertently, its effect can be explained accordingly.

Example 4.80. *Obtain an expression for the short-circuit current amplification of a cross-field machine.*

For a 3-kW cross-field generator, a short-circuit current amplification of 2 is obtained with zero compensation. Its other constants are :

Voltage amplification $A = 50$; $r_d = 5\ \Omega$; $r_c = 1\ \Omega$; $r_f = 100\ \Omega$

Obtain an expression for the output voltage for a field current of 60 mA.

Solution. From Eq. (4.78), $V_d = AV_f - I_d\,[K_1(1 - C) + r_d + r_c]$

Under short-circuit, $V_d = 0$

$\therefore$ $AV_f = I_d\,[K_1(1 - C) + r_d + r_c]$

or $AI_f r_f = I_d\,[K_1(1 - C) + r_d + r_c]$ or $\dfrac{I_d}{I_f} = \dfrac{r_f A}{K_1(1 - C) + r_d + r_c}$

= short-circuit current amplification.

When C = 0, $\dfrac{I_d}{I_f} = 2 = \dfrac{(100)(50)}{K_1 + r_d + 0}$

$\therefore$ $K_1 = 2500 - 5 = 2495$

The output voltage is given by

$$V_d = AV_f - I_d\,[K_1(1 - C) + r_d + r_c]$$

$$= (50)\left(\frac{100 \times 60}{1000}\right) - I_d\,[2495\,(1 - C) + 6]$$

or $V_d = 300 - I_d\,[2495\,(1 - C) + 6]$.

For various values of compensation C, the external characteristics (output voltage versus load current) can be obtained from the above equation.

Example 4.81. *A 3-kW, 300 V, 200 rad/sec, amplidyne has the following constants :*

$$r_f = 50\ \Omega,\ r_a = 5\ \Omega,\ r_c = 1\ \Omega$$

Voltage constants $K_{qf} = 250$ *V/field amp.*

$$K_{dq} = 100 \text{ V/amp.}$$

$$K_{qd} = 80 \text{ V/amp.}$$

Calculate the field current and power gain at rated output. Also obtain these values when the compensation is zero.

Solution. Voltage amplification $A = \dfrac{K_{dq}K_{qf}}{r_q r_f} = \dfrac{(100)(250)}{(5)(50)} = 100.$

For an amplidyne, the voltage equation is $V_d = AV_f - I_d\,(r_d + r_c)$

At rated voltage of 300 V, the rated current is $\dfrac{3000}{300} = 10$ A.

$$\therefore \quad 300 = 100V_f - 10\,(5 + 1) \text{ or } V_f = 3.6 \text{ V}$$

and $$I_f = \frac{3.6}{50} = 72 \text{ mA.}$$

$$\therefore \quad \text{Power gain} = \frac{V_d I_d}{V_f I_f} = \frac{3000}{0.02592} = 11{,}580.$$

For a metadyne with zero compensation,

$$V_d = AV_f - I_d\,[K_1 + r_d]$$

But $$K_1 = \frac{K_{dq} \cdot K_{qd}}{r_d} = \frac{(100)(80)}{5} = 1600$$

$$\therefore \quad 300 = 100V_f - 10\,[1600 + 5] \quad \text{or} \quad V_f = 163.5 \text{ V}$$

and $$I_f = \frac{163.5}{50} = 3.27 \text{ A.}$$

$$\therefore \quad \text{Power gain} = \frac{V_d I_d}{V_f I_f} = \frac{3000 \text{ watts}}{535 \text{ watts}} = 5.61.$$

4.17. SOME WORKED EXAMPLES

In this article, some typical problems relating to dc machines are solved. A few of these have already appeared in one or the other competitive examination.

Example 4.82. *A 230 V dc shunt motor, with an armature-circuit resistance of 0.5 Ω, is excited to give constant main field. At full load, the motor runs at 600 rpm and takes an armature current of 30 A. A resistance of 1 Ω is inserted in series with armature circuit. Now calculate the motor speed at (a) full load torque and (b) twice the full load torque. (c) Also find the motor stalling torque.*

Solution. Here $V_t = 230$ V, $r_a = 0.5\ \Omega$, ϕ = constant, $N_1 = 600$ rpm, $I_{a1} = 30$ A.

Torque $\quad T_e = K_a\,\phi I_a$. Here ϕ = constant, therefore $T_e \propto I_a$

(a) At full load, $\quad I_{a1} = 30$ A

$$\therefore \quad E_{a1} = 230 - 30 \times 0.5 = 215 \text{ V}$$

With resistance $R_{ex} = 1\Omega$ inserted in series with armature circuit, we get

$$E_{a2} = V_t - I_{a1}\,(R_{ex} + r_a)$$

or $$E_{a2} = 230 - 30\,(1 + 0.5) = 185 \text{ V}$$

Now $$\frac{E_{a1}}{E_{a2}} = \frac{N_1 \phi_1}{N_2 \phi_2}. \text{ Here } \phi_1 = \phi_2 = \phi$$

$\therefore$ $$N_2 = \frac{E_{a2}}{E_{a1}} \times N_1 = \frac{185}{215} \times 600 = 516.3 \text{ rpm}$$

(b) At twice the full load torque, $T_L = 2T_e$.

$\therefore$ $$T_e \propto I_{a1}$$

$$2T_e \propto I_{a3}$$

$\therefore$ $$\frac{T_e}{2T_e} = \frac{I_{a1}}{I_{a3}} \text{ or } \frac{1}{2} = \frac{30}{I_{a3}}, \therefore I_{a3} = 30 \times 2 = 60 \text{ A}.$$

Now $$E_{a3} = V_t - I_{a3}\,(1 + 0.5) = 230 - 60\,(1 + 0.5) = 140 \text{ V}$$

$\therefore$ $$\frac{E_{a3}}{E_{a1}} = \frac{N_3 \phi_3}{N_1 \phi_1} \therefore N_3 = \frac{E_{a3}}{E_{a1}} \times N_1 = \frac{140}{215} \times 600 = 390.7 \text{ rpm}$$

(c) At stalling, motor speed reaches zero, therefore motor counter or back emf is zero.

$\therefore$ Stalling current I_{stl} can be obtained from

$$V_t = 0\,E + I_{stl} \times 1.5$$

$\therefore$ $$I_{stl} = \frac{230}{1.5} = 153.33 \text{ A}$$

Now $$\frac{T_{e.stl}}{T_{efl}} = \frac{I_{stl}}{I_{a1}} = \left(\frac{153.33}{30}\right)$$

$\therefore$ $$\text{Stalling torque} = \left(\frac{153.33}{30}\right) \times T_{efl} = 5.11 \times T_{efl} = 5 \times \text{full load torque.}$$

Example 4.83. *A 230 V dc shunt motor runs at 1100 rpm. If a resistance of 10Ω is inserted in series with shunt field, no-load motor speed rises to 1200 rpm at rated terminal voltage.*

(a) Find resistance of shunt field

(b) If resistance in series with field circuit is increased from 10 Ω to 20 Ω, calculate the new motor speed.

Solution. *(a)* Here armature circuit resistance is not specified, so take $r_a = 0$.

$\therefore$ $$V_t = E_a = K_a \phi \omega_m$$

or $$V_t \propto \phi N \quad \text{or} \quad V_t \propto I_f N$$

For $V_t = 230$ V, $$I_{f1} = \frac{V_t}{R_f}, \therefore 230 \propto I_{f1} N_1$$

or $$230 \propto \frac{230}{R_f} \times 1100 \qquad ...(i)$$

When resistance of 10 Ω is inserted in shunt field circuit,

shunt field current $$I_{f2} = \frac{230}{R_f + 10} \text{ and speed is } N_2 = 1200 \text{ rpm}$$

$\therefore$ $$V_t \propto I_{f2} N_2 \quad \text{or} \quad 230 \propto \frac{230}{R_f + 10} \times 1200 \qquad ...(ii)$$

From Eqs. *(i)* and *(ii)*, we get,

$$1100 \times \frac{230}{R_f} = 1200 \times \frac{230}{R_f + 10}$$

$\therefore$ $$R_f = \frac{1100 \times 10}{100} = 110\ \Omega$$

(b) $V_t = E_a \propto I_{f1} N_1$ Here, $I_{f1} = \frac{V_t}{R_f} = \frac{230}{110}$

If shunt field resistance is increased by 20 Ω, then

$$I_{f2} = \frac{230}{R_f + 20} = \frac{230}{130}$$

$$\therefore \quad 230 \propto \frac{230}{130} \times N_2 \qquad \text{...(iii)}$$

From Eqs. *(i)* and *(iii)*

$$\frac{230}{110} \times 1100 = \frac{230}{130} \times N_2$$

$$\therefore \quad N_2 = \frac{1100}{110} \times 130 = 1300 \text{ rpm}$$

Example 4.84. *A 230 V dc shunt motor has an armature resistance of 0.2Ω. The motor drives a constant-torque load and draws an armature current of 50 A from 230 V dc source. An external resistance of 1Ω is inserted in the armature circuit. Calculate (a) the armature current and (b) the percentage reduction in speed.*

Neglect rotational losses and armature reaction.

Solution. *(a)* With insertion of external resistance in the armature circuit, shunt field circuit is not affected. Therefore, shunt field current and therefore shunt field flux ϕ remains constant. For constant-torque load, T_L = motor torque, $T_e = K_a \phi I_a$ or $I_a = \frac{T_L}{K_a \phi}$. Since K_a and ϕ are constant, armature current remains constant at 50 A

(b) Without external resistance, $E_{a1} = 230 - 50 \times 0.2 = 220$ V

With external resistance of 1 Ω inserted in the armature circuit gives

$$E_{a2} = 230 - 50 \times (1 + 0.2) = 170 \text{ V}$$

Now

$$\frac{E_{a1}}{E_{a2}} = \frac{N_1 \phi_1}{N_2 \phi_2} \quad \text{or} \quad \frac{220}{170} = \frac{N_1 \cdot \phi}{N_2 \cdot \phi}$$

$$\therefore \quad \text{Speed } N_2 = \frac{170}{220} N_1 = 0.7727\, N_1$$

$$\therefore \quad \text{Percentage reduction in speed} = \frac{N_1 - N_2}{N_1} \times 100 = \frac{(1 - 0.7727)N_1}{N_1} \times 100 = 22.73\%$$

Example 4.85. *A 220 V dc series motor runs drawing a current of 30 A from the supply. Armature and field circuit resistances are 0.4 Ω and 0.1 Ω respectively. The load torque varies as the square of the speed. The flux in the motor may be taken as being proportional to the armature current. To reduce the speed of the motor by 50%, the resistance in ohms that should be added in series with the armature is...* [GATE : 2017 (I)]

Solution. $V_t = 220$ V, $I_a = 30$ A, $r_a + r_s = 0.4 + 0.1 = 0.5$ Ω

$$\therefore \quad E_{a1} = 220 - 30 \times 0.5 = 205 \text{ V}$$

Here $T_L \propto N^2$. But $T_L = T_e = K_a\, \phi\, I_a$. It is given that $\phi \propto I_a$, therefore $T_e = K\, I_a^2$, but $T_e = T_L$

$$\therefore \quad I_a^2 \propto N^2 \text{ or } I_a \propto N$$

For armature current I_{a1}, $I_{a1} \propto N_1$

New speed $N_2 = \frac{N_1}{2}$ and new armature current $I_{a2} \propto N_2$

From above

$$\frac{I_{a1}}{I_{a2}} = \frac{N_1}{N_2} = \frac{N_1}{N_1/2} = 2;$$

$$\therefore \quad I_{a2} = \frac{I_{a1}}{2} = \frac{30}{2} = 15 \text{ A.}$$

Let R_{ex} be the resistance added in series with armature. Now, counter emf E_{a2} is

$$E_{a2} = 220 - 15\,[(r_a + r_s) + R_{ex}]$$

$$\therefore \quad \frac{E_{a1}}{E_{a2}} = \frac{205}{220 - 15[0.5 + R_{ex}]} = \frac{N_1 I_{a1}}{N_2 I_{a2}} = \frac{N_1}{N_1/2} \times \frac{I_a}{I_{a1}/2} = 4$$

$$\therefore \quad 205 = 4\,[220 - 15\,(0.5 + R_{ex})]$$

$$\therefore \quad R_{ex} = \frac{880 - 205}{60} - 0.5 = 11.25\ \Omega$$

4.18. PERMANENT MAGNET DC (PMDC) MOTORS

In conventional dc (CDC) motors, salient poles are fixed to yoke or stator. Field winding is wound over these poles to produce the required field flux. In PMDC motors, the required field flux is produced by permanent magnets attached to the stator. Rotor of PMDC motor is similar to the rotor of CDC. In other words, rotor of PMDC motor consists of armature core, armature winding and commutator. Stationary carbon brushes are kept pressed on to the commutator surface as in a CDC motor.

PMDC motors have smooth cylindrical shell of uniform thickness. Permanent magnets, magnetized radially, are attached to the outer shell as shown in Fig. 4.97 *(a)*. Here the arrows indicate the direction in which the permanent magnetic material is magnetized. As stated before, rotor has armature winding, commutator and brushes as in CDC motors.

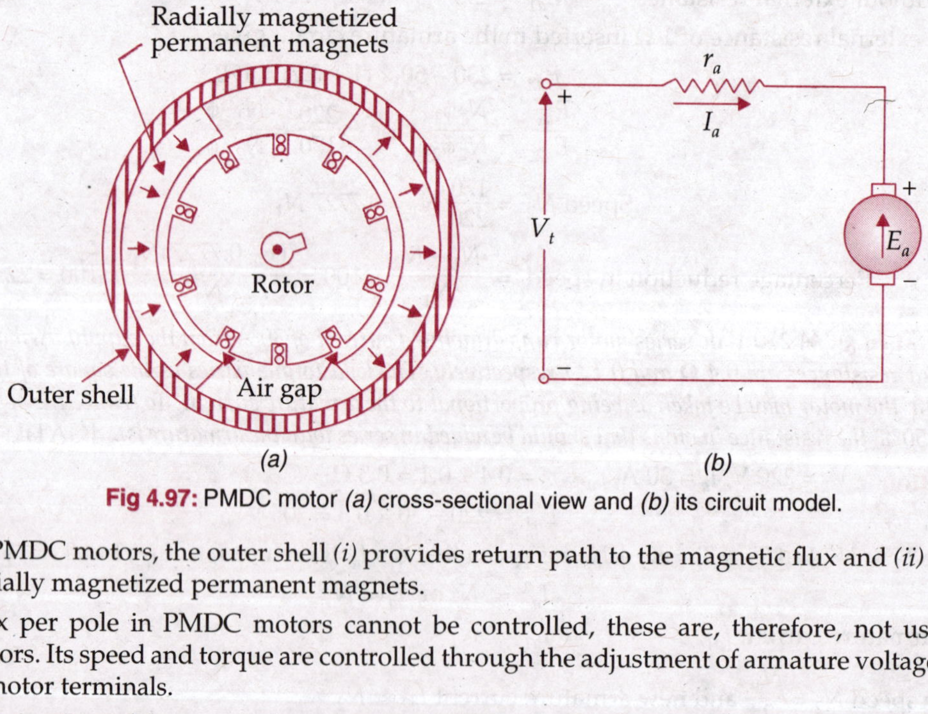

Fig 4.97: PMDC motor *(a)* cross-sectional view and *(b)* its circuit model.

In PMDC motors, the outer shell *(i)* provides return path to the magnetic flux and *(ii)* supports the radially magnetized permanent magnets.

Flux per pole in PMDC motors cannot be controlled, these are, therefore, not used as dc generators. Its speed and torque are controlled through the adjustment of armature voltage applied to the motor terminals.

The circuit model, or equivalent circuit, of a PMDC motor is shown in Fig. 4.97 *(b)*. As field flux in PMDC motor is provided by permanent magnets, the field winding is not shown in the circuit model of this motor. But in the circuit model of a CDC motor, the field winding must always be indicated as in Fig. 4.11.

In a CDC motor, the generated, or counter, emf is given by

$$E_a = K_a \phi \omega_m \qquad ...(4.3)$$

and electromagnetic torque is given by

$$T_e = K_a \phi I_a \qquad ...(4.6)$$

In a PMDC motor, flux ϕ is constant and as a result, above equations can be reduced to

$$E_a = K_m \omega_m \qquad ...(4.80)$$

and $$T_e = K_m I_a = \frac{E_a}{\omega_m} \cdot I_a = \frac{E_a I_a}{\omega_m} \qquad ...(4.81)$$

where $K_m = K_a \phi$ is known as **speed-voltage constant** in V-s/rad or **torque constant** in Nm/A. Its value depends upon the number of field poles, armature conductors etc.

Equivalent circuit of Fig. 4.97 *(b)* gives

$$V_t = E_a + I_a r_a = K_m \cdot \omega_m + I_a r_a \qquad ...(4.82)$$

or $$\omega_m = \frac{V_t - I_a r_a}{K_m} \qquad ...(4.83)$$

Equations governing the performance of PMDC motor are basically the same as for dc shunt motor with constant field. Consequently, the speed and torque of PMDC motor can be adjusted by armature-terminal voltage control, armature rheostat control and chopper control.

The major advantage of PMDC motors is that they require no field current. So the energy required in producing the field flux is saved. Since space for field winding is not needed, PMDC motors are smaller in size and may even cost less than the correspondingly rated CDC motors.

The limitation of PMDC motors is that excessive current in the armature winding may demagnetize the permanent magnets. In addition, the flux density produced in the air gap by permanent magnets is limited. This drawback is, however, overcome to some extent by the development of new magnetic materials like samarium-cobalt and neodymium-iron-boron.

PMDC motors are used extensively in automobiles for windshield wipers and washers, for blowers used in heaters and air conditioners, to raise and lower windows, in slot cars and electric tooth bruhes, in personal computer disc drives etc. As millions of automobiles are manufactured each year, PMDC motors are also produced in millions. PMDC motors have been developed up to about 150 kW for use in industry.

Example 4.86. *A PMDC motor has armature resistance of 1 Ω. When fed from 48 V D.C. source, it runs at a speed of 2400 r.p.m. while taking 0.8 A at no load. Determine (a) the no-load rotational losses of the motor (b) the motor output when running at a speed of 1600 r.p.m. and with source voltage of 40 V D.C. and (c) its stall torque when the source voltage is 20 V D.C.*

Solution. *(a)* From Equation (4.84), the generated e.m.f. E_a is given by

$$E_a = 48 - 0.8 \times 1 = 47.2 \text{ V}$$

At no-load, all the electromagnetic power developed is used to supply the no-load rotational losses.

$\therefore$ No-load rotational losses $= E_a I_a = 47.8 \times 0.8 = 37.76$ W

(b) $E_a = K_m \omega_m$

$\therefore$ Speed-voltage constant, $K_m = \dfrac{47.2 \times 60}{2\pi \times 2400} = 0.188$ V-s/rad

For a speed of 1600 r.p.m., $\omega_m = \dfrac{2\pi \times 1600}{60}$ rad/s

Generated e.m.f. $E_a = K_m \omega_m = 0.188 \times \dfrac{2\pi \times 80}{3} = 31.5$ V

New armature current, $I_a = \frac{V_t - E_a}{r_a} = \frac{40 - 31.5}{1.0} = 8.5$ A

Electromagnetic power developed $= E_a I_a = 31.5 \times 8.5 = 267.75$ W

$\therefore$ Output, or shaft power $= E_a I_a$ – no-load rotational losses $= 267.75 - 37.76 \cong 230.0$ W

(c) When motor stalls, $E_a = 0$ and $V_t = I_a r_a$

$\therefore$ Stall current, $I_a = \frac{20}{1} = 20$ A

Stall torque, $T_e = K_m I_a = 0.188 \times 20 = 3.76$ Nm

4.19. D.C. MACHINE APPLICATIONS

D.C. machine applications involve reconsideration of their operating characteristics, together with their economic and technical evaluation as compared with other competing energy-conversion devices. The outstanding advantage of D.C. machines is that they offer easily controllable characteristics. Their main disadvantages are high initial investment and increased cost of maintenance. In spite of this, D.C. machines still hold a strong competitive position for industrial applications because of their attractive features. In this article, D.C. machine applications are considered briefly.

4.19.1. Generator Applications

The advent of various types of controlled rectifiers, has declined the importance of D.C. generators. Wherever electric energy in D.C. form is required, it has been found much cheaper to convert A.C. to D.C. by means of transformer-rectifier equipment rather than with the use of A.C. to D.C. motor-generator set. The disadvantages of transformer-rectifier equipment are poor power factor, harmonic generation, difficulty in obtaining reversing and regenerative braking. Its advantages, namely less cost, less floor-space, less noise and minimum maintenance ; more than outweigh its disadvantages in this modern age. It does not mean that D.C. generators are not manufactured in the present times. In some applications, D.C. generators are indispensable and some of these applications are dynamometers (for measuring torque etc.), D.C. welding generators, control-type D.C. generators (cross-field generators) for closed loop systems, permanent magnet D.C. generators (*i.e.* tachogenerators) etc. From among the D.C. generators, the commonly used generators are separately-excited generators for wide output-voltage control and cumulatively compounded self excited generators for maintaining constant terminal voltage. Now-a-days, the principal applications of separately-excited D.C. generators are *(i)* to serve as an excitation source for large alternators in power-generating stations, *(ii)* to serve as control generator in Ward-Leonard system of speed control and *(iii)* to serve as auxiliary and emergency power supplies.

The power for electroplating can be obtained from A.C. supply through rectifiers or from D.C. generators. When electroplating is required in expensive equipment, an uninterrupted and constant D.C. voltage is essential. This supply, in practice, is usually taken from several D.C. generators running in parallel. It is because of the fact that A.C. supply through rectifiers used for electroplating may suffer an inadvertent voltage dip, thereby resulting in defective electroplating. As a consequence, expensive equipment under treatment would have to be discarded leading to a huge loss. Therefore, it is essential to employ D.C. generators in parallel for the electroplating of expensive equipment.

4.19.2. Motor Applications

For ordinary industrial drives, dc motors are rarely used. It is because power utility systems deliver ac energy and therefore ac motors are preferred. However, for large size as well as small size industrial drives, where ac motors fail to fulfil the requirement of the drive, dc motors are preferred. It is because dc motors possess excellent torque-speed characteristics and offer a wide range of speed control. Advanced electronics have made possible the availability of ac motors for their use in adjustable speed drives. Yet the versatility and flexibility of dc motors continue to retain their use in industrial electric drives. In view of this, the demand for dc motors would continue undiminished even in the near future. A brief discussion regarding the dc motor applications is given below.

Shunt motors

(i) For a given field current in a shunt motor, the speed drop from no-load to full load is invariably less than 6 to 8%. In view of this, the shunt motor is termed a constant speed motor. Therefore, for constant speed drives in industry, D.C. shunt motors can be employed. But this motor can't compete with constant-speed squirrel cage induction motor, because the latter is more cheaper, rugged and requires less maintenance.

(ii) When constant speed service at low speeds is required, the comparison is usually between synchronous motors and D.C. shunt motors. It is because the construction of high performance polyphase induction motor with large number of poles is difficult. However, for adjustable-speed service at low operating speed, D.C. shunt motor is a preferred choice.

(iii) When the driven load requires a wide range of speed control (both below base speed and above base speed), a D.C. shunt motor is employed, *e.g.* in lathes etc.

(iv) In a shunt motor, if field winding is disconnected from armature and connected to an external voltage source, it becomes a *separately-excited motor*. This motor offers independent armature control and field control. Since separately-excited D.C. motors are easily adaptable to wide range speed and torque control, in high-power applications these are used extensively in steel and aluminum rolling mills and in Ward-Leonard systems of speed control. In low-power applications, separately excited D.C. motor finds wide use as a *control motor*.

A control motor is a low-power rating (less than a few hundred watts) motor, with field excitation held fixed and with its torque T_e proportional to armature current I_a.

Series Motors. The outstanding feature of series motor is the automatic decrease in speed as soon as increased load torque is required. Power taken by a series motor tend to remain constant, because increase in load torque is accompanied by low speed and vice-versa.

(i) Since a series motor can withstand severe starting duties and can furnish high starting torques, it is best suited for driving hoists, trains, excavators, cranes etc. Wound-rotor induction motors compete favourably with series motors, but the choice is governed by the economics. However, for traction purposes, series motor is the only choice. Therefore, series motors are widely used in all types of electric vehicles, electric trains, streetcars, battery-powered portable tools, automotive starter motors etc.

(ii) In order to avoid the pollution in big cities, now battery-driven automobiles are being introduced on a large scale. For such battery-driven automobiles, series motors controlled through choppers are best suited.

Compound Motors

(i) A compound motor with a strong series field, has its characteristics approaching that of a series motor. Therefore, such type of compound motors are used for loads, requiring heavy starting torque which are likely to be reduced to zero. In ordinary series motor, no-load speed becomes dangerously high, but in a compound motor, the no-load speed is limited by the weak shunt field.

(ii) A compound motor with weak series field has its characteristic approaching that of a shunt motor. Weak series field causes more drooping speed-torque characteristic than with an ordinary shunt motor. Such compound motors with more steeper characteristics, are used where load fluctuates between wide limits intermittently. Flywheels attached to the shaft of such compound motors serve as load equalizers. During light loads, flywheels store kinetic energy but during peak loads, the motor speed drops allowing the flywheel to give up some of its stored energy to the load. This has the effect of reducing the power demand from the supply. The type of drives where such compound motors can be employed are rolling mill drive, punching press, planning or milling machine etc.

(iii) When the supply voltage across the motor terminals is likely to vary considerably, such as in traction motors, compound motors are preferred. The series field helps in reducing the fluctuations of the armature current drawn from the supply, because of its inductance and because of series-field m.m.f. effect on the flux and therefore on the counter e.m.f.

(iv) A differential compound motor is almost never used. In this motor, shunt and series fields oppose each other and it is possible that at some state of operation, there may be zero flux in the air gap. When this occurs, motor speed $\left(n \propto \frac{1}{\phi}\right)$ becomes dangerously high and armature current increases to a very high value. This shows a differential compound motor is associated with increased armature current at high operating speed ; this motor may also draw increased armature current during its starting. This increased armature current during starting or during high-speed operation becomes dangerously so high that it may damage the commutator and armature windings. So, a differential compound motor is rarely used in practice.

In general, major cause of using D.C. machines in electromechanical systems is that their dynamic characteristics can be controlled easily through the use of variable voltage across armature and/or field windings. Recent advances in power electronics have, however, made available variable-voltage variable frequency (VVVF) converters of sufficient power level. The drives consisting of VVVF controllers and A.C. machines are now being considered for such applications which were once dominated by D.C. machines. Field-oriented control of ac motors, though complex and more expensive, is now being considered for adjustable speed drives.

In the end, it must be emphasized that choice of a D.C. motor for adjustable speed drives should not be based merely on its merits and demerits. In fact, it is necessary to make specific, analytic, economic and technical comparison of all possible alternatives of dc and ac drives. Operating characteristics of motor and load must be compatible with each other. At the same time, comparative studies amongst various choices must be based on the combination of motor and its associated control equipment. As the D.C. machines are easily adaptable to control strategies, D.C. machines offer versatile energy conversion devices and hence their demand continues undwindled.

Permanent-Magnet D.C. Motors. As stated before, these motors are used in automobiles as starter motors and for windshield wipers and washers, for blowers used in heaters and air-conditioners, for raising and lowering windows, for electric tooth brushes etc. Literally, PMDC motors are manufactured in millions each year to meet the demand of millions of automobiles produced each year.

At last, it may be said about D.C. motor applications that the use of power-semiconductor devices in electric drive systems has strengthened the competitive position of D.C. motors where precise control of speed and/or torque is required.

PROBLEMS

4.1. (*a*) Draw neat diagram of a 4-pole D.C. machine. Label all its parts and mention the material used for each part.

(*b*) A 10 kW, 250 V, 6-pole lap-connected D.C. generator runs at 1200 rpm. Armature has 500 conductors. For full-load armature-ohmic loss of 200 W, find the useful flux per pole. Take 2 V as the brush drop at full-load. **[Ans.** 0.0257 Wb]

4.2. (*a*) Which parts of a D.C machine are laminated if it is to be operated through a power-electronics converter? Name these parts and give their constructional details.

(*b*) A 4-pole lap-connected D.C. generator has no-load generated e.m.f. of 500 V when driven at 1200 r.p.m. Calculate the flux per pole if the armature has 120 slots with 6 conductors per slot.

In case each conductor has a resistance of 0.01 Ω, find the resistance of the armature winding. **[Ans.** (*b*) 0.03472 Wb, 0.45 Ω]

4.3. (*a*) Describe the constructional details of commutator of a D.C. machine.

(*b*) Following statements are made regarding the armature reaction in dc machines:

(*i*) It is stationary in space. (*ii*) It rotates with respect to stator.

(*iii*) It is stationary with respect to armature.

(*iv*) Its peak is along the brush axis.

Explain which of the above statement/s is/are correct.

[Ans. (*b*) (*i*) and (*iv*) correct; (*ii*) and (*iii*) incorrect.]

4.4. (*a*) What are the two functions of a commutator in D.C. machines?

(*b*) Explain how the commutator keeps the armature m.m.f. stationary in space, along the interpolar axis, even though the armature rotates.

4.5. (*a*) In a D.C. machine, the electromagnetic torque is $T_e = K_a \phi I_a$ and the armature generated e.m.f. is $E_a = K_a \phi\omega_m$. Show that the armature constant K_a, appearing in both T_e and E_a expressions, are dimensionally equivalent.

(*b*) In a D.C. machine, electromagnetic torque is $T_e = K_a I_a$ where K_a has the units of Nm/A. The generated e.m.f. is $E_a = K_a \omega_m$ where the units of K_a are volt-s/rad. Show that K_a appearing in T_e and E_a expressions are dimensionally equivalent.

(*c*) A D.C. shunt machine develops an open circuit e.m.f. of 250 V at 1500 r.p.m. Find its developed torque for an armature current of 20 A. **[Ans.** (*c*) 31.831 Nm]

4.6. (*a*) Resistance measured across two adjacent positive and negative brushes of a 6-pole dc machine is 0.06 Ω. Find the effective armature resistance seen from the armature terminals if the dc machine is (*i*) lap wound and (*ii*) wave wound.

[Hint : (*i*) Lap winding has four parallel paths, refer to Chap. 7. (*ii*) Wave winding has only two brushes, refer to Chap. 7.]

(*b*) A 6-pole, 12 kW, 240 V D.C. machine is wave-connected. If this machine is now lap-connected, all other things remaining the same, calculate its voltage, current and power ratings. **[Ans.** (*a*) (*i*) 0.01 Ω (*ii*) 0.06 Ω (*b*) 80 V, 150 A, 12 kW]

4.7. (*a*) E.m.f. generated in one N-turn coil, rotating in a constant field flux ϕ, at any time t is given by

$$e_c = N\omega_r \phi \sin \omega_r t$$

where ω_r = armature speed of D.C. machine in rad/sec.

Use this expression of e_c to derive the following e.m.f. expression for a D.C. generator :

$$E_a = \frac{\phi ZnP}{a} \text{ volts.}$$ **[Hint :** Refer to Art. 3.44.]

(b) A separately-excited D.C. generator, operating with fixed excitation, delivers 450 kW to a D.C. bus at 600 V. Estimate the percentage change in generator speed required so that 180 kW is delivered to D.C. bus. Resistance between bus-bar terminals and the armature terminals is 0.015 Ω and armature-circuit resistance is 0.015 Ω. **[Ans.** *(b)* – 2.1687%]

4.8. *(a)* By using *Blv* concept, derive the following e.m.f. expression for a D.C. machine :

$$E_a = \frac{\phi ZnP}{a} \text{ volts}$$

(b) A 10 kW, 6-pole D.C. generator develops an e.m.f. of 200 V at 1500 r.p.m. The armature has a lap-connected winding. The average flux density over a pole pitch is 0.9 Tesla. The length and diameter of the armature are 0.25 m and 0.2 m respectively. Calculate *(i)* the flux per pole *(ii)* the total number of active conductors in the armature and *(iii)* the torque developed by the machine when the armature supplies a current of 50 A. *[GATE, 1991]*

[Ans. *(b) (i)* 0.02356 Wb *(ii)* 340 *(iii)* 63.745 Nm]

4.9. *(a)* Derive an expression for the electromagnetic torque developed in a D.C. machine by using *BIl* concept.

(b) A 2-pole lap-wound D.C. shunt motor with 360 conductors operates at a constant flux level of 50 m Wb. The motor armature has a resistance of 0.12 Ω and is designed to operate at 240 V, taking a current of 60 A at full load.

(i) Determine the value of external resistance to be inserted in the armature circuit so that armature current does not exceed twice its full-load value at starting.

(ii) The external resistance is completely cut out when the motor reaches its final speed, with the armature current at the full-load value. Calculate the motor speed under these conditions. *[GATE, 1992]* **[Ans.** *(i)* 1.88 Ω *(ii)* 776 r.p.m.]

4.10. *(a)* Develop the circuit model of a D.C. machine. Hence bring out clearly how the e.m.f. and current in the armature conductors of a D.C. motor oppose each other.

(b) A D.C. shunt generator gives an open-circuit voltage of 240 V. When loaded, the terminal voltage falls to 220 V. Determine the load current in case armature-circuit and field-winding resistances are 0.1 Ω and 50 Ω respectively. Neglect the effect of armature reaction.

[Ans. *(b)* 195.6 A]

4.11. *(a)* Prove that in a D.C. generator, generated e.m.f. and current in a conductor are in the same direction, whereas in a D.C. motor, generated e.m.f. opposes the flow of current in a conductor.

(b) In a 6-pole D.C. machine, total armature ampere conductors are 4200, flux per pole is 0.03 Wb. Calculate the total torque developed in this machine.

[Hint : *(b)* $\frac{I_a}{a} Z = 4200$. Use Eqn. (4.4)] **[Ans.** *(b)* 120.32 Nm]

4.12. *(a)* In a D.C. machine, the main field flux passes the armature mainly through the teeth, because the slot portion has longer air gap. As a consequence, flux density in the slot width is much lower than its value in the teeth. Extend this fact to explain the physical process of torque production in D.C. machines.

(b) A 230 V, 10-pole, lap-connected D.C. shunt motor runs at 120 r.p.m. while taking an armature current of 1200 A. Each conductor has active length of 30 cms and armature diameter is 120 cm. Because of the facts stated in part *(a)* above, flux density in the slot is 0.06 T for a total flux per pole of 80 mWb. Calculate the average force on each conductor

(i) if the conductor is housed in the slot and

(ii) if the conductor is placed on a smooth cylindrical iron surface.

[Ans. *(b) (i)* 2.16 N *(ii)* 25.47 N]

4.13. *(a)* Describe, with relevant diagrams, the different methods of excitation of D.C. machines.

(b) A 4-pole compound generator has armature, series-field and shunt-field resistances of 1 Ω, 0.5 Ω and 100 Ω respectively. This generator delivers 4 kW at a terminal voltage of 200 V. Allowing 1 V per brush for contact drop, calculate for both short-shunt and long-shunt connections

(i) the generated e.m.f. and

(ii) the flux per pole if the armature has 200 lap-connected conductors and is driven at 750 rpm. **[Ans.** *(b) (i)* 234.1 V, 235 V *(ii)* 93.64 mWb, 94 mWb]

4.14. *(a)* Explain why the e.m.f. generated in the armature of a D.C. motor is called 'back e.m.f'.

(b) Four terminals of a D.C. shunt machine are available, but these are unmarked. How would you identify the field and armature terminals?

(c) Find the resistance of the load which takes a power of 6 kW from a D.C. generator whose external characteristic is given by the equation $V_t = 300 - 0.5\ I_L$ where I_L is the load current. **[Ans.** *(b)* Low-resistance terminals are armature terminals whereas high-resistance terminals are field terminals *(c)* 13.982 Ω]

4.15. *(a)* In the model of a D.C. machine, field winding and its armature circuit are always drawn at 90° with respect to each other. Why?

(b) How are the series and shunt windings arranged on the pole of a D.C. compound machine?

(c) How will you distinguish between series and shunt windings of a D.C. compound machine?

(d) Discuss the terms commutation and commutation period.

4.16. *(a)* What is meant by armature reaction?

(b) Show that the effect of armature m.m.f. on the main field, is entirely cross-magnetizing.

(c) Under saturated conditions, the effect of armature m.m.f. is to demagnetize the main field. Explain this with the help of developed view of armature conductors and poles.

4.17. *(a)* The effect of armature reaction is to decrease the flux under one pole tip and to increase it under the other pole tip. Explain this with respect to both D.C. generator and motor by using the developed view of armature current sheet and poles.

(b) Explain briefly the four bad effects of armature reaction.

4.18. *(a)* How should the main-pole tips be constructed to minimize the effect of armature reaction on the main field?

(b) If the brushes are shifted in the direction of rotation (forward shift), the flux per pole is reduced in a generator. Explain.

What would happen if the brushes are given a backward shift in a generator?

4.19. *(a)* Explain how the effect of armature m.m.f. on the main field flux can be described with the help of magnetization curve of a D.C. machine.

(b) How can you detect whether the brushes in a D.C. machine are placed correctly along the interpolar axis or not?

(c) In D.C. machines, explain why air-gap length at pole centre is short as compared to air-gap length at pole tips.

(d) What are the various types of brushes and where these are employed?

4.20. (a) Derive expressions for the back ampere turns per pole and cross-magnetizing ATs per pole in case brushes are given a lead of θ° from GNA in case of a D.C. generator.

(b) A 6-pole, wave-wound D.C. generator has armature conductors 360, armature current 80 A, angle of lead 5° from GNA. Calculate (i) back and cross ampere turns per pole (ii) number of series turns per pole to neutralise the demagnetization. Take leakage co-efficient = 1.2.

[**Hint :** (b) $\frac{\text{Series field m.m.f. per pole}}{\text{back ATs per pole}} = 1.2$] [**Ans.** (b) (i) 200, 1000 (ii) 3]

4.21. (a) What is meant by commutation in D.C. machines? Differentiate between good commutation and bad commutation. Enumerate the mechanical and electrical conditions leading to poor commutation in D.C. machines.

(b) Describe the process of commutation in D.C. machines through the reversal of current in a coil.

Hence show that e.m.f. induced in a coil undergoing commutation is given by $\frac{2I_a/a}{T_c}$ where I_a is the armature current and T_c is the commutation period.

4.22. (a) If coil resistance is neglected as compared to the copper-carbon resistance, linear commutation is obtained; if coil resistance is not neglected, resistance commutation is obtained. Explain.

(b) On what four factors, does the current in a commutated coil depend? Discuss.

4.23. (a) Give the concept of reactance voltage in D.C. machines.

Discuss how reactance voltage causes under commutation in D.C. machines.

(b) Discuss resistance commutation qualitatively.

Explain how good commutation is achieved by minimising the reactance voltage.

Describe the role played by resistance commutation in securing good commutation in D.C. machines.

4.24. (a) Sketch the general waveform of armature m.m.f. and flux in a D.C. machine. Where has the flux zero value and maximum value and why?

(b) How is the voltage commutation achieved in D.C. machines?

4.25. (a) What are the interpoles?

Why are interpoles designed to provide m.m.f. more than the armature m.m.f. in the commutating zone?

(b) With the D.C. machine fitted with interpoles, draw the resultant flux density waveform and show therefrom the improvement in the commutation process of both the generator and motor.

(c) What should be the polarity of interpoles with respect to the main poles in a D.C. machine?

4.26. (a) Explain how the flashover between positive and negative brushes may occur in D.C. machines subjected to rapidly changing loads. How is this trouble of flashover overcome by compensating windings?

(*b*) A compensated D.C. machine has 19,000 armature ampere-turns per pole. The ratio of pole-arc to pole-pitch is 0.7 Interpolar air-gap length and flux density are respectively 1 cm and 0.3 T. For rated armature current of 1000 A, calculate the compensating winding conductors per pole and the number of turns on each interpole.

[Ans. (*b*) 26 conductors, 9 turns]

4.27. (*a*) Explain how an arc between adjacent commutator segments may occur in D.C. machines subjected to heavy overloads. Discuss how the occurrence of such an arc can be avoided.

(*b*) Show physical arrangement of the connections of armature circuit with the compensating winding having four conductors in its pole-face slots.

(*c*) A D.C. compound machine possesses both interpole and compensating windings. Draw its schematic diagram indicating each part clearly. Discuss the function of each of the windings shown in the diagram.

4.28. (*a*) Draw the equivalent circuit of a D.C. compound machine for both generating and motoring modes for long-shunt as well as short-shunt connections. Write voltage equations for these circuits defining all the parameters used.

(*b*) In a 220-V compound generator ; the armature, series and shunt windings have resistances of 0.25 Ω, 0.15 Ω and 50 Ω respectively. The load consists of 100 lamps, each rated at 60 W, 220 V. Find the total e.m.f. and armature current when the machine is connected for (*i*) long shunt and (*ii*) short shunt. **[Ans.** (*b*) (*i*) 232.67 V, 31.673 A (*ii*) 232.03 V, 31.755 A]

4.29. (*a*) Explain the methods of improving commutation in D.C. machines.

(*b*) Sketch and comment on the resultant flux density waveform for a D.C. machine fitted with compensating winding and interpoles.

4.30. (*a*) Explain how the effect of armature reaction in D.C. machines can be determined from no-load and load magnetization curves.

(*b*) What useful information can be obtained from the armature characteristic of D.C. generators? Explain.

(*c*) Why does the terminal voltage fall more rapidly in a self-excited shunt generator than in a separately-excited D.C. generator?

4.31. (*a*) Why does the slope of open-circuit characteristic of a D.C. generator change after a certain value of field current?

(*b*) When a D.C. separately-excited or shunt generator is rotated at rated speed with zero field current, why the voltage across their brushes is not zero? In case it is zero, what you would do with the D.C. machine?

(*c*) A 220 V, 1.5 kW, 859 r.p.m. separately-excited D.C. motor has armature resistance of 2.5 Ω and it draws a current of 8 A at rated load condition. If the field current and the armature voltage are fixed at the value of the rated speed at rated load, what will be the no-load speed of the motor? Assume losses remain constant between no-load and full-load operation. *[GATE, 1995]*

[Hint : (*c*) Take $I_a = 0$ at no-load] **[Ans.** (*c*) 944.9 r.p.m.]

4.32. (*a*) What features of a D.C. series generator distinguish it from the other types of D.C. generators? Explain.

(*b*) A D.C. series generator having a total resistance of 0.5 Ω is running at 1000 r.p.m. and delivering 5 kW at a voltage of 100 V. If the speed is raised to 1500 r.p.m. and the load adjusted to 8 kW, find the new field current and terminal voltage.

[**Hint :** *(a)* External characteristic–terminal voltage rises with increase in load–in others it falls etc.

(b) $E_{a1} = k\,N_1\,I_{f1}$, find $k = \frac{1}{400}$ V–A/r.p.m. New armature or field current $= \frac{8000}{V_{t2}}$ and new $E_{a2} = V_{t2} + \frac{8000}{V_{t2}}$ etc.] [**Ans.** *(b)* 49.614 A, 161.245 V]

4.33. *(a)* Explain in detail the manner in which the terminal voltage of a D.C. shunt generator will vary when the load resistance is reduced steadily in stages from infinity to zero. The speed is maintained constant and the resistance in the field circuit is unaltered after the initial adjustment.

(b) A separately excited D.C. gererator has armature circuit resistance of 0.1 Ω and a total drop at brushes is 2 V. When running at 1000 r.p.m., it delivers a current of 100 A at 250 V to a load of constant resistance. If the generator speed drops to 700 r.p.m., with field current unaltered, find the current delivered to load. [**Ans.** *(b)* 69.77 A]

4.34. A D.C. shunt generator is developing rated terminal voltage at some speed. For this generator, answer the following questions and give a brief explanation in support of your answers :

(a) If only the direction of rotation is reversed, will the generator build-up?

(b) In addition to the reversal of direction of rotation, the residual magnetism is also reversed. Will the generator build up?

(c) If only the field winding connections of the original machine are reversed, will the generator build up?

(d) If only the residual magnetism of the original machine is reversed, will the generator build up?

(e) If both the direction of rotation and field winding connections of the original machine are reversed, will the machine build up?

(f) If the brushes are moved in the direction of rotation of the original machine, what will happen to the generator operation?

[**Ans.** *(a)* no *(b)* no *(c)* no *(d)* yes, brush polarity is reversed *(e)* yes, brush polarity is reversed *(f)* commutation is improved and generator terminal voltage falls.]

4.35. *(a)* Explain the voltage build-up process in D.C. shunt generators.

(b) It is found that the voltage of a D.C. shunt generator does not build up. Explain the various possible causes of this failure.

4.36. The open circuit characteristic for a D.C. shunt generator at 800 r.p.m. is given by following data :

I_f, amp.	0	0.2	0.40	0.65	1.02	1.75	3.15	5.00
E_a, volts	10	40	80	120	160	200	240	260

Determine the critical field resistance at

(a) 800 r.p.m. and

(b) 900 r.p.m.

(c) If the field winding resistance is 55 Ω, find the range of field rheostat to vary the voltage from 200 to 250 V, on open circuit at a speed of 800 r.p.m.

(d) Determine the terminal voltage and field current of the generator for a total armature resistance of 0.6 Ω, armature current of 50 A and a speed of 800 r.p.m. Neglect armature reaction. [**Ans.** *(a)* 200 Ω *(b)* 225 Ω *(c)* 59.29 Ω to 9.52 Ω *(d)* 220 V, 4 A]

4.37. A D.C. generator with interpoles is running satisfactorily as a cumulatively compounded generator. The machine is stopped and its residual magnetism is reversed. After this, the connections are made as they were before and the machine is run in the same direction.

(a) Does the machine build-up voltage? Explain.

(b) If answer to part (a) is yes, is the terminal voltage the same as before? Explain.

(c) Is the machine now cumulatively or differentially compounded?

(d) Do the compoles have proper polarity for good commutation?

[**Ans.** (a) Yes, (b) Yes, but the polarity is reversed. (c) Cumulatively compounded generator, (d) Yes.]

4.38. (a) Explain why the magnetization curve for a D.C. generator obtained with increasing values of field current departs from that obtained with decreasing values of field current.

(b) Had there been no saturation in self-excited shunt generator, what would be the terminal voltage at no-load? Explain.

(c) A compounded generator gives over-compounded external characteristic. How can the level-compounded characteristic be obtained for this generator? Explain.

(d) A separately-excited generator can operate satisfactorily over the entire magnetization curve, whereas the self excited generator can operate only over a small range of the magnetization curve. Explain.

[**Hint :** (d) In a separately-excited generator, the field current does not depend on the armature voltage etc.] [**Ans.** (a) Due to hysteresis. (b) Close to residual-flux voltage or infinite voltage. (c) By diverter.]

4.39. (a) Draw the external characteristics of various types of D.C. generators in one figure assuming the same no-load terminal voltage. Discuss the nature of these characteristics and compare them.

(b) A short-shunt cumulatively compounded generator has the following data for its magnetization curve at 1000 r.p.m. :

I_f, *amp.*	0	0.5	1.0	1.8	3.0	4.8	6.8	9.0	12.0	14.0
E_a, *volts*	11	40	80	140	184	220	240	250	274	282

The armature circuit resistance (including brushes) is 0.05 Ω and series field resistance is 0.04 Ω. There are 20 series turns per pole, 1000 shunt turns per pole and armature reaction at rated armature current of 120 A is 451 ATs per pole.

For a shunt field resistance of 45 Ω,

(i) determine the no-load terminal voltage,

(ii) if the speed at rated armature current is 950 r.p.m., calculate the terminal voltage taking the field current the same as found in part (i).

[**Hint :** (b) (ii) The equivalent shunt field current $I_{fe\,q}$ is

$$I_{fe\,q} \times 1000 = 4.95 \times 1000 + 115.05 \times 20 - 451$$

and $V_t = 228 - 120 \times 0.05 - 115.05 \times 0.04 = 217.4$ V] [**Ans.** (a) 222 V, (b) 217.4 V]

4.40. (a) Explain the nature of no-load, external and armature characteristics of a D.C. shunt generator. Why does the external characteristic of this generator turn back as the generator is overloaded?

(b) A belt driven 60 kW shunt-wound generator running at 500 r.p.m. is supplying full load to a bus bar at 200 V. At what speed will it run if the belt breaks and the machine continues to run taking 5 kW from the bus bar? The armature and field resistances are 0.1 Ω and 100 Ω respectively. Brush contact drop may be taken as 2 V. Neglect armature reaction.

[Ans. *(b)* 421.404 r.p.m.]

4.41. (a) Draw the external characteristics of various types of D.C. generators in one figure on the assumption of same rated terminal voltage and the same rated load current. Discuss the nature of these characteristics and compare them.

(b) A 20 kW, 250 V D.C. series generator is running at 1000 r.p.m. under full-load conditions. It is given that field flux per pole $\phi \propto \frac{I}{50+I}$, $r_s = 0.01\ \Omega$, $r_a = 0.015\ \Omega$ and armature demagnetizing ampere turns per pole = 6% of the field ampere-turns per pole. Brush voltage drop is 2 V. Calculate the motor terminal voltage in case the motor draws 100 A at 1050 r.p.m.

[Hint : *(b)* $E_{a1} = 250 + 80 \times 0.025 + 2$, Net field flux $= \frac{80}{130} \times 0.94$ and $\phi_2 = \frac{I_2}{50 + I_2} \times 0.94$.

Also $\frac{254}{E_{a2}} = \frac{1000}{1050} \times 0.923$ etc.]

[Ans. *(b)* 284.45 V]

4.42. (a) Distinguish between external and internal characteristics of a D.C. generator. Explain, with appropriate diagrams, how the internal characteristics can be obtained from external characteristics of the following D.C. generators :

(i) separately-excited generator *(ii)* shunt generator *(iii)* series generator.

(b) A 240 V, 36 kW, D.C. shunt generator has 500 field turns per pole. On no-load, the generated voltage of 240 V is obtained with a field current of 2 A. For maintaining 240 V at full load and at the same speed, the field current required is 3.2 A. Calculate the number of series-field turns per pole required for level compounding. **[Ans.** *(b)* 4 turns]

4.43. (a) Derive the speed-current characteristics of D.C. shunt, series and cumulative compound motors. Sketch these characteristics in one figure on the assumption of *(i)* same speed at no-load and *(ii)* rated speed at rated current. Comment on the nature of these characteristics.

(b) A 4-pole D.C. series motor has wave-connected winding with 600 conductors. Total resistance of motor is 0.8 Ω. When fed from 250 V D.C. source, the motor supplies a load of 10 kW and takes 50 A with a flux per pole of 3 mWb. For these operating conditions, calculate the developed torque and the shaft torque. **[Ans.** *(b)* 28.65 Nm, 27.284 Nm]

4.44. (a) Derive torque-current characteristics of D.C. shunt, series and cumulative compound motors. Sketch these characteristics in one figure on the assumption of *(i)* same torque at no-load and *(ii)* rated torque at rated current.

From these torque-current characteristics; find, giving reasons, the most suitable motor for traction-type loads.

(b) A 5 kW, 250 V D.C. shunt motor takes a no-load armature current of 4 A at rated voltage and runs at 1200 r.p.m. The armature circuit resistance is 0.4 Ω and the field resistance is 250 Ω. At rated load and rated voltage, the motor takes 26 A and the armature reaction weakens the field flux by 3%.

Calculate the full-load speed and the corresponding electromagnetic torque of the motor.

[Ans. *(b)* 1195.3 r.p.m. ; 47.94 Nm]

4.45. *(a)* Derive the speed-torque characteristics of D.C. shunt, series and cumulative compound motors. Sketch these characteristics in one figure on the assumption of *(i)* same speed at no-load and *(ii)* rated speed at rated torque. Comment on the nature of these characteristics.

(b) The field current of a 10 kW, 230 V, 1500 r.p.m. D.C. shunt motor is adjusted so that it runs at a no-load speed of 1600 r.p.m. with an armature current of 2 A. When load on motor is increased, it is observed that armature current is 40 A and speed is 1400 r.p.m. Under these conditions, find the percentage reduction in field flux per pole due to armature reaction. The armature circuit resistance is 1 Ω and supply voltage is 230 V. **[Ans.** *(b)* 4.76%]

4.46. A 230 V, 600 r.p.m. D.C. series motor has a total armature and field resistance of 0.25 Ω. Its magnetization curve at 400 r.p.m. is given as follows :

Induced e.m.f., volts	130	154	172	184	192	198
Field current, amp	25	30	35	40	45	50

At rated voltage and rated speed, the motor takes a full-load current of 36 A. Find the internal starting torque, in case the starting current is limited to 60 A. Assume the demagnetizing effect of armature reaction to be proportional to the square of the current.

[Hint : Plot the magnetization curve at 600 r.p.m. The demagnetizing effect for 36 A is 7.6 A according to $E_a = 230 - 36 \times 0.25 = 221$ volts. For 60 A, the demagnetizing effect is $\left(\frac{60}{36}\right)^2 \times 7.6 = 21.1$ A. Therefore, the net *d*-axis field m.m.f. is equivalent to a field current of 60 – 21.1 = 38.9 A. Now see part *(e)* of Example 4.36] **[Ans.** 260.7 Nm]

4.47. A D.C. shunt motor is connected to a 3-point starter. Explain what would happen if

(a) the starter handle is moved rapidly from OFF to the ON position,

(b) the field circuit is open and an attempt is made to start the motor,

(c) the field circuit becomes open-circuited with the motor running at no-load,

(d) the field circuit becomes open-circuited with the motor running at no-load, with the assumption that the starter is not provided with the no-volt release and the spring,

(e) the starter handle is pulled back to stop the motor,

(f) there is a sudden overload of 100%,

(g) the field excitation is minimum at the time of starting.

[Ans. *(a)* Motor draws large current, resulting in heavy sparking at the brushes. The motor accelerates rapidly and large starting current may overheat the motor.

(b) Motor would not start and the armature would draw heavy current from the source.

(c) to *(g)* Read Art. 4.13]

4.48. A 220 V, 1500 r.p.m. D.C. motor has full-load armature current of 30 A. It is proposed to design a starter which restricts the maximum armature current during starting to 60 A. For design purposes, the minimum current during starting is to be restricted to 30 A, the series resistance in the armature circuit being cut in steps whenever the current falls to 30 A. Assuming that the armature resistance of the D.C. motor is 0.5 Ω, calculate the maximum series resistance used in the starter and the amount of resistance cut during each of the first two steps.

[I.A.S., 1987]

[Ans. 3.167 Ω, 1.834 Ω, 0.9166 Ω]

4.49. *(a)* Explain what would happen if the D.C. motor is directly switched on to the supply without any starter.

(*b*) Explain the function of no-volt release in a three-point starter.

(*c*) Explain the advantages of four-point starter over the three-point starter.

(*d*) What is the difference between a starter and a controller?

(*e*) What would happen if the external resistance for starting the D.C. motor is left in the armature circuit?

4.50. (*a*) Describe, with a neat diagram, the working of a three-point starter used for a D.C. shunt motor.

(*b*) The efficiency of a 7.5 kW, 220 V shunt motor is 90%. The armature ohmic losses are half of the total losses. The normal field current is 1 ampere. Find the magnitude of resistance for each step of a 6 stud starter for this motor.

The maximum armature current is limited to twice the full load armature current.

[**Hint :** (*b*) Total losses = $\left(\frac{1}{0.9} - 1\right) \times 7500 = 833$ W

Line current = $\frac{7500}{0.9 \times 220} = 37.9$ A, $I_a = 36.9$ A, $r_a = \frac{416.5}{(36.9)^2}$ etc.]

[**Ans.** (*b*) 1.0901 Ω, 0.6915 Ω, 0.4386 Ω, 0.2782 Ω, 0.1765 Ω]

4.51. (*a*) Explain the following terms :

Base speed, speed regulation, speed range, constant power drive and constant torque drive.

(*b*) Describe and compare the various methods of speed control of D.C. motors.

4.52. (*a*) For a D.C. motor, the armature-circuit-resistance method of speed control is called a constant torque drive method. Explain.

(*b*) A D.C. shunt motor runs at 750 r.p.m. from 250 V supply and is taking a full-load line current of 60 amperes. Its armature and field resistance are 0.4 Ω and 125 Ω respectively. Assuming 2 V brush drop and negligible armature reaction effect, calculate

(*i*) the no-load speed for a no-load line current of 6 amperes,

(*ii*) the resistance to be added in series with the armature circuit to reduce the full-load speed to 600 r.p.m.,

(*iii*) the percentage reduction in flux per pole needed, in order that the speed may be 900 r.p.m. when the armature current is 30 amperes, with no-added resistance in the armature circuit. [**Ans.** (*b*) (*i*) 822 r.p.m. ; (*ii*) 0.7752 Ω ; (*iii*) 12.5%]

4.53. A D.C. shunt motor takes an armature current of 50 A at its rated voltage of 240 V. Its armature-circuit resistance is 0.2 Ω. If an external resistance of 1 Ω is inserted in series with the armature and the field flux remains unchanged, then calculate :

(*a*) percentage decrease or increase in speed for the same load torque,

(*b*) percentage decrease or increase in speed for half of the load toque.

[**Ans.** (*a*) 21.739% decrease (*b*) 8.7% decrease]

4.54. (*a*) For a D.C. motor, the field-flux-speed control method is called a constant power drive method. Explain.

(*b*) The e.m.f. developed in the armature of a shunt generator at 1155 r.p.m. is 240 volts for a field current of 4.5 amperes and 255 volts for a field current of 5 amperes. The generator is now used as a motor on a 260 V supply and takes an armature current of 75 amperes. Find the motor speed, when the field current is adjusted to 4.8 A. Armature resistance (including brushes) is 0.12 Ω. (*Ranchi Univ.*)

[**Hint :** For a field current of 4.8 A, the e.m.f. generated in the generator armature is 240 + $\frac{255-240}{0.5} \times 0.3$, *i.e.*, $E_{a1} = 249$ V. For a motor field current of 4.8 A, the e.m.f. generated in the armature is $E_{a2} = 260 - 75 \times 0.12 = 251$ V

$\therefore \quad E_{a1} \propto 1155 \times 4.8$ and $E_{a1} \propto n_2 \times 4.8$ etc.] **[Ans.** 1164.3 r.p.m.]

4.55. *(a)* What are the advantages of field-flux control method over the armature-circuit-resistance control method employed for the speed adjustment of D.C. motors?

(b) A D.C. series motor has the following data for its magnetization curve :

Current, p.u.	0.40	0.60	0.80	1.00
Flux, p.u.	0.62	0.80	0.92	1.00

The per unit values are expressed in terms of their respective full-load values. A diverter is used to raise its speed to 1.2 p.u. from full-load speed of 1.00 p.u., at constant full-load torque. Neglecting losses, calculate diverter resistance in terms of series field resistance.

[**Hint :** $V_t = E_{a1} \propto n_1 \phi_1$

Also $V_t = E_{a2} \propto n_2 \phi_2$

Now $n_1 \phi_1 = n_2 \phi_2$ or $\phi_1 = 1.2\phi_2$

$\therefore \quad \phi_2 = 0.833\phi_1$

$\phi_2 = 0.833$ p.u., because ϕ_1 is full load flux.

For constant full load torque $I_{a1}\phi_1 = I_{a2}\phi_2$ or $1 \times 1 = I_{a2} \times 0.833$

$\therefore \quad I_{a2} = 1.2$ p.u.

A flux of 0.833 p.u. requires a field current I_{f2} (from magnetization-curve) of 0.65 p.u.

But $I_{a2} = 1.2$ p.u.

$$\therefore \quad I_{f2} = I_{a2}\frac{R_{di}}{R_{di}+r_s}$$

or $0.65 = 1.2\frac{R_{di}}{R_{di}+r_s}$ etc.] **[Ans.** $R_{di} = 1.182\, r_s$]

4.56. A 4-kW D.C. series motor has four field coils. The motor runs at 900 r.p.m. and takes 20 A from a 230 V D.C. source when field coils are in series under normal operation. Estimate the speed and current taken by the motor if field coils are reconnected in two parallel groups of two in series. Assume that the flux is directly proportional to the current and all losses are neglected. Take the load torque as proportional to

(a) Square of speed *(b)* speed *(c)* speed raised to power zero.

[Ans. *(a)* 1070.4 r.p.m., 33.63 A *(b)* 1134 r.p.m., 31.75 A *(c)* 1273 r.p.m., 28.28 A]

4.57. A 4-pole D.C. series motor runs at a speed of *N* r.p.m. on a fixed D.C. supply with all field coils in series. Estimate the speed at which the motor would run if fed from the same supply with the field coils re-connected in two parallel groups of two coils each. Assume that the load torque varies as the square of the speed, that all losses are negligible and that the magnetization characteristic is linear. *(I.A.S., 1989)*

4.58. A 460-V series motor has its field coils split into two equal halves and takes 40 A when running at 600 r.p.m. with the field coils in series. Determine the speed when the two halves of the field winding are connected in parallel, assuming the load torque to remain constant and the magnetic circuit to be unsaturated. The resistance of the armature circuit is 0.5 Ω and that of the field coils in series is 0.2 Ω. *(I.A.S., 1980)*[**Ans.** 842.55 r.p.m.]

4.59. *(a)* Describe the disadvantages of field-flux control method for the speed control of a D.C. shunt motor.

(b) A D.C. series motor gave the following open circuit curve at a speed of 600 r.p.m. :

Field current, A	10	20	30	40	60	80
Open circuit voltage, V	103.5	158	206	230	259	282

Total resistance of the armature and field circuit is 1 Ω. Plot the speed-torque and current-torque curves of this series motor when connected to 250 V supply.

Find also the speed of the motor when *(i)* armature current is 40 A and *(ii)* the developed torque is 120 Nm. [**Ans.** *(b) (i)* 548 r.p.m. *(ii)* 590 r.p.m.]

4.60. A 200 V D.C. shunt motor takes 27 A at rated voltage and runs at 800 r.p.m. Its field resistance is 100 Ω. If an additional resistance of 20 Ω is inserted in the armature circuit, compute the motor speed and the line current in case load torque varies as the square of the speed.

[**Ans.** 370.66 r.p.m., 7.367 A]

4.61. A D.C. shunt motor with an armature resistance of 0.2 Ω drives a load at 1245 r.p.m., drawing an armature current of 125 A from a 440 V supply. If the excitation is reduced to 75% of the initial value and the total torque developed by the armature remains unaltered, calculate new speed. *(GATE, 1987)* [**Ans.** 1626.68 r.p.m.]

4.62. A 220 V, D.C. shunt machine has the following open circuit characteristic at 1000 r.p.m.

I_f, A	0.25	0.50	0.75	1.00	1.50	2.00
E_a, V	71	133	170	195	220	232

The armature circuit resistance (including brushes) is 0.2 Ω and shunt field resistance is 110 Ω. The shunt field has 1000 turns and rated armature current is 50 A. At rated voltage, if the speed control is carried out by field-flux control, then, neglecting armature reaction, calculate:

(a) the range of external field circuit resistance for a speed variation of 1000 r.p.m. on no-load to 2000 r.p.m. on rated load—assume negligible armature current at no-load;

(b) the series field amperes-turns required to reduce the speed from 1000 r.p.m. at no-load to 913 r.p.m. at rated load; and

(c) the speed at rated load with the series winding in circuit and with the shunt field set to give 2000 r.p.m. at no-load.

[**Hint :** Plot the O.C.C.

(a) At no-load $E_a = 220$ V and I_f from O.C.C. is 1.5 A.

At rated load, $E_a = 220 - 50 \times 0.2 = 210$ V at 2000 r.p.m.

Therefore, at 1000 r.p.m., $E_a = 210 \times \dfrac{1000}{2000} = 105$ V

and the corresponding field current from O.C.C. is 0.38 A etc.

(b) At no-load, $E_a = 220$ V and $I_f = 1.5$ A.

At rated load, $E_a = 220$ V at 913 r.p.m.

Therefore, at 1000 r.p.m., $E_a = 210 \times \dfrac{1000}{913} = 230$ V and the corresponding field current from O.C.C. is 1.857 A. Field ATs at no-load are 1500 and at rated load, 1875.

Therefore, ATs to be provided by series field winding = 1875 – 1500 = 375 ATs.

(c) At no-load speed of 2000 r.p.m., $E_a = 220$ V.

Therefore, at 1000 r.p.m., $E_a = 110$ V

and field current is 0.3875 A.

At rated load, total field ATs are 0.3875 × 1000 + 375.

$$\therefore \text{ Equivalent shunt field current} = \frac{0.3875 \times 1000 + 375}{1000} = 0.7625 \text{ Amp.}$$

Corresponding 0.7625 A, E_a from O.C.C. is 155.5 V at 1000 r.p.m. But at rated load,

$$E_a = 220 - 50 \times 0.2 = 210 \text{ volts.}$$

$$\therefore \quad \text{Speed at rated load} = \frac{210}{155.5} \times 1000 = 1350 \text{ r.p.m.]}$$

[Ans. *(a)* 36.67 Ω to 468.95 Ω]

4.63. A D.C. series motor is driving a fan load where the load torque is proportional to the cube of speed. The resistance of the armature and field in series is 1 Ω and the motor takes 10 A and runs at 1000 r.p.m. when operating from a 200 V supply.

Calculate the value of resistance to be inserted in series with the armature to reduce the operating speed to 800 r.p.m. *(I.A.S., 1988)***[Ans.** 11.751 Ω]

4.64. A 220 V D.C. shunt motor has an armature resistance of 0.5 Ω and field circuit resistance of 220 Ω. It takes a line current of 41 A when delivering full-load torque. If it is desired to raise the speed by 60 percent with the load torque remaining constant, find the additional resistance to be inserted in the field circuit. Assume linear magnetisation characteristic.

*(I.A.S., 1994)***[Ans.** 159.5 Ω]

4.65. A D.C. shunt motor, when fed from 200 V D.C. source, delivers full-load torque to a load at 1000 r.p.m. Its supply voltage is reduced to 100 V, the motor speed becomes 800 r.p.m. with the load torque remaining constant. Calculate the armature voltage drop at rated torque. Assume no magnetic saturation. **[Ans.** 12.5 V]

4.66. Make approximate estimates, giving brief reasons, of the changes in the armature current and speed of a D.C. shunt motor when operating conditions are changed as described below :

(a) With the load torque and field current held constant, the armature voltage is halved.

(b) With field current held constant, the terminal voltage is halved; load torque is proportional to square of the speed.

(c) With the armature voltage and load torque held constant, the field flux is halved.

(d) With the torque held constant, both the armature voltage and field flux are halved.

*(I.A.S., 1987)***[Ans.** With n_1 and I_{a1} as the initial values :

(a) $\frac{n_1}{2}, I_{a1}$ *(b)* $\frac{n_1}{2}, \frac{I_{a1}}{4}$, *(c)* $2n_1, 2I_{a1}$ *(d)* $n_1, 2I_{a1}$]

4.67. A 250-V, D.C. shunt motor has an armature current of 20 A when running at 1000 r.p.m. against some load torque. The armature resistance is 0.5 Ω and brush contact drop is one volt per brush. By how much must the main flux be reduced to raise the speed by 50% if the developed torque is constant? Ignore effects of armature reaction and magnetic saturation.

*(Gate, 1990)***[Ans.** 34.81%]

4.68. Two adjustable-speed D.C. shunt motors have speed-control range of 1500 to 500 r.p.m. In both the motors, speed adjustment is obtained by field-flux control. Motor *A* drives a load requiring constant power over the entire speed range ; motor *B* drives a load requiring constant torque over the entire speed range. Ignore all losses and armature reaction in both the motors.

(*a*) If power outputs are equal at 1500 r.p.m. and armature currents are each 90 A, find their armature currents at 500 r.p.m.

(*b*) If power outputs are equal at 500 r.p.m. and armature currents are each 90 A, find their armature currents at 1500 r.p.m.

[**Hint :** Read Example 4.58 carefully before solving this problem.]

[**Ans.** (*a*) 90 A, 30A (*b*) 90 A, 270 A]

4.69. Repeat parts (*a*) and (*b*) of Problem 4.68 in case speed adjustment is obtained by armature-voltage control, other conditions remaining unchanged.

[**Ans.** (*a*) 270 A, 90 A (*b*) 30A, 90A]

4.70. (*a*) Describe in detail the methods of speed control of D.C. shunt motors. While working with a very weak field, a shunt motor shows tendency (*i*) to flashover between brushes and (*ii*) to hunt. Explain clearly the reasons for these and the methods of avoiding them.

(*b*) For the speed control of a D.C. shunt motor by varying the field flux, show that the field resistance should be changed in small steps in order to avoid objectionable armature current surges.

4.71. (*a*) What is meant by constant power drive and constant torque drive? Explain how a D.C. motor can be adopted for these types of drives.

(*b*) How is the rating of a D.C. motor affected by a decrease in speed?

(*c*) What is the effect of brush lead in a D.C. motor?

(*d*) Which losses of a D.C. shunt motor are constant?

4.72. A D.C. shunt motor is running at 1500 r.p.m. at rated load torque. Discuss what would happen to the motor operation, if the following changes are made :

(*a*) Field terminal are reversed.

(*b*) Supply wires are reversed.

(*c*) Brushes are shifted against the direction of rotation.

(*d*) Brushes are shifted in the direction of rotation.

(*e*) The armature is rewound with a fewer number of turns of thick wire.

(*f*) Some of the field-turns are short-circuited.

[**Ans.** (*a*) Direction of rotation is reversed, commutation unaffected.

(*b*) Direction of rotation is unchanged, commutation unaffected.

(*c*) Motor speed increases and commutation is improved.

(*d*) Motor speed decreases and commutation is worsened.

(*e*) Less armature turns means less turns per coil. This decreases reactance voltage and therefore, the commutation is improved; speed is almost unaffected. With reduction in Z, armature constant K_a decreases and for the same load torque, armature current becomes more.

(*f*) Field m.m.f., therefore, field flux is reduced, motor speed increases. For the same load torque, motor draws more armature current.]

4.73. A 250-V, 1500 r.p.m. D.C. machine has an armature resistance (including brushes) of 0.2 Ω and a brush drop under load of 2.0 volts. The rotational losses for a speed of 1500 r.p.m. and for an armature generated voltage of 250 V are 600 watts. Neglect the field circuit losses.

(a) For an armature current of 30 A and an armature generated voltage of 250 V, find the electromagnetic torque of the motor at rated speed.

(b) If the machine in part *(a)* is working as a generator, determine the shaft power input and the electric power output.

(c) If the machine in part *(a)* is working as a motor, determine electric power input and the shaft power output.

(d) The motor of part *(c)* drives a load requiring constant torque at all the motor speeds. Calculate the motor speed if the armature terminal voltage is halved and the field flux is kept constant.

(e) The motor of part *(c)* drives a load requiring a constant power. Calculate the motor speed if the field flux is reduced to 0.6 of its previous value and the armature terminal voltage is kept constant.

[**Hint:** *(d)* $V_t = E_a + I_a r_a + 2 = 250 + 30 \times 0.2 + 2 = 258$ V.

Constant torque and constant flux require current to remain at 30 A.

$$\therefore \quad E_{a2} = \frac{V_t}{2} - 30 \times 0.2 - 2 = 121 \text{ volts.}$$

$$\therefore \quad n_2 = \frac{1500 \times 121}{250} \text{ r.p.m.}$$

(e) $E_a I_a = \text{constant} = 7500$ W,

But $E_a = 258 - 2 - 0.2 I_a$

$$\therefore \quad E_a = 256 - 0.2 \times \frac{7500}{E_a} \quad \text{or} \quad E_a^2 - 256 E_a + 1500 = 0$$

$$\therefore \quad E_a = 250.00 \text{ V and } n_2 = \frac{1500}{250} \times \frac{250}{0.6} \text{ r.p.m.}]$$

[**Ans.** *(a)* 47.75 Nm, *(b)* 8100 W, 7260 W ; *(c)* 7740 W, 6900 W, *(d)* 726 r.p.m. *(e)* 2500 r.p.m.]

4.74. A 230-V D.C. shunt motor is used for adjustable-speed drive over the range of 0 to 2000 r.p.m. Speed from zero to 1000 r.p.m., are obtained by adjusting the armature terminal voltage from zero to 230 V, with the field current kept constant. Speeds from 1000 to 2000 r.p.m. are obtained by decreasing the field current, with the armature terminal voltage held constant at 230 V. Armature reaction effects and losses may be ignored.

(a) The torque required by the load remains constant over the entire speed range. Show the general form of the curve for armature current and power *versus* speed, over the entire speed range.

(b) Instead of keeping the load torque constant, suppose that the armature current is not to exceed a specified value. Show the general form of the curve for allowable load torque and power *versus* speed, over the entire speed range.

[**Ans.** *(a)* From 0 to 1000 r.p.m. : armature current remains constant at I_a (say) but power rises linearly from 0 to $V_t I_a$.

From 1000 to 2000 r.p.m. : armature current and power, both increase linearly from I_a to $2I_a$ and from $V_t I_a$ to $2V_t I_a$ respectively.

(b) From 0 to 1000 r.p.m. : allowable torque remains constant say T_1 but power rises linearly from 0 to $V_1 I_a$ 1000 r.p.m.

From 1000 to 2000 r.p.m. : allowable torque decreases inversely with speed from T_1 to $\frac{T_1}{2}$ $\left(i.e. \text{ allowable torque} \propto \frac{1}{\text{speed}}\right)$ and power remains constant at $V_t I_a$.]

4.75. A D.C. shunt motor is required to supply a load requiring a constant torque of 120 N-m, over a speed of 500 to 2000 r.p.m.

(a) Explain the three methods of obtaining the required speed range.

(b) For each of the methods of part *(a)*, specify the base speed and the kW rating of the motor.

(c) Compare the merits and demerits associated with each method of speed control.

[**Ans.** *(b)* For armature-circuit-resistance control and armature-terminal voltage control methods, the base speed is 2000 r.p.m. For field-flux control method, the base speed is 500 r.p.m. For each method, the power rating is 25.133 kW.]

4.76. *(a)* Enumerate the various losses in a D.C. machine. Which of these losses are constant? Derive expressions for the efficiency of a D.C. generator and a D.C. motor.

(b) A 6 kW, 230 V, 4-pole wave-connected D.C. motor has 400 armature conductors. At full load, the useful flux per pole is 0.02 Wb and rotational losses are 100 W. Find the full-load speed. [**Ans.** *(b)* 876.86 r.p.m.]

4.77. *(a)* Enumerate the losses occurring in a D.C. shunt motor and state how each loss varies as the load on the machine is altered. Describe a method of determining the efficiency of a shunt motor at various loads without actually putting a load on the motor. Critically examine the assumptions made in the method described.

(b) The speed of a 500 V D.C. series motor coupled to a fan is reduced to one half of full speed by a series resistance. At full speed, the current is 100 A and the load torque is proportional to the square of the speed. Show that the power input is proportional to the cube of the speed and calculate the resistance required assuming that the field is unsaturated and motor losses do not vary. [**Ans.** *(b)* 7.50 Ω]

4.78. Discuss how power input and motor torque get adjusted automatically as load on the shaft of following D.C. motor types is varied :

(a) shunt motor *(b)* series motor *(c)* cumulative compound motor.

[**Hint:** *(a)* Shaft load increases, speed falls, counter e.m.f. falls, armature current rises etc.

(b) Speed falls, $I_a = \frac{V_t}{K\omega_m + (r_a + r_s)}$ rises etc.

(c) Speed falls, $I_a = \left[\frac{V_t}{K\omega_m + (r_a + r_s)} - \frac{K_a}{K}\phi_{sh}\right]$ rises etc.]

4.79. A D.C. shunt motor is running at a certain speed. Discuss the effect on the speed of this motor if its

(i) line voltage is reduced to half

(ii) armature-terminal voltage is reduced to half but its field current is kept constant

(iii) field current is reduced to half but its armature terminal voltage is held fixed.

Neglect armature reaction and all losses. Answer the three parts listed above under the assumption of magnetic saturation *(a)* neglected *(b)* included.

[**Ans.** *(a)* *(i)* No change in speed *(ii)* speed halved *(iii)* speed doubled
(b) *(i)* Speed decreases *(ii)* speed halved *(iii)* speed rises]

4.80. *(a)* What is meant by torque?

(b) What is the difference between speed regulation and speed control?

(c) Distinguish between constant-speed, variable-speed and adjustable-speed motors.

(d) Discuss the significance of back e.m.f. in a D.C. motor.

[Hint: *(a)* Tendency of motor to produce shaft rotation.

(d) Back, or counter e.m.f. *(i)* opposes the applied voltage and *(ii)* limits the armature current to a value just sufficient to meet the power demanded by the shaft load.]

4.81. A D.C. shunt machine gave the following data for its OCC at 1500 r.p.m. :

I_f, A	0.3	0.6	0.9	1.2	1.5	1.8	2.10	2.4	2.7
E_a, V	60	120	180	229	260	282	298	306	310

This D.C. machine, when operated at no-load from 230 V D.C. source as long-shunt compound motor, runs at 1500 r.p.m. The no-load current is negligible. The shunt field winding has 2000 turns as per pole.

Calculate the number of series-field turns per pole required to reduce the speed to 1200 r.p.m. while taking an armature current of 90 A from the mains. This armature current causes an armature loss of 810 W and series-field winding loss of 450 W.

[Hint: At 1200 r.p.m, $E_{a2} = 230 - \frac{810}{90} - \frac{450}{90} = 216$ V and this e.m.f. at 1500 r.p.m. is 270 V which needs a field current of 1.635 A etc.] **[Ans.** 10 turns]

4.82. In Fig. 4.80, current input to each motor, whether in series or parallel, is I_L whereas the D.C. source voltage is V_t. Calculate the ratio of *(a)* speeds and *(b)* torques with motors in parallel to those with motors in series. Does this scheme offer a constant-power or a constant-torque drive under the conditions specified? **[Ans.** *(a)* 2 *(b)* 1. Constant-torque drive]

4.83. *(a)* Discuss the effect of speed and size on the efficiency of D.C. machines.

(b) For a 400 V long-shunt compound generator ; the constant loss, comprising of excitation and no-load rotational loss, is 10 kW. The resistances of the armature, series and shunt fields are respectively 0.1 Ω, 0.05 Ω, and 50 Ω. Find the maximum efficiency and the output at which it occurs.

[Hint: *(b)* $I_a^2\ (r_a + r_s) = 10$ kW etc.] **[Ans.** *(b)* 83.34%, 100.08 kW]

4.84. *(a)* Enumerate the various losses in a D.C. machine. Which of these losses are *(i)* constant *(ii)* proportional to current and *(iii)* proportional to current squared.

(b) In a D.C. motor, hysteresis and eddy-current losses at 1000 r.p.m. are 200 W and 100 W respectively. Find the speed at which the total losses would be reduced to half on the assumption of constant field flux. **[Ans.** *(b)* 581.015 r.p.m.]

4.85. A 150 V D.C. shunt motor runs at no-load at 600 r.p.m. The resistance of the field coils is 25 Ω. Find what resistance must be placed in series with the field coils to increase the speed to 700 r.p.m. at no-load. Neglect armature reaction and armature resistance drop. The magnetization curve for the machine is as under :

I_f, A→	1	2	3	4	5	6
φ, Wb→	0.0044	0.008	0.0102	0.0115	0.0121	0.0124

where I_f = Field current and

φ = Field flux per pole. **[Ans.** 21.15 Ω]

4.86. In a test on a D.C. shunt generator, whose full load output is 200 kW at 250 V, the following figures were obtained :

(a) With the machine at rest, a p.d. of 8 volts produced an armature current of 400 A.

(b) With the motor running at no-load and at rated speed, the line current was 36 A, the field current 12 amperes and the supply voltage 250 V.

Obtain the generator efficiency at full load and half full load.

[**Hint:** $r_a = \frac{8}{400} = 0.02\ \Omega$

For motor at no-load, $I_a = 36 - 12 = 24$ A.

$I_a^2 r_a$ at no-load $= (24)^2 \times 0.02 = 11.52$ W

$\therefore$ Constant losses $= 36 \times 250 - 11.52 = 8988.48$ W.

Generator on full load, $I_a = \frac{200,000}{250} + 12 = 812$ A

$\therefore$ $I_a^2 r_a = (812)^2 (0.02) = 13200$ W.

Total losses $= 8988.48 + 13,200 = 22,188.48$ W

$\therefore$ $\eta_g = \left(1 - \frac{22,188.48}{200,000 + 22,188.48}\right) \times 100$ etc.]

[Ans. 90.019% ; 88.981%]

4.87. *(a)* What is the effect of excitation, speed and load on the losses of a D.C. machine?

(b) A 230-V D.C., shunt motor is taking 5 A when running light (*i.e.* at no-load). The armature resistance (including brushes) is 0.2 Ω and field circuit resistance is 115 Ω. For an input current of 72 A, calculate the shaft output and efficiency. Also calculate the armature current at which the efficiency is maximum. **[Ans.** 14.432 kW, 87.15%, 75.77 A]

4.88. A 600 V D.C. shunt motor drives a 60 kW load at 1000 r.p.m. The field resistance is 100 Ω and armature resistance is 0.15 Ω. Stray-load loss is negligible. In case motor efficiency is 85%, determine

(a) the rotational losses

(b) the speed at no-load and the speed regulation.

[Ans. *(a)* 5118.3 W *(b)* 1026.52 r.p.m, 2.652%]

4.89. Hopkinson's test on two similar D.C. shunt machines gave the following data :

Line voltage 230 V ; Line current, excluding both the field currents, 40 A ; motor armature current 350 A; field currents 5 A and 4.2 A.

Calculate the efficiency of each machine. Armature resistance of each machine is 0.02 Ω.

[Ans. Generator efficiency = 92.855% ; Motor efficiency = 92.844%]

4.90. *(a)* Justify the correctness or otherwise of the statement : "For increasing the speed of D.C. series motor, the 'armature diverter' connection is preferred to the 'field diverter' connection." *(I.A.S., 1989)*

(b) In electric drive schemes, 'field forcing' is recommended for reducing starting time of driving motors. Discuss. *(I.A.S., 1988)*

(c) Explain what happens when the field curent of a shunt wound motor is reduced suddenly by about 5%. *(I.A.S., 1980)*

[**Hint:** *(a)* Armature diverter or shunted armature method is used only for decreasing the speed of D.C. series motor below the base speed.]

4.91. *(a)* "The magnetomotive force due to armature reaction in a D.C. generator can be effectively utilized to result in an equivalent two generators in cascade in one frame and yielding larger power amplification." Justify this statement. *(I.A.S., 1982)*

(b) "A cross-field machine may behave as a constant voltage or a constant current generator depending upon the degree of compensation." Justify on the correctness or otherwise of this statement. *(I.A.S., 1994)*

(c) "Ward-Leonard method of speed control of a D.C. motor provides a smooth control in both the directions." Justify on the correctness or otherwise of this statement. *(I.A.S., 1994)*

[**Hint:** *(a)* The two generators in cascade in one frame yield a cross-field generator.]

4.92. *(a)* In cross-field machines, one pole consists of two polar projections. Explain the reason.

(b) In cross-field generators, the polarity of the output brushes remains unaltered even with reversed direction of rotation. Explain.

(c) A 4-kW, 250 V, 3000 r.p.m. amplidyne has the following constants :

$$r_f = 60\ \Omega,\ r_a = 5\ \Omega,\ r_c = 1\ \Omega$$

Voltage constants, $K_{qf} = 300$ V/field amp

$$K_{dq} = 120 \text{ V/amp},\ K_{qd} = 50 \text{ V/amp}$$

Calculate the field current and power gain at rated output. Also obtain these values when the compensation is zero. [**Ans.** *(c)* 48.056 mA, 28868.39, 27.125 A, 9.061]

4.93. *(a)* Derive an expression for the output voltage of a partially compensated cross-field machine. Obtain therefrom the external characteristics of this machine for different degrees of compensation.

(b) An amplidyne has an input field winding of 100 Ω resistance and 500 turns. It has a two-pole armature with 400 lap-connected conductors. The effective resistance of the quadrature circuit is 4 Ω and of the output circuit is 5 Ω including the compensating winding. The speed is 3000 r.p.m and an excitation of 1 AT on either axis produces a flux of 6×10^{-5} Wb. Calculate the voltage amplification and power amplification. Load resistance is 20 Ω and saturation is neglected.

[**Hint:** *(b)* $\phi_f = \left(\dfrac{V_f}{100} \times 500\right)(6 \times 10^{-5})$ Wb, $E_q = 6\,V_f$, $\phi_q = 4.5 \times 10^{-3}\,V_f$

Power output $= \left(\dfrac{90}{25} \times V_f\right)^2 \times 20$ etc.] [**Ans.** *(b)* 90, 25920]

4.94. *(a)* Explain voltage amplification factor as applied to cross-field machines. Discuss the factors on which it depends.

(b) Discuss the effect of speed on *(i)* voltage amplification factor and *(ii)* external characteristics of amplidyne.

[**Ans.** *(b)* *(i)* V.A.F. $\propto n^2$ *(ii)* external characteristic gets bodily shifted up or down depending upon whether the speed is raised or lowered.]

4.95. What is a cross-field machine? Give its constructional features and explain its working. Derive an expression for the output voltage of an amplidyne. Give any two applications of amplidyne.

4.96. *(a)* Give the constructional details of permanent-magnet D.C. motors. Discuss their advantages and limitations. Where are these motors employed in industry?

(b) Give the equivalent circuit of a PMDC motor. How does it differ form the equivalent circuit of a conventional D.C. motor?

Derive e.m.f. and torque expressions for a PMDC motor from the corresponding expressions used in conventional D.C. motors.

4.97. A small permanent-magnet D.C. motor runs at a no-load speed of 10,600 r.p.m. and takes 10 mA when fed from 6 V D.C. source. Its armature circuit resistance is 6 Ω. Calculate its

(*a*) no-load rotational losses (*b*) stall torque

(*c*) speed to achieve a shaft power 1 W (*d*) efficiency under the conditions of part (*c*).

[**Ans.** (*a*) 0.0584 W (*b*) 5.26×10^{-3} Nm (*c*) 8401 r.p.m. (*d*) 72.876%]

4.98. (*a*) Compare the application of D.C. generators with respect to transformer-rectifier equipment.

Are the D.C. generator being built in the present age? Discuss the applications where the use of D.C. generators is indispensable.

(*b*) Describe the applications of D.C. shunt, series and cumulative compound motors.

How do D.C. motors compete with ac motors? Discuss.

4.99. A 500 V, 25 HP (= 18.65 kW), D.C. shunt motor takes a current of 2.4 A while running light. The field and armature resistances are 650 ohms and 0.57 ohm, respectively. Calculate full-load efficiency, assuming a brush drop of 2 V. (*I.E.S., 2002*) [**Ans.** 89.297%]

4.100. (*a*) A 120 V d.c. shunt motor takes 2 A at no-load. It takes 7 A on full-load while running at 1200 r.p.m. The armature resistance is 0.8 Ω and shunt field resistance is 240 Ω. The no-load speed, in r.p.m., is .... (*GATE ; 2017 (2)*)

(*b*) A 200 V dc series motor, when operating from rated voltage while driving a certain load, draws 10 A current and runs at 1000 r.p.m. The total series resistance is 1 Ω. The magnetic circuit is assumed to be linear. At the same supply voltage, the load torque is increased by 44%. The speed of the motor in r.p.m. is .... (*GATE ; 2018*)

[**Ans.** (*a*) 1241.8 r.p.m. (*b*) 824.56 r.p.m.]

5 Chapter

Polyphase Synchronous Machines

INTRODUCTION

A three-phase synchronous machine is a doubly-excited A.C. machine, because its field winding is energised from a D.C. source and its armature winding is connected to an A.C. source. When working as a motor, the synchronous machine takes in active power from an A.C. source. During its working as a generator, synchronous machine delivers or exports A.C. power. However, the field winding of a synchronous machine always absorbs or takes in power from a D.C. source. Since a synchronous generator delivers A.C. output, it is also known as an *alternator*.

Under steady-state conditions, operating speed of a synchronous machine depends on the frequency of armature currents and the number of field poles and is given by Eq. (3.68) or Eq. (3.69) as under :

$$n_s = \frac{2f}{P} \text{ rpm or } N_s = \frac{120f}{P} \text{ rpm} \quad \text{...(5.1)}$$

where P = number of field poles

n_s = rotor speed in rps (called synchronous speed)

N_s = rotor speed in r.p.m. (called synchronous speed)

and f = frequency of armature currents.

A synchronous generator is universally employed for the generation of three-phase power at all generating stations. The largest-sized electrical machines are polyphase synchronous generators. The highest rating so far for 3-phase alternators, as reported in the literature, is 1700 MW.

The constructional features, of the two types of synchronous machines, are already described in Art. 3.2. The cylindrical-rotor construction of Fig. 3.7 *(b)* is used for two or four pole steam-turbine generators. That is why cylindrical-rotor synchronous generators are called *turbo-generators* or *turbo-alternators*. A cylindrical-rotor synchronous machine is characterised by long core length and small diameter so as to limit the centrifugal forces developed in the high-speed rotor. The salient-pole construction shown in Fig. 3.6 is the most suitable for multipolar slow-speed water-turbine generators. That is why salient-pole synchronous generators are called *hydro-generators*. Most of the synchronous motors are of the salient-pole type. A salient-pole synchronous machine has small core length and large diameter so that large number of field poles can be accommodated on the rotor periphery.

The expression for the generated e.m.f. in a synchronous machine is derived in Art. 3.4.3. It has also been concluded in Art. 3.8 that for the production of electromagnetic torque the relative velocity between the interacting stator and rotor fields must be zero. The object of this chapter is to develop the techniques for the steady-state analysis of polyphase synchronous machines.

5.1. EXCITATION SYSTEMS FOR SYNCHRONOUS MACHINES

In large synchronous machines, the field winding is always provided on the rotor, because of certain advantages described in Art. 3.2. In the present article is given a brief account of the various schemes employed for supplying D.C. excitation to the field winding of large synchronous machines. Some of the more important excitation systems are given below :

(a) **D.C. exciters.** This is an old conventional method of exciting the field windings of synchronous generators. In this method ; three machines, namely pilot exciter, main exciter and the main 3-phase alternator are mechanically coupled and are therefore driven by the same shaft. The pilot exciter is a D.C. shunt generator feeding the field winding of a main exctier. The main exciter is a separately-excited D.C. generator. The D.C. output from the main exciter is given to the field winding of the main alternator through brushes and slip rings as shown in Fig. 5.1.

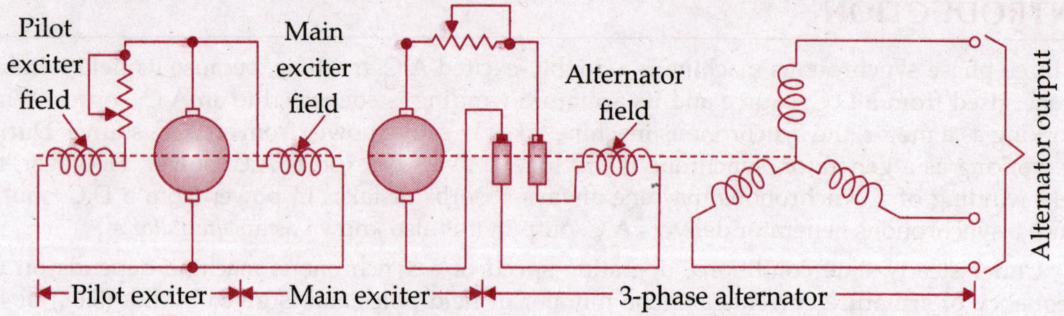

Fig 5.1: D.C. exciter for a synchronous generator.

The conventional method of excitation suffers from cooling and maintenance problems associated with slip rings, brushes and commutators as the alternator ratings rise. The trend toward modern excitation systems has been to decrease these problems by minimising the number of sliding contacts and brushes. This trend has led to the development of static-excitation and brushless-excitation systems.

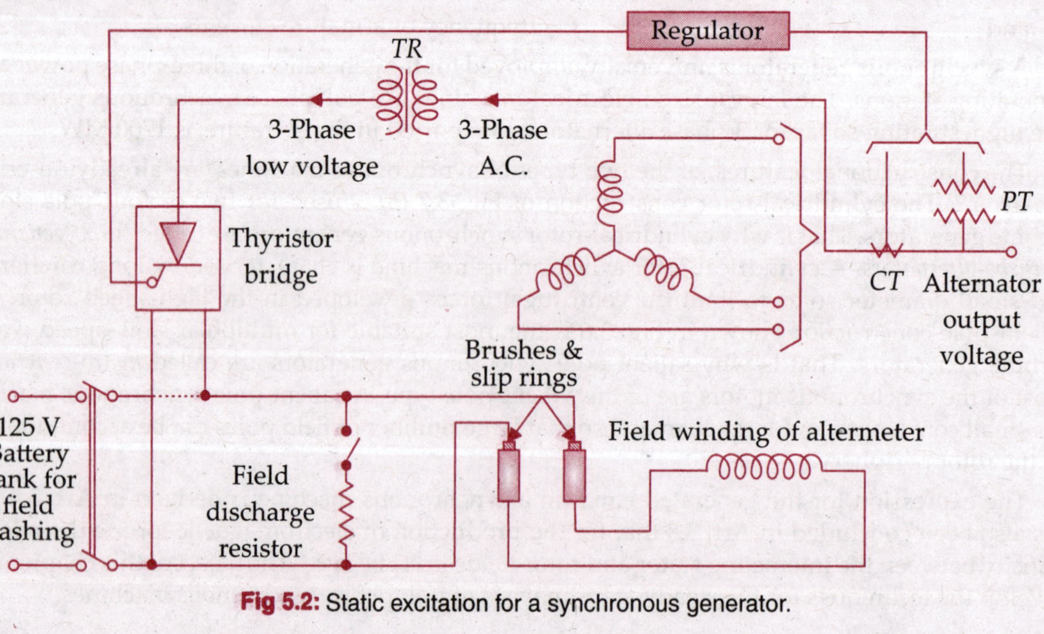

Fig 5.2: Static excitation for a synchronous generator.

(*b*) **Static excitation.** In this method, the excitation power for the main alternator field is drawn from output terminals of the main 3-phase alternator. For this purpose, a 3-phase transformer *TR* steps down the alternator voltage to the desired value. This 3-phase voltage is fed to the 3-phase full-converter bridge using thyristors. The firing angle of these thyristors is controlled by means of a regulator which picks up the signal from alternator terminals through potential transformer *PT* and current transformer *CT* as shown in Fig. 5.2. The controlled power output from thyristor unit is delivered to the field winding of main alternator through brushes and slip rings as shown.

For initiating the process of static excitation, first of all, field winding is switched on to the stationary battery bank to establish the field current in alternator. The alternator speed is adjusted to rated speed. After the output voltage from alternator has built up sufficiently, the alternator field winding is disconnected from battery bank and is switched on to the thyristor bridge output.

A good number of protection devices are installed in the static excitation scheme for any possible fault in the excitation system.

The advantages of static excitation are as under :

(1) The excitation system, with the use of reliable and high-power SCRs, is simple in design and provides fast response characteristics as needed in modern power systems.

(2) Since there is no separate rotating-type exciter, the system is free from friction, windage and commutator loss occurring in the exciter. This makes the system more efficient and in addition, maintenance is reduced.

(3) As exciation energy is taken directly from the alternator terminals, the excitation voltage is proportional to alternator speed. This improves the overall system performance considerably.

(*c*) **Brushless excitation.** This method of excitation is illustrated in Fig. 5.3. In this scheme, main shaft of prime-mover drives pilot exciter, main exciter and the main alternator. Silicon diode rectifiers are also mounted on the main shaft.

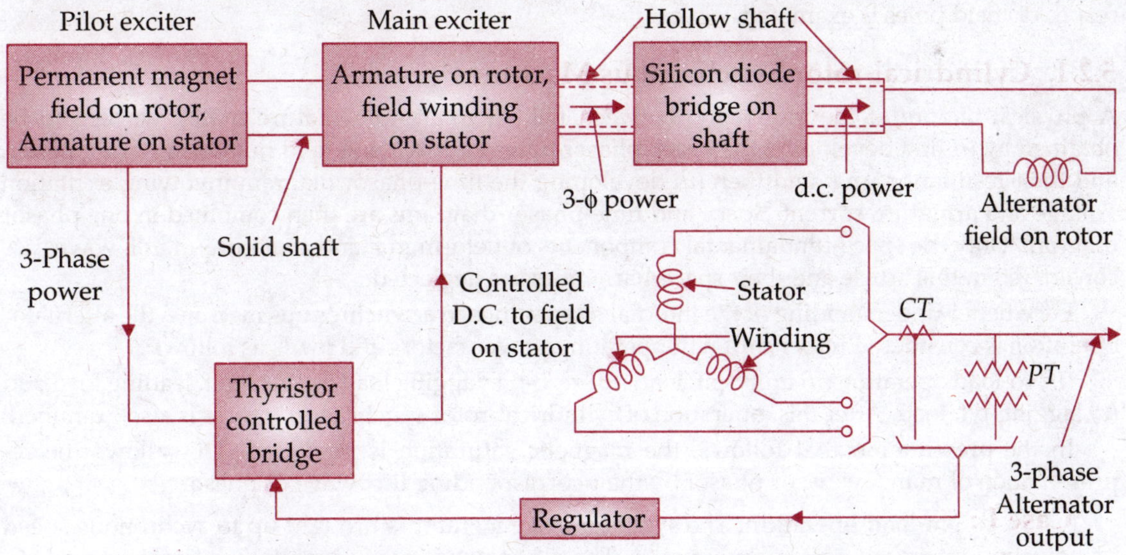

Fig 5.3: Brushless-excitation for a synchronous generator.

Pilot exciter is a permanent-magnet alternator with permanent-magnet poles on the rotor and three-phase armature winding on the stator. Three-phase power from pilot exciter is fed to thyristor controlled bridge placed on the floor. After rectification, the controlled D.C. output is supplied to stationary field winding of main exciter. The frequency of main-exciter output voltage is generally three to four times (150 to 200 Hz), the synchronous generator frequency (50 Hz). The increased frequency is obtained by using more number of poles on the main exciter than on the synchronous generator. The advantage of higher frequency is to reduce the ripple content of dc current supplied to alternator field on rotor. The three-phase power, developed in the rotor of main exciter is fed through hollow shaft to the rotating silicon-diode rectifier mounted on the same shaft. The D.C. power from diode rectifier bridge is delivered, along the main hollow shaft, to the main alternator field without brushes and slip rings.

A signal, picked from alternator terminals through *CT* and *PT*, controls the firing angle of thyristor bridge. This enables the control of field current of the main exciter which eventually governs the alternator output voltage. Since the scheme depicted in Fig. 5.3 does not require any sliding contacts and brushes, this arrangement of exciting the synchronous machine has come to be called as *brushless excitation* system.

For large (500 MW and above) turbo-generator excitation systems, the direct current required by the rotating field winding increases considerably (up to 10 kA or so). In such cases, the brush-gear design becomes more complicated and the reliability of the turbogenerator operation decreases. The only promising solution of feeding the field winding of large turbogenerators is the brushless excitation system. In view of its many advantages, the brushless excitation system is employed in almost all large turbogenerators being designed and manufactured these days.

5.2. FLUX AND M.M.F. PHASORS IN SYNCHRONOUS MACHINES

The object of this article is to examine the interaction between field m.m.f. wave and armature m.m.f. wave. For a cylindrical-rotor synchronous machine, space and time phasor diagrams are developed separately and then combined in one figure for the purpose of analysing the machine performance. For a salient-pole, however, the effect of orientation of armature m.m.f. wave with respect to field poles is examined.

5.2.1. Cylindrical-rotor Synchronous Machines

A physical picture of the interaction between field m.m.f. and armature m.m.f. waves can be obtained by *(i)* first developing the space-phasor diagram involving field m.m.f., armature m.m.f. and their resultant m.m.f. and then *(ii)* developing the time-phasor diagram involving excitation voltage and armature current. Space and time-phasor diagrams are then combined in one phasor diagram. Only the space-fundamental components of field-m.m.f. and armature-m.m.f. waves are considered in this article and their space-harmonics are neglected.

For a better understanding of the internal happenings in a synchronous machine, the alternator operation is considered under different operating power factors and loads as follows :

(i) No-load operation *(ii)* unity-p.f. load *(iii)* zero-p.f. lagging load *(iv)* zero-p.f. leading load and *(v)* lagging-p.f. load. After this, operation of cylindrical-rotor synchronous motor is also examined.

In the presentation that follows, the magnetic saturation is neglected. This allows the representation of m.m.f. wave or phasor by their corresponding flux wave or phasor.

Case I : No-load operation. The synchronous generator is brought up to sychronous speed by adjusting the speed of its prime-mover. The alternator is now separately-excited from a D.C. source. The alternator terminal voltage at no-load is made equal to its rated value by adjusting its field current. The per-phase generated e.m.f., as per Eq. (3.24), is given by

$$E_f = \sqrt{2}\,\pi f N_{ph} k_w \cdot \phi_f \quad ...(5.2)$$

where E_f = no-load voltage, excitation voltage or excitation e.m.f.

$f = \frac{P \cdot n_s}{2}$ = frequency of generated e.m.f.

N_{ph} = series turns per phase

k_w = winding factor

ϕ_f = flux per pole produced by D.C. current in the field winding.

It has already been shown in Eqs. (3.12) and (3.16) that generated e.m.f. lags by 90° the flux that generates it. This is indicated in Fig. 5.4, where E_f is shown lagging ϕ_f by 90°. In this figure, field m.m.f. per pole F_f is equal to $I_f N_f$. As saturation is ignored, field flux phasor ϕ_f is also indicated in phase with field m.m.f. per pole F_f. Axis of field is a long ϕ_f. As field winding m.m.f. F_f and therefore field flux ϕ_f are sinusoidally distributed along the air-gap periphery, these are represented by phasors F_f and ϕ_f in Fig. 5.4.

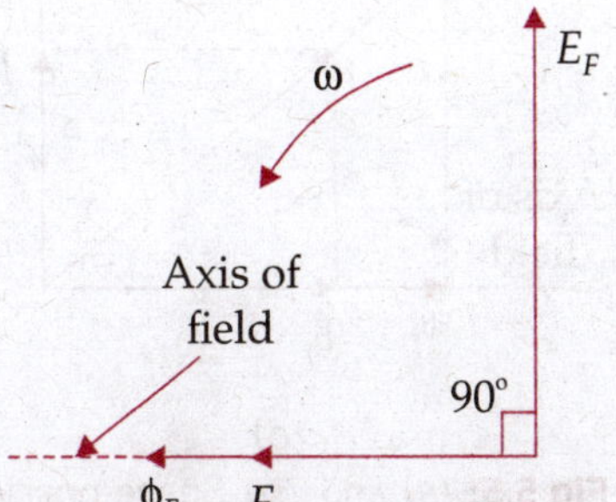

Fig 5.4: Alternator phasor diagram at no-load.

Case II : Unity p.f. load. In order to study the effect of armature m.m.f. wave on the field m.m.f. wave, consider a two-pole cylindrical-rotor alternator of Fig. 5.5 *(a)*. The field winding on the rotor is fed D.C. through brushes and slip rings and the stator carries 3-phase distributed armature winding. As in Art. 3.7, the concentrated full-pitch coils *a a′*, *b b′*, *c c′* on the stator, represent the three-phase windings *a, b, c* in all respects.

The field current indicated by crosses and dots in the field winding on rotor, creates field m.m.f. F_f and field flux ϕ_f which are sinusoidally distributed along the air-gap periphery. As such, both F_f and ϕ_f are repersented by space phasors F_f and ϕ_f as shown in Fig. 5.5 *(a)*, *(b)* and *(e)*. Note that ϕ_f is in phase with F_f as saturation is neglected. The field flux ϕ_f creates *N* and *S* poles on the rotor. Recall that the e.m.f. induced (= *Blv*) in a coil is maximum when its coil-sides are lying in the maximum flux density position. At the instant shown in Fig. 5.5 *(a)*, let phase *'a'* have its coil-side *a, a′* in the maximum flux density position, facing *N, S* poles of the rotor. The e.m.f. induced in coil-sides *a, a′* will, therefore, be maximum. For anticlockwise rotation of rotor, e.m.f. generated in coil-side *a* is indicated by dot and in *a′* by cross. As the coil-sides *b′, c′* are under the influence of field pole *N*, e.m.f. generated in these two coil-sides must be indicated by dot. The magnitude of this e.m.f. would, however, be less than the maximum value. The e.m.f. generated by ϕ_f alone is called the *excitation voltage* and this is indicated in Fig. 5.5 *(a)* by dots and crosses in the armature winding on the stator as discussed above. The magnitude of this e.m.f. is given by Eq. (5.2).

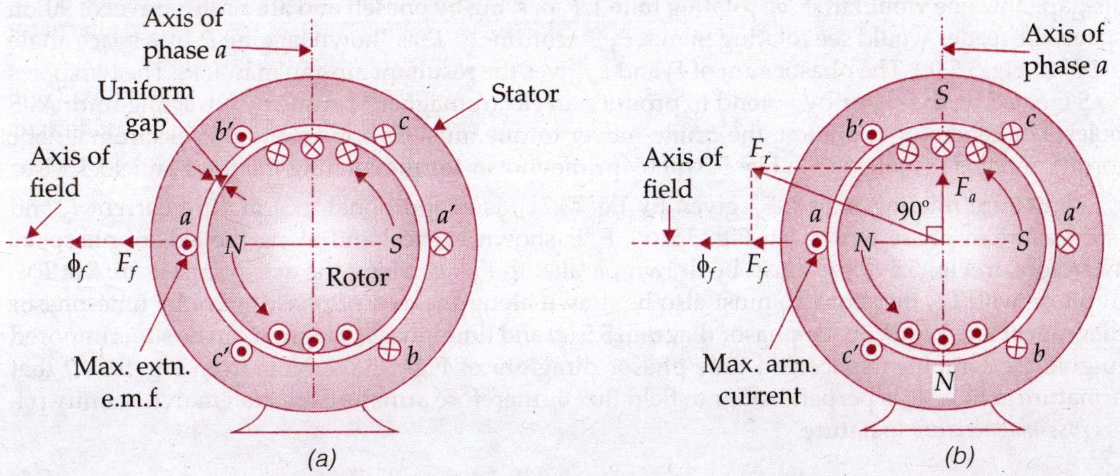

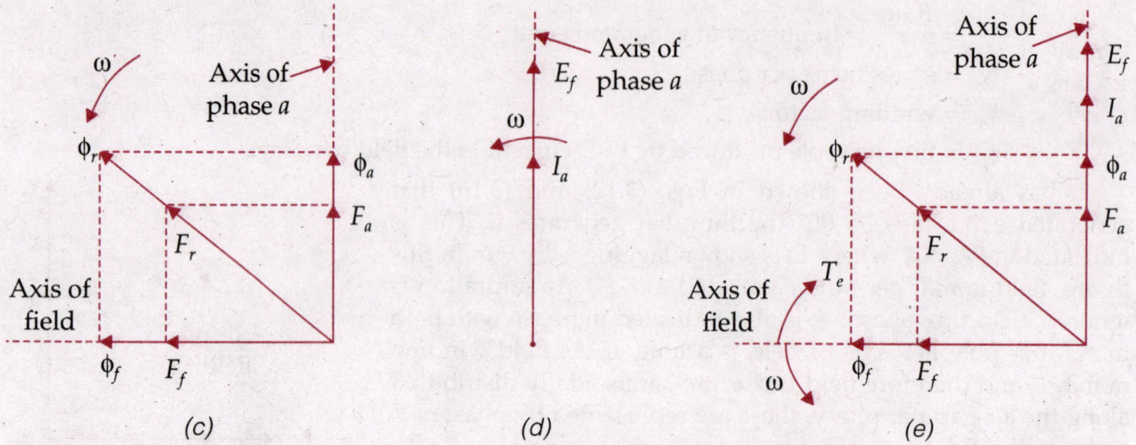

Fig 5.5: *(a)* and *(b)* Space-position of field, armature and resultant m.m.f. phasors in a cylindrical-rotor alternator for unity p.f. load, *(c)* space-phasor diagram, *(d)* time-phasor diagram and *(e)* combined space and time phasor.

When alternator is connected to 3-phase load, 3-phase generated e.m.f. in armature will give rise to 3-phase balanced currents. Let us assume that this armature current I_a is in phase with the excitation e.m.f. E_f . In other words, alternator load is at untiy p.f. with respect to E_f. Unity p.f. means that armature current I_a and excitation voltage are maximum at the same instant of time. In Fig. 5.5 *(a)*, E_f is maximum in phase *'a'* as indicated. At the same instant, armature current I_a is also maximum in phase coil-sides *a, a'*; this is shown in Fig. 5.5 (*b*). Armature current in coil-sides *b, b'* and *c, c'* as indicated in Fig. 5.5 *(b)* is less than maximum. The m.m.f. set up by the armature current is called the *armature-reaction m.m.f.* Recall that for balanced polyphase currents flowing in a polyphase winding, the peak value of the resultant m.m.f. wave is along that phase-axis which carries the maximum current, see Art. 3.7. In view of this, the resultant armature reaction m.m.f. F_a (due to the combined action of 3-phase m.m.fs), is set up along the axis of phase *'a'* because this phase carries the maximum current. It is seen from Fig. 5.5 *(b)* that synchronously rotating armature m.m.f. F_a acts vertically upward (right-hand grip rule) at the instant considered. Since the rotor is also being driven at synchronous speed, the relative velocity between F_f and F_a is zero. Note that for the reference direction of rotation chosen, the field m.m.f. F_f is ahead of F_a by 90° in space and this is depicted accordingly in the space-phasor diagram of Fig. 5.5 *(c)*. In order to draw the space phasor diagram, the reader should imagine oneself seated on the stator tooth or standing in the air-gap–now one would first see rotating m.m.f. F_f passing by oneself and after rotor travel of 90° in space, the reader would see rotating m.m.f. F_a. Accordingly, F_a is shown lagging F_f by a space angle of 90° in Fig. 5.5 (c). The phasor sum of F_f and F_a gives the resultant air-gap m.m.f. F_r. The two poles *N, S* created on the stator by F_a tend to produce an electromagnetic torque by attracting rotor *N, S* poles. For generator operation, the prime-mover torque must be opposite to this electromagnetic torque and this is indicated in Fig. 5.5 *(b)* by prime-mover torque rotating the rotor anticlockwise.

Armature rotating m.m.f. F_a, given by Eq. (3.71), is proportional to armature current I_a and is therefore in phase with I_a. In Fig. 5.5 *(c)*, F_a is shown vertical and along the axis of phase *'a'*. Therefore, in Fig. 5.5 *(d)*, I_a must be drawn parallel to F_a, *i.e.*, along the axis of phase *'a'*. But I_a is in phase with E_f, therefore, E_f must also be drawn along the axis of phase *'a'* in the time-phasor diagram of Fig. 5.5 *(d)*. Space-phasor diagram 5.5 *(c)* and time-phasor diagram can be superimposed to give the combined space and time phasor diragram of Fig. 5.5 *(e)*. Note from Fig. 5.5 *(c)* that armature m.m.f. F_a is perpendicular to field flux ϕ_f, therefore armature reaction m.m.f. at unity p.f. is *cross-magnetizing* in nature.

Case III : Lagging p.f. load. Lagging power-factor loads, having p.f. other than zero p.f. lagging, are more common. So let us consider a general case of armature current I_a lagging the excitation voltage by a time-phase angle ψ° electrical. This means that load p.f. with respect to E_f is cos ψ° lagging. For a two-pole machine, ψ° electrical = ψ° mechanical. In Fig. 5.5 *(a)*, e.m.f. generated in phase-*a* coil-sides *a, a′* is maximum because of the maximum flux-cutting action. For lagging p.f. load having p.f. angle ψ° electrical, the current in coil *a, a′* would attain maximum value after the field poles have moved to a new position ψ° electrical ahead of the maximum e.m.f. position of Fig. 5.5 *(a)*.

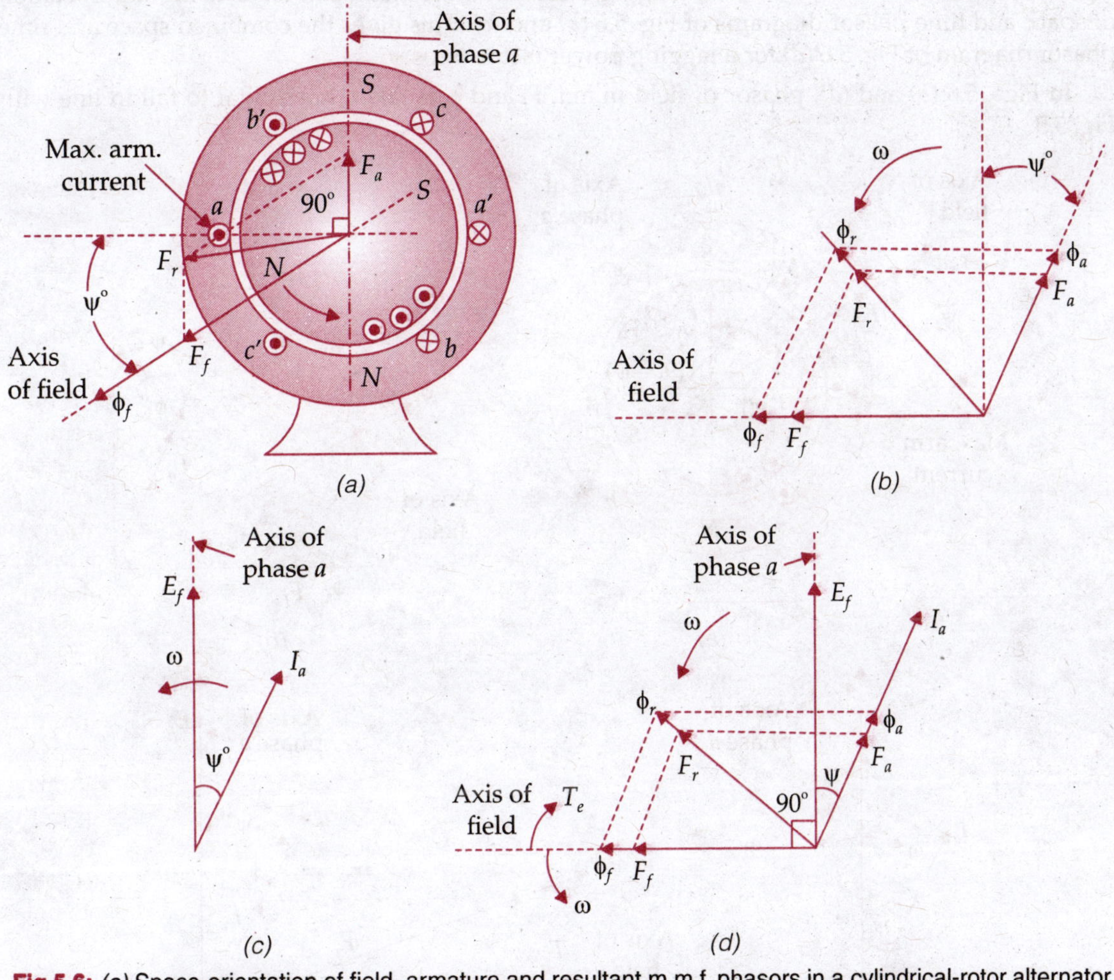

Fig 5.6: *(a)* Space-orientation of field, armature and resultant m.m.f. phasors in a cylindrical-rotor alternator for a lagging p.f. load *(b)* space-phasor diagram *(c)* time-phasor diagram and *(d)* combined space and time phasor diagram.

In other words, by the time armature current in coil *a, a′* attains maximum value with the same polarity (dot in coil-side *a*), the rotor poles *N, S* would have moved forward by ψ° electrical as shown in Fig. 5.6 (a). At the same time, current in coil-sides *b′, c′* would be indicated by dot, but these currents are less than the maximum value. Also, current is indicated by cross in each of the coil sides *b, c*. As before, the resultant of rotating armature m.m.f. F_a is directed vertically upward along the axis of phase-*a*, because this phase carries the maximum armature current at the instant considered. A careful study of Fig. 5.6 *(a)* indicates that armature reaction m.m.f. F_a

lags behind the field m.m.f. F_f by a space angle of (90 + ψ°). Resultant of m.m.fs F_f and F_a gives m.m.f. F_r, this is shown in the space-phasor diagram of Fig. 5.6 *(a)* and *(b)*. Armature mmf F_a is proportional to armature current I_a, therefore, current I_a is drawn parallel to F_a as shown in Fig. 5.6 *(c)*. Excitation emf E_f is shown leading I_a by an angle ψ°, because I_a lags E_f by power-factor angle ψ°. Time-phasor diagram of Fig. 5.6 *(c)* is drawn at the instant excitation emf is maximum in phase *a*. This can happen only when rotor *N* pole is 90° ahead of phase *a* reference axis as shown in Fig. 5.5 *(a)*. Therefore, in the time-phasor diagram of Fig. 5.6 (c), E_f is along the axis of phase *a*. As stated before, excitation e.m.f. lags the field m.m.f. F_f, or field flux ϕ_f, by a time-phase angle of 90°. Also I_a lags E_f by ψ° because load p.f. is cos ψ lagging. Recognition of these facts leads to the superposition of space and time phasor diagrams of Fig. 5.6 *(b)* and *(c)*. This gives the combined space and time phasor diagram of Fig. 5.6 *(d)* for a lagging power factor = cos ψ°.

In Figs. 5.6 *(b)* and *(d)*, phasor of field m.m.f. F_f and ϕ_f is taken horizontal to fall in line with Fig. 5.5.

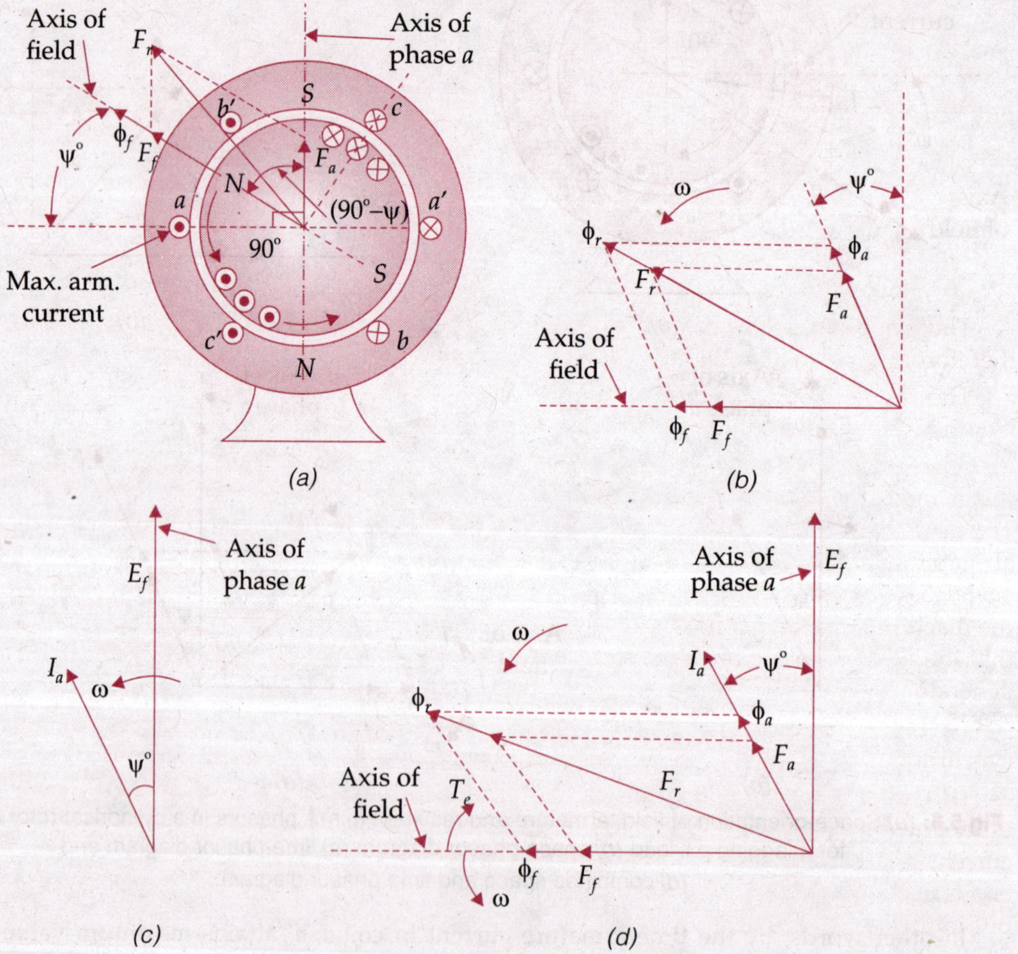

Fig 5.7: *(a)* Space orientation of field, armature and resultant mmf phasors in a cylindrical-rotor alternator for a leading p.f. load *(b)* space-phasor diagram *(c)* time-phasor diagram and *(d)* combined space and time phasor diagram.

Case IV : Leading p.f. load. Let us now consider a case when armature current I_a is leading the excitation emf E_f by a time-phase angle of ψ° electrical. In Fig. 5.5 *(a)*, emf generated in phase-*a* coil sides *a*, *a′* is maximum because of the maximum flux-cutting action. For leading p.f. load having p.f. angle ψ° electrical, the current in coil *a*, *a′* would attain maximum value with the same polarity (dot in coil-side *a*), when the poles are ψ° electrical before the maximum emf position of Fig. 5.5 *(a)*. This is indicated in Fig. 5.7 *(a)*, where rotor poles are shown ψ° prior to the maximum emf position of Fig. 5.5 *(a)*. As before, dots are put in coil sides *b′*, *c′* and cross in coil-sides *b*, *c*. Resultant of rotating armature mmf F_a is vertically upward along the axis of phase *a*, because this phase carries the maximum armature current at the instant considered.

Resultant of mmf F_a and mmf F_f gives mmf F_r; this is shown in the space phasor diagram of Fig. 5.7 *(a)* and *(b)*. In Fig. 5.7 *(b)*, mmf F_f and field flux ϕ_f are taken horizontal for convenience. In Fig. 5.7 *(c)*, I_a is drawn parallel to F_a as before and E_f is shown lagging I_a by angle ψ°. This results in time-phasor diagram of Fig. 5.7 *(c)*. It is seen from Fig. 5.7 *(b)* that mmf F_a lags field mmf F_f by a space-phase angle of (90 – ψ°). As before, excitation emf E_f lags F_f by 90°. Also, I_a leads E_f by ψ°, because internal p.f. is cos ψ°. These facts lead to the combined space and time phasor diagram of Fig. 5.7 *(d)* for a leading pf = cos ψ°.

The resultant, or air-gap mmf F_r is seen to be made up of the phasor sum of field mmf F_f and the armature reaction mmf F_a. Mathematically, it can be written as

$$\overline{F}_r = \overline{F}_f + \overline{F}_a \quad \text{...(5.3)}$$

For a uniform air-gap machine, the reluctance is constant at all angular position of the rotor. If saturation is neglected, then

$$\frac{\overline{F}_r}{\text{Reluctance}} = \frac{\overline{F}_f}{\text{Reluctance}} + \frac{\overline{F}_a}{\text{Reluctance}}$$

or

$$\overline{\phi}_r = \overline{\phi}_f + \overline{\phi}_a \quad \text{...(5.4)}$$

Thus, the waveforms of various fluxes per pole, *i.e.* ϕ_r, ϕ_f and ϕ_a are also sine waves and can, therefore, be represented by phasors as illustrated in Figs. 5.5 *(e)*, 5.6 *(d)* and 5.7 *(d)*.

The above does not hold good for a salient-pole synchronous machine, because its air-gap length is not uniform.

Space-phasor and time-phasor quantities, as usual, are taken to rotate counter clockwise and this is indicated by an arrow marked ω in Figs. 5.5 *(c)*, *(d)*, *(e)* ; 5.6 *(b)*, *(c)*, *(d)* and 5.7 *(b)*, *(c)*, *(d)*. The field mmf wave or field poles have always a tendency to align themselves along the resultant air-gap flux ϕ_r or along the armature-reaction flux ϕ_a, this is shown by an arrow marked T_e in Figs. 5.5 *(e)*, 5.6 *(d)* and 5.7 *(d)*. Since the electromagnetic torque T_e opposes the direction of rotation ω, the machine acts as a generator. It can also be stated by referring to Figs. 5.5 *(b)*, 5.6 *(a)* and 5.7 *(a)* that the field poles must be driven (by the prime-mover) ahead of the resultant air-gap flux, for generator operation.

Cylindrical-rotor synchronous motor : Now operation of three-phase cylindrical-rotor synchronous motor is investigated at different operating power factors.

(I) Unity pf load. Let us consider that a cylindrical-rotor synchronous motor is operating at unity power factor with respect to the excitation emf E_f. For a generator, armature current is output current + I_a, therefore, for a motor, armature current has to be input current-I_a. When the excitation emf is maximum as in Fig. 5.5 *(a)*, armature current for unity power factor would also be maximum but in the **opposite direction** as per the conventions for a synchronous motor. Therefore, in Fig. 5.5 *(b)*, dots must be replaced by crosses in coil-sides *a*, *b′*, *c′* and crosses be replaced by dots in coil-sides *a′*, *b*, *c* so as to obtain Fig. 5.8 *(a)* for a synchronous motor operation. Armature reaction mmf F_a is now vertically downward. The resultant mmf F_r is obtained by phasor sum of field mmf F_f and armature mmf F_a ; *i.e.* $\overline{F}_r = \overline{F}_f + \overline{F}_a$, Fig. 5.8 *(a)*. Space-phasor diagram is drawn in Fig. 5.8 *(b)*. Now armature current I_a is drawn parallel to F_a and – I_a is shown opposite to I_a, Fig. 5.8 *(c)*. For unity pf motor operation, E_f is in phase with – I_a as shown in the time-phasor diagram of Fig. 5.8 *(c)*.

As before, space-phasor diagram of Fig. 5.8 *(b)* and time-phasor diagram of Fig. 5.8 *(c)* are now superimposed to obtain the combined space and time phasor diagram of Fig. 5.8 *(d)*.

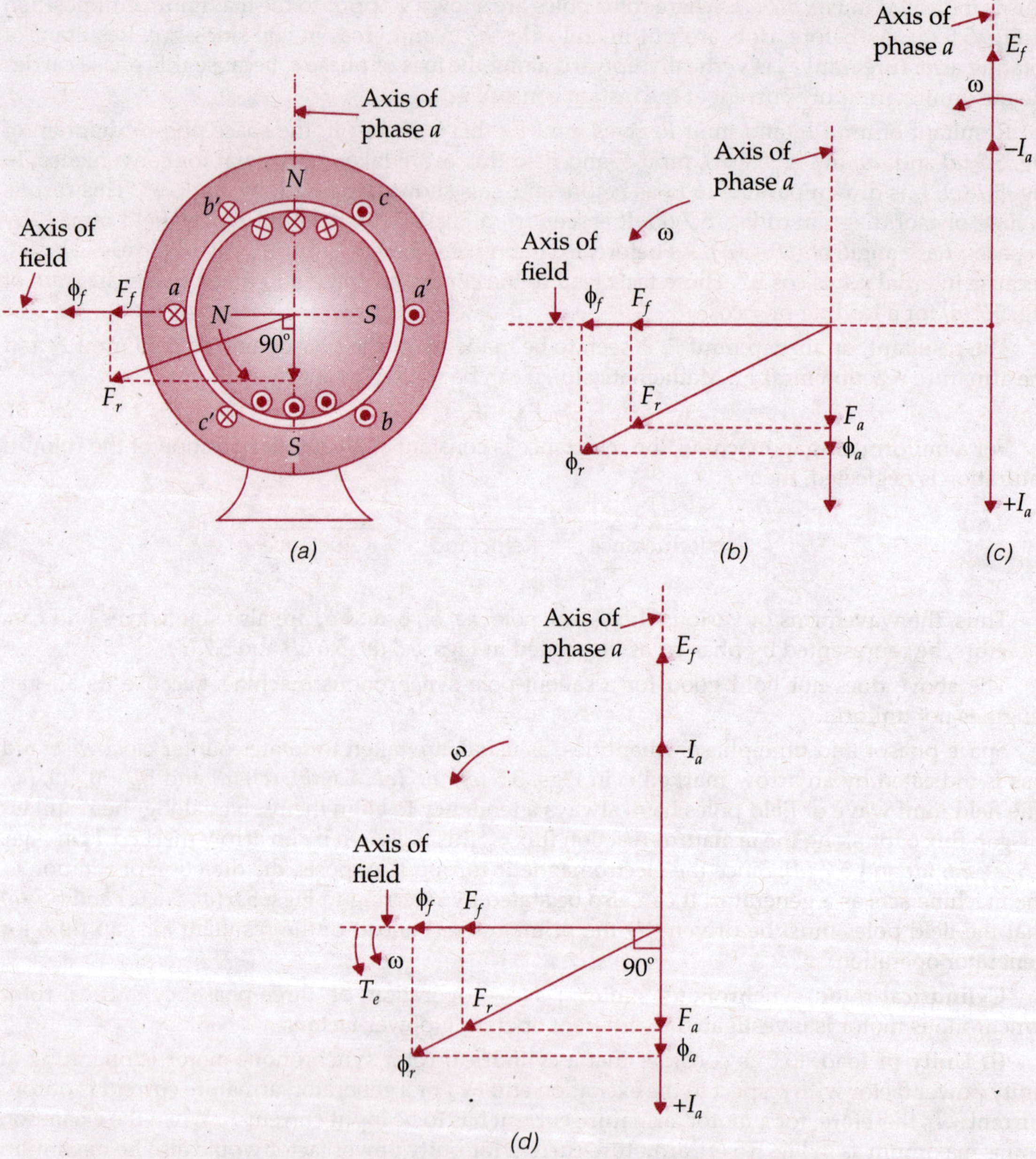

Fig 5.8: *(a)* Space orientation of field, armature and resultant mmf phasors in a cylindrical-rotor synchronous motor for unity pf load *(b)* space-phasor diagram *(c)* time-phasor diagram and *(d)* combined space and time phasor diagram.

In Fig. 5.8 *(a)*, stator *N* pole repels rotor *N* pole but attracts rotor *S* pole causing anticlockwise rotation. Similarly, stator *S* causes anticlockwise rotation. As rotor is rotating anticlockwise, Fig. 5.8 *(a)* pertains to synchronous motor operation.

(II) Lagging pf load : Consider a three-phase synchronous motor operating at a lagging pf load with respect to excitation emf E_f.

As stated before, armature current for a generator is $+ I_a$ and for a motor, armature current is $- I_a$. Combined space and time phasor diagram for a cylindrical-rotor alternator operating at a lagging pf is shown in Fig. 5.6 *(d)*. From this figure, combined space and time-phasor diagram for a cylindrical-rotor synchronous motor can be obtained merely by reversing the direction of armature current as shown in Fig. 5.9 *(a)*. In this figure, $- I_a$ (and not I_a) lags E_f by power-factor angle $\psi°$. So, in this figure, I_a is shown opposite to $- I_a$.

Rotating armature mmf phasor F_a is in phase with armature current I_a. Armature reaction flux ϕ_a is also in phase with F_a as before. Excitation voltage E_f is along the axis of phase *a* and this emf E_f lags field mmf F_f, or ϕ_f, by 90°. The resultant mmf F_r is obtained by the phasor sum of F_f and F_a; *i.e.*, $\bar{F}_r = \bar{F}_f + \bar{F}_a$, Fig. 5.9 *(a)*. Here F_r is ahead of F_f but it lags mmf F_a.

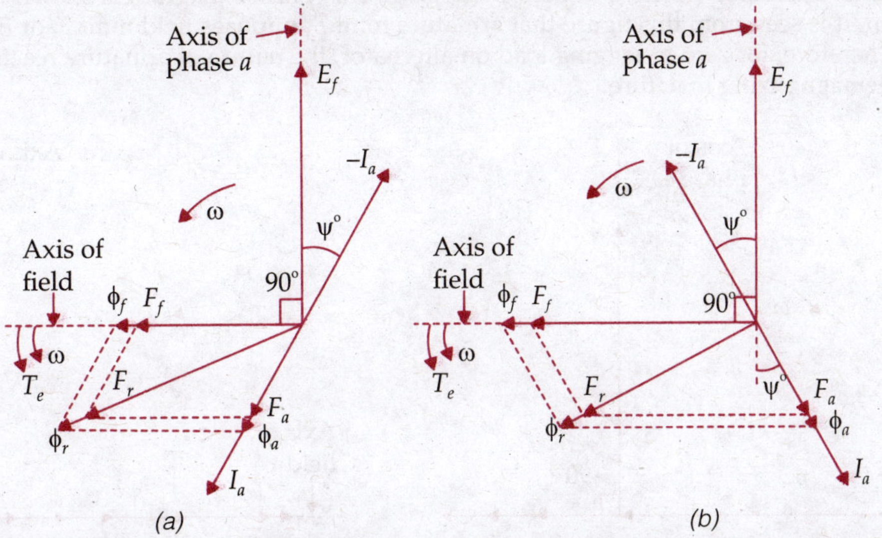

Fig 5.9: Combined space and time phasor diagram for a cylindrical-rotor synchronous motor for *(a)* lagging pf load and *(b)* leading pf load.

(III) Leading pf load : Combined space and time phasor diagram for a cylindrical-rotor alternator working at a leading pf is shown in Fig. 5.7 *(d)*. From this figure, combined space and time phasor diagram for a cylindrical rotor synchronous motor can be obtained by reversing the direction of armature current as shown in Fig. 5.9 *(b)*. Here $-I_a$ (and not $+I_a$) leads E_f by p.f. angle $\psi°$.

As before, resultant mmf F_r is obtained by the phasor sum of F_f and F_a ; *i.e.* $\bar{F}_r = \bar{F}_f + \bar{F}_a$. Here F_r is ahead of F_f but is behind mmf F_a.

Like an alternator, in a cylindrical-rotor synchronous motor also, field poles have a tendency to align themselves along the resultant air-gap flux ϕ_r, this is indicated by an arrow marked T_e in Figs. 5.8 *(d)*, 5.9 *(a)* and 5.9 *(b)*. Since electromagnetic torque T_e aids the direction of rotation, the machine acts as a synchronous motor. It can also be stated that field poles are dragged (by the shaft load) behind the resultant air-gap flux for a synchronous motor operation.

The orientation of armature reaction mmf F_a with respect to field mmf F_f depends on the time-phase angle between excitation emf E_f and armature current I_a. This is summarized as under.

1. For unity pf operation, the space-phase angle between F_a and F_f is 90°, see Figs. 5.5 and 5.8. Therefore armature reaction mmf is cross-magnetizing in nature.
2. The space angle between F_a and F_f is greater than 90° in an alternator operating at a lagging pf, Fig. 5.6 *(d)* and in a synchronous motor working at a leading pf, Fig. 5.9 *(b)*. The

resultant mmf F_r is smaller than F_f. Therefore, armature reaction mmf has demagnetizing effect, *i.e.* resultant mmf is less than field mmf.

3. The space angle between F_a and F_f is smaller than 90° in an alternator operating at a leading pf, Fig. 5.7 *(d)* and in a synchronous motor operating at lagging pf, Fig. 5.9 *(a)*. The resultant mmf F_r is greater than F_f, therefore, armature reaction mmf exerts a magnetizing effect, *i.e.*, resultant mmf F_r is more than field mmf F_f.

Zero pf load on cylindrical-rotor synchronous Machines : If armature current I_a lags or leads the excitation emf by 90° in a synchronous machine, the operation of the machine can be investigated by drawing its phasor diagram under specified operating conditions. For this, one has to refer to any one of the figures 5.6 to 5.9.

(a) **Zero pf lagging load on alternator :** Here pf cos $\psi = 0$, therefore $\psi = 90°$. In Fig. 5.6 *(d)*, if pf angle ψ is taken equal to 90°, then this figure becomes the space and time phasor diagram of an alternator working at zero pf lagging. This phasor diagram is shown in Fig. 5.10 *(a)*. It is seen from this figure that armature mmf F_a **opposes** field mmf F_f or field flux ϕ_f. Therefore, for zero pf lagging load on alternator, the nature of armature reaction mmf is **demagnetizing** in nature.

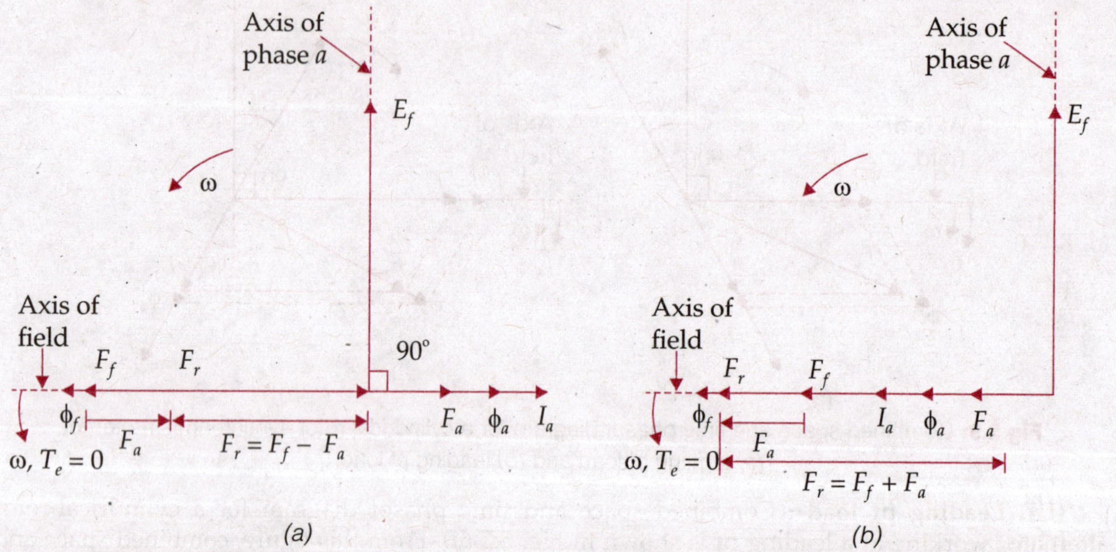

Fig 5.10: Space and time-phasor diagram for an alternator at *(a)* zero pf lagging load and *(b)* zero pf leading load.

(b) **Zero pf leading load on alternator :** Here also $\psi = 90°$. In Fig. 5.7 *(d)*, if pf angle ψ is taken as 90°, then this figure becomes the space and time-phasor diagram of an alternator working at zero pf leading. This phasor diagram is shown in Fig. 5.10 *(b)*. It is seen from this figure that armature reaction mmf F_a **aids** the field mmf F_f. Therefore, the nature of armature reaction mmf for zero pf leading load is **magnetizing** in nature.

(c) **Zero pf lagging load on a synchronous motor :** In Fig. 5.9 *(a)*, if pf angle ψ between E_f and $-I_a$ is made equal to 90°, then the resulting figure would become the space and time phasor diagram for a cylindrical-rotor synchronous motor working at zero pf lagging. This phasor diagram is shown in Fig. 5.11 *(a)*.

It is seen from Fig. 5.11 *(a)* that armature reaction mmf F_a **aids** the field mmf F_f for zero pf lagging load on the synchronous motor. Therefore, nature of armature reaction mmf is **magnetizing** in nature for zero pf lagging load on motor.

(*d*) **Zero pf leading load on a synchronous motor :** Operation of a cylindrical-rotor synchronous motor under these conditions, obtained from Fig. 5.10 (*b*) with $\psi = 90°$, is shown in Fig. 5.11 (*b*). It is seen that armature reaction mmf F_a **opposes** the field mmf F_f or field flux ϕ_f. Therefore, when synchronous motor is operating at zero pf leading conditions, the nature of armature reaction is **demagnetizing** in nature.

It may be summarized from above as under.

If armature current I_a **lags** the excitation emf E_f by 90°, the nature of armature reaction mmf F_a is

(*a*) demagnetizing in an alternator, Fig. 5.10 (*a*).

(*b*) magnetizing in case of synchronous motor, Fig. 5.11 (*a*).

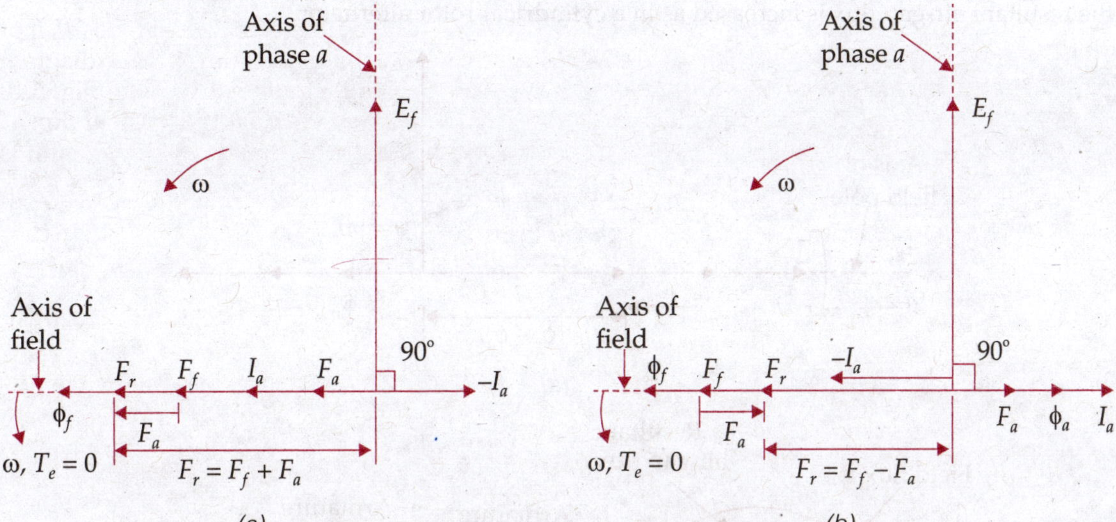

Fig 5.11: Space and time-phasor diagram for a cylindrical-rotor synchronous motor at (*a*) zero pf lagging load and (*b*) zero pf leading load.

In case armature current I_a **leads** E_f by 90°, the nature of armature reaction mmf F_a is

(*a*) magnetizing in case of alternator, Fig. 5.10 (*b*).

(*b*) demagnetizing in a synchronous motor, 5.11 (*b*).

It has been stated before that field poles have a tendency to align themselves along the resultant air-gap flux ϕ_r. For zero pf operation shown in Figs. 5.10 and 5.11, the field poles are already along resultant air-gap flux ϕ_r, therefore no electromagnetic torque is developed. This is indicated in Figs. 5.10 and 5.11 by $T_e = 0$.

5.2.2. Salient-pole Machines

In cylindrical-rotor synchronous machines, the flux produced by armature m.m.f. wave is independent of the spatial orientation of the wave with respect to the field poles. It is because cylindrical-rotor machine has uniform air-gap (neglecting slots) and therefore constant reluctance. In salient-pole machines, the reluctance along the field-pole axis, or direct axis, is much smaller than that along the interpolar, or quadrature, axis. Therefore, in salient-pole machines, the flux produced by an m.m.f. is noticeably greater when peak of m.m.f. wave is aligned with the field-pole axis than when it is in line with the interpolar axis. In other words, the flux produced by an m.m.f. wave in salient-pole synchronous machines depends on the spatial orientation of the armature m.m.f. wave with respect to the field poles.

In salient-pole synchronous generator, if the armature current I_a lags the excitation voltage E_f by 90°, the armature m.m.f. F_a (in phase with and proportional to I_a) is along the field-pole axis and it directly opposes the field flux ϕ_f, Fig. 5.12 *(a)* as in a cylindrical-rotor alternator. In other words, the armature reaction flux ϕ_a for $\psi = 90°$ has a demagnetizing effect on the field flux ϕ_f and consequently the resultant air-gap flux ϕ_r is reduced–this is illustrated in Fig. 5.12 *(b)*. In this figure, the fundamental sine component ϕ_a of the armature reaction flux is shown opposing the fundamental sine component ϕ_f for $\psi = 90°$ and their resultant air-gap flux wave ϕ_r is shown by dashed-dot sine wave. When the armature current I_a leads E_f by 90°, the armature m.m.f. F_a is again along the field-pole axis but it is now directly aiding the field flux ϕ_f (not shown in any figure). In other words, the armature reaction flux ϕ_a for $\psi = 90°$ leading aids the field flux and consequently the resultant air-gap flux is increased as in a cylindrical-rotor alternator.

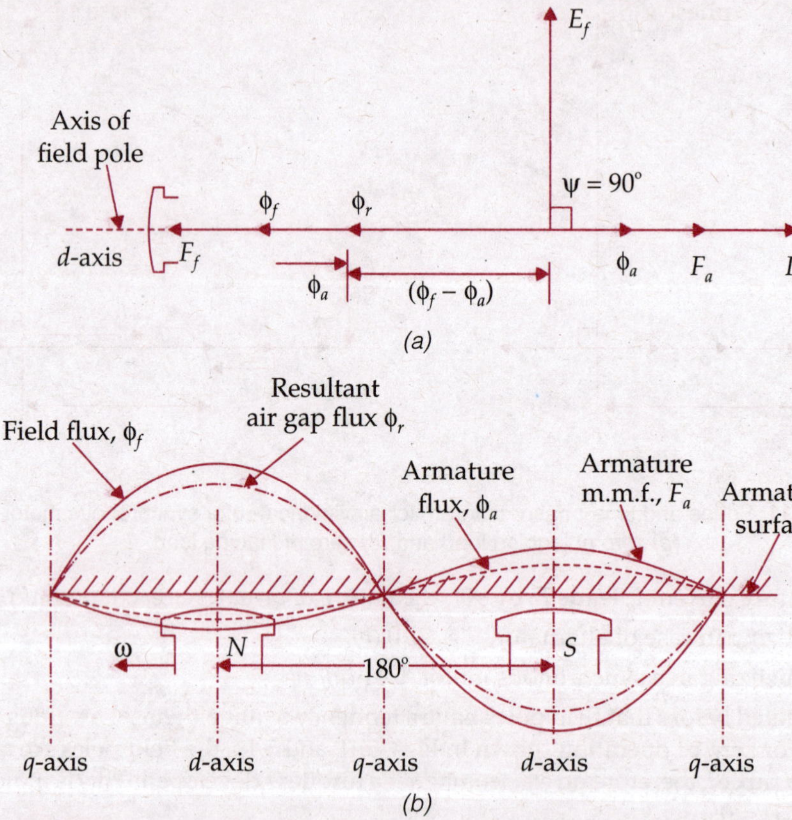

Fig 5.12: Salient-pole synchronous generator air-gap fluxes along direct axis. The flux ϕ_a opposes ϕ_f for $\psi = 90°$ lagging.

In case the armature current is in phase with E_f, the armature m.m.f. F_a would act on an axis 90° away from field, or direct, axis, *i.e.*, along the interpolar axis, Fig. 5.13 *(a)*. In Fig. 5.13 *(b)* are illustrated the fundamental sine component of field flux ϕ_f and sine wave of F_a for $\psi = 0°$. The actual armature flux wave ϕ_a' is obtained by dividing F_a by the air-gap reluctance. Since the reluctance along the interpolar axis is quite large than at the pole tips, the actual armature-reaction flux wave ϕ_a' is saddle-shaped as shown in Fig. 5.13 *(b)*. This flux wave ϕ_a' is seen to consist of a fundamental component ϕ_a and a predominant third harmonic component. The resultant of ϕ_f and ϕ_a' can be obtained by adding their corresponding ordinates and it will be seen that the resultant air-gap flux would be considerably distorted (not shown). Such a distorted flux wave would contain third harmonic flux and as a result, third harmonic e.m.fs are generated in the armature phases but these e.m.fs are zero across the lines. Therefore, when I_a is in phase with E_f, the effect of armature m.m.f. F_a is to distort the field flux wave without appreciably modifying its strength. From above, it can be stated that armature m.m.f. F_a along the direct, or polar, axis is magnetizing or demagnetizing in nature in case time-phase angle between E_f and I_a is 90°. But when F_a is along quadrature axis, it distorts the main field in case time-phase angle between E_f and I_a is zero. In actual practice, I_a lags E_f because of the nature of industrial and domestic loads, consequently armature m.m.f. F_a produces effect both on the direct axis and quadrature axis.

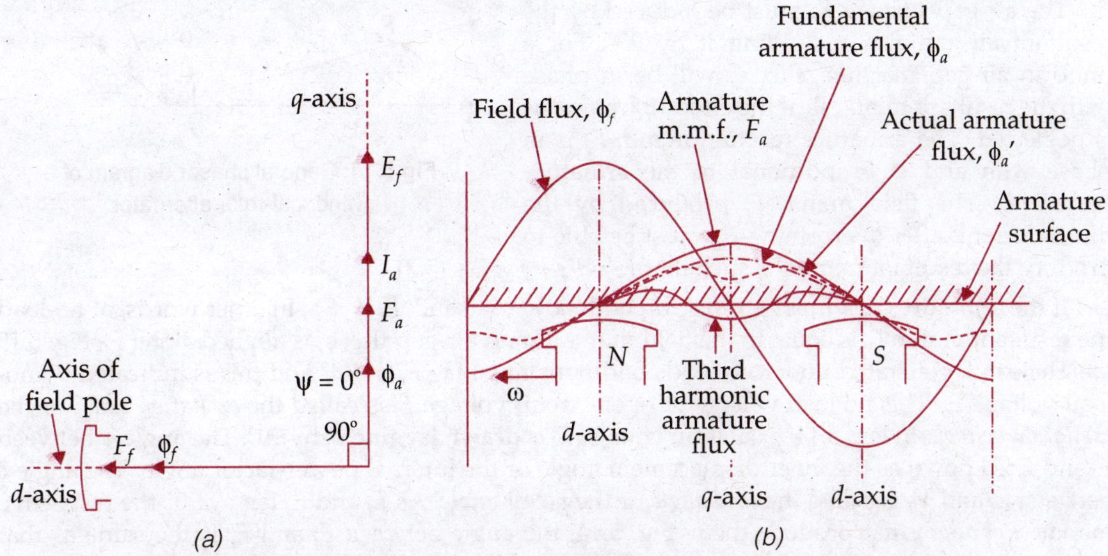

Fig 5.13: Salient-pole synchronous machine air-gap fluxes along quadrature axis. The flux ϕ_a' is cross-magnetizing.

The effect of salient poles can be taken into account by resorting to two-reaction theory. This is discussed in Art. 5.11.

5.3. PHASOR DIAGRAM OF A CYLINDRICAL ROTOR ALTERNATOR

The flux actually existing in the air-gap of a machine is due to the resultant m.m.f. of all the windings. In Art. 5.2, the field m.m.f. F_f and armature reaction m.m.f. F_a have been combined together to give the resultant m.m.f. F_r, in a cylindrical-rotor synchronous machine. The phasor addition of the two m.m.fs. F_f and F_a is possible because of the fact that:

(*a*) these two m.m.fs. are distributed sinusoidally along the air-gap periphery and

(*b*) the relative velocity between the two m.m.fs. is zero at synchronous speed, *i.e.*, the stator and rotor m.m.fs. are stationary with respect to each other.

In order to draw the general phasor diagram, it is assumed that the per phase quantities, *i.e.*, V_t the terminal voltage, I_a the armature current, r_a the armature resistance, x_{al} the armature leakage reactance and cos θ the load power-factor, are known. First of all the terminal voltage V_t^*, with

* Some students do ask in the class as to why V_t is not taken vertical or horizontal. Here V_t is drawn behind excitation voltage so that (V_t + synchronous impedance drop) = E_f turns out to be vertical. This makes field flux ϕ_f, or axis of field, horizontal. When drawing complete phasor diagram involving both e.m.fs and m.m.fs at different operating p.fs, it seems to be convenient to take field-winding axis horizontal.
Now the question arises, why not take field-axis vertical? I must say, it all depends upon the vim and whims of the reader.

armature current I_a lagging behind V_t by the load power-factor angle θ, are drawn. To V_t, are added the armature resistance drop $I_a r_a$ in phase with I_a and the armature leakage reactance drop $I_a x_{al}$ perpendicular to I_a as illustrated in Fig. 5.14. The phasor sum of V_t, $I_a r_a$ and $I_a x_{al}$ gives the perphase e.m.f. E_r, which is called the *air-gap voltage* or the voltage behind leakage impedance.

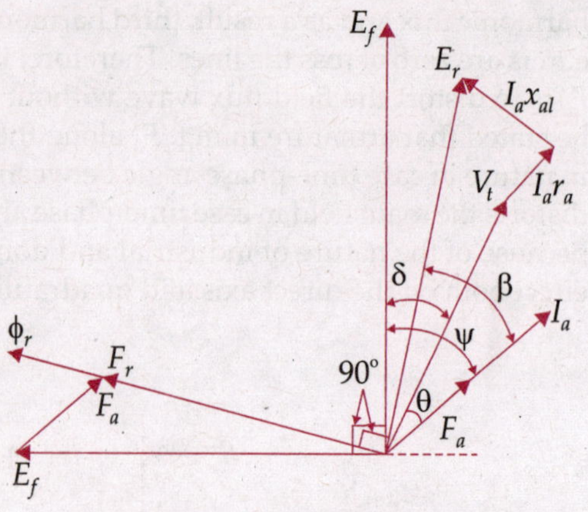

Fig 5.14: General phasor diagram of a cylindrical-rotor alternator.

The air-gap voltage E_r must be induced by the resultant air-gap flux ϕ_r leading it by 90°. For a uniform air-gap machine, flux ϕ_r will be in phase with the resultant m.m.f. F_r, if the effect of hysteresis is neglected. The armature reaction m.m.f. F_a is in phase with and is proportional to the armature current I_a. The field m.m.f. F_f produced by the direct current, after overcoming F_a, must be able to produce the resultant m.m.f. F_r, such that $\bar{F}_r = \bar{F}_f + \bar{F}_a$, Eq. (5.3).

If the armature current is zero (*i.e.*, on no-load) $F_a = 0$ and $\bar{F}_r = \bar{F}_f$. In other words, at no-load the resultant m.m.f. F_r is equal to the field m.m.f. F_f and air-gap flux ϕ_r is aligned along F_f, Fig. 5.15 *(c)*. The e.m.f. generated under no-load conditions must lag F_f by 90° and this is indicated by no-load voltage E_f. This no load voltage or open-circuit voltage E_f is called the *excitation e.m.f.* or the *excitation voltage*. In Fig. 5.14, excitation voltage E_f is drawn lagging F_f by 90°. The angle ψ between E_f and I_a is known as the inner displacement angle or the internal power-factor angle. The angle δ between E_f and V_t is called the *load angle* or the *power angle*. As E_f and E_r lag by 90° the respective m.m.fs. F_f and F_r that produce them, Fig. 5.14, the angle between E_f and E_r is the same as that between F_f and F_r.

5.3.1. The Open-circuit and Short-circuit characteristics of Synchronous Machines

These characteristics are useful for finding out the parameters (or constants) of the synchronous machines and for determining their performance.

For obtaining the open-circuit characteristic (O.C.C.), the alternator is driven at constant rated speed and the open circuit terminal voltage is noted as the field current is gradually increased from zero. Thus the O.C.C. is a graph between the field current I_f or field m.m.f. F_f and the generated e.m.f. E_f. For O.C.C., the final value of E_f should be about 125% of the rated voltage. Fig. 5.15 *(a)* illustrates the circuit diagram for obtaining O.C.C. and Fig. 5.15 *(b)* shows the O.C.C. of the alternator with field current along the abscissa and E_f along the ordinate. The O.C.C. (also called the no-load, saturation, or magnetization characteristic) will not be a straight line, because of saturation in the iron part of the magnetic circuit. At small values of field current or F_f, the air gap requires almost the whole of F_f and m.m.f. required by the iron is almost negligible. But when the m.m.f. has exceeded a certain value, the iron parts require a good amount of m.m.f. and the saturation sets in. In Fig. 5.15 *(b)*, for E_f equal to *oa*, the m.m.f. for the air-gap is *ab* and that for the iron part is *bc*. If it is assumed that the iron part of the magnetic circuit requires zero m.m.f., the relation between E_f and I_f is called the *air-gap line*. Zero m.m.f. for the iron part means that the reluctance is offered by the air-gap alone and that offered by the iron part is zero. The air-gap line is obtained, if the initial straight line portion of O.C.C. is extended as shown in Fig. 5.15 *(b)*. The O.C.C. may be plotted in per unit values, where unit voltage refers to rated voltage and unit field current is the excitation corresponding to unit voltage on the air-gap line.

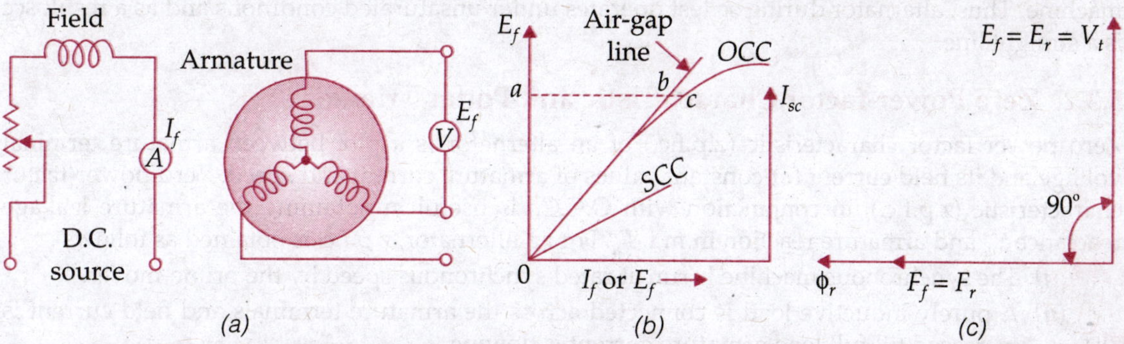

Fig 5.15: *(a)* Circuit diagram for obtaining O.C.C. *(b)* O.C.C. and S.C.C. of an alternator and *(c)* phasor diagram of an alternator on open circuit.

For obtaining the short-circuit characteristic, the machine is driven at rated synchronous speed and the armature terminals are short-circuited through an ammeter, as shown in Fig. 5.16 *(a)*. Now the field current I_f is gradually increased from zero, until the short-circuit armature current has reached its maximum safe value, equal to about 125 to 150% of the rated current. Latter readings may be taken in a short time, in order to avoid armature overheating.

Under short-circuit conditions, the terminal voltage V_t is zero and phasor diagram of Fig. 5.14, reduces to that shown in Fig. 5.16 *(b)*. The air-gap e.m.f. E_r generated by the resultant m.m.f. F_r or air-gap flux ϕ_r is sufficient to overcome the leakage impedance drop $I_a (r_a + jx_{al})$, Fig. 5.16 (b). It can, therefore, be expressed as

$$\bar{E}_r = \bar{I}_a \,(r_a + jx_{al}) \qquad ...(5.5)$$

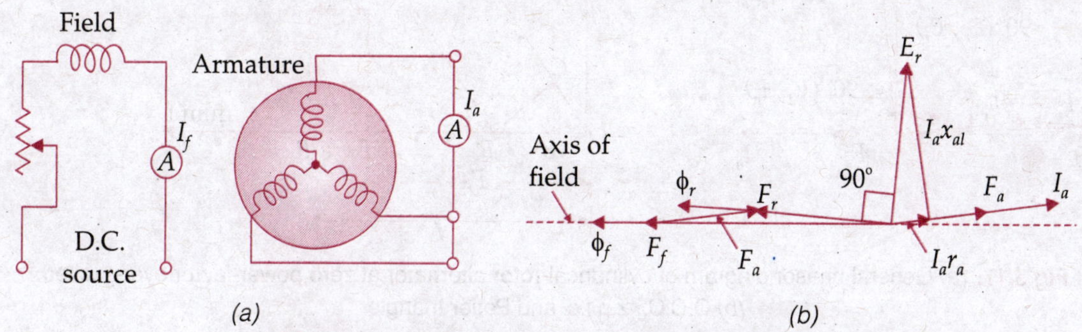

Fig 5.16: *(a)* Circuit diagram for obtaining S.C.C. and *(b)* phasor diagram of the alternator for short-circuit conditions.

Generally x_{al} is much greater than r_a and, therefore, the armature current I_a lags E_r by an angle of nearly 90°. Phasor diagram of Fig. 5.16 *(b)* reveals that F_a is almost opposite to F_f, therefore, F_a is almost entirely demagnetizing in nature. The resultant m.m.f. F_r, almost equal to $F_f - F_a$, is reduced and consequently the resultant air-gap flux is decreased, showing thereby that the saturation under short-circuit conditions does not occur. Therefore, short-circuit characteristic is a straight line through the origin.

Another way of explaining why scc is a straight line is as under:

In a synchronous machine, the value of x_{al} is in between 0.1 to 0.2 per unit and r_a is usually negligible. Taking an average value of x_{al} as 0.15 p.u and $r_a = 0.0$, the magnitude of air-gap e.m.f. E_r at rated armature current, from Eq. (5.5), is 0.15 p.u., *i.e.*, $E_r = 0.15$ p.u. Flux ϕ_r that generates E_r must also be 0.15 p.u. In other words, the resultant air-gap flux ϕ_r during sc test is only about 0.15 of its value under normal-voltage conditions. Such a low value of ϕ_r does not saturate the synchronous machine. Thus, alternator during sc test operates under unsaturated conditions and as a result scc is a straight line.

5.3.2. Zero Power-factor Characteristic and Potier Triangle

Zero power factor characteristic (z.p.f.c.) of an alternator is a plot between armature terminal voltage and its field current for constant values of armature current and speed. Zero-power-factor characteristic (z.p.f.c.), in conjunction with O.C.C., is useful in obtaining the armature leakage reactance x_{al} and armature reaction m.m.f. F_a. For an alternator, z.p.f.c. is obtained as follows :

(i) The synchronous machine is run at rated synchronous speed by the prime-mover.

(ii) A purely inductive load is connected across the armature terminals and field current is increased till full load armature current is flowing.

(iii) The load is now varied in steps and the field current at each step is adjusted to maintain full-load armature current. The plot of armature terminal voltage and field current recorded at each step, gives the zero-power-factor characteristic at full-load armature current.

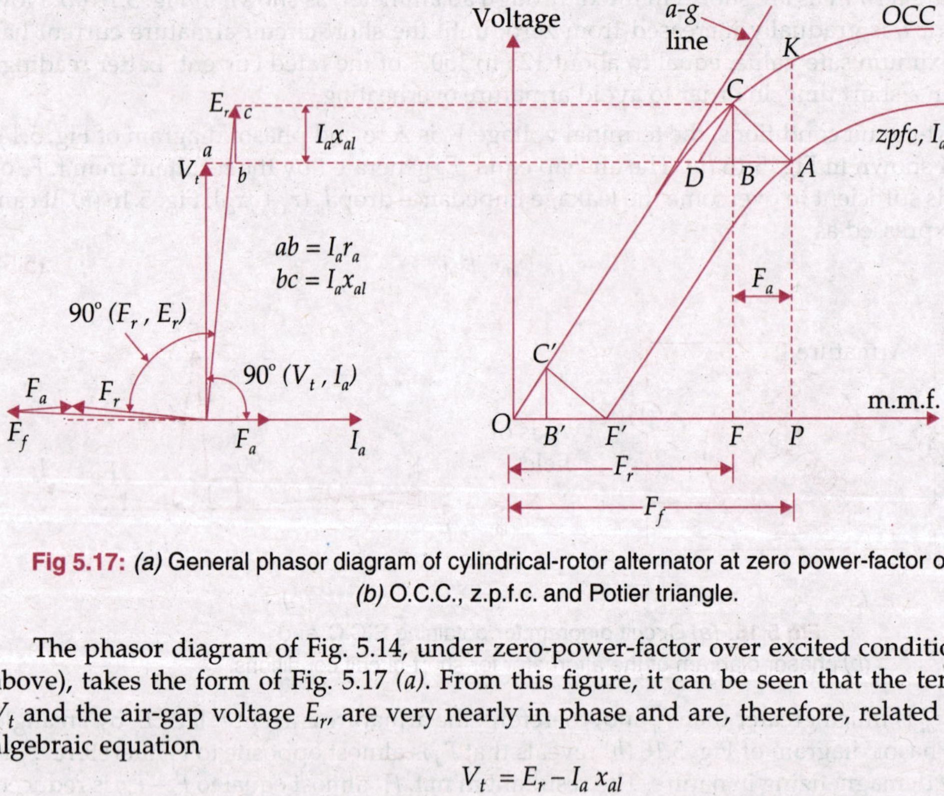

Fig 5.17: *(a)* General phasor diagram of cylindrical-rotor alternator at zero power-factor over-excited. *(b)* O.C.C., z.p.f.c. and Potier triangle.

The phasor diagram of Fig. 5.14, under zero-power-factor over excited conditions (described above), takes the form of Fig. 5.17 *(a)*. From this figure, it can be seen that the terminal voltage V_t and the air-gap voltage E_r, are very nearly in phase and are, therefore, related by the simple algebraic equation

$$V_t = E_r - I_a x_{al}$$

The resultant m.m.f. F_r and the field m.m.f. F_f are also very nearly in phase and are related by the simple algebraic equation

$$F_f = F_r + F_a$$

Assume that O.C.C. gives the exact relation between air-gap voltage E_r and the resultant m.m.f. F_r under load. Also, assume armature leakage reactance to be constant.

The O.C.C. and z.p.f.c are shown in Fig. 5.17 *(b)*. For field excitation F_f or field current I_f, equal to *OP*, the open-circuit voltage is *PK*. With the field excitation and speed remaining unchanged, the armature terminals are connected to a purely inductive load such that full load armature current flows. An examination of Fig. 5.17 *(a)* and *(b)* reveals that under zero power-factor load, the net excitation F_r is OF, which is less than OP (= F_f) by F_a. According to the resultant m.m.f. OF, the air-gap voltage E_r is FC and if $CB = I_a x_{al}$ is subtracted from $E_r = FC$, the terminal voltage $FB = PA = V_t$ is obtained. Since z.p.f.c. is a plot between the terminal voltage and field current I_f or F_f, which has not changed from its no-load value of OP, the point A lies on the z.p.f.c. The triangle ABC so obtained is called the *Potier triangle*, where $CB = I_a x_{al}$ and $BA = F_a$. Thus, from the Potier triangle, the armature leakage reactance x_{al} and armature reaction m.m.f. F_a can be determined.

If the armature resistance is assumed zero and the armature current is kept constant, then the size of Potier triangle ABC remains constant and can be shifted parallel to itself with its corner C remaining on the O.C.C. and its corner A, tracing the z.p.f.c. Thus the z.p.f.c. has the same shape as the O.C.C. and is shifted vertically downward by an amount equal to $I_a\,x_{al}$ (*i.e.* leakage reactance voltage drop) and horizontally to the right by an amount equal to the armature reaction m.m.f. F_a or the field current equivalent to armature reaction m.m.f.

The z.p.f.c. can also be obtained experimentally by connecting an under-excited synchronous motor to the over-excited alternator terminals. The excitation of the alternator and motor are changed in steps so as to keep the alternator armature current constant at its rated value. The graph giving the variation of alternator terminal voltage with its field current, gives the z.p.f.c.

For determining x_{al} and F_a experimentally, it is not necessary to plot the entire z.p.f.c. Only two points A and F' shown in Fig. 5.17 *(b)* are sufficient. The point A (PA = rated voltage) is obtained by actually loading the over-excited alternator by an under-excited synchronous motor, so that the rated armature current flows in the alternator at rated voltage. The other point F' on the z.p.f.c. corresponds to the zero terminal voltage and can, therefore, be obtained by performing short-circuit test. So here OF' is the field current required to circulate short-circuit current, equal to the armature current (generally rated current) at which the point A is determined in the zero (near zero) power factor test.

Now draw a horizontal line AD, parallel and equal to $F'O$. Through point D, draw a straight line parallel to the air-gap line, intersecting the O.C.C. at C. Draw CB perpendicular to AD. Then ABC is the Potier triangle from which

$$BC = I_a\,x_{al} \text{ and } AB = F_a$$

Since the armature current I_a at which the point A is obtained, is known, x_{al} can be calculated.

5.4. VOLTAGE REGULATION OF AN ALTERNATOR

It is defined as the change in terminal voltage, expressed as a precentage (or p.u.) of the rated voltage, when the load at a given power factor is removed, with speed and field current remaining unchanged. Therefore,

$$\text{Voltage regulation} = \frac{E_f - V_t}{V_t} \text{ in p.u.} = \frac{E_f - V_t}{V_t} \times 100 \text{ in percentage.}$$

Here E_f is the no-load excitation voltage and V_t is the full-load terminal voltage at the same speed and field excitation.

For a lagging power-factor load, E_f always increases and for a leading power-factor load, E_f may decrease—consequently the voltage regulation may be positive or negative.

Though the use of automatic voltage regulators have curtailed the importance of computing the voltage regulation of synchronous machines, it is still worth-while to know its value, because of the following reasons :

(i) When the load is thrown off, the voltage rise must be known, since the winding insulation should be able to withstand this increased voltage.

(ii) Voltage regulation determines the type of automatic voltage-control equipment to be used.

(iii) Steady state short-circuit conditions and stability are affected by the voltage regulation.

(iv) Parallel operation of one alternator, with other alternators, is affected considerably by its voltage regulation.

In case of small machines, the voltage regulation can be obtained by actually loading it. In large machines, it may not be possible to obtain the voltage regulation by actual loading because of the cost of dissipating the huge output and also providing the large input. Certain simple tests, involving only small amounts of power, are conducted and from these, the machine constants are determined to compute the voltage regulation. A few methods, for computing the voltage regulation, are described below, where per phase values are used unless otherwise stated.

5.4.1. The Electromotive Force (e.m.f.) Method or Synchronous Impedance Method

This method, though gives inconsistent results for voltage regulation, is quite useful, because it introduces the concept of synchronous reactance. This procedure can be applied to cylindrical-rotor synchronous machines only, because the resultant air-gap flux ϕ_r is not affected by the angular position of the rotor. The iron part of the magnetic circuit is assumed to have constant permeability, *i.e.*, saturation is neglected—this permits the replacement of m.m.f.s by their corresponding fluxes and, therefore, the corresponding e.m.f.s. In short the m.m.fs can be replaced by their corresponding e.m.f.s and it is because of this reason that this procedure of determining voltage regulation is called the e.m.f. method.

Field m.m.f. F_f generates E_f lagging it by 90°, resultant m.m.f. F_r generates air-gap voltage E_r lagging it by 90°, similarly armature reaction m.m.f. F_a must generate armature-reaction e.m.f. E_{ar} lagging F_a by 90°—this is illustrated in Fig. 5.18. Now the phasor sum of $\overline{F}_f$ and $\overline{F}_a$ gives $\overline{F}_r$, similarly the phasor sum of $\overline{E}_f$ and $\overline{E}_{ar}$ must be $\overline{E}_r$ —mathematically it can be written as

$$\overline{F}_r = \overline{F}_f + \overline{F}_a \quad \text{...(5.6 a)}$$

and

$$\overline{E}_r = \overline{E}_f + \overline{E}_{ar} \quad \text{...(5.6 b)}$$

Note that triangle with sides F_f, F_a and F_r is similar to the triangle whose sides are E_f, E_{ar} and E_r.

It is seen from Fig. 5.15 (b) that slope of the air-gap line may be expressed as E_f/F_f or E_f/I_f. If E_f/F_f is taken as K, then $E_f = KF_f$. As E_f lags F_f (or ϕ_f) by 90°, it is possible to express the relation between E_f and F_f in phasor form as

$$\left.\begin{aligned} \overline{E}_f &= -jK\overline{F}_f \\ \text{Similarly,} \quad \overline{E}_r &= -jK\overline{F}_r \\ \text{and} \quad \overline{E}_{ar} &= -jK\overline{F}_a \end{aligned}\right\} \quad \text{...(5.7)}$$

Note that here K is the slope of the air-gap line.

The armature-reaction m.m.f. $\overline{F}_a$ is in phase with, and proportional to, armature current I_a.

$$\therefore \quad \overline{F}_a = C\overline{I}_a$$

where C is a constant, refer to Eq. (3.71)

Substitution of $\overline{F}_a$ in Eq. (5.7) gives $\overline{E}_{ar} = -jCK\overline{I}_a$ ...(5.8)

Further substitution of $\overline{E}_{ar}$ in Eq. (5.6) gives,

$$\overline{E}_r = \overline{E}_f - jCK\overline{I}_a$$

or

$$\overline{E}_f = \overline{E}_r + jCK\overline{I}_a.$$

Fig. 5.18 reveals that phasor sum of V_t, $I_a r_a$ and $I_a x_{al}$ gives air-gap e.m.f. E_r. As an equation, this can be expressed as

$$\bar{E}_r = \bar{V}_t + \bar{I}_a\,(r_a - jx_{al})$$

$$\bar{E}_f = \bar{V}_t + \bar{I}_a r_a + j\bar{I}_{al}\,(x_{al} + CK) \qquad ...(5.9)$$

The tern CK in Eq. (5.9) has the dimension of a reactance, because it appears in bracket with x_{al}. Writing $CK = X_{ar}$,

Eq. (5.8) can be re-written as $\bar{E}_{ar} = -jK\bar{F}_a = -jCK\bar{I}_a = -jX_{ar}\bar{I}_a$ ...(5.10)

Eq. (5.10) reveals that reactance X_{ar} is due to the presence of armature reactions m.m.f. F_a. The total equivalent reactance is $x_{al} + X_{ar} = X_s$ ...(5.11)

where X_s is called *synchronous reactance* of the cylindrical-rotor synchronous machine. The reactance X_{ar}, due to armature reaction m.m.f. is called the *armature-reaction reactance* or the *magnetizing reactance*. Note that X_{ar} is a fictitious reactance and it accounts for the voltage E_{ar} generated by armature reaction m.m.f. F_a. The term $(r_a + jX_s) = Z_s$, is called the *synchronous impedance* of the cylindrical-rotor synchronous machine.

It is seen from Fig. 5.18 that air-gap voltage E_r is given by

$$\bar{E}_r = \bar{V}_t + \bar{I}_a\,(r_a + jx_{al}) \qquad ...(5.12\,a)$$

Examination of Fig. 5.19 reveals that

$$\bar{E}_f = \bar{E}_r + jI_a X_{ar} = \bar{V}_t + \bar{I}_a r_a + jI_a\,(x_{al} + X_{ar})$$

or

$$\bar{E}_f = \bar{V}_t + \bar{I}_a\,(r_a + jX_s) \qquad ...(5.12\,b)$$

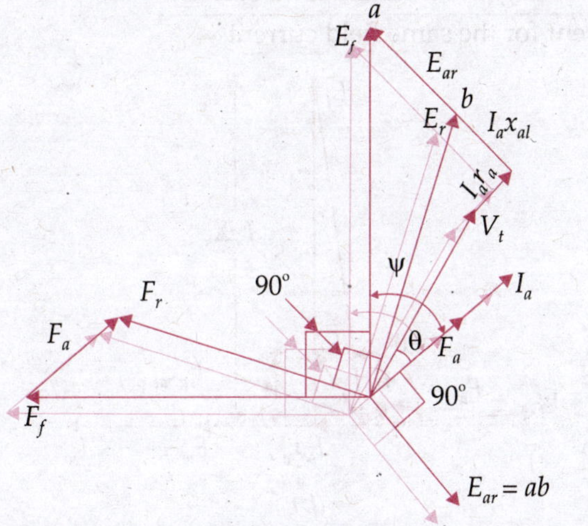

Fig 5.18: Phasor diagram of component mmfs. and corresponding emfs.

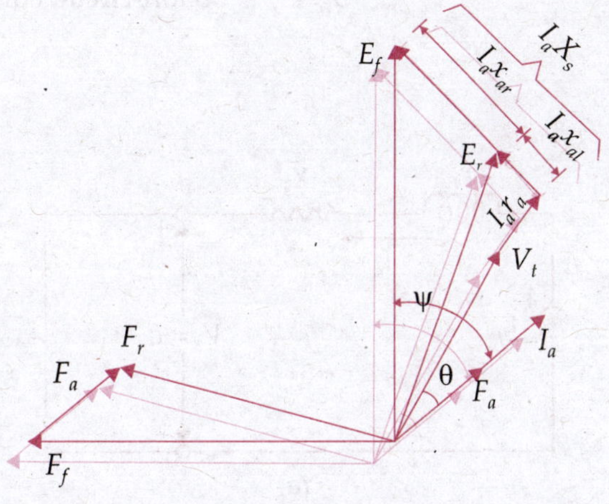

Fig 5.19: Phasor diagram for emf or synchronous-impedance method.

Eqs. 5.12 *(a)* and *(b)* give the equivalent circuit of a cylindrical-rotor synchronous generator as shown in Fig. 5.20 *(a)*. Finally, the equivalent circuit reduces to that shown in Fig. 5.20 *(b)*.

An examination of Fig. 5.19 reveals that $I_a x_{al}$ accounts for armature leakage flux, $I_a X_{ar}$ accounts for the armature reaction m.m.f. F_a (or armature reaction flux) and E_f accounts for the field m.m.f. F_f (or field flux). In short, the synchronous reactance X_s takes into account the entire flux set up by the balanced polyphase armature currents.

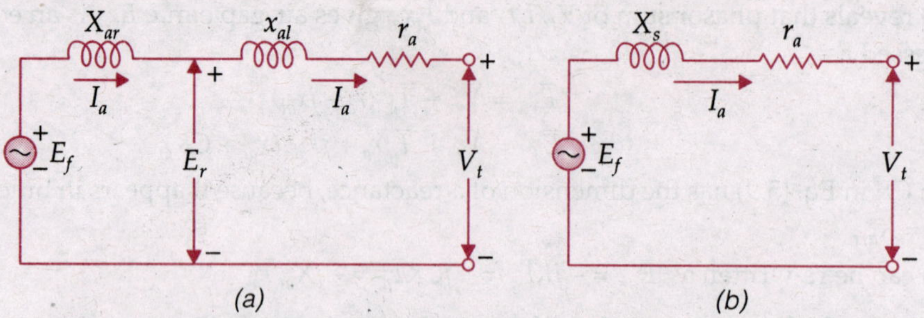

Fig 5.20: Equivalent circuit for a cylindrical-rotor synchronous generator.

For an alternator, the power and, therefore, I_a flows out of the machine. For a synchronous motor, the power and, therefore, I_a flows into the machine. Thus the voltage equation for a synchronous motor can be obtained from alternator voltage equation (5.12) simply by writing $(-I_a)$ in place of I_a. Therefore, the synchronous motor voltage equation is

$$\overline{V}_t = \overline{E}_f + \overline{I}_a (r_a + jX_s) \text{ or } \overline{V}_t = \overline{E}_f + \overline{I}_a Z_s \quad ...(5.13)$$

As before, Z_s is the synchronous impedance for the cylindrical rotor synchronous motor.

Measurement of Z_s and X_s. Open-circuit and short-circuit characteristics are required for the determination of Z_s and X_s.

In open-circuit test, the armature current I_a is zero and $V_t = E_f$, see Fig. 5.15.

In the short-circuit test, entire e.m.f. E_f is consumed in circulating the short-circuit current I_{sc}, through the synchronous impedance Z_s, Fig. 5.21 *(a)* and *(b)*. Therefore,

$$Z_s = \frac{E_f}{I_{sc}} = \frac{\text{Open-circuit terminal voltage for a certain field current}}{\text{Short-circuit current for the same field current}}$$

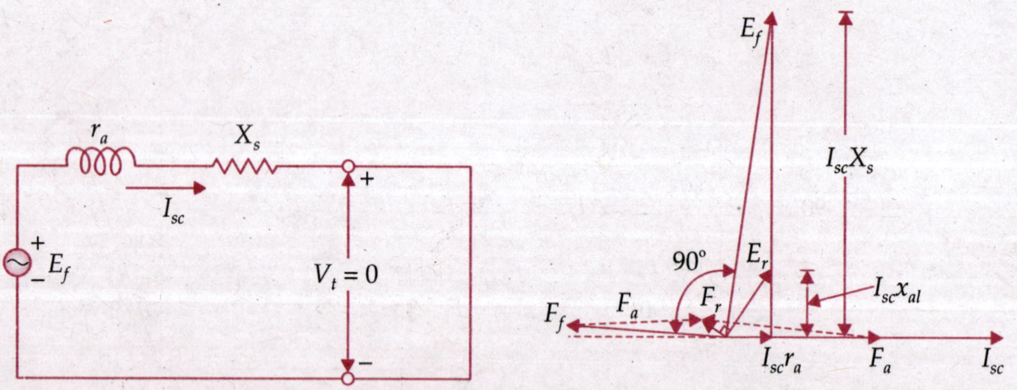

Fig 5.21: *(a)* Equivalent circuit under short-circuit test and *(b)* the phasor diagram under short-circuit test, for a cylindrical rotor alternator.

An open circuit characteristic O.C.C. and short-circuit characteristic scc are shown in Fig. 5.22 *(a)*. It is seen from this figure that for a field current of OC amperes,

$$Z_s \text{ in ohms} = CD = \frac{AC \text{ in volts}}{BC \text{ in amperes}}$$

If there were no saturation, Z_s would be constant. Actually Z_s is variable and it decreases with the onset of saturation in the O.C.C., see Fig. 5.22 *(a)*.

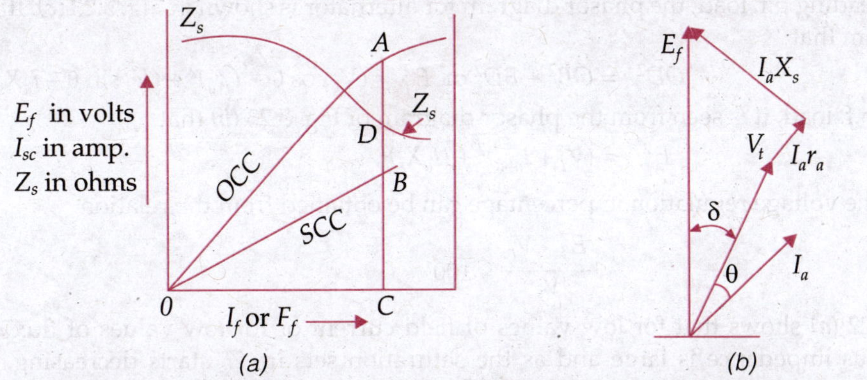

Fig 5.22: *(a)* Determination of synchronous impedance of an alternator and *(b)* its voltage-phasor diagram for a lagging power factor load.

For calculating the voltage regulation, only one value of Z_s can be used and since it is variable with the excitation, considerable care should be used in computing Z_s. Generally the lowest value of Z_s, obtained from the largest possible short-circuit current, is used for determining the voltage regulation. Now

$$Z_s = \sqrt{r_a^2 + X_s^2} \qquad ...(5.14)$$

The D.C. resistance r_{dc} of one phase is measured, as usual, by voltmeter-ammeter method. If the armature winding is star-connected and neutral is not available, then

$$r_{dc} = \frac{1}{2}\,\frac{\text{voltmeter reading}}{\text{ammeter reading}}.$$

In case the armature winding is delta-connected, then

$$r_{dc} = \frac{3}{2}\,\frac{\text{voltmeter reading}}{\text{ammeter reading}}.$$

The effective armature resistance per phase r_a is then calculated from the relation

$$r_a = (1.2 \text{ to } 1.3)\, r_{dc}$$

An accurate method of determining the effective armature resistance is described in Art. 5.17.

After r_a is calculated, X_s can be determined from Eq. (5.14). With the knowledge of r_a and X_s, the voltage phasor diagram of Fig. 5.22 *(b)* is drawn. *With V_t as the reference phasor*, the excitation voltage E_f for any value of I_a, is given by

$$\bar{E}_f = V_t + I_a\, Z_s$$
$$= V_t\,(1 + j\,0.00) + I_a\,(\cos\theta - j\sin\theta)\,(r_a + jX_s)$$
$$= (V_t + I_a\,r_a\cos\theta + I_a\,X_s\sin\theta) + j\,(I_aX_s\cos\theta - I_a\,r_a\sin\theta)$$

$$\therefore \quad E_f = \sqrt{(V_t + I_ar_a\cos\theta + I_aX_s\sin\theta)^2 + (I_aX_s\cos\theta - I_ar_a\sin\theta)^2}$$

If I_a is taken as the reference phasor, then

$$\bar{E}_f = V_t\,(\cos\theta + j\sin\theta) + I_a\,(1 + j\,0.00)\,(r_a + jX_s)$$

$$\therefore \quad E_f = \sqrt{(V_t\cos\theta + I_ar_a)^2 + (V_t\sin\theta + I_aX_s)^2}.$$

The above voltage equation can also be obtained by referring to Fig. 5.23 *(a)*, which is self-explanatory. It is seen from this figure that *OBD* is a right-angled triangle. Therefore

$$OD^2 = OB^2 + BD^2 = (OA + AB)^2 + (BC + CD)^2$$

or

$$E_f^2 = (V_t\cos\theta + I_ar_a)^2 + (V_t\sin\theta + I_aX_s)^2$$

For a leading p.f. load, the phasor diagram for alternator is shown in Fig. 5.23 *(c)*. It is seen from this diagram that

$$OD^2 = OB^2 + BD^2 \text{ or } E_f^2 = (V_t \cos\theta + I_a r_a)^2 + (V_t \sin\theta - I_a X_s)^2$$

For u.p.f. load, it is seen from the phasor diagram of Fig. 5.23 *(b)* that

$$E_f^2 = (V_t + I_a r_a)^2 + (I_a X_s)^2$$

Now the voltage regulation in percentage can be obtained from the relation

$$\frac{E_f - V_t}{V_t} \times 100$$

Fig. 5.22 *(a)* shows that for low values of field current or for low values of flux density, the synchronous impedance is large and as the saturation sets in, Z_s starts decreasing. During the short-circuit test, F_a is almost opposite to F_f—consequently the resultant m.m.f. F_r, responsible for the resultant air-gap flux density, is very small, Fig. 5.21 *(b)*. This results in low value of flux density which is much less than the flux density under actual working conditions—consequently an unsaturated value of Z_s is obtained. As unsaturated value of Z_s is more than the saturated value, voltage regulation computed by e.m.f. method is much higher than the actual value. It is because of this reason that the e.m.f. method is called a *pessimistic method*. This procedure, however, tells us that the voltage regulation would always be less than that computed by this method.

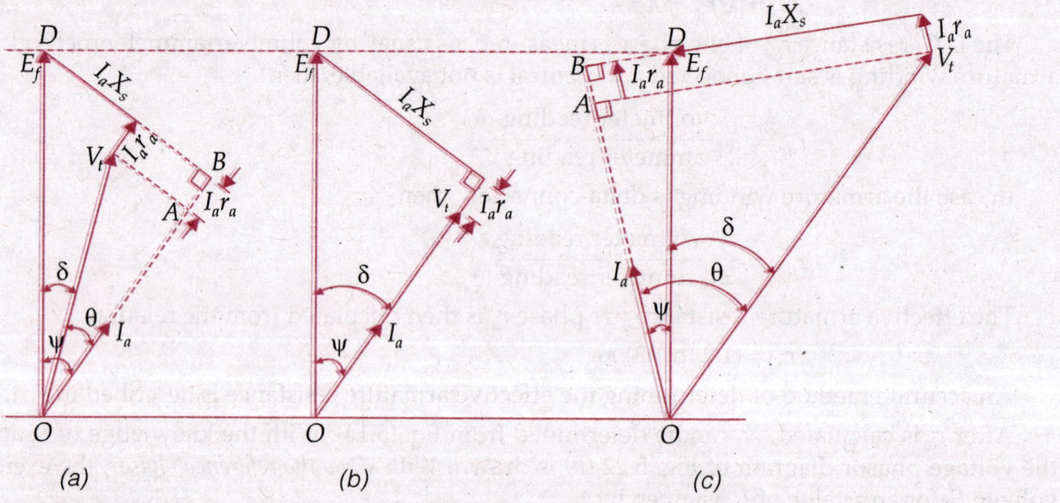

Fig 5.23: Voltage phasor diagram for an alternator at *(a)* lagging p.f. load *(b)* unity p.f. load and *(c)* leading p.f. load.

Under actual operating conditions, the air-gap flux density is quite large, iron is considerably saturated and Z_s should, therefore, be small. In order to compute the voltage regulation under the operating conditions, Z_s should be calculated at largest possible short-circuit current, as stated before.

Range of Synchronous Impedance. It may be worth-while at this stage to know the normal range of the values of synchronous impedance and its components. It is only in the per unit system that values of these parameters lie in the narrow range. The value of armature resistance r_a is usually around 0.01 p.u. It means that voltage drop in the armature resistance at rated armature current is about 1% of the rated voltage. Armature leakage reactance is in the range of 0.1 to 0.2 p.u. and synchronous reactance is of the order of 1.0 p.u. The value of r_a is so low that it can be neglected for all practical purposes for machine ratings above a few hundred kVA. It should, however, be included for the computation of losses, temperature rise and efficiency. It has been found that as the machine size decreases, armature resistance increases whereas synchronous reactance decreases.

The magnitude of synchronous reactance is influenced by air-gap length as under :

Magnetizing reactance, $X_{ar} = \omega L_{ar}$

where L_{ar} = magnetizing inductance

But $$L_{ar} = \frac{N_{ph}^2}{\text{air–gap reluctance}}$$

A synchronous machine with large air-gap has low value of L_{ar} and X_{ar}. In other words, the magnitude of X_{ar} is inversely proportional to air-gap length. Armature leakage reactance x_{al} is usually treated as constant. As x_{al} and X_{ar} are of the order of 0.15 p.u. and 0.85 p.u. respectively, X_{ar} plays a dominant role on X_s. So it can be stated that X_s is inversely proportional to air-gap length.

5.4.2. The Magnetomotive Force (m.m.f.) Method

In the e.m.f. method, all the m.m.fs. were transformed into their corresponding e.m.fs. In the m.m.f. method, the reverse procedure is adopted, *i.e.*, each e.m.f. is replaced by an equivalent m.m.f.; provided all the assumptions of e.m.f. method are invoked here (uniform air-gap and neglect of saturation).

The voltage equation of a synchronous machine, working as an alternator is

$$\bar{E}_f = \bar{V}_t + \bar{I}_a r_a + j\bar{I}_a X_s \quad ...(5.12)$$

For using m.m.f. method, the voltage Eq. (5.12) must now be converted to a new equation involving m.m.fs. only. Examination of Eq. (5.7) shows that division of e.m.f. in volts by $-jK$ gives the value of the corresponding m.m.f. Therefore, division of Eq. (5.12) by $-jK$ converts it into an m.m.f. equation as follows.

$$\frac{\bar{E}_f}{-jK} = \frac{\bar{V}_t + \bar{I}_a r_a}{-jK} + \frac{j\bar{I}_a(x_{al} + X_{ar})}{-jK}$$

or $$\frac{\bar{E}_f}{-jK} = \frac{\bar{E}'}{-jK} - \frac{\bar{I}_a x_{al}}{K} - \frac{\bar{I}_a X_{ar}}{K} \quad ...(5.15)$$

As stated before, K is the slope of air-gap line.

From Eq. (5.7), $\frac{\bar{E}_f}{-jK} = \bar{F}_f$ and similarly let $\frac{\bar{E}'}{-jK}$ be equal to $\bar{F}_{r1}$. The field m.m.f. F_f induces, in the armature winding, an e.m.f. E_f lagging it by 90°, similarly the m.m.f. F_{r1} must induce an e.m.f. E' lagging F_{r1} by 90° as shown in Fig. 5.24.

From Eqs. (5.8) and (5.10), it is seen that $\frac{\bar{I}_a X_{ar}}{K} = \frac{\bar{I}_a CK}{K} = \bar{I}_a C = \bar{F}_a$ armature reaction m.m.f. in phase with I_a. Here armature reaction reactance drop $I_a X_{ar}$ has been transformed into m.m.f. F_a Similarly, armature leakage reactance drop $I_a x_{al}$ can be transformed into equivalent m.m.f. F_{al}, such that $\frac{\bar{I}_a x_{al}}{K} = \bar{F}_{al}$.

As F_a is in phase with I_a, similarly F_{al} is also in phase with I_a.

Introducing these changes, Eq. (5.15) becomes,

$$\bar{F}_f = \bar{F}_{r1} - (\bar{F}_{al} + \bar{F}_a) \quad ...(5.16)$$

Note that the m.m.f. $(\bar{F}_{al} + \bar{F}_a)$ is in phase with the armature current I_a, as illustrated in Fig. 5.24. It is seen from Fig. 5.24 that α is the angle *(i)* by which I_a lags E' and *(ii)* between the normal line to F_{r1} shown dotted and $(F_a + F_{al})$.

Eq. (5.16) can be interpreted by saying that the actual armature reaction m.m.f. F_a, has been increased by an amount F_{al}. This increase in m.m.f. *i.e.* F_{al}, takes into account the effect of armature leakage reactance x_{al}.

For a purely reactive load, the phasor diagram of Fig. 5.24 gets modified to that shown in Fig. 5.25 *(a)*. From this figure, F_{r1} is seen to be nearly equal to the numerical difference between F_f and $(F_a + F_{al})$, *i.e.*, they can be related by simple algebraic equation.

$$F_{r1} = F_f - (F_a + F_{al}) \quad ...(5.17)$$

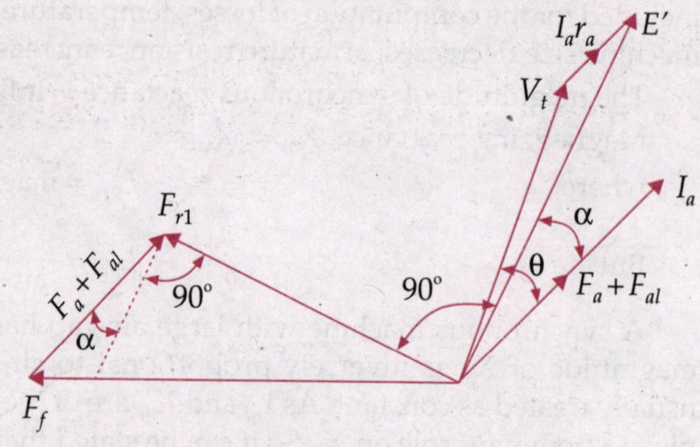

Fig 5.24: Phasor diagram for m.m.f. method.

Terminal voltage V_t is nearly the same as E' in Fig. 5.25 *(a)*. The O.C.C. is again assumed to represent the relation between E' (voltage behind resistance r_a) and m.m.f. F_{r1}. In Fig. 5.25 *(b)*, OP ($= F_f$) is any field excitation, from which $PF = F_a + F_{al}$ has been deducted to give the resultant m.m.f. $F_{r1} = OF$. This m.m.f. F_{r1} induces 90° lagging e.m.f. E' equal to $V_t = FM = PA$. The point A, therefore, lies on z.p.f.c., because it corresponds to the terminal voltage V_t and field m.m.f. F_f or field current I_f. Here z.p.f.c. is seen to be shifted horizontally to the right of O.C.C. by an amount equal to $(F_a + F_{al})$. Thus $(F_a + F_{al})$ can be obtained by measuring the horizontal displacement between O.C.C. and z.p.f.c., such as $MA = OF'$. At point F', $V_t = E' = 0$, consequently F_{r1} is zero and $F_f = F_a + F_{al} = OF'$. Therefore, $(F_a + F_{al})$ is the m.m.f. or field current, required to circulate full-load armature current under short circuit test.

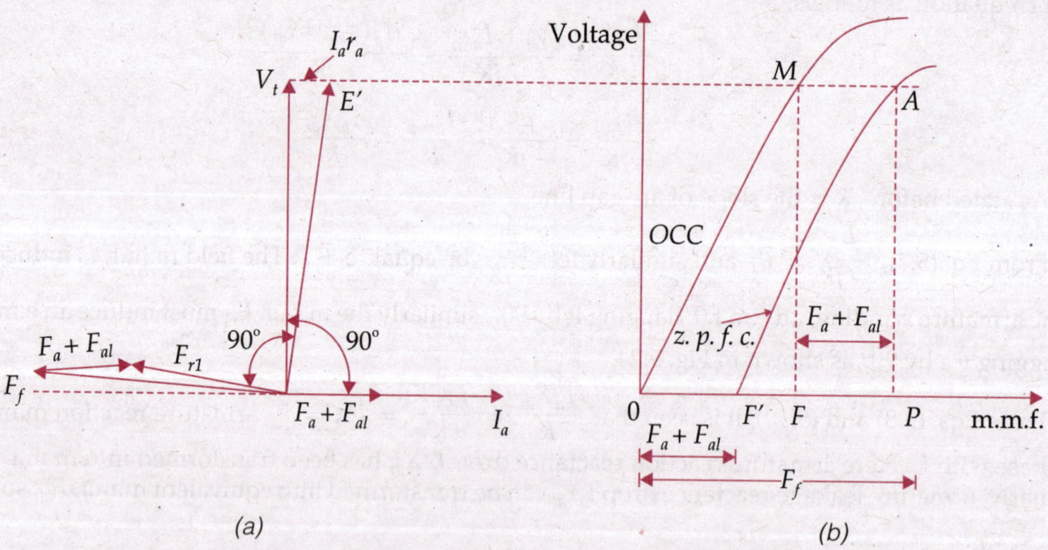

Fig 5.25: *(a)* Alternator phasor diagram for purely reactive load; m.m.f. method *(b)* Determination of $(F_a + F_{al})$ by m.m.f. method.

Hence, in order to obtain voltage regulation by m.m.f. method:

(i) Plot O.C.C. and S.C.C.

(ii) Find $\bar{E}' = \bar{V}_t + \bar{I}_a r_a$ and obtain the corresponding value of F_{r1} from O.C.C.

(iii) Find $(F_a + F_{al})$ from S.C.C.

(iv) Calculate $\bar{F}_f = \bar{F}_{r1} = (\bar{F}_a + \bar{F}_{al})$ as shown in Fig. 5.24. Field m.m.f. F_f can also be obtained from Fig. 5.26 *(a)*, where m.m.f. components in Fig. 5.24 are redrawn by taking F_{r1} horizontal. So, in this figure, take $AB = F_{r1}$. Now draw $BC = (F_a + F_{al})$ at an angle of $(90 + \alpha)°$ with respect to AB as shown. Then AC gives the required value of field m.m.f F_f which is given by the relation

$$F_f = \sqrt{(AB + BC\sin\alpha)^2 + (BC\cos\alpha)^2}$$

Now, corresponding to field m.m.f. F_f, obtain E_f from O.C.C. and thus the voltage regulation of the alternator.

5.4.3. Zero Power Factor Method

This is also called the general method, Potier reactance (or triangle) method of obtaining the voltage regulation. In the e.m.f. method, the phasor diagram involving voltages is used, whereas in m.m.f. method, the phasor diagram involving m.m.fs. is used. For the z.p.f. method, the e.m.fs. are handled as voltages and the m.m.fs. as field ampere-turns or field amperes.

The procedure for z.p.f. method requires the use of general phasor diagram of Fig. 5.14. First of all, determine the air-gap voltage E_r by the relation.

$$\bar{E}_r = \bar{V}_t + \bar{I}_a\,(r_a + jx_{al}) \qquad ...(5.18)$$

According to the magnitude of E_r, obtain F_r from O.C.C. and draw it leading E_r by 90°. The armature reaction m.m.f. F_a and armature leakage reactance x_{al}, can be determined from the Potier triangle, as explained before. Now F_a is drawn in phase with I_a, as shown in Fig. 5.14. Then

$$\bar{F}_f = \bar{F}_r - \bar{F}_a$$

is obtained and corresponding to F_f, excitation voltage E_f is recorded from O.C.C. and the voltage regulation obtained.

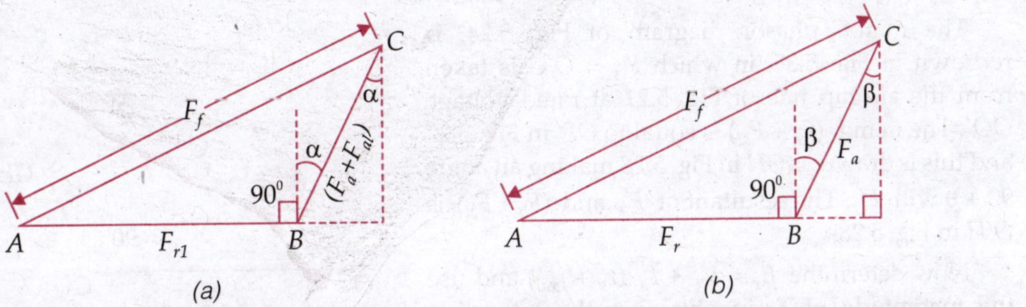

Fig 5.26: Pertaining to the calculation of field m.m.f. F_f for *(a)* m.m.f. method and *(b)* z.p.f. method.

Field m.m.f. F_f can also be obtained by referring to Fig. 5.26 *(b)*, where m.m.f. components in Fig. 5.14 are redrawn by taking F_r horizontal. So, in this figure, $AB = F_r$, $BC = F_a$ and angle β is the angle between E_r and I_a, see Fig. 5.14. Then $AC = F_f$ can be calculated as in Fig. 5.26 *(a)*.

Z.p.f. method requires O.C.C. and z.p.f.c., and gives quite accurate results. Actually, only two points on z.p.f.c. are sufficient, as explained in Art. 5.3.2.

5.4.4. New A.S.A. (American Standards Association) Method

This method is essentially a modification of the m.m.f. method and gives satisfactory results both for cylindrical-rotor and salient-pole synchronous machines.

New A.S.A. method requires O.C.C. and z.p.f.c., though the latter may not be known completely. Only two points *A* and *F'*, are sufficient to be known on the z.p.f.c., Fig. 5.27. The point *A* is obtained by loading the over-excited alternator by an underexcited synchronous motor till full-load armature current at rated voltage is flowing. The point F' is obtained by noting field excitation $(F_a + F_{al})$, required to circulate full-load armature current when the alternator is short-circuited. The armature leakage reactance x_{al} is determined from the Potier reactance drop BC.

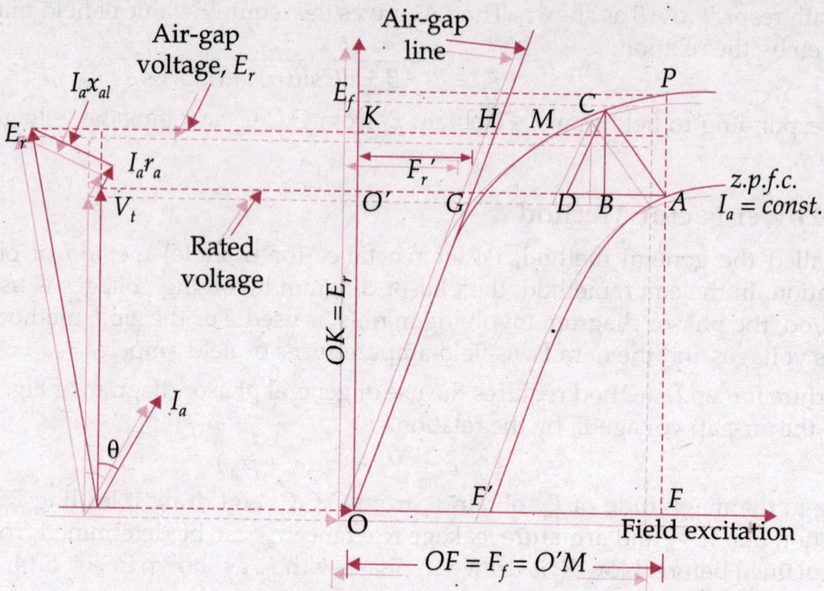

Fig 5.27: Determination of voltage regulation by new A.S.A. method

In well-designed synchronous machines, the ohmic resistance is very small, and in Fig. 5.24 if voltage drop $I_a r_a$ is neglected, then angle θ = angle α.

The m.m.f. phasor diagram of Fig. 5.24, is redrawn in Fig. 5.28, in which $F'_r = O'G$ is taken from the air-gap line of Fig. 5.27 at rated voltage OO'. The m.m.f. $(F_a + F_{al})$ is equal to OF' in Fig. 5.27 and this is drawn as GH in Fig. 5.28 making an angle $90 + \theta$ with F'_r. The resultant of $\bar{F}'_r$ and $(\bar{F}_a + \bar{F}_{al})$ is $O'H$ in Fig. 5.28.

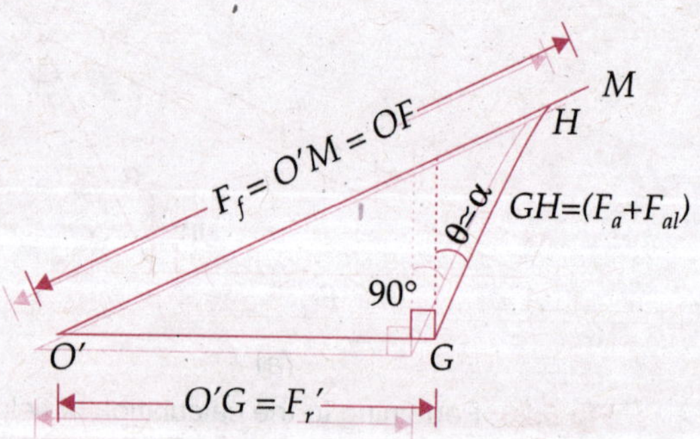

Fig 5.28: Determination of field excitation $O'M$, for new A.S.A. method.

Now determine $\bar{E}_r = \bar{V}_t + \bar{I}_a\,(r_a + jx_{al})$ and use the magnitude of E_r in obtaining the saturation effects. A horizontal line is drawn through K, so that $OK = E_r$. This line intersects the air-gap line at H and the O.C.C. at M. The distance HM, on the field excitation scale, gives the additional excitation that must be added to the unsaturated excitation $O'H$, to determine the total excitation $O'M = F_f$. Now corresponding to $O'M = F_f = OF$, excitation voltage $FP = E_f$ is read from O.C.C. and the voltage regulation obtained.

5.4.5. Saturated Synchronous-reactance Method

In e.m.f. and m.m.f. methods of calculating the voltage regulation, the saturation is neglected. However, under actual operating conditions, the magnet,ic circuit is always in a saturated state. The extent of this saturation under load, can be taken into account by introducing saturation factor K. As in Art. 5.3.2, assume that the flux-condition in the magnetic circuit of the machine under load, is decided by the air-gap voltage E_r and the corresponding resultant m.m.f. F_r as read from O.C.C.

With the help of Eq. (5.18), air-gap voltage E_r is calculated for a certain value of I_a and power-factor at which the voltage regulation is required. For this value of E_r, from Fig. 5.29, the resultant m.m.f. read from O.C.C. is OB and from the air-gap line resultant m.m.f. read is OC. Now the saturation factor k is defined as

$$k = \frac{OB}{OC} \quad \text{...(5.19)}$$

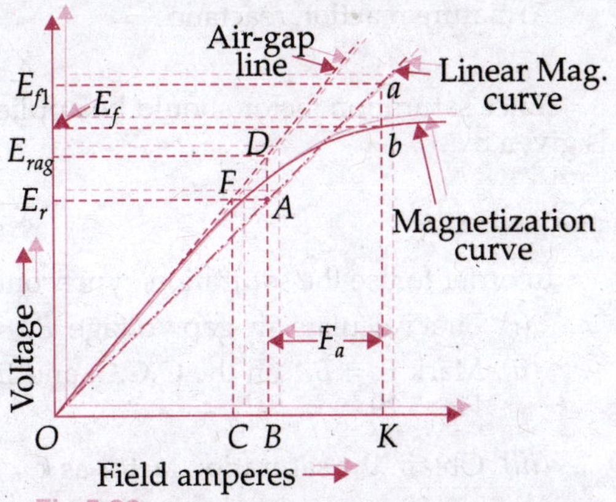

Fig 5.29: Pertaining to the saturated synchronous reactance.

Had there been no saturation, the resultant m.m.f. (or field current) OB, would generate an air-gap voltage E_{rag}. Since two triangles OCF and OBD are similar, the saturation factor can also be written as $k = \frac{OB}{OC} = \frac{BD}{BA} = \frac{E_{rag}}{E_r} = \frac{E_r \text{ from air-line}}{E_r \text{ from O.C.C.}}$ for the same field m.m.f. or field current.

Now the degree of saturation is assumed fixed at the resultant air-gap flux or its associated e.m.f. E_r given by point A in Fig. 5.29. In other words, the machine is linearized at the magnetic state corresponding to the resultant air-gap e.m.f., E_r. The machine operation now follows the linear magnetization curve OAa. Under this assumption, if the armature current is reduced to zero, armature m.m.f. F_a would be zero and as per Eq. (5.3), field m.m.f. $F_f = F_r = OK$. As a consequence, operating point would move from A to a along the linear magnetization curve OAa. The point a is located by the intersection of linear magnetization curve and the ordinate drawn at point K. With linear magnetization curve OAa, the field m.m.f. OK would generate a no-load e.m.f. E_{f1}. Since it does not really happen, E_{f1} has no physical significance. However, the field current OK is a real quantity which is to be calculated. In fact, the construction given in Fig. 5.29 is introduced only for the determination of field current OK. From similar triangles OAB and OaK,

$$\frac{OK}{aK} = \frac{OB}{AB}$$

or field current,

$$OK = \frac{E_{f1}}{E_r}(OB) \quad \text{...(5.20)}$$

The required field current is thus calculated from Eq. (5.20). Then, corresponding to this field currrent of magnitude OK, the excitation e.m.f. $E_f = Kb$ is found from OCC and the voltage regulation obtained.

The synchronous reactance X_s has two components, see Eq. (5.11). The leakage reactance x_{al} remains constant, because the leakage flux path is mainly in air and is almost unaffected by saturation. But the armature reaction reactance X_{ar} is affected by the magnetic saturation because the path of the armature reaction flux is mainly through iron. In view of this, the saturation factor k, should be applied to the magnetizing reactance X_{ar} only. The unsaturated synchronous reactance X_{sag} is calculated as follows :

$$Z_{sag} = \frac{\text{e.m.f. from air-gap line}}{\text{armature current from S.C.C.}}$$

for the same field current. Note that the unsaturated synchronous impedance Z_{sag} remains constant and may be calculated for any value of field current.

Unsaturated synchronous reactance

$$X_{sag} = \sqrt{Z_{sag}^2 - r_a^2} \quad \text{...(5.21 a)}$$

Armature reaction reactance

$$X_{ar} = X_{sag} - X_{al}.$$

Since saturation factor should be applied to X_{ar} only, the saturated synchronous reactance X_{ss} is given by

$$X_{ss} = X_{al} + \frac{X_{sag} - x_{al}}{k}\ \Omega \quad \text{...(5.21 } b\text{)}$$

In order to use the saturation-synchronous-reactance method for voltage-regulation :

(i) First calculate air-gap voltage $\bar{E}_r = \bar{V}_t + \bar{I}_a\ (r_a + j\,x_{al})$.

(ii) Mark $E_r = BA$ on the O.C.C. and find the corresponding voltage BD, on the air-gap line, Fig. 5.29.

(iii) Obtain the saturation factor as $k = \dfrac{BD}{BA}$.

(iv) Calculate X_{sag} from Eq. (5.21 a).

(v) Find saturated synchronous reactance X_{ss} from Eq. (5.21 *b*).

(vi) Draw phasor diagram as illustrated in Fig. 5.22 (*b*), but with X_s replaced by X_{ss} —now calculate E_f and thus the voltage regulation.

If the field excitation is to be determined for given values of terminal voltage, load current and power factor, the foregoing five methods described for voltage-regulation computations, are also helpful. For example, in e.m.f. and saturated synchronous reactance methods, calculate E_f and then the required field excitation F_f, is read from O.C.C. In e.m.f., z.p.f. and new A.S.A. methods, the required field excitation under load is calculated directly under the specified load conditions.

Example 5.1. *A 220-V, 50 Hz, 6-pole star-connected alternator with ohmic resistance of 0.06 ohm per phase, gave the following data for open-circuit, short-circuit and full-load zero-power-factor characteristics :*

Field current, A	0.20	0.40	0.60	0.80	1.00	1.20	1.40	1.80	2.20	2.60	3.00	3.40
Open-circuit voltage, E_f in V	29.0	58.0	87.0	116	146	172	194	232	261.5	284	300	310
Short-circuit current, I_{sc} in A	6.6	13.2	20.0	26.5	32.4	40.0	46.3	59.0	-	-	-	-
Z.p.f. terminal voltage in V	-	-	-	-	-	0	29	88	140	177	208	230

Find the percentage voltage regulation at full-load current of 40 amps at power-factor 0.8 lag by (a) e.m.f. method (b) m.m.f. method (c) z.p.f. method (d) new A.S.A method and (e) saturated-synchronous reactance method.

Compare the results so obtained.

Solution. Rated per phase voltage $V_t = \dfrac{220}{\sqrt{3}} = 127$ V.

Per phase values for O.C.C. and z.p.f.c. are tabulated below and O.C.C., S.C.C. and z.p.f.c. are plotted in Fig. 5.30.

I_f in A	0.2	0.4	0.6	0.8	1.0	1.20	1.40	1.80	2.20	2.60	3.00	3.40
E_f in V	16.73	33.5	50.2	67.0	84.3	99.3	112	134	151	164	173.2	179.0
z.p.f. terminal voltage in V	-	-	-	-	-	0	16.73	50.8	80.8	102	120	132.7

(a) **E.m.f. method.** The values of the synchronous impedance Z_s and synchronous reactance X_s, are tabulated below for different values of excitations (taking E_f from O.C.C. and I_{sc} from S.C.C. for the same field current) :

I_f in A	0.20	0.40	0.60	0.80	1.00	1.20	1.40	1.80
E_f in V	16.73	33.50	50.2	67	84.3	99.3	112	134
I_{sc} in A	6.6	13.2	20.0	26.5	32..4	40.0	46.3	59.0
Z_s in Ω	2.535	2.535	2.51	2.53	2.51	2.48	2.42	2.27
X_s in Ω	2.53	2.53	2.51	2.53	2.51	2.48	2.42	2.27

Here $X_s \cong Z_s$, since r_a is quite small.

For full load and power factor of 0.8 lagging, the phasor diagram is similar to that given in Fig. 5.22 *(b)*. With V_t as the reference phasor,

$$\bar{V}_t = 127 + j0.00, \quad \bar{I}_a = 40\,(0.8 - j0.6) = (32 - j24).$$

$$\therefore \quad \bar{E}_f = \bar{V}_t + \bar{I}_a\,(r_a + jX_s)$$

$$= 127 + (32 - j24)\,(0.06 + j2.27) = 182.92 + j70.16$$

or $$\bar{E}_f = \sqrt{(182.92)^2 + (70.16)^2} = 195.5 \text{ volts.}$$

$$\therefore \text{ Percentage voltage regulation} = \frac{195.5 - 127}{127} \times 100 = 53.9\%.$$

Excitation voltage E_f can also be calculated by referring to Fig. 5.23 *(a)*.

Note that minimum value of Z_s, corresponding to maximum short-circuit current, has been used here.

(b) **m.m.f. method.** Voltage behind armature resistance r_a,

$$\bar{E}' = \bar{V}_t + \bar{I}_a r_a.$$

For convenience, take I_a as the reference phasor.

$$\therefore \quad \bar{E}' = 127\,(0.8 + j0.6) + 40\,(0.06) = 104 + j76.2 \qquad ...(5.22)$$

or $$\bar{E}' = \sqrt{(104)^2 + (76.2)^2} = 129.0 \text{ V}.$$

For $E' = 129.0$ V, the field excitation F_{r1} from O.C.C. is equal to 1.69 A.

From S.C.C., $F_a + F_{al}$ = The field current required to circulate full-load short circuit current = 1.20 A.

From Eq. (5.22), the angle α in Fig. 5.24, is given by

$$\alpha = \tan^{-1}\left(\frac{76.2}{104}\right) = 36.2°.$$

In phasor form, $$\bar{F}_f = 1.69\,[\cos(90 + \alpha) + j \sin(90 + \alpha)]$$

$$= 1.69\,[-\sin\alpha + j\cos\alpha]$$

$$= 1.69\,[-0.591 + j0.807] = -1 + j1.365.$$

$$\therefore \quad \bar{F}_f = \bar{F}_{r1} - (\bar{F}_a + \bar{F}_{al}) = -1 + j1.365 - 1.20 = -2.20 + j1.365$$

or $$F_f = 2.59 \text{ A}.$$

Field m.m.f. F_f can also be computed by referring to Fig. 5.26 *(a)* where = $AB = F_{r1} = 1.69$ A ; $BC = (F_a + F_{al}) = 1.20$ A and α = 36.2°

$$\therefore \quad F_f = \sqrt{(1.69 + 1.20 \sin 36.2)^2 + (1.20 \cos 36.2)^2} = 2.5868 \cong 2.59 \text{ A}$$

Corresponding to $F_f = 2.59$ A, E_f from O.C.C. is 163.5 V.

$\therefore$ Percentage voltage regulation $= \dfrac{163.5 - 127}{127} \times 100 = 28.75\%$.

(c) **Zero power-factor method.** First of all, the Potier triangle *ABC* is drawn as described before. Point *A* corresponds to the rated voltage of 127 V on the z.p.f.c. The line *AD* is drawn parallel and equal to $F'O = 1.2$ A. Then *DC* is drawn parallel to the air-gap line, meeting the O.C.C. at point C. Perpendicular *CB* on *AD*, gives $I_a x_{al}$ drop equal to 30 volts.

$\therefore$ Armature leakage reactance $x_{al} = \dfrac{30}{40} = 0.75\ \Omega$.

The air-gap voltage E_r, from Eq. (5.18), is $\bar{E}_r = \bar{V}_t + \bar{I}_a\ (r_a + jx_{al})$

With I_a as the reference phasor, $\bar{E}_r = 127\ (0.8 + j0.6) + 40\ (0.06 + j0.75)$

$$= 104 + j106.2 \qquad \text{...(5.23)}$$

$$\therefore \quad E_r = \sqrt{(10.4)^2 + (106.2)^2} = 148.6 \text{ volts.}$$

Corresponding to $E_r = 148.6$ V, the field current F_r from O.C.C. is 2.134 A. The armature m.m.f. F_a, from Potier triangle is $AB = F_a = 0.84$ A.

Now the angle between E_r and I_a is, say β in Fig. 5.14, then from Eq. (5.23),

$$\beta = \tan^{-1}\left(\frac{106.2}{104.0}\right) = 45.6°.$$

F_r leads E_r by 90° or I_a by (90 + β).

$$\therefore \quad \bar{F}_r = 2.134\ [\cos (90 + 45.6) + j \sin (90 + 45.6)]$$

$$= (-1.524 + j1.494) \text{ Amp.}$$

$$\bar{F}_a = 0.84 \text{ Amp.}$$

$$\therefore \quad \bar{F}_f = \bar{F}_r - \bar{F}_a = [(-1.524 + j1.494) - (0.84)]$$

$$= -2.364 + j1.494$$

or $\qquad F_f = 2.797$ A.

Field m.m.f. F_f can also be calculated by referring to Fig. 5.26 *(b)* where $AB = 2.134$ A, $BC = F_a = 0.84$ A and β = 45.6°.

$$\therefore \quad F_f = \sqrt{(2.134 + 0.84 \sin 45.6°)^2 + (0.84 \cos 45.6°)^2}$$

$$= 2.7966 \text{ A} = 2.797 \text{ A}$$

For $F_f = 2.797$ A, the excitation voltage from O.C.C. is 169.0 volts.

$\therefore$ Percentage voltage regulation $= \dfrac{169 - 127}{127} \times 100 = 33.1\%$.

(d) **New A.S.A. Method.** The armature leakage reactance x_{al} and the air-gap voltage E_r needed for this method, have already been calculated in part *(c)*.

Corresponding to $E_r = 148.6$ volts, the difference in the field current between the O.C.C. and the air-gap line, in Fig. 5.30, is $HM = 0.366$ A.

The field current, corresponding to the rated per phase voltage of 127 volts on the air-gap line, is $O'G = 1.507 \text{ A} = F'_r$ in Fig. 5.30.

For Fig. 5.28, $\qquad \theta = \cos^{-1}(0.8) = 36.9°$

and $\qquad GH = (F_a + F_{al}) = 1.2$ A.

Now by referring to Fig. 5.28,

$$\overline{O'H} = O'G + (F_a + F_{al}) \sin \theta + j\ (F_a + F_{al}) \cos \theta$$

$$= 1.507 + (1.2)\ (0.6) + j\ (1.2)\ (0.8) = 2.227 + j\,0.96$$

or $$O'H = 2.425 \text{ Amp.}$$

Adding the saturation effect $HM = 0.366$ A to $O'H$, we get

$$O'M = O'H + HM = 2.791 \text{ Amp.}$$

The excitation voltage E_f from O.C.C. corresponding to $O'M = F_f = 2.791$ A, is 169 V.

$\therefore$ Percentage voltage regulation $= \dfrac{169 - 127}{127} \times 100 = 33.1\%$.

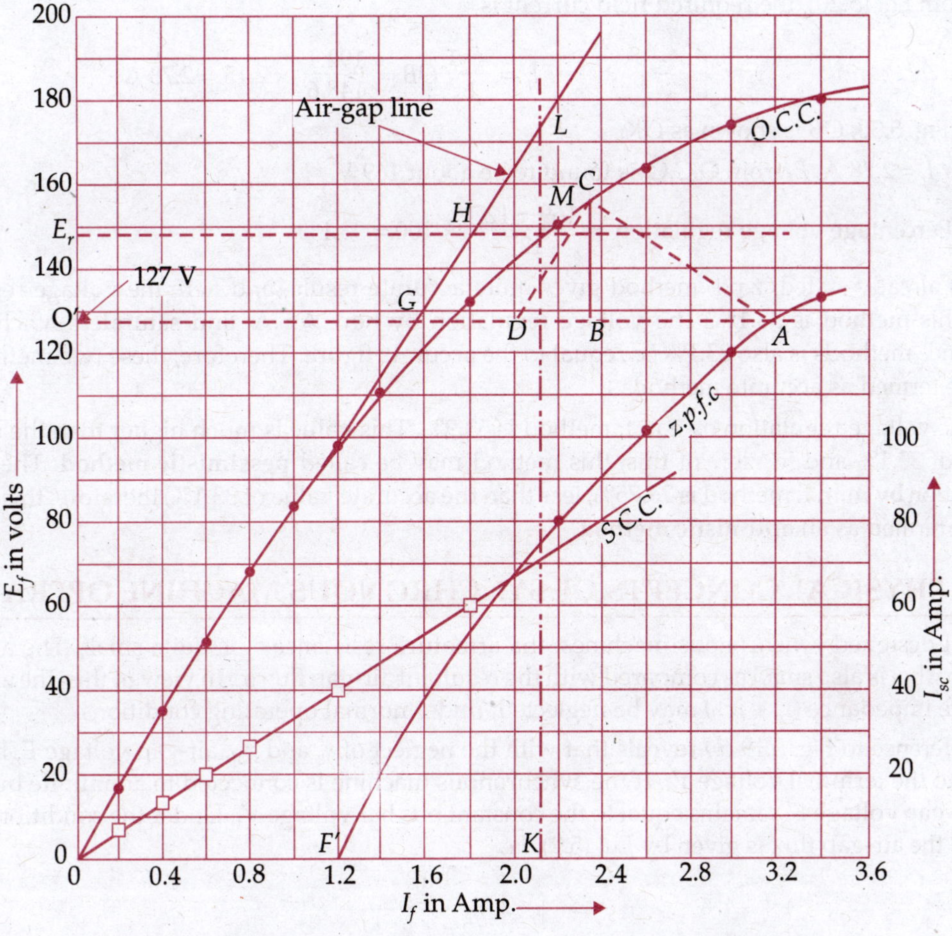

Fig 5.30: Determination of alternator voltage regulation. Example 5.1.

(e) **Saturated synchronous-reactance method.** From part *(c)*, air-gap voltage $E_r = 148.6$ volts. In Fig. 5.30, E_r is marked as KM and corresponding value of E_{rag} from air-gap line is

$$KL = 179.5 \text{ V.}$$

$\therefore$ Saturation factor $$k = \frac{KL}{KM} = \frac{179.5}{148.6} = 1.207$$

From part *(c)*, $$x_{al} = 0.75\ \Omega.$$

Unsaturated synchronous reactance X_{sag}, from air-gap line and S.C.C. is, say for a field current of 1.2 A, $X_{sag} = \dfrac{100.5}{40} \cong 2.50\ \Omega$.

$\therefore$ Saturated synchronous reactance $X_{ss} = 0.75 + \dfrac{2.50 - 0.75}{1.207} = 2.20\ \Omega.$

With the help of part (a), $\bar{E}_f = \bar{V}_t + \bar{I}_a (r_a + jX_{ss})$

With V_t as a reference phasor,

$$\bar{E}_{f1} = 127 + (32 - j24)\,(0.06 + j2.20) = 179.8 + j68.48$$

or

$$E_{f1} = 192.1 \text{ volts.}$$

From Eq. (5.20), the required field current is

$$\therefore \qquad I_f = \frac{E_{f1}}{E_r} OB = \frac{192.1}{148.6} \times 2.15 = 2.78 \text{ A}$$

In Fig. 5.30, *OB* is shown as *OK*.

For $I_f = 2.78$ A, E_f from O.C.C. is found to be about 169 V.

$\therefore$ Percentage voltage regulation $= \dfrac{169 - 127}{127} \times 100 = 33.1\%.$

As already stated, z.p.f. method gives quite accurate results and here the voltage regulation with this method is 33.1%. The voltage regulation by new A.S.A. and saturated synchronous-reactance methods is also 33.1% *i.e.*, equal to the accurate figure. Therefore, these two methods can also be termed as accurate methods.

The voltage regulation by e.m.f. method is 53.9%. This value is much higher than the accurate value of 33.1% and in view of this, this method may be called **pessimistic method**. The voltage regulation by m.m.f. method is 28.75%, less than the accurate value of 33.1%, therefore, this method can be termed as an **optimistic method**.

5.5. PHYSICAL CONCEPTS OF SYNCHRONOUS MACHINE OPERATION

In well-designed synchronous machines, tha armature resistance r_a is quite small. The armature leakage flux is also small as compared with the resultant air-gap flux ϕ_r. In view of this, the armature leakage impedance $(r_a + jx_{al})$ may be neglected, under normal operating conditions.

Reference to Fig. 5.19 *(b)* reveals that with the neglect of r_a and x_{al}, air-gap voltage E_r becomes equal to the terminal voltage V_t. If the synchronous machine is connected to an infinite bus*, then the air-gap voltage E_r remains equal to the constant bus bar voltage V_t. Under the conditions stated above, the air-gap flux is given by Eq. (5.2), *i.e.*

$$\phi_r = \frac{V_t}{\sqrt{2}\pi f k_\omega N_{ph}} \qquad \text{...(5.24)}$$

In the above-expression, $V_t, f, k_\omega N_{ph}$, are all constant, therefore, air-gap flux ϕ_r remains constant and is unaffected by the nature of synchronous machine load.

At no-load, $I_a = 0, F_a = 0$ and load angle δ_{rf} between F_f and F_r is zero—this condition is illustrated in phasor diagram of Fig. 5.31 *(a)*. With the neglect of r_a and x_{al}, torque angle is equal to load angle. For $F_a = 0$, the machine is neither generating nor motoring; under such a condition, the synchronous machine is said to be *floating* on the infinite bus. Let us assume for simplicity that the field current is not varied from its no-load value, this means that F_f or E_f remains constant at their no-load value. For a constant voltage V_t, ϕ_r (or F_r) remains constant as per Eq. (5.24). When the machine is made to work as a generator or a motor, the orientation of ϕ_r does not alter as V_t, the infinite bus voltage, is held fixed.

* An infinite bus is a constant-frequency constant-voltage source.

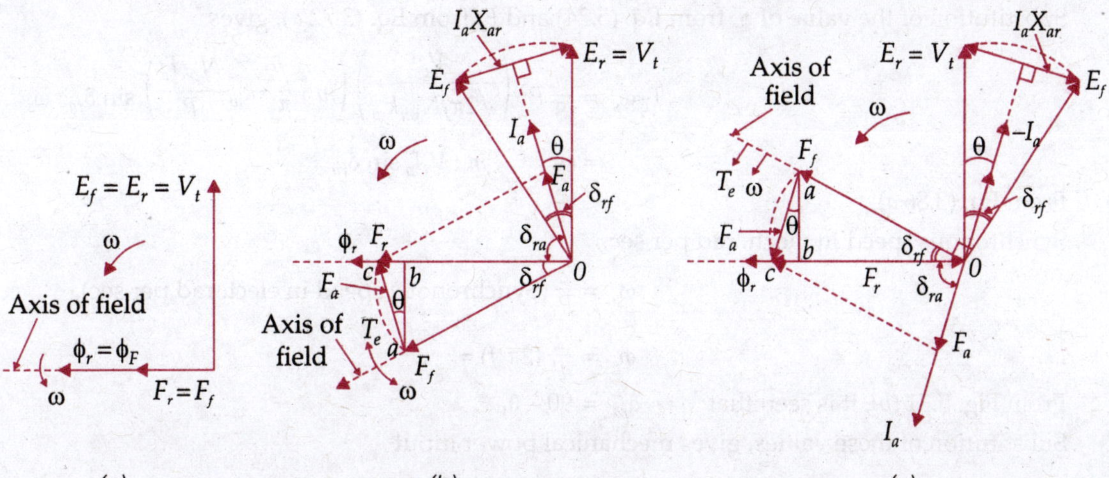

Fig 5.31: Space-phasor and time-phasor diagrams for a synchronous machine *(a)* at no-load *(b)* working as a generator and *(c)* working as a motor.

When the machine shaft is given power from the prime-mover, the field poles are driven ahead of the resultant air-gap flux ϕ_r or resultant m.m.f. F_r. As the field poles are pushed ahead of F_r by the prime-mover torque, the field m.m.f. F_f also occupies a space position ahead of F_r by an angle δ_{rf} as shown in Fig. 5.31 *(b)*. As E_f lags F_f by 90°, E_f occupies a position ahead of V_t by angle δ_{rf}. It is seen from Fig. 5.6 *(d)* that with field poles ahead of F_r, the machine works as an alternator. The appearance of load angle δ_{rf} between F_r and F_f, gives rise to the development of electromagnetic torque, Eq. (3.82),

$$T_e = \frac{\pi}{8} P^2 F_f \phi_r \sin \delta_{rf}. \quad \text{...(5.24 a)}$$

When torque T_e becomes equal to the applied prime-mover torque, the generator works under steady state conditions. It is seen from Fig. 5.31 *(b)* that F_f (equal to F_r under the assumption) is no longer in phase with F_r. Since the m.m.f. relation $\overline{F}_r = \overline{F}_f + \overline{F}_a$ must hold good, armature reaction m.m.f. F_a comes into existence. For developing F_a, a current I_a, in phase with F_a, must flow in the armature winding as shown in Fig. 5.31 *(b)*. Excitation e.m.f. E_f lags F_f by 90°. Also, $E_r = V_t$ lags F_r by 90°. As F_r lags F_f by torque angle δ_{rf}, E_r (or V_t) lags E_f by the same angle δ_{rf}. Since I_a has a component in phase with E_f or V_t, the machine is acting as a generator delivering electrical power to the bus bars. In the manner explained above, the mechanical power input to the synchronous machine is delivered as electrical power output equal to $mV_tI_a \cos\theta$. Here θ is the p.f. angle of I_a with respect to V_t or E_r. Also, $\overline{E}_f = \overline{V}_t + j\,\overline{I}_a X_{ar}$.

For showing that the mechanical power input is equal to the electrical power output $mV_tI_a \cos\theta$; the torque expression including the load angle δ_{ra}, *i.e.*, the load angle between ϕ_r and F_a, must be used.

$$\therefore \quad T_e = \frac{\pi}{8} P^2 F_a \phi_r \sin \delta_{ra} \text{ and } T_e \cdot \omega_s = \left(\frac{\pi}{8} P^2 F_a \phi_r \sin \delta_{ra}\right) \omega_s$$

But armature m.m.f. from Eq. 3.72 *(a)* is

$$F_a = m \frac{2\sqrt{2}}{\pi} k_w \frac{N_{ph} \cdot I_a}{P} \text{ ATs/pole} \quad \text{...(3.72 a)}$$

Substitution of the value of ϕ_r from Eq. (5.24) and F_a from Eq. (3.72 *a*), gives

$$T_e\,\omega_s = \frac{\pi}{8}P^2\left(\frac{V_t}{\sqrt{2}\pi f N_{ph} k_w}\right)\left(m\frac{2\sqrt{2}}{\pi}k_w\frac{N_{ph}I_a}{P}\right)\sin\delta_{ra}\cdot\omega_s$$

$$= \omega_s\,\frac{P}{4\pi f}\;m\cdot V_t I_a \sin\delta_{ra}$$

From Eq. (3.86 *a*),

Synchronous speed in mech. rad per sec.,

$$\omega_s = \frac{2}{P}\text{(Synchronous speed in elect. rad per sec).}$$

i.e.
$$\omega_s = \frac{2}{P}(2\pi f) = \frac{4\pi f}{P}$$

From Fig. 5.31 *(b)*, it is seen that $\delta_{ra} = 90 - \theta.$

Substitution of these values, gives mechanical power input

$$= T_e\,\omega_s = \frac{1}{\omega_s}\cdot\omega_s\cdot mV_t I_a \sin(90-\theta)$$

$$= mV_t I_a \cos\theta = \text{electrical power output.}$$

When external load is gradually put on the machine shaft, the field poles slip back in space, with respect to the air-gap flux ϕ_r which is fixed in space by V_t. When field poles are behind F_r, the machine works as a motor, see Fig. 5.9. Note that the relative velocity between field poles and resultant flux ϕ_r is always zero. The effect of field poles lagging behind the space-phase position of ϕ_r, causes the appearance of load angle δ_{rf} between ϕ_r and F_f as shown in Fig. 5.31 *(c)*. Since the m.m.f. relation $\bar{F}_r = \bar{F}_f + \bar{F}_a$ must hold good again, the armature reaction m.m.f. F_a comes into existence as before. Consequently the armature current I_a, parallel to F_a, must flow in the armature winding, in order to establish F_a. As before, E_f and E_r lag by 90° the m.m.f. F_f and F_r respectively. The machine now acts as a motor, because I_a has a component in phase opposition to E_f or V_t. If all the losses are ignored, the electrical power input $mV_tI_a\cos\theta$ can be shown to be equal to $T_e\,\omega_s$, as before.

In the Figs. 5.31 *(b)* and *(c)*, $ab = F_f\sin\delta_{rf} = F_a\cos\theta = CI_a\cos\theta,\ \therefore\ I_a\cos\theta = \frac{F_f}{C}\sin\delta_{rf}$

Now power
$$P = V_t I_a\cos\theta = \frac{V_t\cdot F_f}{C}\sin\delta_{rf} \qquad ...(5.25)$$

In Eq. (5.25), left hand side $V_tI_a\cos\theta$ gives the active power present in both generating and motoring modes of a synchronous machine. As V_t or E_r is proportional to ϕ_r, the right-hand side of Eq. (5.25) is proportional to $\frac{\phi_r\cdot F_f}{C}\sin\delta_{rf}$ and as per Eq. (5.24 *a*), is proportional to torque. Thus, Eq. (5.25) demonstrates that active power existing in both generating and motoring modes is proportional to the mechanical torque as expected.

In Eq. (5.25), C and V_t are constant. Therefore, for constant F_f, the electrical power variation with load angle δ_{rf} is as shown in Fig. 5.32.

It is also seen from Fig. 5.31 *(b)* and *(c)* that $ob + bc = oc$

or
$$F_f\cos\delta_{rf} + F_a\sin\theta = F_r \qquad ...(5.26\ a)$$

Under no-load, $F_f = F_r$, Fig. 5.31 *(a)*. But as the synchronous machine is loaded electrically or mechanically, F_f gets displaced from F_r in space, though their magnitudes remain unaltered. The resultant m.m.f. F_r is now made up of the combined action of armature

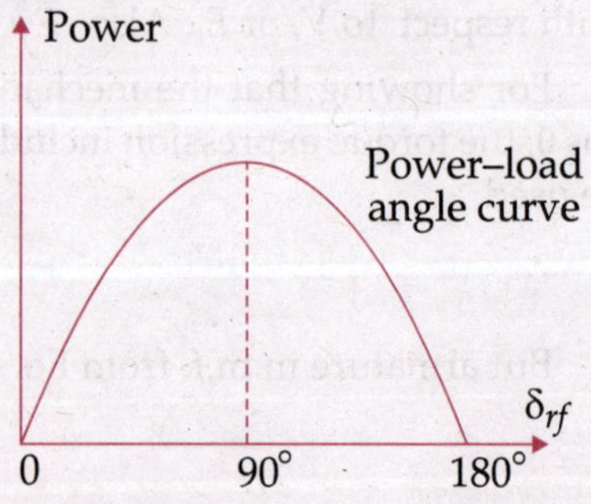

Fig 5.32: Power-load angle characteristic of a synchronous machine.

m.m.f. component $F_a \sin\theta$ and field m.m.f. component $F_f \cos\delta_{rf}$. The other component of armature m.m.f. $F_a \cos\theta$, or the armature current component $I_a \cos\theta$, must adjust itself to meet the torque requirement T_e as per Eq. (5.25).

From Eq. (5.26 *a*), $F_f \cos\delta_{rf} + CI_a \sin\theta = F_r$

or
$$\frac{V_t F_f}{C}\cos\delta_{rf} + V_t I_a \sin\theta = \frac{V_t F_r}{C} \quad \text{...(5.26 } b)$$

Since $I_a \sin\theta$ has a time-phase angle of 90° with respect to V_t, the product $V_t I_a \sin\theta$ represents the reactive power flow in the armature of a synchronous machine.

Eq. (5.25) shows that for constant electrical power $V_t I_a \cos\theta$, $F_f \sin\delta_{rf}$ must remain constant as V_t and C are constant. Let us discuss the effect of varying field m.m.f. F_f or field current I_f. In $F_f \sin\delta_{rf}$, if F_f is increased, δ_{rf} decreases, $\sin\delta_{rf}$ decreases so that $F_f \sin\delta_{rf}$ remains constant. With increase in F_f, δ_{rf} decreases, $\cos\delta_{rf}$ rises, $\frac{V_t \cdot F_f}{C}\cos\delta_{rf}$ rises and therefore $V_t I_a \sin\theta = \frac{V_t \cdot F_r}{C} - \frac{V_t}{C} F_f \cos\delta_{rf}$ = reactive power falls with *increase* in F_f or I_f.

If F_f is decreased, δ_{rf} rises, $\sin\delta_{rf}$ rises so that $F_f \sin\delta_{rf}$ is constant. So, with increase in F_f, δ_{rf} rises, $\cos\delta_{rf}$ decreases, $\frac{V_t F_f}{C}\cos\delta_{rf}$ falls. Therefore, $V_t I_a \sin\theta = \frac{V_t \cdot F_r}{C} - \frac{V_t \cdot F_f}{C}\cos\delta_{rf}$ = reactive power rises with decrease in F_f or I_f.

It is seen from above that reactive power flow in a synchronous machine can be controlled by varying the field excitation F_f or the field current I_f.

A careful examination of Fig. 5.31 *(b)* and *(c)* reveals that as synchronous machine is loaded from floating conditions, alternator begins operating at a leading p.f. whereas the synchronous motor at a lagging p.f. It is also observed from Figs. 5.31 *(b)* and *(c)* that same voltage equation, $E_f = V_t + jI_a X_{ar}$ is applicable to both generator and motor operation. However, in a generator, E_f is *ahead* of V_t and in a motor, E_f is behind V_t.

5.6. SYNCHRONOUS MOTOR PHASOR DIAGRAM

For gaining physical insight into the operation of a synchronous machine, the m.m.f. and flux phasors are very useful. Since these m.m.fs. or fluxes manifest themselves as generated voltages in the armature winding, the voltage phasor diagram of a synchronous machine may only be considered for simplicity. The analysis of the synchronous machine can thus be carried out with the help of its voltage phasor diagram.

In order to draw the synchronous motor phasor diagram, refer to Fig. 5.31. Alternator voltage phasor diagram of Fig. 5.31 *(b)*, is redrawn in Fig. 5.33 *(a)*, but for the lagging power factor and by including the armature leakage impedance $(r_a + jx_{al})$. Note that Fig. 5.33 *(a)* agrees with Fig. 5.22 *(b)*. Here I_a has a component in phase with E_f and the machine is, therefore, operating as a generator. If this machine is made to work as a synchronous motor at the same terminal voltage V_t, the current I_a gets reversed and Fig. 5.33 *(a)* gets modified to that shown in Fig. 5.33 *(b)*. Note that Fig. 5.33 *(b)* corresponds to the conventions adopted in Fig. 5.10 or in Fig. 5.31 *(c)*. Here I_a has a component in phase opposition to E_f, the machine is, therefore, acting as a synchronous motor. Voltage equation,

$$\overline{E}_f = \overline{V}_t + \overline{I}_a (r_a + jX_s)$$

is applicable to both the Figs. 5.33 *(a)* and *(b)*. Although synchronous motor phasor diagram of Fig. 5.33 *(b)* is exact, it is usually customary and simpler, to omit the negative sign with I_a and draw its phasor diagram as shown in Fig. 5.33 *(c)*. This figure reveals that the voltage equation for a synchronous motor is

$$\overline{V}_t = \overline{E}_f + \overline{I}_a (r_a + jX_s)$$

which agrees with Eq. (5.13) already obtained for a synchronous motor.

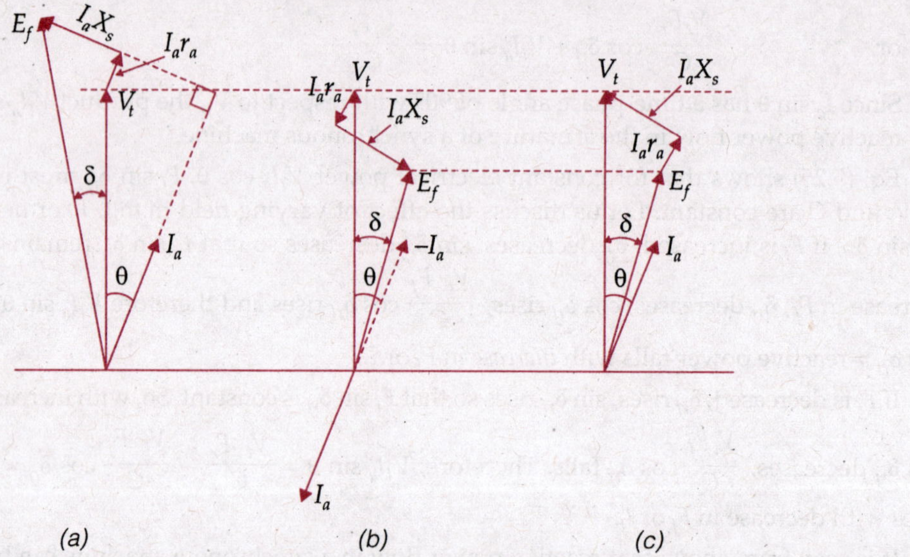

Fig 5.33: *(a)* Alternator voltage phasor diagram. *(b)* and *(c)* synchronous motor voltage phasor diagrams.

It should, however, be remembered that for an *alternator, phasor E_f is always ahead of phasor V_t*, just as field poles are ahead of ϕ_r. *For a synchronous motor, phasor E_f is always behind phasor V_t*, just as the field poles are behind ϕ_r.

It will be helpful at this stage to draw synchronous motor phasor diagrams at different operating p.fs. These are shown in Figs. 5.34 *(a)* to *(c)* for the same V_t and $I_a \cos\theta$. It is seen from these figures that for lagging p.f., Fig. 5.34 *(a)*,

$$E_f^2 = (V_t \cos\theta - I_a r_a)^2 + (V_t \sin\theta - I_a X_s)^2$$

for u.p.f., Fig. 5.34 *(b)*,

$$E_f^2 = (V_t - I_a r_a)^2 + (I_a X_s)^2$$

and for leading p.f., Fig. 5.34 (c),

$$E_f^2 = (V_t \cos\theta - I_a r_a)^2 + (V_t \sin\theta + I_a X_s)^2$$

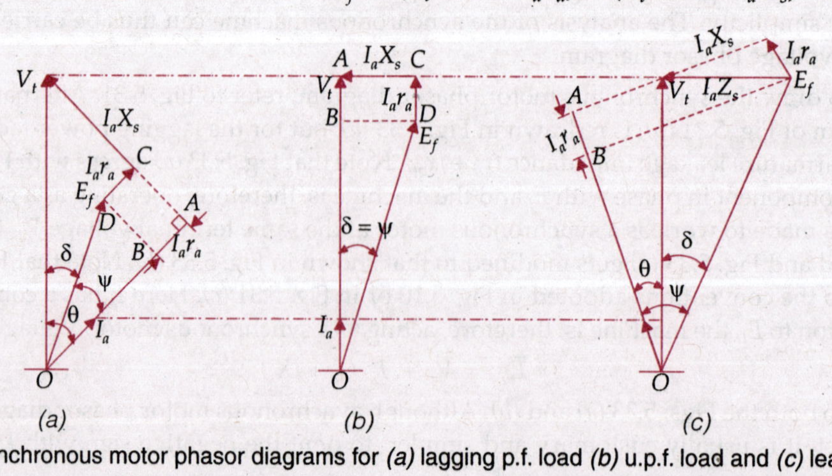

Fig 5.34: Synchronous motor phasor diagrams for *(a)* lagging p.f. load *(b)* u.p.f. load and *(c)* leading p.f. load.

Example 5.2. *An unloaded synchronous motor is connected to an infinite bus. If its O.C.C. and S.C.C. are available, explain how its leakage reactance can be determined.*

Solution. The z.p.f.c. of an alternator, at rated armature current, can be obtained by over-exciting it. For the determination of leakage reactance, only two points need be known on the z.p.f.c. In Fig. 5.17 *(b)*, points *F′* can be obtained from S.C.C. The other point *A* can be obtained by over-exciting the alternator connected to the under-excited synchronous motor—the alternator phasor diagram pertaining to this operation is illustrated in Fig. 5.35 *(a)*. In this figure, V_t represents terminal voltage of the alternator or of the synchronous motor and E_f is the excitation voltage of the alternator.

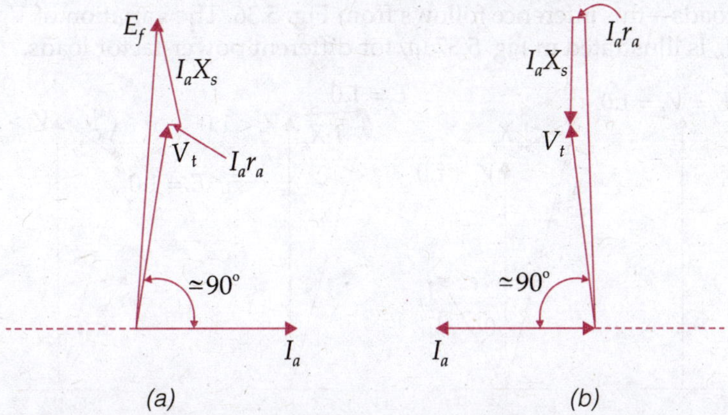

Fig 5.35: Phasor diagram for cylindrical rotor *(a)* over-excited alternator, operating at near z.p.f. and *(b)* over-excited synchronous motor operating at near z.p.f.

In this example, the synchronous motor is connected to a constant-voltage source V_t. If the field current of synchronous motor is increased, E_f increases but V_t remains constant. So, now increase the field current, till the synchronous motor draws rated armature current—under this condition the phasor diagram of Fig. 5.35 *(b)* is obtained. It is seen from Fig. 5.35 *(b)* that the time-phase angle between I_a and V_t is nearly 90°, as it is in Fig. 5.35 *(a)*.

It is seen from above that if an over-excited alternator working at near z.p.f. lagging gives *A* as the operating point in Fig. 5.17 *(b)*, then the same machine working as an over-excited synchronous motor at near z.p.f. leading would give the same operating point.

This is because the small amount of synchronous machine losses have almost negligible effect on the operating point *A*. Once the point A in Fig. 5.17 *(b)* is plotted, the leakage reactance x_{al} can be obtained as explained in Art. 5.3.2.

5.7. OPERATING CHARACTERISTICS OF ALTERNATORS AND THEIR RATINGS

The steady-state operating characteristics of a cylindrical rotor alternator can be obtained from its equivalent circuit shown in Fig. 5.20. Only the main characteristics of practical importance are presented here.

5.7.1. External Load Characteristics

The external load characteristics or the alternator **voltampere characteristics**, represent the variation of armature terminal voltage V_t with armature current I_a, for a constant field current.

Consider the alternator to be running at constant speed and with constant excitation, *i.e.* the alternator has constant E_f. At no-load, $I_a = 0$, therefore, $E_f = V_t = 1.0$, Fig. 5.36 *(a)*. The armature resistance drop, as usual, is neglected for convenience. For a lagging p.f. load, the phasor diagram is shown in Fig. 5.36 *(b)* and V_t is less than E_f.

For unity power-factor load, V_t is again less than E_f but it is more than its value at a lagging power factor load. For a leading power-factor load, V_t is more than E_f. Thus it is seen that the terminal voltage V_t falls on lagging power factor loads and may rise on leading power factor loads—this inference follows from Fig. 5.36. The variation of V_t with I_a for constant E_f or constant I_f, is illustrated in Fig. 5.37 *(a)* for different power-factor loads.

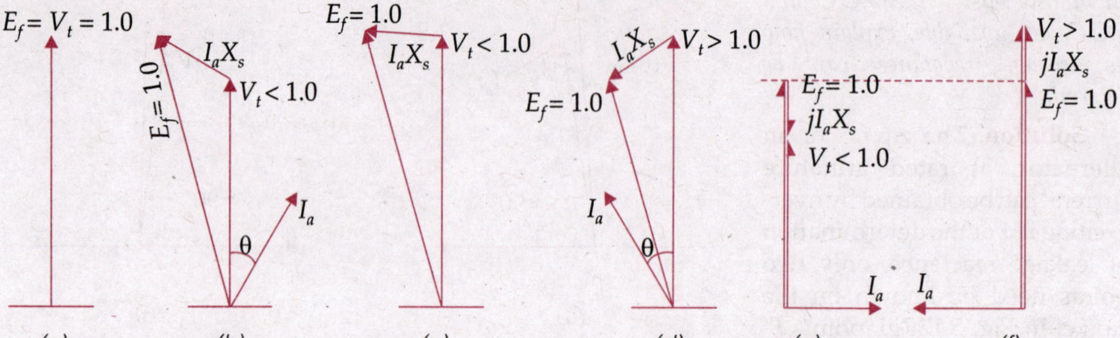

Fig 5.36: Alternator phasor diagrams for constant E_f *(a)* at no load *(b)* for lagging power factor *(c)* at unity p.f. *(d)* for leading p.f. *(e)* z.p.f. lag and *(f)* z.p.f. lead.

The operation of alternator at zero power factor lagging and z.p.f. leading is shown in Fig. 5.36 *(e)* and *(f)* respectively. For z.p.f. loads, it is seen that scalar relation $V_t = E_f \pm I_a X_s$ holds good. As $V_t = E_f \pm I_a X_s$ is the equation of a straight line, the variation of V_t with I_a are straight lines for both z.p.f. lagging and z.p.f. leading loads as shown in Fig. 5.37 *(a)*. For z.p.f. lagging, the algebraic equation is $V_t = E_f - I_a X_s$ and for z.p.f. leading, the algebraic equation is $V_t = E_f + I_a X_s$. For z.p.f. lag, when $V_t = 0$, $I_a = E_f/X_s$. For z.p.f. lead, for the same short-circuit current $\dfrac{E_f}{X_s}$, as during the z.p.f. lag, the terminal voltage for zero p.f. lead is $V_t = E_f + \dfrac{E_f}{X_s} \cdot X_s = 2E_f = 2.00$.

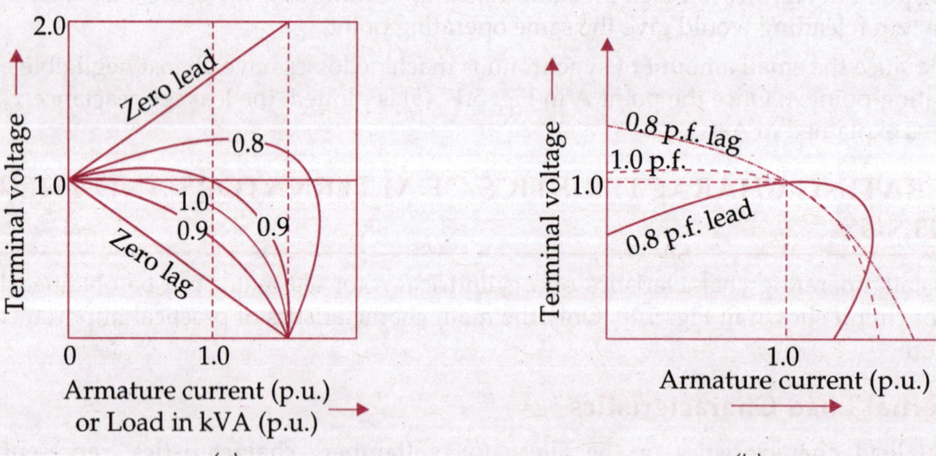

Fig 5.37: Alternator external characteristics with I_f held constant *(a)* at its no-load value and *(b)* at its rated V_t and rated I_a.

With alternator running at rated terminal voltage V_t and at rated current I_a (= 1.0), what happens if load current is reduced to zero? No-load voltage, or excitation voltage, E_f may rise or fall depending upon the load p.f. This is discussed below :

If terminal voltage at rated current is 1.0, then no-load voltage E_f must be more than 1.0 for a lagging p.f. load; this is illustrated in Fig. 5.38 *(a)*. At unity p.f. also, it is seen from Fig. 5.38 *(b)* that

E_f is more than 1.0. However for leading p.f. load, E_f is less than V_t at rated load. The inferences drawn from Fig. 5.38 are shown in Fig. 5.37 *(b)* in the form of $V_t - I_a$ characteristics at different load p.fs under the condition that alternator delivers rated V_t at rated I_a.

5.7.2. Alternator Compounding Characteristics

These characteristics show the variation of field current required to maintain rated terminal voltage, as its load at a specified power factor is increased. In practice, the alternator terminal voltage is held constant by controlling its field current manually or by automatic voltage regulators.

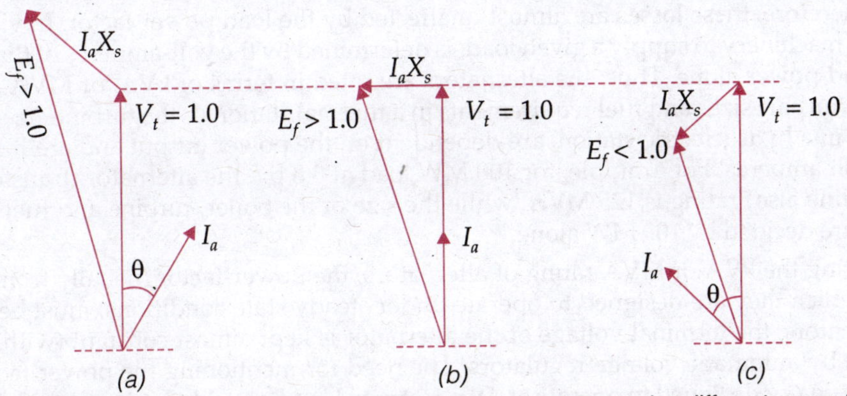

Fig 5.38: Alternator phasor diagrams for constant terminal voltage and at different power factors of *(a)* lagging *(b)* unity and *(c)* leading.

In order to illustrate the variation of E_f or I_f, for maintaining constant voltage V_t, refer to Fig. 5.38. At a lagging p.f., E_f is more than 1.00 if V_t = 1.00. For unity p.f. E_f is a little more than 1.00, but for leading p.f. in Fig. 5.38 *(c)*, E_f < 1.00. In other words, for maintaining constant terminal voltage V_t, the excitation voltage E_f or the field current I_f should be increased for lagging power-factor loads and should be decreased for leading power-factor loads. For unity power-factor loads, the increase in I_f with the increase in I_a is small as compared with 0.8 p.f. lagging loads. Fig. 5.39 illustrates these compounding curves for alternators at 0.8 p.f. lag, unity p.f. and at 0.8 p.f. lead.

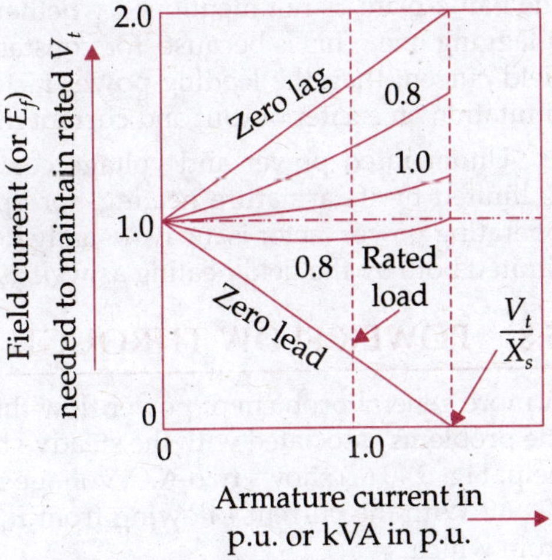

Fig 5.39: Alternator compounding curves for maintaining rated terminal voltage V_t

For zero power-factor lag or lead, the phasor diagrams are already drawn in Figs. 5.36 *(e)* and *(f)* respectively. As $E_f = V_t \pm I_aX_s$ is an algebraic equation for z.p.f. loads, the graph between E_f and I_a is a straight line for maintaining V_t constant. For z.p.f. lag, the algebraic equation is $E_f = V_t + I_aX_s$ and for z.p.f. lead, the algebraic equation is $E_f = V_t - I_aX_s$.

Also, for z.p.f. lag, the armature m.m.f. is direct demagnetizing ; therefore the field excitation or E_f must be increased in order to maintain armature terminal voltage V_t constant. For zero p.f. lead, the armature m.m.f. is direct magnetizing, the field current and therefore E_f must be reduced for maintaining V_t constant. This is shown in Fig. 5.39 for z.p.f. loads also. For z.p.f. lead, when $E_f = 0$,

$I_a = V_t/X_s$. For z.p.f. lag, for the same short-circuit current $\frac{V_t}{X_s}$ as during z.p.f. lead, the excitation voltage for zero p.f. lag is $E_f = V_t + \frac{V_t}{X_s} \cdot X_s = 2V_t = 2.00$ p.u.

5.7.3. Rating of Alternators

The rating of A.C. machinery, such as alternators, transformers (and cables) is determined by their heating and hence by losses in them. These losses are made up of I^2R losses, core losses and a small amount of friction and windage losses. The I^2R losses depend on current and the core losses on voltage, therefore, these losses are almost unaffected by the load power factor. In view of this, rating of A.C. machinery to supply a given load, is determined by the volt-amperes of that load and not by the load power alone. Thus, the alternators are rated in terms of kVA. or MVA. However, the boiler and turbine sizes and fuel requirements in a thermal station or the turbine size and water requirements in a hydroelectric station, are dependent on the power output and are independent of the load volt amperes. For example, for 100 MW load at 0.8 p.f. the alternator (transformer and transmission line also) rating is 125 MVA, while the size of the boiler, turbine and fuel (or water) requirement are decided by 100 MW alone.

While stating the kVA or MVA rating of alternators, the power-factor (usually from 0.8 to 0.9 lagging) for which they are designed to operate under steady state conditions, must be stated. In modern alternators, the terminal voltage of the alternator is kept almost constant (within ± 5% of rated voltage) by automatic voltage regulators. The need for mentioning the power factor arises, because an alternator designed to operate at 0.9 p.f. at rated load, would require more field current, more E_f, when operated at 0.80 p.f. and at rated load, see Fig. 5.39. More field current would result in over-heating of the field system, which is not desirable. If the alternator power factor given on the name-plate, is not mentioned whether it is leading or lagging one, then it should be taken as a lagging one. This is because, for constant terminal voltage, lagging power factors require more field current than the leading power factors, see Fig. 5.39. Thus a lagging power factor places a limitation on exciter output and current in the field coils.

Under rated power and voltage conditions, reactive power flow handled by an alternator is limited by its armature heating, for operating power factors near the rated value. When the operating power factor is away (usually lower) from its designed value, the reactive power flow is limited both by the field heating as well as armature heating.

5.8. POWER FLOW THROUGH AN INDUCTIVE IMPEDANCE

A more general problem of power flow through an inductive impedance is considered here, since the problems associated with the steady-state power flow in many systems, can be studied with its help. Fig. 5.40 (a) shows two A.C. voltage-sources E_1 and E_2 interconnected through an impedance $Z \angle\theta_z$. With the current I flowing from E_1 to E_2, the phasor diagram is as shown in Fig. 5.40 *(b)*, from which

$$\bar{E}_1 = \bar{E}_2 + \bar{I}\,\bar{Z}$$

or

$$\bar{I} = \frac{\bar{E}_1 - \bar{E}_2}{\bar{Z}} = \frac{\bar{E}_1}{\bar{Z}} - \frac{\bar{E}_2}{\bar{Z}} \quad \text{...(5.27)}$$

Eq. (5.27) shows that current $\bar{I}$ is the difference of two currents $\frac{\bar{E}_1}{\bar{Z}}$ and $\frac{\bar{E}_2}{\bar{Z}}$, lagging behind their respective voltages by angle θ_z as shown in Fig. 5.40 *(b)*. Here impedance angle θ_z is given by

$$\theta_z = \tan^{-1}\left(\frac{X}{R}\right)$$

It is seen from Fig. 5.40 (b) that $\alpha_z + \theta_z = 90°$.

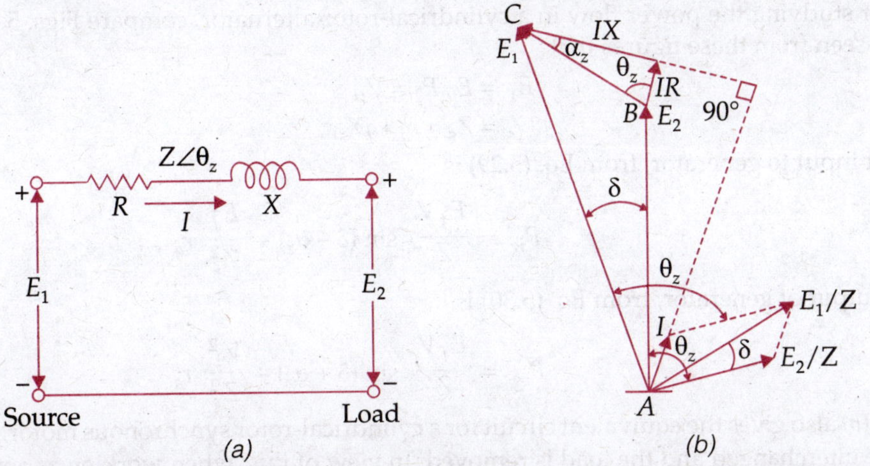

Fig 5.40: *(a)* Circuit for inductive impedance between two voltage and *(b)* its phasor diagram.

The power P_1 at the source end E_1 of the impedance Z, is given by

$$P_1 = E_1 \text{ (component of } I \text{ in phase with } E_1).$$

From Eq. (5.27) and Fig. 5.40 *(b)*, the component of I in phase with E_1 is seen to be $\left[\frac{E_1}{Z}\cos\theta_z - \frac{E_2}{Z}\cos(\delta+\theta_z)\right]$.

$$\therefore \quad P_1 = E_1\left[\frac{E_1}{Z}\cos\theta_z - \frac{E_2}{Z}\cos(\delta+\theta_z)\right]$$

$$= \frac{E_1^2}{Z}\cos\theta_z - \frac{E_1E_2}{Z}\cos(\delta+\theta_z) \quad \text{...(5.28)}$$

Now $\quad \cos\theta_z = \frac{R}{Z},$

and if $\theta_z = (90 - \alpha_z)$ is substituted in Eq. (5.28), we get

$$P_1 = \frac{E_1^2 R}{Z^2} - \frac{E_1E_2}{Z}[\cos\{(\delta - \alpha_z) + 90°\}]$$

$$= \frac{E_1E_2}{Z}\sin(\delta - \alpha_z) + \frac{E_1^2 R}{Z^2} \quad \text{...(5.29)}$$

The power P_2 at the load end E_2 and flowing through the impedance Z, is given by

$$P_1 = E_2 \text{ (component of } I \text{ in phase with } E_2).$$

From Eq. (5.27) and Fig. 5.40 *(b)*, the component of I in phase with E_2 is $\left[\frac{E_1}{Z}\cos(\theta_z - \delta) - \frac{E_2}{Z}\cos\theta_z\right]$

$$\therefore \quad P_2 = \frac{E_2E_1}{Z}\cos(\theta_z - \delta) - \frac{E_2^2}{Z}\cos\theta_z$$

$$= \frac{E_2E_1}{Z}\cos[90 - (\alpha_z + \delta)] - \frac{E_2^2}{Z}\cos\theta_z$$

$$= \frac{E_2E_1}{Z}\sin(\delta + \alpha_z) - \frac{E_2^2}{Z^2}R \quad \text{...(5.30)}$$

The power flow in a cylindrical-rotor synchronous machine is a special case of the above more general problem of power flow through an inductive impedance—this is because the equivalent circuit of this machine is identical with the circuit of Fig. 5.40 *(a)*.

Thus, for studying the power flow in a cylindrical-rotor alternator, compare Figs. 5.40 *(a)* and 5.20 *(b)*. It is seen from these figures that

$$E_1 = E_f, E_2 = V_t,$$
$$Z = Z_s = r_a + jX_s.$$

∴ Power input to generator, from Eq. (5.29) is

$$P_{ig} = \frac{E_f V_t}{Z_s} \sin(\delta - \alpha_z) + \frac{E_f^2}{Z_s^2} r_a \quad \text{...(5.31)}$$

Power output of generator, from Eq. (5.30) is

$$P_{og} = \frac{E_f V_t}{Z_s} \sin(\delta + \alpha_z) - \frac{V_t^2}{Z_s^2} r_a \quad \text{...(5.32)}$$

Fig. 5.20 *(b)* also gives the equivalent circuit for a cylindrical-rotor synchronous motor, provided E_f and V_t are interchanged and the load is removed. In view of this, when working as a motor,

$$E_1 = V_t, E_2 = E_f, \quad Z = Z_s = r_a + jX_s.$$

∴ Power input to motor, from Eq. (5.29) is

$$P_{im} = \frac{E_f V_t}{Z_s} \sin(\delta - \alpha_z) + \frac{V_t^2}{Z_s^2} r_a \quad \text{...(5.33)}$$

Power output of motor, from Eq. (5.30) is

$$P_{om} = \frac{E_f V_t}{Z_s} \sin(\delta + \alpha_z) - \frac{E_f^2}{Z_s^2} r_a \quad \text{...(5.34)}$$

The subscripts *i, o, g* and *m* stand for input, output, generator and motor respectively.

Note that the power at the shaft for a synchronous motor is P_{om} minus the rotational losses (friction, windage and core losses). Here P_{om} is called the mechanical power developed or gross power developed. Similarly the mechanical power input to generator is P_{ig} plus the rotational losses.

The difference between inputs (P_{ig} or P_{im}) and outputs (P_{og} or P_{om}), for either a generator or a motor, must be equal to ohmic loss $I_a^2 r_a$. This can be proved from Eqs. (5.31) and (5.32) or from Eqs. (5.33) and (5.34) as follows. From Eqs. (5.31) and (5.32),

$$P_{ig} - P_{og} = \frac{E_f V_t}{Z_s} [\sin\delta \cos\alpha_z - \cos\delta \sin\alpha_z - \sin\delta \cos\alpha_z - \cos\delta \sin\alpha_z] + (E_f^2 + V_t^2) \frac{r_a}{Z_s^2}$$

$$= \frac{r_a}{Z_s^2}(E_f^2 + V_t^2) - \frac{2E_f V_t}{Z_s} \cos\delta \sin\alpha_z$$

$$= \frac{r_a}{Z_s^2}(E_f^2 + V_t^2) - \frac{2E_f V_t}{Z_s} \cdot \frac{r_a}{Z_s} \cdot \cos\delta$$

$$= \frac{r_a}{Z_s^2}[E_f^2 + V_t^2 - 2E_f V_t \cos\delta]$$

From Δ*ABC* of Fig. 5.40 (b) and with appropriate changes

$(AC)^2 + (AB)^2 - 2(AC)(AB)\cos\delta = (BC)^2$

or
$$E_f^2 + V_t^2 - 2E_f V_t \cos\delta = I_a^2 Z_s^2$$

∴
$$P_{ig} - P_{og} = \frac{r_a}{Z_s^2}(I_a^2 Z_s^2) = I_a^2 r_a = \text{ohmic loss.}$$

Similarly, $$P_{im} - P_{om} = I_a^2 r_a.$$

Generally, armature resistance r_a is negligible and this makes

$$\alpha_z = 0 \text{ and } Z_s = X_s.$$

With these changes, the Eqs. (5.31, 5.32, 5.33 and 5.34), all reduce to

$$P_{ig} = P_{og} = P_{im} = P_{om} = P \text{ (say)} = \frac{E_f V_t}{X_s} \sin \delta \qquad ...(5.35)$$

An examination of Eqs. (5.31), (5.34) and Fig. 5.40 *(a)* reveals that power input to generator is at the terminals where the voltage is E_f and power output of the motor P_{om} is also at the same terminals. The powers P_{ig} and P_{om} should therefore be equal and opposite to each other but with δ replaced by (– δ). This can be verified as under :

$$P_{om} = -[P_{ig} \text{ from Eq. (5.31)}]$$

$$= -\frac{E_f V_t}{Z_s} \sin(-\delta - \alpha_z) - \frac{E_f^2}{Z_s^2} r_a$$

$$= \frac{E_f V_t}{Z_s} \sin(\delta + \alpha_z) - \frac{E_f^2}{Z_s^2} r_a \qquad ...(5.34)$$

Similarly, $$P_{im} = -P_{og}.$$

5.8.1. Maximum Power Conditions

In this section of the article, maximum power flow in both alternators and synchronous motors is studied.

(a) **Maximum power output.** With constant E_f, V_t and Z_s, the condition for maximum power output for a generator or a motor is obtained by differentiating Eq. (5.32) or Eq. (5.34) with respect to δ.

$$\therefore \quad \frac{dP_{og}}{d\delta} = \frac{dP_{om}}{d\delta} = \frac{E_f V_t}{Z_s} \cos(\delta + \alpha_z) = 0 \quad \text{or} \quad \delta + \alpha_z = 90°$$

$$\therefore \quad \delta = 90 - \alpha_z = \theta_z.$$

∴ For maximum power output, load angle δ = impedance angle θ_z.

From Eq. (5.32), maximum power output from a generator is

$$P_{og(max)} = \frac{E_f V_t}{Z_s} - \frac{V_t^2}{Z_s^2} r_a \qquad ...(5.36)$$

and from Eq. (5.34), maximum power out (or maximum power developed) in case of a motor is

$$P_{om(max)} = \frac{E_f V_t}{Z_s} - \frac{E_f^2}{Z_s^2} r_a \qquad ...(5.37)$$

The phasor diagrams, under the conditions of maximum power output, can be obtained from Fig. 5.22 *(b)* for a generator and from Fig. 5.34 *(c)* for a motor, by making $\delta = \theta_z = 90° - \alpha_z$. These are drawn respectively in Fig. 5.41 *(a)* and *(b)*.

In Fig. 5.41 *(a)* for alternator, with line *AB* extended,

$$\angle CBA = \pi - \theta_z - \theta$$

and in ΔABC, $$\angle BCA + \angle CBA + \theta_z = \pi$$

$$\therefore \quad \angle BCA = \pi - \theta_z - \angle CBA = \pi - \theta_z - (\pi - \theta_z - \theta)$$

$$\therefore \quad \angle BCA = \theta, \text{ p.f. angle.}$$

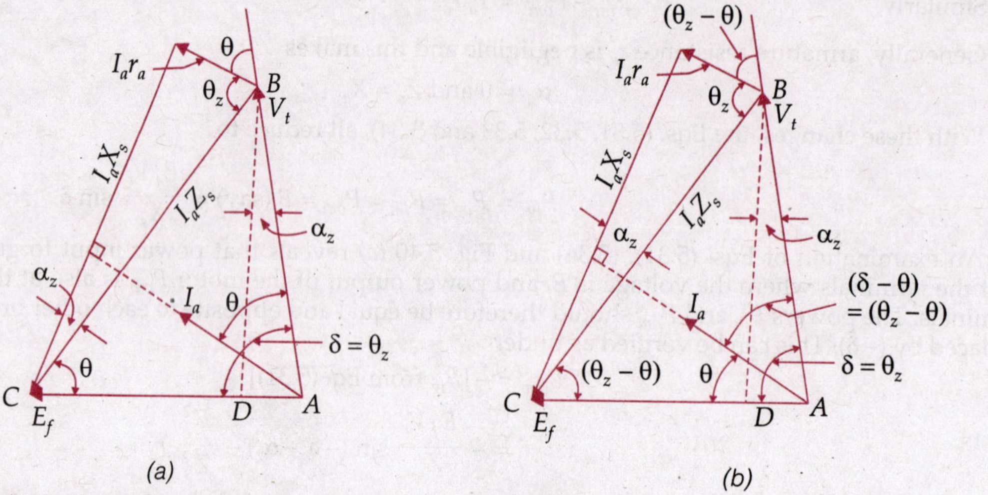

Fig 5.41: Phasor diagrams under maximum power output conditions for *(a)* generator and *(b)* motor.

For synchronous motor in Fig. 5.41 *(b)*, with line *AB* extended,

$$\angle CBA = \pi - \theta_z - (\delta - \theta)$$

In ΔABC, $\angle BCA + \angle CBA + \theta_z = \pi$

$\therefore$ $\angle BCA = \pi - \theta_z - \angle CBA = \pi - \theta_z - (\pi - \theta_z - \delta + \theta)$

$\therefore$ $\angle BCA = \delta - \theta = \theta_z - \theta.$

Now draw *BD* perpendicular to *AC* in Fig. 5.41 *(a)* and *(b)*. Then p.f. at which alternator is operating under maximum power output conditions is given by

$$\cos\theta = \cos\angle BCA = \frac{CD}{CB} = \frac{CA - AD}{CB}$$

$$= \frac{E_f - V_t\cos\theta_z}{I_a Z_s} = \frac{E_f Z_s - V_t r_a}{I_a Z_s^2} \quad \text{...(5.38)}$$

In case θ_z is known, the motor p.f. under maximum power output conditions can be obtained from the relation

$$\cos\angle BCA = \frac{V_t - E_f\cos\theta_z}{I_a Z_s} \quad \text{or } \cos(\theta_z - \theta) = \frac{V}{} - \frac{E_f r_a}{{}_s^2} \quad \text{...(5.39)}$$

Fig. 5.41 *(a)* and *(b)* also gives $\quad I_a Z_s = \sqrt{E_f^2 + V_t^2 - 2E_f V_t \cos\theta_z} \quad$ ...(5.40)

In case Z_s is known, the magnitude of armature current under maximum power output conditions can be obtained from Eq. (5.40).

(b) **Maximum power input.** With constant E_f, V_t and Z_s, the condition for maximum power input to generator or motor can be obtained by differentiating Eqs. (5.31) or (5.33) with respect to δ.

$$\therefore \quad \frac{dP_{ig}}{d\delta} = \frac{dP_{im}}{d\delta s} = \frac{E_f V_t}{Z_s}\cos(\delta - \alpha_z) = 0$$

or $\quad \delta = 90 + \alpha_z = \theta_z + 2\alpha_z = 180 - \theta_z.$

$\therefore$ For maximum power input,

load angle, $\delta = 90 + \alpha_z = 180 -$ impedance angle θ_z.

Maximum power input to generator, from Eq. (5.31), is

$$P_{ig\,(\max)} = \frac{E_f V_t}{Z_s} + \frac{E_f^2}{Z_s^2} r_a \qquad ...(5.41)$$

and maximum power input to motor, from Eq. (5.33), is

$$P_{im\,(\max)} = \frac{E_f V_t}{Z_s} + \frac{V_t^2}{Z_s^2} r_a \qquad ...(5.42)$$

The phasor diagrams, under the conditions of maximum power input, can be obtained from Fig. 5.22 *(b)* for an alternator or from Fig. 5.34 *(c)* for a motor, by making $\delta = 90° + \alpha_z$. These are shown in Fig. 5.42 *(a)* and *(b)*.

In Fig. 5.42 *(a)* for alternator, with line *AB* extended,

$$\angle CBA = \pi - \theta_z - \theta$$

$$\therefore \quad \angle BCA = \pi - \delta - \angle CBA = \pi - \delta - \pi + \theta_z + \theta = -\delta + \theta_z + \theta$$

$$\text{But} \quad \delta = \theta_z + 2\alpha_z$$

$$\therefore \quad \angle BCA = -\theta_z - 2\alpha_z + \theta_z + \theta = \theta - 2\alpha_z$$

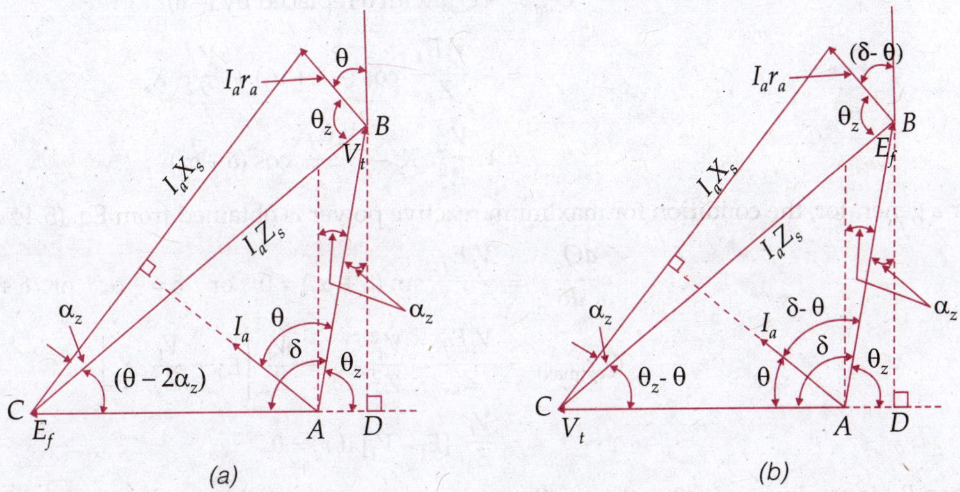

Fig 5.42: Phasor diagram under maximum power input conditions for *(a)* generator and *(b)* motor.

For motor, from Fig. 5.42 *(b)*,

$$\angle CBA = \pi - \theta_z - \delta + \theta$$

$$\therefore \quad \angle BCA = \pi - \delta - \angle CBA = \pi - \delta - \pi + \theta_z + \delta - \theta = \theta_z - \theta.$$

The ΔABC in Fig. 5.42 (*a*) and (*b*) can be analysed for determining the performance of synchronous machine under maximum power input conditions.

From an examination of the phasor diagrams of Fig. 5.23 for an alternator, it is seen that when

(i) $(E_f \cos\delta - I_a r_a \cos\theta) > V_t$, p.f. is lagging
(ii) $(E_f \cos\delta - I_a r_a) = V_t$, p.f. is unity
(iii) $(E_f \cos\delta - I_a r_a \cos\theta) < V_t$, p.f. is leading ...(5.43 *a*)

Further, phasor diagrams of Fig. 5.34 for a synchronous motor reveal that when

(i) $(E_f \cos\delta + I_a r_a \cos\theta) > V_t$, p.f. is leading
(ii) $(E_f \cos\delta + I_a r_a) = V_t$, p.f. is unity
(iii) $(E_f \cos\delta + I_a r_a \cos\theta) < V_t$, p.f. is lagging ...(5.43 *b*)

5.8.2. Reactive Power

So far as the reactive power flow in a synchronous machine is concerned, reactive power is of interest only at the output terminals of a generator and at the input terminals of a motor.

Reactive power at the generator output terminals, from Fig. 5.40, is

$$Q_{og} = E^2 \text{ (component of } I \text{ in quadrature lagging } E_2)$$

$$= V_t \left[\frac{E_f}{Z_s}\sin(\theta_z - \delta) - \frac{V_t}{Z_s}\sin\theta_z\right]$$

$$= \frac{V_t E_f}{Z_s} \sin\,[90 - (\alpha_z + \delta)] - \frac{V_t^2}{Z_s} \sin\theta_z$$

$$= \frac{V_t E_f}{Z_s} \cos\,(\delta + \alpha_z) - \frac{V_t^2}{Z_s^2} X_s \qquad \text{...(5.44 } a)$$

Output terminals for the generator are the same as the input terminals for the motor.

$$\therefore \quad Q_{im} = -Q_{og} \text{ with } \delta \text{ replaced by } (-\delta)$$

$$= -\frac{V_t E_f}{Z_s} \cos\,(-\delta + \alpha_z) + \frac{V_t^2}{Z_s^2} X_s$$

$$= +\frac{V_t^2}{Z_s^2} X_s - \frac{V_t E_f}{Z_s} \cos\,(\delta - \alpha_z) \qquad \text{...(5.44 } b)$$

For a generator, the condition for maximum reactive power is obtained from Eq. (5.44 *a*).

$$\therefore \quad \frac{dQ_{og}}{d\delta} = \frac{V_t E_f}{Z_s} \sin\,(\delta + \alpha_z) = 0 \quad \text{or} \quad \delta = -\alpha_z \quad \text{or} \quad \delta + \alpha_z = 0$$

$$\therefore \quad Q_{og(\max)} = \frac{V_t E_f}{Z_s} - \frac{V_t^2}{Z_s^2} X_s = \frac{V_t}{Z_s}\left[E_f - \frac{V_t}{Z_s}\cdot X_s\right]$$

$$= \frac{V_t}{Z_s}\,[E_f - V_t] \text{ if } r_a = 0$$

When P_{og} is maximum, $\delta = \theta_z = 90 - \alpha_z$, the reactive power under this conditions, from Eq. (5.44 *a)*, is given by

$$Q_{og} = -\frac{V_t^2}{Z_s^2} X_s$$

For a motor, the condition for maximum reactive power is obtained from Eq. (5.44 *b*).

$$\therefore \quad \frac{dQ_{im}}{d\delta} = -\frac{V_t E_f}{Z_s} \sin\,(\delta - \alpha_z) = 0 \quad \text{or} \quad \delta = \alpha_z \quad \text{or} \quad \delta - \alpha_z = 0$$

$$Q_{im(\max)} = \frac{V_t^2}{Z_s^2} X_s - \frac{V_t E_f}{Z_s} = \frac{V_t}{Z_s}\left[\frac{V_t}{Z_s}\cdot X_s - E_f\right]$$

$$= \frac{V_t}{X_s}\,[V_t - E_f] \quad \text{if } r_a = 0$$

When P_{im} is maximum, $\delta = 90 + \alpha_z$, the reactive power under this condition, from Eq. (5.44 *b*), is

$$Q_{im} = \frac{V_t^2}{Z_s^2} X_s$$

Generating mode. If $r_a = 0$, then from Eq. (5.44 *a*),

$$Q_{og} = \frac{V_t E_f}{X_s} \cos \delta - \frac{V_t^2}{X_s} = \frac{V_t}{X_s}(E_f \cos \delta - V_t) \qquad ...(5.45)$$

For a generator, positive values of active and reactive powers indicate their flow *out* of the generator. The flow of reactive power in a generator for different excitations is as under :

(i) When $E_f \cos \delta > V_t$ (overexcited), O_{og} is positive and therefore reactive power flow is outward, *i.e.* generator delivers reactive power just as it delivers active power. Under this condition, alternator operates at a lagging p.f.

(ii) When $E_f \cos \delta = V_t$ (normally excited), $Q_{og} = 0$. The generator neither delivers nor absorbs reactive power. Under this condition, synchronous generator p.f. is unity.

(iii) When $E_f \cos \delta < V_t$ (under excited), Q_{og} is negative, therefore reactive power flow is inward, *i.e.*, generator is absorbing reactive power from the infinite bus. Under this condition, alternator operates at a leading p.f.

Motoring Mode. If $r_a = 0$, then from Eq. (5.44 *b*),

$$Q_{im} = -\frac{V_t E_f}{X_s} \cos \delta + \frac{V_t^2}{X_s} = \frac{V_t}{X_s}(V_t - E_f \cos \delta) \qquad ...(5.46)$$

For a motor, positive values of active and reactive powers indicate their flow *into* the motor. For different excitations, the flow of reactive power in a motor is as under :

(i) When $E_f \cos \delta > V_t$ (overexcited), Q_{im} is negative and therefore reactive power flow is outward, *i.e.*, motor is acting as a generator of reactive power. In other words, the motor is delivering reactive power to the infinite bus and is operating at a leading p.f.

(ii) When $E_f \cos \delta = V_t$ (normally excited), $Q_{im} = 0$, *i.e.*, motor is neither delivering nor absorbing reactive power. Under this condition, synchronous motor operates at unity p.f.

(iii) When $E_f \cos \delta < V_t$ (under excited), Q_{im} is positive and reactive power flow is inward, *i.e.*, motor is absorbing reactive power just as it is absorbing active power. Under this condition, synchronous motor p.f. is lagging.

From above, it can be stated, in general, that *an overexcited synchronous machine, may be generator or motor, delivers reactive power whereas an underexcited one absorbs reactive power. Under normal excitation, it neither absorbs nor delivers reactive power.*

From the relations in Equations (5.35), (5.45) and (5.46), the variation of active and reactive powers can be plotted in case values of E_f, V_t etc. are known. For a synchronous machine, assuming $V_t = 1.0$, $X_s = 1.25$, $r_a = 0$ and $E_f = 2.0$, the active power versus load angle curves are plotted in Fig. 5.43 with the help of Eq. (5.35). For generator, the active, or synchronous, power P is shown positive and for synchronous motor as negative.

Synchronous generator. For generator, the reactive power can be obtained from Eq. (5.45) as under :

$$Q_{og} = \frac{1}{1.25}(2 \cos \delta - 1) = 0.8 (2 \cos \delta - 1)$$

For $\delta = 0°$, $Q_{og} = 0.8$. As this reactive power is positive, the alternator delivers this reactive power and operates at a lagging p.f.

For $\delta = \pi$, $Q_{og} = -2.4$. As this reactive power is negative, the alternator absorbs reactive power and operates at a leading p.f.

For $\delta = 60°$, $Q_{og} = 0$. Therefore, alternator neither delivers nor absorbs reactive power and it operates at unity p.f.

Synchronous motor. For motor, from Eq. (5.46),

$$Q_{im} = \frac{1}{1.25}(1 - 2\cos\delta) = 0.8\,(1 - 2\cos\delta)$$

For $\delta = 0°$, $Q_{im} = -0.8$. As reactive power is negative, the motor delivers this reactive power to infinite bus and operates at a leading p.f. As a result, this reactive power is plotted above the reference line in Fig. 5.43 indicating that motor is delivering this reactive power.

For For $\delta = \pi$, $Q_{im} = 2.4$. As this reactive power is positive, the synchronous motor absorbs this reactive power. It is therefore plotted below the reference line. The motor operates at a lagging p.f.

For $\delta = 60°$, $Q_{im} = 0$. The synchronous motor neither delivers nor absorbs reactive power and it operates at unity power factor.

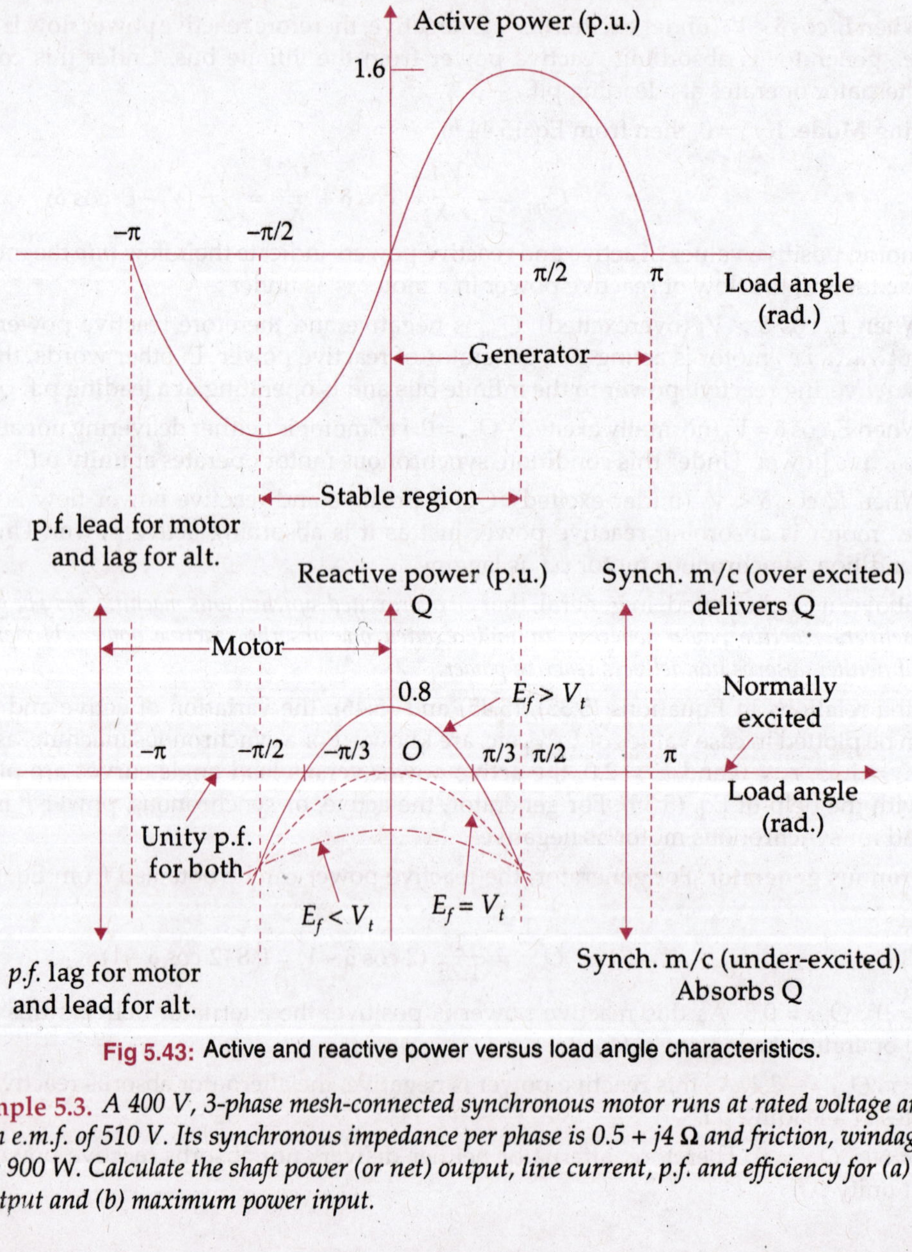

Fig 5.43: Active and reactive power versus load angle characteristics.

Example 5.3. *A 400 V, 3-phase mesh-connected synchronous motor runs at rated voltage and with an excitation e.m.f. of 510 V. Its synchronous impedance per phase is 0.5 + j4 Ω and friction, windage and iron losses are 900 W. Calculate the shaft power (or net) output, line current, p.f. and efficiency for (a) maximum power output and (b) maximum power input.*

Solution. Here

$$V_t = 400 \text{ V}, E_f = 510 \text{ V}$$

$$Z_s = \sqrt{0.5^2 + 4^2} = 4.031\ \Omega$$

$$\theta_z = \tan^{-1}(4/0.5) = 82.87°, \alpha_z = 90 - \theta_z = 7.13°$$

(a) For maximum power output in case of motor, refer to Fig. 5.41 *(b)*. From Eq. (5.37), maximum power output is

$$P_{om(\max)} = \frac{E_f V_t}{Z_s} - \frac{E_f^2}{Z_s^2} r_a = \frac{510 \times 400}{4.031} - \left(\frac{510}{4.031}\right)^2 \times 0.5$$

$$= 42604.2 \text{ watts per phase}$$

$\therefore$ Shaft power output $= P_{om(\max)} -$ F.W. and iron losses

$$= 42604.2 \times 3 - 900 = 126912.6 \text{ W}$$

From Eq. (5.40), $I_a Z_s = [510^2 + 400^2 - 2 \times 510 \times 400 \times \cos 82.87]^{1/2}$

or $I_a = 150.79$ A and line current $= \sqrt{3} \times 150.79 = 261.17$ A

From Eq. (5.39),

$$\cos(\theta_z - \theta) = \frac{V_t Z_s - E_f r_a}{I_a Z_s^2} = \frac{400 \times 4.031 - 510 \times 0.5}{(150.79)(4.031)^2} = 0.554$$

or $(\theta_z - \theta) = 56.36°$ or $\theta = 26.51°$

$\therefore$ p.f. $= \cos\theta = \cos 26.51° = 0.895$ lag

Check. Power input to motor is given by

$$\sqrt{3} \times 400 \times 261.17 \times \cos\theta = 42604.2 \times 3 + (150.79)^2 \times 0.5 \times 3 = 161919.03 \text{ W}$$

or $\cos\theta = 0.895$ lag

$$\text{Efficiency} = \frac{\text{output}}{\text{input}} = \frac{126912.6}{161919.03} \times 100 = 78.38\%.$$

(b) For maximum power input, refer to Fig. 5.42 *(b)*.

From Eq. (5.42), maximum power input to motor is

$$P_{im(\max)} = \frac{510 \times 400}{4.031} + \left(\frac{400}{4.031}\right)^2 \times 0.5$$

$$= 55531.2 \text{ watts per phase}$$

From Fig. 5.42 *(b)*, $I_a Z_s = [510^2 + 400^2 - 2 \times 510 \times 400 \times \cos 97.13°]^{1/2}$

or $I_a = 170.21$ A per phase

Line current $= 170.21 \times \sqrt{3} = 294.8$ A

$\therefore$ Shaft power output $= 55531.2 \times 3 - (170.21)^2 \times 0.5 \times 3 - 900 = 122236.43$ W

From Fig. 5.42 *(b)*,

$$\cos(\theta_z - \theta) = \frac{V_t + E_f \cos\theta_z}{I_a Z_s} = \frac{400 + 510 \cos 82.87}{(170.21)(4.031)} = 0.675$$

$\therefore$ $(\theta_z - \theta) = 47.53°$ or $\theta = 35.34°$

$\therefore$ p.f. $= \cos\theta = \cos 35.34° = 0.816$ lag

Check. Power input $= 400 \times 170.21 \times \cos\theta = 55531.2$ or $\cos\theta = 0.816$ lag

$$\text{Efficiency} = \frac{122236.4}{55531.2 \times 3} \times 100 = 73.37\%.$$

Example 5.4. *A 3300 V, 500 kW, 3-phase, star-connected synchronous motor has synchronous impedance of 0.4 + j5 Ω per phase. The motor works at constant excitation. Core loss, and friction and* *windage losses are 2 kW. For an output of 250 kW, the power factor is 0.8 leading. Calculate armature current and power factor (a) at full load and (b) when the input power is 400 kW.*

Solution. Here $V_t = \dfrac{3300}{\sqrt{3}} = 1905.3$ V, $Z_s = \sqrt{0.4^2 + 5^2} = 5.016\ \Omega$, $\alpha_z = \tan^{-1}\left(\dfrac{0.4}{5}\right) = 4.57°$ and impedance angle $\theta_z = 90 - \alpha_z = 90 - 4.57 = 85.43°$.

For an output of 250 *kW*, the power developed P = 250 kW + friction and windage loss + core loss = 250 + 2 = 252 kW.

But power developed $\qquad P = 3\,[V_t I_a \cos\theta - I_a^2 r_a]$

$$\therefore \qquad \frac{252{,}000}{3} = 1905.3\, I_a \times 0.8 - I_a^2 \times 0.4$$

$$\text{or} \qquad I_a^2 - 3810.6\, I_a + 21{,}000 = 0$$

Its solution gives $I_a = 55.93$ A and 3754.67 A.

Higher value of armature current of 3754.67 A is not feasible. Therefore, $I_a = 55.93$ A

For a leading pf, E_f from phasor diagram of Fig. 5.34 *(c)*, is given by

$$E_f = [(V_t \cos\theta - I_a r_a)^2 + (V_t \sin\theta + I_a X_s)^2]^{1/2}$$

$$= [(1905.3 \times 0.8 - 55.93 \times 0.4)^2 + (1905.3 \times 0.6 + 55.93 \times 5)^2]^{1/2} = 2068.83 \text{ V}$$

(a) At full load, mechanical power developed, $P = 500 + 2 = 50$ kW.

From Eq. (5.34), $\qquad P = 3\dfrac{E_f \cdot V_t}{Z_s} \sin(\delta + \alpha_z) - 3\left(\dfrac{E_f}{Z_s}\right)^2 \cdot r_a$

$$\therefore \qquad \frac{502000}{3} = \frac{2068.83 \times 1905.3}{5.016} \sin(\delta + \alpha_z) - \left(\frac{2068.83}{5.016}\right)^2 \times 0.4$$

$$\text{or} \qquad \sin(\delta + \alpha_z) = \frac{235{,}378.07 \times 5.016}{2068.83 \times 1905.3}$$

$$\text{or} \qquad \delta = 17.43° - 4.57° = 12.86°$$

From Fig. 5.34 *(c)*, $(I_a Z_s)^2 = E_f^2 + V_t^2 - 2E_f V_t \cos\delta$

$$\therefore \qquad I_a = \frac{1}{5.016}[2068.83^2 + 1905.3^2 - 2 \times 2068.83 \times 1905.3 \times \cos 12.86°]^{1/2}$$

$$= 94.46 \text{ A}$$

Now, power input = mechanical power developed + total I^2R loss

$$\therefore \qquad \sqrt{3}\, V_t I_a \cos\theta = 502{,}000 + 3 \times 94.46^2 \times 0.4 = 512{,}707.23$$

$$\therefore \qquad \text{Power factor } \cos\theta = \frac{512{,}707.23}{\sqrt{3} \times 3300 \times 94.46} = 0.9496$$

Here, from Eq. (5.43 *b*),

$$E_f \cos\delta + I_a r_a \cos\theta = 2068.83 \times \cos 12.86 + 94.46 \times 0.4 \times 0.9496 = 2052.8 \text{ V} > V_t.$$

Therefore, $\quad$ power factor = 0.9496 leading

(b) Input power = 400 kW.

From Eq. (5.33), $\qquad P_{im} = \dfrac{E_f V_t}{Z_s} \sin(\delta - \alpha_z) + \left(\dfrac{V_t}{Z_s}\right)^2 \times r_a$

$$\text{or} \qquad \frac{400{,}000}{3} = \frac{2068.83 \times 1905.3}{5.016} \sin(\delta - \alpha_z) + \left(\frac{1905.3}{5.016}\right)^2 \times 0.4$$

$$\therefore \qquad \sin(\delta - \alpha_z) = 0.09623 \text{ or } \delta - \alpha_z = 5.522°$$

$\therefore$ Load angle $\delta = 5.522 + 4.57 = 10.1°$

Also $I_aZ_s = [2068.83^2 + 1905.3^2 - 2 \times 2068.83 \times 1905.3 \times \cos 10.1°]^{½}$

$\therefore$ $I_a = 76.932$ A

$$\sqrt{3}\, V_t I_a \cos\theta = \sqrt{3} \times 3300 \times 76.932 \times \cos\theta = 400{,}000$$

$\therefore$ $\cos\theta = 0.90968 \simeq 0.91$

$$E_f \cos\delta + I_a r_a \cos\theta = 2068.83 \times \cos 10.1 + 76.932 \times 0.4 \times 0.91$$
$$= 2036.77 + 28 = 2064.77 > V_t (= 1905.7)$$

$\therefore$ Power factor = 0.91 leading

Example 5.5. *A 230 V, 4 pole, 50 Hz, star-connected synchronous motor has $r_a + jX_s = 0.6 + j3.0\ \Omega$ per phase. Its field current is so adjusted that motor draws 10 A at u.p.f. from rated voltage source. Now with the field current unchanged, the load on the motor is increased till it draws 40 A from the supply. Find the torque developed and the new p.f.*

Solution. Here $V_t = \dfrac{230}{\sqrt{3}} = 132.8$ V,

$Z_s = \sqrt{0.6^2 + 3^2} = 3.06\ \Omega$

$\alpha_z = \tan^{-1}(0.6/3) = 11.31°$

From the synchronous motor phasor diagram at u.p.f., Fig. 5.44 *(a)*,

$E_f = [(V_t - I_a r_a)^2 + (I_a X_s)^2]^{1/2}$

$= [(132.8 - 6)^2 + (10 \times 3)^2]^{1/2} = 130.3$ V

When load torque is increased with E_f held fixed, E_f falls back, load angle δ increases as shown in Fig. 5.44 *(b)* and the motor begins operating at a lagging p.f. with $I_a = 40$ A. It is also seen from this phasor diagram that

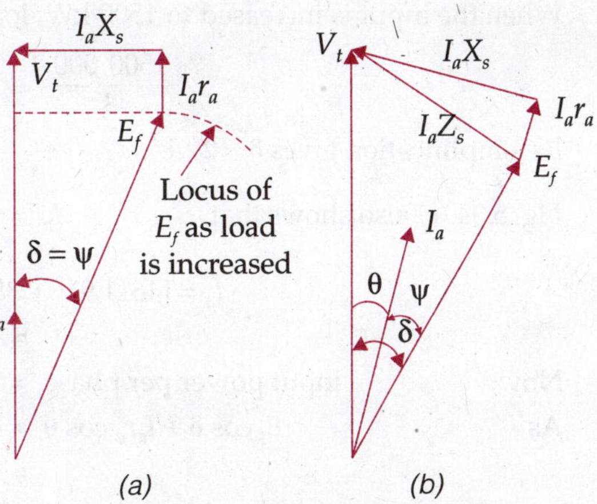

Fig 5.44: Pertaining to Example 5.5.

$$I_aZ_s = (E_f^2 + V_t^2 - 2E_f V_t \cos\delta)^{1/2}$$

or $$40 \times 3.06 = 130.3^2 + 132.8^2 - 2 \times 130.3 \times 132.8 \times \cos\delta]^{1/2}$$

or $$\cos\delta = 0.5673 \text{ or } \delta = 55.44°$$

Power input from Eq. (5.33) is $$P = \frac{130.3 \times 132.8}{3.06}\sin(55.44 - 11.31) + \left(\frac{132.8}{3.06}\right)^2 \times 0.6$$

$$= 5067.48 \text{ W} = V_t I_a \cos\theta$$

$\therefore$ $$\text{p.f.} = \cos\theta = \frac{5067.48}{132.8 \times 40} = 0.954 \text{ lag}$$

Power developed $$= 3(P - I_a^2 r_a) = [5067.48 - 40^2 \times 0.6] \times 3 = 12322.44 \text{ W}$$

Now $$\omega_s T_e = P$$

Here $$N_s = \frac{120 \times 50}{4} = 1500 \text{ r.p.m.}$$

$\therefore$ Gross torque, $$T_e = \frac{12322.44 \times 60}{2\pi \times 1500} = 78.45 \text{ Nm.}$$

Example 5.6. *A 6.6 kV star-connected 3-phase synchronous motor works at constant voltage and constant excitation. Its synchronous impedance is 1.5 + j12 Ω per phase. When the input power is 1000 kW, the p.f. is 0.8 leading. Find the p.f. when input is increased to 1500 kW.* (I.E.S., 1984)

Solution. Here
$$V_t = \frac{6600}{\sqrt{3}} = 3810.6 \text{ V},$$
$$\text{p.f.} = 0.8 \text{ leading}$$
$$I_a = \frac{1000,000}{\sqrt{3} \times 6600 \times 0.8} = 109.35 \text{ A}$$
$$Z_s = \sqrt{1.5^2 + 12^2} = 12.09$$
$$\alpha_z = \tan (1.5/12) = 7.13°$$

The phasor diagram for a leading p.f. load is shown in Fig. 5.34 *(c)* from which it is seen that

$$E_f = [(V_t \cos \theta - I_a r_a)^2 + (V_t \sin \theta + I_a X_s)^2]^{1/2}$$
$$= [(3810.6 \times 0.8 - 109.35 \times 1.5)^2 + (3810.6 \times 0.6 + 109.35 \times 12)^2]^{1/2} = 4611.91 \text{ V}$$

When the input is increased to 1500 kW, load angle δ must increase. From Eq. (5.33),

$$\frac{1500,000}{3} = \frac{4611.91 \times 3810.6}{12.09} \sin (\delta - \alpha_z) + \left(\frac{3810.6}{12.09}\right)^2 \times 1.5$$

Its simplification gives δ = 21.1°

Fig. 5.34 *(c)* also shows that
$$I_a = \frac{1}{Z_s} [E_f^2 + V_t^2 - 2E_f V_t \cos \delta]^{1/2}$$
$$I_a = [4611.91^2 + 3810.6^2 - 2 \times 4611.91 \times 3810.6 \times \cos 21.1°]^{1/2} \left(\frac{1}{12.09}\right)$$
$$= 143.23 \text{ A}$$

Now, input power per phase $= 3810.6 \times 143.23 \times \cos \theta = 500,000$ W or $\cos \theta = 0.9161$

As $E_f \cos \delta + I_a r_a \cos \theta = 4611.91 \times \cos 21.1° + 143.23 \times 1.5 \times 0.9161$
$= 4808.73 > V_t$ (= 3810.6 V), therefore

Synchronous motor is operating at a p.f. = 0.9161 leading (see Eq. (5.43 *b*))

Example 5.7. *A 3-phase, 6-pole, 2.3 kV, 200 kVA, star-connected synchronous motor has synchronous reactance of 12 Ω per phase and negligible resistance. The motor is initially operating at a load of 120 kW with the field current adjusted such that the armature current is minimum. The field current is now increased such that the armature current is increased by 50%. With this field current, the load is reduced to 60 kW. Calculate the new values of armature current and power factor. Neglect all losses.* (GATE, 1988)

Solution.
$$V_t = \frac{2300}{\sqrt{3}} = 1327.95 \text{ V}$$

Minimum armature current corresponds to unity p.f.

$$\therefore \quad 3V_t I_a \cos \theta = 120,000 \text{ W or } I_a = \frac{120,000}{3 \times 1327.95 \times 1} = 30.122 \text{ A}$$

The phasor diagram under u.p.f. is as shown in Fig. 5.45 *(a)*. With the increase in field current, E_f rises to E_{f1} and I_a to I_{a1} such that $I_{a1} = 1.5\, I_a = 1.5 \times 30.122 = 45.183$ A as shown. Under this condition, p.f. $\cos \theta_1$ is given by

$$I_{a1} \cos \theta_1 = I_a \text{ or } \cos \theta_1 = \frac{1}{1.5} = 0.667$$

The magnitude of E_{f1} can be obtained from Fig. 5.45 (*a*) as

$$E_{f1} = [(V_t \cos \theta_1)^2 + (V_t \sin \theta_1 + I_{a1} X_s)^2]^{1/2}$$
$$= [(1327.95 \times 0.667)^2 + (1327.95 \times 0.745 + 45.183 \times 12)^2]^{1/2}$$
$$= 1769.21 \text{ V}$$

When load is reduced to 60 kW with E_{f1} remaining constant, the phasor diagram is as shown in Fig. 5.45 *(b)*. Excitation e.m.f. E_{f1} shifts to new orientation *OC* and load angle reduces from δ_1 to δ_2. The current is seen to become I_{a2} and load angle δ_2.

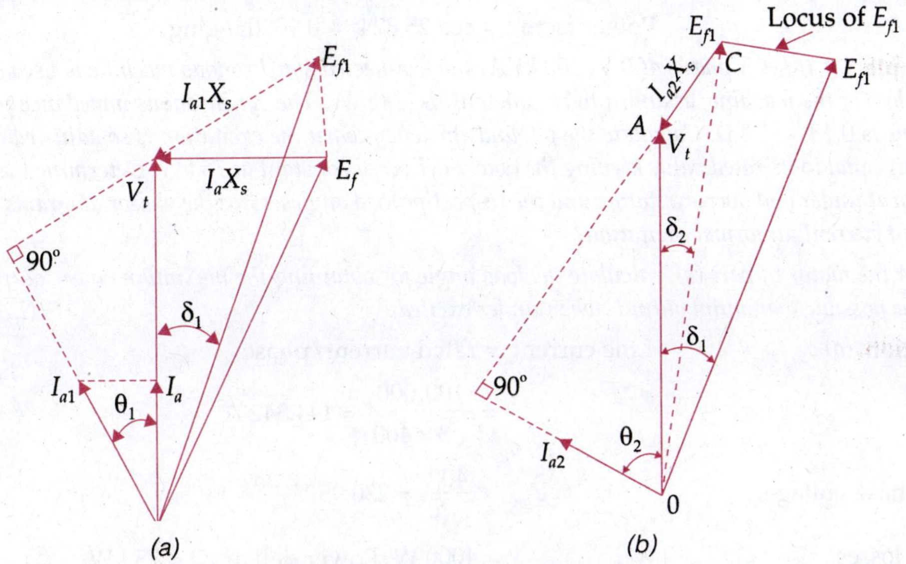

Fig 5.45: Pertaining to Example 5.7.

$$\text{Now} \qquad \frac{E_{f1} \cdot V_t}{X_s} \sin \delta_2 = \frac{60{,}000}{3} \text{ W} \quad \text{or} \quad \delta_2 = 5.863°$$

$$\text{From } \Delta OAC, \qquad I_{a2}X_s = [1769.21^2 + 1327.95^2 - 2 \times 1769.2 \times 1327.95 \times \cos 5.863]^{1/2}$$

$$\text{or} \qquad I_{a2} = 39.02 \text{ A}$$

$$\text{Also} \qquad 3V_tI_a \cos \theta_2 = 60{,}000$$

$$\therefore \qquad \cos \theta_2 = \frac{60{,}000}{3 \times 1327.95 \times 39.02} = 0.386 \text{ lead.}$$

Example 5.8. *A number of alternators are working in parallel with their terminal voltage equal to the rated value. One of the machines, which has a synchronous reactance of 50% and a resistance of 1%, delivers a power output in kW equal to 70% of its rated kVA. If the e.m.f. of this unit equals 1.2 times the terminal voltage, find out the power factor at which the machine is operating.* [I.A.S., 1989]

Solution. It is given that $\frac{I_a r_a}{V_t} = 1\% = 0.01$ and $\frac{I_a r_a}{V_t} = 50\% = 0.50$. Fig. 5.23 *(a)* shows that

$$E_f^2 = (V_t \cos \theta + I_a r_a)^2 + (V_t \sin \theta + I_a X_s)^2$$

$$= V_t^2 \left[\left(\cos\theta + \frac{I_a r_a}{V_t} \right)^2 + \left(\sin\theta + \frac{I_a X_s}{V_t} \right)^2 \right]$$

$$\text{Here} \qquad I_a = 0.7 I_{rated}.$$

$$\therefore \qquad (1.2V_t)^2 = V_t^2 \, [(\cos \theta + 0.01 \times 0.7)^2 + (\sin \theta + 0.5 \times 0.7)^2]$$

$$1.44 = 0.014 \cos \theta + 0.7 \sin \theta + 1.12255$$

or $0.014 \cos \theta + 0.7 \sin \theta = 1.44 - 1.12255 = 0.31745$ ...(i)

$$\text{It is known that} \qquad (A \cos \theta + B \sin \theta) = \sqrt{A^2 + B^2} \sin \left(\theta + \tan^{-1} \frac{A}{B} \right)$$

∴ Eq. (*i*) can be written as

$$0.70014 \sin (\theta + 1.14577°) = 0.31745$$

or $\sin (\theta + 1.14577°) = 0.4535$ or $\theta = 25.824°$

∴ Power factor $= \cos 25.824° = 0.900$ lagging.

Example 5.9. *(a) A 3-phase, 400 V, 100 kVA, star-connected synchronous machine is used as a motor. The stray loss of the machine, assumed to be constant, is 4000 W. The synchronous impedance per phase of the machine is 0.13 + j1.3 Ω. Calculate the p.f. and efficiency when the excitation is so adjusted as to take a line current equal to its rated value keeping the power delivered constant at 75 kW. Determine the excitation e.m.f.s both at under and over-excitation and the respective load angles. Give the phasor diagrams. What will be the input current at normal excitation?*

(b) For the motor in part (a), calculate the load angle for obtaining the maximum power output and the value of the possible maximum output when under excited. *(I.A.S., 1987)*

Solution. *(a)* Line current = rated current/phase

$$= \frac{100,000}{\sqrt{3} \times 400} = 144.342 \text{ A}$$

Per-phase voltage, $V_{ph} = \dfrac{400}{\sqrt{3}} = 230.95$ V

Stray losses = 4000 W, Power delivered = 75 kW

Power developed = 75000 + 4000 = 79000 W

Ohmic losses in armature $3 I_a^2 r_a = 3(144.342)^2 \times 0.13 = 8125.5$ W

Total losses in motor = 4000 + 8125.5 = 12125.5 W

Power input = 75000 + 12125.50 = 87125.5 W

Also $\sqrt{3}\, V_t I_a \cos\theta$ = Power input

∴ Power factor $= \cos\theta = \dfrac{87125.5}{100,000} = 0.8713$ or $\theta = 29.39°$

Efficiency $= \left(1 - \dfrac{\text{losses}}{\text{input}}\right) = \left(1 - \dfrac{12125.5}{87125.5}\right) \times 100 = 86.083\%$

For Fig. 5.34 *(a)*, $V_t \cos\theta = 230.95 \times 0.8713 = 201.23$ V

$V_t \sin\theta = 230.95 \times 0.491 = 113.396$ V

$I_a r_a = 18.764$ V and $I_a X_s = 144.342 \times 1.3 = 187.64$ V

As $I_a X_s > V_t \sin\theta$, the phasor diagram for lagging p.f. is as shown in Fig. 5.46. In this figure, E_f can be obtained from ΔABC.

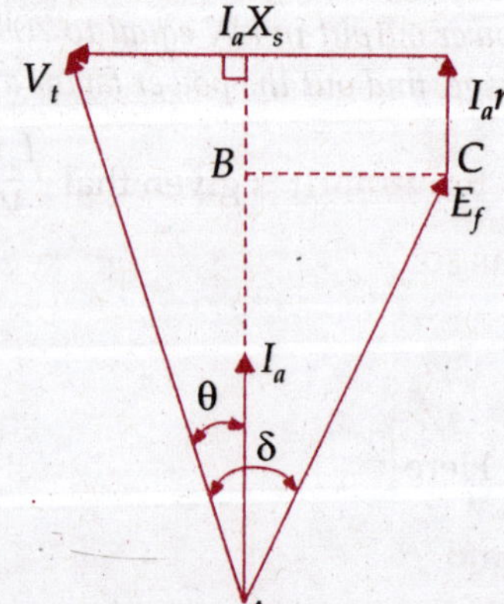

Fig 5.46: Pertaining to Example 5.9.

$$\therefore \quad E_f^2 = (V_t \cos\theta - I_a r_a)^2 + (I_a X_s - V_t \sin\theta)^2$$

$$= (201.23 - 18.764)^2 + (187.64 - 113.396)^2$$

$$= (182.466)^2 + (74.244)^2$$

or $E_f = 196.9924 \cong 197.0$ V

$$\tan(\delta - \theta) = \frac{BC}{AB} = \frac{74.244}{182.46}$$

or $\delta = 22.14 + 29.39° = 51.53°$

For leading p.f. load, it is seen from Fig. 5.34 *(c)* that

$$E_f^2 = (182.466)^2 + (187.64 + 113.396)^2 = (182.466)^2 + (301.036)^2$$

or $$E_f = 352.02 \text{ V}.$$

$$\tan(\delta + \theta) = \frac{301.036}{182.466}$$

or $$\delta = 58.78° - 29.39° = 29.39°$$

$$\text{Input current at normal excitation} = \frac{87125.5}{\sqrt{3} \times 400 \times 1} = 125.76 \text{ A at unity p.f.}$$

(b) For maximum power output, $\delta = \theta_z = \cos^{-1}\dfrac{r_a}{Z_s} = \cos^{-1}\dfrac{0.13}{\sqrt{0.13^2 + 1.3^2}}$

∴ Load angle $\delta = 84.23°$

From Eq. (5.37), maximum power output is given by

$$P_{om} = \frac{E_f V_t}{Z_s} - \frac{E_f^2}{Z_s^2} r_a = \frac{197.0 \times 230.95}{1.3065} - \left(\frac{197}{1.3065}\right)^2 \times 0.13$$

$$= 31866.5 \text{ W/phase} = 95599.5 \text{ Watts (total).}$$

Example 5.10. *A 500 kVA, 3-phase, 6.6 kV, star-connected synchronous motor has synchronous reactance of 0 + j 20 Ω per phase.*

(a) For a load angle of 10°, the motor takes rated current. Find the excitation e.m.fs both at lagging and leading p.f.s.

(b) Find the mechanical power developed and p.f. in part (a).

(c) Find the minimum excitation voltage for delivering 200 kW at rated voltage without falling out of step.

Solution. Terminal voltage, $$V_t = \frac{6600}{\sqrt{3}} = 3810.6 \text{ V}$$

Rated armature current, $$I_a = \frac{500}{\sqrt{3} \times 6.6} = 43.74 \text{ A}$$

(a) Phasor diagram in Fig. 5.47 is drawn with I_aX_s same for both leading and lagging p.fs. It is seen from this figure that

$$(I_aX_s)^2 = E_f^2 + V_t^2 - 2E_fV_t \cos\delta$$

$$(43.74 \times 20)^2 = E_f^2 + 3810.6^2 - 2E_f \times 3810.6 \cos 10°$$

or $$E_f^2 - 7505.42E_f + 13755397 = 0$$

Its solution gives $$E_f = 3180.5 \text{ V and } 4324.9 \text{ V}$$

∴ Excitation e.m.fs are $E_{f1} = 3180.5$ V per phase for lagging p.f. and $E_{f2} = 4324.9$ V per phase for leading p.f. Their corresponding line values are

$$E_{f1} = \sqrt{3} \times 3180.5 = 5508.63 \text{ V}$$

and $$E_{f2} = \sqrt{3} \times 4324.9 = 7490.73 \text{ V}.$$

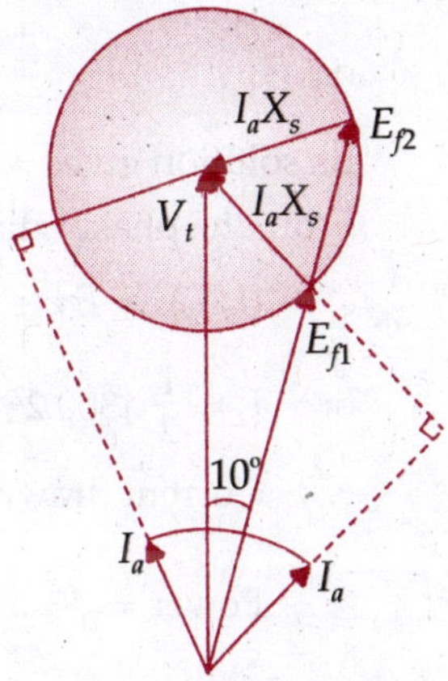

Fig 5.47: Pertaining to Example 5.10.

(b) For lagging p.f. the mechanical power developed is

$$P = 3 \times \frac{3810.6 \times 3180.5}{20} \times \sin 10° = 315682.3 \text{ W}$$

$$\text{Power factor} = \frac{315682.3}{\sqrt{3} \times 6600 \times 43.74} = 0.6314 \text{ lag}$$

For leading p.f., the mechanical power developed is

$$P = 3 \times \frac{3810.6 \times 4324.9}{20} \sin 10° = 429270.4 \text{ W}$$

$$\text{Power factor} = \frac{429270.4}{\sqrt{3} \times 6600 \times 43.74} = 0.8585 \text{ lead}$$

(c) The synchronous motor will fall out of step when $\delta = 90°$.

$$\therefore \quad 200{,}000 = 3 \frac{E_f \times 3810.6}{20} \sin 90°$$

or $E_f = 349.90$ V per phase or 606 V (line).

Example 5.11. *A 3-phase, 415 V, 6-pole, 50 Hz, star-connected synchronous motor has an e.m.f. of 520 V (L – L). The stator winding has a synchronous reactance of 2 ohms/phase, and the motor develops a torque of 220 Nm. The motor is operating off 415 V, 50 Hz bus.*

(a) Calculate the current drawn from the supply and its power factor.

(b) Draw the phasor diagram showing all the relevant quantities. (GATE, 1992)

Solution. Per phase $V_t = \dfrac{415}{\sqrt{3}} = 239.6$ V

Per phase $E_f = \dfrac{520}{\sqrt{3}} = 300.2$ V

Synchronous speed, $\omega_s = \dfrac{4\pi f}{P} = \dfrac{4\pi \times 50}{6}$

$$= \frac{100\pi}{3} \text{ rad/s}$$

$$\text{Torque} = \frac{3}{\omega_s} \cdot \frac{E_f V_t}{X_s} \sin \delta$$

or $220 = \dfrac{3}{100\pi} \cdot \dfrac{520 \times 415}{2} \sin \delta$

Its solution gives $\delta = 12.33°$.

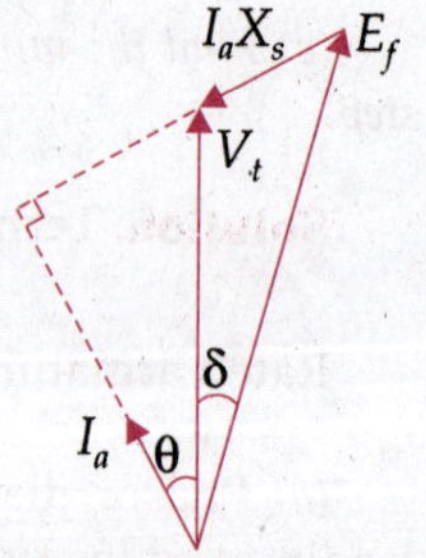

Fig 5.48: Pertaining to Example 5.11.

From the phasor diagram of Fig. 5.48, it is seen that

$$(I_a X_s)^2 = E_f^2 + V_t^2 - 2E_f \cdot V_t \cdot \cos \delta$$

or $I_a = \dfrac{1}{2}\, [300.2^2 + 230.9^2 - 2 \times 300.2 \times 239.6 \times \cos 12.33°]^{1/2} = 41.8$ A

$\therefore$ Current drawn from the supply = 41.8 A

$$\text{Power} = \sqrt{3}\, V_t \times 41.8 \cos \theta = \frac{E_f V_t}{X_s} \sin \delta, \quad \therefore \quad \cos \theta = \frac{E_f}{X_s} \sin \delta \times \frac{1}{\sqrt{3} \times 41.8}$$

$$\therefore \quad \cos \theta = \text{p.f.} = \frac{520}{2 \times 41.8 \times \sqrt{3}} \times \sin 12.33° = 0.7669 \text{ leading.}$$

Example 5.12. *A 3-phase, 50 Hz, 415 V, synchronous machine operates at rated voltage and at a leading power factor of 0.9. Shaft power is 15 kW and the excitation e.m.f. is 400 V. If per-phase resistance is 0.5 ohm, find the synchronous reactance. Neglect mechanical losses of the system.* (GATE, 1995)

Solution. Assuming the synchronous machine to be star connected.

$$V_t = \frac{415}{\sqrt{3}} = 239.6 \text{ V}, E_f = \frac{400}{\sqrt{3}} = 230.95 \text{ V}$$

As E_f is less than V_t and p.f. is leading, it must work as an alternator. For this operation, phasor diagram of Fig. 5.23 *(c)* is applicable.

$$\text{Power input} = \sqrt{3} \times 415 \times I_a \times 0.9 \text{ W}$$

$$\therefore \quad \text{Shaft power} = \sqrt{3} \times 415 \times I_a \times 0.9 - 3I_a^2 \times 0.5 = 15000 \text{ W}$$

or $\quad I_a^2 - 431.27 I_a + 10{,}000 = 0$

Its solution gives I_a = 24.585 A and 406.685 A. The higher value of armature current is not feasible.

$$\therefore \quad I_a = 24.585 \text{ A.}$$

From the phasor diagram,

$$E_f^2 = [(V_t \cos\theta + I_a r_a)^2 + (V_t \sin\theta - I_a X_s)^2]$$

or $\quad 230.95^2 = (239.6 \times 0.9 + 24.585 \times 0.5)^2 + (239.6 \times 0.436 - 24.585 \times X_s)^2$

Its solution gives $\quad X_s = 2.736\ \Omega.$

Example 5.13. *A 3-phase synchronous motor has 80% synchronous reactance and negligible resistance. When connected to bus bars at rated voltage and the excitation adjusted for an e.m.f. of 120%, the machine draws an input kVA of 100%. Find the mechanical power delivered by the motor, neglecting all losses. If for the same load on the motor, the excitation is reduced to generate an e.m.f. of 100%, what would be the input kVA?* *(I.A.S., 1994)*

Solution. Three-phase problems can be solved in per unit by treating them as single-phase problems.

Here X_s = 0.8 p.u., r_a = 0, E_f = 1.2 p.u., V_t = 1.00 p.u. For an input kVA of 100% at V_t = 1.00, $V_t I_a$ = 1.00 and therefore I_a = 1.00 p.u.

As E_f = 1.2 p.u. is more than V_t = 1.00, synchronous motor is working at a leading p.f. From Fig. 5.34 *(c)*,

$$E_f^2 = (V_t \cos\theta - I_a r_a)^2 + (V_t \sin\theta - I_a X_s)^2$$

$$1.2^2 = \cos^2\theta + (\sin\theta - 0.8)^2$$

$$1.44 = \cos^2\theta + \sin^2\theta + 0.64 - 1.6\sin\theta, \text{ or } \sin\theta = \frac{0.2}{1.6} = 0.125$$

Power factor, $\quad \cos\theta = 0.9922$ leading.

Mechanical power developed by the motor

$$= V_t I_a \cos\theta = 1 \times 1 \times 0.9922 = 0.9922 \text{ p.u.}$$

When excitation e.m.f. is reduced to 1.00 p.u. for the same load, then

$$\frac{E_f V_t}{X_s}\sin\delta = 0.9922, \quad \frac{1\times 1}{0.8}\sin\delta = 0.9922 \text{ or } \delta = 52.54°$$

From Fig. 5.34 (c), with r_a = 0,

$$(I_a X_s)^2 = E_f^2 + V_t^2 - 2E_f \cdot V_t \cos\delta$$

$$(0.8 I_a)^2 = 1^2 + 1^2 - 2 \times 1 \times 1 \times \cos 52.54° \text{ or } I_a = 1.1065 \text{ p.u.}$$

$$\therefore \quad \text{Input kVA} = V_t I_a = 1 \times 1.1065 = 1.1065 \text{ p.u. or } 110.65\% \text{ kVA.}$$

Example 5.14. *An alternator, with synchronous reactance of 0.8 p.u. is connected to an infinite bus at rated voltage. With its excitation e.m.f. adjusted to 1.3 p.u., the alternator delivers an output of 0.5 p.u. Neglect all losses.*

(a) Determine the load angle, armature current in per unit and the power factor of the alternator.

(b) The alternator is now made to operate at another value of excitation e.m.f. which results in the same values of power output and armature current. Under these conditions, find the excitation voltage, load angle and the power factor.

(c) Of the excitations in (a) and that obtained in (b), which is more likely to be used in practical situations and why?

Solution. (*a*) It is given that $X_s = 0.8$ p.u., $V_t = 1.0$, $E_f = 1.3$ p.u., $P = 0.5$ p.u.

$$\frac{E_f \cdot V_t}{X_s} \sin\delta = P$$

$$\therefore \quad \delta = \sin^{-1}\left[\frac{0.5\times 0.8}{1\times 1.3}\right] = 17.92°$$

It is seen from the phasor diagram of Fig. 5.49 that

$$(I_a X_s)^2 = E_f^2 + V_t^2 - 2E_f V_t \cos\delta$$

or

$$I_a = \frac{1}{0.8}[1.3^2 + 1^2 - 2\times 1.3\times 1\times \cos 17.92°]^{1/2} = 0.581 \text{ p.u.}$$

Also, $\quad V_t I_a \cos\theta = P$

or

$$\text{p.f.} = \cos\theta = \frac{0.5}{1\times 0.581} = 0.8606 \text{ lagging.}$$

(*b*) Another value of excitation E_{f1} is possible as shown in Fig. 5.49. As I_a, V_t and power are unchanged, the magnitude of p.f. remains the same but it is now 0.8606 leading. Fig. 5.49 shows that

$$E_{f1}^2 = (V_t\cos\theta)^2 + (V_t\sin\theta - I_a X_s)^2$$

$$= 0.8606^2 + (0.5093 - 0.581\times 0.8)^2$$

or

$$E_{f1} = 0.86175 \text{ p.u.}$$

For the same power, $\quad \dfrac{E_{f1}.V_t}{X_s}\sin\delta_1 = P$

$$\therefore \quad \delta_1 = \sin^{-1}\left[\frac{P X_S}{E_{f1}\times V_t}\right]$$

This gives load angle,

$$\delta_1 = \sin^{-1}\left[\frac{0.5\times 0.8}{0.86175\times 1.0}\right] = 27.66°$$

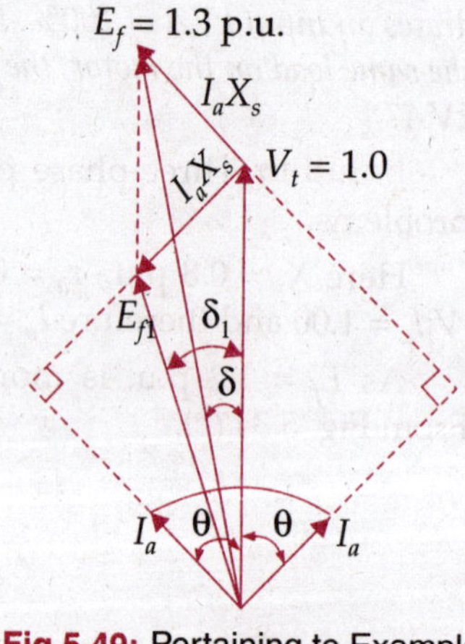

Fig 5.49: Pertaining to Example 5.14.

(*c*) $E_f = 1.30$ p.u. is more likely to be used in practical situations because the alternator, in addition to supplying the active power, must deliver reactive power to the system.

Example 5.15. *A star-connected, 11 kV turbogenerator, with synchronous impedance of 1 + j 10 Ω per phase is connected to an infinite bus at rated voltage. The alternator delivers an armature current of 100 A at unity power factor to the bus bar.*

(a) With the alternator output remaining constant, the alternator excitation is increased by 15%. Find the new values of armature current, load angle and p.f.

(b) With the excitation of (a), discuss how alternator can be made to operate at unity p.f. Under this condition, find the armature current, load angle and power delivered to the bus.

Solution. Per phase $V_t = \dfrac{11000}{\sqrt{3}} = 6351$ V

The phasor diagram at unity p.f. is drawn in Fig. 5.50. This figure gives the excitation e.m.f. as

$$E_f^2 = (V_t + I_a r_a)^2 + (I_a X_s)^2$$

$$= (6351 + 100 \times 1)^2 + (100 \times 10)^2$$

or $$E_f = 6528.05 \text{ V}$$

$$Z_s = \sqrt{1^2 + 10^2} = 10.05\ \Omega,$$

$$\alpha_z = \tan^{-1}\left(\frac{1}{10}\right) = 5.71°$$

Load angle, $$\delta = \tan^{-1}\left(\frac{100 \times 10}{6351 + 100}\right) = 8.81°$$

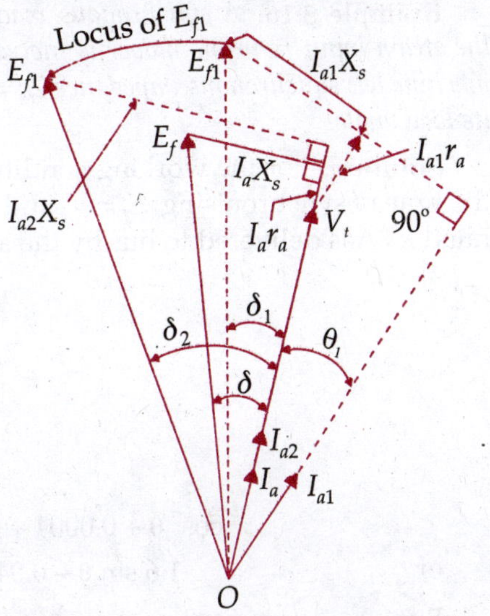

Fig 5.50: Pertaining to Example 5.15.

From Eq. (5.32), per phase power delivered to bus bar is

$$P = \frac{6528.05 \times 6351}{10.05} \sin(8.81 + 5.71°) - \left(\frac{6351}{10.05}\right)^2 \times 1$$

$$= 634947.65 \text{ W}.$$

(a) New value of excitation e.m.f., $E_{f1} = 6528.05 \times 1.15 = 7507.3$ V. With this value of E_{f1}, armature current lags bus-bar voltage V_t by an angle θ_1, Fig. 5.50. As alternator output is constant, the power delivered to bus remains unchanged. From Eq. (5.32),

$$634947.65 = \frac{7507.3 \times 6351}{10.05} \sin(\delta_1 + 5.71°) - \left(\frac{6351}{10.05}\right)^2 \times 1$$

Its simplification gives load angle

$$\delta_1 = 12.59° - 5.71° = 6.88°.$$

Also, $$(I_{a1}Z_s)^2 = 7507.3^2 + 6351^2 - 2 \times 7507.3 \times 6351 \times \cos 6.88°$$

or $$I_{a1} = \frac{1}{10.05}(1422.5611) = 141.55 \text{ A}$$

Power output of alternator = Power input to bus bar

or Power factor $$= \cos\theta = \frac{634947.65}{6351 \times 141.55} = 0.7063 \text{ lagging.}$$

(b) By increasing the steam input to the turbine, the turbogenerator can be made to work at unity power factor. Voltage V_t remains fixed as it is an infinite bus voltage. For more steam input, E_{f1} traces a locus as shown in Fig. 5.50 until unity p.f. is reached. It is seen that

$$E_{f1}^2 = (6351 + I_{a2} \times 1)^2 + (10 \cdot I_{a2})^2$$

or $$7507.3^2 = (6351 + I_{a2})^2 + (10 I_{a2})^2$$

or $101\, I_{a2}^2 + 2 \times 6351\, I_{a2} + 6351^2 - 7507.3^2 = 0$

or $$I_{a2}^2 + 125.76\, I_{a2} - 158657 = 0$$

Its solution gives armature current $I_{a2} = 340.3$ A

Power delivered to infinte bus $= V_t I_a \cos\theta = 6351 \times 340.3 \times 1$

$= 2161245.3$ W per phase

$= 6483735.9$ W for three-phases

Example 5.16. *A synchronous machine is synchronized with an infinite bus at rated voltage. Now the steam input to prime-mover is increased till synchronous machine starts operating at rated kVA. The machine has synchronous impedance $Z_s = 0.02 + j0.8$ p.u. Determine the operating p.f. of the alternator and its load angle.*

Solution. For the working conditions described, the phasor diagram is shown in Fig. 5.51. At the time of synchronising, $E_f = V_t$ and $\delta = 0$. As the steam input is increased, E_f is pushed ahead till rated kVA is delivered to bus by the alternator. The right-angled triangle OAB shows that

$$OB^2 = OA^2 + AB^2$$

$$E_f^2 = (V_t \cos\theta + I_a r_a)^2 + (I_a X_s - V_t \sin\theta)^2$$

$$1^2 = 1^2\left[\left(\cos\theta + \frac{I_a r_a}{V_t}\right)^2 + \left(\frac{I_a X_x}{V_t} - \sin\theta\right)^2\right]$$

$$1 = [(\cos\theta + 0.02)^2 + (0.8 - \sin\theta)^2]$$

$$\cos^2\theta + 0.0004 + 0.04\cos\theta + 0.64 + \sin^2\theta - 1.6\sin\theta = 1$$

or $$1.6\sin\theta - 0.04\cos\theta = 0.6404 \qquad \text{...}(i)$$

But $$A\sin\theta + B\cos\theta = \sqrt{A^2+B^2}\,\sin\left(\theta + \tan^{-1}\frac{B}{A}\right)$$

From Eq. *(i)*, we get

$$\sin\left(\theta - \tan^{-1}\frac{0.04}{1.6}\right) = \frac{0.6404}{\sqrt{1.6^2+0.04^2}} = 0.400125$$

or $$\theta = 23.586 + 1.432 = 25.018°$$

∴ $$\text{Power factor} = \cos 25.018° = 0.9062 \text{ leading}$$

$$Z_s = \sqrt{0.8^2+0.02^2} = 0.8002,$$

$$\alpha_z = \tan^{-1}\left(\frac{0.02}{0.8}\right) = 1.432°$$

Power output of generator, from Eq. (5.32), is

$$\frac{1\times 1}{0.8002}\sin(\delta + 1.432°) - \left(\frac{1}{0.8002}\right)^2 \times 0.02 = V_t I_a \cos\theta$$

$$= 1 \times 1 \times \cos\theta = 0.9062 \text{ p.u.}$$

or $$\delta = 48.171 - 1.432 = 46.74°$$

∴ $$\text{Load angle} = 46.74°.$$

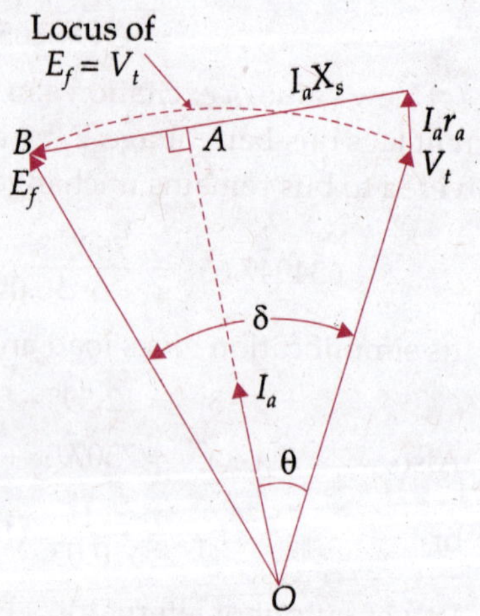

Fig 5.51: Pertaining to Example 5.16.

Example 5.17. *A 4-pole, star-connected, 50 Hz, 11 kV, 40 MVA turbogenerator, with a synchronous reactance of 0.8 p.u., is connected to a power network. This power network can be represented by 11-kV infinite bus with a series reactance of j 0.5 Ω. A voltage regulator adjusts the field current such that alternator terminal voltage remains constant at 11 kV.*

The generator delivers an output of 40 MVA.

(a) Draw the phasor diagram under the conditions specified above.

(b) Find the armature current and the alternator power factor.

(c) Find also the magnitude of excitation e.m.f.

Solution. *(a)* The equivalent circuit for the conditions specified is shown in Fig. 5.52 *(a)*. Phasor diagram is drawn in Fig. 5.52 (b) where V_b = per-phase bus bar voltage = V_t = per phase alternator terminal voltage = $\frac{11000}{\sqrt{3}}$ = 6351 V, excitation e.m.f. = E_f and $CD = I_a X_s$.

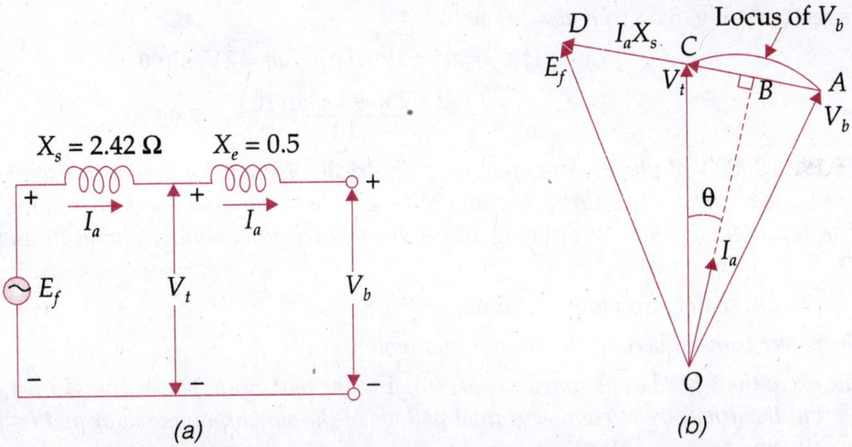

Fig 5.52: *(a)* Equivalent circuit and *(b)* phasor diagram for Example 5.17.

(*b*) Per phase armature current, $I_a = \dfrac{40,000}{\sqrt{3}\times 11} = 2099.52$ A

$$X_s \text{ in ohms} = X_s \text{ in p.u.} \times \frac{V_t}{I_a} = 0.8 \times \frac{11000}{\sqrt{3}} \times \frac{\sqrt{3}\times 11}{40,000} = 2.42\ \Omega$$

Voltage drop $AC = I_a \cdot X_e = 2099.52 \times 0.5 = 1049.76$ V

Power-factor angle, $\theta = \sin^{-1}\dfrac{BC}{OB} = \sin^{-1}\dfrac{1049.76/2}{6351} = 4.74°$

∴ Alternator power factor = cos 4.74° = 0.9966 lagging

(*c*) It is seen from the phasor diagram that

$$E_f^2 = OB^2 + (BC + CD)^2$$

$$= (6351 \times 0.9966)^2 + \left(\frac{1049.76}{2} + 2099.52 \times 2.42\right)^2$$

or $E_f = 8454.9$ V line to neutral

$= 14643.9$ V (line voltage).

Example 5.18. *A 3-phase star-connected 400 V synchronous motor takes a power input of 5472 watts at rated voltage. Its synchronous reactance is 10 Ω per phase and resistance is negligible. If its excitation voltage is adjusted equal to the rated voltage of 400 V, compute the load angle, power factor and the armature current.*

Solution. With $V_t = E_f$, the synchronous motor phase diagram is as shown in Fig. 5.53.

Here $V_t = E_f = \dfrac{400}{\sqrt{3}} = 230.95$ V

Now $\dfrac{E_f V_t}{X_s}\sin\delta = P$

or $\dfrac{400 \times 400}{3 \times 10}\sin\delta = \dfrac{5472}{3}$ or $\delta = 20°$

Thus the motor operates with a load angle of 20°. Fig. 5.53 reveals that I_a lags V_t and $V_t = E_f$ and $r_a = 0$, $\theta = \dfrac{1}{2}\delta = 10°$.

∴ Motor p.f., $\cos\theta = \cos 10° = 0.9848$ lag

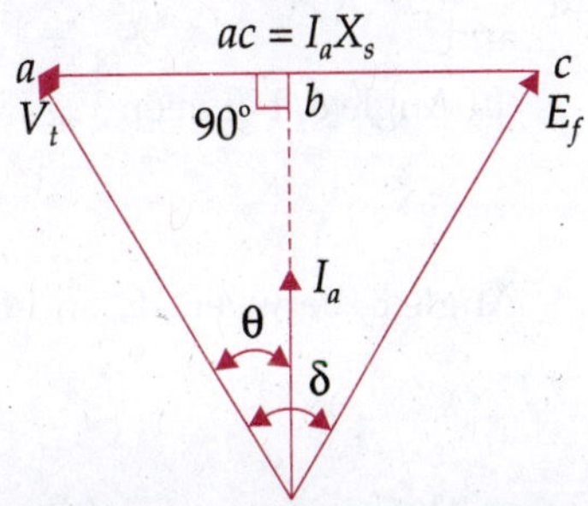

Fig 5.53: Pertaining to Example 5.18.

It is also seen from Fig. 5.53 that $ab = V_t \sin\theta$

$$I_a X_s = ac = ab + bc = 2ab = 2V_t \sin\theta$$

or

$$I_a = \frac{2 \times 230.95 \times \sin 10°}{10} = 7.96 \text{ A.}$$

Example 5.19. *A 2000 V, 3-phase, star-connected cylindrical rotor synchronous motor with synchronous reactance $X_{sm} = 2\ \Omega$ is connected to a turbogenerator with $X_{sg} = 3\ \Omega$, through transmission line of reactance $X_{tr} = 1.5\ \Omega$. The synchronous motor is drawing 100 A at rated terminal voltage and at unity power factor at its terminals.*

(a) Compute the alternator and motor excitation voltages.

(b) Find the power transfer between alternator and motor.

(c) With the excitations fixed as obtained in part (a), find the maximum power transfer between the two machines. Also find the armature current, terminal voltage of the synchronous motor and its power factor under these conditions.

Solution. *(a)* The equivalent circuit for this example is shown in Fig. 5.54 (*a*) and its phasor diagram is drawn in Fig. 5.54 (*b*).

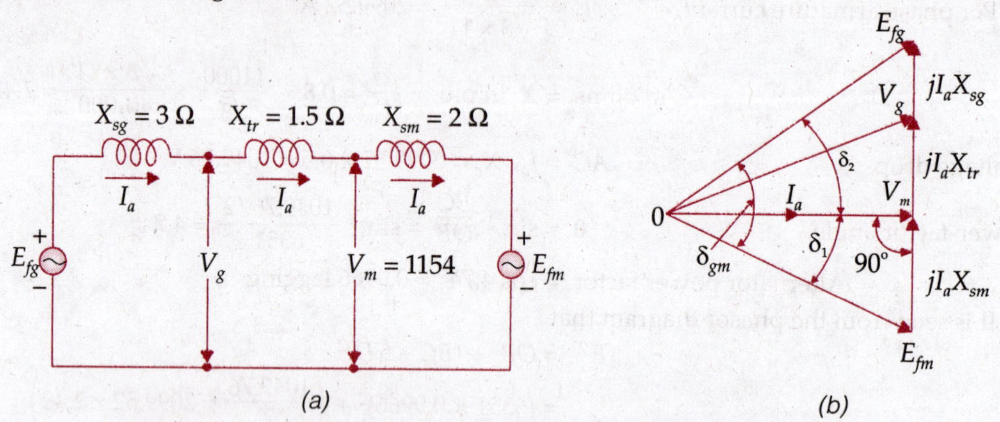

Fig 5.54: *(a)* Equivalent circuit and *(b)* phasor diagram for Example 5.19.

Rated motor terminal voltage per phase

$$V_m = \frac{2000}{\sqrt{3}} = 1154 \text{ V} \qquad I_a = 100 \text{ A.}$$

From phasor diagram of 5.54 (*b*),

$$E_{fm} = \sqrt{V_m^2 + (I_a X_{sm})^2} = \sqrt{(1154)^2 + (100 \times 2)^2} = 1170 \text{ V.}$$

and

$$E_{fg} = \sqrt{V_m^2 + \left\{I_a\left(X_{sg} + X_{tr}\right)^2\right\}} = \sqrt{(1154)^2 + (100 \times 4.5)^2} = 1240 \text{ V.}$$

(b) Angle δ_1 between V_m and E_{fm} is

$$\delta_1 = \cos^{-1}\left(\frac{V_m}{E_{fm}}\right) = \cos^{-1}\left(\frac{1154}{1170}\right) = \cos^{-1}(0.987) = 9°$$

Angle δ_2 between V_m and E_{fg} is

$$\delta_2 = \cos^{-1}\left(\frac{V_m}{E_{fg}}\right) = \cos^{-1}\left(\frac{1154}{1240}\right) = \cos^{-1}(0.929) = 21.8°.$$

∴ The power angle between E_{fg} and E_{fm} is

$$\delta_{gm} = 21.8° + 9° = 30.8°.$$

Power transfer between alternator and motor

$$= \frac{E_{fg} X_{fm}}{X_{sm} + X_{tr} + X_{sg}} \sin \delta_{gm} = \frac{(1240)(1170)}{6.5} \sin 30.8$$

$= 112.1$ kW per phase

$= 336.3$ kW for three-phases.

(c) For maximum power transfer between alternator and synchronous motor, the angle between E_{fg} and E_{fm} must be 90°, as shown in Fig. 5.54 (c). From this phasor diagram:

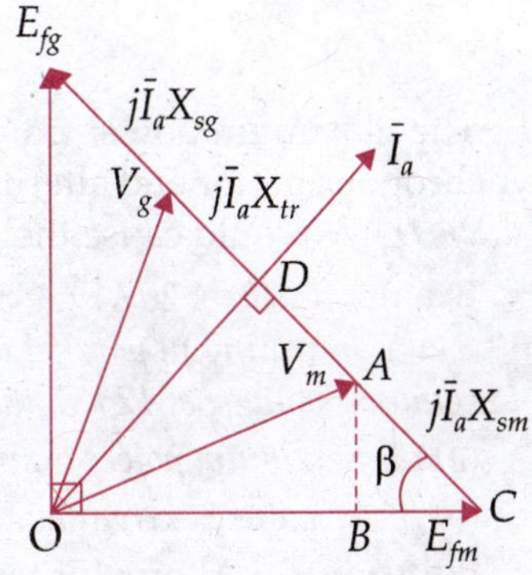

Fig 5.54: *(c)* Phasor diagram for maximum power transfer Example 5.19.

$$I_a (X_{sm} + X_{tr} + X_{sg}) = \sqrt{E_{fm}^2 + E_{fg}^2}$$

$$\therefore \quad I_a = \frac{\sqrt{(1170)^2 + (1240)^2}}{6.5} = 260 \text{ A.}$$

$$\therefore \quad P_{max} = \frac{E_{fm} E_{fg}}{X_{sm} + X_{tr} + X_{sg}} = \frac{(1170)(1240)}{6.5}$$

$= 223.0$ kW per phase

$= 669.0$ kW for 3-phases

From phasor diagram $\quad \beta = \cos^{-1} \dfrac{E_{fm}}{I_a(X_{sm} + X_{tr} + X_{sg})}$

$$= \cos^{-1}\left(\frac{1170}{1690}\right) = 46.2°.$$

$\therefore \quad AB = I_a X_{sm} \sin \beta = (260)(2)(0.721) = 375$ V

and $\quad BC = I_a X_{sm} \cos \beta = (260)(2)(0.6925) = 360$ V.

$$\therefore \quad V_m = \sqrt{(OB)^2 + (AB)^2} = \sqrt{(E_{fm} - BC)^2 + (AB)^2}$$

$$= \sqrt{(810)^2 + (375)^2}$$

$= 892.6$ V line to neutral $= 1546$ V line to line

Synchronous motor terminal voltage V_m can also be obtained from ΔOAC as under :

$$V_m^2 = E_{fm}^2 + (I_a X_{sm})^2 - 2 \cdot E_{fm} (I_a X_{sm}) \cos \beta$$

$$= 1170^2 + (2 \times 260)^2 - 2 \times 1170 \times 520 \times \cos 46.2°$$

$= 892.8$ V line to neutral

It is seen from Fig. 5.54 *(c)* that power-factor angle for synchronous motor is $\angle DOA$ = the angle between motor terminal voltage V_m and its armature current I_a. In ΔOAC,

$$\frac{AC(= I_a X_{sm})}{\sin \angle AOC} = \frac{OA(= V_m)}{\sin \beta}, \quad \frac{260 \times 2}{\sin \angle AOC} = \frac{892.6}{\sin 46.2°}$$

$\therefore \quad \angle AOC = 24.86°$

In right-angled triangle DOC, $\quad \angle DOC = 90 - \beta$.

$\therefore$ Power factor angle $\quad \angle DOA = \angle DOC - \angle AOC$

$= (90 - \beta) - \angle AOC = 90 - 46.2 - 24.86° = 18.94°$

$\therefore \quad$ Synchronous motor power factor $= \cos \angle DOA$

$= \cos 18.94° = 0.9459$ leading

Synchronous motor p.f. can also be obtained as under.

$$\text{Power} = \frac{E_{fm} \cdot V_m}{X_{sm}} \cdot \sin (E_{fm}, V_m) = V_m I_a \cos \theta$$

$$\therefore \qquad 260 \cos \theta = \frac{E_{fm}}{X_{sm}} \sin \angle AOC$$

or
$$\cos \theta = \frac{1}{260}\left[\frac{1170}{2} \sin 24.86°\right] = 0.9459 \text{ leading}$$

The maximum power transfer of 669 kW represents the maximum load that can be put on the synchronous motor and alternator for the two machine system under consideration. A load greater than 669 kW would cause the synchronous motor to loose synchronism.

Example 5.20. *A 20 MVA, 3 phase star-connected alternator, with an impedance of 5 Ω and a resistance of 0.5 Ω, is operating in parallel with constant-voltage 11 kV bus bars. If its field current is adjusted to give an excitation voltage of 12 kV, then calculate :*

(a) the maximum power output from the alternator and

(b) the armature current and power factor under maximum power conditions.

Solution. *(a)* Alternator terminal voltage per phase,

$$V_t = \frac{11,000}{\sqrt{3}} = 6350 \text{ V}.$$

Alternator excitation voltage per phase,

$$E_f = \frac{12,000}{\sqrt{3}} = 6930 \text{ V},$$

Maximum power output from the alternator, from Eq. (5.36) is given by

$$P_{og\,(max)} = \frac{E_f V_t}{Z_s} - \frac{V_t^2}{Z_s^2} r_a$$

$$= \frac{(6930)(6350)}{5} - \frac{(6350)^2}{(5)^2} \times \frac{1}{2} = \frac{6350}{5}[6930 - 635]$$

$$= 7,994,650 \text{ W} \cong 8 \text{ MW per phase} = 24 \text{ MW for 3 phases.}$$

(b)
$$\cos \theta_z = \frac{r_a}{Z_s} = \frac{0.5}{5} = 0.1$$

From Eq. (5.40),
$$I_a Z_s = \sqrt{E_f^2 + V_t^2 - 2E_f V_t \cos\theta_z}$$

$$= \sqrt{(6930)^2 + (6350)^2 - 2(6930)(6350)(0.10)} = 8920.$$

$$\therefore \qquad I_a = \frac{8920}{5} = 1784 \text{ A}.$$

From Eq. (5.38), the power-factor under maximum power conditions is given by

$$\cos \theta = \frac{E_f Z_s - V_t r_a}{I_a Z_s^2} = \frac{6930 \times 5 - 6350 \times \frac{1}{2}}{1784(5)^2} = 0.706 \text{ leading.}$$

5.9. CIRCLE DIAGRAMS OF SYNCHRONOUS MACHINES

The steady state behaviour of a synchronous machine can easily be obtained from its circle diagrams. These diagrams offer quick graphical solution to many synchronous machine problems, though the results are a little less accurate from those obtained analytically.

In this article, the circle diagrams of cylindrical-rotor synchronous motor have only been discussed.

5.9.1. Synchronous Motor Circle Diagrams

Here the excitation-circle and power-circle diagrams for a cylindrical-rotor synchronous motor are developed. These circle diagrams give the *locus of armature current* for different values of load on motor.

(a) **The excitation circles.** The excitation circle diagram gives the locus of armature current I_a, as the excitation voltage E_f and load angle δ are varied. This circle diagram for a synchronous motor is based on its voltage equation,

$$\overline{V}_t = \overline{E}_f + \overline{I}_a\overline{Z}_s \text{ or } \overline{I}_a = \frac{V_t}{\overline{Z}_s} - \frac{\overline{E}_f}{\overline{Z}_s} \qquad ...(5.47)$$

In Fig. 5.55, phasor diagram for voltage equation $\overline{V}_t = \overline{E}_f + \overline{I}_a\overline{Z}_s$ for a lagging pf load is drawn. Now the current phasor $\frac{V_t}{Z_s}$ (= OC) lagging V_t by impedance angle $\theta_z = \tan^{-1}\frac{X_s}{r_a}$ is drawn. Similarly, E_f/Z_s (= OB) lagging E_f by θ_z is shown. Note that angle between $\frac{V_t}{Z_s}$ and $\frac{E_f}{Z_s}$ is power angle δ as it is in between V_t and E_f. Draw CA parallel and equal to OB so that in magnitude $CA = OB = E_f/Z_s$. As per Eq. (5.47), $OC + CA = \frac{\overline{V}_t}{\overline{Z}_s} - \frac{\overline{E}_f}{\overline{Z}_s} = OA = I_a$, armature current. In Fig. 5.55, the orientation of phasor V_t is deliberate so that V_t/Z_s becomes horizontal.

For fixed values of V_t and E_f, V_t/Z_s and E_f/Z_s are constant. If load on motor is increased, power angle δ must increase (power $\simeq \frac{E_f V_t}{X_s}\sin\delta$) to meet the load demand. In Fig. 5.55, this can happen only if tip of phasor E_f/Z_s traces a circle with E_f/Z_s as radius and with C as centre. This circle is called **excitation circle**. As E_f/Z_s executes circle, armature current I_a, pf angle θ and load angle δ vary. This shows that excitation circle gives the locus of armature current for fixed excitation. For different shaft loads, excitation circles define the magnitude and power factor of armature current and load angle.

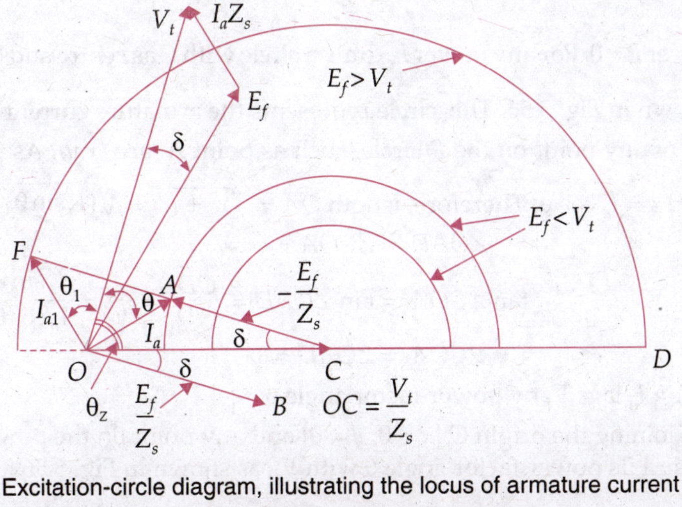

Fig 5.55: Excitation-circle diagram, illustrating the locus of armature current as E_f and δ are varied in a synchronous motor.

For $E_f > V_t$, excitation circle with radius $CD = E_f/Z_s$ is also drawn. For the same load angle δ, F is the operating point on this excitation circle. Therefore, now armature current is $OF = I_{a1}$, pf = $\cos\theta_1$ leading with load angle δ. Therefore, for $E_f > V_t$, the motor operates at a leading pf and for $E_f < V_t$, the motor operates at a lagging pf.

Note that the maximum value of load angle ACO can be equal to θ_z, as proved in Art. 5.8.

(b) **The power circles.** A power circle gives the locus of the armature current I_a, as mechanical power developed and power-factor angle θ are varied.

The power output per phase in case of a synchronous motor is

$$P = V_t I_a \cos\theta - I_a^2 r_a \qquad ...(5.49)$$

where $V_t I_a \cos\theta$ is the per phase power input to a synchronous motor and P is the mechanical power developed including both the iron and mechanical losses. In other words,

$$P = \text{Shaft power} + \text{Iron and mechanical losses.}$$

Eq. (5.49) can be re-written as

$$I_a^2 - \frac{V_t}{r_a} I_a \cos\theta + \frac{P}{r_a} = 0 \qquad ...(5.50)$$

$$\text{or } I_a^2 \cos^2\theta + I_a^2 \sin^2\theta - \frac{V_t}{r_a} I_a \cos\theta + \frac{P}{r_a} = 0 \qquad ...(5.51)$$

Let $x = I_a \sin\theta$ and $y = I_a \cos\theta$. With this substitution, Eq. (5.51) becomes,

$$x^2 + y^2 - \frac{V_t}{r_a} y + \frac{P}{r_a} = 0 \qquad ...(5.52)$$

Eq. (5.52) is the equation of a circle* with its centre at $\left(0, \dfrac{V_t}{2r_a}\right)$.

and $\qquad$ radius $= \sqrt{\left(\dfrac{V_t}{2r_a}\right)^2 - \dfrac{P}{r_a}}$

The construction of power circle diagram is as follows. Draw a vertical line $CO = \dfrac{V_t}{2r_a}$ to scale. Now draw a circle with C as centre and $CO = \dfrac{V_t}{2r_a}$ as radius. This circle represents the armature current locus for power $P = 0$. For any power P, draw a circle with C as centre and $CA = \sqrt{\left(\dfrac{V_t}{2r_a}\right)^2 - \dfrac{P}{r_a}}$ as radius ; this is shown in Fig. 5.56. This circle represents the armature current locus for power P.

The co-ordinate of any point on the P circle, such as point A, are (x,y). As per Eqs. (5.51) and (5.52), $x = I_a \sin\theta$ and $y = I_a \cos\theta$. Therefore, length $OA = \sqrt{x^2+y^2} = \sqrt{(I_a \sin\theta)^2 + (I_a \cos\theta)^2} = I_a$.

Now $\qquad \angle OAD = \angle COA$

$$\therefore \qquad \tan\angle COA = \tan\angle OAD = \frac{OD}{AD} = \frac{x}{y} = \frac{I_a \sin\theta}{I_a \cos\theta} = \tan\theta$$

$$\therefore \qquad \angle COA = \angle OAD = \theta$$

Thus current $OA = I_a$ lags V_t by power-factor angle θ.

Therefore, a line joining the origin O $[x = 0, y = 0]$ and any point on the power circle, gives the armature current I_a and its power-factor angle θ with V_t, as shown in Fig. 5.56.

* The general equation of a circle is $x^2 + y^2 + 2gx + 2fy + c = 0$, with its centre at $(-g, -f)$ and radius $= \sqrt{g^2 + f^2 - c}$.

In Fig. 5.56, when $P = 0$, the radius of power circle $= \dfrac{V_t}{2r_a}$ showing thereby that the zero-power circle passes through origin, marked O in Fig. 5.56. As the power developed P, goes on increasing, the radius of the power circle goes on reducing and maximum power would occur when the radius of power circle is zero, *i.e.*, when

$$\sqrt{\left(\frac{V_t}{2r_a}\right)^2 - \left(\frac{P_{max}}{r_a}\right)} = 0 \text{ or } \frac{P_{max}}{r_a} = \frac{V_t^2}{4r_a^2} \text{ or}$$

$$P_{max} = \frac{V_t^2}{4r_a}$$

Corresponding to the maximum power P_{max}, the power circle of zero radius is the point C itself and the armature current is $\dfrac{V_t}{2r_a}$ · in phase with V_t, *i.e.*, power factor is unity.

Maximum power input

$$= V_t I_a \cos\theta = V_t \frac{V_t}{2r_a} \cdot 1 = \frac{V_t^2}{2r_a}$$

and maximum power output,

$$P_{max} = \frac{V_t^2}{4r_a}.$$

∴ Efficiency at maximum output = 50%.

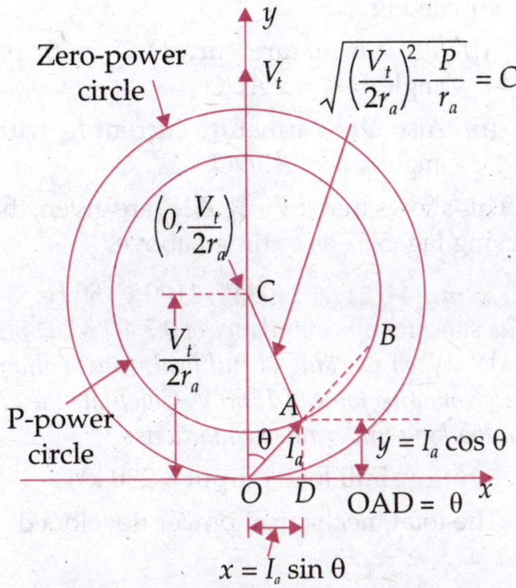

Fig 5.56: Power circle diagram illustrating the locus of armature current for constant mechanical power developed.

An efficiency of 50% is too low a value for a synchronous motor. At this efficiency, losses would be about half of the input and temperature rise would be far above the permissible termperature of the motor. As such, maximum power output of $V_t^2/4r_a$ can never be obtained in practice from a synchronous motor.

Eq. (5.50) when solved for I_a, for given values of power and power factor gives two currents, which are also indicated as OA and OB in the power-circle diagram of Fig. 5.56.

(c) **Superimposition of circle diagrams.** With the superimposition of excitation and power circle diagrams, a quick graphical solution can be obtained for many synchronous motor problems.

Fig. 5.57 shows the superimposition of power and excitation circle diagrams. Here with C as centre, a circle of radius $CO = \dfrac{V_t}{2r_a}$ is drawn. This gives zero-power circle. Now draw another circle with C as centre and with radius $CG = \sqrt{\left(\dfrac{V_t}{2r_a}\right)^2 - \dfrac{P}{r_a}}$.

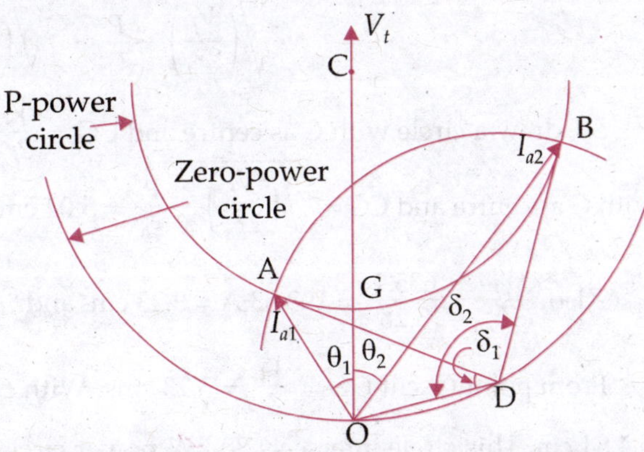

Fig 5.57: Power and excitation circles superimposed.

This is the P-power circle. From point O, cut $OD = \frac{V_t}{Z_s}$. With D as centre, draw excitation circle or arc of radius $DA = \frac{E_f}{Z_s}$ as in Fig. 5.55. This circle interacts P-power circle at points A and B. Join A and B to both points O and D as shown in Fig. 5.57.

Now in Fig. 5.57,

(i) OA = armature current I_{a1} with power factor = $\cos \theta_1 = \cos \angle AOC$ leading and load angle = $\delta_1 = \angle ADO$

(ii) Also OB = armature current I_{a2} with power factor = $\cos \theta_2 = \cos \angle BOC$ lagging and load angle = $\delta_2 = \angle BDO$.

This shows that if V_t, E_f, Z_s, r_a are given, then for power P, I_a, pf and δ can be obtained graphically by using Fig. 5.57 as outlined above.

Example 5.21. *A 230 kW, 1100 V, 50 Hz, 3-phase star-connected cylindrical-rotor synchronous motor has its synchronous impedance of 0.7 + j 3.2 Ω per phase. Its core loss is 6 kW, and friction and windage loss is 4 kW. When working at full load, rated voltage and rated frequency, its field current is adjusted to give an electromotive force of 1650 V. Calculate the armature current, power factor, load angle and power input when working under rated conditions.*

Solution. Full load output = 230 kW.

The total mechanical power developed = shaft power + core loss + friction and windage loss

$$= 230 + 6 + 4 = 240 \text{ kW}$$

$\therefore$ Per-phase developed power, $P = \frac{240}{3} = 80$ kW.

Terminal voltage per phase, $V_t = \frac{1100}{\sqrt{3}} = 635.1$ V

Emf per phase, $E_f = \frac{1650}{\sqrt{3}} = 952.6$ V

Synchronous impedance, $Z_s = 0.7 + j\,3.2 = \sqrt{0.7^2 + 3.2^2} = 3.28\ \Omega$

$\frac{V_t}{2r_a} = \frac{635.1}{2 \times 0.7} = 453.6$ A. Take a scale of 60 A = 1 cm. $\therefore$ $\frac{V_t}{2r_a} = \frac{453.6}{60} = 7.56$ cm.

$$\sqrt{\left(\frac{V_t}{2r_a}\right)^2 - \frac{P}{r_a}} = \sqrt{\left(\frac{453.6}{2 \times 0.7}\right)^2 - \frac{80,000}{0.7}} = 302.5 \text{ A} = 5.04 \text{ cm}$$

So, draw a circle with C as centre and $CO = \frac{V_t}{2r_a} = 7.56$ cm as radius. Now draw another circle with C as centre and $CG = \sqrt{\left(\frac{V_t}{2r_a}\right)^2 - \frac{P}{r_a}} = 5.04$ cm as radius.

Also, $\frac{V_t}{Z_s} = \frac{635.1}{3.28} = 193.63$ A = 3.23 cm and $\frac{E_f}{Z_s} = \frac{952.6}{3.28} = 290.43$ A = 4.84 cm.

From point O, cut $OD = \frac{V_t}{Z_s} = 3.23$ cms. With D as centre, draw excitation circle of radius $\frac{E_f}{Z_s}$ = 4.84 cm. This circle intersects 80 kW power circle at points A and B in Fig. 5.57. Join A and B to both the points O and D as shown in the figure.

Now, in Fig. 5.57, OA = armature current $I_{a1} = 3.06 \times 60 = 183.6$ A, power factor = $\cos \angle AOC = \cos \theta_1 = \cos 23° = 0.92$ lead and load angle $\delta_1 = \angle ODA = 38°$

Also, $I_{a2} = 7.98 \times 60 = 478.8$ A, pf = cos ∠BOC = $\cos \theta_2 = \cos 40° = 0.766$ lead and load angle $\delta_2 =$ 117.5°. Since load angle cannot exceed $\theta_z = 77.7$, point B on power circle gives unstable operation. Therefore, here armature current = 183.6 A, pf = 0.92 lead and load angle = 38°.

$$\text{Power input} = \text{developed power} + \text{total } I^2R \text{ losses}$$
$$= 240{,}000 + 3 \times 183.6^2 \times 0.7 = 310789 \text{ W} = 310.789 \text{ kW}.$$

Example 5.22. *Repeat Example 5.21, if the armature resistance r_a is neglected.*

Solution. Since armature resistance $r_a = 0$, $\dfrac{V_t}{2r_a} \to$ infinity. Similarly $\sqrt{\left(\dfrac{V_t}{2r_a}\right)^2 - \dfrac{P}{r_a}} \to$ infinity.

Thus the power circles become straight lines with centre at infinity. Here $V_t = 635.1$ V, $E_f = 952.6$ V, $X_s = 3.2\ \Omega$

Developed power per phase, $P = 80$ kW

Also input power per phase = $V_t I_a \cos\theta = 80$ kW, because armature resistance is neglected.

$\therefore$ Working component of armature current $= I_a \cos\theta = \dfrac{80{,}000}{635.1} = 125.96\ A$

Scale 60 A = 1 cm, $\therefore\ I_a \cos\theta = \dfrac{125.96}{60} = 2.1$ cm.

Take V_t along y-axis, draw $I_a \cos\theta = OG = 125.96\ A = 2.1$ cm in phase with V_t, see Fig. 5.58. Draw a line through G parallel to x-axis, this horizontal line represents the power of 80 kW per phase. Note that it is also the locus of armature current for different values of excitations.

Take $OD = \dfrac{V_t}{X_s} = \dfrac{635.1}{3.2} = 198.47$ A = 3.31 cm, $\theta_z = 90°$ away from V_t, *i.e.*, along x-axis. With D as centre, draw a curve of redius $\dfrac{E_f}{X_s} = DA = \dfrac{952.6}{3.2} = 297.68$ A ≅ 5 cm. Join A with O and D. Now armature current $OA = I_a = 2.92 \times 60 = 175.2\ A$, pf = cos ∠AOG = cos 28.5° = 0.879 lead and load-angle δ = ∠ADO = 25°, see Fig. 5.58.

Since armature resistance $r_a = 0$, power input = power developed = 240 kW.

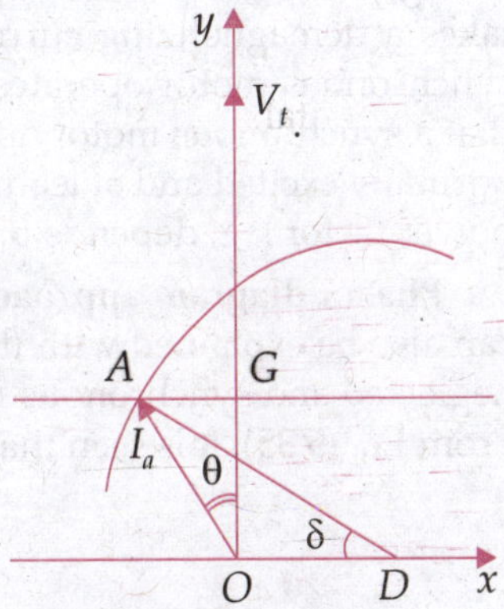

Fig 5.58: Pertaining to Example 5.22.

5.10. POWER FACTOR CONTROL OF SYNCHRONOUS MACHINES

Power factor of synchronous machines can be controlled by the adjustment of their field excitation. In this article, the effect of variation of field current on the operating power factor of synchronous machines is examined first for motors and then for alternators connected to an infinite bus.

5.10.1. Power-factor Control of Synchronous Motors

The object of this article is to present a physical picture of what happens in a synchronous motor, when its field current is varied. The conclusions arrived from this physical understanding, are further supported by synchronous motor phasor diagrams for different field currents.

Physical Concept: It should be remembered at the outset that A.C. electromagnetic devices must draw a magnetizing current from the A.C. source, in order to establish the working flux. This magnetizing current lags the applied voltage by almost 90°. In other words, the function of the magnetizing current or lagging reactive VA, drawn by A.C. electromagnetic device (or an A.C. motor), is to set up the flux in the magnetic circuit of the device.

A synchronous motor is a doubly-excited machine, its armature winding is energised from an A.C. source and its field winding from a D.C. source. When synchronous motor is working at constant applied voltage, the resultant air gap flux as demanded by constant V_t, remains substantially constant as per Eq. (5.24). This resultant air-gap flux is established by the co-operation of both A.C. in the armature winding and D.C. in the field winding. If the field current is sufficient enough to set up the air-gap flux, as demanded by constant V_t, then magnetizing current or lagging reactive VA required from the A.C. source is zero and, therefore, the motor operates at unity power factor. This field current, which causes unity power factor operation of the synchronous motor, is called *normal excitation or normal field current*. If the field current is made less than the normal excitation, *i.e.*, the motor is *under-excited*, then the deficiency in flux (= constant air-gap flux–flux set up by D.C. in the field winding) must be made up by the armature winding m.m.f. In order to do the needful, the armature winding draws a magnetizing current or lagging reactive VA from the A.C. source and as a result of it, the motor operates at a lagging power factor.

In case the field current is made more than its normal excitation, *i.e.*, the motor is *over-excited*, then the excess flux (= Flux set up by D.C. in the field winding—resultant air-gap flux) must be neutralized by the armature winding. The armature can do so only if it draws a demagnetizing component of current from the A.C. source. Since in a motor, the magnetizing current lags the applied voltage by about 90°, the demagnetizing component of current must lead the applied voltage by about 90°. In view of this, the excess flux can be counterbalanced only if the armature takes a demagnetizing current or leading reactive VA from the A.C. source—consequently the synchronous motor operates at a leading power factor. It can, therefore, be inferred from above that a synchronous motor operates at a lagging power factor when underexcited, at unity pf when normally excited and at leading power factor when overexcited. The extent of power factor lead or power factor lag, depends upon the degree of over-excitation or under-excitation.

Phasor diagram approach. The effect of field current on the synchronous-motor power factor can also be explained with the help of its phasor diagram. For simplicity, armature resistance r_a is neglected and synchronous reactance X_s and terminal voltage V_t are assumed to remain constant. From Eq. (5.35), it is seen that the per phase power is given by

$$P = \frac{E_f V_t}{X_s} \sin \delta = V_t I_a \cos \theta.$$

For constant power output, therefore, $E_f \sin \delta$ and $I_a \cos \theta$ must remain constant, because V_t and X_s are constant. This means that as the field current is varied, excitation voltage E_f varies, but component of E_f normal to V_t, *i.e.*, $E_f \sin \delta$ must remain constant. As E_f varies, $I_a X_s$ and therefore armature current I_a also varies, but in such a manner as to keep $I_a \cos \theta$ constant.

When the excitation voltage is E_{f1}, the motor is underexcited and the armature current I_{a1} must lag V_t by p.f. angle θ_1, so that the relation $\overline{E}_f + j\overline{I}_a X_s = \overline{V}_t$, is satisfied. When the excitation voltage is increased to E_{f2} by increasing the field current, the angle must decrease from δ_1 to δ_2 so that $E_{f1} \sin \delta_1 = E_{f2} \sin \delta_2$. In order to satisfy the relation $\overline{E}_f + j\overline{I}_a X_s = \overline{V}_t$ the phasor of armature current must change to I_{a2}, see Fig. 5.59 and the motor, therefore, operates at unity power factor. When the excitation is increased to E_{f3}, the load angle must decrease from δ_2 to δ_3, so that $E_{f3} \sin \delta_3 = E_{f2} \sin \delta_2 = E_{f1} \sin \delta_1$. In order to satisfy the voltage relation $\overline{E}_f + j\overline{I}_a X_s = \overline{V}_t$ again, the phase of armature current I_{a3} is pushed ahead of V_t as shown in Fig. 5.59 and, therefore, the motor now operates at a leading power factor. Note that the active power components of armature currents are equal, *i.e.*, $I_{a1} \cos \theta_1 = I_{a2} \cos \theta_2 = I_{a3} \cos \theta_3$. Fig. 5.59 also reveals that the armature current is minimum at unity p.f. and more at leading or lagging p.fs. This variation of armature current with the changes in field current is plotted in Fig. 5.60 *(a)* for different fixed powers. Since the plot resembles the letter V, these are called *V*-curves of a synchronous motor. Note that *V*-curves show the relation between armature current and field current with constant shaft load and for constant terminal voltage. In Fig. 5.60 *(a)* the unity p.f. dotted curve, joining all the minimum-armature current points, is called unity power factor *compounding curve*. Points to the left of unity pf compounding curve correspond to underexcitation and lagging current operation. Points to the right of unity pf curve correspond to overexcitation and leading current operation. Similarly compounding curves for 0.8 p.f. lag and 0.8 p.f. lead, are shown by dotted curves in Fig. 5.60 *(a)*. The compounding curves for other p.fs. can also be drawn if required. These compounding curves show the manner in which the field current should be varied in order to maintain constant p.f. under changing loads. Note that the synchronous motor compounding curves are similar to the synchronous generator compounding curves of Fig. 5.39.

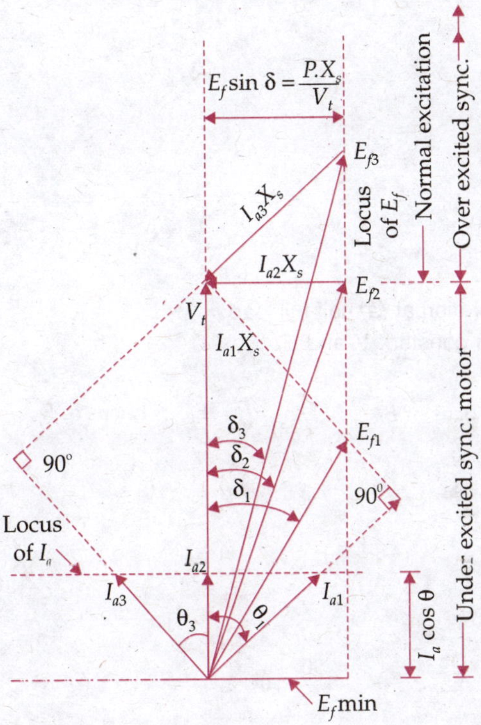

Fig 5.59: Effect of field current on synchronous motor power factor.

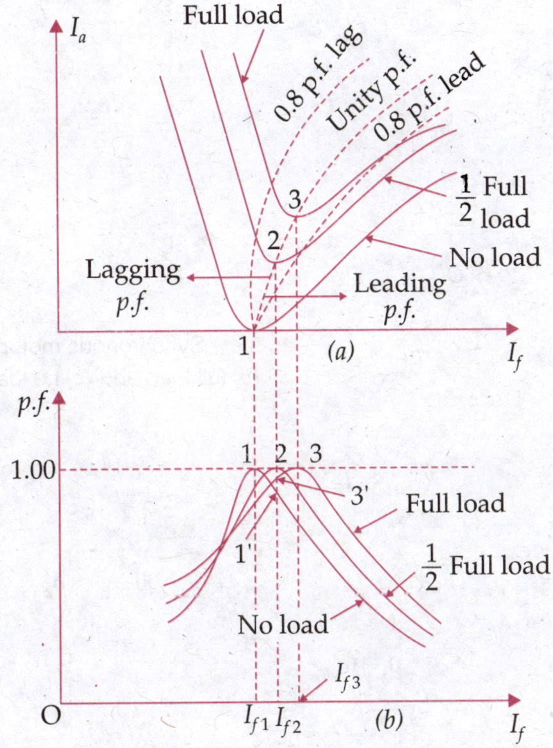

Fig 5.60: Synchronous motor *(a)* V-curves and *(b)* power factor versus field current curves.

In Fig. 5.60 *(a)*, minimum armature currents give motor operation at unity power factor. These points are marked 1, 2 and 3 for operation at no load, half-full load and full load respectively.

If motor power factor is plotted as a function of field current, the curves of Fig. 5.60 *(b)* are obtained. In Fig. 5.60 *(b)*, points 1, 2, 3 denote unity power-factor working. Note that field current I_{f3} for u.p.f. at full load is more than the field current I_{f2} for u.p.f. at half load and I_{f1} for u.p.f. at no load. To the left of points 1, 2, 3, the motor operates at lagging p.f. and to the right of these points, the motor operates at leading pf.

Supposing the motor is operating at half-full load at upf with current I_{a1} and load angle δ_1, Fig. 5.61 *(a)*. If load is increased from half full load to full load, current and load angle must increase to some higher values, say I_{a2} and δ_2 with E_f remaining constant, Fig. 5.61 *(b)*. Here it is seen that pf is lagging. When load is reduced to no load, current and load angle must decrease, say I_{a3} and δ_3 with E_f remaining constant. This is shown in Fig. 5.61 *(c)*. It is seen from this figure that here the pf is leading. Fig. 5.60 *(b)* also provides the same information.

At half-full load, unity pf operating point is 2 and field current is I_{f2}. If load is increased to full load for the same E_f or I_{f2}, the operating point shift to 3′, indicating lagging pf operation at full load. Also, for no load operation, point 2 shifts to 1′ showing leading pf operation.

Supposing the motor is operating at unity pf at full load as shown in Fig. 5.62 *(a)*. When load is reduced to half and also to no load, Figs. 5.62 *(b)* and *(c)* show that motor now operates at leading pfs. Fig 5.60 *(b)* also reveals the same results.

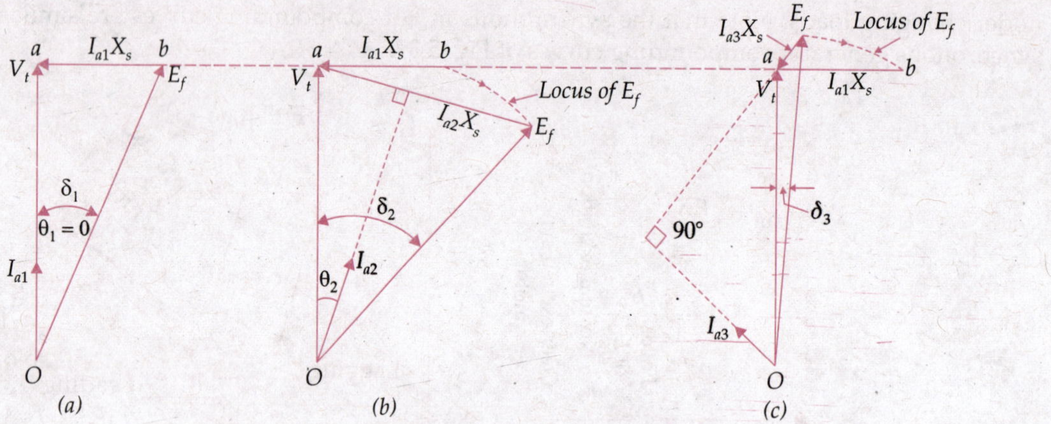

Fig 5.61: Synchronous motor operation at *(a)* half full load *(b)* full load and *(c)* no load for constant V_t and E_f.

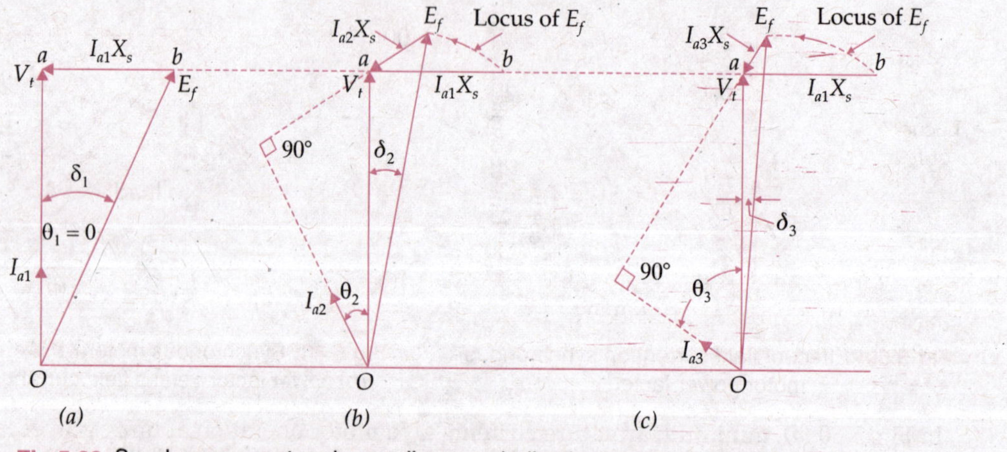

Fig 5.62: Synchronous motor phasor diagrams indicating operation at *(a)* full-load *(b)* half-full load and *(c)* no load for constant V_t and E_f.

Since power factor versus field current plots in Fig. 5.60 *(b)* resemble inverted letter *V*; these are, therefore, often called **inverted V-curves** of a synchronous motor.

The ability of a synchronous motor to operate at leading power factors when overexcited, is utilised for improving the power factor of many supply systems. For example, an industrial organisation having a large number of induction motors, may employ a synchronous motor to improve the power factor of the entire load and thus save the organisation from the low-power factor penalty clause.

It should be remembered that an induction motor must take lagging kVAr from the supply system, in order to set up its working air-gap flux. A single line diagram of a 3-phase induction motor connected to an A.C. source is given in Fig. 5.63 *(a)*. When a synchronous motor is connected in parallel with it ; then this motor, when overexcited, generates leading reactive power and these are supplied locally to meet the lagging kVAr needed by the induction motor. As a result, distribution lines are relieved completely or partially from supplying the lagging kVAr needed by the induction motor. Now the supply lines have to handle reduced kVA and reduced current; this leads to better operation of the overall system, see Art. 5.19. Note that the induction motor is still operating at the same lagging p.f., absorbing same kVAr and kW. It is the combined load, consisting of over-excited synchronous motor and induction motor, that is working now at an improved p.f. In case the demand of lagging kVAr required by induction motor is completely met by the overexcited synchronous motor locally, then the combined load operates at unity p.f.

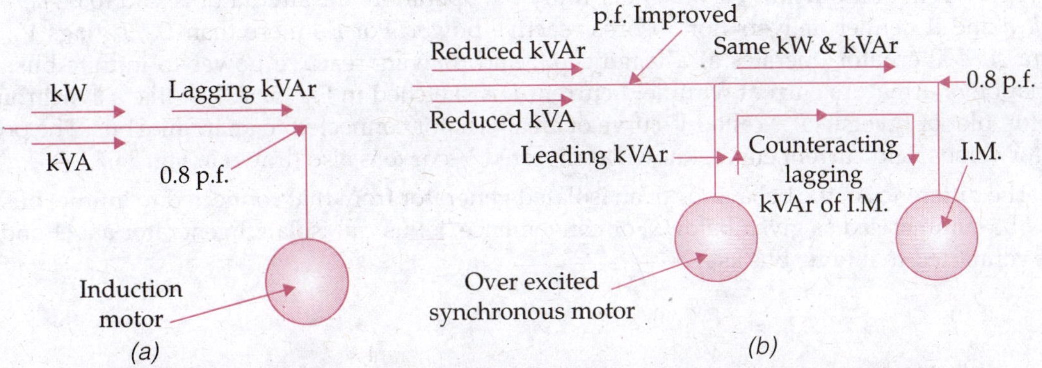

Fig 5.63: *(a)* 3-Phase Induction Motor *(b)* An overexcited synchronous motor in parallel with induction motor.

When the primary function of a synchronous motor is to improve the power factor of the system or to control the flow of kVAr, then the synchronous motor carries no mechanical load on its shaft. Such an unloaded synchronous motor with no shaft extension, is called a *synchronous condenser* or synchronous compensator and is used in large power systems, where static capacitors are uneconomical.

Under ideal conditions, the synchronous motor phasor diagrams for z.p.f. leading and z.p.f. lagging are drawn in Fig. 5.64 *(a)* and *(b)* respectively. As E_f and V_t are in phase, load angle δ is zero and power $P = 0$. From these phasor diagrams, it is observed as under :

(a) As I_a leads V_t by 90° just like a capacitor, synchronous motor behaves like a capacitor bank under z.p.f. leading operation.

(b) As I_a lags V_t by 90° just like an inductor, synchronous motor behaves like an inductor bank under z.p.f. lagging operation.

Fig. 5.65 shows the *V*-curve of an ideal synchronous motor.

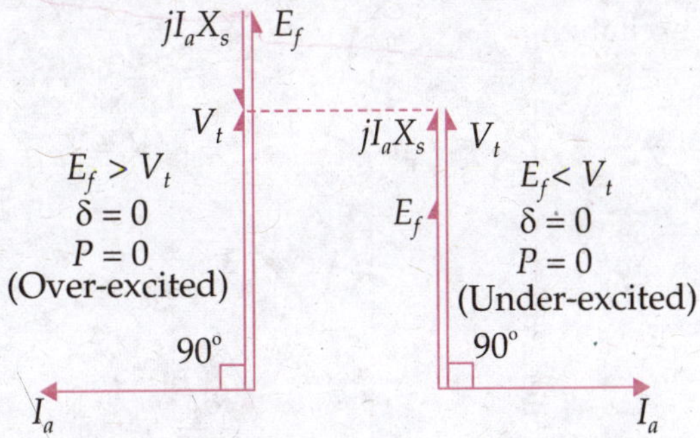

Fig 5.64: Synchronous motor *(a)* zpf leading *(b)* zpf lagging

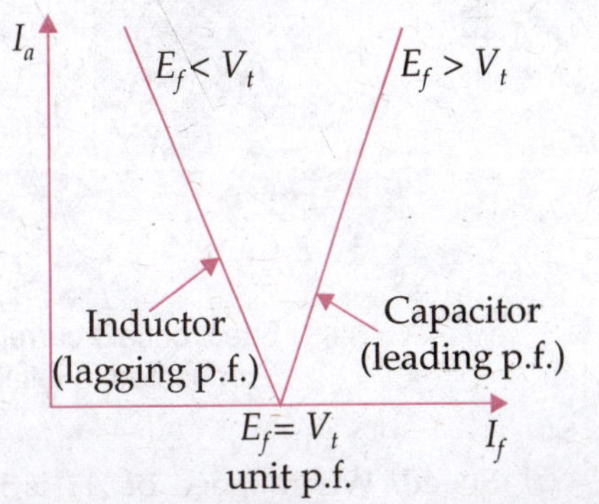

Fig 5.65: Ideal synchronous motor *V*-curve

5.10.2. Power-factor Control of Alternators

For a single alternator, isolated alternator or stand-alone alternator, delivering power to a load, the relevant characteristics are already described in Art. 5.7. In this section of the article, the behaviour of cylindrical-rotor alternator connected to an infinite bus is discussed briefly.

For alternator, the voltge equation is $\bar{E}_f = \bar{V}_t + j\bar{I}_a X_s$ with zero armature circuit resistance. The phasor diagram of Fig. 5.66 is drawn like Fig. 5.59. When excitation e.m.f. is E_{f1}, the alternator is *underexcited* and the armature current I_{a1} is leading $V_t = V_b$ = bus-bar voltage. Therefore, for E_{f1}, underexcited alternator operates at a leading p.f. and absorbs reactive power from infinite bus.

With an increase in field current, excitation e.m.f. rises. For excitation e.m.f. E_{f2}, armature current I_{a2} is in phase with $V_t = V_b$. Under unity p.f. operation, the alternator is said to be *normally excited* and it neither delivers nor absorbs reactive power. For E_{f3} more than E_{f2}, I_{a3} lags V_t. The *overexcited* alternator operates at a lagging p.f. and delivers reactive power to infinite bus. The variation of armature current with field current I_f is sketched in Fig. 5.67. Just like a synchronous motor, plot of I_a versus I_f is called *V*-curve of an alternator connected to an infinite bus. The power factor versus field current curve, known as inverted *V*-curve is also drawn in Fig. 5.67.

The difference in the behaviour of an isolated generator from that connected to infinite bus can now be summarised as given below. For convenience, let us call isolated generator as *A*1 and the one connected to infinite bus as *A*2.

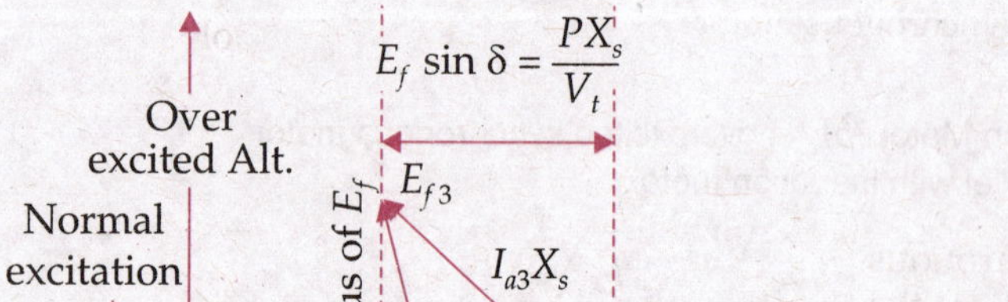

Fig 5.66: Effect of field current on an alternator connected to infinite bus.

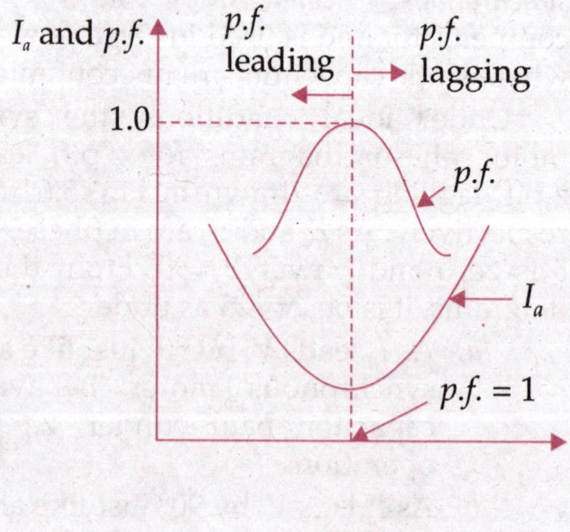

Fig 5.67: V and inverted V-curves for alternator connected to infinite bus.

(i) **Speed.** When speed of *A*1 is increased, its excitation e.m.f. and terminal voltage both rise. Its output frequency also increases with increase in speed and as a consequence its

synchronous reactance also rises. In other words, operating frequency of an isolated generator can be controlled above or below that given on the name plate.

Speed of $A2$ cannot be altered as its operating frequency and, therefore, speed are governed by bus-bar frequency. Further, terminal voltage of $A2$ is fixed by bus-bar voltage.

(ii) **Field excitation.** If field current of $A1$ is increased, its excitation e.m.f. and terminal voltage both rise. Its operating power factor depends upon the nature of load. For example, for heater load, operating p.f. of isolated generator is always unity.

If excitation of $A2$ is increased, its operating p.f. will change from leading to lagging if already operating at a leading p.f., see Fig. 5.66. In other words, for a constant power, alternator V-curves can be obtained only for $A2$ and not for alternator $A1$.

(iii) **Prime-mover input.** If prime-mover input to $A1$ is increased, its operating speed and frequency go up. As a result, its excitation e.m.f., terminal voltage and power delivered to load increase.

When prime-mover input to $A2$ is increased, its excitation e.m.f., terminal voltage and operating frequency cannot alter. But the active power delivered to infinite bus rises because of the increase in load angle as E_f shifts away from infinite bus voltage $V_t = V_b$.

5.11. TWO-REACTION THEORY OF SALIENT-POLE MACHINES

In e.m.f. method of voltage regulation, the armature-reaction m.m.f. F_a is accounted for by means of an equivalent armature-reaction e.m.f. E_{ar}, see Fig. 5.19 *(a)* and therefrom the concept of synchronous reactance X_s is evolved. This is permissible only in case of non-salient pole machines where the air-gap is uniform and the reluctance of the magnetic circuit is substantially constant-whatever orientation of the field poles with respect to the armature m.m.f. wave may be.

In salient-pole machines, the armature m.m.f. cannot be accounted for by introducing one equivalent reactance. This is because the air-gap is not uniform and the reluctance along the polar or direct axis is considerably smaller than that along the interpolar or quadrature axis. Therefore, the cylindrical-rotor theory, based on constant air-gap reluctance, cannot be applied to a salient-pole machine which has different air-gap reluctances along its periphery.

In a salient-pole synchronous machine, the location of armature-winding m.m.f. relative to the field-winding m.m.f. is similar to that obtained in a cylindrical-rotor synchronous machine. In order to recapitulate this, Fig. 5.68 *(a)* is drawn by referring to Fig. 5.5 (a), but with round rotor replaced by salient-pole rotor. In Fig. 5.68 *(a)*, field poles N, S on rotor are shown facing coil-sides a, a'. Therefore, maximum e.m.f. is generated in coil a, a'. For the anticlockwise direction of rotor rotation, the direction of e.m.f. is indicated by dots in the coil-sides (a, b', c') under the influence of N-pole and by crosses in the coil-sides (a', b, c) under the effect of S-pole.

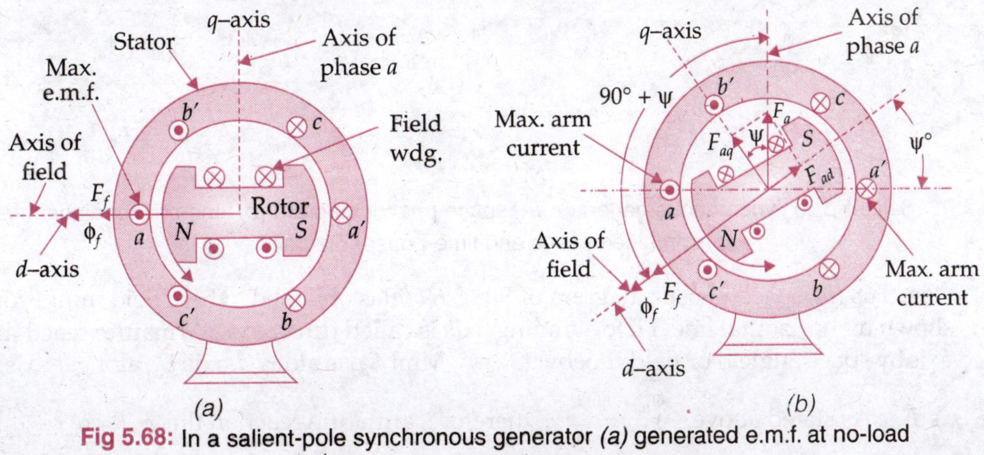

Fig 5.68: In a salient-pole synchronous generator *(a)* generated e.m.f. at no-load *(b)* spatial orientation of F_a relative to F_f

As before, the armature current is assumed to lag excitation e.m.f. E_f by a time-phase angle $\psi°$ so that internal p.f. is cos $\psi°$ lagging. Therefore, current in coil a, a' would attain maximum value after the field poles have moved to a new position $\psi°$ electrical ahead of the maximum e.m.f. position of Fig. 5.68 *(a)*. In other words, by the time armature current in coil a, a' reaches maximum value, the rotor poles N, S would have moved forward by $\psi°$ electrical from its maximum e.m.f. position of Fig. 5.68 *(a)*. This is shown in Fig. 5.68 *(b)*, since coil a, a' representing phase *'a'* carries maximum current, peak of the resultant rotating armature m.m.f. F_a is directed vertically upward along the axis of phase *'a'*. Fig. 5.68 *(b)* reveals that armature m.m.f. F_a lags field m.m.f. F_f by a space angle of $(90 + \psi°)$ as in a cylindrical-rotor alternator of Fig. 5.8. With changes in internal p.f. angle ψ, the reluctance offered to armature m.m.f. F_a varies because of a change in its spatial orientation relative to the field-pole axis or direct axis. This shows that the magnitude of armature reaction flux per pole ϕ_a (= F_a/ reluctance) varies with a change in angle ψ. This difficulty of encountering different reluctances by armature reaction m.m.f. F_a, as the angle ψ changes, can be overcome by resorting to two-reaction theory suggested by Blondel.

According to *two-reaction theory*, the sinusoidal armature m.m.f. F_a is resolved into two sinusoidal components, one F_{ad} along d-axis and the other F_{aq} along q-axis. It is seen from Fig. 5.68 (b) that F_{ad} experiences minimum but constant reluctance along d-axis. Similarly, component F_{aq} encounters maximum but constant reluctance along q-axis. The d-axis component F_{ad} is seen to be demagnetizing in nature in Fig. 5.68 *(b)*. In general, the d-axis component F_{ad} is magnetizing in nature if ψ is an angle of lead and is demagnetizing in nature if ψ is an angle of lag, as in Fig. 5.68 *(b)*, *i.e.*, F_{ad} produces only a change in the field strength. The q-axis component F_{aq} produces only a distortion of the field-flux wave. In a salient-pole synchronous machine, the reluctance along the field-pole axis *i.e.*, d-axis is less than that along the q-axis. In view of this, the component fluxes $\phi_{ad} = F_{ad}$ divided by reluctance along d-axis and $\phi_{aq} = F_{aq}$ divided by reluctance along q-axis are not in the same ratio as are the component mmfs, *i.e.* $\dfrac{\phi_{ad}}{\phi_{aq}} \neq \dfrac{F_{ad}}{F_{aq}}$.

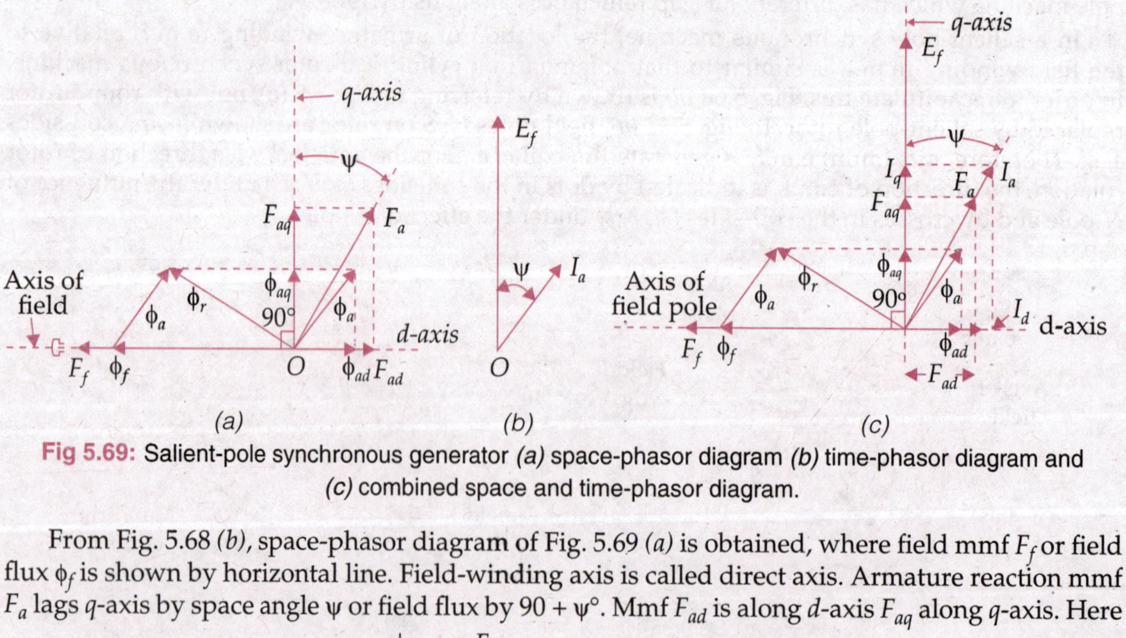

Fig 5.69: Salient-pole synchronous generator *(a)* space-phasor diagram *(b)* time-phasor diagram and *(c)* combined space and time-phasor diagram.

From Fig. 5.68 *(b)*, space-phasor diagram of Fig. 5.69 *(a)* is obtained, where field mmf F_f or field flux ϕ_f is shown by horizontal line. Field-winding axis is called direct axis. Armature reaction mmf F_a lags q-axis by space angle ψ or field flux by $90 + \psi°$. Mmf F_{ad} is along d-axis F_{aq} along q-axis. Here $\bar{F}_a = \bar{F}_{ad} + \bar{F}_{aq}$. As stated above, $\dfrac{\phi_{ad}}{\phi_{aq}} \neq \dfrac{F_{ad}}{F_{aq}}$, therefore, armature reaction flux ϕ_a ($= \phi_{ad} + \phi_{aq}$) and armature reaction mmf F_a (=$F_{ad} + F_{aq}$) are not in phase with each other as shown in Fig. 5.69 *(a)*. In this figure, resultant air-gap flux ϕ_r is the phasor sum of armature reaction flux ϕ_a and main field flux ϕ_f, *i.e.*, $\bar{\phi}_r = \bar{\phi}_f + \bar{\phi}_a$.

Armature mmf F_a is proportional to armature current, therefore, current I_a is drawn parallel to F_a in Fig. 5.69 *(b)*. Current I_a lags E_f by $\psi°$, therefore excitation emf E_f is shown vertical in Fig. 5.69 *(b)*. Fig. 5.69 *(a)* is the space-phasor diagram whereas Fig. 5.69 *(b)* is the time phasor diagram. These two diagrams can be superimposed to obtain space and time phasor diagram of a salient-pole synchronous generator, this is shown in Fig. 5.69 *(c)*.

The armature mmf components F_{ad} and F_{aq} may be thought of, as produced by those components of armature current I_a, which are respectively in time-quadrature and in time-phase with E_f, *i.e.*, F_{ad} and F_{aq} are taken to be produced by I_d and I_q respectively, see Fig. 5.69 *(c)*. From this figure, it is seen that $I_d = I_a \sin \psi$ and $I_q = I_a \cos \psi$. In other words, the armature current I_a is resolved into two components I_d and I_q-the component I_d is in time-quadrature with E_f whereas component I_q is in time-phase with E_f. Excitation voltage E_f lags field flux ϕ_f by 90°.

Armature current I_a lags E_f by internal pf angle $\psi(= \delta + \theta)$ as assumed.

Note that a direct-axis quantity is one whose magnetic effect is along the field pole axis, *e.g.* here F_{ad} is a direct-axis quantity. Since component of armature current I_d, in time quadrature with E_f, produces F_{ad}, I_d is also a *d*-axis quantity. Similarly, a quadrature-axis quantity is one whose magnetic effect is along the interpolar axis and here both F_{aq} and I_q are *q*-axis quantities. It should also be noted that both F_{ad} and F_{aq} are space-phasor quantities whereas I_d and I_q are time-phasor quantities.

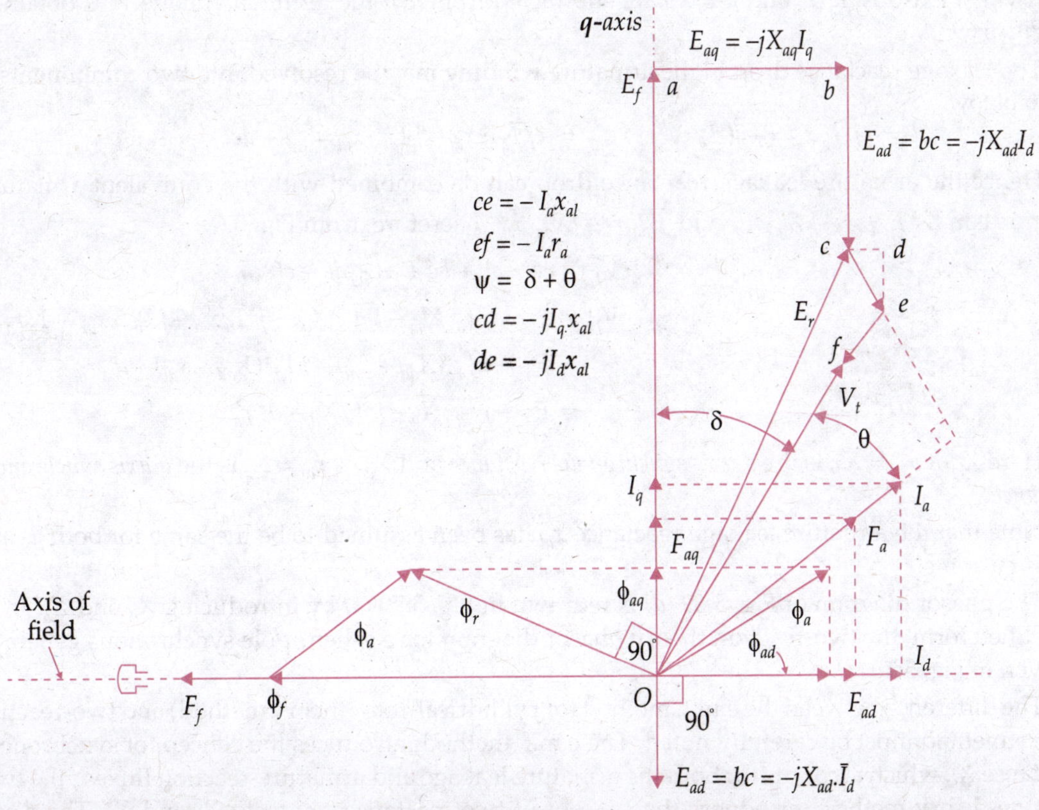

Fig 5.69: *(d)* Salient-pole synchronous generator phasor diagram, based on two-reaction theory.

Two Reaction Theory Phasor Diagram. For obtaining two-reaction theory phasor diagram, Fig. 5.69 *(c)* is drawn again in Fig. 5.69 *(d)*. Now, in this figure, air-gap voltage E_r is shown lagging resultant air-gap flux ϕ_r by 90° as in Fig. 5.18. In Art. 5.4.1, armature mmf F_a is replaced by time-quadrature lagging induced emf E_{ar}, see Fig. 5.18. In an identical manner, the armature mmf components in Fig. 5.69 *(d)* can be replaced by the induced voltages E_{ad} and E_{aq}, lagging in time by 90°, their respective mmf components F_{ad} and F_{aq} (or I_d and I_q). For the sake of clarity in the figure, only E_{ad} is shown lagging F_{ad} by 90°. By neglecting saturation and by referring to Eq. (5.10); E_{ad} the emf induced in the armature winding due to *d*-axis armature mmf component F_{ad} can be written as

$$\bar{E}_{ad} = -j\,K_d\,\bar{F}_{ad} = -j\,K_d\,C\,\bar{I}_d = -j\,X_{ad}\cdot\bar{I}_d$$

Here E_{ad}/F_{ad} is taken equal to K_d. Since E_{ad} lags F_{ad} by 90°, it is possible to write $\bar{E}_{ad} = -j\,K_d\,\bar{F}_{ad}$.

Similarly E_{aq}, the voltage induced in the armature winding due to *q*-axis armature reaction component F_{aq}, is given by

$$\bar{E}_{aq} = -j\,K_q\,\bar{F}_{aq} = -j\,C\,K_q\,\bar{I}_q = -j\,X_{aq}\,\bar{I}_q$$

Here X_{ad}, X_{aq} are proportionality constants similar to the magnetizing reactance X_{ar} of the cylindrical rotor machine, see Eq. (5.10). Thus here X_{ad} and X_{aq} *are respectively the d-axis and q-axis magnetizing reactances* (or armature-reaction reactances) *of a salient pole synchronous machine.*

The phasor sum of E_f, E_{ad} and E_{aq} gives the air-gap voltage E_r just as in a cylindrical-rotor machine, see Eq. (5.6), *i.e.*,

$$\bar{E}_r = \bar{E}_f + \bar{E}_{ad} + \bar{E}_{aq} \qquad ...(5.53)$$

If voltage drops $\bar{I}_a\,r_a$ and $j\,\bar{I}_a\,x_{al}$ are subtracted from $\bar{E}_r$, the terminal voltage V_t is obtained, see Fig. 5.69 *(d)*.

The leakage reactance drop in the armature winding may be resolved into two components as given below.

$$ce = -j\,\bar{I}_a\,x_{al} = -j(\bar{I}_d + \bar{I}_q)\,x_{al} = -j\,\bar{I}_q\cdot x_{al} - j\,\bar{I}_d\cdot x_{al} = cd + de$$

Hence the armature leakage reactance drop can be combined with the equivalent armature-reaction e.m.f.s $\bar{E}_{ad} = -j\,X_{ad}\,\bar{I}_d$ and $\bar{E}_{aq} = -jX_{aq}\,\bar{I}_q$. Therefore, from Fig. 5.69,

$$\bar{V}_t = oa + ab + bc + cd + de + ef$$

$$\therefore \quad \bar{V}_t = \bar{E}_f - j\,\bar{I}_q\,X_{aq} - j\,\bar{I}_d\,X_{ad} - j\,\bar{I}_q\,x_{al} - j\,\bar{I}_d\cdot x_{al} - \bar{I}_a\,r_a$$

$$= \bar{E}_f - j\,\bar{I}_q\,(X_{aq} + x_{al}) - j\,\bar{I}_d\,(X_{ad} + x_{al}) - \bar{I}_a\,r_a$$

$$= \bar{E}_f - j\,\bar{I}_q\cdot X_q - j\,\bar{I}_d\,X_d - \bar{I}_a\,r_a$$

Here $X_{ad} + x_{al} = X_d$, is the *d-axis synchronous reactance* and $X_{aq} + x_{al} = X_q$ is the *q-axis synchronous reactance*.

Note that the armature leakage reactance x_{al} has been assumed to be the same for both *d*- and *q*-axis currents.

The phasor diagram of Fig. 5.69 *(d)* is redrawn in Fig. 5.70 *(a)* by introducing X_d and X_q. In its simplified form, the two-reaction theory phasor diagram for a salient-pole synchronous generator is given in Fig. 5.70 *(b)*.

The difference between the e.m.f. method (or cylindrical-rotor theory method) and two-reaction theory method must be carefully noted. The e.m.f. method introduces the concept of synchronous reactance X_s, which accounts for both the armature leakage and armature-reaction fluxes ; the two-reaction-theory method introduces the concept of two reactances, namely X_d and X_q. The *d*-axis synchronous reactance X_d accounts for the armature leakage flux and the *d*-axis component of armature-reaction flux, whereas X_q accounts for the armature leakage flux and q-axis component of armature-reaction flux. In e.m.f. method, the armature-reaction e.m.f. E_{ar} lags F_a or I_a by 90°; whereas in two-reaction theory method, armature reaction e.m.f. = $\sqrt{E_{ad}^2 + E_{aq}^2}$ lags F_a or I_a by an angle other than 90°.

Fig. 5.70 *(b)* reveals that the phasor sum of $\bar{V}_t$, $\bar{I}_a r_a$, $j\bar{I}_d X_d$ and $j\bar{I}_q X_q$ gives the excitation voltage $\bar{E}_f$. Thus the voltage equation for each phase of a salient-pole synchronous generator is

$$\bar{E}_f = \bar{V}_t + \bar{I}_a r_a + jX_d\bar{I}_d + j\bar{I}_q X_q \qquad ...(5.54)$$

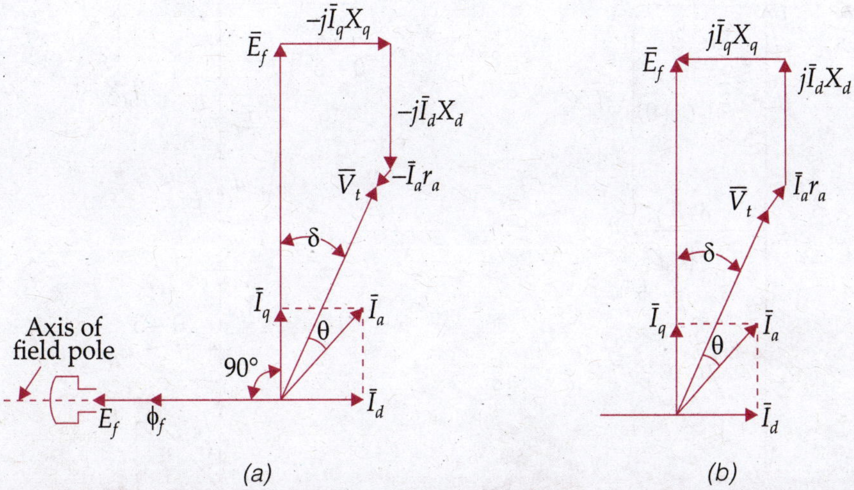

Fig 5.70: *(a)* Two-reaction theory phasor diagram of a salient pole synchronous generator and *(b)* its simplified version.

Analysis of phasor diagram. In order to use the phasor diagram of Fig. 5.70 *(b)*, the armature current I_a must be resolved into its d- and q-axis components. Usually V_t, I_a, power-factor angle θ, X_d and X_q are given in a problem, but for calculating I_d and I_q, the internal power-factor angle (δ + θ) must be known. For this purpose, draw *ab* normal to I_a as shown in Fig. 5.71 *(a)*. Since *ab* is 90° away from I_a, it must be a reactance drop, say I_aX. Draw *ac* perpendicalar to *ob*. It is seen from Fig. 5.71 *(a)* that *oa′b* and *acb* are right-angled triangles and, therefore, ∠*bac* = ∠δ + θ.

$$\therefore \qquad ac = ab\cos(\delta + \theta) = XI_a\cos(\delta + \theta) = de$$

$$\text{or} \qquad XI_q = X_qI_q \qquad [\because I_q = I_a\cos(\delta + \theta)]$$

$$\text{or} \qquad X = X_q$$

Thus in Fig. 5.71 *(a)*, $ab = I_aX_q$. If $ob = E'_f$, then

$$\bar{E}'_f = \bar{V}_t + \bar{I}_a r_a + j\bar{I}_a X_d \qquad ...(5.55)$$

Note that phasors $\bar{E}_f{}'$ and $\bar{E}_f$ are directed along the same line.

Therefore, the phasor sum $\bar{V}_t + \bar{I}_a r_a + j\bar{I}_a X_q$ gives $\bar{E}'_f$ and the angular position of the excitation voltage E_f with respect to V_t, *i.e.*, angle δ is known. From this, the angle (δ + θ) and, therefore, I_d and I_q can be obtained—this is illustrated in Example 5.24. Fig. 5.71 *(a)* also reveals that

$$bd = cd - cb = X_dI_d - X_qI_a\sin(\delta + \theta)$$

$$= X_dI_d - X_qI_d = (X_d - X_q)I_d$$

Eq. (5.54) can now be re-written as $\bar{E}_f = \bar{V}_t + \bar{I}_a r_a + j\bar{I}_a X_q + j\bar{I}_d(X_d - X_q)$ ...(5.56)

Salient-pole synchronous motor phasor diagram. For a synchronous generator, the voltages are generated and the currents are output currents. For a synchronous motor, the voltages are applied and the currents are input currents. Thus the motor voltage equation can be obtained from the generator voltage Eq. (5.54) by writing $-\bar{I}_a$ in place of $\bar{I}_a$. Therefore, the voltage equation for a salient-pole synchronous motor, from Eq. (5.54) is

$$\bar{V}_t = \bar{E}_f + r_a \bar{I}_a + j\bar{I}_d X_d + j\bar{I}_q X_q \quad ...(5.57)$$

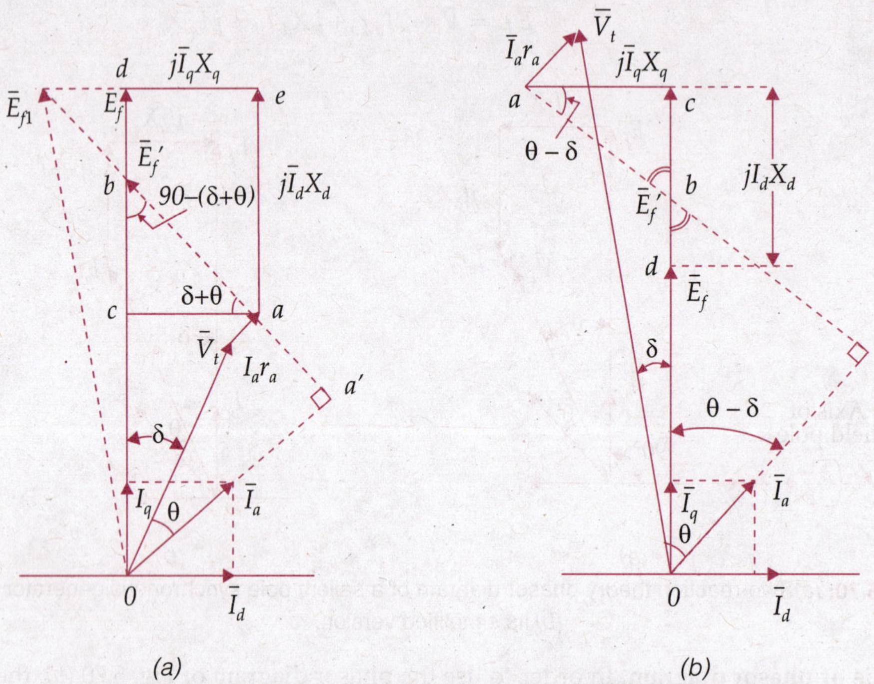

Fig 5.71: Resolving of I_a into its *d*- and *q*-axes components I_d and I_q *(a)* for a synchronous generator and *(b)* for a synchronous motor.

The voltage phasor diagram as per Eq. (5.57), is given in Fig. 5.71 *(b)*. In order to compute E_f from V_t, I_a, r_a, X_d, X_q and power factor angle θ, draw *ab* perpendicular to I_a. As before, *ab* is 90° away from I_a and therefore, *ab* must be a reactance drop, say $I_a X$. Fig. 5.71 *(b)* reveals that

$$\angle abc = 90 - (\theta - \delta) \text{ and } \angle bac = \theta - \delta.$$

$$\therefore \quad ac = ab \cos(\theta - \delta)$$

$$= XI_a \cos(\theta - \delta)$$

$$= XI_q \text{ or } XI_q = X_q I_q$$

$$\therefore \quad X = X_q$$

Therefore, the angular position of E_f can be obtained by computing $ob = \bar{E}'_f = \bar{V}_t - \bar{I}_a r_a - j\bar{I}_a X_q$. This permits the calculation of angle (θ – δ), I_d and I_q. Here again $bd = I_d (X_d - X_q)$. Eq. (5.57) can now be re-written as

$$\bar{V}_t = \bar{E}_f + j\bar{I}_d (X_d - X_q) + j\bar{I}_a X_q + r_a \bar{I}_a \quad ...(5.58)$$

Note, as before, that E_f is ahead of V_t for a generator and E_f is behind V_t for a motor.

Eqs. (5.56) and (5.58) include a term $I_d (X_d - X_q)$ which is due to saliency and this quantity reduces to zero for a cylindrical-rotor synchronous machine in which $X_d = X_q$. This saliency factor in salient-pole synchronous machines is quite appreciable, since X_d is approximately 60% larger than X_q. Even in turbo-generators, small salient-pole effect is present due to the effect of field-winding slots on q-axis reluctance-consequently X_d differs slightly from X_q in cylindrical rotor machines.

It is helpful to further investigate the phasor diagrams of a synchronous machine working at lagging as well as leading power factors. This will certainly lead to a better understanding of the operation of a salient-pole synchronous machine. Fig. 5.71 *(a)* for alternator is redrawn again in Fig. 5.72 *(a)* but with still more details. Thus, for alternator working at a lagging p.f. cos θ,

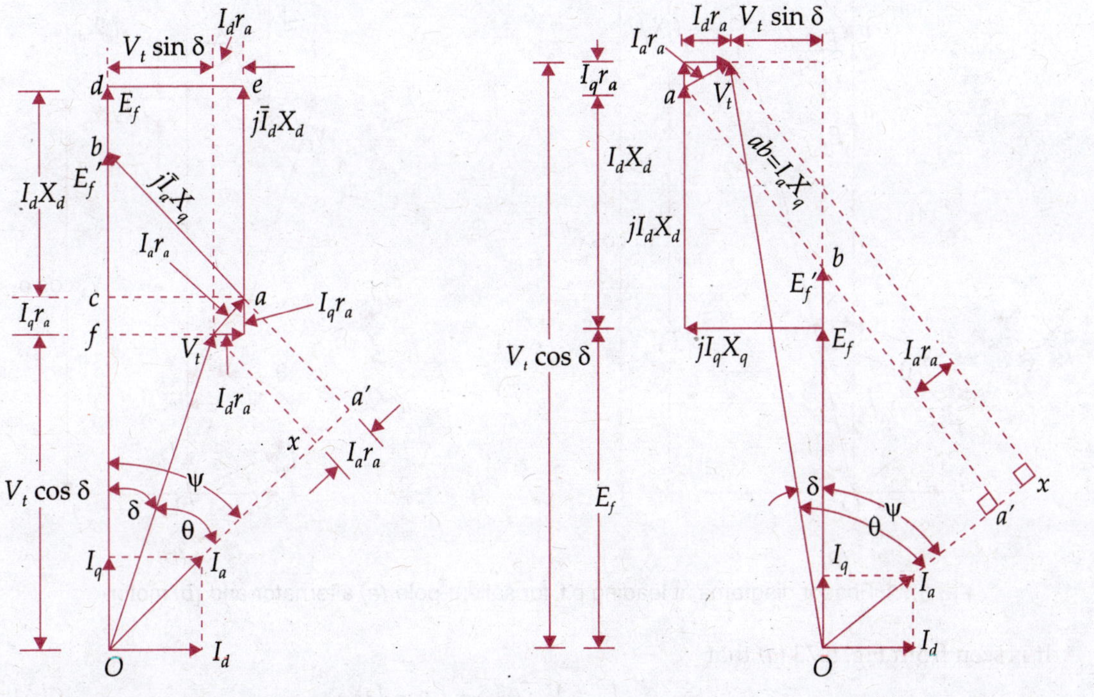

(a) (b)

Fig 5.72: Phasor diagrams at lagging p.f. for salient-pole *(a)* alternator and *(b)* motor.

$$od = of + fc + cd$$

or
$$E_f = V_t \cos\delta + I_q r_a + I_d X_d \quad \text{...(5.59 a)}$$
$$I_q X_q = V_t \sin\delta + I_d r_a \quad \text{...(5.59 b)}$$

From $\Delta oa'b$,
$$\tan\psi = \frac{a'b}{oa'} = \frac{ab + aa'}{a'x + ox}$$
$$= \frac{I_a X_q + V_t \sin\theta}{I_a r_a + V_t \cos\theta} \quad \text{...(5.59 c)}$$

where ψ = internal p.f. angle by which I_a lags E_f. = δ – θ.

For a synchronous motor working at a lagging p.f., Fig. 5.72 *(b)*,
$$E_f = V_t \cos\delta - I_q r_a - I_d X_d \quad \text{...(5.60 a)}$$
$$I_q X_q = V_t \sin\delta + I_d r_a \quad \text{...(5.60 b)}$$

From $\Delta oa'b$,
$$\tan\psi = \frac{a'b}{oa'} = \frac{a'a - ab}{ox - a'x} = \frac{V_t \sin\theta - I_a X_q}{V_t \cos\theta - I_a r_a} \quad \text{...(5.60 c)}$$

where $\psi = \theta - \delta$.

For leading p.f. loads, the phasor diagrams are drawn in Fig. 5.73 *(a)* and *(b)* for an alternator and synchronous motor respectively.

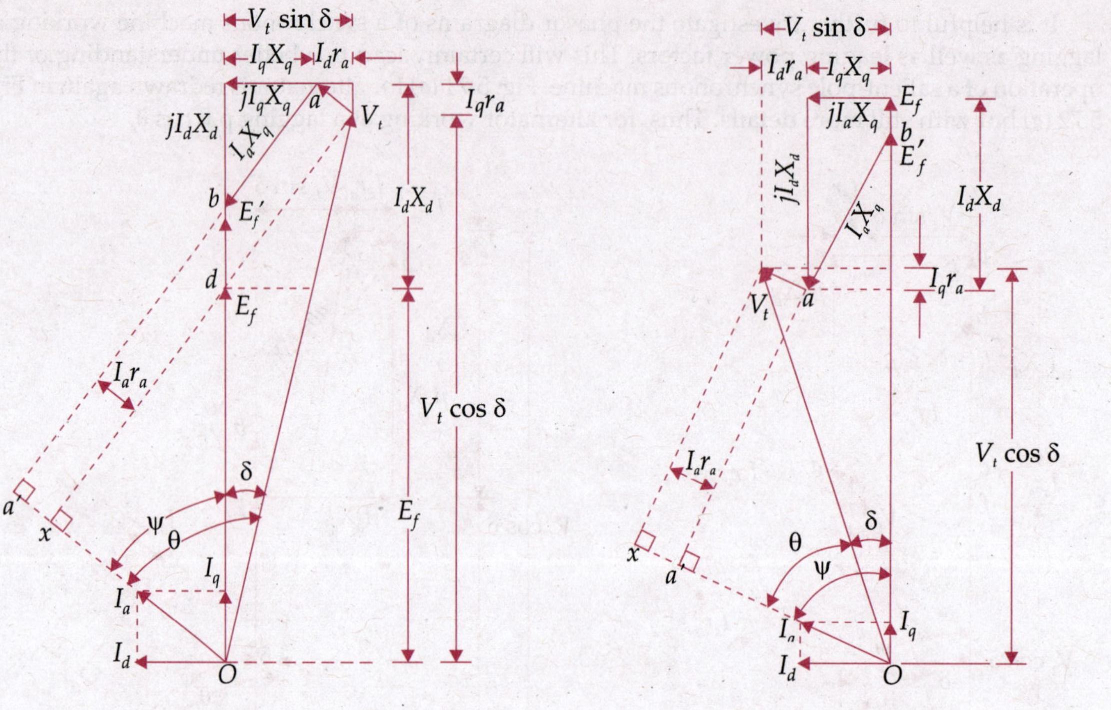

Fig 5.73: Phasor diagrams at leading p.f. for salient-pole *(a)* alternator and *(b)* motor.

It is seen from Fig. 5.73 *(a)* that

$$E_f = V_t \cos\delta + I_q r_a - I_d X_d \quad \text{...(5.61 a)}$$

$$I_q X_q = V_t \sin\delta - I_d r_a \quad \text{...(5.61 b)}$$

$$\tan\psi = \frac{a'b}{oa'} = \frac{V_t \sin\theta - I_a X_q}{V_t \cos\theta + I_a r_a} \quad \text{...(5.61 c)}$$

For Fig. 5.73 (*b*),

$$E_f = V_t \cos\delta - I_q r_a + I_d X_d \quad \text{...(5.62 a)}$$

$$I_q X_q = V_t \cos\delta - I_d r_a \quad \text{...(5.62 b)}$$

$$\tan\psi = \frac{a'b}{oa'} = \frac{a'a + ab}{ox - a'x} = \frac{V_t \sin\theta + I_a X_q}{V_t \cos\theta - I_a r_a} \quad \text{...(5.62 c)}$$

Computation of internal p.f. angle ψ facilitates the determination of I_d and I_q as

$$I_d = I_a \sin\psi$$

and

$$I_q = I_a \cos\psi \quad \text{...(5.63)}$$

Example 5.24. *A salient-pole synchronous generator has the following per unit parameters :*
$X_d = 1.2$, $X_q = 0.8$, $r_a = 0.025$.

Compute the excitation voltage E_f on a per unit basis, when the generator is delivering rated kVA at rated voltage and at power factor of (a) 0.8 lagging and (b) 0.8 leading.

Solution. For this example, refer to Fig. 5.71 *(a)*. With V_t as a reference phasor,

$$\overline{V}_t = 1.00 + j0.00$$
$$\overline{I}_a = 0.8 - j0.60 = 1.00\angle 36.9°$$
$$j\overline{I}_a X_q = j(0.8 - j0.60)(0.80) = 0.48 + j0.64$$
$$\overline{I}_a r_a = 0.020 - j0.015$$

Thus
$$\overline{E}'_f = \overline{V}_t + j\overline{I}_a X_q + \overline{I}_a r_a$$
$$= (1 + j0.00) + (0.48 + j0.64) + (0.020 - j\,0.015)$$
$$= 1.50 + j\,0.625 = 1.625\angle 22.62°$$

∴
$$\delta = 22.62° \text{ and } \angle\delta + \theta = 22.62 + 36.9 = 59.52°.$$

Resolving the armature current I_a into its *d-q* components, we get

$$I_d = 1.00 \sin 59.52° = 0.862 \text{ and } I_q = 1.00 \cos 59.52° = 0.507.$$

Fig. 5.71 (*a*) reveals that E_f' and E_f are along the same line *od*. Thus E_f can be obtained by adding the length $bd = I_d(X_d - X_q)$ numerically to E_f'.

∴
$$E_f = E_f' + I_d(X_d - X_q)$$
$$= 1.625 + (0.862)(0.40) = 1.9698$$

and
$$\overline{E}_f = 1.9698\angle 22.62°.$$

The above solution can also be obtained by referring to Fig. 5.72 *(a)*. From Eq. (5.59 *c*),

$$\tan\psi = \frac{I_a X_q + V_t \sin\theta}{I_a r_a + V_t \cos\theta} = \frac{0.8 + 0.6}{0.025 + 0.8} \text{ or } \psi = 59.49°.$$

∴
$$I_d = I_a \sin\psi = 0.862$$

and
$$I_q = I_a \cos\psi = 0.507$$

Load angle,
$$\delta = \psi - \theta = 59.49° - \cos^{-1} 0.8 = 22.59°.$$

From Eq. (5.59 *a*),
$$E_f = 1 \times \cos 22.59 + 0.507 \times 0.025 + 0.862 \times 1.2 = 1.9701.$$

(b) For the salient-pole synchronous generator, the phasor diagram for a leading power-factor is illustrated in Fig. 5.74. Here again V_t is taken as the reference phasor.

∴
$$\overline{V}_t = 100 + j0.00$$

and
$$\overline{I}_a = 0.8 + j0.60 = 1.00\angle 36.9°$$
$$j\overline{I}_a X_q = j(0.8 + j0.6)(0.8)$$
$$= -0.48 + j0.64$$
$$\overline{I}_a r_a = 0.020 + j0.015$$

Thus
$$\overline{E}'_f = \overline{V}_t + j\overline{I}_a X_q + \overline{I}_a r_a$$
$$= 1. + j0.00 - 0.48 + j0.64 + 0.020 + j0.015$$
$$= 0.54 + j0.655 = 0.849\angle 50.50°$$

∴
$$\delta = 50.50°.$$

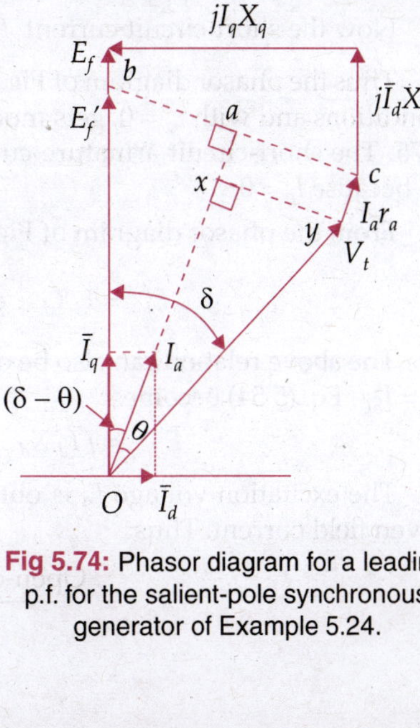

Fig 5.74: Phasor diagram for a leading p.f. for the salient-pole synchronous generator of Example 5.24.

For a leading power factor, the internal power factor angle between I_a and E_f is given by

$$\psi = \angle\delta - \theta$$

∴
$$\angle\delta - \theta = 50.50 - 36.9 = 13.60°$$

Resolution of I_a into its *dq* components, gives

$$I_a = 1.00 \sin 13.6° = 0.235$$

and
$$I_q = 1.00 \cos 13.6°.$$

The excitation voltage E_f is again the numerical sum of E_f' and $I_d(X_d - X_q)$.

$$\therefore \quad E_f = E_f' + I_d(X_d - X_q)$$
$$= 0.849 + 0.235\,(0.4) = 0.943 \text{ p.u.}$$

or $$\bar{E}_f = 0.943\angle 50.5°.$$

Alternatively, from Eq. (5.59 *c*) and Fig. 5.74,

$$\tan\psi = \tan(\delta-\theta) = \frac{ab}{oa} = \frac{cb-ca}{ox+xa} = \frac{cb-yx}{ox+yc} = \frac{I_aX_q - V_t\sin\theta}{V_t\cos\theta + I_ar_a}$$

Here $\psi = \delta - \theta$ is positive as E_f leads I_a, but θ is negative.

$$\therefore \quad \psi = \tan^{-1}\frac{1\times 0.8 - 1\times 0.6}{1\times 0.8 + 1\times 0.025} = 13.63°$$

$$\therefore \quad I_d = 0.235,\ I_q = 0.972$$

From Fig. 5.74, $\delta = \psi + \theta = 13.63 + 36.9° = 50.53°$. From Eq. (5.59 *a*),

$$E_f = 1\times\cos 50.53 + 0.972\times 0.025 + 0.235\times 1.2 = 0.942$$

Now the per unit voltage regulation can be obtained by using the relation $\left(\dfrac{E_f - V_t}{V_t}\right)$.

For a leading power factor, the voltage regulation is seen to be negative.

If required, the field currents, corresponding to the excitation voltage can be obtained from OCC of the salient-pole generator.

Example 5.25. *For a salient-pole synchronous machine, prove that the d-axis synchronous reactance X_d, can be obtained from its OCC and SCC. Neglect armature resistance.*

Solution. Phasor diagram of Fig. 5.70 *(b)* for a salient-pole synchronous generator reveals that with $r_a = 0$,

$$V_t\sin\delta = I_qX_q$$

Under steady state short-circuit conditions, terminal voltage $V_t = 0$.

$$\therefore \quad I_qX_q = V_t\sin\delta = 0 \text{ or } I_q = 0.$$

Now the short-circuit current $\bar{I}_{SC} = \bar{I}_d + \bar{I}_q = \bar{I}_d$.

Thus the phasor diagram of Fig. 5.70 *(b)* under short-circuit conditions and with $r_a = 0$, gets modified to that shown in Fig. 5.75. The short-circuit armature current I_{SC} becomes equal to I_d, because $I_q = 0$.

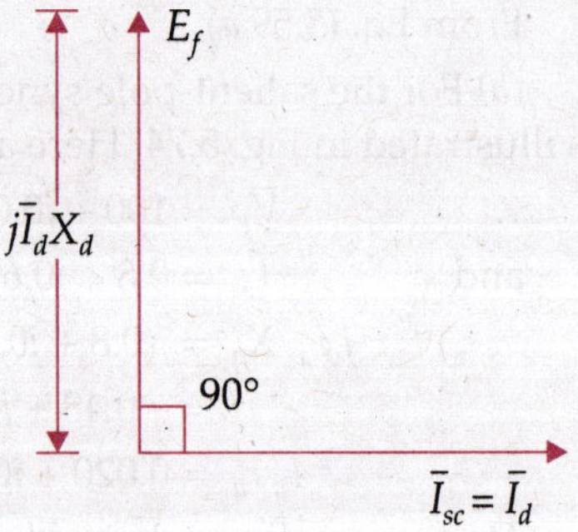

Fig 5.75: Two reaction theory phasor diagram, under short-circuit condition and with $r_a = 0$.

From the phasor diagram of Fig. 5.75, it is seen that

$$E_f = I_dX_d \quad \text{or} \quad X_d = \frac{E_f}{I_d} = \frac{E_f}{I_{SC}}$$

The above relation can also be obtained from Eq. (5.54) for an alternator. With $V_t = 0$, $I_q = 0$ and $I_d = I_{SC}$, Eq. (5.54) becomes

$$\bar{E}_f = j\bar{I}_dX_d \quad \text{or} \quad E_f = I_dX_d = I_{SC}X_d$$

The excitation voltage E_f is obtained from o.c.c. and short-circuit current I_{SC} from s.s.c. for a given field current. Thus

$$X_d = \frac{\text{Open-circuit (or excitation) voltage for a given field current}}{\text{Short-circuit curent for the same field current}}$$

The excitation voltage of the synchronous machine, as given by Eq. (5.2), is

$$E_f = \sqrt{2}\,\pi f k_w N_{ph} \phi_f$$

Since field flux ϕ_f is proportional to field m.m.f. F_f or field current I_f, excitation voltage can be written as

$$E_f = \frac{1}{\sqrt{2}}(2\pi f)\, k_w N_{ph}\,(kI_f) \text{ or } E_f = K\omega I_f$$

and $$X_d = \omega L_d.$$

$$\therefore \quad I_{SC} = \frac{E_f}{X_d} = \frac{K\omega I_f}{\omega L_d} = \frac{KI_f}{L_d} \qquad ...(5.64)$$

Here K is a constant and L_d is the d-axis synchronous inductance of the synchronous machine. Eq. (5.64) shows that for a given field current I_f, the armature short-circuit current remains substantially constant over a wide range of frequency or alternator speed. In view of this, during the short-circuit test, it is not necessary for the alternator speed to be equal to the synchronous speed. However, at considerably lower speeds, the resistance becomes comparable with reactance and the change in armature current is manifested.

Example 5.26. *From the phasor diagram of an over-excited salient-pole synchronous motor (i.e., with armature current leading the terminal voltage), prove the following relations :*

$$\tan\delta = \frac{I_a(X_q\cos\theta + r_a\sin\theta)}{V_t + I_a(X_q\sin\theta - r_a\cos\theta)}$$

and

$$X_q = \frac{V_t\sin\delta - I_a r_a \sin(\delta+\theta)}{I_a\cos(\delta+\theta)}$$

where δ and θ are load and power-factor angles respectively.

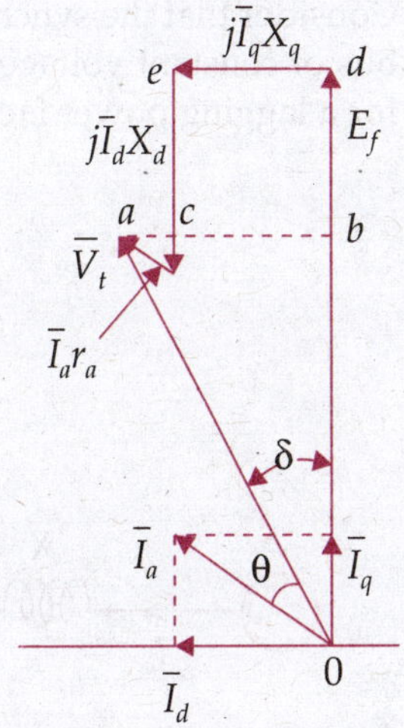

Fig 5.76: Phasor diagram of an overexcited synchronous motor.

Solution. Phasor diagram for an over-excited synchronous motor is drawn in Fig. 5.76.

From the tip of the voltage phasor V_t, *i.e.*, point a, draw ab perpendicular to od. Now $bc = de = I_q X_q$. Since the resistance drop ac is parallel to I_d,

$$ac = I_d r_a.$$

$$\therefore \quad ab = ac + cb = I_d r_a + I_q X_q.$$

From the phasor diagram, it is seen that

$$\sin\delta = \frac{ab}{oa} = \frac{ac+cb}{oa} = \frac{I_d r_a + I_q X_q}{V_t} \qquad ...(5.65)$$

But $$I_d = I_a \sin(\delta+\theta)$$

and $$I_q = I_a\cos(\delta+\theta).$$

∴ From Eq. (5.65), $V_t \sin\delta = r_a I_a \sin(\delta+\theta) + X_q I_a \cos(\delta+\theta)$

or $$V_t\sin\delta = r_a I_a(\sin\delta\cos\theta + \cos\delta\sin\theta) + X_q I_a(\cos\delta\cos\theta - \sin\delta\sin\theta).$$

Collecting sin δ terms on the right hand side and cos δ terms on the left hand side, we get

$$\sin\delta\,[V_t + X_q I_a\sin\theta - r_a I_a\cos\theta] = \cos\delta\,[r_a I_a\sin\theta + I_a X_q\cos\theta]$$

$$\therefore \quad \frac{\sin\delta}{\cos\delta} = \tan\delta = \frac{I_a(X_q\cos\theta + r_a\sin\theta)}{V_t + I_a(X_q\sin\theta - r_a\cos\theta)}$$

Eq. (5.65) readily yields the value of X_q as

$$X_q = \frac{V_t \sin\delta - I_d r_a}{I_q} = \frac{V_t \sin\delta - I_a r_a \sin(\delta+\theta)}{I_a \cos(\delta+\theta)}$$

From above, X_q can be calculated by measuring V_t, I_a, r_a, power input (for computing angle θ) and δ. The load angle δ is usually measured with the help of a stroboscope.

5.12. POWER-ANGLE CHARACTERISTICS OF SYNCHRONOUS MACHINES

In this article, the power expressions are derived in terms of power-angle δ, from the phasor diagrams of cylindrical-rotor and salient-pole machines. The power flow through a non-salient pole synchronous machine is already discussed in Art. 5.8 and the present derivation merely supplements the previous analysis.

Armature resistances of synchronous machines are usually small, these are, therefore, neglected in this article.

5.12.1. Cylindrical-rotor Synchronous Machine

Consider that the synchronous machine is acting as a generator and is feeding power to an infinite bus of constant voltage V_t, as shown in the single line diagram of Fig. 5.77 *(a)*. Its phasor diagram for a lagging power factor and with zero armature resistance, is illustrated in Fig. 5.77 *(b)*.

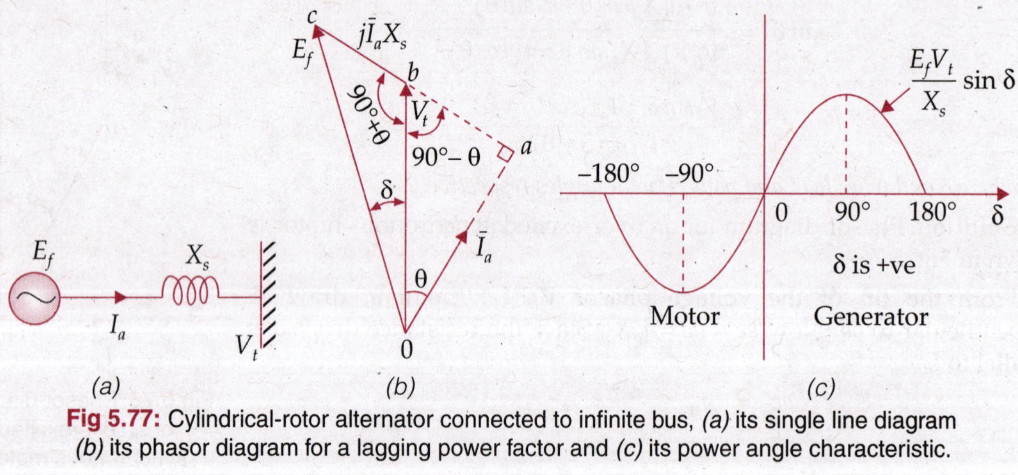

Fig 5.77: Cylindrical-rotor alternator connected to infinite bus, *(a)* its single line diagram *(b)* its phasor diagram for a lagging power factor and *(c)* its power angle characteristic.

The per phase power delivered to the infinite bus is given by

$$P = V_t I_a \cos\theta \qquad \text{...(5.66)}$$

It is seen from Fig. 5.77 *(b)* that $\angle oba = 90 - \theta$ and $\angle obc = 180 - (90 - \theta) = 90 + \theta$.

The triangle *obc* reveals that $\dfrac{bc}{\sin\angle boc} = \dfrac{oc}{\sin\angle obc}$ or $\dfrac{X_s I_a}{\sin\delta} = \dfrac{E_f}{\sin(90+\theta)}$

or $X_s I_a \sin(90+\theta) = E_f \sin\delta$ or $X_s I_a \cos\theta = E_f \sin\delta$

or $I_a \cos\theta = \dfrac{E_f}{X_s}\sin\delta.$

Substitution of value of $I \cos\theta$ in Eq. (5.66) gives,

$$P = \frac{E_f V_t}{X_s}\sin\delta \qquad \text{...(5.67)}$$

Eq. (5.67) agrees with Eq. (5.35) already derived for a cylindrical-rotor synchronous machine.

With the help of Eq. (5.67), the variation of power P with power-angle δ, is plotted in Fig. 5.77 *(c)*. This power *versus* load-angle curve has a sinusoidal shape and is usually called the **power-angle characteristic** of the cylindrical-rotor synchronous machine. The power P, for generator is taken as positive and therefore, for motor as negative. The power angle characteristics for a synchronous machine, running as a generator or motor, are alike if its armature resistance is neglected, see Eq. (5.35).

5.12.2. Salient-pole Synchronous Machine

Consider that the synchronous machine, acting as a generator, is connected to an infinite bus, see Fig. 5.78 *(a)*. Its phasor diagram for a lagging power factor load and with zero armature circuit resistance, is illustrated in Fig. 5.78 *(b)*. The components of V_t in phase with I_d and I_q are $V_t \sin\delta$ and $V_t \cos\delta$ respectively. Since these two components of V_t are in phase with I_d and I_q, the per phase power delivered to the bus is

$$P = I_d (V_t \sin\delta) + I_q (V_t \cos\delta) \qquad \text{...(5.68)}$$

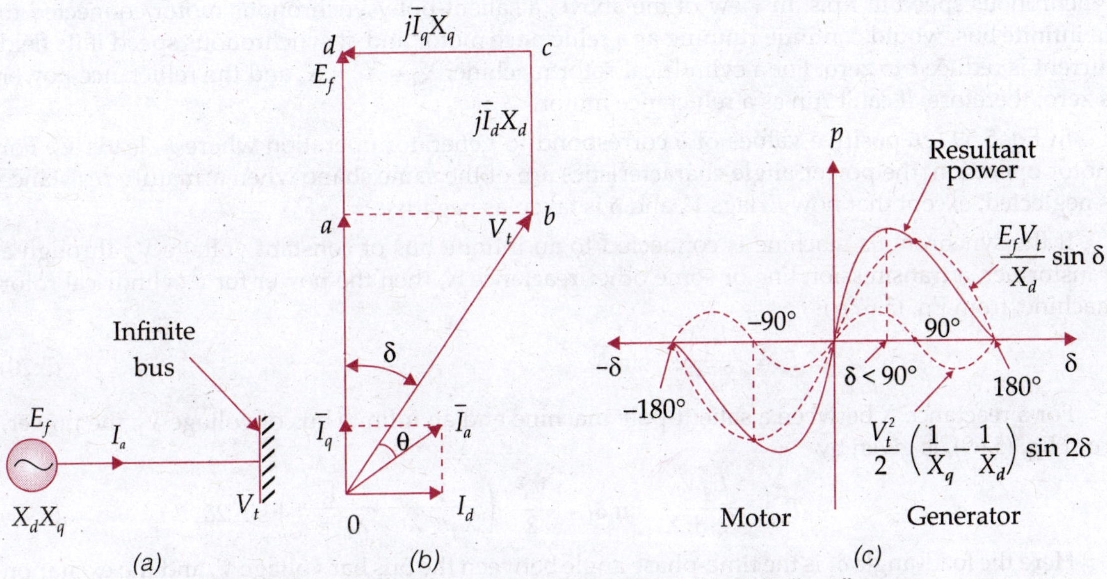

Fig 5.78: Salient pole synchronous generator *(a)* single line diagram *(b)* phasor diagram for a lagging p.f. and *(c)* power-angle characteristic.

From Fig. 5.78 *(b)*,

$$V_t \sin\delta = ab = dc = I_q X_q$$

$$\therefore \qquad I_q = \frac{V_t \sin\delta}{X_q}$$

and

$$V_t \cos\delta = oa = od - ad = od - bc = E_f - I_d X_d$$

$$\therefore \qquad I_d = \frac{E_f - V_t \cos\delta}{X_d}$$

Substituting the values of I_d and I_q in Eq. (5.68) and simplifying, we get

$$P = \frac{E_f V_t}{X_d} \sin\delta + \frac{V_t^2}{2}\left(\frac{1}{X_q} - \frac{1}{X_d}\right) \sin 2\delta \qquad \text{...(5.69)}$$

Eq. (5.69) gives the power *versus* load-angle characteristic of a salient pole machine as shown in Fig. 5.78 *(c)*. The total power consists of a fundamental component $\frac{E_f V_t}{X_d}$ sin δ and a second harmonic component $\frac{V_t^2}{2}\left(\frac{1}{X_q}-\frac{1}{X_d}\right)$ sin 2δ.

The first term in Eq. (5.69) is identical with that obtained for a cylindrical rotor machine. This component of power is called the *electromagnetic power*, because its existence depends on the existence of both the armature winding (with V_t) and the field winding (with I_f). The second term of Eq. (5.69) exists even when the field current is zero, *i.e.*, E_f is zero. This second component of power is present because the armature-reaction flux has a tendency to pass through the field structure along its minimum reluctance path *i.e.*, along the field-pole axis or direct-axis. Since $\frac{V_t^2}{2}\left(\frac{1}{X_q}-\frac{1}{X_d}\right)$ sin 2δ exists because of the different reluctances along *d*- and *q*-axes, it is called the *reluctance power* and the term $\frac{1}{\omega_s}\frac{V_t^2}{2}\left(\frac{1}{X_q}-\frac{1}{X_d}\right)$ sin 2δ is called the *reluctance torque*. Here $\omega_s = 2\pi n_s$ and n_s is the synchronous speed in r.p.s. In view of the above, a salient-pole synchronous motor connected to an infinite bus, would continue running as a reluctance motor and at synchronous speed if its field current is reduced to zero. For a cylindrical rotor machine, $X_d = X_q = X_s$ and the reluctance power is zero, therefore, it can't run as a reluctance motor.

In Eq. 5.59 *(c)*, positive values of δ correspond to generator operation where E_f leads V_t. For motor operation, the power-angle characteristics are of the same shape when armature resistance is neglected, except that now E_f lags V_t and δ is taken as negative.

If the synchronous machine is connected to an infinite bus of constant voltage V_t, through a transformer, a transmission line or some other reactance *X*, then the power for a cylindrical rotor machine, from Eq. (5.67), is

$$P = \frac{E_f V_t}{X_s + X}\sin\delta_1 \quad \text{...(5.70)}$$

For a reactance *X* between a salient-pole machine and an infinite bus of voltage V_t, the power, from Eq. (5.69), is given by

$$P = \frac{E_f V_t}{X_d + X}\sin\delta_1 + \frac{V_t^2}{2}\left(\frac{1}{X_q + X}-\frac{1}{X_d + X}\right)\sin 2\delta_1 \quad \text{...(5.71)}$$

Here the load-angle δ_1 is the time-phase angle between the bus bar voltage V_t and the excitation voltage E_f.

At constant V_t and E_f, the condition for maximum power is obtained by putting $\frac{dP}{d\delta} = 0$. Therefore, for a cylindrical-rotor machine, from Eq. (5.67).

$$\frac{dP}{d\delta} = \frac{E_f V_t}{X_s}\cos\delta = 0 \text{ or } \delta = 90°$$

This shows that the maximum power in a cylindrical-rotor synchronous machine occurs at δ = 90°, as is obvious from Fig. 5.77 *(c)*.

For a salient-pole synchronous machine, from Eq. (5.69),

$$\frac{dP}{d\delta} = \frac{V_t E_f}{X_d}\cos\delta + V_t^2\left(\frac{1}{X_q}-\frac{1}{X_d}\right)\cos 2\delta = 0$$

In this equation, substitute cos 2δ = 2 cos² δ – 1 and then its solution gives,

$$\cos\delta = -\frac{E_f X_q}{4V_t(X_d - X_q)} \pm \sqrt{\frac{1}{2} + \left[\frac{E_f X_q}{4V_t(X_d - X_q)}\right]^2} \quad ...(5.72)$$

Out of the ± signs, only positive sign should be used, because negative sign gives ambiguous results. The value of load angle δ, from Eq. (5.72), is seen to be less than 90°. This shows that for a salient-pole machine, the maximum power occurs at δ < 90°, as can be seen from Fig. 5.78 *(c)*. In order to calculate the maximum power for a salient-pole machine, find angle δ from Eq. (5.72) and substitute it in Eq. (5.69).

Example 5.27. *A 3-phase, 400 V, star-connected synchronous machine is synchronized with an infinite bus at rated voltage. The synchronous machine is now made to deliver a shaft load of 9.5 kW. The machine resistance is negligible and $X_d = 5\ \Omega$ per phase and $X_q = 3.2\ \Omega$ per phase. Friction, windage and core loss total 500 watts. For this shaft output, calculate*

(a) power angle, armature current, p.f. and draw the phasor diagram and

(b) the maximum power output and the corresponding power angle.

Solution. *(a)* Shaft power = 9500 W

Friction, windage and core loss = 500 W

Power developed in the synchronous motor, $P = 9500 + 500 = 10{,}000$ W

Also
$$P = 3\left[\frac{E_f V_t}{X_d}\sin\delta + \frac{1}{2}V_t^2\left(\frac{1}{X_q} - \frac{1}{X_d}\right)\sin 2\delta\right]$$

$$10{,}000 = 3\left[\frac{400^2}{3\times 5}\sin\delta + \frac{1}{2}\left(\frac{400}{\sqrt{3}}\right)^2\left(\frac{1}{3.2} - \frac{1}{5}\right)\sin 2\delta\right]$$

or
$$1 = 3.2\ \sin\delta + 0.9\sin 2\delta$$

By trial and error, δ = 11.623°

With $E_f = V_t = 400/\sqrt{3} = 230.95$ V per phase, the synchronous motor would be operating at a leading p.f. With $r_a = 0$, it is seen from Fig. 5.73 *(b)* that

$$I_d X_d = E_f - V_t\cos\delta$$

or
$$I_d = \frac{230.95 - 230.95\times\cos 11.623°}{5} = 0.947 \text{ A}$$

Also
$$I_q = \frac{V_t \sin\delta}{X_q} = \frac{230.95\sin 11.623°}{3.2} = 14.541 \text{ A}$$

∴ Armature current, $I_a = \sqrt{I_d^2 + I_q^2} = \sqrt{0.947^2 + 14.541^2} = 14.572$ A

Fig. 5.73 *(b)* also shows that $I_q = I_a\cos(\delta + \theta)$

or
$$\delta + \theta = \cos^{-1}\left(\frac{I_q}{I_a}\right) = \cos^{-1}\left(\frac{14.541}{14.572}\right) = 3.738°$$

∴
$$\theta = 3.738 - 11.623 = -7.885°$$

As θ turns out to be negative for a leading p.f. phasor diagram of Fig. 5.73 *(b)*, power-factor angle θ is actually lagging.

∴
$$\text{p.f.} = \cos 7.885 = 0.9905 \text{ lagging.}$$

The phasor diagram for this part is as shown in Fig. 5.79.

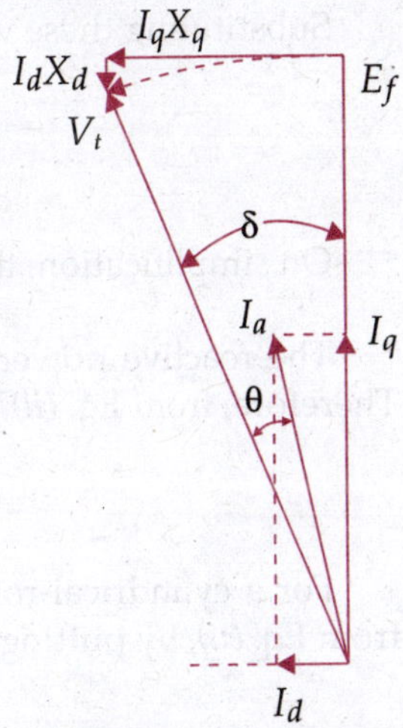

Fig 5.79: Pertaining to Example 5.27.

(b) For maximum power developed, from Eq. (5.72),

$$\cos\delta = -\frac{230.95\times 3.2}{4\times 230.95\times 1.8} \pm \sqrt{\frac{1}{2}+(0.444)^2}$$

$$= -0.4444 \pm 0.8352 \text{ or } \delta = 67°$$

∴ Maximum power developed

$$= 3\,\frac{400^2}{3\times 5}\sin 67° + 3\,\frac{400^2}{3\times 2}\left(\frac{1.8}{5\times 3.2}\right)\sin 134° = 35930.2 \text{ W}$$

∴ Maximum power output = 35930.2 – 500 = 35430.2 W.

Example 5.28. *Show that for a salient-pole synchronous generator, the per-phase reactive power in terms of power angle δ and for a lagging power factor is given by*

$$Q = \frac{E_f V_t}{X_d}\cos\delta - \frac{V_t^2}{X_d} - V_t^2\left(\frac{1}{X_q}-\frac{1}{X_d}\right)\sin^2\delta.$$

Also, determine the maximum reactive power Q, the generator can deliver with fixed excitation. Neglect armature resistance.

Solution. The product of voltage and quadrature lagging component of armature current, gives the reactive power Q.

From the phasor diagram of Fig. 5.78 *(b)*, it is seen that I_d lags $oa = V_t\cos\delta$ by 90°, whereas I_q leads $ab = V_t\sin\delta$ by 90°. Therefore, the reactive power per phase is given by

$$Q = V_t\cos\delta I_d - V_t\sin\delta\, I_q \quad ...(i)$$

Also $V_t\sin\delta = ab = dc = I_d X_q$

$$\therefore \quad I_q = \frac{V_t\sin\delta}{X_q}$$

and $E_f - V_t\cos\delta = ad = bc = X_d I_d$

$$\therefore \quad I_d = \frac{E_f - V_t\cos\delta}{X_d}$$

Substituting these values of I_d and I_q in Eq. *(i)* gives,

$$Q = \frac{V_t\cos\delta(E_f - V_t\cos\delta)}{X_d} - \frac{V_t^2\sin^2\delta}{X_q}$$

On simplification, this gives $Q = \frac{E_f V_t}{X_d}\cos\delta - \frac{V_t^2}{X_d} - V_t^2\left(\frac{1}{X_q}-\frac{1}{X_d}\right)\sin^2\delta$ ...*(ii)*

The reactive power of a salient-pole alternator would be maximum when load angle δ = 0. Therefore, from Eq. *(ii)*, we get

$$\therefore \quad Q_{max} = \frac{E_f\cdot V_t}{X_d}\cos 0 - \frac{V_t^2}{X_d} - 0 = \frac{V_t}{X_d}[E_f - V_t] \quad ...(iii)$$

For a cylindrical-rotor alternator working at a lagging p.f., the reactive power Q is obtained from Eq. *(ii)*, by putting $X_d = X_q = X_s$.

$$Q = \frac{E_f V_t}{X_s}\cos\delta - \frac{V_t^2}{X_s} = \frac{V_t}{X_s}[E_f\cos\delta - V_t] \quad ...(iv)$$

It is seen that Eq. *(iv)* is the same as obtained earlier in Eq. (5.45). This equation shows that when $E_f\cos\delta = V_t$, *i.e.*, under normal excitation, the reactive power Q = 0 and the alternator operates at u.p.f. In case $E_f \cos \delta > V_t$, *i.e.*, the alternator is over-excited, Q is positive–consequently the alternator delivers reactive power to the bus-bars.

If $E_f \cos \delta < V_t$, *i.e.*, the alternator is underexcited, Q is negative, consequently the alternator absorbs or consumes reactive power.

In general, an overexcited generator or motor produces, delivers or exports reactive power to the system network, whereas under-excited synchronous machine absorbs, consumes or imports reactive power from the system network.

Example 5.29. *A synchronous generator is running overexcited with $E_f = 1.40$ p.u. This machine, with a synchronous reactance of 1.20 p.u., is delivering a synchronous power of 0.50 p.u. to the bus.*

If the prime-mover torque is increased by 1%, by how much will the synchronous power P and reactive power Q change?

Solution. For a cylindrical-rotor synchronous machine the synchronous power or the real power is given by

$$P = \frac{E_f V_t}{X_s} \sin \delta$$

i.e.

$$0.5 = \frac{1.4 \times 1}{1.2} \sin \delta \quad \text{or} \quad \delta = 25.4°$$

1% increase in torque means 1% increase in real power.

$\therefore$ dP = 1% of its previous value

i.e.,

$$dP = \frac{1}{100} (0.5) = 0.005 \text{ p.u.}$$

For cylindrical-rotor machine, reactive power from Eq. (5.45) or Eq. (*iv*) is,

$$Q = \frac{E_f V_t}{X_s} \cos \delta - \frac{V_t^2}{X_s}$$

$$\therefore \quad \frac{dQ}{d\delta} = -\frac{E_f V_t}{X_s} \sin \delta$$

But

$$\frac{dP}{d\delta} = \frac{E_f V_t}{X_s} \cos \delta,$$

$$\therefore \quad \frac{dQ}{dP} = -\tan \delta = -\tan 25.4° = -0.475.$$

$$\therefore \quad dQ = -0.475\,(1\%) = -0.475\%.$$

This shows that with 1% increase in prime-mover torque, the active power P is increased by 1% of its pervious value, but the reactive power Q is decreased by 0.475% of its previous value.

Example 5.30. *A synchronous machine has been synchronised with an infinite bus. Now, without changing the field current, the machine is made to deliver real power to the bus. Will it, at the same time, generate or consume reactive power?*

Solution. For proper synchronization, $E_f = V_t$

$\therefore$ Reactive power,

$$Q = \frac{V_t^2}{X_s} \cos \delta - \frac{V_t^2}{X_s}$$

$$= \frac{V_t^2}{X_s} (\cos \delta - 1).$$

Since the real power P is delivered to the bus, the load angle δ can't be zero, *i.e.*, $\cos\delta$ is less than one. This means Q is negative, which shows that the synchronous generator is absorbing or consuming reactive power. The same conclusion can be arrived at from the synchronous generator phasor diagram when $E_f = V_t$.

Example 5.31. *A 400 V, 3 phase star-connected synchronous motor with $X_d = 6\ \Omega$ and $X_q = 4\ \Omega$, is running in parallel with an infinite bus. If its field current is reduced to zero, find the maximum load that can be put on the synchronous motor. Also compute the armature current and power factor at the maximum power. Prove the formula used for reluctance power. Neglect armature resistance.*

Solution. When the field current is reduced to zero, excitation voltage E_f becomes zero. Therefore, the phasor diagram of Fig. 5.71 *(b)*, for $E_f = 0$, gets modified to that shown in Fig. 5.80. Note that the armature resistance r_a is neglected. In this diagram $V_t \cos\delta$ is in phase with I_q and $V_t \sin\delta$ is opposite to I_d. Therefore, the reluctance power is given by

$$P = V_t \cos\delta I_q - V_t \sin\delta I_d$$

It is also seen from the figure that $V_t \sin\delta = I_q X_q$.

$$\therefore \quad I_q = \frac{V_t \sin\delta}{X_q} \text{ and } V_t\cos\delta = I_d X_d$$

$$\therefore \quad I_d = \frac{V_t\cos\delta}{X_d}$$

Substitution of the values of I_d and I_q in P gives

$$P = \frac{V_t\cos\delta\, V_t\sin\delta}{X_q} - \frac{V_t\sin\delta\, V_t\cos\delta}{X_d} = \frac{V_t^2}{2}\left(\frac{1}{X_q} - \frac{1}{X_d}\right)\sin 2\delta.$$

For maximum reluctance power, $\sin 2\delta = 1$, *i.e.*, $\delta = 45°$.

$$\therefore \quad P_{max} = \frac{V_t^2}{2}\left(\frac{1}{X_q} - \frac{1}{X_d}\right)\cdot 1 = \frac{1}{2}\left(\frac{400}{\sqrt{3}}\right)^2\left(\frac{1}{4} - \frac{1}{6}\right)$$

$= 2220$ watts per phase $= 6660$ watts for 3-phases.

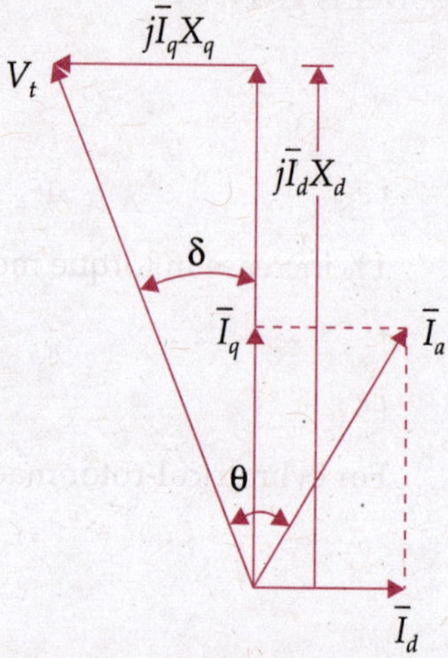

Fig 5.80: Reluctance motor phasor diagram with $r_a = 0$.

The component currents I_q and I_d, corresponding to maximum power and $\delta = 45°$, are

$$I_q = \frac{V_t \sin\delta}{X_q} = \frac{(231)(0.707)}{4}$$

and
$$I_d = \frac{V_t\cos\delta}{X_d} = \frac{(231)(0.707)}{6}$$

$\therefore$ Armature current corresponding to maximum power $= I_a = \sqrt{I_d^2 + I_q^2}$

$$= (231)\ (0.707)\sqrt{\left(\frac{1}{4}\right)^2 + \left(\frac{1}{6}\right)^2} = 49.1 \text{ Amp.}$$

Also, $\sqrt{3}\, V_t I_a \cos\theta = P_{max}$

or $\quad \sqrt{3} \times 400 \times 49.1 \cos\theta = 6660$ W or $\cos\theta = 0.1958$

Therefore, power factor at maximum power is 0.1958 lagging.

Example 5.32. *The synchronous motor of Example 5.31, carries a total load equivalent to 21 kW. If the motor field current is decreased, load angle δ must increase to meet the demand of the load. Find the minimum excitation voltage and the maximum stable load-angle for the given load.*

Solution. $\quad$ Per phase load $= \dfrac{21}{3} = 7$ kW.

$$P = \frac{E_f V_t}{X_d} \sin \delta + \frac{V_t^2}{2}\left(\frac{1}{X_q} - \frac{1}{X_d}\right) \sin 2\delta$$

$$E_f = \frac{P - \frac{V_t^2}{2} \cdot \frac{X_d - X_q}{X_d X_q} \sin 2\delta}{\frac{V_t}{X_d} \sin \delta} \qquad ...(i)$$

Since P and V_t are constants, E_f shall be minimum when $\frac{dE_f}{d\delta} = 0$. The value of $\frac{dE_f}{d\delta}$, from Eq. *(i)* is $\left[\left(\frac{V_t}{X_d} \sin \delta\right)\left(-\frac{V_t^2}{2} \cdot \frac{X_d - X_q}{X_d X_q} 2 \cos 2\delta\right)\right.$

$$\frac{dE_f}{d\delta} = \frac{\left. -\left(P - \frac{V_t^2}{2} \cdot \frac{X_d - X_q}{X_d X_q} \sin 2\delta\right) \frac{V_t}{X_d} \cos \delta\right]}{\left(\frac{V_t}{X_d} \sin \delta\right)^2} = 0$$

or $$-\frac{V_t}{X_d} \sin \delta \cos 2\delta \frac{V_t^2 (X_d - X_q)}{X_d X_q} = \left(P - \frac{V_t^2}{2} \cdot \frac{X_d - X_q}{X_d X_q} \sin 2\delta\right) \frac{V_t}{X_d} \cos \delta.$$

Its simplification gives

$$\cos \delta = \frac{V_t^2}{P} \frac{X_d - X_q}{X_d X_q} \sin^3 \delta \qquad ...(ii)$$

For minimum E_f, Eq. *(ii)* gives the maximum possible value of δ for given P and V_t. The value of δ obtained from Eq. *(ii)*, when substituted in Eq. *(i)*, gives the minimum excitation voltage $E_{f\,min}$.

Substituting the value of P, V_t, X_d in Eq. *(ii)* gives,

$$\cos \delta = \frac{(231)^2}{7000} \cdot \frac{(2)}{24} \sin^3 \delta = 0.634 \sin^3 \delta.$$

Its trial and error solution give δ = 63.2° and this is the maximum stable load-angle. Substitution of this value of δ(= 63.2°) in Eq. *(i)*, gives the minimum excitation voltage as

$$E_{f\,min} = \frac{7000 - \frac{(231)^2}{2} \cdot \frac{2}{24} \sin(126.4°)}{\frac{231}{6} \sin 63.2°} = 199 \text{ V}.$$

Example 5.33. *For a 3-phase salient-pole synchronous motor running as a reluctance motor, derive the following relation under maximum power conditions.*

$$\tan \theta = \frac{X_d + X_q}{X_d - X_q}$$

where θ = power-factor angle of reluctance motor.

Solution. It is seen from the phasor diagram of a reluctance motor, Fig. 5.80 that

$$I_d = I_a \sin(\theta - \delta) \text{ and } I_q = I_a \cos(\theta - \delta)$$

or $$\frac{I_q}{I_d} = \frac{\cos(\theta - \delta)}{\sin(\theta - \delta)} \qquad ...(i)$$

Phasor diagram of Fig. 5.80 also gives

$$V_t \sin \delta = I_q X_q \text{ and } V_t \cos \delta = I_d X_d$$

or

$$\tan \delta = \frac{I_q}{I_d} \cdot \frac{X_q}{X_d} \text{ or } \frac{I_q}{I_d} = \frac{X_d}{X_q} \cdot \tan \delta \quad ...(ii)$$

From Eqs. *(i)* and *(ii)*, we get $\frac{X_d}{X_q} \tan \delta = \frac{\cos(\theta - \delta)}{\sin(\theta - \delta)}$

Under maximum power conditions in a reluctance motor, $\delta = 45°$.

$$\therefore \quad \frac{X_d}{X_q} \cdot 1 = \frac{\cos\theta \times 0.707 + \sin\theta \times 0.707}{\sin\theta \times 0.707 - \cos\theta \times 0.707}$$

or

$$\frac{X_d}{X_q} = \frac{\sin\theta + \cos\theta}{\sin\theta - \cos\theta}$$

or

$$\frac{(\sin\theta + \cos\theta) + (\sin\theta - \cos\theta)}{(\sin\theta + \cos\theta) - (\sin\theta - \cos\theta)} = \frac{X_d + X_q}{X_d - X_q}$$

$$\therefore \quad \frac{\sin\theta}{\cos\theta} = \tan\theta = \frac{X_d + X_q}{X_d - X_q}$$

Under maximum power conditions, reluctance motor operates at a lagging power factor.

Example 5.34. *A 3-phase synchronous generator is delivering a power of 0.9 p.u. to an infinite bus at rated voltage and at p.f. 0.8 lagging. The generator has $X_d = 1.0$ p.u. and $X_q = 0.6$ p.u. Determine the load angle and the excitation voltage.*

In case loss of excitation takes place, will the generator remain in synchronism?

Solution. In per unit system,

$$V_t I_a \cos\theta = \text{Power or } 1 \times I_a \times 0.8 = 0.9$$

$$\therefore \quad I_a = 1.125 \text{ p.u.}$$

It is seen from the phasor diagram of Fig. 5.71 *(a)* with $r_a = 0$, or Eq. 5.59 *(c)* that

$$\tan(\delta + \theta) = \frac{I_a X_q + V_t \sin\theta}{V_t \cos\theta} = \frac{1.125 \times 0.6 + 1 \times 0.6}{1 \times 0.8} \text{ or } (\delta + \theta) = 57.894°$$

$$\therefore \quad \delta = 57.0894° - \cos^{-1}(0.8) = 57.894° - 36.87° = 21.024°.$$

Also

$$I_d = I_a \sin(\delta + \theta) = 1.125 \sin(57.894°) = 0.953 \text{ p.u.}$$

$$\therefore \quad E_f = V_t \cos\delta + I_d X_d = 1 \times \cos 21.024° + 0.953 \times 1.0 = 1.8864 \text{ p.u.}$$

When loss of excitation takes place, $E_f = 0$ and the maximum power is then given by

$$\frac{1}{2} V_t^2 \left(\frac{1}{X_q} - \frac{1}{X_d}\right) \sin 2\delta = \frac{1}{2}\left(\frac{1}{0.6} - \frac{1}{1}\right) \sin 90° = 0.333 \text{ p.u.}$$

With loss of excitation, the maximum power that the reluctance generator can deliver to infinite bus is 0.333 p.u. As this is less than 0.9 p.u., the generator will lose synchronism.

5.13. SYNCHRONIZING POWER AND SYNCHRONIZING TORQUE

The rate at which synchronous power P varies with δ is called the *synchronizing-power coefficient* P_{sy}. It is also known as stiffness of coupling, rigidity factor or stability factor. For a cylindrical-rotor machine, from Eq. (5.67),

$$P_{sy} = \frac{dP}{d\delta} = \frac{E_f V_t}{X_s} \cos\delta \quad \text{...(5.73)}$$

For a salient pole machine,

$$P_{sy} = \frac{dP}{d\delta} = \frac{E_f V_t}{X_d} \cos\delta + V_t^2\left(\frac{1}{X_q} - \frac{1}{X_d}\right) \cos 2\delta \quad \text{...(5.74)}$$

The coefficient P_{sy} is equal to the slope of the power angle curve and its variation with δ is illustrated in Fig. 5.81 for both types of machines.

The synchronizing-power coefficient is a measure of the stiffness of electromagnetic coupling between stator and rotor fields. Too large stiffness of coupling means that the motor tends to follow closely, the variation of speed caused by the disturbance in electric power supply. In case there is no power-supply disturbance, then too much stiffness of coupling would cause the motor speed to remain practically constant, regardless of the mechanical load fluctuations. In view of this, too rigid electromagnetic coupling causes undue mechanical shocks, whenever there are fluctuations in the mechanical load or the supply. Examination of Eqs. (5.73) and (5.74) reveals that P_{sy} is inversely proportional to X_s or X_d and is directly proportional to the excitation voltage E_f. Consequently an overexcited synchronous machine is more rigidly coupled than the one which is underexcited. Large air-gap decreases the value of X_s or X_d, thus a synchronous machine with longer air-gap is more stiffer than the one with smaller air-gap.

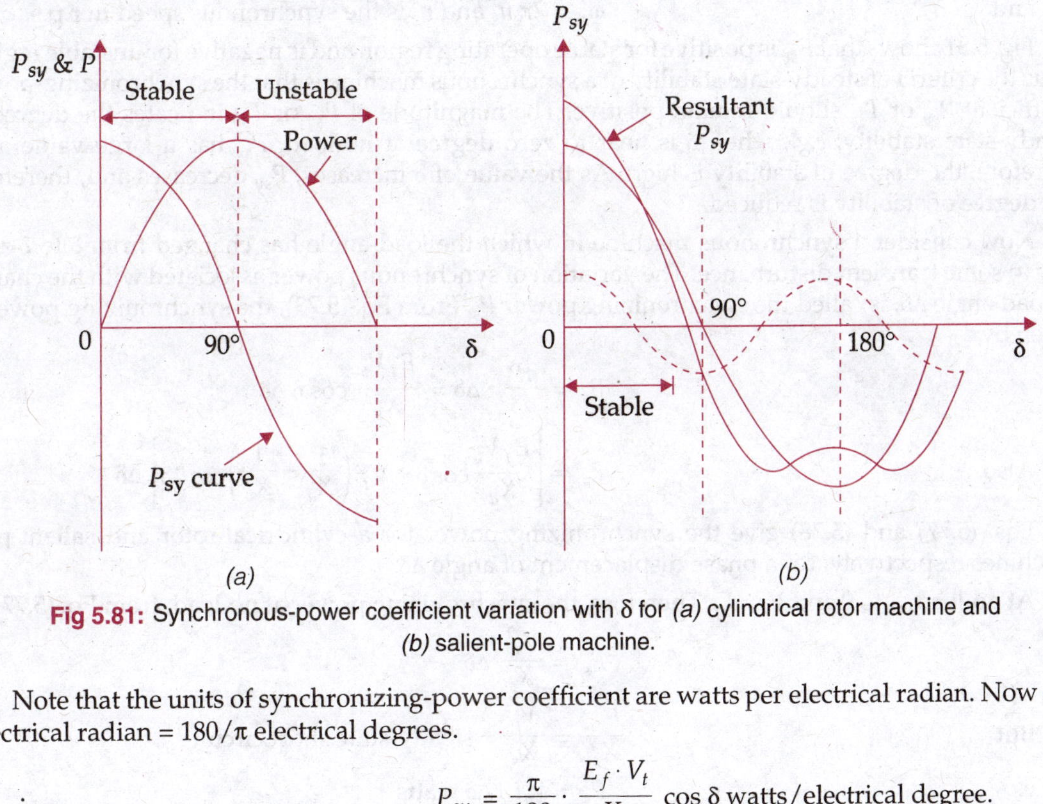

Fig 5.81: Synchronous-power coefficient variation with δ for *(a)* cylindrical rotor machine and *(b)* salient-pole machine.

Note that the units of synchronizing-power coefficient are watts per electrical radian. Now one electrical radian = 180/π electrical degrees.

$$\therefore \quad P_{sy} = \frac{\pi}{180} \cdot \frac{E_f \cdot V_t}{X_s} \cos\delta \text{ watts/electrical degree.}$$

It should be noted that one electrical degree in space is smaller than one mechanical degree in space, for machines with more than two poles. For example, in a 6-pole machine, one electrical degree in space is equal to 1/3 of one mechanical degree in space. In general,

$$\text{One electrical degree in space} = \frac{2}{P}\text{(one mechanical degree in space)}.$$

$$\therefore \qquad P_{sy} = \frac{\pi}{180}\cdot\frac{E_f \cdot V_t}{X_s}\cos\delta \; \frac{W}{\text{elect. deg}}$$

$$= \frac{\pi}{180}\cdot\frac{E_f V_t}{X_s}\cdot\cos\delta \; \frac{W}{\frac{2}{P}\cdot\text{mech. deg}}$$

or
$$P_{sy} = \frac{P\pi}{360}\cdot\frac{E_f V_t}{X_s}\cos\delta \text{ watts/mech. deg.} \qquad \text{...(5.75)}$$

Synchronizing-power coefficient gives rise to synchronizing torque coefficients at synchronous speed. If T_{sy} is the synchronizing torque coefficient, the

$$T_{sy} = \frac{1}{\omega_s}\, m\,\frac{dP}{d\delta} \text{ Nm/elect.rad.}$$

or
$$T_{sy} = \frac{1}{\omega_s}\, m\,\frac{dP}{d\delta}\cdot\frac{P\pi}{360} \text{ Nm/mech.deg.} \qquad \text{...(5.76)}$$

where m = number of phases

and $\omega_s = 2\pi\, n_s$ and n_s is the synchronous speed in r.p.s.

Fig. 5.81 shows that P_{sy} is positive for stable operating region and is negative for unstable region. Thus the criteria of steady-state stability of a synchronous machine is that the synchronizing-power coefficient P_{sy} or T_{sy} should remain positive. The magnitude of P_{sy} or T_{sy} indicates the degree of steady-state stability; *e.g.*, when δ is near to zero degree at no-load, P_{sy} has a large value and, therefore, the degree of stability is high. As the value of δ increases, P_{sy} decreases and, therefore, the degree of stability is reduced.

Now consider a synchronous machine in which the load-angle has changed from δ to δ + Δδ due to some transient disturbance. The variation of synchronous power associated with the change of load angle Δδ, is called the synchronizing power P_s. From Eq. (5.73), the synchronizing power is given by

$$P_s = \frac{dP}{d\delta}\cdot\Delta\delta = \frac{E_f V_t}{X_s}\cos\delta\,\Delta\delta \qquad \text{...(5.77)}$$

Also
$$P_s = \left[\frac{E_f V_t}{X_d}\cos\delta + V_t^2\left(\frac{1}{X_q} - \frac{1}{X_d}\right)\cos 2\delta\right]\Delta\delta \qquad \text{...(5.78)}$$

Eqs. (5.77) and (5.78) give the synchronizing power for a cylindrical-rotor and salient-pole machines respectively, for a phase displacement of angle Δδ.

At no-load, δ ≅ 0 and $V_t = E_f$. Therefore, the synchronizing power at no-load, from Eq. (5.77), is

$$P_s = \frac{V_t^2}{X_s}\,\Delta\delta \qquad \text{...(5.79 a)}$$

But
$$\frac{E_f}{X_s} = \frac{V_t}{X_s} = \text{steady-state short circuit } I_{sc}.$$

$$\therefore \qquad P_s = V_t I_{sc}\,\Delta\delta \text{ watts} \qquad \text{...(5.79 b)}$$

A careful consideration reveals that synchronizing power is transient in nature, *i.e.*, it comes into play only when there is a sudden disturbance in the steady-state operating conditions. In case of generator, a sudden disturbance in prime-mover torque causes the synchronizing power to flow from, or to, the bus, in order to restore the rotor to its previous position. A sudden disturbance in the generator or motor field current, also causes the synchronizing power to come into play, so as to maintain the synchronism. In case of motor, a sudden disturbance in shaft-load torque causes the synchronizing power to flow from or to the motor, so that rotor is brought back to its initial steady position. In short, the synchronizing power comes into play only when the steady-state operating conditions are disturbed. Once the steady state condition is reached after the disturbance, the synchronizing power reduces to zero. Thus the synchronizing power is transient in nature and exists only for the time during which the disturbance persists. The synchronizing power flows from, or to, the bus, in order to maintain the relative velocity between interacting stator and rotor fields zero—once this equality is attained, the synchronizing power vanishes.

The synchronizing power gives rise to synchronizing torque T_s and its magnitude for a small displacement $\Delta\delta$ is given by

$$T_s = \frac{1}{\omega_s} P_s = \frac{1}{\omega_s} m \frac{dP}{d\delta} \cdot \Delta\delta = T_{sy} \cdot \Delta\delta \quad ...(5.80)$$

It may be seen from Eqs. (5.73) and (5.77) that synchronizing power coefficient P_{sy} is equal to the synchronizing power per unit of phase displacement, *i.e.*, $P_s = P_{sy} \cdot \Delta\delta$. Similarly $T_s = T_{sy} \cdot \Delta\delta$.

If armature resistance is not neglected for a cylindrical-rotor machine, then from Eqs. (5.32) and (5.34), the synchronizing power is given by

$$P_s = \frac{E_f V_t}{Z_s} \cos(\delta + \alpha_z) \cdot \Delta\delta \quad ...(5.81)$$

where $\alpha_z = \tan^{-1} \dfrac{r_a}{X_s}$.

5.13.1. Physical Concepts of Synchronizing Power

Consider a synchronous motor connected to an infinite bus with terminal voltage V_t, armature current I_a, excitation voltage E_f and steady-state load angle δ. The angle δ depends on the load on the motor shaft.

Due to some transient disturbance, let the load angle increase from δ to δ + Δδ. This disturbance causes the rotor to shift back by an angle Δδ from its previous position. Since the phasor E_f depends on the rotor position, this small departure Δδ causes the phasor E_f to shift back from its steady-state position *OA* to new position *OB*. The voltage phasor V_t is not affected by transient disturbance, because V_t is the terminal voltage of infinite bus. The small departure Δδ from *OA* to *OB*, causes the appearance of synchronizing voltage $E_s = BA$, see Fig. 5.82.

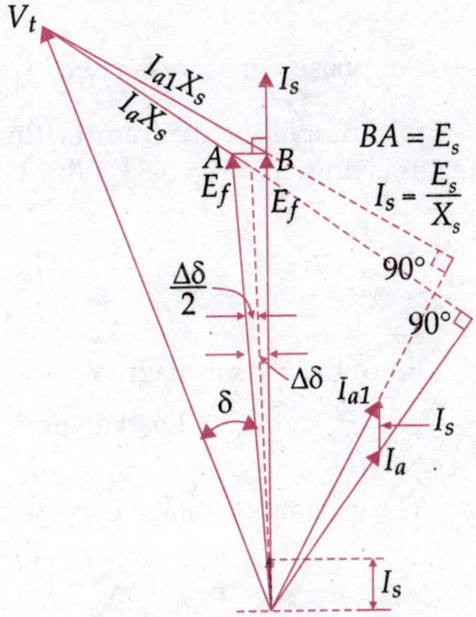

Fig 5.82: Pertaining to the physical concept of synchronizing power.

$$\therefore \quad E_s = BA = 2E_f \sin \frac{\Delta\delta}{2}.$$

When E_f shifts back, I_aX_s drop increases to $I_{a1}X_s$, *i.e.* armature current increases from I_a to I_{a1} and this gives rise to synchronizing current I_s, such that $\bar{I}_{a1} = \bar{I}_a + \bar{I}_s$. Remember that it is the synchronizing voltage E_s that causes the appearance of synchronizing current I_s.

$$\therefore \quad I_s = \frac{E_s}{X_s}^* = 2 E_f \cdot \frac{1}{X_s} \sin \frac{\Delta\delta}{2}$$

* In case the load angle changes from δ to δ + Δδ very rapidly, X_s should be replaced by X_d' or X_d'', depending upon how fast Δδ changes with time.

Note that I_s lags E_s by 90° because only X_s is considered.

Now the angle between V_t and synchronizing current I_s is equal to $\left(\delta+\frac{\Delta\delta}{2}\right)$. Therefore, the synchronizing power flow from bus to the motor is

$$P_s = V_t I_s \cos\left(\delta+\frac{\Delta\delta}{2}\right)$$

or

$$P_s = V_t \cdot \frac{2E_f}{X_s} \cdot \sin\frac{\Delta\delta}{2} \cdot \cos\left(\delta+\frac{\Delta\delta}{2}\right)$$

For small disturbance $\Delta\delta$, $\sin\frac{\Delta\delta}{2} = \frac{\Delta\delta}{2}$ and $\cos\left(\delta+\frac{\Delta\delta}{2}\right) = \cos\delta$.

$\therefore$ Synchronizing power, $$P_s = \frac{E_f V_t}{X_s}\cos\delta \cdot \Delta\delta = \frac{dP}{d\delta} \cdot \Delta\delta = P_{sy} \cdot \Delta\delta.$$

In case load angle decreases from δ to $\delta - \Delta\delta$ due to some disturbance, then synchronizing power would flow from motor to infinite bus.

Example 5.35. *A 20 MVA, 3-phase star-connected 11 kV, 12 pole, 50 Hz salient-pole synchronous motor, with negligible armature resistance, has reactances of $X_d = 5\ \Omega$ and $X_q = 3\ \Omega$. At full load, unity power-factor and rated voltage, compute :*

(a) The excitation voltage.

(b) Power (and check the result).

(c) Synchronizing power per electrical degree and the corresponding torque.

(d) Synchronizing power per mechanical degree and the corresponding torque.

(e) Maximum value of power-angle δ and the corresponding power.

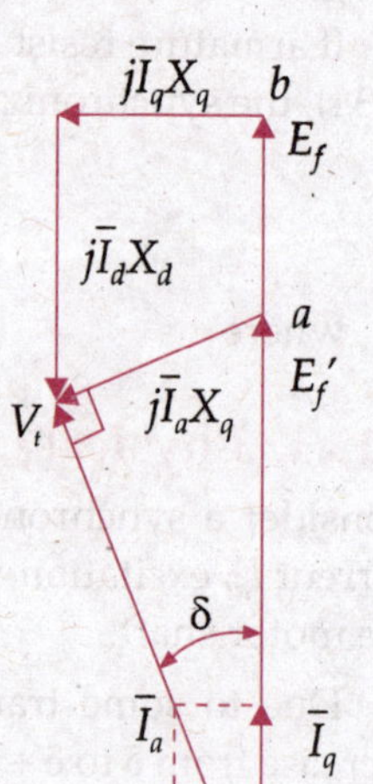

Fig 5.83: Phasor diagram, Example 5.35.

Solution. Per phase terminal voltage, $V_t = \frac{11,000}{\sqrt{3}} = 6,350$ V.

Per phase armature current, $I_a = \frac{20,000}{\sqrt{3}(11)} = 1049$ A.

(a) The phasor diagram of the synchronous motor at unity power-factor is drawn in Fig. 5.83. With V_t as reference phasor,

$$\bar{V}_t = 6350 + j0.00$$

$$\bar{I}_a = 1049 + j0.00$$

$$\therefore \quad j\bar{I}_a X_q = j(1049 + j0.00)(3) = 0 + j3147.$$

From the phasor diagram, $oa = \bar{E}_f' = \bar{V}_t - j\bar{I}_a X_q = 6350 - j\,3147 = 7090\angle -26.4°$.

$\therefore$ Load angle $\delta = 26.4°$.

Now $I_d = I_a \sin\delta = (1049)(0.444) = 466$ A.

The excitation voltage E_f is the arithmetic sum of oa and ab

$$\therefore \quad E_f = oa + ab$$

$$E_f' + I_d(X_d - X_q) = 7090 + 466\,(5-3) = 3022 \text{ volts to neutral.}$$

(b) $$P = \frac{E_f V_t}{X_d}\sin\delta + \frac{V_t^2}{2}\left(\frac{X_d - X_q}{X_d X_q}\right)\sin 2\delta.$$

$$P = \frac{(8022)(6350)}{5}\sin 26.4° + \frac{(6350)^2(5-3)}{(2)(5)(3)}\sin 52.8°$$

$$= 6670 \text{ kW per phase.}$$

For three phases, $P = 6670 \times 3 = 20{,}010$ kW, which is almost equal to the specified 20,000 kW. The small difference springs from the rounding off the calculated values.

(c) Synchronizing power per electrical radian is given by

$$\frac{dP}{d\delta} = \frac{E_t V_t}{X_d} \cos \delta + V_t^2 \left(\frac{X_d - X_q}{X_d X_q}\right) \cos 2\delta$$

$$= \frac{(8022)(6350)}{5} \cos 26.4° + (6350)^2 \left(\frac{2}{15}\right) \cos 52.8°$$

$= 12{,}370$ kW per phase

$= 37{,}110$ kW for 3-phases.

∴ Synchronizing power per electrical degree

$$= \frac{(37{,}110)(\pi)}{180} = 647 \text{ kW}$$

and the corresponding synchronizing torque,

$$T_s = \frac{647 \times 10^3}{\omega_s} = \frac{647 \times 10^3}{2\pi n_s}.$$

But n_s = Synchronous speed in rps $= \dfrac{2f}{P} = \dfrac{100}{12}$

$$\therefore \quad T_s = \frac{647 \times 10^3 \times 12}{2\pi(100)} = 12{,}360 \text{ Nm.}$$

(d) Synchronizing power per mechanical degree

$$= 647 \times \frac{P}{2} = 647 \times \frac{12}{2} = 3882 \text{ kW.}$$

and the corresponding synchronizing torque

$$= \frac{(3882)(10)^3(12)}{2\pi(100)} = 74{,}160 \text{ Nm.}$$

(e) At constant V_t and E_f, the maximum value of power angle is given by Eq. (5.72), *i.e.*

$$\cos \delta = -\frac{E_f X_q}{4V_t(X_d - X_q)} + \sqrt{\frac{1}{2} + \left[\frac{E_f X_q}{4V_t(X_d - X_q)}\right]^2}$$

$$= \frac{-(8022)(3)}{4(6350)(2)} + \sqrt{\frac{1}{2} + \left[\frac{(8022)(3)}{4(6350)(2)}\right]^2} = 0.3775.$$

Thus the maximum value of power angle is $\cos^{-1}(0.3775) = 67.85°$.

$$\therefore \quad P_{max} = \frac{(8022)(6350)}{5} \sin 67.85° + \frac{(6350)^2}{2} \cdot \frac{2}{15} \sin 135.70°$$

$= 11{,}325$ kW per phase

$= 33{,}975$ kW for 3-phases.

Example 5.36. *A 3000 kVA, 3-phase, star-connected, 6,600 volt, 8-pole, 50 Hz alternator has a synchronous reactance of 20% and is running in parallel with infinite bus. Calculate the synchronizing power and the corresponding synchronizing torque per-mechanical degree of phase displacement (a) at no-load and (b) at full load, 0.8 power-factor lagging.*

Solution. Per phase voltage, $V_t = \dfrac{6600}{\sqrt{3}} = 3810$ V

Per phase armature current, $I_a = \dfrac{(3000)(10)^3}{\sqrt{3}(6600)} = 262$ A

Percentage reactance, $X_s = \dfrac{X_s \text{ in ohms}}{V_t / I_a} \times 100$

$\therefore$ X_s in ohms $= \dfrac{20}{100} \times \dfrac{3810}{262} = 2.90$

(a) At no-load, $\delta \cong 0$ and $V_t = E_f$

$\therefore$ Synchronizing power per mechanical degree,

$$P_s = m \cdot \frac{dP}{d\delta} \cdot \frac{\pi P}{360} = 3\,\frac{V_t E_f}{X_s} \cos\delta \cdot \frac{\pi P}{360}$$

$$= \frac{3(3810)^2}{2.90} \cdot \frac{\pi(8)}{360} = 1048 \text{ kW}$$

The corresponding synchronizing torque is

$$T_s = \frac{60}{2\pi N_s} \cdot P_s = \frac{P_s}{2\pi n_s} = \frac{1 \times 8}{2\pi \cdot (100)} (1048)(10^3) = 13{,}340 \text{ Nm}$$

(b) The phasor diagram for an alternator, operating at a lagging power factor is given in Fig. 5.77 (b). With V_t as a reference phasor,

$$\bar{E}_f = 3810 + j262\,(0.8 - j0.6)\,(2.9) = 4310 \angle 8.11°$$

The synchronizing power per mechanical degree is

$$P_s = 3\,\frac{\pi P}{360} \cdot \frac{E_f \cdot V_t}{X_s} \cos\delta$$

$$= 3\,\frac{\pi \times 8}{360} \cdot \frac{(4310)(3810)}{29} \cos 8.11 = 1173 \text{ kW.}$$

The corresponding synchronizing torque is

$$T_s = \frac{1}{2\pi n_s} P_s = \frac{8}{2\pi(100)} (1173 \times 10^3) = 14{,}930 \text{ Nm.}$$

Example 5.37. *A star-connected 8 pole, 50 Hz synchronous motor has synchronous reactance of 11 Ω per phase. On no-load, both the excitation and the terminal voltages are requal to 3.3 kV. Neglect all losses.*

(a) For a sudden disturbance in the shaft-load torque, the rotor falls back in space by one mechanical degree. Calculate the synchrnoizing current, synchronizing power and synchronizing torque tending to restore the rotor to its previous position.

(b) With gradual increase in the shaft load, the rotor slides back in space by one mechanical degree. Calculate the armature current. For an armature current of 30 A, find the angle in mechanical degrees, through which the rotor slips back.

Solution. For this example, refer to Fig. 5.82.

(a) At no-load, $\delta \cong 0$.

$\therefore$ E_f and V_t are in phase.

One mechanical degree in space $= \dfrac{8}{2}$ electrical degrees in space $= \Delta\delta = 4°$

$\therefore$ Synchronizing voltage, $BA = E_s = 2E_f \sin\dfrac{\Delta\delta}{2} = 2\,(3300) \sin\dfrac{4}{2} = 230$ V.

Synchronizing current in the armature, $I_s = \frac{E_s}{X_s} = \frac{230}{11} = 20.91$ A.

Synchronizing power, $P_s = m\ V_t I_s \cos\left(\delta + \frac{\Delta\delta}{2}\right)$

$$= 3\ (3300)\ (20.91)\cos(0 + 2°) = 206.9 \text{ kW}.$$

Synchronous speed, $\omega_s = 2\pi\ n_s = 2\pi \times \frac{2 \times 50}{8} = 25\pi$ rad/sec.

∴ Synchronizing torque, $T_s = \frac{1}{25\pi}(206{,}900) = 2634$ Nm.

(*b*) When the rotor slides back by one mechanical degree, then $I_a X_s$ drop becomes equal to 230 V and the armature current increases from zero to 20.91 amperes.

For an armature current of 30 A, $I_a = 30 = \frac{2E_f \sin\frac{\Delta\delta}{2}}{X_s} = \frac{2 \times 3300}{11}\sin\frac{\Delta\delta}{2}$

or $\sin\frac{\Delta\delta}{2} = \frac{330}{2 \times 3300} 0.05.$

∴ $\Delta\delta = 5.732$ electrical degrees.

∴ The rotor slips back by $\frac{5.732 \times 1}{4} = 1.433$ machanical degrees.

5.14. SYNCHRONOUS MACHINE STABILITY

Any machine system is said to be stable if, under steady state, it is operating in equilibrium and a slight disturbance does not effect the stable operation. The term equilibrium denotes perfect power balance between input and output powers.

A synchronous machine connected to an infinite bus is said to be working in a stable condition, if it is in synchronism or in step with the bus. Unstable operation denotes loss of synchronism or falling out of step.

Stablility. The tendency of a synchronous machine to develop forces so as to maintain synchronism and equilibrium, is called stability.

Stability limit. A stability limit represents the maximum power flow possible, when the synchronous machine is operating with stability.

The terms stability and stability limit are applicable both to steady-state and transient conditions.

Steady state stability limit. It pertains to the maximum power flow possible through a particular point without loss of stability, when the power is increased very gradually.

Assume that the load on synchronous motor is increased gradually, until point C of maximum power is reached. If an additional increment of shaft load is put on the motor, the load-angle δ would increase as demanded by the load. But with an increase in δ beyond that given by point C, the electric power input decreases, as is obvious from the shape of the power-angle curves in Figs. 5.84 and 5.85 for salient-pole and cylindrical-rotor synchronous machines. Since, with the increase of shaft load, the electrical power input has decreased, the motor gets retarded more quickly. As a consequence of it, the angle δ increases further and the motor pulls out of step or loses synchronism. Thus P_m given by the point C is the steady-state (or static) stability limit—the region to the left of point C is stable one.

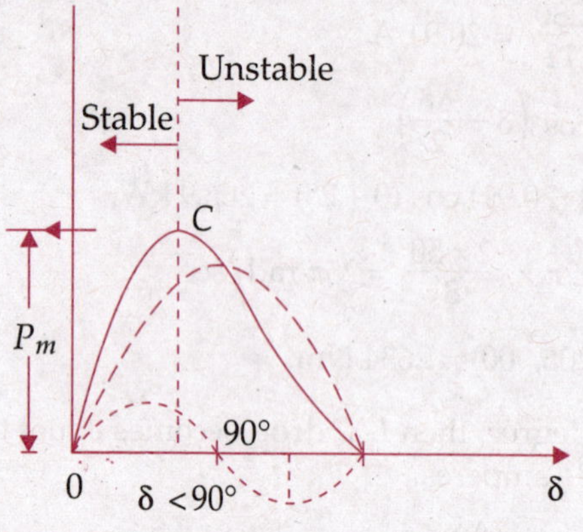

Fig 5.84: Salient-pole synchronous machine power-angle characteristics.

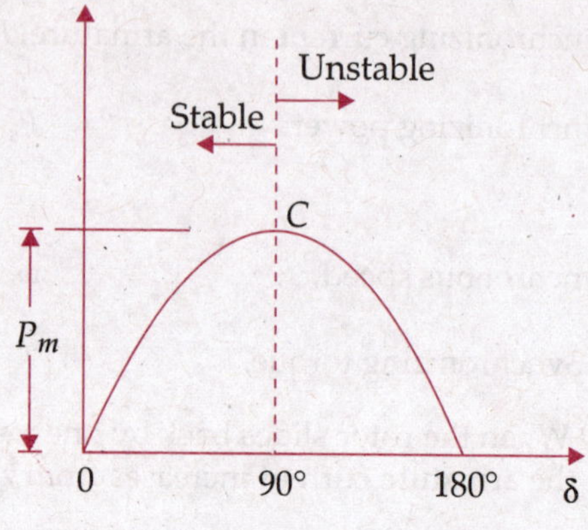

Fig 5.85: Cylindrical-rotor synchronous machine power-angle characteristics.

The steady-state limit can be improved upon as follows :

(i) Synchronous machine excitation should be increased, so that E_f becomes more.

(ii) Reactance should be decreased, *e.g.*, two transmission lines in parallel would reduce the line reactance to half.

(iii) Series capacitors may be used to reduce the line reactance.

Transient stability limit. It refers to the maximum power flow possible through a point without loss of stability, when a sudden disturbance occurs. Sometimes a transient disturbance, such as a sudden increment of load, may cause the loss of stability because of its sudden application, but may be carried without loss of synchronism if it were applied gradually. Usually the disturbances for which the transient stability limit is desired to be known, are caused by a fault, or by switching in or out some circuits in a supply system, or by a sudden increment of shaft load.

Transient stability limit is more important since

(i) it is lower than steady state stability limit and

(ii) the transient disturbances are more common.

The object of studying the transient stability of a synchronous machine is to find whether or not the synchronism is maintained, *i.e.*, whether or not the load angle δ settles down to a steady operating value, after the machine has been subjected to a large disturbance.

The method of determining the transient stability of a system is known as the equal area criterion and has been dealt with in detail in the companion volume, in the chapter on synchronous machines.

5.15. HUNTING AND DAMPER WINDINGS

In this article, physical concepts of hunting in a synchronous machine are described first. Then the use of damper bars in damping out these rotor oscillations, or hunting, is presented.

5.15.1. Hunting

A synchronous machine operates satisfactorily, if the mechanical speed of the rotor is equal to the stator field speed, *i.e.*, if the relative speed between the rotor and stator fields is zero. Any departure from these conditions, gives rise to synchronizing forces, which tend to maintain this equality.

Unloaded synchronous motor operation is illustrated in Figs. 5.86 and 5.87, where all the losses are neglected and load angle δ is assumed zero at no-load. The rotor structure in Fig. 5.86 is shown different from its actual construction, merely for simplicity in showing the rotor oscillations. In the phasor diagram of Fig. 5.87, X_d and X_q are assumed equal for convenience.

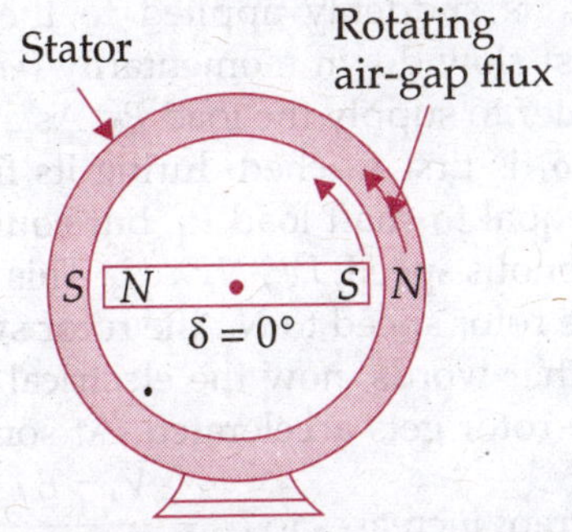

Fig 5.86: Physical interpretation of an unloaded synchronous motor.

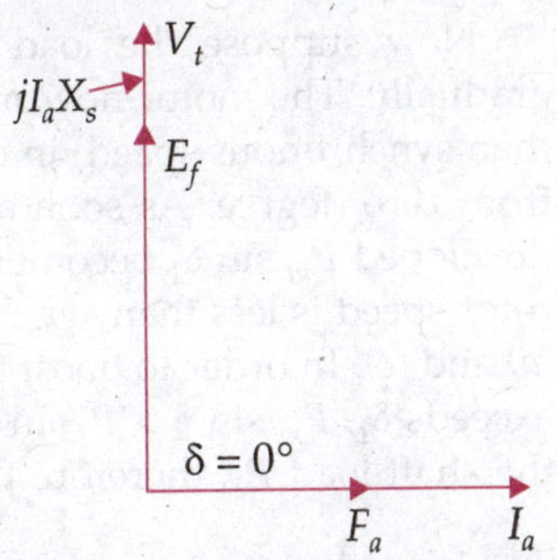

Fig 5.87: Phasor diagram of synchronous motor at no-load.

If the shaft load is put on the synchronous motor in small steps, the load angle would increase gradually from zero. For any shaft load P_1, the load angle would be δ_1 (say), armature current would be I_{a1}, this is illustrated in Fig. 5.88 *(a)*, *(b)* and *(c)*. Under steady state, $P_1 = \frac{E_f \cdot V_t}{X_s} \sin\delta_1 = P_m \sin\delta_1$ and the operating point is *'a'* as indicated in Fig. 5.88 *(a)*, *(b)* and *(c)*. This operating point travels from *'o'* to *'a'* as the load is gradually increased to P_1, Fig. 5.88 *(c)*.

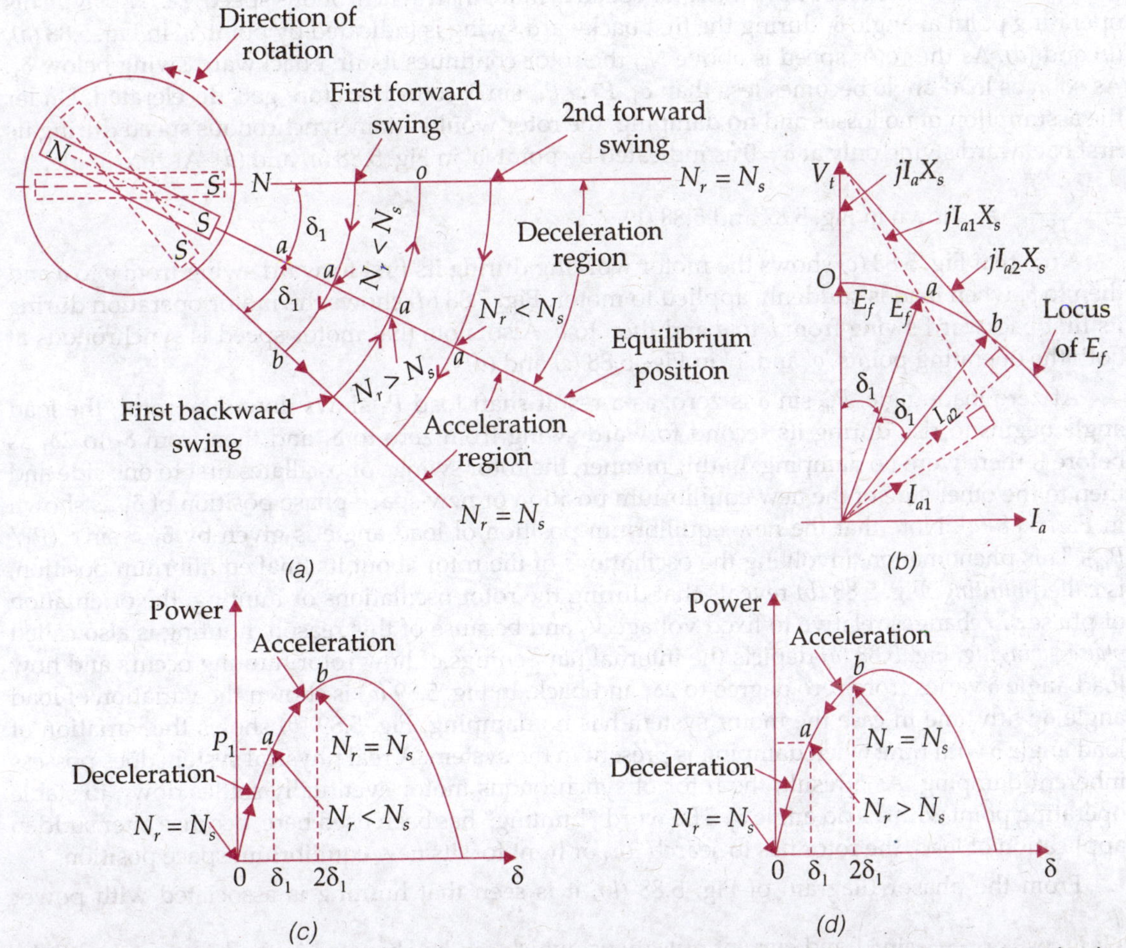

Fig 5.88: Illustrating the rotor hunting in a synchronous motor *(c)* First forward swing *(d)* First backward swing

Now suppose the load P_1 is suddenly applied to the unloaded motor shaft, instead of gradually. The motor now must slow down momentarily (*i.e.*, the rotor speed must become less than synchronous speed) in order to supply the load P_1. As a result, load angle starts building up from zero degree. As soon as δ_1 is first reached during its first forward swing, electrical power developed $P_m \sin \delta_1$ becomes equal to shaft load P_1, but equilibrium is not established, since the rotor speed is less than synchronous speed, *i.e.*, $N_r < N_s$. This is indicated by point *'a'* in Figs. 5.88 *(a)* and *(c)*. In order to boost the rotor speed to N_s, the rotor swings further. As soon as load angle exceeds δ_1, $P_m \sin \delta > P_1$. In other words, now the electrical power input $P_m \sin \delta$ has exceeded the shaft load P_1, therefore the rotor gets accelerated. At some angle $\delta_2 = 2\delta_1$, the rotor attains synchronous speed and the current increases to $I_{a2} = \dfrac{\overline{V}_t - \overline{E}_f}{jX_s}$.

The operation at load angle $2\delta_1$ is indicated by point *'b'* in Fig. 5.88 *(a)*, *(b)* and *(c)*. Note that for the rotor travel from *'o'* to *'a'*, the rotor decelerates ($\because P_m \sin \delta < P_1$) and from *a* to *b*, the rotor accelerates ($\because P_m \sin \delta > P_1$). At load angle $2\delta_1$, point *b* in Fig 5.88(c), $N_r = N_s$ but $P_m \sin \delta$ is still greater than P_1, the rotor therefore continues to accelerate even above synchronous speed. The effect of rotor speeding up above synchronous speed causes the load angle to decrease from $2\delta_1$. After some time, load angle decreases to δ_1, though $P_m \sin \delta_1 = P_1$ at this angle, the equilibrium is not yet established, because now the rotor speed is more than synchronous speed, *i.e.*, $N_r > N_s$. This operating point at angle δ_1 during the first backward swing is indicated by point *'a'* in Fig. 5.88 *(a)*, *(b)* and *(d)*. As the rotor speed is above N_s, the rotor continues its first backward swing below δ_1. As soon as load angle becomes less than δ_1, $P_1 > P_m \sin \delta$, rotor therefore gets decelerated. Under the assumption of no losses and no damping, the rotor would attain synchronous speed during its first backward swing only at $\delta = 0$ as indicated by point *'o'* in Fig. 5.88 *(a)* and *(d)*. At zero angle, $\overline{I}_a = \dfrac{\overline{V}_t - \overline{E}_f}{jX_s}$ as shown in Fig. 5.87 and 5.88 *(b)*.

Note that Fig. 5.88 *(c)* shows the motor working during its first forward swing from *o* to *a* and then to *b*, when load is suddenly applied to motor. Fig. 5.88 *(d)* shows the motor operation during its first backward swing from *b* to *a* and then to *o*. Also, note that motor speed is synchronous at both the operating points *'o'* and *'b'* in Figs 5.88 *(c)* and *(d)*.

At zero load-angle, $P_m \sin \delta$ is zero, as a result shaft load P_1 slows down the rotor, the load angle begins to rise during its second forward swing from zero to δ_1 and then from δ_1 to $2\delta_1$ as before if there were no damping. In this manner, the rotor swings or oscillates first to one side and then to the other side of the new equilibrium position or new space-phase position of δ_1 as shown in Fig. 5.88 *(a)*. Note that the new equilibrium position of load angle is given by $\delta_1 = \sin^{-1} (P_1/P_m)$. This phenomenon, involving the oscillations of the rotor about its final equilibrium position, is called *hunting*. Fig. 5.88 *(b)* reveals that during the rotor oscillations or hunting, the orientation of phasor E_f changes relative to fixed voltage V_t and because of this reason, hunting is also called *phase-swinging*. Fig. 5.88 *(a)* depicts the internal happenings of how rotor hunting occurs and how load angle δ varies from zero degree to $2\delta_1$ and back. In Fig. 5.89 *(a)* is shown the variation of load angle δ with time in case the motor system has no damping. Fig. 5.89 *(b)* shows the variation of load angle δ with time when damping is present in the system. A real physical system does possess inherent damping. As a result, the rotor of synchronous motor eventually settles down to stable operating point with a load angle δ_1. The word "hunting" has been used here, because after sudden application of load, the rotor has to search for, or hunt for, its new equilibrium space position.

From the phasor diagram of Fig. 5.88 *(b)*, it is seen that hunting is associated with power $\left(V_t I_a \cos\theta \text{ or } \dfrac{E_f V_t}{X_s} \sin\delta\right)$ and current pulsations, which can be observed in the laboratory with the help of wattmeter and ammeter. The rotor hunting can also be observed in the laboratory by means of a stroboscope light falling on the rotor shaft. At normal synchronous speed the rotor appears stationary.

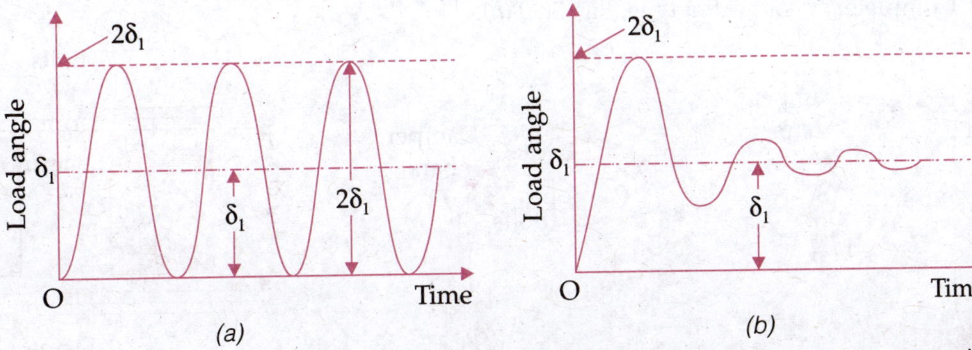

Fig 5.89: Variation of load angle δ, after sudden loading of an unloaded synchronous motor with *(a)* no damping and *(b)* damping present.

In an alternator synchronized with infinite bus, if the gate-opening in case of hydroelectric power stations (or steam-valve opening in case of thermal power stations) is decreased suddenly, the alternator will slow down momentarily thereby decreasing the load angle. Rotor oscillations or hunting will follow before the final equilibrium space position is reached.

Hunting is objectionable, particularly when the synchronous machine is coupled with a system whose torque variations contain harmonics, *e.g.*, air-compressor, reciprocating engine etc. If frequency of the torque component happens to be equal to that of the frequency of free oscillations of synchronous machine the latter may fall out of step. The other bad effects of hunting are as follows :

(i) It produces severe mechanical stress and fatigue in the shaft.

(ii) It causes great surges in current and power flow.

(iii) It increases machine losses and thus the temperature rise of the machine.

The various causes of hunting may be

(a) a sudden change in load,

(b) a fault in the supply system,

(c) a sudden change in field current,

(d) a load or drive containing harmonic torques.

The undesirable phenomenon of hunting, can be guarded against in three ways :

(i) by using a flywheel,

(ii) by designing the synchronous machine with suitable synchronizing power coefficient or stiffness factor and

(iii) by the employment of damper or amortisseur windings and this is discussed below in detail.

5.15.2. Damper Windings

Damper windings consist of low-resistance copper, brass or aluminium bars, embedded in slots in the pole-faces of salient-pole machines. The projecting ends of the bars are connected to short-circuiting strips of the same material as used for the bars. Sometimes interpolar connectors are omitted to form *incomplete type* of damper winding as shown in Fig. 5.90 *(a)*. When strips on both sides of the pole shoes are joined by interpolar connectors as in Fig. 5.90 *(b)*, *complete type* of damper winding is obtained. Fig. 5.90 *(c)* shows how strips are interconnected by interpolar connectors. It is seen from above that damper windings are of two types :

(*i*) Incomplete, non-connected, or open type, Fig. 5.90 *(a)*.

(*ii*) Complete, or connected type, Fig. 5.90 *(b)*.

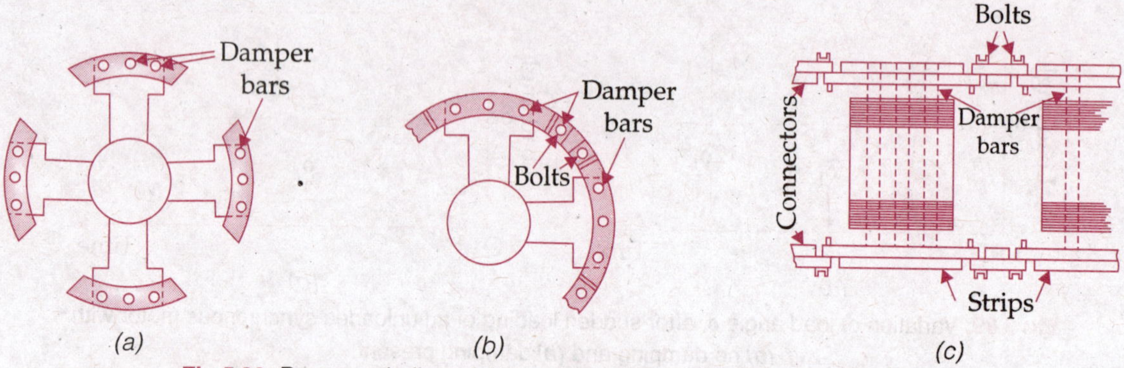

Fig 5.90: Damper windings *(a)* incomplete type, *(b)* and *(c)* complete type.

An additional equivalent rotor circuit, providing the damping effect, may be formed by the bolts and iron of the salient-pole structure. The salient-pole circuit which takes part in damping out the rotor hunting, is called amortisseur circuit. In view of this, damper winding is also called amortisseur winding.

Damper windings are not used on turbo-generators. But the solid-steel rotor cores of such machines, provide path for eddy currents, especially in the quadrature axis, where the iron may form an equivalent rotor circuit, thus producing the same effects as those of damper bars.

Damper bars may form the starting winding for synchronous motors of the salient-pole type. For good starting torque, damper bars should have high resistance. But for large damping effect near synchronous speed, the damper bars should have low resistance. Therefore, a compromise between good starting torque and good damping effect should be made, for obtaining satisfactory operation of the synchronous motor. However, such a problem does not exist in alternators, because the purpose of damper bars in them is merely to damp out rotor oscillations, *i.e.*, hunting. Therefore, low-resistance damper winding can be used in alternators.

It should be noted that when the rotor is running at synchronous speed, the relative speed between damper bars and rotating air-gap flux is zero. Because of zero relative speed, no flux-cutting action takes place and e.m.f. generated in damper bars is zero—consequently no damping torque is developed. The damper winding comes into play only during rotor hunting, when rotor speed departs from synchronous speed.

In order to understand how the damper bars damp out hunting, assume the rotor speed to become 10 r.p.m. less than the synchronous speed of 1500 r.p.m. (say), Fig. 5.91 *(a)*. Under this assumption, the relative velocity between rotor and air-gap field is 10 r.p.m., Fig. 5.91 *(b)*. If *S* pole is assumed on the stator near the damper bar, an e.m.f. shown by a dot* is induced in the bar, Fig. 5.91 *(b)*. This bar current sets up its own flux lines which interact with the *S* pole to produce a torque in the direction of rotation as shown in Fig. 5.91 *(c)*.

* Superimpose a velocity of 10 r.p.m. (so that rotating S pole becomes stationary) from left (L) to right (R) on both S pole and damper bar in Fig. 5.91 (b). Under this condition, S pole comes to a standstill but damper bar moves from L to R at 10 r.p.m. Now apply right hand rule for determining the direction of e.m.f. in the damper bar. According to this rule, thumb is in the direction of rotation, first finger (near the thumb) is in the direction of flux lines and middle finger gives the direction of e.m.f. Note that thumb, first finger are in the same plane but normal (i.e. perpendicular) to each other; the middle finger is normal to the plane of thumb and first finger.

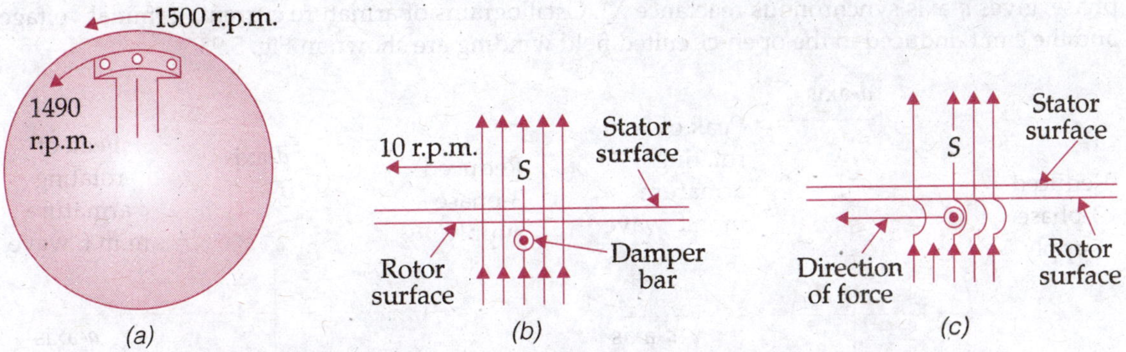

Fig 5.91: Pertaining to the production of torque due to damper bars.

The effect of this torque is to accelerate the rotor, tending to make the two speeds equal. This torque in the direction of rotation, is known as induction motor torque and is produced whenever the rotor speed falls below the synchronous speed.

Likewise, when the rotor speed becomes greater than synchronous speed, induction generator torque (against the direction of rotation) is produced, which tends to retard the rotor and make the two speeds equal. In other words, when the rotor speed falls below the synchronous speed, the slip becomes temporarily positive, induction motor action comes into play and rotor is accelerated—when the rotor speed exceeds synchronous speed, the slip becomes temporarily negative, induction generator action takes place and rotor is retarded.

Thus, when the rotor speed departs from the synchronous speed, the damping torques (motor or generating torques) are brought into play to make the relative speed between rotor and stator fields as zero. The magnitude of these damping torques is approximately proportional to the slip speed, provided the slip is small.

5.16. MEASUREMENT OF X_d AND X_q

The *d*-axis synchronous reactance is determined from o.c. and s.c. tests, as illustrated by Ex. 5.25. The *q*-axis synchronous reactance can be measured by the following three methods:

(a) **Slip test.** From this test, the values of X_d and X_q can be determined. The synchronous machine is driven by a separate prime-mover (or motor) at a speed slightly different from synchronous speed. The field winding is left open and positive sequence balanced voltages of reduced magnitude (around 25% of rated value) and of rated frequency are impressed across the armature terminals. Under these conditions, the relative velocity between the field poles and the rotating armature m.m.f. wave is equal to the difference between synchronous speed and the rotor speed, *i.e.*, the slip speed. A small A.C. voltage across the open field winding indicates that the field poles and rotating m.m.f. wave, are revolving in the same direction—and this is what is required in slip test. If field poles revolve in a direction opposite to the rotating m.m.f. wave, negative sequence reactance would be measured.

At one instant, when the peak of armature m.m.f. wave is in line with the field pole or direct axis, the reluctance offered by the small air-gap is minimum as shown in Fig. 5.92 *(a)*. At this instant the impressed terminal voltage per phase divided by the corresponding armature current per phase, gives *d*-axis synchronous reactance X_d.

After one-quarter of slip cycle, the peak of armature m.m.f. wave acts on the interpolar or *q*-axis of the magnetic circuit, Fig. 5.92 *(b)* and the reluctance offered by long air-gap is maximum. At this instant, the ratio of armature terminal voltage per phase to the corresponding armature current per phase, gives q-axis synchronous reactance X_q. Oscillograms of armature current, terminal voltage and the e.m.f. induced in the open-circuited field winding are shown in Fig. 5.93.

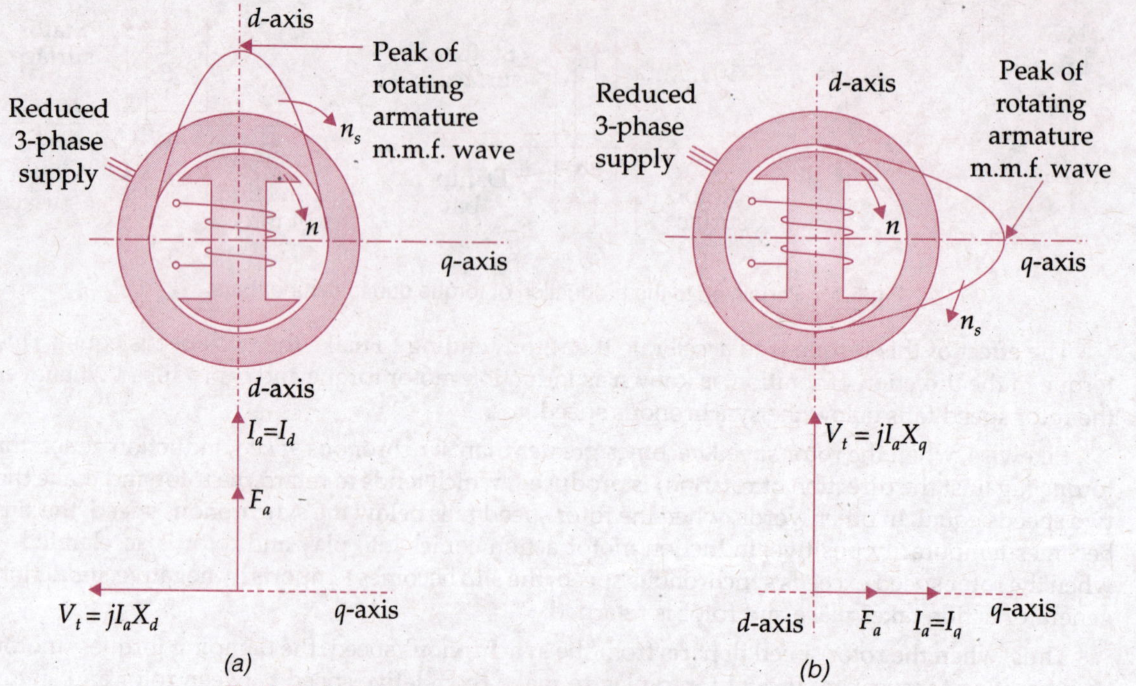

Fig 5.92: Pertaining to the physical concepts of (a) X_d and (b) X_q.

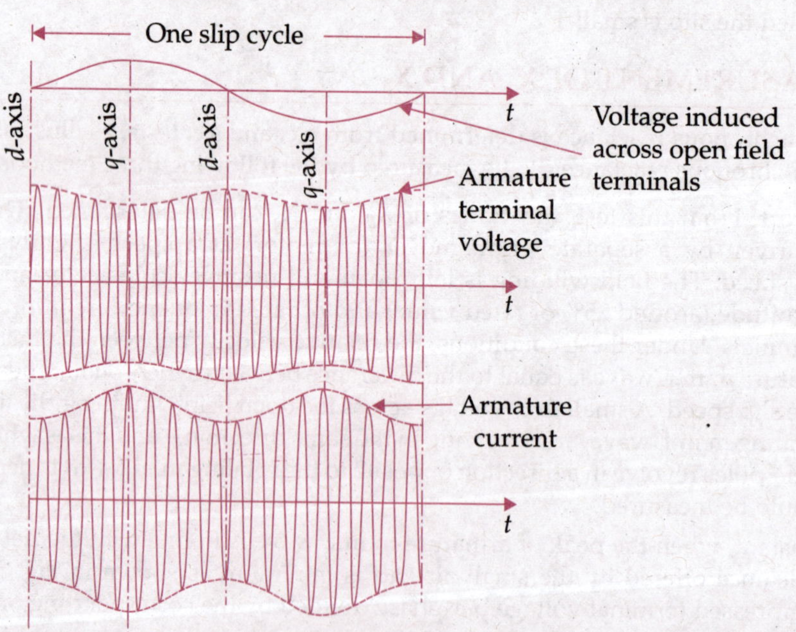

Fig 5.93: Typical oscillograms in slip test.

A much larger slip than would be used in practice, has been shown in Fig. 5.93, merely for the sake of clarity. When the armature m.m.f. wave is along the direct axis, the armature flux passing through open field winding is maximum, therefore, the induced field e.m.f., *i.e.*, $d\phi_a/dt$ is zero. The *d*-axis can, therefore, be located on the oscillogram of Fig. 5.93 where the induced field e.m.f. is zero. When armature m.m.f. wave is along *q*-axis, the armature flux linking the field winding is zero, therefore, the induced field e.m.f. $d\phi_a/dt$ is maximum. Thus the *q*-axis can also be located on the oscillogram. Waveforms of voltage across open field and the armature current in Fig. 5.93 reveal that armature current varies cyclically at twice the slip frequency.

If oscillograms can't be taken, then an ammeter and a voltmeter are used as shown in the connection diagram of Fig. 5.94. The prime-mover (or D.C. motor) speed is adjusted till ammeter and voltmeter pointers swing slowly between maximum and minimum positions. Under this condition, maximum and minimum readings of both ammeter and voltmeter are recorded in order to determine X_d and X_q. Since the applied voltage is constant, the air-gap flux would be constant. When crest of the rotating m.m.f. wave is in line with the field-pole axis, Fig. 5.92 (a), minimum air-gap offers minimum reluctance—consequently the armature current, required for the establishment of constant air-gap flux, must be minimum. Constant applied voltage minus the minimum impedance voltage drop (armature current being minimum) in the leads and 3-phase variac gives maximum armature terminal voltage. Thus the *d*-axis synchronous reactance is given by

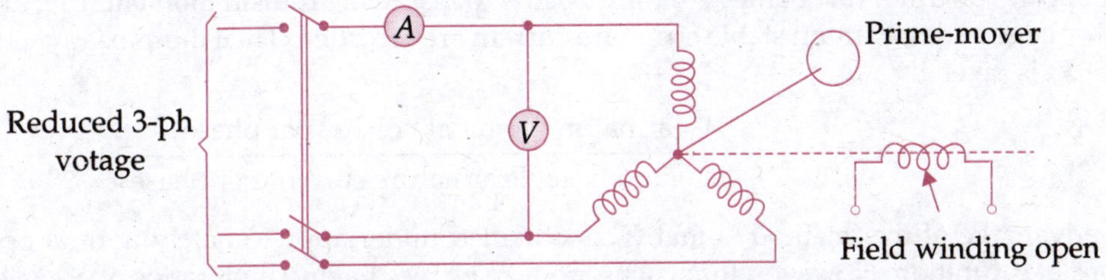

Fig 5.94: Slip-test connection diagram for obtaining X_d and X_q.

$$X_d = \frac{\text{Maximum armature terminal voltage per phase}}{\text{Minimum armature current per phase}}$$

By a similar thought process.

$$X_q = \frac{\text{Minimum armature terminal voltage per phase}}{\text{Maximum armature current per phase}}$$

During slip test, it would be observed that swing of the ammeter pointer is very wide, whereas the voltmeter has only small swing because of the low impedance voltage drop in the leads and 3-phase variac. Since low armature terminal voltages are used, values of reactances obtained are unsaturated values.

When performing this test, the slip should be made as small as possible, otherwise the currents induced in the amortisseur circuits would cause large errors in the measurement of X_d and X_q (lower value of reactances for larger slips). It is 'however' quite difficult to maintain very small slips, as the reluctance torque due to saliency tends to bring the rotor into synchronism with the rotating armature m.m.f. wave. It is because of this reason that the slip test must be conducted at low values of armature terminal voltage so that reluctance torque due to saliency is low.

The advantages of oscillographic method over voltmeter-ammeter method are *(i)* elimination of the inertia effects of voltmeter and ammeter and *(ii)* the possibility of large slip-speed, which in turn allows higher armature-terminal voltages to be applied.

In practice , there may be error in reading the oscillograms. At the same time voltmeter ammeter readings are not very reliable because of their inertia effect. In view of these shortcomings, slip test is conducted only to determine the ratio of X_q/X_d so that any error in the measurement of X_d and X_q gets cancelled. Now, using the value of X_d computed from o.c. and s.c. tests, X_q can be determined as follows :

$$\therefore \quad X_q = \left(\frac{X_q}{X_d}, \text{from slip test}\right)(X_d, \text{ from o.c. and s.c. tests}).$$

(b) **Maximum-lagging-current test.** In this test, the salient pole synchronous machine is made to run as an unloaded synchronous motor, with balanced rated voltage across its terminals. Its field current is then reduced to zero gradually. Reference to Eq. (5.69) shows that for zero field current, E_f is zero, but the reluctance power is not zero. In view of this, even for zero field current, the salient-pole synchronous motor continues running as a reluctance motor at synchronous speed. The direction of the field current is now reversed by a suitable switch. If the reversed field current, *i.e.*, the negative excitation is increased in small steps, armature current must increase due to the fact that armature m.m.f. has to magnetize the machine and has also to overcome the reversed field m.m.f. At some value of increased negative excitation, the rotor falls out of step, *i.e.*, loses synchronism momentarily—after slipping one pole, the rotor is again pulled into step with the next pole of opposite polarity. Just before the rotor begins to lose synchronism momentarily, armature terminal voltage and maximum stable armature current are recorded. Then the *q*-axis synchronous reactance X_q is given by

$$X_q = \frac{V_t(\text{armature terminal voltage per phase})}{I_a(\text{maximum stable armature current per phase})} \quad ...(5.83)$$

The advantage of this method is that X_q is obtained under approximately normal operating conditions of saturation. However, for synchronous machines having high ratios of X_d/X_q or large armature rated currents, the maximum-lagging current test may be conducted at reduced armature voltage, otherwise the maximum stable armature current may become dangerously high.

(c) **Reluctance-motor test.** For this test, the synchronous machine is run as a reluctance motor and its load is then gradually increased, till it steps out of synchronism. When the reluctance motor is on the verge of losing synchronism, *i.e.*, under maximum reluctance power conditions of $\delta = 45°$, the maximum stable armature current, armature terminal voltage and maximum stable armature power are recorded.

If damper winding is present, then the reluctance motor, just after losing synchronism, will continue running as an induction motor at a speed less than synchronous speed and the current drawn will be quite large. In view of this, care should be taken in noting the instrument readings at maximum reluctance power conditions, *i.e.*, just before the rotor begins to lose synchronism.

The reluctance power, for $E_f = 0$ in Eq. (5.69), is given by

$$P = \frac{V_t^2}{2}\left(\frac{1}{X_q} - \frac{1}{X_d}\right)\sin 2\delta$$

For maximum reluctance power, $\delta = 45°$.

$$\therefore \quad P_{max} = \frac{V_t^2}{2}\left(\frac{1}{X_q} - \frac{1}{X_d}\right)$$

Assume

$$\frac{X_d}{X_q} = K$$

$$\therefore \quad P_{max} = \frac{V_t^2}{2 \cdot X_q}\left(1 - \frac{1}{K}\right) = \frac{V_t^2}{2X_q}\left(\frac{K-1}{K}\right) \quad ...(5.84\ a)$$

From Fig. 5.80, Ex. 5.31 and for $\delta = 45°$,

$$V_t \sin\delta = X_q I_q,$$

$$\therefore \quad I_q = \frac{V_t}{\sqrt{2}X_q} \text{ and } V_t \cos\delta = X_d I_d,$$

$$\therefore \quad I_d = \frac{V_t}{\sqrt{2}X_d}$$

Now armature current

$$I_a = \sqrt{I_d^2 + I_q^2} = \frac{V_t}{\sqrt{2}}\sqrt{\frac{1}{X_d^2}+\frac{1}{X_q^2}}$$

$$= \frac{V_t}{\sqrt{2}\cdot X_q}\frac{\sqrt{1+K^2}}{K} \quad \text{...(5.84 b)}$$

Dividing Eq. (5.84 *a*) by Eq. (5.84 *b*), we get

$$\frac{P_{max}}{I_a} = \frac{V_t}{\sqrt{2}}\left\{\frac{K-1}{\sqrt{K^2+1}}\right\} \quad \text{...(5.85)}$$

Since P_{max}, I_a and V_t are measured, K can be determined from Eq. (5.85). The value of K greater than one is retained and consequently X_q can be calculated from Eq. 5.84. Then the value of d-axis synchronous reactance is given by $K \cdot X_q$. An advantage of this method is that the values of X_d and X_q can be found under approximately normal operating conditions of saturation.

Example 5.38. *Find an expression for the reactive power as a function of load angle δ ;*

(a) for a salient-pole synchronous motor working at a lagging power-factor ;

(b) for a salient-pole synchronous-generator with its field current reduced to zero.

Neglect armature resistance for both parts (a) and (b).

Solution. As stated before, the product of voltage and quadrature component of armature current gives the reactive power.

(a) For a salient-pole motor working at a lagging power factor, refer to Fig. 5.71 *(b)* for finding the reactive power.

In this figure, when $r_a = 0$, *oa* becomes equal to V_t.

$$\therefore \quad Q = V_t \cos\delta\, I_d + V_t \sin\delta I_q \quad \text{...(5.86)}$$

Also

$$V_t \sin\delta = X_q I_q, \qquad \therefore\ I_q = \frac{V_t \sin\delta}{X_q}$$

and

$$E_f + X_d I_d = V_t \cos\delta, \qquad \therefore\ I_d = \frac{V_t \cos\delta - E_f}{X_q}$$

Substituting the values of I_d and I_q in Eq. (5.86), we get

$$Q = \frac{V_t \cos\delta\left(V_t \cos\delta - E_f\right)}{X_d} + \frac{V_t \sin\delta V_t \sin\delta}{X_q}$$

$$= -\frac{E_f V_t}{X_d}\cos\delta + \frac{V_t^2}{X_d} + V_t^2\left(\frac{1}{X_q} - \frac{1}{X_d}\right)\sin^2\delta \quad \text{...(5.87)}$$

(b) The phasor diagram for a salient-pole synchronous generator with zero E_f, is shown in Fig. 5.95. The armature current is seen to be leading V_t, therefore, the generator is operating at a leading power factor.

Its reactive power Q is given by

$$Q = -V_t \cos\delta\, I_d - V_t \sin\delta I_q$$

Now $\qquad V_t \sin\delta = X_q I_q, \therefore\ I_q = \dfrac{V_t \sin\delta}{X_q}$

and $\qquad V_t \cos\delta = X_d I_d, \therefore\ I_d = \dfrac{V_t \sin\delta}{X_d}$

$$\therefore \quad Q = -\frac{V_t^2}{X_d}\cos^2\delta - \frac{V_t^2}{X_q}\sin^2\delta$$

$$= -\frac{V_t^2}{X_d} - V_t^2\left(\frac{1}{X_q} - \frac{1}{X_d}\right)\sin^2\delta.$$

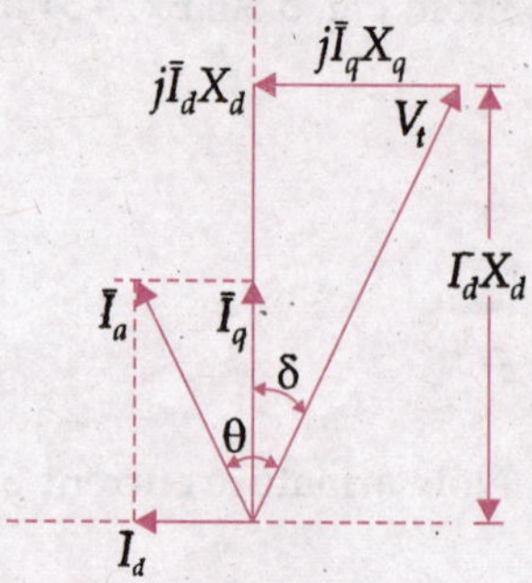

Fig 5.95: Salient-pole synchronous generator phase diagram with $I_f = 0$ and $r_a = 0$.

Example 5.39. *Show that the q-axis synchronous reactance X_q, can be determined from the maximum-lagging current test. Armature resistance and the rotational losses are to be ignored.*

Solution. For negligible armature resistance in a salient-pole synchronous motor, the active and reactive powers are respectively given by Eqs. (5.69) and (5.87). These are re-written here for convenience. Therefore,

$$P = \frac{E_f V_t}{X_d}\sin\delta + \frac{V_t^2}{2}\left(\frac{1}{X_q} - \frac{1}{X_d}\right)\sin 2\delta$$

and

$$Q = -\frac{E_f V_t}{X_d}\cos\delta + \frac{V_t^2}{X_d} + V_t^2\left(\frac{1}{X_q} - \frac{1}{X_d}\right)\sin^2\delta.$$

For negative excitation during the maximum-lagging current test, P and Q are given by

$$P = -\frac{E_f V_t}{X_d}\sin\delta + \frac{V_t^2}{X_d}\left(\frac{1}{X_q} - \frac{1}{X_d}\right)\sin 2\delta$$

and

$$Q = \frac{E_f V_t}{X_d}\cos\delta + \frac{V_t^2}{X_d} + V_t^2\left(\frac{1}{X_q} - \frac{1}{X_d}\right)\sin^2\delta$$

When the motor is just on the verge of falling out of step, $\dfrac{dP}{d\delta} = 0.$

$$\therefore \quad \frac{dP}{d\delta} = -\frac{E_f V_t}{X_d}\cos\delta + V_t^2\left(\frac{1}{X_q} - \frac{1}{X_d}\right)\cos 2\delta = 0.$$

At no-load, angle δ is zero.

$$\therefore \quad \frac{dP}{d\delta} = -\frac{E_f V_t}{X_d} + V_t^2\left(\frac{1}{X_q} - \frac{1}{X_d}\right) = 0$$

or

$$E_f = V_t\left(\frac{X_d}{X_q} - 1\right) \qquad \text{...(5.88)}$$

Since the rotational losses are ignored, the power input is zero, *i.e.*, $V_t I_a \cos\theta = 0$ or $\theta = 90°$ lag. Thus

$$Q = V_t I_a \sin\theta = V_t I_a.$$

For negative excitation and for $\delta = 0$,

$$V_t I_a = Q = \frac{E_f V_t}{X_d} + \frac{V_t^2}{X_d} = \frac{V_t}{X_d}(E_f + V_t)$$

or $$I_a = \frac{1}{X_d}(E_f + V_t) \qquad ...(5.89)$$

Substitution of E_f from Eq. (5.88) in Eq. (5.89) gives,

$$I_a = \frac{1}{X_d}\left[V_t\left(\frac{X_d}{X_q} - 1\right) + V_t\right] = \frac{V_t}{X_q} \text{ or } X_q = \frac{V_t}{I_a}.$$

This result agrees with Eq. (5.83).

Example 5.40. *A salient-pole synchronous machine with 4-pole A.C. winding is coupled to a prime-mover. The machine is running at a speed of 1490 r.p.m. The synchronous machine stator is excited with a current of 50 Hz frequency. Rotor winding of the machine is open. Per-phase voltage and current for phase A of the machine are 30 V, 25 V, 10 A and 6.5 A. Armature resistance is negligible. The name-plate rating of the machine is 20 MVA, 3-phase, star connected, 11 kV, 50 Hz. At full load unity pf and rated voltage, calculate*

(a) the excitation voltage and

(b) the reluctance power developed by the machine.

Solution. Synchronous speed $= \frac{120f}{P} = \frac{120 \times 50}{4} = 1500$ r.p.m.

The synchronous machine is running at 1490 r.p.m., less than the synchronous speed and the rotor winding, *i.e.*, the field winding is open. Voltage readings indicate that the stator is energized from 3-phase, 50 Hz source at reduced voltage. A careful study of the question reveals that this question pertains to slip test on a salient-pole synchronous machine.

Thererfore, *d*-axis synchronous reactance,

$$X_d = \frac{\text{Maximum voltmeter reading per phase}}{\text{Minimum ammeter reading per phase}} = \frac{30}{6.5} = 4.62\ \Omega$$

$$X_q = \frac{\text{Minimum voltmeter reading per phase}}{\text{Maximum ammeter reading per phase}} = \frac{25}{10.0} = 2.5\ \Omega$$

Taking the machine to be working as a synchronous generator, the phasor diagram at unity *pf* is as shown in Fig. 5.96.

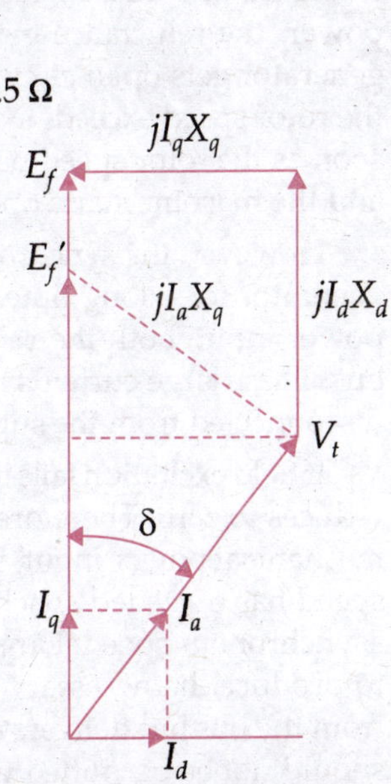

Fig 5.96: Pertaining to Example 5.40.

(a) Full-load armature current, $I_a = \frac{20,000}{\sqrt{3} \times 11} = 1049.76$ A

Per-phase armature voltage, $V_t = \frac{11000}{\sqrt{3}} = 6351$ V

Taking V_t as reference, we get $V_t = 6351\angle 0°$ and $I_a = 1049.76\angle 0°$

$\therefore$ $\bar{E}'_f = \bar{V}_t + j\bar{I}_a X_q = 6351 + j0 + j(1049.76) \times 2.5$

$= 6351 + j2624.4$ V

$\therefore$ $\bar{E}'_f = 6871.88\angle 22.45°$

Therefore load angle, $\delta = 22.45°$

D-axis current, $I_d = I_a \sin\delta = 1049.76 \sin 22.45°$

$= 400.88$ A

Per-phase excitation e.m.f., $E_f = E_f' + I_d(X_d - X_q)$

or $E_f = 6871.88 + 400.88\,(4.62 - 2.5) = 7720.866$ V

Also, $E_f = V_t \cos\delta + I_d X_d = 6351 \times \cos 22.45° + 400.88 \times 4.62 = 7721.74$ V.

∴ Line value of excitation voltage = $\sqrt{3} \times 7720.866 = 13372.54$ V

(*b*) Reluctance power developed by the machine

$$= \frac{V_t^2}{2}\left(\frac{1}{X_q} - \frac{1}{X_d}\right) \sin 2\delta$$

$$= \frac{(6351)^2}{2}\left[\frac{1}{2.5} - \frac{1}{4.62}\right] \sin(2 \times 22.45°) = 2612966.2 \text{ W per phase}$$

∴ Total reluctance power developed by the machine

$$= \frac{3 \times 2612966.2}{1000} = 7838.899 \text{ kW}$$

Example 5.41. *A salient-pole synchronous generator with damper winding, is supplying power to an infinite bus. Explain what would happen if its field circuit gets open-circuited accidentally.*

Solution. Under normal operation, synchronous generator supplies both electromagnetic power $\frac{E_f V_t}{X_d} \sin\delta$ and reluctance power $\frac{V_t^2}{2}\left(\frac{1}{X_q} - \frac{1}{X_d}\right) \sin 2\delta$, to the infinite bus. When open circuit occurs in the field circuit, E_f and, therefore, $\frac{E_f V_t}{X_d} \sin\delta$ reduces to zero, but reluctance power does not become zero. In view of this, the salient-pole generator with an open circuit in the field winding, operates as a reluctance generator at synchronous speed. If prime-mover power input is less than the maximum reluctance power developed $\left[= \frac{V_t^2}{2}\left(\frac{1}{X_q} - \frac{1}{X_d}\right)\right]$ by the reluctance generator, then this generator runs stably at synchronous speed and continues feeding active power to the infinite bus. In case the mechanical power input is more than the maximum reluctance power, the reluctance generator loses synchronism, as soon as the field circuit of synchronous generator gets open-circuited. After the generator has lost synchronism, or has fallen out of step, the rotor speed exceeds synchronous speed, because of the mechanical power input to the rotor. As soon as the rotor speed becomes more than synchronous speed, damper winding comes into play and the machine starts operating as an induction generator feeding power to the bus.

However, the synchronous generator should not be run as a reluctance generator or induction generator for a long time. This is because with failure of excitation and for the same mechanical power input, both the reluctance and induction generators have to deliver large currents to the bus. These large currents may overheat the armature winding, consequently the generator must be disconnected from the supply, within a few minutes of its losing excitation.

If field excitation fails in cylindrical rotor alternator, synchronous power developed by generator reduces to zero. Therefore, the rotor speed becomes more than synchronous speed because of the mechanical power input. Since cylindrical rotor machine is connected to infinite bus and the rotor speed has exceeded synchronous speed, the machine starts working as an induction generator at asynchronous speed. Large currents are set up in the rotor body to interact with stator air-gap flux to produce the necessary electrical torque. The induction generator now absorbs reactive power from the bus but delivers active power to it. Asynchronous operation, in general, is damaging and should not be permitted under any circumstances. However, low-power asynchronous operation as induction generator at about 10% of the rated power is found to be quite safe and such operation may be permitted at thermal stations if required during the night periods. In case low-power asynchronous operation is not required, the governor action comes into play which prevents the rotor speed from reaching dangerously high values.

5.17. EFFICIENCY OF SYNCHRONOUS MACHINES

The various losses in synchronous machines are :

(i) *No-load rotational losses.* (a) friction and windage loss and (b) open-circuit core loss.

(ii) *Field circuit loss.* (c) I^2R loss in the field winding, where R is its resistance.

(iii) *Direct load loss.* (d) I^2R loss in armature winding.

(iv) *Stray load losses.* (e) in iron and (f) in the armature conductors.

The combination of direct load loss and stray load losses is referred to as *short-circuit load loss.*

It is worthwhile to go through Art. 3.9. Note that (i) sum of friction and windage losses is called mechanical loss, (ii) no-load rotational losses are also called fixed losses, ∴ fixed losses = mechanical loss + open-circuit core loss, (iii) open-circuit core loss is also called no-load core loss, sometimes just core loss.

In case armature winding is on stator and field winding on rotor, then open-circuit core loss may also be called stator core loss ; direct load loss as stator I^2R loss and field circuit loss as rotor I^2R loss.

Friction and windage loss can be measured by running the synchronous machine at rated speed with its field winding unexcited. The mechanical power input, W_f required to drive the synchronous machine gives its friction and windage loss. Now when the synchronous machine field winding is excited, the mechanical power input $(W_f + W_2)$ becomes equal to the sum of friction, windage and open-circuit core losses of the synchronous machine. Thus the open-circuit core loss is given by W_2.

The open-circuit core loss, a combination of eddy-current and hysteresis losses is caused by changing flux densities in the machine iron when only the field winding is energised. Since the eddy-current and hysteresis losses are approximately proportional to square of the voltage, the open-circuit core loss also varies approximately as the square of the open-circuit voltage—this variation is illustrated in Fig. 5.97 (a). The variation of no-load rotational losses with field current is as shown in Fig. 5.97 (b). Note that the intercept of no-load rotational losses with the vertical axis in Fig. 5.97 (b), gives the constant friction and windage loss ; because with zero field current, open-circuit core loss is also zero.

The field circuit loss can be determined from $V_f I_f$, where V_f is the applied voltage to the field winding and I_f is the field current. Alternatively field circuit loss = $I_f^2 r_f$.

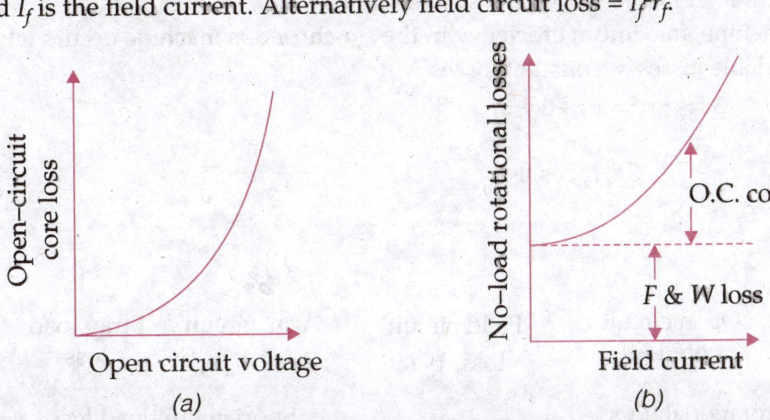

Fig 5.97: Variation of (a) open circuit core loss with open circuit voltage and (b) rotational losses with field current.

Here r_f is the field winding D.C. resistance calculated at 75°C.

The short-circuit load loss is a combination of ohmic loss in the armature winding and the stray load loss. The armature D.C. resistance is measured and corrected for the working temperature rise, usually 75°C. Then the stray load loss is obtained by the following relation :

Stray load loss = (Short-circuit load loss) – (Armature ohmic loss, calculated by using hot value of D.C. resistance).

The variation of short-circuit load loss and stray load loss, with the armature current is shown in Fig. 5.98. Short-circuit load loss is approximately proportional to the square of the armature current.

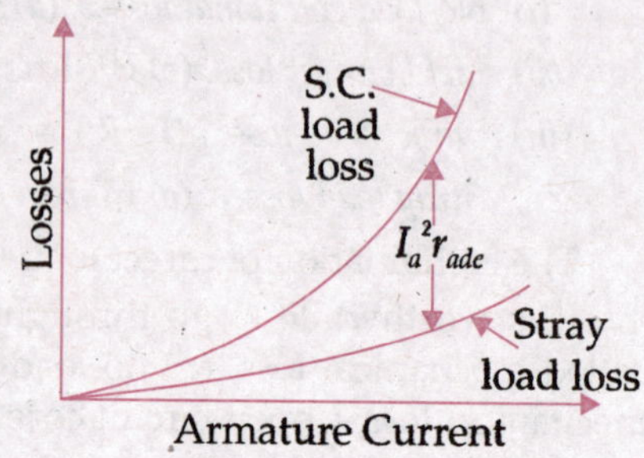

Fig 5.98: Short-circuit load loss and stray load loss curves

The stray load loss consists of two components, namely:

(*i*) iron loss or core loss due to armature leakage flux and

(*ii*) armature ohmic loss due to skin effect and eddy currents in the armature conductors.

In iron parts, the stray load loss caused by the armature leakage flux, is due to the eddy current and hysteresis losses in the teeth, core end-plates, end-covers etc.

A part of the armature leakage flux links the armature conductors and consequently e.m.fs are induced in them. These induced e.m.fs set up circulating currents or eddy currents in the conductors and make the conductor current distribution non-uniform which gives rise to additional ohmic loss. This additional ohmic loss forms a considerable percentage of stray load loss. In A.C. electromagnetic devices, the short-circuit load loss divided by the square of the short-circuit armature current gives its effective resistance $r_{a.eff}$. Thus for a synchronous machine,

$$r_{a.eff} = \frac{\text{Short–circuit load loss}}{(\text{Short–circuit armature current})^2} \quad ...(5.90)$$

The stray load loss and effective armature resistance once computed at rated current are considered to remain constant under normal operating conditions.

The power flow diagrams for a 3-phase alternator as well as for a 3-phase synchronous motor are shown in Fig. 5.99 (*a*) and (*b*) respectively. It is seen from this figure that no-load rotational loss,

$$P_r = \text{friction and windage loss + open-circuit core loss or core loss.}$$

$$P_r + V_f I_f = \text{constant losses}$$

$$\text{Short-circuit load loss} = 3\,I_a^2 \times r_a + \text{stray-load loss.}$$

As in a D.C. machine, maximum efficiency in the synchronous machine occurs when

$$\text{variable losses} = \text{constant losses}$$

or

$$3\,I_{am}^2 \cdot r_a = P_r + V_f \cdot I_f$$

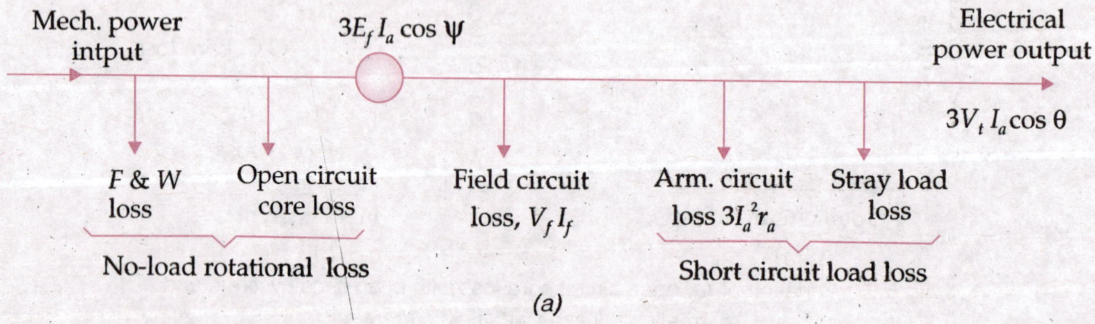

(*a*)

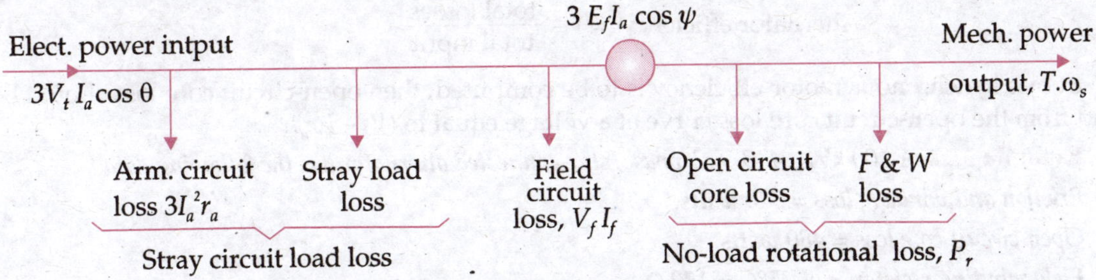

(b)

Fig 5.99: Power flow diagram for *(a)* a 3-phase alternator and *(b)* a 3-phase synchronous motor.

where I_{am} is the armature current at which maximum efficiency occurs in the synchronous machine.

Alternator efficiency in the laboratory. The efficiency of an alternator can be determined in the laboratory by using a D.C. shunt motor as its prime mover and by performing the following tests :

(i) Uncouple the D.C. motor and alternator. Run the D.C. motor alone at rated (= synchronous) speed of the alternator. For the D.C. motor, record armature terminal voltage V_a and armature current I_a. For known value of armature-circuit resistance r_a.

$$V_a I_a = \text{Friction, windage (F.W.) and core loss of D.C. motor, } W_1 + I_a^2 r_a$$

or
$$W_1 = V_a I_a - I_a^2 r_a$$

Note that $V_a I_a$ is the total input to motor armature only ; it is not the total input to dc motor.

(ii) Couple the alternator mechanically with D.C. motor. Run the D.C. motor again at synchronous speed, with alternator field unexcited. Record V_a, I_a again. Now,

$$V_a I_a = W_1 + I_a^2 r_a + \text{F.W. loss of alternator, } W_f$$

or
$$W_f = V_a I_a - (W_1 + I_a^2 r_a)$$

In step *(ii)*, I_a will be different from its value in step *(i)*.

(iii) Repeat step *(ii)* but with alternator excited with normal field current and with armature circuit open.

$$V_a I_a = W_1 + I_a^2 r_a + W_f + \text{open-circuit core loss of alternator, } W_2$$

or
$$W_2 + W_f = V_a I_a - (W_1 + I_a^2 r_a)$$

or
$$W_2 = V_a I_a - (W_1 + I_a^2 r_a + W_f)$$

If $(W_2 + W_f)$ is plotted as a function of alternator field current, then the intercept of this curve on the vertical axis gives W_f. It is because with $I_f = 0$, $W_2 = 0$ and constant loss W_f is obtained, see Fig. 5.97 *(b)*.

(iv) Run the dc motor at rated speed. Perform 3-phase symmetrical short-circuit test on alternator with short-circuit current equal to rated current of alternator. Record V_a, I_a for the dc motor. Now,

$$V_a I_a = W_1 + I_a^2 r_a + W_f + \text{short-circuit load loss, } W_3$$

or
$$W_3 = V_a I_a - (W_1 + I_a^2 r_a + W_f)$$

Since field current is small during balanced 3-phase short circuit test, alternator core loss (approximately proportional to field current) is customarily neglected.

(v) Field-circuit loss is equal to the product of voltage applied to field winding and the normal field current.

Total alternator losses = F.W. loss + open-circuit core loss + short-circuit load loss + field-circuit loss.

$$= W_f + W_2 + W_3 + V_f I_f$$

$$\therefore \quad \text{Alternator efficiency} = 1 - \frac{\text{total losses}}{\text{total input}} \quad \text{...(5.91)}$$

In case synchronous motor efficiency is to be computed, then open-circuit core loss should be read from the open-circuit core loss curve at a voltage equal to $(V_t - I_a r_a)$.

Example 5.42. *A 100 kVA, 440 V, 3-phase, star-connected alternator has the following data :*

Friction and windage loss = 340 watts.

Open-circuit core loss = 480 watts.

Field winding resistance at 75°C = 180 Ω.

Effective armature resistance per phase = 0.02 Ω.

The voltage applied to field winding is 220 V. Calculate the alternator efficiency at 0.8 p.f. and at

(a) half full load and (b) full load.

Solution. Full-load armature current per phase,

$$I_a = \frac{100{,}000}{\sqrt{3} \times 440} = 131.22 \text{ A}.$$

(a) Short-circuit load loss at half-full load $= 3\left(\frac{I_a}{2}\right)^2$ (Effective armature resistance per phase)

$$= 3\left(\frac{131.22}{2}\right)^2 (0.02) = 258.28 \text{ watts}.$$

$$\text{Field-circuit loss} = \frac{(220)^2}{180} = 268.89 \text{ watts}.$$

$$\therefore \quad \text{Total losses} = 340 + 480 + 258.28 + 268.89 = 1347.17 \text{ watts}.$$

∴ Efficiency at half full load, from Eq. (3.88), is

$$= \left(1 - \frac{1347.17}{40{,}000 + 1347.17}\right) \times 100 = 96.742\%.$$

(*b*) Short-circuit load loss at full load = 3 $(131.22)^2$ (0.02) = 1033.12 watts.

$$\therefore \quad \text{Total losses} = 340 + 480 + 1033.12 + 268.89 = 2122.01 \text{ watts}.$$

∴ Efficiency at full load, from Eq. (3.88), is

$$= \left(1 - \frac{2122.01}{80{,}000 + 2122.01}\right) \times 100 = 97.416\%.$$

Example 5.43. *A 40 kVA. 400 V, star-connected synchronous machine has short-circuit load loss of 1.5 kW at rated armature current and at 30°C. At this temperature, the D.C. resistance of the armature is 0.118 Ω per phase. Calculate the effective armature resistance in per unit and also in ohms per phase at 30°C. Find also the ratio of A.C. to D.C. resistance.*

Solution. Rated armature current, $I_{ar} = \dfrac{40{,}000}{\sqrt{3} \times 400} = 57.74$ A

$$\text{Short-circuit load loss in per unit} = \frac{1.5}{40} = 0.0375$$

Effective armature resistance, from Eq. (5.90), is

$$r_{a \cdot eff} = \frac{\text{S.C.load loss in p.u.}}{(\text{armature current in p.u.})^2} = \frac{0.0375}{(1.0)^2} = 0.0375 \text{ p.u.}$$

$$\text{Short-circuit load loss per phase} = \frac{1.5 \times 1000}{3} = 500 \text{ W}$$

Effective armature resistance, $r_{a \cdot eff} = \dfrac{500}{(57.74)^2} = 0.15\ \Omega$ per phase.

The ratio of A.C. to D.C. resistance is given as under :

$$\frac{r_{a \cdot eff}}{r_{a \cdot dc}} = \frac{0.15}{0.118} = 1.2712.$$

Example 5.44. *A 500 kVA, 11 kV, 3-phase star-connected alternator has the following data :*

Friction and windage loss = 1500 W

Open-circuit core loss = 2500 W

Effective armature resistance per phase = 4 ohm

Field copper loss = 1000 W

Find (a) alternator efficiency at half-full load and at 0.8 power factor lagging,

(b) maximum efficiency of the alternator. *(I.A.S., 1999)*

Solution. *(a)* Full-load armature current per phase,

$$I_a = \frac{500}{\sqrt{3} \times 11} = 26.244 \text{ A}$$

$$\text{Short-circuit load loss at half-full load} = 3\left(\frac{I_a}{2}\right)^2 \times r_a + \text{stray-load loss, which is zero here}$$

$$= 3\left(\frac{26.244}{2}\right)^2 \times 4 = 2066.24 \text{ W}$$

$$\text{Total loss at half-full load} = 1500 + 2500 + 2066.24 + 1000 = 7066.24$$

$$\text{Efficiency at half-full load} = \left[1 - \frac{7066.24}{500{,}000 \times \frac{1}{2} \times 0.8 + 7066.24}\right] \times 100 = 96.587\%.$$

(b) For maximum efficiency,

$$\text{variable losses, } 3 I_{am}^2 \cdot r_a = \text{rotational loss + field-circuit loss}$$

$$3 I_{am}^2 \cdot 4 = 1500 + 2500 + 1000 = 5000 \text{ W}$$

The current I_{am} at which maximum efficiency occurs is given by

$$I_{am} = \sqrt{\frac{5000}{12}} = 20.412 \text{ A}$$

$$\text{Output at maximum efficiency} = 3V_t \cdot I_{am} \cdot \cos\theta$$

$$= 3 \times \frac{11000}{\sqrt{3}} \times 20.412 \times 0.8 = 311{,}111.54 \text{ W}$$

$$\text{Total losses at maximum efficiency} = 2 \times 5000 = 10{,}000 \text{ W}$$

$$\therefore \quad \text{Maximum efficiency} = \left[1 - \frac{10{,}000}{311{,}111.54 + 10{,}000}\right] \times 100 = 96.886\%.$$

5.18. OPERATING LIMIT ON SYNCHRONOUS GENERATORS

All electrical devices are designed to operate within certain specified limits. For their optimum performance, these limits should not be exceeded. For alternators delivering power to an infinite bus, the operating limits are active power (dependent upon the prime-mover output), reactive power, power factor, stator and rotor currents and the stability limit. A diagram showing the working limits of various operating parameters of an alternator is called an *operating chart* of a synchronous generator. The practical use of operating chart of an alternator connected to infinite bus is to know the active and reactive powers shared by this alternator and the currents, *p.f.*, excitation and power angle at which it is operating under given load conditions.

An operating chart that gives the maximum reactive power loading allowed on an alternator for fixed values of active power and voltage is called *reactive capability chart* or *curve*. During the planning of a power system, capability curves are useful in the selection of synchronous generators so far as their contribution towards allowable reactive power is concerned. These curves are also helpful during the normal operation to know about the maximum allowable reactive power that can be taken from this alternator for different power loadings and power factors at rated voltage. In this article, first operating chart and then the capability curves of cylindrical-rotor alternator are presented.

5.18.1. Operating Chart

Phasor diagram of an alternator forms the basis for the development of its operating chart. Fig. 5.100 *(a)* shows the phasor diagram of an alternator for lagging power factor. In this figure, armature circuit resistance is neglected as it is usually small in large synchronous generators. Now each side of Fig. 5.100 *(a)* is divided by X_s. So we get $GO = \frac{V_t}{X_s}$, $OM = I_a$ and $GM = \frac{E_f}{X_s}$ in Fig. 5.100 *(b)*. Extend GO to N and draw MP parallel to NO. Also draw MN and PO perpendicular to GO. Here, $ON = PM = I_a \sin \theta$, therefore, $V_t I_a \sin \theta = V_t \cdot (ON)$ = reactive power of alternator. Also $NM = OP = I_a \cdot \cos \theta$ and therefore, $V_t I_a \cos \theta = V_t \cdot (OP)$ = active power of alternator. It is, therefore, seen that line OP perpendicular to GO represents the active power and line ON in phase with GO represents the reactive power of alternator.

For constant I_a, locus of armature current I_a is a circle with radius OM and centre on the point O. For constant field current, excitation circle is drawn with G as the centre and GM as the radius. Load angle δ is in between $GO \left(= \frac{V_t}{X_s}\right)$ and $GM \left(= \frac{E_f}{X_s}\right)$. Power-factor angle θ is between OM and OP or between MN and MO. Based on Fig. 5.100 *(b)*, the operating chart of a cylindrical-rotor alternator is drawn as under :

First of all, draw $GO = \frac{V_t}{X_s}$ on some scale in Fig. 5.101. When $E_f = V_t$, the circle with G as centre and $\frac{E_f}{X_s}$ as radius, passes through the point O.

This circle may be termed as per-unit excitation circle or 100% ext. In this manner, more excitation circles, with G as centre, are drawn as shown in Fig. 5.101.

Now the rated power of alternator is drawn as AB parallel to GO and at a horizontal distance of

$$OP = \frac{\text{per-phase rated power}}{\text{per-phase voltage}}$$

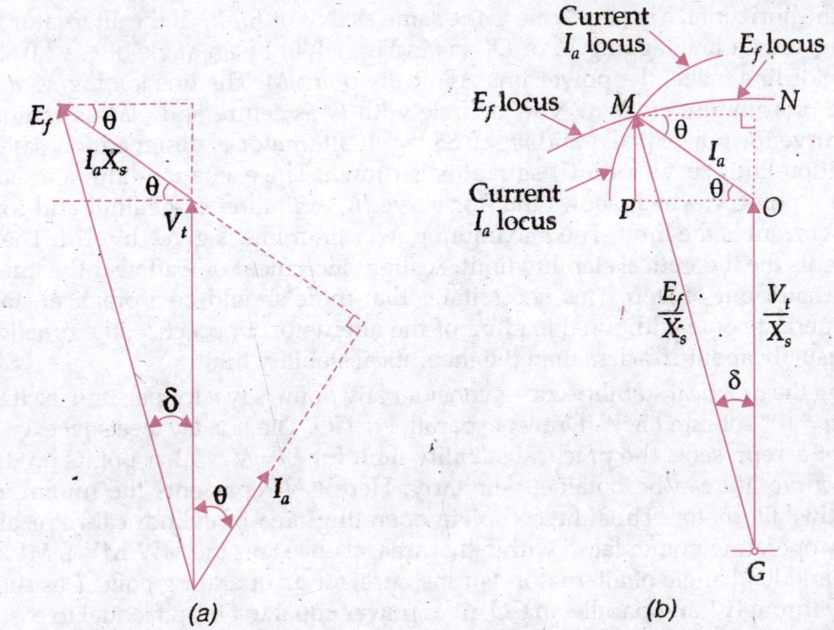

Fig 5.100: Pertaining to the development of operating chart of a cylindrical-rotor alternator.

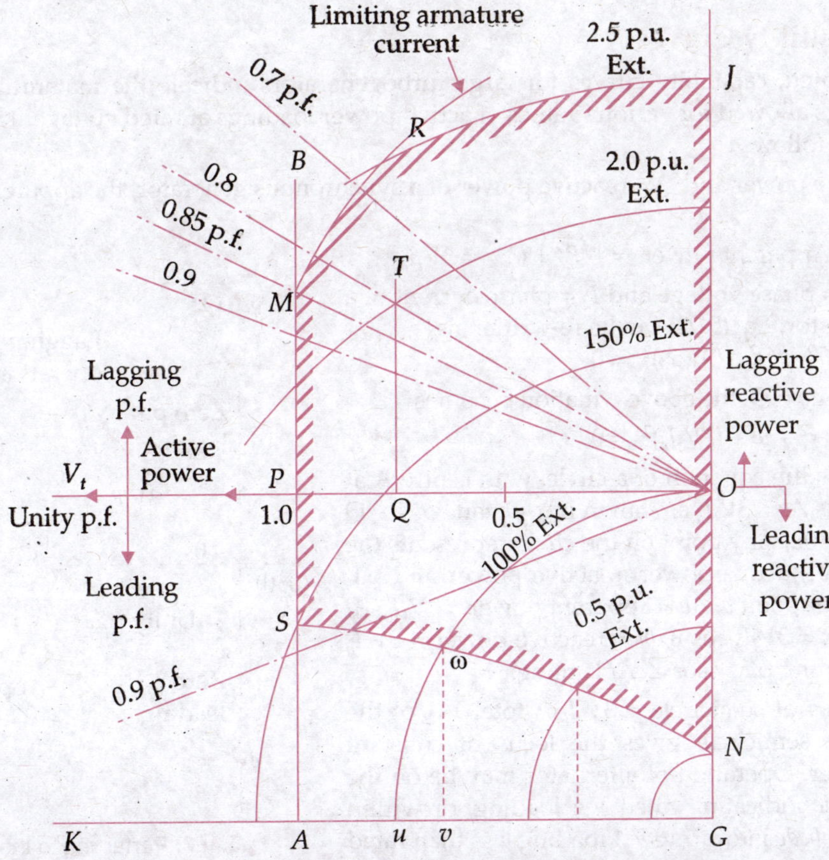

Fig 5.101: Operating chart of a cylindrical-rotor alternator.

Note that the horizontal distance scale is the same as that of E_f/X_s. If the alternator is designed for, say 0.85 lag, then a line lagging V_t or OP (as in Fig. 5.100) by an angle of $\cos^{-1} 0.85$ is drawn. This power-factor line meets the power line AB at the point M. The line joining M with O gives the magnitude of armature current. Now a circle with O as centre and OM as radius gives the current-limit curve for power = GA and pf = 0.85 lag. If alternator is designed for, say $E_f = 2.5\ V_t$, then the excitation-limit curve with GJ as radius is drawn. The excitation-limit and current-limit curves meet at a point R, which shows that for curve JR, excitation is the limit and for the curve RM, armature current is the limit. The maximum power limit line is given by AM. The horizontal line GK represents the theoretical stability limit. A slight increment of load near the line GK would throw the alternator out of step. This necessitates that there should be a practical stability limit which should permit some additional loading of the alternator. In practice, the practical stability limit is taken usually about 10% less than the theoretical stability limit.

For drawing the practical stability curve, consider any point, say u for per-unit excitation on the line GK. Cut μv = 10% of rated MW. Draw vw parallel to GO. The line vw meets pu excitation circle in w. This point w represents the practical stability limit for $E_f = V_t$. Other points on the practical stability-limit curve NS can be obtained similarly. Here GN represents the minimum possible excitation for this alternator. Thus the complete operating area of cylindrical-rotor alternator is $JRMSNOJ$. Any operating point placed within this area, at once tells the MW, MVA, $MVAr$, current, p.f., excitation and load angle of alternator. For instance, for an operating point T as shown in Fig. 5.101, a line TQ through T and parallel to GO gives power equal to OQ, p.f. equal to $\cos \angle QOT$ and armature current equal to 0 T. The VA output is given by (OT) (operating voltage), VAr output is given by (TQ) (operating voltage) and GT represents the excitation. The load angle is equal to TGO.

5.18.2. Capability Curves

As already stated, capability curves for large turbogenerators indicate the maximum reactive-power loadings allowed for various values of active-power loadings at rated voltage. These curves are derived as follows :

If P = active power and Q = reactive power of a synchronous generator, the apparent power is given by

$$\text{Apparent power} = \sqrt{P^2 + Q^2} = 3V_tI_a \quad \text{...(5.92)}$$

where V_t = phase voltage and I_a = phase current of a 3-phase alternator. Eq. (5.92) can be re-written as

$$P^2 + Q^2 - (3V_tI_a)^2 = 0$$

If $x = P$ and $y = Q$, the above equation becomes

$$x^2 + y^2 - (3V_tI_a)^2 = 0 \quad \text{...(5.93)}$$

Eq. (5.93) is the equation of a circle, with centre A at (0,0) and radius $Ab = 3V_tI_a$ as shown in x-y plane or $P - Q$ plain in Fig. 5.102. Any point on the circle represents the apparent power, active power, reactive power and p.f. For example, for point b, Ab = apparent power = $3V_tI_a$, Af = active power = $3V_tI_a \cos\theta$, bf = reactive power = $3V_tI_a \sin\theta$ for operating p.f. = $\cos \angle bAf$ lagging.

Since radius of semicircle = $3V_tI_a$ = total VA of the alternator, the semicircle gives the locus of constant apparent power. Operation of alternator may lie on the semicircle $abcde$ indicating rated VA loading, or within the semicircle $abcde$ indicating VA loading less than rated VA.

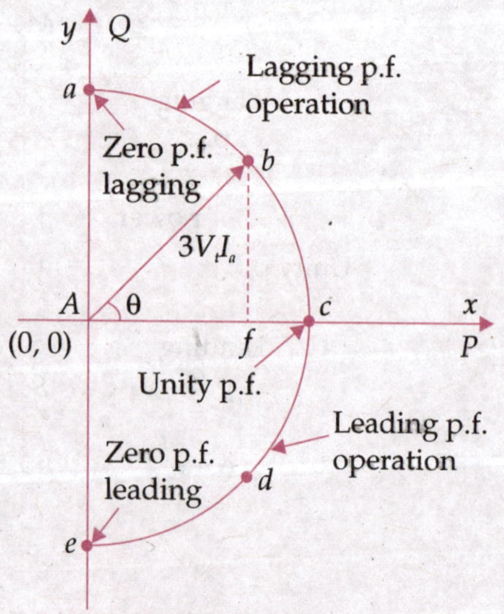

Fig 5.102: Pertaining to the locus of constant apparent power.

The first quadrant operation *abc* of the semicircle corresponds to alternator operation at lagging p.f., because lagging reactive power is taken positive by convention. Therefore, alternator operation in the first-quadrant pertains to lagging p.f. whereas fourth-quadrant operation gives alternator operation at leading power factor. Point *c* in Fig. 5.102 pertains to unity p.f. operation. As the alternator operation moves from *c* towards *a* ; p.f. becomes more lagging progressively and at the point *a*, the p.f. is zero lagging. Similarly, p.f. becomes more leading as the alternator operation moves from *c* to *e* and its value is zero leading at point *e*. Alternator operation at lagging p.f. needs more field current, whereas for leading p.f. operation less field current is required. An increased value of field current would entail more field copper loss and therefore more heating of rotor. This means that field current cannot be permitted to increase at one's whims. There is, therefore, an upper safe limit for the value of field current in the first quadrant operation of alternator. For obtaining these boundary points, consider alternator operation with constant terminal voltage and variable field current (or variable e.m.f. E_f). The field current is limited by a consideration of the rotor-field heating. Three-phase complex power output of a synchronous generator is given by

$$S = P + jQ = 3\,\overline{V}_t\,\overline{I}_a^{\,*} \qquad \text{...(5.94)}$$

With $\quad r_a = 0,\ \overline{E}_f = \overline{V}_t + j\,\overline{I}_a X_s$ for an alternator.

or
$$\overline{I}_a = \frac{\overline{E}_f - \overline{V}_t}{jX_s} = -j\left[\frac{\overline{E}_f - \overline{V}_t}{X_s}\right]$$

$\therefore$
$$\overline{I}_a^{*} = j\left[\frac{\overline{E}_f - \overline{V}_t}{X_s}\right]$$

Substituting the value of $\overline{I}_a^{*}$ in Eq. (5.94), we get

$$P + jQ = j.3\,\overline{V}_t\left[\frac{\overline{E}_f - \overline{V}_t}{X_s}\right] = j\left[\frac{3\overline{E}_f\overline{V}_t}{X_s} - \frac{3\overline{V}_t^2}{X_s}\right]$$

or
$$P + jQ + j\,\frac{3V_t^2}{X_s} = j\left[\frac{3E_f\cdot V_t}{X_s}\right]$$

$$P + j\left[Q + \frac{3V_t^2}{X_s}\right] = j\left[\frac{3E_f\cdot V_t}{X_s}\right] \text{ or } P^2 + \left[Q + \frac{3V_t^2}{X_s}\right]^2 = \left[\frac{3E_f\cdot V_t}{X_s}\right]^2$$

or
$$P^2 + Q^2 + 2Q\cdot\frac{3V_t^2}{X_s} + \left(\frac{3V_t^2}{X_s}\right)^2 = \left[\frac{3E_f\cdot V_t}{X_s}\right]^2$$

$$P^2 + Q^2 + 2\,\frac{3V_t^2}{X_s}\,Q + \left(\frac{3V_t}{X_s}\right)^2\left[V_t^2 - E_f^2\right] = 0 \qquad \text{...(5.95 a)}$$

Let $x = P$ and $y = Q$,

$$\therefore\ x^2 + y^2 + 2\,\frac{3V_t^2}{X_s}\cdot y + \left(\frac{3V_t}{X_s}\right)^2\left[V_t^2 - E_f^2\right] = 0 \qquad \text{...(5.95 b)}$$

This is the equation of a circle with centre at $\left(0, -\dfrac{3V_t^2}{X_s}\right)$ and

$$\text{radius} = \left[0^2 + \left(\frac{3V_t^2}{X_s}\right) - \left(\frac{3V_t}{X_s}\right)^2\left(V_t^2 - E_f^2\right)\right]^{1/2} = \frac{3E_f\cdot V_t}{X_s}$$

Eq. (5.95), the equation of a circle, is represented in PQ plane in Fig. 5.103 with centre at $\left(0, -\dfrac{3V_t^2}{X_s}\right)$ and radius $= \dfrac{3E_f \cdot V_t}{X_s}$. Here only a segment of this circle is shown as *fgbh*. In $\dfrac{3E_f \cdot V_t}{X_s}$, V_t and X_s are constant, therefore radius of the circle is governed by E_f or I_f or the rotor field heating. This means that curve *fgbh* represents the limit of field winding heating. So the alternator operation must fall within this circle so as to limit the heating of rotor field winding.

From Fig. 5.102, locus of constant apparent power $3V_tI_a$ is shown as half circle with radius $3V_tI_a$ and centre (0, 0) in Fig. 5.103. The point of intersection of the two circles, one with radius $3V_tI_a$ and the other with radius $\dfrac{3E_f \cdot V_t}{X_s}$ represents the machine rating ; in Fig. 5.103, this point is *b*. This shows that operation of alternator for lagging p.f. operation must be constrained below the field-heating limit curve *fgb*.

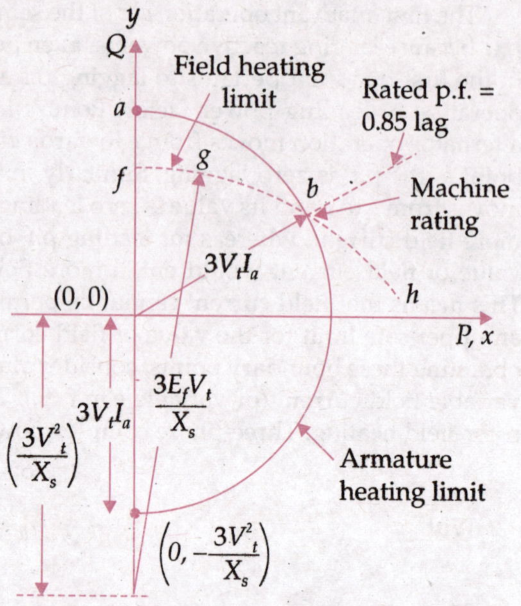

Fig 5.103: Pertaining to the construction of capability curves of a synchronous generator.

In actual practice, an alternator must deliver reactive power to the system. In other words, the alternator must always work in first quadrant of PQ plane so that it can operate at lagging p.f. and deliver active power as well as reactive power to the infinite bus as desired. In order to illustrate the alternator operation in first quadrant, Fig. 5.104 is drawn by referring to Fig. 5.103. In this figure. AB is the field heating limit curve similar to curve *fgbh* of Fig. 5.103 and BC is the armature-heating limit curve, similar to $3V_tI_a$ curve of Fig. 5.103. Point B defines the machine rating at rated p.f. In Fig. 5.104, rated p.f. is taken 0.85 lagging as point *b* in Fig. 5.103.

In Fig. 5.104, the operating region is $OABCO$. This region can, however, be augmented to operating region $OA'B'C'O$ provided alternator is better cooled by external means. For machine-rating point B, OD = acting power loading, OE = reactive power loading so that $\sqrt{OD^2 + OE^2}$ = 1.00 (rated apparent power).

From Fig. 5.104, the maximum reactive-power loading can be obtained for any value of power loading of alternator at constant voltage. For example, for half the rated power output = OF, the maximum reactive power loading is FG under normal cooling. This reactive-power capability can, however, be increased to FH with improved cooling of alternator.

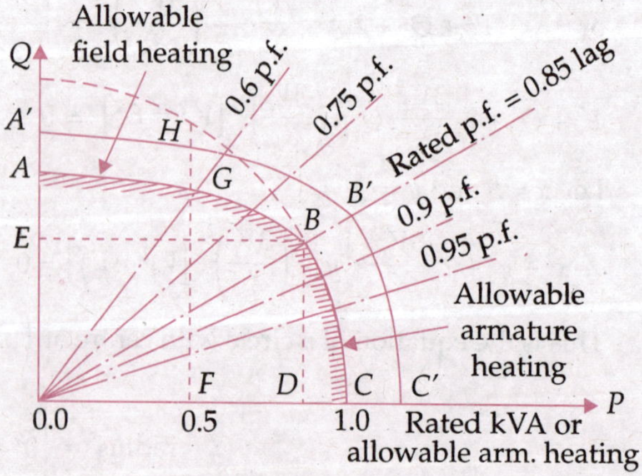

Fig 5.104: Capability curves of a cylindrical rotor synchronous generator.

An examination of capability curves of Fig. 5.104 reveals that *(a)* for pf above rated value, *i.e.*, more than 0.85, field-heating curve AGB in Fig. 5.104 or curve *fgbh* in Fig. 5.103 shift down bodily. As a result, radius

$\frac{3E_f \cdot V_t}{X_s}$ in Fig. 5.103 is reduced, therefore field current required for pf above rated value (here 0.85) is reduced, therefore armature heating is the limiting factor. *(b)* For pf less than rated value (< 0.85), field-heating curve *AGB* in Fig. 5.104 or curve *fgbh* shifts up bodily. As a result, radius $\frac{3E_f \cdot V_t}{X_s}$ in Fig. 5.103 becomes more, therefore field current will have to be increased and thus rotor-field heating is the limiting factor.

Therefore, from rated pf (0.85) to unity p.f., armature heating is the limiting factor. From rated p.f. (0.85) to lower values of p.f., rotor-field heating is the limiting factor.

5.19. POWER FACTOR CORRECTION BY SYNCHRONOUS MOTORS

For the transmission of a certain amount of A.C. power to a load centre, a low power factor would mean greater load current. Such a current would result in greater I^2R loss in the transmission lines, transformers and alternators. As a consequence, the entire energy system would operate at a reduced efficiency. Further, a greater load current at a low power factor would mean poor voltage regulation of the transmission lines, transformers etc. and this would result in an unsatisfactory operation of the utilization devices like induction motors, fluorescent tubes etc. Thus, from the viewpoint of efficiency, voltage regulation and better operation of the utilization devices, load p.f. should be as close to unity as is economically viable.

It has already been discussed in Art. 5.10 that an outstanding advantage of a synchronous motor is its ability to operate at leading p.fs. when overexcited. An examination of Fig. 5.60 reveals that a synchronous motor can be made to operate at unity and leading p.fs. merely by increasing its excitation voltage E_f with the adjustment of its field current. The advantage of this fact is taken in improving the p.f. of an electrical system by counteracting a part or the entire lagging kVAr of the load. A synchronous motor, whose primary function is to improve the p.f. of an electrical system and with no mechanical load on it is called a *synchronous condenser*. A synchronous condenser, installed at the receiving end of a supply line, is used only when static capacitors are found uneconomical.

5.19.1. Synchronous Condenser

As stated above, an overexcited synchronous motor, used primarily for power factor correction and with no shaft load on it, is called a ***synchronous condenser****, or a* ***synchronous capacitor****.* Fig. 5.105 *(a)* shows an elementary energy system network. If V_t is the terminal voltage at point A, E_f is the alternator excitation voltage, *I* is the load current at p.f. cos θ and *X* is the total reactance between E_f an V_t, then phasor diagram for this system is as shown in Fig. 5.105 *(b)*. At the point *A*, the load is *o a* k W proportional to *I* cos θ, the apparent power is *o b* kVA proportional to *I* and load kVAr is *a b* proportional to *I* sin θ. With the installation of a synchronous condenser at *A*, Fig. 5.106 *(a)*, suppose the load p.f. at *A* is improved to unity. Then, lagging kVAr required by the load and equal to *a b* are locally supplied by the synchronous condenser as *o g* = *a b* as shown in Fig. 5.106 *(c)*. In this manner, the energy system network between alternator and point *A* is relieved of lagging kVAr, the current is reduced from *ob* to *oa* and the voltage at point *A* rises from *oc* to *od* for the same E_f as shown in Fig. 5.106 *(b)*. Since the system current has reduced, it would result in decreased I^2R loss and therefore better system efficiency. Thus, with the help of a synchronous condenser, more power $\left(= \frac{E_f V_t}{X} \sin\delta\right)$ can be delivered to load because V_t has increased ; p.f. of the system and its efficiency are improved and consequently the general operation of the load apparatus becomes better.

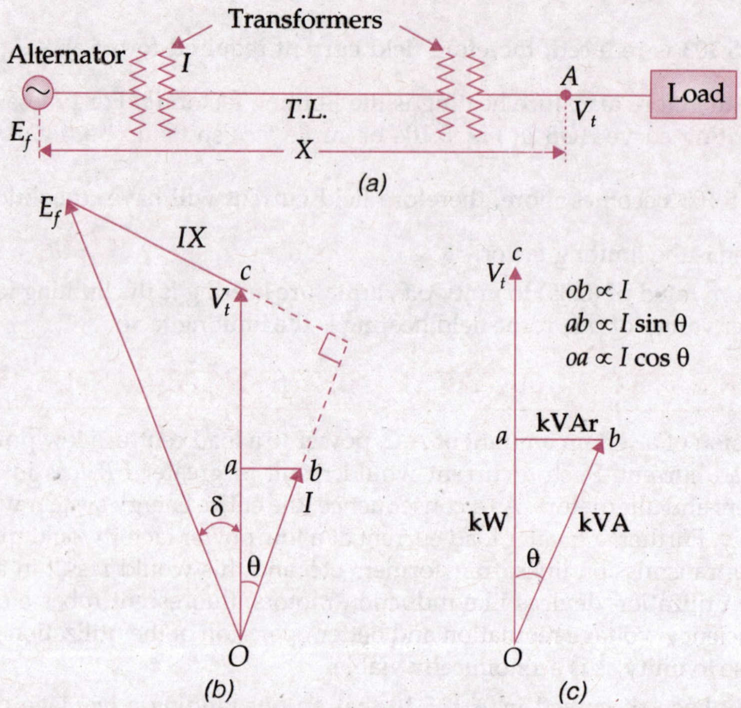

Fig 5.105: *(a)* An elementary energy system network *(b)* its voltage-phasor diagram and *(c)* components of the load kVA.

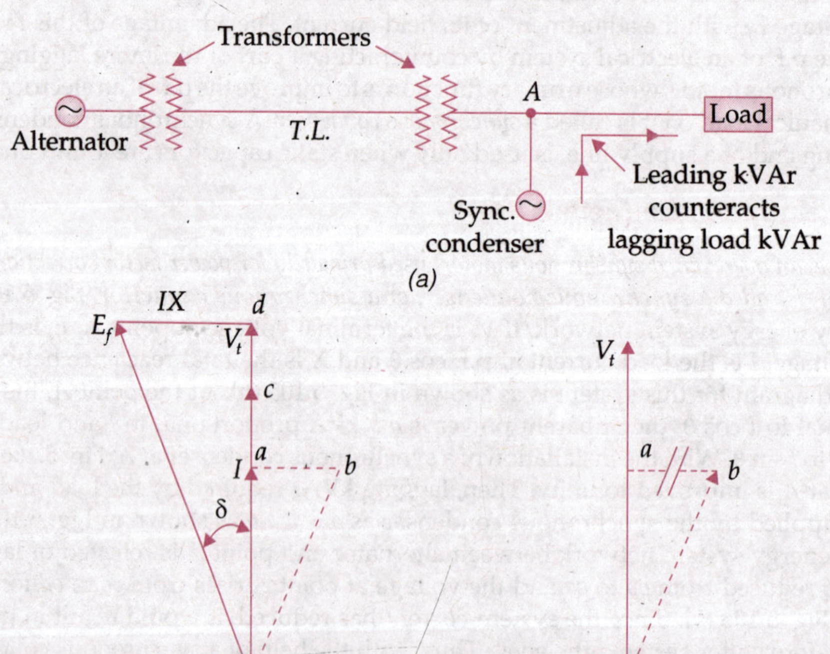

Fig 5.106: *(a)* Total lagging kVAr of the load are supplied locally by synchronous condenser, *(b)* and *(c)* Phasor diagrams.

In case synchronous condenser supplies lagging kVAr somewhat less than *ab* in Fig. 5.106, the p.f. at point *A* would be near to unity and even then the efficiency and voltage regulation would improve. In practice, the p.f. is improved up to about 0.9 or 0.95 lagging, because above this value the cost of the synchronous condenser far outweighs its advantages.

Note that a synchronous condenser is a synchronous motor but designed with a large field current. In view of this large current, a synchronous condenser is usually modified both mechanically and electrically from a synchronous motor. Since there is no mechanical output, there is no shaft extension. Large field current requires greater amount of copper and large area of cross-section of field poles as compared to an ordinary synchronous motor of the same rating.

A synchronous condenser, installed at the receiving end of a supply or at the plant premises, is used only when static capacitors are found uneconomical. It has, however, been found that for higher MVA ratings (20 MVA to 200 MVA or even more) and for higher voltages, synchronous condensers are cheaper and, therefore, preferred over static capacitors.

Example 5.45. *A factory has a total load of 1800 kW at a p.f. of 0.6 lagging. If it is desired to improve the factory p.f. to 0.95 lagging with the installation of a synchronous condenser, then calculate*

(a) the kVA rating of the synchronous condenser and

(b) total kVA of the factory.

Solution. For the solution of such an example, it is convenient to draw its phasor diagram first and then solve it accordingly. For this example, refer to Fig. 5.107.

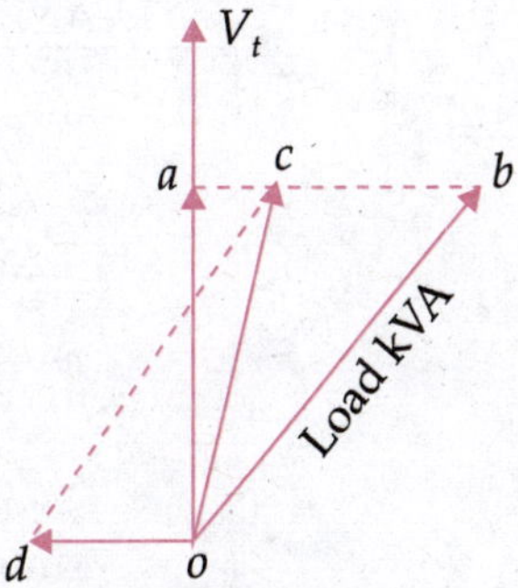

Fig 5.107: Pertaining to Example 5.45.

Load $\quad \text{kVA} = ob = \dfrac{1800}{0.6} = 3000$

$$\angle aob = \cos^{-1} 0.6 = 53.13°$$

$$\angle aoc = \cos^{-1} 0.95 = 18.195°$$

Load $\quad \text{kVAr} = ab = ob \sin 53.13°$

$$= 3000 \times 0.8 = 2400 \text{ kVAr}$$

Combined $\quad \text{kVAr} = ac = oa \tan 18.95°$

$$= 1800 \times 0.329 = 592.2 \text{ kVAr}$$

(a) Synchronous condenser rating

$$od = bc = ab - ac = 2400 - 592.2 = 1807.8 \text{ kVA}.$$

Remember that synchronous condenser rating is in kVA and not in kVAr.

(b) Total resultant kVA of the factory,

$$oc = \sqrt{(oa)^2 + (ac)^2} = \sqrt{(1800)^2 + (592.2)^2} = 1894.91 \text{ kVA}.$$

Note that kVA required by the factory has reduced from 3000 kVA to 1894.91 kVA, but at the expense of a synchronous condenser of 1807.8 kVA rating. If the factory has to purchase an alternator, transformer and cables, their ratings are now only 1849.91 kVA instead of 3000 kVA without synchronous condenser. At the same time, improved p.f. will affect good amount of savings in the energy bill.

5.19.2. Dual-purpose Synchronous Motor

A synchronous motor is used in a factory usually for serving two purposes ; one is to drive a mechanical load and the other is to correct an otherwise low lagging p.f. of the electrical load. The use of induction motors and fluorescent tubes in a factory is more common, but with their use the overall p.f. of the factory becomes low. For a fixed factory load in kW, a low p.f. would mean more kVA demand and as a result the factory has to pay more. In such factories, it is advantageous to install a synchronous motor for correcting the p.f. of the factory and at the same time, for driving a constant-speed load such as a large pump, a D.C. generator etc.

In Fig. 5.108 *(a)*, power triangle *oab* shows load kVA, kW and kVAr for a lagging pf load. In Fig. 5.108 (*b*), power triangle *ocg* shows synchronous motor kVA, kW and kVAr for leading p.f. load. Superimposition of phasor diagrams of Figs. 5.108 *(a)* and *(b)* is shown in Fig. 5.108 *(c)* ; this figure is the combined diagram of load and overexcited synchronous motor. In Fig. 5.108 (*c*), synchronous motor power triangle *ocg* is redrawn as *bde* with *bd* = *oc*, *be* = *og* and *ed* = *gc*. In this figure,

of = *oa* + *af* = combined plant and motor load, kW

fd = *fe* (or *ab*) – *de* = combined plant and motor load, kVAr

od = combined plant and motor load, kVA.

Power factor of the plant = cos ∠*aob*

New improved power factor of plant and load = cos ∠*fod*.

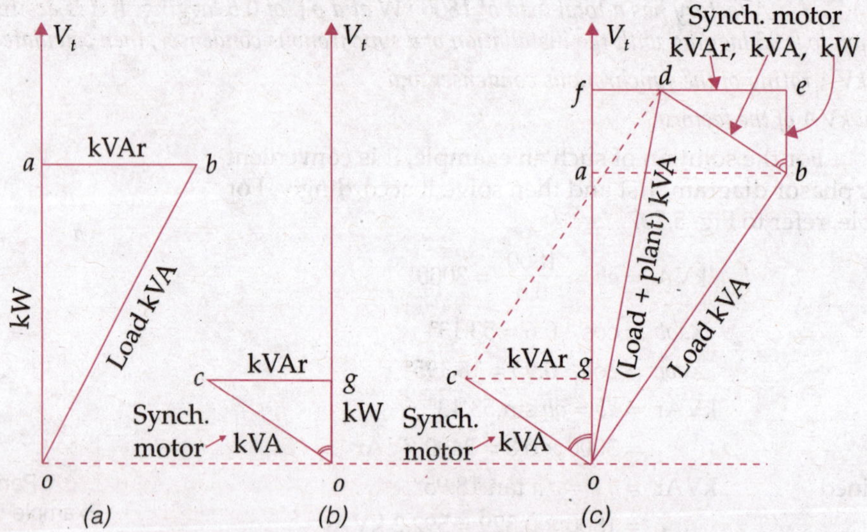

Fig 5.108: Power triangles for *(a)* load only *(b)* overexcited synchronous motor and *(c)* combined load and overexcited synchronous motor.

Example 5.46. *A factory has an average load of 300 kW at a p.f. of 0.6 lagging. A synchronous motor, with an efficiency of 88%, is used to raise the combined p.f. to 0.90 lagging and at the same time supply a mechanical load of 60 kW. Calculate*

(a) total load kVA,

(b) kVA capacity of the synchronous motor and

(c) synchronous motor operating power factor.

Solution. For the solution of this example, refer to Fig. 5.108.

$$\text{Synchronous motor input} = og = af = \frac{60}{0.88} = 68.18 \text{ kW}$$

Combined load, $of = oa + af = 300 + 68.18 = 368.18$ kW.

(a) Total load kVA $\quad od = \dfrac{of}{\text{Combined p.f.}} = \dfrac{368.18}{0.90} = 409.09$ kVA.

(b) $\quad \angle aob = \cos^{-1}(0.6) = 53.13°$

Load kVAr, $ab = fe = oa \tan \angle aob = 300 \tan 53.13° = 400$

$\angle fod = \cos^{-1}(0.9) = 25.84°$

Combined load kVAr, $fd = of \tan \angle fod = 368.18 \tan 25.84° = 178.30$

∴ Leading kVAr supplied by synchronous motor

$$= cg = de = fe - fd = 400 - 178.30 = 221.70$$

Synchronous motor input $= og = be = af = 68.18$ kW

∴ kVA capacity of synchronous motor $= oc = db = \sqrt{(og)^2 + (cg)^2}$

$$= \sqrt{(68.18)^2 + (221.70)^2} = 231.95 \text{ kVA}$$

(c) Synchronous motor operating p.f. $= \cos \angle cog = \dfrac{og}{oc} = \dfrac{68.18}{231.95} = 0.294$ leading.

It is seen from this example that installation of 231.95 kVA synchronous motor reduces the overall load kVA from 500 $\left(= \dfrac{300}{0.6}\right)$ to 409.09 and raises the power factor from 0.6 lag to 0.90 lag.

Example 5.47. *A substation operating at its full load of 1000 kVA supplies a load of power factor 0.71 lagging. Calculate the permissible additional load at this p.f. and the rating of an ideal synchronous condenser to raise the substation power factor to 0.87 lagging.*

Solution. Refer to Fig. 5.109 for this example.

Load kVA, $oa = 1000$

Load kW, $ob = 1000 \times 0.71 = 710$

Load kVAr, $ab = \sqrt{(1000)^2 - (710)^2} = 704.2$

When synchronous condenser is installed, the operating p.f. is improved from $\cos \angle aob = 0.71$ lag to $\cos \angle cod = 0.87$ lag. But note that the load kVA delivered by substation remains

$$oa = oc = 1000 \text{ kVA}.$$

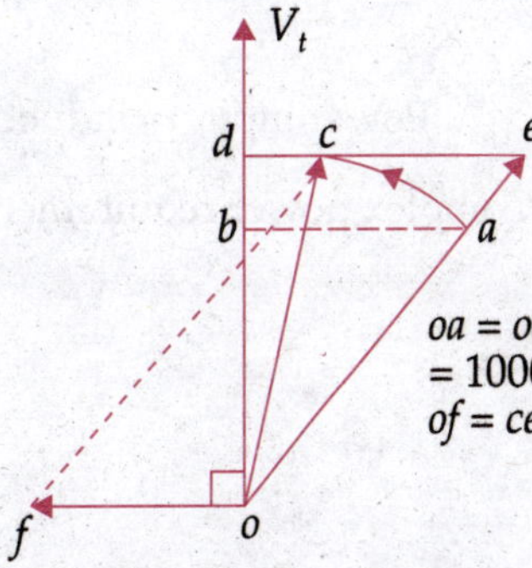

Fig 5.109: Pertaining to Example 5.47.

New power delivered to load, $od = oc \cos \angle cod$

$$= 1000 \times 0.87 = 870 \text{ kW}.$$

Note that the load p.f. remains 0.71 lag. But the combined p.f. of the load and synchronous condenser at the substation terminals is 0.87 lag.

New load kVA, $oe = \dfrac{870}{0.71} = 1225.352$

This means that with the installation of synchronous condenser, total load that can be supplied at p.f. 0.71 lag is 1225.352 kVA. Therefore, permissible additional load at p.f. 0.71 lag is given by

$$ae = oe - oa = 1225.352 - 1000 = 225.352 \text{ kVA}.$$

New load kVAr, $de = \sqrt{oe^2 - od^2} = \sqrt{(1225.352)^2 - (870)^2} = 862.895$

Load kVAr with the use of synchronous condenser,

$$cd = \sqrt{(1000)^2 - (870)^2} = 493.052.$$

∴ Leading kVAr supplied by synchronous condenser,

$$of = ce = de - cd = 862.295 - 493.052 = 369.843$$

∴ Rating of synchronous condenser = 369.843 kVA.

Example 5.48. *An industrial plant takes a load of 4 MW at p.f. 0.8 lagging from a power system network. It has been decided to replace one 400 kW induction motor by a synchronous motor of the same rating in order to raise the plant p.f. The induction motor and synchronous motor both have efficiency of 90%. The induction motor operates at p.f. 0.9 lagging but synchronous motor is designed to operate at p.f. 0.8 leading. Find the new p.f. of the plant. Calculate also the percentage reduction in line current.*

Solution. Let P and Q be the plant load in kW and in kVAr respectively. In Fig. 5.108 (*a*), let $P = oa$ and $Q = ab$.

With V_t as reference, it is known that complex power $= P - jQ$ for lagging pf load and $= P + jQ$ for leading pf load.

From Fig. 5.108 (*a*), $\tan\theta = \dfrac{ab}{oa} = \dfrac{Q}{P}$

$\therefore$ $Q = P\tan\theta.$

$\therefore$ Complex power $= P - jQ = P - jP\tan\theta$

But $\cos\theta = \text{pf}$ or $\theta = \cos^{-1}(\text{pf}).$

$\therefore$ Complex power $= P - jP\tan[\cos^{-1}(\text{pf})]$

Plant load P = 4 MW, pf = 0.8 lag.

$\therefore$ Complex power of plant,

$$A = P - jP\tan[\cos^{-1}(\text{pf})]$$
$$= 4000 - j4000\tan[\cos^{-1}(0.8)]$$
$$A = 4000 - j4000 \times 0.75 = 4000 - j3000 \text{ kVA}$$

$$\text{Power input to induction motor} = \frac{400}{0.9} \text{ kW}$$

$\therefore$ Complex power requirement of induction motor, B

$$= \frac{400}{0.9} - j\frac{400}{0.9}\tan[\cos^{-1}(0.9)]$$
$$= \frac{400}{0.9} - j\frac{400}{0.9} \times 0.484322$$

$\therefore$ $B = 444.44 - j215.25$ kVA

Complex power requirement of synchronous motor, C

$$= \frac{400}{0.9} + j\frac{400}{0.9}\tan[\cos^{-1}(0.8)]$$
$$= \frac{400}{0.9} + j\frac{400}{0.9} \times 0.75$$

$\therefore$ $C = 444.44 + j333.33$ kVA.

Net requirement of plant = plant load, A – IM load removed, B + synchronous motor load added, C

$$= A - B + C = 4000 - j3000 - 444.44 + j215.254 + 444.44 + j333.33$$
$$= 4000 - j2451.42 \text{ kVA} = 4691.424\angle -31.5° \text{ kVA}$$

$\therefore$ New p.f. $= \cos 31.5° = 0.8526$ lag

$$\text{Original line current} = \frac{4000 \times 10^3}{\sqrt{3} \times V_t \times 0.8} = \frac{5000}{\sqrt{3}V_t} \text{ kA}$$

Here V_t = line voltage

$$\text{New line current} = \frac{4691.424}{\sqrt{3}V_t} \text{ kA}$$

$$\text{Percentage reduction in line current} = \frac{5000 - 4691.424}{5000} \times 100 = 6.172\%.$$

Example 5.49. *Sketch the phasor diagram of a 3-phase synchronous machine :*

(a) at the moment of synchronizing

(b) when working as a motor and

(c) when working as a generator, marking the reference directions for voltages and currents in the associated circuit diagrams. Indicate, on the phasor diagrams, the load/torque angle in each case.

Solution, Suppose 3-phase synchronous machine is synchronized with 3-phase infinite bus of voltage V_t. Here E_f, the excitation e.m.f. (or no-load generated e.m.f.) of alternator, is assumed to remain constant.

(a) At the moment of synchronizing, magnitude of E_f = magnitude of V_t. Both E_f and V_t must be in phase, because no power flow takes place and load angle δ is zero, so that $\frac{E_f \cdot V_t}{X_s}$ sin δ is zero. Armature current I_a is, therefore, also zero. The phasor and circuit diagrams, at the moment of synchronizing, are as shown in Fig. 5.110 *(a)*.

(b) When working as a synchronous motor, E_f must lag behind V_t as shown in Fig. 5.110 *(b)*. As a result, armature current I_a starts flowing and the motor operates at a lagging p.f., with voltage equation $\bar{V}_t = \bar{E}_f + j\,\bar{I}_a X_s$. The phasor and circuit diagrams are shown in Fig. 5.110 *(b)*. Note that V_t remains vertical, since V_t is the terminal voltage of the infinite bus.

(c) When it is made to work as a synchronous generator, E_f must be ahead of V_t as shown in Fig. 5.110 *(c)*. The armature current I_a is seen to lead V_t, therefore alternator operates at a leading p.f. with voltage equation $\bar{E}_f = \bar{V}_t + j\,\bar{I}_a X_s$. The phasor and circuit diagrams are illustrated in Fig. 5.110 *(c)*. Here again V_t remains fixed along vertical axis.

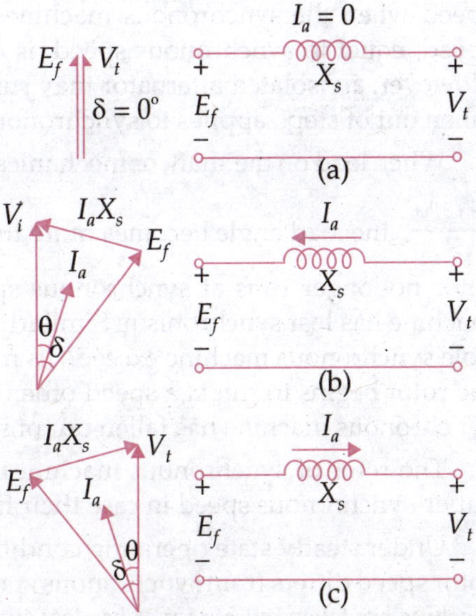

Fig 5.110: Synchronous machine phasor and circuit diagrams *(a)* at the moment of synchronizing *(b)* when working as a motor and *(c)* when working as a generator.

Example 5.50. *An alternator is running at synchronous speed. Its field is now energised from an A.C. source at rated frequency. Discuss the nature of the generated voltage and the alternator performance.*

Solution. When field winding on the rotor is excited with alternating current, an alternating (or pulsating) field is produced. As per Example 3.21, this field can be resolved into two components, one rotating forward at synchronous speed ω with respect to rotor and the other rotating backward at speed ω with respect to rotor. The relative speed between backward rotating field and stationary armature, given by the sum of forward rotor speed ω and backward rotating field speed (– ω) is zero. This component of field, therefore, generates no voltage in the armature.

The relative speed between forward rotating field component and standstill armature is double the synchronous speed, *i.e.*, 2ω. Thus, the frequency of the e.m.f. generated in the armature is 2*f* and the magnitude of per-phase generated e.m.f. is given by

$$\sqrt{2}\,\pi\,(2f)\,N_{ph} \cdot k_w \cdot \frac{\phi_{max}}{2} = \sqrt{2}\,\pi f \cdot N_{ph} \cdot k_w \cdot \phi_{max}$$

where ϕ_{max} is the amplitude of pulsating, stationary field flux produced by alternating current in the field winding of alternator.

Core losses in the armature at double frequency $2f$ would be more. Field iron would also have core losses. Alternator efficiency would therefore be reduced considerably.

Example 5.51. *Discuss what you understand by the statement, "Synchronous machine has lost synchronism or synchronous machine has fallen out of step."*

Solution. Steady-state operation of an alternator or a synchronous motor demands that the relative speed between stator and rotor fields is zero. In other words, rotor must run at synchronous speed when the synchronous machine is connected to an infinite bus. In such cases ; the rotor speed, equal to synchronous speed, is determined by bus-bar frequency and the machine poles. However, an isolated alternator may run at any speed. The statement, "synchronous machine has fallen out of step" applies to synchronous machines connected to an infinite bus.

When load on the shaft, or mechanical input to a cylindrical-rotor synchronous machine exceeds $\frac{E_f \cdot V_t}{X_s}$, the load angle becomes more than 90°, $\frac{E_f \cdot V_t}{X_s}$ sin δ now begins to decrease and therefore rotor no-longer runs at synchronous speed. It is then said that a cylindrical-rotor synchronous machine has lost synchronism. Similarly, when load on the shaft, or mechanical input to a salient-pole synchronous machine exceeds its maximum stable limit (δ approximately between 60° to 85°), the rotor begins to run at a speed other than synchronous speed ; it is then said that a salient-pole synchronous machine has fallen out of step.

The rotor of synchronous machines connected to infinite bus may attain sub-synchronous or super-synchronous speed in case their field current vanishes.

Under steady state operating conditions of synchronous machines connected to infinite bus, if rotor speed differs from synchronous speed due to any reason whatsoever, it is said that *synchronous machine has fallen out of step or has lost synchronism.*

A salient-pole synchronous motor with damper bars and with field current reduced to zero continues running at synchronous speed as reluctance motor. Now if load on the motor exceeds $0.5\ V_t^2 \left(\frac{1}{X_q} - \frac{1}{X_d}\right)$, the reluctance motor loses synchronism and begins to run at sub-synchronous speed as a squirrel cage induction motor with increased line current and poor p.f. The operation of reluctance motor as a squirrel cage induction motor is possible because of the presence of damper bars in the pole faces of salient-pole synchronous machine. In case field current is made zero in a cylindrical-rotor synchronous motor, it may run at reduced speed with motor torque developed due to a combination of eddy-current and hysteresis torques.

The asynchronous operation of a synchronous motor at sub-synchronous speed is damaging and therefore the motor must at once be disconnected from the supply mains.

5.20. SYNCHRONOUS MOTORS

Here first the working principle of polyphase synchronous motors is presented. Then, their methods of starting are described.

5.20.1. Principle of Operation

As stated before, 3-phase synchronous motors are doubly-excited ac machines. When dc current is given to field winding on rotor, alternate *N*, *S* poles are created on rotor. When 3-phase supply is given to 3-phase winding on stator, three-phase currents set up a rotating magnetic field. The speed of this rotating field is synchronous speed n_s. Thus, there are two magnetic fields present in the air gap of this machine. If rotor is driven at synchronous speed by some means, then rotor field also begins to rotate at synchronous speed. If the rotating field set up by 3-phase currents and that produced by dc in rotor winding, rotate in the same direction, then two fields (both running at synchronous speed) are stationary with respect to each other.

Fig. 5.111 *(a)* shows two poles N_1, S_1 produced on stator and rotating at synchronous speed n_s. Field current in rotor winding produces two poles N_2, S_2 on rotor. Since the two fields are rotating at synchronous speed and in the same direction, relative speed between stator poles N_1, S_1 and rotor poles N_2, S_2 is zero. The rotor poles tend to align themselves with stator poles. In case poles of opposite polarity face each other, *i.e.*, if S_2 is near N_1 and N_2 near S_1 as shown in Fig. 5.111 *(a)*, then rotor pole S_2 is attracted by stator pole N_1 and pole N_2 by S_1. There is thus established a magnetic force of attraction between poles of opposite polarity. This leads to **magnetic locking** between stator and rotor poles and an electromagnetic torque is produced. The **basic principle** of synchronous motor operation is that rotor rotates because of strong magnetic attraction (or magnetic locking) between rotating stator poles and rotor poles of opposite polarity.

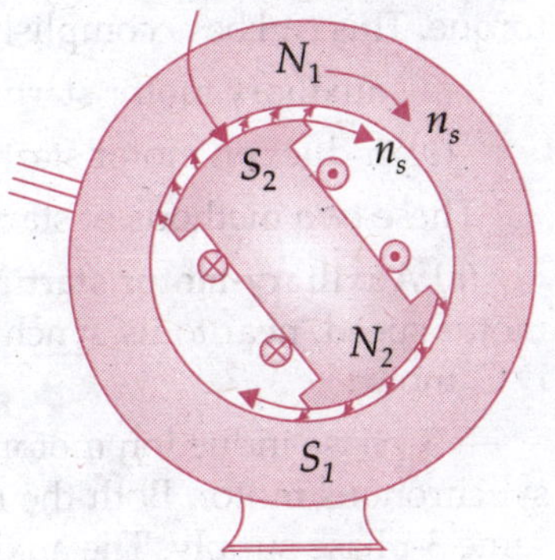

Fig 5.111: *(a)* Illustrating principle of synchronous motor operation.

5.20.2. Starting of Synchronous Motors

When three phase currents are flowing in the 3-phase winding on the stator of a synchronous motor, a synchronously rotating magnetic field is set up. If the rotor is stationary, then relative speed between standstill rotor field and rotating stator field is equal to the synchronous speed. Consequently the torque angle between rotating stator poles and stationary rotor poles is a function of time. An examination of Eq. (3.78) reveals that the electromagnetic torque varies sinusoidally with time—it reverses during each half cycle and therefore, the average value of electromagnetic torque over a complete cycle is zero. Hence a synchronous motor, on its own, has no net starting torque.

For another way of describing that a synchronous motor has no net starting torque, refer to two pole synchronous motor of Fig. 5.111 *(b)* and *(c)*. With three phase currents in the three phase armature winding ; stator *N*, *S* poles rotate at synchronous speed. At the instant shown in Fig. 5.111 *(b)*, stator *N*, *S* poles attract stationary rotor *S*, *N* poles—thus producing a clockwise torque on the rotor. After half a cycle, *i.e.*, after 0.01 sec (= 1/2*f*) for a 50 Hz supply system, stator poles occupy the position shown in Fig. 5.111 *(c)*. Now the stator *N*, *S* poles repel stationary rotor *N*, *S* poles, thus producing a counter-clockwise torque. In Fig. 5.111 *(b)*, the rotor is urged to rotate clockwise, but soon after, *i.e.*, after 0.01 sec, the rotor is urged to rotate anti-clockwise. The rotor due to its inertia can't respond to such quick reversals of electromagnetic torque, consequently the

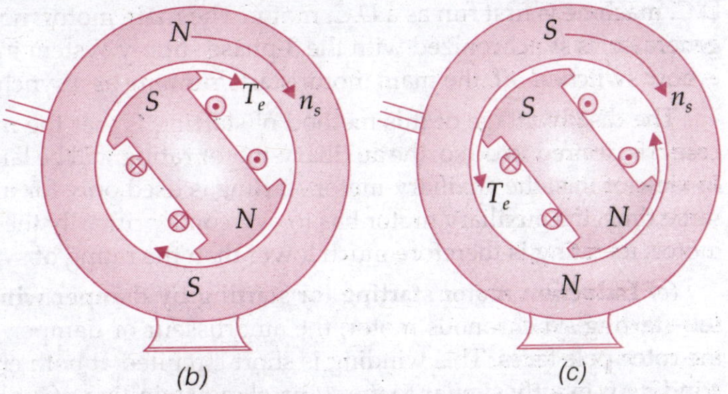

Fig 5.111: Pertaining to the development of starting torque in a synchronous motor.

rotor remains at standstill showing thereby that in a synchronous motor, the net starting torque is zero.

It is seen from above that *(i)* a synchronous motor has no inherent starting torque and *(ii)* development of steady-state torque is possible only when **magnetic locking** between stator and rotor poles takes place in a synchronous motor. This shows that rotor speed must be brought up to a speed equal to rotating stator-field speed for the production of steady-state electromagnetic torque. This can be accomplished by two methods, namely

(a) auxiliary motor starting and

(b) induction motor starting.

These two methods of starting synchronous motors are now described below.

(a) **Auxiliary-motor starting.** The purpose of the auxiliary motor is to bring the synchronous motor speed, near to its synchronous speed. The auxiliary motor may be an induction motor or a D.C. motor.

If 3-phase induction motor is used as an auxiliary motor, then it is mechanically coupled with synchronous motor. Both the motors have the same number of poles and are energised from the same 3-phase supply. The auxiliary 3-phase induction motor brings the main motor speed almost equal to its synchronous speed. At this time, the armature winding of synchronous motor is also energised from 3-phase supply. Now when the field winding of main motor is connected to D.C. source, the field poles get locked with those produced by armature winding. As a result of this, main motor starts running as a synchronous motor at synchronous speed. The auxiliary induction motor can now be disconnected from three-phase supply.

Sometimes an induction motor with two poles, less than the synchronous-motor poles, is used as an auxiliary motor. This induction motor runs the main motor above its synchronous speed. After this, the induction motor is switched off and the synchronous motor armature is switched on to 3-phase A.C. supply. When the speed of the set is just above synchronous speed of the main motor, the field winding is energised from D.C. supply. By the time the field current rises to its constant value, the set attains synchronous speed.

If the synchronous motor is coupled with a D.C. machine, as it is usual in the laboratories, then D.C. machine is first run as a D.C. motor. The main motor, now made to operate as a synchronous generator, is synchronized with the 3-phase supply system in the usual manner. If the D.C. motor is now switched off, the main motor starts running as a synchronous motor.

The disadvantage of this method of starting is that the motor can't be started under load ; in case it is desired to do so, the auxiliary-motor rating will be large, thus increasing the cost of the set. In view of this, the auxiliary-motor starting is used only for unloaded synchronous motors. At the same time, the auxiliary motor has to overcome primarily the inertia of the unloaded synchronous motor, its rating is therefore much lower than the rating of synchronous motor.

(b) **Induction motor starting (or starting by damper winding).** In order to make the motor a self-starting synchronous motor, the amortisseur or damper winding is embedded in the slots in the rotor pole faces. This winding is short-circuited at both ends by metal rings. Thus the damper winding is exactly similar to the squirrel cage winding of 3-phase induction motors.

When armature is excited from 3-phase supply, a rotating magnetic field is established. This rotating field and the damper winding develop induction motor torque; rotor is, therefore, accelerated up to about synchronous speed. Note that the synchronous motor with damper bars in its rotor pole shoes, runs as a squirrel cage induction motor, from standstill up to near its synchronous speed. If the field winding is now energised from a D.C. source, the rotor and stator poles will lock together provided the rotor poles just approaching the stator poles are of opposite polarity as shown in Fig. 5.112. In all other cases (*e.g.* rotor *S* pole ahead of stator *N* pole, rotor *N* pole near stator *N* pole etc.), the rotor and stator poles will not lock together immediately after the instant of closing the field circuit. In view of this, the synchronous motor torque is not constant but consists of induction motor torque plus a sinusoidally time-varying torque of very low frequency, equal to the slip frequency. This pulsating torque causes violent disturbances in the supply current. In case the load torque required is not too great, the positive half cycle of the synchronous motor torque pulls the rotor into synchronism under favourable conditions. Actually pull-in process of a salient-pole synchronous motor is quite complex and will not be discussed here.

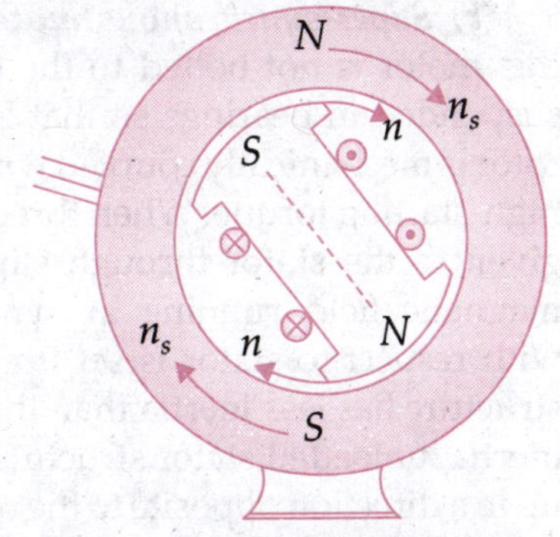

Fig 5.112: Pertaining to the starting of synchronous motors.

Instead of direct-on-line starting, the synchronous motor is sometimes started by star delta starting, reactor starting or auto-transformer starting, in order to limit the starting current.

The field winding has usually a large number of turns as compared to the stator turns. At the time of starting, very high voltage may be induced in the field winding. The stator may be thought of as the primary winding and the field winding as the secondary winding of a transformer. On starting, rotating magnetic field cuts the field winding at synchronous speed and, therefore, high values of e.m.fs. are induced in it. This high value of induced e.m.f. may cause breakdown of the field winding insulation. The voltage induced in the field winding can be limited by short-circuiting the field winding or by connecting it to a resistance whose value is about 7 to 10 times the field winding resistance itself. As rotor speeds up, the induced e.m.f. in the field winding decreases, therefore, the external resistance in the field circuit should be gradually reduced. When the rotor reaches normal speed, external resistance in the field circuit is reduced to zero and field winding is opened; after this the field winding is connected to a D.C. source. Another advantage of short-circuiting the field winding or of connecting it in series with external resistance during synchronous motor starting is that additional torque is developed due to interaction between rotating field and field-circuit m.m.fs. This additional torque adds to the induction motor torque developed by damper bars and in this manner, starting torque is increased. Star-delta starting, reactor-starting or the auto transformer starting also helps in reducing the voltage induced in the field winding.

5.20.3. Starting of Synchronous Motors Against High Torques

Auxiliary-motor starting and induction-motor starting for synchronous motors are employed, when the load requires low rotating torque. For loads requiring high starting torques, the synchronous motor may be started as follows.

(a) ***Synchronous-induction motor.*** The rotor of synchronous induction motor is similar to the rotor of wound-rotor induction motor. At the time of starting, high resistance is inserted in the rotor circuit in order to develop high starting torque as in a wound rotor induction motor. As the motor working as slip-ring induction motor speeds up, the external resistance is gradually reduced to zero. Zero external rotor resistance would cause the rotor speed to be very near to synchronous speed. At this time, rotor short-circuit is removed and rotor winding is switched over to D.C. supply as shown in Fig. 5.113. The rotor poles thus created would be attracted by stator poles and synchronism is thus achieved.

Synchronous induction motor has a larger air-gap than that of a slip-ring induction motor, because the machine must operate as a synchronous motor at normal loads with high stability limit (proportional to air-gap length).

(b) ***Super-synchronous motor.*** The stator of this motor is not bolted to the bed plate, but is suspended in bearings so that it can rotate. The rotor is mechanically coupled with load requiring high-starting torque. When three phase supply is given to the stator through slip rings, rotating magnetic field running at synchronous speed with respect to stator is set up. Since the stator structure has less inertia than the rotor plus load inertia, unloaded stator structure starts speeding up in a direction opposite to the rotating magnetic field while the rotor remains stationary. When the stator speed is near the synchronous speed, the rotor is excited by direct current, thus converting the induction motor into a synchronous motor. Under these conditions, stator is running at synchronous speed n_s (say anticlockwise), stator field is rotating clockwise at speed n_s and rotor is stationary. Now band brake is gradually applied to the stator structure to decrease its speed. If the stator speed decreases by n r.p.m. then the rotor must run at n r.p.m. clockwise in the direction of rotating field so that the relative speed between stator and rotor fields is zero. When the stator structure is brought to rest by band brake, the rotor starts running clockwise at synchronous speed in the direction of rotating field. In this manner, maximum synchronous motor torque equal to the *pull-out* torque, is available for starting the heavy torque load on the rotor shaft. In an ordinary synchronous motor, the pull-out torque is available only when the rotor speed is synchronous. Super-synchronous motors are used in paper and cement mill drives where starting duty is very severe.

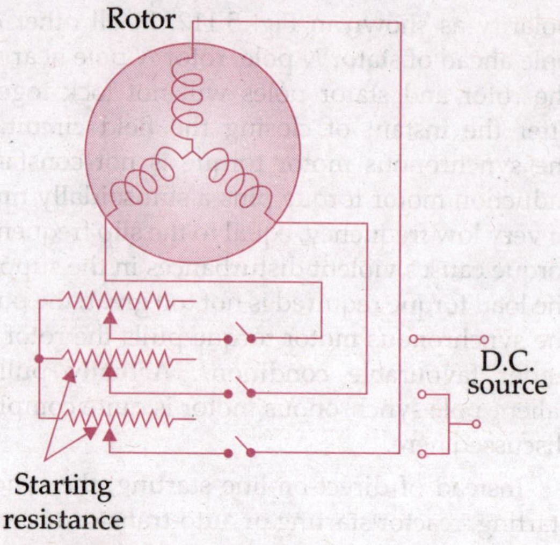

Fig 5.113: Synchronous-induction motor circuit diagram

5.21. SOME WORKED EXAMPLES

In this article, some typical problems pertaining to polyphase synchronous machines are solved. Most of these problems have appeared in one or the other competitive examination.

Example 5.52. *A 150 MVA, 11 kV, four-pole, 50 Hz star-connected alternator with synchronous reactance of 1.2 p.u. is connected to an infinite bus of 11 kV through a reactance of 0 + j 0.20 Ω. A voltage regulator maintains the armature terminal voltage constant at 11 kV at all possible loads. For alternator output power of 90 MW,*

(a) *draw circuit diagram and its phasor diagram for the conditions specified,*

(b) *find the current and its power factor at the alternator terminals,*

(c) *find the magnitude of alternator excitation voltage,*

(d) *find the maximum power that the alternator can deliver to infinite bus.*

Solution. (a) Bus voltage, V_B = phase voltage $= \dfrac{11000}{\sqrt{3}} = 6351$ V

Base current, I_B = phase current $= \dfrac{150 \times 1000}{\sqrt{3} \times 11} = 7873.2$ A

Base impedance, $$Z_B = \frac{V_B}{I_B} = \frac{11000}{\sqrt{3}} \times \frac{\sqrt{3} \times 11}{150 \times 1000} = \frac{11^2}{150} = 0.8067\ \Omega$$

Synchronous reactance, $X_s = 1.2 \times 0.8067 = 0.97\ \Omega$

For the conditions specified, the circuit and phasor diagrams are drawn in Fig. 5.114 *(a)* and *(b)* respectively.

$$\text{Reactance } X_t = \frac{0.2\square}{0.8067\square} = 0.248 \text{ pu}$$

(b) Here $V_b = V_t = 1.0$ pu. Load power, $P = \frac{90}{150} = 0.6$ pu

Now
$$P = \frac{V_b V_t}{X_t} \sin \delta_1$$

$$\therefore \qquad \delta_1 = \sin^{-1}\left[\frac{0.6 \times 0.248}{1 \times 1}\right] = 8.557°$$

In Fig. 5.114 *(b)*, from triangle *OAC*, we get

$$AC = [OA^2 + OC^2 - 2OA \cdot OC \cdot \cos \delta_1]^{1/2}$$

or
$$I_a X_t = \left[V_b^2 + V_t^2 - 2V_b V_t \cos \delta_1\right]^{1/2}$$

$$\therefore \qquad I_a = \frac{\sqrt{1+1-2 \times 1 \times \cos 8.557}}{0.248} = 0.6 \text{ pu}$$

$$= 0.6 \times 7873.2 = 4724 \text{ A}$$

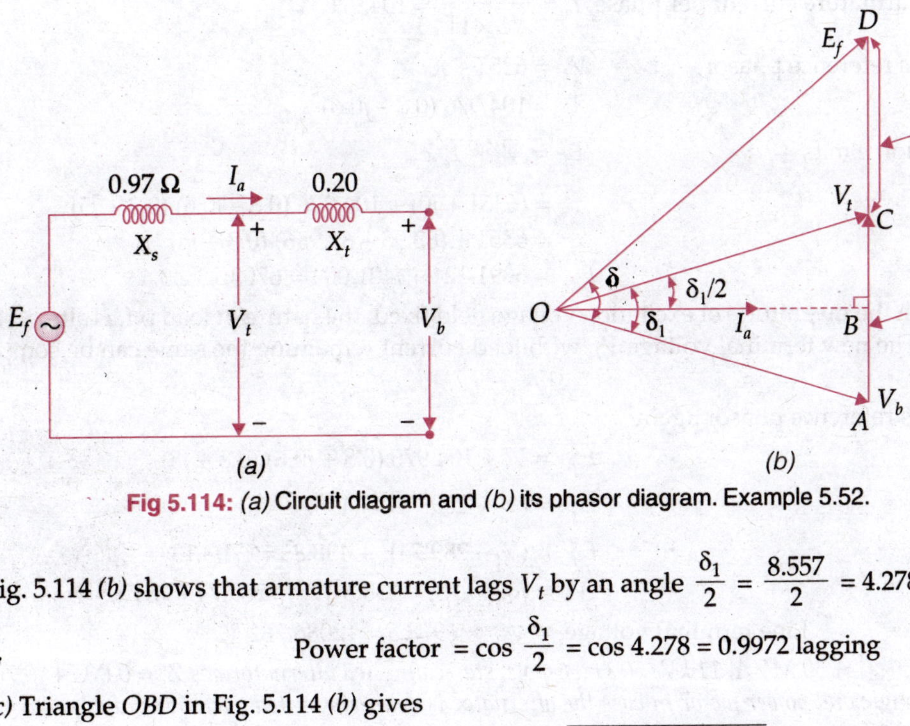

Fig 5.114: *(a)* Circuit diagram and *(b)* its phasor diagram. Example 5.52.

Fig. 5.114 *(b)* shows that armature current lags V_t by an angle $\frac{\delta_1}{2} = \frac{8.557}{2} = 4.278°$.

$$\therefore \qquad \text{Power factor} = \cos \frac{\delta_1}{2} = \cos 4.278 = 0.9972 \text{ lagging}$$

(c) Triangle *OBD* in Fig. 5.114 *(b)* gives

$$E_f = OD = \sqrt{OB^2 + (BC + CD)^2}$$

$$= \left[\left(V_t \cos \frac{\delta_1}{2}\right)^2 + \left(V_t \sin \frac{\delta_1}{2} + I_a X_s\right)^2\right]^{1/2}$$

$$= [(0.9972)^2 + (0.0746 + 0.6 \times 1.2)^2]^{1/2} = 1.275 \text{ p.u.}$$

$$= 1.275 \times 11000 = 14025 \text{ (line voltage)}$$

(*d*) The load angle δ between E_f and V_b can be obtained from triangle *OAD*.

$$\therefore \quad E_f^2 + V_b^2 - 2E_f V_b \cos\delta = [I_a(X_s + X_t)]^2$$

$$1.275^2 + 1 - 2 \times 1.275 \times 1 \times \cos\delta = [0.6\,(1.2 + 0.248)]^2$$

or
$$\delta = \cos^{-1}\left[\frac{1.275^2 + 1 - (0.6 \times 1.448)^2}{2 \times 1.275}\right] = 42.807°$$

∴ Maximum power delivered by alternator to infinite bus

$$= 3.\frac{E_f \cdot V_b}{X_t + X_s}\sin\delta = 3.\frac{1.275 \times 1}{0.248 + 1.2}\sin 42.807$$

$$= 1.795 \text{ pu} = 1.795 \times 150 = 269.25 \text{ MW}.$$

Example 5.53. *A 2000 kVA, 11 kV, 3-phase star-connected alternator has synchronous impedance of $Z_s = 0.3 + j\,5\,\Omega$ per phase. It delivers full load current at a p.f. of 0.8 lagging and normal rated voltage. Compute the terminal voltage for the same excitation and current at 0.8 p.f. leading* (*I.A.S., 1997*)

Solution. Terminal voltage per phase, $V_t = \dfrac{11000}{\sqrt{3}} = 6351$ V

Full-load armature current per phase, $I_a = \dfrac{2000}{\sqrt{3} \times 11} = 104.976$ A

With V_t as reference phasor,
$$V_t = 6351 + j0$$
$$I_a = 104.976\,(0.8 - j0.6)$$

∴ Excitation e.m.f.,
$$E_f = \overline{V}_t + \overline{I}_a Z_x$$
$$= (6351 + j0) + 104.976\,(0.8 - j0.6)\,(0.3 + j5)$$
$$= 6351 + (83.98 - 62.986)\,(0.3 + j5)$$

$$\therefore \quad \overline{E}_f = 6691.124 + j401.004 = 6703.13\,\angle 3.43°$$

Now, with the magnitude of excitation voltage held fixed, the nature of load p.f. is altered to 0.8 p.f. leading. The new terminal voltage V_t, with load current remaining the same can be computed as under :

Take V_t as reference phasor again

$$\therefore \quad \overline{E}_f = V_t + 104.976\,(0.8 + j0.6)\,(0.3 + j5)$$
$$\overline{E}_f = (V_t - 289.74) + j438.8$$

or
$$E_f^2 = (V_t - 289.74)^2 + 438.8^2 = 6703.13^2$$

$$\therefore \quad V_t = [6703.13^2 - 438.8^2]^{1/2} + 289.74 = 6978.5 \text{ V}$$

$$\text{Line terminal voltage} = \sqrt{3} \times 6978.5 = 12086.762 \text{ V}.$$

Example 5.54. *A 30 MVA, 11 kV, 50 Hz, 6-pole, star-connected alternator has $Z_s = 0.005 + j0.70$ p.u. Find the load angle and power factor in case the alternator is delivering rated current at rated voltage with excitation e.m.f. 1.5 p.u.*

Solution. Here $I_a = 1.0$ p.u., $V_t = 1.0$ p.u., $r_a = 0.005$ p.u., $X_s = 0.70$ p.u., $E_f = 1.5$ p.u.

From the phasor diagram of Fig. 5.23 (*a*), we get

$$E_f^2 = (V_t\cos\theta + I_a r_a)^2 + (V_t \sin\theta + I_a \cdot X_s)^2$$

or
$$1.5^2 = [\cos\theta + 0.005]^2 + [\sin\theta + 0.70]^2$$

or
$$2.25 = \cos^2\theta + 0.005^2 + 0.01\cos\theta + \sin^2\theta + 0.49 + 1.4\sin\theta$$
$$= 0.01\cos\theta + 1.4\sin\theta = 0.759975 \cong 0.76$$

As per Example 5.8, the above expression can be written as

$$1.4000357 \sin(\theta + 0.40925) = 0.76 \quad \text{or} \quad \theta = 32.4682°$$

$$\therefore \quad \text{Power factor} = \cos 32.4682 = 0.8437 \text{ lagging}$$

It is also seen from Fig. 5.23 *(a)* that

$$E_f^2 + V_t^2 - 2E_f \cdot V_t \cdot \cos\delta = (I_a Z_s)^2$$

$$\therefore \quad 1.5^2 + 1^2 - 2 \times 1.5 \cos\delta = (0.005^2 + 0.7)^2$$

$$\therefore \quad 0.490025, \delta = \cos^{-1}\frac{3.25 - 0.490025}{3} = 23.075°.$$

Example 5.55. *A salient-pole synchronous generator, with $X_d = 1.2$ p.u. and $X_q = 0.8$ p.u., is connected through an external reactance of 0.10 p.u., to an infinite bus of voltage 1.0 p.u. The generator delivers rated VA at p.f. 0.9 lagging at its terminals.*

(a) Calculate the generator terminal voltage and its armature current.

(b) Calculate the generator load angle and the excitation voltage.

Solution. For the system shown in Fig. 5.115 *(a)*, the phasor diagram is shown in Fig. 5.115 *(b)* where V_b = bus-bar voltage = 1.0 p.u., V_t = generator terminal voltage, I_a = generator current E_f = excitation voltage and δ = generator load angle.

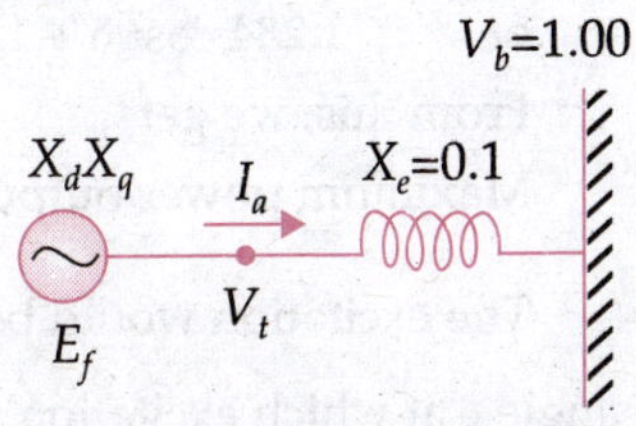

Fig 5.115: *(a)* Pertaining to Example 5.55.

At the generator terminals, $V_t I_a = 1.00$ p.u.

It is seen from the phasor diagram of Fig. 5.115 *(b)* that

$$\overline{V}_t = \overline{V}_b + jI_a \cdot x_e \quad \text{or} \quad \overline{V}_b = \overline{V}_t - jI_a \cdot x_e$$

With V_t as reference phasor,

$$\overline{V}_t = \overline{V}_t, \overline{I}_a = (0.9 - j\,0.436)\, I_a$$

$$\therefore \quad \overline{V}_b = V_t - j\,(0.9 - 0.436)\, I_a \times 0.1$$

$$= V_t - j\,0.09\, I_a - 0.0436\, I_a$$

$$\text{or} \quad \overline{V}_b = (V_t - 0.0436\, I_a) - j0.09\, I_a$$

$$\therefore \quad V_b^2 = (V_t - 0.0436\, I_a)^2 - (0.09\, I_a)^2$$

$$= V_t^2 + 0.0019\, I_a^2 - 0.0872\, V_t I_a - 0.0081\, I_a^2 = 1.00$$

$$\text{or} \quad V_t^2 - 0.0872\,(1) - 0.0062\, I_a^2 = 1.00$$

$$\text{But} \quad I_a = \frac{1.0}{V_t}$$

$$\therefore \quad V_t^2 - \frac{0.0062 \times 1}{V_t^2} - 1.0872 = 0$$

$$\text{or} \quad V_t^4 - 1.0872\, V_t^2 - 0.0062 = 0$$

Its solution gives $V_t^2 = 1.092873$ and $V_t = 1.0454$ p.u.

$$\therefore \quad I_a = \frac{1}{V_t} = \frac{1}{1.0454} = 0.9566 \text{ p.u.}$$

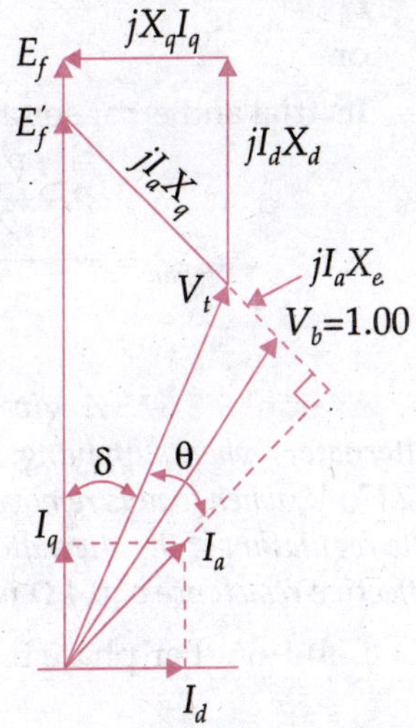

Fig 5.115: *(b)* Pertaining to Example 5.55.

(b) Also $\overline{E}'_f = \overline{V}_t + j\,\overline{I}_a X_q$

With V_t as reference, $\overline{E}'_f = 1.0454 + j\,(0.9 - j\,0.436) \times 0.9566 \times 0.8$

$$= 1.3791 + j\,0.6888 = 1.5415 \angle 26.54°$$

$$\therefore \quad \text{Load angle } \delta = 26.54°. \text{ Power-factor angle } \theta = \cos^{-1} 0.9 = 25.842°$$

$$I_d = I_a \sin(\delta + \theta) = 0.9566 \sin(26.54 + 25.842) = 0.7577 \text{ p.u.}$$

$$\therefore \text{ Excitation voltage, } E_f = \overline{E}'_f + I_d (X_d - X_q) = 1.5415 + 0.7577 \times 0.4 = 1.8446 \text{ p.u.}$$

Example 5.56. *A salient-pole synchronous motor has $X_d = 0.85$ p.u. and $X_q = 0.55$ p.u. It is connected to bus bars of 1.0 p.u. voltage, while its excitation is adjusted to 1.2 p.u. Calculate the maximum power output that the motor can supply without loss of synchronism. Compute the minimum p.u. excitation that is necessary for the machine to stay in synchronous while supplying the full-load torque.* *(I.A.S., 1996)*

Solution. The power output in a salient-pole synchronous motor is given by

$$P = \frac{E_f \cdot V_t}{X_d}\sin\delta + \frac{V_t^2}{2}\left(\frac{1}{X_q} - \frac{1}{X_d}\right)\sin 2\delta$$

$$= \frac{1.2\times 1}{0.85}\sin\delta + \frac{1}{2}\left(\frac{1}{0.55} - \frac{1}{0.85}\right)\sin 2\delta$$

or $$P = 1.412\sin\delta + 0.321\sin 2\delta$$

Power P is maximum when $\dfrac{dP}{d\delta} = 0$

$$\therefore \quad \frac{dP}{d\delta} = 1.412\cos\delta + 0.321\times 2\cos 2\delta = 0$$

$$1.412\cos\delta + 0.642\,[2\cos^2\delta - 1] = 0$$

or $$1.284\cos^2\delta + 1.412\cos\delta - 0.642 = 0$$

From this, we get $\delta = 69.764°$

Maximum power output, $P_{max} = 1.412\sin 69.784 + 0.321\sin 2\times 69.764 = 1.5332$ p.u.

The excitation would be minimum when $\dfrac{dE_f}{d\delta} = 0$. In Example 5.32, it is shown that the load angle δ at which excitation e.m.f. is minimum is obtained from

$$\cos\delta = \frac{V_t^2}{P}\cdot\frac{X_d - X_q}{X_d + X_q}\sin^3\delta = \frac{1}{1}\cdot\frac{0.30}{0.85\times 0.55}\sin^3\delta$$

or $$\cos\delta = 0.6417\sin^3\delta.$$

Its trial and error solution gives $\delta = 63°$

$$\therefore \quad E_{fmn} = \frac{P - \dfrac{V_t^2}{2}\cdot\dfrac{X_d - X_q}{X_d\cdot X_q}\sin 2\delta}{\dfrac{V_t}{X_d}\sin\delta} = \frac{1 - \dfrac{1}{2}\cdot\dfrac{0.30}{0.85\times 0.55}\sin 2\times 63°}{\dfrac{1}{0.85}\sin 63°} = 0.70635 \text{ p.u.}$$

Example 5.57. *A given 3 MVA, 50 Hz, 11 kV, 3-phase, Y-connected alternator, when supplying 100 A at zero p.f. leading has line to line voltage of 12370 V; when load is removed the terminal voltage falls down to 11000 V. Predict the regulation of the alternator when supplying full-load at 0.8 p.f. lag. Assume an effective resistance of 0.4 Ω per phase.*

Solution. Per-phase terminal voltage, $V_t = \dfrac{12370}{\sqrt{3}} = 7142$ V

P.u. – phase excitation voltage, $E_f = \dfrac{11000}{\sqrt{3}} = 6351$ V

Full-load phase current, $I_a = \dfrac{3000}{\sqrt{3}\times 11} = 157.46$ A

For zero p.f. leading, the phasor diagram is shown in Fig. 5.116. It is seen from this diagram that $E_f^2 + V_t^2 - 2E_fV_t\cos\delta = (I_aZ_s)^2$

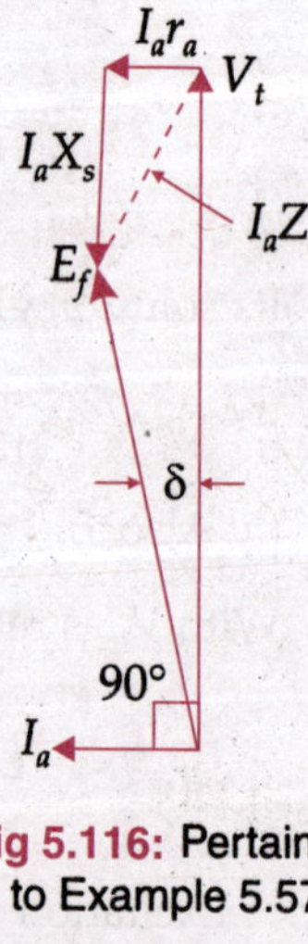

Fig 5.116: Pertaining to Example 5.57.

Here load angle $\delta = 0$.

$$\therefore \quad (V_t - E_f)^2 = (I_a Z_s)^2$$

or
$$Z_s = \frac{V_t - E_f}{I_a} = \frac{7142 - 6351}{100A} = 7.91\ \Omega$$

$\therefore$ Synchronous reactance, $X_s = \sqrt{7.91^2 - 0.4^2} = 7.90\ \Omega$

For 0.8 p.f. lagging, phasor diagram of Fig. 5.23 *(a)* gives

$E_f^2 = (6351 \times 0.8 + 157.46 \times 0.4) + (6351 \times 0.6 + 157.46 \times 7.90)^2 = 5143.784^2 + 5045.534^2$

$\therefore$ Excitation voltage, $E_f = 7211.58$ V

$$\text{Voltage regulation} = \frac{E_f - V_t}{V_t} \times 100 = \frac{7211.58 - 6351}{6351} \times 100 = 13.55\%.$$

Example 5.58. *A star-connected alternator is synchronized with an infinite bus of 11 kV; its steam input is then increased till its output power is 15 MW. Now, when its excitation e.m.f. is increased to 130%, the synchronous machine starts operating at a p.f. of 0.8 lagging. Compute the synchronous reactance of the machine. Neglect armature resistance.*

Determine the power factor, load angle and the armature current of the machine before the excitation e.m.f. is increased. *(I.E.S., 2000)*

Solution. For star-connected alternator,

$$\sqrt{3}\ V_l \cdot I_a \cos\theta = \text{Power}$$

$$\sqrt{3} \times 11000 \times I_a \times 0.8 = 15 \times 10^6 \text{ W}$$

Per-phase armature current, $I_a = \dfrac{15 \times 10^6}{\sqrt{3} \times 11000 \times 0.8} = 984.15$ A

Per-phase bus voltage, $V_b = \dfrac{11000}{\sqrt{3}} = 6351$ V

Under the condition of increased steam input and increased field excitation, the phasor diagram is shown in Fig. 5.117 *(a)*. This diagram gives

$$(OA)^2 + (AB)^2 = OB^2$$

$$(6351 \times 0.8)^2 + (6351 \times 0.6 + 984.15 \cdot X_s)^2 = (1.3 \times 6351)^2$$

or
$$0.8^2 + (0.6 + 0.15496 \cdot X_s)^2 = 1.3^2 \quad \text{or} \quad X_s = 2.74\ \Omega$$

Under the condition of increased steam input, the phasor diagram is shown in Fig. 5.117 *(b)*.

Here
$$3\,\frac{E_f \cdot V_b}{X_s} \sin\delta = 15 \times 10^6$$

or
$$3\,\frac{(6351)^2}{2.74} \sin\delta = 15 \times 10^6 \text{ or } \delta = 19.856°$$

It is seen from the phasor diagram that p.f. $= \cos\dfrac{\delta}{2} = \cos\dfrac{19.856}{2} = 0.985$ leading.

Also,
$$I_a X_s = 2 \times 6351 \sin\frac{19.856}{2}$$

$\therefore$
$$\text{Armature current, } I_a = \frac{2 \times 6351 \sin 9.9325}{2.74} = 799.254 \text{ A.}$$

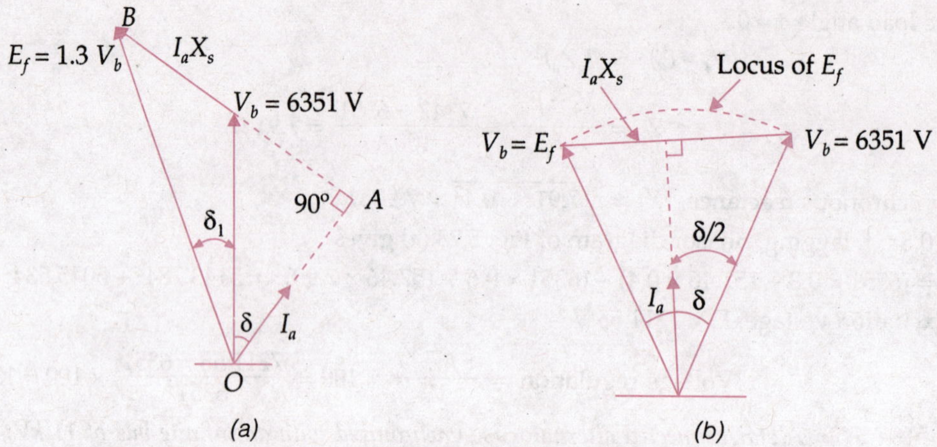

Fig 5.117: Pertaining to Example 5.58.

5.22. SYNCHRONOUS MACHINE APPLICATIONS

Synchronous machines have wide variety of applications as listed below :

Synchronous Generators. Synchronous generators or alternators are used universally for the generation of three-phase power in the whole world.

Large power stations use cylindrical-rotor alternators in thermal stations and salient-pole alternators in hydro-stations. These alternators are the largest size energy-converter devices in the world. Their higher power ratings are in the range of about 1500 MVA or more. It is expected that synchronous generator ratings may rise to several thousand MVA in the near future.

Synchronous generators are also used in ships and air-crafts. The range of ratings and speeds of synchronous generators is very wide. All synchronous generators are invariably three-phase star-connected machines.

Synchronous Compensators. These are also called synchronous condensers. These are overexcited self-driven synchronous machines in ratings up to about 200 MVA. Synchronous compensators are used to generate reactive power and thus improve the system power factor in situations where static capacitors become more expensive.

Synchronous Motors. These are usually made in sizes above about 50 kW, because in small sizes they are more expensive as compared to induction motors.

The main disadvantages of synchronous motors are :

(i) the requirement of D.C. supply for field excitation,

(ii) the starting, synchronizing and control devices are more expensive, and

(iii) the motor is more sensitive to system disturbances.

Its principal advantages are as follows :

(i) An overexcited synchronous motor can generate reactive power to improve the system power factor and at the same time drive a constant-speed load.

(ii) It has high operating efficiency and constant speed.

(iii) For operating speeds less than about 500 r.p.m. and for power requirements from 35 kW up to about 2500 kW; size, weight and cost of synchronous motors are much less than those of induction motors of the same speed and kW rating. It is because of these reasons that synchronous-motor applications are on the rise for such speed and power requirements.

In view of the above, synchronous motors are preferred for driving the loads requiring high powers at low speeds ; for example, large low-head pumps, reciprocating pumps and compressors, rolling mills, pumps, mixers, ball mills, crushers, pulp grinders etc.

The use of synchronous motor for a specific purpose requires the considerations of the following specifications:

(i) **Starting torque.** It pertains to the ability of the motor to accelerate the load.

(ii) **Pull-in torque.** It refers to the ability to pull into synchronism when changing from induction to synchronous motor operation.

(iii) **Pull-out torque.** It pertains to the ability of the motor to remain in synchronism under rated *load* conditions.

PROBLEMS

5.1. *(a)* Give the constructional details of rotor of both salient-pole and cylindrical-rotor synchronous machines.

(b) Describe the various schemes used for exciting large synchronous machines. Which scheme is being preferred these days for exciting very large turbo-generators and why?

5.2. *(a)* Discuss the following giving reasons :

(i) Cylindrical-rotor alternators have small diameter and large core length.

(ii) Salient-pole alternators have large diameter and small core length.

(b) A 415 V, star-connected, 3-phase, 4-pole synchronous generator has 36 stator slots carrying double layer 3-phase windings formed through uniformly distributed coils each short-pitched by one slot. The diameter at the air gap is 20 cm and the effective axial length is 60 cm. The rotor driven at 1500 r.p.m. is excited to result in a sinusoidally varying air-gap flux density distribution in space with a peak value of 0.5 T. Calculate the number of series turns per phase to generate rated no-load voltage. *(I.A.S., 1998)* **[Ans.** *(b)* 38 turns]

5.3. Derive an e.m.f. expression for an alternator from fundamentals showing clearly the expressions for pitch and distribution factors. Find, therefrom, the ratio of induced e.m.fs. of *n*th harmonic to fundamental. Can we adopt short-chording for single-layer winding?

5.4. *(a)* Explain the several means by which an attempt is made to obtain the waveform of the generated e.m.f. in a 3-phase alternator sinusoidal.

(b) The phase e.m.f. of a 3-phase, 50 Hz alternator consists of a fundamental, a 20% third harmonic and a 10% fifth harmonic. The amplitude of the fundamental voltage is 1000 V. Calculate the r.m.s. line voltage when the alternator windings are *(i)* star and *(ii)* delta.

If the reactance per phase at 50 Hz, is 12 Ω, calculate the circulating current when the machine is delta connected. **[Ans.** *(b) (i)* 1230.85 V *(ii)* 710.741 V ; 3.929 A]

5.5. The field-form of a 3-phase, 50 Hz, 10-pole, star-connected alternator has a spatial flux density distribution given by the expression $B = \sin\theta + 0.3 \sin 3\theta + 0.2 \sin 5\theta + 0.1 \sin 7\theta$ T. The machine has 180 slots and has a two-layer winding with 3-turn coils. Each coil spans 15 slots, the coils being connected in 60° groups. The armature diameter is 125 cm and core length 45 cm. Determine

(a) the expression for the instantaneous e.m.f. per conductor,

(b) the expression for the instantaneous e.m.f. per coil and

(c) the r.m.s. phase and line voltages.

[Ans. *(a)* $17.675 \sin \omega t + 5.33 \sin 3\omega t + 3.535 \sin 5\omega t + 1.77 \sin 7\omega t$
(b) $67.61 \sin \omega t + 22.624 \sin 3\omega t + 5.5 \sin 5\omega t - 2.752 \sin 7\omega t$ *(c)* 4200 V, 7195.4 V]

5.6. *(a)* What are the causes of harmonics in the e.m.f. waveforms of synchronous generators and what means are adopted to minimise them?

(b) A 3-phase alternator has 2 slots per pole per phase and coil span of 5 slot pitches. The flux density wave of alternator consists of a fundamental and a 25% third harmonic. Calculate the percentage increase in the phase voltage due to harmonic. [**Ans.** *(b)* 0.893%]

5.7. *(a)* What do you understand by the term space-phase angle?

(b) In a cylindrical-rotor alternator, armature current is in phase with the excitation voltage. Develop the space and time-phasor diagrams for this alternator. Draw these two diagrams in one phasor diagram and show that armature reaction m.m.f. at unity p.f. is cross-magnetizing in nature.

Discuss whether the field poles are ahead or behind the resultant air-gap field.

5.8. Develop and draw space and time-phasor diagrams for a cylindrical-rotor machine in case the alternator operates at an internal power factor of *(a)* zero lagging *(b)* zero leading and *(c)* cos ψ lagging.

Discuss the nature of armature reaction m.m.f. and the development of electromagnetic torque in each of the three cases listed above.

5.9. *(a)* Draw the combined space and time-phasor diagram for a cylindrical-rotor alternator with armature current lagging the excitation e.m.f. Discuss about the various parameters involved in it.

(b) Explain how the diagram of part *(a)* can be applied to a synchronous motor.

(c) Discuss the location of field poles relative to the resultant air-gap m.m.f. in parts *(a)* and *(b)*.

5.10. *(a)* In a salient-pole synchronous machine, explain how the armature flux depends on the spatial orientation of the armature m.m.f. wave relative to the field poles.

(b) Discuss the nature of armature reaction flux in a salient-pole synchronous machine in case armature current *(i)* lags the excitation e.m.f. E_f by 90° *(ii)* leads E_f by 90° and *(iii)* is in phase with E_f.

5.11. *(a)* In case armature terminal voltage, armature current, power-factor angle etc. are known, draw and discuss the general phasor diagram for a cylindrical-rotor alternator showing the various m.m.fs as well.

(b) Explain how open-circuit and short-circuit tests are conducted on a synchronous machine.

(c) What is an air-gap line? Discuss its significance with respect to the magnetization characteristic of an alternator.

5.12. A synchronous generator on load takes armature current at a lagging power-factor angle θ. Its leakage impedance is assumed negligible. For an internal power-factor angle ψ, find out the angle by which

(a) air-gap excitation m.m.f. leads or lags armature m.m.f.

(b) resultant m.m.f. leads or lags armature m.m.f.

(c) excitation e.m.f. leads or lags resultant m.m.f. and

(d) air-gap e.m.f. leads or lags air-gap excitation m.m.f.

[**Ans.** *(a)* leads by $(90 + \psi)$ *(b)* leads by $(90 + \theta)$ *(c)* lags by $(90 - \delta)$ *(d)* lags by $(90 + \delta)$]

5.13. A 3-phase synchronous motor, connected to an infinite bus, is supplying a constant-torque load. Its field current is adjusted to operate it at unity p.f. Neglect leakage impedance.

Now if its field current is increased, explain what happens to the following :

(a) The magnitude of resultant flux wave.

(b) The magnitude of armature current and its p.f.

(c) The magnitude of armature current in phase with V_t.

(d) Rotor movement away from resultant m.m.f. wave or towards it.

(e) The space-phase angle between armature m.m.f. wave F_a and the resultant air-gap m.m.f. wave F_r.

[**Hint.** Refer to Fig. 5.31 *(c)*]

[**Ans.** *(a)* Remains constant. *(b)* I_a increases and p.f. becomes leading. *(c)* Remains unchanged. *(d)* Towards the resultant m.m.f. wave, *i.e.*, in the direction of rotation. *(e)* Angle between F_a and F_r increases from 90° to $(90 + \theta)°$ where θ = p.f. angle]

5.14. A round-rotor synchronous motor on load draws a current at a leading p.f. angle θ. Its leakage impedance is assumed negligible. Find out the angle by which

(a) air-gap excitation m.m.f. leads or lags armature m.m.f.,

(b) resultant m.m.f. leads or lags armature m.m.f.,

(c) excitation m.m.f. leads or lags resultant m.m.f.,

(d) air-gap excitation m.m.f. leads or lags the air-gap e.m.f. and

(e) air-gap e.m.f. leads or lags armature m.m.f.

[**Ans.** *(a)* lags by $(90° + \psi)$ *(b)* lags by $(90° + \theta)$ *(c)* lags by $(90° + \delta)$ *(d)* leads by $(90 - \delta)$ *(e)* lags by $(180 + \theta)$]

5.15. (a) In an alternator, a lagging current has the effect of weakening the main field ; but in a synchronous motor, the effect of lagging current is to strengthen the main field. Explain.

(b) An alternator connected to an infinite bus, is supplying some power at p.f. 0.9 lag. For constant power input from the prime-mover, if the field current is increased, explain what happens to the load angle. Will the rotor move towards the resultant air-gap m.m.f. or away from it? What happens to the magnitude of armature current and power factor? Neglect leakage impedance.

[**Hint.** *(a)* In Fig. 5.14, armature m.m.f. F_a for lagging current, has a component in phase opposition to F_f. For a synchronous motor, Fig. 5.9 shows that armature m.m.f. F_a for a lagging current, has a component in phase with F_f etc.]

[**Hint.** *(b)* Refer to Fig. 5.31 *(b)*]

[**Ans.** *(b)* Load angle decreases and the rotor moves towards the resultant air-gap m.m.f. Armature current increases and power factor becomes more lagging.]

5.16. (a) Draw phasor diagram of a round-rotor alternator on *(i)* open-circuit and *(ii)* short-circuit. Discuss why short-circuit characteristic is a straight line whereas open-circuit characteristic is a curve.

(b) A 300 kVA, 400 V alternator connected in delta is now reconnected in star. Calculate the new voltage, current and kVA ratings. [**Ans.** *(b)* 692.8 V, 250 A, 300 kVA]

5.17. An ideal synchronous machine, with negligible leakage impedance, is connected to an infinite bus. At no-load, the machine is neither generating nor motoring.

(a) Explain how the mechanical power input T_{ws} to the synchronous machine is delivered as electrical power output $mV_tI_a \cos\theta$.

(b) Explain how the application of shaft load causes a synchronous machine to operate as a motor.

Also show that the reactive power flow in a synchronous machine can be controlled by varying its field current.

5.18. Explain how the Potier triangle can be drawn with the help of OCC and any two points on the z.p.f.c.

5.19. *(a)* Discuss the factors that govern the change in terminal voltage of an isolated synchronous generator when feeding its own load.

(b) A 3-phase star-connected alternator is delivering 20 MW and 8 MVAr to an infinite bus at 11 kV. The alternator has synchronous impedance of $0 + j3\ \Omega$. Determine the load angle and the excitation e.m.f. of the alternator. **[Ans.** *(b)* 22.48°, 14265.3 V]

5.20. *(a)* Define the voltage regulation of an alternator.

Is it possible to have the full-load terminal voltage greater than the no-load terminal voltage? Explain.

(b) Why does the armature terminal voltage change as the alternator is loaded?

(c) What is the necessity of computing the voltage regulation of alternators?

(d) Develop the e.m.f. method of determining the voltage regulation and hence show that synchronous reactance consists of two components of reactances.

5.21. *(a)* Explain the method of determining the voltage regulation of an alternator by new ASA method.

(b) Describe how saturated synchronous reactance of an alternator is calculated. Hence, explain the method of determining the voltage regulation by using this saturated reactance.

5.22. *(a)* Compare the results obtained for voltage regulation by e.m.f., m.m.f., z.p.f., new ASA and saturated synchronous-reactance methods.

(b) A 3-phase, 17.32 kVA, 400 V, star-connected alternator is delivering rated load at 400 V and at p.f. 0.8 lag. Its synchronous impedance is $0.2 + j\,2\ \Omega$ per phase. Find the load angle at which it is operating.

Now, with the magnitude of excitation voltage held constant, the nature of rated load p.f. is altered to p.f. 0.8 leading. Determine the new value of terminal voltage and load angle.

[Hint. *(b)* First calculate $E_f (= 267.57\text{ V})$ at 0.8 p.f. lag and then find out V_t at p.f. 0.8 leading.]

[Ans. *(b)* 7.95° ; 502.44 V, 9.25°]

5.23. *(a)* Explain why synchronous impedance method of computing the voltage regulation, leads to a pessimistic value at lagging p.f. loads.

(b) A three-phase, 50 Hz, 2000 kVA, 11 kV, star-connected alternator has a full-load voltage regulation of 10% at 0.8 p.f. lag. Now the speed of the alternator prime-mover decreases to give a frequency of 48 Hz. Determine its effect on alternator rating and also on the voltage regulation at 0.8 p.f. lag. The field and armature currents are assumed unchanged. Neglect armature resistance.

[*(b)* **Hint.** Excitation voltage $\propto I_f : f$. Since I_f is constant, new excitation voltage $E_{f2} = 0.96\ E_{f1}$ and $X_{s2} = 0.96\ X_{s1}$. For negligible armature resistance. Fig. 5.22 *(b)* shows that $V_{t2} = 0.96$, $V_{t1} = 10.56$ kV etc.] **[Ans.** 10.56 kV, 1920 kVA, 10%]

5.24. A 6.6 kV, 3 phase, 50 Hz, star-connected alternator gave the following data for open circuit, short circuit and full-load zero-power factor tests :

I_f *in A*	3.2	5.00	7.50	10.00	14.00
E_f *in kV*	3.10	4.90	6.60	7.50	8.24
I_{sc} *in A*	500	778	1170	–	–
z.p.f. terminal voltage in kV	–	1.85	4.24	5.78	7.00

Per phase armature resistance is 0.2 Ω. Calculate the voltage regulation at full load current of 500 A at 0.8 p.f. lagging by the following methods :

(a) e.m.f. method (b) m.m.f. method

(c) z.p.f. method (d) new ASA method and

(e) saturated-synchronous reactance method.

[Ans. *(a)* 31.77%, *(b)* 13.52%, *(c)* 17.585%, *(d)* 17.45%, *(e)* 17.585%]

5.25. *(a)* An alternator has a synchronous reactance of 20% and negligible resistance. Calculate its voltage regulation when working at full-load *(i)* 0.8 p.f. lag *(ii)* unity p.f. and *(iii)* 0.8 p.f. lead.

(b) The magnetization curve of a 10 kVa, 230 V, 50 Hz, star-connected alternator is as shown in Fig. 5.30. Its synchronous reactance is 1.2 Ω per phase and resistance is negligible.

The terminal voltage of the alternator is to be kept constant at 230 V from no-load to 1.4 times the rated load at 0.8 p.f. lag. Compute the range of field current adjustment which the voltage regulator should carry out.

[Hint. *(a)* From Fig. 5.23 *(a)*, the excitation voltage E_f, with r_a equal to zero and with I_a as reference phasor, can be written as

$$E_f^2 = (V_t \cos \theta)^2 + (V_t \sin \theta + I_a X_s)^2$$

$$= V_t^2 \left[(\cos\theta)^2 + \left(\sin\theta + \frac{I_a X_s}{V_t} \right)^2 \right] = V_t^2 \; [(0.8)^2 + (0.6 + 0.2)^2] = 1.28 \; V_t^2$$

$\therefore$ $E_f = 1.13\, V_t$ etc.] **[Ans.** *(a)* 13.1% ; 1.98% ; – 10.6% *(b)* 1.76 A to 2.26 A]

5.26 A 11 kV, 50 Hz, star-connected cylindrical rotor alternator gave the following data on open circuit :

I_f in A	0	10	15	20	31	39	50	55
E_f in kV	0	5.00	7.50	9.00	11.00	12.00	12.80	13.40

An excitation of 20 A was required to circulate a full-load current of 160 A on short-circuit. For zero-power factor test, an excitation of 66 A was required to circulate 1.25 times the full load current at 11 kV. Estimate the voltage regulation at full load 0.8 p.f. lagging, by z.p.f. method. Neglect armature resistance.

[Hint. Draw o.c.c. and s.c.c. in the usual manner. Plot point *A* corresponding to excitation of 66 A and voltage of 11 kV. Since point *A* corresponds to 1.25 times the full-load current, *i.e.*, 1.25 × 160 = 200 A, *OF′* should be equal to the excitation required to circulate 200 A on short circuit, refer to Fig. 5.17 *(b)*. Here *OF′* = 25 A. From *A* draw a line *AD* parallel and equal to *OF′*. Through *D* draw *DC* parallel to air-gap line. Drop *CB* perpendicular to *DA*. Then *CB* = 1.25 × 160 (x_{al}) and full-load armature m.m.f. = $\frac{AB}{1.25}$. In this problem, x_{al} = 3.90 Ω and full load armature m.m.f. is equivalent to 18.00 A.] **[Ans.** 15.45%]

5.27 A 3-phase star-connected alternator is rated 1600 kVA, 13,500 V. The armature effective resistance and synchronous reactance are 1.5 Ω and 30 Ω respectively per phase. Calculate the percentage regulation for a load of 1280 kW at power factors of *(a)* 0.8 leading, *(b)* unity and *(c)* 0.8 lagging. *(I.E.S., 1986)*

[Ans. *(a)* – 11.991% *(b)* 3.227% *(c)* 18.6%]

5.28. *(a)* Explain the m.m.f. method of determining the voltage regulation of an alternator.

(b) A 30 kVA, 440 V, 50 Hz, 3-phase star-connected alternator gave the following test data :

Field current (A)	2	4	6	7	8	10	12	14
Terminal voltage (V)	155	287	395	440	475	530	570	592
S.C. Current (A)	11	22	34	40	46	57	69	80

Resistance between any two terminals is 0.3 ohm. Find the regulation at full load, 0.8 p.f. lagging by *(i)* synchronous-impedance method and *(ii)* m.m.f. method.

[Ans. *(b) (i)* 50.66% ; *(ii)* 31.496%]

5.29. *(a)* Describe the procedure for determining the voltage regulation of an alternator by saturated synchronous-reactance method.

(b) For an armature leakage reactance of 0.8 Ω in Prob. 5.28 *(b)*, compute the following at rated voltage, rated load and 0.8 p.f. lagging :

(i) Unsaturated synchronous reactance *(ii)* Saturation factor

(iii) Saturated-synchronous reactance and *(iv)* The voltage regulation.

[Ans. *(b)* 7.372 Ω, 1.246, 6.074 Ω, 33.07%]

5.30. *(a)* Explain the method of determining the voltage regulation of an alternator by z.p.f. and new ASA methods.

(b) The following data relate to a 14860 kVA. 3-phase, 50 Hz. 40-pole, star-connected hydroelectric generator :

I_f in Amp	10	15	20.5	25	30	35	40	45
E_f in kV	6.45	9.0	11.0	12.2	13.25	14.0	14.5	15.0

S.C. test. $I_f = 18$ A, $I_{sc} = 780$ A.

Z.p.f. test. $I_f = 52.5$ A, $I_a = 780$ A, $V_t = 11$ kV.

Find the voltage regulation at rated armature current of 780 A at 0.8 p.f. lag by z.p.f. and new ASA methods. Take armature circuit resistance of 0.2 ohm per phase.

[Ans. *(b)* 33.84%, 34.07%]

5.31. *(a)* Why is the e.m.f. method so called?

(b) What are three factors that cause a change of the alternator terminal voltage as it is loaded?

(c) Develop the equivalent circuit of a cylindrical-rotor synchronous machine.

(d) What happens to the value of synchronous reactance X_s if air-gap is increased?

(e) What is the excitation voltage in case of synchronous machines?

(f) For zero-power factor lagging load on an alternator, armature m.m.f. F_a opposes main-field m.m.f. F_f, but for zero-power factor leading load, F_a assists F_f. Explain.

[Ans. *(b)* r_a, x_{al} and X_{ar} (d) X_s decreases because air-gap reluctance increases *(e)* E_f. Its magnitude depends on speed (or frequency), field current,number of armature turns per phase etc.]

5.32. *(a)* If an alternator is not running at synchronous speed, discuss its effect on *(i)* voltage regulation, *(ii)* short-circuit current and *(iii)* open-circuit characteristic. Neglect armature resistance for parts *(i)* and *(ii)*.

(b) In an alternator, less field current is required to reach rated voltage for leading p.f. operation, whereas more field current for lagging p.f. operation. Explain.

(c) Synchronous-impedance method does not give accurate value of voltage regulation of an alternator. Despite this, why it is still used.

[Ans. *(a) (i)* No effect *(ii)* No effect *(iii)* OCC shifts bodily up or down depending on whether speed is more or less than synchronous speed. *(b)* for leading p.f., E_f is less ...]

5.33 A 3-phase alternator is rated at 5 kVA, 110 V, 26.3 A, 50 Hz and 1000 r.p.m. The stator resistance between terminals as measured with D.C. is 0.2 Ω. With no-load and rated speed, the stator line voltage is 160 V for a field current of 4 A. At rated speed, the short-circuit stator current per phase is 60 A for a field current of 4 A. Compute *(a)* synchronous impedance per phase *(b)* voltage regulation at 0.8 p.f. lagging at rated load.

The alternator is star-connected.

[Hint. Take $r_a = 1.25\ r_{dc}$] **[Ans.** *(a)* 1.54 Ω *(b)* 50.08%]

5.34. *(a)* Show how the phasor diagram can be used to demonstrate the conditions of motoring or generating in a synchronous machine.

(b) Draw alternator phasor diagrams for lagging, unity and leading power factors on the assumption of same *(i)* terminal voltage and *(ii)* excitation voltage.

5.35. *(a)* Explain how one can distinguish whether a phasor diagram is for an alternator or a synchronous motor.

(b) Draw phasor diagrams for cylindrical-rotor synchronous motor when working under lagging, unity and leading power factors on the assumption of same *(i)* terminal voltage and *(ii)* excitation voltage.

5.36 Draw the voltage phasor diagram of an alternator and a synchronous motor, so that the same voltage equation, namely $\overline{E}_f = \overline{V}_t + \overline{I}_a\ (r_a + jX_s)$, is applicable to both these machines. Hence draw the commonly used voltage phasor diagram for a cylindrical rotor synchronous motor. How can one distinguish whether the voltage phasor diagram is for an alternator or for a motor?

5.37. *(a)* Draw external and internal characteristics of an alternator. Explain the shape of these characteristics with the help of phasor diagrams.

(b) Explain why alternators are rated in kVA. What is the necessity of mentioning the p.fs. at their name plates?

The p.f. given on the name plate of an alternator is 0.85. Explain whether the alternator is designed to operate at a lagging p.f. or at a leading p.f. **[Ans.** *(b)* Lagging p.f.]

5.38. *(a)* From the equivalent circuit of a cylindrical-rotor alternator, derive an expression for its power input and power output.

(b) A 3-phase star-connected alternator has synchronous impedance of 1 + j 10 Ω per phase. It is operating at a constant voltage of 6.6 kV and its field current is adjusted to give an excitation voltage of 6.4 kV. Find the power output, armature current and p.f. under the conditions of *(i)* maximum power output and *(ii)* maximum power input.

[Ans. *(i)* 3771.91 kW, 501.21 A, 0.6583 lead *(ii)* 3688.75 kW, 553.8 A, 0.5826 lead]

5.39. A 3-phase star-connected non-salient pole synchronous motor connected to 6.6 kV mains has an armature impedance of 2.5 + *j*15.0 Ω per phase. The excitation of the machine gives a generated e.m.f. of 7.0 kV. The iron and friction losses amount to 10 kW. Determine the output of the motor when operating at a load angle of 31° (electrical). *(GATE 1987)*

[Ans. 1431.816 kW]

5.40. A 3300-V, star-connected synchronous motor works at constant terminal voltage and constant excitation. Its synchronous impedance is 1 + *j* 10 Ω per phase. It operates at a p.f. of 0.8 leading when taking 600 kW from the mains. Find the p.f. when the input is increased to 900 kW.

[Ans. 0.9428 lead]

5.41. The synchronous reactance per phase of a 3-phase star-connected 6600 V synchronous motor is 20 Ω. For a certain load, the input is 915 kW at normal voltage and the induced e.m.f. is 8942 V. Determine the line current and the p.f. Neglect armature resistance.

[Ans. 97.055 A, 0.8247 lead]

5.42. A 2200-V, 400 kW, 3-phase, star-connected synchronous motor has a synchronous impedance of 0.3 + *j* 3 Ω. Determine the excitation e.m.f. and the power angle if the motor works at rated load at 0.8 p.f. leading and with an efficiency of 94%. [**Ans.** 2651.6 V, 13.607°]

5.43. A 2000 V, 3-phase, star-connected synchronous motor has synchronous impedance of 0.5 + *j*5 Ω per phase. For an excitation voltage of 3000 V, the motor takes an input of 900 kW at rated voltage. Compute the line current and p.f. [**Ans.** 260.71 A, 0.9965 lead]

5.44. A 11-kV, 3-phase, mesh-connected synchronous motor has synchronous reactance of 10 Ω per phase. Its friction, windage and iron losses are 1000 kW.

(a) The motor excitation is so adjusted that it takes u.p.f. current at a shaft load of 10 MW. Calculate the excitation voltage.

(b) Now the excitation e.m.f. is increased to 12.5 kV and the shaft load is adjusted so that motor again operates at u.p.f. Calculate the shaft load output.

[**Ans.** *(a)* 11493.95 V *(b)* 18592.76 kW]

5.45. A 3-phase star-connected alternator with synchronous impedance of 0 + *j* 5 Ω per phase is connected to an 11-kV system. The alternator power output is found to be 10 MW and reactive power output as 3 MVA. Compute the magnitude of excitation voltage, load angle, line current and power factor. [**Ans.** 13172.54 V, 20.185°, 547.96 A, 0.9578 lead]

5.46. A 2300-V, 3-phase, star-connected, 50 Hz synchronous motor operating at normal voltage is excited to give an excitation voltage of 2400 V. Determine the maximum power developed, armature current and power factor under this excitation. Per-phase synchronous impedance is 1.5 + *j* 21 Ω. [**Ans.** 242.7 kW, 87.853 A, 0.7927 lag]

5.47. From the equivalent circuit of a cylindrical rotor synchronous motor, derive expressions for the power input and power output in terms of load angle, synchronous impedance, excitation voltage etc.

Show that the difference in power input and power output is equal to ohmic loss $I_a^2 r_a$.

5.48. A 10 kVA, 380 V, 4-pole, 50 Hz, star-connected cylindrical rotor alternator has a stator resistance and synchronous reactance of 1 ohm and 15 ohm respectively. It supplies a load of 8 kW at rated voltage and 0.8 power factor lagging.

(a) Draw a phasor diagram of operation.

(b) Express the resistance and synchronous reactance in per unit values with the machine rating as the base.

(c) Calculate the percentage regulation.

(d) What is the terminal voltage if the load is suddenly removed (with the speed and excitation unaltered)? [**Ans.** *(a)* See Fig. 5.23 *(a)*, *(b)* 0.0693 p.u., 1.039 p.u. *(c)* 85.53% *(d)* 705 V]

5.49. A 3-phase, 400 V, 6-pole, 50 Hz, star-connected synchronous motor has synchronous impedance of 0.5 + *j* 8 Ω per phase. Its input current is 10 A at unity power factor for a certain field current. With the field current remaining constant, the load torque is increased until the motor takes an input current of 35 A. Calculate the developed torque and the new power factor. [**Ans.** 179.69 Nm, 0.776 lagging]

5.50. *(a)* Derive an expression for power developed in a cylindrical-rotor alternator in terms of power angle and synchronous impedance.

(b) An alternator, with a synchronous impedance of (0 + *j*1.25) p.u. delivers rated current to infinite busbars at p.f. 0.8 lagging. For the same excitation, find the current and power factor just before falling out of step. [**Ans.** *(b)* 1.80 p.u., 0.8958 leading]

5.51. A 3-phase, 2200 V, 200 kW, star-connected synchronous motor has synchronous impedance of 1.2 + *j* 12 Ω per phase. Its no load rotational loss is 2 kW. *(a)* For an output of 100 kW, the motor excitation is so adjusted as to give the operating p.f. 0.8 leading. Calculate the excitation voltage and the load angle.

(b) With the excitation fixed as found in part (a), the load on the motor shaft is increased to rated load. For this load, find the armature current and power factor.

[**Hint.** (a) $3(V_t I_a \cos\theta - I_a^2 r_a) = 102$ kW or $I_a^2 - 846.8 I_a + 28333.3 = 0$ etc.]

[**Ans.** (a) 2651.60 V, 13.59° (b) 57.79 A, 0.9719 leading]

5.52. A 3-phase, 1000 kW, 3.3 kV, 50 Hz, 4-pole, star-connected synchronous motor receives its supply from a 3-phase, 1500 kVA, 3.3 kV, 8-pole star-connected synchronous generator running at 750 r.p.m. The synchronous reactance per phase of the motor and the generator are 3.5 Ω and 3.0 Ω respectively. Neglecting all losses, determine the maximum torque in Nm that the synchronous motor can deliver. Assume that the excitation of each machine has been separately adjusted to values that would be needed for rated load unity p.f. conditions at their terminals. *(I.A.S., 1990)* [**Ans.** 11621.3 Nm]

5.53. (a) Derive an expression for power developed in a cylindrical-rotor synchronous motor in terms of load angle and synchronous impedance.

(b) A turbo-alternator having a reactance of 10 Ω has an armature current of 200 A at unity power factor, when running on 11000 V, constant frequency bus-bars. If the prime-mover input is not changed but the e.m.f. is raised by 20%, find the value of armature current and power factor. *(I.A.S., 1994)* [**Ans.** 243.3 A, 0.822 lag]

5.54. A 3-phase, turbo-alternator with a synchronous reactance of 10 Ω per phase and negligible armature resistance is connected to 11 kV constant voltage constant-frequency bus-bars and supplies 100 A at unity p.f. to the system. If the turbine power is kept constant and the excitation of the alternator is increased by 25%, what would be the new current and p.f.? Make appropriate assumptions. *(I.A.S., 1994)* [**Ans.** 190.65 A, 0.5245 lag]

5.55. A 3-phase star-connected alternator, rated at 11 kV, 1600 kVA, has negligible armature resistance and a synchronous reactance of 30 Ω per phase. When delivering full-load current at a certain p.f., the voltage regulation of the machine is zero. Estimate the p.f. of the load and the power delivered by the machine. *(I.A.S., 1997)*[**Ans.** 0.9801 leading, 1568.2422 kW]

5.56. For a synchronous machine, excitation e.m.f. = 2.3 p.u., terminal voltage = 1.00 p.u. $r_a = 0$, X_s = 1.5 p.u. Plot the variations of active and reactive powers. Find the maximum values of active and reactive powers and the corresponding load angles. In the reactive-power diagram, indicate the reactive power flow to or from the synchronous machine. At what load angle is the power factor unity?

[**Ans.** P_{max} = 1.533 at δ = 90° ; $Q_{og\,(max)}$ = 0.866 at δ = 0°. Load angle = 64.23°]

5.57. (a) Develop the excitation circles for a cylindrical rotor synchronous motor. How are these circles helpful in studying the steady state behaviour of synchronous motors?

(b) Explain the development of power circles for a cylindrical rotor synchronous motor. Show that :

(i) zero-power circle passes through origin, (ii) $P_{max} = \dfrac{V_t^2}{4r_a}$ and

(iii) efficiency at maximum power output = 50%.

5.58. (a) With regard to synchronous motor V-curves drawn for no load, half full-load and full load conditions, do the following :

(i) Draw unity pf compounding curve. Why is there a bend in this curve?

(ii) What information can be obtained from unity pf compounding curve?

(b) Draw a plot of power factor as a function of field current when synchronous motor is working at no load, half full-load and full load. What are these curves called?

A synchronous motor is working at full load and at unity power factor. From these curves, find the motor pf in case motor load is reduced to half full-load.

(c) A synchronous motor is operating at full load. If load is reduced to half full-load ; explain, with the help of phasor diagrams, what happens to armature current, load angle and power factor.

[**Ans.** *(b)* leading p.f. *(c)* I_a decreases, δ decreases, p.f. leading]

5.59. *(a)* A synchronous motor is operating at half full-load at unity power factor. If motor load is *(i)* increased to full load *(ii)* decreased to a value less than half full load, what happens to armature current, load angle and power factor.

(b) A 3-phase alternator is connected to an infinite bus. Describe how alternator V-curve can be obtained. Illustrate your answer with a phasor diagram.

Point out the difference between the V-curves of a synchronous motor and an alternator.

[**Ans.** *(a) (i)* Both I_a and δ increase, p.f. lagging *(ii)* both I_a and δ decrease, pf leading]

5.60. A 433-V, 3-phase, star-connected synchronous motor has a synchronous reactance of 5 Ω per phase. For a power output of 15 kW, find its minimum armature current, excitation voltage and the power angle. Neglect all losses.

[**Hint.** First calculate I_a, then E_f and δ by using its voltage phasor diagram.]

[**Ans.** 20 A, 466.4 V, 21.83°]

5.61. Explain from physical considerations, how a synchronous motor can be made to operate at leading or lagging power factors. Verify the above conclusions with suitable phasor diagrams.

5.62. *(a)* What do you understand by the terms, normal excitation, under-excitation and over-excitation in connection with synchronous motor operation?

(b) A synchronous motor is running at a certain load. When its field current is increased, its armature current decreases. Before this change, explain whether the motor was delivering or absorbing the lagging reactive kVA.

(c) Repeat part *(b)*, in case an increase in field current causes a corresponding increase in armature current.

[**Ans.** *(b)* Operating at lagging p.f. *i.e.*, motor is absorbing lagging reactive kVA from the bus. *(c)* Delivering lagging reactive kVA to the bus.]

5.63. It is seen from the V-curves of a synchronous motor that for one value of armature current, there are two different values of field current.

(a) Which of these two values of field current would give greater margin of stability?

(b) Out of these two field currents, which would give greater efficiency.

(c) In practice which of these two field currents would be used for synchronous motor operation?

[**Ans.** *(a)* and *(c)* Larger value of field current. *(b)* Lower value of Field current (because it gives lower field-circuit losses.)]

5.64. *(a)* A synchronous motor is operating at 0.2 p.f. lag at half-full load. With E_f, V_t and X_s remaining constant, explain whether its power factor is worsened or improved when it is made to operate at full load.

(b) A synchronous motor is operating at a certain load. Explain how you will find out in the laboratory whether it is operating at a leading or lagging power factor.

(c) The field current of a synchronous motor is adjusted to operate it at unity p.f. at no-load. If the load is increased, keeping E_f, V_t constant, will the synchronous motor be delivering or aborbing reactive power?

[**Ans.** *(a)* p.f. improves *(b)* Decrease field current; if I_a decreases p.f. is leading and if I_a increases p.f. is lagging *(c)* Absorbing lagging reactive kVA or absorbing reactive power.]

5.65. *(a)* In a D.C. shunt motor, counter e.m.f. (or generated e.m.f. E_a) must always be less than the terminal voltage V_t. It is possible in a synchronous motor to have counter e.m.f. or excitation e.m.f. E_f greater than terminal voltage V_t? Explain.

(b) A synchronous machine is running under steady-state conditions at rated voltage and rated frequency. At an excitation voltage of 1.5 p.u., the rated current flows at 0.8 p.f. leading. Is the synchronous machine operating as a motor or a generator? Explain.

(c) A variable ratio three phase transformer is interposed between a synchronous motor and the bus bars. If the synchronous motor terminal voltage is reduced with the help of variable-ratio transformer, the armature current increases. Before this change, was the synchronous motor working at a leading or a lagging p.f.? Explain.

[**Ans.** *(a)* Possible *(b)* Synchronous motor *(c)* Leading power factor.]

5.66. *(a)* Compare the performance of a synchronous generator connected to an infinite bus with that of an isolated alternator operating on its own load.

(b) An alternator, connected to infinite bus, is operating at unity power factor at half-full load. With field current remaining constant, steam input is increased till alternator begins to operate at full load. Under this condition, discuss what happens to power factor and reactive power flow.

(c) An alternator is synchronized to an infinite bus through a variable-ratio transformer. If the alternator terminal voltage is increased with the help of variable-ratio transformer, the armature current increases. Before this change, was the alternator working at a leading or lagging power factor? Explain.

[**Ans.** *(b)* Power factor becomes leading and alternator absorbs reactive power *(c)* Leading p.f.]

5.67. *(a)* Explain why cylindrical rotor theory can't be applied to a salient-pole synchronous machine.

(b) Show that in an alternator,

(i) if armature current lags E_f by 90°, the armature reaction m.m.f. is completely demagnetizing and

(ii) if armature current leads E_f by 90°, the armature reaction m.m.f. is completely magnetising.

(c) Show that when armature current is in phase with E_f, the effect of armature m.m.f. is to distort the field-flux wave, without appreciably modifying its strength.

5.68. *(a)* Explain the two-reaction theory as applied to salient-pole synchronous machines and draw its phasor diagram for a lagging p.f. load.

(b) Explain the difference between cylindrical-rotor theory and two-reaction theory.

(c) How can motor voltage equation be obtained from generator voltage equation for a salient-pole synchronous machine? Draw the voltage phasor diagram for a motor operating at lagging p.f.

5.69. *(a)* A salient-pole synchronous generator with negligible resistance, has the following per unit parameters : $X_d = 0.8$, $X_q = 0.5$

If this generator is supplying rated kVA at rated voltage and at 0.8 p.f. lagging, compute the load angle and the excitation e.m.f.

(b) Now cylindrical-rotor theory is applied to salient-pole machine of part *(a)* by assuming it to have only one reactance equal to X_d. Compute the load angle and excitation voltage by using cylindrical rotor theory and compare the results.

[Hint. *(b)* In Fig. 5.71 *(a)*, E_{f1} is the excitation voltage with cylindrical rotor theory such that $\bar{E}_{f1} = \bar{V}_t + j\,\bar{I}_a X_d$ and the angle between phasor E_{f1} and V_t is the load angle with this theory.

It will be seen that the magnitudes of E_f and E_{f1} are almost equal but the load angles with the two theories are considerably different from each other. In view of this, V_t, I_a, E_f and power over the normal operating range can be computed by simple cylindrical-rotor theory with sufficient accuracy.] **[Ans.** *(a)* 17.1°, 1.603 *(b)* 23.4°, 1.612]

5.70. *(a)* For a cylindrical-rotor alternator working at lagging p.f. show that

$$\tan\delta = \frac{I_a(X_s\cos\theta - r_a\sin\theta)}{V_t + I_a(X_s\sin\theta + r_a\cos\theta)}$$

(b) For salient-pole synchronous motor, working at lagging p.f., show that

$$\tan\delta = \frac{I_a(X_q\cos\theta - r_a\sin\theta)}{V_t - I_a(X_q\sin\theta + r_a\cos\theta)}$$

(c) Find an expression for power in terms of load angle δ, for a salient-pole synchronous motor working at a lagging p.f. Armature resistance may be neglected.

5.71. *(a)* A 3-phase, 30 kW, 433 volts, 50 Hz, star-connected salient-pole synchronous motor is operating at 0.8 p.f. leading and taking 40 A from the mains. If the direct and quadrature axes reactances of the machine are 5 Ω and 3 Ω respectively, calculate the maximum power the motor can develop if its excitation is maintained constant.

[Hint. $E_f = 400.284$ V, $\delta_{max} = 70.875°$]. **[Ans.** 64.4673 kW]

5.72. *(a)* A salient-pole synchronous motor is connected to infinite bus. If its field current is reduced to zero, will it stop or continue running? If the latter, what will be its speed? At what load angle will it fall out of step with zero field current?

(b) A salient-pole synchronous motor with damper bars is connected to an infinite bus system. Its field current is reduced to zero and the load on the synchronous motor is gradually increased. It has been found in practice that after the motor has fallen out of step, it continues running at sub-synchronous speed. Explain how it happens. What will happen to the magnitude of armature current and its p.f.?

[Ans. *(a)* Synchronous speed, δ = 45° *(b)* After falling out of step, it works as an induction motor at sub-synchronous speed. The motor draws large current at a poor p.f.]

5.73. A salient-pole synchronous generator on load draws an armature current at a lagging power-factor angle θ. Find out the angle by which

(a) air-gap excitation m.m.f. lags or leads the armature m.m.f. F_a,

(b) *q*-axis component of armature m.m.f. lags or leads F_a,

(c) *d*-axis component of armature m.m.f. lags or leads F_a and

(d) air-gap excitation m.m.f. lags or leads armature terminal voltage.

[Ans. *(a)* leads by (90 + θ + δ) *(b)* leads by (δ + θ) *(c)* lags by [90 – (θ + δ)] *(d)* leads by (90 + δ)]

5.74. *(a)* Draw the phasor diagram of a salient-pole synchronous generator showing also the field components. Write whether these salient-pole synchronous generators are low-speed or high-speed synchronous machines.

(b) A salient-pole synchronous generator has the following per unit parameters :

$$X_d = 1.00, X_q = 0.60, r_a = 0.02.$$

If this generator is delivering rated kVA at rated voltage and at 0.8 p.f. leading, compute the power angle and the excitation e.m.f. Draw the phasor diagram also.

[Ans. *(b)* 36.87°, 0.82]

5.75. Draw the following phasor diagrams for salient-pole synchronous machines clearly mentioning the parameters involved :

(a) Alternator operating at leading p.f. with power-factor angle θ less than power angle δ.

(b) Alternator operating at leading p.f. with θ > δ.

(c) Synchronous motor operating at lagging p.f. with θ < δ.

(d) Synchronous motor operating at lagging p.f. with θ > δ.

5.76. A 6-pole, 50 Hz synchronous motor is supplied from a 4000 V, 3-phase mains. The motor reactances are $X_d = 10.0\ \Omega$, $X_q = 7.00\ \Omega$. Losses are negligible. The excitation of the loaded motor is so adjusted that the internal generated voltage per phase is 2000 V at a power angle of 20°. Calculate the developed torque, the input current and the p.f. (indicating lag or lead). Draw the complete phasor diagram, showing I_d and I_q with their magnitudes. There are three suggestions regarding the value of the power angle at which maximum power will be developed : *(i)* 20° < δ < 90° *(ii)* δ = exactly 90° *(iii)* δ > 90°. Choose the correct suggestion.

(I.A.S., 1988) **[Ans.** 6629.96 Nm, 114.12 A, 0.8781 lag, 20° < δ < 90°]

5.77. A salient-pole synchronous motor with $r_a = 0$, $X_d = 1.0$ p.u. and $X_q = 0.5$ p.u. is operated on infinite bus-bar of 1.00 p.u. voltage. Show that for 1.00 synchronous power, the excitation voltage is

$$E_f = \operatorname{cosec}\delta - \cos\delta$$

Also derive the condition for load angle when synchronous power is maximum.

$$\left[\textbf{Ans.}\ \cos\delta = -\frac{E_f \cdot X_q}{4V_t(X_d - X_q)} \pm \sqrt{\frac{1}{2} \pm \left[\frac{E_f \cdot X_q}{4V_t(X_d - X_q)}\right]^2}\ \right]$$

5.78. For a 3-phase salient-pole synchronous machine operating as reluctance generator under maximum power conditions, derive the following relation :

$$\tan\theta = \frac{X_d + X_q}{X_d - X_q}$$

where θ = p.f. angle of reluctance generator.

5.79. A 30 kVA, 50 Hz, 4 pole alternator connected to infinite bus at rated voltage has $X_d = 1.00$ p.u. and $X_q = 0.6$ p.u.

(a) For zero excitation, find the output in terms of rated power that the machine can deliver without loss of synchronism.

(b) Under the conditions of *(a)*, estimate the current and p.f.

(c) Find the maximum available torque in Nm.

[Hint. *(c)* Torque in Nm = $\frac{1}{\omega_s}$ (p.u. power) (Rating in VA)]

[Ans. *(a)* 0.333 p.u. *(b)* 1.374 p.u., 0.2424 lag *(c)* 63.662 Nm]

5.80. *(a)* A turbo-generator synchronized with an infinite bus system is supplying its rated power. What happens to the alternator if its field circuit gets open-circuited accidentally?

(b) A turbo-generator synchronized with infinite bus-bar operates at unity p.f. If its field current is reduced to 80% of its previous value, will it be absorbing or delivering reactive power?

[**Ans.** *(a)* With $E_f = 0$, $P = 0$, therefore the alternator supplies no active power to the bus bars, consequently the alternator speeds up to run-away speed. (The run-away speed is defined as the speed which a prime-mover would attain if full load on the prime-mover were suddenly reduced to zero). *(b)* alternator absorbs reactive power.]

5.81. A 3-phase salient-pole synchronous motor, with X_d = 1.00 p.u., X_q = 0.8 p.u., is connected to an infinite bus of rated voltage 1.0 p.u. Calculate the percentage of rated output that this synchronous motor can deliver without losing synchronism with zero field current. Calculate the p.u. armature current and p.f. under these conditions.

[**Ans.** 12.5%, 1.132 p.u., 0.1104 lag]

5.82. *(a)* Derive an expression for the reactive power output from the terminals of a cylindrical-rotor alternator.

(b) A 3-phase, 20 MVA, 11 kV, star-connected alternator has $Z_s = 1 + j\,8\,\Omega$ per phase. Determine the maximum reactive power that can be delivered by this alternator for an excitation voltage of 14 kV.

(c) Repeat parts *(a)* and *(b)* in case armature-circuit resistance of this alternator is neglected.

[**Ans.** *(b)* 4.2091 MVAr *(c)* 4.125 MVAr]

5.83. A cylindrical-rotor synchronous motor is running with constant field current at a lagging p.f. Armature circuit resistance is negligible. Discuss, by means of phasor diagrams, that happens to the magnitudes of load angle, armature current and power factor if the following changes in its operating conditions are made.

(a) Frequency reduced by 10%, both applied voltage and load power constant.

(b) Both applied voltage and frequency reduced by 10%, load torque constant.

[**Hint.** Use the relation $P = \dfrac{E_f V_t}{X_s} \sin\delta$ and the voltage phasor diagram.]

[**Ans.** *(a)* δ remains constant, I_a is increased and p.f. becomes more lagging. *(b)* All the three δ, I_a and p.f. remain unaltered.]

5.84. A synchronous motor runs at a load angle of 20° at rated voltage and at rated frequency. Armature circuit resistance is neglected. For constant field current, compute the value of load angle with the following changes in its operating conditions.

(a) Frequency increased by 10%, load power and applied voltage constant.

(b) Frequency reduced by 10%, load torque and applied voltage constant.

(c) Both applied voltage and frequency reduced by 10%, load power constant.

(d) Both applied voltage and frequency reduced by 10%, load torque constant.

[**Ans.** *(a)* 20° *(b)* 17.93° *(c)* 22.335° *(d)* 20°]

5.85. *(a)* Draw the phasor diagram of a salient-pole synchronous motor working at leading p.f. and obtain therefrom an expression for power in terms of load angle δ. Neglect armature resistance.

(b) A salient-pole synchronous motor has the following per unit constants :

$X_d = 1.25$, $X_q = 1.00$.

Find the excitation voltage when the motor takes rated current (leading) at rated voltage, delivering 0.5 p.u. mechanical power. Ignore all losses.

[Hint. $V_t \sin \delta = X_q I_q$,

$\therefore \quad I_q = \sin \delta$. Also $V_t I_a \cos \theta = 0.5$

$\therefore \quad \cos \theta = 0.5 \quad \text{or} \quad \theta = 60°$.

Now $\quad I_a \cos (\theta + \delta) = I_q = \sin \delta = \cos (90 - \delta)$

$\therefore \quad 60 + \delta = 90 - \delta \quad \text{or} \quad \delta = 15°$

$I_d = I_a \sin (60 + 15) = ...$] **[Ans.** 2.174 p.u.]

5.86. *(a)* Define synchronizing-power coefficient. How is it related with steady-state stability limit of a synchronous machine?

(b) Define synchronizing power. Show that it comes into play only when steady-state operating conditions are disturbed.

5.87. *(a)* Give the physical concepts of synchronizing power.

(b) Show that the synchronizing power per electrical radian of phase displacement for *m*-phase cylindrical rotor synchronous machine is given by

(i) $m \dfrac{V_t^2}{Z_s} \cos \alpha_z$ on no-load and *(ii)* $m \dfrac{E_f V_t}{Z_s} \cos \delta \cos \alpha_z$ on load.

Here E_f, V_t and Z_s are phase values of excitation voltage, terminal voltage and synchronous impedance respectively, δ is the load-angle and $\alpha_z = \tan^{-1} \dfrac{r_a}{X_s}$.

[Hint. *(b)* At no-load $\delta = 0$ and $E_f = V_t$. Also $\sin \alpha_z \cong 0$.]

5.88. A 5 MVA, 11 kV, 50 Hz, 4 pole, star-connected synchronous generator with synchronous reactance of 0.7 p.u. is connected to an infinite bus. Find synchronizing power and the corresponding torque per unit of mechanical angle displacement.

(a) at no-load and *(b)* at full load of 0.8 p.f. lag.

[Ans. *(a)* 249.347 kW, 1587.4 Nm ; *(b)* 354.073 kW, 2254.1 Nm]

5.89. On no-load, the e.m.f. of a 2.2 kV, star-connected, 3-phase, 4-pole, synchronous motor may be considered equal to and in phase with the terminal voltage. If, on the application of load, the e.m.f. induced is retarded by 1 mechanical degree, calculate the armature current and power developed by the motor, taking the synchronous reactance to be 3 Ω per phase and the stator resistance to be negligible. *(I.A.S., 1989)* **[Ans.** 14.7787 A, 56307.13 W]

5.90. A 15 MVA, 11 kV, 50 Hz, 3-phase, 4-pole, star-connected cylindrical-rotor synchronous generator supplies rated output at p.f. 0.9 lagging to an infinite bus-bar. Its synchronous reactance is 0.35 p.u. Determine the synchronizing torque for a shaft displacement of 0.4° (mechanical). Neglect losses and saturation. **[Ans.** 4391.567 Nm]

5.91. *(a)* When will you call any machine system to be operating under stable conditions?

(b) Define the terms stability and stability limit.

(c) Explain steady-state stability limit. How can it be improved for synchronous machines?

5.92. *(a)* Explain the transient stability limit. What is the object of studying the transient stability limit of synchronous machines?

(b) Explain how steady-state stability limit can be depicted on the power circle diagrams.

5.93. (*a*) Describe, with physical concepts, the hunting phenomenon in synchronous machines. Explain why hunting is objectionable. What are the various causes of hunting? How can it be reduced?

(*b*) Explain the action of damper bars in damping out the rotor-oscillations.

(*c*) What is the effect of damper bars, under steady-state operating conditions?

5.94. (*a*) What information do the 'power-load angle curves' of synchronous machines convey and how do they look like for the two types of synchronous machines? Explain why the salient-pole machine is able to remain in synchronism on low load even though there has been a field failure. (*I.A.S., 1983*)

(*b*) Explain the term 'synchronous impedance' and how it affects the value of the load angle for maximum power delivered when the machine acts as a motor. (*I.A.S., 1987*)

(*c*) State and explain the difference between the damper windings of an alternator and induction-start synchronous motor. (*I.A.S., 1985*)

(*d*) In the case of a synchronous motor, describe with the help of phasor diagrams the effect of varying

(*i*) the excitation at constant mechanical load,

(*ii*) the mechanical load at constant value of excitation. (*I.A.S., 1972*)

5.95. (*a*) Describe how slip test can be conducted in the laboratory, for measuring X_d and X_q.

(*b*) Explain why the pointers of ammeter and voltmeter swing during the slip test?

(*c*) Why should the slip be kept as small as possible during the slip test? Discuss.

(*d*) A salient pole synchronous motor is working at no-load with terminal voltage $V_t = 1$ p.u. Now the excitation of the motor is adjusted to give $E_f = 0.6$ p.u. and armature current $I_a = 0.5$ p.u. The ratio $\frac{X_d}{X_q}$ obtained from slip test is 1.6. Determine the values of X_d and X_q. Neglect all losses.

[**Hint.** (*d*) First draw the salient-pole synchronous motor phasor diagram for $\delta = 0$ (at no-load) and with $r_a = 0$]

[**Ans.** (*d*) $X_d = 0.8$ p.u. and $X_q = 0.5$ p.u.]

5.96. Explain clearly the terms direct-axis and quadrature-axis synchronous reactances. How are these determined in the laboratory?

The results of slip test on a star-connected alternator are given below :

$V_{max} = 100$ V, $V_{min} = 96$ V

$I_{max} = 10$ A, $I_{min} = 7$ A.

All are line values. Neglecting resistance, calculate X_d and X_q in ohms. [**Ans.** 8.248 Ω, 5.543 Ω]

5.97. (*a*) Explain maximum-lagging current test for determining *q*-axis synchronous reactance X_q. Show that X_q is given by $\frac{V_t}{I_a}$ in Ω. Here I_a is the maximum stable armature current per phase.

(*b*) Explain the determination of X_d and X_q from reluctance-motor test.

5.98. A 3-phase star-connected synchronous motor has a synchronous reactance of 40% and negligible resistance. When operating with a load of 120 kW, the motor is overexcited so that the armature current is 50% more than the minimum possible at this load. If the load now reduces to 60 kW with the excitation maintained at the earlier-value, what would be the power factor at which the machine operates? Neglect all internal losses in the motor. (*I.A.S., 1991*)

[**Hint.** Load = $\frac{120\text{kW}}{200\text{kW}}$ = 0.6 p.u. V_t = 1.0 p.u. Minimum armature current = $\frac{0.6}{1 \times 1}$ = 0.6 p.u.
Increased armature current = 0.9 p.u. etc. See Example 5.7] [**Ans.** 0.3876 leading]

5.99. *(a)* Enumerate the various losses in synchronous machines. Explain how these losses can be determined.

(b) Experiments conducted on a set of D.C. motor and a 10 kVA 3-phase alternator gave the following data for the power-input to D.C. motor armature :

(i) D.C. motor running alone : 240 watts

(ii) D.C. motor alternator coupled together with later unexcited : 360 watts

(iii) Same as in *(ii)* but with alternator excited : 460 watts

(iv) Alternator s.c. test at rated current : 600 watts.

Calculate the alternator full-load efficiency at 0.8 p.f. leading with its field current and field terminal voltage equal to 0.74 A and 220 V respectively. [**Ans.** 92.777%]

5.100. A 3-phase, 2000 kVA, 11 kV star-connected alternator has the following loss data :

Open circuit core loss at 11 kV = 14 kW

Short circuit load loss at 90 A, 75°C = 10 kW

Friction and windage loss = 16 kW

Field winding resistance at 75°C = 0.31 Ω

For a field current of 110 A, compute the alternator efficiency at rated load 0.8 p.f. lagging. Compute also the effective armature resistance in per unit. [**Ans.** 97.125%, 0.0068 p.u.]

5.101. A 25 kW, 1000 V, 3-phase star-connected synchronous motor is connected to an infinite bus at rated voltage. At no-load, the motor takes a line current of 6 A and 1 kW, when field current is 3 A at 250 V D.C. Armature circuit resistance is 1 Ω per phase. Calculate

(a) no-load rotational loss of the machine

(b) machine efficiency at rated load at p.f. 0.9 lag and

(c) maximum efficiency at p.f. 0.9 lag.

[**Hint.** *(a)* No-load rotational loss = $1000 - 3 \times 6^2 \times 1 = ...$]

[**Ans.** *(a)* 892 W *(b)* 91.68% *(c)* 91.74%]

5.102. *(a)* For the same kVA load, efficiency of an alternator at leading p.f. is more than at lagging p.f. Explain.

(b) A synchronous motor is supplying a constant load. Will its efficiency be greater at 0.8 p.f. lead or 0.8 p.f. lag? Explain.

(c) An alternator has an efficiency of 90 per cent when operating at unity p.f. and at rated kVA. Explain what happens to its efficiency at rated kVA but at 0.8 p.f. lagging.

[**Ans.** *(a)* An alternator operating at leading p.f. requires less field current, therefore, less field-circuit loss and greater efficiency, for the same kVA load. *(b)* Efficiency is greater at 0.8 p.f. lag *(c)* At 0.8 p.f., output decreases (80 per cent of its previous value), no-load rotational losses and s.c. load losses remain unchanged but 0.8 p.f. lag requires more field current—there are, therefore, more field current losses and thus efficiency is decreased.]

5.103. What is an operating chart? What is the basis for the development of operating chart for an alternator?

Describe how an operating chart of a round-rotor alternator is developed from its phasor diagram. Explain how a point within its operating area renders useful information about the alternator output in MW, MVA, p.f., load angle etc.

5.104. What are reactive capability curves of an alternator? Develop the capability curves starting from the locus of constant apparent power of a cylindrical-rotor alternator.

Discuss the quadrant in which alternator operation is more common so far as capability curves are concerned. Is it possible to augment the active and reactive power capabilities of an alternator? Explain.

5.105. *(a)* Explain why the construction of synchronous condensers differs somewhat from those of standard synchronous motors.

(b) When is it desirable to use dual-purpose synchronous motors?

(c) An industrial load of 200 kW is supplied at 11000 V, the p.f. being 0.8 lagging. A synchronous motor is required to meet an additional load of 50 kW and at the same time to raise the resultant p.f. to 0.9 lagging. Find the kVA capacity of the motor and p.f. at which it must operate. **[Ans.** *(c)* 57.75 kVA, 0.8658 leading**]**

5.106. *(a)* What is a synchronous condenser?

(b) What are the advantages of installing a synchronous condenser in an electrical system? Illustrate your answer with an example.

(c) An industrial plant has an average load demand of 800 kW at a p.f. of 0.71 lagging. A synchronous motor of 400 kVA is installed for driving an additional load and for improving the plant power factor. The synchronous motor load is 160 kW at an efficiency of 90%. For synchronous motor operation at rated kVA, calculate the total load kVA and the resultant p.f. **[Ans.** *(c)* 1070.24 kVA, 0.9136 lagging**]**

5.107. *(a)* Show that the use of a synchronous condenser improves the efficiency and regulation of a system.

(b) A consumer has a total load of 2000 kW at a p.f. of 0.8 lagging. If it is required to improve the p.f. to 0.95 lagging, determine the kVA rating of the synchronous condenser for the purpose. *(I.A.S., 1999)* **[Ans.** *(b)* 842 kVA**]**

5.108. *(a)* In Fig. 5.118 *(a)* and *(b)*, explain whether the synchronous machine is working as a generator or a motor, with field winding on the rotor and with the direction of rotation shown. The phasor diagram for each figure should also be drawn indicating p.f. angle, internal p.f. angle, excitation voltage, terminal voltage, armature current etc. for lagging as well as leading p.f. operations. Armature resistance may be neglected.

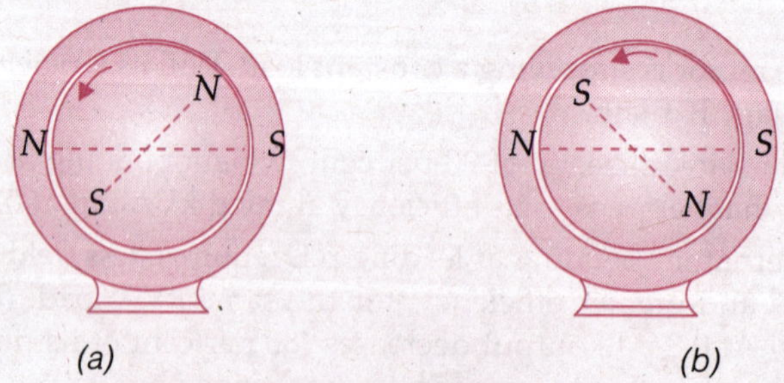

Fig 5.118: Pertaining to Problem 5.108.

(b) In case synchronous machine of part *(a)* is operating at no-load, show the orientation of field poles in relevant diagrams. Draw phasor diagram under these conditions also assuming excitation voltage greater than terminal voltage. Neglect all losses.

[Ans. *(a) (A)* Alternator *(B)* Motor**]**

5.109. *(a)* Data for open-circuit and short-circuit characteristics is available for a 3-phase synchronous machine. In case this machine, connected to an infinite bus, is working as a synchronous motor at no-load, describe how its Potier reactance can be obtained.

(b) A salient-pole synchronous machine is synchronized with an infinite bus at rated voltage, steam input to prime-mover is now increased till the synchronous machine delivers rated kVA to the infinite bus at a load angle of 40°. If *d*-axis synchronous reactance of the machine is 1.2 p.u., find the value of X_q, power factor and power delivered to infinite bus under the conditions specified. Find also the reactive power delivered to the bus.

[**Ans.** *(b)* 0.6544 p.u., 0.8766 leading, 0.8766 p.u., – 0.481 p.u.]

5.110. *(a)* Show that a synchronous motor has no net starting torque.

(b) Describe the methods of starting the synchronous motors against light-load torque.

(c) Explain the methods of starting synchronous motors against high-torque loads.

5.111. *(a)* During the induction-motor starting of a synchronous motor, explain why it is necessary *(i)* to start the motor at reduced voltage and *(ii)* to short-circuit the field winding at the time of starting.

(b) During the induction-motor starting, when the field winding is energised, there may be wide fluctuations in the supply current. Explain how this occurs. Give a method of overcoming this occurrence.

(c) For a synchronous machine, the three-phase winding is on the rotor and field winding is on the stator. The revolving field produced by the 3-phase armature current revolves clockwise. Explain the direction in which rotor must rotate.

[**Ans.** *(b)* It can be overcome by increasing the field current gradually,
(c) Direction of rotor rotation must be anti-clockwise.]

5.112. *(a)* A synchronous motor is supplying a certain load. In order to stop the motor, it is essential to switch-off first the A.C. supply and then its field current. Explain the reason.

(b) An alternator connected to infinite bus is operating at half full-load. An increase of its field current causes a decrease in the armature current. Is the armature current leading or lagging the terminal voltage?

(c) Explain how the graph between p.f. and field current can be obtained from the *V*-curve of a synchronous motor.

[**Ans.** *(a)* *V*-curves indicate that if field current is first reduced to zero, armature current increases to a value much higher than its rated current which is detrimental to both the synchronous motor and the supply system.

(b) Armature current is leading the terminal voltage.

(c) For minimum armature current, I_{min}, p.f. is unity. For any other field current, $I_a \cos \theta = I_{min}$. Since armature current I_a is known from the *V*-curve, p.f. for any value of field current can be calculated.]

5.113. *(a)* Discuss the applications of synchronous generators and synchronous condensers.

(b) Enumerate the advantages and disadvantages of using synchronous motors in industrial applications.

(c) Discuss the industrial applications where synchronous motors are preferred to induction motors.

5.114. The transformer and cable feeding power to an industrial plant have a rating of 1000 kVA and are fully loaded by the plant which draws 1000 kVA at a p.f. of 0.7 lagging. A 100 kW synchronous motor having an efficiency of 90% is to be added to the plant load without increasing the rating of transformer and cable. At what p.f. must the synchronous motor operate? [**Ans.** 0.652 leading]

5.115. A star-connected synchronous machine, with $Z_s = 1 + j10\ \Omega$ per phase, is synchronized with an infinite bus of 11 kV. The machine is made to operate at a leading p.f. of 0.8 with an armature current of 50 A and with terminal voltage ahead of the excitation e.m.f. Calculate the magnitude of excitation e.m.f.

How can this machine be made to operate at unity p.f. without altering its field excitation? Under this condition, find the armature current and load angle. *(I.A.S., 2000)*

[Ans. 6624.97 V, 260.751 A, 23.178°]

5.116. A cylindrical rotor alternator is operating at a lagging pf. Show that $E_f \cdot I_a \cdot \cos\psi$ is equal to $\dfrac{E_f \cdot V_t}{X_s} \sin\delta$, where ψ = internal power-factor angle and δ = load angle. Armature-circuit resistance is neglected.

5.117. A cylindrical-rotor synchronous machine is synchronised with an infinite bus at rated voltage. Now the steam input to the machine is increased till the synchronous machine begins to operate at its rated current. The synchronous machine has $Z_s = 0 + j1.2$ p.u. Calculate the p.f., load angle and the active and reactive powers delivered to the infinite bus under these conditions.

Without any change in the steam input, how can this alternator be made to deliver no reactive power to the bus? Find the excitation voltage and load angle under this condition.

[Ans. 0.8 leading, $\delta = 73.74°$, $P = 0.8$ p.u., $Q = -0.60$ p.u., $E_f = 1.3862$ p.u., $\delta = 43.83°$]

5.118. A salient-pole synchronous machine is synchronized with an infinite bus at rated voltage. Its steam input is then increased till the machine delivers rated current to the bus. The machine has $X_d = 1.0$ p.u., $X_q = 0.8$ p.u. and negligible resistance. Find the load angle, power factor and active and reactive powers under the conditions stated here.

If the machine is made to operate at unity p.f. without altering its steam input, calculate the new excitation voltage and load angle.

[Ans. 48.77°, 0.8761 leading, 0.62807 p.u., – 0.48232 p.u. ; 1.3216 p.u., 35.03°]

6 Chapter

Polyphase Induction Motors

INTRODUCTION

A polyphase induction motor is a singly-excited A.C. machine in the sense that it is supplied power from a single A.C. source. Its stator winding is directly connected to A.C. source, whereas its rotor winding receives its energy from stator by means of induction (*i.e.* transformer action). Balanced polyphase currents in polyphase windings produce a constant-amplitude rotating m.m.f. wave. The stator-produced m.m.f. wave and rotor-produced m.m.f. wave, both rotate in the air-gap in the same direction at synchronous speed. These two m.m.f. waves are thus stationary with respect to each other, consequently the development of steady electromagnetic torque is possible at all speeds but not at synchronous speed. The stator and rotor m.m.f. waves combine to give the resultant air-gap flux density wave of constant amplitude and rotating at synchronous speed. Since an induction motor can't run at synchronous speed, it is called *asynchronous machine*.

The stator of a 3-phase induction motor is essentially similar to that of a synchronous machine. The reader is advised to go through the constructional features of cage-rotor and wound-rotor induction motors already presented in Art. 3.2. Of the two types of induction motors, squirrel-cage induction is the most widely used A.C. polyphase motor because this motor is the simplest in construction, is highly reliable and is maintenance free. Slip-ring induction motor has higher initial cost and involves increased maintenance, it is used where higher starting torque and speed control is desired.

Expressions for the e.m.fs. generated in stator and rotor windings are derived in Art. 3.4.3. The object of this chapter is to develop the techniques for the analysis of polyphase induction machines.

6.1. INDUCTION MOTORS AS A TRANSFORMER

An induction motor is similar to a transformer in many respects. In this connection, consider an induction motor with both its stator and rotor windings in star. The rotor winding is assumed open-circuited so that rotor current is zero and no electromagnetic torque is developed. Application of three-phase balanced voltages at line frequency f_1 to the stator winding, causes the production of a rotating magnetic field. This rotating flux cuts both the stator and stationary rotor conductors at synchronous speed, consequently e.m.fs. of line frequency f_1 are induced in them. Per phase value of the e.m.f. E_1 induced in stator winding is given by Eq. (3.26) as

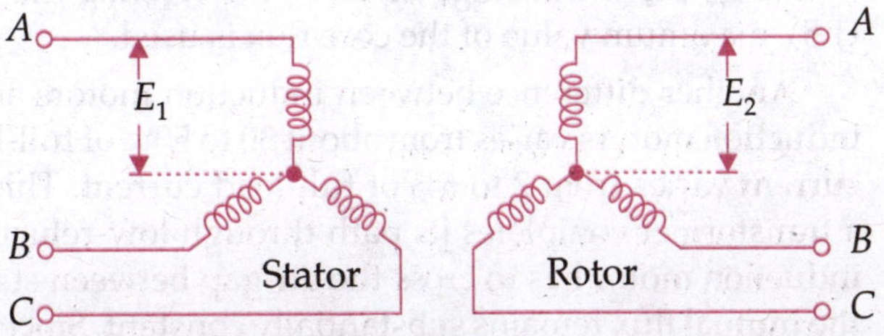

Fig 6.1: 3-phase wound-rotor induction motor with both stator and rotor, in star.

$$E_1 = \sqrt{2}\pi f_1 k_{w1} N_1 \phi \quad ...(6.1)$$

Here N_1 = stator series turns per phase

and k_{w1} = stator winding factor.

Similarly per phase value of e.m.f. E_2 induced in the standstill rotor winding is given by

$$E_2 = \sqrt{2}\pi f_1 k_{w2} N_2 \phi \quad ...(6.2)$$

Here N_2 = rotor series turns per phase

and k_{w2} = rotor winding factor.

Line frequency f_1 appears in the expression for E_2 also, because rotor is at standstill. Here ϕ is the resultant air-gap flux per pole.

The e.m.f. or voltage ratio for the induction machine from Eqs. (6.1) and (6.2) is

$$\frac{E_1}{E_2} = \frac{N_1 k_{w1}}{N_2 k_{w2}} = \frac{N_1'}{N_2'} \quad ...(6.3)$$

Here N_1' and N_2' are called the effective number of stator-series turns per phase and rotor-series turns per phase respectively.

Eq. (6.3) is similar to the voltage ratio of a transformer, see Eq. (1.10). Thus, a woundrotor induction motor at standstill is similar to a transformer at no load. Further, the resultant mutual flux in a transformer is due to the combined action of primary and secondary m.m.fs. ; similarly in induction machines, synchronously rotating air-gap flux (or mutual flux) is due to the combined action of both stator and rotor m.m.fs. In a transformer, mutual flux is pulsating in nature, whereas in a 3-phase induction motor, mutual flux is rotating in nature. In induction machine; the rotating air-gap flux generates counter e.m.f. E_1 in the stator winding similar to the counter e.m.f. induced (by the mutual flux) in the primary winding of a transformer. As the transformer is loaded, the m.m.f. of the secondary current reacts on the primary in order to draw more power from A.C. source, similarly with the increase in shaft load, the rotor m.m.f. reacts on the stator winding in order to extract more power from the A.C. source. A 3-phase induction motor with its rotor blocked behaves similar to a transformer under short circuit. In addition, stator and rotor windings of an induction machine possess resistances and leakage reactances just like the resistances and leakage reactances of the primary and secondary windings of a transformer. In view of these similarities, an induction machine is called a *generalized transformer* and it is for this reason that the stator winding of an induction machine is treated as its primary and the rotor winding as its secondary. Consequently, the phasor diagram and equivalent circuit of a 3-phase induction motor are almost similar to those in a transformer. The subscripts 1 and 2 are used to denote the stator and rotor quantities respectively, as in a transformer.

The voltage ratio of the induction machine includes winding factors $k_{\omega1}$ and $k_{\omega2}$, because the stator and rotor windings are distributed along the air-gap periphery. The transformer primary and secondary windings, being concentrated windings, require no winding factors. In Eqs. (6.1) and (6.2), ϕ is the average value of the rotating flux per pole. In transformer e.m.f. Eqs. (1.3) and (1.5), maximum value of the core flux is used.

Another difference between induction motors and transformers is that the no-load current in induction motors varies from about 30 to 50% of full-load current, whereas in transformers, no-load current varies from 2 to 6% of full-load current. This is because of the fact that the mutual flux in a transformer completes its path through low-reluctance iron core, whereas the mutual flux in an induction motor has to cross the air-gap between stator and rotor. For a constant applied voltage, the mutual flux remains substantially constant. Since the reluctance offered to the mutual flux in an induction motor is more due to the presence of air gap, a constant mutual flux (m.m.f./reluctance) requires more magnetizing m.m.f. and, therefore, more magnetizing current. In induction motors, the magnetizing current (lagging nearly 90° behind the applied voltage) forms a considerable portion of no-load current, that is why induction motors operate at low power factors at no loads. Usually the no-load power factors of induction motors are in the neighbourhood of 0.15 or so. The effect of low value of no-load power factor is to decrease the full-load operating power factor of the induction motor. Thus, for keeping the induction motor magnetizing current low and, therefore, a better no-load and full-load power factors, air gaps in induction motors are kept as small as are mechanically possible.

6.2. PRINCIPLE OF OPERATION

The stator winding of a 3-phase induction motor is connected to 3-phase balanced supply. The flow of 3-phase currents in the 3-phase stator winding produces a rotating magnetic field as discussed in Art. 3.7. The speed of rotating field is the synchronous speed, $n_s = 2f_1/P$ rps. The rotating flux wave cuts the stationary rotor conductors n_s times per sec and therefore e.m.fs. are induced in the rotor conductors. As the rotor circuit is short-circuited, these induced e.m.fs. give rise to current in the rotor conductors. The interaction of these rotor currents with rotating flux wave produces torque in the rotor of a 3-phase induction motor and as a consequence, rotor begins to rotate.

According to Lenz' law, *effect opposes the cause.* Here, effect is the developed torque and cause is the flux-cutting by the rotor conductors. Therefore, as per Lenz's law, the developed torque must oppose (or minimise) the cause, that is flux-cutting action. This is possible only if the developed torque forces the rotor to rotate in the direction of rotating field. When this happens, the relative speed between rotating flux and rotor conductors is reduced and therefore flux-cutting action (times per sec) also gets reduced. For example, if rotor speed is n_r rps in the direction of rotating flux wave, the relative speed between rotating flux wave and rotor conductors becomes $(n_s - n_r)$ rps and the flux-cutting action reduces from n_s times per sec to $(n_s - n_r)$ times per sec as demanded by Lenz's law. This shows that *rotor must rotate in the direction of rotating magnetic field* when 3-phase supply is given to stator of a 3-phase induction motor. If rotor is assumed to run at synchronous speed n_s in the direction of rotating field, then relative speed between stator and rotor fields would be zero, there would be no flux-cutting action, no e.m.f. in rotor conductors, no current in rotor bars and therefore no developed torque. Thus, the rotor of 3-phase induction motor can never attain synchronous speed.

6.3. TORQUE IN THREE-PHASE INDUCTION MOTORS

It has already been stated that for the development of torque in an electric motor, relative velocity between stator field and rotor field must be zero. We shall see how this happens in the two types of three-phase induction motors.

6.3.1. Squirrel-Cage Induction Motor

Fig. 6.2 shows a 2-pole, 3-phase squirrel cage induction motor. When three-phase supply is given to 3-phase winding (not shown) on the stator, a rotating magnetic field is established. This magnetic field produces two poles N_1, S_1 rotating anticlockwise (assumed direction) and at synchronous speed n_s rps. These poles running at synchronous speed generate maximum emf in stationary bars A and B, because these are just under the centre of poles N_1, S_1. Bars under the influence of pole N_1 have emfs indicated by cross * and those under the influence of pole S_1 have emfs indicated by dots. If the magnitude of bar emfs is plotted along the air-gap periphery (*i.e.*, in space), it would be a sine wave. Frequency of the emf generated in stationary rotor bars is equal to stator frequency.

* Direction of emf in bars : Make the pole N_1 stationary, bar A rotates clockwise, now apply right-hand rule.

If rotor is assumed resistive, then bar currents would be in phase with bar emfs. Therefore, bar currents are maximum in bars A and B and have lower values in other bars. Thicker the cross or dot, larger is the value of the current represented in Fig. 6.2. Since the bar currents are induced by the stator rotating field, these rotor bar currents must naturally produce a rotating field running at synchronous speed n_s in the direction of stator field. Relative speed between stator and rotor rotating fields is, therefore, zero.

Right hand grip rule to the bar currents gives the direction of rotor mmf F_2. This F_2 is vertically downwards. As a result, F_2 creates two poles N_2, S_2 on rotor as shown in Fig. 6.2. These two poles rotate anticlockwise at speed n_s. This shows that relative speed between stator and rotor fields is zero. Thus, stator and rotor poles can interact to produce steady torque. In Fig. 6.2, stator pole N_1 attracts rotor pole S_2 but repels rotor pole N_2, thus producing anticlockwise torque. Similarly, stator pole S_1 repels rotor pole S_2 and attracts pole N_2, again producing anticlockwise torque. This shows that total electromagnetic torque developed by the interaction of stator and rotor fields is in the same direction as that of the stator rotating field. As a consequence, starting torque is produced and rotor begins to rotate in the direction of rotating magnetic field. It can, therefore, be stated that 3-phase induction motor is a self starting motor. Eventually, rotor attains a speed somewhat less than synchronous speed n_s.

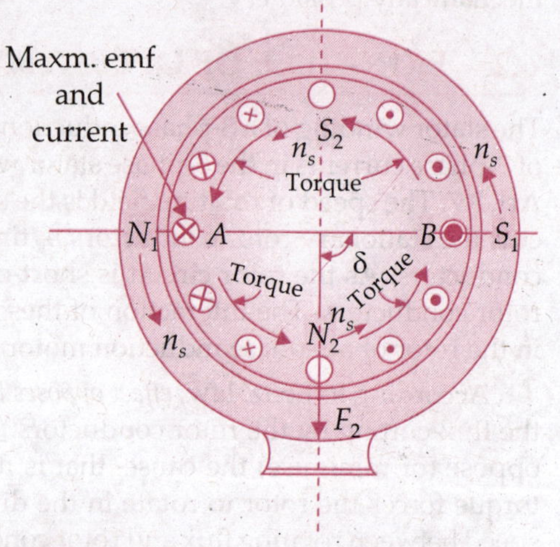

Fig 6.2: Torque in SCIM, rotor resistive.

Actually, the rotor bars are housed in rotor slots. As a result, rotor bars possess considerable amount of leakage reactance x_2 at standstill. Therefore, rotor current in each bar lags behind the generated emf in that bar by rotor power-factor angle $\theta_2 = \tan^{-1} \frac{x_2}{r_2}$. Bars A and B under stator N_1, S_1 poles have maximum emf generated in Fig. 6.2. On account of rotor leakage reactance, currents in bars A and B would attain maximum value only after the poles N_1, S_1 have travelled through an angle θ_2 from its maximum emf position shown in Fig. 6.2. This is illustrated in Fig. 6.3. As before, right-hand grip rule gives the direction of rotor mmf F_2. Mmf F_2 creates two poles N_2, S_2 on rotor as shown in Fig. 6.3. These poles N_2, S_2 rotate at synchronous speed n_s in the direction of stator rotating field. Relative velocity between stator and rotor poles is zero. Therefore stator pole S_1 repels S_2 and attracts N_2. Similarly, stator pole N_1 repels N_2 but attracts S_2, thus producing electromagnetic torque. This starting torque is in the direction of rotating magnetic field.

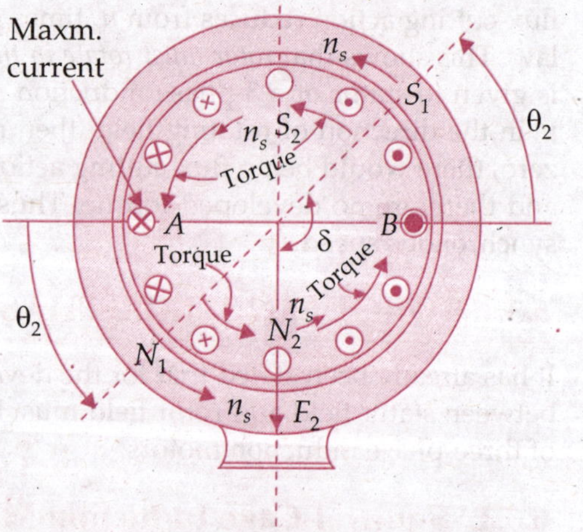

Fig 6.3: Torque in SCIM, rotor reactive

In all rotating electrical machines, magnitude of electromagnetic torque is given by

$$T_e \propto \text{(stator field strength, } S_1\text{) (Rotor field strength, } R_1\text{)} \times \sin \delta$$

where δ = torque angle between stator field axis and rotor field axis, see Art. 3.1.1.

Torque angle δ is 90° in Fig. 6.2 and $(90 + \theta_2)$ in Fig. 6.3. In 3-phase induction motor, $\delta = 90 + \theta_2$ is called *load angle*.

∴ In Fig. 6.2, $T_e = K\,S_1\,R_1 \sin 90° = K\,S_1\,R_1$

In Fig. 6.3, $T_e = K\,S_1\,R_1 \sin(90° + \theta_2)$

$= K\,S_1\,R_1 \cos(\theta_2) < K\,S_1\,R_1$ of Fig. 6.2.

It is seen from above that torque developed in reactive rotor of Fig. 6.3 is less than the torque developed in a resistive rotor of Fig. 6.2.

6.3.2. Slip-Ring Induction Motor

Fig. 6.4 shows a 2-pole, 3-phase slip-ring induction motor. Three-phase winding on stator is not shown. Rotor has two pole, 3-phase winding, with coils *aa′*, *bb′*, *cc′* representing phases *a*, *b*, *c* respectively. When 3-phase supply is given to three-phase stator winding, a rotating magnetic field is established. This magnetic field produces two poles N_1, S_1 rotating anticlockwise at synchronous speed n_s rps. These two rotating poles cut the stationary 3-phase rotor winding at speed n_s; therefore line-frequency emfs are generated. Phase a has maximum emf generated in it, because coil *aa′* representing phase *a* lies under the centre of poles N_1, S_1; where the flux density is peak. Maximum emf in phase *a* is indicated by large cross and dot in coil-sides *a*, *a′* in Fig. 6.4. Coil-sides *b′*, *c′* are under the influence of pole N_1, emf generated in these two coil-sides is less than the maximum value and is indicated by crosses of lower size. Similarly, dots of lower size are shown in coil-sides *b*, *c*. In case rotor circuit is assumed purely resistive, then current in a coil would be in phase with the emf generated in that coil ; these currents are shown in Fig. 6.4. Right-hand grip rule gives rotor mmf F_2 vertically downward. This mmf F_2 creates two poles N_2, S_2 on rotor, rotating anticlockwise at speed n_s. This is shown in stationary rotor in Fig. 6.4. Relative speed between stator and rotor poles is zero, therefore, these poles can interact to produce torque in Fig. 6.4 ; as it is produced in squirrel-cage induction motor of Fig. 6.2. Reader can easily explain it further on their own.

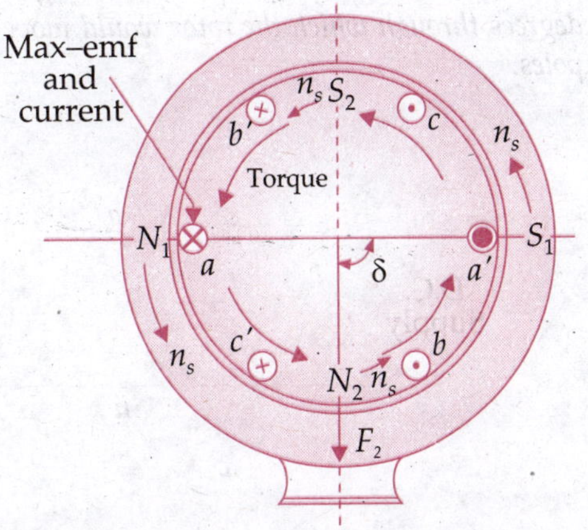

Fig 6.4: Torque in SRIM, rotor resistive.

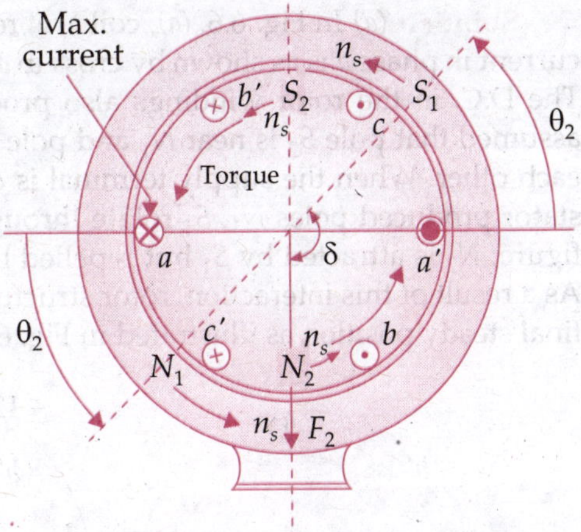

Fig 6.5: Torque in SRIM, rotor reactive.

Actually, rotor winding has leakage reactance x_2. As a result, rotor current in each phase lags behind the generated emf in that phase by rotor power factor angle $\theta_2 = \tan^{-1}\dfrac{x_2}{r_2}$, Fig. 6.5. Now the reader can easily explain it further as it is done in a squirrel-cage induction motor of Fig. 6.3.

It can be summarised from above as follows.

(i) If rotor is resistive, more starting torque T_{est} is produced. Rotor is, however, reactive in nature, therefore starting torque is lower as compared to that produced with resistive rotor.

(ii) In case rotor power-factor angle $\theta_2 = \tan^{-1}\frac{x_2}{r_2}$ at starting is reduced, T_{est} can increase. This can be achieved in slip-ring induction motors only by inserting external resistance R in the rotor circuit. With R, $\theta_2 = \tan^{-1}\frac{x_2}{r_2+R}$ is reduced and therefore starting torque is increased. In other words, starting torque can be controlled in slip-ring induction motors and not in squirrel-cage induction motors.

Example 6.1. *A three-phase, star-connected wound-rotor induction motor is fed from two D.C. sources as shown in Fig. 6.6. The currents in both stator and rotor windings are kept within limits. If the D.C. supply terminal is changed from a phase winding to b phase winding of the stator, find the number of mechanical degrees through which the rotor would move, in case the motor has (a) two poles (b) four poles and (c) six poles.*

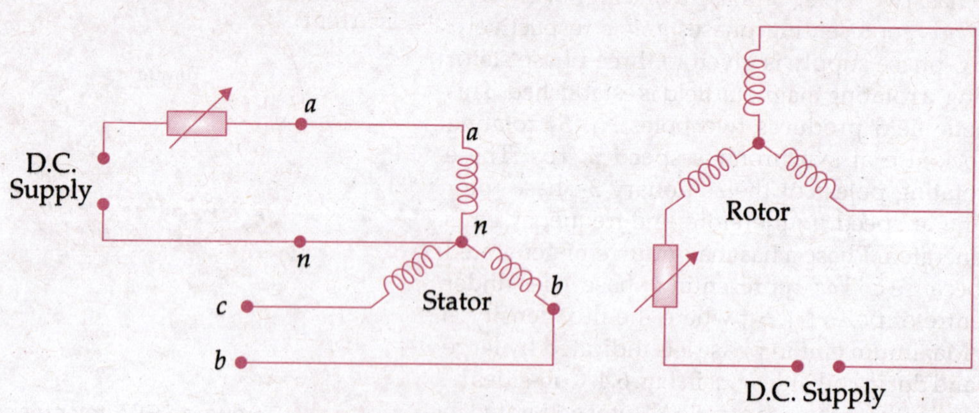

Fig 6.6: Circuit diagram, Example 6.1.

Solution. *(a)* In Fig. 6.6. *(a)*, coil a, a' represents phase a winding. When the direction of direct current in phase a is as shown by cross in a and dot in a', then two stator poles N_1, S_1 are produced. The D.C. in the rotor windings also produces two poles N_2, S_2 as shown. In Fig. 6.6. *(a)*, it is assumed that pole S_2 is near N_1 and pole N_2 is near S_1, because poles of opposite polarity attract each other. When the supply terminal is changed from phase a winding to phase b winding, the stator produced poles N_1, S_1 rotate through 120° elect clockwise as shown in Fig. 6.6. *(b)*. In this figure, N_2 is attracted by S_1 but repelled by N_1, similarly S_2 is attracted by N_1 but repelled by S_1. As a result of this interaction, rotor structure moves through 120° elect clockwise and occupies the final steady position as illustrated in Fig. 6.6. *(c)*.

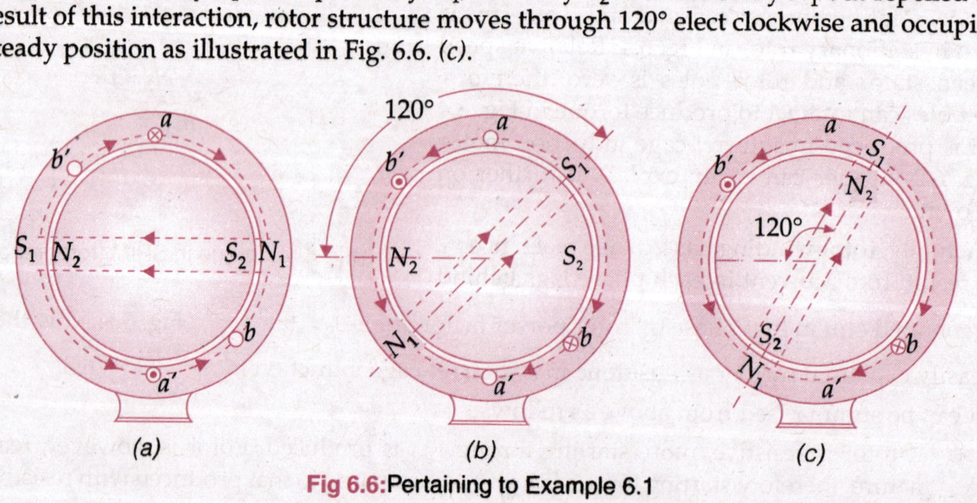

Fig 6.6: Pertaining to Example 6.1

For a 2-pole machine, $\theta_{elec.} = \theta_{mech}$, therefore, the rotor revolves 120 mechanical degrees *i.e.*, through one-third of a revolution.

(*b*) For a *P*-pole machine, $\theta_{elec} = \frac{P}{2}\,\theta_{mech}$

For a 4-pole machine, as the supply is changed from phase *a* winding to phase *b* winding, the rotor again revolves through 120° elect.

$$\therefore \qquad \theta_{mech} = \frac{2}{4}\,(120°) = 60°.$$

Thus in a 4-pole machine, the rotor rotates through 60 mechanical degrees (*i.e.*, 1/6th of a revolution) as the D.C. supply is changed from one phase to the next phase in sequence.

(c) For a 6-pole machine, $\theta_{mech} = \frac{2}{6}\,(120°) = 40°$.

Thus in a 6-pole machine, the rotor revolves through 40 mechanical degrees (*i.e.*, 1/9th of a revolution) as the D.C. supply is changed from one phase winding to the adjacent phase winding.

6.4. ROTOR FREQUENCY

It has been shown that rotor starts running in the direction of rotating magnetic field. At standstill, rotor conductors are being cut by rotating flux wave at synchronous speed n_s, therefore frequency f_2 of the rotor e.m.f. and current is equal to the line frequency f_1. When rotor revolves at a speed of n_r r.p.s., less than n_s in the direction of rotating flux wave, the relative speed between synchronously-rotating flux and rotor conductors becomes $(n_s - n_r)$ rps.

∴ Frequency of rotor e.m.f.

$$= \frac{(\text{poles})\{\text{relative speed between rotating flux and rotor structure in r.p.s}\}}{2} \qquad \text{...(6.4 a)}$$

$$= \frac{P(n_s - n_r)}{2} \qquad \text{...(6.4 b)}$$

The slip has already been defined by Eq. (3.29 *b*) as

$$s = \frac{n_s - n_r}{n_s} = \frac{\text{synchronous speed} - \text{rotor speed}}{\text{synchronous speed}}$$

$$\therefore \qquad n_s - n_r = sn_s = \text{slip speed} \qquad \text{...(6.5)}$$

$$\therefore \text{ Rotor frequency,} \qquad f_2 = \frac{P \cdot sn_s}{2} = s \cdot \frac{Pn_s}{2} = sf_1 \qquad \text{...(6.6)}$$

Thus the frequency of the rotor e.m.f. and current in an induction motor is given by the product of slip *s* and the line frequency f_1. It is for this reason that f_2 is also called the *slip frequency*.

At standstill, rotor frequency is f_1 and the field produced by rotor currents revolves at a speed equal to {2(rotor frequency)}/(rotor poles) $(2f_1/P = n_s)$ with respect to rotor structure. When the rotor is revolving at a speed n_r, the rotor frequency is sf_1 and the rotor-produced field revolves at a speed of $\{2(sf_1)/P\} = sn_s$ in the forward direction with respect to rotor structure. But the rotor is already revolving at a mechanical speed of n_r r.p.s. with respect to stator. Therefore, the speed of rotor field with respect to stator is equal to the sum of mechanical rotor speed n_r and rotor-field speed sn_s with respect to rotor. Thus the speed of rotor field with respect to stator is given by

$$n_r + sn_s = n_s(1 - s) + sn_s = n_s \text{ r.p.s.}$$

But the stator-field speed with respect to stator is synchronous speed n_s r.p.s. This concludes that the stator and rotor fields are stationary with respect to each other at all possible rotor speeds.

Since the relative speed between stator and rotor fields is zero, a steady torque is produced by their interaction as explained before and rotation is maintained.

The rotor of an induction motor can never attain synchronous speed. In case rotor speed is synchronous, the rotor conductors would be stationary with respect to the synchronously-rotating magnetic field. As a result of it, no e.m.fs. would be generated in rotor conductors and, therefore, rotor m.m.f. would be zero. But the existence of rotor m.m.f. as per Figs. 6.2 to 6.5, is essential for production of torque. This shows that the operating speed of the rotor of an induction motor can never be equal to the synchronous speed.

Example 6.2. *A 3-phase, 50 Hz induction motor has full-load speed of 1440 r.p.m. For this motor, calculate the following :*

(a) number of poles

(b) full-load slip and rotor frequency

(c) speed of stator field with respect to (i) stator structure and (ii) rotor structure and

(d) speed of rotor field with respect to (i) rotor structure (ii) stator structure and (iii) stator field.

For parts (c) and (d), answer should be given in r.p.m. and rad/sec.

Solution. *(a)* The use of full-load speed of 1440 r.p.m. in Eq. (3.69) gives

$$1440 = \frac{120 f_1}{P} = \frac{120 \times 50}{P} \text{ or } P = \frac{120 \times 50}{1440} = 4\frac{1}{6} \text{ poles}$$

Since the number of poles must be even and a whole number, the induction motor must have 4 poles. Note that an induction motor runs at a speed, a little less than synchronous speed.

(b) Synchronous speed,

$$N_s = \frac{120 \times 50}{4} = 1500 \text{ r.p.m.}$$

$\therefore$ Slip, $$s = \frac{N_s - N_r}{N_s} = \frac{1500 - 1440}{1500} = 0.04.$$

Rotor frequency, $f_2 = sf_1 = 0.04 \times 50 = 2$ Hz.

(c) (i) Speed of stator field with respect to stator structure

$$= N_s = 1500 \text{ r.p.m.}$$

$$\therefore \quad \omega_s = \frac{2\pi N_s}{60} = \frac{2\pi \times 1500}{60} = 150.08 \text{ rad/sec}$$

(ii) Speed of stator field w.r.t. revolving rotor structure

$$= 1500 - 1440 = 60 \text{ r.p.m.} = \frac{2\pi \times 60}{60} = 6.283 \text{ rad/sec}$$

(d) (i) Speed of rotor field w.r.t. rotor structure

$$= \frac{120(\text{rotor frequency})}{\text{Poles}} = \frac{120 \times 2}{4}$$

$$= 60 \text{ r.p.m.} = 6.283 \text{ rad/sec}$$

(ii) Speed of rotor field w.r.t. stator structure

= (Mechanical speed of rotor) + (Speed of rotor field w.r.t rotor structure)

$$= 1440 + 60 = 1500 \text{ r.p.m.} = 150.08 \text{ rad/sec.}$$

(iii) Since both the stator and rotor fields are rotating at synchronous speed of 1500 r.p.m. with respect to stator structure, speed of rotor field with respect to stator field is zero. Thus the stator and rotor fields are stationary with respect to each other.

Example 6.3. *A properly shunted centre-zero galvanometer is connected in the rotor circuit of a 6-pole, 50 Hz wound-rotor induction motor. If the galvanometer makes 90 complete oscillations in one minute, calculate the rotor speed.*

Solution. One complete oscillation of galvanometer corresponds to one cycle of rotor frequency.

∴ Rotor frequency, $f_2 = sf_1 = \frac{90}{60} = 1.5 \text{ Hz}$

or Slip, $s = \frac{f_2}{f_1} = \frac{1.5}{50} = 0.3$

Rotor speed $= N_s(1-s) = \frac{120 \times 50}{6}(1 - 0.03) = 970$ r.p.m.

Example 6.4. *A 4-pole, 3-phase slip-ring induction motor (SRIM) is used as a frequency converter. Its stator is excited from 3-phase, 50 Hz supply. A load requiring 3-phase, 20 Hz supply is connected to the star-connected rotor through three slip-rings of SRIM.*

(a) At what two speeds the prime-mover should drive the rotor of this SRIM.

(b) Find the ratio of the two voltages available at the slip rings at the two speeds.

(c) Find out whether the phase sequence of 3-phase rotor voltages remain the same at the two speeds.

Solution. *(a)* Speed of stator field with respect to stator structure

$$= \frac{120 f_1}{P} = \frac{120 \times 50}{4} = 1500 \text{ r.p.m.}$$

Speed of rotor field with respect to rotor structure $= \frac{120 \cdot f_2}{P} = \frac{120 \times 20}{4} = 600$ r.p.m. In a 3-phase induction motor, rotor speed, $n_r \pm$ speed of rotor field with respect to *(w.r.t.)* rotor = speed of stator field w.r.t. stator, n_s

or $n_r \pm 600 = 1500$ r.p.m.

For positive sign, rotor must be driven in the direction of stator field at a speed,

$$n_r = 1500 - 600 = 900 \text{ r.p.m.}$$

For negative sign, rotor must be driven against the direction of stator field at a speed,

$$n_r = 1500 + 600 = 2100 \text{ r.p.m.}$$

(b) Rotor e.m.f. at any slip *s* is given by

$$E_{2s} = \sqrt{2}\,\pi\,(sf_1)\,N_2\,\phi\,k_{w2}$$

For $n_r = 900$ rpm, slip $s_1 = \frac{1500 - 900}{1500} = 0.4$

∴ $E_{2s}' = \sqrt{2}\,\pi\,(0.4 f_1)\,N_2\,\phi\,k_{w2}$ ...*(i)*

For $n_r = 2100$ rpm, slip $s_2 = \frac{1500 - 2100}{1500} = -0.4.$

Negative slip means motor is working as an induction generator.

∴ $E_{2s}'' = \sqrt{2}\,\pi\,(-0.4 f_1)\,N_2\,\phi\,k_{w2}$ ...*(ii)*

From Eqs. *(i)* and *(ii)*, we get

$$\frac{E_{2s}''}{E_{2s}'} = \frac{\sqrt{2}\pi(-0.4 f_1)N_2\phi k_{w2}}{\sqrt{2}\pi(0.4 f_1)N_2\phi k_{w2}} = -1.$$

(c) For rotor speed $n_r = 900$ r.p.m. clockwise (say), stator field is running at 600 r.p.m. *clockwise with respect to rotor*. Let the phase sequence of the e.m.fs generated at slip rings be *abc*.

For rotor speed n_r = 2100 r.p.m. clockwise, stator field is running at 600 rpm *anticlockwise with respect to rotor*. Therefore, phase sequence of the e.m.fs. generated at slip rings is reversed, *i.e.*, it is now *acb*.

6.5. ROTOR E.M.F., CURRENT AND POWER

At standstill, the relative speed between rotating magnetic field and rotor conductors is synchronous speed n_s ; under this condition let the per phase generated e.m.f. in rotor circuit be E_2. When the rotor speed is, say 0.4 n_s, slip is 0.6 and the relative speed between rotating field and rotor conductors is 0.6 n_s ; under this condition, the per phase generated e.m.f. becomes $0.6\, n_s \times (E_2/n_s) = 0.6\, E_2$. At a rotor speed of 0.8 n_s, slip is 0.2 and the relative speed between rotating field and rotor conductors is 0.2 n_s, therefore, the per phase generated e.m.f. under this condition becomes $0.2\, n_s \times (E_2/n_s) = 0.2\, E_2$. In general, for any value of slip *s*, the per phase generated e.m.f. in rotor conductors is equal to $sE_2 = s\,[\sqrt{2}\,\pi f_1 k_{w2} N_2 \phi] = \sqrt{2}\,\pi\,(sf_1)\,k_{w2} N_2 \phi$.

Now rotor leakage reactance = 2π (Rotor frequency) (Rotor leakage inductance l_2)

$\therefore$ Rotor leakage reactance at standstill $= 2\pi f_1 l_2 = x_2\ \Omega$.

Rotor leakage reactance at any slip $s = 2\pi f_2 l_2 = 2\pi\,(sf_1)\,l_2 = sx_2\ \Omega$.

Rotor leakage reactance at standstill $= \sqrt{r_2^2 + x_2^2}$.

At any slip *s*, rotor leakage impedance $= \sqrt{r_2^2 + (sx_2)^2}$. ...(6.7)

Per phase generated e.m.f. divided by the per phase rotor leakage impedance gives the per phase rotor current.

$\therefore$ Per phase rotor current at standstill $\dfrac{E_2}{\sqrt{r_2^2 + x_2^2}}$.

Per phase rotor current at any slip *s* given by

$$I_2 = \frac{sE_2}{\sqrt{r_2^2 + (sx_2)^2}} = \frac{E_2}{\sqrt{(r_2/s)^2 + x_2^2}} \qquad ...(6.8)$$

The rotor current I_2 lags the rotor voltage E_2 by rotor power factor angle θ_2 given by

$$\theta_2 = \tan^{-1}\frac{sx_2}{r_2}.$$

Eq. (6.8) can be represented by a simple series circuit as shown in Fig. 6.7. This circuit is usually called rotor equivalent circuit of a 3-phase induction motor. It is seen from this circuit that per phase power input to rotor,

$$P_g = E_2 I_2 \cos\theta_2.$$

But,

$$\cos\theta_2 = \frac{\text{Per phase rotor resistance}}{\text{Per phase rotor impedance}} = \frac{r_2/s}{\sqrt{(r_2/s)^2 + (x_2)^2}}$$

$\therefore$

$$P_g = \frac{E_2}{\sqrt{(r_2/s)^2 + (x_2)^2}} \cdot I_2 \frac{r_2}{s} = I_2^2 \frac{r_2}{s} \qquad ...(6.9)$$

An examination of Fig. 6.7 also reveals that per phase power input to rotor is equal to $I_2^2 \dfrac{r_2}{s}$ as the reactance x_2 consumes no power.

P_g is the power transferred from stator to rotor across the air gap. In view of this, P_g is called the *air-gap power*. The expression for P_g may be written as

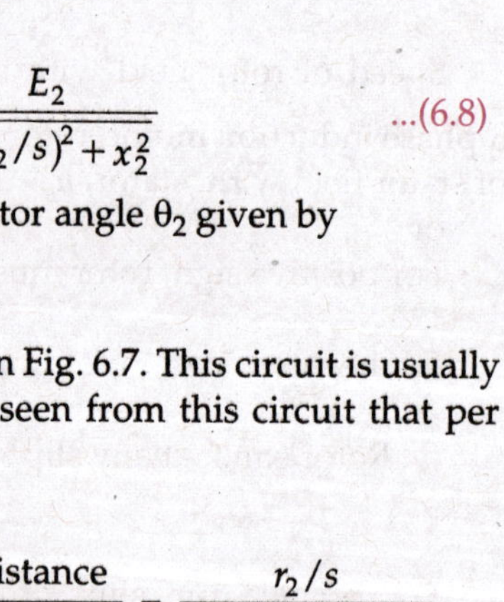

Fig 6.7: Rotor equivalent-circuit of an induction motor.

$$P_g = I_2^2 \frac{r_2}{s} = I_2^2 r_2 + I_2^2 r_2 \left(\frac{1-s}{s}\right) = \text{(Rotor ohmic loss)}$$

$$+ \text{Internal mechanical power developed in rotor } (P_m)$$

$$= sP_g + (1-s) P_g \quad \text{...(6.10 a)}$$

$$\therefore \quad P_m = (1-s) P_g = I_2^2 r_2 \left(\frac{1-s}{s}\right)$$

$$\text{Rotor ohmic loss} = \left(\frac{s}{1-s}\right) P_m = sP_g \quad \text{...(6.10 c)}$$

Eq. (6.9) reveals that rotor ohmic loss = $I_2^2 r_2 = sP_g = s$ (power input to rotor) ...(6.11)

Internal (or gross) torque developed per phase is given by

$$T_e = \frac{\text{Internal mechanical power developed in rotor}}{\text{Rotor speed in mechanical rad. per sec.}}$$

$$\therefore \quad T_e = \frac{P_m}{\omega_r} = \frac{(1-s)P_g}{(1-s)\omega_s} = \frac{P_g}{\omega_s} \quad \text{...(6.12)}$$

Here $\omega_s \,(= 2\pi n_s) = \dfrac{4\pi f_1}{P}$

is the synchronous speed in mechanical radians per second.

Also electromagnetic torque T_e is

$$T_e = \frac{P_g}{\omega_s} = \frac{1}{\omega_s} \cdot \frac{I_2^2 r_2}{s} = \frac{\text{Rotor ohmic loss}}{(\omega_s)\text{ Slip}}$$

$$= \frac{1}{2\pi n_s} I_2^2 \frac{r_2}{s} \quad \text{...(6.13)}$$

The power available at the shaft can be obtained from P_g as follows :

Output or shaft power, $P_{sh} = P_m$ – Mechanical losses (friction, and windage losses)

or $P_{sh} = P_g$ – Rotor ohmic loss – Friction and windage losses

= Net mechanical power output or net power output

Output or shaft torque $$T_{sh} = \frac{P_{sh}}{\text{Rotor speed}} = \frac{P_{sh}}{(1-s)\omega_s} \quad \text{...(6.14)}$$

If stator input is known, then air-gap power P_g is given by

P_g = stator power input – stator I^2R loss – stator core loss.

6.6. LOSSES AND EFFICIENCY

The losses in a 3-phase induction motor are *(i)* fixed losses and *(ii)* variable losses.

Fixed losses : These losses are composed of *(a)* core loss *(b)* bearing friction loss *(c)* brush friction loss in wound-rotor induction motors (WRIMs) only and *(d)* windage loss. These losses are taken to be constant over the normal working range of the induction motor. Friction loss may vary slightly with load and speed. But this loss is also considered constant as the speed varies only by a small amount over the normal working range of the motor.

A 3-phase induction motor under its usual working conditions has very low-frequency currents in the rotor circuit. As a result, rotor core losses, almost proportional to frequency squared, are negligible. The fixed losses or no-load rotational losses (friction, windage and core losses) can be obtained directly by performing no-load test on the induction motor.

∴ Fixed losses = Power input at no load – (stator I^2R loss at no load)

Variable losses : These losses are composed of *(a)* stator ohmic loss *(b)* rotor ohmic loss *(c)* brush contact loss for WRIMs only and *(d)* stray load losses. The stator and rotor ohmic losses can be calculated directly in case A.C. resistances of stator and rotor windings are known. Total ohmic losses can be obtained by performing blocked rotor test on the induction motor. The rotor ohmic loss in a squirrel cage induction motor can only be obtained by subtracting stator ohmic loss from the total ohmic loss measured during the blocked rotor test.

The brush contact loss for WRIM = slip-ring current × 1 volt.

Stray load loss occurs in iron as well as in conductors. Their measurement is very complex. These are usually accounted for by taking efficiency 0.5% less than its calculated value on full load and pro-rata for other loads.

Fig. 6.8 gives the power flow diagram for a 3-phase induction motor. It indicates clearly how power input to stator is distributed in a 3-phase induction motor. Rotor input power, or air-gap power, differs from stator input power by total stator losses. Under normal running conditions, rotor core loss is neglected. The power at the rotor shaft differs from the mechanical power developed by friction and windage losses.

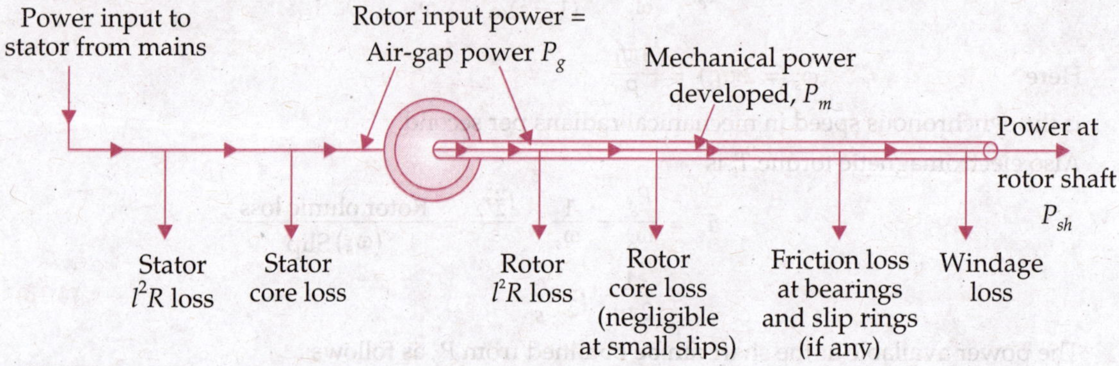

Fig 6.8: Power-flow diagram for a 3-phase induction motor.

The efficiency of a 3-phase induction motor is given by

$$\eta = \frac{P_{sh}}{P_{sh} + P_f + P_{oh}} \times 100$$

where P_{sh} = shaft power

P_f = fixed losses = core loss + friction and windage losses

P_{oh} = stator and rotor ohmic losses + brush contact loss (if any).

Example 6.5. *A 3-phase, 4-pole, 1440 r.p.m., 50 Hz induction motor has star-connected rotor winding, having a resistance of 0.2 Ω per phase and a standstill leakage reactance of 1 Ω per phase. When the stator is energised at rated voltage and frequency, the rotor induced e.m.f. at standstill is 120 V per phase.*

(a) Calculate the rotor current, rotor power factor and torque both at starting and at full load and compare these results.

(b) If an external resistance of 1 Ω per phase is inserted in rotor circuit, calculate rotor current, rotor power factor and torque at the time of starting.

Solution. Here $r_2 = 0.2\ \Omega,\ x_2 = 1\ \Omega,\ p = 4,\ f_1 = 50$ Hz.

∴ Synchronous speed $= \frac{120 \times 50}{4} = 1500$ r.p.m.

Rotor current at starting, $I_{2 \cdot st} = \frac{E_2}{\sqrt{r_2^2 + x_2^2}} = \frac{120}{\sqrt{(0.2)^2 + (1)^2}} = \frac{120}{1.0198} = 117.67$ A

Rotor power factor at starting $= \dfrac{r_2}{\sqrt{r_2^2 + x_2^2}} = \dfrac{0.2}{\sqrt{(0.2)^2 + (1)^2}} = 0.196$ lag

Synchronous speed in radians per second,

$$\omega_s = \frac{2\pi N_s}{60} = \frac{2\pi(1500)}{60} = 50\,\pi \text{ rad/sec.}$$

From Eq. (6.13),

Starting torque, $T_{e\cdot st} = \dfrac{3}{\omega_s}(I_{2\cdot st})^2 \dfrac{r_2}{1} = \dfrac{3}{50\pi}(117.67)^2(0.2) = 52.9$ Nm.

Nameplate speed of 1440 r.p.m. is the full-load (or rated) speed of the motor.

Full load slip, $s = \dfrac{1500 - 1440}{1500} = 0.04.$

Rotor current at full load, $I_{2\cdot fl} = \dfrac{sE_2}{\sqrt{r_2^2 + (sx_2)^2}} = \dfrac{(0.04)(120)}{\sqrt{(0.2)^2 + (0.04 \times 1)^2}}$

$$= \frac{4.8}{0.204} = 23.53 \text{ A.}$$

Rotor power factor at full load, $= \dfrac{r_2}{\sqrt{r_2^2 + (sx_2)^2}} = \dfrac{0.2}{0.204} = 0.98$ lag

Full-load torque, $T_{e\cdot fl} = \dfrac{1}{\omega_s} 3\,(I_{2\cdot fl})^2 \dfrac{r_2}{s} = \dfrac{1}{50\pi} \cdot 3(23.53)^2 \dfrac{0.2}{0.04} = 52.87$ Nm.

Ratio of starting to full-load current $= \dfrac{117.67}{23.53} \cong 5.00.$

Ratio of starting to full-load torque $= \dfrac{52.90}{52.87} \cong 1.00.$

(b) When external resistance is inserted in the rotor circuit, the total rotor circuit resistance becomes $0.2 + 1 = 1.2\ \Omega$ per phase.

$$\therefore \quad I_{2\cdot st} = \frac{120}{\sqrt{(1.2)^2 + (1)^2}} = \frac{120}{1.562} = 76.82 \text{ A}$$

Rotor p.f. at starting $= \dfrac{1.2}{\sqrt{(1.2)^2 + (1)^2}} = \dfrac{1.2}{1.562} = 0.768$ lag

$$\therefore \quad T_{e\cdot st} = \frac{1}{50\pi} 3\,(76.82)^2 \frac{1.2}{1} = 135.25 \text{ Nm.}$$

This example demonstrates that with the insertion of external resistance in rotor circuit, $I_{2\cdot st}$ has decreased, $T_{e\cdot st}$ has increased and rotor power factor at starting has improved. These are the main advantages of wound-rotor induction motor over squirrel-cage induction motor.

Example 6.6. *A 3-phase, 6-pole, 50 Hz induction motor has a full-load speed of 960 r.p.m. with its slip rings short-circuited. The motor drives a constant-torque load.*

If the rotor speed is reduced to (a) 800 r.p.m. and (b) 400 r.p.m. by inserting external resistance in the rotor circuit, compare the rotor ohmic losses at these two reduced speeds with that at full load.

Solution. Constant torque load requires constant electromagnetic torque T_e. Eq. (6.12) shows that for constant torque T_e, air-gap power P_g remains constant because synchronous speed (dependent on poles and frequency) is constant. Eq. (6.11) shows that for constant P_g, rotor ohmic losses are proportional to slip, *i.e.*,

Rotor ohmic loss $\propto$ slip.

$$\text{Now slip at full load} = \frac{1000-960}{1000} = 0.04$$

$$\text{Slip at 800 r.p.m.} = \frac{1000-800}{1000} = 0.20$$

$$\text{Slip at 400 r.p.m.} = \frac{1000-400}{1000} = 0.60$$

$$\therefore \quad \frac{I_2^2 r_2 \text{at 800 r.p.m.}}{I_2^2 r_2 \text{at full load}} = \frac{\text{Slip at 800 r.p.m}}{\text{Full-load slip}} = \frac{0.2}{0.04} = 5.$$

$$\frac{\text{Rotor ohmic loss at 400 r.p.m.}}{\text{Rotor ohmic loss at full load}} = \frac{0.6}{0.04} = 15.$$

Example 6.7. *A 10 kW, 400 V, 3-phase, 4-pole, 50 Hz delta connected induction motor is running at no load with a line current of 8 A and an input power of 660 watts. At full load, the line current is 18 A and the input power is 11.20 kW. Stator effective resistance per phase is 1.2 Ω and friction, windage loss is 420 watts. For negligible rotor ohmic losses at no load, calculate,*

(a) stator core loss ; (b) total rotor losses at full load ; (c) total rotor ohmic losses at full load ;

(d) full load speed ; (e) internal torque, shaft torque and motor efficiency.

Solution. *(a)* At no load, total power input is equal to the sum of stator core loss, friction and windage loss, stator no-load I^2R loss and negligible rotor core loss.

$$\therefore \quad \text{Stator core loss} = \text{Power input at no-load} - \text{Friction and windage loss} - \text{Stator } I^2R \text{ loss at no load}$$

$$= 660 - 420 - 3\left(\frac{8}{\sqrt{3}}\right)^2 (1.2) = 163.2 \text{ W}.$$

(b) Air-gap power at full load, P_g = Stator input at full load – Stator core loss – Stator full load ohmic loss

$$= 11200 - 163.2 - 3\left(\frac{18}{\sqrt{3}}\right)^2 (1.2) = 10{,}648 \text{ watts}.$$

$$\therefore \quad \text{Total rotor loss} = \text{Rotor input power, } P_g - \text{Shaft power}$$

$$= 10{,}648 - 10{,}000 = 648 \text{ watts}.$$

(c) Total rotor loss consists of rotor ohmic loss and friction, windage loss.

$$\therefore \quad \text{Rotor ohmic loss} = 3I_2^2 r_2 = 648 - 420 = 228 \text{ watts}.$$

(d) Now, $3I_2^2 \dfrac{r_2}{s} = P_g$ or $3(I_2^2 r_2) = sP_g$ or $(228) = s_{fl} P_g = s_{fl} (10{,}648)$

∴ Full-load slip, $s_{fl} = \dfrac{228}{10{,}648} = 0.0212$

Full-load speed of rotor, $N_r = N_s (1 - s) = 1500 (1 - 0.0212) = 1468.2$ r.p.m.

(e) Internal torque, $T_e = \dfrac{P_g}{\omega_s} = \dfrac{10648}{50\pi} = 67.79$ Nm.

Shaft torque, $T_{sh} = \dfrac{P_{sh}}{\omega_s(1-s)} = \dfrac{10{,}000}{50\pi(1-0.0212)} = 65.04$ Nm.

$$\text{Efficiency} = \frac{P_{sh}}{\text{Power input}} = \frac{10{,}000}{11{,}200} = 0.892 \text{ or } 89.2\%$$

Example 6.8. *An induction motor has an efficiency of 0.9 when the shaft load is 45 kW. At this load, stator ohmic loss and rotor ohmic loss each is equal to the iron loss. The mechanical loss is one-third of the no-load losses. Neglect ohmic losses at no-load. Calculate the slip.*

Solution. Total losses for an output of 45 kW are

$$= \left(\frac{1}{0.9} - 1\right) \times 45000 = 5000 \text{ W}$$

Total losses= stator I^2R loss + stator core loss + rotor I^2R loss + mechanical loss ...*(i)*

At no load, the losses include mechanical (friction and windage) loss, stator core loss and a small amount of I^2R loss in stator and rotor. As I^2R losses are neglected at no load, we have,

$$\text{no-load losses} = \text{stator core loss + mechanical loss} \quad ...(ii)$$

It is given that mechanical loss is one-third of no load loss or on-load loss is 3 times the mechanical loss. Therefore, from *(ii)*, we have,

$$3 \text{ (mechanical loss)} = \text{stator core or iron loss + mechanical loss}$$

or
$$\text{mechanical loss} = \frac{1}{2} \text{ (stator core or iron loss)}$$

Let stator I^2R loss (= rotor I^2R loss = stator core or iron loss) be A. Then, from *(i)*,

$$\text{Total losses} = A + A + A + \frac{A}{2} \text{ or } 5000 = \frac{7A}{2}$$

$\therefore$
$$\text{Rotor ohmic loss} = A = 1428.57 \text{ W}$$

Air-gap power,
$$P_g = 45000 + 1428.57 + \frac{1428.57}{2} = 47142.86 \text{ W}$$

$\therefore$
$$\text{Slip} = \frac{\text{Rotor } I^2R \text{ loss}}{P_g} = \frac{1428.57}{47142.86} = 0.0303.$$

6.7. INDUCTION MOTOR PHASOR DIAGRAM

When 3-phase supply is given to stator winding of a 3-phase induction motor, a rotating magnetic flux ϕ is produced. Fig. 6.9 shows per-phase applied voltage V_1 and the mutual flux ϕ. Rotating flux ϕ generates emfs E_1 and E_2 in stator and rotor windings respectively. Per-phase emfs E_1 and E_2 lag flux ϕ by 90° as shown.

Emf E_2 sets up rotor current I_2 lagging E_2 by rotor power-factor angle $\theta_2 = \tan^{-1}\frac{sx_2}{r_2}$. Rotor current I_2 produces rotor mmf $F_2 = I_2N_2'$. The rotor mmf reacts on stator and calls for a compensating load component of stator current I_2' such that load component of stator mmf F_1' = rotor mmf F_2.

or
$$I_2'N_1' = I_2N_2'$$

or
$$I_2' = I_2\frac{N_2'}{N_1'} = I_2\frac{N_2.k_{w2}}{N_1.k_{w1}} \quad ...(6.15a)$$

Here N_1' and N_2' are per-phase effective number of stator and rotor turns respectively. In Fig. 6.9, load component of stator mmf $F_1' = I_2'N_1'$ is shown opposing rotor mmf $F_2 = I_2N_2'$. Mutual flux ϕ is produced by the magnetizing current I_m (neglecting hysteresis loss) taken from the supply. Note that ϕ is in phase with I_m under

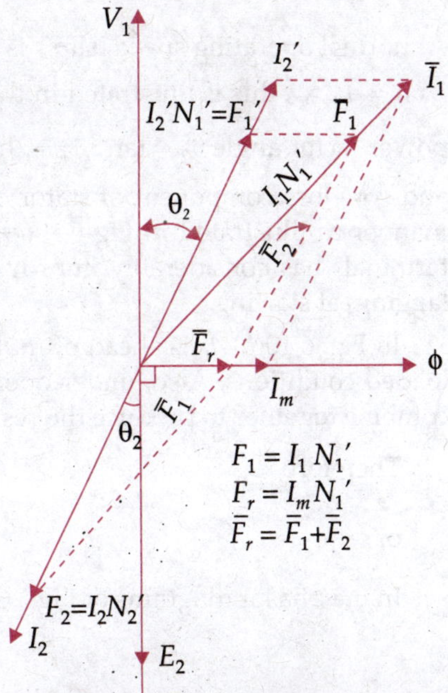

Fig 6.9: Pertaining to induction motor phasor diagram.

the assumption of no hysteresis loss. Magnetizing current I_m produces the resultant air-gap mmf $F_r = I_m N_1'$ and this further produces resultant air-gap flux ϕ.

Resultant mutual flux ϕ is produced by the combined effect of stator mmf $F_1 = I_1 N_1'$ and rotor mmf $F_2 = I_2 N_2'$.

Therefore, resultant air-gap mmf $\overline{F}_r = \overline{F}_1 + \overline{F}_2$ is sufficient to maintain mutual flux ϕ.

Therefore,
$$\overline{I}_m N_1' = \overline{I}_1 N_1' + \overline{I}_2 N_2'$$

$$\text{or } I_m = \overline{I}_1 + \frac{N_2'}{N_1'} \cdot \overline{I}_2 \quad \text{...(6.15}b\text{)}$$

6.7.1. Phasor Diagram At Standstill

Complete induction motor phasor diagram at standstill is drawn in Fig 6.10(*a*), where mmfs are not shown for the sake of clarity. The resultant air-gap flux is drawn horizontal. As before, emfs E_1, E_2 lag ϕ by 90°. At standstill, $E_2 = I_2 (r_2 + jx_2)$ is shown in Fig. 6.10(*a*). Rotor current I_2 lags E_2 by rotor power-factor angle $\theta_2 = \tan^{-1} \frac{x_2}{r_2}$. At standstill, friction and windage loss is zero. Therefore, core loss component of stator no-load current I_0, *i.e.*, I_c is in phase with $\overline{V}_1'$ or $-E_1$. The stator no-load current $\overline{I}_0 = \overline{I}_m + \overline{I}_c$, stator load current is $\overline{I}_1 = \overline{I}_2' + \overline{I}_0$. Current I_2' balances rotor current I_2 so that $\overline{I}_2' N_1' = I_2 . N_2'$. The stator applied voltage V_1 must balance the stator counter emf V_1' $(= -E_1)$ plus stator leakage impedance drop $\overline{I}_1 (r_1 + jx_1)$ as shown in Fig. 6.10(*a*), *i.e.* $\overline{V}_1 = \overline{V}_1' + \overline{I}_a (r_1 + jx_1)$. The power factor angle (between V_1 and I_1) at the stator terminals is very high, *i.e.*, stator power factor, at the time of starting, is very poor in a 3-phase induction motor.

6.7.2. Phasor Diagram at Normal Speed

At normal operating speed, slip s is small. The rotor voltage equation now becomes $s\overline{E}_2 = \overline{I}_2 (r_2 + jsx_2) = \overline{I}_2 \overline{z}_2$, this is illustrated in the phasor diagram of Fig. 6.10(*b*). Current I_2 lags $s\overline{E}_2$ by rotor power-factor angle $\theta_2 = \tan^{-1} \frac{sx_2}{r_2}$. In this figure, $\overline{I}_0 = \overline{I}_m + \overline{I}_{fc}$, where I_{fc} is the friction, windage and core-loss component of stator current. The rest of the phasor diagram is drawn is the same manner as illustrated in Fig 6.10(*a*). Fig. 6.10(*b*) reveals that full-load power factor at the stator terminals has considerably improved (0.8 to 0.9 lagging) from its poor power factor (0.1 to 0.3 lagging) at starting.

In Fig. 6.10(*b*), I_0 is ahead of mutual flux ϕ because of friction, windage and core losses under loaded conditions. Also, under operating conditions, the stator mmf $I_1 N_1'$ and rotor mmf $I_2 N_2'$ combine together to produce the resultant mmf $I_0 N_1'$.

Therefore,
$$\overline{I}_0 N_1' = \overline{I}_1 N_1' + \overline{I}_2 N_2'$$

or
$$\overline{I}_0 = \overline{I}_1 + \frac{N_2'}{N_1'} \cdot \overline{I}_2 \quad \text{...(6.15}c\text{)}$$

In the phasor diagrams of Figs. 6.9 and 6.10, all quantities have per phase values.

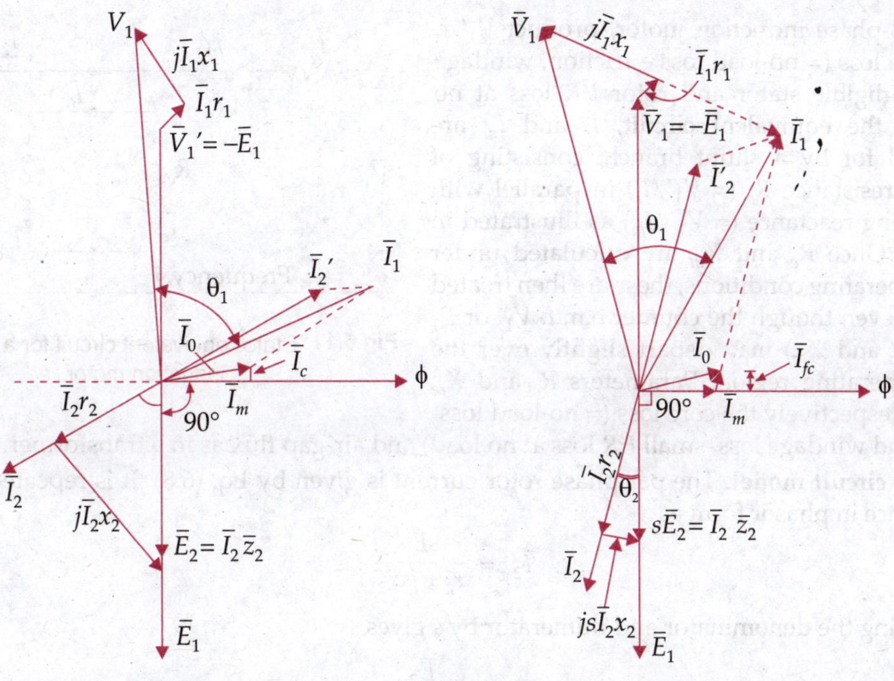

(a) (b)

Fig 6.10: Induction motor phasor diagram at *(a)* standtill and *(b)* at a full-load slip *s*.

6.8. EQUIVALENT CIRCUIT

An induction motor has been shown equivalent to a transformer, naturally induction motor equivalent circuit should be similar to the transformer equivalent circuit. The only difference is on account of the fact that the secondary winding (*i.e.* rotor winding) of an induction motor rotates and, therefore, involves the development of mechanical power. The derivation of induction motor equivalent circuit proceeds in the same manner as in the case of a transformer. All the equivalent circuit parameters have per phase values.

We shall develop here first the circuit model for stator and then for the rotor. These two circuit models are then combined to obtain the equivalent circuit of a 3-phase induction motor.

Stator-circuit model. When a voltage V_1 is applied to the stator terminals of a 3-phase induction motor, a rotating air-gap flux ϕ is established. This flux ϕ generates counter e.m.fs in all the 3-phases of stator (or the primary) winding. The stator terminal voltage V_1 has to overcome counter e.m.f. $\overline{V}'_1 (= -\overline{E}_1)$ and the stator leakage impedance drop $\overline{I}_1 \ (r_1 + jx_1)$. Therefore, just like a transformer, the stator or primary voltage is given by,

$$\overline{V}_1 = \overline{V}_1' + \overline{I}_1 \ (r_1 + jx_1) \qquad ...(6.16)$$

As in the case of a transformer, the stator current I_1 consists of two components. One component I_2' is the load component and counteracts the rotor m.m.f. $I_2 \ N_2'$ completely, see Eq. (6.15*a*). The other component is the exciting or no-load current I_0, whose function is to create the resultant air-gap flux ϕ and to provide the core loss. As in a transformer, the exciting or no-load current I_0 can be resolved into two components, core-loss component I_c in phase with V_1' and a magnetizing component I_m lagging V_1' by 90°. No-load current I_0 in a 3-phase induction motor, as shown in Fig. 6.10, has to create resultant air-gap flux ϕ and to supply the no load losses (= stator core loss + friction, windage loss + small stator and rotor I^2R loss), whereas function of I_0 in a transformer is to create ϕ and to provide only the core loss.

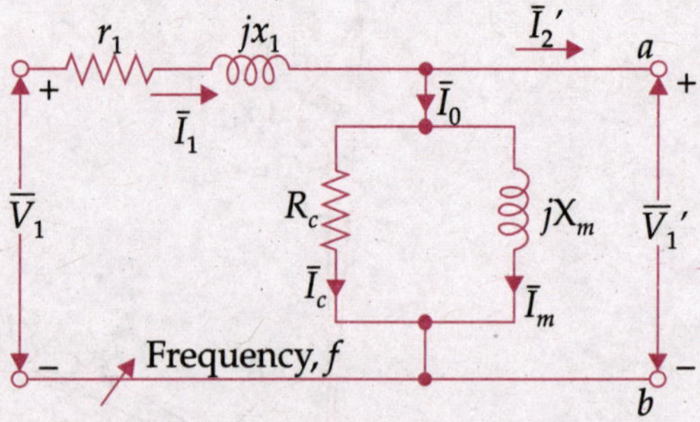

Fig 6.11: Stator equivalent circuit for a polyphase induction motor.

In a 3-phase induction motor, product $V_1' I_c$ gives core loss (= no-load loss – friction, windage loss – negligible stator and rotor I^2R loss at no load). In the equivalent circuit, I_c and I_m are accounted for by a shunt branch, consisting of core-loss resistance R_c (= V_1'/I_c) in parallel with magnetizing reactance (= V_1'/I_m) as illustrated in Fig. 6.11. Once R_c and X_m are calculated under normal operating conditions, these are then treated constant, even though the counter e.m.f. V_1' or E_1 (across R_c and X_m) may depart slightly over the normal operating region. Parameters R_c and X_m simulate respectively the core loss (= no-load loss-friction and windage loss–small I^2R loss at no load) and air-gap flux as in a transformer.

Rotor circuit model. The per phase rotor current is given by Eq. (6.8). It is repeated here for convenience in phasor form as

$$\bar{I}_2 = \frac{s\bar{E}_2}{r_2 + jsx_2} \quad \text{...(6.17)}$$

Dividing the denominator and numerator by *s* gives

$$\bar{I}_2 = \frac{\bar{E}_2}{\frac{r_2}{s} + jx_2} \quad \text{...(6.18)}$$

Note that the magnitude and phase of I_2 obtained from the Eqs. (6.17) and (6.18) are the same. There is, however, a significant difference between these two equations. In Eq. (6.17), slip-frequency generated e.m.f. sE_2, when divided by $r_2 + jsx_2$ gives slip-frequency current, but in Eq. (6.18) line-frequency e.m.f. E_2 when divided by $r_2/s + jx_2$ gives line-frequency current. Equivalent circuits of Fig. 6.12 *(a)* and *(b)* are obtained from Eqs. (6.17) and (6.18) respectively.

In Fig. 6.12 *(a)*, the rotor circuit consists of *(i)* a constant resistance r_2 *(ii)* a variable leakage reactance sx_2 *(iii)* slip frequency emf sE_2 and *(iv)* rotor current I_2 at slip frequency sf_1. This interpretation is in line with the actual physical facts existing in the rotor circuit of a 3-phase induction motor.

In Fig. 6.12 *(b)*, the rotor circuit consists of *(i)* a constant leakage reactance x_2 *(ii)* a variable resistance r_2/s *(iii)* line-frequency emf E_2 and *(iv)* rotor current I_2 at line frequency. This interpretation is useful in drawing the complete equivalent circuit of a 3-phase induction motor which is used for further analysis of an induction motor under different operating conditions.

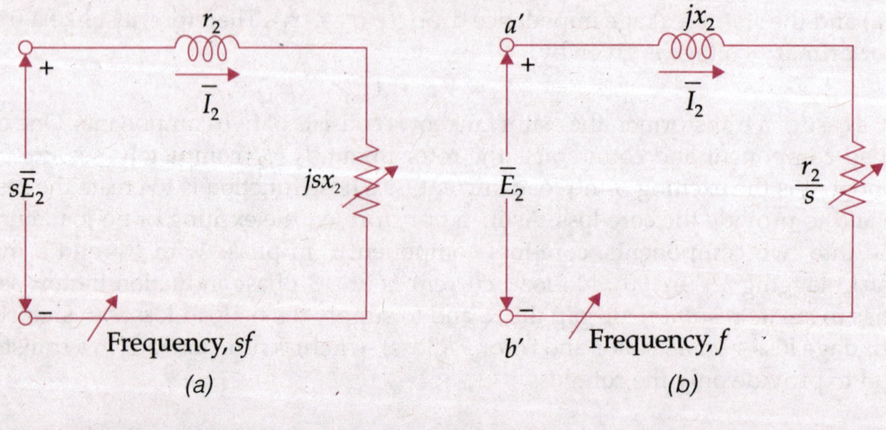

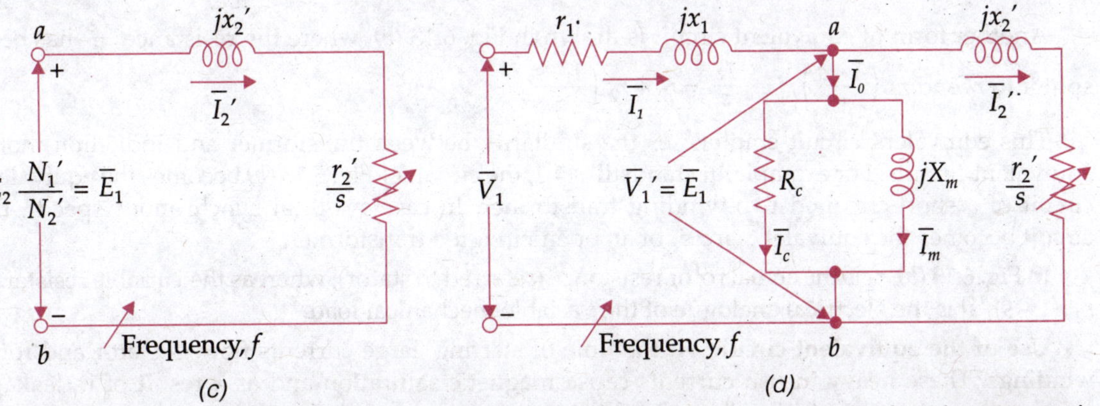

Fig 6.12: *(a)* Actual rotor circuit *(b)* equivalent rotor circuit *(c)* equivalent rotor circuit referred to stator and *(d)* exact induction motor equivalent circuit.

Complete equivalent circuit. The line-frequency e.m.f. E_2 applied to the rotor circuit of Fig. 6.12*(b)*, differs from the magnitude of E_1 or V_1' by the turns ratio, as in a transformer. Therefore, rotor voltage E_2 must be referred to stator or primary. Thus,

$$\text{Rotor voltage when referred to stator} = \frac{E_2}{N_2'} \cdot N_1' = E_1.$$

Similarly, rotor leakage impedance and rotor current I_2 when referred to stator are

$$= \left(\frac{r_2}{s} + jx_2\right)\left(\frac{N_1'}{N_2'}\right) = \frac{r_2'}{s} + jx_2'$$

and $$I_2\left(\frac{N_2'}{N_1'}\right) = I_2' \text{ as in Eq. (6.15}a\text{).}$$

The voltage appearing across terminals *ab* of Fig. 6.12 *(c)* is of the line frequency and has the same magnitude as at the terminals *ab* of Fig. 6.11. These terminals can, therefore, be connected together to give the complete equivalent circuit of an induction motor as shown in Fig. 6.12 *(d)*. Note that in this figure, rotor quantities referred to stator have been primed. A more general equivalent circuit of induction motor has been redrawn in Fig. 6.12 *(a)* where, for simplicity,

(i) prime notation used for referred quantities have been dropped and

(ii) the complex notation (bar over *I*, j with reactance etc.) has been given up.

But one must keep in mind that in Fig. 6.13 *(a)*, all the rotor quantities have been referred to stator side. Note that all the quantities in Fig. 6.13 *(a)* are at stator frequency.

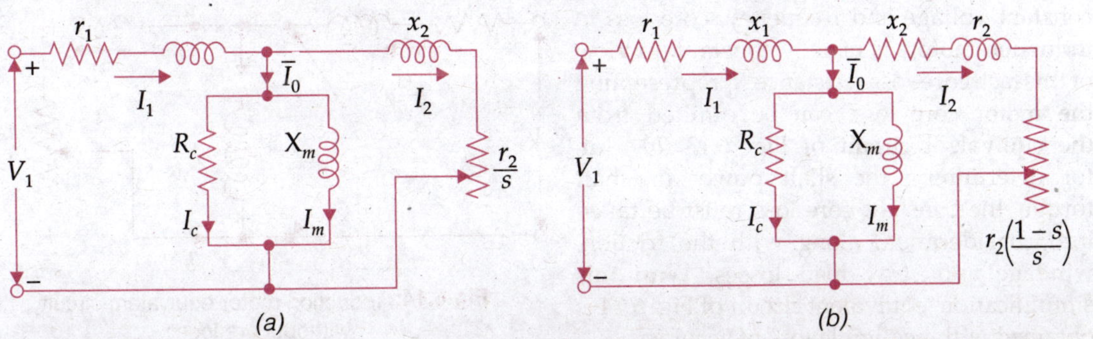

Fig 6.13: *(a)* Equivalent circuit for a polyphase induction motor *(b)* modified form of induction motor equivalent circuit.

Another form of equivalent circuit is drawn in Fig. 6.13 *(b)*, where the resistance $\frac{r_2}{s}$ has been split into r_2 and $r_2\left(\frac{1-s}{s}\right)$, *i.e.*, $\frac{r_2}{s} = r_2 + r_2\left(\frac{1-s}{s}\right)$

This equivalent circuit emphasises the similarity between transformer and induction motor equivalent circuits. For example, at standstill $s = 1$, the circuit of Fig. 6.13 *(b)* becomes the equivalent circuit of a short-circuited two-winding transformer. In case $s = 0$ (at synchronous speed), the circuit becomes the equivalent circuit of an open-circuited transformer.

In Fig. 6.13 *(b)*, r_2 is the actual rotor resistance (referred to stator), whereas the variable resistance $r_2\,[(1-s)/s]$ is the electrical analogue of the variable mechanical load.

Use of the equivalent circuit. At the time of starting, large currents flow in stator and rotor windings. These heavy inrush currents cause magnetic saturation and as a result of it, leakage reactances are less than their values at full-load operating conditions. The rotor frequency varies from line frequency at the time of starting to a low value of slip frequency at full-load speed. Therefore, the distribution of current in the rotor conductors is different at high and low rotor frequencies, consequently the rotor resistance varies significantly over this speed range. In view of this, the equivalent circuit parameters should be determined at those values of rotor frequency and current, at which the performance calculations are to be carried out by using the equivalent circuit.

Note that R_c in the induction motor equivalent circuit does not represent the no-load loss, it represents only the core loss of the induction motor.

6.9. ANALYSIS OF THE EQUIVALENT CIRCUIT

All the important performance characteristics of an induction motor can be determined from its equivalent circuit. Expressions for the air-gap power P_g, internal mechanical power P_m developed in rotor have already been obtained in Art. 6.5.

The use of the exact equivalent circuit of Fig. 6.13 *(b)* is quite laborious. Some simplifications can, however, be made in this equivalent circuit. In transformers, an analysis of the equivalent circuit is carried out either by neglecting the shunt branch consisting of R_c and X_m in parallel, or by moving the shunt branch across the primary terminals. This simplification is however not permissible in case of induction motor equivalent circuits. This is due to the fact that the exciting current in transformers varies from 2 to 6% of full-load current and per unit primary leakage reactances are small ; but in case of induction motors, the exciting current varies from 30 to 50 per cent of full-load current and per unit stator leakage reactances are comparatively higher. On account of this, large errors are introduced in the determination of power and torque, in case the shunt branch is neglected, or connected across the stator terminals in a 3-phase induction motor.

Under normal operating conditions of constant voltage and frequency, core loss in induction motors is usually constant. In view of this fact, core-loss resistance R_c representing the motor core loss, can be omitted from the equivalent circuit of Fig. 6.13 *(b)*. But, for determining the shaft power or shaft torque, the constant core loss must be taken into consideration, along with the friction, windage and stray load losses. With this simplification, equivalent circuit of Fig. 6.14 is obtained with negligible loss of accuracy.

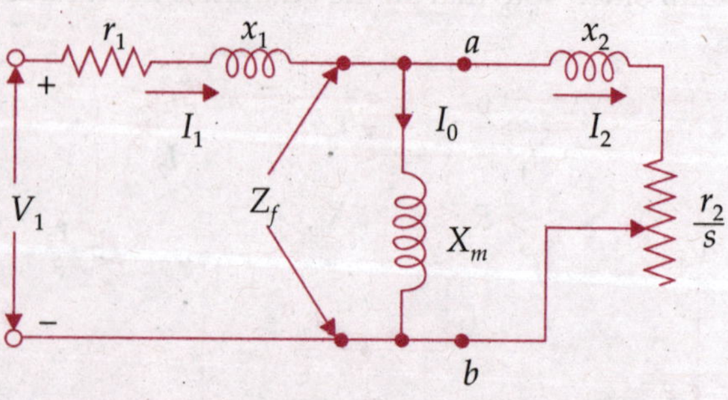

Fig 6.14: Induction motor equivalent circuit without core loss.

The equivalent circuit of Fig. 6.13 *(b)* is redrawn in Fig. 6.15 where the various losses in a 3-phase induction motor are indicated. The shaft power is equal to mechanical power developed in $[r_2 (1 - s)/s]$ minus the mechanical loss (friction and windage losses). In Fig. 6.14, R_c is ignored, but loss represented by R_c, *i.e.*, core loss, must be accounted for along with friction and windage losses while utilizing this equivalent circuit for computation of machine performance.

Note that all the quantities used in the equivalent circuit are per phase quantities.

Steady-state performance parameters of the induction motor, such as current, speed, torque, losses etc. can be computed from the equivalent circuit of Fig. 6.14. In this figure, Z_f is the per-phase impedance offered to the stator by the rotating air-gap field. Note that Z_f includes the reflected effect of rotor leakage impedance $r_2/s + jx_2$ and the magnetizing reactance X_m. From Fig. 6.14,

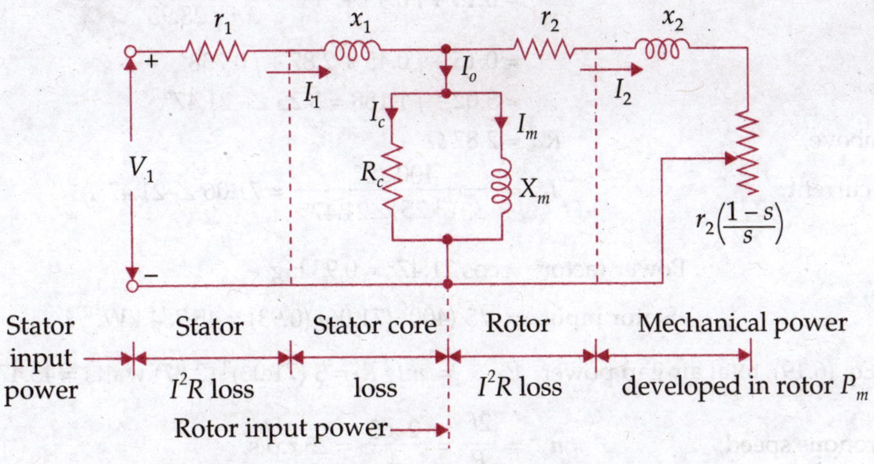

Fig 6.15: Power distribution in a 3-phase induction motor.

$$Z_f = R_f + jX_f = \frac{\left(\frac{r_2}{s} + jx_2\right)(jX_m)}{\frac{r_2}{s} + j(x_2 + X_m)}$$

Impedance Z_1 as seen by the stator applied voltage V_1 is $Z_1 = r_1 + jx_1 + Z_f$

$\therefore$ Stator current, $I_1 = V_1/Z_1$

The total power lost in the parallel combination of $r_2/s + jx_2$ and jX_m is $I_2^2 r_2/s$. Since $Z_f = R_f + jX_f$, the power lost in Z_f is $I_1^2 R_f$ and it must be equal to $I_2^2 r_2/s$

$\therefore$ Per-phase air-gap power, $\quad P_g = I_2^2 \frac{r_2}{s} = I_1^2 R_f$ ...(6.19)

Once air-gap power is known, shaft output, torque, efficiency etc. can be determined by referring to Art. 6.6.

Example 6.9. *A 3-phase, star-connected, 400 volts, 50 Hz, 4-pole induction motor has the following per phase constants in ohms referred to stator:*

$r_1 = 0.15$, $x_1 = 0.45$, $r_2 = 0.12$,

$x_2 = 0.45$, $X_m = 28.5$

Mechanical losses (friction and windage losses) = 400 watts.

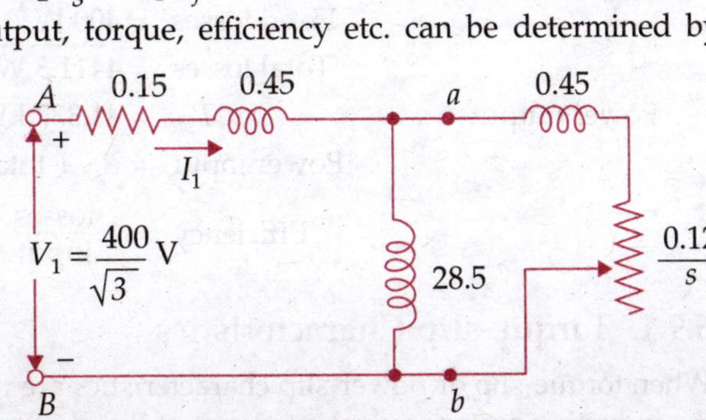

Fig 6.16: Induction motor equivalent circuit, Example 6.9.

Compute the stator current, rotor speed, output torque and efficiency when the motor is operated at rated voltage and frequency at a slip of 4 percent.

Solution. From the equivalent circuit of the induction motor as shown in Fig. 6.16, the impedance offered to the voltage source is

$$\overline{Z}_{AB} = r_1 + jx_1 + \frac{\left(\frac{r_2}{s} + jx_2\right)(jX_m)}{\frac{r_2}{s} + j(x_2 + X_m)} = r_1 + jx_1 + R_f + jX_f$$

$$= 0.15 + j\,0.45 + \frac{\left(\frac{0.12}{0.04} + j\,0.45\right)(j\,28.5)}{3 + j\,28.95}$$

$$= 0.15 + j\,0.45 + 2.87 + j\,0.738$$

$$= 3.02 + j\,1.188 = 3.25\,\angle{-21.47°}.$$

From above, $R_f = 2.87\ \Omega$

Stator current, $I_1 = \dfrac{400\angle 0°}{\sqrt{3}(3.25)\angle 21.47°} = 71.06\ \angle{-21.47°}\text{A}.$

Power factor $= \cos 21.47° = 0.93$ lag

Stator input $= \sqrt{3}\,(400)\,(71.06)\,(0.93) = 45.784$ kW.

From Eq. (6.19), total air-gap power, $P_g = mI_1^2 R_f = 3\,(71.06)^2\,(2.87)$ watts $= 43.476$ kW.

Synchronous speed, $n_s = \dfrac{2f}{P} = \dfrac{2 \times 5}{4} = 25$ r.p.s.

∴ Rotor speed, $n_r = (1 - s)\, n_s = 0.96 \times 25 = 24$ r.p.s., or 1440 r.p.m.

$\omega_s = 2\pi\,(25) = 50\,\pi$ rad/sec

Mechanical power developed, $P_m = (1 - s)\, P_g = (0.96)\,(43.476) = 41.737$ kW

∴ Power output, $P_{sh} = P_m -$ mechanical losses $= 41.737 - 0.40 = 41.337$ kW

$$\text{Output torque} = \frac{P_{sh}}{\omega_r} = \frac{41337}{(1-s)\omega_s} = \frac{41337}{0.96 \times 50\pi} = 274.12\ \text{Nm.}$$

The various losses in the induction motor are as under :

Stator ohmic losses $= 3\, I_1^2 r_1 = 3\,(71.06)^2\,(0.15) = 2272.3$ W

Rotor ohmic loss $= sP_g = (0.04)\,(43476) = 1739$ W

Fixed losses $= 400$ W

Total losses $= 4411.3$ W

Power output $P_{sh} = 41.337$ kW

∴ Power input $= P_{sh} +$ total losses $= 41.337 + 4.411 = 45.748$ kW

∴ Efficiency $= 1 \dfrac{\text{losses}}{\text{input}} = 1 \dfrac{4.411}{45.748} = 0.9036$ or 90.36%.

6.9.1. Torque-slip Characteristics

When torque-slip or power-slip characteristics are required, application of Thevenin's theorem to the induction motor equivalent circuit of Fig. 6.14 reduces the computation labour considerably.

For applying Thevenin's theorem to Fig. 6.14, consider two points a, b as shown. From these two points view towards the voltage source V_1. As per Thevenin's theorem, the circuit consisting of r_1, x_1, X_m and source voltage V_1 can be replaced by an equivalent voltage source V_e and an equivalent impedance $\overline{Z}_e = R_e + jX_e$, as shown in Fig. 6.17, where

$$\overline{V}_e = \frac{V_1(jX_m)}{r_1 + j(x_1 + X_m)} \quad \text{...(6.20)}$$

and

$$\overline{Z}_e = \frac{(r_1 + jx_1)(jX_m)}{r_1 + j(x_1 + X_m)} \quad \text{...(6.21)}$$

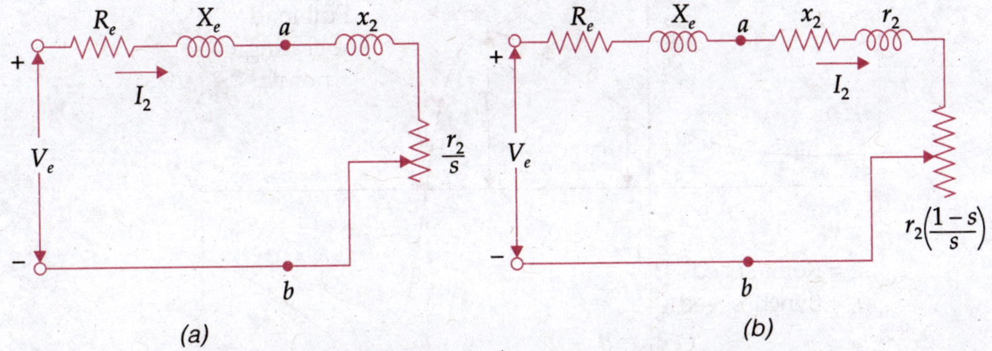

Fig 6.17: Thevenins's equivalent circuits of an induction motor.

Here $\overline{V}_e$ is the voltage appearing across terminals a, b with the rotor circuit disconnected from these two points. Equivalent stator impedance $\overline{Z}_e$ is the impedance viewed from terminals a, b towards the voltage source and with the source voltage short circuited.

For most induction motors, $(x_1 + X_m)$ is much greater than r_1. In view of this, r_1 can be neglected in the denominator of both the Eqs. (6.20) and (6.21), without causing any noticeable error.

Thus,

$$V_e = \frac{V_1 X_m}{x_1 + X_m} = \frac{V_1 X_m}{X_1} \quad \text{...(6.22)}$$

and

$$\overline{Z}_e = R_e + jX_e = \frac{r_1 X_m}{x_1 + X_m} + \frac{jx_1 X_m}{x_1 + X_m}$$

$$= \frac{r_1 X_m}{X_1} + j\frac{x_1 X_m}{X_1} \quad \text{...(6.23)}$$

Here $X_1 = x_1 + X_m$, is the stator self-reactance per phase.

From the equivalent circuit of Fig. 6.17 *(a)*, rotor current is given by

$$\overline{I}_2 = \frac{\overline{V}_e}{\left(R_e + \frac{r_2}{s}\right) + j(x_2 + X_e)} \quad \text{...(6.24 a)}$$

and from Eq. (6.13), the total torque is

$$T_e = \frac{m}{\omega_s} \cdot \frac{V_e^2}{\left(R_e + \frac{r_2}{s}\right)^2 + (x_2 + X_e)^2} \cdot \frac{r_2}{s} \text{ Nm} \quad \text{...(6.24 b)}$$

Hence m is the number of stator phases.

For convenience, Eq. (6.24 *b*) is re-written as,

$$T_e = \frac{K_t}{\left(R_e + \frac{r_2}{s}\right)^2 + X^2} \cdot \frac{r_2}{s} \text{ Nm} \quad \text{...(6.25)}$$

where $$K_t = \frac{mV_e^2}{\omega_s} = \frac{mV_e^2}{2\pi n_s} \text{ and } X = x_2 + X_e.$$

The variation of torque with slip, or speed, of an induction motor can be plotted from Eq. (6.24) for different values of slip s and with the motor connected to constant-frequency voltage source. A general shape of the torque-speed or torque-slip curve is shown in Fig. 6.18. Depending upon the value of slip an induction motor can have the following operating regions or modes :

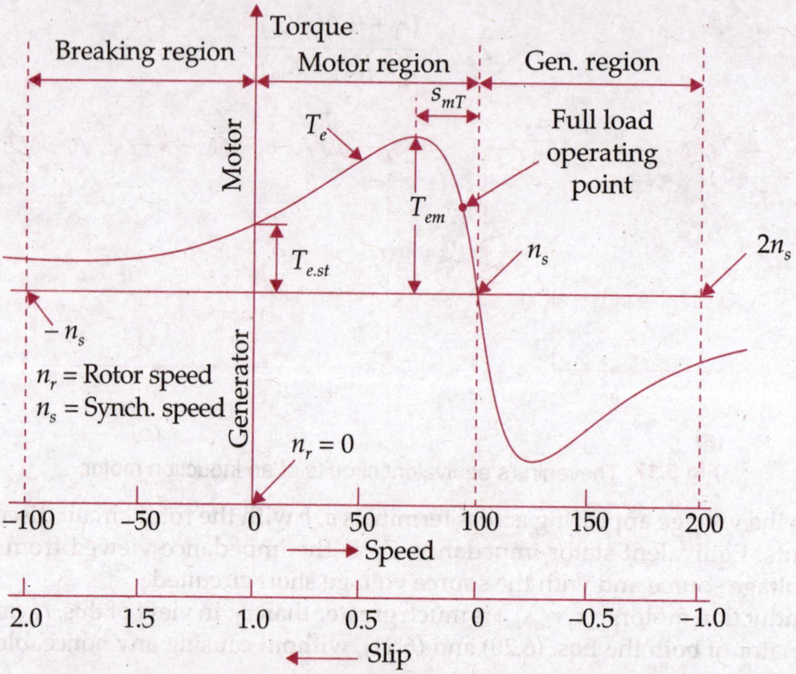

Fig 6.18: Torque-slip curve for an induction machine showing its braking, motor and generator regions.

(a) Motoring Mode : $0 < s \leq 1$.

Under normal operation, rotor revolves in the direction of rotating field produced by the stator currents. As such, the slip varies from 1 at standstill to zero at synchronous speed, *i.e.* $0 < s \leq 1$. The corresponding speed values are zero (s = 1.0) and synchronous speed (s = 0.0).

(b) Generating mode : $s < 0$.

For this operating mode, slip is negative, *i.e.*, $s < 0$. An induction motor will operate in this region only when its stator terminals are connected to constant-frequency voltage source and its rotor is driven above synchronous speed by a prime mover. The connection of stator terminals to voltage source is essential in order to establish the rotating air-gap field at synchronous speed. In case stator is disconnected from voltage source and rotor is driven above synchronous speed by the prime mover, no generating action would take place.

(c) Braking mode : $s > 1$.

For this mode, slip is greater than 1. A slip more than one can be obtained by driving the rotor, with a prime mover, opposite to the direction of rotating field. But such a use in practice is rare. A practical utility of slip more than 1 is obtained by bringing the rotor to a quick stop by braking action, called *plugging*. For obtaining $s > 1$, or for obtaining plugging, any two stator leads are interchanged. With this the phase sequence is reversed and, therefore, the direction of rotating magnetic field becomes suddenly opposite to that of the rotor rotation. The electro-magnetic torque T_e, now acting opposite to rotor rotation, produces the braking action. Thus the motor can be quickly brought to rest by plugging, but the stator must be disconnected from the supply before the rotor can start rotating in the other direction.

All the three regions of operation (braking region, $s = 2.0$ to $s = 1.0$; motor region, $s = 1.0$ to $s = 0$ and generator region, $s = 0$ to $s = -1$) are illustrated in Fig. 6.18.

Maximum internal torque. This is also referred to as *stalling torque, pull-out torque* or *breakdown torque* T_{em}. The condition for maximum internal torque can be obtained by using the *maximum power transfer theorem* of circuit theory. As per Eq. (6.13), torque is maximum when $I_2^2 r_2/s$ is maximum, *i.e.*, when power delivered to r_2/s is maximum. Applying this theorem to Fig. 6.17 *(a)*, power absorbed by r_2/s will be maximum when impedance r_2/s becomes equal to the magnitude of impedance seen by r_2/s towards the voltage source V_e, *i.e.*,

$$\text{when} \qquad \frac{r_2}{s_{mT}} = \sqrt{R_e^2 + (X_e + x_2)^2} = \sqrt{R_e^2 + X^2}$$

$$\text{where} \qquad X = x_2 + X_e.$$

Thus the slip s_{mT} at which maximum torque occurs is given by

$$s_{mT} = \frac{r_2}{\sqrt{R_e^2 + X^2}} \qquad \text{...(6.26)}$$

Substitution of r_2/s_{mT} in place of r_2/s in Eq. (6.25) gives maximum, breakdown torque T_{em} as

$$T_{em} = \frac{K_t[\sqrt{R_e^2 + X^2}]}{[R_e + \sqrt{R_e^2 + X^2}]^2 + X^2}$$

$$= \frac{K_t[\sqrt{R_e^2 + X^2}]}{[R_e^2 + R_e^2 + X^2 + 2R_2\sqrt{R_e^2 + X^2}] + X^2}$$

$$= \frac{K_t[\sqrt{R_e^2 + X^2}]}{2\sqrt{R_e^2 + X^2}[R_e + \sqrt{R_e^2 + X^2}]}$$

$$\therefore \qquad T_{em} = \frac{K_t}{2[R_e + \sqrt{R_e^2 + X^2}]} \qquad \text{...(6.27)}$$

Eq. (6.26) shows that the slip at which maximum torque occurs is directly proportional to the rotor resistance r_2, but Eq. (6.27) indicates that maximum torque T_{em} is independent of r_2. This means that if r_2 is increased by inserting external resistance in the rotor circuit of a wound-rotor induction motor, the magnitude of maximum internal torque is unaffected but the slip at which it occurs is affected proportionally.

Now K_t ($\propto V_e^2$) is proportional to the square of stator voltage V_1, R_e is proportional to stator resistance r_1 and X is proportional to x_1 and x_2. In view of these facts, an examinaton of Eq. (6.27) shows that

(i) T_{em} is directly proportional to the square of the stator voltage

(ii) T_{em} is reduced by an increase in stator resistance r_1 (*i.e.* R_e) and

(iii) T_{em} is reduced by an increase in stator leakage reactance x_1 and rotor leakage reactance x_2.

For obtaining higher value of maximum torque, the air-gap is kept as small as is possible. A small air gap allows more flux to be mutual between stator and rotor windings. As a consequence, leakage fluxes and therefore leakage reactances are reduced and the magnitude of maximum torque becomes more.

Typical torque-slip curves for an induction motor with variable rotor-circuit resistances are obtained from Eq. (6.24 *b*) and are shown in Fig. 6.19 *(a)*. For the load torque curve T_L as shown, the speed is n_1 for a rotor-circuit resistance r_2, speed is reduced to n_2 for $r_2' > r_2$ etc. For rotor-circuit resistance r_2''', Fig. 6.19 (a) reveals that it is not possible to obtain maximum torque during motoring mode of the three-phase induction machine. This value of rotor resistance can, however, give maximum torque only during braking mode of the induction machine. In case the effect of rotor resistance on stator current is to be investigated, then refer to Fig. 6.13 *(a)*. In this figure, if stator impedance and no-load current are neglected, then stator current I_1 is given by

$$I_1 = \frac{V_1}{\sqrt{\left(\frac{r_2}{s}\right)^2 + x_2^2}}$$

At standstill, slip $s = 1$ and $\therefore\ I_{1st} = \dfrac{V_1}{\sqrt{r_2^2 + x_2^2}}$. For rotor resistance r_2, let the starting current I_{1st} be OA, Fig. 6.19 *(b)*. For different values of slips from 1 to 0, variation of stator current I_1 is plotted in Fig. 6.19 *(b)* for rotor resistance r_2. When rotor resistance is increased from r_2 to r_2', starting current I_{1st} reduces to $OB = I_{2\cdot st}$. Variation of I_2 for different values of s is also plotted in Fig. 6.19 *(b)* for r_2'. Similarly, variation of stator current I_1 for resistances r_2'', r_2''' is shown in Fig. 6.19 *(b)*, where $r_2''' > r_2'' > r_2' > r_2$.

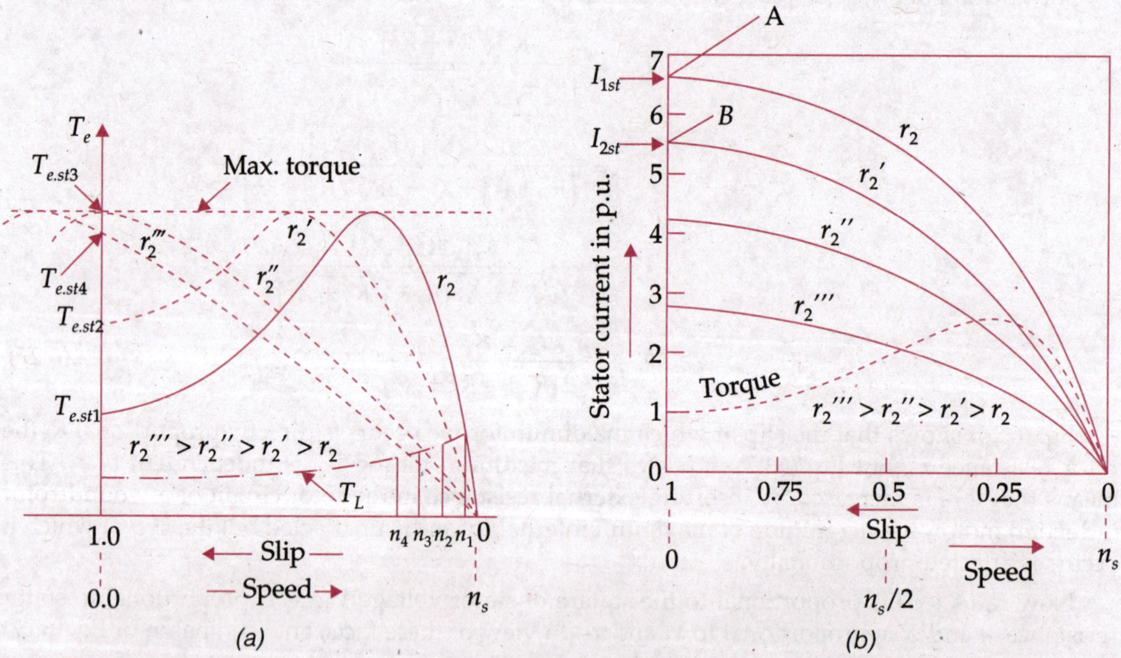

Fig 6.19: *(a)* Induction motor torque-slip curves with different values of rotor-circuit resistances. *(b)* Effect of rotor resistance on stator current versus slip characteristics of a 3-phase induction motor.

From the torque-slip curves of Fig. 6.19 *(a)* and stator current versus slip characteristics of Fig. 6.19 *(b)*, it can be concluded for a wound-rotor induction motor that

(i) the speed of motor can be controlled by varying the rotor-circuit resistance but maximum torque remains unaffected

(ii) the starting torque can be varied by changing the rotor-circuit resistance

(iii) the line current taken by the motor shall also vary with rotor-circuit resistance, Fig. 6.19 (b) shows the effect of rotor-circuit resistance on the stator input current as a function of slip and

(iv) the power factor at starting is also affected by rotor-circuit resistance.

It can be observed from Fig. 6.19 that when rotor circuit resistance is increased, though starting current has reduced, yet the starting torque has increased. For resistance r_2'', starting stator current has decreased, but torque at starting is maximum. For resistance more than r_2'', both stator starting current and starting torque have reduced. Also, with increase in rotor circuit resistance, slip at which maximum torque occurs increases.

In order to get better performance of the induction motor, starting torque is increased by inserting a suitable external resistance in the rotor circuit at starting. As the motor accelerates, external resistance is cut out in steps so as to maintain maximum torque during the accelerating period. Finally, external resistance is reduced to zero and the rotor attains normal speed.

Starting Torque. At starting, slip $s = 1.00$. From Eq. (6.25), starting torque $T_{e\cdot st}$ is given by

$$T_{e\cdot st} = \frac{K_t}{(R_e + r_2)^2 + X^2} \cdot r_2 \qquad ...(6.28)$$

Starting torque T_{est} can be controlled by varying rotor circuit resistance as illustrated in Fig. 6.19. In order to get maximum starting torque, the rotor-circuit resistance must be increased to $\sqrt{R_e^2 + X^2}$, refer to Eq. (6.26) where $s_{mT} = 1.00$. This new value of rotor-circuit resistance can be obtained by inserting external resistance equal to $(\sqrt{R_e^2 + X^2} - r_2)$ in the rotor circuit at the time of starting.

Motor operation near synchronous speed. When slip s is small, r_2/s becomes quite large as compared to other denominator terms of Eq. (6.24 *a*) and consequently these can be ignored. Thus from Eq. (6.24 *a*),

$$I_2 = \frac{sV_e}{r_2} \qquad ...(6.29)$$

and from Eq. (6.25),

$$T_e \cong \frac{K_t}{\left(\frac{r_2}{s}\right)^2} \cdot \frac{r_2}{s} = \frac{sK_t}{r_2} \qquad ...(6.30\ a)$$

$$= sK \qquad ...(6.30\ b)$$

Here $\quad K = \frac{K_t}{r_2}$ is a constant

An examination of Fig. 6.19 (with rotor-circuit resistance r_2) also reveals that under normal operating region of small slips, the torque-slip characteristic is almost a linear one.

If terminal voltage is variable, then from Eq. (6.30*a*)

$$T_e = s\,\frac{mV_e^2}{\omega_s} \cdot \frac{1}{r_2} = K' V_1^2 s \qquad ...(6.31)$$

Here K' is also a constant.

Motor torque in terms of T_{em}. The torque expression of an induction motor can also be expressed in terms of maximum torque T_{em} and the dimensionless ratio s/s_{mT}. In order to get a simple and approximate expression, stator resistance r_1, or the stator equivalent resistance R_e, is neglected.

Division of Eq. (6.25) by Eq. (6.27) gives $\dfrac{T_e}{T_{em}} = \dfrac{2[R_e + \sqrt{R_e^2 + X^2}]}{\left(R_e + \frac{r_2}{s}\right)^2 + X^2} \cdot \dfrac{r_2}{s}$

Since r_1 or R_e is neglected, $$\frac{T_e}{T_{em}} = \frac{2X}{\left(\frac{r_2}{s}\right)^2 + X^2}\cdot\frac{r_2}{s} \qquad ...(6.32)$$

From Eq. (6.26), $$r_2 = s_{mT} X \qquad (\because R_e = 0)$$

Substitution of this value of r_2 in Eq. (6.32) gives

$$\frac{T_e}{T_{em}} = \frac{2X}{\left(\frac{s_{mT}X}{s}\right)^2 + X^2}\cdot\frac{s_{mT}X}{s} = \frac{2}{\left(\frac{s_{mT}}{s}\right)^2 + 1}\cdot\frac{s_{mT}}{s}$$

or $$\frac{T_e}{T_{em}} = \frac{2}{\frac{s_{mT}}{s} + \frac{s}{s_{mT}}} \text{ or } T_e = \frac{2T_{em}}{\frac{s_{mT}}{s} + \frac{s}{s_{mT}}} \qquad ...(6.33)$$

6.9.2. Power-slip Characteristics

The total internal mechanical power developed is

$$P_m = m\,(1 - s)\,P_g = m\,I_2^2\,r_2\left(\frac{1-s}{s}\right) \text{ watts}$$

or $$P_m = \frac{mV_e^2}{\left[R_e + r_2 + \frac{r_2(1-s)}{s}\right]^2 + X^2}\cdot r_2\left(\frac{1-s}{s}\right) \qquad ...(6.34)$$

Maximum power transfer theorem is invoked again to obtain maximum value of internal mechanical power developed. Since P_m per phase is the power delivered to $r_2\left(\frac{1-s}{s}\right)$, internal mechanical power developed is maximum, refer to Fig. 6.17 *(b)*, when

$$\frac{r_2(1 - s_{mP})}{s_{mP}} = \sqrt{(R_e + r_2)^2 + X^2} \qquad ...(6.35\,a)$$

or $$s_{mP} = \left[\frac{r_2}{\sqrt{(R_e + r_2)^2 + X^2} + r_2}\right] \qquad ...(6.35\,b)$$

In order to get maximum power P_m, substitute $\frac{r_2(1 - s_{mp})}{s_{mp}}$ from Eq. (6.35 *a*) in place of $\frac{r_2(1-s)}{s}$ in Eq. (6.34).

$$\therefore \quad P_{mm} = \frac{mV_e^2\sqrt{(R_e + r_2)^2 + X^2}}{[R_e + r_2 + \sqrt{(R_e + r_2)^2 + X^2}]^2 + X^2} \qquad ...(6.36)$$

or $$P_{mm} = \frac{mV_e^2}{2[R_e + r_2 + \sqrt{(R_e + r_2)^2 + X^2}]} \qquad ...(6.36)$$

Note that the denominator of Eq. (6.36) can be obtained from the denominator of Eq. (6.27) if R_e is replaced by $(R_e + r_2)$.

It is observed from Eq. (6.36) that P_{mm} depends on rotor resistance r_2 whereas T_{em} does not.

From Eqs. (6.26) and (6.35), it is seen that s_{mP} is smaller in magnitude than s_{mT}.

Eq. (6.34) shows that at starting, slip $s = 1$ and internal mechanical power developed P_m is zero. The variation of mechanical power developed with slip s is illustrated in Fig. 6.20.

At starting, though the internal mechanical power developed P_m is zero, the starting torque T_{est} is not zero. This is due to the fact that when slip $s = 1$, the air-gap power transferred from stator to rotor is $I_2^2 r_2$ and this all appears as ohmic loss in the rotor circuit and, therefore, the mechanical power developed P_m is zero. However, $T_{e\cdot st} = 1/\omega_s \times I_2^2 r_2$ is not zero.

Fig. 6.20 shows that power P_m during braking region is negative. In other words, power P_m during plugging is returned to the supply. As slip s is more than 1 during plugging, Eq. (6.34) shows that P_m is negative. Note, however, that T_e is positive during plugging or braking region.

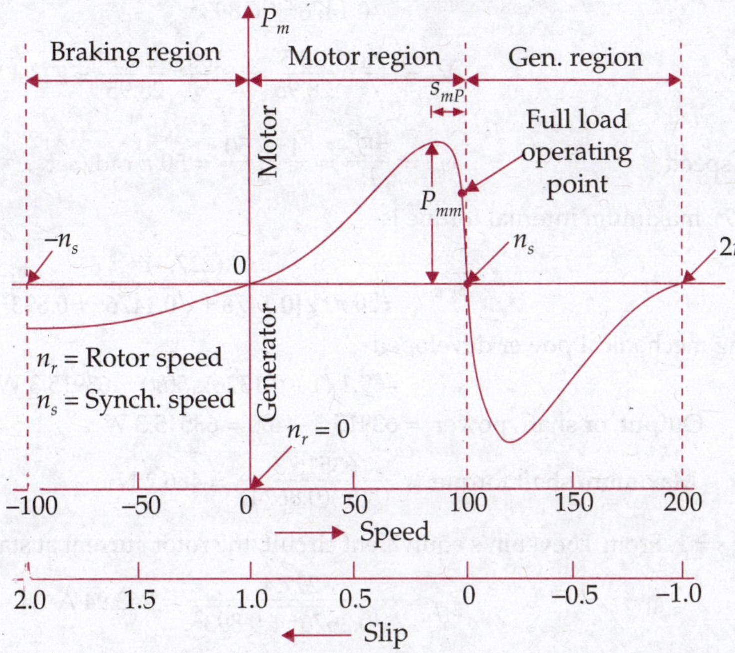

Fig 6.20: Power-slip curve for an induction machine showing its braking, motor and generator regions.

In order to get maximum power output from an induction generator, reference to Fig. 6.20 shows that the rotor must be driven at a speed given by

$$n_s \left[1 + \frac{r_2}{\sqrt{(R_e + r_2)^2 + X^2} + r_2}\right]$$

Example 6.10. *For the motor of Example 6.9, determine (a) the slip at which maximum torque occurs, the maximum torque and the corresponding power output ; (b) the rotor current and the torque at starting; (c) the external resistance to be inserted in the rotor circuit to produce maximum torque at starting ; (d) the internal power developed for a slip of 0.04 and (e) the maximum internal power developed and the corresponding slip.*

Stator to rotor effective turns rotio is 1.2.

Solution. *(a)* Reduce induction motor equivalent circuit of Fig. 6.16 to Thevenin's equivalent circuit of Fig. 6.17 *(a)*, in which

$$\bar{Z}_e = \frac{(0.15 + j0.45)(j28.5)}{(0.15 + j28.95)} \cong \frac{(0.15 + j0.45)(j28.5)}{j28.95}$$

$$\therefore \quad R_e = \frac{(0.15)(j28.5)}{j28.95} = 0.1476\ \Omega$$

and $$X_e = \frac{(0.45)(j28.5)}{j28.95} = 0.443\ \Omega$$

From Fig. 6.17 *(a)*, torque is maximum when

$$\frac{r_2}{s_{mT}} = R_e + j\,(x_2 + X_e) \text{ or } \frac{0.12}{s_{mT}} = 0.1476 + j0.893$$

or $$s_{mT} = \frac{0.12}{\sqrt{0.1476^2 + 0.893^2}} = 0.1326$$

$$V_e = \frac{V_1}{\sqrt{3}}\cdot\frac{28.5}{28.95} = \frac{400}{\sqrt{3}}\cdot\frac{28.5}{28.95} = 227.4\text{ V}$$

Synchronous speed $$\omega_s = \frac{4\pi f}{P} = \frac{4\pi \times 50}{4} = 50\ \pi\text{ rad/sec}$$

From Eq. (6.27), maximum internal torque is

$$T_{em} = \frac{3(227.4)^2}{(50\ \pi)\,2[0.1476 + \sqrt{0.1476^2 + 0.893^2}]} = 469.1\text{ Nm}$$

Corresponding mechanical power developed

$$= 469.1\ (1 - 0.1326)\ (50\pi) = 63915.3\text{ W}$$

$\therefore$ Output, or shaft, power $= 63915.3 - 400 = 63515.3$ W

$\therefore$ Maximum shaft torque $$= \frac{63515.3}{(50\pi)(0.8674)} = 466.2\text{ Nm}$$

(b) At starting $s = 1$. From Thevenin's equivalent circuit, the rotor current at starting is given by

$$I_{2\,st} = \frac{227.4}{\sqrt{0.2676^2 + 0.893^2}} = 243.94\text{ A}$$

Starting torque, $$T_{est} = 3\ (243.94)^2 \left(\frac{0.12}{1}\right)\frac{1}{50\pi} = 136.4\text{ Nm}$$

(c) Let R be the external resistance inserted in the rotor circuit to get maximum torque T_{em} at starting when $s = 1$. From Fig. 6.17 *(a)*, we get

$$\frac{r_2 + R}{1} = \sqrt{R_e^2 + (X_e + x_2)^2}$$

or $$r_2 + R = \sqrt{0.1476^2 + 0.893^2} = 0.9051\ \Omega.$$

$\therefore$ External resistance (referred to stator) which must be inserted in rotor circuit,

$$R = 0.9051 - 0.12 = 0.7851\ \Omega.$$

Actual external resistance that must be inserted in the rotor circuit

$$= \frac{0.7851}{(1.2)^2} = 0.5452\ \Omega.$$

(d) From Eq. (6.34), the internal power developed for a slip of 0.04 is

$$P_m = \frac{3 \times (227.4)^2}{\left[0.1476 + 0.12 + \dfrac{0.12 \times 0.96}{0.04}\right]^2 + .893^2} \times 0.12 \times \frac{0.96}{0.04}$$

$$= 41736.36\text{ W} = 41.736\text{ kW}$$

(e) The slip at which internal power developed is maximum is given by Eq. (6.35) as

$$S_{mP} = \frac{0.12}{[(0.1476+0.12)^2+0.893^2]^{½}+0.12} = 0.114$$

From Eq. (6.36), maximum internal power developed is

$$P_{mm} = \frac{3\times(227.4)^2}{2[0.1476+0.12+\sqrt{0.2676^2+0.893^2}]}$$

$$= 64647.44 \text{ W} = 64.647 \text{ kW}.$$

Example 6.11. *For the three-phase induction motor of Example 6.9, find the maximum internal torque developed under the following conditions :*

(a) 230 V/phase, 50 Hz *(b) 115 V/phase, 50 Hz*

(c) 115 V/phase, 25 Hz *(d) 23 V/phase, 5 Hz*

Solution. The Thevenin's equivalent circuit parameters at 50 Hz from Example 6.10 are :

$$R_e = 0.1476\ \Omega,\ X_e = 0.443\ \Omega,\ r_2 = 0.12\ \Omega,\ x_2 = 0.45\ \Omega$$

$$V_e = \frac{28.5}{28.95}\ V_1 = 0.9845\ V_1$$

Synchronous speed $\omega_r = \frac{4\pi f}{P} = \pi f$ with $P = 4$.

From Eq. (6.27), for $f = 50$ Hz,

$$T_{e\cdot m} = \frac{3}{\pi\times 50}\cdot\frac{V_e^2}{2[0.1476+\sqrt{0.1476^2+0.893^2}]}$$

$$= 9.071\times 10^{-3}\, V_e^2.$$

(a) When supply voltage is 230 V at 50 Hz,

$$V_e = 0.9845\times 230 = 226.44 \text{ V}$$

$\therefore$ $$T_{e\cdot m} = 9.071\times 10^{-3}\times(226.44)^2 = 465.12 \text{ Nm}.$$

(b) For $V_1 = 115$ V at 50 Hz, $V_e = 0.9845\times 115 = 113.22$ V

$\therefore$ $$T_{e\cdot m} = 9.071\times 10^{-3}\times(113.22)^2 = 116.28 \text{ Nm}$$

As expected, maximum torque is $\frac{1}{4}$ of that obtained in part (*a*).

(c) For $f = 25$ Hz, $V_e = 0.9845\times 115 = 113.22$ V

$R_e = 0.1476\ \Omega$ $$X_e = \frac{\left(\frac{1}{2}\times 0.45\right)\left(\frac{1}{2}\times 28.5\right)}{\left(\frac{1}{2}\times 28.95\right)} = 0.2215\ \Omega,\ x_2 = 0.225\ \Omega$$

$\therefore$ $$T_{e\cdot m} = \frac{3}{\pi\times 25}\cdot\frac{113.22^2}{2[0.1476+\sqrt{0.1476^2+0.4465^2}]} = 396.24 \text{ Nm}.$$

(d) When f = 5 Hz, $V_e = 0.9845\times 23 = 22.644$ V

$$X_e = \frac{1}{10}\times 0.443 = 0.0443\ \Omega,\ x_2 = \frac{1}{10}\times 0.45 = 0.045$$

$\therefore$ $$T_{e\cdot m} = \frac{3}{\pi\times 5}\cdot\frac{22.644^2}{2[0.1476+\sqrt{0.1476^2+0.0893^2}]} = 152.96 \text{ Nm}$$

This example demonstrates that even if V/f is kept constant, the maximum torque at lower frequencies is reduced due to the effect of winding resistance.

Example 6.12. *From the equivalent circuit of a polyphase induction motor, obtain the following relations:*

(a) $\dfrac{I_{2\,st}}{I_2} = \sqrt{\dfrac{s^2+s_{mT}^2}{s^2(1+s_{mT}^2)}}$ (b) $\dfrac{I_{2\cdot mT}}{I_2} = \sqrt{\dfrac{1}{2}\left[1+\left(\dfrac{s_{mT}}{s}\right)^2\right]}$.

Here $I_{2\cdot st}$ is the stator load-component of current at starting and $I_{2\cdot mT}$ is the stator load-component of current at maximum torque. Neglect stator resistance.

Solution. *(a)* From the equivalent circuit of Fig. 6.17 *(a)*, the stator load-component of starting current $I_{2\cdot st}$ is

$$I_{2\cdot st} = \frac{V_e}{\sqrt{(R_e+r_2)^2+(X_e+x_2)^2}}$$

The stator load current I_2 at any slip s is

$$I_2 = \frac{V_e}{\sqrt{(R_e+r_2/s)^2+(X_e+x_2)^2}}$$

With negligible stator resistance r_1, $R_e = 0$ and the ratio of I_{2st} and I_2 gives

$$\frac{I_{2\cdot st}}{I_2} = \sqrt{\frac{(r_2/s)^2+X^2}{r_2^2+X^2}} \quad ...(6.37\ a)$$

From Eq. (6.26) with $R_e = 0$, $r_2 = s_{mT}\,X$

Substitution of the value of r_2 ($= s_{mT}$ X) in Eq. (6.37 *a*) gives

$$\frac{I_{2\cdot st}}{I_2} = \sqrt{\frac{(s_{mT}/s)^2X^2+X^2}{(s_{mT}X)^2+X^2}} = \sqrt{\frac{s^2+s_{mT}^2}{s^2(1+s_{mT}^2)}} \quad ...(6.37\ b)$$

(b) Stator load current I_2 with $r_1 = 0$ is $I_2 = \dfrac{V_e}{\sqrt{(r_2/s)^2+X^2}}$.

Current $I_{2\cdot mT}$ corresponding to maximum torque is given by

$$I_{2\cdot mT} = \frac{V_e}{\sqrt{(r_2/s_{mT})^2+X^2}}$$

$$\therefore \quad \frac{I_{2\cdot mT}}{I_2} = \sqrt{\frac{(r_2/s)^2+X^2}{(r_2/s_{mT})^2+X^2}}$$

But $r_2 = s_{mT}\,X$,

$$\therefore \quad \frac{I_{2\cdot mT}}{I_2} = \sqrt{\frac{(s_{mT}/s)^2X^2+X^2}{(s_{mT}/s_{mT})^2X^2+X^2}}$$

$$= \sqrt{\frac{1+(s_{mT}/s)^2}{1+1}} = \sqrt{\frac{1}{2}\left[1+\left(\frac{s_{mT}}{s}\right)^2\right]} \quad ...(6.38)$$

Example 6.13. *A 10 kW, 400 V, 3-phase, 4-pole, 50 Hz slipring induction motor develops rated output (i.e. 10 kW) at rated voltage and frequency and with its slip rings short-circuited. The maximum torque equal* *to twice the full-load torque, occurs at a slip of 10% with zero external resistance in the rotor circuit. Stator resistance, stator core and mechanical losses are neglected. Determine*

(i) slip and rotor speed at full-load torque,

(ii) rotor ohmic loss at full-load torque,

(iii) starting torque at rated voltage and frequency,

(iv) starting current in terms of full-load current,

(v) stator current a maximum torque, in terms of full-load current and

(vi) full-load efficiency.

The rotor resistance is now trebled by inserting external resistance in the rotor-circuit. For the same full-load torque, find

(vii) the slip at maximum torque,

(viii) full-load slip and rotor speed,

(ix) starting torque,

(x) starting current in terms of full-load current,

(xi) rotor I^2R loss at full-load torque and

(xii) developed power at full-load torque and efficiency.

Solution. *(i)* Maximum torque,

$$T_{em} = 2\text{ (full-load torque, } T_{e\cdot fl})$$

$$\therefore \quad T_{em} = 2T_{e\cdot fl} \text{ and } s_{mT} = 0.10$$

From Eq. (6.33),

$$\frac{T_{e\cdot fl}}{T_{em}} = \frac{2}{\dfrac{s_{mT}}{s_{fl}} + \dfrac{s_{fl}}{s_{mT}}} \text{ or } \frac{1}{2} = \frac{2}{\dfrac{0.1}{s_{fl}} + \dfrac{s_{fl}}{0.1}}$$

$$s^2_{fl} - 0.4\, s_{fl} + 0.01 = 0$$

Its solution gives full-load slip, $s_{fl} = 0.0268$ or 2.68%

Rotor speed, $N_r = 1500\,(1 - 0.0268) = 1459.8 \cong 1460$ r.p.m.

(ii) Since the mechanical losses are neglected, see Fig. 6.8, mechanical power developed is P_m = shaft power of 10,000 watts.

$$\therefore \text{ Air-gap power, } \quad P_g = \frac{P_m}{1 - s_{fl}} = \frac{10{,}000}{1 - 0.0268} = 10275.4 \text{ W.}$$

Rotor ohmic loss at full-load torque = $sP_g = 0.0268 \times 10275.4 = 275.4$ watts.

Alternatively, rotor ohmic loss = $P_g - P_m = 10{,}275.4 - 10{,}000 = 275.4$ W.

(iii) Full-load torque,

$$T_{e\cdot fl} = \frac{P_g}{2\pi\, n_s} = \frac{10{,}275.4}{2\pi\,(25)} = 65.42 \text{ Nm.}$$

Now

$$\frac{T_{e\cdot st}}{T_{e\cdot m}} = \frac{2}{\dfrac{s_{mT}}{1} + \dfrac{1}{s_{mT}}}$$

$$\therefore \quad T_{e\cdot st} = \frac{2T_{em}}{\dfrac{0.1}{1} + \dfrac{1}{0.1}} = \frac{2(2T_{e\cdot fl})}{10.1} = \frac{4}{10.1} = (65.42) = 25.91 \text{ Nm}$$

(iv) From Eq. (6.37),
$$\frac{I_{2\cdot st}}{I_{2\cdot fl}} = \sqrt{\frac{s_{fl}^2 + s_{mT}^2}{s_{fl}^2(1+s_{mT}^2)}} = \sqrt{\frac{(0.0268)^2 + (0.1)^2}{(0.0268)^2(1+0.01)}} = 3.844$$

$\therefore$
$$I_{2\cdot st} = 3.844\, I_{2fl}$$

(v) From Eq. (6.38),
$$\frac{I_{2\cdot mT}}{I_{2\cdot fl}} = \sqrt{\frac{1}{2}\left[1+\left(\frac{s_{mT}}{s_{fl}}\right)^2\right]} = \sqrt{\frac{1}{2}\left[1+\left(\frac{0.1}{0.0268}\right)^2\right]} = 2.623$$

$\therefore$
$$I_{2\cdot mT} = 2.623\, I_{2fl}.$$

Note that current $I_{2\cdot mT}$ corresponding to maximum torqure is less than the current $I_{2\cdot st}$ at starting.

(vi) Since stator resistance and stator core loss are neglected, power input = P_g = 10275.4 W.

$\therefore$
$$\text{Efficiency} = \frac{\text{Output}}{\text{Input}} \times 100 = \frac{10,000}{10275.4} \times 100 = 97.32\%$$

(vii) Before the external resistance is inserted in the rotor circuit, we have from Eq. (6.26) with $r_1 = 0$,
$$\frac{r_2}{s_{mT}} = \sqrt{(X_e + x_2)^2} = \sqrt{X^2} = X \text{ or } \frac{r_2}{X} = s_{mT} = 0.10.$$

When the rotor-circuit resistance is trebled,

then
$$\frac{3r_2}{X} = s_{mT1}.$$

$\therefore$ New value of slip at which maximum torque occurs is
$$s_{mT1} = 3\,(0.10) = 0.3 \text{ or } 30\%.$$

(viii) With increase in rotor circuit resistance, maximum torque T_{em} remains unchanged. As full load torque remains same, $T_{em} = 2.T_{e\cdot fl}$. From Eq. (6.33)
$$\frac{1}{2} = \frac{2}{\dfrac{s_1}{0.3} + \dfrac{0.3}{s_1}}$$

Its solution gives full-load slip
$$s_1 = 0.0804$$
$$= 3 \text{ times the previous full-load slip } (= 0.0268)$$

Rotor speed, N_r = 1500 (1 – 0.0804) = 1379.4 r.p.m., less than previous speed of 1460 r.p.m.

(ix)
$$\frac{T_{e\cdot st}}{T_{em}} = \frac{2}{\dfrac{1}{0.3} + \dfrac{0.3}{1}}$$

$\therefore$
$$T_{e\cdot st} = \frac{2}{3.63}\,(2T_{e\cdot fl}) = \frac{4}{3.63}\,(65.42) = 72.09 \text{ Nm.}$$

It is more than previous
$$T_{e\cdot st} = 25.91 \text{ Nm.}$$

(x) From Eq. (6.37),
$$\frac{I_{2\cdot st}}{I_{2\cdot fl}} = \sqrt{\frac{(0.0804)^2 + (0.3)^2}{(0.0804)^2(1+0.09)}} = 3.7$$

$\therefore$
$$I_{2\cdot st} = 3.7\, I_{2\cdot fl}, \text{ less than previous } I_{2.5st} = 3.844\, I_{2fl}.$$

(xi) Any change in the rotor circuit influences the stator through the resistance r_2/s. With r_2 being increased to $3r_2$ and with new full-load slip $s_1 = 3s$, resistance r_2/s remains constant. This implies that all equivalent circuit parameters are constant and the stator is therefore unaware of

any change in the rotor circuit. This means that stator current and power factor, air-gap power and torque remain unchanged so long as r_2/s is constant.

Rotor ohmic loss at full-load torque = $s_1 P_g = 0.0804 \times 10275.4 = 826.14$ W.

(xii) Power developed at full-load torque,

$$P_{m1} = (1 - s_1) P_g = (1 - 0.0804)(10275.4) = 9449.26 \text{ W}.$$

$$\therefore \qquad \text{Efficiency} = \frac{9449.26}{10275.4} \times 100 = 91.96\%.$$

This example illustrates that the effect of introducing external resistance in the rotor circuit is *(a)* to decrease the rotor speed, starting current, output power and efficiency and *(b)* to increase the slip at which maximum torque occurs, rotor ohmic loss and starting torque.

Example 6.14. *A 60 kW, 400 V, 3-phase, 6-pole, 50 Hz wound rotor induction motor has a full-load slip of 0.04 when operating at rated voltage and frequency with rotor winding short circuited at slip rings. The slip at maximum torque is 0.2. Stator resistance and mechanical losses are neglected. Determine (a) the maximum torque and (b) full-load rotor ohmic losses.*

Rotor resistance is now doubled by adding external series resistance in each rotor phase. For the rated power output, determine (c) slip at maximum torque (d) full-load slip and (e) full-load torque.

Solution. Synchronous speed,
$$\omega_s = \frac{2\pi \times 1000}{60} = 104.72 \text{ rad/s}$$

Rotor speed,
$$\omega_r = 104.72\,(1 - 0.04) = 100.53 \text{ rad/s}$$

As mechanical losses are neglected, the mechanical power developed,

$$P_m = 60{,}000 \text{ W}$$

$$\therefore \qquad \omega_r T_{e\text{-}fl} = 60{,}000 \text{ W or } T_{e\text{-}fl} = T_1 = \frac{60000}{100.53} = 596.84 \text{ Nm}$$

(a) As stator resistance in neglected,

$$\frac{T_1}{T_{e\cdot m}} = \frac{2}{\dfrac{s_{mT}}{s_1} + \dfrac{s_1}{s_{mT}}} = \frac{2}{\dfrac{0.2}{0.04} + \dfrac{0.04}{0.2}} = \frac{2}{5.2}$$

where s_1 = full-load slip = 0.04

∴ Maximum torque,
$$T_{em} = \frac{5.2}{2} \times 596.84 = 1551.8 \text{ Nm}.$$

(b) Full-load rotor ohmic losses $= s_1 P_g = \left(\dfrac{s_1}{1 - s_1}\right) P_m = \left(\dfrac{0.04}{0.96}\right) \times 60{,}000 = 2500$ W

(c) It is given that $\dfrac{r_2}{X} = s_{mT} = 0.2$

New slip at maximum torque,
$$s_{mT1} = \frac{2r_2}{X} = 2 \times 0.2 = 0.4$$

(d) As stator resistance is neglected, $T_{em} = 1551.8$ Nm

From Eq. (6.33),
$$\frac{T_2}{1551.8} = \frac{2}{\dfrac{s_2}{0.4} + \dfrac{0.4}{s_2}}$$

where s_2 and T_2 are new full-load slip and torque respectively.

$$T_2 = \frac{1551.8 \times 2 \times 0.4\, s_2}{s_2^2 + 0.16} = \frac{1241.44\, s_2}{s_2^2 + 0.16} \qquad \text{...}(i)$$

It is given that $\omega_r T_2 = 60{,}000 \text{ W or } T_2 = \dfrac{60000}{104.72(1-s_2)}$ ...(*ii*)

From (*i*) and (*ii*), $\dfrac{60000}{104.72(1-s_2)} = \dfrac{1241.44\, s_2}{s_2^2 + 0.16}$

or $s_2^2 + 0.16 = 2.167\,(s_2 - s_2^2) \text{ or } 3.167\, s_2^2 - 2.167\, s_2 + 0.16 = 0$

Its solution gives $s_2 = 0.084$ and 0.6

∴ Full-load slip, $s_2 = 0.084$, the other value being redundant.

(*e*) $104.72\,(1 - 0.084) T_2 = 60{,}000$

∴ Full-load torque, $T_2 = \dfrac{60{,}000}{104.72 \times 0.916} = 625.5 \text{ Nm.}$

Example 6.15. *For a 3-phase induction motor, maximum torque is twice the full-load torque and starting torque is 1.6 times the full-load torque. In order to get a full load slip of 5%, calculate the percentage reduction in rotor circuit resistance. Neglect stator impedance.*

Solution. From Eq. (6.32), $\dfrac{T_{e \cdot st}}{T_{em}} = \dfrac{1.6\, T_{e \cdot fl}}{2.0\, T_{e \cdot fl}} = \dfrac{2}{\dfrac{s_{mT1}}{1} + \dfrac{1}{s_{mT2}}}$ or $s_{mT1}^2 - 2.5\, s_{mT1} + 1 = 0$

Its solution gives $s_{mT1} = 0.5$

From Eq. (6.26), for negligible stator impedance,

$$\frac{r_2}{x_2} = s_{mT1} = 0.5 \quad \text{or} \quad r_2 = 0.5\, x_2.$$

For a full-load slip of 0.05, $\dfrac{T_{e \cdot fl}}{T_{em}} = \dfrac{1}{2} = \dfrac{2}{\dfrac{s_{mT2}}{0.05} + \dfrac{0.05}{s_{mT2}}}$ or $s_{mT2}{}^2 - 0.20\, s_{mT2} + 0.0025 = 0.$

Its solution gives $s_{mT2} = 0.1866$ and from Eq. (6.26), $\dfrac{r_2'}{x_2} = 0.1866$

∴ Rotor-circuit resistance for obtaining a slip of 5%, $r_2' = 0.1866\, x_2$

Thus, reduction in rotor circuit resistance $= 0.5\, x_2 - 0.1866\, x_2$

∴ Percentage reduction in rotor-circuit resistance $= \dfrac{0.5\, x_2 - 0.1866\, x_2}{0.5\, x_2} = 62.68\%.$

Example 6.16. *The rotor of a 3-phase induction motor has 0.04 Ω resistance per phase and 0.2 Ω standstill reactance per phase. What external resistance is required in the rotor circuit in order to get half of the maximum torque at starting? Neglect stator impedance.*

By what percentage will this external resistance change the current and p.f. at starting?

Solution. $\dfrac{T_{e \cdot st}}{T_{em}} = \dfrac{\frac{1}{2} T_{em}}{T_{em}} = \dfrac{2}{\dfrac{s_{mT}}{1} + \dfrac{1}{s_{mT}}}$ or $s_{mT}^2 - 4 s_{mT} + 1 = 0$

or $s_{mT} = \dfrac{4 \pm \sqrt{(4)^2 - 4}}{2} = 3.73 \text{ or } 0.27.$

Higher value of 3.73 is redundant. Therefore, $s_{mT} = 0.27$. For negligible stator impedance, from Eq. (6.26),

$$\frac{r_2'}{s_{mT}} = x_2 \text{ or } r_2' = 0.2 \times 0.27 = 0.054\ \Omega.$$

$\therefore$ External resistance that must be inserted in the rotor circuit

$$= r_2' - r_2 = 0.054 - 0.04 = 0.014\ \Omega.$$

Without external resistance,
$$I_{st} = \frac{V}{\sqrt{0.04^2 + 0.2^2}} = 4.903\text{ V}$$

$$\text{p.f.} = \frac{0.04}{\sqrt{0.04^2 + 0.2^2}} = 0.196.$$

With external resistance,
$$I_{st} = \frac{V}{\sqrt{0.054^2 + 0.2^2}} = 4.827\text{ V}$$

$$\text{p.f.} = \frac{0.054}{\sqrt{0.054^2 + 0.2^2}} = 0.261.$$

Percentage reduction in starting current
$$= \frac{4.903 - 4.827}{4.903} \times 100 = 1.55\%.$$

Percentage improvement in p.f.
$$= \frac{0.261 - 0.196}{0.196} \times 100 = 33.16\%.$$

Example 6.17. *A 3-phase induction motor with $r_2/x_2 = 0.5$, has a starting torque of 25.0 Nm. For negligible stator impedance and no-load current, determine the starting torque in case the rotor-circuit resistance per phase is (a) doubled (b) halved.*

Solution. With negligible stator impedance and no-load current, the starting torque from the induction motor equivalent circuit is given by

$$T_{e\cdot st} = \frac{1}{\omega_s} \cdot \frac{3V_1^2}{r_2^2 + x_2^2} r_2 = 25.00\text{ Nm}.$$

With
$$\frac{r_2}{x_2} = 0.5 \text{ or } x_2 = 2r_2$$

$$T_{e\cdot st} = \frac{1}{\omega_s} \cdot \frac{3V_1^2}{r_2^2 + 4r_2^2} \cdot r_2 = 25 \text{ or } \frac{1}{\omega_s} \cdot \frac{3V_1^2}{r_2} = 25 \times 5 = 125\text{ Nm}$$

(a) When rotor-circuit resistance is doubled, the starting torque is given by

$$T_{e\cdot st} = \frac{1}{\omega_s} \cdot \frac{3V_1^2}{(4r_2^2) + x_2^2} (2r_2)$$

But $\quad x_2 = 2r_2 \quad$ (given)

$$\therefore \quad T_{e\cdot st} = \frac{1}{\omega_s} \cdot \frac{3V_1^2}{(4r_2^2) + 4r_2^2} (2r_2)$$

or
$$T_{e\cdot st} = \left(\frac{1}{\omega_s} \cdot \frac{3V_1^2}{r_2}\right)\left(\frac{1}{4}\right) = \frac{125}{4} = 31.25\text{ Nm}$$

(b) When rotor-circuit resistance is halved, the starting torque is given by

$$T_{e\cdot st} = \frac{1}{\omega_s} \frac{3V_1^2}{\left(\frac{r_2}{2}\right)^2 + x_2^2}\left(\frac{r_2}{2}\right) = \frac{1}{\omega_s} \cdot \frac{3V_1^2}{\frac{r_2^2}{4} + 4r_2^2}\left(\frac{r_2}{2}\right)$$

$$= \left(\frac{1}{\omega_s} \cdot \frac{3V_1^2}{r_2}\right)\frac{2}{17} = \frac{125 \times 2}{17} = 14.706\text{ Nm}$$

Example 6.18. *A 3-phase induction motor has a starting torque of 150% and a maximum torque of 250% of the full-load torque. Neglect stator resistance and assume constant rotor resistance. Compute (a) the slip at maximum torque (b) full-load slip and (c) the rotor current at starting in terms of full-load rotor current.*

Solution. *(a)* $T_{est} = 1.5\, T_{e\cdot fl},\ T_{em} = 2.5\, T_{e\cdot fl}$

From Eq. (6.33), $$\frac{T_{est}}{T_{em}} = \frac{2}{\dfrac{s_{mT}}{1} + \dfrac{1}{s_{mT}}} \text{ or } \frac{1.5}{2.5} = \frac{2s_{mT}}{s_{mT}^2 + 1} \text{ or } s_{mT}^2 - 3.333\, s_{mT} + 1 = 0$$

Its solution gives $s_{mT} = 0.333.$

(b) $$\frac{T_{e\cdot fl}}{T_{em}} = \frac{2}{\dfrac{s_{fl}}{s_{mT}} + \dfrac{s_{mT}}{s_{fl}}}$$

or $$\frac{1}{2.5} = \frac{2}{\dfrac{s_{fl}}{0.333} + \dfrac{0.333}{s_{fl}}} \text{ or } s_{fl}^2 - 1.665\, s_{fl} + 0.111 = 0$$

Its solution gives $s_{fl} = 0.0695.$

(c) From Eq. (6.13), $$T_{e\cdot st} = \frac{1}{\omega_s} \cdot I_{2st}^2\, r_2,\ T_{efl} = \frac{1}{\omega_s} \cdot I_{2fl}^2 \frac{r_2}{s_{fl}}$$

$$\therefore \quad \frac{T_{e\cdot st}}{T_{e\cdot fl}} = \left(\frac{I_{2st}}{I_{2fl}}\right)^2 s_{fl}$$

$$\therefore \quad \left(\frac{I_{2st}}{I_{2fl}}\right)^2 = \frac{1.50}{0.0695} \text{ or } I_{2st} = 4.646\, I_{2fl}.$$

Example 6.19. *In a 3-phase induction motor, leakage reactance is four times the resistance for both stator and rotor circuits. But stator leakage reactance is equal to rotor standstill leakage reactance referred to stator. The motor develops a torque of 200 Nm at a slip of 0.04. Compute the starting and maximum torques. Neglect no-load current.*

Solution. Here $x_1 = x_2 = 4r_1 = 4r_2$

At a slip of 0.04, the torque, from Eq. (6.24 *b*), is

$$T_e = 200 = \frac{3V^2}{\omega_s} \cdot \frac{1}{\left[\left(1 + \dfrac{1}{0.04}\right)^2 + (4+4)^2\right] r_2^2} \cdot \frac{r_2}{0.04}$$

or $$\frac{3V^2}{\omega_s} = 5920 \text{ (Assuming } r_2 = 1.00)$$

$$\therefore \quad T_{e\cdot st} = \frac{3V^2}{\omega_s} \cdot \frac{1}{[(1+1)^2 + (4+4)^2]} = 5920\ \frac{1}{2^2 + 8^2} = 87.06 \text{ Nm}$$

$$s_{mT} = \frac{r_2}{\sqrt{r_1^2 + (x_1 + x_2)^2}} = \frac{1}{\sqrt{1 + 8^2}}\ 0.124$$

$$\therefore \quad T_{em} = \frac{3V^2}{\omega_s} \cdot \frac{1}{\left(1 + \dfrac{1}{0.124}\right)^2 + 8^2} \times \frac{1}{0.124} = 326.63 \text{ Nm}$$

Maximum torque can also be obtained from Eq. (6.27) directly without computing s_{mT}.

From this equation, $$T_{em} = \frac{3V^2}{\omega_s} \cdot \frac{1}{2[1 + \sqrt{1^2 + 8^2}]} = 5920\ \frac{1}{2[1 + \sqrt{65}]} = 326.63 \text{ Nm.}$$

Example 6.20. *A 3-phase wound-rotor induction motor runs at a slip of 5% at full load torque and with its slip rings short circuited. If rotor-circuit resistance is now increased to four times by inserting external non-inductive resistance in the rotor circuit; then determine, at full-load torque, the following parameters in terms of their previous values with rotor resistance r_2 :*

(a) slip (b) rotor current, rotor ohmic loss, rotor p.f. and (c) power output.

Solution. Here subscript A is used for the values when rotor resistance is r_2 and B for the values when resistance is $4r_2$.

(a) From Eq. (6.30),

$$T_e = \frac{sK_t}{r_2}$$

$$\therefore \quad T_{eA} = \frac{0.05\,K_t}{r_2} \text{ and } T_{eB} = \frac{s_B K_t}{4r_2}$$

$$\therefore \quad \frac{T_{eB}}{T_{eA}} = 1 = \frac{s_B K_t}{4r_2}\cdot\frac{r_2}{0.05K_t} = \frac{s_B}{0.2}$$

$$\therefore \quad s_B = 0.2$$

As $s_A = 0.05$, this shows

$$s_B = 4\,s_A$$

(b) From Eq. (6.29),

$$I_2 = \frac{sV}{r_2}$$

$$\therefore \quad I_{2A} = \frac{0.05\,V}{r_2} \text{ and } I_{2B} = \frac{0.2\,V}{4r_2}$$

$$\therefore \quad \frac{I_{2B}}{I_{2A}} = \frac{0.2\,V}{4r_2}\,\frac{r_2}{0.05\,V} = 1 \text{ or } I_{2B} = I_{2A}$$

Thus rotor current at $4r_2$ is the same as I_{2A} with rotor resistance r_2.

Rotor ohmic loss

$$= I_{2B}^2\,(4r_2) = (I_{2A}^2\;4r_2)$$

$$= 4\,(I_{2A}^2\;r_2) = 4 \text{ times the previous loss}$$

Rotor p.f.,

$$(\cos\theta)_B = \frac{4r_2}{\sqrt{(4r_2)^2+(s_B\,x_2)^2}} = \frac{4r_2}{\sqrt{(4r_2)^2+(4s_A\,x_2)^2}}$$

$$= \frac{r_2}{\sqrt{r_2^2+(s_A\,x_2)^2}} = (\cos\theta)_A$$

This shows that rotor p.f. at full-load torque remains unchanged as rotor resistance is changed from r_2 to $4r_2$.

(c)

$$\text{Speed } \omega_A = (1-s_A)\,\omega_s = 0.95\,\omega_s$$

Power output,

$$P_A = T_{eA}\,\omega_A = 0.95\,\omega_s\,T_{eA} \text{ or } \omega_s\,T_{eA} = P_A/0.95$$

Now

$$s_B = 0.20 \text{ and } \omega_B = (1-s_B)\,\omega_s = 0.80\,\omega_s$$

$$\therefore \quad P_B = T_{eB}\,\omega_B = T_{eA}\times 0.80\,\omega_s \qquad (\because T_{eA} = T_{eB})$$

$$= 0.80\,(\omega_s\,T_{eA}) = \frac{0.8P_A}{0.95} \text{ or } P_B = 0.842\,P_A$$

Thus power output with $4r_2$ is reduced from P_A to $0.842\,P_A$.

Example 6.21. *A 3-phase, 50 Hz, 6-pole induction motor has a shaft output of 10 kW at 930 r.p.m. Friction and windage loss amount to 1% of output. Total stator losses are 600 W.*

(a) Determine the rotor input and stator input.

(b) If maximum torque is developed at 800 r.p.m., compute the starting torque with rated-voltage starting.

Solution. *(a)*

$$\text{Full-load slip} = \frac{1000-930}{1000} = 0.07$$

$$\text{Friction and windage loss} = 10{,}000 \times \frac{1}{100} = 100 \text{ W}$$

Mechanical power developed, $P_m = 10{,}000 + 100 = 10{,}100$ W

∴ Rotor input, $P_g = P_m/(1-s) = 10100/0.93 = 10860.2$ W

$$\text{Stator input} = P_g + \text{total stator losses} = 10860.2 + 600 = 11460.2 \text{ W.}$$

(b)

$$s_{mT} = \frac{1000-800}{1000} = 0.20$$

$$T_{e\cdot fl} = \frac{P_g}{\omega_s} = \frac{10860.2 \times 60}{2\pi \times 1000} = 103.71 \text{ Nm}$$

or

$$\frac{T_{e\cdot fl}}{T_{em}} = \frac{2}{\dfrac{0.2}{0.07} + \dfrac{0.07}{0.2}} \quad \text{or } T_{em} = 1.604\, T_{efl}$$

$$\frac{T_{est}}{T_{em}} = \frac{2}{\dfrac{0.2}{1} + \dfrac{1}{0.2}} \quad \text{or } T_{est} = \frac{2}{5.2} \times 1.604 \times 103.71$$

∴ $T_{est} = 63.981$ Nm.

Example 6.22. *A 7.5 kW, 420-V, 3-phase, star-connected, 50 Hz, 4-pole squirrel cage induction motor develops full-load torque at a slip of 4% under rated voltage and frequency conditions. Friction, windage and core losses are to be neglected. The machine has the following impedance data :*

$$r_1 = 1.2\ \Omega,\ x_1 = x_2 = 1.4\ \Omega,\ X_m = 38.6\ \Omega$$

Determine the maximum torque at rated voltage and frequency and the slip at which it occurs. Also calculate the starting torque.

Solution. Thevenin's equivalent circuit parameters, from Eqs. (6.22) and (6.23), are as under :

$$R_e = \frac{1.2 \times 38.6}{38.6 + 1.40} = 1.158\ \Omega, \quad X_e = \frac{1.4 \times 38.6}{40} = 1.351\ \Omega$$

$$V_e = \frac{420}{\sqrt{3}} \times \frac{38.6}{40} = 234.0 \text{ V}$$

As friction, windage and core losses are neglected, the mechanical power developed,

$$P_m = 7500 \text{ W}$$

Now

$$P_m = 3\,(1-s)\,P_g = 3\,(1-s)\,\frac{I_2^2 r_2}{s}$$

From Eq. (6.29),

$$I_2 = \frac{sV_e}{r_2}$$

∴

$$P_m = 3\,(1-s)\,\frac{s^2 V_e^2}{r_2^2}\cdot\frac{r_2}{s} \quad \text{or } 7500 = 3\,(1-s)\,\frac{sV_e^2}{r_2}$$

or

$$r_2 = \frac{3(0.96)(0.04)(234)^2}{7500} = 0.841\ \Omega$$

The slip at which maximum torque occurs is given by Eq. (6.26) as

$$s_{mT} = \frac{0.841}{\sqrt{1.158^2 + (1.351 + 1.4)^2}} = 0.282$$

From Eq. (6.27), $$T_{em} = \frac{3 \times 234^2}{50\,\pi} \cdot \frac{1}{2}\left[\frac{1}{1.158 + \sqrt{1.158^2 + 2.751^2}}\right] = 126.21 \text{ Nm.}$$

From Eq. (6.28), $$T_{est} = \frac{3 \times 234^2}{50\,\pi} \cdot \frac{0.841}{1.999^2 + 2.751^2} = 76.05 \text{ Nm.}$$

Example 6.23. *A 100 kW, 3-phase, 420 V, 6-pole, 50 Hz wound-rotor induction motor, with its rotor winding short circuited, has a full-load slip of 0.04 and the slip at maximum torque of 0.2 when operating at rated voltage and frequency. Neglect stator resistance and rotational losses. Find (a) maximum torque, (b) starting torque and (c) full-load rotor ohmic loss.*

The rotor resistance is now doubled by adding external series resistance. Determine (d) slip at full-load output (e) full-load torque (f) slip at maximum torque.

Solution. *(a)* As rotational losses are neglected, 100 kW is the mechanical power developed.

Therefore, $$P_m = 100 \text{ kW}$$

$$P_g = P_m/(1 - s_{fl}) = \frac{100}{0.96} \text{ kW}$$

Synchronous speed, $$\omega_s = \frac{4\pi f}{P} = \frac{4\pi \times 50}{6} = \frac{100\,\pi}{3} \text{ rad/sec}$$

$\therefore$ $$T_{efl} = \frac{P_g}{\omega_s} = \frac{100{,}000 \times 3}{0.96 \times 100\,\pi} = 994.72 \text{ Nm}$$

$$\frac{T_{efl}}{T_{em}} = \frac{2}{\frac{0.2}{0.04} + \frac{0.04}{0.2}}$$

or $$T_{em} = 2.6\, T_{efl} = 2.6 \times 994.72 = 2586.272 \text{ Nm.}$$

(b) $$\frac{T_{est}}{T_{em}} = \frac{2}{\frac{1}{0.2} + \frac{0.2}{1}} = \frac{2}{5.2}$$

$\therefore$ $$T_{est} = \frac{2}{5.2} \times 2586.272 = 994.72 \text{ Nm.}$$

(c) $$\text{Rotor ohmic loss} = s\,P_g = 0.04 \times \frac{100}{0.96} = 4.167 \text{ kW.}$$

(d) From Eq. (6.30 *a*), $$T_e = \frac{s}{r_2} \cdot \frac{3V^2}{\omega_s}$$

$\therefore$ Full load output is $$T_e \cdot \omega_r = \frac{s}{r_2} \cdot \frac{3V^2}{\omega_s} [\omega_r (1 - s)] = \frac{3V^2 \cdot s}{r_2} (1 - s)$$

$\therefore$ $$T_e \cdot \omega_r = \frac{3V^2 \cdot s}{r_2} (1 - s) = \frac{3V^2 \times 0.04 \times 0.96}{r_2} \quad ...(i)$$

With rotor resistance doubled, full-load output is $\frac{3V^2 s_1}{2r_2} (1 - s_1)$ ...*(ii)*

From *(i)* and *(ii)*, for the same full-load output,

$$\frac{3V^2}{r_2} \times 0.04 \times 0.96 = \frac{3V^2}{2r_2} s_1 (1 - s_1) \text{ or } s_1^2 - s_1 + 0.0768 = 0$$

Its solution gives $s_1 = 0.0888$

(e) $$T_{efl} = \frac{100{,}000 \times 3}{(1 - 0.0838) \times 100\,\pi} = 1042.27 \text{ Nm.}$$

(*f*) With rotor resistance r_2, $s_{mT} = \frac{r_2}{X} = 0.2$

With rotor resistance $2r_2$, $s_{mT1} = \frac{2r_2}{X} = 2 \times 0.2 = 0.4.$

Example 6.24. *The rotor of a 3-phase slip-ring induction motor is rewound with twice as many turns of conductors having half of the cross-sectional area of copper. The arrangement and space factor of the old and new windings are the same. Discuss the effect of this change on different parameters, characteristics and performance of the motor. Neglect stator impedance.*

Solution. Rotor resistance, $r_2 = \frac{\rho L}{A}$

With new winding, $r_2' = \frac{\rho(2L)}{\frac{A}{2}} = \frac{4\rho L}{A} = 4r_2$

Leakage reactance $\propto$ (Number of turns)^2

$\therefore \quad x_2 \propto N_{ph}^2$

With new winding, $x_2' \propto (2N_{Ph})^2$

$\therefore \quad \frac{x_2'}{x_2} = 4 \text{ or } x_2' = 4x_2$

Slip at which maximum torque occurs,

$$s_{mT} = \frac{r_2}{x_2}$$

With new winding, $s_{mT1} = \frac{4r_2}{4x_2} = s_{mT}$

Thus, the slip at which maximum torque occurs remains unchanged.

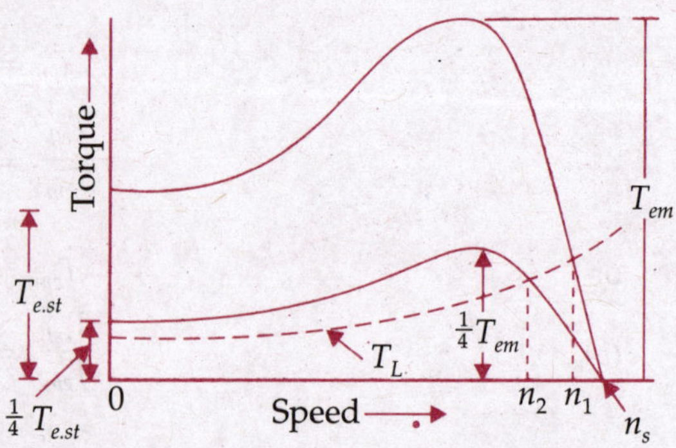

Fig 6.21: Pertaining to Example 6.24.

Starting current, $I_{2 \cdot st} = \frac{V}{\sqrt{r_2^2 + x_2^2}}$

Starting current with new winding,

$$I_{2st}' = \frac{V}{4\sqrt{r_2^2 + x_2^2}} = \frac{I_{2st}}{4}$$

Starting torque, $T_{est} = I_{2st}^2 \, r_2$

With new winding, $T_{est}' = (I_{2st}/4)^2 \times 4r_2 = \frac{1}{4} T_{est}$

From Eq. (6.27), maximum torque,

$$T_{em} = \frac{3V^2}{\omega_s} \cdot \frac{1}{2x_2}$$

With new winding $T_{em}' = \frac{3V^2}{\omega_s} \cdot \frac{1}{2(4x_2)} = \frac{1}{4} T_{em}$

It is seen from above that starting and maximum torques are reduced to 25% of their previous values. For load torque profile T_L as shown in Fig. 6.21, the operating speed drops from n_1 to n_2. The motor would now have reduced efficiency. The motor rating is now reduced to about 25% of its previous rating.

Example 6.25. *A 3-phase, 10 pole, 50 Hz wound-rotor induction motor is to be used as a frequency converter. This induction motor is driven by an adjustable-speed D.C. motor. The output power taken from the rotor slip rings is 48 kW at 0.8 power factor lagging and it remains constant over the output frequency range of 120 to 300 Hz. If all the machine losses, leakage impedance drops and exciting currents are neglected, then calculate*

(a) speed range of D.C. motor,

(b) kVA rating of the induction-motor stator,

(c) the D.C. motor rating and its maximum torque output.

If maximum speed is limited to 2700 r.p.m., then compute

(d) the number of poles for the induction machine and

(e) the new speed range of the D.C. motor.

Solution. *(a)* Speed of the stator field $= \dfrac{120\,f}{P} = \dfrac{120 \times 50}{10} = 600$ r.p.m.

For obtaining rotor frequencies greater than the stator frequency, the rotor should preferably be driven against the direction of stator field. Hence, if rotor speed is N_r r.p.m., then relative speed between stator field and rotor conductors is $(600 + N_r)$ r.p.m. In view of this, the rotor frequency as per Eq. (6.4 *a*) is given by

$$\frac{P\,(600 + N_r)}{120} = f_2$$

For $f_2 = 120$ Hz,

$$\frac{10\,(600 + N_r)}{120} = 120 \text{ Hz},$$

$\therefore$ $N_r = 840$ r.p.m.

For $f_2 = 300$ Hz,

$$\frac{10\,(600 + N_r)}{120} = 300 \text{ Hz}$$

$\therefore$ $N_r = 3000$ r.p.m.

Therefore, D.C. motor speed range is from 840 to 3000 r.p.m.

(b) and *(c)*. At standstill, let the rotor per phase voltage be V_2 and rotor output current as a frequency converter be I_2. Since leakage impedance drops, exciting current and all losses are neglected, per phase electrical output $V_2 I_2$ from the rotor is equal to the per phase electrical input from stator to rotor, *i.e.*, stator volt-amperes per phase $V_1 I_1$ = rotor voltamperes per phase $V_2 I_2$, just like a transformer. As the rotor starts rotating, its per phase voltage becomes sV_2 and its per phase output in volt-amperes becomes $sV_2 I_2$.

In the frequency converter, slip s is greater than 1, therefore, $sV_2 I_2$ is greater than the volt-amperes $V_1 I_1$ supplied by stator. Naturally the rest of power $(sV_2 I_2 - V_1 I_1) \cos\theta$ must be supplied by the D.C. motor.

$\therefore$ Power handled by D.C. motor $= (sV_2 I_2 - V_1 I_1) \cos\theta = (s - 1)\, V_1 I_1 \cos\theta$ watts

$$[\because V_2 I_2 = V_1 I_1]$$

This shows that electrical power output from rotor slip rings is supplied in two ways, namely :

(i) electrically, from stator to rotor by transformer action and

(ii) mechanically, from the D.C. motor shaft.

For $$N_r = 840 \text{ r.p.m.},$$

$$\text{slip } s_1 = \frac{840 + 600}{600} = 2.4$$

and for $N_r = 3000$ r.p.m., $$\text{slip } s_2 = \frac{3000 + 600}{600} = 6.0$$

Rotor kVA output, $$3sV_1I_1 = \frac{48}{0.8} = 60 \text{ kVA}$$

$\therefore$ Stator kVA rating, $$3V_1I_1 = \frac{60}{s} = \frac{60}{2.4} \text{ or } \frac{60}{6.0} \text{ kVA} = 25 \text{ kVA or } 10 \text{ kVA}.$$

Since the stator should be able to handle higher kVA, the stator kVA rating is 25 kVA.

$$\text{D.C. motor rating} = (s - 1)\, V_1\, I_1 \cos\theta = (2.4 - 1)\, 25 \times 0.8 \text{ kW}$$
$$= (6 - 1)\, 10 \times 0.8 \text{ kW} = 28 \text{ kW or } 40 \text{ kW}.$$

$\therefore$ D.C. motor rating is 40 kW.

$$\text{D.C. motor output torque} = \frac{28{,}000 \times 60}{2\pi \times 840} \text{ or } \frac{40{,}000 \times 60}{2\pi \times 3000} = 318.3 \text{ Nm or } 127.3 \text{ Nm}.$$

$\therefore$ Maximum torque output from D.C. motor is 318.3 Nm.

(d) When the maximum speed is limited to 2700 r.p.m., then let the number of induction machine poles may be P_1. Then speed of stator field $= \dfrac{120 \times 50}{P_1}$ r.p.m.

Relative speed between stator field and rotor conductors is $\left(\dfrac{120 \times 50}{P_1} + 2700\right)$ r.p.m.

From Eq. (6.4 *a*), $$\frac{P_1\left(\dfrac{1200 \times 50}{P_1} + 2700\right)}{120} = 300 \text{ Hz}.$$

$$\therefore \quad P_1 = \frac{30{,}000}{2700} = 11\frac{1}{9}$$

But P_1 can't be a fraction, therefore, P_1 must be 12 (a higher even number).

(e) Maximum speed of D.C. motor $$= \frac{12\left(\dfrac{120 \times 50}{12} + N_{r1}\right)}{120} = 300$$

$$\therefore \quad N_{r1} = 2500 \text{ r.p.m.}$$

Minimum speed of D.C. motor $$= \frac{12\left(\dfrac{120 \times 50}{12} + N_{r2}\right)}{120} = 120 \text{ or } N_{r2} = 700 \text{ r.p.m.}$$

Therefore, new speed range of D.C. motor is from 700 to 2500 r.p.m. Note that the ratio of maximum to minimum speed is same $\left(\dfrac{3000}{840} = \dfrac{2500}{700}\right)$ in both the cases.

Example 6.26. *A 3-phase, 50 Hz, 4-pole induction motor has rated output of 10 kW at 1425 r.p.m. and maximum torque is developed at 1200 r.p.m. Calculate the starting torque. Neglect stator resistance and mechanical losses.*

Solution. Slip, $$s = \frac{1500 - 1425}{1500} = 0.05$$

Power output = 10,000 W = power developed, P_m as the mechanical losses are neglected.

$\therefore$ Electromagnetic torque, $$T_e = \frac{P_m}{\omega_s(1-s)}$$

$\therefore$ $$T_{efl} = \frac{10{,}000 \times 60}{2\pi \times 1500\,(1-0.05)} = 67.013 \text{ Nm}$$

Slip at which maximum torque occurs is given by

$$s_{mT} = \frac{1500-1200}{1500} = 0.2$$

Taking s as full-load slip, $$\frac{T_{efl}}{T_{e\cdot m}} = \frac{67.013}{T_{e.m}} = \frac{2}{\frac{0.05}{0.2}+\frac{0.2}{0.05}} \text{ or } T_{e\cdot m} = 142.403 \text{ Nm}$$

For obtaining starting torque, use the relation

$$\frac{T_{e.st}}{T_{e.m}} = \frac{2}{\frac{1}{s_{mT}}+\frac{s_{mT}}{1}} = \frac{2}{\frac{1}{0.2}+\frac{0.2}{1}} = 0.3846$$

$\therefore$ $$T_{e\cdot st} = 0.3846 \times 142.403 = 54.7682 \text{ Nm.}$$

Example 6.27. *An induction motor runs at a slip frequency of 2 Hz when supplied from a 3-phase, 400 V, 50 Hz supply. For the same developed torque, find the slip frequency at which it will run when supplied from a 3-phase 340 V, 40 Hz system. Slip at which the machine develops maximum torque using 50 Hz supply is 0.1. Neglect the stator impedance and assume linear torque-slip characteristic between zero torque and maximum torque in the working region.* (GATE, 1992)

Solution. With stator impedance ignored, the maximum torque in a 3-phase induction motor, from Eq. (6.27), is given by $$T_{em} = \frac{3}{\omega_s}\cdot\frac{V^2}{2x_2}$$

For 400 V supply, $$s_{mT} = 0.1$$

When $f = 50$ Hz, $$\frac{r_2}{X_2} = s_{mT} = 0.1\ \alpha\ \frac{r_2}{50}$$

For $f = 40$ Hz, $$s_{mT1} \propto \frac{r_2}{40}$$. From these relations

$$s_{mT1} = \frac{50}{40} \times 0.1 = 0.125$$

Maximum torque, $$T_{e\cdot m} = \frac{3}{\omega_s}\cdot\frac{V^2}{2x_2} = \frac{3P}{4\pi f}\cdot\frac{V^2}{2(2\pi f l_2)} \text{ or } T_{em} \propto V^2/f^2$$

As torque-slip characteristic is linear between zero torque and maximum torque, the developed torque T_{ed} at a slip of 0.04 is

$$T_{ed} = \frac{T_{e.m}}{s_{mT}} \times 0.04 \propto \left(\frac{400}{50}\right)^2 \times \frac{0.04}{0.1} \qquad \text{...(i)}$$

For 340 V, 40 Hz, $$T_{ed} \propto \left(\frac{340}{40}\right)^2 \times \frac{s}{0.125} \qquad \text{...(ii)}$$

For the same developed torque, from *(i)* and *(ii)*,

$$\left(\frac{400}{50}\right)^2 \times \frac{0.04}{0.1} = \left(\frac{340}{40}\right)^2 \times \frac{s}{0.125}$$

$\therefore$ New value of slip, $$s = 0.0443$$

Slip frequency $$sf = 0.0443 \times 40 = 1.772 \text{ Hz.}$$

Example 6.28. *A 50 Hz, 440 V, three-phase, 4-pole induction motor develops half the rated torque at 1490 r.p.m. With the applied voltage magnitude remaining at the rated value, what should be its frequency if the motor has to develop the same torque at 1600 r.p.m.? Neglect stator and rotor winding resistances, leakage reactances and iron losses.* *(GATE, 1995)*

Solution. Slip,
$$s = \frac{1500 - 1490}{1500} = \frac{1}{150}. \text{ From Eq. (6.24 } b\text{)},$$

$$T_e = \frac{3}{\omega_s} \cdot \frac{V^2}{\left(\frac{r_2}{s} + r_1\right)^2 + (x_1 + x_2)^2} \cdot \frac{r_2}{s}$$

With the neglect of resistances and leakage reactances,
$$T_e \propto \frac{3}{f} \cdot \frac{V^2}{r_2} \cdot s$$

$$\therefore \qquad T_e \propto \frac{3}{50} \cdot \frac{(440)^2}{r_2} \cdot \frac{1}{150} \qquad ...(i)$$

Also
$$T_e \propto \frac{3}{f} \cdot \frac{(440)^2}{r_2} \cdot s \qquad ...(ii)$$

For the same torque, from *(i)* and *(ii)*, we get
$$\frac{3}{f} \cdot \frac{(440)^2}{r_2} \cdot s = \frac{3}{50} \cdot \frac{(440)^2}{r^2} \cdot \frac{1}{150} \text{ or } \frac{s}{f} = \frac{1}{7500} \qquad ...(iii)$$

Synchronous speed,
$$N_s = \frac{120 f}{4} = 30 f$$

and
$$\text{slip, } s = \frac{30 f - 1600}{30f}$$

Substituting the value of s in *(iii)* above,
$$\left(\frac{30f - 1600}{30 f}\right) \frac{1}{f} = \frac{1}{7500}$$

$$f^2 - 7500 f - 400{,}000 = 0$$

Its solution gives $f = 53.7$ Hz.

Example 6.29. *The following data refers to a 12-pole, 420 V, 50 Hz, 3-phase mesh connected induction motor :*

$r_1 = 2.95\ \Omega$, $x_1 = 6.82\ \Omega$, $r_2' = 2.08\ \Omega$, $x_2' = 4.11$ *per phase.*

On no load, the line value of magnetizing current is 6.7 A and the total core loss is 269 W. Determine the p.f., input current, equivalent rotor current and torque developed by the motor at a slip of 3% using exact equivalent circuit. Determine the maximum torque developed and the corresponding speed. *(I.A.S., 1989)*

Solution. The equivalent circuit on no load is as shown in Fig. 6.22 *(a)*.

Per-phase magnetizing current,
$$I_m = \frac{6.7}{\sqrt{3}} = 3.87 \text{ A}$$

Here
$$V_1 = E_1 + I_m (r_1 + jx_1)$$

I_m lags E_1 by 90° and with E_1 as reference,
$$V_1 = E_1 - j\,3.87\,(2.95 + j\,6.82) = E_1 - j\,11.417 + 26.4$$

or
$$V_1^2 = (E_1 + 26.4)^2 + 11.417^2$$

or $$420^2 = E_1^2 + 52.8\,E_1 + 697 + 130.35$$

or $$E_1^2 + 52.8\,E_1 - 175572.65 = 0$$

Its solution gives $$E_1 = 393.45\ V$$

$\therefore$ Magnetizing reactance, $$X_m = \frac{393.45}{3.87} = 101.67\ \Omega$$

The exact equivalent circuit, referred to stator, is now shown in Fig. 6.22 (*b*).

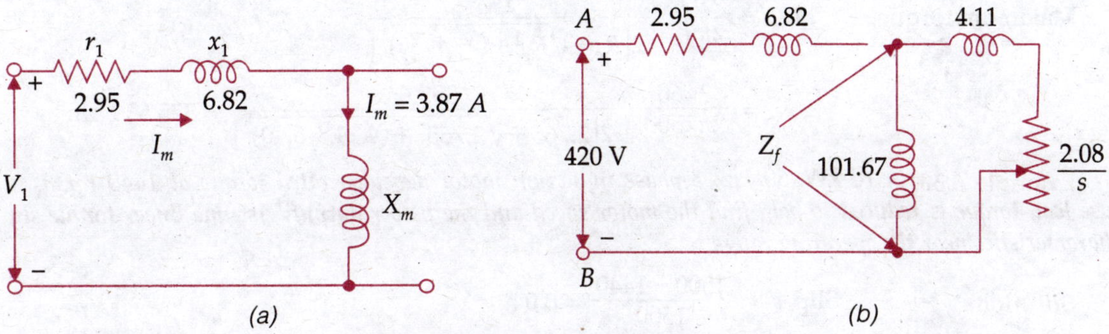

Fig 6.22: Pertaining to Example 6.29.

From this circuit, $$Z_f = \frac{\left(\frac{2.08}{0.03} + j4.11\right)(j101.67)}{(69.33 + j105.78)}$$

$$= \frac{69.452\angle 3.4^\circ \times 101.67\angle 90^\circ}{126.484\angle 56.761^\circ} = 55.83\ \angle 36.64^\circ$$

or $$R_f + jX_f = 44.80 + j\,33.32,$$

$$r_1 + jx_1 = 2.95 + j6.82$$

$$Z_{AB} = 47.75 + j40.14 = 62.38\ \angle 40.05^\circ$$

Input current, $$I_1 = \frac{420\angle 0^\circ}{62.38\angle 40.05} = 6.733\ \angle -40.05^\circ$$

$$p.f. = \cos 40.05^\circ = 0.765 \text{ lag}$$

Equivalent rotor current, $$I_2 = I_1 \frac{jX_m}{\frac{r_2}{s} + j(x_2 + X_m)}$$

$$= 6.733\ \angle -40.05 \times \frac{j101.68}{69.33 + j105.78}$$

$$= 6.733\ \angle -40.05 \times \frac{101.68\angle 90^\circ}{126.484\angle 56.761^\circ} = 5.413\ \angle -6.811^\circ$$

$$\text{Torque} = 3\frac{I_1^2 R_f}{\omega_s} = \frac{3 \times 60}{2\pi \times 500} \times (6.733)^2 \times 44.80 = 116.364 \text{ Nm}$$

Maximum torque can easily be obtained through the use of Thevenin's equivalent circuit,

$$X_1 = x_1 + X_m = 6.82 + 101.67 = 108.49\ \Omega$$

$\therefore$ $$R_e = \frac{r_1 X_m}{X_1} = \frac{2.95 \times 101.67}{108.49} = 2.765\ \Omega$$

$$X_e = \frac{x_1 \cdot X_m}{X_1} = \frac{6.82 \times 101.67}{108.49} = 6.40\ \Omega$$

From Eq. (6.26), slip at which maximum torque occurs,

$$s_{mT} = \frac{r_2}{\sqrt{R_e^2+(x_2+X_e)^2}} = \frac{2.08}{[2.765^2+(4.11+6.40)^2]^{1/2}} = 0.1914$$

Speed at maximum torque = 500 (1 – 0.1914) = 404.3 r.p.m.

From Eq. (6.27),

Maximum torque, $$T_{em} = \frac{3V_e^2}{2\pi n_s}\cdot\frac{1}{2\left[R_e+\sqrt{R_e^2+(x_2+X_e)^2}\right]}$$

$$= \frac{3\times 60}{2\pi\times 500}\cdot\frac{393.6^2}{2\left[2.765+\sqrt{2.765^2+(4.11+6.40)^2}\right]} = 325.55 \text{ Nm.}$$

Example 6.30. *A 10 kW, 50 Hz, 3-phase induction motor develops rated torque at 1440 r.p.m. In case load torque is reduced to half, find the motor speed and the power output. Assume linear torque-slip characteristics near the operating range.*

Solution. Slip, $s = \frac{1500-1440}{1500} = 0.04$

For linear torque-slip characteristics, from Eq. (6.30 *a*),

$$T_e = \frac{3V^2}{\omega_s}\cdot\frac{s}{r_2}$$

As V, ω_s and r_2 are constant, $T_e \propto 0.04$ and $\frac{1}{2}T_e \propto s_1$

$$\therefore \quad \frac{\frac{1}{2}T_e}{T_e} = \frac{s_1}{0.04} \text{ or } s_1 = \frac{1}{2}\times 0.04 = 0.02$$

New motor speed = 1500 (1 – 0.02) = 1470 r.p.m.

Rated torque $= \frac{10{,}000\times 60}{2\pi\times 1440}$ Nm

Power output at half of rated torque $= \frac{1}{2}\cdot\frac{10{,}000\times 60}{2\pi\times 1440}\times\frac{2\pi\times 1470}{60} = 5.104$ kW.

Example 6.31. *A 3-phase, 1455 r.p.m. induction motor drives a load requiring constant torque. In case supply voltage drops to 90%, find what happens to motor speed and losses. Take linear torque-slip characteristic over the working range.*

Solution. Slip $s_1 = \frac{1500-1455}{1500} = 0.03$

From Eq. (6.30 *a*), $$T_e = \frac{3V^2}{\omega_s}\cdot\frac{s}{r_2}$$

For the same load torque, $$T_e = \frac{3V^2}{\omega_s}\cdot\frac{0.03}{r_2} = \frac{3(0.9V)^2}{\omega_s}\cdot\frac{s_2}{r_2}$$

$$\therefore \quad s_2 = \frac{0.03}{0.81} = 0.037$$

Motor speed = 1500 (1 – 0.037) = 1444.5 r.p.m.

At small values of slips, rotor current from Eq. (6.29) is

$$I_{21} = \frac{s_1 V}{r_2} = \frac{0.03V}{r_2}$$

$$\text{Rotor current with reduced voltage, } I_{22} = \frac{s_2(0.9V)}{r_2} = \frac{0.037(0.9V)}{r_2}$$

$$\therefore \quad \frac{I_{22}}{I_{21}} = \frac{0.037(0.9V)}{0.03V} = 1.11$$

$$\frac{\text{Ohmic loss with reduced voltage}}{\text{Ohmic loss with normal voltage}} = \left(\frac{I_{22}}{I_{21}}\right)^2 = (1.11)^2 = 1.2321$$

$$\text{Percentage reduction in speed} = \frac{1455 - 1444.5}{1455} = 0.722\%$$

$$\text{Percentage increase in ohmic loss} = \frac{1.2321 - 1}{1} \times 100 = 23.21\%$$

This example demonstrates that reduction in supply voltage does not materially affect the motor speed but increases the losses and therefore the temperature rise noticeably under the condition of constant load torque.

Example 6.32. *A 7.5 kW, 400 V, 3-phase, 50 Hz, 6-pole squirrel-cage induction motor operates at 4% slip at full load when rated voltage and frequency is applied. Assume a linear relationship between torque and slip in the operating region, calculate the no-load speed of the motor when the supply voltage is reduced to half its rated value. The no-load torque is 6 Nm.* (I.A.S., 1988)

Solution. When torque-slip relation is linear, from Eq. (6.30 *a*),

$$T_e \propto \frac{sV^2}{\omega_s \cdot r_2}$$

$$\text{Full-load torque,} \quad T_{e\,fl} = \frac{7500 \times 60}{2\pi \times 1000 \times 0.96} = 74.604 \text{ Nm}$$

$$\therefore \quad 74.604 \propto \frac{0.04 \times 400^2}{\omega_s \cdot r_2} \text{ and } 6 \propto \frac{s \times 200^2}{\omega_s \cdot r_2}$$

$$\text{or} \quad \frac{6}{74.604} = \frac{s \times 200^2}{0.04 \times 400^2}$$

$$\text{or} \quad s = 0.04 \times 6 \times \left(\frac{400}{200}\right)^2 \times \frac{1}{74.604} = 0.01287$$

$\therefore$ No-load speed of the motor = 1000 (1 – 0.01287) = 987.13 r.p.m.

Example 6.33. *A 6-pole, 50 Hz, 3-phase wound rotor induction motor has its maximum torque of 250 percent of full-load torque at 18 percent slip. The rotor resistance per phase is 1.0 Ω at 50 Hz. The input supply voltage is subject to large fluctuations. Determine the minimum voltage that could be impressed so that the motor can still supply its rated torque.*

Also determine the resistance to be inserted in the rotor circuit so that the motor will develop full-load torque at starting at this reduced voltage.

Assume that the magnetic circuit is unsaturated.

Solution. $T_{em} = 2.5\, T_{efl},\ s_{mT} = 0.18$

$$\text{Also} \quad s_{mT} = \frac{r_2}{x_2} = 0.18, \therefore x_2 = \frac{1.0}{0.18} = 5.55\ \Omega$$

$$\frac{T_{e.fl}}{T_{em}} = \frac{1}{2.5} = \frac{2}{\dfrac{0.18}{s} + \dfrac{s}{0.18}} = \frac{0.36s}{s^2 + 0.0324}$$

where s = full-load slip. $\therefore\ s^2 - 0.9\,s + 0.0324 = 0$

Its solution gives $s = 0.0376$

$$T_{e.fl} = \frac{3}{\omega_s} \cdot \frac{V_2}{\left(\frac{1.0}{0.0376}\right)^2 + 5.5^2} \times \frac{1}{0.0376} = \frac{3}{\omega_s} \cdot \frac{V^2}{27.754}$$

Let the minimum voltage be x V where $x < 1$. The motor can continue supplying its rated torque until $T_{em} = \frac{3}{\omega_s} \cdot \frac{V^2}{2x_2}$, at reduced voltage $= T_{e \cdot fl}$.

$$\therefore \quad \frac{3}{\omega_s} \cdot \frac{(xV)^2}{2 \times 5.55} = \frac{3}{\omega_s} \cdot \frac{V^2}{27.754} \text{ or } x = \sqrt{\frac{11.1}{27.754}} = 0.6324 \text{ or } 63.24\%$$

Let R be the external resistance inserted in the rotor circuit. It is given that starting torque at reduced voltage $= T_{e \cdot fl}$

$$\therefore \quad \frac{3}{\omega_s} \cdot \frac{(0.6324V)^2}{(R+1)^2 + 5.55^2} \times (R+1) = \frac{3}{\omega_s} \cdot \frac{V^2}{27.754}$$

or $\quad 11.1\,(R + 1) = R^2 + 2R + 1 + 30.80$ or $R^2 - 9.1\,R + 20.7 = 0$

Its solution gives $R = 4.55\ \Omega$.

$\therefore$ External resistance required in the rotor circuit = 4.55 Ω.

Example 6.34. *A 3-phase induction motor is designed to operate on 50 Hz and V_1 volts. In case the motor is fed from 40 Hz. 0.9 V_1 voltage source, find the ratio of 50 Hz to 40 Hz operation for the starting currents, starting torques and maximum torques.*

Also find the ratio of V_2 at 40 Hz to V_1 at 50 Hz for the same starting and maximum torques.

Neglect stator impedance and rotor resistance.

Solution. For x_2 at 50 Hz, rotor leakage reactance x_2' at 40 Hz is given by $x_2' = 0.8\,x_2$.

From Eq. (6.24 *a*), with stator impedance and r_2 neglected, we get $I_{2st} = \frac{V_1}{x_2}$.

$$\frac{\text{Starting current at 50 Hz}}{\text{Starting current at 40 Hz}} = \frac{V_1}{x_2} \cdot \frac{0.8x_2}{0.9V_1} = \frac{0.8}{0.9} = 0.889$$

From Eq. (6.24 *b*), with stator impedance and r_2 neglected, we get

$$T_{est} \propto \frac{3}{\omega_s} \cdot \frac{V_1^2}{x_2^2} \text{ or } T_{est} \propto \frac{3}{f} \cdot \frac{V_1^2}{x_2^2}$$

$$\frac{\text{Starting current at 50 Hz}}{\text{Starting current at 40 Hz}} = \frac{3}{50} \cdot \frac{V_1^2}{x_2^2} \cdot \frac{40}{3} \cdot \frac{(0.8x_2)^2}{(0.9V_1)^2} = 0.8\left(\frac{0.8}{0.9}\right)^2 = 0.6321$$

From Eq. (6.27), with stator impedance and r_2 neglected, we get

$$T_{em} = \frac{3}{\omega_s} \cdot \frac{V_1^2}{2x_2} \text{ or } T_{em} \propto \frac{3}{f} \cdot \frac{V_1^2}{2x_2}$$

$$\frac{\text{Maximum torque at 50Hz}}{\text{Maximum torque at 40Hz}} = \frac{3}{50} \cdot \frac{V_1^2}{2 \cdot x_2^2} \cdot \frac{40}{3} \times \frac{2 \times 0.8\,x_2}{(0.9V_1)^2} = \left(\frac{0.8}{0.9}\right)^2 = 0.790$$

For the same starting torque,

$$\frac{3}{40} \cdot \frac{V_2^2}{(0.8x_2)^2} = \frac{3}{50} \cdot \frac{V_1^2}{(x_2)^2} \text{ or } \frac{V_2}{V_1} = \sqrt{\frac{40}{50} \times (0.8)^2} = 0.755$$

For the same maximum torque

$$\frac{3}{40} \cdot \frac{V_2^2}{2(0.8x_2)} = \frac{3}{50} \cdot \frac{V_1^2}{2x_2} \text{ or } \frac{V_2}{V_1} = \sqrt{(0.8)(0.8)} = 0.8.$$

Example 6.35. *A 3-phase, 4-pole, 60 kW, 50 Hz induction motor connected to rated supply voltage and running without load consumes 3 kW. When prevented from rotating it draws rated current at 30% rated supply and takes a power input of 4 kW. Assuming that under rated load conditions, the stator and rotor copper losses are equal and that the mechanical losses are 30% of the no-load losses, determine (a) slip at rated load and (b) starting torque of the motor with rated applied voltage.* (I.A.S., 1991)

Solution. Mechanical loss $= \frac{30}{100} \times 3000 = 900$ W

Stator core loss = Power input at no-load – mechanical loss – stator I^2R loss at no load

Neglecting stator I^2R loss at no load,

stator core loss = 3000 – 900 = 2100 W

Power input during blocked rotor test (for 30% of V_1, with stator core loss neglected)

= stator I^2R loss + Rotor I^2R loss = 4000 W = 4 kW

$$\therefore \quad \text{Stator } I^2R \text{ loss} = \text{Rotor } I^2R \text{ loss} = \frac{4000}{2} = 2000 \text{ W} = 2 \text{ kW}$$

(*a*) At rated load, air-gap power, P_g = Output power + mechanical loss + rotor I^2R loss

$\therefore$ P_g = 60,000 + 900 + 2000 = 62900 W

But rotor I^2R loss $= 2000 \text{ W} = s \cdot P_g$

$\therefore$ Slip at rated load, $s = \frac{2000}{62900} = \mathbf{0.0318}$

(*b*) At rated voltage, power input to motor during blocked rotor test

$$= 4 \times \left(\frac{100}{30}\right)^2 = \mathbf{44.444 \text{ kW}}$$

Air-gap power, P_g = Power input – stator core loss – stator I^2R loss

= 44444 – 2100 – 2000 = 40344 Watt

Synchronous speed, $\omega_s = \frac{4\pi f}{P} = \frac{4\pi \times 50}{4} = 50\,\pi$ rad/s

$$\therefore \quad \text{Starting torque} = \frac{P_g}{\omega_s} = \frac{40344}{50\pi} = \mathbf{256.84 \text{ Nm.}}$$

Example 6.36. *A 3-phase induction motor is designed to operate at 50 Hz and V_1 volts. Its breakdown torque occurs at a slip of 0.2 and its stator impedance is negligible. In case the motor is made to operate from V_1 volts, 45 Hz, find the ratio of starting current, starting torque and maximum torque at 45 Hz operation to their corresponding values at 50 Hz operation.*

Solution. $s_{mT} = \frac{r_2}{x_2} = 0.2$

At 50 Hz, leakage reactance of rotor = x_2

At 45 Hz, leakage reactance of rotor = 0.9 x_2

Subscripts 1 and 2 are used for V_1, 50 Hz operation and V_1, 45 Hz operation respectively.

Starting currents : $I_{st1} = \frac{V_1}{\sqrt{r_2^2 + x_2^2}}$ and $I_{st2} = \frac{V_1}{\sqrt{r_2^2 + (0.9\,x_2)^2}}$

$$\therefore \quad \frac{I_{st2}}{I_{st1}} = \sqrt{\frac{r_2^2 + x_2^2}{r_2^2 + (0.9x_2)^2}} = \sqrt{\frac{s_{mT}^2 + 1}{s_{mT}^2 + 0.9^2}} = \sqrt{\frac{0.2 + 1}{0.2^2 + 0.81}} = 1.1061$$

Starting currents : $$\frac{T_{st.2}}{T_{st.1}} = \frac{V_1^2 \cdot r_2}{r_2^2 + (0.9x_2)^2} \cdot \frac{r_2^2 + x_2^2}{V_1^2 r_2} = \frac{s_{mT}^2 + 1}{s_{mT}^2 + (0.9)^2} = \frac{0.2^2 + 1}{0.2^2 + 0.81} = 1.2235.$$

Maximum torques: With stator impedance neglected,

maximum torque, from Eq. (6.27), is $T_{em} = \dfrac{3}{\omega_s} \cdot \dfrac{V_1^2}{2x_2}$

$$\therefore \qquad \frac{T_{m2}}{T_{m1}} = \frac{3}{\omega_s} \cdot \frac{V_1^2}{2(0.9x_2)} \cdot \frac{\omega_s}{3} \frac{2 \cdot x_2}{V_1^2} = \frac{1}{0.9} = 1.111.$$

Example 6.37. *A 20 kw, 400 V, 3-phase, 50-Hz, Y-connected, 4-pole squirrel-cage induction motor has the following parameters in ohms referred to stator :*

$r_1 = 0.2,\ x_1 = x_2 = 0.45,\ X_m = 18$

When this motor is energised at rated voltage and frequency, it develops full-load internal torque at a slip of 0.04. Mechanical losses are neglected. Calculate

(a) maximum internal torque and internal starting torque at rated voltage and frequency and

(b) slip at maximum torque.

Solution. Here mechanical losses are neglected, therefore power output 20 kW = mechanical power developed, P_m.

$$\therefore \qquad P_m = 20{,}000 \text{ W at a slip of } s = 0.04.$$

$$\therefore \text{ Air-gap power,} \qquad P_g = \frac{P_m}{1-s} = \frac{20000}{1-0.04} = \frac{20{,}000}{0.96}$$

$$\text{Total rotor } I^2R \text{ loss } = s\,P_g = \frac{0.04}{0.96} \times 20{,}000 = 833.33 \text{ W} \quad \text{or} \quad 3\,I_2^2 r_2 = 833.33 \text{ W}$$

$$\text{Per-phase stator voltage}, V_1 = \frac{400}{\sqrt{3}} = 230.95 \text{ V}$$

$$\text{For Thevenin's equivalent circuit, } V_e = \frac{V_1 \cdot X_m}{X_m + x_1} = \frac{230.95 \times 18}{18.45} = 225.32 \text{ V}$$

$$R_e = \frac{0.2 \times 18}{18.45} = 0.195\ \Omega$$

$$X_e = \frac{0.45 \times 18}{18.45} = 0.44\ \Omega$$

From Thevenin's equivalent circuit, rotor current is given by

$$I_2 = \frac{V_e}{(R_e + r_2/s) + j(X_e + x_2)}$$

$$\therefore \qquad 3\,I_2^2 r_2 = 3\,\frac{225.32^2}{\left(0.195 + \dfrac{r_2}{0.04}\right)^2 + (0.44 + 0.45)^2} \times r_2 = 833.33 \text{ W}$$

$$182.77\,r_2 = 0.038 + 625\,r_2^2 + 9.75\,r_2 + 0.7921 \quad \text{or} \quad r_2^2 - 0.2768\,r_2 + 0.001328 = 0$$

Neglecting 0.001328, we get $r_2 = 0.2768\ \Omega$.

(*a*) Synchronous speed, $\omega_s = \dfrac{4\pi \times 50}{4} = 50 \cdot \pi$ rad/sec

Maximum internal torque, from Eqn. (6.27), is

$$T_{e \cdot m} = \frac{3}{\omega_s} \cdot \frac{V_e^2}{2[R_e + \sqrt{R_e^2 + X^2}]}$$

$$= \frac{3}{50\pi} \cdot \frac{225.32^2}{2[0.195 + \sqrt{0.195^2 + 0.89^2}]} = 438.3 \text{ Nm}$$

Initial starting torque,
$$T_{e.st} = \frac{3}{\omega_s} \cdot \frac{V_e^2}{[R_e + r_2]^2 + [X_e + x_2]^2} . r_2$$

$$= \frac{3}{50\pi} \cdot \frac{225.32^2}{[0.195 + 0.2768]^2 + 0.89^2} \times 0.2768 = 264.5 \text{ Nm}$$

(b) Slip at which maximum torque occurs is

$$s_{mT} = \frac{r_2}{\sqrt{R_e^2 + (X_e + x_2)^2}} = \frac{0.2768}{[(0.195)^2 + (0.89)^2]^{1/2}} = 0.3038.$$

Example 6.38. *A 3-phase, 400 V, 50 Hz, 6-pole, 200 kW slip-ring induction motor gave the following data with its slip rings short circuited :*

full load slip = 0.02

rotor I^2R loss at full-load torque = 3 kW.

If rotor circuit resistance is increased to 4 r_2 by inserting external resistances in each rotor phase, then calculate (a) the slip for developing the same full load torque, (b) total rotor ohmic losses at full load torque and (c) power output at full-load torque.

Solution. *(a)* Developed torque is given by $T_e = \frac{1}{\omega_s} \times$ air-gap power

$$= \frac{1}{\omega_s} \times I_2^2 \frac{r_2}{s}$$

∴ Full-load torque,
$$T_{e1} = \frac{1}{\omega_s} \times I_{2 \cdot fl}^2 \cdot \frac{r_2}{s_1}$$

where r_2 = inherent rotor resistance per phase and s_1 is the slip at full-load torque T_{e1}.

With rotor resistance $4r_2$, the full-load torque T_{e2} is

$$T_{e2} = \frac{1}{\omega_s} \cdot I_{2fl}^2 \frac{4r_2}{s_2} \text{ where } s_2 \text{ is the slip for } T_{e2}.$$

For the same full-load torque, $T_{e1} = T_{e2}$

$$\therefore \quad \frac{1}{\omega_s} \cdot I_{2 \cdot fl}^2 \frac{r_2}{s_1} = \frac{1}{\omega_s} \times I_{2fl}^2 \cdot \frac{4r_2}{s_2}. \text{ This gives } \frac{r_2}{s_1} = \frac{4r_2}{s_2}$$

∴ Now value of slip
$$s_2 = \frac{4r_2}{r_2} \times s_1 = 4s_1 = 4 \times 0.02 = \mathbf{0.08}$$

(b) At standstill, per phase rotor emf = E_2 and per-phase leakage reactance = $2\pi f_2 l_2 = x_2$.

At slip s_1, per-phase rotor emf = $s_1 E_2$ and per-phase rotor leakage reactance = $2\pi s_1, f_2 l_2 = s_1 \cdot x_2$

∴ Initial rotor current at slip s_1 is
$$I_2 = \frac{s_1 E_2}{s_1 x_2 + r_2} = \frac{E_2}{x_2 + \frac{r_2}{s_1}} \quad ...(i)$$

With rotor resistance $4r_2$, $s_2 = 4s_1$ and rotor current at slip s_2 is given by

$$I_2 = \frac{4s_1 E_2}{4s_1 \cdot x_2 + 4r_2} = \frac{E_2}{x_2 + \frac{r_2}{s_1}} \quad ...(ii)$$

It is seen from Eqs *(i)* and *(ii)* that effective rotor current with rotor resistance r_2 is equal to that with rotor resistance $4r_2$.

Initial rotor I^2R loss = 3 I_2^2 r_2 = 3 kW (given)

With rotor resistance $4r_2$, new rotor I^2R loss = 3 I_2^2 $(4r_2)$ = 4 × 3 I_2^2 r_2 = 4 × 3 = **12 kW**

(c) Power output $= T_e \times \omega_r$

$$\therefore \quad T_{e.fl} \times \omega_r (1 - s_1) \propto 200 \text{ kW}$$

$$T_{e.fl} \times \omega_r (1 - s_2) \propto P$$

$$\therefore \quad \frac{P}{200} = \frac{1 - 0.08}{1 - 0.02} = \frac{0.92}{0.98}$$

∴ Power output at full load torque, $P = 200 \times \dfrac{0.92}{0.98}$ = **187.76 kW**

Example 6.39. *A 3-phase delta-connected squirrel-cage induction motor has certain equivalent circuit parameters. With the same stator core, the motor is rewound with star-connected windings of same poles for operation at the same supply voltage and frequency to give same rated power output at the same slip. By what factors each of the equivalent circuit parameters would be changed?* *(I.A.S., 1998)*

Solution. Let the subscripts d and y denote respectively the parameters of delta-connected and star-connected windings of 3-phase induction motor.

Let the per-phase values of rated voltage and rated current be V_{1d} and I_{1d} for the stator in delta.

Rating of 3-phase induction motor = $3 V_{1d} I_{1d} \cos\theta$

When stator is rewound in star, rated stator voltage per phase, $V_{1y} = 1/\sqrt{3}\ V_{1d}$ and rated stator current per phase, $I_{1y} = \sqrt{3}\ I_{1d}$, so that rating = $3 V_{1y} I_{1y} \cos\theta = 3 (1/\sqrt{3}\ V_{1d}) \cos\theta = 3 V_{1d} I_{1d} \cos\theta$ remains the same as before.

Per-phase turns in star, $N_{1y} = 1/\sqrt{3}\ N_{1d}$ $\quad \because V_{1y} = 1/\sqrt{3}\ V_{1d}$

Cross-sectional area of conductor in star, $a_{1y} = \sqrt{3}\ a_{1d}$, because $I_{1y} = \sqrt{3}\ I_{1d}$.

∴ Length of conductor in star $L_{1y} = 1/\sqrt{3}\ L_{1d}$

All parameters referred below are per-phase parameters.

(i) Stator resistance in delta, $r_{1d} = \dfrac{\rho \cdot L_{1d}}{a_{1d}}$

Stator resistance in star, $$r_{1y} = \frac{\rho \cdot L_{1y}}{a_{1y}} = \frac{\rho \cdot \frac{1}{\sqrt{3}} L_{1d}}{\sqrt{3} \cdot a_{1d}} = \frac{1}{3}\,\frac{\rho \cdot L_{1d}}{a_{1d}} = \frac{1}{3}\, r_{1d}$$

(ii) **Stator leakage reactance.** It is known that inductance = $\dfrac{N^2}{\text{Rel}}$

∴ Leakage inductance in delta, $l_{1d} = \dfrac{N_{1d}^2}{\text{Rel}}$

Leakage inductance in star, $$l_{1y} = \frac{N_{1y}^2}{\text{Rel}} = \frac{1}{3} \cdot \frac{N_{1d}^2}{\text{Rel}} = \frac{1}{3}\, l_{1d}$$

$$\therefore \quad x_{1y} = \frac{1}{3}\, x_{1d}$$

(ii) **Magnetizing reactance.** For delta connections, magnetizing inductance,

$$L_{m\,1d} = \frac{N_{1d}^2}{\text{Rel}}.$$

For stator in star, magnetizing inductance,

$$L_{m1y} = \frac{N_{1y}^2}{\text{Rel}} = \frac{1}{3} \cdot \frac{N_{1d}^2}{\text{Rel}} = \frac{1}{3} L_{m1d}$$

$\therefore$ Magnetizing reactance, $X_{my} = \frac{1}{3} X_{md}$

As no changes are made in cage rotor, rotor parameters in star remain the same as these are for stator in delta. However, rotor circuit parameters, when referred to stator in star, would reduce to $\frac{1}{3}$ as under :

$$r_{2d}' = r_2 \text{ when referred to stator in delta} = \left(\frac{N_{1d}}{N_{2d}}\right)^2 r_2$$

$$r_{2y}' = \left(\frac{N_{1y}}{N_{2y}}\right)^2 r_2 = \frac{1}{3}\left(\frac{N_{1d}}{N_{2d}}\right)^2 r_2 = \frac{1}{3} r_{2d}'$$

Similarly $x_{2y}' = \frac{1}{3} x_{2d}'$

Equivalent circuit of a 3-phase induction motor with stator winding in delta is shown in Fig. 6.23. With stator rewound in star and for the conditions specified, the equivalent circuit is given in Fig. 6.24. All subscripts and primes are dropped for the sake of convenience.

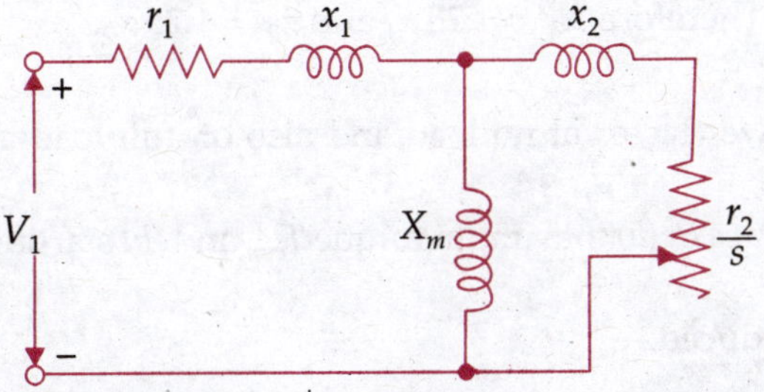

Fig 6.23: 3-phase induction motor equivalent circuit with stator winding in delta

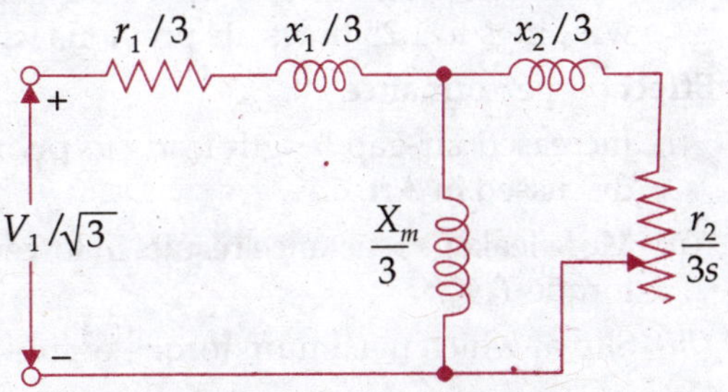

Fig 6.24: 3-phase induction motor equivalent circuit with stator winding in star

Stator core loss (proportional to stator flux) in delta is proportional to (V_{1d}/N_{1d}).

Stator core loss in star $\alpha\ (V_{1y}/N_{1y}) = V_{1d}/\ (\sqrt{3}\ N_{1d})\ \sqrt{3} = V_{1d}/N_{1d}$

This shows that stator core loss remains the same. Stator ohmic loss in delta = $3\ I_{1d}^2\ r_{1d}$

Stator ohmic loss in star $= 3\ I_{1y}^2\ r_{1y} = 3\,(\sqrt{3}\ I_{1d})^2\ \frac{r_{1d}}{3} = 3\ I_{1d}^2\ r_{1d}$

It is seen from above that stator losses for both delta and star connections remain the same. For same power input, therefore air-gap power = $3\,I_2^2\ \frac{r_2}{s}$ is unchanged.

For stator in delta, stator m.m.f. = rotor m.m.f.

$$I_{1d} \cdot N_{1d} = I_2 N_2$$

$\therefore$ Rotor current, $I_2 = \dfrac{I_{1d} \cdot N_{1d}}{N_2}$

For stator in star, $I_{1y} \cdot N_{1y} = I_2 N_2$

$\therefore$ Rotor current, $I_2 = \dfrac{I_{1y} \cdot N_{1y}}{N_2} = \dfrac{\sqrt{3} I_{1d}}{N_2} \cdot \dfrac{N_{1d}}{\sqrt{3}} = \dfrac{I_{1d} \cdot N_{1d}}{N_2}$

This shows that rotor current is the same whether the stator winding is in delta or star. For the same air-gap power $3\ I_2\ r_2/s$, therefore operating slip s is the same in both types of stators.

Example 6.40. *A 3-phase induction motor has an air-gap length of 2 mm. If its air-gap length is increased to 2.5 mm, discuss its effect on the equivalent-circuit parameters as well as on the performance of 3-phase induction motor.*

Solution. With increase in air-gap length from 2 mm to 2.5. mm, the new air-gap length becomes (2.5/2) = 1.25 times its previous gap length. Its effect on equivalent circuit parameters and performance characteristics is examined below :

(a) **Effect on equivalent-circuit parameters**

(i) Stator resistance r_1 and rotor resistance r_2 remain unaffected.

(ii) In a 3-phase induction motor, mutual flux remains practically constant. Therefore, with air-gap length increased by 1.25 times, the magnetizing current must be 1.25 times its previous value so that constant flux is established. Therefore, new magnetizing reactance

$$= \frac{V_1}{1.25 I_{mag}} = 0.8 \text{ (previous value of magnetizing reactance).}$$

$$\therefore \quad X_m' = 0.8\, X_m$$

where prime is used to denote equivalent circuit parameters with increased air-gap length.

(iii) With increased air-gap length, the stator winding and rotor winding get away from each other. The effect of this increased gap is to increase the leakage flux between the two windings to 1.25 times its previous value. Therefore, $x_1' = 1.25\, x_1$ and $x_2' = 1.25\, x_2$.

Effect on performance

(i) Increased air-gap length leads to poor power factor at no load and also on full load as discussed in Art. 6.1.

(ii) More leakage reactance results in lower values of *(a)* maximum torque $T_{e \cdot m}$ and *(b)* starting torque $T_{e \cdot st}$.

(iii) Slip at which maximum torque occurs is reduced.

6.10. OPERATING (OR PERFORMANCE) CHARACTERISTICS OF INDUCTION MOTORS

Steady-state operating characteristics of an induction motor, show graphically the variation of speed, slip, power factor, stator current and efficiency as the shaft power output is varied from no-load to full load. For a given induction motor, the operating characteristics are governed by its rotor resistance, air-gap length and shape of both stator and rotor slots. The object of this article is to describe the nature of the steady-state operating characteristics of induction motors and to examine the factors that govern them. Fig. 6.25 illustrates typical operating characteristics of an induction motor. The shape of these curves is now explained below.

(a) **Speed.** At no load, rotor speed is near to synchronous speed, therefore, the no-load slip is very small. Also, the no-load torque, sufficient to overcome the loss-torque required by friction and windage, is very low. As a result of small no-load torque, the rotor current is also quite small and load angle δ is very near to 90°. When the load torque is increased, electromagnetic torque T_e must increase to meet the load torque ; this can happen only if the rotor current rises. In order that rotor current I_2 rises, the rotor emf $s\, E_2$ must rise, or the slip must increase, in other words, the rotor speed must fall as the load torque is increased. Here E_2 is the rotor emf per phase at standstill.

When slip increases with rise in load torque, rotor speed falls and the rotor current I_2 rises to meet the required load torque. The fall in speed from no load to full load is usually in the range of 2 to 5% of rated speed. In view of this, an induction motor can be said to possess shunt characteristics.

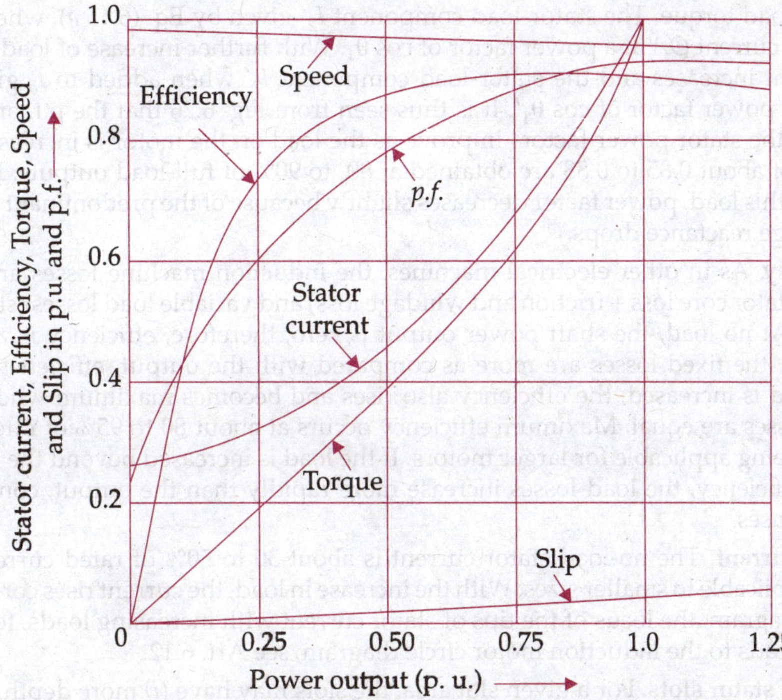

Fig 6.25: Operating characteristics of an induction motor.

(b) **Power factor.** The stator current of a three-phase induction motor is made up of the following three components :

(i) Magnetizing current I_m. This component lags stator voltage V_1 by 90° as in a transformer. Its function is to set up rotating magnetic field. Current I_m is purely reactive in nature.

(ii) Stator-loss component. This component supplies the stator core loss and friction and windage losses.

(iii) Load component. This component balances the rotor m.m.f. as in a transformer.

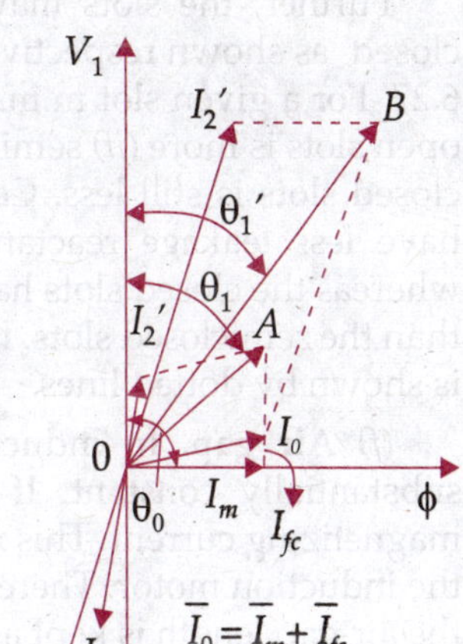

Fig 6.26: Improvement of power factor with increase in load, (bars over V_1, I_1 etc. not shown).

At no load, stator current I_o is shown in Fig. 6.26. The function of I_o is *(i)* to create rotating flux ϕ and *(b)* to provide stator core loss and friction and windage losses.

Current producing rotating flux ϕ is indicated by I_m ; and stator core loss plus friction and windage losses are represented by current I_{fc} in Fig. 6.26 and also in Fig. 6.10 *(b)* ; *i.e.*, $\overline{I}_o = \overline{I}_m + \overline{I}_{fc}$. On account of air-gap in an induction motor, magnetizing current I_m is much higher as compared to current I_{fc}. As a result, no-load current I_o lags the stator voltage by an angle θ_0 in the range of 75° to 85°. Consequently, the stator power factor at no load may be as low as 0.1 to 0.3, the lower values being applicable for large induction motors.

As the motor is loaded, the third, *i.e.*, load, component of stator current rises above its no-load value. The increment of load component of stator current above its no load value is responsible for supplying the load torque. The stator-load component I_2' given by Eq. (6.15 *a*), when added to I_o, gives the stator current *OA* at a power factor of cos θ_1. With further increase of load on the motor, the rotor current increases and the stator-load component I_2' when added to I_o gives the stator current *OB* at a power factor of cos θ_1'. It is thus seen from Fig. 6.26 that the p.f. angle decreases and, therefore, the stator power factors improve as the load on the motor is increased. The stator power factors of about 0.85 to 0.88 are obtained at 80 to 90% of full-load outputs. If the motor is loaded beyond this load, power factor decreases slightly because of the predominant effect of stator and rotor leakage reactance drops.

(c) **Efficiency.** As in other electrical machines, the induction machine losses are made up of fixed losses (= stator core loss + friction and windage loss) and variable load losses (stator and rotor ohmic losses). At no load, the shaft power output is zero, therefore, efficiency is zero. At lower values of loads, the fixed losses are more as compared with the output, efficiency is, therefore, low. As the load is increased, the efficiency also rises and becomes maximum when fixed losses and variable losses are equal. Maximum efficiency occurs at about 80 to 95% of rated output, the higher values being applicable for larger motors. If the load is increased beyond the load resulting in maximum efficiency, the load losses increase more rapidly than the output, consequently the efficiency decreases.

(d) **Stator current.** The no-load stator current is about 30 to 50% of rated current, the larger values being applicable to smaller sizes. With the increase in load, the current rises correspondingly. In the phasor diagram, the locus of the tips of stator current with increasing loads, follows a semi-circle and this leads to the induction motor circle diagram, see Art. 6.12.

(e) **Shape of stator slots.** For a given slot area, the slots may have *(i)* more depth, less width or *(ii)* less depth and more width. Part *(b)* of Example 2.17 reveals that slot leakage flux is directly proportional to slot depth. In view of this, induction motors with deeper slots have more leakage reactance and, therefore, low values of $T_{e.st}$, T_{em}, s_{mT}. Similar thought process can be applied to induction motors with wider slots.

Further, the slots may be open, semi-closed or closed as shown respectively in *(a)*, *(b)* and *(c)* of Fig. 6.27. For a given slot m.m.f., reluctance offered by *(i)* open slots is more *(ii)* semi-closed slots is less and *(iii)* closed slots is still less. Consequently the open slots have less leakage reactance than semiclosed slots, whereas the closed slots have more leakage reactance than the semiclosed slots. In Fig. 6.27, the leakage flux is shown by dotted lines.

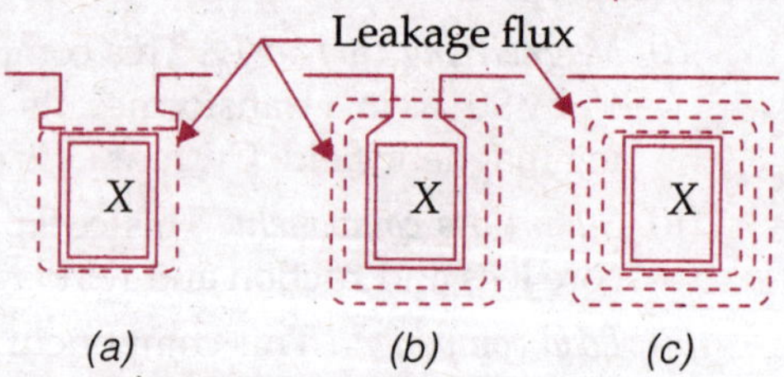

Fig 6.27: *(a)* open *(b)* semi-open and *(c)* closed slots.

(f) **Air gap.** In induction motors, for constant supply voltage, the air-gap flux remains substantially constant. If the air-gap length is increased, then constant flux requires more magnetizing current. This reduces the no-load power factor as well as the full-load power factor of the induction motor. Therefore, in order that an induction motor operates at a better power factor, the air-gap length is kept as small as is mechanically possible. Small air-gap clearance in induction motors necessitates a heavier shaft and high-grade bearings than are required for other types of rotating machines of the same rating and speed.

Open slots in an induction motor has the effect of increasing the air-gap length (1.10 to 1.20 times the actual air-gap length) as a result of which more magnetizing current is required and the operating power factor of the motor is worsened. But an induction motor with open slots has less leakage reactance and, therefore, more $T_{e \cdot st}$, more T_{em} etc. Likewise an induction motor with semi-closed slots or closed slots requires less magnetizing current and, therefore, better operating power factor, but its $T_{e \cdot st}$, T_{em} etc. are reduced. In view of this, at the design stage, a compromise has to be made between $T_{e \cdot st}$, T_{em} and the operating power factor of the induction motors.

6.10.1. Induction Motor Stability

Practically in almost all the motors, the speed drops as the load torque is increased. Mere intersection of motor torque T_e and load torque T_L characteristics, does not guarantee a stable operating point. Stable operation of the system consisting of motor and load is possible if the motor speed decreases with an increase in load torque or *vice versa*.

An induction motor is designed to operate at low values of full-load slips (from 0.02 to 0.05) under normal operating conditions. In Fig. 6.28 *(a)*, the normal operating region extending from s = s_{mT} is shown by solid curve. The region from s = 1 to s_{mT} as shown by dotted curve in Fig. 6.27 *(a)* is rarely used.

In Fig. 6.27 *(b)*, motor starting torque *OA* is more than the load torque *OB*, the motor, therefore, accelerates to the operating point C. If the load torque increases from curve T_{L1} to curve T_{L2}, the operating point shifts from C to D and the motor speed drops from *Oc* to *Od*. It can also be shown that if the load torque decreases, the motor speed increases. This leads to the conclusion that point C is stable one.

For load characteristic T_L as shown in Fig. 6.28 *(c)*, the motor will not start, because starting torque *OA* is less than load torque *OB*. Thus the question of any operating point does not arise.

For load characteristics T_{L1} of Fig. 6.28 *(d)*, C is the stable operating point because an increase of load torque from T_{L1} to T_{L2} shifts the operating point from C to D and the speed is thereby decreased. Such a load characteristic, however, would rarely be used under normal circumstances, because operating point C would result in higher values of slip, high currents, low power factor, more loss and very low efficiency.

For load characteristic T_{L1} as shown in Fig. 6.28 *(e)*, *A* is the stable operating point. If, due to some reason or the other, the load torque decreases suddenly from T_{L1} to T_{L2}, motor torque exceeds T_{L2}—the rotor gets accelerated till the operating point B is reached. After the point *B* is arrived at, if T_{L2} again increases to T_{L1}, the operating point C at reduced speed is obtained. Thus the normal operating region from $s = 0$ to s_{mT} is more stable than the region from s_{mT} to $s = 1$.

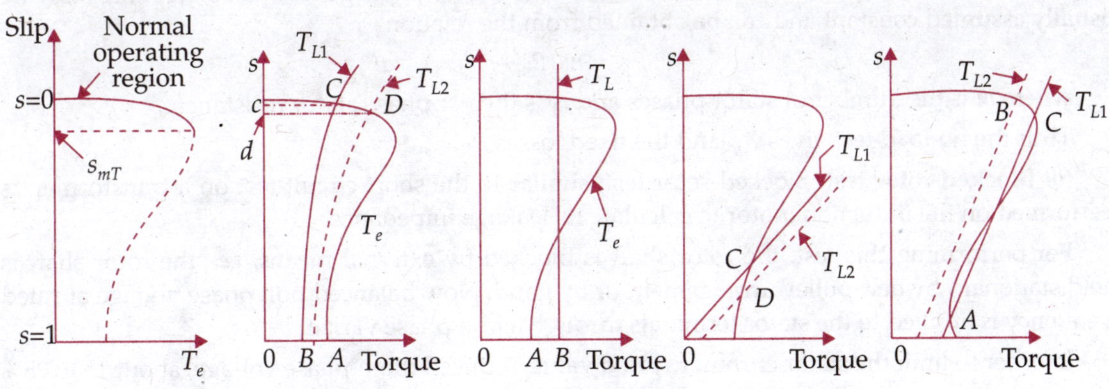

Fig 6.28: Pertaining to the induction motor stability.

It can be concluded from above that stable operation depends on the nature of load torque and motor torque characteristics and the way they intersect. It may also be seen that if $\frac{dT_L}{dn} > \frac{dT_e}{dn}$, the system is stable. In case $\frac{dT_L}{dn} < \frac{dT_e}{dn}$, the system is unstable.

Practically, the region between $s = 0$ and s_{mT} is used. This region is sometimes referred to as stable one, because all types of load-characteristics in this region result in stable-operating points.

Since the speed-torque characteristic in the normal operating region is like that of D.C. shunt motor (low variation of speed from no load to full load), the induction motor is said to possess shunt characteristics.

6.11. DETERMINATION OF EQUIVALENT CIRCUIT PARAMETERS

The equivalent circuit parameters of polyphase induction motors can be determined from no load test, blocked-rotor test and stator winding D.C. resistance. The object of this article is to describe the methods of determining the parameters from these tests.

(a) **No-load test (or running light test).** The induction motor is made to run at no load at rated voltage and frequency. Per phase values of applied stator voltage V_{nl}, input current I_{nl} and input power P_{nl} are recorded.

The no-load slip s_{nl} is very small, therefore, r_2/s_{nl} in Fig. 6.14 is very large as compared to X_m. In view of this, the resultant of parallel branches jX_m and $\left(\frac{r_2}{s_{nl}} + jx_2\right)$ is almost equal to jX_m. This leads to the induction motor equivalent circuit at no load as shown in Fig. 6.29 *(a)*. Thus the no-load reactance X_{nl} seen from the stator terminals is equal to $x_1 + X_m$, *i.e.*,

$$X_{nl} = x_1 + X_m = X_1 \qquad ...(6.39)$$

where X_1 is the stator self-reactance.

From the instrument readings at no load,

stator no-load impedance, $Z_{nl} = \frac{V_{nl}}{I_{nl}}$

and stator no-load resistance, $R_{nl} = \frac{P_{nl}}{I_{nl}^2}$ $\qquad \therefore X_{nl} = \sqrt{Z_{nl}^2 - R_{nl}^2} = x_1 + X_m$

The fixed losses or no-load rotational losses P_R (friction, windage loss and stator core loss) are usually assumed constant and can be obtained from the relation

$$P_R = m\,(P_{nl} - I_{nl}^2 r_1)$$

where m is the number of stator phases and r_1 is the per phase stator resistance.

Thus the no-load test gives X_{nl} and the fixed losses P_R.

(b) **Blocked-rotor test.** Blocked-rotor test, similar to the short-circuit test on a transformer, is performed on the induction motor to calculate its leakage impedance.

For performing this test, the rotor shaft is blocked by external means, *i.e.*, the rotor shaft is held stationary by belt-pulley arrangement or by hand. Now balanced polyphase voltage at rated frequency is applied to the stator terminals through a polyphase variac.

In order to limit the stator current to rated value, reduced three-phase voltage, about 15 to 25% of rated voltage, is applied to stator terminals. At this reduced voltage, core loss ($\propto V^2$) is quite small. Therefore, no-load current I_o or the shunt branch $R_c \parallel X_m$ in Fig. 6.13 *(a)* can be neglected. Thus, equivalent circuit under blocked-rotor conditions is as shown in Fig. 6.29 *(b)*. Per phase values of applied voltage V_{br}, input current (= rated current) I_{br} and the input power P_{br} are recorded. Current I_{br} may be affected by rotor position, in view of this the rotor should be held in a position that gives I_{br} equal to the mean of maximum and minimum current values. Measure the *dc* resistance per phase of the stator winding soon after this test and multiply it by 1.1 to 1.3 in order to obtain the per-phase effective stator resistance r_1.

From the instrument readings during blocked rotor test and Fig. 6.29 *(b)*, the parameters can be obtained as under.

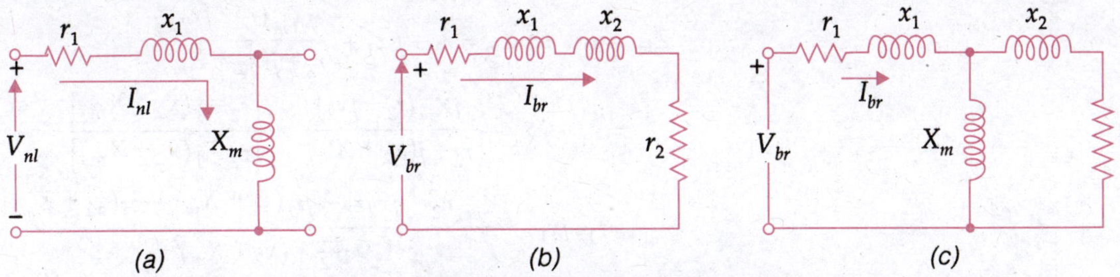

Fig 6.29: Three-phase induction motor equivalent circuit for *(a)* no-load test and *(b)* and *(c)* blocked-rotor test.

Blocked-rotor impedance, $Z_{br} = \dfrac{V_{br}}{I_{br}}$

Blocked-rotor resistance, $R_{br} = \dfrac{P_{br}}{I_{br}^2}$

∴ Blocked-rotor reactance, $X_{br} = \sqrt{Z_{br}^2 - R_{br}^2}$

Here X_{br} is equal to the sum of stator and rotor leakage reactances x_1 and x_2.

$$\therefore \quad X_{br} = x_1 + x_2 \quad \text{...(6.40)}$$

There is no practical method of separating x_1 and x_2. For wound-rotor induction motors, x_1 is assumed equal to x_2, *i.e.*, $x_1 = x_2 = \dfrac{1}{2} X_{br}$.

For squirrel cage induction motors, total leakage reactance X_{br} (= $x_1 + x_2$) can be distributed between stator and rotor as per the following table :

Table 6.1. Empirical Distribution of Leakage Reactance X_{br}

Class of motor		Fraction of X_{br}	
		x_1	x_2
1.	Class A (normal $T_{e\,.\,st}$ and I_{st})	0.5	0.5
2.	Class B (normal $T_{e\,.\,st}$ and low I_{st})	0.4	0.6
3.	Class C (high $T_{e\,.\,st}$ and low I_{st})	0.3	0.7
4.	Class D (high $T_{e\,.\,st}$ and high slip)	0.5	0.5

Once x_1 is known, then from Eq. (6.39), the stator magnetizing reactance can be obtained from no-load stator reactance X_{nl}

$$\therefore \quad X_m = X_{nl} - x_1 \quad \text{...(6.39)}$$

For rotor circuit parameters, the value of x_2 is obtained from Eq. (6.40). The magnitude of x_2 remains substantially constant over the entire operating speed range. However, the effective value of r_2, *i.e.*, $\dfrac{r_2}{s}$ does not remain constant over the entire running range. Therefore, the calculation of r_2 cannot be obtained from $r_2 = R_{br} - r_1$ but requires careful examination.

When slips is small, magnitude of $\dfrac{r_2}{s}$ may be near to X_m and when slip $s = 1$ at standstill, r_2 is quite small as compared to X_m. So, when calculating Z_{br}, X_m must be included and therefore, equivalent circuit during blocked-rotor test of Fig. 6.29 *(c)* must be used. Therefore, from Fig. 6.29 *(c)*, blocked-rotor impedance Z_{br} seen from stator terminals is given by

$$Z_{br} = R_{br} + j\,X_{br} = r_1 + j\,x_1 + \frac{jX_m(r_2 + jx_2)}{r_2 + j(x_2 + X_m)}$$

$$= r_1 + j\,x_1 + \frac{jX_m(r_2 + jx_2)}{r_2 + j(x_2 + X_m)} \times \frac{[r_2 - j(x_2 + X_m)]}{[r_2 - j(x_2 + X_m)]}$$

$$= r_1 + jx_1 + \frac{jX_m[r_2^2 + jx_2r_2 - jr_2(x_2 + X_m) + x_2(x_2 + X_m)]}{r_2^2 + (x_2 + X_m)^2}$$

or
$$Z_{br} = R_{br} + j\,X_{br} = r_1 + j\,x_1 + \frac{jX_m[r_2^2 - jr_2X_m + x_2X_2]}{r_2^2 + X_2^2} \qquad ...(6.41)$$

where $X_2 = x_2 + X_m$ is the rotor self-reactance. Taking the real components of both sides of Eq. (6.41), blocked-rotor resistance R_{br} as seen from stator terminals is

$$R_{br} = r_1 + r_2 \frac{X_m^2}{r_2^2 + X_2^2}$$

For machines of normal design, $X_2 >> r_2$, therefore, r_2 in the denominator can be neglected as compared to X_2.
$$\therefore \quad R_{br} = r_1 + r_2 \left[\frac{X_m}{X_2}\right]^2$$

$\therefore$ Per phase rotor resistance,
$$r_2 = (R_{br} - r_1)\left[\frac{X_2}{X_m}\right]^2 \qquad ...(6.42)$$

Thus X_m from Eq. (6.39), r_2 from Eq. (6.42), r_1 from d.c. resistance per phase of stator winding and x_1, x_2 from Eq. (6.40) and Table 6.1 can be determined from three tests. The equivalent circuit can now be used for computing the motor performance.

During blocked-rotor test, the power input is almost entirely I^2R loss in both stator and rotor windings. For low voltage during this test, the flux density is quite low and core loss is therefore very small. For example, for 20% input voltage, the flux density is about one-tenth of its normal value and the core loss is therefore about one percent of normal core loss, which is quite a small figure.

Note. For large motors (above 20 kW or so), if induction motor characteristics are required near $s = 1$ (*e.g.*, for starting torque etc.) ; then since rotor frequency f_2 is equal to the line frequency, the blocked-rotor test should be carried out at line frequency and with currents equal to those encountered at the time of starting.

In case induction motor characteristics are required near synchronous speed (*e.g.* during normal operation), then rotor frequency is equal to sf_1, therefore, the blocked-rotor test should be carried out at reduced frequency and with normal currents.

Example 6.41. *A 10 kW, 400 V, 4 pole delta-connected squirrel cage induction motor gave the following test results :*

No-load test : 400 V, 8 A, 250 watts.

Blocked-rotor test : 90 V, 35 A, 1350 watts.

The D.C. resistance of the stator winding per phase measured immediately after the blocked-rotor test is 0.6 Ω. Calculate the no-load rotational losses and the equivalent circuit parameters.

Solution. No-load rotational losses or fixed losses are

$$P_R = 250 - 3\left(\frac{8}{\sqrt{3}}\right)^2 \times (0.6 \times 1.20) = 203.92 \text{ watts.}$$

Note that the effective stator resistance per phase is taken equal to 1.2 times its D.C. value.

From no-load test, $$Z_{nl} = \frac{400}{(8/\sqrt{3})} = 86.6\ \Omega \quad R_{nl} = \frac{250}{3(8/\sqrt{3})^2} = 3.91\ \Omega$$

$$\therefore \quad X_{nl} = \sqrt{Z_{nl}^2 - R_{nl}^2} = \sqrt{(86.6)^2 - (3.91)^2} = 86.51\ \Omega$$

From blocked-rotor test, $$Z_{br} = \frac{90}{(35/\sqrt{3})} = 4.454\ \Omega, \quad R_{br} = \frac{1350}{3(35/\sqrt{3})^2} = 1.102\ \Omega$$

$$\therefore \quad X_{br} = \sqrt{(4.454)^2 - (1.102)^2} = 4.316\ \Omega$$

$$\therefore \quad x_1 = x_2 = \frac{1}{2} X_{br} = 2.158\ \Omega.$$

and $$X_m = X_{nl} - x_1 = 86.51 - 2.158 = 84.352\ \Omega$$

$$X_2 = X_m + x_2 = 84.352 + 2.158 = 86.51\ \Omega$$

From Eq. (6.42), per phase rotor resistance is given by

$$r_2 = (R_{br} - r_1)\left(\frac{X_2}{X_m}\right)^2 = (1.102 - 0.6 \times 1.2)\left(\frac{86.51}{84.352}\right)^2 = 0.402\ \Omega.$$

Thus the parameters of the induction motor equivalent circuit are

$$r_1 = 0.72\ \Omega,\ r_2 = 0.402\ \Omega,\ x_1 = x_2 = 2.158\ \Omega \text{ and } X_m = 84.352\ \Omega$$

Example 6.42. *(a) Explain how friction and windage loss can be computed from the no-load test.*

(b) Under normal operation of the induction motor, the rotor core loss is usually negligible. Explain.

Solution. *(a)* The power input to the induction motor at no-load has to supply the stator ohmic loss, stator core loss and friction and windage loss.

The D.C. resistance of the stator winding is measured and its per phase effective value r_1 is calculated from the relation,

$$r_1 = (1.1 \text{ to } 1.3) \text{ (D.C. resistance of one phase)}.$$

For computing the friction and windage loss, the applied voltage to the unloaded induction motor is varied from 1.25 times the rated voltage to about 20% of the rated voltage. The input power, current and voltage are recorded so that a graph can be plotted. The speed, with reduction in voltage, will fall only slightly so that the friction and windage loss remains substantially constant.

From each of the input-power readings, the corresponding stator ohmic loss is subtracted to obtain the stator core loss and friction and windage loss, *i.e.*,

$$P_R = m\,(P_{nl} - I_{nl}^2 r_1)$$

where P_{nl} is the per phase power input, I_{nl} is the per phase stator current and r_1 is the effective per phase stator resistance. The plot of no-load rotational loss P_R with variable stator voltage is shown in Fig. 6.30. The intercept of the P_R curve with the ordinate gives the friction and windage loss, because the core loss is zero for zero applied voltage. In order to get a more accurate value of mechanical loss (friction and windage loss), no-load rotational loss P_R should be plotted against (voltage)². This plot of P_R with (voltage)² is almost linear and, therefore, the extrapolation is easier.

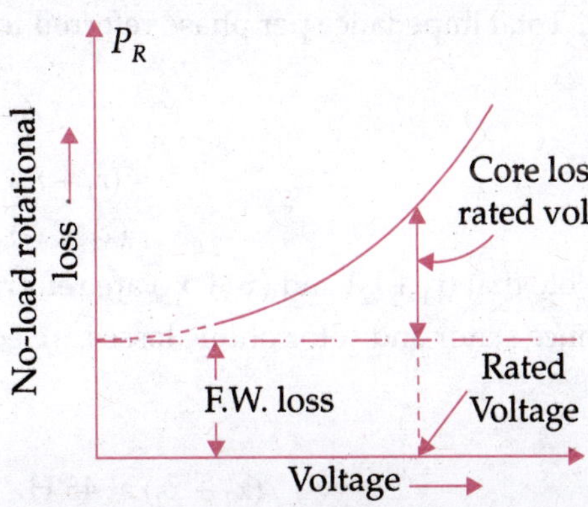

Fig 6.30: Variation of rotational loss with voltage.

(b) Core loss or iron loss consists of eddy-current loss ($\propto B^2f^2$) and hysteresis loss ($\propto B^xf$). At standstill, the rotor frequency is equal to supply frequency *f*, therefore, the rotor core loss is appreciable. As the motor speeds up, the rotor frequency decreases and with it the rotor core loss decreases accordingly. Under normal running conditions, the slip is small (0.02 to 0.05), the rotor frequency is also very small ; consequently the rotor core loss is very low and can, therefore, be neglected.

Example 6.43. *A 420 V, 3-phase, 4-pole, 50 Hz, delta connected squirrel cage induction motor gave the following data for blocked rotor test :*

210 V, 20 A, 5 kW

Stator core loss at rated voltage and frequency is 300 watts. The D.C. resistance measured between any two stator terminals is 0.6 Ω. Determine the starting torque at rated voltage and frequency.

Solution. With the stator winding in delta, the resistance per phase *R* is obtained from the relation $\frac{R \times 2R}{3R} = 0.6$ or $R = 0.9\ \Omega$.

Effective stator resistance per phase = 1.2 × 0.9 = 1.08 Ω

Power input at rated voltage during blocked rotor test $= 5 \times \left(\frac{420}{210}\right)^2 = 20$ kW

Stator current at rated voltage during blocked rotor test $= 20 \times \frac{420}{210} = 40$ A

∴ Air-gap power at rated voltage and frequency, with the rotor blocked, is given by

$$P_g = 20{,}000 - 3\left(\frac{40}{\sqrt{3}}\right)^2 \times 1.08 - 300 = 17972 \text{ W}$$

Synchronous speed, $\omega_s = \frac{4\pi f}{P} = \frac{4\pi \times 50}{4} = 50\pi$ rad/sec.

∴ Starting torque $= \frac{P_g}{\omega_s} = \frac{17972}{50\pi} = 114.413$ Nm.

Example 6.44. *Blocked-rotor test on a 3-phase, 40 kW, 400 V, 50 Hz, 6-pole star-connected induction motor gave the following data : 200 V, 110 A, p.f. = 0.4*

Determine the starting torque for a 3-phase voltage of 380 V at 45 Hz. Neglect magnetizing current and assume stator and rotor ohmic losses equal.

Solution. During blocked-rotor test, per phase voltage, $V_b = 200/\sqrt{3} = 115.5$ V and per phase current, $I_b = 110$ A

∴ Total impedance per phase referred to stator,

$$Z_b = \frac{V_b}{I_b} = \frac{115.5}{110} = 1.05\ \Omega$$

∴ $$(r_1 + r_2) = Z_b \cos\theta_b = 1.05 \times 0.4 = 0.42\ \Omega$$

$$(x_1 + x_2) = Z_b \sin\theta_b = 1.05 \sin[\cos^{-1}(0.4)] = 0.9623\ \Omega$$

Note that $(r_1 + r_2)$ and $(x_1 + x_2)$ are referred to stator.

Since stator and rotor ohmic losses are equal,

$$r_1 = r_2 = \frac{0.42}{2} = 0.21\ \Omega$$

$$(x_1 + x_2) \text{ at 45 Hz} = 0.9623 \times \frac{45}{50} = 0.866\ \Omega$$

Total impedance at 45 Hz $= 0.42 + j\,0.866\ \Omega$

Per-phase voltage at 45 Hz, $V_1 = \dfrac{380}{\sqrt{3}}$ V

$$\text{Starting current} = \frac{380}{\sqrt{3}[0.42 + j0.866]}$$

Synchronous speed, $w_s = \dfrac{4\pi \times 50}{4} = \dfrac{100\pi}{3}$ rad/sec

$\therefore$
$$\text{Starting torque} = \frac{3}{w_s} \cdot \frac{V_1^2}{(\text{impedance at 45 Hz})^2} \cdot r_2$$

$$= \frac{3 \times 3}{100 \times \pi} + \frac{380^2}{3[0.42^2 + 0.866^2]} \times 0.21 = 312.594 \text{ Nm.}$$

Example 6.45. *A 3-phase, 400 V, 50 Hz star-connected induction motor gave the following test results :*

No load : 400 V, 7.5.A, 0.135 power factor

Blocked rotor : 150 V, 35 A, 0.44 power factor

The ratio of standstill leakage reactance of stator and rotor is estimated as 2. If the motor is running at a speed of 960 r.p.m., determine

(a) net mechanical power output (b) the net torque and (c) efficiency of the motor.

Assume stator and rotor ohmic losses to be equal.

Solution. No-load test.

$$Z_{nl} = \frac{400}{\sqrt{3} \times 7.5} = 30.793\ \Omega$$

$$R_{nl} = Z_{nl} \cos\theta_{nl} = 30.793 \times 0.135 = 4.157\ \Omega$$

$$X_{nl} = \sqrt{Z_{nl}^2 - R_{nl}^2} = \sqrt{30.793^2 - 4.157^2} = 30.511\ \Omega$$

Blocked-rotor test.

$$Z_{br} = \frac{150}{\sqrt{3} \times 35} = 2.474\ \Omega$$

$$R_{br} = Z_{br} \cos\theta_{br} = 2.474 \times 0.44 = 1.09\ \Omega$$

$$X_{br} = \sqrt{Z_{br}^2 - R_{br}^2} = \sqrt{2.474^2 - 1.09^2} = 2.22\ \Omega$$

Here $\dfrac{x_1}{x_2} = 2.$

But $x_1 + x_2 = X_{br}$ $\quad \therefore 3x_2 = 2.22\ \Omega.$

This gives $x_2 = 0.74$ and $x_1 = 2 \times 0.74 = 1.48\ \Omega$

$$X_m = X_{nl} - x_1 = 30.511 - 1.48 = 29.031\ \Omega$$

It is given that stator and rotor ohmic losses are equal.

$\therefore$
$$r_1 = r_2 = \frac{R_{br}}{2} = 0.545\ \Omega$$

The exact equivalent circuit for this induction motor is shown in Fig. 6.31 *(a)*.

Thevenin's equivalent circuit parameters obtained from Eqs. (6.22) and (6.23) are given below :

$$V_e = \frac{V_1 \cdot X_m}{x_1 + X_m} \quad \text{where } x_1 + X_m = 1.48 + 29.031 = 30.511\ \Omega$$

Per-phase stator voltage, $V_1 = \dfrac{400}{\sqrt{3}} = 230.95$ V

$$\therefore \quad V_e = \frac{230.95 \times 29.031}{30.511} = 219.75 \text{ V}$$

$$R_e = \frac{0.545 \times 29.031}{30.511} = 0.519\ \Omega$$

$$X_e = \frac{1.48 \times 29.031}{30.511} = 1.408\ \Omega$$

Thevenin's equivalent circuit is as shown in Fig. 6.31 *(b)*.

$$\text{No-load rotational losses} = \sqrt{3} \times 400 \times 7.5 \times 0.135 - 3 \times 7.5^2 \times 0.545 = 609.5 \text{ W}$$

$$\text{Synchronous speed} = 1000 \text{ r.p.m.,}$$

$$\text{slip } s = \frac{1000 - 960}{1000} = 0.04$$

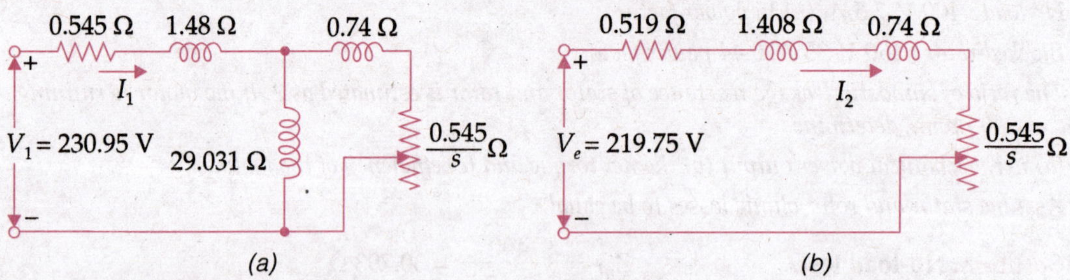

Fig 6.31: Induction motor equivalent circuits pertaining to Example 6.45.

Rotor current at slip $s = 0.04$, from Fig. 6.31 *(b)*, is given by

$$I_2 = \frac{219.75}{\left(0.519 + \frac{0.545}{0.04}\right) + j2.148}$$

Mechanical power developed, $P_m = 3 I_2^2 r_2 \left(\frac{1-s}{s}\right)$

$$= 3\ \frac{219.75^2}{(14.144)^2 + 2.148^2} \times \frac{0.96}{0.04} = 9258.48 \text{ W}$$

(a) Net mechanical power output $= P_m$ – No-load rotational losses

or $P_{sh} = 9258.48 - 609.5 = 8648.98$ W.

(b) Synchronous speed, $\omega_s = \frac{4\pi \times 50}{6} = \frac{100\pi}{3}$ rad/sec

$\therefore$ Net torque, $T_{sh} = \frac{P_{sh}}{\omega_r} = \frac{8648.98}{\frac{100\pi}{3}(1-0.04)} = 86.033$ Nm.

(c) Rotor ohmic losses $= \frac{P_m \cdot s}{1-s} = \frac{9258.48 \times 0.04}{0.96} = 385.77$ W

Stator ohmic losses $= 385.77$ W

No-load rotational losses $= 609.5$ W

Total losses in motor $= 385.77 \times 2 + 609.5 = 1381.04$ W

Power input $= 8648.98 + 1381.04 = 10030.02$ W

$$\therefore \text{Efficiency} = \frac{\text{Power output}}{\text{Power input}} = \frac{8648.98}{10030.02} \times 100 = 86.23\%.$$

Example 6.46. *A 230 V, 20 h.p., 60 Hz, 6-pole, 3-phase induction motor driving a constant torque load at rated frequency, rated voltage and rated horse power, has a speed of 1175 r.p.m. and an efficiency of 92.1%. Determine the new operating speed if a system disturbance causes 10% drop in voltage and 6% drop in frequency. Assume that friction, windage and stray power losses remain constant.* [GATE, 2000]

Solution. Synchronous speed $= \dfrac{120 \times 60}{6} = 1200$ r.p.m.

Slip, $s_1 = \dfrac{1200 - 1175}{1200} = \dfrac{1}{48}$

From Eqn. (6.30), rated torque is given by

$$T_{e \cdot r} = s_1 \cdot \frac{3V_1^2}{\omega_s} \cdot \frac{1}{r_2} = \frac{1}{48} \cdot \frac{3V_1^2}{\omega_s} \cdot \frac{1}{r_2} = A$$

With reduced voltage and lowered frequency, we get

$$T_{e \cdot r} = s_2 \frac{3(0.9V_1)^2}{0.94\,\omega_s} \cdot \frac{1}{r_2} = A = \frac{1}{48} \cdot \frac{3V_1^2}{\omega_s} \cdot \frac{1}{r_2}$$

or $$s_2 = \frac{0.94}{0.81 \times 48} = 0.0242$$

New operating speed $= \dfrac{120 \times 0.94 \times 60}{6}(1 - 0.0242) = 1100.70$ r.p.m.

6.12. CIRCLE DIAGRAM

Induction motor circle diagram is a graphical representation of its equivalent circuit. This means that whatever information can be obtained from the equivalent circuit, the same can also be obtained from the circle diagram. The advantages of circle diagram are its simplicity and quick estimation of the induction motor operating characteristics. Though a computer can rapidly provide the performance characteristics of a 3-phase induction motor from its equivalent circuit, yet the graphical solution through the use of circle diagram is even now popular in several organisations. It is because a circle diagram.

(*i*) gives the results which are sufficiently accurate for practical purposes, despite the fact that an approximate equivalent circuit is used in a circle diagram,

(*ii*) provides a panoramic view of how operating characteristics are affected by changes in the machine parameters, voltage, frequency etc.

A circle diagram shows that the extremities of stator current phasor follow a circular locus as the slip varies from + ∞ to – ∞. In this article, first the development of circle diagram from its approximate equivalent circuit is presented. Then the use of this circle diagram for obtaining performance calculations is described.

(*a*) **Current locus for the rotor circuit.** The rotor circuit voltage equation in phasor form can be written, by referring to its equivalent circuit of Fig. 6.7, as

$$\bar{E}_2 = \bar{I}_2 \frac{r_2}{s} + j\,\bar{I}_2 x_2 \qquad ...(6.43)$$

or $$\frac{\bar{E}_2}{jx_2} = \bar{I}_2 + \bar{I}_2 \frac{r_2/s}{jx_2}$$

or $$-j\frac{\bar{E}_2}{x_2} = \bar{I}_2 - j\,\bar{I}_2 \frac{r_2}{sx_2} \qquad ...(6.44)$$

In Eq. (6.43), rotor current I_2 lags emf E_2 by rotor pf angle $\theta_2 = \tan^{-1} \frac{sx_2}{r_2}$. In Eq. (6.44), $\frac{E_2}{x_2}$ denotes a constant current ; $-j\frac{E_2}{x_2}$ implies that this current lags E_2 by 90° because of $-j$ before E_2. In Fig. 6.32, E_2 is taken along the vertical axis and $-j\frac{E_2}{x_2}$ (= OB) lags E_2 by 90°. It is also observed from Eq. (6.44) that current $-j\frac{E_2}{x_2}$ is made up of two components, these are I_2 and $-jI_2\frac{r_2}{sx_2}$.

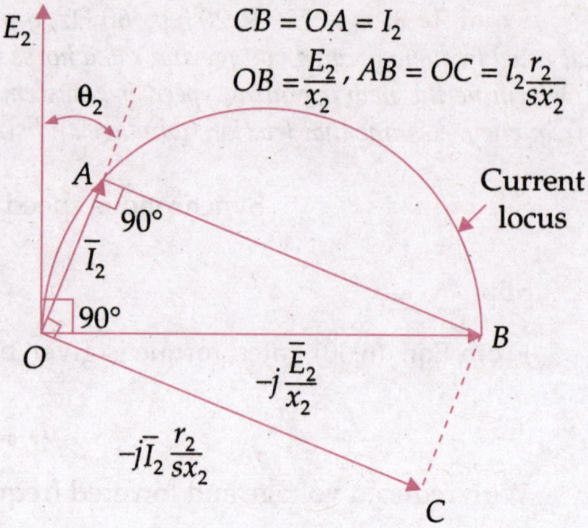

Fig 6.32: Current locus for the rotor circuit of a 3-ϕ induction motor.

Current component I_2 (= OA) lags E_2 by rotor pf angle θ_2 as per Eq. (6.43). Further, $-jI_2\frac{r_2}{sx_2}$ (= OC) lags I_2 by 90° because of $-j$ before I_2, this is shown in Fig. 6.32. Now draw a line AB parallel and equal to OC. Since angle OAB is equal to 90°, the point A must lie on a circle with OB as its diameter.

Since stator current I_1 is equal to the phasor sum of constant no-load current I_o and rotor current referred to stator I_2', total stator current is $\bar{I}_1 = \bar{I}_o + I_2'$. As tip of rotor current I_2 or I_2' traces a circle, the tip of stator current phasor I_1 must also trace a circle. This forms the basis for the induction motor circle diagram.

(b) **Circle diagram from the approximate equivalent circuit.** The shunt branch consisting of R_c and X_m in parallel, see Fig. 6.13 *(a)*, may be connected across the supply terminals, resulting in the approximate equivalent circuit of induction motor as shown in Fig. 6.33. This circuit neglects the stator leakage impedance drop due to I_o and is used sometimes for approximate performance calculations, because it leads to simplicity and reduced labour.

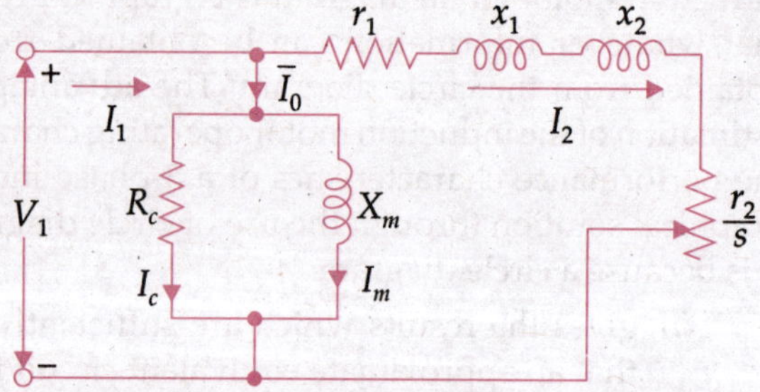

Fig 6.33: Approximate equivalent circuit of an induction motor

The per phase voltage V_1 sends a current I_2 through the series circuit consisting of r_1, x_1, r_2/s and x_2.

$$\therefore \quad \bar{V}_1 = \bar{I}_2\left[\left(r_1+\frac{r_2}{s}\right)+j(x_1+x_2)\right] \quad ...(6.45)$$

The current I_2 lags V_1 by an angle $\theta_2 = \tan^{-1}\frac{x_1+x_2}{r_1+\frac{r_2}{s}}$

Eq. (6.45) can be re-written as, $-j\frac{V_1}{x_1+x_2} = \bar{I}_2 - j\bar{I}_2\frac{r_1+\frac{r_2}{s}}{x_1+x_2}$

As before, $-j\frac{V_1}{x_1+x_2}$ lags V_1 by 90° and $-jI_2\frac{r_1+\frac{r_2}{s}}{x_1+x_2}$ lags I_2 by 90° and I_2 lags V_1 by θ_2 where

$\theta_2 = \tan^{-1}\dfrac{x_1+x_2}{r_1+\dfrac{r_2}{s}}$. This is illustrated in Fig. 6.34 *(a)*, where V_1 is taken along the vertical axis. Here

$OB = \dfrac{V_1}{x_1+x_2}$ is the diameter of the rotor-current locus, $OA = I_2$ lags V_1 by rotor pf angle θ_2 and AB

$= OC = I_2\dfrac{r_1+\dfrac{r_2}{s}}{x_1+x_2}$. At standstill, for V_1 applied voltage, I_2 (= OD) becomes very large and angle θ_2

increases to $\tan^{-1}\dfrac{x_1+x_2}{r_1+r_2}$. This is also shown in Fig. 6.34 *(a)* in which $DB = I_2\dfrac{r_1+r_2}{x_1+x_2}$.

In order to include the effect of shunt branch in the circle diagram, draw magnetizing current $I_m = \dfrac{V_1}{X_m} = OQ'$ and core-loss component of current $I_c = Q'Q = \dfrac{V_1}{R_C}$. Then OQ is the no-load current I_o. The rotor-current locus diagram of Fig. 6.34 *(a)* is repeated again with QB $\left(= \dfrac{V_1}{x_1+x_2}\right)$ as the diameter. In this manner circle diagram of Fig. 6.34 *(b)* is obtained from the approximate equivalent circuit. Here QA is the rotor current I_2, OA is the stator current I_1 and $\cos\theta_1$ is the operating power factor at stator terminals.

Note that $QQ' \times V_1$, in Fig. 6.34 *(b)*, represents the core loss only. However, in addition to core loss, friction and windage loss at no load operation must also be taken into consideration. This is explained next.

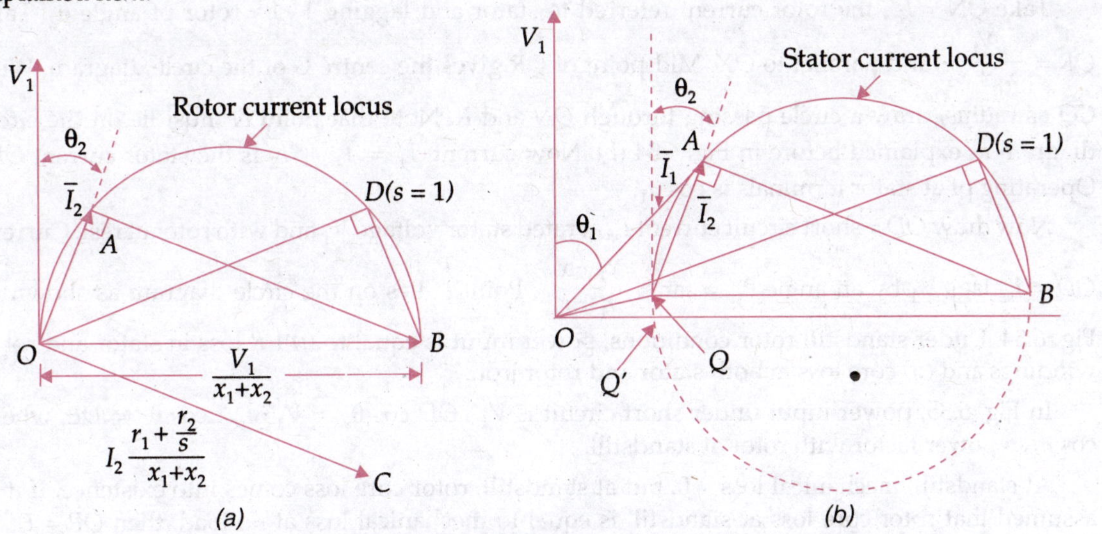

Fig 6.34: Induction motor circle diagram. *(a)* with shunt-branch neglected and *(b)* effect of shunt branch included

(c) **Circle diagram and performance computation.** In Fig. 6.35, draw OQ = no-load current (on some scale, say one cm = 2 *A* etc.) I_o lagging V_1 by no-load pf angle θ_0. Lines OX and QR are drawn perpendicular to voltage phasor V_1 shown vertical. Draw QP perpendicular to reference line OX. Here $QP \times V_1$ = no-load input to stator = friction and windage loss (or mechanical loss) + stator core loss + negligible stator I^2R loss. Power-factor angle θ_0 is given by

$$\theta_0 = \cos_{-1}\frac{\text{No-load power input}}{\sqrt{3}\,(\text{No-load current})\,V_1}$$

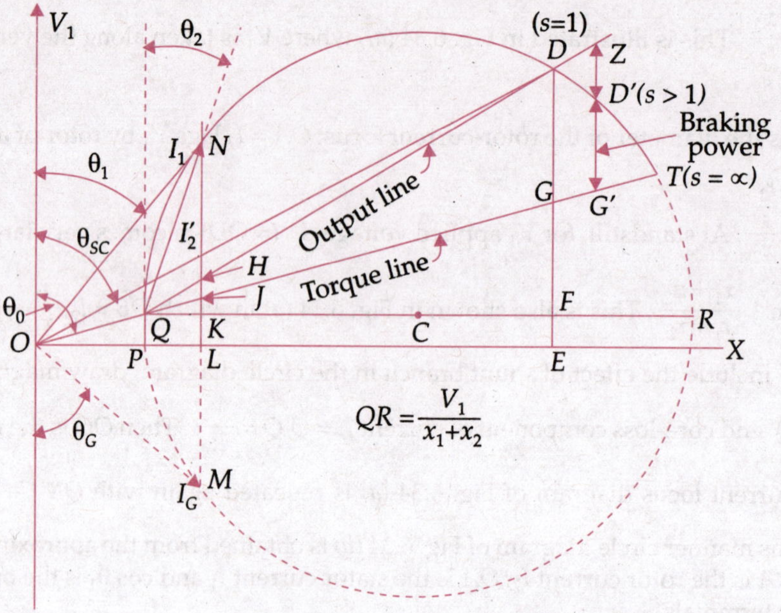

Fig 6.35: Induction motor circle diagram. Stator current locus QND (motor mode), DT (brake mode) and QPMRT (generator mode).

Take QN = I_2', the rotor current referred to stator and lagging V_1 by rotor pf angle θ_2. Take $QR = \dfrac{V_1}{x_1 + x_2}$ and parallel to OX. Mid-point of QR gives the centre C of the circle diagram. With CQ as radius, draw a circle passing through QN and R. Note that point N must lie on the circle diagram as explained before in Fig. 6.34 *(b)*. Now current $\bar{I}_1 = \bar{I}_o + \bar{I}_2'$ is the stator current ON. Operating pf at stator terminals is cos θ_1.

Now draw OD = short circuit current I_{sc} at rated stator voltage V_1 and with rotor at rest. Current $OD = I_{sc}$ lags V_1 by an angle $\theta_{sc} = \tan^{-1} \dfrac{x_1 + x_2}{r_1 + r_2}$. Point D lies on the circle diagram as shown in Fig. 6.34. Under standstill rotor conditions, power input is equal to *(i)* I^2R loss in stator and rotor windings and *(ii)* core loss in both stator and rotor iron.

In Fig. 6.35, power input under short circuit is $V_1 \cdot OD \cos \theta_{sc} = V_1 \cdot I_{sc} \cdot \cos \theta_{sc} = DE$, where $\cos \theta_{sc}$ = power factor with rotor at standstill.

At standstill, mechanical loss = 0, but at standstill, rotor core loss comes into existence. If it is assumed that rotor core loss at standstill is equal to mechanical loss at no load, then $QP = EF$ = constant loss = sum of mechanical and stator core losses. At standstill, power input to stator = DE = stator core and mechanical losses EF (= QP) + stator and rotor I^2R losses. This shows that here $DE - EF = DF$ must be the total stator and rotor ohmic losses. Let G divide DF such that

$$\frac{GD}{GF} = \frac{\text{rotor ohmic loss}}{\text{stator ohmic loss}}$$

. Join Q with D and G as shown.

In Fig. 6.35, stator power input is NL. Also, stator power input NL [rotor ohmic loss HJ + stator ohmic loss JK + constant loss] = NH. Thus, NH is the output power ; therefore, the line joining Q with D and passing through H can be called **output power line.**

Also, torque = $\frac{NJ}{\omega_s}$ at slip s, but torque = $\frac{DG}{\omega_s}$ at standstill. Therefore, here NJ and DG represent torque to scale and therefore, a line passing through J and G can be labelled torque line. Therefore, in Fig. 6.35, QD is the **output power line** and QG is the **torque line.**

In Fig. 6.35, N is the operating point with stator current I_1 and stator pf cos θ_1. From N on the circle diagram, NL is normal to the horizontal line OX. Perpendicular NL intersects the output line at H and torque line at J and QR line at K.

Stator and rotor I^2R losses. In Fig. 6.35, triangles QKH and QFD are similar. Here DF represents the stator and rotor ohmic loss at standstill for stator current OD. Likewise, HK must represent, on the same scale, the stator and rotor ohmic loss for stator current ON.

Further, the triangles QKJ and QFG and also the triangles QJH and QGD are similar ; therefore, KJ = stator ohmic loss for stator current ON and JH = rotor ohmic loss for current ON.

Performance parameters. For the operating point N on the circle diagram in Fig. 6.35, the induction motor performance can be obtained as under.

Star input current = ON Power output = NH

Rotor I^2R loss = HJ Stator I^2R loss = JK

Friction and windage (or mechanical) and core loss = KL

Power input = NL

Now torque is given by

$$\text{Torque} = \frac{\text{Air-gap Power}}{\text{Synchronous speed}}$$

$$= \frac{\text{Power input } NL - [\text{Total mechanical and core losses, } KL + \text{Stator } I^2R \text{ loss } KJ]}{\omega_s}$$

$$= \frac{NL - [KL + KJ]}{\omega_s} = \frac{NL - JL}{\omega_s} = \frac{NJ}{\omega_s}$$

$$\therefore \qquad \text{Torque} = \frac{NJ}{\omega_s} = \frac{\text{Air-gap power or power input to rotor}}{\omega_s} \qquad \text{...(6.46)}$$

$$\text{Slip} = \frac{\text{Rotor I}^2\text{R loss}}{\text{Air-gap power}} = \frac{HJ}{NJ} \qquad \text{...(6.47)}$$

From Triangle OLN, stator pf = cos $\underline{/NOL}$ = cos $\theta_1 = \frac{LN}{ON}$

$$\text{Efficiency} = \frac{\text{Power output}}{\text{Power input}} = \frac{NH}{NL} \qquad \text{...(6.48)}$$

Brake Mode. If slip is made more than 1, then braking action takes place. In Fig. 6.35, D' is a typical operating point for which the slip is more than one. Here the braking torque is $\frac{D'G'}{\omega_s}$ = $\frac{\text{rotor input}}{\omega_s}$. It is also seen that rotor input (= $D'G'$) is less than rotor ohmic loss $Z\,G'$. Brake mode in the circle diagram of Fig. 6.35 is indicated by part of the circle between D (s = 1) and T ($s = \infty$). Note that at T, slip is infinity, rotor current is zero and therefore rotor I^2R loss is zero.

Generator Mode. If rotor speed is made more than synchronous speed, the induction motor starts operating as an **induction generator**. Generator mode is indicated by dotted line from Q to P, lower part of circle, R and to T ($s = \infty$). For operating point M on the lower part, ML = electrical power output from generator and I_G (= OM) is the stator output current. Mechanical power input from prime-mover to drive the machine is MH. Total I^2R losses are HK and constant losses are LK as for the motor mode. Operating pf is $\cos\theta_G = \cos \angle OML$ leading. Here leading pf implies that machine still requires lagging reactive power input to magnetize the machine for producing rotating field. Active power output is ML.

(d) **Circle diagram from test data.** The circle diagram depicting the locus of stator current, can be drawn by using the test data obtained from no-load and blocked-rotor tests and the stator resistance.

No-load and blocked-rotor tests are conducted as explained in Art. 6.11. The rated voltage V_{nl}, current I_{nl} and power P_{nl} are all per phase values for no-load test. Current $I_{nl} = OQ$ is drawn making an angle of θ_o with reference phasor V_1. Here angle θ_o is given by

$$\cos\theta_o = \frac{P_{nl}}{V_{nl}I_{nl}} \quad \text{...(6.49)}$$

or
$$\theta_o = \cos^{-1}\frac{P_{nl}}{V_{nl}I_{nl}}$$

Note that OQ in Fig. 6.36 is drawn to a suitable scale.

In blocked-rotor test, the applied voltage V_{br} is only a fraction of rated voltage. The blocked-rotor test data V_{br}, I_{br} and P_{br} is converted to values that would have been obtained with rated applied per-phase voltage V_1.

$$\therefore \quad I_{sc} = I_{br}\frac{V_1}{V_{br}}$$

$$P_{sc} = P_{br}\left(\frac{V_1}{V_{br}}\right)^2$$

$$\cos\theta_{sc} = \frac{P_{br}}{V_{br}I_{br}} = \frac{P_{sc}}{V_1 I_{sc}} \quad \text{...(6.50)}$$

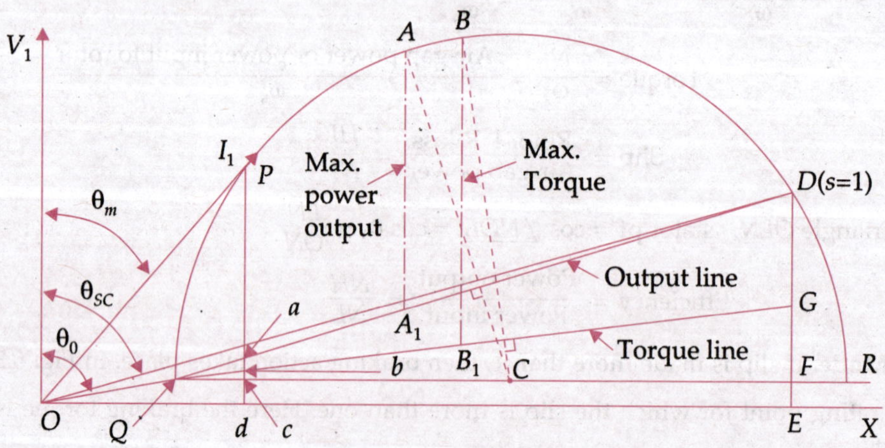

Fig 6.36: Circle diagram from no-load and blocked-rotor tests.

Now $OD = I_{sc}$ is drawn making an angle of θ_{sc} with V_1. Points Q and D on the current locus are, therefore, determined. Lines QR and OX are drawn perpendicular to phasor V_1. Right bisector of the line joining power Q, D meets QR in C which is the centre of locus-circle. With C as centre and CQ as radius, the circle is drawn. Now draw DE perpendicular to OX. Divide DF at G so that

$\frac{DG}{GF} = \frac{r_2}{r_1}$, where r_1 is the effective per phase stator resistance and r_2 is the per phase resistance referred to stator. Now for any operating point P on the circle diagram, the entire performance can be obtained by drawing a perpendicular dP on the line OX. Thus for the operating point P in Fig. 6.36, input current = OP, power output = aP, rotor-ohmic loss = ab, stator ohmic loss = bc, friction-windage and core loss = cd, power input = dP, torque = $\frac{bP}{\omega_s}$, slip = $\frac{ba}{bP}$, power factor = $\frac{dP}{OP}$ and efficiency = $\frac{aP}{dP}$.

If current scale is 1 cm = x amperes, then per phase power scale is 1 cm = xV_1 watts, where V_1 is the per phase voltage.

For obtaining maximum power output, draw, from the centre C of the circle, a perpendicular CA to the output line QD, see Fig. 6.36. Now AA_1, drawn normal to OX, represents the maximum power output to scale.

Maximum torque is obtained by drawing from the centre C of the circle, a perpendicular CB to the torque line QG. Then BB_1, drawn normal to OX, gives the maximum torque to scale.

Maximum power factor can be obtained by drawing a tangent from O to the circle. In Fig. 6.36, I_1 is the stator current corresponding to the maximum power factor $\cos\theta_m$.

Example 6.47. *A 15 kW, 400 V, 4-pole, 50 Hz, 3-phase star-connected induction motor gave the following test results :*

	No-load test	*Blocked-rotor test*
Line voltage	*400 V*	*200 V*
Line current	*9 A*	*250 A*
Power input	*1310 watts*	*7100 watts*

Stator and rotor ohmic losses at standstill are assumed equal.

Draw the induction motor circle diagram and calculate :

(a) line current, power factor, slip, torque and efficiency at full load;

(b) maximum possible power factor and the corresponding line current ;

(c) maximum power output and maximum power input ;

(d) slip at which maximum torque occurs, maximum torque and

(e) starting toque.

Solution. From no-load test, no-load power factor is

$$\cos\theta_o = \frac{1310}{\sqrt{3}\times 400\times 9} = 0.21$$

$$\therefore \qquad \theta_o = 77.88°$$

No-load current $I_o = 9$ A.

From blocked-rotor test, short-circuit power factor is

$$\cos\theta_{sc} = \frac{7100}{\sqrt{3}\times 200\times 50} = 0.41$$

$$\therefore \qquad \theta_{sc} = 65.8°.$$

Short-circuit current at rated stator voltage is

$$I_{sc} = \frac{400}{200}\times 50 = 100 \text{ A.}$$

The circle diagram can now be drawn with the help of above data, as follows :

Scale 6 A = 1 cm

Draw $OQ = 9/6$ cm at an angle $\theta_o = 77.88°$ lagging V_1, and draw $OD = \frac{100}{6}$ cm at an angle of $\theta_{sc} = 65.8°$ behind V_1. Join Q with D to get the output line QD. The right-bisector of QD meets QR in C and this is the required centre of the circle diagram. Note that OX and QR are drawn perpendicular to phasor V_1. With C as centre, draw a circle with CQ as radius. From D, draw DE perpendicular to OX. Since stator and rotor ohmic losses are equal, make $FG = GD$. Join G with Q to obtain the torque line GQ, Fig. 6.37.

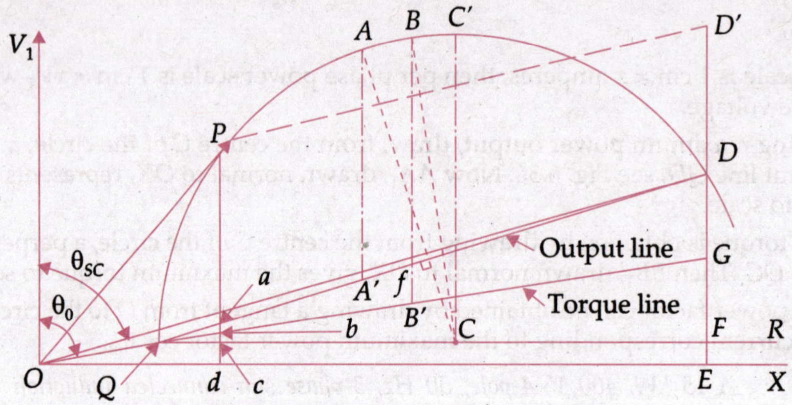

Fig 6.37: Induction motor circle diagram, Example 6.47.

(a) Per phase power scale = xV_1 watts per cm.

Here $\quad V_1 = \frac{400}{\sqrt{3}}$ volts

and $\quad x = 6$ A/cm.

$\therefore$ Per phase power scale $= \frac{400}{\sqrt{3}} \times 6 = 1385.7$ watts/cm.

Full-load power per-phase $= \frac{15{,}000}{3} = 5000$ watts.

In order to get the operating point P, extend FD to D'.

Make $DD' = \frac{5000}{1385.7} = 3.61$ cm.

Now draw $D'P$ parallel to the output-line QD. Join P with O.

$\therefore$ Full-load line current $= OP = 6 \times 6.05 = 36.3$ A

$\therefore$ Full-load power factor $= \cos \angle OPd = \cos \angle POV_1 = \cos 29.5° = 0.87$ lag.

$$\text{Full-load slip} = \frac{ba}{bP} = \frac{2.5}{38.5} = 0.065.$$

$$\text{Full-load torque} = \frac{1}{\omega_s}(bP)\,(\text{per phase power scale}) \times 3$$

$$= \frac{1}{50\pi}(3.85)(1385.7) \times 3 = 101.89 \text{ Nm.}$$

$$\text{Full-load efficiency} = \frac{aP}{dP} = \frac{3.6}{4.45} = 0.809 \text{ or } 80.9\%.$$

(b) In this example, OP (per chance) turns out to be tangent to the circular-locus. Therefore, maximum or best possible operating power factor is 0.87 lag and the line current is 36.3 A.

(c) For maximum power output, draw CA perpendicular to output-line QD. From A draw AA' perpendicular to QR. Then maximum power output is given by

AA' × per phase power scale × 3 = 5.3 × 1385.7 × 3 = 22.03 kW.

For maximum power input, draw CC' perpendicular to QR. Then maximum power input = CC' + Friction-windage and core-losses. But CC' is equal to the radius of circle.

∴ Maximum power input = 8.45 × 1385.7 × 3 + 1310 = 36.437 kW.

(d) For maximum torque, draw CB perpendicular to torque line QG. Draw BB' normal to QR. Then,

$$\text{Maximum torque} = \frac{1}{\omega_s}\,(BB') \times (\text{Per phase power scale}) \times 3 = \frac{1}{50\pi}\,(6.65)\,(1385.7)\,(3) = 176 \text{ Nm.}$$

$$\text{Slip at which maximum torque occurs} \quad = \frac{fB'}{BB'} = \frac{1.58}{6.65} = 0.238.$$

(e) Starting torque,

$$T_{e\cdot st} = \frac{1}{\omega_s}\,(DG)\,(\text{Per phase power scale}) \times 3$$

$$= \frac{1}{50\pi}\,(3.30)\,(1385.7)\,(3) = 87.33 \text{ Nm.}$$

Example 6.48. *A 4.5 kW, 400 V, 50 Hz, 3-phase delta connected induction motor gave the following test results :*

No-load test (line values) : 400 V, 4.2 A, 480 W.

Blocked-rotor test (line values) : 215 V, 15 A, 1080 W.

Rotor resistance referred to stator is 1.2 Ω per phase. Stator and rotor ohmic losses at standstill are assumed equal and stator to rotor phase turns ratio is 2/1.

Calculate the external resistance that must be inserted in series with the rotor circuit in order to obtain (a) maximum torque at starting and (b) 1.25 times the full-load torque at starting.

For both parts (a) and (b), find the corresponding stator currents and power factors also.

If the induction motor is made to work as an induction generator with output current equal to motor full-load current, then find

(c) its power output, operating power factor and efficiency.

Solution. From no-load test, no-load power factor is

$$\cos\theta_o = \frac{480/3}{400\left(\dfrac{4.2}{\sqrt{3}}\right)} = 0.165,\ \theta_o = 80.5°.$$

From blocked-rotor test, short-circuit power factor is

$$\cos\theta_{sc} = \frac{1080/3}{215\left(\dfrac{15}{\sqrt{3}}\right)} = 0.1933,\ \therefore\ \theta_{sc} = 78.86°.$$

Per phase short-circuit current at rated voltage

$$= \frac{400}{215} \times \frac{15}{\sqrt{3}} = 16.11 \text{ A.}$$

$$\text{Per phase no-load current} = \frac{4.2}{\sqrt{3}} = 2.42 \text{ A.}$$

Scale 1A = 1 cm.

Draw the circle diagram as explained in Example 6.47.

(*a*) In order to get the maximum torque, draw *CB* perpendicular to the torque line *QG*. Draw *BB′* perpendicular to *OX*. Then *BB′* gives the maximum torque, Fig. 6.38.

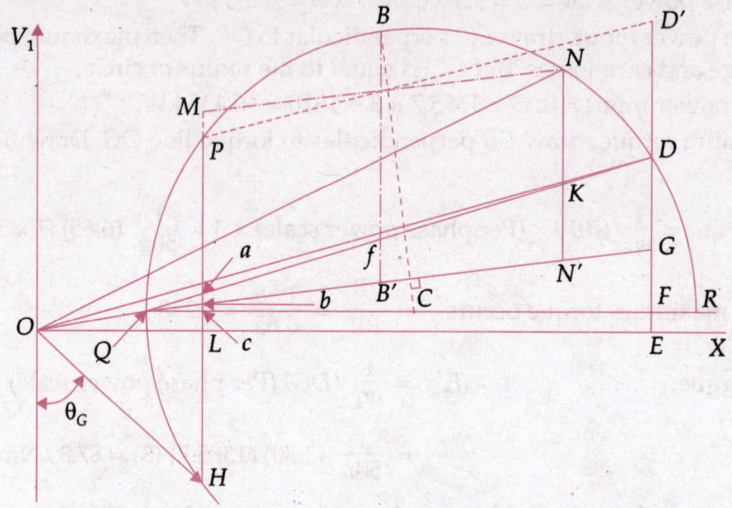

Fig 6.38: Induction motor and generator circle diagram. Example 6.48.

The maximum torque at starting can be obtained only if the operating point at starting is *B* (and not *D*). At this operating point *B*, the internal rotor resistance consumes a loss equal to *fB′*. The remainder of the loss *fB* (at starting) must be consumed by the external resistance to be inserted in the rotor circuit.

$$\therefore \quad \frac{\text{External resistance to be inserted}}{\text{Internal rotor resistance}} = \frac{Bf}{B'f} = \frac{4.6}{1.25}.$$

$$\therefore \quad \text{External resistance to be inserted} = \frac{4.6}{1.25} \times 1.2 = 4.416\ \Omega.$$

External resistance referred to rotor (or actual value of the external resistance) $= \dfrac{4.416}{(2)^2} = 1.104\ \Omega$.

Corresponding to maximum torque at starting, the per phase starting current is $OB = 11.24$ A or the starting line current is $11.24 \times \sqrt{3} = 19.47$ A. The power factor is $\cos \angle OBB' = \cos 45.5° = 0.701$ lag.

(*b*) Per phase power scale $= xV_1 = 1 \times 400 = 400$ W/cm.

$$\text{Full-load power per phase} = \frac{4500}{3} = 1500 \text{ watts.}$$

In order to get the full-load operating point *P* and thus the full-load torque $T_{e\cdot fl}$, extend *FD* to *D′* so that $DD' = \dfrac{1500}{400} = 3.75$ cm. Now draw *D′P* parallel to the output line *QD*. The full-load torque $T_{e\cdot fl}$ is proportional to *bP*. Now extend *bP* to *M* so that $bM = 1.25\ bP$. Draw *MN* parallel to the torque line *QG*. Draw *NN′* normal to *OX*. Now *N* is the operating point at starting so that 1.25 times the full load torque is obtained. As in part (*a*), internal rotor resistance consumes a loss equal to *N′K* and the remainder *KN* is consumed in the external resistance.

$$\therefore \quad \text{External resistance to be inserted} = \frac{NK}{N'K} \times \text{Rotor resistance} = \frac{2.9}{2.1} \times 1.2 = 1.657\ \Omega.$$

$$\text{External resistance referred to rotor} = \frac{1.657}{(2)^2} = 0.414\ \Omega$$

Corresponding to operating point N, per phase starting current is $ON = 14.35$ A or the starting line current is $14.35\sqrt{3} = 24.85$ A. The operating power factor is $\cos \angle ONN' = \cos 58.3° = 0.525$ lag.

(c) Per phase output current when working as an induction generator = OH = 5.35 A.

$$\text{Induction generator p.f.} = \cos\theta_G = \cos 41.3° = 0.75 \text{ leading.}$$

$$\therefore \quad \text{Induction generator output} = 3 \times 400 \times 5.35 \times 0.75 = 4815 \text{ W} = 4.815 \text{ kW.}$$

$$\text{Induction generator efficiency} = \frac{HL}{Ha} = \frac{3.95}{4.90} = 0.80612 \text{ or } 80.612\%.$$

Example 6.49. *A 150 kW, 400 V, 8-pole, 50 Hz, star-connected induction motor has the following impedance parameters in ohms per phase referred to stator.*

$r_1 = 0.02\ \Omega,\ r_2 = 0.04\ \Omega,\ x_1 = x_2 = 0.2\ \Omega,\ X_m = 9.8\ \Omega$

At rated shaft output, it runs with a slip of 4 percent and with an efficiency of 93%.

(a) Calculate the mechanical and core losses at rated load from the data given above.

(b) If this motor is driven as a generator at a slip of 4 percent, determine (i) electric power output (ii) p.f. at the generator terminals and (iii) efficiency.

The induction generator is connected to a distribution system of 400 V.

Solution. (a) From Fig. 6.14,

$$Z_f = \frac{\left(\frac{0.04}{0.04} + j0.2\right)(j9.8)}{1 + j(9.8 + 0.2)} = \frac{-1.96 + j9.8}{1 + j10} \times \frac{1 - j10}{1 - j10}$$

$$R_f + jX_f = \frac{96.04 + j29.4}{101} = (0.951 + j\,0.291)\ \Omega$$

$$r_1 + jx_1 = 0.02 + j\,0.2$$

$\therefore$ Total input impedance,
$$Z = 0.971 + j\,0.491 = 1.088\ \angle 26.824°$$

Stator current,
$$I_1 = \frac{400}{\sqrt{3} \times 1.088} = 212.27 \text{ A}$$

Air-gap power,
$$P_g = 3\, I_1^2\, R_f = 3\ (212.27)^2 \times 0.951 = 128552.1\text{W}$$

Total stator
$$I^2R \text{ loss} = 3\,(212.27)^2 \times 0.02 = 2703.5 \text{ W}$$

Total rotor
$$I^2R \text{ loss} = sP_g = 0.04 \times 128552.1 = 5142.1 \text{ W}$$

$$\text{Total losses} = \left(\frac{1}{n} - 1\right)\text{output} = \left(\frac{1}{0.93} - 1\right) \times 150{,}000 = 11290.3 \text{ W}$$

Total mechanical and core losses = 11290.3 – (2703.5 + 5142.1) = 3444.7 W

(b) When slip $s = -0.04$, from Fig. 6.14,

$$Z_f = \frac{\left(-\frac{0.04}{0.04} + j0.2\right)(j9.8)}{-1 + j10} = \frac{-1.96 - j9.8}{-1 + j10} \times \frac{-1 - j10}{-1 - j10}$$

$$R_f + jX_f = \frac{-96.04 + j29.4}{101} = -0.951 + \text{j}\,0.291$$

$$r_1 + jx_1 = 0.02 + j\,0.2$$

Total impedance,
$$Z = -0.931 + j\,0.491 = 1.0525\ \angle 152.2°$$

$$I_1 = \frac{400}{\sqrt{3}} \times \frac{1}{1.0525\ \angle 152.2°} = 219.43\ \angle{-152.2°} \text{ A}$$

$$\therefore \quad \text{Stator output current} = 219.43\ \angle 27.8° \text{ A}$$

$$\text{Power factor at machine terminals} = \cos 27.8° = 0.8846$$

(i) Electric power output= $\sqrt{3} \times 400 \times 219.43 \times 0.8846 = 134478$ W

(ii) Regarding 134478 W as output power, the induction generator works at a leading p.f. of 0.8846.

(iii)
$$\text{Air-gap power} = 3\,(219.43)^2 \times 0.951 = 137370.6 \text{ W}$$
$$\text{Total stator } I^2R \text{ loss} = 3\,(219.43)^2 \times 0.02 = 2889 \text{ W}$$
$$\text{Total rotor } I^2R \text{ loss} = sP_g = 0.04 \times 137370.6 = 5494.8 \text{ W}$$
$$\text{Total mechanical and core losses} = 3444.7 \text{ W}$$
$$\text{Total losses} = 11828.5 \text{ W}$$

Mechanical power input to drive the induction generator
$$= \text{Power output} + \text{total losses}$$
$$= 134,478 + 11828.5 = 146306.5 \text{ W}$$
$$\text{Efficiency of induction generator} = \frac{134,478}{146,306.5} \times 100 = 91.92\%.$$

6.13. POWER FACTOR CONTROL OF THREE PHASE INDUCTION MOTORS

The best possible power factor of an induction motor operating near its full-load capacity is about 0.86 lag, whereas its no-load power factor varies from 0.1 to 0.3 lag. Since induction motors may be light-loaded for a part of their operating time, their average operating power factor is very low. The reasons that an induction motor always operates at lagging power factors for any value of the load, are as follows :

(i) The magnetizing current, necessary for the production of working magnetic flux, lags the applied voltage by 90°.

(ii) The voltage drops in stator and rotor leakage reactances increase the power factor angle between applied voltage and stator current. Consequently the effect of leakage reactances is to decrease the operating power factor.

At present, major industrial and agricultural loads consist of polyphase induction motors operating at average low power factors. In order to utilize the distribution and feeder circuits better and to decrease the losses in these circuits, a larger operating power factor is essential. The important methods of power factor control of polyphase induction motors are :

(a) by the use of static capacitors across the stator terminals of both the squirrel cage and wound-rotor induction motors and

(b) by the use of auxiliary machines for wound-rotor induction motors.

In this article, only the first method of power factor control of induction motors is considered.

6.13.1. Static Capacitors

This method, which involves the connection of static capacitors across stator terminals of an induction motor, does not alter the inherent motor characteristics. In smaller sizes, controlling the power factor by static capacitors is the simplest and most economical.

In order to study the effect of connecting static capacitors across the stator terminals, refer to Fig. 6.39 *(a)*. Fig. 6.39 *(b)* shows that without the use of static capacitors, the stator current is I_1 and the motor operating power factor is cos θ_1. When capacitors are connected across stator terminals as shown in Fig. 6.39 *(a)*, the current I_c through the capacitors lead the voltage V_1 by 90° (assumed ideal capacitors). The phasor sum of I_1 and I_c gives the current I_1' drawn from the supply. In Fig.

6.39 *(b)*, stator leakage impedance drop is ignored for the sake of simplicity. The power factor of the combination (capacitors and induction motor) improves from cos θ_1 to cos θ_1' and stator current decreases from I_1 to I_1'.

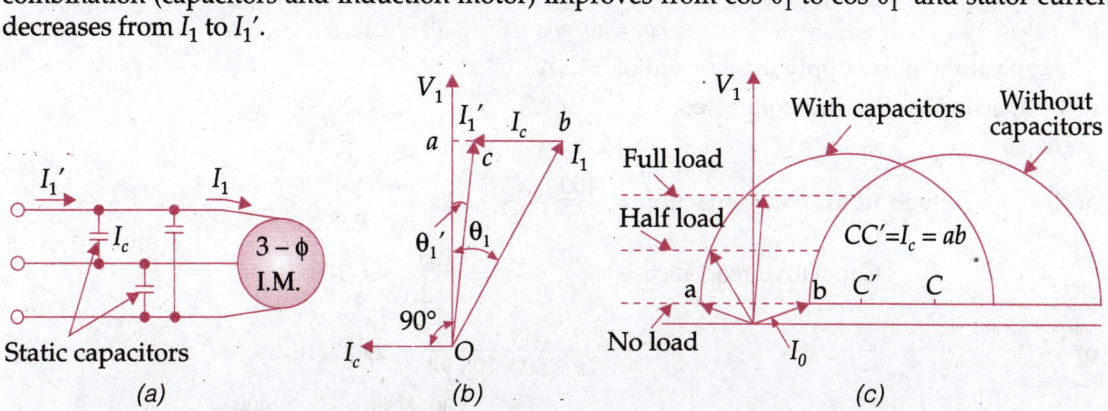

Fig 6.39: Pertaining to the induction motor power-factor control by static capacitors.

The degree of power factor correction at different loads can be appreciated with the help of circle diagram. In Fig. 6.39 *(c)*, the stator current locus of the induction motor is shifted to the left—this shift being equal to the length of the current phasor $\bar{I}_c$. This means that the centre of current locus shifts from C to C′ such that length CC′ = I_c. It is seen from this current locus that with fixed value of capacitance, the degree of power factor correction is different at the various loads. Fig. 6.39 *(c)* reveals that if full-load power factor is nearer to unity, the power factors at no load and half full-load are leading. The leading power factor under certain condition may result in rise of the stator terminal voltage, because the transformer supplying this induction motor may have negative voltage regulation at these loads.

Sometimes the switching on of induction motor and capacitor as a unit may result in self-excitation which may cause serious stator over-voltages or excessive transient torques. The self-excitation of the induction machine can be avoided by limiting the size of the parallel capacitors. A still better way of avoiding self-excitation is to adjust the capacitance with load either manually or automatically.

Example 6.50. *An induction motor operating from a balanced three phase 400 V, 50 Hz supply, takes a line current of 10 amperes at 0.8 p.f. lag. Calculate the per phase value of capacitance and the total kVA rating of the 3-phase capacitor bank which, when connected to the motor terminals, would improve the line power factor to 0.9 lag.*

Solution. It is not given whether the induction motor is star or delta connected, same is the case with 3-phase capacitor bank. Here the induction-motor stator is assumed in star and the capacitor bank is taken to be first star-connected and then delta connected. The above calculations are again repeated with the induction-motor stator in delta. For this example, refer to Fig. 6.39 *(b)*.

(a) **Stator in star.** Per phase current, $I_1 = 10$ A.

With phase voltage as reference, the current in phasor form is

$$\bar{I}_1 = 10\,(0.8 - j\,0.6) = 8 - j\,6 = oa - j\,ab.$$

When the power factor is improved to 0.9 lag, current is I_1', but its real component *oa* is again 8 A. Thus the magnitude of I_1' is given by

$$I_1' = \frac{\text{Real part of } I_1}{\cos\theta_1'} = \frac{8}{0.9} = 8.89 \text{ A.}$$

In phasor form, $$\bar{I}_1' = 8.89\,(0.9 - j\,0.436) = 8 - j\,3.880 = oa - j\,ac.$$

Examination of Fig. 6.39 *(b)* reveals that reactive component of current to be neutralised by capacitor is *cb*.

$$\therefore \qquad cb = ab - ac = 6 - 3.88 = 2.12 \text{ A.}$$

The capacitors must supply this current of 2.12 A.

(i) If capacitor bank is star-connected,

then $$I_c = 2.12 \text{ A}$$

and $$\text{voltage across each capacitor} = \frac{400}{\sqrt{3}} \text{ V.}$$

$$\therefore \qquad \text{Capacitive reactance} = \frac{400}{\sqrt{3} \cdot I_c} = \frac{400}{\sqrt{3} \times 2.12} = 108.94\ \Omega.$$

or $$C = \frac{1}{2\pi \times 50 \times 108.94} = 29.22\ \mu\text{F.}$$

$$\text{Total kVA rating of the 3-phase capacitor bank} = 3I_c \times \frac{400}{\sqrt{3}} = 3 \times 2.12 \times \frac{400}{\sqrt{3}} = 1.469 \text{ kVA.}$$

(ii) When capacitor bank is delta connected, let C be its capacitance per phase. Problems involving balanced star-load in parallel with delta-load should be solved by converting *(i)* star-load into an equivalent delta or *(ii)* delta load into an equivalent star. Then the problem is solved on per phase basis.

As stator is connected in star, it is convenient to convert delta-connected values to equivalent star for this part.

Capacitive reactance for delta-connected capacitor bank,

$$X_\Delta = \frac{1}{2\pi f C}$$

Star-equivalent of delta-connected capacitor bank,

$$X_Y = \frac{X_\Delta}{3} = \frac{1}{2\pi f(3C)}$$

$$\text{Per-phase voltage across } Y\text{-connected bank} = \frac{400}{\sqrt{3}}$$

Per-phase current, $$I_C = 2.12 \text{ A}$$

Per-phase reactance, $$X_Y = \frac{400}{\sqrt{3} \times 2.12} = \frac{1}{2\pi\, 50\,(3C)}$$

or $$C = \frac{\sqrt{3} \times 2.12}{400 \times 2\pi\, 50(3)} = 9.74\ \mu\text{F}$$

$$\text{Total kVA rating of 3-phase capacitor bank} = 3 \times 2.12 \times \frac{400}{\sqrt{3}} \times \frac{1}{1000} = 1.469 \text{ kVA}$$

(b) **Stator in delta.** Per phase current, $I_1 = \dfrac{10}{\sqrt{3}} = 5.77$ A.

In phasor form, $$\bar{I}_1 = 5.77\,(0.8 - j\,0.6) = 4.62 - j\,3.46.$$

When power factor is 0.9 lag, then magnitude of I_1' is $I_1' = \dfrac{4.62}{0.9} = 5.13$ A.

In phasor form, $$\bar{I}_1' = 5.13\,(0.9 - 0.436) = 4.62 - j\,2.24$$

As in part *(a)* $$cb = ab - ac = 3.46 - 2.24 = 1.22 \text{ A.}$$

(i) For star-connected capacitor bank of capacitor *C* per phase,

$$X_Y = \frac{1}{2\pi f C}$$

Delta-equivalent of star-connected capacitor bank,

$$X_\Delta = 3X_Y = \frac{3}{2\pi f C}$$

Per phase voltage across delta-equivalent bank = 400 V

Per phase capacitor current = 1.22 A

$$\therefore \quad X_c = \frac{400}{1.22} = \frac{3}{2\pi \times 50 \times C}$$

$$\therefore \quad C = \frac{1.22 \times 3}{400 \times 2\pi \times 50} = 29.125\ \mu F$$

Total kVA rating of 3-phase capacitor bank = $3 \times 400 \times 1.22 \times \frac{1}{1000} = 1.464$ kVA

(ii) For delta-connected capacitor bank, I_c = 1.22 A

and voltage across each capacitor bank = 400 V

$$\therefore \quad X_c = \frac{400}{1.22} = \frac{1}{2\pi \times 50 \times C}$$

$$\text{or} \quad C = \frac{1.22}{400 \times 2\pi (50)} = 9.708\ \mu F$$

Total kVA rating of 3-phase capacitor bank = $3 \times 1.22 \times 400 \times \frac{1}{1000} = 1.464$ kVA

It is seen from above that for the improvement of power factor of a given 3-phase induction motor, the kVA rating of capacitor bank is the same whether the motor is in star or delta. Also the value of per-phase capacitance *C* for **delta-connected capacitance bank is one-third of that required for star-connected capacitance bank.**

Example 6.51. *A 3-phase, 500 kW, 3.3 kV, 50 Hz, star-connected induction motor works at a full-load power factor of 0.7 lag. A delta-connected capacitor bank is used to raise the full-load power factor to 0.9 lag. Calculate the capacitance of the bank. If each capacitor is rated at 420 V, 50 Hz, compute the capacitance of each unit. The motor efficiency is 86%.*

If this induction motor is fed by a distribution circuit, calculate the percentage saving in the energy lost in this distribution circuit, as the power factor is improved from 0.7 to 0.9 lag.

Solution. Motor per phase input current

$$I_1 = \frac{500}{\sqrt{3} \times 3.3. \times 0.7 \times 0.86} = 145.32 \text{ A.}$$

With per phase stator voltage as the reference phasor, the current in phasor form is

$$\bar{I}_1 = 145.32\,(0.7 - j\,0.714) = 101.72 - j\,103.76.$$

Magnitude of per phase motor current I_1' as the power factor is improved to 0.9 [refer to Fig. 6.39 *(b)*],

$$I_1' = \frac{\text{Real component of } I_1}{0.9} = \frac{101.72}{0.9} = 113.02 \text{ A.}$$

In phasor form, $\bar{I}_1' = 113.02\,(0.9 - j\,0.436) = 101.72 - j\,49.28.$

∴ Reactive component of per phase current that capacitor must supply = Reactive component of $\bar{I}_1$ – Reactive component of $\bar{I}_1'$ = 103.76 – 49.28 = 54.48 A.

Here the induction motor is star-connected and the capacitor bank is delta-connected. Converting delta-connected bank of per-phase capacitance C to an equivalent star-connected bank, we get

$$X_Y = \frac{X_\Delta}{3} = \frac{1}{2\pi f(3C)}$$

$$\text{Per phase voltage} = \frac{3300}{\sqrt{3}}$$

$$\text{Per phase current} = 54.48 \text{ A}$$

$\therefore$ Per-phase reactance
$$X_Y = \frac{3300}{\sqrt{3} \times 54.48} = \frac{1}{2\pi f(3C)}$$

or
$$C = \frac{\sqrt{3} \times 54.48}{3300 \times 2\pi \times 50 \times 3} = 30.34\ \mu\text{F}.$$

Now each capacitor is rated at 420 V, therefore, 8 $\left(\cong \frac{3300}{420}\right)$ such capacitors will have to be connected in series.

$\therefore$ Capacitance of each capacitor $= 30.34 \times 8 = 242.72\ \mu$F.

Let the resistance of the distribution circuit be R ohms per phase.

Then, power lost in the distribution circuit without capacitor bank $= 3\,(145.32)^2 R$ watts.

Power lost when the capacitor bank is installed $= 3\,(113.02)^2 R$ watts.

$$\therefore \quad \text{Percentage saving in the losses} = \frac{3(145.32)^2 R - 3(113.02)^2 R}{3(145.32)^2 R} \times 100 = 39.51\%.$$

In case the capacitor bank is star-connected, then it can be computed that the capacitance of each bank is $30.34 \times 3 = 91.02\ \mu$F. Five such capacitors $\left(\cong \frac{3300}{\sqrt{3} \times 420}\right)$ would have to be connected in series and capacitance of each capacitor should be

$$91.02 \times 5 = 455.10\ \mu\text{F}.$$

6.14. STARTING OF POLYPHASE INDUCTION MOTORS

It is seen from Fig. 6.18 that a 3-phase induction motor has positive finite starting torque T_{est} when slip $s = 1.0$. This means that 3-phase induction motor is a self-starting motor and begins to rotate on its own when connected to a 3-phase source.

At the instant of starting, a 3-phase induction motor behaves like a transformer with short-circuited secondary. Consequently, a 3-phase induction motor takes high starting current if started at full voltage. In order to limit this high starting current to reasonable values, some methods are adopted for the starting of 3-phase induction motors.

In this article, various methods of starting polyphase induction motors are described. First the methods of starting squirrel-cage motors are presented and then the methods of starting wound-rotor motors.

6.14.1. Starting of Squirrel-cage Motors

For cage motors, the choice of any particular method of starting depends on *(i)* size and design of the motor *(ii)* capacity of the power lines and *(iii)* type of the driven load. There are primarily two methods of starting squirrel-cage induction motors : *(a)* full-voltage starting and *(b)* reduced-voltage starting. The full-voltage starting consists of DOL starting only. The reduced-voltage starting has the advantage of reducing the starting current, but it produces an objectionable reduction in the starting torque, on account of the fact that motor torque is proportional to the square of the applied voltage. Despite this, reduced-voltage starting is the most popular method of starting three-phase squirrel-cage induction motors and consists of stator resistor (or reactor) starting, auto-transformer starting and star-delta starting. The various methods are now described in what follows.

(a) **Direct-on line (across-the-line) starting.** As the name suggests, this method involves the direct switching of polyphase stator on to the supply mains. The motor takes low-power factor starting current of 5 to 7 times its full-load current, depending upon its size and design. Such large currents of short duration don't harm the rugged squirrel cage motor, but the high currents may cause objectionable voltage drop in the power supply lines feeding the induction motor. These large voltage drops cause undesirable dip in the supply line voltage ; consequently the operation of other equipments connected to the same supply line is affected considerably. A common example is the momentary dimming of lamp and tube-lights in the home at the instant a refrigerator motor starts.

If the supply system is of sufficient power capacity and the low-power factor starting-current surges don't cause objectionable voltage dips in the supply line voltage, then the direct-on-line starting should be preferred.

The relation between starting torque $T_{e\cdot st}$ and full-load torque $T_{e\cdot fl}$ is now obtained. Let I_{st} and I_{fl} be the per-phase stator currents drawn from the supply mains corresponding to starting and full-load conditions respectively. From Eq. (6.13),

$$T_e = \frac{1}{\omega_s} \cdot I_2^2 \cdot \frac{r_2}{s}$$

$$\therefore \quad \frac{T_{e\cdot st}}{T_{s\cdot fl}} = \frac{I_{2st}^2 \dfrac{r_2}{1}}{I_{2fl}^2 \dfrac{r_2}{s_{fl}}} = \left(\frac{I_{2st}}{I_{2\cdot fl}}\right)^2 \cdot s_{fl} \qquad \text{...(6.51 a)}$$

Eq. (6.51 *a*) is valid in case rotor resistance remains constant. Actually, rotor resistance varies with the freuency of rotor current ; at starting rotor frequency is 50 Hz and at full load it is only a few hertz.

Here I_{2st} and $I_{2\cdot fl}$ are the per-phase rotor currents at starting and full-load conditions respectively. If no-load current is neglected, then

$$I_{st} \times \text{effective stator turns} = I_{2\,st} \times \text{effective rotor turns}$$

or $$I_{st} = I_{2\,st} \text{ (effective rotor to stator turns ratio)}$$

or $$\frac{I_{st}}{I_{fl}} = \frac{\text{(Effective rotor to stator turns ratio)} I_{2\cdot st}}{\text{(Effective rotor to stator turns ratio)} I_{2\cdot fl}}$$

or $$\frac{I_{st}}{I_{fl}} = \frac{I_{2\cdot st}}{I_{2\cdot fl}}$$

Here I_{st} and I_{fl} are the stator current at start ($s = 1$) and at full load (slip = s_{fl}) respectively.

From Eq. (6.51 *a*), $$\frac{T_{e\cdot st}}{T_{e\cdot fl}} = \left(\frac{I_{st}}{I_{fl}}\right)^2 s_{fl} \qquad \text{...(6.51 b)}$$

If V_1 is the per phase stator voltage and Z_{sc} is the standstill per phase leakage impedance referred to stator, then per phase short-circuit current I_{sc} at standstill (or at starting) is $I_{sc} = V_1/Z_{sc}$.

where $$Z_{sc} = (r_1 + r_2) + j\,(x_1 + x_2).$$

Note that here shunt branch of the induction motor equivalent circuit of Fig. 6.13 *(a)* is neglected. Therefore, for direct switching, we have starting current, I_{st} = short-circuit current,

$$I_{sc} = \frac{V_1}{\text{short circuit impedance}} = \frac{V_1}{Z_{sc}}$$

Eq. (6.51 *b*) can, therefore, be written as $\dfrac{T_{e \cdot st}}{T_{e \cdot fl}} = \left(\dfrac{I_{sc}}{I_{fl}}\right)^2 s_{fl}$ ...(6.52)

(b) **Stator resistor (or reactor) starting.** In this method, a resistor or a reactor is inserted in between motor terminals and the supply mains, as illustrated in Fig. 6.40. At the time of starting, some voltage drop occurs across the starting resistor or reactor and, therefore, only a fraction x (less than 1) of the supply voltage appears across the stator terminals. This reduces the per-phase starting current I_{st} drawn by the motor from the supply mains.

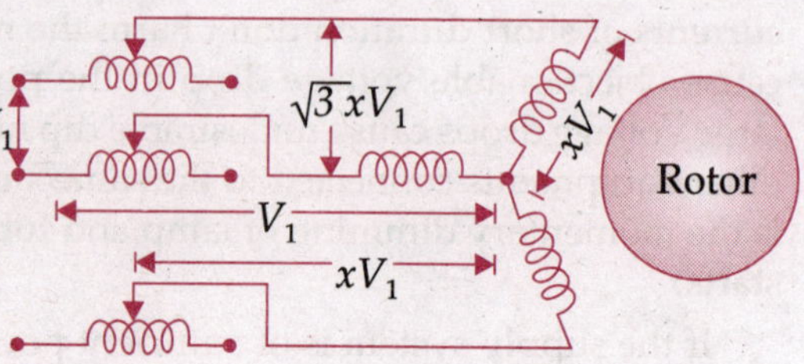

Fig 6.40: Reactor (or resistor) starting of squirrel cage induction motor

As the motor speeds up, the reactor is cut out in steps and finally short-circuited when the motor speed is near to its operating speed. Since per phase voltage is reduced to xV_1, see Fig. 6.40, the per-phase starting current I_{st} is given by

$$I_{st} = \frac{xV_1}{Z_{sc}} = x\, I_{sc} \qquad \text{...(6.53)}$$

As before,

$$\frac{T_{e \cdot st}}{T_{e \cdot fl}} = \left(\frac{I_{st}}{I_{fl}}\right)^2 s_{fl} \qquad \text{...(6.54 a)}$$

or

$$\frac{T_{e \cdot st}}{T_{e \cdot fl}} = x^2 \left(\frac{I_{sc}}{I_{fl}}\right)^2 \cdot s_{fl} \qquad \text{...(6.54 b)}$$

In an induction motor, torque $\propto$ (voltage)^2

$$\therefore \frac{\text{Starting torque with reactor starting}}{\text{Starting torque with direct switching}} = \left(\frac{xV_1}{V_1}\right)^2 = x^2 \qquad \text{...(6.55)}$$

Series reactor is more costly than the series resistor, but the former has lower energy loss and is more effective in reducing the voltage, because the induction-motor power factor at starting is quite low.

(c) **Auto-transformer starting.** A fraction xV_1 of the supply voltage V_1 is applied to the stator terminals at the time of starting, by means of an auto-transformer as shown in Fig. 6.41. This reduces the motor current and also the current drawn from the supply. After the motor has accelerated near to its operating speed, auto-transformer is disconnected and full line voltage is applied to the induction motor by connecting it directly across the supply mains. Note that here x is less than one.

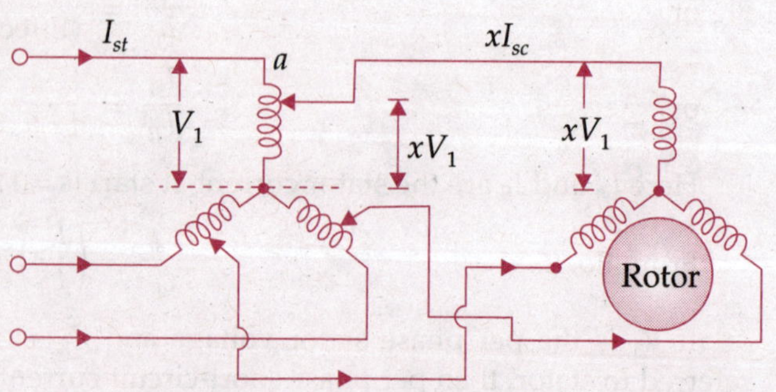

Fig 6.41: Pertaining to auto-transformer starting.

With auto-transformer, per phase starting current in motor winding

$$= \frac{xV_1}{Z_{sc}} = x\, I_{sc} \qquad \text{...(6.56)}$$

If no-load current of auto-transformer is neglected, then per phase output *VA* of auto-transformer must be equal to its per phase input *VA*. That is

$$I_{st} \cdot V_1 = xV_1 \text{ (per phase starting current in motor winding)}$$

or

$$I_{st} \cdot V_1 = xV_1\,(xI_{sc})$$

∴ Per phase starting current from the supply mains,

$$I_{st} = x^2 \cdot I_{sc} \qquad \text{...(6.57)}$$

Eq. (6.56) shows that motor starting current per phase is reduced only to x times the direct switching current I_{sc} ; but the per phase starting current from the supply mains is reduced to x^2 times the direct switching I_{sc}. As per Eq. (6.51 *b*),

$$\frac{T_{e \cdot st}}{T_{e \cdot fl}} = \frac{(\text{Per phase starting current in motor winding})^2}{(\text{Per phase motor full-load current})^2} \cdot s_{fl}$$

From Eq. (6.56)

$$\frac{T_{e \cdot st}}{T_{e \cdot fl}} = \frac{(xI_{sc})^2}{I_{fl}^2} \cdot s_{fl} = x^2 \left(\frac{I_{sc}}{I_{fl}}\right)^2 s_{fl} \qquad \text{...(6.58)}$$

The ratio of starting to full-load torque in terms of both motor starting current I_{st} (= $x^2 I_{sc}$) and short circuit current I_{sc} can be obtained from Eq. (6.58) as follows.

$$\frac{T_{e \cdot st}}{T_{e \cdot fl}} = \frac{(x^2 I_{sc}) I_{sc}}{I_{fl}^2} \cdot s_{fl} = \frac{I_{st} \cdot I_{sc}}{I_{fl}^2} \cdot s_{fl} \qquad \text{...(6.59)}$$

For an induction motor, torque ∝ (voltage)^2

$$\therefore \quad \frac{T_{e \cdot st} \text{ with an auto-transformer}}{T_{e \cdot st} \text{ with direct switching}} = \left(\frac{xV_1}{V_1}\right)^2 = x^2 \qquad \text{...(6.60)}$$

It is seen from Eq. (6.54 *b*) and Eq. (6.58) that starting torque with stator reactor = starting torque with auto-transformer starter.

It is observed from above that with an auto-transformer, the starting current I_{st} from the mains and starting torque $T_{e \cdot st}$ are reduced to x^2 times their corresponding values with direct-on-line starting, see Eqs. (6.57) and (6.60).

(*d*) **Star-delta starting.** This method of starting is used for motors designed to operate normally in delta. The six terminals from the three phases of the stator must be available as shown in Fig. 6.42 *(a)*. Here the terminals are marked *a*, *A* for phase *A* ; *b*, *B* for phase *B* and *c*, *C* for phase *C*. Commercially, the terminals are marked A_1, A_2 for phase *A* ; B_1, B_2 for

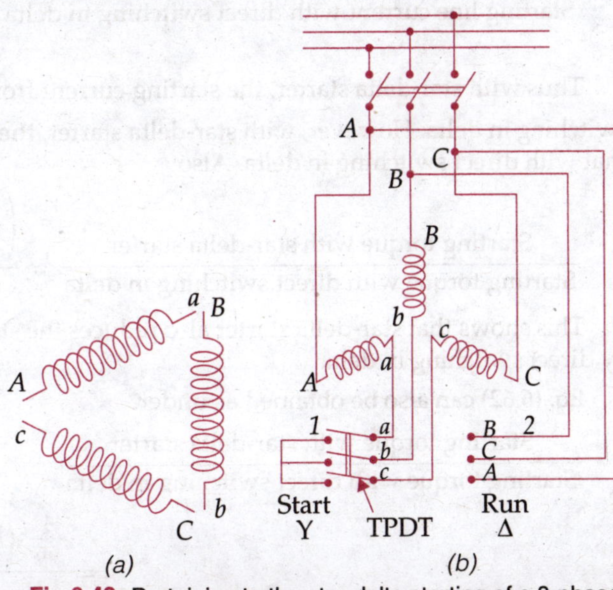

Fig 6.42: Pertaining to the star-delta starting of a 3-phase cage induction motor.

phase B and C_1, C_2 for phase C. Fig. 6.42 *(b)* illustrates a simple schematic diagram of a star-delta starter.

As stated above, three stator terminals are marked A, B, C in Fig. 6.42 *(b)* and the other three stator terminals marked a, b, c are connected to the middle terminals of a triple pole double throw *(TPDT)* switch. The stator phases are first connected in star by throwing the tripple pole double throw *(TPDT)* switch to position 1 and after steady-state speed has reached, *TPDT* is thrown over to position 2, thereby connecting the stator winding in delta, see Fig. 6.42 *(b)*.

In position 1, terminals a, b, c are short circuited. In position 2, terminal a is connected to B ; b to C ; c to A.

Let V_L be the line voltage. Then per phase motor starting current $I_{st \cdot y}$ with stator winding in star is given by $I_{st \cdot y} = V_L / \sqrt{3}\ Z_{sc}$

With stator winding in star, $I_{st \cdot y}$ is also the starting line current with star-delta starter. If the stator winding were delta connected, then with the direct switching, the per phase motor starting current $I_{st \cdot d}$ would be given by $I_{st \cdot d} = V_L / Z_{sc} = I_{sc \cdot d}$

and starting line current with direct switching would be equal to $\sqrt{3}\ V_L/Z_{sc} = \sqrt{3}\ I_{st \cdot d} = \sqrt{3}\ I_{sc \cdot d}$. Here $I_{sc \cdot d}$ is the per-phase short circuit current with motor winding in delta.

From above,
$$\frac{I_{st \cdot y}}{I_{st \cdot d}} = \frac{V_L}{\sqrt{3} Z_{sc}} \times \frac{Z_{sc}}{V_L} = \frac{1}{\sqrt{3}} \quad \text{...(6.61 a)}$$

$$\therefore \quad I_{st \cdot y} = \frac{1}{\sqrt{3}} \cdot I_{st \cdot d} \quad \text{...(6.61 b)}$$

$$\therefore \quad \frac{\text{Starting per-phase current with star-delta starter}}{\text{Starting per phase current with direct switching}} = \frac{1}{\sqrt{3}}$$

Here the subscripts y and d denote star and delta connections of stator winding respectively. From above

$$\frac{\text{Starting line current with star-delta starter}}{\text{Starting line current with direct switching in delta}} = \frac{I_{st \cdot y}}{\sqrt{3} I_{st \cdot d}} = \frac{\frac{1}{\sqrt{3}} \cdot \frac{V_L}{Z_{sc}}}{\sqrt{3} \cdot \frac{V_L}{Z_{sc}}} = \frac{1}{3}$$

Thus with star-delta starter, the starting current from the mains is one-third of that with direct switching in delta. However, with star-delta starter, **the starting current per-phase** is $\frac{1}{\sqrt{3}}$ times of that with direct switching in delta. Also

$$\frac{\text{Starting torque with star-delta starter}}{\text{Starting torque with direct switching in delta}} = \frac{\left(\frac{V_L}{\sqrt{3}}\right)^2}{V_L^2} = \frac{1}{3} \quad \text{...(6.62)}$$

This shows that star-delta starter also reduces the starting torque to one-third of that produced by direct switching in delta.

Eq. (6.62) can also be obtained as under.

$$\frac{\text{Starting torque with star-delta starter}}{\text{Starting torque with direct switching in delta}}$$

$$= \frac{\frac{1}{\omega_s} \cdot (I_{st \cdot y})^2 \cdot \frac{r_2}{1}}{\frac{1}{\omega_s} (I_{st \cdot d})^2 \cdot \frac{r_2}{1}} = \left[\frac{I_{st \cdot y}}{I_{st \cdot d}}\right]^2 = \left[\frac{1}{\sqrt{3}}\right]^2 = \frac{1}{3} \quad \text{...(6.62)}$$

Note that in Eq. (6.62), the relation $I_{st \cdot y} = \frac{1}{\sqrt{3}} I_{st \cdot d}$ from Eq. (6.61 *b*) is used.

In auto-transformer, if the ratio of output voltage to supply voltage is $1/\sqrt{3}$, then both the starting line current, Eq. (6.57), and motor starting torque, Eq. (6.62), are reduced to one-third of their corresponding values with direct switching in delta. This shows that with star delta-starter, a motor behaves as if it were started by an auto-transformer starter with $x = 1/\sqrt{3} = 0.58$, *i.e.*, with 58% tapping.

$$\frac{\text{Starting torque with star-delta starter, } T_{e \cdot st}}{\text{Full-load torque with stator winding in delta, } T_{e \cdot fld}}$$

$$= \frac{\frac{1}{\omega_s}(I_{st \cdot y})^2 \frac{r_2}{1}}{\frac{1}{\omega_s}(I_{fl \cdot d})^2 \frac{r_2}{s_{fl}}} = \frac{\left(\frac{1}{\sqrt{3}} I_{st \cdot d}\right)^2}{(I_{fl \cdot d})^2} s_{fl} = \frac{1}{3}\left(\frac{I_{sc \cdot d}}{I_{fl \cdot d}}\right)^2 \cdot s_{fl} \quad \text{...(6.63)}$$

Star-delta starter is cheap as compared to auto-transformer starter and is, therefore, used extensively. For applications requiring starting torque not exceeding about 50% of rated torque, star-delta starting is the most suitable method. This method is, therefore, used for starting SCIM coupled with pumps, fans, propellors, machine-tools, motor-generator sets etc. For line voltages exceeding 3.3 kV, star-delta starter is not used, because then the stator winding in delta requires large turns making the motor more expensive.

Example 6.52. *(a) Show that the starting torque per line ampere with auto transformer starting is more than that obtained by stator-reactor starting.*

(b) Show that the starting torque of a polyphase induction motor varies (i) linearly with starting line current in case of an auto-transformer starting and (ii) non-linearly with starting line current in case of stator-reactor starting. Hence plot the variation of starting torque with starting line current for an induction motor with $\frac{I_{sc}}{I_{fl}} = 5$ *and full-load slip equal to 0.05.*

Solution. *(a)* Starting torque with an auto-transformer starting = $1/\omega_s$ (per phase starting current in motor winding)^2. $r_2/1 = 1/\omega_s\,(x\,I_{sc})^2\,r_2$; see Eq. (6.56).

Per-phase starting line current I_{st}, from Eq. (6.57), is $I_{st} = x^2 \cdot I_{sc}$.

$\therefore$ $T_{e \cdot st}$ per line ampere with auto-transformer starting is given by

$$= \frac{1}{\omega_s} \frac{(x \cdot I_{sc})^2 \cdot r_2}{I_{st}} = \frac{1}{\omega_s} \frac{(xI_{sc})^2}{x^2 \cdot I_{sc}} r_2$$

$$= \frac{1}{\omega_s} I_{sc} r_2 \quad \text{...(6.64)}$$

$T_{e \cdot st}$ with stator-reactor starting = $1/\omega_s$ (per phase starting current in motor winding)^2 $r_2/1$ = $1/\omega_s \cdot I_{st}^2 \cdot r_2 = 1/\omega_s\,(x\,I_{sc})^2\,r_2$, see Eq. (6.53).

Per-phase starting line current, from Eq. (6.53), is $I_{st} = x\,I_{sc}$.

$\therefore$ $T_{e \cdot st}$ per line ampere with stator-reactor starting

$$= \frac{1}{\omega_s} \cdot \frac{(x \cdot I_{sc})^2 \cdot r_2}{I_{st}} = \frac{1}{\omega_s} \frac{(xI_{sc})^2}{x\,I_{sc}} r_2 = \frac{1}{\omega_s} x\,I_{sc}\,r_2$$

$$\therefore \frac{T_{e \cdot st} \text{ per line ampere with auto-transformer starting}}{T_{e \cdot st} \text{ per line ampere with stator-reactor starting}} = \frac{\frac{1}{\omega_s} I_{sc} r_2}{\frac{1}{\omega_s} \cdot x \cdot I_{sc} r_2} = \frac{1}{x}.$$

Since x is less than 1, starting torque per line ampere with auto-transformer starting is more than that obtained with stator-reactor starting.

(*b*) For auto-transformer starting, from Eq. (6.59),

$$\frac{T_{e \cdot st}}{T_{e \cdot fl}} = \frac{I_{st} \cdot I_{sc}}{I_{fl}^2} \cdot s_{fl} \quad ...(6.59)$$

For stator-reactor starting, from Eq. (6.54 *a*), $\frac{T_{e \cdot st}}{T_{e \cdot fl}} = \left(\frac{I_{st}}{I_{fl}}\right)^2 \cdot s_{fl}$ ...(6.54 *a*)

For an induction motor of given rating, $T_{e \cdot fl}$, s_{fl}, I_{fl} and I_{sc} are dependent on its design, these are, therefore, constant. In view of this, Eq. (6.59) becomes

$$T_{e \cdot st} = \left(\frac{T_{e \cdot fl}}{I_{fl}^2} s_{fl} \cdot I_{sc}\right) I_{st} \text{ or } T_{e \cdot st} = K\, I_{st} \quad ...(6.65)$$

and Eq. (6.54 *a*) becomes

$$T_{e \cdot st} = \frac{T_{e \cdot fl}}{I_{fl}^2} \cdot s_{fl} \cdot I_{st}^2 = K_1\, I_{st}^2 \quad ...(6.66)$$

Eq. (6.65) shows that for an auto-transformer starting, variation of starting torque $T_{e \cdot st}$ with starting line current I_{st} is linear. For stator-reactor starting, Eq. (6.66) shows that $T_{e \cdot st}$ varies non-linearly with I_{st}.

For $\frac{I_{sc}}{I_{fl}} = 5$ and $s_{fl} = 0.05$, various value of $\frac{T_{e \cdot st}}{T_{e \cdot fl}}$ for different values of $\frac{I_{st}}{I_{fl}}$ are given below in tabular form :

	Starting current / Full-load current $= \frac{I_{st}}{I_{fl}}$	*0*	*1*	*2*	*3*	*4*	*5*
$\frac{T_{e \cdot st}}{T_{e \cdot fl}}$	Auto-trans. starting, Eq. (6.59)	0	0.25	0.50	0.75	1.00	1.25
	Stator-reactor starting Eq. (6.54 *a*)	0	0.05	0.20	0.45	0.80	1.25

Note that when $I_{st} = I_{sc}$, starting torque by both the methods are equal. It is also seen from the table and Fig. 6.43 that stator-reactor starting is suitable only in those applications, which require low-starting torques.

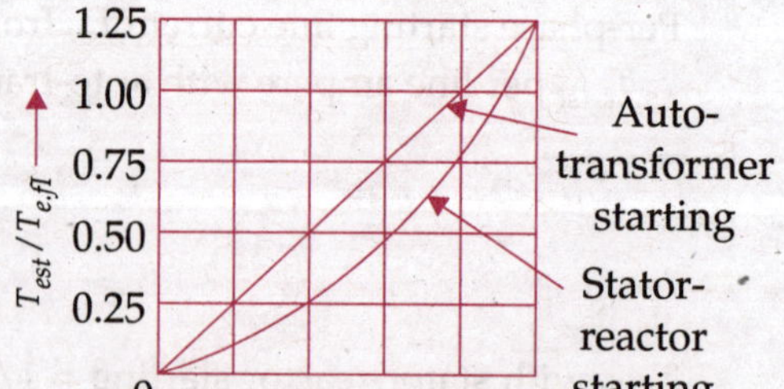

Fig 6.43: Pertaining to Example 6.52.

Example 6.53. *A squirrel cage induction motor has a full-load slip of 0.05. The motor starting current at rated voltage is 6 times its full-load current. Find the tapping on the auto-transformer starter which should give full-load torque at start. Also find the line current at starting.*

Solution. Here motor starting or short-circuit current I_{sc} is $6I_{fl}$. Now from Eq. (6.58),

$$\frac{T_{e \cdot st}}{T_{e \cdot fl}} = x^2 \left(\frac{I_{sc}}{I_{fl}}\right)^2 \cdot s_{fl}$$

$$\therefore \quad 1 = x^2\,(6)^2 \times 0.05 \text{ or } x = \sqrt{\frac{1}{1.8}} = 0.745 \text{ or } 74.5\% \text{ tapping.}$$

From Eq. (6.57), starting line current is

$$I_{st} = x^2 I_{sc} = (0.745)^2 (6I_{fl}) = 3.33\, I_{fl}.$$

Example 6.54. *A 3-phase squirrel cage induction motor, with an applied voltage of 40%, gives a blocked-rotor current of 250% and internal starting torque of 30% of their corresponding rated values. If an auto transformer limits the starting line current to 150% of the motor full-load current, compute the percentage starting torque.*

Solution. 40% of applied voltage V_1, or 0.4 V_1 gives a blocked rotor current of 2.5 times the full-load current. Therefore, rated voltage V_1 would give a blocked-rotor current or short-circuit current I_{sc} equal to

$$I_{sc} = \frac{V_1}{0.4V_1} \times 2.5\, I_{fl} = \frac{25}{4} I_{fl}.$$

It is seen from Eq. (6.57) that per phase starting current from supply mains is, $I_{st} = x^2 I_{sc}$. Since the starting line current I_{st} is limited to 1.5 I_{fl}, we have

$$I_{st} = 1.5\, I_{fl} = x^2 \left(\frac{25}{4} I_{fl}\right) \text{ or } x^2 = \frac{6}{25}.$$

Now for an induction motor,

$$\text{Starting torque} \propto (\text{Voltage})^2$$

It is given that $0.3\, T_{e \cdot fl} \propto (0.4\, V_1)^2$

Also $T_{e \cdot st2} \propto (x\, V_1)^2$

$$\therefore \quad T_{e \cdot st2} = \left(\frac{xV_1}{0.4V_1}\right)^2 (0.30\, T_{e \cdot fl}) = \frac{x^2}{0.16} \times 0.3\, T_{e \cdot fl}$$

$$= \frac{6}{25} \times \frac{1}{0.16} \times 0.3\, T_{e \cdot fl} = 0.45\, T_{e \cdot fl}$$

∴ Starting torque is 45% of full-load torque.

Example 6.55. *A three-phase 440 V distribution circuit is designed to supply not more than 1200 amperes. Assuming that a three-phase squirrel cage induction motor has a full-load efficiency of 0.85 and a full-load power factor of 0.8 and that the starting current at rated voltage is 5 times the rated full-load current, what is the maximum permissible kW rating of the motor,*

(a) if it is to be started at full voltage?

(b) if it is to be started using an auto-transformer stepping down the voltage to 80%?

(c) if it is designed for use with a star-delta starter? *(I.E.S., 1978)*

Solution. *(a)* Maximum permissible line current that the 3-phase induction motor can take from the distribution circuit is 1200 A at the time of starting. It is given that the starting current at rated voltage is 5 times the rated current of the induction motor. Therefore the rated line current of 3-phase induction motor with full-voltage starting is 1200/5 = 240 A. Thus the maximum permissible induction motor rating when started at full voltage

$$= \sqrt{3}\; V_1 I_1 \cos\theta_1 \times \text{Efficiency}$$

$$= \sqrt{3}\; (440)\,(240)\,(0.8)\,(0.85) \text{ watts} = 124.371 \text{ kW}.$$

(b) From Eq. (6.57), maximum permissible starting current from supply mains,

$$I_{st} = 1200 = x^2 I_{sc} = x^2 (5\, I_{fl})$$

or

$$1200 = (0.8)^2 (5\, I_{fl})$$

$$\therefore \quad I_{fl} = \frac{1200}{(0.8)^2 \times 5} = 375 \text{ A}.$$

∴ Maximum permissible induction motor rating

$$= \sqrt{3}\ (440)\ (375)\ (0.8)\ (0.85) \text{ watts} = 194.33 \text{ kW.}$$

(c) A star-delta starter is equivalent to auto-transformer starter with 57.8% tapping.

$$\therefore \quad 1200 = (0.578)^2 (5 I_{fl}) = \left(\frac{1}{\sqrt{3}}\right)^2 (5\, I_{fl})$$

$$\therefore \quad I_{fl} = 720 \text{ A.}$$

∴ Maximum permissible induction motor rating

$$= \sqrt{3}\ (440)\ (720)\ (0.8)\ (0.85) = 373.113 \text{ kW.}$$

Example 6.56. *A 10 kW, 400 V, 3-phase induction motor has full-load efficiency of 0.87 and power-factor of 0.85. At standstill and at rated voltage, the motor draws 5 times its full-load current and develops a starting torque of 1.5 times its full-load torque. An auto-transformer is installed to reduce the starting current and to give full-load torque at starting. Neglecting exciting current of auto-transformer, determine at the time of starting*

(a) the voltage applied to the motor terminals

(b) the current drawn by the motor and

(c) the line current drawn from the supply mains.

Solution. *(a)* The electromagnetic torque T_e is proportional to square of the voltage.

$$\therefore \quad T_{e\cdot st1} = 1.5\, T_{e\cdot fl} \propto (400)^2$$

$$\text{Also} \quad T_{e\cdot st2} = T_{e\cdot fl} \propto (V_1)^2$$

$$\therefore \quad \frac{T_{e\cdot st1}}{T_{e\cdot st2}} = \frac{1.5\, T_{e\cdot fl}}{T_{e\cdot fl}} = \left(\frac{400}{V_1}\right)^2 \text{ or } V_1 = \frac{400}{\sqrt{1.5}} = 326.6 \text{ volts.}$$

(b) For 400 V, the motor starting current = $5\, I_{fl}$

∴ For 326.6 V, the motor starting current = $5\, I_{fl}\, \dfrac{326.6}{400} = 4.0825\, I_{fl}$

Now motor full-load current, $I_{fl} = \dfrac{10{,}000}{\sqrt{3} \times 400 \times 0.87 \times 0.85} = 19.52$ A.

$$\therefore \quad \text{Motor starting current} = 4.0825 \times 19.52 = 79.6904 \text{ A.}$$

(c) On the auto-transformer secondary, the motor current is 79.64 A and the secondary voltage is 326.6 V. Therefore the current on the auto-transformer primary side of 400 V, is given by

$$\frac{326.6}{400} \times 79.64 = 65.03 \text{ A.}$$

∴ Current drawn from the supply is 65.03 A.

Current drawn from the supply mains can also be obtained by using Eq. (6.57). This example can also be solved by first calculating s_{fl} (= 0.06 here) and then using Eq. (6.58) for x etc.

Example 6.57. *A 3 phase squirrel cage induction motor has maximum torque equal to twice the full-load torque. Determine the ratio of motor starting torque to its full-load torque, if it is started by*

(a) direct-on-line starter,

(b) star-delta starter,

(c) auto-transformer starter with 70% tapping.

The per phase rotor resistance and per phase standstill reactance referred to stator are 0.2 Ω and 2 Ω respectively. Neglect stator impedance.

Solution. *(a)* With negligible stator impedance, slip at which maximum torque occurs is given by

$$s_{mT} = \frac{r_2}{x_2} = \frac{0.2}{2} = 0.1$$

Now
$$\frac{T_{e\cdot st}}{T_{em}} = \frac{2}{\frac{s_{mT}}{1}+\frac{1}{s_{mT}}} = \frac{2}{\frac{0.1}{1}+\frac{1}{0.1}} = \frac{2}{10.1}$$

$$\therefore \quad T_{e\cdot st} = \frac{2}{10.1}(2\,T_{e\cdot fl}) = 0.396\,T_{e\cdot fl}.$$

(b) With star-delta starter, starting torque is one-third of that obtained by direct-on-line starter.

$$\therefore \quad T_{e\cdot st} = \frac{1}{3}(0.396\,T_{e\cdot fl}) = 0.132\,T_{e\cdot fl}.$$

(c) With auto-transformer starter, from Eq. (6.62), we get

$$T_{e\cdot st} = (0.70)^2 \times 0.396\,T_{e\cdot fl} = 0.194\,T_{e\cdot fl}.$$

Example 6.58. *A 40 kW induction motor with a star-delta starter is supplied through a feeder from 400 V, 50 Hz main. Owing to the line drop, the starting torque is found to be the same with star as with delta connections. Determine the resistance of the feeder. From a short-circuit test on the motor, when delta-connected, the following data were obtained : V = 200 V; I = 100 A ; power factor = 0.4 (all line values). If a second feeder of the same cross-section is run in parallel with the original one, find the percentage increase in starting torque, obtained with each connection.* *(I.A.S., 1986)*

Solution. Per phase equivalent circuit parameters of the induction motor can be obtained from short-circuit test data :

$$Z_{sc} = \frac{200\sqrt{3}}{100} = 3.464\,\Omega$$

$$R_{sc} = Z_{sc}\cos\theta_{sc} = 3.464 \times 0.4 = 1.386\,\Omega$$

$$X_{sc} = \sqrt{3.464^2 - 1.386^2} = 3.175\,\Omega.$$

Let R be the resistance of each feeder line.

$$\text{Starting torque with star connection} = \frac{3}{\omega_s}\cdot\left(\frac{400}{\sqrt{3}}\right)^2 \frac{1}{[(R+1.386)^2+(3.175)^2]} \times 1.386 \quad ...(i)$$

When the stator winding is connected in delta, balanced delta connection must be replaced by an equivalent star connection so that each phase of the star is in series with each feeder line. Therefore, starting torque with delta connection is given by

$$\frac{3}{\omega_s}\left(\frac{400}{\sqrt{3}}\right)^2 \frac{1}{\left(R+\frac{1.386}{3}\right)^2+\left(\frac{3.175}{3}\right)^2} \times \frac{1.386}{3} \quad ...(ii)$$

From *(i)* and *(ii)*, for the same starting torque,

$$(R+1.386)^2 + (3.175)^2 = \left[\left(R+\frac{1.386}{3}\right)^2+\left(\frac{3.175}{3}\right)^2\right]3$$

Its simplification gives $\quad R = 2\,\Omega.$

Previous starting torque with star connection and with one feeder

$$= \frac{3}{\omega_s}\cdot\frac{(231)^2}{3.386^3+3.175^2} \times 1.386 = 0.0464\text{ K}$$

where $$K = \frac{3(231)^2}{\omega_s} \times 1.386$$

because $$K = \frac{1}{3.386^2 + 3.175^2} = 0.0464.$$

With two feeders in parallel, their effective resistance = 1 Ω.

∴ New starting torque with star connection and with two feeders in parallel

$$= \frac{3}{\omega_s} \cdot \frac{(231)^2}{2.386^2 + 3.175^2} \times 1.386 = 0.0634 \text{ K}$$

∴ Percentage increase in starting torque with star connection

$$= \frac{0.0634\,K - 0.0464\,K}{0.0464\,K} \times 100 = 36.64\%$$

Previous starting torque with delta connection and one feeder

$$= \frac{3}{\omega_s} \cdot \frac{(231)^2}{\left(2 + \frac{1.386}{3}\right)^2 + \left(\frac{3.175}{3}\right)^2} \times \frac{1.386}{3} = 0.1392\,K_1$$

where $$K_1 = \frac{3}{\omega_s} \cdot \frac{(231)^2}{3} \times 1.386$$

New starting torque with delta connection and two feeders in parallel

$$= \frac{3}{\omega_s} \cdot \frac{(231)^2}{\left(1 + \frac{1.386}{3}\right)^2 + \left(\frac{3.175}{3}\right)^2} \times \frac{1.386}{3} = 0.307\,K_1.$$

∴ Percentage increase in starting torque with delta connection

$$= \frac{0.307\,K_1 - 0.1392\,K_1}{0.1392\,K_1} \times 100 = 120.55\%.$$

Example 6.59. *A 40 kW, 3-phase induction motor has standstill impedance of 1.2 + j 3.0 Ω per phase. The motor is fed from 400 V, 50 Hz source through a feeder 500 m long. Determine the minimum allowable cross-section of each conductor of the feeder in order that starting torque shall not be reduced by more than 30% due to voltage drop in the feeder. The machine is started through a star-delta starter. Take resistivity of feeder material as 0.02 Ω/m/mm².*

Solution. Starting torque without feeder $= \frac{3V^2}{\omega_s} \cdot \frac{1}{1.2^2 + 3^2} \times 1.2$ ...(*i*)

Let R be the resistance of each feeder line.

Starting torque when fed through feeder $= \frac{3V^2}{\omega_s} \cdot \frac{1}{(R+1.2)^2 + 3^2} \times 1.2$ ...(*ii*)

Starting torque when fed through feeder should at least be equal to 0.7 times the starting torque as given by (*i*).

From (*i*) and (*ii*), $$\frac{1}{(R+1.2)^2 + 3^2} = \frac{0.7}{(1.2)^2 + 3^2} \text{ or } R^2 + 2.4\,R - 4.4743 = 0 \text{ or } R = 1.232\ \Omega.$$

Now $$\frac{\rho L}{A} = \frac{0.02 \times 500}{A} = 1.232\ \Omega.$$

∴ $$A = 8.117 \text{ mm}^2$$

Thus minimum allowable cross-section of each conductor of the feeder is 8.117 mm².

Example 6.60. *A 10-pole, 3-phase, 50 Hz, delta-connected induction motor takes 120 kW during blocked-rotor test at rated voltage and frequency. Stator ohmic loss is assumed equal to rotor ohmic loss during blocked rotor test.*

(a) Determine the starting-torque if DOL starting is used for this motor.

(b) What would be the starting torque if phase windings are connected in star and DOL starting is used?

Solution. During blocked-rotor test, power input to a 3-phase induction motor appears almost entirely as I^2R loss in both stator and rotor windings.

$\therefore$ Stator I^2R loss + rotor I^2R loss = 120 kW

It is given that stator ohmic loss = rotor ohmic loss during blocked rotor test.

$$\therefore \quad \text{Total rotor } I^2R \text{ loss } = 3\, I_2^2\, r_2 = \frac{120}{2} = 60 \text{ kW.}$$

(a) Synchronous speed,
$$\omega_s = \frac{4\pi f}{P} = \frac{4\pi \times 50}{10} = 20 \cdot \pi \text{ rad/sec}$$

$\therefore$ Starting torque,
$$T_{e \cdot st} = \frac{3}{\omega_s} \cdot I_2^2\, r_2 = \frac{60{,}000}{20\pi} = 954.93 \text{ Nm}$$

(b) With phase windings in star, starting phase current is reduced to $1/\sqrt{3}$ times the starting current when in delta.

$$\therefore \text{ Total rotor ohmic loss, } 3\, I_2^2\, r_2 \text{ when in star} = \frac{60}{(\sqrt{3})^2} = 20 \text{ kW}$$

$\therefore$ Starting torque,
$$T_{e \cdot st} = \frac{3 I_2^2 r_2}{\omega_s} = \frac{20{,}000}{20\pi} = 318.31 \text{ Nm.}$$

Example 6.61. *(a) A 5 kW, 3-phase cage induction motor is fitted with an automatic star-delta starter. On account of faulty operation of the starter, the motor continues running with its winding in star. What is the power capacity of the induction motor when running in star? Assume the motor losses to be negligible.*

(b) What is the drawback of star-delta starter? How can it be overcome?

(c) A 3 phase squirrel cage induction motor is fitted with a star-delta starter. On small loads, if the stator winding is reconnected in star, its operating power factor improves. Explain.

In case a fully-loaded delta-connected induction motor is reconnected in star, explain what happens to its operating power factor, line current and efficiency.

Solution. *(a)* Since the induction motor is fitted with star-delta starter, the motor is designed to develop 5 kW with its stator winding in delta. Let the per phase value of voltage and current for the delta-connected motor be V_1 and I_1 so that $3\, V_1 I_1 \cos\theta_1 = 5$ kW.

When the motor winding is in star, the per phase value of voltage reduces to $\frac{V_1}{\sqrt{3}}$, but the rated phase current remains as I_1. Thus the rating of induction motor when reconnected in star, becomes $3\, \frac{V_1}{\sqrt{3}}\, I_1 \cos\theta_1 = \frac{5}{\sqrt{3}} = 2.887$ kW. It is assumed that the operating power factor of the motor remains unchanged from delta connection to star connection.

(b) In an ordinary star-delta starter, the stator winding is disconnected from the supply mains when changing from star to delta. During this small interval (0.1 to 0.3 sec), the motor speed remains practically unchanged. As soon as the stator is disconnected from the supply, the rotating magnetic field is not allowed to collapse by the currents induced in the rotor bars. This rotating

field now induces voltages in the temporarily open-circuited stator winding and the frequency of these voltages is $f(1-s)$. When the star-delta switch connects the winding in delta across the supply mains, the time phase angle between the supply voltage and the stator-induced voltages may be anywhere between 0° and 180°. In case the time phase angle turns out to be 0°, both the supply voltage and the stator induced voltages are added up algebraically and a large current surge is observed in all the phases.

This drawback can be overcome by using a modified form of star-delta starter, which does not interrupt the current during the change over from star to delta. Such a starter will naturally be more complex and, therefore, more costly.

(c) In Fig. 6.44, *OA* is the no-load current with stator winding in delta, for a phase voltage of V_1. When starter is reconnected in star, the phase voltage becomes $\frac{V_1}{\sqrt{3}}$ and the no-load current reduces to *OB*. Had there been no saturation, *OB* would be equal to $\frac{1}{\sqrt{3}}$ *OA*, but on account of saturation *OB* is much less than $\frac{1}{\sqrt{3}}$ *OA*. Blocked-rotor test gives point *C* with the winding in delta and point *D* with the winding in star. The current locus passing through *C* has a diameter of $\frac{V_1}{x_1+x_2}$ and diameter of that passing through *D* is $\frac{V_1}{\sqrt{3}(x_1+x_2)}$. For any particular power output (less than that given by point *E*), I_1 is the stator current with the winding in delta and I_1' with the winding in star. Note that operating power factor $\cos\theta_1'$ with the winding in star is better than the operating power factor $\cos\theta_1$ with the winding in delta. For power-outputs less than that given by point *E*, the power factor is better with the winding in star. But for power outputs greater than that given by point *E*, operating power factor is better with the winding in delta. At the operating point *E*, power factor is same whether the winding is in star or in delta, see Fig. 6.44 *(b)*. On small loads (30 to 50% of full load) and with the winding in star, various losses (because $OB < OA$ and $I_1' < I_1$) decrease, as a result its efficiency becomes better than that obtained by the winding in delta.

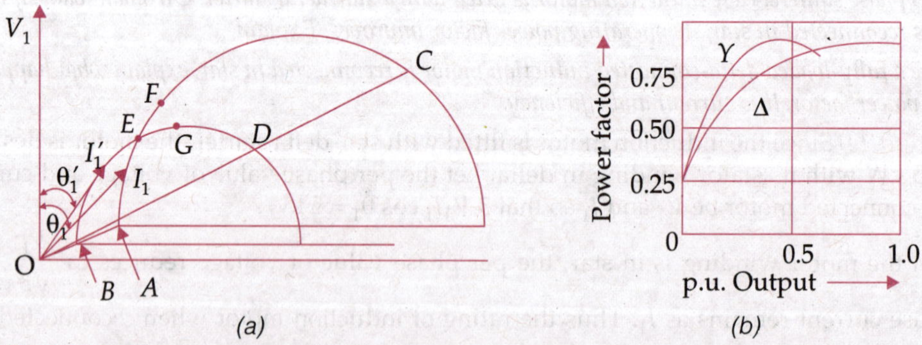

Fig 6.44: Pertaining to Example 6.53. Both the figures illustrate the effect of reconnecting the delta-connected winding in star.

With stator winding in delta, full-load power output is greater than that indicated by point *E*. In Fig. 6.44 *(a)*, let this operating point be *F*. When the stator winding is reconnected in star, the point *F* shifts to *G*, showing thereby that when operating in star at full-load, the power factor becomes poorer as compared to its value in delta and the current increases from *OF* to *OG*. Consequently there are more losses and efficiency in star at full-load is less than its value in delta at full load.

6.14.2. Methods of Starting Wound-rotor Motors

The methods used for starting squirrel-cage motors can also be employed for starting wound-rotor motors, but it is usually not done so because then the advantages of wound-rotor induction motors can't be fully realized.

The simplest and cheapest method of starting wound-rotor induction motors is by means of added rotor resistance, with full-line voltage across the stator terminals. It has already been discussed that at the time of start, the addition of external resistance in the rotor circuit of a wound-rotor induction motor

(i) decreases its starting current

(ii) increases its starting torque (for a suitable external resistance) and

(iii) improves its starting power factor.

The rotor winding terminals of a wound-rotor motor are connected to three slip-rings mounted on but insulated from the shaft. The leads, from the three brushes pressing on these slip rings, are taken to external resistances as shown in Fig. 6.45. At the time of start, the entire external resistance is added in the rotor circuit. As the rotor speeds up, the external resistance is decreased in steps so that motor torque tends to remain maximum during the accelerating period. Finally, under normal operation, the external resistance is fully cut off and the slip rings are short-circuited so that motor now develops full-load torque at low value of slip for which it is designed.

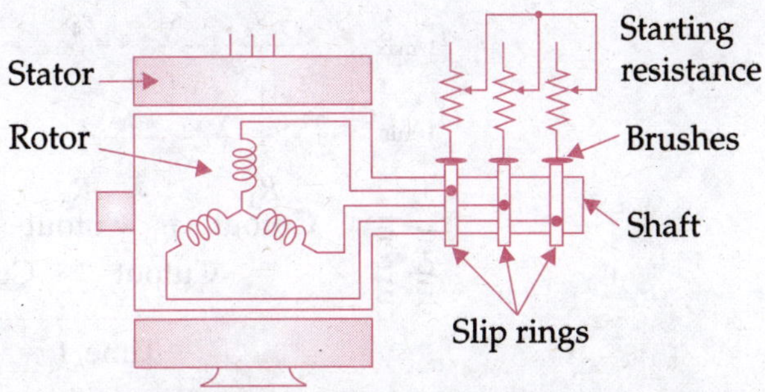

Fig 6.45: Illustrating the addition of external resistance in the rotor circuit of a wound-rotor induction motor.

Calculation of resistance of elements (or sections). Consider one phase of the rotor of a wound-rotor induction motor, with resistance r_2 and standstill leakage reactance x_2. Let R_1, R_2, R_3... R_n be the resistances of the n resistance elements (or sections) and R_1', R_2', R_3',... R_n', R_{n+1}' be the total resistances in each phase of the rotor circuit on 1st, 2nd, 3rd, ..., nth and $(n + 1)$th stud respectively as shown in Fig. 6.46 *(a)*, such that

$$R_1' = R_1 + R_2 + R_3 + R_4 + ... + R_{n-1} + R_n + r_2$$
$$R_2' = R_2 + R_3 + R_4 + ... + R_{n-1} + R_n + r_2$$
$$R_3' = R_3 + R_4 + ... + R_{n-1} + R_n + r_2$$
$$\vdots$$
$$R_{n+1}' = r_2.$$

Note that Fig. 6.46 *(a)* illustrates n-element starter, n-section starter, $(n + 1)$ stud starter or n-step starter.

For calculation of the section resistances, the following assumptions are made :

(i) During starting time, a constant load torque is assumed.

(ii) The stator leakage impedance and its no-load current are neglected.

(iii) Stator current is taken to fluctuate between fixed limits I_{1max} (maximum value) and I_{1min} (minimum value) as shown in Fig. 6.46 *(b)*.

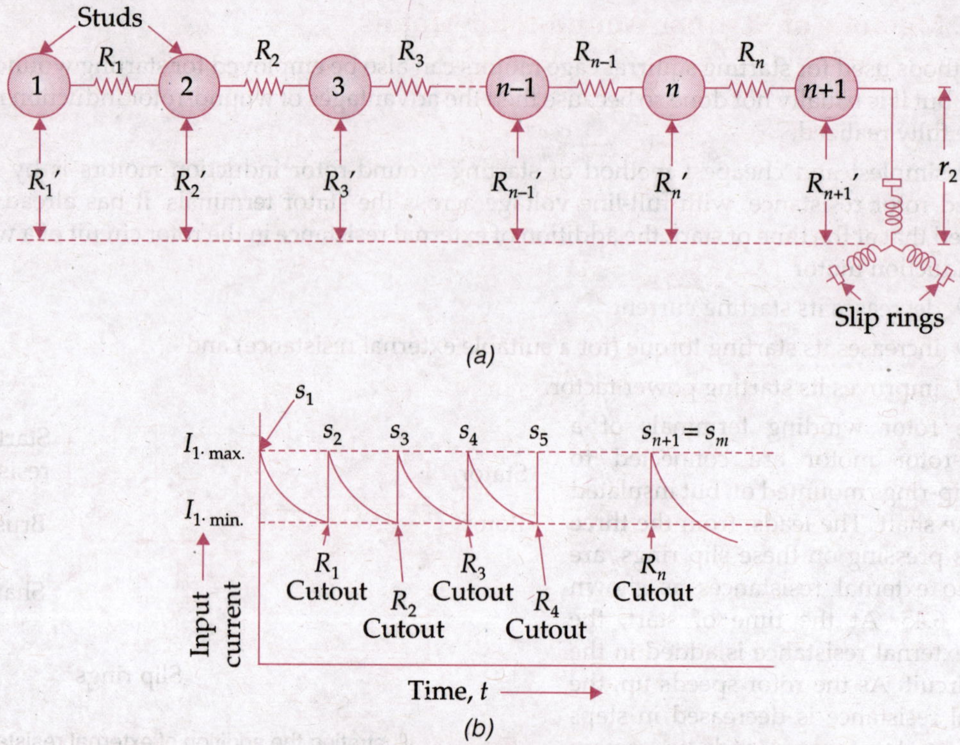

Fig 6.46: *(a)* Pertaining to the design of starter for wound-rotor induction motor *(b)* Variation of input current with time.

At the time of start, the movable handle is at stud 1 and the rotor-circuit resistance is R_1'. When the supply is switched on to the stator, the input current shoots to I_{1max} and its value is given by

$$I_{1max} = \frac{V_1}{\sqrt{(R_1'/s_1)^2 + x_2^2}} \quad ...(6.67)$$

Note that at the time of start, slip $s_1 = 1.00$.

On first stud, R_1' remains in circuit until the motor has started and the current has fallen from I_{1max} to I_{1min}. At the same time, the slip falls from s_1 to s_2

$$\therefore \quad I_{1min} = \frac{V_1}{\sqrt{(R_1'/s_2)^2 + x_2^2}} \quad ...(6.68)$$

As soon as I_{1min} is reached at stud 1, resistance R_1 is cut out by moving the handle from stud 1 to stud 2. During the notching process (the process of moving the handle from one stud to the next stud), the speed is assumed to remain constant, *i.e.*, the slip remains as s_2 but current at stud 2 becomes I_{1max} as illustrated in Fig. 6.46 *(b)*.

$$\therefore \quad I_{1max} = \frac{V_1}{\sqrt{(R_2'/s_2)^2 + x_2^2}} \quad ...(6.69)$$

At stud 2, the speed rises so that the slip falls to s_3 and current decreases to I_{1min}.

$$\therefore \quad I_{1min} = \frac{V_1}{\sqrt{(R_2'/s_3)^2 + x_2^2}} \quad ...(6.70)$$

During the next notching process, *i.e.*, at the third stud when R_2 is cut out,

$$I_{1max} = \frac{V_1}{\sqrt{(R_3'/s_3)^2 + x_2^2}} \qquad \text{...(6.71)}$$

and

$$I_{1min} = \frac{V_1}{\sqrt{(R_3'/s_4)^2 + x_2^2}} \qquad \text{...(6.72)}$$

$$\vdots$$

and so on.

From Eqs. (6.67), (6.69), (6.71) etc., we get

$$I_{1max} = \frac{V_1}{\sqrt{(R_1'/s_1)^2 + x_2^2}}$$

$$= \frac{V_1}{\sqrt{(R_2'/s_2)^2 + x_2^2}} = \frac{V_1}{\sqrt{(R_3'/s_3)^2 + x_2^2}} = \dots .$$

From above it follows that

$$\frac{R_1'}{s_1} = \frac{R_2'}{s_2} = \frac{R_3'}{s_3} = \dots\dots = \frac{R_n'}{s_n} = \frac{R'_{n+1}}{s'_{n+1}} = \frac{r_2}{s'_m} \qquad \text{...(6.73)}$$

where $s_m = s_{n+1}$ is the slip under normal operating conditions when all external resistance in rotor circuit is reduced to zero and the input current is I_{1max}.

From Eq. (6.73), we get

$$\frac{s_2}{s_1} = \frac{s_3}{s_2} = \frac{s_4}{s_3} = \dots\dots = \frac{s_n}{s_{n-1}} = \frac{s_{n+1}}{s_n} = \frac{s_m}{s_n}$$

$$= \frac{R_2'}{R_1'} = \frac{R_3'}{R_2'} = \frac{R_4'}{R_3'} = \dots\dots = \frac{R_{n-1'}}{R_{n-2'}} = \frac{R_n'}{R_{n-1'}}$$

$$= \frac{R_{n+1}'}{R_n'} = \frac{r_2}{R_n'} = \alpha \text{ (say)} \qquad \text{...(6.74)}$$

Since slip $s_1 = 1$, the total resistance in rotor circuit on the first step (or first stud) from Eq. (6.73), is

$$R_1' = \frac{s_1}{s_m}\, r_2 = \frac{r_2}{s_m} \qquad \text{...(6.75)}$$

From Eq. (6.74),

$$R_2' = R_1'\alpha,\ R_3' = R_2'\alpha = R_1'\alpha^2$$

$$R_4' = R_3'\alpha = R_2'\alpha^2 = R_1'\alpha^3$$

$$\vdots$$

$$R_{n+1}' = R_1'\alpha_n$$

or

$$r_2 = R_1'\alpha_n \qquad \text{...(6.76)}$$

Substituting the value of R_1' from Eq. (6.75) in Eq. (6.76), we get

$$r_2 = \left(\frac{r_2}{s_m}\right)\alpha^n \text{ or } \alpha^n = s_m$$

or

$$\alpha = (s_m)^{1/n} \qquad \text{...(6.77)}$$

∴ Resistances of the sections are :

$$R_1 = R_1' - R_2' = R_1'(1-\alpha) \qquad \text{...(6.78)}$$

$$R_2 = R_2' - R_3' = R_2'(1-\alpha) = \alpha R_1'(1-\alpha) = \alpha R_1$$

$$R_3 = R_3' - R_4' = R_3'(1-\alpha) = \alpha R_2'(1-\alpha) = \alpha^2 R_1.$$

Similarly $R_4 = \alpha^3 R_1$

$\vdots$

$$R_n = \alpha^{n-1} R_1 \qquad \text{...(6.79)}$$

The slip $s_m = s_{fl}$ provided $I_{1max} = I_{fl}$. In case I_{1max} is different from I_{fl}, slip s_m should be calculated accordingly and then from Eq. (6.77), α can be obtained. Once R_1' is determined by using Eq. (6.75), first resistance element R_1 is obtained by using Eq. (6.78) and then R_2, R_3, R_4 .. . can be calculated from Eq. (6.79).

Example 6.62. *Calculate the values of resistance elements of a 4-step starter for a 3-phase, 400 V, wound-rotor induction motor. The full-load slip is 3% and the maximum starting current is limited to its full-load value. Rotor resistance per phase is 0.015 Ω.*

Solution. For a 4-step starter, there are 4 sections, *i.e.*, $n = 4$.

Here $s_m = s_{fl} = 3\% = 0.03$.

From Eq. (6.77), $\alpha = (s_m)^{1/n} = (0.03)^{1/4} = 0.416$

From Eq. (6.75), $R_1' = \dfrac{r_2}{s_m} = \dfrac{0.015}{0.03} = 0.5\ \Omega.$

The resistances of the various elements are :

$$R_1 = R_1'(1 - \alpha) = 0.5(1 - 0.416) = 0.292\ \Omega$$

$$R_2 = \alpha R_1 = 0.416 \times 0.292 = 0.121\ \Omega$$

$$R_3 = \alpha^2 R_1 = \alpha R_2 = 0.416 \times 0.121 = 0.051\ \Omega$$

and $R_4 = \alpha^3 R_1 = \alpha R_3 = 0.416 \times 0.051 = 0.021\ \Omega.$

As a check, sum of R_1, R_2, R_3, R_4 and r_2 should be equal to R_1'. Here $R_1 + R_2 + R_3 + R_4 + r_2 = 0.292 + 0.121 + 0.051 + 0.021 + 0.015 = 0.50\ \Omega = R_1'$.

Example 6.63. *Design the 5 sections of a 6-stud starter for a 3-phase slip-ring induction motor. The full-load slip is 2% and the maximum starting current is limited to twice the full-load current. Rotor resistance per phase is 0.03 Ω.*

Solution. In this example, note that slip s_m is to be calculated corresponding to maximum input current = $2 \cdot (I_{2 \cdot fl})$.

Rotor current, $I_2 = \dfrac{E_2}{\sqrt{(r_2/s)^2 + x_2^2}}$

For small values of slips, $\dfrac{r_2}{s} \gg x_2$

In view of this, $I_2 = \dfrac{E_2}{r_2} s$ or $I_{2fl} = \dfrac{E_2}{r_2} s_{fl} = \dfrac{E_2}{r_2}(0.02)$

Since the starting current is limited to twice the full-load current, we have

$$2.0\,(I_{2 \cdot fl}) = \frac{E_2}{r_2}(s_m)$$

or $(2.0)\left[\dfrac{E_2}{r_2}(0.02)\right] = \dfrac{E_2}{r_2}(s_m)$

$\therefore$ $s_m = 0.04.$

Here number of sections, $n = 5$

$\therefore$ From Eq. (6.77), $\alpha = (s_m)^{1/n} = (0.04)^{1/5} = 0.525.$

From Eq. (6.75), $R_1' = \dfrac{r_2}{s_m} = \dfrac{0.03}{0.04} = 0.75\ \Omega.$

$\therefore$ The resistance of the various elements are :

$$R_1 = R_1'(1-\alpha) = 0.75\,(1-0.525) = 0.356\ \Omega$$
$$R_2 = \alpha R_1 = 0.525 \times 0.356 = 0.187\ \Omega$$
$$R_3 = \alpha^2 R_1 = \alpha R_2 = 0.525 \times 0.187 = 0.098\ \Omega$$
$$R_4 = \alpha^3 R_1 = \alpha R_3 = 0.525 \times 0.098 = 0.052\ \Omega$$
$$R_5 = \alpha^4 R_1 = \alpha R_4 = 0.525 \times 0.052 = 0.027\ \Omega$$

Rotor resistance, $r_2 = 0.030\ \Omega$

Total $= 0.75\ \Omega$

As a check, this total resistance is equal to R_1'.

Example 6.64. *A 200 kW, 3300 V, 6-pole, 50 Hz star-connected slip-ring induction motor has a star connected rotor. Stator to rotor turns ratio is 3.2. Rotor resistance and leakage reactance are 0.1 Ω and 1 Ω respectively. Neglect stator impedance and exciting current. Find (a) current and torque at starting on rated voltage and with slip rings short circuited and (b) the external resistance required to reduce the starting current to 50 A with across-the-line starting. Compute also the starting torque under these conditions.*

Solution. r_2 when referred to stator $= (3.2)^2 \times 0.1 = 1.024\ \Omega$

x_2 when referred to stator $= (3.2)^2 \times 1 = 10.24\ \Omega$

$$\omega_s = \frac{4\pi f}{P} = \frac{4\pi \times 50}{6} = \frac{100\pi}{3}\ \text{rad/sec.}$$

(a)

$$I_{st} = \frac{3300/\sqrt{3}}{\sqrt{(1.024)^2 + (10.24)^2}} = 185.14\ \text{A}$$

$$T_{e\cdot st} = \frac{3}{\omega_s} I_{st}^2 r_2 = \frac{3 \times 3}{100\pi} \times (185.14)^2 \times 1.024 = 1005.5\ \text{Nm.}$$

(b) Let R be the external resistance connected in each phase of the rotor circuit.

$$I_{st} = \frac{3300/\sqrt{3}}{\sqrt{(1.024+R)^2 + 10.24^2}} = 50\ \text{A or } R = 35.681\ \Omega$$

$$R \text{ when referred to rotor} = \frac{35.681}{(3.2)^2} = 3.484\ \Omega$$

$$T_{e\cdot st} = \frac{3}{\omega_s} \cdot I_{st}^2 r_2 = \frac{3 \times 3}{100\pi} \times (50)^2 \times (1.024 + 35.681)$$
$$= 2628.8\ \text{Nm.}$$

Note that the effect of external resistance is to decrease the starting current by a factor of 185.14/50 = 3.703 and increase the starting torque by (2628.8/1005.5) = 2.614.

6.15. POLARITY TEST

Usually six terminals from the three phases of an induction motor (or a synchronous machine) are available. If their polarity markings (A_1, A_2 ; B_1, B_2 ; C_1, C_2) are not known, then these can be found out by a polarity test on the induction motor. The object of this article is to describe this polarity test which is, in general, applicable to all 3-phase machines whose six terminals are available. Three methods of performing the polarity test are described here.

(a) **First Method.** In order to perform the polarity test on the induction motor, single-phase supply is given to any one phase, say *A*, of the induction motor and see that the rated current is not exceeded. Mark the terminals of phase *A* arbitrarily as A_1 and A_2 as shown in Fig. 6.47 *(a)*. Now join one terminal of phase *B* with terminal A_2 of phase *A*. Connect a voltmeter of suitable rating across A_1 and the remaining terminal of Phase *B* as illustrated in Fig. 6.47 *(a)*. Since the magnetic axes of phases *A* and *B* are displaced from each other by a space angle of 120° electrical, the voltage induced in phase *B* by transformer action is given by $V_1 \cos 120°$ (ideal case). If the phase *B* polarity, relative to phase *A* polarity, is as shown in Fig. 6.47 *(b)* then voltmeter reading (traversing closed circuit clockwise) would be given by

Voltage drop (going from plus to minus) in phase *B* + Voltage rise in phase

$$A = -(V_1 \cos 120°) + V_1 = -(-0.5\, V_1) + V_1 = 1.5\, V_1.$$

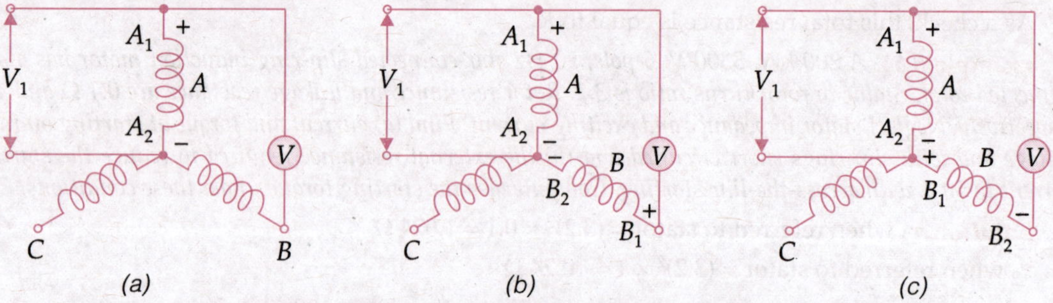

Fig 6.47: First method of polarity test on a 3-phase induction motor.

In actual practice, the magnitude of voltage induced in phase *B* is less than 0.5 V_1 because of the existence of large leakage flux. From this, it can be concluded that if voltmeter reading is more than the supply voltage V_1, then phase *B* polarity markings relative to phase *A* polarity markings are as shown in Fig. 6.47 *(b)*.

In case the phase *B* polarity markings relative to phase *A*, are as shown in Fig. 6.47 *(c)*, then the voltmeter reading would be less than the supply voltage V_1. The same procedure can be adopted for phase C of the induction motor.

With phase *A* excited from single-phase supply, the magnitude of voltage induced in phase *B* or *C* of a wound-rotor induction motor may be around 40% of V_1, because its rotor winding is open-circuited. In case of squirrel cage induction motor, the currents induced in the rotor bars oppose the pulsating flux produced by phase *A* ; consequently the voltage induced in phase *B* or *C* is much less (around 20% of that applied to phase *A*).

(b) **Second method.** In the second method, all the six terminal markings are put on phases *A*, *B* and *C* arbitrarily as shown in Fig. 6.48 *(a)*. Phase *A* is kept isolated. For phases *B* and *C*, any two terminals are connected together and a voltmeter is placed across the remaining two terminals. In Fig. 6.48 *(a)* ; B_1, C_1 are connected together and a voltmeter is placed across B_2, C_2. Now phase *A* is energised by applying single-phase voltage V_1 as shown. The magnitude of voltages induced in phases *B* and *C* by transformer action would be 0.5 V_1. In case voltmeter reads zero, the polarities of phases *B* and *C* would be as marked in Fig. 6.48 *(a)*. In this figure, from B_2 to B_1, there is a voltage drop of 0.5 V_1 and from C_1 to C_2, there is a voltage rise of 0.5 V_1 and this leads to zero voltmeter reading in Fig. 6.48 *(a)*. In case voltmeter reading is not zero (usually much less than V_1) the polarity markings of phases *B* and *C* would be as shown in Fig. 6.48 *(b)*. Same procedure can be repeated for other phases as well.

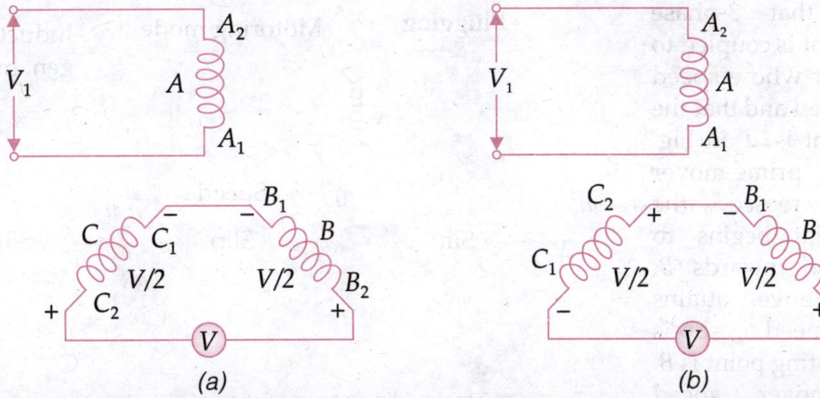

Fig 6.48: Second method of polarity test on a 3-phase induction motor.

(c) **Third method.** For this method, connect any two phases in series, say A and C, as shown in Fig. 6.49 *(a)*. For phases A and C, mark the polarities arbitrarily. Phase B is kept isolated. Apply single-phase voltage V_1 to phases A and C in series as shown. Measure voltage across phase B. If this voltage is not zero (much less than V_1), the polarities of phases A and C are as shown in Fig. 6.49 *(a)*. With V_1 as applied voltage, the voltage across each phase A or C is $V_1/2$. With the polarities as shown in Fig. 6.49 *(a)*, flux ϕ_A is set up by phase A along its winding axis. Similarly, flux ϕ_C is set up by phase C along its winding axis. Their resultant is shown as $\phi_R = \phi$. Since ϕ_R is along the axis of phase B, e.m.f. induced in phase B is not zero. Ideally, this e.m.f. in phase B should be equal to $V_1/2$, but in practice it is much less than $V_1/2$ because of the existence of large leakage flux. Thus if voltage across phase B is not zero, the phase C polarity markings, with respect to phase A, are as shown in Fig. 6.49 *(a)*.

If the polarity markings of phase C, with respect to phase A, are as shown in Fig. 6.49 *(b)*, then fluxes ϕ_A and ϕ_C are set up along their respective winding axis as shown. With $\phi_A = \phi_C = \phi$, their resultant ϕ_R is equal to $\sqrt{3}\,\phi$. As the axis of resultant flux ϕ_R is perpendicular to phase B axis, e.m.f. induced in phase B would be zero. Thus, in case voltmeter placed across phase B reads zero, the polarity markings of phases A and C are as shown in Fig. 6.49 *(b)*. Same sequence of steps can be adopted for other phases as well.

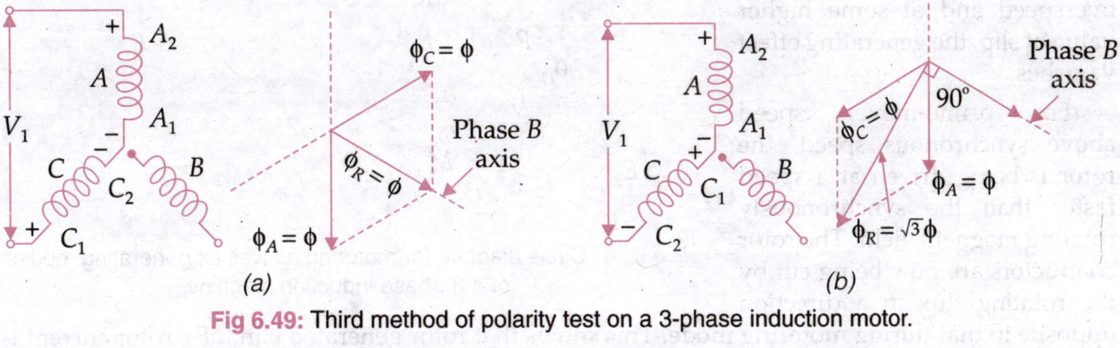

Fig 6.49: Third method of polarity test on a 3-phase induction motor.

6.16. INDUCTION GENERATOR

Fig. 6.50 shows the complete torque-slip (or torque-speed) characteristics of a 3-phase induction motor over its entire slip range of – 1 to 2. During the motoring mode, the operating point lies somewhere near point '*a*' between the points B and A. Here B indicates zero torque at zero slip and A denotes maximum torque at slip s_{mT}.

Suppose that 3-phase induction motor is coupled to a prime-mover whose speed can be controlled and that the operating point is *'a'* in Fig. 6.50. If the prime-mover speed is increased, the operating point begins to travel from *'a'* towards *B*. When prime-mover attains synchronous speed n_s, slip is zero and operating point is *B*. For prime-mover speed above synchronous speed, slip becomes negative. As a consequence, rotor e.m.f. and rotor current as per Eqn. (6.17), torque as per Eqn. (6.25) and power as per Eqn. (6.34), all attain negative values. This implies that for negative slip, electric torque developed is negative, *i.e.*, opposite to the prime-mover torque. Under such a condition, machine must act as a generator and delivers its generated power to the supply mains from which it was taking power when working as a 3-phase induction motor. In other words, when rotor speed is made more than synchronous speed, slip becomes negative and 3-phase induction machine begins to operate as a 3-phase induction generator.

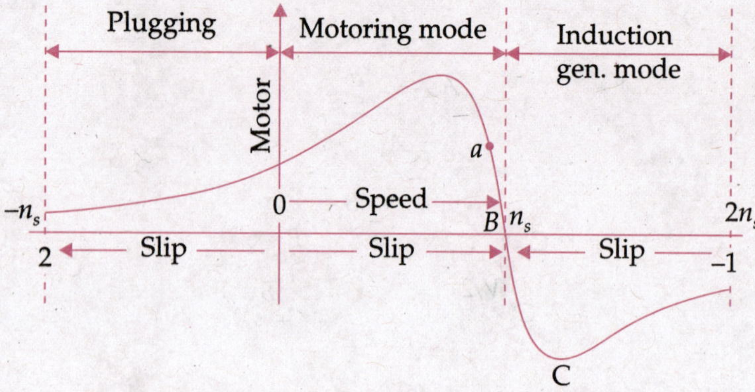

Fig 6.50: Torque-slip characteristics of a 3-phase induction machine showing plugging, motoring and generating modes.

Just as point *A* denotes the maximum torque of a 3-phase induction motor, point *C* indicates the maximum torque that can be applied to induction machine now working as an induction generator. If the prime-mover torque exceeds this maximum torque given by point *C*, induction generator will overspeed and at some higher value of slip, the generating effect vanishes.

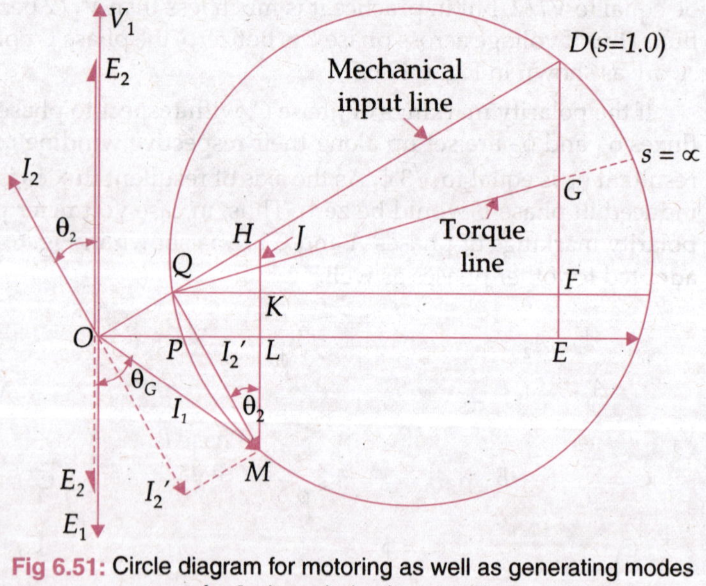

Fig 6.51: Circle diagram for motoring as well as generating modes of a 3-phase induction machine.

For prime-mover speed above synchronous speed, the rotor is being driven at a speed faster than the synchronously rotating magnetic field. The rotor conductors are now being cut by the rotating flux in a direction opposite to that during motoring mode. This shows that rotor generated e.m.f. E_2, rotor current I_2 and hence its stator component I_2' change their signs as shown in Fig. 6.51. The stator current *OM* is now composed of current *OQ* and component I_2' in phase opposition to stator applied voltage V_1, Fig. 6.51. As the speed during induction-generator operation is not synchronous, it is also called an *asynchronous generator*.

In polyphase induction motors, rotating magnetic field is set up by the magnetizing current drawn by the stator from the supply mains. When the speed of the machine is made more than synchronous speed, even then this magnetizing current must be delivered to the induction generator by the supply mains so that rotating flux is established. In other words, induction generator is not a *self-excited machine* and must therefore continue to get its magnetizing current and reactive power from the supply mains to which it was connected to run as a polyphase induction motor. Thus, 3-phase induction generator cannot work in isolation ; it must work in parallel with the bus-bar or other synchronous generator/s, which can supply the magnetizing current and reactive power needed by 3-phase induction generator.

The transition from motoring mode to generating mode can easily be shown on the circle diagram of a polyphase induction machine. In Fig. 6.51, induction motor operation is from point Q, upper part of semi-circle and up to point D where s = 1.0. Induction generator operation is from point Q, lower part of semicircle and up to point s = ∞.

Suppose, 3-phase induction machine is coupled with a loss-less prime-mover (p.m.). With 3-phase induction motor running at no load from a 3-phase source, the operating point is Q. The motor operates at a small value of no-load slip. Under this condition, A.C. source supplies *(i)* quadrature magnetizing current OP and *(ii)* a power component PQ to supply friction, windage and core loss in 3-phase induction motor. Now increase the speed of p.m. so that operating point P is obtained. At this point P, speed is synchronous, all losses are supplied by p.m. and the bus-bar supplies the magnetizing current OP as well as the corresponding reactive power (= $V_1 \cdot OP$) to the 3-phase induction machine.

As the p.m. speed is increased, induction generator begins to deliver active power P to the three-phase electrical system to which it is connected. However, reactive power Q is still withdrawn from the same 3-phase ac mains to create the rotating magnetic field in the induction generator. This means that active power P to electrical system and reactive power Q from the electrical system flow in opposite directions.

When operating point M (at about $s = -0.03$ to -0.05) is reached in Fig. 6.51, then

MH = mechanical power input to induction generator

ML = electrical power output of induction generator

OM = stator current

OL = magnetizing current taken from the bus-bar which has increased from OP to OL

KL = constant losses

KJ = stator ohmic loss

JH = rotor ohmic loss

$\cos \theta_G = \cos \angle (V_1 \cdot OM)$

= leading pf of the induction generator.

6.16.1. Self-excited or Isolated Induction Generator

This type of induction generator does not require an existing A.C. supply system for obtaining its magnetizing reactive power. In the self-excited induction generator, a capacitor bank is connected across its stator terminals as shown in Fig. 6.52. The capacitor bank provides the lagging reactive power of both the induction generator as well as the load. In Fig. 6.52,

Capacitive reactive power,

$Q = Q_1$, reactive power needed by 3-phase induction generator

+ Q_2, reactive power needed by the load.

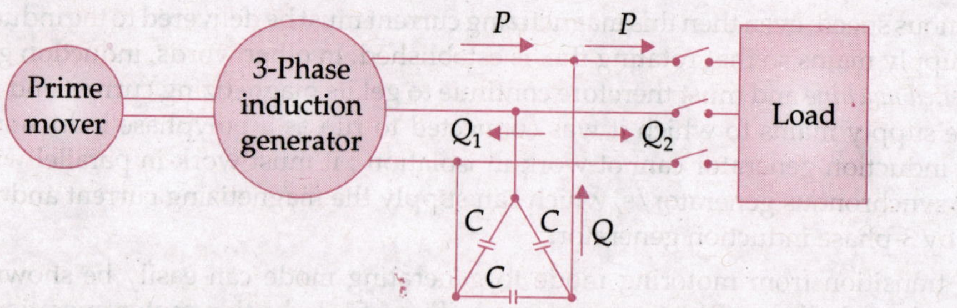

Fig 6.52: A capacitor bank connected across stator terminals of a 3-phase induction generator.

In self-excited induction generator, stator terminal voltage depends upon its magnetization curve as shown in Fig. 6.53 *(a)*. The reactive current of a capacitor depends upon the voltage across its terminals, *i.e.*, capacitor voltage $V_c = I \cdot X_c$ where $X_c = 1/\omega C$ · In Fig. 6.53 *(b)*, load lines of capacitor banks having different capacitances $C_1 > C_2 > C_3 > C_4$ are drawn.

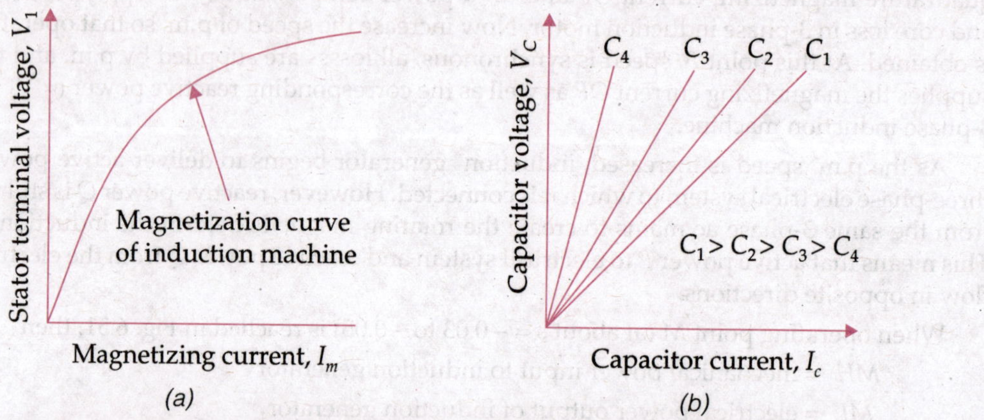

Fig 6.53: Characteristics of *(a)* induction generator and *(b)* capacitor bank.

In Fig. 6.52, capacitor bank is connected across the stator terminals of a 3-phase induction machine. When the rotor of induction machine is run at the required speed, residual magnetism present in the rotor iron generates a small terminal voltage *oa* across stator terminals, Fig. 6.54 *(a)*. This voltage produces a capacitor current *ob*. This current *ob* creates a flux which aids the residual flux, thus producing more flux and therefore more generated voltage *bc* across stator terminals. This voltage *bc* sends a current *od* in the capacitor bank which eventually generates voltage *de*. This cumulative process of voltage build up continues till the saturation curve of induction generator intersects the capacitor load line at point *f*, thus giving a no-load generated e.m.f. of *gf* for magnetizing current I_{m1}. Note that this voltage build up process is similar to that in a D.C. shunt generator.

If the residual flux is absent in the rotor iron, the induction generator will not build up. This problem can, however, be overcome by running the machine as a polyphase induction motor for some time to create residual magnetism.

Note that the voltage build up depends upon the value of capacitor. Higher the value of capacitance, greater is the voltage build up, see Fig. 6.54 *(b)*. In case capacitor load line does not intersect the magnetization curve of induction machine, there would be no voltage build up. In Fig. 6.54 *(b)*, voltage build up for capacitor C_4 does not occur.

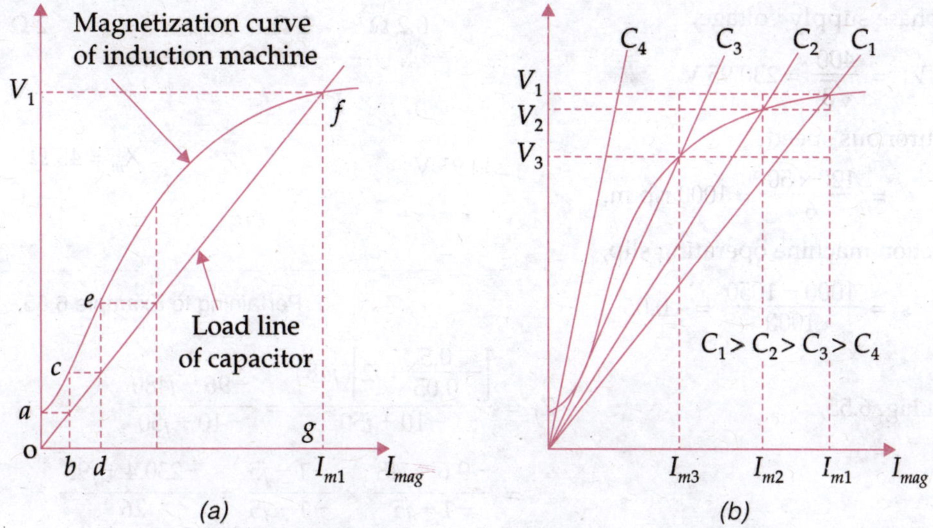

Fig 6.54: *(a)* Voltage build-up process in a 3-phase induction generator and *(b)* No-load voltages V_1, V_2, V_3 for C_1, C_2, C_3.

6.16.2. Applications of Induction Generators

(a) **Externally-excited generators.** This type of generators require a little auxiliary equipment. These are run in parallel with an existing 3-phase system. Thus, voltage and frequency of induction generators cannot be controlled. Only the active power can be regulated through the speed control of prime-mover driving the 3-phase induction generator. These generators don't hunt. The short-circuit current of these generators is limited. It is because a short-circuit at once reduces the excitation and thus short-circuit current gets limited.

Externally-excited induction generators are also used in unattended small remote hydro plants thereby interconnecting a small power station to a large power distribution network.

Their disadvantages are as under :

(i) They require considerable amount of reactive power from the existing supply system.

(ii) Efficiency is relatively poor.

(iii) It can work at leading power factor only.

Induction generator principle is used for regenerative braking of hoists or electric locomotives driven by 3-phase induction motors.

(b) **Self-excited generators.** With depletion of energy sources world wide, every effort is made to convert other forms of unconventional energies into electrical energy. Therefore, energy recovery schemes are becoming an important aspect of present-day industrial processes. In the coastal areas, wind energy is available in abundance. For the conversion of this wind energy into electrical energy, an induction generator coupled with a wind-mill offers an ideal solution.

Example 6.65. *A 400 V, 3-phase, 6-pole, 50 Hz, star-connected induction motor has the following per-phase parameters referred to stator :*

$$r_1 = 0.2\ \Omega,\ r_2 = 0.5\ \Omega,\ x_1 = x_2 = 2\ \Omega,\ X_m = 48\ \Omega$$

This motor drives a hoist. During lowering of the hoist, the load accelerates the motor to a speed of 1050 r.p.m. At this speed, determine (a) the line current (b) power returned to 3-phase supply and (c) the efficiency in case its mechanical and core losses are 600 W.

Solution. The induction motor equivalent circuit, for this example, is shown in Fig. 6.55.

Per-phase supply voltage,

$$V_1 = \frac{400}{\sqrt{3}} = 230.95 \text{ V}$$

Synchronous speed

$$= \frac{120 \times 50}{6} = 1000 \text{ r.p.m.}$$

Induction machine operating slip,

$$s = \frac{1000 - 1050}{1000} = -0.05$$

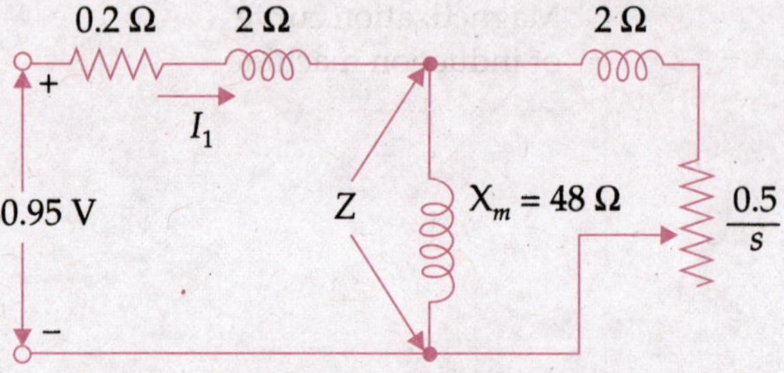

Fig 6.55: Pertaining to Example 6.65.

From Fig. 6.55,
$$Z_f = \frac{\left[-\frac{0.5}{0.05} + j2\right](j48)}{-10 + j50} = \frac{-96 - j480}{-10 + j50}$$

$$= \frac{-9.6 - j48}{-1 + j5} \times \frac{-1 - j5}{-1 - j5} = \frac{-230.4 + j96}{26}$$

$$\therefore \quad Z_f = R_f + j X_f = -8.862 + j\,3.692\ \Omega$$

$$r_1 + jx_1 = 0.2 + j\,2\ \Omega$$

$\therefore$ Total input impedance,
$$Z = -8.862 + j\,3.692 + 0.2 + j\,2$$
$$= -8.662 + j\,5.692 = 10.365\ \angle 146.7°$$

$$I_1 = \frac{V_1}{Z} = \frac{230.95}{10.365\angle 146.7°} = 22.282\ \angle -146.7° \text{ A}$$

Stator line current $= 22.282\ \angle -146.7°$ A

Power factor at stator terminals $= \cos \angle -146.7° = 50.836$

A negative value of p.f. means that power factor is 0.836 leading.

(b) Power at stator terminals $= 3\, V_1\, I_1 \cos \theta_1$

$$= 3 \times 230.95 \times 22.282 \times \cos 146.7° = -12906.24 \text{ W}$$

As power at stator terminals is negative, the induction machine is acting as a 3-phase induction generator and a power of 12906.24 W is being fed back to the 3-phase supply system.

(c) Air-gap power $= 3\, I_1^2\, R_f = 3 \times 22.282^2 \times 8.862 = 13199.62$ W

Total stator I^2R loss $= 3 \times 22.282^2 \times 0.2 = 297.9$ W

Total rotor I^2R loss $= s\, P_g = 0.05 \times 13199.62 = 659.98$ W

Mechanical and core losses $= 600$ W

Total losses in induction generator $= 297.9 + 659.98 + 600 = 1555.88$ W

Mechanical power input to induction generator

= Power delivered to 3-phase source + total losses

$= 12906.24 + 1555.88 = 14462.12$ W

$\therefore$ Efficiency of induction generator
$$= \frac{12906.24}{14462.12} \times 100 = 89.242\%.$$

6.17 APPLICATIONS OF POLYPHASE INDUCTION MOTORS

For loads requiring low starting torques and substantially constant speeds, squirrel-cage induction motor is the best choice, because of its ruggedness, simplicity, low cost and reduced maintenance charges. Squirrel cage motor may be designed with low rotor resistance or with high rotor resistance. As stated before, a high rotor resistance gives better starting conditions but poor running performance. On the other hand, a cage motor with low rotor resistance gives poor starting conditions but better running performance. In view of this, the rotor-circuit resistance should be chosen judiciously at the design stage so that there is a compromise between its starting conditions and running performance.

Squirrel cage motors with relatively low rotor resistance (full-load slip 3 to 5%) are used for fans, centrifugal pumps, most machinery tools, wood-working tools etc. Cage motors with relatively high rotor resistance (full-load slip 3 to 7%) are used for compressors, crushers, reciprocating pumps. Squirrel cage motors with still higher values of rotor-circuit resistance (full-load slip 7 to 16%) are used for intermittent loads like punching presses, shears, hoists, elevators etc.

A wound-rotor induction motor is used for loads requiring severe starting conditions or for loads requiring speed control. A wound rotor induction motor is more expensive than a squirrel cage motor and also it requires more maintenance because of the brushes and slip rings. A wound-rotor motor, also called slip-ring motor, may be used for hoists, cranes, elevators, compressors, rolling mills etc.

The relative advantages of cage motor over a wound-rotor motor of the same power rating, are given below.

(i) A cage rotor requires considerably less conductor material than a wound rotor, consequently I^2R loss in cage rotor is less. Therefore, cage motor is a little more efficient than a wound-rotor motor.

(ii) Wound-motor construction requires slip rings, brushes, short-circuiting devices etc. As a result of it, a wound-rotor motor is costlier than a cage induction motor.

(iii) A squirrel-cage rotor has very small length of overhang, therefore, it has low rotor overhang leakage flux. This has the effect of resulting in low leakage reactance x_2 for a cage rotor than for a wound rotor. Consequently, the diameter of circle diagram for a cage motor is greater than for a wound-rotor motor. This shows that a cage motor has more pull-out torque, greater maximum power output and better operating power factor as compared to a wound-rotor induction motor.

(iv) Cage motor is more rugged and requires no slip rings, brushes etc., therefore, its maintenance charges are low.

(v) Cage rotor can be cooled better because of its bare end-rings.

The disadvantages of cage motor as compared to a wound rotor motor are its small starting torque for very large starting current and its poor starting power factor. In addition to it, the total energy lost during starting of cage motor is much more than with the wound-rotor motor and this fact is very important where frequent starting of large number of motors is required.

It may be worthwhile here to compare the working of an induction motor with a synchronous motor.

S. No.	*Induction Motor*	*Synchronous Motor*
1.	It has inherent self-starting torque.	It has no inherent self-starting torque, therefore some external means must be used to start it.
2.	Its speed falls with increase of load. It can never run at synchronous speed.	It runs at a constant synchronous speed at all possible loads.
3.	It requires no D.C. excitation, i.e., it is a singly excited machine.	It requires both A.C. and D.C., *i.e.*, synchronous machine is a doubly excited machine.

S. No.	Induction Motor	Synchronous Motor
4.	It can operate only at lagging power factors.	It can operate both at leading and lagging power factors.
5.	Speed control is possible.	Under normal circumstances, synchronous motor works with no speed control.
6.	It can be used to supply only mechanical load.	It can be used for delivering mechanical loads and for improving the system power factor.
7.	Its maximum torque is proportional to square of the supply voltage.	Its maximum torque is proportional to supply voltage.
8.	Induction motors with speeds above 500 r.p.m. and ratings below about 120 kW are cheaper than synchronous motors.	Sychronous motors with speeds below 500 r.p.m. and ratings above about 40 kW or with medium speeds from 500 to 1000 r.p.m. and ratings above about 500 kW, are less costly than induction motors.

PROBLEMS

6.1. Describe constructional features of both squirrel-cage induction motor and slip-ring induction motor.

Discuss the merits of one over the other.

6.2. *(a)* Discuss the points of similarities between a transformer and an induction machine. Hence, explain why an induction machine is called a generalized transformer.

(b) Explain why a 3-phase induction motor, at no-load, operates at a very low power factor.

(c) Two 3-phase induction motors *A*, *B* are identical in all respects except that motor *A* has a larger air gap than motor *B*. Explain which of the two motors will have

(i) more no-load current *(ii)* poorer no-load power factor and

(iii) better full-load power factor. **[Ans.** *(c)* : *(i)* and *(ii)* Motor *A*, *(iii)* motor *B*]

6.3. *(a)* Describe the principle of operation of a 3-phase induction motor. Explain why the rotor is forced to rotate in the direction of rotating magnetic field.

(b) Discuss the differences between 3-phase induction motors and transformers.

6.4. A 3-phase induction motor is sometimes called a generalized transformer in so far as voltage and frequency transformations are concerned. As per this statements, discuss how a 3-phase induction motor operates under the following conditions :

(a) Rotor frequency f_2 = stator frequency f_1

(b) $f_2 < f_1$ *(c)* $f_2 > f_1$

(d) rotor generated voltage and rotor current are maximum

(e) rotor e.m.f. E_2 and rotor current are zero

(f) both E_2 and I_2 are minimum *(g)* both E_2 and I_2 are negative.

[**Ans.** *(a)* At standstill *(b)* Under normal running conditions *(c)* Rotor is driven against the direction of rotating magnetic field *(d)* At standstill *(e)* At synchronous speed *(f)* At no-load *(g)* When operating as a 3-phase induction generator]

6.5. Explain the development of torque in a 3-phase squirrel cage induction motor through the interaction of stator and rotor produced poles, in case nature of rotor circuit is *(a)* resistive and *(b)* reactive.

Discuss whether the torque developed in resistive circuit is more or less than that produced in reactive circuit.

6.6. *(a)* Describe the development of electromagnetic torque in a 3-phase slip ring induction motor, through the concept of interaction between poles produced on stator and rotor.

(b) Discuss the conditions under which optimum torque is produced in a 3-phase induction motor.

[*(b)* **Ans.** *(i)* Rotor circuit resistive *(ii)* x_2 as small as possible relative to r_2]

6.7. A 6-pole, 50 Hz, three-phase induction motor is running clockwise with a slip = – 0.10. Find the speed and direction of rotation of

(a) rotor field with respect to stator,

(b) rotor field with respect to stator field,

(c) rotor field with respect to rotor.

[**Ans.** *(a)* 1000 r.p.m., clockwise *(b)* zero r.p.m. *(c)* 100 r.p.m., anticlockwise]

6.8. A 3-phase, 4-pole, 50 Hz induction motor is fed from rated voltage. Discuss the mode of induction motor operation under the following conditions:

(a) Rotor is running at 1200 r.p.m in the direction of rotating field.

(b) Rotor is running at 1200 rpm in a direction opposite to rotating field.

(c) Rotor is running at 2000 rpm in the direction of rotating field.

[**Ans.** *(a)* f_2 = 10 Hz, motoring mode *(b)* f_2 = 90 Hz, braking mode *(c)* f_2 = – 16.67 Hz, generating mode]

6.9. *(a)* The speed of rotor field, with respect to stator, is always equal to synchronous speed at all possible speeds of the induction motor. Explain.

(b) Explain why the rotor of a polyphase induction motor can never attain synchronous speed.

(c) The rotor of a slip-ring induction motor is connected to an A.C. source, whereas its stator winding is short-circuited. If rotating magnetic field produced by rotor winding rotates clockwise, explain the direction in which the rotor must revolve. [**Ans.** *(c)* Anti-clockwise]

6.10. *(a)* A 3-phase slip-ring induction motor (SRIM) has its stator wound with 4-poles but its rotor is wound with 6 poles. Will this induction motor be able to develop torque? Explain.

(b) A SRIM has 3-phase stator winding but 4-phase rotor winding. Both the windings are, however, designed to produce the same number of poles. Will the induction motor be able to run? Explain.

(c) A 3-phase, 50 Hz induction motor has a full-load speed of 960 r.p.m.. Calculate

(i) number of the poles *(ii)* slip frequency

(iii) speed of rotor field with respect to rotor structure ; with respect to stator structure and with respect to stator field.

[**Ans.** *(a)* No *(b)* Yes *(c)* 6 poles, 2 Hz, 40 r.p.m., 1000 r.p.m. and zero r.p.m.]

6.11. *(a)* Show that the voltage generated in the rotor circuit of a 3-phase induction motor at any slip s is equal to s times the voltage generated at standstill.

(b) With the help of rotor equivalent circuit of an induction motor, show that the power transferred magnetically from stator to rotor is given by $I_2^2 \frac{r_2}{s}$ per phase.

(c) Explain the terms air-gap power P_g, internal mechanical power developed P_m and shaft power P_{sh}. How are these terms related with each other? Hence show that

P_g : rotor ohmic loss : $P_m = 1 : s : (1 - s)$

6.12. *(a)* Justify the following statements for a 3-phase induction motor :

(i) Rotor leakage impedance at starting is different from its value at normal running conditions.

(ii) Relative speed between stator field and rotor field is zero.

(iii) Stator current rises as the shaft load is increased.

(b) What are fixed and variable losses in a 3-phase induction motor? Give the power-flow diagram for this motor and discuss the various losses involved in it.

6.13. The stator of a 3-phase, 4 pole-slip-ring induction motor is connected to 50 Hz supply. At the rotor terminals, a frequency of 30 Hz is required. Find the possible speeds at which the rotor must be driven. What is the ratio of slip-ring e.m.f.s at these speeds at no load?

[Ans. 600 r.p.m., 2400 r.p.m., unity]

6.14. A 4-pole, 3-phase, 50 Hz synchronous machine has its rotor directly coupled to that of a 3-phase slip-ring induction motor. Stators of both machines are connected to the same 3-phase, 50 Hz supply. It is desired to use such an arrangement to generate 150 Hz across the rotor terminals of the induction motor. Determine the number of poles for which the induction machine should be wound. Give all possibilities. [*I.A.S.*, 1987] **[Ans.** 8 poles or 16 poles]

6.15. A 3-phase, delta-connected, 4-pole, 50 Hz induction motor has a stator resistance of 0.4 Ω per phase at the operating temperature. For a line current of 20 A, the total stator input is 4000 watts. For negligible stator core losses, find out the internal torque. **[Ans.** 24.45 Nm]

6.16. A 3-phase, 400 V, 50 Hz induction motor takes a power input of 35 kW at its full-load speed of 980 r.p.m. The total stator losses are 1 kW and the friction and windage losses are 1.5 kW. Calculate *(a)* slip *(b)* rotor ohmic losses *(c)* shaft power *(d)* shaft torque and *(e)* efficiency.

[Ans. *(a)* 0.02 *(b)* 680 W *(c)* 31.82 kW *(d)* 310.06 Nm *(e)* 90.91%]

6.17. A 400 V, 3-phase, 6 pole, 50 Hz induction motor draws a power 2 kW at no load and at rated voltage and frequency. At a full-load slip of 3%, the power input to motor is 50 kW and the stator ohmic loss is 1.5 kW. Neglect I^2R loss at no load. If the stator core loss and mechanical losses are assumed equal, then at a slip of 3% calculate *(a)* rotor ohmic loss *(b)* shaft (or output) power *(c)* shaft torque *(d)* internal torque and *(e)* efficiency.

[Ans. *(a)* 1.425 kW *(b)* 45.075 kW *(c)* 443.75 Nm *(d)* 453.60 Nm *(e)* 90.15%]

6.18. A 20 kW, 6 pole, 400 V, 50 Hz 3-phase induction motor has a full-load slip of 0.02. If the torque, lost in mechanical (friction and windage) losses is 20 Nm, find the rotor ohmic loss, motor input and efficiency. Stator losses total 900 watts.

[Hint. $T_{sh} = \dfrac{20{,}000 \times 60}{2\pi \times 1000 \times 0.98} = 194.88$ Nm.

Mechanical torque developed = 194.81 + 20 = 214.88 Nm.

$\therefore \quad P_m = \dfrac{2\pi \times 1000(0.98)}{60}(214.88) = \ldots$]**[Ans.** 450.04 watts, 23402.1 watts, 85.462%]

6.19. A 10 kW, 3-phase, 50 Hz, 4 pole induction motor has a full-load slip of 0.03. Mechanical and stray load losses at full-load are 3.5% of output power. Compute

(a) power delivered by stator to rotor,

(b) electromagnetic (internal) torque at full load, and

(c) rotor ohmic losses at full load. **[Ans.** *(a)* 10.67 kW *(b)* 67.93 Nm *(c)* 320.10 W]

6.20. A 3-phase induction motor has its stator ohmic loss equal to the sum of the mechanical and iron losses. Its rotor ohmic loss is equal to one-third of stator ohmic loss. If its efficiency is 79%, calculate its slip. Take mechanical loss equal to iron loss. **[Ans.** 0.0347]

6.21. The power supplied to a 3-phase induction motor is 40 kW and the corresponding stator losses are 1.5 kW. Calculate the net mechanical power developed and the rotor I^2R loss when the slip is 0.04 per unit. What will be the net power developed if the speed of the above motor is reduced to 40% of the synchronous speed by means of external rotor resistors, assuming the torque and stator losses to remain unaltered? Friction and windage losses may be assumed to be 0.8 kW. [*I.A.S., 1980*] [**Ans.** 36.16 kW, 1.54 kW, 14.6 kW]

6.22. *(a)* Discuss why the speed of a 3-phase induction motor falls as its load torque is increased.

(b) Two wattmeters are connected to measure the power input to a 3-phase induction motor running at no load. One of the two wattmeters gives negative reading. Why? Explain.

(c) Explain why a 3-phase induction motor, in general similar to a transformer, takes more magnetizing current as compared to a transformer.

6.23. *(a)* Explain why slip in a 3-phase induction motor is directly proportional to torque when operating near synchronous speed.

(b) A 4-pole, 20 kW, 50 Hz, 400 V SCIM has a starting torque of 160 Nm and a full-load torque of 120 Nm.

Calculate

(i) starting torque for a stator voltage of 300 V,

(ii) voltage so that motor operates satisfactorily at full load from a 60-Hz source,

(iii) voltage applied to stator so that full-load torque is developed at starting.

[**Hint.** *(b)* Keep $\frac{V}{f}$ constant] [**Ans.** *(b)* 90 Nm, 480 V, 346.14 V]

6.24. *(a)* A 3-phase, 50 Hz source feeds the stators of both 3-phase SRIM having 8 poles and a synchronous motor having 2 poles. The synchronous motor, coupled mechanically with induction motor, runs clockwise whereas the rotating field in 3-ϕ induction motor rotates counterclockwise.

Calculate frequency of the voltages taken from the slip rings of SRIM.

(b) Find the number of synchronous-motor poles and the conditions for obtaining a frequency of 150 Hz from the rotor of SRIM of part *(a)*.

(c) Repeat part *(b)* for obtaining a slip-ring frequency of $16\frac{2}{3}$ Hz.

[**Ans.** *(a)* 250 Hz *(b)* 4 poles, synchronous motor rotation against the direction of rotating field in SRIM *(c)* 6 poles, synchronous motor rotation in the direction of rotating field in SRIM]

6.25. A 4-pole, 3-phase SRIM is coupled mechanically with a synchronous motor having 2 poles. The synchronous motor and stator of the induction motor are fed from 50 Hz voltage source. What will be the frequency of the e.m.fs. at the rotor terminals if the synchronous motor is driven:

(a) in a direction opposite to the induction motor stator rotating field,

(b) in the direction of rotating field in SRIM.

If the frequency of the rotor voltage is required to be 300 Hz, then calculate

(c) the number of poles that the SRIM must have. [**Ans.** *(a)* 150 Hz *(b)* 50 Hz *(c)* 10 poles]

6.26. *(a)* A 3-phase, 6-pole SRIM is directly driven by the shaft of a 4-pole, 3-phase synchronous motor. If stators of both the machines are given a 50-Hz supply, what frequencies are available at the slip rings of SRIM.

(b) A 3-phase, 50 Hz induction motor has a starting torque which is 1.25 times full-load torque and a maximum torque which is 2.5 times full load torque. Neglecting stator resistance and rotational losses and assuming constant rotor resistance, find :

(i) the slip at full and (ii) the slip at maximum torque and

(iii) the rotor current at starting in per unit of full-load rotor current. [I.E.S., 1978]

[**Ans.** (a) 25 Hz or 125 Hz (b) 0.056, 0.268, 4.722]

6.27. Develop the phasor diagram for a polyphase induction motor. How does it differ from the phasor diagram of a transformer?

6.28. Develop the equivalent circuit of a polyphase induction motor. Explain how this equivalent circuit is similar to the transformer equivalent circuit.

When using the induction motor equivalent circuit, what should be kept in mind regarding the equivalent circuit parameters?

6.29. (a) Draw the exact equivalent circuit of an induction motor. What do the various parameters represent?

(b) The shunt branch consisting of R_c and X_m in parallel, is either omitted or moved to the primary terminals during the analysis of transformer equivalent circuit. This, however, is not permissible in the analysis of induction motor equivalent circuit. Explain.

(c) Explain the similarities between the transformer and induction motor equivalent circuits.

(d) Per unit leakage reactances are higher in induction motors than in transformers. Explain.

[**Hint.** (d) Because of the presence of air-gap, induction motor has more leakage flux and, therefore, more leakage reactance.]

6.30. If stator impedance of an induction motor is neglected, show from its equivalent circuit that maximum torque per phase is given by

$$T_{em} = \frac{2}{2\pi n_s} \cdot \frac{V_1^2}{2x_2}$$

and hence show that

$$\frac{T_e}{T_{em}} = \frac{2}{\dfrac{s_{mT}}{s} + \dfrac{s}{s_{mT}}}$$

For small value of slip occurring in the stable operating region prove that

$$T_e = \frac{2T_{em}}{s_{mT}}\, s$$

6.31. (a) Sketch the typical torque-speed characteristic of an induction motor. How is this characteristic modified

(i) if its rotor-circuit resistance is increased,

(ii) if its rotor circuit reactance is increased.

(b) A 3-phase wound-rotor induction motor develops a maximum torque of 4 times the full-load torque at a slip of 0.20. The per phase rotor resistance is 0.04 Ω. The stator resistance and rotational losses are negligible.

(i) Calculate the slip at full-load torque. If the stator resistance were considered, would the value of slip at full-load torque be smaller, same or larger?

(ii) Calculate the value of external resistance that must be inserted in the rotor circuit in order to obtain maximum torque at starting.

[**Hint.** (b) (i) If stator resistance were considered then the slip at which maximum torque occurs, is given by

$$s_{mT} = \frac{r_2}{\sqrt{R_e^2 + X^2}}$$

Since s_{mT} is reduced with the consideration of stator resistance, the full-load slip would be smaller.

(ii) $\frac{r_2}{X} = s_{mT} = 0.2$ or $X = \frac{0.04}{0.2} = 0.2\ \Omega$ etc.]

[Ans. *(a) (i)* See Fig. 6.19 *(ii)* All the three $T_{e \cdot fl}$, T_{em} and s_{mT} are reduced.

(b) (i) 0.0254, smaller. *(ii)* 0.16 Ω].

6.32. *(a)* Sketch the torque-slip characteristic of an induction motor working at rated voltage and frequency. Explain and draw these characteristics, with respect to the normal one, if the following changes are made :

(i) Applied stator voltage is reduced to half at rated frequency.

(ii) Both the applied voltage and frequency are reduced to half.

(b) For a 3-phase induction motor, the rotor ohmic loss at maximum torque is 16 times that at full-load torque. The slip at full-load torque is 0.03. If stator resistance and rotational losses are neglected, then calculate

(i) the slip at maximum torque,

(ii) the maximum torque in terms of full-load torque and

(iii) the starting torque in terms of full load torque.

[Hint. *(b)* $\frac{T_{e \cdot fl}}{T_{em}} = \frac{2}{\frac{s_{mT}}{s_{fl}} + \frac{s_{fl}}{s_{mT}}}$

Now $\frac{T_{e \cdot fl}}{T_{e \cdot m}} = \frac{I_{2 \cdot fl}^2 \frac{r_2}{s_{fl}}}{I_{2 \cdot mT}^2 \frac{r_2}{s_{mT}}} = \frac{I_{2 \cdot fl}^2 r_2}{I_{2 \cdot mT}^2 r_2} \cdot \frac{s_{mT}}{s_{fl}} = \frac{1}{16} \cdot \frac{s_{mT}}{s_{fl}}$

$\therefore \quad \frac{1}{16} \cdot \frac{s_{mT}}{s_{fl}} = \frac{2}{\frac{s_{mT}}{s_{fl}} + \frac{s_{fl}}{s_{mT}}}$ etc.]

[Ans. *(a) (i)* $T_{e \cdot st}$ and T_{em} are reduced to $\frac{1}{4}$, but n_s and s_{mT} remain unchanged.

(ii) $T_{e \cdot st}$ and s_{mT} increase, T_{em} remains same but n_s is reduced to half.

(b) (i) 0.167 *(ii)* 2.874 $T_{e \cdot st}$ *(iii)* 0.934 $T_{e \cdot fl}$]

6.33. *(a)* Show that the maximum internal torque developed by a polyphase induction motor does not depend on the rotor circuit resistance.

(b) A 3-phase squirrel-cage induction motor has a rotor starting current of 6 times its full load value. The motor has a full load slip of 5%. Determine

(i) the starting torque in terms of full-load torque ;

(ii) the slip at which maximum torque occurs ; and

(iii) maximum torque in terms of full-load torque.

[Hint. *(i)* Use Eq. (6.51 *a*). *(ii)* Use Eq. 6.33. **[Ans.** *(b) (i)* 1.8 $T_{e \cdot fl}$ *(ii)* 0.31 *(iii)* 3.18 $T_{e \cdot fl}$]

6.34. *(a)* With stator resistance neglected, the torque-slip characteristic can be obtained from the expression

$$\frac{T_e}{T_{em}} = \frac{2}{\dfrac{s_{mT}}{s_{fl}} + \dfrac{s}{s_{Tm}}}$$

Derive this expression and show that $s = s_{mT}\,[k \pm \sqrt{k^2 - 1}\,]$

where $k = \dfrac{T_{e \cdot m}}{T_e}$

(Use negative sign if $s_{mT} > s$, *e.g.*, $s_{mT} > s_{fl}$ and use positive sign in case $s_{mT} < s$, *e.g.* at starting).

(b) The maximum torque of a 3-phase squirrel-cage induction motor is 4 times the full-load torque and the starting torque is 1.6 times the full-load torque. Neglect stator resistance. Calculate

(i) the slip at the maximum torque *(ii)* full-load slip and

(ii) the rotor current at starting in terms of full-load rotor current.

[Ans. *(i)* 0.21 *(ii)* 0.0267, *(iii)* 7.759]

6.35. *(a)* Sketch the torque-speed curve of a conventional induction motor and indicate how this will change when

(i) the rotor resistance is doubled, keeping stator voltage and frequency unchanged ;

(ii) the applied voltage is halved, the frequency and rotor resistance remain unchanged ;

(iii) both the applied voltage and frequency are halved, rotor resistance remains unchanged. [*I.A.S., 1987*]

(b) A 3-phase induction motor at rated voltage and frequency has a starting torque of 150% and a maximum torque of 200 percent of full-load torque. Neglecting stator resistance and rotational losses, calculate the slip at full load and slip at maximum torque. [*I.A.S., 1984*]

[Ans. *(b)* 0.121, 0.452]

6.36. A 3-phase, 4-pole, 50 Hz, 400 V delta-connected induction motor develops a maximum torque of 240 Nm at a speed of 1200 r.p.m. Stator impedance and rotational losses are assumed negligible. The rotor resistance is 0.2 Ω per phase. Calculate the additional rotor resistance required to give a starting torque of :

(a) 75% of maximum torque at rated voltage and

(b) 75% of maximum torque when the supply voltage is reduced to 360 volts.

[Hint. $s_{mT} = 0.2$; $x_2 = \dfrac{r_2}{s_{mT}} = 1\ \Omega$.

Since r_1 and x_1 are negligible,

$$T_{em} = \frac{1}{\omega_s} \cdot \frac{3V_1^2}{2x_2} = \frac{K}{2}$$

or $$240 = \frac{K}{2} \text{ or } K = 480.$$

(a) If R is the sum of rotor resistance and external resistance, then at starting.

$$T_{e \cdot st} = \frac{1}{\omega_s} \times \frac{3V_1^2}{[R^2 + x_2^2]} \cdot R$$

or $$0.75 \times 240 = \frac{K}{R^2 + 1} R, \text{ etc.}$$

(b) $$0.75 \times 240 = \left(\frac{360}{400}\right)^2 \frac{480}{R^2+1} R, \text{ etc.}$$

[Ans. *(a)* 0.2514 Ω, *(b)* 0.472 Ω**]**

6.37. *(a)* Derive the condition of maximum torque developed in a 3-phase induction motor and hence prove that to increase the starting torque extra resistance must be added in the rotor-circuit.

(b) A 4-pole, 50 Hz, 3-phase induction motor develops a maximum torque at a speed of 1350 r.p.m. and per phase rotor resistance is 0.2 Ω. Calculate the value of external resistance that must be inserted in series with each rotor phase to produce a starting torque equal to half the maximum torque. Neglect stator impedance.

[Hint. *(a)* Condition for maximum torque is

$$s_{mT} = \frac{r_2}{\sqrt{R_e^2 + X^2}} \quad ...(6.26)$$

The external resistance in rotor circuit at starting is $\left(\sqrt{R_e^2 + X^2} - r_2\right)$.

(c) $\frac{1}{2} = \frac{2}{\frac{s_{mT1}}{1} + \frac{1}{s_{mT1}}}$ and $s_{mT1} = \frac{r_2 + \text{added resistance}}{x_2}$**]** **[Ans.** *(b)* 0.336 Ω**]**

6.38. *(a)* Explain the differences between the characteristics of slip-ring and squirrel-cage polyphase induction motors. Sketch a typical characteristic for each.

(b) A 4-pole, 3-phase, 50 Hz induction motor has a full-load slip of 3% and a maximum torque of twice the full-load torque. Clearly specifying any approximations you may need to make, calculate the starting torque of the motor as a percentage of full-load torque.

[*I.E.S., 1975*]**[Ans.** *(b)* 44.24%**]**

6.39. In a 3-phase induction motor, the stator reactance equals the rotor reactance at standstill while each resistance is one-fourth of this value. If the motor develops 220 Nm at 3% slip, what will be its

(a) starting and

(b) pull-out torques. Ignore no-load current. **[Ans.** *(a)* 120.67 Nm, *(b)* 452.737 Nm**]**

6.40. A 6-pole, 50 Hz, 3-phase induction motor has a rotor resistance of 0.2 Ω per phase and a maximum torque of 160 Nm at 875 r.p.m. Calculate :

(a) the torque for a full-load slip of 4% and

(b) the resistance to be added to the rotor circuit to obtain 80% of full-load torque at starting. No-load rotational losses and stator impedance are neglected.

[Ans. 92.89 Nm, 0.192 Ω**]**

6.41. A 4-pole, 3-phase, star-connected slip-ring induction motor is to operate from 400 V, 3-phase, 50 Hz mains. Its rotor has a stand still leakage impedance of 0.4 + *j* 2 ohms per phase. For negligible stator impedance and no-load rotational losses, compute :

(a) maximum torque in newton-metres,

(b) the resistance to be included in the rotor circuit to develop 0.8 of maximum torque at start.

[Ans. *(a)* 254.65 Nm, *(b)* 0.6 Ω**]**

6.42. A 420-V, 6-pole, 50 Hz star connected induction motor has stator impedance of 0.07 + j 0.30 Ω and standstill rotor impedance referred to stator is 0.08 + *j* 0.37 Ω. The magnetizing current is neglected. Determine

(a) the maximum internal power developed and the corresponding slip and

(*b*) the maximum internal torque and the slip at which it occurs.

[Ans. (*a*) 105.427 kW, 0.1044 ; (*b*) 1088.176 Nm, 0.1187]

6.43. (*a*) A 3-phase induction motor has a slip of 4% at normal voltage. Find the slip of the induction motor when developing the same torque but at a voltage 10% less than the normal voltage.

(*b*) A 3-phase induction motor has 5% slip at full-load torque and at normal voltage. The rotor resistance and rotor standstill leakage reactance per phase are 0.1 Ω and 0.6 Ω respectively. What should be the percentage reduction in supply voltage if the motor has to develop full-load torque at 3/4th of normal full-load speed. Neglect stator impedance.

[Hint. (*a*) Use Eq. (6.31)

(*b*) $$T_{e \cdot fl} = \frac{V_1^2}{\left(\frac{0.10}{0.05}\right)^2 + (0.6)^2} \times \frac{0.10}{0.05} = \frac{(xV_1^2)}{\cdots} \times \frac{0.10}{0.2875} \text{ etc.}$$]

[Ans. (*a*) 4.938%, (*b*) 20.356%]

6.44. A 440-V, 3-phase, 4-pole, 50 Hz slip-ring star-connected induction motor has a voltage of 80 V between slip-rings when full-voltage is applied to the stator and the slip-rings are open-circuited with the rotor stationary. The stator current at no-load is 2A at a pf of 0.2 lagging. The rotor is star-connected with a per phase standstill leakage impedance of 0.05 + j 0.25 Ω referred to rotor. For the motor running with the slip-rings short-circuited and at a slip of 5%, calculate

(*a*) the torque developed in Nm,
(*b*) the mechanical power developed,
(*c*) the rotor ohmic loss and
(*d*) the stator current and power factor.

Neglect stator leakage impedance and rotational losses.

[Hint. (*d*) Rotor current at 0.05 slip, $I_2 = 44.81$ A.

Rotor pf at 0.05 slip, $\cos\theta_2 = 0.970$

Rotor current in phasor form, $\bar{I}_2 = I_2(\cos\theta_2 - j\sin\theta_2) = 43.47 - j\,10.89$

Stator current required to balance the rotor current is given by

$$\bar{I}_1{}' = \frac{1}{5.5}\,\bar{I}_2$$

$\therefore$ Total stator current, $\bar{I}_1 = (\bar{I}_1{}' + \bar{I}_0) = \left(\frac{1}{5.5}\bar{I}_2\right) + (0.4 - j\,1.96) = (8.3 - j\,3.94)$ A etc.].

[Ans. (*a*) 38.35 Nm (*b*) 5722.8 watts (*c*) 301.2 watts (*d*) 9.188 A at 0.903 p.f. lagging.]

6.45. (*a*) A 3-phase induction motor has operating p.f. of 0.85 at full-load speed of 960 r.p.m. and at 400 V supply voltage. In case the supply voltage falls to 350 V, find the operating p.f. at the same full-load torque.

(*b*) A 3-phase induction motor has a rotor resistance of 0.5 Ω per phase and rotor standstill leakage reactance of 1.5 Ω per phase. If the ratio of maximum starting torque to full-load torque is 2, find the ratio of actual starting torque to full-load torque for direct starting. Neglect stator impedance and no-load rotational losses.

[Hint. (*a*) $$0.85 = \frac{r_2}{\sqrt{r_2^2 + (0.04\,x_2)^2}}$$

This gives $r_2 = 0.06454\,x_2$.

Slip at reduced voltage = 0.0522 etc.

(*b*) Maximum starting torque can, at the most, be equal to maximum torque $T_{e \cdot m}$.

Here $s_{mT} = 1/3$.

$$\frac{T_{e\cdot st}}{T_{e\cdot m}} = \frac{2}{\frac{1/3}{1}+\frac{1}{1/3}} \text{ etc.}\Bigg]$$

[Ans. *(a)* 0.7775 lag *(b)* 0.6143]

6.46. A 3-phase, 50 Hz, 400-V wound-rotor induction motor runs at 960 r.p.m. at full-load. The rotor resistance and standstill reactance per phase are 0.2 Ω and 1 Ω respectively. If a resistance of 1.8 Ω is added to each phase of the rotor at standstill, what would be the ratio of starting torque with full voltage and the added resistance to the full-load torque under normal running conditions? State assumptions made in your calculations. Can the same starting torque be obtained with another value of the additional resistance? Explain. If the answer is yes, find its value. *[I.E.S., 1979]*

[*Hint.* $T_{e\cdot st} = \frac{3}{\omega_s}\cdot\frac{2}{5}V^2\,;\,T_{e\cdot fl} = \frac{3}{\omega_s}\cdot\frac{5}{26}V^2$ etc.]

[Ans. Assumptions, *(i)* stator impedance and no-load rotational losses ignored and *(ii)* induction motor parameters remain constant. 2.08. Yes, but with an additional resistance of 0.3 Ω].

6.47. A 40 kW, 3-phse slip ring induction motor of negligible stator impedance runs at a speed of 0.96 times synchronous speed at rated torque. The slip at maximum torque is 4 times the full load value. If the rotor resistance of the motor is increased by 5 times, determine

(a) the speed, power output and rotor ohmic loss at rated torque

(b) the speed corresponding to maximum torque.

Neglect mechanical losses. *[GATE, 1993]* **[Ans.** *(a)* 0.52 N_S, 21.67 kW, 20 kW *(b)* 0.04 N_S]

6.48. A 5 kW, 400 V, 50 Hz, 4 pole delta connected 3-phase induction motor is supplied by a cable of negligible inductance. On starting the motor using a star-delta starter, it is found that the starting torque is the same in star as well as delta connection, due to the voltage drop in the feeder resistance. The equivalent circuit parameters of the motor are as follows :

$r_1 = 1\,\Omega$, $x_1 = 4.5\,\Omega$, $r_2' = 1.4\,\Omega$ and $x_2' = 4.5\,\Omega$

Determine the feeder resistance. *[GATE, 1991]* **[Ans.** 5.378 Ω]

6.49. A 400 V, 5- Hz, 3-phase, delta connected, 6-pole induction motor has the following standstill leakage impedances per phase referred to stator :

$z_1 = 1.2 + j\,2.1\,\Omega$, $z_2 = 1.32 + j\,2.2\,\Omega$

Neglecting magnetizing impedance, determine

(a) gross output power at a slip of 0.04,

(b) the change in line current when the stator terminals are switched from star to delta at a slip of 0.4,

(c) the resistance to be added in each rotor phase to obtain a starting torque of 350 Nm.

[Ans. *(a)* 12798.6 W *(b)* 37.105 A, 111.309 A *(c)* 1.08 Ω or 6.98 Ω]

6.50. A 10 kW, 6-pole, 50 Hz, 3-phase induction motor has linear torque-slip characteristics between zero torque and maximum torque. The slip at which maximum torque of 520 Nm occurs is 0.2. For mechanical losses of 600 W, find the speed at which the motor would run when delivering rated shaft power. **[Ans.** 959.5 r.p.m.]

6.51. The normal full-load slip and shaft torque of a 373 kW, 50 Hz, 3-phase induction motor are respectively 1.9% and 2400 Nm. The rotor winding has a resistance of 0.25 Ω and a standstill leakage reactance of 1.5 Ω per phase. Estimate the slip and the power output for the same full-load current when external resistors of 2 Ω per phase are inserted in the rotor circuit. Neglect no-load current. [*I.A.S.*, 1997]

[**Hint.** For solution, refer to Chapter on Polyphase Induction machines in the book "Generalised Theory of Electrical Machines" by the same author.] [**Ans.** 17.1.%, 315.206 kW]

6.52. A 3-phase induction motor has 4-pole star-connected stator winding and runs on 400 V, 50 Hz supply. The rotor resistance is 0.1 Ω and reactance 0.9 Ω. The stator to rotor turns ratio is 1.75 and the full-load slip is 5%. Calculate the full-load power output. Determine also the maximum torque and the corresponding speed.

[*I.A.S.*, 1998] [**Ans.** 121.0806 kW, 184.791 Nm, 1333.5 r.p.m.]

6.53. A 3-phase, 6-pole, 50 Hz, 400 V SCIM has per-phase rotor leakage impedance = 0.8 + j 2.4 Ω at standstill. Rotor copper bars of this motor are replaced by aluminium bars. Determine how the following performance parameters change with respect to their previous values :

Slip at maximum torque, starting torque, maximum torque, full-load slip.

Take resistivity = 2.1μΩ cm for copper and 3.4 μΩ cm for aluminium.

[**Ans.** 1.62, 1.392, 1.0, 1.6188]

6.54. A 3-phase, 5 kW, 400 V, 50 Hz SCIM has the following data :

Flux per pole = 40 mWb, mean conductor length = 18 cm

Copper density = 8.94 gm/cm^3, current density = 4 A/mm^2.

Full-load efficiency = 0.84 and power factor = 0.85.

Compare the amount of copper required for stator winding if the induction motor is designed to operate with stator winding in *(a)* delta and *(b)* star.

[**Ans.** (a) Delta : Total turns = 144, conductor weight = 0.6762 kg.

(b) Star : Total turns = 84, conductor weight = 0.6831 kg.]

6.55. A 3-phase induction motor is designed to operate at rated voltage *V* and rated frequency *f*. In case both source voltage and frequency are respectively changed to *(a)* $\frac{V}{2}, f/2$ *(b)* $V, f/2$ *(c)* $\frac{V}{2}, f$ *(d)* $V, 2f$; find the maximum and starting torques in terms of their rated values. Neglect all stator losses. [**Ans.** *(a)* 1, 2 *(b)* 4, 8 *(c)* $\frac{1}{4}, \frac{1}{4}$ *(d)* $\frac{1}{4}, \frac{1}{8}$]

6.56. *(a)* What are the factors that govern the operating characteristics of polyphase induction motors.

(b) In case of polyphase induction motors, explain why the rotor speed falls as the load torque is increased.

(c) Power factor of a polyphase induction motor is low at no-load, but it improves as the load on the motor is increased. Explain.

6.57. Two squirrel cage induction motors *A* and *B* are identical in all respects, except that they have any one of the following differences in construction :

(a) Motor *A* has open stator slots but motor *B* has semi-closed stator slots.

(b) Motor A has semi-closed rotor slots but motor *B* has closed rotor slots.

(c) Motor *A* has longer air-gap than motor *B*.

For each of the three differences listed above, discuss which of the two motors have :

(i) better starting torque *(ii)* higher breakdown torque

(iii) better full-load power factor and *(iv)* higher full-load speed.

[**Ans.** *(a)* A, A, B, B, *(b)* A, A, B, B, *(c)* A, A, B, B]

6.58. (a) In case of induction motors, explain why the air-gap length is kept as small as is mechanically possible.

(b) Show that polyphase induction motors possess shunt speed-torque characteristic.

(c) A 3-phase squirrel cage induction motor is designed to have rotor copper bars. If, instead of using copper, aluminium is used for rotor bars, explain what happens to its speed, efficiency etc. under normal running conditions.

[**Ans.** (c) Speed is less, T_{em} remains unchanged, s_{mT} increases, rotor ohmic losses increase, output and, therefore, efficiency are reduced.]

6.59. (a) Explain how the equivalent circuit parameters of a polyphase induction motor can be determined from no-load and blocked-rotor tests and per phase stator winding D.C. resistance.

(b) A 400 V, 50 Hz, 3-phase star-connected squirrel-cage induction motor gave the following test results :

No-load or open-circuit test (line values) : 400 V, 9 A, 560 W. Blocked-rotor or short circuit test (line values) : 210 V, 36 A, 4820 W.

The effective stator resistance is 0.72 Ω per phase. Calculate the equivalent circuit parameters. [**Ans.** $r_1 = 0.72\ \Omega$, $r_2 = 0.59\ \Omega$, $x_1 = x_2 = 1.567\ \Omega$, $X_m = 24\ \Omega$]

6.60. (a) What is represented by the circle diagram of an induction motor? What information can be obtained from it?

Derive the current-locus for the rotor circuit of a polyphase induction motor.

(b) Show that the diameter of current-locus circle of a polyphase induction motor is $V_1/x_1 + x_2$, where x_1 is the per phase stator leakage reactance, x_2 is the standstill per phase rotor leakage reactance referred to stator and V_1 is the per phase stator voltage.

6.61. (a) Explain how the circle diagram for a polyphase induction motor can be drawn from its test data.

(b) A 400 V, 3-phase, 8 pole, 50 Hz star-connected induction motor gave the following test results :

No-load test (line values) : 400 V, 10 A, $\cos \theta_0 = 0.2$.

Blocked-rotor test (line values) : 160 V, 30 A, $\cos \theta_{sc} = 0.35$.

If, at full load and rated voltage, the power factor is at its maximum, then calculate full-load current, power factor, torque in newton-meters, speed, power output and efficiency. Stator and rotor ohmic losses are equal.

[**Ans.** 28.75 A, 0.806, 174.224 Nm, 698.7 r.p.m., 12.644 kW, 78.834%]

6.62. A 4 kW, 400 V, 50 Hz, 3-phase, 4-pole delta connected slipring induction motor has stator resistance of 0.36 Ω per phase, rotor resistance of 0.06 Ω per phase and per phase stator to rotor turns ratio of 2. The following data pertains to the line values during light load tests :

No-load	:	400 V, 3.3 A, $\cos \theta_0 = 0.174$
Locked rotor	:	210 V, 16 A, $\cos \theta_{sc} = 0.45$

Draw the circle diagram and compute :

(a) line current, power factor, slip, torque and efficiency at full load,

(b) best operating power factor, maximum power output, maximum torque in Nm and slip at maximum torque.

(c) the external resistance that must be inserted in series with rotor circuit to obtain maximum torque at starting.

[**Ans.** (a) 8.66 A, 0.8434, 0.057, 26.738 Nm, 77.65% (b) 0.852, 6.42 kW, 50.04 Nm, 0.21 (c) 0.2264 Ω referred to rotor]

6.63. *(a)* If no-load power factor angle θ_o for a polyphase induction motor is taken to be equal to 90°, show with the help of circle diagram that the best possible operating power factor is given by $\dfrac{V_1}{V_1 + 2I_0(x_1 + x_2)}$.

(b) Two induction motors *A* and *B* are identical in all respects, except that motor *A* has 6 poles and motor *B* has 4 poles. Explain which motor will possess higher value of best operating (maximum) power factor and also a better full-load power factor.

[Hint. *(b)* Induction motor leakage reactance is directly proportional to the number of poles.]

[Ans. *(b)* Motor B. Consequently slow-speed induction motors (motor *A* here) operate at poor power factors.]

6.64. *(a)* What are the causes of an induction motor operating always at lagging power factors? Explain how the power factor of an induction motor is controlled by static capacitors. Show that for a constant capacitance, the degree of power factor correction is not the same at different loads.

(b) A delta-connected induction motor operating from a balanced 3-phase, 400 V, 50 Hz supply takes a line current of 50 A at 0.76 p.f. lag. Calculate per phase value of the capacitance and total kVA rating of the 3-phase delta-connected capacitor bank which when connected to the motor terminals would improve the line power factor to 0.9 lag.

[Ans. 64.78 μF, 9.768 kVA]

6.65. *(a)* Discuss why the power factor of a 3-phase induction motor is low at *(a)* no-load and *(b)* also under overloads.

(b) A three-phase induction motor rated at 400 V, 50 Hz, coupled to a pump is running at a low power factor of 0.6. The input is 4.5 kVA. It is proposed to improve the power factor to 0.8 by connecting a delta-connected capacitor bank. Find the value of the capacitor per phase. [*GATE, 1994*] **[Ans.** 18.104 μF]

6.66. *(a)* What is the objection to the reduced-voltage starting of polyphase induction motors?

(b) Under what conditions is the direct-on-line starting of polyphase cage induction motors preferred?

(c) The starting period from zero to normal speed is more severe in case of D.C. motors than in induction motors. Explain.

(d) A 3-phase induction motor at normal speed is carrying about half the rated load. If one of the supply-line fuses blows off, will the motor stop or continue running? Explain.

[Ans. *(c)* Large starting currents in case of D.C. motors give rise to commutation difficulties etc. *(d)* Motor will continue running as a single-phase induction motor with more line current and at a slightly reduced speed.]

6.67. A 3-phase induction motor has rotor impedance of $0.03 + j\,0.18\ \Omega$ per phase referred to stator. Full-load slip at rated voltage is 3%. Estimate the percentage reduction in stator voltage to develop full-load torque at half of the full-load speed. Also, determine the power factor. Neglect stator impedance and mechanical losses. **[Ans.** 22.85%, 0.308]

6.68. A 3-phase, 4-pole, 50 Hz induction motor, during the short-circuit test, took 100 A and 30 kW. In case stator resistance is equal to equivalent standstill rotor resistance, compute the starting torque. **[Ans.** 95.493 Nm]

6.69. A 3-phase star-connected, 440 V, 50 Hz, 4-pole induction motor has the following constants in ohms per phase referred to stator side :

$r_1 = 0.294,\ x_1 = 0.503,\ r_2 = 0.144,\ x_2 = 0.209,\ X_m = 13.25$

The stator core losses are negligible.

Total friction and other losses (assumed constant) = 1400 W.

Find the power output in kW and the rated output in Nm if the motor is being operated at rated voltage and frequency with 2 percent slip. *[I.A.S., 1979]* [**Ans.** 21.093 kW, 137.02 Nm]

6.70. A 20 kW, 400 V, 3-phase induction motor has full-load power factor of 0.86 and full-load efficiency of 0.88. With stator winding in delta, short-circuit line current at 200 V is 70 A. If this motor is fitted with a star-delta starter, find

(a) the ratio of starting to full-load line current and

(b) the starting torque in terms of full-load torque, for a full-load slip of 5%.

[**Hint.** *(b)* Use Eq. (6.63)] [**Ans.** *(a)* 1.223 *(b)* 0.2244]

6.71. *(a)* Why is it necessary to employ special starting arrangements for induction motors?

(b) Calculate the relative values of starting currents and starting torques of a 3-phase squirrel-cage induction motor, when it is started by

(i) direct-on-line starter, *(ii)* star-delta starter and

(iii) auto-transformer starter with 60% tapping. [**Ans.** *(b)* $1 : \frac{1}{3} : 0.36$]

6.72. A 3-phase squirrel cage induction motor has a short-circuit current of 5 times the full-load current. Its full-load slip is 5%. Calculate the starting torque as a percentage of full-load torque if the motor is started by

(a) direct-on-line starter, *(b)* star-delta starter,

(c) auto-transformer starter, limiting the motor starting current to twice the motor full-load current. Also find the starting current drawn from the supply, in terms of motor full-load current. What is the percentage auto-transformer tapping in this case?

(d) auto-transformer starter limiting the supply line starting current to twice the full-load current. Find the auto-transformer tapping in this case also.

[**Hint.** *(b)* and *(c)*. Read auto-transformer starter between lines.]

[**Ans.** *(a)* 1.25 *(b)* 0.417 *(c)* 0.20, 0.8 I_{fl}, 40% *(d)* 0.5, 63.2%]

6.73. At rated voltage, a polyphase induction motor develops a starting torque of twice the full-load torque and draws from the supply a starting current of 6 times the full-load current.

(a) The motor is started using a compensator (auto-transformer) which steps down the voltage to 70%. Determine the motor starting current, starting current drawn from the supply and the starting torque.

(b) If the auto-transformer starter limits the starting current from the supply to twice the full-load current, determine the starting torque and auto-transformer tapping.

[**Hint.** From Eq. (6.51). $s_{fl} = \frac{1}{18}$]

[**Ans.** *(a)* 4.2 I_{fl}, 2.94 I_{fl}, 0.98 $T_{e.fl}$ *(b)* 0.667 $T_{e.fl}$, 57.74% tapping]

6.74. A squirrel cage induction motor when started by star-delta starter, develops a starting torque of 0.4 times the full-load torque and takes from the supply a starting current of twice the full-load current. Calculate the supply line current and starting torque if this induction motor is started by

(a) across-the-line starter,

(b) auto-transformer starter with 80% tapping

[**Hint.** Here $s_{fl} = \frac{1}{30}$] [**Ans.** *(a)* 6 I_{fl}, 1.2 $T_{e.fl}$ *(b)* 3.84 I_{fl}, 0.768 $T_{e.fl}$]

6.75. A 3-phase, 10 kW, 400 V squirrel-cage induction motor has a full-load efficiency of 0.87 and a full-load power factor of 0.85. With stator winding in delta, the motor takes a starting line current of 80 amperes at rated voltage. Its full-load slip is 5%. Find the minimum starting current to be taken from the supply in order that starting torque equal to half the full-load torque is developed when started by

(a) an auto-transformer starter,

(b) stator resistor starter.

Calculate the percentage tapping on auto-transformer also.

[**Ans.** *(a)* 47.432 A, 77% tapping *(b)* 61.664 A]

6.76. A 3-phase squirrel cage induction motor has a rotor resistance of 0.3 Ω per phase and a standstill rotor reactance of 2.5 Ω per phase. The ratio of maximum torque to full-load torque is found to be 3. Determine the ratio of actual starting-torque to full-load torque for star-delta starting. State the assumptions made in your calculations.

[**Hint.** With direct switching, $\dfrac{T_{e \cdot st}}{3T_{e \cdot fl}} = \dfrac{2}{\dfrac{0.12}{2} + \dfrac{1}{0.12}}$.

With star-delta starting torque is reduced to one-third of that during direct switching].

[**Ans.** 0.2366]

6.77. A 50 kVA, 440 V, 3-phase, 50 Hz induction motor is provided with a 3-phase step-down auto-transformer starter which steps down the voltage to 50% of the input. Given that the starting current of the motor on rated voltage is 6 times the rated full-load current, estimate the current drawn by the auto-transformer from the mains at starting. What is the starting kVA drawn by the auto-transformer? *[I.A.S., 1987]* [**Ans.** 98.415 A, 75 kVA]

6.78. The starting current of a delta-connected 3-phase induction motor at rated voltage is 5 times the full-load current and the slip at full-load is 5%. The no-load current is negligible.

(a) If an auto-transformer starter is used to limit the starting current from mains to 2 times the full-load current, estimate the starting torque then obtained as a percentage of the full-load torque.

(b) Neglecting stator impedance, determine the slip at which maximum torque occurs in the motor. *[I.A.S., 1991]* [**Ans.** *(a)* 50 per cent *(b)* 0.253]

6.79. A 3-phase, 400 V, 50 A, 4-pole, 1440 r.p.m. induction motor takes a blocked-rotor current of 6 times its full-load current at 0.4 p.f. lag at rated voltage and develops a torque of 1.8 times its full-load torque. If this induction motor is started by an auto-transformer with 60% tapping, then at the time of starting, calculate *(a)* motor power factor *(b)* motor current *(c)* line current *(d)* power input to motor and *(e)* starting torque in terms of full-load torque.

[**Ans.** *(a)* 0.4 lag *(b)* 180 A *(c)* 108 A *(d)* 29.929 kW *(e)* 0.5184 $T_{e \cdot fl}$]

6.80. A SCIM has a starting current of six times the full-load current at a slip of 0.04. Calculate the line current and starting torque in p.u. of full-load values for the following methods of starting :

(a) Direct switching

(b) Auto-transformer starting with motor current limited to 2.0 p.u.

(c) Star-delta starting.

[I.E.S., 2002] [**Ans.** *(a)* 6 p.u., 1.44 p.u. *(b)* 0.67 p.u., 0.16 p.u. *(c)* 2 p.u., 0.48 p.u.]

6.81. *(a)* Why is it not advisable to start wound-rotor induction motors by the methods employed for starting cage induction motors?

(*b*) What are the advantages of inserting external resistance in the rotor circuit of a wound-rotor induction motor at the time of starting?

(*c*) How is the induction motor operation affected if the external resistance in the rotor-circuit is not fully cut off?

(*d*) The resistance measured at the stator-terminals of a polyphase induction motor is 0.2 Ω. For a given line current show that the stator ohmic losses would be same whether it is star or delta connected.

6.82. Calculate the value of the resistance elements of a 5-step (or 6-stud) starter for a 3-phase, 400 V, wound-rotor induction motor. The full-load slip is 2.5% and the maximum starting current is limited to its full load value. Rotor resistance per phase is 0.02 Ω.

Derive any formula used stating the various assumptions made.

[**Ans.** 0.418 Ω, 0.20 Ω, 0.096 Ω, 0.046 Ω, 0.022 Ω]

6.83. Design a 4-step starter for a 3-phase wound rotor induction motor. The full-load slip is 2.5% and the maximum starting current is limited to 1.6 times its full load value. Rotor resistance per phase is 0.02 Ω.

Derive the formula used for calculating the resistance sections and state the various assumptions made. [**Ans.** 0.277 Ω, 0.124 Ω, 0.055 Ω, 0.025 Ω]

6.84. (*a*) Explain any two methods for performing the polarity test on a 3-phase induction motor.

(*b*) A polarity test is performed on a 3-phase, 400 V wound-rotor induction motor. Phase *A* is given 100 V and the voltmeter connected across the two terminals of phases *A* and *B* is seen to record a voltage of 141 volts, with the rotor open circuited. What are the polarity markings of phase *B*, relative to phase *A*?

[**Ans.** (*b*) The two terminals of phases *A* and *B*, which are connected together, have the same polarity markings.]

6.85. (*a*) What is an induction generator? Describe, with the help of circle diagram, the operation of an externally-excited 3-phase induction generator.

(*b*) Discuss the following for a 3-phase induction generator :

(*i*) It operates always at a leading power factor.

(*ii*) Control of load on induction generator and its limit.

(*iii*) Application of SCIM in the generating mode.

(*iv*) It requires reactive power for its operation from an existing supply network.

(*v*) Comparison of the use of induction generator with a synchronous generator.

6.86. (*a*) Explain the principle of operation of a self-excited 3-phase induction generator. Give the condition under which this generator may fail to build up.

(*b*) Give the applications of both externally-excited and self-excited 3-phase induction generators.

6.87. (*a*) Compare the relative advantages and disadvantages of cage-rotor and wound-rotor induction motors of the same power rating.

(*b*) How do you compare the operation of a polyphase induction motor with that of a polyphase synchronous motor?

7

Chapter

Armature Windings

INTRODUCTION

The windings used in rotating electrical machines can be classified as

(a) concentrated windings and *(b)* distributed windings.

In concentrated type of winding, all the winding turns are wound together in series to form one multi-turn coil. Examples of concentrated winding are field windings for salient-pole synchronous machines as well as for D.C. machines. In concentrated coils, all the turns have the same magnetic axis. Primary and secondary windings of a transformer also form concentrated windings.

In distributed type of winding, all the winding turns are arranged in several full-pitch or fractional-pitch coils. These coils are then housed in the slots spread around the air-gap periphery to form phase or commutator winding. Stator and rotor of induction machines, the armatures of both synchronous and D.C. machines have distriuted type of windings.

As stated before in Art. 3.2, the field (or exciting) winding is that which produces the working flux. The armature winding is one in which working e.m.f. is induced by the working flux. The object of this chapter is to serve as an introduction to the study of armature windings for both D.C. and A.C. machines.

Armature windings, in general, are classified under two main heads, namely,

(a) closed windings and (b) open windings.

The closed windings are used only for commutator machines, such as D.C. machines and A.C. commutator machines. The open windings are used only for A.C. machines, like synchronous machines, induction machines, etc. In closed windings, there is a closed path in the sense that if one starts from any point on the winding and traverses it, one again reaches the starting point from where one had started. Open windings terminate at suitable number of slip-rings or terminals. Note that three phase delta connected winding used for A.C. machines, forms a closed circuit. This 3-phase delta can, however, be open-circuited and reconnected in star if desired. Closed windings used for commutator machines can, in no case, be open-circuited.

Some of the terms common to both the closed and open armature windings are described below. A reference to Art. 3.3 is helpful.

(i) **Conductor.** A length of wire which takes active part in the energy-conversion process is called a conductor. In Fig. 7.1 *(a)*, wire length *AB* is one conductor, wire length *DE* (or *ED*) is another conductor.

(ii) **Turn.** One turn consists of two conductors. In Fig. 7.1 *(a)*, two conductors *AB* and *DE* form one turn. The two conductors of a turn are usually a pole-pitch apart, so that generated e.m.fs. in these conductors are additive in nature.

(iii) **Coil.** One coil may consist of any number of turns; *e.g.* in Fig. 7.1 *(a)* one coil has one turn, in Fig. 7.1 *(b)* one coil has two turns. The schematic diagram of a coil having more than one turn is as shown in Fig. 7.1 *(c)*. The number of turns in any particular coil decides its designation, *e.g.* a coil having one turn is called **one turn coil**. Similarly, the coil may be designated as **2-turn coil, 3-turn coil** or ***N*-turn coil** depending on whether it has two turns, three turns or *N*-turns respectively. A **multi-turn (or N-turn) coil** is one which has more than one turn.

(iv) **Coil-side.** One coil with any number of turns has two coil-sides, see Fig. 7.1 where *AB* and *DE* are the two coil-sides.

The number of conductors in any coil-side is equal to the number of turns in that coil. For example, each coil-side of one-turn-coil in Fig. 7.1 *(a)* has one conductor, each coil-side of *N*-turn coil in Fig. 7.1 *(c)* has *N* conductors. Note that *BCD* in Fig. 7.1 is called the end-connection or overhang.

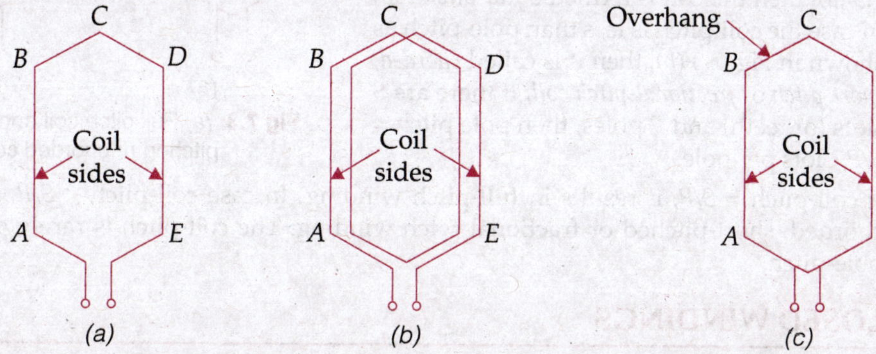

Fig 7.1: Schematic diagram of *(a)* one-turn coil, *(b)* two-turn coil and *(c)* multi-turn coil.

(v) **Single-layer and double-layer windings.** If the winding is so designed that one coil-side occupies the total slot area, then it is called a *single layer winding*, see Fig. 7.2 *(a)*. In case the slot contains even number (may be 2, 4, 6 etc.) of coil-sides in two layers, the winding is referred to as a *two layer winding*, see Fig. 7.2 *(b)* and *(c)*. Single-layer winding is used only in small A.C. machines, whereas double-layer winding is more common above about 5 kW machines.

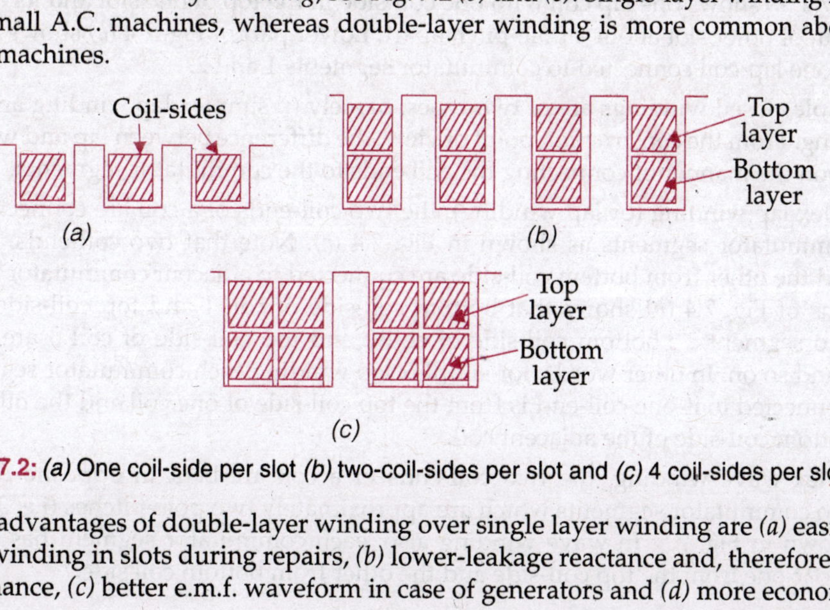

Fig 7.2: *(a)* One coil-side per slot *(b)* two-coil-sides per slot and *(c)* 4 coil-sides per slot.

The advantages of double-layer winding over single layer winding are *(a)* easier to house the winding in slots during repairs, *(b)* lower-leakage reactance and, therefore, better performance, *(c)* better e.m.f. waveform in case of generators and *(d)* more economical.

(vi) **Pole-pitch.** The term pitch indicates a particular method of measurement in terms of coil-sides, teeth etc. A pole pitch is defined as the peripheral distance between identical points on two adjacent poles, see Figs. 3.10 *(a)* and 3.11 *(c)*. Pole-pitch is always equal to 180° electrical.

(vii) **Coil-span or coil-pitch.** The distance between the two coil-sides of a coil is called coil-span or coil-pitch. It is usually measured in terms of teeth, slots or electrical degrees.

(viii) **Chorded-coil.** If the coil-span (or coil-pitch) is equal to the pole-pitch as illustrated in Fig. 7.3 *(a)*, then the coil is termed a *full-pitch coil.* In case the coil-pitch is less than pole-pitch as shown in Fig. 7.3 *(b)*, then it is called *chorded, short-pitch* or *fractional-pitch coil.* If there are S slots (or teeth) and P poles, then pole pitch = S/P, slots per pole.

If coil-pitch = S/P, it results in full-pitch winding. In case coil-pitch < S/P, it results in chorded, short-pitched or fractional-pitch winding. The coil-pitch is rarely greater than pole-pitch.

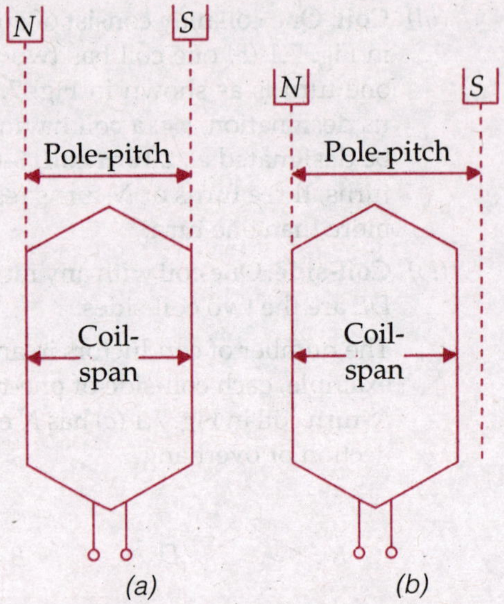

Fig 7.3: *(a)* Full pitch coil and *(b)* short-pitched or chorded coil.

7.1. CLOSED WINDINGS

As has been stated before, closed windings are used for all types of D.C. machines and for A.C. commutator machines. It should be kept in mind at the outset that closed armature windings are always double layer windings. Each coil in double layer winding has its one coil-side in top layer and its other coil-side in the bottom layer. In drawing these windings, the top coil-side is shown with a solid line and the bottom coil-side by a dotted line as illustrated in Figs. 7.4 and 7.5. Upper part of Fig. 7.4 *(a)* shows one lap coil with one coil-side in the top of one slot and its other coil-side in the bottom of other slot about a pole-pitch apart. Lower part of Fig. 7.4 *(a)* shows the schematic diagram of one lap-coil connected to commutator segments 1 and 2.

The simple closed windings are of two types, namely *(i)* simplex lap winding and *(ii)* simplex wave winding. From the construction point of view, the difference between lap and wave windings depends upon the manner of connecting the coil ends to the commutator segments.

In simplex lap winding (or lap winding), the two coil-ends of a coil are connected to the two adjacent commutator segments as shown in Fig. 7.4 *(a)*. Note that two coil-ends, one from top coil-side and the other from bottem coil-side are connected to adjacent commutator segments. An examinations of Fig. 7.4 *(b)* shows that bottom coil-side of coil 1 and top coil-side of coil 2 are connected to segment 2 ; bottom coil-side of coil 2 and top coil-side of coil 3 are connected to segment 3 and so on. In other words, for simplex lap winding each commutator segment has two coil-ends connected to it-one coil-end is from the top coil-side of one coil and the other coil-end is from the bottom coil-side of the adjacent coil.

In simplex wave winding, the two coil-ends of a coil are bent in opposite directions and connected to commutator segments which are approximately two pole-pitches (i.e. 360° electrical) apart as shown in Fig. 7.5. In wave winding also, each commutator segment has two coil-ends connected to it-one from the top coil-side and the other from bottom coil side.

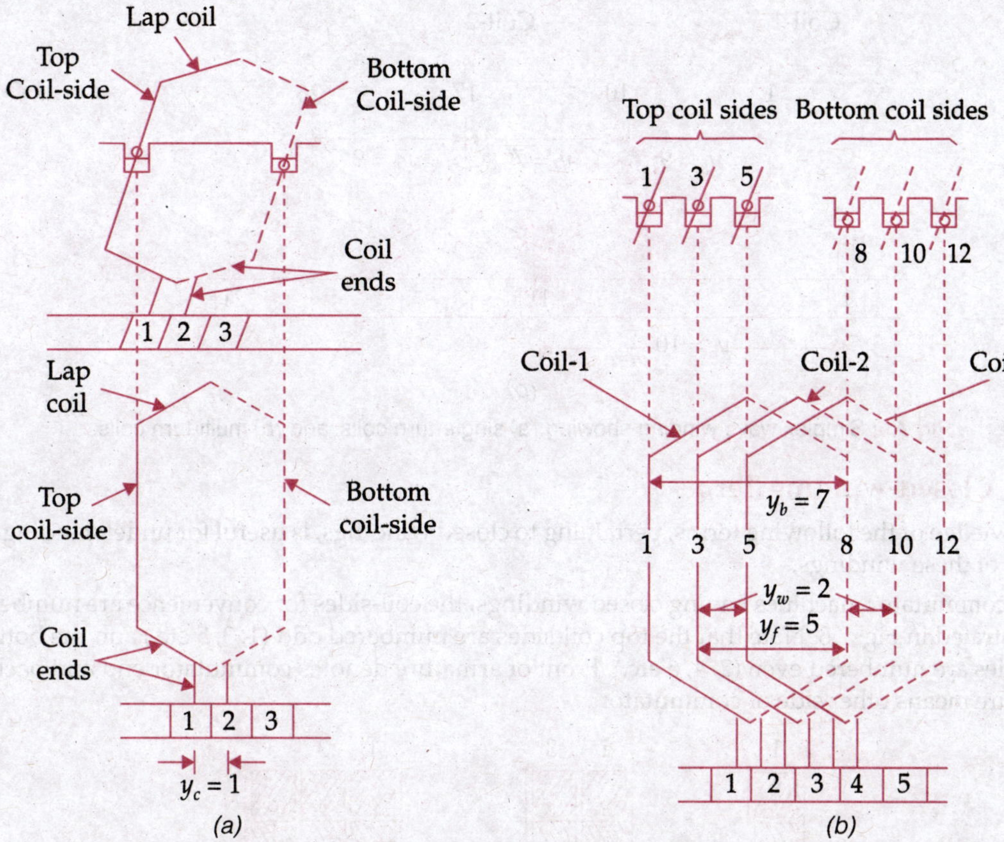

Fig 7.4: Lap-coil connections, *(a)* single multi-turn lap coil and *(b)* three multi-turn lap coils.

Examination of Fig. 7.4 *(b)* reveals that if lap coils are traversed, the movement is forward and backward alternately ; whereas Fig. 7.5 *(a)* reveals that for wave winding, the movement is forward only. In both the lap and wave windings, all the coils are traversed in series.

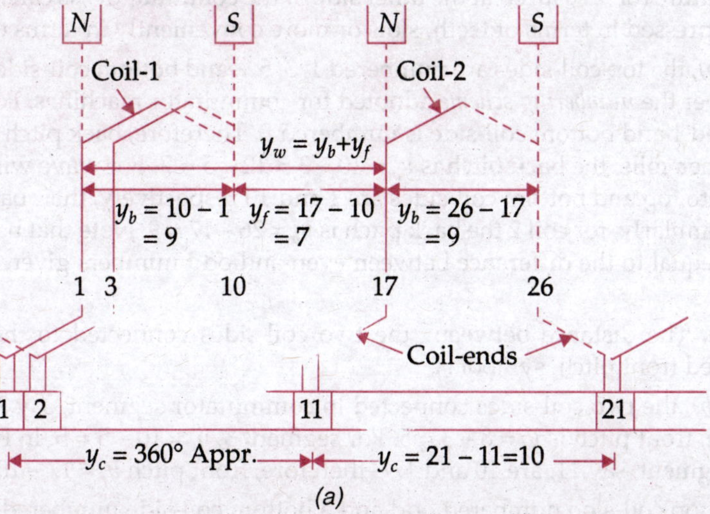

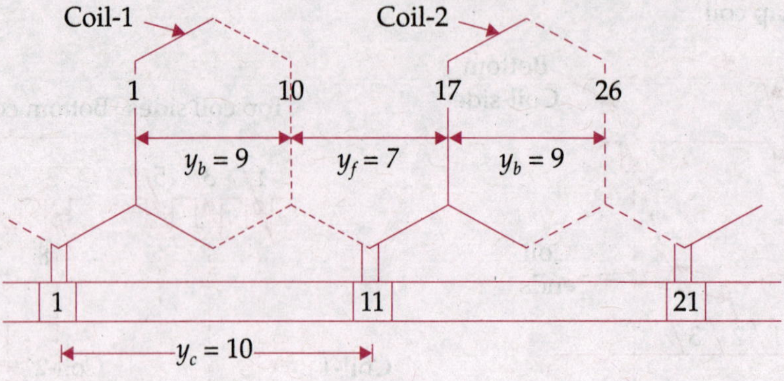

(b)

Fig 7.5: Simplex wave winding showing *(a)* single-turn coils. and *(b)* multi-turn coils.

7.1.1. Closed-winding Terms

A knowledge of the following terms, pertaining to closed windings, is useful for understanding the details of these windings.

In commutator machines having closed windings, the coil-sides for convenience are numbered as illustrated in Fig. 7.6. Note that the top coil-sides are numbered odd (1, 3, 5 etc.) and the bottom coil-sides are numbered even (2, 4, 6 etc.). Front of armature denotes commutator end and back of armature means other side of commutator.

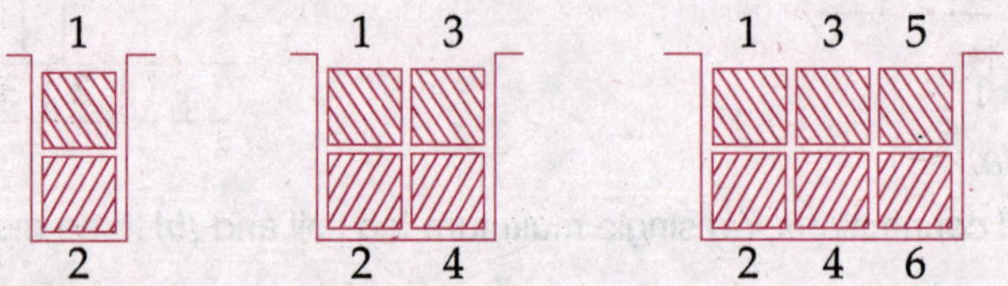

Fig 7.6: Illustrating the method of numbering coil sides in commutator machines.

Back Pitch. The distance between the top and bottom coil-sides of one coil, measured at the back of the armature (or measured at the other side of the commutator), is called back pitch, symbol y_b. It may be expressed in terms of teeth, slots or more conveniently in terms of coil-sides.

In Fig. 7.4 *(b)*, the top coil-sides are numbered 1, 3, 5 ... and bottom coil-sides are numbered, say 8, 10, 12 ...., as per the *numbering scheme* adopted for commutator machines. For coil 1, the top coil-side is numbered 1 and bottom coil-side is numbered 8. Therefore, back pitch for coil 1 is $8 - 1 = 7$; similarly for other coils, the back pitch is $y_b = 10 - 3 = 12 - 5 = 7$. For wave winding in Fig. 7.5, the numbers given to top and bottom coil-sides are 1 and 10 respectively, their back pitch is therefore, $y_b = 10 - 1 = 9$. Similarly, for coil 2 the back pitch is $y_b = 26 - 17 = 9$. Note that back pitch y_b is always odd, since it is equal to the difference between even and odd numbers given to the two coil-sides of the same coil.

Front pitch. The distance between the two coil-sides connected to the same commutator segment, is called front pitch, symbol y_f.

In Fig. 7.4 *(b)*, the two coil-sides connected to commutator segment, say 2, are numbered as 3 and 8, therefore, front pitch is $y_f = 8 - 3 = 5$. For segment 3, $y_f = 10 - 5 = 5$. In Fig. 7.5, the coil-sides connected to segment, say 11, are 10 and 17—therefore, front pitch $y_f = 17 - 10 = 7$.

Note that a top coil-side numbered odd and a bottom coil-side numbered even, are connected to the same commutator segment—this shows that the front pitch y_f is always odd.

Winding pitch. The distance between the two consecutive and similar top, or bottom, coil-sides, as the winding progresses, is called the winding pitch, symbol y_w. It is expressed in terms of coil-sides.

In Fig. 7.4 *(b)*, the consecutive and similar top coil-sides are numbered 1, 3, 5 ... or similar bottom coil-sides are numbered 8, 10, 12 .... Therefore, for Fig. 7.4 *(b)*, winding pitch $y_w = 3 - 1 = 5 - 3 = 10 - 8 = 12 - 10 = 2$. An examination of Fig. 7.4 *(b)* reveals that for simplex lap winding, $y_w = y_b - y_f$.

In Fig. 7.5, the consecutive and similar top coil-sides, as the winding progresses, are numbered 1, 17 or similar bottom coil sides are numbered 10, 26. Therefore, for Fig. 7.5, winding pitch $y_w = 17 - 1 = 26 - 10 = 16$. An examination of Fig. 7.5 reveals that for simplex wave winding, $y_w = y_b + y_f$.

Note that winding pitch y_w is always even, because it is equal to either the difference or the addition of two odd numbers y_b and y_f.

Commutator pitch. The distance between the two commutator segments, to which the two ends of one coil are joined, is called the commutator pitch, symbol y_c. It is always expressed in terms of commutator segments.

For simplex lap winding, the two ends of coil 1 are joined to segments 2 and 1, therefore, $y_c = 2 - 1 = 1$, see Fig. 7.4 For simplex wave winding, the two ends of coil 1 are joined to segments 11 and 1, therefore, $y_c = 11 - 1 = 10$, Fig. 7.5. For simplex lap winding, y_c is always equal to 1. For simplex wave winding, y_c is almost equal to 2 pole-pitches.

7.2. SIMPLEX LAP WINDING

Let C be the number of armature coils and P the number of poles. Since each coil has two coil-sides, total number of coil-sides is $2C$. The back pitch y_b, almost equal to pole pitch, must be odd, therefore,

$$y_b = \text{coil-sides per pole} \pm K \text{ or } y_b = 2C/P \pm K \qquad \text{... (7.1)}$$

where K is a number (integer or fraction) added to $2C/P$ to make y_b an odd integer. Here $2C/P$ is equal to the pole-pitch in terms of coil-sides per pole.

An armature winding may be either *progressive* or *retrogressive.* In progressive lap windings, if coil 1 is placed first, then coil 2 is placed in slots to the right of slots occupied by coil 1, coil 3 in the slots to the right of coil 2 and so on as shown in Fig. 7.7 *(a)*. Thus the progressive winding progresses to the right as seen from the commutator side. Therefore, for the progressive simplex lap winding, the winding pitch is

$$y_w = y_b - y_f = (8 - 1) - (8 - 3) = +2 \text{ and } y_c = +1.$$

In retrogressive lap winding, coil 2 is placed in slots to the left of coil 1, coil 3 in slots to the left of coil 2 and so on, see Fig. 7.7 *(b)*. Thus the winding retrogresses, *i.e.*, progresses to the left as seen from the commutator end. Therefore, for simplex retrogressive lap winding, the winding pitch is

$$y_w = y_b - y_f = [8 - 1] - [8 - (-1)] = 7 - 9 = -2 \text{ and } y_c = -1.$$

Fig. 7.7 *(b)* reveals that coil-ends are crossing in retrogressive lap winding, there are, therefore, more chances of fault and in view of this, it is rarely used.

Hence for a simplex lap winding,

winding pitch, $y_w = \pm 2$

and commutator pitch, $y_c = \pm 1$

The positive sign is used for progressive winding and negative sign is used for retrogressive winding.

In the term "simplex lap winding", simplex refers to the fact that coil 1 is placed in the slots adjacent to coil 2, coil 2 is placed in slots adjacent to coil 3 and so on ; lap refers to the fact that coil

2 laps over coil 1, coil 3 laps over coil 2 and so on for one parallel path. The lap winding is also known as parallel winding.

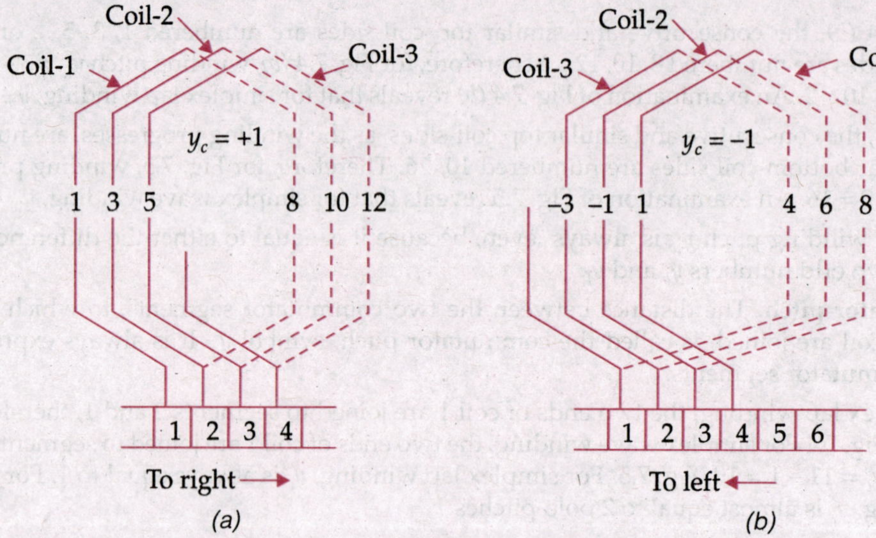

Fig 7.7: Simplex lap winding with single turn coils *(a)* progressive type and *(b)* retrogressive type.

Example 7.1. *For a commutator machine with 6 poles and 40 coils, determine for a simplex lap winding: (a) the number of commutator segments, (b) back pitch and front pitch and (c) commutator pitch.*

Solution. *(a)* Since one commutator segment is required for each coil, the number of commutator segments = number of coils, C = 40.

(b) Back pitch, $y_b = \frac{2C}{P} \pm K = \frac{2 \times 40}{6} \pm K = \frac{40}{3} \pm \frac{1}{3}$.

The back pitch y_b must be odd, therefore,

$$y_b = \frac{40}{3} - \frac{1}{3} = 13.$$

But $y_b - y_f = \pm 2$

$\therefore$ $y_f = 13 - 2 = 11$ for progressive winding.

and $= 13 + 2 = 15$ for retrogressive winding.

(c) Commutator pitch, $y_c = \pm 1$.

Example 7.2. *For a commutator machine with 12 coils and 4 poles, design a progressive simplex lap winding with two coil-sides per slot. Draw the winding diagram also.*

Solution. Number of commutator segments = number of coil, C = 12.

Twelve coils have 24 coil-sides. For two coil-sides per slot,

$$\text{total number of slots} = \frac{24}{2} = 12$$

Back pitch, $y_b = \frac{2C}{P} \pm K = \frac{24}{4} \pm 1 = 7 \text{ or } 5.$

For progressive lap winding, $y_w = y_b - y_f = +2$

$\therefore$ $y_f = 5$ for $y_b = 7$ or $y_f = 3$ for $y_b = 5$.

It is desirable that $\frac{y_b + y_f}{2}$ should be as nearly equal to pole pitch as is possible. In view of this, $y_b = 7$ and $y_f = 5$ should be chosen for this commutator machine, because $\frac{7+5}{2}$ = pole pitch in terms of coil-sides $\left(= \frac{24}{4} \text{coil-sides per poles}\right)$.

For progressive simplex lap winding, commutator pitch, $y_c = +1$.

For drawing the winding diagram in radial form, 12 commutator segments, 12 slots and 24 coil sides are first drawn as illustrated in Fig. 7.8. Now segment 1 is connected to top coil-side 1 and then to bottom coil-side 8 (= $1 + y_b = 1 + 7$).

Note that the coil-side 1 and segment 1 are so numbered that the coils resemble a lap coil. Since $y_c = 1$, the coil-side 8 is connected to segment 2 ($1 + y_c = 1 + 1$). Bottom coil-side is now connected to top coil-side 3 ($8 - y_f = 8 - 5$), then to bottom coil-side 10 (3 + 7), then to top coil-side 5 (10 – 5), then to bottom coil-side 12 (5 + 7) and so on. The winding table written below is helpful in drawing this winding diagram.

$(1 \xrightarrow{+y_b} 8) \xrightarrow{-y_f} (3 \xrightarrow{+y_b} 10) \xrightarrow{-y_f} (5 \xrightarrow{+y_b} 12) \to (7 \to 14) \to (9 \to 16) \to (11 \to 18) \to$ $(13 \to 20) \to (15 \to 22) \to (17 \to 24) \to (19 \to 26$ or $26 - 24$ *i.e.* $2) \to (26 \to y_f$ or $21 \to 21 + y_b$, *i.e.* $4) \to$ $(28 - y_f$. *i.e.* $23 \to 6) \to 1$.

In the winding table (1 → 8) means that the top coil-side 1 is connected to bottom coil-side 8 to form one coil. Same is true for all other coils. Note that winding table does not contain any number greater than 24 (= total number of coil-sides). Each coil-side is used only once in the winding table and the winding closes on itself (starting from 1 and ending on 1).

In this machine with 12 slots and 4 poles, 3 slots are assumed to be under the effect of each pole. For example, 3 slots containing coil-sides 1 to 6 are taken under say *N* pole, next 3 slots with coil-sides 7 to 12 under the adjacent *S* pole and so on. Directions of e.m.fs. and currents in the coil-sides under *N* pole are indicated by, say, cross and those under *S* pole by dot. Now the direactions of currents can be marked by noting that current flows from segments to cross-marked coil-sides and to the segments from dot-marked coil-sides.

A careful examination of winding diagram of Fig. 7.8 reveals that currents leave at the commutator segments 1, 7 and the currents enter at the commutator segments 4, 10. Thus four brushes *A*, *B*, *C*, *D* can be placed in contact with segments 1, 4, 7, 10 respectively as shown. Brushes *A* and *C* have the same polarity, these can, therefore, be joined together, similarly brushes *C* and *D* can be joined. Armature power can be handled at the terminals marked E, F. If *E* and *F* are marked positive and negative respectively, the machine works as a generator as shown in Fig. 7.8 and the direction of rotation is clockwise. In case *E* and *F* are given negative and positive polarities respectively, the machine works as a motor with the direction of rotation anti-clockwise.

If right hand grip rule is applied to coil-sides 1 to 6 and coil-sides 19 to 24, one pole N_1 is created on the armature in between these two coil groups as shown in Fig. 7.8. Now main stator pole *N* repels pole N_1 and main stator pole S attracts pole N_1, therefore, an anticlockwise torque is produced for motoring mode. For generator operation, the armature must be rotated clockwise against the motoring mode.

From brush *A*, one parallel path is through coils *a*, *b*, *c* to brush *B* and the second parallel path is through coils *l*, *k*, *j* to brush *D*. From brush *C*, one parallel path is through coils *f*, *e*, *d* to brush *B* and the second parallel path through coils *g*, *h*, *i* to brush *D*. These parallel paths at any instant, are illustrated in Fig. 7.9. There are thus four parallel paths for a 4-pole machine—in general, for a simplex lap winding, number of parallel paths *a* is equal to the number of poles *P*, *i.e.*, $a = P$. Expression $\phi ZnP/a$ reveals that the generated e.m.f. in lap connected machines (equal to ϕZn) is independent of the number of poles.

An examination of Fig. 7.9 reveals that current handled by each brush is twice the current per parallel path. If I_a = armature current, that for simplex lap winding, current per conductor, I_c = current per parallel path.

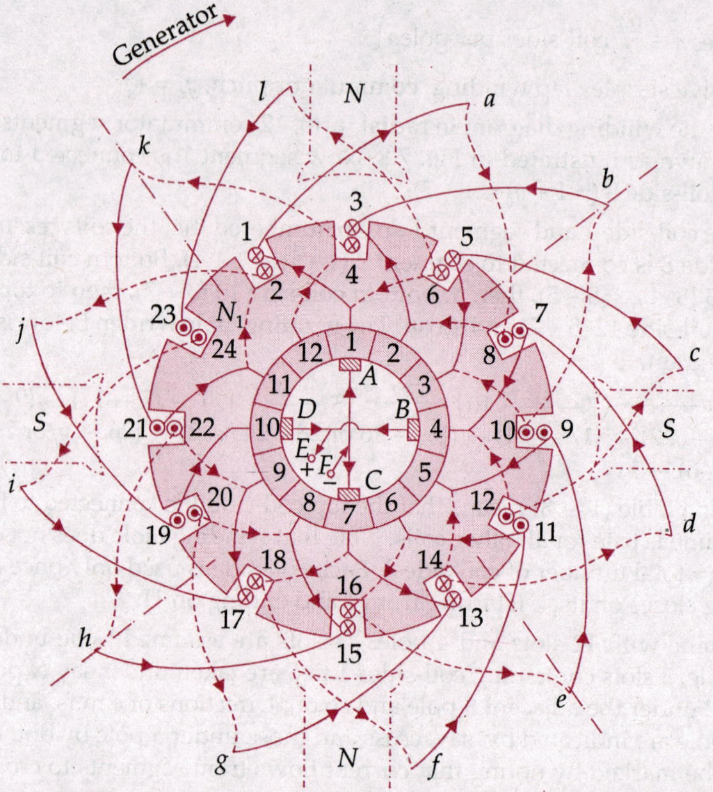

Fig 7.8: Simplex lap winding for 4 poles, 12 slots and two coil-sides per slot, pertaining to Example 7.2.

$$= \frac{I_a}{a} = \frac{I_a}{P}$$

and current per brush (or per brush-set or per brush-arm) $= \dfrac{2I_a}{P}$

It is also seen from Fig. 7.8 that brushes are physically placecd just below the pole centres. Therefore, electrical angle between adjacent brushes is 180°. Note that physical location of brushes under the pole centres is beacause of the diamond shape of the coils, Fig. 7.20. Brushes are actually connected electrically to the coil-sides lying close to the interpolar region. This shows that brushes are displaced 90° electrical away from the main-pole axis. This fact of 90° displacement between main-pole axis and brushes (or brush-axis) is used in the schematic representation of D.C. machines in Chapter 4.

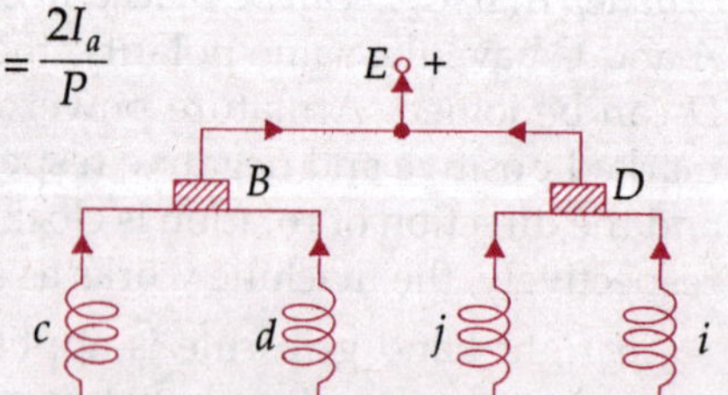

Fig 7.9: Pertaining to Example 7.2.

Example 7.3. *A progressive simplex lap winding is to be designed for a 4-pole, 14-slot, 2 coil-sides per slot D.C. armature. Obtain the following :*

(a) winding table, *(b) winding diagram in radial form and*

(c) position of the brushes on the commutator.

Solution. *(a)* Number of coils, $C = \frac{14 \times 2}{2} = 14.$

Back pitch, $y_b = \frac{2C}{P} + K = \frac{2 \times 14}{2} \pm 0 = 7$

For progressive lap winding,
front pitch, $y_f = y_b - 2 = 7 - 2 = 5.$

The winding table is as written below :

$(1 \to 8) \to (3 \to 10) \to (5 \to 12) \to (7 \to 14) \to (9 \to 16)$
$\to (11 \to 18) \to (13 \to 20) \to (15 \to 22) \to (17 \to 24) \to$
$(19 \to 26) \to (21 \to 28) \to (23 \to 2) \to (25 \to 4) \to (27 \to 6) \to 1.$

(b) The winding diagram in radial form shown in Fig. 7.10, is drawn as explained in Example 7.2.

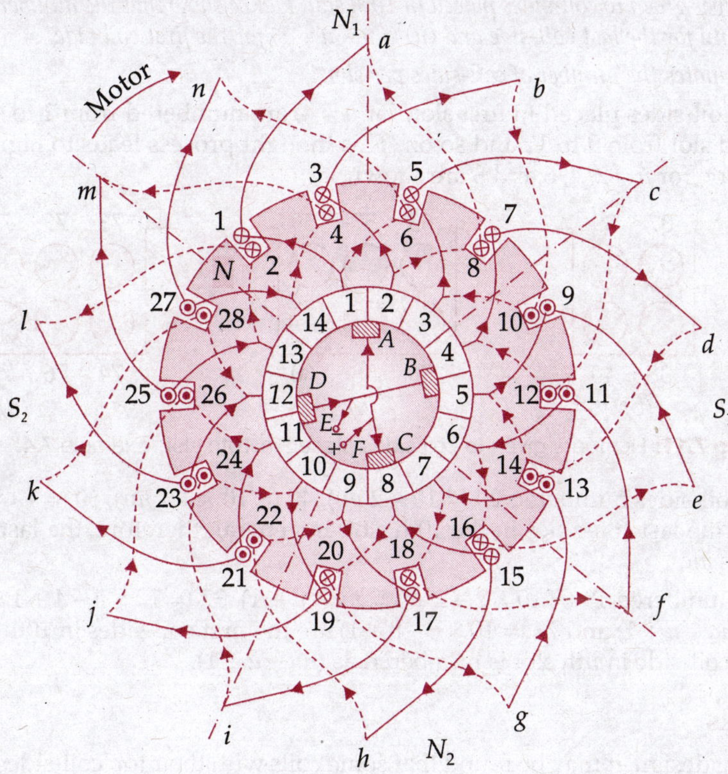

Fig 7.10: Simplex lap winding, 4 poles, 14 slots, 2 coil-sides per slot. Example 7.3.

(c) For a 4-pole, 14-slot D.C. machine, the slots per pole are $3\frac{1}{2}$. Had there been 4 coil-sides per slot, then its two coil-sides (top and bottom) would be taken under the effect of one pole and the remaining two coil-sides of the same slot (top and bottom) under the effect of neighbouring pole. But in the present case, there are only two coil-sides per slot. Here if we take 7 slots under the effect of two north poles and the remaining 7 slots under the effect of two south poles, the position of brushes can be located. In Fig. 7.10, 4-slots containing coil sides 1 to 8 are taken under the effect of main pole N_1. Similarly, 3 slots containing coil sides 9 to 14, again next three slots housing coil-sides 15 to 20 and next 4 slots containing 21 to 28 coil sides are taken under the effect of main poles S_1, N_2 and S_2 respectively. Crosses are shown under north poles and dots under south poles. If right hand

grip rule is applied to coil sides 1 to 8 and coil sides 21 to 28, pole N is created on the armature in between these two groups of coil-sides as shown in Fig. 7.10. Now, main stator pole N_1 repels N pole and main stator pole S_2 attracts pole N, thus producing an anticlockwise torque and therefore motoring action takes place. For generator operation, armature must be driven clockwise against the motoring torque.

Since currents are leaving segments 1 and 2, brush A is shown covering both the segments partly. Same is true for segments 11 and 12 where the currents are entering. Brushes B and C touch segments 5 and 8 respectively. The machine works as a motor because E and F are given negative and positive polarities respectively and the direction of rotation is counter-clockwise.

Example 7.4. *A D.C. machine is designed to have*

(a) 2 coil-sides per slot *(b) 4 coil-sides per slot*

(c) 6 coil-sides per slot and *(d) 8 coil-sides per slot.*

Indicate the number given to coil-sides placed in 10th slot. Hence show that the number given to the coil-side in nth slot is (i) nu for the last coil-side and (ii) (nu – u + 1) for the first coil-side.

Here symbol u denotes the number of coil-sides per slot.

Solution. The coil-sides placed in first slot, for $u = 4$, are numbered from 1 to 4, in second slot from 5 to 8, in third slot from 9 to 12 and so on. This thought process leads to Fig. 7.11, where the coil-sides in 10th slot, for $u = 2, 4, 6$ and 8 are shown.

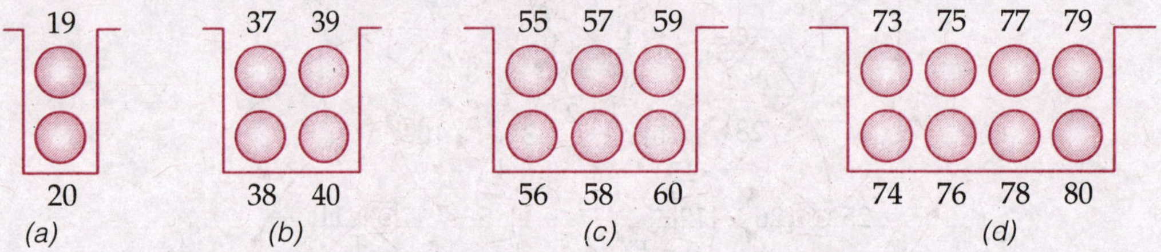

Fig 7.11: Numbers given to coil-sides placed in 10th slot, Example 7.4.

Note that the coil-sides numbered 20 (= 10 × 2 nu), 40 (= 10 × 4 = nu), 60 (= 10 × 6 = nu) and 80 (= 10 × 8 = nu) are the last coil-sides in the 10th slot. In general, therefore, the last coil-side in nth slot is numbered as nu.

The coil-sides numbered 19 (= 10 × 2 – 2 + 1 = $nu - u + 1$), 37 (= 10 × 4 – 4 + 1 = $nu - u + 1$), 55 (= 10 × 6 – 6 + 1 = $nu - u + 1$) and 73 (= 10 × 8 – 8 + 1) are the first coil-sides in 10th slot. In general, therefore, the first coil-side in nth slot is numbered as ($nu - u + 1$).

7.2.1. Split Coils

During the winding design, it may be found that some coils with their top coil-sides together in one slot, may not have their bottom coil-sides together in another slot. Such cases arise only when there are more than two coil-sides per slot. These coils with their top coil-sides in one slot and bottom coil-sides in two different slots, are called *split coils*. So far as commutation is concerned, split coils are helpful but the labour charges increase considerably. Example 7.5 illustrates the condition that must be satisfied if split coils are to be avoided.

Example 7.5. *Work out a suitable arrangement for the simplex lap winding with no split coils, in the following two cases :*

(a) 30 slots, 60 coils, 4 poles. *(b) 20 slots, 60 coils, 4 poles.*

Solution. *(a)* Total coil-sides = 2C = 2 × 60 = 120.

Coil-sides per slot, $$u = \frac{120}{30} = 4.$$

Back pitch, $y_b = \frac{2C}{P} \pm K = \frac{120}{4} \pm 1 = 29 \text{ or } 31.$

For $y_b = 29$, top coil-sides 1 and 3 in slot 1 should be connected to bottom coil sides numbered 1 + 29 and 3 + 29, *i.e.*, 30 and 32 respectively. These coil-slides numbered 30 and 32 are in the bottom layer of slot 8.

For $y_b = 31$, top coil-slides 1 and 3 should be connected to bottom coil-slides 1 + 31 and 3 + 31 *i.e.*, 32 and 34 respectively as illustrated in Fig. 7.12 *(a)*. Since bottom coil-side 32 is in slot 8 and the other bottom coil-side 34 is in slot 9, $y_b = 31$ results in split coils which have to be avoided. Consequently $y_b = 29$ is the only possible back pitch here.

(b) Total coil-sides $= 2C = 2 \times 60 = 120$

Coil-sides per slot, $u = \frac{120}{20} = 6$

Back pitch, $y_b = \frac{2C}{P} \pm K = \frac{120}{4} \pm 1 = 29 \text{ or } 31$

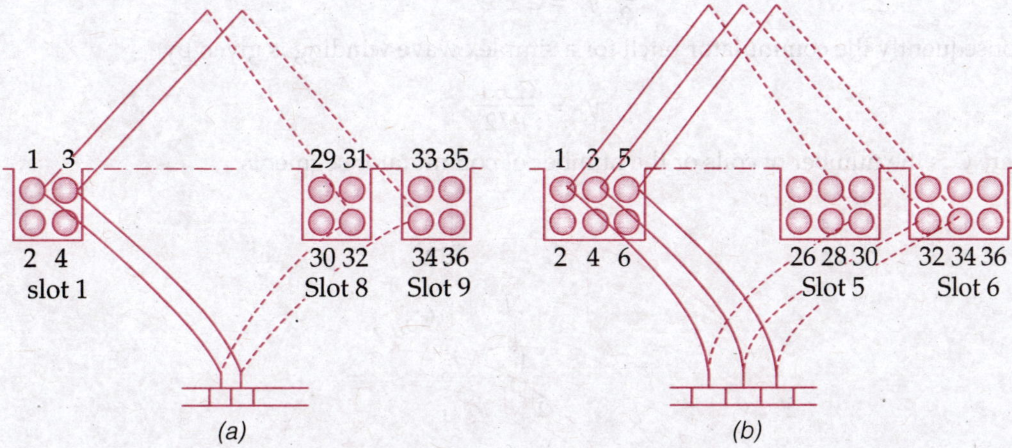

Fig 7.12: Illustrating the split coil, Example 7.5.

For $y_b = 29$, top coil-sides 1, 3, 5 should be connected to bottom coil-sides 30 (1 + 29), 32 (3 + 29) and 34 (5 + 29). Fig 7.12 *(b)* reveals that this back pitch results in split coils. Therefore, $y_b = 29$ is ruled out.

For $y_b = 31$, top coil-sides 1, 3, 5 should be connected to bottom coil-sides 32, 34 and 36 which are in the bottom layer of slot 6.

From parts *(a)* and *(b)*, it may be concluded that split coils or split winding can be avoided for some values of back pitches. In part *(a)*, $\frac{29-1}{4}\left(=\frac{y_b-1}{u}\right)$ is an integer whereas $\frac{31-1}{4}$ is not an integer. In part *(b)*, $\frac{31-1}{4}\left(=\frac{y_b-1}{u}\right)$ is a whole number but $(29-1)/6$ is not an integer. Thus it can be concluded that split coils can be avoided only when $((y_b-1)/u)$ is an integer. Note that for avoiding split coils, there is no restriction on the front pitch y_f.

7.3. SIMPLEX WAVE WINDING

In Fig. 7.5 *(a)*, one end of coil 1 is connected to segment 1 and its other end is connected to segment 11, which is approximately 360° electrical away from segment 1. One end of coil 2 is connected to segment 11 and its other end, for a 4-pole machine, must be connected to a segment just ahead of segment 1 for progressive wave winding or to a segment just before segment 1 for retrogressive wave winding.

Fig. 7.5 *(a)* is reproduced in Fig. 7.13 in a radial form and for progressive wave winding. This figure reveals that for a 4-pole machine, there are two commutator pitches y_c along the commutator periphery. As stated before, the number of commutator segments is equal to the number of coils C. Since the last coil-end of coil 2 must be connected to a segment either ahead (for progressive winding) or before (for retrogressive winding) segment 1, the following relation for a 4-pole machine can be written as

$$2y_c = C \pm 1 \quad \text{or} \quad \frac{4}{2}\, y_c = C \pm 1$$

For a 6-pole machine, there are 3 commutator pitches,

$$\therefore \qquad 3y_c = C \pm 1 \quad \text{or} \quad \frac{6}{2}\, y_c = C \pm 1.$$

Hence, for a P-pole machine there are $P/2$ commutator pitches,

$$\therefore \qquad \frac{P}{2}\, y_c = C \pm 1.$$

Consequently the commutator pitch for a simplex wave winding is given by

$$y_c = \frac{C \pm 1}{P/2} \qquad \text{... (7.2)}$$

Here C is the number of coils or the number of commutator segments.

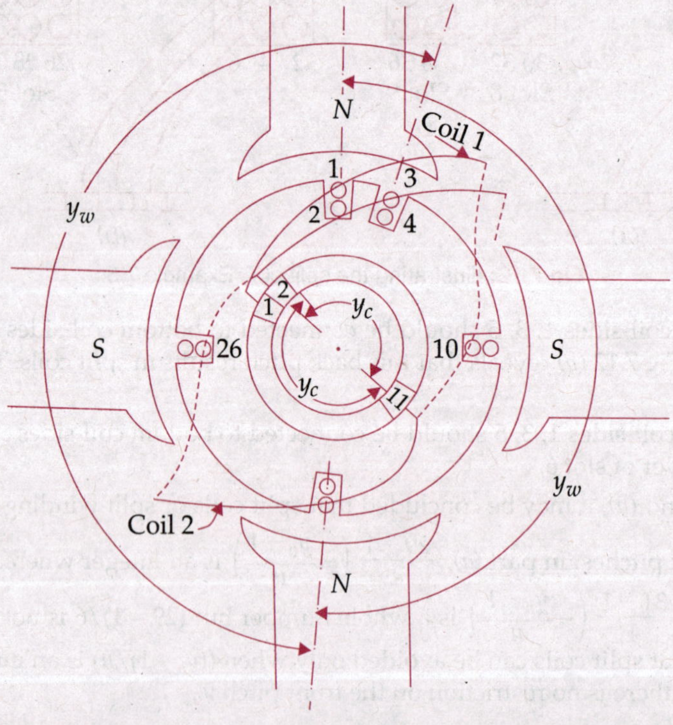

Fig 7.13: Illustrating commutator pitch y_c and winding pitch y_w for progressive simplex wave winding for a 4-pole machine.

An examination of Fig. 7.13 reveals that for a 4-pole machine there are two winding pitches y_w. Since the next coil-side connected to segment 2 must have its top coil-side numbered three (2 more for progressive winding or 2 less for retrogressive winding), the relation between winding pitch y_w and coil-sides 2C for a 4-pole machine, can be wirtten as

$$2\,y_w = 2C \pm 2 \text{ or } \frac{4}{2}\,y_w = 2C \pm 2.$$

For a 6-pole machine, there are three winding pitches,

$$\therefore \qquad \frac{6}{2}\,y_w = 2C \pm 2.$$

Consequently, for a *P*-pole machine,

$$\therefore \qquad \frac{P}{2}\,y_w = 2C \pm 2.$$

$\therefore$ Winding pitch for a simplex wave winding is

$$y_w = \frac{2C \pm 2}{P/2} = 2y_c \qquad \text{... (7.3)}$$

Note that in Eqs. (7.2) and (7.3), positive and negative signs should be used for progressive and retrogressive windings respectively.

As y_c must be an integer, y_w must always be even for wave winding. Also $y_w = y_b + y_f$. Since both y_b and y_f are odd, their sum must always be even—this verifies the above statement.

Wave winding is also known as series winding. The cause of designating it as wave winding is that during the traverse of a parallel path, one moves through the winding in a wavelike progression.

Example 7.6. *Design and draw a simplex wave winding with the following data : 4 poles, 11 slots, 2 coil-sides per slot, progressive winding.*

Solution. Number of coil-sides = 11 × 2 = 22

$$\text{Number of coils} = \frac{22}{2} = 11.$$

For progressive wave winding, the winding pitch is

$$y_w = \frac{2C \pm 2}{P/2} = \frac{22+2}{4/2} = 12.$$

Now $y_w = y_b + y_f = 12$. Since both y_b and y_f must be odd, choose $y_b = 7$ and $y_f = 5$.

For progressive winding, the commutator pitch is

$$y_c = \frac{C+1}{P/2} = \frac{11+1}{4/2} = 6.$$

The winding table for simplex wave winding is as follows :

$$\begin{array}{l} \quad +y_b \quad\;\; +y_f \qquad\quad +y_b \qquad +y_f \qquad +y_b \qquad +y_f \\ (1 \rightarrow 8) \rightarrow (13 \rightarrow 20) \rightarrow (20 + 5 - 22 = 3 \rightarrow 10) \rightarrow (15 \rightarrow 22) \rightarrow (5 \rightarrow 13) \rightarrow (17 \rightarrow 2) \rightarrow (7 \rightarrow 14) \rightarrow \\ (19 \rightarrow 4) \rightarrow (9 \rightarrow 16) \rightarrow (21 \rightarrow 6) \rightarrow (11 \rightarrow 18) \rightarrow 1. \end{array}$$

Note that there are 11 coils and 22 coil-sides. The winding diagram in radial form shown in Fig. 7.14 is drawn as explained in Example 7.2.

In this example, number of slots are not divisible by the number of poles *P*. In view of this, it may be assumed that 3 slots are under the influence of each of the three poles and the remaining 2 slots are under the fourth pole. In Fig. 7.14, 2 slots are taken under the north pole N_1. An examination of Fig. 7.14 shows that at the instant shown, one brush A should touch the segment 3, because two currents are going towards this segment. The only other point where the two currents are going away from each other is at the other end of the commutator—this in indicated by B_1. Since the brushes must touch the commutator segment, the brush *B* can be placed where the two coil-sides of coil *k* are connected. That is, brush *B* may be placed either at segment 6 or at segment 11. In Fig. 7.14, it is shown at segment 11.

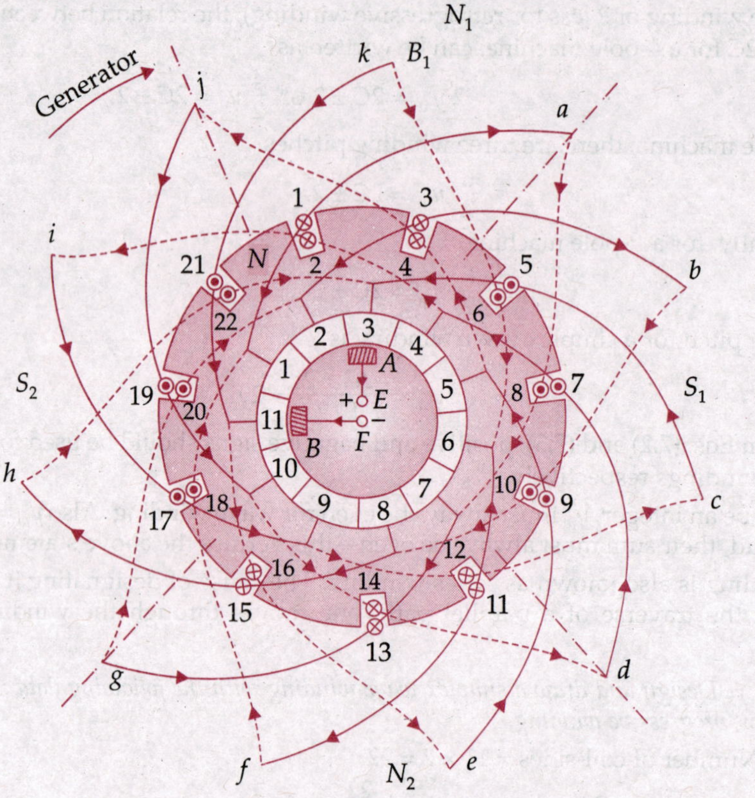

Fig 7.14: Progressive simplex wave winding for 4-poles, 11 slots and 2 coil-sides per slot. Example 7.6.

From brush A, one parallel path is through c, i, d, ... to brush B and other parallel path is through h, b, g .... to brush B as shown in Fig. 7.15. Therefore, in simplex wave winding, two brushes are required and there are only two parallel paths as illustrated in Fig. 7.15. Also the distance between two brushes (or set of brushes) is approximately equal to one pole pitch in terms of commutator segments. In general, for any number of poles, a simplex wave winding has always two parallel paths and a minimum of 2 sets of brushes.

However, in case larger currents are to be handled, the number of brush-sets may be made equal to the number of poles. In such cases, all positive and all negative brushes are connected together respectively as in lap windings. The current handled by brush is then $2I_a/P$. However, in practice, when wave winding is employed, only two brushes (or brush-sets) are used from the viewpoint of economy.

If right hand grip rule is applied to coil sides 1 to 4 under N_1 pole and coil sides 17 to 22 under S_2 pole, then N pole is created on armature in between these two coil groups as shown in Fig. 7.14. Main pole N_1 repels N pole but main pole S_2 attracts N pole, thus creating an anticlockwise torque. For generator operation, armature must be rotated clockwise.

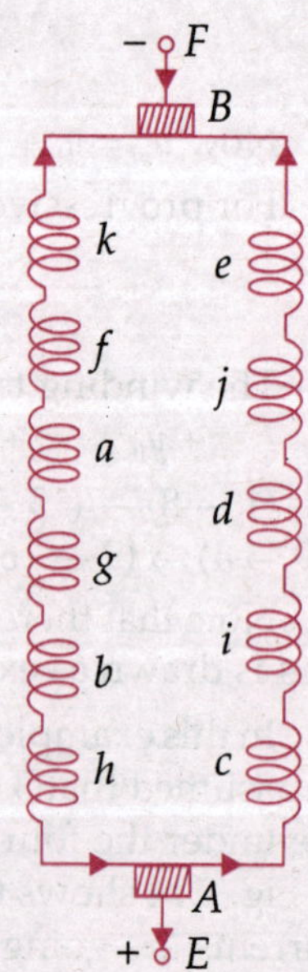

Fig 7.15: Pertaining to Example 7.6.

7.3.1. Dummy Coils

From economy point of view, standard armature laminations are used for different ratings of the commutator machines. When simplex wave windings are used, Eq. (7.2) must be satisfied. If this relation is not fulfilled, then two ends of one (or more) coil may be cut off, insulated and not connected to the commutator segments. This unused and inactive coil, though placed in the armature slots for machanical balance is called a dead or *dummy coil*. In order to have symmetrical armature winding, a dummy coil should be avoided as far as possible. However, it may be used in low-rating commutator machines where armature core with existing number of slots have to be used in order to avoid extra expenditure on new punching tools etc. If dummy coils are to be avoided, then $S/(P/2)$ should not be an integer, this is revealed in Example 7.7.

Examples 7.7 and 7.8 illustrate the use of a dummy coil.

Example 7.7. *Work out a suitable arrangement for simplex wave winding for a commutator machine with 6 poles, 72 slots and 4 coil-sides per slot.*

Solution. Number of coils,
$$C = \frac{72 \times 4}{2} = 144.$$

Commutator pitch,
$$y_c = \frac{C \pm 1}{P/2} = \frac{144 \pm 1}{6/2} = 47\tfrac{2}{3} \text{ or } 48\tfrac{1}{3}$$

For wave winding y_c must be an integer. If all the 144 coils are used, wave winding is not possible, because y_c is not an integer. However, if one coil is made dummy then active coils are 143 and the commutator pitch is now given by

$$y_c = \frac{143 \pm 1}{3} = 48 \text{ or } 47\tfrac{1}{3}.$$

Winding pitch,
$$y_w = \frac{2C \pm 1}{P/2} = \frac{2 \times 143 \pm 2}{3} = 96 \text{ or } 94\tfrac{2}{3}.$$

It shows that only progressive simplex wave winding with one dummy coil is possible.

Now
$$y_w = y_b + y_f = 96.$$

Take $y_b = 49$ and $y_f = 47$, because both need be odd. At the same time, split coils are avoided with $y_b = 49$ since

$$\frac{y_b - 1}{u} = \frac{49 - 1}{4}$$

is a whole number.

Here $72/(6/2) = 24$ is an integer and a dummy coil is essential. It shows that if dummy coils are to be avoided in simplex wave winding, then $S(P/2)$ should not be an integer.

Example 7.8. *Design the winding for a 4-pole armature with 2540 conductors, 127 commutator sectors (or segments) and 32 slots.*

If an induced voltage of 500 V is required, calculate its speed for a field flux of 5 m Wb per pole.

Solution. Conductors per slot × Slots = $z_s \times S = 2540$

∴ Conductors per slot,
$$z_s = \frac{2540}{32} = 79.375$$

Sine z_s must be a whole number, choose $z_s = 80$.

This gives total conductors as 32 × 80 = 2560.

Total number of coils, C = number of commutator segments = 127.

∴
$$\text{Turns per coil} = \frac{2560}{2 \times 127} = 10.08 \cong 10.$$

Since the coil is a multi-turn coil, wave winding should be used.

$$\text{Actual number of coils} = \frac{2560}{2 \times 10} = 128 \text{ coils.}$$

It is essential that actual coils are equal to the number of commutator segments 127. In view of this, one coil must be made dummy, so that there are 127 active coils.

$$\therefore \quad y_c = \frac{C \pm 1}{P/2} = \frac{127 \pm 1}{4/2} = 64 \text{ or } 63$$

$$y_w = \frac{2C \pm 2}{P/2} = \frac{2 \times 127 \pm 2}{4/2} = 128 \text{ or } 126.$$

$\therefore$ $y_b = 65$ and $y_f = 63$ for progressive wave winding and $y_b = 63$ and $y_f = 63$ for retrogressive wave winding.

Since the dummy coil is not in circuit, the number of active conductors is

$$127 \times 10 \times 2 = 2540$$

Now $$E_a = \frac{\phi Z n P}{a}$$

or $$500 = \frac{5 \times 10^{-3} \times 2540 \times n \times 4}{2}$$

or $$n = \frac{500 \times 2}{5 \times 10^{-3} \times 2540 \times 4} \text{ r.p.s.} = \frac{5 \times 60}{254 \times 10^{-3}} \text{ r.p.m.}$$

$$= 1181 \text{ r.p.m.}$$

7.4. MULTIPLEX WINDINGS

In some cases, the number of parallel circuits may not be adequate enough from design considerations. For example in a 10-pole commutator machine, simplex wave winding gives only 2 parallel paths whereas simplex lap winding results in 10 parallel paths. In case the parallel paths required are in between 2 and 10 or more than 10, then multiplex windings are employed.

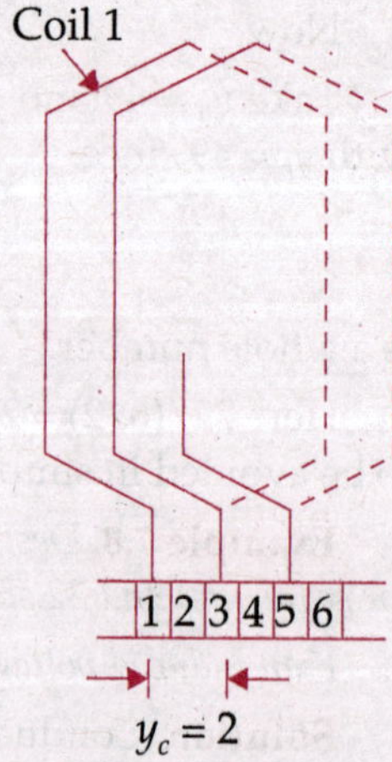

Fig 7.16: Illustrating duplex lap winding.

In *duplex lap winding*, the distance between the segments to which the two ends of one coil are connected is 2, *i.e.*, $y_c = \pm 2$. For example, if one end of coil 1 is joined with segment 1, then for progressive duplex lap winding its other coil-end is connected to segment 3, leaving segment number 2 in between them, see Fig. 7.16. The coil starting from segment 3 has its second coil-end connected to segment 5 and so on.

In *triplex lap winding*, the distance between the segments to which the two ends of one coil are connected is 3 and, therefore, $y_c = \pm 3$.

In duplex wave winding, the last coil-end after travelling once around the commutator, is connected to two segments behind or ahead of the starting point.

$$\therefore \quad y_c = \frac{C \pm 2}{P/2} \qquad \text{... (7.4)}$$

In triplex wave winding, the last coil-end after traversing once around the commutator, is connected to 3 segments behind or ahead of starting point.

$$\therefore \qquad y_c = \frac{C \pm 3}{P/2} \qquad \text{... (7.5)}$$

In general, if m denotes "plex" of the multiplex windings,

then $y_c = \pm m$ for lap winding

and $y_c = \frac{C \pm m}{P/2}$ for wave winding.

In the above expressions for y_c, positive sign is used for progressive winding and negative sign is for the retrogressive winding.

The number of parallel paths a in lap winding is $a = mP$ and in wave winding, $a = 2m$.

Multiplex wave windings are rarely used in D.C. machines.

7.5. EQUALIZER RINGS

For batteries operating in parallel, the circulating currents will flow if their e.m.fs. are unequal. Similarly, in lap-connected machines, the circulating currents will exist if the e.m.fs. generated in the various parallel paths (equal to the number of poles) are not equal. The existence of circulating currents in lap-connected machines may be due to any one or all of the following reasons :

(i) The air gap under different poles may not be the same, due to wear of the bearings or faulty assembly. As a result of it, some poles carry more flux than the other poles and, therefore, different e.m.fs. are generated in the various parallel paths.

(ii) The joints between pole cores and yokes or between pole cores and pole faces may not be identical for all the poles. This results in different reluctances for the various magnetic circuits. Even if the air gap is uniform, the pole flux will be different under the various poles and, therefore, different e.m.fs. are generated in the parallel circuits.

(iii) The different reluctances for each magnetic path may also be due to the impurities or imperfections in the materials constituting the magnetic circuit.

In order to illustrate the detrimental effects of circulating currents, consider a 4-pole lap-connected commutator machine shown in Fig. 7.17. Suppose the full-load current is 200 A. For equal e.m.fs. generated in the parallel paths, the distribution of currents is as illustrated in Fig. 7.17 *(a)*. All the four brushes are handling 100 A of current and each parallel path is carrying 50 A.

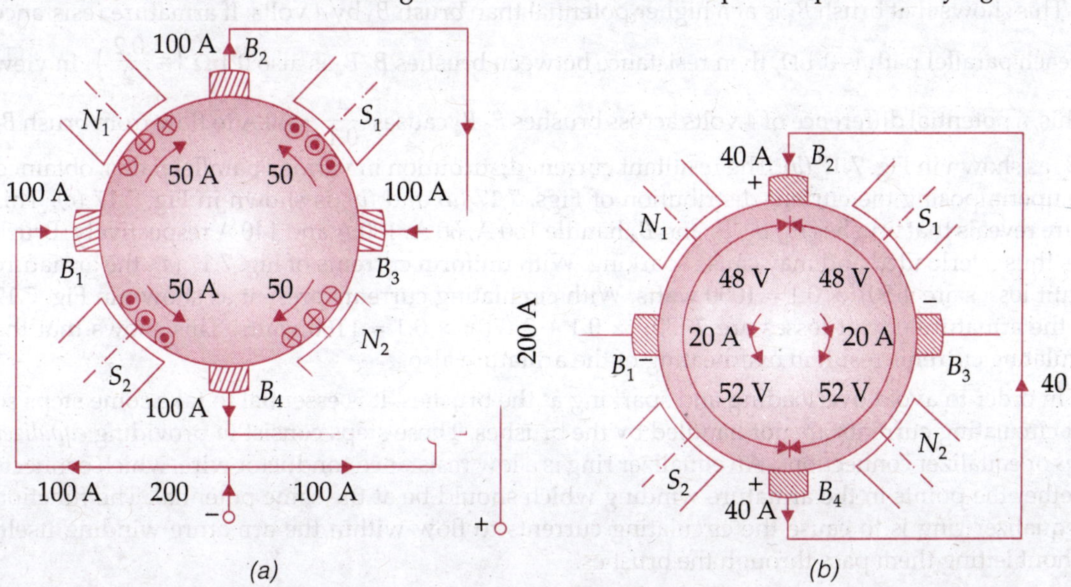

(a) *(b)*

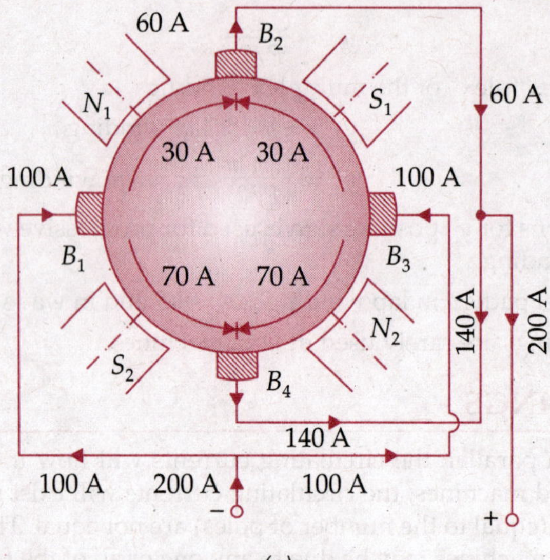

(c)

Fig 7.17: *(a)* Armature current distribution for equal e.m.fs.
(b) Circulating current due to unequal e.m.fs. and
(c) resultant armature current distribution due to unequal e.m.fs.

Now suppose that the air gap under the top pole-pair N_1, S_1 becomes more than that under the bottom pole-pair N_2, S_2, due to wear of the bearings. As a result of this wear, air-gap flux under N_1, S_1 decreases and that under poles N_2, S_2, increases. On account of these different air-gap fluxes, the e.m.f. generated in the parallel paths under N_1, S_1 becomes less and that under N_2, S_2 becomes more. Let these e.m.fs. generated in parallel paths B_1B_2 and B_3B_2 be 48 volts and that in parallel paths B_1B_4 and B_3B_4 be 52 volts as shown in Fig. 7.17 *(b)*. The potential of negative brushes B_1, B_3 remains unchanged, because from B_1 to B_3 or from B_3 to B_1, there is an equal voltage rise and equal voltage fall. From brush B_2 to brush B_4,

$$V_{B2B4} = -48 + 52 = 4 \text{ V}.$$

This shows that brush B_4 is at a higher potential than brush B_2 by 4 volts. If armature resistance for each parallel path is 0.1 Ω, then resistance between brushes $B_2\,B_4$ is also 0.1 Ω $\left(=\frac{0.2}{2}\right)$. In view of this, a potential difference of 4 volts across brushes $B_2\,B_4$ causes $\frac{4}{0.1} = 40$ A to flow from brush B_4 to B_2 as shown in Fig. 7.17 *(b)*. The resultant current distribution in various parallel paths, obtained by superimposing the current distribution of Figs. 7.17 *(a)* and *(b)*, is shown in Fig. 7.17 *(c)*. This figure reveals that brushes B_1, B_2, B_3 and B_4 handle 100 A, 60 A, 100 A and 140 A respectively. Brush B_4 is thus overloaded and may cause sparking. With uniform currents of Fig. 7.17 *(a)*, the armature circuit losses are $4(50)^2 \times 0.1 = 1000$ watts. With circulating currents present as shown in Fig. 7.17 *(c)*, the armature circuit losses are $2\,(30)^2 \times 0.1 + 2\,(70)^2 \times 0.1 = 1160$ watts. This shows that the circulating currents result in overheating of the armature also.

In order to avoid overloading and sparking at the brushes, it is essential to take some steps so that circulating currents are not handled by the brushes. These steps consist in providing *equalizer rings* or equalizer connections. An equalizer ring is a low resistance conductor wire, which connects together the points in the armature winding which should be at the same potential. The function of equalizer ring is to cause the circulating currents to flow within the armature winding itself, without letting them pass through the brushes.

Refer to Fig. 7.18, where the coils connected to brushes B_2 and B_4 have potential difference of 4 V between them. If an equalizer connection is joined to these coils, then circulating current of 40 A will flow through the equalizer *a b c* and then through the armature coils as shown in Fig. 7.18. Though the circulating currents are still present, the brushes are saved from handling these currents. The voltage between brushes B_3B_2 and B_1B_2 becomes 48 + 20 × 0.1 = 50 V and between brushes B_1B_4 and B_3B_4, the voltage is 52 – 20 × 0.1 = 50 V, see Fig. 7.17 *(b)*. Thus the tendency of the circulating currents is to equalize the potential of all parallel circuits—in other words, the circulating currents have the effect of reducing the flux unbalance that was responsible for the initial potential difference. Thus the functions of equalizer rings are

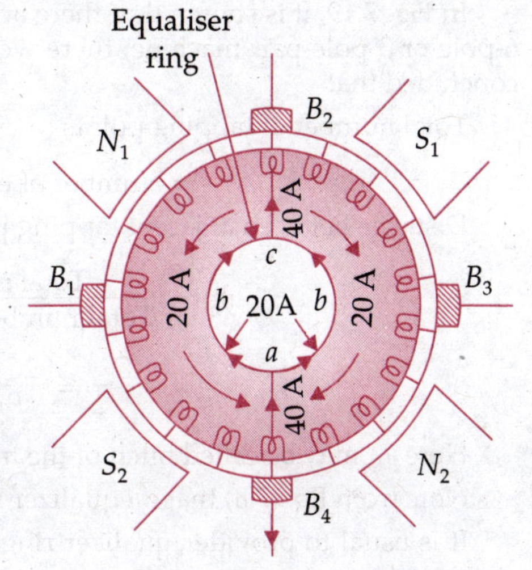

Fig 7.18: Pertaining to equalizer ring.

(i) to save the brushes from handling the circulating currents and

(ii) to reduce the magnetic flux unbalance that causes the potential difference in various parallel paths.

Refer now to Fig. 7.19. Points 1 and 2 on the armature winding are under the centre of poles N_1 and N_2 respectively. These points are two pole-pitches apart and have the same induced e.m.f., if there is no flux unbalance. If points 1 and 2 are short-circuited by an equalizer-ring as shown, then this ring will carry no current and the armature winding remains unaffected. Similarly, points 3 and 4 can be connected by another equalizer-ring as depicted in Fig. 7.19.

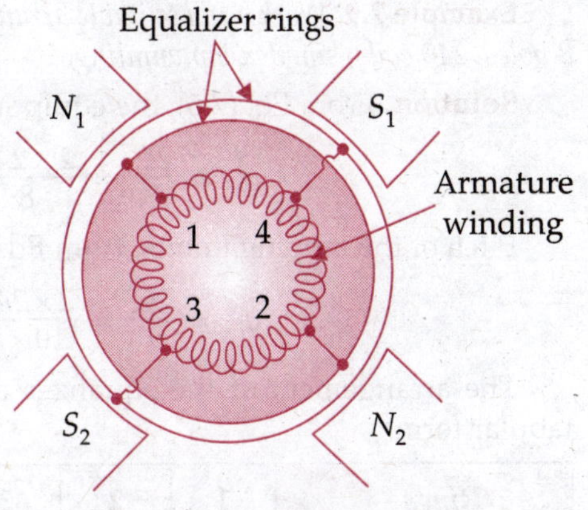

Fig 7.19: Illustrating the method of connecting equalizer rings.

In case there is flux unbalance, then points 1, 2 or 3, 4 will be at different potentials and circulating current will start flowing through the rings and armature coils, without flowing through the brushes.

An examination of Fig. 7.19 reveals that an equalizer ring connects as many coils as there are pole-pairs. In Fig. 7.19, the ring connects 2 coils because there are two pole-pairs. It is also obvious from Fig. 7.19 that any two points two pole-pitches apart, can be joined by an equalizer ring. There is, however, a limit to the number of equalizer rings from the economy point of view. It is usual to employ 10 to 20 rings, the actual number depending on the size of the machine.

From Fig. 7.19, it is seen that the distance between coils (or points) having the same potential is 2 pole-pitches, *i.e.*

$$y_{eq} = 2 \text{ pole-pitches} = \frac{\text{Total number of coils}}{\text{Pole pairs}}$$

$$= \frac{C}{P/2} = \frac{2C}{P} \text{ coils} \qquad \text{... (7.6)}$$

The symbol y_{eq} is called the *equipotential pitch* in terms of coils, because y_{eq} indicates the distance between two adjacent equipotential points.

In Fig. 7.19, it is shown that there are 4 taps, 2 equalizer rings and 2 pole pairs. Likewise for a 6-pole or 3-pole-pair machine, there would be 6 taps and 2 equalizer rings. From this, it may be concluded that

Total number of tapping points

$$= \text{Number of equalizer rings } (r) \times \text{pole-pairs } \left(\frac{P}{2}\right) = \frac{rP}{2} \quad \text{... (7.7)}$$

Distance between adjacent tapping points,

$$y_{tp} = \frac{\text{Total number of coils}}{\text{Total number of tapping points}}$$

$$= \frac{C}{rP/2} = \frac{2C}{rP} = \frac{y_{eq}}{r} \quad \text{... (7.8)}$$

Here y_{tp} may be called pitch of the tapping points in terms of coils.

Note from Eq. (7.8) that if equalizer rings are to be employed, $2C/P$ must be a whole number.

It is usual to provide equalizer rings at the back of the armature, *i.e.*, at the other side of the commutator.

Equalizer rings are not required for simplex wave windings even if there is magnetic unbalance. This is due to the fact that coil-sides in two parallel paths are distributed under all the poles. In view of this, both the parallel circuits are affected equally and there is, therefore, no need of equalizer rings in simplex wave windings.

Example 7.9. *Work out a suitable arrangement of ten equalizer rings for a commutator machine having 8 poles, 240 coils, simplex lap winding.*

Solution. From Eq. (7.6), the equipotential pitch is

$$y_{eq} = \frac{2C}{P} = \frac{2 \times 240}{8} = 60 \text{ coils}$$

Pitch of the tapping points, from Eq. (7.8), is

$$y_{tp} = \frac{2C}{rP} = \frac{2 \times 240}{10 \times 8} = 6 \text{ coils}$$

The arrangement of the equalizer rings and the coils connected to them is given below in tabular form.

Rings →	1	2	3	4	5	6	7	8	9	10
Number of coils connected to the rings	1	7	13	19	25	31	37	43	49	55
	61	67	73	79	85	91	97	103	109	115
	121	127	133	139	145	151	157	163	169	175
	181	187	193	199	205	211	217	223	229	235

Since there are 4 pole-pairs, 4 coils are connected to each equalizer ring. For example ring 2 has coils connected to it which are numbered 7, 67, 127 and 187 in the above table.

Summary. A review of the salient features of lap and wave winding is presented in Table 7.1 below :

Table 7.1: Comparison between Simplex-lap and Simplex-wave Windings

		Simplex-lap Winding	*Simplex-wave Winding*
1.	E.m.f.	$\phi Z n$, does not depend on the number of poles	$\frac{\phi ZnP}{2}$, depends upon the number of poles
2.	Average coil-span	$\frac{2C}{P}$ coil-sides where C = Number of coils	$\frac{2C}{P}$ coil-sides
3.	Back pitch, y_b	$\frac{2C}{P} \pm K$, odd	$(y_w - y_f)$, odd
4.	Front pitch, y_f	$y_b \pm 2$, odd (+ for retrogressive wdg and – for progressive wdg)	$(y_w - y_b)$, odd
5.	Commutator pitch, y_c	± 1	$\frac{C \pm 1}{P/2}$
		+ for progressive and – for retrogressive wdg	
6.	Winding pitch, y_w	± 2	$\frac{2C \pm 2}{P/2} = y_b + y_f$
		+ for progressive wdg and – for retrogressive wdg	
7.	Number of parallel paths, *a*	P	2
8.	Number of brushes	P	2 (For large machines, number of brushes may be equal to P)
9.	Dummy coils	Not needed	May be required
10.	Equalizer rings	may be needed ; then $\frac{2C}{P}$ must be an integer	Not required
11.	Conductor current, I_c = current in each path	$\frac{I_a}{a}$ ...	$\frac{I_a}{2}$
12.	For avoiding split coils (machines having 2 coil-sides per slot)	$\frac{y_b - 1}{u}$ must be an integer	$\frac{y_b - 1}{u}$ must be an integer
13.	Applications	Low-voltage high-current machines	High-voltage low-power machines

Advantages of wave windings over lap windings. Wave windings possess certain advantages over lap windings and these are given below :

(*i*) A wave winding requires only two brushes (or two sets of brushes) whereas lap winding requires brushes equal to the number of poles.

A wave winding may be fitted with as many brushes as the number of poles. In such a case, if one or more brushes develop poor contact with the commutator, the commutator machine continues operating satisfactorily whereas this is not true in case of lap-connected machines.

(ii) Lap-connected machines require equalizer rings for obtaining better commutation, whereas wave windings do not rquire any equalizer ring.

(iii) Since lap-connected machines require more brushes and equalizer rings, these machines are more costly as compared to wave-connected machines.

Lap windings are used on low-voltage medium power (50 to 500 kW) and high power (above 500 kW) machines. Wave windings are used on high-voltage low-power (less than 50 kW) and medium power machines.

The preferred choice of wave windings is due to the fact that wave windings do not require equalizer-rings. As a consequence, wave-wound D.C. machines are less expensive as compared to lap-wound D.C. machines. However, for armature currents more than 400 A, lap winding is the only choice. It is because for armature currents exceeding 400 A, current per path in wave winding would be more than 200 A and such a current leads to poor commutation in wave-wound D.C. machines.

In addition to lap and wave windings, there is another type of winding called *composite winding or frog-leg winding*. It is a combination of simplex lap and multiplex wave windings and requires no equalizer rings. It is beyond the scope of this book to describe frog-leg winding. This type of winding is used mainly on high-power commutator machines.

Example 7.10. *(a) From an outside appearance of the armature of a commutator machine, how would you distinguish whether it is lap- or wave-wound.*

(b) A simplex lap-wound armature has 12 coils, each of resistance 0.1 Ω.

(i) What is the resistance measured between two adjacent commutator segments?

(ii) If one coil gets open-circuited or short-circuited, explain how it can be located.

(c) A commutator machine has Z conductors, 'a' parallel paths and P poles. If each conductor has a length (including overhang) of L metre, area of cross-section of A metre² and a resistivity of ρΩ-m, find the resistance of commutator machine. How are these expressions modified for lap and wave-connected machines?

Solution. *(a)* For a lap-wound armature, if the ends of the coils connected to commutator segments are bent, say, to the left then its other coil-ends, on the other side of commutator, are also bent to the left, see Fig. 7.4. In other words, lap-wound armatures have both their coil ends bent in the same direction.

For a wave-wound armature, if the ends of coils connected to commutator segments are bent, say, to the left, then its other coil-ends, on the other side of commutator, are bent to the right, see Fig. 7.5. In other words, wave-wound armatures have their coil-ends bent in opposite directions.

(b) (i) Resistance of one coil connected to adjacent commutator segments is 0.1 Ω. This coil is in parallel with the remaining 11 series-connected armature coils of total resistance 11 × 0.1 = 1.1 Ω. In other words, one coil of resistance 0.1Ω becomes in parallel with 11 series-connected coils of resistance 1.10 Ω. This can be ascertained by referring to Fig. 7.8. Therefore, the resistance measured between two adjacent commutator segments is

$$\frac{0.1 \times 1.1}{0.1 + 1.1} = 0.0917\ \Omega.$$

(ii) The resistance measured across two commutator segments to which one open-circuited coil is connected, would be that given by the remaining 11 series-connected coils. In view of this, the resistance measured across an open-circuited coil is

$$= 11 \times 0.1 = 1.10\ \Omega$$

With one coil short-circuited, the resistance measured across its two coil-ends (or segments) would be (ideally) zero.

It may be concluded from above that an open-circuited coil is indicated by the highest possible resistance across its two segments ; whereas a short-circuited coil can be located by the lowest possible resistance across its terminals.

(*c*) Resistance of one conductor $= \frac{\rho L}{A} \Omega$

Each parallel path has Z/a conductors.

$\therefore$ Resistance of each parallel path $= \frac{Z}{a} \times \left(\frac{\rho L}{A}\right) \Omega$

Thus, resistance of the commutator machine with number of parallel paths 'a', is given by

$$= \frac{1}{a} \cdot \left(\frac{Z}{a} \cdot \frac{\rho L}{A}\right) = \frac{Z}{a^2} \cdot \frac{\rho L}{A} \Omega$$

For lap-connected machine, $a = P$, its resistance is therefore, equal to $\frac{Z}{P^2} \cdot \frac{\rho L}{A} \Omega$

For wave-wound machine, $a = 2$, its resistance is, therefore, given by $\frac{Z}{4} \cdot \frac{\rho L}{A} \Omega$.

7.6. OPEN WINDINGS OR A.C. ARMATURE WINDINGS

The machines which do not require a commutator, can have their armature windings opened at one or more points. In commutator machines, the turns per coil are limited for obtaining better commutation. But in machines without commutator, there is no such restriction on the choice of number of turns per coil.

Closed or commutator windings are always double layer windings whereas A.C. armature windings may be single layer or double layer. As stated before, single layer windings are used for small A.C. machines, whereas double layer windings are used for machines above about 5 kW.

The main difference between single and double layer windings is in the arrangement of their overhang. In single layer winding, the coils are arranged in groups. Each group has its overhang crossing the overhang of adjacent groups. This is possible only by having individual coil groups of different sizes and shapes. This means that a single layer winding requires a variety of sets of coils with each set differing both in size and shape from the other sets. All this adds to the cost of single-layer windings. Single-layer windings are, therefore, rarely used in modern machines except in small sizes. In single-layer mush windings, however, all the coils have the same shape and size.

In double-layer winding, all coils are of the same shape and size. Each coil has its one coil-side in top half of one slot and other coil-side in the bottom half of some other slot. A special kink, see Fig. 7.20, at each end of the diamond shaped coil allows neat symmetrical arrangement of coils. As a result, the problem of overhang does not exist in double-layer winding as it is in single layer winding. As double-layer winding has identical coils, their fabrication is easier and this leads to reduction in cost.

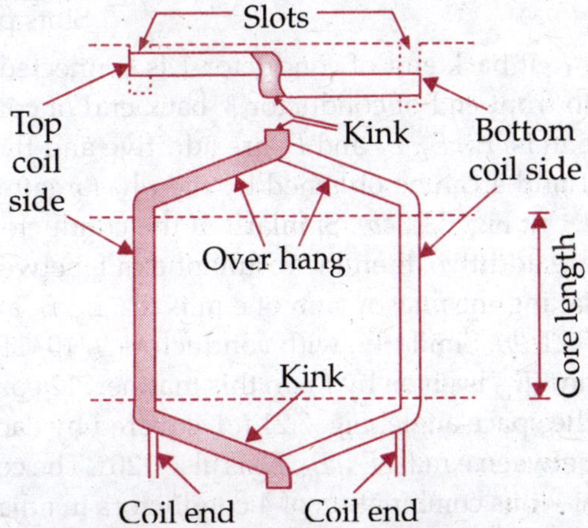

Fig 7.20: Diamond shaped coil.

The advantages of double-layer winding over single-layer winding are as follows :

(a) easier to manufacture and lower cost of the coils,

(b) fractional-slot winding (slot per pole per phase is not an integer) can be used,

(c) chorded-winding is possible,

(d) lower-leakage reactance and, therefore, better performance of the machine and

(a) better e.m.f. waveform in case of generators.

In general, double layer is preferred now-a-days, except in high voltage induction motors with large slot openings and short air-gap lengths.

In A.C. armature windings, the separate coils may be connected in several different manners, but the two most common methods are lap and wave.

In polyphase windings it is essential that

(i) the generated e.m.fs. of all the phases are of equal magnitude,

(ii) the waveforms of the phase e.m.fs. are identical,

(iii) the frequency of the phase e.m.fs. are equal and

(iv) the phase e.m.fs. have mutual time-phase displacement of $\beta = 2\pi/m$ electrical radians. Here m is the number of phases of the A.C. machine.

Phase spread. A knowledge of the phase spread is beneficial for understanding the polyphase winding arrangements. For this purpose, refer to Fig. 7.21, where field winding on the rotor is shown to produce 2 poles and the stator carries 12 conductors housed in 12 slots. Conductor 1 is under the centre of N pole, it has, therefore, maximum e.m.f. E_m induced in it. This e.m.f. can be represented by a phasor of length $E_1 = E_m/\sqrt{2}$, lying along the vertical. Conductor 4 is cutting zero lines of flux and has, therefore, zero e.m.f. induced in it. This can be represented by phasor E_4 since its vertical projection is zero. The e.m.f. generated in conductor 7 is maximum, because it is cutting maximum lines of flux from S pole. The polarity of e.m.f. in conductor 7 will be opposite to that in conductor 1, it is, therefore, represented by $E_7 = E_m/\sqrt{2}$, opposite to E_1. Similarly the e.m.fs. generated in conductors 2, 3, 5, 6 and in conductors 8 to 12 can be represented by phasors E_2, E_3, E_5, E_6 and E_8 to E_{12} as shown in Fig. 7.21 *(a)*.

Here the slot-angular pitch is given by

$$\gamma = \frac{180°}{\text{Slots per pole}} = \frac{180°}{6} = 30°$$

If back end of conductor 1 is connected to back end of conductor 2, front end of conductor 2 to front end of conductor 3, back end of conductor 3 to back end of conductor 4, then all the four e.m.fs. E_1, E_2, E_3 and E_4 are additive and their resultant appearing at the front ends of conductors 1 and 4 can be obtained by the phasor sum of E_1, E_2, E_3 and E_4. This phasor sum is indicated by E_A in Fig. 7.21 *(b)*. Similarly if the conductors 5, 6, 7 and 8 are joined in series so that their e.m.fs. are additive, then the resultant e.m.f. between the front ends of conductors 5 and 8 is obtained by taking the phasor sum of e.m.fs. E_5, E_6, E_7 and E_8. This phasor sum is indicated by e.m.f. E_B in Fig. 7.21 *(b)*. Similarly, with conductors 9, 10, 11 and 12 in series, the phasor sum of e.m.fs. E_9, E_{10}, E_{11} and E_{12} is given by E_c. In this manner, 12 conductors are grouped in three phases A, B, C. Note that the space angle, Fig. 7.21 *(a)*, covered by each phase is 120° and the time phase angle, Fig. 7.21 *(b)*, between e.m.fs. E_A, E_B, E_C is also 120°. The conductors 1, 2, 3 and 4 in adjacent slots, belong to phase A—this combination of 4 conductors in adjacent slots is called *phase-band, phase-belt or phase-group*. Similarly conductors 5, 6, 7 and 8 constitute second phase-belt and conductors 9, 10, 11 and 12 the third phase-belt. In general, the *phase-belt* may be defined as the group of adjacent slots belonging to one phase under one pole-pair. The angle subtended by one phase-belt is called *phase spread*, symbol σ. Thus the phase spread in Fig. 7.21 *(a)* is 120°, because 4 adjacent slots pertaining to any one phase belt cover 4 slot-pitches (= 4 × 30° = 120°).

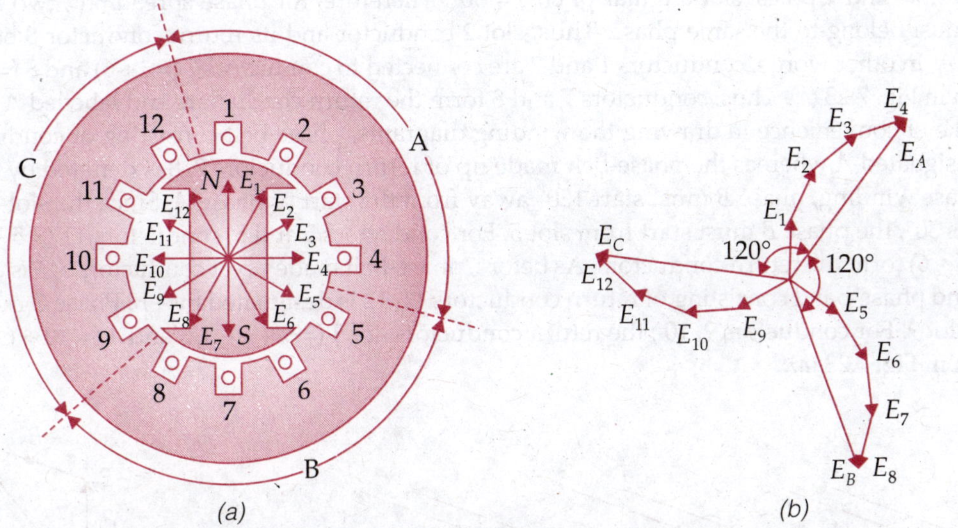

Fig 7.21: Pertaining to 3-phase winding. *(a)* phase spread is 120° and *(b)* time phase angle is 120° between E_A, E_B and E_C.

If conductors 1, 2 are connected in series, then e.m.f. *A* is obtained, see Fig. 7.22 *(b)*. Similarly join 3-4, 5-6, 7-8, 9-10 and 11-12 respectively in series to give voltages *B, C, D, E* and *F* as shown in Fig. 7.22 *(b)*. These 6 voltages form 6 phases with time phase angle of 60° between them. Note that here the phase spread is 60°, because the angle subtended by one phase-belt consisting of two adjacent slots of any one phase is 60°, see Fig. 7.22 *(a)*.

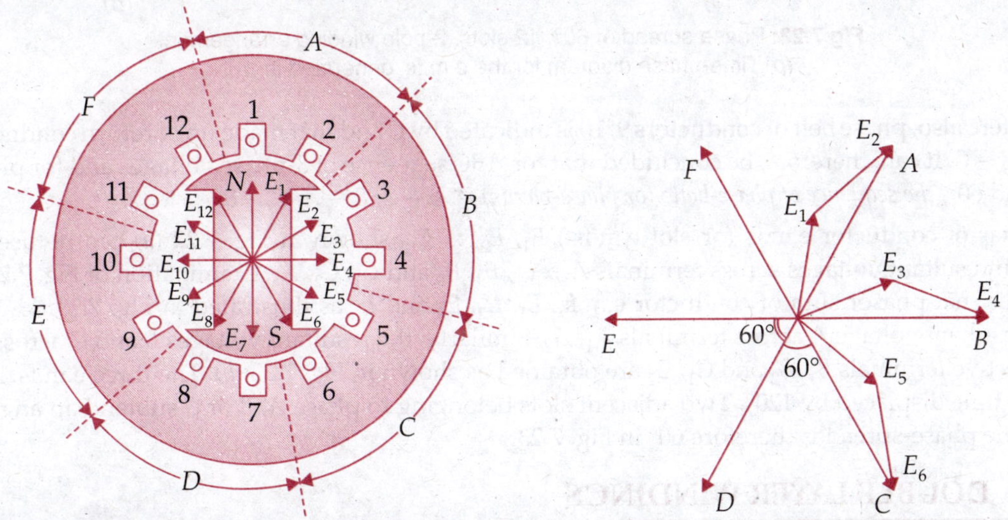

Fig 7.22: Pertaining to 6-phase winding, *(a)* phase spread is 60° and *(b)* time phase angle is 60°.

Sequence of Phase-belts. The developed view of Fig. 7.22 *(a)* is drawn in Fig. 7.23 *(a)* for convenience. The twelve conductors can be used to obtain three-phase single-layer winding having a phase spread of 60°. In Fig. 7.23 *(a)*, coil-pitch or coil-span is taken equal to pole pitch = 12/2 = 6 slots. For this coil-span, conductor 1 should be connected to conductor 7 as shown in Fig. 7.23 *(a)*. For 12 slots and 2 poles, slot-angular pitch $\gamma = 30°$. Therefore, for phase spread 60°, two adjacent slots must belong to the same phase. Thus, slot 2 conductor and its return conductor 8 belong to phase A. In other words, conductors 1 and 2 are connected to conductors 7 (= 1+ 6) and 8 (= 2+6) as shown in Fig. 7.23 *(a)*. Thus, conductors 7 and 8 form the return conductors and labelled A', A'. For the sake of convenience in drawing the winding diagrams, phase-belt consisting of conductors 1, 2 is designated A whereas the phase-belt made up of return conductors 7, 8 is denoted by $-A$. For a 3-phase winding, phase B must start 120° away from the start of phase A. Since the slot-angular pitch is 30°, the phase B must start from slot 5. For conductors 5 and 6, conductors 11 (= 5 + 6) and 12 (= 6 + 6) form the return conductors. As before, phase-belt made up of conductors 5, 6 is denoted by B and phase-band consisting of return conductors 11, 12 is designated by $-B$. Phase C must start from slot 9. For conductors 9, 10 ; the return conductors are 3 (= 9 + 6 – 12) and 4 (= 10 + 6 – 12) as shown in Fig. 7.23 *(a)*.

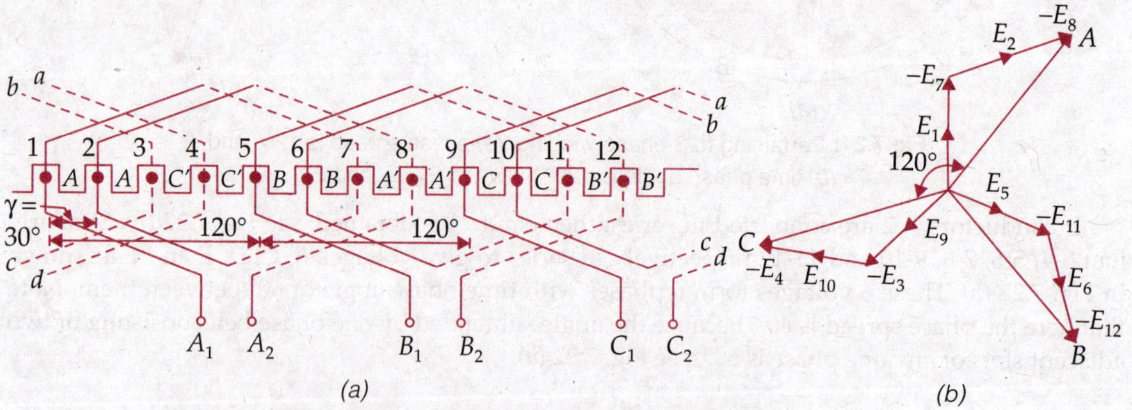

Fig 7.23: Phase spread of 60°, 12 slots, 2-pole winding arrangement.
(b) Time-phase diagram for the e.m.fs. generated in *(a)*.

Here also, phase belt of conductors 9, 10 is indicated by C and that made up of return conductors 3, 4 by – C. It can, therefore, be concluded that for ABC sequence of 3-phase voltages and for phase-spread 60°, *the sequence of phase-belts (or phase-bands) is A, – C, B, – A, C, – B.*

Star of conductor e.m.fs (or slot e.m.fs.) E_1, E_2, ... E_{12} shown in Fig. 7.22 *(a)* can be used to obtain resultant voltages across terminals A_1, A_2 ; B_1, B_2 and C_1, C_2. An examination of Fig. 7.23 *(a)* reveals that phasor sum of conductor e.m.fs. E_1, E_2, E_7 and E_8 as illustrated in Fig. 7.23 *(b)* gives the resultant voltage A across terminals A_1, A_2. Similarly, the resultant voltages B and C across the respective terminals B_1, B_2 and C_1, C_2 are obtained as shown in Fig. 7.23 *(b)*. The three e.m.fs. A, B, C are time displaced by 120°. Two adjacent slots belonging to phase A, B or C subtend an angle of 60°, the phase-spread is therefore 60° in Fig. 7.23.

7.7. DOUBLE LAYER WINDINGS

Synchronous machine armatures and induction-motor stators above a few kW, are wound with double layer windings. If the number of slots per pole per phase q, *i.e.*, S/mP is an integer, then the winding is called an *integral-slot winding*. In case the number of slots per pole per phase, *i.e.*, q is not an integer, the winding is called *fractional-slot winding*. For example, a 3-phase winding with 36 slots and 4 poles is an integral slot winding, because here $q = 36/(3 \times 4) = 3$ is an integer. A 3-phase winding with 30 slots and 4 poles is a fractional-slot winding, because $q = 30/(3 \times 4) = 5/2$ is not an integer. In both the integral and fractional-slot windings, the number of coils C is always equal to the number of slots, *i.e.*, $C = S$. In order to obtain a balanced polyphase winding, it is essential that the number of slots is a multiple of the number of phases.

7.7.1. Integral Slot Windings

Assume that the full-pitch or pole-pitch of a winding is 6 slots per pole. If the coil-pitch is taken to be equal to full-pitch, then upper coil-side (indicated by full line) in slot 1 should be connected to bottom coil-side (shown by dotted line) in slot 7 (= 1 + 6) Fig. 7.24. Since there are 6 slots per pole of 180°, the slot angular pitch is $\gamma = 180°/6 = 30°$. For a phase spread of 60°, slots 1 and 2 must contain coil-sides pertating to phase A. Upper coil-side in slot 2 must be connected to bottom coil-side in slot 8 (= 2 + 6). The winding is further completed for phase A only, for a 3-phase machine, see Fig. 7.24. An examination of this figure shows that slots 7, 8, 13, 14 and 19, 20 (slots 1, 2 also if the winding is completed) contain coil-sides belonging to the same phase A. In general, it can be stated that for *full pitch integral slot winding, each slot contains coil-sides belonging to the same phase.*

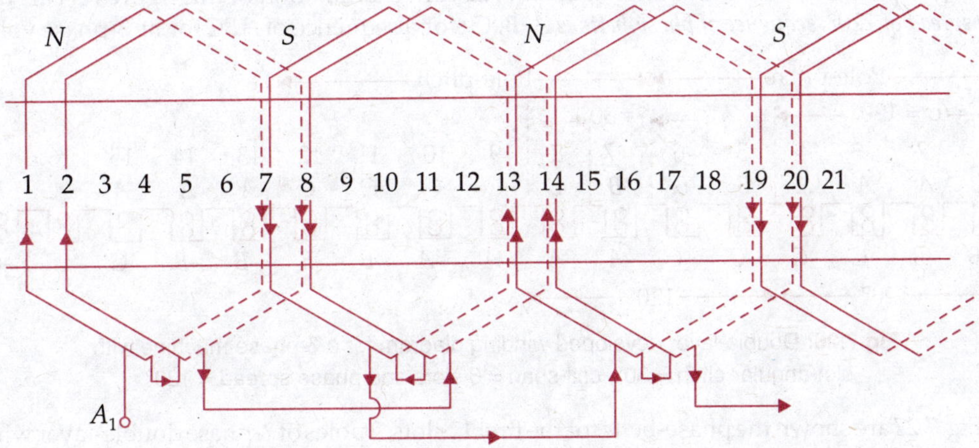

Fig 7.24: Pertaining to the double-layer, full pitch integral slot winding.

Now consider a 3-phase machine with slot-angular pitch $\gamma = 30°$, slots per pole = 6 and coil-span = full-pitch = 6 slots. For phase-spread $\sigma = 60°$, $2(= \sigma/\gamma)$ adjacent slots must belong to phase A. For coil-span = 6, top coil sides in slots 1, 2 should be connected to bottom coil-sides in slots 7 (= 1 + 6), 8 (= 2 + 6). As coil-sides 7, 8 form the return coil-sides for upper coil-sides 1, 2 for phase A, phase-belt 7, 8 is labelled $-A$ and phase-belt 1, 2 as A, Fig. 7.25. Starting of phase B must be space displaced by 120° (= 4 slot-pitches) from the start of phase A. In view of this, phase B must start from slot 5 (= 1 + 4). For 60° phase spread, two slots 5 and 6 must belong to phase B. The top coil-sides in slots 5, 6 should be connected to bottom coil-sides in slots 11, 12. Here also, phase-belt consisting of lower return coil-sides 11, 12 is designated $-B$ and that forming upper coil-sides 5, 6 as B, Fig. 7.25, slots 9, 10 belong to phase C. As the various coils have coil-span = full pitch = 180°, each slot contains coil-sides belonging to the same phase. If the three-phase winding having more than 2 poles is completed, slots 3, 4 would contain return coil-sides for phase C, these phase-belts are therefore labelled $-C$ in Fig. 7.25. It is thus seen that a phase spread of 60° produces a phase-band sequence of $A, -C, B, -A, C, -B$ for a sequence of ABC for 3-phase voltage.

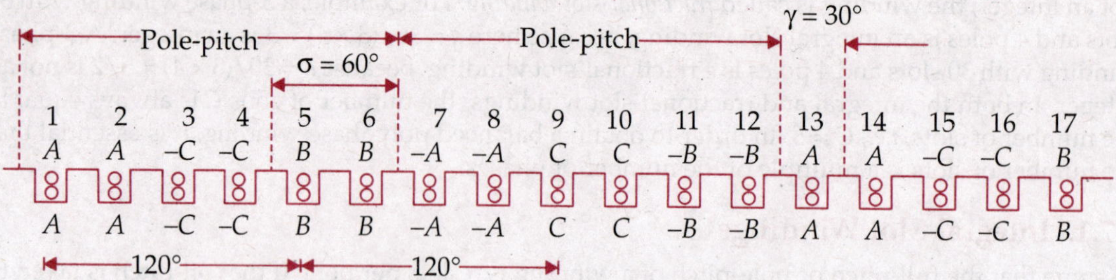

Fig 7.25: Developed winding diagram for a 3-phase machine with double layer, slot-angular pitch = 30°, coil-span = 6 slots and phase spread = 60°.

Consider now a phase spread of 120° for the 3-phase machine with γ = 30°, coil-span = full-pitch = 6 slots. A phase spread of 120° requires 4 (= σ/ γ) adjacent slots for each phase. Therefore, upper coil-sides in slots 1, 2, 3, 4 pertain to phase *A* and its return coil-sides are in slots 7, 8, 9, 10. As before, the phase-belt consisting of upper coil-sides 1, 2, 3, 4 is labelled *A* and the phase-belt formed by lower coil-sides 7, 8, 9, 10 is designated – *A*. Similarly, the arrangements of coil-sides pertaining to phases *B* and *C* is as shown in Fig. 7.26. An examination of this figure reveals that *for a phase spread of 120°, sequence of phase-belts is A, B, C* ; for a sequence of *ABC* for its 3-phase voltages.

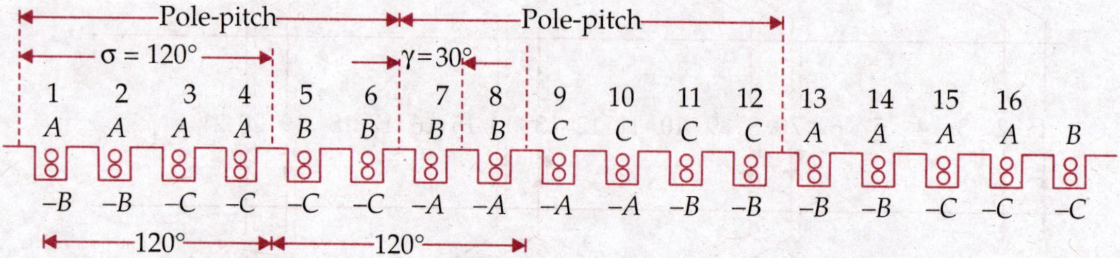

Fig 7.26: Double-layer developed winding diagram for a 3-phase machine with slot-angular pitch = 30°, coil-span = 6 slots and phase spread = 120°.

In Fig. 7.27 are shown the phase-belts for the first 12 slots, 2 poles of 3-phase double-layer winding of Fig. 7.25 having a phase spread of 60°. The phase-belts shown here can be used to illustrate as to how a 3-phase balanced winding can be obtained by their interconnection. For this purpose, left-hand terminal of phase-belt *A* forms its starting terminal A_1. The other end of this phase-belt *A* is connected to right-hand terminal of phase-belt – *A*. The left-hand terminal of phase-belt – *A* forms the end terminal of phase *A*. The same procedure is adopted to interconnect the phase-belts of phases *B*, *C* so as to obtain their respective start and end terminals B_1, B_2 and C_1, C_2 in Fig. 7.27.

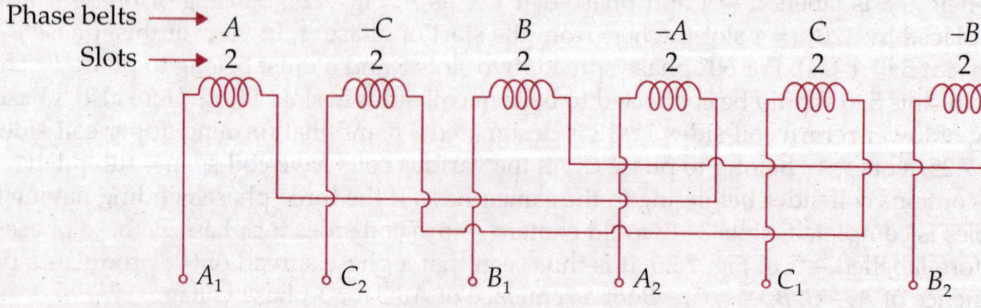

Fig 7.27: Illustrating the inter-connection between the phase-belts of a 12-slot, 2-pole, 60° phase spread, 3-phase machine.

The winding arrangement can also be shown by a simple method, called *clock-diagram method*. In the clock diagram, the arrangement of the coil-sides in both layers is illustrated. The winding arrangement of Fig. 7.25 is drawn in Fig. 7.28 in the form of clock diagram.

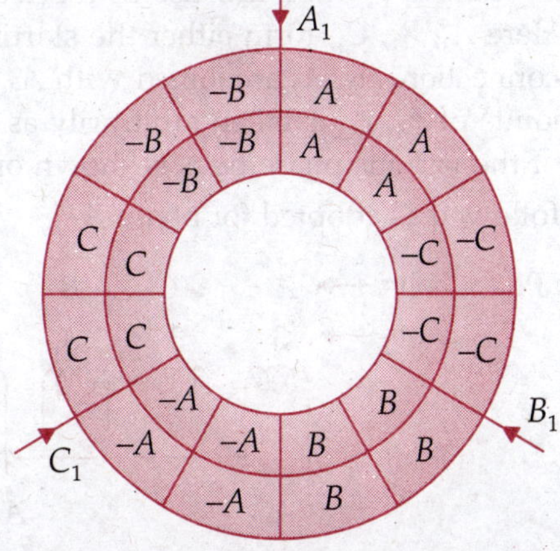

Fig 7.28: Clock diagram for Fig. 7.25.

Consider now another example with 36 slots, 4 poles, full-pitch winding with a phase spread of 60°. Here the slot-angular pitch $\gamma = \dfrac{4 \times 180}{36} = 20°$. Therefore, for a phase spread of 60°, 3 slots $\left(= \dfrac{\text{phase spread}}{\gamma}\right)$ would contain coil-sides belonging to the same phase as shown in the clock diagram of Fig. 7.29. As before, the sequence of the phase belts is $A, -C, B, -A, C, -B$, for one pole pair. The method of interconnection between the various phase belts is shown in Fig. 7.30. Note that there are 4 phase belts for each of the three phases. For the phase A, the terminals A_1, A_2 may be connected either in series or in parallel with the terminals, A_3, A_4 depending upon the operating voltage of the machine. For series connection A_2 and A_3 are joined together giving A_1 and A_4 as the two output terminals, see Fig. 7.30 *(a)*.

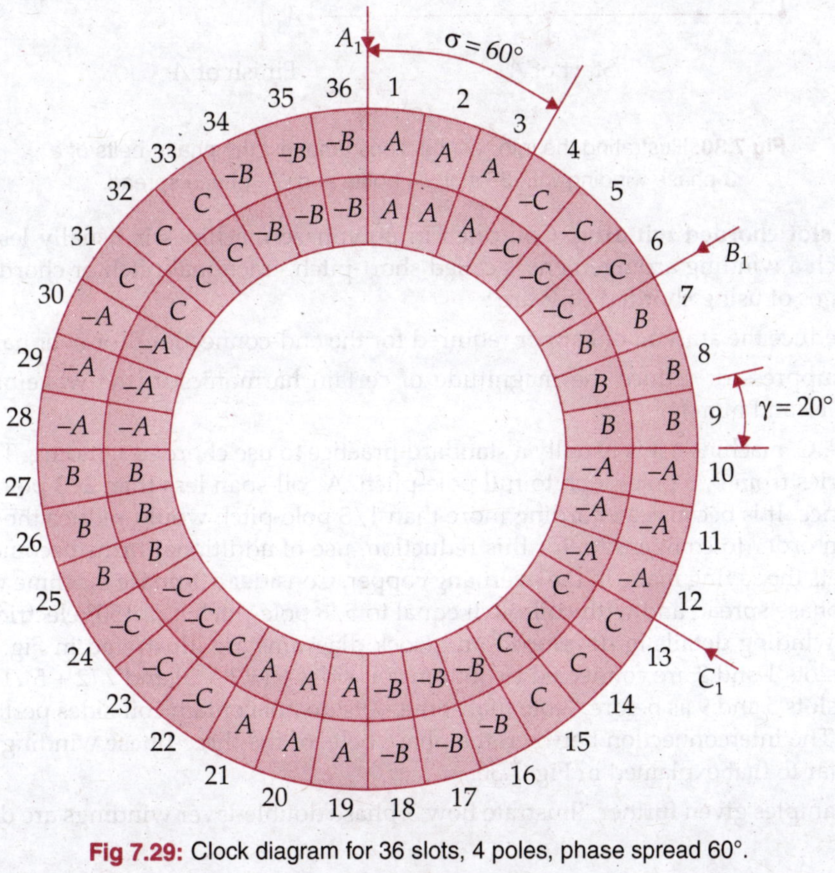

Fig 7.29: Clock diagram for 36 slots, 4 poles, phase spread 60°.

Phases B and C are also connected similarly to give B_1, B_4 and C_1, C_4 as the output terminals. Here A_1, B_1, C_1, form either the starting or the finish of phases A, B, C respectively. For parallel connection, A_1, A_2 are joined with A_3, A_4 respectively as shown in Fig. 7.30 *(b)*. In this figure, the joints of A_1, A_3 is taken arbitrarily as the start of phase A. For clarity sake, the inter-connections of the various phase-belts is shown only for phase A. For phases B and C, the same procedure is followed as adopted for phase A.

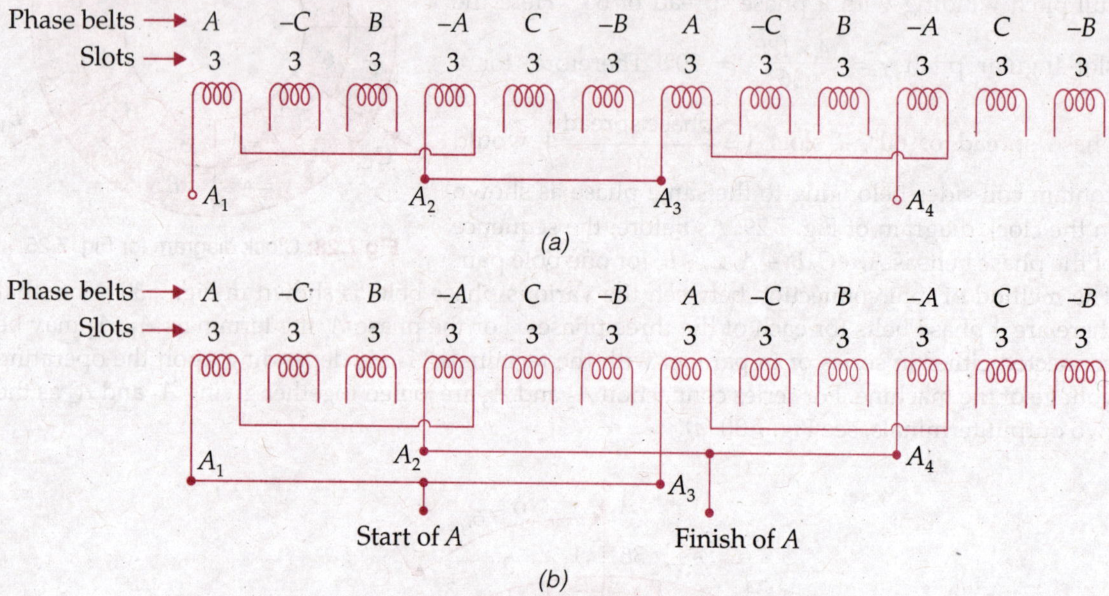

Fig 7.30: Illustrating the inter-connections amongst the phase-belts of a 3-phase winding with 36 slots, 4 poles and 60° phase spread.

Integral slot chorded winding. Coil pitch in polyphase machines is usually less than pole-pitch and such a winding arrangement is called short-pitch, fractional-pitch or chorded winding. The advantages of using chorded coils are :

(i) to reduce the amount of copper required for the end-connections (or over hang) and

(ii) to suppress or reduce the magnitude of certain harmonics in the waveform of phase e.m.fs. and m.m.fs.

In most A.C. machines, it is usually a standard practice to use chorded winding. The coil-pitch generally varies from 2/3 pole-pitch to full pole-pitch. A coil-span less than 2/3 pole-pitch is not used in practice. It is because a chording more than 1/3 pole-pitch would reduce the phase e.m.f. noticeably. In order to compensate for this reduction, use of additional turns becomes necessary and this offsets the saving made in the overhang copper. Consider a 3-phase machine with 12 slots, 2 poles, 60° phase spread and with coil-pitch equal to 5/6 pole-pitch, *i.e.*, 150° electrical, 5 slots or 5 teeth. The winding details in developed and clock diagrams are illustrated in Fig. 7.31. Upper coil-sides in slots 1 and 2 are connected to bottom coil-sides 6 (= 1 + 5) and 7 (2 + 5). Phases B and C start from slots 5 and 9 as before. Note that some slots do not contain coil-sides pertaining to the same phase. The interconnection between the phase belts of the three-phase winding is done in a manner similar to that explained in Fig. 7.30.

A few examples given further, illustrate how 3-phase double-layer windings are designed and drawn.

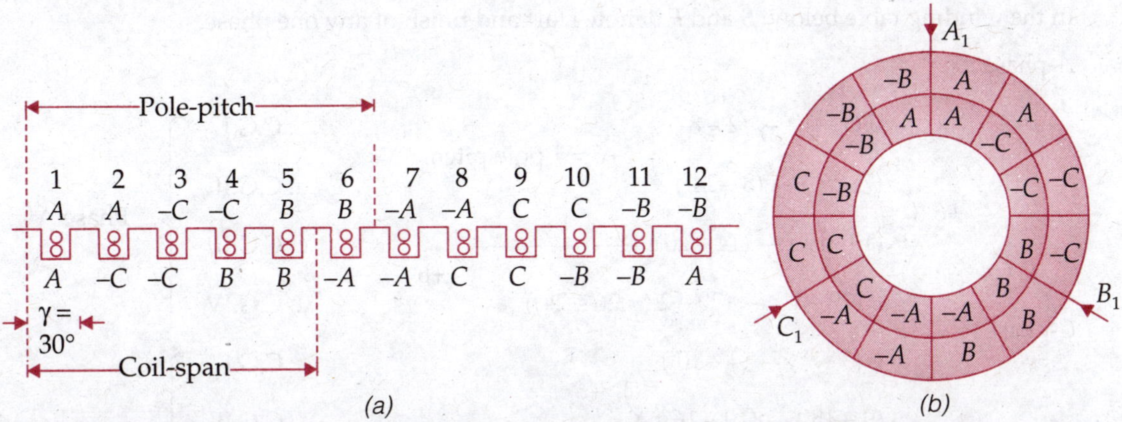

Fig 7.31: Integral slot chorded winding with 12 slots, 2 poles, 60° phase spread and coil-pitch = 5 slots.

Example 7.11. *(a) Make a winding table for the armature of a 3-phase machine with the following specifications :*

Total number of slots = 24, Double-layer winding

Number of poles = 4, Phase spread = 60°

Coil-span = full-pitch

Name the upper coil-side as n and lower coil-side as n′ for nth slot (1 < n < 24).

(b) Draw the detailed winding diagram for one phase only clearly showing the connection of different coil groups.

(c) Show the star of coil-e.m.fs. Draw phasor diagram for narrow-spread (σ = 60°) connections of the 3-phase winding showing coil-e.m.fs. for phases A and B only.

(d) Calculate its distribution factor. [E.M.D. (AMIE : S'98) parts (a), (b) & (d) only]

Solution. *(a)* Slot angular pitch, $\gamma = \frac{4 \times 180}{24} = 30°$

Phase spread, $\sigma = 60°$

Number of adjacent slots in one phase-belt $= \frac{\sigma}{\gamma} = \frac{60}{30} = 2$

$$\text{Coil-span} = \text{full-pitch} = \frac{24}{4} = 6 \text{ slots.}$$

Winding table for the 3-phase armature is prepared below. For double-layer winding, there are two coil-sides per slot ; one upper coil-side and the other lower coil-side. As required, upper coil-sides are named 1, 2, 3, ... and the corresponding lower coil-sides are named 1′, 2′, 3′, ...

For phase A, upper coil-side 1 in slot 1 is connected to lower coil-side 7′ (= 1 + 6) to form one coil. Upper coil-sides 1, 2 form phase-belt *A* and their lower coil-sides 7′, 8′ make phase-belt – *A*, these are called coil-group (C.G.) *I* and so on.

In the winding table below, S and F denote start and finish of any one phase.

A-phase :

$S\ (1-7') \xrightarrow{+6} (2-8')$	... C.G.I	
$\downarrow$ +6 = 1 pole pitch		
$(7-13') \leftarrow (8-14')$	... C.G.II	
$\downarrow$ +6		Phase A
$(13-19') \rightarrow (14-20')$	... C.G.III	
$\downarrow$ +6		
$F\ (19-1') \leftarrow (20-2'(=26-24))$	... C.G.IV	

C-phase :

$F\ (3-9') \rightarrow (4-10')$	... C.G.I	
$\downarrow$ +6		
$(9-15') \leftarrow (10-16')$	... C.G.II	
$\downarrow$ +6		Phase (–C)
$(15-21') \rightarrow (16-22')$	... C.G.III	
$\downarrow$ +6		
$S\ (21-3') \leftarrow (22-4'(=28-24))$	... C.G.IV	

B-phase :

$S\ (5-11') \rightarrow (6-12')$	... C.G.I	
$\downarrow$ +6		
$(11-17') \leftarrow (12-18')$	... C.G.II	
$\downarrow$ +6		Phase B
$(17-23') \rightarrow (18-24')$	... C.G.III	
$\downarrow$ +6		
$F\ (23-5') \leftarrow (24-6'(=30-24))$	... C.G.IV	

Above is the winding table for 3-phase armature winding having 24 slots, 4 poles, phase spread = 60°.

(b) By referring to the above winding table, detailed winding diagram for phase A only is drawn in Fig. 7.32 *(a)*. As shown, phase A starts from top coil-side 1 in slot 1 and finishes at top coil-side 19 in slot 19. Note that the winding is traversed clockwise in coil-groups I and III and anticlockwise in coil-groups II and IV. Terminals A_1 and A_2 are marked as the start and finish respectively for phase A winding.

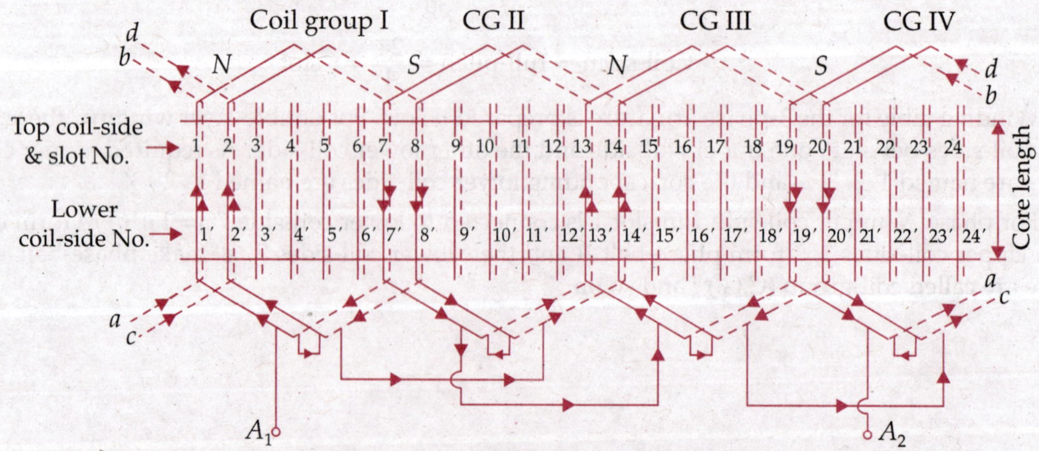

Fig 7.32: *(a)* Detailed double-layer winding diagram for phase *A* for a 3-phase armature having 24 slots, 4 poles, phase spread 60°. Example 7.11.

Phase B would start from top coil side 5, 120° away from the start of phase A. Similarly, phase C would start from top coil side 9, 120° away from the start of phase B or 240° away from the start of phase A.

(c) The star of coil e.m.fs. can be drawn similar to the star of slot e.m.fs. or star of conductor e.m.fs.

Suppose slot 1 is under the middle of north *(N)* pole, then slot 7 (= 1 + coil-span) would be under the middle of south *(S)* pole. Therefore, e.m.f. generated in coil 1 – 7′ is maximum, it is therefore shown by a vertical phasor 1 – 7′ in Fig. 7.32 *(b)*. Further, slot 13 (= 1 + 2 pole-pitches) is under the middle of N pole and slot 19 (= 13 + coil-span) is under the middle of S pole. Thus, coil 13 – 19′ has also maximum e.m.f. generated in it.

Therefore, e.m.f. in coil 13 – 19′ is in phase with the e.m.f. in coil 1 – 7′ and the two e.m.fs. are shown by a vertical phasor marked 1 – 7′, 13 – 19′ in Fig. 7.32 *(b)*. Coil e.m.fs. 2 – 8′, 14 (= 2 + 2 pole pitches) – 20′ are shown by a phasor displaced by slot-angular pitch $\gamma = 30'$ from the e.m.f. phasor 1 – 7′, 13 – 19′. Same procedure is adopted for drawing other coil e.m.fs. in Fig. 7.32 *(b)*.

Phasor diagram for narrow-spread (or phase spread 60°) showing phase voltages A, B, C can be drawn by referring to the winding table made in part *(a)*. For phase A, first obtain the phasor sum of coil e.m.fs. 1 – 7′, 2 – 8′ of coil-group *I*. Now reverse e.m.fs., 8–14′ and 7-13′ of coil-group II and add to *oa* giving *ob* as the resultant e.m.f., Fig. 7.32 *(c)*. Now add coil-e.m.fs. 13 – 19′, 14 – 20′ of coil group *III* to *ob* to get *oc*. Further, reverse coil-e.m.fs. 20 – 2′ and 19 – 1′ of coil-group *IV* and add to *oc* to get *od* as the net phase voltage A in Fig. 7.32 *(c)*. Same procedure is adopted for obtaining phase voltages B and C in Fig. 7.32 *(c)*.

(d) Distribution factor, from Eqn. (3.46), is given by

$$k_d = \frac{\sin \sigma/2}{q \sin \gamma/2}$$

Here $\sigma = 60°$, $\gamma = 30°$, $q = \frac{24}{3 \times 4} = 2$ $\therefore$ $k_d = \frac{\sin 30°}{2 \sin 15°} = 0.96593.$

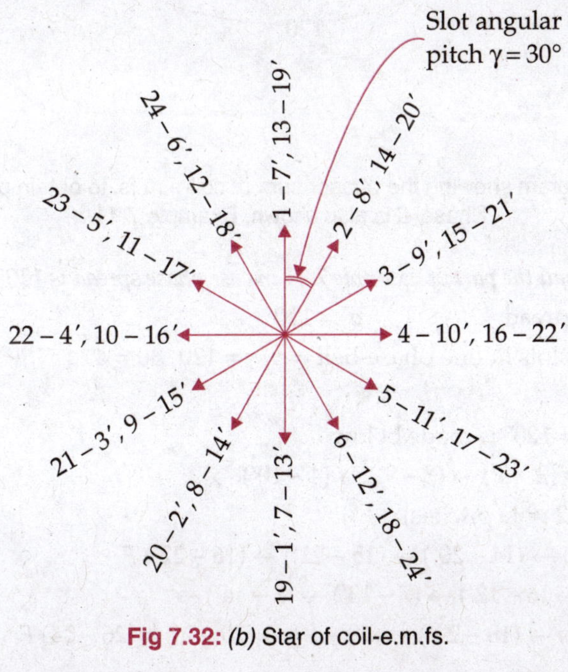

Fig 7.32: *(b)* Star of coil-e.m.fs.

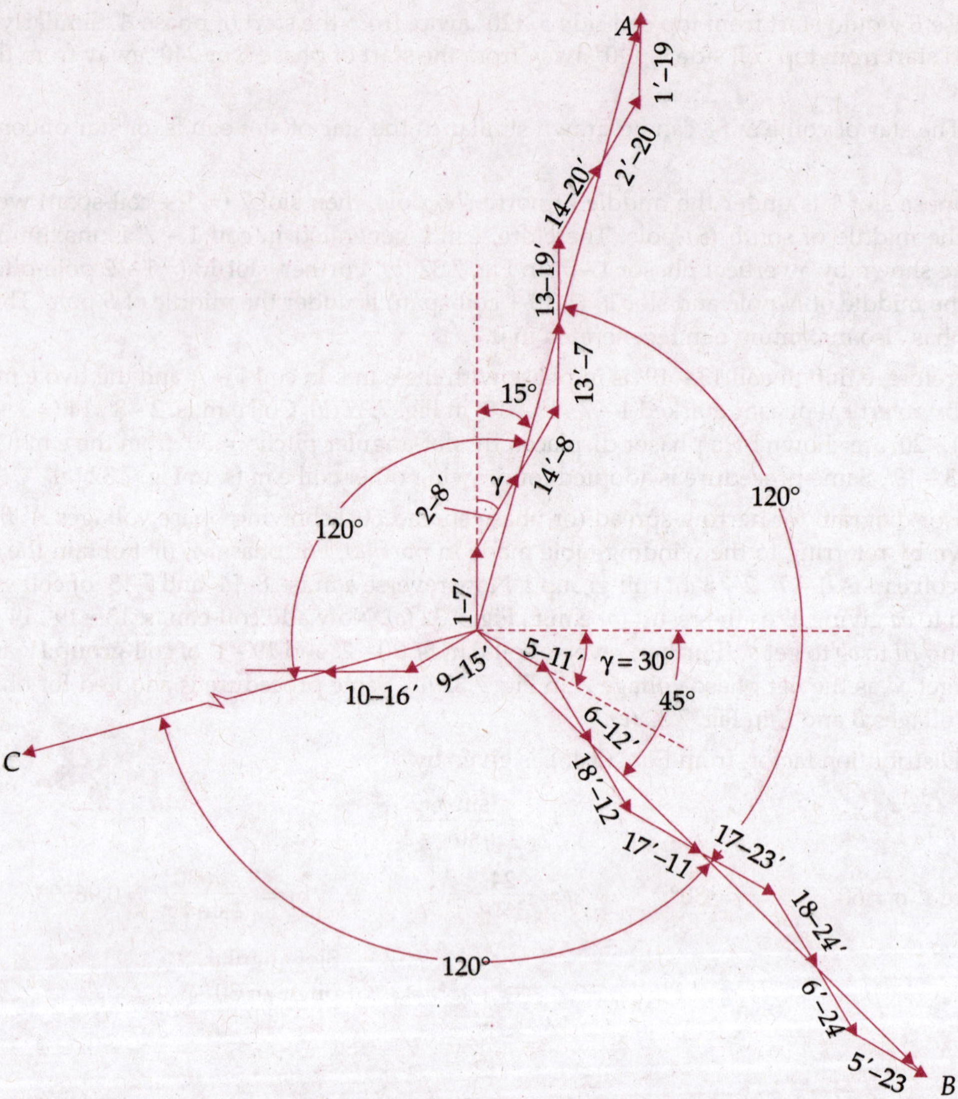

Fig 7.32: *(c)* Phasor diagram showing the phasor sum of coil-e.m.fs. to obtain phase voltages *A* and *B*. Phase *C* is also shown, Example 7.11.

Example 7.12. *Repeat all the part of Example 7.11 in case phase spread is 120°.* [E.M.D. (AMIE : S'98)]

Solution. *(a)* Phase spread, $\sigma = 120°$

Number of adjacent slots in one phase-belt = $\sigma/\gamma = 120/30 = 4$.

Coil-span = 6 slots

Winding table for $\sigma = 120°$ is made below :

A-phase : S (1 – 7′) → (2 – 8′) → (3 – 9′) → (4 – 10′) → ... C.G.I

↓ + 12 (= 2 pole pitches)

→ (13 – 19′) → (14 – 20′) → (15 – 21′) → (16 – 22′) *F* ... C.G.II

B-phase : S (5 – 11′) → (6 – 12′) → (7 – 13′) → (8 – 14′) → ... C.G.I

→ (17 – 23′) → (18 – 24′) → (19 – 1′) → (20 – 2′) = (26 – 24) *F* ... C.G.II

C-phase : S (9 – 15′) → (10 – 16′) → (11 – 17′) → (12 – 18′) → ... C.G.I

→ (21 – 3′) → (22 – 4′) → (23 – 5′) → (24 – 6′) *F* ... C.G.II

(b) Winding diagram for phase *A* is drawn in Fig. 7.33 *(a)*. As shown, phase *A* starts from top coil-side 1 in slot 1 and finishes at bottom coil-side 22′ in slot 22.

(c) Star of the coil-e.m.fs. is the same as shown in Fig. 7.32 (b).

Phasor diagram for wide-spread, *i.e.*, phase spread 120°, showing phase voltages A, B, C can be drawn by referring to winding table prepared in part *(a)* above. For phase *A*, first obtain the phasor sum *oa* of coil-e.m.fs. 1 – 7′, 2 – 8′, 3 – 9′, 4 – 10′ of coil-group *I*. Now add coil-e.m.fs. 13 – 19′, 14 – 20′, 15 – 21′, 16 – 22′ of coil-group *II* to *oa* to obtain *ob* as the resultant phase voltage *A* in Fig. 7.33 (b). Similarly, the phase voltages *B* and *C* can be obtained in Fig. 7.33 (b).

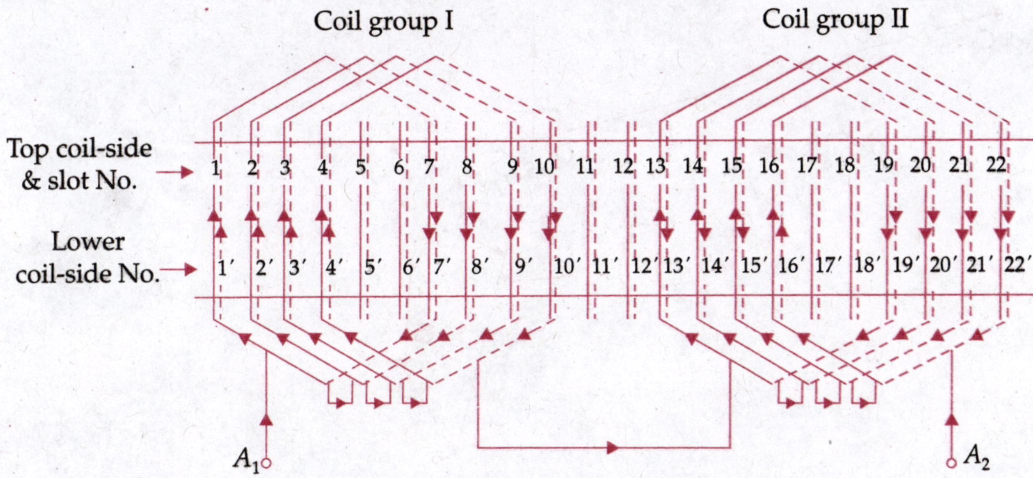

Fig 7.33: ***(a)*** **Double-layer winding for 24 slots, r = 30°, phase spread = 120° for phase *A* only of a 3-phase armature winding.**

(d) Distribution factor, from Eq. (3.46), is given by

$$k_d = \frac{\sin \sigma/2}{q \sin \sigma/2q}$$

Here $\sigma = 120°$, $\gamma = 30°$ $q = \frac{24}{3 \times 4} = 2$ $\therefore\ k_d = \frac{\sin 60}{2 \sin \frac{120}{4}} = 0.866$

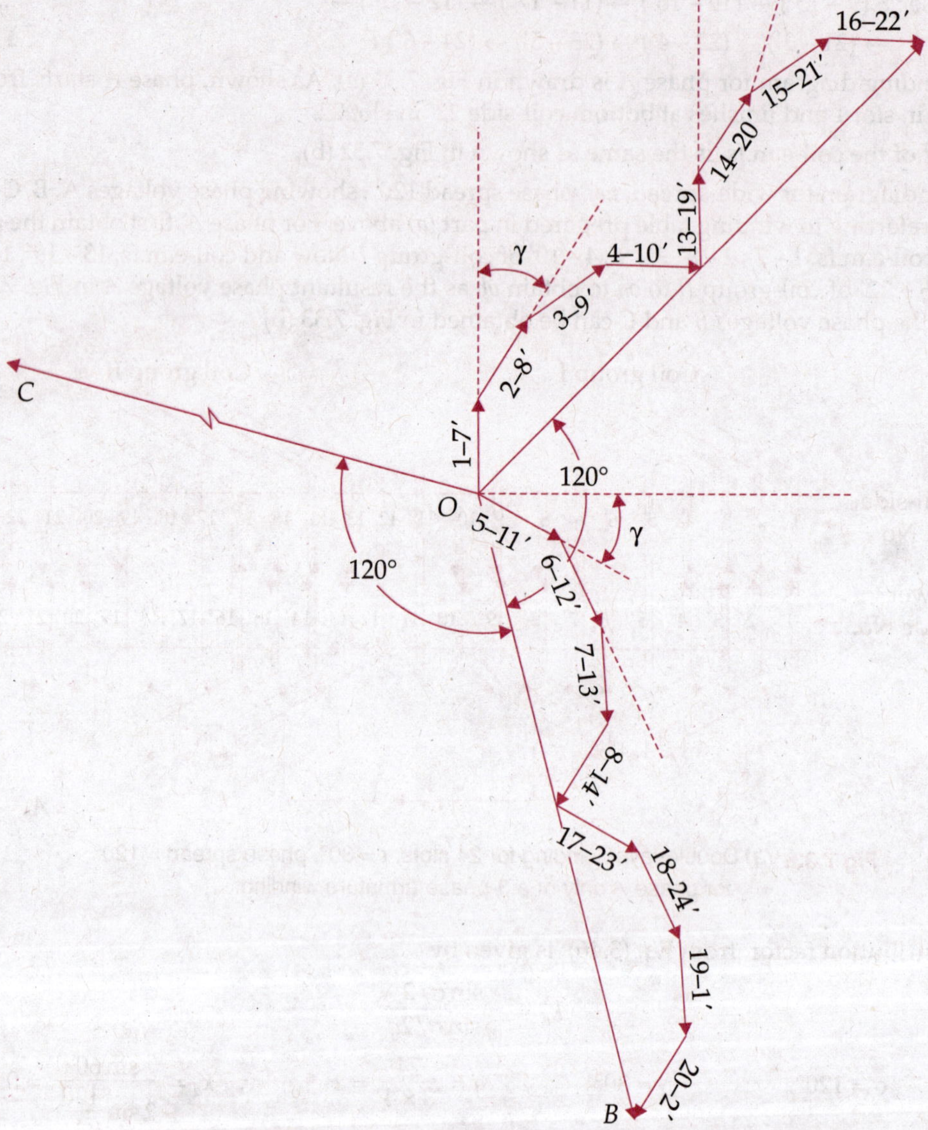

Fig 7.33: *(b)* Phasor diagram showing the phasor sum of coil e.m.fs. to obtain phase voltages *A* and *B*. Phase *C* is also shown, Example 7.12.

Example 7.13. *A 3-phase machine has 4 poles, 9 slots per pole and 4 conductors per slot arranged in two-layer lap-connected winding with coil span closely equal to 80% of the pole pitch. There are to be two distinct circuits per phase arranged for parallel connection. Draw up a winding table, indicating clearly the start and finish of each phase winding and a circuit diagram for parallel connection. Also obtain effective turns per phase.* *[E.M.D. (AMIE : W'98)]*

Solution. Slots per pole = 9

Slot-angular pitch, $\gamma = 180/9 = 20°$

For a phase-spread of 60°, number of adjacent slots belonging to any one phase

$$= \sigma/\gamma = 60/20 = 3$$

Pole pitch = 9 slots

Coil-span = 80% of pole pitch = 80/100 × 9 = 7.2

So take a coil-span of 7 slots.

From above, winding table for this machine is prepared as under. Here *S* and *F* denote start and finish of any one phase. The top coil-sides are labelled 1, 2, 3, ... and bottom coil-sides 1′, 2′, 3′, ...

A-phase :

+7

S (1 – 8′) → (2 – 9′) → (3 – 10′) ... C.G.I

+9 (= 1 pole – pitch)

(10 –17′) ← (11 – 18′) ← (12 – 19′) ... C.G.II

+9

(19 –26′) → (20 – 27′) → (21 – 28′) ... C.G.III

+9

F (28 – 35′) ← (29 – 36′) ← (30 – 1′(= 37 – 36′)) ... C.G.IV

C-phase :

F (4 – 11′) → (5 – 12′) → (6 – 13′) ... C.G.I

+9

(13 – 20′) ← (14 – 21′) ← (15 – 22′) ... C.G.II

+9

(22 – 29′) → (23 – 30′) → (24 – 31′) ... C.G.III

+9

S (31 – 2′) ← (32 – 3′) ← (33 – 4′) ... C.G.IV

B-phase :

S (7 – 14′) → (8 – 15′) → (9 – 16′) ... C.G.I

+9

(16 – 23′) ← (17 – 24′) ← (18 – 25′) ... C.G.II

+9

(25 – 32′) → (26 – 33′) → (27 – 34′) ... C.G.III

+9

F (25 – 5′) ← (35 – 6′) ← (36 – 7′) ... C.G.IV

As required, start and finish of phase windings *A*, *B*, *C* is indicated in the above winding table. It is seen from this winding table that each phase has 4 coil-groups and each coil-group consists of 3 coils forming a phase-band or phase-belt. For phase *A*, coil-group *I* forms phase–belt *A*, coil-group *II* phase-belt – *A*, coil-group *III* phase-belt *A* and coil-group *IV* phase-belt – *A*. For phase *C*, coil-groups *I* and *III* form phase-belt–*C* whereas coil-groups *II* and *IV* form phase-belt *C*. Similarly, for phase *B*, coil-groups *I* and *III* make phase-belt *B* and coil-groups *II* and *IV* form phase-belt – *B*.

The various phase-belts are shown in Fig. 7.34. In Fig. 7.34 *(a)*, the interconnections amongst phase-belts of phase *A* are shown. Terminals A_1', A_1'' are joined together to form the starting point of phase *A*. Terminals A_2', A_2'' together form the finish of phase *A*. Note that there are two distinct parallel paths for phase-*A* winding in Fig. 7.34 *(a)*. One parallel path is from A_1' to A_2' and the second parallel path is from A_1'' to A_2''. Similarly, interconnections amongst phase-belts pertaining to phases B and C are shown in Fig. 7.34 *(b)* and *(c)* respectively. Two distinct parallel paths are also indicated for phases B and C in this figure.

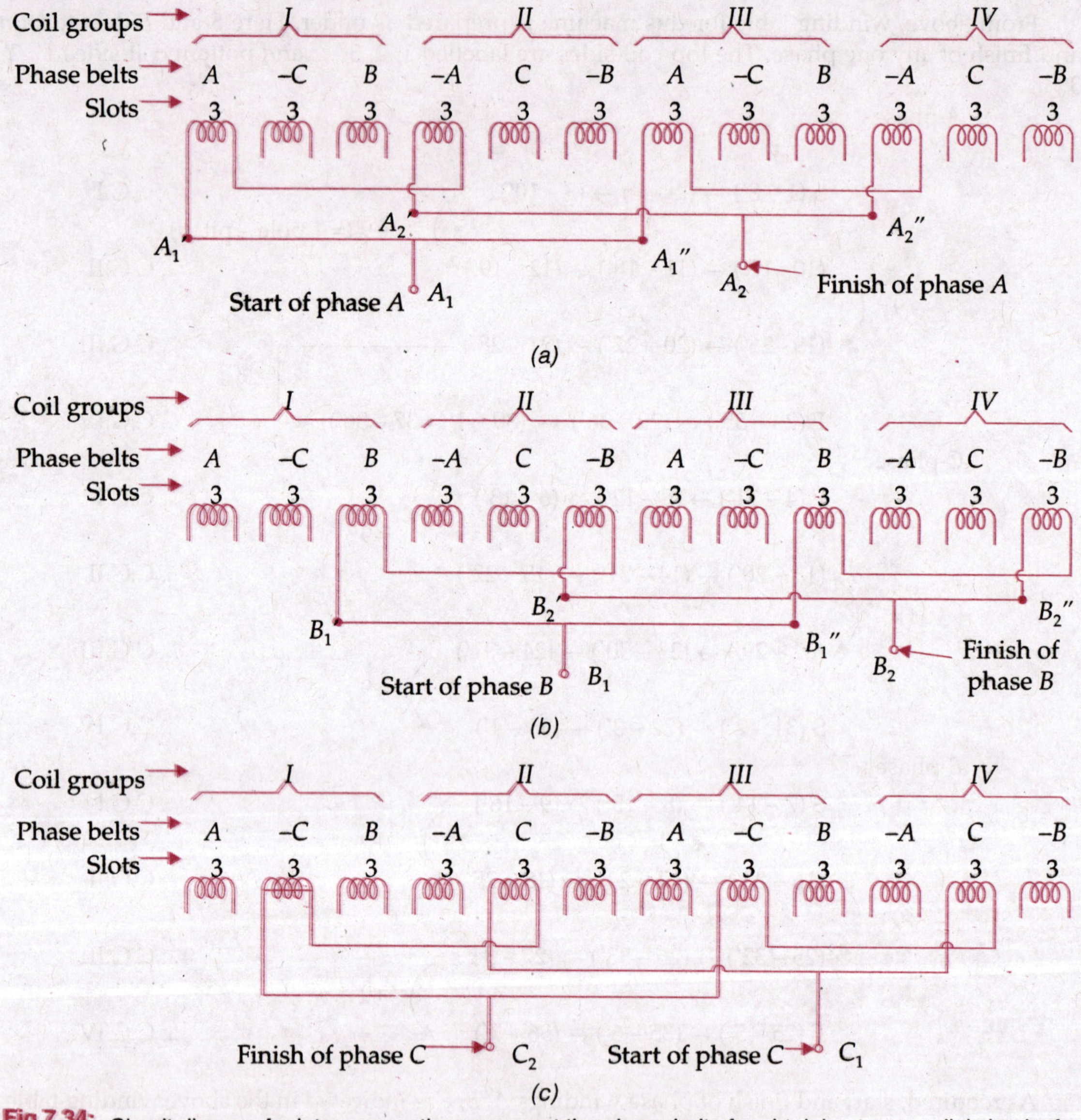

Fig 7.34: Circuit diagram for inter-connections amongst the phase-belts for obtaining two parallel circuits for *(a)* phase-*A*, *(b)* phase-*B* and *(c)* phase-*C* windings.

$$\text{Total turns in the machine} = \frac{9 \times 4 \times 4}{2} = 72$$

Here phase spread $\sigma = 60°$

slots per pole per phase, $q = \frac{9}{3} = 3, \gamma = 20°$

$\therefore$ Distribution factor, $k_d = \dfrac{\sin \sigma/2}{q \sin \dfrac{\gamma}{2}} = \dfrac{\sin 30°}{3 \sin 10°} = 0.9598.$

Coil-span $= 7\,\gamma = 7 \times 20 = 140°$

$\therefore$ Chording-angle, $\varepsilon = 180° - 140° = 40°.$

Coil-span factor, $k_p = \cos \dfrac{\varepsilon}{2} = \cos 20° = 0.9397.$

$\therefore$ Winding factor, $k_w = k_d \times k_p = 0.9598 \times 0.9397 = 0.901924.$

Number of effective turns per phase $= [\text{Turns/phase}] \times k_w$

$$= \frac{72}{3} \times 0.901924 = 21.65.$$

7.8. FRACTIONAL SLOT WINDINGS

In fractional slot windings, the number of slots per pole per phase is not a whole number. But from the view point of symmetry, the number of slots must be divisible by the number of phases, *i.e.*, 3.

The advantages of these windings are as given below :

(i) This winding reduces the high-frequency harmonics in the e.m.f. and m.m.f. waveforms.

(ii) This winding permits the use of already existing slotting numbers for the armature laminations, because here the armature slots need not be a multiple of the number of poles. This avoids additional expenditure on new punching tools etc.

(iii) This winding allows more freedom in the choice of coil-pitch. For example, a machine with 48 slots and 10 poles has $4\frac{4}{5}$ slots per pole and the coil-pitch for a fractional slot winding can be taken as 4 or 3 (always less than the slots per pole).

The restrictions of the fractional-slot winding are that :

(i) it can be used only with double-layer windings and

(ii) the number of parallel circuits is limited (as explained at a later stage in this article).

Let S be the total number of slots (a multiple of 3 for a 3-phase winding) and P be the number of poles. Then the slots per pole per phase, for a 3-phase winding, are $(S/3)/P$. If k is the highest common factor between $S/3$ and P, then slots per pole per phase can be written as

$$\frac{S/3}{P} = \frac{k \cdot S_k}{k \cdot P_k} = \frac{S_k}{P_k}$$

where $S_k = \dfrac{S/3}{k}$ and $P_k = \dfrac{P}{k}$

The ratio S_k/P_k is called the *characteristic ratio* of the fractional slot winding. S_k represents the coils per phase, distributed among P_k successive poles. The highest common factor k between $S/3$ and P represents the number of repeatable sections. Since the repeatable sections may be connected in series or in parallel, k also gives the number of possible parallel circuits in fractional-slot winding. For example, with $S = 48$ and $P = 10$,

$$\frac{S_k}{P_k} = \frac{48/3}{10} = \frac{16}{10} = \frac{2 \times 8}{2 \times 5} = \frac{8}{5}$$

Here highest common factor k is 2, therefore, repeatable sections and the number of possible parallel circuits is 2. The characteristic ratio 8/5 shows that there are 8 coils per phase, distributed among 5 successive poles. In other words, 8 coils belonging to any one phase may be distributed under 5 adjacent poles as follows :

1st pole	2nd pole	3rd pole	4th pole	5th pole
2 coils	1 coil	2 coils	1 coil	2 coils

Since k is equal to 2, the winding pattern under first 5 poles is repeated under the remaining 5 poles. It is however not clear whether under first pole, there would be 2 coils or 1 coil, *i.e.*, the distribution of 8 coils per phase under 5 adjacent poles is not certain.

In order to overcome this difficulty, a coil-group table as shown in Table 7.2 is prepared as outlined below :

1. Calculate the slot-angular pitch, $\gamma = \frac{180 \times P}{S} = \frac{180 \times 10}{48} = 37\frac{1°}{2}$

2. Indicate the beginning of slot number 1 with zero degree. Now fill in the table for the next slot 2, 3, 4, ..., 24 (= 3 S_k) by taking into account the slot-angular pitch. In case the angle exceeds 180°, subtract 180° (equal to one pole-pitch). This step takes care of the location of coils under a particular pole.

3. As the slots are considered progressively, the phase groups for a phase-spread of 60° are located as under :

Phase group A : $0° \le$ angle $< 60°$

phase group C : $60° \le$ angle $< 120°$

phase group B : $120° \le$ angle $< 180°$

As proved before, the sequence of phase groups is $A, -C, B, -A, C, -B$.

With the help of above three steps, the distribution of 8 (= S_k) coils under 5 (= P_k) adjacent poles can be obtained from Table 7.2 which is now prepared as under :

Table 7.2

← Pole-pitch 1 →					
Slot No.	1	2	3	4	5
Angle	0°	$37\frac{1}{2}$	75	112.5°	150°
Phase	A	A	– C	– C	B
← Pole-pitch 2 →					
Slot No.	6	7	8	9	10
Angle	7.5°	45°	82.5°	120°	157.5°
Phase	–A	–A	C	– B	–B
← Pole-pitch 3 →					
Slot No.	11	12	13	14	15
Angle	15°	52.5°	90°	127.5°	165°
Phase	A	A	– C	B	B
← Pole-pitch 4 →					
Slot No.	16	17	18	19	20
Angle	22.5°	60°	97.5°	135°	172.5°
Phase	–A	C	C	– B	–B

Pole-pitch 5					
Slot No.	21	22	23	24	
Angle	*30°*	*67.5°*	*105°*	*142.5°*	
Phase	*A*	*–C*	*– C*	*– B*	

Table 7.2 shows that 8 coils belonging to phase *A* are distributed under 5 successive or adjacent poles as follows :

1st Pole	*2nd Pole*	*3rd Pole*	*4th Pole*	*5th Pole*
2	2	2	1	1

There is another method of determining the distribution of S_k coils under P_k adjacent poles. This method is quite simple and straight-forward. According to this method, a tabular construction, as explained below is adopted.

In this table, number of rows is made equal to the basic pole unit P_k (in this case 5). The total number of columns is made equal to 3 S_k (in the present case 24). The sequence of the phase-belts is obtained by dividing 3 S_k columns in three equal sections *ACB* for a 3-phase 60° phase-spread winding. Start from the extreme left and top square with a cross. Now proceed to the right and go on putting crosses separated from each other by P_k (= 5). After first row, go to the second row and so on. From Table 7.3, it is seen that S_k (= 8) coils belonging to phase *A* are distributed under P_k successive or adjacent poles as obtained from Table 7.2. In Table 7.3, coils pertaining to phase *A* are indicated by 2 crosses in first row for first pole, 2 crosses in the second row for pole number 2 and so on.

Table 7.3: Tabular method of construction for fractional-slot windings

Poles	*A Phase*								*– C Phase*								*B Phase*							
1	×					×					×					×					×			
2		×					×					×					×					×		
3			×					×					×					×					×	
4				×					×					×					×					×
5					×					×					×					×				

It is also seen from both the tables that the coil sequence or slot sequence of phase belts belonging to phase *C* coils is 2 1 1 2 2 and for phase *B* is 1 2 2 2 1.

The basic pole unit of P_k poles for this example may be tabulated as follows :

Poles →	1	2	3	4	5
Phase A	+ 2	– 2	+ 2	– 1	+ 1
Phace C	– 2	+ 1	– 1	+ 2	– 2
Phase B	+ 1	– 2	+ 2	– 2	+1

The clock diagram layout for one layer of the winding (usually upper layer) is shown in Fig. 7.35. The lower layer has the same groupings but is displaced from the upper groups by the coil-pitch. Since slots per pole is a fractional number, the coil pitch can't be full-pitch but it must be same for all coils. With 48 slots and 10 poles, there are $\frac{48}{10} = 4\frac{4}{5}$ slots per pole and the coil-pitch may be chosen either 3 or 4 slot-pitches.

Requirement of symmetry. Even in fractional slot windings, the time-phase angle between the 3-phase voltages must be 120° or $2\pi/3$ radians.

Let S_{ab} and S_{ac} represent the number of slot-pitch displacements between the starting of phase A and the starting of phases B and C respectively. Then

$$S_{ab}\,\gamma = \frac{2\pi}{3} \text{ or } \frac{2\pi}{3} + x\pi$$

and $$S_{ac}\,\gamma = \frac{4\pi}{3} \text{ or } \frac{4\pi}{3} + x\pi$$

Here x may have any integral value. If x = 0, 2, 4 ..., the polarity of the starting phase belts of phases B and C is the same as that of the starting phase belt of phase A. In case x = 1, 3, 5, ..., the polarity of the starting phase belts of phases B and C is opposite to that of phase A. These polarities must be taken into consideration during the inter-connection of the phase belts.

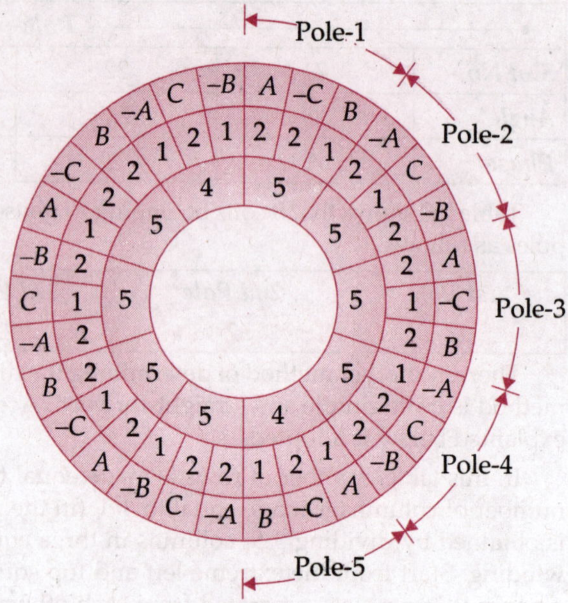

Fig 7.35: Clock diagram for 48 slots, 10 poles, 60° phase spread fractional-slot winding.

Now slots per pole per phase are,

$$q = \frac{S}{3P} = \frac{S/3}{P} \text{ or } \frac{P}{S} = \frac{1}{3q}$$

Slot pitch, $$\gamma = \frac{\pi P}{S} = \frac{\pi}{3q}$$

$\therefore$ $$S_{ab} = \frac{1}{\gamma}\left(\frac{2\pi}{3} + x\pi\right) = \frac{3q}{\pi}\left(\frac{2\pi}{3} + x\pi\right) = q\,(3x+2)$$

$$= \frac{S_k}{P_k}\,(3x+2) \qquad \text{... (7.9)}$$

Similarly, $$S_{ac} = q\,(3x+4) = \frac{S_k}{P_k}\,(3x+4) \qquad \text{... (7.10)}$$

It may be seen from Eqs. (7.9) and (7.10) that if P_k is equal to 3 or a multiple of 3, S_{ab} and S_{ac} can never be whole numbers and, therefore, fractional slot winding is not possible. For example, 33 slots and 6 poles give S_k/P_k equal to 11/6, therefore, fractional slot winding is not possible for these slots and poles.

For illustrating the inter-connection among the various phase belts, the layout of the winding arrangement is as shown in Fig. 7.36.

In the present example, $$\frac{S_k}{P_k} = \frac{8}{5}.$$

$\therefore$ $$S_{ab} = \frac{8}{5}\,(3x+2)$$

For $x = 1$, $$S_{ab} = \frac{8}{3}\,(3+2) = 8.$$

Therefore, the starting of phase B is displaced by 8 slot pitches from the starting of phase A. Since $x = 1$, the polarity of the starting phase belt of phase B must be opposite to the polarity of starting phase belt of phase A, see Fig. 7.36.

Now $$S_{ac} = \frac{8}{5}(3x + 4)$$

For $x = 2$ $$S_{ac} = \frac{8}{5}(3 \times 2 + 4) = 16.$$

This shows that the starting of phase C is displaced by 16 slot pitches from the starting of phase A. Since $x = 2$, the polarity of the starting phase belt of phase C is the same as that of the starting phase belt of phase A, see Fig. 7.36. In this figure, inter-connection of phase A belts is only shown for the sake of clarity. However, starting of phases B and C has been indicated.

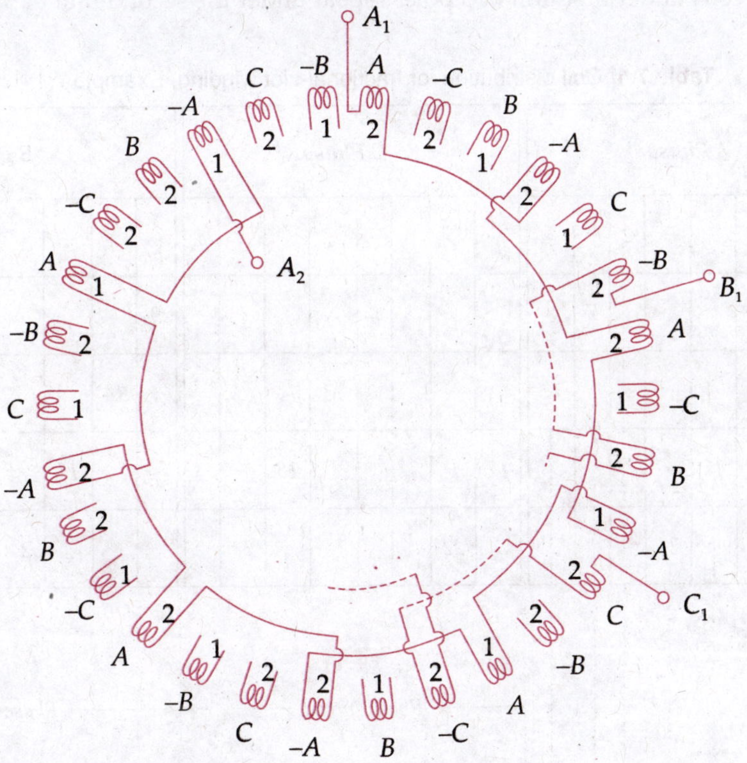

Fig 7.36: Pertaining to the inter-connection of phase belts for a fractional slot winding with 48 slots, 10 poles, 60° phase spread.

From the starting of phase A, slot sequence of the phase A belts is 22211, 22211 for all the 10 poles. Examination of Fig. 7.35 reveals that the slot sequence of the phases B and C belts from their corresponding starting points is the same as for phase A.

Example 7.14. *(a) Develop a winding table for the armature of a 3-phase machine having the following data :*

48 slots, 10 poles, narrow-spread, coil-span = 3 slots.

Name the upper coil-side as n and lower coil-side as n′ for the nth slot.

(b) Draw the coil-e.m.f. star for phase A only.

Solution. (*a*) A table giving the construction for fractional-slot winding of this example is already prepared in Table 7.3. This table is repeated again in Table 7.4, but here *coil-numbers* are written in the boxes instead of crosses. So now start from the extreme left and top square (or box) and write 1. In the next cross of Table 7.3, write 2 and in the next cross in the same row, write 3 and so on, till one unit of 5 poles is completed in Table 7.4. It is seen from this table that for the first unit of 5 poles

(*i*) coils 1, 2, 6, 7, 11, 12, 16 and 21 (total 8) belong to phase *A*,

(*ii*) coils 3, 4, 8, 13, 17, 18, 22 and 23 (total 8) belong to phase (– *C*) and

(*iii*) coils 5, 9, 10, 14, 15, 19, 20 and 24 (total 8) belong to phase *B*.

The winding table 7.5 for phases *A*, *B*, *C* is developed as follows. For phase *A*, connect top coil-side 1 to bottom coil-side 4′ (= 1 + 3), top coil-side 2 to bottom coil-side 5′ (= 2 + 3) and so on. Remember that coils under first unit of 5 poles repeat under the second unit of 5 poles for this 10-pole machine.

Table 7.4: Coil distribution for fractional-slot winding, Example 7.14

Pole ↓	*A Phase*								*–C Phase*								*B Phase*							
1	1					2					3					4					5			
2		6					7					8					9					10		
3			11					12					13					14					15	
4				16					17					18					19					21
5					21					22					23					24				
6	25																							

7.5

15°

22.5°

30°

y = 37.5°

45°

52.5°

Phase spread = 60°

Phase spread

Phase spread

Table 7.5: Development of winding table for fractional-slot winding, Ex. 7.14

Pole	*A Phase*	*– C Phase*	*B Phase*
1.	*S* (1 – 4′) → (2 – 5′)	*F* (3 – 6′) → (4 – 7′)	*S* (5 – 8′)
2.	(6 – 9′) ← (7 – 10′)	(8 – 11′)	(9 – 12′) ← (10 – 13′)
3.	(11 – 14′) → (12 – 15′)	(13 – 16′)	(14 – 17′) → (5 – 18′)
4.	(16 – 19′)	(17 – 20′) ← (18 – 21′)	(19 – 22′) ← (20 – 23′)
5.	(21 – 24′)	(22 – 25′) → (23 – 26′)	(24 – 27′)
6.	(25 – 28′) ← (26 – 29′)	(27 – 30′) ← (28 – 31′)	(29 – 32′)
7.	(30 – 33′) → (31 – 34′)	(32 – 35′)	(33 – 36′) → (34 – 37′)
8.	(35 – 38′) ← (36 – 39′)	(37 – 40′)	(38 – 41′) ← (39 – 42′)
9.	(40 – 43′)	(41 – 44′) → (42 – 45′)	(43 – 46′) → (44 – 47′)
10.	*F* (45 – 48′)	*S* (46 – 1′) ← (47 – 2′)	*F* (48 – 3′)

The information obtained from Table 7.3 can also be derived from Table 7.4 and 7.5.

(b) Slot-angular pitch $\gamma = \dfrac{10 \times 180}{48} = 37.5°.$

Suppose emf in coil 1 is taken vertical in Fig. 7.37. Then, emf in coil 2 would be displaced by one slot angular pitch γ = 37.5° from the emf in coil 1, see Table 7.4. Emfs in coils 1 and 2 are shown in Fig. 7.37 by 0-1 and 0-2 respectively. An examination of Table 7.4 shows that emfs in coils 1, 2 under pole 1 ; emfs in coils 11, 12 under pole 3 (= 1 + 2 pole pitches or 360°) and emfs in coil 21 under pole 5 (= 3 + 2 pole pitches) are positive. Therefore emf 0 1 is shown vertical as assumed. Emf 0-11 is shown at angle 15°, emf 0-12 at an angle 52.5° and emf 0-21 at an angle 30°.

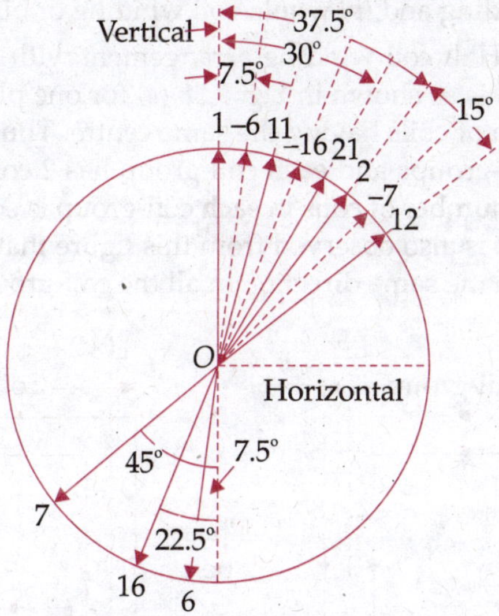

Fig 7.37: Coil-emf star for phase A. Ex. 7.14.

Emfs generated in coils under pole 2 and 4 (= 2 + 2 pole pitches) would be negative. Therefore, emfs in coils 6 and 7 under pole 2 are shown negative as 0-6 at an angle 7.5° + 180° = 187.5° and 07 at angle 45° + 180° = 225°. Emf in coil 16 is shown as 0-16 at an angle 22.5 + 180° = 202.5°. All the eight emfs (1, – 6, 11, – 16, 21, 2, – 7, 12) generated in one 5-pole unit shown in Fig. 7.37 constitute the coil-emf star for phase A.

7.9. SINGLE-LAYER WINDINGS

As stated earlier, single-layer windings (SLWs) are not commonly employed in practice, except for machines of a few kW rating. The three-phase SLWs are of two types, namely *(i)* concentric windings and *(ii)* mush windings. In addition to the disadvantages enumerated earlier, SLWs have the following limitations :

(i) Concentric SLW cannot have chorded coils.

(ii) In concentric SLW, effective coil span is equal to pole-pitch, even though coil-span of individual coils in a coil-group differs from pole-pitch.

(iii) In mush windings, coil-span is constant. In other words, all the coils have the same shape and size.

(iv) In mush windings, coil-span is always odd. This requirement may result in the coils to be chorded. For example, in a 4-pole, 36-slot machine, the coil-span = pole-pitch = 9. In 4-pole, 24-slot machine, coil-span cannot be equal to pole-pitch = 6 slots. A coil-span has to be odd, so a coil-span of 5 slots or 7 slots can be chosen. A coil-span of 5 slots results in chorded coils.

(v) Fractional-slot windings cannot be used for concentric as well as mush windings.

In single-layer windings, one coil-side occupies one slot completely, in view of this, number of coils C is equal to half the number of slots S, *i.e.*, $C = \frac{1}{2}$ S. Now concentric and mush windings are described briefly.

7.9.1. Concentric Windings

These windings are so called because the coils under one pole pair are wound in such a manner as if these have one centre. The concentric winding can further be sub-divided into *(a)* half-coil winding or unbifurcated winding and *(b)* whole-coil winding or bifurcated winding.

(a) **Half-coil winding.** Half-coil winding arrangement with 2 slots per pole per phase and for 60° phase spread is as shown in Fig. 7.38 *(a)* for one phase only. A coil-group may be defined as the group of coils having the same centre. Thus Fig. 7.38 *(a)* reveals that there are two (= $P/2$) coil-groups and each coil-group has 2 coils (= phase spread/slot pitch). In other words, the number of coils in each coil-group is equal to the number of coil-sides in each phase belt. It is also observed from this figure that the coils are connected so that they carry current in the same direction in all the coil-groups, [clockwise in Fig. 7.38 *(a)*].

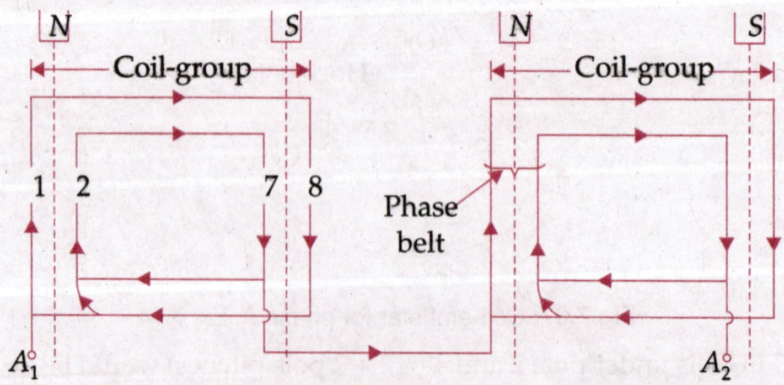

(a)

Fig 7.38: Single layer concentric winding *(a)* half-coil arrangement.

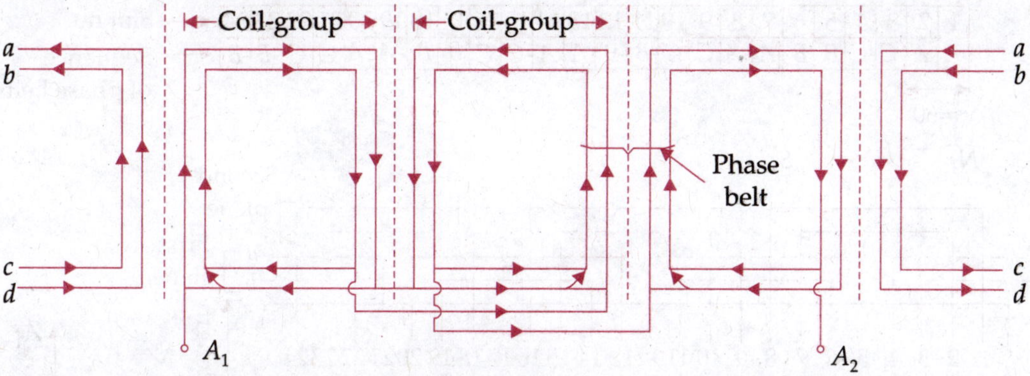

(b)

Fig 7.38: Single layer concentric winding *(b)* whole-coil arrangement.

(b) **Whole-coil winding.** The whole-coil winding arrangement with 4 slots per pole per phase is as illustrated in Fig. 7.38 *(b)* for one phase only. This figure reveals that there are *P* coil-groups and the adjacent coil-groups carry currents in opposite directions [first clockwise and then counter-clockwise in Fig. 7.38 *(b)*]. Note that the number of coil-sides in each phase belt (here 4) are double the number of coils (here 2) in each coil-group.

Example 7.15. *Design and draw (a) half-coil and (b) whole-coil single-layer concentric windings for a 3 phase machine with 24 slots, 4-poles and 60° phase spread.*

Solution. *(a) Half-coil concentric winding.*

Slots-angular pitch, $\gamma = \dfrac{4 \times 180}{24} = 30°$

Full-pitch or pole-pitch $= \dfrac{24}{4} = 6$ slots-pitches.

For a phase spread of 60°, each phase belt must have 2 slots. Coil-side 1 would be joined to 8 (= 1 + 7), 8 to 2 and 2 to 7, so that the average coil-pitch is equal to 6 slot-pitches. Coil-side 7 should be connected to 13 (= 7 + 6) and so on. Phase *B* should start 120° away from the starting point of phase *A*, *i.e.*, from slot number 5 $\left(= 1 + \dfrac{120°}{\gamma} = 1 + 4\right)$. Similarly phase *C* should start from slot 9 (= 5 + 4).

The upper part of Fig. 7.39 illustrates the coil distribution in all the 24 slots. For the instant at which the winding diagram of Fig. 7.39 is drawn, the phasor diagram is as shown in the right of Fig. 7.39. Note that the current enters terminal A_1 and leaves terminals B_1 and C_1. The unbifurcated winding shown in Fig. 7.39 requires two-plane overhang.

(b) **Whole coil concentric winding.** For slot-pitch $\gamma = 30°$ and phase spread $\sigma = 60°$, the number of coils per phase-belt are 2, therefore, the number of coils in each coil-group must be 1. Here the pole-pitch is 6 slot-pitches. The coil-pitch of 6 slot-pitches does not result in proper arrangement of the winding. In view of this, a coil-pitch of 5 is chosen. Therefore, coil-side 1 should be connected to coil-side 6 and 6 to 12 to 7 (= 12 – 5) and so on. As before, phases *B* and *C* start from slots 5 and 9. For the instant at which the winding diagram of Fig. 7.40 is drawn the voltage phasor diagram is the same as that of Fig. 7.39.

Note that the slots allotted to various phases are as follows :

Phase *A* : 1—6, 7—12, 13—18, 19—24

Phase *B* : 5—10, 11—16, 17—22, 23—4

Phase *C* : 9—14, 15—20, 21—2, 3—8

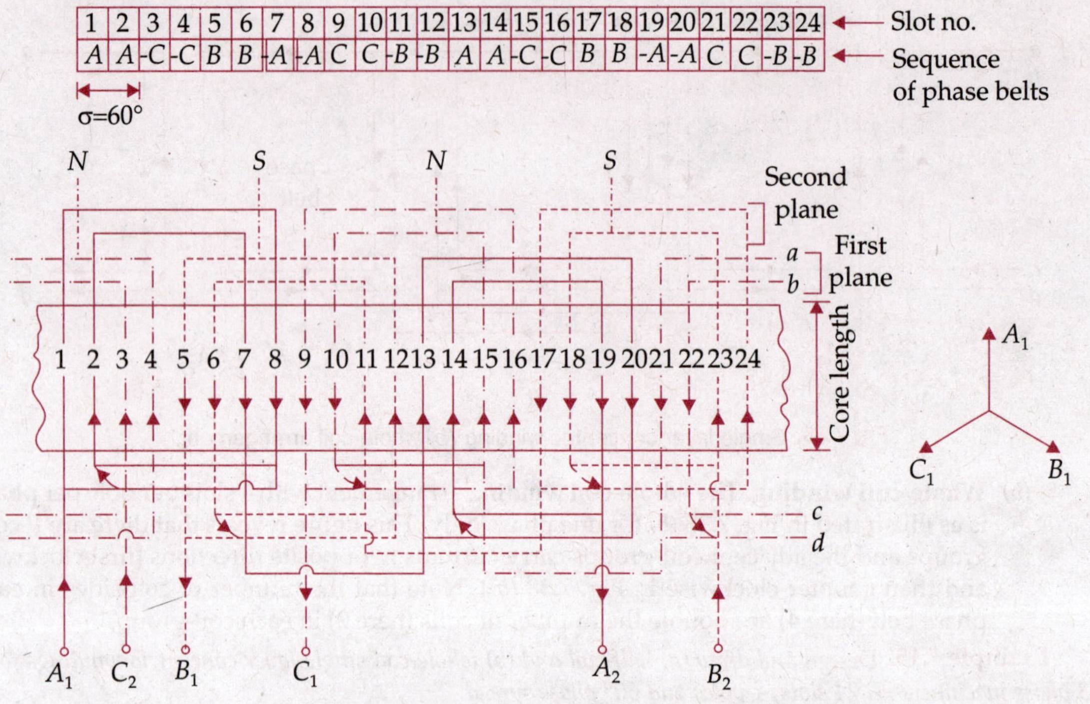

Fig 7.39: Half-coil winding diagram for 24 slots, 4 poles, 60° phase spread single-layer concentric winding (two-plane overhang).

For the sake of clarity, the inter-connections among the coils of phase C are not shown in Fig. 7.40. The bifurcated winding shown in Fig. 7.40 requires three-plane overhang.

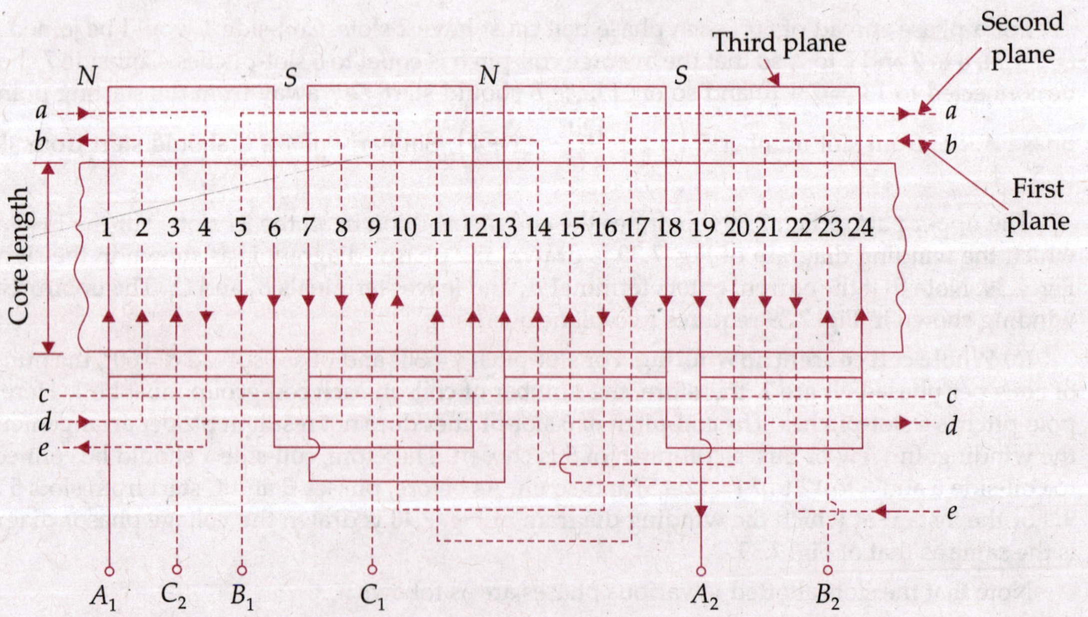

Fig 7.40: Whole-coil winding arrangement of 24 slots, 4 poles, 60° phase spread, single-layer concentric winding (three-plane overhang).

7.9.2. Mush Windings

For single-layer concentric windings, the coil-pitch is not the same for all the coils. However, in mush windings, the coil-pitch is the same for all the coils. The single-layer mush windings are sometimes employed for small 3-phase induction motors.

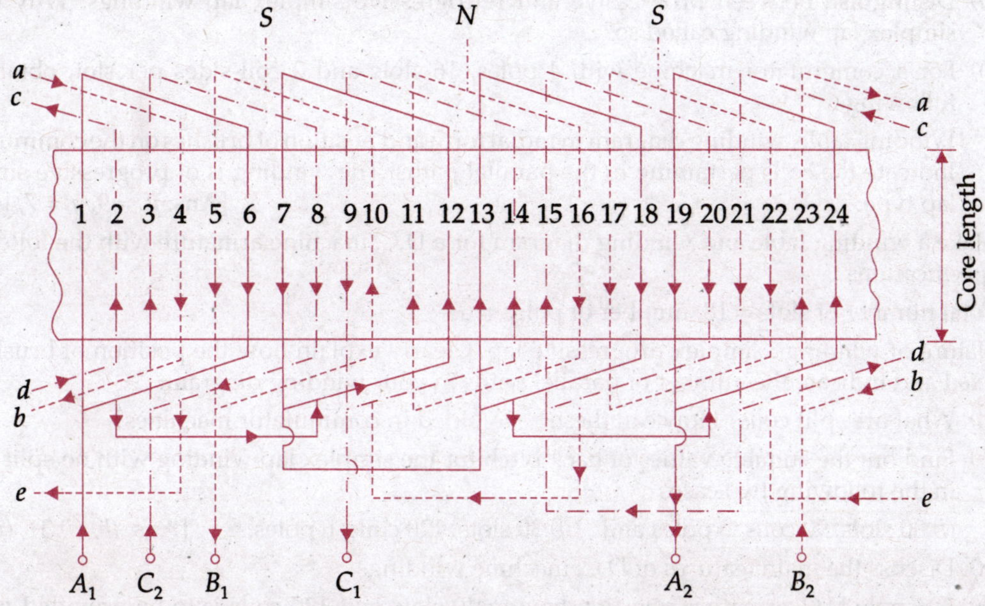

Fig 7.41: Single-layer mush winding diagram or 24 slots, 4 poles and 60° phase spread.

For mush winding, each coil is first wound on a trapezoidal shaped former. Then the short coil-sides are first fitted in alternate slots and the long coil-sides are inserted in the ramaining slots. Since the mush coils can be dropped conductor by conductor into the slots, this winding is suitable for semi-closed slots. If the end connections of the short coil-sides are bent to the left, then the end connections of adjacent long coil-sides are bent to the right. In other words, the end connections in adjacent slots are bent in opposite directions. In this winding, the number of slots per pole per phase must be a whole number. The coil-pitch is always odd. For example, for 24 slots, 4 poles, single-layer mush winding, the pole pitch is 6 slot-pitches. Since the coil-pitch must be odd, it can be taken as 5 or 7. Choosing here a coil-pitch of 5 slot-pitches (chorded coils are preferred), the winding arrangement for the 3-phase is as shown in Fig. 7.41, where for clarity sake, the inter-connections among phase *B* coils are not shown. Here $\gamma = 30°$ and for $\sigma = 60°$, 2 slots must belong to the same phase. For the instant shown in Fig. 7.41, the phasor diagram is the same as in Fig. 7.39.

Note that the method of mush coil inter-connection is the same as for the whole-coil concentric winding. Also note that coil ends of long coil-side 1 are bent to right and those of adjacent short coil-side 2 are bent to the left and so on. The slots allotted to the 3-phases are the same as given in Example 7.15 *(b)*.

PROBLEMS

7.1. *(a)* What are the two general types of armature windings and where are these used?

(b) Explain the following with respect to armature windings :

Conductor, turn, coil, coil-side, single-and double-layer windings, advantages of double-layer windings over single-layer windings, pole-pitch, coil-pitch, full-pitch windings and chorded windings.

7.2. (a) Distinguish between simplex lap and simplex wave windings so far as their construction and number of parallel paths are concerned.

(b) Explain the following with regard to commutator machines :
Numbering scheme, back pitch, front pitch, winding pitch and commutator pitch.

7.3. (a) Distinguish between progressive and retrogressive simplex lap windings. Why is the simplex lap winding called so?

(b) For a commutator machine with 4 poles, 16 slots and 2 coil-sides per slot, obtain the following :

Winding table, winding diagram in radial form and position of brushes on the commutator. Indicate the coils pertaining to the parallel paths. The winding is of progressive simplex lap type. **[Ans.** $y_b = 9, y_f = 7, y_c = 1$]

7.4. Make a winding table and winding diagram for a D.C. machine armature with the following specifications :

Total number of slots = 18, number of poles = 6

Nature of winding : simplex progressive lap. Clearly explain how the position of brushes is fixed and indicate the number of parallel paths in your winding diagram.

7.5. (a) What are split coils? How can these be avoided in commutator machines?

(b) Find out the suitable values of back pitch for the simplex lap winding with no split coils, in the following two cases :

(i) 30 slots, 90 coils, 6 poles and (ii) 30 slots, 120 coils, 6 poles. **[Ans.** (b) (i) 31, (ii) 41]

7.6. (a) Discuss the main features of D.C. machine windings.

(b) A 4-pole D.C. armature winding having 40 slots and 120 coils is to be provided with a simplex-lap winding. Work out a suitable arrangement so that split winding is not used.

7.7. (a) For a simplex wave winding, derive the following relations :

Commutator pitch, $y_c = \frac{C \pm 1}{P/2}$ and Winding pitch, $y_w = \frac{2C \pm 2}{P/2}$

(b) Design and draw a simplex wave winding with the following data :
4 poles, 15 slots, 2 coil-sides per slot, progressive winding.
Indicate the location of brushes on the winding diagram. Show the coils pertaining to the parallel paths also. **[Ans.** (b) $y_c = 8, y_w = 16, y_b = 9, y_f = 7$]

7.8. (a) Explain what is meant by a dummy coil. When does an armature have a dummy coil and what purpose is served by it?

(b) A standard armature with 37 slots and 147 commutator segments is to be used for a 4-pole winding with 1470 conductors. Discuss which type of winding should be employed for this armature. Then workout a suitable arrangement for this winding.

[Ans. (b) Turns per coil = 5, Actual coils = 148, Active coils = 147, y_c = 74 or 73, y_w = 148 or 146, y_b = 73 and y_f = 75 for progressive winding and y_b = 73 and y_f = 73 for retrogressive winding.]

7.9. (a) Enumerate the main point of distinction between simplex lap and simplex wave windings.

(b) A 20 kW, 250 V, 4-pole, lap-connected generator has 288 conductors with single-turn coils. If the armature connections to the commutator are changed to obtain a wave-winding, calculate its effect on current, voltage and power ratings of the machine.

[Hint. (b) Wave-winding would have one dummy coil.]

[Ans. (b) 40 A, 496.53 V, 19.8612 kW]

7.10. (a) What are the advantages of multiplex windings over simplex windings? Distinguish between duplex and triplex windings of both types.

(b) When are the circulating currents present in lap-connected armatures? Explain the causes of their existence.

7.11. (a) In the case of lap-connected armature, illustrate the detrimental effects of circulating currents with suitable diagrams.

(b) What is an equalizer ring? Explain how it performs its two functions?

7.12. (a) A 200 kW, 500 V, 10-pole D.C. machine is lap-wound. Find the current handled by each brush and each parallel path.

(b) A 4-pole D.C. machine has generated e.m.f. of 250 V. If this machine is re-wound with 8 poles, other things remaining unchanged, the magnitude of generated e.m.f. remains at 250 V. Is the machine wave or lap-wound?

(c) Work out a suitable arrangement of 10 equilizer rings for a commutator machine having 6 poles, 120 coils, simplex lap winding.

[Ans. *(a)* 80 A, 40 A *(b)* lap-wound *(c)* y_{eq} = 40 coils, y_{tp} = 4 coils]

7.13. (a) A simplex wave-wound 4-pole armature has 11 coils, each of resistance 0.1 Ω :

(i) What is the resistance measured between two adjacent commutator segments?

(ii) If one coil gets open-circuited or short-circuited, explain how it can be located.

(b) Number of poles, speed of rotation, voltage and power ratings are the same for two machines, one of which is lap-wound and the other is wave-wound. Show that the amount of copper required for the armature winding of each machine is the same.

[Hint. *(b)* Subscripts *L* and *W* are used to denote lap and wave windings respectively.

$$Z_L = \frac{E_a}{\phi n} \text{ and } Z_w = \frac{2}{P} \cdot \frac{E_a}{\phi n} = \frac{2}{P} \cdot Z_L$$

Area of conductor cross-section, $A_L = \frac{I}{a} \cdot \frac{1}{\delta} = \frac{I}{P} \cdot \frac{1}{\delta}$

Also $A_w = \frac{I}{2} \cdot \frac{1}{\delta} = \frac{P}{2} \cdot A_L$

Volume of copper for wave-winding = $A_w Z_w$ ...] **[Ans.** *(a) (i)* 0.16364 Ω *(ii)*0.9 Ω, 0.09 Ω]

7.14. (a) Explain why the number of turns per coil are limited in case of commutator machines.

(b) What would happen if the space of dummy coil is left unoccupied?

(c) Compare and discuss the use of simplex-lap and simplex-wave windings.

7.15. (a) Give the advantages of double-layer windings over single-layer windings.

(b) What are the essential conditions that polyphase windings must possess?

(c) Describe clearly the terms phase-belt and phase-spread as applied to A.C. armature windings, with the help of e.m.f. polygon.

7.16. (a) What are integral slot windings? Show that for full-pitch double layer integral slot winding, each slot contains coil-sides belonging to the same phase.

(b) Prove that a phase spread of 60° produces a sequence of *A*, – *C*, *B*, – *A*, *C*, – *B* in the phase belts, for a 3-phase voltage sequence of *ABC*.

(c) Prove that a phase spread of 120° produces a sequence of *ABC* in the phase-belts for *ABC* phase sequence of the 3-phase voltages.

7.17. (a) What are the merits of using chorded coils?

(b) A 48-slot stator is to be wound for 4-poles, 3-phase, double layer winding and 60° phase spread. Draw a clock diagram to show the position of the phase-belts in each layer for (i) full-pitch coils and (ii) 5/6 pole-pitch coils.

Show the inerconnections amongst the phase-belts of any phase indicating series and parallel schemes.

7.18. (a) What is fractional-slot winding? Why should its armature slots be divisible by 3 in case of 3-phase machines?

(b) Give the merits of fractional-slot windings. Are there any restrictions on this winding?

(c) What is characteristic ratio of fractional-slot windings and what does it signify?

(d) Design and draw a double layer winding for 42 slots, 10 poles, 3 phases and 60° phase spread. Indicate the start of each phase. Show the inter-connection amongst the coils of any one phase.

7.19. (a) Explain whether chorded coils and fractional-slot windings are possible in a single-layer winding.

(b) Design and draw a double-layer winding with 90 slots, 8 poles, 3 phases and 60° phase spread. Indicate the start of each phase. Show the inter-connection amongst the coils of any one phase.

7.20. Justify the following statements :

(a) A phase spread of 60° is more commonly used than a phase spread of 120° in 3-phase machines.

(b) The windings are usually short-pitched.

(c) Fractional-slot windings are quite common in 3-phase A.C. machines.

(d) Fractional-slot winding is not possible if P_k, in the characteristic ratio S_k/P_k, is a multiple of three.

7.21. (a) Prepare a winding table for the armature of a 3-phase machine with the following specifications :

36 slots, double-layer winding, 4 poles, narrow-spread and coil-span = pole-pitch.

Indicate the upper coil-side by n and lower coil-side by n' for nth slot ($1 < n < 36$).

(b) Draw the detailed winding diagram for one phase only clearly showing the connection of different coil groups.

(c) Show the star of coil-e.m.fs. Draw phasor diagram for narrow-spead connections of the 3-phase winding showing coil e.m.fs. for phases A and C only.

7.22. (a) Make a winding table for the armature of a 3-phase machine having the following data :

54 slots, 8 poles, narrow-spread, coil-span = 6.

Name the upper coil-side as n and lower coil-side as n' for the nth slot.

(b) Draw the coil-e.m.f. star for phase A only.

7.23. (a) Distinguish between single-layer concentric and mush windings.

(b) Why are the concentric windings so called? Distinguish between half-coiled and whole-coiled armature windings.

(c) For the same phase voltage, how many turns per coil are there for the whole-coiled winding with respect to the number in a half-coiled winding.

(*d*) Define a coil-group. How are the coils in such a group connected?

(*e*) Explain how the number of coils in a coil-group are determined for half-coil as well as whole-coil windings?

(*f*) Explain how the successive coil-groups are connected in the unbifurcated and bifurcated windings.

[**Ans.** (*c*) Number of coils in whole-coil winding are double of that in the half-coil winding. Therefore, for the same voltage and consequently for the same phase turns, the number of turns per coil in a whole-coil winding is half the number of turns in a half-coil winding.]

7.24. (*a*) Explain how the mush winding is fitted in the armature slots.

(*b*) What is the similarity between whole-coil and mush windings.

(*c*) Design and draw a mush winding for a 3-phase machine with 36 slots, 4 poles, 60° phase spread.

A
Appendix

Magnetic Circuits

Introduction

Coupling magnetic field exists in transformers and practically in all the rotating electrical machinery. In low-power electrical machines, magnetic field may be produced by permanent magnets. But in high-power electrical machinery and transformers, coupling magnetic field is produced by electric current. Thus, an elementary knowledge of the analysis of magnetic circuits is necessary for understanding the working of these devices. The object of this appendix is to develop some basic techniques for the analysis of magnetic-field systems.

A.1 INTRODUCTION TO MAGNETIC CIRCUITS

The complete closed path followed by the lines of flux is called a *magnetic circuit*. Some important terms relating to the study of magnetic circuits are discussed here.

(i) **Magnetomotive force (m.m.f.).** In an electric circuit, the current is due to the presence of electromotive force. By analogy, in a magnetic circuit, the magnetic flux is due to the presence of a *magnetomotive force.*The m.m.f. is created by a current flowing through one or more turns. This shows that m.m.f. is equal to the product of current and the number of turns in the coil.

$\therefore$ m.m.f., $\quad F = NI$ ampere-turns (or ATs)

For the purpose of dimensional analysis, it is expressed in amperes, since the number of turns is a dimensionless quantity. In Fig. A.1, a current of I amperes flows through a coil of N turns. This coil therefore produces m.m.f. = IN ATs.

In this figure, *abcda* is the closed path followed by magnetic flux lines. An examination of coil reveals that there are five turns, *i.e.* $N = 5$ in Fig. A.1. The direction of magnetic flux produced by coil in Fig. A.1 is given by the right-hand grip rule : grip the core *da* by fingers of right hand along the direction of current, the thumb gives the direction of magnetic flux.

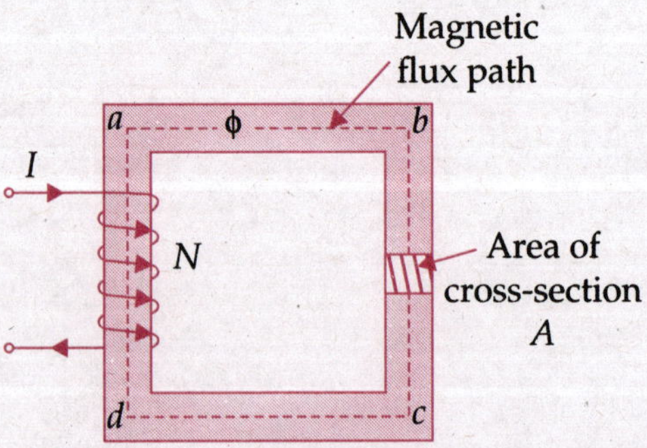

Fig A.1: A simple magnetic circuit with N turns and current I.

(ii) **Magnetic field intensity.** If the magnetic circuit of Fig. A.1 is homogeneous and of uniform cross-sectional area, the magnetomotive force per unit length of magnetic circuit is termed as the *magnetic field intensity*, its usual symbol is H. If l is the mean length of magnetic circuit *abcda* in Fig. A.1, then

$$H = \frac{IN}{l} = \frac{F}{l} \text{ ampere-turns/metre} \qquad \text{[or ATs/m]}$$

(iii) **Permeability of free space.** Suppose a long straight conductor x carries a current I amperes, Fig. A.2. The direction of current is indicated by cross showing that current is away from the observer. The flux lines, given by right-hand grip rule, are in the clockwise direction around the conductor as shown in Fig. A.2. The right-hand grip rule used here is the same as stated above. Therefore, another equivalent way of stating the right-hand grip rule is : with right hand grip the conductor with thumb pointing in the direction of conductor current, the four fingers give the direction of magnetic flux created by the current.

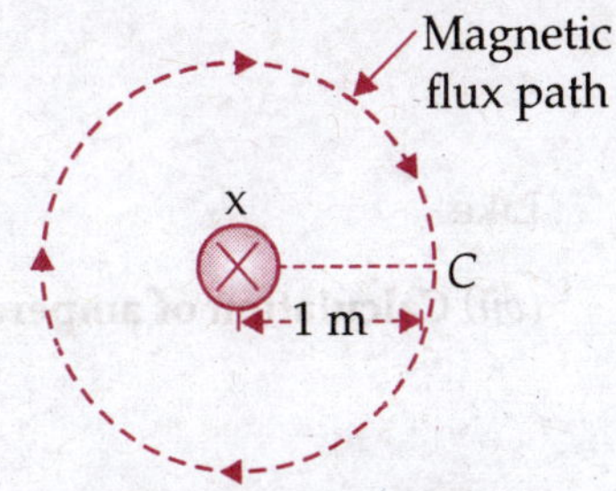

Fig A.2: Pertaining to permeability of free space.

Suppose flux density at C, caused by magnetic field intensity H at x, is B tesla and if C is one metre away from x, then permeability of free space μ_o is given by

$$\mu_o = \frac{B}{H}$$

Note that conductor x and point C are in vacuum (free space), in air or in any other non-magnetic medium.

$$\therefore \quad \mu_o = \frac{B}{H} \text{ for vacuum or non-magnetic materials}$$

$$= 4\pi \times 10^{-7} \text{ henries/m}$$

(iv) **Reluctance.** The opposition offered by the magnetic circuit to magnetic flux is called *reluctance.* Reluctance is analogous to resistance in electric circuit. Just as resistance $R = \rho.l/a$, reluctance Rl is given by

$$Rl = \frac{l}{\mu.A} \text{ AT/Wb} \quad \text{...(A.1)}$$

where l = length of the magnetic path, m

A = area of cross-section normal to flux path, m^2

$\mu = \mu_o \cdot \mu_r$ = permeability (or absolute permeability) of the magnetic material

μ_r = relative permeability of the magnetic material

μ_o = permeability of free space = $4\pi \times 10^{-7}$ H/m

Since resistance $R = \dfrac{l}{\left(\frac{1}{\rho}\right) A}$, absolute permeability μ is analogous to conductivity $\left(\frac{1}{\rho}\right)$.

(v) **Permeance.** Reciprocal of reluctance is called permeance, symbol $\wedge$.

$$\therefore \quad \text{Permeance} = \frac{1}{\text{reluctance}} = \frac{\mu_o \mu_r A}{l} \text{ Wb/AT}$$

(iv) **Magnetic flux and flux density.** Magnetic flux is analogous to current in an electric circuit. As current I = e.m.f/resistance, flux ϕ in webers in a magnetic circuit is given by

$$\phi = \frac{\text{m.m.f.}}{\text{reluctance}} \text{ Wb} \quad \text{...(A.2)}$$

In Fig. A.1, $\quad Rl = \dfrac{l}{\mu_o \mu_r A}$

and m.m.f., $\quad F = IN$

the magnetic flux ϕ is given by $\quad \phi = \dfrac{IN \cdot \mu_o \mu_r \cdot A}{l}$ Wb

Magnetic flux density B is defined as the magnetic flux per unit cross-sectional area of the core. Its unit is Wb/m^2 or Tesla (T).

$$\therefore \qquad B = \frac{\text{magnetic flux}, \phi}{\text{core area}, A} = \frac{IN \cdot \mu_o \mu_r}{l} \qquad \text{...(A.3)}$$

Like $\qquad R = \dfrac{E}{I}$ V/A or Ω, we have $Rl = \dfrac{F}{\phi}$ AT/Wb

(vii) **Calculation of ampere-turns.** In any magnetic circuit, flux ϕ is given by

$$\phi = \frac{\text{m.m.f.}}{\text{reluctance}} = \frac{F \cdot \mu A}{l}$$

Ampere turns required for the magnetic circuit, $F = \phi \times$ Reluctance

$$= \phi \times \frac{l}{\mu A} = \frac{\phi}{A} \cdot \frac{l}{\mu} = \frac{B}{\mu} \cdot l = H \cdot l \qquad \left[\because H = \frac{B}{\mu}\right]$$

= Magnetic field intensity H in AT/m in that part of circuit × length l of that part normal to flux path ... (A.4)

A.2. COMPARISON BETWEEN MAGNETIC AND ELECTRIC CIRCUITS

There are many similarities in magnetic and electric circuits.

The reader is usually more conversant with electric circuits. Thus, a comparison of electric and magnetic circuits in tabular form goes a long way in the better understanding of magnetic circuits.

Table A.1

Electric Circuit	*Magnetic Circuit*
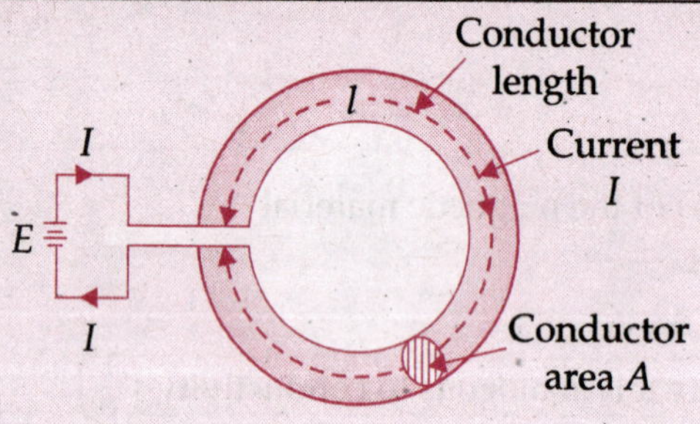 A toroidal copper ring length l, cross-sectional area A is connected to e.m.f. E so that current I flows.	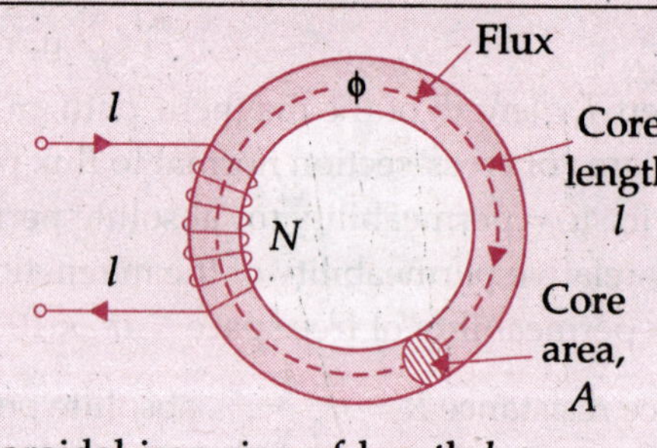 A toroidal iron ring of length l, core area A is excited by a coil of N turns carrying I amperes so that flux ϕ is produced.
Similarities	
1. Closed path for the electric current is called an electric circuit.	1. Closed path for the magnetic flux is called a magnetic circuit.
2. Driving force is e.m.f. E, volts	2. Driving force is m.m.f. $F = IN$ ATs
3. Resistance, $R = \dfrac{\rho \cdot l}{A}$ V/A or Ω	3. Reluctance, $Rl = \dfrac{l}{\mu A}$ AT/Wb
4. Equivalent circuit : 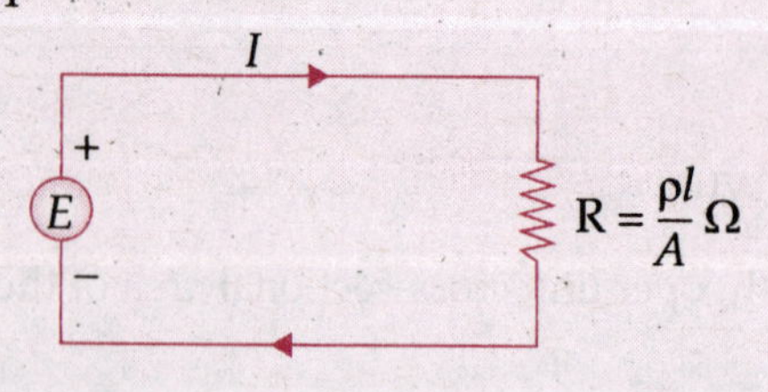	4. Equivalent circuit : 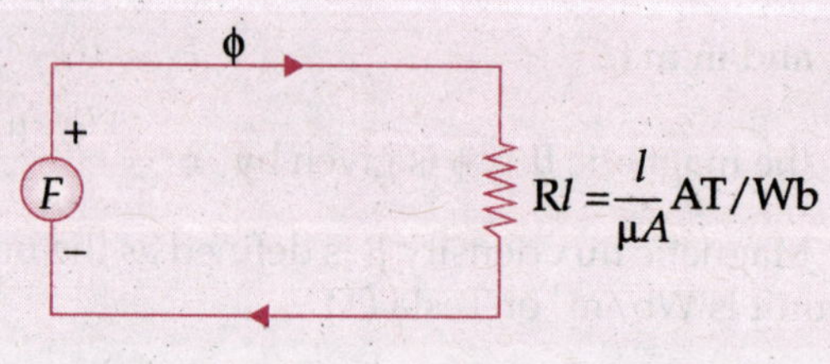

5. Current, $I = \dfrac{\text{driving force}}{\text{resistance}}$ or $I = \dfrac{E}{R}$ A	5. Magnetic flux, $\phi = \dfrac{\text{driving force}}{\text{reluctance}}$ or $\phi = \dfrac{F}{Rl}$ Wb
6. Current density, $J = \dfrac{I}{A}$ A/m^2	6. Magnetic flux density, $B = \dfrac{\phi}{A}$ T (or Wb/m^2)
7. Electric field intensity, $\varepsilon = \dfrac{E}{l}$ V/m Also $\varepsilon = \dfrac{E}{l} = \dfrac{IR}{l} = \dfrac{I}{l} \cdot \dfrac{\rho \cdot l}{A} = \rho \cdot \dfrac{I}{A}$ or $\varepsilon = \rho \cdot J$ V/m	7. Magnetic field intensity, $H = \dfrac{IN}{l}$ AT/m Also $H = \dfrac{IN}{l} = \dfrac{F}{l} = \dfrac{\phi \cdot Rl}{l} = \dfrac{\phi}{l} \cdot \dfrac{l}{\mu A} = \dfrac{1}{\mu} \cdot \dfrac{\phi}{A}$ or $H = \dfrac{1}{\mu} \cdot B$ AT/m
8. Conductivity of current path, $\sigma = \dfrac{1}{\rho}$ so that $J = \sigma . \varepsilon$ A/m^2	8. Permeability of magnetic circuit, μ so that $B = \mu H$ Wb/m^2 or T
Dissimilarities	
1. The electric current actually flows in an electric circuit. For the existence of this current, energy is drawn from the source continuously. This energy gets dissipated in resistance in the form of heat.	1. Strictly speaking, magnetic flux does not flow. Energy is needed for establishing the required flux. Once the requisite flux is created, no more energy is needed in maintaining it.
2. Electrical insulator confines the current to well defined paths.	2. There are no magnetic insulators. Even in the best known magnetic insulator air, the flux can be established.

Example A.1. *A mild steel ring has a mean diameter of 20 cm and a cross-sectional area of 50 cm^2. For a relative permeability of 800, calculate (a) reluctance of the ring and (b) current required in 200-turn coil to produce a flux of 1 mWb in the ring.*

Solution. *(a)* Reluctance $= \dfrac{l}{\mu_o \mu_r A}$. Here $l = \pi D = \pi \times 20$ cm, $A = 50$ cm^2

$$\therefore \quad Rl = \frac{\pi \times 20 \times 10^{-2}}{4\pi \times 10^{-7} \times 800 \times 50 \times 10^{-4}} = 1.25 \times 10^6 \text{ AT/Wb}$$

(b) From Eq. (A.2),
$$1 \times 10^{-3} = \frac{m.m.f.}{1.25 \times 10^6}$$

$\therefore$ m.m.f.,
$$F = 1 \times 10^{-3} \times 1.25 \times 10^6 = 1250 \text{ ATs.}$$

$\therefore$ Current in the coil,
$$I = \frac{F}{N} = \frac{1250}{200} = 6.25 \text{ A}$$

A.3. SERIES AND PARALLEL MAGNETIC CIRCUITS

Like electric circuits, a magnetic circuit may be made up of a series circuit, a parallel circuit or a combination of series-parallel circuits. Such magnetic circuits may be excited by one or more coils. Solution of such magnetic-circuit configurations can be obtained by applying Kirchhoff's m.m.f. or Kirchhoff's flux laws.

A.3.1. Series Magnetic Circuit

Just like a series electric circuit, a series magnetic circuit carries the same flux ϕ in each part of the circuit configuration. Fig. A.3 shows a composite magnetic circuit consisting of three different magnetic materials in series. There is also an air gap as shown. The dimensions are indicated in Fig. A.3. Since the same flux ϕ exists through each part of the magnetic circuit in Fig. A.3, the total reluctance is equal to the sum of four individual circuit reluctances as under :

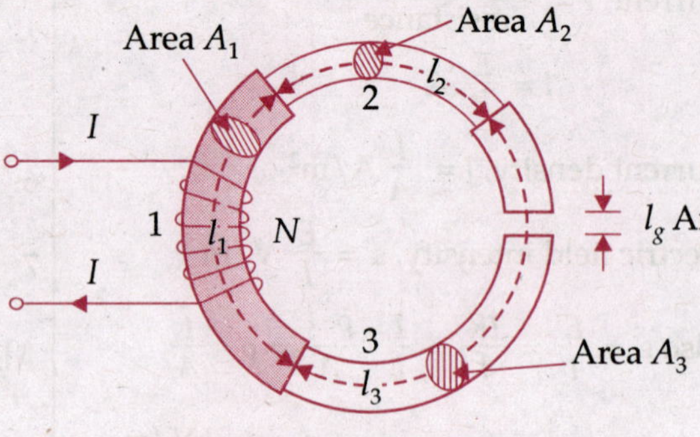

Fig A.3: Composite magnetic circuit

$$\text{Total reluctance,} \quad Rl = \frac{l_1}{\mu_0\mu_{r1}A_1} + \frac{l_2}{\mu_0\mu_{r2}\cdot A_2} + \frac{l_3}{\mu_0\mu_{r3}\cdot A_3} + \frac{l_g}{\mu_0\cdot A_g}$$

Note that μ_r for air is one.

$\therefore$ Total m.m.f. = flux × total reluctance of the series circuit

$$= \phi\left[\frac{l_1}{\mu_0\mu_{r1}\cdot A_1} + \frac{l_2}{\mu_0\mu_{r2}\cdot A_2} + \frac{l_3}{\mu_0\mu_{r3}\cdot A_3} + \frac{l_g}{\mu_0\cdot A_g}\right]$$

$$= \frac{\phi}{A_1}\cdot\frac{l_1}{\mu_0\cdot\mu_{r1}} + \frac{\phi}{A_2}\cdot\frac{l_2}{\mu_0\cdot\mu_{r2}} + \frac{\phi}{A_3}\cdot\frac{l_3}{\mu_0\cdot\mu_{r3}} + \frac{\phi}{A_g}\cdot\frac{l_g}{\mu_0}$$

$$= \frac{B_1}{\mu_0\cdot\mu_{r1}}\cdot l_1 + \frac{B_2}{\mu_0\cdot\mu_{r2}}\cdot l_2 + \frac{B_3}{\mu_0\cdot\mu_{r3}}\cdot l_3 + \frac{B_g}{\mu_0}\cdot l_g$$

$$= H_1\cdot l_1 + H_2\cdot l_2 + H_3\cdot l_3 + H_g\cdot A_g \quad \text{...(A.5 a)}$$

$$\therefore \text{Total m.m.f.,} \quad IN = \text{m.m.f. for magnetic path of length } [l_1 + l_2 + l_3 + l_g] \quad \text{...(A.5 b)}$$

Eq. (A.5*a*) may be re-written as under : $IN - H_1l_1 - H_2l_2 - H_3l_3 - H_gl_g = 0$

In general, Σ m.m.f. around a closed magnetic circuit = 0.

But this statement is similar to Kirchhoff's voltage law for a series electric circuit. Therefore, *Kirchoff's m.m.f. law* for a series magnetic circuit is as under :

Kirchhoff's m.m.f. law (KML) states that algebraic sum of m.m.fs. rises (or falls) taken in a specified direction in a closed magnetic circuit is zero.

A.3.2. Parallel Magnetic Circuit

Consider a parallel magnetic circuit shown in Fig. A.4 *(a)*. Coil *N* carrying a current *I* produces a flux ϕ_1 in path *EFAB*. At point *B*, flux ϕ_1 gets divided into two paths, ϕ_2 and ϕ_3 such that

$$\phi_1 = \phi_2 + \phi_3 \quad \text{or} \quad \phi_1 - \phi_2 - \phi_3 = 0$$

$$\text{In general,} \quad \sum\phi = 0$$

The above statement is similar to Kirchhoff's current law. Therefore, for a magnetic circuit also, total magnetic flux towards a junction is equal to the total magnetic flux away from that junction. In other words, algebraic sum of magnetic fluxes at a junction is zero-this is called *Kirchhoff's flux law* (KFL).

In Fig. A.4 *(a)*, if reluctance of path $EFAB = Rl_1$

reluctance of path $BE = Rl_2$

and reluctance of path $BCDE = Rl_3$,

then equivalent magnetic circuit of Fig. A.4 *(b)* is obtained. From this circuit, it is seen that

total coil m.m.f., $F = IN$ = m.m.f required for path [$EFAB + BE$]

$\therefore \quad IN = \phi_1 Rl_1 + \phi_2 Rl_2$

Also, $F = IN$ = m.m.f. required for path [$EFAB + BCDE$]

$\therefore \quad IN = \phi_1 Rl_1 + \phi_3 Rl_3$

Fig. A.4 *(c)* gives the equivalent electric circuit.

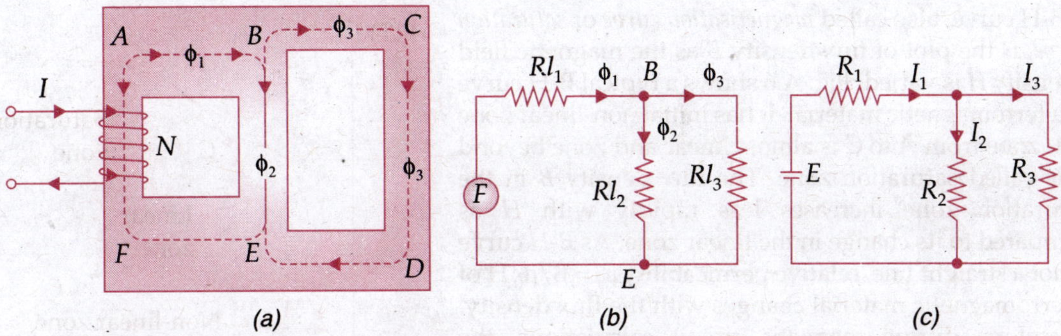

Fig A.4: *(a)* Parallel magnetic circuit. Its equivalent *(b)* magnetic circuit and *(c)* electric circuit.

A.4. LEAKAGE FLUX AND FRINGING

All practical magnetic circuits are so designed that most of the flux produced by an exciting coil is confined to the desired magnetic path of low reluctance. However, a small amount of flux does follow a path through the surrounding air. Fig. A.5 shows a magnetic circuit with a ferromagnetic core. The flux which returns by such paths as *a, b, c* is called *leakage flux*. It does not follow the intended path. Therefore, *leakage flux may be defined as that flux which does not follow the intended path in a magnetic circuit*. Leakage flux does exist in all practical electromagnetic devices. Its effect on the analysis of electrical machinery is carried out by replacing it by an equivalent leakage reactance.

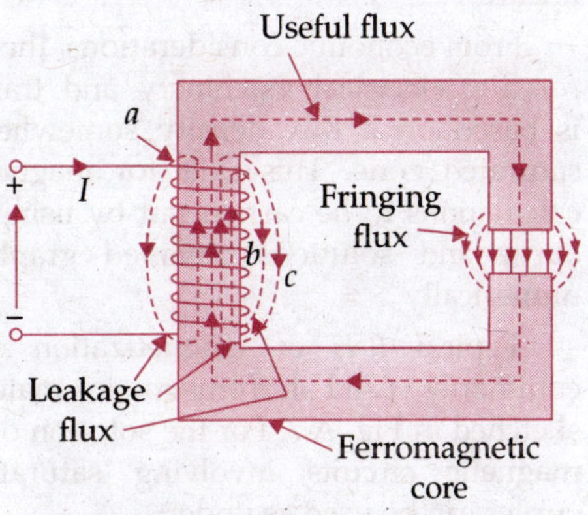

Fig A.5: Fringing of the flux across air gap. Useful and leakage fluxes are also shown.

It is seen from Fig. A.5 that total flux through the exciting winding = usuful flux + leakage flux. A term *leakage factor* gives a measure of the leakage flux. It is defined as

$$\text{Leakage factor} = \frac{\text{Total flux handled by the exciting winding}}{\text{Useful flux}}$$

The value of leakage factor in electrical machinery is in the range of 1.15 to 1.25.

As the magnetic flux lines cross the air gap, these bulge out as shown in Fig. A.5. This bulging out of the flux is called fringing.* Longer the air gap, more is the flux fringing. The effect of fringing flux is to increase the effective cross-sectional area of the air gap. As a result, flux density in the air gap is not uniform and average flux density gets reduced.

* Fringing is like the girl's hair cut short and allowed to hang over her forehead

The effect of fringing can be taken into account empirically by adding one gap length to each of the linear dimensions making up the gap area. For example, if core dimensions are a and b and small gap length is l_g, then effective gap area taking fringing into consideration is $A_g = [(a + l_g) \times (b + l_g)] >$ core area $A_c = a \cdot b$. If core is circular of radius r, then effective gap area $A_g = [\pi(r + l_g)^2] >$ core area $A_c = \pi r^2$.

A.5. B-H CURVE

A B-H curve, also called *magnetisation curve* or *saturation curve*, is the plot of flux density B as the magnetic field intensity H is varied. Fig. A.6 shows a typical B-H curve of a ferromagnetic material. It has initial non-linear zone OA, zone from A to C is almost linear and zone beyond C is called saturation zone. The flux density B in the saturation zone increases less rapidly with H as compared to its change in the linear zone. As B-H curve is not a straight line, relative permeability $\mu_r = B/\mu_0 H$ of a ferromagnetic material changes with the flux density. Therefore, during magnetic circuit calculations, the value of μ_r and H should correspond to the flux density under consideration. In free space or non-magnetic materials, μ_0 is constant, therefore B-H relationship is linear.

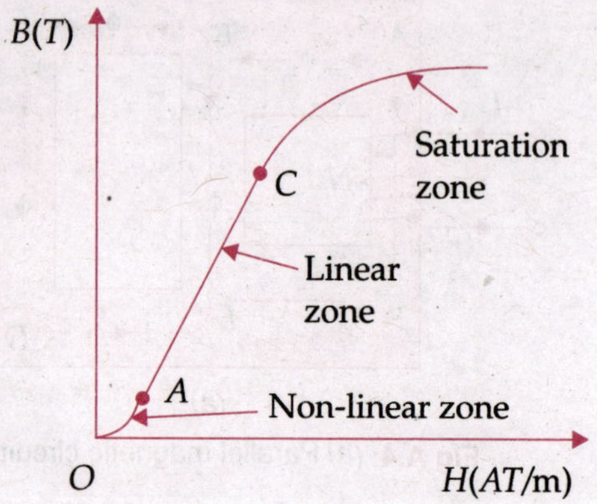

Fig A.6: Typical magnetization curve of a ferromagnetic material.

From economic considerations, the design of rotating electrical machinery and transformers is based on a flux density somewhere in the saturated zone. This calls for magnetic-circuit calculations to be carried out by using real B-H curve and solutions obtained graphically or numerically.

Typical B-H or magnetization curves of commonly used ferromagnetic materials are sketched in Fig. A.7. For the solution of practical magnetic circuits involving saturation, B-H curves can be used as under:

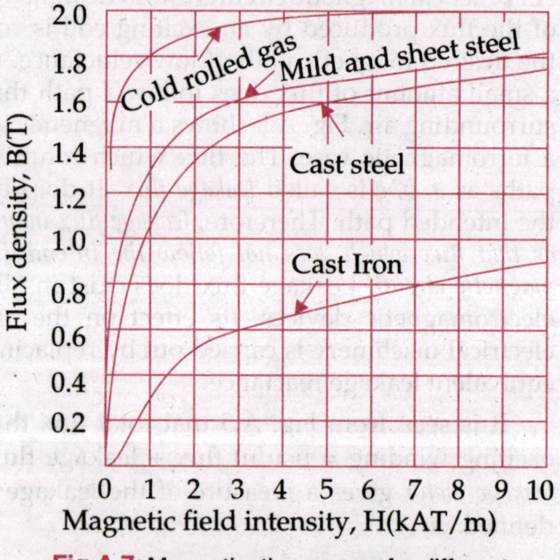

Fig A.7: Magnetization curves for different ferromagnetic materials.

(i) For the magnetic path, flux density B is calculated.

(ii) Corresponding to the above value of calculated B and the core material, find the value of H from the B-H curves of Fig. A.7.

(iii) Find the length l of the magnetic circuit where B is the flux density.

(iv) m.m.f. required for that part of the magnetic circuit = $H \times l$ ATs.

Example A.2. *The magnetic circuit of Fig. A.5 has cross-sectional area of core = 5 × 5 cm², core length = 50 cm, gap length = 4 mm and N = 600 turns. For producing a flux density of 1.2 T, find the exciting current in the coil. Assume relative permeability of iron = 10,000 and neglect fringing.*

Solution. It is seen from Eq. (A.5) that

m.m.f., $IN = H_1 l$ (for iron core) + $H_2 \cdot l_g$ (for air gap)

$$= \frac{B}{\mu_0\mu_r} \cdot l + \frac{B}{\mu_0} \cdot l_g = \frac{B}{\mu_0}\left[\frac{l}{\mu_r} + l_g\right]$$

or
$$600 \times I = \frac{1.2}{4\pi \times 10^{-7}}\left[\frac{50 \times 10^{-2}}{10{,}000} + 4 \times 10^{-3}\right]$$

∴ Exciting current in the coil is given by

$$I = \frac{1.2}{4\pi \times 10^{-7} \times 600}\,[(5 + 400)\,10^{-5}] = 6.446 \text{ A}$$

It may be noted from above that $\dfrac{\text{Reluctance of air gap}}{\text{Reluctance of iron path}} = \dfrac{400}{5} = 80.$

In other words, reluctance of air-gap is 80 times the reluctance of iron path in this example.

Example A.3. *For the magnetic circuit shown in Fig. A.8, l_c = 50 cm, A_c = 2.85 cm dia, l_g = 2 mm and N = 500. Air-gap flux = 0.8 mWb.*

(a) Find the exciting current in the coil in case μ_r = 500. Neglect magnetic leakage and fringing.

(b) Repeat part (a) if flux fringing at air gap is taken into account.

(c) Calculate the exciting current in the coil if magnetization curve for the magnetic circuit has the following data :

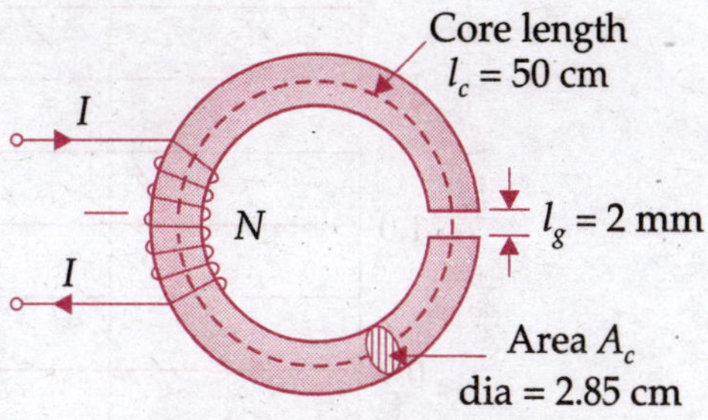

Fig A.8: Pertaining to Example A.3.

H (AT/m)	*1500*	*2210*	*2720*	*3500*	*4100*
B (T)	*0.90*	*1.10*	*1.20*	*1.275*	*1.30*

Neglect magnetic leakage and fringing.

Solution. *(a)* Air-gap length, l_g = 2 mm, μ_r = 500, core area $A_c = \frac{\pi}{4} \times 2.85^2$ cm^2

Gap reluctance, $$Rl_g = \frac{l_g}{\mu_0 A_c} = \frac{2 \times 10^{-3} \times 4}{4\pi \times 10^{-7} \times \pi (2.85)^2 \times 10^{-4}} = 24.9483 \times 10^5 \text{ AT/Wb}$$

Iron-core reluctance $$Rl_c = \frac{l_c}{\mu_0 \cdot \mu_r \cdot A_c} = \frac{50 \times 10^{-2} \times 4}{4\pi \times 10^{-7} \times 500 \times \pi \times (2.85)^2 \times 10^{-4}}$$
$$= 12.474 \times 10^5 \text{ AT/Wb}$$

Total reluctance, $$Rl = Rl_g + Rl_c = 37.4223 \times 10^5 \text{ AT/Wb}$$

But m.m.f. = flux × reluctance

∴ $$I = \frac{\phi \cdot Rl}{N} = \frac{0.8 \times 10^{-3} \times 37.4223 \times 10^5}{500} = 5.9876 \text{ A}$$

(b) When flux fringing is taken into account, the effective gap area A_g

$$= \frac{\pi}{4}(d + 2g)^2 = \pi (r + g)^2 = \pi\left[\frac{2.85}{2} + 0.2\right]^2 = \pi \times 1.625^2 \text{ cm}^2$$

Air-gap reluctance, $$Rl_g = \frac{l_g}{\mu_0 \cdot A_g} = \frac{2 \times 10^{-3}}{4\pi \times 10^{-7} \times \pi \times 1.625^2 \times 10^{-4}} = 19.185 \times 10^5 \text{ AT/Wb}$$

$$I = \frac{\phi}{N}[Rl_c + Rl_g]$$

∴ Coil current, $$I = \frac{0.8 \times 10^{-3}}{500}[12.474 + 19.185] \times 10^5 = 5.0654 \text{ A}$$

(c) As fringing is neglected,

air-gap area A_g = core area $A_c = \pi \dfrac{2.85^2}{4}$ cm^2

Air-gap flux density, $B_g = \dfrac{\phi}{A_c} = \dfrac{0.8 \times 10^{-3} \times 4}{\pi(2.85)^2 \times 10^{-4}} = 1.254$ T

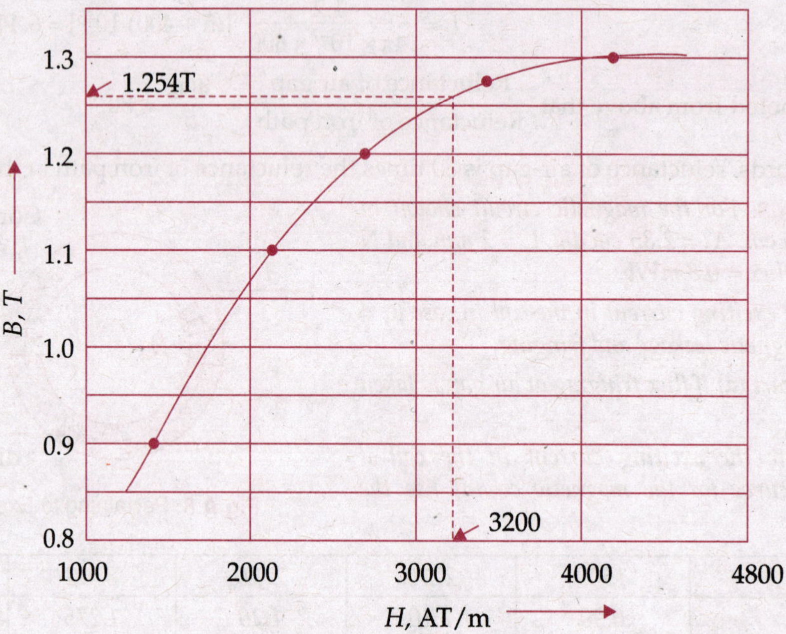

Fig A.9: Pertaining to Example A.3.

Air-gap m.m.f. $AT_g = \dfrac{B_g}{\mu_0} \cdot l_g = \dfrac{1.254}{4\pi \times 10^{-7}} \times 2 \times 10^{-3} = 1995.8$ ATs.

From the magnetization curve plotted in Fig. A.9, for core flux density $B_c = 1.254$ T, magnetic field intensity $H_c = 3200$ ATs/m.

$\therefore$ m.m.f. for core, $AT_c = H_c \times l_c = 3200 \times 0.5 = 1600$ ATs

Total m.m.f. required $= AT_g + AT_c = 1995.8 + 1600 = 3595.8$ ATs

$\therefore$ Exciting current, $I = \dfrac{3595.8}{500} = 7.192$ A.

Example A.4. *A magnetic circuit of cast steel is arranged as shown in Fig. A.10. Various dimensions are also indicated in the figure. The exciting coil, with N = 1000 turns, sets up a flux of 1 m Wb in the central limb. Find the coil current if, for cast steel,*

(a) $\mu_r = \infty$ and (b) $\mu_r = 6000$

Neglect fringing and leakage.

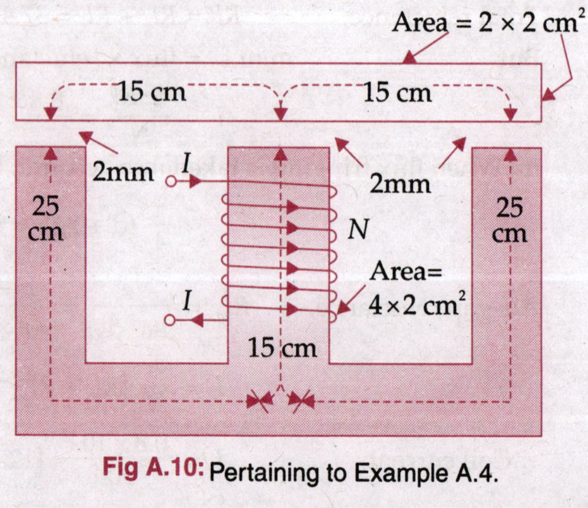

Fig A.10: Pertaining to Example A.4.

Solution. (a) When relative permeability $\mu_r = \infty$, the reluctance offered by cast steel is zero and therefore no m.m.f. (= flux × reluctance) is required by the steel. Reluctance is offered by the air gaps alone. Reluctance Rl_1 offered by each of the air gaps in outer limbs is

$$Rl_1 = \frac{2\times10^{-3}}{4\pi\times10^{-7}\times4\times10^{-4}} = 3.98\times10^6 \text{ AT/Wb}$$

Reluctance Rl_2 offered by air gap in central limb is

$$Rl_2 = \frac{2\times10^{-3}}{4\pi\times10^{-7}\times8\times10^{-4}} = 1.99\times10^6 \text{ AT/Wb}$$

The electrical analog of the magnetic circuit of Fig. A.10 is shown in Fig. A.11 *(a)*. As two reluctances Rl_1 are in parallel, their resultant is $Rl_1/2$ and the circuit gets reduced to that shown in Fig. A.11 *(b)*. For this circuit, Kirchhoff's m.m.f. law gives

$$NI - \text{flux}\left(Rl_2 + \frac{Rl_1}{2}\right) = 0$$

or $\quad 1000\times I = 1\times10^{-3}\,[1.99 + 1.99]\times10^6$

$$\therefore \quad I = \frac{1\times10^{-3}[3.98]\times10^6}{1000} = 3.98 \text{ A}$$

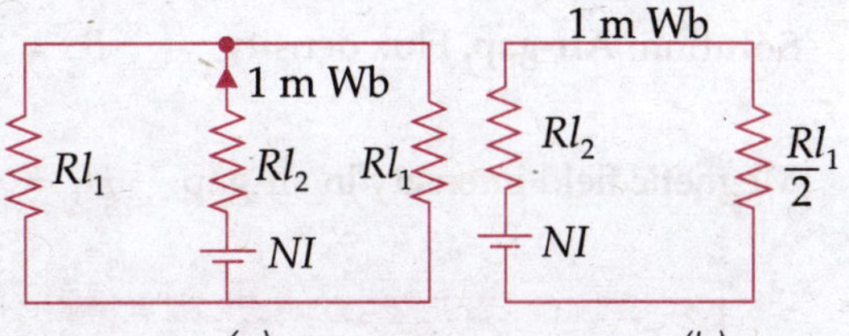

Fig A.11: *(a)* and *(b)*. Electrical analog of magnetic circuit of Fig. A.10.

(b) Relative permeability, $\mu_r = 6000$. Here reluctance of the cast steel cannot be neglected. The electrical analog of the magnetic circuit of Fig. A.10 is now drawn in Fig. A.12 *(a)*, where Rl_{c1} is the reluctance of each of the outer two steel limbs and Rl_{c2} is the reluctance of the central steel core.

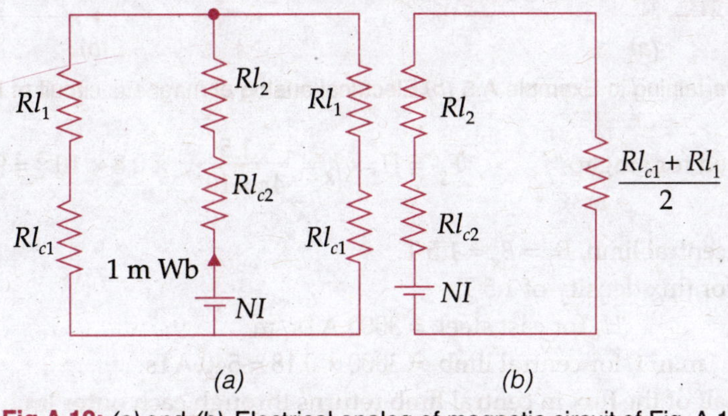

Fig A.12: *(a)* and *(b)*. Electrical analog of magnetic circuit of Fig. A.10.

Reluctance of outer steel core (including the top 15 cm)

$$Rl_{c1} = \frac{(0.25+0.15)}{4\pi\times10^{-7}\times6000\times4\times10^{-4}} = 1.33\times10^5 \text{ AT/Wb}$$

For central steel core, $$Rl_{c2} = \frac{0.15}{4\pi\times10^{-7}\times6000\times8\times10^{-4}} = 0.25\times10^5 \text{ AT/Wb}$$

Resultant of outer reluctances $$= \frac{Rl_1 + Rl_{c1}}{2}\quad\frac{(1.33+39.8)\times10^5}{2} = 20.565\times10^5 \text{ AT/Wb}$$

Fig. A.12 (a) is redrawn in Fig. A.12 (b) for which Kirchhoff's m.m.f. law gives

$$NI - \phi\left[Rl_{c2} + Rl_2 + \frac{Rl_{c1}+Rl_1}{2}\right]$$

or $$IN = 1 \times 10^{-3} [0.25 + 19.9 + 20.565] \times 10^5$$

∴ Exciting current, $$I = \frac{1 \times 10^{-3}}{1000} [40.715 \times 10^5] = 4.072 \text{ A}$$

Example A.5. *A magnetic circuit made of cast steel is shown in Fig. A.13 (a). Central limb has N = 500 turns. Dimensions in mms are indicated in the figure. Cross-sectional area of central limb is 600 mm² and that of each of the two outer limbs is 375 mm². Neglect magnetic leakage and fringing. Calculate the exciting current required to set up a flux of 0.9 mWb in the air gap. The magnetization characteristic of cast steel is given in Fig. A.7.*

Solution. Air-gap. Flux density, $$B_g = \frac{\phi}{A} = \frac{0.9 \times 10^{-3}}{600 \times 10^{-6}} = 1.5 \text{ T}$$

Megnetic field intensity in air gap, $$H_g = \frac{B_g}{\mu_0} = \frac{1.5}{4\pi \times 10^{-7}} \text{ AT/m}$$

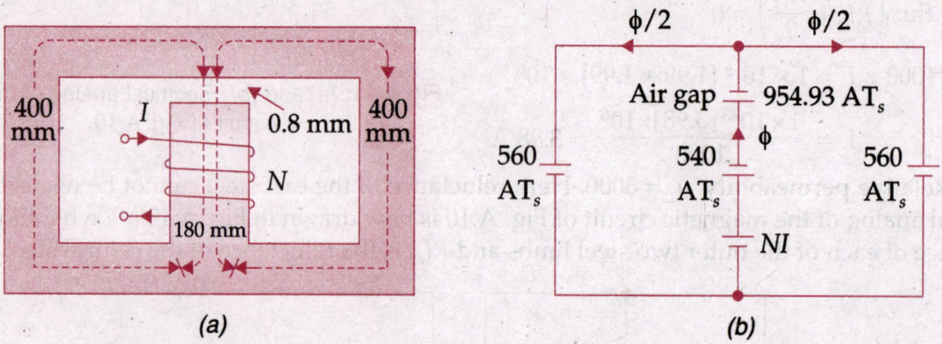

Fig A.13: *(a)* Pertaining to Example A.5 *(b)* Electrical analog of magnetic circuit of Fig. A.13 *(a)*.

∴ m.m.f. required for air gap, $$F_g = H_g \times l_g = \frac{1.5}{4\pi \times 10^{-7}} \times 0.8 \times 10^{-3} = 954.93 \text{ ATs.}$$

Central limb.

Flux density in central limb, $B_1 = B_g = 1.5$ T.

From Fig. A.7, for flux density of 1.5 *T*,

$$H_1 \text{ for cast steel} = 3000 \text{ ATs/m}$$

∴ $$\text{m.m.f. for central limb} = 3000 \times 0.18 = 540 \text{ ATs.}$$

Outer limbs. Half of the flux in central limb returns through each outer limb.

∴ Flux density in outer limb, $$B_2 = \frac{0.9 \times 10^{-3}}{2 \times 375 \times 10^{-6}} = 1.2 \text{ T}$$

For $B_2 = 1.2$ T, the value of H_2 from Fig. A.7 for the outer limb = 1400 AT/m.

∴ $$\text{m.m.f. for each outer limb} = 1400 \times 0.4 = 560 \text{ ATs}$$

Exciting current. Electrical analog of the magnetic circuit of Fig. A.13 *(a)* is drawn in Fig. A.13 *(b)*. Kirchhoff's m.m.f. law for this circuit gives

$$NI - 540 - 954.93 - 560 = 0$$

or $$I = \frac{2054.93}{500} = 4.11 \text{ A}$$

Example A.6. *Magnetic circuit shown in Fig. A.14 is made of cast steel. Dimensions are given in the figure. Cross-sectional area of central limb is 20 cm² and that of each outer limb is 15 cm². The coil has 400 turns. Magnetic leakage and fringing are neglected.*

Calculate the coil current needed to establish a flux of 0.9 m Wb in the air gap.

Solution. The magnetic circuit of Fig. A.14 is redrawn and labelled *a, b, c* etc. so that circuit under consideration can be identified easily.

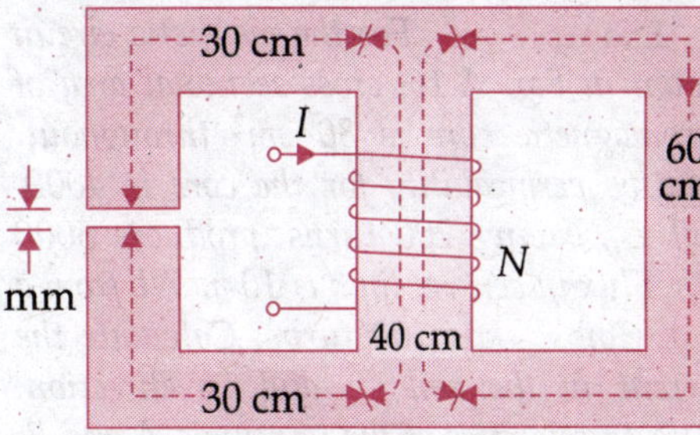

Fig A.14: Pertaining to Example A.6.

As there is no fringing and leakage, flux density in the path *bcda* is the same.

Air-gap flux density,

$$B_g = \frac{0.9 \times 10^{-3}}{15 \times 10^{-4}} = 0.6 \text{ T}$$

∴ Air-gap m.m.f.,

$$F_g = \frac{B_g}{\mu_0} \times l_g = \frac{0.6}{4\pi \times 10^{-7}} \times 1 \times 10^{-3} = 477.46 \text{ ATs.}$$

The flux density in path *bc* or *da* is the same as $B_g = 0.6$ T. From the magnetisation curve in Fig. A.7, $H_{bc} = H_{da} = 575$ AT/m for a flux density of 0.6 T in the cast steel.

∴ M.m.f. for magnetic path $(bc + da) = 575\,(0.3 + 0.3) = 172.5 \times 2 = 345$ ATs.

M.m.f. between junction points *a, b* is F_{ab} = m.m.f. for [*bc* + air gap + *da*]

$$= 172.5 + 477.46 + 172.5 = 822.46 \text{ ATs.}$$

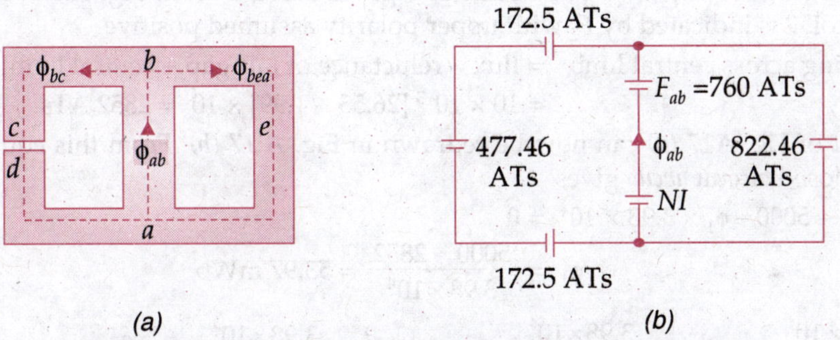

Fig A.15: *(a)* Fig. A.14 labelled *(b)* Equivalent circuit for Fig. A.14.

This m.m.f. of 822.46 ATs acts across the magnetic path *aeb* also.

Therefore, magnetic field intensity in path *aeb* is $H_{aeb} = \frac{m.m.f.}{\text{length}} = \frac{822.46}{0.6} = 1370.77$ ATs.

From cast-steel *B-H* curve in Fig. A.7,

flux density B_{aeb} corresponding to 1370.77 ATs/m is 1.19 T.

∴ Flux in path *bea*, $\phi_{bea} = 1.19 \times 15 \times 10^{-4} = 1.785$ mWb

Use of Kirchhoff's flux law at node *b* gives flux in central limb,

$$\phi_{ab} = \phi_{bea} + \phi_{bc} \text{ (or } \phi_g) = (1.785 + 0.9)\, 10^{-3} = 2.685 \text{ mWb.}$$

Flux density in central limb, $B_{ab} = \frac{2.685 \times 10^{-3}}{20 \times 10^{-4}} = 1.3425$ T

From *B-H* curve for cast steel, magnetic field intensity $H_{ab} = 1900$ AT/m for flux density $B_{ab} =$ 1.3425 T.

∴ m.m.f. for path *ab*, $F_{ab} = 1900 \times 0.4 = 760$ ATs

Equivalent circuit for Fig. A.14 is drawn in Fig. A.15 *(b)*. Kirchhoff's m.m.f. law for this figure gives $NI - 760 - 822.46 = 0$

∴ Coil current, $I = \frac{1582.46}{400} = 3.9562$ A

Example A.7. *For the magnetic circuit shown in Fig. A.16, cross-sectional area of ferromagnetic core is 30 cm² throughout. Relative permeability for the core is 4000. Coil C_1, having 200 turns, produces 5000 ATs. Flux in central limb is 10 m Wb from a to b. Coil C_2 has 100 turns. Calculate the current in the coil C_2 and its direction. Indicate polarities of the terminals A and B. Neglect magnetic leakage and fringing.*

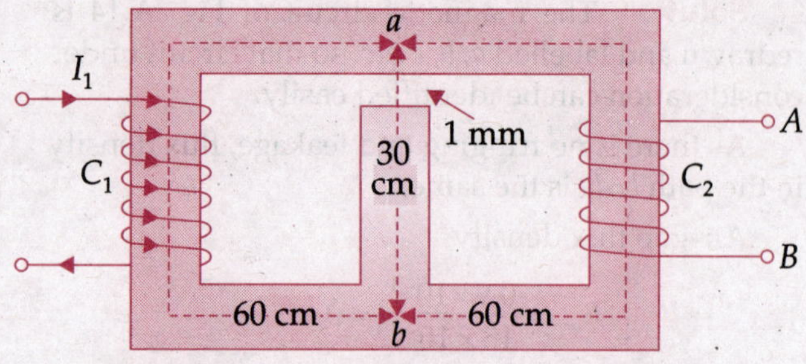

Fig A.16: (a) & (b). Pertaining to Example A.7.

Solution. Reluctance of each outer limb,

$$Rl_1 = \frac{60 \times 10^{-2}}{4\pi \times 10^{-7} \times 4000 \times 30 \times 10^{-4}} = 3.98 \times 10^4 \text{ AT/Wb}$$

Reluctance of central limb, $$Rl_2 = \frac{30 \times 10^{-2}}{4\pi \times 10^{-7} \times 4000 \times 30 \times 10^{-4}} = 1.99 \times 10^4 \text{ AT/Wb}$$

Air-gap reluctance, $$Rl_g = \frac{1 \times 10^{-3}}{4\pi \times 10^{-7} \times 30 \times 10^{-4}} = 26.53 \times 10^4 \text{ AT/Wb}$$

Electrical analog for the magnetic circuit of Fig. A.16 is drawn in Fig. A.17 *(a)* where m.m.f. produced by coil 2 is indicated by F_2 with upper polarity assumed positive.

M.m.f. acting across central limb = flux × reluctance of [air gap + central limb]

$= 10 \times 10^{-3}\,[26.53 + 1.99] \times 10^4 = 2852$ ATs.

The circuit of Fig. A17 *(a)* can now be redrawn in Fig. A.17 *(b)*. From this equivalent circuit, KML for the closed circuit *abcda* gives

$$-2852 + 5000 - \phi_1 \times 3.98 \times 10^4 = 0$$

$$\therefore \quad \phi_1 = \frac{5000 - 2852}{3.98 \times 10^4} = 53.97 \text{ mWb}$$

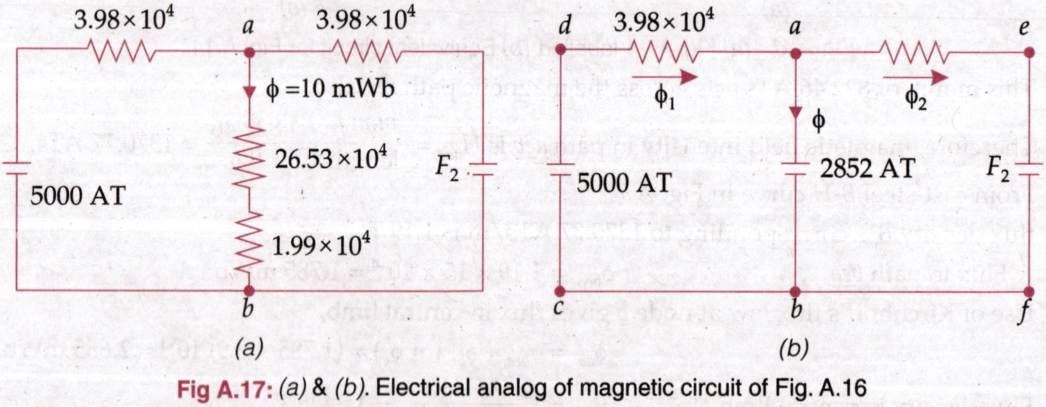

Fig A.17: *(a)* & *(b)*. Electrical analog of magnetic circuit of Fig. A.16

K. flux law at node a gives flux ϕ_2 in the branch *ae* as under:

$$\phi + \phi_2 = \phi_1 \text{ or } \phi_2 = \phi_1 - \phi = [53.97 - 10] \times 10^{-3} = 43.97 \text{ mWb.}$$

Now *K.* m.m.f. law for the circuit *efbae* (upper polarity of F_2 is assumed positive) gives

$$-F_2 + 2852 - 3.98 \times 10^4 \times 43.97 \times 10^{-3} = 0$$

$$\therefore \quad F_2 = 2852 - 1750 = 1102 \text{ ATs}$$

$$\therefore \quad \text{Current in coil } C_2 = \frac{1102}{N_2} = \frac{1102}{100} = 11.02 \text{ A}$$

As m.m.f. F_2 has turned out to be positive, assumed polarity of coil C_2 is correct. In other words, in Fig. A.16, current enters terminal A, passes through coil C_2 and leaves terminal B. Therefore, terminal A is positive and terminal B is negative, *i.e.*, terminals A and B are connected respectively to positive and negative polarities of an external source.

A.6. INDUCTANCE

Self inductance, or inductance, of a coil is defined as the flux linkages with a coil per ampere in the same coil. Its usual symbol is L.

$$\therefore \quad L = \frac{\psi}{I} = \frac{N\phi}{I} \quad \text{...(A.6)}$$

where $\psi = N\phi$ = flux linkages, Wb—turns

ϕ = flux, Wb

N = number of turns in the coil.

But flux $\phi = \dfrac{\text{m.m.f.}}{\text{reluctance}} = NI \cdot \dfrac{\mu_0\mu_r A}{l}$.

Substituting this value of ϕ in Eq. (A.6), we get

$$L = \frac{N}{I} \cdot \frac{NI \cdot \mu_0\mu_r A}{l}$$

$$= \frac{N^2 \cdot \mu_0\mu_r A}{l} = \frac{N^2 \cdot \mu A}{l} = \frac{N^2}{Rl} = N^2\,\Lambda \quad \text{...(A.7)}$$

where Rl and Λ are respectively the reluctance and permeance of the magnetic circuit under consideration.

Inductance has the units of henries or Wb-turns per ampere. Eq. (A.7) shows that inductance is proportional to

(i) square of the number of turns in the coil

(ii) permeability of the ferromagnetic material forming the magnetic circuit and

(iii) cross-sectional area of the magnetic circuit.

Note that inductance is inversely proportional to length of the magnetic path, Eq. (A.7).

Since permeability μ (= B/H) depends upon the saturation of the magnetic circuit, its value is not constant and likewise the value of L $\left(= \dfrac{N^2 \cdot \mu A}{l}\right)$ is not constant. In case a linear relation between B and H is assumed, μ and therefore L can be treated constant.

From Eq. (A.6), $\psi = LI$. Substituting this value in Eq. (0.1), we get

$$e = \frac{d}{dt}(LI) = L\frac{dI}{dt} + I\frac{dL}{dt}$$

$$= \text{transformer e.m.f., } L\frac{dI}{dt} + \text{speed e.m.f., } I\frac{dL}{dt} \quad \text{...(A.8)}$$

Mutual inductance. If magnetic flux produced by a current in one coil is varying with time and links a nearby coil, mutually induced e.m.f. appears across the second coil. This e.m.f. e_2 in second nearby coil is given by

$$e_2 = M\frac{dI_1}{dt}$$

where M = mutual inductance in henries between coils 1 and 2 and

$\dfrac{dI_1}{dt}$ = rate of change of current with respect to time in coil 1.

Example A.8. *For the magnetic circuit of Example A.3, find the inductance L by using the expression* $\frac{N^2}{Rl}$. *(a) for part (a) and (b) for part (c)*

Solution. *(a)* As per Eq. (A.7),
$$L = \frac{N^2}{Rl}$$

From Example A.3, it is seen that total reluctance of the magnetic circuit is

$$Rl = \text{gap reluctance, } Rl_g + \text{iron-core reluctance, } Rl_c$$
$$= (24.9483 + 12.474) \times 10^5 = 37.4223 \times 10^5 \text{ AT/Wb}$$

∴ Inductance,
$$L = \frac{N^2}{Rl} = \frac{(500)^2}{37.4223 \times 10^5} = 0.0668 \text{ H} = 66.8 \text{ mH}$$

Also,
$$L = \frac{N\phi}{I} = \frac{500 \times 0.8 \times 10^{-3}}{5.9876} = 66.80 \text{ mH}$$

(b) In this part, core flux density has been calculated as 1.254 T. For this B_c, magnetisation curve gives magnetic field intensity $H_c = 3200$ AT/m. From this, the relative permeability is calculated.

∴
$$\mu_r = \frac{B_c}{\mu_0 \cdot H_c} = \frac{1.254}{4\pi \times 10^{-7} \times 3200} = 311.844$$

Iron-core reluctance,
$$Rl_c = \frac{l_c}{\mu_0 \times \mu_r \times A} = \frac{50 \times 10^{-2} \times 4}{4\pi \times 10^{-7} \times 311.844 \times \pi(2.85)^2}$$
$$= 20 \times 10^5 \text{ AT/Wb}$$

Total magnetic circuit reluctance,
$$Rl = Rl_g + Rl_c$$
$$= (24.9483 + 20) \times 10^5 = 44.9483 \times 10^5 \text{ AT/Wb}$$

∴
$$L = \frac{N^2}{Rl} = \frac{500^2}{44.9483 \times 10^5} = 55.62 \text{ mH}$$

Also,
$$L = \frac{N\phi}{I} = \frac{500 \times 0.8 \times 10^{-3}}{7.192} = 55.62 \text{ mH}$$

Example A.9. *For the magnetic circuit of Fig. A.16 pertaining to Example A.7, find the inductance of coils C_1 and C_2.*

Solution. Inductance of coil C_1,
$$L_1 = \frac{N_1\phi_1}{I_1} = \frac{200 \times 53.97 \times 10^{-3}}{25} = 0.4318 \text{ H}$$

Inductance of coil C_2,
$$L_2 = \frac{N_2\phi_2}{I_2} = \frac{100 \times 43.97 \times 10^{-3}}{11.02} = 0.39873 \text{ H.}$$

PROBLEMS

A.1. *(a)* Define the terms reluctance, m.m.f. and flux. What are their units? How are these related?

(b) What is a series magnetic circuit? If a series circuit is made up of three different magnetic materials, find the total m.m.f. to be provided by the exciting coil. Hence, define Kirchhoff's m.m.f. law.

(c) For the magnetic circuit shown in Fig. A.8, $I = 2$A, $N = 400$, $l_c = 60$ cms, $\mu_r = 5000$, flux density in core $B_c = 1.2$ T. For no magnetic leakage and fringing, calculate the air-gap length l_g. **[Ans.** *(c)* 0.718 mm**]**

A.2. *(a)* Define a parallel magnetic circuit.

Take a parallel magnetic circuit with an exciting coil. How can coil m.m.f. be calculated for this circuit. Hence, define Kirchhoff's flux law.

(*b*) Give the analogy between magnetic and electric circuits. State the unit of the various terms involved.

A.3. (*a*) "A magnetic circuit consumes energy". Justify the statement

(*b*) For the magnetic circuit of Fig. A.18, $I = 2$ A, N = 600 turns and all dimensions are indicated. Calculate the flux and flux density in the two outer limbs and the central limb. The relative permeability of iron core is infinity.

[**Ans.** (*b*) Outer limbs : $\phi_{cd} = 1.885$ mWb, $B_{cd} = 0.754$ T; $\phi_{ef} = 3.77$ mWb, $B_{ef} = 1.508$ T, Central limb : $\phi = 5.655$ mWb, $B = 1.131$ T]

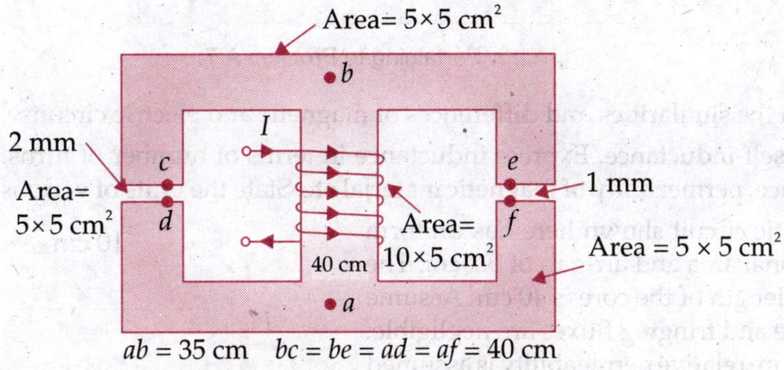

Fig A.18: Pertaining to Problem A.3 (*b*).

A.4. Solve Problem A.3 (*b*) in case relative permeability of iron core is 5000.

[**Ans.** Outer limbs : $\phi_{cd} = 1.668$ mWb, $B_{cd} = 0.6672$ T; $\phi_{ef} = 3.106$ mWb, $B_{ef} = 1.2424$ T, Central limb : $\phi = 4.774$ mWb, $B = 0.9548$ T]

A.5. (*a*) A magnetic circuit is made up of ferromagnetic core and a small air gap in series. Which part of this magnetic circuit would require most of the ampere turns to set up the requisite flux and why?

(*b*) For solving magnetic-circuit problems, use of B-H curve is desirable. Give the reasons.

(*c*) Explain the terms leakage flux and fringing.

A.6. The magnetic circuit shown in Fig. A.19 uses CRGO steel for its core. The mean length of magnetic path is 60 cm and total core area is 10 cm². Coils *A* and *B* with 100 and 200 turns respectively are wound as shown and carry a current of 1 *A* and 1.5 *A* respectively as indicated. For creating a flux of 1.62 mWb in the core, find the current *I* required in the coil C having 250 turns. Neglect leakage flux and take stacking factor 0.9. [**Ans.** 1.136 A]

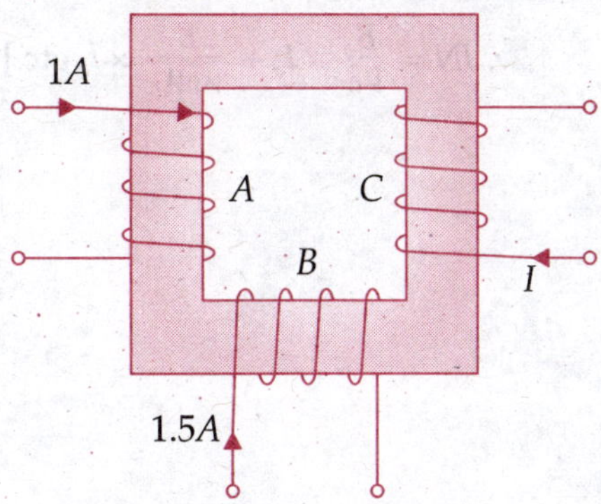

Fig A.19: Pertaining to Problem A.6.

A.7. In the magnetic circuit of Fig. A.20, each outer limb *acb* or *adb*, has a length of 90 cm and a core area of 16 cm² and the corresponding values for central limb are 30 cm and 32 cm². A current of 1 *A* in a 300-turn coil on the central limb produces an air-gap flux of 0.5 mWb. Calculate the relative permeability of the core material. Neglect magnetic leakage and fringing. [**Ans.** 849.445]

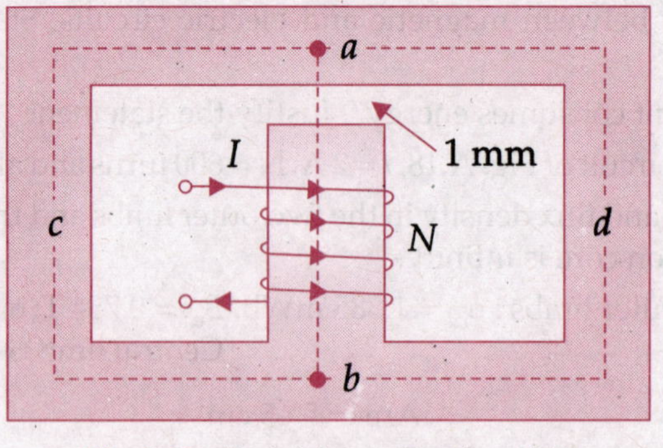

Fig A.20: Pertaining to Problem A.7.

A.8. (*a*) Explain the similarities and differences of magnetic and electric circuits.

(*b*) Define self-inductance. Express inductance in terms of number of turns, permeability of free space, permeability of magnetic material etc. State the units of various terms involved.

A.9. The magnetic circuit shown here has uniform cross-sectional area and air-gap of 0.2 cm. The mean path length of the core is 40 cm. Assume that leakage and fringing fluxes are negligible. When the core relative permeability is assumed to be infinite, the magnetic flux density computed in the air gap is 1 tesla. With same Ampere-turns, if the core relative permeability is assumed to be 1000 (linear), the flux density in tesla (rounded off to three decimal places) calculated in the air gap is [*GATE*, 2019]

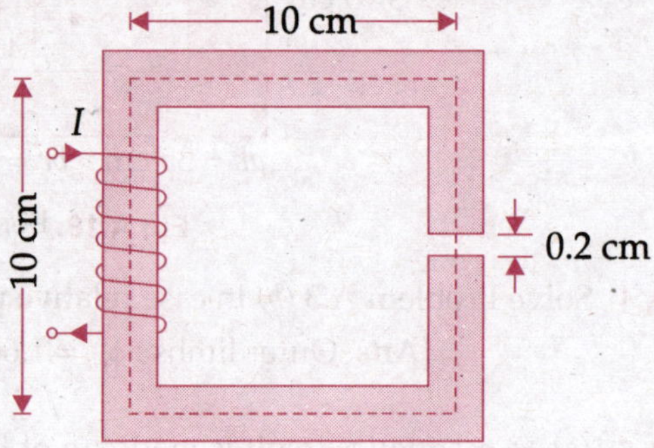

[**Hint.** Air-gap flux density, $B_g = \dfrac{IN \times \mu_0 \times 1}{0.2 \times 10^{-3}} = 1$

$\therefore IN = \dfrac{0.2 \times 10^{-3}}{\mu_0}$. For series circuit, flux density is B,

$\therefore IN = \dfrac{B}{\mu_0} \times l_g + \dfrac{B}{\mu_0 \mu_r} \times l_c$ etc.] **[Ans.** 0.833 T]

B
Appendix

Three-Phase Circuits

It is a well established fact that three-phase systems are more economical and efficient as compared to single-phase systems. It is for this reason that the use of 3-phase devices and systems is almost universal for the generation, transmission, distribution and utilization of high-power A.C. energy.

An *m*-phase balanced system, in general, employs *m* voltages equal in magnitude but phase displaced* from each other by an angle of $360°/m$. For a 3-phase balanced system, 3-phase voltages are equal in magnitude and are displaced from each other by a phase angle of 120°.

At present, three-phase systems are the most popular throughout the world, consequently three-phase circuits are discussed in this appendix.

B.1. GENERATION OF THREE-PHASE VOLTAGES

Fig. B.1 illustrates an elementary 2-pole, 3-phase A.C. generator. Three phases *A*, *B*, *C* of the armature winding on the stator are represented by three coils $a - a'$, $b - b'$ and $c - c'$ respectively. The flux density produced by field winding on the rotor is sinusoidally distributed along the air-gap periphery. For the field-pole orientation shown in Fig. B.1, the flux density at 1 (midway between the poles) is zero ; it rises sinusoidally to peak at 4, decreases sinusoidally to zero at 7 and so on. This sinusoidal variation in flux density *B* is plotted in Fig. B.2 *(a)*.

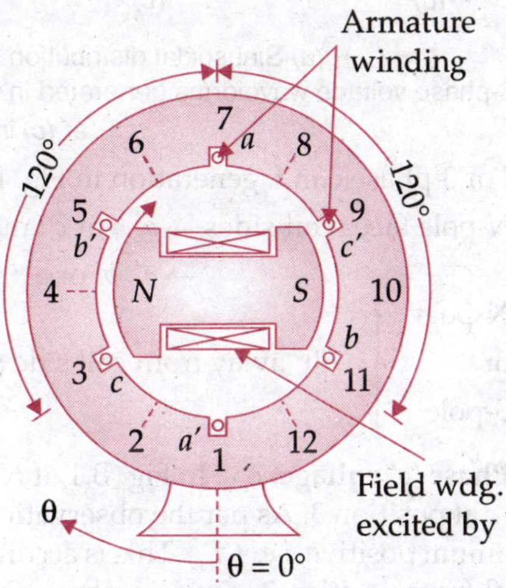

Fig B.1: Elementary 2-pole three-phase A.C. generator.

Phase 'a' voltage, $e_{a'a}$. At the instant shown in Fig. B.1, coil $a - a'$ is experiencing zero flux density, therefore, e.m.f. generated (= *Blv*) in coil $a - a'$ is zero. When field poles rotate 90° clockwise, *N*-pole faces coil-side *a* and *S*-pole faces coil-side *a′*. Therefore, e.m.f. generated in coil $a - a'$ is maximum. After further 90° clockwise travel, *N*-pole faces point 10 and *S*-pole faces point 4, therefore e.m.f. generated is zero. Further 90° clockwise rotation brings *N*-pole facing *a′* and *S*-pole facing a′. As the coil now experiences peak flux density B_p, e.m.f. generated in coil $a - a'$ is maximum but negative. This variation of generated e.m.f. $e_{a'a}$ in phase *a* is drawn in Fig. B.2 *(b)* and is indicated by $e_{a'a}$.

* For m = 2, phase angle = 180°/2 = 90°.

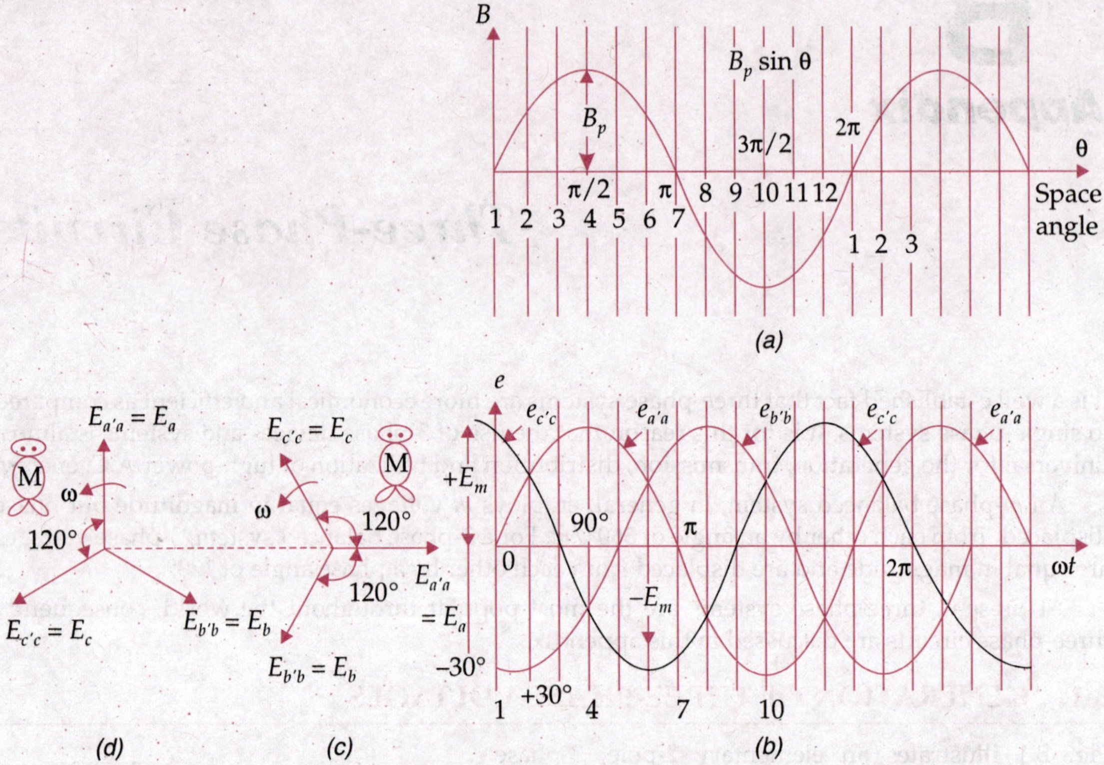

Fig B.2: *(a)* Sinusoidal distribution of flux density along the air-gap periphery of Fig. B.1. *(b)* 3-phase voltage waveforms generated in the windings of Fig. B.1. Phasor diagram of generated voltages at *(c)* instant 1 and *(d)* instant 4.

For 3-phase e.m.f. generation in Fig. B.1, the following may be kept in mind :

N-pole faces coil-sides → *a*, *b* or *c* : maximum positive e.m.f. is generated,

→ *a'*, *b'* or *c'* : maximum negative e.m.f. is generated.

N-pole or S-pole] 90° away from coil side *a*, *b*, *c*, or *a'*, *b'*, *c'* : no e.m.f. is generated.

Phase 'c' voltage, $e_{c'c}$. In Fig. B.1, if *N* – *S* poles are moved 30° anticlockwise, *N*-pole faces coil-side *c* at position 3. As per the observations made above, e.m.f. generated in phase coil *c* would be maximum positive, *i.e.* $+E_m$. This is accordingly shown at $\omega t = -30°$ in Fig. B.2 *(b)*. For 90° clockwise travel from position 3, e.m.f. in phase *c* would be zero, for further 90° clockwise rotation, *N*-pole faces *c'* at position 9, e.m.f. generated in phase *c* is therefore maximum negative and so on. This e.m.f. waveform is drawn as $e_{c'c}$ in Fig. B.2 *(b)*.

Phase 'b' voltage, $e_{b'b}$. From the orientation of *N*, *S* poles shown in Fig. B.1, if poles travel 30° clockwise, *N*-pole faces *b'* at the position 5 and *S*-pole comes across *b* at position 11, therefore, e.m.f. generated in phase coil *b* – *b'* would be maximum but negative. This is accordingly shown as $-E_m$ at $\omega t = 30°$ in Fig. B.2 *(b)*. A travel of 90° clockwise from the position 5 would generate zero e.m.f. in coil *b*. Further 90° clockwise movement of *N*-pole from postion 8 would bring *N*-pole facing coil-side *b* at position 11. Therefore, e.m.f. generated in coil *b* would be maximum positive. This variation of e.m.f. in coil *b* – *b'* is drawn as $e_{b'b}$ in Fig. B.2 (b).

It is seen from Fig. B.2 *(b)* that three e.m.f. waves are displaced 120 electrical degrees in time. It is because the phase windings *a, b, c*, represented by three coils *a a′, b b′, c c′* are displaced 120° in space.

The basic principle of drawing the phasor diagram is that the vertical component of a phasor should be equal to the value of sine wave at the instant considered. In Fig. B.2 *(c)*, the phasor diagram is drawn at $\omega t = 0°$. Here, the vertical component of horizontal phasor $E_{a'a}$ is zero because value of $e_{a'a}$ at $\omega t = 0°$ in Fig. B.2 *(b)* is zero. Vertical component of $E_{b'b}$ is equal to the value of sine wave $e_{b'b}$ at $\omega t = 0°$. Same is true for $E_{c'c}$. At instant 4, when $\omega t = 90°$, $e_{a'a}$ attains maximum value. Therefore, phasor $E_{a'a}$ is shown vertical, because vertical component of $E_{a'a}$ is maximum in Fig. B.2 *(d)*. Likewise $E_{b'b}$ and $E_{c'c}$ are drawn.

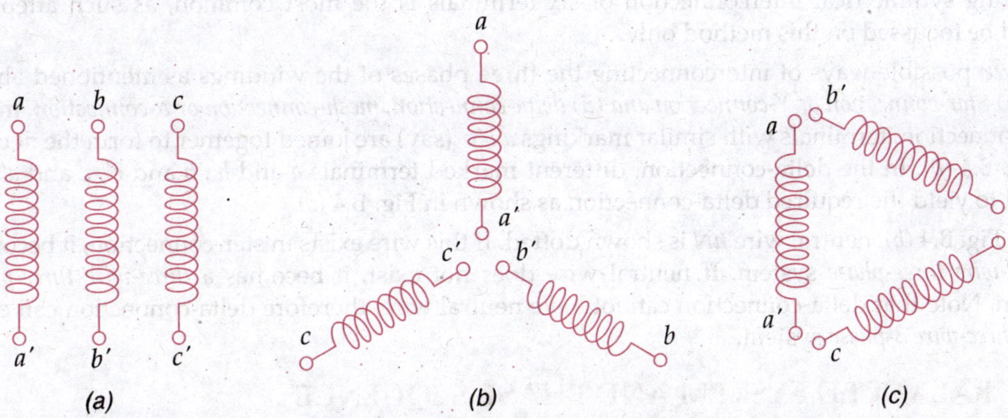

Fig B.3: Schematic representation of 3-phase winding of Fig. B.1.

The three-phase windings $a-a'$, $b-b'$, $c-c'$ illustrated in Fig. B.1 can be represented schematically by three coils *a a′, b b′, c c′* shown in Fig. B.3 *(a), (b)* or *(c)*. The character of each phase winding is identified by two terminal markings. Terminals marked *a′, b′, c′* denote the start (or beginning) of the three windings whereas terminals marked *a, b, c* indicate their finish (or end) respectively.

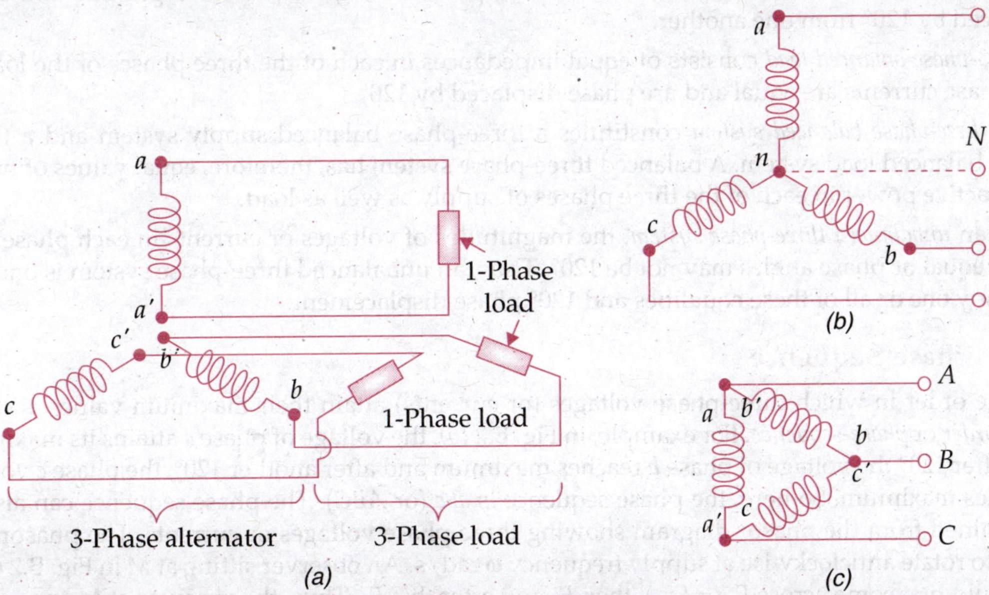

Fig B.4: *(a)* Three-phase alternator connected to three separate 1-phase loads *(b)* Y-connection and *(c)* Δ-connection.

The three-phase voltages generated in the 3-phase windings of an alternator can be utilized as under :

(i) Connect terminals a, a' to one single-phase load ; b, b' to other single-phase load and c, c' to third single-phase load as shown in Fig. B.4 *(a)*. There are thus three separate single-phase systems.

(ii) Interconnect six terminals a, a' ; b, b' and c, c' in such a manner as to obtain either a star connection or a delta-connection.

Out of the two methods mentioned above, one method requiring six leads (with each 1-phase load connected to corresponding 1-phase supply) is rarely used in practice. The other method involving symmetrical interconnection of six terminals is the most common, as such attention would be focussed on this method only.

Two possible ways of interconnecting the three phases of the windings as mentioned above are : *(i) Star-connection or Y-connection and (ii) delta-connection, mesh-connection or Δ-connection*. In the star-connection, terminals with similar markings $a'b'c'$ (say) are joined together to form the neutral n, Fig. B.4 *(b)*. In the delta-connection, different marked terminals a and b', b and c', c and a' are joined to yield the required delta-connection as shown in Fig. B.4 *(c)*.

In Fig. B.4 *(b)*, neutral wire nN is shown dotted. If this wire exists in star-connection, it becomes a *four-wire three-phase* system. If neutral wire does not exist, it becomes a *three-wire three-phase* system. Note that delta-connection cannot have neutral wire, therefore delta-connection can offer only *three-wire 3-phase* system.

B.2. BALANCED SYSTEM AND PHASE SEQUENCE

In the following lines, general features of a balanced system are given and then phase-sequence is discussed.

B.2.1. Balanced System

A *three-phase balanced supply* consists of three-phase voltages equal in magnitude and phase displaced by 120° from one another.

A *3-phase balanced load* consists of equal impedances in each of the three phases of the load so that phase currents are equal and are phase displaced by 120°.

A *three-phase balanced system* constitutes a three-phase balanced supply system and a three-phase balanced load system. A balanced three-phase system has, therefore, equal values of power and reactive power in each of the three phases of supply as well as load.

In an *unbalanced three-phase system*, the magnitudes of voltages or currents in each phase may not be equal or phase angles may not be 120°. Thus, an unbalanced three-phase system is one that lacks any one or all of these equalities and 120° phase displacement.

B.2.2. Phase Sequence

The order in which three-phase voltages (or currents) attain their maximum values is called *phase-order* or *phase-sequence*. For example, in Fig. B.2 *(b)*, the voltage of phase a attains its maximum first, after 120° the voltage of phase b reaches maximum and after another 120°, the phase c voltage becomes maximum. So here, the phase sequence is *abc* (or *ABC*). The phase sequence can also be determined from the phasor diagram showing three-phase voltages or currents. The phasors are taken to rotate anticlockwise at supply frequency ω rad/s. An observer sitting at M in Fig. B.2 *(c)* or *(d)* would first come across E_a $(= E_{a'a})$, then E_b and after this E_c. Thus, the observer at M encounters phase voltages in the order a, b, c ; so the phase sequence of three-phase voltages is *abc*.

If the direction of rotor rotation in Fig. B.1 is revered, the phase sequence of generated voltages would be reversed. It would now become *acb*. So here voltage $e_{c'c}$ would lag $e_{a'a}$ by 120°, and $e_{b'b}$ would lag $e_{c'c}$ by another 120°.

The phase sequence of the voltages across the 3-phase load depends upon the order in which three-phase supply lines are connected to 3-phase load. Phase sequence of the voltages applied to a load can be reversed by interchanging any two supply lines feeding the three-phase load.

Phase sequence *abc* (or *ABC*) is sometimes denoted by RYB (red, yellow, blue). In power stations and substations, RYB is quite popular. Three wires in these stations are of red, yellow and blue colours indicating RYB phase sequence. Three lamps in line RYB are of red, yellow and blue colour. This all leads to an easy identification of any one line in case of a fault in the three-phase system.

B.3. THREE-PHASE GENERATOR CONNECTIONS

As stated before, three windings of an alternator can be interconnected either in star or in delta. These two possible connection schemes are examined in what follows.

B.3.1. Star Connection

For obtaining star connection of three-phase windings, three similar terminals, either *a'*, *b'*, *c'* or *a*, *b*, *c* are joined to form the neutral point. In Fig. B.5 *(a)*, star connection is made by joining together the three terminals *a'*, *b'*, *c'*. The other terminals *a, b, c* form the line terminals. For convenience, three-phase load terminals are denoted by *A, B, C*.

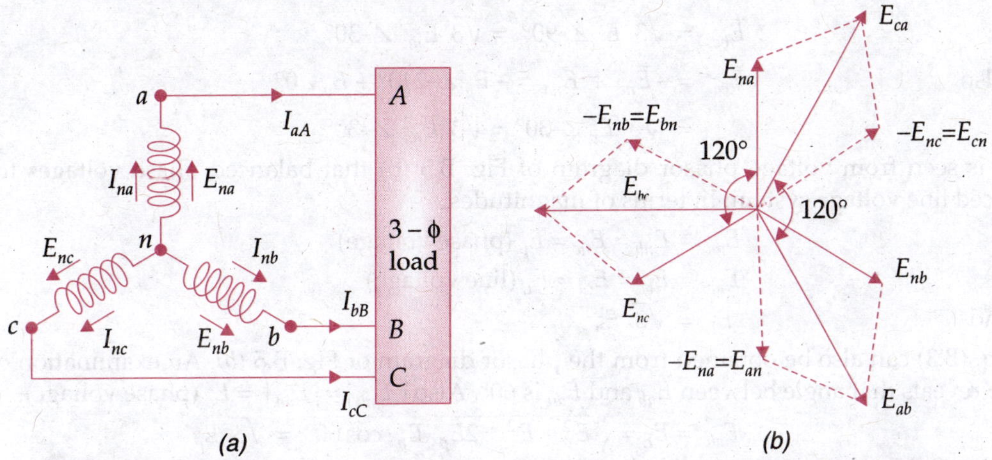

Fig B.5: *(a)* Three-phase star connection and *(b)* phasor diagram for star connection.

In Fig. B.5 (a), phase sequence is *abc*. Double subcript is used here because it makes simpler the job of drawing the circuit and phasor diagrams. For example, voltage E_{na} indicates it exists between the terminals *n* and *a*. It also denotes that voltage rise is taken from *n* to *a*, *i.e.*, from *first subscript to second subscript*.

In Fig. B.5 *(a)*, voltage in each phase is talen positive when acting from neutral point outwards. Therefore, three generated voltages are shown as E_{na}, E_{nb} and E_{nc} in Fig. B.5 (a). The three voltages, corresponding to circuit diagram, are shown as phasors E_{na}, E_{nb}, and E_{nc}, in the phasor diagram of Fig. B.5 *(b)*. These voltages E_{na}, E_{nb}, E_{nc} are called *phase voltages* or *line to neutral voltages*. In magnitude, these are equal, i.e., $E_{na} = E_{nb} = E_{nc} = E_p$, where subscript *p* stands for 'phase'. Note that phasors E_{na}, E_{nb}, E_{nc} are displaced from each other by a time-angle of 120°.

In phasor form, taking phase a voltage as reference,

$$\begin{aligned} \bar{E}_{na} &= E_{na} \angle 0 = E_p \angle 0^\circ \\ \bar{E}_{nb} &= E_{nb} \angle -120^\circ = E_p \angle -120^\circ \\ \bar{E}_{nc} &= E_{nc} \angle -240^\circ = E_p \angle -240^\circ \end{aligned} \quad ...(B.1)$$

The three voltages E_{ab}, E_{bc}, E_{ca} are called line to line voltges or more conveniently line voltages. For a balanced system, $E_{ab} = E_{bc} = E_{ca} = E_L$, where subscript '$L$' denotes line. By using KVL, line voltage E_{ab} is

$$\bar{E}_{ab} = \bar{E}_{an} + \bar{E}_{nb} = -\bar{E}_{na} + \bar{E}_{nb} \quad ...(B.2)$$

From Eq. (B.1),

$$\bar{E}_{ab} = -E_p \angle 0 + E_p \angle -120^\circ$$

$$= -E_p + E_p [\cos(-120^\circ) + j \sin(-120^\circ)] = -1.5 E_p - j \frac{\sqrt{3}}{2} E_p$$

$$= \left[1.5^2 + \left(\frac{\sqrt{3}}{2}\right)^2\right]^{1/2} E_p \cdot \tan \angle \frac{\sqrt{3}}{2} \times \frac{1}{1.5} = \sqrt{3} E_p \angle -150^\circ$$

This shows that line volage E_{ab} lags the reference phase voltage E_{na} by 150° or E_{ab} lags E_{nb} by 30° which can be written as $E_{ab} = \sqrt{3}\, E_{nb} \angle -30^\circ$.

Eq. (B.2) reveals that for obtaining line voltage $\bar{E}_{ab}$, reverse phasor $\bar{E}_{na}$ and add it to phasor $\bar{E}_{na}$; this is illustrated in Fig. B.5 *(b)*. An examination of this figure reveals that $\bar{E}_{ab} = \sqrt{3}\, E_{nb} \angle -30^\circ$.

Similarly,

$$\bar{E}_{bc} = \bar{E}_{bn} + \bar{E}_{nc} = -\bar{E}_{nb} + \bar{E}_{nc}$$

$$= -E_p \angle -120^\circ + E_p \angle -240^\circ = \sqrt{3}\, E_p \angle -90^\circ$$

$$\therefore \quad \bar{E}_{bc} = \sqrt{3}\, E_p \angle -90^\circ = \sqrt{3}\, \bar{E}_{nc} \angle -30^\circ$$

Also,

$$\bar{E}_{ca} = -\bar{E}_{nc} + \bar{E}_{na} = -E_p \angle -240^\circ + E_p \angle 0^\circ$$

$$= \sqrt{3}\, E_p \angle -30^\circ = \sqrt{3}\, \bar{E}_{na} \angle -30^\circ$$

It is seen from voltage phasor diagram of Fig. B.5 (b) that balanced phase voltages form a balanced line voltage system. In terms of magnitudes,

$$E_{na} = E_{nb} = E_{nc} = E_p \text{ (phase voltage)}$$

$$E_{ab} = E_{bc} = E_{ca} = E_L \text{ (line voltage)}$$

and

$$E_L = \sqrt{3}\, E_p \quad ...(B.3)$$

Eq. (B.3) can also be obtained from the phasor diagram of Fig. B.5 *(b)*. An examination of this figure reveals that angle between E_{nb} and E_{an} is 60°. Also $|E_{nb}| = |E_{an}| = E_p$ (phase voltage).

$$\therefore \quad E_{ab} = E_L = \sqrt{E_p^2 + E_p^2 + 2E_p \cdot E_p \cdot \cos 60^\circ} = \sqrt{3}\, E_p \quad ...(B.3)$$

Eq. (B.3) states that *for a star connection, line voltge is equal to $\sqrt{3}$ times the phase voltage.*

KCL at node 'a' in Fig. B.5 *(a)* gives $\bar{I}_{na} = \bar{I}_{aA}$. Also $\bar{I}_{nb} = \bar{I}_{bB}$ and $\bar{I}_{nc} = \bar{I}_{cC}$.

But $I_{na} = I_{nb} = I_{nc} = I_p$ (phase current) and $I_{aA} = I_{bB} = I_{cC} = I_L$ (line current)

$$\therefore \quad I_L = I_p \quad ...(B.4)$$

Eq. (B.4) states that in a star-connected system, **line current = phase current.**

B.3.2. Delta Connection

The three-phase winding of Fig. B.3 *(c)* is connected in delta by joining dissimilar terminals *ab'*, *bc'* *ca'* as shown in Fig. B.6 *(a)*. In this figure, E_{ab}, E_{bc}, E_{ca} are the phase voltages and E_{AB}, E_{BC}, E_{CA} are the line voltages. Since terminals *a, b, c* are directly connected to terminals *A, B, C*, $E_{AB} = E_{ab} = E_{BC} = E_{bc}$ and $E_{CA} = E_{ca}$ or line voltage = phase voltage or

$$E_L = E_p \quad ...(B.5)$$

For delta-connected alternator, voltage phasor diagram is shown in Fig. B.6 *(b)*. Eq. (B.5) stated in words say that for a delta connection, **line voltage is equal to phase voltage.**

In Fig. B.6 *(a)* ; I_{ab}, I_{bc}, I_{ca} are phase currents directed from first subscript to second subscript as shown. The phasor diagram for three currents $\bar{I}_{ab}$, $\bar{I}_{bc}$, $\bar{I}_{ca}$ is drawn in Fig. B.6 *(c)*. KCL at node *'a'* in Fig. B.6 *(a)* gives

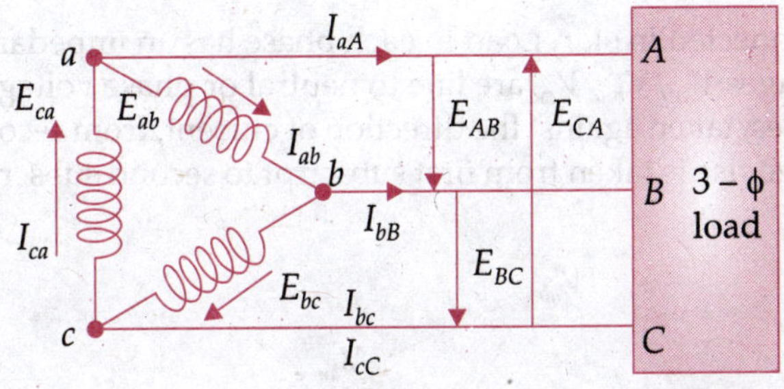

(a)

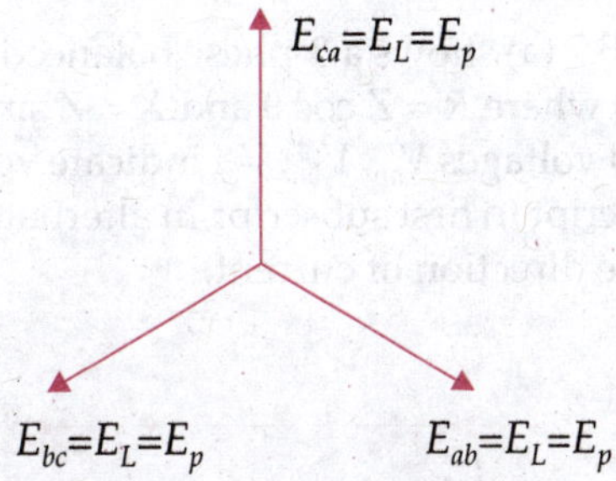

(b)

Fig B.6: *(a)* 3-phase delta connection *(b)* voltage phasor diagram for delta connection.

$$\bar{I}_{ca} \text{ [current entering node } a] = (\bar{I}_{ab} + \bar{I}_{aA}) \text{ [both currents leaving node } a]$$

or
$$\bar{I}_{aA} = \bar{I}_{ca} - \bar{I}_{ab}$$

The above equation states that reverse $\bar{I}_{ab}$ and add it to $\bar{I}_{ca}$ to obtain line current $\bar{I}_{aA}$; this is illustrated in the phasor diagram of Fig. B.6 *(c)*. Taking $\bar{I}_{ca}$ as reference phasor, $\bar{I}_{ca} = I_p \angle 0°$, $\bar{I}_{ab} = I_p \angle{-120°}$ and $\bar{I}_{bc} = I_p \angle{-240°}$.

$$\therefore \quad I_{aA} \text{ (line current)} = \bar{I}_{ca} - \bar{I}_{ab}$$
$$= I_p \angle 0° - I_p \angle{-120°}$$
$$= \left(1.5 + j\frac{\sqrt{3}}{2}\right) I_p$$
$$= \sqrt{3}\ I_p \angle 30°$$
$$= \sqrt{3}\ \bar{I}_{ca} \angle 30° \qquad \text{...(B.6)}$$

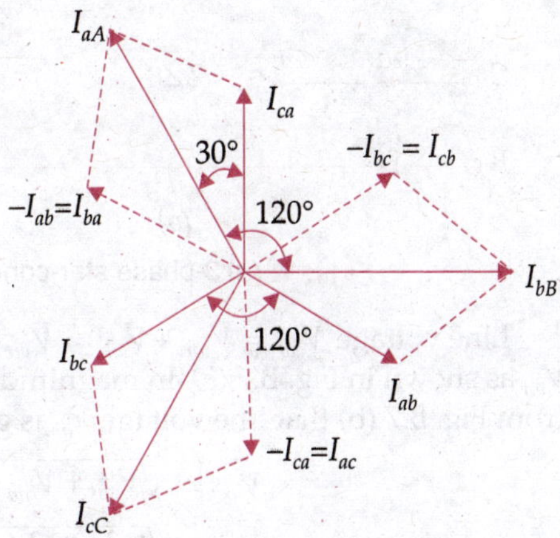

Fig B.6: *(c)* Current phasor diagram for delta connection.

This show that $\bar{I}_{aA}$ leads $\bar{I}_{ca}$ by 30° as shown in Fig. B.6 *(c)*.

Similarly, $\quad \bar{I}_{bB} = \bar{I}_{ab} - \bar{I}_{bc} = \sqrt{3}\ \bar{I}_{ab} \angle 30°$ and $\bar{I}_{cC} = \sqrt{3}\ \bar{I}_{bc} \angle 30°$

Here $I_{aA} = I_{bB} = I_{cC}$= line current, I_L and $I_{ab} = I_{bc} = I_{ca}$ = phase current, I_p.

∴ From Eq. (B.6),

we get
$$I_L = \sqrt{3}\ I_p \qquad \text{...(B.7)}$$

Eq. (B.7), stated in words, says that for a delta connection, line current is $\sqrt{3}$ times the phase current.

Eq. (B.7) can also be obtained from the phasor diagram of Fig. B.6 *(c)*. This phasor diagram reveals that angle between I_{ca} and I_{ba} is 60°. But $|I_{ca}| = |I_{ba}| = I_p$.

$$\therefore \quad I_{aA} = I_L = \sqrt{I_p^2 + I_p^2 + 2I_p \cdot I_p \cdot \cos 60°} = \sqrt{3}\ I_p$$

B.4. THREE-PHASE LOAD CONNECTIONS

If each phase of the load has impedances equal in magnitude and phase angle, the 3-phase load is said to be balanced. Here three-phase balanced loads connected in star and delta are discussed.

B.4.1. Star-connected Load

Fig. B.7 (a) shows a 3-phase balanced load connected in star. Load in each phase has an impedance $Z\angle\theta$ where $R = Z\cos\theta$ and $X = Z\sin\theta$. Voltages V_{an}, V_{bn}, V_{cn} are line to neutral or phase voltages. Load voltages V_{an}, V_{bn}, V_{cn} indicate voltage rises, taken against the direction of current, from second subscript to first subscript-in alternator voltage rise is taken from first subscript to second subscript in the direction of current.

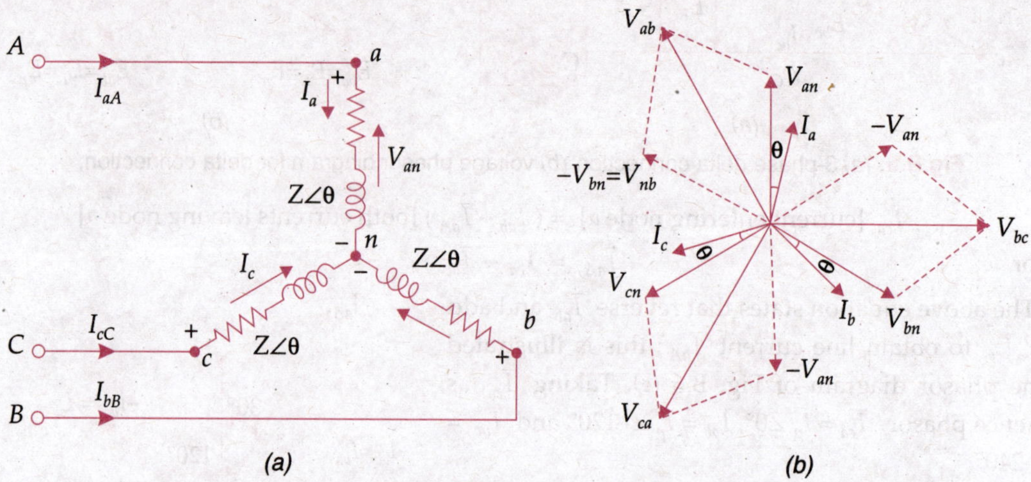

Fig B.7: *(a)* 3-phase star-connected load and *(b)* phasor diagram for circuit *(a)*.

Line voltage $\overline{V}_{ab} = \overline{V}_{an} + \overline{V}_{nb} = \overline{V}_{an} - \overline{V}_{bn}$. So V_{ab} is obtained by reversing V_{bn} and adding it to V_{an} as shown in Fig. B.7 *(b)*. In magnitude, $V_{an} = V_{bn} = V_{cn} = V_p$ (phase voltage). Therefore, it is seen from Fig. B.7 (b) that line voltage V_{ab} is given by

$$V_{ab} = \sqrt{V_{an}^2 + V_{nb}^2 + 2V_{an}\cdot V_{nb}\cdot\cos 60^\circ}$$

$$\therefore \quad V_{ab} = \sqrt{V_p^2 + V_p^2 + 2V_p\cdot V_p\cdot\cos 60^\circ} = \sqrt{3}\,V_p = V_L \text{ (line voltage).}$$

Similarly $\quad \overline{V}_{bc} = \overline{V}_{bn} - \overline{V}_{cn} = \sqrt{3}\cdot V_p$ and $V_{ca} = \overline{V}_{cn} - \overline{V}_{an} = \sqrt{3}\cdot V_p$

Phase current, $\quad \overline{I}_a = \dfrac{\overline{V}_{an}}{Z\angle\theta}$. Taking V_{an} as reference phasor, $\overline{V}_{an} = V_p\angle 0^\circ$

$$\left.\begin{aligned}\therefore \quad \overline{I}_a &= \frac{V_p\angle 0}{Z\angle\theta} = \frac{V_p}{Z}\angle -\theta \\ \overline{I}_b &= \frac{\overline{V}_{bn}}{Z\angle\theta} = \frac{V_p\angle -120^\circ}{Z\angle\theta} = \frac{V_p}{Z}\angle -(\theta + 120^\circ) \\ \text{and} \quad \overline{I}_c &= \frac{\overline{V}_{cn}}{Z\angle\theta} = \frac{V_p\angle -240^\circ}{Z\angle\theta} = \frac{V_p}{Z}\angle -(\theta + 240^\circ)\end{aligned}\right\} \quad \text{...(B.7)}$$

KCL at node '*a*' gives $\overline{I}_{Aa} = \overline{I}_a$

$\therefore$ Magnitude of line current, $\overline{I}_{Aa} = \overline{I}_{Bb} = \overline{I}_{Cc} = \dfrac{V_p}{Z}$.

B.4.2. Delta-connected Load

A 3-phase delta-connected balanced load is shown in Fig. B.8 *(a)*. Load impedance in each phase is $Z \angle\theta$ as in star-connected load.

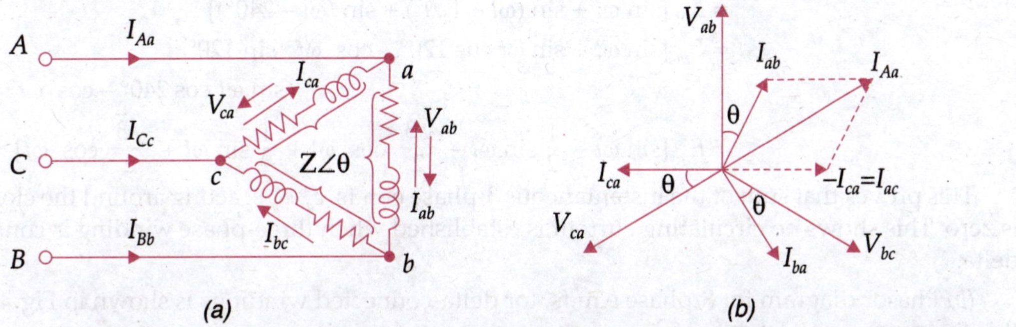

Fig B.8: Three-phase delta-connected load *(a)* its connection diagram and *(b)* its phasor diagram.

Here $V_{ab} = V_{bc} = V_{ca} = V_L$ (line voltage) $= V_p$ (phase voltage). The phasor diagram showing phase, or line, voltages V_{ab}, V_{bc}, V_{ca} and phase currents I_{ab}, I_{bc}, I_{ca} is drawn in Fig. B.8 *(b)*. The phase currents are shown lagging their respective phase voltages by an angle θ. Phase current flows from *a* to *b* whereas voltage rise is taken from *b* to *a* and written as V_{ab} as in star-connected load.

Taking V_{ab} as the reference phasor, we have $\overline{V}_{ab} = V_L \angle 0° = V_p \angle 0°$.

$$\therefore \quad \left.\begin{aligned} \overline{I}_{ab} &= \frac{\overline{V}_{ab}}{Z\angle\theta} = \frac{V_p\angle 0}{Z\angle\theta} = \frac{V_p}{Z}\angle -\theta = I_p \angle -\theta \\ \overline{I}_{bc} &= \frac{\overline{V}_{bc}}{Z\angle\theta} = \frac{V_p\angle -120°}{Z\angle\theta} = I_p\angle -(\theta + 120°) \\ \overline{I}_{ca} &= \frac{\overline{V}_{ca}}{Z\angle\theta} = \frac{V_p\angle -240°}{Z\angle\theta} = I_p\angle -(\theta + 240°) \end{aligned}\right\} \quad \text{...(B.8)}$$

where phase current, $$I_p = \frac{V_p}{Z}.$$

In Fig. B.8 *(a)*, KCL at node *'a'* gives $\overline{I}_{Aa} = \overline{I}_{ab} - \overline{I}_{ca}$. So reverse $\overline{I}_{ca}$ and add it to $\overline{I}_{ab}$ to obtain line current $\overline{I}_{Aa}$ as illustrated in Fig. B.8 (b). In magnitude, $I_{ab} = I_{ac} = I_p$

$$\therefore \quad \overline{I}_{Aa} = \sqrt{I_{ab}^2 + I_{ac}^2 + 2I_{ab}\cdot I_{ac}\cdot\cos 60°}$$

or Line current, $$\overline{I}_{Aa} = I_L = \sqrt{I_p^2 + I_p^2 + 2I_p\cdot I_p\cdot\cos 60°} = \sqrt{3}\ I_p$$

Similarly, $$\overline{I}_{Bb} = \overline{I}_{bc} - \overline{I}_{ab} \text{ and } I_{Bb} = I_L = \sqrt{3}\ I_p$$

and $$\overline{I}_{Cc} = \overline{I}_{ca} - \overline{I}_{bc} \text{ and } I_{Cc} = I_L = \sqrt{3}\ I_p$$

Phasor diagram for delta-connected load is shown in Fig. B.8 *(b)*.

Example B.1. *Prove that (a) sum of the instantaneous e.m.fs and (b) sum of r.m.s value of phasor e.m.fs. acting around the closed delta circuit formed by three-phase winding is zero.*

Solution. *(a)* From Fig. B.2 (b), with time origin taken at $\omega t = 0$ for phase-*a* voltage wave, the instantaneous voltage of phase *a* can be expressed as

$$e_a = E_m \sin \omega t$$

where E_m = maximum (or peak) value of phase voltage.

Since phase-*b* e.m.f. e_b lags e_a by 120°, $e_b = E_m \sin(\omega t - 120°)$

Similarly, $$e_c = E_m \sin(\omega t - 240°)$$

Sum of the instantaneous e.m.fs. acting around the closed delta of Fig. B.4 *(c)* is given by

$$\begin{aligned} e_{net} &= e_a + e_b + e_c \\ &= E_m \sin \omega t + E_m \sin(\omega t - 120°) + E_m \sin(\omega t - 240°) \\ &= E_m [\sin \omega t + \sin(\omega t - 120°) + \sin(\omega t - 240°)] \\ &= E_m [\sin \omega t + \sin \omega t \cos 120° - \cos \omega t \cdot \sin 120° \\ &\qquad + \sin \omega t \cos 240° - \cos \omega t \cdot \sin 240°] \\ &= E_m [\sin \omega t - \frac{1}{2} \sin \omega t - \frac{\sqrt{3}}{2} \cos \omega t + \frac{1}{2} \sin \omega t + \frac{\sqrt{3}}{2} \cos \omega t] = 0 \end{aligned}$$

This proves that sum of the instantaneous 3-phase e.m.fs. e_a, e_b, e_c acting around the closed delta is zero. This shows no circulating current is established when three-phase winding is connected in delta.

(b) Phasor diagram for 3-phase e.m.fs. for delta-connected windings is shown in Fig. B.6 *(b)*. In this figure, magnitude of e.m.f.

$$E_{ab} = E_{bc} = E_{ca} = E_p \text{ or } E_L.$$

Resultant of two phase e.m.fs. E_{ca} and E_{ab}, displaced from each other by 120°, is given by

$$\bar{E}_{ca} + \bar{E}_{ab} = \bar{E}_{cb}$$

This phasor sum $\bar{E}_{cb}$ is shown in Fig. B.9. Phase angle between E_{ca} (= E_p) and E_{ab} (= E_p) is 120°. Therefore, their phasor sum is

$$E_{cb} = \sqrt{E_p^2 + E_p^2 + 2E_p^2 \cos 120°} = E_p$$

Since $E_{cb} = E_p$ is 180° away from $E_{bc} = E_p$, the phasor sum $\bar{E}_{bc} + \bar{E}_{cb} = 0$. This shows that phasor sum of r.m.s value of three e.m.fs. acting around the closed delta is zero.

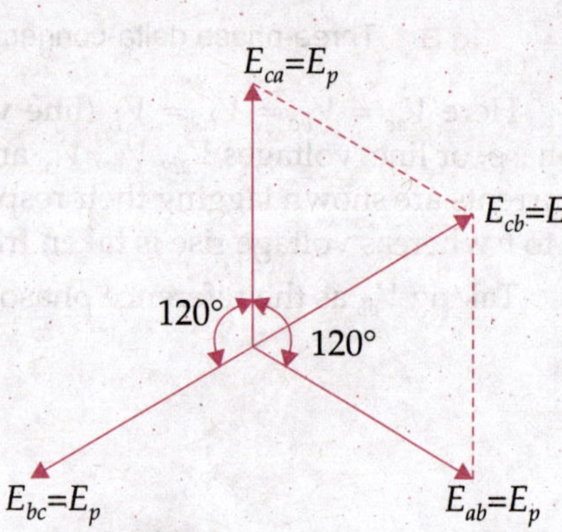

Fig B.9: Pertaining to Example B.1.

Example B.2. *A four-wire 3-phase system is shown in Fig. B.10. Generated e.m.fs. and load constitute a balanced 3-phase system. Find the current in the neutral conductor.*

Solution. Since the three loads have the same magnitude of impedance as well as phase angle, the three load currents are balanced and displaced from each other by a time angle of 120°.

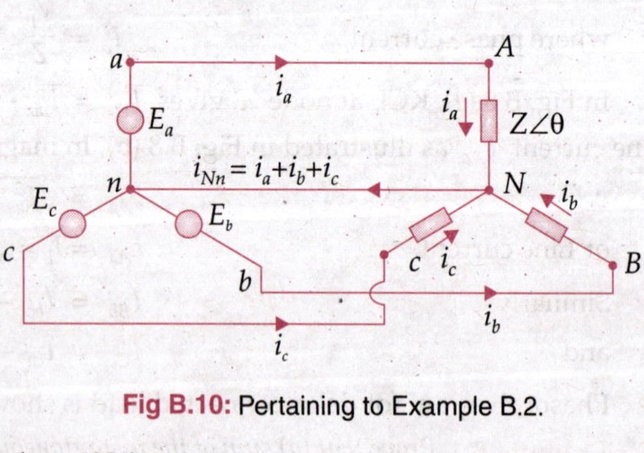

Fig B.10: Pertaining to Example B.2.

Let the current in phase-*a* be expressed with time origin at $\omega t = 0$.

$\therefore$ $\quad i_a = I_m \sin \omega t,\ i_b = I_m \sin(\omega t - 120°)$

and $\quad i_c = I_m \sin(\omega t - 240°)$

Current in the neutral conductor i_{Nn} is the sum of three instantaneous current i_a, i_b and i_c.

$\therefore$ $\quad i_{Nn} = I_m [\sin \omega t + \sin(\omega t - 120°) + \sin(\omega t - 240°)] = 0$ [As in Example B.1].

This shows current in neutral conductor is zero at every instant of time. Hence this conductor can be dispensed with and the 3-phase system of Fig. B.10 would then become a three-wire three-phase star-connected system.

Note. Balanced three-phase circuit problems can be solved on per-phase basis. For this, a single-phase equivalent circuit is formed and the analysis carried out. Then, the single-phase solution is appropriately converted into a 3-phase solution by taking into consideration whether the system is star or delta connected.

B.5. POWER IN THREE-PHASE CIRCUITS

In a balanced 3-phase circuit (star or delta), the phase voltages and currents can be expressed in instantaneous form as under :

Phase voltages:

$$e_a = E_m \sin \omega t$$
$$e_b = E_m \sin (\omega t - 120°)$$
$$e_c = E_m \sin (\omega t - 240°)$$

Phase currents lagging the corresponding phase voltages by an angle θ are

$$i_a = I_m \sin (\omega t - \theta)$$
$$i_b = I_m \sin (\omega t - \theta - 120°)$$
$$i_c = I_m \sin (\omega t - \theta - 240°)$$

Instantaneous power p_a in phase a is

$$p_a = e_a\, i_a = E_m I_m \sin \omega t \times \sin (\omega t - \theta)$$

But
$$\sin A \sin B = \frac{1}{2} [\cos (A - B) - \cos (A + B)]$$

∴
$$p_a = \frac{E_m I_m}{2} [\cos \theta - \cos (2\omega t - \theta)] \qquad \text{...(B.9)}$$

Here
$$\frac{E_m}{\sqrt{2}} = \text{r.m.s phase voltage, } E_p$$
$$\frac{I_m}{\sqrt{2}} = \text{r.m.s phase current, } I_p$$

∴
$$p_a = E_p I_p [\cos \theta - \cos (2\omega t - \theta)]$$

Similarly,
$$p_b = e_b i_b = E_p I_p [\cos \theta - \cos (2\omega t - \theta - 240°)]$$
$$p_c = e_c i_c = E_p I_p [\cos \theta - \cos (2\omega t - \theta - 120°)]$$

Total instantaneous power p is $p = p_a + p_b + p_c$

$$= 3\, E_p I_p \cos \theta - E_p I_p [\cos (2\omega t - \theta) + \cos (2\omega t - \theta - 120°) + \cos (2\omega t - \theta - 240°)]$$

Sum of the three cosine terms, displaced from each other by 120° is zero.

∴
$$p = 3\, E_p I_p \cos \theta \qquad \text{...(B.10)}$$

or
$$p = 3 \text{ [average power per phase]}$$

Eq. (B.10) shows total instantaneous power in a balanced 3-phase system does not depend on time.

For a single-phase system. Eq. (B.9) reveals that instantaneous power, in general, can be expressed as

$$P = EI [\cos \theta - \cos (2\omega t - \theta)]$$

It is seen from above expression for power p that instantaneous power in a single-phase circuit is not constant, whereas it is constant in a three-phase system as per Eq. (B.10). It follows from this that shaft torque developed in single-phase machines is of pulsating nature, whereas shaft torque available from 3-phase machines is constant. This is one of the most important reasons for the universal adoption of three-phase systems for high-power applications.

Thus, power in a balanced star/delta system is given by

$$P = 3\,E_p I_p \cos\theta = 3\,I_p^2 R_p \text{ W}$$

Also $$P = \sqrt{3}\;E_L I_L \sin\theta$$

Similarly, reactive power, $$Q = 3\,E_p I_p \sin\theta = 3\,I_p^2 \cdot X_p \text{ VAr}$$

Also, $$Q = \sqrt{3}\;E_L I_L \sin\theta$$

Here E_p, I_p, θ, X_p are respectively the per-phase values of voltage, current, power-factor angle and reactance.

Total 3-phase apparent power, $$S = \sqrt{P^2 + Q^2} \text{ VA}$$

or $$S = 3\,E_p I_p = \sqrt{3}\;E_L I_L = 3\,I_p^2 Z_p \text{ VA}$$

where Z_p = per-phase impedance

E_L = line voltage, I_L = line current.

Note that θ in Eq. (B.10) is the angle between phase voltage and phase current and is given by

$$\theta = \tan^{-1}\frac{X_p}{Z_p} = \sin^{-1}\frac{X_p}{Z_p} = \cos^{-1}\frac{R_p}{Z_p}$$

B.6 THREE-PHASE CIRCUITS

As stated before, problems pertaining to three-phase balanced circuits can be solved conveniently by forming their equivalent single-phase circuits. The solution obtained from single-phase circuit is then transformed to 3-phase solution.

When load consists of a parallel combination of star-connected as well as delta-connected loads, it is essential that calculations are carried out by converting star-connected load to equivalent delta or delta-connected load to equivalent star. The conversion from star to delta or delta to star is based on the general star-delta transformation used in circuit theory. Thus, in Fig. B.11, equivalent delta-connected impedance Z_d from given star-impedance Z_y is

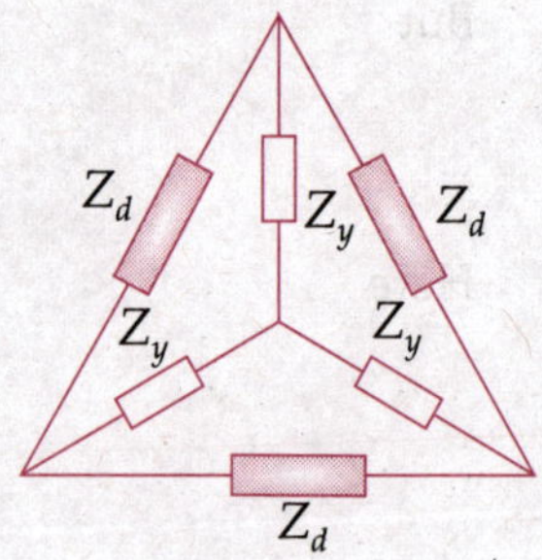

Fig B.11: Star-delta transformation.

$$Z_d = Z_y + Z_y + \frac{Z_y \cdot Z_y}{Z_y} = 3Z_y \qquad \text{...(B.11 (a))}$$

Equivalent star-connected impedance Z_y from known delta-connected impedance Z_d in Fig. B.11 is

$$Z_y = \frac{Z_d \cdot Z_d}{Z_d + Z_d + Z_d} = \frac{1}{3}\,Z_d \qquad \text{...(B.11 (b))}$$

It is obvious from above that a three-phase circuit can be solved by representing the entire three-phase system by star-connected circuits or by delta-connected circuits. It has, however, been found that working with star-connected circuits is more convenient, as such this approach is usually adopted.

Sometimes it is not specified in a problem whether three-phase system is in star or in delta. In such a case, it is common to assume the system to be in star for calculation purposes.

Example B.3. *For a supply voltage of 3-phase, 400V, calculate phase current, line current, power factor, total volt-amperes, total active and reactive powers if a load of impedance = 10 + j 7.5 Ω per phase is (a) star-connected and (b) delta-connected.*

Solution. ***(a)* Star-connected load**

Phase voltage, $V_p = \frac{V_L}{\sqrt{3}} = \frac{400}{\sqrt{3}} = 230.95$ V

Impedance per phase, $Z_p = 10 + j\,7.5 = 12.5\angle 36.87°$

Phase current, $I_p = \frac{V_p}{Z_p} = \frac{230.95}{12.5\angle 36.87°} = 18.476\angle -36.87°$ A

Line current, $I_L = I_p = 18.476$ A

Power factor $= \cos 36.87° = 0.8$ lagging

Total $VA, S = \sqrt{3}\cdot V_L I_L = \sqrt{3} \times 400 \times 18.476 = 12800.173$ VA

Total active power, $P = \sqrt{3}\, V_L I_L \cos\theta = \sqrt{3} \times 400 \times 18.476 \times 0.8 = 10240.14$ W

Total reactive power, $Q = \sqrt{3}\, V_L I_L \sin\theta = \sqrt{3} \times 400 \times 18.476 \times 0.6 = 7680.1$ VAr.

***(b)* Delta-connected load**

Phase voltage, $V_p = V_L = 400$ V

Phase impedance, $Z_p = 10 + j\,7.5 = 12.5\angle 37.87°$

Phase current, $I_p = \frac{V_p}{Z_p} = \frac{400}{12.5\angle 36.87°} = 32\angle -36.87°$ A

Line current, $I_L = \sqrt{3}\, I_p = \sqrt{3} \times 32 = 55.424$ A

Power factor, $= \cos 36.87° = 0.8$ lagging

Total VA, $S = \sqrt{3}\, V_L I_L = \sqrt{3} \times 400 \times 55.424 = 38397.75$ VA

Total active power, $P = \sqrt{3}\, V_L I_L \cos\theta = \sqrt{3} \times 400 \times 55.424 \times 0.8 = 30718.2$ W

Total reactive power, $Q = \sqrt{3}\, V_L I_L \sin\theta = \sqrt{3} \times 400 \times 55.424 \times 0.6 = 23038.65$ VAr

It is seen from the solution of this example that

(i) $\frac{\text{line current in delta}}{\text{line current in star}} = \frac{55.424}{18.476} \simeq 3$ *(ii)* $\frac{\text{power in delta}}{\text{power in star}} = \frac{30718.2}{10240.14} \simeq 3$ and

(iii) $\frac{\text{VA in delta}}{\text{VA in star}} = \frac{23038.65}{7680.1} \simeq 3.$

Example B.4. *A balanced 3-phase star-connected load takes 30 kW at a leading current of 48 A from a 3-phase source of 500 V, 50 Hz. Find the circuit constants per phase.*

Solution. Total power, $P = \sqrt{3}\, V_L I_L \cos\theta$

$30{,}000 = \sqrt{3} \times 500 \times 48 \times \cos\theta$

∴ Power factor, $\cos\theta = \frac{30{,}000}{\sqrt{3} \times 500 \times 48} = 0.7217$ leading (given)

$\sin\theta = 0.6922$

Phase voltage, $V_p = \frac{500}{\sqrt{3}}$ V, phase current, $I_p = I_L = 48$ A

∴ Phase impedance, $Z_p = \frac{V_p}{I_p} = \frac{500}{\sqrt{3} \times 48} = 6.014\ \Omega$

Load resistance, $R_p = Z_p \cos\theta = 6.014 \times 0.7217 = 4.34\ \Omega$

When load current is leading, the other load parameter must be a capacitance.

$$\therefore \quad X_c = Z_p \sin \theta = 6.014 \times 0.6922 = 4.163\ \Omega$$

or
$$\frac{1}{2\pi fC} = X_c = 4.163\ \Omega \text{ or } C = \frac{10^6}{2\pi \times 50 \times 4.163} = 764.616\ \mu\text{F}.$$

Example B.5. *Three star-connected impedances of 10 + j 15 Ω per phase are in parallel with three delta-connected impedances of 12 – j 15 Ω per phase across a 3-phase, 400 V supply.*

(a) Calculate the total line current

(b) Calculate also the power factor, power and reactive power of the combination.

Solution. As stated earlier, it is more convenient to replace delta-connection by an equivalent star-connection for solving such problems, and therefore, same is done here.

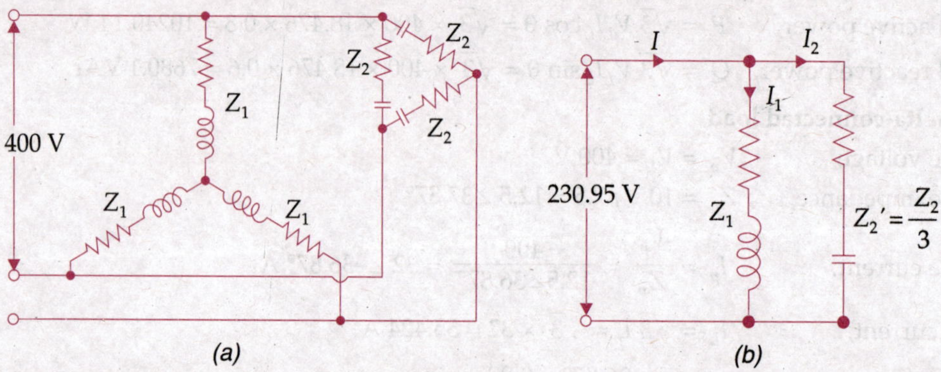

Fig B.12: *(a)* Pertaining to Example B.5 *(b)* equivalent single-phase circuit of Fig. B.12 *(a)*.

(a) In Fig. B.12 *(a)*, star and delta connected loads are shown. Replacing per phase impedance of Δ-connected load by an equivalent *Y*-connected load of Z_2' per phase, we get Fig. B.12 *(b)*, where

$$Z_2' = \frac{Z_2}{3} = \frac{12 - j15}{3} = 4 - j\,5 = 6.4\ \angle{-51.34°}$$

and
$$Z_1 = 10 + j\,15 = 18.03\ \angle 56.31°$$

Phase voltage,
$$V_p = \frac{400}{\sqrt{3}} = 230.95\ \text{V}$$

Current I_1 and I_2 are shown flowing in impedances Z_1 and Z_2' respectively in Fig. B.12 *(b)*.

$$\therefore \quad I_1 = \frac{V_p}{Z_1} = \frac{230.95}{18.03\angle 56.31°} = 12.81\ \angle{-56.31°}\ \text{A}$$

Therefore, phase, or line current in *Y*-connected load = 12.81 A

$$I_2 = \frac{V_p}{Z_2'} = \frac{230.95}{6.4\angle{-51.34°}} = 36.086\ \angle{-51.34°}\ \text{A}$$

∴ Line-current in Δ-connected load = 36.086 A and its phase current = $\frac{36.086}{\sqrt{3}}$ = 20.835 A.

Line current of the combined load, I_L = line current of Y-connected load, I_1 + line current of Δ-connected load, I_2

or
$$\begin{aligned} I_L &= 12.81\ \angle{-56.31°} + 36.086\ \angle{-51.34°} \\ &= (7.106 - j\,10.66) + (22.54 + j\,28.18) \\ &= 29.646 + j\,17.52 = 34.436\ \angle 30.582°\ \text{A} \end{aligned}$$

∴ Total line current, $I_L = 34.436$ A

(*b*) Power factor of the combination = cos 30.582° = 0.861 leading.

Total power of the combination $= \sqrt{3}\, V_L I_L \cos\theta = \sqrt{3} \times 400 \times 34.436 \times 0.861 = 20541.1$ W

Here $\sin\theta = 0.5086$

Total reactive power $= \sqrt{3}\, V_L I_L \sin\theta$

$= \sqrt{3} \times 400 \times 34.436 \times 0.5086 = 12133.8$ VAr

B.7 MEASUREMENT OF POWER IN THREE-PHASE BALANCED CIRCUITS

Power in a 3-phase circuit can be measured by two-wattmeter method. Fig. B.13 illustrates the connection of two wattmeters for the measurement of power in a 3-phase star-connected balanced load. Load phase voltages V_{an}, V_{bn}, V_{cn} are shown as phasors in Fig. B.14 and the corresponding phasor currents I_a, I_b, I_c are drawn lagging the respective phase voltages by a p.f. angle θ.

Wattmeter W$_1$. Current through its coil $= I_a$, Potential difference across the voltage coil

$$= V_{ac} = \overline{V}_{an} + \overline{V}_{nc} = \overline{V}_{an} - \overline{V}_{cn}.$$

So reverse phasor V_{cn} and add to phasor V_{an} to obtain V_{ac}; this is shown in Fig. B.14.

Phase angle between V_{ac} and $I_a = 30 - \theta$

∴ Reading of wattmeter, $W_1 = V_{ac} \cdot I_a \cdot \cos(30 - \theta)$

Wattmeter W$_2$. Current through its coil $= I_b$

Potential difference across its voltage coil $= V_{bc} = \overline{V}_{bn} + \overline{V}_{nc} = \overline{V}_{bn} - \overline{V}_{cn}$

So reverse V_{cn} and add it to V_{bn} to get V_{bc} as illustrated in Fig. B.14.

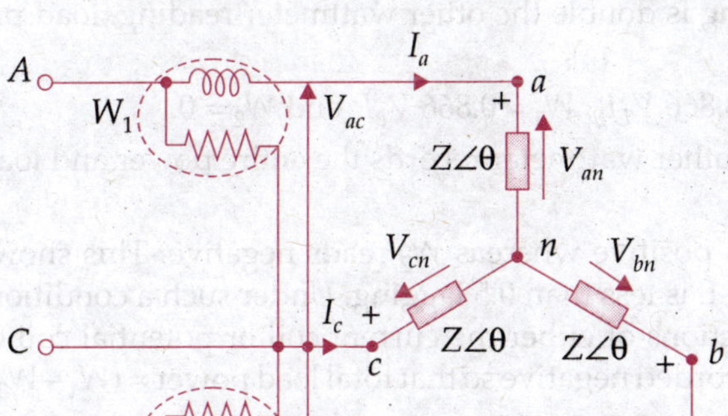

Fig B.13: Measurement of power by two-wattmeter method.

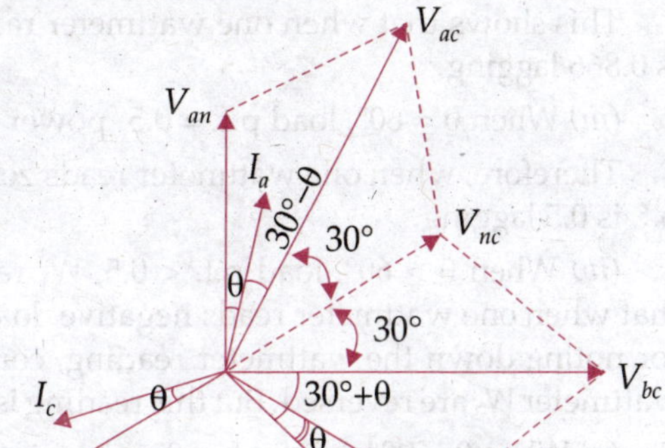

Fig B.14: Phasor diagram for two-wattmeter method.

Phase angle between V_{bc} and $I_b = 30 + \theta$

∴ Reading of Wattmeter $W_2 = V_{bc} I_b \cos(30 + \theta)$

For a balanced load, $I_a = I_b = I_c = I_p = I_L$ (line current)

and $V_{ab} = V_{bc} = V_{ca} = |V_{ac}| = V_L$ (line voltage)

∴ $W_1 = V_L I_L \cos(30 - \theta)$ ...(B.12)

and $W_2 = V_L I_L \cos(30 + \theta)$ ...(B.13)

Sum of two wattmeter readings,

$$W_1 + W_2 = V_L I_L [\cos(30-\theta) + \cos(30+\theta)]$$
$$= V_L I_L [\cos 30 \cos\theta + \sin 30 \sin\theta + \cos 30 \cos\theta - \sin 30 \sin\theta]$$
$$= 2V_L I_L \cos 30 \cos\theta$$
$$= 2V_L I_L \cdot \frac{\sqrt{3}}{2} \cdot \cos\theta$$

$$\therefore \quad W_1 + W_2 = \sqrt{3}\, V_L I_L \cos\theta = \text{total 3-phase power} \quad ...(B.14)$$

Difference of two wattmeter readings, $W_1 - W_2 = V_L I_L [\cos(30-\theta) - \cos(30+\theta)]$

$$= V_L I_L [\cos 30 \cos\theta + \sin 30 \sin\theta - \cos 30 \cos\theta + \sin 30 \sin\theta]$$
$$= 2V_L I_L \sin 30 \sin\theta = V_L I_L \sin\theta \quad ...(B.15)$$

From above, $\dfrac{\text{Eq.}(B.15)}{\text{Eq.}(B.14)} = \dfrac{V_L I_L \sin\theta}{\sqrt{3}\, V_L I_L \cos\theta} = \dfrac{W_1 - W_2}{W_1 + W_2}$

or $\tan\theta = \sqrt{3}\, \dfrac{W_1 - W_2}{W_1 + W_2}$

$$\therefore \quad \text{Load power factor} = \cos\left[\tan^{-1} \cdot \sqrt{3}\frac{W_1 - W_2}{W_1 + W_2}\right] \quad ...(B.16)$$

It is observed from above that

(i) When $\theta = 0°$, load p.f. = 1, power= $\sqrt{3}\, V_L I_L$, $W_1 = V_L I_L \cos 30 = 0.866\, V_L I_L$. Also, $W_2 = 0.866\, V_L I_L = W_1$. Therefore, when both wattmeter readings are equal, load p.f. is unity.

(ii) When $\theta = 30°$, load p.f. = 0.866, power = $1.5\, V_L I_L$, $W_1 = V_L I_L$ and $W_2 = 0.5\, V_L I_L = \dfrac{W_1}{2}$.

This shows that when one wattmeter reading is double the other wattmeter reading, load p.f. is 0.866 lagging.

(iii) When $\theta = 60°$, load p.f. = 0.5, power = $0.866\, V_L I_L$, $W_1 = 0.866\, V_L I_L$ and $W_2 = 0$.

Therefore, when one wattmeter reads zero, other wattmeter records the entire power and load p.f. is 0.5 lagging.

(iv) When $\theta > 60°$, load p.f. < 0.5, W_1 reads positive whereas W_2 reads negative. This shows that when one wattmeter reads negative, load p.f. is less than 0.5 lagging. Under such a condition, for noting down the wattmeter reading, connections of either the current coil or potential coil of wattmeter W_2 are reversed. But this reading is recorded negative so that total load power = $(W_1 - W_2)$.

(v) When $\theta = 90°$, load p.f. = 0, power = 0, $W_1 = 0.5\, V_L I_L$ and $W_2 = -0.5\, V_L I_L$.

So when both wattemter readings are equal but one is positive and the other is negative, the load p.f. is zero.

Note. Out of the two wattmeter readings, the higher reading is taken as positive and the other reading as W_2; except when p.f. = 1.

Example B.6. *Power input to a 3-phase induction motor is measured by two-wattmeter method. For supply mains of 1100 V, 50 Hz ; the two wattmeter readings are 85 kW and 35 kW respectively. Motor efficiency is 0.85. Calculate power input, power factor, line current and shaft power of this motor.*

Solution. Wattmeter readings are $W_1 = 85$ kW and $W_2 = 35$ kW.

$\therefore$ Power input to motor = 85 + 35 = 120 kW

From Eq. (B.16), $\tan\theta = \sqrt{3}\, \dfrac{W_1 - W_2}{W_1 + W_2} = \sqrt{3}\, \dfrac{85 - 35}{85 + 35} = 0.7217$

$$\theta = \tan^{-1}(0.7217) = 35.82°$$

$$\text{Motor p.f.} = \cos 35.82° = 0.81 \text{ lagging}$$

$$\text{Also, power input to motor} = \sqrt{3} \times V_L I_L \cos\theta = 120 \text{ kW}$$

or $$\sqrt{3} \times 1100 \times I_L \times 0.81 = 120{,}000 \text{ W}$$

$\therefore$ Line current, $$I_L = \frac{120{,}000}{\sqrt{3}\times 1100 \times 0.81} = 77.76 \text{ A}$$

Shaft power $$= \eta \times \text{power input to motor.}$$
$$= 0.85 \times 120 = 102 \text{ kW.}$$

Example B.7. *Two wattmeters connected to measure the no-load power input to a 3-phase induction motor indicate 2000 W and 400 W respectively, but the latter reading is obtained after reversing the connections to its current coil. Find the no-load losses of 3-phase induction motor and its no-load p.f.*

Solution. Here $$W_1 = 2000 \text{ W},$$
$$W_2 = -400 \text{ W}$$

$\therefore$ No-load losses of 3-phase induction motor = 2000 – 400 = 1600 W

From Eq. (B.16), $$\tan\theta = \sqrt{3}\,\frac{2000+400}{2000-400} = 2.598$$
$$\theta = 68.948°$$

No-load p.f. of 3-phase induction motor = cos 68.948° = 0.3592 lagging.

Example B.8. *Two wattmeters are used to measure the power input to a balanced star-connected load consisting of C = 100 μF in each phase. The load is fed from 3-phase, 230 V, 50 Hz source. Calculate the reading of each wattmeter and the total power input to the load.*

Solution. For the circuit diagram of Fig. B.13 consisting of C as the load in each phase, the phasor diagram is drawn in Fig. B.15. Here phase currents I_a, I_b are shown leading by 90° their corresponding phase voltages V_{an}, V_{bn}.

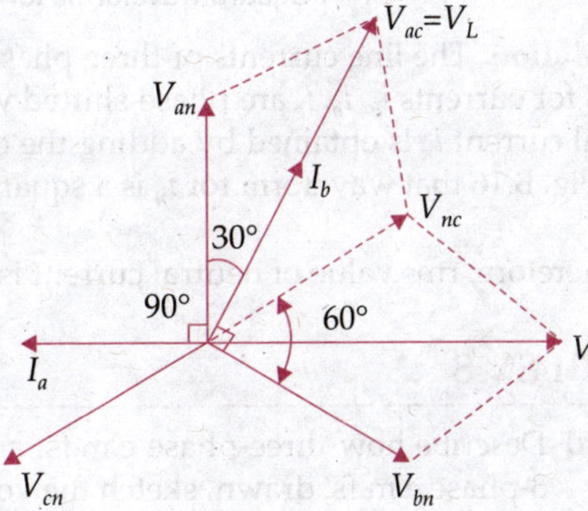

Fig B.15: Phasor diagram pertaining to Example B.8.

Phase voltage, $$V_p = \frac{230}{\sqrt{3}} \text{ V}$$

Phase impedance, $$Z_p = \frac{1}{2\pi fC}$$

or $$Z_p = \frac{10^6}{2\pi \times 50 \times 100} = 31.831\ \Omega$$

Phase current, $$I_a = I_b = I_c = \frac{230}{\sqrt{3}\times 31.831} = 4.172 \text{ A}$$

It is seen from Fig. B.15 that reading of wattmeter W_1 is given by

$$W_1 = V_{ac} \cdot I_a \cdot \cos\,\overline{(V_{ac}, I_a)} = 230 \times 4.172 \times \cos 120° = -479.78 \text{ W}$$

Reading of wattmeter, $W_2 = V_{bc} \cdot I_b \cdot \cos\,\overline{(V_{bc}, I_b)} = 230 \times 4.172 \times \cos 60° = 479.78$ W

Power input to load = $W_1 + W_2 = 0$. The result is as expected, since C consumes no power.

Example B.9. *The line currents of a three-phase four-wire system are square waves with amplitude of 100 A. These currents are phase shifted by 120° with respect to each other. The rms value of neutral current in amperes is ....* [GATE, 2019]

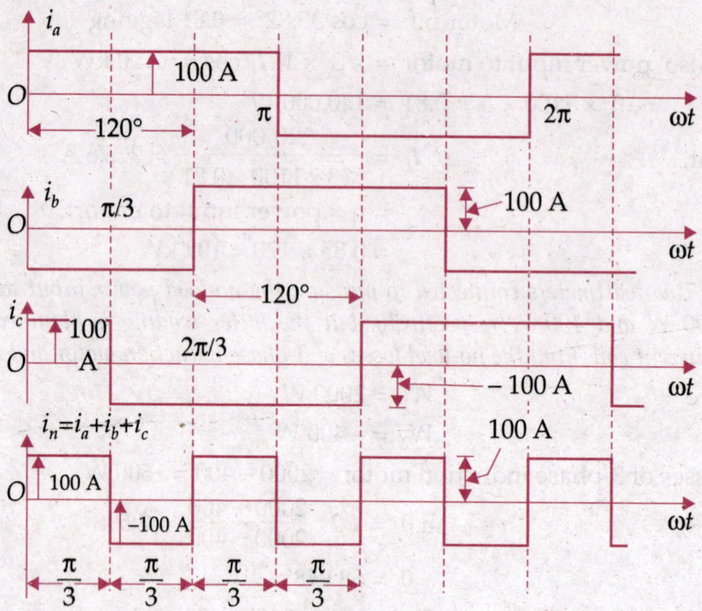

Fig B.16: Square waveforms for line currents i_a, i_b, i_c and neutral current i_n.

Solution. The line currents of three phases *a*, *b*, *c* are shown as i_a, i_b, i_c in Fig. B.16. The square waves for currents i_a, i_b, i_c are phase-shifted with respect to each other by 120°. The wave form for neutral current i_n is obtained by adding the ordinates of three currents i_a, i_b, i_c as shown. It is seen from Fig. B.16 that waveform for i_n is a square wave of amplitude 100 A with periodicity $\pi/3$.

Therefore, rms value of neutral current is $I_n = \left\{\frac{1}{\pi/3}\left[(100)^2 \times \frac{\pi}{3}\right]\right\}^{1/2}$ = **100 A.**

PROBLEMS

B.1. *(a)* Describe how three-phase e.m.fs. are generated in an alternator. From the waveform of 3-phase e.m.fs. drawn, sketch the voltage phasor diagrams at $\omega t = 60°$ and at $\omega t = 120°$.

(b) A 3-phase delta-connected load, with an impedance of $8 + j\,6\ \Omega$ per phase, is fed from 230 V, 50 Hz source. Find the phase current, line current, power factor, apparent power, active and reactive powers of the load.

[Ans. (b) 23 A, 39.836 A, 0.8 lagging, 15870 VA, 12696 W, 9522 VAr]

B.2. *(a)* Distinguish between balanced and unbalanced three phase systems.

(b) What is phase sequence? How can it be reversed for a 3-phase *(i)* generator and *(ii)* load.

(c) Three load impedances, each of $8 + j\,6\ \Omega$, are connected in star and fed from 3-phase, 230 V, 50 Hz supply mains. Calculate phase current, line current, power factor, apparent power, active and reactive powers.

[Ans. *(c)* 13.28 A, 13.28 A, 0.8 lagging, 5290.22 VA, 4232.177 W, 3174.133 VAr]

B.3. *(a)* Derive the relationship between the phase and the line values of em.fs. and currents in a 3-phase star-connected alternator.

(b) A balanced 3-phase delta-connected load takes 50 kW at a lagging current of 90 A when connected to a 3-phase, 400 V, 50 Hz source. Find the circuit parameters per phase.

[Ans. *(b)* $R = 6.172\ \Omega$, $L = 14.64$ mH]

B.4. (a) Deduce the relationship between the phase and the line currents and e.m.fs. of a 3-phase delta-connected alternator.

(b) Three equal impedances, connected in delta, take a power of 30 kW when fed from 3-phase source. If load impedances are reconnected in star, find the new power taken by the load.

[Ans. *(b)* 10 kW]

B.5. Three star-connected impedances of $14 - j\,16\ \Omega$ per phase are in parallel with delta-connected impedances of $30 + j\,24\ \Omega$ per phase across a 3-phase, 400 V source. Calculate the line current, power factor, power and reactive power of the combined load.

[Ans. 21.74 A, 0.9926 lag, 14950 W, 1828.915 VAr]

B.6. Three star-connected inductances, each of 1 H per phase, are connected in parallel with three delta-connected capacitances, each of *C* farads per phase. This combination takes no current from 3-phase, 50 Hz source. Find the value of C. **[Ans.** C = 3.3774 μF]

B.7. (a) Show by means of connection and circuit diagrams that sum of two wattermeter readings measure the total power in a 3-phase, 3-wire circuit. Assume the load to be inductive in nature.

(b) Discuss what happens to two wattmeter readings in case load is capacitive in nature. Illustrate your answer with a phasor diagram.

[Ans. *(a)* $W_1 = V_L I_L \cos(30 - \theta)$, $W_2 = V_L I_L \cos(30 + \theta)$]

(b) $W_1 = V_L I_L \cos(30 + \theta)$, $W_2 = V_L I_L \cos(30 - \theta)$

B.8. (a) Show, with relevant connection and phasor diagrams that the power in a balanced 3-phase circuit can be derived from the reading of two wattmeters.

(b) A 60 kW, 1100 V, 3-phase induction motor operates at full load efficiency 90% and p.f. 0.86. Calculate the reading on each of the two wattmeters connected to measure the full-load input. **[Ans.** *(b)* 44.756 kW, 21.918 kW]

B.9. (a) Explain the following terms :

Three-phase balanced supply, three-phase balanced load, three-phase balanced system, three-phase unbalanced load.

(b) A balanced star-connected load of $10 + j\,20\ \Omega$ per phase is fed from 440 V, 50 Hz supply. The phase sequence is *abc* (or *RYB*). Two wattmeters connected to read the total power have their current coils connected in the *a* and *c* (or *R* and *B*) lines respectively. Draw the circuit and phasor diagrams, derive the expression for each wattmeter reading and calculate the reading of each wattmeter.

[Hint. *(b)* Follow the Art. B.7. Here $W_1 = V_{ab} I_a \cos(30 + \theta)$ and $W_2 = V_{cb} I_c \cos(30 - \theta)$ etc.]

[Ans. *(b)* $W_1 = V_L I_L \cos(30 + \theta)$, $W_2 = V_L I_L \cos(30 - \theta)$; – 299.485 W, 4171.222 W]

B.10. (a) Prove that total power in a 3-phase balanced circuit is $\sqrt{3}\, V_L I_L \cos\theta$ where the symbols used have their usual meanings.

(b) Three identical impedances are fed from 3-phase balanced supply. Prove that power consumption with impedances in delta = 3 × (power consumption with impedances in star).

(c) Power in a balanced three-phase load is measured by two-wattmeter method and it is found that the ratio of two readings is 3 to 1. What is the power factor of the load if

(i) both the wattmeter readings are positive and

(ii) one of the two wattmeter readings is negative. **[Ans.** *(c)* 0.756 lag ; 0.27736 lag]

B.11. *(a)* Sketch the waveform of three-phase voltages taking the voltage of phase *'a'* maximum at $\omega t = 0°$. Write their expressions as a function of time.

(b) Three identical coils are connected in star to a 400 V, 3-phase supply and each takes 1600 W. The power factor is 0.6 lagging. What will be the line current and total power if the same coils are re-connected in delta to the same supply?

If power is measured by two wattmeters with the coils in star, what will be their readings?

[Ans. *(b)* 34.64 A, 14400 W; 4247.65 W, 552.50 W]

B.12. *(a)* The resistance across any two terminals of a balanced 3-phase load is 2 Ω. For a supply voltage of 400 V, the line current is 80 A. Find power factor and per-phase parameters of the load connected in *(i)* star and *(ii)* delta.

(b) Two wattmeters measure the input to a balanced star-connected load of $L = 20$ mH in each phase. For a supply voltage of 400 V, 50 Hz, calculate the reading of each wattmeter and total power taken from the source. Illustrate your answer with a suitable phasor diagram.

[Ans. *(a) (i)* 0.3464 lag, R = 1 Ω, X = 2.7083 Ω *(ii)* 0.3464 lag, $R = 3$ Ω, X = 8.124 Ω

(b) $W_1 = 7352$ W, $W_2 = -7352$ W, total power = 0]

C
Appendix

Objective Type Questions

The multiple choice questions given in this appendix pertain to general electrical-engineering topics and in particular, to the electrical-machinery topics covered in this book. Several questions have been taken from competitive examinations like GATE, IES, IAS etc.

Out of the various alternatives given, choose the most appropriate answer.

ELECTRICAL ENGINEERING

1. The resistance between the opposite faces of 1 meter-cube is found to be 1 Ω. If its length is increased to 2 meters, its volume remaining unchanged, then resistance between the opposite faces of its length is

(*a*) 2 Ω (*b*) 4 Ω (*c*) 1 Ω (*d*) Ω 8

2. Time constant for an *RL* series circuit is given by

(*a*) *R/L* (*b*) 1/*RL* (*c*) *RL* (*d*) *L/R*

3. Time constant for series *RL* circuit is defined as the time taken by the current to reach

(*a*) 36.8% of its final value (*b*) 36.8% of its initial value

(*c*) 63.2% of its final value (*d*) 63.2% of its initial value

4. Time constant for *RC* series circuit is equal to

(*a*) 1/*RC* (*b*) *R/C* (*c*) *C/R* (*d*) *RC*

5. A series *RC* circuits is suddenly connected to a D.C. voltage of *V* volts. The current in the series circuit, just after the switch is closed is equal to

(*a*) zero (*b*) *V/RC* (*c*) *VC/R* (*d*) *V/R*

6. A series *RL* circuit is suddenly connected to a D.C. voltage source of *V* volts. The current in this circuit, soon after the switch is closed, is equal to

(*a*) zero (*b*) *V/L* (*c*) *V/R* (*d*) *VL/R*

7. A series *LC* circuit is suddenly connected to a D.C. voltage source of *V* volts. The current in this circuit at $t = 0^+$, is equal to

(*a*) zero (*b*) *V/L* (*c*) *V/C* (*d*) *VL/C*

8. In the network shown in Fig. C.1, the current through 11 Ω resistor is

(*a*) $\frac{1}{4}$ A (*b*) $\frac{1}{3}$ A (*c*) $\frac{9}{8}$ A (*d*) $\frac{1}{2}$ A

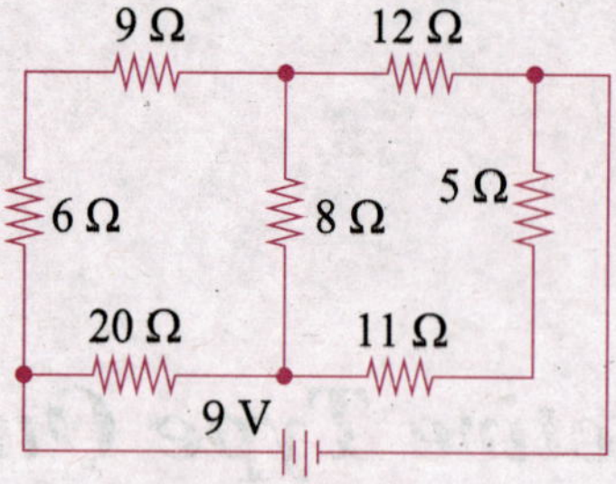

Fig C.1

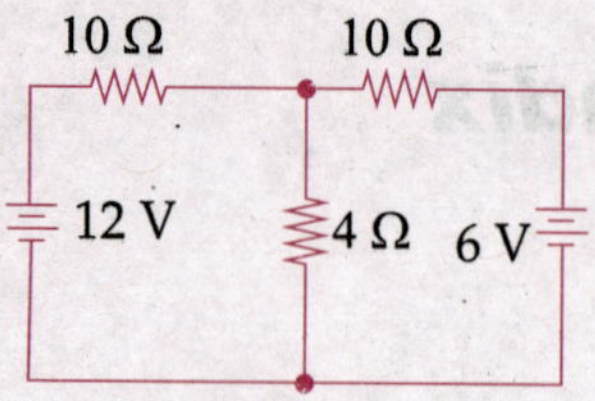

Fig C.2

9. In the network shown in Fig. C.2, the current through 4 Ω resistor is

(a) 2 A (b) 1 A (c) $\frac{1}{2}$ A (d) 1.5 A

10. In the circuit of Fig. C.3, the potential of terminal

(a) *B* is higher than *A* by 5 V (b) *A* is higher than *B* by 5 V

(c) *B* is higher than *A* by 13 V (d) *A* is higher than *B* by 13 V

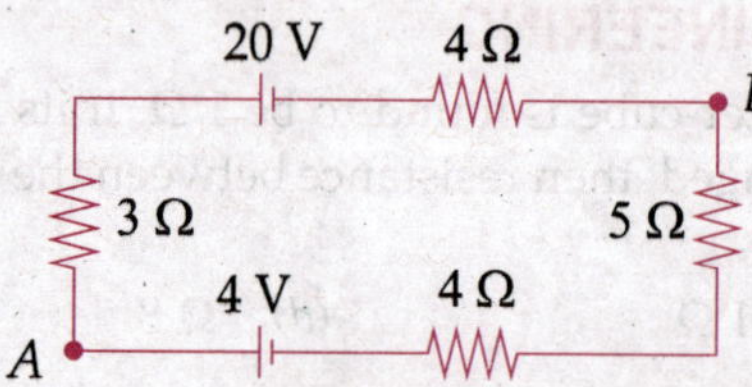

Fig C.3

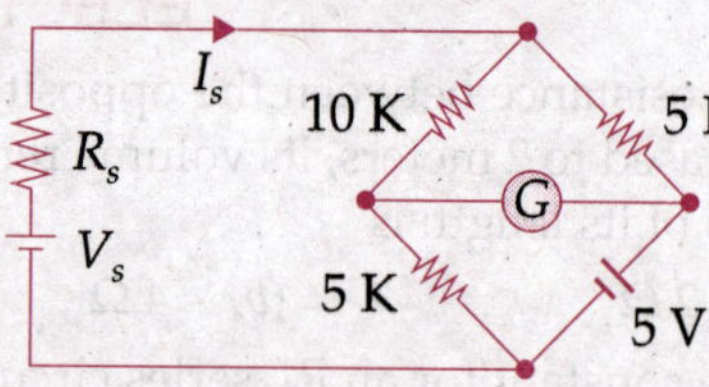

Fig C.4

11. The current through the galvanometer *G* shown in Fig. C.4 is zero. The current I_s through the source is

(a) 1 mA (b) 2 mA (c) 3 mA (d) 4 mA

12. The time constant of the network shown in Fig. C.5 is

(a) 2*RC* (b) 3*RC* (c) *RC*/2 (d) 2*RC*/3

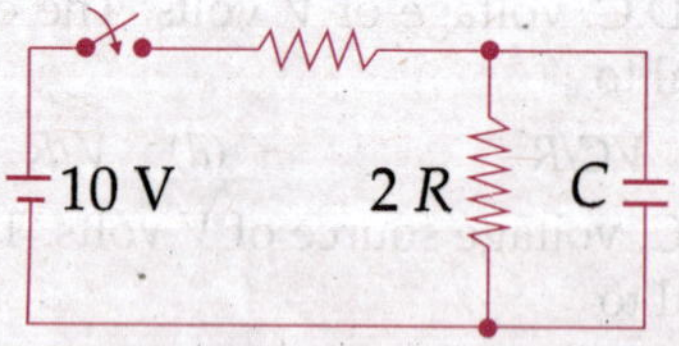

Fig C.5

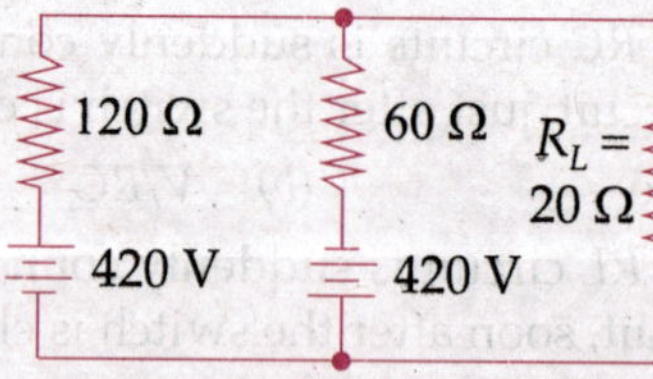

Fig C.6

13. In the circuit shown in Fig. C.6, the magnitude of current through R_L is

(a) 1 A (b) zero (c) 2 A (d) 6 A

14. The Thevenin's impedance across the terminals *AB* or the network of Fig. C.7 is

(a) $\frac{10}{3}$ Ω (b) $\frac{20}{9}$ Ω (c) $\frac{13}{4}$ Ω (d) $\frac{11}{5}$ Ω

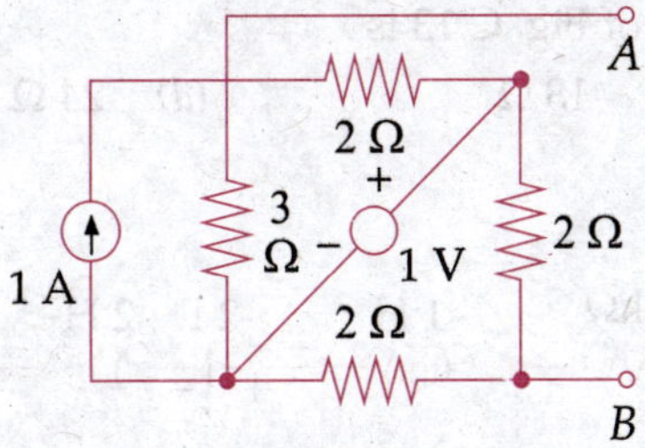

Fig C.7

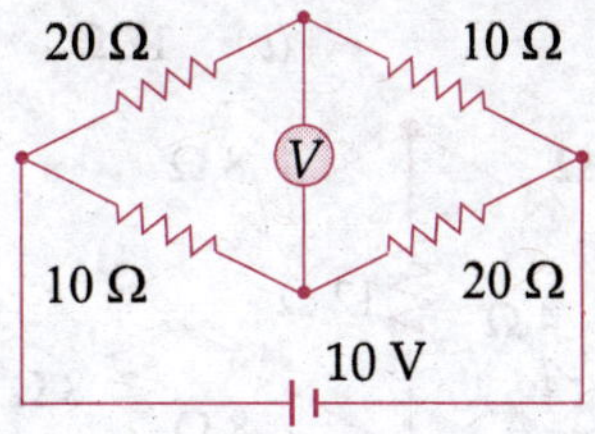

Fig C.8

15. In the bridge given in Fig. C.8, reading of the high-impedance voltmeter is

(a) zero (b) 6.66 V (c) 4.20 V (d) 3.33 V

16. Resistance between terminals A and B of Fig. C.9 is

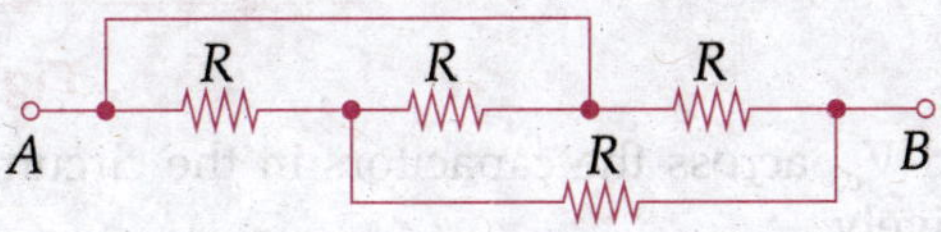

Fig C.9

(a) $\frac{2}{5}R$ (b) $\frac{3}{5}R$ (c) $\frac{2}{3}R$ (d) R

17. Resistance between terminals A and B of Fig. C.10 is

(a) $\frac{2}{5}R$ (b) $\frac{3}{5}R$ (c) $\frac{2}{3}R$ (d) R

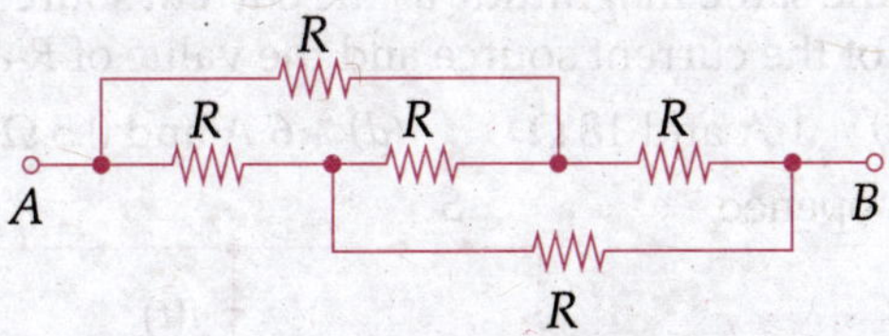

Fig C.10

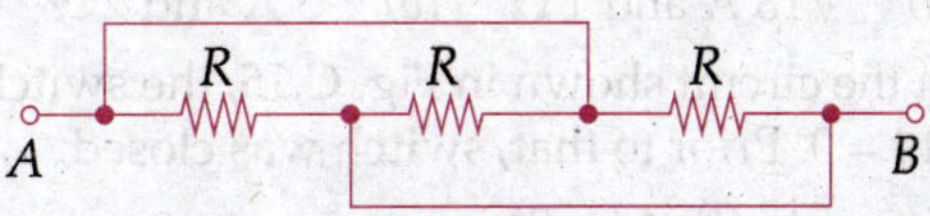

Fig C.11

18. Resistance between terminals A and B of Fig. C.11 is

(a) $\frac{2}{3}R$ (b) $\frac{R}{3}$ (c) R (d) $\frac{3}{4}R$

19. Resistance between terminals A and B of Fig. C.12 is

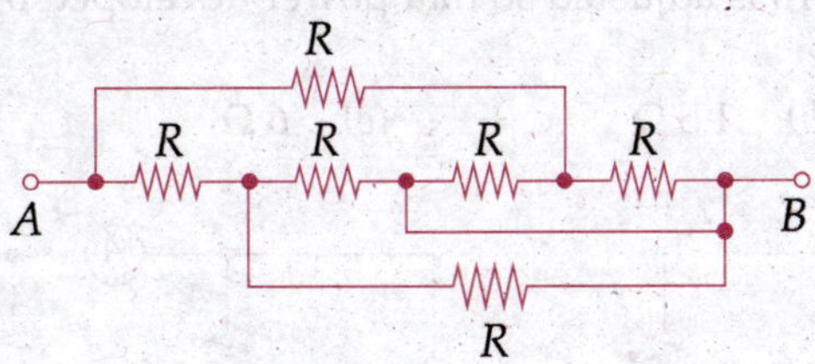

Fig C.12

(a) $\frac{3}{4}R$ (b) $\frac{2}{3}R$ (c) R (d) $\frac{4}{3}R$

20. The effective resistance between points A and B of Fig. C.13 is

(a) 9 Ω (b) 12 Ω (c) 18 Ω (d) 24 Ω

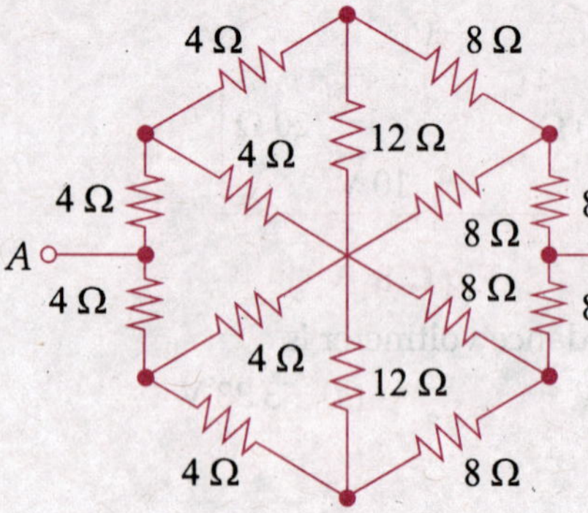

Fig C.13

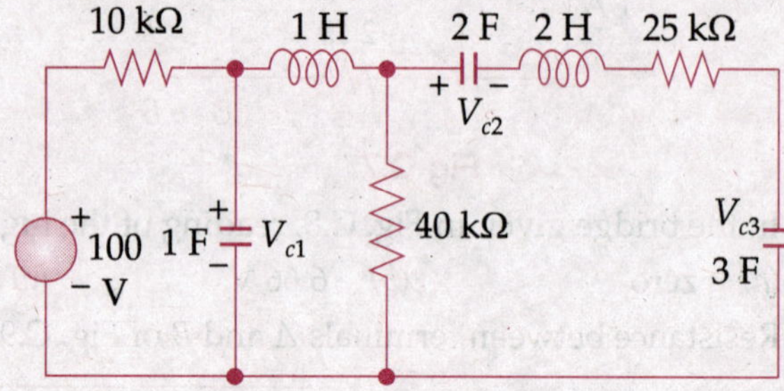

Fig C.14

21. The voltage V_{c1}, V_{c2} and V_{c3} across the capacitors in the circuit shown in Fig. C.14, under steady-state, are respectively

(a) 80 V, 32 V, 48 V (b) 80 V, 48 V, 32 V (c) 20 V, 8 V, 12 V (d) 20 V, 12 V, 8 V

22. Four resistances 80 Ω, 50 Ω, 25 Ω, and R are connected in parallel. Current through 25 Ω resistance is 4 A. Total current of the supply is 10 A. The value of R will be

(a) 66.66 Ω (b) 40.25 Ω (c) 36.36 Ω (d) 76.56 Ω

23. When a resistor R is connected to a current source, it consumes a power of 18 W. When the same R is connected to a voltage source having the same magnitude as the current source, the power absorbed by R is 4.5. W. The magnitude of the current source and the value of R are

(a) $\sqrt{18}$ A and 1 Ω (b) 3 A and 2 Ω (c) 1 A and 18 Ω (d) 6 A and 0.5 Ω

24. In the circuit shown in Fig. C.15, the switch S is opened at $t = 0$. Prior to that, switch was closed.

Current $i\,(t)$ at $t = 0^+$ is

(a) $\frac{2}{3}$ A (b) $\frac{3}{2}$ A

(c) $\frac{1}{3}$ A (d) 1 A

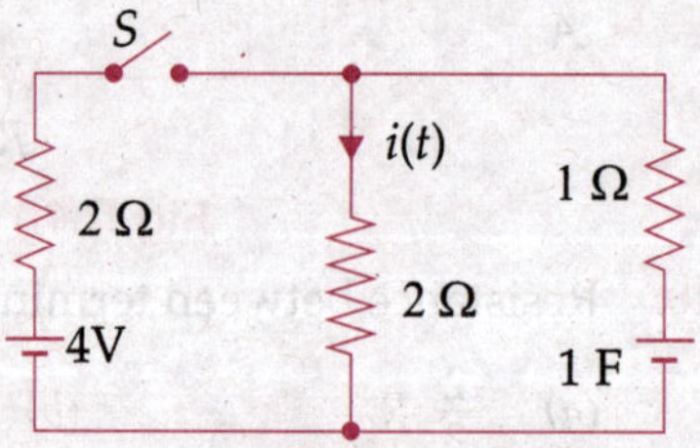

Fig C.15

25. The value of R in Fig. C.16 is adjusted so that power developed by the voltage source is zero. The value of R is

(a) 0 Ω (b) 1.5 Ω (c) 6 Ω (d) 0.667 Ω

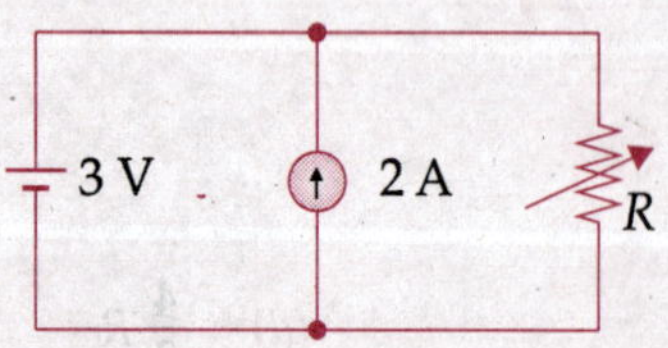

Fig C.16

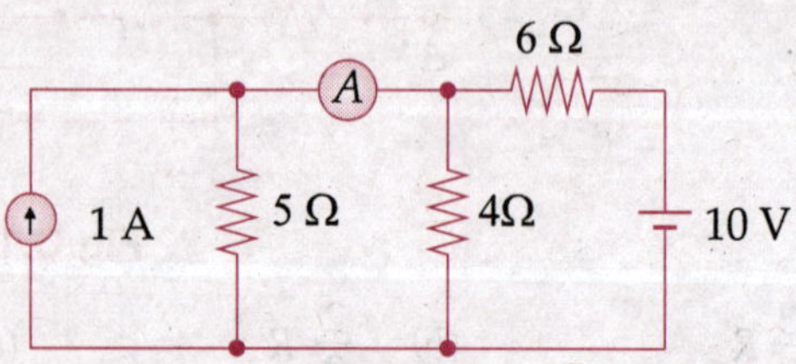

Fig C.17

26. In Fig. C.17, the current through the ammeter is

(a) $\frac{1}{7.4}$ A (b) 0 A (c) $\frac{5}{9}$ A (d) $\frac{2.4}{7.4}$ a

27. A long uniform coil of inductance L henries and associated resistance R ohms is physically cut into two exact halves which are then rewound in parallel. The resistance and inductance of the combination are

(a) R and L (b) 2 R and 2 L (c) $\frac{R}{2}$ and $\frac{L}{2}$ (d) $\frac{R}{4}$ and $\frac{L}{4}$

28. The current flowing through the resistor R_L in the given circuit of Fig. C.18 is

(a) 1 A (b) zero (c) 3 A (d) 5 A

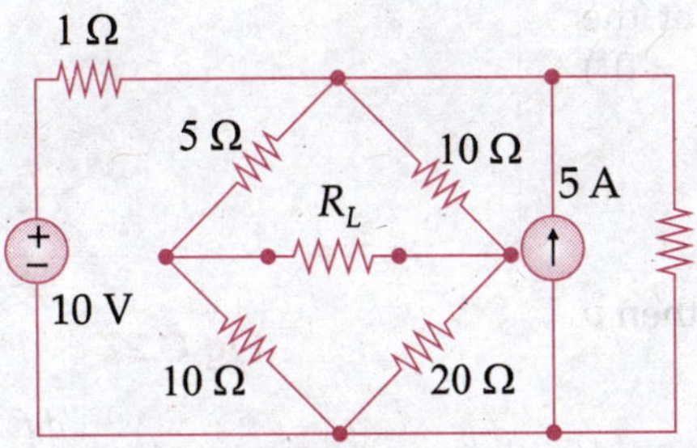

Fig C.18

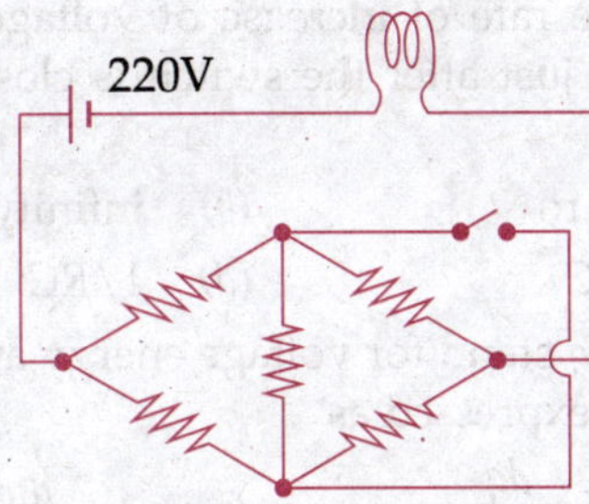

Fig C.19

29. All resistance in the circuit in Fig. C.19 are of R ohms each. The switch is initially open. What happens to the lamp's intensity when the switch is closed? [GATE, 1992]

(a) increases (b) decreases
(c) remains the same (d) answer depends on the value of R.

30. In the circuit of Fig. C.20, the power dissipated in the resistor R is 1 W when only source '1' is present and '2' is replaced by short circuit. The power dissipated in the same resistor R is 4 W when only source '2' is present and '1' is replaced by short circuit. When both the sources '1' and '2' are present, the power dissipated in R will be

(a) 1 W (b) 3 W (c) 4 W (d) 5 W

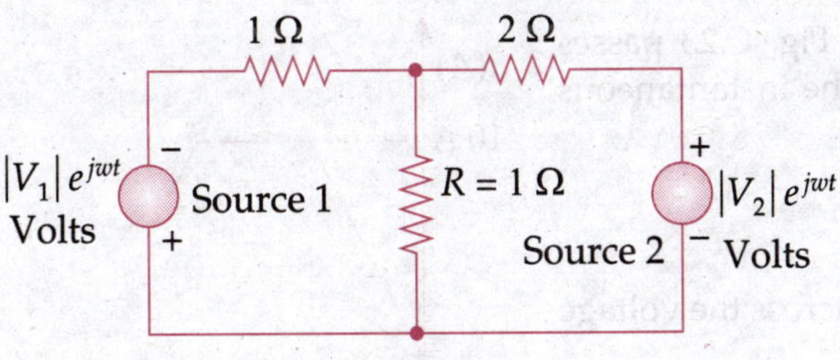

Fig C.20

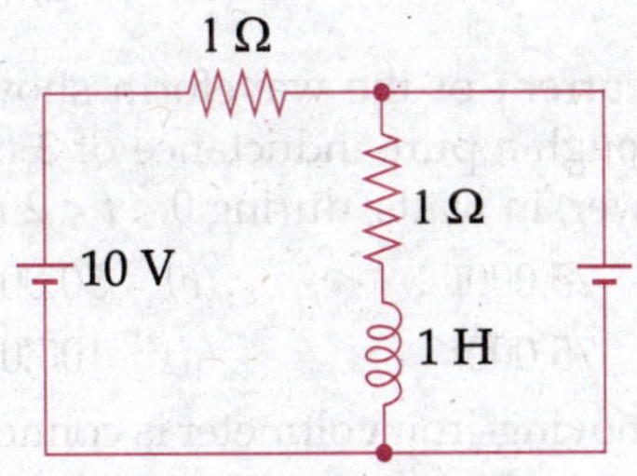

Fig C.21

31. Under steady-state conditions ; the total power dissipated, the energy stored in the inductor and capacitor in Fig. C.21 are respectively

(a) 25 W, 12.5 Ws, 12.5 Ws (b) 50 W, 12.5 Ws, 25 Ws
(c) 50 W, 25 Ws, 25 Ws (d) 100 W, 12.5 Ws, 25 Ws

32. A 0–10 mA PMMC ammeter reads 4 mA in a circuit. Its bottom control spring snaps suddenly. The meter will now read nearly

(a) 10 mA (b) 8 mA (c) 2 mA (d) zero

33. The insulation resistance of a cable of length of 10 kM is 10 M Ω. For a length of 100 kM of the same cable, the insulation resistance will be

(a) 100 MΩ (b) 10 MΩ (c) 1 MΩ (d) 0.1 MΩ

34. An ideal voltage source will charge an ideal capacitor

(a) in infinite time (b) exponentially (c) instantaneously (d) none of the above

35. In the series circuit shown in Fig. C.22, voltage across C starts increasing when the D.C. source is switched on. The rate of increase of voltage across C at the instant just after the switch is closed (*i.e.* at $t = 0^+$) will be

(a) zero (b) infinity

(c) RC (d) 1/RC

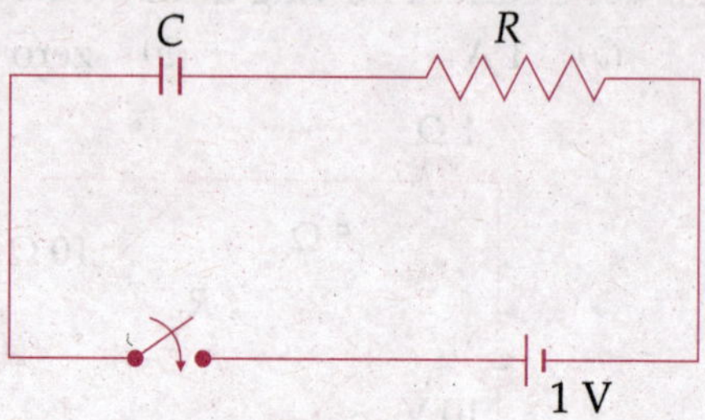

Fig C.22

36. If v, w, q stand for voltage,energy and charge, then v can be expressed as

(a) $v = \frac{dq}{dw}$ (b) $v = \frac{dw}{dq}$ (c) $dv = \frac{dw}{dq}$ (d) $dv = \frac{dq}{dw}$

37. A rectangular pulse of duration T and magnitude I has the Laplace transform

(a) $\frac{I}{s}$ (b) $\frac{I}{s} \cdot e^{-T \cdot s}$ (c) $\frac{I}{s} \cdot e^{-Ts}$ (d) $\frac{I}{s}[1 - \exp(-T \cdot s)]$

38. A voltage waveform $v(t) = 12t^2$ is applied across a 1 H inductor for $t \geq 0$, with initial current through it being zero. The current through the inductor for $t \geq 0$ is given by

(a) $12t$ (b) $24t$ (c) $12t^3$ (d) $4t^3$

39. A current input, $5\ \delta(t)$, is forced through a capacitor C. The voltage $v_c(t)$, across the capacitor is given by

(a) $5t$ (b) $5\ \mu(t).C$ (c) $\frac{5}{C}t$ (d) $\frac{5}{C}\mu(t)$

40. A current of the waveform shown in Fig. C.23 passes through a pure inductance of 3 mH. The instantaneous power, in watts, during $0 < t < 2$ ms, is

(a) $25{,}000t$ (b) $50{,}000t$

(c) $75{,}000t$ (d) $100{,}000t$

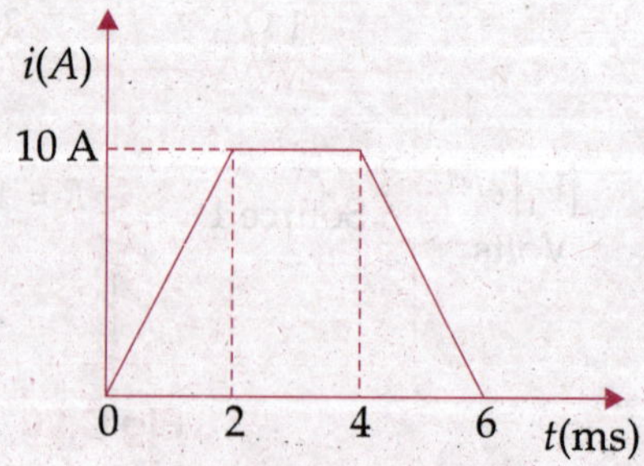

Fig C.23

41. A moving-iron voltmeter is connected across the voltage source whose instantaneous value is

$$v(t) = 5 + 10 \cos(314t + 30°)$$

The reading of the meter is

(a) 15 V (b) 5 V (c) $\sqrt{125}$ V (d) $\sqrt{75}$ V

42. If a capacitor is charged by a square-wave current source, the voltage across the capacitor is

(a) square wave (b) triangular wave (c) step function (d) zero

43. The current passing through a 10-ohm resistor of Fig. C.24 *(a)* has the waveform shown in Fig. C.24 *(b)*. The reading of the PMMC voltmeter connected across the resistor is

(a) 180 V *(b)* 60 V *(c)* 140 V *(d)* 120 V

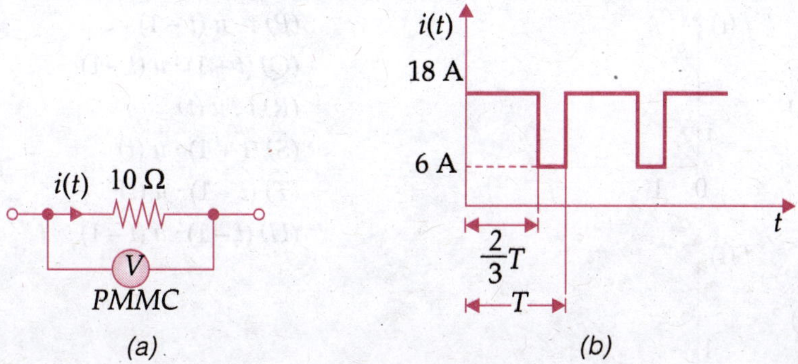

Fig C.24

44. A voltage source with an internal resistance R_s supplies power to load R_L. The power delivered to the load varies with R_L as

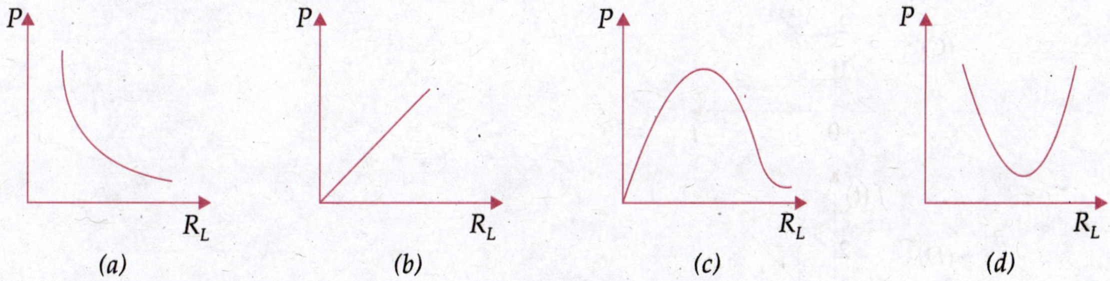

45. A unity feedback system with open-loop transfer function

$$G(s) = \frac{9}{2(s+3)}$$

1. has natural frequency = 9
2. natural frequency = 3
3. damping ratio = 1.2
4. damping ratio = 1/6

From these, the correct answer is

(a) 1, 3 *(b)* 2, 3 *(c)* 1, 4 *(d)* 2, 4

46. In the circuit of Fig. C.25, the inductor current and capacitor voltage are given at a time instant *t*. At this instant, the current *i* and *di/dt* are respectively

(a) + 5 A, – 500 A/s
(b) – 5 A, – 500 A/s
(c) 5 A, 500 A/s
(d) –5 A, 500 A/s.

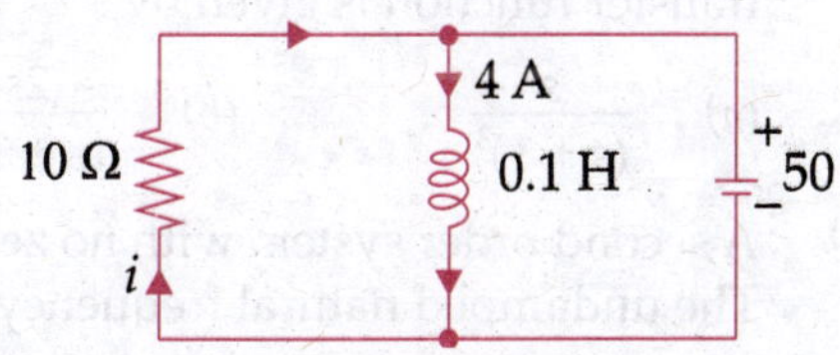

Fig C.25

47. Match the waveform on the left hand side with the correct mathematical description listed on the right-hand side :

Waveforms

(A)

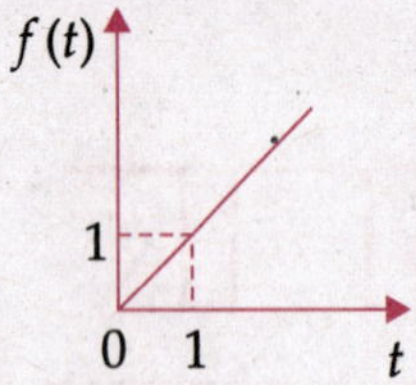

(B)

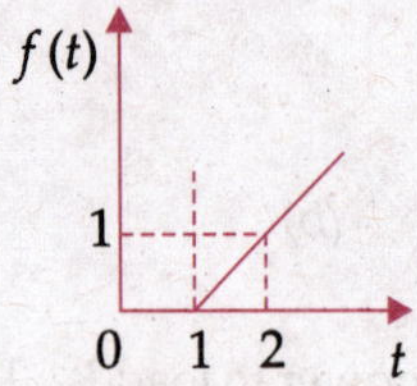

(C)

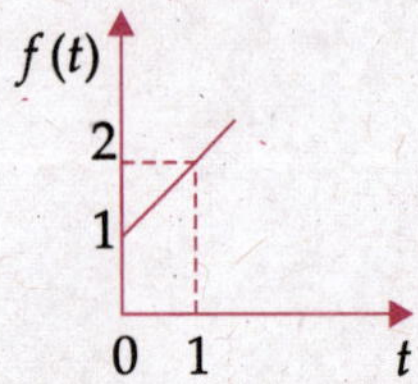

(D)

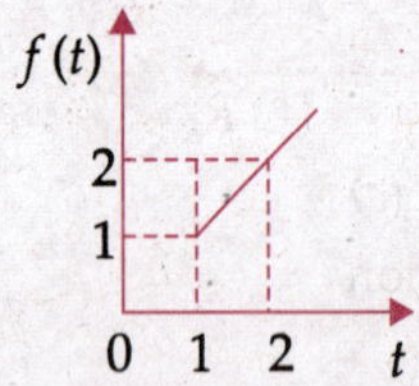

f(t)

(P) $t \cdot u(t-1)$

(Q) $(t+1) \cdot u(t-1)$

(R) $t \cdot u(t)$

(S) $(t+1) \cdot u(t)$

(T) $(t-1) \cdot u(t)$

(U) $(t-1) \cdot u(t-1)$

48. The r.m.s. value of the periodic wave $e(t)$ shown in Fig. C.26 is

(a) $\sqrt{\frac{3}{2}}$ A (b) $\sqrt{\frac{2}{3}}$ A

(c) $\sqrt{\frac{1}{3}}$ A (d) $\sqrt{2}$ A

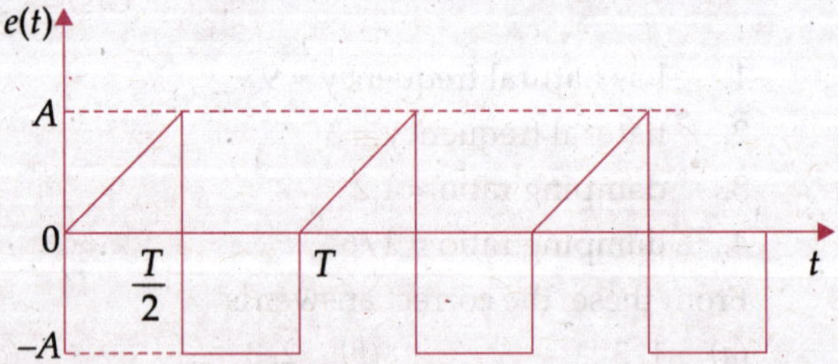

Fig C.26

49. The output of a linear system for a unit step input is given by $t^2 \cdot e^{-t}$. The transfer function is given by

(a) $\frac{s}{(s+1)^3}$ (b) $\frac{2s}{(s+1)^3}$ (c) $\frac{2}{s(s+1)^3}$ (d) $\frac{2}{s(s+1)^2}$

50. A second order system with no zeros has its poles located at $-3+j4$ and $-3-j4$ in the s-plane. The undamped natural frequency and damping factor of the system are

(a) 4 rad/s and 0.75 (b) 3 rad/s and 0.60 (c) 5 rad/s and 0.80 (d) 5 rad/s and 0.60

51. The current through the current coil of a wattmeter is $i = 1 + 2 \sin \omega t$ amperes and the voltage across the potential coil is $v = 2 + 3 \sin \omega t$ volts. The wattmeter reading in watts would be

(a) 8.00 (b) 5.05 (c) 2.00 (d) 0.00

52. Three resistors of value 2 *K*, 5 *K* and 10 *K* are connected in series and a 20 V D.C. supply is applied across the series combination. A voltmeter of internal resistance 10 *K* reads V_1 volts across the 5 *K* resistor and V_2 across the 10 *K* resistor. Which of the following statements is true?

(*a*) $V_1 = 2\,V_2$ (*b*) $V_1 = \frac{V_2}{2}$ (*c*) $V_1 < \frac{V_2}{2}$ (*d*) $V_1 > \frac{V_2}{2}$

53. A series RLC circuit below resonant frequency is

(*a*) resistive (*b*) capacitive (*c*) inductive (*d*) none of these

54. A series RLC circuit above resonant frequency is

(*a*) resistive (*b*) capacitive (*c*) inductive (*d*) none of these

55. The phasor diagram for alternating quantities can be drawn if they have

(*a*) cosine waves (*b*) rectangular waves
(*c*) square waves (*d*) triangular waves

56. Conductance is the reciprocal of

(*a*) inductive reactance (*b*) capacitive reactance
(*c*) resistance (*d*) impedance

57. Admittance is the reciprocal of

(*a*) inductive reactance (*b*) capacitive reactance
(*c*) resistance (*d*) impedance

58. A circuit possesses resistance *R* and inductive reactance *X* in series. Its susceptance is given by

(*a*) X/Z^2 (*b*) X/Z (*c*) R/Z^2 (*d*) R/Z

59. If $V = a + jb$ and $I = c + jd$, then the power is given by

(*a*) $ac + ad$ (*b*) $ac + bd$ (*c*) $bc - bd$ (*d*) $bc + ad$

60. For an RLC series circuit, current at series resonance is

(*a*) maximum at lagging p.f. (*b*) maximum at leading p.f.
(*c*) maximum at unity p.f. (*d*) minimum at unity p.f.

61. For an RLC parallel circuit, current at parallel resonance is

(*a*) maximum at leading p.f. (*b*) maximum at lagging p.f.
(*c*) maximum at unity p.f. (*d*) minimum at unity p.f.

62. The average value of unsymmetrical alternating quantity should be calculated over

(*a*) half cycle (*b*) one cycle
(*c*) two cycles (*d*) complete number of cycles

63. A permanent-magnet moving coil instrument can measure

(*a*) A.C. only (*b*) both D.C. and A.C
(*c*) D.C. only (*d*) pulsating quantities only

64. A moving iron instrument can measure

(*a*) A.C. only (*b*) both D.C. and A.C
(*c*) D.C. only (*d*) pulsating quantities only

65. A dynamometer type of instrument can measure

(*a*) A.C. only (*b*) both D.C. and A.C
(*c*) D.C. only (*d*) pulsating quantities only

66. Rectifier type instrument can measure

(a) A.C. only (b) both D.C. and A.C.
(c) D.C. only (d) pulsating quantities only

67. An electrostatic type of instrument is used for measuring

(a) voltage in D.C. circuit (b) current in D.C. circuit
(c) voltage in both D.C. and A.C. circuits (d) current in both D.C. and A.C. circuits

68. The internal resistance of milliammeter must be low for

(a) higher accuracy
(b) maximum voltage drop across the meter
(c) minimum effect on the circuit resistance
(d) high sensitivity

69. A voltmeter must have very high internal resistance so that it possesses

(a) high accuracy (b) high-voltage range
(c) maximum loading effect (d) minimum current through the meter

70. A material whose resistivity is 0.4 Ω meter must be a

(a) conductor (b) resistor (c) insulator (d) semiconductor

71. The function of a shunt used in the millimeter is to

(a) extend the range and increase the meter resistance
(b) extend the range and reduce the resistance
(c) decrease both the range and the meter resistance
(d) decrease the range but increase the resistance

72. In a fluorescent tube circuit, the function of ballast choke is to

(a) prevent flicker
(b) improve the p.f. of the circuit
(c) suppress the radio interference
(d) provide momentary H.V. to establish the main arc

73. A VTVM has negligible loading effect on the circuit being checked because it has

(a) high resistance range (b) low current range of 50 μA or less
(c) high input resistance of 11 MΩ or more (d) low input resistance

74. A voltage source V with internal impedance $R + jX$ is driving such a load as to have maximum power transfer. Power transfer to load is given by

(a) $\frac{V^2}{R}$ (b) $\frac{V^2}{2R}$ (c) $\frac{V^2}{4R}$ (d) $\left(\frac{V}{R+X}\right)^2 \cdot R$

75. For a sinusoidal waveform, the ratio of average to rms value is

(a) $\frac{2}{\sqrt{2\pi}}$ (b) $\frac{2\sqrt{2}}{\pi}$ (c) $\frac{\pi}{2\sqrt{2}}$ (d) $\frac{\sqrt{2}\cdot\pi}{2}$

76. In the circuit shown in Fig. C.27, voltage V_o

(a) leads current I by 90°
(b) lags current I by 90°
(c) is in phase with I
(d) leads V by some angle less than 90°

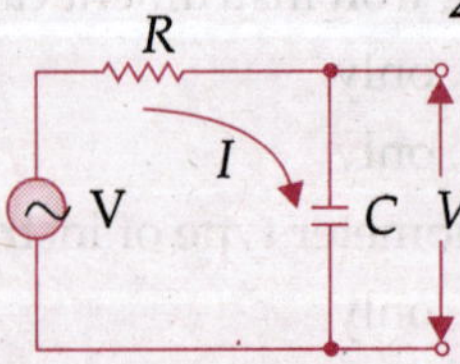

Fig C.27

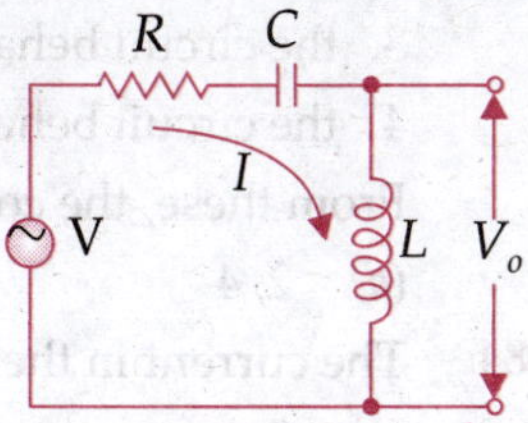

Fig C.28

77. In the circuit of Fig. C.28, voltage V_o

(a) leads current I by 90°
(b) lags current I by 90°
(c) lags current I by some angle less than 90°
(d) leads current I by some angle less than 90°

78. For an A.C. circuit, $v = V_m \sin(\omega t + \alpha)$ and $i = I_m \sin(\omega t + \beta)$. The phase angle between voltage and current waveforms is

(a) $\alpha + \beta$ or $\alpha - \beta$ (b) $\alpha - \beta$ or $\beta - \alpha$ (c) $\beta - \alpha$ or $\beta + \alpha$ (d) $\alpha - \beta$

79. In the figure shown below, ϕ = power-factor angle, W = watts, VA = volt ampere and VAr = volt-ampere reactive for an A.C. circuit. Tick mark the correct figure.

(a)
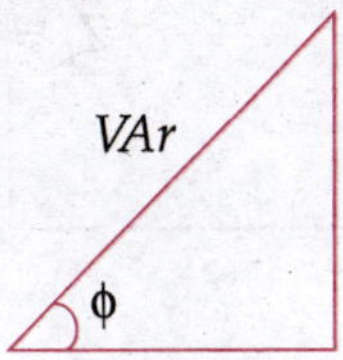

(b)
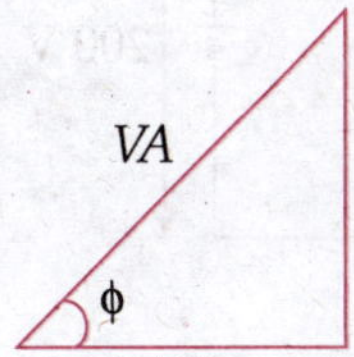

(c)
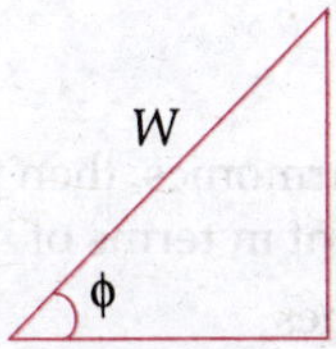

(d)
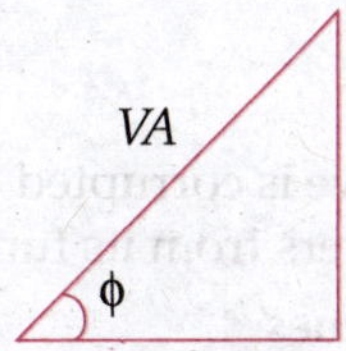

80. A 230 V, 100 W bulb has resistance R_A and 230 V, 200 W bulb has resistance R_B. Here

1. $R_A > R_B$ 2. $R_B > R_A$ 3. $R_A = 2R_B$ 4. $R_B = 2R_A$
5. $R_A = 4R_B$

From these, the correct answer is

(a) 1, 3 (b) 2,4 (c) 1, 5 (d) 1 only

81. In Fig. C.29, the bulb will

(a) light (b) not light
(c) give flickering light (d) light at regular intervals

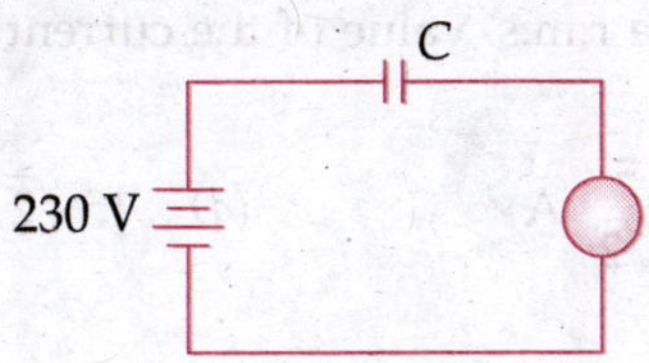

Fig C.29

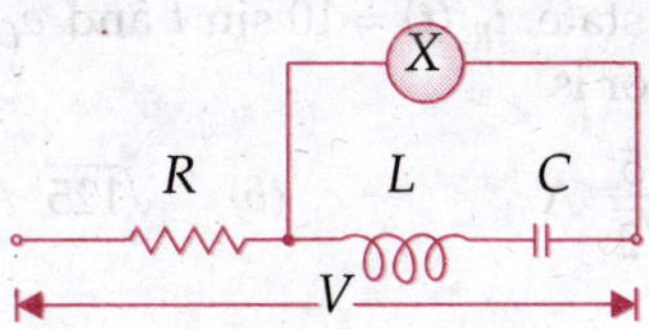

Fig C.30

82. At resonance, reading of voltmeter X in Fig. C.30 will be equal to

(a) V (b) 2 V (c) $\frac{1}{2}$ V (d) zero

83. A coil of resistance R and inductance L is connected in parallel with a capacitor C across an A.C. supply. At resonance,

1. the impedance of the circuit is maximum
2. the susceptance of the circuit is zero

3. the circuit behaves like a pure resistance of value R
4. the circuit behaves like a pure resistance of value L/R

From these, the correct answer is

(a) 2, 4 (b) 1, 2 (c) 2, 3 (d) 1, 2, 4

84. The current in the circuit of Fig. C.31 is

(a) 5 A (b) 10 A (c) 15 A (d) 50 A

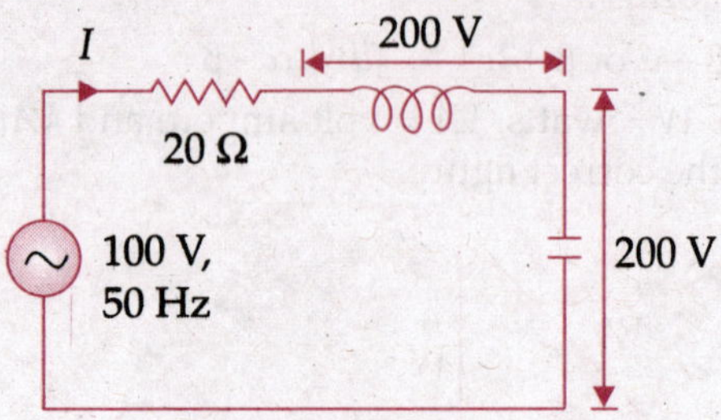

Fig C.31

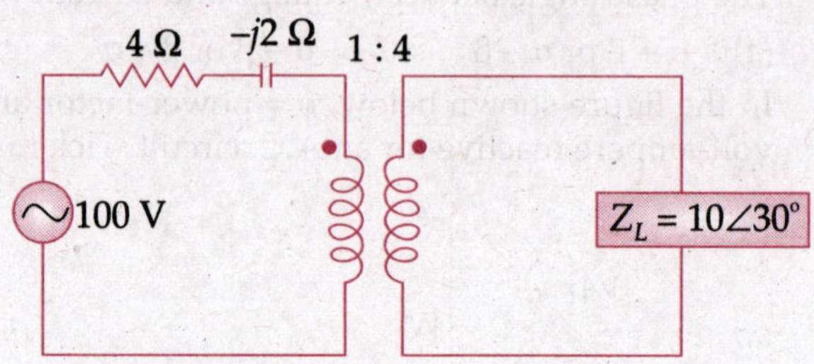

Fig C.32

85. The impedance seen by the source in the circuit of Fig. C.32 is

(a) $(4.54 - j1.687)\ \Omega$ (b) $(4.54 - j2.313)\ \Omega$

(c) $(142.56 + j78)\ \Omega$ (d) $(142.56 - j82)\ \Omega$

86. If the A.C. voltage wave is corrupted with an arbitrary number of harmonics, then the overall voltage waveform differs from its fundamental-frequency component in terms of

(a) only the peak values (b) only the rms values

(c) only the average values (d) all the three measures

87. The voltage phasor of a circuit is $10\angle 15°$ V and the current phasor is $2\angle -45°$ A. The active and reactive powers in the circuit are

(a) 10 W and 17.32 VAr (b) 5 W and 8.66 VAr

(c) 200 W and 60 VAr (d) $20\sqrt{2}$ W and $10\sqrt{2}$ VAr

88. In the circuit shown in Fig. C.33, if the power consumed by the 5 Ω resistor is 10 W, then power factor of the circuit is

(a) 0.8 (b) 0.6 (c) 0.5 (d) zero

89. A part of a circuit consists of a resistor, a capacitor and an inductor as shown in Fig. C.34. At steady state, $i_R(t) = 10 \sin t$ and $v_L(t) = 5 \cos t$. The r.m.s. value of the current through the capacitor is

(a) $\frac{15}{\sqrt{2}}$ A (b) $\sqrt{125}$ A (c) $\frac{5}{\sqrt{2}}$ A (d) $15\sqrt{2}$ A

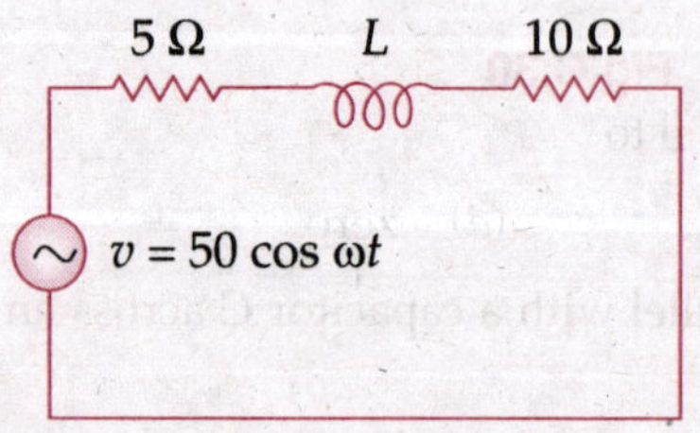

Fig C.33

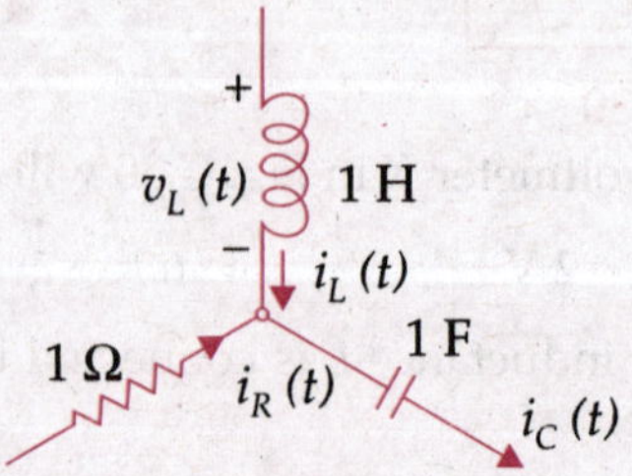

Fig C.34

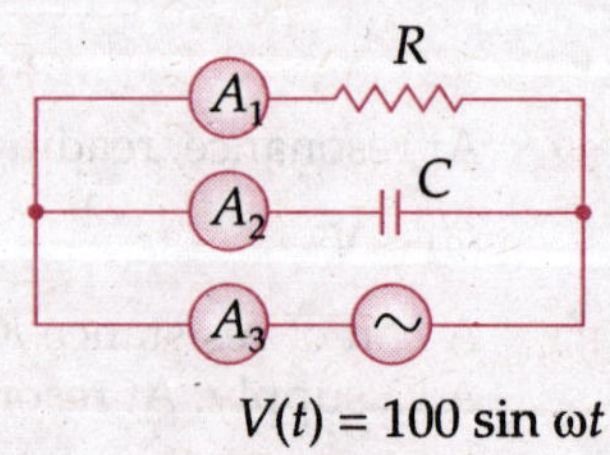

Fig C.35

90. In Fig. C.35 ; A_1, A_2 and A_3 are ideal ammeters. If A_1 and A_3 read 5 A and 13 A respectively, reading of A_2 will be

(a) 8 A

(b) 12 A

(c) 18 A

(d) indeterminate unless the actual values of *R*, C and ω are specified.

91. In a series RLC circuit excited by a voltage = E sin ω*t*, where $LC < \frac{1}{\omega^2}$,

(a) current lags the applied voltage

(b) current leads the applied voltage

(c) current is in phase with the applied voltage

(d) voltage across L and C are equal

92. The response of a series RLC circuit fed from a fixed r.m.s. voltage and variable frequency source is represented graphically in Fig. C.36. Match List I with List II and select the correct answer using the codes given below the lists :

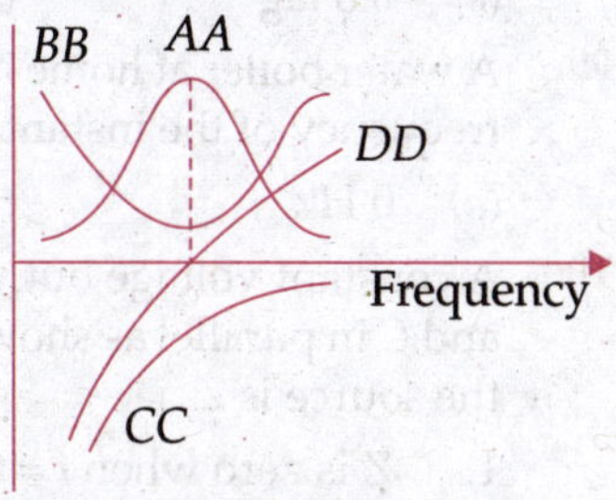

Fig C.36

List I		List II	
A.	AA	1.	current
B.	BB	2.	impedance
C.	CC	3.	capacitive reactance
D.	DD	4.	net reactance
		5.	inductive reactance

Codes :

	A	B	C	D		A	B	C	D
(a)	2	1	3	5	(b)	1	2	3	5
(c)	1	2	3	4	(d)	1	2	4	3

93. A voltmeter, having an internal resistance of 20 kΩ, is connected with two other 20 kΩ resistors across a 200 V, 3-phase mains as shown in Fig. C.37. The reading shown by the voltmeter wil be

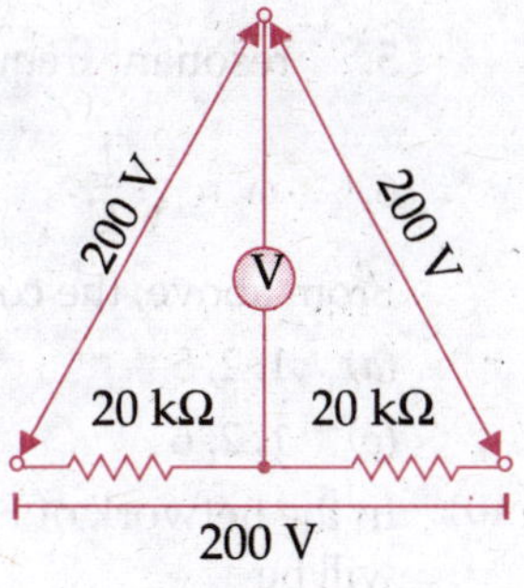

Fig C.37

(a) 115.5 V as the connections are similar to Scott-connection

(b) 173.2 V as the connections are similar to Scott-connection

(c) 115.5 V

(d) 173.2 V

94. At resonance, the parallel circuit of Fig. C.38 constituted by an iron-cored coil and a capacitor behaves like

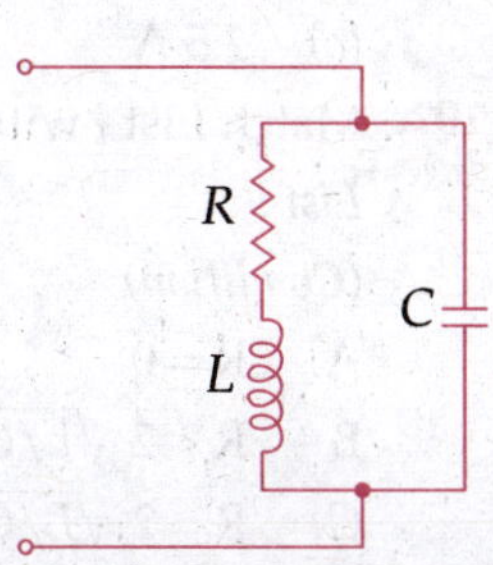

Fig C.38

(a) an open circuit

(b) a short circuit

(c) a pure resistor of value *R*

(d) a pure resistor of value higher than *R*

95. In the circuit of Fig. C.39, currents I_1 and I are respectively

(a) 16 A, 20 A (b) 32 A, 44 A
(c) 32 A, 34.2 A (d) 16 A, 28 A

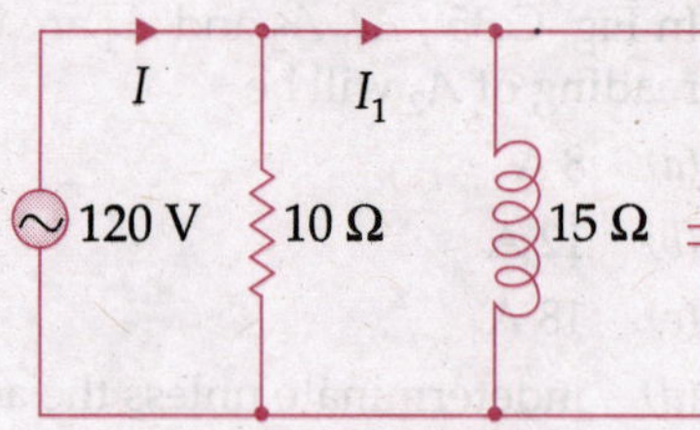

Fig C.39

96. A series RLC circuit has R = 10 Ω, L = 0.01 H and C = 100 μF. The Q factor of the circuit at resonance is

(a) 1.0 (b) 0.316
(c) 0.1 (d) 10

97. Two loads of 10 kW each, are operating at a power factor 0.8 lagging (each). What is their combined power factor?

(a) 0.4 lag (b) 0.64 lag (c) 0.8 lag (d) 1.00

98. Two loads, one of 20 kW at p.f. 0.8 lag and other of 12 kW at p.f. 0.6 lag, are connected in series. Their combined power factor would be

(a) 0.8 lag (b) 0.6 lag (c) 0.7 lag (d) 0.7182 lag

99. A water boiler at home is switched on to the A.C. mains supplying power at 230 V/50 Hz. The frequency of the instantaneous power consumed by the boiler is

(a) 0 Hz (b) 50 Hz (c) 100 Hz (d) 150 Hz

100. A constant voltage but variable frequency A.C. source feeds L and C in parallel as shown in Fig. C.40. The impedance seen by the source is Z.

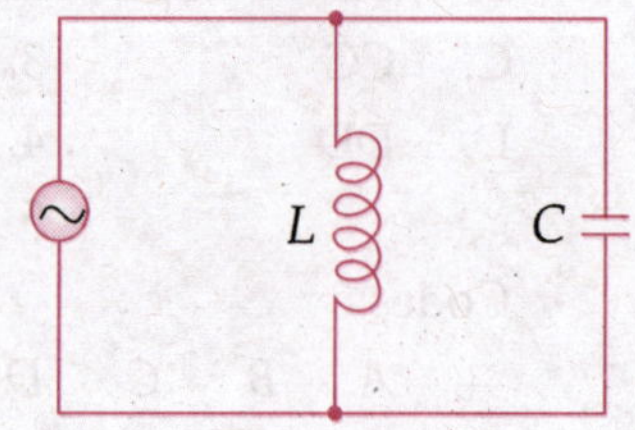

Fig C.40

1. Z is zero when $f = 0$
2. Z is zero when f = infinity
3. Z is infinite when $f = 0$
4. Z is infinite when f = infinity
5. resonant frequency, $\omega_r = \dfrac{1}{\sqrt{LC}}$
6. $\omega_r = \sqrt{\dfrac{L}{C}}$ 7. $\omega_r = \sqrt{\dfrac{C}{L}}$

From above, the correct answer is

(a) 1, 2, 5 (b) 3, 4, 5
(c) 1, 2, 6 (d) 3, 4, 7

101. In the network of Fig. C.41, the current in the 25 Ω resistor will be

(a) 5 A (b) 4 A
(c) 2.5 A (d) zero (*I.A.S., 1993*)

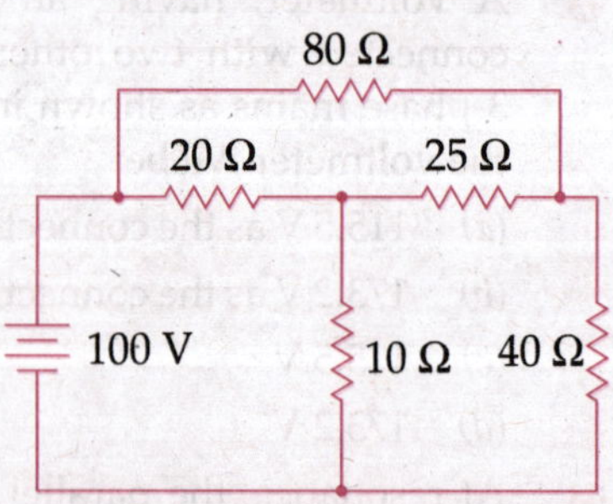

Fig C.41

102. Match List *I* with List *II* and select the correct answer using the codes given below the lists :

List I (*Condition*)	*List II* (*Transient current response*)
A. R = 0	1. Undamped oscillations
B. $R < 2\sqrt{L/C}$	2. Damped oscillations
C. $R = 2\sqrt{L/C}$	3. Critically damped response
D. $R > 2\sqrt{L/C}$	4. Non-oscillatory response

Codes :

	A	B	C	D			A	B	C	D
(a)	1	2	3	4		(b)	1	4	3	2
(c)	3	2	1	4		(d)	3	4	1	2

[I.A.S., 1993]

ANSWERS

1.	(b)	2.	(d)	3.	(c)	4.	(d)	5.	(d)
6.	(a)	7.	(a)	8.	(a)	9.	(b)	10.	(d)
11.	(c)	12.	(d)	13.	(a)	14.	(d)	15.	(d)
16.	(b)	17.	(d)	18.	(b)	19.	(a)	20.	(a)
21.	(b)	22.	(c)	23.	(b)	24.	(a)	25.	(b)
26.	(a)	27.	(d)	28.	(b)	29.	(c)	30.	(a)
31.	(b)	32.	(d)	33.	(c)	34.	(c)	35.	(d)
36.	(b)	37.	(d)	38.	(d)	39.	(d)	40.	(c)
41.	(d)	42.	(b)	43.	(c)	44.	(c)	45.	(b)
46.	(a)	47.	$A \to R, B \to U, C \to S, D \to P$			48.	(b)	49.	(b)
50.	(d)	51.	(c)	52.	(d)	53.	(b)	54.	(c)
55.	(a)	56.	(c)	57.	(d)	58.	(a)	59.	(b)
60.	(c)	61.	(d)	62.	(b)	63.	(c)	64.	(b)
65.	(b)	66.	(a)	67.	(c)	68.	(c)	69.	(d)
70.	(d)	71.	(b)	72.	(d)	73.	(c)	74.	(c)
75.	(b)	76.	(b)	77.	(a)	78.	(b)	79.	(d)
80.	(a)	81.	(b)	82.	(d)	83.	(b)	84.	(a)
85.	(a)	86.	(d)	87.	(a)	88.	(b)	89.	(a)
90.	(b)	91.	(b)	92.	(c)	93.	(c)	94.	(d)
95.	(a)	96.	(a)	97.	(c)	98.	(d)	99.	(c)
100.	(a)	101.	(d)	102.	(a)				

TRANSFORMERS

1. Two windings of a transformer are designated as
   (a) primary and secondary windings
   (b) primary and H.V. windings
   (c) secondary and L.V. windings or primary and L.V. windings
   (d) H.V. and L.V. windings
2. Two transformers *A* and *B*, having identical ratings, are to be designed with flux densities of 1.2 T and 1.4 T respectively. The weight of transformer *A* per kVA would be
   (a) less than that of transformer *B*
   (b) more than that of transformer *B*
   (c) equal to that of transformer *B*
   (d) may be less or more than that of transformer *B* depending upon other parameters
3. In power transformers, core is made up of
   (a) cast iron (b) silicon steel (c) ferrite (d) powdered alloy
4. Consider the following statements :
   1. Air-core transformers are used in gate-triggering circuits of thyristors
   2. Cores made of soft-ferrite are used in pulse transformers
   3. Air-core transformers are used in radio devices
   4. Cores of powdered alloy are used in isolation transformers

   From above, the correct answer is
   (a) 2, 3, 4 (b) 2, 3 (c) 1, 3, 4 (d) 2, 4
5. For a given cross-sectional area of transformer core, stepped cores are used
   (a) to reduce the core loss
   (b) to provide more mechanical strength to the core
   (c) to reduce the conductor material and therefore I^2R loss
   (d) to reduce the magnetizing current
6. In single-phase core-type transformers, L.V. and H.V. windings are arranged as under
   (a) L.V. on one core-limb, H.V. on the other core-limb
   (b) half H.V. near the core and half L.V. outside the H.V. on each limb
   (c) L.V. and H.V. winding sections are sandwiched
   (d) half L.V. near the core and half H.V. outside the L.V. on each limb
7. A 400/200 V, 50 Hz transformer operates at a flux density of 1.2 T when energised from its H.V. side. For this transformer, linear dimensions of core are doubled while the number of turns are halved on both its H.V. and L.V. sides. If this transformer is now connected to 800 V, 50 Hz on its H.V. side, then its flux density would be
   (a) 0.6 T (b) 1.2 T (c) 3.6 T (d) 4.8 T
8. For core-type power transformers, both primary and secondary windings have circular coil sections, because this section
   (a) is easier to wind
   (b) requires minimum conductor material and, therefore, less I^2R loss
   (c) has the strongest mechanical shape
   (d) results in less core material and, therefore, less core loss

9. Transformer action reqires a

(a) constant magnetic flux (b) increasing magnetic flux

(c) alternating magnetic flux (d) alternating electric flux

10. In a single-phase transformer, with subscripts 1 and 2 for primary and secondary windings,

(a) $E_1 N_2 = E_2 N_1$ and $I_1 N_1 = I_2 N_2$ (b) $E_1 N_1 = E_2 N_2$ and $I_1 N_1 = I_2 N_2$

(c) $E_1 N_2 = E_2 N_1$ and $I_1 N_2 = I_2 N_1$ (d) $E_1 N_1 = E_2 N_2$ and $I_1 N_2 = I_2 N_1$

11. The flux involved in the e.m.f. equation of a transformer has

(a) r.m.s. value (b) average value (c) total value (d) maximum value

12. For understanding the behaviour of a transformer, the following laws may be called for

1. Lenz's law
2. Newton's second law
3. Faraday's law of electromagnetic induction
4. Ohm's law
5. Fleming's right-hand rule
6. Right-hand grip rule

From these, the correct answer is

(a) 1, 3, 4 (b) 2, 3, 4, 5 (c) 1, 3, 4, 5, 6 (d) 1, 3, 4, 6

13. In an ideal transfomer, if K is some constant, then the supply voltage V, in terms of its magnetizing current I_m can be expressed as

(a) $jKf\,I_m$ (b) $\dfrac{jK \cdot f}{I_m}$ (c) $-jKf\,I_m$ (d) $-\dfrac{jK \cdot f}{I_m}$

14. In an ideal transformer, the impedance can be transformed from one side to the other

(a) in direct proportion to square of turns-ratio

(b) in direct proportion to turns-ratio

(c) in inverse proportion to square of turns-ratio

(d) in inverse proportion to turns-ratio

15. Distribution transformers are designed to have

(a) core loss $P_c >$ full-load ohmic loss P_{oh} (b) $P_c < P_{oh}$

(c) $P_c = P_{oh}$ (d) P_c negligible as compared to P_{oh}

16. A transformer has sometimes two or more ratings depending upon the use of

(a) the cooling techniques (b) the type of windings

(c) the type of core (d) the type of insulation

17. In a transformer, exciting current is made up of two components ; namely magnetizing current I_m and core-loss current I_c. With negligible leakage impedance drop,

(a) both I_m and I_c lag supply voltage V_1 by 90°

(b) both I_m and I_c are in phase with V_1

(c) I_m lags V_1 by 90° whereas I_c is in phase with V_1

(d) I_m is in phase with V_1 but I_c lags V_1 by 90°.

18. A transformer at no-load is excited at rated voltage. Now a cut is made in the transformer yoke thus creating a small air gap. With this, the transformer core flux

(a) will decrease and magnetizing current I_m will increase

(b) will remain constant and I_m will increase

(c) as well as I_m both will increase

(d) as well as I_m both will decrease

19. If the secondary winding of the ideal transformer shown in the circuit of Fig. C.42 has 40 turns, the number of turns in the primary winding for maximum power transfer to the 2Ω resistor will be

(a) 20 (b) 40 (c) 80 (d) 160

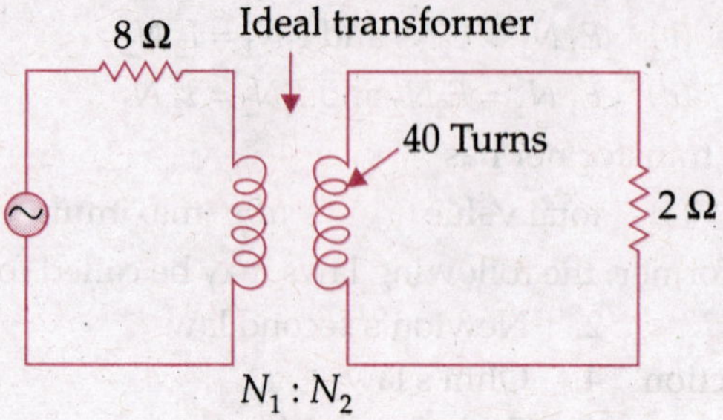

Fig C.42

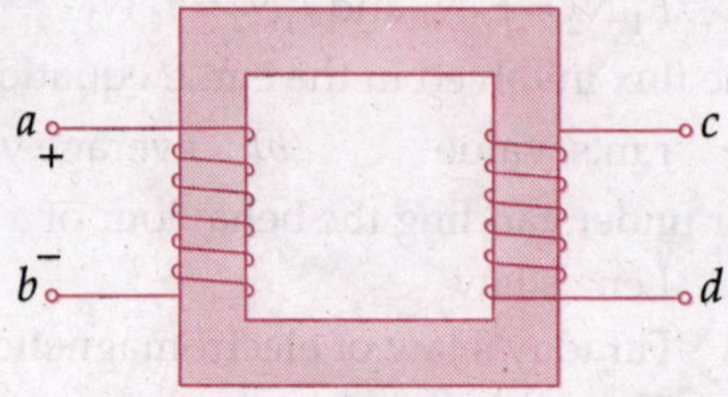

Fig C.43

20. In a single-phase transformer, polarities of terminals *a* and *b* at any instant are shown in the Fig. C.43. At the same instant.

(a) *c* is positive, *d* is positive and flux is clock-wise (*cw*)

(b) *c* is negative, *d* is positive and flux is counterclock-wise

(c) *c* is negative, *d* is positive and flux is *cw*

(d) *c* is positive, *d* is negative and flux is *ccw.*

21. In an oil-filled transformer, oil is provided for

(a) cooling (b) insulation

(c) both cooling and insulation (d) preventing the accumulation of dust

22. Transformers cores are laminated to reduce

(a) eddy-current loss (b) hysteresis loss

(c) both eddy-current and hysteresis loss (d) ohmic loss

23. CRGO laminations in a transformer are used to minimise

(a) eddy-current loss (b) hysteresis loss

(c) both eddy-current and hysteresis losses (d) ohmic loss

24. In case of a power transformer, the no-load current in terms of rated current is

(a) 10 to 20% (b) 2 to 6% (c) 15 to 30% (d) 30 to 50%

25. If a transformer primary is energised from a square-wave voltage source, then its output voltage will be

(a) zero (b) a sine wave (c) a triangular wave (d) a pulsed wave

26. The primary (220 V side) of a 220/6 V, 50 Hz transformer is connected to 110 V, 60 Hz source. The secondary output voltage will be

(a) 3.6 V (b) 3.0 V (c) 2.5 V (d) 1.667 V

27. The no-load current in a transformer lags the applied voltage by

(a) 90° (b) about 75° (c) 0° (d) about 110°

28. A transformer has N_1 and N_2 turns in primary and secondary windings respectively. Its secondary-winding reactance x_2 Ω, when referred to primary, is

(a) $x_2\left(\frac{N_2}{N_1}\right)^2$ (b) $x_2\frac{N_2}{N_1}$ (c) $x_2\left(\frac{N_1}{N_2}\right)^2$ (d) $x_2\frac{N_1}{N_2}$

29. A 400/200 V transformer has total resistance of 0.02 p.u on its L.V. side. This resistance when referred to H.V. side would be

(a) 0.02 *(b)* 0.04 *(c)* 0.01 *(d)* 0.08

30. The leakage flux in a transformer depends upon

(a) the applied voltage *(b)* the frequency

(c) the load current *(d)* the mutual flux

31. The useful flux of a transformer is 1 Wb. When it is loaded at 0.8 p.f. lag, then its mutual flux

(a) may decrease to 0.8 Wb *(b)* may increase to 1.01 Wb

(c) remains constant *(d)* may decrease to 0.99 Wb

32. If, in a transformer P_c = core loss and P_{sc} = full-load ohmic loss, then maximum kVA delivered to the load at maximum efficiency is equal to rated kVA multiplied by

(a) $\frac{P_c}{P_{sc}}$ *(b)* $\left(\frac{P_c}{P_{sc}}\right)^2$ *(c)* $\sqrt{\frac{P_c}{P_{sc}}}$ *(d)* $\sqrt{\frac{P_{sc}}{P_c}}$

33. Two transformers of the same type, using the same grade of iron and conductor materials are designed to work at the same flux and current densities ; but the linear dimensions of one are two times those of the other in all respects. The ratio of kVA ratings of the two transformer closely equals

(a) 16 *(b)* 8 *(c)* 4 *(d)* 2

34. A 3 : 1 transformer has impedance of (1 + *j*5) Ω on the L.V. side and (9 + *j*45) Ω on the H.V. side. The total equivalent impedance at the H.V. terminals is

(a) 18 + *j* 90 Ω *(b)* 2 + *j* 10 Ω *(c)* 10 + *j* 50 Ω *(d)* 8 + *j* 40 Ω

35. A 220/440 V, 50 Hz, 5 kVA, single-phase transformer operates on 220 V, 40 Hz supply with secondary winding open-circuited. Then

(a) both eddy-current and hysteresis losses decrease

(b) both eddy-current and hysteresis losses increase

(c) eddy-current loss remains the same but hysteresis loss increases

(d) eddy-current loss increases but hysteresis loss remains the same

36. The hysteresis and eddy-current losses of a single-phase transformer working on 200 V, 50 Hz supply are P_h and P_e respectively. The percentage decrease in these, when operated on a 160 V, 40 Hz supply are

(a) 32, 36 *(b)* 20, 36 *(c)* 25, 50 *(d)* 40, 80

37. For a single-phase transformer, r_e = total equivalent resistance, x_e = total equivalent leakage reactance, P_c = core loss. The load current at which maixmum efficiency occurs is

(a) $\sqrt{\frac{P_c}{r_e}}$ *(b)* $\sqrt{\frac{P_c}{x_e}}$ *(c)* $\frac{P_c}{r_e}$ *(d)* $\frac{P_c}{x_e}$

38. The maximum efficiency for a transformer occurs at 80% of full load. Its core loss is P_c and ohmic loss is P_{oh}. For this transformer, the ratio $\frac{P_c}{P_{oh}}$ is

(a) 0.8 *(b)* 1.25 *(c)* 0.64 *(d)* 0.8944

39. Frequency of the supply voltage to a transformer at no-load is increased but the supply voltage is held fixed. With this

1. eddy-current loss remains constant but hysteresis loss increases

2. eddy-current loss remains constant but hysteresis loss decreases
3. magnetizing current increases but core-loss current decreases
4. both magnetizing and core-loss currents decrease.

From these, the correct answer is

(a) 2, 3 (b) 2, 4 (c) 1, 3 (d) 1, 4

40. The voltage applied to a transformer primary is increased keeping V/f constant. With this, the core loss will

(a) decrease and magnetizing current I_m will increase
(b) increase and I_m will also increase
(c) remain constant and I_m will also remain constant
(d) increase and I_m will remain constant

41. A 4 kVA, 400/200 V, 1-phase transformer has leakage impedance of $0.02 + j\,0.04$ per unit. This leakage impedance in ohms, when referred to H.V. side is

(a) $0.8 + j\,1.6\ \Omega$ (b) $0.2 + j\,0.4\ \Omega$ (c) $0.08 + j\,0.16\ \Omega$ (d) $1 + j\,2\ \Omega$

42. As the load on a transformer is increased, the core losses

(a) decrease slightly (b) increase slightly (c) remain constant
(d) may decrease or increase slightly depending upon the nature of load

43. For the system shown in Fig. C.44, the phase relation of current I with respect to the voltage V_{AB} is

(a) zero (b) 90° lead
(c) 90° lag (d) 180°

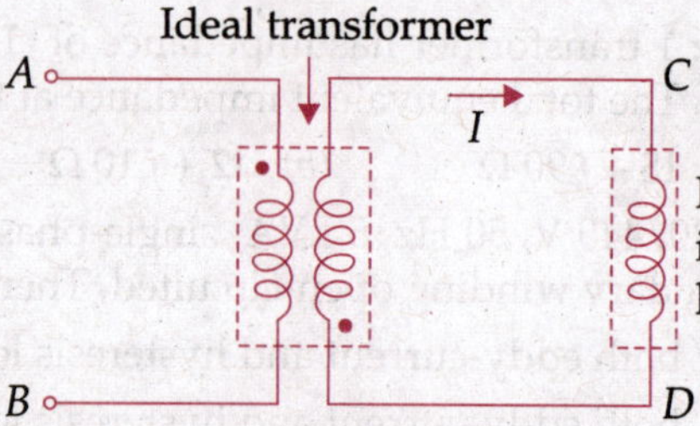

Fig C.44

44. Two transformers X and Y with identical ratings and dimensions have 0.8 mm and 1.2 mm thick laminations respectively. If R_c and X_m are the magnetizing branch parameters in the equivalent circuit, then

(a) R_c values in both are likely to be equal, but X_m of X is likely to be higher than X_m of Y
(b) X_m values in both are likely to be equal, but R_c of X is likely to be higher than R_c of Y
(c) X_m values in both are likely to be equal, but R_c of X is likely to be lower than R_c of Y
(d) R_c values in both are likely to be equal, but X_m of X is likely to be lower than X_m of Y

45. If the applied voltage of a certain transformer is increased by 50% and the frequency is reduced to 50% (assuming that magnetic circuit remains unsaturated), the maximum core flux density will

(a) change to three times the original value (b) change to 1.5 times the original value
(c) change to 0.5 times the original value (d) remains the same as the original value

46. In a transformer, low-voltage winding is placed near the core in case of concentric windings so as to:

1. reduce the leakage flux
2. reduce the insulation requirement
3. reduce the risk of voltage shock in case of insulation breakdown
4. reduce the core loss
5. reduce the total conductor material

From these, the correct answer is

(a) 1, 2, 3, 5 (b) 2, 3, 4, 5 (c) 1, 2, 3, 4, 5 (d) 2, 3, 5

47. Can a 50 Hz transformer be used for 25 Hz, if the input voltage is maintained constant at the rated value corresponding to 50 Hz?
(a) Yes. Since the voltage is constant, current levels will not change
(b) No. Flux will be doubled which will drive the core to excessive saturation
(c) No. Owing to decreased reactance of transformer, input current will be doubled at load
(d) Yes. At constant voltage, insulation will not be overstressed.

48. Voltage applied to the primary of a transformer is kept constant but its frequency is decreased. Under this operation,
(a) magnetizing current increases but core-loss current decreases
(b) magnetizing current decreases but core-loss current increases
(c) magnetizing current and core-loss current both decrease
(d) magnetizing current and core-loss current both increase

49. In a transformer, if primary leakage impedance is neglected, then
1. magnetizing current lags the applied voltage V_1 by 90°
2. core-loss current lags V_1 by 90°
3. no-load current lags V_1 by 90°
4. core-loss current is in phase with V_1
5. no-load current lags V_1 by about 80°
6. magnetizing current lags V_1 by about 80°

From these, the correct statements are

(a) 1, 4, 5 (b) 3, 4, 6 (c) 1, 4 (d) 1, 2, 6

50. A transformer secondary is connected to pure resistive load. The power factor on the primary side will be
(a) near about 0.95 lead (b) near about 0.95 lag
(c) zero (d) unity

51. If supply frequency in a transformer is doubled
(a) hysteresis loss also doubles (b) eddy-current loss doubles
(c) iron-losses double (d) hysteresis loss decreases

52. A 50 Hz transformer having equal hysteresis and eddy-current losses at rated excitation is operated at 45 Hz at 90% of rated voltage compared to rated operating point, the core loss under this condition
(a) reduces by 10% (b) reduces by 19%
(c) reduces by 14.5% (d) remains unchaned [GATE, 1998]

53. For the purpose of analysis, exact equivalent circuit of a transformer is usually replaced by an approximate equivalent circuit. In doing so, errors introduced due to winding ohmic loss and core loss are of differential nature. Due to this, the analysis by approximate equivalent circuit gives fairly satisfactory results. Under the circumstances, which one of the following statements is correct in respect of losses referred to approximate equivalent circuit as compared to exact equivalent circuit?
(a) This accounts for somewhat greater primary winding ohmic loss and less core loss.
(b) This accounts for somewhat less primary-winding ohmic loss and more core loss.
(c) This accounts for somewhat greater secondary-winding ohmic loss and less core loss.
(d) This accounts for somewhat less secondary-winding ohmic loss and more core loss.

54. In a 1-phase transformer, the magnitude of leakage reactance is twice that of resistance of both primary and secondary. With secondary short-circuited, the input p.f. is

(a) $\frac{1}{\sqrt{2}}$ (b) $\frac{1}{\sqrt{5}}$ (c) $\frac{2}{\sqrt{5}}$ (d) $\frac{1}{3}$

55. High leakage-impedance transformers are used for applications such as

(a) power distribution (b) electric toys

(c) fluorescent lamps (d) arc welding

56. In an ideal transformer shown in Fig. C.45,

(a) $V_1 = a\,V_2,\ \bar{I}_2 = -a\,\bar{I}_1$ (b) $V_2 = a\,V_1,\ \bar{I}_2 = -a\,\bar{I}_1$

(c) $V_1 = a\,V_2,\ \bar{I}_2 = \frac{1}{a}\,\bar{I}_1$ (d) $V_1 = a\,V_2,\ \bar{I}_2 = -\frac{1}{a}\,\bar{I}_1$

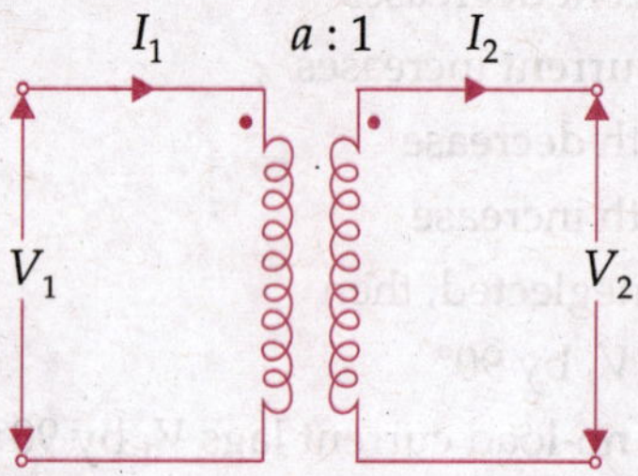

Fig C.45

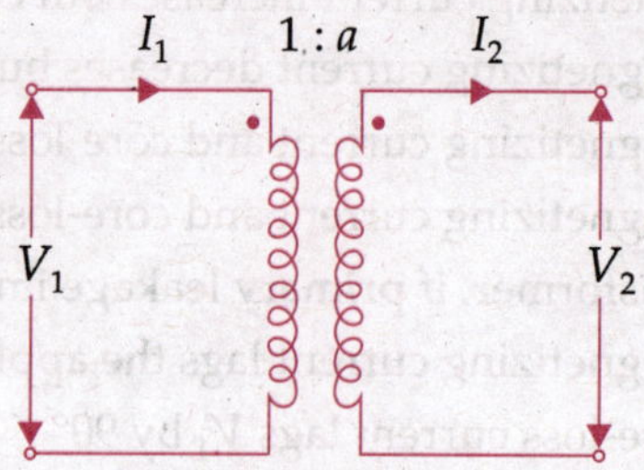

Fig C.46

57. In an ideal transformer shown in Fig. C.46,

(a) $V_1 = a\,V_2,\ \bar{I}_2 = -a\,\bar{I}_1$ (b) $V_2 = a\,V_1,\ \bar{I}_2 = -a\,\bar{I}_1$

(c) $V_1 = a\,V_2,\ \bar{I}_2 = \frac{1}{a}\,\bar{I}_1$ (d) $V_2 = a\,V_1,\ \bar{I}_2 = -\frac{1}{a}\,\bar{I}_1$

58. When compared with power transformer, a distribution transformer has

(a) low %age impedance and high I^2R loss to core-loss ratio

(b) high %age impedance and high I^2R loss to core-loss ratio

(c) high %age impedance and low I^2R loss to core-loss ratio

(d) low %age impedance and low I^2R loss to core-loss ratio

59. Following statements are made regarding the open-circuit test on a 1-phase transformer :

1. It is performed on L.V. side
2. It is performed at rated current
3. It helps in the calculation of equivalent leakage impedance
4. It is performed on H.V. side
5. It is performed at rated voltage
6. It gives magnetizing current and core loss
7. It helps in the determination of voltage regulation
8. It gives turns ratio

From these, the correct answer is

(a) 1, 5, 6, 8 (b) 2, 4, 6, 8 (c) 3, 4, 5, 6, 8 (d) 1, 5, 7, 8

60. Following statements are made regarding the short-circuit test on a 1-phase transformer :

1. H.V. side is short circuited
2. It is performed at rated current
3. It gives the core loss

4. L.V.side is short-circuited
5. It is performed at rated voltage
6. It gives ohmic loss on the side instruments are connected
7. It helps in the calculation of voltage regulation

From these, the correct answer is

(a) 1, 2, 6, 7 (b) 2, 3, 4, 7 (c) 4, 5, 6, 7 (d) 2, 4, 7

61. A 10 kVA, 400/200 V, single-phase transformer with 10% leakage impedance draws a steady short-circuit line current of

(a) 50 A (b) 150 A (c) 250 A (d) 350 A

62. While performing the open-circuit and short-circuit tests on a transformer to determine its parameters, the status of the low-voltage (L.V.) and high-voltage (H.V.) windings will be such that

(a) in O.C., L.V. is open and in S.C., H.V. is shorted
(b) in O.C., H.V. is open and in S.C., L.V. is shorted
(c) in O.C., L.V. is open and in S.C., L.V. is shorted
(d) in O.C., H.V. is open and in S.C., H.V. is shorted

63. A multimeter, for measuring resistance, is connected to one terminal of primary and the other terminal of secondary. The multimeter reading would be

(a) zero (b) infinity
(c) zero or infinity (d) equal to the resistance of the windings

64. For given base voltage and base volt-amperes, the per unit leakage impedance of a transformer is x. What will be the per unit leakage impedance of this transformer when the voltage and volt-ampere bases are both doubled?

(a) $0.5x$ (b) $2x$ (c) $4x$ (d) x

65. At 50 Hz operation, a single-phase transformer has hysteresis loss of 200 W and eddy-current loss of 100 W. Its core loss at 60 Hz operation will be [I.E.S., 1995]

(a) 432 W (b) 408 W (c) 384 W (d) 360 W

66. The hysteresis and eddy-current losses of 1-phase transformer working on 200 V, 50 Hz supply are P_h and P_e respectively. The percentage decrease in these losses when operated on a 160 V, 40 Hz supply would respectively be [I.E.S., 2001]

(a) 32, 36 (b) 20, 36 (c) 25, 50 (d) 40, 80

67. In a transformer, eddy-current loss is 100 watts which is half of the total core loss. If both the thickness of laminations, voltage and frequency are increased by 10%, the new core-loss would be

(a) 256.41 W (b) 231 W (c) 267.41 W (d) 242 W

68. A 220/115 V, 25 Hz, 1-phase transformer has eddy-current loss of 100 W which is half of the no-load loss at rated applied voltage. If this transformer is used with primary connected to 440 V, 50 Hz mains, the total no-load loss would be

(a) 300 W (b) 600 W (c) 1000 W (d) 400 W

69. A 220 V, 50 Hz transformer with 0.35 mm thick laminations has eddy-current loss of 120 watts which is two-third of the total loss at no-load. If this transformer is built with 0.7 mm thick laminations and is worked from 110 V, 25 Hz, then total no-load loss would be

(a) 150 W (b) 510 W (c) 200 W (d) 45 W

70. A transformer, fed from an alternator at 230 V, 50 Hz, has eddy-current loss of 50 W and hysteresis loss of 100 W. If the speed of the prime-mover driving the alternator drops to 80% of its previous speed, then eddy-current and hysteresis losses in the transformer would respectively be

(a) 40 W, 80 W (b) 32 W, 80 W (c) 32 W, 64 W (d) 40 W, 64 W

71. Two windings of a transformer are indicated by terminals *AB* and *CD* as shown in Fig. C.47. When a voltage of 100 V is applied across *AB* with *BD* short-circuited, a voltage of 200 V appears across *AC*. The turns ratio from *CD* to *AB* is

(a) 3 (b) 1
(c) 3 or 1 (d) 2 or 1

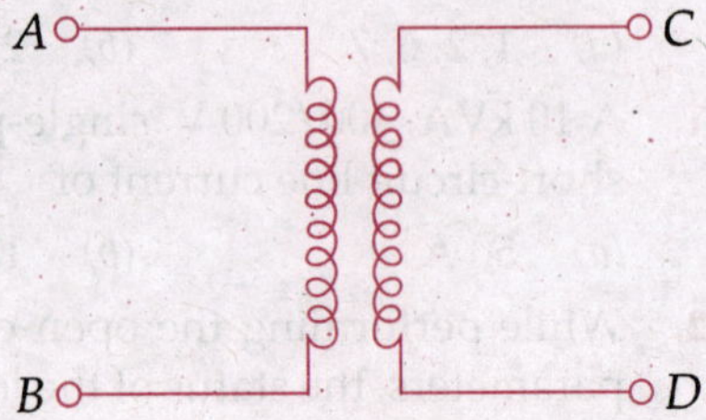

Fig C.47

72. In question 71, if voltage appearing across terminals *AC* is 100 V with input to *AB* as 100 V, then the turns ratio from *CD* to *AB* is

(a) 2 (b) 1
(c) 2 or 1 (d) 3 or 1

73. A 400 V/200 V/200 V, 50 Hz, three-winding transformer is connected as shown in Fig. C.48. The reading of the voltmeter *V* will be

(a) 0 V (b) 400 V
(c) 600 V (d) 800 V

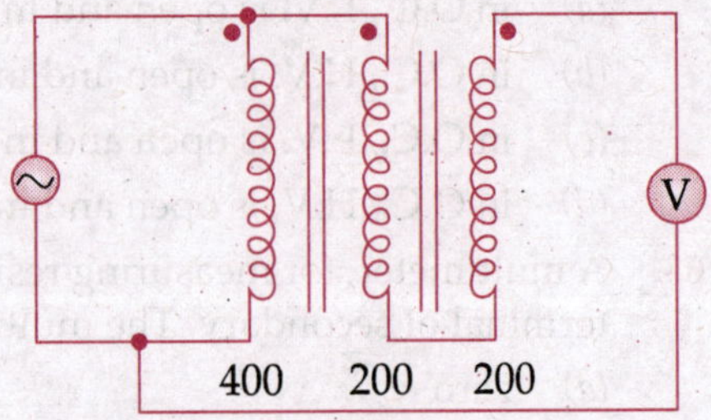

Fig C.48

74. A transformer has leakage impedance of $z_e = r_e + jx_e$. Its maximum voltage regulation occurs at a power factor of

(a) $\frac{r_e}{x_e}$ leading (b) $\frac{r_e}{z_e}$ lagging (c) $\frac{x_e}{z_e}$ leading (d) $\frac{r_e}{z_e}$ leading

75. A transformer has leakage impedance of $z_e = r_e + jx_e$. Zero voltage regulation for this transformer occurs at a p.f. of

(a) $\frac{r_e}{x_e}$ leading (b) $\frac{r_e}{z_e}$ lagging (c) $\frac{x_e}{z_e}$ leading (d) $\frac{r_e}{z_e}$ leading

76. A 1-phase transformer has p.u. leakage impedance of 0.02 + *j* 0.04. Its regulation at p.f. 0.8 lagging and 0.8 leading are respectively be

(a) 4%, 0.8% (b) 4%, – 0.8% (c) 2.4%, – 0.8% (d) 4%, –1%

77. A 10 kVA, 400 V/200 V, 1-phase transformer with a percentage resistance of 3% and percentage reactance of 6% is supplying a current of 50 A to a resistive load. The value of the load voltage is

(a) 194 V (b) 390 V (c) 192 V (d) 196 V

78. In a transformer, $r_{e2} + j_{xe2}$ = equivalent leakage impedance z_{e2}. Its maximum voltage regulation is equal to

(a) r_{e2} at $\frac{r_{e2}}{z_{e2}}$ lagging p.f. (b) x_{e2} at $\frac{x_{e2}}{z_{e2}}$ lagging p.f.

(c) x_{e2} at $\frac{r_{e2}}{z_{e2}}$ leading p.f. (d) z_{e2} at $\frac{r_{e2}}{z_{e2}}$ lagging p.f.

79. Full-load voltage regulation of a power transformer is zero when power factor of the load is near

(a) unity and leading (b) zero and leading (c) zero and lagging (d) unity and lagging

80. A 5 kVA, 250/125 V, 1-phase transformer has leakage impedance of (0.02 + j 0.08) p.u. Its value in ohm referred to H.V. side is

(a) $0.2 + j\,0.8$ (b) $0.25 + j\,1$ (c) $0.02 + j\,0.08$ (d) $0.0625 + j\,0.25$

81. The voltage regulation of a transformer is given by

(a) $\frac{E_2 - V_2}{V_2}$ (b) $\frac{E_2 - V_2}{E_2}$ (c) $\frac{V_2 - E_2}{V_2}$ (d) $\frac{V_2 - E_2}{E_2}$

82. The voltage regulation of a transformer at full-load 0.8 p.f. lagging is 4%. its voltage regulation at full-load 0.8 p.f. leading

(a) will be positive (b) will be negative (c) may be positive (d) may be negative

83. The voltage regulation of a transformer depends on its

1. equivalent reactance
2. equivalent resistance
3. load power factor
4. transformer size
5. load current

From these, the correct answer is

(a) 1, 2, 3, 5 (b) 1, 2, 3, 4, 5 (c) 1, 2, 4, 5 (d) 1, 2, 3, 4

84. The voltage regulation of a transformer at full load and 0.8 p.f. lagging is 2.5 %. The voltage regulation at full load 0.8 p.f. leading will be

(a) – 2.5% (b) zero (c) – 0.9% (d) 2.5%

85. In Sumpner's test on two identical transformers having rated frequency f,

(a) both the primaries and the regulating transformer should be fed from voltage sources of frequency f

(b) both the primaries and the regulating transformer may be fed from voltage source at frequency different from f

(c) both the primaries should be fed from voltage source at frequency f but regulating transformer may be fed at a frequency different from f

(d) both the primaries may be fed from voltage source at a frequency different from f but regulating transformer should be fed at f

86. The efficiency of a transformer at full load 0.8 p.f. lag is 90%. Its efficiency at full load 0.8 p.f. lead will be

(a) somewhat less than 90% (b) somewhat more than 90%
(c) 90% (d) 91%

87. Transformer maximum efficiency, for a constant load current, occurs at

(a) at any p.f. (b) zero pf leading (c) zero p.f. lagging (d) unity p.f.

88. One transformer has leakage impedance of $1 + j4\,\Omega$ and $3 + j11\,\Omega$ for its primary and secondary windings respectively. This transformer has

(a) H.V. primary (b) medium voltage primary
(c) L.V. primary (d) L.V. secondary

89. Transformer at no-load behaves like

(a) a resistor, p.f. = 0 (b) an inductive reactor, p.f. = 0.2 lagging
(c) a capacitive reactor, p.f. = 0.2 leading (d) an inductive reactor, p.f. = 0.8 lagging

90. In a transformer, the tappings are provided on

(a) H.V. side at one end of the winding (b) L.V. side at one end of the winding
(c) H.V. side at the middle (d) L.V. side at the middle

91. In transformers, the windings are tapped in the middle

(a) to avoid the radial forces on the windings

(b) to eliminate the axial forces on the windings

(c) to reduce the insulation level of the windings

(d) to provide a mechanical balance to the windings

92. In transformers, tappings are provided on the H.V. side because

1. it has larger number of turns which allow smoother control of output voltage
2. it has to handle low value of currents
3. it is easily accessible for repairs
4. it requires less insulation

From these, the correct answer is

(a) 1, 2, 3, 4 (b) 2, 3, 4 (c) 1, 2, 4 (d) 1, 2, 3

93. When a transformer winding suffers a short circuit, the adjoining turns of the same winding experience

(a) an attractive force (b) a repulsive force

(c) no force

(d) may be attractive or repulsive depending upon the current directions

94. The relative current directions through the primary (P) and secondary (S) of a 1-phase transformer connected to a resistive load on the secondary side, are indicated in the various cross-sectional views given in Fig. C.49. Which of these are correct representations?

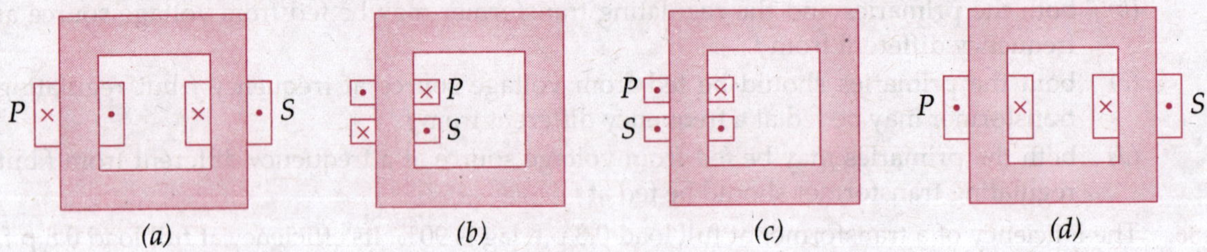

Fig C.49

95. Short-circuit test on a single-phase transformer gave the following data:

30 V at 50 Hz, 20 A, p.f. = 0.2 lag

If s.c. test is performed on 30 V, 25 Hz, then short-circuit current

(a) decreases at a p.f. < 0.2 (b) increases at a p.f. < 0.2

(c) increases at a p.f. > 0.2 (d) decreases at a p.f. > 0.2

96. Open-circuit test on a single-phase transformer gave the following data:

230 V at 50 Hz, 2 A, p.f. = 0.2 lag

If open-circuit test is performed on 230 V, 45 Hz, then no-load current

(a) decreases at a p.f. > 0.2 (b) decreases at a p.f. < 0.2

(c) increases at a p.f. > 0.2 (d) increases at a p.f. < 0.2

97. When short-circuit test on a transformer is performed at 25 V, 50 Hz ; then drawn current 'I'_1' is at a lagging p.f.-angle of ϕ_1. If the test is performed at 25 V, 25 Hz and the drawn current 'I'_2' is at a lagging p.f.-angle of ϕ_2, then

(a) $I_2 > I_1$ and $\phi_2 < \phi_1$ (b) $I_2 < I_1$ and $\phi_2 < \phi_1$ (c) $I_2 > I_1$ and $\phi_2 > \phi_1$ (d) $I_2 < I_1$ and $\phi_2 > \phi_1$

98. Two transformers to be operated in parallel have their secondary no-load e.m.fs. E_a for transformer A and E_b for transformer B. As E_a is somewhat more than E_b, a circulating current I_c is established at no-load which tends to

(a) boost both E_a and E_b with $I_c = \dfrac{\bar{E}_a - \bar{E}_b}{z_{ea} + z_{eb}}$ (b) boost E_a and buck E_b with $I_c = \dfrac{\bar{E}_a - \bar{E}_b}{z_{ea} + z_{eb}}$

(c) buck E_a and boost E_b with $I_c = \dfrac{\bar{E}_a - \bar{E}_b}{z_{ea} + z_{eb}}$ (d) buck both E_a and E_b with $I_c = \dfrac{\bar{E}_b - \bar{E}_a}{z_{ea} + z_{eb}}$

99. Two transformers of identical voltages but of different capacities are operating in parallel. For satisfactory load sharing,

(a) impedances must be equal
(b) per-unit impedances must be equal
(c) per-unit impedances and $\dfrac{X}{R}$ ratios must be equal
(d) impedances and $\dfrac{X}{R}$ ratios must be equal

100. Two transformers of different kVA ratings working in parallel share the load in proportion to their ratings when their

1. per unit leakage impedances on the same kVA base are equal
2. per unit leakage impedances based on their respective kVA ratings are equal
3. ohmic values of the leakage impedances are inversely proportional to their ratings
4. ohmic values of the magnetizing reactances are the same

From these, the correct answer is

(a) 1, 3, 4 (b) 2, 3 (c) 2, 3, 4 (d) 1, 4 [Gate, 1992]

101. Transformers operating in parallel will share a common load in the best possible manner if

(a) the leakage impedances are proportional to their respective kVA ratings
(b) the leakage impedances are equal
(c) per unit leakage impedances are equal
(d) per unit leakage impedances are proportional to their respective kVA ratings

102. The necessary conditions for parallel operation of two 1-phase transformers is that these should have the same

1. polarity 2. kVA rating
3. voltage regulation 4. efficiencies
5. voltage ratio 6. $\dfrac{X}{R}$ ratio

From these, the correct answer is

(a) 1, 2, 3, 4, 5, 6 (b) 1, 2, 5, 6 (c) 1, 5, 6 (d) 1, 3, 5, 6

103. For successful parallel operation of two single-phase transformers, the essential condition is that their

(a) percentage impedances should be equal (b) turns ratio should be exactly equal
(c) polarities must be properly connected (d) kVA ratings should be equal

104. Two transformers operating in parallel have different quality of their leakage impedances. For a load p.f. of 0.8,

(a) both would operate at p.f.s less than 0.8

(b) both would operate at p.f.s more than 0.8

(c) both would operate at the same p.f.s

(d) one would operate at p.f. > 0.8 and the other at p.f. < 0.8

105. Two 1-phase transformer with equal turns ratio have impedances of $(0.5 + j3)\ \Omega$ and $(0.6 + j10)\ \Omega$ with respect to the secondary. If they operate in parallel, how will they share a load of 100 kW at 0.8 p.f. lagging? *[I.E.S., 1992]*

(a) 50 kW, 50 kW (b) 62 kW, 38 kW (c) 78.2 kW, 21.8 kW (d) 85.5 kW, 14.5 kW

106. A single-phase transformer, with kVA rating K, has voltage rating of V_1/V_2. This transformer can be connected as an autotransformer to get two possible voltage ratings of $\frac{V_1+V_2}{V_2}$ and $\frac{V_1+V_2}{V_1}$. The respective kVA ratings as an autotransformer are

(a) $\frac{V_1+V_2}{V_1}K, \frac{V_1+V_2}{V_2}K$ (b) $\frac{V_1+V_2}{V_2}K, \frac{V_1+V_2}{V_1}K$

(c) $\frac{V_1-V_2}{V_1}K, \frac{V_1 V_2}{V_2}K$ (d) $\frac{V_1+V_2}{V_2 \cdot K}, \frac{V_1+V_2}{V_2 \cdot K}$

107. A 400 V/100 V, 10 kVA, two-winding transformer is reconnected as an autotransformer across a suitable voltage. The maximum rating of such a transformer could be

(a) 50 kVA (b) 15 kVA (c) 12.5 kVA (d) 8.75 kVA

108. An autotransformer having a transformation ratio of 0.8 supplies a load of 10 kW. The power transferred inductively from the primary to the secondary is

(a) 10 kW (b) 8 kW (c) 2 kW (d) zero

109. A single-phase transformer has a rating of 15 kVA, 600 V/120 V. It is reconnected as an autotransformer to supply at 720 V from a 600 V primary source. The maximum load it can supply is

(a) 90 kVA (b) 180 kVA (c) 15 kVA (d) 18 kVA

110. In an autotransformer of voltage ratio $\frac{V_1}{V_2}$ and $V_1 > V_2$, the fraction of power transferred inductively is

(a) $\frac{V_1}{V_1+V_2}$ (b) $\frac{V_2}{V_1}$ (c) $\frac{V_1-V_2}{V_1+V_2}$ (d) $\frac{V_1-V_2}{V_1}$

111. A 10 kVA step down autotransformer has voltage ratio of 0.7. The transformed and conducted kVA can be respectively

(a) 3, 7 (b) 7, 3 (c) 5, 5 (d) 3.5, 6.5

112. A supply of 100 V can be obtained from a source of 300 V, by means of a two-winding transformer or an autotransformer. The ratio of weights of conductor material in the autotransformer with respect to two-winding transformer is

(a) 1 : 1.5 (b) 1.5 : 1 (c) 3 : 1 (d) 1 : 3

113. In an autotransformer of voltage ratio V_1/V_2, with $V_1 > V_2$ the conducted power in terms of total power is

(a) $\frac{V_1}{V_2}$ (b) $\frac{V_2}{V_1}$ (c) $\frac{V_1-V_2}{V_1}$ (d) $\frac{V_1-V_2}{V_2}$

114. A 20 kVA, 2300 V/230 V, two winding transformer is to be used as an autotransformer to give 2300 V/2530 V. Its rating will be

(a) 200 kVA with conducted kVA = 20 (b) 200 kVA with conducted kVA = 180
(c) 220 kVA with conducted kVA = 20 (d) 220 kVA with conducted kVA = 200

115. Single-phase supply of 220 V, 50 Hz is to be obtained from 400 V, 50 Hz source. The ratio of weight of conductor material in a two-winding transformer to that required in an autotransformer is

(a) $\frac{20}{9}$ (b) $\frac{9}{20}$ (c) $\frac{20}{11}$ (d) 2

116. A 10 kVA single-phase transformer has core loss of 60 W at rated voltage and ohmic loss of 85 W at rated current. Its maximum efficiency at unity *pf* is

(a) 98.81% (b) 98.52% (c) 98.02% (d) 98.59%

117. An autotransformer has V_1, I_1 as input quantities and V_2, I_2 as output quantities with $V_2 < V_1$. The *VA* conducted from input to output is

(a) $V_1 I_2$ (b) $V_2 I_1$ (c) $V_1 I_1 - V_2 I_2$ (d) $(V_1 - V_2) I_1$

118. An autotransformer has V_1, I_1 as input quantities and V_2, I_2 as output quantities with $V_2 < V_1$. The *VA* transformed from primary to secondary is

(a) $V_1 I_2$ (b) $V_2 I_1$ (c) $V_1 I_1 - V_2 I_2$ (d) $(V_1 - V_2) I_1$

119. The efficiency of a 100 kVA transformer is 0.98 at full as well as half load. For this transformer at full load, the ohmic loss

(a) is less than core loss (b) is equal to core loss
(c) is more than core loss (d) none of the above

120. A 40 kVA transformer has a core loss of 400 W and a full-load copper loss of 800 W. The proportion of full-load at maximum efficiency is

(a) 50% (b) 62.3% (c) 70.7% (d) 100%

121. In a current transformer,

1. primary current is determined by secondary current,
2. primary winding consists of a few turns of thick wire,
3. load across the secondary terminals is called burden,
4. magnetizing impedance is kept small.

From these, the correct answer is

(a) 1, 2, 4 (b) 2, 3, 4 (c) 2, 3 (d) 3, 4

122. In a tap changer, the voltage at consumers terminals is kept within the prescribed limits by varying the

(a) ratio of turns between primary and secondary windings
(b) frequency
(c) flux density in the core
(d) angle between the magnetic axes of the primary and secondary windings

123. In a current transformer,

1. primary current is determined by load current,
2. burden has the units of watts,
3. for obtaining high accuracy in the measurements, core is made from silicon steel,

4. secondary has large number of turns with thin wire,
5. current is stepped down.

From above, the correct answer is

(a) 1, 2, 4 (b) 1, 2, 4, 5 (c) 2, 3, 4 (d) 1, 4, 5

124. When primary winding of a current transformer carries load current, its secondary circuit should never be open-circuited ; otherwise,

1. dangerously high voltage will be induced in both primary and secondary windings,
2. dangerously high voltage will be induced in secondary winding only,
3. large core loss would occur resulting in core heating
4. large core flux may cause presence of residual flux leading to inaccurate future readings.

From above, the correct choice is

(a) 2, 3, 4 (b) 1, 2, 3, 4 (c) 1, 3, 4 (d) 3, 4

125. Read the following statements about instrument transformers.

(a) Load across the secondary terminals of a current transformer is called burden.
(b) Burden on CT has the units of volt-amperes.
(c) Secondary winding of a potential transformer is designed for about 110 V.
(d) all of the above.

126. A 3-phase delta-star transformer has secondary to primary turns ratio per phase of 5. For a primary voltage of 400 V, the secondary voltage would be

(a) 2000 V (b) 80 V (c) 3464 V (d) $80\sqrt{3}$ V

127. A 3-phase star-delta transformer has secondary to primary turns ratio per phase of 5. For a primary voltage of 400 V, the secondary voltage would be

(a) 3464 V (b) 1154.7 V (c) 2000 V (d) 46.2 V

128. A 3-phase delta-star transformer has secondary to primary turns ratio per phase of 5. For a primary line current of 10 A, the secondary line current would be

(a) 2 A (b) 3.464 A (c) 1.633 A (d) 1.155 A

129. A 3-phase star-delta transformer has primary to secondary turns ratio per phase of 5. For a primary line current of 10 A, the secondary line current would be

(a) 50 A (b) 86.6 A (c) 3.464 A (d) 150 A

130. In transformers, the noise or hum is produced primarily due to

(a) improper tightening of core laminations (b) magnetostriction
(c) tank walls (d) loose bolts etc.

131. Match the items on the left-hand side with the most appropriate item on the right-hand side :

Type		*Application*	
A.	Power transformer	1.	Thyristor firing circuits
B.	Distribution transformer	2.	Impedance matching
C.	Pulse transformer	3.	At different city localities
D.	Audio-frequency transformer	4.	At generating stations

132. Which of the following statements are incorrect? *[I.A.S., 1993]*

1. Maximum voltage regulation of a transformer occurs at leading power factor
2. Voltage regulation of a transformer is the maximum when load power-factor (lagging) angle has the same value as the angle of equivalent impedance

3. Voltage regulation of a transformer at zero power factor is always zero
4. Voltage regulation of a transformer can be negative at leading power factor

Select the correct answer using the codes given below:

Codes :

(a) 1 and 3 (b) 2 and 3 (c) 2 and 4 (d) 1 and 4

133. When a short-circuit test is conducted on a single-phase transformer, 30% of the rated voltage is required to allow full-load current. The short-circuit power factor is found to be 0.2. The percentage regulation at UPF is *[I.A.S., 1993]*

(a) 30 (b) 29.5 (c) 15 (d) 6

134. A bank of three identical single-phase 250 kVA, 11 kV/230 V transformer is used to provide 400 V low-tension supply from a 11 kV, 3-phase sub-station. The effective kVA rating of the bank will be *[I.A.S., 1994]*

(a) 250 (b) $250\sqrt{3}$ (c) 500 (d) 750

135. A transformer designed for operation of 60 Hz supply is working on 50 Hz supply system without changing its voltage and current ratings. When compared with full-load efficiency at 60 Hz, the transformer efficiency on full load at 50 Hz will

(a) increase marginally (b) increase by a factor of 1.2

(c) remain unaltered (d) decrease marginally

136. The voltage regulation of a large transformer is mainaly influenced by

(a) no-load current and load power factor (b) winding resistances and load power factor

(c) leakage fluxes and load power factor (d) winding resistances and core loss

137. Fig. C.50 shows an ideal single-phase transformer. The primary and secondary coils are wound on the core as shown. Turns ratio $(N_1/N_2) = 2$. The correct phasors of voltages E_1, E_2, currents I_1, I_2 and core flux ϕ are as shown in *[GATE, 2003]*

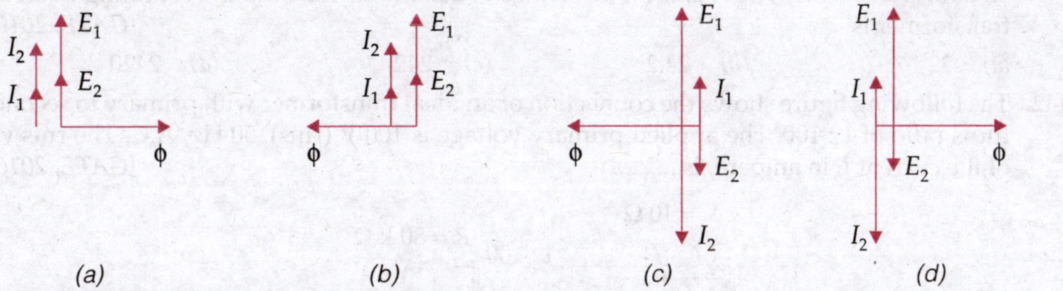

138. Fig. C.51 shows an ideal transformer. The three windings 1, 2, 3, of the transformer are wound on the same core as shown. The turns ratio $N_1 : N_2 : N_3$ is 4 : 2 : 1. A resistor of 10 Ω is connected across winding-2. A capacitor of reactance 2.5 Ω is connected across winding-3. Winding-1 is connected across a 400 V, A.C. supply. If the supply voltage phasor $V_1 = 400\angle 0°$, the supply current I_1 is given by *[GATE, 2003]*

(a) $(-10 + j\,10)$ A (b) $(-10 - j\,10)$ A (c) $(10 + j\,10)$ A (d) $(10 - j\,10)$ A

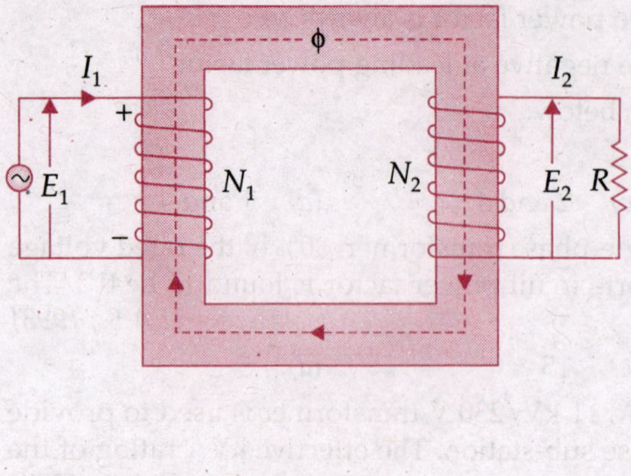

Fig C.50

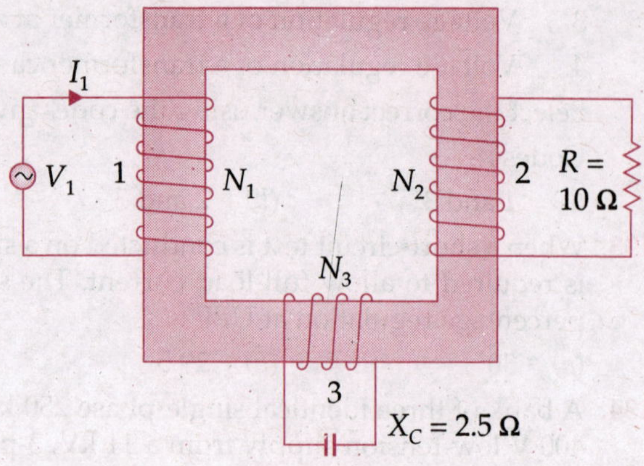

Fig C.51

139. A single-phase transformer has a maximum efficiency of 90% at full load and unity power factor. Efficiency at half load at the same power factor is *[GATE, 2003]*

(a) 86.7% (b) 88.26% (c) 88.9% (d) 87.8%

140. A potential transformer
1. is a step-down transformer,
2. has its secondary winding grounded,
3. has high magnetizing impedance,
4. has its secondary winding designed for very small current.

From above, the correct choice is

(a) 1, 2, 4 (b) 1, 2, 3, 4 (c) 1, 2, 3 (d) 1, 3, 4

141. A single-phase 22 kVA, 2200 V/220 V, 50 Hz, distribution transformer is to be connected as an auto-transformer to get an output voltage of 2420 V. Its maximum kVA rating as an auto-transformer is *[GATE, 2016 (I)]*

(a) 22 (b) 24.2 (c) 242 (d) 2420

142. The following figure shows the connection of an ideal transformer with primary to secondary turns ratio of 1 : 100. The applied primary voltage is 100 V (rms), 50 Hz, A.C. The rms value of the current I, in ampere, is .... *[GATE, 2016 (II)*

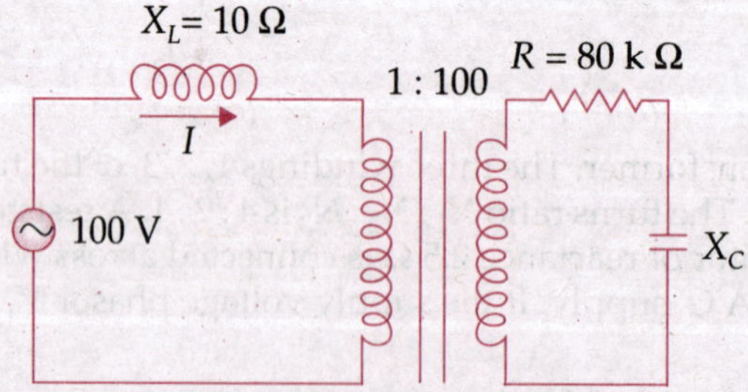

143. Three single-phase transformers are connected to form a delta-star three phase transformer of 110 kV/11 kV. The transformer supplies at 11 kV a load of 8 MW at 0.8 pf lagging to a nearby plant. Neglect the transformer losses. The ratio of phase currents in delta side to star side is

(a) $1 : 10\sqrt{3}$ (b) $10\sqrt{3} : 1$ (c) $1 : 10$ (d) $\sqrt{3} : 10$

[Hint. Per-phase primary VA, $110 \times I_\Delta$ = per-phase secondary VA, $\frac{11}{\sqrt{3}} \times I_y$ etc**]***[GATE, 2016 (II)]*

144. A single-phase 400 V, 50 Hz transformer has an iron loss of 5000 W at the rated condition. When operated at 200 V, 25 Hz, the iron loss is 2000 W. When operated at 416 V, 52 Hz, the value of the hysteresis loss divided by the eddy current loss is .... *[GATE, 2016 (I)]*
[Hint. Iron loss, $5000 = k_h \times f + k_e f^2 = 50\, k_h + 2500\, k_e$ and $2000 = 25\, k_h + 625\, k_e$ etc]

145. In a power transformer, a breather is provided
1. to extract moisture from air going into the tank,
2. to extract moisture from air going into the conservator,
3. to prevent entry of moisture with air,
4. to provide fresh air for increasing cooling effect.

From above, the correct choice is
(a) 1, 3, 4 *(b)* 1, 2, 3 *(c)* 2, 3 *(d)* 2, 3, 4

146. A Buchholz relay
1. is partially filled with oil,
2. is gas actuated device,
3. is current operated device
4. is used in oil-cooled transformers,
5. is placed between tank and conservator.

From above, the correct choice is
(a) 1, 2, 4 *(b)* 2, 4, 5 *(c)* 1, 3, 4, 5 *(d)* 2, 3, 4, 5

147. In a Buchholz relay, which of the following statements is not TRUE.
(a) alarm circuit is actuated by minor fault.
(b) it consists of two floats
(c) it is voltage operated device,
(d) trip circuit is activated by major fault.

148. A conservator,
1. takes care of expansion or contraction of oil in the transformer tank,
2. is an air-tight cylindrical metal drum,
3. is placed below the level of tank top surface,
4. prevents entry of moisture to the tank,
5. is partially filled with oil.

From above, the correct answer is
(a) 1, 2, 5 *(b)* 1, 3, 4, 5 *(c)* 1, 4, 5 *(d)* 1, 2, 4, 5

149. If the primary line voltage rating is 3.3 kV (Y side) of a 25 kVA Y-Δ transformer (the per phase turns ratio is 5 : 1), then the line current rating of the secondary side (in Ampere) is .... *[GATE, 2017 (2)]*

150. A 30 phase 900 kVA,. 3 kV/ $\sqrt{3}$ kV (Δ/Y), 50 Hz transformer has primary (high-voltage side) resistance per phase of 0.3 Ω and secondary (low voltage side) resistance per phase of 0.02 Ω. Iron loss of the transformer is 10 kW. The full load % efficiency of the transformer operated at unity power factor is .... (up to 2 decimal places). *[GATE, 2018]*

151. A single-phase transformer of rating 25 kVA, supplies a 12 kW load at power factor of 0.6 lagging. The additional load at unity power factor in kW (rounded off to two decimal places) that may be added before this transformer exceeds its rated kVA is .... *[GATE, 2019]*
[Hint. 12 kW at pf 0.6 lagging + P kW at unity pf = 25 kVA.
$\therefore\ \frac{12}{0.6}\,[0.6 - j\,0.8] + \text{P} = 25.\ \therefore\ [(\text{P} + 12)^2 + 16^2]^{1/2} = 25$ etc.]

ANSWERS

1. (d)	**2.** (b)	**3.** (b)	**4.** (b)	**5.** (c)
6. (d)	**7.** (b)	**8.** (c)	**9.** (c)	**10.** (a)
11. (d)	**12.** (d)	**13.** (a)	**14.** (a)	**15.** (b)
16. (a)	**17.** (c)	**18.** (b)	**19.** (c)	**20.** (c)
21. (c)	**22.** (a)	**23.** (c)	**24.** (b)	**25.** (d)
26. (b)	**27.** (b)	**28.** (c)	**29.** (a)	**30.** (c)
31. (d)	**32.** (c)	**33.** (a)	**34.** (a)	**35.** (c)
36. (b)	**37.** (a)	**38.** (c)	**39.** (b)	**40.** (d)
41. (a)	**42.** (d)	**43.** (b)	**44.** (c)	**45.** (a)
46. (d)	**47.** (b)	**48.** (d)	**49.** (a)	**50.** (b)
51. (d)	**52.** (c)	**53.** (b)	**54.** (b)	**55.** (d)
56. (a)	**57.** (d)	**58.** (a)	**59.** (a)	**60.** (d)
61. (c)	**62.** (b)	**63.** (b)	**64.** (a)	**65.** (c)
66. (b)	**67.** (a)	**68.** (b)	**69.** (a)	**70.** (b)
71. (c)	**72.** (a)	**73.** (b)	**74.** (b)	**75.** (c)
76. (b)	**77.** (a)	**78.** (d)	**79.** (a)	**80.** (b)
81. (b)	**82.** (d)	**83.** (a)	**84.** (c)	**85.** (c)
86. (a)	**87.** (d)	**88.** (c)	**89.** (b)	**90.** (c)
91. (b)	**92.** (d)	**93.** (a)	**94.** (a) & (b)	**95.** (c)
96. (d)	**97.** (a)	**98.** (c)	**99.** (c)	**100.** (b)
101. (c)	**102.** (d)	**103.** (c)	**104.** (d)	**105.** (c)
106. (a)	**107.** (a)	**108.** (c)	**109.** (a)	**110.** (d)
111. (a)	**112.** (a)	**113.** (b)	**114.** (d)	**115.** (a)
116. (d)	**117.** (b)	**118.** (d)	**119.** (c)	**120.** (c)
121. (c)	**122.** (a)	**123.** (d)	**124.** (a)	**125.** (d)
126. (c)	**127.** (b)	**128.** (d)	**129.** (b)	**130.** (b)
131. $A \to 4, B \to 3, C \to 1, D \to 2$		**132.** (a)	**133.** (d)	**134.** (d)
135. (d)	**136.** (c)	**137.** (d)	**138.** (c)	**139.** (d)
140. (a)	**141.** (c)	**142.** 10 A	**143.** (a)	**144.** 1.4423
145. (c)	**146.** (b)	**147.** (c)	**148.** (a)	**149.** 37.88 A
150. 97.36%	**151.** 7.21 kW			

ELECTROMECHANICAL ENERGY CONVERSION PRINCIPLES

1. An electromechanical energy conversion device is shown in Fig. C.52. The instantaneous value of armature induced e.m.f., bus bar voltage and armature current are respectively e, v and i. T_e, T_a and w_r represent external torque, armature developed torque and angular velocity of shaft respectively. Assume that the given directions of parameters in the given figure are positive. If the device is working in generating mode then

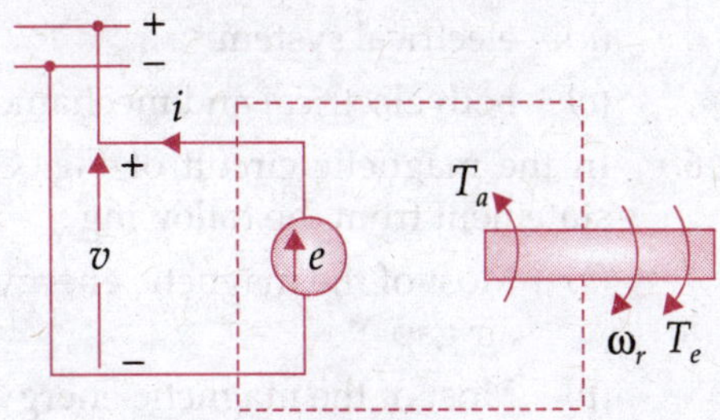

Fig C.52

(a) all parameters will have the positive direction
(b) e, v, T_e and w_r will have negative direction and others will remain in poistive direction
(c) T_a and i will have negative direction and others will remain in positive direction
(d) T_e and w_r will have negative direction and others will remain in positive direction.

2. If W_{fld} = field energy stored, then magnetic force developed in a singly-excited linear magnetic system is given by

1. $f_e = -\dfrac{\partial W_{fld}(\psi, x)}{\partial x}$, saturation may, or may not, be neglected

2. $f_e = -\dfrac{\partial W_{fld}(\phi, x)}{\partial x}$, saturation is included

3. $f_e = +\dfrac{\partial W_{fld}(F, x)}{\partial x}$, saturation is included

4. $f_e = +\dfrac{\partial W_{fld}(i, x)}{\partial x}$, saturation is neglected.

From these, the correct answer is

(a) 1, 2, 3, 4 *(b)* 2, 3 *(c)* 2, 3, 4 *(d)* 1, 2, 4

3. A coupling magnetic field must react with
1. electrical system in order to extract energy from mechanical system
2. mechanical system in order to extract energy from mechanical system
3. electrical system in order to extract energy from electrical system
4. mechanical system in order to extract energy from electrical system
5. both electrical and mechanical systems for electromechanical energy conversion
6. electrical or mechanical system for electromechanical energy conversion.

From these, the correct answer is

(a) 1, 2, 3, 4, 6 *(b)* 1, 4, 5 *(c)* 2, 3, 6 *(d)* 2, 3, 5

4. In a magnetic system, if ψ = flux linkages, then

1. field energy stored, W_{fld} + co-energy, $W_{fld}' = \frac{1}{2}\psi \cdot i$
2. $W_{fld} + W_{fld}' = \psi\, i$
3. $W_{fld} + W_{fld}' = F \cdot \phi$
4. $W_{fld} + W_{fld}' = \phi^2 \cdot Rl$
5. $W_{fld} + W_{fld}' = \frac{1}{2} L\, i^2$

From these, the correct answer is

(a) 1, 3, 4 *(b)* 2, 3, 5 *(c)* 1, 3, 4, 5 *(d)* 2, 3, 4

5. For electromechanical energy conversion process, it is essential that coupling magnetic field reacts on

(a) electrical system (b) mechanical system
(c) both electrical and mechanical systems (d) electrical or mechanical system

6. In the magnetic circuit of Fig. C.53, the coil is excited by a current *I*. Choose the correct statement from the following :

(a) Most of the magnetic energy will get stored in the air gap
(b) Most of the magnetic energy will get stored in the iron core
(c) The magnetic energy stored will be stored almost equally in the iron core and the air gap
(d) All the magnetic energy will be stored in the iron core

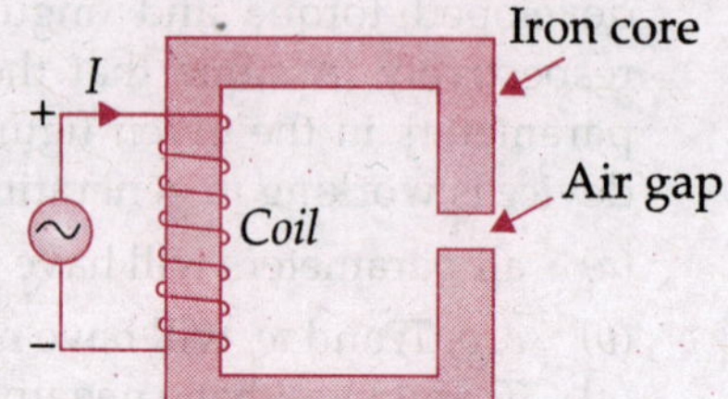

Fig C.53

7. Magnetic stored-energy density in iron is given by

(a) $\frac{1}{2}\phi^2 Rl$ (b) $\frac{1}{2}B^2\mu$ (c) $\frac{1}{2}\frac{B^2}{\mu}$ (d) $\frac{1}{2}\frac{B}{\mu}$

8. The energy stored in a magnetic field is given by

1. $\frac{1}{2}Li^2$ 2. $\frac{1}{2}\phi^2 Rl$ 3. $\frac{1}{2}(\text{m.m.f.})^2 \cdot Rl$ 4. $\frac{1}{2}\psi \cdot i$

From these, the correct answer is

(a) 1, 2, 3, 4 (b) 1, 2, 3 (c) 1, 2, 4 (d) 1, 3, 4

9. A linear magnetic circuit has flux linkages of 1.2 Wb-turns when a current of 10 A flows through its coil. The energy stored in the magnetic field of this coil, in Joules, is

(a) 12 (b) 6 (c) 1.2 (d) 24

10. The electromagnetic force and/or torque, developed in any physical system, acts in such a direction as to tend to

(a) decrease the magnetic stored energy at constant m.m.f.
(b) decrease the magnetic stored energy at constant flux
(c) increase the magnetic stored energy at constant flux
(d) increase the magnetic stored energy at constant current

11. The electromagnetic force, developed in any physical system, acts in such a direction as to tend to

(a) decrease the coenergy at constant m.m.f.
(b) increase the coenergy at constant flux
(c) decrease the coenergy at constant flux
(d) increase the coenergy at constant m.m.f.

12. The electromagnetic torque, developed in any physical system, and with magnetic saturation neglected, acts in such a direction as to tend to

(a) decrease both the reluctance and inductance
(b) increase both the reluctance and inductance
(c) decrease the reluctance and increase the inductance
(d) increase the reluctance and decrease the inductance

13. Electromagnetic force and/or torque, developed in any physical system, acts in such a direction as to tend to
   (a) increase both the field energy and co-energy at constant current
   (b) increase the field energy and decrease the co-energy at constant current
   (c) decrease both the field energy and co-energy at constant current
   (d) decrease the field energy and increase the co-energy at constant current.
14. The developed electromagnetic force and/or torque in electromechanical energy conversion systems act in such a direction that tends
   (a) to increase the stored energy at constant m.m.f.
   (b) to decrease the stored energy at constant flux
   (c) to decrease the coenergy at constant m.m.f.
   (d) to decrease the stored energy at constant m.m.f. [GATE, 1992]
15. The developed electromagnetic force and/or torque in electromechanical energy conversion systems acts in a direction that tends to
   1. increase the coenergy at constant flux
   2. increase the coenergy at constant m.m.f.
   3. decrease the stored energy at constant m.m.f.
   4. decrease the stored energy at constant flux
   From these, the correct answer is
   (a) 2, 4 (b) 1, 3 (c) 2, 3 (d) 1, 4
16. Electromagnetic force or torque developed in any physical system tends to
   1. decrease both field energy and coenergy at constant current
   2. increase both field energy and coenergy at constant current
   3. increase the permeance
   4. decrease the inductance
   5. decrease current at constant flux linkages.
   From these, the correct statements are
   (a) 2, 3, 5 (b) 1, 3, 4 (c) 1, 3, 4, 5 (d) 1, 3, 5
17. A physical system of electromechanical energy conversion consists of a stationary part creating a magnetic field with electric energy input and a moving part giving mechanical energy output. If now the movable part is kept flxed, the entire electrical energy input will be
   (a) stored in the magnetic field
   (b) stored in the electric field
   (c) divided equally between the magnetic and electric fields
   (d) zero
18. An electromagnetic relay has linear magnetic circuit. If the armature moves slowly to shorten the air gap, then
   1. mechanical work done, $W_{mech} = \frac{1}{2}$(electrical energy input, W_{elec})
   2. $W_{mech} = W_{elec}$
   3. field energy stored, $W_{fld} = \frac{1}{2} W_{elec}$
   4. $W_{fld} = W_{mech}$

From these, the correct answer is

(a) 1, 2, 3, 4 (b) 1, 2, 3 (c) 1, 2, 4 (d) 1, 3, 4

19. A magnetic relay has linear magnetization curve at its open and closed positions. If the armature moves slowly from open to closed position, then electrical energy input to the relay

(a) gets stored in the magnetic field

(b) gets converted into mechanical work

(c) gets divided equally between the magnetic and electric fields

(d) gets divided equally between magnetic field and mechanical work

20. Consider the following statments relating to the singly-excited electromechanical system of Fig. C.54. Here, i and ψ are current and flux linkages of the coil respectively. x is the position of the armature from a reference.

1. Magnetic stored energy decreases with increased value of x
2. Force on the armature acts in a direction to increase x
3. Electromagnetic force is equal to the rate of decrease of stored magnetic field energy with displacement at constant flux
4. Force is equal to the rate of increase of coenergy with displacement at constant current Of these statements

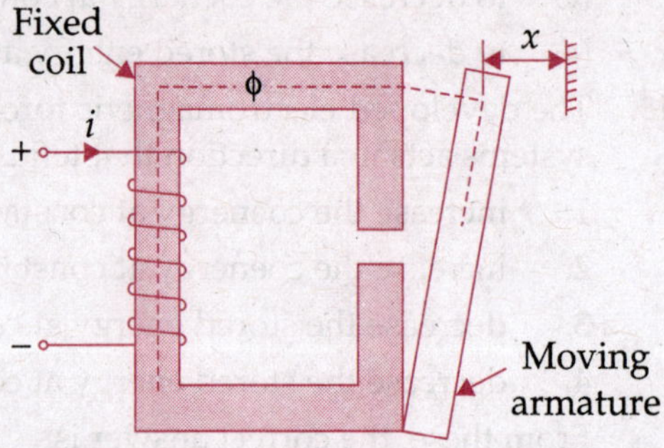

Fig C.54

(a) 1, 3 and 4 are correct (b) 1, 2 and 3 are correct

(c) 2, 3 and 4 are correct (d) 1, 2, 3 and 4 are correct *[I.A.S., 1995]*

21. When a transformer winding suffers a short-circuit, the adjoining turns of the same winding experience

1. an attractive force
2. a repulsive force
3. no force
4. an attractive force proportional to currents
5. a repulsive force proportional to currents
6. an attractive force inversely proportional to distance between adjoining turns
7. an attractive force directly proportional to distance between adjoining turns
8. a repulsive force inversely proportional to distance between adjoining turns

From these, the correct statements are

(a) 1, 4, 6 (b) 1, 4, 7 (c) 3 (d) 2, 5, 8

22. Consider the following statements :

The force per unit length between two stationary parallel wires carrying (steady) currents

1. is inversely proportional to the separation of wires
2. is proportional to the magnitude of each current
3. satisfies Newton's third law

Of these statements

(a) 1 and 2 are correct (b) 2 and 3 are correct

(c) 1 and 3 are correct (d) 1, 2 and 3 are correct

23. Magnetic flux density at a point distant R due to an infinitely long linear conductor carrying a current I is given by

(a) $B = \frac{1}{2\mu\pi R}$ (b) $B = \frac{\mu I}{2R}$ (c) $B = \frac{\mu I}{2\pi R}$ (d) $B = \frac{\mu I}{2\pi R^2}$

24. The energy stored in the magnetic field of a solenoid 30 cm long and 3 cm diameter wound with 1000 turns of wire carrying a current of 10 A is

(a) 0.015 joule (b) 0.15 joule (c) 0.5 joule (d) 1.15 joule

25. In Fig. C.55, a free rotating permanent magnet R lies between the poles of a stator. If D.C. supply is connected to the terminals AB, the rotor will

(a) start rotating
(b) oscillate about the stator-pole axis
(c) align itself with the pole axis of the stator
(d) have no effect

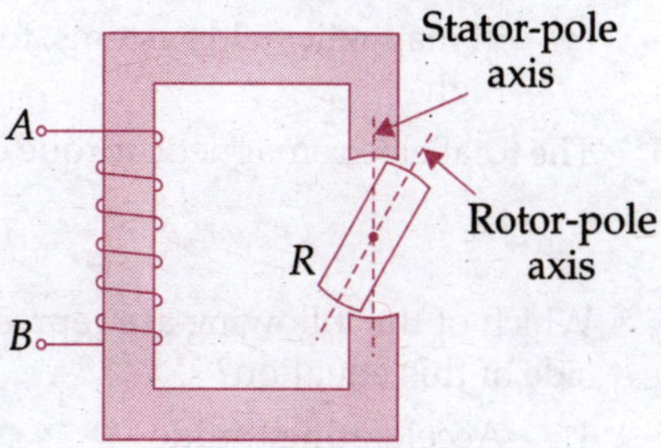

Fig C.55

26. In a simple magnetic relay, armature is in open position. As the armature moves towards the yoke under the influence of magnetic force f_e, air-gap flux density B_g and f_e vary as under :

(a) B_g increases and f_e decreases (b) Both decrease
(c) Both increase (d) B_g decreases and f_e increases

27. In an electric machine, if L = slot length and D = slot depth, then slot leakage flux is proportional to

(a) $\frac{1}{LD}$ (b) LD (c) D/L (d) $\frac{L}{D}$

28. In an electric machine, if Z = conductors per slot and W = slot width, then the slot leakage flux is proportional to

(a) Z/W (b) ZW (c) $\frac{W}{Z}$ (d) $\frac{1}{ZW}$

29. Singly-and doubly-excited magnetic systems are respectively :

(a) loud-speakers and tachometers
(b) synchronous motors and moving-iron instruments
(c) D.C. shount machines and solenoids
(d) reluctance motors and synchoronous motors

30. Reluctance torque in rotating machines is present when

1. air gap is not uniform
2. reluctance seen by stator m.m.f. varies with rotor movement
3. reluctance seen by rotor m.m.f. varies with rotor movement
4. reluctance seen by the working m.m.f. varies with rotor movement

From these, the correct answer is

(a) 1, 2, 3, 4 (b) 4 only (c) 2, 3 (d) 2, 3, 4

31. Electromagentic torque in rotating electrical machinery is present when

(a) air-gap is uniform
(b) stator winding alone carries current
(c) rotor winding alone carries current
(d) both stator and rotor windings carry current

32. All practical electromechanical energy conversion devices make use of the magnetic field rather than the electric field as the coupling medium. This is because

(a) electric field systems present insulation difficulties

(b) electric field systems have more dielectric loss than the magnetic loss for the same power rating of the machine

(c) in electric field systems, for normal electric field strength, the stored energy density is high

(d) in magnetic field systems, for normal magnetic flux density, the stored energy density is high

33. The total electromagnetic torque developed by a motor may be expressed in a general form as

$$T_e = A\frac{d^2\theta}{dt^2} + B\frac{d\theta}{dt} + C$$

Which of the following are represented by the first, second and third terms on the right-hand side of this equation?

1. Accelerating torque 2. Damping torque

3. Friction torque 4. Load torque

Select the correct combination using the following codes :

Codes :

	First term $\left[A\frac{d^2\theta}{dt^2}\right]$	Second term $\left[B\frac{d\theta}{dt}\right]$	Third term [C]
(a)	3	2	1 and 4
(b)	3	4	1 and 2
(c)	1	4	2 and 3
(d)	1	2	3 and 4

34. The general expression for the instantaneous value of the torque of dynamo-electric machine is given by

$$T_e = \frac{1}{2}(i_1)^2\frac{dL_1}{d\theta} + \frac{1}{2}(i_2)^2\frac{dL_2}{d\theta} + i_1 i_2\frac{dM}{d_\theta}$$

where i_1 and i_2 are stator and rotor currents respectively

L_1 and L_2 are stator and rotor windings' self-inductances respectively

M is the mutual inductance between stator and rotor windings and θ is the angular displacement of the rotor.

For a synchronous machine (cylindrical rotor), the torque is given by only the third term of the equation, because

(a) the average value of $(i_1)^2$ and $(i_2)^2$ each is zero

(b) the first and second terms cancel each other

(c) $\frac{dL_1}{d\theta}$ and $\frac{dL_2}{d\theta}$ have positive sign and $\frac{dL_1/d\theta}{dL_2/d\theta} = \frac{(i_1)^2}{(i_2)^2}$

(d) L_1 and L_2 do not vary with respect to θ

35. A rotating electromechanical energy conversion device has uniform air-gap. If δ is the space angle between the axes of stator field and rotor field, then the average torque developed is proportional to (A and B are constants).

(a) $A \sin \delta$ (b) $A \sin 2\delta$ (c) $A \sin \delta + B \sin 2\delta$ (d) δ

36. An electromechanical energy conversion device has cylindrical stator but salient-pole rotor. If δ is the angle between stator field and rotor field, the average torque developed is proportional to (A and B are constants)

(a) $A \sin \delta$ *(b)* $A \sin 2\delta$ *(c)* $A \sin \delta + B \sin 2\delta$ *(d)* δ

37. An electromechanical energy conversion device has cylindrical stator but salient-pole rotor. Rotor is not excited. If δ is the angle between stator field and rotor-long axis, then average torque developed is proportional to (A and B are constants)

(a) $A \sin \delta$ *(b)* $A \sin 2\delta$ *(c)* $A \sin \delta + B \sin 2\delta$ *(d)* zero

38. In an electromechanical energy conversion device, both stator and rotor have salient-pole configuration. Stator carries a winding but rotor is made from ferromagnetic material. If δ is the space angle between the stator-field axis and long-rotor axis, then the average torque developed is proportional to (A and B are constants) :

(a) $A \sin \delta$ *(b)* $A \sin 2\delta$ *(c)* $A \sin \delta + B \sin 2\delta$ *(d)* δ

39. Four singly-excited electromagnetic structures are shown in Fig. C.56 and labelled I, II, III and IV (R : rotor ; S : Stator).

The reluctance torque can be developed in

(a) I and IV *(b)* II and III *(c)* III and IV *(d)* III alone

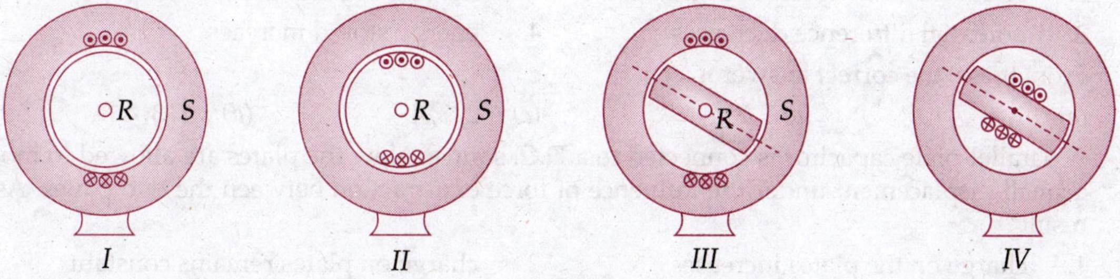

Fig C.56

40. Four electromagnetic rotating machines are shown in Fig. C.57. These are labelled 1, 2, 3 and 4 (R : rotor ; S : stator)

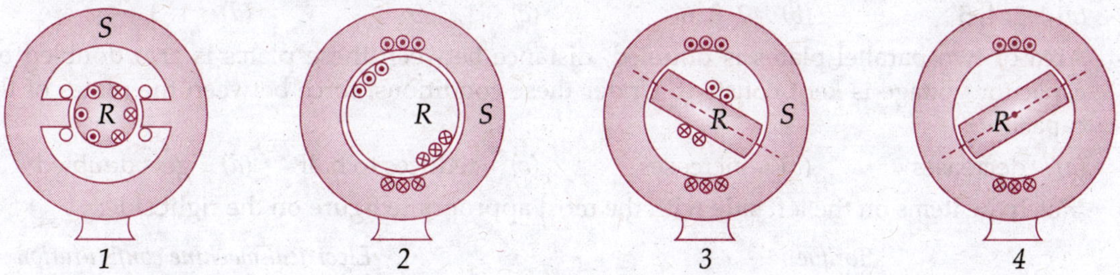

Fig C.57

These machines may produce electromagnetic torque (EMT), reluctance torque (RT) or both EMT and RT.

Use the following codes to choose the correct combination

Codes :	*EMT is produced in Figs.*	*RT is produced in Figs.*
(a)	1, 3, 4	3, 4
(b)	1, 2, 3, 4	1, 3, 4

(c)	1, 2, 3	1, 3, 4
(d)	1, 2, 3	1, 2, 3

41. A parallel-plate capacitor has a capacitance of 10 μF. If the linear dimensions of the plates are doubled and distance between them is also doubled, then new value of capacitance would be

(a) 10 μF (b) 20 μF (c) 5 μF (d) 40 μF

42. A parallel-plate capacitor is charged and then the D.C. supply is disconnected. Now the plate separation is allowed to decrease due to force of attraction between the two plates. As a consequence

1. charge on the plates increases
2. charge on the plates remains constant
3. capacitance C increases
4. capacitance C remains constant
5. potential difference increases
6. potential difference decreases
7. energy stored decreases
8. energy stored increases

From these, the correct answer is

(a) 1, 3, 6 (b) 2, 4, 8 (c) 2, 3, 6, 7 (d) 2, 4, 5, 8,

43. A parallel-plate capacitor is charged and then the D.C. supply is disconnected. The plate-separation is then increased. Between the plates,

1. electric-field intensity is unchanged
2. flux density decreases
3. potential difference decreases
4. energy stored increaes

From these, the correct answer is

(a) 1, 4 (b) 2, 4 (c) 2, 3, 4 (d) 1, 3, 4

44. A parallel-plate capacitor is connected to a D.C. source. Now the plates are allowed to move a small displacement under the influence of force of attraction between the two plates. As a result

1. charge on the plates increases
2. charge on plates remains constant
3. energy stored increases
4. energy stored remains constant
5. electric-field intensity is unchanged
6. flux density increases

From these, the correct answer is

(a) 2, 4, 5 (b) 2, 3, 6 (c) 1, 3, 5 (d) 1, 3, 6

45. Area of two parallel plates is doubled, distance between these plates is also doubled but capacitor voltage is kept constant. Under these conditions, force between the plates of this capacitor

(a) decreases (b) increases (c) reduces to half (d) gets doubled

46. Match the items on the left side with the most appropriate figure on the right side:

Torque	*Electrical machine configuration*
(a) Only reluctance torque is developed	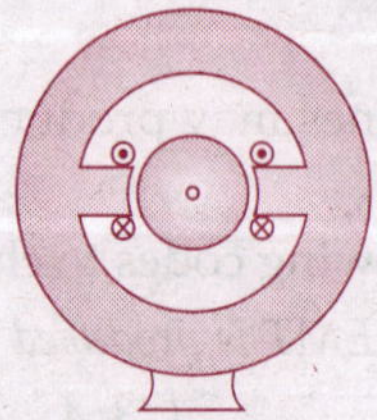 1

(*b*) Electromagnetic torque alone is developed

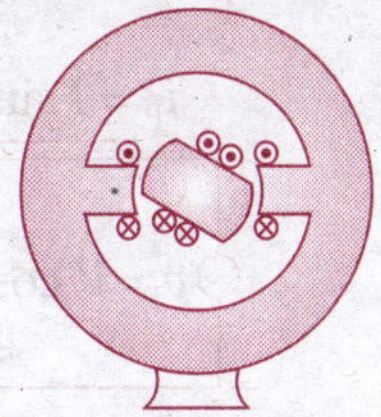

(*c*) No torque is developed

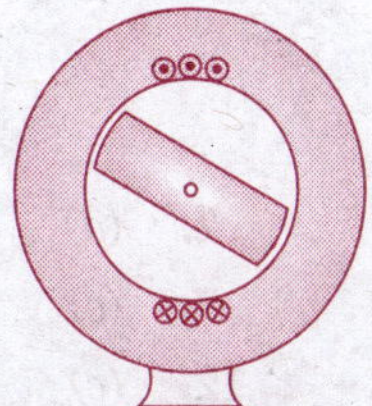

(*d*) Both electromagnetic and reluctance torques are developed

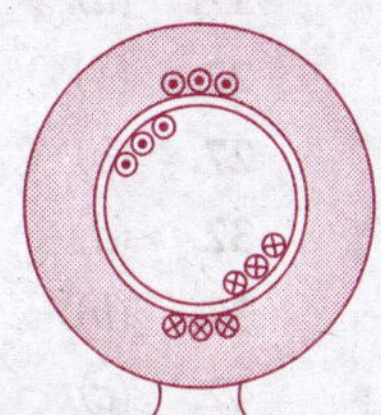

Ans. $A \rightarrow, B \rightarrow, C \rightarrow, D \rightarrow$

47. Two conductors are carrying forward and return current of + *I* and – *I* as shown in Fig. C.58. The magnetic field intensity $\overline{H}$ at point *P* is *[GATE, 2003]*

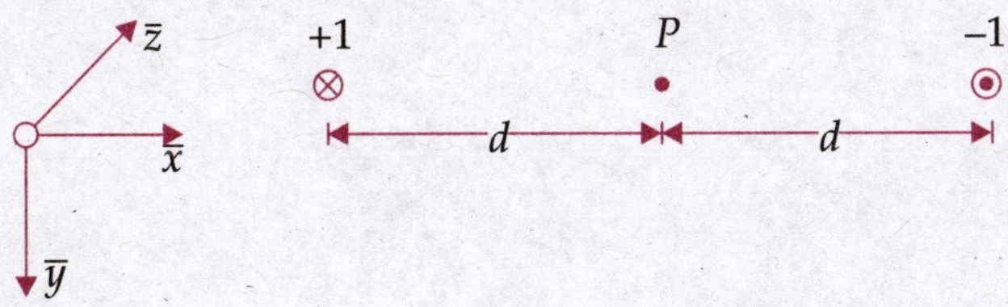

Fig C.58

(*a*) $\dfrac{I}{\pi d}\,\bar{y}$ (*b*) $\dfrac{I}{\pi d}\,\bar{x}$ (*c*) $\dfrac{I}{2\pi d}\,\bar{y}$ (*d*) $\dfrac{I}{2\pi d}\cdot\bar{x}$

48. A parallel plate capacitor has an electrode area of 100 mm^2, with a spacing of 0.1 mm between the electrodes. The dielectric between the plates is air with a permittivity of 8.85×10^{-12} F/m. The charge on the capacitor is 100 V. The stored energy in the capacitor is *[GATE, 2003]*

(*a*) 8.85 pJ (*b*) 440 pJ (*c*) 22.1 nJ (*d*) 44.3 n J

49. A transformer with toroidal core of permeability μ is shown in the figure below. Assuming uniform flux density across the circular cross-section of radius r << R, and neglecting any leakage flux, the best estimate for the mean radius R is *[GATE, 2018]*

(*a*) $\dfrac{\mu V r^2 N_p^2 \omega}{I}$ (*b*) $\dfrac{\mu I r^2 N_p N_s \omega}{V}$ (*c*) $\dfrac{\mu V r^2 N_p^2 \omega}{2I}$ (*d*) $\dfrac{\mu I r^2 N_p^2 \omega}{2V}$

[Hint. $I\,N_p$ (maximum. m.m.f.), Rel = $\dfrac{2\pi R}{\mu \cdot \pi r^2}$, Flux $\phi_m = \dfrac{I N_p \mu\, r^2}{2R}$ Also $\phi_m = \dfrac{V}{\omega N_p}$ etc.]

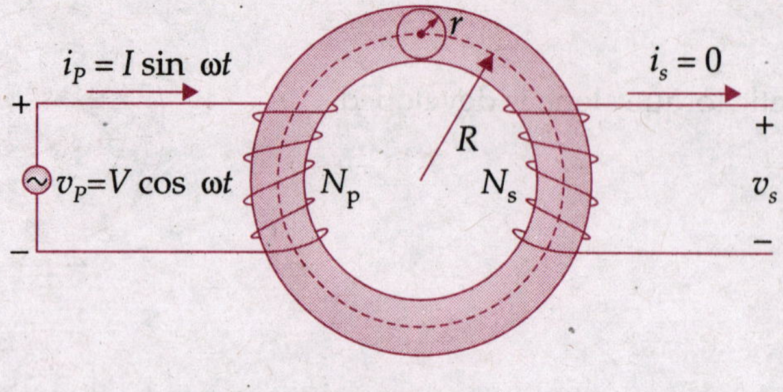

ANSWERS

1. *(a)*	**2.** *(d)*	**3.** *(c)*	**4.** *(d)*	**5.** *(d)*
6. *(a)*	**7.** *(c)*	**8.** *(c)*	**9.** *(b)*	**10.** *(b)*
11. *(d)*	**12.** *(c)*	**13.** *(a)*	**14.** *(b)*	**15.** *(a)*
16. *(a)*	**17.** *(a)*	**18.** *(d)*	**19.** *(d)*	**20.** *(c)*
21. *(a)*	**22.** *(d)*	**23.** *(c)*	**24.** *(b)*	**25.** *(c)*
26. *(c)*	**27.** *(b)*	**28.** *(a)*	**29.** *(d)*	**30.** *(d)*
31. *(d)*	**32.** *(d)*	**33.** *(d)*	**34.** *(d)*	**35.** *(a)*
36. *(c)*	**37.** *(b)*	**38.** *(b)*	**39.** *(d)*	**40.** *(c)*
41. *(b)*	**42.** *(c)*	**43.** *(a)*	**44.** *(d)*	**45.** *(c)*
46. $A \to 3, B \to 4, C \to 1, D \to 2.$		**47.** *(a)*	**48.** *(d)*	**49.** *(d)*

BASIC CONCEPTS OF ROTATING ELECTRICAL MACHINES

1. The torque angle δ is defined as the angle between
(a) stator field axis and resultant field axis (b) rotor field axis and resultant field axis
(c) stator field axis and rotor field axis (d) stator field axis and mutual field axis

2. The interaction torque depends on
1. stator field strength 2. rotor field strength
3. torque angle δ 4. sin δ 5. cos δ
From these, the correct answer is
(a) 1, 2, 4 (b) 1, 2, 5 (c) 1, 2, 3 (d) 1, 2

3. Armature winding is one in which working
(a) flux is produced by field current (b) flux is produced by the working e.m.f.
(c) e.m.f. is produced by the working flux (d) e.m.f. is produced by the leakage flux

4. Large synchronous machines are constructed with armature winding on the stator because stationary armature winding
1. can be insulated satisfactorily for higher voltages
2. can be cooled more efficiently 3. would lead to reduced slip-ring losses
4. would have no slot harmonics 5. would have reduced armature reactance
From these, the correct answer is
(a) 1, 2, 3, 4 (b) 1, 2, 3, 5 (c) 1, 2, 3, 4, 5 (d) 1, 2, 4, 5

5. A pole pitch in electrical machines is
(a) = 180° electrical (b) = 180° mechanical
(c) > 180° electrical (d) < 180°electrical

6. For a *P*-pole machine, the relation between electrical and mechanical degrees is given by
(a) $\theta_{elec} = \frac{2}{P} \cdot \theta_{mech}$ (b) $\theta_{elec} = \frac{4}{P} \cdot \theta_{mech}$ (c) $\theta_{mech} = \frac{P}{2} \cdot \theta_{elec}$ (d) $\theta_{elec} = \frac{P}{2} \cdot \theta_{mech}$

7. A coil consists of
(a) two conductors (b) two coil-sides (c) two turns (d) four turns

8. One turn consists of
(a) two coil-sides (b) two conductors (c) four conductors (d) four coil-sides

9. In A.C. rotating machines, the generated or speed e.m.f.
(a) is in phase with the working flux ϕ (b) leads ϕ by 90°
(c) lags ϕ by 90° (d) lags ϕ by 180°

10. A winding is distributed in the slots along the air-gap periphery
1. to add mechanical strength to the winding
2. to reduce the amount of conductor material required
3. to reduce the harmonics in the generated e.m.f.
4. to reduce the size of the machine
5. for full utilization of iron and conductor materials
From these, the correct answer is
(a) 1, 3, 4, 5 (b) 1, 2, 4, 5 (c) 1, 2, 3, 5 (d) 1, 3, 5

11. Consider the following statements about the chorded coils :
   1. chorded coils reduce the magnitude of output voltage
   2. chorded coils lead to reduction in harmonics
   3. chorded coils give better generated e.m.f. waveform
   4. chorded coils require more conductor material
   5. in chorded coils, coil span < 180° electrical
   6. in chorded coils, coil span may be less or more than 180° electrical.

   From these, the correct statement is

   (a) 1, 2, 3, 4, 5 *(b)* 1, 2, 3, 5 *(c)* 1, 2, 3, 4, 6 *(d)* 2, 3, 5

12. If B_p = peak value of sinusoidal flux-density wave, L = armature core length, D = armature diameter, P = number of poles, then
   1. Flux per pole, $\phi = \frac{2}{P} \cdot B_p \cdot LD$
   2. Average flux-density, $B_{av} = \frac{2}{\pi} \cdot B_p$
   3. $\phi = \frac{4}{P} \cdot B_p LD$
   4. $B_{av} = \frac{3}{\pi} \cdot B_p$
   5. $B_{av} = \frac{P\phi}{\pi DL}$
   6. $B_{av} = \frac{P \cdot \phi}{\pi rl}$

   From these, the correct answer is

   (a) 1, 2, 5 *(b)* 2, 3, 5 *(c)* 2, 3, 6 *(d)* 3, 4, 5

13. The belt factor is defined as the ratio of
   (a) arithmetic sum of coil e.m.fs. to the phasor sum of coil e.m.fs.
   (b) phasor sum of e.m.f. per coil to the arithmetic sum of e.m.f. per coil
   (c) phasor sum of coil e.m.fs. to the arithmetic sum of coil e.m.fs.
   (d) phasor sum of coil e.m.fs. to the per phase voltage

14. A fraction-pitch winding is used to reduce
   1. amount of copper in the winding
   2. size of the machine
   3. harmonics in the generated e.m.f.
   4. cost of the machine

   From these, the correct answer is

   (a) 1, 2, 3, 4 *(b)* 1, 2, 3 *(c)* 2, 3, 4 *(d)* 1, 3, 4

15. The pitch factor, in rotating electrical machinery, is defined as the ratio of resultant e.m.f. of a
   (a) full-pitched coil to that of a chorded coil
   (b) full-pitched coil to the phase e.m.f.
   (c) chorded coil to the phase e.m.f.
   (d) chorded coil to that of a full- pitched coil

16. For a 3-phase uniformly distributed and narrow-spread winding, the distribution factor is

   (a) 0.9 *(b)* 0.955 *(c)* 0.827 *(d)* 0.97

17. The armature winding of a 2-pole, 3-phase alternator for each phase is distributed in a number of slots per phase. The r.m.s. value of the voltage per phase is less than the r.m.s. value of the voltage per coil multiplied by the number of coils in series because the
   (a) r.m.s. value of the voltage in different coils of the phase is different
   (b) equal r.m.s. voltages in different coils of the phase has mutual phase difference
   (c) maximum value of the induced voltage in different coils of the phase are different
   (d) different coils of the phase pass through different saturated regions of the magnetic circuit.

18. A 3-phase, 4-pole alternator has 48 stator slots carrying a 3-phase distributed winding. Each coil of the winding is short chorded by one slot pitch. The winding factor is given by

(a) $\dfrac{\cos 7.5}{16}$ (b) $\dfrac{\cot 7.5}{8}$ (c) $\dfrac{1}{8\sin 7.5}$ (d) $\dfrac{\cot 7.5}{16}$

19. The windings for a 3-phase alternator are :

1. 36 slots, 4 poles, span 1 to 8
2. 72 slots, 6 poles, span 1 to 10
3. 96 slots, 4 poles, span 1 to 21

The windings having pitch factor of more than 0.97 are

(a) 1 and 2 only (b) 2 and 3 only (c) 1 and 3 only (d) 1, 2 and 3

20. Consider the following statements regarding the design of distributed armature winding in a 3-phase alternator :

1. It reduces the phase-belt harmonics
2. It increases the utilization of the armature iron and copper
3. It increases rigidity and mechanical strength of the winding
4. It reduces copper in the overhang of the winding

Which of these statements are correct?

(a) 1, 3, and 4 (b) 2, 3, and 4 (c) 1, 2, and 3 (d) 1, 2, 3 and 4

21. If the dimensions of all the parts of a synchronous generator, and the number of field and armature turns are doubled, then the generated voltage will change by a factor of

(a) 1 (b) 2 (c) 4 (d) 8

22. Two 3-phase A.C. generators are such that one has twice the linear dimensions of the other. The field windings of each are excited to give identical sinusoidal air-gap flux density waveform. Both have the same number of stator slots and identical winding patterns. The conductors per slot in big generator is K times that of the smaller one. The value of K to get equal no-load voltage at same frequency is

(a) 8 (b) 4 (c) $\dfrac{1}{2}$ (d) $\dfrac{1}{4}$

23. Two transformers of the same type, using the same grade of iron and conductor materials, are designed to work at the same flux and current densities ; but the linear dimensions of one are two times those of the other in all respects. The ratio of kVA ratings of the two transformers closely equals

(a) 16 (b) 8 (c) 4 (d) 2

24. For eliminating nth harmonic from the e.m.f. generated in the phase of a 3-phase alternator, the chording angle should be

(a) $n \times$ full-pitch (b) $\dfrac{1}{n} \times$ full-pitch (c) $\dfrac{2}{n} \times$ full-pitch (d) $\dfrac{3}{n} \times$ full-pitch

25. For eliminating nth harmonic from the e.m.f. generated in one phase of a 3-phase alternator, the coil-span (pitch of the coils) must be

(a) $\dfrac{n-1}{n} \times$ full-pitch (b) $\dfrac{2n-1}{n} \times$ full-pitch

(c) $\dfrac{n}{n+1} \times$ full-pitch (d) $\dfrac{2n}{n+1} \times$ full-pitch

26. For eliminating 5th harmonic from the phase e.m.f. generated in an alternator, the coil-span in terms of full-pitch (or pitch fraction) would be

(a) $\frac{4}{5}$ (b) $\frac{5}{4}$ (c) $\frac{5}{6}$ (d) $\frac{6}{5}$

27. In 48 slot, 4-pole, 3-phase alternator, the coil-span is 10. Its distribution and pitch factors are respectively
(a) 0.9717, 0.966 (b) 0.9822, 0.9814 (c) 0.9577, 0.9814 (d) 0.9577, 0.966

28. In an alternator, frequency per revolution is equal to
(a) number of poles (b) twice the number of poles
(c) speed in r.p.s. (d) number of pole-pairs

29. A 6-pole machine is rotating at a speed of 1200 r.p.m. This speed in mechanical rad/sec and electrical radians per sec is respectively
(a) $40\pi, \frac{40\pi}{3}$ (b) $120\pi, 40\pi$ (c) $20\pi, 60\pi$, (d) $40\pi, 120\pi$

30. The short-pitch winding for an alternator gives
1. improved waveform of the generated e.m.f. per phase
2. reduced value of self-inductance of the winding
3. increased rating of machine
4. reduced tooth ripples
5. increased total generated e.m.f.
6. saving in winding copper

From these, the correct answer is
(a) 1, 2, 4, 5, 6 (b) 1, 2, 6 (c) 1, 2, 4, 6 (d) 1, 3, 4, 6

31. A 3-phase machine has integral slot winding with fundamental distribution factor k_{d1}. For slot harmonics, the distribution factor is
(a) less than k_{d1} (b) more than k_{d1} (c) equal to k_{d1}
(d) depends upon the number of slots and poles

32. Consider the following statements :
1. breadth factor for third harmonic k_{d3} is more than that for fundamental k_{d1}
2. $k_{d3} < k_{d1}$
3. k_{d3} may be less or more than k_{d1} depending upon the number of slots and poles
4. coil-span factor for third harmonic $k_{p3} > k_{p1}$ (coil-span factor for fundamental)
5. $k_{p3} < k_{p1}$
6. k_{d3} may be less or more than k_{p1} depending upon the number of slots and poles.

From these, the correct answer is
(a) 2, 5 (b) 1, 4 (c) 3, 6 (d) 1, 3, 4, 6

33. In order to minimise both fifth and seventh harmonics, the coil-span in three-phase A.C. machines must be
(a) 144° (b) $\frac{6}{7}$ th of pole pitch
(c) $\frac{5}{6}$ th of pole pitch (d) 120°

34. A synchronous machine has full-pitch coils having coil-span of 12 slots. For eliminating third harmonic, the coil-span should be
(a) 6 slots (b) 8 slots (c) 9 slots (d) 10 slots

35. Machine A has 60° phase spread and machine B has 120° phase spread. Both the machines have uniformly distributed winding. The ratio of distribution factors of machine A to machine B is

(a) 0.866 (b) 1.1 (c) 1.55 (d) 1.155

36. The e.m.f. generated in an alternator depends upon

1. speed
2. maximum flux per pole
3. series turns per phase
4. phase spread
5. coil-span
6. type of alternator

From these, the correct answer is

(a) 1, 2, 3, 4, 5 and 6 (b) 1, 3, 4, 5
(c) 1, 2, 3, 5, 6 (d) 1, 3, 4, 5, 6

37. A 3-phase alternator is wound with a 60 degree phase spread armature winding and develops 300 kVA. If the armature is reconnected utilizing all the coils for single-phase operation with a phase spread of 180 degree, the new rating of the machine is

(a) 100 kVA (b) 200 kVA (c) 250 kVA (d) 300 kVA

38. A 3-phase alternator is wound with a 60 degree phase-spread armature winding and develops 300 kVA. If the armature is reconnected utilizing all the coils for two-phase operation, the new rating of the machine would be

(a) 282.8 kVA (b) 259.8 kVA (c) 200 kVA (d) 173.2 kVA

39. The armature of a single-phase atlernator is completely wound with T single-turn coils distributed uniformly. The induced voltage in each turn is 2 V (r.m.s.). The e.m.f. of the whole winding is [GATE, 1998]

(a) 2 T volts (b) 1.11 T volts (c) 1.414 T volts (d) 1.273 T volts

40. The armature of a star-connected alternator is uniformly wound with T coils, each coil having N full-pitched turns. The generated e.m.f. per conductor is 2 V (r.m.s.). The per-phase e.m.f. is

(a) $\frac{3}{\pi} NT$ volts (b) $\frac{4}{\pi} NT$ volts (c) $\frac{6}{\pi} NT$ volts (d) $\frac{2}{\pi} NT$ volts

41. A 6-pole alternator with 36 slots carries a 2-phase distributed winding. Each coil is short-pitched by one slot. The winding factor is given by

(a) $\frac{\cot 15°}{3\sqrt{2}}$ (b) $\frac{\cot 15°}{4}$ (c) $\frac{\cot 15°}{2\sqrt{2}}$ (d) $\frac{\cot 15°}{6}$

42. The chording angle for eliminating 5th harmonics should be

(a) 30° (b) 34° (c) 36° (d) 35°

43. IF E_1, E_3 and E_5 are respectively the r.m.s. values of fundamental, third and fifth harmonic voltages generated in each phase of a star-connected alternator, then the line voltage is

(a) $3\sqrt{E_1^2+E_3^2+E_5^2}$ (b) $\sqrt{3}\sqrt{E_1^2+E_3^2+E_5^2}$

(c) $\sqrt{3}\sqrt{E_1^2+E_3^2}$ (d) $\sqrt{3}\sqrt{E_1^2+E_5^2}$

44. In a 3-phase A.C. machine, phase e.m.f. is E_1 and output is P_1 for a narrow-spread, whereas phase e.m.f. is E_2 and output is P_2 for a wide-spread. Here E_1, E_2, P_1 and P_2 are related as under :

(a) $E_1 = E_2$; $P_1 = 1.15\, P_2$ (b) $E_1 = 1.15\, E_2$; $P_1 = 1.15\, P_2$
(c) $E_2 = 1.15\, E_1$; $P_1 = 1.15\, P_2$ (d) $E_2 = 1.15\, E_1$; $P_2 = 1.15\, P_1$

45. M.m.f. produced by one N-turn coil carrying a current i is

(a) reactangular of amplitude $\frac{Ni}{2}$ (b) trapezoidal of amplitude $\frac{Ni}{2}$

(c) rectangular of amplitude Ni (d) trapezoidal of amplitude Ni

46. Peak value of fundamental component of m.m.f. produced by one N-turn coil carrying a current i is

(a) $\frac{4}{\pi} \cdot Ni$ (b) $\frac{2}{\pi} Ni$ (c) $\frac{1}{\pi} Ni$ (d) $\frac{1}{2\pi} Ni$

47. A winding of 20 full-pitched series turns, distributed over a band of 60° under each pole, carries a current of 3A. The winding produces a uniform current sheet of density (in ATs per electrical rad.) of

(a) $\frac{180}{\pi}$ (b) $\frac{120}{\pi}$ (c) $\frac{90}{\pi}$ (d) $\frac{30}{\pi}$

48. A sinusoidal current sheet in a rotating electrical machine has peak value along q-axis. The peak value of sinusoidal m.m.f. would be

(a) in phase with current peak (b) 90° lagging the current peak

(c) 90° leading the current peak

(d) may lag or lead depending upon the type of machine

49. A uniformly distributed winding on the stator has three full-pitched coils, each coil having N turns and each turn carrying a current i. The m.m.f. produced by this winding is

(a) sinusoidal in waveform with an amplitude $3Ni$

(b) sinusoidal in waveform with an amplitude $3Ni/2$

(c) trapezoidal in waveform with an amplitude $3Ni$

(d) trapezoidal in waveform with an amplitude $3Ni/2$

50. The armature m.m.f. wave in a D.C. machine is

(a) sinusoidal and depends on the speed (b) square and independent of speed

(c) triangular and depends on speed (d) triangular and independent of speed

51. The armature m.m.f. wave in a D.C. machine is triangular and

1. rotates with respect to stator 2. is stationary with respect to stator

3. rotates with respect to armature 4. is stationary with respect to armature

From these, the correct answer is

(a) 2 alone (b) 3 alone (c) 1, 4 (d) 2, 3

52. A 3-phase star-connected winding is fed from symmetrical 3-phase supply with their neutrals connected together. If one of the three supply lines gets disconnected, then the revolving m.m.f. wave will have a

(a) constant amplitude, but subsynchronous speed

(b) varying amplitude, but synchronous speed

(c) constant amplitude, but supersynchronous speed

(d) varying speed and a speed fluctuating around the synchronous speed

53. If F_1 is the constant amplitude of fundamental rotating m.m.f. wave, then for the space harmonics of order $6k + 1$ (where $k = 1, 2, 3 ...$), the harmonic m.m.f. wave is of

(a) constant amplitude and stationary in space

(b) constant amplitude and rotates along F_1

(c) varying amplitude and rotates along F_1
(d) constant amplitude and rotates against F_1

54. The fifth harmonic m.m.f. wave, produced by 3-phase currents flowing in 3-phase balanced winding, rotates with respect to the fundamental field (N_s = speed of fundamental m.m.f. wave) at a speed of
(a) $\frac{5}{6}N_s$ (b) $\frac{6}{5}N_s$ (c) $\frac{4}{5}N_s$ (d) $\frac{5}{4}N_s$

55. The seventh harmonic m.m.f. wave, produced by 3-phase currents flowing in 3-phase balanced winding, rotates with respect to the fundamental field (N_s = speed of fundamental m.m.f. wave) at a speed of
(a) $\frac{6}{7}N_s$ (b) $\frac{7}{6}N_s$ (c) $\frac{8}{7}N_s$ (d) $\frac{7}{8}N_s$

56. In a D.C. machine ; Z, P, I_a and a are respectively the number of conductors, number of poles, armature current and number of parallel paths. The peak value of fundamental component of armature m.m.f. wave is
(a) $\frac{8}{\pi}\left[\frac{Z}{2P}\cdot\frac{I_a}{a}\right]$ (b) $\frac{8}{\pi^2}\left[\frac{Z}{P}\cdot\frac{I_a}{a}\right]$ (c) $\frac{4}{\pi}\left[\frac{Z}{2P}\cdot\frac{I_a}{a}\right]$ (d) $\frac{8}{\pi^2}\left[\frac{Z}{2P}\cdot\frac{I_a}{a}\right]$

57. In a rotating machine,
1. $R \cdot \sin(\omega t + \alpha)$ is the backward rotating m.m.f.
2. $R \cdot \sin\alpha$ is the standing m.m.f.
3. $R \cdot \sin(\omega t + \alpha)$ is the backward rotating m.m.f.
4. $R \sin\omega t \cdot \cos\alpha$ is stationary m.m.f.
5. $R \cdot \cos\omega t \cdot \cos\alpha$ is stationary m.m.f.
6. $R \cdot \sin(\omega t + \alpha)$ is pulsating standing m.m.f.

From these, the correct answer is
(a) 2, 3, 5 (b) 1, 2, 4, 5 (c) 2, 3, 4, 5 (d) 1, 4, 6

58. Chording and distribution of armature windings in rotating machines
1. result in reduction of air-gap m.m.f. harmonics
2. need more number of turns for a given voltage
3. result in an increase in the number of effective turns
4. result in the requirement of less copper in the overhang
5. result in the reduction of slot harmonics

From these, the correct answer is
(a) 1, 2, 5 (b) 1, 3, 4 (c) 2, 3, 5 (d) 1, 2, 4

59. A 3-phase, 4-pole, 50 Hz squirrel cage induction motor has stator bore diameter of 0.5 m. If its stator is cut and laid out flat, the speed of travelling field (take π = 3.2) is
(a) 20 m/s (b) 30 m/s (c) 40 m/s (d) 50 m/s

60. Consider the principle that the torque in a rotating machine is proportional to peak of stator m.m.f (F_s), rotor m.m.f. (F_r) and the angle between them (δ). Following statements relate to F_s, F_r and δ in different machines :
1. δ is fixed in D.C. machine.
2. F_s is fixed in D.C. shunt machine
3. δ is variable in induction machine
4. F_r is fixed in synchronous machine
5. F_r is variable in D.C. machine
6. F_r is fixed in induction motor

7. Resultant of F_s and F_r is fixed in synchronous motor :

Of these statements :

(a) 1, 2, 3, 4 and 6 are correct (b) 1, 2, 3, 5 and 7 are correct
(c) 2, 3, 5, 6 and 7 are correct (d) 1, 2, 4, 5 and 7 are correct

61. Output rating of

1. induction motors is in H.P.
2. A.C. motors is in kW
3. A.C. generators is in kVA
4. D.C. motors is in kW
5. synchronous motors is in kVA
6. D.C. generators is in kVA

From these, the correct statements are

(a) 1, 3, 4, 5 (b) 1, 2, 3, 4 (c) 2, 3, 4, 6 (d) 2, 3, 4

62. If ϕ_m is the maximum value of flux due to any one phase, then resultant flux in 2-phase and 3-phase A.C. machines would respectively be given by

(a) ϕ_m and 1.5 ϕ_m; both rotating (b) ϕ_m and 1.5 ϕ_m; both stand still
(c) ϕ_m, standstill and 1.5ϕ_m rotating (d) 1.5ϕ_m and 2ϕ_m ; both rotating

63. In all rotating electrical machines, electrical torque is developed when relative speed between stator field and rotor field is

(a) zero
(b) equal to rotor speed
(c) equal and opposite to rotor speed
(d) dependent upon the type of electrical machine

64. No-load rotational losses in electrical machines consist of

(a) Friction and windage (*F* and *W*) losses (b) stator core, *F* and *W* losses
(c) rotor core, *F* and *W* losses (d) no-load core, *F* and *W* losses

65. Consider the following statements regarding efficiency of electrical machines :

1. Efficiency should be calculated by measuring output and input
2. Efficiency is maximum when constant losses = variable losses
3. Electrical machines are designed to have maximum efficiency at full load
4. Electrical machines are designed to have maximum efficiency at near about full load
5. Efficiency should be calculated by measuring the losses
6. Efficiency is maximum when constant losses = x (variable losses)

From these, the correct answer is

(a) 1, 3, 6 (b) 2, 4, 5 (c) 1, 2, 3 (d) 4, 5, 6

66. If P_i be the iron loss and P_o be the ohmic loss on full load, then which of the following conditions has to be satisfied to obtain maximum efficiency at 3/4 full load?

(a) $P_0 = 3\,P_i/4$ (b) $P_0 = 4P_i/3$ (c) $P_0 = 16\,P_i/9$ (d) $P_0 = 9\,P_i/16$

67. For estimating the power rating of an electric drive, its losses can be considered to be proportional to

(a) power (b) $(\text{power})^2$ (c) $(\text{power})^3$ (d) torque

68. In rotating electrical machines, the insulation temperature limit for class B type is

(a) 105°C (b) 130°C (c) 150°C (d) 180°C

69. The duty cycle of a motor is as under :

Load :	20 kW	10 kW	Rest
Duration :	120 s	120 s	60 s

The continuous rating of the motor suitable for above motor-load application would be

(a) 20 kW (b) 16.4 kW (c) 14.14 kW (d) 15.81 kW

70. A machine attains a termperature rise of 60% of its final temperature rise in one hour. Its heating time constant is

(a) 1.0914 hr (b) 0.9163 hr (c) 0.513 hr (d) 1.9581 hr

71. In a 3-phase induction motor, if the angular speed of the stator feld is ω and the actual angular speed of the rotor is ω_r and the stator induced e.m.f. is given by $e_s = N_1 \omega K_{ws} \cdot \phi$. sin ωt, (N_1 = stator turns per phase), then the rotor e.m.f. with N_2 as the rotor turns/phase will be (K_{ws} = stator winding factor and K_{wr} = rotor winding factor), [I.A.S., 1997]

(a) $e_r = N_2 \omega K_{wr} \cdot \phi \cdot \sin \omega t$

(b) $e_r = N_2 \omega_r k_{wr} \phi \sin \omega_r t$

(c) $e_r = N_2 (\omega - \omega_r) K_{wr} \cdot \phi \cdot \sin (\omega - \omega_r) t$

(d) $e_r = N_2 (\omega + \omega_r) K_{wr} \cdot \phi \sin (\omega + \omega_r) t$

72. In hydrogen-cooled synchronous machines

1. pressure inside the machine is more than atmospheric pressure
2. pressure inside the machine is less than atmospheric pressure
3. heat-storing capacity of hydrogen is more than that of air
4. windage loss decreases
5. fire-hazard inside the machine is minimized because hydrogen content is more than 70%.

From these, the correct answer is

(a) 2, 3, 4, and 5 (b) 1, 3, 4 and 5 (c) 1, 3, and 5 (d) 1, 4, and 5

73. Match List I with List II and select the correct answer from the codes given below :

List I (Type of load torque on motor)	List II (Applications)
A. continuous loads	1. punch press
B. pulsating loads	2. sluice gates
C. impact loads	3. centrifugal pumps
D. short-time loads	4. reciprocating pumps

Codes :

	A	B	C	D
(a)	1	2	3	4
(b)	3	4	2	1
(c)	3	4	1	2
(d)	3	1	4	2

74. The worst type of load on a supply system is

(a) rolling mill load (b) pumping load

(c) motors in paper mill (d) arc furnace load [I.A.S., 2002]

75. List I represents the different types of electric motors, whilst list II gives some of their characteristics.

	List I		*List II*
A.	D.C. series motor	1.	constant speed
B.	D.C. shunt motor	2.	high-starting torque
C.	3-phase induction motor	3.	fairly constant torque
D.	Synchronous motor	4.	lower-starting torque
		5.	pulsating torque
		6.	very poor stability

Use the following codes to choose the correct answer :

Codes :

	A	B	C	D		A	B	C	D
(a)	1	3	4	1	*(b)*	1	2	3	5
(c)	2	1	4	6	*(d)*	4	3	1	2

76. Match the items in the left-side column with the most appropriate item in the right-side column:

	Power losses		*Dependent upon*
A.	No-load rotational loss	1.	Square of load
B.	Hysteresis and eddy-current losses	2.	Rotor rotation
C.	Brush contact loss	3.	Value of flux
D.	Stray load loss	4.	Load

Ans. A →, B →, C →, D →

77. The sinusoidal distributed balanced 3-phase windings shown in Fig. C.59 are supplied with balanced 3-phase currents :

$$i_A = I_m \sin(\omega t - \pi/6)$$

$$i_B = I_m \sin\left(\omega t - \frac{5\pi}{6}\right)$$

$$i_C = I_m \sin(\omega t + \pi/2)$$

At the angular in start $\omega t = \frac{\pi}{2}$, the value of angular position θ of the rotating m.m.f. F with respect to phase A axis will be

(a) $-\pi/2$ *(b)* $\pi/2$ *(c)* $\pi/6$ *(d)* $-\frac{\pi}{6}$

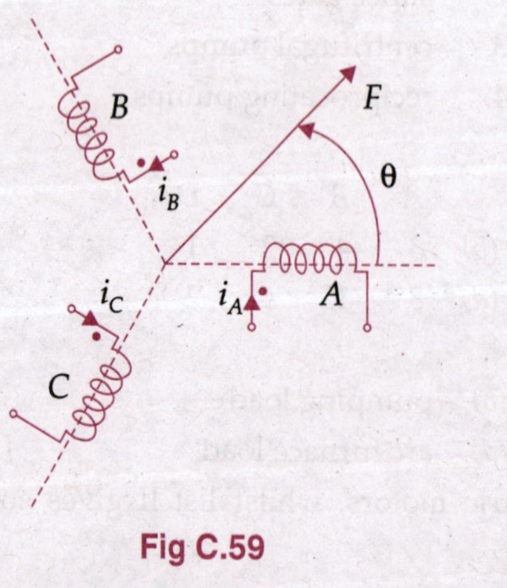

Fig C.59

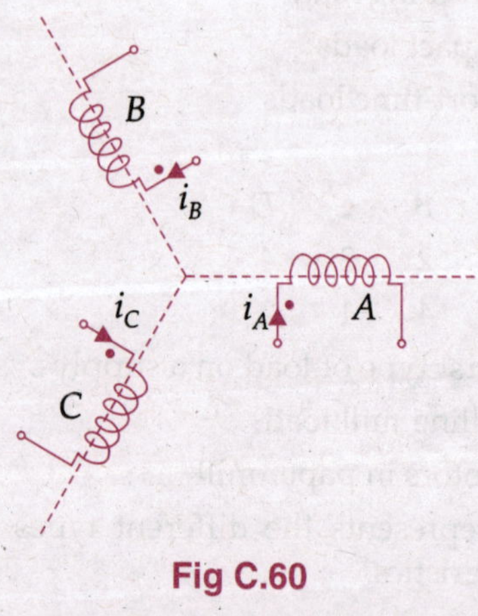

Fig C.60

78. Sinusoidal distributed balanced 3-phase winding in Fig. C.60 is supplied with balanced 3-phase currents :

$$i_A = I_m \sin(\omega t + \pi/6)$$
$$i_B = I_m \sin(\omega t - \pi/2)$$
$$i_C = I_m \sin(\omega t + 5\pi/6)$$

The rotating m.m.f. would be directed along the axis of phase C when ωt equals

(a) $\frac{\pi}{6}$ *(b)* $-\frac{\pi}{3}$ *(c)* $\frac{2\pi}{3}$ *(d)* $\frac{\pi}{3}$

79. Following are some of the properties of rotating electrical machines :

P Stator winding current is D.C., rotor winding current is A.C.

Q Stator winding current is A.C., rotor winding current is D.C.

R Stator winding current is A.C., rotor winding current is A.C.

S Stator has salient poles and rotor has commutator

T Rotor has salient poles and sliprings and stator is cylindrical

U Both stator and rotor have polyphase windings

D.C. machines, synchronous machines and induction machines exhibit some of the above properties as given in the following table. Indicate the correct combination from this table :

	D.C. machines	*Synchronous machines*	*Induction machines*
(a)	P, S	Q, T	R, U
(b)	Q, U	P, T	R, S
(c)	P, S	R, U	Q, T
(d)	R, S	Q, U	P, T

[GATE, 2003]

80. When stator and rotor windings of a 2-pole rotating electrical machine are excited, each would produce a sinusoidal m.m.f. distribution in the air-gap with peak values F_s and F_r respectively. The rotor m.m.f. lags stator m.m.f. by a space angle δ at any instant as shown in Fig. C.61. Thus, half of stator and rotor surfaces will form one pole with the other half forming the second pole. Further, the direction of torque acting on the rotor can be clockwise or counter-clockwise.

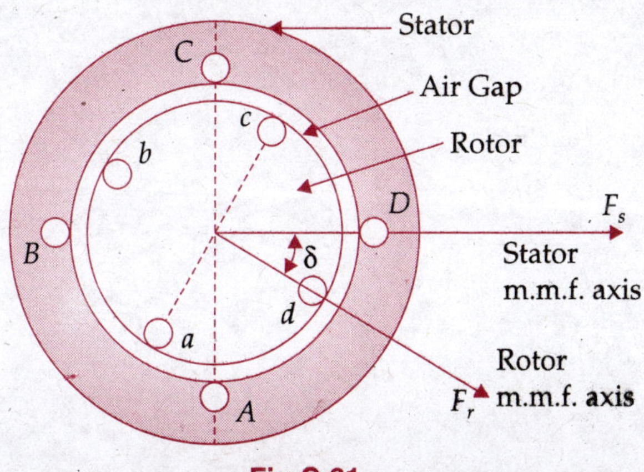

Fig C.61

The following table gives four sets of statements as regards poles and torque. Select the correct corresponding to the m.m.f. as shown in Fig. C.61. *[GATE, 2003]*

	Stator surface ABC forms	*Stator surface CDA forms*	*Rotor surface abc forms*	*Rotor surface cda forms*	*Torque is*
(a)	*North pole*	*South pole*	*North pole*	*South pole*	*Clockwise*
(b)	*South pole*	*North pole*	*North pole*	*South pole*	*Counter-clockwise*
(c)	*North pole*	*South pole*	*South pole*	*North pole*	*Counter-clockwise*
(d)	*South pole*	*North pole*	*South pole*	*North pole*	*Clockwise*

ANSWERS

1. *(c)* **2.** *(a)* **3.** *(c)* **4.** *(b)* **5.** *(a)*
6. *(d)* **7.** *(b)* **8.** *(b)* **9.** *(c)* **10.** *(d)*
11. *(b)* **12.** *(a)* **13.** *(c)* **14.** *(d)* **15.** *(d)*
16. *(b)* **17.** *(b)* **18.** *(b)* **19.** *(c)* **20.** *(c)*
21. *(d)* **22.** *(d)* **23.** *(a)* **24.** *(b)* **25.** *(a)*
26. *(a)* **27.** *(d)* **28.** *(d)* **29.** *(d)* **30.** *(b)*
31. *(c)* **32.** *(a)* **33.** *(c)* **34.** *(b)* **35.** *(d)*
36. *(b)* **37.** *(b)* **38.** *(a)* **39.** *(d)* **40.** *(b)*
41. *(a)* **42.** *(c)* **43.** *(d)* **44.** *(b)* **45.** *(a)*
46. *(b)* **47.** *(a)* **48.** *(c)* **49.** *(d)* **50.** *(d)*
51. *(d)* **52.** *(d)* **53.** *(b)* **54.** *(b)* **55.** *(a)*
56. *(d)* **57.** *(a)* **58.** *(d)* **59.** *(c)* **60.** *(b)*
61. *(d)* **62.** *(a)* **63.** *(a)* **64.** *(d)* **65.** *(b)*
66. *(c)* **67.** *(b)* **68.** *(b)* **69.** *(c)* **70.** *(a)*
71. *(c)* **72.** *(d)* **73.** *(c)* **74.** *(d)* **75.** *(c)*
76. $A \to 2, B \to 3, C \to 4, D \to 1.$ **77.** *(d)* **78.** *(b)* **79.** *(a)*
80. *(c)*

D.C. MACHINES

1. In D.C. machines, the armature windings are placed on the rotor because of the necessity for
   (a) electromechanical energy conversion (b) generation of voltage
   (c) commutation (d) development of torque
2. In D.C. machines, the field system has to be provided on stator unlike synchronous machines wherein it could be on any member, because
   (a) it reduces field structure iron losses
   (b) it gives more uniform air-gap flux distribution
   (c) commutator action is not possible otherwise
   (d) D.C. machines are comparatively low rating machines. [I.A.S., 1996]
3. In D.C. machines, the space distribution of air-gap flux density wave at no load is
   (a) sinusoidal (b) co-sinusoidal (c) flat-topped (d) rectangular
4. A commutator in D.C. machines can
   1. provide half-wave rectification 2. provide full-wave rectification
   3. convert A.C. to D.C. 4. convert D.C. to A.C
   5. provide controlled full-wave rectification
   From these, the correct answer is
   (a) 2, 3, 4 (b) 1, 2, 3 (c) 2, 3, 5 (d) 2, 3, 4, 5
5. In D.C. machines, the space waveform of the air-gap flux distribution affects
   (a) torque but not the voltage (b) voltage but not the torque
   (c) both the torque and voltage (d) neither the voltage nor the torque
6. In D.C. machines, the field-flux axis and armature-m.m.f. axis are respectively along
   (a) direct axis and indirect axis (b) direct axis and interpolar axis
   (c) quadrature axis and direct axis (d) quadrature axis and interpolar axis
7. The brush-axis of a bipolar D.C. motor is rotated by 90°. The effect of this rotation on the back e.m.f. E_b and the torque developed T_d would be such that
   (a) both E_b and T_d are unchanged (b) E_b is zero, but T_d is unchanged
   (c) E_b is unchanged, but T_d is zero (d) both E_b and T_d are zero [I.A.S., 1995]
8. Five cells are connected in series in a row and then four such rows are connected in parallel to feed the current to a resistive load of 1.25 Ω. Each cell has an e.m.f. of 1.5 V with internal resistance of 0.2 Ω. The current through the load will be
   (a) 3.33 A (b) 23.33 A (c) 5 A (d) 1 A
9. Consider the following statements regarding the magnetization characteristics of a D.C. generator :
   1. It represents the variation of field flux with field current.
   2. Variation of open-circuit terminal voltage with field current is independent of speed
   3. It is non-linear from zero to rated field current
   4. It helps to determine the critical field resistance at a given speed
   5. It always starts from the origin
   Which of these statements are correct?
   (a) 1 and 4 (b) 1, 2 and 5 (c) 2, 3, and 4 (d) 3 and 5

10. A D.C. shunt generator builds up to a voltage of 220 V at no-load while running at its rated speed. If the speed of the generator is raised by 25% keeping the circuit conditions unaltered, then the voltage to which the machine would build up will
(a) not change and remain at 220 V
(b) increase to 1.25 times 220 V
(c) increase to value lying between 220 V and 1.25 times 220 V
(d) increase to a value greater than 1.25 times 220 V. *[I.A.S., 1995]*

11. The armature core of a D.C. machine is laminated to minimise
(a) hysteresis loss (b) eddy-current loss
(c) mechanical loss (d) temperature rise

12. The commutator segments of D.C. machines are made up of
(a) brass (b) copper
(c) hard-drawn copper (d) copper alloy

13. Consider the following statements regarding D.C. machines :
1. Possible resistance of shunt-field winding is 1 Ω
2. Possible resistance of series-field winding is 1 Ω
3. Electrographite brushes are used for 230 V, 10 A machines
4. Copper-graphite brushes are used for 230 V, 10 A machines
5. Possible armature-circuit resistance is 1 Ω

From these, the correct statements are
(a) 1, 4 (b) 2, 3, 5 (c) 2, 4, 5 (d) 1, 3, 5

14. A 4-pole D.C. generator runs at 1500 r.p.m. The frequency of current in the armature winding is
(a) 25 Hz (b) 50 Hz (c) zero Hz (d) 100 Hz

15. In normal D.C. machines operating at full-load conditions, the most powerful electromagnet is *[GATE, 1990]*
(a) field winding
(b) armature winding
(c) interpole winding
(d) interpole and compensating windings together

16. A self-excited shunt generator fails to build up, because
1. the field circuit is open 2. the armature circuit is open
3. the residual magnetism is absent 4. the direction of rotation is wrong

From these, the correct answer is
(a) 3 only (b) 1, 3 (c) 1, 2, 3 and 4 (d) 1, 2 and 3

17. A D.C. shunt generator builds up 230 V when driven in clockwise direction. In case it is driven in anticlockwise direction, other things remaining unchanged, then the voltage build up is
(a) 230 V (b) somewhat less than 230 V
(c) somewhat more than 230 V (d) not possible

18. A separately-excited D.C. generator, running at rated speed, has 6 volts across its armature terminals with no field current. When field winding is excited with one ampere, the voltage builds up to 250 V at no-load. In case field current is reduced to zero, with the speed remaining unaltered, the armature terminal voltage would be

(a) 6 V (b) less than 6 V (c) more than 6 V (d) zero

19. A D.C. shunt generator, when driven without any excitation, showed an open circuit voltage of 12 V. When the field winding was excited, the voltage dropped to zero. It happened bacause

(a) field resistance was higher than critical resistance
(b) there was no residual magnetism in the field circuit
(c) field winding was wrongly connected
(d) there was a break in the armature circuit

20. A D.C. shunt generator having a shunt field of 50 Ω was generating normally at 1000 r.p.m. The critical resistance of this machine was 80 Ω. Due to some reason, the speed of the prime-mover became such that the generator just failed to generate.

The speed at that time must have been

(a) 1000 r.p.m. (b) 800 r.p.m. (c) 625 r.p.m. (d) 500 r.p.m.

21. A D.C. shunt generator, when commissioned after a major repair of the field system, failed to build up voltage. It was because

(a) field resistance was higher than critical resistance
(b) field system lost residual magnetism
(c) field winding was wrongly connected
(d) there was a break in the armature circuit

22. A 230-V D.C. series generator is driven at its rated speed. The no-load voltage across its armature terminals would be

(a) 230 V (b) some what more than 230 V
(c) somewhat less than 230 V (d) 6 V

23. A short-shunt cumulatively-compounded D.C. generator builds up a voltage of 220 V at no-load at rated speed. If it is operated as a differentially compounded generator, other things remaining the same, it would build up

(a) 6 V (b) 220 V
(c) more than 220 V (d) somewhat less than 220 V

24. A belt-driven cumulatively-compound D.C. generator is delivering power to the D.C. mains. If the belt snaps then the machine will run as a

(a) cumulative compounded motor in the same direction
(b) differentially compounded motor in the same direction
(c) cumulative compounded motor in the opposite direction
(d) differentially compounded motor in the opposite direction

25. In a D.C. machine,

1. physically, the brush axis is along the direct axis
2. physically, the brush axis is along the interpolar axis
3. schematically, the brush axis is along the direct axis

4. schematically, the brush axis is along the quadrature axis
5. armature m.m.f. is directed along the brush axis

From these, the correct statements are

(*a*) 1, 4, 5 (*b*) 1, 3, 5 (*c*) 2, 3, 5 (*d*) 2, 4, 5

26. The direction of generated e.m.f. in the armature coil of a D.C. machine is

1. the smae as that of the current in a generator
2. the same as that of the current in a motor
3. opposite to that of the current in a generator
4. opposite to that of the current in a motor

From these, the correct answer is

(*a*) 1, 3 (*b*) 2, 3 (*c*) 2, 4 (*d*) 1, 4

27. The counter (or back) e.m.f. in a D.C. machine is

1. the same as generated e.m.f. in a D.C. motor
2. proportional to field flux and armature speed
3. not the same as generated e.m.f. in a D.C. motor
4. inversely proportional to field flux
5. proportional to number of armature conductors
6. constant from no-load to full load

From these, the correct answer is

(*a*) 1, 2, 5 (*b*) 2, 4, 5, 6 (*c*) 2, 3, 6 (*d*) 3, 4, 5

28. A 220-V D.C. machine has an armature resistance of 1 Ω. If the full-load current is 20 A, the diference in the induced voltages when the machine is running as a motor and as a generator is

(*a*) 20 V (*b*) zero (*c*) 40 V (*d*) 50 V

29. The external load characteristics of a D.C. generator at rated speed is assumed to be linear and is as shown in Fig. C.62. The load circuit comprises only resistance. When the load current is 50 A, the value of the load circuit resistance will be

(*a*) 0.9 Ω (*b*) 1.0 Ω

(*c*) 1.9 Ω (*d*) 2.0 Ω

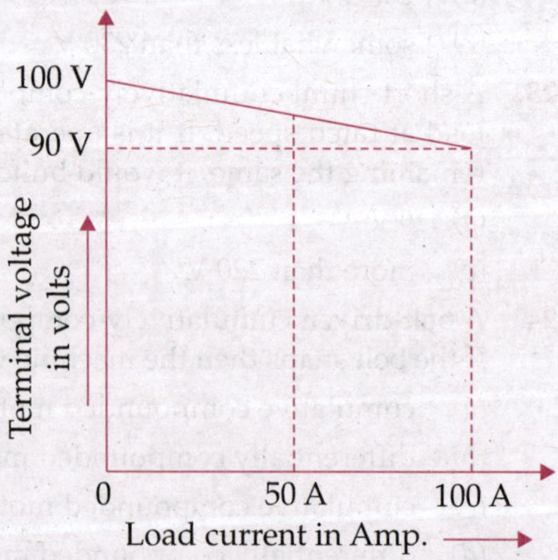

Fig C.62

30. A separately-excited D.C. motor has an armature resistance of 0.5 Ω. It runs off a 250 V D.C. supply drawing an armature current of 20 A at 1500 rpm. The torque developed for an armature current of 10 A, for the same field current, will be

(*a*) 15.28 Nm (*b*) 15.92 Nm

(*c*) 15.6 Nm (*d*) 16.55 Nm

31. A bipolar D.C. machine with interpoles has a main-pole flux of ϕ per pole and an interpole flux of ϕ_i per pole. The yoke of the machine is divided into four quadrants by the main-pole axis and the commutation axis.

The flux-distribution in the quadrants will be

(a) $\frac{1}{2}(\phi + \phi_i)$ in all the four quadrants

(b) $\frac{1}{2}(\phi - \phi_i)$ in all the four quadrants

(c) $\frac{1}{2}(\phi + \phi_i)$ in two diametrically opposite quadrants and $\frac{1}{2}(\phi - \phi_i)$ in the remaining two quadrants

(d) $\frac{1}{2}(\phi + \phi_i)$ in two adjacent quadrants and $\frac{1}{2}(\phi - \phi_i)$ in the remaining two quadrants

[I.A.S., 1996]

32. The residual magnetism of a self-excited D.C. generator is lost. To build up its e.m.f. again

(a) the field winding must be replaced

(b) the armature connection must be reversed

(c) the field winding connection must be reversed

(d) field winding must be excited by low voltage D.C. supply *[I.A.S., 1993]*

33. The armature m.m.f. of a D.C. machine has

(a) triangular space distribution and rotates at the speed of armature

(b) trapezoidal space distribution and is stationary in space

(c) stepped distribution and rotates at the speed of armature

(d) triangular space distribution and is stationary in space

34. The flux is maximum in the following part of a D.C. motor :

(a) pole core (b) under the interpole

(c) under leading pole tip (d) under trailing pole tip

35. The armature m.m.f. in a D.C. machine is

1. stationary with respect to field poles
2. stationary with respect to armature
3. rotating with respect to field poles
4. rotating with respect to armature

From these, the correct answer is

(a) 1, 4 (b) 1, 3 (c) 2, 3 (d) 2, 4

36. The type of D.C. generator used for arc welding purposes is a

(a) series generator (b) shunt generator

(c) cumulatively compounded generator (d) differentially compounded generator

37. The magnetic circuit of a D.C. shunt generator with negligible armature resistance and brush contact voltage drop remains unsaturated when it delivers full-load current at rated terminal voltage. The brushes are kept in the interpolar axis and speed is maintained constant. When the load is switched off, the terminal voltage would *[I.A.S., 1993]*

(a) remain the same (b) increase (c) decrease (d) become zero

38. Fig. C.63 shows the cross-section of a 2-pole D.C. machine. Corresponding flux density and m.m.f. waveforms will be *[I.E.S., 1995]*

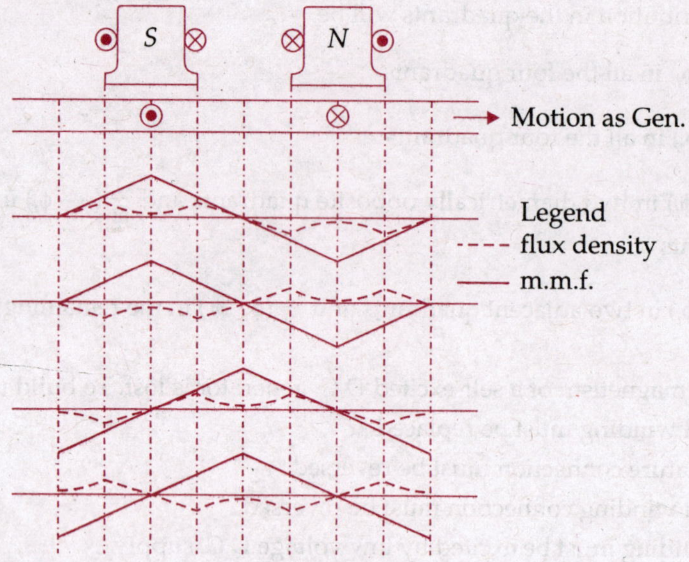

Fig C.63

39. In a loaded D.C. generator, if the brushes are given a shift from the interpolar axis in the direction of rotation, then the commutation will

(a) improve with fall of terminal voltage V_t

(b) deteriorate with fall of V_t

(c) improve with rise in V_t (d) deteriorate with rise in V_t

40. In a loaded D.C. motor, if the brushes are given a shift from the interpolar axis in the direction of rotation, then the commutation will

(a) improve and the speed falls (b) deteriorate and the speed rises

(c) deteriorate and the speed falls (d) improve and the speed rises

41. In a D.C. machine, the demagnetizing effect of armature reaction is due to *[I.A.S., 1995]*

(a) component of armature m.m.f. along field axis

(b) non-sinusoidal nature of armature m.m.f.

(c) magnetic saturation in half of the field pole

(d) uneven air-gap length

42. Which of the following factors improve commutation in a D.C. machine?

1. High contact resistance of brushes
2. High inductance of the coils undergoing commutation
3. Shifting of brushes in the direction of rotation for a generator and in the opposite direction for a motor
4. Narrow width for the commutation bars.

Select the correct answer using the codes given below :

Codes :

(a) 1, 2 and 3 (b) 1 and 3 (c) 2, 3 and 4 (d) 1, 2 and 4

43. In a D.C. generator operating on load with its brushes on the geometrical neutral axis (GNA), the magnetic netural axis (MNA) is shifted in the direction of rotation.

Now, if the brushes are given a lead of 90° (electrical), then the MNA will

(a) shift forward by 90° (b) shift forward by more than 90°

(c) shift forward by less than 90° (d) coincide with the GNA *[I.A.S., 1996]*

44. The volt-ampere equation for a long-shunt compound motor is given by

(a) $V_t = E_a + I_a r_a$ (b) $V_t = E_a + I_a (r_a + r_s)$

(c) $V_t = E_a - I_a r_a$ (d) $V_t = E_a + I_a r_a + I_L r_s$

45. Consider the following statements about commutating poles which are fitted on most large D.C. shunt motors :

1. The commutating poles are placed in the geometric neutral plane and their number is usually equal to the number of main poles
2. The winding on the commutating poles is connected in series with the shunt-field winding on the main poles
3. The polarity of the commutating pole must be that of the next main pole further ahead
4. The commutating poles neutralize the reactance voltage produced in the coil undergoing commutation.

Of these statements,

(a) 1, 2 and 3 are correct (b) 1, and 4 are correct

(c) 2, 3 and 4 are correct (d) 1, 2 and 4 are correct

46. Consider the following statements :

Interpoles in D.C. machines

1. reduce armature reaction effects in the interpolar region
2. have the same dimensions as main poles
3. have their windings connected in series with the armature
4. have same number of turns as the armature
5. have the polarity same as that of the main pole ahead in a motor

From these, the correct statements are

(a) 1, 2 and 3 (b) 1, 3 and 5 (c) 1, 2, 3 and 5 (d) 1 and 3

47. Consider the following statements :

1. Interpole windings are connected is series with armature winding
2. Polarity of interpoles must be the same as that of the main poles in advance
3. Distortion of the main field under the pole shoes is not affected by the use of interpoles

From above, the correct answer is

(a) 1 and 2 (b) 2 and 3 (c) 1 and 3 (d) 1 alone

48. The introduction of interpoles in between the main poles improves the performance of a D.C. machine, because *[I.A.S., 1997]*

(a) the interpoles produce additional flux to augment the developed torque

(b) the flux waveform is improved with reduction in harmonics

(c) the inequality of air-gap flux on the top and bottom halves of the armature is removed

(d) a counter e.m.f. is induced in the coil undergoing commutation

49. In D.C. machines,

1. reactance voltage is proportional to armature current

2. reactance voltage is proportional to core length
3. reactance voltage is due to self-flux of the coil undergoing commutation
4. armature-cross flux is neutralized by interpolar flux
5. interpolar m.m.f. is more than armature m.m.f. in the interpolar zone

From these, the correct answer is

(a) 1, 2, 3, 4 (b) 1, 2, 5 (c) 2, 3, 4 (d) 1, 3, 5

50. The interpoles in D.C. machines have a tapering shape in order to
(a) reduce the overall weight
(b) reduce the saturation in the interpole
(c) economise on the material required for interpoles and their windings
(d) increase the acceleration of commutation

51. If two 8-pole D.C. machines of identical armatures are wound, one with lap winding and the other with wave winding, then
(a) wave-wound machine will have more rated current and more voltage
(b) lap-wound machine will have more rated voltage and more current
(c) lap-wound machine will have more rated voltage and less current
(d) wave-wound machine will have more rated voltage and less current

52. If the applied voltage to a D.C. machine is 230 V, then the back e.m.f., for maximum power developed, is
(a) 115 V (b) 200 V (c) 230 V (d) 460 V

53. A D.C. shunt generator has full-load voltage regulation of 10% at rated speed of 1000 r.p.m. If it is now driven at 1250 r.p.m., then its voltage regulation at full load would
(a) be more than 10% (b) be less than 10%
(c) remain unchanged (d) be 12.5%

54. Two D.C. machines *A* and *B*, using the same conductor material, have armature circuit resistances of 0.4 Ω and 1.2 Ω respectively. Of the two machines,
(a) *A* is bigger than *B* for the same current rating
(b) *A* is bigger than *B* for the same voltage rating
(c) *B* is bigger than *A* for the same current rating
(d) both are of the same size for the same current rating

55. A 10 kW, 230 V, D.C. shunt machine has four terminals brought out through four leads. For this machine
(a) both the windings have thin leads
(b) both the windings have thick leads
(c) armature winding has thin leads whereas field winding has thick leads
(d) armature winding has thick leads whereas field winding has thin leads

56. There are two 2-pole D.C. machines. Main field axis of machine *A* is horizontal and that of *B* is vertical. It is preferable to purchase
(a) machine *A* (b) machine *B*
(c) any of the two machines (d) none of these

57. A compound D.C. generator is delivering full load current at terminal voltage of 230 V. Its series-field winding gets short circuited. If its terminal voltage

1. becomes more than 230 V, it is overcompounded generator
2. becomes more than 230 V, it is differentially compounded generator
3. becomes less than 230 V, it is overcompounded generator
4. becomes less than 230 V, it is differentially compounded generator
5. becomes less than 230 V, it is level compounded generator

From these, the correct answer is

(a) 1, 4, 5 *(b)* 2, 3, 5 *(c)* 1, 4 *(d)* 2, 3

58. D.C. generators are usually designed to develop armature voltages not exceeding 650 V because of the limitations imposed by

(a) field winding *(b)* armature winding
(c) commutator *(d)* starters

59. In a D.C. series generator, the terminal voltage with increase in load will

(a) decrease
(b) increase gradually and then stay at rated voltage
(c) increase to rated voltage and then may decrease
(d) remain nearly constant

60. Consider the following statements :

For a level compounded D.C. generator to run at constant voltage, the series field m.m.f. must effectively compensate

1. armature reaction m.m.f.
2. armature resistance drop
3. brush contact voltage drop

Which of these statements is/are correct?

(a) 2 alone *(b)* 1 and 2 *(c)* 1 and 3 *(d)* 1, 2 and 3

61. A separately-excited D.C. machine, having an armature resistance of 2 ohms was working on a 220 V supply and drawing 10 A armature current from the source when the supply voltage suddenly dropped to 200 V. Assuming that the field circuit source voltage remained unaffected, how will the armature current of the machine react to the change? *[I.A.S., 1994]*

(a) It will initially rise to 11 A and then settle down to 10 A
(b) It will fall momentarily to 9.09 A and then slowly attain 10 A
(c) It will reduce to zero first and then settle back to 10 A
(d) It will remain unaffected by the change and continue to be 10 A

62. Under which of the following conditions is a D.C. motor provided with compensating winding? *[I.A.S., 1993]*

1. Wide range of speed control above normal
2. Wide range of steady load variation with no speed control
3. Wide range of rapid variation in load

Select the correct answer using the codes given below :

Codes :

(a) 1, 2 and 3 *(b)* 2 and 3 *(c)* 1 and 2 *(d)* 1 and 3

63. The following statements ralate to compensating winding *(CW)* and interpole winding *(IW)* of a D.C. machine :

1. *CW* neutralizes the armature reaction under a pole pitch

2. IW is connected in series with armature circuit
3. IW produces m.m.f. in the commutating zone only
4. CW m.m.f. is directed along the brush axis
5. m.m.f. produced by IW is equal to armature m.m.f.

From these, the correct statements are

(a) 1, 2, 3, 4 and 5 (b) 1, 3, 4, 5 (c) 2, 3, 4, 5 (d) 2, 3, 4

64. If the speed of a D.C. motor increases with load torque, then it is a

(a) series motor (b) permanent magnet motor
(c) differentially compounded motor (d) cumulatively compounded motor

65. If the field of a D.C. shunt motor gets opened while the motor is running, then the

(a) speed of motor will be reduced
(b) motor will attain dangerously high speed
(c) armature current will drop
(d) armature will oscillate about original speed as the mean speed

66. A D.C. cumulatively compounded motor delivers rated load torque at rated speed. If the series field is short-circuited, then the armature current and speed will *[I.A.S., 1994]*

(a) both increase (b) both decrease
(c) increase and decrease respectively (d) decrease and increase respectively.

67. A cumlatively compounded D.C. motor delivers rated load power at rated speed. If the series field is short-circuited, then

(a) both armature current I_a and speed ω_m increase
(b) I_a remains constant but ω_m increases
(c) I_a increases and ω_m decreases
(d) both decrease

68. A 240 V D.C. series motor takes 40 A when giving its rated output at 1500 r.p.m. Its resistance is 0.3 Ω. The value of resistance which must be added to obtain rated torque at 1000 r.p.m. is

(a) 6 Ω (b) 5.7 Ω (c) 2.2 Ω (d) 1.9 Ω

69. A D.C. shunt motor is running at 1200 r.p.m. when excited with 220 V D.C.. Neglecting the losses and saturation, the speed of the motor when connected to a 175 V D.C. supply is

(a) 750 r.p.m. (b) 900 r.p.m. (c) 1050 r.p.m. (d) 1200 r.p.m.

70. A 440 V D.C shunt motor has a no-load ($I_a = 0$) speed of 2000 r.p.m. It is running at 1000 r.p.m. at full load torque, reduced armature voltage and full field. If load torque is reduced to 50% of rated value with armature voltage and field voltage held constant at previous values, the speed increases to 1050 r.p.m. The armature voltage drop at full load (neglecting armature reaction effect) is

(a) 16 V (b) 18 V (c) 20 V (d) 22 V

71. A D.C. series motor drawing an armature current of I_a is operating under saturated magnetic conditions. The torque developed in the motor is proportional to

(a) $\dfrac{1}{I_a}$ (b) $\dfrac{1}{I_a^2}$ (c) I_a^2 (d) I_a

72. A D.C. shunt motor having unsaturated magnetic circuit runs at 1000 r.p.m. with rated voltage. If the applied voltage is reduced to half of the rated voltage, the motor will run at

(a) 2000 r.p.m. (b) 1000 r.p.m. (c) 750 r.p.m. (d) 500 r.p.m.

73. A 240 V D.C. shunt motor with an armature resistance of 0.5 Ω has a full-load current of 40 A. Find the ratio of stalling torque to the full-load torque when a resistance of 1 Ω is connected in series with the armature

(a) 4 (b) 12 (c) 6 (d) 8 [GATE, 1998]

74. If speed of a D.C. shunt motor is increased above its rated speed, then its counter e.m.f.

(a) increases (b) decreases
(c) remains unchanged (d) first increases and then decreases

75. A D.C. shunt motor drives a load torque at rated voltage and rated excitation. If the load torque is doubled, the motor speed would

(a) increase slightly (b) decrease slightly (c) become half (d) become double

76. A D.C. shunt motor is required to drive a constant power load at rated speed while drawing rated armature current. Neglecting saturation and all machine losses, if both terminal voltage and the field current of the machine are halved, then

(a) the speed becomes 2 p.u. but armature current I_a remains at 1 p.u.
(b) the speed remains 1 p.u. but I_a becomes 2 p.u.
(c) both speed and I_a become 2 p.u.
(d) both speed and I_a remain at 1 p.u.

77. A D.C. shunt motor runs at a no-load speed of 1140 r.p.m. At full load, armature reaction weakens the main flux by 5% whereas the armature circuit voltage drops by 10%. The motor full-load speed in r.p.m. is

(a) 1080 (b) 1203 (c) 1000 (d) 1200

78. A permanent-magnet D.C. commutator motor has a no-load speed of 6000 r.p.m. when connected to a 120 V D.C. supply. The armature resistance is 2.5 Ω and other losses may be neglected. The speed of the motor with supply voltage of 60 V developing a torque 0.5 Nm is

(a) 3000 r.p.m. (b) 2673 r.p.m. (c) 2836 r.p.m. (d) 5346 r.p.m.

79. A D.C. shunt motor has external resistance R_a and R_f in the armature and field circuits respectively. Armature current at starting can be reduced by keeping

(a) R_f maximum and R_a minimum (b) R_a maximum and R_f maximum
(c) R_a minimum and R_f minimum (d) R_a maximum and R_f minimum

80. While starting a D.C. shunt motor

(a) reduced armature voltage V_a and reduced field voltage V_f should be applied and full-regulator resistance R_r should be included in the field circuit
(b) reduced V_a but full V_f should be applied and R_r should be zero
(c) rated V_a and rated V_f should be applied and R_r should be zero
(d) rated V_a and rated V_f should be applied and R_r should be maximum

81. Consider the following statements :

If the terminal voltage of a D.C. shunt motor, with unsaturated magnetic circuits, is halved with the load torque varying as the square of speed, then

1. speed is halved
2. speed remains unaltered
3. armature current is doubled
4. armature current remains unaltered

Of these statements

(a) 1 and 3 are correct (b) 1 and 4 are correct
(c) 2 and 3 are correct (d) 2 and 4 are correct

82. Consider the following statements regarding the speed control of D.C. motors: *[I.E.S., 2001]*

1. Ward-Leonard method is suitable for constant-torque drives
2. Ward-Leonard method is suitable for constant-power drives
3. Field-control method facilitates speed control below base speed
4. Armature-resistance control method is more efficient than Ward-Leonard method
5. Field-control method is suitable for constant-torque drives
6. Armature-resistance control method is suitable for constant-torque drives.

From these, the correct answer is

(*a*) 1, 2, 6 (*b*) 1, 2, 5 (*c*) 1, 4, 6 (*d*) 1, 3, 5

83. The lower limit of speed in a Ward-Leonard method of speed control is governed by

1. losses in both the machines
2. residual magnetism of the generator
3. armature circuit resistance of both the machines
4. speed of the generator-prime mover

From these, the correct answer is

(*a*) 2, 4 (*b*) 2 only (*c*) 2, 3, 4 (*d*) 1, 2, 3, 4

84. A D.C. shunt motor is run under the following conditions :

1. Normal voltage with no additional resistance in armature or field circuits
2. 50% normal voltage with no additional resistance in armature or field circuits
3. Normal voltage with a small external resistance in the armature circuit of a value equal to the armature resistance
4. Normal voltage with some additional resistance in the field circuit.

Normal speed of the motor would increase in the sequence

(*a*) 1, 2, 3, 4 (*b*) 1, 4, 3, 2 (*c*) 2, 1, 4, 3 (*d*) 2, 3, 1, 4

85. Consider the following statements :

To control the speed of a D.C. shunt motor above the base speed over a reasonably wide range, the motor must

1. have compensating winding
2. have interpole winding
3. be started using a 3-point starter
4. be started using a 4-point starter

Of these statements

(*a*) 1, 2 and 4 are correct (*b*) 1, 2 and 3 are correct
(*c*) 1 and 3 are correct (*d*) 2 and 4 are correct

86. A D.C. shunt motor delivers rated load power at rated speed. If motor terminal voltage is reduced to half (neglect saturation and armature reaction), then

(*a*) speed ω_m, armature current I_a and motor torque T_e remain constant
(*b*) ω_m remains constant, both I_a and T_e are doubled
(*c*) both ω_m and T_e remain constant, I_a is doubled
(*d*) both ω_m and I_a are doubled, T_e remains constant

87. The field windings of a D.C. compound motor are connected in short-shunt configuration. If the series and shunt field windings are interchanged by mistake and the motor is connected to rated voltage,

(a) series winding gets overloaded
(b) shunt winding gets overloaded
(c) both windings get overloaded
(d) neither of the two windings gets overloaded

88. Read the following statements regarding D.C. motors :
1. Direction of rotation of a shunt motor can be reversed by interchanging its supply terminals
2. Additional resistance in the field circuit of a shunt motor decreases its speed
3. Additional resistance in the field circuit of a shunt motor increases its armature current for a constant torque load
4. Direction of rotation of a shunt motor can also be reversed by interchanging its armature terminals
5. A D.C. series motor should never be run at no-load

From these, the correct answer is
(a) 2, 3, 4 (b) 1, 3, 4, 5 (c) 3, 4, 5 (d) 1, 3, 4

89. A separately-excited D.C. generator feeds a D.C. shunt motor. If the load torque on the motor is halved approximately
(a) armature current of both motor and generator are halved
(b) armature current of motor is halved and that of generator is unaltered
(c) armature current of generator is halved and that of motor is unaltered
(d) armature currents of both motor and generator remain unaltered.

90. In a coal mine, Ward-Leonard method of speed control as shown in Fig. C.64 is used to lift the coal from the pit through a crane and bucket arrangement. After lifting the coal to desired level and emptying at the dumping ground, the bucket has to be lowered into the pit. The action to be taken at this stage is to reverse the

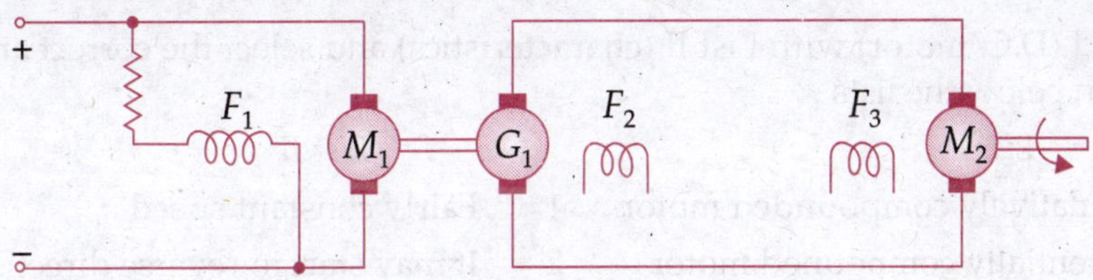

Fig C.64

(a) direction of current in F_2 and slowly increase it
(b) current in F_3 and slowly decrease it
(c) supply terminal of M_1
(d) direction of current in F_1 and slowly increase it

91. A D.C. series motor drives a load. The motor is unsaturated and the load torque is proportional to speed squared. For a speed of 400 r.p.m., motor line current is 20 A. For a speed of 800 r.p.m., the line current will be
(a) 20 A (b) 28.28 A (c) 40 A (d) 80 A

92. Take the normal values as unity, the approximate values of current and speed of a D.C. shunt motor under the conditions of List 1 are given in List 2. Match the two lists and select the correct answer using the codes given below the lists :

	List 1		*List 2*	
			Armature Current	*Speed*
A.	Terminal voltage halved, field current and load torque constant	1.	0.5	0.5
B.	Terminal voltage halved, field current and power output constant	2.	1.0	0.5
C.	Field flux doubled, armature voltage and load torque constant	3.	2.0	0.5
D.	Field flux halved, armature voltage halved and power output constant	4.	2.0	1.0

Codes :

	A	*B*	*C*	*D*		*A*	*B*	*C*	*D*
(a)	1	3	2	4	*(b)*	2	3	1	4
(c)	2	1	4	3	*(d)*	1	2	3	4

93. If the armature of a D.C. motor is supplied from a constant current source, and its field from a constant voltage source, then the speed-torque characteristics of the motor will be

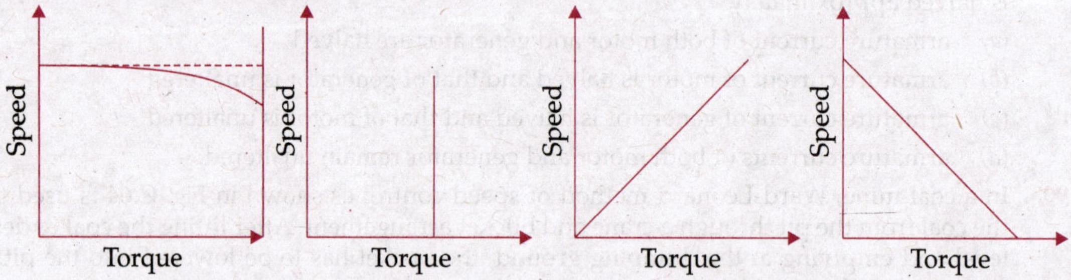

(a) *(b)* *(c)* *(d)*

94. Match List I (D.C. motor) with List II (characteristics) and select the correct answer using the codes given below the lists :

	List I		*List II*
A.	Cumulatively compounded motor	1.	Fairly constant speed
B.	Differentially compouned motor	2.	It may start in reverse direction
C.	Series motor	3.	Definite no-load speed
D.	Shunt motor	4.	Never started without load

Codes :

	A	*B*	*C*	*D*		*A*	*B*	*C*	*D*
(a)	2	3	1	4	*(b)*	3	2	4	1
(c)	1	3	2	4	*(d)*	4	1	3	2

95. In machine-tool drive applications, the speed of a separately-excited D.C. motor is required to be controlled both below and above the rated speed of the motor. Which one of the following methods is best suited for this purpose? (V_a : armature voltage ; I_f : field current and $I_{f \cdot r}$: field current at rated speed).

(a) $I_f = I_{f \cdot r}$; V_a variable *(b)* V_a fixed, I_f variable

(c) V_a and V_f variable with $I_f \leq I_{f \cdot r}$ *(d)* V_a and V_f variable with $I_f \geq I_{f \cdot r}$

96. The following lists relate to speed control of D.C. motors. Match List I and List II, and select the correct answer using the codes given below the lists :

	List I		*List II*
A.	Armature voltage control	1.	Speeds above base speed
B.	Field current control	2.	Speeds below base speed
C.	Use of diverter resistance	3.	Poor motor efficiency
D.	Rheostatic control	4.	Speed control of series motor

Codes :

	A	*B*	*C*	*D*		*A*	*B*	*C*	*D*
(a)	1	2	3	4	*(b)*	2	1	4	3
(c)	4	1	3	2	*(d)*	2	3	1	4

97. A 2-pole series motor with its two field coils connected in series runs at a speed of 500 r.p.m. If the field coils are re-connected in parallel and assuming that the torque is constant and the magnetic circuit is unsaturated, the new speed will be

(a) 250 r.p.m. *(b)* $\frac{500}{\sqrt{2}}$ r.p.m. *(c)* $500\sqrt{2}$ r.p.m. *(d)* 1000 r.p.m.

98. The function of a D.C. motor starter is to

(a) start the D.C. motor *(b)* limit the starting current

(c) increase the starting torque *(d)* avoid dips in the supply voltage

99. D.C. shunt motor should not be stopped by forcing the starter handle back to the OFF position by hand to avoid

(a) heavy sparking at all the studs as handle travels to OFF position

(b) dangerous sparking at the last stud as handle travels to OFF position

(c) dangerous to the operator due to heavy sparking

(d) both *(a)* and *(b)*

100. Three-point starter for D.C. shunt motor is not used where wide speed control above rated speed is required because

(a) the motor may stop at high speed *(b)* the motor may stop at low speed

(c) hunting may occur in the motor *(d)* motor may attain dangerously high speed

101. Consider the following statements :

At starting, the field excitation of a D.C. shunt motor is kept at its maximum value to reduce

1. sparking at brushes
2. accelerating time
3. starting current
4. voltage dip in the supply

Of these statements,

(a) 1 and 2 are correct *(b)* 2, 3 and 4 are correct

(c) 1, 3 and 4 are correct *(d)* 1, 2, 3 and 4 are correct

102. If the field circuit of D.C. shunt motor, equipped with 3-point starter, gets interrupted accidentally, while running normally, then the *[I.A.S., 1994]*

(a) starter arm will fly back to the off position

(b) speed of the motor will rise dangerously

(c) armature winding will draw heavy current

(d) motor will continue to run normally.

103. Consider the following statements : *[I.A.S., 1995]*

A D.C. shunt-motor starter ensures that

1. armature current is under limit during starting
2. field flux is maintained at the maximum value
3. acceleration time is controlled
4. field failure is prevented
5. starting torque is always more than the load torque

Of these statements

(a) 1, 2, 3 and 5 are correct *(b)* 1, 2, 3 and 4 are correct

(c) 1 and 4 are correct *(d)* 1, 3 and 4 are correct

104. Which one of the figures given here best represents the variation in armature current *I* and speed *N* with time during the starting of a D.C. shunt motor?

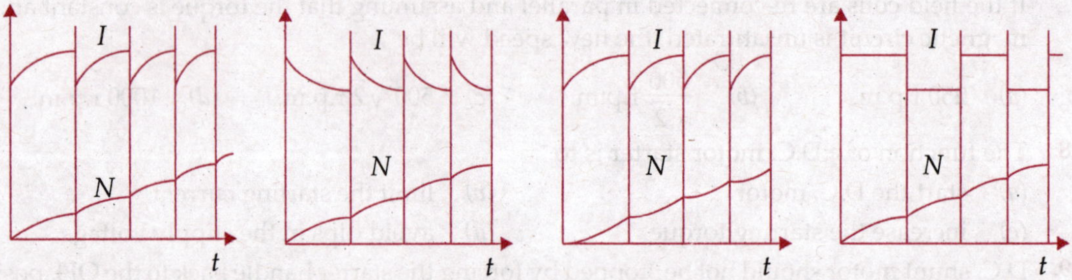

(a) *(b)* *(c)* *(d)*

105. A D.C. shunt motor is started at no-load and its rated speed is noted as 1000 r.p.m. during winter. After 5 hours of continuous no-load running, its speed would

(a) become somewhat more than 1000 r.p.m.

(b) become somewhat less than 100 r.p.m.

(c) remain 1000 r.p.m.

(d) reduce to 950 r.p.m.

106. In D.C. machines, constant loss is composed of

(a) iron loss and mechanical loss

(b) friction, windage *(FW)* and iron loss and field circuit loss

(c) iron loss and field circuit loss

(d) *FW* and stray load loss

107. The efficiency of a D.C. shunt generator is maximum when

(a) magnetic loss is equal to the mechanical loss

(b) field ohmic loss is equal to the constant loss

(c) stray load loss is equal to the armature circuit loss

(d) armature circuit loss is equal to the sum of no-load rotational loss and field circuit loss

108. A D.C. generator has an efficiency of 90% for an output voltage and current of 250 V and 18 A respectively. If this machine is made to operate at the same speed as a D.C. motor with an input voltage of 250 V and current of 18 A, the efficiency of the motor would be

(a) 90% *(b)* 91.12% *(c)* 88.88% *(d)* 87.12%

109. A 200 V D.C. shunt motor delivers an output of 17 kW with an input of 20 kW. The field winding resistance is 50 Ω and the armature-circuit resistance is 0.04 Ω. Maximum efficiency will be obtained when total armature ohmic losses are equal to

(a) 2632 W *(b)* 3000 W *(c)* 3680 W *(d)* 5232 W

110. The winding of a large D.C. series motor and their functions are given below :

	Winding		*Functions*
A.	series field winding	1.	to avoid field distortion under the pole
B.	shunt field winding	2.	to avoid sparking
C.	commutating-pole winding	3.	to generate working flux
D.	compensating winding	4.	to avoid runaway speeds at no-load

Select correct answer using the following code :

	A	*B*	*C*	*D*		*A*	*B*	*C*	*D*
(a)	1	2	3	4	*(b)*	2	3	4	1
(c)	3	4	1	2	*(d)*	3	4	2	1

111. A D.C. series motor fed from rated supply voltage is overloaded and its magnetic circuit is saturated. The speed-torque characteristic of this motor will be approximately represented by which curve of Fig. C.65.

(a) curve *A* *(b)* curve *B*

(c) curve C *(d)* curve *D*

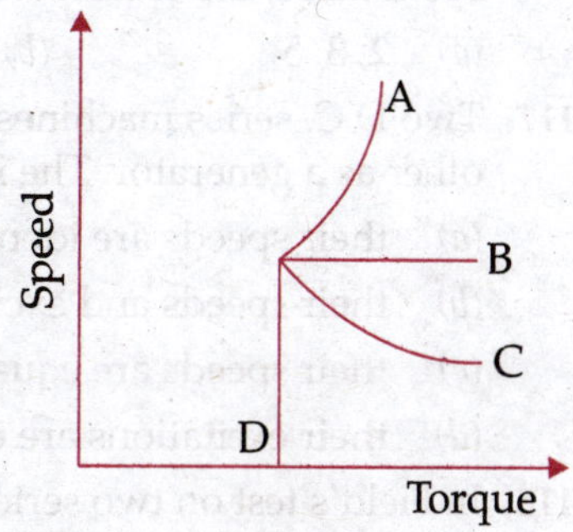

Fig C.65

112. Consider the following statements :

Permanent magnet D.C. motors used in casette-tape recorders have

1. magnets on stator and armature on the rotor
2. magnets on rotor and armature on the stator
3. electronic commutation and no brushes
4. mechanical commutation and brushes
5. automatic speed governors

Of these statements

(a) 1, 3 and 5 are correct *(b)* 1, 4 and 5 are correct

(c) 2, 3 and 5 are correct *(d)* 1 and 4 are correct

113. In Swinburne's method of testing D.C. machines, the shunt machine is run as a

(a) motor at no-load at rated speed and rated voltage

(b) generator at no-load at near rated speed and rated voltage

(c) generator at full load at rated speed and rated voltage

(d) generator at no-load at rated speed and rated terminal voltage

114. In Hopkinson's method of testing D.C. machines, the power taken from the mains has to supply

(a) the losses in the motor only *(b)* the losses in both the machines

(c) the input to both the machines *(d)* the input to motor and not to the generator

115. Two D.C. shunt machines are coupled mechanically and electrically.One D.C. machine is run as a motor and the other as a generator. Their no-load rotational losses are equal because

1. their speeds are equal
2. their speeds and excitations are equal
3. generator iron losses are more than the motor iron losses
4. motor armature current is less than the generator armature current
5. motor has more stray load losses than those in the generator

From the above, the correct answer is

(a) 1, 2, 3, 5 (b) 1, 2, 4, 5 (c) 1, 2, 5 (d) 1, 3, 5

116. In Hopkinson's test on two D.C. shunt machines

1. armature currents of both the machines are equal
2. generator armature current is less than that in the motor
3. their speeds are equal
4. their field currents are equal
5. stray load losses in motor are more than those in the generator

From these, the correct answer is

(a) 2, 3, 5 (b) 1, 3, 5 (c) 2, 3, 4 (d) 1, 3, 4, 5

117. Two D.C. series machines are mechanically coupled. One machine is run as a motor and the other as a generator. The iron and friction loss will be identical when

(a) their speeds are identical
(b) their speeds and excitations are identical
(c) their speeds are equal and back e.m.fs. are half of the supply voltage
(d) their excitations are equal and back e.m.fs. are half of the supply voltage

118. In Field's test on two series machines

1. generator field current I_{fg} is more than motor field current I_{fm}
2. $I_{fg} = I_{fm}$
3. Armature voltage of generator V_{tg} is more than armature voltage of motor V_{tm}
4. $V_{tg} < V_{tm}$
5. From these, the correct statements are

(a) 1, 3 (b) 1, 4 (c) 2, 4 (d) 2, 3

119. Match List I and List II and select the correct answer from the codes :

List I	*List II*
A. Voltage-drop test	1. Efficiency
B. Hopkinson's test	2. Separation of iron and friction losses
C. Swinburne's test	3. Open and short-circuited armature coils
D. Retardation test	4. Temperature rise

Codes :

	A	B	C	D		A	B	C	D
(a)	3	1	4	2	(b)	2	4	1	3
(c)	3	4	1	2	(d)	2	1	4	3

120. A rotating amplifier that can be used as a constant current source is

(a) metadyne (b) amplidyne (c) regulax (d) rototrol

121. An amplidyne develops an output voltage of 100 volts at 1000 r.p.m. If its armature is now driven at 2000 r.p.m., its output voltage would be

(a) 100 V (b) 200 V (c) 400 V (d) 50 V

122. The polarity of the output voltage in a cross-field generator can be altered by

(a) reversing the direction of rotation
(b) reversing both the direction of rotation and field current
(c) reversing the direction of field current
(d) reversing either the direction of rotation or the field current

123. In a 2-pole cross-field generator,

1. there are 4-polar projections
2. there are only 2-polar projections
3. there are four interpoles
4. there are only two interpoles
5. the number of brushes = 4
6. the number of brushes may be 2 or 4

From these, the correct answer is

(a) 1, 3, 5 (b) 2, 4, 6 (c) 1, 4, 5 (d) 1, 4, 6

124. Typical characteristics of a D.C. series motor, operating under loaded condition, are shown in Fig. C.66. List I gives the identification of these characteristics, while List II gives the description of important load characteristics of D.C. motor working on load

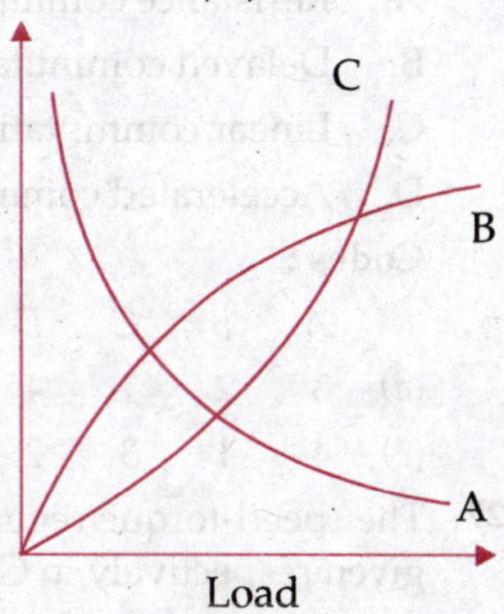

Fig C.66

List I (see figure, curves labelled)	*List II*
A. A ...	1. Efficiency Vs load
B. B ...	2. Torque Vs load
C. C ...	3. Current Vs load
	4. Speed Vs load

Match List I with List II and select the correct answer using the codes given below :

Codes :

	A	B	C		A	B	C
(a)	4	2	3	(b)	2	3	1
(c)	3	2	1	(d)	4	1	2

125. In a D.C. machine, reactance voltage

1. is produced due to self-inductance of the coil undergoing commutation
2. is the sum of e.m.fs. induced by self and mutual fluxes linking the coil undergoing commutation
3. causes delayed commutation
4. can be neutralized by transformer e.m.f. induced by interpole-flux
5. can be compensated by voltage commutation

From these, the correct statements are

(a) 1, 3, 4 (b) 2, 3, 4 (c) 2, 3, 5 (d) 2, 3, 4, 5

126. Commutation characteristics of D.C. machines are shown in Fig. C.67. Match List I with List II and select the correct answer by using the codes given below :

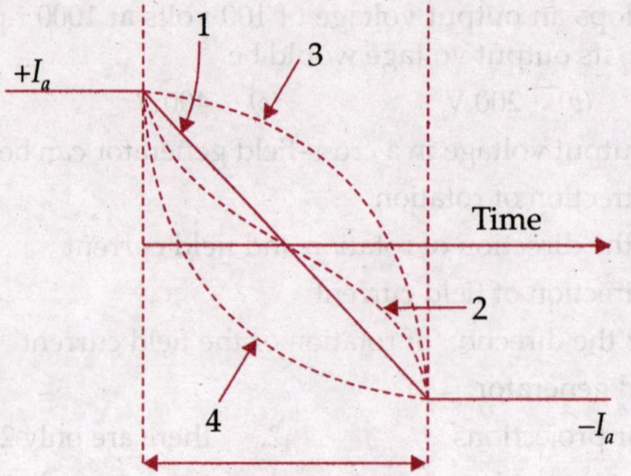

Fig C.67

	List I		*List II*
A.	Resistance commutation	1.	straight line 1
B.	Delayed commutation	2.	curve 2
C.	Linear commutation	3.	curve 3
D.	Accelerated commutation	4.	curve 4

Codes :

	A	*B*	*C*	*D*		*A*	*B*	*C*	*D*
(a)	3	2	1	4	*(b)*	3	2	4	1
(c)	4	1	3	2	*(d)*	2	3	1	4

127. The speed-torque regimes in a D.C. motor and the control methods suitable for the same are given respectively in Group II and Group I *[GATE, 2003]*

	List I		*List II*
P.	Field control	1.	Below base speed
Q.	Armature control	2.	Above base speed
		3.	Above base torque
		4.	Below base torque

The match between the control method and the speed/torque regime is as follows :

(a) P-1 ; Q-3 *(b)* P-2 ; Q-1 *(c)* P-2 ; Q-3 *(d)* P-1 ; Q-4

128. To conduct load test on a D.C. shunt motor, it is coupled to a generator which is identical to the motor. The field of the generator is also connected to the same supply source as the motor. The armature of the generator is connected to a load resistance. The armature resistance is 0.02 p.u. Armature reaction and mechanical losses can be negelected. With rated voltage across the motor, the load resistance across the generator is adjusted to obtain rated armature current in both motor and generator. The p.u. value of this load resistance is *[GATE, 2003]*

(a) 1.0 *(b)* 0.98 *(c)* 0.96 *(d)* 0.94

129. A D.C. series motor driving an electric train faces a constant power load. If is running at rated speed and rated voltage. If the speed has to be brought down to 0.25, the supply voltage has to be approximately brought down to *[GATE, 2003]*

(a) 0.75 p.u. *(b)* 0.5 p.u. *(c)* 0.25 p.u. *(d)* 0.125 p.u.

130. A 220 V D.C. series motor runs drawing a current of 30 A from the supply. Armature and field circuit resistances are 0.4 Ω and 0.1 Ω respectively. The load torque varies as the square of the speed. The flux in the motor may be taken as being proportional to armature current. To reduce the speed of the motor by 50%, the resistance in ohms that should be added in series with the armature is .... (Give the answer up to two decimal places). *[GATE, 2017 (1)]*

[**Hint.** $\dfrac{E_{a1}}{E_{a2}} = \dfrac{N_1\phi_1}{N_2\phi_2} = \dfrac{N_1 I_{a1}}{N_2 I_{a2}} = \dfrac{N}{N/2} \times \dfrac{30}{15} = \dfrac{205}{E_{a2}}$ etc.]

131. A 220 V, 10 kW, 900 rpm separately excited D.C. motor has an armature resistance $R_a = 0.02\ \Omega$. When the motor operates at rated speed and with rated terminal voltage, the electromagnetic torque developed by the motor is 70 Nm. Neglecting the rotational losses of the machine, the current drawn by the motor from 220 V supply is *[GATE, 2017 (2)]*

(a) 34.2 A *(b)* 30 A *(c)* 22 A *(d)* 4.84 A

[**Hint.** $T_e = \dfrac{E_a I_a}{\omega_m} = \dfrac{(220 - I_a \times 0.02) \times I_a \times 60}{2\pi \times 900} = 70$ Nm . ∴ I_a...]

132. A 120 V D.C shunt motor takes 2 A at no load. It takes 7 A on full load while running at 1200 rpm. The armature resistance is 0.8 Ω and the shunt field resistance is 240 Ω. The no-load speed in rpm is .... *[GATE, 2017 (2)]*

133. A separately-excited dc motor has an armature resistance $R_a = 0.05\ \Omega$. The field excitation is kept constant. At an armature voltage of 100 V, the motor produces a torque of 500 Nm at zero speed. Neglecting all mechanical losses, the no-load speed of motor (in radian/s) for an armature voltage of 150 V is .... (up to 2 decimal places). *[GATE, 2018]*

[**Hint.** At zero speed, $E_a = 0$, ∴ $100 = I_a \times 0.05$. Also at zero speed, $T_e = K_m I_a$ or $500 = K_m \times 2000$ etc.]

134. A 200 V D.C. series motor, when operating from rated voltage while driving a certain load, draws 10 A current and runs at 1000 rpm. The total series resistance is 1 Ω. The magnetic circuit is assumed to be linear. At the same supply voltage, the load torque is increased by 44%. The speed of the motor in rpm (rounded to the nearest integer) is .... *[GATE, 2018]*

[Hint. $\phi \propto I_a$, ∴ $T_e = k_a \phi I_a$ or $T_e \propto I_a^2$ or $T_e \propto 10^2$. New torque $1.44\ T_e \propto I_{a1}^2$ etc.]

ANSWERS

1. *(c)*	**2.** *(c)*	**3.** *(c)*	**4.** *(a)*	**5.** *(d)*	**6.** *(b)*	**7.** *(d)*	**8.** *(c)*	**9.** *(a)*	**10.** *(b)*
11. *(b)*	**12.** *(c)*	**13.** *(b)*	**14.** *(b)*	**15.** *(a)*	**16.** *(c)*	**17.** *(d)*	**18.** *(c)*	**19.** *(c)*	**20.** *(c)*
21. *(b)*	**22.** *(d)*	**23.** *(b)*	**24.** *(b)*	**25.** *(a)*	**26.** *(d)*	**27.** *(a)*	**28.** *(c)*	**29.** *(c)*	**30.** *(a)*
31. *(c)*	**32.** *(d)*	**33.** *(d)*	**34.** *(c)*	**35.** *(a)*	**36.** *(d)*	**37.** *(a)*	**38.** *(c)*	**39.** *(a)*	**40.** *(c)*
41. *(c)*	**42.** *(b)*	**43.** *(d)*	**44.** *(b)*	**45.** *(b)*	**46.** *(d)*	**47.** *(c)*	**48.** *(d)*	**49.** *(b)*	**50.** *(b)*
51. *(d)*	**52.** *(a)*	**53.** *(a)*	**54.** *(b)*	**55.** *(d)*	**56.** *(a)*	**57.** *(b)*	**58.** *(c)*	**59.** *(c)*	**60.** *(d)*
61. *(c)*	**62.** *(a)*	**63.** *(d)*	**64.** *(c)*	**65.** *(b)*	**66.** *(a)*	**67.** *(b)*	**68.** *(d)*	**69.** *(d)*	**70.** *(d)*
71. *(d)*	**72.** *(b)*	**73.** *(a)*	**74.** *(c)*	**75.** *(b)*	**76.** *(b)*	**77.** *(a)*	**78.** *(b)*	**79.** *(d)*	**80.** *(b)*
81. *(c)*	**82.** *(a)*	**83.** *(c)*	**84.** *(d)*	**85.** *(a)*	**86.** *(c)*	**87.** *(d)*	**88.** *(c)*	**89.** *(a)*	**90.** *(a)*
91. *(c)*	**92.** *(b)*	**93.** *(b)*	**94.** *(b)*	**95.** *(c)*	**96.** *(b)*	**97.** *(d)*	**98.** *(b)*	**99.** *(b)*	**100.** *(a)*
101. *(d)*	**102.** *(a)*	**103.** *(a)*	**104.** *(b)*	**105.** *(a)*	**106.** *(b)*	**107.** *(d)*	**108.** *(c)*	**109.** *(a)*	**110.** *(d)*
111. *(b)*	**112.** *(d)*	**113.** *(d)*	**114.** *(b)*	**115.** *(d)*	**116.** *(a)*	**117.** *(b)*	**118.** *(c)*	**119.** *(c)*	**120.** *(a)*
121. *(c)*	**122.** *(c)*	**123.** *(a)*	**124.** *(d)*	**125.** *(c)*	**126.** *(d)*	**127.** *(b)*	**128.** *(c)*	**129.** *(b)*	

130. 10.75 Ω **131.** *(b)* **132.** 1241.8 rpm. **133.** 600 rad/sec. **134.** 825 rpm

POLYPHASE SYNCHRONOUS MACHINES

1. A synchronous machine has its field winding on the stator and polyphase armature winding on the rotor. When running under steady-conditions, its air-gap field is

1. stationary with respect to stator
2. rotating at synchronous speed N_s with respect to stator
3. rotating at N_s in the direction of rotor rotation
4. rotating at double the N_s with respect to rotor
5. rotating at N_s with respect to rotor
6. rotating in a direction opposite to rotor rotation

From these, the correct answer is

(a) 2, 5 *(b)* 1, 4, 6 *(c)* 2, 4, 6 *(d)* 1, 3, 5

2. A synchronous machine has its field winding on the rotor and polyphase armature winding on the stator. When running under steady conditions, its air-gap field is

1. stationary with respect to stator
2. rotating at synchronous speed N_s with respect to stator
3. rotating at double the N_s with respect to rotor
4. stationary with respect to rotor
5. rotating at N_s in the direction of rotor rotation

From these, the correct answer is

(a) 2, 5 *(b)* 1, 4, 5 *(c)* 2, 3, 4 *(d)* 2, 4, 5

3. The maximum possible speeds in r.p.m. at which an alternator can be driven to generate voltages at 60 Hz and 50 Hz are respectively :

(a) 2000, 2400 *(b)* 3000, 3600 *(c)* 2400, 2000 *(d)* 3600, 3000

4. Two mechanically-coupled alternators deliver power at 50 Hz and 60 Hz respectively. The highest speed of the alternators is

(a) 3600 r.p.m. *(b)* 3000 r.p.m. *(c)* 600 r.p.m. *(d)* 500 r.p.m.

5. Match List I with List II and select the correct answer using the codes given below the lists :

List I *[Parts of a turbogenerator used in thermal power plants]*	*List II* *[Materials from which these parts are made]*
A. Stator core	1. Copper
B. Rotor core	2. Copper alloy
C. Stator windings	3. Silicon steel
D. Slip rings	4. Mild steel
	5. Aluminium

Codes :

	A	*B*	*C*	*D*		*A*	*B*	*C*	*D*
(a)	3	5	2	1	*(b)*	4	5	1	2
(c)	4	3	1	2	*(d)*	3	4	1	2

6. Consider the following statements :

The synchronous generators used in thermal power stations have

1. cylindrical rotors
2. slip rings and brushes
3. laminated rotor
4. stator slots in multiple of 6
5. 3-phase star-connected stator windings

Which of these statements are correct?

(a) 1, 2, 3 and 4 (b) 1, 2, 3 and 5 (c) 3, 4 and 5 (d) 1, 2, 4 and 5

7. The most appropriate speeds in r.p.m. of generators used in thermal, nuclear and hydro-power plants would respectively be

(a) 3000, 300 and 150 (b) 3000, 3000 and 300
(c) 1500, 1500 and 3000 (d) 1000, 900 and 750

8. In a synchronous generator operating at zero power factor lagging, the effect of armature reaction is [I.A.S., 1995]

(a) magnetizing (b) demagnetizing
(c) cross-magnetizing (d) both magnetizing and cross-magnetizing

9. Match List I with List II and select the correct answer using the codes given below the lists :

List I (Load p.f.)	List II (Nature of armature flux in an alternator)
A. Zero leading	1. Demagnetizing
B. Unity	2. Magnetizing
C. Zero lagging	3. Cross-magnetizing
D. Zero with armature terminals suddenly short-circuited	4. Initially constant, demagnetizing

Codes :

	A	B	C	D		A	B	C	D
(a)	1	2	4	3	(b)	2	3	1	4
(c)	4	3	1	2	(d)	2	1	3	4

10. Open circuit (O.C.) and short-circuit (S.C.) tests on an AC generator are conducted under which of the following conditions?

1. O.C. test at nominal flux and S.C. test at nominal current
2. O.C. test at reduced flux and S.C. test at reduced current
3. O.C. test at zero armature current and S.C. test at reduced flux
4. O.C. test at zero current and S.C. test at nominal flux

Select the correct answer using the codes given below :

Codes :

(a) 1 and 3 (b) 2 and 3 (c) 1 and 4 (d) 2 and 4

11. The zero-power-factor characteristic for the Potier diagram can be obtained by loading the alternator using

(a) lamp load (b) synchronous motor
(c) water load (d) D.C. motor

12. Match List I (methods of full-load regulation of 25 *MVA* alternator at 0.8 p.f. lagging) with List II (% regulation) and select the correct answer using the codes given below the lists :

List I		*List II*	
A.	e.m.f.	1.	13%
B.	m.m.f.	2.	18%
C.	z.p.f.	3.	32%

Codes :

	A	*B*	*C*		*A*	*B*	*C*
(a)	3	1	2	*(b)*	1	3	2
(c)	2	3	1	*(d)*	1	2	3

13. Read the following statements about a cylindrical-rotor alternator :

1. E.m.f. generated by armature reaction m.m.f. lags armature current by 90°
2. Armature reaction due to intermediate lagging p.f. is partly cross-magnetizing and partly magnetizing
3. Air-gap voltage leads terminal voltage
4. Air-gap voltage lags the field flux by 90°
5. Armature reaction m.m.f. lags the field flux by (90° + internal p.f. angle)

From these, the correct answer is

(a) 1, 2, 3, 5 *(b)* 1, 3, 5 *(c)* 2, 3, 5 *(d)* 2, 3, 4, 5

14. The power factor of an alternator under short circuit conditions is almost near

(a) zero leading *(b)* zero lagging *(c)* unity

(d) zero leading or zero lagging depending upon the type of alternator

15. Consider the following statements regarding synchronous machines :

1. In an alternator, armature m.m.f. leads the field flux
2. In an alternator, air-gap flux lags the field flux
3. In a synchronous motor, armature m.m.f. leads the field flux
4. In a synchronous motor, air-gap m.m.f. lags the armature m.m.f.
5. In an alternator, field flux lags the armature current.

From these, the correct answer is

(a) 2, 3, 4 *(b)* 1, 3, 4 *(c)* 2, 3, 4, 5 *(d)* 1, 3, 4, 5

16. In a 3-phase cylindrical-rotor alternator,

(a) field m.m.f. leads the air-gap flux and air-gap flux leads the armature m.m.f.

(b) the armature m.m.f. leads the air-gap flux and the air-gap flux leads the field flux

(c) the armature m.m.f. leads the air-gap flux and the air-gap flux lags the field flux

(d) field m.m.f. leads the air-gap flux and air-gap flux lags the armature m.m.f.

17. Read the following statements about a cylindrical-rotor alternator :

1. Armature reaction m.m.f. due to 0.8 lagging p.f. current is partly cross-magnetizing and partly demagnetizing
2. the field poles lead the resultant air-gap flux
3. the field poles have a tendency to go away from the resultant air-gap flux
4. terminal voltage lags the field flux by 90 + δ.

From these, the correct answer is

(a) 1, 2, 4 (b) 1, 2, 3, 4 (c) 2, 3, 4 (d) 1, 3, 4

18. Potier reactance of an alternator is almost the same as

(a) Field winding reactance (b) total armature reactance
(c) leakage reactance of field winding (d) armature leakage reactance

19. Which one of the following methods would give a higher than actual value of regulation of an alternator :

(a) z.p.f. method (b) m.m.f. method (c) E.m.f. method (d) ASA method

20. The four methods of calculating voltage regulation of a 3-phase alternator are :

1. E.m.f. method
2. Saturated synchronous reactance method
2. New ASA method
4. m.m.f. method

The correct sequence of the ascending order of the values of regulation obtained by these methods is

(a) 3, 4, 2, 1 (b) 4, 3, 1, 2 (c) 3, 4, 1, 2 (d) 4, 3, 2, 1

21. The flux per pole in a synchronous motor with the field circuit ON and the stator disconnected from the supply is found to be 25 mWb. When the stator is connected to the rated supply with the field excitation unchanged, the flux per pole in the machine is found to be 20 mWb while the motor is running on no load. Assuming no-load losses to be zero, the no-load current drawn by the motor from the supply.

(a) lags the supply voltage (b) leads the supply voltage
(c) is in phase with the supply voltage (d) is zero

22. A 3-phase alternator delivers power to a balanced 3-phase load of power factor 0.707 lagging. It is observed that the open-circuit e.m.f. phasor leads the corresponding terminal voltage phasor by 15°. Neglecting the effect of harmonics, the angle between the axis of the main-field m.m.f. and the axis of armature m.m.f. will be [I.A.S., 1997]

(a) 30° electrical (b) 60° electrical (c) 90° electrical (d) 150° electrical

23. A 3-phase, 400 V, delta-connected alternator has a synchronous impedance of $(0 + j20)$ ohms per phase. If it delivers a balanced load of 12 KVA at zero power factor leading, then the percentage voltage regulation of the alternator is equal to

(a) – 50 (b) + 50 (c) – 150 (d) 150 [I.A.S. 1997]

24. A 3-phase alternator has negligible stator resistance. A short-circuit test is conducted on this alternator. At a particular speed, a field current of I_{f1} is required to drive the rated armature current. If the speed of the alternator is reduced of half, the field current required to maintain rated armature current [GATE, 1993]

(a) would be equal to I_{f1} (b) would be equal to $2\ I_{f1}$
(c) would be equal to $I_{f1/2}$ (d) cannot be predicted due to insufficient data.

25. In a 3-phase cylindrical-rotor synchronous machine :

1. effect of armature reaction is taken care of by magnetizing reactance
2. synchronous reactance is equal to the sum of mutual and leakage reactances
3. effect of armature reaction is taken care of by armature-reaction reactance
4. synchronous reactance is made up of magnetizing and leakage reactance.

From these, the correct answer is

(a) 2, 3, 4 (b) 2, 3 (c) 3, 4 (d) 1, 3, 4

26. The full-load voltage regulation of an aternator is 6% at 0.8 p.f. lagging and at rated speed of 1200 r.p.m. Its full-load regulation at 0.8 p.f. lagging and at 1100 r.p.m. would be (assuming negligible armature resistance)

(a) less than 6% (b) more than 6% (c) 6% (d) 5.5%

27. A cylindrical-rotor synchronous generator will deliver maximum power output when

(a) load angle = synchronous impedance angle

(b) load angle = internal power-factor angle

(c) load angle = 90° (d) input power factor is unity.

28. A 3-phase synchronous generator is operating at constant load while the excitation is adjusted to give unity p.f. current. If the excitation is now increased, the p.f. will

(a) become leading (b) become lagging (c) remain at unity (d) become zero.

29. The impedance value of a generator is 0.2 p.u. on a base value of 11 kV, 50 MVA. The impedance value for a base of 22 kV, 150 MVA is

(a) 0.15 p.u. (b) 0.20 p.u. (c) 0.3 p.u. (d) 0.24 p.u.

30. In Fig. C.68, the characteristic that corresponds to the variation of synchronous reactance of a synchronous machine with the field current is

(a) curve A (b) curve B

(c) curve C (d) curve D

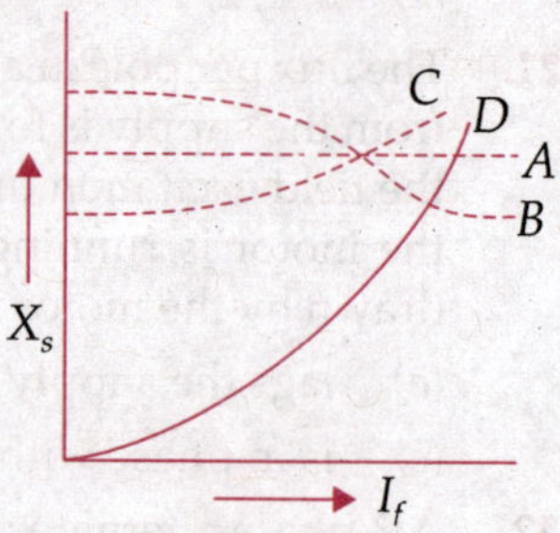

Fig C.68

31. A round-rotor alternator has a leakage reactance of 10%, armature-reaction reactance of 90% and negligible armature resistance. With the machine initially running at rated speed and terminal voltage of 1.0 p.u., a 3-phase short circuit is applied. The sustained armature current will be

(a) 1.25 p.u. (b) 1.11 p.u. (c) 1.0 p.u. (d) 0.9 p.u.

32. A synchronous generator with synchronous reactance of 1.3 p.u. is connected to an infinite bus whose voltage is 1 p.u., through an equivalent reactance of 0.2 p.u. For maximum output of 1.2 p.u., the alternator e.m.f. must be

(a) 1.5 p.u. (b) 1.56 p.u. (c) 1.8 p.u. (d) 2.5 p.u.

33. Consider the following statements for a 3-phase alternator designed to operate at p.f. 0.85:

1. For p.f. > 0.85 lag, armature heating is the limiting factor.
2. For p.f. > 0.85 lag, rotor-field heating is the limiting factor.
3. For p.f. < 0.85 lag, armature heating is the limiting factor.
4. For p.f. < 0.85 lag, rotor-field heating is the limiting factor.

From these, the correct statements are

(a) 1, 3 (b) 1, 4 (c) 2,3 (d) 2, 4

34. Consider the following statements :

Modern alternators are designed for large air gap to have

1. large inherent regulation
2. very stable parallel operation
3. higher stability limit
4. sinusoidal m.m.f. distribution

Which of these statements are correct?

(a) 1, 2 and 3 (b) 2, 3 and 4 (c) 1, 2 and 4 (d) 1, 3 and 4

35. A single-phase, 2000 V alternator has armature resistance and reactance of 0.8 Ω and 4.94 Ω respectively. The voltage regulation of the alternator at 100 A load at 0.8 leading power factor is

(a) 7% (b) – 8.9% (c) 14% (d) 0%

36. A turbo-alternator set feeds power to a 3-phase constant-voltage, constant-frequency bus. If the steam supply to the set is cut off, then the set will

(a) continue to run at rated speed in the same direction
(b) continue to run at a reduced speed in the same direction
(c) run at rated speed in the reversed direction
(d) come to stop

37. Consider the following statements for lagging power-factor load :

1. In a cylindrical-rotor synchronous machine (CRSM), armature reaction flux ϕ_a is in phase with armature current I_a
2. In a salient-pole synchronous machine (SPSM), armature reaction m.m.f. F_a is in phase with I_a
3. In a SPSM, ϕ_a is in phase with I_a
4. In a CRSM, ϕ_a lags I_a
5. In a SPSM, ϕ_a lags F_a

From these, the correct statements are

(a) 1, 2 and 3 (b) 2, 4 and 5 (c) 1, 2 and 4 (d) 1, 2 and 5

38. A 3-phase cylindrical-rotor synchronous generator, with its armature resistance and leakage reactance being neglected, is synchronized to an infinite bus and its field excitation is kept constant therafter. Now the machine is loaded by supplying mechanical input to the shaft so that the load angle δ reaches a value of 60°. Under this condition, the operating pf would be

(a) 0.866 leading (b) 0.866 lagging (c) 0.5 leading (d) 0.5 lagging

39. A 100 MW water-turbine is coupled to 125 MVA, 3-phase alternator rated for 0.8 lagging power-factor operation. The losses of the alternator are negligible. For delivering a load of 90 MW at 0.5 power factor lagging, consider the following statements :

1. The set cannot deliver the load
2. The alternator will be overloaded
3. The turbine will be overloaded
4. The turbine will not be overloaded
5. The alternator will not be overloaded
6. The set can deliver the load.

From these, the correct statements are

(a) 4, 5 and 6 (b) 1, 2 and 4
(c) 1, 2 and 3 (d) 3, 5 and 6

40. The phasor diagram of a synchronous machine connected to an infinite bus is shown in Fig. C.69. The machine is acting as a

(a) generator and operating at a lagging p.f.
(b) generator and operating at a leading p.f.
(c) motor and operating at a leading p.f.
(d) motor and operating at lagging p.f.

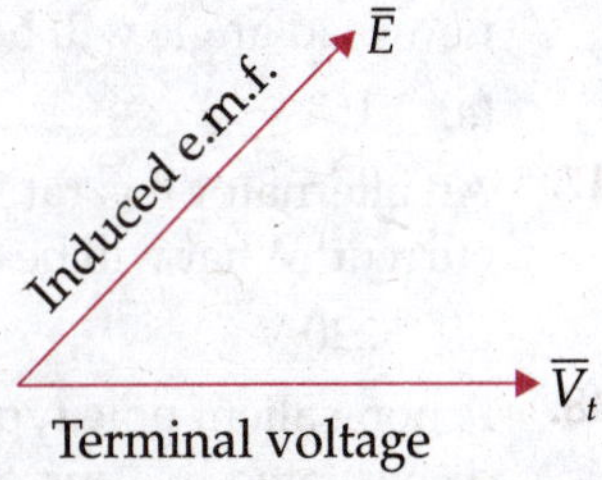

Fig C.69

41. A star-connected synchronous generator has synchronous impedance of 0 + j 5.0 Ω. It delivers a zero p.f. leading current of 20 A at 400 V. Its excitation e.m.f. is

(a) $400 + j\sqrt{3} \times 100$ (b) $400 - j\sqrt{3} \times 100$ (c) $400 - \sqrt{3} \times 100$ (d) $400 + \sqrt{3} \times 100$

42. The torque angle of a synchronous machine operating from a constant voltage bus, is usually defined as the space angle between *[GATE, 1992]*

(a) rotor m.m.f. wave and stator m.m.f. wave

(b) rotor m.m.f. wave and resultant flux-density wave

(c) stator m.m.f. wave and resultant flux-density wave

(d) stator m.m.f. wave and resultant m.m.f. wave

43. A 3-phase synchronous motor with negligible losses is connected to the supply at rated frequency and constant terminal voltage V_t. The induced e.m.f. of the motor is designated as E_f. If the motor is now gradually loaded to its rated power, adjusting its excitation to obtain, say 0.8 lagging p.f. operation, then E_f phasor would be

(a) less than V_t phasor and also lead V_t-phasor

(b) greater than V_t phasor and also lead V_t-phasor

(c) less than V_t phasor and also lag V_t-phasor

(d) greater than V_t-phasor and also lag V_t- phasor

44. Fig. C.70 depicts the load characteristics of an isolated 3-phase alternator, running at constant speed. Match the following sets of operating conditions with the given characteristics. Disregard the effects of saliency, saturation and stator resistance *[GATE, 1992]*

(a) Constant excitation and non-zero leading p.f.

(b) Constant excitation and zero p.f. leading

(c) Constant terminal voltage and zero p.f. leading

(d) Constant terminal voltage and non-zero leading p.f.

Ans. $a \rightarrow$, $b \rightarrow$, $c \rightarrow$, $d \rightarrow$

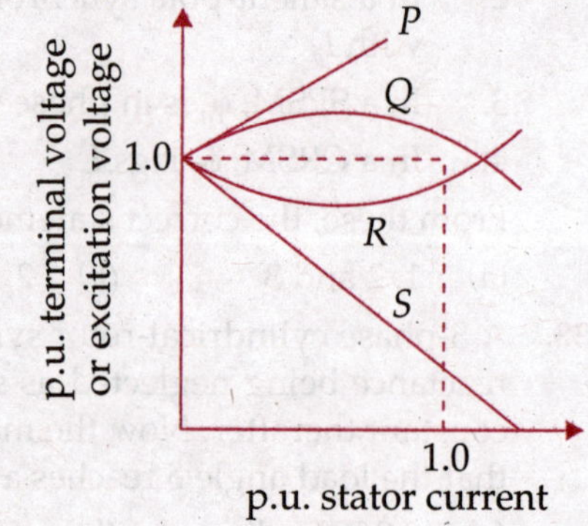

Fig C.70

45. A 3-phase synchronous generator, with negligible armature resistance, operates at a lagging p.f. and delivers constant power to an infinite bus. If its excitation is increased, then (δ = power angle and cos θ = power factor)

(a) δ decreases and cos θ tends to become unity

(b) δ decreases and cos θ tends to become more lagging

(c) δ increases and cos θ tends to become unity

(d) δ increases and cos θ tends to become more lagging

46. A synchronous motor with negligible armature resistance runs at a load angle of 20° at rated frequency. If supply frequency is increased by 10%, keeping other parameters constant, the new load angle will be

(a) 16° (b) 18° (c) 20° (d) 22°

47. An alternator has rated field current of 2 A. It develops 220 V at rated speed for 1 A exciting current. What will be the terminal voltage at rated speed and rated field current at no load?

(a) 220 V (b) 420 V (c) 440 V (d) 480 V

48. A non-salient pole type of 3-phase, 50 Hz, 415 V, 4-pole synchronous motor on rated full load draws rated line current at 0.9 p.f. lead. Under these conditions, the ratio of pull-out torque to the developed torque on full-load is 2.5. The measurable torque angle will be

(a) 23.56° (b) 20° (c) 30° (d) 25.84°

49. A synchronous motor on load draws a current at a leading p.f. angle ϕ. If the internal p.f. angle, which is the phase angle between the excitation e.m.f. and the current in the time-phasor diagram, is ψ, then the air-gap excitation m.m.f. lags the armature m.m.f. by

[GATE, 1995]

(a) ψ (b) $\frac{\pi}{2} + \psi$ (c) $\frac{\pi}{2} - \psi$ (d) $\psi + \phi$

50. A 3-phase, 400 V, 50 Hz, synchronous motor is operating with a load angle 25°. If load on the motor is doubled, keeping other parameters constant, the new load angle will be

(a) 50° (b) 51.5° (c) 53.4° (d) 57.7°

51. A cylindrical-rotor synchronous motor, with negligible armature resistance, operates at

1. unity p.f. if $E_f \cos \delta = V_t$
2. lagging p.f. if $E_f \cos \delta > V_t$
3. lagging p.f. if $E_f \cos \delta < V_t$
4. zero p.f. leading if $E_f > V_t$
5. zero p.f. lagging if $E_f > V_t$

From these, the correct answer is

(a) 1, 3, 4 (b) 1, 2, 4 (c) 1, 3, 5 (d) 1, 2, 5

52. In a cylindrical-rotor synchronous motor, if E_f = excitation e.m.f. and V_t = terminal voltage, then it is possible to have

1. $E_f = V_t$
2. $E_f > V_t$
3. $E_f < V_t$ just like a D.C. motor
4. E_f ahead of V_t
5. E_f behind V_t

From these, the correct answer is

(a) 1, 2, 3, 4 and 5 (b) 1, 3, 4 and 5 (c) 3 and 5 (d) 1, 2, 3 and 5

53. A synchronous motor operates at 0.8 p.f. lagging. If the field current of the motor is continuously increased :

1. the p.f. decreases upto a certain value of field current and thereafter it increases
2. the armature current increases upto a certain value of field current and thereafter it decreases
3. the power factor increases upto a certain value of field current and thereafter it decreases
4. the armature current decreases upto a certain value of field current and thereafter it increases

From these, the correct answer is

(a) 1, 2 (b) 3, 4 (c) 1, 3 (d) 2, 4

54. A synchronous machine is floating on an infinite bus at no load. If its excitation is varied, then it will operate as (assume $r_a = 0$),

1. an alternator with $E_f < V_t$ at z p.f. leading
2. an alternator with $E_f < V_t$ at z p.f. lagging
3. as a motor with $E_f > V_t$ at z p.f. leading
4. as a motor with $E_f > V_t$ at z p.f. lagging
5. as an alternator with $E_f > V_t$ at z p.f. lagging
6. as an a motor with $E_f < V_t$ at z p.f. lagging

From these, the correct answer is

(a) 1, 3, 6 (b) 1, 3, 5, 6 (c) 2, 4, 5, 6 (d) 2, 3, 5, 6

55. A turbogenerator connected to an infinite bus is operating at 0.8 p.f. lagging. If its excitation is increased, then it would

1. feed more leading kVAr to the bus
2. feed more lagging kVAr to the bus
3. feed more real power to the bus
4. start operating at p.f. < 0.8

From these, the correct answer is

(a) 2, 4 (b) 1, 3, 4 (c) 1, 4 (d) 2, 3, 4

56. A cylindrical-rotor synchronous machine is delivering a constant load. When its excitation is varied (δ = load angle, θ = p.f. angle and armature circuit resistance = 0), then

(a) $E_f \sin\delta$ = constant and $I_a \sin\theta$ = constant

(b) $E_f \cos\delta$ = constant and $I_a \cos\theta$ = constant

(c) $E_f \cos\delta$ = constant and $I_a \sin\theta$ = constant

(d) $E_f \sin\delta$ = constant and $I_a \cos\theta$ = constant

57. A cylindrical-rotor alternator on load draws a current at a leading pf angle θ and with an internal p.f. angle ψ. Under this operating condition, electrical angle between field axis and armature-reaction axis is

(a) $90 + \psi$ (b) $90 + \theta$ (c) $90 - \theta$ (d) $90 - \psi$

58. A synchronous machine is operating at constant load and at unity power factor. If its excitation is increased, then it operates as

1. a generator at a leading p.f.
2. a motor at a leading p.f.
3. a generator at a lagging p.f.
4. a motor at a lagging p.f.
5. exporter of reactive power
6. absorber of reactive power

From these, the correct answer is

(a) 2, 4, 6 (b) 1, 2, 5 (c) 2, 3, 5 (d) 3, 4, 6

59. Which of the following limits the reactive power output of a synchronous generator?

1. Armature current
2. Field current
3. Load angle
4. Prime-mover input *[I.A.S., 1993]*

Select the correct answer using the codes given below :

Codes :

(a) 1 and 2 (b) 2 and 3 (c) 3 and 4 (d) 1 and 4

60. A synchronous motor, fed from infinite bus, is delivering half full-load. If an increase in field current causes an increase in the armature current, then the motor will *[I.A.S., 1994]*

(a) deliver reactive power and active power to the bus

(b) absorb reactive power and active power from the bus

(c) absorb reactive power from the bus and deliver active power to the bus

(d) deliver reactive power to the bus and absorb active power from the bus

61. Which of the following will change in a 3-phase synchronous motor, as a consequence of excitation variations? *[I.A.S., 1996]*

1. Pull-out torque
2. Torque angle
3. Magnitude and power factor of stator current
4. Output power

Select the correct answer using the codes given below :

Codes :

(a) 1 and 3 (b) 2 and 4 (c) 2, 3 and 4 (d) 1, 2 and 3

62. Power factor of a synchronous motor varies when

1. applied voltage is varied
2. field excitation is varied
3. load is changed
4. supply frequency is changed

From these, the correct answer is

(a) 1, 2, 3, 4 (b) 2, 3 (c) 2 only (d) 2, 3, 4

63. A 3-phase synchronous motor, connected to an infinite bus, is operating with normal excitation. With decrease in load,

1. armature current decreases
2. p.f. becomes lagging
3. p.f. becomes leading
4. load angle decreases
5. reactive power flows from motor to bus
6. reactive power flows from bus to the motor

From these, the correct answer is

(a) 1, 2, 4 (b) 3, 4, 5 (c) 2, 4, 5 (d) 1, 2, 4, 6

64. Consider the following statements :

1. A grid-connected induction generator always supplies leading reactive power to the bus
2. An overexcited synchronous motor draws current at a lagging p.f.
3. An underexcited synchronous generator connected to an infinite bus works at a leading p.f.
4. The torque angle of a synchronous machine is the angle bewteen the excitation voltage and the gap voltage

Of these statements :

(a) 1 and 2 are correct (b) 3 and 4 are correct

(c) 1, 3 and 4 are correct (d) 1, 2, 3 and 4 are correct

65. A cylindrical-rotor synchronous machine operates as a

1. generator at lagging p.f. if $(E_f \cos \delta + I_a r_a \cos \theta) > V_t$
2. generator at leading p.f. if $(E_f \cos \delta + I_a r_a \cos \theta) < V_t$
3. motor at leading p.f. if $(E_f \cos \delta + I_a r_a \cos \theta) > V_t$
4. motor at unity p.f. if $(E_f \cos \delta - I_a r_a \cos \theta) = V_t$
5. generator and also generating reactive power if $(E_f \cos \delta + I_a r_a \cos \theta) > V_t$

From these, the correct answer is

(a) 1, 3, 4 (b) 2, 3, 5 (c) 2, 3, 4 (d) 1, 3, 5

66. The two-reaction phasor diagram of a salient-pole synchronous generator is considered, where

I_a = armature current per phase,

x_{al} = armature leakage reactance per phase

X_d = *d*-axis synchronous reactance,

X_q = *q*-axis synchronous reactance

V_t = generator terminal voltage, taken as reference

The voltage in phase with quadrature axis will be the phasor sum of

(a) $V_t + I_a r_a + I_a x_{al}$ (b) $V_t + I_a r_a + I_a X_d$

(c) $V_t + I_a r_a + I_a X_q$ (d) $V_t + I_a r_a + I_a (X_d + X_q)$

67. A synchronous motor is operating on no load at unity power factor. If the field current is increased, the p.f. will become

(a) leading and the current will decrease (b) lagging and the current will increase

(c) lagging and the current will decrease (d) leading and the current will increase

68. In a salient-pole synchronous machine,

(a) both I_d and I_q are in phase with E_f

(b) I_q is in phase with E_f and I_d is at 90° to E_f

(c) I_d is in phase with E_f and I_q is at 90° to E_f

(d) both I_d and I_q are at 90° to E_f

69. For a salient-pole synchronous machine with negligible armature resistance,

1. $E_f = V_t \cos\delta + I_d X_d$; generator at a lagging p.f.
2. $E_f = V_t \cos\delta - I_d X_d$; motor at a lagging p.f.
3. $E_f = V_t \cos\delta + I_d X_d$; motor at a leading p.f.
4. $E_f = V_t \cos\delta - I_d X_d$; generator at a leading p.f.

From above, the correct statements are

(a) 1, 3 (b) 2, 4 (c) 1, 2 (d) 1, 2, 3, 4

70. The power-angle characteristic of a salient-pole synchronous machine contains a second harmonic terms, because

(a) the air-gap flux density has a second harmonic component

(b) the frequency has a second harmonic component

(c) of the slot harmonics

(d) of the difference in reluctance of air gap in the direct and quadrature axes.

71. In salient-pole machines, the air-gap length under the poles is not kept constant so as to

(a) obtain a sinusoidal distribution of the main field flux

(b) obtain a sinusoidal distribution of the armature m.m.f.

(c) minimise the effect of armature m.m.f. on the main field flux

(d) obtain better cooling.

72. Consider the following statements regarding the cylindrical-rotor synchronous machine :

1. Phasor addition of stator and rotor m.m.fs. is possible because both are stationary with resect to each other
2. Armature leakage reactance and armature reaction m.m.f. can be computed from occ and one point on z p.f.c.
3. Accurate value of voltage regulation is given by zero p.f. method
4. Armature leakage reactance and armature reaction m.m.f. can be obtained from occ and two points on z p.f.c.
5. Field m.m.f. required to circulate rated armature current during short-circuit test is equal to armature reaction m.m.f.
6. For z p.f. lagging load on alternator, magnitude of terminal voltage V_t = magnitude of $(V_t + I_a r_a)$.

From above, the correct statements are

(a) 1, 2, 3, 5 (b) 1, 3, 4, 6 (c) 1, 2, 3, 6 (d) 1, 3, 4, 5, 6

73. For a synchronous machine, the amplitudes of electromagnetic and reluctance powers are respectively P_1 and P_2. The respective values of synchronous and synchronizing powers for round-rotor machine A and salient-pole machine B are as under :

(a) $A : P_1 \sin \delta, P_1 \cos \delta \,;\, B : P_1 + P_2 \sin 2\delta, P_1 \cos \delta + P_2 \cos 2\delta$

(b) $A : P_1 \cos \delta, P_1 \sin \delta \,;\, B : P_1 \sin \delta + P_2 \sin 2\delta, P_1 \cos \delta + P_2 \cos 2\delta$

(c) $A : P_1 \cos \delta, P_1 \sin \delta \,;\, B : P_1 \sin \delta + P_2 \sin 2\delta, P_1 \cos \delta + 2P_2 \cos 2\delta$

(d) $A : P_1 \sin \delta, P_1 \cos \delta \,;\, B : P_1 \sin \delta + P_2 \sin 2\delta, P_1 \cos \delta + 2P_2 \cos 2\delta$

74. The maximum power in cylindrical and salient-pole synchronous machines is obtained respectively at load angles of

(a) 90°, 90° (b) < 90°, 90° (c) 90°, < 90° (d) > 90°, 90°

75. A synchronous motor, fed from an infinite bus, is working at half-full load. If an increase in its field current causes a reduction in the armature current, then the motor is

(a) delivering reactive power to the bus at leading p.f.

(b) delivering reactive power to the bus at lagging p.f.

(c) absorbing reactive power from the bus at leading p.f.

(d) absorbing reactive power from the bus at lagging p.f.

76. A synchronous generator, connected to an infinite bus, is working at half-full load. If an increase in its field current causes a reduction in the armature current, then the generator is

(a) delivering reactive power to the bus at leading p.f.

(b) delivering reactive power to the bus at lagging p.f.

(c) absorbing reactive power from the bus at leading p.f.

(d) absorbing reactive power from the bus at lagging p.f.

77. A 3-phase synchronous motor is operating at a load angle 20° and with excitation voltage equal to applied voltage. The synchronous reactance drop in terms of excitation voltage will be

(a) 69.46% (b) 34.73% (c) 32.9% (d) 38.2%

78. A 3-phase synchronous motor, connected to an infinite bus, operates at a leading p.f. For constant load torque, if excitation is increased,

(a) load angle δ and power-factor angle θ both decrease

(b) δ and θ both increase

(c) δ increases but θ decreases

(d) δ decreases but θ increases

79. A synchronous generator connected to an infinite bus is overexcited. Considering only the reactive power, from the point of view of the system, the machine acts is [GATE, 1998]

(a) a capacitor (b) an inductor (c) a resistor (d) as RL circuit

80. In a salient-pole synchronous machine, load angle δ can be obtained from a knowledge of [θ = p.f. angle and $r_a = 0$]

(a) V_t, I_a, X_d, θ (b) V_t, I_a, X_q, θ (c) $V_t, I_a, X_d, X_q, \theta$ (d) E_f, I_a, X_q, θ

81. A salient-pole synchronous generator delivers about 20% of rated power to an infinite bus. If its field excitation fails,

(a) the machine will deliver reduced active power to the bus

(b) the machine will deliver reduced active and reactive power to the bus

(c) the machine will absorb reactive power from the bus but will deliver reduced active power

(d) the machine will run as an induction motor and will absorb both active and reactive power from the bus

82. In a round-rotor alternator, reactive power is maximum at a load angle of

(a) 90° (b) 180° (c) 0° (d) 45°

83. In a cylindrical-rotor alternator, maximum reactive power output is

(a) $\frac{3V_t}{X_s}(E_f - V_t)$ (b) $\frac{3V_t}{X_s}(V_t - E_f)$ (c) $\frac{3E_t}{X_s}(E_f - V_t)$ (d) $\frac{3E_f}{X_s}(V_t - E_f)$

84. Under the conditions of maximum active power output, in a round-rotor alternator, the reactive power output is

(a) $\frac{3V_tE_f}{X_s}$ (b) $-\frac{3E_f^2}{X_s}$ (c) $-\frac{3V_t^2}{X_s}$ (d) $\frac{3V_t^2}{X_s}$

85. Under the conditions of maximum load on a cylindrical-rotor synchronous motor, the reactive power input to the motor is

(a) $-\frac{3V_tE_f}{X_s}$ (b) $-\frac{3E_f^2}{X_s}$ (c) $-\frac{3V_t^2}{X_s}$ (d) $\frac{3V_t^2}{X_s}$

86. In modern large sized synchronous machines, the synchronous impedance and operating load angle are respectively

(a) 0.2, 40 (b) 0.6, 30° (c) 1, 40° (d) 0.5, 40°

87. Lists I and II pertain to the operation of salient-pole synchronous machine at rated speed. Match the two lists using the codes given below the lists

List I (*from the phasor diagram*)	*List II* (*Operating as*)
A. $V_t \cos\delta < E_f$	1. generator at lagging p.f.
B. $V_t \cos\delta > E_f$	2. motor at lagging p.f.
	3. generator at leading p.f.
	4. motor at leading p.f.

Codes :

	A	B		A	B
(a)	1, 2	3, 4	(b)	1, 3	2, 4
(c)	2, 3	1, 4	(d)	1, 4	2, 3

88. A cylindrical-rotor synchronous motor is switched on to the supply with its field windings shorted on themselves. It will [GATE, 1996]

(a) not start

(b) start but not run at synchronous speed

(c) start as an induction motor and then run at synchronous speed

(d) start and run as a synchronous motor

89. The rotor oscillations of a synchronous motor about its new equilibrium position, corresponding to new load suddenly thrown off or suddenly applied, is called

1. hunting 2. crawling 3. phase swinging

From these, the correct answer is

(a) 1 only (b) 1 and 2 (c) 1 and 3 (d) 3 only

90. During a disturbance on a synchronous machine, the rotor swings from A to B before finally settling down to a steady state at point C on the power angle curve. The speed of the machine during oscillations is synchronous at point (s). *[GATE, 1996]*

(a) A and B (b) A and C (c) B and C (d) only at C

91. When a 3-phase synchronous motor is running at synchronous speed, the damper winding produces

(a) damping torque (b) eddy-current torque
(c) torque aiding the devloped torque (d) no torque

92. Damper winding is provided in a polyphase synchronous motor in order to

1. dampen out the noise of the machine 2. prevent hunting
3. provide a starting torque
4. provide a cylindrical structure to reduce wind friction

From these, the correct answer is

(a) 2 only (b) 1, 2 and 4 (c) 2, 3 and 4 (d) 2 and 3

93. A synchronous motor is running from an infinite bus of voltage V_1 in steady state at about 50% of its rated load with a power angle δ_1 between V_1 and E_f (induced voltage). The load is suddenly decreased to 25%. E_f attains its new steady-state power angle δ_2 with V_1 by initially

(a) falling behind and making a complete rotation
(b) advancing and making a complete rotation
(c) falling behind, followed by oscillation about δ_2
(d) advancing, followed by oscillation about δ_2

94. A 3-phase synchronous motor connected to an infinite bus is operating at half full-load with normal excitation. When the load on synchronous motor is suddenly increased

(a) its speed will first decrease and then become synchronous
(b) its speed will first increase and then become synchronous
(c) its speed will fluctuate around synchronous speed and then become synchronous
(d) its speed will remain unchanged

95. In synchronous machines, damper windings are used to

1. help in starting the motor 2. run it as an induction motor
3. help in reducing the hunting 4. increase efficiency
5. provide induction motor torque at subsynchronous speed
6. provide induction motor torque at supersynchronous speed

From these, the correct statements are

(a) 1, 3, 5, 6 (b) 1, 2, 3, 4, 5 (c) 1, 2, 3, 6 (d) 1, 3, 5

96. Function of damper bars in a synchronous machine is to

(a) prevent rotor from running at subsynchronous speed
(b) prevent rotor from running at supersynchronous speed
(c) prevent rotor from running at synchronous speed
(d) reduce the rotor oscillations about the operating point

97. A synchronous motor having a synchronous speed of 1500 r.p.m. slows down to 1490 r.p.m. due to sudden load on the motor shaft. Assuming a south pole on the stator near the damper

bars labelled 1, 2, 3 and 4 as shown in Fig. C.71, the direction of induced force on conductor 3 is

(a) F_1 (b) F_2 (c) F_3 (d) F_4

98. A salient-pole synchronous motor is running with normal excitation. If the excitation is reduced to zero

(a) it becomes an induction motor (b) it becomes a reluctance motor
(c) it remains a synchronous motor (d) the motor would stop

99. If the excitation is kept constant in an alternator, then the excitation voltage variation with speed would be

(a) first linear and then curved upwards
(b) first linear and then horizontal
(c) linear
(d) first curved and then linear

100. A salient-pole synchronous motor is running clockwise at no load. If its field current is reduced to zero and then reversed, then

(a) the motor would stop
(b) the motor would run in the reversed direction
(c) the rotor slips by one pole-pitch and continues running at synchronous speed
(d) the rotor slips by one pole-pitch and speed would be less than synchronous speed

101. A salient-pole synchronous motor runs under steady-state conditions at no load with armature current I_a. If the field circuit gets open-circuited, then

(a) the motor stops and I_a becomes very high
(b) it continues to run at the same speed and I_a increases
(c) it continues to run at the same speed and I_a decreases
(d) it runs at a slower speed as an induction motor and I_a increases.

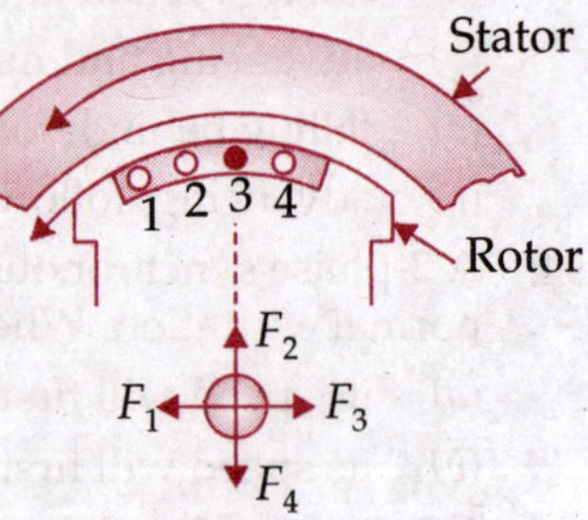

Fig C.71

102. A single-3-phase alternator in the laboratory is not run at synchronous speed. It would produce no effect on its

(a) occ (b) scc (c) occ and scc (d) z pfc

103. For providing a load power of 100 MW at 0.8 p.f., ratings of alternator, its prime-mover, boiler and the transformer should respectively be

(a) 100 MW, 125 MVA, 125 MA, 125 MVA
(b) 125 MVA, 100 MW, 100 MW, 125 MVA
(c) 125 MVA, 100 MW, 125 MVA, 125 MVA
(d) 125 MVA, 125 MVA, 100 MW, 125 MVA

104. An isolated 3-phase alternator delivers a unity p.f. rated load at terminal voltage $V_t = 11$ kV for a field current of 20 A. For maintaining constant V_t, the field current required for rated loads of 0.8 p.f. lag and 0.8 p.f. lead would respectively be

(a) > 20 A, < 20 A (b) > 20 A, > 20 A (c) < 20 A, < 20 A (d) < 20 A, > 20 A

105. The name plate of an alternator indicates an operating p.f. of 0.85. The nature of this p.f. is

(a) lagging so that excitation e.m.f. E_f > terminal voltage V_t and alternator absorbs reactive power Q

(b) lagging so that $E_f > V_t$ and alternator delivers Q
(c) leading so that $E_f < V_t$ and alternator absorbs Q
(d) leading so that $E_f < V_t$ and alternator delivers Q

106. A synchronous motor and an alternator are delivering about 5% of their rated power at unity p.f. If these machines are loaded to their rated capacity, then their armature currents
(a) decrease, motor operates at lagging p.f. and alternator at leading p.f.
(b) increase, motor operates at a leading p.f. and alternator at lagging p.f.
(c) increase, both operate at lagging p.f.s.
(d) increase, motor operates at lagging p.f. and alternator at leading p.f.

107. An alternator and a synchronous motor of the salient-pole type are operating at leading p.f.s. Their excitation e.m.f. E_f is respectively given by
(a) $V_t \cos\delta - X_d I_d$, $V_t \cos\delta + X_d I_d$
(b) $V_t \cos\delta + r_a I_q - X_d I_d$, $V_t \cos\delta + I_a r_a + X_d I_d$
(c) $V_t \cos\delta - r_a I_q - X_d I_d$, $V_t \cos\delta + r_a I_q + X_d I_d$
(d) $V_t \cos\delta + r_a I_q - X_d I_d$, $V_t \cos\delta - r_a I_q + X_d I_d$

108. Slip test is performed to determine
(a) slip
(b) direct-axis reactance and quadrature-axis reactance
(c) positive sequence reactance and negative sequence reactance
(d) sub-transient reactance

109. While conducting a 'slip' test for the determination of direct and quadrature axis synchronous reactances X_d and X_q of a salient-pole machine, the rotor of the machine is run with a slip 's' and the stator supply frequency 'f'. The frequency of
1. voltage induced across open field terminals
2. envelope of the armature terminal voltage
3. envelope of the armature current
4. armature current

will be respectively
(a) sf, sf, sf and f
(b) sf, f, sf and f
(c) f, sf, f and f
(d) f, (1 – s) f, (2 – s) f and f

110. Squirrel-cage bars placed in the rotor pole faces of a 3-phase alternator help in reducing the hunting
1. above synchronous speed only
2. below synchronous speed only
3. at synchronous speed only

From above, the correct answer is
(a) 1 and 2
(b) 1 and 3
(c) 2 and 3
(d) only 3

111. A synchronous machine, connected to an infinite bus, is working at a certain load angle. A sudden increment in load angle causes synchronizing power to flow from
1. infinite bus to motor
2. motor to infinite bus
3. infinite bus to generator
4. generator to infinite bus

From these, the correct answer is
(a) 1, 4
(b) 2, 4
(c) 2, 3
(d) 1, 3

112. In a slip test on a synchronous machine, match the following :

	Armature flux	Voltage in field winding	Armature current	Reactance
1.	Maximum	Maximum	Maximum	X_q
2.	Maximum	Maximum	Minimum	X_d
3.	Maximum	Zero	Minimum	X_d
4.	Minimum	Maximum	Minimum	X_d
5.	Minimum	Maximum	Maximum	X_q

From these, the correct answer is

(a) 1, 4 (b) 2, 5 (c) 3, 4 (d) 3, 5

113. In a slip test on a salient-pole synchronous machine, the e.m.f. induced in the field winding is:

1. zero for X_d
2. zero for X_q
3. maximum positive for X_q
4. maximum negative for X_q
5. maximum positivie for X_d

From these, the correct answer is

(a) 1, 3, 4 (b) 1, 3, 5 (c) 1, 4, 5 (d) 2, 3, 4

114. A synchronous condenser is

(a) an over-excited synchronous motor driving a mechanical load
(b) an ordinary capacitor bank
(c) an over-excited synchronous motor with no shaft extension
(d) an over-excited synchronous motor without mechanical load

115. A 3-phase overexcited synchronous motor is installed near a 3-phase induction motor (IM) with a view to improve the power factor. With this installation,

(a) IM p.f. improves and its current decreases
(b) IM p.f. does not change but its current decreases
(c) IM p.f. improves but its current does not change
(d) IM p.f. and its current do not change, p.f. of the combination improves.

116. A 3-phase induction motor draws 1000 kVA at a p.f. of 0.8 lag. A synchronous condenser is connected in parallel to draw an additional 750 kVA at 0.6 p.f. lead. The p.f. of the total load supplied by the mains is

(a) unity (b) 0.707 lag (c) 0.707 lead (d) zero

117. A synchronous motor operating at rated voltage draws 1.0 p.u. current at 1.0 p.f. The machine parameters are : synchronous reactance 1.0 p.u. ; armature resistance, negligible. Apart from supplying this rated power, if the motor has to supply an addional leading reactive power of 0.8 p.u., then the field current has to be increased by

(a) 42% (b) 46% (c) 52% (d) 60%

118. While starting a 3-phase synchronous motor, its field winding should be

(a) kept open (b) short-circuited
(c) connected to a D.C. source (d) none of these

119. An ideal synchronous motor has no starting torque because the

(a) rotor is made up of salient poles
(b) relative velocity between the stator and rotor m.m.fs. is zero
(c) relative velocity between the stator and rotor m.m.fs. is not zero
(d) rotor winding is highly inductive

120. During the starting of a 3-phase synchronous motor by damper bars, the field winding is usually short circuited so that starting torque is equal to

(a) induction motor torque

(b) induction motor torque plus an additional torque produced by short-circuited field winding

(c) electromagnetic torque produced by the interaction of armature and field-winding m.m.fs.

(d) reluctance torque due to rotor saliency

121. In an alternator, no-load rotational loss and short-circuit load loss are respectively made up of

(a) [Friction, windage (FW) plus open-circuit core loss (CL)] ; [stray load loss (SLL) plus open-circuit loss]

(b) [FW] loss ; [SLL plus direct load loss (DLL)]

(c) [FW plus field circuit loss] ; [SLL plus DLL]

(d) [FW plus CL] ; [SLL plus ohmic loss in armature winding]

122. In synchronous machines, the stray load losses are caused by

1. eddy current in the armature conductors
2. armature leakage flux as hysteresis loss in teeth, core, end plates etc.
3. skin effect in the armature conductors
4. armature leakage flux as eddy-current loss in teeth, core, and plates etc.

From these, the correct answer is

(a) 1, 2, 4 (b) 1, 3, 4 (c) 1, 2, 3, 4 (d) 2, 3, 4

123. Polyphase synchronous motor is preferred over polyphase induction motor for a load requiring

(a) 600 kW at 3000 r.p.m. (b) 600 kW at 1500 r.p.m.

(c) 600 kW at 1000 r.p.m. (d) 600 kW at 500 r.p.m.

124. For driving a 750 kW compressor, a synchronous motor is preferred because :

1. it will result in lower noise and vibration
2. it will help attain compressor pressure faster
3. of the possibility of operating at better p.f.
4. the starting torque requirement is low

Of these statements

(a) 1 and 2 are correct (b) 2 and 3 are correct

(c) 1, 2 and 3 are correct (d) 3 and 4 are correct

125. Match List I with List II and select the correct answer using the codes given below the lists :

List I (*Synchronous machines*)	*List II* (*Phasor diagrams*)
A. Underexcited alternator	1. 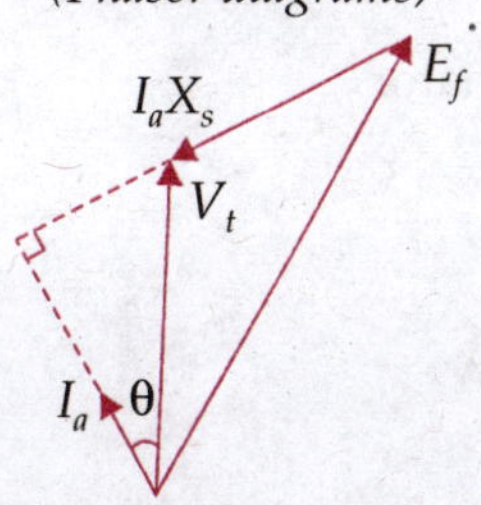

B. Underexcited synchronous motor 2.

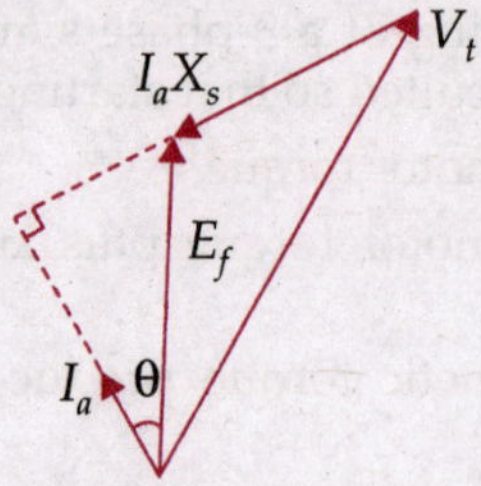

C. Overexcited alternator 3.

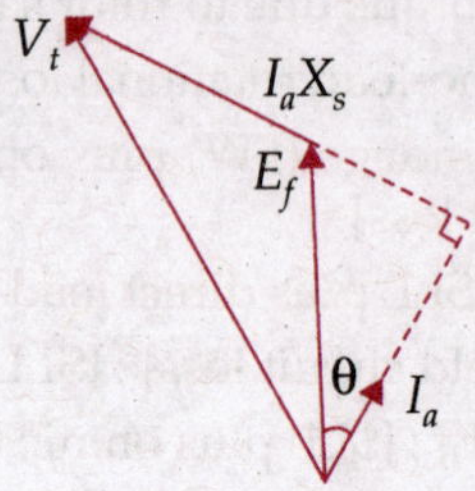

D. Overexcited synchronous motor 4.

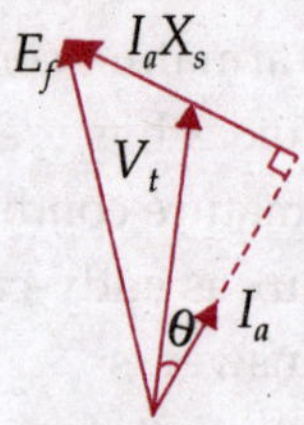

Codes :

	A	B	C	D		A	B	C	D
(a)	1	2	3	4	(b)	2	3	4	1
(c)	2	3	1	4	(d)	3	2	4	1

126. Match List I with List II and select the correct answer using the codes given below the lists :

List I *(Synchronous machine operation)* — *List II* *(Phaor diagrams)*

A. At the moment of synchronizing 1.

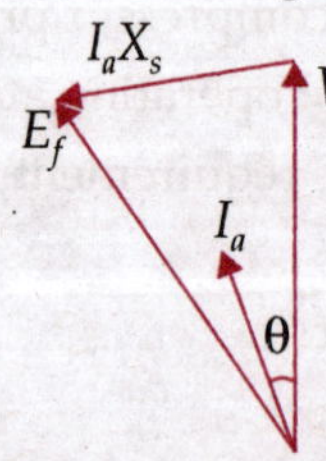

B. As an alternator 2.

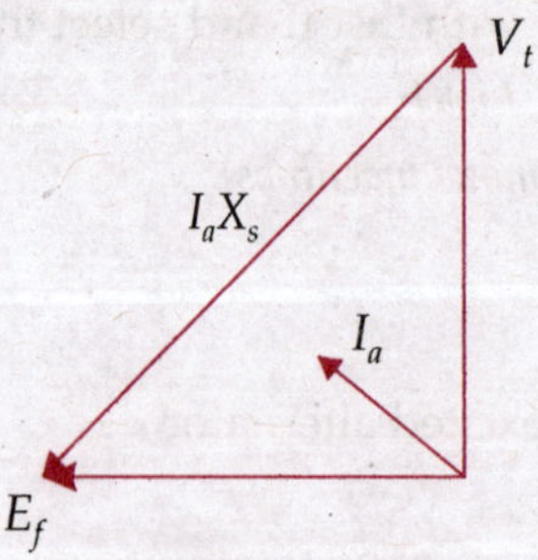

C. As a synchronous motor 3.

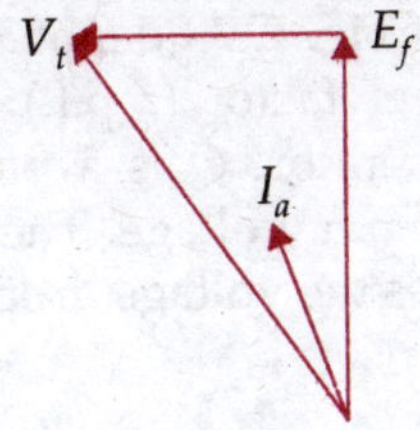

D. At the moment of losing synchronism 4.

Codes :

	A	B	C	D		A	B	C	D
(a)	4	3	2	1	(b)	4	1	2	3
(c)	3	4	1	2	(d)	4	1	3	2

127. Consider the following statements regarding the operation of 3-phase synchronous machines depicted in Fig. C.72 *(a)*, *(b)* and *(c)*.

1. Machine of Fig. *(a)* is operating as a synchronous motor at some load
2. Machine of Fig. *(a)* is operating as an alternator at some load
3. Machine of Fig. *(b)* is operating as a synchronous motor at some load
4. Machine of Fig. *(b)* is operating as an alternator at some load
5. Machine of Fig. *(c)* is operating as a synchronous motor at no load
6. Machine of Fig. *(c)* is operating as an alternator at no load

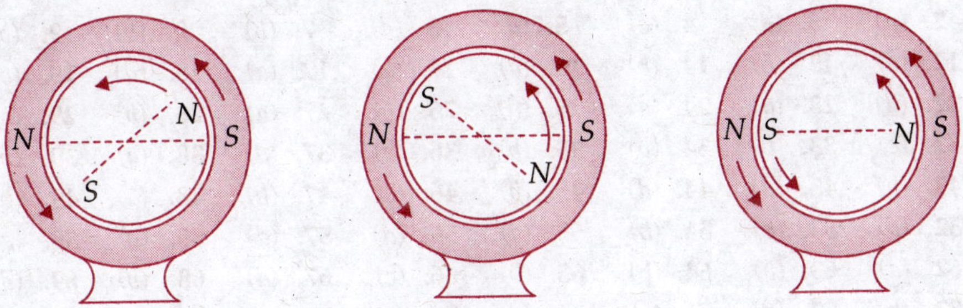

Fig C.72

From these, the correct statements are

(a) 2, 3, 5, 6 *(b)* 1, 4, 5 *(c)* 1, 4, 6 *(d)* 2, 3, 6

128. A stand alone engine driven synchronous generator is feeding a partly inductive load. A capacitor is now connected across the load to completely nullify the inductive current. For this operating condition [GATE, 2003]

(a) the field current and fuel input have to be reduced

(b) the field current and fuel input have to be increased

(c) the field current has to be increased and fuel input left unaltered

(d) the field current has to be reduced and fuel input left unaltered.

129. Curves X and Y in Fig. C.73 denote open circuit and full-load zero power factor (z p.f.) characteristics of a synchronous generator. Q is a point on the z p.f. characteristic at 1.0 p.u. voltage. The vertical distance PQ in Fig. C.73 gives the voltage drop across

[GATE, 2003]

(*a*) synchronous reactance

(*b*) magnetizing reactance

(*c*) Potier reactance

(*d*) leakage reactance

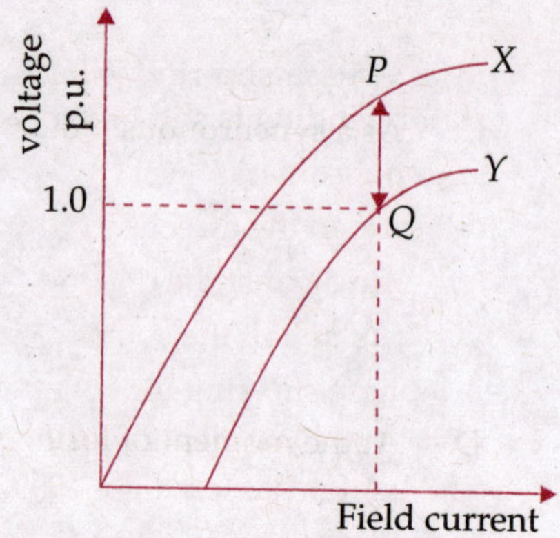

Fig C.73

130. A round-rotor generator with internal voltage $E_1 = 2.0$ p.u. and $X = 1.1$ p.u. is connected to a round rotor synchronous motor with internal voltage $E_2 = 1.3$ p.u. and $X = 1.2$ p.u. The reactance of the line connecting the generator to the motor is 0.5 p.u. When the generator supplies 0.5 p.u. power, the rotor angle difference between the machines will be

[GATE, 2003]

(*a*) 57.42° (*b*) 1° (*c*) 32.58° (*d*) 122.58°

131. A 25 kVA. 400 V, Δ-connected, 3-phase, cylindrical rotor synchronous generator requires a field current of 5 Δ to maintain the rated armature current under short-circuit condition. For the same field current, the open-circuit voltage is 360 V. Neglecting the armature resistance and magnetic saturation, its voltage regulation (in % with respect to terminal voltage), when the generator delivers the rated load at 0.8 p.f. leading, at rated terminal voltage is ....

[GATE, 2017 (2)]

ANSWERS

1. (*b*)	**2.** (*d*)	**3.** (*d*)	**4.** (*c*)	**5.** (*d*)	**6.** (*d*)	**7.** (*b*)	**8.** (*b*)	**9.** (*b*)	**10.** (*a*)
11. (*b*)	**12.** (*a*)	**13.** (*b*)	**14.** (*b*)	**15.** (*a*)	**16.** (*a*)	**17.** (*a*)	**18.** (*d*)	**19.** (*c*)	**20.** (*d*)
21. (*b*)	**22.** (*d*)	**23.** (*a*)	**24.** (*a*)	**25.** (*d*)	**26.** (*c*)	**27.** (*a*)	**28.** (*b*)	**29.** (*a*)	**30.** (*b*)
31. (*c*)	**32.** (*c*)	**33.** (*b*)	**34.** (*b*)	**35.** (*b*)	**36.** (*a*)	**37.** (*d*)	**38.** (*a*)	**39.** (*b*)	**40.** (*b*)
41. (*c*)	**42.** (*b*)	**43.** (*d*)	**44.** (*d*)	**45.** (*b*)	**46.** (*c*)	**47.** (*b*)	**48.** (*a*)	**49.** (*b*)	**50.** (*d*)
51. (*a*)	**52.** (*d*)	**53.** (*b*)	**54.** (*b*)	**55.** (*a*)	**56.** (*d*)	**57.** (*d*)	**58.** (*c*)	**59.** (*a*)	**60.** (*d*)
61. (*d*)	**62.** (*a*)	**63.** (*b*)	**64.** (*b*)	**65.** (*b*)	**66.** (*c*)	**67.** (*d*)	**68.** (*b*)	**69.** (*d*)	**70.** (*d*)
71. (*a*)	**72.** (*b*)	**73.** (*d*)	**74.** (*c*)	**75.** (*d*)	**76.** (*c*)	**77.** (*b*)	**78.** (*d*)	**79.** (*a*)	**80.** (*b*)
81. (*c*)	**82.** (*c*)	**83.** (*a*)	**84.** (*c*)	**85.** (*d*)	**86.** (*c*)	**87.** (*d*)	**88.** (*b*)	**89.** (*c*)	**90.** (*a*)
91. (*d*)	**92.** (*d*)	**93.** (*c*)	**94.** (*c*)	**95.** (*d*)	**96.** (*d*)	**97.** (*a*)	**98.** (*b*)	**99.** (*c*)	**100.** (*c*)
101. (*b*)	**102.** (*b*)	**103.** (*b*)	**104.** (*a*)	**105.** (*b*)	**106.** (*d*)	**107.** (*d*)	**108.** (*b*)	**109.** (*a*)	**110.** (*a*)
111. (*a*)	**112.** (*d*)	**113.** (*a*)	**114.** (*c*)	**115.** (*d*)	**116.** (*a*)	**117.** (*b*)	**118.** (*b*)	**119.** (*c*)	**120.** (*b*)
121. (*d*)	**122.** (*c*)	**123.** (*d*)	**124.** (*c*)	**125.** (*b*)	**126.** (*d*)	**127.** (*a*)	**128.** (*d*)	**129.** (*a*)	**130.** (*c*)
131. – 14.56%.									

POLYPHASE INDUCTION MOTORS

1. In a 3-phase slip-ring induction motor, 3-phase balanced supply is given to the rotor and stator winding is short-circuited. The rotor would
   (a) not run
   (b) run in the direction of rotating field
   (c) run against the direction of rotating field
   (d) run at half the synchronous speed
2. A 3-phase slip-ring induction motor (SRIM) has 4-pole stator and 2-pole rotor. With its stator energised from 50 Hz source, the rotor would run at a no-load speed
   (a) somewhat less than 1500 r.p.m. (b) somewhat less than 3000 r.p.m.
   (c) somewhat less than 2000 r.p.m. (d) of zero r.p.m.
3. The effect of increasing the air-gap length in a 3-phase induction motor (IM) is to
   1. reduce the pulsation loss 2. improve the power factor
   3. reduce the air-gap flux 4. worsen the power factor
   5. reduce the torque 6. increase the efficiency
   From these, the correct statements are
   (a) 1, 4, 5 (b) 1, 3, 4, 5, 6 (c) 2, 3, 5, 6 (d) 1, 3, 4, 5
4. The rotor of an IM cannot run at synchronous speed, because if it did so then
   1. rotor e.m.f. would be zero 2. rotor current would be zero
   3. rotor torque would be zero 4. rotor p.f. would be unity
   5. stator core loss would be zero 6. rotor core loss would be zero
   From these, the correct statements are
   (a) 1, 2, 3, 4, 5 (b) 1, 2, 3, 4, 6 (c) 1, 2, 3, 5 (d) 1, 2, 3, 5, 6
5. A 3-phase 50 Hz squirrel-cage induction motor (SCIM) has its stator rewound for 6 poles without any alteration in the rotor. The motor would now run at a speed
   (a) < 1000 r.p.m. (b) < 1500 r.p.m. (c) < 1200 r.p.m. (d) zero r.p.m.
6. A 3-phase SCIM, designed to operate with stator in star, requires *W* kg of copper for its stator winding. if this motor is rewound with stator in delta, with current and flux densities, kW and voltage ratings remaining the same, then weight of stator copper would be
   (a) $\sqrt{3}$ *W* kg (b) $\frac{1}{\sqrt{3}}$ *W* kg (c) *W* kg
   (d) more or less than *W* kg depending upon other design parameters
7. If the rotor of a 3-phase IM is assumed purely resistive, then electromagnetic torque in the motor is
   (a) minumum with load angle 0° (b) minimum with load angle 90°
   (c) optimum with load angle 90° (d) optimum with load angle 0°
8. If the rotor of a 3-phase IM is assumed inductive, then the electromagnetic torque developed in the motor is
   (a) optimum with load angle $\delta = 0°$ (b) optimum with $\delta = 90°$
   (c) optimum with $\delta = 0°$ (d) zero with $\delta = 180°$
9. A 3-phase, 4-pole, 50 Hz IM runs at a speed of 1440 r.p.m.
   1. Its slip is 0.04

2. Its rotor field rotates at 60 r.p.m. with respect to rotor
3. Its rotor field rotates at 60 r.p.m. with respect to stator field
4. Its rotor runs at a speed of 60 r.p.m. with respect to stator field
5. Its rotor field rotates at a speed of 1500 r.p.m. with respect to stator

From these, the correct statements are

(a) 1, 2, 4, 5 (b) 1, 2, 3, 4, 5 (c) 1, 2, 5 (d) 1, 2, 4

10. The stator of a 3-phase, 4-pole, SRIM is fed from 50 Hz source and its rotor from 30 Hz source. The motor will run at

1. 1500 r.p.m. 2. 900 r.p.m. 3. 600 r.p.m. 4. 2400 r.p.m.
5. 2100 r.p.m.

From these, the correct answer is

(a) 3 only (b) 4 only (c) 1, 2, 5 (d) 3, 4

11. The relative speed between the magnetic fields of stator and rotor under steady-state operation is zero for a

1. D.C. machine 2. 3-phase induction machine
3. 3-phase synchronous generator 4. 3-phase synchronous motor

From these, the correct statements are

(a) 1, 2, 3, and 4 (b) 3 and 4 (c) 2, 3 and 4 (d) 1, 3 and 4

12. The m.m.f. produced by the rotor currents of a 3-phase IM

(a) rotates at the speed of rotor in the air gap
(b) is at standstill with respect to stator m.m.f.
(c) rotates at slip speed with respect to stator m.m.f.
(d) rotates at synchronous speed with respect to rotor

13. If the rotor p.f. of a 3-phase IM is 0.866, then spatial displacement between the stator magnetic field and rotor magnetic field will be

(a) 30° (b) 90° (c) 120° (d) 150°

14. The stator of a 6-pole, 3-phase IM is fed from a 3-phase, 50 Hz supply which contains a pronounced 5th time harmonic. The speed of the 5th space harmonic field produced by the fifth time harmonic in the stator supply will be

(a) 1200 r.p.m. (b) 1500 r.p.m. (c) 1000 r.p.m. (d) 5000 r.p.m.

15. A 6-pole, 50 Hz wound-rotor induction motor (WRIM) when supplied at the rated voltage and frequency with slip-rings open circuited, developed a voltage of 100 V between any two slip rings. If the rotor is driven by external means at 1000 rpm opposite to the direction of stator field, the frequency of voltage across slip rings will be

(a) zero (b) 50 Hz (c) 100 Hz (d) 200 Hz

16. A 6-pole, 3-phase WRIM is driven by another machine at 1800 r.p.m. The rotor of the induction machine is connected to a 50 Hz system. If the mechanical rotation of the rotor is in the same direction as the rotor winding flux rotation, then frequency of the stator voltage will be

(a) 50 Hz (b) 140 Hz (c) 150 Hz (d) 200 Hz

17. The absolute speed of the magnetic field in space of a 3-phase rotor-fed IM is

(a) synchronous speed, N_s (b) rotor speed, N_r
(c) $(N_s - N_r)$ (d) $N_s + N_r$ *[I.E.S., 1996]*

18. A voltmeter gives 120 oscillations per minute when connected to the rotor of an IM. The stator frequency is 50 Hz. The slip of the motor is

(a) 2% (b) 2.5% (c) 4% (d) 5% [I.E.S., 1995]

19. Choose the correct statement from the following as the load on a 3-phase IM is increased from no-load to full-load ;

	power factor	*efficiency*	*slip*
(a)	increases	increases	increases
(b)	decreases	increases	increases
(c)	decreases	decreases	decreases
(d)	increases	decreases	decreases

20. In a 3-phase IM, if P_g represents the air-gap power, then

	rotor ohmic loss		*mechanical power developed*
(a)	$s\,P_g$	...	$(1+s)\,P_g$
(b)	$(1-s)\,P_g$	...	$s\,P_g$
(c)	$s\,P_g$	...	$(1-s)\,P_g$
(d)	$s\,P_g$	...	$P_g/(1-s)$

21. The variable resistance representing the mechanical load in the equivalent circuit of a 3-phase IM is given by

(a) $r_2\,(s-1)$ (b) $r_2\left(\frac{1}{s}-1\right)$ (c) $r_2\left(1-\frac{1}{s}\right)$ (d) $r_2\,(1-s)$

22. If ω_s = synchronous speed in mechanical rad/s, then torque in a 3-phase IM is given by

(a) $\dfrac{3I_2^2 r_2}{s\cdot\frac{P}{2}\cdot\omega_s}$ (b) $\dfrac{3I_2^2\cdot r_2}{s\cdot\omega_s}$ (c) $\dfrac{3I_2^2 r_2}{\omega_s}$ (d) $\dfrac{3I_2^2 r_2}{s}$

23. If stator impedance of a 3-phase IM is neglected, then the maximum torque (V_1 = stator phase voltage) is given by

(a) $\dfrac{3}{\omega_s}\cdot\dfrac{V_1^2}{x}$ (b) $\dfrac{3}{\omega_s}\cdot\dfrac{V_1^2}{r_2}$ (c) $\dfrac{3}{\omega_s}\cdot\dfrac{V_1^2}{2r_2}$ (d) $\dfrac{3}{\omega_s}\cdot\dfrac{V_1^2}{2x_2}$

24. At low values of slips, the torque in a 3-phase IM is given by (V_1 = stator phase voltage)

(a) $T_e\,\alpha\,\dfrac{V_1^2}{r_2}\,s$ (b) $T_e\,\alpha\,\dfrac{V_1^2 r_2}{s}$ (c) $T_e\,\alpha\,V_1^2 r_2\,(1-s)$ (d) $T_e\,\alpha\,\dfrac{V_1\,s}{r_2}$

25. In a 3-phase SRIM, T_{em} = maximum torque, s_{mT} = slip at maximum torque and $T_{e\cdot st}$ = starting torque. The following statements are made for this IM, when resistance is added in the rotor circuit :

1. T_{em} remains constant, $s_{mT} > 1$, $T_{est} < T_{em}$
2. T_{em} remains constant, $s_{mT} < 1$, $T_{est} < T_{em}$
3. T_{em} remains constant, $s_{mT} = 1$, $T_{est} = T_{em}$
4. T_{em} remains constant, $s_{mT} > 1$, $T_{est} > T_{em}$

From these, the correct answer is

(a) all are correct (b) 1, 2, 3 (c) 2, 3 (d) 2, 3, 4

26. Three-phase induction motors with open slots have

1. more starting torque T_{est}, more starting current I_{st} and improved p.f.
2. more T_{est}, more I_{st} and worsened p.f.

3. more T_{est}, more breakdown torque and improved p.f.
4. more T_{est}, more breakdown torque and worsened p.f.
5. more T_{est}, more slip at which maximum torque occurs

From these, the correct answer is

(a) 1, 3 (b) 1, 3, 5 (c) 2, 4 (d) 2, 4, 5

27. A SCIM drives a constant-torque load. If supply voltage reduces to $\frac{1}{\sqrt{2}}$ times its previous stator voltage, then slip and current get modified by factors of

	slip	current		slip	current
(a)	2	2	(b)	$\sqrt{2}$	2
(c)	2	$\sqrt{2}$	(d)	$\sqrt{2}$	$1/\sqrt{2}$

28. In a 3-phase IM, stator impedance is neglected. If supply voltage and frequency are decreased by keeping V/f constant, then maximum torque T_{em} and the slip s_{mT} at which maximum torque occurs would change as under :

(a) T_{em} increases and s_{mT} decreases (b) T_{em} decreases and s_{mT} increases
(c) T_{em} remains constant and s_{mT} increases (d) T_{em} remains constant and s_{mT} decreases

29. In case of 3-phase IM, shaft power is 2700 W and mechanical losses are 180 W. At a slip of 4%, the rotor ohmic losses are

(a) 115.2 W (b) 120 W (c) 108 W (d) 105 W

30. Semiclosed slots or totally enclosed slots are used in 3-phase induction motors, essentially to

(a) improve starting torque (b) increase pull-out torque
(c) increase efficiency (d) reduce magnetizing current and improve p.f.

31. The rotor power output of 3-phase IM is 15 kW and the corresponding slip is 4%. The rotor ohmic loss will be [I.E.S., 1997]

(a) 600 W (b) 625 W (c) 650 W (d) 700 W

32. A 3-phase IM connected in star takes 20 A from the supply mains. When connected in delta, the motor shall take from the supply mains a current of

(a) $20\sqrt{3}$ A (b) $\frac{20}{\sqrt{3}}$ (c) 20 A (d) 10 A

33. Breakdown torque of a 3-phase IM of negligible stator impedance is

1. $\propto V_1$ 2. $\propto V_1^2$ 3. $\frac{1}{x^2}$ 4. $\propto x^2$
5. $\propto \frac{1}{2x_2}$ 6. $\propto \frac{1}{f}$ 7. $\propto \frac{1}{P}$ 8. $\propto P$

From these, the correct answer is

(a) 2, 5, 6, 8 (b) 2, 5, 6, 7 (c) 1, 3, 6, 7 (d) 2, 4, 6, 8

34. A 3-phase IM is loaded. Match the consequent changes indicated in list II with the parameters indicated in list I and select the correct answer using the codes given below the lists :

List I		*List II*	
A.	Power factor	1.	Increase
B.	Slip	2.	Decrease
C.	Effective rotor resistance		
D.	Magnetizing current		

Codes :

	A	B	C	D		A	B	C	D
(a)	1	1	1	2	(b)	2	2	2	1
(c)	1	1	1	–	(d)	–	1	1	–

35. A 3-phase SRIM is fed from the rotor side with stator winding short circuited. The frequency of the currents flowing in the short-circuited stator is

(a) slip frequency
(b) supply frequency
(c) zero
(d) frequency corresponding to rotor speed

36. A 3-phase IM has rotor resistance R_2, standstill rotor induced e.m.f. E_2 and stator to rotor effective turns ratio of m. In an equivalent circuit of this machine, the rotor circuit resistance is shown as $m^2 \cdot R_2/s$, where s is the slip. This implies that the value of the equivalent rotor circuit voltage will be *[I.E.S., 1993]*

(a) E_2 *(b)* $s E_2$ *(c)* $m E_2$ *(d)* $ms E_2$

37. Match List I with List II and select correct answer using the codes given below the lists : *[I.E.S., 1996]*

List I (*Apparatus*)	*List II* (*Equivalent circuit*)
A. 3-phase IM on load	1. 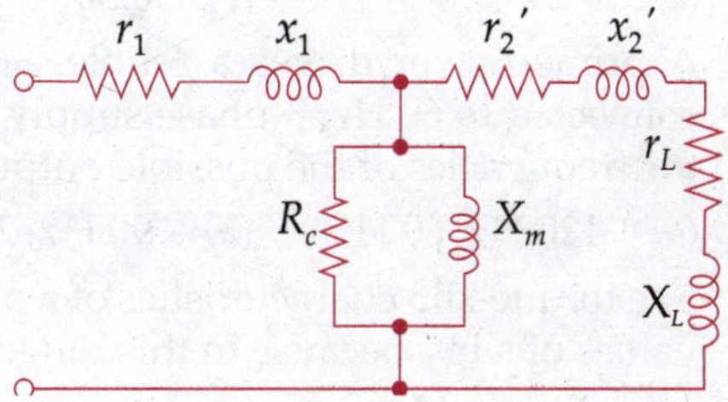
B. Synchronous generator	2. 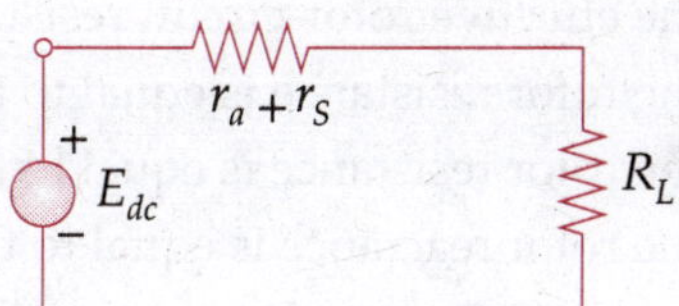
C. Single-phase transformer on load	3. 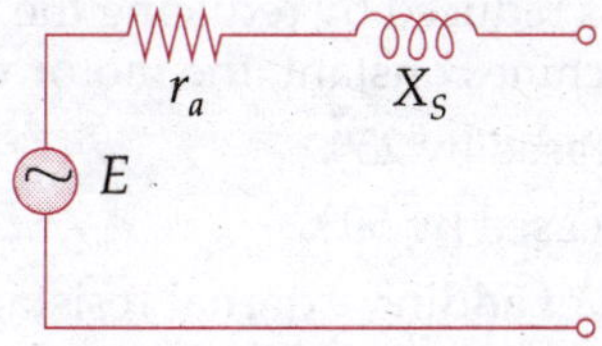
D. D.C. series motor	4. 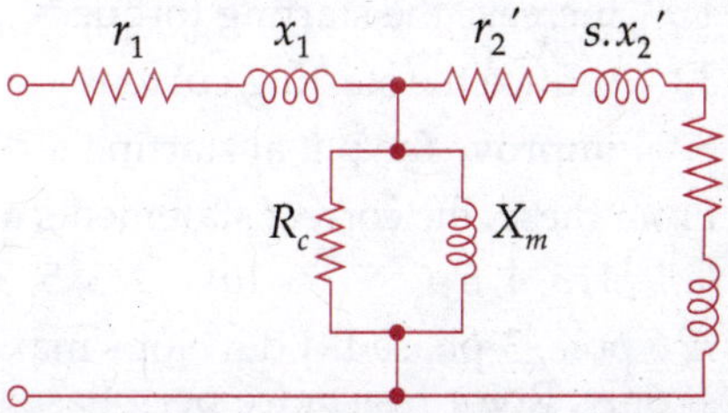

5. 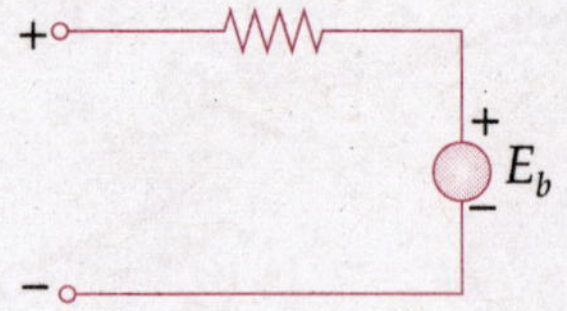

6. 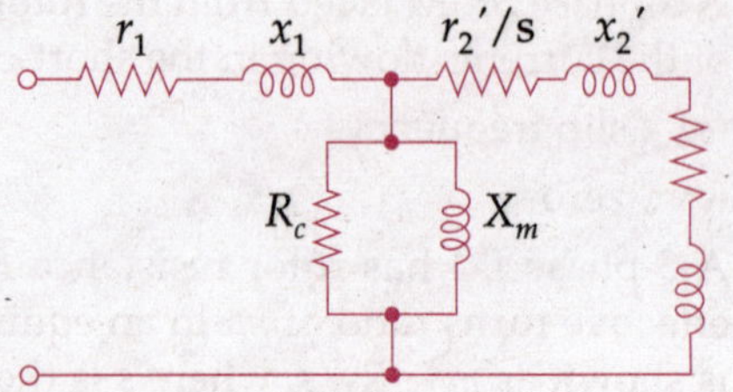

Codes :

	A	B	C	D		A	B	C	D
(a)	1	2	3	4	(b)	2	3	1	5
(c)	6	3	1	5	(d)	6	3	4	2

38. A 3-phase IM is driving a constant torque load of 1 p.u. at 5% slip. It has a maximum torque of 2 p.u. at 10% slip. Torque-speed variation in stable zone is assumed to be linear. For the stable operation of the motor, the minimum p.u. supply voltage is approximately.

(a) 0.25 *(b)* 0.50 *(c)* 0.707 *(d)* 0.80

39. A prime-mover drives a 6-pole, 3-phase induction frequency converter. The converter is connected to 60 Hz, 3-phase supply on the primary. If the prime-mover speed is 3000 r.p.m., the frequencies of the possible outputs from the converter are

(a) 120 Hz, 60 Hz *(b)* 90 Hz, 210 Hz *(c)* 176 Hz, 86 Hz *(d)* 180 Hz, 210 Hz

40. The torque-slip characteristics of a polyphase induction motor becomes almost linear at small values of slips, because in this range of slips,

(a) the effective rotor-circuit resistance is very large compared to the rotor reactance

(b) the rotor resistance is equal to the stator resistance

(c) the rotor resistance is equal to the rotor reactance

(d) the rotor reactance is equal to the stator reactance

41. The speed of a 3-phase IM is controlled by controlling its supply frequency. If the speed of the machine is reduced by reducing the frequency by 50% of the rated frequency ; to keep the flux in the machine constant, the motor voltage compared to rated voltage must be

(a) increased by 25% *(b)* increased by 50%

(c) decreased by 50% *(d)* decreased by 25%

42. The effect of adding external resistance in the rotor circuit of 3-phase SRIM is to

1. increase the starting torque
2. decrease or increase the starting torque
3. reduce the starting current
4. reduce the maximum torque
5. improve the p.f. at starting

From these, the correct statements are

(a) 1, 3, 4, 5 *(b)* 2, 3, 5 *(c)* 2, 3, 4, 5 *(d)* 2, 4, 5

43. A 6-pole, 3-phase IM develops maximum torque at 1000 r.p.m. when operated from a 60 Hz supply. Rotor resistance per phase is 1.2 Ω. Neglect stator impedance. The speed at which it will develop maximum torque when operated from 50 Hz source is

(a) 1200 r.p.m. *(b)* 1000 r.p.m. *(c)* 800 r.p.m. *(d)* 960 r.p.m.

44. A 6-pole, 3-phase IM develops the maximum starting torque at 1000 r.p.m. when operated from a 60 Hz supply. Rotor resistance per phase is 1.2 Ω. Nelgect stator impedance. The external resistance to be connected in series with each rotor phase, for developing maximum starting torque on 50 Hz supply is

(a) 6 Ω *(b)* 4.8 Ω *(c)* 7.2 Ω *(d)* 5 Ω

45. A SCIM having a rated slip of 4% on full load has a starting torque the same as full-load torque. The starting current is

(a) equal to full-load current *(b)* twice the full-load current
(c) four times full-load current *(d)* five times full-load current

46. Approximate phasor diagrams of a 3-phase induction machines for different operating conditions are indicated in List I (with usual notations). Match List I with the operating conditions given in List II and select the correct answer using the codes given below the lists :

List I	*List II*
A. 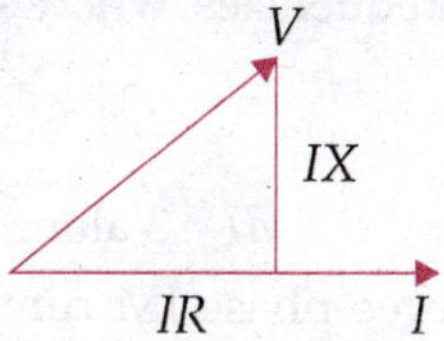	1. Full-load generating
B. 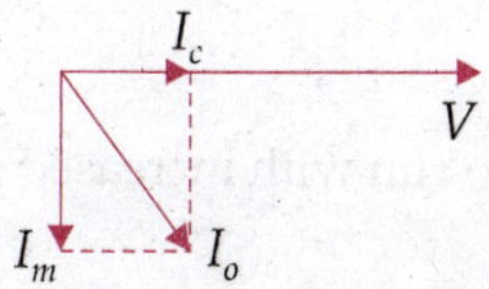	2. Blocked rotor
C. 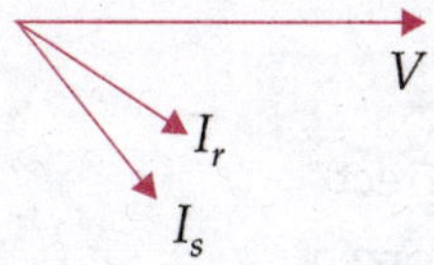	3. Full-load motoring
D. 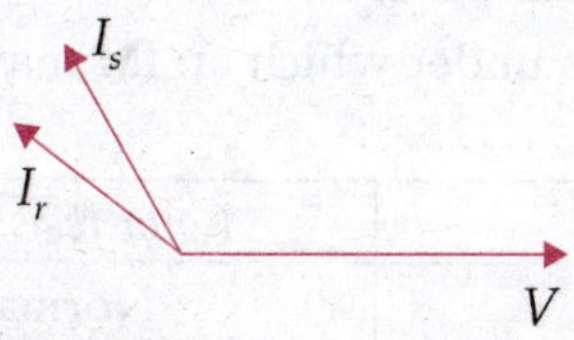	4. No-load

Codes :

	A	B	C	D		A	B	C	D
(a)	2	4	1	3	*(b)*	2	3	4	1
(c)	2	4	3	1	*(d)*	4	2	3	1

47. The slip of a 3-phase IM can be measured by

1. actually measuring the rotor speed
2. stroboscopic method
3. comparing rotor and stator supply frequencies
4. connecting a centre-zero galvanometer in the rotor circuit.

From these, the correct statements are

(a) 1, 2, 3, 4 *(b)* 1, 2, 3 *(c)* 1, 3, 4 *(d)* 2, 3, 4

48. Consider the following statements : *[I.A.S., 1997]*

As a 3-phase IM is loaded from no-load to rated load

1. there is an improvement in the power factor
2. the torque increases almost in proportion to slip
3. the air-gap flux falls sharply

Of these statements

(a) 1, 2 and 3 are correct (b) 1 and 2 are correct
(c) 2 and 3 are correct (d) 1 and 3 are correct

49. A 3-phase IM is connected to a 3-phase supply. One of the line fuses is blown out when the motor is running. Consequently,

1. the motor will come to a standstill
2. the motor will continue to run at the same speed with line current unchanged
3. the motor will continue to run at a slightly reduced speed with an increased current
4. the rotor current will have both sf and $(2 - s)f$ component frequencies, where s is slip and f is the supply frequency.

From these, the correct answer is

(a) 1 alone (b) 2, 4 (c) 3, 4 (d) 3 alone

50. Consider the following statements about the operation of a three-phase IM running at full load : *[I.A.S., 1996]*

If one of the supply line fuses blows off, the motor will

1. stall
2. continue to run with increased slip
3. continue to run with normal supply current
4. continue to run with excessive supply current

Of these staements

(a) 1 alone is correct (b) 3 alone is correct
(c) 2 and 3 are correct (d) 2 and 4 are correct

51. The chart given below indicates four different conditions under which an IM may be called upon to operate, with a constant shaft load.

	Applied voltage	*Frequency*	*Rotor resistance*
1.	Normal	Normal	Normal
2.	80%	Normal	Normal
3.	80%	80%	Normal
4.	Normal	Normal	80%

The operating conditions which lead to increasing values of running slips will be in the sequence *[I.A.S., 1996]*

(a) 1, 4, 3, 2 (b) 1, 4, 2, 3 (c) 4, 1, 3, 2 (d) 4, 1, 2, 3

52. Which one of the following can be obtained by the equivalent circuit of an electrical machine? *[I.A.S., 1993]*

(a) Temperature rise in the cores
(b) Complete performance characteristic of the machine
(c) Type of protection used in the machine
(d) Design parameters of the windings

53. If a 400 V, 50 Hz star-connected 3-phase SCIM is operated from a 400 V, 75 Hz supply, the torque that the motor can now provide while drawing rated current from the supply

(a) reduces (b) increases (c) ramains the same
(d) increases or reduces depending upon the rotor resistance

54. Neglecting the shunt branch from the equivalent circuit of a 3-phase IM, the slip at which maximum torque occurs is given by

(a) $\frac{r_2}{x_2}$ (b) $\frac{r_2}{\sqrt{r_1^2+(x_1+x_2)^2}}$ (c) $\frac{x_2}{\sqrt{(r_1+r_2)^2+x_1^2}}$ (d) $\frac{r_2}{x_1+x_2}$

55. With negligible stator impedance, the condition for the development of maximum power in a 3-phase IM is

(a) $\frac{r_2(1-s)}{s}=r_2$ (b) $\frac{r_2(1-s)}{s}=x_2$ (c) $\frac{r_2(1-s)}{s}=\sqrt{r_2^2+x_2^2}$ (d) $\frac{r_2(1-s)}{s}=0$

56. In a 3-phase IM, electrical torque T_e at any slip s and maximum torque T_{em} at slip s_{mT} are related as under :

(a) $\frac{T_e}{T_{em}}=\frac{2s\cdot s_{mT}}{s^2+s_{mT}}$ (b) $\frac{T_e}{T_{em}}=\frac{2\,s_{mT}}{s^2+s_{mT}^2}$ (c) $\frac{T_e}{T_{em}}=\frac{2s}{s^2+s_{mT}^2}$ (d) $\frac{T_e}{T_{em}}=\frac{s\cdot s_{mT}}{s^2+s_{mT}^2}$

57. A 3-phase SCIM is running at slip s with synchronous speed N_s clockwise and rotor speed N_r. If its two supply leads are interchanged, then at that instant

1. slip is $(2-s)$
2. speed of air-gap field with respect to stator is (N_s+N_r) clockwise
3. speed of air-gap field with respect to rotor is (N_s+N_r) anticlockwise
4. speed of air-gap field with respect to stator is N_s anticlockwise
5. effective rotor resistance increases
6. stator current decreases

From these, the correct answer is

(a) 1, 3, 4, 5, 6 (b) 2, 3, 4, 5, 6 (c) 1, 3, 4, 5 (d) 1, 2, 4, 5

58. No-load current of a 3-phase IM in terms of its rated current is

(a) 10 to 20% (b) 2 to 6% (c) 20 to 30% (d) 30 to 50%

59. No-load and full-load pfs of a 3-phase IM are respectively of the order of

(a) 0.2, 0.85 (b) 0.5, 0.8 (c) 0.7, 0.9 (d) 0.3, 0.95

60. Two 3-phase SCIM have efficiency of 82% and 92% and their no-load p.f.s. of 0.1 and 0.3 These two motors *A* and *B* have the following values for their p.f.s. and efficiencies :

(a) Big motor *(BM)* A : 0.1, 82% ; smaller motor *(SM)* B : 0.3, 92%
(b) *BM A* : 0.1, 92% ; *SM B* : 0.3, 82%
(c) *BM A* : 0.3, 92% ; *SM B* : 0.1, 82%
(d) *BM A* : 0.3, 82% ; *SM B* : 0.1, 92%

61. Motor *A* has deeper and narrow slots, whereas motor *B* has shallow and wider slots. Induction motor *A*, as compared to motor *B*, has

1. less pull-out torque
2. less starting torque
3. less operating speed
4. better operating p.f.

From these, the correct answer is

(a) 1, 2, 3, 4 (b) 1, 2, 4 (c) 1, 3, 4 (d) 2, 3, 4

62. A centre-zero ammeter connected in the rotor circuit of a 6-pole, 50 Hz SRIM makes 45 complete oscillations in one minute. In r.p.m., the rotor speed and speed of stator field with respect to rotor are respectively

(a) 985, 15 (b) 970, 1000 (c) 985, 985 (d) 985, 970

63. The no-load speed of a 3-phase, 50 Hz IM is 1485 r.p.m.. The number of alternations per minute which the rotor e.m.f. will make and the speed of rotor m.m.f. with respect to rotor would respectively be

(a) 0.5, 1485 r.p.m. (b) 30, zero r.p.m. (c) 15, 15 r.p.m. (d) 30, 15 r.p.m.

64. For a 3-phase, 50 Hz, SCIM, rotor leakage reactance at standstill is twice of its resistance. The frequency of the supply at which maximum torque is obtained at starting is

(a) 50 Hz (b) 25 Hz (c) 100 Hz (d) 75 Hz

65. A 3-phase, 50 Hz IM takes a power input of 30 kW at its full-load speed of 1440 r.p.m.. Total stator losses are 1 kW. The slip and rotor ohmic losses at full load are

(a) 0.02, 600 W (b) 0.04, 580 W (c) 0.04, 1160 W (d) 0.04, 1200 W

66. A 3-phase SCIM has its copper bars replaced by aluminium bars. With this change, motor characteristics would be as under :

(a) starting torque T_{est} and maximum torque T_{em} would be same, slip s_{mT} at maximum torque would be more

(b) T_{est} more, T_{em} same, s_{mT} more

(c) T_{est} same, T_{em} more, s_{mT} same

(d) T_{est} more, T_{em} less, s_{mT} more

67. Match the correct values of slips for the three operating regions of a 3-phase IM :

	Generating region	*Motoring region*	*Braking region*
(a)	(– 1) to 0	0 to 1	1 to 2
(b)	2 to 1	1 to 0	0 to (– 1)
(c)	0 to – 1	0 to 1	0 to (– 1)
(d)	(– 1) to 0	1 to 0	0 to1

68. A 3-phase SRIM with negligible stator impedance operates on a balanced 3-phase A.C. supply. Consider the following statements in this regard :

The maximum torque developed by the motor

1. is independent of the value of the rotor-circuit resistance
2. is directly proportional to the square of the supply voltage
3. occurs at a slip whose value is independent of the value of the rotor resistance.

Of these statements

(a) 1, 2 and 3 are correct (b) 1 and 2 are correct

(c) 2 and 3 are correct (d) 1 and 3 are correct *[I.A.S., 1993]*

69. The stator of a 4-pole, 3-phase induction machine is supplied from 3-phase, 50 Hz supply and a prime-mover drives its rotor at a speed of 750 r.p.m. The slip-rings of the machine are open-circuited. The frequency of the voltage across any two slip rings is :

1. 50 Hz 2. 75 Hz 3. 100 Hz 4. 25 Hz

From these, the correct answer is

(a) 1, 2 (b) 1, 3 (c) 2, 3 (d) 2, 4

70. In a 4-pole, 3-phase, 50 Hz induction machine, the slip-rings of the machine are open-circuited. The frequency of the voltage across slip rings is 75 Hz. The rotor is driven at a speed of

1. 750 r.p.m. 2. 1500 r.p.m. 3. 2250 r.p.m. 4. 3750 r.p.m.

From these, the correct statements are

(a) 1, 4 (b) 1, 3 (c) 2, 3 (d) 2, 4

71. A 4-pole, 50 Hz 3-phase synchronous motor and 8-pole, 50 Hz, 3-phase SRIM are coupled to each other mechanically and operate on the same 3-phase, 50 Hz supply system. The slip rings of the induction machine are left open-circuited. The frequency of the voltage across any two slip rings would be

1. 50 Hz 2. 100 Hz 3. 150 Hz 4. 25 Hz

From these, the correct answer is

(a) 2, 3 (b) 2, 4 (c) 1, 3 (d) 1, 4

72. The stator of a 3-phase, 6-pole SRIM is connected to 50 Hz source but its rotor is energised from 20 Hz source. The rotor would run at a speed of

1. 1600 r.p.m. 2. 600 r.p.m. 3. 1400 r.p.m. 4. 400 r.p.m.

From these, the correct answer is

(a) 2, 3 (b) 2, 4 (c) 1, 3 (d) 1, 4

73. If two IMs *A* and *B* are identical except that the air-gap of motor '*A*' is 50% greater than that of motor '*B*', then

(a) the no-load p.f. of *A* will be better than that of *B*

(b) the no-load p.f. of *A* will be poorer than that of *B*

(c) the core losses of *A* will be more than those of *B*

(d) the operating flux of *A* will be smaller than that of *B*. [I.A.S., 1997]

74. Consider the following statements regarding the equivalent circuit parameters of an IM :

1. Leakage reactance is dependent on supply current
2. Magnetizing reactance is dependent on the air-gap flux
3. Core loss is dependent on the input voltage and frequency
4. Rotor resistance is dependent on the speed

Of these statements

(a) 2 and 3 are correct (b) 1, 3 and 4 are correct

(c) 1, 2, 3 and 4 are correct (d) 1, 2 and 4 are correct [I.A.S., 1993]

75. The rotor of a 4-pole 3-phase SCIM is replaced by a 3-phase, 4-pole wound rotor. When fed with normal supply, the machine will

(a) not run

(b) run at very low speed

(c) run at slightly lower than normal speed

(d) run at slightly higher than normal speed

76. A 3-phase stator winding of a SCIM is fed by 3-phase ac supply at a frequency *f*. If the rotor speed is N_r and synchronous speed is N_s, then the absolute speed of resultant flux in space is

(a) N_s, irrespective of rotor speed N_r
(b) $(N_s + N_r)$ if the flux rotates in the same direction as the rotor
(c) $(N_s - N_r)$ if the flux rotates in the same direction as the rotor
(d) N_r, irrespective of N_s.

77. Rotor of a 3-phase SRIM is fed from 3-phase balanced supply with its stator winding short-circuited. If N_s = synchronous speed, N_r = rotor speed, f = supply frequency and s is the slip, then

1. frequency of stator currents is $s\,f$
2. frequency of stator currents is $(2 - s)\,f$
3. speed of stator field with respect to stator is N_s
4. speed of rotor field with respect to rotor is N_s
5. speed of rotor field with respect to rotor is $(N_s + N_r)$
6. speed of air-gap field with respect to stator is $(N_s - N_r)$

From these, the correct answer is

(a) 2, 5, 6 (b) 1, 4, 6 (c) 1, 3, 5 (d) 1, 5, 6

78. Rotor of a 3-phase SRIM is fed from 3-phase balanced supply with its stator winding short-circuited. Synchronous speed is N_s and if rotor rotates clockwise at a speed N_r, then

1. speed of air-gap field with respect to (w.r.t) stator is $(N_s - N_r)$ anticlockwise
2. speed of air-gap field w.r.t. stator is $(N_s - N_r)$ clockwise
3. speed of air-gap field w.r.t. rotor is N_s anticlockwise
4. speed of rotor-produced field w.r.t. rotor is $(N_s + N_r)$ anticlockwise
5. speed of air-gap field w.r.t. rotor is N_s clockwise

From these, the correct statements are

(a) 1, 3, 4 (b) 1, 2, 4 (c) 2, 3, 5 (d) 1, 4, 5

79. For SCIM, reactor starting is preferred over resistor starting because reactors

1. improve the p.f. at starting
2. increase starting torque
3. incur lower energy loss
4. are more effective in reducing the voltage

From these, the correct answer is

(a) 1, 3, 4 (b) 2, 3, 4 (c) 1, 3 (d) 3, 4

80. Consider the following statements :

Star-delta starter is used in 3-phase IM because it

1. mitigates (lessens) heating of the motor winding
2. ensures permissible minimum starting current
3. is regulated by electricity authority
4. ensures smooth run up to full load

Of these statements

(a) 1, 2 and 3 are correct (b) 2, 3 and 4 are correct
(c) 1, 3 and 4 are correct (d) 1 and 2 are correct

81. As compared to DOL starting, a cage IM with star-delta starting shall have

(a) more starting torque (b) more starting current
(c) reduced starting current (d) smooth acceleration

82. A 3-phase SCIM is started with a star-delta starter. The ratios [GATE, 1990]

$$X = \frac{\text{Line current at start with star} - \text{delta starter}}{\text{Line current at start with direct switching in delta}}$$

and
$$Y = \frac{\text{Starting torque with star} - \text{delta starter}}{\text{Starting torque with direct switching in delta}}$$

are respectively,

(a) $\frac{1}{3}, \frac{1}{\sqrt{3}}$ (b) $\frac{1}{\sqrt{3}}, \frac{1}{3}$ (c) $\frac{1}{3}, \frac{1}{3}$ (d) $\frac{1}{\sqrt{3}}, \frac{1}{\sqrt{3}}$

83. If the auto-transformer tapping K is less than 1, then the starting torque in a 3-phase SCIM when started with this auto-transformer starter would be

(a) $K \times$ starting torque T_{est} with direct switching

(b) $K^2 \times T_{e \cdot st}$ (c) $\frac{1}{K} \cdot T_{est}$ (d) $\frac{1}{K^2} \cdot T_{e \cdot st}$

84. A starting torque of 100 Nm is developed in a 3-phase SCIM by an auto-transformer starter with a tapping 40%. If the tapping of the auto-transformer is changed to 80%, then the starting torque would be

(a) 400 Nm (b) 200 Nm (c) 50 Nm (d) 25 Nm

85. The following starting method for a 3-phase SCIM is inferior in view of the poor starting torque per ampere of the line-current drawn :

(a) Direct-on line starting (b) Auto-transformer method of switching

(c) Series-inductor method of starting (d) star-delta starting

86. A 3-phase delta-connected SCIM has a starting current I_d and a starting torque T_d at rated voltage. If the starting current and starting torque while the motor is started through star-delta starter and auto-transformer (with 60% voltage) starter alternatively are I_y, T_y and I_{aut}, T_{aut} respectively, then $\frac{I_y}{I_d} : \frac{I_{aut}}{I_d} : \frac{T_y}{T_d} : \frac{T_{aut}}{T_d}$ is equal to [Pr. I.A.S., 2000]

(a) $\frac{1}{\sqrt{3}} : 0.6 : \frac{1}{\sqrt{3}} : 0.6$ (b) $\frac{1}{3} : 0.6 : \frac{1}{3} : 0.36$

(c) $\frac{1}{3} : 0.36 : \frac{1}{\sqrt{3}} : 0.6$ (d) $\frac{1}{\sqrt{3}} : 0.36 : \frac{1}{3} : 0.36$

87. For SRIM, the rotor-resistance starting is preferred over reduced-voltage starting because it

1. decreases its starting current 2. increases starting torque

3. improves starting p.f. 4. decreases maximum torque

From above, the correct answei is

(a) 1, 2, 3 (b) 2, 3, 4 (c) 1, 2, 3, 4 (d) 1, 2, 4

88. When started by means of an auto-transformer with 50% tapping, supply current at start of a $3-\phi$ SCIM is I_{aut} and when started by means of a star-delta starter, the supply current at start is I_y. The ratio of $\frac{I_{aut}}{I_y}$ is

(a) 1.33 (b) 0.813 (c) 1.5 (d) 0.75

89. A 3-phase, 12 pole, 50 Hz wound-rotor induction motor (WRIM) is to be used as a frequency converter. This IM is driven by adjustable speed D.C. motor. Assume the field of IM to be

rotating clockwise. For an output frequency range of 100 to 300 Hz at the slip rings, speed range of D.C. motor would be :

1. 1500 to 2500 r.p.m. clockwise
2. 1500 to 3500 r.p.m. clockwise
3. 500 to 2500 r.p.m. anticlockwise
4. 1000 to 3000 r.p.m. clockwise
5. 1500 to 3500 r.p.m. anticlockwise

From these, the correct answer is

(*a*) 2, 3 (*b*) 1, 4 (*c*) 1, 5 (*d*) 2, 4

90. During the no-load test, the power input to a 3-phase IM has to supply

(*a*) core loss, friction and windage (FW) loss

(*b*) small ohmic loss and FW loss

(*c*) small ohmic loss, core loss and FW loss

(*d*) small ohmic loss, FW loss and stray load loss

91. During blocked-rotor test on a 3-ϕ IM, the power input to 3-phase IM has to supply

(*a*) ohmic loss (*b*) ohmic loss and core loss

(*c*) core loss (*d*) ohmic loss, core loss and friction and winding loss

92. The diameter of the circle diagram for a 3-ϕ IM is given by (V_1 = stator phase voltage)

(*a*) $\dfrac{V_1}{x_1}$ (*b*) $\dfrac{V_1}{r_1+r_2}$ (*c*) $\dfrac{V_1}{x_1+x_2}$ (*d*) $\dfrac{V_1}{x_2}$

93. The following tests are conducted on a 3-phase IM :

1. Running-light test 2. Blocked-rotor test 3. Stator-resistance test

The complete circle diagram of a 3-phase IM can be drawn with the help of :

(*a*) test 2 alone (*b*) tests 2, 3 (*c*) tests 1, 2, 3 (*d*) tests 1, 2

94. A star-delta starter is equivalent to an auto-transformer starter with a tapping of

(*a*) 86.6% (*b*) 57.73% (*c*) 57% (*d*) 58%

95. Wattmeter readings during the no-load test on a 3-phase IM give :

1. stator I^2R loss
2. stator core loss
3. rotor core loss
4. friction and windage loss

From above, the correct statements are

(*a*) 1, 2, 3, 4 (*b*) 1, 2, 4 (*c*) 2, 3, 4 (*d*) 1, 3, 4

96. Wattmeter readings during blocked-rotor test on a 3-phase IM give :

1. stator I^2R loss
2. stator core loss
3. rotor core loss
4. friction and winding loss
5. rotor I^2R loss

From these, the correct statements are

(*a*) 1, 2, 5 (*b*) 1, 2, 3, 5 (*c*) 1, 4, 5 (*d*) 1, 5

97. The power input to a 415 V, 50 Hz, 6-pole, 3-phase IM running at 975 r.p.m. is 40 kW. The stator losses are 1 kW and friction and windage losses are 2 kW. The efficiency of the motor is

(*a*) 92.5% (*b*) 91% (*c*) 90.06% (*d*) 88%

98. The approximate value of efficiency of a three-phase IM running at a slip '*s*' is given by [*I.A.S., 1998*]

(*a*) $\dfrac{1}{1+s}$ (*b*) $\dfrac{s}{1+s}$ (*c*) $\dfrac{1-s}{1+s}$ (*d*) $\dfrac{s}{1-s}$

99. Consider the following statements :

The e.m.f. induced in the rotor of a 3-phase IM is proportional to the

1. relative velocity between stator field and rotor conductors
2. voltage applied to the stator
3. slip

of these statements

(a) 1, 2 and 3 are correct (b) 1 and 2 are correct

(c) 2 and 3 are correct (d) 1 and 3 are correct

100. A 3-phase IM requires a starter

(a) because there is no back e.m.f. induced in the stator winding during starting

(b) because the motor does not possess an inherent starting torque

(c) because the induced secondary voltage and hence the currents in the windings are abnormally high during starting

(d) to increase the starting torque.

101. To improve the power factor of a 3-phase IM, the capacitor bank should be connected in delta to make

(a) capacitance calculation easy (b) capacitance value small

(c) the connection elegant (d) the p.f. correction more effective.

102. For the improvement of p.f. in a 3-phase IM, the star-connected capacitor bank has a capacitance of C_s and VA rating of VA_s. If the capacitor bank is delta-connected, then its capacitance C_d and VA rating VA_d will respectively be

(a) $C_d = C_s, VA_d = \frac{1}{3} VA_s$ (b) $C_d = \frac{1}{3} C_s, VA_d = \frac{1}{3} VA_s$

(c) $C_d = \frac{1}{3} C_s, VA_d = VA_s$ (d) $C_d = 3C_s, VA_d = VA_s$

103. Induction generators deliver power at

(a) unity p.f. (b) zero p.f. lagging (c) leading p.f. (d) lagging p.f.

104. A 3-phase induction machine runs at supersynchronous speed. For self-excitation, the machine

(a) draws real power from the mains

(b) draws reactive from the mains

(c) feeds reactive power to the mains

(d) generates e.m.f. due to rotor residual magnesium

105. In a self-excited induction generator, to keep the frequency of generated voltage constant with the increase in load, the speed of the induction machine should be

(a) increased (b) decreased

(c) maintained less than the rated synchronous speed

(d) maintained more than the rated synchronous speed

106. A 3-phase induction motor draws active power 'P' and reactive power 'Q' from the grid. If it is operated as a generator, P and Q will respectively be

(a) positive and negative (b) negative and negative

(c) positive and positive (d) negative and positive

107. Consider the following statements :

If a 3-phase SCIM operates at a slip of – 0.05 (i.e. minus 0.05), then the machine will

1. draw electrical power from the mains
2. draw mechanical power through the shaft
3. deliver electrical power to the mains

Of these statements

(a) 1, 2 and 3 are correct (b) 1 and 2 are correct
(c) 2 and 3 are correct (d) 1 and 3 are correct

108. A 3-phase induction machine operates on 3-phase fixed frequency ac mains at a per unit slip of 1.5. Consider the following statements regarding the operating conditions of the machine: *[I.A.S., 1994]*

1. It draws electrical power from the mains.
2. It draws mechanical power through the shaft
3. It delivers electrical power to the mains
4. It delivers mechanical power through the shaft

Of these statements

(a) 1 and 2 are correct (b) 1 and 4 are correct
(c) 2 and 3 are correct (d) 3 and 4 are correct.

109. A 2.3 kV, 3-phase, 50 Hz SCIM has starting current of 600 A and starting torque of 640 Nm. The per unit tapping of auto-transformer to reduce the starting current from mains to 150 A and the corresponding starting torque would respectively be

(a) 0.5, 160 Nm (b) 0.25, 40 Nm (c) 0.6, 230.4 Nm (d) 0.4, 102.4 Nm

110. A 3-phase SCIM with an applied voltage of 40% gives a blocked-rotor current of 240%. Its full-load slip is 0.05. Per unit starting torques with direct-on-starter and auto-transformer with 50% tapping are respectively given by

(a) 0.9, 0.45 (b) 0.9, 0.225 (c) 1.8, 0.9 (d) 1.8, 0.45

111. The power factor of a delta-connected 3-phase, 50 kW, IM is 0.4 when delivering 35% of its rated load. If its stator is reconnected in star with the same load on the shalf, then its

(a) p.f. is improved, stator current decreases
(b) p.f. is improved, stator current increases
(c) p.f. is worsened, stator current increases
(d) p.f. remains unchanged, stator current decreases

112. No-load test on a 3-phase IM was conducted at different supply voltages and a plot of input power versus voltage was drawn. This curve was extrapolated to intersect the *y*-axis. This intersection point yields *[GATE, 2003]*

(a) core loss (b) stator copper loss
(c) stray load loss (d) friction and windage loss.

113. A 3-phase IM is driving a constant torque load at rated voltage and frequency. If both voltage and frequency are halved, following statements relate to the new condition if stator resistance, leakage reactance and core loss are ignored *[GATE, 2003]*

P The diference between synchronous speed and actual speed remains same

Q The airgap flux remains same

R The stator current remains same

S The p.u. slip remains same

Among the above, correct statements are

(*a*) All (*b*) *P*, *Q* & *R* (*c*) *Q*, *R* & *S* (*d*) *P* & *S*

114. A 3-phase SCIM takes a line current of 100 A when started by direct switching. If an auto-transfromer with 50% tapping is used, the motor-line current and the supply-line current would respectively be

(*a*) 50 A, 25 (*b*) 25 A, 50 A (*c*) 50 A, 50 $\sqrt{3}$ A (*d*) 50 $\sqrt{3}$ A, 50 A

115. A 3-phase, star-connected SRIM is fed from 400 V, 50 Hz source. Stator to rotor effective turns ratio is 2. At a rotor speed of 1440 r.p.m., the rotor induced e.m.f. per phase would be

(*a*) 4.62 V (*b*) 46.2 V (*c*) 8.0 V (*d*) 9.24 V

116. Torque developed (E_2, I_2, $\cos\theta_2$ are rotor circuit parameters and ω_s = synchronous speed) in a 3-phase IM is given by

1. $\frac{3}{\omega_s}\cdot E_2 I_2 \cos\theta_2$

2. $\frac{3}{\omega_s}\cdot I_2^2 r_2\left(\frac{1-s}{s}\right)$

3. $\frac{3}{\omega_s}\cdot I_2^2\,\frac{r_2}{s}$

4. $\frac{3}{\omega_s}\cdot\frac{V_1}{\sqrt{\left(r_1+\frac{r_2}{s}\right)^2+(x_1+x_2)^2}}\cdot\frac{r_2}{s}$

5. $\frac{3}{\omega_s}\cdot\frac{V_1^2}{\sqrt{\left(r_1+\frac{r_2}{s}\right)^2+(x_1+x_2)^2}}\cdot\frac{r_2}{s}$

From these, the correct answer is

(*a*) 1, 2, 5 (*b*) 1, 3, 5 (*c*) 1, 2, 4 (*d*) 3, 5

117. With stator impedance neglected, starting torque of a 3-phase IM is proportional to

1. $\frac{r_2}{r_2+x_2}$

2. $\frac{r_2}{r_2^2+x_2^2}$

3. $\frac{x_2}{r_2^2+x_2^2}$

4. V_1

5. V_1^2

6. $\frac{1}{\omega_s}$

7. ω_s

From these, the correct answer is

(*a*) 1, 4, 7 (*b*) 1, 5, 6 (*c*) 3, 5, 7 (*d*) 2, 5, 6

118. An increase in the number of poles of a 3-phase IM results in

(*a*) decrease in maximum p.f. (*b*) increase in maximum p.f.

(*c*) no-change in maximum p.f. (*d*) cannot be depicted

119. When the supply voltage to a 3-phase SCIM is reduced by 20%, the maximum torque will decrease by

(*a*) 10% (*b*) 20% (*c*) 36% (*d*) 40%

120. If a 3-phase 350 V, 50 Hz SCIM is operated on 420 V, 60 Hz supply, then

1. starting torque T_{est} will increase

2. maximum torque T_{em} will increase

3. T_{est} will decrease

4. $T_{e\cdot m}$ will remain constant

5. operating speed will be more

6. operating slip will be less

From these, the correct statements are

(*a*) 1, 2, 5, 6 (*b*) 3, 4, 5, 6 (*c*) 1, 4, 6 (*d*) 2, 3, 5, 6

121. Starting torque of a 3-phase IM varies as

(a) f (b) $\frac{1}{f}$ (c) $\frac{1}{f^2}$ (d) $\frac{1}{f^3}$

122. Maximum torque in a 3-phase IM varies as

(a) f (b) $\frac{1}{f}$ (c) $\frac{1}{f^2}$ (d) $\frac{1}{f^3}$

123. In a 3-phase SCIM, applied voltage is reduced to x times its rated value. Then, its starting line current from mains and starting torque by auto-transformer starting would reduce respectively from their corresponding direct switching values by a factor of

(a) x, x (b) x, x^2 (c) x^2, x^2 (d) x^2, x

124. Out of the several characteristics shown in Fig. C.74, identify the appropriate ones to match the following for a 3-phase induction motor : [GATE, 1996]

	x-axis	y-axis	
A.	Load	efficiency	(P) curve I
B.	Speed	current	(Q) curve II
C.	Speed	power factor	(R) curve III
			(S) curve IV
			(T) curve V

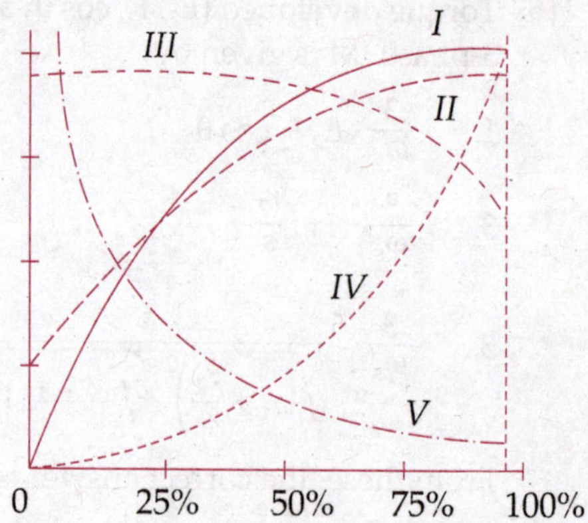

Fig C.74

Codes :

	A	B	C		A	B	C
(a)	R	R	P	(b)	P	R	Q
(c)	P	Q	T	(d)	Q	P	S

125. A 3-phase IM with stator in star draws a line current of 10 A. When connected in delta, it would draw a line current of

(a) 10 A (b) $\frac{10}{\sqrt{3}}$ A (c) 30 A (d) $\frac{10}{3}$ A

126. The most common application of 3-phase induction generator can be in a

(a) steam-power station (b) hydro-power station
(c) wind-power station (d) nuclear-power station

127. Two 3-phase SCIMs are identical in every respect except that the slot depths in machine A are more than those in machine *B*. However, slot areas in both the machines are the same. Machine *B*, as compared to machine *A* will have

(a) more pull-out torque but poor p.f. (b) more pull-out torque and better p.f.
(c) less pull-out torque and poor p.f. (d) less pull-out torque but better p.f.

128. A 3-phase, 20 kW, 400 V, 1470 r.p.m., 50 Hz SCIM develops a torque of 100 Nm at a speed of 1400 r.p.m. If the motor is connected to a 30-Hz supply ; for keeping the same air-gap flux, the supply voltage and the speed for the same load torque would respectively be

(a) 240 V, 840 r.p.m. (b) 240 V, 800 r.p.m. (c) 240 V, 780 r.p.m. (d) 240 V, 750 r.p.m.

129. A 3-phase SCIM has full-load efficiency of 0.8 and a maximum efficiency of 0.9. It is operated at a slip of 0.6 by applying a reduced voltage. The efficiency of the motor at this operating point is [GATE, 1998]

(a) less than 0.4 (b) greater than 0.6

(c) in the range of 0.8 ± 0.1 (d) none of the above

130. A 3-phase, 4-pole, 400 V, 50 Hz squirrel-cage induction motor is operating at a slip of 0.02. The speed of the rotor flux in mechanical rad/sec, sensed by a stationary observer, is closest to [GATE, 2017 (2)]

(a) 1500 (b) 1470 (c) 157 (d) 154

ANSWERS

1. (c)	2. (d)	3. (a)	4. (b)	5. (a)	6. (c)	7. (c)	8. (d)	9. (a)	10. (d)
11. (a)	12. (b)	13. (c)	14. (d)	15. (c)	16. (b)	17. (c)	18. (c)	19. (a)	20. (c)
21. (b)	22. (b)	23. (d)	24. (a)	25. (b)	26. (d)	27. (c)	28. (c)	29. (b)	30. (d)
31. (b)	32. (c)	33. (a)	34. (a)	35. (a)	36. (c)	37. (c)	38. (c)	39. (b)	40. (a)
41. (c)	42. (b)	43. (c)	44. (b)	45. (d)	46. (c)	47. (a)	48. (b)	49. (c)	50. (d)
51. (c)	52. (b)	53. (a)	54. (b)	55. (c)	56. (a)	57. (c)	58. (d)	59. (a)	60. (b)
61. (b)	62. (a)	63. (d)	64. (b)	65. (c)	66. (b)	67. (a)	68. (b)	69. (d)	70. (a)
71. (c)	72. (a)	73. (b)	74. (c)	75. (c)	76. (a)	77. (d)	78. (a)	79. (d)	80. (a)
81. (c)	82. (c)	83. (b)	84. (a)	85. (c)	86. (b)	87. (a)	88. (d)	89. (a)	90. (c)
91. (a)	92. (c)	93. (c)	94. (b)	95. (b)	96. (d)	97. (c)	98. (c)	99. (b)	100. (c)
101. (b)	102. (c)	103. (c)	104. (b)	105. (a)	106. (d)	107. (c)	108. (b)	109. (a)	110. (d)
111. (a)	112. (d)	113. (b)	114. (a)	115. (a)	116. (b)	117. (d)	118. (a)	119. (c)	120. (b)
121. (d)	122. (c)	123. (c)	124. (b)	125. (a)	126. (c)	127. (a)	128. (b)	129. (a)	130. (c)

ARMATURE WINDINGS

1. Closed windings are used for

   1. A.C. machines 2. 3-phase delta-connected machines
   3. A.C. commutator machines 4. D.C. commutator machines

   From these, the correct answer is

   (a) 1, 3 (b) 2, 4 (c) 1, 4 (d) 3, 4

2. A multi-turn coil has

   (a) multi-coil-sides (b) one-coil-side (c) two coil-sides (d) four coil-sides

3. Open windings are used for

   1. D.C. machines 2. A.C. machines
   3. A.C. commutator machines 4. D.C. commutator machines

   From these, the correct answer is

   (a) 1 alone (b) 2 alone (c) 2, 4 (d) 3 alone

4. Closed windings may be

   1. single-layer winding 2. double-layer winding
   3. triple-layer winding

   From these, the correct answer is

   (a) 2 alone (b) 3 alone (c) 1 alone (d) 2, 3

5. Open windings may be

   1. single-layer winding 2. double-layer winding
   3. triple-layer winding

   (a) 1 alone (b) 2 alone (c) 1, 2 (d) 2, 3

6. For C armature coils and P poles in a D.C. machine, the back pitch for simplex-lap winding is

   (a) $\frac{2C}{P} + K$ (b) $\frac{2C}{P} - K$ (c) $\frac{2C}{P} \pm K$ (d) $2\,C\,P \pm K$

7. For a simplex-lap winding, the winding pitch is equal to

   (a) + 1 (b) – 2 (c) ± 1 (d) ± 2

8. For simplex-lap winding, the commutator pitch is equal to

   (a) + 1 (b) ± 1 (c) – 1 (d) ± 2

9. A D.C. machine has 6 coil-sides per slot. The number given to the first coil-side in 8th slot is

   (a) 43 (b) 37 (c) 48 (d) 47

10. If y_b is the back pitch and u is the number of coil-sides per slot, then split coils can be avoided if the following quantity is an integer

    (a) $\frac{y_b+1}{u}$ (b) $(y_b + 1)\,u$ (c) $\frac{y_b-1}{u}$ (d) $(y_b - 1)\,u$

11. For C coils and P poles, the commutator pitch for simplex-wave winding is

    (a) $\frac{C \pm 1}{P/2}$ (b) $\frac{C+1}{P/2}$ (c) $\frac{C-1}{P/2}$ (d) $\frac{C \pm 2}{P/2}$

12. For C coils and P poles, the winding pitch for simplex-wave winding is

    (a) $\frac{2C+2}{P/2}$ (b) $\frac{2C \pm 2}{P/2}$ (c) $\frac{2C-2}{P/2}$ (d) $\frac{2C \pm 1}{P/2}$

13. For simplex wave and lap windings, the back pitch y_b and front pitch y_f are as follows :
(a) y_b is odd, y_f is even (b) y_b is even, y_f is odd
(c) both y_b and y_f are odd (d) both y_b and y_f are even

14. A D.C. machine with 6 poles and 4 parallel paths has
(a) simplex lap winding (b) simplex wave winding
(c) duplex lap winding (d) duplex wave winding

15. The number of commutator segments in a D.C. machine is equal to the number of
(a) coil-sides (b) turns (c) coils (d) slots

16. In lap windings, the function of equalizer rings are
1. to save the armature winding from circulating currents
2. to save the brushes from carrying circulating currents
3. to save the commutator from handling circulation currents
4. to reduce the magnetic unbalance under different poles
5. to save the armature core from eddy currents

From these, the correct statements are
(a) 1, 2, 3, 4 (b) 2, 4 (c) 1, 3, 5 (d) 2, 3, 5

17. If dummy coils are to be avoided in simplex-wave winding, the following should not be an integer :
(a) S/P (b) $\frac{S}{P} \pm 1$ (c) $\frac{2S}{P}$ (d) $\frac{S}{P} \pm 2$

18. If equalizer rings are to be provided in dc machines, then following should be an integer :
(a) $\frac{2C+1}{P}$ (b) $\frac{C}{P}$ (c) $\frac{C \pm 1}{P/2}$ (d) $\frac{2C}{P}$

19. A 6-pole lap-connected D.C. generator has 480 conductors and armature circuit resistance is 0.06 ohm. If the conductors are reconnected to form wave winding, other things remaining unchanged, the value of the armature circuit resistance will be
(a) 0.01 Ω (b) 0.06 Ω (c) 0.36 Ω (d) 0.54 Ω

[GATE, 1992]

20. A 4-pole lap-wound D.C. generator has a developed power of P watts and brush voltage of E volts. Two adjacent brushes of the machine are removed as they are worn out. If the machine operates with the remaining brushes, the developed voltage and power that can be obtained from the machine are
(a) E, P (b) $E/2, P/2$ (c) $E, P/4$ (d) $E, P/2$

21. The dummy coil in a D.C. machine is used to
(a) eliminate reactance voltage
(b) reduce armature reaction
(c) provide mechanical balance to the armature
(d) reduce harmonics generated in armature

22. In A.C. machine, double-layer winding is preferred over single-layer windings because
1. it needs less copper
2. it gives high induced e.m.f. for the same amount of copper

3. if requires one size of the coils
4. it is economical
5. it possesses lower leakage reactance

From these, the correct answer is

(a) 1, 3, 5 *(b)* 2, 4, 5 *(c)* 3, 4, 5 *(d)* 1, 4, 5

23. **For C coils and P poles, the winding pitch for the two types of D.C. armature windings are :**

	Simplex-lap winding	*Simplex-wave winding*
(a)	+ 2	$\frac{2C \pm 2}{P/2}$
(b)	− 2	$\frac{2C + 2}{P/2}$
(c)	± 2	$\frac{4C \pm 4}{P}$
(d)	± 2	$\frac{2C - 2}{P/2}$

24. **For C coils and P poles, the commutator pitch for the two types of D.C. armature windings are:**

	Simplex-lap winding	*Simplex-wave winding*
(a)	± 1	$\frac{2C \pm 2}{P}$
(b)	+ 1	$\frac{C \pm 1}{P}$
(c)	− 1	$\frac{2C + 2}{P}$
(d)	± 1	$\frac{C \pm 1}{P}$

25. **For C coils and P poles, the distance between the coils connected by an equalizer ring is**

(a) C/P *(b)* C/2 *(c)* 2 C/P *(d)* C/2 P

26. **In a P-pole D.C. machine with armature current I_a, the current per brush arm for a lap-connected winding is**

(a) $\frac{I_a}{P}$ *(b)* $\frac{I_a}{2P}$ *(c)* $\frac{2I_a}{P}$ *(d)* $\frac{I_a}{4P}$

27. **An 8-pole D.C. machine has simplex-lap connected 1000 armature conductors, 4 turns per coil and 2 coil-sides per slot. The number of slots in this machine are**

(a) 125, equalizers not possible *(b)* 125, equalizers possible

(c) 250, equalizers possible *(d)* 250, equalizers not possible

28. **Armature of an 8-pole D.C. machine has 15 slots with 4 coil-sides per slot. This machine**

1. will have dummy coil/s if wave winding is used
2. will have equalizer rings if lap winding is used
3. has $y_b = 7$ and $y_f = 5$ for lap winding with no split coils
4. has $y_b = 9$ and $y_f = 7$ for lap winding with no split coils

From these, the correct answer is

(a) 1, 2, 4 *(b)* 1, 2, 3 *(c)* 2, 3 *(d)* 1, 4

29. A 4-pole lap-connected D.C. generator has a developed power of P watts and brush voltage of E volts. One brush of the machine is removed as it is worn out. If the machine operates with the remaining brushes, the developed voltage and power that can be obtained from the machine are

(a) E, P (b) $E/2, P/2$ (c) $E, P/4$ (d) $E, P/2$

30. A 6-pole lap wound D.C. generator has a developed power of P watts and brush voltage of E volts. Three adjacent brushes of the machine are removed as they are worn out. If the machine operates with the remaining brushes, the developed voltage and power that can be obtained from the machine are

(a) E, P (b) $E, \frac{2P}{3}$ (c) $\frac{E}{P}, \frac{2P}{3}$ (d) $E, P/3$

31. A 6-pole lap-wound D.C. generator has a developed power of P watts and brush voltage of E volts. Two adjacent brushes of the machine are removed as they are worn out. If the machine operates with the remaining brushes, the developed voltage and power that can be obtained from the machine are

(a) E, P (b) $E, \frac{P}{2}$ (c) $E, P/3$ (d) $E, 2P/3$

32. A 6-pole lap wound D.C. generator has a developed power of P watts and brush voltage of E volts. One brush of the machine is taken out as it worn out. If the machine operates with the remaining brushes, the developed voltage and power that can be obtained from the machine are

(a) E, P (b) $E, \frac{2P}{3}$ (c) $\frac{E}{2}, \frac{2P}{3}$ (d) $E, P/3$

33. Consider the following statements regarding A.C. machine windings :

1. Phase spread (σ) of 60° produces a phase-belt sequence of A, B, C
2. Phase spread of 120° produces a phase-belt sequence of A, B, C
3. Generated e.m.f. with $\sigma = 60°$ is 15% more than with $\sigma = 120°$
4. Phase spread of 60° produces a phase-belt sequence of $A, -C, B-A, C, -B$
5. Output with $\sigma = 60°$ is 15% less than with $\sigma = 120°$
6. In integral-slot chorded winding, each slot has top and bottom layers belonging to the same phase.

Of these statements

(a) 2, 3, 4 are correct (b) 1, 5, 6 are correct
(c) 1, 2, 3, 4 are correct (d) 2, 3, 5 are correct

34. A 3-phase machine has 39 slots and 6 poles. This machine can have

(a) integral slot winding (b) integral-slot chorded winding
(c) fractional-slot winding (d) none of these

35. For a 3-phase fractional-slot winding with P poles, the number of parallel paths is

(a) P (b) $2P$ (c) $P/2$ (d) none of these

36. For a 3-phase machine with P poles, consider the following statements :

1. The number of parallel paths for integral-slot winding is $P/2$
2. The number of parallel paths for integral-slot chorded winding is $P/2$
3. The number of parallel paths for 54 slots and 10 poles is 2
4. The number of parallel path for 54 slots and 8 poles is 4.

From these, the correct statements are

(a) 1, 2, 4 (b) 1, 3 (c) 1, 2, 3 (d) 1, 4

37. Fractional-slot winding is used in

(a) turbogenerators (b) hydrogenerators

(c) fractional-kW motors (d) squirrel-cage induction motors

38. A 3-phase, 10 pole low-speed water-turbine alternator has 144 slots. The spacing between the starting of phase *A* and that of phase *B*, in terms of slot-pitches, are

(a) 15 (b) 24 (c) 48 (d) 14

39. A 3-phase, 16-pole alternator has 84 slots. Polarity of the starting of phase-belt of phase *B* with respect to phase *A* and its displacement from phase-A starting are

(a) same polarity, 7 pitches (b) opposite polarity, 14 slot-pitches

(c) opposite polarity, 7 slot pitches (d) same polarity, 14 slot-pitches

40. For a 3-phase machine having double-layer winding, mark the correct statement

	Full-pitched winding	*Chorded winding*
(a)	Each slot has coil-sides belonging to the same phase	Each slot has coil-sides belonging to the same phase
(b)	Some slots have coil-sides belonging to different phases	Each slot has coil-sides belonging to different phases
(c)	Each slot has coil-sides belonging to different phases	Some slots have coil-sides of different phases and some from the same phase
(d)	Each slot has coil-sides belonging to the same phase	Some slots have coil-sides of the same phase and some from different phases

41. In single-layer and double-layer windings, the number of coils *C* is related to the number of slots *S* by the following relations respectively

(a) C = S, 2 C = S (b) 2 C = S, C = S (c) 2 C = 3 S, C = S (d) 2 C = S, 3 C = S

42. For the use of mush windings in 3-phase induction motors,

1. the slots should be open
2. coil-pitch, in terms of slots, must be odd
3. the slots should be semi-closed
4. coil-pitch, in terms of slots, may be odd
5. the maximum recommended voltage is 440 V
6. the coil-pitch, in terms of slots, may be even
7. the maximum recommended voltage is 600 V

From these, the correct answer is

(a) 2, 3, 5 (b) 3, 4, 5 (c) 1, 4, 6, 7 (d) 3, 6, 7

43. Whole-coil and mush windings are similar because their

(a) coils are interconnected in the same manner

(b) coil-pitches are the same

(c) phase spreads are equal

(d) slot-pitches are equal

44. In most A.C. machines, it is usually a standard practice to use

(a) fractional-slot winding with full-pitch coils

(b) integral-slot winding with chorded coils
(c) fractional-slot winding with chorded coils
(d) integral-slot winding with full-pitch coils

45. Match List-I (type of winding) with List II (feature) and select the correct answer using the codes given below the lists :

	List I		List II
A.	Fractional-slot windings	1.	Only two-third of the pole-pitch is occupied by the winding
B.	Chorded and distributed windings	2.	Effect of slot harmonics are reduced or even eliminated
C.	Damper windings	3.	Effect of phase-belt harmonics are reduced
D.	Single-phase windings	4.	Additional asynchronous torque capability in projected pole motors

Codes :

	A	B	C	D		A	B	C	D
(a)	2	3	4	1	(b)	2	3	1	4
(c)	3	2	1	4	(d)	3	2	4	1

46. Match List I with List II and select the correct answer by using the codes given below the lists:

List I (Windings)		List II (Associated terms)	
A.	Closed windings	1.	Dummy coil
B.	Open windings	2.	Fractional-slot winding
		3.	Mush winding
		4.	Split coils
		5.	Phase spread 180°
		6.	Parallel paths

Codes :

	A	B		A	B
(a)	1, 4, 5, 6	2, 3, 6	(b)	1, 4, 6	2, 3, 5
(c)	1, 4, 6	2, 3, 6	(d)	1, 4, 5	2, 3, 6

47. A 4-pole, 3-phase, double-layer winding is housed in a 36-slot stator for an A.C. machine with 60° phase spread. Coil span is 7 slot pitches. Number of slots in which top and bottom layers belong to different phases is *(GATE, 2003)*

(a) 24 (b) 18 (c) 12 (d) 0

48. A 3-phase A.C. machine, with 54 stator slots and 10 poles, has its 9 coils, pertaining to phase A, distributed under 5 adjacent poles as under (take double-layer winding and phase spread = 60°) :

	Ist Pole	2nd Pole	3rd Pole	4th Pole	5th Pole
(a)	1	2	2	2	2
(b)	2	1	2	2	2
(c)	2	2	1	2	2
(d)	2	2	2	1	2

49. A 3-phase A.C. machine, with double-layer winding, has 54 stator slots wound for 10 poles. Its 27 slots are distributed under 5 adjacent poles as follows (take phase spread = 60°) :

	Ist Pole	2nd Pole	3rd Pole	4th Pole	5th Pole
(a)	6	6	5	5	5
(b)	6	5	6	5	5
(c)	5	5	5	6	6
(d)	5	6	5	6	6

50. **A 4-pole, 3-phase, double player winding is housed in a 36-slot stator for an A.C. machine with 60° phase spread. Coil span is 8 slot pitches. Number of slots in which top and bottom coil-sides belong to different phases is**

(a) 24 *(b)* 18 *(c)* 12 *(d)* 0

ANSWERS

1.	*(d)*	**2.**	*(c)*	**3.**	*(b)*	**4.**	*(a)*	**5.**	*(c)*
6.	*(c)*	**7.**	*(d)*	**8.**	*(b)*	**9.**	*(a)*	**10.**	*(c)*
11.	*(a)*	**12.**	*(b)*	**13.**	*(c)*	**14.**	*(d)*	**15.**	*(c)*
16.	*(b)*	**17.**	*(c)*	**18.**	*(d)*	**19.**	*(d)*	**20.**	*(c)*
21.	*(c)*	**22.**	*(c)*	**23.**	*(c)*	**24.**	*(a)*	**25.**	*(c)*
26.	*(c)*	**27.**	*(a)*	**28.**	*(d)*	**29.**	*(d)*	**30.**	*(d)*
31.	*(b)*	**32.**	*(b)*	**33.**	*(a)*	**34.**	*(d)*	**35.**	*(d)*
36.	*(c)*	**37.**	*(b)*	**38.**	*(b)*	**39.**	*(d)*	**40.**	*(d)*
41.	*(b)*	**42.**	*(a)*	**43.**	*(a)*	**44.**	*(c)*	**45.**	*(a)*
46.	*(a)*	**47.**	*(a)*	**48.**	*(d)*	**49.**	*(b)*	**50.**	*(c)*

THREE-PHASE CIRCUITS AND MAGNETIC CIRCUITS

1. A mild steel ring with mean diameter of 20 cm has core area of 10 cm^2. For a relative permeability of 500, the reluctance of the ring in AT/Wb is
   (a) 1×10^6 (b) 0.1×10^6 (c) 0.01×10^5 (d) 10×10^6
2. Magnetic flux, flux density and magnetic field intensity have the following units respectively:
   (a) Wb, Wb/m^2, Wb/m (b) Wb, Wb/m, Amp. turns
   (c) Lines, Wb/m^2, Amp. turns/m (d) Wb, Wb/m^2, Amp.turns/m
3. A magnetic circuit with relative permeability of 100 has a core cross-section of 5 cm^2 and mean core length of 25 cm. The coil has 120 turns with an m.m.f. of 1000 AT. The magnetic core flux is
   (a) 0.5 m Wb (b) 0.25 mWb (c) 0.75 mWb (d) 1 mWb
4. The magnetic flux in a homogeneous toroidal core excited by a coil with a given number of turns carrying a fixed current is
   1. proportional to cross-sectional area of the toroid
   2. proportional to the diameter of the toroid
   3. inversely proportional to cross-sectional area of the toroid
   4. inversely proportional to diameter of the toroid

   From these, the correct answer is
   (a) 1, 3 (b) 2, 3 (c) 1, 4 (d) 2, 4
5. A toroidal ferromagnetic ring is uniformly wound with copper wire of certain turns. A D.C. voltage V_1 is applied across the winding to cause a uniform flux density in the ring. If the linear dimensions of the ring, number of turns and length of mean turns are doubled without changing the gauge of the wire, the D.C.-voltage required to be applied across the new winding to produce the same flux density will be
   (a) $\frac{V_1}{2}$ (b) V_1 (c) $2\,V_1$ (d) $4\,V_1$
6. In the magnetic circuit shown in Fig. C.75, the areas of cross-section of limbs B and C are, respectively, 0.01 m^2 and 0.02 m^2. Air gaps of lengths 1.0 mm and 2.00 mm, respectively, are cut in limbs B and C.

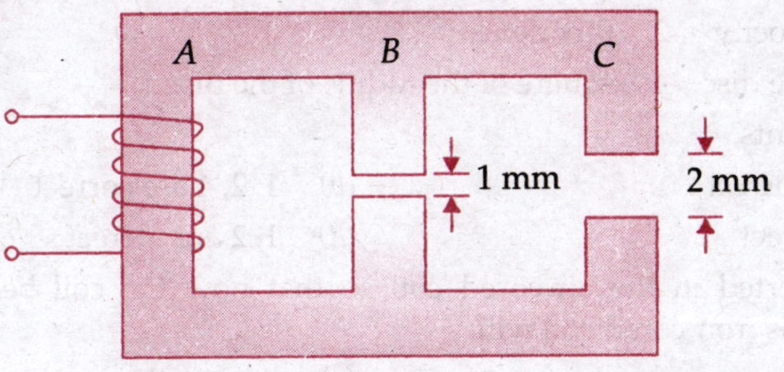

Fig C.75

   If the magnetic medium can be assumed to have infinite permeability and the flux in limb B is 1.0 Wb, the flux in the limb A is *[GATE, 1990]*
   (a) 3 Wb (b) 1.5 Wb (c) 2 Wb (d) 4 Wb
7. The current in a coil wound over a ferromagnetic core is gradually increased to 2 A and then reduced to 1 A and then the current in it is again increased to 2 A. The variation of magnetization of the core will be as shown in

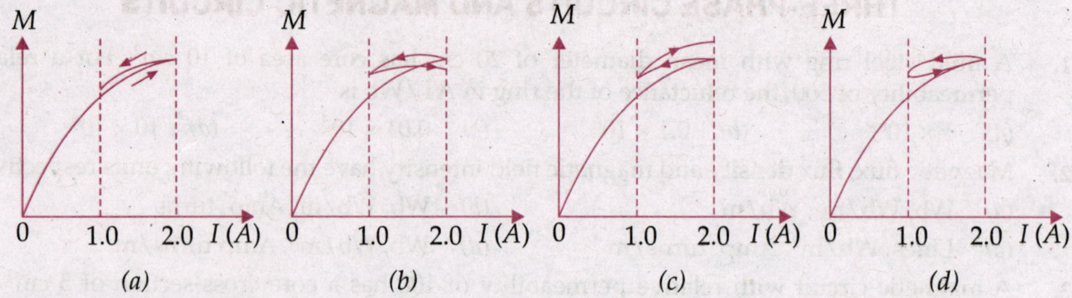

8. "In all cases of electromagnetic induction, an induced voltage will cause a current to flow in a closed circuit in such a direction that the magnetic field which is caused by that current will oppose the change that produces the current", is the original statement of

(a) Lenz's law (b) Faraday's law of magnetic induction

(c) Fleming's law of induction (d) Ampere's law

9. The laws of electromagnetic induction (Faraday's and Lenz's law) are summarized in the following equation : [GATE, 1998]

(a) $e = i R$ (b) $e = L \dfrac{di}{dt}$ (c) $e = -\dfrac{d\psi}{dt}$ (d) none of above.

10. A coil rotates at a constant speed in a uniform magnetic field that is oriented along the x-axis. Induced e.m.f. in the coil will be maximum when the axis of rotation of the coil

(a) coincide s with the x-axis

(b) lies in the $x-y$ plane making an angle of 45° with both x-and y-axes

(c) lies in the $z-x$ plane making an angle of 45° with both z-and x-axes

(d) lies in the $y-z$ plane

11. Consider the following statements relating to a circular disc rotating in a traverse magnetic field B Wb/m^2 as shown in Fig. C.76.

The e.m.f. generated across outer rim A and centre O is proportional to

1. angular velocity 2. flux density

3. radios of the disc 4. square of the radius of the disc

Of these statements

(a) 1, 2, 3 are correct (b) 1, 2, 4 are correct

(c) 2, 4 are correct (d) 1, 2 are correct

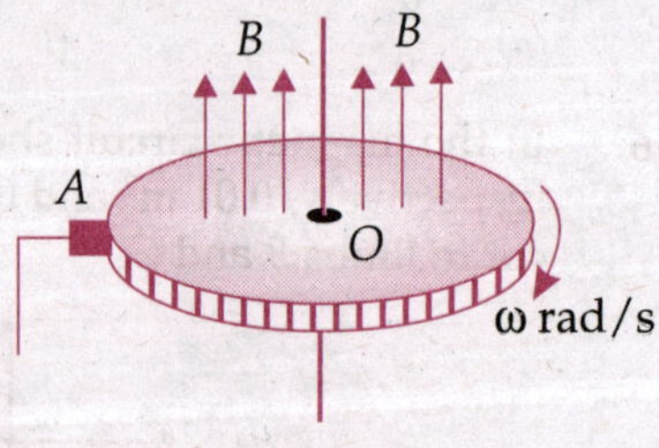

Fig C.76

12. Iron-core is inserted in the air-cored coil so that now the coil becomes iron-cored coil. Inductance of this iron-cored coil will

(a) increase (b) decrease (c) remain the same

(d) increase or decrease depending upon the coil configuration

13. A coil with 60 turns wound over a ferromagnetic core having relative premeability 400 has an inductance of 50 mH. If coil turns are doubled and the core is replaced by a new ferromagnetic core having relative permeability 600, the new inductance would be

(a) 0.03 H (b) 0.3 H (c) 3 H (d) 0.15 H

14. The phase sequence of a 3-phase alternator will reverse if

(a) the field current is reversed keeping the direction of rotation same

(b) the field current remains the same but the direction of rotation is reversed

(c) the field current is reversed and the number of poles is doubled

(d) the number of poles is doubled without reversing the field current

15. Three resistances, each of R Ω, are connected in delta. Their equivalent star value for each resistance is

(a) R *(b)* 3 R *(c)* R/3 *(d)* 2 R

16. Three capacitances, each of C farads, are connected in delta. Their equivalent star value for each capacitance is

(a) C *(b)* 3 C *(c)* C/3 *(d)* 2 C

17. In a certain magnetic circuit, a current of 1 A produces a flux of 1 Wb. If linear dimensions of the magnetic circuit are doubled, then for producing the same flux, the current would be

(a) $\frac{1}{2}$ *A* *(b)* 1 *A* *(c)* 2 *A* *(d)* $\frac{1}{4}$ *A*

18. An iron-cored choke, with 1 mm air-gap length, takes 1 A when fed from a constant-voltage source of 230 V. If its air-gap length is increased to 10 mm, then the magnetic flux produced by the choke would

(a) decrease and the current would also decrease

(b) remain constant and the current would decrease

(c) decrease and the current would increase

(d) remain constant and the current would increase

19. For a solenoid shown in Fig. C.77,

(a) end *A* becomes north pole if *C* has positive polarity

(b) end *B* becomes north pole if *D* has positive polarity

(c) end *B* becomes south pole if *C* has positive polarity

(d) end *A* becomes north pole if *D* has positive polarity

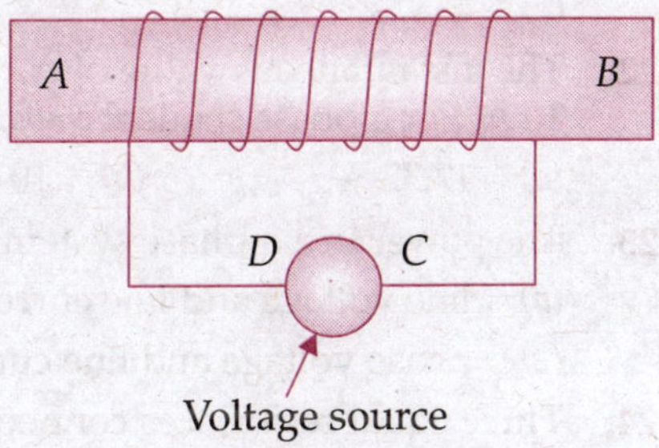

Fig C.77

20. Match List I with List II and give the correct answer by using the codes given below the lists :

List I *(Motion of permanent magnet)*	List II *(Direction of e.m.f. in stationary coil)*
A. 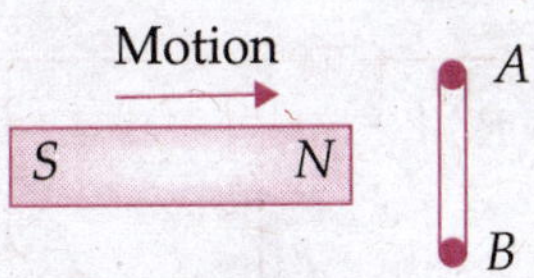	1. No e.m.f. in the coil
B. 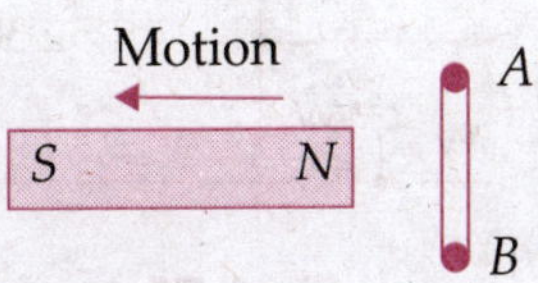	2. Cross in coil-side *A* and dot in coil-side *B*

C. 

3. Dot in coil-side A and cross in coil-side B

D. 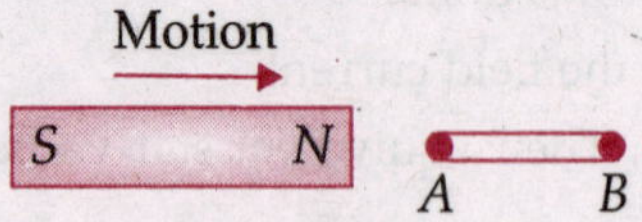

Codes :

	A	B	C	D		A	B	C	D
(a)	1	2	3	3	*(b)*	2	3	3	1
(c)	2	3	1	3	*(d)*	2	3	1	1

21. Match List I with List II and select the correct answer by using the codes given below the list :

List I *(Magnetic Circuit)*	List II *(Electric circuit)*
A. Magnetic flux density	1. Current
B. Magnetic field intensity	2. Conductivity
C. permeability	3. Electric field intensity
D. Magnetic flux	4. Current density

Codes :

	A	B	C	D		A	B	C	D
(a)	4	3	2	1	*(b)*	1	2	3	4
(c)	4	2	1	3	*(d)*	4	3	1	2

22. The instantaneous value of currents in both phases b and c of a 3-phase balanced system are 10 A. For a phase sequence *abc*, the instantaneous value of current in phase *'a'* is

(a) 17.32 A *(b)* 10 A *(c)* 20 A *(d)* 34.64 A

23. The power in a 3-phase system is given by $\sqrt{3}\, V_l I_l \cos\theta$. Here θ is the p.f. angle between

(a) line voltage and line current *(b)* line voltage and phase current
(c) phase voltage and line current *(d)* phase voltage and phase current

24. Three equal resistances connected in star take a line current of 5 A when fed from 400 V, 50 Hz source. If the load resistances are reconnected in delta, the line current would now be

(a) 5 *A* *(b)* $5\sqrt{3}$ *A* *(c)* $\frac{15}{\sqrt{3}}$ *A* *(d)* 15

25. A star-connected balanced load takes P watts from a balanced 3-phase supply. If the star-load is reconnected in delta across the same 3-phase supply, the power consumed will be

(a) P *(b)* $3P$
(c) $\sqrt{3}\,P$ *(d)* $P/3$

26. The input voltage to the 3-phase, 50 Hz A.C. circuit shown in Fig. C.78 is 100 V. For a phase sequence of *abc* (or RYB), the wattmeters would read

(a) $W_1 = 1732$ W and $W_2 = 0$ W
(b) $W_1 = 866$ W and $W_2 = 866$ W
(c) $W_1 = 1154.72$ W and $W_2 = 577.36$ W
(d) $W_1 = 577.36$ W and $W_2 = 1154.74$ W

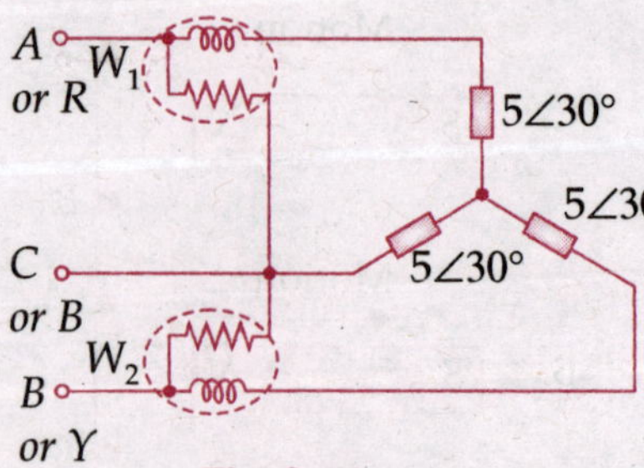

Fig C.78

27. Input to the 3-phase, 50 Hz A.C. circuit shown in Fig. C.79 is 100 V. For a phase sequence of *abc* [or RYB], the wattmeters would read

(a) $W_1 = 1732$ W and $W_2 = 0$ W

(b) $W_1 = 866$ W and $W_2 = 866$ W

(c) $W_1 = 1154.72$ W and $W_2 = 577.36$ W

(d) $W_1 = 577.36$ W and $W_2 = 1154.72$ W

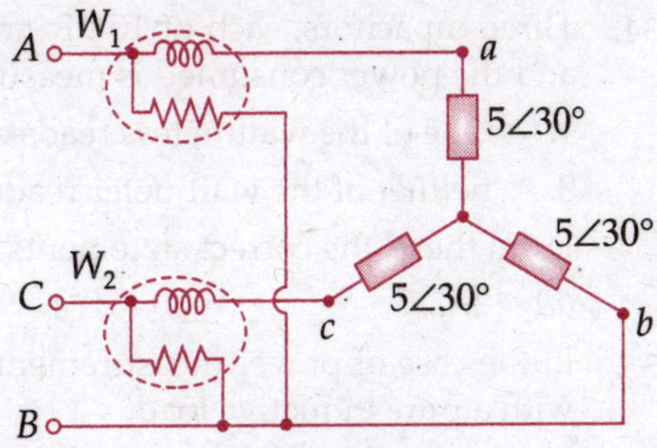

Fig C.79

28. In a two-wattmeter method of measuring power, one of the wattmeters reading is zero watts. The power factor of the circuit is

(a) zero (b) 1

(c) 0.5 (d) 0.866

29. The power delivered to a 3-phase load can be measured by the use of two wattmeters only when the

(a) load is unbalanced

(b) load is balanced

(c) three-phase load is connected to the source through three wires

(d) three-phase load is connected to the source through four wires

30. The minimum number of wattmeters required to measure the real power in an *n*-phase system with unbalanced load is

(a) n (b) $n - 1$ (c) $n + 1$ (d) $n - 2$

31. Three-phase power can be measured by two-wattmeter method in case of

1. balanced load and balanced source
2. balanced source with 3-phase, 3-wire unbalanced load
3. unbalanced source with 3-phase, 3-wire balanced load
4. balanced source with 3-phase, 4-wire unbalanced load
5. unbalanced load and unbalanced source

From these, the correct answer is

(a) 1 only (b) 2, 3 and 5 (c) 1, 2, 3, 4 and 5 (d) 1, 2, 3 and 5

32. Measurement of power and power factor of a 3-phase system by two-wattmeter method can be obtained in case of

1. balanced load and balaned source
2. balanced source with 3-phase, 3-wire unbalanced load
3. unbalanced source with 3-phase, 3-wire balanced load
4. balanced source with 3-phase, 4-wire unbalanced load
5. unbalanced load and unbalanced source

From these, the correct answer is

(a) 1 only (b) 2, 3 and 5

(c) 1, 2, 3, 4 and 5 (d) 1, 2, 3 and 5

33. R.m.s. value of the voltage across the 100 ohm resistor after the switch *S* is closed in the 3-phase circuit shown in Fig. C.80 is (use Thevenin's theorem)

[GATE, 1992]

(a) 230.95 V (b) 115.475 V

(c) 400 V (d) 284.23 V

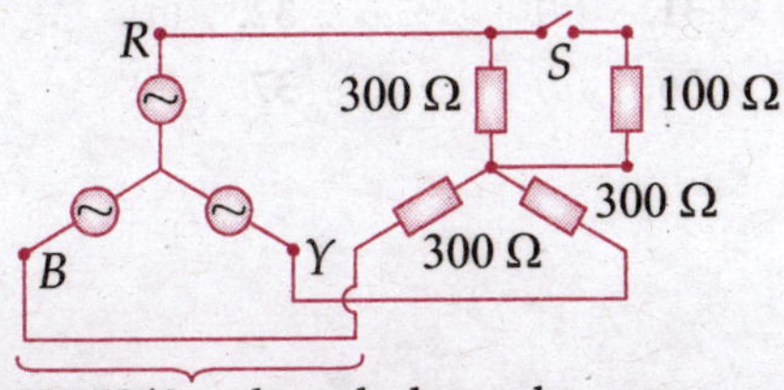

Fig C.80

34. Three capacitors, each of 10 μF, are connected in star across a 3-phase, 400 V, 50 Hz supply and the power consumed is measured by two wattmeter method. Under the conditions

1. One of the wattmeters reads zero
2. both the wattmeters read zero
3. neither of the wattmeter reads zero
4. the total power consumed is zero

From these, the correct statements are

(a) 2, 4 (b) 1, 4 (c) 3, 4 (d) 2, 3

35. In the case of power measurement by two-wattmeter method in a balanced 3-phase system with a pure inductive load [I.A.S., 1993]

(a) both the wattmeters will indicate the same value but of opposite sign
(b) both the wattmeters will indicate zero
(c) both the wattmeters will indicate the same value and of the same sign
(d) one wattmeter will indicate zero and other some non-zero value

36. Two wattmeters used to measure power of a 3-phase balanced load read W_1 and W_2. The reactive power drawn by the load is

(a) $W_1 + W_2$ (b) $W_1 - W_2$ (c) $\sqrt{3}\ (W_1 + W_2)$ (d) $\sqrt{3}\ (W_1 - W_2)$

37. For the balanced Y-Y connected 3-phase circuit shown in the figure below, the line-line voltage is 208 V rms and the total power absorbed by the load is 432 W at a power factor of 0.6 leading. The approximate value of the impedance Z is [GATE, 2017 (2)]

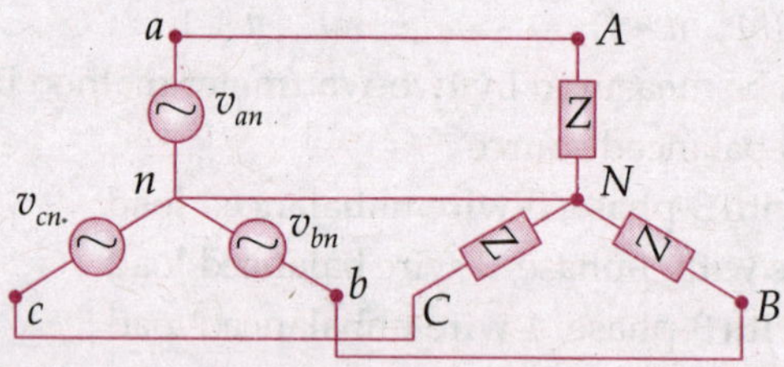

(a) 33 $\angle -53.1°$ (b) 60 $\angle 53.1°$ (c) 60 $\angle -53.1°$ (d) 180 $\angle -53.1°$

ANSWERS

1. (a)	**2.** (d)	**3.** (b)	**4.** (c)	**5.** (d)
6. (c)	**7.** (b)	**8.** (a)	**9.** (c)	**10.** (d)
11. (b)	**12.** (a)	**13.** (b)	**14.** (b)	**15.** (c)
16. (b)	**17.** (a)	**18.** (d)	**19.** (d)	**20.** (d)
21. (a)	**22.** (c)	**23.** (d)	**24.** (d)	**25.** (b)
26. (c)	**27.** (d)	**28.** (c)	**29.** (c)	**30.** (b)
31. (d)	**32.** (a)	**33.** (b)	**34.** (c)	**35.** (a)
36. (d)	**37.** (c)			

D
Appendix

Short-Answer Type Questions

In has been observed that one question is usually compulsory in a question-paper. This compulsory question is invariably of the short-question short-answer type. In this appendix, an attempt is made to familiarise the candidates with the pattern of such type of questions.

Thousands of such questions can be prepared. The readers are advised to make such short-questions on their own and jot-down the short-answer there and then as they go through the text-book diligently. This practice will, at the same time, prepare them for their viva-voce examinations as well as for the job-interview questions.

TRANSFORMERS

1. What are the functions of a transformer?

Ans. The function of a transformer can be any one of the following :

(i) To decrease or increase the voltage and current levels from one circuit to another circuit.

(ii) To match the load impedance with the source impedance for maximum power transfer to the load.

(iii) To isolate one circuit from another or to stop the flow of D.C. while A.C. is permitted to flow to the load.

2. What do you understand by step-down and step-up transformers?

Ans. When the output voltage is lower than the input voltage, it is called a step-down transformer. When the output voltage is higher than the input voltage, it is known as a step-up transformer.

3. Is it possible for any voltage winding in a transformer to serve as its primary?

Ans. Yes. If H.V. winding is connected to A.C. source, it becomes a step-down transformer with H.V. winding as its primary. If L.V. winding is energised from A.C. source, it becomes a step-up transformer with L.V. winding as its primary.

4. Why is it that e.m.fs. induced in the primary and secondary windings of a transformer are in phase with each other?

Ans. It is because the same magnetic flux linking both the primary and secondary windings induces e.m.fs. in primary and secondary windings.

5. What is the transformation ratio in transformers?

Ans. As per IS, there is no clear-cut definition for the transformation ratio of transformers. However, some books take $\dfrac{N_1}{N_2} = \dfrac{E_1}{E_2} = \dfrac{V_1}{V_2} = \dfrac{I_2}{I_1} = a$ as the transformation ratio, while the others take $\dfrac{N_2}{N_1} = \dfrac{E_2}{E_1} = \dfrac{V_2}{V_1} = \dfrac{I_1}{I_2} = a$ as the transformation ratio.

6. How can the iron loss be minimised in a transformer?

Ans. The iron loss in a transformer is made up of hysteresis loss and eddy-current loss. Hysteresis loss is reduced by using cold-rolled-grain-oriented electrical steel for the transformer core. Eddy current loss is minimised by using thin sheets (0.35 mm) of laminations for preparing the transformer core.

7. How can core-loss be measured in a transformer?

Ans. It can be measured by performing open-circuit test on the transformer. In this test, H.V. winding is left open circuited. The voltage applied to L.V. winding is gradually increased to its rated value. Now the wattmeter reading gives the open-circuit core loss in the transformer.

8. How can ohmic loss be measured in a transformer?

Ans. It can be measured by performing short-circuit test on the transformer. In this test, L.V. winding is short circuited. The voltage applied to H.V. winding is gradually increased till the ammeter records the rated current of H.V. winding. Now the wattmeter reading gives the ohmic loss or I^2R loss in the transformer.

9. Which equivalent circuit parameters can be determined from the open-circuit test on a transformer?

Ans. These parameters are core-loss resistance R_c and the magnetizing-reactance X_m.

10. Which equivalent circuit parameters can be obtained from the short-circuit test on a transformer?

Ans. These parameters are

(i) resistances r_1 and r_2 of the primary (*P*) and secondary (*S*) windings respectively and

(ii) leakage reactances x_1 and x_2 of *P* and *S* windings respectively.

11. What is the order of magnitude of no-load current in a transformer?

Ans. It varies from 2 to 6% of full-load current.

12. What are the two components of exciting current in a transformer? What is the function of each of these components?

Ans. The exciting (or no-load) current of a transformer has two components; namely magnetizing current I_m and the core-loss current I_c.

The function of magnetizing current I_m is to produce the necessary m.m.f. to create the required mutual flux in the core. The function of core-loss current is to provide for the core loss in the transformer.

13. A single-phase, 3000/1000 V 10 kVA transformer has its leakage impedance of 2%. What voltage should be applied to the H.V. side for performing short-circuit test at rated current?

Ans. Here $z_{ea} = 2\% = 0.02$, Rated current = 1.00 p.u. = I_1

$\therefore$ Applied voltage $= I_1 z_{ea} = 1 \times 0.02 = 0.02$ p.u. $= 0.02 \times 3000 = 60$ V

14. Can a 1-phase, 110 V, 50 Hz transformer operate at 200 Hz? State the conditions.

Ans. Here $\frac{V}{f} = \frac{110}{50} = \frac{V_1}{200}$ or $V_1 = \frac{110}{50} \times 200 = 440$ V.

If the transformer is fed from 440 V, 200 Hz ; it will operate satisfactorily.

15. How are the transformer losses affected if p.f. of a given load is varied?

Ans. For low value of load p.f., primary and sacondary winding currents become more ($\because$ current $\propto$ Load/p.f.). Therefore, ohmic loss increases as the load p.f. is lowered. Core loss, however, remains unaffected because B_m, f are not altered by load p.f.

16. How is the voltage regulation of a transformer affected by a change in its operating frequency?

Ans. In a transformer, voltage regulation is given by $I_2\, r_{e2} \cos \theta_2 + I_2\, x_{e2} \sin \theta_2$. With increase in frequency, x_{e2} increase, voltage regulation also becomes more. With decrease in frequency, voltage regulation would become lower.

17. An autotransformer has the voltage ratio V_1/V_2 where $V_1 > V_2$. Calculate the fraction of power transferred inductively. [P.T.U., 2001]

Ans. Inductively transferred $VA = \left(1 - \dfrac{V_2}{V_1}\right) \times$ Total input VA

$$\therefore \quad \frac{\text{Power transferred inductively}}{\text{Total input power}} = \left[\frac{V_1 - V_2}{V_1}\right] = \left[1 - \frac{V_2}{V_1}\right] = [1 - k]$$

Where $k = \dfrac{V_2}{V_1}$ and $k < 1$.

18. A 2/1 ratio two-winding transformer is connected as an auto-transformer to a given voltage ratio 2/3. Calculate its kVA rating as an auto-transformer compared to a two-winding transformer. [P.T.U., 2002]

Ans.
$$\frac{\text{kVA ratings as an auto} - \text{transformer}}{\text{kVA rating as a two} - \text{winding transformer}} = \frac{1}{1-k}$$

where $k < 1$
$$= \frac{1}{1 - \frac{2}{3}} = 3 \text{ as } k = \frac{2}{3}.$$

19. Two coils with self-inductance of 1 H and 4 H have mutual inductance of 1 H. Find their coupling factors and the coefficient of coupling. [P.T.U., 2002]

Ans. Self-inductance of coil 1, $L_1 = \dfrac{N_1^2}{Rl} = 1\text{ H}$

Self-inductance of coil 2, $L_2 = \dfrac{N_2}{Rl} = 4\text{ H}$

$$\therefore \quad \frac{L_1}{L_2} = \left(\frac{N_1}{N_2}\right)^2 = \frac{1}{4} \text{ or } \frac{N_1}{N_2} = \frac{1}{2}$$

This gives coupling factor k_1 for coil 1 $= \dfrac{N_1}{N_2} \cdot \dfrac{M}{L_1} = \dfrac{1}{2} \times \dfrac{1}{1} = \dfrac{1}{2} = 0.5$

$$k_2 = \frac{N_2}{N_1} \cdot \frac{M}{L_2} = 2 \times \frac{1}{4} = \frac{1}{2} = 0.5$$

Coefficient of coupling, $k = \sqrt{k_1 k_2} = \sqrt{0.5 \times 0.5} = 0.5$

20. Two mutually coupled coils act as an ideal transformer. Find the nature of its core reluctance. [P.T.U., 2002]

Ans. An ideal transformer should have linear magnetization curve. This means that its permeability is constant. Reluctance is given by

$$R_l = \frac{L}{\propto_0 \propto_r \cdot A}$$

For an ideal transformer, L and A are constant and here $\mu_0\, \mu_r$ is also constant, therefore reluctance for a magnetic circuit is constant.

21. If P_i and P_o represent iron loss and full-load ohmic loss, then find the fractional load at which maximum transformer efficiency occurs. [P.T.U., 2002]

Ans. For maximum transformer efficiency, variable ohmic loss = constant iron loss i.e., $n^2 P_o = P_i$

$\therefore$ Fractional load at which maximum efficiency occurs,

$$n = \sqrt{\frac{P_i}{P_o}}.$$

22. What happens in a transformer if its core is prepared from high-permeability ferromagnetic material? *[P.T.U., 2002]*

Ans. For a magnetic circuit, $\text{reluctance} = \dfrac{\text{length}}{\mu_0 \mu_r \cdot A}$

So a core with high permeability has low reluctance. The core flux, determined by the applied voltage and frequency, is constant

$$\therefore \quad \text{Flux} = \frac{\text{m.m.f.}}{\text{Rel}} = \text{constant}$$

For low reluctance, magnetizing m.m.f. is low, therefore magnetizing current is low. Thus, a transformer having high-permeability core would require low value of magnetizing current.

23. A 1000 kVA, 50 kV/40 kV, single-phase autotransformer is fully loaded. Find the current in the common section of the winding.

Ans. Current from source, $I_1 = \dfrac{1000}{50} = 20$ A

Load current, $I_2 = \dfrac{1000}{40} = 25$ A

$\therefore$ Current in common section of the winding = $I_2 - I_1 = 25 - 20 = 5$ A.

24. Why is transformer core laminated? *[P.T.U., 2001]*

Ans. So as to reduce the eddy-current loss.

25. Compare hot-rolled and C.R.G.O. laminations as used in a transformer.

Ans. For hot-rolled (h.r.) 0.35 mm thick laminations, the iron loss for $B_m = 1.3$ T of 50 Hz varies from 1.63 to 2.02 W per kg of core material.

Iron loss for 0.35 mm thick C.R.G.O. laminations for $B_m = 1.65$ T of 50 Hz varies from 0.89 to 1.11 watts per kg of core laminations. This shows that iron loss in a core made of C.R.G.O. laminations is less than it is for the core of H.R. laminations.

As C.R.G.O. laminations allow more B_m, e.m.f. per turn = $\sqrt{2}\,\pi f B_m A_i$ is more, therefore, number of turns in L.V. and H.V. windings are less. At the same time, more B_m reduces size of the transformer.

ELECTROMECHANICAL ENERGY CONVERSION PRINCIPLES

1. Based on the principle of conservation of energy, write an energy balance equation for a motor. Also, write briefly about the various energy terms involved.

Ans. Energy balance equation for a motor is as under :

{Total electrical energy input to motor} = {Mechanical energy output at the shaft} + {Total energy stored} + {Total energy dissipated}

(i) Total electrical energy input to motor = (Applied voltage) (current) (time)

(ii) Mechanical energy output at shaft = Torque × speed × time

(iii) Total energy stored

= Energy stored [in magnetic field, $\frac{1}{2} LI^2$ + in mechanical system, $\frac{1}{2} J\omega_r^2$]

(iv) Total energy dissipated = Energy dissipated as [I^2R loss in windings + magnetic-core loss + friction and windage loss].

2. Write the following expressions :

(a) W_{fld} in terms of ϕ and R **(b) W_{fld} in terms of ψ and i**

(c) W_{fld} in terms of L and i

(d) field energy density in terms of B and H and also μ and B.

Ans. (a) $W_{fld} = \frac{1}{2}\phi^2 Rl$ (b) $W_{fld} = \frac{1}{2}\psi i$

(c) $W_{fld} = \frac{1}{2} Li^2$ (d) $W_{fld} = \frac{1}{2} HB = \frac{1}{2}\frac{B^2}{\mu}$ J/m^3

3. The armature of a simple magnetic relay moves through a virtual displacement dx in the direction of magnetic force f_e. As a consequence, the magnetization curves at locations g_1 and $(g_1 + dx)$ measured from the open position are as shown in Figs. D.1 *(a)* and *(b)*.

Write an expression for mechanical work done $f_e \cdot dx$ from a physical consideration of Fig. D.1 *(a)* and obtain therefrom an expression for magnetic force f_e.

Ans. In Fig. D.1 *(a)*, area *oaho* represents field energy *decrement* from *oaheo* to area *oheo*.

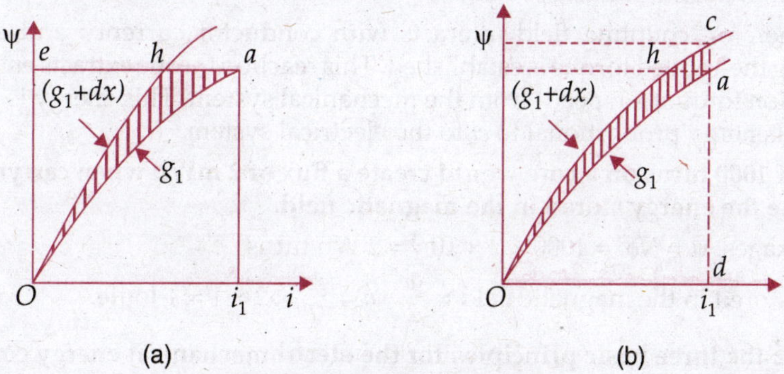

Fig D.1: Pertaining to Probs 3 and 4

∴ Mechanical work done, $f_e \cdot dx$ = area *oaho* = decrease in field energy stored after virtual displacement dx in the direction of f_e, at constant ψ

or $$f_e \cdot dx = -\,dW_{fld} \text{ at constant } \psi$$

∴ Magnetic force, $$f_e = -\frac{\partial W_{fld}}{\partial x}(\psi, x) = -\frac{\partial W_{fld}}{\partial x}(\phi, x)$$

4. Repreat Prob. 3 for Fig. D.1 (b).

Ans. In Fig. D.1 (b), area *oacho* represents *an increase* in coenergy from area *oado* to area *ohcado*.

∴ Mechanical work done, $f_e \cdot dx$ = area *oacho* = increase in coenergy after virtual displacement dx in the direction of f_e, at constant current

or $$f_e \cdot dx = +\,dW_{fed}' \text{ at constant current}$$

∴ Magnetic force, $$f_e = +\frac{\partial W_{fld}'}{\partial x}(i, x) = +\frac{\partial W_{fld}'}{\partial x}(F, x)$$

5. What do you understand by coenergy? *[P.T.U., 2002]*

Ans. Coenergy has no physical significance. It is given by the relation,

coenergy, W_{fld}' = electrical energy input − field-energy stored, W_{fld}

i.e., $W_{fld} + W_{fld}'$ = electrical energy input

For a linear magnetic system,

$$W_{fld}' = \frac{1}{2}\psi i = \frac{1}{2}\phi^2 \cdot Rl = \frac{1}{2}F^2 \cdot \Delta = \frac{1}{2}Li^2$$

Expression for coenergy is useful in the calculation of magnetic forces.

$$\therefore \qquad f_e = \frac{\partial W_{fld}'(i,x)}{\partial x}$$

For a doubly-excited linear magnetic system, $f_e = \frac{\partial W_{fld}'(i_1,i_2,x)}{\partial x}$

For a doubly-excited rotary magnetic system, $T_e = \frac{\partial W_{fld}'(i_1,i_2,\theta)}{\partial \theta}$

6. For an electromechanical energy conversion process, reaction of coupling magnetic field on electrical or mechanical system is essential. *[P.T.U., 2001]*

Ans. In a motor, coupling magnetic field reacts with the electrical system. As a result, reaction e.m.f. *e* opposing the applied voltage is established. An electrical energy proportional to *ei* is extracted from the electrical system and energy proportional to (torque) (speed) is delivered to the mechanical system.

In a generator, coupling field interacts with conductor current *i* and a reaction torque opposing the applied torque is established. This reaction torque extracts energy proportional to (reaction torque) × (speed) from the mechanical system. This energy is then delivered as electrical energy proportional to *ei* to the electrical system.

7. A coil of 1000 turns on a core would create a flux of 2 mWb when carrying a current 1 A. Calculate the energy stored in the magnetic field. *[P.T.U., 2002]*

Ans. Flux linkages, $\psi = N\phi = 1000 \times 2 \times 10^{-3} = 2$ Wb turns

Energy stored in the magnetic field $= \frac{1}{2}\psi i = \frac{1}{2} \times 2 \times 1 = 1$ Joule.

8. What are the three basic principles for the electromechanical energy conversion?

Ans. The three basic principles are induction, interaction and alignment.

Induction pertains to the e.m.f. induced in a coil when this coil links changing flux linkages. **Interaction** pertains to the development of force or torque when fields produced by stator as well as rotor interact with each other.

Alignment pertains to the development of reluctance force or torque. This torque is present when the reluctance seen by the working flux changes with the rotor movement.

9. Derive an expression for the lifting force of an electromagnet.

Ans. The electromagnet and the ferromagnetic material to be lifted are separated by an air-gap of length *x*.

Field energy density in the air gap, $W_{fld} = \frac{1}{2}\frac{B^2}{\mu_o}$ J/m^3

If *A* is the cross-sectional area of the electromagnet normal to the flux path, then field energy stored is

$$W_{fld} = \frac{1}{2}\frac{B^2}{\mu_o} \cdot Ax \text{ Joules}$$

$\therefore$ Lifting force,

$$f_e = \frac{\partial W_{fld}}{\partial x} = \frac{1}{2}\frac{B^2}{\mu_o} \cdot A \text{ Newtons.}$$

10. How is the reluctance torque produced in a rotating machine? *[P.T.U., 2001, 2002]*

Ans. In rotating electrical machines, reluctance torque is produced when the reluctance, seen by the working flux, changes with the rotor movement.

BASIC CONCEPTS OF ROTATING ELECTRICAL MACHINES

1. Why are salient-pole alternators more suitable for low-speed operation?

[M.U., April 1996]*

Ans. For low-speed operation, rotating machine requires more number of poles $\left(=\frac{120f}{\text{speed}}\right)$.

Large number of poles can however be accommodated on a spider having large diameter. The field poles are either dovetailed or bolted to the outside periphery of spider. In order that field poles experience low centrifugal forces, the spider must be driven at low speed. This shows that salient-pole alternators are more suitable for low-speed operation.

2. Why are non-salient pole alternators more suitable for high-speed operation?

[M.U., April 1996]*

Ans. For low-speed operation, more number of poles cannot be accommodated on cylindrical-rotor construction. Only two or four poles can be economically provided on the cylindrical-rotor surface. But two or four poles means high-operating speed of alternator. At the same time, non-salient pole rotor is made from fabricated steel, it can therefore withstand more centrifugal forces. This shows that non-salient-pole alternators are more suitable for high-speed operation.

3. What type of alternators will be used *(a)* for hydraulic turbines and *(b)* for steam turbines as prime-movers?

[M.U., Nov. 1996]

Ans. *(a)* Hydraulic turbines have best operating characteristics at low speeds, these are therefore best suited for driving salient-pole alternators. These alternators are usually called hydrogenerators.

(b) Steam turbines have superior operating characteristics at high speed, these are therefore used for driving non-salient-pole alternators called turbogenerators.

4. In a D.C. machine, which of the following parts are rotating and which are stationary?

Yoke, armature, brushes, commutator, field poles, interpole winding, end-covers.

Ans. In a D.C. machine, rotating parts are : armature and commutator and stationary parts are : yoke, brushes, field poles, interpole winding and end-covers.

5. What are the two types of 3-phase induction motors? Which type is generally preferred and why?

[M.U., No. 1996]

Ans. The two types of 3-phase induction motors are

(i) squirrel-cage induction motor (SCIM) and

(ii) slip-ring induction motor (SRIM).

Three-phase SCIM is generally preferred because it is rugged in construction, requires less maintenance and is economical as compared to 3-phase SRIM.

6. Why are the rotor slots skewed in 3-phase induction motors?

Ans. Skewing of rotor slots leads to quieter and smoother operation of 3-phase induction motors.

7. Why is an induction motor called so?

Ans. It is because stator winding delivers energy to the rotor by means of induction, *i.e.*, transformer action.

8. Write expressions for the flux per pole, in a rotating electrical machine, in terms of B_p as well as B_{av} and number of poles P. Write about the parameters involved.

* M.U. stands for Madras University.

Ans. Flux per pole, $\phi = \frac{4}{P} \cdot B_p \cdot l \cdot r$

Also, $\phi = \frac{2\pi rl}{P} \cdot B_{av}$

where B_p = peak flux density in T, under each pole

B_{av} = average flux density in T, under each pole

l = core length and r = radius of core.

9. Discuss nature of field flux in which a full-pitched *N*-turn rotating coil is found to consist of

(a) rotational e.m.f. only

(b) both rotational e.m.f. as well as transformer e.m.f.

Ans. (a) Coil is rotating in field flux that does not vary with time but is sinusoidally distributed along the air-gap periphery.

(b) The field flux is time varying in nature and is sinusoidally distributed along the air-gap periphery.

10. Write an expression for the e.m.f. generated at no-load in one phase of a 3-phase synchronous generator. Name the various parameters involved. *[M.U., April 1999]*

Ans. $E_{ph} = \sqrt{2}\,\pi\, f N_{ph} \cdot \phi \cdot k_w$

where E_{ph} = No-load generaed e.m.f. in one-phase. It is also called excitation e.m.f. E_f;

N_{ph} = series turns per phase ; ϕ = flux per pole ; f = rotational frequency

and k_w = winding factor.

11. Write an expression for the e.m.f. generated in one rotor-phase of a 3-phase induction machine. Name the various parameters involved in it.

Ans. Rotor e.m.f. per phase, $E_2 = \sqrt{2}\,\pi\,(sf) \cdot N_{ph2} \cdot \phi \cdot k_{w2}$

where s = slip ; f = stator supply frequency ; N_{ph2} = rotor series turns per phase ; ϕ = flux per pole and k_{w2} = rotor winding factor.

12. Write an expression for the angular slot pitch in electrical degrees in a rotating electrical machine.

Ans.

$$\text{Slot-angular pitch} = \frac{180 \cdot P}{\text{Total number of slots}} \cdot \text{Electrical degrees}$$

where P = number of poles

13. Can a D.C. generator be converted into an alternator? Give reasons for your answer. *[M.U., April 1996]*

Ans. Yes, it can be converted into an alternator by tapping the armature winding at intervals of 120° electrical from the other side of commutator. As the armature winding is closed on it self, the alternator so obtained would be delta-connected.

14. Define belt factor. *[M.U., April 1996]*

Ans. It is defined as :

$$\frac{\text{phasor sum of coil e.m.fs}}{\text{arithmetic sum of coil e.m.fs}} = k_d = \frac{\sin\frac{q \cdot \gamma}{2}}{q \sin\frac{\gamma}{2}},$$

where q = slots per pole per phase and γ = slot-angular pitch.

15. What are the other names for belt factor?

Ans. Distribution factor and breadth factor.

16. Define pitch factor. *[M.U., April 1996]*

Ans. It is defined as under :

$$\frac{\text{resul an t e.m.f. of a chorded coil}}{\text{resul tan te.m.f. of a full} - \text{pitched coil}} = k_p = \cos\frac{\varepsilon}{2}$$

where ε = chording angle.

17. What is the distribution factor for a uniformly distributed 3-phase winding having a phase spread of *(a)* 60° *(b)* 120°?

Ans. For a uniformly distributed winding, distribution factor is given by

$$k_d = \frac{\sin\sigma/2}{\sigma/2} \quad \text{where } \sigma = \text{phase spread}$$

(a) For $\sigma = 60°, \quad k_d = \dfrac{\sin\dfrac{30}{\neq}}{30\times\dfrac{\neq}{180}} = 0.955$

(b) For $\sigma = 120°, \quad k_d = \dfrac{\sin 60°}{60\times\dfrac{\pi}{180}} = \dfrac{3}{\pi}\sin 60° = 0.827.$

18. What is the meaning of "electrical angle"? How is it different from mechanical angle? Can they be equal? *[M.U., April 2001]*

Ans. Electrical angle is a measure of one cycle of e.m.f. wave or current wave. In electrical engineering, one cycle = 360° electrical.

In a 2-pole machine, one revolution is equal to 360° mechanical. It one conductor completes one revolution in a 2-pole field, one cycle (or 360° electrical) of e.m.f. is generated. Therefore, in a 2-pole rotating machine, electrical degrees are equal to mechanical degrees.

In a *P*-pole machine, $\frac{P}{2}$ cycles $\left(or\frac{P}{2}\times 360° \text{ electrical}\right)$ are generated in one revolution (= 360° mechanical). So we can get $\frac{P}{2}\times 360°$ electrical from 360° mechanical by multiplying 360° mechanical by $P/2$.

$$\therefore \qquad \theta_{elec} = \frac{P}{2}\cdot\theta_{mech}.$$

19. What is the peak value of fundamental m.m.f. wave produced by one *N*-turn full-pitched coil carrying a current *I*?

Ans. Amplitude of square wave $= \dfrac{Ni}{2}$

Peak value of fundamental m.m.f. wave $= \dfrac{4}{\pi}\cdot\dfrac{NI}{2}$ ATs.

20. Three *N*-turn coils having the same magnetic axis are excited by 3-phase balanced currents. Write an expression for resultant m.m.f. wave.

Ans. Resultant m.m.f. wave, $\qquad F_R = 0.$

21. Three *N*-turn coils, having their magnetic axes displaced from each other by 120°, are excited by 3-phase balanced currents. Write an expression for the resultant m.m.f. wave and identify the terms used.

Ans. Resultant travelling m.m.f. wave $= \dfrac{3}{2}\, I_m N\cos(\alpha - \omega t).$

where I_m = maximum value of phase current

N = series turns per coil

ω = angular frequency of supply voltage

α = space angle along the air-gap periphery.

22. List the harmonics which are called *(a)* belt harmonics and *(b)* triplen harmonics.

Ans. *(a)* The odd harmonics of the order 5, 7, 11, 13 etc are called belt harmonics.

(b) The odd harmonics of order 3, 9, 15 (multiple of three) are called triplen harmonics.

23. What is the maximum value of flux in a revolving field of a three-phase motor with relation to the flux produced by one phase? *[P.T.U., 2000]*

Ans. If the flux produced by one phase of a 3-phase induction motor has peak value ϕ_m, then maximum value of the revolving flux is $\frac{3}{2}\phi_m$.

24. Calculate the effective voltage in one phase of an alternator, given frequency = 50 Hz, turns per phase = 240, flux per pole 2.08 × 10⁶ Maxwells. *[P.T.U., 2002]*

Ans. Effective voltage in one phase is $E_{ph} = \sqrt{2}\,\pi f \cdot \phi\, N_{ph} \cdot k_w$.

The winding factor k_w is usually taken as 0.955.

Also $\phi = 2.08 \times 10^6 \times 10^{-8} = 2.08 \times 10^{-2}$ Wb

∴ $E_{ph} = \sqrt{2} \times \pi \times 50 \times 2.08 \times 10^{-2} \times 240 \times 0.955 = 1058.9$ V.

25. What are the methods of reducing the space harmonics in a machine? *[P.T.U., 2002]*

Ans. Plot of flux-density wave along the air-gap periphery of a rotating electrical machine may be sinusoidal or non-sinusoidal.

Fourier series analysis of non-sinusoidal flux density wave would consist of fundamental component plus other higher order harmonic components. These higher-order harmonics in the flux density wave are called space harmonics.

The methods adopted for reducing these space harmonic in a machine are as under :

(i) Distributing the winding in slots *(ii)* Using the fractional-pitch windings

(iii) Skewing the slots *(iv)* Using fractional-slot windings.

26. Explain the term 'synchronous speed'. Mention the factors on which it depends. *[M.U., Ap. 1997 ; P.T.U., 2002]*

Ans. Synchronous speed is the speed of rotating magnetic field produced when polyphase currents are applied to a polyphase winding. Synchronous speed N_s is given by

$$N_s = \frac{120f}{P} \text{ r.p.m.}$$

This shows that synchronous speed depends on the supply frequency f given to polyphase windings and the number of poles P for which polyphase winding is designed.

27. Why is the e.m.f. induced in a distributed A.C. winding lower than in a concentrated winding? *[P.T.U., 2002]*

Ans. In a conentrated winding, the e.m.f. induced in various coils gets added up arithmetically. For example, assume two concentrated coils. If r.m.s. value of e.m.f. generated in coil 1 is E_1, then total generated e.m.f. in both the coils of the concentrated winding would be $2E_1$. Now assume these two coils to be distributed in two adjacent slots. Let the angle between the slots be $\gamma°$. If r.m.s. value of e.m.f. generated in coil 1 is E_1, then r.m.s. value of generated e.m.f. in coil 2 would also be E_1 but this e.m.f. would be displaced from coil 1 e.m.f. E_1 by an angle $\gamma°$, so that the resultant e.m.f. is $[(E_1 + E_1 \cos \gamma)^2 + (E_1 \sin \gamma)^2]^{1/2}$. But this e.m.f. is less than $2E_1$. This shows that e.m.f. induced in a distributed A.C. winding is less than in a concentrated winding.

28. How is a sinusoidal voltage developed in a synchronous machine? *[P.T.U., 2002]*

Ans. First of all, attempt is made to make the field flux density sinusoidal. This is done by having

(i) non-uniform air-gap under the salient poles

(ii) distributing the field winding in slots appropriately

(iii) skewing the pole faces

Further, the voltage wave can be made sinusoidal by

(i) distributing the armature winding in slots *(ii)* using chorded coils

(iii) using fractional-slot winding *(iv)* using skewed slots.

29. State the fundamental law of generator action. *[P.T.U., 2002]*

Ans. The fundamental law of generator action is that there should be relative motion between flux density wave and armature winding. This relative motion can be achieved by

(i) rotating the magnetic field with respect to stationary armature winding, or

(ii) rotating the armature winding with respect to stationary magnetic field.

30. Why do we come across sinusoidal voltages and currents in electrical engineering?

or

Why should the output voltage from a polyphase alternator be sinusoidal?

Ans. The following reasons favour the use of sinusoidal waves in electrical engineering.

(i) For sinusoidal waves, hysteresis and eddy-current losses are less ; electrical equipment has, therefore, high efficiency. Non-sinusoidal waves, like square waves, triangular waves etc. consists of fundamental component as well as several harmonic components. These harmonics give rise to increased iron losses ; electrical equipment has therefore reduced efficiency.

(ii) Mathematical calculations involving sine and cosine functions are simpler. Therefore, design as well as analysis of electrical systems is much less laborious.

D.C. MACHINES

1. List the names of five parts of the rotor of a D.C. machine.

Ans. Armature shaft, armature spider, armature core, armature winding, commutator.

2. List the names of eight parts of the stator of a D.C. machine.

Ans. Yoke, field poles, field winding, interpoles, interpole winding, compensating winding, brushes and brush arms, end covers.

3. What is the advantage of using fractional-pitch windings in D.C. machines?

Ans. In order to save the amount of copper required for the armature winding.

4. Name the three basic types of D.C. generators.

Ans. Shunt generators, series generators and compound generators.

5. Name the four types of D.C. compound generators.

Ans. These are overcompounded D.C. generator, level (or flat) compounded D.C. generator, undercompounded D.C. generator and differential compounded D.C. generator.

6. What is meant by good voltage regulation (VR), poor VR, negative VR, positive VR and zero VR.

Ans. Good VR means minimum change in terminal voltage from no-load to full-load.

Poor VR means maximum change in terminal voltage from no-load to full-load.

Negative VR means (terminal voltage at full-load) > (terminal voltage at no-load).

Positive VR means (terminal voltage at full-load) < (terminal voltage at no-load).

Zero VR means (terminal voltage at full-load) = (terminal voltage at no-load).

7. Name the D.C. generators having good VR, poor VR, negative VR, positive VR and zero VR.

Ans. Undercompounded D.C. generator has good VR.

Differential-compounded D.C. generator has poor VR

Overcompounded D.C. generator has negative VR

Shunt, undercompounded and differential compounded generators have positive VR

Level-compounded D.C. generator has zero VR

8. What is voltage commutation? *[P.T.U., 1998]*

Ans. Good commutation achieved through the use of interpoles is called voltage commutation. All modern machines of larger sizes attain voltage commutation by the use of compoles.

9. What is the function of no-volt release in a three-point starter? *[P.T.U., 1998]*

Ans. The function of no-volt release is to stop the D.C. motor. This is achieved by bringing the starter handle back to OFF position in case magnetic force of no-volt release, or hold-coil, becomes less than the spiral-spring force.

10. What is magnetisation curve in reference to a D.C. shunt generator? How is it obtained? *[P.T.U., 1998]*

Ans. The magnetisation curve in reference to a D.C. shunt generator is the plot of armature generated e.m.f. E_a at no load and the field-winding current at a constant speed.

The magnetisation curve of a D.C. shunt generator is obtained by running it as a separately-excited D.C. generator at rated speed. Now E_a, from residual magnetism voltage up to about 1.1 to 1.25 times the rated voltage is obtained by varying its field current I_f gradually. The plot of E_a versus I_f at rated speed gives the magnetisation curve of a D.C. shunt generator.

11. List the causes of delayed commutation in D.C. machines. *[P.T.U., 2000]*

Ans. During commutation, current in the commentated coil reverses. The delayed commutation in D.C. machines is caused by e.m.f. induced in the commutated coil

(*i*) by self-inductance of the coil itself and

(*ii*) by mutual flux produced by the neighbouring coils.

12. Armature-circuit resistance control method controls the speed of D.C. machines below the base speed only. Explain. *[P.T.U., 2002]*

Ans. Motor speed,

$$\omega_{m1} = \frac{V_t - I_a(r_a + R_g)}{K_a\phi} \quad ...(i)$$

where R_g is the external resistance inserted in the armature circuit for speed control. With no external resistance R_g,

$$\omega_{m2} = \frac{V_t - I_a r_a}{K_a\phi} = \text{base speed} \quad ...(ii)$$

It is seen from Eqn. *(i)* that when R_g is changed, speed control is obtained. An examination of Eqs. *(i)* and *(ii)* reveals that armature speed with R_g in circuit, ω_{m1} < base speed ω_{m2}.

Thus, speed control below base speed can only be obtained by the armature-circuit resistance control method.

13. Give two applications of D.C. shunt motor and D.C. compounded generator. *[P.T.U., 2000]*

Ans. D.C. shunt motors are used where wide-speed and torque-control is essential. So it is used *(i)* in lathes and *(ii)* in rolling mills when separately excited.

D.C. compounded generators are used for maintaining constant supply voltage at the load terminals. Differentially-compounded generators are used for welding purposes.

14. Why are interpoles designed to provide m.m.f. more than the armature m.m.f. in the commutating zone. *[P.T.U., 2001]*

Ans. The interpolar m.m.f. does two tasks, *(i)* it neutralises the armature cross flux in the commutating zone and *(ii)* in addition, it provides extra interpolar flux in the commutating zone so as to induce rotational e.m.f. in the commutated coil in such a direction as to nullify the reactance voltage.

15. What feature of a D.C. series generator distinguish it from other D.C. generators? Explain *[P.T.U., 2001]*

Ans. External characteristic for a D.C. series generator distinguishes it from other D.C. generators. Observe carefully that external characteristic of

(a) a D.C. series generators starts from residual magnetism voltage and rises to rated voltage as it is loaded

(b) other D.C. generators start from rated terminal voltage at no-load and may have drooping or rising external characteristics depending upon the type of D.C. generator.

16. Four terminals are available in the terminal box of a D.C. machine. How will you decide the terminals for field winding and armature winding?

Ans. Take a multimeter. Two terminals, indicating high resistance (about 100 to 250 Ω) belong to field winding. The other two terminals showing low resistance (around 1 Ω) belong to armature winding.

17. At full load, the resultant flux in a D.C. machine gets reduced from its no-load value. Give two reasons.

Ans. *(i)* Armature reaction flux distorts the main field flux, under one pole tip it gets reduced while under the other pole tip, it gets augmented

(ii) The degree of augmentation is less than the degree of reduction in the pole-tip flux. There is, therefore, a net reduction in the resultant flux.

18. What is the purpose of interpoles and compensating windings in D.C. machines? *[P.T.U., 2002]*

Ans. For interpoles read the answer in Q. NO.14.

The purpose of compensating winding is to create an m.m.f. which neutralises the armature m.m.f. under the pole faces of field poles only.

19. Define compensating factor in cross-field machines. *[P.T.U., 2002]*

Ans. The degree of compensation or compensating factor in cross-field machines is defined as under :

$$\frac{\text{Effective compensating windings turns}}{\text{Effective } d-\text{axis armature turns}} = C$$

20. Explain the function of commutator in a D.C. motor. *[P.T.U., 2002]*

Ans. A commutator in D.C. motor performs the following two functions :

(i) D.C. supplied at the armature terminals is converted to A.C. in the armature winding by means of commutator.

(ii) It renders the armature m.m.f. stationary in space along the q-axis even though the armature rotates.

21. On what factors does the flux distribution in the air-gap of a D.C. generator depend? *[P.T.U., 2002]*

Ans. The flux distribution in the air-gap of a D.C. generator depends

(i) on the main field flux distribution

(ii) on the armature reaction flux waveform

(iii) on the length of the air gap and

(iv) on whether the magnetic circuit is saturated or not.

22. What do you mean by geometric neutral axis and magnetic neutral axis in a D.C. machine? *[P.T.U., 2002]*

Ans. Geometric neutral axis (GNA) is the same as brush axis of a D.C. machine. GNA is always at an angle of 90° (electrical) away from the main-field (or direct) axis. GNA passes through zero of the main-field flux density wave at no-load.

Magnetic neutral axis (MNA) passes through zero of the resultant flux-density wave at full load or at any load. At no-load, MNA coincides with GNA. When D.C. machine is loaded, MNA gets shifted toward the direction of rotation for a generator and against the direction of rotation for a motor.

POLYPHASE SYNCHRONOUS MACHINES

1. What factors determine the choice of the two types of synchronous machines?

Ans. Type of fuel or energy source available at the site of location determines the choice of synchronous machines. For example, if coal is available, the cylindrical-rotor synchronous machine is the only choice.

2. How will you distinguish between the two types of large synchronous generators from their appearance?

Ans. A synchronous generator possessing large core length and small diameter would be a cylindrical-rotor synchronous machine. A synchronous machine having low core length and large diameter must be a salient-pole synchronous generator.

3. What is meant by armature reaction of a synchronous machine? *[M.U., April, 1997]*

Ans. By armature reaction of a synchronous machine, we mean how armature flux produced by 3-phase armature winding affects the distribution of main-field flux created by D.C. in the field winding.

4. What is the effect of armature reaction in an alternator working at zero power factor lagging load?

Ans. For zero p.f. lagging in an alternator, armature reaction flux is entirely demagnetizing in nature.

5. Calculate the pitch factor for the following winding :

36 stator slots, 4 poles, coil-span 1 to 8 *[M.U., April, 1997]*

Ans. Pole pitch = 9 slots, coil span = 7 slots

Slot angular pitch, $\gamma = \dfrac{4 \times 180}{36} = 20°$

Chording angle, $\varepsilon = 2$ slots-pitches $= 2 \times 20° = 40°$

$\therefore$ Pitch factor $= \cos 40°/2 = \cos 20° = 0.9397.$

6. When the load on an alternator is varied, its terminal voltage is also found to change. Why?

Ans. As the load on an alternator is altered, the voltage drops in *(i)* armature resistance, $I_a\, r_a$ *(ii)* armature leakage reactance, $I_a \cdot x_{al}$ and *(iii)* armature reaction reactance $I_a \cdot X_{ar}$ also alter. With this, the terminal voltage of alternator, $V_t = E_f - I_a\,(r_a + j\,x_{al} + j\,X_{ar}) = E_f - I_a\,(r_a + j\,X_s)$ also varies.

7. Why is the voltage regulation of an alternator negative for leading power-factor loads?

[M.U., April, 1997 ; P.T.U., 2002]

Ans. For leading p.f. loads on the aternator, the armature reaction is magnetizing in nature. In other words, for leading p.f. loads, armature reaction flux aids the field flux ϕ_f so that the resultant air-gap flux ϕ_r gets augmented. As a consequence, air-gap voltage E_r exceeds E_f or armature terminal voltage V_t exceeds E_f. Voltage regulation is, therefore, negative.

8. What is meant by alternators on infinite bus-bars? *[M.U., April, 1996 ; P.T.U., 2002]*

Ans. An infinite bus-bar means a source whose terminal voltage and frequency remains constant irrespective of whether a new voltage source is connected to it or a load is put on it. Thus, alternators on finite bus bar means that their terminal voltage and frequency remain constant, equal to the bus-bar voltage and frequency.

9. Does a change in the excitation of a synchronous motor affect its speed and power factor?

[M.U., April, 1996]

Ans. With change in synchronous motor excitation, *(i)* there is no change in motor speed, *(ii)* power factor of the synchronous motor, however, changes. If already working on lagging p.f., an increase in excitation makes the motor p.f. unity and then leading. If already working on leading p.f., a decrease in excitation changes the motor p.f. to unity and then lagging.

10. What is meant by synchronizing power? *[M.U., Nov., 1996]*

Ans. Synchronizing power is the power that comes into play when rotor speed departs from synchronous speed momentarily. Depending upon whether the load angle decreases or increases suddenly to cause the rotor speed to vary from synchronous speed, synchronizing power flows in order to maintain synchronism. This power flow is transient in nature.

11. Why are synchronous motors not self-starting? *[M.U., Nov., 1996 ; P.T.U., 2001]*

Ans. In case of three-phase synchronous motor, electromagnetic torque is given by

$T_e \propto$ (stator field strength) (rotor field strength) $\sin \delta$

where δ = torque angle between stator poles and rotor poles.

With the rotor stationary, when 3-phase supply is given to stator, a rotating magnetic field is set up. As a result, the torque angle δ between rotating stator poles and stationary rotor poles varies with time. Let this angle δ as a function of time be expressed as $\delta = \omega t$, then Torque $\propto$ (stator field strength) (rotor field strength) $\sin \omega t$. The torque given by above expression varies sinusoidally with time. Its value reverses during each half cycle ; average value of this torque over a complete cycle is zero. Thus, a synchronous motor has no self-starting torque.

12. Why is Potier method of voltage regulation accurate? *[M.U., April, 1997]*

Ans. In e.m.f. method of voltage regulation (VR), m.m.fs. are transformed to their corresponding e.m.fs., so an error is introduced in doing so. Similarly, in m.m.f. method of VR, e.m.fs. are transformed into corresponding m.m.fs. and likewise an error is introduced. But in Potier method, e.m.fs. are handled as voltages and m.m.fs. are held as field ampere-turns. No errors are thus introduced due to transformation of e.m.fs. to m.m.fs. or vice-versa. Potier method (also called zero p.f. method) is, therefore, accurate method of calculating VR of alternators.

13. Why will a 3-phase synchronous motor always run at synchronous speed? *[M.U., April, 1997]*

Ans. Stator poles and rotor poles of synchronous motor are magnetically locked. This locking is possible only if relative speed between field poles and synchronously rotating armature poles is zero. Therefore, in order to maintain this magnetic locking between poles of opposite polarity, the rotor must run at synchronous speed.

14. How is the effect of armature reaction accounted for in computing the voltage regulation of an alternator? *[M.U., Oct., 1999]*

Ans. It is accounted for by armature-reaction reactance or armature-magnetizing reactance of the alternator. The voltage generated by armature reaction m.m.f. is taken care of by voltage drop in X_{ar}.

Therefore, $$E_f = V_t + I_a\,[(r_a + j\,(x_{al} + X_{ar})].$$

15. Write the expression for synchronizing power. *[M.U., April, 1999]*

Ans. The synchronizing power expression is

$$P_s = \frac{E_f \cdot V_t}{X_s} \cos\delta \cdot \Delta\delta$$

for a cylindrical-rotor synchronous machine and

$$P_s = \left[\frac{E_f \cdot V_t}{X_d} \cos\delta + V_t^2 \left\{\frac{1}{X_q} - \frac{1}{X_d}\right\} \cos 2\delta\right] \cdot \Delta\delta$$

for a salient-pole synchronous machine.

16. Damper winding is used in salient-pole structure normally. Explain why? *[P.T.U., 2002]*

Ans. Provision of slots in salient-pole of a synchronous machine is easy. Damper windings can therefore be conveniently inserted in these slots. Rotor of cylindrical-rotor synchronous machines are made from solid steel where slot cutting is laborious. At the same time, solid-steel rotor core provides path for eddy currents producing the same effect as that of damper winding.

17. Name three important characteristics of a 3-phase synchronous motor not found in a 3-phase induction motor. *[M.U., April 1998]*

Ans. *(i)* A 3-phase synchronous motor has no inherent starting torque whereas a 3-phase induction motor possesses inherent starting torque.

(ii) A 3-phase synchronous motor always runs at constant speed, equal to synchronous speed ; whereas speed of a 3-phase induction motor varies as it is loaded.

(iii) A 3-phase synchronous motor can operate at lagging, unity and leading power factors, whereas a 3-phase induction motor always operates at lagging power factors.

18. What is a synchronous condenser? *[M.U., April 2000]*

Ans. A synchronous condenser is an overexcited synchronous motor whose primary function is to improve the power factor of an electrical system. It does so by delivering reactive power to the A.C. system. A synchronous condenser has no shaft extension, because it is not designed to deliver any mechanical load.

19. Why are X_d and X_q values different for salient-pole alternator whereas they are same for smooth rotor machines? *[M.U., Oct., 1999 ; April 2000]*

Ans. In a 3-phase synchronous machine, $L = \frac{N_{ph}^2}{Rl}$ · Also $X_d = \omega L_d$ and $X_q = \omega L_q$.

In a 3-phase saline-pole synchronous machine,

d-axis synchronous inductance $L_d = \frac{N_{ph}^2}{Rl_d}$ and q-axis synchronous inductance $L_q = \frac{N_{ph}^2}{Rl_q}$. As air-gap length along d-axis is minimum, Rl_d is minimum and therefore L_d is more or X_d is high. Likewise, air-gap length along q-axis maximum, Rl_q is more and therefore L_q is less or X_q is low. This shows why $X_d > X_q$ in a salient-pole synchronous machine.

In a smooth-rotor synchronous machine, air-gap is uniform, therefore $Rl_d = Rl_q$ and hence $X_d = X_q = X_s$, synchronous reactance.

20. Name any two methods of starting a synchronous motor. *[M.U., Oct.,1999]*

Ans. *(i)* Starting of a synchronous motor by means of damper winding.

(ii) Starting of a synchronous motor first as slip-ring induction motor and then as a synchronous motor.

21. Give the reasons for flat-topped flux density wave in the air gap of a salient-pole synchronous machine. *[P.T.U., 2002]*

Ans. Fig. D.2 *(a)* shows south *(S)* pole of a salient-pole synchronous machine. In Fig. D.2 *(b)* is shown the m.m.f. variation over a pole-pitch. Note that m.m.f. waveform has constant amplitude $I_f N_f$ extending over the distance from dot to cross. For uniform airgap under the pole, reluctance is constant. Therefore, flux density under the pole is constant (α $I_f \cdot N_f$/reluctance) as shown in Fig. D.2 *(c)*. Actually, the gap length at the pole centre is minimum and is more at the pole tips. As a result, the flux density waveform of Fig. D.2 *(d)* is obtained. In actual practice, fringing of

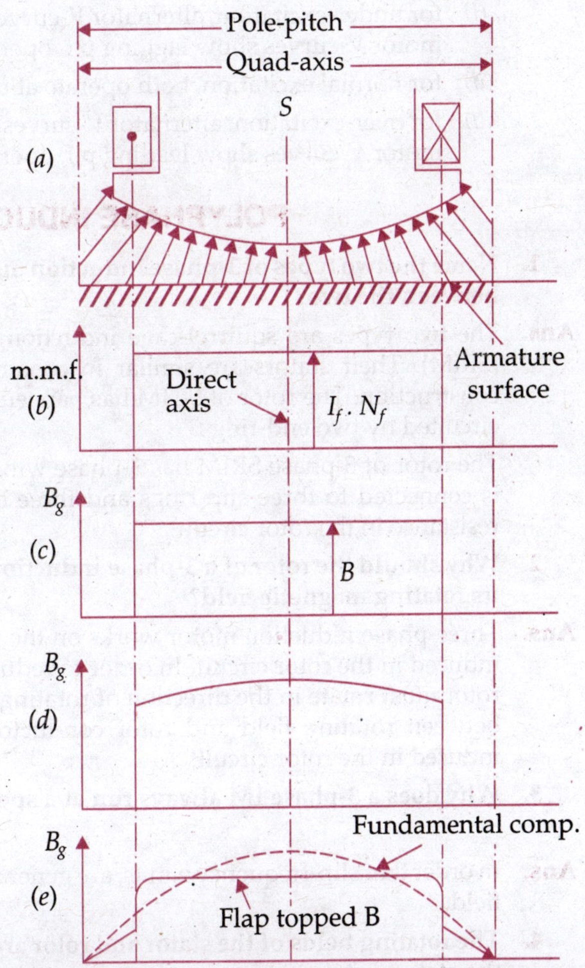

Fig D.2: Flux-density waveform in a salient-pole machine with D.C. excitation

pole flux does occur as shown in Fig. D.2 *(a)*. As a result, a real plot of the flux-density distribution under *S* pole is as shown in Fig. D.2 *(e)*. It is seen that it is fringing of the pole flux that makes the flux-density variation under one pole of a salient-pole synchronous (or D.C.) machine a flat topped wave.

22. Describe the operating condition at which an alternator will give negative voltage regulation. *[P.T.U., 2002]*

Ans. When excitation voltage E_f is less than the terminal voltage V_t, the alternator voltage regulation would be negative. This can happen when alternator is delivering a capacitive load.

23. Can *V*-curves be plotted for alternator operation? How will they differ from *V*-curves of a synchronous motor? *[P.T.U., 2002]*

Ans. *V*-curves can be plotted for an alternator connected to an infinite bus. For a constant load on alternator, field current is varied and for each value of field current, armature current is recorded. Plot of field current along *x*-axis and armature current along *y*-axis gives V-curve of an alternator. The shape of these curves is similar to the V-curves of a synchronous motor. However,

(i) for under-excitation, alternator *V*-curves show leading p.f. operation and synchronous motor *V*-curves show lagging p.f. operation ;

(ii) for normal excitation, both operate at unity p.f. and

(iii) for over-excitation, alternator *V*-curves reveal lagging p.f. operation and synchronous-motor *V*-curves show leading p.f. operation.

POLYPHASE INDUCTION MOTORS

1. Name the two types of 3-phase induction motors. What are the differences in construction between the two?

Ans. The two types are squirrel-cage induction motor (SCIM) and slip-ring induction motor (SRIM). Their stators are similar in construction. However, their rotors have different construction. The rotor of SCIM has bars embedded in rotor slots and these bars are short circuited by two end-rings.

The rotor of 3-phase SRIM has 3-phase winding housed in rotor slots. This rotor winding is connected to three slip-rings and three brushes which allow the insertion of external resistance in the rotor circuit.

2. Why should the rotor of a 3-phase induction motor rotate in the same direction as that of its rotating magnetic field? *[M.U., Oct., 2000]*

Ans. Three-phase induction motor works on the principle that slip-frequency voltages must be induced in the rotor circuit. In order to reduce the rate of flux-cutting by rotor conductors, rotor must rotate in the direction of rotating magnetic field. In this manner, relative speed between rotating field and rotor conductors is reduced and slip-frequency e.m.fs. are induced in the rotor circuit.

3. Why does a 3-phase IM always run at a speed less than the synchronous speed? *[M.U., Oct., 2000]*

Ans. In order that slip-frequency e.m.fs. are generated in the rotor circuit by the rotating magnetic field.

4. The rotating fields of the stator and rotor are stationary with respect to each other. Justify the statement. *[M.U., April, 2001]*

Ans. Stator field rotates at synchronous speed,

$$n_s = \frac{2f_1}{P} \text{ r.p.s.}$$

Rotor speed = speed of rotor with respect to stator = n_r r.p.s.

Frequency of rotor currents = sf_1 Hz

Speed of rotor field with respect to rotor = $\frac{2 \cdot sf_1}{P} = s \cdot n_s$ r.p.s.

∴ Speed of rotor field with respect to stator

= speed of rotor with respect to stator + speed of rotor field with respect to (w.r.t.) rotor

$= n_r + s \cdot n_s = n_s(1-s) + sn_s = n_s$ r.p.s.

∴ Speed of stator field w.r.t. stator = speed of rotor field w.r.t. rotor = n_s

This shows rotating fields of the stator and rotor are stationary w.r.t. each other.

5. What is the effect of introducing resistance in the rotor circuit of a 3-phase IM?

[M.U., April, 2001]

Ans. (i) The effect is to increase the starting torque ; maximum torque, however, remains constant. In case rotor circuit resistance is quite large, starting torque may get reduced; under such a case maximum torque may occur at a slip more than one.

(ii) The effect is also to alter the motor operating speed.

6. Why is the efficiency of a 3-phase IM less than that of a 3-phase transformer?

[M.U., Oct., 2000]

Ans. For the same rating, a 3-phase IM has losses more than those in a 3-phase transformer. This increment is due to the presence of friction and windage losses in a 3-phase IM. As a result, 3-phase IM efficiency is less than that of a 3-phase transformer.

7. List out the tests necessary to draw the circle diagram of a 3-phase IM.

Ans. These tests are *(i)* running-light test, *(ii)* blocked-rotor test and *(iii)* voltmeter-ammeter test for the measurement of stator D.C. resistance.

8. How can the direction of rotation of the 3-phase IM be reversed. *[M.U., April, 1996]*

Ans. It can be reversed by interchanging any two supply lines feeding the 3-phase induction motor. With this, the direction of rotating field gets reversed and likewise direction of rotor rotation is reversed.

9. How do the change in supply voltage and frequency affect the performance of a 3-phase induction motor? *[M.U., April, 1996]*

Ans. With change in supply voltage V_1 only :

(i) starting torque, proportional to V_1^2, changes

(ii) maximum torque $\propto V_1^2$ changes

(iii) operating speed also changes and

(iv) starting current and operating current both change.

With change in supply frequency f_1 only :

(i) synchronous speed = $\frac{2f_1}{P}$ and therefore operating speed both change

(ii) starting torque as well as maximum torque also change.

When both supply voltage V_1 and supply frequency f_1 change such that V_1/f_1 remains constant, then

(i) starting torque increases but

(ii) maximum torque remains constant and

(iii) operating motor speed changes.

10. State the condition for maximum torque in a 3-phase induction motor.

[M.U., Nov., 1996]

Ans. If the shunt branch of the equivalent circuit of a 3-phase IM is neglected, then the condition for maximum torque occurs when resistance $\frac{r_2}{s}$ becomes equal to the impedance seen by $\frac{r_2}{s}$ towards the voltage source V_1, *i.e.* $\frac{r_2}{s_{mT}} = \sqrt{r_1^2 + (x_1 + x_2)^2}$

11. Why do you require starters for the starting of 3-phase induction motors?

[M.U., Nov., 1996]

Ans. The object of using starters for the starting of 3-phase IMs is to limit the starting current to safe values so that voltage dip in the line voltage is not objectionable to other consumers connected to the same line.

12. Write down the torque of a 3-phase IM. *[M.U., April, 1997]*

Ans. In case shunt branch is neglected, then torque expression is given by

$$T_e = \frac{3}{\omega_s} \cdot \frac{V_1^2}{\left(r_1 + \frac{r_2}{s}\right)^2 + (x_1 + x_2)^2} \cdot \frac{r_2}{s} \text{ Nm}$$

where ω_s = synchronous speed, rad/s

$r_1 + jx_1$ = stator leakage impedance per phase

$r_2 + jx_2$ = rotor leakage impedance per phase

and s = operating slip

13. What is the effective rotor resistance under running conditions? Using this term, define air-gap power, rotor power developed and rotor ohmic loss for a 3-phase IM.

Ans. It is $\frac{r_2}{s}$.

Air-gap power $= 3\, I_2^2 \frac{r_2}{s}$ watts

Rotor power developed $= 3\, I_2^2 \frac{r_2}{s}(1 - s)$ watts

Rotor ohmic loss $= 3\, I_2^2\, r_2$ watts

14. Name the four types of starters used for 3-phase IM.

[M.U., April, 1997, April 1999, April 2000]

Ans. 1. Direct-on line starter
2. Stator-reactor starter
3. Auto-transformer starter
4. Star-delta starter

15. The starting torque of given SCIM can't be altered, when the applied voltage is constant. Why?

Ans. Starting torque in a 3-phase IM is given by

$$T_{e \cdot st} = \frac{3}{\omega_s} \cdot \frac{V_1^2}{(r_1 + r_2)^2 + (x_1 + x_2)^2} \cdot r_2 \text{ Nm}$$

Now, in a given 3-phase SCIM ; r_1, r_2, x_1 and x_2 cannot be changed. In case applied voltage V_1 is also constant, then expression for $T_{e \cdot st}$ reveals that starting torque cannot be altered.

16. What is an induction generator? What are its limitations? *[M.U., April, 2001]*

Ans. When a 3-phase IM is made to run at a speed higher than its synchronous speed by means of a prime-mover coupled with it, the 3-phase IM becomes a 3-phase induction generator. Its limitations are :

(i) it cannot run in isolation, it must take reactive power from an existing supply network,

(i) its output voltage and frequency cannot be controlled and

(ii) it always operates at a leading p.f.

17. How is it possible to get frequencies lower than the supply frequency in a 3-phase WRIM?

Ans. By rotating the rotor of WRIM by a prime-mover at a speed lower than the synchronous speed n_s. If rotor is made to revolve at $n_r < n_s$, in the direction of rotating field, then rotor frequency f_2 of the voltage at slip rings is given by

$$f_2 = \frac{P(\text{relative speed between rotating field and rotor in r.p.s.})}{2}$$

$$= \frac{P(n_s - n_r)}{2} \text{ Hz which is lower than the supply frequency } f_1 = \frac{P \cdot n_s}{2}.$$

18. How frequencies greater than the supply frequency can be obtained with the use of a 3-phase SRIM.

Ans. By running the rotor against the direction of rotating magnetic field by means of a prime-mover. If rotor speed in n_r r.p.s. and rotating-field speed n_s, then relative speed between rotor conductors and rotating field would be $(n_s + n_r)$ r.p.s. This gives rotor frequency f_2 of the voltage at slip rings as

$$f_2 = \frac{P(n_s + n_r)}{2} \text{ Hz which is higher than the supply frequency } f_1 = \frac{P \cdot n_s}{2}$$

19. Explain the term skewing. *[P.T.U., 2002]*

Ans. Skewing means angular twist of the slot away from the shaft axis. The angular twist is done through one slot pitch in order to eliminate the effect of slot harmonics. This, in effect, leads to *(i)* the elimination of parasitic torques and therefore a uniform torque-speed curve and *(ii)* the reduction in vibration and noise so as to result in a quieter motor operation.

20. What determines the generated voltage in the rotor when the latter is locked so that it cannot rotate? *[P.T.U., 2002]*

Ans. With the rotor locked, the voltage generated in rotor is given by

$$E_2 = \sqrt{2}\,\pi f_1 \cdot N_{ph\,2} \cdot \phi \cdot k_{w2}$$

Therefore, E_2 is dependent upon supply frequency f_1, series turns per phase $N_{ph\,2}$, rotor-winding factor k_{w2} and rotating flux per pole ϕ.

21. Give three reasons for the preference of fractional-pitch stator windings in 3-phase induction motors. *[P.T.U., 2002]*

Ans. (i) To reduce the amount of copper required for the stator winding.

(ii) To reduce the m.m.f. harmonics produced by the stator winding.

(iii) To make the torque-slip characteristic a smooth curve so as to avoid the crawling.

ARMATURE WINDINGS

1. Name the types of D.C. armature windings.

Ans. Simplex lap winding and simplex wave winding.

2. Why are fractional-pitch windings used in D.C. machines?

Ans. To reduce the amount of copper required for the armature winding of D.C. machines.

3. Where do we prefer the use of lap windings and wave windings.

Ans. Lap windings are employed in high-current and low-voltage D.C. machines. Wave windings are preferred in low-current and high-voltage D.C. machines.

4. Design a suitable winding for 48 slots, 3-phase, 6-pole A.C. machine.

Ans. Here slots/pole/phase, $q = \frac{48/3}{6} = \frac{16}{6} = \frac{8}{3}$. As q is not an integer, only fractional-slot winding can be used for this A.C. machine.

Now $$S_{ab} = \frac{8}{3}(3x + 2) \text{ and } S_{ac} = \frac{8}{3}(3x + 4)$$

In $\frac{8}{3}$, the denominator is 3 ; therefore S_{ab} and S_{ac} cannot become integers. This shows that no A.C. type winding is feasible for this 3-phase machine having 48 slots and 6 poles.

5. Define full-pitched and short-pitched coils. *[P.T.U., 2002]*

Ans. A coil having its coil-span equal to one pole-pitch (*i.e.* 180° electrical) is called a full-pitched coil.

A coil with its coil-span less than one pole-pitch of 180° electrical is called a short-pitched coil.

6. Differentiate between lap winding and wave winding. *[P.T.U., 2002]*

Ans. (*i*) A lap winding has parallel paths a = number of poles P, whereas wave winding has only two parallel paths.

(*ii*) A lap winding may require equalizer rings but these are not needed in wave winding.

(*iii*) A wave winding may have dummy coil/s but lap winding does not require any dummy coils.

(*iv*) In lap winding, winding pitch $y_w = y_b - y_f = \pm 2$, whereas in wave winding, $y_w = y_b + y_f$.

7. Calculate commutator pitch for two-circuit simplex-wave winding having 4 poles and 129 commutator segments. *[P.T.U., 2002]*

Ans. Commutator pitch for simplex-wave winding is given by

$$y_c = \frac{C \pm 1}{P/2} = \frac{129 \pm 1}{4/2} = \frac{130 \text{ or } 128}{2} = 65 \text{ or } 64$$

Thus, commutator pitch may be 64 or 65.

8. Resistance of one conductor for a D.C. machine is 10 mΩ. Find the armature circuit resistance if the D.C. machine with 640 conductors and 8 poles is (*a*) lap-connected and (*b*) wave-connected.

Ans. (*a*) For lap-connected D.C. machine, $r_a = \frac{Z}{P^2}$ (resistance of one counductor)

$$= \frac{640}{8^2} \times 10 \times 10^{-3} = 0.1\ \Omega$$

(*b*) For wave-wound D.C. machine, $r_a = \frac{Z}{4}$ (resistance of one counductor)

$$= \frac{640}{4} \times 10 \times 10^{-3} = 1.6\ \Omega.$$

9. Discuss why phase-spread of 60° is preferred over a phase-spread of 120°.

Ans. For phase spread, σ = 60°, distribution factor = 0.955 and for phase spread, σ = 120°, distribution factor = 0.827.

Therefore, for obtaining the same generated voltage, copper required for armature winding with 120° phase spread would be (0.955/0.827) = 1.15 times the copper required with 60° phase spread.

THREE-PHASE CIRCUITS AND MAGNETIC CIRCUITS

1. What is meant by phase-sequence of a 3-phase system?

Ans. The order in which the currents or voltages in the three phases attain their maximum values is called phase sequence of a 3-phase system.

2. How are the 3-phase systems connected? Write down the relationship between line and phase values for these systems.

Ans. The three-phase systems can be connected either in star or in delta.

If V_L and I_L are line values and V_P and I_P are phase values, then for star-connection, $V_L = \sqrt{3}\ V_P$ and $I_L = I_P$ and for delta connection, $V_L = V_P$ and $I_L = \sqrt{3}\ I_P$.

3. What do you understand by three-phase balanced load?

Ans. A 3-phase balanced load had equal impedance in each of its 3-phases so that phase currents are equal and are phase-displaced by 120°.

4. What is unbalanced 3-phase load?

Ans. An unbalanced 3-phase load may have different voltages or currents in each phase, or the phase angles may not be 120°.

5. Power in a 3-phase balanced load is measured by two-wattmeter method. Write expression for each of the two wattmeter readings.

Ans. The reading of one wattmeter, $W_1 = V_L I_L \cos(30 - \theta)$

and reading of the other wattmeter, $W_2 = V_L I_L \cos(30 + \theta)$

where V_L and I_L are line value and θ is the load power-factor angle.

6. During 3-phase power measurement by two-wattmeter method, one wattmeter reads zero. What is the nature of the load p.f.?

Ans. The wattmeter which gives lower reading is W_2.

$\therefore \quad W_2 = V_L I_L \cos(30 + \theta)$

Here $\quad W_2 = 0 = V_L I_L \cos(30 + \theta) = V_L I_L \cos 90°$

$\therefore \quad 30 + \theta = 90° \text{ or } \theta = 60°$

$\therefore \quad \text{Load p.f.} = \cos 60° = 0.5 \text{ lagging.}$

7. During 3-phase power measurement by two-wattmeter method, two wattmeter readings are equal but of opposite sign. What is the nature of load p.f.?

Ans. Here $\quad W_1 = -W_2$

or $\quad V_L I_L \cos(30 - \theta) = -V_L I_L \cos(30 + \theta)$

$$= V_L I_L \cos(30 + \theta - 180°)$$

$\therefore \quad 30 - \theta = \theta - 150° \text{ or } \theta = 90°$

This gives load p.f. $= \cos 90° = 0$ $\therefore$ Load p.f. is zero lagging.

8. Three resistors, each of 20 Ω, are connected in star across 3-phase, 400 V mains. Find the power delivered to load.

Ans.
$$\text{Per-phase current} = \frac{400}{\sqrt{3} \times 20} \text{ A}$$

$$\text{Power delivered to load} = 3\left(\frac{400}{\sqrt{3} \times 20}\right)^2 \times 20 = 8000 \text{ W} = 8 \text{ kW.}$$

9. Three resistors, each of 20 Ω, are connected in delta across 3-phase, 400 V mains. Find the power delivered to load.

Ans. $$\text{Per-phase current} = \frac{400}{20}\text{ A} = 20\text{ A}$$

$$\text{Power delivered to load} = 3\,(20)^2 \times 20 = 24000\text{ W} = 24\text{ kW}.$$

10. A 3-phase balanced load is connected to 3-phase mains once in star and then in delta. Find the ratio of line currents in star to that in delta.

Ans. Line current with load in star, $$I_{LS} = \frac{V_L}{Z}\cdot\frac{1}{\sqrt{3}}\text{ A}$$

Line current with load in delta, $$I_{Ld} = \frac{V_L\cdot\sqrt{3}}{Z}\text{ A}$$

$$\therefore \quad \frac{I_{LS}}{I_{Ld}} = \frac{V_L}{Z}\cdot\frac{1}{\sqrt{3}}\times\frac{Z}{V_L\cdot\sqrt{3}} = \frac{1}{3}.$$

11. What is meant by 'lines of force' in a magnetic field?

Ans. Lines of force indicate the existance of magnetic field in the neighborhood of a magnetic pole. These are taken to emanate from *N* pole, traverse the surrounding medium, re-enter the *S* pole and pass through the magnet from *S* pole to *N* pole. Note that lines of force must form a closed loop.

12. What do you mean by flux in a magnetic field?

Ans. In a magnetic field, all the lines of force taken together is given the name flux or magnetic flux. Its usual symbol is ϕ and its unit is weber.

13. What is magnetomotive force?

Ans. Magnetomotive force (m.m.f.) drives flux in a magnetic circuit. An *N*-turn coil carrying a current *I* amperes has m.m.f. equal to *IN* ampere-turns.

14. What is reluctance?

Ans. Releuctance is the resistance offered to the establishment of magnetic flux in a magnetic circuit. It is given by

$$Rl = \frac{L}{\mu A}$$

where L = length of the magnetic path along the flux lines,

A = area normal to the flux path,

and μ = permeability of the medium.

15. What is inductance?

Ans. Any circuit associated with magnetic lines of force possesses inductance or self-inductance. Its presence in a circuit is felt only when current is changing.

It may thus be stated that inductance is the property of a circuit by virtue of which an e.m.f. is induced in the circuit itself by the changing current.

16. What is magnetic leakage flux? *[P.T.U., 2001]*

Ans. The flux in a magnetic circuit that does not follow the designed path is called magnetic leakage flux.

17. Explain *B-H* curve.

Ans. The *B-H* curve, also known as magnetisation curve or saturation curve, shows the manner in which the flux density *B* changes as the magnetic-field intensity *H* is varied. A typical shape of *B-H* curve for iron is sketched in Fig. D.3. The shape of *B.H* curve depends upon the magnetic material only and

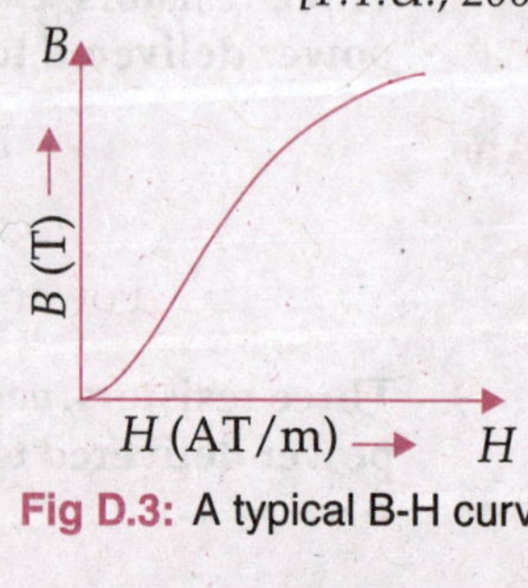

Fig D.3: A typical B-H curve.

not on the dimensions of material. This curve is used for the graphical analysis of magnetic circuit problems.

18. State the Faraday's law. *[P.T.U., 2001]*

Ans. Faraday's law states that an e.m.f. is induced in a coil when the magnetic flux linking the coil changes with time. It is expressed as

$$e = N\frac{d\phi}{dt} = \frac{d\psi}{dt}$$

where e = e.m.f. induced, N = number of turns in the coil, ϕ = flux and ψ = flux linkages with the coil.

19. A conductor of length 1 metre moves at right angles to a magnetic field of flux density 1 Wb/m^2 with a velocity of 25 m/s. Calculate the e.m.f. induced in the conductor. *[P.T.U., 2001]*

Ans.
$$e = Blv = 1 \times 1 \times 25 = 25 \text{ V}$$

20. The area of the face of a pole-shoe is 1.5 cm^2 and the total flux is 0.18 mWb. Calculate the flux density in air gap. *[P.T.U., 2001]*

Ans. Flux density,
$$B = \frac{\phi}{A} = \frac{0.18 \times 10^{-3}}{1.5 \times 10^{-4}} = \frac{1.8}{1.5} = 1.2 \text{ Wb/m}^2$$

21. A cross-bar, 2 m long, is kept on the roof rack of a truck traveling at 90 kmph. If the vertical component of earth's magnetic field is 4 × 10^{-5} T, find the e.m.f. induced at the two ends of cross-bar.

Ans.
$$e = Blv = 4 \times 10^{-5} \times 2 \times \frac{90{,}000}{3600} = 2 \times 10^{-3} = 2 \text{ mV}$$

22. One 800-turn flat coil with an area of 5 × 10^{-2} m^2 is rotating in a magnetic field of flux density 60 mWb/m^2 at 1500 r.p.m. Find the value of the e.m.f. induced in the coil when plane of the coil is parallel to the field.

Ans. e.m.f. induced,
$$e = N\phi\omega$$

where $\phi = 5 \times 10^{-2} \times 60 \times 10^{-3} = 3 \times 10^{-3}$ Wb

$$\omega = \frac{2\pi \times 1500}{60} = 50\pi \text{ rad/s and } N = 800 \text{ turns.}$$

$$\therefore \quad e = 800 \times 3 \times 10^{-3} \times 50\pi = 377 \text{ V}$$

23. Repeat Quest. 22 in case plane of the coil is inclined at 30° to the magnetic field.

Ans. $e = N\phi\omega \sin\theta = 800 \times 3 \times 10^{-3} \times 50\pi \times \sin 30° = 188.5$ V

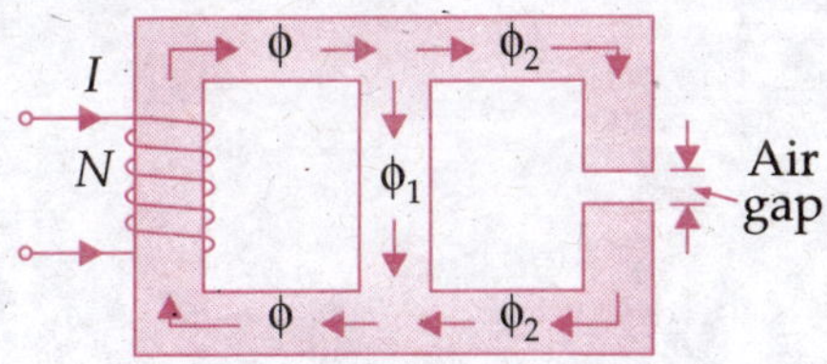

Fig D.4: Pertaining to Prob. 24.

24. Draw analogous electric circuit for the magnetic circuit shown in Fig. D.4. *[P.T.U., 2001]*

Ans. The analogous electric circuit is as drawn in Fig. D.5 where m.m.f., J = IN and

Rl = reluctance of path carrying flux ϕ

Rl_1 = reluctance of path where flux is ϕ_1

Rl_2 = reluctance of path carrying flux ϕ_2 and

Rl_g = air-gap reluctance.

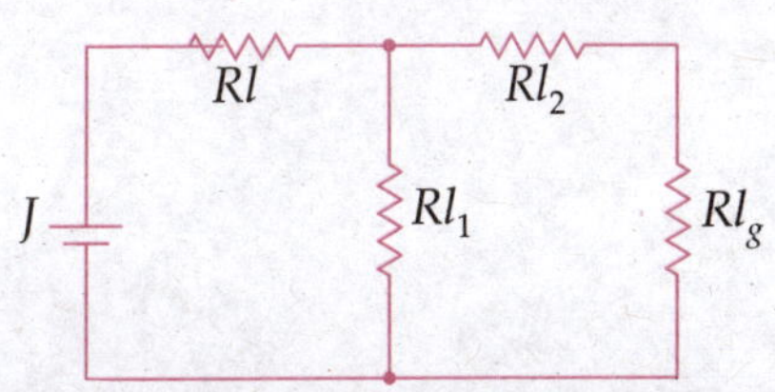

Fig D.5: Analogous electric circuit for Prob. 24.

25. Mention the ways of obtaining change of flux linkages with a coil.

Ans. There are three methods of obtaining the change in flux linkages with a coil. These are as under :

(i) relative motion between coil and the constant flux

(ii) relative motion between coil and the time-varying flux

(iii) coil is stationary but the magnetic flux linking the coil is time-varying.

26. Write expressions giving the magnitude of *(i)* dynamically-induced e.m.f. and *(ii)* statically-induced e.m.f. Give more common names of these e.m.fs.

Ans. *(i)* Dynamically-induced e.m.f. is given by $e = Blv$, where the symbols used have their usual meanings. This e.m.f. is commonly known as speed e.m.f. or rotational e.m.f.

(ii) Statically-induced e.m.f. is given by $e = N\dfrac{d\phi}{dt} = \dfrac{d\psi}{dt}$. This e.m.f. is usually more commonly known as transformer e.m.f.

E
Appendix

Appendix

E.1. TABLE OF CONSTANTS AND CONVERSION FACTORS

Constants

Permeability of free space, $\mu_0 = 4\pi \times 10^{-7}$ H/m
Permittivity (capacitivity) of free space $\varepsilon_0 = 8.854 \times 10^{-12}$ F/m
Gravitational acceleration, $g = 9.807$ m/s^2.

Conversion Factors

Quantity	*S.I. Unit*	*English unit*	*C.G.S. unit*
Length	1m	3.281 ft. = 39.37 in	100 cm
Mass	1 kg	2.205 lb. (mass)	1000 gm
Force	1 N	0.2248 lb.	10^5 dynes
Torque	1 Nm	0.738 lb. ft.	10^7 dyne cm
Energy	1 J = 1 Ws	0.738 ft. lb.	10^7 ergs
Power	1 W	1.341×10^{-3} hp.	—
Moment of inertia	1 kg m^2	23.73 lb. ft^2	10^7 g cm^2
Magnetic flux	1 Wb	10^8 lines	10^8 maxwells
Magnetic flux density	1 Wb/m^2 = 1 T	64.5 kilolines/in^2	10^4 gauss
Magnetic field intensity	1 A/m = 1 A turn/m	0.0254 A/in	0.004 π oersted

E.2. THE GREEK ALPHABET

Letter	*Capital*	*Small*
Alpha	Α	α
Beta	—	β
Gamma	—	γ
Delta	Δ	δ
Epsilon	—	ε
Zeta	—	ζ
Eta	—	η
Theta	—	θ
Iota	—	τ
Lambda	Λ	λ
Mu	—	μ
Nu	—	ν
Xi	—	ξ
Pi	—	π
Rho	—	ρ
Sigma	Σ (sum of)	σ
Phi	—	ϕ
Psi	—	ψ
Omega	Ω (ohm)	ω

Index

D

E

U

V

W

Z